A COMMENTARY

ON

THE HOLY BIBLE

THE MACMILLAN COMPANY
NEW YORK · CHICAGO
DALLAS · ATLANTA · SAN FRANCISCO

**THE MACMILLAN COMPANY
OF CANADA, LIMITED**
TORONTO

A

COMMENTARY

ON

THE HOLY BIBLE

BY VARIOUS WRITERS

EDITED BY

The Rev. J. R. DUMMELOW M.A.

QUEENS' COLLEGE, CAMBRIDGE

COMPLETE IN ONE VOLUME

WITH GENERAL ARTICLES AND MAPS

NEW YORK

THE MACMILLAN COMPANY

1954

Nineteenth Printing, 1954

PREFACE

A few words will suffice to explain the purpose and plan of the present volume, which has been specially written to meet the wants of the ordinary Bible reader.

The Bible is the inspired record of God's gradual revelation of Himself, His Nature, Character, and Will,—a revelation made in the first instance to a people who were chosen to be the guardians of this treasure and to communicate it in due time to the rest of mankind,—a revelation consummated in the Person, Life, and Work of Jesus Christ. In this light it is regarded by at least a third of the human race, who have accepted it as a sure guide through time to eternity. It therefore demands and deserves constant and reverent study, which will be richly repaid by an ever-growing appreciation of its beauties, and a clearer perception of its spiritual power and truth.

Yet it is often forgotten that 1800 years have elapsed since the last pages of the Bible were written, that it deals with events of the remote past, with races moved by ideas and influenced by a civilisation very unlike our own, and that the language of its larger half has ceased to be a living speech for more than two thousand years. Even the translation which is in common use—the Authorised Version—was made 300 years ago, at a time when Christian scholars had only just become conversant with Hebrew, and when no one thought of employing for critical purposes those ancient Versions, such as the Septuagint, which throw so much light on both text and interpretation. It is also only within recent years that travellers have familiarised themselves and others with Eastern scenes and customs, and have become acquainted with the literature, history, religion and archæology of the nations connected with Israel.

It is therefore evident that the reader who possesses only the text of the Bible is greatly hampered by ignorance of the circumstances under which the various books were originally composed, the mental habits of the people to whom they were addressed, and the actual needs which they were designed to meet. Oftentimes he fails to realise that the prophecy, psalm, or epistle was sent forth in response to contemporary circumstances, as urgent and vital as any we experience. Hence arises an inadequate apprehension of the intense reality of the message delivered. Spiritual help may, no doubt, be derived from its perusal—that being the main purpose for which God's providence has preserved it,—but even this will be less efficacious than if there had been caught a more distinct echo of the original bearing and significance of the record.

The One Volume Commentary is an attempt to meet such needs as have been indicated, and to provide, in convenient form, a brief explanation of the meaning of the Scriptures. Introductions have been supplied to the various books, and Notes which will help to explain the principal difficulties, textual, moral or doctrinal, which may arise in connexion with them. A series of Articles has, also, been prefixed, dealing with the larger questions suggested by the Bible as a whole. It is hoped that the Commentary may lead to a perusal of many of the books of Holy Scripture which are too often left unread, in spite of their rare literary charm and abundant usefulness for the furtherance of the spiritual life.

PREFACE

The Authorised Version has been commented on as being still in general use, but pains have been taken to indicate the innumerable passages where the Revised Version leads to a better understanding of the original.

In recent years much light has been thrown upon questions of authorship and interpretation, and the contributors to this volume have endeavoured to incorporate in it the most assured results of modern scholarship, whilst avoiding opinions of an extreme or precarious kind. Sometimes these results differ from traditional views, but in such cases it is not only hoped, but believed, that the student will find the spiritual value and authority of the Bible have been enhanced, rather than diminished, by the change.

The Editor desires to express his gratitude to the many well-known biblical scholars who have responded so readily to his appeal for help, and by their encouragement and contributions have made the production of the Commentary possible. He regrets that the problem of space, which has confronted him from beginning to end, has allowed him to assign to them only sufficient room for the briefest and simplest treatment of their several books.

For the conception and methods of the work the Editor is alone responsible. He has been induced to undertake the task from a belief that, notwithstanding the many commentaries in existence, there is still room for another more suited to the needs and means of the general public. To treat so vast a subject in so small a space must inevitably evoke criticism, but he trusts that even within the limits of a single volume, much will be found to remove difficulties, to strengthen faith, and to lead to a wider study and fuller comprehension of the Word of God.

CONTRIBUTORS

OLD TESTAMENT

AYLES, Rev. H. H. B., D.D., Rector of Barrow, Suffolk.

CURTIS, E. L., Ph.D., D.D., Professor of Hebrew Language and Literature, Yale Divinity School.

DAVISON, Rev. W. T., D.D., Professor of Theology, Richmond, Surrey.

DUMMELOW, Rev. J. R., General Editor.

*EDIE, Rev. W., M.A., B.D., formerly Examiner for the Degree of B.D., St. Andrews.

GREEN, Rev. E. T., M.A., Professor of Hebrew, St. David's College, Lampeter.

JORDAN, Rev. W. G., B.A., D.D., Professor of OT. Criticism, Queen's University, Ontario.

KENNETT, Rev. Canon R., B.D., Regius Professor of Hebrew, Cambridge.

KENT, C. F., Ph.D., Professor of Biblical History and Literature, Yale University.

LOFTHOUSE, Rev. W.F., M.A., Professor of OT. Languages and Philosophy, Handsworth College, Birmingham.

McFADYEN, Rev. J. E., D.D., Professor of Old Testament in the United Free Church College, Glasgow.

*MOULTON, Rev. W. J., M.A., Professor of OT. Languages and Philosophy, Headingley College, Leeds.

PATON, Rev. L. B., D.D., Professor of OT. Exegesis, Hartford Seminary, Conn.

*PATRICK, Rev. J., B.D., B.Sc., formerly Examiner for Degrees in Divinity, St. Andrews.

*RAGG, Rev. Canon L., M.A., sometime Warden of the Bishop's Hostel, Lincoln.

ROBINSON, G. L., Ph.D., Professor of OT. Literature and Exegesis, McCormick Theological Seminary, Chicago.

SANDERS, Frank K., Ph.D., D.D., Director of the Bureau of Missionary Preparation, New York; formerly Dean of the Yale Divinity School, New Haven.

*STOTT, Rev. G. G., M.A., B.D., Examiner for Degrees in Hebrew and Theology, St. Andrews.

STREANE, Rev. A. W., D.D., Fellow of Corpus Christi College, Cambridge.

*TAYLOR, Rev. J., Litt.D., Vicar of Winchcombe.

WADE, Rev. G. W., D.D., Professor and Senior Tutor, St. David's College, Lampeter.

WELCH, Rev. A., B.D., Glasgow.

WOODS, Rev. F. H., B.D., Rector of Bainton, Yorks; sometime Fellow and Tutor, St. John's College, Oxford.

NEW TESTAMENT

*ADENEY, Rev. W. F., D.D., Principal of the Lancashire College, Manchester.

CAMPBELL, Rev. J., M.A., B.D., Monquhitter.

CURTIS, Rev. W. A., D.D., Litt.D., Professor of Systematic Theology, University of Edinburgh.

*FINDLAY, Rev. G. G., D.D., Professor of Biblical Literature and Exegesis, Headingley College, Leeds.

FULFORD, Rev. H. W., M.A., Fellow and Dean (formerly), Clare College, Cambridge.

*HARRIS, Rev. C., D.D., Vicar of Claverley; Examining Chaplain to the Bishop of Llandaff.

MEYRICK, Rev. F., M.A. (the late), Rector of Blickling, Norfolk.

NAIRNE, Rev. A., D.D., Professor of Hebrew, Cambridge.

PALMER, Rev. Frederick, D.D., Managing Editor of the Harvard Theological Review.

PEAKE, A. S., D.D., Dean of the Faculty of Theology in the University of Manchester.

PLUMMER, Rev. A., D.D., sometime Master of University College, Durham.

ROPES, Rev. J. H., D.D., Bussey Professor of NT. Criticism and Exegesis, Harvard University.

SLATTERY, Rt. Rev. C. L., D.D., Bishop of Massachusetts.

SMITH, Rev. G. ABBOTT, D.D., Professor of OT. and NT. Literature, Diocesan Theological College, Montreal.

SMITH, Rev. H., M.A., Lecturer at St. John's College, Highbury.

STURGES, Rev. M. C., M.A., sometime Lecturer in Theology, Cavendish College, Cambridge.

CONTRIBUTORS, ETC.

ARTICLES

CONDER, Colonel, R.E., D.C.L., LL.D.

FREW, Rev. D., B.D., formerly Black Theological Fellow, Glasgow University.

PATERSON-SMYTH, Rev. J., LL.D., Litt.D., Rector of St. George's, Montreal.

PULLAN, Rev. L., M.A., Fellow and Tutor, St. John's College, Oxford.

And other Contributors marked thus * on previous page.

ABBREVIATIONS

AV = Authorised Version.
RV = Revised Version.
RM = Margin of RV.
OT. = Old Testament.
NT. = New Testament.
cp. = compare.
f. = following.
Heb. = Hebrew.

Gk. = Greek.
MSS = Manuscripts.
VSS = Versions.
WH. = Westcott and Hort's text.
LXX = The Septuagint, an ancient Greek translation of the Old Testament.
HDB. = Hastings' Dictionary of the Bible, a valuable work of reference.

COLLECT

BLESSED Lord, who hast caused all holy Scriptures to be written for our learning; Grant that we may in such wise hear them, read, mark, learn, and inwardly digest them, that by patience, and comfort of thy holy Word, we may embrace, and ever hold fast the blessed hope of everlasting life, which thou hast given us in our Saviour Jesus Christ. Amen.

CONTENTS

GENERAL ARTICLES

CONTENTS

COMMENTARY

MAPS

(At end of Volume)

GENERAL INTRODUCTION TO THE BIBLE

THE Bible is the source as well as the result of inspiration. The utterances of the men of old, at the suggestion or under the guidance of the Holy Spirit, live and move again, with informing, uplifting, redeeming power, under the blessing of the same Spirit, in the hearts and lives of men. Every detail regarding it therefore is interesting.

1. **Titles.** The Bible is not one book, but many. The original form and meaning of the word itself bear this out. *Biblos* in Greek means 'book,' so called from *byblos*, the inner bark of the papyrus reed on which early writings were inscribed. *Biblos* is used in Mt 1¹, but in Lk 4¹⁷ a diminutive form *biblion* is used with the same meaning. The early Greek Christians called their Scriptures *Ta Biblia*, i.e. the books *par excellence*. So they were called for centuries. Later, however, the Latin form *biblia*, although plural, was mistaken for a feminine singular, this idea being doubtless helped by the increasing view that the Scriptures were a complete whole— the unique Word of God to the world. In this way the word as a singular acquired popular vogue, and ultimately the Jewish and Christian sacred books, which had been known at first chiefly as 'the Scriptures' (*hai graphai*), became familiar in all the languages of Europe as 'the Bible.'

The term 'Testament,' familiar to us in the phrase, 'Old and New Testaments,' is due probably to some misunderstanding of the Greek word *diathēkē*. This term is used by the Greek translators of the Old Testament to render the Hebrew word *Berith*, 'covenant,' which originally had a very general significance, and referred to decisions or judgments and agreements of different kinds. As these, however, were usually accompanied by religious observances and sanctions, the word 'covenant' came to have a specially religious sense, and was applied to the decisions or judgments of God, and His agreements with His chosen people, or their outstanding representatives. Thus we have His 'covenant' with Noah, Abram, etc., and the new 'covenant' which He made with men in Christ. Under the former the patriarchs of Israel and their descendants came under obligation to render God obedience and service ; while He, on His part, undertook to requite them with His blessing and favour. Israel's failure to keep the covenant of works necessitated the covenant of grace under which forgiveness and

righteousness are secured through faith in Christ. It is in this sense the word is used by St. Paul (2 Cor 3⁶). Only once (Heb 9¹⁶,¹⁷) is it possible that it may refer to a *disposition* or *will*. But this is the sense of the Latin word *testamentum* used to render it, viz. a will, or disposition (of property). An attempt was made to supplant this word *testamentum* by another word, *instrumentum*, meaning an authoritative document. But the former survived and gave to us the familiar words, 'the Old and New Testaments,' meaning the *covenants* or agreements made by God with His people in the Jewish and Christian times respectively.

2. **Language.** The Bible was written in the language of the people among whom it first appeared. The language of the Old Testament is Hebrew.

Hebrew is written from right to left. In a modern Hebrew Bible the pages run also from right to left, and the writing is in square characters (consonants), with small signs and dots attached variously for vowels. Originally Hebrew had no vowels, and the difficulty of reading it must have been to a beginner very great. Thus DBR might be *dābhār*, 'a word,' or *dibber*, 'he spoke,' or *dōbhēr*, 'a speaker,' or *dōbhēr*, 'pasture,' or *debher*, 'pestilence.' The vowel system, as will be seen hereafter, was only introduced in the sixth century A.D. in order to preserve the correct pronunciation. This explains one of the difficulties still experienced in the interpretation of the OT. Scriptures. It is sometimes doubtful whether the correct vowels have been added to the consonants of the original text, and, if not, what others should be substituted for them.

Hebrew includes Aramaic, a kindred dialect with distinctive peculiarities. Parts of the Old Testament, viz. Ezr 4⁸⁻⁶¹⁸ 7¹²⁻²⁶ Jer 10¹¹ Dan 2⁴⁻7²⁸, are written in Aramaic, while isolated words and phrases occur in many other parts of the Old Testament, due either to the local peculiarities of the original writer, or more probably to careless copyists. The common speech of our Lord and His disciples is generally believed to have been some form of Aramaic, and a more careful study of this dialect has already thrown much light on their teaching. The allusions to Hebrew in the New Testament (Jn 5² 19¹³,¹⁷ Ac 21⁴⁰ 22², etc.) are mainly to Aramaic.

The term 'Chaldee,' sometimes applied to the Aramaic portions of the Old Testament, is a misnomer. Chaldea is Babylonia, and Chaldee is the language of the Babylonian inscriptions.

In the third century B.C. there began to be made at Alexandria a Greek version of the Old Testament. It is called the Septuagint version from the traditional belief that seventy scribes (Lat. *Septuaginta*) were employed in its production. This version was probably completed some time before the Christian era, and is of great value in the study of the Old Testament (see art. 'Literature of the Period between Old and New Testaments ').

The language of the New Testament is Greek, a particular form hitherto known as Hellenistic Greek. Recent discoveries have, however, proved conclusively that, in form and in substance, it was simply the language of the Greek-speaking world of New Testament times. The modes of expression in the Septuagint, in the Epistles of St. Paul, and in the Gospels are not peculiar to Christianity or its message, but are due to the style of speech common in that age. Some parts of the Gospels may have been originally in Aramaic, but this is disputed.

3. Divisions. We have already seen that the two main divisions of the Bible are the Old and New Testaments. As it stands in our English Bible, **the Old Testament** consists of thirty-nine books, but these are only reckoned as twenty-four in the Hebrew Bible, 1 and 2 S, 1 and 2 K, 1 and 2 Ch, Ezra, Neh, and the twelve (so-called) Minor Prophets, being each reckoned as one book. The Hebrew divisions are on large lines. The first five books are known as the *Tôrah* (i.e. 'Law ') ; then come the *Nebhîim* (i.e. 'Prophets '), subdivided into Earlier (four books) and Later (four books) ; while the third great division is the *Kethûbhîm* (i.e. 'writings,' called in the Septuagint, 'Hagiographa '). The following table shows the grouping of the various books in the Hebrew Bible :—

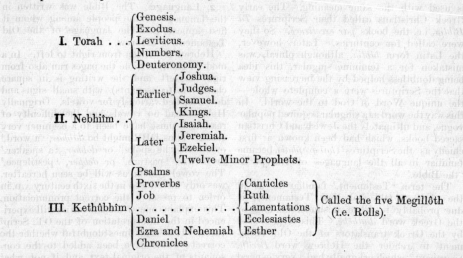

I. Torah . . .		Genesis. Exodus. Leviticus. Numbers. Deuteronomy.	
II. Nebhîim . .	Earlier	Joshua. Judges. Samuel. Kings.	
	Later	Isaiah. Jeremiah. Ezekiel. Twelve Minor Prophets.	
III. Kethûbhîm		Psalms Proverbs Job . . . . Daniel Ezra and Nehemiah Chronicles	Canticles Ruth Lamentations Called the five Megillôth Ecclesiastes (i.e. Rolls). Esther

Hagiographa means 'sacred writings,' a paraphrase of *Kethûbhîm*. The five *Megillôth* were so called because each was written on a separate roll. They were read yearly at the Jewish festivals : Canticles at the Passover ; Ruth at Pentecost ; Ecclesiastes at the Feast of Tabernacles ; Esther at the Feast of Purim ; Lamentations on the anniversary of the destruction of Jerusalem.

A later grouping of the Hebrew books given by Josephus enumerates twenty-two, being designed to correspond with the twenty-two letters of the Hebrew alphabet. This was accomplished by reading Ruth as part of Judges, and Lamentations as part of Jeremiah.

4. Arrangement. From the grouping of the Hebrew Bible given above, it will be seen that not only the divisions, but also the arrangement of the books differs considerably from those adopted in our English Bible. The latter follows the Latin Vulgate, which in turn is based on the Septuagint. Here the division is according to subject-matter : Law (five books), History (twelve books), Poetry (five books), and Prophecy (seventeen books). This arrangement proves, however, on examination to be superficial and inadequate. It is even less satisfactory than the order in the Hebrew Bible. Modern scholars have striven rather to obtain some historical arrangement of the books ; their aim being to enable students to read the various writings in the light of contemporary events. A sketch of the prophetical books in their historical order, given by the late Prof. A. B. Davidson, illustrates at once the advantages and the difficulties of such an arrangement. ' (1) Prophets of the Assyrian Age—Amos, Hosea, Isaiah (740–700), Micah, Nahum, Zephaniah ; (2) prophets of the Babylonian age—Habakkuk, Jeremiah (626–580), Ezekiel (593–576) ; (3) prophets of the Exile and Restoration—Isaiah xl–lxvi (550), Haggai, and Zechariah (520), Malachi (420) ; the age of Joel and Obadiah is uncertain ; while Jonah is late.' In the case of the other two great divisions of the Old Testament the difficulties would be much greater (see under ' Canon,' § 5).

The arrangement of the **New Testament**, on the other hand, is easily explained. The books, twenty-seven in number, fall readily into six groups : (1) The Gospels, (2) The Acts of the Apostles, (3) The Epistles of St. Paul, (4) The Epistle to the Hebrews, (5) The General Epistles, (6) The Book of the Revelation. This order fits in, more or less, to a comprehensive scheme showing the origin of Christianity in Jesus Christ, its progress under the Apostles, early Christian letters unfolding its doctrines and ideals, and finally its consummation in apocalyptic vision. This arrangement, however, is not chronological— St. Mark being probably the earliest of the Gospels, while some of the Epistles of St. Paul were written still earlier.

It is necessary to add that the arrangement of chapters and verses has nothing to do with the original book. It was an artificial invention of the middle ages. The first printed Bible with chapters appeared in 1525, and the first Bible with verses in 1551. While very convenient for reference, this arrangement often obscures the sense and needlessly interrupts the narrative. The chapters and verses have therefore by the Revisers of 1885 been relegated to the margin.

5. The Canon. Every introduction to the Bible uses the phrase ' Canon of the Old Testament,' or ' Canon of the New Testament,' or ' canonical books.' What is meant by these phrases ? The word ' canon ' is Greek, and denoted originally a measuring-rod or line. Later it came to mean a *standard* of measurement, and last of all the space covered by such a measure. The term ' canon ' came to be used in connexion with the books of the Bible about the fourth century of our era, to indicate either that these books were the standard of faith, or that they occupied a special place, where they were marked off from all other books. Usually the Canon means the collection of books in the Old and New Testaments as opposed to those books (see Apocrypha) which were left out, and on this subject two questions are suggested. (1) Why were such collections made ? (2) What principles guided the choice of book ?

Taking the first question as it applies to the Old Testament, we find the subject involved in some obscurity. As early at least as the days of Samuel there existed the ' schools of the prophets,' where the training was not only religious but scholastic. In these schools were preserved the first records of Israel's history. The compilation and arrangement of these records would be the work of later generations, and how this was done we cannot now say for certain. We may, however, take the great divisions of the Old Testament as indicating how the Canon was formed. The process was gradual. In all likelihood the Pentateuch was the only part recognised as canonical when Ezra read the Tôrah to the people (Neh 8). This is supported by the fact that the Samaritans, who formed themselves into a separate community about that period, possess only the Pentateuch. The work of Ezra answers the first question asked above. Ezra and Nehemiah were social and religious reformers. They desired clear and definite guidance for the people, and so they set up the Pentateuch as the standard of faith and morals. Meanwhile the works of the various prophets would be preserved along with the histories, and these would be added to the Pentateuch at a later date. Later still, and only after much discussion, was the third great division, the Kethûbhîm, added. The claim of the prophetic books to a place in the Canon would readily be admitted in an age when the living voice of the prophet was no longer heard. The purpose of the Kethûbhîm would vindicate a place for the Psalms, so necessary for the service of the second Temple, and for the Megillôth as read at the various festivals.

The general principles on which the books were chosen to form the Canon were threefold. (1) They were books that had been in existence for a considerable time and were well known ; or, (2) they were books associated with some great name, e.g. the books of Moses, the Psalms of David, the Proverbs of Solomon ; or, (3) they were books closely connected with national history or with national festivals.

In all the books admitted into the Canon, it was of course believed that the voice of God was to be heard, as He had spoken to the fathers, saints, and prophets of the Hebrew race, that is to say, as He had at no time spoken to men of other lands : or that His power was to be realised as it had been exhibited not only in the experiences of individual lives, but in the general history of the nation. This presence of God in the books, or the inspired element as we would call it, rendered them unique and sacred in their eyes.

The exact date of the fixing of the Old Testament Canon is uncertain. It could hardly have been earlier than the end of the second century B.C., while even as late as the second century

A.D. the Jewish rabbis were still discussing the claims of such books as Ecclesiastes and Canticles to a place in the Canon.

The history of the **New Testament** Canon is somewhat different. It is now generally admitted that all the books of the New Testament as we know them, were in existence before or soon after the end of the first century A.D. But not for many years did the New Testament, as a complete whole, receive recognition. So long as the Apostles lived there was no apparent need of any written word concerning Jesus Christ and the gospel. The first Christians believed that the Spirit of God descended upon them to lead them into all truth. They further believed that the end of all things was at hand. And these two beliefs made needless the setting up of any written standard of authority. So late as the middle of the second century a Christian leader, Papias, bishop of Hierapolis, expresses in writing his preference for the spiritual gifts as superior to any written testimony. But when the fervour of the Apostolic age began to lose its first glow, and when Christianity went forth to do battle with pagan philosophy, the early Christian records became more precious. Justin Martyr about 150 A.D. tells how 'Memoirs of the Apostles'—doubtless the Gospels—and the prophets of the Old Testament were read on the Lord's Day. By the end of the second century the Syriac Version of the New Testament included all the books in our Canon, except 2 and 3 John, 2 Peter, Jude, and Revelation; while in the West, by this time, all the books found acceptance within the Canon, except Hebrews, James, and 2 Peter. Eusebius, writing about 325 A.D., divides the books of the New Testament into three classes: those universally acknowledged as authoritative (*Homologoumena*), those whose authority was disputed (*Antilegomena*), spurious books (*Notha*). The disputed books were James, Jude, 2 and 3 John, 2 Peter, Hebrews, and Revelation. The spurious books were the Gospel of Peter, the Acts of Paul, and various other Gospels and Apocalypses, most of which are now lost. It is well to point out that in regard to the disputed books the question at issue was their authority as standards in the Church. Opinions were divided. In the East opposition to Revelation lingered even in the fourth century; while in the West the book whose authority was longest disputed was the Epistle to the Hebrews. The subject was much discussed at many councils of the Church, and it was not till the third council of Carthage in 397 that the Canon of the New Testament was finally settled in its present form.

6. The Text of the Bible. A comparison of an English Bible in the Revised Version with one in the Authorised Version reveals at once many changes. Some are due to the progress of the English language, but many others are due to what scholars call various readings in the text. The text is the original Hebrew of the Old Testament and the original Greek of the New Testament. Formerly an idea largely prevailed that this text was an unchanging, unchangeable thing, preserved miraculously from ancient times. The preservation of the Bible is certainly one of the greatest miracles. When we reflect that the Bible had existed for a thousand years before printing was invented in Europe, that all copies had to be made laboriously by hand, and that thousands of copyists must have been employed, the wonder is not that there are various readings of the text, but that these are comparatively few and unimportant. The text of the Bible was preserved by human hands, working under human limitations, but the hand of God is in it too.

7. The Text of the Old Testament. One of the old arguments against the authenticity of the Old Testament was, that writing could not have been known so early ; but this argument has vanished. We now possess tablets written in the fifteenth century B.C. by governors of cities in the south of Palestine to their masters, the kings of Egypt ; while inscriptions in Egypt itself carry us back at least five thousand years before the Christian era.

Scholars now agree that parts of the Old Testament may have existed in writing a thousand years before the Christian era. These were probably copied at first on skins in the form of rolls—*megillôth*. Early Hebrew differed considerably in form (as seen in the Moabite Stone—about 850 B.C.) from modern Hebrew, in which the characters are square. In the work of transcription through all these centuries down to the age of printing many slips would undoubtedly be made. For many centuries no vowel signs were used at all, and the consonants were written without any spaces between words. The scribes who copied were undoubtedly very careful, but sometimes the same consonant was written twice. Sometimes, of two consonants of the same form one was omitted ; or a word might occur twice in one verse, and the scribe going on to the second as he copied the first would omit the intervening words. About the third century A.D. certain consonants began to be used to express unchangeably long vowels. This was called *scriptio plena*, i.e. full writing. About the middle of the sixth century, when the Jews were much scattered, the danger arose that the proper pronunciation of Hebrew would be lost. A set of scribes called Massoretes, i.e. Traditionists, introduced a complete system of points to indicate the vowels as traditionally pronounced. Long before that time the consonantal text had come to be regarded by the Jews as absolutely sacred in every jot and tittle. The Massoretes were most careful to change nothing in this text—where change was obviously necessary they placed notes to that effect in the margin. So sacred was the text that everything was reproduced; letters written large were written large, those small were kept small; even signs unknown, some of them probably due to accident, were faithfully copied. Thus thousands of copies of the Hebrew Scriptures must have been made, at first on skins, and later on papyrus. But thousands perished in these early centuries. The Jews themselves in superstitious reverence hid away many copies that were thus lost for ever. They also destroyed all worn copies lest the sacred text should suffer. In the early persecutions of the Christians under the Roman emperors the most strenuous attempts were made to stamp out Christianity by destroying its literature, which included both Old and New Testaments. Even more zealous were the followers of Mahomet, in their mad career of conquest, to extirpate all religious books except the Koran. The result is that the oldest part of the Hebrew Bible now in existence is a section of the prophetical books made in 916 A.D., while the oldest complete MS of a whole Bible belongs to the eleventh century A.D., and we have very few MSS to guide us as to readings of various texts. We can, however, get much help from the versions.

(a) There is Aquila's Greek version. Aquila was a learned Jewish proselyte who made a word-for-word translation of the Hebrew text in the second century A.D.

(b) Symmachus, an Ebionite, also made a translation into Greek in the same century.

(c) Theodotion revised the Septuagint version about the same time.

(d) Very important too, for comparison, is a version of the Scriptures in Syriac made from the Hebrew and Septuagint probably as early as the second century, and known as the Peshitto, i.e. the plain version.

(e) We have also fragments of an old Latin version made mainly from the Septuagint.

(f) More important than the old Latin is the translation of the Old Testament made by St. Jerome. This was made mainly from Hebrew into Latin about the end of the fourth century A.D., and is now universally known as the Vulgate.

It must be noted, however, that although many various readings exist, the vast majority are of small importance, and bear testimony both to the marvellous accuracy of the Jewish scribes, and to the miraculous preservation of these Scriptures through many vicissitudes. In recent years much patient and laborious

study has been given to the Old Testament towards what may be called the reconstruction of the text, wherein scholars making abundant use of Hebrew, Targums (i.e. the marginal explanations given in Aramaic by early Jewish rabbis), and versions, and even going behind all these, have sought to reproduce more accurately the various books of the Old Testament.

8. The Text of the New Testament. The story of the text of the New Testament may be told more briefly, although the subject is more complicated. The New Testament was written in Greek, and when we want to get at the original words of any text our materials are threefold.

(1) Early MSS in Greek. Of these the most famous are the following : (a) The Sinaiticus (known as $\aleph$, *Aleph*), found by Tischendorf in the Convent of St. Catherine on Mount Sinai in 1859. It was made, probably, not later than 350 A.D., and contains the Old Testament (Septuagint) and whole of the New Testament. It is now in the Imperial Museum at St. Petersburg. (b) The Alexandrinus (known as A), presented to Charles I by the Patriarch of Constantinople in 1627. It belongs to the fifth century, and contains the Old Testament (Septuagint) and nearly all the New Testament. It is now in the British Museum. (c) The Vatican (B. 4th cent.) containing the Old Testament (Septuagint)—not complete—and the New Testament down to Heb 9 14. It is now in the Vatican at Rome, and includes the General Epistles ; but the Pastoral Epistles, Philemon, and Apocalypse are wanting. These are the three chief MSS ; while almost equally important are the MSS known as C, D, and D₂.

(2) Quotations from the Early Fathers. These include Clement of Rome, Tatian, Justin Martyr, Irenæus, and Origen in Greek, and Tertullian, Cyprian, Ambrose, and Augustine in Latin. The difficulty with such quotations is that the writer often quotes from memory, and gives the sense rather than the words. These quotations are also as liable to error in transcription as the New Testament itself.

(3) Versions of the New Testament. Among the more important is the Diatessaron of Tatian, a harmony of the Four Gospels interwoven with texts (the word *diatessaron* means 'according to four') made about 170 A.D. Tatian was a disciple of Justin Martyr, and his work survives both in an Arabic version, and also in a commentary on the Diatessaron by Ephraim the Syrian. In addition we have the Peshitto version, the Old Latin, and the Vulgate, all mentioned in connexion with the Old Testament ; while, as in the case of the Old Testament, there are less important versions in Armenian, Egyptian, and Gothic.

The Hebrew Scriptures were printed in 1488,

but no edition of the Greek New Testament appeared till 1514. This was the work of editors acting under Cardinal Ximenes. Erasmus produced a different version in 1516, and the so-called 'received text' was the work of R. Stephens (1550), and was printed by the Elzevirs at Leyden in 1624. Since that time great progress has been made in collating MSS, and several noteworthy editions have been issued, including those of Tischendorf (1860), Westcott and Hort (1881), and Nestlé (1901).

The work of the scholar who seeks to know the mind of the New Testament writers is much more difficult than similar work in the Old Testament. To begin with, the writers of the Gospels report in Greek (although they may have had some Aramaic sources) the sayings of Jesus Christ, who for the most part probably spoke Aramaic. Nor is it likely that these writers or their copyists had any idea that their records would go beyond the early Churches, with which they themselves were familiar.

The same applies to St. Paul. His letters, now so valued, were messages intended only for the Churches to which they were addressed. Those who first copied them would not regard them as at all 'sacred' in our sense of the word.

Nor even in later centuries do we find that scrupulous regard for the sacred text which marked the transmission of the Old Testament. A copyist would sometimes put in not what was in the text, but what he thought ought to be in it. He would trust a fickle memory, or he would even make the text accord with the views of the school to which he belonged. Besides this, an enormous number of copies are preserved. In addition to the versions and quotations from the early Christian Fathers, nearly four thousand Greek MSS of the New Testament are known to exist. As a result the variety of readings is considerable.

But while we can see how intricate and difficult is the task of the New Testament scholars, we must remember, on the one hand, that the vast majority of the differences are unimportant, and, on the other hand, that where they are important we have in the providence of God such range of material as no age has ever possessed for learning the truth. We can still search the Scriptures in perfect confidence that they will testify of Christ, and that their testimony is true.

9. English Versions. The first attempts to render the Scriptures in English are represented by some extant translations and paraphrases of the Psalms and other books dating from a very early time. About the end of the fourteenth century (1382) the complete version of Wyclif was made from the Latin Vulgate, the Gospels being his own work, and

the rest of the Bible (including the Apocrypha) being done by some of his followers. The Reformation and the invention of printing together stimulated the production of versions, and the following appeared during the sixteenth century : Tyndale's New Testament, Pentateuch, and other books of the Bible (1525–1535); Miles Coverdale's complete English Bible (1535) ; Matthew's Bible (1537), made up out of the earlier versions, and published as an 'Authorised Version' with the Royal licence ; the Great Bible (1539), a revision of Matthew's ; the Geneva Bible (1560), published by the exiled reformers in Geneva during the reign of Queen Mary, and long popular with the common people, being still known as the 'Breeches' Bible from its rendering of Gn 3 [7] ; and the Bishops' Bible (1568), produced by episcopal scholars, mostly bishops, and vulgarly termed the 'Treacle' Bible, from its rendering of Jer 8 [22]. In 1604 a conference was convened by James I at Hampton Court, to set in order things amiss in the Church, and one result was a new translation of the Scriptures, done by six committees of divines, two sitting at Westminster, two at Cambridge, and two at Oxford, the whole work being finally revised by a general committee. This version appeared in 1611, and gradually displaced the previous versions, winning its way with learned and unlearned alike by its faithfulness to the original languages and its peculiar felicities of English style. It is the version still generally used, and known as the 'Authorised' version. In the latter half of the last century it became increasingly felt that the new materials which had accumulated upon the Bible in the way of early MSS, versions, and quotations from ancient writers necessitated a fresh translation of the text, and on the suggestion of the Convocation of Canterbury, this was undertaken by two companies of translators, one for the Old Testament and the other for the New. With them were associated two similar companies of American scholars, and the result of their joint labours was the Revised Version, of which the New Testament was published in 1881, and the Old in 1885. It retains so far as possible the character and style of the Authorised Version ; but it corrects its mistranslations, substitutes modern English words for words that have become obsolete or archaic, arranges prose matter in paragraphs and poetry in lines according to modern usage, and introduces such changes in the text as are required by the new sources of information that have come to light. It is thus of great value, not to scholars only, but to all who desire to get closer to the original language of the Scriptures than the limited range of authorities used by previous versions could render possible.

HEBREW HISTORY TO THE EXILE

1. The unique value of Hebrew History. In every record of human progress the story of the Hebrew people must always take the foremost place. Whilst other peoples have ruled over vaster empires, and left behind them far greater monuments in literature or in art, it is to this race that we owe the Christian religion. If it is true that on the secular side our intellectual life is rooted in Greece and Rome, on the religious side it is rooted in Israel. So long as men recognise the abiding value of religion as the answer to their deepest need, they will turn with inexhaustible interest to the story of the first beginnings and the gradual development of the people whose faith has conquered the civilised world.

2. Need of a Special Statement. There are special reasons why a separate sketch of the history of the Hebrews is required. The Bible narratives differ from secular history in that all other interests are entirely subordinated to the religious one. Hence public events of the utmost importance are lightly passed over, whilst whole chapters are devoted to the records of spiritual experience. Moreover, as the detailed expositions of this volume show, books from widely differing ages lie side by side with very slight indications of date. Further still, recent archæological discoveries have enabled us to understand, as never before, the place that Israel filled among the surrounding nations. In this brief sketch a twofold aim has been followed :—(1) The exhibition of the history of the Hebrews in its relations to the great world-movements of other peoples. (2) The setting forth of the emergence and growth of the great ideas which culminated in Jesus Christ.

3. Origin of the Hebrews. The Hebrews belong to the Semite branch of the human race, a branch whose original home, in all probability, was in Arabia. Pressing north and west these peoples established themselves in Western Asia, above all in Mesopotamia, between the Tigris and the Euphrates. Here, in the third and fourth millenniums B.C., the earliest records show them as settled nations, highly developed both in civilisation and in religious beliefs and practices. About 2400 B.C. the rulers of the ancient city of Babylon succeeded in establishing their supremacy over the greater part of this region, and founded a dynasty of which Hammurabi was the most famous member (see art. 'Laws of Hammurabi'). Seeing that Hammurabi is now generally identified with Amraphel (Gn 14¹), we are

thus able to fix the date of Abraham, circ. 2250 B.C. Some scholars incline to bring Hammurabi's date down as low as 1900 B.C. We are safe in saying that the Patriarchal period reaches back to the beginning of the second millennium B.C.

For a discussion of the historicity, in broad outline, of the Bible narratives about Abraham, reference must be made to the intro. to Gn 12–25. The fact there emphasised that we have a right to see in Abraham the founder of the distinctive religion of Israel makes the question as to the religious influences amongst which he grew up one of vital interest. Were there present in the world before his day any tendencies towards a pure faith ?

We find that all the records of this period are permeated with religion. Religion was the mainspring of intellectual activity, priests were the leaders in all departments of thought. This religion, at first sight, offers a picture of hopeless confusion. Gods of the sky, gods of the earth, gods of the deep, families of gods, fathers and mothers, sons and daughters, local gods of cities and hills, gods directing and involved in all the powers of nature confront and bewilder us. The whole effect is that of a crass polytheism, full of degrading superstition. Yet when we look a little closer higher thoughts are not wanting. Looking upwards to the sky, familiar to Orientals in a degree altogether unknown to us, the Babylonian thinkers watched the movements of the heavenly bodies and saw in them the seats of the great gods. To them the whole universe was divided into three regions. First came the northern heavens, in which the pole-star burned continually , then the broad belt of the zodiac spanning the skies, within which all the movements of sun, moon, and planets were confined ; lastly, the southern depths. Over these regions the three great gods, Anu, Bel and Ea presided. Similarly in the zodiac itself there was a threefold division, ruled over by moon, sun, and Venus the evening star. Again and again it seemed as though the thought of one supreme God, of whom all others were manifestations, was about to break forth. So Sin the moon-god is hailed in lofty strains—

'Lord, the ordainer of the laws of heaven and earth,
　Whose command may not be broken.
In heaven who is supreme ? Thou alone, thou art supreme !
On earth who is supreme ? Thou alone, thou art supreme ! '

Similarly as the local deities became more and more absorbed into the conquering Marduk of Babylon ; or, as in the 'penitential psalms,' the worshipper seems led out far beyond the limits of his creed, we come again to the very verge of a new revelation. Yet the step across that verge was never taken. In the highest thoughts of Babylonia the gods seem rather pale abstractions than living persons with distinctive characters. It is here that the Bible narrative of Abraham finds its place. Living in the midst of all this movement of thought he heard in his own conscience and heart a deeper voice speaking to him, found that he could enter into real communion with a God who was indeed a Person, and for the sake of that intercourse forsook his home and wandered out into Canaan. The strange figure of Melchizedek suggests that there may have been others who found something of the same truth. Yet Abraham alone was able to pass on his faith to those that followed him. If so he was the first to understand that religion means personal communion with God. We have no means of judging how far his faith led him into a theoretical monotheism, nor how high his conceptions of morality were. But if he was led to make the great step that has been described, then he was truly ' the father of the faithful,' and we understand why the course of subsequent revelation followed the line of his descendants, rather than any other. Here the Father who had always been seeking those who would worship Him ' in spirit and truth' found at last one who could understand His message.

4. Israel and Egypt. After an indefinite period, during which the Hebrews lived as nomads in the pasture lands between Hebron and Beersheba, in the district afterwards known as the Negeb, or south-country of Judah (Gn 22 19 28 10), they passed on to Goshen, an alluvial region on the border of Egypt. Egypt at this time was under the rule of the Hyksôs, or Shepherd kings, probably themselves of Semitic origin, who had established a dynasty there which lasted till the sixteenth century B.C. The favour with which the Hebrews were received is easily explained by their racial affinities with the ruling house. When the Hyksôs had been expelled, not later, probably, than 1530 B.C., a new king arose who knew not Joseph (Ex 1 8), and the oppression began. It is now fairly well established that the Pharaoh of the oppression was Ramses II, who has been identified as the builder of the treasure city Pithom (Ex 1 11).

5. The Exodus. Converging lines of evidence make it probable that the date of the exodus was not later than 1180 B.C. ; it may have been as early as 1250 B.C. Before that time Palestine had been, as the Tel el Amarna tablets show, an Egyptian province, and the

control of Egypt was too strong to admit of the Hebrew conquests. Afterwards came a time of royal weakness and general anarchy, when the hold on the outlying parts of the empire was greatly relaxed. The reign of Ramses III (1180–1148 B.C.) has been suggested as the most likely period for the desert wanderings. Merenptah, son of Ramses II, is most probably the Pharaoh of the exodus.

For a discussion of the plagues and of the route from Goshen, reference must be made to the Commentary. The Passage of the Red Sea, however explained, left an abiding mark on the national memory. As Cornill says : ' This overwhelming moment created the people of Israel ; they never forgot it. Here they recognised the God of their fathers, who with strong hand and outstretched arm had saved His people, and brought them out of the house of bondage, out of Egypt.'

6. The Religious Teaching of Moses. For some time after this deliverance Israel remained in the neighbourhood of Sinai, and here the great work of Moses, the religious reorganisation of the people, was achieved. After all the critical discussion of the various sources of the Pentateuch, it remains abundantly clear that under the guidance of Moses a covenant between Jehovah and the people of Israel was concluded at Sinai (Ex 34 10, etc.). This covenant was no merely national bond. It was the outcome of the free moral choice of the God of their fathers, who, moved by pity, had rescued them from Egypt, and was ready to save them in the future. As the Commentary states, there is no reasonable ground for denying the Decalogue in its primitive form to Moses ; hence it is possible to summarise the faith of Moses as follows :

(a) He believed in a personal God, who had revealed Himself in former days to the fathers, and who was once more manifesting Himself to His people. This God, whose sacred name was Jehovah, was not bound to the Hebrews because of any blood relationship or any external necessity—the relationship between Him and them rested upon His own free determination ; hence Israel was the people of Jehovah because He had chosen them. No other nation had ever had such a thought about its god.

(b) He believed in a God whose fundamental attributes were righteousness and mercy. The strength of this God was greater than that of the mighty power of Egypt; but it was not brute force—it was always used to serve moral ends.

(c) He taught that this God, having concluded His covenant with the people, demanded on their side righteous conduct, justice, and brotherly kindness between man and man ; hence he insisted on the indissoluble bond between religion and morality

So whilst for the time of Moses, and for long after, the religion of Israel remained a national one, there were hidden in his teaching the germs of a universal religion. His great fundamental ideas were often forgotten, and sometimes buried beneath the corruptions of heathenism ; yet it was these truths that enabled the religion of Israel to resist the influences of Canaan, and to outlast even the nation itself. The victory of his teaching is the sufficient proof of the justice of his claim to be the specially chosen messenger of God.

7. The Conquest of Canaan. Much of the wilderness period was spent in Kadesh-Barnea, in the desert S. of Canaan, out of reach of the Egyptians (Nu 13²⁶ Dt 1⁴⁶). But meanwhile events had been making possible the invasion of Canaan. Many alien races, amongst them the pirates from the West known to us as the Philistines, had been sweeping down on Palestine. Ramses III, in a great expedition, reasserted the Egyptian power, but this was the last intervention of Egypt for some centuries. Egypt lost Syria, which now became the home of many independent city states, and the way was open for a resolute assault upon the Land of Promise. The first campaigns were on the E. of the Jordan, where an Amorite kingdom had been established, with its capital at Heshbon. Its king, Sihon, was defeated and slain, and his territory occupied (Nu 21²¹⁻²⁵). Moses having now died was succeeded by Joshua, and with the passage of the Jordan opposite to Jericho the invasion was begun (Josh 1–3). Combining the accounts in Joshua with those in Jg 1 (see the Commentary), we gather that the people, by united victories under Joshua, gained a foothold in the land. After his death, since much remained unconquered, expeditions were undertaken by separate tribes, Judah and Simeon, Joseph, Zebulun, Asher, Naphtali, and Dan (Jg 1). In the end the maritime cities of Phœnicia and Philistia remained independent, and strong fortresses such as Taanach, Megiddo, Bethshean (1²⁷), secured to their former inhabitants the richest inland plain, the valley of the Kishon, while such citadels as Ajalon (1³⁵), Jebus (1²¹), and Gezer (1²⁹) shut off Judah and Simeon almost completely from the rest of the Israelites. The recent explorations of Palestine have proved conclusively the truth of this representation, since they make it clear that the development of these Canaanite cities went on unbrokenly for nearly two centuries after the invasion. Proofs of this statement must be sought in the many publications of the Palestine Exploration Fund.

8. The Period of the Judges. The date assigned to the exodus reduces this period to less than 200 years, seeing that it closes about 1050

B.C. (see Intro. to the book of Judges). The deliverances achieved by Deborah and Barak (Jg 4, 5) and by Gideon (Jg 6–8), show that the people still rallied to the name of Jehovah. Nevertheless the religion of the conquered country exercised a powerful influence over the victors. Many altars standing on high places, formerly consecrated to local deities, were now adapted to the worship of Jehovah. This became the fruitful source of many later evils, as the writings of the prophets so clearly show. Still, on the whole, Ewald's statement remains true : 'The people learned by perpetual struggle to defend valiantly their new home and the free exercise of their religion, and were thereby preparing for coming generations a sacred place, where that religion and national culture might unfold itself freely and fully.' Deborah's Song (Jg 5), admitted generally as a product of this age (see Commentary *in loco*), is a striking proof both of the national consciousness of unity, and of the vigour of the true faith in Jehovah. The period closes with the oppression of the Philistines. This bold and warlike race, much resembling the Danes in the early history of England, were greatly superior in military art to the Hebrews. They seem to have conceived the idea of subduing to their sway the whole of Israel. Shamgar (3³¹) and Samson (12 f.) were popular heroes who by single-handed deeds of daring destroyed many marauding bands. But the Hebrews were quite unable to resist an organised attack. With the loss of the sacred ark at Aphek near Mizpah (1 S 4), the doom of the nation seemed sealed. The Philistine rule was extended over the whole centre and south of Israel, their head-quarters were established at Geba in Benjamin, even the use of military weapons is said to have been forbidden to the Israelites (1 S 13³, ¹⁹⁻²³).

9. Samuel and the Founding of the Kingdom. In this crisis there arose a man who has a double claim to honour, as the first of the order of prophets, and as the founder of the monarchy. The narratives about Samuel are, as the Commentary shows, derived from sources of unequal value. His victories (1 S 7¹³) cannot have been nearly so decisive as one source represents them. In a time of great national humiliation he was led to see that a king was needful to weld the disorganised tribes into a whole, so as to enable them to face their enemies. In his patriotic aims he was seconded by the wandering bands of prophets, who were enthusiastic adherents of Jehovah. This resort to a monarchy, though not ideal (1 S 8), was in the situation the only wise choice. In Saul, a Benjamite of great personal prowess, the destined leader was found. After a brilliant feat of arms, by which Jabesh-Gilead was rescued from the Ammonites (1 S 11), he succeeded in rallying to himself all the tribes (11 14, 15). Saul's reign was an almost continuous struggle against the Philistines. Starting from the E. he gradually regained the highlands of Judah and the centre of Palestine (1 S 14, 17, etc.). At the close of his reign, weakened by his quarrel with David, and with his mind clouded by his recurring melancholia, he died in battle on Mt. Gilboa, in the plain of Jezreel, a fact which shows that the Philistines had again penetrated into central Israel (1 S 31). The date of this battle is about 1017 B.C.

10. The Reign of David. After a seven years' interval, during which David reigned as king of Judah at Hebron, and Saul's adherents made Mahanaim, across the Jordan, their centre (2 S 2 4, 8, 11), the murder of Ishbosheth (2 S 4 5-7) opened the way for David's accession as king of a united people (2 S 5 1-3). His reign is marked by the complete conquest of the Philistines, who henceforth play little further part in the history (2 S 5 17-25 8 1), by conquests over the surrounding peoples, which marked the real foundation of an Israelite empire (8 2-14 and c. 10), and by the capture of Jerusalem, and the transference thither of the ark (2 S 5 6-10 6 12-19). At this time Assyria was weak, the northern empire of the Hittites had disappeared, and Egypt was divided and powerless. All this explains the rapid growth under David and Solomon.

11. Solomon. Solomon's reign was marked by the building of the Temple, and great commercial prosperity; but his attempts to reduce the free yeomen of Israel to the status of the subjects of an Oriental king caused deep dissatisfaction, and was one main cause of the disruption as soon as his strong hand was removed (1 K 4 21-28 5 13 11 26, etc.).

12. Religion in the Early Monarchy. The religious conditions of this period may be gathered from many scattered notices. The strict law of the central sanctuary, which afterwards concentrated all sacrificial worship at Jerusalem, was unknown. Samuel sacrificed at Mizpah (1 S 7 9), built an altar at Ramah (7 17), sacrificed on the high place there (9 12), also at Gilgal (11 15), and at Bethlehem (16 5). We may gather from 14 35 that Saul built more than one altar to Jehovah in token of his loyalty. So in 20 6 there is a most natural reference to the yearly sacrifice for Jesse's family at Bethlehem. The simple and unforced way in which these notices are given shows that they are not dealing with exceptions, but relating the normal practice : see on Ex 20 24. At the same time prophets such as Nathan maintained the moral character of the claims of Jehovah, and were treated with the utmost respect (2 S 12 1-15). With the founding of David's kingdom the hope was raised of the perpetual kingdom of Jehovah, which plays so great a part in the writings of the later prophets (2 S 7 1-17).

13. Disruption of the Kingdom, 937 B.C. With the disruption of the kingdom after Solomon's death Judah was left relatively small and insignificant, and was further weakened by the invasion of Shishak of Egypt (1 K 14 25, 26). Egyptian lists in the temple of Amon at Karnak record this raid. From the fact that Ephraimite cities also are said to have paid tribute, it is supposed that for a time both Israel and Judah became tributary to Egypt; but there is no record of any warlike operations against Northern Israel. For a time the two kingdoms were at war, Israel being the stronger. A fateful step was taken when Asa, king of Judah, invited the help of Benhadad, king of Syria, against Baasha (1 K 15 18-21), circ. 900 B.C. The condemnation of this action (2 Ch 16 7-9) is fully justified, as it resulted in the first invasion of Israelite territory by Syrian armies. After repeated revolutions, a strong dynasty was founded by Omri, 889 B.C. (1 K 16 23-28). Omri built Samaria as his capital. Under him peace was made between Israel and Judah, and the royal houses were afterwards allied by marriage. The Moabite Stone, with Mesha's inscription, shows that he subjugated Moab. References to him on Assyrian monuments prove that he was regarded as the founder of the kingdom of Israel. The silence of the Bible narratives as to the more brilliant exploits of his reign is a striking illustration of the indifference of the Hebrew writers to purely secular interests.

14. Jehovah or Baal. In the reign of Ahab, Omri's son, came the great conflict between Elijah and the priests of Baal. As a matter of state policy Jeroboam had erected golden bull-shaped images of Jehovah at Bethel and at Dan. The official religion of the Northern Kingdom was therefore a corrupted form of the worship of Jehovah. It is precarious to argue, as is often done, that Elijah's silence, so far as our records go, as to this bull-worship, is a proof that he found nothing offensive in it. The higher conscience of Israel was always against any form of image-worship. Even in Northern Israel there were probably altars where the purer worship of Jehovah was maintained : cp. Elijah's complaint 1 K 19 10, and his action 1 K 18 30. But when Ahab's Phœnician wife Jezebel, princess of Zidon, sought to establish the worship of the Tyrian Baal and persecuted the adherents of Jehovah (1 K 16 31-33 18 4), Elijah came forward as the champion of Jehovah. The question was no longer that of a pure or debased worship of Jehovah, but the life and death alternative—Jehovah or Baal. This explains the relentless severity with which Elijah pushed home his victory (1 K 18⁴⁰), and the part taken by Elisha in instigating the revolution which resulted in the overthrow of Omri's house and the accession of Jehu (2 K 9).

15. The Syrian Wars. This time of religious conflict was marked by long-continued wars with Syria, which had lasted since the invasion referred to during the reign of Baasha. The kings of Israel appear to have been reduced to the position of vassals (1 K 20³), and in 854 B.C. Benhadad of Syria, with Ahab, who is said by the monuments to have furnished a contingent of 2,000 chariots and 10,000 men, was defeated at Karkar, near Hamath, by Shalmaneser II of Assyria. Afterwards Ahab succeeded in asserting his independence against Syria, and won several victories (1 K 20). Syria at this time was weakened by successive Assyrian campaigns against Damascus, in 850, 849, and 846. In 842 Shalmaneser received tribute from Jehu (see the Black Obelisk of Shalmaneser in the British Museum), and in 839 again defeated Hazael of Damascus. At this point an insurrection in Assyria, headed by Shalmaneser's son, who drove that king to take refuge in North Babylonia, gave Syria a respite and enabled the kingdom to recover its strength. Repeated invasions of Israel followed, reducing the people to the last extremity (2 K 10³², 13³⁻⁷ 14²⁶). Then, under Ramman-Nirari of Assyria (812–783), Damascus was once more subdued, and under Joash and Jeroboam II the lost prestige of Israel was recovered, and all the captured territory regained (2 K 13²⁵ 14²⁵⁻²⁸). In these victories Elisha appears as a watchful and fearless patriot (2 K 13¹⁴⁻²⁰). Thus in the reign of Jeroboam II (782–741) Israel enjoyed a period of prosperity which had had no parallel since the days of Solomon.

The legitimate succession in the Southern Kingdom, which had acted as the ally of Israel both against Syria and Moab (1 K 22 2 K 3), was interrupted by the usurpation of Athaliah (2 K 11), but restored through Jehoiada (11⁴ᶠ.). Amaziah, breaking the alliance with Israel, was disastrously defeated by Joash (14⁸⁻¹⁴). But under Uzziah (790–749) Judah recovered her position, and defeated the Philistines (2 Ch 27⁶), whilst the army was reorganised (27¹³,¹⁴), and frontier towers built as barriers against the desert nomads (27¹⁰).

16. The Decadence of Israel. With the death of Jeroboam the Northern Kingdom's brief period of prosperity passed away. Repeated revolutions weakened the strength of Israel (2 K 15¹⁰⁻¹⁴). Meanwhile, under Tiglath-pileser III (called Pul in 2 K 15¹⁹), Assyria resumed her aggressive policy, and Menahem of Israel became tributary to him (15¹⁹,²⁰). In 734–3 Pekah of Israel, in alliance with Rezin of Syria, invaded Judah, apparently to coerce Judah to join a coalition against Assyria (2 K 15³⁷ 16⁵ Isa 7). Judah was saved by the intervention of Assyria, and Northern Israel devastated (2 K 15²⁹). Pekah's murderer, Hoshea, was recognised as a vassal king by Tiglath-pileser (so the monuments). But Hoshea's intrigues with So of Egypt (17⁴) brought speedy retribution. Shalmaneser IV marched into Israel, but died during the siege of Samaria. His work was completed by his successor, Sargon, and in 722 Samaria was captured and the Northern Kingdom finally destroyed.

17. The Teaching of the Prophets. A bright light is thrown on this period by the utterances of Amos and Hosea. Amos, appearing in Jeroboam's reign, reasserted with tremendous force that the moral claims of Jehovah extended not only over Israel, but over the surrounding peoples. Utterly repudiating the ritual worship of Bethel, he declared the approaching ruin of the nation. The one hope that he saw for the future was in the restoration, after heavy chastisement, of the kingdom under a Davidic king (9¹¹: see Commentary *in loco*).

Hosea, whose ministry lay in the dark days after Jeroboam's death, and whose tragic personal history is the key to his message (see Commentary), sounds another note, but repeats Amos's prophecy of doom. He treats the bull-worship as sheer idolatry : ' of their silver and their gold have they made them idols ' (8⁴). The fact that it is the love rather than the righteousness of God which Hosea emphasises only makes his threatenings more terrible ; yet beyond the storm he also sees the abiding kingdom of God, and believes in its permanence (3⁵, etc.).

The importance of the testimony of these two prophets is supreme. They come forward not as innovators, but as restorers of the ancient faith. Their teaching is in essence one with that of Moses ; but the boldness with which they present Jehovah as the God of the universe, and their unwavering conviction that no past privileges can save Israel from the consequences of her breaches of the law of righteousness, broaden and deepen the foundations of the true religion. It must be said that it is extremely hard to believe, as is suggested, that Hosea was the first to denounce the image-worship of Jehovah. At any rate, he shows not the slightest consciousness that he is making any new declaration when he says of the calf in Samaria, ' The workman made it, and it is no god ' (8⁶).

18. Judah during the Assyrian Period. With the fall of Northern Israel Judah was left dependent for its existence on Assyria. Despite the protests of Isaiah, Ahaz freely imitated both the customs and religion of the conquerors (2 K 16 10-18). His son, Hezekiah (720–692 B.C.), succeeded to a troubled inheritance. In the south the Ethiopian kings of Egypt were growing in strength, and sought alliance with him. This policy was strongly denounced by Isaiah (30 1-7, 31 1-4), who counselled entire abstention from world-politics and simple trust in Jehovah. Hezekiah, however, pursued the policy of alliances. He carried on negotiations with Merodach-Baladan (2 K 20 12-19), who from 721–710 B.C. had succeeded in establishing himself in Babylon, formed a league against Assyria with Tyre, Sidon, Ashkelon, and Ekron, and looked for help from Egypt. The victorious advance of Sennacherib, Sargon's successor, broke up this coalition. Egypt was defeated at El-tekeh, near Ekron, and Hezekiah, after the loss of forty-six cities and many subjects, only secured the safety of Jerusalem by the payment of a huge-ransom (2 K 18 14-16). The Bible narratives that follow are extremely confusing. In the monuments nothing is said of any disaster to Sennacherib's army, and some have conjectured that this happened in a later, unrecorded campaign ; yet the fact that Jerusalem remained untaken needs explanation. The most probable explanation is, that after receiving Hezekiah's ransom, a section of the Assyrian army returned and treacherously demanded the surrender of the city ; then the main body, lying on the borders of Egypt, was smitten with plague, and Sennacherib retired to his own land. This deliverance (701 B.C.) was foretold by Isaiah (31 5 37 33-35), who held that Jerusalem, God's own city, could not be taken.

19. The Religious Teaching of Micah and Isaiah. Two prophets throw light on this period. Micah the countryman, denouncing fiercely the social wrongs of the peasantry, prophesied the downfall of Jerusalem (3 12) ; yet he believed in the permanence of the divine rule, and looked for another king like David to come from the heart of the people and restore the ruined state (5 2 f.).

Isaiah looked for repeated punishments, from which only a remnant should escape (6 11-13, etc.: cp. the name of his son Shear-jashub = 'a remnant shall return,' 7 3). Yet his hope of a better kingdom is borne witness to by his prophecy of Immanuel (7 13-16), and the magnificent promise of the Prince with the four names (9 6,7), who will reign in an age of millennial peace and blessing, and who is called 'a shoot out of the stock of Jesse' (11 1-10).

In Hezekiah's reign partial attempts were made to destroy the high places and concentrate the worship at Jerusalem, but the work must have been very incomplete (2 K 18 4-22, etc.).

20. The Reaction under Manasseh. Manas-

seh's long reign (692–641 B.C.), though for the most part externally prosperous, was marked by a recrudescence of heathenism, in which much of Isaiah's work was undone (2 K 21 1-17). Towards the close of his reign he appears to have become involved in the revolt against Assyria of the viceroy of Babylon, and to have been taken to Babylon to expiate his crime before his suzerain, Assurbanipal (2 Ch 33 11-13).

The survival of the true faith is witnessed to by the book of Deuteronomy, probably compiled during this reign, and possibly by the last two chapters of Micah (see Commentary).

21. The Reign of Josiah. Josiah (639–608), succeeding his murdered father Amon, began his reign under unfavourable auspices. The invasion of Western Asia by hordes of Scythians probably gave rise to the gloomy anticipations of Zephaniah, who looked for the coming of the day of universal judgment. But these invasions, seriously shaking the power of Assyria, really left Judah free to follow her own destiny. The first prophecies of Jeremiah belong also to this period (see Commentary). An earnest attempt at religious reform was greatly helped by the providential finding of the Book of the Law, 621 B.C., almost certainly Deuteronomy (2 K 22 8, etc.). On the basis of this book all the high places where Jehovah was worshipped with semi-heathenish accompaniments were destroyed, and the Temple at Jerusalem made the one central sanctuary (2 K 23 4-15).

Meanwhile Assyria was tottering to its fall, and, while Nineveh was besieged by Babylonians and Medes, Pharaoh-Necho of Egypt marched northwards to make his bid for the empire of the world. In resisting his progress Josiah was defeated and slain at Megiddo, 608 B.C. (2 K 23 29, 30). In the following year Nineveh fell, and by his defeat of the Egyptians at Carchemish, on the Euphrates, Nebuchadrezzar of Babylon became master of the world, 605 B.C. During the brief period of Egyptian supremacy in Palestine Jehoahaz was deposed and Jehoiakim made king (2 K 24 31-35). Rebelling against Babylon three years later Jehoiakim was deposed and carried to Babylon (2 K 24 1 2 Ch 36 6). Three months later his successor Jehoiachin was taken after him, together with the flower of the nation, including Ezekiel, 597 B.C. (2 K 24 8-16).

The prophetic teaching during this period is found in Nahum, with his fierce exultation over the doom of Nineveh, and Habakkuk, who looking out over a ruined world and finding each successive conqueror equally guilty, yet declares with invincible assurance, 'the just man shall live by his faithfulness' (2 4). The central part of Jeremiah's heroic ministry also falls here.

22. The Fall of Jerusalem. Rejecting warnings of Jeremiah, Zedekiah, the last king of Judah, involved himself in many plots against Babylon (Jer 27 1-11 Ezk 17 15). The inevitable result followed. Jeremiah had long since foretold the destruction of Jerusalem and almost paid the price of his daring with his life (Jer 26). Now, after a siege of nineteen months, from January 588 to July 586, the city was taken and destroyed by Nebuchadrezzar, and the Temple burnt (2 K 25).

Jeremiah's noble personality is the chief glory of these closing years. Despite his repeated declarations of the ruin of Jerusalem, he looks forward to the time when once more it shall be 'the throne of Jehovah' (3 17). Despite his word about Jehoiakim, 'no man of his seed shall prosper, sitting upon the throne of David, and ruling any more in Judah' (22 30), he can still hope that Jehovah will raise up a righteous branch unto David (23 5). His hope in the kingdom of God was deeper than his despair. But his grandest word of all came, as it seems, from his prison. There, while the Babylonian armies surrounded Jerusalem, he was inspired to speak of the new covenant, which God Himself would write on the hearts of the people, when all from the least to the greatest should know Him, and, pardoned and restored, enjoy His favour (31 31-34).

Thus this great history closes with a note of hope, and a conception of religion that, far below all externalism, rests on the personal and intimate relationship between the individual soul and its God. Though the hopes of the prophets of a glorious kingdom in Jerusalem under a righteous Ruler were never realised, they have been fulfilled in a far deeper sense than those who uttered them ever dreamed by the King whose kingdom is 'not of this world,' who sealed the new covenant with His own blood. So we claim that the faith of the prophets, embodied in many forms and figures, has outlived them all and is triumphant in the world to-day. Jesus took the faith which they held, ennobled it and purged it, and through His life and death established a kingdom which will never pass away. Looking backwards we see that all history is one, knit together by the guiding, inspiring controlling Spirit of God. Looking forward we believe still, with more assured faith than ever, in the perfect establishment of that kingdom so long desired, so wistfully looked for, against which the gates of hell shall not prevail.

INTRODUCTION TO THE PENTATEUCH

1. Divisions and Contents. *Pentateuch* is a Greek word meaning the 'fivefold volume,' and has been used since the time of Origen (third century A.D.) as a convenient designation for the first five books of the Old Testament. It serves to remind us that these constitute really one volume in five parts. In the Old Testament itself this is called 'The Law,' or 'book of the Law,' to which is sometimes added 'of God' or 'of Moses': see e.g. Neh 8 1, 2 f. 9 3 13 1. Later Jewish writers call it the 'book of the Law,' or the 'Five Fifths of the Law.' In Hebrew manuscripts the division into five books is not so strongly marked as in the English Bible, the Pentateuch being treated as one and divided into a number of larger and smaller sections, which are numbered consecutively from Genesis to Deuteronomy. The five larger sections are usually named by the first word or first important word in each. Thus Genesis is called *B'reshith*, i.e. 'In the Beginning'; Exodus is *Shemoth*, i.e. 'Names'; Leviticus is *Vayyikra*, i.e. 'And He called'; Numbers is *Vay'dabber*, i.e. 'And He spake,' or, *Bammidbar*, i.e. 'In the Wilderness'; and Deuteronomy is *D'barim*, i.e. 'Words.' Sometimes titles more particularly descriptive of their contents are applied to the books; thus Leviticus is styled the 'Law of the Priests,' Numbers the 'Fifth' (part) 'of Numberings,' and Deuteronomy the 'Second Law.' The English titles are taken from the Vulgate Latin Version, which again derived them from the Septuagint. The fivefold division of the Pentateuch is thus shown to be earlier than the origin of the Septuagint, and is probably as old as the time of Nehemiah. It is older than the division of the Psalter, which was arranged in five books on the model of the Pentateuch.

As the book of Joshua displays a certain affinity with the Pentateuch both in spirit and literary style, and forms its natural continuation and complement, modern scholars speak of a Hexateuch, or 'sixfold volume,' and regard the books from Genesis to Joshua as six parts of a complete whole.

For details of the **Contents of the Pentateuch** reference should be made to the introductions prefixed to the separate books in the Commentary. It will suffice here to say that they are made up of two elements, history and legislation. The theme is the Kingdom of God upon the earth, and its gradual revelation and embodiment in Israel as the chosen people, both in its external (historical) and internal (legislative) aspects. The Song of Moses (Dt 32) and such Psalms as 105, 106 may be regarded as giving a summary of this history. From the way in which the Pentateuch opens it might have been supposed that its aim was to outline the history of the whole human race. But it soon appears that the account of the creation of the world, the entrance of sin, and the rise and spread of the races, is only preliminary to the main subject. Little by little the history is narrowed down till at Gn 12 we come to Abraham, who is chosen as the progenitor of the people to whom God will specially reveal Himself. From this point the Pentateuch, and indeed the entire Old Testament, becomes a history of the Hebrew nation. In the third generation from Abraham his descendants to the number of seventy, with their households, migrate from Canaan to Egypt. There they increase in spite of all obstacles till they become a great nation. The book of Exodus tells of their deliverance from Egypt by the hand of Moses. They come into the Sinaitic peninsula on their way to the promised land, and there they enter into a solemn covenant with Jehovah on the basis of the Law given to them at Mount Sinai. Practically the whole of Leviticus is occupied with legislation, the purpose of which is to mark this nation off from all others as the 'peculiar people' of Jehovah, a 'kingdom of priests' and a 'holy nation.' The book of Numbers continues the history of the sojourn in the wilderness, until they come to the borders of Canaan, and is interspersed with numerous laws. Deuteronomy contains the discourses addressed to the people by Moses before his death. It consists largely of laws, and closes with an account of the solitary death of the great leader and Lawgiver. The book of Joshua relates the entrance into Canaan, and its conquest by the Israelites under the leadership of Joshua, the successor of Moses.

2. The Mosaic Authorship. The question of the authorship of the Pentateuch, or rather of the Hexateuch, has been the subject of much discussion in modern times, and scholars are still carefully investigating the subject. The traditional view was that Moses was the author of the five books which bear his name in our Bibles; and until comparatively recent times this belief was accepted without question or inquiry regarding its grounds. A thorough study of these books, however, has led many to the conclusion that this view of their authorship does not fit in with the facts, and that another view is necessitated by the evidence which the books themselves present.

Two arguments are often brought forward for the Mosaic authorship which demand some notice. (*a*) One is the fact that our Lord when quoting the Pentateuch refers to it as the work of Moses: cp. Mt 19 8 Mk 7 10 12 26 Lk 24 44 Jn 5 45-47 7 19. Regarding this it has sometimes been pointed out that these references by our Lord do not compel us to believe that Moses wrote the whole of the Pentateuch, but only that certain parts of it were derived from him, which indeed many of the foremost scholars admit. But another answer may be given, and that is that our Lord did not come to deal with questions of literary authorship, but to bring men salvation ; that He appeals to the Pentateuch entirely for the practical purposes of quickening men's consciences and reproving their sins ; and that He called it the Law of Moses because that was the name by which it was commonly known. It may be accepted as a guiding principle in the study of the Scriptures, that the subjects of divine revelation are not matters such as biblical authorship or physical processes, which men can discover by the exercise of their faculties, but only those truths of God's love and His purposes of salvation ' which the angels desire to look into.' The force of our Lord's teaching, it is hardly necessary to add, is not affected by the view taken of the authorship of the Pentateuch. (*b*) The other argument for the traditional view is, that Jewish tradition consistently ascribes the composition of the Pentateuch to Moses. With reference to this point it must be remembered that there is no trace of the existence of this tradition until a comparatively late period, and that it is unsupported by any strong evidence. It must also be noted that as a whole the Five Books are anonymously written, and that there is no passage in the Old Testament which claims Moses as their author. The 'Law of Moses' indeed is frequently spoken of, and it is unquestionable that Israelitish law did originate with him ; but this expression is not evidence that Moses was the writer of the Pentateuch as we have it, or that the laws which it contains represent throughout his unmodified legislation. On the other hand, there are parts of these books which are expressly ascribed to him ; e.g. (1) the account of the defeat of Amalek (Ex 17 14); (2) the book of the Covenant, Ex 20–23 (Ex 24 4, 7); (3) the Renewed Covenant, Ex 34 10-26 (cp. Ex 34 27) ; (4) the Lists of Stations on the March in Nu 33 (33 2) ; (5) the law spoken of in Dt 31 9, 11, 24-26 ; (6) the Song of Moses, Dt 32 : cp. also Josh 1 7, 8 8 31, 35 23 6 24 26. These

passages indicate that Moses wrote and laid up for preservation records of certain important events and laws.

It is also to be kept in view that many of the laws preserved in the Pentateuch relate to circumstances which imply a nomadic life in tents, pointing to a period contemporary with Moses: cp. e.g. Lv 14 3 with 14 34 16 20-22 Nu 10 1-7.

There is no difficulty in understanding the rise of the belief in the Mosaic authorship or in sympathising with the feelings which suggested it. Apart from Moses it would be impossible to account for the religion of the Old Testament. It was to him that the decisive creative revelation of Jehovah's nature and His relation to Israel came. It was he who laid the foundations of the ideas, laws, and institutions, which made Israel the nation in which all the families of the earth have been blessed. The later developments of faith, custom, and ritual require him at the beginning as their primary explanation. And if he was thus under God the originator of the beliefs and practices which lie at the root of Old Testament religion, it is difficult to avoid the conclusion that he put into writing some of its laws and some narratives of leading events to guide the conduct and inspire the patriotism of the people whom he had welded into a nation.

On close examination, however, it must be admitted that the Pentateuch reveals many features inconsistent with the traditional view that in its present form it is the work of Moses. For instance, it may be safely granted that Moses did not write the account of his own death in Dt 34. The statement in Dt 1 1 that Moses spoke these words ' beyond (RV) Jordan in the wilderness ' (see note there) is evidently made from the standpoint of one living in Canaan, which Moses never did ; and when we read that the ' Canaanite was then in the land' (Gn 12 6 13 7), and that ' these are the kings that reigned in Edom before there reigned any king over Israel ' (Gn 36 31), it is difficult to resist the impression that the speaker was living in the one case after the conquest, and in the other after the establishment of the monarchy. In Gn 14 14 and Dt 34 mention is made of Dan ; but the territory did not receive that name till it was conquered by the Danites, long after the death of Moses (Josh 19 47 Jg 18 29). Again, in Nu 21 14, 15 there is quoted as an ancient authority ' the book of the Wars of the Lord,' which plainly could not have been earlier than the days of Moses. Other passages which can with difficulty be ascribed to him are Ex 6 26, 27 11 3 16 35, 36 Lv 18 24-28 Nu 12 3 Dt 2 12.

Of course such things do not amount in themselves to a disproof of the Mosaic authorship, but they naturally lead to the question : 'On what authority does this belief rest, that Moses is the author of the Pentateuch in its present form?' And it appears that no authority could be cited except the late tradition of the Jewish Church. Therefore men have thought themselves at liberty to investigate the matter, and a careful examination has led many scholars to the conviction that the writings of Moses formed only the rough material or part of the material, and that in its present form it is not the work of one man, but a compilation made from previously existing documents. In this connexion it must be remembered that editing and compiling is a recognised mode of authorship in Old Testament history. Just as St. Luke tells us (Lk 1 1) that, before our Four Gospels were written, there were many earlier accounts of our Lord's life already in existence, so the Old Testament writers tell us of similar accounts already written of the facts which they record. And not only so, but they distinctly indicate that they used these earlier accounts in composing their own books. It is most interesting to find embedded in the existing books fragments of the old literature of ancient Israel, as geologists find the fragments of the lost animal life of early ages embedded in the rocks of to-day. See, for example, 'the book of the Wars of Jehovah' (Nu 21 14), 'the book of Jasher' (2 S 1 18), 'the books of Gad and Nathan' (1 Ch 29 29), 'the books of Shemaiah and Iddo' (2 Ch 12 15). Here we have evidence of the existence of sources of information to which editors and compilers of later days had access. We find also several ancient poems incorporated in the sacred text, e.g. Gn 4 23 f. Ex 15, 17 16 Nu 21 17, 18, 27 f. Jg 5, etc., and it is probable there were other early writings available besides those which can now be traced. There is thus nothing strange in the suggestion that the books of the Pentateuch were based on preëxisting materials.

3. Composition. The following are the main grounds of the conviction that the Pentateuch is not the original work of one man, but a compilation from previously existing documents.

(1) In the historical parts we find duplicate accounts of the same event, which do not always agree in detail. Sometimes the two accounts are set down side by side ; sometimes they are fused together more or less completely ; but in many instances no attempt has been made either to remove or to reconcile their differences. Thus two distinct and independent accounts of the Creation are given, one in Gn 1–2 4, the other in Gn 2 4-25. Two accounts of the Flood may be detected on a careful reading of Gn 6–9. Again, we find two sets of instructions for the ob-

servance of the Passover in Ex 12, one in vv. 1–13, the other in vv. 21–27. We may also instance the contrasts between such passages as Gn 27 1-45 and 27 46-28 9, where Rebekah is actuated by one motive in the former and by quite another in the latter ; Gn 28 19 and 35 9-15, where the name is given to Bethel in very different circumstances ; Gn 35 10 and 32 28. Compare also Ex 3 1-6 1 with 6 2-7 13, where the latter section takes no account of the former, but begins the story of the mission to Pharaoh anew, as if 3 1-6 1 had never been written.

(2) Similarly in the legislative portions of these books we find apparent contradictions, and these not in minor or insignificant details, but in fundamental enactments ; and the only way in which we can solve the problem thus presented is by understanding that in these books (especially Exodus to Deuteronomy) we have the records of laws laid down at various periods of the national history, and dealing with radically different conditions of life. In Ex 20–23, e.g., we have a set of laws which are evidently suited to the circumstances of an agricultural and pastoral community scattered over a considerable tract of country with their flocks and herds. This legislation is of a very simple and practical nature, based on the fundamental principles of truth and righteousness, and having reference to a primitive state of society. Thus the worship is very simple ; altars are to be built of earth or of rough stones *at any place* where God has blessed them (20 24-26); firstlings and first fruits are to be offered *on the eighth day* (22 28-30); the law of injuries is 'eye for eye, tooth for tooth, life for life' (21 1-21); murder is to be atoned by the death of the culprit, but the altar gives refuge to the homicide by accident (21 12-14); special reference is made to oxen and sheep, to vineyards and fields of corn, and restitution for damage done to these is commanded (21 33-23 7). Again, the poor are provided for by the produce of the fields every seventh year (23 10, 11); the seventh day is appointed as the sabbath—a day of rest for man and beast (23 12); three feasts are to be kept—two of them agricultural—the feast of unleavened bread in memory of the exodus, and those of harvest and ingathering. The laws are suited to the conditions of life experienced by the Israelites in the wilderness, and in their earlier days in Canaan.

In the book of Deuteronomy we find a more advanced type of legislation, applying evidently to different circumstances. Many injunctions, indeed, are repeated, but many others are changed. The principles are the same as in the older legislation, but the rules are largely modified. Deuteronomy is the Mosaic Law applied to the altered conditions of a later and more complex age. Thus the worship is to be *centralised in one place*, and *local* altars are to be abolished (Dt 12⁴⁻⁶, ¹³⁻²⁸), because of abuses that had sprung up in connexion with them ; firstlings are to be offered *once a year* instead of on the eighth day, and in place of the local altars cities of refuge are provided for 'him who killeth his neighbour unawares' (Dt 19²). The conditions of life are different from those in Ex 20–23 ; the people dwell in cities, not in the camp (Dt 13¹²⁻¹⁵ 17² 21⁶, etc.) ; a commercial element has entered into the nation (23¹⁹,²⁰ 25¹³⁻¹⁶), and intercourse with foreigners has brought new dangers to religion (13⁶,⁷ 17³,⁴).

Again, in the book of Leviticus, with parts of Exodus and Numbers, we find another type of legislation, founded still upon the same Mosaic principles, but more elaborate, more priestly, more rigid than that of Ex 20–23 or that of Deuteronomy. Here we find detailed rules for the ritual of the Temple, for the consecration of priests, for many points in ordinary life and conduct. Many of these are found in the other codes ; but many are new (e.g. the feasts in Lv 23), and indicate the result of a long process of development. The worship is highly developed and centralised in the Temple ; the altar is an elaborate structure (Ex 27¹⁻⁸) ; the duties of priests and Levites are carefully detailed, and the Levites are distinguished from the priests as their servants (Nu 8¹⁹ 18¹⁻⁷).

(3) Different parts of the Pentateuch exhibit marked differences of vocabulary and literary style. Many of these differences, especially of vocabulary, can only be appreciated by those acquainted with Hebrew ; but any one can see that the book of Deuteronomy is written in a much more rhetorical style than, say, the book of Leviticus, and can appreciate its lofty and inspiring eloquence. Again, in one set of passages, of which Gn 1–2⁴ is a type, the Almighty is called God (Hebrew *Elohim*), while in another set, of which Gn 2⁴⁻²⁶ is an example, He is designated LORD (Hebrew *Jehovah*) ; and there are many other points of difference which are most satisfactorily explained by the theory that the writer of the Pentateuch, as we have it, made use of and incorporated into his work documents originally separated.

Following up the clue given by these differences, scholars have endeavoured to disentangle the separate documents from which it is suggested that the Pentateuch was compiled, and we shall now give a brief outline of the results of their investigations.

4. Sources.

(*a*) There is first what we may call the Primitive source (itself resting upon older written authorities), usually denoted by the symbol JE. It has sometimes been called the Prophetic document, because it reflects the same ideas found in more developed forms in the writings of the prophets, especially their religious and moral teaching. By some, again, it is styled Pre-prophetic, as earlier in date than the prophets, and simpler in its outlook.

It begins at Gn 2⁴, and may be said to supply all the more detailed and picturesque narratives in Genesis, and Exodus, part of Numbers, and the first twelve chapters of Joshua. To it we owe entirely the narratives of the Fall and Cain and Abel, the details of Abraham's trials and wanderings, of Sodom and Gomorrah, of Isaac and Rebekah, of Jacob's fraud, his journey to Haran and his successful career, and of the life of Joseph. A feature in this Primitive source is its fondness for antiquities. It reaches back into a remote past, and delights to record the traditions and history that centred round the great figures of the race. It is this document that preserves the early legislation already referred to (Ex 20–23) with its permission of local sanctuaries ; that gives us the ten commandments, and that records the ancient songs of Lamech, of Moses, and of the conquering Israelites (Nu 21¹⁴⁻¹⁵,¹⁷⁻¹⁸,²⁷⁻³⁰). It makes use of the term 'Jehovah' for God from the very outset of its narrative. Plausible attempts have been made to analyse it into two components, J and E ; but for these reference must be made to larger works. In any case, the parallel threads are closely allied, and may for our purpose be treated as a unity.

This source presents a very simple, vivid, and picturesque narrative, and is characterised among other things by its naïvely anthropomorphic conception of God, i.e. it speaks of God in language that is strictly appropriate to man only. For example, it represents God as planting a garden and walking in it in the cool of the day (Gn 2⁸ 3⁸), as coming down in order to see what men are doing on the earth (Gn 11⁵ 18²¹), as shutting the door of the ark behind Noah (Gn 7¹⁶), as smelling the sweet odour of sacrifice (Gn 8²¹), and as experiencing the emotions to which men are subject (cp. e.g. Gn 6⁶), etc. This bold way of speaking about God, it may be remarked here, is not due to any irreverence or familiarity, but is the outcome of an intensely religious spirit that is completely possessed by the consciousness of God's immediate presence and power in the world. The Primitive narrative, too, is not careful to conceal the moral faults of the patriarchs. The English reader will form an idea of its style and characteristics from such passages as Gn 2⁴ᵇ–3²⁴ 9²⁰⁻²⁷ 11¹⁻⁹ 18, 19, 20, 22, 24, 27, and practically the whole of the history of Joseph.

It seems probable that the older written authorities underlying this Primitive or Prophetic narrative were drawn up not later than 750 B.C., and perhaps even a century earlier; they themselves in their turn being founded on writings like 'the book of the Wars of the Lord,' and 'the book of Jasher,' as well as on traditions handed down from generation to generation in the tribes of Israel. The early prophets make frequent and confident appeals to events of past history and to promises of God to the fathers which are recorded in this Primitive narrative: cp. Hos 9 10 11 1 12 3, 4, 9, 12 Am 2 9 3 1 5 25.

(b) There is, secondly, the Priestly document (usually designated P). This work is so called because it regards the history of Israel from the priestly point of view, and because it contains the greater part of the priestly and ceremonial legislation in Exodus, Leviticus, and Numbers. It is written in a somewhat dry and formal style, with little descriptive colour or poetic grace; but in parts (e.g. the story of Creation) its diction is dignified and worthy of the subject. It gives an outline of the history of Israel from the earliest times; though this is usually of the slightest, many incidents detailed at length in the Primitive document receiving a bare mention, and long periods being passed over with little more than a list of the names of the leaders who lived at the time: cp. Gn 11 10. It is only when the writer comes to some epoch-making event or to the origin of some well-known institution that he enters into particulars (e.g. Gn 17 1-27 Ex 12 1-20). This writing, however, gives a systematic account of the rise and progress of Israel as a theocracy, paying special attention to the laws and institutions, and showing great interest in everything pertaining to the Ceremonial Law, the division of the nation into tribes, and the partition of the promised land among them (cp. e.g. Nu 1–4 Josh 13 15–14 5 15 1-13, 20-62, and most of 17–22). It abounds in genealogies (e.g. Gn 5 6 9-22 46 6-27), inventories (Ex 25–31), and chronological details (e.g. Gn 11 10 f.). A favourite expression, usually beginning a list, is 'These are the generations of..' (Gn 2 4 5 1 6 9 10 1 11 10 25 12 36 1).

This Priestly document avoids all anthropomorphic representations of God, and in this respect is in striking contrast to the Primitive writing JE, which represents God as thinking and acting like a man: cp. Gn 18, 19 Ex 24 4 f. In P God's revelations take the form, not of visible appearances, but of speech (Gn 1 28 6 13 Ex 6 1 12 1); except on the one occasion of the supreme revelation on Mount Sinai (Ex 24 16 25 22). A feature of its references to God is that it makes use of the name Elohim (God) for God almost exclusively (El Shaddai, Gn 17 1 28 3 35 11 48 3) until Ex 6 3, where God reveals His name Jehovah (the LORD) to Moses. The writer of this document evidently belonged to the priestly class; his aim was entirely a religious one; he sought to show from a sketch of Israel's history that 'God was in the midst of her.'

Scholars are of opinion that this document was drawn up, in the form in which it is embedded in the Pentateuch, for the guidance of the priests and others after the return from the captivity in the days of Ezra. The worship is regarded in it as completely centralised in Jerusalem; the priests are exclusively the descendants of Aaron, and the Levites are distinct from them; the system of sacrifices and feasts is much more developed than even in Deuteronomy (see under (c)); the idea of God is purer and less akin to that of a magnified man. The Priestly document thus exhibits signs of the discipline and purification which the nation experienced in the exile and is appropriately dated at the close of that event.

(c) The third document underlying the Pentateuch (or rather the Hexateuch) is the book of Deuteronomy, usually cited as D, and identified in its main parts with the Law-book discovered in the Temple by Hilkiah in the eighteenth year of King Josiah, 621 B.C. (2 K 22). This book has a strongly marked literary style, being smooth, redundant, and rhetorical: cp. e.g. Dt 11, 12. It insists on the worship of the one God at the one sanctuary, and is characterised by a lofty spiritual, moral, and humanitarian tone. In many respects it differs from the earlier legislation of the Primitive document; but always in matters of detail. Its laws are suited to a later age and to a more complex condition of society than those of JE; the worship is centralised in Jerusalem, because the local shrines had been abused; and the centralisation of the worship necessitated many changes in detail. Thus Deuteronomy, or the Second Legislation, is simply the development of the first; it is the Mosaic principles applied to new conditions. It is animated by the same spirit as the older law, inspired by the same desire for purity of worship, for singleness of heart, for holiness of life.

It is supposed that these three documents— the Primitive writing, the Priestly writing, and the book of Deuteronomy—were welded together somewhat in this way. The first attempts to write a history of Israel probably originated in the schools of the prophets in the ninth century B.C.; and in the Primitive writing JE we have the finished result. About the same time as JE was composed, the Second Legislation (D) was set down in writing and made public as recorded in 2 K 22. This was afterwards combined with the earlier writing, which gave it a historic background. Then during, or immediately after the exile, the ritual law was drawn up in accordance with priestly traditions, and given an appropriate setting in a historical framework, the result being the Priestly writing (P). Finally a later historian, taking these as his authorities, wove them together into a complete whole, connecting them by notes and explanations, where these were necessary; not putting the history in his own words or presenting it from his own standpoint as a modern historian would do, but piecing together the sections of the sources which referred to the same events, and thus preserving not only the history, but the very words in which it had reached him, for all coming generations. In this writer's work we have the Pentateuch of the Old Testament Scriptures.

This, then, is a brief outline of the views held by most scholars who have devoted themselves to the thorough study of these books of the Bible. Such a theory of the composition of the Pentateuch, while it may surprise us at first sight, will give us larger ideas of God's working and inspiration, and will strengthen rather than disturb our faith. For

it will remove many difficulties in the interpretation of these books, and explain those contradictions of which we are all conscious when we read them. When we realise that God did not teach Israel only by Moses, but 'at sundry times and in divers manners' by teachers and leaders whom He inspired according to the work He gave them to perform, we shall have worthier ideas of His government of the world and of His watchful care over His people. The fact that the legislation of the Pentateuch was given not all at one time, but to different generations, according to their circumstances and needs, surely teaches us, as perhaps nothing is better fitted to teach us, that 'He that keepeth Israel neither slumbers nor sleeps.' And the view of the books which scholars suggest to us shows us that His inspiration wrought not through one but through many, and that in every age of Israel's history there were men inspired by the spirit which animated their master, Moses, eager to make known to their fellows how great things God had wrought, and longing to win them to loyalty and devotion to Him who was the God of Abraham and Isaac and Jacob, and who desired still to be their God.

THE CREATION STORY AND SCIENCE

MANY of the difficulties felt in connexion with the Bible story of creation arise from a misunderstanding of the bearing of modern science upon it. A few general considerations, therefore, may help to obviate them.

(a) There is a vague idea in many minds that science demands a much greater antiquity for the world than the Bible account will allow. This impression has probably been gathered from the statement in the margin of many Bibles that creation took place in the year 4004 B.C. It is well, therefore, to be reminded that this marginal note is not a part of the Bible. It originated in calculations, both Jewish and Christian, which are now admitted to have been based upon imperfect knowledge. The sacred writer in Genesis does not commit himself to any definite limits of time, but simply speaks of the creation as taking place 'in the beginning,' and this phrase is elastic enough to cover the modern scientific position.

(b) Another difficulty is caused by the apparent antagonism between modern scientific theories and the statement of Gn 1 that the work of creation was completed in six days. Attempts have been made, from several points of view, to get rid of this antagonism, by taking the language of Scripture in a figurative sense. For example, it has been suggested by some that the sublime panorama of creation was flashed into some primeval prophet's consciousness in a series of visions that occupied a space of six days ; and by others that the days are not to be interpreted as natural days of twenty-four hours each, but as age-long periods of time corresponding to the successive stages in the evolution of the world. Whatever truth there may be in these suggestions, and however helpful they may be to many minds, others may be able to obtain a more satisfactory rendering of the Bible account of creation, by looking at it in the light of the three following considerations. (1) The story was written in the very childhood of our race, when human knowledge was only at the dawn, and men's minds were awakening for the first time to the problems of life and the world. It was inevitable, therefore, that it should be cast in a simple and childlike form, if it was to be at all intelligible to those among whom it appeared ; and the wisdom of giving it such a setting has been more than justified by the impression it has left, and still continues to make, upon the thought of the world. (2) It is now widely admitted that the Genesis account of creation contains elements of belief which existed, perhaps thousands of years before the book of Genesis was written, among the peoples of Babylonia and Assyria. The connexion between the traditions of these early nations and the story of Genesis is still a matter of discussion, but one thing has emerged clearly from their comparison. Whatever elements the sacred writer in Genesis may have in common with the Babylonian and Assyrian beliefs, he has been able to redeem and purify them from their baser form, and invest them with the presence and power of a Sovereign God, the one only Creator of heaven and earth. (3) The purpose of the writer in Gn 1 is not scientific but religious. His scientific knowledge may be bounded by the horizon of the age in which he lived, but the religious truths he teaches are irrefutable and eternal. To put the matter in another way : The scientific account of creation has been written by the finger of God upon the crust of the earth, and men are slowly spelling it out ; but the religious account of creation is written in the first chapter of Genesis, in letters that all can read. Both accounts are from God, and should be received accordingly. As Dr. Marcus Dods has said : ' The greatest mistake is made when men seek in the one record what can only be found in the other, when they either refuse to listen to the affirmations of nature because they seem to disagree with what is found in the Bible, or when they are content with the teaching of nature, as if nature could tell us all we need to know about ourselves, about the world, and about God.' What was necessary in the primitive world to save men from grovelling, debasing polytheism was the knowledge that it was God, holy and good, who made all things, and that the crown and summit of His work was man ; and this is the knowledge set forth in the book of Genesis. The real question for us is then : ' Does the story of Genesis so accomplish what seems to be its purpose, that only inspiration from God can account for it ?' To ask : 'Is it a completely scientific account of creation?' is to raise an issue that is scarcely fair.

(c) These considerations must be kept in mind, for they are equally helpful, in dealing with the further difficulty that has arisen in connexion with the theory of evolution, and the marvellous discoveries with which it has been associated. Science is now teaching that the order and beauty of the world are not the result of one directly creative act, but the outcome of a long and gradual process, continued probably over myriads of years ; and that the varied life of nature is not as it was fixed 'in the beginning,' but as it has been evolved, through age-long periods and many lower stages, from original germs. On the face of it, this teaching seems to conflict with the teaching of the Bible, and in particular to throw suspicion upon the story of creation as given in Genesis. It was thus it was received at first ; but in recent years, as men have gone back to the old creation story, and pondered it afresh, in view of the teaching of science, their difficulties and perplexities have largely disappeared. Besides making allowances for the considerations already urged under (b), they have come to see that creation would be just as divine and miraculous, if it were slow and gradual, as it would be if it were sudden and complete. The power necessary to originate and support a ceaseless and prolonged process of development in the world would be no less than that required to bring it into being in a moment, and sustain it in its ordered course. Doubtless, God could instantaneously make a mighty oak ; but it is no less wonderful that He should make it gradually, causing it to grow out of the little acorn, of which we can carry a dozen in the hand, yet every one of which contains within it a germ endued with power to carry on a succession of mighty oaks through ages to come. To realise this is to advance a long way in the solution of the difficulty arising from the theory of evolution, and rob it of its power to disturb a genuine faith in the Bible. A further reflection, however, may be called in to support the mind of the biblical believer. Not only is evolution itself only a theory, which may in the future undergo modification, and may possibly be displaced by some other theory, but even if it is a true and final account of the origin of created things, the old creation story of Genesis is, to say the least, not incompatible with it. The process of creation, as unfolded in Genesis, when viewed in the light of the new scientific teaching, reveals a law of continuous development, which is at least a foreshadowing of the process of evolution. And so the apparent irreconcilability between them becomes largely reduced, if it does not indeed altogether disappear. 'These,' we read, 'are the generations of the heavens when they were created.' 'The inspired historian saw no Almighty hand building up the galleries of creation : he heard no sound of hammer nor confused noise of workmen : the Spirit of the Lord moved upon the face of the deep : chaos took form and comeliness before his inspired vision : and the solar system grew through a succession of days to its present order and beauty.' At last, when all things were ready—after how many myriads of years we know not—man came forth, the summit of the whole creation, for 'God breathed into his nostrils the breath of life, and he became a living soul.'

GENESIS AND THE BABYLONIAN INSCRIPTIONS

DURING the last thirty years a considerable amount of light has been thrown on the first few chapters of Genesis by the recovery and interpretation of an extensive Babylonian literature. The Assyrian king, Assurbanipal, who reigned in the middle of the seventh century B.C., caused copies of immense numbers of documents from other libraries in the country to be made for his library at Nineveh, some of these writings dating from many hundred years earlier. They comprised works on religion, history, mathematics, law, magic, and astronomy. The copies, like the originals, were on tablets of fine clay, inscribed, whilst in a soft state, with wedge-shaped (cuneiform) characters, and then burned in a furnace till they became hard and dry. These clay tablets are of all sizes, from an inch to more than a foot long, and the museums of Europe and America now possess thousands of them, derived from Assurbanipal's library and other places. Excavations are still being carried on, with the result that every year sees a large addition to the recovered treasures. In 1872 Mr. George Smith discovered on some of the tablets, which may now be seen in the British Museum, accounts of the Creation and the Flood, written from the religious standpoint of the Babylonians. Many similarities were at once observed between them and the early chapters of Genesis. This will not cause surprise, for the Hebrew and Babylonian peoples were allied branches of the great Semitic race, and it was natural that their ideas respecting the origin of the world, and their traditions as to its primitive history, should have much in common. But these Babylonian records, which have thrown so much light on the character of the early narratives of Genesis, have at the same time done more than anything else to confirm the real divine inspiration of the latter, and their peculiar religious worth. The biblical narratives, when compared with these kindred legends, present differences which are even more striking than the resemblances. And it is these differences which reveal their spiritual value. The Babylonian stories are full of grotesque and polytheistic ideas, while those of the Bible speak only of the one living and true God. Compared with the former, the Scriptures are incomparably truer and grander from a religious point of view. They conveyed to the Hebrews, and they still convey to us, the worthiest conceptions of God and of His relation to the world and

men. They are a standing witness to the fact that the nation of Israel enjoyed a peculiar revelation of the true God. If the 'folk-lore' of the Hebrews, like that of all other peoples, was inconsistent at many points with our modern knowledge of nature and history, yet it was so purified among them, under the guidance of the Spirit of God, from all taint of heathenism, that, as it stands in the opening chapters of Genesis, it contains nothing inconsistent either with the religion of Jehovah or with the fuller revelation of Jesus Christ.

1. The Babylonian Account of the Creation. Two Babylonian legends of the Creation are known. The longer and more important is inscribed on seven tablets, some of which are imperfect. According to it, all things were produced at the first from Tiamat, a personification of the primeval chaos, represented as a huge dragon. The gods came into being in a long succession, but at length enmity arose between them and Tiamat, who created monsters to oppose them. Merodach, a solar deity, known also as Bel, and regarded as the supreme god and patron deity of Babylon, was chosen as the champion of the gods. He vanquished Tiamat, cut her body in two, and with one half of it made a firmament supporting the upper waters in the sky: see on Gn 1 6-8. Merodach then fixed the signs of the zodiac in the sky as the stations of the great gods, and also placed the moon in the heavens to determine the months. The next part of the tablets is mutilated, but describes the creation of the heavens. The seventh tablet contains a hymn to Merodach.

The following are a few passages from the Babylonian Creation epic, extracted mainly from T. G. Pinches' translation—

' When, above, the heaven was not named,
Beneath, the earth did not record a name,
The ocean (*Apsu*) the primeval was their begetter,
The tumult Tiamat was mother of them all,
Their waters in one united together.
Then were the gods born,
Lahmu Lahamu came forth,
Ansar, the god Anu ' . . .

The rest is fragmentary.

The second, third, and fourth tablets describe the conflict between Merodach and Tiamat. The victory of the former appears to signify the conquest of light and order over darkness and chaos. Then follows the formation of the firmament from the body of

Tiamat and creation of the heavens, as a habitation for the gods—

'He cleft her like a fish into two parts,
The half of her he set up and made a covering for the heaven,
Set a bar before it, and stationed a watchman,
Commanding him not to let the waters escape.'
'Then Bel (i.e. Merodach) measured the extent of the abyss,
A palace he founded in its likeness, Esarra ;
The palace Esarra which he made (is) the heavens,
A habitation for Anu, Bel, and Ea.'

The fifth tablet describes the creation and arrangement of the heavenly bodies.

'He (Merodach) made stations for the great gods,
Stars their likeness—he set up the Zodiac,
He ordained the year, defined divisions,
Twelve months, each with three stars, he appointed,
He caused the moon to shine, ruling the night : ' etc.

In spite of certain obvious parallelisms of thought, the first chapter of Genesis, it will be be seen, is greatly superior to the Babylonian account of the beginning of the world. It has a striking symmetry of arrangement, and a simple dignity which contrasts favourably with the childish and grotesque elements of the other narrative. But, above all, its religious teaching differs from that of the Babylonian story as day from night. Here we have no multitude of divinities, but one living and true God. Here we have no primeval matter from which the gods arise, but 'In the beginning, God.' Here the heavenly bodies are not deities to be worshipped, but the handiwork of God. Here man is at the head of creation, because he shares the image of God.

2. The Babylonian Flood Legend bears more directly upon the narrative of Genesis. One version of it has been preserved by Berosus ; but it is now known to us in a fuller and more authentic form, from the series of cuneiform tablets discovered in the library of Assurbanipal. These tablets contain an ancient Babylonian epic, the hero of which is Gilgamesh, whose adventures are related in twelve books. The eleventh book tells how Gilgamesh visited the deified hero Ut-napistim (or Pir-napistim), and heard from him the story of the flood and of his deliverance from it. The four gods, Anu ('Lord of the ocean of heaven'), Bel ('Lord of the air'), Ninip ('the god of man'), and Ennugi resolved to destroy mankind with a deluge. The god Ea ('Lord of the earth') warned Ut-napistim, who worshipped him, to escape by building a ship, and told him what to say to those who should ask him what he was doing. Ut-napistim built the ship, made it watertight with pitch, stored it with food and drink, and brought into it all kinds of living creatures along with his family, his workmen, and a pilot. The sun-god Shamash

fixed the time of the flood. A wild storm of wind and rain raged for seven days and caused the gods to flee to heaven and to cry out in alarm. Istar (Ashtoreth = 'Venus') interceded for men, and the rain ceased. Ut-napistim looked out from his ship and saw land in the distance. The ship grounded on a mountain in the land of Nizir, E. of the Tigris, and after seven days Ut-napistim sent forth in succession a dove, a swallow, and a raven. The first two came back, but the latter did not return. Ut-napistim thereupon sent out all the animals and offered a sacrifice on the mountain top. The gods gathered around it like flies. Istar came and held up the 'signets' which Anu had made. She took an oath by her 'necklace' that she would always remember this time, and asked that Bel might not be allowed to come to the sacrifice. Bel came, however, and was angry at Ut-napistim for his escape. But Ea reproached Bel for having caused the flood, and advised him to take some other means (lions, hyænas, famine, pestilence) for checking human population in future. Bel was appeased, conferred immortality on Ut-napistim and his wife, and gave them an abode 'afar at the mouths of the rivers.'

A few extracts from the tablets will show the parallelism of ideas in the Babylonian and Hebrew accounts.

'Surippak, the city which thou knowest,
Lies (upon the bank) of the Euphrates,
That city was old, and the gods within it.
The great gods decided in their hearts to make a flood,
There was their father Anu
Their counsellor, the warrior Bel'...

The god Ea warns Ut-napistim to save himself—

'Surippakite, son of Umbara-Tutu,
Forsake thy house, build a ship,
Leave what thou hast, see to thy life,
Take up the seed of life into the midst of the ship.'

. . . .

A vivid description of the storm is given—

'At the appearance of dawn in the morning
There arose from the foundation of heaven a dark cloud:
Ramman thundered in the midst of it. . .
Then came Ninip casting down destruction,
The Anunnaki (spirits of the earth) raised their torches,
With their brilliance they illumined the land:
Everything bright to darkness turned
In heaven the gods feared the flood,
They fled, they ascended to the heavens of Anu ;
The gods kennelled like dogs, crouched down in the enclosures.

. . . .

Six days and six nights the wind blew,
The deluge and flood overwhelmed the land,
The seventh day when it came, the storm ceased

The sea shrank back, the evil wind ended,
Like palings the marsh reeds appeared.
I opened my window, the light fell on my face,
I fell back dazzled, I sat down, I wept.
I noted the region, the shore of the sea,
The ship had stopped at the land of Nisir,
I sent forth a dove, and it left,
But there was no resting-place, and it returned.
I sent forth a swallow, etc.,
I sent forth a raven, and it left,
It ate, it waded, it croaked, it did not return.
I sent forth (the animals) to the four winds,
I made an offering on the peak of the mountain,
Seven and seven I set incense-vases there.
The gods smelled a sweet savour,
They gathered like flies over the sacrificer.'

As in the Creation story the immense religious and moral superiority of the biblical account must be manifest to every reader. There is no multitude of gods, divided in counsel, crying out in fear, wrangling like children, and changing from capricious hate to capricious favour. The unity of God, His hatred of evil, His love of righteousness, His mercy and faithfulness appear instead of the vain conceptions of the heathen.

One or two interesting questions arise as to the general relationship between the biblical and the Babylonian accounts of the Creation and the Flood. Was the one set of traditions directly derived from the other, and if so which was the original one, and when did the borrowing take place ? Or must both sets be traced to a common source which was prior to either of them ? That the Babylonian accounts were derived from the Hebrew ones is most unlikely. The Creation and Flood tablets discovered in 1872 were taken from the library of the Assyrian king Assurbanipal, who lived 668–626 B.C. This date shows that the traditions recorded on the tablets were current in Babylonia almost a century before the exile. Further, the literature preserved in Assurbanipal's library consists almost entirely of *copies* of Babylonian documents, belonging in all likelihood to a time before the beginnings of the Hebrew nation. The local colouring of the narratives, too, points clearly to Babylonia as their original home. If, on the other hand, the Hebrews obtained the traditions from the Babylonians, it can-

not have been during the exile, since the Primitive document, which has an account of the Flood, was drawn up before that time. As the Tel el Amarna tablets show that Palestine was under the influence of Babylonian culture in the second millennium B.C., it is possible that the traditions in question may have passed from the Babylonians to the Canaanites, and from them to the Hebrews after the Conquest. But as Abraham, the ancestor of the Hebrews, himself came from Babylonia, it is in every way more natural to suppose that the biblical narratives are to be traced to their source through some such direct channel. There still remains the question as to how the difference between the Hebrew and the Babylonian traditions *in their present form* is to be explained. Were the polytheism and superstition of the Babylonian stories present in them from the first, and simply eliminated among the Hebrews before the narratives passed into the Bible ? Or have the present Babylonian legends degenerated from a purer original, of which the Bible has more faithfully preserved the religious tone ? Probably the truth lies midway between these two views. On the one hand, both the evidence of the Babylonian records and the analogy of other religious systems, suggest that the gross polytheism reflected in the Babylonian stories, as we have them, was preceded by a higher and simpler belief, approaching to monotheism. On the other hand, we cannot assume a primitive religion so exalted as to do away with the reality of the revelation in the after history of Israel which the Old Testament records. The Hebrew nation was set apart not merely to preserve or revive ancient truth, but to receive a progressive unfolding of God's character and will. The Babylonian and biblical accounts of primitive times are best regarded as two streams of tradition flowing from one source (itself Babylonian)—each in its own direction. The former has lost whatever religious value the tradition originally had ; while the latter has preserved whatever truth the source contained, and has developed it still further under the guidance of God's Spirit, in the course of the revelation which has been completed in Jesus Christ.

THE LAWS OF HAMMURABI

In Gn 14 we read of a certain 'Amraphel, king of Shinar,' who was contemporary with Abraham. It is generally agreed that this Amraphel is identical with Hammurabi, the sixth king of the First Dynasty of Babylon, under whom the kingdom was first united, with Babel as its capital. It has long been known that a code of laws existed in ancient times bearing the name of the 'Judgments of Hammurabi.' Fragments of the code had been discovered on tablets dating from the reign of Assurbanipal (Sardanapalus : ? Asnapper, Ezr 4 10), king of Assyria, 668–625 B.C., and now preserved in the British Museum and the Berlin Museum. But our knowledge of this most ancient code of laws was enormously enhanced by the discovery made by the French Exploration Society in Dec. 1901–Jan. 1902 at Susa (Shushan, Esth 1 2, Gk. Persepolis, capital of an old Elamite kingdom, and rival of Babylon) of a block of black diorite about 8 ft. high, containing on one side 16 and on the other 28 columns of writing, amounting in all to 3654 lines. When deciphered this monument was found to contain the long-lost CODE OF HAMMURABI. At the top there is a fine representation of King Hammurabi receiving his laws from the Sun-god Shamash.

The value of this Code of Laws lies in its antiquity. It is the 'oldest (known) code of laws in the world.' It is perhaps a thousand years older than the time of Moses, and the laws themselves must have been in operation long before their codification and promulgation by Hammurabi. Old as it is, it discloses a very highly advanced state of civilisation. We find a central government with organised local administration. We find professional men, priests, lawyers, and doctors, business men and tradesmen, farmers, brickmakers, builders, carpenters, tailors, merchants, boatmen, as well as a host of slaves. The duties of each class are determined, and fees, wages, rents, and prices are regulated by statute. Over and over again we are impressed by what seems the curiously 'modern' spirit of many of these ancient regulations. To the student of the Bible this code is particularly interesting. Abraham came from Ur of the Chaldees, and if the identification of Hammurabi with Amraphel is correct, the ancestor of the Hebrew people in all probability not only knew these laws, but may have found them to some extent in operation in Canaan, where Babylonian influence was preponderating. The Laws of Hammurabi, therefore, may have formed part of the original tradition of

the Hebrew race. Already the question of the relationship between the Mosaic legislation and that of this great Oriental ruler, and the possible dependence in parts at least of the former upon the latter, have been much discussed, and given rise to a considerable literature.

In the space at our disposal we can only refer to a few of the more interesting features of this ancient code, particularly those to which a parallel may be traced in the Law of Moses.

Curiously enough, considering that Babylonia is the home of magic and witchcraft, the code opens with two judgments directed against sorcery. 'If a man weave a spell and put a ban upon a man and has not justified himself, he .. shall be put to death.' With this we may compare Ex 22 18. The next section prescribes an ordeal by water. 'If a man have put a spell upon a man and has not justified himself, he upon whom the spell is laid .. shall plunge into the holy river, and if the river overcome him, he who wove the spell shall take his house. If the holy river makes that man to be innocent and has saved him, he who laid the spell upon him shall be put to death.' The same ordeal is prescribed in § 132 in the case of a wife suspected of infidelity, with which should be compared Nu 5 12 f. Then follows a long series of offences punishable by death, including the intimidation or bribing of witnesses, housebreaking, theft, and reset of stolen property, etc. Of these we may cite § 21, 'If a man has broken into a house, one shall kill him before the breach and bury him in it (?)' ; cp. Ex 22 1-4. § 14, 'If a man has stolen the son of a freeman, he shall be put to death' : cp. Ex 21 16. The same penalty is prescribed against harbouring a runaway slave. An interesting series of sections follows dealing with the duties and rights of officers or constables employed on active service as royal or public messengers, a kind of postal system. The laws relating to agriculture are most explicit. The rent of a garden is a tithe of the produce, the crop of the fifth year being divided between the owner and the tenant. § 54 reads, 'If a man has neglected to strengthen his bank of the canal .. and the waters have carried away the meadow, the man in whose bank the breach has been opened shall render back the corn which he has caused to be lost.' In § 57 we find a law similar to that in Ex 22 5, 'If a shepherd has caused the sheep to feed on the green corn .. without the consent of the owner of the field .. he shall give 20 *gar* of corn per *gan* to the owner of the field.' In § 112 a law dealing with deposits is laid down similar to that in Ex 22 7f., the penalty being in some cases fivefold, in others threefold. § 125 reads, 'If a man has given anything of his on deposit, and where he gave it, either by housebreaking or by rebellion, something of his has been lost along with something of the owner of the house, the owner of the house .. shall make good and render to the owner of the goods, and the owner of the house shall seek out whatever of his is lost and take it from the thief.' § 128 f. deal with marriage, divorce, adultery, etc. § 128, 'If a man has married a wife and has not laid down her bonds, that woman is no wife.' A woman taken in adultery is to be drowned along with the man : cp. Lv 20 10 Dt 22 22. Incest is, in general, punishable with death.

The law of retaliation and restitution exhibits close analogies to that in Exodus. Thus, 'If a man has caused the loss of a gentleman's (i.e. noble's) eye, his eye one shall cause to be lost.' 'If a man has made the tooth of a man that is his equal to fall out, one shall make his tooth to fall out': cp. Ex 21 24-27. Injury in the case of a poor man is compensated with a money payment. Again, 'If a man has struck a man in a quarrel and has caused him a wound, that man shall swear, "I do not strike him knowingly," and shall answer for the doctor': cp. Ex 21 18,19. 'If a man has struck a gentleman's daughter and caused her to miscarry, he shall pay ten shekels of silver. If that woman has died, one shall put to death his daughter': cp. Ex 21 22,23. §§ 215-223 prescribe the fees which a doctor is entitled to charge for operations, and the penalties, amounting to the cutting off both hands, in the event of the operation proving fatal. The following are closely analogous to enactments in the Mosaic Law. 'If a builder has built a house for a man and has not made strong his work, and the house he built has fallen and he has caused the death of the owner of the house, that builder shall be put to death': cp. Dt 22 8. If it is the son or slave who has been killed, then the son or slave of the builder is put to death. 'If a wild bull in his charge has gored a man and caused him to die, that case has no remedy. If the ox has pushed a man, by pushing has made known his vice, and he has not blunted his horn, has not shut up his ox, and that ox has gored a man of gentle birth and caused him to die, he shall pay half a mina of silver. If a gentleman's servant, he shall pay one-third of a mina of silver': cp. Ex 21 28-32. 'If a man has caused an ox or sheep which was given him to be lost, ox for ox, sheep for sheep, he shall render to their owner.' 'If

in a sheepfold a stroke of God has taken place or a lion has killed, the shepherd shall purge himself before God and the accident to the fold the owner of the fold shall face it': with this cp. Ex 22 9-13. 'If a man has struck his father, his hands one shall cut off': cp. Ex 21 15. Lastly, there may be cited, as giving an interesting glimpse of the police regulations in those early days, § 109, 'If a wine merchant has collected a riotous assembly in her house and has not seized those rioters and driven them to the palace, that wine merchant shall be put to death.'

Such are a few examples culled from this most interesting and wonderful code of laws, 4000 years old, and yet in many ways so modern in spirit. To read it is to be impressed with a feeling of reverence for this old-world ruler, who with justifiable pride says in the preamble of the code that he 'established law and justice in the land and made happy the human race in those days.' 'In that day I, Hammurabi, the glorious Prince, the Worshipper of my God, decreed justice for the land, for witness, plaintiff, and defendant ; to destroy the wicked tyrant and not to oppose the weak, like unto the Sun-god, I promulgated.'

With regard to the relationship existing between this code and the laws promulgated by Moses at Sinai, reference may be made to what is said in the Introduction to the book of Exodus, § 2. In the present state of our knowledge it is hazardous to dogmatise. There are resemblances, but there are also differences. The resemblances do not necessarily imply direct derivation, for most of the enactments which exhibit them are such as might be promulgated by any lawgiver possessed of a high sense of justice and humanity. On the other hand, when all due allowance has been made for the possibility of suggestions being received from the earlier code, the differences are decided, and numerous enough to argue the independence and originality of the Law of Moses. On the whole, it is more merciful than that of Hammurabi ; it takes less account of the social distinctions between the 'gentleman,' the 'poor man,' and the 'slave'; it bases its demands upon the sense of indebtedness and responsibility to the Most High God. It is true, Hammurabi ascribes his legislation to the Sun-god ; and he whom he 'ignorantly worshipped' under this symbol may in reality have been 'the true light which lighteth every man that cometh into the world.' In that case, his code of laws is simply another illustration of the great truth that God 'in times past suffered all nations to walk in their own ways ; nevertheless he left not himself without witness.'

HEATHEN RELIGIONS REFERRED TO IN THE BIBLE

EVERY careful reader of the Bible notices the number and variety of the forms of idolatry with which the Israelites came into contact. Nor was it a mere external contact. Idolatry and the pollutions attendant on it appealed with too much force to something in the people's own character. Nothing short of the great calamity which destroyed their national life in the year 586 B.C. could have rid them entirely of the taint.

There has been much diversity of opinion as to the origin of those forms of heathenism which prevailed amongst the races with which the Hebrews were related. Some have found their main root in the worship of dead ancestors. Others have discerned many tokens of the adoration of animals supposed to be related to the communities which worshipped them. Others, again, have found, most deeply seated of all, the belief in a world of spirits, suggested by dreams and uncanny experiences, spirits manifesting their power in nature, dwelling in trees or animals, animating springs and rivers, moving in wind and storm. But the beliefs of each race must be studied separately, and when this is done more than one cause may perhaps be found to have been at work.

Joshua is represented (24 2) as reminding the Israelites that their fathers 'dwelt of old time beyond the River, even Terah, the father of Abraham, and the father of Nahor : and they served other gods.' That carries our thoughts to the religion of the land from which Abraham was believed to have emigrated. And there, in **Babylonia,** two types of faith and practice may be noted. First, the recognition of an immense number of deities, each with a distinct name and individuality. There is a clay tablet still in existence, inscribed on each side with six columns of writing, each column containing more than one hundred and fifty lines, and on almost every line the name of a deity ! These deities were conceived of as possessing human form and human attributes. The greater of them were exceedingly mighty, but were actuated by the same passions as ordinary men, and performed, on a larger scale, the deeds which a Babylonian would have wished to emulate. They were magnified men. On the other hand, they were impersonations of the forces of nature. To one of them the motions of the sun were ascribed, to another the changes of the moon, to another tempests.

Every city had its patron god, and when one city acquired mastery over its rivals their deities had to take a lower rank. The three who stood first were Anu, the god of heaven ; En-lil (afterwards called Bel), god of the earth and of mankind ; Ea, who presided over the abyss of waters. Next came the moon-god, Sin ; the sun-god, Shamash ; Rammân, god of the atmosphere. The rise of Babylon to supreme power gave to its local deity, Marduk, the headship of the gods. He was then identified with the older Bel, and Nebo, the god of Borsippa, became his minister because Borsippa sank into a kind of suburb of the capital (Isa 46 1). With the exception of Ishtar the Babylonian goddesses were utterly devoid of importance. She presided over love, magic, and battle. At Erech, where her principal shrine was situated, she was served by a community of unmarried priestesses, who sacrificed their chastity for her glory. Originally Ishtar was the goddess of the morning and the evening star. In this connexion we may notice the worship offered to the heavenly bodies. This spread from Babylonia westwards. 'The chariots of the sun,' 2 K 23 11, remind us of the chariot of the sun, to which sacrifices were brought, at Sippara in Babylonia : see also 2 K 23 5 Ezk 8 16.

The other, gloomier strain in the religion of Babylon was probably derived from an older stratum of the population. It came from the belief in a vast world of spirits, unnamed and unidentifiable, mostly hostile to man and easily provoked by unwitting offences. These demons were hideous in shape and features. An ill-omened word was sufficient to bring down their wrath. Charms and incantations were needed to avert or remove their displeasure. Hence the majority of the clay tablets from the buried libraries of Babylonia, so far as they have hitherto been read, are covered with formulas of incantation. The populace was deeply impressed by this darker side of their religion, and must therefore have been made very gloomy and unhappy by it. And there is much in the history of religion amongst the Hebrews to remind us of these superstitions. The teraphim were images representing dead ancestors, from whom counsel was sought (RV of Gn 31 19, 34 1 S 19 13, 16 Ezk 21 21 ; in all which passages AV has the inadequate word 'images'). The ephod (certainly an image at Jg 8 26 f.) was consulted as an oracle (1 S 14 18 RM, 23 9 30 7). The necromancers plied their unholy trade of raising the dead (Dt 18 11 1 S 28 7 Isa 8 19f.). The wizards and sorcerers found many dupes (Lv 19 31 20 6 2 K 21 6 23 24).

As a whole the religion of **Assyria** closely resembled its parent in Babylonia. But there was a strong tendency to concentrate faith and devotion on the one god Asshur, who represented the State, who is glorified by the kings in terms which a Hebrew might have applied to Jehovah, whose predominant qualities, however, are martial ones, for he is praised above all else for the victories he gives to the king, his son and servant.

The student of **Egyptian** religion finds it composed of three tangled threads which are so closely and so confusedly interlaced that it is most difficult to separate them, and impossible to keep them apart. The highest element is that connected with the name of Osiris, who appears to have been originally a deified human king. He was the god of the other world and of the resurrection. The requirements for admission to that happy world were such as a Christian moralist would have no hesitation in subscribing to. But their effect was sadly marred by the value ascribed to amulets, spells, words. And the inveterate habit of deifying the Pharaoh involved a painful servility which lowered and degraded every subject. The letters written to him from governors of distant cities begin after this fashion : ' To the king, my lord, my god, my sun, the sun who cometh from the heavens .. I fall down before the feet of the king my lord seven times and twice seven times, back and breast.' Secondly, there was the adoration of the sun-god Ra, which, so far as the official cult was concerned, swallowed up the rest ; all the other deities coming to be regarded as forms and manifestations of him. This has led some modern scholars to write as though the Egyptians believed firmly and always in One Almighty God. But there was a vagueness about the belief which rendered it quite unlike what we mean when we speak of the unity of God, a changefulness, a phantasmagoric character which must have made it hard to grasp the truth. On the whole, it chiefly meant the adoration of the forces of nature. Attention was called to the lower, not the highest, in God. The power displayed in the universe, even if it be almighty, is not so high a thing as righteousness and love. Thirdly, originating no doubt in the least cultivated stratum of the population, but adopted perforce by the priests, there was the deification of animals—cats, lions, bulls, jackals, crocodiles, and the rest. The educated may have looked on these as symbols of the deity: to the unlearned they were actually divine. It seems most probable that Aaron's golden calf (Ex 32 1-6) and the two set up by Jeroboam (1 K 12 28, 29) were not suggested by the worship of the bull Apis at Memphis, or Mnevis at Heliopolis. To many primitive peoples the bull has been an apt emblem of creative power : Aaron and Jeroboam intended that Jehovah should be worshipped by means of this image. In later days, however, when the Hebrews were anxious to gather materials for their religion from every quarter, Egypt contributed the forms ' of creeping things and abominable beasts ' which Ezekiel in his vision saw portrayed on the walls of the Temple (Ezk 8 10).

Every **Phœnician** town had its divine lord, who was in many cases called Baal, which means owner, possessor. Thus there are inscriptions bearing the names Baal of Tyre, Baal of Sidon, Baal of Tarsus, Baal of Lebanon, Baal of Heaven. There are also such designations as Eshmun, Tanith (goddess of Carthage), Melkarth (of Tyre). The sun, certain springs, rivers, mountains, and trees were held sacred. Sacrifices were offered on elevated spots—the 'high places' of the Bible—as being nearer heaven. Two foul enormities were perpetrated. First, the sacrifice of children. The image of El at Carthage (the most famous of Phœnician colonies) was of metal, and was heated inside : the child placed in its arms rolled into the flames below. In days of gloom and fanaticism the Hebrews were only too ready to make the same dread sacrifice (Dt 12 31 2 K 16 3 23 10 Jer 19 5 Mic 6 7). More loathsome still was the sacrifice of honour. Reference has already been made to the licentiousness practised at Erech in Babylonia. The goddess of that place, Ishtar, was welcomed by the Phœnicians under the name Ashtoreth. She was the chief deity of Sidon (1 K 11 5, 33 2 K 23 13), and was regarded as the patroness of sexual passion. The ceremonial weeping for Adonis, which is one of the outstanding features of Phœnician worship, came from the same source, and resembled it in character. In Babylonia, Tammuz (the god of spring vegetation, slain by the fierce sun of summer) was mourned by Ishtar. In Phœnicia, Adonis, the husband of Ashtoreth, killed by the wild boar's tusk, was annually lamented. All the women of the town of Byblus went in a mad procession to Aphaka in the Lebanon, where rites of so shameful a nature were celebrated that Constantine the Great eventually abolished them by force. Similar unholy customs found a footing in Israel. The women wept for Tammuz (Ezk 8 14 Zech 12 11). See also 1 K 14 24 15 12 2 K 23 7 Gn 38 21, 22 RM, Hos 4 14, etc. Dt 23 17, 18 shows how deeply such practices were resented by the representatives of a better faith.

In **Canaan** itself the conditions closely resembled those in Phœnicia. The local gods were entitled Baalim, Baals of the several towns and districts; each of them credited with the fertility of his own domain (Hos 2 5-8). There were also many Ashtoreths (1 K 7 4 Jg 2 13 10 6). High places abounded, and the Hebrew immigrants succumbed to the fatal fascination which hung around them. At the high place, near the altar, stood an asherah—wrongly translated 'grove' in our AV,—a sacred post, fixed in the ground to represent the tree which in earlier times had been believed to be animated by the life of the Deity. There was also a mazzebah, or pillar, wrongly translated 'image' in such passages as Dt 16 21 Hos 3 4 10 1, 2. At first the pillar would be a natural stone (Gn 28 18, 22), in which the divine being was supposed to dwell. Afterwards it was shaped into the form of an obelisk. A still later development of the mazzebah, derived from Phœnicia and connected with sun-worship, is the sun-pillar of Isa 17 7 27 9 2 Ch 14 2, etc. Grave immoralities were common at the high places (Hos 4 13 Am 2 7).

Little is known about the religions of **Syria** on the one hand, or the smaller nations by which Israel was surrounded on the other. The Syrians of Damascus recognised Hadad as their greatest god. He seems to have been considered a sun-god, but was frequently identified with Rammân, the god of the atmosphere, whom the Assyrians greatly venerated. Besides him were Shamas, El, Resheph (god of fire), Rekeb-el, etc. The main object of worship to the **Moabites** was Chemosh, and it would appear from 2 K 3 27 that he was thought to be most surely moved by human sacrifices. On the Moabite Stone, which contains an inscription of Mesha (2 K 3 4, 5), a contemporary of Ahab, Ishtar-Chemosh, as well as Chemosh, is mentioned. This points to an identification of the two, and although Chemosh was a male deity there was nothing to prevent the identification, seeing that in Babylonia itself Ishtar was sometimes regarded as of both sexes, and in Arabia was masculine—so shifting and uncertain were these shadowy products of the imagination! The **Ammonites** served Milcom, which is but another form of the word for 'king,' or of the name Molech which meets us so often in the Old Testament. But we are not warranted in asserting that the children burnt in the valley of Hinnom (2 K 23 10) were immolated to the Ammonite god: in v. 13 he is a distinct being; in v. 10 Molech is a name for Jehovah. Yet the strong expression, 'Milcom the abomination of the children of Ammon,' indicates that there were most objectionable details in the ritual of his worship. The **Edomite** deities of whom we read bear foreign names. Hadad came from Syria, Â from the farther East. Dagon was supreme in **Philistia**. He was the

god of agriculture, and also gave his people victory over their enemies (Jg 16 23, etc.). At Ekron Baal-zebub (lord of flies) was revered and consulted (2 K 1 2, 3): why this title was given him remains uncertain. Ashtoreth also had a temple in one of the Philistine cities (1 S 31 10).

This is not the place for discussing the voluminous subject of the **Greek** and **Roman** religions. When Israel first felt the impact of the former, it had become a mixed product, imbued with many elements drawn from Oriental sources. Antiochus IV, the Greek monarch of Syria, attempted to force it on the Jews (168 B.C.). No wonder that they rose in revolt. The Temple at Jerusalem 'was filled with riot and revellings by the heathen, who dallied with harlots within the sacred precincts' (2 Mac 6 4). Again, at a later period, when we come across the name of a Greek goddess, Artemis, or, as our Bible calls her, Diana of the Ephesians (Ac 19 28), she is Oriental rather than Greek in character. Her image, with its numerous breasts, symbolises the sustaining and reproductive forces of Nature: her worship is defiled by wild and immoral orgies. At Daphne, too, near Antioch in Syria, where the Greek god Apollo was honoured and oracles from him were sought, 'all that was beautiful in nature and in art had created a sanctuary for a perpetual festival of vice.' It is not a Christian, but one of the worthiest of the heathens who, in the fourth century of our era, writes concerning the great annual festival at Antioch, that it 'consists only of the perpetuation of all that is impure and shameless and the renunciation of every lingering spark of decency.'

It is hardly too much to say that when the Jews came under the yoke of Rome the religion of **Rome** might be summed up as being the worship of the Roman State. The city was deified, so was the emperor. And so it was that all the munificent charities of Herod the Great towards his subjects could not atone in their eyes for the insult he offered to their religion by building at Cæsarea a temple to Rome and another to Augustus. Thousands of Jews were ready to die rather than acquiesce in Pilate's placing the standards of the legions with the image of the emperor on them in the Holy City. They knew that the soldiers worshipped those images. The distinctive feature in the religion of their rulers was worship of self, reverence for power, a consecration of human pride.

The unpopularity of the Jew in and about the Christian era was largely due to the uncompromising intolerance with which he bore himself towards the faiths and rituals of his neighbours. This had been aroused in him by the sad lessons of experience and the teachings of his sacred books. It may be that a modern reader sometimes wonders whether the lawgivers and prophets of the Old Testament are not too bitterly contemptuous or too fiercely severe in their language concerning idolatry. But it is to be remembered that they were engaged in a life and death struggle. If Monotheism, the faith in One Only God, had not made unyielding resistance, it would have been submerged in the floods of 'gods many and lords many.' Then the soul of man would have known no settled peace. There is no security for him who has propitiated one god, but with whom another perchance is angry. Think of the confusion and uncertainty implied in the Babylonian's prayer :

'May the god whom I know not be appeased !
May the goddess whom I know not be appeased !
May both the god I know and the god I know not
  be appeased !'

And confusion of the intellect also follows. An intelligent grasp of the order of the universe cannot coexist with a belief that the universe has been made and sustained by a plurality of independent powers. The uniformity of Nature depends on the unity of God. The adoration of the forces of Nature which underlies so much ancient idolatry also distracts attention from the highest elements in the Nature of God. The best we can learn of Him is that He is a living Person, holy, just, and good. And, as we have sufficiently seen, the worship in question led directly to licentiousness. If pictorial representations of the reproductive forces of Nature were constantly depicted on the walls of heathen temples ; if the Higher Beings were unchaste ; if impurity was part of their service, what chance was there for morality ? Rightly does the Wisdom of Solomon assert (14 27) :

'For the worship of those nameless idols
Is a beginning and cause and end of every evil.'

Again, when a man—king or emperor, king of Babylon or Assyria, Pharaoh of Egypt, Antiochus Theos (God) of Syria, or the irresponsible ruler of Rome—is held as divine, and temples are dedicated to his honour when dead, or even whilst still alive, this is an impregnable barrier to liberty and progress. The religion of the Old Testament has conferred an inestimable boon on humanity by insisting on the unity and unapproachable majesty of Him before whom all mankind are equal, and by repudiating in His name all that is impure and cruel. The religion of the New Testament has softened down all harsher features and satisfied all legitimate cravings for One higher than man, yet in closest touch with him, by its revelation of the God-Man, the Mediator, the Way, the Truth, and the Life.

INTRODUCTION TO HEBREW PROPHECY

1. Place of the Prophetic Books in the Canon. The second, or prophetic, division of the Jewish Canon of the Old Testament comprises the books of Joshua, Judges, 1 and 2 Samuel, and 1 and 2 Kings ('the Earlier Prophets'), as well as the more strictly prophetic books ('the Later Prophets'). The second of these groups forms the special subject of this Introduction, in the course of which, however, it will appear why the historical books above mentioned were also placed in the prophetic portion of the Canon. The 'Later Prophets' include Isaiah, Jeremiah, Ezekiel, and the book of the Twelve Prophets. The last-named collection consists of the books from Hosea to Malachi, which, on account of their comparative brevity, are generally known as the 'Minor Prophets.' Daniel is not among the prophetic books, but belongs to the third division of the Canon.

2. Early History of Prophecy. The prophetic books of the Old Testament may all be placed in the period between the middle of the eighth and the end of the fifth century B.C. But prophecy in Israel dated from much earlier times. The prophetic gift is ascribed to Moses (Dt 34 10 Hos 12 13), to Miriam (Ex 15 20), to Deborah (Jg 4 4), and to Samuel (1 S 3 20). From the time of Samuel onwards there was a succession of prophets, like Nathan, Gad, Ahijah the Shilonite, Shemaiah, Jehu the son of Hanani, etc., who appeared as the counsellors and monitors of David and the subsequent kings. In the beginning of the eighth century Micaiah, Elijah, and Elisha played a prominent part as prophets, though they have left no books bearing their names. In early times the prophet was called a 'seer,' and was consulted in times of perplexity, even upon matters of practical interest, receiving a present in return for his services (1 S 9 6-9). In those days we find also companies of prophets, who were the subjects of a sort of ecstasy, which appears to have been contagious (1 S 10 10-12 19 18-24). It would seem that Samuel organised these enthusiasts, placing himself at their head, and making Naioth in Ramah their centre. In later times there was a prophetic guild, known as 'the sons of the prophets,' with branches in various places, such as Bethel and Jericho (2 K 2 2, 3, 15). The canonical prophets, however, had little direct connexion with these professional communities, which became in the end the nurseries of false prophecy. Amos in particular affirms his independence of them (Am 7 14).

The 'seer' of early Israel performed functions somewhat akin to those of the soothsayers of other nations. Divination, however, and all allied practices were sternly discouraged by Jehovah's revelation of Himself to Israel; and as time went on the work of the true prophets became more and more ethical and spiritual. There were prophets of heathen gods, who worked themselves into frenzy by various physical means (1 K 18 19-29), and there were also false prophets who claimed to speak in the name of Jehovah. But though prophecy in its beginnings had elements found also in the superstitious institutions of Israel's neighbours, and though even in later times it had its heathen parallels and its native counterfeits, yet in its genuine and fully developed form it was a unique phenomenon, and a channel of the loftiest and most direct divine revelation.

3. Arrangement of the Prophetic Books. These books are not placed in our Bibles according to their order of time. The three longer books come before the twelve shorter ones, and even the latter do not form a strictly historical series. Further, the books of Isaiah and Zechariah each contain the work of more than one author, and belong to more than one period. The table on the following page indicates how the canonical prophets may be historically grouped.

The books of Joel and Obadiah are of uncertain date. Some place them among the earliest prophets, and others after the exile. The same is true of Zech 9-14. The prophet Jonah lived in the eighth century B.C. (2 K 14 25), but the book which bears his name is now regarded as post-exilic.

4. The Prophet's Inspiration and Work. The popular definition of a prophet is 'one who predicts the future.' This was the conception which heathen nations had of their inspired oracles, and it has very largely prevailed in the Christian Church regarding the Old Testament prophets. But such a view is narrow and misleading. The prophet is 'one who speaks for God'—a *forth*-teller rather than a mere *fore*-teller. This is seen from Ex 7 1, where Aaron's relation to Moses as his spokesman is compared with the prophet's relation to God. The prophets were men who claimed to have received from Jehovah the truths which they spoke in His name. The

PERIOD.	ISRAEL.	JUDAH.	CENTURY.
Assyrian	Amos, circ. 760–750 B.C. Hosea, circ. 750–737	Isaiah, circ. 740–700 B.C. Micah, circ. 724 and onwards Zephaniah, circ. 627 Nahum, circ. 610–608	Eighth Seventh
Chaldean	In Jerusalem . . . . In Babylon	{ Habakkuk, circ. 605–600 { Jeremiah, circ. 626–586 { Ezekiel, circ. 593–573 { Isaiah 13–14, 34, 35, 40–66, circ. 540	Sixth
Persian		Haggai, } circ. 520 Zechariah, 1–8 } Malachi, circ. 460–450	 Fifth

bestowal of their prophetic gift is described in the phrase 'The word of Jehovah came.' The standing formula with which they prefaced their messages was, 'Thus saith Jehovah.' The prophet's inspiration was the process by which the truth was brought home to him by the Divine Spirit. Though inscrutable by us it was an undoubted reality to his consciousness. God's word to him was distinct from his own thoughts and desires (Jer 14, 15), as well as from the illusions of dreams (Jer 23 28). It came with a self-attesting and irresistible power (Jer 23 29, 30 Am 3 8). It compelled the prophet to utter it in spite of all natural hesitation and fear (Jer 20 9). The divine message might be presented in visionary form (Isa 6 Ezk); or suggested by some sight of everyday life (Jer 18 5, 6); or by some special circumstance to which God's inspiration gave a new meaning (Jer 32 8). It might be uttered in plain words, or in parables, or in symbolic actions, but in every case it was a declaration made in God's name.

The work of the prophets was threefold.

(1) They were first of all, and chiefly, **preachers to their contemporaries.** They addressed themselves to the political, social, and religious conditions among which they lived. A great part of their writings, which is unintelligible without a knowledge of these conditions, becomes in the light of this knowledge full of living interest and meaning. Each book, and each prophecy, must be placed in its historical setting. This may be done by the aid of the historical books of Scripture, taken along with the allusions to dates and events which the prophecies contain, and with the internal evidence they furnish as to the state of things they have in view. The prophetic books often supplement the historical ones, so that a complete picture of the state of Israel at any period can be got only by combining the particulars obtained from the two sources of information. When their writings are read in this way the prophets appear in their true light as preachers of righteousness, whether as political counsellors, or as advocates of social or religious reform.

(2) They were also **interpreters of the past.** They reviewed the earlier history of Israel, and showed the divine meaning which their countrymen were slow to discern in it. Thus Jeremiah drew a moral from the desolation of Shiloh (Jer 7 12-15), and Ezekiel repeatedly told the story of Israel's past rebelliousness, and of God's patient love (Ezk 16, 20). This prophetic interpretation of the past was necessary, because the popular one was often greatly at variance with it. Thus in Jer 44 the prophet traces the fall of Jerusalem to Israel's idolatry (vv. 2–6), while the people ascribe their troubles to their discontinuance of the worship of the queen of heaven (v. 18). The great lesson which the prophets drew from the history of Israel was the connexion between sin and calamity on the one hand, and between obedience and prosperity on the other. And as the historical books of the Old Testament emphasise the same truth above everything else they are simply an expansion of this side of the prophets' work. They were written from the point of view of the prophet rather than from that of the mere historian. The title 'the Earlier Prophets,' which has been given to some of them, expresses their true character.

(3) The prophets were, lastly, **predictors of the future.** While this has often been wrongly regarded as their sole function, it was a real, though subordinate, element of their work. Prophetic prediction was of two kinds.

(a) Some predictions were **definite,** and related

to the near future. Thus, when the Assyrian power appeared in Western Asia, Amos and Hosea foretold that it would be the instrument of Israel's downfall. When Sennacherib's invasion of Judah took place, Isaiah predicted that king and people would be brought into great peril through their trust in earthly alliances, but that in the end they would be humbled, would seek God's help, and would obtain deliverance. When Nebuchadrezzar besieged Jerusalem, both Jeremiah and Ezekiel announced that the capture of the city was inevitable, and that the exile, though certain, would only last for a limited time. When Cyrus had begun his career of victory, the author of Isa 40–46 foretold that he would conquer Babylon, and would deliver the Jews from captivity. Such predictions related to persons already alive, to nations already existing, to the issues of movements already in progress. They cannot be explained as triumphs of mere human foresight and sagacity, and must be traced to the prophets' divine inspiration. At the same time they were not wholly unintelligible and miraculous revelations of isolated future events. They were the inferences which the prophets were enabled to draw from the great truths about God's character and God's purpose with Israel which had been revealed to them. The essence of the prophets' inspiration lay in their grasp of these principles, and in their power of applying them to the situations in which they lived.

In the view of New Testament writers, some definite predictions of the prophets extended much further than has been indicated, and included references to particular events of the remote future. Thus Hos 11[1], which is primarily a description of the deliverance of Israel from Egyptian bondage, is interpreted as a prediction of our Lord's flight into Egypt (Mt 2[15]). Jer 31[15], which is primarily a picture of the grief of Rachel (viewed as the ancestral mother of Israel) at the departure of the exiles from Ramah (see Jer 40[1]), is regarded as a prediction of the massacre at Bethlehem (Mt 2[18]). And Mic 5[2] foretells, not only the coming of a ruler of David's line who will deliver Judah from the Assyrians (see vv. 5, 6), but the birth of Christ at Bethlehem (Mt 2[6]). It is scarcely to be thought that these secondary fulfilments of their utterances were actually present to the minds of the prophets : still the suggestiveness, and even the legitimacy, of interpreting their prophecies in this way—as foreshadowings of events in the life of our Lord—can hardly be denied without incurring the danger of setting arbitrary limits to the free working of the Spirit of God.

(b) Other predictions were of a more general kind, and had to wait for their fulfilment till a more distant future. In them the prophets

presented their inspired ideals of a perfect king (Isa 11[1-10] 32[1-8]), of a nation penitent and forgiven, united and restored (Ezk 36, 37), of a righteous Servant of the Lord first suffering and then triumphant (Isa 53), of a divine Shepherd (Ezk 34), of a world-wide kingdom of God (Isa 60 Mic 4[1-7]), of a new and spiritual relationship between God and His people (Jer 31[31-34]). Such prophecies are usually termed 'Messianic,' because they point forward to Jesus Christ, and to the religious conditions of New Testament times.

In our Lord's day the expectation of a great deliverer, known as the Messiah (or the Christ), was current among the Jews, and was undoubtedly based on Old Testament prophecy. It is true that none of the prophets applied the term Messiah to a single distinct figure in the future. This was rather done by Jewish writers in the period between the Old and the New Testament. But the ideals of the prophets furnished the basis of the conception of the Messiah, which was adopted by our Lord as true, and which, according to His own teaching, was realised in Himself and His work (Mt 11[2-6] Lk 4[17-21] Jn 4[25, 26]). The argument from prophecy in defence of the truth of Christianity has lost none of its value, though it can no longer be stated in the terms which were formerly used. Its force depends not on isolated predictions of single occurrences in the far future, but on the many converging lines of spiritual anticipation along which the prophets gazed into the coming time, and which all meet in Jesus Christ.

5. The False Prophets. The nature of true prophecy receives additional illustration when it is compared with the spurious form of prophecy which accompanied it like a shadow. The professional prophets appear to have largely degenerated into this 'false' class. Their peculiar garb became a symbol of deception, and their self-mutilations made them objects of suspicion (Zech 13[4, 6]). The phrase, 'the burden of the Lord,' was on their lips conventional and misleading (Jer 23[33-40]). The false prophets spoke in the name of Jehovah, but without any real inspiration from Him (Jer 23[21] Ezk 13[6]). In some cases they may have been conscious impostors, or deliberate time-servers, but in most cases they were probably sincere in believing their own words. Yet their messages were often in direct contradiction to those of the real prophets. Thus Ahab's prophets foretold the success of his expedition against Ramoth-gilead (1 K 22[6]). Hananiah foretold the speedy return of the Jewish exiles from Babylon (Jer 28[1-4]). Prophets in Babylon said the same thing (Jer 29[8, 9] Ezk 13[16]). How, it may be asked, were the people to distinguish between the false prophets and the true ? Various tests are indicated in Scripture. When predictions were in question, the simplest test was that of fulfilment (Dt 18 21, 22), but this could not be applied until the fulfilment had taken place. A deeper principle is suggested in Jer 28 8, 9. True prophets, as a rule, had messages of warning to deliver. One who foretold peace was therefore to be regarded with suspicion, and was not to be believed until the event justified his prediction. Thus the nature of the message was to be taken into account in judging of its truth. This principle is further developed in Jer 23 22. The true prophet is the man who denounces sin, and seeks to turn men away from it. The conflict between the false prophets and the true really arose from the different conceptions which they had about God's character and His relation to Israel. The false prophets held that He was a purely national God, and so was bound to protect and favour His people in all circumstances ; while the true prophets knew Him as the one living God, ruling the whole world in righteousness, who had chosen Israel to be a righteous nation, and could not but punish them if they fell into sin (Am 3 1, 2).

6. Interpretation and Fulfilment of Prophecy. Though the test of fulfilment could not always be applied to a prophet's predictions by his contemporaries, it can be applied by us, and we can see that in a great many cases, and, indeed, on the whole, the words of the prophets about the future have come true. Yet there are some predictions which have not been, and cannot now be, literally fulfilled, and there are certain principles of interpretation which have a special bearing upon these, and which also hold good of the prophetic writings in general.

(1) The language of the prophets is often poetic and figurative. The picture of the transformation of nature, for example, in Isa 11 6-8, is an imaginative description of universal peace, and is not to be understood in a literal sense. The same thing is true of a great many other passages.

(2) The predictions of the prophets were conditional. They were made to enforce the appeal for righteousness in the present. They foretold the consequences of sin on the one hand, and of righteousness on the other. Judgments might be averted by repentance. Blessings might be forfeited by disobedience. This principle is clearly laid down in Jer 18 7-10, and is of universal application. The 'if' is implied even when it is not expressed. Thus Jonah's prediction that Nineveh would

be destroyed in forty days was not fulfilled, yet Jonah was not a false prophet, because the threat was only made on the supposition that Nineveh remained impenitent. Such predictions, it has been said, were made not that they might, but that they might not, be fulfilled.

(3) The prophets' view of the future was limited by the circumstances of their own time. As Perowne justly remarks, ' Prophecy never seems wholly to forsake the ground of history. However extended the vista which stretches before him, that vista begins at the prophet's feet. The present is his home and starting-point, though he may make " all ages " his own.' Hence the prophets conceived of God's kingdom as continuing under the national form in which they knew it. Their descriptions of the future are often expressed in terms of a state of things which was destined to change and pass away. Thus Micah speaks of Jerusalem as the centre of God's kingdom of Peace (4 1, 2). Ezekiel conceives the future divine kingdom as a restored Israel, with its Temple and sacrifices (chs. 40–48), and of its enemies as the same nations that have vexed Judah in the past (28 25, 26). Even Jeremiah's new covenant is to be made with the House of Israel and the House of Judah (31 31). Much that was literal in the minds of the prophets themselves can therefore be only figurative for us. The permanent spiritual meaning has to be separated from the transient external form in which it is expressed.

(4) It follows from this that the prophets' view of the future often takes no note of what may be called historical perspective. That is to say, their view of the future kingdom of God is so vividly present to their mind that any intervening stretch of time is disregarded. For all of them the Golden Age lies just beyond the horizon of their own times. Isaiah's pictures of it are attached to his predictions of deliverance from Assyria. Ezekiel and the author of Isa 40–66 represent it as following the return from Babylon. Messianic prophecy of an ideal kind is constantly combined with more definite predictions regarding the near future. Thus the King whom Isaiah describes as Immanuel is one who is to appear in the prophet's own time, to share the hardships of the Assyrian invasion, and finally to conquer the oppressor ; but he is spoken of in exalted language, which was not applicable to any king of Judah, and has only been truly realised in Jesus Christ. See also art. ' Messianic Hope.'

THE MESSIANIC HOPE

STRICTLY speaking the Messianic hope is Israel's expectation of a Messiah, the confident assurance of men of faith, inspired in them by the prophets, that a king and deliverer of the line of David would be sent by God to save them from their oppressors, to roll back the overwhelming tide of calamities that had swept over the nation, and to usher in an era of peace and prosperity such as the world had never seen before. But in a wider application of the term we may take it to indicate the belief in future divine deliverance and blessedness apart from the specific kingly idea. The whole subject is vague and various in its earlier appearances. The hope takes first one form, then another. While one school of religious teachers—that of the prophets—cherishes it, another school, consisting of the authors of the Wisdom literature, ignores it. But then this school. not itself a Messianic idea, but a thought which Christians have seen to be realised and consummated in Jesus Christ quite as much as that of the kingly deliverer. To put the case another way, our Lord gathers up into Himself a number of scattered hopes and ideas of Israel, fulfilling them all in His own way, which if it is not always the way expected by the earlier dreamers, differs from that only by being more complete, more perfect, more lofty.

With this general notion of the whole subject we shall be prepared to map out its distinct branches, and trace the development till the scattered rays of the earlier revelation are drawn together and focussed in the Gospel history.

In the first place, we have a sacred character in the early Israelite kingship. This is brought out very vividly by the primitive account of Samuel's anointing of Saul (1 S 9 16). Here we see the king chosen by God, to be anointed by God's prophet in sign of the divine appointment, and so commissioned to deliver the nation from its enemies. Thus the throne was established with high hopes. But those hopes were doomed to a speedy disappointment. Saul went his own way, and Samuel in anger told him that God had rejected him. Then the same process was repeated in the selection and anointing of David, and with happier results. The second king of Israel, from being first a great warrior, became also in course of time a great monarch. The nation was not only saved from the ravages of petty marauding neighbour-tribes, it extended its boundaries, and seemed to promise to become a great world-empire. For a time men's eyes were dazzled by the glamour of this secular imperialism. But before long they were undeceived. Solomon's reign was even more magnificent than his father's. But it proved to be costly and burdensome. The issue was, that under his ill-advised and obstinate son there was a fatal revolt, and the Israelites became two nations. The subsequent history of these two kingdoms is of the usual mixed character. Some kings were good and great: others were bad and mischievous. By the time of Isaiah people had come to look back on the golden glory of a splendid past, magnified by the sentiment of antiquity. The ideal David was now a much greater personage than the real David had been. The dreadful crimes with which the national hero had stained his career were forgotten. Only his successful achievements were remembered. Then there appeared the hope that a second David would come, and do for the later age what the founder of the kingly line had done in his day. Since Assyria was a more powerful and menacing foe than Philistia had been, a greater David would be needed to overthrow the Assyrians than the warrior king who had mastered the Philistines. At this stage the prophets came to the aid of the nation with inspired utterances that met the popular need, but elevated the popular hope above its merely political outlook. Isaiah cried, 'And there shall come forth a shoot out of the stock of Jesse, and a branch out of his roots shall bear fruit : and the spirit of the Lord shall rest upon him, the spirit of wisdom and understanding, the spirit of counsel and might, the spirit of knowledge and of the fear of the Lord ; and his delight shall be in the fear of the Lord,' etc. (Isa 11 1-9). This great oracle is the earliest clearly expressed, definite prophecy of the Messiah as the Son of David. Hints and suggestions of coming deliverance have appeared earlier, and mystic thoughts have gathered about promising sovereigns ; but now at length we have the distinct promise of a Second David. The religious value of this prophecy is seen in its elaborate portraiture of the moral and spiritual character of the Messiah. He is more than a conquering ruler. He is the righteous ruler, just, merciful, pacific, because he is possessed by the fear of the Lord

Now in the light of this great utterance, which is the key to the Messianic ideas of Israel, we can go back to two earlier obscure oracles. The first is in Isa 7, where we read of the promised birth of Immanuel. The difficulty about this passage is that it is deeply embedded in contemporary history ; it plainly indicates a near approaching birth. Some have thought the reference is to a coming son of Isaiah himself, some to a young prince to be born in the palace. But when we go on to the second of these earlier oracles we find the mysterious child acclaimed with the most magnificent titles as, ' Wonderful, Counsellor, Mighty God, Everlasting Father, Prince of Peace' (Isa 9⁶). These are the greatest things said of the Messiah anywhere in the Old Testament. Can they be applied to a child of Isaiah's day ? Yet the oracle of c. 9 seems to refer back to that of c. 7, which is plainly contemporary.

The solution of the difficulty that here emerges will be found in an explanation of an important feature of Messianic prophecy. We have to distinguish between its ideas and the local, temporal, personal application of them. The prophets were inspired to perceive the ideas which shone out on them as luminous stars in the firmament. But it was not given them to know ' the times and the seasons.' Even our Lord confessed that He did not know the divinely appointed day or hour of His Second Advent. Much less is it to be supposed that Old Testament prophets were endowed with an exactness of foresight in this matter that was denied to the Son of Man Himself. Accordingly, it should be no surprise to us that they looked for the Deliverer much earlier than He appeared. Being men of large enthusiasm, some of them were ready to hail one young promising prince or another as the very man in whom God's rich promises, that they saw so clearly and believed in so truly, were to be fulfilled. In this way Isaiah may have dreamed that the child to be born in the Syrian crisis, described in c. 7, would possess all the high qualities named in c. 9, and therefore appear as the victorious and pacific ruler portrayed in c. 11. History did not verify the dream. God was educating His people, even His prophets, through the illusions due to their own limited vision. But there was no illusion in the ideas of the prophecy ; the illusion was confined to their historical setting and personal embodiment.

Here we come to the wonderful vitality of the Messianic hope. Disappointment did not kill it, did not even permanently damp its ardour. Various persons were supposed to realise the idea—Hezekiah, Zerubbabel, even the pagan Cyrus, and later the patriot Judas Maccabæus. They all did some good things in accordance with it. But the idea was too great for any of them. So it had to be confessed in the end with every case that the expectation had been disappointed. Still it survived ; it moved on ; it hovered above the prophets and the people—a divine idea, trying patience by its tardy tarrying, still firing hope by its invincible vitality.

It is in view of this remarkable combination of faith and disappointment that we must view many of the passages of Scripture that are commonly reckoned Messianic, although they are not prophetic in form. For instance, the second Psalm has been assigned by scholars to various personages—David, Solomon, Jehoshaphat, Ahaz, Hezekiah, Alexander Jannæus. Its glorious divine kingship was never fully realised by any of these men. Yet we cannot set it down to the adulation of a courtier. This is not the language of flattery ; it is an utterance of faith. The Psalmist is not merely trying to express exuberant loyalty. Trusting in God he sees clearly that what he here portrays must be accomplished in the person of God's true king. When he describes the king as God's Son, he has not attained to a vision of the mystery that St. Paul and St. John perceived in the incarnate Christ, but he is carried forward on luminous clouds of hope that will some day descend in the blessings of the definite Christian revelation. Similarly, Psalm 72 has been applied to Solomon, to Hezekiah, to others. It is fully true of none of them. These great kings partially realised its ideas, but the full realisation awaited a Christ who was never seen till Jesus was born.

Sometimes what perhaps we may call the Messianic hope shrinks to little more than an assurance of an unending line of kings in the family of David. Psalm 89 seems to be written in this spirit. Even here it is remarkable that the hope clinging to the stock of David should be so persistent and confident.

On the other hand, there is a large class of prophecies that have no connexion with the idea of a personal Messiah, but still predict redemption and deliverance. Some of these prophecies centre in ' the day of the Lord.' Here it is God Himself who is the Deliverer. There seems to be no room for any human agent, nor does he seem to be needed. A prince of the House of David, *who was no more than this*, could not accomplish all that was needed. The evils of the times were too vast and the hopes of the golden age of the future too brilliant for any man, even the greatest king, though chosen and anointed by God, to master or achieve. The Jews had been disillusioned with regard to the confidence they had placed in the throne of David. It had cost them much, and it had not secured them the boons they had been promised with it. Accordingly, they turned from it in weariness and despair, till their hopes were kindled in another quarter. God and God alone was to be the Redeemer of Israel. This is the dominant note of the second Isaiah, during the captivity when human help had proved a disappointment. Then we read, 'Fear not, thou worm Jacob, and ye men of Israel ; I will help thee, saith the Lord, and thy Redeemer is the Holy One of Israel' (Isa 41 14 RV). The idea of the day of the Lord is much earlier than this. Amos warns of God's coming to judgment ; Zephaniah sees a day of God's vengeance. The common thought is that the enemies of Israel will be smitten, and God's people rescued and exalted. That is the most elementary idea of redemption. But a deeper note is frequently struck by the prophets. The judgment is on Israel ; God's own people will be sifted and tried ; only a remnant will be spared. Then the great hope of the future goes on with the remnant.

These two ideas—the idea of David's glorious son, and the idea of God's direct interference and rectification of affairs—are never united in the Old Testament. They are two broken lights that await their combination in the full-orbed Christian revelation.

Three other important ideas that were not reckoned at the time to be Messianic may here be noted. The first is the conception of the prophet of the future (Dt 18 18). This is never connected with the Messiah in the Old Testament, as it is in the New, where Jesus first appears as a prophet, and is afterwards hailed as the Christ.

The second of these associated ideas is the great thought of the suffering servant of the Lord in the second Isaiah. The prevalent judgment of scholars, after very much discussion of the subject, is that whoever this strange personage may be—whether Jeremiah, or Israel, or the pious remnant of Israel—it is scarcely probable that he was thought of in the first instance as the Messiah. A late tradition, little heeded by the Jews, makes mention of two Messiahs—the triumphant Son of David, and the suffering Son of Joseph But this cannot be traced back to the authorship of the prophecy. Here, however, we have to apply the principle that has been our guide all along. The idea is great, and true, and inspired by God. It matters little what was the prophet's original application of it, except as a question of history and literary interpretation. The vital fact is that we have the idea.

In the third place, we have Jeremiah's prediction of the new covenant : see Jer 31 31-34. This is not associated with the Messiah by the prophet himself. But it is the most typical anticipation of the spirit and character of Christianity anywhere to be found in the Old Testament ; and it is a promise of the good time coming, that is to say, the Messianic era. As such it was adopted by Jesus in the institution of the Lord's Supper, and applied to the gospel by the Apostles.

When we consider the fulfilment of Messianic prophecy by Jesus Christ, we must see that He did not attempt to do this in the outward way of the earlier expectation any more than to satisfy the hopes of contemporary Jews for a new and greater David, a later Maccabæus, to break the yoke of the pagan oppression. But He came as the king, because He introduced the kingdom of God as a rule over society by means of inward influences ; as the Deliverer, because He came to save from the sin that was worse than its chastisement, and at the same time as the supreme Prophet or Revealer of God's will, the Suffering Servant of the Lord, and the Founder of the new covenant. That Jesus claimed to be the Messiah cannot be denied without tearing the gospel story to threads. Wrede was the most conspicuous scholar to make the denial ; but he has been amply answered. That our Lord was in fact the Messiah will be admitted by those who perceive that the spiritual essence of the Messiahship is its vital element, and note how, while He cast aside the trappings of its external form, He added to it the great ideas of the Day of the Lord and the divine Redeemer, as well as the prophetic, suffering, and covenant element, none of them joined to the Messiah in the Old Testament, but all enriching it in His fulfilment of that hope.

This subject is discussed in Drummond, 'The Jewish Messiah'; Stanton, 'The Jewish and the Christian Messiah' ; Briggs, 'Messianic Prophecy,' 'The Messiah of the Gospels,' and 'The Messiah of the Apostles'; Schürer, 'Jewish People in the Time of Christ'; Castelli, 'Il Messia secondo gli Ebrei'; Dalman, 'Der leidende und der sterbende Messias.'

THE HISTORY, LITERATURE, AND RELIGIOUS DEVELOPMENT OF THE JEWS IN THE PERIOD BETWEEN THE TESTAMENTS

1. SUMMARY OF JEWISH HISTORY

FROM THE CAPTIVITY TO THE FALL OF JERUSALEM, 70 A.D.

1. Introductory. Some account of Jewish history is necessary to bridge the gap between the two Testaments, and throw light upon allusions of New Testament writers and the state of affairs in their time. The starting-point is the disruption of the Davidic kingdom after the death of Solomon. That event was keenly felt in Judah, which could not forget the glories of the undivided monarchy nor cease to hope for their revival. Except for a short alliance in the time of Jehoshaphat, a relation of hostility was maintained with the revolted tribes; and, as the years passed, both kingdoms wasted their strength, not only in warring with the Syrian kings, but in mutual aggressions and internal revolutions.

2. Fall of Israel. The northern kingdom, whose growing idolatry and moral declension had provoked the denunciations of Amos and Hosea, was the first to fall before the foreign invader. In 738 B.C. the great Assyrian power, which had long menaced their independence, 'came into the land,' and in 722 B.C. captured Samaria, the capital from Omri's time. The leading inhabitants (27,290) were exiled by the Assyrian king, Sargon, to Mesopotamia and Media, and their places filled by foreigners from the Euphrates plain, from whom were descended the Samaritans of later times.

3. Captivity of Judah. Though subjected to tribute, Judah escaped a similar fate through the action of Hezekiah, prompted by the prophet Isaiah. In 701 B.C. Sennacherib, the successor of Sargon, sent an army against Jerusalem, and demanded its surrender; but it was successfully held against him. For a while political opinion was divided in Judah— one party advocating alliance with Assyria or Egypt, another, which included the prophets, seeking to foster national sentiment and keep clear of foreign complications. Manasseh was of the former persuasion, and, as a docile tributary of the Assyrian king, corrupted the people by the introduction of strange worship and customs. Josiah, however, reversed this policy, and by the promulgation and enforce-

ment of the Deuteronomic laws accomplished a national reformation. In his time the Assyrian empire began to break up before the growing power of the Babylonians, and Necho II of Egypt seized the opportunity to annex southern Syria. In the hope of achieving the independence of his country, Josiah gave him battle at Megiddo, in the plain of Jezreel (608 B.C.), but fell on the field. Shortly afterwards the victorious Babylonians, under Nebuchadrezzar II, advanced against him, and putting him to rout at Carchemish, on the Euphrates (605 B.C.), asserted their supremacy over Judah and the rest of Syria. Twice thereafter the Jews, encouraged by Egypt, rebelled against their new masters. On the first occasion, Nebuchadrezzar invested Jerusalem, and, compelling the young king Jehoiachin to submit, sent him captive to Babylon with the noblest of his people. Among the exiles was the prophet Ezekiel, who reckons from this event (597 B.C.) the years of the 'Babylonian captivity.' On the second occasion (586 B.C.) more severe measures were taken. Jerusalem, which had withstood Nebuchadrezzar for a year and a half, was given to the flames, and its walls destroyed. Seventy of the leaders were executed, and king Zedekiah, with some 15,000 of the principal inhabitants, deported to Babylon; while the vacant lands were given to the poorer classes left behind. To escape the troubles of the time many of the remaining Jews, including the prophet Jeremiah, migrated to Egypt.

Judah was left in a forlorn condition, but the indomitable spirit of the people soon evinced itself in an attempt at reorganisation. An old system of division into families and clans was revived, and to the heads of these, as elders, was entrusted the administration of affairs. Among the pious-minded submission, penitence, and the desire of amendment became the prevailing feelings, from which new confidence sprang that God would arise for the judgment of the nations and the vindication of His people (Lam 2–5, Zech 7 f.). Of the exiles in Babylonia, many accommodated themselves to their new surroundings, and, becoming immersed in commerce, were lost to the nation, like the northern tribesmen whom Sargon had deported, and of whom no more is heard. Others, however, remaining faithful to their ancient traditions, cherished the love of Zion and the memories of their native land. So far as possible they maintained the worship and customs of the past—not sacrifice (for they were dwellers in an unclean land), but circumcision, fasting, the observance of the sabbath, and prayer (Ps 137, Isa 40 31 55 6, 7 58 2, 3, 13, 14 Jer 29 4-9 Ezk 36 Dan 3, 6 10). At the same time, they gave themselves increasingly to the study and multiplication of their sacred books, so that the order of the Scribes grew into great importance. Adversity, accepted as a chastisement of God, served to deepen and purify their patriotic and religious feelings (Ps 51).

4. The Persian Dominion. In 538 B.C. the Babylonian empire fell before the irresistible prowess of Cyrus II of Persia. The change of dominion was hailed with delight by the devout Jews, and proved the prelude of better things to them. The religion of Cyrus (Zoroastrianism) permitting him to respect and safeguard other religions, he at once despatched Sheshbazzar—a prominent Jew—to Jerusalem, with a company of his compatriots, and authority to rebuild the Temple. The work was opposed and obstructed by the Palestinian Jews and their neighbours, the Samaritans, but eventually completed in 515 B.C. Associated with it were the prophets Haggai and Zechariah, Zerubbabel, the Persian governor of Judah, and Joshua the high priest. It was found impossible, however, to order and maintain the Temple worship satisfactorily, and the situation in Jerusalem became worse than before. Not until the time of Nehemiah and Ezra (circ. 446–430 B.C.) was the deliverance of the people completed, and their life and religion organised upon a stable basis. Then a large number of Babylonian Jews returned to Jerusalem; the walls were rebuilt; the people put definitely under the Divine Law, with the Temple as the centre of worship; and the charge of affairs, so far as permitted by the Persian satrap at Damascus, given to the elders or heads of families, with the high priest at their head. The improvement in their condition was so manifest, that the Samaritans copied their constitution, adopting the Pentateuch, and establishing a rival temple with a high priest on Mount Gerizim (Jn 4 20).

The next hundred years are involved in considerable obscurity, but it may safely be inferred that the regulations of Nehemiah and Ezra remained in force, and that the office of high priest grew in dignity and importance. Comparatively few in numbers, and limited to a territory of 10 or 15 m. radius round their capital, the Jews preserved their exclusiveness, and

kept up the worship and customs of their fathers.

5. Alexander the Great and his Successors. The conquests of Alexander the Great (334–323 B.C.) put an end to the Persian dominion. By successive victories at the Granicus (334 B.C.) and Issus (333 B.C.), and a series of campaigns in Egypt and the East, he made himself master of Asia. Jerusalem seems to have come peaceably into his possession. Josephus, in his 'Antiquities.' tells a story of Jaddua the high priest, and the leading inhabitants, going forth in pomp to meet him, and being received with reverence and emotion ; but this is generally regarded as a romance of later years. In any case, he showed himself favourable to the Jews, and settled some of them, with special privileges, in his new capital, Alexandria, where they afterwards grew into a large and prosperous colony. With Alexander, it must be noticed, came a body of new ideas and Western ways of life, which eventually permeated the thoughts and habits of the peoples whom he conquered. The Greek language and literature became widely known, and the arrangements and constitution of the Greek cities were generally adopted. At first these Hellenistic tendencies, as they were called, were resisted at Jerusalem ; but in course of time they gained a footing there as elsewhere, and exerted considerable influence upon the current of events.

After Alexander's death in 323 B.C., a period of fierce fighting ensued amongst his generals for the possession of his dominions. Out of the confusion two new kingdoms emerged, Egypt and Syria, between which Palestine lay, as a debatable land, and was the cause of protracted contention. After the battle of Ipsus, however, in 301 B.C., it passed finally to Egypt.

6. The Ptolemies. The founder of the Greek dynasty in Egypt being Ptolemy, it became a rule with his successors to bear that name and a surname added for the sake of distinction. Under the first three Ptolemies, the Jews were contented and prosperous, and extended their settlements in Egypt, where they were freely permitted to build synagogues, and practise their religious rites. The result was to bring them into closer touch and sympathy with Hellenism. The Jewish emigrants, for social and religious reasons, kept themselves in communication with Jerusalem, and occasionally resorted to it for the great feasts ; consequently they could hardly avoid transmitting Greek tendencies and influences to their own people. To this period belongs the original nucleus of the Septuagint version of the Holy Scriptures, the Pentateuch at least having been translated into Greek by Egyptian Jews, in the reign of Ptolemy II Philadelphus (284–247 B.C.).

Peace, however, was broken, and the conœntion over Palestine renewed, when Ptolemy IV Philopator filled the throne of Egypt. The weakness and dissoluteness of this king seemed to offer a favourable opportunity to Antiochus III of Syria, commonly called the Great, and he opened war upon him. To the joy of the Jews, Antiochus was signally defeated at Raphia (217 B.C.), and for a time had to relinquish his plans. On the death of Philopator, and the accession of his infant son Ptolemy V Epiphanes, the Syrian king resumed the war, and in 198 B.C. gained a decisive victory over the Egyptians at Panium, near the sources of the Jordan. The Jews, now suffering from the degeneracy and misgovernment of Egypt, welcomed the change of dominion, and assisted Antiochus to oust the Egyptian garrison from Jerusalem.

7. The Seleucidæ. The first Greek king of Syria, one of the best of Alexander's generals, had been Seleucus ; and his successors for a while took either his name or that of Antiochus, while the dynasty as a whole is known as the Seleucidæ. Antiochus the Great, the new overlord of Palestine, was the fifth in succession from the founder. He made no attempt to interfere with the privileges which the Jews had enjoyed under the rule of Egypt, but on the contrary, conferred further favours upon them, and allowed them the free exercise of their religion. The effect, however, of the Syrian supremacy was to introduce disunion among the Jews, and involve them in troubles such as they had not yet experienced. Antioch, the Syrian capital, was a great centre of Hellenism ; and the intercourse with it, of which the new conditions admitted, opened fresh channels for the entrance of Hellenising principles into Judah. Soon there arose a powerful Greek party in Jerusalem, and conflicts ensued with those who still cherished the national ideals, and contended for the righteousness of the law. After the death of Antiochus the Great, his son Seleucus IV Philopator (187–175 B.C.) accentuated the situation in Jerusalem by repressing the patriotic party, and attempting to plunder the Temple. In the time of his successor Antiochus IV Epiphanes (175–164 B.C.), matters came to a head. Onias, the high priest and leader of the orthodox party, drove the sons of Tobias and their Hellenising adherents out of Jerusalem ; Epiphanes intervened, and replaced Onias with creatures of his own, first Jason, then Menelaus ; Onias retired to Egypt, with many others of the devout, and at Leontopolis founded a new Jewish temple (170 B.C.). Jerusalem now seethed with discontent ; and, a report obtaining ground that Epiphanes had died campaigning in Egypt, a rising took place, in which many of the supporters of Menelaus were put to death. Epiphanes, on his return from Egypt, set himself not only to extinguish the revolt, but to prevent its recurrence. Besides treating the insurgents with merciless severity, he entered the Temple and despoiled it of its treasures and sacred vessels, recast the service according to the forms of the Greek religion, and set up an image of the Greek god Zeus, probably bearing his own features. At the same time, he remodelled the little state after the pattern of a Greek republic, and appointed over it a royal commissioner. Not so much, perhaps, from real hostility to the Jewish religion, as from the desire to extirpate the cause of disaffection and rebellion, torture and death were decreed against those who persisted in their Jewish practices, and refused to sacrifice to the heathen god.

At this point we come upon what is generally considered the most sublime moment in Jewish history. Many of the old patriotic party, now called the Hasidim, or 'righteous ones,' willingly gave up their lives, rather than betray their principles, thus setting a noble example for the martyrs of future ages. Some of them escaped to the wilder parts of the country, and, if taken on the sabbath, refused to defend themselves, lest they should desecrate the holy day. Passive submission was their answer to the hatred and cruelty of their persecutors. Human endurance, however, is not unlimited, and at length they stood at bay, and made a brave struggle for freedom. The first blow was struck at Modin, between Beth-horon and Lydda, by Mattathias, an old country priest, and head of the house of Hashmon. His anger rising at the sight of a Jew offering heathen sacrifice, he cut him down, as well as the Syrian officer, Apelles, who was with him. Fleeing to the wilderness, with his five sons, he gathered others round him, and raised the standard of revolt.

8. The Maccabees. On the death of Mattathias in 166 B.C., his son Judas, known as Maccabæus, or 'the hammer,' took over the leadership, and in less than two years, by a series of remarkable victories, at Beth-horon, Emmaus, and Beth-zur, cleared Judah of the Syrians, except for the garrison in the citadel (Acra) at Jerusalem. On 25 Dec. 165 B.C., the Temple was rededicated, and its worship restored—an event commemorated in the Feast of the Dedication, still observed by the Jews. In 163 B.C. Lysias, the regent of Syria for the young king, Antiochus V Eupator, advanced with an overwhelming force to relieve the garrison in the Acra, but Judas was able to make honourable terms with him, according to which the fortresses of Judah were to be dismantled, but the rights of the Jewish religion conserved. This settlement deprived the war of its religious character, and many of the Hasidim laid down their arms; but Judas was not content with it, and determined to continue the struggle, till political liberty was achieved. Resisting the elevation to the high priesthood of Alcimus, a flagrant Helleniser and nominee of the Syrian king, he gained a further victory over the Syrian general Nicanor, but in 161 B.C. was himself defeated by Bacchides, and fell in battle, at Eleasa.

Jonathan, the brother of Judas, succeeded to the leadership, and, after the death of Alcimus (160 B.C.), had full charge of affairs. An adroit and vigorous man, he made good use of the opportunity, offered by the troubles that thickened round the Syrian government, to win advantages for the Jewish state. Treacherously done to death in 144 B.C. by the Syrian general Trypho, he was followed by Simon, another son of Mattathias, who forced the Syrian garrison to withdraw from Jerusalem, and thus delivered his country from the last vestige of foreign control. With great solemnity, he was appointed by the people to the threefold office of high priest, commander-in-chief, and ethnarch; and the first Jewish coins were struck in his name (141 B.C.).

9. Independence. In the breaking up of the Syrian kingdom, Simon was able to consolidate the new Jewish state, extend its influence, and secure for it the friendship of the Romans. In 135 B.C. he, and two of his sons, were murdered at the castle of Dok near Jericho, by his ambitious son-in-law, Ptolemæus; and his third son, John Hyrcanus, took his place. In spite of the attempts of the Syrians to regain their supremacy, Hyrcanus maintained the independence of the state, and extended its narrow limits by the conquest of (1) Samaria, where he destroyed the temple on Mount Gerizim, and (2) Idumæa, whose inhabitants he compelled to accept the Law, and submit to circumcision. In his time, the Hasmonæan house began to lose the confidence of the orthodox, patriotic party, now called the Pharisees, and to cultivate closer relations with the Sadducees, the party of cosmopolitan ideas and worldly ambition.

Hyrcanus was succeeded by his son Aristobulus I, who assumed the title of king, and imitated the style of a foreign court. He only reigned a year (103 B.C.), but managed to annex Iturea (the Galilee of the Gospels) and compel its people to embrace Judaism. His brother, Alexander Jannæus (103–76 B.C.), a fierce and warlike king, extended still further the frontiers of the kingdom, and made Judæa the dominant power in Palestine. With him the house of Hashmon reached its greatest height, and began that downward course, which ended in its complete collapse.

His character and conduct, ill-suited to a high priest, made him hated by the Pharisees, on whom he inflicted many cruelties, and some 3,000 of whom sought safety in flight. At his death he bequeathed his high priesthood to his son Hyrcanus, and his political power to Alexandra his wife, whom he is said to have urged to peace with the Pharisees. Under her the Pharisees controlled affairs, and the kingdom, which equalled in power and extent the old Davidic dominion, had peace and rest; but at her death (67 B.C.) a fierce and prolonged contest for supremacy ensued between her sons, Aristobulus and Hyrcanus: the former, an active and daring man; the latter, feeble and irresolute, and almost entirely in the hands of a prominent Idumæan called Antipater. The Romans having now established themselves in Asia, both parties sought by presents and promises to enlist them in their favour. In 63 B.C. appeals were made at Damascus to the Roman general Pompey, who promptly marched upon Jerusalem, and, installing Hyrcanus as high priest, with a small territory subject to tribute, sent Aristobulus and his two sons to Rome. Thus, after eighty years of freedom, Judæa again came under foreign domination.

10. The Roman Dominion. (1) The Herods. For the next twenty years Hyrcanus (II) was high priest, but Antipater really exercised the power accorded under the Roman governor of Syria. During this time certain towns on the coast and in Peræa were released from Jewish control, and formed themselves into a league, under the name of the Decapolis (Mt 4 25). The attempts of Aristobulus and his sons, on escaping from Rome, to recover the crown, only added to the authority of Antipater. On his death by poison at the hands of a Jewish notable in 43 B.C., the government was divided between his sons Herod and Phasael, who received the titles of tetrarchs. Shortly afterwards the Parthians invaded Syria, and driving the Romans before them put Antigonus, son of Aristobulus, on the Jewish throne. Phasael was captured and killed; Hyrcanus had his ears cropped, to disqualify him for the high priesthood; Herod fled to Rome, where he was favourably received, and nominated by the Senate king of the Jews. Returning to Judæa with Roman help, Herod soon recaptured Jerusalem, and had Antigonus put to death (37 B.C.); thereafter maintaining his position till the dawn of the Christian era.

The material splendours of the reign of Herod have gained him the name of 'the Great,' but he was unscrupulous and cruel in his character, and dissolute in his life. To secure his power, he ingratiated himself adroitly with successive parties at Rome; and, on one pretext or another, killed out the survivors of the Hasmonæan house, including his own wife Mariamne and her two sons. Political intrigue and brutal murder were leading characteristics of his reign. At the same time, he aimed at magnificence, and executed many public works, besides restoring order and encouraging intercourse throughout the kingdom. Posing as a Hellenistic king, he built new cities upon Greek lines, such as Sebaste (27 B.C.), on the site of the old Samaria, and Cæsarea (22–10 B.C.), which became the second city of the kingdom. He also added a theatre and amphitheatre to Jerusalem, and built temples, porches, and baths in foreign cities. One of his greatest works was the rebuilding of the Temple at Jerusalem, which was begun in 20 B.C., and was not quite finished in the time of our Lord (Jn 2 20). In other ways he tried, but without success, to conciliate his Jewish subjects, respecting their traditions, and using his influence to protect their settlements abroad. To the end he was hated, especially by the Pharisees, who gave themselves more than ever to the minute observance of the Law, the study of the prophecies, and the hope of the Messianic kingdom.

On the death of Herod in 4 B.C., his dominions were divided, with the consent of the Romans, between his three sons : Archelaus becoming ethnarch of Judæa and Samaria ; Herod Antipas, tetrarch of Galilee and Peræa; and Philip, tetrarch of the region beyond Jordan. In 6 A.D. Archelaus was removed for misconduct, and his principality put under the charge of a Roman Procurator—so called from the original function of collecting the imperial taxes.

(2) Procurators. The following were procurators of Judæa and Samaria (6–41 A.D.): Coponius, M. Ambivius, Annius Rufus, Valerius Gratus (15–26), Pontius Pilate (26–36), Marcellus (36, 37), and Marullus (37–41). Wittingly and unwittingly, they often offended the susceptibilities of the Jews ; and, apart from the extortion which they generally practised, the duties and taxes which they were authorised to exact were a continual grievance. Pontius Pilate, whose condemnation of Christ has covered him with lasting infamy, aroused such exasperation otherwise that he was summarily recalled. The seat of the procurators was at Cæsarea, but Pilate happened to be at Jerusalem for the great feast, when the outburst against Christ took place. The outcome of the procuratorial system was widespread discontent, which was fomented by the Zealots—a new party aiming at revolution, and the establishment of the Messianic kingdom by force.

(3) Herod Agrippa. For a short time, a reversion took place to the old monarchical form of government, as it had existed in the time of Herod the Great. In 34 A.D. Philip, the tetrarch of the north, died ; and in 37 A.D. his dominions were given to Agrippa, a grandson of the Great Herod, with the title of king. To these were added in 40 A.D. the tetrarchy of Herod Antipas, the murderer of John the Baptist, whose misdoings and ambition were punished by his banishment to Gaul. A year later, the procuratorship of Judæa and Samaria was abolished, and Agrippa's dominions were extended to include these provinces, so that he now held sway over the whole of his grandfather's kingdom. His policy was to please the Pharisees, without offending the Romans ; consequently he conformed to Pharisaic practices, respected Jewish prejudices and traditions, and persecuted as schismatic the early Christian Church (Ac 12 1-19). After a reign of three years, he died suddenly at Cæsarea (Ac 12 23) ; and, his son Agrippa II being set aside as too young for rule, the whole kingdom was placed under procurators, subordinate to the governor of Syria.

(4) Palestinian Procurators. The order of these was : Cuspius Fadus (44–46 A.D.), Tiberius Alexander (46–48 A.D.), Ventidius Cumanus (48–52 A.D.), Felix (52–60 A.D.), Porcius Festus (60–62 A.D.), Albinus (62–64 A.D.), and Gessius Florus (64–66 A.D.). Under them the condition of things that had prevailed under the former procurators was accentuated ; misunderstanding, oppression, and extortion ripening the hatred and disaffection of the Jews. Alexander, though of Jewish descent, was an implacable tyrant ; Felix was so cruel and intolerant that lawlessness grew rampant, and the Zealots, increasing in numbers and daring, and now called Sicarii, from the weapon (sica) which they carried, kept the country seething with revolt ; Florus strained the patience and endurance of the people to the breaking point.

Cæsarea was the scene of the first outbreak. In that Gentile city there was a large colony of Jews, who at this time had settlements all over the civilised world, in Babylonia, Asia Minor, Upper and Lower Egypt, Greece, and Italy. The Jews of Cæsarea, having been deprived of their civil rights, were insulted and maltreated in the streets, and forced to quit the town. Florus chose this critical moment to plunder the Temple treasure and the upper city of Jerusalem, and put many of the inhabitants to death. Retaliations followed, and soon throughout the country Jew and Gentile were locked in deadly strife. The procurator appealed for help to the Governor of Syria, Cestus Gallius, who marched to his relief with 23,000 men, and, quickly subduing Galilee, appeared before Jerusalem. Forced to retreat, he was followed by the Jews, and defeated at

Beth-horon with heavy loss. Rome now sent her most experienced general, Vespasian, with a large increase of forces, to carry on the war. During the summer of 67 A.D. he brought the country districts into subjection, and took many of the smaller towns, Josephus, the historian, being one of the prisoners captured. Jerusalem he let alone for the time, as panic and fanaticism were there doing their deadly work, and thinning the ranks of the defenders. With the help of 26,000 Idumæans, the Zealots had secured complete control, and the consequent feuds and murders, aggravated by pestilence and famine, were fast bringing the city to a terrible pass. In the summer of 69 A.D. Vespasian was proclaimed emperor at Rome, and his son Titus took over the conduct of the war. Jerusalem fell to him in August of 70 A.D., after a four months' siege of terrible suffering and almost incredible orgies of rage and bloodshed. Titus would have spared the Temple and city, but they were set on fire by his soldiers, and burned to the ground. Most of the inhabitants were massacred ; those who survived were sold into slavery, or reserved to grace the conqueror's triumph at Rome.

Thus was fulfilled the warning of Christ forty years before (Lk 19$^{42-45}$).

Three fortresses held out for a while, but were ultimately taken : Machærus, to the E. of the Dead Sea, Herodeion and Massada to the W. The last-mentioned, which stood on an almost inaccessible mountain-top, was only captured after a prolonged siege (73 A.D.), and then the besiegers found to their horror that all the defenders had committed suicide together.

(5) The end. Judæa became a colony under a Roman governor, the condition of the inhabitants resembling that of their brethren of the Dispersion. Without political rights, without their Sanhedrin, without their Temple and priests, they were like strangers in a strange land. Once again, in Hadrian's time, they rebelled and, under the leadership of Simon Bar-Kocheba, resisted the Roman power for over three years (132–135 A.D.) ; but the revolt was stamped out in blood, and Jerusalem turned into a Gentile city, under the name of Ælia Capitolina, into which the Jews were forbidden to enter. Here their history closes, so far as their association with the land of their fathers is concerned.

2. LITERATURE OF THE PERIOD BETWEEN THE OLD AND NEW TESTAMENTS

According to the theory of the Jewish Church, direct revelation ceased with the prophets ; hence no books were admitted into the Old Testament Canon which were known to have been produced after the time of Ezra and the Great Synagogue. A considerable body of religious literature is extant, belonging to the period that supervened before the rise of the New Testament Canon. Emanating from centres so widely diffused as Egypt, Palestine, and Babylonia, it is not only interesting in itself, but an indispensable source of information upon the course of contemporary thought and events. The books of which it is composed vary in character, from the narrative and legendary to the didactic and prophetic, but as a whole reflect the later developments of social and religious life among the Jews, their national vicissitudes, and the foreign influences to which they were subjected. They thus help to bridge the chasm between the Old Testament and the New, and throw light upon the preparation proceeding in the world for the advent of the Christian faith, and the environment in which it originally found itself.

Many of them are distinguished from the canonical Scriptures by their manifest inferiority of thought and style, which betrays itself in a want of freshness and originality, and a tendency to rhetorical and artificial ex-

pression. Reverence for the past is a prevailing feature of these books ; and this appears, sometimes, in the modification and enlargement of Old Testament narratives and the imitation of books like Proverbs and Job : at other times, in exaggerated accounts of the doings of Jewish heroes, and fulsome estimates of their characters. Not infrequently, however, they rise to a higher level ; and not only, as in 1 Maccabees, contain reliable, historical matter of the utmost importance, but also, as in Wisdom and Ecclesiasticus, exhibit a felicity of diction and grasp of religious truth which put them on a level with some of the books of the Canon. The higher elements of their teaching, the hopes they originated or sustained, and their anticipations of New Testament thought and phraseology, will be indicated in the review of the development of Jewish religion that follows this article (p. lxvi).

I. THE APOCRYPHA

1 Esdras.	Song of the Three Holy
2 Esdras.	Children.
Tobit.	History of Susanna.
Judith.	Bel and the Dragon.
The rest of Esther.	Prayer of Manasses.
Wisdom.	1 Maccabees.
Ecclesiasticus.	2 Maccabees.
Baruch.	

This is a collection of books importan

enough to have had canonical authority claimed for them. They have never, however, been able to secure more than the general approval of the Jewish or the Christian Church. Among the Alexandrian Jews they were held in such high repute as, with the exception of 2 Esdras, to be embodied in their (Greek) version of the Old Testament Scriptures. Some of the early Christian Fathers, notably Augustine, accepted and used them as sacred literature, thereby establishing a tradition in the Roman Church, which led to the recognition of their canonicity at the Council of Trent. In connexion with this view, the term deutero-canonical is sometimes applied to them : it indicates that they belong to a second canon of Scripture only slightly, if at all, inferior to the first. On the other hand, the Palestinian Jews rigidly excluded them from the Hebrew Canon, and were followed in their unfavourable estimate by the great Christian scholar Jerome. Generally speaking, his position with respect to them is that which prevails in the modern Reformed Church : they may be read for edification, as they contain valuable lessons for the conduct of life, but they are not to be used as a basis of doctrine.

The term, 'Apocrypha,' by which they are known, is derived from the Greek, and means 'secret' or 'hidden.' It used to be applied to the doctrinal writings of religious and philosophical sects, which were concealed from the world, and even withheld from many of their own members. Originally, therefore, there was nothing objectionable about it : it simply implied that the books so designated were confined in their use to a limited circle ; but, as some of them were found to assume an authorship to which they were not entitled, and as all of them had their claims of canonicity rejected, the word acquired a disparaging sense, and 'apocryphal' came to be an equivalent for spurious or false. This no doubt has affected the estimate put upon these books, and the treatment they have received ; though their uncertain origin and uncanonical authority in no way detract from their historic significance and usefulness. Some of the books of the Canon are in similar case so far as uncertainty of origin is concerned. Like them, the 'apocryphal' books must be considered on their merits, when it will be found that they are of great value both from the religious and historical point of view. They are the oldest and most important witnesses to the period that succeeded the Captivity ; they help to bring its great movements of thought and activity before us ; they provide an independent testimony to the place and influence which the canonical books of Scripture had already acquired among the Jews ;

and they show us, in actual operation, that fusion of Hellenistic language and culture with Jewish speech and modes of thought, which is reflected in the New Testament, and which prepared the way for the expansion and development of the Christian religion.

(1) The First Book of Esdras

Esdras is the Greek form of 'Ezra,' the name of the great Jewish scribe, with whom two of the canonical books are intimately concerned. These are frequently conjoined in a sequence with the two apocryphal books, which then become 3rd and 4th, 1st and 4th, or 1st and 3rd Esdras respectively. The English usage, however, which follows the method of the Geneva Bible, is to give the names of Ezra and Nehemiah to the canonical books, and call the apocryphal 1st and 2nd Esdras. This arrangement is sufficiently convenient, and is warranted by the fact that the apocryphal books exist only in Greek and Latin versions, not in Hebrew or Chaldaic.

For the most part, 1 Esdras is a compilation from the canonical Scriptures, probably done by various hands. The passages transcribed, with unimportant alterations, are the last two chs. of 2 Chronicles, considerable portions of Ezra, and Nehemiah 7^{73}–8^{13} ; all dealing with the destruction and rebuilding of the Temple, and the promulgation of the Law by Ezra. There is, however, an original section (chs. 3–5^6), in which a striking incident or legend is introduced. Zerubbabel, at the Persian court, gives such an exhibition of wisdom, as to secure the favour of king Darius, and the return of the captive Jews. In a contest of wits, he carries off the palm by his eloquent praise of truth, and vindication of the superiority of its power over that of wine, the king, or woman. 'Great is the earth,' he says, 'high is the heaven, swift is the sun in his course... Is he not great that maketh these things ? therefore great is the truth, and stronger than all things... With her there is no accepting of persons or rewards... Neither in her judgment is any unrighteousness ; and she is the strength, kingdom, power, and majesty of all ages. Blessed be the God of truth.' To this all the people answer, 'Great is Truth, and mighty above all things' ; which, with some slight variation, has passed into a proverbial expression (4^{33-41}).

The date of this book cannot be determined with certainty, as there is no external evidence of its existence earlier than Josephus (100 A.D.). It is supposed, however, to have been written in Alexandria, about the end of the second or the beginning of the first century B.C. Its emphatic representation of the favour shown to the Jews by the Persian kings would suggest, as the aim of the author. the desire to obtain similar benefits from the king of Egypt, but there is hardly support for the view that the occasion was the building of the Temple of Onias for the Jews of Alexandria in 170 B.C.

(2) The Second Book of Esdras

As cast in a prophetic rather than a historic mould, this book differs widely from the foregoing, and used to be called 'the Revelation of Ezra.' It is a combination of three distinct writings, or an original writing supplemented by two considerable additions from different hands. There are 16 chs. in all, but the first and last pairs form sections by themselves, and are evidently of later date than the main body of the work. Their affinities with New Testament thought and phraseology suggest for each of them a Christian source: cp. 1 30-33 with Mt 23 37f., 2 13 with Mt 25 34, 15 8 with Rev 6 10, and 16 54 with Lk 16 15. The burden of these chs. is the rebuke of Israel for her rebellions, and the summoning of the Gentiles to the enjoyment of the blessings forfeited by her, with denunciations of judgment, quite in the vein of the Old Testament prophets, upon the nations that provoke and withstand God. They are probably as late as the third century A.D.

Chs. 3–14, which form the larger section of the book, are of purely Jewish origin, though they were known from early times to the Christian Church. They describe a series of revelations and visions purporting to have been communicated to Ezra in the thirtieth year of the Babylonian captivity. Depressed with the sorrows of his people and doubts of the righteous government of God, he is visited by the angel Uriel, who reproves his sadness, and throws light upon the moral mysteries of the world. In three revelations and five visions Uriel shows him that, though the purposes of God are unsearchable, his Providence is surely working for the defeat of evil and the triumph of good. Iniquity may succeed for a time, but it has its appointed limit, and when the signs indicated in the visions are fulfilled, the Son of God, the Anointed One, shall appear and reign. The powers of the heathen shall be broken, and the lost tribes of Israel gathered together again into their city of Zion. Meantime Ezra is to have the Law written out for the people, and seventy books of mysteries prepared for those worthy to participate in the secret things of God. In several places there are noteworthy references to the Messiah (7 27f. 12 31f. 13 32, 37, 52), and in one passage (7 29) a curious statement regarding His death: 'after these years shall my son Christ die, and all men that have life.'

A clue to the date of the book is afforded by the vision of the eagle (11 1–12 51), the wings and heads of which are evident allusions to successive emperors of Rome. The last to whom reference is made is Domitian; in his reign accordingly the composition of the book is generally placed (81–96 A.D.). The destruction of Jerusalem by Titus, and the consequent troubles of the Jews, may account for the melancholy of the writer and his choice of subject. Some remains of a Greek version are extant; but since the discovery of a missing fragment by Professor Bensly, in 1875, the whole exists in a Latin translation, and on this account is sometimes called the Latin Esdras as distinguished from the other or Greek Esdras.

(3) The Book of Tobit

This is a religious tale, cast in very pleasing form. It may have had a historical basis, but that would be of little importance in comparison with its purpose. The scene is laid in Nineveh, in the time of the Assyrian captivity. Tobit, a pious, God-fearing man, of the tribe of Naphtali, loses his eyesight, and falls into such other grievous misfortunes as cause him to pray for death. Calling to mind ten talents of silver which he had left with a kinsman in Media, he sends his son Tobias for them, accompanied by a stranger hired for the journey. At Ecbatana they lodge in the house of Raguel, whose daughter Sara is in great distress and desirous of death, owing to the slaying of her seven successive husbands on the wedding night by the evil spirit Asmodeus. Tobias marries her, and she is delivered from the power of the evil spirit. The ten talents of silver are recovered, the eyesight of Tobit is miraculously restored, and both households enjoy renewed prosperity—all through the instrumentality of the travelling companion of Tobias, who proves to be the angel Raphael, sent by God in answer to the prayers of Tobit and Sara.

The story was doubtless intended to encourage and comfort the Jews of foreign lands, and stimulate their observance of the Law. Incidentally, considerable emphasis is laid upon almsgiving (e.g. 4 7-11 12 8, 9), and the marriage of Tobias may be introduced to point the advantages of Jews intermarrying with their own people.

It is difficult to assign a date to the book, but various indications suggest either the second or the beginning of the first century B.C. It seems to have had a Hebrew original, but there is no Hebrew text extant earlier than the LXX version.

(4) The Book of Judith

This is another historical romance, though different in kind from that of Tobit. Judith, the heroine, a pious and beautiful widow, performs a deed of daring for her people not unlike that of Jael in the book of Judges.

Her native city of Bethulia (said in 4^6 7^3 to be over against Esdraelon, though identified by some modern scholars with Jerusalem, on the interpretation of the name as 'House of God'), being besieged by Holofernes, the general of Nebuchadnezzar, she determines to effect its deliverance. Making her way with a single attendant into the camp of Holofernes, she captivates him with her beauty, and secures his favour ; then, when he is filled with wine, she cuts off his head, and returns with it to the city. The courage of the besieged is roused to such a pitch that they rush out upon the enemy, and put them to complete rout.

The story has been a frequent subject of art, and may have had its origin in some actual occurrence ; but as it stands, it can hardly be historical. Its general features are improbable, and it contains many historical and geographical misconceptions. Its purpose evidently is to animate the patriotic zeal of the Jews, and confirm them, not only in the observance of their own Law and customs, but in their resistance of foreign oppression. The time of the Maccabean struggle would accord well with its spirit, and many are disposed to ascribe its composition to that period, about the middle of the second century B.C. Others bring it down a century later—to the time of Hyrcanus II—and find veiled allusions in the high qualities with which the heroine is credited to queen Alexandra, a strong supporter of the Pharisees (76–67 B.C.). It probably belongs to one or other of these periods.

(5) The rest of the Book of Esther

In the LXX version of the canonical book of Esther a number of passages appear which are not in the Hebrew text. These interpolations were probably introduced in the Jewish schools of Alexandria, in which it was not unusual to work up traditional narratives into longer form and embellish them with striking details. Collected together by Jerome, and placed at the end of his translation of Esther, they now form the apocryphal book. Besides amplifying the scriptural story, they evidently aim at giving it a more distinctly religious turn, by ascribing the deliverance of the Jews from their Gentile enemies to the intervention of God in answer to the prayers of Mordecai and Esther. In the six and a half short chapters of which the supplement consists these prayers are given, as well as a dream of Mordecai, and two letters of Artaxerxes the king—one commanding a wholesale destruction of the Jews, and another revoking that order and enjoining the thirteenth day of the twelfth month Adar to be kept as a memorial feast.

These additions are generally supposed to belong to the first or second century B.C. It is easy to see why the Alexandrian Jews would admit them into their Canon. They illustrated the care of God over His people in foreign lands, and made up by the frequent mention of His name for the marked absence of it in the older book.

(6) The Wisdom of Solomon

This is a book of great interest and importance. As its title indicates, it belongs to the class of 'Wisdom' literature, of which it is one of the most striking examples. In it may be seen the stream of revealed truth coming into contact with the current of heathen speculation, and the 'wisdom' idea of Old Testament times passing into the later Logos doctrine. The ascription of its authorship to Solomon is, of course, an example of a common literary device of the period, and implies no intention of imposing upon the readers. The adoption of Solomon's name is only meant to suggest the character and scope of the work. It was quite in accordance with ancient usage, to affix to an original production the name of a great predecessor, in whose spirit it might be presumed to be written, or whose work it professed to continue. In the present instance, neither the author's contemporaries nor his future critics were likely to be deceived by the sponsorship assumed.

The book is a hymn in praise of Wisdom, and falls naturally into two parts. (1) Chs. 1–9. Wisdom is regarded in a speculative aspect ; its origin and effects are discussed, and the pursuit of it is earnestly commended to men. Beginning with an exhortation to seek Wisdom, these chapters then lay down the conditions of success—purity of thought, truthfulness of speech, and uprightness in deed. The position of the Materialist is canvassed, and shown to be the result of voluntary ignorance of God, and the introduction of death and sin into the world through the envy of the devil. This leads on to an elaborate contrast of the righteous with the wicked, in regard to their families, their length of life, and fate in the world to come. Wisdom is then eulogised as the true guide of life ; her properties are represented under the figure of a bride, and men, especially rulers, are enjoined to seek and pray for her after the example of Solomon.

(2) Chs. 10–19. Wisdom is discussed in its historical aspect, as exhibited in the history of Israel. First, a sketch is given of the lives of the fathers from Adam to Moses, to illustrate the effects of the guidance of Wisdom ; this is followed up by warnings against the neglect of it, drawn from the punishments that overtook the Egyptians and the Canaanites ; then the revolting character and results of idolatry are described, and a comparison is instituted between the Israelites

and the Egyptians, greatly in favour of the former, which is kept up to the end of the book.

Its apparently abrupt termination has suggested the idea that part of it has been lost, and a supposed difference of manner between the two sections has been taken to betray a difference of authorship; but it is doubtful whether there are sufficient grounds for either surmise. The book is generally regarded as complete, and the work of one person—a Jew of Alexandria, probably writing about the period 217–145 B.C., though the date of his composition is sometimes put considerably before and after that period. The style throughout is in keeping with the sustained loftiness of its thought, and both alike are influenced by the fusion of Hebrew and classical learning that took place in Egypt before the dawn of the Christian era. On the one hand, the point of view is Jewish, and the more valuable elements of the ancient faith are justified and enforced. Occasional Hebraic phrases are also used, and expressions and ideas borrowed from the Old Testament, as well as the name of Solomon, and the manner of the canonical writings previously assigned to him. On the other hand, the language is Greek, of a pure and polished character, sometimes rising into strains of great eloquence; and there are frequent allusions to Greek customs and ideas, which could only come from one intimately acquainted with the culture of the West. Thus in 2^8, the revellers crown themselves with garlands; in 4^2, conquerors in a strife are rewarded with a wreath; in 13^{15}, every household has its gods; in 14^1, every ship has its protecting deity; and in 19^{21}, manna is termed 'ambrosial food.' Again, there are evident references to Platonic and Stoic philosophy, in the 'formless matter' (11^{17}) out of which the world is created; in the application of the phrase 'understanding spirit' to Wisdom (7^{22}); in the enumeration of the four cardinal virtues (8^7), and elsewhere. There are many compound words peculiar to the book, such as 'infant-slaying' (11^7), 'child-killing' (14^{23}), 'ill-labouring' (15^8), and 'sounding-around' (17^4); and the word 'Protoplast,' now used as a scientific term, probably appears in it for the first time ($7^1 10^1$). There are, also, some felicitous expressions that have now become current in religious speech; for example, 'a hope full of immortality' (3^4), and 'the souls of the righteous are in the hand of God' (3^1).

The purpose of the book was to vindicate the essentials of the Jewish faith against materialism, idolatry, and speculative philosophy, and encourage the Alexandrian Jews to adhere to the religion of their fathers, in spite of the seductions of heathenism, and the ad-

verse circumstances in which they were placed. That it had its effect in this direction, even to succeeding generations, may be seen from the influence it has exerted upon the New Testament. Some of the books, such as the Gospel of John and Hebrews, show considerable affinities of thought with it, while most of them reflect its phraseology. The combination 'grace and mercy' ($3^9 4^{15}$) reappears in 1 Tim 1^2 and elsewhere; the expression 'for truly they perhaps err while they seek after God, and have the will to find Him' (13^6) is almost the same as 'that they should seek the Lord if haply they might feel after Him, and find Him' (Ac 17^{27}); and the likeness between 5^{17-20} and Paul's description of the Christian armour in Eph 6^{13-17} is too exact to be accidental: cp. also 3^5 with Rev 3^4 16^6, 7^{26} with Heb 1^{13}, 13^2 with 1 Cor 8^5, etc.

(7) The Wisdom of Jesus, the Son of Sirach, or Ecclesiasticus

The former of these two titles is the more ancient, being that of the LXX version, and indicates the character and authorship of the book. The latter, which means 'pertaining to the Church' or 'Churchly,' is the title given to it from the fourth century onward, on account of the use made of it in the worship and instruction of the Western Church: it appears in the Latin and English versions. The shorter forms 'Proverbs' and 'Ben-Sira' are also found.

It is a book of the same class as the preceding, having for its subject the praise and inculcation of Wisdom; but it is written upon more practical lines, and from a more distinctively Hebraistic point of view. In style and thought it stands between the Wisdom books of the Old Testament Canon and the book of Wisdom in the Apocrypha. Its closest affinities are with the book of Proverbs. It starts from the same general conception of Wisdom, and follows a similar method in applying it by means of short, pithy sayings, to moral conduct and behaviour. It broadens and develops the standpoint of Proverbs, but not to the same extent as the Wisdom of Solomon, nor does it exhibit the same speculative bias and admixture of Greek philosophical notions. The one is the native, Palestinian type of later Wisdom thinking: the other is its cosmopolitan, Alexandrian expression.

There is no apparent plan in the book of Ecclesiasticus. It is a series of reflections upon life, some doubtless original, some simply gathered, rather than a reasoned treatise. Its contents, however, may be roughly divided into two unequal sections. (1) Chs. 1–43. This section opens with a chapter in praise of Wisdom, and closes with a sublime and powerful passage upon the works of Nature. The intervening chapters are devoted to the discussion of Wisdom, mostly in its practical bearings, a great variety of topics being introduced, such as obedience to parents, regard for the poor, friendship, prudence, envy, pride, boastfulness, women, and money. These are sometimes called the Sayings of the Wise. They represent the kind of instruction that was needed in the circumstances of the time. The decay of the national idea, consequent upon the exile, had given rise to questions of individual behaviour and responsibility, which had not been pressing at the time the older canonical books were written. Something was needed to supplement the word of revelation, and this the son of Sirach undertakes to supply. Many of the sentiments are exalted enough, but others merely worldly wise, and some rather repellent to the modern mind. Even at their lowest, however, they seldom fail to be interesting for the light they shed upon contemporary life and thought.

(2) Chs. 44–51. This section passes in review the great names of Hebrew history, and eulogises the bearers of them for their faithfulness to God and the Law. The names of Ezra, Daniel, and Mordecai are omitted from the list, and in a kind of Epilogue the feeling of the time to the Samaritans is shown in a passing reference to them as 'a nation which my heart abhorreth' (50 25, 26). It closes with an appendix in the form of a prayer or thanksgiving, the genuineness of which has been disputed, but which is perhaps the author's own afterthought.

If there are any traces of Greek influence in the book, they are confined to a few general conceptions, such as the identification of virtue with knowledge, and the emphasis laid upon moderation in action. These may quite well be accounted for by the Hellenistic atmosphere that prevailed even in Palestine itself. The thought is predominantly Jewish, and of a period antecedent at least to the rise of the Maccabees. Wisdom is viewed in its later scriptural significance, as the knowledge of God, and the guide and inspiration of life; God is regarded as the universal Lord, the Creator and Governor of the whole world of men and things; no account is taken of intermediate beings, except in quotations from the Old Testament; prominence is given to the Law, but there is no indication of a belief in the resurrection, and no definite Messianic anticipation; the rewards of a good life are still to be found in temporal prosperity and posthumous fame.

This is quite in agreement with the authorship which the book itself claims, and the date which is accordingly assumed for it. Unlike the rest of the Apocrypha, it carries its real author's name with it. In 50 27, he calls himself 'Jesus the son of Sirach of Jerusalem'; and there is a preface to the book containing further details. According to it, the book was composed by Jesus, in Hebrew, and translated into Greek by his grandson (the writer of the preface), in the thirty-eighth year of Euergetes, king of Egypt, in which country the translation is also stated to have been made. This is generally understood to refer to Ptolemy VII Physcon (170–116 B.C.), the thirty-eighth year of whose reign would give 132 B.C. as the date of the translation. Going back two generations, we come to the first quarter of the century, in which accordingly the composition of the original must be placed. Corroboration of this date is found in the fact that the list of great men mentioned in the book closes with Simon the high priest, understood to be Simon II (218–198 B.C.); and the account given of him is so circumstantial as to suggest most strongly actual knowledge on the part of the author. This interpretation of the preface is sometimes disputed, on the strength of an ambiguity in the Greek, and the references applied to a previous Euergetes and Simon; but the probabilities are all in favour of it. Nearly one-half of the original Hebrew text, it may be mentioned, has been discovered in recent years.

The preface of the translator, besides helping to solve the questions of date and authorship, throws a valuable light upon the authority and contents of the Old Testament Canon in his day. He speaks of it as the Law, the Prophets, and the rest of the books.

There are no direct citations from Ecclesiasticus in the New Testament; but various passages seem to show an acquaintance with it: cp. 29 12 f. with Lk 12 19 f., 2 1-5 with Jas 1 2-4, and 5 11 with Jas 1 19. Later writers, however, frequently appeal to it; and John Bunyan, in his 'Grace Abounding,' relates how he was 'greatly enlightened and encouraged' by the passage: 'Look at the generations of old, and see; did ever any trust in the Lord, and was confounded? or did any abide in His fear, and was forsaken? or whom did He ever despise, that called upon Him? For the Lord is full of compassion and mercy, longsuffering, and very pitiful, and forgiveth sins, and saveth in time of affliction' (2 10, 11). Here, as at 18 10-13, the conception of God's forbearance approaches very close to the thought of Ps 103.

(8) The Book of Baruch

In this book, which is not to be confounded with the Apocalypse of Baruch, several documents are brought together under the name of Baruch, the faithful friend and secretary of the prophet Jeremiah. Most of it professes to have been written by him, at Babylon, five years after Jerusalem was destroyed by the

Chaldeans; but linguistic and historical considerations alike preclude this. It consists at least of two distinct sections and a supplementary chapter, each in all probability emanating from a different hand. (1) 1–3[8]. After a short historical introduction, a confession of sin is put into the mouths of the captive Jews, and a prayer that God will forgive them their offences, especially that of disregarding the prophets. (2) 3[9]–5[9]. A discourse is addressed to the Israelites scattered among the nations, ascribing their afflictions to their disobedience to God the fountain of Wisdom, and comforting them with the hope of a glorious restoration. There is no organic connexion between these two sections, and they even appear to have been originally written in different languages—the one in Hebrew, and the other in Greek. Both of them, however, adopt the prophetic style of utterance : the first being largely modelled upon Jeremiah and Daniel, the second upon Job and Isaiah. It is difficult to assign dates to them. If, as seems most probable, the mention of the fall of Jerusalem is an allusion to its destruction by the Romans, and not, as is sometimes supposed, to its capture by Antiochus Epiphanes, the former section would require to be placed after 70 A.D. On the other hand, the latter section may be somewhat earlier. Its closing verses bear some resemblance to a passage in the Psalms of Solomon, which are usually referred to the middle of the first century B.C., so that it is generally put subsequent to that, or about the beginning of the Christian era. The combination of the two sections, as we have them in the book of Baruch, could not take place much before the end of the first century A.D. It does not seem to have been held in much esteem by the Jews.

The supplementary chapter (6) purports to be a letter written by Jeremiah, the prophet, to the Jews about to be led captive to Babylon. It, too, is unauthentic, being most likely the production of an Alexandrian Jew of the first century B.C. It is a curious piece of writing, and deals chiefly with the folly of idolaters and the impotency of idols. Probably it was suggested to the writer by the letter mentioned in Jer 29[1], and offered a safe medium for the conveyance to his fellow-countrymen of a warning against the dangers and temptations which surrounded them in Egypt.

(9) The Song of the Three Holy Children

This and the two following pieces, each of a single chapter, appear in the Greek Bible as additions to Daniel. They illustrate the tendency of the Jewish schools, especially in Alexandria, to weave moral and religious legends round the striking names of sacred

history. Nothing is known of their origin, which may have been quite independent of the canonical book : in any case, they were incorporated with it before the beginning of the Christian era.

The Three Holy Children are Shadrach, Meshach, and Abed-nego, under their Hebrew names of Ananias, Misael, and Azarias (Dan 1[6,7]). Their Song is inserted in the Greek Daniel between vv. 23 and 24 of the third chapter, at the point where they 'fell down bound into the midst of the burning fiery furnace.' It consists of (a) (vv. 1–22) a prayer of Azarias, which is quite general in its terms, and makes confession and supplication for Israel as a whole, after the manner of Dan 9 and Ezr 9 ; (b) (vv. 23–27) a connecting narrative which, in its description of the preservation of the three Hebrews from the flames that consume some of the Chaldeans, seems to give the answer to the prayer ; (c) (vv. 28–68) a thanksgiving or invocation to creation in all its different orders to praise and bless the Lord.

The last section, which is the Song proper, has only one reference to the deliverance which purports to be the occasion of it. It is largely dependent upon such thanksgiving Psalms as 103[20f.], 136, 148, and Ecclus 43. Under the name of 'The Benedicite,' or 'The Song of the Three Children,' it was sung in the Christian Church as early as the fourth century. It is still used in the Anglican Church at morning service as an alternative canticle to the 'Te Deum.'

(10) The History of Susanna

In the Greek Daniel, this story stands as a supplement to the twelve canonical chapters. It tells how Daniel, in his youth, by his great wisdom, delivered the chaste and beautiful Susanna from condemnation to death upon a shameful charge. The story recalls Ahab and Zedekiah, the two evil prophets of Babylon, who roused the anger of Jeremiah (29[20-23]), and who are frequently mentioned in later Jewish writings. It may have been intended to reprobate iniquity in high places, or simply to glorify the wisdom of Daniel. Shakespeare must have had it in mind, when he made Shylock exclaim, 'a Daniel come to judgment' ('Mer. of Ven.' IV, 1).

(11) The History of the Destruction of Bel and the Dragon

Here are given two further stories of the wisdom and piety of Daniel. They are attached to the Greek text of the canonical book as a concluding or fourteenth chapter. In the first (vv. 1–22), Daniel exposes the deceit practised by the priests of Bel, in pretending that the god devours the large daily offerings of food and wine, while they and their wives and children steal in by a secret entrance, and consume them during the night. The result is that the priests and their families are put to death, and Daniel is permitted to destroy Bel and his temple. The second story (vv. 23–42) tells of the destruction of a sacred dragon, to which the Babylonians paid divine honours. The Jewish hero feeds it with indigestible materials, which cause it to burst, and he is thrown into a den of lions at the instigation of its enraged worshippers. There he remains unharmed for six days, and is supported by food brought miraculously from Judæa by the prophet Habakkuk. On his release, his enemies are given to the lions, and at once devoured. This was supposed by the later Jews to be quite a different incident from that preserved in the canonical book.

The Greek title of the double narrative is, ' From the prophecy of Habakkuk, the son of Jesu, of the tribe of Levi.' Its aim is to contrast the impotence of idols with the omnipotence of God, and expose the futility and absurdity of worshipping them. It may have been suggested by the references of Jeremiah (10^{14} 51^{34}) to the falsehood of images, and the dragon-like voracity of Nebuchadrezzar, king of Babylon.

(12) The Prayer of Manasses

This is a short confession of personal sin, and fervent supplication for the divine forgiveness, cast in a very beautiful form. It purports to be the prayer of the penitent Manasseh, king of Judah, during his imprisonment in Babylon (2 Ch 33$^{11-13}$); but, with the exception of one expression, ' I am bowed down with many iron bands,' there is nothing that applies distinctively to him. There is no mention of specific sins that might have been expected to form the chief burden of his confession. The ascription of the prayer to him was probably suggested by 2 Ch 33^{18,19}, which states that his prayer was written, along with his acts, ' in the book of the kings of Israel.' and ' among the sayings of the seers.' Already in existence, it may have had the name of Manasseh affixed to it, on the strength of this passage; or it may have been expressly composed for insertion in the canonical Scriptures at this place. It is largely dependent upon biblical phraseology and ideas, and is poetical in form. It is supposed to have had a Hebrew or Aramaic original.

(13) The First Book of the Maccabees

There are four books of the Maccabees in all—so called from the name of the family that rose to supreme power in Judæa during the second century B.C.—but only two of them are in the Apocrypha and claim consideration in this section.

1 Maccabees is a history of the forty years (175–135 B.C.) during which, under the famous family, the Jews carried on their struggle for religious freedom and political independence. Its general reliability, fulness of detail, and accuracy in regard to dates, render it of the highest value for the knowledge of the period. After a brief introduction upon the conquests of Alexander the Great and the origin of the Syrian empire, it follows the course of events, almost in strict chronological order, from the persecutions of Antiochus Epiphanes, to the death of Simon, the third of the Maccabæan brothers. (a) (1^{10}-2) An account of the sufferings of the Syrian persecutions is given, and the revolt described which Mattathias initiated at Modin. (b) (3–9^{22}) The heroic efforts and achievements of Judas Maccabæus are detailed (167–161 B.C.), including his recovery of the Temple and dedication of a new altar to God. (c) (9^{23}–16) The further fortunes of the nation are followed, through the reign of Jonathan (160–143 B.C.), to their climax under Simon (143–135 B.C.). A brief mention of John Hyrcanus, Simon's successor, brings the book to a close.

The narrative hardly ever fails to be interesting, being written in simple, succinct style, with due proportion observed throughout, and numerous graphic touches that suggest a contemporary knowledge of places and events. The only exceptions that have been taken to its general trustworthiness are, the statement in 1^6 that Alexander parted his dominions among his generals while yet alive, the reference to the Roman Senate in 8^{15,16}, and a tendency to exaggerate the numbers of the Syrians in the various battles opposed to the Jews. Except in the wonderful successes of the Jews, in view of the statements of the odds against them, there is no appearance of a miraculous element; and seldom, as in other books of the kind, is the flow of the narrative interrupted by the personal reflections of the author. One outstanding feature of the book is the method of dating events from the beginning of 'the kingdom of the Greek'; that is to say, from the foundation of the Seleucid dynasty in Syria (312 B.C.). There is no such accurate reckoning upon the line of a recognised era in previous Jewish literature.

The composition of 1 Maccabees is usually assigned to the beginning of the first century B.C. On the one hand, it is said, the terms of friendliness and admiration in which it refers to the Romans (c. 8) necessitate the dating of it some years before the capture of Jerusalem by Pompey (63 B.C.), and, on the other hand, the last verses of the book (16^{23,24}), in which it asserts that ' the rest of the acts of John (Hyrcanus) are written in the chronicles,' imply that his reign (135–105 B.C.) was concluded before it was composed. The latter inference, however, is sometimes disputed, on the ground that the verses quoted embody a stereotyped formula, with which the author merely rounds off his book, and which he might quite well have used, though he wrote in the time of Hyrcanus. The tone of the book, it is argued, its remarkable accuracy, and certain specific references, require an earlier date, and so it is placed at the beginning of the reign of Hyrcanus, or between 135 and 125 B.C.

There is little doubt that it was originally written in Hebrew by a Palestinian Jew. This was the opinion of Origen and Jerome, and it is confirmed by the number of Hebrew idioms in the Greek text and occasional evidences of mistranslation and transliteration of proper names. The interest, too, of the author in Palestine, and his minute acquaintance with its topography go to corroborate it. Other facts regarding the author may be gathered by inference from his book. It is plain that he was a patriotic Jew, devoted to the customs and religion of his country. He was also intimately acquainted with political affairs, being probably a man of rank, who moved in the highest circles. At the same time, he must have been a loyal adherent of the Hasmonæan family, whose deeds he extols, and to whom he ascribes the prosperity and glory of Israel. That he refrains from the mention of the name of God, generally substituting for it the term 'heaven,' is only in accordance with the practice of his time, arising from the growing view of God's transcendence ; but his silence upon the resurrection, coupled with his uniform reverence for the Jewish priesthood, suggests that, of the two rising parties, he belonged to that of the Sadducees. He has no references to the Messianic hope, unless we count as such the remark that follows the statements of the laying up of the stones of the old altar (4 46), and of the appointment of Simon as governor and high priest for ever (14 41) : 'until there should arise a faithful prophet.'

(14) The Second Book of the Maccabees

This book also purports to be a Maccabæan history, but is in no way related to the first book ; on the contrary, though covering part of the same period, it seems written in entire ignorance of it, and is quite unlike it in character and style. Its narrative begins shortly before the accession of Antiochus Epiphanes to the Syrian throne (175 B.C.), and ends with the defeat and death of Nicanor, and the triumph of Judas Maccabæus (161 B.C.). In the intervening chapters are related, with considerable detail, the unsuccessful attempt of Heliodorus to plunder the Temple treasury, the intrigues of the leaders at Jerusalem for the high priesthood, the desecration of the Temple by Antiochus, the subsequent calamities of the great persecution, and the wars by which Judas achieved the freedom of his country.

The author makes no pretence to originality, but asserts that his book is merely an abridgement of an earlier work in five volumes by Jason of Cyrene (2 23). Of Jason and his history nothing certain is known, though the probabilities are that he wrote in Greek, somewhere about the end of the second century B.C., and drew his materials from oral sources. The method of his abridger seems to have been to leave out large sections of the original work, and embody others very much as he found them. Of him we may almost certainly conclude, from the style of his Greek, and the earliest allusions to his compilation, that he was a Jew of Alexandria ; and certain characteristics, in which he differs from the author of 1 Maccabees, suggest that he belonged to the Pharisaic party. Besides his unhesitating mention of the divine name, he has clear references to the belief in a resurrection (7 9, 14 12 43), and the practice of prayers for the dead ; and he loves rather to exalt the glory of the Lord, who uses all men as His instruments, than dwell upon the prowess of the Maccabæan heroes. The date of his work is uncertain ; but, as it was known to Philo and the author of the Epistle to the Hebrews (cp. 2 Mac 6 18–7 42 with Heb 11 35 f.), it cannot be placed later than the beginning of the Christian era.

Prefixed to the history proper, which only begins at 2 19, are two letters which profess to have been sent by the Jews of Palestine to their brethren in Egypt.

II. APOCALYPTIC WRITINGS

Baruch.	Testament of Twelve
Enoch.	Patriarchs.
Ascension of Isaiah.	Psalms of Solomon.
Jubilees.	Sibylline Oracles.
Assumption of Moses.	

The name Apocalypse, which is derived from the Greek word for 'revelation,' is applied to a number of Jewish and early Christian works, to mark their distinctive character. The aim of these works is to solve the problem involved in the apparent discordance of events with the moral government of God. The Jewish thinker, who believed in the righteousness of God, and the rewards promised to the keeping of the Law, could not rest in the actual condition of things, when the servants of God were subjected to calamity and oppression, and the heathen enjoyed prosperity and power. A method had to be sought of reconciling the sufferings of the righteous with the demands of the religious conscience. This was found by the Apocalyptists in a moral and religious interpretation of the history of the world as a whole. Contact with the great empires of East and West had broadened their minds, and made them acquainted with the larger movements of human history: throughout it all, in the fate of individuals as in the rise and fall of nations, they saw the gradual unfolding of a divine purpose, of which the future held the complete fulfilment. The righteousness of God would be abundantly justified, and His faithful people vindicated in the eyes of the heathen. In a series of visions or revelations, generally attached to the name of an ancient prophet, they gave a rapid sketch or outline of the world's history, and depicted the glorious consummation to be confidently expected.

The variety of style and contents in these writings is considerable. Some are addressed to the Gentiles, by way of showing the excellence of the Jewish faith, and the danger of neglecting its claims ; others are written for the comfort and encouragement of the author's co-religionists. Some are almost entirely mystical and apocalyptic ; others are largely taken up with the exposition and enforcement of the Law. Some point generally to a revival of the glory and dominion of Israel ; others anticipate more definitely a world-wide Messianic kingdom, and a resurrection life, while the nature and duration of these are also differently conceived by different writers. As a whole, they had an undoubted influence upon the development of Jewish life and thought, and so have an appreciable value for the historian. On the one hand, they helped to prepare the higher minds of Judaism for the reception of the gospel, with its world-denying precepts, and its glorious outlook upon the future. On the other hand, they stimulated the patriotic zeal of those who strove time after time to throw off the Roman bondage, and ultimately brought destruction upon the Jewish nation.

Two examples of apocalyptic literature have been admitted into the Canon—the book of Daniel in the Old Testament and the Revelation of John in the New. In the Apocrypha, 2 Esdras comes under the same denomination ; but there are many others of which those cited above are the more important.

(1) The Apocalypse of Baruch

In points of doctrine, as well as in other characteristic features, this book bears a strong resemblance to 2 Esdras. It purports to be a prophecy of Baruch, son of Neriah, uttered shortly before the Chaldean invasion of 586 B.C., and foretelling the destruction of Jerusalem, and its subsequent restoration. There are seven distinct sections in it, mostly composed of prayers and visions, with connecting narrative portions, and separated from each other, except in one instance, by the observance of a fast. The concluding chapters embody a letter of Baruch to the tribes in captivity. This letter has been known for a considerable time, but the book, as we now have it, was only discovered in a Latin version so late as 1866. It seems to have come, through Syriac and Greek versions, from a Hebrew original. Besides the fact that part of it appears to have been written before the fall of Jerusalem to the Romans in 68 A.D., and part of it afterwards, there are other grounds for concluding that it is a composite work, by various hands, produced at intervals between 50 and 100 A.D. It has a strongly Pharisaic cast of thought, and its language is occasionally reminiscent of the New Testament.

(2) The Book of Enoch

The assumption of Enoch's name for apocalyptic purposes was probably suggested by the statement of $Gn 5^{24}$. His supposed intercourse with God would furnish sufficient reason for ascribing to him revelations of things present and future, of things on earth and in heaven. A considerable body of apocalyptic literature seems to have been put forward in early times as proceeding from him, and portions of it that have been preserved now form the book called by his name. These are generally believed to have been written in Palestine during the last two centuries B.C., but the Hebrew or Aramaic original has disappeared, and the complete text is only known in an Ethiopic version.

The contents of Enoch are supposed to fall into five sections, all by different hands, and varying in date from 170 B.C. almost to the beginning of the Christian era. Interspersed through these are passages purporting to be written by Noah, and evidently interpolated by the editor from another Apocalypse circulating under that patriarch's name. The general theme is the overthrow and judgment of the enemies of God and His people, and the final establishment of the divine kingdom in righteousness and power. In one vision, seventy angels or shepherds are commissioned to watch in turn over Israel, but proving unfaithful to their trust, as the national history is adduced to show, they are cast with their adherents into an abyss of fire. Enoch visits heaven, and learns much of the destiny of men and angels ; he also penetrates the recesses of nature, and discovers its secret processes. In the middle of the book there is a series of three allegories (chs. 37–70), belonging, as some think, to the period 90–60 B.C., and certainly not later than the reign of

King Herod. With the usual apocalyptic matter, there is in them a striking and original presentation of the person of the Judge, who is to redress the oppressions and injustices of the world. He is no mere descendant of David, but the Elect or Righteous One, the Christ or the Anointed, and still more 'the Son of Man who hath righteousness, with whom dwelleth righteousness, and who revealeth all the treasures of that which is hidden, because the Lord of Spirits hath chosen him' (46[1-3]). All four titles were subsequently applied to Jesus by Himself or His early followers. In addition to this, however, there are many other indications of the esteem in which the book of Enoch was held in the primitive days of Christianity. The language of the New Testament reflects it in quite a number of passages, and in one place it is directly quoted (Jude vv. 14 f.). Its doctrine, too, bears distinct traces of its influence, especially in connexion with the belief in the resurrection, the rewards and punishments of the future, the ministry of angels, and the nature and activities of demons. Among the earliest Fathers of the Church, the book of Enoch was quoted with approval, and the Epistle of Barnabas even ascribes to it canonical authority.

A few years ago, a book came to light, called 'The Secrets of Enoch,' which contains further fragments of Enochic Apocalypse. From the language in which it is written it is called the Slavonic Enoch, to distinguish it from the older Ethiopic book. Some of it seems to have been drawn from Hebrew originals, but the greater part of it has evidently been composed in Greek, about the beginning of the Christian era. It describes the mysteries revealed to Enoch during his wanderings in the seven heavens, and is chiefly valuable for the light it sheds on the New Testament, some of the ideas of which, such as the millennium and the sevenfold division of the celestial regions, appear in it for the first time.

(3) The Ascension of Isaiah

This book, of which an Ethiopic version is the only complete text, comprises (a) an account of the martyrdom of Isaiah, (b) a short Apocalypse, in which the history of the early Church (50–80 A.D.) is outlined, and (c) a vision of Isaiah, in which he visits the seven heavens, and learns amongst other things of the coming advent, crucifixion, and resurrection of the Saviour. The first part was probably written by a Jew about the beginning of the first century A.D.; the other two parts are of Christian authorship, and belong to the second half of the century. Heb 11[37f.] is probably a reference to this book

(4) The Book of Jubilees

This Apocalypse is cast in the form of a homiletic commentary upon the book of Genesis, after the manner of the Jewish Haggadic teaching. Passing in review the period from the creation of the world to the institution of the Passover, it gives a rendering of the patriarchal history from the standpoint of the Jewish theologian of the century before the Christian era. The leading aim of the author is to emphasise the antiquity of the Law and the Levitical ordinances by carrying back their observance, even with heightened strictness, to the earliest times. At the same time he seeks to excuse or smooth over statements and facts that were calculated to give offence to the Hellenic mind ; for example, the expulsion from Eden, the curse upon Cain, the deceit of Abraham and Jacob, and the severities inflicted upon the Canaanites by the Israelites on their entrance into the Promised Land. There is no doctrine of the resurrection taught in the book, though there are evident references to the immortality of the soul. The title of Jubilees is given to it from its system of time-reckoning, which is based upon Jubilee cycles of forty-nine years each. It is also called, from its subject-matter, 'The Little Genesis'; not because it is shorter than the canonical book, which it is not, but on account of its inferior authority.

Though the only entire text extant is the Ethiopic version, it has evidently been written originally in Hebrew, and by a Pharisee. The date cannot be fixed more definitely than within the period of fifty years on either side of the birth of Christ. On the one hand, it assumes the existence of the Temple, and so must have been written before the fall of Jerusalem in 68 A.D. ; and on the other hand, it quotes largely from a section of the book of Enoch, which is regarded as not later than 60 B.C., and may have seen the light any time thereafter. It is of considerable value, not only for the study of Pharisaism and the New Testament, but also for the determination of the Hebrew text of Genesis.

(5) The Assumption of Moses

In this book, Moses, knowing that he is about to die, entrusts to the care of Joshua a collection of prophecies. These relate to the history of Israel, and subsequent chapters work over that history, from the apocalyptic point of view, down to the time when Judæa became a Roman province. A statement by the author (c. 6) is significant for the determination of the date. He says that the sons of Herod should reign for a shorter time than their father ; and as three of them reigned for longer periods, the book must have been written during their lifetime, and therefore not later than 30 A.D. The author was probably a Pharisee, and wrote in Hebrew, though the book is chiefly known to us in a Latin version.

(6) The Testament of the Twelve Patriarchs

Here the twelve sons of Jacob are represented as delivering their dying instructions to their descendants. Each in turn goes over the story of his life, and points the moral of it; exhorts his children to emulate his virtues and shun his vices; and utters a prediction of the calamities and oppressions that will come on account of sin. The mixed nature of the contents favours the theory that the book is based upon an original Jewish writing, largely interpolated by later Jewish and Christian hands. The oldest portions probably belong to the second century B.C., but the interpolations extend from that date well into the Christian era. Our chief authority for it is a Latin translation of the thirteenth century. It has the same system of time-reckoning as the book of Jubilees, and agrees with it in many of its biographical details.

(7) The Psalms of Solomon

These eighteen Psalms, fictitiously ascribed to Solomon in the usual literary sense, evidently emanate from one, or possibly two, of the later Pharisees. It is certain that they were originally written in Hebrew, though they are known to us now only in versions. In figurative language which is easily interpreted, they depict the course of events in Jerusalem from its capture by Pompey in 63 B.C. to his death fifteen years afterwards. The Hasmonæan princes who welcomed him to the city are denounced as usurpers of the throne of David; the defeat and massacre of the party of Aristobulus (II) are described, and the subsequent calamities depicted; while Pompey is portrayed as a dragon, who would assume divine power and rule the world, but dies miserably on the shores of Egypt, with none to bury him. Not only in his rendering of events, but in his religious views and references, the author betrays his affinities with the Pharisees rather than with the Sadducees. The former are the 'saints' and 'righteous'; the latter are 'proud sinners' and 'transgressors.' The theocratic view of the Jewish state is emphasised, and righteousness chiefly presented as fulfilment of the Ceremonial Law. Throughout the book there are the usual warnings of judgment, but there are also distinct anticipations of a resurrection of the dead to rewards and punishments. The Messianic hope is clearly defined only in the last

two Psalms, which suggests the necessity of ascribing them to a different author than the others; but the whole collection may be safely assigned to the period with which it deals, 70–40 B.C.

(8) The Sibylline Oracles

Sibyls in the ancient world were supposed to be inspired prophetesses, unconnected with any official order, through whom the gods revealed their thoughts and indicated their will. Their utterances were held in great esteem, especially at Rome, where upon momentous occasions they were consulted by the authorities. It is not surprising that the Jews of Alexandria, and after them the early Christians, sought to gain attention to their distinctive principles and beliefs by adopting a Sibylline style and guise. These were more likely to attract the notice of the Gentile world than the assumed authorship of one of their own prophets or patriarchs.

The writings thus put forth as Sibylline Oracles form a heterogeneous collection, extending over several centuries and by many different hands. Originally they consisted of fourteen books, but only twelve now exist. The third book probably contains the nucleus round which the rest of the collection was gathered, and which may have been produced as early as the middle of the second century B.C. It gives an apocalyptic review of the history of Israel from the building of Babel to the time of Antiochus Epiphanes, and closes with a prediction of the coming glory and prosperity of the Messiah's kingdom. The other books pursue a similar vein, with a large admixture of Christian elements and frequent veiled allusions to the Roman power. They are of varying dates, some of them being supposed to be even as late as the second and third centuries of the Christian era.

Besides the above there are other apocalyptic writings, bearing the names of Adam, Abraham, Moses, Elias, Zephaniah, etc.; but these are not of sufficient importance to require separate treatment.

III. THE SEPTUAGINT

References have already been made to the ancient Greek version of the Old Testament, which originated among the Jews of Alexandria. It is called 'The Septuagint' (LXX), from a tradition that persisted in Egypt regarding its inception. The story is told in a fictitious Jewish letter of the Ptolemaic period, purporting to have been written by Aristeas, a courtier of Ptolemy Philadelphus (284–247 B.C.). It relates how that Egyptian king sent to Jerusalem for seventy-two learned men—being six from each of the tribes—and set them to work upon a translation of the Hebrew

Scriptures for the great library of Alexandria, and how, without collusion, they agreed upon their renderings and completed their version in seventy-two days, which thereafter became the authorised Scripture of all the Greek-speaking Jews. In part, no doubt, the story is apocryphal, and in later years it received still further embellishments ; but the main elements of it may be perfectly true. It is highly probable that the Pentateuch at least was translated at the instigation of Philadelphus, who was a great patron of learning, and had the laws of all nations collected for his library. In that case, his Jewish subjects would readily receive the new version as supplying the want that had arisen from their general adoption of the Greek tongue. The remaining books (which, as we have seen, included most of the Apocrypha) were translated at different times by various hands between the reign of Philadelphus and the beginning of the Christian era. The translator of Ecclesiasticus (132 B.C.) refers to a Greek version of ' the Law and the Prophets and the rest of the Books,' but does not specify the writings comprised under the last-mentioned section. Philo, the Jewish philosopher of Alexandria, about the time of Christ, shows an acquaintance with the whole of the Old Testament Scriptures, with the exception of three or four books. About the end of the third century A.D. three recensions or critical revisions of the Septuagint appeared, which were the work of Hesychius, Lucian, and Eusebius. These form the basis of the manuscripts from which our text is derived.

The diversity of hands employed upon the Septuagint is patent from the contents, which exhibit great variety of style and merit. On the whole, the Pentateuch reaches the highest degree of excellence, being a careful and scholarly rendering of the original : among the other books, the historical generally stand upon a higher level than the poetical. Some of the translations are done in very good Greek ; others are faulty, and abound in idioms carried over from the Hebrew. Some evince considerable capacity, but omit, alter, or expand, from mere arbitrariness, or the desire to avoid irreverence and the wounding of Jewish or Egyptian susceptibilities ; others are more conscientious, but frequently misread, mistranslate, or merely transliterate the original. Some aim at a correct reproduction of the Hebrew text ; others are more of a paraphrase or commentary than a translation. The order of the books, too, and in some instances even the order of the various chapters, differs from that in the Hebrew text known to us ; and the Apocryphal additions interspersed throughout accentuate the divergence. In spite of these discrepancies, and the problems which they raise, this ancient translation of the Old Testament Scriptures is of great interest and value. It is supposed to be the earliest translation of any considerable extent from one language into another ; and that alone would render it remarkable. Apart from that, however, it is of immense service, if it is not indeed indispensable, for the determination and elucidation of the text both of the Old and the New Testament. As evidently the translation of an ancient text of the Old Testament, now lost, it not only corroborates but enables us to correct the received text. On the other hand, as the Authorised Version circulating in Palestine, in the time of our Lord and the New Testament writers, it helped to shape their language, and affords a key to its interpretation. There is no doubt also, that in making the Hebrew Scriptures known to the Gentile world, it had its influence in preparing the way for the reception of the gospel.

IV. OTHER REMAINS

3 Maccabees.	Logia.
4 Maccabees.	Didache.
Josephus.	

(1) 3 Maccabees

The only justification for the title of this book is that, like the genuine Maccabæan writings, it deals with the sufferings of the Jews under foreign persecution. The scene of its story is not even laid in the Maccabæan age, but in the reign of Ptolemy IV Philopator (222–204 B.C.). The Egyptian king is miraculously prevented from entering the Temple at Jerusalem, and afterwards frustrated by successive divine interpositions, from wreaking his vengeance upon his Jewish subjects. A similar story is related by Josephus of Ptolemy VII Physcon, and it may have had a foundation in fact. All that can be said of the date of the book is that it was written between 100 B.C. and 100 A.D.

(2) 4 Maccabees

This book derives its title from the fact that the greater part of it is taken up with reflections upon the story of the martyrs in 2 Mac 6 18–7 41. The purpose of the author, according to his own showing (1 1), is to prove that ' the pious reason is absolute master of the passions.' His work falls into two parts, (a) a discourse upon the general philosophic question, and (b) a restatement of the story of the Maccabæan martyrs, with the lessons to be drawn from it. Evidently he is a devout Jew, desirous of fortifying the faith of his brethren against the seductions of pagan philosophy. Incidentally he evinces his belief in universal immortality, and a state of future rewards and punishments. It is presumed that he belonged to Alexandria or some other Hellenistic city, and wrote about the beginning of the Christian era.

(3) The Works of Josephus

Flavius Josephus was born at Jerusalem in 37 A.D., and lived at least to the end of the century. He received a superior education, and rose to such esteem among the Pharisaic patriots that, on the outbreak of the war with Rome, he was appointed governor of Galilee. In the subsequent operations he distinguished himself by his wisdom and courage, but was taken prisoner by Vespasian, and ultimately retired to Rome, where he devoted himself to literary pursuits. His works are (1) 'The History of the Jewish Wars,' giving an outline of events from the time of Antiochus Epiphanes, and a full account of the struggle in which he himself had been engaged ; (2) 'Jewish Antiquities,' relating the story of his country from the earliest times to the close of Nero's reign ; (3) a 'Treatise against Apion,' which is chiefly valuable for its copious extracts from profane historical writers ; and (4) his 'Autobiography,' which is an elaborate vindication of his defence of Galilee during the war.

For centuries the works of Josephus were almost the only source of information possessed by the Christian world upon Jewish history, and even yet they are of great value in this respect. They are written in good Greek style, with a wonderful freedom from bias, though occasionally they may soften down statements and facts in deference to the Roman audience they were expected to secure.

(4) The Papyrus Logia

Several papyrus fragments have come to light in recent years, containing short collections of the sayings (logia) of Jesus. The first was published by Bickell in 1885 from the collection of the Archduke Rainer, and is simply a parallel to Mk 14 26-30. The second was published in 1897 by Grenfell and Hunt, who had discovered it at Oxyrhynchus. It gives six sayings and the first word of a seventh ; three of them being parallels to Lk 6 42 4 24 Mt 5 14, and three new and distinctive. Harnack supposes the second group to be extracted from the 'Gospel according to the Egyptians,' but there is no definite agreement yet as to the origin of either of them, and the same may be said of those still more recently discovered.

(5) The Didache

The 'Didache (Teaching) of the Twelve Apostles' was first printed in 1883 from a Greek manuscript of 1056, discovered at Constantinople. It consists of two distinct parts : (a) a number of moral precepts, called 'The Doctrine of the Two Ways,' which does not refer to any of the Gospels, and may have had a Jewish origin ; and (b) a collection of Church rules for discipline and worship, in which use has probably been made of the Gospel of Matthew. It is generally assigned to the period 80–110 A.D., but in its present form may be as late as the middle of the second century.

In addition to the above, the names, and sometimes a few fragments of Apocryphal Gospels, Acts, and Epistles, have come down from the early days of the Christian Church. Of these it may be sufficient to mention : the Gospels according to Peter, the Hebrews, and the Egyptians ; the book of James usually called 'Protevangelium' ; The Acts of Pilate, and of Paul and Thecla ; the Abgarus Letters ; the Epistles of Paul to the Laodiceans, the Alexandrines, and the Corinthians (the third).

3. DEVELOPMENT OF JEWISH RELIGION IN THE PERIOD BETWEEN THE OLD AND NEW TESTAMENTS

Though founded on divine revelation, and essentially conservative, the religion of the Jews did not escape modification from the ordinary human influences to which it was subjected. As encountered in the New Testament, it exhibits considerable variation from the prevailing type of Old Testament times. The intervening centuries had been characterised, not only by great political movements and momentous social changes, but also by a high degree of intellectual activity ; and these have left their mark upon the national religion. Old beliefs and practices have undergone a change of emphasis, if not a complete transformation ; new ideas have been introduced, and become the starting-points of fresh developments. The process is reflected in the literature of the period (of which an account has been given) ; and some knowledge of it is necessary for the appreciation of the attitude of Jesus and the Apostles towards the religion of their day.

1. The Doctrine or Idea of God. During the exile this central element of belief was purged of the heathen corruptions and accretions to which in former days it had been liable. After many warnings and chastisements, the people learned in national humiliation and personal suffering to adore the God of their fathers as the one supreme God of

the world, and to dissociate His worship from the impure rites of the heathen. Idolatry was abjured and never again permitted to corrupt their faith, or foul the stream of their devotion. Even the severities of persecution—as in the instance of Antiochus Epiphanes—served only to confirm their attachment to the unity and spirituality of God.

As the sense of national abandonment and desolation increased, and the ideal methods of Greek thought gained ground among Jewish theologians, the tendency appeared to refine upon this idea, and remove God entirely from the world of material things. What is called the transcendent view of God became predominant ; that is to say, He was regarded as so far exalted above the world as to be out of touch or communication with men. He who had formerly tabernacled with His people and spoken familiarly to the prophets, seemed now to dwell in a far-off heaven where no personal intercourse could be had with Him. This conception colours the literature of the period, which generally abstains from expressions that would suggest human passions or parts in God, and even avoids the mention of His name. Strongly imbued with it, the Jews of the time of Jesus resented the familiarity with which He spoke of God as Father, and asserted His interest in the humblest human concerns.

2. The Law. The sublimation of the idea of God was accompanied by an increasing reverence for the Divine Law. When God had retired within the clouds, and discontinued His communications with His people, the knowledge of His will could only be obtained indirectly, through His actions and utterances in the past. No longer having the living voice to guide them, they could but fall back upon the written word ; and the more perplexing and painful their circumstances, the more necessary it became for them to search and study it. Stimulated by the exile, the regard for the Law was deepened and confirmed by subsequent calamities, and grew to a passion with the Pharisaical section of the nation, as the chains of foreign oppression were riveted upon them, and the shadow of impending dissolution fell upon the national life. It became, not only the basis of the civil polity, but the sovereign rule and standard of private conduct ; and the scribes, whose special function was to expound and enforce it, rose to a position of great power and prominence.

In a previous article it has been shown how the various parts of the Pentateuch were probably conjoined to form a rule of religious practice and belief. By the third century B.C., the prophetic books had been gathered together and invested with almost equal authority. Other books were subsequently added which were believed to date from the prophetic period,

and the Old Testament Canon was finally completed and closed by the end of the first century of our era. Alongside this written standard of faith and practice, there was an ever-growing body of oral tradition, which was supposed to have been delivered to Moses on Sinai, and handed down—through Joshua, the elders, and the prophets—to the men of the Great Synagogue (Ezra—291 B.C.), and the schools of the scribes. It consisted of two parts, called *Halakah* or ' walking,' and *Aggadah* or ' teaching '; the former supplementing and defining the written Law, the latter explaining it and illustrating it with narrative matter. The whole was the care of the scribes, who in general united with the Pharisees in the scrupulous observance of its numerous minute and exacting precepts. It is the ' tradition of the elders' referred to in the Gospels (Mt 15² Mk 7³, etc.), and was probably in Christ's mind when He spoke of the sayings of ' them of old ' (Mt 5²¹), and the burdens of the Pharisees ' grievous to be borne ' (Mt 23⁴ Lk 11⁴⁶). In the early centuries of our era, this oral Law, with the amplifications and discussions which had gathered round it, was gradually committed to writing at two different centres, and formed what are called the Babylonian and Palestinian Talmuds.

3. Individuality. With the new conception and predominating influence of the Law, the emphasis was shifted from the national to the personal point of view. Hitherto the people as a whole had been the chief object of religious consideration : the duties and privileges of the nation, its errors and backslidings, had been the main occupation of the religious mind : now the way of thinking is reversed, and the responsibilities and claims of the individual come into prominence. The virtual abolition of the nation at the exile awakened the individual sense of sin, and stimulated individual effort to regain the favour of God. The hope was still cherished that the nation would be restored ; indeed, as their outlook upon the world and mankind was widened by their Babylonian experiences, a larger vision began to flit before the devout—the overthrow of the heathen empires, and the recognition of the God of Israel by all the inhabitants of the earth. This, however, was only to be realised by the righteousness of individual men : it was to be the reward of the faithful keeping of God's Law. On the return to Jerusalem, political claims were practically given up, and the community was rearranged and constituted upon a religious, not a national, foundation. Its head was the high priest : its centre the Temple worship : its members individually paid the Temple tax, made acknowledgment of sin, and promised obedience to the Divine Law. The result was to develop and strengthen the individual conscience, and make piety a personal concern (witness the narratives of Daniel and Susanna) ; also, as time went on, to beget a proselytising spirit, which encouraged and even compelled men of other nationalities to accept the Jewish faith. To understand the persistence of Judaism, especially among the Dispersed, it must be remembered that, from the exile onwards, except during the period of the Hasmonæan supremacy, the Jewish people were a religious fellowship, rather than a political combination ; a body of individuals held together by a common rite (circumcision), a common faith, training, and worship.

4. Angels and Demons. The doctrine of God's transcendence and absolute supremacy over the world left room for a development of belief in the action of intermediate beings between Him and men. Accordingly we find in the later Jewish literature statements about angels and demons, compared with which the references in preëxilic writings are meagre and obscure. In the earlier books of the Old Testament superhuman beings other than God are occasionally introduced, and even the name 'angels' is applied to them ; but they have not the definite doctrinal signification of later times, which regarded them as helpful and harmful spirits, entering into close relations with men, and influencing their lives. To the contemporaries of Jesus they were real heavenly messengers, or equally real messengers of Satan, countless in numbers, but divided into ranks, and occasionally bearing specific names. The development of this belief was probably encouraged by the contact of the Jews with other nations, and especially with the Persians, in whose religion the hierarchies of good and evil spirits had been set forth with great elaboration. The movement, however, so far retained its native character that Satan and his hosts were never, as in Persian dualism, coördinated with God and the angels, but always relegated to an inferior position. The belief, as a whole, was rejected by the Sadducees (Ac 23⁸), but it was fully shared by the Pharisaic party, and among the Essenes had an exaggerated importance given to it. To some extent it was countenanced by Christ. He accepted the belief in the existence of spirits, but disfavoured some of the notions popularly associated with it, and in particular claimed for Himself and the Comforter, or Holy Spirit, the sole power of imparting divine revelation and blessing.

5. Wisdom. Along with the belief in angels and demons, there grew up an idea of the divine 'wisdom' which is closely related to it. This idea is responsible for the tone and character of a section of the contemporary literature, embracing the book of Job, some Psalms, Proverbs, Ben-Sira or Ecclesiasticus, Ecclesiastes, and the Wisdom of Solomon, which are hence called the Wisdom Books. Here again the roots were planted in the days before the exile, but the growth was stimulated and brought to fruit by the reflexions and foreign influences of later times. The idea probably had its origin in the general conception of human sagacity, and the need of sympathy with the thought and will of God for its higher manifestations. Wisdom thus became associated with the Word of God, which by an easy extension of its meaning was applied to His whole message or revelation to men. In this sense it was personified in a kind of poetical way, and not only had divine attributes ascribed to it, but was regarded as having been seen by the prophets (Isa 2¹). The Wisdom Books take up the process at this point, and carry forward the personification upon more definite and elaborate lines. Wisdom is the agent or messenger of God, through whom He reveals His will to men, and gives expression in the world to His benevolence and power (Prov 8). She is His first creation, and the friend of all who love Him (Ecclus 1⁴⁻¹⁰) ; her thoughts are more than the sea, and her counsels profounder than the great deep (Ecclus 24²⁹). In vivid style, the Wisdom of Solomon describes the origin and character of Wisdom, recounts her praises, and expatiates upon her benefits (chs. 7, 8, 9).

That this way of thinking took firm hold of the Jewish mind is evident from the Targums or Aramaic expositions of the Old Testament, which were current in the early Christian age. In them, the Word of God (*Memra*) appears almost as a real person, standing in the place of God Himself, as the vehicle of His selfexpression, and the agent through whom He executes His purposes. Exalted above the world, He yet communicates with it, and acts upon it, through His Word. A somewhat similar doctrine, though more largely marked by the influence of the Greek theory of ideas, was developed in Alexandria by the Jewish philosopher Philo. Accepting the Jewish conception of the transcendence of God, he found in the Word (*Logos*) of Old Testament Scripture the power, or medium, through which His reason and energy still come into touch with the world. The Logos is His first-born Son, the highest Angel, even a second God : through Him the world of men and things is created and preserved. The widespread currency of these speculations, and the allegorical method of Scripture interpretation by which they were supported, are reflected in the New Testament, especially in such books as the Epistle to the Hebrews and the Fourth Gospel. In the prologue to the latter, the author seizes an idea familiar to his contemporaries and containing anticipations of the truth, and applies it in his own way to Him who is the Light and Life of men.

6. Hellenism. At various other points the influence of Greek thought may be traced in the later beliefs of the Jews. In spite of their exclusiveness, the Hellenistic movement which overspread the civilised world in the wake of the conquests of Alexander the Great did not leave them untouched ; and for centuries thereafter, especially in the Dispersion, they were largely affected by the close contact into which they were brought with the great speculative nation of the West. Their knowledge of its language and familiarity with its customs and ideas inspired them with a new breadth of thought which appears, not only in the later Jewish literature, but throughout the New Testament. The Wisdom of Solomon, for instance, is largely Greek in its way of thinking, and uses phraseology borrowed from the schools of Greek philosophy. It enumerates with approval the four cardinal virtues of Greek morality (8^7) ; it speaks in Platonic terms of a creation of the world from formless matter instead of from nothing (11^{17}) ; it calls manna ambrosial food (19^{21}), and pictures virtue crowned with a wreath like the victor in the athletic games (4^2). Similarly the book of Revelation (7^9), in its description of the saints, uses a figure taken from the Greek contests, and St. Paul draws illustrations of Christian virtues and ideas from the circus and racecourse, which in former times were abhorred and avoided by the Jews. These are indications of a considerable interchange of thought, in the course of which, not only moral and political ideas, but philosophical and religious conceptions, were communicated and received. To the Greeks the Jews are said to have been indebted for the distinction between the kingdom of heaven and the kingdom of the world, and they certainly found in the Greek thinkers clear and definite statements of great truths, like the immortality of the soul and the rewards and punishments of the future life, which had been but faintly outlined and suggested by their own religious teachers. The greatest consequences, however, of the familiarity with Western language and thought were the undermining of the old division between the Jew and Gentile, and the preparation of the world for the preaching of the universal gospel. Only in the light of it is it possible to understand the wonderful success that attended the labours of St. Paul and other Apostles of the Cross.

7. The Messianic Hope. The circumstances of the Jews conjoined with their new thoughts of God and mankind to bring eschatological ideas into prominence : that is to say, ideas relating to the Last Things. So far as the world in general was concerned, these gathered round the Messianic Hope—the expectation of a God-sent Deliverer, who would restore the vanished greatness of Israel, and establish the rule of God's people in righteousness and power. The foundations of this expectation were laid in Old Testament prophecy, in which also numerous suggestions were afforded for the fulness of colour and detail which it eventually assumed. The earlier as well as the later prophets had their visions of the salvation of Israel from all internal and external evils, and the complete reconciliation of the nation to God, with the consequent blessings of devotion and obedience. Their descriptions vary, according to the age in which they lived, and the circumstances of the people ; but the stress invariably falls upon the realisation of God's undisputed sovereignty, and the beneficent results of the holiness and submissiveness of the nation. Hints are given of a great outstanding figure, through whom the purpose of God is to be accomplished : he is 'a prophet like unto Moses,' 'a king of David's line,' 'the servant of the Lord' ; but the conception as often is that God will employ no intermediate personality, but intervene Himself. The Old Testament, indeed, has no precise or uniform doctrine of the Messiah's person ; it does not even employ the term Messiah ('Anointed') in the particular sense that afterwards attached to it—though Jew and Christian alike, in later years, could find in it prophetic anticipations of their own beliefs (see art. 'Messianic Hope').

After the exile, the prospect of national greatness and prosperity was too dim and distant to serve as a practical religious or political stimulus. The contact of the Jews with other nations, too, broadened their ideas of the world, and corrected the perspective in which the movements of history had appeared to them. As the scribes succeeded the prophets, and the sense of individuality took the place of the old national sentiment, the bulk of the people fell back upon an external religiosity, which lacked the confidence and inspiration of former days. At the same time, there were not wanting more reflective spirits, that still cherished the ancient hope, and saw nothing in the altered circumstances of the time to exclude the possibility of God's intervention. Transcendent as He was, could He not bend the firmament of heaven, and come down for the restoration of His penitent people ? Could He not arise for the shaking of the heavens and the earth, and the overthrow of the throne of kingdoms ($Hag 2^{21}$) ? Side by side with the study of the Law, there went an anxious scrutiny of the promises and predictions of the prophets, with the result that a new and grander form of the old expectation took possession of many minds. In this form it was to be fulfilled by supernatural power, and with a world-wide significance ; the heathen empires were to be overthrown ;

the dispersed of Israel gathered to their own land; the worship of Jehovah reëstablished at Jerusalem, and all the inhabitants of the earth made to do Him reverence. This is the view of Daniel, and there are sufficient references to it in other books of the period to prove its persistence both before and after the Maccabæan struggle. So far, however, no symptoms appear of the prominence of the idea of a personal Messiah, so characteristic of later Jewish thought, and during the rise and supremacy of the Hasmonæan family, the hope itself of a future ideal kingdom fell into almost utter abeyance. At first, the fierceness of the struggle for independence monopolised the thoughts of the Jews, and discouraged reflexion upon ideal eventualities; then the success of their cause secured to them such freedom and prosperity as served to withdraw their minds from the future. They were content to enjoy the good already attained, and postpone further questions till a new prophet should arise among them (1 Mac 14 41).

A marked change is noticeable early in the century immediately preceding the birth of Christ. The Hasmonæan house was tottering to its fall: the excesses and feuds of its princes were bringing hopeless ruin upon themselves, and confusion and distress upon their country; the Pharisees and other kindred spirits repudiated the actual government of the land, and turned for consolation to the old hope of an ideal kingship. Under the Hasmonæan rule, their sentiment of nationality had been revived and accentuated; now that their confidence had been betrayed and their hopes disappointed, they threw themselves with new ardour into the old prophetic expectations of a divinely-established kingdom. The feeling of the time is indicated in the ninetieth chapter of the book of Enoch, and still more clearly in the Psalter of Solomon. In the latter, for the first time, the name and person of the Messiah are distinctly set forth. Probably the idea of a Messianic king had been shaping itself for some time in the Jewish mind; thereafter it possessed it with increasing force, as the centre of religious hope, and the theme alike of theological study and devout reflexion. Under the tyranny of the Herods and the Roman Procurators, it took on almost a feverish intensity, the people praying and longing for the consolation of Israel, and eagerly watching the signs of the times for the evidences of the Messiah's advent, and the coming of God's kingdom (Lk 1, 2, etc.). The hold it had obtained upon the popular imagination is abundantly evidenced in the pages of the New Testament. It helps to explain the effects of the preaching of John the Baptist, and the favour with which the contemporaries of our

Lord regarded His early ministry: it also throws light upon the vehemence with which Christ was ultimately rejected, when He failed to exhibit the expected characteristics of the Messiah, and proclaimed a spiritual kingdom which conflicted with preconceived notions. Later on, it led them to try those conclusions with the Roman power, which eventuated in their national effacement.

8. Personal Immortality. No greater advance was made during the period than in the determination and development of those eschatological ideas which bear upon the future life and condition of the individual soul. The stimulus to this advance may be found, not only in the new emphasis laid upon individuality, and the Persian and Greek influences already noticed, but still more, perhaps, in the internal condition of the country, which was distracted by political and religious factions. In the strife and commotion of the time, the sudden reversal of fortune, and the eclipse of the hopes of national power and greatness, it was natural for the Jews to turn to the thought of a life after death, in which all inequalities would be adjusted, and all wrongs redressed. Especially would this thought be cherished in times of persecution, when they were called to sacrifice their lives for their country and their faith. Belief in a future dispensation of judgment is a condition of the martyr spirit, and was probably found necessary to support the fortitude of the early martyrs of the Jewish faith.

The Old Testament has little to say upon the subject of individual immortality. In some of the later books, such as the Psalms (16, 17, 49, 73), and Job (14 13-15 19 25-29), suggestive hints are given of a continued existence beyond the grave; and it is possible to see in the accounts of the translation of Enoch and Elijah at least the faint anticipation of the later view of death; but in general the faith of the Hebrew people does not seem to have been attracted by the prospect of a future life. It seldom rose above the consideration of earthly things, the continued enjoyment of which is the blessing they expect from God. The salvation for which they long is mostly of a national and temporal kind: deliverance from the ordinary calamities of life, or from the fear and power of their enemies. When they think at all of the future life, it is as a state of deprivation and loss, compared to which their earthly present life is an incalculable boon. They can see in it only the grim shadows and terrors of Sheol—an uncertain state of bodiless existence, into which death gathers good and bad alike, and from which even the most fervent piety and trust in God will not avail for deliverance.

Starting from this slender basis of eschatological belief, Jewish thought was now led to richer and clearer conceptions of things to come. To begin with the cardinal idea, there was undoubtedly a steadily-growing sense and assurance of personal immortality. This is a conclusion forced upon us by a comparison of the confident utterances of the Apocryphal and Talmudic writers with the vaguer references of the Old Testament Scriptures. Even the words 'immortal' and 'immortality' seem now to have come into general use, as if the ideas conveyed by them formed part of the intellectual furniture of the ordinary Jew. Men certainly looked for a continued conscious existence after death as different as could be from the dim and shadowy condition expressed in the old popular conception of Sheol. Very soon, too, the idea of immortality became filled up with a wealth and intensity of meaning, which raised it to a prominent place in the regulation and government of life. There became associated with it, at least, two supplementary conceptions, which went to render it more tangible and effective: the thoughts of a resurrection of the body, and of a future distribution of rewards and punishments. Both of these, with some variations, have been adopted into the Christian system, and have exercised an untold influence upon modern thought.

It seems to have been about the time of the Maccabæan wars that the belief in immortality came to be most strongly felt, and to include the resurrection of the body as an essential part. Twenty years before these wars the greatest teacher of the time—the Son of Sirach—could speak of departure from the world in strains of pathetic hopelessness (Ecclus 41 1-4 17 27-32); but during them the tone is completely changed, and afterwards we have the most precise utterances regarding the resurrection (Dan 12 2 Ps Sol 7 16). In the second book of Maccabees (c. 7) we find the seven sons and their mother witnessing before the persecuting king to the hope of resurrection to eternal life, and (14 46) Razis, at his death, throwing his entrails upon the people, and calling upon the Lord of life and spirit to restore him those again. Other references might be given (Ps Sol 13 9 14 2 15 13 Enoch 90 23 91 10, etc.); but perhaps the best evidence of this belief, subsequent to the time of the Maccabees, is the fact that in the time of Christ it was a current popular doctrine, rejected apparently as an innovation by the Sadducees, but strenuously advocated by the Pharisees, and acquiesced in by the great bulk of the nation who held with them.

The idea of the resurrection, as it presents itself in the thought of the period, exhibits considerable variety of form, if not a definite process of development. At first it seems to have been restricted to the godly, and anticipated as an accompaniment of the establishment of the Messiah's kingdom. That kingdom had been delayed, but those who had lived in the hope of it, and had been overtaken by death before its realisation, would be raised to life again at the Messiah's advent, and share in the Lord's salvation. This is the view taken in the Psalter of Solomon.

Afterwards there arose, as part of the generally accepted Jewish belief, the doctrine of a universal resurrection to judgment before the divine throne and a life of eternal retribution. Judging from 2 Esdras (7 27 f.), written towards the close of the first century of our era, this view was probably current in the time of Christ. In some quarters it was combined with the more limited view, so that both a particular and a universal resurrection were anticipated: a resurrection of the just, at the coming of the Messiah, to participation in the blessings of His earthly reign; and, afterwards, at the end of the world, a resurrection of the remainder of mankind to judgment and retribution. Evidences of this combination, in connexion with the Second Coming of Christ, are to be found in the New Testament, and especially in the eschatological ideas of the author of Revelation. As time went on, however, the hope of the individual tended to dissociate itself from the national Messianic expectation, and become entirely independent of it. Reaching forward to a blessedness, of which after all the Messianic blessedness could only be the prelude, it gradually withdrew the thoughts of men from the Messianic hope, and gathered them about itself. Apparently, uniformity of belief on the nature of the resurrection life had not been attained at the close of our period; in the time of Christ and afterwards questions regarding it still continued to be keenly agitated (Mt 22 23-33 Ac 23 6 1 Th 4 13-18).

The other adjunct to the idea of immortality —the thought of a future distribution of rewards and punishments—seems also to have come into prominence about the time of the Maccabæan wars. Like the belief in the resurrection of the body, no trace of it is to be found in the book of the Son of Sirach. At first it meets us in the simple undeveloped form of a division of the future world into two opposite states of happiness and misery, corresponding to the simplest moral classification of men as good and bad. The book of Wisdom says, 'the souls of the righteous are in the hand of God, and there shall no torment touch them'; 'having been a little chastised, they shall be greatly rewarded'; 'but the ungodly shall be punished according to their own imaginations' (3 1, 5, 10 5 14-16, etc.). The same conception appears in the books of the Maccabees (e.g. in the words of the martyrs before the king, 2 Mac 7 35-37). This is the first vague form of the belief in future retribution ; but it could not have been long till it acquired definiteness and precision, for we find from the rabbinical traditions that a tolerably elaborate theory on the subject was in existence by the time of Christ. The two divisions of the future world were called Paradise (or sometimes, metaphorically, Abraham's Bosom) and Gehenna—a name derived from the valley in the neighbourhood of Jerusalem, which served as a common sewer and receptacle for the bodies of executed felons. To Paradise, the righteous were admitted without delay immediately after death ; but all others were consigned to Gehenna for longer or shorter periods, according to the degree of their iniquity. The former class was supposed to include only the true Israelites—those who believed the whole Law, and regulated their conduct according to its precepts ; but occasionally it was extended to embrace men of other creeds and nations who lived holy and righteous lives. The other class was composed of Gentiles and imperfectly righteous Israelites—that is to say, Israelites, who neglected or despised the Law and committed sin with their bodies. For them a retribution of suffering was reserved amid the gloom and misery of Gehenna. It is, however, to be noticed that the punishments of Gehenna were seldom, if ever, considered to be of endless duration ; they were rather regarded as terminable in their nature and reformative in their effects. Between the two opposite states of the future world there was but a short space, which might be bridged over by the repentance and amendment of the sinner ; hence it was believed that the less sinful Jews confined in Gehenna—those who were not irredeemably bad—passed upward into Paradise after enduring pain for a period sufficient to purge them from sin and bring them to repentance. It is probable, also, that both Gehenna and Paradise were sometimes regarded as divisions of an intermediate state —the old Sheol—from which the righteous and those who had repented of their unrighteousness passed ultimately to the blessedness of Heaven. About the fate of the remainder— the incurably wicked—the common opinion seems to have been that they were annihilated, but this is not so clearly established as to be beyond dispute. Certain rabbinical expressions are supposed to suggest a belief in endless punishment for the finally unrepentant. But against this it is urged that, if such a belief existed, it must have been dropped in later years ; for the teaching of the Talmud as a whole is decidedly against the idea of everlasting damnation, and in favour of a temporary punishment even for the worst of sinners.

Christ did not dispute these current conceptions of His time, but occasionally made use of them in His teaching ; for example, in the parable of the rich man and Lazarus, and in His promise to the thief upon the cross (Lk 16 19 f. 23 43). Doubtless, too, they underlie His sayings about 'the many stripes and the few' (Lk 12 47, 48), 'the payment of the uttermost farthing' (Mt 5 26), and 'the more tolerable judgment upon the sins of ignorance' (Mt 11 22 f.). (His general attitude to the future life is discussed in art. 'Teaching of Jesus Christ.')

9. Worship and Practice. During the exile a more spiritual note began to pervade Jewish worship. Deprived of the ritual and sacrifices of the Temple, the better spirits of the nation, while maintaining the circumcision rite and the observance of the sabbath, betook themselves to more frequent prayer and meditation on the Law of God. It is probable, too, from the religious zeal afterwards exhibited by the exiles, that they met together periodically in local assemblies for mutual edification and encouragement. This, at any rate, is the origin generally assumed for the well-known institution of the **Synagogue,** which was already regarded as ancient in New Testament times (Ac 15 21). In the circumstances of the exile, worship could only be an affair of scattered individuals, not of the nation as a whole ; consequently it lost much of its official aspect, and acquired a more personal character.

After the Return, a rearrangement and elaboration of the Temple services took place. The daily sacrifices of a yearling lamb, morning and evening, were reëstablished and maintained without intermission—except for a short period during the persecution of Antiochus Epiphanes—until the fall of Jerusalem. Burnt offerings and sin offerings were appointed for the sabbaths and new moons and the great annual feasts. In course of time several other festivals were added to those that had been in existence before the exile—of these the chief were the Feast of Purim, supposed to celebrate the frustration of Haman's plots against the Jews of Persia (Esth 9 23-32), and the Feast of the Dedication, commemorative of the restitution of the Temple worship by Judas Maccabæus in 165 B.C. The sacrifices on all these occasions were no longer provided by royal munificence, but by individual contributions from the Jews scattered over the world ; consequently they took on a more representative character, and became the symbols of a widespread religious fellowship. At the same time, as an effect of the increased study of the prophets, a deeper religious spirit was infused into them ; they were regarded as well-pleasing to

God, not so much for any virtue in themselves as in the expression they gave to pious and penitent feeling. It had come to be seen that God cared more for the doing of His will than for the blood of bulls and of goats (Pss 40 6 f. 50 7 f. Prov 21 3 Ecclus 34 18-35, etc.). Jesus, though He sets less value on the sacrifices than the Jewish teachers of His time, did not interfere with them, but in this, as in other respects, conformed to the ordinary practices of the Law (Lk 2 41 f. Mk 14 12 f. Jn 2 13 f. 5 1 f. 7 2 f.).

Other elements of worship were introduced or emphasised, which detracted from the prominence of the sacrifices, and gave the laity, as distinct from the priests, a larger interest in the services. This was partly the result and partly the cause of the multiplication of synagogues as local places of worship apart from the Temple, one of which, and sometimes more, were to be found in every considerable Jewish community. Both in the Synagogue and the Temple, the Law was read and expounded for the popular benefit: in later times, the prophets also (Lk 4 17), and other Old Testament books; while sacred songs (many of which are preserved in the book of Psalms) were chanted or sung, generally by trained choirs, but yet as the praises of the congregation. Prayer was an important element in the worship, as well as in the individual life; with praise and thanksgiving, it accompanied every offering of incense or sacrifice. There were several stated forms of it for public use, the chief of which were 'The Eighteen Benedictions,' a short recension of which is called 'The Habinenu,' and 'The Kaddish.'

In keeping with the eschatological ideas of the time, the practice seems to have grown up in the second century B.C. of making sacrifices and prayers for the dead. It may have been suggested by the heathen custom of making oblations at the graves of the departed; but it differs from it in the fact that, according to the higher ideas of the Jewish religion, the offerings were made, not to the souls of the dead, but on behalf of them to God. In the form of prayer alone, without the accompaniment of sacrifice, the practice afterwards passed into the early Christian Church. The origin of it cannot be exactly determined, but it is easy to see how natural it was to pious Jewish minds, that had come to a strong and earnest faith in the immortality of the soul, the resurrection of the body, and the purifying purposes of the punishments of Gehenna. They might well believe that the souls that had been benefited by their prayers in this world might still be helped by them in the world beyond the grave. An instance of such prayers has been supposed to occur in Ps 132,

assuming the post-Davidic date of the Psalm. 'Lord, remember David and all his afflictions'; but we cannot lay much weight upon that. For the first time, the usage comes clearly into view in the history of the Maccabæan wars, where a case of it is found on a tolerably large scale (2 Mac 12 40-45). The teaching of the Jewish schools was quite in accordance with it; and there is reason to believe that, during the life and ministry of Christ, though He is practically silent about it, prayers for the dead were offered in the synagogues, and repeated by the mourning relatives. In Jewish cemeteries of the first and second centuries after Christ, inscriptions have been found bearing witness to the usage; and a trace of it may appear in the New Testament in St. Paul's prayer for Onesiphorus (2 Tim 1 18).

Except in small devout circles, such as those in which the gospel of Christ found a ready soil, Judaism, towards the close of our period, degenerated into pure legalism and formality. The doctrine of God's transcendence had begotten harsh conceptions of His nature, and arbitrary ideas of His judgments; caprice and partiality, rather than love, were ascribed to Him; His requirements were supposed to be contained in the Law and the traditions of the elders, which by this time had become a vast conglomerate of precepts bearing upon the minutest actions and circumstances of life. Only the strictest observance of the Pharisaic rules could make a man righteous before God; but that need not be more than an external observance, and so the religious life came to be divided between the performance of rites and ceremonies, in which purifications played a great part, and punctilious attention to matters of outward conduct. The whole Pharisaic system aimed at making clean the outside of the cup and platter; it tithed mint and rue and all manner of herbs, but passed over judgment and the love of God (Lk 11 39-42). Expedients were devised to atone for the shortcomings of those who failed in their efforts to keep the whole Law: exceptional suffering and works of surpassing merit, especially almsgiving, even the good works and virtues of ancestors and friends were regarded as compensating for personal deficiencies. Under such a system a healthy spiritual life was hardly likely to be fostered; its only outcome could be, as the New Testament shows, pride and hypocrisy on the one hand, and hopelessness on the other. Jesus protested against it till His lips were closed on the cross, and in striking contrast to it presented that pure moral teaching and profound spiritual faith which have since conquered the world.

THE LIFE OF JESUS CHRIST

In the estimation of His followers, Christ's life is the central fact in the history of the world. This is indicated externally in their manner of computing time, and dating other events, with reference to it. More particularly, however, they regard it as the most significant fact for their personal lives, the basis of their individual thinking and behaviour in the world. Christianity revolves so closely round the person and work of Christ that a knowledge and understanding of His life are requisite for the comprehension of Christian truth. Besides, as a life of absolute purity and devotion to God, it presents not only the perfect standard for moral conduct, but the ideal type of religious aspiration and devotion. It deserves, therefore, the closest, most reverent study ; and in such study the following short sketch may be helpful, as bringing the various details of the Gospels together, and arranging them so far as possible in chronological order.

1. The accepted date of **Christ's birth** is wrong by several years. In reality He was born in B.C. 6 or 7, at a little village 5 m. S. of Jerusalem, called Bethlehem. There His mother gave Him birth in a stable, there being no room for her in the inn. His mother, Mary, and His reputed father, Joseph, were devout Jews of the tribe of Judah. They claimed descent from the royal house of David, but, like others of his descendants, were in poor circumstances. According to the Gospel narrative, based probably on the testimony of Joseph and Mary, Joseph was not in a literal sense the father of Jesus. Before their marriage Jesus had already been miraculously conceived by His mother, in accordance with an angel's message. A marvel so stupendous, which, if alleged of an ordinary person, could not be credited, is rendered credible, and almost natural, by the extraordinary subsequent career of Jesus. There is no need to enlarge upon the subject in this place, as it is fully discussed in the Commentary upon St. Matthew's Gospel. See on Mt 1 18-25.

2. **Childhood and Youth of Jesus.** When Jesus was born, Herod the Great ruled Judæa and all Palestine. Soon afterwards he died (B.C. 4), and his kingdom was divided among his sons. Archelaus received Judæa, Samaria, and Idumæa ; Herod Antipas received Galilee and Peræa ; Herod Philip received Trachonitis and Ituræa. These princes were not independent, but subject to Rome. While Jesus was quite young, Archelaus was banished to Gaul for misgovernment, and Judæa was placed under direct Roman government (A.D. 5). Antipas and Philip were allowed to retain their dominions.

Joseph had intended to settle permanently in Bethlehem, that being the proper home of the Messiah (Mic 5 2), but the hostility first of Herod the Great, from which he took refuge in Egypt, and afterwards of Archelaus, caused him to alter his plans. He returned to Nazareth, his own city, in the dominions of Antipas, and brought up Jesus to his own trade, which was that of a carpenter, or possibly a smith.

Jesus did not enter a rabbinical academy, but doubtless received the usual education of a Jewish boy in the synagogue of Nazareth. This consisted of reading, writing, and perhaps the elements of arithmetic. Schooling began at the age of six or seven. Before this age Jewish fathers were accustomed to teach their sons the Shema (Dt 6 4), certain proverbs, and certain verses from the Psalms. In school the children sat on the ground, and repeated the words of the lesson after the master until they knew it. Great attention was paid to pronunciation and learning by heart. The principal study was the Law, of which Leviticus was taken first, as containing the information about legal observances most necessary for a boy approaching manhood to know. The boys were very anxious to read well, because the best readers were allowed to read the lessons from the Law in the synagogue services.

The Jewish system of education was entirely different from the Greek. The Jewish schoolmasters were scribes, trained in the narrowest ideas of traditional rabbinism. They rigidly excluded from the curriculum all secular subjects, and every Gentile influence. Jewish boys had no sports or athletics like the Greeks, though we read that they played with one another in the streets (Mt 11 16). It may be safely affirmed that Jesus grew up entirely uninfluenced by Greek culture, although it is probable that, owing to the presence of so many Gentiles in Galilee, He found it necessary to learn the Greek language. Some have maintained that He was acquainted only with the vernacular Aramaic (called Hebrew in the New Testament), but it is more probable that He was bilingual, speaking Aramaic or Greek according to circumstances.

It is doubtful whether Jesus during His whole life ever read any other book than the Bible. With this He was intimately acquainted

In His recorded discourses, He quotes nearly every book of the Old Testament, and shows a profound knowledge of its spirit and meaning.

Only one incident of His childhood is recorded (Lk 2 41), but it is interesting as showing that even at twelve years of age He possessed the consciousness of His divine Sonship (Lk 2 49). The childhood of Jesus was marked by no miracle. Like other children He grew in wisdom and stature (Lk 2 52). He showed exceptional, but not superhuman ability (Lk 2 47). Passing through every stage of human life, He showed the virtues and capacities suitable to each. There is no scriptural support for the common idea that from the moment of the Incarnation His human nature possessed all knowledge and every possible perfection. On the contrary, the Scripture teaches that the growth of His human mind in grace and knowledge was real, and that He was subject to real temptations like other men.

Jesus was brought up with several other children, who are called His brothers and sisters. These were either children of Joseph by a former wife, or children of Joseph and Mary born after Jesus, or, as some would prefer to believe with Jerome, cousins of our Lord (see on Mt 12 47-50). They appear to have been jealous of the superior talents of Jesus, and for some time refused to believe in Him (Jn 7 5). After the Resurrection they were converted, and two of them, James and Jude, became prominent Christians.

3. The Ministry of Jesus. No teacher ever achieved so much in so short a time as Jesus. His ministry did not exceed two years and six months (according to some authorities three years and six months), and yet in that short time He founded a Church strong enough to survive the greatest political and social revolutions, and enlightened enough to adapt itself to the continual advance of human knowledge. Christianity to-day is as new as it was two thousand years ago. It already embraces more than a third of the human race, and is still extending its sway over the hearts and lives of men.

The plan of Christ's ministry is quite definite and clear. He felt that His first duty was to offer Himself to the Jewish authorities at Jerusalem, and to the nation at large, as the promised Messiah. This He accordingly did (Jn 2 13-3 36). But He knew from the first that they would reject Him. His ideal of what the Messiah was to be, and theirs, were too far asunder for any other result to follow. They sought an earthly king to lead a revolt against foreign domination, and to found a world-wide Jewish state. He sought a kingdom not of this world. Gradually the nation which at first received Him favourably became estranged, and He devoted Himself more and more to training the Twelve for their future work. The outlook of Jesus was never confined to the limits of Judaism. He looked forward to the conversion of all the nations, and laid His plans accordingly (Mt 8 11 Jn 10 16 Mt 28 19). The idea of the Catholic Church is due, not to St. Paul, but to Jesus.

4. The Localities of the Ministry. Roughly speaking, Jesus spent a year teaching in Judæa, a year (some say two years) in Galilee, and six months in Peræa and other places. The Synoptic Gospels do not describe the Judæan ministry, and very rarely allude to it (Mt 23 37 Lk 4 44 RM and Westcott and Hort). The omission is, no doubt, remarkable, but is capable of a simple explanation. Eight months of the Judæan ministry took place before the death of the Baptist and the public appearance of Jesus in Galilee, and were relatively unimportant. The rest of the Judæan ministry consisted of occasional visits to Jerusalem. On these visits Jesus probably took with Him the Apostle John, who had a house at Jerusalem, leaving Peter and the rest behind in Galilee to carry on His work. Hence the Synoptists, who depend upon St. Peter, omit the Judæan ministry, while St. John, who alone witnessed it, alone records it.

5. The Baptism. Jesus was baptised by John the Baptist, who claimed to be the Forerunner of the Messiah, in the latter half of A.D. 26. After the Baptism, both John and Jesus saw a vision of a dove descending upon Jesus, and heard a voice from heaven saying: 'This is my beloved Son, in whom I am well pleased.' This sign convinced John that Jesus was the Messiah and the Son of God, and henceforth he openly proclaimed the fact. The recognition of Jesus as the Messiah by John, which is most explicit in the Fourth Gospel, was of the greatest assistance to the future ministry of Jesus. John was universally recognised as a prophet, and his words carried weight (Mt 21 26, etc.). From the disciples of John Jesus obtained His first and most influential followers (Jn 1 35-42).

6. The Temptation. After His Baptism, Jesus retired to the wilderness to prepare for His ministry by a period of seclusion. He was wholly occupied in meditation, fasting, and prayer. Here He overcame the temptation, suggested to Him by the Evil One, to take the easy and pleasant road to success by falling in with the ideas of the multitude, founding an earthly kingdom, and using His miraculous powers for unworthy ends. He resolved to live a life of self-denial, humility, and suffering, and to appeal for the spread of His principles, not to force, or to popular favour, but to the religious instincts of pious and holy minds. His should be a Kingdom of Truth (Mt 4 1).

7. The First Disciples. After the Temptation Jesus returned to the neighbourhood of the Baptist, and several of the Baptist's disciples attached themselves to Him. They were Peter, John, Andrew, Philip, and Bartholomew (Nathanael). They joined Him in the belief, or rather in the hope, that He was really the Messiah. But they did not commit themselves irrevocably at first. They followed Him, but did not entirely abandon their ordinary avocations. It was not till the end of a year of personal experience of what Jesus was, that they left all and followed Him (Jn 1 35 Lk 5 11).

8. Sketch of the Ministry. The Synoptic Gospels ignore chronology, and it is only by the help of the Fourth Gospel that anything like a chronological scheme of our Lord's ministry can be constructed. Following St. John, we may divide the ministry into eight periods.

(1) *From the Baptism, September* A.D. 26, *to the First Passover of the Ministry, April* A.D. 27. This period of about six months embraces the Baptism, the Temptation, the gathering of the first disciples, and the first miracle at Cana. The early part of the period was spent in the wilderness, the later part in Galilee. The life of Jesus was still more private than public, but the faith of His little band of disciples was growing, and His position as a teacher or rabbi was beginning to be recognised (Jn 1 29–2 12).

(2) *From the First Passover of the Ministry, April* A.D. 27, *to December of the same year*. This period of eight months was spent entirely in Judæa. At the Passover He cleansed the Temple for the first time, prophesied His death and resurrection in words afterwards quoted against Him at His trial (Mt 26 61), converted a leading member of the Sanhedrin, and afterwards spent several months in Judæa teaching and baptising. He made many converts, but was not satisfied with their faith or earnestness. The apparent success of Jesus roused the envy of the disciples of John, who was obliged to rebuke them, and to renew His strong testimony to Jesus' Messiahship (Jn 2 13–3 36).

(3) *From December* A.D. 27 *to the Feast of Purim, March* A.D. 28. This period of three months was passed chiefly in Galilee. The hostility of the Pharisees, due to the success of Jesus, drove Him from Judæa. On His way to Galilee He passed through Samaria, where he made a number of converts, thus for the first time extending His work beyond the limits of Judaism. This return to Galilee marks the beginning of the active Galilean ministry, which the Synoptists so graphically record (Mk 1 14 f.). At this period John was cast into prison, so that the eyes of all Galilee

were now concentrated upon Jesus. Making Capernaum His head-quarters, He went on preaching tours through Galilee, proclaiming the kingdom of God, casting out devils, and healing the sick. A profound impression was produced. He was everywhere taken for a prophet, and it began to be the popular belief of Galilee that He must in truth be the Messiah. To this period, generally called the great Galilean ministry, in which the success of Jesus was most pronounced, are to be assigned the second miracle at Cana (Jn 4 46), the final call of the Apostles (Mt 4 19 Lk 5 11), the choice of the Twelve, the Sermon on the Mount, much of the teaching by parables, and numerous miracles worked at Capernaum and throughout Galilee. The bulk of the work of Jesus recorded by St. Matthew and St. Mark belongs to this period. So crowded is it with incidents, and so extensive are the journeys which Jesus is said to have undertaken, that some suppose that it cannot have been compressed within the narrow limits of three months, and assign a year and three months to it. Towards the end of the period the Apostles were sent on a preaching tour (Mt 10 5).

The whole period was one of intense activity and full of hope and promise. Although Jesus did not openly call Himself the Messiah (the Christ), He assumed an authority which could only be justified on that assumption. Apparently He avoided the title, because in the minds of the Jews it was inseparably connected with the idea of a temporal king and a temporal kingdom. But among the Samaritans, whose idea of the Messiah was not political, He showed no such reticence, and openly declared Himself to be 'the Christ' (Jn 4 26). In the Fourth Gospel, which does not describe the Galilean ministry, Jesus appears to be less reluctant to allow Himself to be recognised as the Messiah than He does in the Synoptics.

(4) *From the Feast of Purim, March* A.D. 28, *to the Second Passover, April* A.D. 28. This period of about a month began with a visit to Jerusalem to keep the Feast of Purim (Jn 5 1), but was chiefly spent in Galilee. At Jerusalem Jesus healed a man at the pool of Bethesda, and delivered an important discourse asserting His lordship over the sabbath, His equality with the Father, and His power to raise the dead. His words caused great offence, and henceforth plots were formed against His life. While Jesus was at Jerusalem the Apostles were engaged on their mission of healing and preaching in Galilee (Mt 10 5). Returning from Jerusalem, Jesus rejoined the Apostles, who reported with joy the success of their mission (Lk 9 10). Then followed the feeding of the five thousand on the E. of the Lake (Jn 6 1), an event recorded

by all the evangelists. This is the really critical point of the ministry. Hitherto, at least in Galilee, all had been most favourable. Now a change began. The multitudes for whose benefit the miracle was wrought were for the most part enthusiastic Galileans, journeying to Jerusalem to keep the Feast of the Passover. They insisted that Jesus should be conducted to Jerusalem and proclaimed king. Jesus refused, and in so doing displeased not only the multitudes but even the Apostles. On the next day He offended His followers still more by declaring in the synagogue at Capernaum that He was the living bread that came down from heaven, and that those who would have eternal life must eat His flesh and drink His blood. At this many of His followers left Him, but the Apostles, though grievously disappointed, stood firm. For the Passover which followed, the second (or, as some think, the third) of the ministry, Jesus does not seem to have visited Jerusalem (Jn 7 1). See Jn 5 1–6 71.

(5) *From the Second Passover, April* A.D. 28, *to the Feast of Tabernacles in October of the same year.* This period of about six months embraces the second and closing period of the Galilean ministry. The time was spent partly in Galilee proper, and partly in extensive excursions through Phœnicia, and the districts of Cæsarea Philippi and Decapolis. The period is one of opposition, disappointment, and gloom, during which Jesus withdraws more and more from public life, and devotes Himself to His disciples.

The Pharisaic party, which Jesus had deeply offended a month before by His speech at the Feast of Purim, now sent emissaries into Galilee to undermine His influence with the people, who were already beginning to be dissatisfied with Him for reasons of their own. A stormy encounter took place, in which Jesus denounced their pedantic traditions which in effect made void the Law of God (Mk 7 1 f.). Nevertheless He still went on a tour through the land of Gennesaret, and perhaps through the whole of Galilee, and healed multitudes of sick (Mk 6 53-56). Perhaps at this period He visited Nazareth for a second time, and was again rejected (Lk 4 16). At last He determined to leave Galilee and to undertake a tour through heathen territory. But first He pronounced a doom of woe upon those Galilean cities in which so many of His mighty works had been wrought, and wrought in vain (Mt 11 20). The motive for this extensive journey was probably not so much to undertake new work among the heathen, though this to some extent was done, as to be alone with the Apostles and to prepare them for His death. Passing through the land of Tyre and Sidon, He healed the

daughter of the Canaanitish woman (Mk 7 24), and then made a circuit to the other side of the sea of Galilee (Decapolis), where the population was mainly heathen. Here He performed certain cures and fed the four thousand, who probably were mainly Gentiles. Then, crossing to Bethsaida, He healed a blind man (Mk 7 31–8 26). Finding the Pharisees still active, and the country hostile (Mk 8 11), He started on another tour to Cæsarea Philippi, in the extreme N. of Palestine. Here occurred the great confession of St. Peter, in which in the face of apparent failure the Apostle expressed his faith not only in Jesus' Messiahship, but in His Divinity (Mt 16 16). Jesus, deeply moved, declared him to have fully merited the honourable surname, which at their first meeting had been bestowed upon him (Jn 1 43). Then followed the announcement of the Passion and of the Resurrection; the Transfiguration; and a secret return to Capernaum (Mk 9 33). Here occurred the miracle of the coin in the fish's mouth (Mt 17 24), the incident of the little child taken into Jesus' arms (Mk 9 33), and the conversation with His brethren, in which they taunted Him with the failure of His mission, and the present obscurity of His life (Jn 7 2 f.).

(6) *From the Feast of Tabernacles, early in October* A.D. 28, *to the Feast of Dedication in December of the same year.* See Jn 7 10–10 22. Jesus went up to Jerusalem secretly to keep the Feast of Tabernacles, skirting the borders of Samaria (Lk 9 52), and healing ten lepers on His way (Lk 17 11). Finding a certain amount of support at Jerusalem, He ventured from His retirement, and publicly asserted His claims to divine dignity. On one occasion He narrowly escaped stoning (Jn 8 59). The only miracle recorded at this period is the healing of the man born blind. It is generally supposed that Jesus spent the whole of this period, which consisted of nearly three months, in Jerusalem.

(7) *From the Feast of the Dedication, December* A.D. 28, *to the Raising of Lazarus, March* A.D. 29. This period of about three months was chiefly spent in Peræa. At the Feast of the Dedication Jesus again nearly lost His life, and was obliged to retreat into Peræa, beyond Jordan. Here He preached and made many converts, the way having been prepared for Him by the preaching of John the Baptist: see Jn 10 22-42. This period is full of incidents, and is not unlike the earlier Galilean ministry in character. Here, as in Galilee, Jesus was continually opposed by the scribes and Pharisees. To this period are to be assigned the successful mission of the Seventy (Lk 10 1 f.), the question of divorce (Mk 10 2), the blessing of little children (Mk 10 13), the interview with the rich young ruler (Lk 18 18), and the message of Jesus to Herod (Lk 13 31). The **period**

culminates in the great miracle of the raising of Lazarus (Jn 11[1]).

(8) *From the Raising of Lazarus, March* A.D. 29, *to the Crucifixion, April* A.D. 29. This period of about three weeks was passed chiefly in retirement at Ephraim. From this place He returned to Jerusalem, to keep the last Passover and to suffer death, by way of Jericho and Bethany : see Jn 11[54]-12[11]. At Jericho he healed two blind men (Mt 20[29]), and stayed with Zacchæus (Lk 19[1]). On the sabbath before the Passover He arrived at Bethany, and there in the evening Simon the leper entertained Him at a banquet (Jn 12[1] Mk 14[3]). On Sunday (Palm Sunday) He entered in triumph into Jerusalem as the Messiah. His bold action rallied to His side once more His Galilean supporters. His recent miracle of the raising of Lazarus had also made a sensation in Jerusalem itself. He could, if He had so willed, have led a successful revolution ; but He would not, and His supporters gradually deserted Him (Mt 21[1f.]). Nevertheless, Jesus taught daily in the Temple, and was heard with intense earnestness from morning to night (Lk 21[38]). In the Temple He healed many who were blind and lame, and so great was the enthusiasm that even the children cried, 'Hosanna to the Son of David' (Mt 21[14]). On Monday Jesus, who had spent the night at Bethany, cursed the fig-tree (Mt 21[18]). He then cleansed the Temple for the second time (Mk 11[15]). On Tuesday His authority to teach was challenged by the Sanhedrin (Mt 21[23]), and Jesus spoke the parables of the Two Sons (Mt 21[28]), the Wicked Husbandmen (Mt 21[33]), and the Wedding Garment (Mt 22[1]). He also solved the question of the Tribute Money (Mt 22[15]), confounded the Sadducees (Mt 22[23]), and denounced in the strongest terms the general teaching of the scribes and Pharisees (Mt 23[1]). The chief event of the day, which practically closed the ministry, was the great prophecy of the fall of Jerusalem and the end of the world, pronounced on the Mount of Olives (Mt 24[1]). See also Jn 12[20-50].

Wednesday was passed in retirement with the Apostles. On this day, if not before, Judas betrayed Jesus, for thirty pieces of silver (Mt 26[14]). On Thursday evening, a day earlier than the proper day for the Passover, Jesus celebrated the Last Supper, and instituted the Holy Communion (Jn 13[1] Mt 26[17]). This day is commonly called Maundy Thursday, from the 'Command' (*Mandatum*) given by Jesus to His disciples to wash one another's feet. That night He was arrested, and in the early morning of Friday was tried before the Sanhedrin, Pilate, and Antipas. His crucifixion, death, and burial were followed by the Jewish Passover, which in that year coincided with the sabbath day. Saturday (Easter Eve) was passed by Jesus in the abodes of the dead. According to the usually accepted view (which, however, is not entirely free from difficulties), He visited both the place of bliss (Lk 23[43]) and the place of misery (1 Pet 3[18f.]). In the latter He preached (1 Pet 3[19] 4[6]) ; perhaps also in the former.

9. The Resurrection and Ascension. Early on Easter Sunday morning Jesus rose from the dead, in His true body, which was, however, transformed into a glorious and spiritual body, and for forty days appeared at intervals to the disciples, proving the reality of His Resurrection, and instructing them in the things pertaining to the kingdom of God. Then, having given to the Apostles a commission to convert the world, He ascended into heaven in their presence from the Mount of Olives, and sat down at the right hand of God, henceforth to rule over the universe (Ac 1[1-11]). From heaven he sent down the Holy Spirit at Pentecost, and it is believed by Christians that He will one day come in person to judge mankind according to their works.

THE TEACHING OF JESUS CHRIST

THE teaching of Jesus, though not given in systematic form, but in such instalments as were suited to the needs and capacities of the hearers, will be found to form a uniform and consistent whole.

In external form it is thoroughly Jewish and rabbinical, as parallel passages from the rabbis adduced in the Commentary on St. Matthew will abundantly prove. In particular it makes free use of parables, a form of instruction familiar to the rabbis, but employed by Jesus more systematically and effectively than by them. In substance, however, the teaching is not Jewish, but in the widest sense human, and as such equally adapted to all times and conditions of society. To secure this universality Jesus refrained from constructing a detailed code of morals, and from issuing a directory of worship. He laid down principles of conduct and principles of worship, leaving the disciples to work out their practical application for themselves. The teaching of Jesus was thus of a stimulating character. It forced men to think. It did not supply a cut and dried solution of moral problems, but supplied the point of view from which the true solution might be attained. Often the teaching was purposely paradoxical and seemingly contradictory, in order to indicate that moral principles ought not to be reduced to practice without thought, and without due consideration of the competing claims of other principles (Mt 5^{39-42} Lk 14^{26}, etc.). Sometimes the paradoxical form was due to the 'ideal' or 'absolute' character of the teaching (Mt 5^{33-37}). The Sermon on the Mount in particular is of this character. It is a sketch of perfect behaviour in a perfect society, and its precepts cannot be applied to the world as it now is without qualification. Yet there may come a time when the principles of that Sermon may be put in practice without any qualification whatever.

The teaching of Jesus was authoritative teaching. Whereas the sages of Greece regarded their opinions as guesses at truth, and the prophets of Israel spoke only as the voice of God from time to time reached them, Jesus taught with an authority which was inherent in His person. He revised not only the details of the Ceremonial Law by His own authority, but even the Decalogue itself (Mt $5^{21 f.}$), and in general adopted such an attitude towards the whole Old Testament revelation as no prophet had ever assumed. From the beginning of His ministry His hearers 'were astonished at His doctrine, for He taught them as one having authority and not as the scribes' (Mt 7^{28}).

1. **The Fatherhood of God and human sonship.** Without any doubt the leading religious doctrine of Jesus was the Fatherhood of God. This idea, rarely and in a more limited sense expressed in the Old Testament, and seldom, if ever, in any other religion, was made by Jesus the foundation of His teaching. That 'God is love,' and cares with the intensity and impartiality of a father's affection for every individual soul that He has created, is the essence of the gospel (Mt 10^{31}). But according to Jesus God is 'Father,' not primarily because He is the Father of angels and men, but because He is the Father of His only-begotten Son (Jn 3^{35}). From all eternity God loved the Son, and the Son loved God, so that even if the universe had never been created, God would still have been eternally a God of love (Jn 17^{24}). Men become the 'sons of God' in the higher spiritual sense not directly, but through their relation to Jesus Himself (Jn 14^{21}). By faith in Jesus and the new birth of water and the Spirit they become sons of God and heirs of eternal life. Of course, in a general way, men by nature belong to God, and so may be called His children, inasmuch as He is the author of their life and being, the source of all the powers and capabilities they possess. This natural relationship, however, does not make them, in a true and proper sense, the sons of God; it only constitutes the ground and possibility of their becoming such, and still leaves it open to them to become something quite opposite and contradictory. For real filial relationship with God, something more is needed than the derivation of our being from Him: mutual understanding and acknowledgment, community of will, interest, and activity. This was made possible in Christ. Himself the everlasting Son of God, He turned the hearts of God's human (or natural) children to their Father, and opened the floodgates of His love to them. He taught them to claim and exercise their birthright in God. He put into their hands the charter of their divine sonship. He signed and sealed it with His blood. 'As many as received Him, to them gave He power to become children of God, even to them that believe on His name' (Jn 1^{12}). It is only to be expected, then, that

Jesus should always sharply distinguish His own Sonship from the sonship of other men. He says, 'My Father and your Father,' and 'My God and your God,' never 'our Father' and 'our God.' To maintain, as is sometimes done, that the Sonship of Jesus was only a sense of human sonship strongly developed, is to contradict not simply an isolated passage here and there, but the whole tenor of Christ's teaching.

The life of sonship which the baptised Christian enjoys begins with repentance, and a complete surrender of the will to Jesus as a divine Saviour. Without this surrender of the life to Him, to be moulded absolutely according to His holy will, the unique blessedness and power of Christianity cannot be experienced. Only through faith in Christ can men in the full sense 'come to the Father.' 'I am the way and the truth and the life: no man cometh unto the Father but by me': 'He that loveth Father or mother more than me, is not worthy of me': 'No man having put his hand to the plough, and looking back, is fit for the kingdom of God' (Jn 14 6 Mt 10 37 Lk 9 62). The great sacrifice which Christianity demands is the sacrifice of the will. He who has learnt to merge his own will in the will of God, and to take delight only in that which is well pleasing to Him, has learnt the great secret of Jesus, and is filled with the inward joy of sonship.

2. The Motive of Love. God being thus the loving Father of men, it followed of necessity that men should regard one another as brothers. The chief stress, therefore, in Christian morality is laid upon love (Mt 22 37). This love shows itself in various ways. (1) In ready forgiveness. Just as God is always ready to forgive for Christ's sake every penitent sinner, so He insists that the forgiven sinner should forgive his brother also, not only unto seven times, but unto seventy times seven (Mt 6 15 18 22). (2) In avoiding unkind criticism. Christians are warned to 'judge not,' that they be not judged (Mt 7 1). (3) In a peaceful disposition. 'Blessed are the peacemakers, for they shall be called sons of God' (Mt 5 9). (4) In active benevolence. This is often inculcated in an extreme and paradoxical form—'Give to him that asketh thee, and from him that would borrow of thee turn not thou away' (Mt 5 42). 'Sell that ye have and give alms' (Lk 12 33); but it receives its perfect expression in the Golden Rule, 'Therefore all things whatsoever ye would that men should do to you, do ye even so to them; for this is the law and the prophets' (Mt 7 12). (5) In loving enemies and persecutors. Christ speaks of this as a chief and distinctive mark of Christian perfection (Mt 5 43). (6) In not resisting or resenting injuries. 'Resist not him that is evil, but who-

soever smiteth thee on thy right cheek, turn to him the other also' (Mt 5 39). Throughout Christ's teaching constant stress is laid upon conduct, and especially upon the duties of practical benevolence. The final judgment will be according to works, works being regarded as the only trustworthy indication of a living faith, and the works which Christ approves are thus described : 'I was an hungered, and ye gave me meat; I was thirsty, and ye gave me drink; I was a stranger, and ye took me in; naked, and ye clothed me; I was sick, and ye visited me; I was in prison, and ye came unto me.' For those who do such works the kingdom of heaven is reserved (Mt 25 34).

3. The General Type of Christian Character. Christianity has approved a type of character in most respects the very opposite of that which is approved by the world : instead of pride, humility; instead of standing upon one's rights, submission to wrong; instead of ambition, contentment. Gentleness, meekness, patience, sympathy, the power of rejoicing in tribulation, and of extracting pleasure from pain, are the gifts of Christianity to the world. The Christian ideal is sometimes depreciated as lacking in manliness and courage, but in truth it requires much more manliness to be humble than to be proud, much more courage to turn the cheek to the smiter than to smite again. Another great note of the Christian character is truthfulness and sincerity. According to Christ a Christian man's word should be as good as his oath. This is the meaning of the paradoxical saying, 'Swear not at all,' etc. (Mt 5 34). But perhaps the best general description of a Christian man's character is to say that he is a single-minded man. He cannot have one foot in the world and the other in the Church, he cannot serve God and mammon. He must have one main purpose in life to which all others are to be subordinated : 'Seek ye first the kingdom of God and his righteousness, and all these things shall be added unto you' (Mt 6 33).

4. Christ and Wealth. Christ regarded wealth as the great means by which the world binds men to its service. Detachment from wealth, therefore, is a necessary preliminary to being a Christian. In some cases, where the love of wealth was strong, Christ counselled its complete abandonment (Mt 19 21). From this detachment from wealth flow inward peace and absence of care. 'Be not anxious for your life, what ye shall eat, or what ye shall drink, nor yet for your body, what ye shall put on' (Mt 6 25). Although Christ warned His followers against the peril of wealth, and exhorted them to give liberal alms, there is no ground for the opinion that He regarded community of goods as a necessary mark of a Christian society. Accordingly the surrender of wealth has always been regarded by Christians as a counsel of perfection, not as a precept (Mt 19 21).

5. The Future Life. The moral teaching of Christ is based on the idea that this life is a state of probation for another. He taught His disciples not to seek their reward in this life, but in the next, when all the injustices of this world will be redressed, and all sorrows swallowed up in fulness of joy. Not as if the Christian has absolutely no reward in this world. Communion with God through Christ is itself joy unspeakable, and may be called 'eternal life,' yet its full fruition will not be experienced until the final consummation of all things. This assurance of a blessed immortality transforms the face of the world to a Christian. Pain, unhappiness, and even injustice, become part of a cleansing discipline, by which God prepares his soul for eternity. Pain is transfigured, injustice is meekly borne.

6. Death. To some extent, in speaking of death and the future world, Christ accommodated His language to the ideas in the minds of His hearers. It is unsafe, therefore, to build up specific views upon a literal interpretation of every reference, however casual, which He made to the subject. The following ideas, however, may be deduced with considerable probability from the general trend of His utterances. At death the souls of men do not pass at once to their final reward, but into a state (called 'Hades' in the RV, and 'hell' in the Apostles' Creed) in which they await the Judgment and the Resurrection. Yet even in this condition there is, as it were by anticipation, a distinction made. The souls of the just enjoy such a measure of felicity that they can be spoken of as in 'Paradise' or 'Abraham's bosom.' From this it has been inferred that their state is one of progressive sanctification and glory, culminating in the resurrection. It was an inference of this kind that originated the practice of praying for the dead, which had already gained ground in the Jewish Church (see 2 Mac 12 42-45) before the time of our Lord, and seems to have been carried forward by some of the primitive Christians into the worship of the Church of Christ: cp. 2 Tim 1 16-18 4 19. The souls of the wicked, on the other hand, pass into a state of unhappiness, which is a foretaste of their future woe (Lk 16 23). Whether the pains endured by them are in some cases remedial, being intended to effect the reformation of those who are not absolutely hardened in sin, is not distinctly revealed, but has been largely entertained as a pious hope. It was believed in the primitive Church, and is still held by many Christians, that good men among the heathen who die without a knowledge of Christ are given an opportunity of Christian instruction in the other world, or at least are admitted to the 'more tolerable judgment.' There is a statement in 1 Peter that may be interpreted in the light of this hope. He says that Christ Himself, when He descended into 'hell,' preached the gospel to the dead (1 Pet 3 19 4 6).

7. The Resurrection. At the Last Day Christ will raise from the dead by His own power (Jn 5 28) both the just and the unjust (Jn 5 29). The resurrection body, though not materially identical with the present body, will be in some sense continuous with it. It will be a glorious and spiritual body, fitted, not for an earthly life, but for a new and higher state of existence (Mt 22 30). In the Judgment Christ will sit as Judge 'because He is the Son of man' (Jn 5 27), and it is He who will give the sentence (Mt 25 34) of eternal glory or eternal woe (Mt 25 46).

8. Eternal Punishment. Of late years current ideas of future punishment have undergone extensive revision. The prevalence of more enlightened views of the character of God, and the more general recognition of the distinction, very strongly marked in the New Testament, and now in the RV made evident even to the English reader, between Hades and Gehenna, have led in some quarters to more hopeful views, and almost everywhere to less positive and dogmatic assertions, regarding the ultimate fate of those who at death do not seem to be in a state of grace. Nevertheless, eternal punishment (though many of the notions associated with it may be given up) is still believed in, at least as a possibility. The doctrine seems to be taught by our Lord Himself (Mt 25 46 Mk 9 48, etc.), and the attempts to eliminate it from the Gospel, or to explain it away, have not been very successful. It seems, in fact, to be an almost necessary deduction from the generally accepted truths of the immortality of the soul and the freedom of the will. If the soul is free to choose between good and evil, and cannot die, it follows of necessity that the soul which makes evil a permanent part of its nature will be permanently excluded from fellowship with God. That is the very essence of eternal punishment. Eternal punishment is not, as has been sometimes represented, an arbitrary vindictive act of God, but a result which follows naturally, in certain cases, from the known nature of man and the known nature of God. God cannot, even if He would, make a man good by force, because the very essence of goodness consists in its being voluntarily embraced. If a man deliberately embraces evil and identifies himself with it permanently, even God cannot save him. Of the exact nature of this punishment nothing is revealed, except that there may be degrees of it suited to the various degrees of delinquency (Lk 12⁴⁷). It is possible that an essential part of it, in the case both of angels and men, will be the loss of free will. This view provides for the ultimate extinction of moral evil.

9. Eternal Bliss. Of the nature of the final reward of the righteous, which is expressly stated to be eternal (Mt 25⁴⁶), we can speak only in the most general terms. The language of Christ which describes it is in all cases figurative (Mt 8¹¹ 25¹⁰, etc.). Nevertheless it seems to be indicated that there will be degrees of blessedness (Jn 14²), and perhaps of authority (Lk 19¹⁷) in heaven. Some have imagined that heaven will be a state of passive contemplation or ecstatic worship, but it seems more likely that contemplation will be united with practical activity suited to the capacity of each individual soul (Lk 19¹⁷,¹⁸). Christ taught that the future life of the blessed will be lived in a transfigured and glorified universe (Mt 19²⁸), an idea which is in harmony with the doctrine of the resurrection of the body. Heaven is uniformly conceived in the New Testament as a society or city. Its citizens find their happiness not merely in the contemplation, worship, and love of God (though this is their supreme delight), but in the loving fellowship which they enjoy with one another. Heaven is a perfect society, of which the basis is perfect love—love of God and love of all God's creatures.

10. Other teaching of Christ. Large portions of the teaching of Christ are entirely passed over in this article, which simply aims at supplementing what is stated elsewhere. The title 'Son of God' which He claimed at His trial, is discussed in the article 'The Person of Jesus Christ'; the title 'Son of man,' which was His favourite designation of Himself, is discussed in a note on Mt 8²⁰. The 'Kingdom of God,' or 'of heaven,' one of the leading religious ideas of Christ, is dealt with in the Introduction to St. Matthew and in the prefatory remarks to the Sermon on the Mount (Mt 5). For Christ's teaching about His Death, which He regarded as an atonement for the sins of the world, and as establishing a new covenant between God and the human race, see on Mt 20²⁸ 26²⁸, and article 'The Atonement.' For His teaching upon the Law and the Old Testament, see Mt 5¹⁷⁻¹⁹ 22³⁷⁻⁴⁰ Lk 16¹⁶ 24⁴⁴ 26⁵³ Jn 5³⁹,⁴⁰, ⁴⁵⁻⁴⁷. For public and private prayer, see Mt 6⁵⁻¹⁵ 7⁷⁻¹¹ Lk 11⁵⁻⁸ 18¹⁻⁸ ⁹⁻¹⁴ Jn 14¹³,¹⁴ 16²³,²⁴ Mt 21¹³,²¹,²² 26⁴⁰,⁴¹ Jn 4²¹,²⁴. For the sabbath day, see Mt 12³⁻¹² Mk 3⁴ Jn 7²¹⁻²⁴ Lk 13¹⁵,¹⁶. For fasting, see Mt 6¹⁶⁻¹⁸ 9¹⁵. On almsgiving, see Mt 5⁴² 6¹⁻⁴ 25³¹⁻⁴⁶ Lk 12³³,³⁴ 14¹²⁻¹⁹,²¹⁻²³ 10³⁰⁻³⁷ 21³,⁴ 16⁹. For repentance, see on Mt 4¹⁷ 21²⁸⁻³² Lk 5³¹,³⁶ 13²⁻⁵ 15¹⁰,¹⁷⁻²⁰ 16³⁰,³¹ 24⁴⁶,⁴⁷. On gratitude, see Lk 7⁴⁰⁻⁴⁷ 8³⁹ 17¹⁷,¹⁸. On hypocrisy, see Mt 23. On marriage, see Mt 5²⁷⁻³² 19⁴,¹². On Church and State, see Mt 22²¹. On scepticism, see Mt 14³¹ 17¹⁷⁻²⁰ Jn 3¹⁸,¹⁹ 4⁴⁸ 8²⁴ 15²²⁻²⁴. On the work of the Holy Spirit, see Jn 3³ᶠ. 14¹⁶⁻¹⁸,²⁶ 15²⁶ 16⁷⁻¹⁴. On Satan and demonic possession, see on Mt 4²⁵. On missionary work, see Mt 28¹⁸⁻²⁰ Lk 24⁴⁶⁻⁴⁹. On the Church, see Mt 16¹⁸ 18¹⁷. On the Sacraments, see Mt 26²⁶⁻²⁹ 28¹⁹ Jn 3⁵ 6³¹ᶠ.

THE SYNOPTIC PROBLEM

THE chief, and also the most difficult, critical question connected with the Synoptic Gospels is their relation to one another and to their presumed sources. Prolonged investigations, extending over more than a century, have not yet reached final results, but a considerable consensus of opinion inclines to the following conclusions.

1. That St. Mark is the oldest of the synoptists, and has been used by St. Matthew and St. Luke, who have incorporated the bulk of his Gospel into their own with comparatively few alterations.

The evidence for this is extremely strong. In the first place, the whole of St. Mark's Gospel, except from thirty to forty comparatively unimportant verses, is contained either in St. Matthew or in St. Luke, and most of it in both; whereas large portions of St. Matthew and St. Luke, and those very important ones, are peculiar to each of those Evangelists. Hence, if there was borrowing at all, it must have been from St. Mark. The other possibilities will not bear examination. St. Mark did not copy from St. Matthew, for he would not have omitted the Nativity, the Sermon on the Mount, and such parables as the Unmerciful Debtor, the Labourers in the Vineyard, the Ten Virgins, the Talents, and the Sheep and the Goats. St. Matthew did not copy from St. Luke, for he would not have omitted the parables of the Good Samaritan, the Rich Fool, Dives and Lazarus, and the Prodigal Son. Finally, St. Luke did not borrow from St. Matthew, for he would not have omitted those striking parables of St. Matthew which have been already mentioned.

We shall now prove that there was actual borrowing, and, in order to do so, shall quote and comment on a few parallel passages.

Mk 13 14	Mt 24 15, 16
But when ye see the abomination of desolation standing where he ought not (let him that readeth understand), then let them that are in Judæa flee unto the mountains.	When, therefore, ye see the abomination of desolation, which was spoken of by Daniel the prophet, standing in the holy place (let him that readeth understand), then let them that are in Judæa flee unto the mountains.

Here we have an author's comment (viz. 'let him that readeth understand') verbally identical in the two Gospels, and inserted at precisely the same point in our Lord's speech. As it is impossible to believe that the two Evangelists hit upon the same comment and inserted it at the same place *by accident*, we must conclude that one of them copied from the other.

Mk 6 16, 17	Mt 14 1-3
But Herod when he heard thereof, said, John, whom I beheaded, he is risen. For Herod himself had sent forth and laid hold upon John, and bound him in prison for the sake of Herodias, his brother Philip's wife, etc.	At that season Herod the tetrarch heard the report concerning Jesus, and said unto his servants, This is John the Baptist, he is risen from the dead, and therefore do these powers work in him. For Herod had laid hold on John and bound him, and put him in prison for the sake of Herodias, his brother Philip's wife, etc.

Here the death of John the Baptist is introduced and described by both Evangelists at the same point in the history, but out of its true historical order. Nothing but copying will account for this.

Mk 1 16	Mt 4 18
And passing along by the sea of Galilee, he saw Simon, and Andrew the brother of Simon, casting a net in the sea; for they were fishers.	And walking by the sea of Galilee, he saw two brethren, Simon who is called Peter, and Andrew his brother, casting a net into the sea, for they were fishers.

Observe here the comment upon the narrative ('for they were fishers') made by both Evangelists. We cannot conceive that it occurred to them to make such a remark just at this point independently.

Mk 3 19	Mt 10 4	Lk 6 16
And Judas Iscariot, which also betrayed him.	And Judas Iscariot, who also betrayed him.	And Judas Iscariot, which was the traitor.

It cannot be an accident that the three Evangelists concur at this point in calling Judas a traitor any more than it can be an accident that, at the arrest of Jesus, all three Evangelists are careful to remind us that Judas Iscariot was 'one of the Twelve' (Mk 14 10 Mt 26 14 Lk 22 3).

Mk 5 24	Mt 9 19	Lk 8 42
And he went with him, and a great multitude followed him, and they thronged him. And a woman, which had an issue of blood twelve years, and had suffered many things of many physicians, etc.	And Jesus arose and followed him, and so did his disciples. And behold a woman which had an issue of blood twelve years, etc.	And as he went the multitude thronged him. And a woman having an issue of blood twelve years, which had spent all her living upon physicians, etc.

Observe here how all three Evangelists break off the story of Jairus's daughter precisely at the same point to describe the cure of the woman with an issue, who, they all agree, had been ill twelve years.

Mk 1 32	Mt 8 16	Lk 4 40
And at even, when the sun did set, they brought unto him all that were sick a d them that were possessed with devils.	nd when even was come, they brought unto him many possessed with devils.	And when the sun was setting, all they that had any sick with divers diseases brought them unto him.

Here we have a clear indication that it is St. Mark's Gospel which is used by the other two ; for of St. Mark's two expressions to describe the close of day ('even' and 'when the sun did set'), St. Matthew adopts one and St. Luke the other. Cases of this kind occur throughout the Gospel history. St. Mark's account of the common incidents is generally the longest and the richest in detail, and what is found is that some of St. Mark's details are in St. Matthew, and some of them in St. Luke, and not all in both.

Two other considerations tend to confirm the priority of St. Mark : (1) St. Mark's order of events is always supported either by St. Matthew or by St. Luke, whereas St. Matthew's deviations from St. Mark's order are never supported by St. Luke, nor St. Luke's by St. Matthew's ; (2) the close resemblances between St. Matthew and St. Luke are generally confined to the incidents which they record in common with St. Mark. Their accounts of the Nativity have practically nothing in common, and the differences between their versions of the Sermon on the Mount are very great.

2. The version of St. Mark used by St. Matthew and St. Luke was probably the present Greek Gospel. For a long time it was customary to attribute the resemblances of the three Synoptic Gospels to a supposed 'original Mark'; but recent research has demonstrated that this 'original' Mark resembled the present St. Mark so closely that the simplest view is to suppose them identical, as accordingly is now very generally done.

3. Oral tradition probably exercised some influence over the composition of the Synoptic Gospels, especially of the First and Third ; but the resemblances are altogether too close to allow us to suppose that the principal common source was mere oral tradition. The 'original Mark' was certainly *written*, for the author of it once addressed his *readers* (Mk 13 14 = Mt 24 15, see above), and St. Luke refers to numerous written sources (Lk 1 1).

4. There is much less agreement among critics as to the sources of St. Matthew and St. Luke in those portions of their works which are not parallel with St. Mark. These sources would include (1) oral tradition ; (2) in the case of St. Luke, at least, personal researches and enquiries in Palestine ; (3) earlier documents which, though numerous, were probably rather fragmentary (Lk 1 1). A very early writer, Papias, who flourished about 130 A.D.,

speaks of St. Matthew as having compiled 'the oracles' in the Hebrew (or Aramaic) tongue. The exact meaning of 'oracles' is doubtful, but the tendency of modern criticism is to suppose that St. Matthew's Hebrew 'Logia' was a collection of our Lord's discourses, rather than a continuous narrative. These 'logia' of St. Matthew, in the form of a Greek translation, were probably used by the author of the First Gospel, perhaps even incorporated entire, so that it is not without reason that the present Gospel is called 'according to Matthew.' Whether the 'logia' were also used by St. Luke, and if so to what extent, is a difficult question. St. Luke and St. Matthew have about 200 verses common to them alone. The question is whether St. Luke's deviations from St. Matthew in these verses, which are generally very considerable, are not altogether too great to allow the supposition that he used a common document. The reader will be able to form his own judgment upon this matter by comparing the parallel passages, a complete list of which is given in the following table.

Mt.	Lk.	
3 7-10, 12.	3 7-9, 17.	Preaching of John.
4 3-11.	4 3-13.	Temptation.
5 1-6, 10-12.	6 20-23 . 25.	Sermon on the Mount.
5 13.	14 34, 35.	,, ,,
5 18.	16 17.	,, ,,
5 25, 26.	12 57-59.	,, ,,
5 38-48.	6 27-30, 32-36.	,, ,,
6 3, 4.	14 13, 14.	,, ,,
6 9-13.	11 1-4.	,, ,,
6 19-21.	12 33, 34.	,, ,,
6 22, 23.	11 34-36.	,, ,,
6 24.	16 13.	,, ,,
6 25-34.	12 22-32.	,, ,,
7 1, 2.	6 37, 38.	,, ,,
7 3-5.	6 41, 42.	,, ,,
7 7-11.	11 9-13.	,, ,,
7 12.	6 31.	,, ,,
7 13, 14.	13 23, 24.	,, ,,
7 15-20. } 12 33-37. }	6 43-45.	,, ,,
7 21.	6 46.	,, ,,
7 22, 23.	13 25-27.	,, ,,
7 24-27.	6 47-49.	,, ,,
8 5-13.	{ 7 1-3, 6-10. } { 13 28, 29. }	Centurion's servant.
8 19, 20.	9 57, 58.	'The foxes have holes.'
8 21, 22.	9 59, 60.	'Let the dead bury their dead.'
9 32-34. } cp. 12 22-24. }	11 14, 15.	The deaf demoniac.
9 36-38.	10 2.	'The harvest truly is plenteous.'
10 5-16.	10 1-12.	Charges to the Twelve and the Seventy.
10 24-33.	6 40 12 2-9.	,, ,,

Mt.	Lk.	
10 34-36.	12 51-53.	Charges to the Twelve and the Seventy.
10 37,38.	14 26,27.	" "
10 39.	17 33.	" "
10 40,41.	10 16.	" "
11 1-6.	7 18-23.	John sends disciples.
11 7-11.	6 24-28.	Christ's opinion of John.
11 12-14.	16 16.	" "
11 16-19.	7 31-35.	" "
11 20-24.	10 12-15.	'Woe to thee, Chorazin.'
11 25-27.	10 21,22.	'I thank thee, Father.'
[12 9-14.	14 1-6.]	?
12 27,28,30.	11 19,20,23.	Beelzebub.
12 38-42.	11 29-32.	The sign of Jonah.
12 43-45.	11 24-26.	The house swept and garnished.
13 16,17.	10 23,24.	'Blessed are your eyes.'
13 33.	13 20,21.	Parable of the Leaven.
15 14.	6 39.	Blind leaders of the blind.
16 2,3.	12 54-56.	'Ye can discern the face of the sky.'
17 19,20.	17 5,6.	Faith as a grain of mustard-seed.
18 7.	18 1.	'Woe to the world because of offences.'
18 12-14.	15 3-7.	The lost sheep.
18 15,16,21,22.	17 3,4.	'If thy brother sin.'
19 28.	22 28-30.	Judging the twelve tribes of Israel.
[21 31,32.	7 29,30.]	?
21 44.	20 18.	'He that falleth upon this stone.'
[22 1-10.	14 15-24.]	?
23 4-7,12,13.	11 43,45,46,52. 14 11. }	Woe to the Scribes and Pharisees.
23 28-33.	11 37-44,47,48.	" "

Mt.	Lk.	
23 34-36.	11 49-51.	Woe to the Scribes and Pharisees.
23 37-39.	13 34,35.	'Jerusalem, Jerusalem, that killest the prophets.'
24 26-28.	17 23,24,37.	Sayings about the Second Advent.
24 37-39.	17 26,27.	" "
24 40,41.	17 34-36.	" "
24 43-51.	12 39-46.	" "
25 14-30.	19 11-28.	The Talents and the Pounds.

It will be noted that the common matter is mainly, though not exclusively, sayings and discourses, and that its order and arrangement in the two Gospels is generally very different. This variation in order and arrangement, which is extreme, constitutes a real objection to the view that the authors of the First and Third Gospels both used the 'logia,' at least as a principal common source. When they copy St. Mark, they preserve, as a rule, not only his words, but also his order and context, but when they are supposed to copy the 'logia,' they deal much more freely with the words, and, as to the order and context, they either take no account of them at all, or differ from each other. Even if we admit that St. Matthew's habit was to collect our Lord's sayings into large masses, and St. Luke's to preserve the separate sayings in their original context, there still remain numerous divergences of order and context, which are most difficult to account for on the hypothesis of a single common source.

It seems most natural to suppose that if St. Luke used the 'logia,' he used them only to a limited extent, and is indebted for his knowledge of our Lord's sayings mainly to other sources.

THE DYNASTY OF THE HERODS

1. Herod I (The Great). The Herods were not Israelites by race, but Idumeans. Herod I's grandfather, Antipater (Antipas), was the chief ruler of Idumea. His father, also called Antipater (or Antipas), embraced the Jewish religion when Idumea was taken by John Hyrcanus, and Herod I was consequently brought up a Jew. In 47 B.C. his father was made procurator of Judæa by Julius Cæsar, and he immediately assigned subordinate jurisdictions to his four sons. Herod received Galilee, which he governed with great vigour, putting down brigandage with a strong hand. In 40 B.C. the Roman senate, at the instigation of Antony, made Herod king of Judæa, but it was not till 37 B.C. that he succeeded in establishing himself in Jerusalem, the people being still strongly attached to the Asmonean dynasty which had ruled in Palestine for 126 years. At last Herod captured Jerusalem, and signalised his triumph by massacring the whole Sanhedrin except two persons, and putting to death all the adherents of the rival prince Antigonus. Antigonus himself was beheaded by Antony. Herod was a wise, far-seeing, firm, and enlightened ruler, altogether free from Jewish narrowness and prejudice, and inclined to adopt the learning and culture of the Romans and Greeks. On the other hand, he was suspicious, cruel, selfish and implacable. Towards the end of his life, when he was afflicted by a painful disease, his thirst for blood amounted almost to insanity. Among his victims were his tenderly loved wife Mariamne, her brother Aristobulus, her grandfather Hyrcanus, and his own sons Alexander, Aristobulus, and Antipater. The great work of his lifetime was the building of the Temple, which was begun in 20 B.C., and was not completely finished till 65 A.D., just before the outbreak of the war with Rome. On his deathbed (4 B.C.) he ordered the principal Jews to be shut up in the circus at Jericho, and slaughtered as soon as he had breathed his last, in order that there might be some real mourners at his funeral. He had ten wives, and numerous children.

2. Herod Antipas was the son of Herod I by Malthake, a Samaritan. By the will of his father he received the tetrarchy of Galilee and Perea, which yielded a yearly revenue of 200 talents. He married the daughter of Aretas, king of Arabia Petræa, but was guilty of an intrigue with Herodias, his brother Philip's wife, whom he afterwards incestuously married, in spite of the expostulations of John the Baptist, whose execution Herodias managed to procure by an artifice which is recorded only in the Gospels. Antipas was a great friend of Tiberius, in whose honour he built and named the city of Tiberias. In 38 A.D. he was banished to Lugdunum in Gaul, and eventually died in Spain. Herodias voluntarily shared his exile.

3. Herod Archelaus was also the son of Herod I and Malthake, and was junior to Antipas. In spite of this, his father's will assigned to him a superior position, giving him the government of Judæa and the title of king. He was extremely unpopular in Judæa, and when he sailed to Rome to ask to be confirmed in his kingdom, his subjects sent a message after him, requesting that he might be removed from the kingdom, and Judæa placed under direct Roman government. To this circumstance our Lord alludes, Lk 19 12-27. Augustus assigned to Archelaus Judæa, Samaria, and Idumea, with the title of ethnarch, not king. In 6 A.D. he was deposed by Augustus for tyranny, and banished to Vienna in Gaul. His dominions were placed under the government of a Roman procurator, and this arrangement continued till 41 A.D. We are told, Mt 2 22, that Joseph avoided entering the territory of the tyrant Archelaus, and retired to Nazareth to live under the government of the milder Antipas.

4. Herod Philip I, called Herod by Josephus, and Philip in the Gospels (Mt 14 3 Mk 6 17 Lk 3 19), must be carefully distinguished from Philip, tetrarch of Iturea and Trachonitis (Lk 3 1). He was the son of Herod I by the second Mariamne, daughter of Simon the high priest. Owing to his mother's treason, he was left out of his father's will, and lived all his life as a private gentleman, chiefly at Rome. He was the first husband of Herodias, who divorced him to marry her uncle Antipas.

5. Herod Philip II, generally known as Philip the tetrarch, was the son of Herod I and Cleopatra of Jerusalem. He was brought up with Archelaus and Antipas at Rome. His father's will assigned to him certain territories to the N. and E. of the Sea of Galilee (Batanea, Trachonitis, Auranitis), and the title of tetrarch. St. Luke calls him tetrarch of Iturea and Trachonitis (Lk 3 1). He reigned from 4 B.C. to 34 A.D., and was celebrated for his moderation, justice, and good government.

He built Cæsarea Philippi, and Bethsaida Julias, whither our Lord on one occasion retired to avoid Antipas (Lk 9 10). His wife was Salome, daughter of Herod Philip I and Herodias. Since he was childless, his dominions were annexed on his death to the Roman province of Syria.

6. Herodias (see Mt 14 1 Mk 6 14 Lk 3 19) was the daughter of Herod I's son Aristobulus, and his niece Berenice. She first married her uncle Herod Philip I, by whom she had a daughter Salome, who danced before Antipas and pleased him. Afterwards she divorced him and married his brother Antipas, who for her sake put away his wife, and thus provoked a disastrous war with his indignant father-in-law. Herodias procured the death of John the Baptist, and shared her husband's exile. She was sister to Herod Agrippa I.

7. Herod Agrippa I, called Agrippa the Great by Josephus, was the son of Aristobulus and Berenice, and grandson of Herod I. He was brought up at Rome on terms of the closest intimacy with the imperial family, and was particularly friendly with Caligula and Claudius. When Caligula became emperor in 37 A.D. he at once gave Agrippa the tetrarchy of Philip, who had died in 34 A.D., and in 38 A.D. added to this the tetrarchy of the exiled Antipas (Galilee and Peræa). In 41 A.D., in return for great services rendered to Claudius, he received in addition Judæa and Samaria, and the title of king. He now ruled over all the dominions of Herod the Great. He constantly lived in Jerusalem, and kept the Mosaic Law with the utmost strictness, allowing no day to pass without offering sacrifice. His zeal for the Law caused him to persecute the Church (Ac 12). He died in 44 A.D. The account of his end given by Josephus is in substantial agreement with that of St. Luke. His wife was named Cypros, and among his children by her were Herod Agrippa II, Bernice, and Drusilla.

8. Herod Agrippa II, son of Herod Agrippa I and Cypros, was only 17 years old when his father died, and Claudius, thinking him too young to govern the kingdom, made it once more a Roman province. In 48 A.D. Claudius assigned to him the small kingdom of Chalcis, and in 53 A.D. gave him in exchange for this the tetrarchies of Philip and Lysanias, with the title of king. Nero added to his dominions certain cities in Galilee and Peræa. He was entrusted with the general oversight of the Temple, and to him is due the credit of completing it. His capital was Cæsarea Philippi, which he enlarged and renamed Neronias, in honour of Nero. He advised his countrymen not to rebel against Rome, and when war broke out sided with the Romans. After the fall of Jerusalem, 70 A.D., he received a considerable accession of territory. His later years were spent in Rome, where he died, about 100 A.D., the last of the Herodian dynasty. Although 'expert in all customs and questions which are among the Jews,' and well able to form an opinion as to the orthodoxy of St. Paul's opinions (Ac 25, 26), he was of vicious life.

9. Berenice, or Bernice, see on Ac 25 13.

10. Drusilla, see on Ac 24 24.

ABRIDGED GENEALOGY OF THE HERODS TO ILLUSTRATE THE NT.

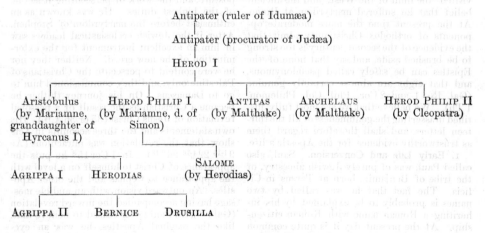

Antipater (ruler of Idumæa)

Antipater (procurator of Judæa)

HEROD I

Aristobulus (by Mariamne, granddaughter of Hyrcanus I)	HEROD PHILIP I (by Mariamne, d. of Simon)	ANTIPAS (by Malthake)	ARCHELAUS (by Malthake)	HEROD PHILIP II (by Cleopatra)

SALOME (by Herodias)

AGRIPPA I   HERODIAS

AGRIPPA II   BERNICE   DRUSILLA

THE LIFE AND WORK OF ST. PAUL

Of all the personalities of the apostolic age St. Paul shines brightest. Modern opponents of Christianity have, indeed, interpreted him very differently. They have never solved the problem that he presents to them. Some of them assert that he did little more than succeed in corrupting Christianity. Others regard him as the real founder of Christianity in spite of the positive evidence which he gives to show he was only its disciple. A few have had the audacity to assert that none of the Epistles which bear his name were the product of his pen. But even those who maintain this incredible theory cannot deny that St. Paul made a profound impression upon the mind of early Christendom. No one indeed would have taken the trouble to forge Epistles in his name if it had not already been venerated and loved as the name of one of the very foremost missionaries of Christ. All indeed admit, whether they are Christians or not, that no person of the apostolic age laboured more successfully than St. Paul.

Our sources for a knowledge of his life are the Acts written by his companion St. Luke, and St. Paul's own letters. Early traditions also preserve a few facts of value. Then there seem to be a few genuine traits in the apocryphal 'Acts of Paul and Thekla,' a romance of the second century, and there is no reason for doubting the statement of St. Clement that he visited 'the limit of the West,' and the ancient belief that he suffered martyrdom at Rome. At the present time the more moderate opponents of orthodox Christianity admit that the evidence of the second century is too strong to be brushed aside, and say that none of the Epistles can be safely called pseudonymous, and that eight are almost certainly genuine (Gal, Ro, 1 and 2 Cor, Phil, Col, Philemon, 1 Th). We believe that we are most fully justified in asserting the genuineness of all the thirteen letters, and shall therefore regard them as trustworthy evidence for the Apostle's life.

1. **Early Life and Conversion.** Saul, also called Paul, was of purely Jewish ancestry, of the tribe of Benjamin, born at Tarsus in Cilicia. The fact that he was called by two names is probably to be explained by his inheriting a Roman name with Roman citizenship. At the present day it is quite common for Jews to have a Jewish and a Gentile name, and as 'Saulos' in Greek bears the ignoble sense of 'waddling,' it was not likely to be used in Gentile circles. Like all Jewish boys,

Paul learnt a trade, in his case that of making tents, for the manufacture of which the hair of the Cilician goat was peculiarly fitted. His father was apparently well-to-do, and Paul was carefully educated. He studied rabbinical theology under Gamaliel at Jerusalem, and his literary method and style show a strong rabbinical and Pharisaic influence. He was, nevertheless, not uninfluenced by the broader and more Greek type of Judaism prevalent at Alexandria. His character was charged with zeal, courage and emotion. His physical powers were not equal to his intellectual. His presence was not imposing, his health was uncertain, and the 'thorn in the flesh' of which he speaks, signifies some humiliating ailment which was most likely of an hysterical or even epileptic character. His early life was guileless, but his education developed within him an overpowering sense of the majesty of God's law, and with a sense of the meaning of the law there came also a sense of the meaning of sin. The commandment which was destined to be 'unto life' he found to be 'unto death.' The knowledge that sin was forbidden, and that sin was possible, led him into a severe inward conflict (Ro 7: see Liddon's and Sanday and Headlam's Commentaries).

The consciousness of inward failure seems to have stimulated his outward zeal for the Law. He regarded Christianity as a vile imposture, and the work of persecuting it as one of the highest duties. He was known as an enthusiast before the martyrdom of Stephen. After it the Jewish ecclesiastical leaders saw in him an excellent instrument for the extermination of the new creed. Neither they nor he were content to persecute the Christians of Palestine only, and they commissioned him to go to Damascus. On his journey thither he became a Christian as the result of a personal revelation of Jesus Christ (35 or 36 A.D.). His own statements and the three accounts in Acts show that the revelation was miraculous (Ac 9 1-16 22 4-16 26 9-18). In 1 Cor 15 8 he puts the appearance of Christ to himself on a level with the appearance to Cephas and the other Apostles. An outward vision with an audible message having accompanied the inward revelation (Gal 1 16), St. Paul never ceased to believe that, like the original Apostles, he was an eye-witness of the risen Christ. With this vision he connected his call to be an Apostle to the Gentiles. And in writing to Corinth he assumes that his enemies could not well admit the outward vision and then deny his apostolic vocation.

2. Beginning of Missionary Career. After three days spent at Damascus the future Apostle of the Gentiles was baptised by Ananias. And now, as a member of the Christian Church, he began to proclaim in the synagogues that 'this Jesus is the Son of God.' But the great mental strain which he had undergone soon made rest imperative. He retired for three years to Arabia, and then returned with new force to Damascus. In consequence of Jewish plots against his life, he went to Jerusalem in order to become acquainted with St. Peter (38 A.D.). He remained there only fifteen days, and, in accordance with his policy not ' to confer with flesh and blood,' saw none of the apostles except Peter and James, ' the Lord's brother.' Ac 9 26-30 shows us that it was Barnabas who introduced him to these apostles. He was conveyed by the disciples to the seaport of Cæsarea Stratonis, and thence took ship for Tarsus (Gal 1 21, 23 Ac 9 30 11 25, 26). He appears to have spent about seven years in Syria and Cilicia, and made converts there : cp. Ac 15 23.

Summoned by St. Barnabas to Antioch, St. Paul took a leading position in this important Church. The next year, 46 A.D., he was sent with Barnabas to take alms from Antioch to the needy Christians of Judæa (Ac 11 30). After this the Holy Spirit singled out the two friends to begin the definite evangelisation of the Roman empire, 47 A.D. In company with John Mark, they set out for Cyprus, where they won a triumph in the conversion of Sergius Paulus, the Roman proconsul. They then set sail for Perga on the mainland, and, though deserted by John Mark, began boldly to preach in South Galatia. St. Paul persevered in preaching first to the Jews. They replied by hunting him from city to city. The missionaries everywhere found that the Gentile proselytes heard them gladly, the heathen Gentiles also showed that they were willing to receive the gospel. The romantic and perilous adventures of the missionaries were not in vain. Churches were founded at Pisidian Antioch, Iconium, Lystra, Derbe, and probably in other places. It was already clear that God 'had opened to the Gentiles a door of faith,' and that St. Paul had a special vocation to convert men who were not of his own race.

3. The Council at Jerusalem, 49 A.D. The influence of St. Paul was now to receive a fresh acknowledgment. A revelation (Gal 2 2) directed him to go from Antioch to Jerusalem, where he laid before the Apostles the gospel that he preached among the Gentiles. It was a time of acute crisis. Certain Judaising converts of the original apostles maintained that the promises of the gospel only belonged to those who observed the Mosaic Law. St. Paul had asserted the justification of all Gentiles who believed on Jesus Christ, without the Law. He saw that if the Gentiles had to be circumcised, it meant that the Gentile had to become a Jew in order to become a Christian, and the gospel was then not primary but secondary. The 'pillar' apostles supported St. Paul. They gave him the ' right hands of fellowship,' and he returned to Antioch with complete liberty to act as the appointed head of the mission to ' the uncircumcision.' All risk of Christianity becoming a mere sect of Judaism was now removed.

4. Second Missionary Journey, 49–52 A.D. Ac 15 36–18 22 gives us an account of this journey, which was marked by the Apostle's greatest missionary successes, by the earliest of his letters now extant (1 and 2 Th), and by the extension of the gospel to Europe. It began with a rupture between St. Paul and St. Barnabas, occasioned by St. Paul's refusal to be accompanied by Mark, with whom, however, he was afterwards reconciled. In company with Silas, a Jewish Christian of Roman citizenship, he visited the Churches which he had founded on his first journey. At each place the decisions of the Council of Jerusalem were communicated to the faithful (Ac 16 4, 5). At Lystra St. Paul took as an assistant Timotheus, whom he circumcised, as he was the son of a Jewess. The Holy Spirit forbade the missionaries to preach in the province of Asia, and a vision summoned St. Paul to Europe. At the seaport of Troas he was joined by St. Luke, who has told us the story (St. Luke uses the pronoun ' we ' in 97 vv. of Acts. They are 16 10-17 20 5-15 21 1-18 27 1–28 16). They crossed to Macedonia and began to preach at Philippi. Hitherto, with the exception of Antioch, St. Paul had not preached in any really large town since his mission began. Henceforward he was to preach mainly in great centres of population. He was cruelly opposed at Philippi, the first town where we find that the relations between the missionaries and the civil authorities became a difficulty. As afterwards at Ephesus, the opposition was not religious or political, but came from the mercenary hatred of men whose interests were bound up with superstition. At Thessalonica and Berœa St. Paul won staunch converts, in spite of a deadly persecution directed against him by the Jews of Thessalonica.

From Berœa he went to Athens, the educational centre of Greece, where he delivered an earnest address on the hill of the Areopagus. One member of the court of the Areopagus was converted, but the intellectual men of Athens were not sufficiently conscious of their inward moral failure to receive the gospel seriously. The huge city of Corinth, the commercial capital of Greece, offered a very different field. It was notorious for the sensuality of the rich and the misery of the poor. While there St. Paul lived as a poor man with the poor, and made it his determination to preach nothing but 'Jesus Christ, and Him crucified.' Protected by Roman law, he won many converts, including some persons of distinction. While at Corinth he wrote twice to the Thessalonians. The second journey closed with a visit to Jerusalem. It was probably soon after this visit that an incident happened which showed the vitality of the Judaising party in the Church. They no longer denied that the uncircumcised believers were Christians, but they tried to gain a distinct and higher status for the circumcised. When St. Paul went from Jerusalem to Antioch in 52 A.D., St. Peter, fearing to offend these Judaisers, was guilty of pretending to believe that he agreed with them. He refused to eat with uncircumcised Christians. St. Paul then openly rebuked him for this 'dissembling' (Gal 2[11]), i.e. for acting in a manner contrary to his true convictions. (Some authorities place this incident earlier, shortly before the Council of Jerusalem, 49 A.D.: see on Ac 15. It is still debated among scholars whether St. Paul ever visited North Galatia, or whether 'the Phrygian and Galatian country' (Ac 16[6]) means one district known by two different names, extending from Iconium to Pisidian Antioch, Phrygian racially and Galatian politically. For list of authorities on either side see HDB. vol. iii. pp. 706, 707.)

5. Third Missionary Journey, 52–56 A.D. The Judaisers took their revenge by visiting the Churches founded by St. Paul, where they presented themselves with 'letters of commendation,' pretending that they represented the original Apostles, and came to supply the defects of St. Paul's teaching. In the meantime St. Paul visited Galatia and Phrygia, made a long stay at Ephesus, and went to Macedonia and Greece. During these few years St. Paul reached the pinnacle of his power. Forced, against his will, to engage in controversy, he wrote the four Epistles, 1 and 2 Corinthians, Galatians, and Romans, which rank among the greatest masterpieces of all literature. The whole period was one of difficult but victorious conflict. In Acts 19 we are told the dramatic story of the riot at Ephesus, where the craftsmen who made images of Artemis stirred up the mob to expel him. On leaving Ephesus he brought the gospel to Troas, and went on to Macedonia, Illyria, and Greece, making Corinth his real goal. He had previously visited it 'in sorrow' from Ephesus (2 Cor 2[1] 13[1,2]), but was compelled to return there on account of renewed controversies. These controversies occasioned the Apostle the greatest anxiety, and

though 2 Corinthians shows that his anxiety was partly allayed before he left Macedonia, he continued his journey, and arrived at Corinth at the end of 55 A.D. He stayed there three months (Ac 20[3]), during which he wrote the Epistle to the Romans. Wishing to return to Syria, he was prevented by a plot of the Jews from taking ship at Corinth for Syria. He therefore went round by Philippi, where he spent the Easter of 56 A.D., and Troas. St. Luke describes the journey in Acts 20 and 21. St. Paul met with a friendly reception from St. James and 'all the elders' at Jerusalem, a fact which shows that there was no split among the leaders of the Church, however much the partisans of those leaders might differ. Recognised in the Temple by certain Asiatic Jews, the Apostle was attacked by a hostile mob, and after defending himself in an address to the people and another address to the Sanhedrin, he was sent to the Roman procurator Felix at Cæsarea.

6. Period of Imprisonment, 56–61 A.D. The course of proceedings taken against St. Paul is made perfectly intelligible by St. Luke. St. Paul was a Roman citizen, and the Roman procurators were too just to deliver him to the Jews, though Felix was not above hoping for a bribe. St. Paul finally determined to cut the matter short by appealing to the emperor, an appeal which the procurator Festus could not disregard. The voyage to Rome is described by St. Luke with picturesque accuracy, and shows St. Paul manifesting that easy ascendency over his fellows which he always gained in unprejudiced surroundings. At Rome the Jewish leaders did not oppose him, but the majority of the Jews deserted him. He remained at Rome until 61 A.D., living in his own hired house under the supervision of a soldier. During this period he wrote Colossians, Philemon, Ephesians and Philippians. They do not show the same exuberance of argument as the four preceding Epistles. But their tenderness and devotion, their combination of authority and humility, their insight into the true significance of Christ and of the Church, prove that St. Paul was still advancing 'from strength to strength.'

7. Conclusion. St. Paul was released from his first imprisonment at Rome, as he seems to have hoped would be the case when he wrote Philippians (1[26] 2[24]). He had long wished to visit Spain (Ro 15[28]), and though his Epistles do not record such a visit, St. Clement of Rome, writing about 95 A.D., speaks of him as going 'to the limit of the West,' which in a Roman writer probably means Spain. From the Epistles to Timothy and Titus we learn that he returned to the East. His last Epistle is 2 Timothy, written with winter in prospect and when the first stage of his last trial was over. He had been lately at Troas and in Crete, and probably at Miletus and Corinth. 1 Timothy was apparently written from Macedonia on the way to Corinth, and the letter to Titus was written from Corinth when he was expecting to spend the next winter at Nicopolis opposite to Italy (Tit 3 12). He must have been arrested soon after the letter to Titus was despatched. According to the traditions of the primitive Church he was beheaded about three miles from Rome on the Ostian Way, close to the place now occupied by the great basilica of St. Paul. The basilica contains his tomb, marked by an inscription of the fourth century. The year of his death was probably 64 A.D., though it was formerly dated 67 A.D. The year of his conversion was probably 36 A.D. No Christian in all history accomplished as much work in a period of twenty-eight years.

SURVEY OF THE EPISTLES OF ST. PAUL

1. **Form of St. Paul's Writings.** We have from the hand of the Apostle Paul thirteen Epistles—addressed four of them to individual helpers, and the rest to Christian societies of his foundation or lying within the circuit of his mission (Romans, Colossians). They are primarily not treatises upon religious doctrine, nor homilies enforcing specific duties, but letters of a friend to his friends, of the absent missionary and pastor to his flock. They are selections from a larger correspondence, and in several instances (notably 1 and 2 Cor) imply letters and messages from the other side. The acquaintance and mutual affection of the parties, their common interests in Christ, supply the basis of the communications. They are essentially personal documents, originating in the relationship between writer and readers ; from this standpoint the questions, of theology or morals or church administration, that arise in them should be approached, as being the questions of the hour to the correspondents. In the Epistles we watch the vital Christian problems emerging in the experience of the earliest Churches and taking shape and colour from their constitution and surroundings. These writings give to the subjects of which they treat the actuality and living interest that attach to the career of the Apostle of the nations engaged in his missionary labours and in the shepherding of his strangely mingled flock.

With this personal origin is connected the incidental nature of St. Paul's writings. The Apostle took up the pen to supply the lack of his presence (1 Th 2 17), when his field of labour became too wide to admit of frequent visits to the Churches. He wrote for the most part upon the spur of the moment (Romans was an exception)—on occasion of recent news, in response to some message or enquiry, in self-explanation and in expression of the thankfulness or solicitude concerning his readers that occupies his mind : see, e.g., 1 Th 3 8 1 Cor 1 11 7 1 2 Cor 1 8 7 6 13 10 Phil 2 12 4 10 Col 1 4, 8 2 1 Philemon v. 10, etc. Yet through these disconnected and seemingly casual letters, thrown off in the intervals of travel, in prison, or from the Apostle's winter-quarters, there runs one master purpose, one all-embracing conception of human life and of the things of God.

2. **Style of the Epistles.** The saying that ' the style is, the man ' holds especially of epistolary writings. The letters of a gifted man are often more attractive than his laboured work, because they are written in freedom of heart and are the frank and unstudied expression of himself. In this quality of St. Paul's Epistles is found at once their charm and their difficulty. His 'epistolary style is the most personal that ever was—a rapid conversation reported verbatim and without correction' (Renan). There is nothing in literature that reflects more vividly the personality of the writer than some of these Epistles.

Now St. Paul's is not an easy style, for he was not a man framed to take things easily. Life was for him a continual struggle, both without and within. Beneath his restless missionary activity and the calm of his prison-days, there went on in him an unceasing effort to 'apprehend that for which he was apprehended by Christ.' He is ' travailing in birth ' not only over his wayward offspring in the faith, but over the grand 'mystery of God,' of which he is the appointed dispenser, striving to explore the unsearchable riches and sound the unfathomed depths of the love revealed in Christ. The strain of the author's mind is manifest in the involved sentences of which some of his greatest passages consist —such as Ro 5 12-21 Gal 2 3-10, or Eph 1 3-14. With broken, impetuous utterance he sweeps us breathless through his long-drawn periods, until he reaches his lofty climax and the tangled path lies clear beneath our feet. St. Paul was a pioneer in religious thought, opening a way for the truth of the gospel to the conscience and intellect of the Gentile world. The difficult task has left its mark on his writings, like the lame thigh that witnessed to wrestling Jacob's victory. This subtle and eager thinker was at the same time a man of ardent feeling. In many places the entanglement of St. Paul's style is due to contending currents of feeling, to the quick play of emotion in his singularly mobile nature: see, e.g., 1 Cor 4 14-21 2 Cor 5 11-15 7 5-9 Gal 4 12-20. Logic and sentiment, passion and severe thought, are fused in his utterance to form a combination of singular pliancy, tenderness, and strength. In his grammatical constructions and the connexion of phrase with phrase there is frequent uncertainty arising from the throng and press of his thoughts; the thoughts themselves are clear and luminous. His leading terms are as crystalline in definition, as they are massive and profound in significance. The great watchwords of St. Paul's doctrine were framed to last for ever.

A native of Tarsus, St. Paul knew Greek from childhood; the niceties of its idiom come to him instinctively. The groundwork of his dialect was not, however, the literary Greek of the times, but the vernacular of every-day speech. Behind the Greek dress there lived in him a Hebrew spirit. Saul's youth had been spent 'at the feet of Gamaliel' (Ac 22 3), and his mind formed by the rabbinical discipline (Gal 1 14). He draws freely on the language and ideas of the Old Testament, following, though not slavishly, the Septuagint Greek Version which was in the hands of his readers. His imagery is mainly borrowed not like that of Jesus from nature and the open fields, but from the scenes of city life and the throngs of men. The Apostle's mind was fertile and plastic in expression; each group of Epistles contains its distinctive locutions. He has his mannerisms and idiosyncrasies, but is tied to no hackneyed formulæ; his speech reflected the colour of its surroundings, and suited itself to the constituency addressed. Compare from this point of view the stateliness and measured argument of Romans with the incisiveness, poignancy, and pathos of Galatians and 1 and 2 Corinthians, the affectionate frankness and spontaneity of 1 Thessalonians and Philippians, and the playful familiarity of the little letter to Philemon.

3. The Matter of the Epistles. St. Paul's letters were cast in the epistolary mould of the time. The salutation 'Grace and peace' is adapted from the ordinary courtesies of greeting. The salutation, variously expanded and qualified, serves sometimes to strike the keynote of the Epistle, as in Romans and Galatians. A thanksgiving is next offered to God for the Christian worth of the correspondents (Galatians is the signal exception), commonly supplemented by an appropriate prayer; in Ephesians the opening acts of praise and prayer swell into a principal part of the letter. After the introductory devotions, the writer's purpose comes into view; where his object is theological, we may look for some fundamental statement of principle at this point: see Ro 1 16,17 Col 1 15, etc. The specific truth thus asserted is expounded and vindicated as need may require; and its exposition is followed up by moral and practical exhortation. Details of personal news, messages, and greetings, with a final benediction, close the letter. Such is the order of the doctrinal Epistles—Romans, Galatians, Ephesians, Colossians, and 2 Thessalonians. Where, however, the writer's main business is personal and practical, no such plan suggests itself: the explanations, discussions, or expostulations called for by the occasion naturally occupy the foreground, while directions of a more general bearing come in afterwards; and theological passages occur here and there, wherever the handling of the matter strikes upon the underlying principles of the Gospel. Such is the case with Philippians, and the two Epistles to the Corinthians.

The contents of the Epistles may be arranged, therefore, under the following heads: personal, theological, ethical, administrative, and devotional. These constituent elements are combined with perfect freedom; no strict line can be drawn between them. The proportion in which they are blended, and the preponderance of the one strain or the other, give to each letter its complexion. Romans is above all the theological Epistle; 2 Corinthians, Philippians, and Philemon are intensely personal; in 1 Corinthians and the Pastorals the practical and administrative interests predominate, with a large infusion of the ethical and doctrinal; in 1 Thessalonians the personal and ethical; in 2 Thessalonians, Colossians, and Ephesians doctrine and ethics are equally balanced, with a conspicuous development of the devotional vein in the last named; Galatians is the best example of the union of the personal, theological, and moral in St. Paul's writings, the theological dominating the other two.

The chapter- and verse-divisions—a modern invention of convenience—must be ignored by the reader who wishes to understand St. Paul's Epistles; the paragraphic arrangement of the Revised Version is preferable. Furnishing himself with a preliminary outline, and noting difficult expressions for later examination, he should read each document right through and allow it to make its complete impression, as he would treat a letter from a friend, returning to the salient passages and critical points of the Epistle, in order to fasten upon his mind its essential import.

4. Order and Connexion of the Epistles. The accepted order of St. Paul's letters has prevailed from early times. Originally they formed a distinct volume (to which Hebrews was attached), under the title of 'The Apostle,' with the several letters headed, 'To the Romans,' 'To the Corinthians 1,' and so on. First came the nine letters addressed to (seven) Churches, then the four to (three) friends—the two sections being arranged in the order of size and importance, not of time.

(*a*) The first four in the traditional succession form a coherent group, in which First and Second Corinthians and Romans followed consecutively at intervals of a few months. The date of Galatians is disputed; but it clearly belongs in character and subject-matter to this group, and is akin to Romans (56–57 A.D.).

(*b*) The next three, along with the little note to Philemon, fall into a later group; amongst these Colossians and Ephesians are synchronous and 'twin' Epistles, Philemon coming in as a private enclosure accompanying the former. Philippians stands somewhat apart, in character as in destination, from its neighbours; opinions differ as to whether it preceded or followed them. These four were prison-letters—issued (Philippians certainly, the rest almost certainly) from Rome during the years 60–61 of St. Paul's first captivity there.

(*c*) 1 and 2 Thessalonians, separated only by a few months, are the oldest of St. Paul's extant writings, having been written shortly after the Apostle's mission in Thessalonica (Ac 17), while he was labouring at Corinth in the latter period of his Second Missionary Journey, probably during 50–51 A.D. (Ac 18).

(*d*) The three Pastoral Epistles presuppose St. Paul's acquittal in Rome from the charges against which he had 'appealed to Cæsar' at Festus' tribunal (Ac 25), the extension of his missionary course to a period which lay outside the narrative of the Acts, his re-arrest and approaching martyrdom in Rome (2 Tim). They are dated in the year 64, on the presumption that the Apostle fell in the great Neronian persecution, or about 67 by those who think it likely that he escaped this storm, and who recognise the lengthened course of ministry necessary to account for the new complexion of the Pastoral Epistles, if brought within his life-time. Their succession was: 1 Timothy, Titus, 2 Timothy.

(*c*), (*a*), (*b*), (*d*) is therefore the historical order of the four groups. Their composition extended over some sixteen years: (*c*) 50–51, (*a*) 55–57, (*b*) 61–62, and (*d*) about 67 (? 64) A.D.

5. Course of Thought in the Epistles. The general course of St. Paul's thought in the later part of his life is revealed by the tenor and outstanding features of the several groups of his letters. When the earliest of them was written, the Apostle was midway in his career, and had been a Christian believer and preacher for at least fourteen years; his mind was ripe, his doctrine in all essentials complete. The progress marked in the Epistles, while indicating certain changes of inward experience and the growth inevitable in an active mind, was principally due to the advance of the Apostle's mission, the development of his Churches and the trials through which they passed. As time goes on, his preoccupations become increasingly those of the pastor and teacher, rather than the missionary and evangelist; compare 1 Thessalonians at the beginning with 1 Timothy at the end of the series of Epistles. His work as Gentile Apostle and Church-founder was exposed to three chief assaults—the first of these proceeding from Jewish Christians of Pharisaic temper, who desired to subject all believers in Christ to the Law of Moses; the second from the reaction of heathen idolatry and immorality upon Gentile converts. The second group of the Epistles marks the crisis of the former struggle, which was decisive for St. Paul's authority, and gave shape to his characteristic doctrines of Justification by faith and Redemption through the cross; in Galatians we witness the climax, in Romans the practical conclusion of this controversy. 1 and 2 Corinthians, during the same period, illustrate most vividly the dangers of relapse to paganism; 1 Thessalonians earlier, and Ephesians later, witness to the same effect. A more subtle type of error betrayed itself at Colossæ, and reappears in the evils denounced by the Pastorals of the last group—viz. the perversion of Christian truth by Greek 'philosophy' (Col 2⁴,⁷ 1 Tim 6²⁰), from which sprang the imposing Gnostic systems of the second century. This movement had its source in the conception of the evil of matter and the consequent separation of God from the finite world—an idea which precluded any real incarnation or atonement, and perverted the whole ethics of Christianity; its working is seen already in the denial at Corinth of bodily resurrection (1 Cor 15). The Gnostic tendency took sometimes an ascetic (Col 2²⁰⁻²³ 1 Tim 4³⁻⁵), sometimes an antinomian turn (2 Tim 3¹⁻⁹ Tit 1¹⁴⁻¹⁶) in morals. Some Jewish ingredients entered into this amalgam, which originated probably in the attempt to assimilate the gospel to Essenic or Alexandrian theosophy. As the Apostle's doctrine of Salvation were wrought out in the heat of the legalist controversy (Galatians, Romans), so the incipient Gnosticism served, by contradiction, to bring into relief his conception of the person of Christ and the nature of the Church, and to develop his ethical principles (Colossians, Ephesians, Philippians).

The dangerous illness from which the Apostle suffered in the year 56, between the date of 1 and 2 Corinthians, formed a crisis in his life, and materially affected his views of the future. Previously he had written as one expecting the Lord's coming within the present generation (1 Th 4 15-17 1 Cor 7 29-31 15 52), though guarding himself against positive assertion on the subject or fixing of the date (1 Th 5 2 2 Th 2 1, etc.); from this time he anticipates his own death; the *parousia* recedes into the background, and a wider prospect opens out for the Church and for the progress of humanity (see 2 Cor 1 9 5 1-8 Phil 1 21-23 2 Tim 4 6 Eph 2 7 1 Tim 1 16 2 6 2 Tim 2 2). The influence of Rome probably counted for a good deal in the direction of St. Paul's thought and work. The memory of the impious emperor Caius Caligula (37–41 A.D.) and the popular Cæsar-worship of Asia Minor supply a clue to the mystery of the Antichrist in 2 Th 2. On the other hand, St. Paul's conception of the universal Church under the headship of Christ owed something of its breadth and grandeur to the spectacle of the world-empire unfolding before his eyes. His mission was laid out on an imperial scale ; he planted his Churches at the strategic points of Roman commerce and administration. By the time St. Paul (in the words of 2 Tim 4 7) had 'fought his fight' and 'finished his course,' he had carried the gospel through every land from Syria to Spain, and through every class of Gentile society from the slave to the emperor. This outward progress was matched by the development of his doctrine. His spirit has penetrated to the depths of the mystery of Christ ; his inspired logic and force of character have won for the gospel a decisive victory over the Jewish and the pagan reaction, and over the antagonism of philosophic thought. He sees himself the recognised 'herald' of Christ to the nations, the 'teacher of the Gentiles in faith and truth' (1 Tim 2 7); his teaching is embodied in a line of organised Churches extending through the empire. The permanence of the gospel and its propagation amongst mankind are guaranteed ; 'a pillar and ground' are set up, on which 'the truth' will stand for ever (1 Tim 3 15).

6. Characterisation of the Epistles. There is a *crescendo* and *diminuendo* of vigour and fulness of thought in the sequence of the four groups : I. the forenoon ; II. the noontide ; III. the afternoon ; IV. the evening Epistles.

I. (*a*) 1 THESSALONIANS : *a missionary's letter to young converts*, whom he had left in the infancy of their faith ; full of tender recollection and solicitude ; consoling, edifying, non-controversial ; comparatively simple in style. Its chief warning is against heathen impurity (4 1-8). The one error corrected is due to a too eager expectation and narrow view of Christ's Second Advent (4 13-5 11). The full 'gospel' set forth in Romans is implied in 1 Th 4 14 5 9, 10.

(*b*) 2 THESSALONIANS deals with the continued unsettlement of the Church in regard to the Second Advent (1 5-2 12), and the consequent neglect of secular labour (3 6-15).

II. (*a*) 1 CORINTHIANS *is the Epistle of the doctrine of the Cross in application*, and holds in the practical sphere a place similar to that of Romans in the theological. Its first part (chs. 1–6) arises out of disquieting news received from Corinth (see 1 11, 12 5 1) ; its second part from questions put to the Apostle in a letter from the Church (chs. 7–16). In the piercing light that shines from Calvary the manifold problems confronting the Apostle of the Gentiles are surveyed ; Greek wisdom and Corinthian vice, church parties and rival ministries, and disorders in worship, spiritual gifts and their use and abuse, great social questions such as marriage and slavery, lighter matters of diet and dress, the restoration of the body and the final state of the dead, are all discussed in their bearing on the relationship of men to Christ and upon principles deduced from 'the word of the cross' (1 17 2 2). This 'word' embraces the truths of the resurrection of Jesus along with His death (15 3, 4) of the new life in the Spirit and the union of the believer with the dying and exalted Saviour (1 30 2 12 3 16 6 19, etc.).

(*b*) 2 CORINTHIANS : *St. Paul's apologia pro vita sua.* Since 1 Corinthians much has happened—'fightings within, fears without' : the Apostle's all but fatal sickness (1 9 4 7-5 8), a revolt quelled with difficulty and followed by a revulsion of loyal feeling toward him (2 5-11 7 2-16), changes in his plans bringing the reproach of vacillation (1 15-18), the coming to Corinth of Judæan emissaries who disparage him and set up as his rivals (3 1 10 12 11 4, 12-15). Chs. 1–7, addressed to the reconciled majority (see 2 6), are St. Paul's *defence of his ministry* before the Church ; chs. 10–13, *the vindication of himself* against his adversaries. The interjected chs. 8, 9 urge a more liberal contribution for Jerusalem : cp. 1 Cor 16. This letter best reveals St. Paul as a minister of Christ and a man amongst men—the wealth of his heart, the ascendency and fire of his genius, and the charm of his disposition.

(*c*) GALATIANS is St. Paul's *vindication of the gospel against legalism.* 'Another gospel' (1 6) is being preached with seductive effect (3 1) in Galatia : the Judaisers at Corinth assailed St. Paul's authority ; here they impugn his doctrine, by insisting on circumcision as essential to the full Christian status (3^{1-4} $5^{3,4}$), thus seeking to bring Gentile believers under the Mosaic yoke and incorporate them in Judaism. The legalists appealed to the authority of St. Peter and the Jerusalem Church, from which (they asserted) St. Paul had received his knowledge of Christ. The Apostle exposes their statements by telling, in chs. 1 and 2, how he received his commission from Jesus Christ, and had won from the mother-church the recognition of Gentile liberties. 3^1–5^{12} is the core of the Epistle, demonstrating the salvation of men by faith in Christ crucified only, and the subordinate and preparatory office of Mosaism. 5^{13}–6^{10} is an ethical homily addressed to the faults of the readers, and 6^{11-16} a trenchant summary of the letter. In historical interest and controversial power Galatians ranks first amongst the Epistles.

(d) ROMANS is the most abstract and objective of the Epistles : *the grand exposition of God's plan of salvation for mankind*. St. Paul will soon visit Rome, where he claims authority as Apostle to the Gentiles. In this Church, which has existed for some years, he has already a number of friends ($1^{5,10-15}$ 15^{15-29} 16^{1-16}). At this crisis of his work, it is well to deliver a full manifesto in face of the 'other gospel' with which he has been in conflict; he will thus best introduce himself at Rome, and counteract by anticipation the legalist propaganda. Chs. 1–8 unfold in positive, systematic, and deliberate fashion 'the word of the cross,' which Galatians argued negatively and polemically, and which 1 and 2 Corinthians have assumed and built upon. Chs. 9–11 discuss the difficulty raised by the repudiation of the gospel on the part of the Jewish people, who had a prior claim to it (1^{16})—a distressing problem to the Apostle personally, and a very serious objection to his argument. Chs. 12^{1-15} 13 is a digest of Christian ethics, social and civil, based on the consecration of the body and the 'renewal of the mind' under Christ's all-embracing law of love. The rest of the letter is of personal and local interest.

The above are 'the four evangelical Epistles,' containing the heart and sum of the Apostle's teaching.

III. (a) COLOSSIANS, like Galatians, is controversial. This is *the Epistle of the exaltation of Christ*, whose headship of the Church is affirmed to rest upon His anterior headship over the created universe (1^{15-20}). The right understanding of Christ's lordship in the realms of nature and grace, and of the boundless scope of His atonement (1^{18-20} $2^{9,10}$), leaves no room for the angel-mediations and ritual appliances by which the Colossian error-

ists would have supplemented the Redeemer's work : see p. xciii above, and Intro. to Colossians. In the ethical half of the letter (3^{1-4^6}), each duty is enforced by the lordship of Christ: family relationships are dwelt upon with an emphasis new in the Epistles (3^{18}–4^1) : cp. p. xciii.

(b) PHILEMON should be attached to Colossians. This exquisite little note—a specimen probably of many such—reveals St. Paul's character in private life. It appeals for the reception by his master of Onesimus, a runaway slave now converted to Christ, 'as a brother beloved.'

(c) EPHESIANS is *the Epistle of the glory of the Church*, regarded as Christ's body and His bride. Ephesians and Colossians are kindred in thought and language ; the former reads as the complement and continuation of the latter. Yet there is a marked difference of manner—Colossians being polemical, incisive, sometimes very abrupt and obscure ; Ephesians the most calm, expansive, and diffuse of St. Paul's writings. He has dismissed the Colossian error from his mind, and gives himself up to the train of meditation on the glory of Christ and the Church which the controversy has occasioned. In richness of ethical and hortatory matter (4^1–6^{20}), transfused with theological thought, Ephesians resembles Romans, to which Colossians and Ephesians stand next in point of doctrinal importance.

(d) PHILIPPIANS is, above all, *the Epistle of heart-fellowship*. Its simplicity and discursive freedom remind us of 1 Thessalonians. As 2 Corinthians discloses the loftiness of the writer's character and the supernatural powers of the ministry, Philippians reveals the depths of his inner faith and communion with Christ It supplies essential matter for the Apostle's biography. 2^{5-11} is a passage of surpassing theological interest. This is the most serene and beautiful of St. Paul's writings.

IV. The three PASTORALS are *letters on Church discipline*. In 1 TIMOTHY and TITUS the Apostle's delegates, at Ephesus and in Crete, are instructed about the appointment of elders (or bishops) and deacons, the stress being laid on qualifications of character. They are exhorted as to their own conduct in the ministry, especially in face of the heretical and vicious teaching now coming into vogue. The like admonitions, mingled with personal reminiscences and forebodings of the writer's death, occupy 2 TIMOTHY—St. Paul's 'swan song.' These are conservative and valedictory Epistles ; 'guard the good deposit,' 'speak the things that become the sound doctrine,' are their watchwords.

7. Summary of Doctrine. *The Godhead.* 'To us there is one God, the Father, of whom are all things and we for Him' (1 Cor 8^6). This 'one God' is known as 'The Father of our Lord Jesus Christ'—ours through Him; there is 'one mediator between God and men, the man Christ Jesus, who gave Himself a ransom for all' (1 Tim 2 5, 6). Christ appears by the Father's side as the 'one Lord Jesus Christ, through whom are all things and we through Him' (1 Cor 8 6). In Him, 'the Son of God's love,' 'dwells all the fulness of the Godhead' (Col 1 13 2 9); in Him, since He 'came in the likeness of men,' a complete and sinless humanity is realised (Gal 4 6 Phil 2 7, 8, etc.). The interests and destinies of mankind are lodged with Him, for salvation and for judgment (Ro 5 21 2 Cor 5 10, etc.). In the end 'every knee shall bow' to Him; Christ will then 'deliver up the kingdom to God even the Father,' and 'the Son Himself will be subject to Him that subjected all things unto Him, that God may be all in all' (Phil 2 10, 11 1 Cor 15 24-28). The divine Lordship of Christ does not impair, but vindicates, the unity of the Godhead. This is equally true of the Deity of the Holy Spirit, whom the Apostle associates with the Father and the Son in the benediction of 2 Cor 13 14 and elsewhere. 'The Spirit' is God dwelling and working in the soul and in the Church (1 Cor 2 12 3 16 6 19 Ro 8 26 Gal 4 6 Eph 2 21, etc.). He comes to men as the 'Spirit of God's Son,' and is the witness of their 'adoption' in Christ, the 'earnest of their inheritance,' the agent of their sanctification, the imparter of all gifts and powers of grace (Ro 8 14-17 Gal 5 16-25 2 Cor 1 21-22 Eph 1 13, 14 1 Th 4 7, 8 1 Cor 12 4-11, etc.). As the Holy Spirit wrought in the resurrection of Jesus, He will be the means of 'quickening the mortal bodies' of those in whom He dwells (Ro 8 6-11). Grace—'the grace of God,' 'of our Lord Jesus Christ'—is the conspicuous attribute of the Godhead in Christianity.

Sin and Redemption. Except 'the one man Jesus Christ,' who is God's 'own Son,' 'all have sinned and are destitute of the glory of God' (Ro 3 23 8 3). The sin of mankind, calling forth 'God's wrath,' has brought both Gentiles and Jews to their present shameful and guilty state (Ro 1 18–3 20); it is 'laying up in store' for the impenitent a dreadful retribution (Ro 2 5 1 Th 1 10, etc.). From Adam downwards our race has been in bondage under 'the law of sin and death' (Ro 5 12-14 7 23, 24 8 2). The law of Moses, which expressed in a more definite and imperative form the universal law of God engraved on the human conscience (Ro 2 14-16 3 9, 19 5 13), has served to provoke and aggravate, rather than to prevent, transgression (Ro 3 15 7 7-24 Gal 3 19, etc.). In the fulness of time, when the law had done its work, 'Christ redeemed us from its curse'; 'He was made sin for us, who knew no sin, that we might become God's righteousness in

Him' (Gal 3 13 2 Cor 5 21). Our Lord in 'the death of the cross' submitted on His brethren's behalf to the judicial consequence of human sin, meeting in its course that holy 'wrath' which deals out death to transgressors. So dying 'one for all,' He offered 'a propitiatory sacrifice in His blood' and effected 'reconciliation (atonement)' for mankind—a fact certified by His resurrection (Ro 3 22-26 4 25 5 8-11 2 Cor 5 18, 19). Faith in Him who thus 'died and rose again' for us, makes the individual man participator in the common salvation and brings 'peace with God' (Ro 3 22, 25 5 1, 2 Eph 2 13-18, etc.); faith is the trustful and submissive hand of the sinner meeting God's outstretched hand of grace in Christ. The act of God in saving 'him who is of faith in Jesus,' St. Paul speaks of as 'justification.' By this he means not merely the (negative) forgiving of past sins, but the (positive) giving to the sinner of the status of a righteous man (Ro 5 15-17), who is for Christ's sake counted for and treated as righteous, his past sin being regarded as though it had not been (Ro 4 3-8 5 2 2 Cor 5 21 Col 2 14), and is set thereby in the way of becoming righteous in life and conduct (Ro 6 4, 18 8 4). Hence justification implies 'adoption,' the receiving of the alien into the divine household, his endowment with 'the Spirit of God's Son,' and his investiture with the inheritance of God's children (Ro 8 16, 17, 31-34 Gal 4 4-7 Eph 1 5). In view of Christ's 'propitiation,' this restitution of the sinner is not merely an act of love on God's part : He is 'just' though He 'justifies the ungodly' (Ro 3 26 4 5), and His action is *legal* in the highest sense (Ro 3 27-31). The 'redemption that is in Christ Jesus' includes with the soul the body, won also for God by the price of His blood (1 Cor 6 20); of its recovery from the grave, completing man's salvation, the resurrection of Jesus gives pledge (Ro 3 24 8 16-23 Eph 1 7, 14 1 Cor 15 20, 23, 45-57 ·1 Th 4 14 2 Tim 1 10, etc.).

The New Life in Christ. 'Justification' through faith in the death of Christ leads to 'sanctification' by union with the living Christ (Ro 6 1-11). All believers in Christ are 'saints' (1 Cor 1 2 6 11, etc.), however defective their saintship; they were consecrated to God in the act of saving faith (Ro 6 18, 22), and regard themselves as no longer 'their own' (1 Cor 6 19, 20). They practically 'live to God,' in so far as faith identifies them with Christ; they 'have coalesced with Him by the likeness' first 'of His death' and then 'of His resurrection' (Ro 6 4-11 Col 3 1-4, etc.). All human relations and earthly events are transformed for the man who is 'in Christ Jesus' (2 Cor 5 15, 16); he 'knows no one' merely 'after the flesh,' for he is a man of the Spirit, 'renewed in the spirit of his mind' (Eph 4 23, 24), and carries spiritual estimates and aims into everything (Ro 8 9 Gal 5 25, etc.). 'The law of Christ,' summed up in the two commands of love to God and man, rules his whole conduct (Ro 5 5 12 9, etc.). Impurity is shunned as a defilement of 'the temple of God' and an outrage upon the Holy Spirit (1 Cor 6 19 1 Th 4 8); lying is impossible amongst those who are 'members one of another' (Eph 4 25); unkindness contradicts the example of Christ's self-sacrifice (Eph 4 31–5 2): these are examples of the ethical logic of 'the word of the cross.' The obligations of the family and the state are not destroyed for the Christian, but assume a deeper meaning and a new sanctity. Even his eating and drinking are done to the glory of God (1 Cor 10 31 Col 3 17, etc.). 'All things' become his servants and 'work together for his good' (1 Cor 2 21-23 Ro 8 28, etc.). For himself, his supreme desire is to be 'sanctified completely' (1 Th 5 23), to be 'conformed'—in spirit now, in body hereafter—'to the image of God's Son' (Ro 8 29 Phil 3 9-21); for others, that they may be saved from sin and finally 'presented perfect in Christ' (Ro 10 1 Col 1 28 2 Tim 2 10, etc.). Thus his entire being is 'rooted and built up,' and wrapped up, 'in Christ,' the Head and Soul of redeemed humanity (Gal 2 20 Col 2 6, 7 3 11 Eph 4 10 1 Cor 8 6 11 3, etc.).

The Church. The Christian redemption is as truly social as personal; Christ 'loved me and gave Himself up for me'; He also 'loved the Church and gave Himself up for her' (Gal 2 20 Eph 5 25). 'The saints and faithful brethren' addressed in the Epistles belong, all of them, to the Christian community and owe allegiance to it (Gal 6 2 Eph 5 21 1 Cor 12 12-27, etc.); they were 'called into the fellowship of God's Son, Jesus Christ our Lord' (1 Cor 1 10). In earlier letters we read of this or that local Church, or 'churches of God.' Gradually the idea of 'the Church,' as the 'body of Christ' and 'habitation of God in the Spirit,' which embraces the particular Churches and consists of all without distinction who 'hold fast the Head,' grows upon St. Paul's mind (Gal 3 26-28 Col 3 11); we see it completely formed in Ephesians (2 21 22) and the Pastorals (1 Tim 3 15 2 Tim 2 20). The Church is necessary to Christ as the body to the head; in Eph 1 23 she is called His 'fulness' or 'complement'; He 'cherishes' her, as the husband does his spouse (Eph 5 23-32). The Church is no mere temporal, provisional institute; through 'all the generations of the age of the ages' she shares the glory of Christ, and will appear in her splendour of holiness at the Lord's coming (Eph 3 21 5 27). 'Our gathering together unto Him,' in the perfected fellowship of the redeemed, is the goal of Christian hope (2 Th 2 1, etc.).

The grace given to individuals is corporate property. Each Christian must 'look on the things of others' and 'by love serve' his brethren; no feeblest limb of the body of Christ is without its use (Eph 4 7, 16, 25 Gal 5 13 Phil 2 1-5 1 Cor 12 14 f.). Christ, who 'emptied Himself' and 'humbled Himself unto death' for His brethren's sake, is the Christian model (Ro 14 3 Phil 2 5-8). The various 'ministries' with their specific 'gifts of grace' (*charisms*), exist for the common benefit, and must be controlled for this end by the spirit of love (1 Cor 12 4–14 40); their object is to furnish and enable 'the saints' for their 'work of ministry,' and to promote a mutual edification through the entire fabric of the Church (Eph 4 11 16). Hence it is character and soundness of faith, not ability, for which St. Paul is supremely anxious in his instructions to Timothy and Titus about appointments to Church-office. Christian teachers and pastors 'have no lordship over the faith' of the flock; they must 'commend themselves to every conscience of men in the sight of God' (1 Cor 10 15 2 Cor 1 23 4 2 2 Tim 2 15). At Christ's tribunal they will 'give account,' as being His 'servants and stewards of the mysteries of God' (1 Cor 4 1-4 2 Cor 5 9). Fidelity to Christ, possession of His 'mind,' and a love for men that dictates unlimited self-denial, distinguish the gospel minister (1 Cor 2-4, 9, 2 Cor 12 15 Ro 1 14, 15 9 3). The Apostle lays stress upon the ordinances of Baptism and the Lord's Supper in respect both of their doctrinal significance and their covenantal force (Ro 6 3, 4 1 Cor 10 16-22 11 23-34), while he attaches small importance to his personal administration of them (1 Cor 1 16,17).

The Kingdom of God, and the Consummation. The thought of 'the kingdom of God and of Christ' retires in the Epistles somewhat behind that of 'the Church,' but it was never displaced in the Apostle's mind. He took over the Old Testament Messianic conception of 'the kingdom,' as it was transformed by Jesus. The Church consists of the 'citizens' of God's kingdom (Eph 2 19 Phil 3 20); 'the kingdom' embraces the entire order of things determined by the will of God in Christ, including the natural and secular provinces of life, which are bound up with the economy of grace (Ro 13 1-5 Col 3 22–4 1 1 Tim 4 3-5 6 15). Creation and redemption are parts of one scheme, and Christ is their unifying principle (Col 1 15-18).

The history of God's kingdom pursues a hidden 'purpose of the ages,' conceived in His prescient wisdom and executed according to 'the good pleasure of His will,' which centres in the mission of Christ and is revealed by the preaching of the gospel to mankind (Ro 16 25-27 Eph 3 2-11 2 Tim 1 9,10, etc.). The throne of this kingdom is 'the heart' (Ro 10 10 2 Cor 4 6 Col 3 15); its power is that of 'the Spirit'; its wealth lies in 'righteousness and peace and joy in the Holy Ghost' (1 Cor 2[4] 4[20] Ro 14[17]). It is destined, however, to dominate all mundane affairs (1 Cor 3[21, 22] 6[2] 15[25]), and to liberate nature along with 'the children of God' 'from the bondage of corruption' (Ro 8[19-23]). The Satanic powers regnant in heathenism, and all evil men, are the enemies of God and of Christ (Eph 6[10-13] 1 Cor 10[20-22], etc.); these constitute, in alliance, a 'dominion of darkness' warring against 'the kingdom of the Son of God's love' (Col 1[13]); they are doomed to an utter overthrow. 'Death, the last' of Christ's foes, is in course of abolition (1 Cor 15[26, 54-57] 2 Tim 1[10]).

The Apostle oftenest speaks of 'the kingdom of God' in the light of its future consummation, as matter of hope and 'inheritance' (2 Th 1[5] 1 Cor 6[9], etc.). 'The fashion of this world is passing' (1 Cor 7[29 31]); at 'the revelation,' or 'coming (parousia) of our Lord Jesus Christ,' it will vanish (1 Cor 1[7] 2 Cor 5[1] 1 Th 3[13] 2 Th 2[1], etc.). God's kingdom will then come in its 'glory' (1 Th 2[12])—the manifested 'glory of God' streaming through the world (Ro 5[2] Tit 2[13]), and centring in the person of the enthroned Christ (Phil 2[11] 2 Th 2[8, 14] 1 Tim 6[14]). But there are those to whom Christ's 'appearing' will bring shame and ruin (1 Th 5[2, 3] 2 Th 2[8-10]); for He comes the second time as Judge. 'All must be manifested before Christ's tribunal,' where doom will be pronounced on 'the works of darkness' (1 Cor 4[5] 2 Cor 5[10] Ro 2[16]). 'The day of the Lord' to the impenitent is 'a day of wrath and revelation of the righteous judgment of God' (Ro 2[5, 6, 8, 9]). The risen saints, approved at His coming, will be 'conformed' to Christ's 'body of glory' (Phil 3[21] Col 3[1-4] 1 Cor 15[49]). For Christians living in the flesh at His return the Apostle anticipates a transformation, without dissolution, of the 'earthy' into the 'heavenly' or 'spiritual body'; they will 'put on' the latter 'over' the former, so that 'the mortal' part of them will be 'swallowed up of life' (1 Cor 15[51-55] 2 Cor 5[1-5] 1 Th 4[15-17]). In Christ's resurrection the Apostle sees the 'firstfruits' of the glory destined for 'those who are Christ's at His coming' (1 Cor 15[20, 23] 2 Cor 4[10-14] 2 Tim 2[11, 12])—'a weight of glory' irradiating all created nature, with which their severest tribulations 'are not worthy to be compared' (Ro 8[17-21]). Meanwhile, the saints 'dying in the Lord' pass away to be 'with Christ,' in a state 'very far better' than their present toil and warfare (Phil 1[21-23] 2 Cor 5[8]). 'God, all things in all,' is the goal to which creation and redemption move (1 Cor 15[28]).

8. Authenticity and Integrity of the Epistles. The Pauline authorship of Romans, 1 and 2

Corinthians, and Galatians has never been denied, except by a few eccentric scholars. 1 Thessalonians, Philippians, and Philemon are added to the list of *homologumena*, as documents which, though questioned for a while during the last century, have vindicated their genuineness by the clearness with which they reflect the personality of the Apostle. The other six are still counted as *antilegomena*—Colossians being the least disputed of them, the three Pastorals the most, while 2 Thessalonians is held in considerable suspicion, and Ephesians in still more. Adverse critics recognise a Pauline nucleus in the personal data of Titus and 2 Timothy. Some regard Colossians and 2 Thessalonians—perhaps 1 Timothy —as Pauline in basis, but interpolated. Ephesians must be treated as genuine or pseudonymous in its entirety. A good and sufficient defence can be made for St. Paul's full authorship in each case: see the several Introductions.

Where Pauline authenticity is maintained, the *unity* of some Epistles is called in question. The difference in tone between 10[1]–13[10] and the rest of 2 Corinthians leads some able interpreters to regard this section as imported from another Epistle of Paul to Corinth—possibly the lost 'letter' of 2[3,4] and 7[8]. 2 Cor 6[14]–7[1], again, is a paragraph that fits badly into its context, and that seems suitable to the earlier letter alluded to in 1 Cor 5[9]. It has been asked, moreover, whether the long chain of greetings found in Ro 16 may not have been attached to a copy of this Letter, or of the principal parts of it, sent to some other Church than Rome—say to that of Ephesus, where the Apostle had laboured for three years. The triple ending of this Epistle (in 15[33] 16[20] and 16[25-27]), and the absence of the words 'in Rome' (1[7]) from certain ancient copies, decidedly suggest the hypothesis of a manifold destination : see Intro. to Ro.

It is to be noted that the most important of the thirteen Letters are the most certainly authentic. Whatever else may be denied, no one can reasonably doubt that there was such a man as Paul the Apostle of Christ Jesus, who wrote letters that are in our hands to Christian societies in Asia Minor, Corinth, and Rome, within thirty years of his Master's death. This is an historical fact of immense importance ; for these Epistles contain all the vital truths of Christianity, and exhibit them as living and transforming powers in society. These documents presuppose the person and teaching, the death and resurrection of the Lord Jesus. Without the Christ of the Four Gospels, the Paul of the Epistles is unintelligible.

BELIEF IN GOD

THE central subject of the Bible is God. The Book opens with an account of His creation of the heavens and the earth (Gn 1 1), and concludes with a description of the 'new heavens and earth' (Rev 21)—the ideal to which creation is moving, and wherein God Himself shall be the immediate source of illumination and the object of worship.

Throughout the Bible God is referred to as almighty, all-wise, all-holy, the eternal creator, sustainer, and moral governor of the universe. He is represented as entering into special relations with his highest creature, man, who is created in His image, after His likeness (Gn 1 26, 27), to be His vicegerent upon earth (Gn 1 26-28), and to increase in sympathy and fellowship with Himself. Man has, however, abused His highest gift of free-will, and so introduced sin into the world, a blot upon the fair creation, and a hereditary taint upon his own stock. Henceforth God's relation to man is changed. The glad love of pure beneficence becomes the wistful love of redemptive purpose. And in due time is chosen out for specially intimate relations with God, a single tribe—the 'seed of Abraham.' Israel is 'elected,' i.e. chosen out for special privilege and guidance, not from any motives of favouritism, but in order that he may be the vehicle of blessing to all mankind. To Israel—and through Israel to all men—is given an even deeper and clearer revelation of the character and will of God—that revelation which we see running through all the Old Testament, and reaching its climax in Jesus Christ: cp. Heb 1 1-5 f. Different misconceptions are successively purged away as opportunity occurs. At Sinai any lingering taint of idolatry and crude anthropomorphism is purged by the revelation of the ten commandments, and the natural tendency to irreverent, easy-going approach to the Almighty is met by the elaborate system of strict ceremonial. The prophets of the eighth century B.C. point out the futility of ceremonial reformation apart from righteousness of character, and go far towards removing the still-prevailing misconceptions by which the LORD was regarded as the tribal God of Israel, pledged to protect and support them, irrespective of their deserts. The LORD is 'exalted in judgment' (Isa 5 16), and no respecter of persons. Special closeness involves special responsibility (Am 3 2). Side by side with this comes a universalising tendency, a growing realisation of the one God's equal rule

and care of all mankind (Am 9 7 Isa 2 2, 3 19 18-25), which finds strong emphasis in some of the later Psalms (cp. e.g. Pss 96, 100, 117), and in the book of Jonah.

Meanwhile the discipline of suffering and perplexity, which had its effect upon the Hebrew people throughout their history, but most markedly during the Babylonian exile, purified and spiritualised the conception of the meaning of religion and of life ; carried forward the thoughts of the faithful more and more wistfully to a future life, in which righteousness should be vindicated and the balance of happiness redressed ; and while it brought home to them the weakness and impurity of human nature, intensified the desire for personal holiness and communion with God ; and, finally, gave occasion for the portrayal of the 'Suffering Servant of the LORD' (Isa 41-53) gathering up into Himself at once human penitence and divine redemption—that most wonderful figure in all the Old Testament, which is strikingly typical of the central Figure of the New Testament.

The statements about God in Holy Scripture are uttered with an air of authority, dogmatically ; not as the result of a long chain of reasoning : 'The LORD said ' this—' did ' that—or more emphatically, in the form of a message, ' Thus saith the LORD.' The teaching of the Bible is not the result of deductive or inductive reasoning. No direct arguments are adduced to prove the existence of God—that is assumed throughout. His attributes may be the subject of argument ; His existence, never. His justice, His wisdom, His power may be momentarily obscured by the mystery of evil in the world—as in the book of Job. Incidentally we may get arguments dealing with the nature of the Deity, as e.g. the interesting *à fortiori* argument from creature to Creator in Ps 94, 'He that made the eye, shall he not see ? ' etc., which logically carried out becomes an inference of Personality in God from man's personality—there are arguments such as these either stated or suggested in Holy Scripture, but the existence of God never comes within their scope. It lies behind all else ; it is the fundamental conception in the light of which all else is viewed. Not only in the Pentateuch and the Prophets and the Psalms, but in the historical narratives— in the brief and apparently barren records of the accession, regnal years, and death of the various kings, it is made clear that God's Hand is at work throughout guiding the course of events, and that He is the ever-present Judge by whom the actions of king and subject alike are weighed. Even in the book of Esther, in which the divine Name never once occurs, no doubt is left upon the mind as to the providential overruling of events both great and small. Nay, in those books which are least formally theological—Job, Proverbs, and Ecclesiastes, the works of the 'wise men,' the humanists or philosophers of Israel—the thought of God is present from first to last. They do not grope and search after Him like the great pagan thinkers. They set out, not to discover, but to recognise Him; to learn from His dealing with nature and human nature more about that divine Personality who is the primary presupposition of all their system, and with whom their heart holds sacred communion even while the intellect stands baffled before the insoluble problems involved in His permission of evil in the world He rules.

The Bible, as we have said, does not offer arguments to prove the existence of the Deity, but it offers something which is far more valuable to most of us than any abstract proof. It gives us a concrete, experimental, descriptive theology. It shows us a picture of the world with God at work in it, which the devout, appreciative soul instinctively recognises as true. It offers us, largely in the concrete form of narrative and history, a theory of the universe which, rightly understood, is found to meet the demands of hearts and minds alike: revealing a God whose character is such and whose relation to man is such that in Him both our needs and our aspirations find satisfaction. At the same time it incidentally provides a theory of human nature (see especially Gn 1–3) that affords the only satisfactory key to the *raison d'être* of those needs and aspirations—the explanation of man's actual littleness and his potential greatness.

We will consider first the message of the Bible to man's heart, and then its message to his understanding.

The needs and aspirations of heart and spirit can only be satisfied by personal communion with the Deity, such as the Psalter so wonderfully delineates (see especially Pss 16, 17, 63, 73), a communion which attains its fullest expression in the religion of the New Testament.

This heart-knowledge is after all, to each individual who has it, the most direct form of evidence for the existence of God—the personal intercourse with Him of our personal spirit—the communion in virtue of which we can say, 'I know that there is a God *because I know Him*. I experience in prayer and sacrament and meditation a conviction of His reality and His presence which is quite as real to me as is the conviction that those things exist which I can touch and see. This conviction is clearest and strongest when I am at my best, and I attribute all that is best and highest in my character to such communion, as thousands have done before me.'

This is the kind of 'knowledge of God' that cries aloud to us from the Psalms and Prophecies, and underlies the other writings of the Old Testament. And the perfection of this communion is to be found in Jesus Christ, as portrayed for us in the Synoptic Gospels (Lk 10^{22}; cp. Mk 13^{32}), but especially in St. John (5$^{19f.}$ 10^{15,30} 14^{11}, etc.), and reaches its climax in the great high-priestly prayer of Jn 17. After our Lord's Ascension and the descent of the Holy Spirit, it takes the form, for Christ's members, of a fellowship with the blessed Trinity, Father, Son, and Holy Ghost (2 Cor 13^{14}; cp. 1 Jn 1^3).

Being, however, in one sense, a purely personal and individual matter, this sense of communion is commonly thought to be too subjective to be adduced as an argument for the existence of God. It is always open to an objector to say, 'You assert that you have this feeling; I am willing to admit your sincerity, but you may be the victim of illusion. All I can say is that I have no such feeling myself.' To such an assertion it seems perhaps inadequate to reply, 'If you will but assume first provisionally (as we have to assume many things in practical life) that existence which you cannot demonstrate, and then act upon the assumption, conviction will come with experience.' Yet such a reply may be enforced and corroborated with all the weight of more than nineteen centuries of personal experience. Generation after generation of martyrs and saints have testified in the strongest possible manner to their conviction that 'God is, and is a rewarder of them that diligently seek Him' (Heb 11^6), and have been ready to seal the conviction with their life's blood.

That such evidence is not without scientific value, is very strongly argued by no less a scientist than the late G. J. Romanes, who speaks of those who would ignore it as untrue to the principles of an impartial Agnosticism. Still it fails to appeal to a large class of enquirers, who look for a more definitely intellectual proof and one less intimately associated with personal feeling and emotion.

There are such **arguments for the being and character of God,** and some of them have come down to us from very ancient times. It may be admitted that they do not—either singly or even in combination—amount to demonstrative proof; yet they form, as we shall see, a very strong presumption in favour of belief in just such a God as the Bible claims to reveal.

We will now briefly sketch the more important of these types of argument, and then we may be better able to estimate the extent to which the Biblical revelation corresponds to, and completes, man's intellectual search after God. We must remember, however, at the outset that these traditional arguments are not the originating cause of man's belief, even where belief is found outside the influence of revelation, rather, they represent an intellectual analysis or justification of a belief already existing. As far back as Cicero in the first century B.C., or even earlier, pagan thinkers had observed that religion in some form or other is a universal trait in human nature. And though in modern days apparent exceptions of 'atheistical tribes' have been adduced to prove the contrary, the trend of anthropological science may be said on the whole to support the judgment of antiquity. There may indeed be savages (though the point has not been proved) among whom no definite trace of religious observance can be discerned; but are they normal representatives even of undeveloped humanity? Is there no such thing as degradation? And have not even these poor savages some vestige at least of the religious faculty? for that is all our argument really requires. The worldwide progress of Christian missions to the heathen seems to testify quite triumphantly that no race or tribe of men, however degraded and apparently atheistic, lacks that spark of religious capacity which may be fanned and fed into a mighty flame.

Granted, then, that the religious faculty is practically universal among mankind, what is the significance of this fact? From ancient times it has been regarded as an argument—often (wrongly) as a proof—that God exists. It is called the argument 'from the general consent of mankind': in Latin, *argumentum e consensu gentium*. The whole world, it is urged, must surely be right—*securus judicat orbis terrarum.*

Of a truth it is exceedingly unlikely, if (as we must presume) the world is rational, that a phenomenon so universal as religion, so intimately and intricately interwoven with the central facts of human life and progress, should be founded on illusion. But the outward expression of the religious principle in different ages and climes exhibits so much variety, inconsistency, and vagueness, that we ought not perhaps to speak of this argument (at least in this, its broader and vaguer form) as directly evidencing the existence and character of God. What it really amounts to is, as has been well said, 'an evidence that there are evidences.' If the religious instinct is observed to be practi-

cally universal, it will be worth while to see whether it is not essential to human nature. And this quest leads us to the formal arguments for God's existence. The grounds of this religious instinct will be found to lie partly in man's relation to the external world, partly in the constitution of human nature itself.

The consideration of the external world around him, even in its broadest aspect, leads man up to the thought of an Eternal Cause; the study of its phenomena in detail with its marvellous intricacy of harmonious interaction produces the impression of design, and leads to the thought of a Designer—i.e. of an Eternal Cause that is intelligent and free. Reflexion on his own consciousness and the fact that the external world corresponds in a mysterious way to his own thought leads to the idea of a primal and Universal Consciousness embracing all reality and forming, as it were, a meeting-place between Thought and Things. Lastly, his own moral nature—conscience, with its authoritative voice, clearly distinguishable from mere wish, taste, desire, and self-interest—speaks to him of a Universal Lawgiver, supreme and perfect, to whom alone the 'categorical imperative' of the inner monitor can be adequately referred. The Eternal Cause is thus found to be endowed with all the attributes characteristic of personality as seen in man.

Of the first of these arguments little further need be said. Man finds in himself a principle of causality in the light of which he interprets the external world. He cannot help regarding the succession of phenomena which he observes as effects—attributing each to some cause. When he examines that again he discovers it to be no true or absolute cause, but itself the effect of something further back, and so on. He finds in himself the nearest approach to a *vera causa:* yet he would recognise the absurdity of calling himself self-caused. And the mind cannot rest in an endless chain of cause-effects. There must be, it feels, if you go far enough back, a *real* Cause, akin, in some way, to man's own power of origination, yet transcending it—a cause that owns no cause—no source of being—but itself. And to this Eternal Cause all things, including man himself, must be ultimately referable.

The third argument, again, in favour of a Universal Consciousness, which has several different forms, is too abstruse for the ordinary reader, requiring for its appreciation some degree of metaphysical training. The second and the fourth—the 'Design' and 'Conscience' arguments—demand a somewhat fuller treatment here, being specially important in view of the light thrown on them by recent scientific theory.

The **Design-argument** is perhaps the most ancient and the most popular of all. It is never actually formulated in the Bible, for the Bible, as we have seen, never treats God's existence as the subject of argument. But its basis, the marvellous harmony of the created world, is the theme of more than one of the Psalms (cp. e.g. Pss 19, 104, 147, 148) ; and St. Paul comes very near to stating the argument in so many words, when he says (Ro 1 [20]) in depreciation of pagan superstitions and immorality, that the 'everlasting power and divinity' of the Creator are clearly discernible from His works.

Granted that the very existence of the world implies an Eternal Cause, what can we learn about that Cause ? The nearest thing to a true first Cause of which I have experience, is my own personality : hence there is a presumption that the world's first Cause will be *at least* what we know as personal. But that presumption is not all we have to go upon. There are definite indications in nature, when more closely observed, that make it impossible to regard the Eternal Cause as a merely mechanical originator of the world-process, that stamp it—or rather Him—as intelligent and free, a nature like my own rational nature, only far above and beyond it.

Everywhere in nature we see the *teleological* principle (as it is called) at work, i.e. we see means adapted to ends, and the present subordinated to the future. This adaptation of means to ends manifests itself in a bewilderingly complex way—in each individual member of the great organism, in the lesser and greater groups, and in the whole. Everywhere, in fact, I see traces of *purpose* and *design*—for such adaptation speaks to me irresistibly of these. My only direct experience of like phenomena is in my own personality, and so I am led to infer a Designer.

Some, however, have thought that this inference is invalidated by a closer scrutiny of those means by which the evolution of physical organisms is effected, according to modern scientific theory. Evolution, they say, has upset the Design-argument altogether. The marvellously adjusted interaction of forces and interests which we observe in nature is not, as we have hitherto supposed, a perfect piece of elaborate machinery fresh from the Designer's Hand. It has a history behind it, and a history which we have only just begun to trace aright. The present state of things is not the result of a serene and orderly procession wherein every member has found its due and rightful place. On the contrary, it is the result in every department of a struggle for existence fierce and unintermitted, in which only a small proportion—'the fittest'—have survived. Nature's waste products, far outweighing her successes —how do they affect the Design-argument ?

Again, we can see in part the actual means by which this relative progress in evolution has been made. On the one hand, there is the principle of *Variation*, whereby the offspring always varies in some degree from the parent, and, on the other hand, that of *Natural Selection*, which results in the survival of the type best fitted to survive. Where, then, is there room for Design and a Designer ? The answer seems to be that the origin or root-principle of evolution has not yet been disclosed. What is it that produces the Variation which Natural Selection fixes and makes the basis of an upward step ? The choice seems to lie between God and—chance. That chance, or some non-rational force, could work on such definitely 'teleological' lines, could produce such ordered and systematic results, is a theory harder to believe than the theistic theory. And the difficulty of it is rather enhanced than otherwise by recent scientific discovery. For if a mechanically regular world in which neither failures nor waste products had place, would produce the impression of design and purpose, much more forcibly are we driven to the same conclusion when we see order growing out of chaos, peace out of strife, and apparently intractable material moulded to artistic perfection. The background of struggle, pain, decay and seeming waste may be in itself difficult to account for ; but the result shows that behind the working of the principles of Variation and Natural Selection there must be intelligence, will, purpose.

The Design-argument may have been stated, in the past, in such a way as to expose it to the criticism of scientists ; but the argument itself—especially when broadly and generally treated—has only gained strength and illumination from the modern view of nature's working methods ; for 'Evolution,' as Asa Gray said to Darwin, ' has brought back teleology to science.'

The **Moral argument**—that drawn from the phenomena of Conscience—has been similarly assailed, but with no better success. Attempts have been made to discredit the authoritative character of conscience by claiming for it a non-moral origin. Conscience, it is urged, is the result of a long and complicated process of evolution, and really represents not the divine voice of an inward monitor, but the outcome of ages and ages of racial self-interest. To reduce it to a principle of *individual* self-interest is obviously absurd considering how frequently conscience and immediate self-interest are found to be ranged on opposite sides. But the interest of the community or the race is a different thing. Generation after generation has, as it were, mechanically impressed upon its members the tendency to act in a direction salutary to the race, so that at last this unselfish or 'altruistic' principle has become a sort of instinct or second nature, varying indeed in its range, intensity, and degree of enlightenment, but a constant characteristic of man as man.

This line of argument is supported by the consideration that there are traces of apparently conscientious action in animals customarily regarded as irrational, and that conscience in mankind exhibits extremely various and inconsistent results in different circumstances and stages of civilisation.

But to treat conscience and the moral argument on these lines involves a misconception of the scope of Natural Science. The scope of Natural Science, properly so called, does not include the *origin* of things nor the purpose and *end* of their being. It is merely concerned with a description of their present state and the discovery and analysis of the process by which they arrived thereat. Conscience is what it is, quite independently of the process by which it may have been evolved ; just as man is man—an intelligent, rational, moral, spiritual being, whatever may have been the stages whereby the physical side of him climbed up from the humblest places of the realm of organic life. Undoubtedly the truer view of things is the teleological—that which sees in the humble beginning the germ of a great future—and not the view which refuses to man and conscience their proper names because there may have been a time when they were far removed from their present stage of development.

As for the startlingly inconsistent ways in which conscience vents itself in action, that only emphasises the one underlying principle, the principle expressed in the words ' I ought.' The *subject-matter* of conscience and its practical range of influence may vary indefinitely according to the surroundings, circumstances, and moral attainment of its particular possessor, and it is on this side that we speak of conscience as capable of education and enlightenment ; but the *form* of conscience remains constant. It may be stronger or weaker according to the measure of its use, but it remains in essence ever the same ; a principle of moral constraint, recognising in extreme cases no human tribunal whatever—not even the expressed will or the obvious immediate interest of society in general, and witnessing to an obligation that can only have reference to a Universal Moral Ruler and Lawgiver, whose will is regarded as at once morally perfect and absolutely without appeal.

Whatever, then, may be the history of the evolution of conscience, the testimony of man's moral nature would seem to be direct and unmistakable. It points to an Eternal Cause of the Universe and of mankind characterised not merely by creative power and wisdom, but also by moral holiness.

Is it corroborated by the testimony of history ? for if the actual ordering of the world of mankind clearly contradicts the testimony of conscience, we may still be tempted to treat that testimony as illusory.

Bishop Butler has shown convincingly that though the government of the world represents a scheme imperfectly comprehensible to us, yet there exist quite undeniable marks of moral rule—tokens that the Power which guides the world is, in more modern phrase, ' something — not itself — which makes for righteousness.' The rise and fall and the succession of empires ; the advance and decadence of races, tribes, families ; the fortunes of individual men—all these, while they present many puzzling and inexplicable features, about which we shall have more to say later on—bear witness on the whole to the righteousness of Him who sits on the world's throne.

On the physical side of human nature, where we should expect things to work themselves out most mechanically, the moral law is perhaps most clearly vindicated. Immoral conduct produces its own punishment in so large a number of cases that sin and suffering have sometimes been regarded as simply and in every case, cause and effect. Experience teaches us, however—and the Bible teaches it too, in the book of Job—that not all which we commonly regard as evil—all pain, suffering or material loss—is the direct consequence of moral wrong-doing in the individual who suffers. And Christ Himself expressly discountenances this attribution of suffering to sin, as its necessary cause (Lk 13 $^{2, 3, 4}$). Indeed, suffering is not always an evil, as things are now, though we rightly look upon it as belonging to an imperfect state of existence. Sometimes it seems to be the consequence of virtue and intended to stimulate the aspiring soul to still higher ideals.

In history, the most striking picture of moral government is to be found in the fortunes of Israel. Here we are leaving Natural Religion and bordering upon Revelation. But if the Bible picture of Hebrew history be taken as substantially true, it will be found to supply a key to history in general, and to justify the believer's conviction that Old Testament history differs from secular history not so much in its subject-matter as in its treatment—that it is unique not mainly because the Chosen People were uniquely nurtured, guided, and disciplined, but because here alone the veil is lifted and the true issues of personal and national conduct are made plain as they appear to Him whose hand has guided the history of mankind from its beginning until now. For this reason, in spite of our enormous advance in historical method, and of the advantage that comes from an indefinitely wider horizon, it may be boldly said that the historians of to-day can never hope to surpass or even to equal the fundamental grasp of truth achieved in the early and unscientific efforts of the inspired historians of Israel.

Revelation. 'Natural Religion,' as it is called—i.e. the witness of human nature to God—needs Revealed Religion to complete it. Man's mind, dwelling on external nature, is led up to the thought of an immensely wise, mighty and beneficent Creator and Ruler. But there are many considerations which tend to depreciate the design-argument and rob it of its force. Man needs some direct assurance from outside the circle of his ordinary thought, to combat the problems raised by the presence of anomaly, failure, and waste, to say nothing of pain.

Again, man's nature bears on it the impress of moral law, and would lead him up to belief in an all-holy Universal Lawgiver. Yet there is much in the facts of human society that would draw him in a quite opposite direction. No one can read the Psalms or the book of Job, no one can face honestly the facts of human society around him to-day, without feeling something of the almost overwhelming difficulty that is involved in the spectacle of successful wickedness, unpunished oppression, and unmerited suffering.

We need some more direct assurance than conscience itself can give us if we are to exclaim with real conviction—

> 'God's in His heaven ;
> All's right with the world.'

And it is natural to ask : If there be a God such as human nature seems to suggest or demand, could He not—would He not find some means of making Himself known to His rational creatures ?

The presupposition of the Bible is that he has found such means, and supplemented and completed Natural Religion by direct Revelation. This Revelation is focussed in the divine-human figure of Jesus Christ, foretold and expected in the Old Testament, present to teach and work in the New, and ever abiding by His Spirit in the Church.

The fact of divine revelation is, of course, denied by Atheism : but apart from revelation altogether, Atheism is self-condemned by its presumption. To prove a negative is confessedly a difficult task in any field, and the Atheist claims to have proved it in the widest field of all—the universe—and in face of the many-sided testimony of Nature and Human Nature. To be justified in a flat and categorical denial of the existence of a deity I must be furnished with a full knowledge of the universe both as a whole and in its details, so as to be competent to declare that nowhere in all the realms of things existing is there any trace of evidence which might even probably tell in favour of Theism. None but a mind practically infinite, omnipresent, and all-knowing could compass this. And so it might be suggested that the Atheist really claims for himself the divine qualities and attributes of which he denies the existence in a God.

Another line of thought antagonistic to revelation goes by the name of Agnosticism. It dwells on the obvious limitations of our mental powers, which find themselves baffled in every department when they attempt to pass beyond a certain point ; and says that the circumscribed human mind, excellent as it is in its own sphere, can never hope to comprehend the Infinite, the Absolute. 'The Power,' it says, 'which the universe manifests to us, is inscrutable.' It dwells also on the difficulties and anomalies in nature ; on the darker side of evolution—its aspect of failure, struggle and decay ; on the darker side of human nature—the presence of evil, especially of moral evil, in the world ; and says these so far balance the tokens of goodness observable, that we cannot be sure, if there be a government of the world, whether it is one that really 'makes for righteousness.'

There is considerable justification for the emphasis laid by Agnosticism on these two factors in human life ; but it is just in regard to them that Revelation is our greatest help. The problem of evil scarcely falls to be discussed here : but it may be remarked that, while a very real and pressing problem, it can be seen, in the light of Revelation, to be no insuperable obstacle to faith. With regard to the other point, the inadequacy of our faculties, it may be said at once that Natural Religion does fall short of certainty and completeness, and that this is fully admitted in the Bible. There is a sense in which the God of the Bible is 'incomprehensible,' 'inscrutable.' He is as high above man in His ways and thoughts as heaven is above earth (Isa 55 9). His essential inaccessibility is expressed as a 'dwelling in the thick darkness' (1 K 8 12), or in 'light inapproachable' (1 Tim 6 16). 'No man hath seen God at any time . .' (Jn 1 18) ; 'No man knoweth who the Father is save the Son' (Lk 10 22). Again, man as we know him is, of himself, utterly incapable of any true knowledge of God : the natural man is incapable of discerning the things of the Spirit (1 Cor 2 14).

At the same time no duty is more persistently impressed on their hearers by the prophets than 'to know the LORD.' To its neglect are ascribed the woe and failures of the Chosen People (Isa 1 3 5 13 Hos 4 6), and its presence is a guarantee of righteous conduct. In the New Testament the knowledge of the Father and the Son is identified with 'everlasting life' (Jn 17³). What is the meaning of this apparent contradiction? Fallen man, though sin has blurred in him the image of his Creator, retains still the potentiality of that communion for which he was created; and though he cannot of his own initiative 'by searching find out God' (Job 11⁷), he can still, by penitent coöperation with Divine grace, attain to a true knowledge of One who has been seeking him ever since the first days of alienation in Paradise (Gn 3⁹), and has revealed Himself to receptive hearts in times past 'by divers portions and in divers manners' (Heb 1¹). In Himself essentially inscrutable, God wills to be known with the knowledge of personal communion. He has given man the capacity for such communion, and though man has rejected Him, God has devised means that His banished be not outcast from Him: cp. 2 S 14¹⁴. The greatest prophet of the Old Testament portrays in wonderful words this paradox of divine condescension (Isa 57¹⁵). The New Testament presents it to us in concrete form, in the Messiah on whom the wistful gaze of Prophet and Psalmist had for centuries been fixed. Then was given once and for all a revelation of God and of Man together in a single life.

The revelation of God in Jesus Christ has stood the test of many generations as corresponding to the highest aspirations and most urgent demands of human nature. Consideration of its characteristics shows it is just the revelation that man needs. On the one hand, it is a revelation of the *character of Almighty God*, as in the highest and supremest sense 'our Father.' On the other hand, it is a revelation of *Ideal Manhood:* the bewildered question of ages about the meaning, purpose, and destiny of the human life is cleared up in the New Testament. What He tells us, in the Sermon on the Mount and elsewhere, about our duty and our hopes in this life and beyond the grave—what He shows us in His own person of communion with the Heavenly Father, and successful resistance of temptation in the strength of that communion—what He shows us of absolute self-surrender, even to the point of death, of triumph through suffering, and of new life and glory after the grave—all these are essential parts of His Revelation. But the Revelation is no bare presentation of truth and of an ideal utterly inaccessible to weak and fallen man. Grace as well as Truth came by Jesus Christ (Jn 1¹⁷). And what differentiates this from all other so-called Revelations is that, while the ideal it holds up before man is uniquely lofty—nothing less than *perfection* (Mt 5⁴⁸)—it supplies at the same time the motive force necessary for arriving at the ideal.

The Revelation of Truth by itself might well generate despair. Its most characteristic effect has always been the production of a *sense of sin:* resulting from the felt contrast between the absolute holiness of Almighty God, required by Him in man, and exhibited actually in the Man Christ Jesus, and the tale that conscience tells us of our own impurity and pollution. This terrible contrast—viewed in the light of God's revealed Love—would by itself produce an unspeakably bitter remorse; but that remorse is transformed into penitence by the further revelation of *Grace*—i.e. of the means which Divine Love has devised for man's restoration. And so the sense of sin leads to 'Conversion.' In the Bible teaching about Atonement—culminating in the Self-offering of Christ—we see the true Representative of Mankind removing the barrier set up by sin, opening once more the avenue of access to God, and so rendering possible to man a sacramental sharing of the divine life and strength. Here find their satisfaction that instinct and yearning that led to the primitive institution of *sacrifice*, as old apparently and as universal as the human race. In the teaching about the Incarnation—'the Word made flesh'—the Son of God taking upon Him not an isolated individual human personality, but *our nature* in a universal way, so as to become true representative man; we find the fulfilment of the true idea underlying those strange dreams, clothed often in unworthy guise which find expression in the 'Incarnation Myth' of Hindoo and other religions. While in the outcome of the Incarnation—the incorporation of human personalities one by one as members into the body of Christ, that incorporation which renders the atoning sacrifice effectual in each one—we see realised the ideal of the *social* instinct: all other social 'membership' being but a poor metaphor beside the living membership in the Church, 'which is His Body.'

Finally, the Revelation in both its sides receives a magnificent corroboration, when we see the life of Christ reproduced really, if not completely, in the thousands of His followers who, conscious of their own shortcomings, have yet been able to say with lips and life at once, 'I live, yet not I but Christ liveth in me' (Gal 2²⁰). 'I can do all things through Christ which strengtheneth me.'

THE PERSON OF JESUS CHRIST

1. Present Position of Christianity. Christianity is now the religion of at least a third of the human race. So rapid has been its advance during the past century, and so hopeful are its present prospects, that the remarkable prophecy of its Founder, that the whole world would ultimately be converted, is already within measurable distance of fulfilment. To investigate the origin of so remarkable a movement, and to attain to a clear conception of the character and personality of its great Founder, is the purpose of the present article.

2. What is Christianity? Among the nations of the West, even those who reject Christianity as a creed, still revere Jesus of Nazareth as the noblest and purest, and probably the greatest character which has ever appeared on the scene of history. 'About the life and sayings of Jesus,' says John Stuart Mill, 'there is a stamp of personal originality combined with a profundity of insight, which .. must place the prophet of Nazareth, even in the estimation of those who have no belief in His inspiration, in the very first rank of the men of sublime genius of whom our species can boast... Religion cannot be said to have made a bad choice in pitching on this man as the ideal representative and guide of humanity ; nor even now would it be easy even for an unbeliever to find a better translation of the rule of virtue from the abstract into the concrete than to endeavour so to live that Christ would approve our life.' 'Jesus,' says Renan, 'is in every respect unique, and nothing can be compared with Him. Be the unlooked-for phenomena of the future what they may, Jesus will not be surpassed. Noble Initiator, repose now in Thy glory ! Thy work is finished, Thy divinity established. A thousand times more living, a thousand times more loved since Thy death than during the days of Thy course here below, Thou shalt become the corner-stone of humanity, insomuch that to tear Thy Name from this world would be to shake it from its very foundations. No more shall men distinguish between Thee and God.'

To Christians, however, Jesus is more even than this. A few, generally called Unitarians, are satisfied with regarding Him as the greatest of human prophets, but to the immense majority of Christians, in this as in every preceding age, He is the divine Son of God, who took our nature upon Him to redeem it, and after suffering upon the Cross, rose from the dead, and ascended into heaven, where, seated upon the throne of the universe, He receives a homage indistinguishable from that paid to the eternal Father.

3. The Christian Doctrine of the Incarnation. The belief that the historical person Jesus Christ is the eternal Son of God made man, and that accordingly (to use the words of an ancient hymn), He is 'God of the substance of the Father, begotten before the worlds, and man of the substance of His mother, born in the world ; perfect God and perfect man, of a reasonable soul and human flesh subsisting, equal to the Father as touching His Godhead, and inferior to the Father as touching His manhood,' is called the doctrine of the Incarnation. The idea of incarnation as a mode of manifestation of the divine nature is not altogether peculiar to Christianity. It is characteristic of several Eastern religions, particularly of those of India. According to the teaching of Brahmanism, Vishnu, one of the triad of supreme gods, became incarnate many times. His best-known incarnation is the ninth, in which he appeared as Crishna, literally 'the black one.' After achieving various heroic exploits, such as the avenging of the murder of his parents, and the slaying of the serpent Caliga, he was put to death by being shot with an arrow, leaving behind him the prediction that thirty years after his death the iron age would begin. The resemblance, however, of these Eastern incarnations to that of Jesus Christ is altogether superficial. Those were temporary, Christ's was permanent. In those the incarnate god practices without shame every species of vice ; Christ's life was sinless, and a perfect model for imitation. In those no salvation is achieved, except occasionally from the oppression of some earthly tyrant ; in Christ salvation from sin and eternal life are offered to all mankind. Puerile, vulgar, unspiritual, degrading, and limited in scope, the incarnations of other religions cannot for a moment compare with the splendour of the Incarnation of Christ, the aim of which is to atone for sin, to destroy the power of evil, and to raise the whole human race into fellowship with God.

4. The Reasonableness of the Incarnation. The Incarnation is not accepted by Christians simply because it is taught in the Bible, or because it is part of the traditional creed of the Church, but because it is itself intrinsically reasonable and in harmony with the highest and best ideas about God and man.

(1) *It harmonises with the idea that man is made in God's image.* All the higher forms of religion assume that the nature of God and the nature of man are closely analogous. The gift of reason, the knowledge of right and wrong, the freedom of the will, the desire of holiness, and the instinctive seeking after God which is found to some extent even in the most degraded races, are regarded as indicating that there is a real spiritual affinity between the Creator and the creature. The nature and character of God are manifested to some extent in the works of physical nature, but far more fully and adequately in the rational and spiritual nature of man, which, even in its fallen state, is the most God-like thing known to us. It is, therefore, altogether credible that human nature should be chosen as the medium of God's final revelation to the human race. An ideally perfect human life, lived under human conditions, and in the midst of ordinary human difficulties, is a far more satisfying and morally fruitful revelation than a number of abstract propositions about God written in a book.

(2) *The Incarnation reveals God's love more effectually than any other kind of revelation.* That God truly loves His creatures is in theory a truth of natural religion, but the present order of nature contains so much which seems to contradict it, that a special revelation intended to confirm it is urgently needed. The earthquake, the tornado, and the pestilence, overwhelm in a common destruction the saint and the sinner. Nature seems an adamantine system of blind resistless forces, which roll on for ever, careless of human needs and human tears or groans. What, therefore, is imperatively required in a revelation designed to satisfy human needs is some definite and tangible proof, other than words, that nature is ruled by a personal Being friendly to the human race, and attentive to the needs of individual men. Such proof is offered by the Incarnation. God did not simply send a message from heaven announcing that He is friendly to the human race ; He sent His own Son to live a human life, to struggle like other men against sin, to suffer human sorrow, toil and disappointment, and finally to die a martyr's death. In Christ God shows His sympathy with our sufferings by suffering with us ; ' for we have not a high priest that cannot be touched with the feeling of our infirmities, but one that hath been in all points tempted as we are, yet without sin.'

But it was not only in suffering, but also in acting, that Jesus Christ manifested the love of God. He ' went about doing good, and healing all who were oppressed with the devil, for God was with him.' He restored reason to the insane, sight to the blind, muscular power to the paralysed, life to the dead. Every miracle which He wrought was a miracle of benevolence, intended to convince men that the Father whose nature He came to manifest, was truly a lover of men, and truly kind and just.

(3) *The Incarnation is the most adequate way that we can imagine of atoning for sin.* The chief barrier between God and man is sin, and the religious instinct of our race recognises that man cannot of himself remove that barrier. Superficial thinkers sometimes affirm that no reconciliation with God is necessary, or that, if it is, it can be effected by human penitence. There is truth in this, but only a half-truth. It is quite true that penitence is the natural and fitting atonement for sin. Thus when one human being sins against another, penitence is accepted as an adequate atonement. Even in the case of a sin against God, a really adequate repentance would be an adequate atonement. But the awakened conscience of man knows that this is impossible. His penitence for sin, like all his other virtuous acts, is weak and ineffectual, and he needs some transforming power which will make his penitence perfect. The Incarnation provides for this. The Incarnate Son of God as head of the human race, and as responsible for it, renders to God adequate sorrow for the sins of the world, and gives individual men, through their union with Him, grace to attain deeper and deeper penitence, until in the end their penitence will become perfect, and God will accept it as adequate.

(4) *The Incarnation is designed to make sinless perfection possible, not at once, but in due course.* It effects this not simply by the inspiring influence of Christ's perfect example, but by means of constant supplies of supernatural grace given to those who are really walking by faith. According to the Christian theory, Christ by virtue of His holy Incarnation becomes the new ancestor of the human race. As by our natural birth and training we inherit the evil nature and sinful tendencies of our ancestors, so by our new and spiritual birth we are made partakers of Christ's holy and sinless human nature, and in its strength are enabled to obtain complete victory over sin. This sounds mystical, and to some minds fanciful, but it represents the central and vital religious experience of Christians. All who have advanced far in the religious life testify that through Christ they have been brought into vital union with God, and have received a new strength against the powers of evil.

(5) *The Incarnation achieves most perfectly the supreme end of religion, the complete union between the worshipper and the object of worship.* In Christ human nature is personally united to God, and since individual believers are related to Christ as members to the head,

or as branches to the trunk, they are thereby brought into supernatural union with the life of God. In this world the full fruition of the divine life is not attained; but in the world to come, when human nature has been perfected through suffering, and cleansed from all stain of sin, every true believer will see God as He is, and will be united to Him perfectly by knowledge and love, and will so fully partake of His nature as to be in a manner deified.'

(6) *The Incarnation emphasises human solidarity and human brotherhood.* The humanity of Christ is not individual or racial, but universal. He is the ideal of humanity as a whole realised, and in Him races and individuals are brought into spiritual fellowship with one another, and form one Church, family, or brotherhood. The Incarnation saves men not as individuals, but as members of the body of Christ, and makes the performance of social duties indispensable to admittance into the Kingdom of Heaven.

4. Christ's Deity. Having shown the reasonable character of the Christian doctrine of the Incarnation, we shall now proceed to state briefly the direct evidence for Christ's Divinity.

(1) *Christ's Divinity was accepted by the earliest believers, not only of the Gentile, but also of the Jewish-Christian Churches.*

The Pauline Epistles, of which all except the Pastorals are practically undisputed, fall between the dates 51 A.D. (1, 2 Th) and about 67 A.D. (2 Tim). From them it appears that as early as twenty years after the Ascension the doctrine of Christ's Deity was already firmly established in the Church. It is not argued about or proved, but assumed as one of those fundamental ideas about which Christians are agreed. Thus it is stated that He existed before He was born into the world (1 Cor 10 [4, 9]), and indeed before all creation (Col 1 [17]), in a state of equality with God (Phil 2 [6]); that He created the world as the Father's agent, and still sustains it in existence (Col 1 [16, 17] 1 Cor 8 [6]); that to redeem the human race He became man (Gal 4 [4]), and died upon the Cross (Col 1 [20]); that He dwells in believers as the source of their spiritual life (2 Cor 13 [5]); that He is the Son of God (Ro 8 [32]), and actually God (Ro 9 [5] Tit 2 [13] RV), and therefore to be worshipped with divine honours by angels and men in His divine and human natures (Phil 2 [10]). Prayer to Him is so much a matter of course, that Christians are spoken of as 'those that call upon His name' (1 Cor 1 [2]). A certain real subordination of Christ to the Father, as being His Son, St. Paul admits (1 Cor 15 [28]), but He constantly unites His name with that of the Father on terms of equality as the author of grace, blessing, and all well-being (2 Cor 13 [14]). That in all the Churches founded by St. Paul, Jesus was reverenced as a Divine Being, can scarcely be doubted by any careful reader of his Epistles.

But now perhaps it will be said, 'How can we be sure that St. Paul's view was shared by the other Apostles? Is it not possible that the Twelve regarded Jesus as a purely human Messiah, and that it was St. Paul who first introduced into the Church the idea that He was divine?' We are fortunately not without the means of answering this question. The Pauline Epistles themselves furnish us with important evidence. From them we learn that though the relations between St. Paul and the Twelve were not always harmonious, and that theological disputes at times waxed hot, yet those disputes were about questions of inferior moment (e.g. the obligation of Circumcision and of the Ceremonial Law, the position of Gentile Christians in the Church, the relative authority of St. Paul and the Twelve), and that on all matters of fundamental importance the parties were agreed. We learn that the Apostle of the Gentiles laid before the pillars of Jewish Christianity a statement of the gospel which he preached, that they declared themselves satisfied, demanded no modifications whatever in his doctrine, and gave him 'the right hands of fellowship' as an Apostle of the true faith (Gal 2 [1-10]). In accordance with this, St. Paul uniformly assumes that his own gospel and that of the Twelve is identical (see, e.g., 1 Cor 15 [11], 'Therefore whether it were I or they, so we preach, and so ye believed'), which he could not have done unless there had been agreement upon the crucial doctrine of Christ's person, and His relationship to God and man.

But we have still more definite evidence than this. The leader of the Twelve has left an Epistle, which was unquestioned in the early Church, and which is supported by testimonies so numerous and so ancient, that to reject it is most hazardous. From Clement of Rome (95 A.D.), Polycarp (110 A.D.), and Papias (130 A.D.), a long line of definite and coherent testimony establishes the antiquity and authority of the First Epistle of Peter. This document presents a view of the person of Christ in essential agreement with that of St. Paul. According to this Epistle, Christ existed before His nativity, for it was He who inspired the Old Testament prophets (1 [11]). His death has a supernatural efficacy, being an atoning sacrifice, which procured for mankind the remission of sins (1 [2, 8] 2 [21, 24] 3 [16]). He is now at God's right hand, invested with supreme authority over the universe, so that even the angels obey Him (3 [22]). He will come again to judge the world ($1^{7,13}$ $4^{5,12}$ 5^3). He is the centre of Christian love and devotion (1^8). He is the one Mediator through whom the Father can be approached in worship and prayer (2^5 4^{11}). He is mystically united to His people, and present in their hearts ($3^{15,16}$ $5^{10,14}$). Salvation is given through Him, and through faith in Him (1^9 5^{10}). The absolute Divinity of Christ is especially apparent in 1^{11}, where the Holy Ghost who inspired the ancient prophets, is declared to be the Spirit of Christ. Less certain is the doxology (4^{11}), which, though it probably refers to Christ, may perhaps refer to the Father. It is clear, therefore, that St. Peter's doctrine of the person of Christ closely resembles that of St. Paul, and that not only in the Gentile, but also in the Hebrew Churches a very high conception of Christ's person was taught. Such other evidence as we have points in the same direction. The strongly attested, and in ancient times undisputed, First Epistle of John regards Christ as existing with the Father before His Incarnation as His 'Logos,' or 'Word,' and sharing His eternal divine life ($1^{1,2}$), as manifested in the flesh to destroy the works of the devil, to take away sin, and to give eternal life to men (1^2 3^5 4^2 3^8), as atoning by His death for the sins of the whole world, and by His blood cleansing the soul from sin (1^7 2^2, etc.), and as so inseparably one with the Father, that both are equally the objects of saving faith (2^{23-25}, etc.). The disputed, but very ancient and probably genuine Epistle of James, coördinates Christ with God quite in the manner of St. Paul (1^1), calls Him 'the Lord of glory' (2^1), a title suggestive of superhuman dignity and power, and looks for His Second Coming to Judgment ($2^{8,9}$). The Epistle to the Hebrews, which, though not by an Apostle, was written by a disciple of the Apostles, regards Christ as eternal (1^{12} 13^8), as the agent of the Father in creation ($1^{2,10}$), as the sustainer of the universe (1^3), as the superior of the angels and the object of their worship (1^{4-6}). The early speeches of St. Peter in Acts, recorded by a companion of St. Paul, represent Christ as 'Lord of all,' i.e. of the whole universe (10^{36}), as the Dispenser of the Holy Spirit (2^{32}), as the Prince or Author of life (3^{15}), as the sole Mediator between God and men, and only giver of salvation (4^2), as sinless (3^4 7^{52}), and as the future judge of quick and dead (10^{42}). Already at this early period Christ was invoked in prayer by the Church of Jerusalem (Ac 7^{59}, probably also 1^{24}), and Christians were described as those 'who call upon the Name' of Jesus (9^{14}).

(2) *Christ taught His own divine Sonship.* The prevalence of such a type of teaching in the Apostolic Church renders it certain that Jesus must have claimed for Himself a far higher place in the system of religion which He came to found, than has been claimed by the founders of other religions. Whereas such teachers as Gautama, Mahomet, and Confucius have claimed faith in their doctrines, not in their persons, Jesus evidently claimed faith in His person, and submission to His authority, of an altogether unique kind. Our direct knowledge of the teaching of Jesus is almost confined to the Four Gospels. Of these the Second is universally recognised to be based upon the reminiscences of St. Peter, the First to have behind it (at least in its reports of our Lord's discourses) the authority of St. Matthew, and the Third to have been compiled by a companion of St. Paul from authentic sources. As to the Fourth Gospel there is less agreement among critics. Its direct authorship by St. John is strongly maintained in this Commentary in accordance with the prevailing opinion among English scholars, but as there is less agreement upon the point among German critics, and we wish to reach absolutely unquestionable results, we shall only use its testimony in this article to corroborate the statements made by other authorities.

St. Mark's Gospel contains hardly any of our Lord's discourses, and therefore very little that bears directly upon our present enquiry. Nevertheless, it is clear even from this Gospel that Jesus claimed superhuman dignity. He was put to death as a blasphemer for claiming to be not merely the Messiah, but the Son of God, and prophesying His future session at God's right hand, and Second Coming to Judgment (Mk 14^{62}). To His death He attributed a significance unintelligible on the assumption that He was a mere human being. His death, He taught, was 'a ransom for many (10^{45}), a propitiation for sin, and the establishment of a new covenant between God and man (14^{24}). Even while admitting His ignorance as man of the day and hour of His Second Coming, He assigned to Himself a position in the scale of being above the angels, and second only to that of the Supreme Father Himself ('But of that day or that hour knoweth no one, not even the angels in heaven, neither the Son, but the Father,' 13^{32}, where notice the absolute use of the title 'the Son' as in the Fourth Gospel).

St. Mark's evidence is confirmed by the more copious evidence of the discourses of Jesus, recorded in the First and Third Gospels. Here we find Jesus demanding unlimited faith in His own Person—a faith so intense, and a devotion so consuming, that none but God can rightly claim it (Lk 14^{26} Mt $10^{14,15,32,33,37,40}$ 11^{28}). He speaks with an authority higher than that of a prophet ; by His own authority revising the Mosaic Law, even the sacred words spoken by God Himself on Sinai (Mt 5 21f.). Specially insistent is His claim to be the future judge of the world. It is found even in the Sermon on the Mount, which is sometimes stated to be a purely ethical discourse (Mt 7 22, 23), and again and again in the discourses which follow (Mt 16 27 Lk 12 8, 40 Mt 25 31). It often occurs in the parables, the most characteristic of the utterances of Jesus, and the least capable of alteration or perversion, e.g. in the parable of the Tares ('Let both grow together until the harvest, and in the time of harvest *I* will say to the reapers, Gather ye together first the tares, and bind them in bundles to burn them : but gather the wheat into my barn. . . So shall it be in the end of the world. The Son of man shall send forth His angels. and they shall gather out of His kingdom all things that cause stumbling and them that do iniquity, and shall cast them into the furnace of fire ; there shall be the weeping and gnashing of teeth,' Mt 13 30, 40-42); also in the parable of the Ten Virgins, where it is undoubtedly Christ Himself who pronounces the sentence of exclusion (Mt 25 12), and in the parable which follows it, where Christ is represented as going into a far country, and then returning and recompensing His servants according to their behaviour during His absence (Mt 25 14f.; cp. Lk 19 12f.). More striking still is the description of the Last Judgment (Mt 25 31f.), where the Son of man sits on the throne of His glory, summons all nations into His awful presence, separates the good from the wicked as a shepherd divideth his sheep from the goats, and says to the former, ' Come, ye blessed of My Father, inherit the kingdom prepared for you from the foundation of the world,' and to the latter, ' Depart from me, ye cursed, into the eternal fire which is prepared for the devil and his angels.'

Specially instructive, as illustrating the sense in which Jesus called Himself the Son of God, is Mt 11 27 = Lk 10 22, ' All things have been delivered unto Me of My Father ; and no one knoweth the Son save the Father ; neither doth any know the Father save the Son, and he to whomsoever the Son willeth to reveal Him.' In this passage, which is admitted on all hands to belong to the original ' Logia' of St. Matthew, the point of greatest significance is neither the omnipotence granted to the Son, nor the fact that He alone knows the Father, but the remarkable statement that the nature of the Son is so transcendent, that it is apprehended by the Father alone. Is it not clear that a Being so exalted that He shares the Father's omnipotence, and is incapable of being understood by any but Him is no creature, but is the Father's *alter ego*, His consubstantial Son, and the sharer of His throne and attributes ?

The divinity of Christ is so clearly the doctrine of the Synoptic Gospels that there is no need to adduce in its support the evidence of the baptismal formula (Mt 28 19). The testimony for and against the genuineness of that formula has been given with considerable fulness in the Commentary, and it has been shown that the balance of evidence is decidedly in its favour ; but whether it is original or whether it is a later addition, the doctrine which it represents, the essential divinity of the Founder of Christianity, is certainly original, and forms an important part of the teaching of Christ Himself in the oldest strata of our oldest authorities. It is certainly not the fact, as is sometimes asserted, that the doctrine of Christ's divinity is a later addition to the simplicity of the primitive Gospel.

5. Further evidence for Christ's Deity. We have shown that the doctrine of the Incarnation is in full harmony with what we know of the divine nature and of human nature, and is therefore reasonable. We have also shown that the New Testament teaches this doctrine, affirming that the Founder of Christianity, Jesus Christ, is both God and man. We shall conclude with a few plain reasons for accepting this belief, reminding the reader that a full discussion would require a treatise, not a short article like the present.

(1) *Christ's sinlessness.* If Jesus Christ was really God, His life must have been one of absolute holiness and beneficence. And this was really the case. His goodness is shown in part by the excellence of His moral and religious teaching, which is not derived from other teachers, but is stamped with the impress of His own beautiful personality. The best rationalist opinion confesses this. Keim speaks of ' the complete domination' in His life, ' of the idea of moral good,' and adds, ' The life of Jesus, both in public and private, was in an eminent degree holy and pure, and allows us as such to infer a previous unsullied youth striving towards the noble and the exalted. The small defects that have been detected are no sins . . and vanish like a drop in the ocean of brilliant and superhuman achievement... We are still able to retain the strong and joyful conviction that it was Virtue herself who trod the earth in Him, and that the dolorous confession made by antiquity of the impossibility of sinlessness and of the non-existence of the ideal of virtue and wisdom found in Him its refutation and its end.' Similarly Strauss says : ' This intuition of a God good to all [as expressed in the Sermon on the Mount] Jesus could only have drawn out of His own being ; it could only have emanated out of that universal benevolence which was the fundamental characteristic of His own nature, and by which He felt

Himself in perfect harmony with God. . . The dominant feature of His character was that love which embraces all creatures, and He makes of that the fundamental characteristic of the Divine Essence.'

The goodness of Jesus is affirmed in the strongest language by those who have the best right to pronounce upon it—those, namely, who for nearly three years were brought into the closest daily contact with Him. Thus St. Peter represents Him as absolutely sinless : 'A lamb without blemish and without spot' (1 Pet 1 19) ; 'who did no sin, neither was guile found in His mouth : who, when He was reviled, reviled not again' (1 Pet 2 22, 23) ; 'Christ also suffered for sins once, the righteous for the unrighteous, that He might bring us to God' (1 Pet 3 18) ; with which we may compare St. Peter's confession (Jn 6 69 RV), 'We have believed and know that Thou art the Holy One of God.'

St. John, the bosom friend of Jesus, who knew Him even more intimately than St. Peter, speaks of Him as sinless : 'Jesus Christ the righteous' (1 Jn 2 1) ; 'If ye know that He is righteous, ye know that every one also that doeth righteousness is begotten of Him' (1 Jn 2 29) ; 'We know that He was manifested to take away sins ; and in Him is no sin' (1 Jn 3 5).

Even the traitor Judas recognised the goodness of Jesus, for 'he repented himself,' and said, 'I have sinned in that I have betrayed the innocent blood' (Mt 27 3, 4).

The goodness of Jesus is also affirmed by those who were in no way connected with Him : by Pilate ('I am innocent of the blood of this just person,' Mt 27 24 ; 'Why, what evil hath He done ?' Mk 15 14 ; 'I find no fault in this man,' Lk 23 4, 14, 22 Jn 18 38 19 4, 6, 12) ; by Pilate's wife ('Have thou nothing to do with that just man,' Mt 27 19) ; by one of the thieves ('This man hath done nothing amiss,' Lk 23 41); by the centurion ('Certainly this man was righteous,' Lk 23 47).

Specially to be noted in this connexion is the fact that Jesus was without that consciousness of sin which exists in the holiest of men in proportion to their holiness. This is a point of deep significance. The general opinion of mankind has pronounced sinlessness impossible. Demosthenes attributed it to the gods alone. Cicero had never found or heard of a perfectly wise man. Mahomet expressly disclaimed sinlessness, and recorded in the Koran God's command to him, 'Pray for the forgiveness of thy sins.' Gautama is not represented as having been sinless from the first, but as gradually attaining it. Socrates detected in his evil heart the germs of all the vices. Moses was guilty of serious sin (Ex 2 12). 'Isaiah was a man of unclean lips' (Isa 6 5).

Elijah confessed, 'I am not better than my fathers' (1 K 19 4). St. Peter wept tears of penitence (Mk 14 72). St. Paul confessed himself the chief of sinners (1 Tim 1 15). St. John, one of the most blameless of all the New Testament characters, says, 'If we say that we have no sin, we deceive ourselves, and the truth is not in us ; but if we confess our sins, He is faithful and just to forgive us our sins, and to cleanse us from all unrighteousness. If we say that we have not sinned, we make Him a liar' (1 Jn 1 8). Jesus, on the other hand, never recognised in Himself the least moral blemish (for Mk 10 17, see the Commentary). The most explicit statements of His sinlessness are found in the Fourth Gospel (Jn 8 46 14 30 8 29 10 11 17 4), but the synoptic evidence is really as strong. The claim to be the personified Moral Law of the human race, and in particular to be not one of the subjects of judgment but the Judge, implies sinlessness. So does His claim that His death is a propitiatory sacrifice for the sins of the whole world (Mk 10 45). Quite decisive also is the passage (Mt 11 28) where, after declaring that 'no man knoweth the Father, save the Son,' He says, 'Come unto Me, all ye that labour and are heavy laden, and I will give you rest. Take my yoke upon you and learn of Me ; for I am meek and lowly in heart : and ye shall find rest unto your souls.' An invitation like this could never have been addressed, without extreme arrogance and impiety, by a sinner to fellow-sinners.

We have, therefore, in Jesus the absolutely unique case of a man of unexampled holiness, and yet without any consciousness of sin. This harmonises well with, and indeed suggests the belief, that the personality of Jesus was not merely human, but superhuman.

(2) *Christ's miracles.* From human nature we expect works of human capacity, from superhuman nature works of superhuman capacity. A natural Christ may, perhaps, afford to dispense with miracles. A supernatural Christ cannot. From a supernatural Christ supernatural works are imperatively and rightly demanded, and, if they are not forthcoming, sober reason will be inclined to conclude that the 'supernatural' Christ is not supernatural. Now the ministry of Christ is simply full of mighty works which exceed human capacity, and can only be regarded as miracles. The credibility of these miracles is discussed in a special article, to which the reader is referred ; all that we have here to do is to point out their bearing upon the doctrine of Christ's person. Every unprejudiced mind which has come to the conclusion that they are true will surely admit, (1) that they harmonise with and confirm the view that Christ's personality was superhuman : and

(2) that they must be regarded as setting the stamp of divine approval upon the teaching of Jesus, part of which was, as we have shown, His Divine Sonship. This is particularly the case with regard to the Resurrection. Jesus was put to death as a blasphemer, because He reaffirmed at His trial His claim to be the Son of God. God the Father, by raising Him from the dead, proclaimed to the world that this claim was true. St. Paul, therefore, is perfectly justified in saying that Jesus was ' declared to be the Son of God with power, according to the spirit of holiness, by the resurrection of the dead ' (Ro 1⁴) : see art. ' The Resurrection.'

(3) *Christ's influence upon the world.* The moral and spiritual influence of Jesus Christ upon the world during the last two millenniums has been so exceedingly great as to harmonise thoroughly with the view that He was a divine person. ' It is needless,' says a judicious writer, ' to attempt to prove that the supreme attractiveness of the Person of the Founder of Christianity has imparted to the Church the whole of its vitality. To this fact all history bears witness. Nor is its testimony less certain that of all the influences that have been exerted in this earth, that of Jesus has been the most potent. Enumerate all the great men who have ever existed, whether kings, conquerors, statesmen, patriots, poets, philosophers, or men of science, and their influence for good will be found to have been as nothing compared with that which has been exerted by Jesus Christ. . . He who was in outward form a Galilean peasant, who died a malefactor's death, has founded a spiritual empire which has endured for eighteen centuries of time, and which, despite the vaticinations of unbelievers, shows no signs of decrepitude. Commencing with the smallest beginnings, His empire now embraces all the progressive races of men. Those by whom it has not been accepted are in a state of stagnation and decay. It is the only one which is adapted to every state of civilisation.

' It differs from all other states and communities in that it is founded neither on force nor on self-interest, but on persuasion and the supreme attractiveness of the character of its Founder... History affirms that Jesus has not only been a great man among great men, or even the greatest of them, but that He stands at an immeasurable height above them. He is the one only catholic man, the one ideal of humanity, for whose presence in and action on history none of the known forces that energise in the moral and spiritual worlds can account. What is the necessary inference from this ? I answer that, as those forces which have energised in man from the day of his appearance on this earth have failed to produce His fellow, we must be in the presence of a moral miracle.'

(4) *The argument from Christian experience.* The argument which looks weakest upon paper, but which is really in many ways the strongest, is the argument from the experience of believers. What keeps people Christian, and adds to the number of Christ's adherents, is the fact that He really does give to His followers that joy, and peace, and blissful communion with God, and victory over the powers of evil, which He declared that He would. Those who come to Jesus in faith do not find Him wanting. They receive from Him spiritual life and vital power. Their characters are gradually transformed, and they become capable of acts of heroism and exalted virtue, which without Christ they could not possibly perform. Their souls are filled with serenity and peace beyond human understanding, which not even the fiercest storms of life can seriously disturb. Labouring and heavy laden they go to their Lord, and in Him find rest unto their souls.

(5) *The great dilemma.* We have been led to the conclusion that the Founder of Christianity, who is revered not only by Christians but also by most Freethinkers as the best of men, and the greatest of religious and moral reformers, claimed to be divine. This conclusion is supported by such varied and convergent evidence, that real doubt upon the subject is precluded. We are therefore brought face to face with a very serious dilemma : either the Author of Christianity was divine, or He was not good (*aut Deus aut homo non bonus*). Of attempts to evade this dilemma the following are the chief. (*a*) It has been maintained that Jesus was insane. We reply that it is strictly impossible that a system of religion and morality which has commended itself to the intellect and conscience of the highest races of the earth can have been originated by a madman. (*b*) It has been maintained that Jesus believed Himself to be divine, not because He had any internal knowledge of the fact, but because He interpreted the Old Testament prophecies, especially those of Daniel, as indicating that the Messiah would be a Divine Person. We reply that no mere man who interpreted the prophecies in this way, could (unless he was insane) possibly imagine Himself to be the Messiah.

The dilemma, then, cannot be evaded. Either Christ was divine, as He claimed to be, or He was a deceiver. A deceiver He cannot have been, because He founded the purest system of religion and morals that has ever been presented to the world. He must, therefore, have been divine, as the Apostles themselves, and the Church ever since their day, have believed.

The notes on Lk 2⁴⁰ Mk 13³² and Phil 2⁷ should be consulted.

THE TRINITY

ALTHOUGH the exact theological definition of the doctrine of the Trinity was the result of a long process of development, which was not complete till the fifth century or even later, the doctrine itself underlies the whole New Testament, which everywhere attributes divinity to the Father, the Son, and the Spirit, and assigns to them distinct functions in the economy of human redemption. The New Testament mainly contemplates the relations of the Divine Persons to man and the universe, regarding the Father as Creator, the Son as Mediator and Redeemer, and the Spirit as Sanctifier (the 'economic' Trinity); but hints are not wanting that this threefold function in creation and redemption is an outward manifestation of certain inward and eternal distinctions in the Godhead Itself (the 'essential' Trinity). In the early Church the Monarchians, and especially the Sabellians, laid such exclusive stress upon the 'economic' Trinity, that they denied that there are any real distinctions in the Godhead at all, and taught that Father, Son, and Spirit are only three different modes in which the One Personal God reveals Himself and acts upon man. The main current of Christian thought, however, has always held firmly to the belief that the terms Father, Son, and Holy Spirit represent eternal and necessary distinctions, and those of a personal and ethical as well as of a merely metaphysical kind, within the Divine Substance. Christians have seen in the doctrine of the Trinity not only an intellectual, but also a moral and spiritual revelation of the highest importance.

1. **Personality Human and Divine.** Theism regards God as personal, and Christianity as tri-personal, but the term 'person,' as applied to God and to the 'Persons' in God, is not used in quite the same sense as that in which it is used of human beings. The first distinction is that human personality is finite, and Divine Personality infinite. This constitutes so enormous a difference, that some thinkers deny that God can be conceived of as personal. Personality, they say, is essentially finite; it is a definite thing marked off and distinguished by certain boundaries from other things, and if those boundaries are removed, personality ceases to be. Moreover, they maintain, even if personality could be predicated without contradiction of God, it is of the nature of a limitation or imperfection, and therefore could not be appropriately attributed to a Perfect Being.

We reply that though limitation characterises the imperfect personality of man, it is no part of the essential idea of personality. When a being is spoken of as 'personal,' it is meant among other things less important (1) that he is intelligent, (2) that he is self-conscious, (3) that he possesses will. Now not one of these qualities implies, of itself, any limitation or imperfection. It is as easy to conceive a perfect intelligence, knowing all actual and possible things, as to conceive a limited intelligence like man's. Intelligence, therefore, in a perfect and infinite degree can be legitimately predicated of God. Self-consciousness, again, is implied in perfect intelligence; for if a perfectly intelligent Being did not know Himself, His intelligence would be limited. Will, in like manner, is capable of real perfection; it does not necessarily imply any limitation of nature. It is as easy to conceive of a Will absolutely free and infinitely powerful, as to conceive of a limited will like man's. It is perfectly legitimate, therefore, to say that God possesses a Will adequate to His Intelligence—that is, that He is able to achieve all that is possible. Personality, therefore, being potentially infinite, can be ascribed, not only without contradiction, but with propriety and truth, as the least inadequate term known to us, to the Infinite and Absolute God.

The second distinction is that, whereas human personality stands outside and excludes every personality except its own, the Divine Persons of the Trinity mutually pervade, interpenetrate, include, and contain one another. This wonderful quality (technically known as *perichorēsis, circumincessio,* or *circuminsessio*) cannot be distinctly conceived of by us from lack of any analogous experience among human persons. Perhaps the best way of gaining some faint glimpse of what it means, is to start with the idea of human sympathy, and to imagine it infinitely deepened and extended. If it were possible in the case of two friends, for the one not only to know the thought or feeling or resolution present in the mind of the other, but also to feel it in his own mind as his own thought or feeling or resolution, we should have a human analogy, real though extremely inadequate, of the far closer and more exalted union and communion which subsist among the Divine Persons.

2. **The Trinity and the Divine Self-Consciousness.** In man self-consciousness only arises when the self distinguishes itself from

h

the not-self, i.e. when the thinking subject has present to its consciousness some object of thought distinct from itself.

Now the doctrine of the Trinity indicates that what is true of man is true also of God. From eternity the Father and the Son were personally distinct beings, knowing one another and themselves as such, and consequently for the Trinitarian there is no difficulty in understanding how God was self-conscious even before the world was created, i.e. before there was any created not-self from which He could distinguish Himself.

3. The Trinity and God's Moral Perfection. Since Christ taught the supremacy of love and the duty of universal benevolence, it has come to be felt and acknowledged with increasing clearness, that love is the most beautiful of human virtues, and the most adorable of the Divine Perfections. But perfect love is only possible between equals. Just as a man cannot satisfy or realise his powers of love by loving the lower animals, so God cannot satisfy or realise His love by loving man or any creature. If God is truly Love, in the full sense of that term, He must have always possessed some equal object of His love, some *alter ego*, or, to use the language of Christian theology, a consubstantial, co-eternal, and co-equal Son.

4. The Trinity and Social Life. An ideally perfect life is a social life. A life lived in the exercise of friendship, social intercourse, and benevolence, is a far higher life than that of a recluse, who seeks to attain perfection in solitude. If, therefore, the life of the Godhead is as perfect as can be conceived, it must be a *social life*—that is to say, there must exist within the Divine Unity a plurality of Persons, among whom the most perfect fellowship exists. This conception of the Godhead as a Perfect Society, characteristic of Trinitarianism, is ethically more fruitful, and practically more stimulating than that of Unitarianism, which regards God as an isolated Person, incapable of social life, or of any real love but self-love. The Trinitarian, and the Trinitarian alone, is able to discern perfect love realised in his object of worship, and to recognise in the essential Nature of the Godhead, the perfect pattern of the Family, of the Church and of the State.

5. The New Testament Doctrine. The leading Trinitarian texts in the New Testament are discussed in the Commentary. Reference should be made to Mt 3[13f]. 28[19] Lk 1[35] Jn 14, 15, 16 (especially 14[16] 15[26] 16[13-15]), 1 Cor 12[3-6] 2 Cor 13[13] 1 Pet 1[1,2] (1 Jn 5[7]). For the Deity of the Son, see art. 'Person of Jesus Christ.' For the Deity and Personality of the Holy Ghost, see also Jn 14[16-26] 15[26] 16[7] 20[22] Ac 2[33] Ro 8[26] Gal 4[6].

MIRACLE

1. Introductory. The attitude of the opponents of supernatural religion towards Miracle has changed very considerably during the last two centuries. The old frontal assault of the Deists, routed by men like Butler and Paley with weapons that are now largely out of date, has been succeeded by flank attacks, (1) from the direction of historical and literary criticism, and (2) from that of a more modern natural science. First a vigorous attempt was made by the celebrated Tübingen school of critics to discredit the documentary evidence, and the New Testament passed through a severe fire of criticism from which it issued stronger than ever. The old traditional and uncritical views, though modified at points, were in general deliberately and distinctly confirmed. As a result of this fierce attack the relation of the documents to the traditional Christian faith remains unaltered, and their unique value as historical evidence of the first importance has been established on a new basis. Criticism of a more or less hostile tendency and of a progressively searching character still continues, and from time to time throws important light on some aspect of the problems concerned. But the trustworthy character of the New Testament documents as a whole may be regarded as established permanently, on firmer ground than ever before.

After the New Testament, the Old. We are all familiar with the recent controversies raised by what is called 'the Higher Criticism'; and we may readily admit that it has modified very considerably our views of the external history and development of the documents in question. It has not, however, shaken our belief in inspiration, nor impaired the value of the Old Testament writings as the record of the earlier stages of God's progressive revelation to mankind. On the contrary, we may thankfully admit that the assured results of criticism, as distinct from its unverifiable speculations, have made clearer the stages of that revelation, and have given back to us the human aspect of the Bible without taking away the divine.

We shall be justified, then, in approaching our subject in the simplest and most straightforward way, taking for granted the general trustworthiness of the documents, though ready, as we go along, to deal with any special points that may come up before us.

If the Bible really contains, as we believe, the record of God's revelation of Himself to men, we should expect it, while clearly in touch with every-day human life, to abound in traces of its special origin and purpose. We should expect it to offer us frequent glimpses of a higher order of things, beyond the range of our ordinary perception—to exhibit, in fact, a miraculous element.

And such, indeed, is the case. The purpose of this article is to emphasise and illustrate this fact: to show that the Miraculous is too closely interwoven into the texture of the Bible to be removable; then to consider the cause and purpose of its presence there, and its place as an integral and essential part of Revelation. Thus we may find ourselves in a position to meet the objections that are often urged against the possibility of Miracle, on the ground that it contradicts the scientific principle of Natural Law. A general treatment alone will be possible here. For further suggestions the reader is referred to the notes on the various passages in which the most important miracles are recorded.

2. Miracle inseparable from the Bible. When we assert that Miracle is an integral part of the Bible we mean that the miraculous considered generally—whatever may be thought of particular instances—is too closely interwoven into the texture of the Bible to be removable without destroying the character of the records.

The consideration of the claims of individual miracles is quite another question. We are not compelled to put all miracles on the same footing, either as regards their importance or as regards their attestation. We may be willing to admit that the evidence for the different events recorded in the Bible, or the evidence that such and such recorded events were miraculous, varies considerably.

For instance, the external attestation of our Lord's Resurrection is stronger than that available for any other of the biblical miracles, or indeed for any other event of ancient history. On the other hand, the documentary evidence for His Virgin birth is less strong, though it has the combined and (in general) harmonious witness of two obviously independent narratives, and receives full corroboration from the otherwise unaccountable difference between His recorded life and character and that of any other human being. In the case of the Old Testament the external evidence is, throughout, naturally less abundant. But here also we find varying degrees of attestation. That an exodus from Egypt, in some sense miraculous, took place in the time of Moses, is a fact which—as the many and varied references testify—has stamped itself too clearly upon the Hebrew consciousness to be seriously questioned, save by those who deny the miraculous altogether, and even they would probably admit a basis of historic fact. But the miracle of the 'sun standing still,' as popularly understood, is scarcely referred to again in the canonical books, and the poetical setting of the passage puts the problem of the actual miracle on an entirely different footing from the fact of the battle in which the miracle is thought to have occurred : see note on Josh 10 12. Similarly, it has been suggested (and the context gives some colour to the idea) that the incident of the ass speaking occurs in a dream of Balaam's, after which he arose and 'went with the princes of Balak' (Nu 22 35). Again, the story of Jonah is by many regarded as an allegory of God's dealings with the Jewish Church, of which it certainly supplies a fruitful parable. Individual miracles, then, may be treated each on its own merits according to the evidence available. The question before us is a wider one.

Can the miraculous element as a whole be regarded as an accidental or non-essential adjunct to the Bible ? Can the miracles be explained away altogether or one by one, or is there an 'irreducible minimum' which refuses to be explained away ?

Now there are two ways in which an attempt may be made to explain away miracles altogether. (1) By the first, they are regarded as the result of a superstitious tendency to 'supernaturalise' distant events ; (2) by the second, as the outcome of an unscientific tendency to regard as miraculous all that contemporary knowledge cannot explain. We do not deny that each of these explanations may possibly be applicable to some of the more obscure events usually regarded as miraculous, but we do deny emphatically that they have any general application to the miracles of the Bible.

(1) If the first argument were sound, we should expect to find the miraculous element concentrated in, if not confined to, the earlier portions of Revelation, so as to give the impression that the idea of miracle belongs to the dawn of Hebrew thought. But this is far from being the case. Miracle is not found exclusively or chiefly in the earlier or more obscure portions of the Old Testament, nor is it confined within the limits of the Old Testament, but occupies a like or even a more important place in the New. And in particular the miraculous is so intricately interwoven into the life of Christ that the attempt

to disentangle it from the Gospels necessitates such a grievous mutilation of the records as would change their entire character. If the Gospel material be reduced to the comparatively small residuum of matter which is common to all three synoptists, Miracle would still be there ; and, indeed, the Gospels denuded of the supernatural would be as inexplicable as the long discourse in the sixth chapter of St. John would be if deprived of the miracle of the ' Five Thousand ' which forms, as it were, its text. If the point of view of the writers themselves and their contemporaries counts for anything, we cannot fail to observe that the first preachers of the gospel boldly staked the truth of Christianity on the fact that Christ was risen, and regarded themselves in a special sense as ' witnesses of the Resurrection ' (an essential qualification for apostleship, as in the case of Matthias : see Ac 1 22 and cp. 2 32 3 15 4 20, 33, etc.). While St. Paul, in whose life and teaching the Resurrection plays a supremely important part—as he himself testifies, according to the narrative of the Acts, at Antioch, Thessalonica, and Athens, and before the Sanhedrin, Felix, Festus, and Agrippa—adduces, in an important argument on this subject addressed to the alert and critical Corinthians, more than five hundred witnesses for the fact of the miracle (1 Cor 15 6).

Taking the Bible, then, as it stands, it may be confidently stated that the miraculous element is as strong (or stronger) in the later portions as in the earlier. But the question is complicated by the date of the documents. Are not the miracles, it may be asked, concentrated in those documents, whether earlier or later in the Bible series, which may be supposed to have been written at the furthest distance of time from the events which they record ?

It would be easy to show, did space permit, that, even on the hypotheses adopted by the majority of modern 'Higher Critics,' this is not the case. In the Old Testament, e.g., the record of the Mosaic miracles does not come down to us wholly or mainly through the group of documents called by the critics the 'Priestly Traditions '; the older 'Prophetic Narratives' supply a full account of the Flood, Egyptian Plagues, Crossing of the Red Sea, and many more. The miracles of the Kingdom period, again, are not confined to the book of Chronicles, which is rightly regarded as much later, in its present form, than the book of Kings ; on the contrary, the most striking and significant instances occur in one of the undoubtedly oldest sections of the latter book—in the narrative of Elijah and Elisha.

As regards the New Testament, the case is even stronger, for it is at least far from improbable that the last of its books was written before the first century of the New era was well passed, while the earliest (1 Th) may be confidently dated at no more than twenty-five years after the Crucifixion.

And so, whether we consider the narratives in their biblical order, or regard them in relation to the nearest ascertainable date of the documents which record them, we find that in neither way is the view supported which would regard Miracle as the outcome of that superstitious tendency which leads a later age to magnify far distant events—especially events connected with crises in the national history—and endue them with a supernatural colouring.

So far from the supernatural being confined to those documents which originated at a period furthest distant from the events they record, the most stupendous miracle of all, and the most important, viz. Christ's Resurrection, is attested by evidence which may, without any straining of language, be called contemporaneous.

(2) We now have to face the second objection. Admitting that the events occurred, and occurred to a large extent in the manner recorded, may not the supernatural interpretation of them be questioned? Even the descriptions of contemporaries or eye-witnesses are sure to take colour from the age in which they originate. Must we not take into consideration the absence of scientific knowledge of nature's laws characteristic of early ages, and especially the unscientific character of the Hebrew mind—its notorious tendency to ignore secondary causes, and find the immediate working of the finger of God in all events alike? May it not be true that events described in the Old Testament as involving the direct interposition of the Almighty might, with the fuller knowledge of a later and more scientific generation, be traced to the working out of natural forces, and be characterised, not as miracles, but as unusually striking coincidences? May not, e.g., the drying up of the Red Sea and of Jordan be explained as due to the combined action of known natural forces, acting only more powerfully than has otherwise been observed? Have we not, in many at least of the Egyptian plagues, rather an emphasising of phenomena already common in Egypt, than an entirely new experience? Do not the majestic accompaniments of the lawgiving at Sinai recall the associations of a volcanic eruption, or a more than ordinarily lengthy and terrific electric disturbance? Or again, to tread on still more sacred ground, may not many of Christ's miracles of healing, whether in cases of demoniacal possession or otherwise, be explained as exhibiting an unusually intense form of that many-sided influence of mind over both mind and matter with which modern mental science has made us familiar?

In attempting to meet this form of objection, we shall, as in the former case, be ready to admit the possibility that it may apply in some cases. Let each be judged, as far as possible, on its own merits, when the principle has been allowed. We shall maintain, however, two positions: first, that the objection does not cover the whole ground, and, secondly, that it misconceives what we mean by Miracle.

(a) It does not cover the whole ground. So far, at any rate, as science has yet gone, many of the miracles, and some of them among the most strongly attested, remain outside its range. There is an irreducible minimum which is not amenable to such explanation. It will be sufficient to take the New Testament. Here we find that, while many of Christ's miracles of healing find some sort of analogy in modern scientific treatment of hysteria and the like—and may thus be possibly regarded as miraculous rather in their inexplicable anticipation of the results of later human progress, than in anything else—many also are admitted by medical experts to involve, if true, such organic changes in the patient as cannot be accounted for by reference to any power of mind over matter known to modern science. Further, there are the miracles wrought upon Nature, e.g. the turning of the water into wine, the feeding of the 4,000 and 5,000, the stilling of the storm, the walking on the sea, which physical science confessedly cannot as yet explain; and above all, there is the central miracle of the Resurrection so uniquely attested.

(b) It is a misconception of the meaning of Miracle as we understand it, to suppose that the defender of the miraculous is concerned to prove a contradiction of Law as such, or to minimise or exclude the operation, in these cases, of secondary causes. He does not argue in favour of a contradiction of Law, for according to his own belief the Author of miracles is also the Author of Nature and its laws. Neither does he hold a brief against secondary causes. If there be such a thing as Miracle, working definite effects upon the external world, then it will be true of miraculous as of non-miraculous events that they are capable, in their measure, of scientific description.

The physical condition, e.g., of Naaman, or of the blind man healed by Christ at Bethsaida (Mk 8 22-26) would have been capable, no doubt, of medical diagnosis at any stage of the cure. The only factor which would remain outside the range of medical science would be the force that originated the series of reactions which resulted in physical soundness.

Again, to take an instance of a rather different kind. The miracle of the stoppage of

Jordan's waters (see on Josh 3 16) is curiously paralleled by an Arabic narrative of the middle ages, which records a similar stoppage in the same river, and accounts for it as the result of a damming up of the stream by an extensive landslip higher up. It is at least possible that a scientific account of the great event recorded in the book of Joshua would trace it to secondary causes of a similar kind. What physical science could not do would be to explain Joshua's foreknowledge of this very remarkable natural phenomenon, and its co-incidence with the needs and purposes of the Israelite army.

Many other miracles of the Old Testament may be similarly treated and with a similar result. We may strip them of much of their 'portentous' clothing—of that which our present habit of thought is inclined to regard as crude and arbitrary. We may explain this as the outcome of a mode of speech, graphic, figurative, poetical, insulted by translation into the prose of hard fact. We may make full allowance for the imaginative tendency of the Oriental mind : its pictorial and dramatic genius. But we shall not even so get rid of the miraculous. The miracles are not miracles merely or chiefly because of their intrinsic character. Their claim to be miraculous lies rather in the moment of their occurrence, and its obvious relation to the necessities and proprieties of the great scheme in which they are set, and in the fact that, in so many cases, they could be predicted. And the belief that they involved the personal interposition of the Deity for a definite purpose, is not shaken in the least by the consideration that the Author of Nature may have chosen to interpose by the employment of those natural forces through which He normally works.

3. Miracle essential to the Biblical Revelation. So far we have seen that miracle is practically inseparable from the Bible ; that the miraculous element in Holy Scripture cannot be explained away as being simply a superstitious and unscientific interpretation of events which a later age could have explained satisfactorily on a basis of physical science. And in the course of our enquiry we have seen hints at least that there is some reason for this stubborn and unremovable presence of the miraculous.

If we can make clear to ourselves what is the place of Miracle in the Bible, and what is its relation to Revelation, we may also go far towards finding an answer to the further problems that arise in connexion with the relation of Miracle to Natural Law.

In theology and biblical exegesis there has been a change of ideas corresponding in some degree to that which has marked the last century in the matter of physical science.

The old mechanical conception of the universe which finds expression in Milton's description of creation, has given place to an *organic* conception. The world, we say now, is less fitly symbolised by Paley's 'Watch' than by a living organism—growing, developing, progressively fulfilling the law of its being, and in consequence witnessing more rather than less convincingly to the divine wisdom and power and purpose of its Originator and Sustainer, who is also its immanent principle of life. Similarly the problem of the miraculous has received a new setting. Miracles are not now regarded in the old way as external credentials to Revelation—a sort of artificial adjunct or added appendix. The evidential value of the miraculous may be fully recognised, but at the same time it is viewed as an organic part of the Revelation itself. The miracles of Christ, e.g., as we now see, were not isolated manifestations of supernatural power put forth simply and solely to excite wonder and astonishment, and as it were to compel belief. He refused, very definitely, to work a miracle of this kind (Mk 8 11 and parallels). Rather they are the outcomes of His wonderful and gracious character, integral portions of His teaching ; touches which, if removed, would leave a blank which would be felt in the complete, harmonious, and supremely natural if also supernatural portrait which the evangelists have artlessly combined to paint for us. And the supreme miracle, as we shall see shortly, is Christ Himself. His 'mighty works' were, of course—and some of them especially—tokens of His divinity. The Resurrection, e.g., is classed as such by St. Paul (in Ro 1 4 : cp. Jn 5 36 10 25, 38 Mt 11 2-5). They were signs, not to compel belief—for compelled belief is no longer faith—but signs to stimulate and strengthen and develop the germ of faith already present, and to transform it into assured conviction. Thus St. John (2 11) speaks of Christ's first miracle at Cana—which was obviously a sign of sympathy and kindness—as being also a manifestation of His glory ; but the manifestation is to the inner circle of His disciples. Similarly Christ Himself enumerates His characteristic miracles of healing, together with other works, as credentials of His Messiahship. But the evidence, be it observed, is addressed to St. John the Baptist.

This view of Miracle as an integral part of Revelation may explain to some extent the difference in character between the miracles of the Old Testament and those of the New. The Revelation, as we are observing more and more, is a *progressive* one, a gradual unfolding of divine truth to man, in divers parts and divers manners (Heb 1 1), as he was able to bear it. Will not the miraculous element, then, show itself progressive too ? Shall we be surprised if some of the Old Testament miracles, e.g. the shadow on Ahaz' dial, or the transformation of Moses' rod, seem to lack the obvious appropriateness and the richness of spiritual teaching and symbolism that shine forth from the recorded works of Christ ?

If miracles are *acted teaching*, should we not expect those which belong to an earlier and more elementary stage of Revelation to be of a simpler and more elementary sort ? One might venture to say that just as divine commands could be laid on Abraham and Joshua, in the childhood of morality, which could not be laid on us : so miracles could be wrought and be helpful in an earlier stage which in a later—such as our own age—would be simply a stumbling-block to belief. Yet even the earliest, and, if we may so say, 'crudest' of Old Testament miracles display a marked superiority, from this point of view, to many of the meaningless and ludicrous 'miracles' of the Apocryphal Gospels and mediæval hagiologies.

The accepted view of the universe has advanced, and Natural Science has taught us so well the lesson that the Almighty is a God of Law and order, that we instinctively suspect as unworthy of Him anything which seems to verge on the arbitrary or capricious. Many of the Old Testament miracles, if wrought to-day, would be as inappropriate as in their context they were appropriate. Let us consider for a moment some broad facts about them. At first sight they seem quite incidental and unsystematic. Possibly a progress may be dimly discerned, allowing for exceptions. The miracles, e.g., of the ninth century B.C.—especially the more beneficent miracles recorded of Elijah and Elisha, seem more like those of Christ than the Mosaic miracles of some seven centuries earlier. These earlier ones, again, adapted as they are to the special circumstances of their occasion, have a more exclusively general appeal to masses of people, while the later ones involve more individual dealing.

Other indications of law and system are to be found in the miracles of the Bible. Chief among these is their *threefold grouping*. The miracles are, for the most part, concentrated in three epochs, epochs when a vindication of God's supremacy was specially to be looked for ; and they are grouped around those three figures which find places together on the mysterious Mount of Transfiguration : Moses—Elijah—Christ.

(1) The first or Mosaic group ushers in the redemption from Egypt, the giving of the divine Law, and the foundation of the Hebrew theocracy. (2) The second marks a new crisis, when owing to the religious innovations of Ahab and Jezebel the worship of the true God

in Israel was first formally menaced by a new and hostile cult actively supported by the Court. (3) The third group is the climax of all. The miracles of Jesus Christ, with their peculiar appeal to reason, affection and conscience, throw back a flood of light upon the obscurer miracles of the Old Testament. ' The central point,' as Dr. Sanday has said, ' in the Old Testament revelation was that God is a *living God;* that the world is not a dead world, but instinct with life, which is all derived from Him. The New Testament takes up this and tells us that Christ the Word was the Light and Life of men.'

The miracles of the Old Testament certainly exhibit God as a living God, and culminate in the Incarnate Life—the Christ of the Gospels, whose career on earth issues in a Resurrection and Ascension which have brought new life to the world. And in this supernatural figure we see Miracle exhibited to us most naturally and in closest contact with all that we instinctively recognise as highest and noblest. His character is indeed the supreme wonder of all : more marvellous than any of those particular miracles which were, after all, but partial 'signs' of the fulness that was in Him. Whether we read it in the pages of the Gospels, or in St. Paul's description (1 Cor 13) of Love at work, we perceive in it an ideal perfection combining all the recognised manly virtues with those usually thought of as womanly. We mark its union of opposites—patience, gentleness, meekness, with a sternness and a force unequalled in history ; the cosmopolitan breadth of ideas found in one brought up in what would naturally have been the narrowest surroundings. Its superhuman claims are combined with an unparalleled humility and reasonableness ; its superhuman powers are controlled always and focussed on His mission, never employed for His own material comfort or the earthly advancement of His followers. Above all, there is the ideal morality exhibited, as even opponents admit, in His life and teaching, and the marvellous fact that none of His many recorded sayings, whether in the ethical sphere or in any other, have become obsolete or subject to revision in the subsequent growth of human knowledge.

But if Christ on earth is a wonder, still more is Christ ascended. It is the character of Christ as exhibited and developed in the history of His Church, impressing itself fruitfully on successive ages and on divers races, at home in each and bringing out the best in each regardless of diversity of clime, race, tradition, antecedents, and civilised status ; it is the vital power of Him, exercised in the tremendous if familiar phenomenon of conversion, which persists to-day to prove that the age of miracle is *not* past. Believers see in this but the fulfilment of His own recorded promise, 'Greater things than these shall' the believer 'do'; 'because I go to the Father' (Jn 14 12).

That systematic and rhythmical sequence of miracle which is represented by the names, Moses, Elijah, Christ, does not suddenly come to an end with the close of the New Testament, though its character, as we have seen, tends to change with the changing requirements of successive ages. To us children of a practical, matter-of-fact, and scientific century 'signs and wonders' like some of those in the Bible would be a hindrance and not a help, even had we the strength of faith necessary to evoke them. Yet He who after His Ascension wrought 'many signs and wonders' 'by the hands of the Apostles' (Ac 2 43 5 12) and 'confirmed the word with signs following' (Mk 16 20; cp. Ac 4 29, 30), has continued by moral and spiritual miracles to give evidence of His living presence throughout the centuries, according to the terms of His recorded promise, 'Lo, I am with you alway, even unto the end of the world' (Mt 28 20).

4. Miracle essential to Revelation as such. We may claim, perhaps, to have shown that Miracle is essential to the biblical Revelation. May we not go further, and say that it would seem to be essential to Revelation considered in the abstract—that is, to any conceivable method by which God might reveal Himself to man in a manner more direct and more unmistakable than is afforded by His revelation of Himself in the course of nature? On this subject it was formerly considered enough to observe that a divine message could only be sufficiently accredited by obviously supernatural accompaniments, and that therefore miracles were appended to Revelation as its necessary 'credentials.' Such a statement is, however, from a modern point of view, far from satisfactory.

We can no longer (as was pointed out above) look upon miracles as an external appendix added to Revelation by way of credentials. Miracle, we should say, has a great credential value, but its witness is intrinsic—from within; it witnesses to the truth of Revelation by witnessing to the character of the person revealed. The miracles of Christ hold a supreme place as the work of Incarnate God; but the other miracles also as emanating from the one personal Deity may be expected to bear the stamp of a personal consciousness and will. We know that a succession of phenomena in nature can be diverted by the action of our own human wills, and that without any real breach of Nature's laws. This is done, for instance, whenever a surgeon performs a successful operation, or a physician using his

knowledge of *materia medica* arrests the natural course of a disease. So, too, without any real contradiction of the system of Law which He has established for the working of the universe, the Personal Creator and Ruler of all things may be conceived as 'interposing' —either directly or by means of His creatures —and so diverting or interrupting what would otherwise have been the inevitable course of events. Such interposition, if definite and striking in its external results, would be what we know as Miracle. It would differ from the action of our limited minds and wills in many points: notably in the range of its power and influence and in the constant perfection of its purpose. These exclude the element of capriciousness that makes the action of our wills so often unaccountable and out of harmony with the course of nature.

In this conception of Miracle as a *display of personality* is to be found, we believe, the true solution of the various problems with which the question is encumbered. It helps us to understand, by the analogy of our own volition, what else would look like the introduction of a capricious principle into a world where we have been accustomed to see Law reigning: it helps us, moreover, to realise the place and purpose of miracle as evidencing, in the only way possible, the *personal* character of the Ruler of the universe: and it supplies a link between what we regard as the ordinary works of Providence—the normal phenomena which the world's process exhibits—and those abnormal phenomena inexplicable by our accustomed methods, which we call miracles. Both alike are manifestations of a personal mind and will and power, working according to the law of a perfect nature; but the one class of manifestations is deliberately intended to supplement—and interpret—the other.

So we are led back again to Christ as the supreme miracle and the revealer of the ultimate naturalness, if we may so speak, of the supernatural. For He in whom meet heaven and earth, the human and the divine, expresses uniquely in His recorded miracles as in His words and life, the perfect character of Him 'whom no man hath seen, nor can see,' yet concerning whom He Himself hath said: 'He that hath seen me hath seen the Father.' In the Incarnate what we ordinarily call Miracle is, as it were, normal; for in Him is God personally revealed to man, personally acting under conditions of human life.

5. Miracle and Natural Law. But since it is reverence for Natural Law that is responsible for most of the modern distrust of Miracle, it will be necessary to enter a little more fully into the relation between Miracle and Natural Law.

Of course the whole structure of modern science is built upon the foundation of the uniformity of Nature. If things happen anyhow, as in a nightmare, then there can be no use in attempting to study Nature at all. And if the presence of Miracle disturbs the uniformity of Nature and introduces absolute chaos into the world, we can forgive people for refusing to consider the possibility of the miraculous. But is it true that a belief in Miracle contradicts the reign of Law in Nature? As a matter of fact, the average believer in Miracle speaks and acts in his daily life as one who believes also that Nature is normally constant and uniform. His expectations, his forecasts, his plans imply just as steady and practical a reliance on this principle as do those of the veriest sceptic. And why? Because the very possibility of Miracle depends on the fact of uniformity. Miracle needs the ordinary working of Natural Law as its background. It does not exclude Natural Law, but it is relative to it. If all things were unaccountable, where would be place for Miracle? St. Augustine had arrived at a really profound conception of the relation of Miracle to Natural Law, when he suggested that all God's ordinary works are wonderful —miraculous—but that, since familiarity has so blunted men's minds that they fail to appreciate the yearly miracle of harvest and vintage, the Lord of Nature who, year by year, by natural processes which He has ordained, multiplies bread-substance for hungry men, and turns rain-water into wine to gladden man's heart, once on a time saw fit to do these things by a momentary act of that Will to which one day is as a thousand years.

Miracles, if they occur at all, must be, as St. Augustine saw, the work of the same Lawgiver who day by day exhibits to us the orderly wonders of Nature's processes. But if this be so it follows that miracles themselves must conform to Law, albeit some higher law than those with which physical science is conversant. Nature and conscience alike demand that we should regard God as the author 'not of confusion, but of peace' (1 Cor 14 33), i.e. as self-consistent because absolutely perfect. It is true that there is a disturbing element in the world ; that there is a principle at work absolutely contrary to the principle of Law—what the Bible calls *sin*. 'Sin,' as St. John says, 'is lawlessness' (1 Jn 3 4). But sin is not a positive entity, a created thing ; it is rather the abuse of a choice offered to man by his Maker, and offered of necessity if man was to be a free agent. The possibility of *choosing* to do right necessarily involves the possibility of choosing to do *wrong*. How far human or angelic sin is responsible for the anomalies in

the physical world which occasionally perplex and baffle the student of Natural Law, we are not here concerned to consider. There is one consideration, however, suggested by the presence of this disturbing factor. If Miracle seems arbitrary and violent, may it not be because some forcible method is necessary to redress the balance already upset by the introduction of evil into a world originally ' very good ' ?

And further, may not this forcible redressing of the balance, if such it be, be still performed in accordance with some higher principle of Law ?

The analogy of human personal action suggested above may help us here. When the physician—acting, it must be remembered, in accordance with the laws of medical science —restores the body to health, although he forcibly interrupts a series of physical processes which apart from him must have worked themselves out, he is really ranged on the side of the natural and normal. And it may perhaps be worthy of remark that the abnormal conditions which his skill and determination have fought and conquered are often directly, more often, probably, indirectly, the result of human sin. May we not say then that in the sphere of biblical miracle ' the real intervention is not the intervention of grace, but that of the sin which required it ' ?

We have seen above that there are traces of law and system discernible in the miracles of the Bible viewed generally, and that in the case of many of them the entire physical results may have been achieved by a disposition of natural forces at a particular time and for a particular purpose. There are other cases, however, where such an explanation seems inadequate to account for the result. These cases cannot, it is true, be referred to Natural Law ; but may they not be glimpses of a higher system which, for want of a better name, we must call 'Supernatural Law'? Nature herself supplies us with an illustration (and it is more than a mere illustration) which may enable us to realise the probability and, so to speak, naturalness of there being above and beyond the laws which our reason is able to discover, a higher *stratum* of law such as must appear to our ordinary intelligence supernatural, miraculous.

In external Nature we see four different worlds ; the higher in each case built upon the lower, in a sense including it, and yet remaining for ever distinct from it and apparently inaccessible to it.

(*a*) First there comes the *Inorganic* World —chemical elements and their products—dead matter. This is subject to its own elementary laws of gravitation, cohesion, and the like.

(*b*) Above that stands the *Organic* World,

which takes up the inorganic into its cell-structure, and is in this respect amenable to the laws of Matter ; but has in it, besides, potentialities and conditions of existence wholly unknown to the inorganic, and is subject, in consequence, to a fresh set of laws which do not touch the lower sphere—the laws of organic life.

(c) Higher up we have *Animal* Life, with its own peculiar gifts, conditions, laws of growth, nutrition, locomotion, etc. ; (d) and higher up, again, the rational, self-conscious, moral life of *Man*.

Each member of this ascending series of worlds is supernatural and miraculous from the point of view of those below it, while subject in a real sense to the laws governing its inferiors. None is lawless, arbitrary, capricious in reality, though the higher you go up the scale, the more *appearance* there is of absence of law and uniformity. The truth is that they are subject to ever higher, grander, more complex, more mysterious laws.

The teaching of the Bible seems to be that above these familiar orders of the inorganic, the organic, the animal, and the rational as known in man, there is yet another order, (e) the sphere of the purely spiritual, glimpses of which appear now and again to us as 'miracles.' These glimpses are possible, because man is himself on one side a spiritual being, made 'in the image of God,' and so akin to the supernatural world. They appear to him miraculous, because his intelligence, which lives and moves habitually in the natural world, is not at home yet in the spiritual. They are given because the Ruler of that supernatural world is Ruler also of the natural, and desires personal contact and communion with His rational creature, man.

If the relation of the supernatural to the natural world be such as our illustration suggests—if, that is, the former interpenetrates and completes while it also transcends the latter, we should expect that, though the laws to which miracles conform be beyond our reason as such, there would yet be something in them which would appeal to us as reasonable, and would have contact at least with the principle of Law as we see it working in the world around us. This we have already, to some extent, found to be the case, and deeper consideration will confirm the impression that the Bible miracles may be explained as instances rather of the controlling action of a higher law than of sheer violation of the lower.

One further suggestion may be made in this connexion—not as though it would cover the whole field of Miracle or offer in any sense an adequate explanation of all the miraculous phenomena of the Bible.

We have already spoken of some of the miracles of Christ as involving an inexplicable anticipation of the results of later human progress ; and surely it is true to say that a marked anticipation of a distinctly later stage of the advance of humanity is in itself of the nature of Miracle. It would have been nothing short of a miracle—e.g. if any one had made use of wireless telegraphy in the days of Queen Anne—because it would have been an advance quite out of touch with anything else in the conditions and circumstances of the time. From this point of view the mighty works of Christ would lose nothing of their miraculous character if it could be shown that modern or future medical science could produce identical results. The system of religion and morality set forth by Christ —which is intrinsically far more important than the miracles usually so called—gathers up into itself all the yearnings and gropings of the ancients, and at the same time represents the goal towards which the ethical advance of humanity has been gradually moving, so that His words have 'never passed away' like the utterances of other ancient teachers. May not His wonderful dealings with matter and with mind in like manner represent the capacity of *perfect* humanity—the goal towards which mankind is moving intellectually and scientifically by the help of the accumulated experience of centuries ? This, as we have seen, would render them no less miraculous ; and it strikes out a line of thought that has a much wider reference, including in its scope the Old Testament as well as the New. For if an inexplicable advance, out of all proportion to the contemporary development of the race, be miraculous, what claims may not be made for the Law, Prophecy, and History of the Old Testament.

Conclusion. Man moves on the borderland of the rational and spiritual worlds. He belongs in part to both. The higher is his heritage as much as the lower ; but of the first he enjoys as yet but rare glimpses. One great purpose of the Bible's miraculous record, culminating as it does in that Resurrection miracle without which subsequent history is inexplicable, is to warn us against the spirit which would discredit and reject those priceless glimpses when they are presented, and elect to live always on the lower plane.

Such a despising of man's birthright is not possible to those for whom the statements of the Christian creed represent historic facts. Christ, the Incarnate Deity, at once natural and supernatural ; Christ crucified, risen, ascended, glorified, has achieved for them perpetual access to the higher realm ; they 'see heaven open and the angels of God ascending and descending upon the Son of man' (Jn 1[51]).

THE RESURRECTION

IT cannot be said of the Resurrection, as is sometimes said of other miracles, that it lacks an adequate motive. The greatest of all questions that it concerns man to know, is whether there is or is not a future life. 'It matters,' says Pascal, 'to the whole of life to know whether the soul is mortal or immortal.' If a supernatural revelation is possible at all (and all who believe in a Personal God who loves His creatures, must believe that it is), a revelation on the subject of a future life is of all others the most credible. For in the presence of this great question all human knowledge is bankrupt. Science can only trace the history of the conscious soul to the moment of death. The human heart may yearn for immortality, philosophy may speculate about it, but neither can prove it. Socrates more than any other man applied himself to prove the immortality of the soul, but when the death-sentence was passed upon him, he could only say : 'The hour of departure has arrived, and we go our ways, I to die, and you to live. Which is better God only knows.'

The Christian Church claims to have received from God a special revelation upon this great question. According to her settled belief, God raised her Founder from the dead for the special purpose of revealing to mankind (1) the existence of a future life, and (2) the nature of that life.

1. **The Character of the Evidence.** The evidence for the Resurrection is of a kind which appeals primarily to the spiritual faculty of spiritual men. Those who already know and love God, who feel in their souls a yearning for eternal communion with Him, and a deep sense that the injustices, disappointments, and failures of this life point to a future life in which God's righteousness and love will be finally vindicated, will be drawn to examine attentively the evidence for the Resurrection of Jesus Christ. Those, on the other hand, who are living without faith in a personal God, and to whom Nature therefore manifests only a series of unvarying mechanical laws, will either reject the evidence without examination, or, if they examine it, will pronounce it insufficient. Yet, although the final decision will depend largely upon a man's general attitude towards spiritual and moral truth, the Resurrection claims to be a historical fact, and therefore the evidence for it, so far as it is historical, admits of being tested by the same canons of criticism as other historical

evidence. It is the duty of Christians, therefore, to subject the evidence for the Resurrection to the most rigid scrutiny, a scrutiny all the more penetrating and searching in proportion as the practical results which follow from the alternative decisions of the question are momentous.

2. **The Documents.** All modern criticism, except that which is carried to the point of perversity, acknowledges the genuineness of the chief Epistles of St. Paul, and since that Apostle was converted soon after the Resurrection (according to Harnack as early as 30 A.D., and certainly not later than 36 A.D.), his Epistles will be admitted to be a valuable witness as to what the belief of the first Christians was upon this subject. That the Resurrection of Jesus was firmly believed not only in the Churches founded by St. Paul, but also in those founded by the original Apostles, is manifest from these writings. The leading passage is 1 Cor 15$^{3f.}$, in which St. Paul rehearses the fundamental articles of the Christian faith. Of the Resurrection he says (see RV): 'For I delivered unto you first of all [this was in 50 A.D., about twenty years after the event] that which also I received, how that Christ died for our sins according to the Scriptures ; and that He was buried ; and that He hath been raised [the perfect represents the permanence of the result] on the third day according to the Scriptures ; and that He appeared to Cephas [i.e. Peter], then to the Twelve [in reality to the eleven, but 'the Twelve' is a recognised title of the apostolic body] ; then He appeared to above five hundred brethren at once, of whom the greater part remain until now, but some are fallen asleep ; then He appeared to James ; then to all the Apostles ; and last of all, as unto one born out of due time, He appeared to me also... Whether then it be I or they, so we preach, and so ye believed.'

We learn from this passage that the Resurrection of Jesus Christ was regarded as one of the foundation doctrines of Christianity, and that faith in it was taught to all converts 'first of all,' or more literally, 'among the first or most important truths' of the new faith ; that St. Paul's teaching upon this subject was identical with that of the other Apostles ; and that more than five hundred private Christians (most of whom were still alive when St. Paul wrote) could testify that they had seen the risen Lord. So far from the Resurrection being based, as is sometimes alleged, on the all but unsupported evidence of a single hysterical woman, there is no mention of any appearances to women at all. The list is clearly an official one of appearances to the Church and its officers. There is an appearance to St. Peter, the leader of the Apostles; one to the Twelve, the recognised heads of the Christian community ; one to James the Lord's brother, destined soon to rule the great mother-church of Jerusalem ; one to all the Apostles, i.e. to other leading men besides the Twelve, perhaps to the whole Seventy (Lk 10¹) ; one to the whole Church, on which occasion over five hundred were present ; and one to St. Paul, the founder of Gentile Christianity. It is important to notice that two of these appearances were to unbelievers. The unbelief of James is particularly noted in the Gospels (Jn 7⁵ Mk 3²¹ Mt 15³⁷), and it was probably this appearance which effected his conversion (Ac 1¹⁴). As to St. Paul, his companion and biographer tells us that he was ' yet breathing out threatenings and slaughter against the disciples of the Lord' (Ac 9¹), when the risen Lord appeared to him outside the gates of Damascus. Taken altogether, the evidence to which St. Paul alludes in this passage represents a truly impressive mass of testimony. This is the opinion not only of defenders of traditional views, but even of recent negative criticism. Schmiedel, for example, says, ' This passage must be regarded as the earliest account of the appearances of the risen Jesus ; unquestionably it goes back to the communications made by Peter during the fifteen days' visit of Paul, three years after the conversion of the latter' (Gal 1¹⁸) ; Weizsäcker says, ' Paul's knowledge of these things must have come from the heads of the primitive Church' ; Wernle says, ' In the very earliest time St. Paul obtained this information from St. Peter' ; Keim says, ' Paul wishes in pious earnestness to give the truth. . . It is beyond doubt that the facts were really experienced and believed as they were faithfully related to him, and as he has again faithfully reported them. . . Paul's help supplies the whole question with its fixed point, its Archimedean fulcrum.'

The important evidence of St. Paul is confirmed by the first-hand evidence of St. Peter. St. Peter's First Epistle is one of the best attested of all ancient documents, and since its contents are in harmony with its reputed date and authorship, we need have no hesitation in accepting its evidence. Its testimony to the Resurrection is remarkably strong. For St. Peter the Resurrection is not a speculation, but a most certain fact, the basis of the Christian's hope. ' Blessed,' he says, ' be the God and Father of our Lord Jesus

Christ, who according to His great mercy begat us again into a living hope by the Resurrection of Jesus Christ from the dead' (1³). And again, ' God raised Him from the dead, and gave Him glory ; so that your faith and hope might be in God' (1²¹). The testimony of two other Apostles can be added. The Gospel of St. Matthew, whether it be directly by that Apostle, or based upon his original Hebrew ' Logia,' apparently rests upon his authority. Its testimony to the Resurrection is quite explicit (Mt 28). The Gospel of St. John, though questioned in modern times by certain schools of criticism, was in ancient times universally accepted, and is in truth attested by weighty evidence, both internal and external, as the work of the Apostle. Its writer offers a personal testimony to the Resurrection, and gives a detailed account of three appearances of the risen Lord which he himself beheld.

Besides these primary authorities the secondary witnesses are of great importance. St. Luke, probably a Gentile of Antioch, during his long sojourn at Cæsarea (Ac 24²⁷) from 56–58 A.D., had ample opportunities of consulting the actual eye-witnesses, and we have every reason to suppose he did so (Lk 1¹⁻⁴). His Gospel and Acts must therefore be regarded as valuable authorities Their testimony to the Resurrection is unmistakable. As for St. Mark, his position as secretary and interpreter to St. Peter (cp. 1 Pet 5¹³) gave him exceptional opportunities of knowing the truth. Unfortunately the conclusion of his Gospel has been lost, but it is certain that his narrative was written from the point of view of a believer in the Resurrection and that in its complete form it contained an account of that event (Mk 16⁶, etc.).

3. The Number of Appearances. It is implied by the sacred writers that the appearances of the risen Lord were numerous (Jn 21²⁵ Ac 1³). At least ten or eleven are definitely mentioned.

(1) To Mary Magdalene (Jn 20¹⁶ ; cp. Mk 16⁹).

(2) To the other women (Mt 28⁹).

(3) To Peter (Lk 24³⁴ 1 Cor 15⁵).

(4) To two disciples on their way to Emmaus (Lk 24¹⁵).

(5) To the ten Apostles without Thomas (Lk 24³⁶ Jn 20¹⁹).

(6) To the Apostles with Thomas (Jn 20²⁶).

(7) To seven disciples, among whom were Peter, Thomas, Nathanael, James, and John (Jn 21¹).

(8) To the eleven disciples on a mountain in Galilee (Mt 28¹⁶), with which is probably to be identified—

(9) The appearance to over 500 brethren at once (1 Cor 15⁶).

(10) To James the Lord's brother (1 Cor 15 [7]).

(11) To the Apostles on the occasion of the Ascension (Ac 1 [4]).

(12) To St. Paul (Ac 9 [3], etc.).

4. Alleged Discrepancies in the Evidence. The above passages taken together represent an impressive mass of cumulative evidence, the weight of which would not be sensibly diminished, even if it could be shown that discrepancies exist between the narratives. For it is one of the established rules of historical criticism that the disagreement of the witnesses in matters of detail, does not invalidate their testimony to the main facts which they agree in relating. Up to a certain point, indeed, the presence of discrepancies in different narratives is rather a favourable indication than otherwise, because fictitious narratives, intended to win credit as history, would inevitably be precise, chronological, and harmonious not only in reality, but in appearance.

The only question is whether the discrepancies in the accounts of the Resurrection are so numerous and important, as to throw discredit upon the history as a whole. The chief difficulties are the following. St. Luke and St. John mention two angels, St. Matthew and St. Mark only one. According to the synoptists, the angels were seen by the women; according to St. John by Mary Magdalene only. According to St. Luke and St. Matthew, news was brought by the women that the tomb was empty, and that Jesus had risen; according to St. Mark, 'they said nothing to any one, for they were afraid'; whereas, according to St. John, news of the empty tomb (but not of the Resurrection) was brought by Mary Magdalene only, though there is a hint (Jn 20 [2]) that other women also had been present. Again the words of the angel announcing a Galilean appearance are given in substantial agreement by St. Matthew and St. Mark; but in St. Luke an important change is made. The word Galilee is retained, but the reference to a Galilean appearance is obliterated, probably because it is not St. Luke's design to record any appearances in Galilee.

These are all the discrepancies of any moment which can plausibly be alleged against the scriptural narratives. They relate almost entirely to the proceedings of the women on the morning of the Resurrection, and are easily explained by the fact that the women were so much startled by the appearance of the angel (Mt 28 [8] Mk 16 [8] Lk 24 [5]), that they were unable to give an entirely consistent account of their experience: cp. Lk 24 [11]. As to the often repeated statement that the authorities contradict one another as to the locality of the appearances, some placing them in Judæa and others in Galilee, we can only say that no sufficient reason has been shown why there should not have been appearances in both localities. The biblical writers, at any rate, recognise no such incompatibility. Not one of them says that the appearances were all in one locality. St. Matthew records one appearance in Jerusalem and one in Galilee; St. John three in Jerusalem and one in Galilee; while St. Paul does not mention the locality of any of the appearances.

The discrepancies, therefore, are too slight to discredit the narratives as a whole. This is the opinion even of many leaders of modern rationalism—of F. C. Baur, for example, who says, 'For the disciples the Resurrection was as real as any historical fact—whatever may have been the medium of this persuasion'; and of Mr. Macan, who says, 'Two broad facts may be taken as certain—that Paul and the other Apostles had certain visions, and that, in consequence of these visions, they believed that Jesus had risen from the dead.'

5. The interpretation of the facts. Various attempts have been made to explain the facts which have just been described, most of them without supposing that a miracle occurred. The chief are—

(1) *The theory of fraud.* This is the oldest. Soon after the Resurrection the Jews spread a report that the disciples had stolen Christ's body, and pretended that He had risen (Mt 28 [13-15]). This calumny is alluded to by Justin Martyr, Tertullian, and Origen; is found in the heathen Acts of Pilate, and the mediæval Jewish Toledoth Jeshua; and was advocated by the German rationalist Reimarus (1694–1767). In our day even rationalists reject this theory as 'repellent and disgraceful' (Keim). It is acknowledged on all hands that so pure an ethical movement as Christianity cannot have originated in conscious fraud.

(2) *The theory of the natural disappearance of the body.* The body is supposed to have been removed by some person or persons unknown (e.g. the gardener, unknown Galilean disciples, Mary Magdalene, the Sanhedrin, Pilate, etc.). But these unknown persons would either have produced the body, or at least have explained that they had removed it, as soon as the Apostles began to proclaim that Christ had risen from the tomb.

(3) *The theory of apparent death.* It is alleged that Jesus did not die upon the cross, but fainted, and after burial revived and came out of the tomb, thus giving rise to the belief that He had risen from the dead. This theory, once the usual one among rationalists, is now nearly, if not quite, obsolete. Strauss (1864) says of it: 'A man half-dead, dragging Himself in languor and exhaustion out of His tomb, with wounds requiring careful and continuous medical treatment—could He, in such a state, have

produced upon the minds of the disciples the impression that He was victor over death and the grave, the Prince of Life—an impression which nevertheless was the source and spring of all their subsequent activity ? '

(4) *The theory of subjective visions.* This view, now the accepted one among rationalists, was already stated, nearly in its modern form, by Celsus (A.D. 170), who says, ' Who beheld the risen Jesus ? A half-frantic woman, as you state, and some other person, perhaps, of those who were engaged in the same system of delusion, who had either dreamed so, owing to a peculiar state of mind, or, under the influence of a wandering imagination, had formed to himself an appearance according to his own wishes, which has been the case with numberless individuals ' (see Origen, ' Against Celsus,' ii. 55). Modern advocates of this view maintain that they can account for the appearances by the ordinary laws of psychology, without introducing supernatural agency. Hallucinations are known to occur, (*a*) to persons afflicted with certain physical diseases, (*b*) to insane persons, (*c*) to persons, not insane, but suffering from certain disorders of the nervous system, (*d*) to healthy persons intensely preoccupied with an idea which they have allowed to obtain exclusive possession of their minds. (*e*) It is also maintained by good authorities, but is not yet generally accepted, that the thought of one mind acting ' telepathically ' (i.e. without any material means of communication) upon the thought of another mind of a certain type of psychological sensitiveness may induce a visual hallucination.

Now it cannot be fairly said that the appearances of the risen Christ can be explained on any of these principles. For as to (*a*) none of the perceivers were sick ; as to (*b*), none of them were insane ; as to (*c*), even if it be supposed that Mary Magdalene and St. Paul suffered from some form of nervous ailment, this cannot be said of the Twelve, or of James, or of the five hundred brethren ; as to (*d*), the disciples were certainly not intensely preoccupied with the idea of the Resurrection. The ignominious death of Jesus had scattered His followers, and thrown them into the deepest despondency. They were in the position of men who, having placed implicit trust in a leader, were beginning to wonder whether, after all, they had not made a great mistake. All the Gospels represent our Lord's prophecies of His Resurrection as falling upon deaf ears (Mt 16 22 Mk 9 10 Jn 20 9, etc.), and depict the despondency of the disciples (Mt 26 56 Mk 16 10), and their unwillingness to believe the good news (Mt 28 17 Mk 16 11, 12, 14 Lk 24 11, 25, 37, 38 Jn 20 25).

As to (*e*), if hallucinations can be telepathic-

ally induced at all (and this is doubtful), this can only happen to persons of a very rare and quite abnormal psychological sensitiveness. To suppose that the nervous systems of the Twelve and of the five hundred were all so abnormally ' sensitive,' that the visions of Mary Magdalene could be ' telepathically ' communicated to them all, surpasses credence. Nor is this all. Recent research has demonstrated (see the voluminous evidence collected by the Psychical Research Society) that visual phantoms hardly ever speak, and, when they do, never more than a word or two. But the risen Lord spoke every time that He appeared, and carried on long conversations with the disciples. On the significance of the empty tomb, of the handling, and of the eating—all which circumstances are inconsistent with the theory we are considering —more will be said in the next sections.

(5) *The theory of objective visions, or of a ' spiritual resurrection.'* Many who reject the traditional belief in a corporeal resurrection, and yet desire to find a mediating position between that and the purely negative view, adopt the theory of objective visions. They suppose that, after Jesus had been put to death, His body did not rise, but that His glorified and immortal spirit was allowed by God to appear to the disciples, as a token that the teaching of Jesus had been ratified by the divine approval, and that, in particular, human immortality is a fact. This theory, often spoken of as that of a ' spiritual resurrection,' approximates very closely in practical effect to that usually denominated ' orthodox,' and deserves sympathetic and respectful consideration. Our objection to it is, that while it removes none of the real difficulties involved in the older view, it introduces new and greater difficulties of its own. The great difficulty of believing in our Lord's Resurrection is its miraculous character. The theory of objective visions tries to eliminate the element of miracle by denying our Lord's corporeal, while admitting His spiritual, Resurrection. But even on such a view the Resurrection of Jesus remains a miracle. It is as much a breach of the order of nature, and, therefore, as much a miracle, for a disembodied spirit to return and hold conversations with living persons, or for God to send ' a telegram from heaven ' (Keim), as for a corpse to rise. It is a mistake to think that the philosophic objections to miracles apply exclusively, or even with especial force, to physical miracles. They apply equally to all miracles. It is more difficult, doubtless, to determine the limits of natural possibility in the case of mind than in the case of matter ; but when those limits are plainly transcended, as they are when the facts require the hypotheses of spirit return and of telegrams from heaven to be entertained, the philosophic

objections against alleged psychical miracles are as strong as those against alleged physical miracles. The half-hearted Rationalism, therefore, which accepts a spiritual, while denying a corporeal resurrection, is as incapable as Orthodoxy of removing the great stumbling-block of miracle, and is under the additional disadvantage of being forced to deal with the evidence in a thoroughly arbitrary way. It is compelled, for instance, to disbelieve what even Schenkel regarded as incontrovertible, that the tomb was empty on the third day, and that the risen Jesus, in order to convince the disciples that He was not a phantom, allowed Himself to be handled, and ate before them.

(6) *The theory of a corporeal resurrection.* Upon the whole, no theory will be found to satisfy the facts, except the traditional one of a bodily resurrection. On the morning of the third day the tomb was empty. This fact, in spite of recent denials in the interest of the theory of a spiritual resurrection, stands firm. It is attested not only by Luke, who had good sources of information, but also by Mark (that is, by Peter), by Matthew, by John, by the Jews (Mt 28 [13]), and apparently by Paul also, for that is the natural conclusion to draw from the fact that he mentions the burial in connexion with the Resurrection (1 Cor 15 [4]). To deny a fact so amply attested is not sound criticism. The tomb, then, was empty, and, since the removal of the body either by the disciples or by the Jews is (as we have shown) an inadmissible hypothesis, we must conclude that the body of Jesus rose to a new life. Other evidence points in the same direction. Thus the risen Lord sought to dispel the idea which the Apostles at first entertained, that He was a disembodied spirit, by offering Himself to be handled, and by showing the wounds in His hands, feet, and side (Lk 24 [37f.] Jn 20 [20f.]) ; also by eating before and with the disciples (Lk 24 [42] Ac 10 [41] ; cp. Ac 1 [4] RM, Mk 16 [14]). It is no sufficient reply to this to say that the risen body could pass through solid matter (Jn 20 [19, 26]), could appear and vanish suddenly (Lk 24 [31, 36]), could transport itself instantaneously from place to place (cp. Lk 24 [31-34]), and therefore must have been a phantom or spirit. If we adopt the usual view, that at the Resurrection the body of Jesus was transfigured, and became a glorious and spiritual body, no longer limited by the laws and conditions of ordinary matter, no contradiction arises. We shall suppose that our Lord's risen body belonged naturally to the sphere of heaven, not to that of earth, and that it was by way of condescension and to confirm the faith of the disciples, that He made it visible to earthly eyes, tangible to human hands, and capable of eating earthly food. His risen body was not like that of the widow's son or of Lazarus, but like that of the saints in glory (1 Cor 15 [35f.]).

6. The Permanent Significance of the Resurrection. From many points of view the Resurrection is the most important event in human history, and a large treatise would hardly exhaust its many-sided significance. Only the briefest outline of its bearing upon human life and thought can be given here.

(1) The Resurrection has brought new hope and happiness into the world by the light it throws upon human immortality (1 Pet 1 [3, 4]). This is recognised even by rationalists. For example, John Stuart Mill says : ' The beneficial effect of such a hope (in human immortality) is far from trifling. It makes life and human nature a far greater thing to the feelings, and gives greater strength as well as solemnity to all the sentiments which are awakened in us by our fellow-creatures, and by mankind at large. It allays the sense of that irony of Nature which is so painfully felt when we see the exertions and sacrifices of a life culminating in the formation of a wise and noble mind, only to disappear from the world when the time has just arrived at which the world seems about to begin reaping the benefit of it. The truth that life is short and art long is from of old one of the most discouraging parts of our condition ; this hope (of immortality) admits the possibility that the art employed in improving and beautifying the soul itself may avail for good in some other life, even when seemingly useless for this.'

(2) The Resurrection makes it possible to vindicate God's justice and benevolence in the government of the world. If this life is all, God cannot be regarded as perfectly just and benevolent, because he frequently permits the righteous to be afflicted, and even to be unjustly put to death, while the wicked go unpunished and enjoy worldly prosperity. But if, as the Resurrection indicates, there is a life beyond the grave in which all earthly wrongs are righted and all wickedness adequately punished, the moral character of God can be successfully vindicated.

(3) The Resurrection indicates that the future life will be not that of the soul only, but of the soul united to a suitable organ or ' body.' Christians regard matter as possessed of an intrinsic excellence of its own. It has reached its present perfection as the result of many ages of cosmical development, and therefore it is probable, on the theory that there is a final goal to which all creation moves, that matter as well as spirit will be ultimately perfected and glorified (cp. Ro 8 [18-25] 2 Pet 3 [13] Rev 21 [1]), and that in the future life we shall be surrounded by a ' material ' environment of some kind. Unless hereafter we possess bodies,

it is difficult to understand how we shall even recognise one another, and unless there are beautiful objects, it is difficult to understand how the soul will enjoy, as Plato says it will, the contemplation of perfect beauty for ever.

(4) The Resurrection sets the seal of the divine approval upon the Teaching of Jesus, and in particular

(5) Declares Him to be the Divine Son of God.

On the last two points see art. 'The Person of Jesus Christ.'

THE ATONEMENT

THE meaning of the word 'atonement' becomes plain when it is divided into syllables, 'at-one-ment.' It signifies the setting at one of those who have been estranged. 'We actually find the word "onement," reconciliation, in old authors' (Skeat).

In the New Testament the word only occurs in Ro 5 11 AV, but in RV it has disappeared even from that passage, and is replaced by 'reconciliation' : cp. Ro 5 10 11 15 2 Cor 5 18 f. where the Greek word is the same as in Ro 5 11.

The word 'atonement' is really taken from the Old Testament, where it occurs about fifty times, generally in conjunction with the verb 'to make.' Thus Ex 30 15, 'to make an atonement for your souls' ; Lv 9 7, 'make an atonement for thyself, and for the people,' etc. It is given there as the translation of a form of a Hebrew word, which literally means 'to cover,' and describes the effect of the sacrifices of the Jews in 'covering,' i.e. removing sin and uncleanness, and so restoring communion between God and man. Therefore, used of the death of Christ, the word may be taken to imply that Christ's death was sacrificial, and that its effect is to do away with that separation between God and man which has been brought about by sin.

Although the word 'atonement' is absent from the New Testament (RV), yet the thought runs throughout the sacred volume. Thus in Mk 10 45 Christ speaks of giving 'his life a ransom for many,' and in Mk 14 24 says, 'This is my blood of the New Testament, which is shed for many.' In Jn 1 29 the Baptist proclaims, 'Behold the Lamb of God, which taketh away the sin of the world' ; in Ro 5 10 St. Paul says, 'When we were enemies we were reconciled to God by the death of his Son' ; and in 1 Pet 1 19 we read of being redeemed 'with the precious blood of Christ, as of a lamb without blemish, and without spot.' Cp. Jn 3 14 f. 6 51 10 11, 15 12 24 15 13 Ro 3 24 f. 4 25 8 3, 32, 34 1 Cor 1 30 6 20 7 23 15 3 2 Cor 5 18 f. Gal 1 4 3 13 4 f. Eph 1 7 2 16 5 2 Phil 2 8 f. Col 1 14, 20 f. 2 14 1 Th 5 10 1 Tim 2 6 Tit 2 14 Heb 7 27 9 11 f. 26 f. 10 10 f.

12 24 13 10 f. 1 Pet 1 2 2 24 3 18 1 Jn 1 7 2 2 3 5, 16 4 10 Rev 1 5 5 6, 9 7 14 14 3 f.

In these passages the teaching of the New Testament may be clearly discerned. It may be briefly summed up thus : Christ died for us ; He became a Ransom, and redeemed us ; He became a Propitiation for our sins ; He became a 'curse' for us, and was 'made sin' on our behalf ; by His death, by the shedding of His blood, by the giving of His life, by His Cross come forgiveness, cleansing, the taking away of sin, eternal life.

Although the connexion between His death and our salvation is so clearly stated in the New Testament, when we ask in what manner the death of Christ brings about our forgiveness, no precise answer is given in Scripture ; and yet it seems impossible for man to rest satisfied without an answer. His heart may find rest and peace with God in the Cross of Christ, but, none the less, his mind calls out for an explanation of the mystery of the Cross. Various attempts have been made to supply this intellectual need.

It was thought in the earlier Christian centuries that the death of Christ was a ransom paid to Satan, that mankind might be released from bondage to him. Afterwards it was taught that Christ gave up to God His sinless life in payment of the debt which man had incurred to God, by not rendering the obedience and honour due to Him. Again, it was held that God satisfied His justice by inflicting on Christ the punishment which the sins of mankind deserved ; or, that Christ suffered to show God's justice, bearing a punishment instead of us, that we might recognise the wickedness of sin.

Whatever support these theories may still obtain, they present such difficulties to modern religious thought as necessitate an advance to something more satisfactory. We cannot think either that God would punish the innocent, or that for the sake of punishment inflicted on the innocent He could justly spare the guilty. We cannot think that there can be anything formal and fictitious about our rela tion to God. These unsatisfying theories have largely come from unduly pressing, in a literal manner, the details of metaphors which should be interpreted broadly and freely. The metaphors of 'ransom' and 'redemption' are meant to express the greatness of Christ's self-sacrifice, and its purpose and effect in delivering us from sin and its consequences. The metaphors of 'propitiation,' 'reconciliation,' and 'justification,' are meant to express, not that God needs to be appeased, but that the effect of the work of Christ, when taken into the heart of sinful man, is to do away with the barrier which sin has built between him and God, and to bring him back to God in penitence and obedience. Christ in His sacrifice was at one with the mind of the Father. God did not hate the world, but 'so loved the world that He gave His only-begotten Son.'

In opposition to the penal theories, some have supposed that the death of Christ became the means of our salvation simply by giving us such a manifestation of God's love as would win our hearts, and lead us to surrender ourselves in love and gratitude to Him. This theory contains a measure of truth, but does not seem to take sufficient account of the representation of the death of Christ as a sacrifice offered to God for our sins to 'shew God's righteousness.'

The meaning of the Atonement must be found in the facts. The great fact, of course, was the death of Christ. It was His death on which the main stress was laid both by Christ Himself and by His apostles. It is not said that His life was lived for the remission of sins, but that His blood was shed for that purpose.

Now, historically considered, the death of Christ was a natural event. The manner of His death was the natural consequence of the life which He lived. The outstanding feature of His life was its deliberate and unceasing submission to the will of His Father in every point. The human society in which He lived, the human social organism by which He was surrounded, sought to bring Him into line with its own will, its own desires ; and those desires were self-centred, self-seeking. At the same time, the human nature which He shared with us had the natural feelings of man, which shrink from pain and sacrifice, and which desire self-gratification. So that, as has been said, He had 'all the external machinery' for disobedience. But the will of human society, and the temptations of human nature, beat upon Him in vain. His life was, all through, the complete representation, the perfect realisation, of the will of God.

Such a life naturally led to the Cross. The sinful passions of man, which could not bend Christ to yield to them, rose against Him in hatred, and put Him to death. Thus, on the part of men, the Crucifixion was a murder. But on the part of Christ, the death of the Cross was the culmination of His righteous life, the crowning act of assent to the will of God. It was a 'death unto sin.' It was the refusal of sin, carried to its last and victorious extremity.

Looked at in this way, then, the death of Christ was the perfect display of righteousness, the complete achievement of union with the Divine will, the absolute condemnation of human sin.

But the life and death of Christ were more than individual. He was not one among many, but the man of all men, the son of man, the second Adam, the perfect representative of the human race. He was made in all points like unto His brethren, that He might express, before man and before God, what the thoughts and wishes and acts of man should be. His life was an offering to God, and that not merely for Himself, but for others, as expressing the return to God of sinful humanity. It was the beginning of a new and reformed order of things for human nature. In the life and death of Christ, the best man, the natural leader of men, spoke to God for man. It remained for the rest of mankind to utter their 'Amen' to that perfect prayer.

Christ, then, is the elder brother of the human race, bound to mankind in such intimate relationship that some have liked to think that the Son of God would have become Incarnate even if man had not sinned. But since mankind has sinned, the righteousness and holiness and love for man of the Son of God must have produced in Him sorrow for the sin of man. A sinner's sorrow for his sin, when it is true, is penitence. Christ was sinless. But seeing that His relationship to man is so intimate, and His love for man so great, we can imagine that His sorrow for man's sin would be filled with shame, and be that true penitence which man himself did not rightly feel. For as a loving and saintly mother suffers shame and penitence for the sin of her son, so even more, and to an infinite degree, would the loving and holy Son of God feel shame and penitence for the sin of mankind which He 'bore' when He identified Himself with our sins in such a manner that it is said that He was 'made sin' (2 Cor 5 21). The burden of our sins thus borne upon His heart would explain His agony in the garden and His cry of desolation upon the Cross.

Accordingly, Christ accepted the Cross

when it came in His way, instead of escaping from it. He did so, not only because it was the culmination of His union with the will of the Father, but also because in the shame of that death, and in its utter emptying of Himself before God, He expressed the true penitence of man for the sin of man.

Thus the death of the Cross was a double sacrifice offered in man's name. It expressed the sacrifice of self to the holy and righteous will of God, and the sacrifice of true penitence and righteousness. This sacrifice, joined as it was to self-sacrificing love, was 'the noblest act that God had ever looked upon.' It was acceptable to God, 'an offering and a sacrifice to God for an odour of a sweet smell' (Eph 5 2).

But how could a sacrifice of penitence and righteousness, offered by Christ, alter the relationship in which we stand to God? The answer is to be found, partly, in the union between Christ and the human race, through which, in an ideal and sacramental way, 'one died for all, therefore all died' (2 Cor 5 14). Practically and actually, for each individual the answer is to be found in the union of the believer with Christ. As St. Paul makes clear

in his Epistles, he who has faith in Christ can be justified, i.e. accepted by God, because his face is set in the right way, because the seed has been sown which bears the fruit of life. Faith is more than abstract belief. It is even more than trust. It is that loving adhesion to Christ which loves all He is and all He did, which 'loves the Crucified because of the Cross and the Cross because of the Crucified.' Therefore the character of the believer is altered by his faith. He enters into the meaning of Christ's Cross and makes it his own. He, too, takes up his Cross and follows Christ. He, too, seeks the will of God, through his union with Christ, even at the cost of 'cutting off his hand' or 'plucking out his eye.' He, too, dies to the sin of the world, in his heart and will and life. He shares the righteousness of Christ as well as His repudiation of sin. And he can do all this, not only through the transforming power of loving faith, but also because the Holy Spirit, which is the Spirit of the Crucified, is given to him, reproducing Christ in Him, and changing him 'into the same image.' He of whom this has become true is one with Christ in God.

INSPIRATION

THE word 'inspire' means 'breathe into.' In the Authorised Version Wisd 15 11 illustrates this meaning, 'Forasmuch as he knew not his Maker, and Him that inspired into him an active soul, and breathed in a living spirit.' The word 'inspiration' occurs twice in the Authorised Version : (1) Job 32 8, 'But there is a spirit in man : and the inspiration of the Almighty giveth them understanding'; and (2) 2 Tim 3 16, 'All Scripture is given by inspiration of God, and is profitable for doctrine.' The last instance is, however, doubtful, and we shall probably do well to accept the rendering of the Revised Version, 'Every Scripture inspired of God is also profitable,' an interpretation which agrees with some of the oldest English versions. We must content ourselves with noticing that in any case this verse shows how the word 'inspire,' like many other words, gradually passed from a physical to a spiritual meaning. St. Paul's phrase corresponds with that of St. Peter, who speaks of the prophets as 'moved by the Holy Ghost' (2 Pet 1 21).

Inasmuch as every faithful Christian is moved by the Holy Ghost who dwells within him, it is possible to speak of every Christian as inspired. But this does not imply that the Holy Spirit grants to every Christian the same degree of insight into truth, or that there is no progress in the apprehension of different parts of truth, or that the Holy Spirit bids every man to manifest his inspiration in the same way. To assume that it does, is to raise needless difficulties in the interpretation of the Bible, which clearly exhibits, not only varying degrees of inspiration, and different ways of manifesting it, but also individual and general progressiveness in the apprehension of divine truth. Bearing this in mind, then, we must enquire what is meant by the inspiration of the writers of the Bible.

Speaking broadly, the Christian means by their inspiration an impulse from God causing certain persons to write, and directing them how to write, for the edification of others. Though it is closely connected with *revelation*, it is not identical with it. By revelation God makes known to a soul truths which were unknown to it before. But it is not at all necessary that an inspired writer should receive any new truths by way of revelation. Thus St. Mark was inspired to write his Gospel, but he was inspired to write down truths which were already familiar to him and to others through the instructions given by St. Peter. While the

Church has continuously witnessed to her belief in the inspiration of those Scriptures which she decided to include in the Canon, she has never defined the method of inspiration by saying how the Holy Spirit acted upon the natural faculties of the writers. Therefore the method of inspiration may still be regarded as, in a certain sense, an open question. But it is, nevertheless, not so open as to be unaffected by certain definite limits which we must now consider.

The nature of inspiration must be ascertained (1) by a careful and exact study of the Holy Scriptures themselves : their own testimony as to their origin, design, and authority must be scrupulously observed. (2) From the action of the Church with regard to Holy Scripture and its meaning. To learn what inspiration is, we must not only see how the books were written, but also see their effect on the life of the Church and the testimony which the Church gave to them. (3) The Christian must ascertain the meaning of inspiration by submission to it. The man whose own life is not under the influence of the Holy Spirit cannot expect to understand inspiration. And a Christian can only learn to look upon the Scriptures from the right point of view in proportion as he acts as a member of that divine society which produced the Scriptures and set its seal to them.

Fidelity to the above principles will keep us from the extreme theories which men have constructed with regard to the divine and the human elements in the Bible respectively. By saying 'extreme,' we do not mean that any opinion which is called 'extreme' is necessarily wrong, or that any opinion which is called 'moderate' is necessarily right. It is our duty to accept a doctrine, not because it is moderate, but because it is true. And the more extreme theories about the Bible must be rejected, not because they are extreme, but because they are false. They either lay such an emphasis on the divine element in the Bible as to make the human element unreal, or they lay such an emphasis on the human element as to leave no room for the divine element. Thus they offer a striking parallel to certain errors with regard to the Person of our Lord. In early times the Gnostics, Apollinarians, and Monophysites allowed our Lord no true human nature, while certain of the Adoptionists and all the Nestorians insisted so strongly upon the human nature as to limit or even eliminate the divine. One extreme was sometimes an actual reaction against the other. So it has been with the Bible. At the time of the Reformation there was among Protestants a strong tendency to appeal to the Bible against the traditions of the Church. And in order to make the appeal as effective as possible every attempt was made to safeguard the divine authority of the inspired books. This attempt led to some extraordinary exaggerations. Many scholars were led to adopt the opinion of a Jew named de Rossi, who held that the little points in the Hebrew Bible denoting the vowels were inspired, a theory which de Rossi defended by holding that the origin of the vowels was communicated to Adam in Paradise and transmitted to Moses. In 1675 A.D. some Swiss Protestants actually made the divine inspiration of the vowel-points a doctrine of their articles of religion. The result was that people pinned their faith on separated passages in the Bible instead of its general teaching, and derived from it maxims for condemning historical and scientific enquiries which the authors of the Bible would not have condemned themselves. Thus the Old Testament was quoted to support slavery when circumstances no longer justified its retention, and a line of poetry was employed to condemn Galileo for asserting that the earth moves round the sun. It is to be feared that many men were turned away from the doors of Christian churches for not accepting claims made for the Bible which the Bible does not make for itself.

Then came the reaction. Atheists and Agnostics began to lecture on the 'mistakes of Moses,' assuming that if they could show that Moses committed some errors in science, their Christian hearers would give up Christ. Rationalistic writers deliberately tried to erase everything that is supernatural in the Old Testament, and all the miracles in the New Testament were treated as legendary wonders rising from a desire to enforce some pet theory held by the evangelists, or from a love of the marvellous in the minds of ignorant peasants. Thus the divine element in the Bible was either wholly denied or was reduced to such guidance as might be granted by God to any man in any place.

The true and middle way is for us to see the divine element of inspiration in the human element of human words and thoughts.

The Human Element. This can be recognised (a) in the coöperation of human minds with the mind of the Holy Spirit. The Psalmist who unburdened his soul in Ps 51 must have been deeply conscious that he was himself imploring forgiveness, and like other humble saints may have been scarcely aware that the Divine Spirit was prompting his prayer. In the same way the prophets were perhaps often unaware of the full divine meaning which God intended their words to bear ultimately. When the Psalmist says, 'They pierced my hands and my feet,' and when Hosea says, 'When Israel was a child then I loved him, and called my son out of Egypt,' we need not suppose that they were at all conscious that their words would correspond with the experiences of the Messiah.

The human element can be recognised (b) in the materials employed by the sacred writers, and in the manner in which they are combined. The writers used various sources of information as modern writers do. Thus in Nu 21 14 we find a reference to a 'Book of the Wars of the Lord,' and in Samuel, Kings, and Chronicles several documents are quoted. Even in the New Testament the writers felt at liberty to rearrange or modify earlier inspired writings, for St. Luke and St. Matthew both appear to have absorbed much of St. Mark's Gospel, and St. Luke has endeavoured to make the Greek more elegant. Again, the fact that Mk 16 9-20 and Jn 7 53-8 11 were probably not written by those evangelists themselves does not affect their inspiration. The Church has recognised them as true, and has connected them with the sacred narrative that embraces them.

The human element can be recognised (c) in those occasional statements which appear to be inaccuracies. St. Jerome says plainly that there is an error both in Mt 13 35 and in Mt 27 9, points which are well known to modern students. When different narratives have been combined we find some apparent contradictions; thus in Gn 32 28 and 35 10 we find two different explanations of the name Israel. In spite of such contradictions the biblical histories are of immense value even as histories, and apart from the precious instructions which they convey with regard to faith and morality.

The human element can be recognised (d) in the fact that the inspiration of the books and of the authors is progressive. Only to our Lord Jesus Christ was the Holy Spirit given 'without measure.' The inspiration of all other teachers was intermittent (Jer 42 7 1 Cor 7 10). They received different measures of enlightenment. Inspiration was commensurate with the medium through which it passed, and with the development of the minds for whose benefit it was originally given. We can readily admit, for example, that in the imprecatory Psalms the writers were probably so goaded by the persecution and cruelty which they experienced at the hands of their enemies, that those necessary ideals of religion—mercy and forgiveness—were, for a time at least, quite obscured. In a less degree, the human limitations of circumstances and environment probably influenced such books as the Song of Solomon,

Ecclesiastes and Esther, although each of these has a place and purpose in the Old Testament well understood by every student of Jewish history. The value of many of the laws of the Old Testament consists not in the fact that they afford a moral standard for all time, but in the fact that they afforded the best moral standard for their own age and prepared for the best moral standard in the future. And the history of the Old Testament shows us how God made use of imperfect men, and of literary methods which belonged to the child-mind of the race. But though these are earthen vessels, they contain heavenly treasure.

The Divine Element. This is (*a*) discernible in prophecy, which is a characteristic of the New Testament as well as of the Old. St. John in the Revelation (22⁹) is shown to be among the prophets as Isaiah and Amos had been. The prophets were filled with the certain conviction that their inspiration came not from within them, but from without. The call of Moses (Ex 3, 4) shows that he is forced to be a prophet against his will. Isaiah receives his call with reluctance and self-abasement. It is the same with Jeremiah. We find repeatedly in the prophets that an irresistible impulse came upon them, and that after some deep communion with God they felt forced to speak. Ac 2¹⁷,¹⁸ shows that the Apostles on the day of Pentecost knew the same kind of impulse, and in Gal 1¹⁶ St. Paul testifies to an inward revelation similar to that given to Moses. The inspiration was sometimes regarded as an ' answer ' from God like an answer to prayer (Jer 23³⁵ Mic 3⁷). Sometimes the inspiration implied a direct command to write (Isa 8¹ Jer 36²⁸ Rev 21⁵). The prophets are ' men of God,' ' interpreters.' They always insist on morality and religion in closest union, interpreting current events in the light of God's will. They foretell the fall of the Jewish state as St. John foretold the fall of Rome, and they insist that the destroying powers are instruments of God. But their teaching about the nature of God and the duties of the people are coördinate with an inspired outlook into the future. The prophets are ' seers,' and the predictive element in their teaching is essential (see Isa 1, 5, 6 Hos 11 Am 2). They foretell the punishment of the wicked, the kingdom of God that is to come, and the perfect king. We cannot always say that all the details of the prophecies have been fulfilled, but we can often say that these details are a setting and shrine of the brilliant truths which have come to pass.

(*b*) The divine element can be discerned in the laws and in the worship of the Bible. The strong commands and prohibitions of the Decalogue lay down conditions that are necessary for the human race, and show us that a violation of the laws which are for the good of human society is an offence against God, who constituted human society. The elaborate regulations of external worship had a divine purpose in teaching man his need of the Saviour and in foreshadowing the priestly work of Christ. In the prayers and praises of private or of public worship which we read in the Old Testament we find a spiritual joy and self-humiliation which are unparalleled in other literature.

(*c*) The divine element can be discerned in the history of the Bible. The events of history are, in a sense, the words of God, and the inspired historians interpret these words. The intention of God, in the development or decline of Israel and Judah and the nations around them, was grasped by the writers and described for the religious education of the world. The traditions and fortunes of the race are represented to us as illustrating God's dealings with man, ' God's judgment on sin ; His call of a single man to work out a universal mission ; His gradual delimitation of a chosen race ; His care for the race ; His overruling of evil to work out His purpose.' To the historians of the Old Testament, as in a far deeper sense to the historians of the New, their records were not a series of disconnected facts, or the tale of a physical and material continuity. They were the story of God's purpose in establishing His own kingdom.

(*d*) The divine element can be discerned in the action of the word of God upon the souls of men. We are sometimes told that we ought to read the Bible like any other book. This is true with regard to the language and grammar of the Bible. But it is not true with regard to the matter which the Bible contains. For the Bible is not like any other book. It bears the stamp of the divine, and it gathers round the person and word of Jesus Christ, who is the central figure of human history. The Bible tells us how the world can be regenerated, and how we can be saved. The remedy for its frequent misuse is not to read it less, but to read it more, and to read it with greater reverence. We need forgiveness : where can we find language better than the Lord's Prayer, and Ps 51 ? We need courage : what words are better than ' The Lord is my shepherd ' ? We need comfort : where can we find it better than in the story of Him who bore our griefs ? We need recalling to the great simplicities of the moral life : what can we do better than ponder the words of the Sermon on the Mount ?

THE STUDY OF THE BIBLE

I. Function of Conscience in Bible Study

God has given to men a conscience as well as a Bible. They are made to correspond with each other, as the eye is made to correspond with the light and the light to correspond with the eye. The chief function of the Bible is to develop the conscience. One great function of the conscience is to interpret the Bible. If you read your Bible, ignoring this function of conscience, you will misinterpret it.

Conscience is constituted to appreciate the distinction between right and wrong, between ought and ought not. If we make two lists —if truth, fairness, generosity, self-sacrifice be put in one list, and falsehood, unfairness, meanness, selfishness in the other, we are compelled by conscience to label the one set ' ought ' and the other ' ought not.' We cannot help it. No one in his senses could reverse these labels. We know that if practising the first set bring pain, and the second set pleasure, yet we cannot reverse our decision. Nay, more, we feel certain that the distinction belongs not to this earth alone—that the ought and ought not stretch to the furthest planets, to the angels of God, to God Himself. Wrong would be no less wrong if it were attributed to God. No revelation, no external portent, could persuade us of the opposite. If even a voice from heaven should declare to us that lying and dishonesty were right, we should, as St. Anselm says (' Cur Deus Homo,' I. 12), be forced to believe not that they were right, but rather that the voice which spoke was not God. We must carry this belief into our Bible reading ; that is true faith. Faith in God means faith in a Person, faith in a character ; faith in an infinite justice and love and nobleness and generosity—faith in a God to whom it would be absolutely impossible to do what was unfair or ungenerous to any man.

Therefore, if we are offered a certain interpretation in Scripture that clashes with men's highest sense of what is generous and fair, we must not ignore that clashing. We must refuse to accept that interpretation for the present till we have enquired more about it. For example, if we are told that in the 'hardening of Pharaoh's heart' God punished Pharaoh for something that Pharaoh could not have helped, we must decline that interpretation. If we read in Ro 9 St Paul's famous passage about election, and if any man

should explain it to mean that God destines some men to eternal heaven and some to eternal hell, not for anything of good or evil in them, but for His own glory to magnify Himself, we are bound to reject such a meaning without hesitation. This is not a question of doubting the Bible, but of doubting men's interpretation of it. True faith will not accept an interpretation that is dishonouring to God. It is as if a schoolboy got a letter from his father containing a passage capable of an evil meaning. A companion suggests such a meaning. The boy, though he does not understand the passage, instinctively rejects that interpretation as unworthy his father's character If he can find no other meaning he prefers to leave the passage a mystery for the present.

It is very necessary to say this ; yet it is necessary also to add a grave caution against the attitude that would make every man set up his own judgment as to what he would believe or disbelieve. It is not at all safe to judge from the recoil of this or that man's individual conscience, lest there may be in it anything abnormal. It is only when one can feel sure that a certain interpretation of Scripture, though otherwise possible, clashes with the best men's sense of what is right and true, that he is justified in rejecting it.

Such humble, prayerful, yet fearless use of conscience soon sets us asking questions which lead to important results. For we begin to find in the Old Testament utterances that fall below the level of the enlightened Christian conscience, and actions that one feels would not win the approval of Christ. We find permission of slavery, plurality of wives, divorce, etc. We find fierce, vengeful words in the imprecatory Psalms. Conscience insists on our questioning these things, and the more conscience is enlightened by the main teaching of the Bible the more will it insist on such questioning.

II. The Divine and Human in the Bible

There are two answers. First, that in the Bible the divine and human are blended (see art. ' Inspiration '). We must not regard the Bible as an absolutely perfect book in which God is Himself the author using human hands and brains only as a man might use a typewriter. God used men, not machines— men with like weakness and prejudice and passion as ourselves, though purified and ennobled by the influence of His Holy Spirit; men each with his own peculiarities of manner and disposition—each with his own education or want of education—each with his own way of looking at things—each influenced differently from another by the different experiences and discipline of his life. Their inspiration did not involve a suspension of their natural faculties; it did not destroy their personality, nor abolish the differences of training and character; it did not even make them perfectly free from earthly passion; it did not make them into machines—it left them men.

Therefore we find their knowledge sometimes no higher than that of their contemporaries, and their indignation against oppression and wrong-doing sometimes breaking out into desire of revenge. This would not surprise us in the least in other good men who were, we knew, striving after God and righteousness. It surprises us in the Bible, because of our false preconceptions; because it is in the Bible we do not expect the actors to be real and natural; because of our false theory of Verbal Inspiration we are puzzled when the divine is mingled with the human. We must learn that the divine *is* mingled with the human.

We cannot draw a line between the divine and the human. We cannot say of any part, 'This is divine,' or 'That is human.' In some parts, as the Gospels, there is more of the divine; in others, as the Chronicles, more of the human. It is as a mine of precious ore where the gold is mingled with the rock and clay—the ore is richer in one part than another, but all parts in some degree are glittering with gold. It is as sunlight through a painted window—the light must come to us coloured by the medium—we cannot get it any other way. In some parts the medium is denser and more imperfect, in others the golden glory comes dazzlingly through. It is foolish to ignore the existence of the human medium through which the light has come; it is still more foolish to ignore the divine light, and think that the tinted dome is luminous itself, that the light of heaven has only come from earth. Both must be kept in mind—the divine and the human—if the Bible is to be rightly understood.

III. PROGRESSIVENESS OF REVELATION

And the other answer to the questionings of conscience is this—that we must think of human life as the great school of God, where gradually, patiently, through all the ages He has been training humanity for nobleness of life. The Old Testament is to be read not as a series of perfect precepts equally applicable to all men in all ages of the world, but rather

as the story of God's gradual education of humanity. It was like our gradual education of our children to-day. We begin with the lowest rudiments of knowledge. Very crude and imperfect conceptions must satisfy us at first. Though all the glory of the highest knowledge lie before the child by and by, yet he can only partially receive it now until his mind has grown. Perhaps a better illustration of the attitude of the Old Testament is seen in the attitude of the missionary to-day in dealing with the lower races of heathendom. He knows how little is to be expected from them at first. He has to tolerate and overlook much that grieves him. He must be content to move slowly. He rejoices at every effort after good, even though it be largely mixed with evil. He gives warm approval to acts which for these poor savages really mean progress upward, though to the Christian world at home they may seem worthier censure than praise. He believes that God is helping men by His Holy Spirit, even though error and wrong-doing yet remain. By and by, when some of his converts have grown into noble, faithful strugglers after Christ, will they not look back on the early training and the early notions as on a lower stage that they have long since passed, and yet confess that it was a necessary stage in their progress upward?

Such was God's progressive education of the race. Many things in the early stages were overlooked or 'winked at' (Ac 17^{30}). Slavery was not at once swept away, but its cruelties were forbidden and its abuses checked —divorce was not absolutely prohibited, but laid under stringent regulations. When we read of these evils so allowed to exist—when we find, as in the Psalms, the lofty teachings and burning aspirations after God now and then marred by the fierce prayer for vengeance on the wicked—we must remember that we are judging men in the lower classes of the great school of God, and that the presence of His Spirit with men did not necessarily involve absolute perfection in teaching and conduct. Notice in the Sermon on the Mount how clearly our Lord teaches this progressiveness of revelation: 'Ye have heard that it was said to them of old time . . but I say unto you,' etc.: see Mt 5$^{17, 21, 27, 33, 38, 43}$ RV.

IV. THE BIBLE IN THE TWENTIETH CENTURY

In the beginning of this new century there are other questions arising about the Bible besides those already referred to. There are questions of scientific accuracy, and questions as to the 'Higher Criticism,' as it is called. People have learned that the first chapter of Genesis cannot be reconciled with science; that the stories of the Creation and the Flood had existed as legends of other races long before the Bible was written. They have learned that there are certain books of Scripture which bear on the face of them marks of being not original work, but compilations from earlier lost documents. And most of these things that they have learned are true. There is no doubt that the ordinary Bible reader will be compelled in the new century to shift his point of view. We have learned much during the past fifty years which has thrown new light on the meaning of parts of our Bible, which has at any rate made doubtful some of our old views and interpretations of it. But we must learn not to be disturbed at changing our view-point, and we especially must try in educating the younger generation to prepare them for changes which must come. For example, we must not insist that the Bible teaches as God's infallible truth that the world was created in six literal days, and finished off on Saturday night as a carpenter would finish his week's work, or that the order of Creation *must* be accurately given in the first chapter of Genesis. We cannot teach positively that the story of the Fall is an exactly literal narrative of facts. Some people think that it is, and others, who are certainly no less holy and no less learned, think that it is an ancient allegory embodying a deep and vital truth. We must keep an open mind about many such things as these. We must endeavour in our Bible study to be thoroughly real and thoroughly truthful, 'to assert nothing as certain which is not certain, nothing as probable which is not probable, and nothing as more probable than it is.' We must keep in mind that God's way of helping the world to the light may have been very different from what we thought it was, and that it is a dangerous thing to put in the place of inspiration certain popular notions as to what inspiration should be. We must therefore seek to let in the light on all sides, however it may ultimately modify our preconceived notions of inspiration. And if we do so we shall find by and by that the result will be not loss, but great gain to the Bible.

There is a story of an ancient land where a fire once swept over the hills destroying the flowers and the foliage and changing the familiar aspect of the scene. But as the people were grieving for their loss they discovered that the fire which had destroyed the flowers and the foliage had opened by its heat deep fissures in the rocks, disclosing to their view rich veins of silver—so it shall be with us if we face the new questions wisely. If by the searching fire of literary and scientific criticism we lose some cherished traditional notions, we shall gain in a deeper knowledge of truth. We shall gain in knowledge of the nature and limits of inspiration and in under-standing God's methods of communication with men, and we shall be saved from many of the errors and misapprehensions that are turning men away from the Bible to-day.

And for the questions of the Higher Criticism, if we believe that the Old Testament story is true, that the inspired men who wrote it had access to sources of knowledge in the past, why should it matter if the books in their present form were written much later than we thought, or that they are the result of compiling and editing again and again under the mysterious free supervision of the Spirit of God? We do not all believe that all the statements of Higher Criticism will ultimately be accepted—many of them are being already relinquished and forgotten—but no doubt there will ultimately remain a residuum of established fact which must modify in some measure our views about the Bible. And we do not believe that in that residuum of fact will be anything to prevent thoughtful men from believing in the divine origin of the Bible.

In these times of questioning and doubt about the Old Testament there are some reassuring thoughts that men should keep before them. First think of the wonder of this, that any set of old documents always open to scrutiny and question should have been accepted as of divine origin and yielded to by men as having authority to impose on them commands often disagreeable to them. What gave them that authority? There seems no possible answer but that they possessed it of themselves; they commanded the position they held by their own power. Men's moral sense and reason combined to establish them. Where there were no miracles or portents, no external voices from heaven to compel allegiance, men must have received these books largely because of their appeal to the God-given conscience within. That is to say, the authority of the Scriptures through all the ages primarily rests on the conviction which they themselves produced that they came from God. That conviction forces itself on us still to-day. In the records of other nations we see the chief stress laid on power and prosperity and comfort and wealth. In these strange records goodness is the only thing of importance. The chief business of prophet and historian and legislator seems to be to rebuke men for sin and point them to holiness. Look at the wonderful national poems and hymns: 'Have mercy on me, O God, after Thy great goodness' (Ps 51); 'Praise the Lord, O my soul' (Ps 103); 'The Lord is my shepherd' (Ps 23), and think of the dark, horrible history of the outside world at the time that all these wonderful national poems were written. Then notice the compulsion that seemed laid upon the prophets, the mysterious Spirit striving with them, enlightening them, compelling them to speak of God's righteousness. Hear the constant iteration, 'The Word of the Lord'; 'Thus saith the Lord.' Surely these are not the phenomena of ordinary human history! Then see how the whole Bible centres in Jesus Christ. The Old Testament tells of the preparation for Christ; the New Testament tells that when that preparation was complete 'in the fulness of time God sent forth His Son.' Jesus Christ as it were stands between the Old Testament and the New, and lays His hand on them both. The Old Testament, He insists again and again, is the Word of God, and bears witness of Him. The New Testament is the story of the words and works of Himself and of the Apostles sent forth by Him. And both together form this Bible of ours, which beyond all the books of the world has proved its power to turn men towards righteousness. We never hear man speak of the power and peace and hope that come from the study of the Latin classics, or of lives wrenched round from darkness to light by any other teaching than that of the Bible.

Therefore let us rest our hearts on these foundations and be at peace, while men are questioning and finding out for us what we did not know before about the inspired Word of God.

V. HINTS AND SUGGESTIONS FOR STUDY

1. **On using Common Sense.** The old objection is often repeated that the Bible is like a 'nose of wax' that can be turned every way; that one can gather all sorts of contradictory teaching from its pages. Yes, if you read it foolishly; for the Bible is no formal system of teaching with every precept accurately defined and limited, and every exception carefully pointed out. It deals with broad principles rather than with particular precepts. We are trusted to apply these principles ourselves to the practical guiding of our lives. Sometimes its commands are of universal application; sometimes they apply only to such special cases as are before the writer; sometimes they are figurative and intended to prescribe the spirit and temper of our lives, such as 'Give to him that asketh thee,' etc. The same caution is needed about the types and prophecies of the Old Testament. If man will not diligently use the common sense that God has given him he must make mistakes in reading the Bible. The inspired writers express themselves quite freely, and usually without showing any anxiety to prevent misunderstandings. They seem to assume that their readers will be sensible people. They see no need of constantly guarding and qualifying their statements, and reminding us that they are to be taken in connexion with other statements made elsewhere.

There are many ways in which this absence of common sense shows itself. There is the thoughtless habit of quoting all parts of the Bible as Scripture, whether they be the words of our Lord or the words of Bildad the Shuhite and Zophar the Naamathite, in the book of Job, who are afterwards represented as condemned and contradicted by God. There is the habit often indulged in by preachers of twisting the obvious meaning of words, and the commoner and more dangerous habit of quoting for the support of doctrines isolated texts utterly regardless of the context or of the circumstances under which they were originally uttered. One might as well take as a general proposition a single sentence of a letter without considering the context or the writer, or the purpose of the letter or the person to whom it was written. Thus people put St. Paul and St. James in opposition with regard to Faith and Works. It is quite natural that two teachers, or even the same teacher at different times, should make these different statements. A preacher dealing with penitents who in their misery were trying to win God's favour by piling up good deeds might very wisely tell them that God desired not this, but that they should come with simple trustful faith, as a little child to its father. But just as wisely might he, in dealing with people who justify frequent lapses into impurity and meanness and ill-temper by talking much about their faith and their resting on the finished work of Christ and not on their own righteousness—just as wisely might he insist as indignantly as St. James that faith without works is dead.

2. **On Taking Pains.** Using common sense implies taking considerable pains in one's reading. Take two readers, say, of the Epistle to the Galatians. The first makes no attempt to get into touch with his author. He begins each day at the beginning of his daily chapter. Quite possibly, owing to faulty chapter division, this may begin in the middle of an argument, or not be at all the logical commencement of the subject discussed; so he reads over the chapter feeling very hazy as to its meaning. As he has read the previous chapter in the same hazy way, he never thinks of looking back to find the connexion; thus he wastes a good deal of time, turns away dissatisfied, or contents himself with culling out one or two disconnected texts. The other reader takes pains. He knows that to understand any man's letter one must find out its drift and purpose, and get in touch with the writer and his original readers; so he looks into the Acts of the Apostles to find out St. Paul's connexion

with these Galatians. Then he reads over the whole Epistle two or three times for a general view of it. He notices its severe, indignant tone. He sees that the writer is hurt and offended about the fickleness of his converts and their reception of false teachers who oppose him. He seems very self-assertive as to his position. Perhaps this is all that a first or second perusal of the Epistle reveals. But this sets him thinking. He has kept clear of commentaries, trying to get his view of the Epistle by himself. But now he turns to his commentary, and with its assistance he goes back again to the Acts of the Apostles. He finds reason to believe that after Paul had left Galatia, his constant opponents, the emissaries of the Judaising party, had come proclaiming (as in the case recorded Ac 15), 'Except ye be circumcised and obedient to the Law ye cannot be saved.' The reader at once understands the vexation of the Apostle at these fickle converts deserting him for false teachers, and putting in jeopardy the whole future of Christianity in that region. With this key he turns back again to his perusal of the Epistle, and it becomes at once full of life and interest. Let this hint suffice. We cannot go further with the subject in our limited space.

3. Devotional Study. Surely it is not necessary to say that one should study regularly—should study with the object of growing acquainted with God, and with the purpose of finding God's will and doing it when he has found it. Still less is it necessary to say to any honest Bible reader study prayerfully, though it may be well to suggest to him the habit of reading his regular portion first, and then on his knees trying to turn it into prayer, so that there should be not only God's speaking to him, but also his speaking back to God in God's inspired words.

All these things are matters of course to a devout reader. What, perhaps, he is most in need of is a help towards meditation. In Liddon's 'Clerical Life and Work' there is a valuable section on this subject which has much helped the writer. So few know how to read their Bible profitably, especially few

know how to meditate on it. Let us very diffidently suggest what a meditation should be. Not the leaning lazing on your elbow with the Bible open before you, reading the verses silently, and letting the thoughts frequently wander; it is no such listless dreaming over the text; it is an act of the whole soul rising in the fulness of its energy towards God—memory, imagination, intellect, will, fully engaged; it is the soul placing itself in the presence of Jehovah; it is an effort after the Vision of God.

First of all, let your imagination play freely on the passage. Think of the actor or writer. Put yourself in his place. Try to enter into the feeling of the formalist Pharisees, the jealous scribes, the ignorant mob, and especially of the great loving heart of Him who loved and understood and watched over them all. Try, as you read a passage of St. Paul, to 'put yourself in the place' of the writer, with his keen, highly-strung nature, now glad, now despondent, now vexed and dissatisfied, but always with every thought full of loyalty to his Master. This use of the imagination will help you to the heart of the passage. Then the intellect is summoned before God to enter into His message, to grapple with the subject and select the leading thought in it.

This is but preparatory; then bring the will to bear on it—Will to love the highest, Will to imitate the noblest, Will to cast yourself down in lowly adoration before all the love and self-sacrifice told of God, of Jesus Christ.

Get the habit of doing it—if not once a day, then once a week; but as often as you can. Select the fittest portions—the story of the Passion, the words of Christ, the prayers of St. Paul for his beloved people. Thus let the soul linger in the presence of God, laying the inmost being before Him, and entering into reverent and affectionate yet trustful conference with Him. Lie low before Him. Let Him speak to your soul, and speak back to Him, face to face, as a man speaketh to his friend. Take a great deal of trouble to learn and acquire the habit of meditation. It is there the soul learns most to blame itself and to adore and love its Lord

THE ELEMENTS OF RELIGION

THE opening pages of the Bible reveal to us the elements of religion, in language which, though figurative, is unmistakable in its import. We are told of the Creator who called the universe into being (Gn 1 1 f.), and formed man 'in His own image' (Gn 1 26, 27), with the gift of free-will. We are told how man abused this gift, and, seeking a false independence, fell under the bondage of sin and death (Gn 3 ; cp. Ro 5 12 f.): a bondage from which divine succour alone could redeem him. The law-books, especially Leviticus, emphasise this need of divine help, in their doctrine of Sacrifice, laying stress on the awful holiness of God (Lv 11 45 19 2 20 7, etc.), and man's need of purification and self-surrender ; while the Psalmists and Prophets dwell on the inner spiritual character of repentance and of that obedience of the heart to God's moral law, without which sacrifice is worse than a mockery (1 S 15 22 Pss 40 6 51 16, 17 Isa 1 11 f. Hos 6 6).

Some of these thoughts are found, in a more or less incomplete or distorted form, in every religion. The dependence on an unseen spiritual being, or beings ; the consciousness of broken communion ; the consequent need of some new, heaven-given means of access —these ideas, as well as the simpler and more childlike thought of tribute or of free-will offerings of homage and thankfulness, lie at the root of those sacrificial customs in which religion has always expressed itself even among pagans. The Bible's teaching about religion, if we compare it with what we can learn of contemporary heathen customs, and especially those of the pagan Semites, seems to take up these common ideas, to purify and transfigure them, and make them the vehicle of a doctrine valuable for all ages.

1. **The Covenant of God with Man.** One of the leading conceptions of the Old Testament —the one, in fact, from which the volume derives its name—is that of a Covenant between God and man (Covenant with Noah, Gn 6 18; with Abraham, Gn 12 1-3 17 1-14 22 16-18 ; with Jacob, Gn 28 13-15; with the people of Israel. Ex 24 7 34 10, 27 Lv 26 9 Dt 29 9-15 31 24-30; with David, Ps 89 3, 28, 33-39);—a Covenant which, as St. Paul points out (Gal 3 15 f., especially v. 17), is prior to the Law, and superior to it. Herein the Almighty condescends to pledge Himself, that if man fulfil certain conditions, He, on His part, will pardon his sins and bless him. The true inner meaning of this Covenant is manifested in that *New* Covenant (of

which the Old is but a shadow), foretold by prophets (Jer 31 31 f. ; cp. Heb 8 8-12 and 2 Cor 3 6), and announced by Christ in His institution of the Lord's Supper, in the words : 'This is my blood of the New Covenant,' or 'This cup is the New Covenant in my Blood' (Mt 26 28 Mk 14 24 Lk 22 20 1 Cor 11 25).

2. **Covenant and Sacrifice.** The Covenant of which the Bible speaks is made with sacrifice (Ex 24 5 f. Ps 50 5 Heb 9 15 f.). Its principle is an Atonement (At-one-ment) between man and God (Leviticus, especially c. 16, Day of Atonement, and Heb 9). The sacrifices of the Old Covenant, in their three leading types of sin-offering (Lv 4–6), Burnt-offering (Lv 1 3 f.), Peace-offering (Lv 3 1 f.), while revealing the true character of man's relation to God, and ministering in a provisional way to the devotional needs of the faithful, led up to the great Atonement of the New Covenant, in which all their defects were remedied, and their imperfections removed. The Sin-offering teaches that communion is broken and that access to God can only be reopened by the shedding of life-blood (Lv 17 11), symbolising expiation and cleansing ; the Burnt-offering, in which the entire sacrifice is consumed upon the altar, speaks of that unreserved self-surrender which is the only homage God can accept from man; the Peace-offering, in which priest and offerer feast together at 'God's board' symbolises the life of joyful communion between man and his Maker.

3. **Christ's Sacrifice of Atonement.** All these conceptions are realised completely in our Lord's self-offering as displayed to us in the New Testament. He gives Himself as an atonement for sin (Ro 3 25 1 Jn 2 2 4 10), as an offering of perfect obedience to the Father (Phil 2 8), as a gift of communion and life to His members (Jn 6 32 f. 10 10 11 25 14 6 Col 3 4). What are, after all, but types and shadows (Heb 10 1 ; cp. Col 2 17) in the Old Testament, the New Testament reveals in real substance. For instance, the victim in the Old Covenant was unconscious and unwilling : Christ offers Himself of His own free-will (Jn 10 17, 18), and looks forward to the dread moment with wistful yearning (Lk 12 50). (So false, we may notice in passing, is that idea of the Atonement which pictures it as an angry Father punishing an innocent Son.) Again, the victim under the Old Covenant was only by a sort of 'legal fiction' identified with the offerer, who laid his hand on the beast's head, and pre-

sented its life instead of his own (Lv 1⁴). But Christ's offering is in a very real sense identical with those on whose behalf it is made. The Victim is indeed Himself the offerer; offering, however, as representative of all mankind. When St. John tells us that the Word was made flesh (Jn 1¹⁴), he speaks of an incarnation in which the Son of God took upon Him not the physique of an individual man, but assumed our human nature in a general way; an assuming which is the more universal in its effects because of the omnipotence and omnipresence of the Person who assumed it. Christ thus becomes, as St. Paul teaches, a second Founder of the race—the 'Second Adam' (1 Cor 15⁴⁵⁻⁴⁷ Ro 5¹²⁻²¹). In this character, as being truly, and by no fiction, representative of the whole race, He was able to offer up to Almighty God the threefold sacrifice of expiation, homage, and communion on behalf of all mankind. Further, what He thus accomplished for all of us, He is able, if we are willing, to accomplish in each one of us individually: His divinity effectuating in detail, through the power of His Spirit, what His perfect humanity achieved once for all. Thus the redemption and sanctification which His Atonement brings to individual souls by His indwelling is no more a 'legal fiction' than His self-offering on behalf of all. 'Christ in you,' says St. Paul, is 'the hope of glory' (Col 1²⁷). His victorious might, working in those who are united to Him as members of His Body, and blending their wills with His, is able to transform them, step by step, into His own likeness, as He, literally, grows to maturity in them: and the effect of righteousness thus produced, is then quite truly both His and ours—He is, in fact, 'our righteousness' (1 Cor 1³⁰). Dwelling in us, He frees us not only from the guilt of sin by His expiatory death, of which He makes us partakers (Ro 6³,⁴ 2 Cor 4¹⁰ Col 2¹²,²⁰ 2 Tim 2¹¹), but also from its bondage and its taint, by the power of His resurrection life (Col 2¹³ᶠ· 3¹ᶠ·). His Holy Spirit, by whom He indwells in the believer, transforms the soul from glory to glory, making it a 'mirror' of the Lord's perfection (2 Cor 3¹⁷,¹⁸).

4. Material Pledges of the Atonement. Sacraments. As in the Old Covenant God deigned to work by material pledges, so also in the New. Here again, however, we have no longer symbol but reality. 'Except a man be born anew—be born of water and the Spirit,' says our Saviour, 'he cannot see—he cannot enter into—the kingdom of God' (Jn 3³,⁵,⁷). And later on He bids His followers 'make disciples of all the nations, baptising them into the name of the Father and of the Son and of the Holy Ghost' (Mt 28¹⁹). Again, He says: 'I am the bread which came down

from heaven .. the bread of life .. the bread which I will give is my flesh for the life of the world .. except ye eat the flesh of the Son of Man and drink His blood, ye have not life in yourselves' (Jn 6³⁴,⁴¹,⁴⁸,⁵¹,⁵³). And later on He takes up bread and wine in His Holy Supper, saying, 'This is my body,' 'this is my blood,' 'do this in remembrance of me'; and speaks of His Blood as that of the 'New Covenant' (Lk 22¹⁹,²⁰ and parallels). So it is that the two great Sacraments of the Gospel, though they have been the subject of much discussion, especially since the Reformation, are recognised by all Christians as having a special importance in relation to the New Covenant, as pledges of our union with the Incarnate Redeemer. That He should use such humble material means as vehicles of spiritual blessing is not only appropriate to our own composite nature—part matter and part spirit —but of a piece also with the marvel of His Incarnation, whereby heaven and earth are wedded together: cp. Jn 1⁵¹. The Sacraments are rightly considered as moral instruments for the conveying of God's grace in Christ to us. What God offers us therein is no mechanical or magical power, still less a mere symbol or fiction, but an indubitable spiritual boon. The effect upon ourselves depends on the attitude of our own souls. Repentance, faith, obedience are the requisites for a right reception of either of these Sacraments, as they are necessary conditions of a right relation to God: and these requisites are themselves gifts of the Holy Spirit, to be won by earnest prayer.

5. Infant Baptism. Those many Christians who practise infant baptism, do so because they believe (1) that it is in accordance with the mind of Christ and a proper understanding of the sacred rite, and (2) that its significance and effect are secured by the pledges of the sureties that as the child develops he shall be taught what are the privileges and responsibilities of a member of Christ and the initial gift be fostered by 'the nurture and admonition of the Lord' (Eph 6⁴).

The adult who is admitted to baptism takes these pledges upon himself, promising to forsake sin, to accept trustfully the revelation of God's mercy in Christ, and to walk in the path of the divine commandments. In pagan lands it is usually as a result of preaching (cp. Ro 10¹⁴,¹⁵) that the light dawns upon him, and he experiences what we know as 'Conversion'; then, after fuller instruction, he is brought to the baptism of the Covenant.

6. Conversion. This phenomenon of conversion often happens, and sometimes in a striking way to those who have been brought up in Christian surroundings, and those who have been baptised in infancy. The grace of God in them has been so far quenched by contending influences—worldliness, carelessness, vicious passions, or the like—like the seed in thorny ground whose growth is choked by worldly cares and riches (Mt 13 22). At last the Voice of God makes itself heard ; with conviction of sin and sincere repentance union with Christ is realised and the divine forces of the indwelling Spirit are brought into play. The result is seen in a fruitful life of communion with God. This conversion is not to be confused with the gift of baptism. In adults converted from alien beliefs it normally precedes baptism, as in the case of St. Paul (Ac 9 3f. and v. 18 22 6f. and v. 16), while in those who are baptised as infants it naturally follows the rite. In some cases, as in that of St. Paul, the conversion comes in a single moment ; in others it is a gradual process, more or less continuous, of more intimate approach to God. Often it has a kind of rhythmical or recurring character, marked by definite stages in the external or internal life of the individual, as at confirmation and at first communion, in times of sickness or bereavement, or on the occasion of marriage or parenthood—these crises forming steps in a more or less regular evolution of the spiritual life.

For all alike conversion in some sense is necessary, and for all alike it involves the individual realisation of our relation of sonship to the heavenly Father. 'Except ye be converted,' says the Saviour, 'and become as little children, ye shall in no wise enter into the kingdom' (Mt 18 3).

7. Religious Duties. The typical duties on which our Lord lays stress in His Sermon on the Mount—Fasting (Mt 6 16-18), Almsgiving (Mt 6 1-4), and Prayer (Mt 6 5-15)—cover the whole field of the religious life, representing respectively the three aspects of our Lord's atoning sacrifice, as sin-offering, burnt-offering, and peace-offering.

(1) **Prayer.** Prayer is the soul's communion with its Maker. Its importance and something of its nature are revealed to us by our Lord's example (we are told of His spending long hours alone in prayer, Mt 14 23 Lk 6 12 Mk 1 35), by His precepts (Mt 9 38 Lk 21 36 Mk 7 7f. 11 22f., etc.), and by the pattern prayer which He has given us (Mt 6 9-13 Lk 11 2-4). It is the outpouring of the child's soul to the heavenly Father, with whose will the child's will is blent. In a wide sense it is an attitude, not necessarily expressed in words, so that St. Paul can say, 'Pray without ceasing' (1 Th 5 17). Yet that there is something more in prayer than a mere spiritual self-surrender —a 'Thy will be done'—is clear from Christ's words and works. Always in submission to the all-wise will of the Father, He encourages

us to ask for definite things. For spiritual blessings, first of all, where there can be no doubt about God's will, and the only necessary condition is faith (Lk 11 13 ; cp. 1 Cor 12 31 14 1). But not for spiritual blessings only. In His agony He prayed definitely to have the 'cup' removed, if it were the Father's will (Lk 22 42 ; cp. Heb 5 7). In His model prayer He bids us, after the petitions of which God is the subject, to ask for daily bread (Mt 6 11). In His works of healing He Himself answers the prayers of parents and friends for the restoration of their loved ones to health (Mt 8 5f. 9 2f. and v. 18f. 14 35, 36 15 22f., etc.).

In modern times people have often been puzzled about prayer. Science has taught us that God works in the world by law and system, and that everything works together in an extremely complicated interaction. What place is there then, it is asked, for individual prayers ? If I ask for a definite thing for myself or my friend, even though it be not what we commonly call a 'miracle,' am I not presuming, and presuming in vain, to beg for a breach of the laws by which God works ?

The answer is, first of all, that if God works by law and system, marshalling the forces of nature in harmonious interaction, the force of the prayer of faith is not *outside* that system, but is one of its most potent factors. Furthermore, we ask all subject to God's will, confessing our own ignorance ; and as we advance in the knowledge and love of Him, our own wills inevitably become more and more attuned to His, and it becomes growingly impossible that we should approach Him with extravagant and unworthy petitions. Again, as St. Augustine observes, we are bidden to ask all in the name of Jesus (Jn 15 16 16 23, 26), the Saviour : anything asked in ignorance which would, if granted, run counter to God's redemptive purposes, we shall expect to be withheld, as not being really in the Saviour's name. Finally, as we suggested above, Christ makes it quite clear that it is normal and right for the faithful to ask for such things as they need, and gives us many object lessons, in His works of mercy on earth, of answers to the prayer of faith in what must have seemed like desperate cases. It is noticeable also that He frequently combined with the physical boon prayed for, a corresponding spiritual boon, adding the healing of the soul to that of the body (Mt 9 2-6, etc.).

The prayer of which our Lord is specially speaking in the Sermon on the Mount is that private intimate communion with God which the 'Father who seeth in secret' is pledged to recompense (Mt 6 6). This aspect of prayer is emphasised in contrast to the ostentatious praying in the streets of the contemporary Pharisees (Mt 6 5), and is not, of course, meant to condemn those regular meetings for prayer in which the corporate life of God's people expressed itself alike in the Old Covenant and the New.

(2) **Fasting.** Fasting—the spirit of the sin-offering—i.e. of purification and self-discipline, and almsgiving—the spirit of the burnt-offering, i.e. of self-surrender, are, like prayer, assumed and taken for granted in the Sermon on the Mount, the necessity of unostentatious sincerity being similarly emphasised.

Self-discipline, the inner principle of fasting, is rendered necessary by the disorder in our nature wrought by sin. Not even an apostle can do without it: 'I keep under my body,' says St. Paul, 'and bring it into subjection' (1 Cor 9 27 ; cp. 2 Cor 6 5 11 27). It is, in fact, that renunciation of the world, the flesh, and the devil which from the earliest ages has accompanied Christian baptism, and represents the penitent coöperation of man with the Holy Spirit in the work of self-purification. It naturally expresses itself in acts of self-denial, a mark of Christ's sincere disciples (Mt 16 24), and still more, perhaps, in the glad acceptance of God's manifold discipline in life.

(3) **Almsgiving.** Self-surrender, the inner principle of almsgiving, is the recognition that all we have and are is doubly due to God, who has first, as Creator, granted us our existence, and then, as Redeemer, bought us with a price (1 Cor 6 20 7 23)—the precious blood of Jesus Christ.

8. In these practices we realise our union with Christ. Thus in the three principles represented by fasting, almsgiving and prayer, the believer is united with the Saviour in His threefold act of atonement ; and by the power of the divine indwelling his sinful body is progressively purified and assimilated to the stainless humanity of Christ, his warped will is brought more and more into line with that perfect will, his whole life is caught up into an ever closer communion with the life of God. And thus individual believers are gathered up into the pure offering of a redeemed humanity, the sacrifice which He offered up once for all upon the Cross, and effectuates successively and in detail in those whom He unites to Himself. The sanctification of individual Christians is thus a kind of propagation of Christ Himself, and is a little type of that great corporate perfection of the whole body of the redeemed of which St. Paul speaks as the coming to a perfect, i.e. full-grown, Humanity, the measure of the stature of the fulness of Christ (Eph 4 13).

9. Penitence : Sins of Believers. It would be misleading however, to describe this process of sanctification as one of steady and undevi-

ating advance. As there have been retrograde moments and periods of decline and disloyalty in the Church in general (both under the Old Covenant and under the New), so too the individual Christian life is often a perplexing mixture of ascents and downfalls. The Old Testament is full of such instances, alike in the Church and in the individual. The frequent backslidings of the nation are paralleled by the failures of patriarchs like Israel himself, and of subsequent saints of eminence like Moses and David—grave, though incidental failures, which do not affect the favourable character of the final verdict. In the New Testament the mention of the single name of Peter is sufficient to show the possibility of defection after an intimate walk with Christ, and the certainty of a full restoration after sincere repentance.

There is, indeed, a passage in the Epistle to the Hebrews which speaks of a form of disloyalty after which renewal is impossible (Heb 6 4-6), and our Lord Himself has words of deepest solemnity about a blasphemy against the Holy Spirit 'which hath never forgiveness' (Mk 3 29). We shall be justified in identifying these two sins—a deliberate and wilful ranging oneself against known truth—and in distinguishing from this unforgivable offence the constant instances of frailty in the redeemed for which Christ expressly invites us to ask pardon (Mt 6 12, 14). For though the New Testament speaks of believing members of Christ as 'saints' or holy people (e.g. Ro 1 7 15 26 16 15 1 Cor 1 2 6 1 14 33, etc., etc.), and St. John, speaking of the believer ideally considered, says that 'whosoever is begotten of God doeth no sin' . . 'cannot sin' (1 Jn 3 6, 9) ; yet the Lord clearly contemplated in the faithful some deviations from the path of perfection, else He would not have inserted into His model prayer the clause 'forgive us our trespasses.' Nor can we forget that St. John, in the same Epistle just quoted, speaks clearly and strongly to believers about the forgiveness and cleansing that can be won by confession of sins (1 Jn 1 9, 10). The Christian consciousness has rightly regarded confession of sins as a normal part of private as well as public devotions, and a necessary condition of continuance in God's grace. It is especially appropriate as a preparation for the reception of Holy Communion, and has been so recognised by all Christian denominations. Confession accompanied by contrition and purpose of amendment, by which the soul renews from time to time its renunciation of the world, the flesh and the devil, wins, so Scripture assures us, the forgiveness of the Father and restoration to effective communion with Him.

10. Eternal Life. The communion of the

spirit with God in Christ, which the New Testament, taking up the language of the Old, describes as 'knowledge' of God (Hos 4[1] 6[3,6] Jn 17[3] Phil 1[9] Col 1[10], etc.), is called by St. John 'Eternal Life' (Jn 17[3]); a phrase by which the Apostle clearly means, not a future gift, but a present possession. It is a gift, no doubt, but imperfectly appropriated here—the 'crown' of it, its full and triumphant fruition, is to be attained by the faithful after death (2 Tim 4[8] Rev 2[10]); yet it is nevertheless a real possession on this side of the grave. Even the Psalmists of the Old Testament recognised this truth, and the fact of present communion with God was to them the supreme argument for a future life (Pss 16[8-11] 17[15]); an argument clinched by our Lord when He said the God of Abraham, Isaac and Jacob is not a God of the dead, but of the living, for all live unto Him (Lk 20[37, 38]). Just as the phrase 'kingdom of God' or 'of Heaven' is used sometimes of the Church militant and imperfect (e.g. Mt 13[24 f. 47 f.]), and sometimes of the perfect, triumphant Church of the future (Mt 25[34])—and rightly so, because these are really two different stages of the same thing; so too with 'Eternal Life.' It begins as soon as Christ is appropriated, as soon as the believer is first united to His triumphant resurrection life; it is to be consummated when the Son of man shall come in His glory.

11. Death and Judgment, Heaven and Hell. Over against Life stands Death, the penalty incurred by man as the result of his wilful breach with God: 'in the day that thou eatest thereof thou shalt surely die' (Gn 2[17]). The death thus spoken of in Scripture is not primarily or exclusively the physical dissolution of the body, but rather that death of body and soul together of which Christ speaks in such solemn and mysterious tones (Lk 12[5]). If God is Life and man's eternal life consists in close and constant communion with Him, it needs no dogmatic statement to make clear the terrible character of a permanent alienation from Him. The language of Scripture is forcible enough on this head (Mt 25[41, 46] Mk 9[48]); but there is no more powerful aid to the realisation of the appalling alternative than the consideration of the extent of the Saviour's sufferings for our redemption. The value of the redemption can only be estimated by an appreciation of the price paid. It is thus that Christ's passion, from the agony in the garden to the death on the Cross, has always been the strongest stimulus to conversion; it draws us with a twofold cord of love and fear—fear of that ineffable doom which it cost so much to avert, and love to Him who for love of us willingly paid the price. The Cross is the only adequate measure of the hatefulness of sin and of the horror of

its consequences. Those consequences are not to be regarded as belonging entirely to the future, any more than are the consequences of saving union with the Redeemer. As it was said in the Old Testament that 'in the day that' man disobeyed 'he should surely die,' so also in the New Testament we are told by St. John that 'he that hath not the Son of God hath not the life' (1 Jn 5[12]), and that 'he that loveth not abideth in death' (1 Jn 3[14, 15]). In both cases, however, the consummation, whether of life or death, lies beyond the grave, and Scripture describes the eternal future of mankind as following upon a Judgment in which all alike are to pass before Christ's throne (Ro 14[10] 2 Cor 5[10]). This is clear from our Lord's own words as well as from those of His Apostle (Mt 25[31, 32]). The Judgment is represented as preceded by the general resurrection of the dead, at Christ's Second Coming (Jn 5[28, 29]).

12. Paradise. If we ask what is the condition, meanwhile, of those who have passed away from this life, our Lord's words to the penitent robber: 'To-day shalt thou be with me in Paradise' (Lk 23[43]), to which the parable of Dives and Lazarus (Lk 16[20 f.]) form a kind of commentary, suggest to us a state in which the believer's soul is in a special sense 'with Christ,' in a more intimate relation than is possible for us here: a state to which St. Paul seems to be looking forward when he says that 'to depart and be with Christ' is far better (Phil 1[23]). This 'waiting state' (Heb 11[39, 40]; cp. Rev 6[9]) of the faithful has as its background in the parable the 'torment' of Dives, which seems, correspondingly, a foretaste of that 'Gehenna of fire' (Mk 9[43-48]), under the symbolism of which our Lord refers to the eventual condition of the permanently wicked—the 'fire prepared,' He says, 'for the devil and his angels' (Mt 25[41]). Any attempt to reveal to us in our present state either the joys of heaven or the woes of hell must necessarily be couched in figurative language; but the language of Scripture on this subject, though to be interpreted with caution, is certainly of a kind to be received with the utmost seriousness; and when all has been said, no more appalling definition can be given of the state of the lost than that it is one of wilful, permanent, and absolute alienation from God who is Life and Love.

13. Faith in Christ. It was to save us from this doom that the Redeemer was given, 'for God so loved the world, that He gave His only begotten Son, that whosoever believeth in Him should not perish, but have everlasting life' (Jn 3[16]). This belief in Him —not a mere intellectual assent to certain doctrines, but a going forth of the whole nature in trustful homage—brings with it of necessity a fervent love, and with the love a patient submission and obedience. Thus the doctrine of St. James is complementary to that of St. Paul, and though in a sense faith is the one thing needful, because it opens the soul to accept God's grace, and thus makes His entry into us possible ; yet faith without works is not only dead but inconceivable (Jas 2 17f.).

Faith, as we have said, is God's gift to those who desire it and are ready to receive it. It is in all ages a requisite to the effective working of the Holy Spirit in man's soul ; even as in the days of our Lord's ministry it was an indispensable condition without which even He could do no mighty works on men (Mt 13 58).

It is perhaps to stimulate faith that certain difficulties—like the problems of evil and of suffering—are allowed to remain unsolved for us, and certain eventualities unrevealed. Enough is told us to command our trust and to justify the venture of belief. If all were clear, there would be no place for the discipline of faith ; we would walk, not by faith, but by sight (2 Cor 5 7 ; cp. Jn 20 29 1 Pet 1 8).

Such are the leading elements of the Christian religion ; and if, like its individual professors, it is to be judged by its fruits, we need have no fear of the result. To compare it, not merely with the polytheistic religions which once held sway in Europe, but with its great contemporary rivals for the homage of mankind—Buddhism and Mohammedanism— is to gain a fresh appreciation of its superiority, and be confirmed in our conviction of its truth. Consider what the Church has done for Europe and for Western civilisation during the nineteen centuries of her existence. She leavened the great Roman Empire when it was festering with moral corruption, and so prolonged and purified the good influence of its ideals of law and government. When the knell of the old Empire as mistress of the world sounded, and the northern barbarians rushed in upon her borders, the Church took up her task of taming and civilising these barbarians, offering to each race and people from the inexhaustible treasury of Christ's perfect humanity the gifts specially adapted to develop its own peculiar character, and thus under her influence nationality slowly came into view ; that spirit to which modern Europe owes so much of her best. And what she has done for individual nations, bringing some sort of order out of chaos, she is doing gradually for the comity of nations, leavening the public opinion of the world in favour of peace and justice.

In the social sphere, her teaching has transformed the family, especially in regard to the status of woman, has abolished slavery, and has brought out what the ancient world never dreamed of, the infinite worth of the individual personality, while inculcating at the same time the highest altruistic ideals of universal brotherhood and membership in a common Body. In the sphere of knowledge, where the Christian Church is often blamed as a reactionary and obscurantist influence (a blame which, no doubt, is well deserved in certain cases), she has on the whole exercised a salutary check upon wild and fantastic speculation, while supplying at the same time the strongest possible stimulus to research, declaring the wonders of creation and of human nature to be a mirror of the glory and beauty of its Creator. The religion of the Bible is one which, while it fixes our ultimate gaze on the world to come (2 Cor 4 18), gives a new and inexhaustible interest to God's visible creation, in which it reads a record of His everlasting power and divinity (Ro 1 20), and, above all, to the study of mankind—history, anthropology, and kindred studies—for there are written the records of His educative and redemptive dealings with the being whom He formed in His own image (Gn 1 26, 27).

PALESTINE

PALESTINE is a little country, no bigger than Wales; but it was in the centre of the ancient civilised world, and the highway of the nations led along its borders from Egypt to Assyria. It was a mountain land, with fresher climate than either the Delta or the plains of Babylonia, and it was rich in corn and oil. It was therefore always coveted by the kings of Egypt and Assyria; and though it had no ports, yet in the immediate N. the Phœnicians developed a great sea-traffic, and sent out colonies to Africa and Europe.

The land from Dan to Beersheba—i.e. from N. to S.—was about 150 m. long, and contained 6,000 sq. m. W. of Jordan and 4,000 to the E. in Moab, Gilead, and Bashan. Western Palestine consists of a chain of mountains rising generally not more than 3,000 ft. above the sea, having a wide plain on the W. and the deep Jordan valley on the E. The mountains are of limestone, the plain of good soil, bordered by sand dunes or by crumbling sandy cliffs. In Lower Galilee the ridge of Carmel juts out NW., and the range of Gilboa runs further E., leaving the triangular inland plain of Esdraelon between them, bounded on the N. by the hills of Nazareth and of Lower Galilee, with Tabor as an outlier on the E. N., again, are the mountains of Upper Galilee, sloping down to the narrow plains and hills between Accho and Tyre. In the centre of the land Ebal and Gerizim are among the highest summits, divided by the narrow valley of Shechem. Between the mountains of Jerusalem and Hebron and the plains of Sharon and Philistia is the region of the foot-hills, called the Shephelah in the Bible. This continues N. to Carmel. The western spurs, which receive the W. winds from the sea, are clothed with copses; the foot-hills are covered with olive groves, while the plains are fit for corn. The Hebron mountains—and, indeed, most of those throughout the country—are green with vineyards; but the appearance of the hills, especially round Jerusalem and Shechem, is rugged and barren. The land is well supplied with springs throughout. The eastern steep slopes are very rocky and bare, and on this side, towards the S., the desert of Judah is a waste of white ridges with tall precipices above the Dead Sea. On the S. the mountains fall from Hebron to the rolling grassy downs of Beersheba.

There are several perennial streams in Sharon; and under Carmel the boggy Kishon, rising at Tabor, enters the sea in the only bay S. of Tyre. There are others, again, flowing to the Jordan, of which the chief are the waters of Ænon, NE. of Shechem, and the stream in the Valley of Jezreel. The Jordan rises near Dan, at the foot of Hermon, and runs through the papyrus swamps of the Huleh lake to the pear-shaped Sea of Galilee, which is flanked by precipices mirrored in its waters. Thence, still descending, it reaches the Dead Sea, which is 1,300 ft. below the Mediterranean. It winds through a thicket of tamarisks and other low trees, never being broader than about 30 yds., and having some 30 fords, the last opposite the plain of Jericho; but the current is rapid, especially near the mouth. The Dead Sea is 10 m. wide and 40 m. long, and on either side sheer precipices rise sometimes 1,000 ft. above the water.

The country E. of Jordan includes half the Jordan Valley, which has on an average a total width of 10 m. Very steep slopes lead up to a plateau which stretches E. to the Syrian Desert. These slopes are sandstone below and hard limestone higher up. In Moab the plateau is bare and treeless, but in Gilead, to the N., the hills are covered in parts with woods of fir and oak. The only real forest in Western Palestine has now been sadly thinned, but presented twenty years ago a dense wood of oaks between Nazareth and Carmel. In Gilead, where there are many beautiful streams, especially the Jabbok, opposite Shechem, the scenery is at times park-like, at times presents only grey mountain slopes. N. of this, again, are the rich corn plains of Bashan, and the basalt regions of Golan and Argob, with their extinct volcanoes; while far to the E. the 'Hill of Bashan' rises over the plains.

There is thus much variety of scenery in Palestine, and while the plains are hot and fever-stricken in summer and autumn, the hills are healthier and cooler, especially when the W. wind blows daily in June from the sea. The climate of Palestine is like that of Southern Italy. In spring the plains are gay with flowers, and the Jordan Valley is carpeted with bright colours. In autumn all is brown and grey, parched by the summer sun and the searching E. winds of May and October. But the country is famous in the East for its fruits; and figs, grapes, pomegranates, melons, and apricots are found in all parts of it. It is a 'good land,' ruined only by the evil deeds of man. Amid the copses the traveller often lights on the wine-presses and vineyard towers, which betoken former cultivation.

Palestine is capable of supporting ten times

its present population, and could well have held the numbers which we are told dwelt there in the days of the Hebrews. All the ancient fauna of the Bible—beasts, birds, and reptiles—still remain, except the lion, whose bones are found in the Jordan gravel beds ; the wild bull (miscalled by Greek translators the 'unicorn'), which was still hunted in Lebanon in 1130 B.C. ; and the bear, which is now only found on the snowy slopes of Hermon, 9,000 ft. above the sea. Even the fallow-deer has been found among the oaks of Tabor, and the roebuck in the copses of Carmel and Galilee, and in the woods of Gilead. The antelope runs in herds in the plains ; the ibex leaps among the 'rocks of the wild goats' in the Desert of Judah. The 'coney,' or hyrax, has there, too, its home in the cliffs ; the leopard and wolf haunt the Jordan, and the fox, jackal, and hyena are common, as are all birds of prey, and the wild doves which fill the oak woods ; while the partridge runs in the higher hills. The trees of Palestine are also the same as of old, though the 'apple' is rarely found in the S. Even Leviathan—the crocodile—survives in the Crocodile river S. of Carmel, though Behemoth—the elephant—is unknown. In the sixteenth century B.C. there were, however, herds of wild elephants on the Euphrates, as mentioned in the annals of Thothmes III, and the great beast was no doubt well known when Solomon and Hezekiah had thrones of ivory and Ahab made an ivory shrine.

We may turn briefly to consider the chief towns of the country noticed in the Bible. In the mountains W. of Jordan Hebron was the chief city of the S., standing in a flat mountain vale surrounded by vineyards, and having under the floor of its Mosque the ancient rock sepulchre which appears to have been that of the Patriarchs.

Jerusalem—which was already a strong city of Amorites in Joshua's time—occupied a defensible position, surrounded, except on the N., by deep ravines. The old city occupied two spurs on the W., separated by interior valleys from the Temple ridge, which sank gradually to Ophel—the priests' quarter, walled-in later—beyond which on the E. was the gorge of the Kidron, with its precipices ; and E. again the chalky slopes of Olivet dotted with olives. All that now remains of ancient Jerusalem are the ramparts of Herod's outer Temple enclosure, and part of the western wall and its great tower—also of the same age. The old city was rather larger than the present walled town ; and after 30 A.D. it had extended N. to include a total of 300 acres, requiring a new third wall on this side. Exploration shows that the traditional site of Calvary, in the Cathedral, is the summit of a knoll, with a steep southern slope, which appears to have formed the citadel of the lower city ; and it is practically impossible that this should not have been very early included in Jerusalem. The more probable site of Golgotha is the hillock outside the N. gate of the city, to which Jewish tradition still points as the site of the ancient place of execution.

Passing N. by Bethel, a hamlet on the grey rocks, we reach the ancient capital at Shechem, close to which on the E. is Jacob's Well—one of the few spots where we can feel certain of the presence of Christ ; it is now preserved in the ruins of a Crusaders' church. In Shechem the last remnant of the Samaritans preserve their ancient copies of the Law, and yearly observe the Passover on Gerizim. W. of this, Samaria, in the low hills, presents the ruins of Herod's temple and colonnades on a long, low hillock. Thence we pass to the small brown plain of Dothan, with its well, at the site still keeping the ancient name ; and so on to Jezreel on a spur of Gilboa, where we find remains of wine-presses to the E., where was Naboth's vineyard. A little to the N. is Shunem with its lemon gardens and springs ; and on the N. of the volcanic peak of Moriah, is the hamlet of Endor with its cave, and Nain, a little village to the W., hard by. The only other towns needing notice in the N. are Accho, on the N. side of its bay, a city mentioned on monuments very early ; and Tyre, with its two harbours N. and S., now a fair-sized place, and no longer a ruin. Sidon, which has a larger port, is beyond the limits of the Holy Land.

On the sea-coast Gaza alone—on its hillock surrounded by long olive avenues—is left as a city, out of the five towns of the Philistines. Ascalon, on the shore, is a ruin half covered with sand, with remains of the walls built by Richard Lion Heart. Ashdod, on a hill of red sand, is but a mud village, as is Ekron further N. The site of Gath is probably the present Tell es Sâfi, at the mouth of the valley of Elah. Lachish is a Tell, or mound, further S., where remains have been excavated dating back to Joshua's time. Joppa remains the port of Jerusalem (connected now by rail), and is a considerable place, famous for its orange groves. In the plain of Sharon to the N., Cæsarea is now a ruin with a few cottages, and remains of the walls, the theatre, the race-course, and the temple of Herod's time, extending beyond the walls of the small Crusader city. In the Jordan Valley, Jericho is represented by mounds of sun-dried brick, close to the hills at 'Ain es Sultân, N. of the Valley of Achor (Wady Kelt) ; while a solitary tamarisk in the plain to the E. marks the site of Gilgal. The only other town W. of the river is Beth-shean, N. of the Valley of Jezreel, now a mud hamlet, but with walls, theatre, and temple, of the Roman age.

E. of Jordan, all Moab lies in ruins ; and these, though retaining their ancient names, are mostly of the Christian period, such as those at Dibon, Medeba, Heshbon, Rabbath-Ammon, and Gerasa. The hill slopes, however, are strewn with cromlechs and standing stones, probably of the Canaanite age. Mahanaim in Gilead is a ruin in the circular hollow plain on the hills, and is now called Mukhmah; while, N. of the Jabbok, Ramoth Gilead stands on a high hill at the present village of Reimûn, and Sûf further N. may be the Mizpeh of Jacob and Jephthah. Mizpeh in Benjamin is not to be confused, and is probably the present ruined mound Tell Nasbeh, S. of Bethel, near Geba, and Ramah, and Michmash with its deep ' Valley of Thorns,' and its cliffs Seneh and Bozez. In Bashan there are also few villages ; and the sites of Ashtaroth Karnaim (Tell 'Ashterah), and Edrei (Adrà) are ruined mounds. This region is full of fine houses and temples, now overthrown, which bear dated Greek inscriptions of the second and third centuries A.D. —these have no connexion with the old cities of Og and Sihon ; but further E., at Siâ, is a temple, which by its inscriptions is known to have been built for Herod the Great, to the god Baal Shemim. Damascus by the rushing Abana, beyond the limits of Palestine, is still a city under Hermon, with some 250,000 inhabitants. Banias, at the source of Jordan, above Dan (Tell el Kâdy), represents Cæsarea Philippi ; and the scenery, where the river bursts full-grown from the rocky cave with its Greek shrine of Pan, is amongst the most picturesque in Palestine, tall poplars lining the river, while the ruins of the Crusader castle tower over the village, and the snowy Hermon dome rises to the N.

The scenery of the New Testament is mostly connected with Lower Galilee. Nazareth was a remote village, otherwise unnoticed in history, lying in a hollow plateau on the hills, with a cliff behind it to the N. It is now a thriving town. Tiberias, which was a new city in the days of Christ, is now a walled town on the W. of the Sea of Galilee, and the remains of older walls, enclosing a larger area, are traced on the slopes above.

Chorazin with its ruined synagogue is a certain site, N. of the lake, as is Magdala, a village near the shore on the W., N. of Tiberias. The site of Capernaum has been disputed, Christian tradition placing it at Tell Hûm (Caphar-Ahim of the Talmud) on the N. shore, where too are remains of a synagogue ; while Jewish mediæval tradition places it further W., at the ruin of Minyeh, on the shore in the Plain of Gennesaret—a small recess at the foot of the mountains. The latter site seems best to meet the requirements of the account by Josephus, who speaks of the Fountain of Capernaum as watering the Gennesaret plain. As to Bethsaida, there appears to have been only one place so named—at the mouth of the Jordan where it enters the lake, and E. of the river. It is now called et-Tell, and a sort of delta has been formed which now makes the mouth of the river nearly a mile further S.

The site of the Baptism at Bethabara was only a day's journey from Cana of Galilee (now Kefr Kenna), N. of Nazareth, and it was also about two or three days from Bethany (Jn 1 $^{28, 35, 45}$ 2 ^{2} 10 ^{40} 11 $^{6, 17}$) on the Mount of Olives. Thus the Christian tradition which places it E. of Jericho appears to be incorrect ; and the name occurs only once in Palestine, at the great ford of 'Abârah, not far S. of the Sea of Galilee. This situation fulfils all requisites in a satisfactory manner. Other doubtful sites, such as Gergesa and Ephraim, need not be discussed ; but the fact that Dalmanutha stands (Mk 8 ^{10}) instead of Magdala may be explained by the latter being the Hebrew term for ' tower,' while the former is probably an Aramaic name, meaning ' place of the fort.' Aramaic was the common tongue of Palestine when the Gospels were written, and probably the language spoken by Christ Himself.

The last scenes of His ministry are connected with Bethany, now a little stone village on the S. slopes of the central top of Olivet, where is an old ruined castle, once guarding the Benedictine Nunnery of Queen Milicent of Jerusalem. The first scene of His life is laid at Bethlehem, which is now a well-built Christian town not far S. of Jerusalem, on a long spur with terraced sides planted with olives. The cathedral here is the oldest church in the world ; the pillars of its basilica are those erected by Constantine. The rocky grotto beneath, with its rock-cut manger, is the traditional stable by the inn—the only sacred site of Gospel history mentioned earlier than the fourth century A.D. by Christian writers ; for it was known to Justin Martyr and Origen, as well as to Jerome. Such rock stables often occur in ruined towns of the Hebron mountains ; and the site is at least possible.

Space does not allow further description of places like Adullam, Debir, Gezer, Megiddo, Antipatris, Bezek, Taanach. and other cities recently rediscovered with many more ; for of some 600 towns in Palestine noticed in the Bible at least 400 are well known; and about 150 of them were not to be found on any map before the survey of Palestine was carried out between 1872 and 1882 A.D.

BIBLE ANTIQUITIES

The most distinctive characteristic of Bible study during the past century has not been criticism (which began in the eighteenth century), but rather discovery. The comparative method, as in other studies, has gradually taken the place of older forms of comment ; and a mass of independent and reliable information has come to light, in an unexpected manner, due to scientific exploration of Eastern lands, and of their hidden treasures. For more than twelve centuries Western Asia was practically closed to the scholar and explorer by Moslem fanaticism ; but when at length the increase of civilisation, and of facilities for travel, enabled Europeans to study the realities of Eastern life on the ground, unhoped-for treasures, forgotten civilisations, languages, and scripts, which had, for thousands of years, been preserved under the sands of Egypt, or the foundations of Asiatic palaces, were gradually recovered, and made available by the zeal of explorers and the genius of scholars. Through such discovery the study of the Bible has been placed on an entirely new basis ; and, while many of the theories of the eighteenth and earlier centuries have thus been rendered obsolete, the testimony of monuments so preserved has more and more served to confirm the history, and to explain the ideas and customs, of the Hebrews and of their neighbours, as described in both the Old and the New Testament, by the light of original and entirely independent evidence. We have probably not as yet by any means exhausted the possibilities of such study ; and almost every year now adds some welcome detail to the total of our knowledge, through research in Palestine, in Egypt, in Mesopotamia, or in Asia Minor, and through the better understanding of the languages and written characters of the monuments, in which such records are preserved as contemporary accounts of events noticed in the Bible.

Before about 1820 A.D. only Greek, Roman, and a few Phœnician monuments, of late date, were available to the scholar ; and study was chiefly devoted to the comparison of manuscripts and versions of the Scriptures, which only carry us back to 916 A.D. for the Hebrew, and to the fourth and fifth centuries of our era for the Greek, Syriac, and Samaritan manuscripts. Egyptian hieroglyphs, and cuneiform tablets, had, it is true, excited the curiosity of observers even in the middle ages, but it was not until 1822 that an impetus was given to such study through the decipherment of the Egyptian by Champollion, the famous French scholar. Already in 1812 the first Hittite monuments had been described by Burckhardt at Hamath ; yet their importance, and the wide diffusion of this civilisation, remained unsuspected till about twenty years ago. In 1835 Sir Henry Rawlinson began the study of cuneiform, which by his genius was developed into a new special science ; but it was not till 1888 that proof of the civilisation of Canaan, in the time of Moses and Joshua, was afforded by the recovery of the political correspondence of Asiatic kings and chiefs with the Pharaohs, found at the village of Amarna, between Memphis and Thebes in Egypt. The discoveries of E. Chantre (1893) and of Dr. H. Winckler (1907), in Cappadocia, have added cuneiform texts which give us the history of Hittites, Egyptians, and Babylonians in wonderful detail in the fifteenth and fourteenth centuries B.C.

The modern scholar no longer relies on second-hand information derived from Greek or Roman writers, who were often ignorant of the realities of foreign civilisations ; or on the corrupted text of Josephus, the Hebrew historian, and of Manetho, the Egyptian chronicler of Ptolemaic times ; or on the few fragments of Berosus the Babylonian. He can study the original sources on monuments of granite, basalt, and limestone, or in pottery tablets and in papyri, as easily as the later Phœnician texts, or the coins of Palestine, Persia, Greece, and Rome. Languages the existence of which had been entirely forgotten —such as the Akkadian (in Chaldea), the Assyrian, the Egyptian, the Sabean (in Arabia), the ancient Persian, Vannic, and Lycian—have been recovered ; and have been explained by aid of living tongues, such as Turkish, Arabic, Coptic, etc. ; while others, found later, still form the subject of discussion among scholars, such as the Hittite and cognate dialects, which have only recently come to light.

Egyptian research, while receiving perhaps more general attention than any other branch, still suffers from the fragmentary nature of the information recovered, and from the absence of systematic chronicles. We know that the civilisation of the Delta was very ancient, but the age in which it first arose is still uncertain within some two thousand years. From about 1600 to 1200 B.C. the Egyptians were masters of the great trade-route, through

Palestine and Syria, to Mesopotamia. Monuments of Rameses II occur (about 1330 B.C.) at Sidon, Beirut, and even in Bashan, where also an inscription of Seti I (about 1400 B.C.) has quite recently been found ; but as yet we have only a single allusion to the Hebrews in Egyptian texts, namely, to the attack on 'Israel' in Palestine by Mineptah after 1300 B.C. On the other hand, the most important contribution to early Bible history as yet recovered is found in the Canaanite letters, already mentioned as preserved in Egyptian archives ; and in these we have probably the earliest monumental notice of the Hebrews in the fifteenth century B.C., at the time of Joshua's conquest of Palestine.

Babylonian and Assyrian monuments contain much more that has direct bearing on the Bible than is found in Egypt. The chronicles of Babylon preserve an exact chronology, back to the date of the founding of that great city about 2250 B.C. ; and the existence of Chaldean kings many centuries earlier has been ascertained, although the earlier chronology, before the date above given, still remains very uncertain. From the ninth century B.C. onwards the names of kings of Israel and Judah occur in the records of their Assyrian contemporaries who are noticed in the Old Testament ; and texts of Nebuchadnezzar, others referring to the Belshazzar of the book of Daniel, and later, Persian inscriptions of Darius and Artaxerxes serve to illustrate and to confirm biblical history. The famous excavations of Layard at Nineveh, which led to the recovery of most of this information, were first undertaken in 1845 ; but quite recent explorations by Americans at Nippur (Calneh) in Chaldea, south of Babylon ; by Germans at Babylon itself, and in North Syria ; by French Government Expeditions at Tell Loh in Chaldea, at Shushan (east of the lower course of the river Tigris), and in Cappadocia, immediately north of Syria, have materially added to our general knowledge of the earliest ages of civilisation in Western Asia.

Phœnician records are generally too late to be of assistance in respect to Bible history, though interesting as showing the influence of Hebrew speech on this famous maritime nation, which held the shores from Tyre northwards under Lebanon. In the fifteenth century B.C. the Phœnicians spoke the same language used in Babylonia and Assyria, and wrote in the cuneiform character, then commonly employed throughout Western Asia ; but their later inscriptions, about the fourth century B.C., are in alphabetic characters, and in a dialect closely akin to Hebrew, while the texts of the Samala ruins (in the extreme north of Syria), in the eighth century B.C.,

give an Aramaic dialect, whence the later Palmyrene and Syriac are derived.

Palestine has so far only yielded three very ancient texts, namely, the Moabite Stone (ninth century B.C.), the Siloam inscription (before 703 B.C.), and a cuneiform tablet of the fifteenth century B.C., found at Lachish, in which Zimrida—a local governor whose letters also occur in the Tell el Amarna collection—is noticed. The Galilean synagogues of the second century A.D. present square Hebrew texts, and one somewhat earlier occurs on the tomb of the Beni Hezir at Jerusalem ; but as yet very few ancient inscriptions—even including coins and seals—have been found in the Holy Land.

Hittite monuments present a very archaic art, with human figures which are recognised to be Mongolic, wearing a peculiar costume, and long pigtails like the Tartars. These carvings occur at Hamath and Aleppo in North Syria, accompanied by a distinct hieroglyphic system of writing ; and they are probably as old as 2000 B.C. They are found in the region where, as we know from other monuments, the Hittites lived from the earliest times down to the reign of Nebuchadnezzar (600 B.C.) ; but they extend also all over Asia Minor ; and two examples have been found in Babylon itself, while Hittite seals have been recovered in Nineveh. The Hittites themselves were confined to North Syria and Cappadocia, but this class of antiquities belongs to a race evidently akin to the ancient Akkadians of Babylonia, of which the Hittites formed only one tribe or branch among many others.

Greek antiquities in Western Asia are valuable for comparative purposes, in studying the New Testament. The most important example is the stone found in Jerusalem, which presents a text prohibiting any Gentile from entering the inner courts of Herod's temple. It was standing in place in the time of our Lord, and of St. Paul. Other texts witness the existence of a Greek-speaking population in Decapolis (east of the Sea of Galilee, within the province of Bashan) in the same age. Others again, further east, belong to the pagan temple of Siâ, built by a subject of Herod the Great. It is well known that the technical expressions used, especially in the Acts of the Apostles, agree in a very remarkable manner with the wording of Greek texts, and of classic writings, which refer to the government of Syria and Asia Minor by the Romans in the first century of our era. The Greek papyri from Egypt have also added much that is interesting to our knowledge of early Christianity.

Palestine Exploration has been an important feature in the general development of the comparative method of Bible study. The first scientific enquiry into geography in Palestine, undertaken in 1838 by the famous American explorer Dr. Robinson, substituted for the contradictory (and sometimes ignorant) traditions of the Latin and Greek Churches a real study of Bible topography on the ground, with the identification of ancient sites, where the old names still remain almost unchanged in modern Syrian speech. In 1864 the survey of Jerusalem was carried out by Sir C. W. Wilson, K.C.B., and in 1867–70 important excavations on the Temple hill, and in the city, were made by Sir Charles Warren, K.C.B. The survey of Western and Eastern Palestine by the present writer followed (1872–1882); and about 150 Bible towns were then discovered, which had not appeared on older maps. The survey of Sinai, begun in 1867, with later researches, has done much to clear up disputed questions as to the story of the exodus. But in addition to geographical research, the study of archæology in Palestine has dispelled many false conceptions, and has brought to light many indications of ancient civilisation, both Hebrew and Canaanite, although at present the task of excavation, at sites other than Jerusalem, has only been recently begun, and much remains still to be done. At Lachish, and at the probable site of Gath, at Gezer, at Taanach in Galilee, and elsewhere, English, American, and German explorers have recently laid bare the foundations of ancient cities, in south and north

alike. They have recovered inscriptions, Hebrew weights and gems and coins, remains of early Canaanite idols, and other valuable indications of the early civilisation of the country which illustrate Bible statements. The destruction of Canaanite idolatrous emblems by the Hebrews renders it impossible to find such remains, on the surface, in the Holy Land; and it is only by excavation that they can be recovered.

The general result of such practical work has been to confirm the historical statements of the Bible as a whole, whenever these can be compared with contemporary records. The history of Babylonia is accurately traced to the days of Abraham; and the civilisation of Canaan, as described in the time of Moses and Joshua, is proved by the Egyptian chronicles of victory, and by the extant remains, which equally attest the early wealth and culture of the Hebrew kings. We find, moreover, that records on permanent materials—stone or brick—existed as early as the time when Moses wrote the tablets of the Law; that gems were then carved, and tents with golden pillars used; that ancient scribes were able to preserve their records correctly through the lapse of more than a thousand years, and were careful and faithful in copying their yet older authorities; and in general, that there is nothing that suggests any anachronism or misrepresentation in the picture of ancient civilisation preserved to us in the Pentateuch.

HEBREW CALENDAR, COINS, WEIGHTS AND MEASURES

CALENDAR

THE growth of the Hebrew Calendar cannot be traced here, but its general form in later times may be given. The year, determined by the recurrence of the seasons, was divided into twelve months, according to the changes of the moon, numbering alternately twenty-nine and thirty days. There is some difference of opinion as to when the year was supposed to begin at different epochs of Hebrew history. Before the exile, it may have begun in autumn ; but afterwards there seems to have been a double arrangement, by which the civil year was reckoned to begin in autumn and the sacred year in spring. The months are usually indicated in the Old Testament by numbers, as the 'first' month ; but the following names gradually became affixed to them. Abib, or Nisan, corresponded approximately to our April, and the others in order were : Zif, Sivan, Thammuz, Ab, Elul, Tishri or Ethanim, Bul, Chisleu, Tebeth, Shebat, and Adar. The month was divided into weeks of seven days each, the last, not the first as with us, being the sabbath day of rest. The day was reckoned from sunset to sunset, and was divided into watches or hours, according as night-time or daytime was in question.

MONEY

The earliest Jewish coins were struck in the time of Simon Maccabæus, about 140 B.C., but Persian, Egyptian, and Phœnician money was in use before that, and later on Greek and Roman coins were in circulation. Of course, from very early times, various precious metals were used as means of exchange, either in the lump or in the form of rings, the value being determined by the weight as shown by the balance. The following are the principal values of gold and silver as estimated by the weight :—

	EARLY HEBREW.			JEWISH.	
	£	s.	d.	s.	d.
Light Shekel, silver		1	8	1	2
Heavy Shekel, silver		3	4	2	4
Light Manah, silver	4	3	4		
Light Manah, gold	66	13	4		
Light Talent, silver	250	0	0		
Light Talent, gold	4000	0	0		

Coins were not in use before 700 B.C., and none are noticed in the Bible before the time of Ezra. In Ezr 2 69 and Neh 7 70, 71, 72 we find *darkĕmōn*, and in 1 Ch 29 7 Ezr 8 27 *adarkōn*, probably the same piece of money, and translated 'dram' in the Authorised Version and 'daric' in the Revised Version. It is a foreign word, probably of Persian origin, the Persians having a 'daric' which weighed 130 grains. In the New Testament the following words are to be noticed, belonging to the Greek or Roman coinage :—

Mite (*Lepton*), Mk 12 42, the smallest Jewish (bronze) coin = $\frac{1}{4}$ farthing.

Farthing (*Kodrantes*), Mt 5 26, $\frac{1}{4}$ Roman *As* = $\frac{1}{2}$ farthing.

Farthing (*Assarion*), Mt 10 29, the Roman *As* = a halfpenny or cent.

Penny (*Denarius* or *Denarion*), Mt 18 28, etc., a Roman coin = $8\frac{1}{2}d$.

Piece of silver (*Drachmē*), Lk 15 8, a coin of Antioch = the denarius.

Tribute money (*Didrachmon*), Mt 17 24, equivalent to two drachms of Antioch = 1s. 4d.

Piece of silver (*Argurion*), Mt 26 15, equal in value to three denarii, or 2s. $1\frac{1}{2}d$.

Piece of money (*Stater*), Mt 17 27, same value as last.

WEIGHTS

Light Shekel = 160 grains.

Heavy Shekel = 320 grains.

Light Manah = 50 Light Shekels = 8,000 grains = 1 lb. 4 oz. 13 dwt. 8 grs.

Heavy Manah = 100 Shekels = 16,000 grains.

Light Talent = 3,000 Light Shekels = 480,000 grains.

Heavy Talent = 3,000 Heavy Shekels = 960,000 grains.

Bekah = $\frac{1}{2}$ Shekel.

Rebah = $\frac{1}{4}$ Shekel.

Gerah = $\frac{1}{20}$ Shekel.

Talent, or Kikkar = 60 Manahs.

MEASURES OF LENGTH

The Egyptians had a cubit of 20·6 inches, and used, later, one of about 21·6 inches. The ancient Akkadians of Chaldea used a unit of 10·5 inches ; we do not know if this was used by Babylonians and Assyrians. The length of the Siloam tunnel (1,200 cubits) shows that, in Hezekiah's age, the Hebrew cubit cannot have exceeded 17 inches. According to Maimonides the building cubit was 16 inches, and the smaller cubit 13·3 inches, equal to half of an Arabic *Draâ*, or 'arm.'

The word cubit means a 'forearm.' The cubit was divided as follows :—

Barley corn	. .	·33 inches.
Finger	. . .	·66 ,,
Palm	. . .	2·66 ,,
Hand	. . .	5·33 ,,
Span	. . .	8·00 ,,
Foot	. . .	10·66 ,,
Small cubit	. .	13·33 ,,
Building cubit	. .	16·00 ,,
Large cubit	. .	18·66 ,,

SQUARE MEASURE

The Hebrew square measure (Ex 27 9, 12) was based on a square of 50 cubits, so that a Kor of land (with a 16-inch cubit) would be 3·03 acres, or very close to the Arabic Feddan, or 'yoke' of land, of 3·3 acres.

DRY MEASURE

According to the rabbis the Hebrew Lôg was equal to the contents of six hen's eggs,

and held 6,000 grains weight of water. This measure agrees closely with that used in Egypt.

Lôg	24	cubic inches	0·69	pints.
Cab	96	,, ,,	2·76	,,
Omer	172·8	,, ,,	4·96	,,
Hin	288	,, ,,	1·04	gallons.
Seah	576	,, ,,	2·08	,,
Ephah	1728	,, ,,	6·20	,,
Kor	17280	,, ,,	62·00	,,

LIQUID MEASURE

This, as described by Josephus, agrees with Greek measures :—

	HEBREW.			GREEK.	
	cub. in.				
Lôg	32·7	0·81 pts.	1 Xesta	0·94 pts.
Cab	130·8	3·24 ,,	4 Xestæ	3·76 ,,
Omer	236·0	6·70 ,,	7 Xestæ	6·58 ,,
Hin	393·0	1·40 gals.	2 Choas	1·39 gals.
Seah	785·0	2·90 ,,	1½ Modii	2·80 ,,
Bath	2353·6	8·40 ,,	1 Metretes	8·40 ,,
Kor	23536·0	84·00 ,,	10 Metretes	84·0 ,,

BIBLE CHRONOLOGY

FOR the period before the Call of Abraham no chronology is possible, and for many years after that event, indeed until the times of the kings, the dates are more or less doubtful. The duration of the Oppression and of the rule of the various Judges as given in the book of Judges is greatly in excess of the interval probably to be assigned to them ; but it is likely that many of the events described were really contemporaneous, not successive. The dates assigned to the successive Hebrew kings are based upon the length of their reigns as given in the books of Samuel and Kings, corrected so far as possible by the evidence of

the Assyrian inscriptions which, in the matter of Chronology, are of great value.

Dates.	Events.
B.C. ?2300	Abraham.
?1700	Joseph.
	Descent into Egypt.
?1250	Moses.
	The exodus.
1200–1050	Period of the Judges.
1040	Saul.
1017	David.
977	Solomon.
973	Foundation of Temple.
937	Division of Monarchy.

AFTER DIVISION OF MONARCHY

Dates.	Israel.	Judah.	Dates.	Israel.	Judah.
B.C. 937	Jeroboam I.	Rehoboam.	B.C. 875	Ahab.	
		Invasion of Shishak.	854	Ahab at battle of Karkar.	
920	. . . .	Abijah.	853	Ahaziah.	
917	. . . .	Asa.	852	Jehoram (Joram).	
915	Nadab.		851	. . . .	Jehoram.
914	Baasha.		843	. . . .	Ahaziah.
900 (890)	Elah.		842	Jehu.	Athaliah.
899 (889)	Zimri.			Pays tribute to Assyria.	
899 (889)	Omri.		836	. . . .	Joash.
	Foundation of Samaria.		815	Jehoahaz.	
876	. . . .	Jehoshaphat.	798	Joash.	

BIBLE CHRONOLOGY

Dates.	Israel.	Judah.	Dates.	Israel.	Judah.
B.C. 796	. . . .	Amaziah.	B.C. 722	Fall of Samaria.	
789	. . . .	Azariah (Uzziah).	720	. . . .	Hezekiah.
782	Jeroboam II.		701	. . . .	Invasion of Sennacherib.
739	. . . .	Jotham.			
741	Zechariah. Shallum.		692	. . . .	Manasseh.
			641	. . . .	Amon.
740	Menahem.		639	. . . .	Josiah.
738	Pays tribute to Assyria.		608	. . . .	Battle of Megiddo Jehoahaz.
736	Pekahiah.		608	. . . .	Jehoiakim.
735	Pekah.		607	. . . .	Fall of Nineveh.
734	. . . .	Ahaz.	605	. . . .	Battle of Carchemish.
	Alliance with Rezin of Syria against Judah.		604	. . . .	Nebuchadrezzar, king of Babylon.
	Invasion of Tiglath-pileser, king of Assyria.		597	. . . .	Jehoiachin. Zedekiah.
729	Hoshea.		586	. . . .	Fall of Jerusalem.

LATER EVENTS

B.C. 586–538   Period of the exile in Babylon.
538   Capture of Babylon by Cyrus.
536   Return of the Jews from exile.
536–330   Period of Persian dominion.
515   Building of Second Temple completed.
458   Ezra's arrival at Jerusalem.
445   Nehemiah's first visit.
433   Nehemiah's second visit.
330   Conquest of Persia by Alexander.
322   Beginning of Greek (Ptolemaic) dynasty in Egypt.
312   Beginning of Greek (Seleucid) dynasty in Syria.
320–198   Period of Ptolemaic dominion.
197–167   Period of Syrian dominion.
167   Revolt of the Maccabees.
165   Temple services resumed.
160   Judas Maccabæus (166–160) falls in battle.
143   Jonathan (160–143) put to death.
142–135   Simon High-Priest and Prince.
134–104   Hyrcanus I.
103   Aristobulus I, king.

B.C. 102–76   Jannæus.
75–67   Alexandra.
66–63   Hyrcanus II and Aristobulus II.
63   Jerusalem taken by Pompey. Beginning of Roman dominion.
62–40   Hyrcanus II under Roman sovereignty.
40   Parthian invasion.
40–37   Antigonus.
37–4   Herod the Great.
7–6 ?   Birth of Jesus Christ.
B.C. 4–A.D. 6   Archelaus ethnarch of Judæa, etc.
A.D. 6–41   Roman Procurators in Judæa.
26–36   Pontius Pilate Procurator of Judæa.
26–29   Ministry of Jesus.
29   Death of Jesus.
29–61   The story of the Acts of the Apostles.
41–44   Agrippa I (grandson of Herod), king of Judæa.
44–70   Second Period of Roman Procurators.
64   Fire at Rome. Persecution by Nero.
70   Destruction of Jerusalem.

THE COMMENTARY

GENESIS

INTRODUCTION

1. Title and Contents. Genesis is the first of the five books which compose 'The Pentateuch' and deal with the history and religion of the Hebrews before their final settlement in Canaan. It is known in Hebrew as 'B're-shith' ('In the beginning'), from the word with which it opens. 'Genesis' is a Greek word meaning 'origin' or 'beginning,' and is the name applied to it in the LXX version. It has passed into general use as an appropriate description of the contents.

The book is divided into two main sections: chs. 1–11, giving an outline of the Hebrew traditions regarding the early history of the world and man; and chs. 12–50, containing an account of the lives of Abraham, Isaac, Jacob, and Joseph, in their bearing upon the origin of the Hebrew race. More particularly, its contents may be summarised as follows. Part 1. The Primeval History: (a) chs. 1–5, the story of Adam and his descendants; (b) chs. 6–11, the story of Noah and his sons. Part 2. The Patriarchal History: (a) chs. 12–26, the lives of Abraham and Isaac; (b) chs. 27–36, the life of Jacob; (c) chs. 37–50, the life of Joseph. The first eleven chapters may be regarded as an introduction, designed to show the relation of the Hebrew race to other nations, and connect their history with that of the world. The real history of the book commences with the twelfth chapter, where the call of Abraham marks the beginning of an epoch. As a whole, the book presents an account of the origin and rise of the Hebrew nation, written from a religious point of view, to show how God chose them to be His peculiar people, and made with them those covenants and promises which were fulfilled in their later history.

2. Religious value. While recognising the progressiveness of revelation, and finding the standard of Christian morals in the New Testament rather than in the Old, we must still regard the book of Genesis as 'profitable for teaching, for reproof, for correction, for instruction which is in righteousness.' Certain great fundamental truths of the religious and moral life are woven into the texture of its narratives, and the lessons to be derived from them have lost little or nothing of their original significance and force. That God is one, the Source of all that is, the Supreme Lord and Ruler of the world; that what He creates and does is all 'very good'; that He does not brook disobedience to His will, but punishes the sinner, while He rewards them that diligently seek and serve Him: these are some of the ideas on which it insists, ideas which lie at the root of all morality and religion. It has even a gospel to proclaim, for the love and grace of God are brought out conspicuously, not only in His normal relations with man, but amid the ruin and havoc wrought by sin. He holds communion with the creature whom He has created in His own image; He loves and cares for him in his state of innocence or rectitude; He has mercy on him when he has sinned and forfeited the blessings of Paradise. Throughout the book there is a conception of God as one, holy, spiritual, and an insight into His relationship with man and the world, neither of which can be paralleled in ancient literature. Some of its earlier portions have points of resemblance to the primitive traditions of other nations, but they are clearly distinguished from them in their representations of moral and religious truths. They may be cast in simple language, and embody ideas of their time; but, unlike the ancient mythologies, they are never immoral or unreal, and they trace everything to the thought and action of a living, personal God.

The teaching of Genesis, then, is still applicable in Christian times. It is the more valuable that it is enforced, not by precept merely, but by concrete examples in personal and family life. Its characters are real men, not fictitious heroes or demigods. And God is actually in touch with them, working out His purposes in the events of their lives. He is the God of Abraham, Isaac, and Jacob; in all the incidents of their careers, in the general march of human history in which they bear their part, we see Him moving and acting with merciful, redeeming aim. The promise that 'the seed of the woman shall bruise the head of the serpent,' the covenant with Noah after the Flood, the choice and call of Abraham, the covenants with him and his successors, the election of the Hebrew nation and its progressive consolidation into a theocracy or kingdom of God, are all indications of His underlying purpose to redeem the whole world from the effects of 'man's first disobedience.' Genesis thus graphically and realistically depicts the beginning and partial development of that long and patient process which culminated in the work of Christ.

3. **Authorship.** Until recently, Genesis, like the rest of the Pentateuch, was regarded as the work of Moses. This view was accepted on the authority of Jewish tradition, which generally seeks to attribute the sacred books of the nation to the most famous names in its history. The tradition, however, did not arise until a comparatively late period; and, in the absence of corroboration, its evidence can hardly be regarded as conclusive. The book itself is anonymous, and contains nothing to suggest a Mosaic authorship. On the contrary, it bears traces of having been put together in its present form, many years after the death of the great Hebrew patriot, when the Canaanite was no longer in the land (Gn 12 6), and the Jewish monarchy indeed had been established (Gn 36 31). Dual accounts are sometimes given of the same event, and different passages exhibit such diversity of literary and other characteristics as to point to an origin in independent sources. Accordingly the view is now largely entertained that Genesis is the work of an unknown editor who had access to documents containing the traditions and early records of the Hebrew race, and welded them together into a whole. For a fuller discussion of the subject, reference should be made to art. 'The Origin of the Pentateuch.' Of the three documents there mentioned as underlying the Pentateuch, only two are to be met with in Genesis, viz. the so-called Primitive and Priestly documents. The latter supplies the framework of the book, and the various parts of the former are dovetailed into it, as it were, by way of heightening the effect, and giving more detailed information.

As is pointed out in the general article, the difference of style in the two documents is clearly marked. The Primitive document is lively and picturesque, and abounds in descriptive touches, which lighten up the narrative, and impart a living interest to the people and places described. The Priestly document, on the other hand, is written in a more formal manner: it is much taken up with chronologies and genealogies, and loves to dwell upon covenants and religious ordinances. In illustration of these characteristics, the Priestly account of the end of the Flood in Gn 8 1-5

may be compared with the picturesque description of the same event taken from the Primitive document in 8 6-12; also the appearance of God to Abraham in c. 17 with the accounts of similar appearances in 16 7-14 and 18 1-8, 16. The two threads of narrative, Primitive and Priestly, are supposed to have been based upon older written accounts compiled from oral traditions, and to have been put together, to form the present book of Genesis, in the days of Ezra.

4. **Analysis.** The framework of the book is marked by the repetition of the formula, 'These are the generations of,' a phrase which occurs ten times, and always at the beginning of a new section, except in 2 4, where it is put at the end of the first account of the Creation, to which it properly belongs. The instances of its occurrence, with the references, are these : 2 4 (of the Creation) ; 5 1 (of Adam) ; 6 9 (of Noah) ; 10 1 (of Shem, Ham, and Japheth) ; 11 10 (of Shem) ; 11 27 (of Terah) ; 25 12 (of Ishmael) ; 25 19 (of Isaac) ; 36 1, 9 (of Esau) ; 37 2 (of Jacob). The passages derived from the Priestly document which constitutes the framework are roughly as follow : in Part 1 (chs. 1–11) : 1 1–2 4a 5 1-32 6 9-22 7 6–8 5 8 13-19 9 1-17 8 28-10 7 10 20-23, 31-32 11 10-32 ; in Part 2 (chs. 12–50) : (a) the history of Abraham and Isaac, 16 15-17 27 21 1-6 23 1-20 25 7-20 26 34-35 ; (b) the history of Jacob, 27 46-28 9 34 (parts) 35 9-15, 23-29 36 ; (c) the history of Joseph 37 1-2a 46 6-27 47 5-11 48 3-7 49 28-33 50 12-13. The Primitive document is traced in these passages : in Part 1, 2 4b-4 6 1-8 7 1-5 8 6-12, 20-22 9 18-27 10 8-19, 24-30 11 1-9 ; in Part 2, (a) 12 1-16 15 18 1-20 18 21 7-22 24 24 1-25 6 25 21-26 33 ; (b) 27 1-45 28 10-33 20 34 (parts) 35 1-8, 16-22 ; (c) 37 2b-46 5 46 28-47 4 47 12-48 2 48 8-49 27 50 1-11, 14-26.

The discovery of the composite character of Genesis, it may be added, need not be regarded as affecting the question of the inspiration of the book. That question remains practically the same, whether Genesis be the work of one or of several hands. The dates assigned to the parts of which it is supposed to be composed, as well as to the recasting of them in their present form, are all embraced within the age of the prophetic activity in Israel ; and the whole bears all the marks of true and genuine inspiration. In this respect Genesis will stand comparison with any of the historical books of the Old Testament. God, it must be remembered, 'at sundry times and in divers manners spake in time past unto the fathers by the prophets' (Heb 1 1).

CHAPTERS 1–2⁴ᵃ

THE CREATION

'The foundation of foundations and pillar of all wisdom is to know that the First Being is, and that He giveth existence to everything that exists!' Thus wrote Moses Maimonides, a Jewish scholar of the 12th cent. A.D., concerning whom the Jewish proverb runs: 'From Moses to Moses there arose none like Moses.' He had in his mind the opening chapter of the Bible, the object of which is to lay this foundation ; to declare the existence of the One God ; to teach that the Universe was created by Him alone, not by a multitude of deities ; that it is the product of a living, personal Will, not a necessary development of the forces inherent in Matter ; that it is not the sport of Chance, but the harmonious result of Wisdom. The writer, and the Blessed Spirit who guided him, had but one object in view, to insist on the two truths which underlie all others, the Unity of God and the derivation of all things from Him.

If we remember that, we shall be relieved of a difficulty which has greatly troubled devout and thoughtful men. Many are the essays and books which have been written on the discrepancies between the scientific account of the mode in which our globe came into being, and the account given in this first chapter of the Bible. Astronomy has shown it to be highly probable that, millions of years ago, an inconceivably immense mass of glowing gas gradually cooled down and took the form of a rotating sphere. This threw off the planets, our earth amongst the number. The central part is now the sun. The earth by slow stages grew fit to be the abode of life. Assuming that the astronomers are right, or, indeed, on any reasonable supposition, the sun and moon were not created later than the earth, on the Fourth Day (1 ¹⁶, ¹⁷). Again, Geology has proved that animal life cannot be dated later than vegetable (1¹¹, ¹² compared with 1²⁴), and the remains of animals found in the rocks testify by their structure to their feeding on other animals, not on fruit and herbs (1³⁰). But such discrepancies do not detract from the real value of our narrative, which is intended to teach Religion, not Science. For the exercise and training of human faculties God, in His Wisdom and Goodness, has left men to find out physical truths by the use of the powers He has given them. The biblical writer availed himself of the best ideas on the subject then attainable, put them into a worthy form, freed them from all disfigurements, stamped them with the impress of Religion. And the miracle of it is that the result continues valid and precious for all time, a noble presentation of the Unity and Spirituality of God, of the Omnipotence of His Will and of the Wisdom of His operations. (For a fuller consideration of this subject see art. 'Creation Story and Science.'

The question will be asked, whence did the OT. writer derive his ideas about the creation of the world which we find in this passage ? It used to be generally supposed that they were given to him by direct revelation of God. Some competent authorities maintain that, if not appearing for the first time in his work, they were at least original to the nation to which he belonged. Something may be said for this view, but the majority of scholars, upon historical and literary grounds, incline to the opinion that they were more or less derived. All the great nations of antiquity, it is argued, endeavoured to account for the origin of the world, and there are striking similarities in the pictures they drew. There is little doubt that the Hebrews were deeply affected by Babylonian influences, political and literary, and the Creation Story written on the clay-tablets of Babylonia has so many features in common with that before us as to warrant the conclusion that there is a historical connexion between them.

In an article 'Genesis and the Babylonian Inscriptions,' extracts are given from the Babylonian stories of the Creation and the Flood, and the relationship of the two accounts is discussed. It is sufficient to say here that nowhere is the force of inspiration more manifest than in the way the whole subject is treated in the Bible. The Babylonian poem describes the Creation as an episode in the history of the gods; the Bible places it in its right position as the first scene in the drama of human history : the former represents the deities themselves as evolved from Chaos ; the latter assumes God to be before all things, and independent of them : the former loses itself in a confused, conflicting medley of deities ; to the latter there is but One God: the wild grotesqueness of the one story is in startling contrast with the gravity, dignity, and solemnity of the account with which we have been familiar from childhood, which has also its message for our maturer years.

The present passage is full of the characteristics which mark the Priestly source. See on 2⁴ᵇ and art. ' Origin of the Pentateuch.'

1–3. Render, ' In the beginning, when God created the heavens and the earth — now the earth was waste and void, and darkness was over the deep, and the spirit of God was brooding over the waters — then God said: Let there be light.' On this rendering ' Creation ' is not ' out of nothing,' but out of pre-existing chaos. Vv. 1 and 3 tell how, when God determined on the creation of the ordered universe the first work was the formation of light as essential to life and progress. The first half of 2⁴ was probably prefixed originally to v. 1. See on 2¹⁻³.

2. God] Heb. *Elohim.* The word probably signifies 'strength,' but the etymology is obscure; cp. Arabic *Allah.* The Heb. word is plural in form, but as a rule it is significantly followed by verbs in the singular, except when used of heathen gods. The plural form may be used to express the variety of attributes and powers which are combined in the divine nature, or it may indicate that with the Hebrews one God had taken the place of the many gods who were worshipped by their heathen kindred. **Created]** Heb. *Bara;* a word used only of the creative action of God. **The heaven and the earth]** the ordered universe as contrasted with the dark watery waste of v. 2. The creation of the heaven and the earth did not precede the work of the six days, but comprised it, cp. 2¹. There was no 'heaven' until the second day. With the whole v. cp. Col 1¹⁶, ¹⁷, Heb 3⁴ 11³. **Without form** (RV 'waste') **and void]** The word rendered void is *bohu.* It reminds us of the Phœnician myth that the first men were the offspring of 'the wind Kolpia and his wife Baau which is interpreted Night,' and of the yet earlier Babylonian Bau, 'the great mother,' who was worshipped as the bestower of lands and flocks on mankind, and the giver of fertility to the soil. **The deep]** Heb. *tehom:* the mysterious primeval watery mass which, it was conceived, enveloped the earth. The Babylonians personified it as Tiamat, the dragon goddess of darkness whom Merodach must conquer before he can proceed to the higher stages of creation. **The Spirit** (RV 'spirit': lit. 'breath' or 'wind') **of God]** In the Bab. myth the gods are first evolved from the primeval deep: here the Divine agency is described as working on formless matter from the beginning. **Moved]** rather, 'was brooding' with life-giving power as a bird on her nest.

3–5. First day :— Creation of Light.

3. And God said, Let there be light] A sublime sentence ! ' By the word of the LORD were the heavens made.' Light and darkness are regarded as two objects, each occupying a place of its own (Job 38¹⁹). Light is created on the first day, the luminaries on the fourth. Not as an explanation, for this it is not, but merely as an illustration, it may be remembered that, according to the generally approved modern theory, the matter composing our solar system existed at first in the shape of an inconceivably vast mass of fiery vapour, which gradually cooled down and took the form of a rotating sphere. This threw off the planets, our earth amongst the number. The central part is now the sun. So that light in itself

may be regarded as prior to the specific lights that stood related as luminaries to the earth. The earth by slow stages grew fit to be the abode of life.

4. Good] i.e. perfect for the purpose for which God designed it.

5. And the evening, etc.] RV ' and there was evening and there was morning, one day.' In the endeavour to bring the Creation story into harmony with the ascertained results of science, it is often maintained that the writer meant indefinite periods of time by the term ' days.' But the science of Geology was entirely unknown to the ancients, and it is not legitimate to read a knowledge of modern discoveries into these ancient records. The author meant days in the sense of v. 16. Evidently, he had in mind the Jewish week, which he regarded not only as prefigured, but rendered obligatory by God's example in creating the world, as God worked six days, and rested the seventh : so the week was to consist of six working days, and a Sabbath day of rest. At the same time the writer intended to show that there was an orderly process in the work of creation. Note that **evening** is put before **morning,** probably because the Jewish day began at sunset.

6–8. Second day :— Creation of the Firmament.

6. The firmament] the sky, heavens. The word means something ' solid ' or ' beaten out,' like a sheet of metal. The ancients supposed that the sky was a solid, vaulted dome stretched over the earth, its ends resting on the mountains, and the heavenly bodies fastened to its inner surface. It served as the throne of God, cp. Ex 24¹⁰ Ezk 1²⁶. Its purpose here was to divide in two the primeval mass of waters. Above, it supported the upper waters which fell upon the earth through ' the windows of heaven' (7¹¹) in the form of rain ; below were the waters on which the earth rested, and from which it emerged. These waters were supposed to form a subterranean abyss which supplied the springs and seas ; for the idea cp. Gn 7¹¹ 49²⁵ Dt 33¹³ Job 38¹⁶ Ps 24² Prov 8²⁸, also Ex 24¹⁰ Ezk 1²⁶. This thought of the division of the primeval ocean into an upper and lower portion is represented in the Babylonian story by the cleaving of the body of Tiamat.

9–13. Third day :— Separation of land and water. Creation of vegetation.

9. Let the dry land appear] by emerging from the lower waters which were now gathered into seas. See Ps 104⁶⁻⁸. **11, 12. Grass . . herb yielding seed . . tree yielding fruit]** a simple and popular classification of the vegetable world. **Whose seed is in itself]** RV ' wherein ' (i.e. in the fruit) ' is the seed thereof.' **After his kind]** i.e. according to their several species.

14-19. Fourth day : — Creation of sun, moon, and stars.

The special value of this part of the story lies in its opposition to the worship of the heavenly bodies as deities, which was such a prominent feature of heathenism in Babylonia and elsewhere. Here they are declared to be created for the service of man, fulfilling a definite purpose. That purpose was threefold: (a) ' to divide the day from the night ' ; (b) to be ' for signs, and for seasons, and for days, and years,' i.e. to give the means of reckoning time ; (c) ' to give light upon the earth.'

14. Lights] rather, ' luminaries,' to hold and distribute the light created on the first day. **In]** rather, ' on ' or ' before ' the firmament; 30 vv. 17-20. See on v. 6. **Signs . . seasons . . days . . years]** For some of the modes in which the heavenly bodies were believed to serve as signs see 2 K 20 8-11 Isa 7 11 Jer 10 2 Joel 2 30 Mt 2 2 24 29. The seasons of the year are of course determined by them. The sun and moon rule the day and night; the length, temperature, etc., of day and night depending on their positions.

20-23. Fifth day : — Creation of fishes and birds.

20. Let the waters] render, ' let the waters swarm with swarms of living creatures,' animal-culæ, insects, fish, etc. **Fowl that may fly]** RV ' let fowl fly.' **21. Great whales]** Heb. denotes rather creatures like serpents, croco-diles, etc. **22. Blessed them]** As animate creatures they received a divine blessing, which suggests God's pleasure in the creation of beings capable of conscious enjoyment.

24-31. Sixth day : — Creation of animals and man.

26. Let us make man] the crowning work of creation and its highest development. The plural form ' us,' which occurs again 3 22 11 7 and Isa 6 8, has been interpreted of the Holy Trinity, but this would be anticipating a doctrine which was only revealed in later ages. The thought is perhaps that of God speaking in a council of angelic beings, or the form of the word may indicate a plural of majesty : see on ' God ' v. 1. The point of the expres-sion, however, is that it marks a closer relation of God to man than to the rest of His creation. It is not ' Let man be made ' but ' Let us make man.' **Man]** Heb. *adam*, the name of the race which becomes the name of the first man.

In our image, after our likeness] The likeness to God lies in the mental and moral features of man's character, such as reason, personality, free will, the capacity for com-munion with God. These distinguish man from the animals with which on the physical side he has much in common, and inevitably ensure his dominion over them (cp. Ps 8 5, 6). When the perfect Image of the Father (Heb 1 3)

had fully manifested His character, it beca ne possible to declare, in yet more adequate la i-guage, what true likeness to God is (Eph 4 24 Col 3 10).

27. Male and female] There is nothing in this account of the Creation to suggest that the sexes were not simultaneously created : contrast 2 21-23, which is from the earlier document. **29, 30.** The writer of the Priestly narrative here represents men and animals as living only on vegetable food. We seem to trace the thought of a primitive golden age, when the animals did not prey on each other, but lived at peace together : cp. Isa 11 6-9 65 25 Hos 2 18. It is he also who records the permission to use animal food after the Flood (9 2, 3). But the parrallel narrative from the Primitive document refers to the keeping of flocks (4 2, 4, 20), and takes no notice of any prohibition of animal food. **31. Very good]** Certain systems of philosophy and morality, ancient and modern, have proceeded on the assumption that evil is inherent in matter, and therefore that God and the world are antagonistic. This idea is quite foreign to the Scriptures, which teach that ' every creature of God is good.' Genesis teaches that evil enters the world from without : see on 3 1.

2 1-3. Seventh day : — God ceases from His work and sanctifies the day on which He rests.

Vv. 1-3 clearly belong to the first narrative of the Creation, of which they form the natural conclusion. The first part of v. 4, ' These are the generations of the heavens and of the earth when they were created,' has probably been transposed from its original place before 1 1, as in all other cases the phrase stands at the beginning of the section to which it refers, cp. 5 1 6 9 10 1. The second account of Creation begins in the latter half of v. 4, and should have formed the commencement of c. 2.

1. All the host of them] i.e. ' all the contents of heaven and earth.' **2. He rested on the seventh day]** God ceased (as the word means) from His creative work.

3. God blessed the seventh day and sanctified (RV ' hallowed ') **it]** This is adduced in Exodus as the ground for the observance of the sabbath (see Ex 20 8-11 notes, 31 17 Heb 4 4). It was separated from ordinary days, and set apart as a day for rest, and at a later time for holy observance. Further instructions as to its use will be found in Ex 31 13 35 2. The Babylonians observed the 7th, 14th, 19th, 21st and 28th days of the lunar month, as days when men were subjected to certain re-strictions: the King was not to eat food prepared by fire, nor offer sacrifice, nor consult an oracle, nor invoke curses on his enemies. But the weekly sabbath came to have a peculiar religious significance among the

Hebrews, which is not evident among other nations; and by its regular recurrence every seventh day it was dissociated from its connexion with the moon, and with lunar superstitions.

4. These are the generations of the heavens and of the earth when they were created] i.e. this is the history of their creation. See on vv. 1–3. The phrase 'These are the generations' occurs ten times in Genesis, viz. 2⁴ 5¹ 6⁹ 10¹ 11¹⁰ 11²⁷ 25¹² 25¹⁹ 36¹ 37².

CHAPTERS 2⁴ᵇ–3²⁴

PARADISE AND THE FALL

In this famous passage we possess a wealth of moral and spiritual teaching regarding God and man. The intention of the writer is evidently to give an answer to the question: How did sin and misery find their way into the world? As is natural among Orientals he put his reply into narrative form; and though it is generally accepted that the details are to be interpreted symbolically rather than literally, yet they are in marvellous agreement with the real facts of human nature and experience. Adam is the representative of the human race. The story of his temptation, fall, and consequent forfeiture of Paradise shadows forth some of the greatest mysteries of the human lot — the strangely mingled glory and shame of man, his freedom of action, the war between the law in his members and the law of his mind. It thus comes to have a universal significance and shows each man, as in a mirror, his own experience. When he reads this narrative, his conscience says to him, like a prophet of God: 'Thou art the man; the story is told of thee!'

In c. 2 the nature of man is unfolded. It has two sides, a higher and a lower; on the one hand, he is connected with the material world, as made of dust of the earth: on the other hand, he is related to God, who breathes into his nostrils the breath of life. He stands above the animal creation by his endowments of reason, discrimination, and language; he gives names to the beasts. The ideal relationship of the sexes appears in the creation of woman from the side of man, and his delight in finding in her an adequate companion and helper. Special emphasis is laid upon the moral and spiritual aspects of human nature. Man is created with the faculty of holding free and trustful communion with God, and with the power of exercising freedom of choice. It is chiefly in virtue of these high prerogatives that he can be said to be created in the image of God. Liberty of choice, however, or free will, is a perilous gift. It may be used either rightly or wrongly, and so there arises the possibility of temptation, of sin, of a 'fall': see on 2¹⁴.

C. 3 shows how man misuses his freedom. He is tempted by a mysterious power of evil, and falls before the temptation. Immediately the direst results ensue, both for his inward and outward condition. 'The fruit of man's first disobedience' is seen at once in his consciousness of guilt, his interrupted communion with God, his miserable state, and even the altered condition of the world in which he dwells. Yet God does not abandon him. He continues His care over him, and comforts him with the promise of final victory over the power of evil. See on 3¹⁵ for the significance of this passage in the light of Christianity.

It is to be expected that, in externals at least, the Bible narrative should resemble the traditions of other Oriental peoples. Accordingly we find, as in the case of the Creation and Flood narratives, that certain parallels to the Paradise story existed among the ancient Babylonians. This, and the further fact that Eden is placed in the vicinity of the Euphrates, have been taken to suggest that the Hebrews brought the original tradition with them from their home in the plains of Babylonia. The Bible narrative, however, differs from all others in its worthy conception of the divine nature, its freedom from polytheistic and heathen associations, and its embodiment of such profound religious truths as stamp it with the mark of inspiration.

The passage (2⁴ᵇ–3²⁴) now under consideration begins with a second account of the Creation forming an introduction to the story of man's temptation and fall. Some scholars regard this account as simply complementary to that given in c. 1. They maintain that it is not a separate story of the Creation, but a continuation of the former, with special reference to man's position in the universe. There are strong reasons, however, for regarding 2⁴ᵇ⁻²⁵ as a narrative independent of 1–2⁴ᵃ. (a) The primeval chaos, the creation of man and woman, vegetation and animals, are described, but there are striking differences in the two accounts. (b) The Creator is no longer called 'God' (Elohim) but 'The LORD God' (Jehovah Elohim), a fact which first suggested that the Pentateuch was compiled from different sources, and gave its name 'Jehovistic' to the continuous Primitive document of which this passage forms the commencement. (c) The writer speaks of the universe and its Author in different terms to those of c. 1. God is regarded as intimately concerning Himself with men rather than in His transcendental power; and this concern of His is expressed in terms which are properly applicable to the only living persons we directly know, viz. men. This anthropomorphism runs through the whole of the Paradise story (cp. 2⁷, ⁸, ¹⁹, ²¹ 3⁸). (d) The lordship of man over creation is expressed, not by setting him up as the goal to which all tended (cp. 1²⁶ᶠ·), but by representing him as the first created, before plants or herbs (2⁴⁻⁸), the being for whom the animals were afterwards made, and finally woman as a fitting mate. (e) The formal, orderly style of c. 1, which characterises the Priestly document, is exchanged here for the imaginative, poetical style which marks the Primitive (cp. 2 8, 9, 15, 19, 3 1-6, 7, 8). (f) Finally, if the two accounts of Creation had been originally the work of one writer, he would surely have explained that he was describing the same event from different standpoints, giving reasons for so doing. But he does not, and it is reasonable to conclude from all the variations which have been pointed out, that we possess two accounts of the Creation and of the origin of man upon earth, drawn from different sources.

4ᵇ–7. Render, 'In the day that the Lord God made earth and heaven, when no plant of the field was yet in the earth; and no herb of the field had yet sprung up .. the Lord God formed man,' etc. Vv. 5, 6, from 'For the Lord God,' thus form a parenthesis.

4. The Lord God] Where Lord is thus printed in capitals in the English Bible it stands for the Heb. JHVH, the sacred divine name which was probably pronounced 'Yahweh.' In later times the word was considered to be too sacred to be uttered; the title Adonai (i.e. My Lord) was substituted in reading, and thus the true pronunciation was lost. Hebrew was originally written without vowel-signs; when these were added to the MS text, the vowels of the name as read (Adonai) were attached to the consonants JHVH, and thus the artificial form 'Jehovah' was produced, which has come into common Christian use. See on Ex 3¹³ for the significance of the word, which means perhaps 'The Self-existent' (or 'Self-unfolding'). Yahweh (Jehovah) is the proper name of the God of Israel rather than a title, and as such was used by other nations who regarded Jehovah as the tribal God of the Jews (cp. Isa 36²⁰); the name also occurs on the Moabite stone set up by Mesha (2 K 3⁴). The American revisers have substituted 'Jehovah' for 'the Lord' throughout the OT. In Gn 2 and 3 Jehovah is joined with Elohim ('the Lord God'). The latter name was probably added by the editor who combined the narratives in order to show that the Jehovah of this section (the God of Israel) is the same as the Elohim (the Creator of the world) of the previous one. **The earth and the heavens]** RV 'earth and heaven.' Note the difference in the order from that in 1¹. The centre of interest in this c. is man on the earth.

6. Mist] The kindred word in the Assyrian language denotes the annual inundation of the Euphrates; see on v. 8 and on 3⁷.

7. Man] Heb. *adam* as in c. 1. AV renders the word as a proper name frequently in chs. 2–4; RV gives 'man' throughout except 3¹⁷ 4²⁵. **Ground]** Heb. *adamah.* A connexion is thus suggested between the two words, but the derivation of Adam is uncertain. **Formed man of the dust of the ground]** The lowly origin of man, and his derivation on the physical side from the lower elements of creation, are here implied. To 'become a living soul' means no more than to possess the principle of life possessed by the animals; cp. v. 19, where the Heb. for 'living creature' is the same as for 'living soul' here. But it is not said of the animals that God breathed into their nostrils the breath of life, only of man: this implies that man stands in a special relation to God, and may be taken as referring to the gift of those spiritual faculties by which he holds communion with God, and possesses a 'likeness' to Him; see on 1²⁶.

8. A garden] LXX renders by 'Paradeisos' (a Persian word meaning 'a park'), hence the English 'Paradise.' **Eastward]** i.e. of Palestine, such as Babylonia would be. **Eden]** The Heb. word *eden* means 'delight,' but there is a Babylonian word *edinu,* meaning 'plain,' and there may be a reference to the great plain in Babylonia between the Tigris and the Euphrates. In the southern portion of this plain an ancient hymn placed a garden of the gods wherein 'a dark vine grew .. its appearance as lapis lazuli.'

9. Every tree] The garden was planted with trees, like a king's pleasure park. The trees are specially mentioned, partly because they were to provide man's food, and partly because attention is directed to two of them for a particular reason. As life was to be sustained by them, so immortality was to be received through the fruit of the tree of life, and knowledge of good and evil with death in the end were the possible consequences of eating of the forbidden tree. The garden was divinely planted, and the trees had miraculous powers of good and evil. **The tree of life]** The Egyptians believed that in the blissful fields of Alu in the other world grew the tree of life, which the stars gave to the departed that they might live for ever; cp. also Rev 22².

10–14. There are many theories regarding these rivers. Perhaps the most likely is that the ancients, with their very limited notions of geography, regarded the four great rivers known to them, Euphrates, Tigris, Indus **(Pishon)** and Nile **(Gihon)**, as having a common source in some large lake in Eden. **Cush** will then be Ethiopia. It is possible, however, that the main river stands for the Persian

Gulf, which was anciently called 'The Salt River,' and the **four heads** were four streams connected with it, viz. (1) the Euphrates; (2) the Hiddekel, which the Persians called the Tigra, and Greeks the Tigris ; (3) the Gihon, which is said to 'compass' the land of Cush, the country of the Kashshu in W. Elam, and which may therefore be the Kerkha, which once ran with the Euphrates and Tigris into the Persian Gulf ; and (4) the Pishon, which has not been identified. **Havilah**] the sandy region of N. Arabia, and thus not far from the other localities. **Bdellium**] an odoriferous transparent gum. **Onyx**] RM 'beryl.' Vv. 10–14 are regarded by many as a later addition to the narrative.

15. Dress] i.e. cultivate. **Keep**] i.e. protect (from the beasts).

17. Knowledge of good and evil] i.e. moral consciousness issuing in moral judgment ; the power to distinguish between good and evil, not in act only but in consequence as well. This faculty is necessary, in order that man may reach moral maturity. The narrative implies that it would have come gradually to man, through the teaching of God, and without the loss of his own uprightness. It is a faculty which is developed from within, not conferred from without. By discipline and self-control man gains character and moral strength, or the knowledge of good and evil, and the power to discriminate between them. Hence 'the fruit of the tree of the knowledge of good and evil' is forbidden to man, not given to him like that of the others. It can impart the knowledge of good and evil at once, without a prolonged process of discipline or education ; but the attainment of it in this summary way is made an act of disobedience, perhaps to assist man's moral development by affording a test of his self-control. Man's freedom of choice, however, makes it possible for him to disobey, and so come to the required knowledge by a wrong way ; for the knowledge of good and evil is bought dearly by doing ill.

Shalt surely die] Man, it is implied, was created mortal, but had the privilege of attaining immortality by means of the tree of life. But by eating of the tree of the knowledge of good and evil man forfeited his liberty to eat of the tree of life (see 3²²⁻²⁴). This implies that the physical is the consequence of the moral death. 'Some of the older expositors observe that the troubles and sufferings to which man became liable through sin, are nothing else than disturbances of life, the beginning of death' (D.).*

18–25. Now the other animals and woman are formed. The order of Creation is not the same as in 1²⁴⁻²⁷.

18. Help meet] This is not one word but two, the former being the noun and the latter the qualifying adjective on which the main emphasis lies. Man might have many helps ; the vegetable and animal creation might minister to his welfare and comfort. But though these are 'helps,' they are not 'meet,' i.e. suitable for him. Only a creature like himself can be an adequate companion; and so woman is formed: see v. 20. **19.** The giving of a name implies a power of discrimination and reflection not possessed by the lower animals. Even proper names in the Scriptures are usually significant and descriptive of some quality supposed to be possessed by the person who bears it. Cp. e.g. the importance attached to the 'name' by which God is known : see on Ex 3¹³. **21.** The symbolical account of the creation of woman teaches the close relationship of the sexes, and the dependence of woman on man. **23. This is now**] Render, 'This time it is bone of my bones,' etc. It is Adam's cry of delight at finding a congenial, sympathising companion, after failing to find one among the animals (v. 20). **She shall be called Woman**] The similarity of the English words 'man,' 'woman' (wife-man) is also found in the Hebrew *Ish, Ishshah*. **24.** The creation of one man and one woman in the ideally perfect state of Eden implies that monogamy is the ideal of the married life. Polygamy and divorce were later accommodations to man's 'hardness of heart.' But 'from the beginning' (i.e. in the original purpose of the Creator) 'it was not so' (Mt 19⁴,⁸). **25.** See on 3⁷.

CHAPTER 3

The Temptation and the Fall of Man

This chapter describes how 'by one man sin entered into the world and death by sin' (Ro 5¹²). Although there is here no ambitious attempt to search out the origin of evil in the universe, the biblical account of the Fall pierces the depth of the human heart, and brings out the genesis of sin in man. The description, as already said, is true to life and experience.

There is no certain Babylonian counterpart to the biblical narrative of the Fall.

1. The serpent] The writer here sets himself to answer the question how evil came into the heart of man, who was created pure. His answer is that it came from without; it did not originate with man. And herein lies the hope of victory. The wrong approaches us from outside ourselves, and is not the native product of our own heart. There are present in our world beings and objects which, consciously or unintentionally, draw us towards that which is wrong; channels of sense, intellect, aspirations by which we may be touched

* A. von Dillmann, the greatest of all commentators on Genesis.

The narrative tells us that man was tempted by some evil power, whose personality remains in the background. But this power must have made use of a medium, which could not have been another human being, seeing there were as yet only Adam and Eve. That it was an animal was therefore a natural assumption. On two grounds the writer was left to fix upon the serpent as the medium of the temptation. One was the natural habits of the creature, its stealthy movements, its deadly venom, and the instinctive feeling of repulsion which the very sight of it provokes. These things are all suggestive of the insidious approach and fatal power of temptation. The other was the fact that already the serpent in older mythologies was associated with the powers of darkness. In Babylonian belief Tiamat, the power of darkness and chaos, and the opponent of the god of light, was represented as a gigantic dragon, also known as Rahab and Leviathan (Job 9 13 RV 26 12 RV Ps 74 13, 14 89 10 Isa 27 1 Am 9 3); while to the Persians the serpent was the emblem of Angra-Mainyu, the hostile god. In later times, when the power of evil was more definitely personified by the Israelites as Satan, the serpent remained as the symbol under which he was popularly conceived. See e.g. Rev 12 9 20 2.

There can be no doubt that our author intended to teach that an actual serpent was the tempter. As one of our deepest thinkers puts it : 'There was an animal nature in Eve to which the animal nature in an inferior animal could speak.' We who have been taught that 'our wrestling is not against flesh and blood, but against the principalities, against the powers, against the world-rulers of this darkness, against the spiritual hosts of wickedness in the heavenly places,' are almost irresistibly led to think of the serpent as a mere agent of him that is called the Devil and Satan (Rev 12 9); but we shall miss something of the instructiveness of the narrative if we do not, in the first instance, take the simple view originally intended. St. Paul, we must remember, adhered to it : 'The serpent beguiled Eve in his craftiness' (2 Cor 11 3).

And he said] An ancient Jewish legend represents all the animals as having had the gift of speech, and using one language, until the day when Adam was expelled from Eden. **The woman**] She is first addressed, as an easier prey to temptation (cp. 1 Tim 2 14). Observe that the serpent exaggerates the prohibition, and suggests that it is an undue curtailment of liberty. Sin usually begins as a revolt against authority. **2, 3.** The woman denies that the prohibition extends to every tree. It applies only to one, and its object is man's own safety. She also adds that the danger is such that they are forbidden

even to touch the tree. Evil is to be kept at arm's length. **4.** The serpent grows bolder on seeing that the woman is willing to argue the matter, and now flatly denies the truth of the divine warning. It is due not to a solicitude for man's safety, but to an ulterior motive, the envy or jealousy of God. The serpent avers that the threatened penalty will not be exacted, that God has selfishly kept out of their sight a great boon which men may gain ; that He is unwilling to see them rise too high. So the serpent sows discord between man and his Maker, by misrepresenting God's character.

5. As gods] RV 'as God.' It probably means here, as divine beings, like the angels. Cp. v. 22. **6.** 'Our great security against sin consists in our being shocked at it. Eve gazed and reflected when she should have fled' (Newman). Here we see the physical basis of temptation, the lust of the flesh, which 'when it hath conceived bringeth forth sin' (Jas 1 15). **She gave also unto her husband**] It is not in malice, but with a sincere view to his advantage, that she persuades the man to eat of the fruit.

7. They knew that they were naked] The serpent's promise (v. 5) is fulfilled, but not in the way expected. 'To the pure all things are pure' (cp. 2 25), but the act of sin is immediately followed by the sense of guilty shame. 'To innocence, standing in undisturbed union with God, everything natural is good and pure (2 25). So soon as, however, by the act of disobedience, the bond of union with God is broken, and the sensuous nature of man has released itself from the dominion of the spirit which rests in God, it stands there naked and bare and calls forth in its possessor inevitably the feeling of weakness, unworthiness and impurity' (D.). The first result of disobedience is the awakening of conscience. 'They lost Eden and they gained a conscience' (Newman). The whole story of the Fall is a parable of every sinner's experience. In every temptation there are an exciting cause without and an answering inclination within : every act of submission to temptation is a choice exercised by the will : and the result of sin is an uneasy conscience and a haunting sense of shame. **Aprons**] RM 'girdles.' There is a Jewish legend to the effect that at the moment of the Fall the leaves dropped off all the trees but the fig.

8-13. Conscience is a witness-bearer to God. Accordingly the accusing voice of conscience is followed by that of God in judgment.

8. On the anthropomorphism of this v. see intro. to 2 4-3 25. **Cool of the day**] lit. 'in the evening breeze,' i.e. in the evening when the heat of the day is tempered with a cool breeze, enabling Orientals to walk abroad ; cp. Gn 24 63 Song 2 17. **Adam**] RV 'the man' :

see on 2⁷.   **Hid themselves**] Hitherto they have been able to meet God in trustful simplicity : now conscious guilt moves them to hide from His presence. But the attempt is vain.   **10.** The man's answer shows that a change has come over him. He was not wont to be afraid of God.

11. The question does not imply that God does not already know what has occurred. But He compels the man to make a full confession.   **12.** Instead of frankly confessing his sins, the man lays the blame upon the woman. Observe also that he even tries to lay part at least of the blame upon God Himself (**whom Thou gavest** *to be* **with me**). This is a most life-like touch in the picture of the moral state which sin produces.   **13.** The woman in turn blames the serpent. Man is always inclined to blame the outward incitement to sin, rather than the inward inclination.

14-19. The Judgment.

14. The serpent, being the tempter and prime mover in the transgression, is judged first. It would appear that the writer conceived of the serpent as originally walking on feet. Its crawling in the dust, and taking dust into its mouth with its food (cp. Isa 65²⁵ Mic 7¹⁷ and the figurative expression 'to lick the dust,' Ps 72⁹ Isa 49²³) are marks of its degradation.

15. Nature's social union is also broken. The serpent race is an object of abhorrence, even though many kinds of serpents possess a remarkable beauty and grace. The curse, however, goes beyond this. There is a mingling of the literal and the allegorical in the sentence. The serpent, as representing the spirit of revolt from God, will continue to be the tempter of man. Man and the power of evil will be at constant feud.   **It shall bruise thy head, and thou shalt bruise his heel**] cp. Ro 16²⁰. While each will hurt the other, it is here implied that man will have the best of the serpent in the end. The seed of the woman means the human race as sprung from her. But in the course of history it becomes more and more evident that mankind is unable of itself to gain the complete victory over evil. This has been achieved by One alone, in whom this word of hope has been fulfilled. It is, therefore, with justice that Christians read in this promise the Protevangelium, or first proclamation of the Good Tidings of the final victory over sin. It is in Christ that the seed of the woman crushes the serpent.

16. The woman is now judged. Her doom is pain, chiefly the pain of child-bearing, and a position of subjection to and dependence on man. There is abundant evidence in human nature of the close connexion of sin and suffering, though our Lord warns us against uncharitably arguing back from the fact of

suffering to previous sin, in special instances, and in the case of others. See e.g. Lk 13¹⁻⁵ Jn 9¹⁻³, and cp. the whole argument of ħhe book of Job. In the case of child-bearing, it is not unreasonable to suppose that the pain and danger connected with it have been increased by the accumulated wrongdoing of mankind. Among the lower animals the process of birth is much easier.

17. The judgment on the man. Work had already been appointed as the duty of men (2¹⁵). But it was not laborious. The change from innocence to sin is marked by the change of order from the keeping of the garden to the tilling of the ground (v. 23). Henceforth work is to be done under adverse conditions. The connexion between the sin of man and the productiveness of the earth is not so easily traced, but the conditions of labour are undoubtedly made harder by the evils and inequalities of human society due to man's sin and selfishness.   **19. Till thou return unto the ground**] The story does not assume that man was created physically immortal. But the inevitable certainty of death is now seen to increase the sadness of his earthly lot. It is sin which gives death its sting (1 Cor 15⁵⁶) ; and though the Redemption of Christ has not abolished physical death, yet it gives victory over death, by removing the guilt and fear that make it so appalling and hopeless : cp. Heb 2¹⁴,¹⁵.   **20. Eve**] Heb. *Havvah*, 'life.'

21. God does not cease to care for man, even though he has rebelled against Him : cp. Mt 5⁴⁵.

22-24. Now that man has used his power of free-will to disobey God and become alienated from Him, a perpetuation of his sinful life would have been a curse rather than a blessing. Physical immortality which, according to the writer, he might have gained by eating of the tree of life, is therefore denied to him. But the blessing forfeited 'by one man's offence' is restored 'by the obedience of one' (Ro 5¹²⁻²¹). In Christian thought Adam is 'a figure of Him that was to come.' Adam and Christ are the originators of two different streams of humanity ; and as those descended from Adam by physical generation inherit the consequences of his disobedience, in virtue of an undoubted law or principle of heredity, or of the solidarity of the human race, so those regenerated in spirit through Christ enjoy the fruit of His perfect obedience, and have a right to the tree of life. 'As in Adam all die, even so in Christ shall all be made alive.'

24. Cherubims] RV 'the Cherubim' (plur. of 'Cherub'). These mystic beings are mentioned as attendants of God in various passages of the OT. (Ps 18¹⁰ Ezk 1 and 10). Here they appear as the guardians of God's abode : cp.

Ezk 28 13-17, also on Ex 25 18 32 4. When the Psalmist says that 'Jehovah rode upon a cherub and did fly,' he is obviously describing a thunderstorm with its swift storm-clouds ; and when he goes on to speak of the 'brightness before Him,' he suggests a connexion between the flaming sword of this v. and the lightning-flash.

To keep the way of the tree of life] Man, it would appear, had not yet eaten of the tree of life, not having felt the need of it. But now, when his knowledge of evil has brought him the fear of death, and he has realised the value of this tree, he is prevented even from approaching it. The tree of life, however, though denied to man on this side the grave, will be found by those who overcome in the conflict with evil, in the midst of the Paradise of God (Rev 2 7 22 2).

CHAPTER 4

Cain and Abel. The Descendants of Cain

The narrative, which forms part of the Primitive document, impressively shows how sin, having once appeared, became hereditary in the human race, and speedily developed into its most revolting form. Its details enable us to see how jealousy, when indulged, leads to hatred and murder, and violates not only the ties of humanity but those of family affection ; how the sinner casts off all regard for the truth and for his natural obligations ; how progress in sin adds to the misery of man's lot ; and 'conscience doth make cowards of us all.' The truths taught are, that God looks on the hearts of His worshippers, seeks to restrain the sinner ere he yields to passion, marks the death of the innocent, and graciously mitigates His punishment when His mercy is sought.

The story is but loosely attached to that of Paradise. It assumes that there is already a considerable population in the world, for no explanation is given whence Cain got his wife, or who were the people whose vengeance he feared. It presupposes the institution of sacrifice, of which nothing has been said previously, and of blood revenge. Various solutions of these difficulties have been suggested, but scholars now generally suppose that the story occupied originally a later position among the traditions than that in which we find it.

1. Adam] RV 'the man.' **Cain**] Heb. *Kayin,* 'a spear,' in Arabic 'smith' (see v. 22). Here connected with *Kanah,* 'gotten,' or 'acquired.' The Hebrews attached a great importance to names, which were mostly regarded as descriptive of some characteristic in the thing or person on whom they were bestowed. In the giving of a name, or in

explaining one already given, strict regard was not paid to the actual derivation of the word. It was enough if the name resembled in any way a word which might be taken as applicable to the subject : cp. Abel, Noah (5 29), Babel (11 9), and the names of Jacob's sons in chs. 29, 30. **From the** LORD] RV 'with *the help of* the LORD.'

2. Abel] perhaps from the Assyrian *ablu,* 'a son.' Here it may be connected with Heb. *hebel,* 'a breath,' a fitting name for one whose life was so brief : see on v. 1. **3.** On the nature and origin of sacrifice see Intro. to Leviticus.

4. And the LORD **had respect,** etc.] The characters of the brothers rather than their offerings are kept chiefly in view. Many passages show that the decisive reason why a worshipper is accepted or rejected lies in the disposition with which he draws nigh (cp. 1 S 15 22 Isa 1 11-17 Ps 50 8-15 Heb 11 4). The manner in which God's approval was declared is not mentioned, but see Jg 6 21 1 K 18 38 2 Ch 7 1. Possibly the contrast between his toilsome life in tilling the soil and the easier existence of Abel, makes Cain envious.

7. We may paraphrase thus, 'If thou doest well, is there not lifting up of the countenance, banishment of depression and gloom ? And if thou doest not well, Sin is at the door, crouching in readiness to spring on thee and make thee a prey, but thou must resist its promptings' (RM 'Unto thee shall be its desire, but thou shouldest rule over it'). What is suggested is that, if a sullen and jealous disposition is harboured, it will only require opportunity to tempt to malice and cruelty.

8. And Cain told (RV) **Abel**] Heb. 'said unto.' LXX and other versions insert here 'Let us go into the open country,' showing Cain's intention to murder. In his case the harboured jealousy tempted him not merely to take an opportunity of using violence, but to make one. **9.** Cain sounds a much lower depth of depravity than his parents. Besides the guilt of murder, there is the impudent denial that he has harmed Abel, and the repudiation of responsibility for his safety.

10. Crieth unto Me] The thought of great evils crying to God is frequently met with in Scripture : cp. 18 20 19 13. The ground, which has been unwillingly obliged to drink the blood of Abel, is represented as refusing to tolerate his murderer, or to make him an adequate return for his toil : cp. Job 16 18 31 38-40. In Heb 12 24 the blood of Jesus, which appealed for men's pardon, is contrasted with that of Abel, which demanded retribution.

11. The earth] RV 'the ground.' Cain is banished from the ground which he had formerly tilled and had now polluted, to the wide world (v. 12), a sterner punishment than that of Adam and Eve. **14. From Thy face shall I be hid**] Cain supposes that God's presence and protection are limited to his old home. **Vagabond**] RV 'wanderer.' **Whosoever findeth me**] See prefatory remarks.

15. Sevenfold] Vengeance should be taken upon seven of the murderer's family : cp. 2 S 21⁸. **Set a mark upon Cain**] RV 'appointed a sign for Cain.' Perhaps it was some token to assure him of safety, like the rainbow at the Flood. Others take it that Cain was marked in some way to show that he was under God's protection. **16. Went out from the presence of the LORD**] from the land he had before inhabited. See on v. 14. **Nod**] The word, which means 'wandering,' is by some regarded as merely a figurative expression for a nomadic life, but Cain appears to have built a city there (v. 17).

17–24. The descendants of Cain. In these vv. is traced the origin of the different forms of civilisation and culture. Their religious value lies in the fact that the inventions are attributed to men, whereas in heathen mythologies they were thought to be due to various deities.

It will be observed that great similarity exists between the names of the descendants of Adam in this c. and those given in c. 5. The two accounts come from different documents, and although the names differ somewhat in form and order, it is now generally supposed that they are merely two versions of the same traditional list of the Patriarchs before the Flood. The most important difference is that, whereas in c. 5 Seth and Enos are given as the son and grandson of Adam, and Cainan (whom we may identify with Cain) appears as the great-grandson, in the present c. Seth and Enos are put in a supplementary list (vv. 25, 26) and Cain appears as Adam's son. If the list in c. 5 is correct and the Cain of this c. be identified with Cainan there, it is evident that there must have then existed a considerable population of his tribe. And this is indeed presupposed in v. 14 where Cain expresses his dread of Abel's avengers, and in v. 17 where he is said to have built a city.

17. Builded a city] The 'city' of course would be a collection of huts surrounded by a defensive palisade. **19.** The first mention of polygamy in the Bible. The custom of having more than one wife does not seem to have been uncommon among the Hebrews, and we find legislation on the subject in Dt 21¹⁵⁻¹⁷ ; but the divine intention was that a man should have but one wife : cp. 2²⁴ Mt 19⁵.

20. The father] i.e. 'originator' ; the first to lead a pastoral life. **21. Organ**] RV 'pipe.'

22. Tubal-cain] i.e. 'Tubal the smith' : see on 4¹. **An instructer of every artificer in**] RV

'the forger of every cutting instrument of. Brass**] rather, 'copper' (RM), or bronze.

23. I have slain, etc.] RM 'I will slay a man for wounding me, and a young man for bruising me.' On this rendering it would seem that Lamech, rejoicing, perhaps, in his son's invention of weapons, boasts that he would be able to amply repay any one who injured him. The words of Lamech are metrical and are the first instance of poetry in the Bible. Hebrew poetry does not depend on rhythm as with us, but in parallelism of ideas in each couplet, as may be traced in this instance ; see Intro. to Psalms. **24.** See v. 15 and note. **25, 26.** A supplementary note mentioning the birth of Seth and Enos : see on v. 17. **Seth**] 'appointed' or 'substituted.' **Enos**] 'man.'

26. Then began men to call upon the name of the LORD] The Primitive or Jehovistic document uses **Jehovah** as the name of the God of Israel from the first ; but the Priestly document speaks of the name being first revealed to Moses. See Ex 3¹⁴ 6². What is here suggested is, either that Enos worshipped God as Jehovah (reading 'he began to call'), or that in his day men began to worship Jehovah by public invocation and sacrifice.

CHAPTER 5

THE DESCENDANTS OF ADAM TO NOAH

The purpose of the historian in giving the names and ages of the antediluvian Patriarchs was, no doubt, to show the glorious ancestry of the chosen race, and to account for the period between the Creation and the Flood. This, according to the Hebrews, was 1656 years. (See on 10³².) Various attempts have been made to explain the great ages attributed to these Patriarchs, but they are purely conjectural, and the view now generally held is that the Hebrews, like all other ancient nations, had a tradition that the forefathers of the race were vastly longer lived than their descendants. The golden age of the Hebrew lay in the past ; and he attributed in pre-eminent degree to his ancestors in these far-off days the blessing he valued most of all—length of days upon the earth.

The similarity of the lists of names in chs. 4 and 5 has been discussed in a note on 4¹⁷. C. 5 continues the narrative of the Priestly document which we met with in 1¹–2⁴ᵃ, as appears from (a) the recurrence of 1²⁷,²⁸ in vv. 1, 2, (b) the phrase 'the generations of' characteristic of P (see on 2⁴ᵃ), (c) the divine name God, and (d) the formal statistical style of the chapter.

1. The generations of Adam] i.e. the genealogy of Adam's descendants, cp. 2⁴ and note. **2. Called their name Adam**] This shows that the word 'Adam' was originally applied to the race, and was not a proper name. In the previous v. it is so used for the first time in the Priestly narrative.

3. His own likeness] as he himself was created in the likeness of God.

21–24. Enoch] the one figure which breaks the formality of this c. His conduct is mentioned in a way which implies that the majority of men lived differently. In all his actions he recognised the duty which he owed to God ; from none of his thoughts was God absent ; he lived in communion with Him. The meaning of the expression **He was not ; for God took him,** is, no doubt, correctly given by the writer of Heb 11, as that Enoch never died, but was translated to heaven, like Elijah, as a reward for the holiness of his life. In Jewish tradition Enoch's walking with God was taken to mean initiation into the mysteries of the universe, and the secrets of the past and future. A whole circle of apocalyptic literature was ascribed to him in the post-exilic days, which is embodied in the so-called book of Enoch. This book is quoted in Jude 14 as the work of 'Enoch the seventh from Adam.' **23. The days of Enoch**] It is noteworthy that the life of Enoch is the shortest mentioned in this c.

29. Noah] here connected with *nahem*, 'to comfort.' The name is really derived from *nuah*, 'to rest.' The comfort may refer to the invention of wine, which is attributed to Noah in 9 20-27, a passage perhaps from the same source as the present one.

CHAPTER 6 1-4
THE SONS OF GOD AND THE DAUGHTERS OF MEN

1–4. This fragment seems to have been placed here as an instance of the wickedness which necessitated the Flood. Stories of unions between deities and the women of earth, which resulted in gigantic and corrupt races, were common to many nations of antiquity ; and it is now generally held that we have here traces of a similar tradition among the Hebrews, which had survived to the writer's day. But though the passage retains signs of these primitive ideas, it is free from the polytheistic and impure features which are found in the pages of heathen mythology. Probably such passages as 2 Pet 2 4 Jude 6 f., which speak of the fall of the angels, are based on these verses.

2. The sons of God] This expression occurs in other passages, e.g. Job 1 6 38 7 Dan 3 25 RV, where it is evident that the angels are meant, and this seems the only possible explanation here. It used to be supposed that the 'sons of God' meant the Sethites, who became corrupted by marriage with the Cainites. But the phrase

is nowhere else used to describe them, and, as Bishop Ryle remarks, 'the popular assumption that Cain's descendants were pre-eminently wicked has no foundation either in c. 4 or c. 6.' Nor could such unions have produced the race of giants mentioned in v. 4. The religious idea suggested is that the wickedness that prevailed was too great to be entirely of mere human origin. **3.** The general meaning is that God now sets a limit (**an hundred and twenty years**) to human life, which up to this time had been indefinitely long. **My spirit**] refers to the spirit of life with which the fleshly nature of man had been endowed. It will not sustain man for ever (RV) in this world.

4. There were giants] RV 'the Nephilim were.' The Nephilim, a race of giants, famous in popular legend, are represented as being men of renown at the same time as these angels formed unions with the daughters of men. They are alluded to by the spies (Nu 13 33 RV) as ancestors of the giant races of Canaan : and this is probably what is referred to by the words **and also after that.**

CHAPTERS 6 5–9 17
THE FLOOD

This narrative records the judgment of God upon the sinful forefathers of mankind, and His preservation of a righteous family, in whom the divine purposes for men might be carried out. The spiritual teaching of Noah's deliverance has always been recognised by Christians, who see in the ark a symbol of the Church into which they are admitted by baptism, God thereby graciously providing for their deliverance from the wrath and destruction due to sin. The story of the Flood was fittingly used by our Lord and the NT. writers to convey lessons of judgment (Mt 24 37 Lk 17 26 2 Pet 3 5-7), righteousness (2 Pet 2 5), repentance (1 Pet 3 20), and faith (Heb 11 7).

No section of these early chs. of Genesis has excited more interest than the account of this terrible catastrophe. Traditions of a great primeval deluge, similar to the one here recorded, exist in the annals of many nations besides the Hebrews. Of these the Babylonian Flood story is the most closely allied to the Bible narrative. Josephus and Eusebius both preserve fragments of a history of Chaldea which was written by Berosus, a priest of Babylon 250 B.C., and which he had gathered from the archives of the temple of Bel at Babylon. Among these fragments is a record of the Flood story as it occurred in his country. Two thousand years later, in 1872, Mr. G. Smith of the British Museum discovered fragments of a tablet of baked clay at Nineveh, inscribed in the cuneiform character, and of greater antiquity than the chronicle of Berosus, which strikingly confirm the latter's account of the Flood. As is well known, the Hebrews and Babylonians belonged to the same Semitic stock, and the ancestors of the Hebrew race came from Babylonia. A comparison of the biblical and Babylonian stories shows clearly that they are two versions of the same narrative, although great differences exist in the religious standpoint. See art. 'Genesis and the Babylonian Inscriptions.'

The question has been discussed whether the Flood was limited in its extent to the early home of man and the birth-place of the tradition, viz. Central Asia, or whether it was world-wide. Various scientific objections to a universal immersion of the earth have been brought forward, such as its inconsistency with the existing distribution of animals, the impossibility of the different species of animals finding accommodation in the ark, the want of sufficient moisture in our world, either in the form of vapour or in that of water, to cover the highest mountains, and the disturbance to the solar system which would have been caused by the sudden creation of the amount required. In considering these objections, we must remember that the impression of a general divine judgment would be quite adequately produced by the submergence of the comparatively small district inhabited at the time by man ; also, that the preservation of the record could only be due to the survivors, whose ideas of the extent of the catastrophe were drawn from their personal experiences, and the limited geographical knowledge of the time. In this way the statements of 6 ^{17} and 7 $^{4, 21-23}$ may be satisfactorily accounted for. 'The language relating to the catastrophe is that of an ancient legend, describing a prehistoric event. It must be judged as such. Allowance must be made, both for the exaggeration of poetical description and for the influence of oral traditions during generations, if not centuries, before the beginnings of Hebrew literature' (Bishop Ryle). We need not hesitate, therefore, to accept the opinion now generally held that the Flood was only local in its extent.

The scene of the Flood is indicated by the traditions. Both mention the mountainous range on the borders of Armenia, Mesopotamia and Kurdistan as the region where the ark rested. The Babylonian account also places the building of the 'ship' at Shurippak, a city on the Euphrates. This district was the original home of both Hebrews and Babylonians; and it is reasonable to conclude that the two accounts preserve the tradition of a calamitous occurrence in the early annals of their race, which left a lasting impression upon the two peoples, and which they both regarded as a divine visitation.

A word must be added regarding the natural phenomena which occasioned the catastrophe. The chief cause may have been, in addition to excessive rains, an earthquake which drove the waters of the Persian Gulf over the lowlying plains of Babylonia, turning them into an inland sea. Something of this kind is suggested in 7 ^{11}. The same agency may have driven the ark towards the mountains. Such upheavals of ocean beds, or subsidences of the earth, resulting in a disastrous inrush of the ocean, have occurred in modern times. In 1819, in a district known as the Runn of Cutch in India, 2,000 sq. m. of land were turned into an inland sea, owing to sudden depression of land followed by an earthquake.

The whole story emphasises the righteousness of God, who is 'of purer eyes than to behold iniquity,' His stern punishment of sin, and His abundant mercy towards them that fear Him.

The narrative of the Flood affords an illustration of the composite character of Genesis. Many difficulties in the story are removed if we assume that the narrator made use of two distinct traditions. To the Priestly document may be assigned 6 $^{9-22}$ 7 $^{6, 11, 13-16a, 18-21, 24}$ 8 $^{1 2a, 3b, 13a, 14-19}$ 9 $^{1-17}$. This furnishes the groundwork of the story; the vv. assigned to the Primitive document are 7 $^{1-5, 7-10, 12, 16b, 17, 22, 23}$ 8 $^{2b, 3a, 6-12, 13b, 20-22}$. In 7 $^{7-10}$ the Primitive account has been modified by the introduction of some expressions from the Priestly narrative. The following are the chief points in which the two versions of the Flood story differ from each other. According to the Priestly narrative only one pair of every kind of creature is preserved in the ark; the cause of the deluge is the opening of the fountains of the great deep as well as of the windows of heaven; the waters prevail for a hundred and fifty days; it is five months after the beginning of the Flood when the ark rests on the mountains of Ararat; more than two months still pass before the mountain tops are visible; other two months elapse before the waters disappear; and almost two months more before the ground is perfectly dry; God's promise is, that He will not again destroy the earth with a Flood. According to the Primitive document, seven pairs of all clean beasts and fowls, and one pair of all unclean animals, are taken into the ark; the Flood is caused simply by a prolonged rain which lasts for forty days and nights; forty days after the rain ceases, Noah sends forth a raven and a dove; seven days later, the dove is sent out a second time, and again after other seven days ; the ground is then dry ; God promises to curse the ground no more, and to maintain the fixed order of all natural seasons. God's covenant with Noah is peculiar to the former, and Noah's sacrifice to the latter account.

6. It repented the LORD] The writer, as in c. 3, interprets God's acts from man's point of view, and explains them on the analogy of human motives. See on 11⁵. **9. Perfect**] i.e. 'upright,' a man of integrity. **13. With the earth**] rather, 'from the earth.'

14–16. The Hebrew word for **ark** means a 'vessel,' that which contains anything. It was shaped like a chest, with a flat bottom and a roof. If the **cubit** measured 18 in., the ark was 450 ft. long, 75 ft. broad, and 45 ft. in depth; and therefore smaller than many modern steamships. It had three decks, and was divided into compartments. It was built of **gopher wood**, which was probably the cypress; and was coated with pitch. The **window** of v. 16 (RV 'light,' RM 'roof') was probably an open space for light and air left all round the ark, just under the roof, which was supported at intervals by posts. **16. In a cubit**, etc.] RV 'to a cubit shalt thou finish it upward,' i.e. a space of 18 in. was to be left. **18. My covenant**] see on 9⁹. **19. Every living thing of all flesh**] This comprehensive command is limited in the Primitive narrative (7²) to clean animals (such as sheep, oxen, and goats), and to beasts that are not clean (which by analogy means domestic animals, such as camels, asses, horses, etc.), and fowls. The inclusion of all living animals in the ark is the explanation which the tradition had to give, to account for a fact, otherwise inexplicable on its theory of a universal flood; namely, the presence in the world of so many different species of animals after such a destructive event.

CHAPTER 7

THE FLOOD (continued)

2. By sevens] RV 'seven and seven,' or seven pairs. The clean animals might be used for food, and would also be required for sacrifice. Observe that in 6¹⁹ this distinction between clean and unclean is not noticed, and that there also the animals are chosen in single pairs, 'two of every sort.' Lists of 'clean' and 'unclean' animals are given in Lv 11. **11. The second month**] The year is here supposed to begin in autumn (cp. Ex 34²²), so that the second month would be Marchesvan (middle of Oct. to middle of Nov.). That was about the beginning of the rainy season in Palestine. **The great deep**] See on the ancient Semitic conception of the world, 1⁶. Evidently some vast inrush of water is intended, beyond heavy rains. **16. Sit-napisti** says, 'I entered into the midst of the ship and shut my door.' In our narrative Provi-

dence is nearer at hand, **The LORD shut him in.** **20. Fifteen cubits upward**] The waters are supposed to be 15 cubits higher than the loftiest mountains. The ark is conceived as immersed up to 15 cubits; so that whenever the waters decreased, the ark grounded on a mountain-top (8⁴).

CHAPTER 8

THE FLOOD (continued)

4. The mountains of Ararat] Ararat is the Assyrian 'Urardhu,' the country round Lake Van, in what is now called Armenia; but the word also signifies 'highlands,' and perhaps it is a general expression for the hilly country which lay to the N. of Assyria. Mt. Masis, now called Mt. Ararat (a peak 17,000 ft. high), is not meant here. **11. The olive leaf** indicated that the tree was above water, and as the olive does not grow at a great elevation, the inference was that the waters had greatly abated.

21. The LORD smelled a sweet savour] A common expression for the favourable acceptance of an offering, cp. Lv 1⁹,¹³,¹⁷.

I will not again curse, etc.] An acknowledgment of man's innate propensity to evil. If wicked thoughts, desires, and actions were always to be followed by the judgments they merit, disaster would never be far off (Isa 1⁵).

22. Practically there are but two seasons in the land where this was written : one may be called Seed-time, Cold, Winter (middle of Sept. to middle of March) ; the other, Harvest, Heat, Summer (the rest of the year).

CHAPTER 9

THE DIVINE BLESSING AND COVENANT. NOAH AND THE VINE. THE CURSE OF CANAAN

1–7. The primeval benediction of man (1²⁸) is now repeated and enlarged. Animal food is allowed (cp. 1²⁹), but blood is forbidden. The blood makes the life manifest, as it were, to our senses, and the life belongs to God, and must, therefore, be offered to Him.

5, 6. The ground of the sacredness of human life here is the existence of the divine image in man. It is not conceived as being wholly destroyed by sin.

9. My covenant] This word occurs some two hundred times in the OT., and the idea lies at the root of the whole conception of law among the Jews. Covenants, as made between men, form the beginnings of civilised government : cp. 26²⁶ 31⁴⁴, etc. The word is also used of the relation of God to man ; of His justice, His unchangeable nature, and His protecting power, on the one side, and the corresponding duties devolving upon man, especially as embodied in the law of Moses, on the other. A series of covenants (with Abraham and his successors, with Israel in the wilderness, with David) runs through OT. history. The particular idea in the covenant with Noah is that of the uniform working of God in Nature (cp. 8 22), and of His loving care for His creation. On these two ideas are based all physical science, which could not exist if there were no laws of nature, and all religion, which otherwise would become mere superstitious dread of unseen powers. Jeremiah (31 31-34) speaks of a new covenant which is to take the place of the covenant of the exodus. The New Testament claims that this new covenant has been introduced by Christ (Lk 22 20 1 Cor 11 25 2 Cor 3 6 Heb 8). Hence the two divisions of the Scriptures are properly not 'Testaments' but 'Covenants.'

13-17. We are not to understand that the bow was now first created. From the beginning a rainbow would be formed, whenever the sunshine and the rain met together. But it was now designated to be the token of God's gracious promise, and its use for this purpose is in harmony with the feelings which it naturally excites. The rain-storm is on us, but the sun is in the skies : the dark background brings out the glorious arc of colour. Man need not yield wholly to depression, for he knows that the clouds will pass. Hindoo mythology calls the rainbow Indra's war-bow, laid aside by him after he had vanquished the demons. Scandinavian legend speaks of it as a bridge built by the gods to join heaven and earth. It is also alluded to in the Babylonian narrative of the Flood.

18-27. Noah and the Vine. The curse of Canaan.

The purpose of the passage is (1) to explain by a story the origin of the cultivation of the vine, and (2) to set forth the moral and religious position of Israel among the other nations of the world. On the ground of the mention of Canaan instead of Ham in vv. 25, 27, it has been suggested, with some probability, that in the Primitive document the sons of Noah were originally Shem, Japheth and Canaan, and that the explanations in vv. 18, 22 (**Ham the father of Canaan**) were introduced to harmonise the story with the Priestly document, which speaks of Shem, Ham and Japheth.

18, 19. These vv. are a link, inserted to connect the incident with the account of the Flood. **20.** Noah is represented as the first cultivator of the vine. **21.** Noah's intoxication was not due to deliberate excess, but was his practical discovery of the properties of wine. The story therefore contains nothing inconsistent with the character already ascribed to him. **25.** Canaan represents the nations of Palestine subdued by Israel. The justification of the conquest lay in the impure character

of their worship, which was foreshadowed in the immodest conduct of their ancestor.

26. The LORD God of Shem] RV 'the LORD (Jehovah), the God of Shem.' Shem was the ancestor of Israel, and these words assert Israel's unique position and calling, as the chosen people of the true God. **Canaan shall be]** RV 'let Canaan be' : so in v. 27.

27. God shall enlarge] RV 'God enlarge Japheth.' Japheth represents the remaining peoples of the world. They have a share in God's favour, even though they do not know Him in His true character as Jehovah. **He shall dwell]** RV 'let him dwell,' in friendly alliance. We may see in the words a forecast of the days when the descendants of Japheth should come to worship the LORD God of Shem : cp. Isa 60 3, 5.

CHAPTER 10
THE NATIONS DESCENDED FROM NOAH

This section gives the origins and situations of the nations of the world, as their relationships were conceived by the early Hebrews. Before passing to the history of the chosen race, the author traces the ties by which the rest of mankind are united with his own people, and shows the position of Israel among the nations. Each nation is regarded as a unity, and is summed up in the person of its supposed ancestor. The nations being treated as individuals, it follows that their mutual relations are put in terms borrowed from family life ; Gomer is the 'son' of Japheth, and so on. But this relationship is not to be understood literally. The names are in many cases plainly national (the Jebusite, the Canaanite, etc.). Others are well-known names of countries (Mizraim or Egypt, Asshur, etc.) ; and nearly all appear elsewhere in OT. in a geographical sense (see especially Ezk 27 and 38 1-13). We may therefore consider that the arrangement is determined chiefly by geographical considerations, nations in proximity to each other being regarded as related. Thus the races assigned to Japheth (vv. 2-5) are all in the N., those to Ham in the S. (vv. 6-20), whilst Shem's descendants (vv. 21-31) are in the centre. These come last because it is this line which is followed out in the sequel. The classification of the nations is a rough and approximate one, made in far distant days when the science of ethnology was unknown. The limitations of the Hebrew author's knowledge of the extent of the world are also apparent. The nations mentioned are mainly those which were grouped round the Mediterranean Sea, and are generally known as Caucasian, no reference being made to Negro, Mongolian or Indian races. But it may be truly said that the list upon the whole proves itself to be an excellent historico-geographical monument of an age from which we no longer have other comprehensive sources of information. While the groundwork of the section is from the Priestly document, this has been combined with extracts from the Primitive document (10 8-19, 21, 24-30), which do not perfectly harmonise with it. Thus Sheba (10 28) and Havilah (10 29) are descendants of Shem, while in 10 7 they are Cushites, descended from Ham. The identification of the following names is uncertain : Abimael, Almodad, Anamim, Casluhim, Diklah, Gether, Hadoram, Hul, Jerah, Lud, Ludim, Mash, Obal, Resen, Sabtechah, Salah. The notes on the names follow the groupings of the text.

2–5. The sons of Japheth. These are nations mostly N. or W. of Palestine. **Gomer]** the Cimmerians, near the Crimea. **Ashkenaz]** perhaps, Phrygia. **Riphath]** perhaps, Paphlagonia on S. borders of the Black Sea. **Togarmah]** Armenia. **Magog]** supposed to be Scythians, cp. Ezk 38 2, where they are associated with Gomer. **Madai]** the Medes. **Javan]** Ionian Greece. **Elishah]** some coast or island in the Greek seas (Ezk 27 7) : Crete, Cyprus, and Greece (Hellas) have been suggested. **Tarshish]** Though often mentioned in OT., the identity is quite uncertain. Suggestions are either Tarsus in Cilicia, Tartessus in S. Spain, or the Etruscans of Italy. **Kittim]** Citium, the modern Larnaca in Cyprus. **Dodanim]** (in 1 Ch 1 7 Rodanim) Rhodes. **Tubal]** the Tibareni ; **Meshech]** the Moschi, both SE. of the Black Sea. **Tiras]** uncertain. Perhaps the Turusha, a seafaring people mentioned in Egyptian inscriptions, or the Tyrseni, a people dwelling on the shores of the Ægean Sea.

5. It is likely that this v. in its complete form ran : ' Of these were the coasts and islands of the peoples divided. These are the sons of Japheth, in their lands, each according to his language, after their families, in their peoples.' Cp. vv. 20, 31.

6, 7, 13-19. The sons of Ham.

6. Ham] a name for Egypt. The 'sons of Ham' means the nations connected with Egypt geographically or politically. They were all S. of Palestine. **Cush]** Ethiopia or Nubia, S. of Egypt. **Phut]** probably the 'Punt' of Egyptian inscriptions, on the E. African coast.

7. Seba . . Havilah . . Sabtah . . Raamah . . Sheba . . Dedan . .] all countries bordering on the African or Arabian coasts of the Red Sea.

8-12. This paragraph interrupts the connexion. Before and after it are simple genealogies. The **Cush** of v. 8 is thought to be distinct from the African **Cush** cf v. 7, and to stand for the Kashshu or Cossæi, who were the dominating power in Babylonia between the 16th and 13th centuries B.C.

8. Begat] was the progenitor of. **Nimrod]** the one personal figure of the chapter. Here his name is proverbial as that of a mighty hunter (v. 9). He founds both Babylonian and Assyrian civilisation (vv. 10–12). There is no trace of Nimrod as an historical character on the monuments, and it has been suggested that the name (as if from *marad*, ' to rebel ') was a deliberate mutilation and corruption of that of Merodach, the god of Babylon, made by one who wished to deny his divine character. If this was the case, the heathen deity who caught Tiamat in his net has been transformed in the Bible story into a mere human huntsman, a creature of the true God (cp. before **Jehovah**, v. 9), and the ancient cities that boasted of their divine origin are traced to a human founder. **10. Babel]** Babylon. **Erech]** Warka, on the left bank of the Euphrates. **Accad]** the ancient name of N. Babylonia ; also a city, the capital of Sargon I, the earliest historical ruler of all Babylonia. **Calneh]** probably the same as Nippur, the modern Niffer, recently excavated by the Pennsylvanian expedition. **Shinar]** an ancient name for S. Babylonia.

11. Out of that land went forth Asshur] RV ' out of that land he (Nimrod) went forth into Assyria.' This v. correctly indicates that Assyria owed its civilisation to Babylonia : it was also politically dependent until the 10th cent. B.C. **Nineveh]** the modern Kouyunjik on the Tigris, the ancient capital of Assyria. Its ruins have been excavated in recent years, and numbers of tablets, inscriptions, and carvings collected from its palaces. **The city Rehoboth]** RV ' Rehoboth-ir ' (' broad spaces of the city ') : probably a suburb of Nineveh. **Calah]** the modern Nimrûd, 20 m. S. from Kouyunjik. **Resen]** not known. **The same is the (RV) great city]** i.e. Nineveh and the other three together formed the ' great city.'

13, 14. The descendants of Mizraim. **Mizraim]** the Hebrew name for Egypt. The plural form is supposed to indicate Upper and Lower Egypt. **Lehabim]** Libya, W. of Egypt. **Naphtuhim]** perhaps N. of Lower Egypt. **Pathrusim]** S. or Upper Egypt. The clause ' Whence went forth the Philistines ' (RV) should be placed after **Caphtorim**, or people of Crete, with whom the Philistines are elsewhere said to be connected (Jer 47 4 Am 9 7). They settled on the SW. coast of Canaan, and gave the name Palestine to the country.

15-19. Canaan] Phœnicia and Palestine. The Canaanites were a Semitic race, speaking a language near akin to Hebrew. They are here assigned to Ham, perhaps contemptuously, or possibly because Palestine was a province of Egypt previous to the exodus. **Sidon]**

the Phœnician seaport.   **Heth**] The Hittites are now well known from Egyptian and Assyrian inscriptions to have been a powerful nation to the N. of Palestine, with Carchemish on the Euphrates and Kadesh on the Orontes as their chief cities. An offshoot of the nation is found at Hebron : cp. Gn 23³ 25¹⁰. **The Jebusite**] the tribe in and around Jerusalem : cp. Josh 15 ⁸, ⁶³ 2 S 5 ⁶⁻⁹.   **The Amorite**] one of the most powerful Palestinian tribes. In Assyrian and Egyptian inscriptions they are called the *Amurru*, and "Amorite" seems to have been a general term for the old inhabitants of Canaan : see on 12⁵. According to Nu 13²⁹ they dwelt chiefly in the mountainous districts. Sihon and Og were Amorite kings. **The Girgashite**] perhaps connected with Gergesa, near the Sea of Galilee. **The Hivite**] a petty tribe of Central Palestine. **The Arkite**] the tribe connected with the Phœnician city of Arka, 12 m. N. of Tripolis. **The Sinite**] probably connected with a city called Sin, near Lebanon. **The Arvadite**] Arvad was a city built on an island off the Phœnician coast (now Ruwad). **The Zemarite**] Sinsyra, S. of Arvad. **The Hamathite**] Hamath was a city on the Orontes. The 'entering in of Hamath' was the northern limit of Palestine. Most of these tribes were afterwards driven out by the conquering Israelites. **19. The border of the Canaanite**] from Zidon in the north, to **Gaza**, a Philistine city in the direction of Gerar. The other cities mentioned in v. 19 were probably, but not certainly, at the S. end of the Dead Sea.

21–31. The sons of Shem. The nations connected racially or geographically with the Hebrews.

Shem also, the father of all the children of Eber] Attention is thus called to Shem as the ancestor of the Hebrews ('children of Eber'). The Amarna tablets speak of a tribe called the *Habiri* invading Canaan in the days of Joshua, and many scholars identify them with the Hebrews. **The brother of Japheth the elder**] RV 'the elder brother of Japheth.' This is mentioned to show that though Shem is put last, he was not the youngest. **22. Elam**] NE. of Babylonia. Its capital was Susa. **Asshur**] Assyria. **Arphaxad**] RV 'Arpachshad': uncertain. Some connect it with the Kasdim or Chaldeans who lived on the Persian Gulf and became rulers of Babylonia. **Lud**] uncertain, possibly Lydia in Asia Minor. **Aram**] Syria, NE. of Palestine. Damascus was a Syrian kingdom. The Jews in later times spoke Aramaic.

23. Uz] probably near Edom, see Job 1¹.

25. Peleg] 'divided.' **In his days was the earth divided**] alluding perhaps to the dispersion of man described in c. 11.

26–30. The sons of **Joktan** represent various Arabian tribes.

Hazarmaveth] Hadramaut in S. Arabia. **Uzal**] the capital of Yemen. **Sheba** and **Havilah**] See prefatory remark and on v. 7. **Ophir**] a famous region, the locality of which is still in dispute. Some place it in E. Africa in Mashonaland, where remarkable remains of ancient mining works have been found, some in India, and some in S. Arabia. **Mesha**] NE. Arabia. **Sephar**] SW. Arabia. **Unto Sephar,** etc.] RM 'toward Sephar, the hill country of the East.'

CHAPTER 11

THE TOWER OF BABEL. THE DESCENDANTS OF SHEM TO ABRAHAM

We have here the ancient Hebrew explanation of the diversity of human language, and of the wide dispersion of the human race. Babylon is represented as the original centre of human civilisation after the Flood. The splendid buildings of Babylonia were among the most remarkable achievements of human power and pride. But they were repugnant to the Jews as being associated with idolatry, and their erection is here regarded as rebellion against Jehovah, who confounds the language of the builders, and brings about their dispersion. 'The story emphasises the supremacy of the One God over all the inhabitants of the world, and ascribes to His wisdom that distribution into languages and nations which secured the dissemination of mankind .. and provided for the dispersion of civilising influences into different quarters of the globe. Above all, it teaches that rebellion against God is the original source of discord. The gift of Pentecost, as the Fathers saw, is the converse of the story of the Tower of Babel. The true unity of the race, made known in Christ (cp. Col 3¹¹) is confirmed by the utterance of the Spirit which is heard by all alike. The believer "journeys" not away from God's presence, but draws nigh to Him by faith' (Bishop Ryle). The narrative is from the Primitive source.

1. It used to be conjectured that Hebrew was the primitive language of mankind, but it is now known that that language is only one branch, and that not the oldest, of the Semitic group of languages including Assyrian. Aramaic, Phœnician and Arabic. **2. From the east**] RM 'in the east.' The writer is in Palestine. **Shinar**] S. Babylonia.

3. Brick .. slime (RM 'bitumen')] These were the regular materials of ancient Babylonian architecture, as the remains of the oldest cities still show. There was no stone available in these alluvial plains.

4. A city and a tower] The principal

building in every ancient city was its temple, and the chief feature of a Babylonian temple was its ziggurat or stage-tower. The remains of these towers are the most prominent of the mounds which mark the sites of ruined cities. The pile of vitrified brick near Babylon, known as Birs Nimrûd, is the best known example of such a ziggurat, and early travellers supposed it to be the biblical Tower of Babel. The most famous temple-tower, however, and the one which probably gave rise to the tradition here, was that of E-Sagila, the temple of Bel in Babylon, built of brick in seven stages, the topmost of which formed a shrine for the god. It was of extreme antiquity, and was restored and beautified by Nebuchadnezzar.

Whose top may reach unto heaven] cp. Dt 1 28. The expression 'Whose top is in the heavens' has been found on inscriptions concerning these storied towers, but it seems as if the writer regarded the enterprise as an impious attempt to scale heaven. **Let us make us a name**, etc.] The tower was meant to procure renown for its builders, and to serve as a centre and bond of unity, so that none would think of leaving it. The writer seems to indicate the intention of establishing a universal empire.

5. The LORD came down, etc.] The words are meant to teach that God is concerned in men's doings. But 'it is not to be thought from such modes of expression that human characteristics are intended to be ascribed to the Creator. In any age it is necessary to describe the unknown by the help of the known ; and as the mysterious personality of God must ever be incomprehensible to men, there is no means in which we can represent His relations to us, except by using words borrowed from our own faculties, emotions, and modes of action' (Geikie). **6, 7.** God is here represented as dreading lest men make themselves so powerful as to become His opponents. The v. is a good example of the anthropomorphism characteristic of the Primitive document.

7. Us] God is conceived as taking counsel with the angels His attendants : cp. 3 22.

9. Babel] as if from *balal*, 'to confound.' The true etymology, however, is *Bab-ilu*, 'gate of God.' See on 4 1.

10-32. The descendants of Shem to Abraham.

The formal list here is the continuation of that in c. 5, and both belong to the Priestly document. The early period of the world's history from the Creation to Abraham is thus represented in the form of a genealogical table. The figures given here cannot be regarded as literally historical. Only 300 years are reckoned to have elapsed between the Flood and the birth of Abraham (say 2200 B.C.), whereas the beginnings of Babylonian civilisation can be traced back to 5000 B.C. As in c. 5, the number of generations is ten, a number which is common in the lists of other ancient nations. It may have been suggested by the ten fingers, as indicating completeness. We may therefore regard the present list as a conventional arrangement for bridging over the interval between the Flood and the beginnings of the Hebrew race, based on ancient tradition. It will be observed that the ages assigned to the Patriarchs enumerated in this c. are much lower than those in c. 5. There is a continuous reduction from the 600 years of Shem to the 138 of Nahor. The names of the generations from Shem to Eber have already been given in 10 22-25, and the latter's Arabian descendants in the line of Joktan were there traced. Now (vv. 18-26) his successors in another line are followed, until the point of supreme interest is reached in the Birth of Abraham.

14. Eber] the ancestor of the Hebrews. See on 14 13. **26.** For the meaning of **Abram** and **Sarai** (v. 29) see on c. 17. **27. Haran**] son of Terah. The Jewish Book of Jubilees declares that he was burnt to death, whilst attempting to save some of the images of the gods, when Abraham burnt the house in which they were.

31. Ur of the Chaldees] or 'Ur Kasdim.' The Chaldeans lived in S. Babylonia. The modern Mugheir, near the Euphrates, 125 m. NW. of the Persian Gulf, marks the site of an ancient city called Uru, which is by many identified with the Ur of this passage. But in the Accadian inscriptions the whole province of Accad or N. Babylonia was called Uri. Haran, the town (see next note), was also in this district, and the difficulty of explaining why Terah made the long journey of 600 m. from Mugheir disappears, if the Ur of Genesis may be identified with Uri. The family of Terah was evidently a pastoral one, and it was natural that they should make a new settlement from time to time.

31. Haran] (the Roman *Carrhœ*) was a city in Mesopotamia. It was an ancient seat of the worship of the moon god Sin. Caravan roads led from Haran to Syria and Palestine. Terah, who had intended to settle in Canaan, remained at Haran, and died there. C. 12 tells us how Abraham received the divine command to leave his home and relatives, and, in reliance on God's promise, to settle in a new country, there to found a race who should preserve the knowledge of the true God, and prove a blessing to all mankind.

32. The days of Terah were two hundred and five years] According to the Samaritan text Terah was 145 years old when he died. As Terah was 70 at the birth of Abram (11 26) and the latter left Haran when he was 75, the Samaritan text confirms the statement in Ac 7⁴ that Abram waited till after his father's death to leave Haran.

CHAPTERS 12–25

The History of Abraham

At this point the specific purpose of the writer of the Pentateuch begins to appear more clearly. Speaking generally, that purpose is to trace the development of the kingdom of God in the line of Israelitish history. To this subject the preceding chs. of Genesis have formed an introduction, dealing with universal history, and indicating the place of Israel among the other nations of the world. The narrative now passes from universal history to the beginnings of the chosen people and their subsequent fortunes. The connecting link is furnished in the person of Abraham, and interest is now concentrated on him, and the promises made to him.

Abraham is one of the very greatest figures in the religious history of the human race. Three great religions look back to him as one of their spiritual ancestors, and accept him as a type of perfect faith and true religion, viz. the Jewish, the Mohammedan, and the Christian. The world owes to him its first clear knowledge of the true God, His spiritual and holy nature, and the way in which He is to be served and worshipped. How much of this Abraham may have brought with him from Ur of the Chaldees we do not know. Recent discovery points to a very close connexion between the religions of Babylonia and Israel. That need not surprise us, nor does it impair the truth and value of the biblical narrative. Every religious system, not excepting Christianity itself, is based upon the foundations of the past. What we find in Abraham is a new point of departure. Religious beliefs, opinions, laws, and ideals, which he inherited, are, by a power which we cannot explain but can only define as the inspiration of God, purified and elevated, with the result that religion starts afresh with him on a higher level. The affirmation of the truth of monotheism and the rejection of human sacrifice in the worship of God would, apart from other considerations, make Abraham rank among the foremost religious reformers the world has seen.

In recent times an attempt has been made to date the beginnings of Israel's religion from Moses, and to represent the patriarchs as 'shadows in the mist' of antiquity of whose personal existence and religious views nothing can be said with certainty. In particular the attempt has been made to reduce Abraham, Isaac, and Jacob to later personifications of ancient tribes. The patriarchs, it is said, were not individuals but tribes, and what are represented as personal incidents in their lives are really events, naïvely and vividly described, in the history of the various tribes to which the nation of Israel owed its descent. In some cases such personification of tribes may be admitted ; e.g. Canaan, Japheth, and Shem clearly represent tribes in the blessing of Noah (Gn 9²⁵⁻²⁷ 10¹⁻³²), cp. also intro. to Gn 49. The same is true of Ishmael in Gn 16¹², and of Esau, who is called Edom in Gn 25³⁰ 36¹,⁸,¹⁹. But admitting that there may be an element of truth in this theory, and that the biographies of the patriarchs may have been idealised to some extent by the popular feelings and poetical reflection of later times, the view that sees in the story of the patriarchs nothing that is personal and historical is certainly extreme and improbable. Popular imagination may add and modify but it does not entirely create. It requires some historical basis to start from. That basis in the case of Abraham and the other patriarchs is popular oral tradition, and that this preserved a genuine historical kernel cannot be denied. The amount of personal incident, the circumstantiality, the wealth of detail contained in the patriarchal narratives, can only be rightly accounted for on the ground that Abraham, Isaac, and Jacob were real historical personages, leaders of distinct national and religious movements, who made their mark upon the whole course of subsequent history. Some time ago, when an utterly impenetrable veil of obscurity hung over all contemporary profane history, the biblical narrative of the patriarchs could find no corroboration elsewhere. But of late a flood of light has been thrown upon ancient Assyria, illuminating the very period to which Abraham belongs. A background has been provided for the patriarchal age ; and our increasing knowledge of Babylonian civilisation and religion goes to substantiate the historical nature of the stories of Abraham and the other patriarchs, and shows that they might well be the products of such a country and such an age. We may go further, and say that later Jewish history seems to require such a historical basis as the patriarchal narratives furnish, as its starting-point and explanation. Abraham, and not Moses, is the father of the Jewish nation, and the founder of its distinctive religion. It was no new and unknown God in whose name Moses spoke to his brethren in Egypt. He was able to appeal to Israel in the name of a God who had already revealed Himself, in the name of 'the God of their fathers, the God of Abraham, the God of Isaac, and the God of Jacob.' See Ex 3⁶ 4⁵, and note on the former passage.

The sections of the history of Abraham (chs. 12–25) which are attributed to the

Priestly source are the following : 11 27-32 12 5 13 6, 11b, 12 16 1-3, 15, 16 17 1-27 19 29 21 1b, 2b-5 23, 25 7-17. Those which form part of the Primitive narrative are : 12 1-4, 6–13 5, 7-11a, 12b-18, 14, 15, 16 4-14, 18, 19 (except v. 29), 20, 21 (mostly), 22, 24, 25 1-6, 18-34. They afford a good example of the characteristic differences in style of the two sources, as explained in the art. 'Origin of the Pentateuch.'

CHAPTER 12

THE CALL OF ABRAHAM. THE REMOVAL TO CANAAN. THE VISIT TO EGYPT

1. Had said] RV 'said,' when he was in Haran. In what manner the call came to Abraham, whether through some outward incident which he recognised as the prompting of Providence, or through the suggestions of the Divine Spirit in his inmost soul, we do not know. Anyhow he regarded it as divine and authoritative, and it was too definite to be misunderstood. **Get thee out of . . and from . . and from**] The repetition emphasises the complete severance of all connexion with his early home and friends. **A land that I will shew thee**] The fact that the land was not named increased the demand on Abraham's faith and made his self-surrender the more absolute ; cp. Heb 11. **2. Thou shalt be a blessing**] RV 'Be thou a blessing,' i.e. the very embodiment of blessing : blessed thyself, and the source of blessing to others.

3. In thee shall all families of the earth be blessed] or, 'bless themselves.' Through Abraham and his descendants men everywhere would come to know God as One and Holy, and to long for 'the Desire of all nations.'

4. Lot went with him] Haran, Lot's father, was dead, 11 28. **5. They went forth to go**] Haran, the starting-place, was some 300 miles from Canaan. They would go through Syria, halting perhaps at Damascus (see 15 2), then proceeding southwards through Bashan to the fords of the Jordan S. of the Sea of Galilee, and thence to Shechem in the centre of Palestine. **The souls that they had gotten**] i.e. their slaves. **The land of Canaan**] the ancient name of Palestine. At this time much of Syria and Canaan was ruled by the Amorites, who were for centuries the dominant race.

6. Sichem] RV 'Shechem.' The term 'the place of Shechem' intimates that this was an ancient sanctuary, and this is confirmed by 35 4 Dt 11 29 27 4 Josh 8 33 24 26. The 'terebinth (or turpentine tree) of the director' (as we may render plain of Moreh) points to the same conclusion. Most likely there was a grove of trees, the rustling of whose leaves was interpreted as an oracle (cp. 2 S 5 24). Oracles of this kind were much resorted to. **The Canaanite**] see on 13 7.

7. The LORD appeared unto Abram] see on v. 1. The faith of Abraham, in leaving Haran in obedience to the divine call, is now rewarded by the definite promise of possession of the land by his descendants. **There builded he an altar**] thus consecrating the place to God, who had there manifested Himself to him. The building of an altar was the recognised act of worship : cp. 8 20 13 18, etc.

8. Beth-el] 5 m. S. of Shechem ; see on 28 19. **Hai**] or, Ai, near Bethel.

9. The south] or, 'the Negeb,' the district between Palestine and the wilderness N. of Sinai. It forms a transition from the cultivated land to the desert ; and, though not fertile, yields much pasture for flocks ; see Josh 15 21-32.

10-20. Abraham's visit to Egypt. Owing to a famine, to which Palestine is sometimes liable if the winter rains fail, Abraham moves down to Egypt. There, owing to the inundations of the Nile and the system of irrigation practised, crops rarely failed, and neighbouring countries had their wants supplied : cp. Ac 27 6, 38. Egypt was already a highly civilised country in Abraham's time. Many of the pyramids were built long before his day.

The patriarch on this occasion appears in a very unfavourable light. Admitting the great dangers which threatened him at the hands of a licentious despot, admitting also that among Easterns duplicity is admired rather than scorned, the readiness he showed to risk his wife's honour in order to secure his own safety, and his lack of trust in God's protection, are inexcusable. But we esteem our Bible all the more for its candour in not hiding the faults of its greatest characters. Of only One can it be said that He was 'without sin.'

13. Thou art my sister] Sarah was Abraham's half-sister (20 12). By this prevarication he doubtless thought the danger to himself would be less than if he had confessed that she was his wife.

15. Pharaoh] the official title of the kings of Egypt ; cp. Pharaoh-Necho (2 K 23 29). It is the Egyptian word *Pr'o*, 'great house,' which was originally applied to the royal palace and estate, and afterwards to the king : cp. our use of the word 'Court' to designate the king and his household. It is probable that at this time Egypt was governed by Asiatic conquerors known as the Hyksôs, or Shepherd kings ; see Intro. to Exodus. **16.** It is usual in the East to give presents to the bride's relatives on such occasions, to make, in fact, payment for the bride ; cp. Ex 22 16 Ruth 4 10. **Camels**] It is doubtful if these were used by the ancient Egyptians. Perhaps the Semitic conquerors of Egypt may have introduced them from Asia at this period. **17.** Cp. Ps 105 14, 'He suffered no man to do them wrong ; yea, he reproved kings for their sakes.'

CHAPTER 13

THE RETURN OF ABRAHAM FROM EGYPT,
AND HIS SEPARATION FROM LOT

1. Into the south] see on 12[9].

5, 6. There was not sufficient pasturage and water (especially after the recent famine and drought) for the two encampments with their flocks and herds, which doubtless numbered many thousands.

7. The Perizzite] 'dweller in open villages.' It is thought by some that they were the original inhabitants of the country who had been subdued by Canaanite invaders. The words **dwelled then in the land** indicate that the writer lived long after the conquest of Canaan. **8, 9.** Abraham's offer was marked by a generosity towards his nephew, and a readiness to leave his own future entirely in God's hands, which called forth at once the divine approval: see vv. 14–17.

10. If they were standing on the 'mountain east of Bethel' (12[8] 13[3]), Lot would look eastward over the fertile Ghôr or Jordan valley, whilst in all other directions only the barren limestone hills of Judea would be visible. **Garden of the Lord]** Eden. **As thou comest unto]** i.e. in the direction of. **Zoar]** Zoar was a city near the Dead Sea: see on 14[3]. But the Syriac text reads 'Zoan,' i.e. Tanis, a city in the Nile Delta.

11–13. Lot's choice showed that he cared chiefly for worldly prosperity; the evil reputation of his neighbours did not affect his decision, which proved a fatal one: see chs. 14 and 19. The sacred narrative now becomes confined to the history of Abraham and his direct descendants.

12. Land of Canaan] see on Nu 13[21].

14–17. The promises of c. 12 are confirmed to Abraham, only more fully and definitely.

18. Plain] RM 'terebinths'; see on 12[6]. **Mamre]** an Amorite chief. It is evident from 14[13] that Abraham now settled down among this community of Amorites, and entered into a confederacy with them.

Hebron] an ancient city 20 m. S. of Jerusalem, earlier called Kirjath-Arba, 23[2]. From its connexion with Abraham it soon came to be regarded as a holy place. Joshua appointed it to be one of the six cities of refuge, and assigned it to the Levites. For 7 years it was the seat of David's kingdom (2S5[1-5]). It is now called *el-Khalil*, 'the friend,' after Abraham, 'the friend of God' (Isa 41[8]). Hard by is the cave of Machpelah where the patriarchs were buried.

CHAPTER 14

THE BATTLE OF THE KINGS, AND THE
CAPTURE AND RESCUE OF LOT

Chedorlaomer, king of Elam, had subdued the Canaanites of the Jordan valley some years before the events narrated in this chapter. The latter had rebelled, and a campaign for their fresh subjugation was undertaken, which included a general punitive expedition from Syria to the Gulf of Akaba.

Within the last few years Assyrian tablets of great antiquity have been found, throwing considerable, if indirect, light on this narrative, and helping to determine its date. The cuneiform inscriptions on them refer to a series of campaigns by the kings of Elam NE. of Chaldea, perhaps about 2150 B.C. Their conquests extended over the vast territories, which became later the Babylonian and Assyrian empires, and included Syria and Canaan. The names Amraphel, Arioch, and (perhaps) Chedorlaomer occur in these inscriptions, and help to give a historical setting to the present narrative. The Tel el Amarna tablets discovered in Egypt testify to the dominion exercised by these northern nations over Syria and Canaan some centuries later, perhaps whilst Israel was still in Egypt; see on Nu 13[17].

1. Amraphel] king of Shinar or Babylonia. He eventually expelled the Elamites who had invaded his territory. Amraphel has by many authorities been identified with *Hammurabi* of the inscriptions. A tablet of laws issued by this monarch was discovered at Susa in 1902, and has been translated: see art. 'Laws of Hammurabi.' **Arioch]** identified with *Eriaku*, king of Larsa (Ellasar), on the left bank of the Euphrates in S. Babylonia. He was a contemporary and rival of Amraphel, and of Elamitic family. **Chedorlaomer]** A name read by Prof. Sayce as *Kudurlaghgamal* was found on a tablet of Hammurabi in 1896. This reading is, however, questioned. The element *Kudur* (perhaps 'servant') is found in the names of other Elamite kings, e.g. *Kudur-Nahundi*, and 'bricks have been found at Mugheir (Ur) due to a king *Kudur-Mabug* who calls himself *Adda-Martu*, "ruler of the west country," viz. Canaan' (D.). **Tidal]** identification uncertain. **Of nations]** RV 'Goiim'; perhaps the Heb. word is intended to describe the *Guti*, a powerful nation N. of Babylonia.

2. The five towns (Pentapolis) mentioned here lay round the Dead Sea. The kings were mere chieftains, tributaries of Chedorlaomer, who now threw off his yoke.

3. The vale of Siddim which is the Salt Sea] The words imply that what had been the fertile vale of Siddim was covered, in the author's time, by the Salt (Dead) Sea. It is a disputed question whether this vale in which were the 'cities of the plain,' was situated at its N. or S. end. 'For the N. end, it is argued that Abraham and Lot looked upon the cities from near Bethel (13[10]), whence it would be impossible to see the S. end of the Dead Sea; that the name "Circle (or plain) of Jordan" is inapplicable to the S. end ; and that the presence of five cities there is impossible. On the other hand, at the S. end of the Dead Sea there lay, through Roman and mediæval times, a city called Zoara by the Greeks and Zughar by the Arabs, which was identified by all as the Zoar of Lot. Jebel Usdum, at the SE. end, is the uncontested representative of Sodom. The name *Kikkar* ("circle") may surely have been extended to the S. of the Dead Sea ; just as to-day, the *Ghôr* (lower Jordan valley) is continued a few miles to the S. of Jebel Usdum. Jewish and Arab traditions fix on the S. end ; and finally the material conditions are more suitable there than on the N. end to the description of the region both before and after the catastrophe, for there is still sufficient water and verdure on the E. side of the Ghôr to suggest the Garden of the Lord, while the shallow bay and long marsh at the S. end may, better than the ground at the N. end of the sea, hide the secret of the overwhelmed cities' (G. A. Smith). The Dead Sea, which is about 46 m. long by 9 m. wide, is now nearly divided in two parts towards the S. end by a tongue of land jutting from the E. shore. This tongue probably once joined the opposite shore, and formed the S. limit of the Sea: but it is conjectured that, by the action of an earthquake, a subsidence took place, and, as Prof. Smith hints, what had been the fertile vale of Siddim became a desolate lagoon. The saltness of the water (26 per cent. as compared with the 4 per cent. of the ocean) is due to the presence of a mountain of rock salt (*Jebel Usdum*) at the S. end of the sea. Fish cannot live in it, not so much owing to its saltness as to the excess of bromide of magnesium ; and the extreme buoyancy of its waters is well known. The position of this salt mountain, taken in connexion with 19 26 and the occurrence of bitumen pits at the S. end (see on v. 10), supports the theory of the position of the cities just mentioned. The name 'the Dead Sea' occurs nowhere in the Bible, and has not been found earlier than the 2nd cent. A.D.

4. They] i.e. the Canaanite chieftains. They refused to pay tribute.

5 f. The Campaign of Chedorlaomer. Passing Hamath in Syria, and Damascus, the invaders first attacked the **Rephaim**, a race of great stature, who lived in the Bashan district, E. of Jordan. Their chief city was **Ashteroth Karnaim**, meaning, perhaps, 'Ashtaroth of the two horns.' 'Ashtoreth, the goddess of the Zidonians, and associated commonly with Baal in worship (1 K 11 5 2 K 23 13), was the female or productive principle in nature. She is identified with Ishtar (Assyria) and Astarte (Greece and Rome). Sometimes she is regarded as the Moon-goddess (Baal = Sun, cp.

Gn 14 5), sometimes as Venus, the goddess of love. Her image of wood, cp. Dt 16 21 2 K 23 15, was called an Asherah (AV "grove ")' ('Camb. Compn. Bible'). **Zuzims**] or Zamzummims, in the country between the rivers Arnon and Jabbok: cp. Dt 2 20. **Ham**] Perhaps Rabbath Ammon to S. of Bashan, or Hameitat, 6 m. S. of the Dead Sea. The Peshitto and the Vulgate render 'among them' for **in Ham**. **Emims**] They held what became the land of Moab: cp. Dt 2 10 f. **Shaveh Kiriathaim**] i.e. 'the plain of Kiryathaim.' It is mentioned on the Moabite Stone, but the site is disputed: cp. Nu 32 37. **6.** Proceeding S. the invaders smote the **Horites**, cave-dwellers in the mountainous district of Seir, afterwards held by the Edomites, descendants of Esau. This district extends from the Dead Sea to the Gulf of Akaba. The wonderful rock city Petra may have been hollowed out by them. Thence they proceeded to Elath, near the wilderness of **Paran**, the scene of the forty years' wandering, known as Et-Tih: see on 21 21. Turning to the north-west further victories were gained over the Amalekites at Kadesh Barnea, called also **En-Mishpat** ('well of judgment'), and over the Amorites at **Hazezon-tamar**, or Engedi, on the W. side of the Dead Sea. **8-10.** The vale of Siddim was now reached, and was the scene of a fierce battle with the five Canaanite kings. **10. Slimepits**] Wells of inflammable bitumen, a mineral pitch allied to naphtha. Masses of bitumen are still thrown up in the S. portion of the lake. The Canaanite armies seem to have been snared in the slimy substance. **The king of Sodom .. fell there**] This refers rather to his army, as we find him welcoming Abraham on his return (v. 17). **12.** Lot with his wealth would be a desirable prisoner.

13. The Hebrew] Abraham may have been so called from his ancestor Eber (11 14). As the Heb. *ibrī*, however, means ' of the country beyond,' the title may have been given to him by the Canaanites because he had come from across the Euphrates.' LXX renders, 'Abraham the crosser.' In OT. the word generally occurs in the mouth of foreigners or in connexion with them: cp. Gn 40 15 43 32 1 S 13, 14, and some scholars consider it probable that the present narrative may come from a Canaanite source. The Jews called themselves ' Israel,' ' Israelites.' **Plain of Mamre**] i.e. Hebron: see on 13 18.

14. This number of able-bodied men in Abraham's household shows that he was now a chieftain of great importance. He also had allies in the venture: see v. 24. **14. Dan**] known in Abraham's day as Laish. It was near the sources of the Jordan, some 30 m. N. of the Sea of Galilee. In later days part of the tribe of Dan settled there (Jg 18 27-29).

15. The Elamite army was doubtless much larger than Abraham's following, but the attack from different quarters in the darkness created a panic, similar to that caused by Gideon's men (Jg 7). **Hobah**] N. of Damascus.

17. The king of Sodom] see on v. 10. **The king's dale**] unknown. Perhaps the place where Absalom set up a pillar: see 2 S 18 18. Josephus says it was near Jerusalem.

18. Melchizedek] The word may mean 'Sidik' (a deity) 'is my king,' although in Heb 7 the Jewish writer in connexion with his argument explains it as 'King of righteousness.' In Josh 10 3, five hundred years later, we find another king of Jerusalem whose name has the same termination, viz. Adonizedec, i.e. 'Sidik is my lord.' Melchizedek was king of Salem, the chief town of the Jebusites, known to us as Jerusalem. The Amarna letters (1400 B.C., written in cuneiform characters on clay tablets) which passed between the rulers of Egypt and their officers in Canaan (at that time tributary to Egypt), show that its name was then *Uru-Salim*, 'the city of peace.' Among these tablets are letters from its king Ebed-tob to the Pharaoh of the time, in one of which he states that his office was not an hereditary one, but that he owed his position to the Egyptian king. Cp. Heb 7 3, 'without father or mother.'

Brought forth bread and wine] to refresh Abraham and his party.

He was the priest of the most high God] This Canaanite chieftain was both king and priest, a combination not uncommon in those days: cp. Jethro (Ex 18 12). 'He (Melchizedek) is designated priest of El Elyon, **the most high God**, whom Abraham, as we see from v. 22, could in a general way acknowledge as his god. This agrees very well with the findings of the history of religions. There is abundant evidence for the name *El* or *Il* as the oldest proper name of deity among the Babylonians, Assyrians, Phœnicians, and Sabeans, . . among foreign peoples he was early pushed into the background by younger gods who only expressed particular aspects of his being . . but Melchizedek in his worship still held fast to him as the old sovereign god, the ruler of the universe' (D.). **20.** Abraham, recognising in Melchizedek a priest of the true God, receives his blessing, and gives him as God's representative a tithe (tenth part) of the spoils he has just taken as a thank offering. Other instances of the payment of tithes are Gn 28 22 Lv 27 30 Nu 31 31 f. 2 S 8 11.

21. Give me the persons, and take the goods to thyself] The victor used to keep the whole booty, including prisoners who became his slaves. The king of Sodom proposes that Abraham should restore the captives but keep the spoil. **22–24.** Abraham nobly refuses to keep anything for himself, but claims their share of the spoils for his Amorite allies. Possibly the character of the Sodomites made any transaction with them odious to him.

22. I have lift up mine hand] a form of swearing: cp. Ex 6 8. **The LORD, the most high God**] *Jehovah El Elyon*. Note that Abraham prefixes Jehovah to the title used by Melchizedek, 'as if to claim for Him the exclusive right to supreme divinity.'

23. Shoelatchet] or 'sandal thong': i.e. a thing of the least value.

NOTE. Melchizedek is referred to again twice in the Bible (Ps 110 4 Heb 5–7), and each time as a type of the priesthood of Christ. 'The Melchizedek type of priesthood is, first, a *royal* priesthood (*king* of righteousness); second, a *righteous* priesthood (king of *righteousness*); third, a priesthood promotive of peace, or exercised in the country of *peace* (king of Salem = king of *peace*); fourth, a *personal*, not an inherited, dignity (without father, without mother, i.e. so far as the record is concerned); fifth, it is an *eternal* priesthood (without beginning of days or end of life—so far as the record is concerned)' (HDB. art. 'Hebrews'). See on Heb 5, 6, 7.

CHAPTER 15

GOD PROMISES AN HEIR TO ABRAHAM AND THE LAND OF CANAAN FOR HIS DESCENDANTS. THE PROMISE IS RATIFIED BY A COVENANT

The passage is from the Primitive source. A somewhat similar account from the Priestly narrative is given in c. 17. The repetition shows the importance attached by the compiler of Genesis to these records of the promises as testifying to the divine purposes for the Hebrew people.

1. Vision] probably a trance, with the senses dormant, but the mind awake to spiritual impressions: cp. Nu 24 3, 4, 15, 16. **Fear not**] It is thought that Abraham was depressed at the thought (1) of his childlessness, and (2) of the powerful enemies he had made through the rescue of Lot. To remove the latter fear God promises Himself to be his **shield**. **Thy exceeding great reward**] RM 'thy reward shall be exceeding great.' **2. What wilt thou give me**] of what avail are these promised possessions, with no child to inherit them? **The steward, etc.**] RV 'he that shall be possessor of my house,' i.e. the heir, would be Eliezer of Damascus, a servant. The Damascenes have always boasted a connexion with Abraham.

4. Abraham is assured that his heir should be a child of his own begetting. **5. He brought him forth**] This was probably part of the vision. **Tell the stars**] i.e. count them.

6. He counted it to him for righteousness] Faithful Abraham gave up his own will to the will of God, did not seek to force his way in the world (14 22), but awaited God's blessing in His good time. And this attitude of trust and submission was esteemed by God. St. Paul quotes this passage to show that mankind are accepted by God through their faith apart from any observance of the Mosaic law, which indeed had not at the period referred to in this passage come into existence. See Ro 4 and 5 Gal 3 Heb 11 Jas 2.

8. Abraham asks for some pledge of the fulfilment of the promises. **9.** God condescends to confirm the promise of the possession of the land by a visible sign. Abraham is directed to make the usual preparations observed in old times when two parties were about to make an important covenant or alliance : cp. Jer 34 18. Certain animals and birds used in sacrifice were slain, and the bodies of the former divided in two parts : hence the expression to 'strike' or 'cut' a covenant. The two parties then passed between the parts, met in the middle, and took an oath of agreement, the position signifying that if they were false to the covenant they merited a similar fate to that of the slain animals.

10. The birds divided he not] see on Lv 1 17. Probably they were put opposite one another. **11. Fowls**] RV 'birds of prey' : an omen of the troubles which his descendants must encounter before entering into their possession. **12. An horror of great darkness**] lit. 'a terror, even great darkness,' preceding the wondrous sight of v. 17.

13. Abraham is given a glimpse of the fortunes of his descendants. **A land that is not theirs**] i.e. Egypt. Centuries must elapse before the family of Abraham had grown into a nation fit to take possession of Canaan. Much of this time was to be spent in Egypt, where trials and afflictions would discipline them to become the consecrated nation who were to preserve the knowledge of Jehovah.

Four hundred years] see on Ex 12 40. The **four generations** of v. 16 taken in agreement with this v. must mean periods of a hundred years each, but there are no data by which we can verify or correct the figures. **15. Go to thy fathers**] see on 25 8. **16. The iniquity of the Amorites is not yet full**] The Amorites here stand for the races of Canaan generally. They are to be spared for 400 years, until their idolatry and gross vices have exhausted the forbearance of God : cp. Dt 7 1 and Intro. to Joshua. **17. Burning lamp**] probably 'torch,' though the meaning is uncertain. The ratification of the covenant now took place by a bright light enveloped in cloud, the symbol of God's presence, passing between the victims :

cp. Ex 3 2,3 40 34, etc. God gave the promise of the inheritance of the land : Abraham's part was continued trust, patience, and obedience.

18. The river of Egypt] probably the Wady el Arish on the border of Egypt. In the days of Solomon the promise was fulfilled (1 K 4 21, 24). **19. Kenites and Kenizzites**] Tribes of the Negeb and Southern Desert. The Kenites were widely spread from Midian to Naphtali : cp. Jg 1 16 4 11. **Kadmonites**] of the Syro-Arabian Desert. **20, 21. Perizzites**] see on 13 7. **Rephaims**] see on 14 5. The others were peoples of Canaan : see on 10 16.

CHAPTER 16

The Circumstances connected with the Birth of Ishmael

1, 2. Abraham was now eighty-five years old, Sarah was seventy-five, and the promise of an heir seemed no nearer fulfilment. Despairing of offspring herself, Sarah persuades Abraham to take her Egyptian maid Hagar as a secondary wife, intending, according to ancient custom, to regard the issue as her own. But her lack of faith in God's promises was productive of very unhappy consequences. **4. Hagar**] The Arabs claim descent from Hagar through Ishmael. Her name, which means 'flight,' is akin to the word Hegira, used of the flight of Mohammed from Medina to Mecca (622 A.D.), an event from which the Mohammedans date their era.

Her mistress was despised in her eyes] because she was fruitful while Sarah was barren : cp. Hannah and Peninnah (1 S 1 6). It was accounted a great disgrace and a sign of God's displeasure to be without offspring : cp. 30 23.

5. My wrong be upon thee] i.e. May the blame for the wrong done to me (by Hagar's conduct) fall on thee.

7. The angel of the LORD] see on Ex 3 2. **Shur**] The word means 'wall' and was probably applied to the chain of fortresses on the NE. frontier of Egypt. The Desert of Shur was the wilderness bordering on these fortresses which were built to keep out Asiatic invaders. **7, 8.** Hagar might flee from the presence of Sarah, but not from the knowledge and sight of God. He finds her, and addresses her, as He did Adam, when he concealed himself in the Garden of Eden : cp. 1 8,9.

10. A promise fulfilled in the Arab race : see on v. 4. **11. Ishmael**] 'El (God) hears.' **12. A wild man**] RV 'as a wild-ass among men.' The wild ass is of an untameable nature, ever roving : cp. Job 39 5f. Such was Ishmael, and such are his Arab descendants. **He shall dwell in the presence of all his brethren**] i.e. shall preserve his independence, though close to them ; a true forecast of the history of Ishmael's descendants. But another translation gives, 'He shall dwell to the east of his brethren.' **13. Have I also here,** etc.] Hagar realises that she still lives though God has looked upon her.

14. Beer-lahai-roi] 'the well of the living one who hath seen' God : see on c. 21 for St. Paul's references to Hagar.

CHAPTER 17

The Covenant of Circumcision

This c. is from the Priestly document, of which it shows marked characteristics : see preface to c. 15.

1. Ninety years old and nine] Ishmael was now thirteen years old, and Abraham probably expected no other heir. But his faith was to be put to a further test. **The Almighty God**] Heb. *el Shaddai*: the name of power shows the ability to perform what was promised. **Walk before me, and be thou perfect**] i.e. always conscious of My presence, and living a pious, whole-hearted, upright life. These are the conditions required by God in connexion with the covenant about to be made. **2.** God, on His part, promises to make Abraham the ancestor of many nations, and to give Canaan to his descendants.

4, 5. The patriarch's name in Babylonia had been *Abram*, meaning, perhaps, 'exalted father,' or, according to others, 'Ram (the lofty one) is father'; cp. Hiram, 'Ram is brother.' Under the form *Abu-Ramu* it appears to be a recognised proper name in the Assyrian inscriptions. On entering into a new relationship with God by covenant, of which the sign was circumcision, the patriarch received a new name, 'Abraham.' This is probably a variation on 'Abram,' but its meaning is unknown, the popular explanation 'father of multitude' being considered untenable. In commemoration of this event Jewish children receive their name when admitted to the covenant by circumcision (Lk 1 59), as do Christian children when baptised into the Church of Christ. The 'many nations' of vv. 4 and 6 included not only Israelites but also Ishmaelites, Edomites (through Esau), Midianites (by Keturah), Arabs (by Hagar).

10. This is my covenant] i.e. this is the sign of the covenant, viz. circumcision. Note that both parties undertake obligations here as contrasted with the covenant in c. 15.

Circumcision] (lit. 'cutting round') is the removal of the foreskin. The rite has always been practised by the Jews from Abraham's time to the present day. Other ancient nations also observed the ceremony, such as the Egyptians and Phoenicians, but not the Philistines, Babylonians, Greeks or Romans. It is still observed, not only by Mohammedan nations who claim to be descended from

Abraham, but by the Abyssinian, Egyptian, Polynesian and other peoples. Among these latter the rite is generally performed about the age of ten or twelve years, as a preliminary to marriage, and as admitting to full civil and religious tribal privileges. With the Hebrews circumcision had a special significance. They regarded it as a sign of the covenant between God and His people, and they alone of all nations circumcised their infants, thereby devoting them from their birth to Jehovah. With them, too, the shedding of the blood of that part upon which depends the perpetuation of life was the symbol of the continuous consecration of the nation from one generation to another. The spiritual significance of the rite is frequently insisted on by the inspired writers. The outward sign must be accompanied by the putting away of fleshly and sinful desires: cp. Dt 10 16 Ro 2 28, 29.

The Acts of the Apostles and the Epistles to the Romans, Galatians, and Colossians witness to the desire of the Jewish Christians to impose the obligation of circumcision on their Gentile brethren, and to the struggle in which St. Paul was successful in freeing his converts from the yoke of Judaism.

11. The flesh of your foreskin] better, 'the foreskin of your flesh.' **12. Eight days old**] Until the eighth day children were considered unclean, and so unfit to be offered to God. **12, 13.** The law of circumcision applied to all male members of Jewish households, who were henceforth regarded as Israelites, and shared in the national and religious privileges of the chosen race. **14. That soul shall be cut off from his people**] This expression seems usually to mean that the offender is to be excommunicated, or cut off from all connexion with the Hebrew community, and from any share in the blessings of the covenant, nor could he claim protection for life or property : cp. Ex 12 15, 19 Nu 9 13 19 13. But the sentence of death seems sometimes to be added in the case of presumptuous sins, such as the sacrificing of children to Moloch, and the deliberate nonobservance of the sabbath : see Ex 31 14 Lv 20 1-6 Nu 15 30-36. 'Cutting off' in such cases is plainly equivalent to putting to death.

15. Sarah's name, like Abraham's, is changed on admission to the covenant. Sarah means 'princess' : the exact meaning of Sarai is doubtful. **18.** Abraham was unwilling that Ishmael should be deposed from his position as heir: but God would prosper him also (v. 20). **19. Isaac**] i.e. he laughs. The name would recall an event which made Abraham laugh with joy and probably also with wonder. **20. Twelve princes**] see 25 12 f. **25.** Ishmael was circumcised when thirteen years old, the age still observed by Mohammedans: cp. on 17 10.

CHAPTER 18

THE VISIT OF THE ANGELS TO ABRAHAM.
THE JUDGMENT OF SODOM ANNOUNCED.
ABRAHAM INTERCEDES ON ITS BEHALF

In this beautiful narrative the writer dwells on the unique revelations of God's purposes with which Abraham was favoured. In after times the patriarch received the title of ' the friend of God ' (2 Ch 20⁷ Isa 41⁸ Jas 2²³). The c. is from the Primitive document. The religious lessons, the vivid description, and the consciousness of God's immediate presence and interest in the affairs of men are all characteristic of that source. See on 11⁵ Ex 24¹⁰ and Intro. Exodus, § 3, for the anthropormorphisms of the c.

1. In the plains of Mamre] RV ' by the oaks of Mamre,' i.e. Hebron : cp. 13¹⁸.

2. Three men] heavenly visitors, angels, as appears from 19¹. With one, God identifies Himself (v. 13).

3. My Lord] This was only a title of respect; it is not LORD, i.e. Jehovah. Abraham was entertaining angels unawares (Heb 13²).

4. The difficulty of procuring the necessaries of life when travelling in the East causes the duty of hospitality to be observed to an extent unknown to ourselves. Lane, in 'Modern Egyptians,' says that we have here a perfect picture of the manner in which a modern Bedawee sheikh receives travellers arriving at his encampment. He immediately orders his wife or woman to make bread; slaughters a sheep or some other animal, and dresses it in haste ; and bringing milk and any other provisions that he may have ready at hand, sets all before his guests. If these be persons of high rank, he stands by them while they eat, as Abraham did in this case. The ready hospitality of Abraham is in striking contrast with the conduct of the Sodomites to the same visitors. **Wash your feet**] since they only wore sandals. **6. Measure**] Heb. *Seah*, nearly a peck and half. From Mt 13³³ it seems that three measures made a batch of bread. **Cakes**] thin biscuits of meal, baked on an iron plate on the heated hearthstone. **7. A calf**] Owing to the hot climate only fresh meat can be used, but it is tender if cooked at once. Animal food is very rarely eaten except at festivities, or on the arrival of a distinguished visitor. A quick method usually practised is to broil slices of meat on skewers. **8. Butter**] rather, ' curdled milk,' which is very refreshing and still constantly drunk in Palestine and Arabia. Cp. Jg 5²⁵. The Arabs make butter by shaking cream in a leather bag : but owing to the heat it does not get firmly set.

10. According to the time of life] RV ' when the season cometh round,' ' at the time reviving.' i.e. ' when this time revives, a year from

now' (D.) : cp. 2 K 4¹⁶,¹⁷. **12. Laughed**] in unbelief, not in joy. **14. Is any thing too hard, etc.**] Cp. the Angel Gabriel's words to Mary, 'With God nothing shall be impossible' (Lk 1³⁷).

17–21. God reveals to Abraham the purpose of the visit to Sodom. It was essential that His servant as founder of a great nation should understand God's dealings with nations generally ; that He is concerned in their affairs, and that whilst ' slow to anger and of great kindness' He is a righteous God who will by no means clear the guilty. **19. I know him. that he will command**] rather, ' I have known Him in order that He may command,' etc. To ' know' means to take notice, of regard. 'The mission of Israel was to preserve a pure faith and pure morals amid the corruptions of mankind till the Messiah should come.' **20. Cry**] i.e. evil report. **21. I will go down now, and see**] The expression means that in His visitations on men God acts with absolute justice and a perfect knowledge of all the circumstances. **I will know**] the whole truth. **22. Stood yet before the LORD**] as if to stay His departure until he had interceded for Sodom, and especially with a thought for his kinsman Lot, who dwelt there.

23–32. We have here ' the effectual fervent prayer of a righteous man,' humble, yet earnest, and even bold. In his anxious sympathy for others Abraham forgot, perhaps, that ' the love of God is broader than the measures of man's mind,' but he was right in believing that God allows His purposes to be influenced by prayer and repentance : cp. Jon 3. For we observe that God's sentence upon Sodom was not yet passed (v. 21) ; He would grant the prayer of His servant if the necessary conditions were forthcoming. They were not, however, as the people of Sodom were universally depraved ; but Abraham learned that God prefers mercy to judgment, and that those who have the least claim on His mercy receive it, as was the case with Lot and his family. Nor should we overlook another side of this narrative, viz. the value of a good man. Ten righteous men in Sodom will save the city. So our Lord calls His disciples ' the salt of the earth,' Mt 5¹³. Another point to be noted is that while Abraham thought all along that the righteous would perish with the wicked unless the whole city was saved, God distinguished between the innocent and the guilty, and saved four persons.

CHAPTER 19

THE DESTRUCTION OF THE CITIES OF THE PLAIN

1. The visit of the two angels (who are ' the men' of c. 18) may be regarded as the final test of Sodom. If they were hospitably received and honourably treated they might still be spared.

In the gate] The entrance gate of walled Eastern cities is a great place of resort. In front of it the market was held and justice administered. See Ruth 4 2 S 15 2 Am 5 10-15 Job 31 21 Dt 21 19 Jer 38 7.
2. We will abide in the street all night] To sleep out of doors is no hardship in a hot climate. Lot shows that he retained, at all events, the virtues of hospitality and of bravery in the defence of strangers.　**3. Unleavened bread**] bread made quickly without yeast : cp. Ex 12 39.
4, 5. The causes which led to the fall of Sodom are alluded to in Ezk 16 49, 50. See also Christ's comparison of the punishments of Sodom and Capernaum (Mt 11 20).　**7. Do not so wickedly**] So St. Peter speaks of 'just Lot vexed with the filthy conversation of the wicked,' 2 Pet 2 7. But Lot himself was only relatively righteous.　**8.** Lot's sense of the sacred duty of hospitality was no excuse for neglecting his still greater duty of caring for his daughters' honour.　**9.** He will needs be a judge] Evidently Lot had reproved them before this.
11. Blindness] probably confused or indistinct vision : cp. 2 K 6 18.
14. Sons in law] By comparing this expression with vv. 8 and 16 it seems that the men were only betrothed, not married, to Lot's daughters. Indeed, RV has 'were to marry' instead of 'married.'　**17. The mountain**] the mountains of Moab, E. of the Dead Sea.　**18-22.** The motive of Lot's request is uncertain. He either feared that there would not be time to reach the mountain, or he was reluctant to leave the place where he had long lived ; the latter view seems perhaps most in accordance with his character.
21. Zoar was spared, not because its insignificant size excused its sinfulness, but as a refuge for Lot.　**22. Zoar**] 'littleness,' perhaps at the SE. end of the Dead Sea, but position disputed. It is called Bela in 14 2.
24. A consideration of the probable nature of this awful visitation will explain the vivid statement of the text. As was pointed out in c. 14, the whole neighbourhood of the Dead Sea abounds in sulphur and bitumen, furnishing the materials for the terrible conflagration which ensued. Probably a convulsion of the earth released some springs of naphtha which flowed through the cities and ignited. In our own days when the petroleum springs at Baku in the Caspian become accidentally ignited, they burn for days. The note on 14 3 explains in what sense the site of the guilty cities can be said to be covered by the waters of the Dead Sea. Their destruction was due to the agency of fire, not of water. The latter condition of this once fertile and populous district is referred to in Dt 29 23 and 2 Esdras 2 8, 9.

On the religious significance Dean Payne Smith says : 'Though God used natural agencies in the destruction of the cities of the plain, yet what was in itself a catastrophe of nature became miraculous by the circumstances which surrounded it. It was thus made the means not merely of executing the divine justice, of strengthening Abraham's faith, and of warning Lot, but also of giving moral and religious instruction for all time.'
26. She became a pillar of salt] This may mean that she was overwhelmed in the rock salt of the district which was thrown up by the earthquake : see on 14 3. The story of Josephus that this particular 'pillar' of salt was still to be seen in his day may be explained by the presence of cones of salt which are to be seen standing detached from the salt mountain of Usdum at the SW. end of the Dead Sea : see on 14 18. Our Lord alludes to the fate of Lot's wife as a warning to His followers against clinging too closely to the world (Lk 17 32).
29. God remembered Abraham] i.e. his intercession for Lot : see c. 18.
30-38. The only explanation of the shameful conduct of Lot's daughters, if understood literally, is to be found in their motive, which was probably based on the strong views entertained by Orientals regarding childlessness and the extinction of the family ; they seem also, from v. 31, to have really thought that they were the sole survivors of the terrible catastrophe just narrated. The Moabites and Ammonites settled to the E. of the Dead Sea. They afterwards became bitter enemies of Israel who first came into contact with them when nearing Canaan at the end of the wanderings. See Nu 21-25, also Jg 3 1 S 11 14 47 2 S 8 2 2 K 3 2 Ch 20 Isa 15 Jer 48 Zeph 2 8. Some scholars, however, look upon this story as the expression of the Hebrews' hatred of their two neighbours and enemies. Many of the customs of these people were doubtless abhorrent to the purer-minded Israelites ; and their feelings are expressed in this account of a current belief among the people of a later age.

CHAPTER 20
ABRAHAM AT GERAR

1. Abraham leaves Mamre (Hebron) for Gerar, SW. of Philistia. It seems from 21 34 that he remained in that district for some years.　**2. She is my sister**] Twenty years earlier Abraham had used the same device in Egypt and now again he incurs a rebuke from one outside the Covenant. See 12 11-20 and notes.　**Abimelech**] perhaps, 'Molech is my father,' in honour of the false god. Cp. Abijah, 'Jehovah is my father.'
4. Wilt thou slay also a righteous nation]

Abimelech's people, at all events, had not been guilty of any sin. **5. In the integrity of my heart**] Abimelech was 'not consciously violating any of his own rules of morality.' Had he known that Sarah was Abraham's wife he would not have taken her into his harem.

7. He *is* **a prophet**] i.e. one to whom God reveals His will, and who in turn declares it to men ; and so one who can mediate between God and man, as in this case: see on Ex 7 1.

11–13. Abraham explains that he was only following an arrangement made with his wife when they first came among the licentious Canaanites. **12.** Cp. 12 13. Sarah was daughter of Terah by another wife, and so was half-sister to Abraham. It is thought that these marriages between relatives in early days were partly intended to keep the blood of the family or tribe pure and unmixed.

16. Thy brother] ironical. **Behold, he is,** etc.] RV 'Behold, it is for thee a covering of the eyes to all that are with thee ; and in respect of all' (MG or, 'before all men') 'thou art righted.' Apparently this means that the gift was to render those with Sarah willing to overlook the wrong to which she had been exposed.

CHAPTER 21

BIRTH OF ISAAC. DISMISSAL OF HAGAR AND ISHMAEL. COVENANT BETWEEN ABRAHAM AND ABIMELECH

8. Weaned] in his second or third year, as is usual among Orientals.

9. Ishmael had no doubt been regarded as Abraham's heir until the birth of Isaac. The change in his prospects may account for his conduct, which St. Paul uses to illustrate the persecution of the Christians by the Jews (Gal 4 29). Proud of their natural descent as children of Abraham, the Jews scorned the idea that God could regard others as His spiritual children and allow them to share in their privileges and blessings : see Gal 3, 4. The story affords painful evidence of the jealousies and unhappiness caused by polygamy.

12. In Isaac shall thy seed be called] i.e. the promises should centre in Isaac.

14. Beer-sheba] 30 m. S. of Hebron.

15. Bottle] (RM 'skin'): made of the skin of a sheep or goat. All openings are sewn up and made watertight with pitch except the neck, which is tied up when the skin is full. **17, 18.** Formerly (16 7, 8) God sought out Hagar to reprove her, and bid her go back upon her course : now He appears to her to comfort her, and to supply her needs and those of her child. In both ways, He displays His grace. **19.** A miraculous supply of water is not suggested here. God enabled Hagar to see an existing spring of water.

21. Wilderness of Paran] Et-Tih, the country between Canaan and the Peninsula of Sinai. The descendants of Ishmael, Bedouin Arabs, still possess the country. It was the scene of the wanderings of the Israelites: cp. Dt 1 19 Nu 10 12.

22–34. Abraham was still living in the neighbourhood of Abimelech, king of Gerar: see c. 20. He was now regarded as a chieftain of great importance (cp. 23 6), and the king here seeks to enter into a covenant of friendship with him. Abraham takes the opportunity to secure his right to a well which he had made. Abimelech acknowledges Abraham to be the rightful possessor by accepting the seven lambs which he offers. The place was henceforth called **Beer-sheba,** 'well of the seven,' or 'well of the oath,' because the covenant had been ratified by the sacred or perfect number seven which was the usual number of things sworn by. Some very ancient wells have been discovered at Beer-sheba which marks the southern limit of Palestine. **33. A grove**] RV 'a tamarisk tree': see on 12 6.

CHAPTER 22

THE OFFERING OF ISAAC ON MOUNT MORIAH

In this narrative we have the crowning proof that Abraham was willing to resign all that was dearest to him at the bidding of God, even that son on whose life depended the fulfilment of the divine promises. But his trial must be also regarded as the occasion of bringing about an advance in the moral standard of the men of his time, which was gradually to become universal. In Abraham's day the sacrifice of the firstborn was a common practice among the Semitic races, and was regarded as the most pleasing service which men could offer to their deities. It was the 'giving of their firstborn for their transgression, the fruit of their body for the sin of their soul' (Mic 6 7). The horrible custom was even practised by the Jews in the dark days of Ahaz and Manasseh : cp. 2 K 23 10 2 Ch 28 3 33 6, and the cases of Jephthah (Jg 11) and Mesha, king of Moab (2 K 3 27). The custom probably prevailed among the tribes in whose midst Abraham dwelt, and it was borne in upon him that he should show his devotion to God in this way also. Regarding the suggestion, however it was made, as coming from God, he did not hesitate or delay, though his heart must have been wrung by the very thought. He had covenanted to give up his own will to the will of God, and in fulfilment of his obedience he was willing to sacrifice his own son. Self-sacrifice is the supreme test of faith, and Abraham was not found wanting : cp. Heb 11 17-19. The will, however, was taken for the deed, and regarded as sufficient proof of his loyalty and obedience. And Abraham, and through him the world, learnt that, far from desiring human sacrifice, Jehovah abhors it: that His worship is to be attended by mercy and justice and humanity in His followers, and that the most acceptable offering is a life of obedience and faith and love.

1. Tempt] RV 'prove,' i.e. put his faith and obedience to the proof.

2. The land of Moriah] only mentioned again 2 Ch 3 1, 'Then Solomon began to build the house of the LORD at Jerusalem in Mount Moriah.' Beneath the dome of the Mosque of Omar, which now stands on the site of the Jewish Temple, is the rock which is traditionally supposed to have been the scene of the sacrifice. It is uncertain whether the two places are to be identified, but we may gather from v. 14 that the writer wished Jerusalem to be understood here. The Samaritans assert that Mt. Gerizim was the scene of the event, regarding Moriah as Moreh in Sichem.

5. Abraham's assurance that he would return with Isaac indicates his hope that God would in some way preserve his son to him. 'He accounted that God was able to raise him up even from the dead: from whence also he received him in a figure' (Heb 11 19). He could not believe that the solemn promises respecting his son would fail of fulfilment.

6. Fire] embers from the hearth carried in a vessel. **10.** By this action Abraham in spirit and intention completed the sacrifice and showed his faith and obedience.

13. The substitution of the ram involves a recognition of God's right to demand sacrifice for His sake, and preserves the spirit which prompted Abraham's act, while at the same time it indicates the objectionableness of human sacrifice.

14. Jehovah-jireh] 'The LORD will see.' **In the mount .. seen**] Render, 'In Jehovah's mount (the Temple hill) He is seen,' i.e. 'He sees' the needs of His worshippers and 'is seen' by revealing Himself to them and 'providing' (as RV renders) for their wants. The words received their highest fulfilment when God withheld not His only Son, but freely gave Him up for men in this very place. **15–18.** Abraham's victory of faith is rewarded by a confirmation of the promises already made to him: cp. Heb 6 13.

20–24. The family of Nahor. The names are to be identified with tribes on the eastern borders of Canaan. **21. Huz**] RV 'Uz.' Cp. 10 23, where Uz is given as the name of a son of Aram. Job is described as of the land of Uz, and his friend Elihu is called a Buzite. **Aram**] probably the Syrians. **24. Concubine**] a secondary but lawful wife. By such alliances the influence and importance of the

family in early times were increased. Regarding these names as those of tribes, what is suggested here is that the last four were related to the main group somewhat distantly.

CHAPTER 23

DEATH OF SARAH AND PURCHASE OF THE
BURYINGPLACE OF MACHPELAH BY ABRAHAM

This section is from the Priestly source and dwells on the legal transaction.

2. Came] rather, 'went in,' perhaps from his own tent to that of Sarah. **3. Stood up from before his dead**] To sit upon the ground was the posture of mourning: cp. Job 2 13 **Sons of Heth**] i.e. the Hittites: see on 10 15.

6. After true Eastern custom, there was excessive courtesy in the transaction, but a large sum was in the end required. 'In Damascus, when a purchaser makes a lower offer than can be accepted, he is answered, "What, is it a matter of money between us? Take it for nothing, friend, it is a present from me"' (Delitzsch).

9. The cave of Machpelah] This spot, over which now stands the great Mohammedan mosque at Hebron, is generally admitted to be the original buryingplace of the Jewish patriarchs, and the spot where their remains still rest. It is most religiously guarded by the Mohammedans (who regard Abraham as the founder of their race through Ishmael) from all intrusion. The cave is a double one, and visitors are permitted entrance only to the upper storey, where there is little to see except counterfeit tombs. 'Only one European, Pierotti, an Italian architect in the service of the Sultan, has succeeded, at the risk of his life, in entering the lower cavern. He noticed there sarcophagi of white stone, the true tombs of the illustrious dead, in striking corroboration of the statement of Josephus, that these were of fair marble, exquisitely wrought' (Geikie). **Machpelah**] is not the name of the cave, but the name of the locality in which the piece of land containing the cave was situated: cp. vv. 17, 19.

9. For a possession, etc.] RV 'in the midst of you for a possession of a buryingplace.' Abraham wished that the Hittites should be present as witnesses of the purchase.

10. And Ephron dwelt] RV 'Now Ephron was sitting.' **12. Bowed**] in thanks for granting his request. **13. In the audience of the people**] The Hittites were thus witnesses to the agreement. **15. Four hundred shekels of silver**] Reckoning the shekel at half-a-crown, this would be about £50, but the purchasing power of silver was much greater in those days. **16. Current money**] Note that the word 'money' is not in the original. The word 'shekel' means 'weight,' and it is believed that, in these early days, rings of silver of a marked weight were used, and not coins bearing a definite value. Abraham probably weighed them to show they were of full value. ' Coined money was not known to the Hebrews before the Captivity, when first Persian and then Greek or Syriac currency was employed, till Simon the Maccabee (about 140 B.C.) struck Jewish coins, especially shekels and half shekels, specimens of which have been preserved to us ' (Kalisch).

19. Abraham and Sarah, Isaac and Rebekah, Jacob and Leah, were all buried here.

CHAPTER 24

THE MARRIAGE OF ISAAC AND REBEKAH

A charming picture of patriarchal marriage customs. It is very characteristic of the Primitive source.

2. Put .. thy hand under my thigh] a form of taking an oath, only mentioned again in 47 29. ' It is from the thighs that one's descendants come, so that to take an oath with one hand under the thigh would be equivalent to calling upon these descendants to maintain an oath which has been fulfilled, and to avenge one which has been broken' (D.). Modern instances are recorded of Egyptian Bedouins acting similarly in making a solemn asseveration.

3. Marriage with Canaanites was afterwards strictly forbidden (Ex 34 11-16). **4. My country]** Haran, in Mesopotamia, where Nahor's family still lived. **5–8.** Isaac was on no account to leave Canaan, the land promised by God as his inheritance.

10. The sending of a deputy instead of Isaac himself is quite in accordance with Eastern custom. The Jews of the present day employ a professional matchmaker, the *Shadchan*, who arranges all the preliminaries of the marriage contract. **For all the goods of his master *were* in his hand]** RV ' having all goodly things of his master's,' i.e. presents for the bride and her family : see 53.

Mesopotamia] (from Gr *mesos*, ' middle,' and *potamos*, ' river ') Heb. *Aram-Naharaim*, i.e. ' Aram (or Syria) of the two rivers,' the country lying between the Khabour and the Orontes.

City of Nahor] Haran. **12–14.** Throughout this beautiful story the direct guidance of God in all that happened is emphasised.

16. Went down to the well] To this day there is but one well of drinkable water at Haran, and the women still fill their waterskins at it. It bears every mark of great age and wear. **22. Earring]** rather, 'nose-ring.' It hung from the left nostril. Such rings are still the betrothal present in Arabia : see on rings at Ex 32 2. **24.** See 22 23.

49. Turn to the right hand, or to the left] i.e. ' to search in other families for the woman

he desires ' (D.). **50. Speak .. bad or good]** say ' yes ' or ' no.' **53.** See on Gn 12 16. **58. Wilt thou go with this man ? And she said, I will go]** ' In W. Asia marriage consists in the betrothal or the contract, sometimes written, but more commonly verbal, of the parties concerned, after which nothing remains but the removal of the bride from her father's house to that of the bridegroom or of his father. Isaac married Rebekah by proxy through a simple verbal contract' (Van Lennep). **59. Her nurse]** Deborah. Her death is mentioned in 35 8. In 29 24, 29 we have other instances that a handmaid formed part, if not all, of the bride's dowry.

62. Lahai-roi] near Beer-sheba : see 16 14. **63. Meditate]** naturally, on the bride he had not seen and whose coming he awaited. But the Syriac version reads, ' to walk in the fields.' **64. She lighted off]** to show respect. **65. She took a vail]** It is the custom for the bride to appear veiled before the bridegroom until they are married : cp. 29 23-25

CHAPTER 25

THE SONS OF ABRAHAM BY KETURAH. DEATH AND BURIAL OF ABRAHAM. DESCENDANTS OF ISHMAEL. BIRTH AND YOUTH OF ESAU AND JACOB

1. It is not known at what period of his life Abraham took Keturah as his secondary wife or concubine ; for it is clear from v. 6 and 1 Ch 1 32 that she only held that position. Some of the names of Keturah's children have been identified in Arabia as tribes. **2. Midian]** The Midianites became a considerable nation, spreading over the country S. and SE. of Palestine from Moab to the Gulf of Akaba. **6. Concubines]** Hagar and Keturah : see on 22 24. **Sent them away .. eastward]** towards Arabia, where they founded nations.

8. Gave up the ghost] an expression taken from the Genevan Bible. The Hebrew word means simply ' to die,' lit. ' come to an end.' **Was gathered to his people]** joined his ancestors in the unseen world. The expression cannot refer to the actual burial of Abraham with his forefathers, since they lay at Haran and Ur. We may probably see in it a vague belief in future existence. Cp. David's words on the death of his son (2 S 12 23, also Gn 35 29).

13. The descendants of Ishmael settled generally in N. Arabia, and with the Joktanites (10 26), or ' pure Arabs,' of Arabia Felix, formed the great Arab race scattered over Syria and the shores of the Persian Gulf. **Nebajoth]** the Nabateans became an important people after the death of Alexander the Great. Their chief town was Petra in Idumæa. The name became synonymous with Arabians, and all the land between the Euphrates and the Gulf of Akaba was at one time called Nabatene.　**Kedar**] a people often mentioned in OT. : they dwelt between Arabia and Babylonia.　**16. Towns and castles**] RV ' villages and encampments.' The Arabs may be distinguished as ' nomad ' (wandering, pastoral) and ' agricultural ' (with fixed habitations) ; the distinction is already marked in this passage.　**18. Havilah**] near the Persian Gulf.　**Shur**] the desert between Egypt and Palestine. The lands to S. and E. of Palestine generally are meant.　**Before Egypt, as thou goest toward Assyria**] rather, ' E. of Egypt in the direction of Assyria,' i.e. in N. Arabia.　**He died in the presence of**] see on 16 ^{12}.

19. Isaac] ' In Genesis Isaac appears throughout as the pale copy of his father. He is the son of promise and inherits his position, and the possessions and the blessings won by his father. He follows in Abraham's footsteps without his strength of character and purpose. In quietness and patience he faithfully preserves his inheritance, serves his father's God, and in turn like Abraham is guided, preserved, and blessed by him ' (D.).　**20. Padan-aram**] ' the plains of Syria,' the same as Mesopotamia. **22. The children struggled**] significant of the contests to come, between the brothers, and the nations descended from them, Israel and Edom. If *it be* **so, why** *am* **I thus** ?] i.e. perhaps, If I have conceived, what is the significance of these struggles ? but RV gives ' If *it be* so, wherefore do I live ?' since I suffer such pain. **Enquire of the LORD**] 'Nothing is more natural than that the Hebrew author intended to intimate that Rebekah enquired of God through Abraham the prophet, her father-in-law, who still survived ' (Kalisch).

23. Note the poetical form of the oracle. See RV.　**Shall be separated,** etc.] or ' From thy womb they will separate from one another,' i.e. be at variance from their birth.　**The elder shall serve the younger**] the descendants of the elder son (the Edomites) would be subject to those of the younger (the Israelites). See on 27 ^{40}. The knowledge of this prediction explains in some measure the later conduct of Rebecca and Jacob.　**25. Esau**] meaning uncertain. Some render ' hairy.'

26. Jacob] i.e. following at the heel. See Esau's allusion to the name (27 ^{36}), giving it a sinister sense, as suited to Jacob's plotting nature. The words Jacob and Joseph, compounded with -*el* or -*ilu* (= god), have been found as names in Assyrian inscriptions earlier than this period.

27. Cunning] i.e. clever.　**Plain**] RM ' quiet ' or ' harmless.'　**Dwelling in tents**] preferring home pursuits.　**28.** The evil of such marked preferences in families appears plainly in the narrative.　**29. Sod**] or ' seethed,' i.e. boiled.　**30. Red pottage**] lit. ' red stuff.' Esau in his haste did not define

its nature. It was a mess of lentils (34). It is said that such pottage is, or was, distributed at the mosque at Hebron in memory of the event.　**Edom**] i.e. ' red.' Probably here, as in many other instances in these ancient narratives of Genesis, we have the popular derivation of the names of well-known people and places. Edom is so called from the ' red ' colour of its sandstone cliffs. Here Esau afterwards settled: see c. 36.

31. Sell me . . thy birthright] The birthright included the headship of the family, a double portion of the inheritance (Dt 21 ^{17}), priestly rights (in these early days), and in the family of Abraham heirship to the covenant privileges. Perhaps all that was involved in the birthright here, however, was the double inheritance ; as in 27 ^{36} it is directly contrasted with the blessing which involved the primacy in the family (27 $^{28, 29}$).

The character of Esau has many attractive features ; but he cared only for the pleasure of the moment and was without any lofty spiritual aspirations. His generous, warmhearted spirit attracts sympathy at first sight, when contrasted with the wiles of the cold, calculating Jacob. But judged by a higher standard Esau appears plainly as a worldly, irreligious man, indifferent to his parents' wishes, uninterested in the divine covenant, and unmindful of the privileges and responsibilities which were to distinguish his race : cp. 26 ^{34} 27 ^{46}. His character is summed up in Heb 12 ^{16,17}, where he is called a ' profane,' i.e. unconsecrated or common person.

The character of Jacob is in marked contrast to that of Esau. Craftiness and subtilty, even meanness and deceit, mark many of his actions ; but, on the other hand, his patient endurance, strength of character, and warmth of affection call forth admiration. Long years of suffering and discipline were needed to purify his character from its baser elements, and make him worthier of the divine blessing. And certainly he was worthier than his brother, for he believed in and sought after his father's God, held spiritual things in reverence, and in the chief turning-points of his life, at Bethel, Haran, and Penuel, showed a conviction that God was with him to bless and guide. He stood out at last as one who has conquered himself, and proved himself to be worthy of the divine favour and patience, Israel, a prince with God. These considerations help us to understand why Jacob rather than Esau was selected as heir to the promises. See also Ro 9.

CHAPTER 26
ISAAC AT GERAR

Many of the notes on chs. 20, 21 are applicable to this c. It is thought probable that the present narrative is in the main a repetition from another source of events already recorded.

2. Go not down into Egypt] to get food as Abraham did. The covenant blessing is renewed and the possession of Canaan assured to Isaac. He is encouraged to stay in Canaan in dependence on God. **7. My sister**] The expression might mean cousins.

12. An hundredfold] Though very large, such a crop is not unknown. Isaac's obedience in not going to Egypt had its reward.

15. It is said that Arabs still fill up the wells on pilgrimage roads, if they do not receive the toll they demand. The conduct of Abimelech's people was a violation of the agreement of 21 25-31. Geikie, in his 'Hours with the Bible,' gives some interesting information respecting wells in Palestine :—

'The upper porous limestone of the central hills, and indeed of Palestine generally, allows the rain to a large extent to filter through it to an underlying sheet of hard limestone, which slopes towards the sea, forming a shelf on which the water flows in a subterranean stream below the whole coastplain from N. to S. Hence it is only necessary to sink a well to reach a copious supply of living water.'

20-22. Esek] 'contention.'   **Sitnah**] 'Enmity.'   **Rehoboth**] 'enlargement,' i.e. room to settle.   **26-31.** Isaac and Abimelech make a covenant to abstain mutually from aggressions.   **30.** See on 27 3.

33. Shebah] RV 'Shibah,' i.e. 'oath,' in allusion to the covenant. See on 21 31.

34. Here we have another proof of Esau's indifference to the family traditions and covenant obligations. Both Abraham and Isaac strongly condemned marriage with the inhabitants of the land who were outside the covenant of promise : see 24 3 28 1.

CHAPTER 27

JACOB BY SUBTILTY OBTAINS THE BLESSING

Urged on by his mother, Jacob attempts by unworthy means to secure the blessing of the firstborn with all the privileges it involved. But the wrongdoing of the actors in the story was soon followed by the suffering which assuredly waits on sin. To quote Delitzsch : '(a) Isaac suffers for his preference for Esau, which was not determined by the will of God but by his weak affection : (b) Esau suffers for despising the blessing of the firstborn : (c) Rebekah suffers for her connivance, by separation from her favourite son whom she never saw again. (d) Jacob, from the time when he confirmed himself in the possession of the sinfully acquired birthright by sinfully acquiring the blessing, had to endure a long strain of hardship and disappointments which made him feel how

he had sinned against his father and brother. Yet these were at the same time the means of his education by which his ignoble nature was to be done away, and himself made worthy of being one in the line of those who inherited the promises.' This c. belongs to the Primitive narrative.

1. Isaac was old] He was about 120, and both he and Esau thought that his death was at hand (vv. 2, 41). According to 35 27-29 he lived sixty years longer ; and Jacob and Esau, their old strife put away, were present at his burial: but it must be noted that that passage is from a different (the Priestly) source, which has a different chronology from the Primitive document.

4. That my soul may bless thee before I die] In purposing to give the blessing to Esau, his firstborn son, Isaac was acting in opposition to the expressed decree of God: see 25 23.

5-14. Rebekah knew that the blessing was to be Jacob's ; she therefore used this device to prevent an injustice from being done, and to obtain the fulfilment of God's purpose. That, however, she should have left to God to carry out in His way. Such 'pious frauds' are the outcome of a weak faith in the wisdom and method of the divine providence. The present narrative disproves the worldly maxim that 'the end justifies the means.'

11. Hairy man] see 25 25.   **15. Goodly raiment**] RV 'the goodly raiment,' his better clothes which were at home in his tent.

28, 29. The blessing as here recorded refers first to the fruitful land the supposed Esau would inherit, and then to his lordship over his brethren and other tribes. In 28 3, which belongs to the Priestly source, the 'blessing of Abraham' is expressed in another form characteristic of that source. **28. The dew of heaven**] greatly valued in hot climates where rain often does not fall from April to September.

33. Yea, and **he shall be blessed**] Isaac evidently feels that the purposes of God are not to be thwarted by his own preferences, and does not withdraw the blessing from Jacob.

36. Supplanted] see on 25 26.   **39. Shall be the fatness**] rather, 'Shall be away from the fatness.' Read thus, the prophecy is in agreement with the general barrenness of Edom or Seir, where the descendants of Esau dwelt.

40. Shalt serve thy brother] Throughout OT. history we read of the subjugation of the Edomites to Israel, varied by their throwing off the yoke in troublous times : see 2 S 8 14 1 K 11 1 Ch 18 13 2 Ch 21. About 100 B.C. the Maccabean prince, John Hyrcanus, subdued the Edomites and compelled them to receive circumcision, after which they formed one people with the Jews. Herod, the Edomite, ruled Judæa in our Lord's day.

41. Days of mourning] see on v. 1.

44. Tarry with him a few days] It was twenty years before Jacob returned from Haran ; and Rebekah, so far as we know, never saw him again.   **45. Deprived also of you both**] of Jacob by death, and of Esau through punishment as a murderer.

46. This verse must be read in connexion with 28 1 ; 27 46–28 9 are from the Priestly source and continue the narrative of 26 34, 35, without any reference to 27 1-45. Rebekah suggests to Isaac as the reason for Jacob's departure that it was desirable that Jacob, as the acknowledged heir, should seek a wife among his relatives at Haran, as Isaac had done before him (c. 24). Esau's heathen marriages had evidently caused his parents much unhappiness : see 26 34, 35 and notes.

CHAPTER 28
Jacob departs for Padan-aram. His Dream at Bethel

1-4. Isaac bids Jacob seek one of the daughters of his uncle Laban in marriage, and assures him that the blessings and promises bestowed on Abraham should fall to him as heir.

6-9. Esau's marriage, though well meant, was only a union with the seed of the Egyptian bondservant, and therefore not one of the pure Hebrew race.

10. After journeying for some days, Jacob reaches the district in the mountains of Ephraim, where Abraham had rested, when entering Canaan, and built an altar (12 8). The strata of limestone rock, of which the hills around are composed, take the form of steps rising above each other, and we can well believe that as Jacob lay down to rest, their form lent shape to the vision which followed. In his dream he sees a ladder, or, rather, a ' staircase,' uniting earth and heaven, and on it angelic messengers ascending and descending. Doubtless this was to assure him that, although he was in distress and fleeing for his life, he was yet the object of God's love and care. He was to learn that all that should happen to him in the future was a part of the working out of the divine providence. Our Lord alludes to this passage in Jn 1 51.

16. Jacob perceives that, though he has left his father's home at Beer-sheba, his father's God is still watching over him. In these early days the idea of Jehovah as the God of the universe, and not of the nation only, was not realised : cp. Jg 11 23, 24.

18. The stone] Jacob set up the stone as marking the spot hallowed by God's presence, and consecrated it by pouring oil upon it. On his return to Palestine (c. 35) he set up an altar by it in fulfilment of his vow in this c.

The belief that a stone or pillar was the abode of deity was common among primitive peoples. The stone which Jacob set up was the symbol of the presence of the divine spirit, which he probably believed to be in some way connected with it, seeing that he called the stone ' God's house.' Jacob shared the beliefs of his age, and his idea of God, like his character, was only gradually purified. In consequence of the abuse of these sacred stones in the worship of the Canaanites, their erection was forbidden by the Law ; cp. Lv 26 1, where ' standing image ' should be rendered ' pillar ' or ' obelisk,' also Dt 12 3. There is a well-known tradition that Jacob's stone was brought in after ages to Scotland, and finally placed under the coronation chair in Westminster Abbey. But the fact that ' all the rock at Bethel is limestone, whereas the stone in the Abbey is common granite ' (Harper), removes any foundation for the legend.

19. Beth-el] ' the house of God.' In the period of the Judges, Bethel became the chief religious centre of the northern tribes. The ark was stationed there (Jg 20 18); it was frequented as a place for sacrifice, and for consulting the divine oracle (Jg 20 18, 26 RV). Under Jeroboam I it became the religious capital of the Northern Kingdom. Here and at Dan the golden calves were set up (1 K 12). Under Jeroboam II the sanctuary reached the summit of its renown, but the worship was corrupt, and was denounced by Amos and Hosea: see Am 3 14 4 4 Hos 10 15 RV.

19. Luz] an old Canaanite city, afterwards called Bethel because of its proximity to that sanctuary.   **20–22.** The first vow mentioned in Scripture. Jacob vows that in return for God's protecting care, if he is spared to return, he will regard this stone as a holy spot, and set apart a tithe of all he gains to religious purposes. In Am 4 4 it is said that it was customary to pay tithes at Bethel, a practice based perhaps on this occurrence.

CHAPTER 29
Jacob in Mesopotamia with Laban

The divine care and blessing promised to Jacob at Bethel (28 15) are illustrated in the narrative of the sojourn of the patriarch at Haran, which apparently lasted for twenty years (31 41), after which he returned to the land of promise, blessed with a numerous family, and rich in goods. But equally marked is the severe discipline to which he was subjected in order that the darker features in his character might be purified, and that he might learn to put his reliance, not in unworthy scheming, but in simple faith in the love and blessing of the God of Abraham and Isaac.

1. The land of the people of the east] a

general term for the lands eastward of Palestine, here e.g. Mesopotamia: cp. Job 13.

3. A well often belonged to two or three families. The opening was covered with a heavy stone which could only be moved by the united efforts of the shepherds of their several flocks. By this device it was impossible for one, more than another, to obtain an undue share of the precious water. **4. Haran**] see on 11 31. **5. The son of Nahor**] rather, 'grandson.' Laban was the son of Bethuel (28 5). **11. Wept**] with joy at finding himself among friends again.

15. What shall thy wages be?] Laban was a covetous man and, as will be seen, took every advantage of Jacob to retain his services. **17. Leah** was **tender-eyed**] rather, 'weak-eyed,' perhaps from ophthalmia, so common in the East. Leah means 'gazelle,' **Rachel,** 'ewe.' **18.** Jacob had no rich gifts to offer for Rachel, such as Abraham sent for Rebekah (24 53). He therefore offered his services. Kitto says that 'personal servitude to the father is still in some places in the East, including to this day Palestine, the price paid by young men who have no other means of providing the payment which a father has always been entitled to expect for his daughter, as compensation for the loss of her domestic services.' **22. A feast**] the wedding feast. **23–25.** Jacob the deceiver is now the deceived. The bride would be closely veiled (see 24 65), and, it being night, Leah successfully connived at her father's deception. **24.** The female slave was a usual part of the bride's dowry. **26.** The custom which Laban pleaded was not uncommon. Among the Hindoos it is a law not to give the younger daughter in marriage until the elder is married. **27. Fulfil her week**] i.e. celebrate Leah's bridal festivities for the usual seven days : cp. Jg 14 12. **28.** At the end of the seven days Jacob received Rachel as his wife: but he had to serve Laban for her other seven years. Though the blame in the matter rests with Laban rather than Jacob, who must have regarded Rachel as his true wife, we shall see, as in the case of Abraham, the unhappiness and jealousy which too often attended such double unions. **31. Hated**] The word means no more than that Jacob preferred Rachel: see v. 30.

32–35. Reuben] 'behold, a son.' But the writer derives the name from *Raah beonyi,* 'looked on my affliction': see on 4 1. **Simeon**] 'hearing.' **Levi**] 'joined.' **Judah**] 'praise.'

CHAPTER 30

JACOB'S CHILDREN. HIS STRATAGEM TO INCREASE HIS PROPERTY

1. Rachel envied her sister] To be childless

was regarded as a great reproach: cp. Lk 1 25. Fruitfulness meant an addition of strength and prosperity to a family. **3.** By this symbolic act Bilhah's children would be legally regarded as Rachel's: cp. 16 1 note. **6. Dan**] 'judging.' God had judged her case and decided in her favour by giving her, after a fashion, a child. **8. Great wrestlings**] lit. 'wrestlings of God,' an emphatic expression : cp. 10 9 and 13 13. **Naphtali**] 'my wrestling.' Rachel regarded this child as a victory over her more fruitful sister. **11. A troop cometh**] RV 'Fortunate !' **Gad**] RM 'Fortune.' **13. Asher**] 'happy,' or 'blessed.' **14. Mandrake**] or 'love apple.' A dwarf plant with large grey leaves and whitish-green blossoms. It yields in the spring a yellow fruit like a small tomato, and was believed to produce fruitfulness. **18–24.** Note double derivations of names, due to the two traditions. **18. Issachar**] 'there is a reward' or 'hire. **20. Zebulun**] assonant with **Zabal,** 'to dwell.' It may also mean 'endowed.' **21. Dinah**] 'judgment,' the feminine corresponding to Dan. Perhaps Leah chose this name for the same reason that Rachel called her son Dan: see on v. 6. Jacob had other daughters (37 35), but probably Dinah is mentioned because of the episode in c. 34.

22. At last Rachel receives a son, though not by her human devices, but by God's grace and favour. **24. Joseph**] i.e. may God add a son. 'Taking away' the reproach of childlessness is another meaning.

27. Learned by experience] RV 'divined': by omens, etc. Laban does not want to lose Jacob.

31–43. Jacob by a stratagem possesses himself of a large portion of his uncle's flocks. The natural craftiness of the patriarch comes out very strongly in the transaction, but Laban undoubtedly had already obtained Jacob's services for fourteen years by mean and unworthy devices, and had given him no opportunity of enriching himself, nor had he assisted his daughters (31 15, 16). **32.** As sheep are usually white, and goats either black or brown, Jacob proposes that Laban should keep these, whilst the few speckled or spotted ones should fall to him as his wage. **33.** Jacob stakes his reputation that Laban shall never find any white sheep or black goats in his (Jacob's) flocks. **35. Ringstraked**] 'striped.'

35–42. It would appear that Laban, after sorting out Jacob's speckled sheep and goats from his own pure ones, gave the former in charge of his sons to be kept at a distance from his own, thereby hoping to prevent there being any more spotted ones born in his own flock, which he would have to give to Jacob. Jacob meanwhile had to remain and look after Laban's flocks. But Jacob had other plans for increasing his possessions. By the device described in vv. 37, 38 (which he only employed when the stronger ewes were breeding, v. 41), he brought it about that Laban's pure ewes produced speckled lambs, which he claimed as his own. In addition he arranged to keep these speckled kids and lambs in view of Laban's ewes with the same result (v. 40), thus gradually acquiring flocks of his own.

36. Betwixt himself and Jacob] Note that *LXX* and Samaritan versions read 'between them (i.e. Jacob's flock) and Jacob.'

37. Poplar .. hazel .. chesnut] rather, 'storax,' 'almond,' 'plane.'

CHAPTER 31
Jacob's Return from Haran

4-13. Jacob attributes his prosperity to God's favour. **14-16.** Rachel and Leah point out that their father had no claim on them, since Jacob had won them by his services, and Laban had given them no share in the profits he had made through their husband's labours. They agree to leave their home.

19. The images] Heb. *teraphim.* These were figures of metal, wood, or clay of varying sizes, apparently in human form. They probably answered to the 'Lares and Penates,' or household gods of the Romans, which were supposed to ward off danger from the home and to bring luck. This would explain Rachel's reason for stealing them. Laban speaks of them as 'my gods' in v. 30. There is an interesting reference to them in 1 S 19 13, 16. From Ezk 21 21 RV it is clear they were connected with magic and soothsaying. It has been suggested that in some cases the teraphim were mummied human heads, perhaps of ancestors, and were consulted in some way as an oracle. Whatever they were, it is not probable that their possession by the Jews interfered seriously with belief in and worship of God, though we find their use rightly denounced as superstitious. The following passages refer to the teraphim : Jg 17 5 1 S 15 23 RV 2 K 23 24 RV Hos 3 4 Zech 10 2 RV. Payne Smith remarks on 'the tendency of uneducated minds, even when their religion is in the main true, to add to it some superstitions, especially in the way of fashioning for themselves some lower mediator.'

21. The river] the Euphrates. **Gilead**] Hebrew territory E. of the Jordan.

24. Either good or bad] cp. 24 50. God warns Laban to restrain his feelings.

27. Tabret] i.e. 'tambourine.' **30. My gods**] see on v. 19. **34. The camel's furniture**] a sort of palanquin or basket-seat bound upon the camel. **40. Frost by night**] Hot as the days are in the East, it often becomes very cold when the sun goes down. **42. The**

fear of Isaac] the God whom Isaac feared and reverenced. **43-52.** Laban and Jacob conclude a covenant of friendship. 'The narrative .. is disconnected, and full of duplications, and is certainly the result of a union of several sources' (D.). The main features are the erection of a great stone as a memorial pillar by Jacob, and the collection of a heap of stones on which the covenant meal was held : cp. 26 30. The cairn of stones and pillar were erected as witnesses to Jacob's promise that he would not ill-treat Laban's daughters, and to an agreement pledging both Jacob and Laban to regard Mt. Gilead as a boundary which neither must cross with hostile motives. The narrative was of special interest in after times as the original settlement of the border between Israel and Syria (represented by Jacob and Laban).

47. Jegar-sahadutha .. Galeed] We have here the popular etymology of the name Gilead. Both words in the text mean 'heap of witness,' the former being Aramaic, the latter Hebrew. The double designation is due to the fact that the place is regarded as a boundary between Syria and Israel. It may be remarked here that Hebrew is but one branch of a great family of languages spoken in Western Asia between the Mediterranean and the Euphrates, to which the general name of Semitic is applied. This is usually divided into (1) the South Semitic, which includes Arabic, classical and modern, and Ethiopic ; and (2) the North Semitic. The latter again comprises three main branches, viz. (a) Assyrian-Babylonian in the East, the language of the cuneiform inscriptions ; (b) Aramaic, in the northern parts of Mesopotamia and Syria ; it is to this dialect, incorrectly styled Chaldee, that the first name in the text belongs, and in it certain parts of Ezra and Daniel are written. From Isa 36 11 we gather that it was used as the diplomatic language in the 8th cent. B.C. ; and it ultimately took the place of Hebrew as the language of Palestine. The language of the Jewish Targums is a form of Aramaic, and so too is Syriac. The third branch of the North Semitic language is (c) the Canaanitic, which comprises Hebrew, and closely connected with it, Phœnician or Punic From this table it appears that Abraham coming from the East would find in Canaan a dialect very closely akin to that with which he was familiar, and that he (or his descendants) adopted it. In all probability his native dialect was Aramaic, spoken at Haran in Mesopotamia. Or he may have spoken the language of Assyria, which, as the Tel el Amarna tablets show, was the official language of communication between Palestine and Egypt in the 15th cent. B.C.

49. Mizpah] 'outlook place.' **54. Did**

eat bread] in token of friendship. **55.** It is pleasant to read of this happy ending to years of strife.

CHAPTER 32

The Approach of Esau. Jacob Wrestles with the Angel

1. The angels of God] God had given Jacob, by an angelic vision, a pledge of His watchful love, when he left his home (28 12). Now that he was returning to Canaan after twenty years, and with dangers at hand, God renews this assurance by another heavenly vision. **2. God's host**] Heb. *Mahanaim*. It was an important city in Gilead. **3. The land of Seir**] or Edom, S. of the Dead Sea, where Esau settled (36 8). **6, 7.** Esau's large retinue alarms Jacob, since their parting had been a hostile one.

9–12. Jacob's prayer is a pattern of humility, earnestness, and faith in God's promises. **10. With my staff**, etc.] When Jacob first left Canaan he was a lonely wayfarer with no companion but his staff : now, blest by God, he returns with a numerous family and large possessions.

22. The ford Jabbok] i.e. 'wrestler.' Read, 'the ford of the Jabbok,' a stream which flows from the neighbourhood of Rabbath Ammon into the Jordan opposite Shechem.

24–32. The writer of this passage, it can hardly be doubted, was thinking of a physical wrestling. Like the men of his day, he had not reached the idea of the purely spiritual nature of God, and could only conceive of Him in a materialistic way. Practically, it is thus God is still thought and spoken of, as pure spirit is a condition of being which it is hardly possible for us to understand. In the narrative there is portrayed a spiritual experience through which Jacob passed at a critical moment of his life, and in which he received the final lesson that humbled and broke down his self-will, and convinced him that he could not snatch the blessing from God's hand, but must accept it as a gift of grace.

28. Israel] 'Perseverer with God.' 'As the name was to the Hebrews the symbol or expression of the nature, the change of name is significant of the moral change in the patriarch himself ; he is no longer Jacob the Supplanter, the Crafty one, the Overreacher, but Israel the Perseverer with God, who is worthy also to prevail' : cp. Hos 12 4. 'The incident serves to explain further the name *Penuel*, "Face of God" ; "for," said Jacob, "I have seen God face to face, and yet my life is preserved" (in allusion to the belief that no one could "see God and live," Ex 19 21 33 20 Jg 6 22 13 22). The narrator deduces also from this incident the custom of not eating in animals the muscle corresponding to the one which was strained

in Jacob's thigh ; it was treated as sacred through the touch of God.' See HDB. art. 'Jacob.' **As a prince hast thou power**] RV 'Thou hast striven.' **29. Wherefore is it,** etc.] i.e. Surely you must know who I am.

CHAPTER 33

1–16. Jacob and Esau meet peaceably. **17–20.** Jacob settles in Canaan. **3. Bowed seven times**] in token of submission to Esau. **4.** Jacob's prayer (32 11) is answered, and Esau, whatever his original purpose, now shows his brother only goodwill and affection. **10. I have seen thy face**, etc.] i.e. I find thee as favourable to me as God is, alluding, no doubt, to the name Peniel (32 30).

11. My blessing] RV 'my gift' : the present which accompanied expressions of goodwill. So Naaman said to Elisha, 'I pray thee, take a blessing of thy servant' (2 K 5 15). **12–16.** Jacob was unwilling to refuse Esau, and yet thought it most prudent to keep apart from his hasty brother. He therefore made an excuse and crossed the Jordan into Canaan.

17. Succoth] 'booths,' S. of the Jabbok and on the E. side of Jordan. Succoth and Penuel are mentioned together in Jg 8. **18. To Shalem, a city of Shechem**] RV 'in peace to the city of Shechem.' But there is a village called Salim 3 m. E. of Shechem. Here Jacob settled for some eight or ten years. The well which he dug still exists, though nearly choked with stones, some 1¼ m. from Nablous. It was here that Christ conversed with the woman of Samaria (Jn 4). **19. Pieces of money**] Heb. *Kesitah*, probably bars or rings of silver of a certain weight. See on 23 16, also Job 42 11. **20. El-elohe-Israel**] i.e. El (God) is the God of Israel (Jacob's new name).

CHAPTER 34

The Dishonour done to Dinah, and the Crafty Revenge of Simeon and Levi

1. Went out to see the daughters of the land] According to Josephus there was a festival among the Canaanites at Shechem. **7. Folly**] The term is frequently applied in the moral sense as equivalent to immorality: see Dt 22 21 Jg 20 6 2 S 13 12, and frequently in Proverbs, as 7 7f. A world of argument lies in the scriptural identification of wickedness and folly. The moral man is the wise man. **In Israel**] The author anticipates the national name. **12. Dowry and gift**] The former was the price paid to the relatives for the bride, the latter the gift to the bride.

13–17. Simeon and Levi professed to have scruples in giving their sister to one who was of an uncircumcised race, but they had another motive: by procuring the circumcision of the tribe they were able to carry out their revenge when the Shechemites were suffering from the effects of the rite. **25. Simeon, Levi,** and **Dinah** were all children of Leah.

29. Little ones] rather, 'household,' servants, etc. **28–30.** The murder of the Shechemites was a treacherous and cruel act. Jacob was deeply incensed at it, and on his deathbed (c. 49) denounced and cursed the murderers, though at the time he was chiefly concerned for the consequences of their conduct. **30. Make me to stink**] i.e. to be in bad odour, as we say : cp. Ex 5²¹.

CHAPTER 35

JACOB JOURNEYS BY WAY OF BETHEL TO HEBRON. DEATH OF RACHEL AND OF ISAAC

1. Jacob is commanded to go to Bethel and fulfil the vow he had once made there (28²⁰,²²). **2. Strange gods**] Perhaps the idols of some of Jacob's people who had come with him from Haran, such as the teraphim which Rachel carried off (31¹⁹). **Be clean, and change your garments**] rites symbolising purification from idolatry. **4. Earrings**] worn superstitiously as charms, and often inscribed with magical formulæ. **The oak**] It was here perhaps that Joshua, hundreds of years later, bade the Israelites put away the strange gods which were among them (Josh 24²³⁻²⁶). **5.** They were divinely protected from any revenge the Shechemites may have meditated. **7. El-beth-el**] 'the God of Bethel,' or 'the God of the House of God.' **8. Allon-bachuth**] 'oak of weeping.' Deborah and Eliezer (c. 24) are good examples of the honourable position assigned to servants in times of patriarchal simplicity. Deborah means 'bee.' **9–13.** These vv. give the origin of the names 'Israel' and 'Bethel' from the Priestly source. Note the absence of anthropomorphisms as compared with the account in 32²²⁻³². **14. A pillar**] see on 28¹⁸. **A drink offering**] a libation of wine in token of thankfulness. Under the Law meat and drink offerings accompanied the burnt sacrifice. **16. Ephrath**] or Bethlehem, 4 m. S. of Jerusalem : cp. 48⁷ Mic5². **18. Ben-oni**] 'son of my sorrow.' **Benjamin**] perhaps ' son of my right hand,' that being the fortunate side, and so a name of better omen. Another rendering is ' son of days,' i.e. of Jacob's old age **21. Tower of Edar**] lit. ' tower of the flock,' probably between Bethlehem and Hebron. The name is used symbolically of Jerusalem in Mic4⁸. **22.** By this crime Reuben, the eldest son, forfeited the birthright (49³,⁴) like Simeon and Levi before him : see on 34²⁸. **27.** Jacob rejoins his father after thirty years' separation. **City of Arbah**] Hebron :

see 23². **28, 29.** Isaac was buried in the cave at Machpelah, 49³¹.

CHAPTER 36

THE GENERATIONS OF ESAU

' The amount of detail here arises from the fact that Edom was always counted Israel's brother, and of great importance in the history of Israel. The Horites (" cave-dwellers ") were originally in the mountainous country of Seir (v. 20) ; the Hebrews under Esau entered and amalgamated with them. Esau married the Horite Aholibamah, and his son Eliphaz, the Horite Timna. They then became rulers of Seir to Akaba ; God gave it them as Canaan to Israel ' (D.). See Dt 2⁵.

1. Esau, who is Edom] i.e. Esau, who was called Edom, and gave to his land his name : see on 25³⁰. **2.** The names of the wives of Esau given here vary from those mentioned in 26³⁴ 28⁹. The difficulties have never been explained, and are generally attributed to two irreconcilable traditions. **Zibeon the Hivite**] a clerical error : read ' Horite.' Zibeon was doubtless a Horite or dweller in Mt. Hor : see v. 20. It was by the marriage mentioned here that Esau acquired his influence among the Horites, the aboriginal inhabitants of Seir : see on 14⁶. **8, 9.** The fact is dwelt on that the Edomite nation was descended from Esau. **Mount Seir**] a chain of mountains extending from the Dead Sea to the Gulf of Akaba. Mt. Hor is towards the centre of the range. Aaron was buried there : see on Nu20²²ᶠ. **12. Amalek**] This does not mean that the great tribe of the Amalekites was descended from Edom, but that a branch became attached to the Edomites. **15. Dukes**] RM ' chiefs.' **24. The mules**] ' the hot springs.' Such springs exist near the Dead Sea, and are much prized by the desert wanderers for their medicinal qualities. **31.** This v. shows the early development of the monarchy in Edom, and also that there were kings in Israel in the author's lifetime. **37. River**] either the Euphrates or the Wady el Arish : see on 15¹⁸.

CHAPTER 37

JOSEPH IS HATED BY HIS BRETHREN AND SOLD INTO EGYPT

With the exception of a few passages chiefly in chs. 46 and 49, the rest of the book of Genesis is taken from the Primitive source.

The chief event with which the rest of Genesis is concerned, namely, the migration of Israel to Egypt, displays the working out of God's purposes declared in Gn 15. In Egypt the chosen race grew in peace from a tribe to a nation, instead of having to encounter the hostility of the Canaanites as their numbers increased and their aspirations became known. In Egypt, too, they came in contact with a highly civilised and law-abiding nation, and learnt from them much of the highest value for the future.

There are many points in the history of Joseph which remind us of Christ, e.g. in his being the loved son of his father, in his being sent to his brethren who hated and rejected him, in his humiliation and glory, and in the benefits he conferred on those among whom he came to dwell.

2. The generations of Jacob] i.e. the history of Jacob's descendants, especially of Joseph. **Their evil report**] RV 'the evil report of them.' The sins of Jacob's sons in chs. 34, 37, 38 afford plain evidence of their lawless characters. **3. A coat of** *many* **colours**] RM 'a long garment with sleeves,' i.e. reaching to the ankles and wrists, and worn by persons of distinction. The ordinary coat had no sleeves and reached only to the knees.

5. Joseph dreamed] The fact of the dreams indicates a contemplative disposition in Joseph : their character foreshadows his future pre-eminence among his brethren. **10. Thy mother**] According to 35^{19}, Rachel was already dead : but critics assign that passage to a different source.

13. Jacob was living at Hebron, but he had land at Shechem : see 33$^{18, 19}$. **15. In the field**] i.e. in the open country. **17. Dothan**] 12 m. N. of Shechem. It was on the caravan route between Syria and Egypt. This explains the passing of the merchants.

21 f. The narrative in this chapter appears to be drawn from two sources which give somewhat varying accounts of the way in which Joseph was rescued and sold without any attempt to harmonise them. In one it is Judah who defends him and Ishmaelites who buy him ; in the other it is Reuben and Midianites.

24. A pit] These pits or, rather, cisterns are generally dry except in the rainy season. They are much smaller at top than bottom, that they may be the more easily closed. Some are 80 to 100 ft. deep : cp. Jer 38^6.

25. Spicery, balm, and myrrh] fragrant gums from various trees, used in Egypt for making incense, and for embalming. **28. Twenty pieces of silver**] ' The price, in later times, of a male slave from five to twenty years old, the medium price being thirty shekels of silver or £4 ' (Edersheim). **29.** Reuben had evidently been absent during this transaction. **34. Sackcloth**] a coarse material made of goats' hair, and worn next the skin in token of the affliction of the soul.

35. The grave] the Heb. 'Sheol' means the place of departed souls. **36. Sold him**] Syrian slaves were highly valued by the Egyptians. **Potiphar**] probably means ' the gift of Ra,' the sun-god of the Egyptians.

Captain of the guard] i.e. of the bodyguard who protected Pharaoh's person and executed criminals : but some render 'chief of the butchers.'

CHAPTER 38
The History of Judah

The sins recorded in this chapter testify eloquently to the great need the world had of the Greatest of the descendants of Judah, who came to teach the virtue of purity and the sanctity of family life. The honesty and truthfulness of the historian are shown in his not concealing the dark spots in the history of Judah, whose descendants attained to such greatness. The direct purpose of the narrative is to show the ancestry of David, who was descended from Pharez the son of Judah by Tamar : see Ruth 4^{18} Mt 1^3.

1. Adullamite] Adullam was in the lowland of Judah, SW. of Jerusalem. **8.** The law in Dt 25$^{5-10}$, respecting the duty of a surviving brother to marry his deceased brother's widow in order to continue the race, will fully explain the circumstances here detailed. To inculcate observance of this law was probably the aim of the historian. Had Judah given Shelah to Tamar, as he admitted he should have done according to ancient custom, the events recorded here would not have happened : see also Mt 22$^{23 f.}$ **13. Timnath**] on the Philistine border of Judah. **14. An open place**] RV ' the gate of Enaim,' near Adullam.

15. Harlot] RM Heb. *Kedeshah*, ' that is, a woman dedicated to impure heathen worship : see Dt 23^{17} Hos 4^{14}.' The surrender of their chastity as the greatest sacrifice women could make was common in heathen worship. At Corinth in St. Paul's day it is known that this shocking practice formed part of the ritual at the temples dedicated to Aphrodite.

18. Bracelets] rather, ' cord ' by which the seal was suspended round the neck.

26. The reason of Tamar's action may be found in the strong desire for the perpetuation of the family, so often observed in the sacred narrative.

27-30. This incident testifies to the importance and privileges attached to the firstborn. **Pharez**] ' breach.' **Zarah**] perhaps ' scarlet,' but uncertain.

CHAPTER 39
Joseph in the House of Potiphar

5. Overseer] rather, ' house-steward.' **6.** Potiphar left everything under Joseph's control except his own food. There may be here an allusion to the strict caste laws of Egypt : cp. 43[32] 46[34].

7. Joseph was yet but a youth, when temptations are strongest, and he was far removed from all the restraining influences of home. But He who was 'the fear of Isaac' (31[42]) was 'the fear of Joseph' also, and his resolute resistance to temptation teaches that the prospect of earthly advantage or pleasure should never for a moment close our ears to the voice of conscience.

A papyrus has been found called 'The Tale of Two Brothers,' which gives in Egyptian form some incidents similar to this narrative.

8. Wotteth] RV 'knoweth.' **9. And sin against God**] Other passages (e.g. 40[8] 41[16 51, 52] 42[18] 50[19, 20]) show that Joseph 'made the consciousness of God's presence and intervention in his affairs, a vital principle of his actions, the law of his life' : cp. Neh 5[15].

20. It is probable from the lightness of Joseph's punishment that Potiphar was not altogether convinced of his steward's guilt.

CHAPTER 40
Joseph interprets the Dreams of Pharaoh's Officers

1. Butler] rather, 'cupbearer,' a high court official : cp. Neh 1[11] 2[1]. **Baker**] rather, 'cook.' It is conjectured that these officials were accused of plotting to poison Pharaoh.

8. No professional interpreter was available : see on 41[8]. **Do not interpretations, etc.**] i.e. It may be that God who sent the dreams will give me the interpretation of them. **9-11.** Grape juice mixed with water is used as a refreshing drink in the East. Among the inscriptions on the temple of Edfu is one in which the king is seen with a cup in his hand, and underneath are the words, 'They press grapes into the water and the king drinks.' **16. White baskets**] rather, 'baskets of white bread.' **17. Bakemeats**] i.e. confectionery. **19. Hang thee on a tree**] rather, 'impale thee on a stake' after being beheaded. Hanging as a form of punishment is not referred to, except in the book of Esther, the scene of which is laid in Persia. **The birds shall eat,** etc.] The Egyptians held that after a stay of 3000 years in the unseen world, the soul re-entered its former body, and commenced a fresh existence on the earth. They therefore took the greatest pains to preserve the bodies of the dead : see on 50[2]. For a body to be devoured by the birds, as Joseph foretold, would be regarded as a terrible doom.

CHAPTER 41
The Dreams of Pharaoh and the Advancement of Joseph

1. Pharaoh] It is believed that a dynasty of Asiatic (perhaps Bedouin) conquerors, known as the Hyksôs or Shepherd kings, were now in power in Egypt. Their rule lasted for 500 years, until 1700 or 1600 B.C., when a native Nubian dynasty from Thebes expelled the invaders. The court was at Zoan on the eastern frontier of Egypt. The elevation of Joseph to an almost royal position, and the welcome extended to his kinsmen, were natural at the hands of a dynasty who were Asiatic like himself, but very improbable had a native dynasty who hated foreigners been in power : see on Ex 1[8].

1. The river] Heb. *Yeor*, i.e. the Nile. As is generally known, the fertility of Egypt depends entirely upon the amount of water which overflows the banks when the Nile is at its highest. Without that river the land would be a desert, the rainfall being extremely slight. In recent years great improvements have been made for maintaining the water at a normal height always. Large 'barrages' or dams have been erected at Assouan, by the island of Philœ, for this purpose. The artificial irrigation of Egypt is alluded to in Dt 11[10], where see note.

2, 3. The seven well favoured kine] coming up out of the Nile signified an abundant overflow for seven years and consequent plenty for Egypt, but the **ill favoured** ones the reverse. **Meadow**] RV 'reed grass' which grows by the Nile. **5. Seven ears .. upon one stalk**] This many-eared wheat is still grown in Egypt. Specimens have been found in mummy cases of very early periods. **6. The east wind**] the parching SE. wind from the desert ; see on Ex 10[21].

8. Magicians] RM 'sacred scribes.' They were the literary caste of Egypt, writing the hieroglyphics, or sacred writings, and learned in the interpretation of dreams and astrology. They attended at the Court of the Pharaohs, and their duty was 'to guide every act of the king's life, and to interpret the will of the gods as shown in visions, omens, or signs in the heavens. They did not affect to speak by direct inspiration in giving their interpretations, but confined themselves to consulting the holy books and to performing magical rites' (Geikie). See on Ex 7[11].

14. He shaved *himself*] so as to be ceremonially clean in Pharaoh's presence, a distinctively Egyptian trait. 'The Hebrews regarded their beard with peculiar pride, cultivated it with care, touched it at supplications, often swore by it, and deemed its mutilation an extreme ignominy : hence, in mourning, they shaved their beards and hair' (Kalisch). The Egyptians, on the other hand, never allowed the hair to grow unless they were in mourning, or prisoners, or belonged to the poorer classes. To be shaved was regarded as essential to ceremonial purity, as well as to cleanliness : see on Ex 8 16. The great beards and head-dresses with which Egyptian kings are represented on the monuments are artificial. There is an ancient Egyptian wig in the British Museum, and the strap by which the beard was held on the chin may be observed on the monuments.

16. Render, ' It is not I but God who will answer what will profit Pharaoh.'

25. The dream of Pharaoh *is* one] i.e. both dreams have the same significance. The narrative here is a striking fulfilment of the words in 39 2, ' The LORD was with Joseph.'

34. Joseph's suggestion was that a fifth part of the corn crop should be required of the people for the next seven years to be stored up by the government ; this would keep a quantity in the country which would otherwise have been sold to other lands. The corn tax was already an important part of Egyptian revenue, and its increase in years of such abundant plenty would be no hardship.

38. Pharaoh felt that Joseph's wisdom had a divine source. **40.** Pharaoh makes Joseph his grand vizier or prime minister, only reserving to himself the supreme authority.

42. Ring .. vestures .. chain] ' The speculative mind of the Oriental invests everything with a symbolical significance ' (Kalisch). The ring was Pharaoh's signet or seal, showing that Joseph was invested with full power as to edicts and commands. The king and the priestly order only wore the finest linen vestures. The chain round the neck from which the scarabæus, or beetle, the emblem of immortality, was suspended, was also a mark of rank. **43. They cried**] i.e. the grooms who ran before the chariot, as is done to the present day in Egypt. **Bow the knee**] *Abrek*, the word used here, is still the cry to the camel to kneel. **44.** The exaltation of Joseph, who was a Hebrew, is less remarkable if the Pharaohs of this period were themselves of Asiatic descent. See on v. 1.

45. Zaphnaph-paaneah] meaning, perhaps, ' God, the Living One, has spoken.' It is a word of Egyptian origin, but not found earlier than the 9th cent. B.C. **Asenath**] ' One belonging to the goddess Neith, the Egyptian Minerva, goddess of wisdom.' **Poti-pherah**] ' One given by Ra the sun-god.' **On**] or Heliopolis, ' city of the sun,' was 7 m. NE. of Cairo. It was the centre of the sun (Ra) worship. A great granite obelisk of the twelfth dynasty is all that remains standing of the temple of the sun, but a similar monolith known as ' Cleopatra's needle ' was brought from Alexandria to London in 1878, and erected on the Thames embankment. It had originally been one of the obelisks at Heliopolis. It is held that these obelisks were the symbol of Ra, the fertilising sun-god. In Jer 43 13 On is called Beth-shemesh, ' house of the sun.'

This marriage, no doubt, exalted Joseph in the eyes of the Egyptians, but there is abundant evidence that he did not forsake the faith of his fathers on account of these new ties.

46. Thirty years old] he was seventeen when sold into Egypt (37 2). **51, 52. Manasseh**] ' causing to forget.' **Ephraim**] ' fruitful.' The first name suggests that Joseph felt in his present prosperity compensation for his early trials. **54. Seven years of dearth**] A similar visitation took place between the years 1064–1071 A.D., and this also was caused through the failure of the Nile. There is a record on the monuments of a great famine in Egypt 3000 B.C. In Canaan such a scarcity would be due to insufficient rainfall.

56. Over all the face of the earth] an expression for the countries near Egypt, such as Arabia, Palestine, and parts of Africa. **And Joseph opened all the storehouses**] Dr. Brugsch has discovered a tomb at El-Kab with an inscription which very possibly refers to this famine. Its occupant seems to have been one of the distributors of corn during the famine years. The following extract refers to it : ' I collected the harvest, for I was a friend of the harvest god. I was watchful at the time of sowing, and now when a famine came lasting many years I issued corn to the city to each hungry person.'

CHAPTER 42

The First Visit of Joseph's Brethren to Egypt

1. When Jacob saw] The caravans which travelled from Egypt to Syria would bring the news to Hebron. **3.** Dr. Thomson, in ' The Land and the Book,' says he has often met large parties with their donkeys going from Palestine to Egypt in time of drought for food. Jacob's sons no doubt took servants with them and many asses.

8. Joseph, now a middle-aged man, now dressed as an Egyptian, and spoke in Egyptian through an interpreter (v. 23). His brethren, on the other hand, would not have changed in appearance. **9. Ye *are* spies**] Egypt was always liable to attack from Asia, and fortresses were built along that frontier to repel invasion. By suggesting that they were foreigners who were spying out **the nakedness of the land,** i.e. how far it was open to attack from hostile nations, Joseph had an opportunity of enquiring about his family. We may believe also that, though well-intentioned towards his brethren, he sought to bring their sin home to them. **11. We *are* all one man's sons .. thy**

servants are no spies] This was a strong argument. No father would have risked the lives of all his children at once on such dangerous work as that of spies. **13.** *Is* not] i.e. is not alive, meaning Joseph. **14.** Joseph perseveres in this charge in order to have a pretext for getting Benjamin to Egypt. He hoped too, perhaps, that his father would follow when his favourite son had left him.

15. By the life of Pharaoh] a common Egyptian oath: cp. 'As I live saith the Lord,' also 2 K 2⁴. **18. I fear God**] 'and so will not punish on mere suspicion' (D.).

21. Conscience arouses in the brethren the fear that the day of reckoning, so long delayed, has come at last.

27. The inn] This would be no more than a mere shelter or camping place. Even now, when journeying in out-of-the-way parts in the East, travellers take their own food and bedding with them. **36. All these things are against me**] So Jacob thought; but Providence was working out a merciful provision for the welfare of himself and his family.

CHAPTER 43
The Second Visit to Egypt

11. Balm] or 'balsam,' with healing properties. **Honey**] This was grape-honey, a syrup made of grapes and diluted with water for a drink. It is still exported from Hebron to Egypt. Syria is famous for its pistachio **nuts** and **almonds** which do not grow in Egypt.

12. Double money] (1) to repay that put in the sack, and (2) to purchase fresh stores.

18. Again the guilty conscience which dreads every fresh event. **30. Bowels**] regarded as the seat of the affections by the Hebrews: cp. 2 Cor 6¹².

32. The distinctions observed here were due to the existence of various castes among the Egyptians. As with the Hindoos, it was unheard of for a man of one caste to eat from the vessels used by another.

34. He *sent* **messes**] 'Mess' is derived from Lat. *missum*, 'sent': so a dish of meat sent. To do this is an Eastern mark of honour : 2 S 11⁸. Sometimes the host personally puts a particularly choice morsel into the guest's mouth. Joseph's love for Benjamin is thus markedly shown.

CHAPTER 44
The Final Test of Joseph's Brethren

2. Put my cup . . in the sack's mouth of the youngest] Joseph evidently did this as an excuse for keeping Benjamin with him. Perhaps, too, it was a test of the brethren whether they would act as cruelly in deserting their youngest brother as they had dealt with himself. However, they came nobly out of the

trial, and a complete reconciliation took place.

5. Whereby indeed he divineth] Divination by means of bowls of water was very prevalent among the ancients. They appear to have had a superstitious fancy that if one gazed long into a cup, he would see future events reflected in its contents. Bowls have been found in Babylon, inscribed on the inner surface with magical words and exorcisms against evil spirits. In the method of divination called hydromancy 'water was poured into a glass or other vessel and pieces of gold, silver, or precious stones might be thrown in ; then observations were made of the results, of the figures, etc., which appeared, with the expectation of learning the future or the unknown by this means' (D.). At the storming of Seringapatam, during the Indian mutiny, the notorious Tippoo Saib is said to have consulted the divining cup just prior to his death in battle.

18–34. Nothing could be more affecting and generous than Judah's words, especially if the brethren believed that Benjamin had stolen the cup, and yet refused to accuse him, and took the blame on themselves.

CHAPTER 45
Joseph makes Himself known to his Brethren. Pharaoh invites Jacob and his Family to settle in Egypt

5–7. Joseph declares that the events of the past all witnessed to the providential care of God. **6. Earing**] i.e. ploughing, cognate with Lat. *aro*, 'I plough.' The word is now obsolete. **8. A father to Pharaoh**] a title of honour and respect : cp. Isa 22²¹.

10. The land of Goshen] This was a fertile district of N. Egypt, lying to the E. of the Nile between Zagazig and Tel-el Kebir, 40 m. NE. of Cairo. The railway from Alexandria to Suez now runs through it. There have been discovered in this neighbourhood the remains of a town, called on its monuments Gesem. The land of Goshen was probably the same as the 'field of Zoan' (Ps 78¹²) and the 'land of Rameses' (47¹¹). **18, 19.** The district of Goshen was well suited to the pastoral habits of the Hebrews. There is a papyrus of the time of the Pharaoh Merenptah, some centuries later than the present events, which refers to permission given to some tribes of nomad Asiatics (Shasu) to 'pass the fortress Etham in the land of Succoth near the town Pithom to pasture their cattle in that territory.' All these places were in the land of Goshen.

19. Wagons] Those depicted on the monuments had two wheels and were drawn by oxen. **20. Regard not your stuff**] Do not trouble to bring all your belongings with you

24. See that ye fall not out by the way] Joseph perhaps feared that his brothers might reproach one another for their treatment of him, and so quarrels might arise.

CHAPTER 46

THE DESCENT OF JACOB INTO EGYPT
THE GENEALOGICAL TABLE OF THE ISRAELITES

1-4. On reaching Beersheba, the southern boundary of the Promised Land, Jacob offers sacrifices to God. In return God assures him of His continued favour and of the fulfilment of the promises made to Abraham. **4. Put his hand upon thine eyes**] i.e. close them in death. **5. Little ones**] rather, ' household servants and their families.'

6-27. This passage is from the Priestly source, and shows its characteristic fondness for genealogies. **27. Threescore and ten**] This number included Jacob and Joseph and his two sons. See on Ex 1 5 as to the total number of those that went down to Egypt.

28-34. Joseph was anxious to settle his people in Goshen both because the land was rich in pasture and because their calling was distasteful to the Egyptians. **34. Every shepherd is an abomination to the Egyptians**] The reasons for this dislike are disputed. ' Herdmen are represented on the monuments as uncouth and ill clad. They led a rough, unsettled life in the marshes, and seem to have been regarded as pariahs by the scrupulously clean Egyptians ' (D.).

CHAPTER 47

JOSEPH PRESENTS HIS BRETHREN AND HIS FATHER TO PHARAOH. HE MAKES EXTENSIVE CHANGES IN THE LAND TENURE OF EGYPT

6. Rulers over my cattle] The superintendence of the royal flocks and herds would be a position of importance. **9. Few and evil, etc.**] Abraham was 175 years and Isaac 180 years old at their death. Jacob, therefore, regarded his years as comparatively few. The ' evil ' times in his life are not difficult to trace. **11. Land of Rameses**] or Raamses. Evidently identical with the ' land of Goshen ' (vv. 4 and 6). The name here is probably anticipatory of the time of the great Rameses, who made his court at Zoan : see on Ex 1 11.

14-25. From being owners of the land the people became tenants of the crown. They remained on the land, paying one-fifth of the produce for state requirements, and retaining four-fifths for their own use. In such a fertile land as Egypt these conditions must be regarded as much more favourable than in some Eastern states in the present day, such as Turkey and Persia, where the peasants have to hand over from a half to three-fourths of the produce of the land to the government. See Dillmann, and on v. 25.

16, 17. When Joseph took the people's cattle which they were unable to support in the dried-up Nile valley, he probably removed them to Goshen (cp. v. 6) until the famine was ended. **18. The second year**] not of the famine, but the year after they had given up their cattle. **21.** It is now generally held that the v. should be rendered (with the LXX, Vulgate, and Samaritan texts), ' As for the people, he made bondmen of them from one end,' etc. (RM). The people became the tenants of the crown : see on vv. 14-25.

22. The priests were already provided for by the state ; it was therefore unnecessary for them to sell their land. It is said that in later times the king, the soldiers, and the priests each owned one-third of the land.

23. ' The peculiar system of Egyptian land tenure, which is here attributed to Joseph, is so far in accordance with the evidence of the monuments that whereas in the Old Empire the nobility and governors of the nomes (district) possessed large landed estates, in the New Empire (which followed the expulsion of the Hyksôs), the old aristocracy has made way for royal officials, and the landed property has passed out of the hands of the old families into the possession of the crown and the great temples ' (D.).

25. The people were satisfied with Joseph's stipulations. They would be much better off when holding their land direct from the state under definite conditions, than when suffering from the exactions of small feudal rulers, who were a great infliction in Egypt.

29. Put . . thy hand, etc.] see on 24 2.

31. Bowed himself upon the bed's head] perhaps better, ' worshipped, leaning on the top of his staff,' as in Heb 11 21. The Hebrew words for ' bed ' and ' staff ' are very like each other.

CHAPTER 48

JACOB BLESSES MANASSEH AND EPHRAIM, THE SONS OF JOSEPH

He adopts them as his own sons with privileges equal to the others, thus making them heads of distinct tribes. By so doing he gives to Joseph, the eldest son of Rachel, whom he probably regarded as his true wife, the position of firstborn with a double portion of his inheritance. From the time of Moses we find Ephraim and Manasseh giving their names to tribes (Nu 1), which received territory on the conquest of Canaan.

3. Luz] or Bethel : see on 28 19. **6. Any** other children of Joseph would be reckoned as belonging to the tribes of Ephraim or

Manasseh.   **7. By me**] RM 'to my sorrow.' The mention of Rachel here may be only a fond reminiscence called forth by the presence of her grandchildren. But the v. would be perhaps more appropriately placed after 49³¹, where Jacob is speaking of the burial of his ancestors and of Leah.

13, 14. Joseph had so arranged his sons that Manasseh, as the first-born, would receive his father's right hand in the act of blessing ; but Jacob, 'guiding his hands wittingly' as taught by God, transferred that honour to the younger Ephraim, thus prophetically declaring the future superiority of that tribe : see v. 19. Owing to its preëminence the northern kingdom of Israel was often called Ephraim by the prophets, e.g. Isa 11 Ezk 37.

22. Portion] RM 'mountain slope' (Heb. *shechem*). The reference is to Shechem in the mountainous territory of Ephraim. Jacob gives Shechem to Joseph as his advantage over the others. The acquiring of Shechem by Jacob by force of arms represents a different tradition to that mentioned in chs. 33, 34.

CHAPTER 49

Jacob Blesses his Twelve Sons

It is generally considered that in its present form, this c. gives us indeed the last utterances of the dying patriarch respecting the future of his sons, but with additions and developments of a later date. As it stands we have not the broken utterances of a dying man, but an elaborate piece of work full of word-plays and metaphors (see on vv. 8, 13, 16), and of those parallelisms in the vv. which are the chief feature of Hebrew poetry (cp. vv. 11, 15, 22, 25). It is in fact a poem, in which the fortunes of the tribes, which are impersonated by their ancestors, are delineated as they were at one special period, viz. after the Conquest of Canaan, when their territories had been finally settled, and their political importance or weakness had become recognised. Judah and, perhaps, Joseph are alluded to as ruling tribes (vv. 10, 26). No reference is made to the times of the exodus or the captivity, but only to the beginnings of the monarchy ; and it was probably during this period that the original Blessing was developed in its present poetical form. This conclusion is strengthened when we find the word 'Israel' used of the nation, not of the person, and also that facts happening after the Conquest of Canaan are alluded to as past events : cp. vv. 14, 15. It is also significant that many definite political and geographical details are given, in a way which is inconsistent with the general character of the predictions of the Hebrew prophets on such matters. With the Blessing of Jacob should be compared that of Moses in Dt 33 and notes there.

1. Which shall befall you] what will be the fortunes of the tribes descended from you.

In the last days] RV 'in the latter days,' i.e. in the future.

3, 4. The prediction concerning **Reuben**. Reuben was Jacob's eldest son, but the tribe never attained to any distinguished position. It was situated on the E. side of Jordan, and exposed to many attacks from the peoples surrounding them. 'Even so early as under the Judges the tribe showed itself indifferent to the national struggles (Jg 5¹⁵ ᶠ·), and it continued to isolate itself more and more until in the period of the early monarchy it had practically disappeared as part of Israel' (D.). See Dt 33⁶.   **3. Excellency**] rather, 'preeminence.'   **4. Unstable**] rather, 'unrestrained,' descriptive of ungoverned passion. Reuben's sin is mentioned in 35²².   **Excel**] rather, 'have the preëminence.'

5–7. The prediction respecting **Simeon** and **Levi**. Simeon and Levi were both sons of Leah ; but they also were **brethren** in the cruelty of their attack on the Shechemites (34²⁵). The scattered state of both these tribes in their after history is well known. When the territories were assigned in the days of Joshua, Simeon only had some cities within the possessions of Judah : see Josh 19¹⁻⁹. The Levites as priests had forty-eight towns given them throughout the country, but had no inheritance of land, Josh 21¹⁻⁴⁰ : cp. also the picture in Jg 17–19 of the wandering Levites.   **5. Instruments of cruelty, etc.**] better, 'their swords are weapons of violence.'

6. Secret] RV 'council,' referring to the treachery of c. 34.   **They slew a man**] see 34²⁵,²⁶.   **They digged down a wall**] RV 'they houghed an ox,' by cutting the sinew of the thigh: perhaps a reference to the Shechemites' cattle which they raided (34²⁸), maiming in their destructiveness those which they could not carry off.

8–12. Judah now receives the chief blessing which his elder brothers Reuben, Simeon, and Levi had forfeited. He is assured of the headship of the tribes and a fruitful territory.

8. The name **Judah** ('praise') suggests the honour in which the tribe would be held. **Thy hand,** etc.] The tribe of Judah took a leading part in the conquest of Canaan and was first to secure their territory : cp. on Nu 2¹. In the time of David they held the headship of Israel.   **9.** The tribe is compared for its bravery to a lion. The figure of a lion on a pole became the standard of Judah, and our Lord Himself is called 'the Lion of the tribe of Judah' (Rev 5⁵) owing to His descent from David.   **10. A lawgiver**] RV 'the ruler's staff.'   **From between his feet**] This most probably refers to the custom of planting the sceptre or staff of a prince or chieftain in the ground between his feet as he sat.

This verse has always been regarded by both Jews and Christians as a remarkable prophecy of the coming of the Messiah. The Versions generally read *Sheloh* instead of *Shiloh*, and the words until Shiloh come (AV) should then be, 'till he come whose it is' (RM). The Jewish Targums paraphrase thus: 'until the time when the King Messiah comes to whom it belongeth.' On the rendering given above, the whole verse foretells that Judah would retain authority until the advent of the rightful ruler, the Messiah, to whom all peoples would gather. And, broadly speaking, it may be said that the last traces of Jewish legislative power (as vested in the Sanhedrim) did not disappear until the coming of Christ and the destruction of Jerusalem, from which time His kingdom was set up among men.   Gathering of the people] RV 'obedience of the peoples.' Note the world-wide rule implied.   11, 12. These verses dwell on the fertility of the land of Judah. There were famous vineyards at Hebron and Engedi, as well as pasture lands about Tekoa and Carmel.

13. Zebulun shall dwell] The blessing is connected with the word Zebulun, 'dwelling.' The land of this tribe was between Asher and Naphtali. It may have touched the coast-land of Phœnicia represented here by Sidon. So in Dt 33 19 it is said that Zebulun should 'suck of the abundance of the sea,' profiting by maritime traffic : cp. Ezk 27.

14, 15. Issachar occupied part of Galilee and the fertile plain of Jezreel.   Between two burdens] RV 'between the sheepfolds': as at Jg 5 16, which see. 'The bright side of the saying is that Issachar will become a robust and hardy race (a strong ass) and receive a pleasant country inviting to repose. The dark side is that through his tendency to gain and comfort he will rather submit to the yoke of foreign sway than risk his people and possessions by warlike efforts (a servant unto tribute)' (Delitzsch). A number of Cana-anite towns maintained themselves independent and powerful in this tribe.

16. Again a play on the name of the tribe, for Dan means 'judge.' Though small in territory it should retain its tribal independence and self-government : cp. Dt 33 22.

17. Dan shall be a serpent] or, 'May Dan be,' etc., a wish for the tribe's success in war: cp. the conquest of Laish, Jg 18 27. The territory of Dan lay between Ephraim and Simeon. The Danites were hard pressed by the Philistines, and part of the tribe emigrated to Laish in the N. of the Holy Land, and called it Dan.   An adder in the path, that biteth the horse heels] 'What the poet por-

trays is not as in the case of Judah an open contest decided by superior strength, but the insidious efforts of the weaker against the stronger' (D.).

18. The connexion of this verse with the preceding is uncertain. Kalisch says, 'the poet, identifying himself with the oppressed and embarrassed tribe, utters in its name, with mingled reliance and resignation, the fervent prayer "In hope of Thy help, O Lord."'

19. The name Gad is here connected with a Hebrew word meaning a troop or marauding band. The Gadites were settled E. of Jordan, in the land of Gilead. They were much oppressed by the Ammonites whom Jephthah conquered : see Jg 10 and 11: cp. Dt 33 20.

20. The tribe of Asher settled along the productive land on the coast between Mt. Carmel and Lebanon.   Shall be fat] Asher was famous for its produce of olive oil: see on Dt 33 24.

21. A more probable rendering of this v., supported by LXX, is 'Naphtali is a spreading terebinth producing beautiful branches.' The tribe was settled in a fertile district between Lebanon and the Sea of Galilee: cp. Dt 33 23.

22–26. The blessing of Joseph. The branches are Ephraim and Manasseh.

23. The archers] perhaps Canaanite and Arab peoples bordering on these tribes.

24. From thence, etc.] or, 'By the name of the Shepherd, the Stone of Israel.' The name 'Rock' is often given to God in OT.: cp. Moses' Song, Dt 32 4, 18, 31, and Pss 89 94 95.

25. Blessings of heaven] Earthly prosperity of all kinds, rain and sunshine from heaven, springs from the earth, fruitfulness both of man and beast.   26. The blessing of Moses on the tribes of Ephraim and Manasseh, Dt 33 13, may be studied in connexion with this difficult v. Render with RM, 'The blessings of thy father have prevailed above (exceed) the blessings of the ancient mountains, the desirable things of the everlasting hills.' 'The meaning is that the blessings comprised things higher than merely the admirable products of the lovely mountain country (Ephraim, Gilead, Bashan), i.e. doubtless power, respect, honour, and political consequence, and, above all, the promises. In bestowing these on Joseph, Jacob makes him his father's successor, and names him *Nazir* among his brethren, one separated and consecrated, a prince' (D.).

27. Benjamin was a very warlike tribe. Saul, the first king of Israel, was a Benjamite; and so was that other Saul who 'fought a good fight' under his great Captain, 2 Tim 4 7.

33. He .. was gathered unto his people] his shade joined those of his forefathers in the other world. The expression may be held to embody a rudimentary hope of immortality : see on 25 8.

CHAPTER 50
The Burial of Jacob, and Death of Joseph

2. For the importance attached by the Egyptians to the preservation of the corpse see on 40 19. The process, which was so thorough that mummies of Joseph's time may be seen in our museums in a state of good preservation, was briefly as follows. The brain and intestines were removed, and the stomach cleansed and filled with spices (embalmed). The body was then steeped in a mixture of salt and soda (called *natron*), for forty or more days, to preserve it from decay. Next, it was bound up in strips of linen smeared with a sort of gum ; and finally it was placed in a wooden case, shaped like the human body, and deposited in a sepulchral chamber.

4. When the days of his mourning were past] It could not have been that cause which prevented Joseph from going personally to Pharaoh. 'More probably it was not usual to take steps in a matter which personally concerned the minister, without the mediation of other exalted personages' (D.).

10. Threshingfloor of Atad] unknown.

Beyond Jordan] i.e. E. of Jordan, implying that the writer is in Canaan: see on Dt 1 1.

11. Abel-mizraim] 'the meadow of Egypt.' 'The name may be historically explained owing to the long period of Egyptian domination in Palestine in pre-Mosaic times, as we learn from the Tel-el Amarna letters, but the narrator connects the name with Ebel, "mourning"' (D.).

19. *Am* **I in the place of God ?]** i.e. to judge or to punish.

20. The selling of Joseph by his brethren had been a sinful action, but through his coming to Egypt God had brought about a great blessing to many. So He often brings good out of evil, though evil is not to be done in order that good may come. Joseph himself here sums up the great lesson of his career, so far at least as his brethren are concerned.

23. Were brought up upon] RV 'were born upon.' Joseph took the newborn children on his lap and so recognised them as his descendants: see 30 3.

25. Cp. Heb 11 22, 'By faith Joseph when he died made mention of the departure of the children of Israel, and gave commandment concerning his bones.' Joseph's instructions were carried out at the time of the exodus (Ex 13 19) and his body was buried at Shechem: see Josh 24 32.

EXODUS
INTRODUCTION

1. Title and Contents. The second book of the Pentateuch is designated in Hebrew, from its opening words, *Elleh Shemoth*, 'These are the names,' or simply *Shemoth*, 'The names.' *Exodus* is the Latin form of the title prefixed to the book by the Greek translators of the OT. It means 'exit' or 'departure,' and refers to the main event which the book records, viz. the departure of the Israelites from the land of Egypt.

The book of Exodus continues the narrative of Genesis and carries it down to the erection of the Tabernacle at Sinai, in the first month of the second year of the departure from Egypt. It is mainly historical, but contains important legislative matter. It falls naturally into three great divisions: **Part 1. Israel in Egypt : their Oppression and Deliverance, chs. 1–15** 21. In this section the events leading up to the deliverance of the Israelites by the hand of Moses are described. **Part 2. The March from the Red Sea to Mount Sinai, chs. 15** 22**–18** 27. **Part 3. Israel**

at Sinai, chs. 19–40. This last section really extends from Ex 19 to Nu 10 10, and covers in all a period of eleven months. During this time the people were encamped in the vicinity of Mt. Sinai, and were engaged in receiving that Law, both of morals and ceremonies, which was the basis of the covenant between them and Jehovah, and the foundation of their distinctive national and religious life.

2. Origin and Composition. The question as to the authorship of the Pentateuch is discussed in a separate article. Here it will suffice to say a few words as to the confirmation given to the history and legislation contained in Exodus from other sources.

With regard to the **historical** part of the book, while it cannot be said that the residence of the Israelites in Egypt and their departure from it are directly confirmed by the records of profane history and the monuments, what we know from the latter as to the history and condition of Egypt in early times at least leaves room for the biblical account and harmonises with it. (a) The Pharaoh of the Oppression is usually supposed to have been Rameses II, and the Pharaoh of the exodus his son and successor Merenptah, who began to reign about the year 1300 B.C. Reckoning back 430 years, the extent of the sojourn in Egypt, we reach a time when Egypt was ruled by an alien dynasty, called the 'Hyksôs' or Shepherd kings. These were of Asiatic origin, and would be naturally inclined to favour the Hebrews. There can be little doubt that the Pharaoh to whom Joseph was Prime Minister was one of these Hyksôs kings. A famine is recorded to have occurred during the reign of one of the last of this dynasty, Apepi, who may have been the Pharaoh of Joseph. But the Hyksôs were expelled by a native Egyptian dynasty who would look with disfavour on everything Asiatic. This revolution, with the consequent change of treatment afforded to the Hebrew settlers in Egypt, agrees with what is said at the beginning of the book of Exodus that 'there arose up a new king over Egypt, which knew not Joseph.' See 1⁸ and note in the commentary there. (b) Again we read that the Israelites built for Pharaoh store cities, Pithom and Raamses. The former has been discovered at Tel el Maskhuta, and is found to have been a store city built by Rameses II and dedicated to Tum, the god of the setting sun. The site of Raamses has not been discovered, but the city is mentioned in the Egyptian texts as having been built by Rameses II (see on 1¹¹). (c) Egyptian history is silent on the plagues and the incidents accompanying the exodus, but that is not surprising when we take into account the little that we know of the history of Egypt, and the improbability that the monuments would be employed to perpetuate the memory of such untoward events. The biblical account, however, is full of local colour. The plagues are just such as might well occur in Egypt, being for the most part aggravations of evils natural to the climate of Egypt, and owing much of their force to the fact that they strike at the superstitions of the Egyptians. (d) The route of the exodus and the various halting-places are not fully identified, but so far nothing has been discovered that cannot be harmonised with the biblical account. The discovery that the Red Sea at one time extended much further north than it does at present, removes much of the difficulty formerly attaching to the account of its crossing. So far, then, the biblical account has been confirmed instead of contradicted by modern discovery. It is not unreasonable to expect that, as discovery proceeds, further confirmation will be obtained and obscurities removed. For the present we have every reason to believe that in the main the story

of the origin of the Israelitish nation is trustworthy.

As regards the **legislation** contained in Exodus, it is generally admitted that at least the Ten Commandments, the Book of the Covenant (chs. 20–23), and the laws in c. 34, may well go back to the time of Moses. To what extent the laws he promulgated were modified and expanded in later times, we may never be able precisely to determine; but the investigations of most recent times seem to point to the possibility of ascribing more, instead of less, of the legislation of Israel to Moses than was formerly allowed. It has been usual, e.g. to argue that the legislation of the Pentateuch is too advanced to have originated at such an early period as the exodus. But the force of this argument is considerably weakened when it is found that the legislation of Israel, both moral and ceremonial, has many points of contact with that of the earlier civilisations of Babylonia and Egypt. It has come to light in recent times that Babylonian and Egyptian influences extended over Canaan and the Sinaitic peninsula before the time of the exodus, and that Babylonia and Egypt had much to do with each other at a very early date. Consequently, laws and practices, which were supposed to have first come into existence at a comparatively late period in the history of Israel may really have been introduced much earlier. See on Nu 13²¹. The question of the originality of the legislation of Moses has quite recently come prominently to the front as a result of investigations and discoveries made in connexion with the earlier religions of Egypt and Babylonia. It is an undeniable fact that many of the laws and rites of the Pentateuch bear a resemblance to what we find among these other nations of antiquity. The Babylonians, e.g. observed laws of 'clean and unclean'; they kept the seventh day rest; they knew of peace offerings, heave offerings, and sacrifices for sin. The Egyptians practised circumcision and offered incense; the description of the tabernacle is full of allusions to Egyptian customs; the strict rules for the purifying of priests, the ephod of the high priest, the pomegranate decoration of the hem of his robe, his breastplate and his mitre, had all their counterpart among the Egyptians. The newly discovered Code of Hammurabi displays many features similar to the legislation of Moses: see art. 'Laws of Hammurabi.' Of course resemblance does not prove derivation; but even should it have to be admitted that many elements in the moral and ceremonial law of the Israelites were taken from other civilisations, this need occasion neither surprise nor dismay. God is not the God of the Hebrews only; 'He has made of one blood all nations of men to dwell on all the face of the earth,' and it is not strange that the Gentiles who have not the (Mosaic) Law, should 'do by nature the things contained in the Law' (Ro 2 14). What is distinctive in the Mosaic legislation is the new spirit which it exhibits. It is emphatically ethical; and it lifts morality to a higher plane, in accordance with its fundamental conception of a spiritual and holy God, who enters into a covenant relationship with His people on a moral basis. The aim of the Mosaic legislation was 'not so much to create a new system as to give a new significance to that which had already long existed among Semitic races, and to lay the foundation of a higher symbolism leading to a more spiritual worship.' The glory of the Mosaic law, and its indefeasible claim to divine inspiration, reside in the fact that it took existing customs and ceremonies and infused into them a new spirit, elevating, purifying, and transforming them.

3. Religious Value. It is well nigh impossible to overestimate the religious value of the book of Exodus. Nowhere else save in the Christian revelation is there to be found so sublime a conception of the nature of God, or a loftier and purer idea of morality as springing out of man's relationship to Him. In the OT. itself Exodus holds a fundamental position. It depicts the early civic and religious development of a people destined to occupy a unique place among the nations, and to exert upon the world the very greatest spiritual influence. In this book we see the beginning of the fulfilment of the promise made to Abraham, the original ancestor of the Hebrew people, 'in thy seed shall all the nations of the earth be blessed.' The events which it records in connexion with the birth of the nation, and its deliverance from bondage, stamped themselves indelibly on the memory and imagination of succeeding generations, and are frequently employed by prophets and psalm-writers, to enforce lessons of duty and faithfulness, trust and hope, warning and encouragement : see e.g. Hos 2 15 12 9 13 4 Am 2 10 Mic 6 3, 4 Ps 78 12 f. 81 8 f. 105 23 f. 106 114 136. Much of the subsequent teaching of the OT. is but the interpretation and enforcement of the spiritual and moral truths communicated to Israel at the time of the exodus.

The great underlying idea of the book is that of revelation. God is everywhere represented as in the act of self-manifestation. He manifests His power over nature, in Egypt, at the Red Sea, and at Mt. Sinai. In every event His hand is discernible. 'He made known His ways unto Moses, His acts unto the children of Israel.' He constantly speaks to Moses, giving to His servant His counsel in times of emergency, and the knowledge of

His nature and will to be communicated to the people. We cannot read the book without being impressed with the writer's conviction that God, while exalted far above the comprehension of His creatures, who are able to see, not His face, but only His 'back parts' (33 23), does not dwell remote from the world, but is everywhere present and active in nature and in history. This sense of the personal agency of God is expressed frequently in a very bold and anthropomorphic way, somewhat startling to us with our more abstract and spiritual conception of the divine nature and the method of its operations : see e.g. 4 24 14 24, 25 24 10, 11. In their more fervid utterances, OT. writers in general do not hesitate to transfer human conditions, actions, and passions to the Divine Being, though the extent to which they do so diminishes with the course of time. The frequency with which this form of thought appears in Exodus is an eloquent testimony to the intensity of religious feeling that pervades the book. To us, whose conception of God tends always to be more and more abstract and attenuated, this insistence on the truth of the nearness of God and His active interference in the world of human affairs is not the least necessary and valuable lesson conveyed by the book of Exodus.

Another characteristic and fundamental idea of the book is that Israel is the chosen people of Jehovah. It is nowhere asserted that Jehovah is the God of the Hebrews only. He rules over the land of Egypt, and He is the Creator and Lord of nature. All the earth is His (19 5). But He has chosen Israel to be 'a peculiar treasure' unto Him above all people (see on 19 3-6), and He enters into a covenant with them on the basis of the moral law (24 3-8). This idea of the election, or selection, of Israel runs all through the OT., and even passes over to the Christian Church under the 'new covenant' (see on 19 6). It is essentially an election, not to privilege, but to duty. Israel is chosen, enlightened, instructed, disciplined, in order to communicate to the world the knowledge of God and prepare the way for the perfect revelation of His grace in Christ. It is a noble idea, that of a theocracy, a 'kingdom of God,' a people who are each and all 'priests' unto God (19 6). Hence the duty of personal holiness and national righteousness ; hence the minute ceremonial system, with its detailed prescriptions regarding the tabernacle, its furniture, the priesthood, sacrifice, etc., all emphasising the lesson that God is holy and must be served and worshipped by a holy people.

The book of Exodus has been in all ages a source whence both Jews and Christians have drawn lessons of encouragement and warning, applicable to the individual soul no less than to the Church of God. The bondage in Egypt, the deliverance, and the experiences of Israel in the wilderness, have very naturally been regarded as types of man's deliverance from the bondage of sin and error, and of God's grace and providence in guiding, defending, and supplying the wants of His people all through the pilgrimage of life. In Israel men have seen themselves, their need of redemption, their sin and weakness, their continual dependence on God, and their proneness to forget and mistrust Him to whom they owe everything; while in the record of God's gracious dealings with Israel they have read their own experience of the power and grace of the Covenant God whose name is still 'The LORD, the LORD, a God full of compassion and gracious, slow to anger, and plenteous in mercy and truth; keeping mercy for thousands, forgiving iniquity and transgression and sin: and that will by no means clear the guilty,' and whose promise to those who trust in Him is still, 'My presence shall go with thee, and I will give thee rest' (Ex 34 6,7 RV 33 14).

PART 1
(Chs. 1–15 21) ISRAEL IN EGYPT: THEIR OPPRESSION AND DELIVERANCE

CHAPTER 1
OPPRESSION OF THE ISRAELITES

5. Seventy souls] Jacob himself is included in the number : cp. Gn 46 8-27. Of the seventy, sixty-eight were males. If to the direct descendants of Jacob we add the wives of his sons and grandsons, and the husbands of his daughters and grand-daughters, and all their servants with their families, it appears that the total number of those who entered Egypt was very considerable, several hundreds if not thousands. This fact, as well as the acknowledged prolificness of the Hebrew nation, serves to account for their rapid increase in Egypt. At the time of the exodus they must have numbered about three millions : see on 12 37. **7.** Observe the number of words denoting increase. The land is the land of Goshen in the Delta of the Nile.

8. This verse marks the turn of the tide in the fortunes of Israel. Hitherto they have been tolerated and honoured ; now they are feared and oppressed. The change of treatment is here said to be connected with a change in the government of Egypt. As mentioned in the Introduction, Egypt for several hundred years was ruled by an alien dynasty, called the Hyksôs, or Shepherd kings. These were Asiatics, and would therefore naturally tolerate the Hebrew race with whom they may have had affinity. But the Hyksôs were at length expelled, and a native dynasty once more occupied the throne of Egypt. It is usually supposed that this new dynasty is meant by the new king .. which knew not Joseph. One of the most famous kings of the nineteenth dynasty was Rameses II (about 1340 B.C.). He was a great architect, and many monuments remain to attest his greatness, such as the temples at Luxor, Abydos, etc. He is generally held to be the Pharaoh of the Oppression, and his son and successor (Merenptah or Mineptah) the Pharaoh of the exodus: see on 14 28. Against this, however, is to be considered the fact that this Merenptah has left monuments in which he records that he has invaded Palestine and destroyed the Israelites, who are represented as living there at his time. Accordingly the oppression and exodus of the Israelites are by some placed much earlier than the time of Rameses and Merenptah, as early as the 15th cent. B.C.

11. Treasure cities] store cities, situated on the frontier, and serving both as strongholds for defence against invasion and as military depots of provisions and arms. **Pithom**] i.e. the 'Abode of the Setting Sun,' has been identified with Tel-el Maskhuta, between Kassassin and Ismaïliyeh. The walls of this ancient city are found to have been constructed of bricks made of Nile mud and chopped straw. **Raamses**] or Rameses, has not yet been identified, but is supposed to have been situated at the modern Tel-el Kebir. It was in existence at the time of Joseph, as appears from Gn 47 11, so that it was probably repaired or enlarged at a later date. **12. The more they multiplied**] The whole history of the exodus and sojourn in the wilderness is designed to show that nothing can destroy the people of Israel, or thwart the divine purpose with regard to them. **14. Service in the field**] This refers to the construction of irrigation canals and embankments, as well as to the making of bricks for building. With what rigour the system of forced labour was employed may be judged from the fact recorded by Herodotus that 120,000 workmen lost their lives in the construction of a canal connecting the Nile and the Red Sea in the time of Pharaoh Necho. In modern times Mohammed Ali's canal from the Nile to Alexandria cost 20,000 lives.

15-22. Failing to weaken or diminish the Israelites by such severe labour, the Egyptian king has recourse to a more direct method, that of infanticide. He orders the slaughter of all the Hebrew male children at birth. This also fails, Pharaoh's own daughter becoming one of the links in the chain of deliverance

4

With Pharaoh's edict may be compared that of Herod ordering the Massacre of the Innocents of Bethlehem (Mt 2¹⁶).

15. The names of only two of the midwives have been preserved. These two were probably connected with the royal palace. **16. Stools**] RV 'birthstool.'

19. There was, no doubt, some truth in what the midwives said, though their womanly instincts led them to evade the unnatural command of the king. **21. Made them houses**] i.e. blessed them with marriage and many descendants : cp. Ruth 4¹¹ 2 S 7²⁷ 1 K 11³⁸.

CHAPTER 2
BIRTH AND EARLY LIFE OF MOSES

1. The names of the father and mother of Moses were Amram and Jochebed respectively (see 6²⁰). Two children were born to them before Moses. The oldest was a daughter called Miriam (i.e. Mary), who was a young woman at the time when Moses was born (see v. 8); and the second was a son, Aaron, who was born three years before Moses (see 7⁷) and presumably before Pharaoh's exterminating edict : cp. Nu 26⁵⁹. **2. Hid him three months**] This defiance of the king's edict is called an act of faith in Heb 11²³. **3. Ark of bulrushes**] a chest made of the stalks of the papyrus reed which grew at the side of the Nile and in marshy places. The stalks and leaves of papyrus were employed in the manufacture of various articles, such as boats (Isa 18²), sails, mats, ropes, and paper. This last, which gets its name from the papyrus, was made of thin strips of the inner bark pasted together, and compressed. The slime used as a watertight coating for the ark was bitumen, imported into Egypt from Mesopotamia and the vicinity of the Dead Sea ; it was employed as mortar in building and as a preservative in the process of embalming. **5. Daughter of Pharaoh**] Josephus calls her Thermutis, but Eusebius calls her Merris. The Nile was regarded as a sacred river, and bathing in its waters was part of a religious ceremony : cp. 7¹⁵. **10**. The mother kept the child probably till he was weaned, which would be two or perhaps three years. He was then adopted by Pharaoh's daughter and would receive the education of an Egyptian prince. St. Stephen says that 'Moses was learned in all the wisdom of the Egyptians and was mighty in words and in deeds.' Josephus says that Moses became general of the Egyptian army and defeated the Ethiopians, also that Pharaoh's daughter, having no child of her own, intended to make him her father's successor. The name Moses, which she gave him, is an Egyptian, not a Hebrew word, and means 'child' or 'son.' It

appears in names like Rameses, Thothmes, etc. It is only therefore by a play upon words that it is connected with the Hebrew word mashah, ' to draw out.'

11. In those days] According to Ac 7²³ Moses was at this time ' full forty years old.' This incident shows that the patriotism of Moses had not been destroyed by his Egyptian upbringing, also that he was by nature possessed of an impatient and ardent spirit which required the long discipline of the sojourn in Midian to school him into that strength and forbearance necessary in a leader of men : see on 3¹¹. At the same time, it is made clear that his countrymen were not yet ready for emancipation. **15. Land of Midian**] The south-eastern part of the peninsula of Sinai. There is reason to believe, however, that the home, or headquarters, of the Midianites, who were probably a nomadic tribe, lay outside the peninsula on the E. side of the Gulf of Akaba : see Gn 37²⁵ and on Nu 22⁴. **16**. The priest or prince of Midian. In early times, before the multiplication of ritual necessitated a separate religious order, the head or chief of the clan performed priestly functions : see on 19²². He is called Reuel in v. 18 and Jethro in c. 18, while in Jg 4¹¹, and perhaps also in Nu 10²⁹, he is called Hobab. On this apparent confusion see the note there. **17**. In the East wells are of great importance, and frequent disputes arise over rights of watering : see e.g. Gn 26²⁰⁻²². **21**. Moses stayed in Midian forty years (cp. 7⁷), so that his life falls into three equal portions. The first forty years he spent in Egypt (Ac 7²³), the second forty in Midian, and the last forty in the wilderness (cp. Dt 34⁷). It may be observed, however, that in Scripture forty is frequently used as a round number. Here the forty years signify a generation : so that Moses simply waited in Midian till a new set of people arose in Egypt : see e.g. Gn 7⁴ Ex 24¹⁸ 34²⁸ Nu 13²⁵ 14³³ 1 S 17¹⁶ 1 K 19⁸. With the preparatory sojourn of Moses in Midian may be compared that of the Baptist in the wilderness (Lk 1⁸⁰) and of St. Paul in Arabia (Gal 1¹⁷). **Zipporah**] see on Nu 12¹. **22. Gershom**] The name is derived either from the Heb. ger, ' a sojourner,' and sham, ' there,' or from the verb garash, ' to expel.' In either case it shows that the heart of Moses was with his countrymen in Egypt. Another son, Eliezer, is mentioned in 18⁴ : cp. 1 Ch 23¹⁶,¹⁷.

23. The king of Egypt] see on 1⁸.

24. His covenant] see Gn 12⁷ 15¹⁸ 17¹⁻¹⁴ 26³,⁴ 28¹³⁻¹⁵. When it is said here, as elsewhere, that God remembered His covenant, it is not implied that He had previously forgotten it, but that the opportunity had now come of fulfilling His merciful purpose. **25. Had respect unto**] RV 'took knowledge of.'

CHAPTER 3

THE CALL OF MOSES AND HIS COMMISSION TO BE THE DELIVERER OF ISRAEL

1. Horeb] The names Horeb and Sinai seem to be synonymous, though it has been suggested that Horeb is the name given to the entire mountain range, while Sinai denotes the particular mountain where the Law was given. Assuming that the Pentateuch is composed of different documents, it is better to believe that Horeb is the name used by one set of writers and Sinai by another. Horeb is here called **the mountain of God** by anticipation. The reason of the appellation follows in c. 19. At the same time, it is not improbable that there was a sanctuary on Mt. Sinai from earliest times, connected with the worship of the Babylonian moon-god Sin. **2. Angel of the LORD**] i.e. of Jehovah (see on v. 13). In v. 4 it is Jehovah Himself who speaks ; in 23 20, 21, 22 divine attributes are ascribed to the 'angel of the Lord,' God's 'name' is in him (see on 3 13), and his voice is identified with that of God. It would therefore appear that the Angel of Jehovah is not a created angel but Jehovah Himself in the act of self-manifestation : see on 'my presence' in 33 14. On the other hand, there are passages like 32 34 where the angel seems to be distinguished from Jehovah, the explanation being probably that the mere manifestation of God gives rise to a distinction between what He is in Himself, and what He is in His special appearance. In this distinction between God in Himself and God in self-manifestation, we may see an adumbration of the Incarnation of God in Christ. By many, the Angel of the Lord is identified with the Second Person of the Trinity. It is to be observed that on this occasion Moses saw no human form : cp. Dt 4 15. **In a flame of fire**] Fire is a frequent emblem of God in the Scriptures on account of its illuminating, purifying, and destructive properties, and appears as the accompaniment and indication of His presence : see 13 21 19 18 24 17 Dt 4 24 Ps 97 3 Ezk 1 4 Ac 2 3, etc. On this occasion the bush, though enveloped in flame, was not consumed. This may be symbolical of the graciousness of God who spares the unworthy and restrains the fierceness of His anger while He communicates with them : see on 24 9-11. **5.** Every place where God manifests Himself is holy. To take off the shoes is an ancient as well as modern way of expressing reverence in the East. The Mohammedan takes off his shoes when he enters the mosque. The action symbolises the removal of the defilement caused by sin or contact with the world on entering the presence of Him with whom 'evil cannot dwell.'

6. The patriarchs are mentioned to show that it is no new or unknown God who speaks, but One who made a covenant with the fathers of the nation and who still remembers it. These words are cited by our Lord as a proof that God's people continue to live after death : cp. Mk 12 26, 27. **Moses hid his face**] cp. the act of Elijah, 1 K 19 13, and see on 19 9 33 18. Reverence is not only due to God, but is the first condition of receiving divine truth. God manifests Himself to the lowly. **8. Flowing with milk and honey**] A proverbial expression indicating fertility and abundance. On the tribes inhabiting Canaan see on Gn 10 Nu 34 1-15. **11.** With the hesitation of Moses compare that of Jeremiah, Jer 1 4-8. Forty years before Moses was more self-confident (cp. Ac 7 25). In the long sojourn in Midian he learned to mistrust himself, and was on that account all the more fitted to be the instrument of Him whose 'strength is made perfect in weakness.' Moses here puts forward four excuses, each of which is in turn overborne. He pleads (1) that he is personally unfit (vv. 11, 12), (2) that the Israelites will not know who sent him (vv. 13–22), (3) that they will not believe that Jehovah has sent him (4 1-9), and (4) that he does not possess the gift of persuasive eloquence (4 10-17). **12. I will be with thee**] The guarantee of fitness and success : cp our Lord's promise, Mt 28 20. **A token**] The token was still in the future : cp. 1 S 2 34 2 K 19 29 Isa 7 14. Experience corroborates the ventures of faith. For the fulfilment of this sign see c. 19.

13. What is his name?] The name of God is His revealed character : see 23 21 34 5-7. Here God reveals Himself by the name Jehovah. As already explained (Gn 2 4) the word ' Jehovah' is the result of a combination of the consonants of the original name (the consonants alone are written in ancient Hebrew) and the vowels of its substitute 'Adonai.' Most scholars believe that the original form of the name was 'Jahve' or 'Yahve.' Now this resembles in form the third person singular masculine imperfect of a Hebrew verb, and is here connected with the verb hawa or haya, 'to be.' God calls Himself 'Ehyeh,' i.e. I AM. When He is named by others, He is 'Jahve,' i.e. He is. The name denotes the absolute self-existence of God. He alone truly exists : cp. Dt 4 35 Isa 45 6 Rev 1 4. Some scholars, however, prefer to take the word as a future, ' I will be,' in which case the name expresses rather the faithfulness of God, the assurance that He will be with His people as their helper and deliverer. Others, again, take the word to be the causative form of the verb, in which case it will mean, ' He who causes to be,' ' the Creator': see RM and on 6 3 **15. My memorial**] i.e. my name, the designation by which I will be remembered.

16. Elders of Israel] The heads or representatives of the tribes and families. It appears from this that even in Egypt the Israelites had some kind of organisation. In the Pentateuch, when the people of Israel are addressed, it is frequently the 'elders' who are meant. They are the usual medium of communication between Moses and the people, and act as the representatives of the latter : see e.g. 17⁵ 19⁷ Dt27¹ 31⁹,²⁸.

18. God of the Hebrews] To the Israelites God is 'Jehovah, the God of your fathers' (v. 16), a designation which would appeal to their hearts as it reminded them of God's covenant with their forefathers and His faithfulness to it. See on v. 6. But to Pharaoh He is simply 'the God of the Hebrews.'

Three days' journey into the wilderness] i.e. most probably to Horeb, the 'wilderness' being a general term for the region lying between Egypt and Palestine. There was no intention to deceive Pharaoh in this request. Had Pharaoh been willing to grant the people entire release this would have been asked at first. But God, knowing that Pharaoh was not willing to let them go, enjoined Moses to make only this moderate request, so as to emphasise the obstinacy of the king.

19. No, not by a mighty hand] This means either 'in spite of the fact that I will lay My hand heavily upon him' ; or better, with a slight change of reading, as LXX has it, 'unless I lay My hand heavily upon him.'

22. Shall borrow] RV 'shall ask.' The word is the common Hebrew verb meaning 'to ask,' as used e.g. in Jg5²⁵ 1K3¹¹ 2K2¹⁰ Ps122⁶, where there is no idea of asking under a promise of giving back what is received. **Spoil**] The same word is rendered 'recover' in 1S30²², which suggests that if there was any 'borrowing' it was on the part of the Egyptians, who had been taking the labour of the Israelites without any recompense. For the fulfilment, see c. 12³⁵,³⁶.

CHAPTER 4

Signs Attesting the Commission of Moses. His Return to Egypt

Moses still hesitates, and now objects that the people will not believe him when he tells them that Jehovah has sent him. He is granted the power of working three signs by way of substantiating his commission.

2. A rod] probably his shepherd's staff.

3. Fled from before it] A graphic trait, showing that the change was real, and that Moses was not prepared for it. **4. By the tail**] Snake charmers usually take snakes by the neck to prevent them biting. It is much more dangerous to seize them by the tail. When Moses did so with impunity his own faith would be strengthened as well as that of the people : cp. our Lord's promise. Mk16¹⁸. **6. Leprous as snow**] i.e. as white as snow. Leprosy was common in Egypt. The form here meant is that in which the skin becomes glossy, white, and callous. This is the worst form of leprosy and was regarded as incurable. This incident, taken together with the fact that the white leprosy was most common among the Israelites, may have given rise to the tradition, related by the Egyptian priest and historian Manetho, and quoted by Josephus, that Moses was a leper, and that the Israelites were expelled from Egypt because they were afflicted with the same disease.

9. The river] the Nile. This sign is similar to the first of the plagues (see 7²⁰), with the difference that here only part of the water is changed on being poured out on the dry land.

10. Moses now pleads his want of eloquence. Jewish tradition says that he had an actual impediment in his speech, being unable to pronounce the labials. His words here, however, do not necessarily imply any positive defect of this kind. He wishes to be excused, and urges that a more eloquent man than he is required to persuade the king of Egypt to release Israel, and the Israelites also to trust themselves to the guidance of Jehovah. For this he is rebuked, but not excused. Aaron is given to him as spokesman. **12.** Cp. Jer1⁶⁻⁹ Lk21¹⁴,¹⁵. **13, 14.** This request is equivalent to a refusal to go. Moses says, 'send some one else, but not me.' Accordingly 'the anger of Jehovah was kindled against him.' His punishment takes the form of diminished privilege. Aaron henceforth shares in his distinction. **The Levite**] This means not merely the 'descendant of Levi,' but 'the priest,' as the tribe of Levi was afterwards consecrated to the service of the sanctuary. The title is here used by anticipation.

16. Cp. 7¹. **Instead of God**] Because Aaron would receive God's message at the mouth of Moses. **17. Signs**] RV 'the signs,' i.e. the appointed signs.

18-26. Moses takes leave of Jethro and returns with his wife and children to Egypt.

19. Cp. Mt2¹⁹. **20. His sons**] Only one has been previously mentioned, but a second had been born in Midian : see 2²².

21. I will harden his heart] God proposes to harden Pharaoh's heart, in order to have the opportunity of displaying His power in the deliverance of His people, and exhibiting His character to the Egyptians. Some take the expression as due to the Eastern and fatalistic way of regarding all that happens in the world as the result of the direct intervention of God. On this interpretation it is simply synonymous with 'Pharaoh's heart was hardened' (7²²), and 'Pharaoh hardened his heart' (8¹⁵). Where we speak vaguely of the operation of moral and physical laws and of secondary causes, the Oriental frankly says that 'God did this.' He says 'kismet': 'it was fated to be': see on v. 24. We prefer to say that the hardening of Pharaoh's heart was due to his own obstinacy in refusing to yield to the warnings he received; the Eastern moralist means the same when he says that God hardened his heart. The inevitable result is regarded as the divine purpose. It happens in accordance with laws which God Himself has ordained. 'He will not' leads inevitably to 'he cannot': cp. Ro 1²⁸. It should be observed that this, however, is not equivalent to a denial of moral responsibility. It is a man's own fault if he allow himself to be entangled in this chain of inevitable consequences. He is, therefore, responsible for the ultimate hardening of his heart through repeated acts of wilful transgression: see on 10³. **22. Israel is my son,** *even* **my firstborn**] This expresses God's choice of Israel as His peculiar people: cp. Dt 14¹,² Hos 11¹ Jer 31⁹, and see on 19⁵. The term 'firstborn' indicates the high honour conferred upon Israel, and at the same time contains a hint of the ultimate inclusion of the Gentiles also in the covenant. **23. For the fulfilment of** this warning see 12²⁹,³⁰.

24. In the inn] RV 'lodging-place,' not necessarily a building. **Sought to kill him**] This probably means no more than that Moses was struck with some grievous sickness and was in danger of death. It is another example of the Eastern way of attributing whatever happens to the direct interposition of God, referred to in the note on v. 21. It would appear from this mysterious incident that Moses had neglected to circumcise his youngest son, on account perhaps of the mother's objection to the rite. Circumcision was not peculiar to the Israelites, but they alone circumcised infants. What Zipporah objected to, therefore, may not have been the rite itself, but its performance at such an early age. But now seeing the danger her husband was in, and recognising that his sickness was the chastisement of disobedience, she overcame her reluctance and performed the ceremony herself, with the result that Moses' life was spared (v. 26). The incident is designed to show the importance of circumcision as the sign of the covenant between God and His people and the sin and danger of neglecting it. **25. A sharp stone**] Even in later times than this flint knives were employed in circumcision, being regarded as purer than knives of metal: see Josh 5², where 'sharp knives' should be 'knives of flint,' as in RV. Flint knives were

used by the Egyptians in opening bodies for embalming. They are said to be carried by the Bedouin of the Syrian desert at the present day. **A bloody husband** *art* **thou to me**] RV 'a bridegroom of blood.' As the Jews to this day call a circumcised child a 'bridegroom of the circumcision' it is possible that Zipporah's exclamation was addressed to the child. It is usually, however, understood as addressed to Moses, whom his wife reproaches as being the cause of bloodshed. **26. He let him go**] i.e. God let Moses go, removed his sickness and allowed him to recover. It was probably at this time that Moses sent his wife and children back to the house of his father-in-law. They rejoined him at Sinai after the exodus from Egypt: see 18²,⁵.

27. The mount of God] Horeb or Sinai: see on 3¹. The two brothers had not met for forty years previous to this.

CHAPTERS 5–11
THE CONTEST WITH PHARAOH

CHAPTER 5
INCREASE OF THE OPPRESSION

1. Pharaoh] probably P. Merenptah. See on 1⁸. His court may have been at Zoan or Tanis during the events that ensued: cp. Ps 78¹²,⁴³. **The LORD God of Israel**] Heb. 'Jehovah the God of Israel': see on 3¹³,¹⁸. Similarly in the next v. Pharaoh says, 'Who is Jehovah?..I know not Jehovah.' Jehovah not being known and worshipped in Egypt, Pharaoh does not acknowledge His right to command him. **3. See on 3¹⁸. 4. Let the people**] i.e. hinder them, as in Isa 43¹³ Ro 1¹³ 2 Th 2⁷. **6. The taskmasters** are the Egyptian officials, and the **officers** (lit. 'scribes') are the Hebrew clerks under them whose duty it was to keep an account of the bricks made: see v. 14. **7. Straw to make brick**] The bricks were made of Nile mud to which chopped straw was added to give it consistency. They were sometimes stamped with the name of the reigning king. Some have been found bearing the name of Rameses II, the father of Merenptah, and wooden stamps and moulds have also been discovered. **8. The tale**] i.e. the number, as in 1 S 18²⁷ 1 Ch 9²⁸. To 'tell' in Old English means to count, and is used in this sense in Gn 15⁵ 2 Ch 2² Ps 22¹⁷ 48¹² 147⁴, etc. The counter of votes in Parliament is still called the 'teller.'

12. Stubble instead of straw] RV 'stubble for straw.' The word rendered 'straw' means straw cut into short pieces and mixed with chaff. This required little labour, if any, to make it fit for use in brickmaking. What is called 'stubble' is not what we know by that name, but includes all kinds of field rubbish, small twigs, stems, roots of withered plants, etc., which were used for fuel. To make this fit for brickmaking it had not only to be gathered, but chopped up and sorted, thus entailing double labour on the part of the Israelites. **21. Our savour to be abhorred**] i.e. as we say ·to be in bad odour': cp. Gn 34 30. **22.** The faith of Moses was severely tried, seeing that what he had done by God's commandment had the effect of making matters still more grievous for the Israelites meanwhile. But the opening words of the next c. show that their 'present affliction will work a far more exceeding weight of glory.'

CHAPTER 6
The Renewal of the Promise. Genealogies of Reuben, Simeon, and Levi

1. The **strong hand** is the hand of Jehovah, not of Pharaoh. So RV renders, 'by a strong hand,' i.e. under the compelling force of Jehovah's judgments: see on 3 19.

3. The name of God Almighty] Heb. *El Shaddai*, which occurs first in the revelation made to Abraham (Gn 17 1; cp. also 28 3 48 3). It is here said that God was not known in the patriarchal times by the name Jehovah. This constitutes a difficulty, as the name has been already used in passages earlier than this, e.g. in Gn 2 4 3 4 11 1-9, etc. Two explanations have been given : (1) The use of the name Jehovah in these earlier passages may be due, not to the speakers themselves, but to the writer of those parts of the book of Genesis in which it is found, to whom it was familiar, and who used it by anticipation. (2) While the name Jehovah may have been known from earliest times, its full spiritual significance may not have been revealed or apprehended till the time of Moses. Traces of the antiquity of the name Jehovah may be found in its employment by Abraham as part of a proper name : see Gn 22 14. The name of Moses' mother, Jochebed (Ex 6 20), also contains the name Jehovah as its first element.   **5.** See on 2 24.

6. Redeem] deliver from oppression.

7. See on 19 5, 6.   **12. Uncircumcised lips**] Circumcision is the sign of consecration, so that 'uncircumcision' is used metaphorically of what is unclean or inadequate to the service of God : see on Lv 19 23.

14–27. The object of this section is to indicate the genealogy of the deliverers, Moses and Aaron. The family of Levi is therefore given in detail. Those of Reuben and Simeon are prefixed merely to show the position of the family of Levi among the sons of Jacob, and are therefore summarily described.

14. Hanoch] the Hebrew form of Enoch.
20. Jochebed] 'Jehovah is glory': see on

v. 3. Observe that marriage with a father's sister was not forbidden before the giving of the Law : see Lv 18 12. It is not improbable that the genealogy of Amram has been shortened here by the omission of certain names. Joshua, who was a younger contemporary of Moses, was of the tenth generation from Joseph : see 1 Ch 7 20-27. The designation 'daughter of Levi' applied to Jochebed in 2 1 may, therefore, be equivalent to 'descendant of Levi.' But see Nu 26 59, where Miriam's name is also inserted : see on 2 1.   **26. Their armies**] Israel left Egypt as an organised host : see on 3 16, and see 12 17, 51 13 18.

CHAPTER 7
The Rod of Moses turned into a Serpent. The First Plague

1. A god to Pharaoh] see on 4 16.   **Thy prophet**] A prophet is a spokesman. The prophets of God are those who declare His will. In doing this they may foretell His judgments and predict the future ; but prediction is a secondary feature of prophecy, and is not contained in the original and proper sense of the word in which it is used here, where Aaron is called the prophet or mouthpiece of Moses. To prophesy sometimes means to declare God's praise in song. Thus Miriam is called a prophetess in 15 20, Eldad and Medad are said to have prophesied in Nu 11 25 (see note there), Deborah was a prophetess (Jg 4 4 5 1), and in 1 Ch 25 1-3 the sacred musicians in the temple are said to 'prophesy with harps': cp. also 1 S 10 10 19 20 f. 1 Cor 14 1 f.   **4, 5.** The purpose of the miraculous events connected with the exodus was not only the deliverance of the Israelites, but the manifestation of Jehovah's character to the Egyptians : see on 4 21.

7. See on 2 21.   **9. Thy rod**] Moses had entrusted his rod to Aaron : cp. v. 15, which is spoken to Moses.

11. Magicians] lit. 'engravers, sacred scribes': cp. Gn 41 8 RV. They are depicted on the monuments with a quill pen on their heads and a book in their hands. A belief in magic was universal in Egypt and had a most potent influence in every department of thought and conduct. The magicians were a recognised body of men whose services were very frequently employed to interpret dreams, to avert misfortune, or to bring discomfiture upon an enemy : cp. on Nu 22 5. Here Pharaoh calls his magicians to a trial of strength with Moses and Aaron, and they are able to imitate some of the wonders. In the end, however, they confess themselves beaten (8 19). According to Jewish tradition two of the magicians who 'withstood Moses' were called Jannes and Jambres : see 2 Tim 3 8.   **12. They became serpents**] Serpent charming is still practised in Egypt and has been described by several travellers. What was done on this occasion was probably a clever piece of sleight of hand. The magicians when they were called in might know what was expected of them, and be prepared to imitate what was done by Aaron.

13. He hardened Pharaoh's heart] This should be 'Pharaoh's heart was hardened,' as in RV. The Heb. is the same here as in v. 22 : see on 4²¹.

14–25. The First Plague :—The Water of the Nile turned into Blood.

The Nile was regarded as a god to whom worship and sacrifice were offered. The defilement of its waters, therefore, was a severe blow to the religious prejudices of the Egyptians. It was also a great calamity, as the Nile was the source of all the fertility of Egypt, and its fish were largely used for food, some kinds being regarded as sacred. **15. He goeth out unto the water**] either to bathe or to pay his devotions to the sacred river : see on 2⁵.

19. Streams . . rivers] the various canals and branches of the Nile. **20, 21.** At the annual rising of the Nile its waters frequently turn a dull red colour owing to the presence of mud, vegetable débris, and minute animalcules. This plague, therefore, like the following, may have been an aggravation of a natural phenomenon. It is to be observed, however, that whereas the natural discoloration of the water has no pernicious effect on the fish of the Nile, these all died under the plague.

22. The magicians probably obtained some water by digging near the Nile (see v. 24), and in some way were able to convince Pharaoh, who of course was willing to be convinced, that they could imitate the sign wrought by Moses and Aaron. Their sign, however, must have been on a much smaller scale, seeing that all the Nile water was already transformed. **25.** The plague lasted seven days. Nothing is said of its removal.

CHAPTER 8

The Second, Third, and Fourth Plagues

1–15. The Second Plague :—Frogs.

This plague, like the first, was not only in itself loathsome, but an offence to the religious notions of the Egyptians. The frog was a sacred animal, and regarded as representing the reproductive powers of nature. At least one divinity was represented with a frog's head. This sacred sign became an object of abhorrence under this plague. This also was an aggravation of a natural phenomenon, but its supernatural nature was attested by its sudden occurrence in accordance with a previous intimation (v. 2). **3. Ovens**] These were large earthenware jars or pots about 3 ft. high, which were heated by being

filled with burning brushwood. The dough was baked by being laid in thin layers on the hot sides of the jar. Sometimes the oven consisted of a hole dug in the ground outside the house and plastered with clay. It was heated in the same manner as before, and after the fuel was withdrawn, the oven was wiped out and the dough pressed to the hot sides. **Kneading-troughs**] wooden bowls. **7.** The plague would not be difficult to imitate, seeing the frogs abounded everywhere. But the magicians could not remove the plague.

9. Glory over me] RV 'Have thou this glory over me': an expression of courtesy equivalent to 'I am at your service.' **13. The frogs died**] They did not return to the Nile, but remained to pollute the land. The removal of the plague in a manner intensified it.

16–19. The Third Plague :—Lice.

16. Lice] RM 'sandflies,' or 'fleas.' Opinion has been divided both in ancient and modern times as to the nature of these insects. From the fact that they are here said to have attacked the beasts as well as man, and to have come out of the dust, it has been inferred that they were gnats or mosquitoes. Several kinds of small stinging insects are known to breed in the sand, and these pests are particularly prevalent after the fall of the Nile and the drying up of the pools. On the other hand, RV has good authority for retaining the rendering 'lice' in the text. Rawlinson says that lice in N. Africa constitute a terrible affliction, and he quotes Sir S. Baker to the effect that 'at certain seasons it is as if the very dust of the land were turned into lice.' It will be observed that the third plague came without warning. **18.** The magicians fail to imitate this plague, and acknowledge its supernatural origin. They said, 'This is the finger of God,' or 'of a god.' This does not amount to an acknowledgment of Jehovah. They may have been thinking of their own gods.

20–32. The Fourth Plague :—Flies.

21. Swarms of *flies*] The nature of the pests is not indicated, as the Heb. word means simply 'swarms.' The LXX calls them 'dog-flies': cp Isa 7¹⁸. A general opinion is that they were beetles, of a peculiarly destructive sort. If this is correct, then the plague was again a severe blow to the religious notions of the Egyptians. The beetle was sacred, and was regarded as the emblem of the Sun-god. 'It was sculptured on monuments, painted on tombs, engraved on gems, worn round the neck as an amulet, and honoured in ten thousand images' (Geikie). A colossal figure of a scarabæus beetle is in the British Museum. **22.** It is implied here that hitherto the Hebrews had suffered along with the Egyptians. But now the exemption of the Hebrews from the plagues would show that it was the God of the Hebrews who was working on their behalf, and not one of the gods of the Egyptians as the magicians had suggested (v. 19). **24. Was corrupted]** MG ' was destroyed.' **25. In the land]** of Egypt. Pharaoh was unwilling to lose the services of the Hebrews.

26. The abomination of the Egyptians] Animal worship was very prevalent in Egypt, certain kinds of animals being regarded as peculiarly sacred and on no account to be slaughtered. For the Israelites to sacrifice cattle, sheep, and goats would be to outrage the religious feelings of the Egyptians, and might lead to war and bloodshed. That Moses had good grounds for his fear on this account cannot be questioned. Diodorus, the historian, tells of a Roman ambassador who was put to death for accidentally killing a cat. A modern instance of the danger of offending religious prejudices may be seen in the Indian Mutiny, which is said to have been occasioned by the serving out of greased cartridges to the Bengal troops. The end of the cartridge was usually bitten off before being inserted in the musket, and of this these men, who were Hindus and forbidden by their religion to eat cow's flesh, had a superstitious abhorrence. **27.** See on 3 18. **29. Deal deceitfully]** see vv. 8, 15.

CHAPTER 9

THE FIFTH, SIXTH, AND SEVENTH PLAGUES

1-7. The Fifth Plague :—Murrain, i.e. cattle plague.

Visitations of cattle plague are not uncommon in Egypt. An outbreak in 1842 carried off 40,000 oxen. The miraculous nature of the plague recorded here consisted in its occurring at a set time (v. 5), and in the exemption of the cattle of the Israelites, and of the cattle that were housed. This plague was, so far, the most destructive in its effects, entailing a much more serious loss of property than the former.

3. Cattle] A general term including the species mentioned in this verse. **In the field]** Those that were housed escaped, to suffer afterwards from the plague of hail : see vv. 19, 25. The words in v. 6, **all the cattle .. died,** are to be understood with this limitation. Horses were a comparatively recent importation into Egypt, and chiefly used in military operations. They are frequently mentioned in the OT. in connexion with Egypt : see e.g. Gn 47 17 Ex 14 9 Dt 17 16 note, Isa 31 1.

8-12. The Sixth Plague :—Boils.

This plague affected both man and beast,

and, unless we may suppose that the narrative is condensed, was sent without warning.

8. Furnace] i.e. the brick-kiln. The scattering of the fine ashes upon the wind was probably intended to be symbolic of the spread of the disease. **9. Boil breaking forth** _with_ **blains]** An inflamed swelling with pustules. In Dt 28 27 it is called the 'botch of Egypt.' Certain skin diseases are communicated to man from cattle, and the sixth plague may have been connected in some way with the preceding. **11. Could not stand before Moses]** i.e. could not withstand Moses. They were attacked themselves, and could neither imitate nor remove the plague. **12. Hardened the heart of Pharaoh]** see on 4 21.

13-35. The Seventh Plague :—Hail.

14. All my plagues] Pharaoh must not think that God has exhausted His means. There are others which will prove sufficient for His purpose. **15, 16.** Better with RV, ' For now I had put forth my hand, and smitten thee .. and thou hadst been cut off .. but in very deed for this cause have I made thee to stand ' (i.e. have preserved thee alive), ' for to shew thee my power, and that my name may be declared throughout all the earth.' God might have delivered His people by summarily destroying Pharaoh and all his subjects, but He has restrained the full extent of His vengeance for His greater glory : cp Ro 9 22, 23 Isa 48 9. **18. Very grievous hail]** Hail and thunderstorms are not unknown in Egypt, but are rare and seldom dangerous. Since the foundation thereof] i.e. since it was inhabited : cp. v. 24. **20.** Some of the Egyptians, at all events, had been impressed with the previous plagues, and had come to believe the predictions of Moses. **23. Fire ran along upon the ground]** RV 'ran down unto the earth.' Hailstorms are frequently accompanied with electrical disturbances.

25. Brake every tree] Broke the bough so that, in the case of fruit trees, there could be no prospect of fruit. **27. I have sinned this time]** I acknowledge this time that I have sinned. **28. For** _it is_ **enough]** RV ' for there hath been enough.' **31. Flax]** Largely grown for making linen which was worn by the priests, and used, among other purposes, for swathing mummies. The word rendered boiled, i.e. podded, is explained in RM as meaning ' was in bloom.' It means, rather, ' was in bud.' Flax flowers as a rule in February, and barley comes into ear about the same time. Wheat is a month later than barley, and spelt (here incorrectly called rie, which is not grown in Egypt) is sown and ripens at the same time as wheat. The condition of the crops indicated here fixes the time of the plague at about the end of January.

CHAPTER 10

THE EIGHTH AND NINTH PLAGUES

1–20. The Eighth Plague :—Locusts.
2. See on 7 [4, 5].   **3.** This question shows that Pharaoh was responsible for the hardening of his heart : see on 4 [21].   **4–6.** Travellers are unanimous in bearing witness to the terrible ravages caused by a visitation of locusts. They fly in dense swarms, sometimes miles in length, so that the air is darkened with them. Wherever they alight they devour every green thing, not sparing the bark of trees. For a description of a locust plague see Joel 1 [1-7] 2 [1-11], where the locusts are compared to an army of horsemen.   **10. Let the LORD be so with you . .**] This is spoken in scorn, and is equivalent to a refusal to let them go.   **Evil** *is* **before you**] i.e. your intentions are evil : cp. Ps 101 [3].   **11. Ye** *that are* **men**] Pharaoh means to keep the women and children as a pledge that the others will return : cp. v. 24.   **13. An east wind**] Locusts are known frequently to have come from the East, being bred in Syria and Arabia. In this instance they were removed by a west wind which carried them into the Red Sea (v. 19).   **17. This death**] A graphic description of the desolation caused by the plague.
19. Red Sea] The Gk. name, given perhaps on account of the red coral which lines its floors and sides. The Heb. name is *Yam Suph*, which means ' Sea of Reeds.'
21–29. The Ninth Plague :—Darkness.
21. This plague, like the third and sixth, was sent without warning. It is not said how the darkness was produced, but in all probability it had a natural basis, like the other plagues. It resembles the darkness caused by the khamsin, a S. or SW. wind, excessively hot and charged with fine dust, which blows about the time of the vernal equinox. The darkness is often local, covering a belt or strip of the country. The unusually dense gloom would excite the superstitious fears of the Egyptians, who worshipped the sun-god Ra. For a vivid description of the terrors of this plague, see book of Wisdom, c. 17.
24. Cp. the former concession of Pharaoh in v. 11. He is now willing to let the people go, but wishes to retain their flocks, in order to ensure their return.   **26. We know not with what we must serve the LORD**] a reason for taking all their flocks with them. The feast was new, and they did not know what they might require.
29. The present interview does not terminate with these words, but is continued in the next c. Moses leaves the presence of Pharaoh at c. 11 [8]. The first three vv. of c. 11 may be regarded as a parenthesis.

CHAPTER 11

THE TENTH PLAGUE THREATENED

2. Borrow] RV ' ask ' : see on 3 [22].
4. Moses is here speaking to Pharaoh. This v. is the continuation of 10 [29].   **About midnight**] The particular night is not specified, though it is implied that it is the night following the day on which this interview takes place. On the other hand, 12 [3, 6] prescribes a four days' preparation for the Passover. But see on 12 [1].
5. Firstborn] The Heb. word means the firstborn male. The death of the firstborn may be regarded as a punishment for the slaughter of the Hebrew children (see 1 [16, 22]) and the oppression of Israel, the ' firstborn of Jehovah ' (see on 4 [22, 23]).
Behind the mill] What is meant is the hand-mill, which consisted of two circular stones about 18 in. in diameter lying one above the other. The upper stone is turned round a pivot, which rises from the centre of the lower, by means of a handle fixed near its circumference. The grain is poured into a funnel-shaped hole in the upper stone surrounding the central pivot, and the meal escapes between the two stones at the circumference. The mill rests on the ground, and the maid-servant sits ' behind the mill.' Sometimes two servants turned the stone, in which case they sat facing each other, each grasping the handle : cp. Mt 24 [41]. Grinding was considered menial work, fit only for women and slaves : cp. Jg 16 [21] Isa 47 [1, 2] Lam 5 [13].
7. Move (lit. ' whet ') **his tongue**] a proverbial expression : cp. Josh 10 [21].
9, 10. These vv. sum up the purpose and effect of the preceding series of nine plagues.

CHAPTER 12

THE INSTITUTION OF THE PASSOVER. THE TENTH PLAGUE, AND THE DEPARTURE OF ISRAEL

1. In the land of Egypt] These words suggest that what follows was written independently of the foregoing narrative, and an examination of this c. shows that it contains two separate accounts of the institution of the Passover, one extending from vv. 1–20, the other from vv. 21–28. The latter is the proper continuation of c. 11.
2. The beginning of months] The exodus is regarded as an ' epoch-making ' event (cp. Jg 19 [30] 1 K 6 [1]), and to mark its importance the month in which it occurs is to be reckoned the first month of the ecclesiastical year. This is the month Abib (see 13 [4] 23 [15] 34 [18] Dt 16 [1]), i.e. the month of ripening ears, and corresponds to the end of March and the beginning of April. After the exile it was called by the Babylonian name of Nisan : see e.g. Neh 2 [1]

Esth 3 7. The sacred feasts were computed from this date : see Lv 23 4, 5, 15, 24. The civil year began in autumn with the first day of the seventh month after Abib, called by the Babylonians Tishri and in OT. Ethanim : see 1 K 8 2. With this change of reckoning may be compared the reckoning of the Christian Year, which begins with Advent, and of the Christian Week, which begins with the Lord's Day.

3. Unto all the congregation] by means of their representatives : see on 3 16.   **A lamb**]. The word may also mean a kid, but practically a lamb was always chosen : cp. v. 5.

4. Too little] According to Josephus the lower limit was fixed at ten persons. He also says that in his time (between the death of Christ and the destruction of Jerusalem) 250,000 lambs were sacrificed at the Passover and partaken of by 2,700,000 people.

5. In accordance with the principle that whatever is offered to God must be the best of its kind, the law of sacrifice required that the sacrificial animal should be a male (the superior sex) and without blemish : see intro. to Lv 21 and on Lv 22 17-25. So Christ ' offered Himself without spot to God ' (Heb 9 14) as a ' lamb without blemish and without spot ' (1 Pet 1 19).

6. Keep it up until the fourteenth day] This is to ensure that no blemish shall pass undetected.   **In the evening**] lit. ' between the evenings,' i.e. probably between sunset and darkness. Darkness was supposed to begin when three stars became visible. Josephus says that the time of sacrifice was from three to five in the afternoon. Observe that the Passover lamb was sacrificed and the blood sprinkled on the doorposts by each head of a household, there being at this time no tabernacle nor order of sacrificing priests. In later times the lamb was killed in the temple court by the head of the household and the blood poured out at the altar, after which the lamb was carried home to be eaten : cp. Lv 17 3-6 Dt 16 5-7.   **7. Upper door post**] RV ' lintel.' The shedding of the blood signified the offering of the life to God. The sprinkling of the lintel was not only a sign to the destroying angel, but an indication that atonement had been made on behalf of the inmates of the house.   **8. Roast with fire**] The flesh of sacrificial animals which were eaten by the offerers was usually boiled : cp. 1 S 2 13, 14. In the present case the roasting was probably to ensure haste (v. 39) and to prevent the dismemberment of the animal : see vv. 9, 46.

And unleavened bread ; _and_ **with bitter** _herbs_] Leaven, as causing fermentation and corruption, is regarded as unclean, and its use in sacrificial meals is accordingly forbidden. In NT. it is used as a symbol of sin and moral uncleanness : see 1 Cor 5 8 and on v. 14. The bitter herbs, probably some kind of wild lettuce or endive, were meant to symbolise the bitter bondage which the Israelites had endured in Egypt : see 1 14.   **9. His head with his legs, and with the purtenance** (RV ' inwards ') **thereof**] The entrails were taken out, cleansed, and replaced, and the lamb was then roasted whole : cp. v. 46, ' neither shall ye break a bone thereof.' The unmutilated lamb symbolises the unity of Israel. St. John sees in it also an emblem of the unbroken bones of Christ : see Jn 19 36.   **10.** This prohibition is meant to prevent what remains of the sacrifice from being profaned. Burning was the regular mode of disposing of the remains of every sacrificial animal : see 29 34 Lv 4 12 7 17.   **11.** The passover is to be eaten with every indication of haste.   **With your loins girded**] To gird up the loins is to gather up the long flowing skirt of the outer robe under the girdle, so as to leave the limbs free in working or running : see 1 K 18 46 Lk 12 37 17 8. At the present day (as in the time of Christ) the Jews eat the Passover in a recumbent posture to signify that there is no longer need of trepidation, God having given His people rest and security.   **It** _is_ **the LORD'S passover**] Heb. _pesach_, Gk. form _pascha_. The English rendering ' passover ' represents not amiss both the sound and the sense of the Hebrew name. The rite commemorated the ' passing over ' of Jehovah, i.e. His sparing of His faithful people. The word is used in this sense in Isa 31 5.   **12. Against all the gods of Egypt**] The gods of Egypt would be powerless to avert the judgment of Jehovah. As in Egypt many deities were worshipped in the form of animals, the destruction of the firstborn of beasts would be felt as the execution of a judgment upon these gods.

14. For ever] The Jews still keep the feasts of the Passover and Unleavened Bread. They now offer no sacrifice, seeing that Jerusalem has passed from their possession, but they look forward to the time when they will return to Jerusalem and the sacrifice be resumed. Each celebration is closed with the pathetic words, expressive of undying faith and hope, ' Next year in Jerusalem!' To Christians the death of Christ gathers up and fulfils all that was signified by the Jewish Passover, and therefore supersedes it. 'Christ our passover hath been (RV) sacrificed for us; therefore let us keep the feast' (RM 'keep festival,' i.e. the festival of unleavened bread which followed the passover) '. . with the unleavened bread of sincerity and truth': 1 Cor 5 7, 8. Here Christ is regarded as typified in the paschal lamb, as He is also in the Fourth Gospel (19 36), which places the Crucifixion at the time of the

Passover, and regards the fact as significant; His death redeems His people from their spiritual bondage; His blood, sprinkled on their hearts, delivers them from the guilt and consequences of sin. The old Passover sacrifice is fulfilled, once for all, in His sacrifice of Himself, which is commemorated, not repeated, in the sacrament of Holy Communion. That sacrament, accordingly, takes the place of the Passover. It differs from it in so far that it is not a recurring sacrifice, but the continual remembrance of the one great sacrifice offered by Christ, the true Passover lamb. The sacrifice is past, and Christians now live in the time of unleavened bread, and must therefore put away from them the 'leaven of malice and wickedness.'

15. The seven days beginning with the Passover are to be kept as a feast of unleavened bread. The Passover (*pesach*) and feast of Unleavened Bread (*mazzoth*) are really distinct, but as they were always celebrated in succession the name Passover is sometimes used to cover both: cp. Lk 22¹. **Shall be cut off**] This does not necessarily mean put to death, but excommunicated and cast out of the congregation of Israel. A person so cut off becomes like one of a heathen nation. He is reduced to the level of an uncircumcised person, being outside the covenant and having no more part in the privileges of the chosen people: see on Gn 17¹⁴, and cp. Mt 18¹⁷ Eph 2¹². **16. An holy convocation**] The word denotes a gathering of the people for a religious purpose: see Nu 10²⁻¹⁰. The abstention from work enjoined here is not so strict as on the sabbath and the Day of Atonement: cp. Lv 23⁸ with vv. 3, 28, and with Ex 35³. **19. A stranger**] a foreigner who had entered the congregation by circumcision, a proselyte, in contradistinction to 'one born in the land,' i.e. the land of Canaan (another indication of later date), a native Israelite. **22. Hyssop**] supposed to be wild marjoram, which grows in Egypt and Sinai and Palestine. Its powder, which has a pungent aromatic flavour like that of mint, is used as a condiment. It was supposed to have cleansing properties, and a bunch of hyssop was frequently used in ceremonial sprinkling, for which it was naturally suitable, several stalks growing from one root: cp. Lv 14⁴ Ps 51⁷ Nu 19⁶. **26. What mean ye by this service?**] To this day, at the Jewish celebration of the Passover, the youngest child present who is able to do so is made to ask this question, which is answered by a recitation of the circumstances attending the original institution of the feast. An interesting description of a modern Passover will be found in Zangwill's 'Children of the Ghetto,' c. 25.

The Tenth Plague:—Death of the First-born.

29. At midnight] the Passover night, following the 14th day of Abib. The Jewish day is reckoned from sunset to sunset: see on 11⁴.

31–42. The Departure from Egypt.

32. Bless me also] intercede for me, that no further plague come upon me for your sakes. **34. Before it was leavened**] This shows the haste with which they departed: see v. 39. On the kneading-troughs see on 8³. **35. Borrowed**] RV 'asked,' as in 3²² 11². **36. Lent unto them .. *required*]** RV 'let them have what they asked.' **37. Rameses**] see on 1¹¹. Succoth has been identified with the Egyptian Thuku, the region whose capital was Pithom: see on 1¹¹. **Six hundred thousand on foot *that were* men**] i.e. of twenty years old and upwards, fit for war. This implies a total of perhaps three millions. On the number see intro. to Nu 1, and on 14²¹. **38. A mixed multitude**] of foreigners and Egyptians who were associated with the Israelites through marriage and as slaves. We read of these again in Lv 24¹⁰ Nu 11⁴. **Very much cattle**] On the resources of the wilderness and its ability to support a multitude of people with flocks and herds, see intro. to Nu 1.

40. Four hundred and thirty years] This agrees with the prophetical statement in Gn 15¹³. But the Samaritan text of the OT. and LXX after the words 'in Egypt' here add 'and in Canaan,' thus making the 430 years run from the immigration of Abraham into Canaan, and reducing the stay in Egypt after the immigration of Jacob to 215 years. St. Paul accepts the LXX chronology (see Gal 3¹⁷), and it is supported by the genealogy in Ex 6¹⁴⁻²⁰, which allows only four generations between Jacob and the father of Moses. But it is difficult to believe that the descendants of Jacob could have increased so much in 215 years, and there is reason to think that the genealogical table in c. 6 has been abridged : see on 6²⁰. On the whole, it seems more reasonable to accept the reading of the Heb. text represented by the English version, and understand the 430 years as running from the descent of Jacob into Egypt. **41. The self-same day**] on the 15th day of Abib : see v. 29. **42. A night to be much observed**] This rendering rests on the injunction in v. 14. The Heb. is literally 'a night of watching unto the LORD,' i.e. a night of vigil or watch-festival. **43–49.** These directions regarding the lawful participants in the Passover seem to be introduced here in consequence of what is said about the 'mixed multitude' in v. 38. The Passover is only for those who through circumcision have entered into the covenant with Jehovah. Similarly, in the Christian church baptism, which corresponds to circumcision as an initiatory rite, is necessary to partaking of the Lord's Supper. **46**. See on vv. 9, 10. **49. One law**] i.e. of the necessity of circumcision to participation in the Passover.

CHAPTER 13

THE CONSECRATION OF THE FIRSTBORN.
THE MARCH TO ETHAM

1-16. The Consecration of the Firstborn.

All Israel was holy unto the LORD : see on 19 [5,6]. But the firstborn of man and beast were specially consecrated to Him, as the part representing the whole. There was a special fitness in the consecration of the firstborn, seeing they had been spared in the destruction which overtook the Egyptians. The firstborn of mankind were to be consecrated to the service of Jehovah as priests ; the firstborn of animals were to be offered in sacrifice, if clean animals ; if not, they were to be redeemed at a price. Afterwards the whole tribe of Levi was consecrated to the priestly service in lieu of the firstborn : see Nu 3 [40-51]. The firstfruits of the field were also claimed by Jehovah : see e.g. 22 [29].

2. Openeth the womb] What is claimed is the firstborn male. **8.** See on 12 [26].

9. A sign .. upon thine hand] a figurative expression meaning that they were never to lose sight of this duty. In later times the Jews understood this injunction literally, and to this day at times of prayer they attach to their left arm and forehead small cases containing pieces of parchment inscribed with certain passages of the Law. These cases are called in NT. ' phylacteries ' : see further on Dt 6 [8].

12. Matrix] the womb. **13.** The **ass** is here mentioned as a representative of ' unclean ' domestic animals (see Lv 11 [2f.]) which could not be offered in sacrifice. For such, a **lamb** was to be substituted ; if not, its neck must be broken. This would ensure its redemption, as every one would prefer parting with a lamb to losing an ass. Human sacrifices are strictly forbidden, therefore firstborn males must be redeemed. The tribe of Levi was substituted for them, and in addition the sum of five shekels was paid as the redemption price of each firstborn male : see Nu 8 [16] 18 [15,16]. To this day the Jews solemnise the ' redemption of the firstborn ' on the thirtieth day after birth. This was the rite performed by Joseph and Mary on behalf of the child Jesus as recorded in Lk 2 [22,23].

17-22. The March to Etham.

17. The most direct route to Canaan from Raamses in the Eastern Delta where the host had mustered, would have been northeastwards along the Mediterranean coast. This would have implied a journey of not more than 150 or 200 miles. But it would immediately have brought them into collision with the Philistines, a very warlike tribe inhabiting the southwestern part of Canaan, and would have been too great an obstacle for the people's strength and faith. Accordingly the route of march was deflected southeastward into the peninsula of Sinai. The further object of leading the people to Mt. Sinai to be instructed in the Law is not expressly stated here, but neither is it excluded. **18. Harnessed**] RV ' armed ' in organised array : see on 6 [26].

19. See Gn 50 [25] Josh 24 [32]. **20. Succoth**] see on 12 [37]. **Etham**] not identified. It was probably one of the frontier fortifications. The **wilderness** is probably that of Shur (cp. 15 [22], and see on Gn 16 [7]). In Nu 33 [8] it is called the ' wilderness of Etham.'

21. There was only one **pillar**, which in daylight had the appearance of smoke and by night glowed with fire : see 14 [20,24]. It was the symbol of the divine presence with the host (see on 3 [2]), and was their signal and guide on the march : see 40 [34-38], and cp. Nu 9 [15-23]. It is clearly understood here to be miraculous. It was usual to carry fire signals at the head of an army on the march in early times. **Go by day and by** (RV) **night**] It is suggested that the Israelites marched during part of the night as well as by day : cp. Nu 9 [21].

CHAPTER 14

CROSSING THE RED SEA

2. At Etham the Israelites reached the Egyptian frontier, travelling in a northeasterly direction. Instead of crossing the frontier to the E. side of the Bitter Lakes they are commanded to turn southwards, keeping the Red Sea on their left. The reason for this change of route may have been a repulse by the garrison of one of the line of fortresses on the E. border of Egypt. None of the places mentioned here has been identified with certainty. There is even a doubt as to what is meant by **the sea**. Some have understood it to be the Mediterranean, in which case the host must have turned northwards, and the supposed Red Sea (Heb. ' sea of reeds ' ; see on 10 [19]) would be the Serbonian Lake, a large bog lying on the shore of the Mediterranean between Egypt and the SW. extremity of Canaan. It is usual, however, to understand by the ' sea of reeds ' what is now called the Gulf of Suez. There is little doubt that at the time of the exodus the Gulf of Suez extended much further north than it does now, and that the modern Lake Timsah and the Bitter Lakes were connected with each other and the Gulf of Suez by necks of shallow water which in certain conditions might be swept almost dry. It is pretty certain that the Israelites crossed at some point north of the modern Suez.

3. The **wilderness** is the Egyptian wilderness, a tract of desert land lying between the Nile and the Red Sea. To the south, in front of the advancing host, rose an impassable mountain chain, so that they found themselves **entangled in the land.** **7.** The Egyptian chariots were low two-wheeled cars open behind and drawn by two horses abreast. Each chariot contained a driver and a warrior, sometimes two. The **chosen chariots** were probably those of the king's bodyguard. The Hittites are known to have brought 2,500 chariots into the field against Rameses II.

8. With an high hand] Confidently, boldly. **9. Horsemen**] It is doubtful whether the Egyptians at this time used cavalry. The horsemen may be the charioteers.

11. No graves in Egypt] cp. Nu 14 1-3.

14. Hold your peace] The victory will be entirely the work of Jehovah. It is the part of His people to trust in Him and cease from murmuring: cp. Isa 30 15 2 Ch 20 15-17.

19. Angel of God] see on 3 2, and cp. 13 21.

21. In delivering His people, as in bringing the plagues on the Egyptians, God may have made use of natural means. A strong east wind blowing all night, and acting with the ebbing tide, may have laid bare the shallow neck of water joining the Bitter Lakes to the Red Sea, allowing the Israelites to cross in safety: see on v. 2. Indeed, an Egyptian tradition says that Moses waited for the ebb tide in order to lead the Israelites across. The real difficulty in connexion with the passage of the Red Sea lies not in the baring of the sea bottom, but in the fact that the Israelitish host must have numbered about three millions: see on 12 37. This enormous multitude, encumbered as it was with young and old herds of cattle, must have taken a long time to cross the soft floor of the estuary. It is not impossible, however, that the number stated was the total of those who escaped from Egypt, but that they left in several companies, that led by Moses being the main detachment: see on Nu 1.

22. A wall unto them] This need not mean that they stood up like a wall, but that the water on each side was a defence, preventing a flank attack by the enemy: cp. for this use of the term 'wall' 1 S 25 16. **24. In the morning watch**] between 2 a.m. and 6 a.m., the last of the three watches into which the Hebrews divided the night, in earlier times: cp. Lam 2 19 Jg 7 19 1 S 11 11. The Roman division was into four watches: see Mk 13 35 Mt 14 25. It is here implied that the previous part of the night sufficed for the passage of the Israelitish host: see on v. 21.

25. Took off] RM 'bound': made them stick fast. They became clogged with the soft ooze in the sea bed. **27. The sea returned**] In 15 10 this seems to have been effected by a change of wind. **28. And all the host**] RV 'even all the host.' It is not said that Pharaoh himself perished. The supposed discovery in modern times of the mummy of Merenptah is no argument against his being the Pharaoh of the exodus or against the truth of this narrative. Even though he did lead his host in person into the middle of the sea and perished with the others his body might afterwards have been recovered and preserved: see on 1 8. **31.** This notable deliverance naturally made a deep impression upon the Israelites. It justified their faith in Jehovah and it also confirmed the right of Moses to be regarded as their leader. **And believed the LORD, and his servant Moses**] But when they turned away from the scene of their deliverance and faced the stern realities of the desert march, they were only too ready to give way to mistrust and murmuring: cp 15 24 16 2,3 etc.

CHAPTER 15
THE SONG OF MOSES

On the further shore of the Red Sea the Israelites celebrate their deliverance in a magnificent hymn of praise. It consists of three strophes or stanzas of increasing length, viz. vv. 2–5, 6–10, 11–18. The first v. is introductory and may have been repeated as a chorus after each stanza: see on v. 21. On the structure of Hebrew poetry see Introduction to the Psalms. In language and style the song bears many marks of high antiquity. There can be little objection to attributing the first two stanzas at least to Moses. The third presupposes the conquest and settlement in Canaan: see on vv. 13–19. The original song may have been modified and expanded at a later date, with a view to being used as a festal song at the Passover when the deliverance from Egypt was celebrated.

1. The LORD] Jehovah—so throughout the song, in which the might of Israel's God is contrasted with the powerlessness of the Egyptian idols: see e.g. vv. 3, 6, 7, 11.

2. I will prepare him an habitation] RV 'praise him.' **8. Blast of thy nostrils**] referring to the east wind (14 21). The whole v. is figurative and highly poetical.

10. See on 14 27. **11. The gods**] see on v. 1, and on 7 4,5. At this period the gods of other nations might be conceived as real beings, though infinitely inferior to Jehovah. Gradually, however, the Hebrews rose to the truth of one God, the so-called gods of the nations being nonentities: see on 20 3 32 1, and Ps 96 5 115 4 f. Isa 41 29. **12. The earth**] a general term including the sea. **13 Thy holy habitation**] The land of Canaan is meant, or perhaps more particularly Mt. Moriah, where the Temple was erected. This is an indication that the Song assumed its present form after the occupation of Canaan. **14. The people**] heathen nations dwelling in the wilderness and in Canaan. **Palestina**] properly the land of the Philistines. The name was afterwards extended to the whole land of Canaan. **15. Dukes**] leaders, princes, rulers. **16. Purchased**] Jehovah's proprietorship in them was secured by redemption. Hence His claim upon their gratitude and obedience : cp. e.g. Dt 4 34-40 and the ground on which the Ten Commandments are based, Ex 20 2, where see note : cp. also 2 Cor 5 14, 15 1 Pet 1 18, 19.

17. Mountain of thine inheritance] The highlands of Canaan : cp. Jer 2 7. *In the place*

.. in **the Sanctuary**] The fixed abode of the ark is meant here, perhaps Shiloh its first resting-place: see Josh 18 1. **19.** This v. is a later addition indicating the occasion on which the Song was composed. Its insertion here suggests that the Song had a separate existence prior to its incorporation in the book of Exodus. It is unnecessary where it now stands.

20. Miriam the prophetess] the sister of Moses : see on 2 1. As Aaron was the elder of the two brothers, she is here described as his sister. On the meaning of the term ' prophet ' see on 7 1 Nu 11 25. **Timbrel**] i.e. tambourine, still used by Eastern women to accompany their singing and dancing. **21. Answered them**] The pronoun is masculine. Miriam and the women sang the refrain to the stanzas sung by the men. With these triumphal strains the first part of the book of Exodus closes.

PART 2

(Chs. 15 22–18) MARCH FROM THE RED SEA TO MOUNT SINAI

CHAPTER 15 (continued)

Leaving the shore of the Red Sea, the Israelites enter the peninsula of Sinai, the triangular area lying between the two northern arms of the Red Sea. The centre of the peninsula is a vast limestone plateau of an average elevation of 2,000 ft. above the sea level. It is almost waterless, and bare of vegetation save in the ' wadies,' or watercourses, at certain seasons. To the south the point of the peninsula is occupied by the exceedingly rugged mountain district of Sinai. To the north stretches the wilderness of Paran, lying between the peninsula and the southern part of Canaan, and having on its western side the wilderness of Shur, and on its eastern the wilderness of Sin. The peninsula of Sinai was inhabited from very early times by various wandering tribes. During their sojourn there, the Israelites fell in with the Amalekites and the Kenites. The Egyptians are known to have worked copper mines in certain districts, and to have maintained fortresses for the protection of the miners. Recent travellers assert that the present barrenness of the peninsula is due largely to neglect, and that there are evidences of its having at one time supported a considerable population. This fact has an important bearing on the credibility of the Scripture narrative, according to which the Israelites spent some forty years in the peninsula. See intro. to Nu 1. **22. Wilderness of Shur**] Between the coast of the Gulf of Suez and the high central tableland is a strip of level country. The northern half is part of the wilderness of Shur. The southern part is called the wilderness of Sin

in 16 1. The Israelites march southwards along this narrow maritime plain.

23. Marah] lit. ' bitterness ' : cp. Ruth 1 20. This station is by some identified with Ain Suweirah, 30 m. S. of the present head of the Gulf of Suez. The bitterness of the springs in this district is attested by all travellers. It is caused by the abundance of natron in the soil. **25. The LORD shewed him a tree**] There are certain plants whose bark and leaves are employed to sweeten bitter water. Lesseps mentions a kind of thorn found in the desert possessing anti-saline properties. Here, as in the case of the Plagues in Egypt, the miracle was effected by means of a natural agent. The miracle consisted in God's directing Moses at this particular juncture to the use of the right means. The tree would not have been employed had it not possessed the property required. **He made for them a statute**] The subject is most probably God, not Moses. God used this occasion to teach the people that such troubles as the present were intended to ' prove ' them, i.e. to test their loyalty to Him, and that if they stood the test He would protect and provide for them. **26. That healeth thee**] lit. ' thy physician.' The term is employed with reference to the ' healing ' of the noxious waters : cp. Ps 103 3 107 19, 20.

27. Elim] The word means ' trees.' Elim is probably the modern Wady Ghurundel, ' where there is a good deal of vegetation, especially stunted palms, acacias, and tamarisks, and a number of water-holes in the sand.' The minuteness of the description in this v. suggests the testimony of an eye-witness. There would be no occasion for it in a fictitious narrative.

CHAPTER 16

THIRD MURMURING. SENDING OF THE MANNA

1. Pursuing their march southward, the Israelites come at the end of the first month after their departure from Egypt to the **wilderness of Sin,** forming the SW. border of the peninsula : see on 15 22. All the stations in the march are not mentioned. In Nu 33 10 allusion is made to an 'encampment by the Red Sea' between Elim and the wilderness of Sin. It must be remembered also that, owing to the vast extent of the host, there must have been a simultaneous encampment at different places. From Elim, the Israelites might have gone by a more direct route to Sinai, but this would have led them past the copper mines among the mountains, where there was an Egyptian garrison.

2. This was the third murmuring. The first was at Pi-hahiroth (14 10-12), the second at Marah (15 24). The supplies which the Israelites had brought with them out of Egypt being now exhausted, they expect to perish with hunger, and begin to regret having left Egypt, where, with all their hard bondage, they had been well fed : see on Nu 11 4, 5.

4. A certain rate every day] RV 'a day's portion every day' : see vv. 16–21. **That I may prove them**] The miracle had a moral purpose. It was intended not merely to satisfy their hunger, but to teach them dependence upon God and obedience to Him. The goodness of God should lead to repentance (Ro 2 4). **5. The sixth day**] the day before the sabbath, an indication that the sabbath was known previous to the giving of the law at Sinai : see on Ex 20 8. On the method of preparing the manna, see Nu 11 8.

6. Ye shall know] by the quails.

9. Before the LORD] This common phrase denotes the place where God specially manifests Himself : see vv. 33, 34. Here it seems to mean at the pillar of fire in front of the host. **10. Toward the wilderness**] As they are at present in the wilderness, this must mean 'towards the interior of the wilderness,' in the direction of the march and the guiding pillar. **The glory of the LORD**] Here a special radiance is meant. God's self-manifestation is frequently accompanied with an appearance of fire : see on 3 2, and cp. 19 18 24 17 29 43 40 34. **13. Quails**] The quail is a bird belonging to the partridge family, about 7 in. long, and of a buff colour. Its flesh is considered a great delicacy. Quails are migratory. In spring vast flocks pass northwards from the interior of Africa to Syria, crossing the peninsula of Sinai in their flight. They also cross the Mediterranean in great numbers. In a single season, 160,000 have

been netted on the small island of Capri. Quails always fly with the wind. After a sea flight they are easily captured, as they fly low their bodies being heavy and their wings wet : see on Nu 11 4-31. Here, again, God employed a natural means in providing deliverance for His people. The miracle did not consist in a new creation, but in the timely arrival and vast quantity of the quails.

15. It *is* **manna**] Heb. 'what is it?' so rightly in RV. What is now known as manna is a sweet gum which exudes from various shrubs and from the tamarisk tree, and is used medicinally. None of its varieties corresponds to the description given here. These are found only in small quantities, in special localities and at certain seasons, from about May to August ; they are not suitable for food, and cannot be cooked as manna was (see v. 23 Nu 11 8). Moreover, the manna of commerce can be kept for an indefinite time (cp. v. 20). What is meant here is clearly a miraculous substance. Whether, again, the miracle took place on the basis of a natural product cannot with certainty be made out. This is not improbable in the light of the previous wonders. Our Lord employs the manna as a type of Himself, as giving eternal life to those who believe in Him : see Jn 6 31-58. St. Paul calls it 'spiritual meat,' and regards it as a type of the Lord's Supper wherein the faithful are made partakers of the life that is in Christ : see 1 Cor 10 3 f.

16. An **omer** is a little more than seven pints. Ten omers make an ephah, which is, roughly, equal to a bushel : see v. 36. The pint measure is called a 'log' : see e.g. Lv 14 10.

18. Mete] i.e. measure : cp. Mt 7 2. The total quantity of manna amounted exactly to an omer per head. This is evidently regarded here as miraculous, and designed to check want of trust and greed on the one hand and over anxiety on the other. Those who gathered too much wasted their labour, and those who gathered too little were at no disadvantage. St. Paul cites this fact as an incentive to brotherly charity ; the rich ought to make up the deficiency of the poor : see 2 Cor 8 14, 15.

20. God's gift is spoiled by selfish and miserly hoarding. **21. Every morning**] cp. the petition 'Give us this day our daily bread.'

22. See on v. 5. The divine sanction of the sabbath is shown by the cessation of the manna on that day as well as by the double quantity sent on the previous day. The people are to observe the sabbath by resting from the labour of gathering manna : see v. 30. Those who faithlessly and disobediently persist in looking for manna find none. **29. Let no man go out of his place**] Jewish legalists interpreted this commandment to mean strictly that throughout the sabbath day a man must maintain the same posture in which he was found at its commencement. As this was practically impossible it was held to be allowable to walk on the sabbath day a distance not exceeding 2,000 ells, which was supposed to be the distance from the centre of the camp to its circumference. **31. Coriander]** an annual plant much cultivated in the East. The seeds have an aromatic flavour, and are used as a seasoning in cookery and also medicinally. **Wafers]** thin cakes.

32-34. These vv. seem to be a later insertion, as they presuppose the erection of the tabernacle (vv. 33, 34). There would be no need to gather a pot of manna for preservation till the end of the wanderings and the cessation of the manna.

34. The Testimony] the Law which 'testifies' to God's will, inscribed on the two tables of stone and deposited in the ark (Ex 25 16), which is accordingly called the 'ark of the testimony' (Ex 25 22 Nu 4 5) and sometimes simply 'the testimony'; see Nu 17 4. The tent containing the ark is called the 'tent or tabernacle of the testimony': see Nu 9 15. The pot of manna is here said to have been deposited **before** the testimony; but according to Heb 9 4 it was in the ark. The pot of manna was a favourite symbol among the Jews. From the remains of the synagogue at Capernaum it seems that a pot of manna was carved on the lintel of the door of that synagogue. This must have given point to our Lord's discourse on the 'bread of life' there: see Jn 6 24 f. **35.** See Josh 5 10-12.

CHAPTER 17
REPHIDIM. MURMURING FOR WATER.
OPPOSITION OF AMALEK

Leaving the maritime plain the Israelites now strike inland, and after halting at Dophkah and Alush (see Nu 33 12, 13) they come to Rephidim. This is usually identified with the modern Wady Feiran, lying about 20 m. N. of Sinai. It is one of the oases of the peninsula, very fertile and usually well watered. On this occasion the brook was dry.

1. After their journeys] RV 'by their journeys' (RM 'stages'). **2. Tempt the LORD]** challenge His power and willingness to provide for them, put Him to the proof by their unbelief: cp. v. 7; see also Nu 14 22 20 13 Dt 6 16 Mt 4 7. Their unbelief was the less warranted as they had lately experienced God's providence in supplying their wants. This is the fourth murmuring: see on 16 2.

5, 6. The elders] as representing the people (see on 3 16), are to be the witnesses of the miracle. The people, perhaps on account of their sin, are to stand at a distance: cp. 19 17. **Thy rod]** see on 4 2, 20. The **river** is the

Nile: see 7 20. **6. Horeb]** see on 3 1. Tradition identifies the rock with a great detached fragment under the ridge of Ras es-Sufsafeh. This, however, is a long way from the supposed site of Rephidim. At the same time Moses and the elders are represented as going **on before the people,** so that the people obtained the water not at the rock, but some distance down the stream that flowed from it. If the stream continued to flow for some time, as seems natural to suppose, perhaps during the eleven months of the sojourn in that neighbourhood, the people would drink it at various points. This is probably the origin of the rabbinical legend, alluded to by St. Paul (1 Cor 10 4), that the rock followed the Israelites on their march. The apostle spiritualises the rock, making it a type of Christ, from whom flows a perennial stream of grace to His people. **7. Massah]** 'trial' or 'proving.' **Meribah]** 'chiding.' The names are formed from the words used in v. 2. Meribah is the name given to the place where water was again provided (see Nu 20 13), but to distinguish it from the present Meribah it is called Meribah-Kadesh in Dt 32 51. Some commentators hold that the account given here and that in Nu 20 refer to the same occurrence. The resemblances are striking, but there are also manifest points of difference.

8. Amalek] The Amalekites, here described collectively in the singular number, were a nomadic tribe, very fierce and warlike, roaming over the desert country S. of Canaan, including the Sinaitic peninsula where the Israelites first encountered them. They probably regarded the Israelites as their rivals for supremacy. They gave them much trouble, not only at various times during the desert wanderings (see e.g. Nu 13 29 14 25, 43-45), but down to a late period of their history: see Jg 6 3 1 S 15 1-8 30 1 Ch 4 43. **9.** The first mention of **Joshua.** He was an Ephraimite, the son of Nun. He appears here as captain of the host, and later as the personal attendant of Moses (24 13 32 17 33 11). He was one of the spies sent to view the land of Canaan (Nu 13 8 14 6), and was afterwards chosen as the successor of Moses: see Nu 27 18-23 and on v. 18. His name was originally Oshea, 'help' or 'salvation' Moses afterwards changed his name to Joshua, 'Jehovah is my salvation.' The Gk. form of Joshua is Jesus: see Mt 1 12. In Ac 7 45 Heb 4 8 Joshua the son of Nun is meant: see Intro. to Joshua. **10.** According to Jewish tradition, **Hur** was the husband of Miriam: see on 31 2. **11.** The holding up of Moses' hands signified an appeal to God in intercession. His holding up the 'rod of God' in his hand was, at the same time, an appeal to his fighting men to remember what God had already done for them. The rod was associated with many wonderful deliverances, notably that at the Red Sea, so that the sight of it would inspire the warriors with courage and hope. On both grounds one can understand how it was that the fortune of the battle corresponded to the steadfastness with which Moses held up his hands. The story illustrates the value of prayer, in particular of intercessory prayer, and, at the same time, the necessity of prayer being accompanied with believing effort. Moses praying on the hill while the people are fighting in the valley is also an emblem of Christ interceding in the heavenly places for His people struggling upon earth : see Heb 4 14-16. **14. Write this .. in a book**] Written records, contemporary with the events described in them, were no doubt preserved for many generations, and would afford material for future historians. One of these early records was called the 'Book of the Wars of Jehovah' : see on Nu 21 14.

15. Built an altar] for the double purpose of offering sacrifices of thanksgiving, and of commemorating the victory by means of a monument : cp. Gn 33 20 35 7 Josh 22 26, 27. **Jehovah-nissi**] 'Jehovah is my banner,' meaning, ' under His banner, in His name and strength, I fight and conquer ' : cp. Ps 20 5-7.

16. For he said] RV 'and he said.' The words following are literally, ' because a hand upon the throne (of) Jah,' which may be rendered, ' because his (i.e. Amalek's) hand is against the throne of Jehovah, (therefore) will the LORD,' etc.

CHAPTER 18
THE VISIT OF JETHRO
1. On the name Jethro, see 2 16, and on

Midian, 2 15. **2. Sent her back**] see on 4 26. **3, 4.** See on 2 22. **5. The mount of God**] Horeb or Sinai : see on 3 1.

11. See on 15 11. The second half of the v. is obscure. RV reads, 'yea, in the thing wherein they (the Egyptians) dealt proudly against them (the Israelites).' **12.** The **burnt offering** was wholly consumed upon the altar, and signified the complete devotion of the offerer to God : see Lv 1. The **sacrifices** were peace offerings, and were consumed by the offerers in token of fellowship with God and each other : see Lv 3 and on Nu 22 40. **Before God**] at the place consecrated by the offering of the sacrifices : see on 16 9 and 19 22.

15. To enquire of God] This phrase is explained by the words that follow at the end of the next v., I do make *them* know the statutes of God, and his laws: cp. 18 99. Already we see that the decisions given by Moses are regarded by the people as possessing divine sanction. **19. And God shall be with thee**] RV 'and God be with thee,' i.e. may God grant thee the needed wisdom.

21. Hating covetousness] A judge must be above bribery. Bribery was, and still is, a common Oriental vice, and is frequently referred to in Scripture : cp. 23 8 18 83 12 3 Ps 15 5 Isa 1 23 Am 5 12 Mic 3 9-11. **23. If .. God command thee** *so*] Jethro does not presume to dictate to Moses. The matter must be referred to God for sanction : cp. Dt 1 9-18. **To their place**] Each one to his tent, satisfied with the expeditious settlement of his case, instead of waiting all day, as hitherto : see v. 13.

25. According to Dt 1 13 it appears that Moses left the selection of the ' able men ' to the people. Cp. Ac 6 3.

PART 3
(Chs. 19-40) ARRIVAL AT SINAI AND SOJOURN THERE

CHAPTER 19
PREPARATION FOR THE GIVING OF THE LAW
1. The same day] the 15th day of the month: cp. 12 18, 29 16 1. Marching slowly, with long halts at the various stations on the route, the host took two months to traverse the 150 m. between Egypt and Sinai. Here they remained eleven months (see Nu 10 11, 12), during which time the nation entered into a formal covenant with Jehovah on the basis of the moral law received from God by Moses, and promulgated by him.
Wilderness of Sinai] This must not be confounded with the ' wilderness of Sin ' (see on 16 1). The wilderness of Sinai is generally identified with the modern Wady Er-Rahah, a plain fully 2 m. long by half-a-m. wide, ' enclosed between two precipitous

mountain ranges of black and yellow granite, and having at its end the prodigious mountain block of Ras es-Sufsafeh,' which Dean Stanley and others take to be the mount on which the Law was given. Ras es-Sufsafeh is some 7,000 ft. in height, and rises sheer from the plain ' like a huge altar.' Some, however, believe that the actual mount of the Law was another peak of the same mountain mass S. of Sufsafeh, called Jebel Musa, the traditional site. The whole district has been described as one of the most awe-inspiring regions on the face of the earth, and as such it accorded well with the dread revelation of the divine majesty here given to Israel.
4. I bare you on eagles' wings] God's grace and care were the source of Israel's duty of obedience and loyalty: see on 15 16. The image here employed to illustrate the watchful

solitude of God is true and beautiful. When the eaglets first attempt to fly, the parent bird is said to hover round them and beneath them, so as to support them on its expanded wings when they are exhausted: see Dt 32 11. **Brought you unto myself**] i.e. to Sinai, the 'mount of God,' where He was about to make a special revelation of Himself. It is possible, however, to take the words in a spiritual sense, as denoting the divine nurture and education of the Israelites in the fuller knowledge of the true God: see on vv. 5, 6.   **5. If ye will obey**] Although God's grace preceded the covenant (see previous v.), the latter was made upon condition of perfect obedience. But as the law only serves to accentuate man's feeling of inability to keep it, it becomes a 'schoolmaster to lead to Christ,' and the redemption that is by faith in Him: see Ro 7 22-25 Gal 3 23, 24.   **A peculiar treasure**] a private and treasured possession. In later times the Jewish nation presumed upon their privilege as a chosen people, and believed in their unconditional possession of God's favour. From this false security it was the task of the prophets to rouse them: see e.g. Jer 7 4-16 Mt 3 9 8 11,12 21 31.   **Above all people**] RV 'from among all peoples.' All the earth is the Lord's, but Israel belongs to Him in a special degree: cp. 33 16 Am 9 7.   **6. A kingdom of priests**] a kingdom of which every member is consecrated to the service of God, and so 'a holy nation': see on Lv 20 24. The designation expresses also the high calling of Israel. They are to be the medium of communicating the knowledge of the divine nature and will to the world. In general, it may be allowed that the Jewish nation has fulfilled its destiny. It has taught the world true religion. Through its rejection of the Messiah its sacred function has passed over to the Christian church, to which St. Peter transfers the titles given to Israel in these two vv. : see 1 Pet 2 9 Rev 1 6.

7. The elders] see on 3 16.   **9. In a thick cloud**] No one, not even Moses, is able to gaze upon the unveiled majesty of God: see 3 6 33 20 Lv 16 2 Jg 13 22. Hence when He appears it is in a cloud, which becomes the symbol and vehicle of the divine presence: see 13 21, also Nu 11 25 1 K 8 10, 11 Isa 6 4 Mt 17 5 26 64 1 Th 4 17 Rev 1 7.   **And believe thee**] The superior favour shown to Moses as the direct recipient of the divine revelation would attest his authority. See on Nu 12 7, 8.

10. Sanctify them] bid them sanctify themselves. The outward preparation consisted in washing their persons and clothes, and in abstinence from sexual intercourse: see v. 15 and cp. Lv 15 16-18. These outward purifications symbolised the inward purity required in those who draw near to God: see Isa 1 16 Ps 51 6, 7 1 Pet 3 21.   **12. Set bounds unto the people**]

This was intended to impress the people with the unapproachable holiness of God. They could only draw near to God in the person of the mediator whom God Himself had chosen. The NT. writers emphasise the superior privilege of Christians, who enjoy access into the holiest through Christ 'the mediator of the new covenant': see Heb 10 19-22 12 18-24.

13. They shall come up] not the mass of the people, but their privileged representatives: see vv. 23, 24, and cp. 24 1, 2.   **22. The priests**] The Levitical priesthood was not yet instituted, but among the Hebrews, as among other nations of antiquity, there were those, mainly the heads of tribes and families, who exercised priestly functions. Melchizedek was prince and priest in Jerusalem at the time of Abraham (Gn 14 18), and Jethro was both prince and priest of Midian, and offered sacrifice as such (Ex 2 16 3 1 18 1, 12).

CHAPTER 20

THE TEN COMMANDMENTS (vv. 1–21).

Chs. 20–23, containing (1) the Decalogue (Gk. = 'Ten Words' or 'Commandments') and (2) a code of laws regulating the religious and social life of the people, and called the Book of the Covenant (see 24 7), form perhaps the most important part of the Pentateuch. It is the nucleus of the entire Mosaic legislation, and in all probability existed for long as a separate document.

1–17. The Decalogue. In c. 34 28 Dt 4 13 this is called the 'Ten Words' or 'Commandments.' It is also called the 'Testimony' in Ex 25 16 (see on 16 34), and the 'Covenant' in Ex 34 28 Dt 9 9. These words were uttered in the hearing of the awe-struck people (19 9 20 19 Dt 4 12), and afterwards graven by the finger of God on two tables of stone (31 18 Dt 4 13). On witnessing the apostasy of the people Moses broke these tables (32 19), but they were afterwards replaced by another pair on which the same words were written (34 1 Dt 10 1,4). When the ark was made the two tables of the testimony were deposited in it (Dt 10 5 Heb 9 4). As the ark itself stood in the innermost sanctuary of the tabernacle, this position of the Tables of the Law bore emphatic witness to the great truth that the beginning and end of all religious observances is the keeping of the commandments of God: cp. Mt 19 17 Ro 2 25 1 Cor 7 19.

Two versions of the Ten Commandments are preserved in the Pentateuch, the second, exhibiting a few variations. being given in Dt 5 6-21. Most scholars agree that the version given in Exodus is the older and purer of the two, the variations in Deuteronomy being due to the characteristic ideas and style of the writer of that book. The main divergences occur in the fourth and fifth commandments. There is a good deal to be said for the view that the commandments as originally promulgated were shorter than either form, that they consisted merely of the precepts without the reasons annexed, the second e.g. reading simply, 'Thou shalt not make unto thee any graven image,' and the fourth, 'Remember the sabbath day to keep it holy': see on v. 11. That the commandments, at least in this terser form, are really Mosaic, there is no reasonable ground to doubt.

The Ten Commandments were inscribed on two tables and divided into two parts, but opinions differ as to their enumeration and arrangement. The Jews themselves regard v. 2, usually called the Preface, as the First Word, and maintain the number ten by uniting vv. 2–6 (the first and second) and calling these the Second Word. The Roman Catholics and Lutherans combine the first two, and split up the tenth. Our common enumeration is that of Philo and Josephus, who are followed by the Greek and Reformed Churches. As to their arrangement, some have assigned five commandments to each table; while others have divided them in the proportion of four to six. According to the latter division the first four are religious, defining the duties man owes to God ('Thou shalt love the Lord thy God'); the last six are moral, defining the duties men owe to each other ('Thou shalt love thy neighbour as thyself'). On the other hand, seeing that in ancient times filial duty was regarded more as a religious than a moral obligation, there is something to be said for placing the fifth commandment on the first table: see on 21 15.

Christians, while freed from the obligations of the Mosaic law of ceremonies, are still bound, bound more than ever (see Ro 6), to 'the obedience of the commandments which are called moral.' What our Lord did with regard to the Ten Commandments was (1) to sum them up under the two obligations of love to God and love to our neighbour, which, again, are the two sides of the one law of universal Love ('love is the fulfilling of the law'); (2) to widen and deepen their scope, making them apply not only to the outward act, but to the inner spirit and motive, and (3) to change them from mere negative commands to abstain from certain sins to positive obligations, which are never exhausted and involve a perpetual advance in holiness where mere abstention from evil acts implies moral stagnation: see Mt 22 37-40 5 17-48.

2. Redemption is the ground of obedience which springs, not from fear, but from gratitude and love: see Ro 12 1 2 Cor 5 14 1 Jn 4 19. This evangelical truth of obedience springing from gratitude is the great theme of the book of Deuteronomy, where it is reiterated over and over again : see e.g. Dt 4 32-40 and Intro. to that book, § 3.

3. Before me] RM 'beside me.' Monotheism is implied rather than expressly enunciated here. It was only gradually that Israel rose to the truth that there is but one God. Israel was led to this truth along the way of practice. By ceasing to worship other gods they would cease to believe in their existence. It is true still that the sure result of discontinuing the worship of God is the denial of His existence : see on 15 11 32 1.

4. If the first commandment implies the truth of God's unity, the second implies that of His spirituality. Israel is forbidden to worship even the true God under any external form. God is not like anything that human hands can make. In Egypt the Israelites had been familiar with the worship of images.

The water under the earth] This refers to the belief of the time that the earth was a flat disk (Isa 40 22) resting on an abyss of waters : see Gn 1 6 7 11 Ps 24 2. **5. A jealous God**] Human jealousy is usually of an ignoble kind, the fruit of suspicion. But there is a holy jealousy, the pain of wounded love. The heart of God is grieved when His love is rewarded with indifference and unfaithfulness. He will brook no rival in the affections of His people : see Dt 32 16,21 Ps 78 58 Isa 42 8, and on c. 34 15.

Unto the third and fourth *generation*] RV 'upon . .' It is a law of the divine government that the penalty of one man's sins is shared by those connected with him : cp. Josh 22 20. If this seem hard it must be remembered that the law cuts both ways. The benefits of a man's good deeds are likewise distributed over a large area. We cannot enjoy the one result without taking the risk of the other. The law relates, however, only to the consequences of sin, not its guilt. The latter adheres to the sinner personally : cp. Ezk 18 2-4.

6. Unto thousands] i.e. unto a thousand generations, as in Dt 7 9. It is implied here that God's mercy in rewarding righteousness infinitely transcends His anger in punishing the sinful. The consequences of righteousness are more enduring and far-reaching than those of iniquity.

7. This prohibition applies strictly to perjury or false swearing, the breaking of a promise or contract that has been sealed with an oath in the name of God. He will not allow His name to be associated with any act of falsehood or treachery. His **name** must not be taken **in vain**, i.e. lightly or heedlessly. This forbids also the careless or profane use of the divine name and titles. Jesus extended the scope of this commandment so as to prohibit the use of oaths entirely. A man's mere word should be his bond : see Mt 5 33-37.

8. What is laid down here is not the institution of the sabbath rest, but its strict observance. The sabbath rest was known to the Babylonians before this time, and there are indications of its being previously known to the Israelites : see on 16⁵. Hence, probably, the use of the word **remember.** To keep it holy] The seventh day is to be distinguished from other days (the root meaning of the word rendered ' hallow ' is to separate : see on Lv 20²⁴), by abstinence from labour. Nothing is said here as to the religious observance of the day. But after the institution of the Levitical priesthood, the morning and evening sacrifices were doubled on the sabbath (see Nu 28⁹,¹⁰), and in later times the day was naturally that on which a ' holy convocation ' was held : see Lv 23³ Isa 66²³. After the exile, when synagogues were established, divine service was always celebrated on the sabbath.

9. It is sometimes forgotten that the fourth commandment ' enforces the six days' work as well as the seventh day's rest.' **10. Shalt not do any work**] such as gathering manna (see on 16²²), lighting a fire (35³), gathering sticks (Nu 15³²⁻³⁶), agricultural labour (cp. Ex 34²¹), carrying burdens (Neh 13¹⁵⁻¹⁹), buying and selling (Neh 10³¹). The Jewish legalists developed the negative side of this precept to such an extravagant and absurd extent that the sabbath, instead of being a day of rest, became the most laborious day of the seven. The philanthropic motive for its observance (cp. 23¹² Dt 5¹⁴) was almost entirely lost sight of till our Lord said, ' The sabbath was made for man, and not man for the sabbath ' (Mk 2²⁷). **Thy manservant**] The command is specially addressed to heads of families and employers of labour, and requires (1) that they must themselves rest from labour, and (2) allow those in their employment to rest also. **11.** In Dt 5¹⁴,¹⁵ another reason is given for the observance of the sabbath rest, in accordance with the philanthropic spirit which pervades the whole of that book : cp. 23¹². Both reasons are probably later amplifications of the original commandment. **Blessed .. and hallowed it**] consecrated it to Himself with a special blessing upon it. The unusually frequent mention in OT. of the duty of observing the sabbath is an indication of its importance. It is often referred to as constituting along with circumcision the sign of the covenant between God and Israel : see on 31¹³.

12. This is the ' first commandment with promise' (Eph 6²). The promise has been understood by some as applying to the nation as a whole. Undoubtedly the nation takes its character from the home, and well-ordered family life is the prime condition of national welfare and stability : see on Dt 21¹⁸. But the promise is also to the individual. ' Righteous-

ness tendeth to life ' (Prov 11¹⁹). A promise of long life and material prosperity is frequently attached in OT. to moral precepts : see e.g. 23²⁵ᶠ· Lv 26 Dt 7¹²ᶠ· 28 Ps 1 34¹²ᶠ· 37. The doctrine of present rewards and punishments had an important educative value at a time when the truth of a future life was not yet clearly revealed. But the manifest exceptions which experience of human life afforded to this simple view of the divine government proved a great trial to faith, as the book of Job in particular shows, and such passages as Ps 73 Jer 12¹,², etc. That faith was able even in these circumstances to triumph over doubt is shown e.g. in Hab 3¹⁷,¹⁸ Ps 73²³⁻²⁶, in which it may be said that the high-water mark is reached of a trust in God that is superior to and independent of all outward circumstances. In later times, when the belief in a future life was more consistently held, it was only natural that the rewards and penalties should be regarded as in many cases postponed to find their full completion in the next world : see on Dt 22⁷.

13–16. These commandments are given to safeguard a man's life, domestic peace, property, and reputation. For the way in which our Lord extended the scope of the sixth and seventh commandments so as to apply not merely to the outward act but to the inner thought and motive lying at its root, see Mt 5²¹⁻³⁰.

16. It is noteworthy that of the ten commandments, two (the third and the ninth) refer to sins of speech. For the penalty prescribed in cases of false witness, see Dt 19¹⁵⁻²¹. The spirit of the ninth commandment forbids all lying and slander.

17. Of all the commandments, the tenth is the one that goes deepest. What is condemned is not an action, but a thought or desire : cp. Prov 4²³ Mt 15¹⁸⁻²⁰. This commandment shows that the Decalogue is more than a mere code of civil law. Human laws cannot take cognizance of the thoughts of the heart.

19. The Decalogue was given in the hearing of the people. The following commandments were given to them through their mediator Moses : see vv. 21, 22, c. 21¹.

CHAPTERS 20²²–23³³

THE BOOK OF THE COVENANT

This section comprises a number of laws designed to regulate the life of an agricultural community living under comparatively simple conditions. The laws are mainly of a civil order with a small admixture of rudimentary religious enactment (see e.g. 20²³⁻²⁶ 23¹⁰⁻¹⁹). The principle of their arrangement is not clear, but the three sections 21¹²⁻³⁶ 22¹⁻²⁷ 23¹⁻⁸ seem to be amplifications of the sixth, eighth, and ninth commandments of the Decalogue respectively. The Book of the Covenant occupies an intermediate position between the brief and general principles enunciated in the Decalogue and the minute and detailed legislation set forth elsewhere in the Pentateuch. For the relationship between the legislation of Moses and that of earlier civilisations, see Intro. § 2, and art. ' Laws of Hammurabi.'

23. RV is preferable, ' Ye shall not make *other gods* with me ; gods of silver, or gods of gold, ye shall not make unto you.' This is a repetition of the first and second commandments. **24. An altar of earth**] i.e. of the simplest form and material, as a precaution against idolatrous representations : cp. v. 25 Dt 27 5, 6. On the different kinds of sacrifice see Lv 1–7, and on 18 12. **Record my name**] lit. ' cause my name to be remembered,' by some special manifestation of power or grace. A plurality of sacrificial places is here expressly sanctioned, and the historical books of OT. record numerous instances of altars being erected and sacrifice offered in many different places down to the reformation of king Josiah, which took place in the year 621 B.C. In the book of Deuteronomy a plurality of sacrificial places is condemned, and worship restricted to a central sanctuary : see on Dt 12 4, 13 f. **25.** See on v. 24. **26.** With the same object, to prevent exposure of the person, it is afterwards prescribed that the priests be provided with linen drawers while officiating at the altar : see 28 42, 43. The top of the altar of burnt offering, which was four and a half ft. high, was reached, according to tradition, by means of a sloping ramp of earth : cp. 27 5, and see on Lv 9 22.

CHAPTER 21

The Book of the Covenant (continued)

1–11. Regulations regarding the Treatment of Hebrew Slaves.

Slavery was universal in ancient times, and the Mosaic Law does not abolish it. Among the Hebrews, however, slavery was by no means the degrading and oppressive thing that it was among other nations. Manstealing, upon which modern systems of slavery are based, was a crime punishable by death (see v. 16), and the Law of Moses recognises the right of a slave to just and honourable treatment. A Hebrew slave might occupy a high position in his master's household and be regarded as a trusty friend, as the case of Eliezer shows (Gn 24). He could not be bound for more than six years at a time ; in the seventh year he obtained his freedom if he desired it (see v. 2) ; he might hold property and come to be able to redeem himself (Lv 25 49) ; he was protected from the violence of his master (vv. 20,

21) ; he could claim compensation for bodily injury (vv. 26, 27) ; and he was entitled to the sabbath rest (20 10). If a Hebrew girl became her master's concubine he could not sell her to a foreigner, but must let her be redeemed (v. 8) ; if his son married her he must treat her as a daughter (v. 9) ; if he took a second wife he must not degrade her, but use her as liberally as before (v. 10). In general the Hebrew master was to treat his slave rather as a brother or hired servant than as a chattel, and the principle which was to govern his treatment was the humane precept ' thou shalt not rule over him with rigour ; but shalt fear thy God ' (Lv 25 43). These laws, it is true, apply to the slave who was an Israelite, but the lot of even the foreign slave who had been captured in war was only a little less favourable. If it be asked why the Mosaic Law did not at once abolish slavery the answer must be that the time was not ripe for that. Christ Himself did not abolish it ; and His apostles tolerated it (see 1 Cor 7 20-24 and the Epistle to Philemon). Christianity did not violently overthrow existing social institutions or abolish class distinctions. But it taught the brotherhood of all men, and by quietly introducing the leaven of justice, humanity, and brotherly love into society, gradually abolished the worst social abuses and made slavery impossible.

2. If thou buy an Hebrew servant] A man might voluntarily sell himself for debt (Lv 25 39), or he might be judicially sold for theft (see 22 3), or he might be sold by his parents (v. 7). If the year of Jubilee fell before the seventh year of his servitude he went free then : see Lv 25 40, 41. Life-long compulsory servitude was therefore unknown. **3. If he were married**] before coming into slavery. If he married after becoming a slave, the case contemplated in the next verse, he would do so subject to the consent of his master, in which case the wife and children remained with the master. **5.** Slavery may be preferable to freedom. This shows the mild nature of slavery among the Hebrews. **6. Unto the judges**] RV ' unto God.' The expressions are really identical, for the judges would be the priests, or the high priest, and the transaction would take place at the sanctuary and have the sanction of the divine judgment: see on 22 8, 28 RV. **Bore his ear**] The fastening of the ear to the doorpost signifies his perpetual attachment to the house of his master : cp. Dt 15 17. The ear is pierced as being the organ of hearing and, therefore, of obedience.

7. To be a maidservant] The word denotes a slavewife, a consort of inferior rank, like Hagar (Gn 16 3). Her position was permanent. She did not go out at the end of six years, which would have been a degradation. If she were the wife of the master of the house, she was to be treated as a wife ; if of the son, as a daughter. If she were dismissed, it must be in an honourable way (vv. 8, 11), and without repayment of the purchase money.

10. Polygamy, like slavery, was tolerated by the Law of Moses. Its cessation in Christian lands has naturally followed the nobler teaching of Christianity regarding woman : cp. the remarks on the cessation of slavery.

12–17. Three Offences Punishable by Death, viz. murder, manstealing, and the smiting or cursing of parents.

13. For the appointment of cities of refuge as an asylum in the case of accidental homicide, see on Nu 35 9-34. **14. From mine altar]** The altar seems to have been the place of refuge at first : see 1 K 1 50 2 28 f. **15. Smiteth]** not necessarily with fatal effect. Reverence towards parents was regarded in ancient times as more a religious than a social duty, and a breach of the fifth commandment, like blasphemy, was a capital offence : see intro. to the Decalogue, and cp. Dt 21 18 f. **16.** Mansteal-ing is to be punished as severely as murder. **17.** Cursing, like blessing, is always looked upon as efficacious. It is a solemn appeal to God, who will not permit His name to be taken in vain. He will not respond to the child who invokes His power to the injury of a father or mother. And such an impious appeal is itself a serious crime.

18–32. The Law of Compensation for Injury to Life or Limb.

19. Shall . . be quit] i.e. of the charge of murder. But he must pay for the injured man's loss of time and medical treatment.

21. He *is* **his money]** The master himself loses by his servant's inability to work, and is sufficiently punished in this way. If the injury is of a permanent nature the slave is entitled to his freedom: see vv. 26, 27.

23. *Any* **mischief]** beyond the loss of the child (v. 22). The law of retaliation ('like for like') is common to all early stages of civilisation: cp. e.g. art. 'Laws of Hammurabi.' It is a rough and ready kind of justice, but it involves many difficulties and is generally abandoned in favour of a system of fines and penalties. It should be observed that the law of retaliation is not the same as private revenge. The equivalent penalty is inflicted by the judge, not by the injured person: cp. Lv 24 17-21 Dt 19 15-21. Christ refers to this passage in the Sermon on the Mount (Mt 5 38 f.), forbidding the spirit of revenge, and enforcing the duty of forbearance in imitation of the heavenly Father. **28.** The following enactments are a good illustration of the spirit of even-handed justice displayed by the Mosaic Law : cp. Gn 9 5. **His flesh shall not be eaten]** This would serve to emphasise the

horror connected with such an accidental death. It was also in accordance with the law forbidding the eating of blood as unclean. An ox killed by stoning would not be bled : see on Lv 17 10-16, and cp. 22 31. **29.** In this case the owner is morally responsible and is liable to be put to death. The death penalty may, however, be commuted by a fine, the amount of which would be fixed by the relatives of the person killed, with probably an appeal to the judges. **32.** The silver shekel was in value a little more than half-a-crown. The ordinary price of a slave, therefore, was about £3 10s.: cp. Zech 11 12, 13 Mt 26 15. From the latter passage it will be seen that our Lord's life was reckoned of the same value as that of a slave.

33–c. 22 15. Law of Compensation for Injury to Property.

34. The dead *beast* **shall be his]** It is assumed that he has paid the full value of the live animal.

CHAPTER 22

The Book of the Covenant (continued)

1. Four sheep] The larger compensation required in the case of the ox is probably due to the fact that it is an animal used for labour, and of proportionately higher value, therefore, than a sheep: cp. 2 S 12 6. **2. Breaking up]** RV 'breaking in.' **3. If the sun be risen upon him]** i.e. if the housebreaking be committed in daylight. The nocturnal burglar is more dangerous and cannot be so easily detected. In a case of daylight robbery it is less necessary to resort to extreme measures for defence. In English law a similar distinction is made between housebreaking by night and by day.

5. Of the best of his own field] This is a case of wilful damage. In the next v. the damage is accidental, such as might result from the burning of weeds or thorns, in which case an exact equivalent only is required.

7. Deliver unto his neighbour] This practice was common in days when there were no banks. Otherwise, treasure might be buried in a field: cp. Mt 13 44. **8. Unto the judges]** RV 'unto God.' See on 21 6. **11. Oath of the LORD]** an oath invoking Jehovah as witness. On the solemn nature of such oaths, cp. 20 7.

13. Let him bring it] i.e. what remains of it, in order to show the cause of the injury.

15. It came for his (i.e. 'its' ; see on Lv 25 5) **hire]** RM 'it is reckoned in its hire.' The owner is understood to have taken the risk of injury into account in fixing the price of hire.

16–31. Miscellaneous Laws.

16, 17. Endow her] RV rightly, 'pay a dowry for her' : e.g. to her father. The dowry was not the portion brought by the wife into the husband's house, but the price paid by the bridegroom to the father or brothers of the bride, by way, it would seem, of compensation to the bride's family for the loss of her services: cp. Gn 34 12, also Gn 29 18. Seeing that among the Hebrews, as among the Arabs at the present day, a woman who has been unchaste has almost no chance of marriage, the seducer, it is here enacted, must marry her, or, if the father object, make good the dowry. In Dt 22 29 the dowry is fixed at fifty shekels. The seduction of a betrothed damsel is punishable with death: see on Dt 22 23f.

18. A witch] RV 'sorceress.' The word is the same as that in 7 11. Sorcery, or the pretended holding communication with evil spirits, is a form of idolatry or rebellion against Jehovah, and punished as such: see v. 20, and cp. Dt 18 10f. Lv 19 26, 31.

21. Cp. Lv 19 33, 34. The Mosaic Law repeatedly emphasises the duty of kindly consideration of the weak and oppressed, the afflicted and the poor. God is the champion and the avenger of all such: cp. Ps 146 7-9.

25. If thou lend money to *any of* **my people** *that is* **poor by thee]** RV 'to any of my people with thee that is poor': interest is forbidden on loans to a fellow Israelite, but is expressly allowed in dealing with a foreigner: see Dt 23 19, 20, and cp. Lv 25 35. The loans referred to here are loans without interest. The Israelites are commanded to help the poor by giving them free loans, the wisest form of charity. Commercial loans, for trading purposes, are not contemplated at all, and were in all probability unknown among the Israelites in early times and in a primitive state of society.

26. While the taking of interest is forbidden, the taking of a pledge for repayment of a loan is sanctioned, and frequent reference is made in Scripture to the practice: see e.g. Am 2 8 Job 22 6 24 9 Dt 24 6. The outer garment of the Israelite (the *simlah*) is a kind of cloak or plaid about 4 ft. square, which may be used as a coverlet by night. In the case of a poor man this might be the only thing he could give as a pledge, in which case he is to be allowed the use of it each night: cp. Dt 24 12, 13, and for a similar humane precept, v. 6 of that chapter.

28. The gods] RV 'God.' RM 'judges' is also possible : see on 21 6. But cp. St. Peter's injunction (1 Pet 2 17).

29. The first of thy ripe fruits] RV 'the abundance of thy fruits,' etc. : see on 13 1-16. **30. On the eighth day]** The minimum age of a sacrificial animal is eight days. The animal must be in a fit condition, which it could hardly be during the first week : cp. Lv 22 27. The eighth day was also prescribed for the circumcision of children : see Gn 17 12.

31. Holy men] See on 19 5, 6, 10. The numerous regulations with regard to outward

purity, of which one example is given here, were intended to be a symbol and a reminder of that purity of heart which God's people must exhibit. **Torn of beasts]** This prohibition rests on the general law that the blood, as the seat of life, belongs to God and must not be eaten. The flesh of such an animal would not be properly drained of blood : see on 21 28.

CHAPTER 23
THE BOOK OF THE COVENANT (concluded)

1-19. Miscellaneous Laws.

1. Raise] RV 'take up,' i.e. give ear to. This is an extension of the ninth commandment : cp. the Arabic proverb, 'In wickedness the listener is the ally of the speaker.'

2. To decline after] RV 'to turn aside after.' **3. Countenance]** Give undue favour to. As judgment is to be without fear (v. 2), so is it to be without favour, whether of rich or poor : cp. v. 6.

4, 5. Thine enemy's ox] The Mosaic Law inculcates the duty of kindness to animals : see e.g. 20 10 Lv 22 27, 28 Dt 22 6, 7 25 4. In Dt 22 1-4 it is a friend's beast that is to be relieved. Here it is the beast of an enemy : cp. Mt 5 43, 44.

8. Gift] A bribe in any form : see on 18 21

10, 11. On the law of the Sabbatical Year see on Lv 25 1-7. **12.** On the reason annexed to the fourth commandment, see on 20 10, 11.

14-17. The Three Great Annual Feasts are Passover and Unleavened Bread in the month of Abib, Feast of Weeks or Pentecost fifty days afterwards, and Feast of Booths or Tabernacles, here called Feast of Ingathering, at the end of the agricultural year : see on Lv 23 4-22, 33-43. **15. None shall appear before me empty]** As these festivals are all commemorative of God's goodness they are to be celebrated with thankfulness and rejoicing. And in token of their gratitude the people are to present gifts and entertain the poor : cp. Dt 16 16, 17 Neh 8 10. The same principle underlies the custom of making offerings of money as a part of Christian worship. It is expressive of the worshipper's thankfulness for all the divine mercies, temporal and spiritual, of which he is the recipient, and must never be omitted. **17. Three times in the year]** These annual pilgrimages served to maintain a conscious unity of race and worship.

18. Leavened bread] see on 12 8. Fat, like blood, must not be eaten, but burnt upon the altar : see on 29 13.

19. Thou shalt not seethe, etc.] This prohibition may be intended to preserve the natural instinct of humanity : cp. Dt 22 6, 7. But it more probably refers to a superstitious practice of using milk prepared in this way to sprinkle fields, as a charm against unfruitfulness : see Dt 14 21, where the prohibition is connected with the law of unclean meats. On account of this law, the Jews to this day abstain from mixing meat and milk in the same dish ; nor will they partake of the one, except at a considerable interval after the other.

20-33. The Book of the Covenant closes with an exhortation in which a promise is made of God's presence, guidance, and help in overcoming their enemies, of wide dominion, and of material prosperity, on condition that they serve Jehovah alone and make no covenant with the heathen nations or their gods.

20. On the Angel of Jehovah, see on 3 2.

25. See on 20 12. **28. Hornets**] The hornet is a large and fierce kind of wasp. It is doubtful whether the promise here is to be understood literally or figuratively (cp. also Dt 7 20 Josh 24 12). It seems to be taken literally in Wisdom 12 8. But it is more probably a figurative way of describing the terror which would fall upon the nations on hearing of the victorious march of Jehovah's people : see the previous v. and Dt 2 25, and cp. Dt 1 44 Ps 118 12 Isa 7 18. Or the ' hornets ' may be intended to describe the Egyptians, who were frequently at war with the inhabitants of Canaan. Rameses III is known to have broken the power of the ancient kingdom of the Hittites, which would be about the time of the Israelites' sojourn in the wilderness, supposing the exodus to have taken place towards the end of the nineteenth dynasty.

29, 30. The book of Judges shows that the conquest of Canaan was effected gradually.

31. The sea of the Philistines] the Mediterranean ; the **river** is the Euphrates. These bounds were reached in the reign of Solomon : see 1 K 4 21, and cp. Gn 15 18 Dt 11 24.

32, 33. The commandment to expel the Canaanites and to destroy their idols and places of worship was only partially fulfilled, with the result that the evil influence of Canaanitish idolatry and immorality made itself felt over and over again in the history of Israel and was the cause of its final overthrow : see Josh 16 10 17 12, 13 Jg 1 19, 27-36 1 K 11 1-10 14 22-24 2 K 12 3 17 6-23. With this passage cp. 34 12-17 Nu 33 50-56 Dt 7 ; and see on Nu 25 16-18.

CHAPTER 24

The Ratification of the Covenant

1. And he said] The first two vv. of this c. are a continuation of the narrative from 20 21, which was interrupted by the insertion of the Book of the Covenant, originally a separate document. C. 23 33 is continued in v. 3. **Nadab, and Abihu**] the two oldest sons of Aaron : see 6 23. **Seventy of the**

elders] a selection from the heads of the tribes and families : see on 3 16. **3. And Moses came and told the people**] after he had ascended the mountain and received the ' words and the judgments ' contained in chs. 20 22–23 33 : cp. 21 1. **4. And Moses wrote**] see on 17 14. The altar symbolised the presence of Jehovah, the twelve pillars represented the twelve tribes of Israel. These pillars were single unhewn stones which were smeared with the blood of the sacrificial animal or with the oil of a vegetable offering : see on Gn 28 18. The use of pillars is an evidence of the antiquity of the rite of sealing the covenant recorded here, as they were afterwards forbidden owing to their association with heathen worship : see Dt 16 22, and see on 34 13. **5.** See on 18 12. **6.** The sprinkling of the altar with half the blood and of the people with the other half (v. 8) signified that both parties, Jehovah and Israel, entered into fellowship and bound themselves by the terms of the covenant, the people promising obedience and Jehovah promising His help and blessing. See 23 20-31. In the New Covenant the blood of Christ takes the place of the blood of the sacrificial animal, and by faith in His sacrifice, Christians enter into communion with God : see Mt 26 28 Heb 9 11-28 1 Pet 1 2. **8. Concerning all these words**] RM ' upon all these conditions.'

9-11. The ratification of the covenant is concluded with a sacrificial meal (v. 11), which usually followed the peace offering and symbolised the harmonious relationship existing between the offerers and God : see Lv 3. At this meal, which took place on the mount, the representatives of the people were vouchsafed a vision of God Himself, not as previously with terror-inspiring accompaniments of thunder, lightning, and smoke (20 18, 19), but in grace, mercy, and peace. The sight of God, otherwise fatal in its effects (see 33 20 and on 19 9), does not injure them. God does not smite them ; on the contrary they are able to eat and drink in His presence, having entered into covenant relationship with Him (v. 11).

10. They saw the God of Israel] A very bold anthropomorphic way of describing the experience of these favoured persons, which the Gk. (LXX) Version, made many centuries later, avoids by translating ' they saw the place where God stood.' At the same time it is noticeable that the sacred writer evinces a great reserve in speaking of this vision of God. He makes no attempt to describe the appearance of God, only what was under His feet. Similarly Isaiah, who says that he too ' saw the Lord,' describes only the accompaniments of his vision (Isa 6) : see 33 18, 19, 23 In Dt 4 12 Moses is represented as reminding the people that they 'saw no similitude' of God at Horeb ; and in Jn 1 18 (cp. 5 37 6 46) we read that 'no man hath seen God at any time.' The apparent inconsistency between these passages and the present is to be accounted for on the principle of the progressiveness of revelation. Divine truth can only be communicated to men in the measure and in the manner in which they are able to receive it. In early times men were like children in regard to spiritual things, which therefore could only be apprehended by them under material forms of expression. The essential and permanent truth underlying the present representation is that the majesty and the will of the invisible God were brought vividly home to the minds of these men by means of the Moral Law, and that this Law was not a discovery by Moses but a thing revealed to him by God. Cp. what is said on anthropomorphisms in Intro. to Exodus, § 3.

A paved work of a sapphire stone] The ancients regarded the sky as a solid vaulted dome stretched over the earth : see on Gn 1 6-8.

Body of heaven in *his* **clearness**] RV 'the very heaven for clearness.'

12. Moses receives another command to come up into the mount and receive the tables of the Law and other directions connected with the outward service of religion.

Tables of stone] From Dt 5 22 we learn that these contained the Ten Commandments, and the same is implied in c. 34 28, which relates to the second tables, doubtless exact copies of the first which Moses broke. The other regulations which follow in c. 25, etc., seem to have been given orally. The words **which I have written** should perhaps follow **tables of stone**. The expression may be understood as indicating the immediate divine origin of the Law (cp. 31 18).   **13. Minister**] servant, attendant ; cp. Lk 4 20 RV Ac 13 5.

14. Said unto the elders] not merely the seventy spoken of in v. 1, but all the representatives of the people. They are to see that the camp is not removed from the plain during the absence of Moses.   **15. Moses went up**] Joshua accompanied him part of the way, and seems to have awaited his return somewhere on the mountain side : see 32 17.

18. Forty days and forty nights] The later account adds that during this time he neither ate nor drank (Dt 9 9). On the number forty see on 2 21.

(Chs. 25–31) THE TABERNACLE AND THE PRIESTHOOD

CHAPTER 25

THE VESSELS OF THE SANCTUARY

Chapters 25–31 are taken up with prescriptions regarding the Construction of a Tabernacle, i.e. a tent, to form the visible dwelling-place of Jehovah in the midst of His people, the place where He would meet them and receive their worship. The entire structure consisted of three parts. There was an outer Court, 100 cubits by 50, open to the sky, the sides of which were composed of curtains supported on pillars. The entrance was at the eastern end; inside, facing the door, was the altar of burnt offering, and behind that the brazen laver. Within this court and towards the western end was a covered tabernacle, divided by a hanging curtain into two chambers. The outer of these, called the Holy Place, contained the Table of Shewbread, the Candlestick, and the Altar of Incense. The Inner chamber, the Holy of Holies, or Most Holy Place, contained the Ark of the Covenant which supported the Mercy seat and the two golden Cherubim. The three parts, of which the entire structure was composed, were of increasing degrees of sanctity. Into the outer court came the worshippers when they brought their offerings. Into the Holy Place went the priests to perform their sacred offices; while into the Most Holy Place, which was the immediate Presence Chamber of Jehovah, went the high priest alone, and that only once a year on the great day of Atonement with special ceremonial. It has been questioned whether a tabernacle of this somewhat elaborate design and costly workmanship could have been erected by the Israelites in their present circumstances. This difficulty, however, has been exaggerated. In Egypt the Israelites were familiar with arts and manufactures, and they left Egypt with spoil of precious metals (11 2 12 35, 36). Another difficulty has been discerned in the fact that no references to such an elaborate structure occur in the historical books previous to the time of Solomon. Some scholars accordingly hold that many of the details described here are of an ideal nature, the prescription of what ought to be rather than of what actually was carried out, 'the attempt of a devout and imaginative mind to give concrete embodiment to some of the loftiest and purest spiritual truths to be met with in the whole range of scripture.' This difficulty, like the other, is of a negative kind, and we should be careful not to over-estimate it. In any case, the symbolism underlying the construction of the tabernacle with its furniture and ritual is unmistakable. The costliness of the materials teaches the lesson that God is to be served with the best that man can give. The harmony and exact proportions of its parts are a reflection of the harmony and perfection of the divine nature. The increasing degrees of sanctity which characterise the Court, the Holy Place, and the Holy of Holies, emphasise the reverence due by man to Him whose dwelling is in the high and holy place, and who yet condescends in His grace to tabernacle with man and to accept his imperfect worship

1–9. Gifts of materials for the tabernacle. **2.** 'God loveth a cheerful giver' (2 Cor 9 7). **3. Brass**] rather, 'bronze,' an alloy of copper and tin: see on Dt 8 9.   **4. Blue,** etc.] the yarns of which the hangings were to be woven by the women: see 35 25 39 1.   **5. Rams' skins dyed red**] red leather made of sheep skins.   **Badgers' skins**] RV 'sealskins,' RM 'porpoise-skins.'   **Shittim wood**] RV 'acacia wood.' The acacia (Heb. *shittah*, plur. *shittim*) is the characteristic tree of the Sinaitic peninsula. The wood is very durable and much used in furniture making.   **7.** On the ephod see 28 6 f.

8. That I may dwell among them] Strictly speaking, God cannot be said to dwell in one place more than in another. But as men realise His presence most vividly when they are consciously engaged in His worship, the place of worship becomes in a special sense a 'meeting-place' with God (see v. 22) and a 'house, or dwelling-place, of God': cp. Gn 28 17. The expression is anthropomorphic at the best, and is felt to be inadequate as the spiritual nature of God is more fully realised: see Jn 4 20-24. In later times Jewish writers avoided saying that 'God dwells' in any place, even in heaven itself. They said that He 'makes His Shekinah to dwell' there. The 'Shekinah' is the manifestation of God, especially in the bright cloud (see 40 34, 35). The word is connected with the Heb. word for dwelling (*mishkan*) used in the next verse.

9. Pattern] This does not imply any visible or material model. It expresses the fact that Moses, during his long retirement with God on the mount, was divinely directed as to the most fitting way in which God might be worshipped. This inspiration does not exclude the exercise of the natural faculties, but presupposes them as the basis on which it may operate: see on 31 4. Nor does it exclude the appropriation, under divine sanction, of ideas suggested by certain features in the ritual of other nations with which Moses was already acquainted. See Intro. to Exodus, § 2, near the end.

Tabernacle] lit. 'dwelling.' Here it seems to denote the entire fabric. The name is applied in particular to the sacred tent, standing in the midst of the court: see 26 1.

10–22. The Ark of the Testimony.

10. Ark] i.e. a chest or coffer. A cubit is about 18 in. Such sacred arks were well known to the Egyptians and Assyrians. They contained some image of the deity worshipped, and were carried with great pomp in processions at national festivals. It is significant of the spiritual nature of the Hebrew religion that the ark made by Moses contained no image, but instead a copy of the Moral Law. After the conquest of Canaan the ark remained for a long time at Shiloh (Josh 18 1 1 S 3 3), and was at last brought by David to his capital at Jerusalem (2 S 6 1 Ch 13). Solomon placed it in the temple which he built (1 K 8 1), after which there is no further record of it. It may have been carried off by Shishak to Egypt (1 K 14 26) or by Nebuchadnezzar to Babylon (2 K 25 8-17). There seems to have been no ark in the second temple.

11. Crown] i.e. a 'rim' or 'moulding' which projected above the top edge of the ark to keep the 'mercy seat' in its place.   **16. Testimony**] see on 16 34.   **17. Mercy seat**] RM 'covering.' This is not to be regarded as a mere lid or covering of the ark, but has an independent significance. It is the golden throne of God where the people's sins are 'covered,' i.e. expiated or forgiven : see on Lv 1 4.

18. Two cherubims] 'Cherubim' is the Heb. plural of 'cherub.' The exact form of these cherubim is doubtful. Some suppose they were winged bulls such as are represented on Assyrian monuments as guardian spirits at the doors of temples or houses : cp. Gn 3 24. Others take them to be of human form. They figure very often in Hebrew sacred art. They were introduced into the pattern of the curtain which screened off the Holy of Holies (26 31). In Jewish thought the cherubim occupy the highest rank among the angels of heaven, and are the bearers or upholders of the throne of Jehovah, who is accordingly said to sit upon or between the cherubim (2 K 19 15 Ps 18 10 80 1 99 1). In Ezk 10 the cherubim are identified with the four living creatures of c. 1 (see Ezk 10 20 and cp. Rev 4 6 f.). The figures of the cherubim upon the mercy seat were of course small ; those in Solomon's temple were of colossal dimensions (2 Ch 3 10-13).   **19. Of the mercy seat**] RV 'of one piece with the mercy-seat.'   **20. Toward the mercy seat shall the faces . . be**] This is probably what is alluded to in 1 Pet 1 12.   **22. I will meet with thee**] Hence the tabernacle is called the 'tent of meeting,' i.e. the place where Jehovah meets with Moses and Israel, not the place where worshippers assemble, as the AV rendering 'tabernacle of the congregation' seems to imply : see 29 42, 43 33 7.

23–30. The Table of Shewbread.

The ark alone stood in the innermost chamber. The table here described, on which lay twelve loaves (see on v. 30), stood in the second chamber, the Holy Place. On the Arch of Titus, still standing in Rome, there are sculptured the Table of Shewbread and the

Golden Candlestick which the Emperor Titus carried off from the Temple of Herod after the destruction of Jerusalem in the year 70 A.D. These were not the original table and candlestick, but were no doubt exact copies of them.

25. Border] The representation of the table on the Arch of Titus referred to above shows a narrow rail running round the table about halfway down the legs, keeping them in position. This is probably what is meant here by the ' border.' **27. Over against**] RV ' close by.' The rings would be nearly halfway down the legs. **29.** The **dishes** were the plates on which the loaves were brought to the table ; the **spoons** were small vessels to hold the incense which was laid upon the bread (Lv 24⁷) ; the **covers** (RV ' flagons ') and **bowls** held the wine of the drink offering which accompanied every meal offering. For **to cover withal** read with RV ' to pour out withal.' **30. Shewbread**] lit. ' bread of the presence,' RM ' Presence-bread.' This consisted of twelve loaves of unleavened bread, which were laid upon the table, in the presence of God, and changed every sabbath day. It was a kind of thank-offering, expressive of man's constant indebtedness to God for his daily bread : see on Lv 24⁵⁻⁹.

31–40. The Golden Candlestick.
This also stood in the Holy Place. Being made of pure gold, it is called the ' pure candlestick ' in 31⁸, etc. It was really a lampstand. From a central shaft three curved arms sprang on each side, one above the other, rising to the same height as it. On each of these seven supports rested a lamp, in shape like a bowl or saucer. The shaft and the arms were ornamented with representations of almond buds and blossoms, introduced three times into each arm and four times into the shaft (v. 34).

31. Bowls] (RV ' cups ') are the open leaves surmounting the **knops** or ' calyx ' of the flower. The topmost bowl held the lamp. On the oil, see on 27²⁰, ²¹, and cp. Lv 24¹⁻⁴ Nu 8¹⁻⁴.

Shall be of the same] RV ' of one piece with it ' : so in vv. 35, 36.

33. Candlestick] the central shaft, which may have had in all seven knops.

37. The lampstand stood on the south side of the Holy Place with its arms parallel to the wall. On these the lamps, in the form of oval-shaped saucers, were placed crosswise with their nozzles pointing northwards, so that they cast their light **over against** the lampstand, i.e. on the space in front of it. **38.** The **tongs** are the snuffers ; the **snuffdishes** are for receiving and removing the pieces of charred wick. **39.** A talent of gold is estimated at about £6,000 of our money : see on 38²⁴.

CHAPTER 26
THE TABERNACLE PROPER
This, which in the Hebrew is called ' the

dwelling ' (see on 25⁹), consists of an oblong tent, 30 cubits long, 10 broad, and 10 high, and stands within the ' court of the tabernacle ' (27⁹⁻ᶠ.). It is formed of a frame of open woodwork, over which are spread four layers of coverings, the undermost being of linen embroidered with figures of cherubim, the second of goathair cloth, the third of ramskin, and the outermost of sealskin. Internally, therefore, the tabernacle had the appearance of rows of panels enclosing a pattern of cherubim. The tabernacle was divided into two chambers by means of a veil suspended from the roof at a distance of 10 cubits from the back wall. The innermost chamber, or Holy of Holies, was therefore in shape a perfect cube of 10 cubits in the side. The roof, of which nothing is said, is best understood as flat. At the time of the conquest and settlement in Canaan, we hear of a tabernacle being set up at Shiloh, where it seems to have remained during the time of the Judges (Josh 18¹ Jg 21¹⁹ 1 S 1³). In the time of David it seems to have been at Nob (1 S 21¹), and afterwards at Gibeon (1 Ch 21²⁹), where it was at the beginning of Solomon's reign (2 Ch 1¹³). After the building of Solomon's temple we hear no more of it, its furniture being then transferred to the more permanent building.

1–14. The Coverings.
1–6. The undermost covering. This is of linen ornamented with cherubim of ' cunning work,' i.e. of tapestry or embroidery. Ten pieces of material, each 28 × 4 cubits, are sewn together in two sets of five (v. 3), which are then joined at their edges by means of loops and golden ' taches,' i.e. clasps (vv. 4–6), to form one large covering 40 cubits long and 28 wide. Of this length, 30 cubits are taken up with the roof, leaving 10 cubits to hang down the back. The front is left open, to be afterwards closed with a separate hanging (v. 36). Of the breadth, 10 cubits form the roof, leaving 18 to hang down and form the two sides. The covering, it will be observed, does not reach the ground at the sides, but this is not necessary, as there is a base running all round supporting the wooden frame (v. 19). **7–13.** The second covering. This is of goathair and is spread over the first. By joining eleven pieces, each 30 × 4 cubits, a covering is obtained 44 cubits long and 30 wide. The ampler width allows this covering to reach the ground at the sides. The extra length of 4 cubits is partly taken up by doubling back the edge a distance of 2 cubits, leaving 2 cubits the distribution of which is not clear (vv. 12, 13). **14.** The outer coverings. Over the goathair covering are spread two others, one of red leather made of ramskin, and the other, the outermost, of sealskin : see on 25⁵. The purpose of these opaque and heavy curtains is to exclude the light.

15–30. The wooden framework supporting the coverings.

15. The **boards,** as they are here called, are not solid, as then they would have been very heavy, and the cherubim embroidered upon the inner covering would not have been visible at all. It is best, with Professor Kennedy, to take them to be open frames consisting of two uprights connected with cross rails. These frames are 10 cubits in height and $1\frac{1}{2}$ in width, and are kept upright by being let down with tenons and mortises into sockets (v. 19), which rest side by side upon the ground, and form a continuous base or plinth all round. Rigidity is secured by means of long bars running round the structure (v. 26). **18.** The length of the side being 30 cubits, twenty frames are required for each side. **22. Sides**] RV 'hinder part': the W. end is meant. The tabernacle is 10 cubits in width, measured from curtain to curtain. As only six frames, amounting to 9 cubits, are required for the end, it would appear that 1 cubit was taken up with the thickness of the side frames with their stiffening bars. The frames were probably 6 in. deep and the bars 3 in.

23, 24. The exact meaning of these vv. is obscure, but they suggest that the two corners of the back wall were strengthened by means of an extra frame in the form of a sloping buttress. In v. 24 read with RV, 'they shall be double beneath, and in like manner they shall be entire unto the top thereof unto one (or, the first) ring.' The foot of the additional frame would be set back a little, giving the appearance of being 'double beneath,' and the frame would slope in to the top of the upright, where it would be fastened to it.

25. Eight boards] i.e. six upright and two extra for the sloping buttresses.

26–28. In order to give rigidity to the upright frames five bars are run along the three sides of the tabernacle through rings attached to the frames. The middle bar runs from end to end ; the others, it is implied, do not (v. 28).

27. The two sides westward] RV 'the hinder part westward,' as in v. 22.

31–33. The dividing veil. This is of the same material as the inner covering, linen tapestry, embroidered with cherubim, and is supported upon four pillars at a distance of 10 cubits from the back wall or 20 cubits from the entrance (see on v. 33). It screens off the Most Holy Place.

33. Under the taches] under the joining of the covering forming the roof which was at a distance equal to five widths of the material counting from the entrance : see on vv. 1–6.

36. The **hanging** curtain forming the door, RV 'the screen.' This closes the tabernacle on the E. side, and is supported by five pillars dividing the entrance into four equal spaces.

CHAPTER 27

Thr Altar of Burnt Offering. The Court of the Tabernacle. The Oil for the Lamps

1–8. The Altar of Burnt Offering.

This is a hollow chest of acacia wood overlaid with bronze, and stands within the court, midway between the outer entrance and the door of the tabernacle.

1. The approximate size of the altar is $7\frac{1}{2}$ ft. square and $4\frac{1}{2}$ ft. high : see on 20²⁶.

2. The horns] The form and significance of these horns are doubtful. They were very important, and seem to have been regarded as the most sacred part of the altar (cp. Am 3¹⁴). The blood of sin offerings was smeared upon them (Lv 4¹⁸), and this was done also at the consecration of the priests (Ex 29¹² Lv 8¹⁵). Criminals clung to them as an asylum (1 K 1⁵⁰ 2²⁸). Whether sacrificial victims were bound to them is doubtful, as the text is corrupt in the only passage where this practice seems to be alluded to (Ps 118²⁷). It has been suggested that the horns of the altar have some connexion with the worship of Jehovah in the form of a bull : cp. 32⁴. **Of the same**] RV 'of one piece with it.'

4. A grate] The position and purpose of this grating are not clear. It may have been a grating suspended by rings inside the altar, allowing the ashes, blood, and fat of the victims to drain off into the earth with which in all probability the hollow altar was filled. Or it may have been intended to carry the fire, or the victims over the fire. Some take it to be a piece of ornamental open-work extending downwards on each side, from the ledge to the ground, or the ledge itself : see on v. 5.

5. Compass of the altar] RV 'ledge round the altar.' This seems to have been a kind of projecting step or narrow platform running round the altar halfway up, on which the officiating priests stood.

9–19. The Court of the Tabernacle.

This is a sacred enclosure, open to the sky, surrounding the tabernacle, formed of a fence of linen curtains 5 cubits in height suspended on pillars of bronze. In form it is an oblong 100 cubits by 50. The Court is open to all worshippers. **10. Fillets**] Probably rods connecting the pillars with each other.

14. The hangings of one side] The entrance is in the middle of the E. side and is 20 cubits wide, leaving 15 cubits at each side of it. **19. Pins**] Tent pegs.

20, 21. The Oil for the Lamps.

20. Pure olive oil beaten RV] Oil extracted by beating olives in a mortar without heat. It is the purest kind of oil. **To burn always**] As there was no window in the tabernacle it is probable, though nowhere asserted, that the lights burned day and night: cp. Lv 24$^{1-4}$ Nu 8$^{1-4}$.

21. Tabernacle of the congregation] RV 'tent of meeting.' So always; see on 25^{22}. **Before the testimony**] see on 16^{34}. **Order it from evening to morning**] This may mean that the lamps were trimmed evening and morning: see on the preceding v.

CHAPTER 28
The Priestly Garments

1. All Israel is a 'kingdom of priests' (see on 19^6), but for the special service of the sanctuary Aaron and his descendants are selected and solemnly consecrated: see Lv 8, 9. Nadab and Abihu died (Lv 10) and the priesthood was continued in the descendants of Eleazar and Ithamar: see 1 Ch 24$^{1-6}$, and on Nu 25^{12}. **2. Holy garments**] The garments are holy because they are specially set apart and consecrated for use in the sanctuary. **3. Whom I have filled with the spirit of wisdom**] God is the source not only of all spiritual grace, but of every intellectual faculty and artistic gift: cp. Isa 28$^{23-29}$ Jas 1^{17}, and see on 31^4.

6–12. The Ephod.

This is a kind of waistcoat, made of variegated material, supported by straps passing over the shoulders and bound round the waist with a girdle. On each of the shoulder-straps is an onyx stone engraved with the names of six tribes of Israel. On the front of the ephod and attached to it by means of gold chains and rings is a pouch called the 'breastplate' (v. 15^f.).

6. The **gold** was in the form of threads worked into the pattern; see on 39^3. **Cunning work** is again embroidery as in 26^1. **8. Curious girdle**] RV 'cunningly woven band': i.e. embroidered.

9–12. The engraving of gems was an art well known to the Egyptians. The **names** were those of the twelve tribes. In v. 12 the stones are called **stones of memorial unto the children of Israel**. The high priest wore these stones when he ministered before the Lord, as the representative of the people. They served as a kind of visible supplication of His gracious remembrance. **13. Ouches**] The word, which is properly 'nouche,' means a rosette or button of gold filigree in which the stone is set.

14. The **chains** are for attaching the breastplate to the ephod: see vv. 22–25.

15–30. The breastplate] This is really a pouch, one span, or half a cubit, square, made of the same material as the ephod, and ornamented on the outside with twelve jewels set in four rows, each stone being engraved with the name of a tribe. The pouch is intended to hold the Urim and Thummim, by means of which God's judgments are declared (see on v. 30), and is therefore here called **the breastplate of judgment**.

16. Doubled] so as to form a pouch.

17–21. It is not easy to identify the stones mentioned in this and the following vv., the meaning of the Hebrew words being doubtful. The stones in the first row are probably a red jasper, a yellowish green serpentine, and an emerald. In the second row a red garnet, a lapis lazuli, and an onyx. In the third row a yellow agate, a black and white agate, and an amethyst. In the fourth row a yellow jasper, a beryl, and a dark green jasper. With this list of stones may be compared that in Ezk 28^{13}, and that in Rev 21^{19,20} (the foundations of the walls of the heavenly Jerusalem).

22. Chains at the ends *of* **wreathen work**] RV 'chains like cords, of wreathen work.'

30. The Urim and the Thummim] The literal meaning of these words is given in RM, 'the Lights and the Perfections.' The Urim and Thummim are nowhere described, but there can be no doubt that they were material objects, as they are said to be **put in the breastplate**, which was a pocket: cp. also Lv 8^8. From 1 S 28^6 we learn that the Urim (and Thummim) served as one of three ways by means of which the divine will might be ascertained: cp. Nu 27^{21}. In all probability they were two images or jewels, engraved with distinguishing characters, used in casting lots. In this connexion 1 S 14$^{38-42}$ is instructive. V. 41 in our Hebrew text there is evidently mutilated. The Gk. and Lat. versions read, 'If the iniquity be in me or Jonathan my son, give Urim; and if the iniquity be in the people, give Thummim.' On the casting of lots see on Nu 26^{55}, and cp. Lv 16^8 1 S 23$^{9-12}$ 30^{7,8} Ac 1^{26}.

31. The robe of the ephod] This is a frock or cassock, woven entirely of blue, without sleeves, drawn over the head, and worn under the ephod. Its chief characteristic is a row of golden bells attached to the skirt which sounded when the high priest moved, and enabled the people to follow him with their thoughts and prayers when he went into the Holy Place as their representative before God.

32. Habergeon] A sleeveless jacket.

33. Hem] RV 'skirts.' The **pomegranate** is a tree with a fruit like an apple, with a juicy pulp and full of seeds (hence the name, which means grained or seeded apple), extensively cultivated and highly prized in the East. The Heb. name is *rimmon*, which enters into many place-names. The pomegranates here are embroidered on the skirt of the robe. The bells are hung upon it.

35. His sound] i.e. its sound: see on Lv 25^5. **That he die not**] To enter God's presence carelessly is profanation and punishable with death.

36–38. The mitre] This is made of fine linen, and is in the form of a turban. Fastened in front of it is a plate of pure gold with the inscription HOLINESS TO THE LORD (RV ' HOLY TO THE LORD ').

38. The iniquity of the holy things] The ' holy things ' are the offerings of the people. As no offerings are ever worthy of God, their acceptance by Him is an act of grace. The high priest, when he enters the divine presence in the manner prescribed by God Himself, ' bears the iniquity of the holy things,' which are accepted in spite of the unworthiness necessarily attaching to them. For the lofty ideal of the sanctification, not only of what is used in divine service in the narrower sense of the term, but in every department of what is called secular life, see Zech 14 20, 21.

39. The coat is different from the robe (see 29 5). It is an under-garment or shirt of fine linen fastened with an embroidered girdle.

40. Bonnets] RV ' headtires': close fitting caps, probably of a different shape from the turban of the high priest. **41. Anoint them**] see on 29 7. **Consecrate**] lit. ' fill the hand.' The expression probably refers to some symbolic action indicating the giving of authority at a ceremony of installation to a sacred office : cp. 29 24.

CHAPTER 29

THE CONSECRATION OF THE PRIESTHOOD

Cp. Lv 8 9. The form of consecration consists of four things, (1) ablution (v. 4), (2) investiture with the holy garments (vv. 5–9), (3) anointing with holy oil (v. 7), and (4) offering of sacrifices (vv. 10 f.).

1. Without blemish] see on 12 5.

2. Unleavened bread] see on 12 8. **Tempered**] RV ' mingled.' Oil is a common ingredient of cakes in the East: see e.g. 1 K 17 12, and cp. Lv 2 5, 6.

4. Wash them with water] A symbolic action representing the need of inward purity in those who approach God. Washing is frequently enjoined as an act of ceremonial purification: see e.g. 30 17-21 Lv 11 25 14 8 15 13, etc., and cp. Mk 7 3, 4. The symbol is retained in Christian baptism: cp. 1 Pet 3 21.

6. Holy crown] the golden plate with the sacred inscription: see 28 36.

7. Anointing oil] This oil was specially prepared: see 30 23-25. Anointing with oil is an act symbolising a special consecration to the service of God. Jacob anointed the stone at Beth-el with oil (Gn 28 18; cp. 31 13 35 14), and the tabernacle and its furniture were also anointed (see 30 26-29 Lv 8 10, 11). Priests were consecrated by anointing (as here) and also kings (see 1 S 10 1 16 13 2 K 11 12), who are accordingly called the ' Lord's anointed ' (1 S 26 11 2 S 1 14 Ps 2 2 89 38, 39). The Hebrew word for ' anoint ' is *mashach*, whence is derived the word Messiah, which is used figuratively to describe one who is consecrated by God for a

special purpose: cp. e.g. Isa 45 1. In a unique sense it denotes *the* Messiah or Christ, the latter word being the Greek equivalent of the Hebrew term: see Isa 61 1 Lk 4 18. In NT. Christians are called the anointed of God, as having received the unction of the Holy Spirit: see 2 Cor 1 21 1 Jn 2 20, 27.

10–37. The sacrifices of Consecration.

These signify the self-surrender to God of those on whose behalf they are presented, symbolised by the laying of the hands upon the head of the victim and its subsequent slaughter: see on Lv 1 4. **10. The bullock**] is for a sin offering on behalf of Aaron and his sons. For the significance of this sacrifice see Lv 4. **12.** Cp. Lv 4 7. **Upon the horns of the altar**] see on 27 2.

13. The internal fat, like the blood, is regarded as the seat of life, and must always be offered to God by burning upon the altar: see on 23 18 and Lv 3 3. The **caul** *that is* **above the liver**] RV ' caul upon the liver,' is the fatty covering of that organ. **14. Shalt thou burn**] see Lv 4 11, 12, and on Lv 4 26.

15. One ram] one of the two already mentioned (v. 1), to be a whole burnt offering. It is entirely consumed upon the altar: see on Lv 1. **17. Unto his pieces, and unto his head**] RV ' with its pieces, and with its head.' The dismemberment of the victim is to secure its rapid consumption upon the altar.

18. A sweet savour] This phrase is frequently employed in connexion with sacrifices to indicate gracious acceptance on the part of God to whom they are offered: see e.g. Gn 8 21, and cp. Ex 5 21.

19. The other ram] called in v. 22 the ram of consecration, lit. ' of filling (the hand).' See on 28 41. Its blood is used to sprinkle Aaron and his sons and their garments ; its most sacred parts are waved in their hands, and then burnt upon the altar ; after which the flesh is boiled and eaten by them at a sacrificial feast. The ritual here resembles that of the peace offering, for which see on Lv 3.

20. This action symbolises the purification and consecration of the bodily faculties to the service of God. A similar ceremony was performed at the cleansing of a leper: see Lv 14 14, 17.

21. The head of Aaron is already anointed (v. 7), so that this sprinkling with blood and oil may refer only to the garments of himself and his sons. It is uncertain whether any save the high priest was anointed upon the head. In Lv 4 3, 5, 16 ' the anointed priest ' is the high priest (cp. Lv 21 10). On the other hand, Ex 28 41 enjoins the anointing of Aaron's sons, which, however, may refer to this second anointing.

22. The rump] RV rightly, ' the fat tail.' The tail of one species of the Syrian sheep is very long and broad, weighing sometimes from ten to fifteen pounds, and requiring to be supported on a little wheeled carriage. It is considered a great delicacy, its fat being used for cooking instead of butter.

23. The meal offering which usually accompanies a peace offering: see Lv 2 7 11-21.

24. Put all in the hands of Aaron] thus inducting him and his sons into the duties of their office. The 'waving' consisted in moving the offerings horizontally in the direction of the sanctuary, in token that they were first presented to God and then returned by Him to the officiating priests. This ceremony was performed at the presentation of a peace offering (Lv 7 28-34), of the first fruits of harvest (Lv 23 11, 12), and of the two loaves at the Feast of Weeks (Lv 23 20), and also in connexion with the cleansing of a leper (Lv 14 12, 24): see also on Nu 8 21. **26. It shall be thy part**] The law of the **wave offering** prescribes that the breast should be assigned to the officiating priest; on this occasion to Moses: see Lv 7 28-34. After their consecration the ceremony is performed by the priests, who receive the breast and right shoulder as their portion. See vv. 27, 28. **27. Heave offering**] 'Heaving' and 'waving' seem to refer to the same ceremony of presenting the parts first to God.

29. Shall be his sons' after him] cp. Nu 20 26. Here 'sons' is a general term signifying descendants. The priesthood was hereditary in the family of Aaron. **30. Shall put them on seven days**] see on v. 35.

31. The characteristic feature of the peace offering was the sacrificial meal partaken of by the offerers, expressive of their communion with God and one another : see on Lv 3. **In the holy place**] In the court before the door of the tent of meeting : see Lv 8 31.

33. Stranger] One not a priest, a layman : cp. 30 33 Lv 22 10 Nu 1 51 3 10 : see also on 12 19.

34. See on 12 10. **35.** The ceremony is to be repeated each day for seven days : cp. Lv 8 33, and for the fulfilment of the injunction, Lv 8 9. **36. When thou hast made**] RV 'when thou makest,' or, rather, ' by thy making.' The altar was consecrated by anointing : see Lv 8 10, 11, and see on v. 7.

37. Shall be holy] see on Lv 2 3.

38–42. The Daily Sacrifice. Every morning and evening a lamb is to be offered as a burnt offering on behalf of the whole community as an act of public worship : see on Lv 1. It is accompanied with a meal offering and a drink offering, which are sacrifices of thanksgiving. It was offered regularly from the time of its institution down to the destruction of Jerusalem, except for a short period (168–165 B.C.) during the wars of the Maccabees.

40. Tenth deal] tenth part of an ephah : see on 16 16. A **hin** is about a gallon and a half. **41. Meat offering**] RV ' meal offer-

ing ' : see Lv 2. **42. Tabernacle of the congregation**] RV 'tent of meeting' : see on 25 22. **43. Sanctified by my glory**] see 40 34, and on 3 2 16 10.

CHAPTER 30

THE ALTAR OF INCENSE. THE RANSOM MONEY. THE LAVER. THE ANOINTING OIL. THE INCENSE

1–10. The Altar of Incense. The use of incense in worship was probably due to the worshipper's desire to honour God by offering to Him what he enjoys himself. 'Ointment and perfume rejoice the heart' (Prov 27 9). It served also to counteract the strong smell of burning flesh, and was therefore usually presented as an accompaniment of sacrifice, and offered either in censers (Lv 10 1 16 12 Nu 16 17), or on an altar erected for the purpose, as here. In Scripture incense is an emblem of prayer, probably because its smoke ascends to the clouds, where God is supposed to dwell : see e.g. Ps 141 2 Rev 5 8 8 3. The existence of this altar of incense at the time of Moses has been disputed. In about one hundred places mention is made of ' the altar ' as if there was only one, that of burnt offering ; no mention is made of an altar of incense in Lv 16, where it might have been expected ; it is not alluded to among the furniture of Solomon's temple ; and the directions given here for its construction would have stood more naturally in c. 25 or 26, where the omission is somewhat strange. It is accordingly supposed that this passage, and others where an altar of incense is spoken of, are of later date : see on v. 6. Indeed, the whole of chs. 30, 31 is believed by some to be a later addition. Observe the solemn conclusion at the end of c. 29.

2. On the **horns**, see on 27 2. **Of the same**] see on 25 31.

3. Pure gold] Hence this altar is called ' the golden altar' (39 38 40 26 Nu 4 11 Heb 9 4 RM, etc.), to distinguish it from the altar of burnt offering, which is called the ' brazen altar' (39 39). **Crown**] i.e. rim or moulding, as in 25 11.

6. Before the vail] This means outside the veil and, therefore, in the Holy Place, not in the Holy of Holies, where it would be inaccessible save once a year, when the High Priest entered on the Day of Atonement (Lv 16) : see on 40 5. In Heb 9 4, however, it is said to have stood within the Holy of Holies. There seems to have been some doubt, therefore, as to its position in the tabernacle, a fact which is reflected in the construction of this v., which is overloaded and apparently self-contradictory. The altar is before the veil, and it is also before the mercy seat. The LXX omits the words ' before the mercy seat .. testimony.' This confusion corroborates the view that this altar did not belong to the original furniture of the tabernacle : see on vv. 1–10.

9. Strange incense] i.e. incense prepared differently from that prescribed in vv. 34–38 : see on Lv 10 1. **Meat offering**] RV 'meal offering' : see on Lv 2. **10. Make atonement upon it**] RV 'for it.' Owing to the imperfection of all human worship, the altar itself needs to be cleansed with a special rite : see on 28 38 29 36. The reference here is to the ceremonial of the yearly Day of Atonement, for which see Lv 16. **Most holy**] see on Lv 2 3.

11–16. The Ransom Money. It is here enacted that, when a census is taken, every person above the age of twenty shall pay half a shekel as his ransom. At the time of a census the people would be impressed with the great privilege of membership in God's chosen nation, and at the same time with their unworthiness to be reckoned in a 'kingdom of priests' : see on 19 5,6. This need of atonement underlies the payment of a money ransom, which is here called a 'ransom, or atonement, for your souls.' It is to be distinguished from the money given as a redemption for the firstborn, for which see 13 13. For the use made of the ransom money, see 38 25-28.

12. When thou takest the sum] A census of the people was probably in contemplation at this time, and was made twice during the forty years' sojourn in the wilderness : see Nu 1 and 26. Whether it was done regularly does not appear. In time the half shekel became an annual tax devoted to the maintenance of the public sacrifices in the Temple : see e.g. Mt 17 24. **Plague**] as the result of disobedience. **13. Half a shekel**] A silver shekel was equal to fully half-a-crown. The **shekel of the sanctuary** seems to have been a standard weight, and was probably preserved by the priests in the sanctuary.

14. Twenty was the age when liability to military service began (Nu 1 3). **15. All** give alike, for it is a ransom for the soul or life, and all souls are equal in the sight of God. **16. For the service of the tabernacle**] see 38 25-28.

17–21. The Laver. This was of bronze (see on 25 3), and stood in the court of the tabernacle between the altar of burnt offering and the door of the sanctuary, and held the water required for the ablutions of the priests (vv. 19–21 ; see on 29 4). According to 38 8 it was made of the mirrors of the serving women : see on Nu 4 11. Solomon's Temple had ten lavers (1 K 7 27-43).

22–33. The Holy Anointing Oil.

23. Calamus] The word means 'reed' or 'cane.' Several species of aromatic reed are

known in the East. **24. Cassia**] a kind of cinnamon of a very pungent flavour. **An hin**] about a gallon and a half. **25. Apothecary**] RV 'perfumer.' In the warm East ointments and perfumes are greatly employed as cosmetics, and the art of preparing these is carried to a high degree of perfection. Among the Jews there was a guild of perfumers in later times. **29. Most holy**] see on Lv 2 3. **32. Upon man's flesh shall it not be poured**] It must be reserved for the priests, and not used as an ordinary unguent : see v. 33. **33. Stranger**] one who is not a priest, as in 29 33. **Cut off**] see on 12 15.

34–38. The Incense.

34. Stacte] a kind of gum, probably myrrh. **Onycha**] part of the shell of a shell fish. It burns with a pungent odour. **Galbanum**] a gum resin. **Frankincense**] a fragrant gum obtained by slitting the bark of an Indian tree, which was also to be found in ancient times in Arabia : see e.g. Isa 60 6 Ezk 27 22. The substance called in modern times 'common frankincense' is obtained largely from fir trees. The English word means 'pure incense.' **35.** RV 'and thou shalt make of it incense, a perfume after the art of the perfumer, seasoned with salt, pure and holy.' Salt, as preventing corruption, is the symbol of purity and durability ; it was used with all sacrifices both animal and vegetable : see Lv 2 13 Ezr 6 9 Ezk 43 24 Mk 9 49. Among the Arabs salt is the emblem of fidelity and lasting friendship. To have 'eaten salt' with a person, and so partaken of his hospitality, is equivalent to a pledge of mutual and indissoluble amity. Hence in OT. a 'covenant of salt' is one that cannot be broken : see Lv 2 13 Nu 18 19 2 Ch 13 5, and cp. Ezr 4 14 (AM) and Mk 9 50.

37. This particular compound is not to be used for any profane purpose : cp. the similar direction in the case of the holy anointing oil (vv. 32, 33).

CHAPTER 31

THE APPOINTMENT OF BEZALEEL AND AHOLIAB. THE KEEPING OF THE SABBATH

2. By name] indicating a very special call : cp. 33 12 Isa 43 1 45 1,3,4 Jn 10 3. **Bezaleel**] RV 'Bezalel' : see 1 Ch 2 18-20. For the identification of the grandfather of Bezaleel with the Hur of Ex 17 10 there is nothing beyond the similarity of names. **3.** See on 28 3.

4. To devise cunning works] Divine inspiration does not reduce man to a mere machine or passive instrument. It is compatible with originality of invention. This applies not only to the mechanical arts as here, but also to intellectual gifts. It heightens and purifies, but does not supersede the normal faculties. Observe that 'cunning' is used here in its etymological sense of 'knowing' or 'skilful.' See Ps 137[5].

10. Cloths of service] RV 'finely wrought garments,' a general term including what follows : see 39[1, 41].

12–17. The reason why the injunction to observe the sabbath is repeated here and again in 35[1-3] before the account of the carrying out of the preceding instructions is probably the close connexion of the worship of the tabernacle with the observance of the day of rest.

13. A sign] Like circumcision the sabbath is a sign or sacrament marking the covenant relation between Jehovah and His people. Cp. for circumcision Gn 17[11] Ro 4[11], and for the sabbath Ezk 20[12] Isa 56[4, 6]. Ancient profane writers frequently refer to these two things as the distinguishing characteristics of a Jew.

14. Shall be put to death .. shall be cut off] The two expressions are not always synonymous ; see on 12[15].

18. Two tables of testimony] cp. 16[34] 25[16]. Written with the finger of God] see on 24[12].

CHAPTER 32
THE IDOLATRY OF THE PEOPLE

1–6. The historical narrative is here resumed from 24[18]. Becoming impatient at the prolonged absence of Moses on the mount (forty days, 24[18]), and despairing of his return, the people prevail upon Aaron to make a god to go before them. From the earrings of the men and women he accordingly makes a golden bull, to which divine honours are paid.

1. Unto Aaron] Aaron and Hur had been left in charge by Moses ; see 24[14]. **Make us gods]** RM 'a god.' The Hebrew word for God has a plural form. In making this demand it is doubtful whether the people intended to abandon the worship of Jehovah altogether, or wished simply to have a visible representation of Him, in other words, whether their sin was a breach of the first commandment of the Decalogue or the second. The words of Aaron in vv. 4, 5 seem to indicate that he at least regarded the golden bull as an image of the true God ; but in v. 8 the people are charged with deserting Jehovah for another god. The one sin naturally leads to the other. The worship of God by means of images degrades God, and the image gradually usurps His place in the mind of the worshipper. See on 15[11] 20[3, 4].

2. Earrings] RV 'rings.' Taken by itself the word may mean either earrings or nose-rings. Here the former are expressly intended, but in 35[22] both may be included. Among Eastern peoples earrings were formerly worn both by men and women (' your sons ' here ; cp. Jg 8[24]), not only as ornaments but as amulets or charms. In modern times men have discontinued the use of earrings, and nose-rings are worn only by the Bedouin women.

4. After he had made it] read with RV, 'and made it.' The **calf** was really a bullock. It is usually supposed that the symbol was derived from the worship of the Egyptians. But it was a living bull, not an image, that was worshipped in Egypt. More probably, therefore, the symbol was connected with the worship of the Chaldeans and Assyrians, of which some traces may have survived among the descendants of Abraham. A common image with the Assyrians is that of a bull with wings and a human head, emblematic of strength and wisdom. See on the cherubim, 25[18], also 1 K 12[28].

5. A feast to the LORD] i.e. to Jehovah. See on v. 1. Feasting was a common accompaniment of sacrifice ; see on 24[9-11]. On the nature of the **play** in this case see vv. 18, 19, 25, where we learn that it included singing and dancing. Cp. Ex 15[20, 21] Jg 21[19-21] 2 S 6[12-14] 1 K 18[26 mg.] Isa 30[29].

7–14. God tells Moses of the sin of the people and of His purpose to destroy them. At the intercession of Moses they are spared.

7. Thy people which thou broughtest out] By their own act the people have broken the covenant bond uniting them to Jehovah. In v. 11 Moses pleads that they are the people of Jehovah. **9. Stiffnecked]** This common metaphor is taken from a stubborn ox that refuses to submit to the yoke. Cp. Zech 7[11] Hos 4[16] (RV 'stubborn heifer'), Jer 17[23] Neh 3[5] Ps 75[5]. **10.** Cp. the promise made to Abraham in Gn 12[2]. The people having judged themselves unworthy of the promise (cp. Ac 13[46]), a fresh start will be made with Moses who will be the founder of a new nation. Cp. Nu 14[12].

11. In a spirit of noble generosity Moses effaces himself and intercedes with all his soul for the people. See on v. 31. He does not minimise their sin (cp. v. 31), but with a holy boldness he pleads (1) that they are God's own people whom He has redeemed from Egypt (v. 11, cp. 33[13]), (2) that their destruction will be misunderstood by the Egyptians (v. 12), and that (3) it will make the promises to Abraham of no effect (v. 13). **12.** See on Dt 32[27], and refs. there. **13. Israel]** This name is employed rather than Jacob because it suggests the ' prince that had power with God and prevailed ' : see Gn 32[28].

15–29. The suppression of the idolatry. **15,16.** See intro. to c. 20 and on 24[12]. **17. Joshua]** see on 24[15]. **19. And brake them]** The people had already broken the law contained in them which was the basis of the covenant.

20. Burnt it] It was probably not solid, but consisted of a wooden core overlaid with gold: cp. Isa 40[19, 20] 44[12-19]. The total abolition of the idol is indicated in the threefold treatment of burning it, reducing it to powder and casting it into the water: cp. Dt 9 21. This last action was more than a means of dispersing the very atoms of which it was composed. The people were made to drink the water, a grim symbol of retribution, with which may be compared the procedure in connexion with the 'water that causeth a curse' in Nu 5 23, 24: see also 2 K 23 6.

22. Mischief] RV 'evil': Aaron tries to put the whole responsibility on the people. He pleads that they intimidated him. **24. There came out this calf**] as if by accident, a manifestly poor apology. Observe that Aaron's two pleas of compulsion and accident are in various forms most commonly adduced in palliation of wrongdoing. From Dt 9 20 we learn that Aaron's abetting of the people's sin evoked the severe displeasure of God, and that his life was only spared on the intercession of Moses.

25. *Were* **naked**] RV 'were broken loose.' For the use of the word in the literal sense see e.g. on Nu 5 18. Here it is most probably used in the metaphorical sense of 'unruly': cp. 2 Ch 28 19. Read on with RV, 'for Aaron had let them loose for a derision among their enemies,' i.e. not with the intention, but with the result, that they became a derision. The lapse of professedly religious people is not only sinful, but brings religion itself into disrepute.

26. Who *is* **on the LORD'S side?**] The contrast between the characters of Moses and Aaron is strikingly brought out all through this narrative. Aaron appears as timid and compliant; while Moses is rigidly loyal, fearless, ready to stand alone if need be on the Lord's side, impulsive (v. 19) and yet wholly unselfish (v. 32). Observe that it is the sons of Levi, members of the same tribe to which Moses belongs, that come to his call.

29. Consecrate yourselves] lit. 'fill your hands'; see on 28 41. For **upon** read with RV 'against.' The claims of kinship must yield to those of God and duty: cp. Mt 10 37 Lk 14 26 and Mt 12 46-50. The zeal of the Levites is rewarded with a **blessing,** by which doubtless is meant the priesthood: see on Dt 33 9, and cp. the similar reward of Phinehas, Nu 25 12.

30-35. Intercession of Moses.

30. Make an atonement] Something more was required than the punishment that had been inflicted on a portion of the people.

32. If thou wilt forgive their sin] This form of sentence is used in Hebrew to express an earnest desire or passionate entreaty, and is equivalent to 'O that thou wouldest' . . or 'O if thou wouldest but' .. Cp. e.g. Ps 95 7 RV, 'To-day, O that ye would hear,' and 1 Ch 4 10, 'O that thou wouldest bless me,' lit. 'If thou wilt bless me.' **If not, blot me .. out**

of thy book] The figure is taken from the registers in which the names of citizens were enrolled: see e.g. Isa 4 3 Jer 22 30 Ezk 13 9. So God is represented as having a book in which are inscribed the names of those who are to be preserved alive. When He blots out a name that person dies. The Book is therefore a Book of Life: cp. Ps 69 28 Dan 12 1 Lk 10 20 Phil 4 3 Rev 3 5 13 8 20 12 22 19. The Jews believe that on New Year's Day God determines who shall live and who shall die in the course of the year, and that the decision is made final ten days afterwards on the Day of Atonement. Moses's prayer, therefore, is an expression of his willingness to bear the penalty of the people's sin. For a similar instance of absolute self-sacrifice cp. St. Paul's words in Ro 9 3. **33. Whosoever hath sinned**] cp. Ezk 18 4.

34. Mine Angel] see on 3 2. The angel here seems to be distinguished from God Himself: see 33 3. On the other hand, the angel is virtually identified with God, for God's 'presence' goes with them (33 14). **I will visit their sin upon them**] Though the people were not at once destroyed they did not escape all the consequences of their sin.

CHAPTER 33

THE INTERCESSION OF MOSES (continued)

6. By the mount Horeb] RV 'from mount Horeb onward': this implies that they ceased wearing their ornaments. Their humiliation was lasting. **Horeb**] i.e. Sinai: see on 3 1.

7. Moses took the tabernacle] RV 'Moses used to take the tent, .. and he called it, The tent of meeting': see on 25 22. The tent here is most probably not the Tabernacle whose construction is prescribed in chs. 25–31. The words describe the practice of Moses before its erection, the account of which follows in chs. 35–40. **9. Descended**] from the top of the mount. After the erection of the Tabernacle the cloud rested upon it: see 40 34-38. **10. Worshipped**] bowed themselves to the ground.

11. Face to face] A peculiar privilege: cp. 19 9 Nu 12 6-8 Dt 34 10. Verse 23 shows that the expression 'face to face' is not to be pressed literally, but to be understood as distinct from a revelation by means of dreams or visions : see especially Nu 12 6-8. **Joshua**] see on 17 9. The priests and Levites were not yet formally consecrated to the service of the sanctuary.

12-17. The promise of God to go with the people is renewed.

12. Thou hast not let me know] The whole of this passage from v. 7 may be independent of what goes before (cp. the expression 'used to take' in v. 7). Otherwise we must suppose that Moses has not clearly understood the meaning of the promise 'I will send an angel before thee' in v. 2. **I know thee by name**] see on 31 2.   **13. Thy way**] thy purpose. **Thy people**] see on 32 7, 11.

14. My presence] lit. 'my face.' The expression is equivalent to 'myself in person': cp. e.g. 2 S 17 11, where the words are literally 'and that thy face go into battle.' The 'angel of God's presence' (cp. Isa 63 9) is not the angel that stands in the presence of God but in whom the personal presence of God is manifested: see on 3 2. **Will give thee rest**] i.e. a peaceful settlement in Canaan: cp. Dt 3 20 Josh 21 44 23 1.   **16. Separated**] see on 19 4-6 Nu 23 9.

18–23. A divine manifestation asked and promised. **18. Shew me thy glory**] What Moses asks, not out of curiosity but as a confirmation of the promise in v. 14, is impossible. No man can look upon God's unveiled glory and live (v. 20 : see on 19 9 24 9-11). Even the angels cannot do so (Isa 6 2).   **19. My goodness**] A revelation is vouchsafed, but it is one accommodated to human capacity. It is not further described, but probably consisted in the proclamation in the following chapter, vv. 6, 7. This gracious veiling of the ineffable glory and the revelation of God in mercy are both fulfilled in the person of Christ : see Jn 1 14 2 Cor 4 6.   **23. My back parts**] Not the full manifestation of the divine radiance, but its afterglow. The most that human faculties can comprehend of God even in their exalted moments is a faint reflection of His essential glory : cp. 1 Cor 13 12.

CHAPTER 34
THE RENEWAL OF THE COVENANT

In token that the people are forgiven, God renews His covenant relation with them. The conditions are the same as before. The Decalogue is inscribed on two fresh tables, and the main provisions of the ceremonial law are repeated. **1. Which thou brakest**] There is no reproach in these words. Moses is nowhere blamed for his righteous indignation. He was 'angry and sinned not.'   **3.** See on 19 12, 13. **5.** See on 33 19. On the **name** of **The LORD** see on 3 13.

6. RV 'The LORD, the LORD, a God full of compassion and gracious, slow to anger, and plenteous in mercy and truth': this is perhaps the highest utterance of revelation, and is frequently quoted by OT. writers : see e.g. Neh 9 17 Ps 86 15 103 8 145 8 Joel 2 13 Jon 4 2, also Nu 14 18. The divine attributes here proclaimed are not God's dread majesty and power, but His mercy and truth. He is merciful, but He cannot overlook transgression. **7. That will by no means clear** *the guilty*]

i. e. will not allow the guilty to pass unpunished. The same words are rendered in 20 7 'will not hold him guiltless,' and in Jer 30 11 'will not leave unpunished.' **Visiting the iniquity of the fathers**] see on 20 5.

12–17. The warning against idolatry is solemnly repeated, and the people are forbidden to make covenant or intermarry with their idolatrous neighbours in Canaan. See on 23 32, 33 and on Nu 25 16-18.   **13. Images**] RV 'pillars,' or 'obelisks': see 24 4. **Groves**] i.e. 'things graven,' RV 'Asherim.' The Canaanitish shrine contained an altar, near which stood a stone pillar and an *Asherah* (plur. *Asherim*). The latter was a wooden pole or stump of a tree planted in the ground: see Jg 6 26 1 K 15 13 2 K 17 10 23 7, and on 1 K 14 15. Immoral rites were practised at these shrines in honour of the reproductive forces of nature.

14. Whose name *is* **Jealous**] on **name**, see on 3 13, and on **Jealous**, on 20 5.

15. Whoring after their gods] The covenant bond between Jehovah and Israel is frequently compared with a marriage (see e.g. Jer 3 14 Hos 2 19, 20), and idolatry, which is unfaithfulness to Jehovah, is regarded as adultery, a view all the more natural seeing that idolatry and immorality so frequently went together (see on 'groves' v. 13 and on Lv 19 29). For this conception of idolatry, see e.g. Lv 17 7 Nu 14 33 Jer 3 1-20 13 27 Hos 2 (especially vv. 13, 16) Ezk 20 30, 31. In NT. the Church is called the Bride of Christ. See Eph 5 23-32 Rev 19 7-9 21 2, 9, 17.

18–26. See on 23 12-19.   **21. Earing**] i.e. ploughing. At these busy and critical seasons there would be a special temptation to work upon the sabbath day.

24. Desire thy land, when thou shalt go up] i.e. take advantage of your absence to despoil your homes. God will protect their property while they are worshipping Him.

28–35. Moses descends from the Mount with the new Tables.

28. Similar fasts are recorded of Elijah (1 K 19 8) and of our Lord (Mt 4 2) : see on 2 21. **He wrote**] The subject is God : see v. 1.

29. Wist not] knew not. **Shone while he talked with him**] RV 'shone by reason of his speaking with him.' His face was lit up with a radiance which was the reflection of the divine glory, and served to attest the message he delivered to the people. Compare what is said of our Lord at His Transfiguration (Mt 17 2) and of Stephen at his martyrdom (Ac 6 15 7 55). The present instance is a fine illustration of the power of unconscious influence. The Heb. verb rendered 'shone' in this passage is derived from the word meaning 'horn,' which is used figuratively to denote rays or flashes of light proceeding from a luminous object (see e.g. Hab 3 4 with mg.). The Vulgate

(Latin version) accordingly says of Moses' face that it was *cornuta*, which has led to the curious representation of Moses with horns, as seen in early art.

33. *Till* Moses had done speaking with them] RV 'when Moses had done speaking with them.' Moses usually wore the veil, only putting it off when he entered the presence of God or spoke to the people. An interesting reminiscence of this is said to be seen in the Jewish synagogue, where the priest, in pronouncing the Aaronic benediction (Nu 6 24-26), veils his face with his *tallith* (see on Nu 15 37-41), 'lest the utterance of the words should bring up the glory that shone in the face of Moses and strike the people dead.' St. Paul refers to this incident in 2 Cor 3 7-18, and evidently understands that Moses wore the veil in order to hide the *fading* of the glory in his face (see vv. 7, 13). He accordingly sees in Moses' action an illustration of the inferiority of the Jewish dispensation as compared with the Christian. The glory of the former was fading, transitory, and partly obscured ; that of the latter is permanent, unobstructed, ever increasing, and shared by all.

35 1-3. The Sabbath Law. See 31 15, and on 20 8-11.

3. Kindle no fire] an act involving work. This law is observed by pious Jews at the present day. They have fires in their houses on the sabbath, but they employ a gentile to light and tend them : see on 12 16.

CHAPTERS 35 4-40 38
AN ACCOUNT OF THE CONSTRUCTION OF THE TABERNACLE AND ITS FURNITURE.

This section is an almost verbal repetition of chs. 25-31, describing the carrying out of the commands in those chapters by Moses and the people.

4-29. Moses invites the people to contribute the materials required, which they do with great liberality : cp. 36 5-7. See on 25 1-9.

22. Tablets] RV 'armlets,' or 'necklaces' : cp. Nu 31 50. **23. Red skins of rams]** i.e. leather of rams' skins dyed red, as in 26 14. **30-35.** See on 31 1-11.

CHAPTER 36
THE WORK BEGUN. THE LIBERALITY OF THE PEOPLE

Cp. 1 Ch 29 6-9 Ezr 2 68-70 Neh 7 70-72.

8-38. The construction of the Tabernacle : see c. 26.

8. Made he them] The subject down to 38 31 is Bezaleel : cp. 37 1 38 22.

CHAPTER 37
1-9. The Ark and Mercy seat : see 25 10-22.
10-16. Table of Shewbread : see 25 23-30.
17-24. The Candlestick : see 25 31-40.

25-28. The Altar of Incense : see 30 1-5. This is mentioned here in its natural position along with the other furniture of the Holy Place. **29.** The Holy Oil, and the Incense : see 30 22-38.

CHAPTER 38
THE HOLY FURNITURE

1-7. The Altar of Burnt Offering : see 27 1-8.

8. The Laver : see 30 17-21. Read with RV 'mirrors of the serving women which served at the door of the tent of meeting.' What service these women rendered is not said. They are only mentioned once again, in 1 S 2 22. They may have helped in the liturgical part of the worship by their singing and dancing. The Heb. word which indicates their service here is used of the Levites in Nu 4 23 8 24.

9-20. The Court of the Tabernacle : see 27 9-19.

21-31. The Sum of the Precious Metals.

21. Ithamar] the youngest of the four sons of Aaron : see 6 23, and on 28 1. **24.** The gold shekel is estimated to have been worth about £2 of our money, and the gold talent, which contained 3,000 shekels, about £6,000. The silver shekel was worth fully 2s. 6d., and the silver talent about £400. **26.** The number of persons given here is identical with the result of the census taken in the second month of the second year : see Nu 1 46. This suggests that the computations recorded here were made not exactly at this time but after the erection of the tabernacle. It is to be observed that the silver mentioned here is not that contributed voluntarily but what was obtained as ransom money (30 11-16). The latter amount may for some reason have been substituted for the former in this passage.

CHAPTER 39
THE MAKING OF THE HOLY GARMENTS

See c. 28, where the order is slightly different.

1. Cloths of service] RV 'finely wrought garments,' as in 31 10.

2-7. The Ephod : see 28 6-12.

8-21. The Breastplate : see 28 15-30.

22-26. The Robe of the Ephod : see 28 31-35.

27-29. The Other Garments for the Priests : see 28 39-43.

30, 31. The Plate for the Mitre (v. 28) : see 28 36-38.

30. Holy crown] see on 29 6.

32-43. The completion of the work and its approval by Moses. Everything must be in accordance with the pattern shown him in the Mount (25 8, 40).

38. The golden altar] the Altar of Incense : see on 30 3. **39. The brasen altar]** the Altar of Burnt Offering : see 27 2.

CHAPTER 40

The Tabernacle erected

1-16. Moses is commanded to uprear the Tabernacle and consecrate it, together with its furniture, and the priests by anointing them.

2. On the first day of the first month] i.e. of the month Abib (see on 12 2, 41) in the second year after the exodus from Egypt (v. 17). They left Egypt on the fifteenth day of Abib, and arrived at Sinai in the third month : see 19 1.

4. The things . . to be set . . upon it] i.e. the shewbread (see v. 23 and on 25 30).

5. Before the ark] in a line with it but outside the Holy of Holies : see v. 26, and see on 30 6. **9. Anoint the tabernacle]** cp. 30 26-29.

12. See 28 41 29 4, 7.

17-33. The Uprearing of the Tabernacle.

19. The tent over the tabernacle] Heb. 'the tent over the dwelling.' See on 25 9, 26 intro.

20. The testimony] the two tables of stone : see on 16 34. **21. Vail of the covering]** RV 'veil of the screen' : see on 26 3-33.

28. Hanging *at* **the door]** RV 'screen of the door' : see on 26 36.

29. Moses offers the first daily sacrifice (29 40). **33. The court round about the tabernacle]** see 27 9-19.

34-35. The Dwelling being prepared, the cloud descends and the glory of the Lord occupies the sanctuary.

34. A cloud] RV 'the cloud' : it is the same cloud that has been so frequently mentioned already : see 13 21, 19 9 and note there, 33 9. **The glory of the LORD]** see 16 10 24 17.

35. Cp. Lv 16 2 1 K 8 10, 11 2 Ch 5 13, 14 7 2.

36-38. See on 13 21, and cp. Nu 9 15-23.

LEVITICUS

INTRODUCTION

1. Title and Contents. The title Leviticus is prefixed to this section of the Pentateuch in the Greek Version of the OT., but it is not particularly appropriate, as the Levites are hardly mentioned in the book. Jewish writers call it *Vayikra* (Heb. 'and He called'), from its opening word, or the 'Law, or Book, of Priests,' or the 'Book of Offerings.' It may be described as a manual of religious ceremonies composed for the guidance of priests and worshippers. Its specific character is evident at a glance. It differs from the other books of the Pentateuch in being almost entirely a book of laws. There is very little narrative, and historical indications are scanty. Reference is made to Mt. Sinai as the scene where some at least of the laws were promulgated (25 1 26 46 27 34) ; in some passages it is implied that Israel is still leading a camp-life in the wilderness (4 12 14 3 16 10) ; the consecration of Aaron and his sons is described in detail (8–10) ; and two incidents are narrated illustrating the punishment following a breach of the regulations (Nadab and Abihu, 10 1-7, the blasphemer, 24 10-16). With these few exceptions, which are more apparent than real, the incidents being introduced simply as illustrations (see on 24 16), the contents of Leviticus consist entirely of laws, and these mainly of a ceremonial character (see intro. to c. 17).

The twenty-seven chapters forming the book

fall into four well-marked divisions as follows. **Part 1. The Law of Sacrifice, chs. 1–7.** This again consists of two sections : (a) Directions addressed to the Worshippers regarding the five main types of sacrifice, viz. the Burnt Offering (c. 1), the Meal Offering (c. 2), the Peace Offering (c. 3), the Sin Offering (4–5 13), and the Guilt Offering (5 14–6 7), and (b) Directions addressed to the Priests in connexion with these sacrifices, which are dealt with in the same order, except that the Peace Offering comes last. **Part 2. The Consecration of the Priesthood, chs. 8–10.** This comprises the consecration of Aaron and his sons (c. 8), their installation into office (c. 9), and the death of Nadab and Abihu (c. 10). **Part 3. The Law of Clean and Unclean, leading up to the ritual of the Day of Atonement, chs. 11–16.** This division treats of the uncleanness of certain meats (c. 11), of childbirth (c. 12), of leprosy (chs. 13, 14), of sexual discharges (c. 15), and the ceremonial of the Day of Atonement (c. 16). **Part 4. The Law of Holiness, chs. 17–26.** This is a miscellaneous collection of laws, many of them of a moral and religious character. It treats of sacrifice and eating of blood (c. 17), unlawful marriage and unchastity (c. 18), various moral and social duties, such as justice, kindness, purity, etc. (chs. 19, 20), duties of priests and matters of ritual (chs. 21, 22), the sacred seasons (c. 23), the shewbread and law of blasphemy (c. 24), the Sabbatical Year and Year of Jubilee (c. 25), and concludes with exhortations to keep the law (c. 26). The book closes with a chapter on Vows and Tithes with the manner of their commutation, in the form of an appendix (c. 27).

2. Origin and Composition. The general question of the authorship of the Pentateuch is treated in a separate article, to which reference should be made. It will suffice to say here that, while much of the legislation contained in the book of Leviticus is of Mosaic origin, the book in its present form bears evidence of having been put together out of separate collections of laws. It is observed e.g. that the literary style is not uniform throughout, chs. 17–26 occupying in this respect a position quite by themselves (see the introductory note to this section in the commentary); that laws relating to the same subject are not always placed together ; that sometimes the same laws are repeated in different parts of the book ; and that the contents appear in the form of groups, many of which are provided with separate headings and conclusions (see e.g. 7 ^{37,38} 11 ^{46,47} 13 ^{59} 14 $^{54-57}$ 15 ^{32,33} 26 ^{46}, and the introductory notes to chs. 21 and 25). Such features make it tolerably certain that in its present form Leviticus is ' a collection of smaller collections, or a collection added to from time to time.' It need not be thought surprising that this is so. In itself, ritual is subject to the law of change and development, and many regulations, originally framed for a people leading a nomadic life in the wilderness, would require modification when that people dwelt in cities, built their temple, and led a settled agricultural life. We may believe, therefore, that some details in these laws are of later date than others, and that what we have in the book of Leviticus is the final form of a process of collection, editing, and adaptation carried on subsequently to the time of the great Lawgiver. The book is, in fact, a codification of laws originating in the Mosaic legislation. At what time it was cast into its present form we may never be able to determine with certainty. It may be that it was done under the influences which led to the restoration of the Temple in the sixth century B.C., and that the book was used as a kind of liturgy of the Second Temple. But we are not obliged to believe that the laws themselves originated at this later date. Some of them, as was said above, imply that they were given to a people leading a camp-life in the wilderness. At whatever time they were finally collected and incorporated in the Pentateuch, in substance the laws in Leviticus are derived from Moses. In other words, the contents are much older than the vessel in which they are contained.

3. Religious Value. To the ordinary reader of the Bible the book of Leviticus may seem dry and uninteresting. It treats of matters which for Christians have lost direct interest, and of a system of religious observances which they have never known. Its laws, being mainly of a ceremonial nature, have little or no practical bearing on the life of the present day. For this reason readers of the Bible may be inclined to pass it by. Yet Leviticus is anything but an uninteresting book. To the student of comparative religion it is of the greatest possible value. Its religious rites and social customs have numberless points of contact with those of other early nations, and it is interesting and instructive to observe how primitive customs were adopted and transformed, purged in many cases of immorality, cruelty, injustice, and idolatry, transfused with a new spirit, and made to subserve a moral and spiritual purpose. The ceremonial legislation of Leviticus is certainly not the final stage in the progress of revelation, but it marks a great step forward, and prepares the way for better things. Its moral teaching, its insistence on the duty of justice and mercy, of kindness to the poor and strangers, to the weak and slaves, and even to the lower animals, of chastity and truthfulness, is not without its application to the present day, while beneath its forms and ceremonies, its laws of clean and unclean, its ritual purifications, its sacrifices and sacred festivals, its tithes and offerings, it is not difficult to read similar lessons of religion and morals in type and figure. The entire system is penetrated with the thought that Israel is called to be a holy people consecrated to the service of a holy God. Its spirit is expressed in the words, ' Ye shall be holy, for I the Lord your God am holy.' That its minute and multifarious regulations served to impress upon the hearts of the devout in Israel a sense of the holiness and grace of God, of the hatefulness of sin, of the need of cleansing and restoration, cannot be doubted. It may be that the Israelites did not altogether escape the danger, incidental to the observance of all ceremonial laws, of formalism, hypocrisy, and contentment with an external standard of religion ; it may be that at times they fell far short of their ideal ; still no people had ever a loftier conception of the nature of God and of their relationship to Him and consequent obligation to lead a life of righteousness. A holy God, dwelling amid a holy people in a holy land—it would be unfair to say that there were not many in Israel who saw this truth beneath the surface of ceremonial, and were by its means prepared for the coming of Him who ' *is* the end of the law for righteousness to every one that believeth ' (Ro 10 ^{4}).

PART 1

(Chs. 1–7) THE LAW OF SACRIFICE

WHAT is recorded here is not the institution of the rite of sacrifice, which is assumed to be already in existence (see 1²), but its regulation in matters of detail. It did not originate among the Israelites ; it is a primitive and universal custom, based apparently upon a natural instinct, and found in one form or other in all parts of the world. Sacrifice is an act of worship, whereby the offerer either expresses his sense of the harmony and communion existing between himself and his god, or endeavours to restore these when by any means they have been destroyed. In all probability the former idea is the earlier, and the origin of sacrifice is to be found in the conception that the god of a tribe stands in a very close relationship to it, and in some respects has a common life and interests with it. In primitive times the god was conceived in a crude and material form. He was supposed to require food and drink (see on 3¹¹). And, as eating and drinking together is a common token of good relationship, it may well be that sacrifice in its primitive form was regarded as a common meal partaken of by the Deity and his worshippers in good fellowship. Part of the offering was eaten by the latter, and the portion for the god was laid out, and left for him, in some place where he was supposed to dwell. As the god came to be regarded as a more or less ethereal being, means were taken to send his portion to him, as it were, by converting the solid parts into smoke by burning and pouring out the liquids, wine, blood of the sacrificial victim, etc., and letting them sink into the earth. Traces of this primitive idea of sacrifice, as a feast or common meal partaken of by the god and his worshippers, may be discovered among the Israelites in Bible times : e.g. in the sacrificial feast which followed the making of the covenant between Jehovah and His people in Ex. 24 (see on vv. 9–11), and in the feast at the 'high place' to which Saul went (1 S 9¹³ᶠ·). See also the note on the Shewbread (Lv 24⁵⁻⁹) and on the Peace Offering (Lv 3) ; and see for a protest against this materialistic conception of God Ps 50⁸⁻¹⁵.

Alongside of this idea, and perhaps growing out of it, is that which regards the sacrifice as a gift made to the god to procure his favour or appease his vengeance. The worshipper makes his offering as before, by burning or by libation ; but hopes, in consideration of its value, to procure protection from danger, deliverance from calamity, or success in enterprise. This was probably the meaning of the Burnt Offering in Lv 1, and of such human sacrifices as are referred to in Lv 18²¹ (see note there and references).

It is probably not the earliest but the latest view of sacrifice which sees in it a means of expiating the sins of the offerer. When God has come to be regarded as a holy Being to whom all sin is offensive, the sinner feels himself to lie under His wrath and curse. He is conscious that the good relationship that ought to exist between himself and the Deity has been interrupted by his transgression, and seeks a means of restoring harmony. He finds this in the offering of sacrifice, which is said to have a 'covering' efficacy : see on Lv 1⁴. Wherein this atoning efficacy lay is not certain. Some have found it in the idea of substitution. The offerer feels that his life is forfeited by his sins, but believes that he is graciously permitted to substitute a victim, to which his sins are in some way transferred, and which dies in his stead : see on Lv 1⁴ 16⁸, ²⁰⁻²², and cp. 17¹¹. Others have held that the efficacy of the atoning sacrifice consists in its being an expression of the offerer's feelings and desires, his penitence, humility, and prayer for forgiveness, and that it is the latter that procures the remission of his sins. In the Levitical system the idea of expiation and atonement is specially emphasised in the Sin Offering and Guilt Offering (see Lv 4–6⁷ and notes there, and cp. what is said on the ritual of the Day of Atonement, Lv 16).

In considering the various forms of sacrifice prescribed in Leviticus, it must be borne in mind that the book is a collection or codification of the law of ritual, and contains therefore regulations dating from different times. Of the five main types specified (see Intro. § 1, and the notes prefixed to chs. 1–4), the first three, the Burnt Offering (c. 1), the Meal Offering (c. 2), and the Peace Offering (c. 3) are, generally speaking, sacrifices expressive of harmony between the worshipper and God ; they are sacrifices of joy, of wholehearted devotion, of thanksgiving. The other forms of sacrifice, the Sin and Guilt Offerings (chs. 4–6⁷), are expressive of the sense of interrupted communion ; they are sacrifices of atonement and expiation. In them the sense of sin comes more into prominence.

The Levitical system of sacrifice underlies the worship of the OT. Like all systems of rites and ceremonies it was liable to abuse. From the writings of the prophets we learn that a common fault of Israel was to place reliance on the performance of the outward ceremony, and to neglect the weightier matters of the law. It was not the least part of

87

the work of the prophets to counteract the tendency to formalism, perfunctoriness, and externality, and to remind the people of Israel that 'to obey is better than sacrifice,' that God 'desired mercy and not sacrifice, and the knowledge of God more than burnt offerings,' and that 'the sacrifices of God are a broken spirit.' At the same time, the entire nation could hardly ever be blind to the fact that 'gifts and sacrifices could not make him that did the service perfect as pertaining to the conscience.' OT. forms of expiation accordingly have an anticipatory function, and find their fulfilment in the NT., wherein we are taught that Christ shed His blood 'for the remission of sins,' and that He 'put away sin by the sacrifice of Himself.' He is the 'Lamb slain from the foundation of the world.' In His death the whole endeavour of God's saving love, represented and illustrated in the OT. sacrifices, reaches its attainment, and other sacrifices are superseded. They are rendered needless because the goodwill of God to men is fully expressed in the incarnation, life, sufferings, and death of His only begotten Son, and because Christ has offered to God the only real sacrifice for the sins of humanity, in His life of perfect obedience, crowned by His death of free and absolute submission to the will of God.

CHAPTER 1
THE BURNT OFFERING

. This is mentioned first as being the most general form of sacrifice. Its characteristic feature is the consumption of the entire animal by fire upon the altar, for which reason it is also described as the 'whole burnt offering' (1 S 7⁹, cp. Ps 51¹⁹). The victims are oxen, sheep, or goats, for which, in the case of poor persons, turtle doves or young pigeons may be substituted (v. 14). The animal must be a male, i.e. of the superior sex, and without blemish (v. 3). The ritual of the sacrifice is as follows. (1) The animal is presented at the door of the tabernacle by the offerer, who solemnly dedicates it by laying both his hands upon its head (v. 4). (2) It is then slaughtered, by the offerer himself it would appear (v. 5). (3) The blood is caught in a bowl by the priest in attendance and flung round the altar (v. 5). (4) The carcase is then skinned and divided, the entrails and legs washed with water, and the whole, with the exception of the skin, which falls to the priest (7⁸), laid upon the altar and burned (vv. 6–9). In the case of pigeons, their small size and moderate quantity of blood necessitate some differences of detail (vv. 14–17).

The Burnt Offering, being wholly consumed upon the altar, signified the complete self-surrender of the offerer to God. It was the

sacrifice of devotion, and formed therefore the main element of individual and collective worship. It was offered in daily service, morning and evening, on behalf of the entire community (the 'continual burnt offering': see on Ex 29³⁸⁻⁴²).

1. Tabernacle of the congregation] RV 'tent of meeting': see on Ex 25²². **2. Children of Israel]** The instructions in chs. 1–6⁷ are for the laity. Those addressed to the priests follow in chs. 6⁸–7³⁸. **Offering]** RV 'oblation': the general name for a sacrifice or votive offering. The Heb. word is *Corban*, which means a thing 'brought near' or presented: see Mk 7¹¹ RV. **3. Male without blemish]** What is offered to God must be the best of its kind : see on 22¹⁷⁻²⁵ and on Ex 12⁵. **4. Put his hand upon the head]** This signifies the surrender of the animal to God, and, though this is not so clear, the transference of the offerer's guilt to it. In doing so he made a confession of his sins: cp. 3². **Make atonement]** lit. 'put a covering over him,' i.e. screen his unworthiness, protect him in the presence of the holiness of God. **5. He shall kill]** The subject is the offerer. The blood represents the life, and is sprinkled upon the altar in token that the offerer yields his life to God, in expiation of his sins and in consecration to His service.

11. Northward] On the E. side was the place for ashes and refuse (v. 16); on the W. stood the laver and the Holy of Holies; the ascent to the altar was on the S. side. The N. side, accordingly, was the most convenient place of slaughter. **17. A sweet savour]** see on Ex 29¹⁸.

CHAPTER 2
THE MEAL OFFERING

The rendering of AV **meat offering** is liable to misunderstanding, as meat now suggests flesh meat. But this is a vegetable, or bloodless, sacrifice, a consecration to God of the produce of the field. Its principal constituent is fine flour, which may be presented either raw (vv. 1–3), or baked into cakes in the oven (v. 4), or in a pan (vv. 5, 6), or boiled in a pot (v. 7). The meal is mixed with oil and salt, as when used for food, but no leaven or honey must be used, as these cause fermentation and are symbolical of uncleanness (v. 11). As an offering of firstfruits, parched ears of wheat or barley are presented along with oil (vv. 14, 15). Incense is always an accompaniment of a meal offering (vv. 2, 15). Part of the meal offering and all the incense are burned upon the altar (vv. 2, 9, 16). What remains becomes the portion of the priests, and is eaten by them in the sanctuary (v. 3, 6¹⁶). A meal offering might be presented independently, but was frequently an accompaniment of an animal sacrifice (Ex 29 40 Nu 15 1-15). A meal offering might be used as a substitute for a sin offering in the case of a poor person, but without oil or frankincense (5 11-13). A special form of meal offering is the Shewbread: see 24 5-9 Ex 25 30.

1. Frankincense] see on Ex 30 1-10, 34-38.

2. Memorial of it] the term applied to that part of a meal offering burned upon the altar (cp. 24 7), so called probably as intended to bring the offerer to the favourable remembrance of God. But the exact meaning is doubtful: cp. Ps 20 3 Ac 10 4.

3. A thing most holy] The materials of the offerings are of two degrees of holiness. Some, as e.g. the peace offerings, are 'holy' (23 20) and may be eaten in any clean place by the priests and their families (10 14 22 10-13 Nu 18 11); others, as the sin and guilt offerings (6 17, 25-28 7 1-6) and the shewbread (24 9), are 'most holy,' and may only be eaten in the court of the tabernacle by the priests alone (Nu 18 9, 10). The latter, moreover, communicate 'holiness' to whatever comes in contact with them: cp. Ex 29 37 Lv 6 18, 27-29. **13. Salt of the covenant**] see on Ex 30 35.

CHAPTER 3
THE PEACE OFFERING

This form of sacrifice takes its name from a Heb. word meaning a 'requital' or giving of thanks, and is therefore called by some the Thank Offering. It is an animal sacrifice, the characteristic feature of which is the disposal of the carcase. The kidneys and the internal fat, and, in the case of sheep, the fat tail also, are offered to God by burning upon the altar (vv. 3–5). The choice parts, the breast and the right thigh, fall to the lot of the priests after being dedicated to God in a peculiar way by waving them before Him (see on 7 28-34). The rest of the flesh is eaten by the offerer and his family at a sacrificial meal (7 15, 16). The Peace Offering represents, it is thought, the earliest form of sacrifice, in which the Deity and the worshippers exhibit their good relationship by sharing a common meal. It is therefore the sacrifice expressive of harmony between God and His people. It is a feast of communion: see e.g. Ex 24 9-11.

2. Lay his hand] see on 1 4. Whereas at this point in the sacrifice of a burnt offering, the offerer made a confession of his sins, in the case of the peace offering he uttered a prayer of thanksgiving. This indicates the difference in the signification of the two sacrifices.

3. The internal fat, along with the blood, is regarded as the seat of life and possessing a peculiar sanctity. It must, therefore, never be eaten by man, but always offered to God by burning: see Ex 23 18 29 13 Lv 3 16-17 7 22-27 17 10-16.

4. Caul above the liver] see Ex 29 13.

5. Upon the burnt sacrifice] There would always be some portion of the daily burnt sacrifice smouldering upon the altar. The peace offering is to be laid upon it. The fire never went out: see 6 9, 12, 13.

9. The whole rump] RV 'the fat tail entire': see on Ex 29 22.

11. Food of the offering] a general epithet applied to sacrifices: cp. 21 6 22 25 Nu 28 2, 24 Ezk 44 7 Mal 1 7 (where the altar is called the 'table of the Lord'). For a protest against this anthropomorphic conception of God as requiring food for His sustenance or delight see Ps 50 8-15.

CHAPTER 4
THE SIN OFFERING (4 1–5 13) AND THE GUILT OFFERING (5 14–6 7)

These are later and specialised forms of the Burnt Offering. They presuppose a state of matters in which the good relationship between God and the offerer has been interrupted by sin, and the purpose of both is to make atonement for, or cover, the sin of the guilty person or persons. The difference between the two seems to be that while the sin offering is provided for those offences which could not be undone or repaired, the guilt offering is provided for those cases where reparation and restitution are possible, a fine or penalty being imposed on the transgressor in the latter instance (5 16 6 4, 5). The ritual of the two sacrifices is different. While the victim of the guilt offering is usually a ram (5 15) and sometimes a he-lamb (Nu 15 24), the victim of the sin offering varies according to the rank of the offender. For the high priest it is a young bullock (4 3), for the congregation the same (4 14) or a he-goat (Nu 15 24), for a ruler a he-goat (4 23), and for an ordinary person a she-goat (4 28), a ewe-lamb (4 32), a pigeon (5 7), or a meal offering (5 11). The important feature of the sin offering is the manipulation of the blood. Part of it is applied to the horns of the altar of incense and the rest poured out at the base of the altar of burnt offering. But when the sin offering is on behalf of the high priest or congregation, part of the blood is also carried into the tent and sprinkled seven times before the veil of the sanctuary (4 5, 6, 16, 17). On the great Day of Atonement the sprinkling takes place within the veil, on or before the mercy seat (16 14: see notes on that chapter).

2. Through ignorance] RV 'unwittingly.' The word applies to sins not only of ignorance but also of weakness and rashness. It must, however, be observed that the Levitical law provides no sacrifice for deliberate or presumptuous sins, sins committed 'with a high hand' (Nu 15 30, cp. Heb 10 26 f.). **3. The priest**

that is anointed] i.e. the high priest : see on Ex 29 21. **According to the sin of the people**] RV 'so as to bring guilt on the people.'

Horns] see on Ex 27 2. **Altar of sweet incense**] see on Ex 30 1-10.

15. Elders of the congregation] The representatives of the people. **26.** The flesh of the sin offering for a ruler or ordinary person is eaten by the priests (6 26), who, however, must not eat their own sin offering nor that of the congregation which is to be entirely burned (4 11, 12, 21 6 30). **35. According to**] RV 'upon' : see on 3 5.

CHAPTER 5

THE SIN OFFERING AND THE GUILT OFFER-
ING (continued)

1–6. Special cases in which it is proper to offer a Sin Offering. Such are the withholding of testimony (v. 1), touching a carcase or unclean person or thing (vv. 2, 3), making rash oaths (v. 4). **1. Sin, and hear**] RV 'sin, in that he heareth' : cp. Prov 29 24 Jg 17 2. **2.** See 11 27, 28, 31-40 15 7 f. *If* **it be hidden from him**] Vulgate renders, 'if he forgetteth his uncleanness,' i.e. omits to make the prescribed ablutions.

7–13. Substitutes for the goat or lamb of the Sin Offering in cases of poverty. The Mosaic Law is always considerate of the poor, and makes special provision for such in sacrifices of atonement and purification, so that a man's poverty may be no excuse for his remaining under sin or disability connected with ceremonial impurity, or any bar to his obtaining forgiveness : see also 1 14-17 12 8 14 21 f. **11. Ephah**] about a bushel.

5 14–6 7. The Guilt (or Trespass) Offering. Two cases are mentioned in which it is proper to bring a guilt offering. The first (v. 15) is that of a person who occasions loss to the sanctuary by either consuming or keeping back some 'holy thing' (see on 2 3). He is required to restore the value of the thing plus one fifth by way of a penalty (v. 16), and to present a guilt offering. The second case is that of a person who causes loss to his neighbour. The same is required of him (6 4-7), see Nu 5 5-10. **15. Shekel of the sanctuary**] a standard weight of silver, equal to rather more than half-a-crown in value : see Ex 30 13. **16. The fifth part**] the usual proportion in cases of restitution : see 26 13-31.

CHAPTER 6

1–7. These vv. should be reckoned as part of c. 5. The Hebrew chapter begins at 6 8. Our chapter and verse divisions are a late invention, dating from the 13th and 14th centuries. **2.** RV 'deal falsely with his neighbour in a

matter of deposit, or of bargain (or pledge), or of robbery' : cp. Ex 22 7 f.

6 8–7 38. Directions addressed to the Priests regarding the ritual of Sacrifice : see on 1 2.

9–13. The Burnt Offering. The daily or continual burnt offering is meant : see on c.1. The private or occasional burnt offering is referred to in 7 8. **9. It is ..**] RV 'The burnt offering shall be on the hearth upon the altar all night unto the morning' : the offering of devotion to God must never cease.

14–18. The Meal Offering. This again is the daily meal offering presented along with the daily burnt offering : see intro. to c. 2. **17. Most holy**] see on 2 3. **19–23.** The Meal Offering for the High Priest, presented daily, morning and evening (v. 20), by Aaron and his successors in office on their own behalf (v. 22). **20. In the day when he is anointed**] meaning on and from that day, as appears from the term 'perpetual' in v. 20 and the statement in v. 22. **23.** The priest does not eat of his own sacrifice: see on 4 26.

24–30. The Sin Offering. **26. Shall eat it**] i.e. unless it is the sin offering for himself : see on v. 23. **30. Reconcile**] make atonement, as in 1 4.

CHAPTER 7

DIRECTIONS TO THE PRIESTS (continued)

1–10. The Guilt Offering. Vv. 8–10 refer to private offerings and the priest's share in them. **11–21.** The Peace Offering. Three kinds of peace offerings are distinguished here, viz. the thank offering (v. 12), and the votive and free will offerings (v. 16). The former, as its name implies, would be presented after a benefit had been received ; the latter, while the benefit was still expected, as an accompaniment of supplication.

12. The animal sacrifice is accompanied with a meal offering of four kinds of cakes, one of which is leavened. Of each of these one cake is heaved before the Lord (see on Ex 29 24) and appropriated by the priests, the others are eaten by the offerer along with his share of the peace offering : see intro. to c. 3. **21. Shall be cut off**] excommunicated : see on Ex 12 15. **22–27.** Prohibition to eat fat or blood. The fat is the internal fat : see on 3 3. **28–34.** The Priest's share of the peace offerings. This consists of the choice portions, the breast and right thigh which are first heaved or waved before the Lord: see Ex 29 24. **35.** *Portion* **of the anointing**] RM 'Portion.' Vv. 35–38 form a conclusion to the first part of the book of Leviticus, that dealing with Sacrifices.

PART 2

(Chs. 8–10) The Consecration of the Priesthood

CHAPTER 8

The Consecration of Aaron and his Sons

This chapter relates the fulfilment of the injunctions given in Ex 29 1-37.

CHAPTER 9

Installation of Aaron and his Sons

The ceremonial of consecration is repeated daily for seven days (8 33 ; see Ex 29 35). On the eighth day Aaron and his sons formally assume office. Aaron first sacrifices for himself (vv. 7–14) and then for the people (vv. 15–21). The solemn blessing of the people follows (vv. 22, 23), after which fire from the Lord descends and consumes the sacrifices upon the altar (v. 24).

7. Aaron did not approach the altar till called on by Moses to do so, showing that he did not take this honour to himself, but that it was the call of God by Moses: cp. Heb 5 4, 5. 'No man taketh this honour unto himself, but he that is called of God, as was Aaron.'

8. Aaron, having now been consecrated, discharges the priestly duties. During the seven days of his consecration these were performed by Moses : see 8 15. **11. The flesh and the hide he burnt**] They were wholly burned because the sacrifice was offered by Aaron on behalf of himself : see on 4 26.

22. The form of the Benediction is given in Nu 6 22-27. As Aaron is here said to have **come down**, the benediction seems to have been pronounced from the top of the altar, or from its ledge : see Ex 20 26 27 5 RV.

23. Moses takes Aaron into the tent of meeting, in order to induct him into the duties connected with it, and to hand over the sacred furniture to his charge. **Glory of the Lord**] cp. Ex 40 34, 35.

24. This was not the first kindling of the sacred fire, as there was already fire upon the altar (v. 10, etc.). But instead of the sacrifices burning for a long time they were suddenly consumed before the eyes of the people. This was accepted by them as a token that God not only accepted these sacrifices but also approved the consecration of Aaron and his sons to the priesthood : cp. Jg 6 20, 21 1 K 18 36, 39 2 Ch 7 1-3.

CHAPTER 10

Sin and Death of Nadab and Abihu

An illustration of the necessity of a punctilious observance of the regulations. We have no means of ascertaining the precise nature of the trespass committed by the two eldest sons of Aaron. In view of Lv 16 12 (cp. Nu 16 46 Rev 8 5) we may suppose that the sin lay in the use of common fire, instead of fire taken from the altar. But the phrase **strange fire** is wide enough to cover any breach of the laws regulating the preparation and use of incense (see Ex 30 1-10, 34-38). Lv 16 1, 2 might also lead us to infer that Nadab and Abihu presumptuously penetrated into the Holy of Holies. Vv. 16–20 of the present chapter show that the trespass was committed on the day of their entering upon office (cp. 9 1 f.). From the fact that the prohibition against the use of wine by priests on duty follows immediately upon this incident (vv. 8, 9) it has been inferred by later Jewish writers and many modern commentators that Nadab and Abihu sinned when in a state of intoxication. There is, however, no real ground for this supposition, as vv. 8, 9 form a separate and disconnected fragment.

3. Them that come nigh me] i.e. the priests (cp. Ex 19 22 Ezk 42 13 43 19). The greater the privilege the greater the responsibility. Judgment begins at the house of God (1 Pet 4 17). **Held his peace**] acknowledged the justice of the penalty.   **4.** See Ex 6 22. It would not have been unlawful for the surviving brothers to perform this office (see 21 1-3), but probably to spare their feelings the cousins of Aaron were selected for the duty.   **6, 7. Uncover not your heads**] RV 'Let not the hair of your heads go loose.' Aaron and his sons are forbidden to exhibit the usual signs of mourning, dishevelled hair and rent garments, or to interrupt their priestly functions, as an object lesson of submission to righteous judgment.

8, 9. The priests were not absolutely forbidden the use of wine, but only when performing their priestly duties : see prefatory remarks, and cp. Ezk 44 21.   **10.** It was the duty of the priests to instruct the people in their religious duties, and to set an example to them : cp. Ezk 44 23.

16–20. Goat of the sin offering] i.e. the people's sin offering (9 15). Aaron's own sin offering had been burned in accordance with the law (9 8-11). But instead of eating the flesh of the people's sacrifice, as prescribed in 6 26, he had burned it also. When charged with contravening the law, Aaron pleaded that he and his sons had felt themselves to be defiled by the death of Nadab and Abihu, and that it would have been inconsistent for them to eat the sin offering, an act which signified the acceptance of the people by God and their full communion with Him. Moses admitted the justice of the plea in the exceptional circumstances.

PART 3

(Chs. 11–16) The Law of Clean and Unclean

This section deals with the subject of ceremonial uncleanness and the method of its purification. Four main types of uncleanness are referred to, viz. that of meats (11 1-23), of carcases (11 24-40), of leprosy (chs. 13, 14), and of certain bodily functions and conditions (chs. 12, 15). The effect of ceremonial uncleanness is that it disqualifies a person for the worship of God. Its duration varies according to the cause, from a few hours, as in the case of touching the carcase of a clean beast (11 39), to eighty days, as in the case of a woman who has given birth to a girl (12 5). The ritual of purification consists of washing the body, sometimes also the clothes, and in the case of greater defilement, the offering of sacrifice.

The distinction of clean and unclean did not originate at the time of Moses, nor is it confined to the Hebrews. It is to be found in all religions, particularly in their earlier stages. It is not easy to account for it. The restrictions may be due to a natural instinct of aversion from disgusting objects and conditions. Or they may rest upon reasons of health; for undoubtedly many of them possess sanitary advantages. Or, as many believe, a religious idea may lie at the root of them, certain objects being regarded as the seat of evil spirits. Whatever be the origin of these regulations, they were adopted by Moses and made to subserve a sacred purpose. Things ceremonially unclean were used as types of moral defilement. The outward purifications served to impress upon the hearts of the people the need of absolute purity in the service of Jehovah. They were a constant reminder of the precept, 'Ye shall be holy; for I *am* holy' (see e.g. 11 44,45). And if it be the fact that at least some of the 'unclean' animals were worshipped by the Canaanitish tribes, then these regulations served still further to guard the people of Jehovah from the contaminating influences of their surroundings: see 20 25, 26.

CHAPTER 11
Law of Clean and Unclean Meats

The animals whose flesh may or may not be eaten are treated in four classes, viz. large land animals (vv. 3–8), water animals (vv. 9–12), birds (vv. 13–19), winged creeping things (vv. 20–23).

3. Of the large land animals, those are clean which both chew the cud and divide the hoof. Unless they satisfy both these conditions they are unclean and cannot be eaten. The practical effect of this is to exclude all beasts of prey. The flesh of animals that chew the cud is undoubtedly more wholesome than that of those which live on prey. With this list of animals should be compared that in Dt 14, where a list of clean animals is given.

4. The **camel's** foot, though divided above, is united beneath into a broad sole.

5. Coney] The word means a rabbit. But the animal meant here is the rock-badger, which somewhat resembles a guinea-pig, and is common in Palestine. **6.** The **hare** does not really chew the cud, but the action of its jaws resembles that of ruminants.

7. Swine are uncleanly in their habits and food, and the use of their flesh is believed to be the cause of certain diseases in man. The Jews still abstain from eating it.

8. All dead bodies defile. But it should be observed that contact with a living unclean animal did not defile. The ass e.g. was unclean for food, but was the common beast of burden among the Israelites.

9–12. Water animals. The condition of cleanness here is the possession of fins and scales. It follows that shellfish and eels are forbidden as food.

13–19. Birds. No signs are given to distinguish clean from unclean birds. The latter are specified, being mostly birds of prey and feeders on carrion. **13. Ossifrage**] RV 'the gier eagle,' the largest of the vulture tribe. The name 'ossifrage,' which means the 'bone-breaker,' is derived from the practice of the bird in dropping the bones of its prey from a height on to a rock so as to break them and get at the marrow. The **ospray** is the 'short-toed eagle,' the commonest of the eagle tribe in Palestine.

14–19. Vulture] RV 'kite.' **Kite**] RV 'falcon.' **After his kind**] i.e. including others of the same species. **Owl**] RV 'ostrich.' **Cuckow**] RV 'seamew.' **Swan**] doubtful ; RV has 'horned owl.' **Lapwing**] RV 'hoopoe,' a bird of foul habit.

20–23. Fowls that creep] Read with RV, 'All winged creeping things.' What are meant are insects and small reptiles that move horizontally, **go upon** *all* **four**. Four kinds of locusts are exempted and may be eaten. The locust resembles a large grasshopper, and is still eaten in the East. It is usually prepared by being thrown into boiling water, after which the head and wings are removed and the body dried in the sun.

24–40. Uncleanness contracted by contact with dead bodies.

28. Until the even] till the close of the day. The Hebrews reckon the day from sunset to sunset.

29. Tortoise] Jewish authorities regarded the tortoise as a clean animal. What is meant here is probably a kind of lizard. So RV.

30. The names here are uncertain. RV renders, 'the gecko, and the land-crocodile, and the lizard, and the sand-lizard, and the chameleon.'

33. An earthen vessel, being porous, is supposed to absorb the uncleanness so that it cannot be removed with washing. **35. Oven**] an earthenware jar or pot: see on Ex 8³. **36. Pit**] RM 'cistern.' The water in wells and reservoirs, being frequently changed, is not polluted. **That which toucheth**] or, 'he that toucheth.' **37, 38.** The seed in growing undergoes many changes, which are supposed to throw off the uncleanness. But if the seed is wet it may be penetrated by the defiling fluid. **42. Whatsoever hath more feet**] rather, 'hath many feet.' Insects like caterpillars and centipedes are intended.

44. Sanctify] the root meaning of the Heb. words for 'sanctify,' 'hallow,' 'holy,' is that of separation: cp. v. 47. The holiness spoken of here is rather physical than moral; but in keeping themselves free from ceremonial defilement, the people learned to avoid what is morally impure, in accordance with the principle implied in the words, 'first that which is natural, afterward that which is spiritual.'

The composite nature of this c. appears from the position of vv. 29, 30, 41–45, which belong to vv. 20–23. Vv. 46, 47 form the conclusion to the whole.

CHAPTER 12
UNCLEANNESS CONNECTED WITH CHILDBIRTH

The functions of reproduction are in early stages of religion regarded with superstitious dread. The enactments in this c. and the related regulations in c. 15 had an important place in teaching the lesson of purity in sexual relationships.

3. Cp. Gn 17¹⁰⁻¹⁴. The purifications prescribed in this c. are for the mother alone and not for the child, who does not seem to have been regarded as unclean, unless the rite of circumcision involved the idea of the purification of the child. Uncircumcision and uncleanness are frequently identical: cp. 19²³. **4.** On the eighth day the mother is readmitted to society, but is still debarred from the services of the tabernacle till forty days after the birth. **5.** In the case of the birth of a girl the two periods of uncleanness (see last note) are exactly doubled, the reason doubtless being the opinion of the ancients that the derangement of the system is greater. **8.** Cp. Lk 2²⁴, which shows that the Virgin Mary offered the poor woman's sacrifice.

CHAPTER 13
UNCLEANNESS CONNECTED WITH LEPROSY

It is tolerably certain that the leprosy of the OT. is not the leprosy of the Middle Ages, which is still to be found in the East. The latter is a terrible and loathsome disease, called *elephantiasis*, in consequence of which the skin thickens, the features are distorted, and the very limbs mortify and drop off from the body. The leprosy of the Bible is a skin disease, known as *psoriasis*, in which the skin and hair grow white, and which is accompanied with scab and flaky scales which peel off. It is doubtful whether it was infectious or not. Some varieties may have been so; but it is to be observed that when the disease entirely covered the body the person was pronounced clean and could mix in society. Leprosy is regarded in the Bible as a type of sin in its loathsomeness and disfiguring and corrupting effects, and its treatment was in many points symbolical.

3. Plague] i.e. plagued spot. **4. Shut up him**] i.e. place him in quarantine: separate the affected person from the society of others and the service of the tabernacle.

9–17. The case of the reappearance of leprosy after it has been cured. **11. Shall not shut him up**] there is no need for quarantine as the case is undoubtedly one of leprosy. **13.** When the eruption is complete, the disease is supposed to have reached its crisis, and to be discharging itself externally in dry scales.

18–23. The case of leprosy developing from a healed boil.

24–28. The case of leprosy arising from the inflammation following a burn.

29–37. Leprosy in the hair of the head or beard. In this case the hair turns yellow instead of white (v. 30).

38. Another form of leprosy in the shape of white spots. This is harmless, and the affected person is not unclean.

40–44. Leprosy in the bald head.

45. These are the signs of mourning for the dead (cp. 10⁶ 21¹⁰ Ezk 24¹⁷ Mic 3⁷), leprosy being regarded as a living death and the severest token of the divine displeasure : cp. Nu 12¹².

47–59. The leprosy of garments. What is described here is not the leprosy that attacks the human being, but a mildew or fungus causing discoloration and corrosion and bearing a superficial resemblance to leprosy : cp. the leprosy of houses, 14³³⁻⁵³. The regulations regarding this so-called 'leprosy' were no doubt valuable for sanitary reasons ; but they would also serve to 'teach the Hebrew to hate even the appearance of evil.' Cp. what St. Jude says (v. 23) of the Christian 'hating even the garment spotted by the flesh.'

48. Warp, or woof] This translation is doubtful. The words probably mean as in RM, 'woven or knitted stuff,' referring to material not yet made into garments.

CHAPTER 14
The Purification of the Leper. The Leprosy of Houses

When a leper has been cured of his plague, and has satisfied the priest that his cure is complete, he is required to go through a ceremonial purification before being readmitted to his place in society. The ritual of purification consists of three parts. (1) Two living birds are brought, with a rod of cedar wood, a piece of scarlet wool, and a bunch of hyssop, to the priest, who kills one of the birds over water. The living bird and the cedar rod, to which the hyssop is tied with the scarlet thread, are dipped in the blood, which is then sprinkled upon the man seven times. The living bird is then let loose. (2) The man then washes his clothes, shaves off all his hair, and bathes. After seven days he repeats this and is ready for the last act of his purifying. (3) On the eighth day he presents himself with his sacrifices at the door of the tent of meeting. A guilt offering, a sin offering, and a burnt offering are made, the right ear, thumb, and great toe of the man are touched, first with blood and then with oil, and he is once more ceremonially clean.

4. Later usage required the birds to be sparrows. Cedar wood (probably not the cedar of Lebanon but a kind of juniper) may have been chosen on account of its antiseptic property, and hyssop (see on Ex 12 22) for its aromatic qualities. In later times, at least, their use was regarded as symbolical, in the one case of the pride which was supposed to be the cause of visitation by the disease, in the other of the humility which was an essential condition of its removal. The scarlet wool may have betokened the healthy blood now coursing in the veins of the erewhile leper. The same materials were employed in the ritual for purification after contact with dead bodies : see Nu 19 6 and cp. Ps 51 7.

7. The release of the living bird signified the removal of the uncleanness, perhaps also the restored liberty of the leper. Cp. the release of the goat on the Day of Atonement, 16 21, 22. **10.** A **tenth deal** (i.e. part) of an ephah, which was called an omer, was about four pints, the ephah being rather more than a bushel. A **log** is about a pint. **12. Wave them**] see on Ex 29 24. The offering of these sacrifices shows that leprosy was regarded as a punishment of sin. **14.** The anointing of these members signified their reconsecration to the service of God, and the readmission of the leper to the privileges of the tabernacle.

33–53. The leprosy of houses. This, like the leprosy of garments (see 13 47-59), bears only an external resemblance to the leprosy of human beings. It is a fungus or discoloration making its appearance on the walls of houses : see on 13 47-59. The legislation here is prospective : cp. the mention of 'the camp' in v. 3 with that of 'the city' in v. 40. The section may be post-Mosaic. It stands by itself ; its natural position would be after 13 59.

CHAPTER 15
Uncleanness connected with Sexual Discharges

The subject of this c. is related to that of c. 12 : see intro. there. Here three natural (vv. 16, 17, 18, 19–24) and two abnormal (vv. 1–15, 25–30) conditions are dealt with. Though not in themselves sinful, they render the person ceremonially unclean, and the enactments with respect to them would tend to purity of morals, being a reminder that all uncleanness is hateful to God, and that He is to be glorified in our bodies as well as in our spirits.

8. This case is provided for, as spitting upon a person was, and still is, a common expression of contempt among Orientals.

12. See on 11 33. **13. Is cleansed**] i.e. physically. **Shall be clean**] i.e. ceremonially.

CHAPTER 16
Ritual of the Day of Atonement
(See also 23 26-32 Nu 29 7-11 Ex 30 10.)

This solemn ceremonial took place once a year on the tenth day of the seventh month (Tishri = September). It was enacted by the high priest alone, but the whole nation indicated its interest and participation in it, by resting from all manner of work, by keeping a very strict fast, and by assembling for an 'holy convocation.' The ritual of the Day of Atonement marked the culminating point of the Levitical system, and was calculated to impress the minds of the worshippers in a peculiar degree. Most of the other sacrifices and purifications were occasional and personal, but this was the yearly atonement for the nation as a whole, including the priesthood itself, and the yearly purification of the sanctuary and its parts from the defilement of the sins of the people in whose midst it stood. It gathered up and included all the separate and individual sacrifices of the year, and restored to the nation the holiness it had lost. It was but natural that Christians should see, in its peculiarly striking and solemn ritual, a foreshadowing and illustration of the atonement wrought by Christ, through the one sacrifice of Himself, and His entering into the Holy Place, there to appear in the presence of God for His people. This is pointed out by the writer of the Epistle to the Hebrews : see Heb 4 14 6 20 9 11-28, which should be read in this connexion.

A great deal has been made of the fact that there is no mention of the actual observance of the Day of Atonement till after the exile, from which it has been inferred that its institution is of post-exilic date. But the argument is not convincing. The connexion with the death of Nadab and Abihu (see v. 1), and the mention of Azazel (see v. 8 and note), indicate that the ritual of this c. rests on a very ancient basis. And not only are the pre-exilic books silent on the Day of Atonement, but the post-exilic contain no reference to it either, which shows the precarious nature of the argument from silence.

The Day of Atonement is still the great day of the Jewish sacred year, and is observed with much solemnity as a day of humiliation and repentance : see on Ex 32 32.

3–5. The first act of the high priest is to choose the sacrificial victims, to bathe himself, and exchange his distinctive vestments for a garment of white linen, the garment of the ordinary priest.

6–11. He then presents the sin offering for himself and for his house, and casts lots between the two goats of the sin offering for the people, one of which is to be slain and the other let loose. He then sacrifices his own sin offering.

8. For the scapegoat] RV 'for Azazel.' This word does not occur elsewhere in OT. The parallel, **for the LORD**, suggests that it should be taken as a proper name, and left untranslated. The word **scapegoat** in AV is not a translation, but indicates merely the use to which this goat is to be put. Azazel is understood to be the name of one of those malignant demons with which the superstition of the Israelites peopled the wilderness and all waste places (see Isa 13 21 34 14, and cp. Mt 12 43 Mk 1 13). The sending of the sin-laden goat to him (vv. 21, 22) signified the complete removal of the sins of the people and the handing them

over, as it were, to the evil spirit to whom they belonged : cp. the ceremony connected with the cleansing of lepers (14 6, 7). This rite may have been intended, at all events it would serve, to counteract any disposition to honour and worship such evil spirits (cp. 17 7).

12–14. The high priest next enters the Holy of Holies with incense and the blood of his sin offering, which he sprinkles once on the mercy seat and seven times in the space before it, thus making atonement for himself and his house.

15–19. He then goes out into the court and sacrifices the goat on which the lot fell ' for Jehovah,' and brings its blood as before into the Holy of Holies to make atonement for the sanctuary and its parts, and cleanse them from the sins which mingle even with the best service that man can offer to God.

20–22. He now takes the goat destined ' for Azazel,' and laying his hands on its head confesses over it the sins of the people, after which a man standing in readiness leads the goat away into the wilderness and releases it. In the time of the Second Temple the goat was destroyed by being precipitated from a rock 12 m. from Jerusalem.

23–28. He finally bathes and resumes his distinctive vestments and offers the two burnt offerings for himself and the people, in token of entire reconsecration to the service of God. At the same time he burns the fat of the two sin offerings, the flesh of which is taken outside the camp and there consumed. In later times the high priest at this point read in the hearing of the people prescribed portions of the Law, viz. Lv 23 26 f. Nu 29 7-11, concluding with a series of benedictions.

29. Afflict your souls] i.e. observe a fast : see Ps 35 13 Isa 58 3, 5. This is the only fast enjoined in the Mosaic Law. After the exile fasting was a common religious usage : see e.g. Ezr 8 21 Neh 9 1 Esth 4 3 Zech 8 19 Mt 9 14-17 Lk 2 37 18 12 Ac 13 2, 3 14 23. In Ac 27 9 the reference is to the Day of Atonement which was called ' The Fast' *par excellence.*

34. He] i.e. Aaron.

PART 4

(Chs. 17–26) THE LAW OF HOLINESS

This section of Leviticus occupies a position by itself, being distinguished from the rest of the book both by style and contents. A few only of its main characteristics may be noticed here. (1) Among a large number of phrases almost, if not entirely, peculiar to this part of the Pentateuch is the constantly recurring expression ' I am Jehovah,' or ' I am Jehovah your God,' or ' I your God am holy.' This ' divine I,' as it has been called, occurs forty-seven times in these chapters, and only

six times elsewhere from Genesis to Joshua, but is found again seventy-eight times in Ezekiel. See Intro. § 2. (2) A second distinguishing feature of this section is its more rhetorical style and the comparatively large number of hortatory passages, somewhat in the manner of Deuteronomy : see e.g. c. 26. (3) A third characteristic is the high spiritual tone of these chapters. Compared with the rest of the book we find here less ritual and more religion, morality, and humanity. The duty of holiness is repeatedly emphasised and grounded on the holiness of God Himself. The oft-recurring key note of the whole is ' Ye shall be holy, for I the Lord your God am holy.' It is for this reason that the title 'Law of Holiness' has been applied to this part of Leviticus. Some other fragments bearing a similar character outside these chapters have been assigned to the same collection, e.g. Ex 31 $^{13f.}$ Lv 11 (especially vv. 43–45) Nu 15 $^{37-41}$.

It has long been observed that there is a considerable resemblance both in leading ideas and phraseology between this 'Law of Holiness' and the book of Ezekiel. That Ezekiel knew and used this Law Book seems beyond dispute, but that he is also its author is not made out.

CHAPTER 17
RULE OF SACRIFICE. PROHIBITION AGAINST EATING BLOOD

1–9. The first part of this Law prescribes that all oxen, sheep, and goats, slaughtered for food, must first be presented to Jehovah at the sanctuary. This seems to presuppose a time when the Israelites used but little flesh food, and were not widely scattered, which must have been either during the wanderings in the desert, or immediately after the return from exile, when there was only a small community in the vicinity of Jerusalem. This raises the question of the date of the composition of the Law of Holiness, and scholars are still divided upon it. The law is repealed in Dt 12 ^{15}, where it is implied that different conditions of life prevail.

7. The object of this enactment was to counteract the tendency to offer sacrifice to those demons of the wilderness which were worshipped in the form of he-goats, for so the RV renders the word here translated **devils** : see note on Azazel in 16 ^{8}. **Gone a whoring**] see on Ex 34 ^{15}.

10–16. Prohibition against eating blood or fallen carcases. The law against eating blood agrees with natural instincts and is here connected with a religious idea : see on 3 ^{3}.

15. The law against eating what dies of itself is a corollary of the former. The flesh of such an animal cannot be thoroughly drained of blood : cp. Ex 22 ^{31} Dt 14 ^{21}. **16. Bear his iniquity**] bear the penalty of his transgression.

CHAPTER 18
LAW OF FORBIDDEN DEGREES OF MARRIAGE, AND OF CHASTITY

3. Some of the unions here forbidden as incestuous were permitted among the nations of antiquity. The early Egyptians, e.g. permitted marriage with a full sister. Abraham married his half-sister (Gn 20 ^{12}), a practice here forbidden (vv. 9, 11). **6. Uncover** *their* **nakedness**] i.e. marry.

8. Father's wife] This is not the same as 'mother' in the previous v. so that polygamy is here presupposed. It was common, perhaps universal, in the East at the time of Moses. The Mosaic Law did not seek all at once to abolish polygamy, which might have been the occasion of great hardship in the circumstances. But it certainly discouraged it, and by regulating and restraining it prepared the way for its gradual extinction : cp. the remarks on slavery among the Hebrews at Ex 21.

16. This law was not absolute, the so-called levirate marriage, or marriage with the widow of a deceased brother, being not only permissible but almost compulsory : see on Dt 25 ^{5}.

18. In her life *time*] This implies that after the death of the first wife a man might marry her sister. It is not a law against polygamy but only against a special form of it, viz. marrying two sisters. The restriction is professedly made in the interests of domestic peace and happiness. For **to vex** *her* RV reads, ' to be a rival *to her* ' : cp. the case of Leah and Rachel, the wives of Jacob, who were sisters (Gn 29, 30).

21. Cp. 20 $^{1-5}$. **Molech**] ('king') the fire-god of the Ammonites and Canaanites, and especially of the Phoenicians, to whom children were sacrificed in burnt-offering. **Pass through** *the fire*] see 1 K 11 $^{5-7}$ 2 K 3 ^{27} 23 ^{10} 2 Ch 33 ^{6} Jer 7 ^{31} 32 ^{35}. The idea underlying child-sacrifice is probably that of propitiating the deity by offering the most valued possession : see 2 K 3 ^{27}, and cp. the case of Abraham and Isaac (Gn 22 ^{12}). The penalty of this most inhuman form of worship was death by stoning : see 20 ^{2}. It should be observed that the exact meaning of the expression ' pass through the fire' is uncertain. The rite may have been a kind of ordeal by which it was sought to ascertain the mind of the deity by observing whether the child passed through the fire unscathed or not.

CHAPTER 19
VARIOUS LAWS, MAINLY OF A MORAL AND HUMANE CHARACTER

This c. was very naturally regarded by Jewish authorities as an embodiment of the Decalogue. It will be observed that in general the precepts in vv. 3–8 correspond to those of the first table of the Decalogue (' Thou shalt love the Lord thy God '), and those in vv. 9–18 to the second table (' Thou shalt love thy neighbour as thyself '). In this c. alone the characteristic phrase ' I am the LORD ' (i.e. Jehovah) occurs no fewer than sixteen times. It is the divine seal set to the enactments of the law.

5–8. See 7 $^{15-18}$.

9. Kindly consideration of the poor is part of that holiness which God requires and which is the reflection of His own. He is the champion of the weak and oppressed : see on Ex 22²¹, and vv. 33, 34. This injunction is not applicable to the time of the sojourn in the desert ; it presupposes a settled agricultural life in the land of Canaan : see on Dt 24²⁰.

13. Cp. Dt 24¹⁴,¹⁵ Mal 3⁵ Jas 5⁴. **14.** The sin is that of intention, and is seen by Him who 'trieth the hearts.' **15.** Justice must be administered impartially, no favour being shown to a poor man because he is poor (cp. Ex 23³), or to a rich man because he is rich.

16. Stand against the blood of thy neighbour] This may mean generally any conduct imperilling a neighbour's life. But its connexion here with the sin of slander suggests that what is specially meant is the procuring of a sentence of condemnation by means of false witness : cp. Ex 23¹,⁷. **17. Upon him**] RV 'because of him,' on his account, i.e. by cherishing ill-will against him in secret.

18. Thou shalt love thy neighbour as thyself] This is the 'royal law' (Jas 2⁸) and the principle underlying the second table of the Decalogue : see Mt 22³⁵⁻⁴⁰. The word **neighbour** was interpreted in a narrow sense as equivalent to a fellow Israelite or at most to a stranger living in the midst of Israel. Our Lord removed all such limitations and applied the law universally : see Lk 10²⁹⁻³⁷.

19. Such mixtures are forbidden, as not only in themselves contrary to the divinely appointed order of nature, but as opening the door to the unnatural sins mentioned in 18²²,²³ Ro 1²⁶,²⁷ : see on Dt 22⁵. There may be an allusion here to the practice of magic, in which unnatural mixtures played an important part.

20. In the case of a betrothed free woman, both persons were put to death as adulterers, betrothal being regarded as sacredly as marriage itself : see on Ex 22¹⁶.

23. Uncircumcised] i.e. unconsecrated, unclean, and therefore not to be used for the first three years. In the fourth year the fruit is to be dedicated to God, after which the owner is free to enjoy the use of it. Besides impressing the duty of gratitude to God for the fruits of the earth this law is one of practical value. For the metaphorical use of the term 'circumcise' see 26⁴¹ Ex 6¹² Dt 30⁶ Jer 4⁴ 6¹⁰ 9²⁶ Ac 7⁵¹ Ro 2²⁸,²⁹ Phil 3³.

26. Use enchantment] charms or incantations. **Observe times**] RV 'practise augury,' perhaps by watching the clouds or the flight of birds : see on Dt 18¹⁰.

27. The practices in this and the following verses were commonly employed among idolatrous nations. The rounding of the corners of the head and beard may refer to the Arabian custom of presenting the first locks as an offering to the deity : see Jer 9²⁶ 25²³ 49³², with the marginal readings in each case:

cp. the practice of the Nazirite (Nu 6⁵,¹⁸). Oaths by the hair of the head were common (cp. Mt 5³⁶), and a usual Mohammedan oath is still 'by the beard of the prophet.'

28. Cutting the flesh and tattooing the skin are closely connected with cutting the hair as an idolatrous rite : cp. Jer 16⁶ 48³⁷ 1 K 18²⁸ Zech 13⁶.

29. This, too, was a degrading accompaniment of idol worship among the Canaanites, and even among the Greeks. Idolatry and immorality always went hand in hand: see on Ex 34¹³,¹⁵, and cp. Isa 57⁵⁻⁹ Hos 4¹³ Ro 1²³⁻²⁹.

31. That have familiar spirits] necromancers who profess to hold communication with the dead: cp. Ex 22¹⁸ Dt 18¹¹ 1 S 28⁷ᶠ.

33, 34. See on v. 9.

35. Meteyard] i.e. measuring rod. **36.** The **ephah** (about a bushel) and the **hin** (about a gallon and a half) are used here as representative measures: cp. Ezk 45¹⁰ᶠ.

CHAPTER 20

PENALTIES ATTACHED TO THE SINS SPECIFIED ABOVE

1–5. See 18²¹ and note.
6. See 19³¹.
9. See Ex 21¹⁷.
19–21. See 18⁶⁻²³.
27. See 19³¹.

CHAPTER 21

LAWS RELATING TO THE PRIESTHOOD AND SACRIFICE

The principle laid down in this and the following c. is the far reaching one, that whatever comes near or is presented to God must be perfect of its kind: see on Ex 12⁵. Priests, therefore, must be free from physical defects or ceremonial impurity, and sacrifices must be without blemish.

That this section is put together from different sources is shown by the interchange of the singular and plural and of the second and third persons (cp. e.g. 21⁴,⁵,⁸), by the introduction of fresh headings (21¹,¹⁶ 22¹,¹⁷, ²⁶), and by the fact that in the body of the laws the 'seed of Aaron' is spoken of, whereas in the headings and conclusions it is his 'sons.'

1–3. As contact with the dead defiles, priests are forbidden to attend to the funeral rites of any save their nearest relatives. But this exception does not apply to the high priest (see v. 11): see on 10⁴.

5. See on 19²⁷,²⁸. **6. Bread of their God**] see on 3¹¹. **7. Profane**] having lost her chastity.

10. Uncover his head] RV 'let the hair of his head go loose.' The law is more strict with regard to the high priest. The higher the office the greater the responsibility.

12. Go out of the sanctuary] i.e. intermit

his sacred duties : cp. 10 6, 7. **Crown**] RM 'consecration.'

16–24. No priest with any physical defect may officiate at the altar, though he may partake of the sacrificial gifts (v. 22) which fall to the lot of the priests for their maintenance.

18. Flat] RM 'slit.'   **22.** See on 2 3.

CHAPTER 22
Laws relating to the Priesthood and Sacrifice (continued)

1–6. The holy things may not be eaten by priests otherwise qualified, but ceremonially unclean, nor by any persons outside the priestly family.

10. Stranger] i.e. one not a priest, nor a member of a priest's family, even though he be an Israelite: see Ex 29 33. A slave purchased outright is considered to be a member of the family (v. 11).

14. Unwittingly] not knowing, perhaps, that it was a holy thing: see on 4 2 5 14. **With the holy thing**] this must mean its equivalent.

17–25. Sacrifices also must be without blemish. It was a frequent complaint that this law was not strictly observed, and that God was dishonoured with offerings that were mean and imperfect: cp. e.g. Mal 1 8, 13, 14, and see for an example of a better spirit 2 S 24 24.

19. At your own will] RV 'that ye may be accepted.'

27. See on Ex 22 30.   **28.** This prohibition probably rests on humanitarian grounds. The Mosaic Law enjoins kindness to animals.

29. See on v. 19.

CHAPTER 23
The Sacred Seasons

These are the Sabbath (v. 3), Passover and Unleavened Bread (vv. 5–14), Feast of Weeks, or Pentecost (vv. 15–22), Feast of Trumpets (vv. 23–25), Day of Atonement (vv. 26–32), and Feast of Booths or Tabernacles (vv. 33–43).

3. The sabbath] see on Ex 20 8-11.

5–8. Passover and Feast of Unleavened Bread. Passover, Pentecost, and Tabernacles were the three great annual festivals which followed the seasons of the year and the operations of agriculture. For the institution of the Passover see Ex 12 1-14, and for the sacrifices proper to the Feast of Unleavened Bread see Nu 28 16-25. These two parts of the double festival were quite distinct. The Passover was celebrated on the fourteenth day of Nisan beginning at sunset, and was followed by the Feast of Unleavened Bread, which lasted for seven days. Hence the name of the **feast of unleavened bread** is sometimes used to include both festivals, as in Lk 22 1.

9–14. The beginning of the grain harvest was celebrated during the Feast of Unleavened

Bread, when a sheaf of new corn was waved before the Lord, as an acknowledgment of His bounty, and a consecration of the harvest to Him.

11. Wave the sheaf] see on Ex 29 24.

13. Tenth deals .. hin] see on 14 10 19 36.

15–21. Feast of Weeks. Fifty days or seven weeks after the last festival, the Feast of Weeks, called in Gk. 'Pentecost' from the word for 'fifty,' began with the presentation of two loaves made of the new wheat and leavened in the ordinary way, signifying that harvest was completed. Hence this feast, which lasted only a single day, is called also the Feast of Harvest in Ex 23 16. For the sacrifices offered see vv. 18, 19 Nu 28 26-31.

22. See on 19 9.

23–25. Feast of Trumpets. This was celebrated on the first day of the seventh month (Tishri), which was New Year's Day according to the civil reckoning : see on Ex 12 2. For the special ritual of this Feast see Nu 29 1-6.

26–32. Day of Atonement : see c. 16.

33–43. Feast of Booths or Tabernacles. This feast, called also the Feast of Ingathering (Ex 23 16), was observed from the 15th to the 22nd Tishri (in October), and marked the end of the agricultural year, when the combined produce of the whole year, the vintage as well as the grain harvest, had been secured : cp. Dt 16 13. It was celebrated with great rejoicing (v. 40) as the national 'harvest home,' the people camping out in booths constructed of branches upon the roofs of their houses and in the streets during the seven days, in commemoration of the sojourn in the wilderness, v. 43: see on Ex 23 15, and cp. Hos 12 9.

CHAPTER 24
Oil for the Lamps. The Shewbread.
Laws on Blasphemy

1–4. Oil for the Lamps in the Tabernacle. On the construction of the Lampstand see Ex 25 31-40, and with the present passage cp. Ex 27 20, 21 and notes there.

5–9. The Table of Shewbread is described in Ex 25 23-30 (see notes there). On this table, which stood in the Holy Place, twelve new unleavened loaves were laid each sabbath day, and after lying for seven days were removed and eaten by the priests, fresh loaves being again substituted. These loaves, the number of which corresponded to that of the tribes of Israel, are called the 'bread of the Presence,' as being laid before God, or 'bread of the pile' as being arranged in two rows (v. 6), or 'the continual bread,' as lying continually before God (Nu 4 7). The shewbread was a kind of meal offering (see intro. to c. 2), and the rite probably had its origin in the crude notion that the deity required food like his worshippers (cp. on 3 11). In the Levitical law, however, it attained a higher significance. It was an acknowledgment that man owes his ' daily bread ' to God. It was a kind of perpetual grace over meat.

10–23. Punishment of a Blasphemer. A half-Israelite blasphemes the name of Jehovah. As there is some uncertainty whether such a person is subject to the same penalty as full-born Israelites the matter is referred to God, and the decision is given that there is one law for the stranger and for the home-born.

10. See on Ex 12 38. **11. Blasphemed the name** *of the* LORD] RV 'blasphemed the Name,' i.e. blasphemed Jehovah. The peculiar expression is due to some copyist who shrank, out of a feeling of reverence, from inserting the name of Jehovah in this connexion : see on Ex 3 13. **14. Lay their hands**] devoting him to death and solemnly dissociating themselves from complicity in his guilt : cp. Dt 17 7.

16. As well the stranger] This is the important legal point which the above incident is inserted to illustrate : cp. v. 22. **17–22.** Cp. Ex 21 12 f. and notes there.

CHAPTER 25
THE SABBATICAL YEAR. THE YEAR OF JUBILEE

The matters treated in this chapter are closely related to those in c. 23, and their separation is another indication that we are dealing with a book made up of different elements. Observe again the change of number in vv. 14, 17 and the interruption caused by vv. 18–22. Cp. what is said above in intro. to c. 21.

1–7. The law of the Sabbatical Year : see also Ex 23 10, 11 Dt 15 1-11 31 9-13. This law rests on the principle that the land inhabited by the Israelites is not theirs in absolute possession. It really belongs to God ; ' the land *is* mine ; for ye *are* strangers and sojourners with me ' (v. 23). To keep the people in mind of this, it is enacted that every seventh year the land has to lie fallow. Only the spontaneous produce of that year is to be enjoyed, and that not selfishly or for profit ; it is to be shared with the poor and strangers (Ex 23 11). Everything is to be common. Slaves are to be set free if they desire their freedom (Ex 21 2-6), and debts are to be remitted to Israelites (Dt 15 1-3). It is promised that the harvest of the sixth year will be sufficiently abundant to provide for the wants of the people till they reap again (vv. 20–22). The Sabbatical Year began with the first day of Tishri : see on 23 23. How far these enactments were actually carried out it is difficult to say. There is no mention of their observance during pre-exilic times, so that they may have been allowed to become a dead letter, a supposition confirmed by what is said in 2 Ch 36 21. They were renewed under Nehemiah (Neh 10 31).

5. This v. is interesting as containing the only example of the word ' its ' in AV. Elsewhere the word ' his ' is used as the possessive of the neuter pronoun. In the AV of 1611 it is printed ' it ' ; ' that which groweth of it owne accorde.'

Year of rest unto the land] As customs similar to this are found in other countries, it is probable that it is a survival of a communistic age. At the same time, it was a benefit to the land. Thus we have another example here of the Lawgiver adopting a primitive custom and investing it with the sanctity of religion. Cp. what is said in intro. to chs. 11–15, and see also Intro. to Exodus.

8–55. The Year of Jubilee. This rests on the same principle as the Sabbatical Year : see above. In the fiftieth year, i.e. after a period of 7×7 years, the land is to lie fallow, and Hebrew slaves with their families are to be emancipated without price, as in the Sabbatical Year (vv. 39–55). A new and distinctive feature, however, makes its appearance. In the Year of Jubilee all property reverts naturally to the original owner, who through poverty may have been obliged to sell it at some time during the previous period (vv. 13–28). The freehold of agricultural land could never, therefore, be sold in perpetuity (v. 23), and in cases of sale the purchase price was regulated according to the number of years still to run till the Year of Jubilee (vv. 14–16). The only exception was house property in a walled city (vv. 29 f.). The case of the Levitical cities is specially dealt with (vv. 32–34).

The Year of Jubilee was thus, as it were, the ' new birth ' of the whole nation, when property was redistributed, and the inequalities arising in the previous period were removed. It was a remarkable social law, putting a check upon ambition and covetousness, preventing the acquisition of huge estates, and adjusting the distribution of wealth in the various classes of the community. The incidents of Ruth (c. 4) and of Naboth (1 K 21) show that the law against the alienation of land was in force in early times : cp. Jer 32 6 f. That it was not unnecessary in later times appears from such passages as Isa 5 8 Mic 2 2.

9. The Year of Jubilee began on the Day of Atonement, and was ushered in with the blowing of trumpets ; hence its name (Heb. *jobel* = a ram's horn trumpet). **23. For ever**] RV 'in perpetuity.' **25.** A kinsman could redeem his relative's property at any time at a price calculated according to the years still to elapse before the Jubilee. **26. And himself . .**] RV ' and he be waxen rich and find sufficient to redeem it.' **28. Restore** *it* **to him**] RV ' get it back for himself.' **32.** The Levites were granted forty-eight cities to dwell in, v th suburbs for their cattle : see Nu 35.

35–38. See on Ex 22²⁵.

39–46. See on Ex 21¹⁻⁶. Only foreigners could be bought as slaves for ever.

47–54. The converse case of a Hebrew sold to a foreigner.

CHAPTER 26
CONCLUDING EXHORTATIONS

Similar exhortations are found at the conclusion of other codes of laws, as in Ex 23²⁰ f., and frequently in Deuteronomy, e.g. in c. 28. The leading ideas and phraseology are the same in all. There is the same insistence on the holy character of Jehovah, the same demand for holiness on the part of His people, the same promises on condition of obedience, and the same warnings against being led astray by the evil example of the idolatrous nations among whom they dwell.

1, 2. These two vv. have no connexion with what follows, except that they form the fundamental principles of the Hebrew religion, and on them rests the entire body of the Levitical legislation : see on Ex 24⁴ 34¹³.

3–13. Promise of prosperity attached to obedience.

4. In a country like Palestine rain in the proper season is an indispensable condition of prosperity and plenty. Hence it is frequently referred to in the OT. as a special mark of the divine favour : see on Dt 11¹⁰, and cp. Ezk 34²⁶ Isa 55¹⁰, ¹¹ Hos 6³. There are two rainy seasons in Palestine. The former rain falls in October-November when the seed is sown, and the latter rain in March-April before harvest.

5. There will be no scarce season.

10. Because of the new] i.e. to make room for the embarrassing abundance. 12. Cp. 2 Cor 6¹⁶⁻¹⁸. God's presence among, and delight in, His people are the cause of all the material blessings spoken of.

14–39. The penalty of disobedience.

This is described in the form of a climax of which the steps are vv. 14–17, 18–20, 21–22, 23–26, 27–39. 19. The rain will be withheld, and the ground in consequence become like brass for hardness ; see on Dt 28²³, and for an instance, 1 K 17¹. 26. The staff of your bread] RV ' your staff of bread ' : i.e. the bread which is your staff or support : cp. Ezk 4¹⁶ 5¹⁶ 14¹³. Owing to the scarcity one oven will be sufficient to bake the bread of ten families.

29. This actually took place more than once : see on Dt 28⁵³⁻⁵⁷.

30. High places] places of worship, usually on an eminence. The name is sometimes applied to places used for the worship of Jehovah, but in later times the ' high places ' were condemned as idolatrous. Images] RV ' sun-images,' images of the sun-god worshipped by the Phœnicians and Babylonians : see 2 K 23¹¹ 2 Ch 14⁵ 34⁴,⁷, and cp. Ezk 6⁴,⁵.

31. Savour of your sweet odours] i.e. sacrifices : see on Ex 29¹⁸. 34. The land lying desolate will then enjoy the rest of the sabbaths and Sabbatical years refused to it by a disobedient people : see 25¹⁻⁷, and cp. 2 Ch. 36²¹. 36, 37. A highly imaginative description of the inherent weakness of all wrong-doing, and of the cowardice which is the result of an evil conscience : cp. Dt 28⁶⁵⁻⁶⁷ Prov 28¹.

40–45. God desireth not the death of the sinner, and therefore every threat of punishment for disobedience is followed by a promise of mercy, on condition of repentance and amendment : cp. the way in which the prophecies of Amos and Micah conclude.

41. Uncircumcised hearts] unclean, not consecrated to God : see on 19²³.

46. The conclusion of the Law of Holiness (see intro. to chs. 17–26). The following chapter is of the nature of an appendix.

CHAPTER 27
VOWS AND TITHES AND THEIR REDEMPTION

1–29. Law of vows and their redemption.

The making of vows is a very ancient and universal practice connected with prayer. In order to secure his desire the suppliant adds a vow to his prayer. Vows may be either positive or negative. A man may promise either to devote something to God, or to abstain from some comfort or necessary of life. Instances of the latter, vows of abstinence, are to be found in Nu 6¹⁻²¹ 30 1 S 14²⁴ Ps 132²⁻⁵, and of the former in Gn 28²⁰⁻²² Jg 11³⁰,³¹ Nu 21¹⁻³. The present chapter deals with positive vows. The votive offering may be a human being (vv. 2–8), an animal (vv. 9–13), a house (vv. 14, 15), or a piece of land (vv. 16–25).

2–8. Human beings vowed to Jehovah must not be offered to Him in sacrifice. They must be redeemed, a certain sum of money being paid into the sanctuary as an equivalent.

2. Singular vow] a special vow devoting himself or any of his family to God. 3. Fifty shekels] about £6 10s : see on 5¹⁵.

9–13. If a man dedicates an animal and wishes to redeem it, he must pay its estimated value and one-fifth more. 9. Whereof men bring an offering] i.e. one of the sacrificial animals, a bullock, sheep, or goat. 10. See Mal 1¹⁴.

11. As it is unlawful to sacrifice unclean animals they must be redeemed and the equivalent value plus a fifth paid into the sanctuary. 14, 15. The redemption of a dedicated house follows the same rule.

16–25. The redemption of a dedicated piece of land is complicated by the law of Jubilee (c. 25). Its value is reckoned according to the amount of seed required to sow it (v. 16), and a reduction made in proportion to the number of years till the next Year of Jubilee (v. 18). The owner may redeem it at this price plus one fifth. If he does not, it goes to the sanctuary at the Year of Jubilee (vv. 20, 21). But if the dedicant of the land has himself bought it from a third person, then at the Jubilee it reverts to the latter, and the dedicant must recompense the sanctuary by paying its redemption value calculated as before (vv. 22–24).

16. Homer] ten ephahs, or nearly eleven bushels. The value of barley is here stated to be about £6 10s. **23. In that day**] The estimated value of a purchased piece of land must be paid in a lump sum. The estimated value of a hereditary possession, it would appear, was paid in yearly instalments. This practically meant that, till the Jubilee, the dedicant paid to the sanctuary a yearly rent of one shekel per homer of seed that he used. **26–29.** Exception to the Law of Redemption of Vows. **26.** Firstlings, which already belong to God (Ex 13 2), cannot be vowed again without mockery. **27.** Firstlings of unclean animals must be redeemed in the usual manner. In Ex 13 13 34 20 the law is that such must either be redeemed with a lamb or killed. The law seems to have varied at different times. **28.** Devoted things are those consecrated

to God by an extreme form of vow, the ban or curse, requiring their destruction or inalienable devotion to the sanctuary : see Nu 18 14 Dt 13 17 Josh 6 17, 21 1 S 15 3, 9, 20. This form of vow is specially laid upon the spoil of conquered nations. The NT. equivalent is the 'anathema' or excommunication : see Ro 9 3 1 Cor 5 5 16 22 1 Tim 1 20. **29. Devoted of men**] see Ex 22 20, where the Hebrew is 'shall be devoted.' There the 'devotion of men' is the solemn judicial penalty of idolatry. This was probably the only ground of devoting human beings. The case of Jephthah's daughter is doubtful : see Jg 11 30-40.

30–33. The Law of Tithes and their Redemption. Tithes belong to God as the real owner of the land : see on 25 1-7. They are a kind of rent paid by the people as His tenants. Being already God's, tithes cannot be made the subject of vows. Tithes of agricultural produce may be commuted for their money value plus one fifth (v. 31). The tithe of cattle cannot be redeemed (vv. 32, 33). **32. Passeth under the rod**] of the owner as he counts his cattle. Every tenth beast as it comes, whether good or bad, is to be set apart as belonging to God : cp. v. 10. The tithes were given to the Levites for their maintenance, and they in turn tithed their own tithes : see Nu 18 20-32.

NUMBERS

INTRODUCTION

1. Title and Contents. The English title of this book is a translation of that given to it in the Greek version of the Hebrew Bible. It is called Numbers because it tells of two numberings of the Israelites, one near the beginning and the other near the end of the sojourn in the wilderness (chs. 1 and 26). The title is not particularly applicable seeing that the account of these numberings occupies only a small part of the book. A better title is that given to it by the Jews, who call it 'In the Wilderness,' from the fifth word of the opening verse in the Hebrew Bible.

Numbers contains a brief summary of the experiences of the Israelites in the wilderness and covers a period of nearly forty years, extending from the encampment at Sinai to the arrival at the border of Canaan. The contents fall readily into three main divisions.

Part 1. The Camp at Sinai and Preparations for Departure, chs. 1–10 10. This section

includes the first numbering of the people, the order of the camp and the march (1–4) ; laws regarding lepers, marital jealousy, and the vow of the Nazirite (5, 6) ; the offerings of the princes for the service of the tabernacle (7) ; regulations regarding the lighting of the golden lamps and the consecration of the Levites (8) ; the celebration of the Passover in the wilderness (9 1-14) ; the cloudy pillar and the use of the silver trumpets (9 15–10 10).

Part 2. The Journeyings from Sinai to the Plains of Moab, chs. 10 11–22 1. These chapters cover the main period of the wanderings and give, not a full narrative of events, but a few outstanding incidents in these thirty-nine years, interspersed with various laws. Thus we have the departure from Sinai and the murmuring at Taberah and Kibroth-hattaavah where quails are sent (10 11–11 35) ; the jealousy of Miriam and Aaron against Moses (12) ; the sending of the spies from Kadesh, the discouragement of the people and sentence of forty years' wandering in the wilderness (13, 14); laws regarding offerings and sabbath observance (15); the rebellions of Korah, Dathan, Abiram, and On (16); the blossoming of Aaron's rod and the duties of priests and Levites (17, 18); the method of purification for those defiled by the dead (19); the death of Miriam, the murmuring at Meribah, and the giving of water from the rock (20 1-13); opposition of the Edomites and death of Aaron (20 14-29); defeat by the Canaanites, plague of fiery serpents, and conquest of the Amorites (21); arrival at the plains of Moab (22 1).

Part 3. In the Plains of Moab, chs. 22 2–36. This section relates the experiences in the plains of Moab and in the country E. of the Jordan, and includes the story of Balaam (22–24); relapse of the people into idolatry (25); the second numbering (26); law of inheritance, and designation of Joshua as the successor of Moses (27); law of offerings, sacred seasons (28, 29), and vows (30); fight against Midian (31); the assignment of land on the E. side of Jordan to two and a half tribes (32); a list of stations on the march (33 1-49); directions as to the treatment of the Canaanites and the division of the land (33 50–34); appointment of Levitical cities and cities of refuge (35); additional laws regarding inheritance (36).

2. Origin and Composition. The book of Numbers is manifestly a continuation of the story of the Pentateuch, and exhibits the same general literary characteristics as the rest of the books. As a combination of law and narrative, rather than a legislative code, it is more akin to Exodus than Leviticus, and sometimes follows it in ancient lists of OT. books. The circumstantiality of the narrative in many points, and the fact that many of the regulations in Numbers are only suitable to a life in the desert, while others are professedly prospective in their application (see e.g. 15 2 34 2), are indications that the groundwork of the book is of primitive origin. The statement in 33 2 is important as showing that Moses himself made a record of the wanderings, and that it was preserved to later times. It is interesting also to observe that Numbers incorporates several poetical pieces of great power and beauty which are of undoubted antiquity: see 21 14,15,17,18, 27-30 and the utterances of Balaam in chs. 23, 24.

In its present form, however, the whole book can hardly have been written by Moses. C.12 3 is most naturally understood as the judgment of a later writer on the character of Moses, who is not likely to have written this v. himself. Several times the phrase 'beyond Jordan' is used to denote the E. side, implying that the writer was living in Canaan. But Moses never crossed the Jordan; he died on the E. side: see on 21 13 22 1 Dt 1 1. The capture of Havoth-jair (32 41) did not take place till long after the death of Moses, as appears from Jg 10 3, 4. The words 'while the children of Israel were in the wilderness' (15 32) are written from the standpoint of a later time. These things do not, of course, imply that the whole book was a late composition; they can be explained as additions and interpolations in the original work.

3. Religious Value. What has been said as to the permanent religious value of the narrative and legislation of Exodus and Leviticus applies to the corresponding portions of Numbers and need not be repeated here. It is enough to point out that the writer of the book is no mere chronicler of events. He is an interpreter of the history of his people. In every event he sees the finger of God, ruling and guiding His chosen people, providing for their wants, bearing with their sins and infirmities, keeping His covenant with them, and preparing them by means of a long discipline for serving Him and being His witness to the world. Moses and Miriam, Caleb and Joshua, Phinehas and Balaam, are types of character from which we have still something to learn. The description of the camp and the congregation, the distribution of the duties and the provision for sacred ceremonial, are, like the description of the Heavenly Jerusalem in the book of Revelation, valuable, as giving an ideal picture of organised religious life. The Christian reader will recognise, in many of the experiences of God's people in the 'great and terrible wilderness,' types and illustrations of spiritual truths which are unchanging and eternal. The guidance by means of the pillar of cloud and fire (9 15-23), the supply of manna and of water (11, 20), the intercession of Aaron when he stood between the living and the dead till the plague was stayed (16 46-50), the sacrifice of the red heifer (19), the brazen serpent (21), the appointment of the cities of refuge (35), the exclusion from the land of promise of those whose faith failed them (14) and of Moses himself (20 12 27 12-14), the victory of God's people over the evil powers of the unseen world (22–24)—in the words of the Apostle, 'all these things happened unto them for ensamples: and they are written for our admonition, upon whom the ends of the world are come' (1 Cor 10 11).

PART 1

THE CAMP AT SINAI AND PREPARATIONS FOR DEPARTURE (Chs. 1–10 10)

CHAPTER 1

THE FIRST NUMBERING OF THE PEOPLE

At Sinai Moses receives the command to take the number of the males over twenty years of age in the eleven secular tribes, the tribe of Levi being enumerated separately (1 47-49 3 14-39). The result shows a total of 603,550 (cp. Ex 12 37 38 26 Nu 11 21). The result of the second numbering, made in the plains of Moab thirty-eight years afterwards (c. 26), is 601,730. The credibility of these figures has been disputed on two grounds. First, on this reckoning, the entire population, including men, women, and children, must have been at least three millions, and it is difficult to conceive how this large company could have been supported in the wilderness for forty years, not to mention the difficulty of marshalling and conducting them on their marches. The difficulty is a real one, but it is exaggerated by the traditional view, not supported by Scripture, that the Israelites were continually marching, and that they always moved as one company. To speak of them 'marching through the wilderness' is misleading: cp. 9 22. They may have occupied a great part of the peninsula of Sinai, encamping in detachments and moving about in search of pasture, though not simultaneously. The marches mentioned in Numbers may have been those of the main body under Moses: see intro. to 10 11–22 1. As to the resources of the wilderness, these must not be judged by its present condition. The word 'wilderness' does not mean a barren tract, but an uninhabited country which may be very fertile. And traces exist to show that this 'wilderness' not only could but did support at one time an extensive population. Moreover, unless miracles are prejudged to be impossible, account must be taken of the miraculous provision made for the sustenance of the Israelites till the time that they entered Canaan. The second objection is that the number of first-born males is stated in 3 43 to have been 22,273, again exclusive of the tribe of Levi. But this is a very small number in proportion to the total number of males. In answer to this it may be said that what is meant is the first-born males under twenty years of age at the time of the census, or those that had been born since the departure from Egypt. On the whole, while there are undoubtedly difficulties connected with these figures in Nu 1 and 26, our knowledge of the circumstances is too limited to enable us summarily to reject them as incredible : see on Ex 14 21.

16. The renowned] rather, 'the called'; chosen representatives. **18. Polls**] i.e. heads. **47–54.** The Levites are not included in the general census. The tribe of Levi is separated for the service of the tabernacle, and being exempt from military service is enumerated separately: see c. 3. **50. Tabernacle of testimony**] the tent containing the ark: see on Ex 16 34. **51. Stranger**] here one who is not a Levite: cp. 3 10 and Ex 29 33. **53. Wrath**] cp. 16 46 1 Ch 27 24.

CHAPTER 2

THE DISPOSITION OF THE TRIBES IN THE CAMP AND ON THE MARCH

The camp is in the form of a hollow square, each side of which is occupied by three tribes. On the E., the position of honour (cp. 3 38), is Judah, with whom are associated Issachar and Zebulun; on the S. is Reuben, with Simeon and Gad; on the W. is Ephraim, with Manasseh and Benjamin; on the N. is Dan, with Asher and Naphtali. In this arrangement regard seems to have been paid to family relationship. The priests and Levites form an inner square surrounding the tabernacle, which occupies the centre of the camp.

CHAPTER 3

THE LEVITES, THEIR DUTIES AND NUMBER

Although Aaron and his family belong to the tribe of Levi (Ex 2 1) the term 'Levites' is usually employed, as here, to denote the non-Aaronite Levites. The family of Aaron is set apart for the priesthood (Ex 28 Lv 8, 9), and the Levites are designated as their assistants, occupying an intermediate position between the priests and the congregation. They have charge of the tabernacle and its furniture, taking it down, carrying it during the march, and setting it up again. Their services in the tabernacle are not defined, but they would doubtless perform the humbler duties connected with the sacrifices, etc. In later times they were also doorkeepers and musicians in the Temple. See Neh 11, 12 1 Ch 6 31, 32, 48 15 16. The reason why this particular tribe was chosen for these offices, in addition to the fact that Moses and Aaron themselves belonged to it, seems to have been their zeal for the honour of Jehovah at the time of the worship of the Golden Calf (Ex 32 26-29). The subject of the Levites is continued in chs. 8 and 16–18.

4. On **Nadab** and **Abihu** see Lv 10.
10. Stranger] see on 1 51. **13.** See Ex 13 2, 12 f. **43.** See intro. to c. 1. **47.** See on Ex 30 13. Cp. Nu 18 16.

CHAPTER 4

THE DUTIES OF THE LEVITES ON THE MARCH

2. Kohath seems to have been the second son of Levi (3[17]), but his family is mentioned first, because Moses and Aaron belonged to it (3[19]; cp. Ex 6[18, 20]), and because it had charge of the most sacred furniture, the ark, etc.

3. From thirty years old] In 8[24] we read that the time of service was from the age of twenty-five. And in 2 Ch 31[17] Ezr 3[8] it is from the age of twenty: cp. 1 Ch 23[3, 24-27]. The practice seems to have varied at different times.

4–20. The Kohathites carry the ark and the sacred vessels of the tabernacle.

5. The **covering veil** is the curtain which screened off the Holy of Holies: see Ex 26[33].

7. The continual bread] i.e. the shewbread: see on Lv 24[5-9]. **11. The golden altar**] i.e. the altar of incense. In v. 13 **the altar** is the altar of burnt offering (see on Ex 30[1-10]).

15. Lest they die] cp. 2 S 6[6, 7]. **18. Cut not off**] see that you do not expose them to any risk of death by touching the most holy things: cp. Ro 14[15]. **20. They shall not go in**] i.e. the Kohathites.

21–28. The Gershonites take charge of the curtains of the tabernacle and the court. As these were of great weight two ox-wagons were employed in their transport: see 7[7].

29–33. The Merarites take charge of the framework of the tabernacle and employ four ox-wagons: see 7[8].

34–49. The numbers given here are those of the Levites on active service, between thirty and fifty years of age. The total number of the tribe was given in 3[39].

CHAPTER 5

VARIOUS CEREMONIAL LAWS

1–4. On the seclusion of lepers and unclean persons, see Lv 13–15.

5–10. On the law of restitution, see Lv 5[14-6[7]], to which the present passage is a supplement, providing that if the injured person dies and has no kindred to whom the price of restitution may be paid, it has to be given to the priest. Vv. 9, 10 prescribe that the heave offerings (see on Lv 7[28-34]) are the perquisite of the particular priest who officiates at the sacrifice, and are not to be distributed among the priests generally.

11–31. On Marital Jealousy.

A wife suspected of unfaithfulness is required to undergo a trial by ordeal. A potion is prepared by the priest, which she must drink, after taking an oath of purgation (vv. 19–24). If she is innocent the potion is harmless, but if guilty it injures her, thereby bringing her guilt to light (vv. 27, 28). Trial by ordeal is of the nature of an appeal to God to reveal the innocence or guilt of a suspected person. During the middle ages it was frequently resorted to in Europe under sanction of the church and the law. The most common forms of ordeal were those by fire, by water, and by wager of battle. The difference between these and the ordeal prescribed here is that the latter is not in itself injurious, but depends for its efficacy on the direct interposition of God.

13. No witness] The ordeal is prescribed for cases of doubt. To other cases the law of Lv 20[10] applies. **15.** Cp. Lv 2[1]. **17. Holy water**] This is the only place where this phrase is found, and it is not explained. Water from the laver is probably meant: see Ex 30[17-21]. **18. Uncover the .. head**] rather, as in RV, 'let the hair .. go loose,' a common sign of mourning: see Lv 10[6] 13[45]. **Bitter water**] so called as being the instrument of the curse.

CHAPTER 6

THE LAW OF THE NAZIRITE. THE PRIESTLY BENEDICTION

1–21. The Law of the Nazirite.

A Nazirite (from Heb. *nazir*, ' to separate') is a man or woman ' separated,' i.e. consecrated to Jehovah by means of a special vow of abstinence. The word has no connexion with 'Nazarene,' which means an inhabitant of Nazareth. During the period of his vow the Nazirite comes under a threefold obligation, (1) to abstain strictly from wine and all products of the vine, whether intoxicating or not (vv. 3, 4); (2) to let his hair grow (v. 5); and (3) to avoid all ceremonial defilement through contact with a dead body, even that of a near relative (v. 7). If he is accidentally defiled by the sudden death of any one beside him, he must perform rites of purification, and reconsecrate himself, counting as null whatever part of the period of the original vow may have elapsed (vv. 9–12). At the expiration of his vow he presents certain sacrifices (vv. 13–17), shaves his head and offers his hair upon the altar, and returns to ordinary life (vv. 18–21). The Nazirite's vow may either be for a limited period, which is the case supposed in this passage, or for life. The antiquity of the rite is shown by what is related of Samson (Jg 13[5]), and of Samuel (1 S 1[11]), who are usually regarded as lifelong Nazirites. It is also referred to in Am 2[12]. The Nazirite was not a hermit, but a very active devotee of Jehovah. He was very jealous for the Lord God of Israel, and while the vow of consecration and abstinence may sometimes have been undertaken for private and personal reasons, as e.g. to obtain the fulfilment of a desire, it was in many cases the expression of a religious and patriotic zeal, which sought to protect the primitive simplicity of Israel from the corrupting and enervating influences of heathen civilisations and religions. In this respect the Nazirites had much in common with the prophets, with whom they are classed in Am 2[11,12], as being 'raised up' by Jehovah Himself. In NT. references to the Nazirite vow are supposed to be found in Lk 1[15] (John the Baptist), in Ac 18[18] (St. Paul), and 21[24].

5. See on Lv 19[27]. **7. The consecration of his]** RV 'his separation unto.' **9. Die .. by him]** i.e. beside him. **Head of his consecration]** his unshorn locks were the visible sign of his vow of consecration. **14, 15.** The burnt offering betokened his entire dedication to God; the sin offering was presented for the sins he may have committed unwittingly during the period of his consecration; and the peace offering was an expression of his thankfulness for having been able to complete his vow. On the meaning of these sacrifices, see Lv 1, 3, 4. **18.** This denotes the completion of his vow: cp. Ac 18[18]. **21. Beside** *that* **that his hand shall get]** RV 'beside that which he is able to get,' i.e. in addition to any other offerings which it may be in his power to make.

22-26. The Priestly Benediction. It is part of the duty of the priests to bless the people in the name of Jehovah: see Dt 10[8] 21[5], and see on Lv 9[22,23]. The priestly benediction consists of three double clauses of increasing length and intensity, in each of which the sacred name is used. Cp. the three-fold Christian benediction in 2 Cor 13[14]. Ps 67 is evidently modelled on this benediction; cp. also Ps 4[6] 29[11] 31[16] 80[3,7,19]. **25. Make his face shine]** show favour. **26. Lift up his countenance]** take gracious notice of him. **27. Put my name upon]** This may mean simply to pronounce Jehovah's name over the people in blessing and thus mark them as His by covenant relation, as the Christian minister does when he baptises 'into the name of Christ.' But in OT. the 'name of Jehovah' is His revealed character; see on Ex 3[13]. So that to 'put Jehovah's name' upon a person is to declare to him the presence and nature of Jehovah. The priest does this when he blesses the people. He gives them the assurance of Jehovah's presence and favour.

CHAPTER 7
THE OFFERINGS OF THE PRINCES AT THE DEDICATION OF THE ALTAR

The twelve princes, each representing his tribe, presented gold and silver vessels for use in sacrifices, sacrificial animals, and wagons and oxen for the transport of the tabernacle: see 4[29-49]. The dedication of these offerings occupied twelve days, and was a service of thanksgiving.

13. Charger] a large dish, as in Mt 14[8]. **89. To speak with him]** i.e. with Jehovah.

CHAPTER 8
THE LIGHTING OF THE GOLDEN LAMPS. THE CONSECRATION OF THE LEVITES

1-4. See on Ex 25[31-40] 27[20,21]. **5-26.** This is the fulfilment of the injunction in 3[5-13]. **7. Water of purifying]** RV 'of expiation.' This ceremonial cleansing symbolised the inward purity required in those who bore the vessels of the Lord. **11. Offer the Levites ..** *for* **an offering of the children of Israel]** RV 'offer (lit. 'wave') the Levites .. for a wave offering, on the behalf of the children of Israel.' The Levites were solemnly set apart by the representatives of the people laying their hands upon them, and they were also 'waved' before the Lord as being that portion of the nation specially devoted to the service of God. How the 'waving' was done is not certain, whether the Levites were led backwards and forwards by Aaron in the direction of the Holy of Holies, or whether Aaron merely waved his hands over them: see on Ex 29[24]. **16.** The Levites are accepted as the substitutes in the service of the tabernacle for the firstborn among the children of Israel, who are now redeemed by a money payment of five shekels: see Ex 13[13] and cp. 18[15,16]. **19. Plague]** see on 1[53]. **When .. come nigh]** RM 'through coming nigh.' **24. Twenty and five years]** see on 4[3].

CHAPTER 9
RULES ABOUT THE PASSOVER. THE CLOUD AS GUIDE

1-5. The Passover of the second year. This Passover took place before the events narrated in c. 1: cp. 9[1] with 1[1]. The repetition of the injunction to keep the Passover was necessary, because the law in Exodus did not contemplate the possibility of a Passover in the wilderness: see Ex 12[25]. **6-14.** The Supplementary Passover. Certain persons who were unable to celebrate the Passover at the proper time, because of a ceremonial defilement (v. 6), are enjoined to observe a supplementary Passover on the fourteenth day of the second month (vv. 9[r.]). This was called 'The Little Passover.' **13. Cut off]** see on Lv 7[21]. **14. Stranger]** one who is not a Hebrew by birth but has been admitted into the nation by circumcision, a proselyte; see Ex 12[19,48]. **15-23.** The cloudy pillar as a signal on the march. This passage is parallel to Ex 40[34-38]: see on Ex 13[21]. **22.** It is clear from this v. that the people were not continually marching during their sojourn in the wilderness: see intro. to c. 1

CHAPTER 10–1-10

THE USE OF THE SILVER TRUMPETS

This section, like the last, is connected with the breaking up of the camp, one of the uses of the silver trumpets being to give the signal for the departure. **2. Of a whole piece]** RV 'of beaten work.' **9. If ye go to war]** see e.g. 31 6 2 Ch 13 12, 14. **10.** See Lv 23 24 2 Ch 5 12 Ezr 3 10.

PART 2

JOURNEYINGS FROM SINAI TO MOAB (Chs. 10 11–22 1)

After a stay at Sinai of nearly a year (cp. Nu 10 11 with Ex 19 1) the signal is given for the breaking up of the camp. This second division of the book of Numbers relates the wanderings in the wilderness, and covers a period extending from the second to the fortieth year of the exodus : see Nu 33 38 Dt 1 3. But as the events recorded in 10 11–14 45 took place during the first few months after leaving Sinai, and the death of Aaron in 20 22 was in the fortieth year, very little space is given to the events of the intervening thirty-eight years of desert life, more especially as chs. 15, 18, 19 are taken up with laws. There are indeed but two events recorded in that long period, viz. the rebellion of Korah and his company, with which is connected the blossoming of Aaron's rod (16, 17), and the death of Miriam and murmuring of the people at Kadesh (20 1-13). It appears, therefore, that while the period of sojourn in the wilderness was of supreme importance, by way of preparing the people socially and religiously for the occupation of the land of promise, it was uneventful. In all probability the Israelites led a fairly settled life, some of them scattered at a considerable distance from the headquarters of the camp, and moving about not always as one body but in separate detachments : see on 9 15-23. During the greater part of this period Kadesh seems to have been their headquarters. See on 13 26 20 1, and cp. Dt 1 46. It was only near the end of this period that a concerted and continuous march was made from Kadesh to the plains of Moab (c. 21).

CHAPTER 10 11-36

THE DEPARTURE FROM SINAI

12. Paran] see on Ex 15 22. They do not actually reach Paran till 12 16.

29. In Ex 2 18 Moses's father-in-law is called Reuel and in 3 1 4 18 Jethro. Here Hobab is called the son of Reuel (or Raguel), and therefore apparently the brother-in-law of Moses. But in Jg 4 11 (RM) and perhaps here, too, he is called the father-in-law of Moses. There is therefore much uncertainty as to these names and relationships, which is increased by the fact that the word rendered father-in-law is of wide application. It has been supposed that the name Reuel in Ex 2 18 has been inserted by mistake, and that Hobab, otherwise called Jethro, was the son of Reuel and the father-

in-law of Moses. He was a Midianite and well acquainted with the country through which the Israelites were to pass. The service he rendered to them was not forgotten in after times, so that it may be inferred that he yielded to the pressing invitation of Moses : see Jg 1 16 1 S 15 6.

35. When the ark set forward] i.e. whenever it set forward. Every stage of the journey was begun and ended with this prayer of invocation. Ps 68 recalls this march of the people through the wilderness with God at their head to ensure victory.

CHAPTER 11

MURMURING AT TABERAH AND AT KIBROTH-HATTAAVAH

1. In the uttermost parts of the camp] What is meant is that the fire began, where probably the murmuring began, at the extremity of the camp, perhaps among the 'mixed multitude' (cp. v. 4). **3. Taberah]** 'burning.' **4. The mixt multitude]** see Ex 12 38, where, however, a different word is used. **Fell a lusting]** longed for the delicacies of Egypt (v. 5). **Wept again]** This may refer to the story in Ex 16. **15. My wretchedness]** i.e. the failure of my attempts to lead this people : cp. the despairing complaint of Elijah in 1 K 19 4 and of Jeremiah in Jer 15 10. **16.** Later Jewish writers saw in this command of God the origin of their Sanhedrim, or Council of Seventy, who regulated the affairs of the nation in later times : cp. Mk 15 1. **18. Sanctify]** see Ex 19 10, 15.

25. They prophesied] This does not mean that they were able to predict the future, but that they broke out into the praise of God, and declared His will and goodness, while in a state of spiritual exaltation and ecstasy : see on Ex 7 1. **26. Were written]** enrolled among the seventy. The fact that Eldad and Medad also received the spirit shows that the spirit of God is not limited to certain places or individuals, and that He is no respecter of persons : cp. Ac 10 34, 35, 44-48.

28. Cp. Mk 9 38, 39. **29.** A good example of the magnanimity and unselfishness of Moses : see on 27 15.

31. Two cubits *high* **upon the face of the earth]** The simplest interpretation of these words is that the quails were flying at this height (about 3 ft.) above the ground, which allowed the people to capture them easily.

Quails usually fly low, and with the wind (see on Ex 16 13). **32.** A **homer** is about ten bushels. The quails were spread out to dry for preservation. **33.** The plague was probably due to surfeit : cp. Ps. 78 26-31 106 13-15.

34. Kibroth-hattaavah] 'the graves of lusting' : this and **Hazeroth** were between Sinai and Kadesh.

CHAPTER 12
The Jealousy of Miriam and Aaron

In this scene Miriam is the chief actor : the punishment falls on her alone. Aaron seems to have been led away by her (cp. Ex 32 22-25). The controversy arose in connexion with Moses' marriage with an Ethiopian, but the sequel, to which no reference is made to this matter, shows that the real reason of the strife is the jealousy of Miriam and Aaron over the superior position of their younger brother (vv. 2, 6-9).

1. The Ethiopian woman] Heb. 'the Cushite woman.' This can hardly be Zipporah, who was a Midianite (Ex 2 16, 21). Moses, it appears, had married again. Marriage with the Canaanites was forbidden (Ex 34 16), but not with the Egyptians (see Dt 23 7, 8). **2.** Miriam is called a prophetess in Ex 15 20 : see note there and cp. Ex 4 14-17. **3.** Moses made no retort to the criticism, thus exhibiting true greatness.

6-8. The superior favour shown here to Moses consists (1) in the direct manner in which God reveals His will to him, and (2) in his position of general authority. **12.** Leprosy was a living death, and contact with a leper involved the same defilement as with a dead body ; see Lv 13 45. **14.** The prayer is heard, but Miriam is obliged to submit to the customary seclusion and purification, in order that the people may know of her sin and punishment, and take warning.

CHAPTER 13
The Sending of the Spies and their Report

8. Oshea] RV 'Hoshea,' meaning 'help' or 'salvation.' Joshua, or Jehoshua (v. 16), means 'Jehovah is my help' : see on Ex 17 9.

17. Southward] RV 'by (RM 'into') the South' : lit. 'into the Negeb' : see on Gn 12 9. The spies, however, really went northward on this occasion, first through the Negeb, and then through the mountainous district lying N. of it, here called 'the mountain,' afterwards the 'hill-country of Judah,' to the W. of the Dead Sea. **20. Time of the firstripe grapes**] i.e. about the end of July. **21.** The **wilderness of Zin** lay N. or NE. of the wilderness of Paran, and may have formed part of it. Its chief town was Kadesh-Barnea (v. 26). **Rehob** and **Hamath** were in the extreme N. of the country : see Jg 18 28 Nu 34 8.

The spies traversed the entire land from S. to N. The length of Canaan is about 180 m., and its average breadth between the Mediterranean Sea and the River Jordan about 40 m. The country may be regarded as consisting of three strips running N. and S. There is (1) the Maritime Plain extending inwards from the coast to a distance of from 4 to 15 m., very fertile, and including the famous Plain of Sharon and the Lowlands of the Philistines. (2) Behind this rises the 'Hill Country,' forming, as it were, the backbone of the Holy Land, and falling precipitously on the E. down to (3) the valley of the Jordan and the Dead Sea, which divides the land of Canaan from the Highlands of Gilead and Moab E. of the Jordan. See art. 'Palestine.' In the earliest monumental records which we have, this land is called the 'land of the Canaanites' or the 'land of the Amorites,' from which it may be inferred that these were the tribes originally inhabiting it. At a very early period the Hittites, a powerful kingdom to the N. of Canaan, established themselves in the country and have left monuments of their influence. At the time of the Israelitish Conquest the land was inhabited by a mixture of tribes. Of these, the principal were the Canaanites (i.e. probably 'Lowlanders'), dwelling in the Maritime Plain and the valley of the Jordan, the Hittites and the Jebusites in the S., in what was afterwards called Judæa, the Hivites to the N. of these in what came to be known as Samaria, and still further N. the Perizzites. The Amorites (i.e. probably the 'Highlanders') were found in the N. and also in the S. to the E. of the Jordan. The Philistines had also obtained a settlement in the southern part of the Maritime Plain : see Dt 2 23. Till recently it was thought that, prior to the Conquest by the Israelites, Canaan was an unknown and uncivilised country. We know now that long before that time, as early as 3500 B.C., Babylonian kings ruled over Canaan, and that the Babylonian language and civilisation were spread over the country. After the Babylonian influence came the Egyptian. At Tel-el Amarna in Egypt there has been discovered a great number of tablets dating about 1400 B.C., i.e. not long before the Conquest of Canaan by the Israelites. These tablets prove to be mostly letters to the king of Egypt from tributary princes in Canaan written in the Babylonian language. From them we learn that about the time of the exodus Canaan was subject to Egypt, and that instead of being a country of semibarbarians, it possessed a highly developed civilisation, in the ruling power at least. 'At that period Canaan had already behind it a long civilised past. The country was filled with schools and libraries, with richly furnished palaces, and workshops of artisans.

The cities on the coast had their fleets, partly of merchantmen, partly of warships, and an active trade was carried on with all parts of the known world.' But at the time of the exodus Egypt was beginning to lose its hold of the country. The native tribes were restless and rebellious, and Canaan was ready to be 'the prey of the first resolute invader who had strength and courage at his back.' These facts, recently discovered, throw a flood of light upon the Israelitish Conquest of the country. They explain how it was possible for the Israelites to enter and take possession of it. And they are valuable also as proving that long before the Captivity, as early as the exodus, the Israelites were in close contact, not only with Egyptian, but with Babylonian civilisation and religion.

23. The brook (mg **valley**) **of Eshcol**] lay a little to the N. of Hebron, in a district still renowned for its fertility, and especially for its vineyards. The cluster of grapes was carried by two men, not so much on account of its weight as its size, in order that it might not be crushed. **26. To Kadesh**] see on v. 21. This was the most important station of the journey. The people remained here for the greater part of thirty-eight years between the sending of the spies and the entrance into Canaan: see on 20 1. According to Dt 1 19, 22 the spies were sent out from Kadesh. **32. Eateth up the inhabitants**] This refers to the warlike character of the inhabitants, who devour each other in strife. **33. The giants**] Heb. the Nephilim. The word is found only here and in Gn 6 4. The report of the spies is of course exaggerated, but the original inhabitants seem to have been of unusual stature and strength: cp. Dt 2 11 1 S 17 4-7, and on 21 33-35.

CHAPTER 14
DISCOURAGEMENT OF THE PEOPLE AND SENTENCE OF FORTY YEARS' WANDERING

9. Bread for us] cp. 13 32 22 4 24 8. **12.** Cp. Ex 32 10 f., where a similar promise is made and where Moses shows the same self-effacing spirit. **13.** Cp. Josh 7 9 2 S 1 20 Ps 79 10. **17. Let the power of my LORD be great**] i.e. in the eyes of the heathen, when they see Israel possessing the land. **18.** See on Ex 34 6, 7. **22. These ten times**] a round number indicating full measure: cp. Gn 31 7.

33. Shall wander] RV 'shall be wanderers.' Better, 'shall be shepherds,' lead an unsettled life instead of occupying the land. The forty years are reckoned from the time of the departure from Egypt. See Dt 2 14. **Bear your whoredoms**] suffer the penalty of your faithlessness. **34. My breach of promise**] RV 'my alienation' from you; RM 'the revoking of my promise.' **40. The mountain**] the

Hill-country by way of which the spies had gone. The people presume to disobey the command of v. 25. **45. Unto Hormah**] This was about 25 m. NE. of Kadesh. They must therefore have marched considerably to the N. of Kadesh: see on 21 3.

CHAPTER 15
LAWS REGARDING VARIOUS OFFERINGS

1-16. Meal and Drink Offerings. The offerings here referred to are those presented along with other sacrifices (see on the Meal Offering, Lv 2), and an enactment is made regulating the proportion of meal, oil, and wine to be used along with a lamb (vv. 4, 5), a ram (vv. 6, 7), and a bullock (vv. 8-10) respectively. These laws seem to have been given at Kadesh during the long sojourn there. **4. Tenth deal**] i.e. the tenth part of an ephah, which is about a bushel. A **hin** is about a gallon and a half: see Ex 16 16 29 40. **14. Stranger**] see on 9 14.

17-21. The Offering of the First Fruits. **20. Your dough**] Probably a coarse kind of meal: cp. Ezk 44 30.

22-31. Additional Laws regarding Sin Offerings (1) for the congregation (vv. 22-26) and (2) for the individual (vv. 27-31). **30. Presumptuously**] lit. 'with a high hand,' wilfully : see on Lv 4 2. **Reproacheth the LORD**] bringeth a reproach upon the Lord: i.e. causeth His name to be dishonoured.

32-36. The Punishment of the Sabbath Breaker.

This incident is designed to illustrate vv. 30, 31. It tells how the man who reproached the Lord, by breaking the sabbath commandment, was utterly cut off, i.e. put to death, as the Lord commanded Moses.

38. Fringes in the borders of their garments] RM 'twisted threads.' The original form of these is uncertain. Judging from later times, they would be, not ornamental festoons running along the edge of the garment, but tassels attached to each of its four corners by a thread of blue. A religious importance was attached to the wearing of these tassels. They were a visible reminder to the Jews of their obligation to keep the commandments of Jehovah (v. 39). In all probability what we have here is the hallowing of an ancient custom, as these tassels seem to have been worn by the early Persians, among others. The Jews attached an ever-increasing importance to these symbolical ornaments of dress: cp. Mt 14 36 9 20 23 5. The modern survival is the Jewish *tallith*, or prayer-cloth, consisting of a strip of cloth with fringes on its border, which is thrown over the shoulders during the service in the synagogue. **39. All the commandments**] The Rabbis enumerated

613 commandments in the Law. It so happens that the numerical value of the letters in the Hebrew word for **fringe** (*zizith*) is exactly 600. To make this number up to 613 the tassel was made of eight threads with five knots. In this way each tassel represented the 613 commandments, and the wearing of it was said to be of equal merit with the keeping of the whole law. This is a good example of Rabbinical interpretation and of external scrupulosity. **Go a whoring**] see on Ex 34 15.

CHAPTER 16
The Rebellion of Korah, Dathan, Abiram, and On

This incident is similar to that recorded in c. 12, and while it illustrates the difficulties Moses encountered in his leadership, owing to the jealousy of those under him, it served to confirm him (v. 28) and Aaron (c. 17) in the position assigned to them. It is now generally agreed that this c. is composed of two narratives interwoven with each other. The one describes a rebellion led by Dathan, Abiram, and On against the civil authority of Moses (vv. 1, 2, 12–15, 25–34); while the other describes a different sort of rebellion, headed by Korah and 250 princes of the congregation, against the ecclesiastical leadership of Moses and Aaron. This separation of the c. into two distinct narratives reduces it to order and serves to explain, not only the literary inequalities, but also the differences of fact ; such as e.g. in the one case the refusal to obey the summons of Moses, and in the other the compliance with it (cp. v. 12 with 18, 19) ; the difference in locality, in the one case the sanctuary, and in the other the tents of Dathan and Abiram (v. 18 and 25, 26) ; and the different fate of the two companies, in the one case death by earthquake, and in the other by fire from the Lord (vv. 31–34 and 35).

4. The action may denote the dismay of Moses, but more probably his praying for guidance: cp. vv. 22, 45, 20 6. **5. To Korah**] not to Dathan and Abiram, whose rebellion is distinct from this : see above. **11. Against the LORD**] not merely against Aaron, of whose privileges Koran and his company are envious. **13.** Dathan and Abiram are envious of the position of Moses. They complain that, instead of bringing them into a land flowing with milk and honey, as he had led them to believe he would do, he was taking them away from it into a wilderness (vv. 13, 14). **Except thou make thyself**] RV 'But thou must needs make thyself also.' **14. Put out the eyes of these men**] blind them to the real state of matters. The English equivalent would be to ' throw dust in the eyes.' **19. All the congregation**] This shows the serious nature

of Korah's rebellion. The people were in sympathy with it. The claim put forward by Korah was plausible, and flattered the multitude : see v. 3. **22.** The God of the spirits of all flesh must know the thoughts and intents of the heart and be able to judge the real instigator of the evil. The **one man is** Korah: cp. for the thought Gn 18 23. **28. Hath sent me**] i.e. Moses. Dathan's rebellion is directed against Moses as that of Korah against Aaron. On the sending of Moses see Ex 3. **Not . . of mine own mind**] The mark of the true messenger or prophet of God is that he does not speak of his own initiative: cp. Nu 24 13 1 K 22 13, 14 Jer 1 5-10 Mt 10 19, 20. The false prophet, on the other hand, runs where he is not sent and speaks ' out of his own heart' : see Ezk 13 2 Jer 14 14 23 25-32. **30. Quick**] i.e. alive. **The pit**] Heb. *Sheol*, usually rendered ' the grave.' **32. Their houses**] their households, as in 1 2 Gn 7 1. The sons of Korah, however, did not perish : see 26 11.

36–39. The censers used by Korah and his company are collected and made into a covering for the altar, as a memorial of their sin and punishment, and a warning to others against profaning holy things : cp. Jude v. 11. **37.** Eleazar is commanded to do this, not Aaron, who, as high priest, must not defile himself with contact with the dead: see Lv 21 11. **38. The altar**] the altar of burnt offering, which was overlaid with brass : see on Ex 3 1-10.

41–50. The people now turn upon Moses and charge him with being the occasion of this calamity. Their unreasonable murmuring is punished with a plague, which is only stayed by means of the intervention of the high priest. **46.** Incense was usually offered, not alone, but as an accompaniment of a sacrifice. On this occasion the plague had begun, and incense was the readiest sacrifice that could be offered. It is symbolical of prayer and intercession : see on Ex 30 1-10. Observe that the unauthorised offering of incense by the rebels was provocative of the divine indignation, while in the hands of Aaron, the appointed high priest, it was accepted as an atonement, and procured the grace of forgiveness. **48.** A striking picture, illustrating the efficacy of believing prayer (cp. Jas 5 15, 16) and the way in which Christ by the offering of Himself has stayed the plague of sin and death : cp. Eph 5 2.

CHAPTER 17
Aaron's Authority Confirmed

Korah and his followers having questioned the authority of Aaron and the claim of his family to the priesthood, the matter is put beyond the possibility of further doubt by the Blossoming of Aaron's rod.

2. A rod] The common symbol of authority: cp. Ps 110[2]. **4. The testimony**] i.e. the ark in which the 'testimony' is kept : see on Ex 16[34]. **8–11.** On the morrow Aaron's rod is found to have put forth almond buds and fruit, while the others show no sign of life. In this way the exclusive right of the tribe of Levi and family of Aaron to exercise the priestly functions is decided. Aaron's rod is ordered to be laid up before the ark as a token to succeeding generations. **8. Yielded almonds**] Observe that the three stages of vegetable life are simultaneously visible, blossoms, buds, and fruit. As the almond tree blossoms in January when other trees are bare and before its own leaves appear, it is used to symbolise the way in which God fulfils His promises when men least expect it : see Jer 1[11, 12], and cp. Isa 11[1] 53[2] Mt 4[13-16].

10. Before the testimony] According to Heb 9[4] the rod was kept in the ark. This, however, is nowhere asserted in OT. and may be a later tradition: cp. 1 K 8[9]. **12, 13.** The people are awe-struck and impressed with the danger of approaching the sanctuary in any unauthorised manner.

CHAPTER 18
The Duties and Maintenance of Priests and Levites

1. The priests are responsible for the iniquity of the sanctuary and the priesthood, i.e. for their profanation at any time by unauthorised persons and by the sins of the priests themselves. On the Day of Atonement the high priest offers sacrifices to make atonement for himself and the sanctuary : see on Lv 16. **2. Levi**] 'joined' : see Gn 29[34].

8–19. The provision for the maintenance of the priests. The priests receive part of the meal offerings (Lv 2[3]), the sin and guilt offerings, except when these are presented by the priests on their own behalf (Lv 4[26]), the heave portion of the peace offerings (Lv 3), the first fruits of oil, wine, and wheat (vv. 12, 13), devoted things (v. 14 ; see on Lv 27[21-28]), firstlings of clean animals, the redemption price of the firstborn of men and unclean beasts (vv. 15–18), and the tithe of the tithe paid to the Levites (vv. 25–28). **9. Most holy**] see on Lv 2[3]. **16.** See 3[47] Lv 27[6]. **Shekel**] see on Ex 38[24]. **19. Covenant of salt**] i.e. an indissoluble covenant : see on Ex 30[35].

20–24. The priests and Levites have no inheritance in the land of promise. By way of compensation the tithes are given to the Levites, who in turn give a tithe to the priests (v. 26). **20.** Those who are separated to the service of God are taught to depend on Him. He sends no one into warfare at his own charges : see 1 Cor 9[7-14].

25–32. The Levites are to tithe their own tithe and present it to the priests as a heave offering, as the ordinary Israelites do with the produce of their fields. The remainder they are allowed to enjoy in the same manner as others : cp. Lv 27[30f]. **31. In every place**] not restricted, as in the case of the priests, to the holy place : see on Lv 2[3].

CHAPTER 19
The Sacrifice of the Red Heifer

In order to provide a special means of purification for those who are defiled by contact with a dead body, a preparation called the 'water of separation' is made from the ashes of a red heifer and other ingredients. The origin of this rite may have been connected with the large number of deaths recorded in 16[49]. Josephus, however, connects it with the death of Miriam (20[1]).

1–10. A red heifer is slaughtered outside the camp and its blood sprinkled in the direction of the sanctuary seven times (vv. 1–4). The entire carcase is burnt in the same place along with cedar wood, hyssop, and scarlet wool, and the ashes are collected and preserved for use in purifying (vv. 5, 6, 9). Those who take part in the ceremony contract defilement (vv. 7, 8, 10). **2.** Sacrificial animals are usually males. The use of a female in this case may be intended to symbolise the imparting of new life to those who have been defiled by contact with death. The same thought may underlie the regulation as to colour, red being the colour of blood which is the token of life : cp. Lv 17[11]. The words **without spot** probably mean 'without blemish.' **4. Directly before**] RV 'Toward the front of' ; i.e. in the direction of the sanctuary. **6.** See on Lv 14[4].

9. Water of separation] RV 'water of impurity,' i.e. water for the removal of (ceremonial) impurity : see on 8[7].

11–16. The persons for whom this 'water of impurity' is provided are those who have touched a dead body or anything connected with it.

11. Owing to the mystery connected with death a dead body is regarded, not only among the Jews but among other nations of antiquity, as eminently dangerous and communicating defilement in the highest degree. Moreover, such ceremonial defilement is easily associated with the idea of sin, as death is the wages of sin. **12. With it**] i.e. with the 'water of impurity.'

17–22. The method of purification. The ashes of the heifer are mixed with water from a running stream or spring, and sprinkled upon the unclean person or thing. This is done on the third day after the defilement has been contracted. On the seventh day the unclean person washes his clothes, bathes, and resumes his place in society at even. The penalty of neglect is excommunication. The various parts of the expiatory rite lend themselves easily to symbolical interpretation. The connexion of sin and death, the need of cleansing, and the ever-ready means of purification, are all exemplified. The writer of the Epistle to the Hebrews draws a parallel between the heifer, whose ashes were sanctified to the purifying of the flesh from the defilement arising from contact with dead bodies, and Christ who, also without spot, offered Himself without the camp to God to purge the conscience of believers from dead works, i.e. from works which cause death. See Heb 9 13, 14 13 11, 12.

CHAPTER 20
DEATH OF MIRIAM. MURMURING AT MERIBAH. DEATH OF AARON

1. Miriam dies while the people are at Kadesh (see on 13 21, 26). **The first month** is the first month of the fortieth year. As the people came to Kadesh in the second year (see 13 26), they must have remained in the vicinity of Kadesh during the interval, or what is recorded here is a second arrival at the same place : cp. Dt 2 14. **2–13.** Murmuring at Meribah. **3. When our brethren died**] This probably refers to the deaths following the rebellions of Korah and of Dathan and Abiram (c. 16). It implies that these occurrences were recent. **6. Fell upon their faces**] see on 16 4. **8. The rod**] Seeing he took the rod **from before the LORD** (v. 9) it has been thought that Aaron's rod is meant : cp. 17 10. But it was more probably Moses' staff which was associated with former dangers and deliverances : see Ex 4 17 7 17 14 16 17 5, 9.

12. Ye believed me not] The root of Moses' sin was unbelief. He doubted the power of God, or His willingness to bear longer with these **rebels** (v. 10), and instead of speaking to the rock, as he was commanded to do, he struck it twice : cp. Ps 106 33. The punishment was severe, but want of faith on the part of the leaders could not be overlooked or unpunished, because the people had seen it, and might be led away by the evil example : see on 12 14. **To sanctify me**] God is always holy and His essential holiness cannot be increased. But the obedience and praise of His people cause His holiness and grace to be more widely known and acknowledged. Similarly God is said to be 'magnified,' as in Lk 1 46 : cp. the petition 'Hallowed be Thy name.' **13. Meribah**] 'strife.' In 27 14 Dt 32 51 it is called Meribah of Kadesh to distinguish it from the Meribah of Ex 17 7 (see note there).

14–21. The people prepare for the last stage of the journey to Canaan. The direct route to the N. is blocked by the Canaanites

(21 1). On the E. are the Edomites who are the kindred of the Israelites, being descended from Esau the brother of Jacob. Moses accordingly sends messengers to the king of Edom asking a passage through his country to the E. side of Canaan, but the request is refused.

14. Thy brother] see above, and cp. Dt 23 7 Gn 25 30 36 8, 9. The unnatural hostility of the Edomites on another occasion is the subject of the book of Obadiah (see vv. 10–12) ; cp. also Am 1 11. **16. Sent an angel**] see Ex 3 2 14 19. **17. The king's** *high* **way**] Edom lay on the direct route connecting Egypt with Babylonia. The **king's way** here, however, is not a proper name, but signifies the most direct route. They promised not to trespass or injure the country in passing through it.

22–29. Death of Aaron. Turning southward so as to go round the country of the Edomites by way of the N. end of the Gulf of Akaba (see 21 4), the Israelites reach Mt. Hor. Here Aaron dies and is buried. Mt. Hor is identified by most travellers with a precipitous mountain nearly 5,000 ft. high, forming the principal elevation in the range of Mt. Seir. The wonderful rock city of Petra (or Sela), the capital of Edom, lay at its eastern base. A small mosque on the summit now marks the traditional site of Aaron's burial-place. **24. Gathered unto his people**] This may suggest the continuance of life after death along with those who have gone before : see Gn 15 15. **Ye rebelled**] The same word is applied to Moses and Aaron as Moses had applied to the people at Meribah (v. 10). The leaders, as well as the people with whom they were impatient, were 'rebels.'

26. This signifies the succession of Eleazar to the priesthood. The ceremony of putting on the sacred robes was an important part of the consecration of the high priest. See Lv 8 7-9 Ex 29 29, and cp. the action of Elijah, 1 K 19 19 2 K 2 13-15. **28.** Moses also died on the top of a mountain : see Dt 34 1. Aaron died on the first day of the fifth month in the fortieth year of the exodus at the age of 143 : see 33 38, 39.

29. The death of Aaron removed the second greatest figure from among the Israelites, and their first high priest. The writer of the Epistle to the Hebrews contrasts the human priesthood, which is imperfect by reason of its being constantly interrupted by death, with the 'unchanging priesthood' of Him 'who ever liveth to make intercession' for His people : see Heb 7 23-28.

CHAPTER 21
THE BRAZEN SERPENT. CONQUEST OF BASHAN

1–3. The southern Canaanites repulse the Israelites, but are eventually destroyed.

1. King Arad] RV 'king of Arad.' The name of this place still survives in *Tell Arad*, some ruins about 16 m. S. of Hebron and about 50 m. N. of Kadesh. **The way of the spies**] RV 'the way of Atharim.' The word is evidently the name of a place. It has not been identified. **2. Destroy**] lit. 'devote.' See on Lv 27 26-29. **3.** This took place much later : see Josh 12 14 Jg 1 16, 17. Had they been victorious on this occasion the Israelites would naturally have marched directly northwards into Canaan ; but, being repulsed, they retreated southwards, having registered this vow which was ultimately fulfilled. **Hormah** means a 'devoted thing.' It is from the same root as the verb in v. 2.

4-9. The Brazen Serpent. Retreating southwards the people are discouraged and give way again to murmuring. Venomous serpents are sent among them. Moses is commanded to make a brazen serpent, and all who look to it in faith are healed. **4. To compass**] to go round : see on 20 22-29. **The Red Sea**] i.e. the arm now called the Gulf of Akaba. **Because of the way**] They were now marching away from Canaan instead of towards it. **5. This light bread**] or, 'this vile food.' The manna is meant : cp. 11 6.

6. Fiery serpents] i.e. serpents whose sting caused violent inflammation. Venomous sandsnakes are still found in this locality.

8. Upon a pole] RV 'upon a standard.' This brazen serpent was long preserved by the Israelites, and ultimately became an object of superstitious veneration, in consequence of which Hezekiah ordered it to be destroyed (2 K 18 4).

9. When he beheld the serpent of brass, he lived] rather, 'when he looked to it,' i.e. not casually but of purpose and with faith. The lifeless image of the serpent that had caused the pain and death of so many was a symbol of the victory over these things that God gives to those who trust in Him. The Jewish commentators recognise here an illustration of the power of faith. 'The serpent neither killed nor preserved alive, but if the Israelites lifted up their eyes and turned their hearts to their Father in heaven they were healed ; if not, they perished.' Similarly in the book of Wisdom (16 6,7), the brazen serpent is called 'a token of salvation to put them in remembrance of the commandment of Thy law, for he that turned toward it was not saved because of that which was beheld, but because of Thee, the Saviour of all.' The brazen serpent raised upon the pole, for the healing of those who were ready to die, is a striking emblem of the Saviour 'lifted up' on the Cross, for the salvation of all who are wounded by 'that old serpent the devil,' and who look in faith to Him : see Jn 3 14.

10-15. Journey to the Arnon.

12. Zared] The Zered flowed into the Dead Sea at its southern extremity. **13. The other side of Arnon**] This means the S. side of the river Arnon, as the story is narrated from the standpoint of one living in Canaan : see Intro. and 22 1. The Arnon flows into the Dead Sea about the middle of its E. side. It is the boundary between the Moabites on the S. and the Amorites on the N. The Israelites did not go through Moab, as the passage was denied to them, but went round it on the E. side, crossing the upper courses of the Arnon : see v. 11, and cp. Jg 11 17,18.

14. As the Moabites afterwards crossed the Arnon and took possession of part of the land of the Amorites, this ancient fragment of poetry from the 'book of the Wars of the Lord' indicates the original boundary of Moab. The 'book of the Wars of the Lord,' which is mentioned only here in the OT., was probably a collection of war songs, illustrating what Jehovah did for His people by the hand of Moses. The other poetical fragments in this c. (vv. 17, 18, 27-30) are, in all probability, from the same collection. **What he did in the Red Sea**] RV 'Vaheb in Suphah.' The words are names of localities now unknown. Some verb is to be supplied before them, such as 'they subdued.'

16-20. Passage through the land of the Amorites from the Arnon to Pisgah at the N. end of the Red Sea. During this march the people seem to have suffered from want of water. The 'Song of the Well' celebrates the finding of water at Beer. 'Beer' means 'well.' **20. Jeshimon**] rather, 'the Jeshimon,' the plain lying to the NE. of the Dead Sea.

21-30. Conquest of the Amorites and Song of Triumph.

21. Cp. the similar request and refusal in 20 14-21.

24. *Was strong*] This seems to give the reason why the Israelites did not follow up their conquest of the Amorites by entering the land of Ammon. LXX, however, reads, 'the border .. was Jaazer,' a town mentioned in v. 32.

27. In proverbs] This Hebrew word is sometimes rendered 'parable.' It is applied to a by-word or taunt song : see 1 K 9 7 Jer 24 9 Isa 14 4 Job 27 1 and Nu 23 7,18 24 3,15, 20, 21, 23. The opening words of the song are an ironical challenge to the former inhabitants to return to Heshbon, which has been captured and destroyed. 'Come if you can,' they say, 'and dispossess us and repair the city of your king.' The next two vv. refer to the fact stated in v. 26. The haughty conqueror of Moab is now himself subdued. This song is quoted in Jer 48 45, 46. **28.** Read with RV 'fire went out .. it consumed.' The fire is the fire of war. **29. Chemosh**] the sun-god of the Moabites to whom human sacrifices were sometimes offered : see 2K3 27, and see on Gn22 Jg11 30f. The name occurs frequently on the Moabite Stone, a valuable relic dating from the 9th century B.C. and discovered at Dibon (see next note), on which Mesha, king of Moab (see 2K3 4), celebrates his victories over the Israelites, and attributes them to the favour of his god Chemosh. Solomon himself built a high place for Chemosh : see 1K11 7. The words here should read ' he (i.e. Chemosh) gave his sons as fugitives,' i.e. he abandoned them so that they fled. **30. We**] the Israelites. **Dibon** is near the Arnon (v. 13). The locality of **Nophah** is unknown. **Medeba** is a few miles S. of **Heshbon.** The concluding words of the song are obscure, and may be rendered, ' and we laid waste so that fire raged unto Medeba.'

33–35. Conquest of Bashan. Bashan was the northernmost part of the country E. of the Jordan, stretching from the river Jabbok in the S. to Mt. Hermon in the extreme N. This extensive district was celebrated for the richness of its vegetation, being ranked in this respect with Lebanon, Carmel, and Sharon : see Isa33 9 Jer1 19 Nah1 4. Its giant oaks and vast herds of wild cattle are frequently referred to by the sacred writers : see Dt32 14 Isa2 13 Ezk27 6 39 18 Zech11 2. In early times it was inhabited by a race of giants, from whom Og was descended (Gn14 5 Dt3 11 ; see on 13 33). The ruins of the Giant Cities of Bashan remain to testify to the strength of its former inhabitants. See additional notes on Dt3. After its final conquest it was occupied by the half tribe of Manasseh : see Nu32 33 Dt3 13.

PART 3

IN THE PLAINS OF MOAB (Chs. 22–36)

CHAPTER 22

BALAAM

The Israelites now enter upon the last stage of their journey to Canaan. They are within sight of the land of promise, being encamped at the northern end of the Dead Sea, near the mouth of the Jordan. Up to this point they have surmounted every obstacle and conquered the tribes on the east side of the river. But now, at the end of the journey, a graver danger faces them. Balak, king of Moab, finding that he cannot prevail against them with carnal weapons, has recourse to magical arts, hoping in this way to destroy them. He sends to the Euphrates for the famous magician Balaam to come and ' curse Israel.' As the sequel shows it is all in vain. Not even the powers of darkness can stop the victorious march of Jehovah's people. The whole incident is designed to show that Israel by the grace of God is proof, not only against the sword of the enemy, but also against the evil powers of the unseen world. There is no enchantment against Israel. God is for them, and nothing can be against them. They are able to wrestle, not only against flesh and blood, but against spiritual wickedness in high places.

1. The district in which the Israelites are encamped is called the **plains of Moab,** as it formed part of the territory of the Moabites before their conquest by the Amorites (21 26). **On this side Jordan**] The Hebrew is ' beyond Jordan.' So RV : see on 21 13.

4. Elders of Midian] The home of the Midianites is usually supposed to have been within the Sinaitic peninsula towards the S. or SE. : see Ex2 15 31. Here they are found

to the E. of the Jordan, associated with the Moabites in their attempt to bar the progress of the Israelites : cp. Gn36 35 Nu25 6. Their conquest is described in Nu31.

5. RV 'sent .. to Pethor, which is by the River, to the land of the children,' etc. The ' River ' is the Euphrates. The ancient Chaldeans and Babylonians, like the modern Arabs, had a firm belief in the existence and influence of demons. They also believed that certain persons had the power of controlling these demons by means of magic spells and incantations, and these magicians or soothsayers were frequently employed to discover secrets, to foretell the future, to bless an undertaking, or bring ruin upon an enemy. Balaam's fame as a man of this sort had travelled far beyond the limits of his own land, as is shown by the embassy of the king of Moab : see on Ex7 11. **7. Rewards of divination**] the presents made to Balaam to secure his offices. In 2Pet2 15 Balaam is said to have loved ' the wages of unrighteousness.'

8–21. Balaam, being warned by God in a dream, refuses to go ; whereupon Balak sends a more pressing invitation with promise of a larger reward. Balaam hesitates, but at length yields, having received permission to go, but to speak only as God directs him. **8.** Balaam has been blamed for hesitating here. This, however, is unjust. On the occasion of the first message from Balak he was honestly in doubt whether he ought to go or not, and it is to his credit that he would do nothing till he had learned what the mind of God was. It was otherwise, however, on the second occasion (v. 19), when he dallied with the tempting offer, in the hope that God would change His purpose, and allow him to go and do as Balak wished. If the words the LORD, i.e. Jehovah, in this v. were really used by Balaam, and are not due to the historian, then it would appear that Balaam knew the God of Israel and worshipped Him. This is by no means impossible. Balaam lived in the land from which Abraham went out (see Gn 11 28-31 24 4-10), and he was no doubt aware of the history of Abraham's descendants, more especially if he was connected with the Midianites (see 31 8). It need occasion no surprise that God made use of this semi-heathen soothsayer to declare His will. It is but an illustration of the truth that the Spirit of God is not bound : cp. Am 9 7. Throughout the whole incident Balaam appears as the somewhat unwilling medium whereby God chooses to confirm His unchangeable purpose towards Israel. He stands midway between the true prophet of Jehovah and the heathen magician or soothsayer.

12. They *are* **blessed**] see Gn 22 17, 18 Nu 6 27.

18. This is said in good faith. But Balaam is moved by the tempting offer of Balak ; and, while He does not mean to disobey God, he is not without hopes of inducing God to change His mind. He does not yet know that Jehovah's 'kindness shall not depart nor His covenant of peace be removed.' **20.** Balaam is allowed to go, but only on condition that he will speak the word that God gives him.

22-41. On the way Balaam receives a warning not to go beyond the word of the Lord. **22. God's anger was kindled because he went**] This seems to contradict what is said in v. 20, that God gave him permission to go. But that permission was conditional. He might go, but he must speak only what is given him to say. Balaam gladly seizes the opportunity of going, for he is hankering after the reward. For the present he ignores the condition. In his heart he hopes to evade it and satisfy Balak. But God, who is the discerner of the thoughts and intents of the heart, sees the double-mindedness of Balaam, and gives him to know that there must be no trifling. Unless he really means to be obedient he must stay at home. On the 'angel of the Lord ' see on Ex 3 2.

31. Opened the eyes of Balaam] Up to this point Balaam has been like a blind man. He has been determined to have his own way. But now he sees it is useless trying to deceive God or fight against Him. Like Saul he finds it is ' hard to kick against the pricks ': cp. Ac 9 4-6. The refusal of his erstwhile docile ass to carry him further is the God-employed means of bringing the obstinate prophet to his senses. How this was done it is vain to speculate. Some explain away the incident of the vision and the ass speaking e.g. as a dream which Balaam had before starting, or a vivid impres-

sion made upon him by the liveliness of his own thoughts ; but evidently the writer of the narrative believed in the reality of both. In this he simply occupies the standpoint of his age.

34. Balaam is now convinced that it is useless hoping to satisfy Balak, and wishes simply to have nothing more to do with the matter. But this is not the will of God. Balaam must go as His messenger and bless His people.

40. Offered oxen] most probably in sacrifice. It was usual to offer sacrifice at the beginning of any momentous undertaking, or on the arrival of an important visitor : see Gn 31 54 1 K 19 21 1 S 16 5.

41. Baal] 'owner ' or ' lord '; the name of a deity, usually identical with the sun, and worshipped by a number of early Semitic tribes, including the Phœnicians. The place of worship was commonly the top of a hill. There was a sanctuary of Baal in this neighbourhood on Mt. Peor : see 25 3. **The utmost** *part*] Balak showed Abraham the whole extent of the Israelites, probably to justify his alarm at their presence, and exhibit the instant necessity of cursing this formidable army.

CHAPTER 23
BALAAM (continued)

1-10. First Utterance of Balaam.

1. On the meaning of these sacrifices see on 22 40. Balak may have intended these sacrifices for Baal, but Balaam at all events thinks of the God who spoke to him at Pethor and whose angel met him on the way (see v. 4). **3. I will go**] to inspect the omens, to see what indications are visible of God's will : cp. 24 1 Lv 19 31. **To an high place**] RV 'to a bare height': see on 22 41. **7.** Balaam is constrained to bless Israel as God has manifestly done. This is plain from three signs, (1) the separation of the people (v. 9), (2) their number (v. 10), and (3) their righteousness (v. 10). **Aram**] the ancient name of Mesopotamia.

9. The people shall dwell alone, etc.] rather, ' Behold a people that dwelleth alone and is not reckoned among the nations !' Balaam singles out what was, and is still, a distinguishing characteristic of the Hebrew people, viz. their separateness from other nations. They were chosen of God in Abraham their ancestor, and throughout the long course of their history have been distinguished from other nations, both by their religion and manner of life. To this day, though they have no country, they are still a separate nation : see Ex 19 5,6 33 16 Lv 20 24, 26, and frequently in the prophets, e.g. Isa 43 21 Am 3 2.

10. The righteous] The people of Israel are called ' the righteous ' because God, who is Himself righteous, has called them to be the same. The Heb. word for ' righteous ' is

Jashar, and Jeshurun is a poetical name given to Israel in Dt 32¹⁵ 33⁵, ²⁶ Isa 44². It is possible that the title given to a collection of national poetry, the book of Jashar (see Josh 10¹³ 2 S 1¹⁸ : see on 21¹⁴) contains the same idea. Balaam's words mean that Israel's fate will be enviable, and the opposite of what Balak desires it to be. His own fate was miserable : see 31⁸. The death of the righteous is only attained by those who are willing to lead the life of the righteous. **12.** Cp. 1 K 22¹³,¹⁴.

13–26. Balaam's Second Utterance.

13. Seeing that Balaam had been impressed with the multitude of Israel (v. 10), Balak now restricts the prophet's view of the host, in the hope that he may be prevailed upon to curse it : see on 22⁴¹. **14. Zophim]** 'watchers' or 'lookers-out.' It is from the same Heb. root as Mizpah (see Gn 31⁴⁹). **Pisgah** is probably the general name for the mountain range lying to the NE. of the Dead Sea, of which Nebo (Dt 34¹), Peor (v. 28), and Zophim are peaks. In Dt 32⁴⁹ this mountain range is called Abarim. Zophim may be so called simply as being a point of outlook, but it is possible to see in the name a reference to the practice of watching the omens from elevated situations.

18. Balaam declares that God's purpose to bless Israel cannot be altered (vv. 19, 20). With them He is well pleased (v. 21). It is He who is bringing them out of Egypt, and with Him as Leader and Defender they are certain to be victorious (vv. 22–24). **19.** Balak is wrong in thinking to induce God by means of enchantments to alter His purpose : cp. 1 S 15²⁹ Isa 54¹⁰ Ro 11²⁹ Tit 1² Heb 6¹³⁻¹⁸ Jas 1¹⁷.

21. The shout of a king] is not the shout raised by a king, but the shout raised at the presence of a king. Israel rejoices in having God as their king : see Ex 15¹⁸ Dt 33⁵ Isa 33²². **22. God brought]** rather, 'It is God, and no other, that is bringing them out of Egypt.' They are here under the divine direction : cp. Ex 20² 29⁴⁶ Lv 19³⁶. **Unicorn]** RV 'the wild ox,' or 'buffalo: cp. Dt 33¹⁷. **23.** The rendering of AV gives the sense 'it is useless to employ the powers of enchantment against this people ; they are proof against all such weapons.' But the right rendering is rather, 'there is no enchantment *in* Jacob,' i.e. this people has no need to employ magical arts in its defence, as you, Balak, are doing now, for they have God for their protector. **According to this time]** better, ' at this time,' ' now.'

24. A great lion] Heb. 'a lioness.'

25. What Balak means is, ' If you will not curse them, I forbid you to bless them.'

28. Peor] is a peak of the mountain range of Moab. See on v. 14. On **Jeshimon** see on 21²⁰.

CHAPTER 24

BALAAM (continued)

1–9. Balaam's Third Utterance.

1. To seek for enchantments] lit. ' to meet omens': see on 23³. **Toward the wilderness]** i.e. towards the plain where the Israelites were encamped: see 21²⁰ 22¹. **2. The spirit of God came upon him]** cp. 1 S 19²⁰. The following utterances are introduced in a more solemn manner (see vv. 3, 4, 15, 16), and are prophetic of the future.

3. Hath said] The English here is too commonplace to represent the original, which is in a very lofty and impassioned strain. ' Oracle of Balaam, son of Beor ; oracle of the man whose eyes are opened ; oracle of him who hears the words of God, who sees the vision of the Almighty, falling upon his face with his eyes open.' The first word rendered ' opened ' is of uncertain meaning. It may mean 'closed,' in which case it implies that Balaam's eyes are closed to earthly sights but open to the heavenly. Or it may refer to his previous condition. Hitherto scales have been upon his eyes, but now he sees the vision of the Almighty. **4. Falling** *into a trance*] rather, ' falling upon his face.' There is no word in the original corresponding to the words ' into a trance.' He falls to the ground, overpowered by the Spirit of God that comes upon him: cp. 1 S 19²⁴ Ezk 1²⁸ Dan 8¹⁷,¹⁸ Ac 9⁴ Rev 1¹⁷.

6. The images in this and the next v. are those of fruitfulness and vigour. The **lign** (i.e. the wood-) **aloe** is a large spreading tree much prized for its aromatic qualities (Prov 7¹⁷ Song 4¹⁴), and the **cedar** is the king of trees (1 K 4³³ Ps 104¹⁶): cp. Ps 1³ Ezk 31³⁻⁵. **7. He shall pour the water]** better, ' water shall flow from his (i.e. Israel's) buckets, and his seed (i.e. his posterity) shall be in abundance of water.' Israel will always flourish. The literal and the metaphorical are here combined : cp. Gn 49²²,²⁵ Dt 33¹³, and see on Lv 26⁴. **Agag]** the dynastic name of the Amalekite kings: cp. 1 S 15³². The kingdom of Israel will surpass that of Amalek. **8.** See on 23². The subject of the second half of the v. is Israel, who is compared to a ravening lion, the king of beasts.

9. Blessed *is* he, etc.] cp. Gn 12³ 27²⁹.

10–14. Balak in anger dismisses Balaam, who before departing predicts the destruction of Moab and other nations by Israel.

15–24. Balaam's Fourth Utterance: a prediction of the dominion of Israel and the downfall of Moab, Edom, Amalek, and Asshur.

17. I shall see him, etc.] This should be rendered ' I see him ' (i.e. the Israel of the future, and specially the Star who is to rise among them) ' . . I behold him . . A Star is risen out of Jacob . . ' To the eye of Balaam, in his spiritual ecstasy, the future stands out as the present. **A Star**] A common symbol of a brilliant ruler: cp. Isa 14[12] 9[2] Mt 24[29] Rev 22[16] and the expression 'hosts of heaven.' For the sceptre as the symbol of authority see Gn 49[10] Ps 110[2]. This prediction refers in the first place to David, who 'smote Moab and Edom' (2 S 8[2, 14], cp. Ps 60[8f.]), but applies also to 'David's greater Son.' From early times the Jewish commentators have interpreted the prophecy as Messianic. The name Barcochba (i.e. 'Son of a star') was assumed by one who claimed to be the Messiah, not long after the time of our Lord, taking the title no doubt from this prophecy of Balaam. Christians will see in the words of Balaam a prophecy of Jesus, the true Messiah, the King of kings and Lord of lords. He Himself, and not the star which was seen at His birth (Mt 2[2]), is the fulfilment of the prediction. **Children of Sheth**] RV 'the children of tumult,' as in the parallel passage Jer 48[45], where another word from the same root is used. **18. Seir**] the name given to the land of the Edomites : see Gn 36[8, 9] Dt 2[4]. **His enemies**] the enemies of Israel, or rather of the Ruler here spoken of. The fulfilment of this prophecy is recorded in 2 S 8[14]. Cp. also Isa 63[1-4], and see on 20[8, 9].

20. First of the nations] probably in rank ; but see on Ex 17[8]. The next clause reads ' but his end (shall come) to destruction ': cp. Ex 17[14, 16], and for the fulfilment of the prediction see 1 S 14[48] 15[7, 8] 30[17] 2 S 8[12] 1 Ch 4[43].

21. The Kenites] Unlike the tribes previously mentioned the Kenites were always friendly to the Israelites, and consequently the words of Balaam foretelling their destruction are more of sympathy than of threatening. Hobab, the father-in-law of Moses, was a Kenite, and his descendants settled alongside the tribe of Judah in the S. of Canaan (Jg 1[16] 4[11]) : see also 1 S 15[6] 30[26, 29] 1 Ch 2[55]. Of their subsequent history nothing is known. See on v. 22. **Thy nest**] The Heb. word for nest is *ken*, so that there is here a play upon the name of this tribe.

22. The rendering is doubtful. We may translate, 'Nevertheless the Kenite shall be wasted. How long ? Asshur (i.e. Assyria) shall carry thee away captive.' Or, ' But the Kenite shall not be wasted until Asshur shall carry thee (i.e. Israel) away captive.'

24. Chittim] the dwellers in Cyprus or in the islands of the Mediterranean generally. They are said to have emigrated from Phœnicia. In Gn 10[4] the Chittim are said to be descended from Javan, the ancestor of the Ionian (i.e. the Greek) races. In Dan 11[30] the 'ships of Kittim' are those of the Romans, so that Chittim may be a general designation of the Western races, and Balaam's words a

prediction of the overthrow of the Eastern monarchies (**Asshur** = the Assyrians or Persians, and **Eber** = the Hebrews or Syrians) by the empires of the West. **He also**] most probably the conquering nation, the Chittim It may, however, refer to Asshur or Eber.

These last prophecies of Balaam, on Amalek, the Kenites, the Chittim, Asshur, and Eber, have all the appearance of being an appendix, and are supposed by many to be a later addition to the original prophecies regarding Israel.

CHAPTER 25
IDOLATRY AND IMMORALITY OF THE ISRAELITES AT SHITTIM. THE ZEAL OF PHINEHAS

1-5. The Israelites, who have just been exhibited as proof against enchantments, are not able to resist the temptations to idolatry, and its connected sin of immorality, arising from their proximity to the tribes of Moab and Midian. In 31[16] their apostasy is attributed to the counsel of Balaam (see also Rev 2[14]), who is afterwards put to death for it (Nu 31[8] Josh 13[22]). But it is difficult without violence to reconcile this conduct on the part of Balaam with his former attitude towards Israel, and his utterances regarding them. Moreover, the last verse of the preceding chapter is evidently intended to mark his return to the Euphrates and his disappearance from the subsequent history of Israel. It seems almost beyond doubt that there was from early times a double tradition regarding this famous soothsayer. According to one, Balaam is a Mesopotamian soothsayer who becomes the instrument of God in blessing His people and foretelling their future greatness ; according to the other, he is a Midianitish counsellor who sets himself to seduce the people of Jehovah and suffers the extreme penalty of his error. **1.** Shittim] ('the acacias') is the name of the encampment in the plains of Moab : see 33[49] and cp. Josh 2[1].

3. Baal-peor] There appears to have been a sanctuary of Baal on the top of Mt. Peor : see on 22[41] 23[14]. **4. The heads**] the ringleaders. **Hang them up**] Some shameful form of execution, followed by impalement : see on Dt 21[22].

6-18. The zeal of Phinehas in slaying with his own hand an Israelite and his Midianitish concubine is rewarded with the promise of the permanence of the priesthood in his family : cp. Ex 32[26-29] and notes there.

This incident while related to the foregoing is distinct from it. Literary evidence shows that vv. 6-18 are from a different source from vv. 1-5. Observe that in the one case the punishment is slaughter (v. 5), and in the other plague (v. 9), and that the source of temptation in the one case is Moab and in the other Midian : see on vv. 16-18. **6.** *Were* weeping] on account of the plague (v. 8). **8.** There is no previous mention of a plague having broken out, and the word can hardly apply to the slaughter in v. 5. We are here dealing with a separate incident. **11. Zealous for my sake**] lit. 'jealous with my jealousy.' God, as the Redeemer of Israel, has a special claim upon their reverence and affection. When they turn to other gods His love is wounded, and He is jealous with a holy jealousy : see on Ex 20⁵.

13. An everlasting priesthood] Phinehas succeeded to the high priesthood after his father's death (Jg 20²⁸), and the succession remained in his family till the time of Eli, when it passed for some reason to the house of Ithamar. Solomon, however, restored the high priesthood to the descendants of Phinehas (1 K 2³⁵). This action of Phinehas in defending the purity of the religion of Israel at a critical moment was rewarded, not only with this blessing from the Lord, but with the grateful admiration of succeeding generations. In Ps 106 we read that his zeal was 'counted unto him for righteousness unto all generations for evermore,' words which St. Paul applies to Abraham himself (Ro 4²² Gal 3⁶). In Ecclus 45²³⁻²⁶ he is called the 'third in glory' after Moses and Aaron, and his example is quoted in 1 Mac 2²⁶. So blessed is the memory of the just.

16–18. Commandment is given to vex the Midianites (i.e. count them as dangerous adversaries) and to smite them. For its fulfilment see c. 31. Injunctions like this, which were ordered to be carried out with extreme severity, were given in the interests of Israel and the purity of religion and morals. In no other way could that 'separateness' be maintained which Balaam recognised as one of the distinctions of the Israelites (see on 23⁹). For the Christian parallel see 2 Cor 6¹⁴⁻¹⁸ and cp. 5²⁹,³⁰.

The omission of any reference to the Moabites in this passage bears out what is said above as to the different sources of vv. 1–5 and 6–18.

CHAPTER 26
The Second Numbering of the People

The first took place thirty-eight years before (see c. 1) at Mt. Sinai. The people are shortly to enter Canaan, and this second enumeration is made in view of the prospective division of the land among the twelve tribes : see vv. 52–56. The total result shows a decrease of 1,820. While Manasseh has increased by no less than 20,500, Simeon has decreased by the extraordinary amount of 37,100. The latter tribe may have suffered most severely in the recent plague, seeing that Zimri was a Simeonite (25¹⁴).

55. The casting of lots is of the nature of an appeal to God, and was resorted to in order to detect a culprit (Josh 7¹⁴ 1 S 14⁴² Jon 1⁷), to select an office-bearer (1 S 10²⁰ 1 Ch 24⁴,⁵ Ac 1²⁶), or to make a division of property as here (cp. Mt 27³⁵). See also Lv 16⁸ and the note on Urim and Thummim, Ex 28³⁰. In the case before us, lots were cast to determine the locality of each tribe's inheritance, but its size was regulated by the number of the names, the relative fertility of each locality being also no doubt taken into consideration. The twelve lots, which would be tablets of wood or stone, each inscribed with the name of a tribe, were probably put in an urn ; and, as the name of each portion of land was called out, the high priest or representative of a tribe (see 34¹⁶⁻²⁹) drew a lot, and the tribe whose name was drawn inherited that territory. The precise boundaries would be adjusted afterwards, according to the population shown by the census. **64, 65.** See 14²²⁻³².

CHAPTER 27
The Law of the Inheritance of Daughters. Joshua appointed as the Successor of Moses

1–11. According to 26⁵³ (cp. v. 2) the land was to be apportioned to the males. Zelophehad, of the tribe of Manasseh, had died leaving no sons (26³³); and his daughters, fearing that they would have no inheritance, request that they and their sons should succeed to the inheritance of their father, and thus perpetuate his name. Their claim is pronounced to be just, and it is enacted that daughters should inherit where there are no sons, and, failing daughters, the nearest relatives of the father. It was afterwards further enacted (c. 36) that daughters succeeding to an inheritance must marry within their own tribe, in order that the property should remain in that tribe and not be alienated to another. **3. Died in his own sin**] These words have led Jewish commentators to identify Zelophehad with the man who was stoned for sabbath breaking (15³²⁻³⁶). But their meaning rather is that Zelophehad had not forfeited his inheritance by any specially heinous act of transgression, but had died the common death of all men (cp. 16²⁹).

12–23. Moses receives intimation of his approaching death, and Joshua is appointed leader in his place. **12.** This command is repeated in Dt 32⁴⁸ᶠ. and its fulfilment related in Dt 34. In the interval before his death, Moses delivered the concluding laws contained in the book of Numbers and the addresses in the book of Deuteronomy. The conquest of the Midianites seems also to have taken place in this interval, if at least the order of the narrative corresponds to the actual order of events (see c. 31). **Mount Abarim**] see on 23 24. **13. Gathered unto thy people**] see on 20 24. **14. To sanctify me**] see on 20 12. **15.** Moses stifles his personal feelings of disappointment and grief, and thinks only of the flock he is leaving behind. This noble self-effacement was conspicuous on other occasions: see Ex 32 32 Nu 11 29 14 12, 13. If the work goes on, he is content that God should bury the workman: cp. Ro 9 1-3 Phil 1 18. **17.** To **lead out** (to pasture) and to **bring in** (to the fold) is the work of the shepherd: cp. Jn 10 3, 4.

18. The spirit] i.e. the necessary qualification : see on Ex 28 3 31 4. **Joshua** had no doubt learned much from his close association with Moses as his attendant: see Ex 24 13 32 17 33 11 Nu 11 28. He had also some experience as leader of the army of Israel (Ex 17 9 f.). Moreover, he had given evidence of his faith and courage at Kadesh, being the only one save Caleb who was prepared to go forward in reliance on the divine promises and help (Nu 14 6 f.). **Lay thine hand upon him**] in token of consecration: cp. Ac 6 6 13 3 1 Tim 4 14 2 Tim 1 6. Observe that the three marks of a regularly consecrated minister of God are present here, viz. the call of God, the necessary gifts, and a public and solemn ordination to office. **19. Give him a charge**] see Dt 31 7, 8, 23. **21. Urim**] see on Ex 28 30.

CHAPTER 28
Laws regarding Sacrifices and Festivals

1, 2. The general laws regarding the sacrifices proper to the feast days had already been given at Sinai (Lv 23). Their repetition with certain details here probably indicates that these laws had been neglected. Some of them, indeed, were only intended to be observed after the settlement in Canaan, which was now in the near future. Moreover, the generation to whom they were spoken at Sinai had passed away. Hence their repetition here to the younger generation. **2. My bread**] or 'my food': see on Lv 3 11.

3–8. The daily morning and evening burnt offering with its proper meal and drink offering : see on Ex 29 38 f.

9, 10. The Sabbath Offering is double that of ordinary days.

11–25. The Festival of the New Moon is frequently mentioned alongside that of the sabbath: see Am 8 5 2 K 4 23 Isa 1 13 56 2, 3 Hos 2 11. It was a festival of great antiquity, dating from the time when the moon was an object of adoration. The Hebrews were forbidden to worship the moon (Dt 17 3), but the Festival of the New Moon was retained and transformed into a festival in honour of the Creator. Additional sacrifices were offered, and the silver trumpets were sounded during the performance of the sacrificial rites (Nu 10 10).

The day was observed as a day of rest, and was celebrated with great joyfulness. A special importance attached to the new moon of the seventh month: see 29 1-6.

16–25. On the Passover Offering see Ex 12 and cp. Lv 23 4-8.

26–31. The Day of the First Fruits is also known as the Feast of Weeks or Pentecost : see on Lv 23 9-22.

CHAPTER 29
Religious Ordinances of the Seventh Month

The seventh month (*Tishri* = September-October) was the first month of the civil year (see on Lv 23 23-25), and this c. describes the three sacred festivals which fell during that month.

1–6. The Feast of Trumpets on New Year's Day : see Lv 23 23-25.

7–11. The Day of Atonement, the tenth day of the month : see Lv 16.

12–38. The Feast of Tabernacles, beginning on the fifteenth day of the month and lasting eight days. The sacrifices proper to this feast are unusually numerous, a feature expressive of its joyous nature, as the Feast of Harvest Thanksgiving : see Lv 23 33-43.

CHAPTER 30
The Law of Vows

This c. deals with the subject of Vows, which is also treated in Lv 27, where see notes. A vow made by a man is binding (v. 2). But a woman is not considered to have an independent right to make a vow. So long as she is unmarried she is under the jurisdiction of her father, and on her marriage she comes under that of her husband. The assent, therefore, of her father or husband must be given or implied in order that her vow may be binding. **2. Vow a vow .. or swear an oath to bind his soul**] The former is a positive vow or vow of performance ; the latter is a negative vow or vow of abstinence : see on Lv 27.

3–5. Case of an unmarried woman.

6–8. Case of a woman who has entered into a vow while unmarried, but who marries before her vow is fulfilled. The husband has the power either to confirm his wife's vow, or disallow it when he hears of it. The words in v. 6 should read 'if she be married to a husband while her vows are upon her.'

9. Case of a widow, or divorced woman. Her vow is binding.

10–15. Case of a married woman. Her vow to be binding must be ratified by her husband.

CHAPTER 31
War against Midian

This c. contains an account of the fulfilment of the decree of extermination passed upon the Midianites as being the occasion of Israel's apostasy in the plains of Moab : see on 25 16-18.

6. The holy instruments and the trumpets] On the use of the silver trumpets in time of war see on 10 9. It is not clear whether the ark was taken into battle on this occasion. It is possible to translate ' the holy instruments, even the trumpets.' On other occasions, however, the ark accompanied the army as a token of God's presence and blessing. See 1 S 4 4-7 and cp. Nu 14 44. In Dt 20 2-4 the priests are commanded to encourage the host on the edge of battle. The choice of Phinehas on this occasion may be due to his previous zeal for Jehovah against the Midianites : see 25 7, 12.

8. Kings of Midian] from Josh 13 21 we learn that these were princes or chiefs, and that they were tributary to Sihon, king of the Amorites. Balaam by remaining among the Midianites shared their fate. But see on 25 1-5.

13-18. The male children are put to death in order that the race of idolaters may be extirpated. The older women are also slain as having been the prime cause of the apostasy, and likely to lead the people astray at a future time. The women-children, or young females, are spared, and are taken as slaves or wives, being probably adopted into the Hebrew nation as proselytes : cp. Dt 21 10-14. For the reason of such wholesale slaughter see 33 55 Dt 20 17, 18 Josh 23 13 and on 25 16-18.

19-24. On this purification by means of the ' water of separation ' see 19 11-16.

25-47. The spoil is divided equally between the warriors and those who remained in the camp. Part of each portion is dedicated to the sanctuary. The warriors dedicate the five-hundredth part of their spoil which is given to the priests (v. 29). The non-combatants dedicate the fiftieth part of their share, which, being a larger proportion, is given to the Levites who were more numerous than the priests (v. 30). **29. Heave offering**] see on Lv 7 28-34 Nu 8 11. **32. The rest of the prey**] RV ' over and above the booty ' : see v. 50.

48-54. The officers make a voluntary offering as a thanksgiving for victory. **50. Tablets**] RV ' armlets or necklaces ' : cp. Ex 35 22. **Make an atonement**] cp. Ex 30 11-16.

CHAPTER 32

ALLOTMENT OF TERRITORY TO THE TRIBES OF GAD AND REUBEN AND THE HALF-TRIBE OF MANASSEH

1-5. The tribes of Reuben and Gad request that the land of Gilead lying on the E. side of the Jordan be assigned to them, on the ground that it is very fertile and therefore particularly well adapted to their large flocks and herds. These two tribes were associated as neighbours in the camp and on the march (2 10-16), hence their desire to be settled near each other.

1. Gilead lay to the S. and W. of Bashan, and shared the characteristic fertility of that region : see on 21 33-35.

6-15. Moses understands their request as indicating a disinclination on the part of these two tribes to enter the promised land. He reminds them that their fathers suffered the penalty of a similar faintheartedness at Kadesh (c. 14) and, fearing that the example of Reuben and Gad may discourage the rest of the people, he refuses their request.

16-33. The two tribes assure Moses that they will not separate themselves at present from the rest of the people, but will go over Jordan with them, and assist in the conquest of Canaan. After that they will return and settle on the E. side. Moses is satisfied with this assurance, and enjoins Eleazar and Joshua to see that the two tribes fulfil their promise before receiving the inheritance they desire. **28.** Moses lays this injunction on Joshua his successor, as he himself will not live to pass over Jordan : see 27 12-23.

33. The half tribe of Manasseh is not said to have made any request similar to that of the Reubenites and Gadites ; but, seeing that they had been specially engaged in the conquest of Gilead (v. 30), a place was assigned to them also in that district : cp. Dt 3 13-15.

34-42. These vv. are inserted here by way of anticipation. The building, or rather the repairing of these cities, for some of them at least are mentioned as already existing (21 30 33 3), took place after the conquest of Canaan : cp. v. 41 with Jg 10 3, 4. In Josh 22 1-9 we read that, after fulfilling their promise, the two and a half tribes were dismissed to their inheritance by Joshua with his blessing. Owing to their position on the eastern frontier of the holy land they were the first to be carried into captivity by the king of Assyria (1 Ch 5 26), so that it was not an unmitigated advantage to them to obtain this fertile district.

CHAPTER 33

THE JOURNEYINGS OF THE ISRAELITES FROM EGYPT TO THE PLAINS OF MOAB

The greater part of this c. is occupied with a list, drawn up by Moses himself (v. 2), of the Encampments of the Israelites in their journey from Egypt to Canaan. In all, forty stages are enumerated. Many of the names are otherwise unknown, and in places the stages do not coincide with those mentioned in the books of Exodus, Numbers, and Deuteronomy. These differences are, no doubt, due in part to the fact that places change their names in the course of time. At this distance it is exceedingly difficult to identify the route of march, more especially as many of the names were not names of cities or conspicuous landmarks, and therefore very liable to be forgotten.

3-15. Egypt to Sinai. This part of the journey is narrated in Ex 12³⁷–19² where all the names occur except **Dophkah** and **Alush** (vv. 12, 13).

16-18. Sinai to Rithmah. **Rithmah** is not mentioned elsewhere ; but, seeing that it is the station after **Hazeroth,** it is supposed to be the same as Kadesh (cp. 12¹⁶ 13²⁶). *Rothem* in Hebrew means 'juniper' or broom, and there is a Wady Abu Retamat, abounding in broom, near the site of Kadesh, so that the identification may be regarded as in all probability correct. This is the first arrival at Kadesh, in the second year of the exodus ; the second arrival at the same place in the fortieth year is noted in v. 36 : see on 13²⁶ 20¹.

19-36. Encampments during the thirty-eight years, and return to Kadesh. The names in vv. 19–29 are not mentioned elsewhere and have not been identified. With vv. 30-33 cp. Dt 10⁶,⁷. **Ezion-geber** (v. 36) is on the sea at the northern extremity of the Gulf of Akaba (cp. 1 K 9²⁶ 22⁴⁸).

37-49. From Kadesh to the Plains of Moab. The narrative of this journey is contained in Nu 20, 21. With the names in vv. 11–49 cp. Nu 21¹⁰⁻²⁰.

45. Iim is the same as **Ije-abarim** (v. 44), the second part of this word, which means 'The Heaps, or Ruins, of Abarim,' being dropped.

50-56. Command to expel all the inhabitants of Canaan and to destroy their idols and places of worship, so that no inducements to idolatry may remain : see on Ex 23³², and cp. 25¹⁶⁻¹⁸ Dt 7. **52. Pictures**] RV 'figured stones.' On the **high places** see on 22⁴¹ Lv 26³⁰. **55.** Cp. Josh 23¹³ Jg 2³.

CHAPTER 34

THE BOUNDARIES OF THE LAND OF PROMISE
On the land and the tribes inhabiting it see on 13²¹.

3-5. The southern border : this started from the S. extremity of the Dead Sea, here called the **Salt Sea** (v. 3), and proceeded in a SW. direction to the **ascent of Akrabbim,** i.e. 'of scorpions' (v. 4), a row of cliffs about 8 m. distant ; thence it passed by way of Kadesh-Barnea to the **River of Egypt,** where it reached the Mediterranean Sea (v. 5). The 'River of Egypt' is not the Nile but a brook, now identified with the Wady el-Arish, flowing into the sea about 20 m. S. of Gaza. It is frequently mentioned as the SW. border of Canaan : see 1 K 8⁶⁵ 2 K 24⁷ 2 Ch 7⁸ Isa 27¹². This southern boundary was also the boundary of Judah and Simeon : see Josh 15¹⁻⁴ 19⁹.

6. The western border was formed by the Mediterranean Sea, the **Great Sea.**

7-9. The northern border : the places mentioned on this line are unknown. Mt. Hermon is too far E. to be identified with **mount Hor,** which is probably some spur of the Lebanon range.

10-12. The eastern border was formed by the **Sea of Chinnereth** (afterwards called the Lake of Gennesaret, Sea of Galilee, or Lake of Tiberias), the River Jordan, and the Dead Sea.

13-15. See c. 32.

16-29. A list of the persons entrusted with the division of the land W. of the Jordan, one being chosen from each of the tribes interested, in addition to Eleazar and Joshua. The names are all new with the exception of that of Caleb (v. 19).

CHAPTER 35.

THE LEVITICAL CITIES. THE CITIES OF
REFUGE

1-8. The Levitical Cities.

The tribe of Levi received no part of the land of Canaan as their inheritance (18²⁰⁻²⁴ 26⁶²). By way of compensation they received the tithes for their support (18²¹). It is here further provided that 48 cities with their suburbs be allotted to them out of the inheritance of the other tribes, for the maintenance of themselves and their herds. The carrying out of this injunction is recorded in Josh 21, where it is also noted that the priests (the sons of Aaron) received 13 of these cities (v. 4). The people, as well as the priests and Levites, benefited by this arrangement, for the latter being dispersed throughout the land were able to instruct the people in the law and worship of God. On the duty of the priests and Levites to teach the people see Lv 10¹¹ Dt 17⁸,⁹ 33¹⁰ 2 Ch 19⁸⁻¹⁰. It would appear that the law of the Levitical cities was never strictly carried into practice.

4, 5. There is a difficulty in understanding these measurements. Perhaps the simplest explanation is to say that the area of the city itself is disregarded. The city being conceived as a mathematical point, 1,000 cubits measured on either side give a square 2,000 cubits in the side. The Greek version has 2,000 cubits in v. 4. If this is right there is no difficulty at all. The city would be surrounded on all sides by a strip of land 2,000 cubits in width.

6, 9-15. The Cities of Refuge. (See also Dt 19¹⁻³ Josh 20.) In primitive times, before the machinery of justice was organised, the duty of avenging a murder devolved upon the nearest relative of the murdered person. Duty required him to pursue the murderer and slay him with his own hand. This law was not repealed by Moses, but certain restrictions were placed upon it in the interests of humanity and justice. Of the Levitical cities, six were marked out as Cities of Refuge to which a man who had killed another accidentally (vv. 11, 22–25) might flee and be safe from the 'avenger of blood.' This provision did not apply to wilful murderers, who were not to escape the death penalty (vv. 16–21). The names of the cities are given in Josh 20 7, 8. Three were on the W. side of Jordan and three on the E. The reason why Levitical cities were selected for this purpose was, not merely that these were regarded as possessing a sacred character, but that they were inhabited by men who knew the law, and who could decide in doubtful cases between wilful murder and accidental homicide (v. 24 Dt 19 12,17). Dt 19 3 provides that the principal roads leading to these cities of refuge be kept open, so that the innocent fugitive might have every facility in reaching the place of sanctuary (see note there). For the Christian application of this law of asylum see on v. 25. **12. Stand before the congregation**] As a wilful murderer might flee to one of these cities in the hope of escaping with his life, a trial must be held to ascertain whether the murder was wilful or accidental.

16–21. If the trial shows that the murder was committed wilfully, the murderer is to be handed over for execution at the hands of the avenger of blood.

22–29. If the trial shows that the murder was accidental (see Dt 19 4, 5) the murderer's life is spared. But he must stay within the bounds of the city till the death of the high priest, when he is at liberty to go. If he stray outside the bounds before that time he does so at the peril of his own life. **25. Unto**

the death of the high priest] The amnesty declared to the man-slayer on the death of the high priest, which marks the close of one period and the beginning of a new, is an appropriate symbol of that redemption from the sins of the past wrought by Christ, and that new life of liberty into which they enter who believe in Him : cp. Heb 6 18-20.

30–32. Murder is such a serious crime that it cannot be atoned for by the payment of a money fine ; nor can the man who has unintentionally killed another purchase his release from the city of refuge before the death of the high priest. St. Peter reminds Christians that they were not redeemed with silver or gold but with the precious blood of Christ (1 Pet 1 18, 19).

CHAPTER 36
THE LAW REGARDING HEIRESSES

According to 27 1-11 it was decided that, if a man left no sons, his daughters might inherit his property. But if the daughters married into another tribe, the property would go with them, and so be alienated from the tribe to which they formerly belonged. If it were sold after their marriage, it would revert at the year of Jubilee, not to the original tribe, but to that into which it had been transferred by marriage. To obviate this diminution of the lands originally assigned to each tribe, it is here enacted that no heiress shall marry outside the tribe of her father.

DEUTERONOMY

INTRODUCTION

1. Title and Contents. The title of this book is the English form of a Greek word meaning 'repetition of the law.' It is found in c. 17 18, where it was used by the Greek translators of the OT. (LXX) to represent three Hebrew words more exactly rendered in the English Version 'a copy of this law' (see note). The Jews call the book by the first two words in the original rendered ' These are the words.' The LXX title, though based on a mistranslation, is not altogether inappropriate, seeing that much of the legislation given in Deuteronomy is found elsewhere, and the historical portion is largely a *résumé* of what is narrated in the previous books. The scene of the book is in the Plains of Moab, and the time is the interval between the close of the Wanderings in the Wilderness and the Crossing of the Jordan. It opens with

the first day of the eleventh month of the fortieth year of the exodus (1 3) ; and, as the Israelites crossed the Jordan on the tenth day of the first month of the following year, after thirty days' mourning for Moses in the Plains of Moab (see 34 8 Josh 4 19), it follows that the period covered by Deuteronomy is not more than forty days.

The greater part of the book is taken up with a series of discourses spoken to the people by Moses before his death. In these discourses Moses reviews the events and experiences of the past forty years, and founds on them repeated exhortations to gratitude, obedience, and loyalty to Jehovah. The divisions of the book are as follows. **Part I. First Discourse,** chs. 1–4 43, comprising a brief survey of the history of Israel from Mt. Sinai to the Jordan (chs. 1–3), and concluding with an earnest appeal to the people to keep the commandments of Jehovah and remain faithful to His covenant (4 1-40). Three vv. of a historical nature (4 41-43) are then introduced. **Part 2. Second Discourse, chs. 4 44–28**, which is mainly legislative. It begins with a repetition of the Decalogue and an exhortation to cleave to Jehovah and abstain from idolatry (4 44–11), after which follows a series of laws regulating the religious and social life of the people (chs. 12–26). This section forms the nucleus of the book. C. 28 belongs to this section, and contains a sublime declaration of the consequences that will follow the people's obedience to, or transgression of, the law. C. 27, which prescribes the ceremony of the ratification of the law in Canaan, seems to interrupt the discourse. **Part 3. Third Discourse, chs. 29, 30**, in which the covenant is renewed and enforced with promises and threatenings. **Part 4. Chs. 31–34**. These chapters are of the nature of appendices, and comprise Moses' Charge to Joshua, and Delivery of the Law to the Levitical Priests (31 1-13); The Song of Moses, with accompanying historical notices (31 14–32); The Blessing of Moses, which, like the Song, is in poetical form (33); and, lastly, an account of the Death of Moses (34).

2. Origin and Composition. The book of Deuteronomy was certainly in existence in the year 621 B.C. The 'Book of the Law,' discovered in the Temple at Jerusalem in that year by Hilkiah the priest, is generally agreed to have included, if it was not identical with, our Deuteronomy. See 2 K 22 8-20 and notes there. There is no reason to believe that this was not a genuine discovery of a lost work, and its identification with at least the main part of Deuteronomy (chs. 5–26, 28) is inferred from the fact that the reformations instituted by Josiah are such as the law of Deuteronomy would require, e.g. the prohibition of the worship of heavenly bodies (cp. 2 K 23 4, 5, 11 with Dt 17 3), and of other superstitious and idolatrous practices (cp. 2 K 23 6, 13, 14 with Dt 12 2, 3); and the centralisation of worship at Jerusalem (cp. 2 K 23 8, 21-23 with Dt 12 4-28 16 5-7. Cp. also 2 K 23 7 with Dt 23 17, 18, 2 K 23 24 with Dt 18 10, 11, 2 K 23 8, 9 with Dt 18 6-8, and the language in which Josiah's reformation is spoken of in 2 K 23 2, 3 with the general style of Deuteronomy, e.g. 29 1, 9, 25 30 10 31 24). Assuming the practical identity of the book found by Hilkiah with our Deuteronomy, the question remains how old the book was at the time of its discovery. Like the rest of the Pentateuch, Deuteronomy professes to set forth the words and laws of Moses, and is ascribed by tradition to him. This tradition is not lightly to be set aside. It cannot any longer be denied that the art of writing

was practised in the time of Moses, and recent discoveries have shown that writing was employed in Palestine even before his day. That Moses himself left written works is not only in itself likely, but is expressly asserted in several places : see e.g. Ex 17 14 24 4, 7 34 27 Nu 33 2, and especially Dt 31 9, 26, where he is said to have written the Law, and delivered it to the custody of the priests. That in view of his approaching death the great Leader and Lawgiver of Israel should have addressed to the people such exhortations and warnings as are found in this book is also what might be expected. On the other hand, many biblical scholars are persuaded, from a careful study of the book, that it could not have been written by Moses, at least in its present form. It is marked by a distinctive literary style, apparent even to a reader of the English Version, who cannot fail to be struck with the frequent recurrence of characteristic phrases and with the general richness of its rhetorical passages, unlike what is found elsewhere in the Pentateuch. Deuteronomy also contains indications that the writer, or compiler, lived subsequently to the time of Moses and the conquest of Canaan. See e.g. the account of the death of Moses in c. 34, and cp. notes on 2 12 3 14 33 4 34 10-12. The use of the phrase 'beyond Jordan' suggests that the writer lived in Western Palestine, which Moses never did (see note on 1 1). The 'law of the Kingdom' in c. 17 14-20, it is said, could not have been composed before Solomon and other kings gave examples of the hurtful luxury here described, and other parts of the legislation of Deuteronomy, notably that relating to the centralisation of worship at Jerusalem (see 12 4-28), are at variance with what is prescribed elsewhere (cp. Ex 20 24), and do not seem to have been recognised in the earlier history of the nation. See also notes on 14 22 15 19, 20. In this connexion, however, we must reckon with the possibility of laws being promulgated but remaining a dead letter for a long period. It has to be kept in view, moreover, that the book itself professes to be a 'repetition of the law.' In view of the conflict of critical opinion it seems best to regard it as a reformulation of the laws of Moses, designed to meet the changing needs and circumstances of a time subsequent to its original publication.

3. Religious Value. Whatever difference of opinion may exist as to the date of Deuteronomy, there can be none as to its surpassing religious value. It is one of the most beautiful books of the Bible, furnishing some of the finest examples of Hebrew sacred eloquence, and breathing in every chapter an intensely devout and religious spirit. Its aim is professedly practical and hortatory, viz. to enforce upon Israel the unique claim of Jehovah to their gratitude, obedience, love and loyalty. In this respect the teaching of Deuteronomy resembles that of the 'prophets,' in its insistence, viz. by means of exhortation and warning, upon Israel's duty of maintaining the covenant relationship between the people and Jehovah. The people are 'holy to Jehovah,' who has chosen them to be a special people to Himself (7⁶), and they ought to cling to Him alone. Over and over again they are reminded of the great things He has done for them, of His free grace in their election and redemption, and of their unbroken experience of His providential care and kindness towards them. His grace is always adduced as the prime reason and motive why they should cleave to Him with whole-hearted devotion and keep His commandments and beware of the seducing influences of their own prosperity and their neighbours' idolatry. The argument is always the same, the evangelical argument, 'We love Him because He first loved us'; 'I beseech you by the mercies of God.' See e.g. 4 7-9, 32-40 6 20-25 7 7-11 29 2-17, etc. The same motive of gratitude for unde-

served mercies underlies the repeated exhortations to humanity and kindly consideration of the poor, the afflicted, strangers, and even the lower animals. See e.g. 14 22-29 15 7-11 16 10-17 23 17, 18, 22 26 1-11. The love of God to Israel, calling forth a responsive love to God and to humanity, that is the theme of this most profoundly religious and ethical book; and nowhere else is the blessedness of an obedience which is rooted in love and gratitude set forth more eloquently or persuasively.

The book of Deuteronomy seems to have been an especial favourite of our Lord. He resisted the threefold assault of the Tempter in the wilderness with quotations from this book (see Mt 4 and Dt 8 3 6 13 10 20 and notes); and He answered the question as to the 'first and greatest commandment' in the Law by referring to Dt 6 4,5. The Jews selected Dt 6 4-9 for daily recitation as their creed, finding in these words the highest expression of the unity and spirituality of God, and of the whole duty of man to his Maker, Preserver and Redeemer.

PART 1
FIRST DISCOURSE (Chs. 1–4 43)

The long sojourn in the wilderness is now drawing to a close. The Israelites are encamped in the Plains of Moab within sight of the Promised Land. Moses, feeling that his death is approaching, delivers his final charges to the people. In the first, he reviews briefly the history of Israel from Mt. Sinai to the Jordan, dwelling on the goodness of God, and making it the basis of an earnest appeal to the people to remember all that He has done for them, and to keep His commandments.

CHAPTER 1
INTRODUCTION. REVIEW OF THE JOURNEY
FROM SINAI TO KADESH

1–5. Introduction.
1. On this side Jordan] RV 'beyond Jordan,' i.e. on the E. side. The writer speaks from the standpoint of Canaan, as also in v. 5, 3 8 4 41, 46, 49 : see Intro. to Numbers, § 2. The plain is the Arabah, the valley running N. and S. of the Dead Sea. The Red sea] Heb. *Suph*, the name of some place on the Gulf of Akaba.
6–46. Review of the journey from Sinai to Kadesh on the border of Canaan.
6. Horeb] the name given in Dt to Mt. Sinai. The name Sinai occurs in this book only in the Blessing of Moses (33²). 7. The plain] see on v. 1. The hills] RV 'hill country,' the elevated ridge in the centre of Palestine. The vale] the maritime plain. The south] the *Negeb*. See on Nu 13 17, 21. 9. This seems to refer to what is recorded in Ex 18 13-26.
22. See Nu 13. It would appear that the

sending of the spies was suggested by the people, and that Moses referred the matter to God for confirmation : cp. Nu 13 1. 37. For your sakes] Had the unbelief of Moses gone unpunished, the people would have been hardened in their own transgression. For their sakes, therefore, it was impossible to overlook it : see on Nu 20 12. 46. Many days] see on Nu 13 26 20 1.

CHAPTER 2
REVIEW OF THE JOURNEY (continued)

1. The Red sea] i.e. the Gulf of Akaba. On Mt. Seir see Nu 20 22-29. 4. Through the coast] RV 'through the border,' as in v. 18. The Edomites, however, refused to give them a passage through their country : see Nu 20 14-21. The Israelites accordingly went southward towards Elath and Ezion-geber at the N. end of the Gulf of Akaba (see v. 8 and on Nu 20 22), and so round Edom to the country of the Moabites. 9. The Moabites and the Ammonites (v. 19) were related to the Israelites. being descended from Lot, the nephew of Abraham (Gn 19 37, 38). The Edomites were descended from Esau, the brother of Jacob. Ar] the capital of Moab, lying on the river Arnon, which formed the northern border of the country (Nu 21 15, 28).
10-12. These vv. form an antiquarian parenthesis, like vv. 20–23. 10. The Emims (RV 'Emim,' i.e. the 'terrible ones') and the Horims (RV 'Horites,' i.e. the 'cave-dwellers') are mentioned in Gn 14 5, 6. The tribes E. of the

Jordan seem to have been of great stature : see on Nu 21 33-35. **12. As Israel did**] These words must have been written after the occupation of Canaan.

13. On the **Zered** see Nu 21 12.

20. The **Zamzummims** (RV 'Zamzummim') are probably the same as the Zuzim in Gn 14 5.

23. The **Avims** (RV 'Avvim') dwelt in the SW. of Canaan, in the neighbourhood of Gaza, here called **Azzah**. **Hazerim**] RV 'in villages.' **Caphtorims**] the Philistines who came from Caphtor, usually identified with Cyprus or Crete: see Gn 10 14 Am 9 7 Jer 47 4.

CHAPTER 3
REVIEW OF THE JOURNEY (concluded)

1–11. The conquest of Og, king of Bashan. See Nu 21 33-35. **5.** The ruins of these cities remain to this day: see on Nu 21 33.

9. Sirion] means 'glittering like a polished shield,' and corresponds, therefore, to the name Mt. Blanc. The Hermon range is mostly covered with a cap of snow. In 4 48 Hermon is also called 'Sion,' which means the same as Sirion, if indeed it is not a clerical error for that word. **10. Salchah**] still existing under the name of Salkhad, a large town on the E. border of Bashan, lying on the great road from Galilee to the Persian Gulf.

11. The **bedstead of iron** of the giant king was in all probability his sarcophagus of black basalt which the Arabs still call 'iron.' Several such sarcophagi have been discovered E. of the Jordan. Conder believed that he discovered Og's 'bedstead' in the form of a huge stone throne at Rabbath. The word rendered 'bedstead' properly means a couch or divan: see e.g. Am 3 12 6 4.

14. This took place later (see Jg 10 3, 4, and cp. Intro. to Numbers, § 2), and its insertion here indicates the work of a later hand, like the expression **unto this day**: cp. v. 12. See on Nu 32 41. **17. Chinnereth**] the Lake of Gennesaret, or Sea of Galilee. The **plain** is again the Arabah: see on 1 1. **Ashdod-pisgah**] RV 'the slopes of Pisgah': cp. 4 49.

18–20. See on Nu 32.

23–28. See on Nu 27 12-23.

CHAPTER 4 1-43
EXHORTATIONS TO OBEDIENCE

This c. contains the practical part of the discourse. Having briefly rehearsed the experiences of the Israelites in the wilderness up to the present point, Moses closes with an eloquent appeal not to forget what they had seen and learned, but to keep the commandments of the Lord. The argument is quite evangelical. Jehovah of His own free grace has chosen and redeemed this people, they ought, therefore, to love and serve Him alone: cp. Joshua's exhortation in Josh 24.

3. Because of Baal-peor] see Nu 25 1-9.

10. See Ex 19, 20, 24 3-8. At Mt. Sinai the people entered into a national covenant with Jehovah their Redeemer, promising to keep the Law delivered unto them there.

15. The foundation of true religion and morals is a right conception of the nature of God. In the first and second commandments of the Decalogue Israel had been taught the truths of the unity and spirituality of God. They are specially exhorted here to keep themselves from idolatry. **16–18.** This prohibition probably refers to the animal worship of the Egyptians with which their fathers had been familiar in their bondage. **19.** There may be allusion here to the worship of the Persians and Chaldeans. The Israelites fell into this form of idolatry: see e.g. 2 K 17 16 21 3.

24. Cp. 9 3 Heb 12 29. On the nature of the divine jealousy see on Ex 20 5.

25. Remained long in the land] lit. 'slumbered in the land.' The word expresses not only long continuance but a loss of vigour, a gradual weakening of first impressions due to unbroken peace and prosperity. Those who have no changes are apt to forget God (Ps 55 19). Prosperity sometimes acts like a narcotic and sends the soul to sleep: cp. 6 10-13 8 10-20 32 15 ; see also 2 Ch 12 1 26 16 32 25. **28.** Bodily subjection to their heathen conquerors would lead to spiritual bondage. They would be 'given over to a reprobate mind': see Ro 1 24-28.

29–31. These vv. indicate the nature of true repentance. It is not merely sorrow for past sins and their consequences, but a seeking God with all the heart, and obedience to His voice. Such repentance procures the divine mercy, for God does not forget His part of the covenant, however His people forget theirs. 'The gifts and calling of God are without repentance,' i.e. they are irrevocable: see Ro 11 29 Heb 6 17.

32–38. These vv. state the ground of Jehovah's choice of Israel. It is purely an election of grace and love. Hence Israel ought to cleave to Him. No other nation has been so highly favoured by Jehovah. **38.** The Israelites did not take possession of the land of their enemies by their own might. Jehovah went before them into battle: cp. 8 17, 18.

41–43. The appendix to the First Discourse. On the Cities of Refuge see Nu 35 9-34 and notes there, and cp. also c. 19 Josh 20 1-9. The cities appointed here are those E. of the Jordan. In c. 19 those in Canaan are referred to. On the phrase **on this side Jordan** see on 1 1. **Bezer** was the southernmost of the three. It is mentioned on the Moabite Stone as having being rebuilt by Mesha: see on Nu 21 29. Its site has not been identified. It is probably the same as the Bozrah mentioned in Jer 48 24. **Ramoth in Gilead** played an important part in the wars between the kings of Damascus and Israel. It was the scene of the death of Ahab (1 K 22) and the anointing of Jehu (2 K 9).

Golan gave its name to the district E. of the Sea of Galilee, still known as the Jaulan. The precise locality of the city is unknown.

PART 2
SECOND DISCOURSE (Chs. 4⁴⁴⁻²⁸)

This is the longest of the three discourses, and fills over twenty-five chs. The opening vv. (4⁴⁴⁻⁴⁹) are in the form of an introduction : chs. 5–11 are mainly hortatory : the following chs. (12–28), which form the nucleus of the book of Deuteronomy, are taken up with a special code of laws.

CHAPTER 4 (continued)

45. After they came forth] RV 'when they came forth.' It was really in the fortieth year of the exodus. **46.** See on 1¹. **48.** On **Mount Sion,** see on 3⁹. **49. Springs of Pisgah]** RV 'slopes of Pisgah' : see on 3¹⁷.

CHAPTER 5
THE REPETITION OF THE DECALOGUE

This c. repeats the Law of the Ten Commandments given on Mt. Sinai with the circumstances of its delivery : see Ex 20, and the notes there. **3.** Their fathers who had heard the Law given at Sinai were actually dead. But as the covenant had been made not with individuals, but with the nation of Israel, Moses could say that it was made **not with our fathers, but with us.** The expression is really equivalent to ' not only with our fathers but also with ourselves.' **6.** This is the ground on which obedience to the Law is due. God's free grace is the first fact in the covenant. On the Ten Commandments see on Ex 20¹⁻¹⁷. **14, 15.** In Exodus the obligation to keep the sabbath is made to rest on the fact of the divine creation of the world ; here it rests on the divine redemption of Israel. In the former case the reason annexed to the commandment is universal, in the latter national. In both cases the commandment is the same, and it is possible that the original form of the Decalogue gave only the commandment without any reason attached to it : see Ex 23¹² and on Ex 20¹⁰, ¹¹. **23–33.** Cp. Ex 20¹⁸⁻²¹. **24. And he liveth]** This is a special token of the divine favour, because usually man cannot bear the immediate revelation of the divine majesty : cp. Ex 33²⁰ 19²¹ 20¹⁹ Jg 6²³ 13²² Isa 6², ⁵, and on Ex 24⁹⁻¹¹. **29.** The proper attitude of man towards God is not only one of reverence but of obedience. **31.** Man needs, and God Himself provides, a Mediator.

CHAPTER 6
PRACTICAL EXHORTATIONS

To the repetition of the Decalogue Moses adds in the following chs. a practical exhortation to obedience founded on the special relation of Jehovah to Israel as their Redeemer (6–11). C. 6 particularly insists upon the remembrance of God's statutes and the training of the children in them.

4, 5. Our Lord calls these words ' the first and great commandment.' They express the highest truth and duty revealed to the Hebrew nation : the truth of God's unity and uniqueness ; the duty of loving and serving Him with every faculty of the being. Consequently they became the Jewish Confession of Faith ; and under the name of the ' Shema ' (the first word of v. 4 in the Hebrew) are still recited, along with Dt 11¹³⁻²¹ and Nu 15³⁷⁻⁴¹, as the first act of worship in the Jewish synagogue, and twice a day by every adult male Jew. **5.** Love goes deeper than fear. It is the fulfilling of all law, and includes obedience. Both in the OT. and in the New it is the effect of God's greatest love in redemption. ' We love Him because He first loved us.' **8, 9.** Cp. 11¹⁸⁻²⁰. From early times the Jews understood this injunction literally ; and in the time of our Lord a great importance was attached to three ' memorials,' or visible reminders of this obligation to keep the Law of Jehovah. One was the ' zizith ' or ' fringe ' which was worn on the corners of the outer garment : see on Nu 15³⁷⁻⁴¹. The others were the ' tephillin ' and the ' mezuza,' the use of which was founded on this passage of Deuteronomy. The ' tephillin ' were two small boxes, about a cubic in. in size, containing each a piece of parchment, on which were written in a special form of handwriting the four passages, Ex 13¹⁻¹⁰, ¹¹⁻¹⁶ Dt 6⁴⁻⁹ 11¹³⁻²¹. One was fastened inside the left forearm and the other on the forehead, to be **a sign upon the hand and a frontlet between the eyes.** They were worn at prayer on week days, and sometimes enlarged, as by the Pharisees of our Lord's time, to suggest particular devotion to the Law (Mt 23⁵). The Hebrew name ' tephillin ' means ' prayers ' ; but they were also called in Gk. ' phylacteries ' or ' protectors,' from their supposed power to ward off evil spirits. The ' mezuza ' was a small oblong box containing the passage Dt 6⁴⁻⁹ and was affixed to the right-hand door-post of the house and of each inhabited room, in accordance with the injunction in Dt 6⁹. It had a beautiful significance as a reminder of the presence of God in the house, and the obligation of all the inmates to keep His holy law, but has also been degraded into a mere charm to keep off evil spirits during the night.

10-13. Cp. 8 10-14 and see on 4 25. **13. Swear by his name**] Jehovah, the God of truth, is to be recognised as the unseen witness of all agreements between a man and his neighbour, and the avenger of all falsehood : cp. the Third Commandment.

16. They **tempted** God at Massah by insisting that He should prove His presence among them in the way that they prescribed : see Ex 17 7. But man must beware of dictating to God, in unbelief and presumption. Our Lord refused to demand from God a special token of His presence and care, and quoted this warning against the tempter : see Mt 4 7. It is to be observed that our Lord not only took all His answers from the Scriptures, but from the same portion of Deuteronomy, viz. chs. 5–10 : see 8 3 6 13 10 20.

20–25. Cp. v. 7. The keeping of the Law is required by the fact of redemption, and is rewarded with the divine blessing. **25. Our righteousness**] Obedience increases merit. For a particular instance see on 24 13.

CHAPTER 7

PRACTICAL EXHORTATIONS (continued)

In this c. the people are warned against temptations to idolatry and enjoined to avoid contact with their idolatrous neighbours : see on Ex 23 32, 33 Nu 25 16-18.

1. On the tribes inhabiting Canaan see on Nu 13 21. **5. Images**] RV 'pillars,' or obelisks. **Groves**] RV 'Asherim' : see on Ex 34 13. **6. Special people**] RV 'peculiar people' : see on Ex 19 5.

13. On the promise of material prosperity as the reward of obedience, see on Ex 20 12.

19. Temptations] 'provings' or trials, the afflictions that test and reveal character : see 8 2, and cp. Jas 1 2, 12. **20. The hornet**] see on Ex 23 28. **25. Nor take** *it* **unto thee**] Achan did so and brought trouble upon himself and Israel : see Josh 7. **26. Abomination**] i.e. an idol, as in 16 22. **A cursed thing**] RV 'a devoted thing,' a thing laid under the ban of extermination. The verb from the same root is rendered **utterly destroy** in v. 2 : see on Lv 27 28.

CHAPTER 8

PRACTICAL EXHORTATIONS (continued)

The people are reminded of God's goodness to them at the time of the exodus and during their sojourn in the wilderness. They are exhorted to humility and obedience, and warned against worshipping strange gods.

2, 3. The events of the wanderings were intended to teach Israel humility and dependence on God alone : see on 7 19. **3. Which thou knewest not**] see Ex 16 15. **But by every** *word*, etc.] If necessary God can sustain human life apart from the usual means. The Saviour had this trust in God and refused to create bread for himself : see Mt 4 4. **4.** God who gives the life provides also the raiment and the bodily health : see Mt 6 25-34. Jewish commentators understood this description literally, but it is evidently poetical and rhetorical.

6–20. A warning against pride and self-sufficiency : see on 4 25.

7–9. The gifts of God in the rich and beautiful land of Canaan are a motive to thankfulness and obedience, but may become a temptation to forgetfulness and pride : see on 4 25. **9.** Iron is found in various parts of Palestine, especially in the N. Basalt (see on 3 11) is found E. of the Jordan. Copper, here called **brass**, is found in the Lebanon range and to the E. of the Dead Sea. We do not read of the Jews working mines in Canaan, but the writer of the book of Job was acquainted with mining operations, and gives a graphic description of the process in c. 28, which should be read in RV. **16. At thy latter end**] i.e. by bringing them into the land of promise if they stood the test. **18.** Cp. 1 Ch 29 12-14.

CHAPTER 9

PRACTICAL EXHORTATIONS (continued)

The rebellions and provocations of the wilderness are recalled, to show the people that it is not of their own merit that they are to inherit the promises, nor by their own strength that they are to dispossess the inhabitants of Canaan, but by the grace and power of God.

8. Also in Horeb] Even at Horeb, in view of those awe-inspiring tokens of the divine majesty, and at the very time when the Law was being promulgated, the people corrupted themselves : see Ex 32 and notes. **9. I neither did eat bread nor drink water**] In Ex 34 28 this fact is recorded in connexion with the second writing of the Law. **17. And brake them**] The action symbolised the breaking of the covenant through the sin of the people.

18. I fell down] i.e. in intercession : see on Nu 16 4. The words **as at the first** refer probably to the intercession on the mount spoken of in Ex 32 11 : cp. 32 31.

22–24, giving other instances of the people's rebellion, seem to be a parenthesis. V. 25 takes up the thread of v. 21.

CHAPTER 10

PRACTICAL EXHORTATIONS (continued)

1–5. The renewal of the broken covenant : see Ex 34.

6–9. These vv. are evidently a parenthesis.

The death of Aaron took place thirty-eight years after the departure from Sinai, but previous to the delivery of this discourse : see on Nu 20 22-29. The notice of Aaron's death seems to be inserted here to show that the sin of Aaron and the people did not bring the priesthood to a close. The covenant was re-newed, and Aaron was spared for nearly forty years to minister as the high priest ; and on his death the priesthood was continued in his family. In Nu 33 30-33 the same places are mentioned as being visited in a different order. In all probability the children of Israel visited these places twice. **8. At that time**] Not at the time of Aaron's death, but during the sojourn at Sinai : see Ex 32 26. The Levites here include the family of Aaron who were specially set apart to the priesthood : see on Nu 3.

11. In spite of the perversity and rebellion of the people they are permitted by God's grace to continue their journey and possess the land of promise. This verse marks the freeness and fulness of the divine forgiveness. God's covenant of peace is not removed. **12.** Notwithstanding all that the people have done God does not demand of them any-thing more than their plain duty, in view of their past experience of His goodness : cp. Mic 6 8. **13.** The path of duty is also that of safety and welfare. **14, 15.** Although God is Lord of heaven and earth, He has singled out this small nation (7 7, 8) for His special favour. **16.** See on Lv 19 23. **17, 18.** Great as God is, He cares for the lowly : see Ps 138 6. ' Be ye therefore merciful even as your Father is merciful.' **20.** This was our Lord's third answer to the tempter : see Mt 4 10 and on 6 16. **22.** This is another ground of gratitude and obedience.

CHAPTER 11
PRACTICAL EXHORTATIONS (concluded)

Some injunctions to obedience, with the blessing it entails, and the curse that follows disobedience. **1. Therefore**] There should be no break here : see on 10 22. **2. Seen the chastisement**] i.e. experienced for yourselves the discipline or instruction of the Lord. The word refers not only to the punishment of the Egyptians but also to the experiences of the Israelites. **6.** There is no mention here of Korah : see on Nu 16.

10, 11. The fields in Egypt require to be watered artificially. The water is raised from the lakes or from the Nile by means of pumps worked by the foot. But the expression **wateredst** *it* **with thy foot** may refer to the practice of diverting the water into numberless little channels by breaking down the separat-ing ridges, or by opening and shutting the sluices, with the foot. The land of Canaan requires no such human devices to render it fruitful. It **drinketh water of the rain of heaven.** It enjoys the direct blessing of God. A common Palestinian salutation during rain is, ' May God protect you while He is blessing the fields.' **14. First rain**] see on Lv 26 4.

18-21. See on 6 8, 9.

21. Heaven upon the earth] RV ' the heavens above the earth.'

24. Cp. Josh 1 3, 4. The **wilderness** is the wilderness of Judah in the S. ; **Lebanon** is the northern boundary ; the **Euphrates** is in the E. ; and the **uttermost sea** (lit. ' the hinder sea ') is the Mediterranean in the W. In describing the cardinal points the Hebrew stood with his face to the E. or sunrising. Hence in the Hebrew language ' in front ' means the E., ' behind ' means the W., as in this verse, while ' the right ' is the S. : see on Ex 23 31.

26-32. The Blessing and the Curse. See c. 27 and notes there.

28. Other gods, which ye have not known] i.e. who have not revealed themselves in deeds of deliverance and kindness, as Jehovah has done, and who have no claim upon your re-verence and obedience. The argument is always the same, though repeated in various forms. Israel's past experience of God's free grace in their election and redemption is the ground of their love and fear of Jehovah.

29. Put the blessing, etc.] This refers either to the erection of the stones inscribed with the blessings and the curses, or to the placing of the two companies mentioned in 27 12, 13, one to bless and the other to curse. **Ebal** and **Gerizim** are the most conspicuous of the hills of Samaria, being fully 3,000 ft. high. Ebal is on the N., Gerizim on the S.; and they are separated by a very deep ravine running E. and W. The summits command a view of the whole land. It was here that Abraham received the promise which was fulfilled 400 years later on the same spot : see Josh 8 30-35. The Samari-tans afterwards erected a temple on Mt. Gerizim, which became the rival of the temple at Jerusalem : see Jn 4 20, 21. The Passover is still celebrated yearly on its summit. **30. The champaign**] i.e. the plain, RV ' Arabah ' : see on 1 1.

Plains of Moreh] RV ' oaks of Moreh ': see Gn 12 6. The Samaritans claim that Moreh and Moriah (Gn 22 2) are the same, and that the sacrifice of Isaac therefore took place on Mt. Gerizim. They also assert that Mt. Geri-zim was the meeting-place of Abraham and Melchizedek (Gn 14). The **Gilgal** mentioned here is not the Gilgal lying between the Jordan and Jericho (see Josh 4 19), but another place of the same name near Shechem, in the centre of the country. The name means ' circle of (sacred) stones,' a ' cromlech.'

CHAPTER 12

THE ABOLITION OF IDOLATROUS PLACES.
THE CENTRALISATION OF WORSHIP.
ABSTINENCE FROM BLOOD

The larger section of the Second Discourse begins here and extends to the end of c. 26. It consists of a code of laws, and constitutes the nucleus of the whole book : see on 4 44-49. So far as any orderly arrangement can be discovered, chs. 12–16 are taken up with the more strictly religious duties ; chs. 17–20 with civil ordinances ; and chs. 21–26 with social and domestic regulations.

1–3. An injunction to destroy all traces of Canaanitish idolatry : see on 7 1-5.

4–28. No sacrifice to be made to Jehovah unless at the one place which He Himself prescribes. This law of the centralisation of worship is one of the main arguments employed by critics in support of the theory of the late origin of the book of Deuteronomy. The practice of sacrificing at local shrines, it is said, was universal till the time of Josiah, and could hardly have been so if there had been an earlier prohibition : see Intro. § 2.

4. Ye shall not do so] i.e. worship Jehovah in the places where the Canaanites worshipped their gods. **7.** Ye shall eat] The reference is to the sacrificial meal at which part of the offerings were eaten by the worshippers : see on Lv 3. **15.** This is a slight modification of the law prescribed in Lv 17 3, 4, where see note. **16.** On the prohibition to eat blood see Lv 3 3 17 10-16. **31. Every abomination**] see on Lv 18 21.

CHAPTER 13

WARNINGS AGAINST TEMPTATIONS TO
IDOLATRY

The people are warned against three possible sources of temptation to idolatry, viz. the false prophet (vv. 1–5), an erring member of the family (vv. 6–11), and an apostate city (vv. 12–18). In each case the tempter or tempters must be put to death without mercy. **2.** A sign or a wonder is not enough to establish the credentials of a prophet. If he seeks to turn the people from the worship of Jehovah, he confesses himself thereby a tempter to evil, and must be put to death : cp. Mt 24 24 2 Th 2 9 Rev 13 13, 14. **6.** Even should the tempter to apostasy be the nearest and dearest, no mercy must be shown to him (v. 8) : cp. the zeal of the Levites (Ex 32 25-29) and of Phinehas (Nu 25 7,8) and our Lord's words, Mt 10 37 Lk 14 26. The same principle is enunciated in Mt 5 29, 30.

12–18. An instance of this may be read in Jg 19, 20. **13. Men of Belial**] RV 'base fellows' or 'sons of worthlessness.' Belial is not a proper name: cp. 15 9 mg Jg 20 13 RM 1 S 25 25

1 K 21 13. **16. The street** is the open square or market-place of the city. The word rendered **every whit** is the same as that used to denote the 'whole burnt offering,' so that the clause may be translated 'as a whole burnt offering to Jehovah thy God.'

17. Cursed thing] RV 'devoted thing' : see on 7 26 Lv 27 26-29.

CHAPTER 14

DISFIGURINGS FOR MOURNING FORBIDDEN
CLEAN AND UNCLEAN MEATS SPECIFIED

1. Practices connected with idolatry : see on Lv 19 27, 28.

2. The foundation of the entire moral and ceremonial law is contained in this and the preceding verse. Israel is the people whom Jehovah has chosen and called His children. As such they must be holy : see intro. to Lv 17–26.

3–20. On the law of clean and unclean beasts, see Lv 11 and notes. **5.** The **pygarg** is probably a kind of antelope. The exact meaning of the Hebrew word is doubtful, as it only occurs in this passage. As the **chamois** is unknown in Palestine, a species of wild mountain sheep is probably meant.

21. That dieth of itself] For the meaning of this prohibition see on Lv 17 10-16. On the prohibition to seethe a kid in its mother's milk see on Ex 23 19.

22. The produce of the soil is to be tithed and the tithe eaten at the central sanctuary, except when this is inconvenient on account of distance (v. 24), in which case the tithe is to be turned into money, and spent on a sacrificial feast to which the Levites are to be invited (vv. 25–27). Every third year the whole tithe is to be devoted to charity. According to the law in Nu 18 21 the tithe is given to the Levites exclusively. It has been supposed that the tithe in Deuteronomy is a second tithe, different from that in Numbers, and made after the first, or Levite's tithe, has been deducted from the produce. But, as no mention is made of more tithes than one, the different destination of the tithes may be considered as indicating different stages of legislation. In later times, however, a distinction was made between the first and second tithes, the first being devoted to the Levites, and the second consumed by the offerer.

CHAPTER 15

THE SABBATICAL YEAR

This c. deals with the year of release, or the Sabbatical Year, and should be compared with Lv 25. In addition to the rest for the land and the manumission of Hebrew slaves in the seventh year, it prescribes a release of debts (vv. 1–5) ; only, however, so far as Hebrew creditors are concerned, and proper loans, not money due on account of purchase (vv. 3, 8, 9).

4. Save when there shall be] RV 'Howbeit there shall be.' The law is intended to prevent poverty. **10.** 'The Lord loveth a cheerful giver.' **11.** The ideal state of matters is contemplated in v. 4 : here we have the actual fact. There will always be poor people, but poverty will be exceptional, if this injunction is conscientiously carried out : see vv. 4, 5.

12-18. See also Ex 21 2-6 Lv 25 39-46. The subject of slavery is connected with that of poverty, as it is implied here that the poor person has been sold as a slave for debt. Every seventh year the slave has to be released. He is not to be sent away empty, as the probable result would be a return to slavery. He is to be liberally **furnished**, so as to be in a position to earn a livelihood and make a fresh start in life. This is a very wise as well as humane prescription.

16. If a slave elect to remain in the master's service instead of accepting release, a formal compact must be made to that effect. In Ex 21 6 the ceremony is performed in public before the magistrates ; here it seems to be private. The boring of the ear and the fastening it to the doorpost with the awl signified that the person was permanently attached to the house and was bound to obey the words of his master : cp. on Ex 21 6.

19, 20. In Nu 18 15-18 the firstlings of clean beasts are the perquisite of the priests. Here they are to be eaten by the owner and his household annually at the central sanctuary. Much ingenuity has been expended in the attempt to reconcile these two regulations. The simplest explanation is that they belong to different stages of legislation.

21. Whatever is offered to God must be the best of its kind : cp. 17 1, and see on Lv 22 17-25.

CHAPTER 16
INJUNCTIONS REGARDING FEASTS, JUDGES, GROVES, AND IMAGES

1-8. On the Passover see Ex 12 Lv 23 4-8 Nu 28 16-25, and the notes on these passages. It will be observed that the general law of 12 5 (see on 12 4-28) is here applied to each of the three great annual festivals : see vv. 2, 11, 15. **3. Bread of affliction]** So called from the circumstances in which the festival was instituted and which the unleavened bread and bitter herbs were meant to symbolise : see Ex 12 8. **8. Solemn assembly]** see Lv 23 36.

9-12. On the Feast of Weeks see on Lv 23 15-21 Nu 28 26-31. **10. With a tribute of a freewill offering of thine hand]** better, 'after the measure of a freewill offering of thine hand,' i.e. according to thine ability as God has prospered thee, as in v. 17. **11.** The

joyous nature of this festival is emphasised here. The people are to present thank-offerings and remember the poor : cp. v. 16. **13.** On the Feast of Tabernacles see on Lv 23 33-43 Nu 29 12-38. **16. Shall not appear . . empty]** To 'appear before God' is to visit the sanctuary for worship : e.g. Ps 42 2,4. On this injunction to bring an offering see on Ex 23 15, and cp. Ps 96 8.

18. This is the beginning of the subdivision that deals mainly with civil matters. See heading of c. 12. **19.** See on Ex 23 8.

21. Grove of any trees] RV 'Asherah of any kind of tree': see on Ex 34 13. **22. Image]** RV 'pillar' : see on Ex 24 4 34 13.

CHAPTER 17
THE PUNISHMENT OF IDOLATRY. CONTROVERSIES TO BE SETTLED BY PRIESTS AND JUDGES. ELECTION AND DUTIES OF A KING

1. Cp. Lv 22 17-25. **2. Wickedness]** idolatry, as in 4 25. **5. Unto thy gates]** see on Gn 19 1.

7. The hands of the witnesses] This regulation, by throwing the responsibility of the execution upon the witnesses, would act as a safeguard against false evidence : see on Lv 24 14.

8-13. Difficult cases are to be referred to a supreme court of judicature, consisting of the priests and the chief magistrate, whose decision is final. This court is to sit at the central sanctuary : see 2 Ch 19 8-11. **10. Inform thee]** rather, 'direct thee.' The common Heb. word for 'law' is derived from this verb and means really 'direction.'

14-20. The Law of the Kingdom. It is to be observed that the people are not commanded to appoint a king, as in the case of the judges (16 18). But the desire for a king is anticipated and is not disapproved. The kingdom is theocratic, i.e. the king is the vice-gerent or representative of God and is chosen by Him. The law of the kingdom is the law of God (vv. 18-20). The Church and the State are identical. **14. Like as all the nations]** cp. the actual words of the people in 1 S 8 20. **15. Not . . a stranger]** i.e. a foreigner, a non-Israelite : because Israel is the peculiar people of Jehovah. The Jews were always intolerant of foreign authority : cp. Mt 22 17. Messiah when He came was to rid them of the foreign yoke : see Ac 1 6.

16. Not multiply horses] The horse is here forbidden, not as an article of luxury but as an instrument of warfare, in which the kings of Israel are not to trust: cp. Ps 20 7 33 16,17 147 10. Canaan was not suitable for cavalry, and the conquest of the country was effected by infantry, whose superiority was due to the hilly nature of the country. Solomon imported horses from Egypt (1 K 10 26,28), and similar reliance upon Egypt was a frequent snare to the Israelites against which the prophets raised a warning voice : see Isa 31 1 Ezk 17 15. Horses were also dedicated to the sun-god by the idolatrous kings of Israel : see 2 K 23 11, and on Ex 9 3. **17.** Solomon transgressed this commandment with precisely the result here foretold : 1 K 11 1-4, and cp. Neh 13 26.

18. A copy of this law] i.e. not merely the law of the kingdom contained in vv. 14–20, but the entire Deuteronomic law which is in the custody of the priests : see on 31 9, 24-26. At the coronation of Josiah the 'testimony' was put into his hands (2 Ch 23 11) ; and to this day, when a Christian monarch is crowned, the Bible is delivered to him with the words : 'We present you with this book, the most valuable thing that the world affords. Here is wisdom ; this is the royal law : these are the lively (i.e. living) oracles of God,' signifying that the law of God is to be the rule of his kingdom. In LXX the words **a copy of this law** are represented by the single word 'deuteronomion,' from which the title of the whole book is derived : see Intro. § 1.

20. And his children] an indication that a hereditary dynasty is not inconsistent with divine choice.

CHAPTER 18
The Priestly Dues. Character and Work of the True Prophet

1–8. The Priestly dues : see on Nu 18.

4. This is the only place where the priests are said to receive the **first of the fleece** : cp. Nu 18 12.

9–14. Condemnation of superstitious and magical practices.

10. Pass through the fire] The context here seems to imply that this was a method of divining or obtaining an oracle from a god: cp. on Lv 18 21. **Useth divination**] a general term, but applied specially to the casting of lots : see e.g. Ezk 21 21. **Observer of times**] RV 'One that practises augury': the meaning of the word is uncertain. **An enchanter**] one who observes omens, watches for signs in the sky or in the flight of birds. **Witch**] RV 'sorcerer,' one who practises magic by means of drugs and spells : cp. on Ex 22 18. **11. Charmer**] one who **ties knots**, weaves magic spells and curses. **Consulter with familiar spirits, or a wizard**] lit. 'one who consults a ghost or familiar spirit,' probably a ventriloquist who professes to hold communication with subterranean spirits. **Necromancer**] one who inquires of the dead : cp. Lv 19 31 20 27.

15. This is closely connected with what precedes. Israel has no need to employ such arts of divination as other nations use. Jehovah Himself will communicate His will to them through the prophets whom He raises up and instructs. See Isa 8 19. The singular number here, **a Prophet**, does not refer to a particular individual, but to a succession of prophets. Israel will never want a prophet to communicate to them God's will. This prophecy found its ultimate fulfilment in Christ, the perfect revealer of God's grace and truth and the new law-giver, and is applied to Him by St. Peter and St. Stephen : see Ac 3 22 7 37.

18. This v. contains the definition of a prophet. He is one who speaks the word of God and interprets to men the divine will : see on Nu 11 25, and cp. the words of our Lord in Jn 14 10. **20. That prophet shall die**] For an instance see Jer 28 15-17.

21, 22. At no time is it easy to distinguish the true from the false prophet. Different prophets in Israel not unfrequently contradicted each other. One test of the true prophet, but not the only one, is proposed here, viz. the fulfilment of prediction. Manifestly this test could only be applied to predictions of the immediate future. But the prophet sometimes prophesied of things that were afar off (Ezk 12 22-27) so that his words could not be verified by those to whom they were addressed. The ultimate criterion of the true prophet is the moral character of his utterance. Conscience is the true judge. Our Lord reproached His generation because they insisted on seeing signs and wonders before they would believe.

CHAPTER 19
The Cities of Refuge. Punishment of Deceit and False Witness

1–13. On the Cities of Refuge see Nu 35 9-34 and notes there. **2. In the midst of thy land**] Those on the E. side of the Jordan have already been assigned : see on 4 41-43. **3. Prepare thee a way**] It was the duty of the Sanhedrim, or chief council of the Jews, to maintain the roads to these cities in good repair, and to have finger-posts where necessary with the words 'Refuge, Refuge' inscribed upon them, so as to afford every facility to the fugitive.

8. Enlarge thy coast] i.e. thy border, to the limits mentioned in 1 7 11 24. The condition of such enlargement is stated in the next v.

9. Three cities more] i.e. besides the three mentioned in vv. 2, 7, and those in 4 41-43. The additional three would be in the newly added territory beyond the usual limits of the kingdom. There is no evidence to show that they were actually appointed.

14. Cp. 27 17 Job 24 2 Prov 22 28 23 10 Hos 5 10. The landmark was usually a stone, or heap of stones, which in the absence of hedges or walls defined the boundary of a man's field. Its removal was equivalent to theft.

15–21. The law of false witness. Cases of suspected false witness are to be investigated and punished by the supreme court : see on 17 8-13. **21.** See on Ex 21 23 and cp. Lv 24 20.

CHAPTER 20
Laws of Warfare

1. Horses and chariots] The army of the Israelites was chiefly composed of infantry : see on 17 16. **2. The priest**] It is implied that the priests accompany the hosts of Israel into battle : see on Nu 10 9. Hence the Heb. phrase 'to consecrate a war, or warriors,' usually rendered to 'prepare' : see Joel 3 9 mg. Isa 13 3.

5-9. From Nu 1 3 it would appear that all able-bodied men from twenty years of age were liable to military service. But the evils of compulsory service were obviated by the rule laid down in this passage exempting certain classes. There was (1) the man who had built a new house or planted a vineyard, and had as yet got no return for his outlay. The law exempting him for a time was an encouragement to those who by personal outlay increased the material resources of the country. (2) A man who was betrothed or newly married was exempted for a year (cp. 24 5). (3) The fearful and fainthearted were discharged. Fear is infectious, and the presence of such persons in the host would be a source of weakness and danger. For an instance of the observance of this rule see Jg 7 3. It is implied that a sense of honour will protect this law from being abused.

10. War is to be regarded as the last resort, and only to be employed when negotiations for peace have been tried and failed. In the event of victory, only the fighting men are to be put to death ; women and children are to be spared, except in the case of neighbouring idolatrous tribes. **16.** Cp. 7 1-5.

19, 20. Fruit-trees are not to be used for bulwarks and battering rams. The words at the end of v. 19 should probably be read as in RV, 'for is the tree of the field man, that it should be besieged of thee ?' i.e. the tree does no harm and is not to be treated as an enemy. Wanton destruction is not permissible even in war.

All these rules were designed to mitigate as far as possible the evils of war. There is to be no destruction of human life and property beyond what is actually necessary. The conduct of war is to be guided with reason and mercy.

CHAPTER 21
Expiation of Undetected Homicide. Marriage of Captive Women. Punishment of a Rebellious Son

The last sub-section of the Second Discourse begins here, containing a variety of social and domestic regulations.

1-9. The Expiation of Undetected Homicide. The cases of accidental and open, wilful murder have been already provided for in c. 19. This passage treats the case of undetected homicide. Murder pollutes the land and must be expiated. When the murderer cannot be discovered the responsibility of making atonement rests with the city nearest to the scene of the crime. For the ancient Babylonian practice in such circumstances see art. 'Laws of Hammurabi.' **4. For rough valley** read 'valley with running water,' and for **strike off the heifer's neck** read 'break the heifer's neck.' **Eared** means 'ploughed' as in Ex 34 21. The proper satisfaction for the crime of murder would be the death of the murderer : see 19 13 ; but as he cannot be discovered, the heifer takes his place. The unworked heifer and the untilled land probably suggested complete severance from human life, and symbolised the unnaturalness of the crime of murder.

6. The washing of the hands is a protestation of innocence. Cp. the action of Pilate in Mt 27 24. **7.** The elders, in the name of all the citizens, take an oath of purgation. The publicity and solemnity of the ceremony must have had a powerful effect upon the public conscience, and in some cases no doubt assisted in the discovery of the murderer.

10-14. On the Marriage of Captive Women. This rule does not apply to Canaanitish women, whom the Israelites were forbidden in any circumstances to marry : see 7 3 19 16-18.

12. These are rites indicative of purification : see Lv 14 8 Nu 6 9. The captive comes from a heathen people, and this ceremony symbolises the renouncing of her former life and her adoption into Israel. **13.** The woman is to be honourably treated. Even if divorced she must not be sold as a slave but allowed to go back to her people.

15. Succession to hereditary property is a fruitful cause of discord in a family, as is also the favouritism of parents : cp. the case of Isaac and Rebekah (Gn 25 28). A polygamous society is specially liable to disturbance from these causes. **Beloved** and **hated** are relative terms, meaning simply that one is preferred to the other. For a similar use of the terms see Mal 1 2, 3.

17. A double portion] The usual right of the firstborn. An estate was divided into a number of parts exceeding the number of children by one, and the extra share fell to the firstborn. **18.** Children have rights, as the last passage shows, but they have also duties. The punishment of an incorrigible son is very severe. The State is regarded as having an interest in the proper upbringing of children and as exercising its authority when that of the parents is powerless : see on Ex 20 12 21 15, 17.

22, 23. And thou hang him] The hanging followed the execution. See on Nu 25⁴ and cp. Josh 10²⁶ 2 S 4¹². The **tree** was a stake on which the dead body of the criminal was impaled, in token of infamy. The dead body must be taken down before nightfall because it is 'the curse of God.' The words rendered, **he that is hanged** *is* **accursed of God,** are somewhat ambiguous. They mean either he 'is accursed in the sight of God, i.e. cursed by God,' or 'is an insult or reproach to God.' Jewish commentators take them in the latter sense. The dead body pollutes the land and is an insult to God: it must therefore be taken down. St. Paul quotes the words in Gal 3¹³ in the former sense, viz. that the fact of hanging is an evidence of the divine curse resting upon the person. The Jews of the apostle's time, like those of later times, argued from the 'offence of the cross.' Seeing that Jesus was hanged on a tree, He could not be the Son of God: He was manifestly the object of divine displeasure. St. Paul boldly admitted the fact, but reasoned differently from it. The curse, he said, was vicarious. Christ 'was made a curse for us,' thereby redeeming us from the curse of the Law.

CHAPTER 22

LAWS REGARDING LOST PROPERTY, DISTINCTION OF SEX IN APPAREL, AND CHASTITY

1–4. Law of Lost Property: see Ex 23⁴ and note.

5. 'God is not the author of confusion,' and the natural distinctions He Himself has appointed ought to be respected. Whatever contravenes the law of nature contravenes the law of God: cp. the principle laid down by St. Paul in 1 Cor 11³⁻¹⁶. Immodesty leads to immorality. There may be an allusion here to the unchaste practices connected with certain idolatrous rites in which the sexes exchanged dress.

6, 7. To take the old bird as well as the young would be wanton cruelty. Kindness to animals is part of the law of God: see on Ex 23⁴,⁵,²¹ Lv 22²⁸. It is to be observed that the same reward is attached to this commandment as to some of what may be considered the 'weightier matters of the law': see e.g. 5¹⁶,³³. Rabbi Akiba, referring to this promise of long life, supposes the case of a man who climbs a tower and takes the young from a nest, sparing the dam in accordance with the commandment given here. But on his way down he falls and breaks his neck. To the question, 'Where is the **going well and prolonging of days** in this case?' the Rabbi answers, 'In the world where all goes well, and in that world where all is abiding.' He holds that the truth of the resurrection of the dead is implied in all the promises of reward attached to the keeping of the Law: cp. on Ex 20¹².

8. The roofs of Eastern houses were flat, and used not only for drying grain (Josh 2⁶), but as an open-air parlour when coolness or privacy was sought: see e.g. 1 S 9²⁵,²⁶ 2 S 11² Dan 4²⁹ ᵐᵍ. Ac 10⁹. The injunction here is a corollary of the sixth commandment, and contains a principle capable of wide application.

9–11. Cp. v. 5 and see on Lv 19¹⁹.

12. See on Nu 15³⁷⁻⁴¹. The law is applied spiritually by St. Paul in 2 Cor 6¹⁴.

13–30. On the Law of Chastity see on Lv 18, 19.

23. Betrothal consisted in the settlement and payment of a dowry by the bridegroom to the father or brothers of the bride, and in presenting the bride with certain gifts: see on Ex 22¹⁶. It was regarded as sacredly as marriage itself. After betrothal, the bride was under the same restrictions as a wife, and if unfaithful was punished as an adulteress.

24. Here the betrothed damsel is called a wife: cp. Mt 1²⁰. **28.** See on Ex 22¹⁶. The even-handed justice of the Mosaic Law is worthy of note. It deals with equal strictness with both the sinning persons.

CHAPTER 23

LAWS REGARDING ADMITTANCE TO THE CONGREGATION, CLEANLINESS IN THE CAMP, UNCHASTITY, USURY, AND VOWS

1. Shall not enter into the congregation of the LORD] i.e. not merely as priests (see Lv 21¹⁶⁻²⁴) but as ordinary members of the nation of Israel, all of whom are 'holy unto the Lord.' The reference in this v. is probably to the self-mutilation practised by the devotees of certain heathen gods, and alluded to by St. Paul in Gal 5¹²: cp. 14¹. **2. A bastard** is understood by the Jewish commentators to mean here, not one born out of wedlock (Jephthah was such, Jg 11¹), but the child of adultery or incest. **Even to his tenth generation**] i.e. not at all. Similarly in v. 3: see Neh 13¹. **11. Evening cometh on**] A new day begins with the evening.

12–14. Sanitation and morality are both of the utmost importance for an army in camp. Cleanliness is next unto godliness: cp. 2 Cor 6¹⁶⁻7¹. **15.** A foreign slave is probably meant; see v. 16. **18.** From its connexion here the word **dog** seems to denote a person who practised immoral conduct as an idolatrous rite: see on Lv 19²⁹, and cp. Rev 22¹⁵.

19. Thy brother] i.e. a fellow Israelite. In v. 20 **stranger** means foreigner. The Jews have always been noted as money lenders: see on Ex 22²⁵.

21–23. On vows see Nu 30, and cp. Eccl 5⁴, ⁵

24, 25. Jewish commentators limit the

application of this rule to harvest labourers, thus making it analogous to that prohibiting the muzzling of the ox 'when he treadeth out the corn' (Dt 25⁴). But there seems no reason for limiting the natural interpretation of the precept, which like the law of the gleaner (24¹⁹⁻²²) is prompted by a spirit of generosity towards wayfarers and poor persons. The restrictions at the end of vv. 24, 25 would protect the law from abuse. The Pharisees did not accuse our Lord's disciples of the sin of theft but of working on the sabbath day, rubbing the ears of corn being equivalent in their opinion to harvesting : see Mt 12¹ᶠ.

CHAPTER 24
LAWS REGARDING DIVORCE, PLEDGES, MAN-STEALING, LEPROSY, JUSTICE, AND GLEANING

1–4. The Law of Divorce. The right of the husband to divorce his wife is here acknowledged but is guarded against abuse. There must be some good reason for the separation ; it must be done in a legal and formal manner : and it is final. If the woman is divorced a second time, or becomes a widow after re-marriage, she is not free to marry her first husband.

1. Some uncleanness] RV 'some unseemly thing.' The Heb. is literally 'nakedness of a thing,' an expression also used in 23¹⁴. The vagueness of the language gave rise to endless disputes among Jewish teachers. In the time of our Lord, opinion was divided between the school of Shammai who held that it meant unchastity, and the school of Hillel who understood the expression in a much wider sense as referring to almost any cause of displeasure on the part of the husband, such as an ill-cooked meal or the sight of a more beautiful woman. The Pharisees asked the judgment of our Lord upon the matter and He decreed in favour of the stricter interpretation. He acknowledged no ground for divorce except that of adultery, and even this is a doubtful exception (neither Mark nor Luke gives the qualifying words 'except for fornication'; see Mk 10¹¹). He characterised the Mosaic law of divorce as a concession to the 'hardness' of men's hearts, and went back to the original ordinance of God in creating one man and one woman as evidence of the divine idea of the inviolability of the marriage bond : see Mk 10²⁻¹² Mt 19³⁻⁹ 5³¹,³² Lk 16¹⁸. The **bill of divorcement** contained the sentence, 'And thou art permitted (to be married) to another man.' **4.** The infinitude of the divine mercy is beautifully illustrated in Jer 3¹, where God takes back those who have broken His covenant and have repented. His ways are higher than our ways (see also Hos 1–3). **5.** See on 20⁵⁻⁹.

6. On the nature of the Eastern hand-mill

see on Ex 11⁵ 22²⁶,²⁷. The mill is an indispensable domestic utensil ; and, as neither oi the stones is of any use without the other, to take one away would inflict a cruel hardship. It would be to 'take a man's life,' i.e. his means of livelihood. **7.** See Ex 21¹⁶. **8, 9.** See Lv 13, 14 Nu 12. Miriam, though she was the sister of Moses, had to comply strictly with the laws regulating the separation and purification of lepers.

10. Not go into his house] The debtor must be allowed to select himself the article that he will give as a pledge for a loan. Whatever it be, the creditor must accept it, and not force his way into the house to see what is there and perhaps carry off something that the poor man cannot spare. If the man is so poor that he has nothing save his blanket to give in pledge, it must not be kept overnight (vv. 12, 13 ; see on Ex 22²⁶). **13. Righteousness]** In the Rabbinical language the word for 'alms' is 'righteousness.' To give alms is the righteous act *par excellence :* see Mt 6¹ and mg. **15.** Another humane principle of far reaching application. **16.** For an instance of the observance of this rule see 2 K 14⁶, and cp. Ezk 18²⁻⁴,¹⁹,²⁰.

20. When thou beatest thine olive tree] In gathering olives the fruit is brought to the ground either by shaking the boughs or beating them with a long palm branch. At the present time the trees are beaten on a certain day announced by a crier, after which the poor are allowed to glean what is left. A similar permission holds good in the case of vineyards and cornfields : see on Lv 19⁹. Gleaning is a beautiful and kindly custom still surviving to some extent in Palestine, but fast disappearing before the introduction of modern methods of harvesting, which are not unnaturally regarded with disfavour by the poorer classes.

CHAPTER 25
ORDINANCES REGARDING THE INFLICTION OF STRIPES, THE RAISING OF SEED TO A BROTHER, MODESTY, AND FAIR DEALING

3. *And* **not exceed]** In order to keep within the limit it was usual to inflict thirty-nine stripes : see 2 Cor 11²⁴. The milder beating was with a rod. A severer form of this punishment was scourging, inflicted with a whip of thongs into which pieces of iron were inserted. In the time of our Lord beating was inflicted in the synagogue upon ecclesiastical offenders : see on Mt 10¹⁷ Ac 26¹¹. While the culprit was being beaten the words in Dt 28⁵⁸,⁵⁹ Ps 78³⁸ were read. **4.** In threshing, the sheaves were spread out upon a hard beaten piece of ground (the threshing floor), and over them a pair of oxen dragged a wooden sledge or harrow about 5 ft. square, upon which the driver stood to add weight to it. In 1 Cor 9⁹⁻¹⁴

1 Tim 5 17, 18 St. Paul applies this precept to the duty of supporting those who preach the gospel : see on Ex 23 4, 5.

5-10. Marriage of a brother's widow. Among the Jews it was regarded as a great calamity that the family line should become extinct. If a man died childless, his name perished and his property passed to the families of his brothers. To obviate this was the purpose of this law of the levirate marriage (Lat. *levir* = a husband's brother). The duty of marrying a brother's widow was not enforced, but the refusal to do so was regarded as disgraceful. Failing a brother the duty devolved upon the nearest male relative. See on Lv 18 16, and see Ruth 2 20 3 9-13 4. **9.** The loosing of the shoe and handing it over signified an act of transfer or renunciation. In this case it was a mark of discredit : cp. Ruth 2 7, 8. A Bedouin formula of divorce is ' She was my slipper and I have cast her off.'

13-16. Ancient weights were pieces of stone or metal which the merchant kept in a bag. An unscrupulous merchant might have two sets of weights in his bag, a heavier for buying and a lighter for selling : see Mic 6 11 Prov 16 11, and cp. Lv 19 35, 36.

17-19. See Ex 17 8-16, and for the fulfilment of the injunction 1 S 14 48 15, 27 8, 9.

CHAPTER 26
The Presentation of Firstfruits and of Tithes

1-11. Presentation of the Firstfruits, as a Thank-offering for the mercy of God in delivering the nation from Egypt and in giving them a good land and fruitful seasons.

5. A Syrian] Jacob is meant. His mother came from Aram-naharaim (Gn 24 10), and he himself spent fourteen years in that country (Gn 28 1-5 29-31). The term implies a suggestion of disparagement. For his **going down to Egypt** see Gn 46. **11.** Having dedicated their firstfruits the people were free to enjoy what remained.

12-15. On the tithe of the first and second year see on 14 22, 27, and on the tithe of the third year see on 14 28, 29. The latter was the poor's tithe, and was stored up and distributed among the needy. **13. Brought away the hallowed things**] RV ' put away,' wholly parted with them. The ' hallowed things ' are the tithes which were consecrated to Jehovah and could not be lawfully retained by the owner.

14. As the presence of a dead body was ceremonially defiling in the highest degree, the offerer here declares that neither he nor his tithe was defiled in this way. The words **given thereof for the dead** are understood by Jewish commentators to mean that the offerer **had** not used any part of the tithe to provide

a coffin or grave-clothes for a dead person. More probably, however, they refer to the practice, common in Egypt e.g., of making a funeral feast. Thomson, in ' The Land and the Book,' says it is customary after a funeral to send presents of corn and food to the friends in the name of the dead : cp. Jer 16 7 (cp. RV) Hos 9 4. The Egyptians also placed food on the tombs of the dead, but it is doubtful whether this custom obtained among the Jews, although we read in the apocryphal book of Tobit (4 17) : ' Pour out thy bread on the tomb (or, burial) of the just.' In any case the declaration in this passage means that the tithe has not been in any way ceremonially defiled.

16. These statutes] i.e. those contained in chs. 12–26, to which vv. 16-19 here form the hortatory conclusion.

CHAPTER 27
Ceremonies to be observed on reaching Canaan

This chapter has probably been misplaced, as it seems to break the connexion between c. 26 and c. 28. It ordains four ceremonies to be observed after the people have entered Canaan : the Law to be written on stones on Mt. Ebal : an altar to be erected there : the covenant ratified on Ebal and Gerizim : and twelve curses pronounced by the Levites.

1. Elders] Elsewhere the elders are addressed along with the people. Here they are associated with Moses in exhorting the people to obedience.

2, 3. The plaster was intended to make a smooth surface, on which the inscription may have been painted in accordance with the Egyptian custom. Or the writing may have been impressed on the clay when it was soft and the clay afterwards dried or baked in the sun, like the tablets and cylinders of Babylonia. On the fulfilment of the injunction given here see Josh 8 30-35 and on 11 29, 30.

5. Cp. Ex 20 24, 25 and notes there.

9, 10. The Levites are addressed here because it was their duty to pronounce the blessings and the curses, to which the people responded with ' Amen.'

11-13. On Ebal and Gerizim see 11 29, 30. It need not be supposed that six tribes spoke the blessings from the top of Gerizim and the other six the curses from the top of Ebal. According to the Jewish writers the priests and Levites stood in the valley between the two heights and spoke both the blessings and the curses from there (see v. 14), and **all the people** answered with a loud Amen. The valley between the hills is not more than 60 rods wide at the eastern end, and all travellers in Palestine remark upon the wonderful distance at which sounds are audible, on account of the unusual clearness of the air. Our Lord frequently spoke to large multitudes in the open air.

12. To bless] The words of the blessings are not given but may be inferred from the nature of the curses: cp. 11 26-32.

15. Cursed *be* **the man**] There is no verb in the Hebrew, and it might be more correct to say 'cursed is the man.' The words are a declaration of fact rather than an imprecation. The seeming harshness of many expressions in the Psalms e.g. may be explained in this way. The speaker does not always utter his own wish, but declares the inevitable result in God's righteous government of a certain line of conduct. **In** *a* **secret** *place*] cp. 13 7. It is seldom that sin is bold enough to show its head, at least in its beginning. But 'the eyes of the Lord are in every place beholding the evil and the good.'

18. To take advantage of a neighbour's ignorance or credulity is sin: cp. Lv 19 14.

26. Cp. Gal 3 26. As no mere man is able perfectly to keep the whole law, St. Paul argues that part at least of the purpose of the Mosaic Law was to teach men to despair of obtaining righteousness 'by the works of the law,' and to drive them, as it were, to seek a righteousness imputed by God on condition of faith: see Ro 3 19-31 4 9-25 Gal 3 19-24.

CHAPTER 28
The Blessing and the Curse

This c. properly follows 26 19, and concludes the second discourse. It enforces the injunctions given, by exhibiting the blessings associated with the keeping of them, and the curses entailed upon disobedience.

1–14. The Blessings for Obedience.

5. Store] lit. 'kneading-trough' as in Ex 12 34. The **basket** is that used for holding bread: see Gn 40 17 Lv 8 2 Mt 14 20.

7. Seven ways] (at once), a proverbial saying expressing a disorderly rout.

12. See on Lv 26 4 and on c. 11 10.

15–48. The Curse for Disobedience.

22. The sword] rather, 'drought.'

23, 24. A graphic description of long-continued drought. In Palestine the E. wind is hot and dry ; and, blowing from the desert, is often full of fine sand-dust which gives the

sky the appearance of burnished metal. When this wind (called the 'sirocco') is strong, it produces the terrible sand storm so destructive to life, when 'the rain of the land is powder and dust': see on Lv 26 19. **26. Fray**] frighten, or scare: cp. 1 S 17 44 2 S 21 10. **27. The botch of Egypt**] the boil with which the Egyptians were plagued: see Ex 9 9. **Emerods**] hæmorrhoids, as in 1 S 5 6. What is meant is probably the Oriental bubonic plague. **28.** They will be afflicted with mental as well as bodily diseases.

30–34. These troubles are the consequences of defeat in war and oppression by foreign nations. For a historical instance see Jg 6 3-6.

34. For the sight of thine eyes] i.e. on account of what you see. **36. Serve other gods**] see on 4 28. **37.** Cp. 1 K 9 7-9.

38. Cp. Hag 1 6-11. **40. Shall cast its fruit**] i.e. unripe. **42.** See on Ex 10 4-6.

49. The Chaldeans or Assyrians are meant: see Jer 5 15 Hab 1 6-8.

53–57. This crowning horror of a long-continued siege actually took place during the siege of Samaria by the Syrians (2 K 6 26-29), in the siege of Jerusalem by Nebuchadnezzar (Lam 4 10), and later in the final overthrow of Jerusalem by Titus, as recorded by Josephus in his 'Wars of the Jews.' **58.** The **name of** God is His revealed character: see on Nu 6 27. The name here, **Jehovah thy God**, expresses what God is in Himself, and what He is to Israel. He is the eternal and self-existent God who has made Israel His people.

64, 65. These words were fulfilled at the exile, and even more literally at the destruction of Jerusalem during the Roman supremacy. Since that time the Jews have been repeatedly persecuted and driven from one country to another ; but, wonderfully enough, they have always preserved their identity. They still present the strange spectacle of a nation without a country: see on Nu 23 9. **65. The failing of the eyes** indicates the gradual extinction of hope: cp. v. 32. **68.** After the capture of Jerusalem the Roman general Titus sent a great many captives to the Egyptian mines.

No man shall buy you] This does not mean 'shall redeem you,' but 'purchase you as slaves.' They would be exposed for sale as slaves, and no man would consider them worth the buying.

PART 3
Third Discourse (Chs. 29, 30)

CHAPTER 29
Exhortations and Warnings

In this chapter the covenant is renewed and enforced with a reminder of God's goodness and the consequences of disobedience.

3. Temptations] i.e. provings or trials : see

on 7 19. **4.** The people have not laid these things to heart. For the form of expression see on the 'hardening of Pharaoh's heart' (Ex 4 21). **6. Not eaten bread**] but manna. They have been entirely dependent on God, and His care in providing for them should teach them humility and obedience. The goodness of

God should lead to repentance. **11. Your little ones**] Children share the privileges and responsibilities of the covenant into which they enter by circumcision. **15. With** *him* **that is not here**] i.e. with succeeding generations : see on 5³. **18. A root that beareth gall and wormwood**] The reference is to any one who secretly entices his neighbours to idolatry : see 13⁶,¹³, and for an instance Josh 7¹³,²⁵. The words are used in Heb 12¹⁵.

19. Imagination] RV 'stubbornness.' **To add drunkenness to thirst**] i.e. the commission of the sin to the desire to commit it. RV, however, renders the words 'to destroy the moist with the dry,' which seems to be a proverbial expression, like 'root and branch,' indicating the destruction of the whole nation. The sinner perishes not alone in his iniquity, but involves others along with him. The LXX seems to understand the phrase in this sense, for it has 'lest the sinner destroy the innocent along with him.' Achan again furnishes an illustration. See Josh 22²⁰. **23.** Contrast the description of the good land that Jehovah intends His people to enjoy, Dt 8⁷,⁹. **24.** Cp. Jer 5¹⁹ 22⁸,⁹.

29. The meaning of this v. seems to be, 'we know not the entire nature and extent of the divine judgments ; it is enough for us and for our children to have heard the commandments of God and to do them.'

CHAPTER 30
PROMISES AND APPEALS

A promise of restoration, even after abandonment and rejection, is held out, on condition of repentance ; and an appeal is made to the people to choose the way of obedience and life rather than that of disobedience and death.

6. Circumcision is the sign of the covenant. To circumcise the heart is to consecrate it to God : cp. on Lv 19²³. **11. Hidden**] RV 'hard,' lit. 'wonderful.' God's law is not unintelligible or impracticable. It is a revealed thing (see 29²⁹). All that is essential in revelation is plain ; it is within the compass of human understanding and will. St. Paul applies these words to the law of righteousness by faith : see Ro 10⁶. **15-20.** An earnest appeal to the people to choose the way of obedience and life. **20. He** *is* **thy life**] To love God is life : cp. Prov 8³⁵,³⁶.

PART 4
THE LAST WORDS OF MOSES (Chs. 31–34)

CHAPTER 31
FAREWELL EXHORTATIONS OF MOSES TO THE PEOPLE AND JOSHUA. HE DELIVERS THE LAW TO THE PRIESTS. THE ASSEMBLING OF THE CONGREGATION

1. These words] i.e. the following words. **2. Go out and come in**] i.e. perform the office of a leader : see on Nu 27¹⁷. **3.** Jehovah is the real Leader of the hosts of Israel : Joshua is the human instrument : cp. Nu 23²². **9. This law**] i.e. the Deuteronomic law, especially that contained in chs. 12–26 : see intro. to c. 12. **10.** The Feast of Tabernacles was at the beginning of the year of release : see on Lv 23²³⁻⁴³, and cp. Lv 25⁹. On the reading of the law at this season see e.g. Neh 8. **14.** Cp. Nu 27¹²⁻²³ and notes. **16. Go a whoring**] see on Ex 34¹⁵. **19. A witness for me**] When the threatened punishment had fallen, the song would remain to testify that God, who foresaw their apostasy, had warned them against it : see v. 21. The song would also be a means of bringing them to repentance. **26. In the side of**] i.e. beside. The tables with the Ten Commandments were kept in the ark : see on Ex 16³⁴.

CHAPTER 32
THE SONG OF MOSES

The theme of this noble Song is the goodness of Jehovah in choosing Israel and bringing

them into a rich land. When they provoke Him with their forgetfulness and unfaithfulness, He disciplines them. But He does not utterly reject them ; when they repent He takes part with them against their enemies and delivers them. It will be observed that the exodus begins and concludes with a Song of Moses : see Ex 15¹⁻¹⁸. Ps 90 is also attributed to him.

1-6. Heaven and earth are called to witness the perfect righteousness and faithfulness of Jehovah which Israel has requited with ingratitude.

2. As the dew] in its gentleness and beneficent results : cp. Isa 55¹⁰,¹¹ Ps 133³ Job 29²²,²³. **3. Name of the LORD**] i.e. His character : see on 28⁵⁸. **4. The Rock**] This frequent name of Jehovah expresses His absolute and unwavering faithfulness : see e.g. Ps 18². Observe the number of words in this v. all emphasising this attribute of the divine character, and serving to throw into stronger relief the fickleness of Israel. **5.** The first part of this v. is obscure, and various emendations have been suggested. RV has 'they have dealt corruptly with him (i.e. with Jehovah), they are not his children, it is their blemish ; they are a perverse and crooked generation,' which seems to express the general meaning of the original.

7-14. Think of the goodness of Jehovah in choosing Israel, rescuing them in the wilderness, and bringing them into a rich land. **8.** Jehovah is not the God of Israel only, but of all the nations of the earth. He has, however, a special favour towards Israel ; and, when He divided the world among the nations, He left room for the people whom He had chosen.

9. The converse is also true. Jehovah is the portion of His people : see e.g. Nu 18 20 Ps 16 5, 6 73 26 142 5 Jer 10 16. **10.** He found him] like a lost child or wandering sheep. Led him about] RV 'compassed him about.' **11.** The image is that of the old eagle encouraging her timorous young to fly. So Jehovah disciplined Israel in the wilderness, preparing the people for their life in Canaan : see on Ex 19 4. **12.** *There was* **no strange god with him**] i.e. with Jehovah. He did everything for Israel. No other god, therefore, has any claim upon their gratitude and obedience. **14. Rams .. of Bashan**] see on Nu 21 33-35. **Fat of kidneys of wheat**] the finest and most nourishing of wheat, the kidneys being enclosed in the best fat of the animal : cp. Nu 18 12, where the Heb. is 'all the fat of .. '

15–18. All this grace Israel has requited with forgetfulness and unfaithfulness.

15. Jeshurun] (cp. 33 5, 26 Isa 44 2) is a poetical name for Israel, meaning probably 'the righteous one': see on Nu 23 10. Prosperity made Israel self-willed and forgetful : see on 4 25, and cp. 8 10-18. **16. Jealousy**] see on Ex 20 5. **17. Unto devils, not to God**] RV 'unto demons which were no God': cp. v. 21. The 'demons' may mean the divinities worshipped in Assyria in the form of colossal bulls : cp. Ps 106 37.

19–33. In consequence of this perversity Jehovah is provoked and corrects them in His anger. **20. No faith**] i.e. no faithfulness or fidelity. They have broken their covenant with Jehovah. **21. Vanities**] i.e. false gods : see e.g. Isa 41 29 44 10 Jer 8 19 10 15 1 Cor 8 4. **Not a people**] i.e. most probably an undisciplined horde of barbarians, whom God will permit to gain the mastery over Israel. In Ro 10 19 this passage is applied to the Gentiles, whose acceptance of the gospel will have the effect of provoking the jealousy of the chosen people and moving them ultimately to follow their example. **22. Lowest hell**] RV 'pit': Heb. *Sheol.* God's righteous indignation reaches to the deepest and remotest part of the universe : cp. Am 9 2. **27. Behave themselves strangely**] RV 'misdeem,' draw a false conclusion from Jehovah's treatment of Israel by taking credit to themselves for its humiliation : see Nu 14 15-17 and note there, and cp. 9 28. **28. They**] Israel. **29. Their latter end**] the consequences of their conduct.

30. Shut them up] delivered them into the hand of their enemies. **31. Their rock**] the gods of the heathen.

32. Their vine] The analogy with **their rock** in v. 31 suggests that the reference is to the enemy, but more probably it is to Israel itself, whose apostasy is thus severely condemned. Israel is frequently compared to a vine of God's planting, which instead of bearing fruit is either fruitless (Hos 10 1) or bears wild grapes (Isa 5 2-7). Sodom and Gomorrah are types of wickedness, and the vines ascribed to them may be no specific plants, but figurative growths or outcomes. **33. Dragons**] i.e. serpents.

34–43. When Israel is reduced to extremities Jehovah will be merciful to them and avenge them. **34. This**] referring to the vengeance of God (v. 35), which for the present is laid up in store against the day when it will be manifested. **35.** RV 'vengeance is mine and recompence, at the time when their foot shall slide.' **36. Shut up, or left**] i.e. left at large, a proverbial expression meaning everybody: see 1 K 14 10 21 21 2 K 9 8 14 26. **37.** Cp. Jg 10 14 Jer 2 28. **39. No god with me**] This is almost equivalent to 'no god beside me.' Jehovah alone is able to work and save : cp. Isa 43 10-13. **40. Lift up my hand**] The usual attitude of taking an oath : see Gn 14 22 Nu 14 30 mg. Rev 10 5, 6. **I live for ever**] rather, 'As I live for ever.' **41. Mine enemies**] the heathen. **42. From the beginning .. enemy**] RV 'from the head of the leaders of the enemy.' **43.** Read, with RM, 'Praise His people, ye nations, for .. He will make expiation for His land, His people (or, for the land of His people),' i.e. He will make atonement for the blood shed in the land by the slaughter of those who shed it. Then those who witness this righteous judgment will recognise that Israel is the people of Jehovah and will bless, or congratulate, them.

44. Hoshea] see on Ex 17 9.

48–52. See Nu 27 12-14 and notes there. On the death of Aaron see Nu 20 22-29.

CHAPTER 33
THE BLESSING OF MOSES

This chapter contains the last words or 'swan-song' of Moses. Immediately before his death he takes farewell of the people, and blesses each of the tribes in turn, as Jacob had done on his deathbed: see Gn 49. The two blessings should be compared ; see also on v. 4.

2–5. Introduction, describing the majestic appearance of Jehovah to His chosen people. **2.** Cp. Jg 5 4 Hab 3 3. **Seir**] Edom (see on Nu 20 22-29). **Mount Paran**] the S. boundary of Canaan. The appearance of Jehovah is described as a sunrise. The glory of His Presence appeared on Mt. Sinai, His beams smote the top of Mt. Seir, and glowed upon Mt. Paran. Read, 'He came forth from the midst of (not, with) the myriad shining saints that encircle His throne : at His right hand was a burning fire for them.' The last clause is difficult and very probably corrupt. **3. All his saints**] i.e. Israel's saints. **They sat down at thy feet**] as disciples listening to the words of their teacher. **4.** This v. may be interpolated. Moses could hardly have written it himself. The superscription in v. 1 seems also to indicate that a later writer has written down the Blessing of Moses. **5. He was king**] Jehovah, not Moses: cp. on Nu 23 21. On Jeshurun see 32 15.

6. Reuben is the eldest of the sons of Jacob. There is a difficulty in the second half of this v., in which AV has inserted a negative not in the original. It may be better to read with RV 'yet let his men be few.' In the earlier blessing of Jacob it is said that Reuben will not endure, or have preëminence, on account of his misdeed (Gn 35 22). Owing to their position on the E. of the Jordan the Reubenites had a somewhat precarious hold of their territory. The Ammonites were troublesome (Jg 10, 11); on the Moabite Stone (see on Nu 21 29) most of the Reubenite cities are said to be occupied by the Moabites ; and Tiglath-Pileser carried them captive to Assyria (1 Ch 5 6, 22, 26 2 K 15 29. This constant danger of extinction may be alluded to here. But the text may be corrupt, and some words may have dropped out. Some MSS of LXX insert Simeon as the subject of the second clause. It will be observed that he is not otherwise mentioned at all, though the omission may be explained by the fact that the tribe of Simeon was absorbed in that of Judah (Josh 19 9).

7. Let his hands .. for him] RV 'with his hands he contended for himself' (or, 'for it,' i.e. the people). Judah was the champion of the tribes: see e.g. Jg 1 1 20 18.

8. On the **Urim** and **Thummim** see Ex 28 30. Jehovah is addressed in this v., and Levi is meant by **thy holy one**. Three privileges of the priestly tribe are referred to in this blessing, viz. the use of the Urim and Thummim, the teaching of the Law, and the presentation of incense and sacrifice (v. 10 : see on Nu 18, 35 18, 9-15). **Whom thou didst prove, etc.**] At Massah and Meribah the people certainly proved and strove with Jehovah. But unless there is a change of person here, and again in v. 10, it would appear that the person addressed is still Jehovah, who is represented as having proved and contended with Levi there, in the persons of Moses and Aaron. See Nu 20 12 and Dt 8 2. **9.** This v. refers to the separation of the tribe of Levi to their sacred duties. They have no lot or inheritance among their brethren. There may be a particular reference to the exceptional zeal of Levi mentioned in Ex 32 26-29: cp. for the thought Mt 10 37

Lk 9 59-62. **11. Them that rise against him**] such as Korah: see Nu 16.

12. The beloved of the LORD] is Benjamin, and the subject of the second and third clauses is Jehovah, as in AV. The v. refers to the fact that Zion, the dwelling-place of Jehovah, was in the land of Benjamin. Jerusalem was on the border line between Benjamin and Judah, so that Jewish writers speak of the Temple being in Benjamin while its courts were in Judah. Hence, Jehovah is here said to dwell between Benjamin's **shoulders**, i.e. mountain slopes.

13. The fertility of the land of Joseph is also emphasised in the earlier blessing of Jacob : see Gn 49 22-26. The **precious things of heaven** is the rain, and the **deep that coucheth beneath** is the springs of water. The words **for the dew** should perhaps be read ' from above.' **14. Things put forth by the moon**] RV 'things of the growth of the moons,' i.e. probably of the months, things put forth month by month, according to their season. **16. Good will of him that dwelt in the bush**] Jehovah revealed Himself in the bush as the Deliverer of Israel : see Ex 3 2, 6-8 The latter part of the v. is identical with that of Gn 49 26. **17.** Read, ' His firstling bullock, majesty is his, and his horns are the horns of the wild ox.' Ephraim is meant, and is compared to a wild ox : see on Nu 23 22.

18. Thy going out] The reference is to the commercial intercourse between Zebulun and foreign nations. The phrase is almost equivalent to ' exports.' Zebulun seems to have had an outlet to the Mediterranean Sea ; cp. the next v. and also Gn 49 13 Isa 9 1. Nazareth was in the land of Zebulun. **In thy tents**] Issachar was an inland tribe. It possessed the Plain of Jezreel, or Esdraelon, a district of extraordinary fertility and the granary of Palestine. Issachar is accordingly represented as rejoicing in its tents, i.e. pursuing a peaceful agricultural life (Gn 49 14, 15).

19. The people] RV 'peoples,' their heathen neighbours who trade with them, particularly the Phœnicians. These they are here said to **call unto the mountain** where they offer **sacrifices of righteousness**, i.e. sacrifices that are offered rightly. It would appear that in the land of Zebulun and Issachar there were certain mountain sanctuaries where sacrificial feasts were held to which these tribes were wont to invite their neighbours, and that these gatherings were a source of commercial advantage to them. **The abundance of the seas** refers to the maritime commerce mentioned above, and the **treasures hid in the sand** have been supposed to refer to the manufacture of glass for which the sands at the mouth of the river Belus, which flows into the Bay of Acre, were famous. The Roman historian

Pliny says indeed that it was here that glass was first invented or discovered by some sailors who lit a fire upon the sand and accidentally produced glass.

20. He that enlargeth Gad] i.e. Jehovah who has given him the wide territory E. of the Jordan : see Nu 32. The Gadites are compared to a lion, as in 1 Ch 12⁸. **With the crown**] RV 'yea the crown.' **21. The first part**] Gad chose the part E. of the Jordan which was first conquered and also the first to be allotted : see Nu 32. The next clause should read, 'for there was a ruler's (or commander's) portion reserved.' Gad obtained a portion suitable for such a warlike tribe. It was a 'commander's share,' or what might be called a 'lion's share' : see v. 20. **He came with the heads of the people,** etc.] The Gadites, true to their promise, crossed the Jordan with the other tribes and assisted them in the conquest of the land : see on Nu 32¹⁶⁻²³.

22. RV 'Dan is a lion's whelp that leapeth forth from Bashan.' This depicts the stealth and violence of the Danites in war or in marauding expeditions : see e.g. their capture of Laish, Jg 18. The forest and ravines of Bashan were the haunts of wild beasts: see on Bashan, Nu 21³³⁻³⁵.

23. Naphtali touched the Sea of Galilee on the E. and included some of the richest land and most beautiful scenery in Palestine. The Plain of Gennesaret was specially luxuriant. Josephus calls it the 'ambition of nature.' The **west** should be the 'sea,' i.e. the Sea of Gennesaret or Galilee, not the Mediterranean in the W.

24. The first clause should probably read, 'Blessed above sons be Asher.' Northern Galilee has always been distinguished for the cultivation of the olive. Jewish writers say, 'In Asher oil flows like a river' : cp. Gn 49²⁰. In ancient times this district was one of the main sources of the supply of olive oil (cp. 2 Ch 2¹⁰), and even now great quantities are exported to Constantinople and elsewhere. The expression **dip his foot in oil** refers to the ancient custom of treading the olives to obtain the oil. Cp. Mic 6¹⁵. Stone presses, however, were also used for this purpose. Remains of them are still to be seen in the neighbourhood of Tyre. **25. Thy shoes**] rather, 'thy bars' or bolts, referring to the impregnable fortresses guarding the mountain passes of Galilee. Asher, lying in the N., was the gate of Canaan. **Thy strength**] A word of very doubtful signification, not found elsewhere. It means, perhaps, 'rest' or 'security,' and the clause will then imply that Asher's security will never be disturbed.

26. On **Jeshurun,** see v. 5. **In thy help**] rather, 'for thy help.' The clouds are said to be the chariot of God : see Ps 68³³, ³⁴ 104³

Nah 1³. **27. Refuge**] RV 'dwelling-place' : cp. Ps 90¹. Jehovah protects Israel both above and beneath.

28. RV 'Israel dwelleth in safety, the fountain of Jacob alone, in a land of corn and wine ; yea, his heavens drop down dew.' Israel separated from all other nations (see on Nu 23⁹) dwells securely in a rich land. For the expression **fountain of Jacob,** see Ps 68²⁶ Isa 48¹. **29. Thine enemies shall be found liars unto thee**] RV 'shall submit themselves unto thee.' The idea is that of conquered nations cringing before their victors and protesting (perhaps feigning) submission.

CHAPTER 34
THE DEATH OF MOSES

In obedience to the divine command (32⁴⁸⁻⁵²) Moses ascends to the top of Mt. Nebo, whence he views the Land of Promise. Thereafter he dies and God buries him. No man knows of his sepulchre.

1-4. Dan is used to indicate the extreme N., as in the phrase 'from Dan to Beersheba,' though it was not till the time of the Judges that the Danites settled in that district : see Jg 18²⁸, ²⁹. The **utmost sea** (lit. 'hinder, i.e. western, sea' : see on 11²⁴) is the Mediterranean. The **south** is the Negeb : see on Nu 13¹⁷. Zoar lay at the SE. end of the Dead Sea. There is no need to suppose that there was anything miraculous in this vision of the whole land. From the mountains of Moab travellers tell us that they can see the entire valley of the Jordan with Mt. Hermon at the extreme N. Lebanon and Carmel are visible, and the Mediterranean, 50 m. distant, can be seen like a silver streak in the glittering sunshine. Such extensive views are favoured by the exceptional clearness of the atmosphere in Palestine : see on 27¹¹⁻¹³.

5. It is implied here that Moses was alone. But Josephus says that he was accompanied to the top of the hill by 'the senate, and Eleazar, and Joshua.' After viewing the land Moses dismissed the senate, and 'as he was about to embrace Eleazar and Joshua was still discoursing with them a cloud stood over him on a sudden and he disappeared in a certain valley.' With this compare the departure of Elijah, 2 K 2¹¹. Jewish writers take literally the words at the end of this v., **according to the word of the LORD,** and say that God 'kissed him and he slept.'

6. He buried him] i.e. God buried him. This probably means no more than what is expressed in the second half of the v. that his sepulchre was never known. God alone knew where His servant was buried. Fuller quaintly says that God not only buried Moses, but buried his sepulchre also lest it should become a shrine of idol-worship to future generations.

Later Jewish legend says that Michael, who was supposed to be the angel who conducted pious souls to Paradise, came into conflict with Satan as to the disposal of the body of Moses. Whether Satan was regarded as trying to prevent the body of Moses being honoured, or as seeking to seduce the people into paying too much honour to it, is uncertain. The legend is referred to in the Epistle of Jude, v. 9, and the quotation there is made from a Jewish history called 'The Assumption of Moses.' A great many legends about Moses are circulated among the Mohammedans. The words unto this day indicate that the writer of this account of the death of Moses lived long after its occurrence.

7. An hundred and twenty years old] see on Ex 2 21.

8. The usual period of mourning seems to have been thirty days : see Nu 20 29 Gn 50 3, and cp. 21 13. Of these the first seven were more stringently observed : see Gn 50 10. In addition to the natural manifestations of grief, mourning in the East was, and still is, accompanied with a great deal of ceremony : see e.g. Jer 9 17, 18 16 6-8 Ezk 24 16, 17 Mt 9 23. The mourning for Moses was doubtless very genuine. Like many another great person, he was better appreciated after his death than during his lifetime. In his life he was much tried by the murmuring, disobedience, and jealousy of those for whom he lived, but these same people made great lamentation for him when he was dead.

9. 'God buries the workman but carries on the work.' See on Nu 27 18-23.

10–12. RV 'There hath not arisen a prophet since in Israel like unto Moses' : cp. Nu 12 6-8. The words point to a time considerably later than the death of Moses (cp. v. 6, 'unto this day'), when his real greatness could be appreciated and his superiority to all the great prophets and leaders who succeeded him could be rightly estimated.

JOSHUA

INTRODUCTION

1. The Book. In this book we have the record of the Conquest of Canaan by the people of Israel and of their settlement in the land. The value of the book consists chiefly in (1) its description of a critical period in the history of the Hebrews. The war not only gave them a dwelling-place among the peoples of the earth, but carried a step further the consolidation of the tribes into a nation. The elements of unity were already theirs, the chief of them being their common acknowledgment of Jehovah as their God. Their brotherhood in blood was consecrated and maintained by their brotherhood in religion. The discipline of the wanderings in the wilderness, the perils encountered in the successful attempts to obtain a lodgment in the land, and the hardships of the war endured by the Israelites side by side, served to strengthen the bond of union and to develop the sense of nationality. As is always the case with strong men, their noble qualities were brought out in the presence of difficulties. (2) The book is also valuable for its revelation of the Hand of God in the movements of men. He did not give them the land He had promised them without causing them to fight for it. But the gift is recognised in this book as none the less His. He sanctions their advance. He directs their movements. He makes them victorious. He allows them to be defeated. He makes them conquerors in the end. The book enables us to see a little into the way in which God works out His purposes in human affairs.

2. The life and character of Joshua. Son of Nun, of the tribe of Ephraim, he bore originally the name of Hoshea (Nu 13 8, 16 Dt 32 44), which was changed by Moses to the more significant form Jehoshua ('Jehovah (is) salvation'). His intimate relation to Moses—like that of Elisha to Elijah—afforded an unique education for the future leader of Israel, who had been divinely designated (Dt 1 37, 38) as successor to the great Lawgiver, and was solemnly consecrated by him to that office by the laying-on of hands (Nu 27 18-23, cp. Dt 31 14-23). The echo of Moses' charge, 'Be strong and of a good courage' (Dt 31 23), is still ringing in his ears as he takes up his work in the plains of Jordan; the 'grace' of that 'laying-on of hands,' showing itself (Dt 34 9) in a spirit of wisdom and a bearing that won the unquestioning obedience

of the wayward host (Josh 1 16-18 Nu 27 20), is upon him from first to last. His authority is strengthened (Josh 3 7 4 14) by the miracle of Jordan, his courage renewed by the vision of the Heavenly Captain (5 13-15). Even his temporary dismay at the rout before Ai is token of his absolute reliance on divine aid, and of his knowledge of the fortunes and tendencies of war (see on 7 6). The swiftness with which he deals his successive blows upon southern (c. 10) and northern (c. 11) confederacy bespeaks an alert and intrepid general; the impartiality with which he conducts the assignment of the tribal territories exhibits him as an ideal judge and ruler; and finally the tender severity of his admonition to Achan (7 19 f.) gives us a glimpse of the true priestly heart beating beneath the warrior's mail. In his unswerving faith and obedience to the call, in the incorruptible righteousness of his administration, in the gentle severity of his rebuke, as well as in his life's work, Jesus (Heb 4 8) the son of Nun is a veritable type of Jesus the Son of God.

3. The Conquest of Canaan. The book of Joshua opens with the crossing of the Jordan by the forces of Israel and the establishment of a great headquarters' camp at Gilgal. By invading Western Palestine by the ford near Jericho instead of advancing round the S. of the Dead Sea, Joshua was able to drive a wedge between the Canaanites on the N. and those in the S. of the country, and thus to prevent a union of all the tribes against him. The first attack was made upon Jericho. This was the key to Western Palestine, for it was on the way to all the passes of importance into the interior. Jericho taken, Ai, another town on the principal road to the W., soon followed. The Gibeonites by a trick secured an alliance with the conqueror, who marched to attack the kings of the S. and defeated them in a pitched battle at Bethhoron, afterwards overrunning their country and destroying their towns. Thereafter the victorious leader turned his attention to the kings of the N. and defeated them in a great battle near the waters of Merom. After that, according to the chronicler, 'the land rested from war.'

The conquest thus outlined was, however, far from complete. The enemy may have been routed but was not destroyed. The towns may have been overthrown, but many of them were probably soon re-fortified. And the complete subjugation of the enemy was accomplished slowly and with difficulty, not by a general campaign, but by individual tribes fighting for themselves and gradually extending their borders. We have illustrations of this in such accounts as that of Caleb driving out the sons of Anak from Hebron (15 14), and that of the children of Joseph contending with difficulty against the Perizzites and the Rephaim (17 14-18). The country was difficult for warfare, being mountainous, and favoured the defenders. The Israelites having no chariots could not meet their enemies in the plains (17 16), and the valleys thus remained long in possession of the Canaanites. And in many cases the advance was slow and the success uncertain: see e.g. 17 12, 13, and cp. Jg 1.

The inhabitants of Canaan at the time of the invasion, generally described as Canaanites, were divided into a number of petty kingdoms, and had no bond of union save hatred of the invaders. Amongst their divisions were the Amorites, Jebusites, Hivites, and suchlike; also there seem to have been here and there in the land surviving elements of an aboriginal people represented by the Rephaim and the sons of Anak. Their moral and religious condition is indicated by such passages as Dt 9 5 and Lv 18. It was so vicious and depraved as to render dangerous, if not indeed impossible, any association with them on the part of the Israelites. Uncompromising opposition to them was the only practical attitude for a people led by Jehovah, and holding His law. Hence arose the moral necessity for that order for their extermination, which has sometimes been a stumbling-block to the religious mind. The attempt to carry out that order had an effect for good upon the Israelites, in so far as it engaged them in a work of moral and spiritual sanitation: the failure to carry it out completely left open to them a source of weakness and danger, from which sprang many of their subsequent corruptions and defections from the pure worship of Jehovah.

The Canaanites were an agricultural people,
somewhat more advanced than the Israelites in the arts of civilisation. The conquest of them, accordingly, meant for Israel a certain material progress, and an entry into conditions which constituted in many ways an ideal nursery of religion. They passed from a nomadic and pastoral state to the more complex stage of a settled, agricultural condition, with possibilities of village and city life. The division of the conquered territory and the settlement of the Israelite tribes upon it occupy chs. 13-21 of the book of Joshua, which have consequently been called the 'Domesday Book of the Old Testament.'

4. Authorship. The title of the book is no indication of authorship, but like Judges and Samuel has reference to the principal figure in the history. The hero of the book is undoubtedly Joshua, with whose deeds it is largely occupied. Joshua is said to have written a record of the covenant with God, which the people made shortly before his death (24 26), in 'the Book of the Law of God'; and some of the chroniclers of a later date may have borrowed from his own words some of the passages which have come down to us. This, however, is mere speculation. What is agreed by scholars is that the book is a compilation, similar to the Pentateuch, of which it is the continuation. Indeed, 'The five books of Moses' so-called and the book of Joshua form a whole usually termed the Hexateuch. In its present form the book belongs to the same date as the Pentateuch, and the same older sources—the Primitive, the Priestly, and the Deuteronomic—are its basis. These sources contain traditions which were doubtless handed down either orally or in writing from the days in which the great deeds recorded were done, and in one case, at any rate, they give a quotation from the book of Jasher, a collection of songs of very early date (10 12,13); and we need have little hesitation in accepting the outline of the history given in the book as substantially historical.

Analysis. The book falls naturally into three parts: chs. 1-12, The Conquest; chs. 13-21, The Division of the Land; chs. 22-24, Closing Scenes.

PART 1

The Conquest (Chs. 1-12)

CHAPTER 1

Joshua by Divine Commission Succeeds Moses

Chs. 1 1-5 12 record the preparations for the Holy War.

1. Now (better, 'and') **after the death of Moses .. it came to pass**] These words clearly mark the book which follows as a sequel to
Deuteronomy. The book of Judges begins with a precisely similar phrase.

The LORD spake unto Joshua] This formula 'the LORD spake,' which so constantly recurs in the first books of the Bible, corresponds to the more direct formula of the prophets, 'Thus saith the LORD.' It is a characteristic feature of the OT., distinguishing the literature of the Hebrews from that of other nations of antiquity, and marking their claim to express in a very special way the will of Almighty God. It is, in fact, one of the most obvious indications of that which we call 'inspiration.' We may not of course be able, in a given instance, to define the exact mode in which the divine will was communicated. Was it by the Urim and Thummim, or in a dream? Or was it rather an inner conviction borne in upon the soul, voiceless but clear and definite, such as is no uncommon experience with those who are in the habit of communing with God? But the importance of the phrase lies less in any hint of the manner of the revelation than in its testimony to the fact of it. However it came, the thought was recognised as an utterance of God. **Minister**] Joshua had been Moses' attendant and right-hand man—his 'chief of staff.'

4. Boundaries S. and SE., 'the wilderness'; N., Lebanon; NE., the Euphrates; W., the Mediterranean or 'Great Sea.' These, the providential (Gn 15 18 Ex 23 31), and in some sense natural, boundaries of the territory of Israel, were only attained for a brief period during the reigns of David and Solomon. **All the land of the Hittites**] see on Gn 10 15.

8. This book of the law] This obviously refers to the 'law' described in Dt 31 9 as written by Moses and delivered to the Levites and elders. That it embraces a considerable nucleus of the Pentateuchal legislation (including, of course, the bulk of Ex 20–23) few critics would deny.

11. Prepare you victuals] Joshua has the general's eye for the commissariat.

12 f. See Nu 32 20-32 for Moses' injunction to the two and a half tribes, and their promise to obey.

14, 15. On this side Jordan] In both places RV rightly translates 'beyond Jordan,' i.e. on the E. side of Jordan. A little point, but important as showing that the writer (or editor) of this passage was one who resided W. of Jordan.

CHAPTER 2
The Two Spies at Jericho

Joshua himself had been one of twelve sent by Moses on a similar errand, some thirty-eight years before (Nu 13). The incident, natural in itself, acquires a special interest as bringing before us for the first time Rahab, the great-great-grandmother of David, and so human ancestress of our Saviour (Mt 1 3-6, cp. Ruth 4 18-22). It affords incidentally a signal instance among Gentiles of belief in the power of the true God (2 11 f.), which is rewarded (6 25), like the similar attitude of Ruth the Moabitess (Ruth 1 16), with incorporation into Israel and into the direct line of Israel's Hope.

1. Shittim] i.e. 'Acacias.' The district referred to is the part of the Jordan basin opposite Jericho, where acacias still are found. **An harlot's**] 'We know nothing of her after-conduct, but we may well believe that the faith which an apostle could praise (Heb 11 31 Jas 2 25) was accompanied by a true conversion' (HDB. art. 'Rahab'). See on v. 10 and 6 25.

6. She had brought them, etc.] Then, as now, the flat roofs of Eastern houses were used for such purposes as drying flax stalks. The flax would be ripe (cp. Ex 9 31, 32) shortly before wheat harvest.

7. The fords] Clearly, therefore, there were fords in the neighbourhood of Jericho. The account of the miraculous crossing in chs. 3, 4 cannot be based on ignorance of that fact. At the present time fords are said to be comparatively rare in the southern reaches of Jordan.

9. Your terror is fallen upon us] Cp. Ex 15 14-16. Compare 5 1 for a similar panic produced by the crossing of Jordan.

10 f. Rahab had followed the career of Israel with fascinated interest. She is represented as knowing and using the covenant name of 'Jehovah' and as recognising His universal sovereignty. Her whole attitude is in striking contrast to that of her fellow-countrymen.

16. The mountain] the limestone ridges full of caves, NW. of Jericho.

24. Do faint] RV here (and in 2 9 and Ex 15 15) 'do melt away.'

CHAPTER 3
The Passage of Jordan

This is the initial miracle of Joshua's leadership. Its moral effect upon the Israelite host is suggested in 3 7 and 4 14; that wrought upon the Canaanites in 5 1 (which properly belongs to this section of the book). **3. The ark of the covenant of the LORD your God**] see Ex 25 10-22 and 37 1-9. It was the authoritative symbol of the Divine Presence (cp. Ex 23 20 f.), and as such led the van in the desert marches (Nu 10 33-36). **The priests the Levites**] cp. Dt 18 1. Not that all the Levites were originally priests, as some have interpreted that passage: see e.g. Nu 3 5-10 for the relation of the Levites in general to the 'sons of Aaron.'

4. Two thousand cubits] 3,000 ft.; the ancient Hebrew cubit = 18 in.

15. Jordan overfloweth all his banks] The rank jungle, which fills the bed (150 ft. deep) that Jordan has hollowed out at the bottom of the rift, down which it flows, marks the extent of the April floods. The space is from 200 yards to 1 m. broad, and is what Jeremiah calls (12 5 49 19 50 44) the 'Pride' or 'Swelling' of Jordan. In Ecclus 24 26 we find a proverbial phrase, 'full as . . Jordan in the time of harvest' (RV).

16. We should probably render 'a great way off, at the city Adam, which is beside Zaretan.' The incident of the stoppage of Jordan's waters is not without parallel in history, if we may trust the Arabic historian Nowairi (see Sayce, 'Early Hist of Hebr.,' p. 249). According to his account the water was dammed up by a landslip from midnight on Dec. 8, 1267, 'till the 4th hour of the day.' The narrative is very artless, and whether it be true or simply an echo of the book of Joshua, enables us to conceive how the miracle of the crossing may have happened ; for miracle it still remains, even if wrought out at the will of the author of nature by natural means : being a clear exhibition of personal providential purpose in connexion with the great plan of Israel's mission to the world. The position of **Adam** has been identified with Tel Damieh (a place mentioned, curiously, in Nowairi's narrative), near the mouth of the Jabbok. **Zaretan** may probably be the 'Zarthan' of 1 K 7⁴⁶.

CHAPTER 4
The Double Memorial of the Passage of Jordan

The main subject of the c. is the memorial cairn set up at Gilgal, which is described in two sections, 4¹⁻⁸ and 4²⁰⁻²⁴, separated by the record in a single v. (4⁹) of another cairn set up in the midst of Jordan, and by a long parenthesis (4¹⁰⁻¹⁹) describing in an expanded form the crossing already narrated in 3¹⁴⁻¹⁷. The repetitions are most satisfactorily explained on the hypothesis that the narrator has incorporated extracts from more ancient sources in his narrative.

5. Pass over before the ark] Apparently the twelve, who with the rest of the host have already crossed to the W. bank, are bidden to return to where the priests are still standing with the Ark in the midst of Jordan, to set up a cairn of twelve stones (4⁹) on the spot in the river bed and to take up a stone each in addition and return with it to the bank again.

12. As Moses spake] see Nu 32²⁰ᶠ.

19. The tenth *day* **of the first month**] i.e. Abib or Nisan (March-April). They would reach their camp at Gilgal just in time to select the Paschal Lamb (Ex 12³) to be slain on the fourteenth day : see 5¹⁰.

24. That ye might fear] RV 'that they may fear.'

CHAPTER 5
Renewal of Circumcision and Celebration of the Passover

The two incidents recorded in 5²⁻¹²—Circumcision and the Passover—represent the final stage in the preparation of the people for the Holy War. The Circumcision was a necessary preliminary (Ex 12⁴⁴, ⁴⁸) to the Passover Feast, besides marking for the new generation a reversal of the sentence of 'excommunication' virtually pronounced in Nu 14³³, ³⁴ ; and the Passover—the first recorded celebration since the first anniversary of its institution (Nu 9⁵)—was signalised also by the cessation of the extraordinary 'sacrament' of Manna. Thus the period of the Wanderings is definitely brought to a close.

1. Amorites] represent, roughly speaking, the inhabitants of the highland districts. **Canaanites**] = 'lowlanders,' in the specialised sense, the dwellers on the maritime plain. **Until we were passed over**] RM 'until they were passed over.' It was always thus read by the Jews.

2–9. Renewal of the Rite of Circumcision. This was necessary, because all those who had come out of Egypt already circumcised (except, of course, Joshua and Caleb) had died in the wilderness ; while the new generation of males had not been circumcised by the way (5⁷). This omission of the rite was of course not necessitated by the journeyings, which were certainly not continuous. It was more probably a deliberate disciplinary regulation, as a sign of the broken covenant : see prefatory remarks.

2. Sharp knives] RV 'knives of flint.' LXX curiously relates (in an addition to 24³⁰) that these knives were buried with Joshua in his tomb. Flint knives were used for religious purposes by the Egyptians.

9. The reproach of Egypt] This may mean that the Egyptians, laying great stress on circumcision themselves, regarded the fact of uncircumcision as a reproach. **Gilgal**] mg. 'Rolling.' This etymology, like that of 'Babel' in Gn 11⁹, is now generally recognised as unscientific. It is rather a play on words than a derivation. Yet though the word 'Gilgal' probably signified originally a sacred 'circle' of stones—analogous to the druidic circle found in Britain—it certainly meant, to the Hebrews, the rolling away of reproach.

10. Kept the passover on the fourteenth day] of Nisan, as ordained in Ex 12⁶. They had probably selected the lambs four days before, immediately on their arrival at the camp (see on 4¹⁹); and had rested quietly for three full days after the circumcision. This is the third recorded Passover ; the second (Nu 9⁵) being the first anniversary of the institution. There are only three subsequent observances of the Passover recorded in the OT., viz. Josiah's (2 K 23²¹⁻²³), Hezekiah's (2 Ch 30), and that of the returned exiles (Ezr 6¹⁹ᶠ·), and all of these are after the discovery of the Book of the Law by Hilkiah in 621 B.C. But a notice in 2 Ch 8¹³ ascribes to Solomon similar observances, and critics admit (cp. HDB. art. 'Passover') that unrecorded observances may have gone on all along.

11. On the morrow] The feast of Mazzoth, or Unleavened Bread, was a distinct festival (cp. Lv 23 5, 6) of seven days' duration, following on the one-day feast of the Passover. The two came naturally, in the course of centuries, to be regarded as a single festival, to which either title could be applied (cp. e.g. Lk 22 1).

12. The manna ceased] see prefatory note.

13–15. Vision of the Heavenly Captain.

13. A man] clearly, as elsewhere in Holy Scripture (cp. e.g. Gn 18 2 32 24 Dan 9 21 Zech 1 8 Ac 1 10), an angelic being, to be identified with the promised guide of Ex 23 20-23 (cp. Ex 33 2). Of this angel the LORD says (Ex 23 21): 'My name is in him'; and in Isa 63 9 he is called 'the angel of his presence' (see on Ex 3 2).

CHAPTER 6
THE CAPTURE OF JERICHO

This chapter describes the first and perhaps most decisive action in the war. The impression it produced (6 27) no doubt did much to decide the fortunes of subsequent campaigns. The strange method adopted, by divine injunction, for the reduction of the city, with its jubilee trumpets and its elaborate symbolic use of the number seven, was clearly intended to leave no doubt that the enterprise from first to last was in higher hands than Joshua's. Various attempts have been made to explain the fall of Jericho by natural causes. For instance, it has been suggested that the demonstration of the army in force round the city was intended to distract the attention of the enemy from the sapping and mining operations which were being pushed forward, and which culminated in its fall on the seventh day. Again, an earthquake has been suggested; but if such took place, it was providentially timed, and was capable of prediction by Joshua. The narrator regards the event as entirely miraculous, a direct intervention of Jehovah on behalf of His people. Such also was the tradition in Israel, and it is accepted by the writer of the Epistle to the Hebrews (11 30): 'by *faith* the walls of Jericho fell down.'

3. Ye shall compass] The injunction was calculated to produce derision among the enemy, and so would be a discipline of humiliation for the Israelites. It would also put the Canaanites off their guard and hand them over an easy prey at the critical moment.

4. Rams' horns] rather, 'trumpets of jubilee' or 'loud trumpets.' It is the same word *yobel* used in Lv 25 9. **Seven** is a sacred number among the Semites, and in the Bible signifies 'perfection.' The symbolism is very emphatic here.

9. Rereward] RV 'rearward'=rearguard. **Going on, and blowing**] blowing continually.

17. Accursed] Heb. *Kherem*='devoted,' i.e. irredeemably devoted (Lv 27 28, 29) to the LORD. LXX has 'anathema,' the word which St. Paul uses in Ro 9 3 and elsewhere. It appears to denote a form of consecration, but that invariably with a view to destruction. In Lv 27 21, 28, 29 devoted things are excluded from redemption. In v. 21 the word is translated in AV 'utterly destroyed.'

20. The wall fell down flat] see note at beginning of chapter. This was not the first of Israel's sieges. They had already taken the cities of the Amorites, including Heshbon, which was strongly fortified (Nu 21).

23. And left them] lit. 'and caused them to rest.'

25. She dwelleth in Israel *even* **unto this day**] Unless Rahab's descendants are meant, this must be the touch of a contemporary chronicler (cp. 5 1 and 6 26). On Rahab and her incorporation into Israel, see note at beginning of c. 2. Apparently she had long been prepared (see on 2 10) to adopt Israel's religion, and thus the greatest obstacle was removed. Yet her case, like that of Christ's other foreign ancestress Ruth, remains exceptional, and prefigures, as it were, the world-wide extent of the Messiah's kinship with man.

26. This 'inspired curse' of Joshua was fulfilled, after the lapse of some six centuries, in the reign of Ahab (1 K 16 34). Hiel the Bethelite incurred it, being the first, apparently, to attempt a complete rebuilding and fortification of the accursed city, although informal settlements seem to have been there from the first. It is mentioned, e.g. in Josh 18 21, as one of ten 'cities' of Benjamin, and again in the time of David (2 S 10 5). Here we have another note of comparatively early date. If the writer of this passage had known of the fulfilment, he would surely have recorded it.

CHAPTER 7
REPULSE AT AI, DUE TO ACHAN'S SIN

The capture of Jericho is followed by an attempt upon Ai, a place of strategic importance, as commanding a main entrance into the interior of Canaan westward; the upper entrance into the valley of Aijalon being commanded by Ai and Bethel. This c. has an interest of its own, as exhibiting Joshua in a new light, as the spiritual guide, drawing out, with the mingled sweetness and severity of a father (v. 19), the sinner's detailed confession (see on v. 20). The incident of Achan's sin and its effects upon the fortunes of Israel is an illustration (a) of the penalty of solidarity —the inevitable spread of the results of sin and pollution from a single member to the whole body ; (b) of the conditional nature of God's promises of success. In contrast to the many previous assurances, it is announced that the presence of God is to be withdrawn absolutely (v. 12) unless the 'accursed thing' be removed. Further, at the very beginning of the Holy War, Israel is taught—and we through Israel—that exceptional temptations do not excuse a lowering of the standard of conduct on the part of God's soldiers.

6 f. Joshua's extreme despondency is really a mark of his soldiery capacity. He was general enough to know the immense moral effect of even a slight success or reverse at the beginning of a war. Moreover, no one who had Joshua's sense of divine mission and vocation, as represented e.g. by the message of 1 2-9 and the vision of 5 13 f., could fail to interpret the reverse as implying some mysterious cause of divine displeasure. And though Joshua is chidden for the faithlessness of his despondency (7 10), his uneasiness is at the same moment (7 11) justified and explained.

20. There is a special interest about this confession of Achan's, because its wording is practically identical with that of the traditional form of confession which seems to have been used by those who brought sin and trespass offerings. A particular confession is enjoined in such passages as Lv 5 5 Nu 5 6,7. The form was as follows : 'I have sinned, I have done perversely, I have rebelled, and thus' (here follows detailed confession) 'have I done, but I return in penitence before Thee, and let this victim be my expiation.'

21. This verse throws an interesting light on the wealth of Jericho, and the extent of her commerce.

25. And all Israel stoned him with stones, and burned them with fire] This inclusion of Achan's household in the punishment is one of the moral problems of the book. Edersheim ('Bib. Hist.' art. 'Joshua,' p. 69 note) interprets the use of the singular number in 7 25a as showing that Achan was the only *person* stoned ; the plural number following (7 25 b) referring to his cattle and property only. Others emphasise the fact (not brought out in the narrative) that his family must have been privy to the crime ; or dwell on the 'entail' of divine visitation pronounced in the second commandment (Ex 20 5). The last view agrees best with the passage as it stands, which suggests in a very striking way the sufferings people bring upon their children by their sins.

CHAPTER 8
The Conquest of Ai. The Covenant Confirmed upon Mt. Ebal

1–29. The Taking of Ai. Edersheim explains that Joshua detailed a corps of 30,000

men, of whom 5,000 were placed W. of Ai in a wood. The 25,000 pitched N. of Ai, and subsequently moved forward into the valley below the city. Then came the feigned attack and retreat eastward, the signal from Joshua, and the assault by the ambush from the rear. It should be noted, however, that there are two accounts of the ambush, one in vv. 3, 9, in which 30,000 are said to have been concealed, and the other in vv. 10–12, in which only 5,000 are said to have been in hiding. These discrepancies in figures are very common.

15. By the way of the wilderness] i.e. toward the Jordan valley. **17. Or Bethel]** omit, as LXX.

30–35. The Covenant confirmed upon Mt. Ebal, near Shechem. At the first opportunity the law of Jehovah is proclaimed as the law of the land.

31. As Moses . . commanded] see Dt 11 29, and, more fully, Dt 27. **An altar of white stones]** see Ex 20 25. **Burnt offerings]** representing entire oblation of the offerer to God : wholly consumed on the altar. **Peace offerings]** representing communion with God. God was the Host, and the offerer and his friends feasted with Him at His table. **32. The stones]** i.e. the stones when plastered : see Dt 27 2-4. **A copy of the law]** Obviously not the whole Pentateuch, or even the legislative matter contained in it ; but the Law of the Blessings and Cursings : see Dt 27.

CHAPTERS 9–12

In chs. 9–11 inclusive we have the account of two great campaigns, in which Joshua successively defeats a confederacy of the petty kings of southern Palestine under the king of Jerusalem, and a combination of the northern chiefs under Jabin, king of Hazor. C. 12 concludes the narrative of the conquest, with a summary of the successes of Moses on the E. and of Joshua on the W. of Jordan. Critics have been much exercised by the apparent contrast of this narrative of the invasion with that in Jg 1. There we have—in the case of Judah and Simeon at least—independent tribal action. Here there is no word of anything but a general action of Israel, under Joshua's leadership, resulting (11 23) in a conquest of the 'whole land.' The solution of the difficulty may perhaps be (a) that these chapters give us the account of two grand campaigns complete and successful in themselves, but involving a prolonged guerilla warfare and a number of local enterprises, such as those mentioned in Judges. Or it may be (b) that there is in these rounded accounts of the northern and southern conquests something of historical foreshortening ; for we must remember that in 11 18 it is described as a 'long' war (see on 11 16-23). Or possibly a combination of these two explanations may give the true solution.

CHAPTER 9

The League with the Gibeonites

C. 9 forms an introduction to the narrative of the Southern campaign (c. 10). The Gibeonite cities were important enough both politically and geographically (see on 9¹⁷ and 10²) for their defection to frighten the surrounding kinglets into concerted action against Israel.

1, 2. The petty kings combine against Israel. **3. Gibeon**] 2 m. N. of Jerusalem. For its importance see on 10²,¹⁰. **14. Took of their victuals**] thus accepting their specious story, and incidentally committing themselves, according to Eastern rule of hospitality, to at least a temporary friendship. **Asked not counsel by Urim and Thummim**] as e.g. we find them asking in Jg1¹. **17. Now their cities were**] All these four cities have been identified in the territory afterwards occupied by Benjamin and the N. border of Judah. **20. Lest wrath come upon us**] Centuries later we are told (2 S 21) that the Israelites of David's time felt this 'wrath' when Saul had broken his ancestral compact with Gibeon. **21. Hewers of wood**, etc.] This is the description of the normal function of resident aliens in Dt 29¹¹. From vv. 23, 27 we find that their tasks were mainly, though not entirely, concerned with the sacrificial worship of the House of God.

CHAPTER 10

The Conquest of Southern Canaan

This c. narrates the successful campaign against the five confederate chiefs of the S., who are roused by the fall of Jericho and Ai and the alliance with Gibeon, and combine under the leadership of Adonizedek of Jerusalem to retaliate upon the Gibeonites. Bringing succour, as in duty bound, to his new allies, Joshua encounters the confederate forces in Beth-horon. By divine aid he inflicts on them a signal defeat, captures and slays all five kings, and follows up his success by a prompt reduction of six Amorite strongholds in swift succession. A concluding paragraph (10⁴⁰⁻⁴³) describes the work of conquest so far, as summary and complete.

1. Adonizedek] The name recalls that of his famous predecessor Melchizedek, the contemporary of Abraham : see on Gn 14¹⁸. **2. Because Gibeon was a great city**] commanding the chief pass to the western plains and but a few miles from Jerusalem : see on v. 10. **3, 4.** Of the confederate cities three were subsequently reduced by Joshua : see on vv. 29–38. **5. Amorites**] a general name for the mountain tribes.

6–14. Battle of Gibeon (or Beth-horon) : Joshua, summoned by the Gibeonites to their aid, defeats the Amorites. **10.** The pass of **Beth-horon** leading to the valley of Aijalon is of great strategic importance, being the main outlet from Gibeon and Jerusalem towards the coast. 'Throughout history,' says G. A. Smith, 'we see hosts swarming up this avenue or swept down it in flight.' **Azekah .. Makkedah**] between Philistia and the hill-country of Judah. **11. Great stones from heaven**] a hailstorm, in which the hand of God is discerned.

12–14. Then spake Joshua] This celebrated passage (as will be seen in RV) consists of (1) a prose introduction, v. 12ᵃ ; (2) a poetical fragment quoted from the book of Jasher, vv. 12ᵇ, 13ᵃ ; and (3) a prose comment on that quotation, 13ᵇ 14.

The four lines from the book of Jasher run, literally, as follows :—

Sun, be thou dumb upon Gibeon ;
   And thou, moon, in valley of Aijalon !
And the sun became dumb, and the moon stood,
   Till the people were avenged on their foes.

Taken by themselves these four lines might refer to an eclipse, or to a prolongation of the darkness of the hailstorm (see v. 11). The sun is spoken of as 'dumb' when not shining, as in Dante's 'Inferno,' 1. 60, the sunless shade is 'dove il sol tace' (where the sun is speechless). At first sight the comment in vv. 13ᵇ 14 seems decisive against this interpretation. But Edersheim regards these vv. as themselves (substantially) quoted from the book of Jasher ; in which case they would be poetical and figurative, and other writers boldly take them as a later gloss, written at a time when the figurative language of the poem was misunderstood. In favour of this view is the fact that there are no certain references to this event as miraculous in the other books of the OT. ; and it is not till c. 180 B.C. (Ecclus 46⁴) that we find the first clear mention of the miracle as making 'the sun go back' ; an interpretation which was followed by the author of the 'Psalms of Solomon' (18¹⁴) c. 50 B.C., and by Josephus, and has been the 'traditional' one till lately. This interpretation of the incident, which makes it involve a literal 'staying of the sun,' i.e. in modern language, an arresting of the earth's rotatory motion, has not unnaturally tried the faith of many who, while accepting the doctrine of God's omnipotence, feel that such a kind of interpretation contradicts what God Himself has taught them about the orderly working of His universe. Whether we regard the divine answer to Joshua's prayer as given in the form of a prolongation of the daylight, in spite of the hailstorm (see Edersheim), or (perhaps better) as prolongation of the storm darkness, we must not forget that the record is poetry and not prose, and the inspired language of the passage ancient and oriental, not modern, western, and scientific.

13. The Book of Jasher] *Yashar*='Upright' or 'Pious.' The book was presumably a collection of national heroic songs. Elsewhere it is quoted by name only in 2 S 1[18] (David's elegy over Saul and Jonathan). Possibly we may ascribe to the same source other poems, like the Song of Deborah (Jg 5), which has itself a later prose commentary attached to it (Jg 4).

24. Put their feet upon the necks] The monuments of Assyria and Egypt afford graphic parallels. **26. Slew them and hanged them]** The hanging was an additional insult wreaked on the corpse: cp. Dt 21[22, 23].

29. Libnah] in the lowlands of Judah: also **Lachish** (v. 31), **Gezer** (v. 33) and **Eglon** (v. 34). **36. Hebron]** (*El Khalil*, 'the friend' of God) Abraham's city in the mountain of Judah, and one of the six Levitical cities of refuge (20[7]). **38. Debir]** also called Kirjath-Sepher, and falling, like Hebron, to Caleb. It lay in the hill-country of Judah, or in the Negeb (15[15-19]), perhaps on the border.

40-43. On these divisions of the country see on c. 15. A summary like this must not be pressed too literally, but read in the light of other narratives like Jg 1. The meaning is that Joshua's work was thorough, as far as it went; that it was carried out in a spirit of absolute loyalty to the divine commands (cp. Dt 20[16, 17]); and that all its success (v. 42) was due to the divine leadership and assistance. **40.** The campaign in southern Palestine included the **hills** of Judah, the **south**, i.e. the Negeb, the **vale** (RV 'the lowland'), i.e. the Shephelah, and the **springs** (RV 'the slopes') between the hill-country and the Shephelah. **41. Goshen]** in the mountain of Judah (15[51]).

CHAPTER 11
The Campaign in the North

Here there is no trace, as in the former case, of miraculous interposition. Joshua's generalship, courage, swiftness and loyalty are the prominent factors in the achievement. Yet it is made clear here (vv. 6-8) as ever, that those qualities attained their object because they were under the direct guidance of the God of Israel.

1. Jabin] king of Hazor. **Hazor]** may be Tell el-Hurrawiyeh, 2½ m. S. of Kedesh-Naphtali. **Shimron]** (=Shimron-meron 12[20]) is Semûnieh, W. of Nazareth. **Achshaph]** el Yasîf, the port of Accho. Hazor is again a powerful Canaanite centre in the time of Deborah (Jg 4)

and its king bears the same name, or title, Jabin (= wise) and may have been of the same dynasty. **2, 3.** RV 'that were on the north, in the hill-country, and in the Arabah south of Chinneroth, and in the lowland, and in the heights of Dor on the west, to the Canaanite on the east . .' The 'Arabah S. of Chinneroth' means the plain S. of the lake of Gennesaret (Lk 5[1]). **Dor]** near Mt. Carmel. **3. The Canaanite on the east and on the west]** The name 'Canaanite' is more probably geographical than racial. It means 'lowlanders.' In the Amarna tablets (14th cent. B.C.) the Land of Canaan means the Phœnician coast; in later Egyptian monuments it includes all W. Syria. **5. Waters of Merom]** Probably Lake Huleh, a marshy lake near the sources of the Jordan. **6. Thou shalt hough, etc.]** To 'hough' or 'hock' = to hamstring a horse. This was done, no doubt, during the battle, to stop the charge. The chariots were destroyed afterwards.

16-23. General retrospect of Joshua's campaigns. This paragraph covers the preceding chs. as well as c. 11[1-15]. The war, which has been presented to us in graphic sketches following one another in swift succession, is said to have been a 'long' one (v. 18), and the natural inference from 14[7-10] (where see note) is that it lasted seven years. **16.** The mountain country and Negeb (dry southern uplands) and Shephelah (low hills skirting the mountains) first mentioned are those of Judah (see on 10[40]), from which the inference has been drawn that the writer was a native of that tribe, because he does not qualify the terms. Then follows the Arabah (deep valley of Jordan), and finally the mountain of Israel and its Shephelah, i.e. the N. Israelite part of this central range and the low hills (valley) between it and Carmel. The stretch of country described reaches from Halak in Edomite territory S. of the Dead Sea to Baal Gad at the foot of Hermon, N. of Lake Huleh. **22. The Anakims]** This hill-tribe had by their stature made an alarming impression on the original spies (Nu 13[28-33]; cp. Josh 14[12]). It was from Gath that Goliath came (1 S 17[4]) and other giants (2 S 21[18-22]).

CHAPTER 12
A Review of the Victories of Moses and Joshua

This c. concludes the whole section of the book which deals with the conquest of Canaan. The following chs. narrate the partition of the conquered and some unconquered land. The original account of these conquests is to be found in Nu 21[21-35], and of the assignment to the 2½ tribes in Nu 3[2]. A fuller description of the territory is given in c. 13[1-33], where see notes.

1-6. Moses' conquests E. of Jordan. Kingdoms of Sihon and Og. **3. Sea of Chinneroth**] the OT. name for the Sea of Galilee. **Salt sea**] the Dead Sea.

7-24. Joshua's conquests W. of Jordan—thirty-one kings. **7.** The N. and S. limits are given as in 11 [17], only in reverse order. **On this side Jordan on the west**] RV 'beyond Jordan westward.' **9. One**] i.e. one king.

21. Taanach . . Megiddo] see on Jg 5 [19].

23. The nations] RV 'Goiim.' **24. Tirzah**] (probably = Teiasir) NE. of Shechem. It was afterwards the capital of the Northern Kingdom, from the time of Jeroboam (1 K 14 [17]) till the 6th year of Omri, who moved the centre of government to Samaria (1 K 16 [23]).

CHAPTERS 13-21
THE SETTLEMENT

The summaries of c. 12 mark the end of one section of the book, and the opening words of c. 13 as clearly introduce the beginning of another.

This central portion, embracing chs. 13-21, has been called ' The Domesday Book of the Old Testament,' and is invaluable as a groundwork for modern scientific explorers. ' The Book of Joshua ' (writes Col. Conder) ' is the great geographical book of the Old Testament, and the study of its geography is important, as showing that it was written in Palestine by an author who was familiar with the whole land. . . A proportion of about three-quarters of the towns mentioned in this book are more or less certainly known, having either never been lost, or having recently been recovered by exploration, through the survival of the ancient name to our own time, or by other indications —as, for instance, in the case of Lachish, where other indications are confirmed by the discovery of a tablet referring to Zimrida (who is known to have been the ruler of Lachish about 1480 B.C.) which has been dug up in the ruins of the city.'

It may be noted that in chs. 13-22 the Priestly narrative is predominant ; just as the Primitive is in chs. 1-12, although some of the most interesting incidents, e.g. Caleb's inheritance (14 [6-15] 15 [14-19]), are from the earlier source. The section may be thus analysed :—(a) 13 [1-33] Territories of the Eastern Tribes. (b) 14 [1]-19 [51] Territories of the Western Tribes.

CHAPTER 13
TERRITORIES OF THE EASTERN TRIBES

1-7. These vv. describe the land which, though still unconquered, is to be assigned to the 9½ tribes. It includes the W. and N. borders of Palestine. Wellhausen ('History of Israel ') remarks, ' The conquest was at first but an incomplete one. The plain which fringed the coast was hardly touched : so also

the valley of Jezreel with its girdle of fortified cities stretching from Accho to Beth-shean. All that was subdued in the strict sense of the word was the mountainous land, particularly the southern hill-country of Mt. Ephraim ; yet even here the Canaanites retained possession of not a few cities, such as Jebus, Shechem, Thebez.'

2. Geshuri] Distinct from the Geshurites of v. 13 and 12 [5]. We should perhaps read ' the people of Gezer,' S. of Ephraim.

3. Sihor] the Wâdy el Arish, or Brook of Egypt. **4. Aphek**] in Asher. **5. Giblites**] Gebal was at the foot of Lebanon, on the coast.

7, 8. The LXX has a much more intelligible reading—' And now divide this land for an inheritance to the nine tribes and the half tribe of Manasseh, from Jordan to the great sea and toward the sunsetting shalt thou give it : the great sea shall be the border (v. 8). To the tribes and the half tribe of Manasseh, Reuben and Gad, gave Moses on the other side of Jordan, toward the sun-rising. . .'

8-33. The territory of the two tribes and a half, including territory previously taken from Moab by Sihon (Nu 21 [26]) : cp. Nu 32 [1-3, 33-42]. Reuben had from the Arnon on the S. to Heshbon (=Hesbân), a little north of the Dead Sea. Gad had the eastern side of the Jordan valley, from the N. boundary of Reuben to the Sea of Galilee (**Sea of Chinnereth**) and the western slopes of Mt. Gilead ; Manasseh had the eastern half of Mt. Gilead, all the great plateau of Bashan, running up to the range of Hermon.

14. He gave none inheritance] assigned no district as a tribal territory, gave them only scattered cities within the lots of the other tribes. **The sacrifices of the LORD**] (in v. 33, simply ' the LORD ') cp. Nu 18 [20-32]. Their professional absorption in spiritual things made it, however, all the more necessary that their material wants should be provided for (see 1 Cor 9 [13, 14] for an enunciation of this principle and its application to the Christian ministry). Accordingly we find their promised cities duly assigned to the Levites in c. 21 (cp. Nu 35).

15-23. Territory of Reuben : see on vv. 8-33. **16, 17. Plain**] RM ' table-land.' The plateau of Mâdebah includes the sites of Hesbân, the ancient capital, **Dibon** (= Dhîban, where the famous 9th cent. B.C. monument of Mesha, known as the ' Moabite Stone,' was discovered in 1868) and other towns of Reuben. Dibon (Nu 32 [34] 33 [45]) was actually occupied by Gad.

22. The reference to the slaying of Balaam comes in strangely here : but it occurs also in Nu 31 [8] in a parallel context. Evidently there is here trace of a very ancient document.

24-28. Territory of Gad : see on vv. 8–33.

26. Ramath-mispeh] possibly the later Ramoth Gilead (Raimûn), N. of the Jabbok. **Debir**] not the Debir of 10 38 or 15 7. The Hebrew is Ledebir, which may be the Lo-debar of 2 S 9 4. **27. Sea of Chinnereth**] i.e. the Sea of Galilee.

29-31. Territory of the half-tribe of Manasseh. **33.** See on v. 14.

CHAPTERS 14–19
TERRITORIES OF THE WESTERN TRIBES

Chs. 14–19 inclusive describe the allotment of territories to the Western Tribes. There are two assignments. The first, embracing Judah and Joseph, is described as taking place at Gilgal (14 6) under the auspices of Eleazar and Joshua and the 'heads of the fathers' (14 1). Judah (15), Ephraim (16), and Manasseh (17) each occupy a single c. The second assignment, to the seven remaining tribes, takes place apparently at a later date (18 3), after an elaborate survey (18 6, 8, 9) of the territory available. Its scene is Shiloh, and Joshua alone is named as presiding. It is noticeable (see further note on the assignment of the territory) that the details of the seven territories are much more meagre than those of the others, except in the case of Benjamin. C. 14 itself is introductory, partly (14 1-5) to the whole of the 5 chs. following ; partly (14 6-15) to the first assignment (chs. 15–17), recording Caleb's request for Hebron and its favourable reception. This latter section (14 6-15) is of special interest in that it affords incidentally one of the few definite chronological data available for this period (see on 14 10).

CHAPTER 14
THE PORTION OF CALEB

1-5. Introductory Section.

1. Eleazar the priest] The mention of the priest in association with the leader, to whom he is here given precedence, is one of the characteristics of the Priestly narrative.

4. The children of Joseph were two tribes, etc.] This reckoning, with the subtraction of Levi, makes a total of twelve still. Practically, however, Simeon became absorbed in Judah, and each half-tribe of Manasseh came to count as a complete tribe.

6-15. The inheritance of Caleb : see 15 13-19.

6. Thou knowest the thing, etc.] The promise to Caleb occurs in Nu 14 24, and is referred to again in Dt 1 36. On Caleb see on 15 13. **10. These forty and five years**] The notes of time given here and in 14 7 are interesting. Caleb was 40 years old at Kadesh : 45 years have intervened since then, and he is now 85. Allowing 38 years for the penal wanderings, we get 7 years as the period

covered by the war of conquest up to this date.

12-15. Hebron assigned to Caleb : on Hebron see on 10 36, and on Caleb's possession of it, 15 13 f. and note. On the Anakim see on 11 22. **12.** RV 'it may be that the LORD will be with me and I shall drive them out': cp. 5 14 and Jg 1 20. It is a brave man's word (cp. 14 11). Caleb welcomes the task the more for its peril, and the hard work confronting him adds value to the inheritance. **15. The name of Hebron,** etc.] LXX 'Now the name of Hebron was formerly the city of Argob : this was the metropolis of the Anakim' : and similarly in 15 13 21 11 for 'father of Anak' LXX reads 'metropolis of Anak.' This may be the true sense.

CHAPTERS 15–19
THE ASSIGNMENT OF THE TERRITORY

It has been noticed that there are many incidental features in this narrative which point to a contemporary document. Thus in the lot of Judah we have a full description, both of the frontier-lines (15 1-12), and also of the chief cities contained within them (15 21-62) : and the same is true of Benjamin (18 11-28). But these are the tribes which seem to have conquered their territory soonest and most completely. Ephraim and Manasseh, on the contrary, have only their boundaries mentioned without any list of cities (16). As a matter of fact, the children of Joseph seem to have had more difficulties with the Canaanites (17 12, 16, cp. Jg 1 27) than had Judah and Benjamin. Again, Simeon (19 1-9) and Dan (19 40-48) have no boundaries mentioned, only cities, because they originally settled in the territory of Judah and Benjamin. Finally, the accounts of the territory of the remaining tribes, Zebulun, Issachar, Asher, Naphtali (19 10-39), are defective, as is natural if at the date when the document was originally drawn up, these territories were not yet completely conquered : cp. Jg 1 30-33. But if the document be strictly contemporary, it must be regarded as closing with 19 46.

CHAPTER 15
THE LOT OF JUDAH

1-12. The boundaries of Judah's lot. There is a valuable descriptive note on this section and on 15 20-63 in Black's Commentary on 'Joshua' in the Smaller Cambridge Bible.

2-4. The S. Frontier. This coincides, of course, with the S. Frontier of the whole land as given in Nu 34 3-5. **4. The river of Egypt**] RV 'brook of Egypt,' not the Nile, but the Wâdy el Arish : cp. 15 47.

5. The E. Frontier, viz. the Dead Sea.

5-11. The N. Frontier. Cp. the account in 18 15-20 of the S. Frontier of Benjamin.

This is by far the most complicated of the four frontiers, but its line can be fairly well traced. It leaves the Jordan some 4 m. N. of the Dead Sea, and runs W., then SW. past Jerusalem, W. again near Bethlehem, and NW. as it descends to the maritime plain. **7. Debir**] This cannot be the same as the Debir of 11 21 15 15, 49. Perhaps the reading here should be 'toward the wilderness.' **The going up to** (RV 'the ascent of') **Adummim**] This was the steep pass on the road from Jericho to Jerusalem. **En-rogel**] a spring near Jerusalem which supplies the Pool of Siloam. **8. Valley of the giants**] RV 'vale of Rephaim,' SW. of Jerusalem. **9. Kirjath-jearim**] 7 m. NW. of Jerusalem. **10. Mount Seir**] in Judah, distinct from the Mt. Seir in Edom. **Beth-shemesh .. Timnah**] in Dan. **11. Jabneel**] on the coast, known later as Jamnia (cp. 1 Mac 4 15 2 Mac 12 8), in later days a famous seat of Jewish learning. **12.** The W. Frontier, viz. the Mediterranean. Practically, however, the Philistines held the coast for many centuries.

13–19. The inheritance of Caleb. This passage is repeated in Jg 1 10-15, where, however, the expulsion of the Anakim from Hebron, attributed (11 21-23) to Joshua and Israel, and here (cp. 14 12) to Caleb, is ascribed more vaguely to Judah. For further instances of parallels or quasi-parallels, with the book of Judges see on 15 63 19 47 24 28. **13. Caleb**] = 'dog.' He seems to have been of Edomite origin (14 6). He was by no means a solitary instance of an alien adopted into the tribe of Judah. In the ancestry of David himself we find the Canaanitess Rahab and the Moabitess Ruth. **Father of Anak**] LXX has 'metropolis of Anak': see on 14 15. **15. Debir**] see on 10 38. **17. Othniel**] (= 'Lion of God'). For his subsequent career see Jg 3 9-11.

20–62. The cities of Judah.

20–32. Cities in the Negeb, or 'south country': see on Gn 12 9.

33–47. Cities in the Shephelah, or 'lowland' (not as AV 'valley'): the fertile undulating tract between the central ridge and the maritime plain.

48–60. Cities in the 'Mountain,' i.e. the rocky backbone of Judah, the limestone watershed between the Mediterranean and the Dead Sea. Mt. Ephraim is its continuation northwards.

59. LXX inserts here a list of 11 cities (including Tekoa and 'Ephrata which is Bethlehem') which seems to have dropped out of the Massoretic text.

61, 62. Cities in the 'Wilderness,' i.e. the steep and barren slopes between the Mountain and the Dead Sea eastward.

63. The Jebusites dwell with the children of Judah at Jerusalem unto this day] The parallel passage in Jg 1 21 has 'Benjamin' for 'Judah,'

which may be an earlier form. At first sight this v. seems to belong to a time anterior, or at latest to the time when David (2 S 5 6 f.) captured from the Jebusites the citadel of Zion. But that capture did not mean expulsion, as is clear from the later incident of Araunah (2 S 24 16; cp. 1 Ch 21 15. Cp. also the mention of Jebusites as late as Zech 9 7); and in a sense it may be true that Judahite and Jebusite only began to live together in Jerusalem when David made it his capital, though Jg 1 21 may represent an earlier state of things.

CHAPTER 16
THE LOT OF JOSEPH

Chs. 16, 17 describe the territories of Ephraim and the W. half of Manasseh. Vv. 1–4 of c. 16 give the general frontiers of the combined tribes, the rest of the c. (16 5-10) the frontiers of Ephraim as distinct from W. Manasseh. The territory allotted to the two tribes comprised the central and most fertile part of Palestine. The S. border ran from Jericho through Bethel to Beth-horon and the sea; and the N. border from Mt. Carmel. along the S. border of the Plain of Esdraelon to the Jordan.

1. RV 'the lot .. went out from the Jordan at Jericho, at the waters of Jericho on the east. even the wilderness, going up from Jericho through the hill-country to Bethel.' **2. From Beth-el to Luz**] see on Gn 28 19. **6.** The border between Ephraim and Manasseh passed from Jericho westward to Michmethah near Shechem (17 7), and thence to the river Kanah which falls into the Mediterranean N. of Joppa. **9.** RV 'together with the cities which were separated for the children of Ephraim in the midst of the inheritance of the children of Manasseh.' **10. Serve under tribute**] The Canaanite had to take up the forced service of a labourer: cp. 17 13 and Jg 1 28, 33, 35.

CHAPTER 17
THE LOT OF JOSEPH (continued)

Inheritance of Western Manasseh. The Complaint of the children of Joseph, and Joshua's Reply.

1–6. The inheritance of Manasseh especially (vv. 2 f.) of the Western half-tribe. **1. The father of Gilead**] The expression is rather geographical than strictly genealogical, according to Oriental usage. Cp. the table of the generations of the sons of Noah in Gn 10.

3 f. The daughters of Zelophehad] Their case comes up for judgment before Moses in Nu 27 1-7 and again in Nu 36 1-12. Their contention was recognised as just (Nu 36 4).

7–13. The frontiers of Western Manasseh. See on c. 16. **8, 9.** *Belonged* **to the children of Ephraim**] cp. 16 8, 9.

11-13. The Canaanites still held a chain of fortified cities in the N. from Beth-shean on the E. to Accho on the coast. **13. Put the Canaanites to tribute**] RV 'to task-work': cp. 16 10. The remark indicates that the conquest proved exceedingly difficult in some parts of the country, and that the Canaanites long held their own.

14-18. This passage, which is from the Primitive source, supports the testimony of Judges (see on 18 13) that much of the final settlement was left to individual tribal effort. It also throws light on the character of the children of Joseph. The spirit of self-aggrandisement and self-importance here displayed made Ephraim the great rival of Judah throughout history. It shows itself still more vehemently in the period of the Judges, both in their 'chiding' of their kinsman Gideon the Manassite (Jg 8), and their quarrel with Jephthah (Jg 12). Joseph and Judah are alike prominent in the patriarchal blessing (Gn 49 8, 22), and are alike in their growth during the period of wanderings. Joseph increased from 72,000 to 85,200, and Judah from 74,600 to 76,500; while the total for all Israel was lower at the second census by nearly 2,000 (cp. Nu 1 and Nu 26). After Othniel's time until the rise of David, Judah sinks into unimportance; while Ephraim, as the tribe of Joshua, and the home of the national sanctuary (Gilgal, Shechem and Shiloh), takes a foremost place. And it was no doubt the jealous memories of past glories in which Joseph had been supplanted by David's tribe, that made Ephraim take so prominent a part in the revolt of the northern tribes under Jeroboam.

15. If thou *be* **a great people**] Joshua shows tact and firmness in dealing with his own tribesmen as with all the rest. There is a mixture of encouragement with salutary rebuke in his reply, and also practical common-sense. 'Persevere and have confidence in yourselves: ultimately you will prevail over the Canaanites, better equipped though they are for warfare in the plains. Meanwhile you can at least make yourselves clearings in the forest highlands formerly occupied by the pre-Canaanite Rephaim.' **Mount Ephraim**] covers all the later Samaria (cp. Jer 31 5, 6) including Ramah and Beth-el (Jg 4 5) and Shechem (Josh 20 7). The name seems to have spread from the hill-country immediately N. of Benjamin. **18.** The **outgoings** of Mt. Ephraim are valleys, broad, fertile, and of easy gradients.

CHAPTER 18
THE SECOND ALLOTMENT. INTRODUCTION.
THE TERRITORY OF BENJAMIN

1-10. These vv. supply an introduction to the second allotment in general, and agree with the passages which, in common with Jg 1, view the conquest as gradual and partial. The seven tribes still hang back through 'slackness' (v. 3), while Judah and Joseph are already in possession.

5. Judah shall abide, etc.] In the final allotment the S. border of Benjamin coincided with the N. border of Judah as far as Kirjath-jearim; the lowlands and plains W. of that were given to Dan (19 40).

11-20. The lot of Benjamin. It had, as boundaries, Ephraim to the N. and Judah to the S.: the Jordan was the E. border, and Beth-horon to Kirjath-jearim the W. Jerusalem (Jebus) was within its borders.

13. Luz, which *is* **Beth-el**] see on Gn 28 19.

14. And compassed the corner of the sea] RV 'and turned about on the west quarter.'

15. Nephtoah] a fountain near Jerusalem. The S. boundary is the same as the N. boundary of Judah (15 5-9), but traced here from W. to E.

16. Jebusi] RV 'the Jebusite,' meaning Jerusalem. The Benjamin border passed S. of Jerusalem. It is often forgotten that this city, though bordering upon Judah, was really in the territory of Benjamin. **19. Beth-hoglah**] N. end of the Dead Sea.

21-28. The cities of Benjamin. The most famous of them are Jericho, Ramah (1 S 1 19), Mizpeh (1 S 7 5), Jerusalem, and Gibeath or Gibeah.

CHAPTER 19
THE SECOND ALLOTMENT (continued). THE
TERRITORIES OF SIMEON, ZEBULUN, IS-
SACHAR, ASHER, NAPHTALI, DAN. THE
INHERITANCE OF JOSHUA

1-9. The lot of Simeon. Observe that no borders are named, and the lot includes towns previously taken by Judah (15 31-32): see v. 9. This tribe was settled in the Negeb, or 'south country,' that slopes away from the Hebron range towards the desert, bounded on the W. by the Mediterranean and on the E. by the Dead Sea and the Valley of Edom.

10-16. The lot of Zebulun: in the low hills W. of Nazareth and E. of Accho.

17-23. The lot of Issachar: comprising the plain of Esdraelon. **22. Tabor**] Here Zebulun, Issachar, and Naphtali had a common border.

24-31. The lot of Asher: the coast and low hills, from Carmel to Tyre.

32-39. The lot of Naphtali: the high mountains of upper Galilee, and plateau E. of Mt. Tabor to the W. shores of the Sea of Galilee, and the Jordan Valley N. of it.

40-48. The lot of Dan: (a) the original inheritance (19 40-46); (b) the later acquisition in the N. (19 47-48). The territory in the S. lies W. of Benjamin along the two parallel valleys that lead through the Shephelah to the sea, viz. Aijalon and Sorek. The song of

Deborah (Jg 5 17) seems to imply that the Danites had then reached the coast, but the maritime plain was probably never fully occupied by them, and what they had held of it was soon abandoned in favour of a new colony (19 47, 48).

In LXX our v. 48 follows 46, where it is more naturally in place, and both it and v. 47 (which follows it in LXX) contain additional matter about the Danites' struggle with the Amorites, which fits in well with Jg 1 34, where we are told that 'the Amorites forced the children of Dan into the hill-country; for they would not suffer them to come down into the valley.' This obviously gives the reason for the expedition northward.

47. The taking of **Leshem** (called in Judges 'Laish') is related in Jg 18 7, 27-29.

49-51. Concluding section : Joshua's own inheritance. Joshua and his comrade Caleb (15 13), the sole representatives of the generation of the exodus, receive each a special 'inheritance' of his own choice. **50.** According to the word of the LORD] cp. Nu 14 24,30 with Josh 14 9,10. Timnath-serah] cp. 24 30; called Timnath-heres in Jg 2 9, probably Kefr-Hâris, 9 m. S. of Shechem.

CHAPTER 20
THE APPOINTMENT OF CITIES OF REFUGE

The allotment of the tribal inheritance is followed by the appointment of six cities of refuge previously provided and in part assigned by Moses, according to the terms of the Sinaitic law concerning manslaughter : cp. Ex 21 13 Nu 35 6f. These are enumerated in the following order :—W. of Jordan : Kedesh (N.), Shechem (central), Hebron (S.) ; E. of Jordan : Bezer (S.), Ramoth-Gilead (central), Golan (N.). Geographical considerations must have had the first place ; the six cities are so placed as to give nearly equal facilities of access from all parts of Palestine. But it is interesting to observe that the three western cities were ancient traditional sanctuaries. This is inferred from the name of Kedesh (= Holy) and known of the other two. The same may be true of the eastern cities also.

This chapter has a special interest as introducing us to a phase of Hebrew Law typical of many of the Mosaic ordinances. Moses was inspired not so much to produce a system entirely novel as to take up the Semitic customs already in existence, and regulate and purify them. So here, the primitive law of blood-revenge, which laid on the kin of the slain the duty of taking vengeance on the slayer, and which often failed to distinguish between intentional and unintentional homicide, is regulated by the formulation of a clear distinction corresponding to our 'wilful murder' and 'manslaughter,' and by the pro-

vision of definite asylums for the unintentional manslayer.

1-9. The Cities of Refuge.

2. Whereof I spake . . by the hand of Moses] cp. Ex 21 13 Nu 35 6f. Dt 4 41f.

3 Unwittingly] manslaughter, as we should say, as distinct from murder. See the elaborate rules and distinctions drawn out in Nu 35 16-28. Note that this is not the ordinary, almost universal, principle of 'Sanctuary,' by which any criminal whatsoever could claim the protection of some holy place, as e.g. Joab tried to do (1 K 2 28), when he fled to the tabernacle and caught hold of the horns of the altar. It will be observed that Solomon did not respect the Sanctuary in that case.

9. Until he stood before the congregation] The purpose is to provide every homicide a fair trial : see Nu 35 12, 24-25. If he is found guilty of murder, the City of Refuge is no sanctuary to him ; if only of manslaughter (cp. 20 6), it is a safe asylum to him till the death of the high priest, after which he is free to return home.

CHAPTER 21
THE ASSIGNMENT OF FORTY-EIGHT CITIES TO THE LEVITES

2. The injunction to Moses was given in the plains of Moab, and is recorded in Nu 35 2-5.

3-8. Number and localities of the cities distributed to each of the families of Levi.

9-42. Detailed specification of the cities :— Cities of the Aaronites (Priests) in Judah and Benjamin (9-19) ; of the Kohathites in Ephraim, Dan, and W. Manasseh (20-26); of the Gershonites in E. Manasseh, Issachar, Asher, and Naphtali (27-33) ; of the Merarites in Zebulun, Reuben and Gad (34-42).

43-45. Conclusion of the 'Domesday Book'; fulfilment of God's promises of possession and rest. This section is somewhat difficult to reconcile with the situation revealed at the beginning of the book of Judges ; but it must be remembered that this passage is from the later Priestly source, while the previous section is from an earlier document.

CHAPTERS 22-24

These chapters form a section by themselves, and give some closing scenes of Joshua's life, as well as his two farewell discourses to the people.

CHAPTER 22
DISMISSAL OF THE TWO AND A HALF TRIBES. THE ALTAR SET UP AT ED, AND THE CONTROVERSY IT RAISED

1-9. The dismissal of the tribes.

10-34. The controversy at Ed. Here, as in Nu 25 7-9, we see Phinehas playing a prominent part, and the contrast between the scenes is instructive. Swift, stern, and relentless when occasion demanded, he appears in Numbers as the hero who, by prompt execution of judgment, stayed the plague at Shittim (cp. Ps 106 [30]) ; here, on the other hand, though not unmindful of that crisis (22 [17]), he shows tact and gentleness, and under circumstances of the utmost delicacy and tension, helps to avert a disastrous civil war.

12. At Shiloh] the natural place to assemble for so solemn an undertaking. The idea of the tribes is that their brethren are falling into the sin of apostasy (cp. 22 [16] Lv 17 [8, 9] Dt 12 [5-7]), and that therefore it is incumbent on them to enforce the provisions of Dt 13 [12-18]. These provisions, however, included a careful and searching investigation (Dt 13 [14]) before the declaration of exterminating war upon the offenders. **17. The iniquity of Peor]** the occasion of Phinehas' former intervention : see Nu 25. **22. The LORD God of gods]** the original most impressively combines Hebrew names of God : *EL ELOHIM JEHOVAH.*

CHAPTER 23

THE FIRST FAREWELL ADDRESS OF JOSHUA

This discourse was probably delivered at Shiloh or Timnath-Serah. Unlike the Second Discourse, which is mainly a historical retrospect, it dwells chiefly upon the political future of Israel, laying special emphasis on their separateness, and the danger of social and religious intercourse with the remnant of the Canaanites. C. 23 is from the same source as c. 1 and Dt 27.

4. These nations that remain] Like c. 13 [2-7], to the substance of which it probably refers, this passage serves to modify the unqualified character of such summaries of conquest as 10 [40-43] 11 [23] 21 [43-45]. **10. One man of you shall chase a thousand]** RM 'hath chased,' cp. Dt 32 [30]. **15. All evil things]** RV 'all the evil things,' with definite reference to Dt 28 [15-68]. Cp. also Lv 26 [14-39].

CHAPTER 24

JOSHUA'S SECOND AND FINAL FAREWELL

This discourse (24 [1-15]), with Israel's response (24 [16-24]), and consequent renewal of the Covenant (24 [25-28]), occupies the bulk of the chapter. The book is then brought to a conclusion in three short paragraphs, recording (a) the death and burial of Joshua (24 [29-31]), (b) the burial of Joseph's bones (24 [32]), and (c) the death of Eleazar (24 [33]).

1-15. This last address of Joshua, which is admitted by critics to be of great antiquity, recalls, both in spirit and in substance, Samuel's discourse in 1 S 12. But whereas the latter begins with the work of Moses and Aaron, Joshua starts further back and traces the hand of Providence from the call of Abraham out of idolatrous Mesopotamia, thus enforcing a strict renunciation of any lingering idolatry among his contemporaries (cp. 24 [14, 23]). Through patriarchal times he draws his hearers on to the sojourn in Egypt (24 [4]) ; then he refers to the miraculous exodus (24 [5-7]) ; next he recounts the wanderings in the wilderness, and the victories E. of Jordan (24 [7-9]) ; and concludes with the passage of Jordan, and the subsequent conquests (24 [11f.]). Finally Joshua offers them the great choice—loyalty or disloyalty to the LORD who has done so much for them (24 [14, 15]). His own choice is made.

1. To Shechem] the scene of the blessings and cursings of c. 8 [30-35]. It is here hallowed afresh by a solemn renewal of the Covenant (24 [25]). **3. The other side of the flood]** RV 'from beyond the River,' i.e. Euphrates.

6, 7. And ye came unto the sea, etc.] The full and graphic description of this great miracle is remarkable in so concise a speech. Does it not evidence an eyewitness ? Joshua was old enough to lead the host against Amalek that year (Ex 17 [9]), and therefore old enough to be impressed by it. He may well have been—as Caleb was—38 years old at the time (see on 14 [10]). **11. And ye went over Jordan]** Here we pass into the history narrated in the book of Joshua. **12. The hornet]** Either the Israelite invasion was actually preceded by a plague of hornets, insects whose sting is exceedingly painful and may soon be fatal ; or the hornet is used as a type of the dread which the rumour of their victories spread in advance of them.

14, 15. These very definite references to idolatry imply that previous warnings had failed of their effect. Indeed, we learn from the later historical books that it was not until the Captivity that Israel completely forsook the worship of false gods. There were apparently temptations to three distinct forms of idolatry : (a) the ancestral worship of their Mesopotamian forefathers, represented by the 'teraphim' which Rachel stole from Laban (Gn 31 [19, 30], cp. Gn 35 [2, 4]) ; (b) the animal-worship to which the Israelites had been accustomed in Egypt (v. 14), of which the 'golden calf' or Apis-bull of Ex 32 is a type ; (c) the local Baalim of the Canaanite tribes, which proved, as the book of Judges shows, a constant snare to Israel in succeeding generations.

16-24. The People's Response.

18. Drave out . . all the people] A general statement, in line with 10 [40, 43] 11 [23] 21 [43-45], but to be taken together with statements of a qualifying character like 13 [2-7] and 23 [4].

19. Ye cannot serve the LORD : for he *is* **an holy God]** an extreme statement meant to startle them into a sense of the awful responsibility of intercourse with One who has revealed Himself to be All-Holy : cp. Lv 19 ². The whole elaborate scheme of the Levitical sacrifices and ceremonies seems to have this as its primary object, and to bring home to careless minds the inaccessibility of the Deity except to clean hearts and lives.

25–28. Renewal of the Covenant.

26. A great stone] A pillar such as Jacob had set up (Gn 28 ¹⁸) as a memorial of his vision at Bethel, and again (Gn 31 ⁴⁴) as a witness of his covenant with Laban. Moses had set up twelve such pillars (Ex 24 ⁴) as a memorial of the original Covenant at Sinai ; and now a similar monument is erected by Joshua to mark the renewal of that Covenant. On the other hand, an idolatrous ' pillar ' or ' obelisk' (Dt 16 ²² RV) was expressly forbidden. **An oak**] RV ' the oak,' i.e. of Gn 12 ⁶ RV, etc.

29–33. Death and burial of Joshua. Burial of Joseph's bones. Death of Eleazar. Repeated in substance Jg 2 ⁶⁻⁹.

31. All the days .. the elders] The generation old enough to realise and remember the events recorded in this book. These words must not be pressed too rigidly. They assure us that Joshua's inspiring influence was felt up to, and even after, his death. But the next generation (Jg 2 ¹⁰) fell away. A grandson of Moses and contemporary of Phinehas (cp. Jg 20 ²⁸) took a leading part in Danite idolatry (Jg 18 ³⁰ RV). **32. Ground which Jacob bought**] see Gn 33 ¹⁹.

33. Eleazar the son of Aaron died] The traditional Jewish theory being that Joshua wrote the book that bears his name, it was supposed that vv. 29–31 were added by Eleazar, and this v. by ' Phinehas and the Elders.'

JUDGES

INTRODUCTION

1. The Times. In the order of the Bible, the book of Judges follows that of Joshua. But there is a great difference between the two. Joshua tells us of a carefully planned attack by the whole people of Israel upon the seven nations who inhabited Canaan, and its complete success ; and the bulk of the second half of the book is occupied by the distribution of the territory among the twelve tribes. At the beginning of Judges we find the Israelites either setting out on the conquest of parts of Canaan, or dwelling in an only half-conquered country, side by side with the Canaanites ; they are subject to a long series of attacks from enemies inside and outside the country ; united action between the different tribes is at best rare and never complete ; and the book closes with two episodes which have nothing to do with foreign foes, but in which the wildness and even savagery of the period (including general lawlessness, massacre, treachery, mutilation and human sacrifice), clear enough in each of the earlier narratives of the book, is placed in peculiarly strong relief.

The picture, however, is an entirely natural one. The Israelites had been living the life of desert nomads; and when they invaded the rich sown lands of Canaan, to which other tribes from the desert had already found their way, they preserved something of the character of Bedouin raiders. Under a recognised leader like Joshua, they could combine and gain victories as striking as they were transitory ;

when Joshua was dead, they were as ready to split into independent tribal groups, and to refuse to ' come up to the help of Jehovah.' Thereupon they either became slaves where they had been conquerors, or fell beneath the hands of fresh invaders in their turn.

But their nomad character was quickly lost. From shepherds they soon turned into farmers like the Canaanites. In language and even in religious observances there was little to separate the old inhabitants from the new-comers. But there was one difference. The Canaanites worshipped local deities or Baals ; Israel had one God, Jehovah (AV ' the LORD,' really a proper name). He had led them out of Egypt. A common and undisputed allegiance to Him bound together the twelve tribes and severed them from every one else. To forget Him was to fall into the loose and dangerous ways of the Canaanites ; to turn to Him was to unite in politics, in social order and in religion. (See sections 6 and 7.)

2. The Book. The contents of the book fall into three divisions: 1–3 ⁴, 3 ⁵–16 ³¹, and 17–21. The first is introductory, striking the keynote of the book—ease, forgetfulness, disobedience, enslavement, repentance, deliverance, and ease once more. The second describes in more or less detail the various occurrences of these mutations under the Judges. The third, an appendix, contains an account of the early migrations of the Danites, and the feud between Benjamin and the rest of the nation. These divisions are not the work of a single hand. Like the other historical books of the OT., Judges is a compilation. The unknown author of the book as it now stands evidently had before him much material which is now lost (cp. Josh 10 13 2 S 1 17), and he preserved this or made selections from it as he thought best. Thus, c. 5 is certainly a triumph-song going back to the time of Deborah herself. The tone of the first division is almost entirely moralising or religious. Similar passages are inserted in the second division, pointing the moral of each disaster ; but in the body of the narratives this moralising element is absent, while to the story of Abimelech there is no moral at all. This tendency is often spoken of as 'deuteronomic,' because it finds its fullest expression in the book of Deuteronomy, under whose special influence, it is supposed, Judges, like other historical books, was put into its present shape. In the third division the writer has taken over two ancient stories, without adding his own reflections to them save in isolated notes. To a modern reader this may seem an uncritical attempt to make history instructive. But there can be no doubt that history, rightly understood, is calculated to instruct ; and in the case of the Hebrews, to forget the commands of the national God, and to drift into social and domestic relations with the Canaanites, was simply to invite disaster. Thus the real meaning of the older Hebrew narratives (themselves by no means devoid of religious feeling) is explained for the reader by means of the religious insight of the later compiler.

3. The Name. The word 'judge' implies to us something very different from what it implied to a Hebrew. The Hebrews, unlike the ancient Babylonians with their elaborate codes, knew nothing of the complex machinery of the law-court ; disputes were settled by the head of the family, the elders of the tribe or of the village or town, or by the priests ; later on, in the more serious cases, by some person of national influence, and even by the king. The procedure was informal, and regulated at most by custom and a general sense of what was right. The sentence could only be enforced when public opinion was behind it. But a man who was qualified by age or experience, or both, or by special nearness to Jehovah, to settle disputes, could also do something more ; men would naturally look to him for counsel, guidance, deliverance. To judge was thus to lead and to govern. In this sense, after our period, Samuel was said to judge Israel (1 S 7 6 : see also 1 S 8 2). It is in this sense that Deborah, Gideon, Jephthah, and the other heroes of this book are judges. In each case their rise is the result of divine selection. Deborah is a prophetess, and she

summons Barak to her side ; Gideon is called by the angel of Jehovah ; the spirit of Jehovah comes mightily upon Samson (Jg 4 6 6 11 13 25). The result of this is some signal achievement against the common foe ; after which, the people, having learnt to trust the wisdom of their 'judge' in war, willingly follow it in peace (Jg 8 22 12 7). All the judges mentioned in this book appear to have been military leaders ; later, however, we find the peaceful Eli holding this office for the nation ; and Samuel, who used to go 'on circuit' to a certain number of towns (1 S 7 16), though he was constantly asked for advice in a war, is never said to have acted as general. Of the extent of the judges' authority we know nothing ; after their victories have been gained, the historian tells us no more about them. But Saul and even David in his earlier years seem to have been little more than very powerful 'judges' ; the son of Gideon himself gains the title of king with no great difficulty (Jg 9 6). The main business of a Hebrew king, from David onwards, as of an Indian rajah or a Mohammedan caliph, was to lead his people in war, settle their quarrels, and protect the poor. No one could do this satisfactorily unless he were a strong personality ; in the rough period of our book, the only way of impressing the community was by warlike prowess. But no greater service than settling disputes without fear or favour could be rendered ; and the noblest function of the Messiah Himself was to judge the poor and needy, to break in pieces the oppressor, and bring forth judgment to the Gentiles (Ps 72 4, 12 Isa 11 4 42 1, 3).

4. The Dates. Where there is no fixed era, chronology is necessarily obscure. The historian of Hebrew antiquity could of course give us no dates; he could at most tell us the duration of the lives of men or of periods of time. Dealing with times long past, of which exact chronological records were not easily obtainable, it is not surprising if the various writers are not always exact themselves, and if their notices of time do not always agree. The period of Judges, we know, extends from the death of Joshua, a certain number of years after the forty years which followed the exodus, to about the birth of Samuel, i.e. perhaps two generations before the accession of David to the throne of Judah. The exodus is now generally placed about 1250 B.C. David came to the throne about 1000 B.C. But in 1 K 6 1 the interval between the exodus and the founding of the Temple in the 4th year of Solomon, i.e. 44 years after David's accession, is said to be 480 years. From the numbers given in Judges, the interval would appear to have been still greater. Othniel, Ehud, Barak, Gideon and Samson are accountable for 220 years (40, 80, 40, 40, 20) ; the 'minor judges' (Shamgar, Tola, Jair, Ibzan, Elon and Abdon, so called because their story is not given in detail) Jephthah, Abimelech, and the periods of oppression amount to 190. (See Chronological Table.) If we add to these 40 years each for Moses (Dt 2^7, etc.), Eli (1 S 4^{18}) and David (1 K 2^{11}), with more years still for Joshua, Samuel and Saul, we shall get a period nearer to 580 than 480. It has accordingly been pointed out that the round numbers (40, 80, 20) are probably not intended to be taken as exact, but as = a generation, two generations, and half a generation respectively, although the other figures appear to be based on precise records. It has further been suggested that the years of oppression are not to be counted in with the rest, and also that some of the judges (though the book itself gives no hint of this, probable as it would seem) were synchronous with others. Many ingenious manipulations of the figures have been made to reach a result agreeing with the 480 years of 1 K 6 ; but this number may very possibly be an exaggeration, and in any case it is not easy to see how such a period as that of the Judges could ever have lasted much longer than 200 years. The two certain facts seem to be that, even through those wild years, in the case of some of the judges, more or less exact records were preserved, and that the periods of peace were very much longer than those of foreign oppression and war.

5. The Oppressors. Our book makes it clear that while the Israelites failed to conquer the whole country, they kept a firm hold on one part, the central mountain range W. of the Jordan. The desert wanderers, on entering Palestine, were forced to become mountaineers. In the plain of Esdraelon, which cut like a wedge into this range, as well as up and down the country elsewhere, were the Canaanites, with their walled towns and formidable chariots. To the W., in the low lands between the mountains and the sea, were the Philistines. E. of the Jordan valley (which was too tropical to be largely inhabited), on rolling uplands of corn and forest and heath, were the lands assigned to Reuben, Gad (Gilead) and Manasseh, but really much more in the power of Ammon and Moab. Further to the E., on the borders of the desert, were wandering but powerful tribes of Midianites, Amalekites, and others. Far across the desert to the E. were the great powers of Assyria and Babylon ; to the N. were Syria and the empire of the Hittites, while beyond the southern desert was Egypt. During this period, however, all these powers were, for various reasons, engaged within their own borders ; and Palestine, which had in

previous centuries been the battle-field of their armies, and was to be so again, was left unmolested. The oppressors of Israel, therefore, were people little if at all stronger than herself. Entrenched within her mountains, she ought to have feared nothing from Moab, Ammon and Midian. The Canaanites, though they had the doubtful advantage of wealth, and by their strongholds in the plain of Esdraelon could for a time prevent Israelite unity, never regained footing in the hill-country ; nor had they any political cohesion among themselves.

All these peoples (except the Midianites) were closely allied in race with Israel ; the Philistines, who had a better political organisation than any of their neighbours, and who did not practise circumcision, are often thought to have come from Crete, and therefore not to be Semites at all. Their hostility was by far the most serious ; Israel never succeeded in really menacing any one of their five cities ; Samson himself never led an Israelite force into their territory ; and it was the impossibility of making head against them, even under the guidance of Samuel, that led the Hebrews to change the leadership of the judge for the more settled rule of a king (1 S 8). Apart from the Philistines, Israel had more to fear from peace than war. An enemy, once repelled, never throughout this period attacked her again ; and, placed as she was between foes inside and outside her territory, she could yet lift up her eyes unto the hills, and know that her help came from thence.

6. The Historical Value of the Book. What then is to be made of these fragmentary records of invasion, foray, muster and vengeance ? Far more than appears on the surface. When Israel followed Joshua across the Jordan, she was a collection of tribes ; when Samuel handed over his authority to Saul, she was a nation. During those wild years were being forged the bonds of a nationality which has survived unprecedented shocks till the present day. Not even at the time of Saul was the nation complete ; Judah is curiously isolated from his brethren, and in the song of Deborah is never mentioned (1^2 : cp. Dt 33^7). Ephraim is regarded as the leading tribe, though his *rôle* was by no means the most glorious (8^{1,2}). But these repeated shocks of invasion did what nothing else could have done. Consciousness of a common foe gave Israel the consciousness of a common aim, destiny, and religion. This book shows more clearly than any other that the history of Israel was an evolution, a progress. National unity, indeed, might seem no further advanced under Samson than under Barak. But this is an error. The Judges made a wider appeal than to their own tribes alone ; the Hebrews were learning that they were brothers ; and this sense of brotherhood, however strangely manifesting itself, is shown clearly throughout the book.

But can we credit all the marvellous exploits, it will be asked, of individual judges ? When these are examined in detail, they offer comparatively little difficulty. True, there may be exaggeration, as so often in Hebrew writers, in the numbers ; and is it not natural that other details should be magnified when told round the camp-fire or at the village gate ? Our ideas of accuracy, it must be remembered, were unknown in the 10th cent. B.C. In the case of Samson, this tendency to glorify the exploits of a beloved champion was more marked, and reminds us of the stories told of William Tell. On the other hand, there is not an episode that is not full of most graphic and striking touches ; c. 5 is one of the finest lyrics inside or outside the Bible ; the last four chapters contain most valuable material for the religious and social history of the Hebrews ; nor is there a book in the Bible which shows us more clearly the strength and the weakness of the Hebrew nature, its rugged independence and its readiness to assimilate, the meanness and cowardice that it was prone to show, and the courage, the resolution, and the tragedy of its chosen heroes.

7. The Religious Value of the Book. What have these early stories to do with our religious life ? Is not their morality far below that of the present day ? Are not the historical conditions completely different from our own ? Do we not know far more of God than their boldest spirits could ever teach us ? These three questions suggest the following answers: (a) In the primitive character of the morality of the book lies much of its value. The Israelites were not completely different from their neighbours. They could be rash, cruel, vengeful (like the men of the Scottish clans), and even licentious ; a prophetess could exult in an act which to us spells sheer treachery (see on 5 24) ; and for their cruelties they could, like their neighbours, assume divine sanction (e.g. c. 20). Yet in spite of this, they knew that Jehovah was their God ; and, unlike the other gods, He had a definite character; certain kinds of conduct He hated, others He loved. And this knowledge gradually taught them the love of truth, justice, humanity, purity, and the deep piety that breathes in Pss 23 and 84. In our book one can watch this love just beginning to grow. If the nation that produced Jg 20 could also produce, first Jg 5, and, later on, Isa 53, what can be deemed impossible for the Spirit of God ?

(b) The conditions of life in ancient Israel were very different from our own ; but the principles were the same. Racial animosity and greed are as strong to-day as then. National peril always rose from the desire to ·get on ' or to follow the line of least resistance. National strength lay in self-forgetting enthusiasm for a common cause and devotion to the commands of God. It lies nowhere else to-day. Further, history shows that wherever there is a faith like Gideon's, whether in a Judas Maccabæus, a Wilberforce, or a Mazzini, the results are just as surprising, and just as beneficent.

(c) The God we worship is not merely ' the God of Abraham, of Isaac, and of Jacob.' He is ' the God and Father of our Lord Jesus Christ.' But the lesson that God can only be worshipped aright when the whole nation recognises its unity and the duty of mutual care and protection, is not learnt yet. The fatal distinction between God's interest in the religious life and in the social well-being of His people, we must learn to reject. Religion, patriotism and national health are unmeaning apart from each other ; and all alike are impossible unless the cause of disaster is traced to disobedience and sin. The victories of the Hero-judges, as the Epistle to the Hebrews asserts, are victories of faith ; this faith is also ours ; and of this faith the ' author and perfecter' is Jesus (Heb 11 32 12 2).

LIST OF OPPRESSIONS AND JUDGES

	Yrs. of Oppressions.	Yrs. of Judges
Oppression under Chushan-rishathaim	8	—
Peace under Othniel	—	40
Oppression under Eglon (Moab)	18	—
Peace after Ehud's deliverance	—	80
Oppression under Jabin (Canaan)	20	—
Peace after Barak's victory	—	40
Oppression under Midianites and allies	7	—
Peace after Gideon's victory	—	40
Abimelech's ' reign '	—	3
Tola	—	23
Jair	—	22
Oppression under Ammonites	18	—
Peace under Jephthah	—	6
Ibzan	—	7
Elon	—	10
Abdon	—	8
Oppression under the Philistines	40	—
Activity of Samson	—	20
Totals	113	299

Total length of Oppressions and Deliverances reckoned consecutively	412

PART 1

INTRODUCTORY (Chs. 1–3⁴)

Division 1, Chs. 1–2⁵.

This section of the book contains a brief recapitulation of the early conquest of Palestine, told from a somewhat different point of view from that of Josh 7–21, and supplying much that is there not mentioned. From these vv. it is clear that Palestine was not conquered in one great invasion ; and the whole of the book shows Israel to be only in very precarious possession of the land. The narrative in Joshua emphasises the influence over the whole collection of tribes wielded by the Ephraimite hero, Joshua himself ; Jg 1–2⁵ narrates the movements of separate tribes, leaving some of them (Issachar, Levi and Benjamin) unmentioned. It would seem that after the main body of Israelites had crossed the Jordan, captured Jericho, and made Gilgal their headquarters, the larger number of them, under Joshua, faced northwards, while Judah and Simeon remained in the south, and, for some time, were almost detached from the main body. The actual narratives of this division of Part 1 deal with (1) the conquest of Adoni-bezek by Judah and Simeon (1¹⁻⁸) ; (2) conquests of Othniel in the south (1⁹⁻¹⁵) ; (3) further conquests of Judah and Simeon (1¹⁶⁻²¹) ; (4) capture of Bethel (1²²⁻²⁶) ; (5) limits to the conquests of Manasseh, Ephraim, Zebulun, Asher, Naphtali and Dan (1²⁷⁻³⁶) ; (6) the moral, delivered by the angel at Bochim (2¹⁻⁵).

CHAPTER 1

THE CONQUESTS OF JUDAH, SIMEON, AND OTHER TRIBES

1–8. Conquests of Judah and Simeon.

1. After the death of Joshua] This joins the beginning of Judges to the end of Joshua ; but in what follows the author refers to events which must have preceded the partition of Josh 13 f., and the campaigns of Josh 10, 11. **Asked the LORD**] 'Consulted the oracle of the Lord' : cp. 18⁵ 20¹⁸. See also Ex 28³⁰ Nu 27²¹. **2. The land**] the S. part of Palestine. **3. Simeon**] The towns of Simeon (Josh 19¹⁻⁹) are also attributed to Judah (Josh 15²⁶⁻³⁶, ⁴²). Later, Simeon ceases to exist as an independent tribe. **My lot**] Each tribe has had a part of Canaan allotted to it, whose conquest it is to attempt. Judah is chosen to make the first inroad.

4. Perizzites] see on Gn 13⁷. **Canaanites**] in its special sense of 'lowlanders' : cp. Gn 13⁷ 34³⁰. **Bezek**] lying on the road from Gilgal to South Palestine. **5. Adoni-bezek**] (perhaps the same as Adoni-zedek of Josh 10¹) **is** king of Jerusalem, which city also lies in

the path of Judah and Simeon to Judah's 'lot.' **6. Cut off**] to make them unfit for warfare. **7. Kings**] chiefs or sheikhs of a city or even village. **They**] his own people.

8. Jerusalem] The city was not held, but remained in the possession of the Jebusites till the time of David (2 S 5⁶⁻⁹). Not till then would Judah really dominate Southern Palestine (cp. v. 21, and c. 19¹²).

9–15. Conquests of Othniel in the south.

9. The **mountain** denotes the central ridge, stretching from N. of Jerusalem to Hebron ; the **south**, the wild country S. of Hebron, called in Hebrew the *Negeb*, and the **valley** (RV 'lowland') the maritime plain to the W. **10. Hebron**] see on Gn 13¹⁸. **Kirjath-arba**] 'city of four' (quarters). In Josh 14¹⁵ 15¹³,¹⁴, however, Arba is regarded as a personal name ; he is 'the father of Anak,' or 'a great man among the Anakims' (a primitive gigantic race, of which Sheshai, etc., are names of divisions or clans). **11. Debir**] in the Negeb. **Kirjath-sepher**] 'Book-city.' **He**] should be Caleb (see Josh 15¹³), to whom (Josh 14⁶⁻¹⁵) Moses had promised this territory. **13.** Othniel is also the hero of the deliverance from Chushan-rishathaim (3⁹ᶠ.).

15. Blessing] a present (cp. Gn 33¹¹) or solemn token of paternal affection. **Thou hast given me**] RV, better, 'thou hast set me in.' **A south land**] RV 'the land of the South' ; for the most part a waterless region, where springs would be precious. **Upper and nether springs** are proper names.

16–21. Further conquests of Judah and Simeon.

16. The Kenite] Hobab (cp. 4¹¹, elsewhere called Jethro : cp. also Ex 2¹⁸). The Kenites are joined (in Gn 15¹⁹) with the Kenizzites, Caleb's tribe (Kenaz, v. 13), a Bedouin people in firm league with Israel : see 4¹⁷ and 1 S 15⁶. They do not, like Judah, attack the Canaanites. **City of palm trees**] Jericho, which, with Gilgal, was Israel's base of operations. **Arad**] SE. of Hebron. **Among the people**] A more probable reading is 'with the Amalekite,' i.e. not actually in Judah. **17. Zephath**] not known. **Hormah**] 'utter destruction.' To 'destroy utterly' is to put under a ban, or exterminate : cp. Josh 6¹⁷ ᵐᵍ. ('devoted,' i.e. to destruction). **18.** These, with Gath and Ashdod, are the five Philistine cities. The LXX reads 'did not take,' which accords with subsequent references to the Philistines.

19. Chariots of iron] Always an object of dread to the light-armed Israelites (cp. 4³), but useless in the hill-country, where the Israelites were more firmly established.

Could not] The Lord being with Judah, they should have been able to drive them out. Probably their faith failed at sight of the iron chariots. The Hebrew, indeed, does not say 'could not drive them out,' but 'there was no driving out.' **21.** Cp. Josh 15 ^{63}.

22–26. Capture of Bethel.

22. House of Joseph] i.e. Ephraim and Manasseh, the leading division of the nation. Later writers use Ephraim as a synonym for the ten northern tribes (e.g. Hos 11 ^{8} Isa 28 ^{3}).

23. Descry] RV 'spy out.' **Beth-el**] 9½ m. N. of Jerusalem. See Gn 28 ^{19} 35 ^{6}. **26. Hittites**] see on Gn 10 $^{15-19}$. **Luz**] Evidently a different city from that mentioned in v. 23.

27–36. Limits to the conquests of Manasseh, etc.

27. These towns are all in the plain of Esdraelon (see on c. 4), by their hold upon which the Canaanites drove a wedge between the Israelites of Northern and Central Palestine. **Beth-shean** is at the E. of the plain, **Taanach** and **Megiddo** (recently excavated and revealing a wealth of Canaanite remains) on the S., **Ibleam** on the SE., and **Dor** on the coast. **Would dwell**] i.e. succeeded in dwelling. **28. Tribute**] RV 'taskwork.' So Israel had been treated in Egypt. **29. Gezer**] On the edge of the maritime plain ; later on, taken by Egypt and given to Solomon (1 K 9 ^{15}). Here also extensive remains have been found, demonstrating the pagan worship carried on by its inhabitants. **30. Kitron . . Nahalol**] unknown. **31. Accho** (Akka), **Zidon** (Saida), and **Achzib** (Ez-Zib, N. of Akka) are all on the coast : the other towns are unknown. **33. Beth-shemesh** ('house of the sun'), not the well-known Beth-shemesh in Judah : cp. Josh 19 ^{38}. **Beth-anath** (house of the goddess Anāth) is perhaps a town 6 m. N. of Kadesh-naphtali.

34. Dan fails in securing a foothold : later, the Danites make an expedition northwards (c. 18) and Ephraim gains an entrance into the territory from which they are driven (v. 35). **Amorites**] see on Gn 10 ^{16}. **35. Mount Heres**] 'the mountain of the sun.' **Aijalon**] 12 m. W. of Jerusalem ; the scene of Joshua's great victory (Josh 10 ^{12}). **Shaalbim**] possibly 3 m. to the N. **36. Coast**] RV 'border.' The ascent of (RV) **Akrabbim** (scorpions) is said in Josh 15 ^{3} to be on the border of Judah and Edom. **Amorites** is probably a mis-reading for 'Edomites.' The spot lies on a line between Hebron and Petra, the Edomite capital. As it stands, this v. has no connexion with its context. **36. The rock**] should be, as RM, 'Sela,' i.e. Petra in Edom.

CHAPTER 2

PROLOGUE TO THE STORY OF THE JUDGES

1–5. The moral of the preceding notices, delivered by an angel at Bochim.

1. An angel of the LORD] RV 'the angel.' Cp. 6 ^{11,22} 13 ^{3,21}, where it is plain (from 6 ^{14,16} 13 ^{22}) that the angel is thought of as God Himself (see on 6 ^{14}). The word translated 'angel,' however, means simply 'messenger': cp. 6 ^{8}.

Gilgal] the site of the first Hebrew camp after the crossing of the Jordan (Josh 4 ^{19}). **Bochim**] 'weepers' (v. 4), but LXX here reads 'Bethel' (1 ^{23}), which was later the abode of the ark (20 ^{27}). Allon Bacuth, 'weeping tree,' was near Bethel (Gn 25 ^{8}). **Covenant**] see Gn 15 ^{18} 17 ^{19} Dt 4 ^{13} 8 ^{18} 29 ^{1} 31 ^{16}, etc.

Division 2, Chs. 2 ^{6}–3 ^{4}.

A return to the later scenes of Joshua's life, to connect it with the stories of the Judges. C. 2 $^{6-10}$ is very similar to Josh 24 $^{28-31}$. The history of Israel in this period is here interpreted as a succession of punishments for disobedience, and deliverance after repentance, a point of view which is not emphasised in the individual stories, but not inconsistent with them. Israel's only chance of existence in Canaan lay in its adherence to the one bond of union, the worship of Jehovah. The introduction divides into three parts : 2 $^{6-10}$, historical prologue ; 2 $^{11-23}$, interpretation of the history ; 3 $^{1-6}$, Israel's actual relations with the Canaanites.

6–10. Historical Prologue.

6. Cp. Josh 24 ^{28}. Evidently the beginning and not the end of conquest is here referred to. In the OT. Canaan is never regarded as a land of rest. **9. Timnath-heres**] 'territory of the sun': probably near Shechem. In Josh 24 ^{30} the letters of 'heres' are transposed, to avoid the suggestion of idolatrous association (cp. also Jg 8 ^{13} and RV there). **Gaash**] unknown.

11–23. The religious interpretation of the history of the Judges.

11. Baalim] RV 'the Baalim,' i.e. the local gods worshipped by the Canaanites. Baalim is the plural of Baal, which means 'lord' (cp. 8 ^{33}). Each place might thus have its patron god. Jehovah was never thought of by the Hebrews as a local deity in this sense.

13. Ashtaroth] RV 'the Ashtaroth,' properly the feminine counterpart of 'the Baalim.' In Babylon, the goddess Ashtoreth appears as Ishtar (with attributes corresponding in part to Aphrodite or Venus). How easily the worship of the native deities, the Baals, the Ashtoreths, in their sacred groves, would lead to licentiousness is obvious (see on Gn 38 ^{15}).

17. A whoring] Adultery and fornication are common figures for unfaithfulness to Israel's 'lord,' Jehovah, cp. Hos 1–3 Ezk 16, 20, Mt 12 ^{39}. The succeeding stories make it clear that it was by uniting the Hebrews in a religious war that the Judges caused the local cults to be put aside. **18. It repented the LORD**] cp. 1 S 15 ^{11} Ps 90 ^{13} Zech 8 ^{14} : on the other hand, 1 S

15²⁹ Jer 4²⁸ Ezk 24¹⁴. Here the word really means 'pity.' **20. Covenant]** Josh 23¹⁶ c. 2¹. In Joshua the ark is constantly called 'the ark of the covenant' (Josh 3³, etc.). **22. Prove]** cp. 3¹,². Such an expression shows how easily a test may become a temptation. **23. Neither delivered he, etc.]** a later addition : the whole passage deals with what occurred after the death of Joshua.

CHAPTER 3
The Story of the Judges. Othniel. Ehud. Shamgar

1–6. Israel's actual relations with the Canaanites. **1. Wars of Canaan]** i.e. those waged by Joshua, after whose death (2²¹) the career of victory was made to cease by Jehovah. **2.** A third reason for the survival of the heathen in Canaan, in addition to those given in 2¹f. and in 2²² 3¹. **3. Philistines]** see Intro. § 5. The

Philistines occupied the lowland in the SW. Their five cities formed a confederacy : see 16⁵, etc., and 1S6¹⁶f. At the death of Samuel their power extends far into central Palestine (1S31¹⁰). **All the Canaanites]** in the more restricted sense, the lowlanders of the SW. bordering on the Philistines. **Hivites]** read 'Hittites' : see on Gn 10¹⁵⁻¹⁹. **Baal-hermon]** In the similar passage in Joshua we read 'Baal-Gad under Hermon' (13⁵), a place on the W. side of Hermon. **The entering in of Hamath]** Hamath was a powerful city of the Hittites on the Orontes (modern Hamā). The 'entrance' to it is the hollow country between Lebanon and anti-Lebanon, on the plain at the N. end of Lebanon : cp. 2S8⁹ 1K8⁶⁵ Am6¹⁴, where it is regarded as the true northern frontier of Israel. **5.** See on 1¹⁻⁴ 3³. To these six 'nations' of Canaan the Girgashites are often added. **6.** Cp. Ex34¹⁶ Neh13²⁵.

PART 2
HISTORY OF THE JUDGES (Chs. 3⁵–16³¹)

On this, the main section of the book, see Intro. § 2 and List of Oppressions and Judges. The larger part of the book is concerned with six of the Judges, one of whom is not properly a Judge at all (Abimelech), and in the case of another (Samson) isolated forays are recorded, but no actual deliverance.

7–11. Chushan-rishathaim and Othniel. **7. The groves]** RV 'the asheroth.' The word (another plural) means the sacred poles set up near an altar, which were common in Semitic worship (even Solomon's temple had 'pillars': see on 1K7²¹). Here, however, actual goddesses seem to be intended, perhaps regarded as symbolised by the poles. **8. Chushan-rishathaim]** The Heb. word means 'Ethiopian of double iniquity.' The real name must be hidden behind this expression. **Mesopotamia]** see on Gn 24¹⁰. **9. Othniel]** cp. 1¹³. **10. The Spirit of the LORD]** used here and elsewhere of the inspiration which makes a man capable of great and apparently superhuman exploits and achievements : 6³⁴ 11²⁹ 14⁶ 15¹⁴ : cp. also Ex31³. **12–30.** Eglon and Ehud. **12. Moab]** the high plateau on the E. of the Dead Sea : cp. 2K3²⁴. **13. Ammon]** N. of Moab : the Amalekites (Gn36¹²) are called Edomites. They occupied the desert between Sinai and S. Palestine. The Kenites formed one of their nomad clans, but on the whole their enmity to Israel was constant : cp. 1S15²f.; hence their readiness to join Eglon's invasion. **City of palm trees]** cp. 1¹⁶ : Jericho, which was thus not entirely

destroyed (Josh 6²⁶). It would command the roads from central to southern Palestine. **15. Lefthanded]** lit. 'lamed in his right hand.' Hence the success of his ruse : but 20¹⁶ seems to show that ambidexterity is all that is meant : cp. also 1Ch12². **Present]** i.e. tribute. **16. Dagger]** RV 'sword,' about 14 in. in the blade. Being on his right thigh (convenient for his left hand) the guards would not notice it. **17. Brought]** RV 'offered,' as in v. 18. **19. Quarries]** RM 'graven images,' perhaps carved stones. Once beyond these (cp. v. 26), though only 2 m. from Jericho, Ehud knew that he was safe. **20. Summer parlour]** RM 'upper chamber of cooling' : a room on the flat roof of an Oriental house ; in this case enclosed so that the interior was not visible from outside. **22.** No meaning can be obtained from the Heb. words at the end of this v. **23. Locked]** i.e. bolted (as in the East at present). **26. Seirath]** unknown. **27. Mountain]** i.e. hill-country. The men of Ephraim (Joshua's tribe) are recognised as the leaders in Israel : cp. 8¹. **28. Toward Moab]** RV 'against the Moabites,' i.e. to prevent their returning. **29.** For the expression ten thousand, cp. 1⁴ 4⁶ 7³ 20³⁴. **30. Fourscore]** two full generations. **31. Shamgar]** the first of the 'minor' Judges. The name is mentioned in 5⁶, though not as a 'saviour.' No Philistine oppression is mentioned till later. **An ox goad]** would be an efficient substitute for a spear—a six-foot staff tipped with a spike : cp. 15¹⁴f. and 2S23²¹.

CHAPTER 4

DEBORAH AND BARAK

This deliverance is described a second time in the early poem in c. 5 (see on 5¹). No other narrative describes more clearly the religious gathering of the clans, and the prowess of the hardy mountaineers when united. The plain of Esdraelon (see Intro. § 5) is one of the famous battle-fields of history. It drives like a wedge from the coast within 10 m. of the Jordan; but it is dominated by hills on all sides, and is almost closed by them at its western end. In c. 5 all the tribes are mentioned either as uniting or refusing to appear, save Judah and Simeon. Subsequently we hear no more of such united efforts.

1–3. Oppression by Jabin.

2. Jabin] In Josh 11 ¹⁻³ Jabin is defeated by Joshua at the waters of Merom, near the head of the Jordan valley, and Hazor is burned. In c. 5 Jabin is not mentioned, and Sisera is apparently regarded as king. **Hazor]** from Josh 19³⁶, probably near Kadesh-naphtali. **Harosheth of the Gentiles]** or 'foreigners' is thus distinguished from Hebrew Harosheth. Site doubtful; probably not far from Megiddo, or at the W. end of the plain. **3. Chariots]** They would be well-nigh irresistible on the plain. The Israelites, living in the hills, had none until Solomon's time.

4–24. Defeat and Death of Sisera.

4. Judged] not in the technical sense used in this book, but of the deciding of disputes (v. 5). **5. Mount Ephraim]** see on 3²⁷. Deborah's own tribe would seem to have been Issachar (5¹⁵). **Dwelt]** RV 'sat,' as judge, to decide cases. **Deborah]** 'bee.' **6. Barak]** 'lightning': cp. the Carthaginian name Hamilcar Barca. **Kedesh-naphtali]** i.e. Kadesh (i.e. the shrine) of Naphtali; now Kades, 4 m. from the upper end of the waters of Merom. **Mount Tabor]** 1,843 ft. high: it commands the plain of Esdraelon from the NE. **Ten thousand men]** cp. vv. 10, 14, 3²⁹ 5⁸, etc. In this c. only the two tribes Naphtali and Zebulun are mentioned: in c. 5 as many as six gather to Barak's standard. Naphtali and Zebulun, bordering on the plain, are the most concerned. **9. Sell]** cp. 2¹⁴ 3⁸ 4². **A woman]** i.e. Jael.

10. Went up] to Tabor. The flat summit of this conical hill made an excellent position from which the Israelites could charge down to the plain. **11. The Kenites]** cp. 1¹⁶. **Father in law]** is correct, not (as RV) 'brother in law.' The modern traveller Porter noticed the black tents of nomads near Kedesh. **Plain]** RV 'oak'; evidently a prominent tree on the N. of the edge of the plain of Esdraelon. **13. Kishon]** This river rises in the high ground to the SE. of the plain, and flows right through it in a northwesterly direction. From Tabor on the NE. the

Israelites would dash down and drive the Canaanites back upon its banks : in rainy weather the whole plain would be further intersected by the Kishon's tributaries. In 1799, after the battle of Mt. Tabor, numbers of fugitive Turks were swept away by the torrent and drowned. **15. Fled away]** northward to Kedesh, while Barak's host hurries westwards.

18. Mantle] RV 'rug,' or perhaps 'tent-curtain.' **19. Bottle of milk]** i.e. a lamb- or goat-skin. C. 5²⁵ adds 'butter.' 5²⁶ seems (though not certainly) to imply that Sisera is killed as he stands drinking. **21.** The **nail** or tent-pin was of wood : to drive it into the ground when camping was the women's work. On the morality of the act see on 5²⁴. **22.** If Barak came up immediately, he must have left the main body of the pursuers almost as they left the battle-field. **24.** The Israelites now proceed to do on a small scale what, after the victories of Joshua, they had refused to do on a large one.

CHAPTER 5

DEBORAH'S TRIUMPH SONG

This song celebrates the victory of c. 4; but from the point of view, not of a later annalist, but of a contemporary poet—very possibly (though see v. 12) the prophetess herself. The lyric outburst is one of the finest in any language ; its style (though many of the words are now very obscure) is typical of the best Hebrew poetry. Its independence of c. 4 may be inferred from the variations it exhibits. Sisera is represented as king : the majority of the tribes, not Zebulun and Naphtali only, are summoned : and the manner of Sisera's death is different. It says much for the fidelity of the compiler that he did not attempt to 'edit' these apparent discrepancies.

1–5. Introductory.

1. For the avenging of Israel] RV 'for that the leaders took the lead in Israel.' The Hebrew word most probably has to do with 'letting loose' ; perhaps, 'with the streaming locks of warriors.' **3.** A good instance of the 'parallelism' of Hebrew poetry ; parallel, and sometimes almost identical thoughts are placed side by side. Abundant instances can be found in almost every Psalm. For the **kings** and **princes,** cp. Ps 2² Hab 1¹⁰. **4. Seir]** the mountainous region which extends from the E. of the Dead Sea to the head of the Red Sea. The northern half of it was inhabited by Edom. Towards the southern end of it is Sinai (v. 5). Jehovah is still thought of as dwelling in the desert, where He had first revealed Himself to Israel, and where He delivered them from Egypt. Cp. Ps 18⁷ Isa 64¹ Hab 3¹⁰.

6–11. The Oppression.

6. Shamgar] mentioned (if he is the same man) in 3³¹ ; here, the reference can hardly be to a Judge and deliverer. So with Jael ; perhaps another individual is intended ; or the correct name has fallen out of the text.

Unoccupied] Because of the insecurity of the country. **7. The villages**] RV 'rulers'; the word occurs in v. 11, and probably means 'peasantry.' The great trade routes were empty, and even rural life stagnated. **8.** The first two clauses are very obscure ; the second should perhaps be 'the barley-bread failed.'

10. Speak] (RV 'tell') means properly 'meditate upon it.' Of the three classes addressed, the first consists of magistrates or leading men, the second (**in judgment** should be, as RV, 'on rich carpets') of the wealthy, the third of the people. **11.** The words in italics, supplied by the translators, help us to make sense of this v., though they cannot be considered certain. In contrast to v. 6 there is now deep peace throughout the whole country-side.

12–23. The gathering of the tribes, and the battle.

12. Captivity] either 'thy captives' or 'thy captors' ; cp. Ps 68 18 Eph 4 8. **13.** RV is more probable ; 'then came down a remnant of the nobles and of the people.' The two clauses are joined as in vv. 2 and 9. **14.** RV 'out of Ephraim *came down* they whose root is in Amalek.' This seems to suggest that Amalek once possessed the land of Ephraim ; but see on 12 15. The largest and smallest tribes are mentioned together, as in Hos 5 8. **Machir**] a clan of Manasseh (apparently used here for the whole tribe) which is generally connected with Gilead. **Pen of the writer**] RV 'marshal's staff' ; the 'writer' is the officer who musters the troops.

15. He was sent] RV 'into the valley they' (the men of Issachar) 'rushed forth at his feet.' Reuben dwelt in N. Moab, E. of the Dead Sea ; in the later history the tribe is never heard of, as, from this v., is not surprising. **For the divisions**] RV 'by the watercourses' (so in v. 16). **17. Gilead**] i.e. 'the people living in Gilead.' Reuben and Manasseh have been already mentioned ; hence, Gad. **Dan**] would seem to have already migrated to the N. and to have connected itself with the seafaring Phœnicians (18 7). For **Asher**, see 1 31. **Breaches**] RV 'creeks,' or harbours.

19. Kings] the petty chiefs of districts and towns among the Canaanites. **Taanach .. Megiddo**] see on 1 27. **20, 21.** The very forces of nature were in alliance against Canaan. Kishon, though second to the Jordan (35 m. long from source to sea), is often, in parts, dry in the summer. Like other mountain-fed streams, it rises rapidly after a storm ; here, its torrents sweep away the Canaanite chariots. **21. Strength**] Abstract for concrete. **22.** RV 'Then did the horsehoofs stamp by reason of the pransings.' This v., describing the battle, would seem naturally to precede vv. 21 f., describing the rout.

23. Meroz] an unknown place. The mention of Jael immediately after suggests that the villagers of Meroz might have done what Jael did with such success.

24–27. The Death of Sisera.

24. Sisera, according to the code of the times, on entering Jael's tent, was entitled to protection. Could a prophetess, it has been asked, invoke a blessing on an act of sheer treachery ? (cp. 4 17). There may have been extenuating circumstances of which we are ignorant ; more probably the v. is simply an utterance of the poet's joy at an act without which the victory would have been imperfect, and might have proved fruitless : see Intro § 7. **Women in the tent**] Bedouin women nomads. **25, 26.** These vv. say nothing about Sisera's lying down to sleep, and they suggest that he was killed in the act of drinking (note 'smote off' instead of 'smote through') : but (see v. 27) this is not absolutely necessary.

25. Butter] Properly sour milk or curds. **Lordly dish**] A bowl fit for nobles. **27.** The repetition is highly effective.

28–30. Ironical representation of the expectation at Sisera's home.

28. Cried] in eager, half-anxious tones. **30. Have they not sped ?**] rather, 'Do they not find ?'—the form of the word denotes an unfinished action, which accounts for the delay. **A damsel** *or* **two**] rather, 'A slave-girl, two slave girls, for each brave man.' **Prey**] RV 'spoil.' **Needlework on both sides**] means two pieces of needlework (for each man). RV 'embroidery.'

31. Final prayer. The last clause is added by the editor.

CHAPTER 6
GIDEON AND THE MIDIANITES

The story of Gideon, which runs from 6 1 to 8 33, is more detailed than that of Deborah and Barak ; and, from the details, it would appear that different traditions have been used. Gideon, at the bidding of an angel, calls his clan together, and after reducing them to 300 men, and receiving the encouragement of a dream, surrounds the camp of the Midianites and throws them into a panic. The Ephraimites complete the defeat. The two kings of Midian are then pursued beyond Jordan and slain Gideon is offered the kingdom, but refuses it, and lives to old age in honour and peace.

1–6. The Midianites oppress Israel.

1. Midian] These desert nomads are regarded by the Hebrews as akin to them (Gn 36 35 ; cp. Ex 2 15-21). They are found in the neighbourhood of the peninsula of Sinai, and also wander northwards : on this occasion they pour westwards across the Jordan into the more fertile lands of Palestine. Like modern Bedouins they raid and harry and destroy, but make no permanent conquest. That the Israelites did not desert their homes is plain from v. 11, etc. **3. Amalekites**] see on 3 13. **Children of the east**] other tribes living on the borders of the eastern desert. **4. Unto Gaza**] i.e. the whole country from the Jordan to the coast. Gaza was a Philistine town on the SW. of Palestine which they did not venture to pass. **5. Grasshoppers**] RV 'locusts.'

8–10. The Israelites rebuked by a Prophet. **8. A prophet**] who brings a similar message to that of the angel in 2 1-3. The prophet is the spokesman of Jehovah. See Intro. to Samuel. The spirit of the prophetic message is always (a) moral, (b) national. **10. Amorites**] see on Gn 10 16.

11–40. The call of Gideon, and the tests by which it was proved.

11. Angel] see on 2 1. **Ophrah**] in v. 24 'Ophrah of the Abi-ezrites.' Presumably, this Ophrah is near Shechem. Abi-ezer is a division of Manasseh (Josh 17 2). **Wheat by the winepress**] RV 'in'; i.e. for concealment. The usual threshing-floor is in an exposed place : the winepress is a shallow pit in the ground, from which the grape-juice runs into two deeper vats. There would have been but little wheat to thresh. **13. My Lord**] not as LORD, the divine name, but equivalent to 'Sir.' **14. The LORD**] Here the angel is identified with Jehovah : cp. 13 22. **15. Poor**] RV 'the poorest.' Joash, however, can defy the 'city,' v. 31. **17. That thou talkest**] RV 'that it is thou that talkest.' The angel has not, however, told Gideon who he is ; probably this clause was not in the original narrative (cp. v. 22). **23.** The last clause of v. 21 should apparently follow rather than precede this v. **24. Jehovah–shalom**] 'Jehovah is peace' (v. 23) ; cp. Ex 17 15.

25. The altar .. that thy father hath] Joash is the priest and custodian of the village sanctuary. The 'grove' should be the pole or 'asherah' at its side. Such an attack would naturally be resented by the villagers. **26. Ordered place**] RV 'orderly manner.' **31.** To avoid giving up his son (whom the men did not venture to take by force), Joash asks, 'Will *you* be so presumptuous as to plead for Baal ? That would be impiety worthy of instant death.' Baal can defend himself. **32.** Other names compounded with Baal ('lord,' used as equivalent to Jehovah) exist, viz. Ishbaal and Meribbaal. For 'Baal,' 'bosheth' (shame) is at times substituted by later scribes (2 S 11 21). See also on 1 Ch 8 33 2 S 2 8. From the form of the name it should rather mean 'Baal (or Jehovah) founds.'

33. Were gathered together] on the E. of Jordan, for another raid into Palestine, and 'went over' the river. **The valley of Jezreel**] leads up from the Jordan to the plain of Esdraelon. Jezreel is the modern Zerin.

34. Cp. 13 25. **Came upon**] lit. 'clothed itself with Gideon.' In the strength of this inspiration he assembles not only his own clan and fellow-tribesmen, but the men of neighbouring tribes, all of whom would be threatened by the raid.

37. Gideon's tests. Wool retains moisture for a specially long time.

CHAPTER 7
THE ROUT OF MIDIAN

1–7. Gideon's choice of his Followers. **1.** The sites here mentioned are doubtful. **Moreh**] said to be near Shechem (Gn 12 6 Dt 11 30). After the battle Gideon crosses the Jordan by the fords one would take if travelling from Shechem eastwards. **3. Gilead**] is E. of the Jordan : some other locality must be meant. For the return of the timid, cp. Dt 20 8.

5. Probably an arbitrary test. It is as easy to find abstract reasons for choosing those who stooped down as for rejecting them. The test in 12 6 is very different.

8–25. The Rout of Midian.

11. The author frankly admits that, in spite of 6 34, Gideon is afraid to take the bolder course.

13. A cake of barley bread] apparently a disk-like cake baked in the ashes: representing the Israelite peasants, as the tent represents the Midianite nomads.

15. Worshipped] bowed down before God. **16. Lamps**] RV 'torches.'

18. *The sword*] These words do not occur in the Heb. in this v. but are supplied from v. 20. Jehovah is the true leader of the Israelite host.

19. The middle watch] i.e. when the night was about a third through: well before midnight.

22. These places cannot be identified, but were probably in the Jordan valley, towards a point E. of Shechem.

23. See 6 35. Probably those who had left Gideon before the surprise now hurry in pursuit of the flying foe. They did not, however, as it would seem, actually join Gideon (8 4).

24. Ephraim] the leading tribe has not yet been mentioned. **Beth-barah**] not certainly identified; probably a tributary of the Jordan, the Wady Fārah, which the Ephraimites would be able to reach before the fugitives. The latter—thus prevented from moving further southwards—would be enclosed between the two rivers, and helpless. Cp. Isa 9 4.

25. Two princes] RV 'the two princes.'

Oreb] 'Raven.' **Zeeb**] 'Wolf.' **Other side Jordan**] This is an anticipation of the next c. (v. 4).

CHAPTER 8
THE PURSUIT OF THE KINGS. GIDEON'S SUBSEQUENT CAREER AND DEATH

1. Cp. c. 12. Ephraim claimed to be the leading tribe ; later the name was often used as a synonym for the northern kingdom. The natural jealousy of the tribe was appeased by Gideon's ready wit ; one might have suspected that, making such claims as these, they would not have left Gideon to take the initiative.

2. Gleaning and **vintage**] note the contrast between these. **Abi-ezer**] Gideon substitutes this for his own name. **4.** Having driven the Midianites into the arms of Ephraim, Gideon turns eastwards. V. 10 implies that a very considerable section of the foe had escaped the trap and was still formidable. **5. Succoth**] like Penuel (Gn 33 ^{17}) must be E. of the Jordan, near the Jabbok. **6.** The chiefs of Succoth evidently doubt whether Gideon is really victorious as yet.

9. Tower] Where a city had no walls, a central stronghold was frequent. In the middle ages the church tower sometimes served this purpose: cp. 9 ^{46}. **10. Karkor**] unknown. The other two places are probably SE. of the Jabbok. The Midianites were making for the desert (cp. Nu 32 $^{35, 42}$). For the numbers cp. 7 ^{13}. Gideon's first levy is said to have numbered 32,000 (7 ^{3}). **11. The way of them that dwelt in tents**] i.e. the road usually taken by the nomads. **12. Secure**] i.e. free from anxiety, as in the camp W. of the Jordan (c. 7). **13. Before the sun** *was up*] RV 'from the ascent of Heres,' i.e. from the way up to Heres (see on 2 ^{9}). **14. Described**] RM 'wrote down' a list of the chief men. The **elders** are heads of families ; the **princes** (cp. v. 6) are the military leaders. **16. Taught**] if right, bitterly ironical. All the early versions read 'threshed,' or 'carded,' as v. 7 implies.

18. This private wrong of Gideon's is now mentioned for the first time. **Tabor**] see on 4 ^{6}. **19.** According to the law of blood revenge, the nearest relative is bound to avenge the victim's death (cp. Nu 35 ^{19}). **20. Jether**] is the same name as Jethro (Ex 4 ^{18} 1 K 2 ^{5}). To be slain by a boy would be a further indignity for the two chiefs, who meet their death with barbarian courage. **21. Ornaments**] RV 'crescents': cp. v. 26.

22-35. Gideon's subsequent career and death.

22. The fame of Gideon's exploit makes his countrymen desire that he should become an hereditary monarch and not merely a judge. See Intro. to Samuel.

26. *Shekels*] A shekel is rather less than

half an ounce. The whole weight would thus be nearly seventy pounds. **Collars**] RV 'pendants.' **27. Ephod**] see 17 ^{5}. An image of some sort used in consulting the will of Heaven. **28. Forty years**] cp. 5 ^{31}. **29. Jerubbaal**] i.e. Gideon : see 6 ^{32}.

33-35. The Israelites lapse into idolatry after Gideon's death.

33. Baalim] RV 'the Baalim": see on 2 ^{11}. **Baal-berith**] i.e. Baal of the Covenant. The alliance between the Canaanites and the Hebrews would naturally be cemented by a common worship, which would involve the latter in idolatry : cp. 9 ^{46} (El-berith).

CHAPTER 9
THE STORY OF ABIMELECH

This c. breaks the regular order of the book, since Abimelech is not thought of as a judge, and the Canaanites are not here regarded as oppressors. The story, however, throws a valuable light on the way in which Israel fell into unfaithfulness, when free from the yoke of foreign oppression.

1-6. The rise of Abimelech.

1. As being born out of regular wedlock, Abimelech would be brought up at first in his mother's family, and reckoned as belonging to it (v. 2). It seems to have been of considerable position in Shechem. **Shechem**] still, as in Gn 34, chiefly Canaanitish, in spite of being Joseph's burial-place (Josh 24 ^{32}). **Threescore and ten** *pieces* **of silver**] between seven and eight pounds sterling. **4. Vain**] worthless : hired mercenaries of no character. **5. On one stone**] as if they had been sacrificial animals (1 S 14 $^{33 f.}$). **6. Millo**] apparently a Shechemite family, or a town near Shechem (v. 20). The word has a different meaning in 1 K 9 ^{15} 2 K 12 ^{20}. **King**] Abimelech is no Israelite king, but simply the ruler over the single city of Shechem ; nothing implies that the Hebrews recognised this royalty. **Plain**] RV 'oak': cp. Gn 35 ^{4} Josh 24 ^{26} 1 S 11 ^{15}. **Pillar**] like the 'asherah,' a regular feature of a Canaanite shrine.

7-21. Jotham's parable and flight.

7. Gerizim] Shechem lies between Gerizim (nearly 3,000 ft. high) on the S. and Ebal on the N.

8-15. Jotham's Fable. Its connexion with the moral which Jotham wishes to point is somewhat loose, and perhaps it was a popular story ; but it sufficiently expresses Jotham's hatred and contempt ; feelings which find further vent in the sarcasm of the prayer in 16-20. Cp. the fable of Jehoash in 2 K 14 ^{9}. The fruit-trees render the real service ; the bramble desires the empty honour.

21. Beer] not known. The name means 'Well' (cp. Beer-sheba).

22-33. The Conspiracy of Gaal.

22. Over Israel] at most over the Manassites

who were connected with the Canaanites of Shechem. **23. God sent**] cp. 1 S 16¹⁴ and 1 K 22¹⁹. For the general attitude which regards God as the source of good and evil alike, cp. Am 3⁶ Job 2¹⁰. This evil spirit, however, obviously comes as an inevitable retribution upon Abimelech, in fulfilment (as the writer means to imply) of Jotham's curse (v. 57). **25.** The main eastern and northern roads both pass through Shechem. Since Abimelech probably took toll from the merchants who used them, these highway robberies would injure his treasury and his reputation alike. **26.** Gaal is introduced quite abruptly; vv. 26–41 are really in parenthesis: the main narrative is continued at v. 42. **Ebed** means 'slave'; probably the name was Obed, 'servant' (of God). **27. Made merry**] RV 'held festival': see on 21²¹. Gaal seizes his opportunity at this time of excitement. **28. Him**] in each case Abimelech. **The son of Jerubbaal**] and therefore no true Shechemite. For **serve,** etc., it would make better sense to read 'Ye are servants of the men of Hamor,' etc. **Hamor**] cp. Gn 33¹⁹. **29. And he said**] we should read (continuing Gaal's speech) 'and I would say.' Gaal is not interviewing Abimelech (v. 30), who is at Arumah (v. 41). **31. Privily**] RV 'craftily,' or as RM 'at Tormah,' which perhaps stands for Arumah. **32. The field**] the usual expression for the open country: cp. v. 36. **33.** The whole atmosphere reeks with intrigue and cruelty: an eloquent comment on the Canaanite character.

34–49. The Conspiracy is stamped out.

35. The entering of the gate] the usual meeting-place. Gaal does not suspect that Zebul has discovered his plot, and is not on his guard. **37. Plain of Meonenim**] lit. 'oak of the soothsayers.' Cp. Gn 12⁶ Jg 4⁵. Trees in Palestine often served as landmarks; a conspicuous tree is still regarded as endowed with sanctity. **38.** Zebul now throws off the disguise. **41. Arumah**] is unidentified. Gaal has awakened no real enthusiasm; but neither has Abimelech. **42.** The main narrative is continued from v. 25. **45.** To 'sow with salt' (Dt 29²³) is to make utterly desolate.

46. The tower of Shechem] This appears to be a place outside Shechem (perhaps like Millo, v. 20), whose inhabitants fear a fate similar to that of Shechem itself. **Hold**] a rare word for 'hiding place,' as in 1 S 13⁶; here, perhaps, meaning some strong and spacious chamber in the temple. **The god Berith**] RV 'El-berith': see on 8³³. **48. Zalmon**] probably a neighbouring hill. The hill in Ps 68¹⁴ is thought to be E. of Jordan in the Hauran range.

50–57. The Death of Abimelech.

50. Thebez] 13 m. NE. of Shechem. **51. Top**] RV 'roof,' which would probably be flat, with a parapet. **53. A piece of a millstone**] RV 'an upper millstone,' detachable from the lower; such stones weighed about 27 pounds. The mill is of course worked by hand. **All to brake**] RV 'brake.' 'To brake' is really one word, meaning 'smashed' or 'broke in.' **54. Armourbearer**] cp. 1 S 14⁶ 31⁴. The king's attendant has just time to give him a mortal wound. **55. Men of Israel**] see on v. 22. The Israelites have supported Abimelech against their common foes. **56. Rendered**] RV 'requited.'

CHAPTER 10
THE AMMONITE OPPRESSION

1–5. The Minor Judges, Tola and Jair.

1. Defend] RV 'save.' **Tola**] see on Gn 46¹³ Nu 26²³ 1 Ch 7¹. **Shamir**] unknown. Issachar appears at this time to have had no territory of its own. **3. Jair**] see Nu 32⁴¹ Dt 3¹⁴ 1 K 4¹³. Gilead is the country E. of the Jordan to which Jephthah also belongs, and which was specially open to attack. **4. Havoth-jair**] i.e. tent-villages of Jair: cp. 1 Ch 2²². **5. Camon**] unknown.

6–18. The Ammonite oppression. These vv. serve as an introduction to the story of Jephthah, and also, in part (vv. 6, 7), to those of Samson and Samuel. They repeat the lessons of c. 2, and, like that passage, remind us throughout of the tone of Deuteronomy. The sequence of thought is the same; faithlessness, oppression, repentance, deliverance.

6. Baalim and Ashtaroth] see on 2¹¹⁻¹³. **7. The children of Ammon**] see Gn 19³⁸, where they are said to be akin to the Hebrews. They claimed the land between the Arnon and the Jabbok, E. of Jordan, which the tribes of Reuben and Gad had partly possessed, and which includes a large part of Gilead (v. 8). **The Amorites** were the aboriginal inhabitants of this, as of the hill-country W. of the Jordan. **9.** The Ammonite raids extended to the central strongholds of Palestine (cp. 12¹); but c. 11 makes it clear that the brunt of their 'oppression' was felt in Gilead. **11.** See v. 6. The two lists partially coincide. **The Amorites**] Perhaps a reference to Nu 21²¹f. **Ammon**] So far no deliverance from these has been described. **12.** We know nothing of a Zidonian oppression. **Amalekites**] see 3¹³ and 6³,³³, also Ex 17⁸. **Maonites**] LXX has 'Midianites.' The Maonites lived S. of the Dead Sea: cp. 2 Ch 20¹ RV, 26⁷. **17. Mizpeh**] of Gilead, the scene of the compact between Jacob and Laban (Gn 31⁴⁹). The name means 'watch-tower.'

CHAPTER 11
JEPHTHAH'S VICTORY OVER THE AMMONITES. HIS RASH VOW

1–11. The Choice of Jephthah.

1. As the son of a harlot, Jephthah has no legal standing in the tribe. **Gilead begat**] Throughout the rest of the narrative Gilead is the name of a place, not a person (cp. 12⁷). Here Gilead's 'sons' represent the legitimate tribesmen. **3. Tob**] must have been near Gilead, probably to the NE. (cp. 2 S 10⁶). **Vain men**] see on 9⁴. 'Broken men,' such as came to David at the cave of Adullam (1 S 22²). **Went out**] on forays. **9.** Jephthah insists on being more than a hired captain : he will be reinstated in the tribe, and placed at its head permanently : cp. 1 S 11¹⁵.

11. Before the LORD] in the holy place at Mizpeh, so that there would be no going back from the bargain.

12–28. Jephthah and the Ammonite chieftain. For this appeal to the enemy's sense of right cp. Nu 20¹⁴ᶠ·, an event to which Jephthah here refers.

13. See on 10⁷. **Restore**] The possessions of Israel are still in dispute. **18.** Jephthah points out that Israel made a wide detour so as to leave the real territory of Moab free ; he does not refer specifically to Ammon, but in the following vv., as here, he seems to have Moab specially in his mind. The two peoples were akin to one another : cp. Gn 19³⁷,³⁸. **19.** See Nu 21²¹ᶠ. Heshbon is 16 m. E. of the Jordan, and 12 m. S. of the capital of Ammon. The Amorite territory had belonged to Moab formerly (Nu 21²⁶). **20. Coast**] RV ' border,' i.e. territory. **Jahaz**] cp. Nu 21²³ Dt 2³² ; a Moabite city. **22. The wilderness**] the Eastern desert. **23.** Jephthah's argument (see on v. 19) is that no land had been taken from Moab or Ammon, only from the aboriginal Amorites.

24. Chemosh] properly, the god of Moab. The Ammonite god was Milcom (1 K 11³³, etc.). It has been inferred that Jephthah, or the narrator of Jephthah's words, believed in the existence and power of Chemosh as in that of Jehovah : but this cannot be held to be certain : see also v. 27. An interesting commentary on this passage is to be found in an inscription of Mesha, king of Moab (2 K 3⁴ᶠ·), who ascribes all his defeats to the wrath of Chemosh, and his conquests over Israel to Chemosh's goodwill. **25.** RV rightly puts the stop at the end of the v. V. 26 begins a fresh question : see Nu 22²ᶠ. **26. Aroer**] on the N. bank of the Arnon, like **Heshbon** and **Jahaz**, is a Moabite town. The Ammonite town, Rabbath-Ammon, is unmentioned. **Three hundred years**] The different periods hitherto mentioned in the book amount to 301 years.

29–33. Jephthah's Victory over Ammon.

29. The Spirit of the LORD] cp. 7³⁴. In v. 11 Jephthah and all the people are already at Mizpeh. If these words stand in the right place, they must refer to further journeys

taken by Jephthah to rouse the whole people, previous to attacking the Ammonites.

30, 31. Cp. the vows of Jacob (Gn 28²⁰), Hannah (1 S 1¹¹), Absalom (2 S 15⁸). **Whatsoever**] RM 'whosoever.' Who would have been more likely to come out to meet the returning captain than his only daughter ? Mesha, king of Moab, sacrificed his eldest son in the stress of a siege (2 K 3²⁷), and that the rite of child-sacrifice was not unknown in Israel is shown by 2 K 16³ 21⁶ Jer 7³¹ Ezk 16²⁰ 20²⁶ Mic 6⁷, etc. Cp. also Gn 22. **33. The plain of vineyards**] should be a proper name, Abel-cheramim (so RV).

34–40. The fulfilment of Jephthah's vow. The tragic story is told with consummate art and noble reticence. There is no reason to doubt its literal truth.

34. Came out to meet him] cp. Ex 15²⁰ 1 S 18⁶. **35. Thou**] The pronoun is emphatic. Jephthah had had troubles enough both from his kinsmen and his foes. When his daughter comes out to meet him, the full significance of his self-imposed vow bows him strengthless to the ground. **36.** His daughter divines what is in his mind : for she could hardly have learned of his vow beforehand (v. 34).

37. Bewail my virginity] The greatest grief of a Hebrew woman consisted in being childless. The writer leaves us in no doubt of her fate. **40. Lament**] RV ' celebrate.'

CHAPTER 12

The Ephraimites quarrel with Jephthah. His Death

1–6. Jephthah and Ephraim. Once more the members of the leading tribe find themselves left out of the victory, and complain : cp. 8¹. Jephthah deals with them differently from Gideon.

1. Northward] RM 'to Zaphon,' a town near Succoth : cp. Josh 13²⁷. **2. When I called you**] It would seem that Jephthah had done more than simply rouse Gilead : see on 11²⁹. **4.** Jephthah now makes use of the headship promised him in 11¹¹. The second part of the v. is unintelligible. As it stands, it refers to some further taunt of the Ephraimites. But 'fugitives' means, in the original, 'survivors' : and the Gileadites are regarded in the genealogies as an offshoot of Manasseh, to whom, indeed, the land of Gilead is assigned. **5. The passages**] RV 'fords.' Ephraim had invaded Gilead, and the Gileadites took advantage of a dialectical peculiarity to identify every Ephraimite fugitive. Some exaggeration of numbers seems indisputable.

8–15. The Minor Judges, Ibzan, Elon, Abdon.

8. Bethlehem] Probably in Zebulun, mentioned in Josh 19¹⁵. **9. Thirty**] cp. 10⁴. **11. Elon**] in Nu 26²⁶ the name of a clan ;

possibly in the cases of **Ibzan** and **Abdon** also the hero and his family are confused. **15. Pirathon**] Possibly the modern Ferata, SW. of Shechem. **Amalekites**] Probably the Amalekites had made a settlement in Mt. Ephraim.

CHAPTER 13
THE STORY OF SAMSON

Except for 15²⁰ and 16³¹, Samson has none of the characteristics of a Judge. His exploits against the Philistines are all solitary, and though they doubtless afforded relief to the Israelites, they left no permanent result. We learn much more of the internal organisation of the Philistines than of any of the other foes of Israel ; and it was their continued and formidable opposition which, under the will of Jehovah, really welded Israel into a single nation in the times of Samuel and Saul. Samson could not accomplish this ; his hatred of the Philistines is undying ; but its causes are private rather than national; and his fate is the direct result of his unwillingness to break off all relations with them. He is a warning rather than an example ; but such stories as his could not fail to be popular.

1. The Philistine Oppression : see on 3³.

2-25. The Birth and Parentage of Samson. **2. Zorah**] in Josh 19⁴¹ a Danite city; it lies some 17 m. W. of Jerusalem. Later, the Danites migrated northwards (c. 18), and Zorah was reckoned as belonging to Judah (Josh 15³³ 2 Ch 11¹⁰). **Family**] properly, clan.

3. Angel of the LORD] cp. 2¹ 6¹¹.

4, 5. Wine nor strong drink] These are forbidden to the Nazirites (Nu 6³), and here to the mother of the future Nazirite : cp. also Am 2¹². **Unclean**] regarded as unfit for food: we may compare our English attitude to horse-flesh. **No razor**] In Nu 6 the 'Nazirite,' or religious devotee, is under restrictions only for a time ; he takes the condition on himself voluntarily ; at the close of the period he cuts off his hair and devotes it to God (cp. Ac 18¹⁸). Here the state begins before birth, and is to last till death. Samson himself does not appear to abstain from wine (14¹⁰). Nothing is here said of the connexion between Samson's hair and his strength.

6. Man of God] The woman, apparently like Gideon (see on 6¹⁵), does not recognise her visitor as supernatural, though she feels him to be inspired. She does not venture, like her husband, to ask the stranger's name. **12. Now let thy words, etc.**] i.e. granted that this takes place, how shall we, etc. **How shall we**] RV 'what shall be the manner of the child, and *what shall be* his work ?' **15.** Cp. 6¹⁷ᶠ. **16.** The last words give the reason for v. 15. **18. Secret**] RV 'wonderful,' i.e. above your comprehension ; cp. Gn 32²⁹.

22. Cp. 6²²ᶠ. Isa 6⁵. No man can hope to see God and live. Note the sound wisdom of the woman's answer.

24, 25. Samson] i.e. probably 'Sun's man' : cp. the name of the Bethshemesh, 'place of the Sun,' just opposite Zorah. **Move**] a rare word, meaning to disturb or stir up : cp. 14¹⁹ 15¹⁴, also 3¹⁰ 6³⁴ 11²⁹. In Samson's case the narratives suggest a peculiar frenzy of strength and rage. **Camp of Dan**] RV, as a proper name, 'Mahaneh-dan,' which was near Kirjath-jearim, in Judah (c. 18¹²). **Eshtaol**] 1½ m. E. of Zorah.

CHAPTER 14
THE MARRIAGE OF SAMSON

1-5. Samson chooses a wife among the Philistines. He and his parents go down to Timnath.

2. Timnath] some 4 m. SW. of Zorah, allotted to Dan (Josh 19⁴³) ; it was retaken by the Philistines in the reign of Ahaz (2 Ch 28¹⁸). **Get her for me to wife**] It was customary for parents to conduct the negotiations and pay the dowry : cp. Gn 34⁴⁻¹². **3.** Cp. Gn 24³ 26³⁴ 27⁴⁶. **4. It** *was* **of the LORD**] God purposed to use Samson as a weapon against the Philistines.

6-9. The slaying of the Lion.

6. Cp. 13²⁵ ; for the exploit, cp. 1 S 17³⁴ 2 S 23²⁰. **8. A swarm of bees .. in the carcase**] probably it had dried up under the hot sun.

10, 11. The bridal feast. **11. When they saw him**] Many Greek MSS, by a slight change, read 'since they feared him,' a natural explanation of this choice of what was practically a 'body-guard.' Cp. Mt 9¹⁵, 'the children of the bride-chamber.'

12-20. Samson's Riddle and its consequences.

12. Thirty] one for each of his new companions. **Sheets**] RV 'linen garments.'

15. Called] i.e. invited us to your feast. **To take that we have**] RV 'impoverish us.'

16. She does not dare to tell her husband the real reason of her curiosity. **17. Lay sore upon him**] RV 'pressed him sore.'

19. Ashkelon] on the coast of the Philistine country. There is, however, a village of the same name about an hour S. of Timnath (mentioned in 'Survey of Western Palestine') to which perhaps Samson rushed off. To leave the bride like this is an insult, which her father at once avenges by giving her to the 'best man' : cp. 15².

CHAPTER 15
SAMSON SLAUGHTERS THE PHILISTINES

Samson, being denied his wife, burns the corn of the Philistines. He is delivered up to them by the men of Judah, but bursts his bonds, and slaughters many of the Philistines.

1, 2. Samson is denied his wife.

1. Wheat harvest] i.e. about May : cp. 4 f. The reason for the last clause is given in 14 19, 20. **2.** The father still desires to be conciliatory to one who might prove so valuable a son-in-law.

3–8. Samson's Revenge.

3. More blameless than, etc.] RV 'blameless in regard of .. when I do them a mischief.' Samson means that the Philistines have now clearly put themselves in the wrong. **4. Foxes**] RM 'jackals.' **6.** See 14 15. **7. Though ye have done**] RV 'if ye do.' **8. Top, etc.**] RV 'cleft of the rock of Etam.' Samson leaves his own tribe for the neighbouring territory of Judah.

9–13. The action of the men of Judah. **9. Lehi**] The name means 'jawbone,' perhaps from some resemblance in its shape. The site is not definitely known. **10, 11.** Each party represents the other as the aggressor. Observe Judah's dread of the Philistines. It is not difficult, with such a spirit, to understand foreign domination. Nor is one tribe under any obligation to assist a member of another.

14–20. Samson's Deliverance and Slaughter of the Philistines.

14. The Spirit] see on 13 25. **Loosed**] RV 'dropped.' **15. New**] i.e. fresh : not dry or brittle : such might easily be found lying on the ground. **A thousand men**] cp. 3 31 and 2 S 23 11. **16.** In the Hebrew this v. reads as two jingling lines, with a pun on 'ass' and 'heaps.' **17. Called that place**] RV 'that place was called.' Properly, Ramath means 'height.' The name was 'Jawbone height' : by another pun the meaning 'Jawbone-throw' is suggested. **19. That** *was* **in the jaw**] RV 'that is in Lehi,' a hollow (Heb. 'mortar') in the ground close to the scene of the slaughter. The 'caller' (Heb. *hakkōrē*) is the name for the partridge : cp. 1 S 26 20. **20. He judged**] cp. prefatory note to c. 13.

CHAPTER 16
SAMSON'S ESCAPE FROM GAZA. DELILAH'S TREACHERY. SAMSON'S DEATH

1–3. Samson and Gaza.

1. Gaza] 2 m. from the coast, and the last town of Palestine on the coast road to Egypt. Here Samson would be a whole day's journey from his mountain home, in his enemies' territory.

2, 3. They appear not to have surrounded the house, but waited to kill him when he found the gates closed in the morning. He suspects their plan, and does not wait till morning. The two gates would turn on pins, and be made by locks or bars into one piece, which Samson lifts up and carries off. The distance from Gaza to Hebron (one of the highest points in the rugged land of Judah) is nearly 40 m.

4–22. Samson's capture through the treachery of Delilah.

4. A woman] For the third time Samson's reckless daring in love brings him into danger. **Sorek**] a long and fertile 'wady' or glen, running W. from near Jerusalem to the plain : cp. Gn 49 11. Zorah and Timnah are both in this valley. **5. The lords of the Philistines**] see on 3 3. **Wherein his great strength** *lieth*] properly 'by what means his strength is great.' The 'lords' fancy he must have some amulet or magical device. **Afflict**] properly, 'torment.' **Pieces**] i.e. shekels. The amount to be paid by each is about £150.

7. Whether Samson suspects or not, he plays upon her credulity. The supposed secret of the 'green withs,' i.e. the undried bowstrings made from the intestines of animals, has all the more verisimilitude because of the sacred (and magical) number seven (cp. v. 13). The Philistines are deceived as readily as Delilah.

11. Occupied] RV 'wherewith no work hath been done' : cp. Lk 19 13 (AV).

13, 14. The v. is incomplete. LXX helps us to fill the gap, thus : 'if thou weavest .. web, and beatest up with the pin, my strength will fail ; so while he slept Delilah did so, and she beat up the web with the pin, and said.' Delilah wove the long hair into an unfinished piece of stuff left on the upright loom : the pin was used for 'beating up' the cloth (in this case, the hair) tight and firm. **Went away with the pin of the beam**] 'pin' should here be omitted : Samson pulls the posts of the loom out of the ground. **15. Thine heart**] thy mind or knowledge ; cp. vv. 17, 18.

18. Delilah sees at once that Samson is no longer tricking her, and she makes the Philistines equally confident. The belief in the importance of the hair (see on 13 5) was widespread in antiquity. **19. Afflict**] how is not explained. He is still asleep. **20. Departed**] when he was robbed of the hair which it was his duty to preserve. **21.** See 2 K 25 7. Grinding was women's work.

23–31. Samson's Last Exploit and Death.

23. Dagon] the chief Philistine god (1 S 5). **25–29.** He would make sport enough by being what he was, blind and in chains. **Pillars**] Two columns on which rested the roof of a large verandah, perhaps attached to the temple. After being in the court in front, in the sight of all, both below and above, he is brought to rest against these. **28. My two eyes**] RM 'for one of my two eyes.' A stroke of grim humour quite in keeping, at this supreme moment, with the character of Samson. **29. On which it was borne up**] RV 'leaned on them.'

31. The Philistines had no wish, and perhaps no spirit, to interfere with Samson's burial in his own country. Milton has brought out the tragic elements of this wild story at the end

of 'Samson Agonistes.' **Judged**] see intro. to c. 13.

PART 3

THE MIGRATIONS OF THE DANITES, AND THE FEUD BETWEEN BENJAMIN AND THE OTHER TRIBES (Chs. 17–21)

This concluding section is really an appendix. Instead of describing a further deliverance, it recounts two tribal stories in which the rough manners and primitive religious ideas of the time are shown with most valuable and vivid detail. Redundancies and discrepancies in the narratives (see on 17³ 18¹⁷) as well as differences in the language, suggest that more than one account has been used in each of the stories. This is no sign, however, that they are not historical ; and they must probably be placed earlier rather than later in the general framework of the period.

CHAPTER 17
THE STORY OF MICAH

This story, which is continued in the following c., is undoubtedly a very old one. In striking contrast to many other narrative portions of the Old Testament, there is in the body of this narrative no condemnation of the image-worship to which the Danites attached such importance, nor of their mode of securing it. We can but wonder the more at the heights which the religion of Israel was to climb from such beginnings as this. Cp. Josh 19⁴⁷.

1–6. Micah's idols.

1. Ephraim] see on 3²⁷. **2. Eleven hundred**] see on 16⁵. **Taken**] as appears from the following clause, stolen. The mother's curse (though she is ignorant of the thief) will not allow Micah to rest till the money is restored. **3, 4.** As the text stands, Micah restored the money twice over. This can hardly be correct. ' Yet ' (v. 4) should be ' and,' as in RV. Observe that the images are to be made in honour of Jehovah. **3. Graven image**] specifically, an idol carved out of wood or stone, or, generally, any kind of idol. 'Molten image' was added, not (as it would seem) to denote a second idol (' they ' in v. 4 should be 'it' ; see also 18³⁰,³¹), but to show that the idol was covered over with the silver. **5. House of gods**] i.e. a private shrine. In Heb. the word for ' god ' may be read either as singular or plural. **Ephod**] see on 8²⁷. The ephod is often connected with oracular responses (cp. 1S23⁶⁻⁹ : also Ex28 Lv8) ; the priest in charge of it can make inquiry of Jehovah. **Teraphim**] cp. Hos3⁴ : also Gn31¹⁹ 1S15²³ 19¹³ᶠ. The word is plural in form, and seems to denote household idols of some kind : cp. 18²⁴. **Consecrated**] Took

into his employment for the performance of religious duties : cp. v. 10, 18⁴ 1S7¹. **6.** Cp. 18¹ 19¹ 21²⁵.

7–13. The engagement of the Levite. **Levite**] The word denotes not his tribe but his calling. **Sojourned**] The regular term used in connexion with a ' resident alien ' who intends at some time to return to his home.

10. Father] cp. 2K2¹² 6²¹ : also Gn45⁸ ; a title of respect, which might be quite consistent with the priest's being supported as a son (v. 11). **13.** The professional knowledge of the Levite, in matters of ritual, gives him (and his employer) an advantage over others who might be selected as priests.

CHAPTER 18

THE DANITES GO IN QUEST OF AN INHERITANCE. THEY ROB MICAH OF HIS IMAGES, CAPTURE AND SETTLE IN LAISH, AND SET UP IDOL-WORSHIP THERE

1–10. The Danite Spies.

2. From their coasts] RV ' from their whole number.' For **Zorah** and **Eshtaol** see on 13²⁵. **3. They knew**] They recognised him as a Levite from the prayers he was saying. **Makest**] RV ' doest.' **6. Before the LORD**] i.e. under Jehovah's care. **7. Laish**] In Josh 19⁴⁷ the name appears as Leshem. Later on it was called Dan, from its new inhabitants (cp. v. 29, and c. 20¹). It lay near Lebanon and the sources of the Jordan in the extreme N. of Palestine, and was about 40 m. from Sidon, the famous commercial city on the seacoast. The rest of the v. implies that the residents were a colony from Zidon. **Put** *them* **to shame**] The Hebrew here gives no intelligible sense. **Business**] RV ' dealings.' **With** *any* **man**] LXX (in some MSS) reads ' with Syria ' whose capital, Damascus, was about as distant as Sidon. **10. Secure**] as always in AV, 'free from care or apprehension.'

11–31. The Danite Expedition to Laish.

11. Six hundred men] cp. 20⁴⁷ ; a very small number when compared with those given in 20¹⁵,¹⁷ or 15¹⁵ 16²⁷. Yet it would seem that the larger part of the tribe went northwards. **Appointed**] RV ' girt.' **12. Mahaneh-dan**] see on 13²⁵ ; they then turn northwards.

16. The gate] of the village. **17.** An amplification of v. 15 ; further repeated in v. 18. Here and in v. 18 ' graven image ' and ' molten image ' are understood as two distinct objects. In vv. 20, 30, 31 the 'molten image' is left unmentioned. **19.** See on 17[10]. **21. Carriage**] RV 'goods': cp. Ac 21[15] (what is carried: cp. the word 'luggage'). The armed men marched last, expecting pursuit. **28.** See on v. 7. The building of one city on the ruins of another was common, as excavations at Gezer and Lachish have made clear. **Beth-rehob**] unknown. **29. Israel**] Jacob: see Gn 35[10].

30. The possession of this image was evidently an important thing. **Jonathan**] This must refer to the young Levite, who has been hitherto unnamed, unless his name has dropped out of the text previously. **Manasseh**] RV 'Moses.' This, the true text, was altered in later times, to save Moses from any connexion with such a priesthood as this. **Captivity**] Probably the depopulation of Northern Israel by Tiglath-Pileser in 734 B.C. **31. In Shiloh**] NE. of Bethel, where the ark was kept in the 'house of God' (1 S 1–4). The destruction of this 'house' is mentioned in Jer 7[12] 26[9]. Possibly it was destroyed by the Philistines. In 1 S 22[11] the priesthood settled formerly at Shiloh appears at Nob.

CHAPTER 19
THE WICKEDNESS OF GIBEAH

A Levite and his concubine meet with foul treatment at Gibeah, a town of Benjamin. The indignation of the other tribes is roused against the Benjamites.

This c. gives the cause of the war between the rest of the tribes and Benjamin, with which the remainder of Judges is concerned. It is difficult to determine the period to which this war should be assigned. In c. 20 there is no recognised leader or judge in Israel, but all the tribes (quite differently from elsewhere) act together 'as one man' (20[1-11]); and the numbers given (20[2, 15-25]) imply a very large population; though an army approaching half a million in number seems unthinkable. On the other hand, it is hard to believe that Benjamin could have suffered such a disaster as this within a generation or two of Saul's accession to the throne. Probably we have an old story, dating from the wild days before Saul (19[1] 20[28]), part of which at least (20, 21[1-14]) was retold at a much later period, when the exact details had been lost and were replaced by the writer's conceptions of the past: see on 20[28]. **1. When** *there was* **no king**] see on 17[6]. **A certain Levite**] see on 17[7]. **3. He rejoiced**] feeling the separation to be a disgrace. **10. Jebus**] see 1[21]: also Josh 15[8] 1 Ch 11[4]. The journey from Bethlehem would not take more than two hours. **12.** See on 1[7,8]. Did they remember the story of Sodom (Gn 19)? **13. Gibeah . . Ramah**] both N. of Jerusalem. **14.** There is hardly any twilight in

Palestine. **15.** Gibeah thus proves as inhospitable as they feared Jerusalem would be.

16. The field] i.e. the open country surrounding the village. **18. The house of the LORD**] LXX reads 'my house,' which is preferable.

19. Note the politeness of the phrases 'thy handmaid' and 'thy servants.' The traveller needs nothing except actual house-room. An inn is only the modern substitute for the hospitality on which originally travellers were compelled to rely. This hospitality the stranger from Ephraim (cp. Lk 10[33]) insists on providing fully. **22. Sons of Belial**] The Hebrew means simply 'worthless men' or 'rascals.' Belial is not a proper name: cp. 1 S 1[16].

23. The old man dreads being compelled to violate the laws of Eastern hospitality. **29.** Cp. 1 S 11[7].

CHAPTER 20
THE SLAUGHTER OF THE BENJAMITES

The Levite recounts his wrongs to a full assemblage of the tribes, who decree punishment upon Benjamin. Their first two attacks are unsuccessful, but the third results in the almost total extermination of the Benjamites.

1-11. The Israelites assemble at Gibeah.

1. Congregation] This word is only used in the later books of the OT. after Israel had ceased to be a exile to be a nation: see intro. c. 19). **Dan**] see on 18[29]. **Beer-sheba**] the southernmost point of Palestine, 28 m. SW. of Hebron. See Gn. 21, 26 1 S 8[2] Am 5[5].

2. Four hundred thousand] contrast 5[8].

3. Mizpeh] not the place in Gilead mentioned in 11[11], but on a hill about two hours' journey NW. from Jerusalem.

12-29. The defeats of the Israelites.

12. The responsibility for the outrage is regarded as resting on the whole tribe. **15.** In vv. 44-47 only 25,600 men are accounted for. LXX here reads 25,000, and neglects the 700 men of v. 16. **16.** See on 3[15]. **18.** Cp. 1[2]. Bethel (RV) would be some four hours' distance to the N. After this journey the whole army marches back to Gibeah. **23.** This v., placed in brackets, should really precede v. 22, on which v. 24 properly follows. **25.** In these two battles the Israelites thus lose a tenth of their whole number. **26. House of God**] RV 'Bethel.' **Burnt offerings . . peace offerings**] Sacrifices in which the whole was consumed on the altar, and sacrifices in which part was eaten by the worshippers at a common meal.

27, 28. This parenthesis is added to explain why Bethel was visited, and not Shiloh, as might have been expected from the statements made in Josh 18[10] and 1 S 4[3]. If the note about Phinehas is correct, these events must have taken place in the first generation after Joshua.

30-48. The destruction of Benjamin.
31. The same stratagem as that which had proved successful at Ai (Josh 8 16). **House of God**] RV 'Bethel,' as in v. 26. **33. Baal-tamar**] unknown.

35. The LORD] Israel's success is really Jehovah's. This v. anticipates the end of the story. In the whole narrative there is a good deal of misplacement (e.g. vv. 37, 39) and redundancy (e.g. vv. 31, 32). V. 36 commences what is really a second account of the battle, with a very much fuller conclusion. **37. Drew** *themselves* **along**] 'moved forward.' **42. The wilderness**] i.e. to the more desolate region lying to the E. **43. With ease**] RV 'at *their* resting place,' or, as RM, 'at Menuhah.' **The sunrising**] i.e. the E. **45. Rimmon**] 3 m. E. of Bethel. **Gidom** is unknown. **48. The men of** *every* **city**] RV 'the entire city,' or, as RM, 'the inhabited city.'

CHAPTER 21
WIVES ARE GIVEN TO THE BENJAMITE SURVIVORS

1-6. The lamentation for Benjamin.

1. Had sworn] see on 17 2. All the women and children in Benjamin have been massacred: cp. v. 16. **2. House of God**] RV 'Bethel,' as in 20 26, 31. **4. Burnt offerings and peace offerings**] see on 20 26. **5.** Lit. 'the great curse had been pronounced upon,' etc. **6. Repented them**] see on 2 18.

7-25. The Benjamites provided with wives.
8. Jabesh-gilead] i.e. Jabesh in Gilead; cp. 1 S 11 31 11-13. Probably about 10 m. SE. of Beth-shean or Beisan. **12. Shiloh**] see on 18 31. Hitherto, Bethel had been the head-quarters. **13. Call peaceably**] RV 'proclaim peace.' **14.** 200 survivors were still left unprovided for. **19. Shechem**] see on 9 1. **Lebonah**] 3 m. NW. of Shiloh. Shiloh thus lies off the main road, and soon loses its early importance. **21. To dance**] see on 9 27; also 2 S 6 14. The act, like the whole feast, was regarded as religious.

22. No clear sense can be obtained from the Heb. The general meaning must be, 'allow the men to keep these girls, since we did not find wives for them in Jabesh-gilead; and as your daughters were taken from you by force, you have not broken your oath.'

RUTH

INTRODUCTION

THE book of Ruth is one of the most delightful stories ever penned. It carries us without an effort into an old-world realm altogether unlike our work-a-day life. Whilst we read it the customs of that other realm seem quite familiar to us. And how admirably are the actors in the story depicted ! We are made intimately acquainted with Orpah and Ruth ; with the girl who accompanies her mother-in-law on the homeward journey as far as the border of the two countries, professes her intention to go the whole way, only waits to be dissuaded, weeps, kisses, turns back ; and with the girl who forsakes fatherland, kindred, and ancestral worship, because of her deep love for the bereaved and the dead. The character of Naomi, too, is 'instinct with life.' In the difficult position of mother-in-law she knows how to win the tender love of the two younger women, and the open secret of her influence is the unselfishness which declines Orpah's offer and devotes itself to Ruth's interests. And Boaz is provided with an excellent foil in the person of the anonymous kinsman. The latter is a keen and calculating individual, eager to

hear of anything to his advantage, but quick to drop it the moment he is told of a fly in the ointment. The former is quietly ready to respond to any call of duty, yet willing to give up the satisfaction of doing it to one who may have a stronger claim. Modest and humble, he is at the same time beloved and respected. Consider, too, how different an impression is made on us by the critical point in the book, the hinge on which the whole turns, c. 3, from that which would be made by a modern writer treating such a theme ! The course pursued on that occasion is so entirely alien to our ideas and customs. Yet it is described with so skilful a hand, or, rather, with so pure a heart, that no thought of evil can obtrude itself. And the type of piety which it recommends so strongly by merely describing it is singularly engaging. It is so thoroughly unaffected, human and real. Contrast the profound feeling and perfect simplicity of 1 16, 17 with the stilted and unnatural paraphrase in the Talmud. There the older woman says, 'We are forbidden to go beyond the limits of a sabbath day's journey': Ruth replies, 'Where (i.e. as far as) thou goest I will go ' : ' It is not allowed amongst us for two persons of different sexes to be alone together ' : ' Where thou lodgest I will lodge ' : ' Six hundred and thirteen commandments have been given us ' : ' Thy people is my people ' : ' The worship of other gods is prohibited to us ' : ' Thy God is my God ' : ' The courts are allowed to put men to death in four ways ' : ' Where thou diest I will die ' : and so forth. The ancient Jewish commentator saw more clearly the spirit of the book when, after feeling a little puzzled at finding in this Scripture no legal or ceremonial prescriptions, he concluded that it was composed to teach us ' how great is the reward of human kindness.'

It is generally agreed that the book, though embodying old traditions, is of later date than the scenes it describes. The period of the Judges lay far behind (1¹): the customs of an earlier time required explanation (4⁷). The purity of its thought and style lead some scholars to favour a pre-exilic date ; but the majority are disposed to place it either during or after the exile. From the stress which the author lays on the Moabitish origin of Ruth, it has been inferred that he was an opponent of the rigorous measures adopted by Ezra and Nehemiah against intermarriage with foreigners (Ezr 9¹ Neh 13²³). If he did live in the time of that great struggle, and was in some measure influenced by it, he scarcely allows this to appear. Other objects ascribed to him are, to illustrate the life of David, and to enforce the duty of the next-of-kin marrying a childless widow ; but if either of these were in his mind at the start, they were almost forgotten in the interest of the scenes and actions with which he deals. He could never have produced so beautiful a work if he had been writing a pamphlet with a special didactic aim. He simply tells the story of a woman's fidelity and its reward, to show us his ideal of the ' Excellent Woman ' and to make us feel that God did not forget her.

' How sweet an ended strife !
How sweet a dawning life ! '

As a scholar of the last generation has said : ' The book of Ruth presents us with a simple story of domestic life—such as has happened, and is happening over and over again in this world—the familiar story of a daughter's affection and a young wife's happiness... In Ruth we see a daughter clinging to a parent in her age, with all the unselfishness of true-hearted affection ; volunteering to share her lowliness and her distress ; finding favour for her piety with the Lord and also with men ; chosen by Boaz to be his wife ; from obscure poverty taken to an honourable bed ; the young lonely widow of the first chapter, changed in the last into a joyful mother of children.'

It is interesting to remember that when St. Matthew traces the genealogy of Joseph he is careful to say (1⁵) that Boaz begat Obed of Ruth ; and St. Luke has evidently the same line of descent in view when he mentions Boaz, Obed, Jesse, David, Nathan among the ancestors of the mother of our Lord (3³¹,³²).

Ruth occupies the second place amongst the ' Megilloth ' or ' Rolls,' the five short writings kept separate from the rest, each on its own roll, and read in the synagogue on five great days of the Jewish Calendar. It is used on the second of these occasions, at the Feast of Pentecost, the great Harvest Festival. For such an occasion it would be difficult to find a more appropriate lesson than these chapters, which put in so pleasing a light the labours and the charities of the harvest season.

CHAPTER 1
THE EXILE AND THE RETURN OF NAOMI

1. Beth-lehem-judah] two hours' journey S of Jerusalem, is to be distinguished from Bethlehem in Zebulun (Josh 19¹⁵). It was but a short distance from Moab, which, in the days here referred to, was a fertile, highly cultivated country. Travellers still speak of it as a land of streams. Nothing short of the compulsion of famine could have induced a Hebrew to migrate into this foreign country where he would have no right of citizenship, this unclean land where Jehovah could not be worshipped.

2. The name **Elimelech** means ' my God is King.' **Naomi,** or, as it ought to be written, ' Noomi,' means ' pleasant.' The two sons, **Mahlon** (' sickly') and **Chilion** (' wasting away'), evidently owe their names to the fate which overtook them. It is not quite certain how we should understand the names of their wives. **Orpah** was taken by some of the Jewish commentators as signifying ' the back of the neck,' and explained by her having turned her back on Naomi. **Ruth** may be ' friend ' or ' refreshment ' : the Talmud takes the latter view, ' because David sprang from her, who refreshed the Holy One with songs and praises.' **Ephrathah** is another name for Bethlehem, or perhaps the name of the district of Bethlehem.

4. The author of our book sees nothing wrong in their marrying Moabite wives. In this he agrees with earlier ideas and customs (Jg 14 ¹f. 16 ⁴f. 2 S 11 ³³ 1 K 7 ¹⁴), not with such enactments as Dt 23 ³f., or such stern proceedings as Ezra and Nehemiah took when they compelled the Jews to abandon their foreign wives (Ezr 9, 10 Neh 13 ²³⁻³⁰), or the Targum here, which says, ' And they transgressed the commandment of the Lord and married strange women.'

8, 9. The young widow would naturally return to her **mother's house,** for she would live in the women's part of the house or tent

(Gn 24 28, 67 Jg 4 17 Song 3 4). The belief of that age was that men would receive in this life an exact recompense for their good and evil actions : see especially Ps 18 24, 26. These two good women were to find **rest** after the troubles and disappointments of their Hebrew marriages.

11-13. If Naomi had other sons the obligation of marrying their deceased brother's widow would devolve on one of them. This Levirate law (from *Levir* = ' a brother-in-law ') has been observed in many quarters of the globe, in India, Madagascar, Brazil, etc. Amongst the Hebrews the two objects which it aimed at were, to prevent the extinction of the dead man's name, and to save the property belonging to a family from being broken up and dispersed among other families. The firstborn son of the new marriage was considered to be the child and heir of the dead (Gn 38 Dt 25 5-10). Naomi asks : **Would ye stay for them from having husbands?** or, more literally : ' Would ye shut yourselves up from having husbands ? ' For the widow, awaiting the second marriage, must remain at home in seclusion (Gn 38 11).

14, 15. Possibly Orpah did not intend going beyond the necessary courtesy of accompanying her mother-in-law to the border of the two countries. Then she would return to her people and ' her god ' (RV). Chemosh was the national god of Moab (Nu 21 29 1 K 11 7, etc.).

16-18. Ruth's impassioned declaration reminds us of the Druze sheikh, who, on parting with Mrs. Burton, exclaimed, ' Allah be with you and your house ! I would we had never seen you, because of this parting. If you loved a stone I would put it in my bosom, and if you hated the moon I would not sit under its rays.' According to ancient ideas a god and his people were inseparable : if Ruth determined to go over to Naomi's fatherland and race she necessarily accepted their deity : if David was driven out of Israel he was thereby bidden, ' Go, serve other gods ' (1 S 26 19). Moreover, it was an even more cherished privilege then than now to be interred with one's relatives: the phrase for a desirable kind of burial was, ' to be gathered to one's fathers.' In Ezk 32 17-32 it is implied that the various nations inhabit separate localities in the invisible world. Ruth cleaves to her mother-in-law as Elisha to Elijah (2 K 2 2-6).

19-22. Every one in the little town knew her. Yet how much she had altered. The women, of course, knew her best, and they exclaimed, ' *Is* this **Naomi** ? ' She repudiated the old name, renaming herself **Mara,** ' Bitter,' because **the Almighty,** who is here called Shaddai, had dealt bitterly with her. The same expression occurs in Job 27 2. The exact force of the divine name Shaddai is uncertain. Except in the book of Job we always

meet it in conjunction with the general name God, ' God Shaddai.' Ex 6 3 regards it as an ancient title. Jehovah **testified** against Naomi by treating her as a sinner, for suffering was always regarded as an evidence of guilt. When the widow's son dies she cries out to Elijah : ' Art thou come to call my sin to remembrance, and to slay my son ? ' (1 K 17 18). We have no ground for assuming any particular transgression on Naomi's part : the Targum is clearly wrong in fixing on the migration to Moab. How unlike Naomi's fortunes to those of Abraham, who from being alone became a multitude (Isa 51 2), and those of Jacob, who with nothing but a staff in his hand crossed the Jordan, and returned in two bands (Gn 32 10) ! Barley harvest begins early in April.

CHAPTER 2
RUTH THE GLEANER

1. Boaz] (' quickness ') was a kinsman of Elimelech's. We are not informed of the precise degree of relationship. Here and at 3 2 he is designated an ' acquaintance.' It is by no means certain that we are to think of him as ' a mighty man of wealth '; the phrase here employed sometimes points out a capable, active man (1 K 11 28 Neh 11 14). The Targum is of course wrong in explaining it by ' a man strong in the Law '—an explanation which reminds us of Apollos, ' mighty in the scriptures ' (Ac 18 24).

2, 3. Ruth will not sit with folded hands. Like any other poor person she has a right to glean (Lv 19 9f, 23 22 Dt 24 19), but the landowner can make the exercise of this right easier or more disagreeable. Hence she is not sure where her task will be prosecuted, and it seems a piece of rare, though undesigned, good fortune that she lights on the portion of the field which belongs to Boaz. The portions belonging to different owners were not separated by walls, hedges or ditches, but by a stone, a stoneheap, or a marked tree (Dt 19 14).

4-6. These ancient forms of salutation were distinguished by politeness, heartiness, and religious feeling (cp. Gn 43 29 Jer 19 20 f. 2 K 4 29 Ps 129 7,8). The Arabic formula now is ' God be with you ' : in Egypt the first speaker cries ' Peace be on you,' and the reply comes, ' On you be peace, and the mercy of God and His blessings, ' or simply ' On you be peace.'

7. Ruth's good qualities appear at every turn : she was careful to ask leave ; she worked steadily all through the long, weary day, not resting during its hottest hours. The last words of this verse are now corrupt : the original statement was ' she has not rested at all,' or ' she has not been home at all '; 3 7 shows that there was no building in the field to rest in.

8, 9. His **maidens** were the women-servants
who went over the ground after the reapers,
reaping being done in so slovenly a manner in
the East that much would be wasted if this supplementary work were not performed. The
note on v. 3 indicates how easy it would be to
stray into another's field. The **young men**
are the harvesters who come together from all
parts of the country, and, away from the
restraints of their own homes, are apt to be
free of speech, and loose in conduct.

10-12. She throws herself prostrate on the
ground, as Orientals have always done before
their superiors. She acknowledges herself a
foreigner, destitute of right or claims. But
Boaz sees only the heroism implied in her
having committed herself to the uncovenanted
kindness of a strange people. And he commends the wisdom and piety which have brought
her to take refuge under the protecting wings
of Jehovah the God of Israel (Dt 32 11 Ps 36 8
57 2 91 4 Lk 13 34).

13. With joyful surprise she exclaims, **Let
me find favour in thy sight** ! or, rather, 'I find
grace in thy sight!' There is something very
beautiful in the literal meaning of the words
rendered ' Thou hast spoken friendly ' : it is
'Thou hast spoken to the heart' (Isa 40 2
Jer 19 3) : the words are so friendly that they
fall on the heart like dew. And this is all
the more wonderful to her, seeing that, as a
foreigner, she does not stand on a level even
with his women-servants. 'Make me as one
of thy hired servants' (Lk 15 19).

14. Vinegar and water was the customary
drink of Roman soldiers and slaves. The
harvesters in Palestine still dip their bread in
vinegar and find it very refreshing. Parched
corn is also a favourite article of food : the
ears are gathered when not quite ripe, and are
roasted on an iron plate, or are thrust in small
bundles into a fire of dry grass and thorns ;
there is a milky and yet crusty flavour about
it which makes pleasant eating. ' She did eat,
and was sufficed, and left thereof' (RV).

15-18. As a special favour she is to be
allowed to glean not only where the sheaves have
been removed, but amongst them as they stand.
Curiously enough she is represented at v. 7
as requesting this. The reapers are also to
pluck out ears as they gather them up for
binding and let them drop as if by accident.
No wonder that when she had beaten it out
with a stick (Jg 6 11 Isa 28 27) she had about a
bushel of grain. As one has seen poor women
taking home food for their children from some
feast which has been given them, so the thrifty,
affectionate Ruth carries to Naomi the parched
corn which had remained over from her
unexpected midday meal.

19-23. Ruth now learns for the first time
that Boaz is related to them, a near kinsman,

one of those who have the right to buy back
for them the land that has been parted with.
If an Israelite was compelled by poverty
to dispose of his property, such a kinsman
could compel the purchaser to sell it back
(Lv 25 25, 47, 48) ; the object of the law being
to preserve each family in possession of its
land. Naomi felt that Providence was not
only showing loving-kindness to her daughter-
in-law and herself, but also to her husband
and sons, by bringing about the prospect of
the land which had once belonged to them
again being called by their name. Her deep-
seated piety comes out too ; the bitterness of
1 20 yields immediately to faith, hope, and
gratitude. And her practical wisdom is seen
in the injunction not to vex this kind-
hearted man by failing to make use of his
offered kindness. Wheat-harvest is two or
three weeks later than barley.

CHAPTER 3
THE APPEAL TO BOAZ

1. Marriages are always arranged by the
parents in Eastern lands ; here, of course, the
mother-in-law must intervene.

2-7. Grain is winnowed in the evening, to
avoid the heat of the day and take advantage
of the cool sea-wind, which blows in Palestine
from 4 p.m. to half-an-hour before sunset.
As a rule the threshing floor, which is an
open space of clean, hard, dry ground, is on
an elevated spot. But at Beth-lehem it was
necessary to go ' down ' to it, because the
town is on the summit of the ridge and higher
than any of the surrounding eminences. Ruth
is to wash and anoint herself and put on the
simlah, the long outer robe of ceremony, for
this was to be a formal and important visit.
Every precaution, too, was to be taken to
ensure Boaz being in a genial frame of mind ;
the day's work was to be at an end, and he
was to have eaten and drunk : cp. Gn 27 4, 25,
and David's assumption that even Nabal
would be generous during the feast of sheep-
shearing (1 S 25 5-8). Naomi had entire confidence in the honour of her kinsman, and
although the procedure which she devised is
alien to all our thoughts and customs, it is
conceived and carried out without a spot of
impure intention. To this day the Syrian
farmer lies down under the shelter of a heap
of threshed corn to protect it from thieves,
or sleeps close by with his family in a little
hut erected for the purpose.

8-18. At midnight the sleeper was startled.
He bent forward to ascertain what was there,
and the swift, curt question, **Who** *art* **thou?**
reveals his alarm. Her request is : **Spread
thy skirt** (or, thy wing) **over thine handmaid,**
i.e. Become my guardian and protector by
marrying me (Ezk 16 8), according to the duty

of a near kinsman. The law in Dt 25 required that a brother should do this, if he and the deceased had dwelt together on the land belonging to the family. The right or duty was subsequently extended to more distant relatives. Boaz looked on this appeal as an even greater loving-kindness than Ruth had shown to Naomi, seeing that he was no longer young, and younger men would willingly have married her. The Rabbinical commentary on this book goes curiously astray in fixing his age as 80 and hers as 40. All the 'gate' of his people knew that she was an 'excellent' woman. They had discussed her in the gate of the city, which was the place of concourse, consultation and gossip, like the Gk. agora (Ac 17 17, 18), and the forum of the Romans. But ready as he was to take up the position of Goel (see on Job 19 25), he would not encroach on the stronger claim which another man had. For this night she must remain where she was, lest mischief should befall her at the hands of some of the roisterers who were especially likely to be abroad at that season of the year (Song 5 7). Yet she must leave whilst it was still too dark for a man to discern his friend if he met him ; no breath of scandal must touch their good name. **Let it not be known,** said Boaz, **that the woman came to the threshing floor.** The 'mantle' (RV) here mentioned is not the same as the *simlah* of v. 3 ; most likely it was the veil of cotton cloth or coarse muslin which rests on the head and falls down the back of Bedouin and peasant women, and is often used by them for carrying such things as vegetables. The present of three-fifths of a bushel of barley is at one and the same time an out-pouring of his liberality and a precaution against the suspicion which might have been roused if any one had met her ; they were to be led to think that she had been to fetch grain. The AV is correct in stating that she now went into the city ; he came later (4 1). It would almost seem as though her mother-in-law could not at the first moment see who she was : **Who** *art* **thou, my daughter ?** But perhaps the question really meant, 'How hast thou fared ?'

CHAPTER 4
The Marriage of Boaz and Ruth. The Birth of their Child

1. Boaz **went up** from the threshing floor to the open space by the city-gate, where the business he had in hand would have to be done, where, too, he would catch the other kinsman on his way out to the field. The author does not know this man's name, and therefore contents himself with calling him 'So and So.'

2. Ten was considered a perfect number

(Jer 6 27 1 S 25 5 2 S 18 15): where ten Jews live there should be a synagogue ; these ten elders are heads of the community, sheikhs, as they would be called to-day.

3–5. Elimelech was not their **brother** in the strict sense, but was a member of the same family (Gn 13 8 1 S 20 6, 29 2 S 19 13). Naomi had already sold the land. Ruth's being under the necessity of gleaning shows that her mother-in-law was no landowner: 2 18 is an eloquent testimony to their poverty. The kinsman had now the opportunity of buying it back for them, and it is plain from v. 5 that this transaction would take the form of a purchase from Naomi : the presence of the elders and the other inhabitants, 'them that sit here,' would make it a valid bargain. But if he bought the land he must also purchase Ruth as his wife. There can be no doubt that Boaz said: 'Thou must also buy Ruth': Ruth has nothing to do with the sale ; see also v. 10. The money which the bridegroom used to give to the bride's family was compensation for the loss of her valuable services. And at the present time in Syria 'No marriage is strictly legal among the Mussulmans without a *Mahr* or settlement from the bridegroom to the bride. It may consist of only a few silver pence, still it must be made.' Jacob's services to Laban were prices paid for Leah and Rachel.

6. The kinsman draws back. The Rabbinic commentator thought that he was afraid of dying by God's judgment for marrying a Moabite, as Mahlon and Chilion had perished. But his motive seems to have been an unwillingness to encroach on his own property for the sake of a son by Ruth, who would be heir of the newly acquired land and would not be accounted his child.

7–10. In the case described at Dt 25 9 the woman removes the shoe of the man who declines to act ; here the man himself takes it off: there, by that symbolic act, she takes away the right he will not exercise ; here, he renounces it. At Ps 60 10 108 10 the shoe thrown over the land is a sign that possession is taken: see on Am 2 6 8 6. Similar customs have existed amongst the Hindoos, the ancient Germans, and the Arabs. When an Arab divorces his wife, he says: 'She was my babuj (slipper) and I cast her off.' Boaz declares it to be his purpose to prevent the name of the dead from being cut off : if Ruth should bear a son he would be the representative of Mahlon, and men would remember the father's name whilst they called the child Ben-Mahlon, Mahlon's son.

11, 12. No Hebrew woman could desire a better fortune than to resemble the two wives of Jacob from whom the entire people had sprung. And the wish of the Bethlehemites for Boaz was that he might win a name which should be famous amongst them as the head of a powerful and illustrious house. Perez, whom they go on to mention, was the child borne by Tamar to Judah, when the latter unwittingly did her the justice (Gn 38) which Boaz was so willing to render to Ruth. The cases were also parallel as regards the respective ages of the man and the woman.

13–16. It was an honour and a mark of divine favour to have a son, a discredit and curse both to husband and wife to be without: 'He who has not left a son to be his heir, with him the Holy One—blessed be He—is angry.' This son would take upon him all the duties of near kinsman to Naomi. He would be a 'restorer of life' (RV), reviving the fainting soul, inspiring fresh hope, joy, courage (Ps 19 8 Prov 25 13 Lam 1 16). His mother had been better to Naomi than seven (i.e. any number of) sons. And now the grandmother puts the child in her bosom, to indicate that he belonged to her (Gn 30 3 50 23), as a Roman father took up the child from the ground and thus owned him.

17. The women are still to the front. As a rule the father or mother named the child. But it is the neighbours who here call him **Obed**, 'Servant,' anticipating that he would minister to all the wants of the aged woman who had been a true mother to Ruth. The book originally ended with the simple intimation of the manner in which all good wishes were fulfilled in him : 'He is the father of Jesse, the father of David.' The verses which follow may have been borrowed from 1 Ch 2 9-15 : in any case they were added later to bring out clearly the place of Boaz and David in the line of Judah. It is interesting to notice that notwithstanding 4 5,10, though in agreement with 1 Ch 2 12, they do not regard Obed as Mahlon's son, but give him to Boaz.

THE FIRST AND SECOND BOOKS OF
SAMUEL

INTRODUCTION

1. Scope and Contents. The two books of Samuel were in the original Hebrew reckoned as one, and classed, like Judges, among 'the earlier prophets.' In LXX they are divided and called the first two 'books of the kingdoms' : a title which the Vulgate altered to 'books of the kings.' Our own translation keeps the original name and the later division. The whole work embraces the history of the chosen nation from the end of the period of the Judges to the beginning of the reign of Solomon (1 K 1, 2 really belong to the period covered by the books of Samuel and in LXX are counted as 2 S 25, 26). The two books fall into three broad divisions, viz. 1 S 1–14, 1 S 15–2 S 8, and 2 S 9–24 ; giving the stories (1) of Israel under the Philistines and Samuel ; (2) of Saul and the rise of David ; and (3) of David's reign over all Israel. The whole period is about a century (see § 6) ; at its close we find ourselves in an atmosphere completely different from that in which we start, though the change is made entirely natural by the narrative.

The first of the three sections opens with the birth, consecration and call of Samuel (chs. 1–3), and passes to the death of Eli and his sons (c. 4), the captivity and restoration of the ark (chs. 5, 6), and the deliverance from the Philistines (c. 7). The Israelites then demand a king ; Samuel protests and warns (c. 8) ; Saul is revealed to Samuel as the future king, anointed, and accepted (chs. 9, 10) ; a victory over Ammon strengthens Saul's position (c. 11) ; and Samuel formally retires from leadership (c. 12). The Philistines are attacked and defeated (chs. 13, 14), but Saul, for his disobedience after the conquest of Amalek, is rejected (c. 15).

The second section introduces us at once to David ; he is secretly anointed (16 1-13) and brought before Saul (c. 16 14-22). He is victorious over Goliath (c. 17), and wins first Saul's favour and then his jealousy (c. 18). This is followed by a long and detailed account of Saul's pursuit of David, who is soon reduced to live the life of an outlaw (chs. 19–26), and at last takes refuge with the king of Gath (c. 27). Meanwhile, Saul is compelled to face the Philistines on Mt. Gilboa (c. 28); David is expelled from the Philistine army, and sacks Ziklag (chs. 29, 30) ; and Saul is defeated and slain (c. 31). David is then anointed as king of Judah (2 S 1), and gradually wears down the rivalry of Israel (chs. 2–4) ; he is made king of the whole nation, captures Jerusalem, defeats the Philistines (c. 5), and brings the ark to his new capital (chs. 6, 7).

In the third section we find him first showing courtesy to Meribbaal (c. 9), and subduing

Ammon and the Syrians (c. 10). Then follows the Bathsheba episode (11–12 25), with the final conquest of Ammon (12 26-31). Absalom, revenging Amnon's crime, is banished, and recalled (chs. 13, 14) ; his usurpation of the throne leads to his defeat and death, and to David's unopposed return (chs. 15–19). Sheba's revolt is subdued (c. 20). The avenging of the Gibeonites (21 1-14) and sundry exploits of David's heroes (21 14-22) are related ; two psalms of David are given (22–23 7), and another list of David's heroes (23 8-39) ; and the book closes with an account of the census and repentance of David (c. 24). The revolt of Adonijah, which clouded the last days of David, is related in 1 K 1, 2.

2. Structure of the Book. As stated above, 1 and 2 Samuel fall into three divisions ; but none of these divisions have been written as they stand. Each (like so many other books of the Old Testament) is a compilation from earlier documents. Within the first two sections we meet constantly with different accounts of the same events, coupled with differences in the point of view. This will be clear from the following :—

1 S 1–15. (a) Chs. 1–4 contain the story of Samuel's childhood, 7 and 8 his position as recognised head of all Israel—a point of view which is maintained in 10 17-27, 12, 15. (b) On the other hand, 9, 10 1-16 give a separate version of Saul's accession, and 11, 13, 14 follow continuously on 10 16 ; the account of Saul's rejection in 13 8-14 being quite distinct from that of 15. Hannah's song in 2 (which inspired some of the noblest thoughts of the Magnificat) contains conceptions which are inconsistent with what we know of the more primitive religion of this early period, and is probably a later poem, here ascribed to Hannah. The account of the ark in 5 and 6 has no notes of time, except that it must follow the battle of Aphek : it reminds us strongly of the narratives in Judges. Of the two main divisions of this section, the second (b), which is chiefly occupied with Saul, must be the earlier. From 13 20, etc., we can hardly think that such a total defeat of the Philistines as is implied in 7 13 f. took place at so early a period.

1 S 16–2 S 8. In this section we find double narratives of David's introduction to Saul, Saul's offer of a daughter of his to David, and David's sparing of Saul's life. The inconsistencies thus resulting (of which the most noticeable is that while David is brought to Saul as a young warrior in 16, he appears in 17 as a shepherd lad of whom Saul is quite ignorant) may be avoided if we place together 16 14-23 18 6-29 (with the exception of vv. 14–19) 19 11-17 21 1-10 22–23 14 25–27, 29, 30. The rest of 16–31 reads almost as one continuous nar-

rative. There is less difficulty about the first 8 chs. of 2 Samuel : the whole section concludes with a general summary of David's power and prestige ; and in c. 2 we have an undoubted poem of David himself.

2 S 9–24. Chs. 9–20 form a very clear and picturesque narrative, which is quite self-consistent, and must have been written near to the events which it describes. For the distinctness in its portraiture of minor characters as well as of David himself, and for its faithful description of the dark as well as the bright side of the court of Israel's great and beloved king, it is unequalled among all the fine narratives of the Old Testament 21–24 form an appendix ; 21 1-14 would seem to refer to the earlier years of David's reign ; the two psalms (the first of which is almost identical with Ps 18) are strangely wedged in between the notices of David's 'mighty men' ; 24 should at any rate find a place in 9–20, and 1 K 1, 2 should properly follow 2 S 20.

3. The Rise and Growth of the Monarchy. To our minds the word 'king' suggests a definite constitution. Even an absolute monarch must govern according to fixed laws. To the Hebrews, the idea of such a constitution was foreign. The growth of our European monarchical constitutions has been controlled by two factors : the military organisation of the Teutonic nations, and the Roman Law. The Hebrews had nothing corresponding to either of these. In the time of the Judges (see Intro. to Judges) we find the nation composed of a number of tribes largely independent of each other, though held together (as were the ancient Greek states) by certain moral and religious customs, and also by a common faith in Jehovah, the national God. From time to time military leaders of strong personality ('Judges') arise ; but the sphere of their influence is limited, and only in one case (Gideon and Abimelech) is there any attempt to establish the principle of heredity.

The great difference between the Judges and Saul is that, unlike the former, the latter is solemnly chosen by all Israel at a gathering presided over by the moral and religious head of the nation, Samuel. Saul is simply a military leader, chosen to offer an otherwise impossible resistance to the Philistines. It was thus the Philistine oppression which welded the Israelites, under Saul's leadership, into a nation. His first 'kingly' act is to summon the whole nation to arms (1 S 11 7, cp. Jg 19 29) : when he sacrifices, it is as the head of the army (1 S 13 9) : he, like the Judges, receives guidance and command from Jehovah, though, unlike them, indirectly through Samuel : his military leadership, absolute from the side of the nation, is thus strictly limited from the side of Jehovah.

What was the effect of his rule on Israel's internal life ? We are merely told that he put away soothsayers and diviners out of the land (1 S 28⁹). This in itself implies a great deal ; it does not imply, however, that the king was expected to make new laws, but only to enforce the old ones ; at most, like Asa (1 K 15¹³) and Hezekiah (2 K 18⁴), he was a reformer.

If Jonathan had survived the battle of Gilboa, the whole course of Israel's history might have been different. As it was, Saul's son was at once accepted as king by the greater part of the nation (2 S 2⁹). Not until Ish-bosheth's death was David acknowledged as king of all Israel. He began where Saul left off, as recognised military head of the nation. Unlike Saul, he needed no prophet to place him on the throne ; but, like Saul, he gained and held his position by his personal popularity (2 S 3³⁶). At first he is nothing more than the warrior ; and all through his reign he is a ' man of war ' (2 S 17⁸). But by his conquest of Jerusalem and his removal thither of the ark, he becomes the religious head of the nation also, appointing and supervising the priests (2 S 8¹⁸ 20²⁶ ; cp. 1 K 2³⁵). He is now in a position to form foreign alliances and to institute an elaborate and thoroughly Oriental court life (2 S 5¹³). He is also the fountain of justice (2 S 12⁵ 14⁴ᶠ·) ; but while he enforces the traditional law, he does not make fresh laws. The basis of his internal authority (like that of the Roman emperors) is military supremacy: when this is broken he must take refuge in flight (2 S 15¹⁴). He has his captains and high officers (2 S 20 ²³⁻²⁶). He numbers and taxes his people (2 S 24²), but they have free right of access and complaint (2 S 14⁵ 24³), and he acknowledges the moral authority of the prophets (2 S 12²⁵ 24¹¹). He is throughout the father and the shepherd more than the monarch of his people : he is Jehovah's representative in their midst. He made the kingship what it remained for four centuries, a rule limited by no written laws (save perhaps that of 1 S 10²⁵, which is only ' constitutional ' in a restricted sense), but distinctly limited by the extent of the king's military prowess and authority, and moral influence with his people, by the laws of the nation (cp. 1 K 21³), and by the will of Jehovah as expressed by the prophets.

4. The Beginnings of Prophecy.

It is generally agreed that the root from which comes the Hebrew word for ' prophet ' (*nabi*) means to ' announce' or ' forth-tell.' The Hebrew prophets, however, were ' forth-tellers ' of a special kind. Their messages always had to do with the nation and with Jehovah, the nation's God and protector. They were the heralds at once of patriotism, national unity, and religion. We meet them very early in

' bands ' or ' schools ' (1 S 10 ⁵⁻¹⁰) ; they seem to wander up and down the country excitedly proclaiming their message; and they have often been compared to Mahommedan dervishes. We are expressly told that Samuel was not held to be a prophet in this technical sense ; but he organised the prophetic bands (1 S 19²⁰), and this organisation lasted on till the times of Elijah and Elisha (e.g. 1 K 20³⁵ 2 K 6¹). These ' bands ' probably gathered round some teacher or leader of influence. We have no information as to their mode of life and means of support. Possibly, when thus ' banded' together, they bore to Samuel the same relation as Wycliffe's preachers bore to Wycliffe himself. But from the reign of David, and even (according to Jg 6⁸) much earlier, we meet with individual prophets, whose function is to recall the nation, or more often the king, to obedience to the will of Jehovah ; in many cases they announce the punishment which is to follow upon disobedience (cp. 2 S 7² 12²⁵ 24¹¹). In later times both Elijah and Elisha are credited with miraculous powers ; but Elisha is the only prophet whose activity seems to have been as much private as public. Later still, in the middle of the 8th cent., the great series of the ' writing ' prophets begins with Amos ; but in the last stages of the history of the prophetic order, as in the first, the prophet is one who appears suddenly from retirement or seclusion, charged with a special message to people or king, like an embodied conscience.

Hence, prophecy is not the opponent of monarchy ; it is rather the divinely appointed means for keeping monarchy true to its task. In the reign of Saul, Samuel performed this function (cp. 1 S 15³⁻²³ ; and see § 6). His condemnation of the Israelite demand for a king is quite distinct from the general attitude of the prophets, who accepted the kings as Jehovah's appointed servants ; but, like the later prophets, Samuel claimed that the prophetic word was to receive even from the king absolute and unquestioning obedience. It is easy to see from the above how completely the books of Samuel justify their place in the Hebrew canon as prophetic books. They describe and emphasise the ideals of the prophets, and are full of the prophetic spirit— the deep conviction that Jehovah is Israel's God, and that to Jehovah's service Israel is irrevocably bound.

5. The Ark and the Priesthood.

In the books of Samuel the ark appears as the seat or dwelling-place of Jehovah ; where the ark is, there in some special sense is Jehovah Himself (see also Josh 3, 4, 6 Jg 20²⁷). It is placed in Shiloh, the centre of worship, where the sacred tent (' temple,' 1 S 1⁹) is set up. After Israel's defeat by the Philistines it is (to the dismay of the Philistines) taken to battle, but captured and carried off to various Philistine cities, in each of which it causes plagues. It is then returned to Kirjath-jearim, where Eleazar is 'sanctified' 'to keep' it (1 S 3–7). After the conquest of Jerusalem David brings the ark thither (2 S 6). In Israel its presence brings blessing : to foreigners, or those who touch it profanely, it causes disaster. Later, it is brought into Solomon's temple, after which it disappears from history (Jer 3 16). Probably the ark was, in form, a throne, on which Jehovah was regarded as sitting.

Priests (as in Jg 17, 18) are men specially consecrated to superintend worship and guard sacred places and objects (1 S 21 6 ; cp. 2 K 25 18). Both Eli and his degenerate sons are priests at Shiloh (1 S 2 13-15). The Philistines also have priests for their god (1 S 5 5 6 2). The priest, wearing his official symbol—the ephod —consults Jehovah on behalf of the worshipper (1 S 14). The office is hereditary (1 S 14 3 2 S 8 17), and we also find a number of priests dwelling together (1 S 22 19). We read of men being consecrated to serve apparently as priests (1 S 7 1 2 S 8 18). After the ark was established at Jerusalem, we find the priests in close connexion with the royal court (2 S 8 17 15 35 19 11 20 25). Later, Solomon, like subsequent kings, is anointed by the priest (1 K 1 39), as Saul and David had been anointed by Samuel (1 S 10 1 16 13) ; the king is 'the Lord's *anointed*,' and the same word (Messiah, 'anointed ') is applied *par excellence* to the ideal king of the future.

The priests, like the prophets, thus stand in a direct relation to the monarchy as soon as the monarchy is established. Their presence is not, however, essential to worship. Saul sacrifices at Gilgal (1 S 13 8), and he is blamed, not for dispensing with a priest, but for not waiting for Samuel. Samuel sacrifices at Bethlehem (1 S 16 3) and David at Jerusalem (2 S 6 13-17).

6. Samuel. The foregoing discussion has been necessary in order to avoid obscurity, otherwise inevitable, in the portraiture of the leading characters and events in these books. Without it, we should find difficulty in defending them from the charge of carelessness and inaccuracy ; with it, we can pass behind the actual narratives to something like the reality which the Israelites so lovingly handed on from generation to generation.

To take the case of Samuel first. In one instance (a), he is a little-known seer, who, however, has the insight to recognise the need of a king, and to find the fitting man in the youthful Saul. In the other (b), he is the acknowledged leader of Israel (a kind of civil Judge), whose headquarters are at Mizpah, and who bitterly resents Israel's wilfulness in repudiating the traditional theocracy. There can be little doubt that (a) gives the more

correct picture ; but it is easy to see how the Samuel of (a), who at a critical time takes the decisive step in the history of the nation, was elevated in the memory of Israel into a position higher than that of Deborah or Eli, and almost recalling the glory of Moses. The dread of the monarchy, so clearly set forth in (b), but absent in (a), reminds us of the attitude taken up towards it by the prophets Hosea, Jeremiah and Ezekiel. In 1 S 9 9, the actual title of 'prophet' is denied to Samuel; but his relation to the kingdom after the accession of Saul is very similar to that of Isaiah to Ahaz and Hezekiah, just as his position previously had been similar to that of the earlier Judges. His action is uniform, consistent and highminded; and there is every reason for the veneration with which he came to be regarded in after years (Ps 99 6 Jer 15 1).

He has been called 'the last of the Judges and the first of the Kings.' In reality, he was neither a judge (in the sense in which Ehud and Jephthah were Judges) nor a king. But he found Israel a loosely knit body of tribes ; he left it a united people. Recognised as he was by the whole nation, he made a national monarchy possible ; and at the foundation of it he laid firmly the conception of the responsibility of the national ruler to God.

7. Saul. In the case of Saul, as of Samuel, we find two distinct views of his character. He is first shown as a brave and vigorous hero, ably seconded by his son ; for his 'rejection,' the incidents of 1 S 13 9 and even 15 9 hardly seem sufficient cause. As the melancholy of 1 S 16 14 deepens on him, his character becomes less and less favourable ; he is morose, jealous, cunning, violent, though not without gleams of a better nature (1 S 24 17) ; and in the tragic isolation of his last days he reminds us of Macbeth. Yet it is noteworthy that from his accession onwards, his position is never seriously challenged, as was that of David himself subsequently. From his first years, he sets himself to the great business of his reign, the long struggle with the Philistines ; he inflicts upon them blows they have never suffered before, and though he finally falls before them (or under the mental disease which paralysed his powers), his successor is able to bring all serious danger from them to an end. After the appearance of David, the interest of the book in Saul's career apart from David comes to an end ; but it is noteworthy that not even in Judah did David, for all his charm and reputation, succeed in producing any real disloyalty to Saul. If, in his last days, he had recourse to necromancy, he had zealously enforced the laws against superstition in earlier times ; and our judgment on his persistent hostility to David must be modified by David's own verdict upon his 'loveliness and pleasantness,' which throughout his life kept his people true to his rule. On the length of his reign, see § 9.

8. David. The strongest argument for the truthfulness of the portrait of David is that so much therein is repellent not only to our feeling, but to that of Israel also. He is pre-eminently a warrior (a 'man of war,' 1 S 16 18 1 Ch 28 3), with a true warrior's resourcefulness and perception of the need of the moment ; relentless towards his foes, yet possessed of a peculiar personal charm which endeared him to his own people and to strangers alike ; he can make himself at home with Achish of Gath, and one of his closest followers in later years is Ittai, another Gittite Philistine. He has notable skill in music (1 S 16 18 ; cp. Am 6 5). It is probable that his large harem was formed in part as the result of political considera-tions ; in weakness and irresolution in dealing with his own family, he is like many other-wise vigorous Oriental monarchs—as also in his liability to sudden outbursts of strong feeling, both evil and good (2 S 11 2 12 5, 13). He pushed the frontiers of Israel to their furthest extent —an achievement which was the easier since at this time both Egypt and Assyria and Babylon were occupied within their own borders, and never approached Palestine ; he developed the simple rule of Saul (cp. 1 S 22 6) into the royalty of a court and a capital ; but subsequent events showed that he did not destroy the rivalry between the southern and northern halves of the kingdom. Curiously enough, the strength of Absalom's rebellion was in the king's own tribe of Judah. He was exalted by the affectionate memory of later years into the Saint and the Psalmist. It is no wonder that in thinking of the glorious future king of Israel, men should neglect David's degenerate successors and form the picture of their ideal, as 'a son of David,' on the frank generous character and strong vigorous rule of the man whom, in spite of all his faults, they felt to be after God's own mind (1 S 13 14). Not only was he 'prudent in speech' and 'of a comely person,' but 'Jehovah was with him' (1 S 16 18).

9. The Chronology of the Period. The biblical writings themselves give us the lengths of various periods (judgeships and reigns) and of the intervals between events (e.g. 1 K 6 1). In the Assyrian canon we are able to fix the exact year of certain events ; working back from these, and reckoning the reigns of David and Solomon as each equal to 40 years (2 S 5 4 1 K 11 42),* we arrive at 1017 B.C. as the date of David's accession and the death of Saul. The events of David's reign cannot well have been comprised in any shorter

time. The Old Testament does not mention the length of Saul's reign ; the 40 years of Ac 13 21 are certainly too long; Saul can hardly have been older than 60 (if so old) at the battle of Gilboa, while almost at the beginning of his reign his eldest son is a powerful warrior. His actual age at his accession is wanting in the Hebrew text (1 S 13 1), and the narrative of his reign suggests a very much shorter period than David's. We should therefore date his accession between 1040 and 1030 B.C.

For the length of Samuel's judgeship we have no information ; he is introduced to us as already occupying his position ; possibly he obtained it quite gradually after the death of Eli (of the date of this event, also, we are in ignorance). From 1 S 7 2 (RM) it might be inferred that for 20 years after the deposi-tion of the ark at Kirjath-jearim, Israel was satisfied with Jehovah and Samuel ; hence we should place the beginning of Samuel's office in 1060–1050 B.C.; and as he would hardly have been much less than 30 years old when he became Judge, or than 50 years old when he committed the kingdom to Saul, we must place his birth somewhere about 1085 B.C.

10. The Religious Significance of the Book. The main religious lesson of the book is similar to that of Judges ; it is that Israel's safety as a nation lies in union under the guidance of Jehovah and resistance to foreigners. Of this union, the kingship is a symbol. As we have seen, there are two views of the origin of the kingship in the elevation of Saul to the throne ; but that of 1 S 15 (as a defection from loyalty to Jehovah) is certainly not maintained, or even referred to, later on in the book. Both Saul and David were firm worshippers of Jehovah ; in spite of their moral lapses, we hear nothing in their reigns of that falling away into idolatry which is so common both before and after. The references (without any suggestion of blame) to the 'teraphim' (1 S 19 13-16; contrast 15 23) and to the offering of sacrifices in other places besides the central sanctuary, and by others than priests, as well as the omission of all those ritual details which fill the pages of the parallel narrative in Chronicles, show that the religious ideas of the time (as also of the time in which the book was written) are still somewhat primi-tive (cp. also 1 S 16 14, 'the evil spirit from Jehovah,' and 2 S 24 1 contrasted with 1 Ch 21 1, 'the Satan stood up'). But though we are still in the childhood of Israel's religion, it is a childhood that is full of promise ; for it rests, with a loving confidence which is unshaken, on the firm mercy and judgment (Ps 101 1) of Israel's God.

---

* Forty, however, is probably a round number: cp. Intro. to Judges. 'Forty,' in 2 S 15 7, is possibly a mistake for 'four' (so RM). In any case, it is too much.

11. Date, Text, etc. A few miscellaneous points remain to be considered. When was the book written ? This question must mean, in view of § 2, when did the two books reach their present form ? It is impossible to reply with certainty ; the bulk of the three large narratives must have been written comparatively soon after the events they refer to, though we can have no means of knowing when the poetical additions were actually made. Apart from these, there is very little to suggest a date later than the 8th cent.

What is its relation to Chronicles ? The reader will easily see the similarities and the differences in the two parallel narratives. That Chronicles was written at a far later date is shown, apart from internal evidence, by its place in the Hebrew canon, almost at the end, and not, like Samuel, among the 'prophets'— a fact which is emphasised in the name which the book bears in the Septuagint, 'things left out.' These omissions are for the most part lists and genealogies and details connected with the ark or (later on) the Temple, which are either new, or much more fully given in the later book (cp. 1 Ch 11 26 f. 12 15 with 2 S 6 12-19 16 37-43 and the additions in c. 21). On the other hand, some of the most interesting and vividly narrated events in Samuel are passed over entirely, especially anything (except David's numbering of Israel) which is to the disadvantage of the king himself (including the story of Bathsheba and the whole rebellion of Absalom). In the earlier

book, Israel is as important as Judah, apart from the fact that David's prominence gives special weight to the southern tribe ; in the later book (written long after the disappearance of the northern kingdom) Israel is of no importance at all. It is certain that the books of Samuel were among the sources used by the Chronicler, and the smaller additions seem intended either to be didactic, or to fill up apparent gaps in the earlier narrative. See Intro. to Chronicles. A careful comparison with Chronicles will bring out very clearly the impartiality and thoroughness of the books of Samuel.

Have we the best text of Samuel before us ? This question is suggested by the fact (pointed out several times in the notes) that the text is often very corrupt, and also by the divergences constantly to be observed in the Greek translation (the Septuagint—LXX). This Greek translation is itself found in three types of text ; where they agree, we may conclude, with Prof. H. P. Smith, that they represent an ancient Hebrew text. This text (now only recoverable through the Greek translation) would seem to have been free from several errors contained in the Hebrew text from which our own translation has been made. It is, however, unsafe to argue that because a reading is simpler, it is therefore more correct ; in some cases, the reading of our text has been misunderstood ; but in others, we must certainly make corrections by the help of the Greek version.

---

1 SAMUEL

CHAPTER 1

THE BIRTH OF SAMUEL

Hannah, the childless wife of Elkanah, is grieved by her childlessness, and prays for a son. Her prayer is heard, and in gratitude she consecrates her child to the service of Jehovah.

1. Ramathaim-zophim] Ramathaim ('double height') probably denotes the district in which Ramah ('height') was the chief town. It was at Ramah that Samuel was born, lived, laboured, died, and was buried. As Ramah was a common name in a hilly country like Palestine, Zophim is here added to denote that this Ramah was in the land of Zuph (9 5). But even so, the exact position of Ramah has not been determined with certainty. **Mount Ephraim]** RV 'the hill country of Ephraim.' **Ephrathite]** RV 'Ephraimite.'

2. Two wives] The reason was probably the

barrenness of Hannah, which Elkanah would consider a disgrace. Thomson states that at the present day in the East it is considered sufficient reason for a divorce. But here, as elsewhere in OT., we find evidence of the unhappiness which polygamy often produced.

3. Yearly] lit. 'from time to time.' The Law commanded every male to appear before God three times in the year, and there are strong reasons for assigning a very early date to the practice. Of course, the phrase 'from time to time' can mean 'from year to year,' when the context so defines it (as in Ex 13 10); but otherwise there is no justification for so limiting it. **LORD of hosts]** This title of God occurs here for the first time, and its use was probably occasioned by the warlike character of the book. As used in the books of Samuel, 'the hosts' are the armies of Israel (17 45), but afterwards the idea was extended to the hosts of angels (Ps 103 20, 21). **Shiloh]** Joshua set up the Tabernacle there (Josh 18¹), as being central and in the territory of his own tribe. For its position, see Jg 21¹⁹. **And the two sons of Eli, Hophni and Phinehas, the priests of the LORD,** *were* **there**] rather, 'and there the two sons of Eli, Hophni and Phinehas, were priests to the LORD.'

5. A worthy portion] LXX reads 'But unto Hannah he gave a single portion.' Elkanah gave portions to Peninnah and to each of her sons and daughters. But in spite of his love for Hannah, he only gave her a single portion, because she had neither son nor daughter. The Heb. text, as it stands, cannot be translated. The **portion** was the part of the sacrifice consumed by the offerer and his family : see Lv 7. **6. Her adversary**] i.e. Peninnah. The word is a common one in Arabic to denote a rival, or fellow-wife. **7.** *As* **he did so**] Probably the true text is 'So it happened.' **Did not eat**] refused to take any part in the festival, of which the sacrificial meal was a principal feature (cp. c. 9).

9. Eli the priest] i.e. the chief priest. How Eli had attained this rank we do not know, for he was descended from Ithamar the younger son of Aaron, and not from Eleazar the elder son. It has been supposed that in those troublous times the office was bestowed upon him on account of his ability and piety. **Upon a seat by a post**] RV 'upon his seat by the door post,' where he could see all who went in or out : cp. 4¹³. **11.** See Nu 6 respecting the Nazirite vow. **16. A daughter of Belial**] lit. 'a daughter of worthlessness,' i.e. a worthless woman. 'Belial' came to be used as a name for Satan (2 Cor 6¹⁵). **Grief**] RV 'provocation.'

20. Samuel] The name Samuel is here connected with the verb *saal*, 'to ask'; but this seems only to have been a popular etymology. Most probably Samuel means 'name of God' : cp. v. 28.

21. His vow] Perhaps Elkanah had vowed an offering to God if Hannah had a son, which he now fulfilled : cp. Lv 7¹⁶. **22. Until the child be weaned**] After this the ordinary attendants at the Tabernacle would be able to take charge of him. In the Korân the usual time for weaning is stated to be the age of two years. **23. His word**] LXX 'thy word.' No mention has been made in the preceding account of any promise of God. **24. Three bullocks**] Probably one bullock was for the burnt-offering, which accompanied the dedication of Samuel, another was for Elkanah's usual sacrifice, while the third was the thank-offering he had vowed (v. 21). **28. Lent**] RV 'granted,' as in Ex 12³⁶. **And he worshipped the LORD there**] These words interrupt the connexion and are rightly omitted by LXX.

CHAPTER 2
HANNAH'S SONG OF THANKSGIVING. THE SIN OF ELI'S SONS

1-10. The Song of Hannah. This beautiful poem has been well called the 'Magnificat of the Old Testament.' The song of the Virgin Mary (Lk 1⁴⁶⁻⁵⁵) is clearly modelled on it very closely. In each case there is the rejoicing over the exaltation of the poor and despised and the humiliation of the rich. But there is a world of difference between Mary's quiet and restrained gratitude and calm confidence in God's mercy, on the one hand, and the exultant and almost fierce triumph of this song. V. 5 has doubtless led to the attribution of the song to Hannah; but in its general tone it seems more suitable to some public person, and v. 10 (unless it be an interpolation) suggests a later date in Israel's history. Compare the expressions of national triumph in the songs of Moses (Ex 15¹⁻¹⁸) and Deborah (Jg 5).

1. Mine horn is exalted] The figure is that of an animal carrying its head high: cp. Ps 112⁹. **My mouth is enlarged**] The idea is that of speaking with confidence and derision: cp. Isa 57⁴. **Salvation**] In the Bible this word denotes help or deliverance of any kind. **2. Holy**] The Holiness of God in the OT. denotes positively the completeness of the divine nature and negatively God's unlikeness to anything else. **Rock**] This is a frequent metaphor to express the strength and unchangingness of Jehovah. The name also conveys the idea that the strength of God is a refuge for His people (Ps 91²). Rocks, as capable of easy defence, were often used as places of refuge. **3. Weighed**] i.e. estimated. The idea is the same as in Prov 21². **5. Seven**] the number of completeness, perfection. **6. Grave**] Heb. *Sheol*, the place where departed spirits were believed to be gathered at death. **Bringeth up**] restores to life those who were at the point of death. **8. Pillars**] the great men of the state on whom it depended for its stability: cp. Gal 2⁹ Rev 3¹². **9. Saints**] RV 'holy ones': rather, 'pious ones, those who love God.' **10. His anointed**] a common name for the Jewish king.

12. Knew] This verb in the Bible has often the added idea of appreciation, recognition of character, affection.

13-17. The sons of Eli were guilty of a two-fold sin. (*a*) Instead of being content with their allotted portion (Lv 7³¹ᶠ·) they took all they could get of the offerer's portion. (*b*) They dishonoured God by making their claims take precedence of His. The blood and the fat were to be consumed on the altar immediately after slaughtering (Ex 23¹⁸), but they claimed their share before this had been done. After the fat had been conveyed to God the sacrificial flesh was boiled, but Eli's sons demanded their portion raw with a view to its being roasted: see HDB. art. 'Sacrifice.'

16. *If* any man] RV 'if the man,' i.e. the offerer. **Presently**] i.e. immediately, at once.

17. For men abhorred] rather, 'for the men (i.e. the sons of Eli) despised.'

18. But Samuel] Throughout this section Samuel is contrasted with the profligate sons of Eli. **Linen ephod**] the usual priestly garment (1 S 22 18). **20. For the loan which is lent**] rather, 'in return for the petition which was made for (i.e. for the benefit of) the LORD,' i.e. in place of Samuel, the man-child who, if born, was to be given to the LORD.

22. Assembled *at*] RV 'did service at.' It is probable that these women were permanently connected with the Tabernacle: cp. Ex 38 8.

Lay with the women] There is no doubt that the surrender of their chastity was regarded by the women of Canaan and Syria as the highest sacrifice they could make in honour of their gods. The sons of Eli introduced these immoral rites into the worship of Jehovah, and hence the severity of their condemnation.

25. In the original, point is given to Eli's rebuke by the fact that the word here used for 'judge' (*Elohim*) also means 'God.' The judge was regarded as the representative of God: see Ps 82 6. If it is a case of men, God has appointed some one to settle the matter; but when God Himself is the offended party, no higher power exists to whom the case can be submitted. God is both adversary and judge.

Would slay them] lit. 'wished to slay them.' In the OT. the direct intervention of God is assumed, and His ever-present agency realised as a determining fact. We say that after a man has persisted for long years in sinful habits, he finds it impossible to alter. The Bible expresses the same truth by stating, first that the sinner (e.g. Pharaoh) hardens his own heart, and then that God hardens the sinner's heart. The punishment of the wicked is considered to be as much in accordance with God's will as the reward of the righteous.

27. A man of God] a common name for a prophet. With the books of Samuel we come to a period when God guides His people by human agency rather than by direct communication. **Did I plainly appear?**] RV 'Did I reveal myself?' It is an impassioned question, 'Did I or did I not?' **Thy father**] i.e. Aaron.

In Pharaoh's house] LXX reads 'In bondage to Pharaoh's house.' **28. Give..all the offerings**] see Lv 2, 6, 7.

29. Kick ye at] The figure is that of a pampered and intractable animal: cp. Dt 32 15. **Sacrifice and..offering**] bloody and unbloody sacrifices. **Honourest thy sons above me**] Eli

should have removed his sons from a position they disgraced. But he could not bring himself to humiliate them and lower his own position in the sight of the people.

30. When Abiathar, the descendant of Eli, fled to David (22 20), Zadok, a descendant of Eleazar, may have been made chief priest by Saul. He appears soon after, and it is not known how or when the office was bestowed on him. David divided the dignity between the two (2 S 8 17), but Abiathar was deposed by Solomon (1 K 2 27), and the priesthood remained with Zadok and his descendants down to the time of the exile. Thus the prophet's threat was fulfilled.

31-35. It is keenly disputed to what events these vv. refer. The simplest explanation is that v. 31 refers to the massacre of the priests at Nob, vv. 32, 33 to the deposition and consequent poverty of Abiathar, and v. 35 to Zadok.

31. Cut off thine arm] destroy thy power, as Ps 10 15. **32. An enemy** *in my* habitation] lit. 'affliction of habitation.' The context seems to show that the reference is to Eli's own dwelling. While Israel increased in wealth and prosperity in the reign of Solomon, Eli's family were to fall into poverty and obscurity.

33. Those who did not die young would pass their life in vexation and grief. **Thine eyes.. thine heart**] rather as LXX, 'his eyes..his heart.' **Shall die in the flower of their age**] LXX reads 'shall die by the sword of men.'

35. I will build him a sure house] i.e. I will give him a continuous posterity: cp. 25 28 2 S 7 16. **Mine anointed**] the king (singular), really referring to the long line of kings who were to follow David. **36. Put me into**] rather, 'attach me to,' 'make me a hanger on.'

CHAPTER 3

THE CALL OF SAMUEL

1. Precious] RM, 'rare': see Isa 13 12. There was no prophet then. **Open**] rather, 'published, widely announced': cp. 2 Ch 31 5.

3. Ere the lamp of God went out] The lamp ('the seven-branched candlestick') burned all night in the sanctuary, so that the time was early morning: cp. Ex 27 21. Samuel seems to have been sleeping in some chamber near the ark. Cp. RV, 'was laid down *to sleep*, in the temple of the LORD, where the ark of God was.' On the ark see Intro. § 5. **10. Came, and stood**] the Voice became a Vision.

13. Made themselves vile] LXX reads 'Because his sons cursed God.' See on 2 S 12 14.

15. Doors] The Tabernacle was no longer a mere tent, but at this time had been replaced by a substantial building. This was a natural consequence of its occupying a fixed position.

18. It *is* **the LORD**] So Eli was at heart loyal, though he had shown culpable weakness.

19. Let none of his words fall to the ground]
i.e. accomplished all his predictions. For
the idea cp. Dt 18 21, 22. **20. Established]**
i.e. accredited, approved. **Prophet]** see Intro. § 4.

21. In Shiloh by the word of the LORD]
These words are wanting in LXX, and the
connexion gains greatly by their omission.

**C. 4 1a. And the word of Samuel came to all
Israel]** This clause should really form the
conclusion of c. 3 as it does in RV. Samuel
proclaimed to all his countrymen the revelation he had received.

CHAPTER 4
CAPTURE OF THE ARK BY THE PHILISTINES.
DEATH OF ELI

The reason which led to 4 1a being detached
from its proper context is that without it this
c. seems to begin with inexplicable abruptness.
The explanation of this lack of connexion is
that the editor is now using a different document. This section is in no sense a continuation of the preceding. It does not proceed
with the history of Samuel, whose name does
not even occur in it, but relates the journeyings of the ark. Alike in style and in conception it is totally distinct from the section
which precedes and the section which follows
it. In many respects it resembles the history
of Samson more closely than any other part
of OT.

1. The Philistines] see on Jg 3 3. **Eben-
ezer]** 'stone of help.' The place is called by
the name familiar to the readers of the book,
though it did not actually receive the name
till later (7 12). The positions of Eben-ezer
and Aphek have not been determined with
certainty.

3. The ark of the covenant] so called
because it was a sign and proof both of God's
covenant and of His presence.

4. RV 'which sitteth upon the cherubim.'
This does not imply that there were figures
of cherubim upon the ark (1 K 8 6), but refers
to the general glory of Jehovah. The cherubs
are heavenly beings regarded as standing in
Jehovah's presence (cp. the seraphim of Isa 6),
and, in Ezk 1, 10, as of composite form. Cp. also
Ps 18 10. In Solomon's temple two winged
cherubs stood in the most holy place (1 K 6 24).

The two sons of Eli] This notice is intended to remind us why the arrival of the
ark produced no result.

6. Hebrews] This is the general name for
Israelites when foreigners are the speakers
(Gn 39 14). **8.** The Philistines are not quite
accurate in their history, but the mistake is
not at all unnatural.

15. Ninety and eight] This number is
interesting as showing how mistakes arise.
In the original it was denoted by two letters.

The LXX, losing sight of one, reads 90 The
Syriac, confusing 9 with 7, reads 78. The
Hebrew explains the cause of the other two
readings.

19 f. The narrative is somewhat obscure.
Apparently Phinehas' wife dies in giving birth
to her child ; before her death, she cries out
'I-chabod,' which is thus given as the child's
name. V. 22 simply repeats v. 21.

21. I-chabod] 'no glory.' The glory was
that of the presence of God, the visible sign
and symbol of which was the ark.

22. Departed] lit. 'gone into exile.' The
ark had gone into a foreign land.

CHAPTER 5
THE ARK AMONG THE PHILISTINES

1. Ashdod] on an elevation overlooking the
Philistine plain midway between Gaza and
Joppa, and 3 m. from the Mediterranean. Its
importance consisted in the fact that it com-
manded the high road from Palestine to
Egypt.

2. Dagon] seems to have been worshipped
in all the Philistine cities. His name is probably merely the Canaanite pronunciation of
the word for 'corn,' and designates him as
the god of agriculture. The Philistines were
not a maritime people, like the Phœnicians,
but depended on agriculture. Stanley writes :
'The most striking and characteristic feature
of Philistia is its immense plains of cornfields. . . These rich fields must have been the
great source alike of the power and value
of Philistia.' **They brought it]** The Philistines considered that their god, Dagon, had
shown himself stronger than Jehovah, and so
they brought him the symbol of his conquered
rival.

3. Fallen upon his face] in an attitude of
homage. **Set him in his place]** they would
think it was an accident. **4.** This time all
possibility of accident was excluded. *The
stump of* **Dagon]** AV is right in thinking that
some word must have fallen out of the Hebrew
text.

6. In c. 6 we have a plague of mice as well
as of hæmorrhoids. Some regard the introduction of this second plague as due to a
scribe. On the other hand, LXX inserts a
notice of the mice also in 5 6, 10 6 1. Wellhausen thinks that 'mice' are symbolical of
misfortune in general, and do not denote
a second plague. Herodotus attributes the
disaster which overtook Sennacherib's army
and the deliverance of Jerusalem in 701 B.C.
(2 K 19 35-37) to a host of mice, which destroyed
the bowstrings of the Assyrian soldiers : cp.
on 6 5.

12. So the protest of the Ekronites was not
attended to. The Philistines were unwilling
to part with their trophy.

CHAPTER 6

THE PHILISTINES RETURN THE ARK TO ISRAEL

2. The diviners] The Philistines appear to have been notorious for their attachment to divination : see on Isa 2⁶. **3. The trespass offering** was always brought to atone for some wrong done to, or some right withheld from, God or man. **5.** Aristotle relates that in harvest entire crops were sometimes destroyed in a single night by the ravages of field-mice.

7. The **new cart** and the **kine** who had worn **no yoke** were signs of respect. **9.** Under ordinary circumstances the cows would not have left their calves. **Beth-shemesh**] the modern Ain-Shems, on the N. border of Judah.

18. Even unto the great *stone*] Read with LXX, ' And the great stone, whereon they set down the ark of the LORD, is a witness unto this day.'

19. It is very probable that in this v. LXX has preserved the original text : ' But the sons of Jechoniah rejoiced not with the men of Beth-shemesh, when they gazed (with gladness) at the ark of the LORD, and he smote among them 70 men.' All editors are agreed that the 'fifty thousand' is a gloss which has crept into the text. The Hebrew phrase here used is not the correct method of expressing 50,070.

21. Kirjath-jearim] see on Jg 18¹². For the further account of the ark cp. 2 S 6.

C. 7¹. This v. is the conclusion of the narrative, and should really form part of c. 6.

We should have expected the ark to be taken back to Shiloh ; perhaps Shiloh had fallen into the hands of the Philistines, who now overran Israel (cp. 14⁶,¹⁹). At any rate, we hear no more of Shiloh as a national meeting-place ; for the time, whatever national unity exists centres round Samuel.

CHAPTER 7

SAMUEL DELIVERS ISRAEL FROM THE PHILISTINES

The narrative in this c. is taken from a different source from the account which precedes.

2. Twenty years] The time is reckoned till Israel's repentance and not to the removal of the ark by David (2 S 6²). **3, 4.** These vv. appear to be anticipatory and in order of time to follow vv. 5, 6. **4. Baalim and Ashtaroth**] see on Jg 2¹¹,¹³. **5. Mizpeh**] in Benjamin.

Pray] Samuel was noted as a man of prayer (cp. Ps 99⁶).

6. Poured *it* **out**] The symbolism of the act is uncertain. The most probable explanation is that of the Targum, that it represented the pouring out of their hearts in repentance be-

fore the LORD : cp. 2 S 23¹⁶ Lam 2¹⁹. **7. Went up against Israel**] for the object of the assembly at Mizpeh was to throw off the Philistine yoke.

9. A burnt offering wholly] RV 'a whole burnt offering.' The offering of the whole animal symbolised the self-dedication of the worshipper. **12. Eben-ezer**] see on 4¹.

13. All the days of Samuel] The words naturally mean ' all the time he acted as judge.' This must be understood as the optimistic notice of a later writer. The narrative of c. 14 shows that Israel did not succeed in recovering from the Philistine oppression : see also on 7¹ 9¹⁶. **14. The coasts thereof**] i.e. the districts round the towns. **Amorites**] i.e. the old Canaanite inhabitants of the hill-country : see on Jg 1³⁴. Israelite and Canaanite made peace in front of a common enemy.

15. All the days of his life] The attitude of Samuel towards Saul in the matters of (a) his sacrifice and (b) Amalek show that he retained some authority even after Saul was elected king.

16. He instituted what in modern language would be called ' courts of assize.' **Gilgal**] probably the famous site near Jericho.

CHAPTERS 8-14

See on 9¹. There are clearly two accounts of the institution of the kingship. In c. 8, the wish for a king is regarded as a sign of disloyalty to the real King, Jehovah, and, as such, Samuel protests against it. In chs. 9–10¹⁶, Jehovah himself chooses Saul to deliver his people from the Philistines : cp. Intro. § 2.

CHAPTER 8

THE PEOPLE DEMAND A KING

1. Judges] They would be subordinate to their father. When the son of a Judge was influential and popular, he might easily succeed to his father's position : cp. Abimelech in Jg 9¹f.

5. Like all the nations] This was the sin of the people. God intended that they, unlike other nations, should be a peculiar people, governed directly by Himself.

6. Displeased Samuel] They had shown themselves forgetful of their relation to God and ungrateful to Samuel himself. But in spite of this, he simply leaves the decision with God. **7. For**] Samuel was not to hesitate, for the matter was one which concerned God rather than himself. **8. Which they have done**] LXX adds ' to me,' an addition which is required by the contrast with ' to thee.'

11. It does not follow that a Jewish king was actually like this description, but an Oriental despot was, and Israel had asked for a king like other nations. In later years,

Hebrew monarchy sank very low, both in
Judah and Israel : cp. the tone both of Hosea
and of Ezekiel (45 9 46 18). **13. Confectionaries**]
RM 'perfumers' : cp. Ex 30 25. **15. Officers**]
Heb. ' eunuchs.'

CHAPTER 9
SAUL AND SAMUEL MEET

For the picture of Samuel in this c., as a
person of local rather than national importance, cp. Intro. § 6. On early prophecy, see
Intro. § 4.

C. 9 1–10 16 comes from a different source
from c. 8 : see intro. there. The author of
this section gives no hint that the choice of a
king was displeasing to God. But we meet
with the views of c. 8 again when we come to
10 17f.

1. Power] RV 'valour.' **4, 5.** The districts of Shalisha, Shalim, and Zuph have not
been identified. **5. Take thought**] rather,
' be anxious.' **6. In this city**] probably
Ramah.

9. This v. is probably an explanatory note
by the editor, though some regard it as a
scribe's insertion. **Seer**] Heb. *roeh*, a comparatively rare word, in this sense. ' They
were called " seers " for no other reason
than because they were thought to " see "
what for the rest of men was hidden, the
secrets either of the present or of the future ' ;
e.g. in the present case, the matter of the
asses. **Prophet**] The Heb. word is *nabi*, and
is probably connected with the Assyrian *nabu*,
' to call ' or ' name.' The prophet was the
' spokesman ' of Jehovah : see art. ' Hebrew
Prophecy.'
13. This refers to the solemn sacrificial
meal after the peace offering : cp. Ex 24 5, 11
Lv 7. **14. Came out against them**] rather,
' came out to meet them.' **20. On whom** *is*
all the desire] RV ' for whom is all that is
desirable in Israel. Is it not for thee ? '
cp. Hag 2 7 RM. **21. The least of all the
families**] This is Eastern hyperbole and must
not be taken literally : cp. Jg 6 15. **24. And** *Samuel* **said**] The word ' Samuel '
is not in the original. ' And the cook took
up .. and said.' What follows is the garrulous
talk of the cook. **Since I said**] the Heb. is
simply ' saying ' (i.e. Samuel).
25, 26. LXX is the more probable : ' And
when they were come down from the high
place into the city, they spread a couch for
Saul on the housetop, and he lay down. And
it came to pass about,' etc. At the present
day in the East multitudes sleep on the roofs
of houses. **26. Samuel called Saul to the top**]
RV ' Samuel called to Saul on the housetop.'
Saul had been sleeping on the roof, and now
Samuel calls to him to descend.

CHAPTER 10
SAUL IS ANOINTED KING BY SAMUEL

1. LXX is probably right in reading at the
end of this v. 'and this is the sign that the
LORD hath anointed thee to be captain ' (RV
' prince ') ' over his inheritance.' **2. Rachel's
tomb**] was not far from Bethlehem (Gn 35 19, 20).
3. Plain] RV ' oak.'
5. The hill of God] The word is really
' Gibeah,' which was Saul's own home. It is
here called ' God's Gibeah ' because Samuel
had established a school of the prophets there.
Cp. the common term for a prophet, ' man of
God ' (e.g. 1 K 17 18). **They shall prophesy**]
RV ' they shall be prophesying,' lit. acting as
prophets. Music was a recognised means of
promoting the exaltation of spirit necessary
for inspiration (2 K 3 15). **6. Be turned into
another man**] fitted for his new career : see
v. 9.
8. This command appears to have been
given during the Philistine war narrated in
c. 13 : cp. 13 8. Here it interrupts the connexion.
9. Another heart] The heart is not, with the
Hebrews, opposed to the head, as with us. The
term is used for the general bent both of mind
and character. Saul has a new conception of
himself and of his life given to him. This
is quickly followed by a sudden outburst of
' prophesying,' here obviously used in the
sense of ecstatic exaltation of utterance.
Saul's liability to be carried out of himself
(like his namesake of Tarsus) is also made
clear in his fits of melancholic brooding and
sudden passion (cp. 18 10, 11, where for ' prophesied ' RM reads ' raved '). See also Intro.
§ 7.
11. *Is* **Saul also among the prophets ?**] i.e.
has he joined a school of the prophets ? He
was not the sort of young man to adopt such
a life. Another explanation of the saying is
given in 19 24.
12. Who *is* **their father ?**] Prophecy did not
descend from father to son, so that there was
no reason for surprise in finding the son of
Kish among the prophets.
17. At this point the other narrative is
resumed (see on 8 1).
19. Thousands] The word may very possibly
mean simply ' families ' : cp. v. 21. We can
hardly imagine this to mean that the whole
Hebrew population of Palestine was present.
20. The Hebrews considered that in elec-
tions by lot, the decision was made by God
(Josh 7 18 Prov 16 33). **22. Stuff**] i.e. the baggage : cp. 16 11.
25. The manner of the kingdom] This was
a legal document intended to bind both king
and people, and probably to guard against the
abuses mentioned in c. 8. The power of the

Hebrew monarch was, in some respects, narrowly limited. **26. A band of men**] Probably the original text was 'the men of valour,' in contrast to 'the worthless men' of v. 27. Note the simplicity and absence of ceremonial in the new royalty : cp. 11 4 and Intro. § 7.

27. See intro. to c. 11.

CHAPTER 11
SAUL SUBDUES THE AMMONITES

This c. is entirely in the spirit of the narratives in Judges ; from v. 15, it seems to be independent of c. 10 ; but v. 12 points back to 10 27, which is perhaps distinct from vv. 17–24 ; even the ceremony at Gilgal may have been a 'renewal' (v. 10), in the renewed popular enthusiasm, of the ceremony at Mizpeh. But see on 12 12.

1. Nahash] It is very doubtful if this is the Nahash of 2 S 10 2. **3. Come out**] a usual term for 'surrender.' **5.** So Cincinnatus was found by the messengers of the State with his oxen. **6.** Cp. Jg 6 34 11 29 14 6, etc., used of a sudden access of fierce patriotic zeal. Both cause and effect are slightly different in 10 10. **7. Fear of the LORD**] i.e. a dread inspired by the LORD ; RM 'a terror from the LORD.' **9.** i.e. before noon : cp. v. 11.

10. Their object was to make the attack come on the Ammonites as a complete surprise. **13.** Saul possessed many good and generous impulses (24 17 26 21). **15. They made Saul king**] see prefatory note.

CHAPTER 12
SAMUEL RESIGNS HIS JUDGESHIP

This c. is a continuation of 10 17-24, and the scene of the events recorded is the great national assembly at Mizpeh. Notice, however, the reference to Nahash (c. 11) in v. 12.

2. My sons] cp. 8 1-5. **3. His anointed**] i.e. Saul the anointed king. This becomes the regular title of the king : cp. 24 6-10 26 9-11, etc. The word is identical with 'Messiah' or (in its Gk. form) 'Christ.' **6.** It is the LORD] LXX reads 'the LORD is witness.' **Advanced**] RV 'appointed,' i.e. made them the leaders of Israel. **9. Into the hand of Sisera**] see Jg 4. **Into the hand of the king of Moab**] see Jg 3. **11. Jerubbaal**] see Jg 6. **Bedan**] LXX reads 'Barak.' **Jephthah**] see Jg 11. **Samuel**] must be a later insertion either by the editor or by a scribe. **12. When the LORD your God was your king**] cp. 8 7 Jg 8 23. This is not quite in accord with the narrative of c. 11 as it stands, where Saul has already been chosen king (v. 12), and where the attack on Nahash results from his own vigorous initiative.

14. RV 'If ye will fear .. and serve him, and hearken .. and be .. followers .. well.'

15. Against your fathers] i.e. in the times of the Judges.

17. Wheat harvest] This shows that this occurred between the middle of May and the middle of June. In Palestine a summer thunderstorm is very unusual : cp. Prov 21 1. Prof. G. A. Smith writes : 'In May showers are very rare, and from then till October, not only is there no rain, but a cloud seldom passes over the sky, and a thunderstorm is a miracle.'

21. For] The first 'for' in this v. is rightly omitted by LXX. 'And turn ye not aside after vain things which,' etc. **Vain things**] i.e. idols. **22. For his great name's sake**] The idea is explained in Ex 32 12.

CHAPTER 13
SAUL'S WAR AGAINST THE PHILISTINES

1. The age of Saul at his accession has fallen out of the text and also one of the two numbers representing the length of his reign. Our present text is 'Saul was . . years old when he began to reign, and he reigned . . and two years.' We have no means of recovering the former number. For the latter Keil, with great probability, conjectures 22 : see on 2 S 2 10 and Intro. § 9. **2. Michmash**] still retains its ancient name ; it is a village 9 m. from Jerusalem, and is just N. of a narrow pass leading to Geba ; hence it was a thoroughly well-chosen strategic position ; cp 14 4. **3. And the Philistines .. Hebrews hear**] The text is probably corrupt. Driver emends to 'And the Philistines heard saying The Hebrews have revolted,' and puts 'And Saul blew the trumpet throughout all the land' at the beginning of v. 4. **4. Gilgal**] Cornill would read 'Gibeah' here. **5. Thirty thousand**] LXX has '3,000' ; the chariots were less in number than the horsemen ; cp. 2 S 10 18 1 K 10 26. **6. The people did hide themselves**] The prompt action of the Philistines quite quenched the ardour of the undisciplined peasants with Saul.

8. Saul at Gilgal would be anxious lest the Philistines should seize Geba and the heights. **Samuel had appointed**] The reference is probably to 10 8.

9. It is, to say the least, doubtful whether Saul offered the sacrifice with his own hands, or whether he caused it to be offered. At any rate, his offence was not in his offering sacrifice, but in his unwillingness to obey the directions of God and of God's representative, the prophet. It must be admitted that Saul's position was a difficult one ; but this single act was really an index to a weakness in his character : see, however, on 14 24.

14. After his own heart] David's actions were by no means all of them the actions of an ideal character ; but he is presented in the narratives as maintaining on the whole an attitude towards God very different from that of Saul : cp. 16 1.

16. Abode in Gibeah] Saul with his reduced

numbers was compelled to abandon the other two positions and to concentrate his forces at Gibeah. **17. The spoilers**] i.e. bands sent out to ravage the country immediately concerned in the insurrection. This unwise weakening of the Philistine forces gave the Israelites their opportunity. **Ophrah**] a town in Benjamin. **Shual**] Position unknown, as is also that of **Zeboim** in the next v. **18. Beth-horon**] on the border of Benjamin and Ephraim, was on the direct road from Michmash to Philistia. **21. Yet they had,** etc.] RM proposes, 'When the edges of the mattocks .. and of the axes were blunt.' We can hardly imagine that the text as it stands is to be taken literally after the narrative of 13 f. **23. To the passage**] RV 'unto the pass.'

CHAPTER 14
JONATHAN'S EXPLOIT. THE BATTLE OF
MICHMASH. A SUMMARY OF SAUL'S REIGN

3. Ahiah] RV 'Ahijah,' probably merely another form of Ahimelech (21 [1]). Melech (king) was one of the titles of Jah or Jehovah. **4. Between the passages**] RV 'between the passes.' **9.** It has been suggested that the reply would show that the Philistines were brave men, and Jonathan would give up the enterprise as impossible ; but in view of v. 6, it is better to take the sign as a purely arbitrary one : cp. Jg 7 [4 f]. **14. An half acre of land .. plow**] RV 'half a furrow's length in an acre of land,' i.e. half the length of one of the sides of an acre. **15.** There was a trembling both in the (fortified) camp and in the (open) country ; all the people, both garrison and plundering bands, trembled. **16. Behold, the multitude .. one another**] LXX reads, 'Behold the multitude melted away' (i.e. dispersed in confusion) 'hither and thither.' **18.** LXX reads, 'Bring hither the ephod. For he wore the ephod.' It was the Urim and Thummim in the ephod and not the ark which was used to discover the will of God : see 23 [9] 30 [7]. **19. Withdraw thine hand**] Saul had not patience to wait : cp. 13 [9]. **24.** The purpose of this ' taboo ' on food was probably to secure by fasting the continued presence of Jehovah with the victorious army. Israel's battles were Jehovah's, and Saul's motive, according to the ideas of his time, was religious. The people acquiesce : cp. Jg. 21 [18] **25. All** *they of* **the land**] Heb. ' all the land.' Saul's success had made all the country rise against the foreigners. **27. His eyes were enlightened**] lit. ' became bright,' a sure sign of health and vigour. He had been weary with the day's exertions, and now recovers. **31. Aijalon**] see on Jg 1 [35]. It was the natural route by which the defeated Philistines would retreat to their own country. **32. Eat**

them **with the blood**] in direct opposition to the command of God : Gn 9 [4] and Lv 20 [26]. This prohibition to eat with the blood is still carefully observed by strict Jews. **33. Transgressed**] RV 'dealt treacherously,' i.e. disobediently, as if they had been enemies of Jehovah. **34.** The stone would allow the blood to run down from the carcase. **35. Built an altar**] to commemorate his victory : cp. Ex 17 [15] Josh 22 [34] ; or in reference to v. 33 ; the word for ' altar ' means, properly, ' place for slaughtering.' **41. Give a perfect** *lot*] RV ' shew the right.' **43.** *And,* **lo, I must die**] rather, ' Here am I, I will die.' Jonathan does not flinch. This ' taboo,' or ' ban,' which Saul had placed upon the taking of food (see on v. 24) is regarded with as much reverence as Jephthah's vow (Jg 11 [35]) ; but Jonathan's life, unlike that of Jephthah's daughter, is important to the whole nation, and Saul finds that his power is very strictly limited by the popular will. **45. Rescued**] Heb. ' ransomed.' This does not mean that another person was killed in Jonathan's place. The ransom paid might be the life of an animal or a sum of money (13 [13, 15]). **47–51.** These vv. form a conclusion to the life of Saul, after which the editor turns to another section of his history, ' Saul and David.' **47.** The disastrous ending of the life of Saul must not blind us to his many virtues. The earlier part of his reign was a series of successes. To the end the nation was contented with his rule, and it remained faithful to his dynasty even after his death. See Intro. § 7. We know nothing from other sources as to any expedition against Zobah, and the victories over the Philistines would appear to be more sweepingly stated than seems warranted by the last disastrous battle on Mt. Gilboa. This brief summary aptly illustrates the fragmentary and episodic nature of the history of Saul. **48. Gathered an host**] RV ' did valiantly.' **49.** The two daughters are mentioned because of the important part they play in the later history. **51.** Probably the v. originally ran, ' and Kish the father of Saul and Ner the father of Abner were the sons of Abiel.' Saul and Abner were first cousins.

CHAPTER 15
SAUL'S VICTORY OVER AMALEK. HIS
DISOBEDIENCE AND REJECTION

Amalek had attacked Israel at Rephidim (Ex 17 [8 f.]) and opposed their entrance into Canaan (Nu 14 [45] : cp. Dt 25 [7 f.]). They are mentioned as allies of the Midianites in Jg 7 [12]. The Amalekite nomads probably occupied a large tract of the wilderness S. of Judah.

This c. evidently comes from a different

source from the preceding, which concludes the history of Saul. It forms the connexion between the history of Saul and that of David. We have no means of determining to what part of Saul's reign it belongs.

3. Utterly destroy] lit. 'devote' (to Jehovah). The first idea of the word (*herem*) is that the object is dedicated to Jehovah, and so forbidden to common use: see Josh 6 18. We meet with the same root in *harem* (the women's apartments), and *haram* (the sacred enclosure at Mecca): cp. Lv 27 29. **4. Telaim**] probably the same as Telem (Josh 15 24), a town in S. Judah. Men of Judah are thus summoned to the expedition. **5. A city of Amalek**] RV 'the city of Amalek,' i.e. the capital. **6. Kenites**] see on Jg 4 17. They formed a nomad tribe, living partly in and partly outside Palestine.

7. From Havilah *until* **thou comest to Shur**] cp. Gn 25 18. Havilah was the eastern boundary of the district inhabited by the Amalekites, but its position is uncertain. **Shur** (*Wall*) was originally the name of the wall built to protect the eastern frontier of Egypt, and was then applied to the neighbouring part of the desert (Ex 15 22). **8.** The Amalekites subsequently sack Ziklag (1 S 30); but from this time onwards they cease to be formidable.

11. It grieved Samuel] RV 'Samuel was wroth.' He was annoyed at the course events were taking : cp. 2 S 6 8 Jon 4 1. It is characteristic of the Bible that it mentions the failings of its heroes and saints. **12. Carmel**] a town in Judah, 7 m. S. of Hebron. It lay directly in Saul's way on his return from smiting the Amalekites. **A place**] RV 'a monument' (to commemorate his victory) : cp. 2 S 18 18.

17. RM 'Though thou be little in thine own sight, art thou not head of the tribes of Israel?' i.e. the excuse, even if genuine, was not valid.

22, 23. These words are in poetic form, as we can see by the parallelism. See Intro. to Psalms.

22. For the views expressed in this v. cp. Ps 40 6f. 51 16, 17 Isa 1 11f. Jer 6 20 Hos 6 6 Am 5 21f. Mic 6 6f. The Israelite was not left to imagine, like the heathen, that sacrifices were what God chiefly desired. **23.** Samuel goes behind Saul's pretended motive, sacrifice, to his real disobedience. **Iniquity**] RV 'idolatry.' **Idolatry**] RV 'teraphim': see on 19 13.

24, 25. Saul's feeling was not true repentance, but merely a desire to propitiate Samuel and secure his apparent adhesion : see v. 30.

32. Delicately] RM 'cheerfully.' **Surely the bitterness**, etc.] Since Saul had spared his life, Agag thought he was secure.

35. Came no more to see Saul] As a prophet he had no longer any message for the rejected king, although as a man he mourned for the failure of a career that had once seemed so promising.

The execution of Agag seems to us mere butchery; but, to both Samuel and Saul, Agag, like the rest of Amalek, had been put under the 'ban,' and hence his death, even in cold blood, was a religious necessity. According to the ideas of the time, Saul had had no right to give any 'quarter.' Nor is it right to judge the ancient Hebrews by what are happily our higher standards of conduct.

CHAPTER 16
DAVID IS ANOINTED KING OVER ISRAEL

From c. 16 on, the interest centres in David rather than in Saul.

1. Oil] probably consecrated oil for anointing. **2. If Saul hear** *it*] Saul's action, recorded in 22 18, 19, shows that Samuel's fears were far from baseless. **Say, I am come to sacrifice**] Samuel was not asked to prevaricate. God relieved him of his difficulty by giving him a definite command. **4. Beth-lehem**] originally Ephrath (Gn 48 7), 5 m. S. of Jerusalem. **Trembled**] For Samuel had been wont to move from one town to another to punish offences (7 16). **5. Sanctify yourselves**] This was done by washing themselves and removing all ceremonial defilement. **He sanctified Jesse and his sons**] This gave Samuel an opportunity for private conversation.

6. Said] to himself, thought. **10. Again, Jesse made seven**] RV simply, 'And Jesse made seven.' The sons already named are included in the seven. **11. We will not sit down**] probably to the feast which followed the sacrifice : cp. 1 S 9. **12. Ruddy**] This colouring is much admired in the East where most are dark-skinned. **Of a beautiful countenance**] lit. 'fair of eyes.' In those hot countries bordering on the desert, multitudes are disfigured by ophthalmia, as was Leah (Gn 29 17 RV). **13. In the midst of his brethren**] Probably they thought Samuel had anointed him as his follower, or to become in time a prophet like himself.

13, 14. The Spirit of the LORD came upon David . . departed from Saul] The special grace conferred by anointing passed from the rejected Saul to the new king : cp. 10 6.

15. An evil spirit from God] apparently a gloomy, suspicious melancholy bordering on madness. To the Hebrew, every visitation, alike of good and evil, is directly from Jehovah : cp. 1 K 22 22 Am 3 6.

22. Stand before me] i.e. be one of my servants : cp. 1 K 10 8.

CHAPTER 17
DAVID SLAYS GOLIATH

17 1–18 5 is evidently taken from a different document from 16 14-23. In 16 14-23 David is a man of war, and skilful in speech, and an expert harper, and has already become

Saul's musician and armourbearer. In c. 17 he is still a shepherd lad, who is personally unknown to Saul. LXX tries to get rid of the difficulty by omitting several vv., but the attempt is not altogether successful.

1. Shochoh] identified with Shuweikeh, 'a strong position isolated from the rest of the ridge,' W. of Bethlehem. It was fortified by Rehoboam (2 Ch 11⁷). **Azekah**] mentioned in Josh 15³⁵ in connexion with Shochoh.

4. Six cubits and a span] about 9½ ft. **5. Brass**] This is really copper : cp. Dt 8⁹. **Five thousand shekels**] It is uncertain what was the weight of the shekel at this time. **6. Target**] RV 'javelin.' **10. I defy**] rather, 'I have insulted.' **12. An old man**] It is intended to explain why Jesse sent his sons to the war but did not go himself. **15. Went and returned**] RV 'went to and fro.'

17. Parched *corn*] ears of corn plucked just before they are ripe and roasted in a pan or on an iron plate. It is still a common article of merchandise. **18. Take their pledge**] 'bring back from them some proof that you have fulfilled your mission.' **20. Trench**] RV 'place of the wagons.' It was a rude rampart or barricade formed of wagons. **22. His carriage**] i.e. what he was carrying : cp. Ac 21¹⁵. **25. Free**] from forced labour or contributions : cp. 8¹¹ᶠ. **28. The wilderness**] answered to our 'downs' or 'common.' It was land suitable for grazing cattle, but not divided up into fields.

37. The LORD be with thee] RV 'shall be.' It is an encouragement rather than a prayer. **38. Armed David with his armour**] RV 'clad David with his apparel.' This was probably some close-fitting garment worn under the armour, or on occasion without it. **39. Assayed**] LXX 'wearied himself' : cp. Gn 19¹¹. **Proved**] He was not accustomed to wearing heavy armour, and it soon became burdensome. **43. Staves**] i.e. with a mere stick (v. 40) instead of weapons. **46.** In true Oriental fashion David replies to the Philistine's brave words with equally bold language, heightened to something far bolder by his confidence in Jehovah.

52. The valley] LXX reads 'Gath.' This strong fortress of the Philistines, like that of Ekron, checked the pursuit (cp. the end of the v.). Gath was not far W. of Shochoh, and therefore it would seem that at Shaaraim the stream of fugitives would part, some going on southwards to Gath, others northwards to Ekron. **54. Brought it to Jerusalem**] But Jerusalem was still a non-Hebrew city (2 S 5⁴ᶠ). A little later we find the sword of Goliath at Nob (21⁹), and hence some think that Nob is intended here. Stanley and Robinson place Nob on the Mount of Olives.

Others think that David brought the head of Goliath to Jerusalem at a later period (2 S 5⁷). Another reference to Goliath should be noted, which implies the existence either of other traditions, or of more than one Philistine champion of the name (2 S 21¹⁹).

CHAPTER 18

THE LOVE OF JONATHAN FOR DAVID

Vv. 6–30 of this c. seem to be connected with 16¹⁴⁻²³ and not to be taken from the same document as 17¹–18⁵. LXX omits a large part of this section and only retains vv. 6–8ᵃ 12ᵃ 13–16, 20–21ᵃ 22–26ᵃ 27–29ᵃ. In this case the LXX text gives an easy and straightforward account, and many suppose that it is the original. But the character of the LXX omissions in c. 17 renders this a little doubtful.

6. Cp. Ex 15²⁰ Jg 11³⁴ Ps 68¹¹ (RV). **7. Played**] lit. 'sported.' The word is used of festive sports and especially of festal dancing : cp. 1 Ch 15²⁹. **8. But the kingdom**] The knowledge of his deposition rankled in Saul's mind. **10. Prophesied**] The words 'prophet' and 'prophesy' are applied in OT. to the servants of the gods of Canaan as well as to the servants of Jehovah : cp. 1 K 18¹⁹. The behaviour of these Canaanite prophets must have greatly resembled the possession of Saul (1 K 18²⁸). The word 'prophesy' includes such wild outbreaks of frenzy as well as the calm utterances of Isaiah. In the case of Saul this frenzy was regarded as produced by an evil spirit from God.

16. Went out and came in] i.e. lived in an open public manner in contrast to Saul's seclusion which was the natural result of his melancholy. **17.** Every battle fought by Israel was an act of religious worship to Jehovah : cp. 25²⁸. **18. What** *is* **my life**] RM 'Who are my kinsfolk ?' The word denotes a division of the tribe larger than a 'father's family.' **21. In** *the one of* **the twain**] RV 'a second time.' It is an example of regal and rather caustic wit. The first time was when Merab was offered (v. 19). **23. A poor man**] This would suggest that David's lack of patrimony had been made an excuse for not giving Merab to him : but see intro. note to the c. This v. is plainly inconsistent with vv. 19–21. **25. Dowry**] In ancient times some payment was made to the father by the intending bridegroom (Gn 34¹² Ex 22¹⁶), a relic of still earlier days, when a wife was either bought from her parents or captured from foes. But service might be rendered instead of payment in money (Gn 29²⁰). **26. And the days were not expired**] This appears to refer to the time, not previously mentioned, within which the exploit was to be performed. **28. Michal Saul's daughter**] LXX 'all Israel.'

CHAPTER 19

SAUL'S HATRED OF DAVID. DAVID ESCAPES TO SAMUEL

2. Until the morning] RV 'in the morning.'
6. It was difficult for David to estimate correctly Saul's feelings towards him, because the king's repentance was real while it lasted, and because much might be ascribed to his madness.
10. That night] David would probably flee at once : hence LXX may be right in joining these words to v. 11, 'And it came to pass that night that Saul sent.'
13. An image] RV 'the teraphim.' 'Teraphim,' like 'Elohim,' is a plural of dignity and denotes a single image, but the origin of the word is unknown. Such images, derived from Canaanite paganism, appear to have been in human form and to have varied in size ; for, while Michal's could pass for a man, Rachel's could be hidden under the camel's furniture (Gn 31³⁴). Usually, perhaps, the teraphim was a half-length image, or a head only. Teraphim were used for the purpose of divination (Ezk 21²¹ Zech 10²), and Rachel probably stole her father's teraphim, lest he should discover which way she had fled. **Pillow of goats'** *hair*] A word from this root occurs in 2K 8¹⁵, so that it appears to have been some covering made of goats' hair, which was placed over the face of a sleeping person, probably to keep off the mosquitoes. In this case it served as a disguise. **For his bolster**] RV 'at the head thereof.' **With a cloth**] Heb. 'with the garment,' i.e. the mantle, which was regarded as the most indispensable article of dress (v. 24) by day and was used as a covering by night. So Saul's messengers would easily recognise it.
14. Apparently Michal allowed the messengers to get some view of the recumbent figure.
15. Bring him up to me in the bed] As an Eastern bed is merely a mattress, this could be easily done : cp. Mk 2⁴. **17.** Michal pretends that David coerced her into contriving his escape.
18. Came to Samuel] David naturally turned to him for advice and direction. **Naioth**] Evidently the name of some locality in Ramah, but whether a building or a district it is impossible to determine. **23.** Once more the influence of the Spirit fell on Saul for his good. **24. Naked**] i.e. without his outer garment : cp. Isa 20². *Is* **Saul also among the prophets ?**] see on 10¹¹. Observe that the religious frenzy is contagious : cp. Intro. § 4.

CHAPTER 20

THE FRIENDSHIP OF DAVID AND JONATHAN

4. Thy soul] a pathetic periphrasis for 'thou.'
5. The new moon] Many nations of antiquity appear to have observed the day of the new moon as a religious festival. For its observance in Israel cp. 2K 4²³ Isa 1¹³ Am 8⁵ (where it is coupled with the sabbath) Nu 10¹⁰. Vv. 25 and 27 imply that David, like Abner, ate regularly at Saul's table. **6. A yearly sacrifice**] This refers to the ordinary annual festival of the family. Such family festivals were very widespread both among European and Semitic peoples. **8. A covenant of the LORD**] i.e. in which God had been invoked as a witness and the breach of which He would punish.
12. About to morrow any time] RV 'about this time to-morrow.' *Or* **the third** *day*] probably a gloss.
14, 15. That I die not: but *also*] LXX has an attractive reading: 'If I die, thou shalt not cut off thy kindness': cp. 2S 9¹.
16. At the hand of David's enemies] David's enemies are a euphemism for David himself. Jonathan shrinks from invoking retribution on his friend or suggesting in so many words the possibility of his breaking the covenant.
19. Thou shalt go down quickly] LXX reads 'Thou shalt be greatly missed,' and the whole clause means ' thou shalt be greatly missed on the third day.' **The business**] i.e. some matter well known to David and Jonathan. **The stone Ezel**] LXX 'this mound.'
25. Jonathan arose, and Abner sat] Jonathan gave up his rightful place and Abner took it.
26. He *is* **not clean**] i.e. some ceremonial defilement has happened to him which prevents him from sharing in the festival: cp. Jn 18²⁸.
30. Mother's nakedness] She would become the wife of the new king : cp. 2S 12⁸. **41. Out of** *a place* **toward the south**] LXX 'from beside the mound.'

CHAPTER 21

THE FLIGHT OF DAVID

David first of all flees to Nob, where Ahimelech supplies him with food and gives him the sword of Goliath. He next takes refuge with Achish at Gath.
1. Nob] see on 17⁵⁴. **Alone**] He had no escort or retinue.
3. Better, 'Now, therefore, what is under thine hand ? Five loaves ? Give them into mine hand.' **4. Hallowed bread**] i.e. the shewbread. It was removed every sabbath and fresh loaves substituted.
5. Better, 'of a truth women have been kept from us as is usual, when I go on an expedition.' *The bread is* **in a manner common**] The meaning is obscure. RV 'though it was but a common journey ; how much more then to-day shall their vessels be holy ?' i.e. their wallets and utensils were clean when they started and there had been no chance of defiling them since, although their journey was

an ordinary one. Ewald understands 'the vessels' to refer to the young men's bodies, as in 1 Th 4 4. They were ceremonially clean, so that they might partake of holy things. **6.** This incident was referred to by our Lord (Mt 12 3). **10. Fled that day]** He feared that Doeg would give information and that pursuit would begin at once. **Gath]** This connexion with Gath brought David some of his most faithful followers. **13. Feigned himself mad]** to allay suspicion. Easterns have a religious awe of madness and would not think of injuring those so afflicted. **Scrabbled]** i.e. scratched, made meaningless marks. LXX 'beat,' 'drummed' is much more forcible. **15. In my presence]** rather, 'to my annoyance.'

CHAPTER 22

David in the Cave of Adullam. Saul's Slaughter of the Priests at Nob

1. Adullam] probably in the valley of Elah between Philistia and Hebron. **2. Four hundred]** They soon increased to six hundred (23 13). Cp. the description given of Jephthah's band in Jg 11 3.

5. Gad] is here mentioned for the first time. After David's accession he became the king's seer (2 S 24 11). He was sent to rebuke David for his sin in numbering the people, and after his death wrote a history of his reign (1 Ch 29 29). From 2 Ch 29 25 he appears to have been concerned in arranging the temple service. **Forest of Hareth]** not known.

6. In Ramah] RM 'on the height.'

14. Goeth at thy bidding] RV 'is taken into thy council.' **15. Did I then begin?]** RV 'Have I to-day begun?' Ahimelech had been accustomed to place his services at David's disposal. **17. Footmen]** Heb. 'runners'; they ran before the king's chariot (8 11) and sometimes carried news from one place to another. On occasion they acted as executioners, but this was not their special office. **19.** Saul probably wished to make an example which would deter others from rendering David any assistance.

20. Abiathar shared in all David's wanderings and was made by him joint priest with Zadok. But he shared in Adonijah's rising and was deposed by Solomon.

CHAPTER 23

David delivers Keilah and afterwards retires to the Wilderness of Ziph and Maon

6. *With* an ephod in his hand] This is inserted to explain how it was that David was able to enquire of the LORD : see on 14 18.

9. Secretly practised] RV 'devised.' There was no secrecy about Saul's methods.

14. Ziph] identified with *Tell Zif,* a rounded hill, 4 m. SE. of Hebron. **15. In a wood]**

RM 'in Horesh.' But the true rendering is doubtful. If a proper name, it was more probably a mountain than a wood (cp. vv. 14, 19), and the word may mean either. **17. That also]** Saul knew that Jonathan was willing to rank second.

19. Jeshimon] RV 'the desert.' It is the dreary desert of southern Judah : see Nu 21 20.

25. Maon] mentioned in Josh 15 55 in connexion with Carmel and Ziph. It is a lofty conical hill 7 m. S. of Hebron. **28. Selahammahlekoth]** i.e. 'the rock of divisions.'

29. This v. should be joined to the next c. **En-gedi]** A well-watered spot on the E. edge of the desert of Judah. It still bears the name Ain Jidi. 'En' means 'well.'

CHAPTER 24

David spares Saul's Life at Engedi

We have a similar incident narrated in c. 26, and some critics hold that the two are merely varying accounts of the same event. But it is to be noticed that almost every detail that could vary, does vary. Nor is there any difficulty in supposing that David spared Saul's life twice.

2. Rocks of the wild goats] Some cliffs near Engedi, so called because wild goats congregated there. They are still numerous in this district. **3. Sheepcotes]** These were rough, stone walls, built to protect the sheep from wild beasts. Thomson writes : 'There is scarcely a cave in the land .. but has such a cote in front of it.'

4. It is probable that we should translate 'Behold the day on which the LORD saith to thee,' i.e. they interpret the opportunity as a manifest sign of God's intention that Saul should be slain. **7. Stayed]** The word is a very strong one and shows that David had to exert all his authority. **10.** Rather, 'The LORD delivered thee to-day into mine hand and bade me kill thee': see on v. 4. **19. The LORD reward thee good]** Gleams of his former high character still show themselves in Saul.

CHAPTER 25

Death of Samuel. The Incident of Nabal. David and Abigail

1. Paran] That part of the desert between Sinai and Palestine which bordered on Judah. **2. Possessions]** rather, 'occupation,' 'business.' **Carmel]** see on 15 12. **Great]** has frequently the meaning of 'rich' : cp. 2 S 19 32.

Shearing his sheep] A special occasion for festivity and entertainment : cp. v. 36, 2 S 13 23.

Of the house of Caleb] This district of the S. of Judah had been conquered and settled by Caleb. It is called 'the south of Caleb' in 30 14. **6. To him that liveth** *in prosperity*] Vulgate has 'to my brethren.' **8. A good day]** This is the ordinary Heb. phrase for a

13　　　　　　　193

festival. **11. My water**] Water is precious
in these dry lands : cp. Jg 1 15. But LXX
reads ' my wine.'

16. A wall] The protection from Arab
robbers deserved some recognition from those
who lived near the desert. Precisely the same
demand is made at present by Bedouin sheikhs
living on the borders of civilisation. **25. Folly**]
i.e. wrong-headed and foolish obstinacy and
churlishness. The Heb. is the feminine form
of 'Nabal': cp. 2 S 3 33. **27. Blessing**] RV
' present ' : cp. 30 26 mg. Gn 33 11. **28. Fighteth
the battles of the LORD**] David had rescued
the inhabitants of Keilah from the Philistines
(23 5), and protected the dwellers in the S. of
Judah from the desert nomads (v. 16).

29. A man] The reference is to Saul.

Bound] i.e. safely bound up, so that not one
is lost. **In the bundle of life**] rather, ' in the
bundle of the living,' i.e. in the number of
those whose lives are guarded and protected
by God. **With**] ' in the custody of.'

31. Causeless] Abigail ventures to hint that
Nabal's answer was not a sufficient reason for
the vengeance David proposed to take.

33. Thy advice] RV ' thy wisdom.'

39. Communed with Abigail] RV ' spake
concerning.' It is the technical term for ' asking any one's hand in marriage ' : cp. Song 8 8.

44. Saul considered that David, as an outlaw, had forfeited his wife. But David himself never acknowledged this, and claimed
Michal as his wife as soon as he had the
power (2 S 3 14).

CHAPTER 26
DAVID SPARES SAUL'S LIFE A SECOND TIME

1. Hachilah] near the wilderness of Ziph :
see 23 19. **4. Was come in very deed**] Heb.
' was come to Nakon.' Nakon = ' a set place '
(RM), though it may have been the corruption
of a place-name, such as Maon.

6. Hittite] So he belonged to one of the
original inhabitants of the country. We
might expect to find some of them among
David's followers : cp. 22 2. Uriah, another
Hittite, played an important part in David's
history. **Abishai**] is here mentioned for the
first time. He saved David's life in one of
the Philistine wars (2 S 21 17), was implicated
in the murder of Abner (2 S 3 30), shared the
command of the army (2 S 10 10), and remained
faithful to David in Absalom's rebellion.

8. At once] RV ' at one stroke.'

19. Let him accept an offering] cp. Gn 4 7.
The idea in this v. is simply that if Jehovah
had prompted Saul's action, Saul was doing
right, and David would seek pardon by an
offering. **Go, serve other gods**] This seems to
suggest that David limited the rule of Jehovah to the land of Israel as the rule of Chemosh was limited to Moab : cp. Jephthah's

reference to Chemosh in Jg 11 24. In the older
Hebrew thought, Jehovah was specially present in Palestine (though cp. Jg 5 4). Hence
it seemed difficult and almost impossible to
worship the true God in a heathen land, since
when a Hebrew became naturalised elsewhere,
he would conform to the religion of his new
home.

20. Before the face] RV ' away from the
presence of,' i.e. let not my blood be shed
without Jehovah requiring it : cp. Gn 4 10.

A flea] LXX ' my soul.' The Heb. reading
is due to a recollection of 24 14.

CHAPTER 27
DAVID FLEES TO GATH, AND OBTAINS ZIKLAG
FROM ACHISH

2. David's position now as the captain of
600 men was quite different from what it was
in 21 10 f. **7. A full year and four months**]
The phrase probably means ' about four
months,' lit. ' days and four months.'

8 The Geshurites] were the inhabitants of
a district in the S. of Philistia : see Josh 13 2.
They must not be confused with the Geshurites
who lived E. of the Jordan. The tribes mentioned here were constant enemies of Israel
whom David took the opportunity to exterminate. **9. Left**] The tense of the verb denotes David's habitual practice. He never left
any one alive to tell the tale.

10. Made a road] RV ' made a raid.' **The
south of the Jerahmeelites**] Jerahmeel was one
of the divisions of the tribe of Judah (1 Ch 2 9).
The barren south was naturally named after the
fertile lands on which it bordered : the ' south
of Judah,' ' of Jerahmeel,' and so on. The
deception was that Achish understood that
David had smitten the Hebrew inhabitants of
the lands bordering on the desert, whereas he
had smitten the nomad tribes who dwelt in
the actual desert. **11. To bring** *tidings* **to
Gath**] RV ' to bring them to Gath ' in order to
sell them as slaves.' So *will be* **his manner**]
RV ' so hath been his manner all the while he
hath dwelt.'

CHAPTER 2
SAUL AND THE WITCH OF ENDOR

Vv. 3–25 come from another document and
interrupt the connexion, as will be seen if
the account is read without them. In order
of time their proper position is after c. 30.
In 29 1 the Philistines are still in Aphek ; in
29 11 they advance to Jezreel, where we find
them in 28 4. In 28 3-25 we have come to the
eve of the battle, the account of which follows
in c. 31. **2. Keeper of mine head**] i.e. captain
of my body-guard.

3. This v. is inserted to explain what follows.
By **familiar spirits** (Heb. *ob*) some form of witchcraft is intended. In v. 7 the woman is said to

be ' the mistress of an ob.' In Lv 20 27 the *ob* is said to be in the man or woman : cp. 2 K 23 24.

The wizards] From Lv 20 27 it is quite clear that this word denotes not the magician, but the spirit controlled by the magician. It is often joined to ' ob,' and means, etymologically, ' possessed of knowledge,' (i.e. of the future or the unseen) : cp. our modern clairvoyants.

4. Shunem] in the plain of Jezreel, 4 m. from Mt. Gilboa. **Gilboa**] a mountain range on the E. side of the valley of Jezreel.

6. Dreams] These are always regarded in the Bible as one method of divine revelation : see Nu 12 6. **Urim**] see on Ex 28 30. The ephod and the Urim had gone down with Abiathar to David (23 6). **Prophets**] We may compare with this 15 35. The action of Samuel was apparently followed by the rest of the prophets. **7. En-dor**] 4 m. S. of Mt. Tabor, and 10 m. from Mt. Gilboa.

11, 12. This woman would seem to have been what is now called a ' medium ' ; she sees (very possibly having become entranced) a figure, and Saul from her description at once concludes that it is Samuel. Very possibly Saul saw nothing at all ; the words he heard may have come from the woman. Indeed, the LXX translator (who very probably knew as much about such matters as we do) wishing to mark that the words really came from the woman in her trance, spoke of her as a ventriloquist : cp. also Ac 16 16, where the girl, liable to fall into a state of secondary consciousness, is said to have a ' spirit of divination.' To attribute words so spoken to a spirit either internal or external to the medium, was the only course possible to a Hebrew or Jewish narrator.

13. Gods] RV ' a god,' for Saul immediately said, ' What form is he of ? ' We must remember that Elohim in Hebrew is more general than the word ' god ' is with us, and is, in fact, used generally for ' supernatural beings,' or even ' spirits ' : see Ps 82 6. **16. Is become thine enemy**] LXX ' is on the side of thy neighbour.' This is based on a probable emendation. If ' neighbour ' is right, it must be taken in the sense of rival ' (which originally meant almost the same thing). **17. To him**] LXX ' to thee.'

19. Moreover . . the Philistines] LXX omits. **To morrow** *shalt* **thou and thy sons** *be* **with me**] i.e. in Sheol, the place of departed spirits.

CHAPTER 29
DAVID DISALLOWED FROM FIGHTING WITH THE PHILISTINES

1. Jezreel] the plain between Gilboa and Little Hermon. **3. He fell** *unto me*] i.e. ' deserted to me.'

4. An adversary] Heb. *satan*. Satan, the evil spirit, is always entitled ' the Satan,' i.e. the Adversary (Job 1 2 Zech 3 1).

6. As the LORD liveth] Achish would recognise that Jehovah was the national god of Israel and that He existed as well as Dagon (cp. 1 K 17 12).

11. The Philistines went up to Jezreel] The Philistines could not attack Saul's position on Mt. Gilboa from Shunem (28 4), and accordingly they went round Jezreel to attack by the easier slopes there.

CHAPTER 30
THE AMALEKITES RAID ZIKLAG, AND ARE PURSUED BY DAVID

2. Slew not any] They would be valuable as slaves. **6. Spake of stoning him**] They probably thought he had been negligent in leaving Ziklag without a guard. **8. Enquired at the LORD**] by means of the Urim in the ephod : see on Ex 28 30. **13. My master left me**] The life of a slave was of little more importance than that of a horse.

14. The Cherethites] Cherethite is used with Pelethite, perhaps another name for Philistine : see v. 16 and Zeph 2 5. It is very possibly connected with Crete, the country from which the Philistines were believed to have come (Am 9 7). David had the capacity of turning foes into faithful friends and soldiers. **16. Dancing**] RV ' feasting,' i.e. enjoying themselves merrily. **17. Twilight**] This is probably the evening twilight.

20. The LXX has no word corresponding to ' David ' : ' and they took all the sheep and oxen (i.e. those belonging to the Amalekites) and drave them before the other cattle (i.e. those belonging to David's followers) and said, This is David's spoil.' In repentance for their former attitude (v. 6), they resolved only to keep what had been taken from them by the Amalekites, and to surrender the other spoil to David.

26. He sent of the spoil] In gratitude for their goodwill when he was a hunted outlaw. David's action was also due to policy. He wished them to be ready to accept his rule, when the time came.

CHAPTER 31
DEFEAT OF THE ISRAELITES AT MT. GILBOA. DEATH OF SAUL

6. And all his men] LXX omits. **7. The valley**] of Jezreel. **10. The house of Ashtaroth**] at Askelon : cp. 2 S 1 20.

Beth-shan] between the Gilboa and little Hermon ranges. **11.** They thus showed their gratitude for former kindness : see c. 11.

12. Burnt them] The action of the men of Jabesh was probably due to their fear that the Philistines would remove the bodies.

13. Under a tree] RV ' under the tamarisk tree.' It was evidently some well-known tree : cp. Gn 35 4 Jg 4 5.

2 SAMUEL

CHAPTER 1

THE LAMENT OF DAVID OVER SAUL AND JONATHAN

1. There is no break between the two books of Samuel; they really form one continuous narrative. This v. is a continuation of 1 S 30, which describes David's successful attack upon Ziklag. He had not heard of the events narrated in 1 S 31.

2. With his clothes rent, etc.] In 1 S 4 12, which describes the arrival of the messenger at Shiloh with tidings of the capture of the ark, these were the same indications that he was the bearer of evil tidings.

8, 9. The Amalekite's account contradicts 1 S 31 4 and is also improbable in itself. The man was probably lying in the hope of currying favour with David. **10.** For the practice of wearing signs of royalty, when going into battle, see 1 K 22 30. **Bracelet**] In the Assyrian sculptures warriors are often represented with such ornaments.

18. *The use of* **the bow**] RV '*the song of* the bow,' lit. 'the bow.' The text of this v. is doubtful, but if the words are right, 'the bow' will be the title of the lamentation following. There is, however, no warrant for this in Hebrew usage. Some see an allusion to v. 22, 'the bow of Jonathan.' **The book of Jasher**] RV 'Jashar,' mentioned also in Josh 10 13. It was apparently a book of martial or historical poetry. Jashar is probably a name of Israel. We get it in Dt 32 15 under the form Jeshurun: the word properly means 'righteous.'

21. Fields of offerings] fields bearing produce, from which firstfruits are offered. **Not .. anointed with oil**] It is doubtful if this refers to Saul or his shield. Shields were greased to preserve the leather and to prevent spears from sticking: cp. Isa 21 5.

22. In this figurative language, the bow is represented as drinking the blood of the slain and the sword as eating the fat of the mighty: cp. Dt 32 42 Isa 34 6. **Turned not back**] i.e. empty, as the parallel clause shows.

24. Scarlet .. gold] These were the ordinary ornaments of a Hebrew woman: cp. Jer 4 30.

25. O Jonathan, *thou wast* **slain in thine high places**] RV 'Jonathan is slain upon thy high places.' The address is to Israel.

27. The weapons of war] The parallel clause shows that these are Saul and Jonathan themselves, regarded as the sword and bow of the nation. It is remarkable that this poem makes no distinction between Saul and Jonathan, but praises the courage, the success, and the patriotism of both alike. The gloomy picture of Saul given in the later chs. of 1 Sam must not be allowed to efface the courage and determination of his struggle with Israel's foes. On the other hand, the genuine grief expressed in this lament (which cannot be anything else than authentic) over the father as well as the son, shows David's chivalry in a very pleasing light.

CHAPTER 2

DAVID MADE KING OVER JUDAH, ISH-BOSHETH OVER ISRAEL. ASAHEL SLAIN BY ABNER

1. Shall I go up?] The defeat and death of Saul had entirely changed David's position. He had, for some time to come, nothing to fear from Abner, who was occupied elsewhere (vv. 8, 9). The Philistines would not molest him, as he was their vassal. But even so, he asks God's wishes, before he takes the decisive step. **Hebron**] There were several reasons which rendered Hebron suitable. It was fairly central, was a celebrated town, and David had friends there (1 S 30 31). It was 14 m. distant from his birthplace, Bethlehem. No other town in Judah, while Jerusalem was still in Canaanite hands, had the same claim.

5. This was probably an attempt to gain over Jabesh-gilead, the capital of eastern Palestine, and to add the trans-Jordanic tribes to his little kingdom of Judah. If so, it failed for the present. But during his flight from Absalom, it was in eastern Palestine that David found refuge.

8. Ish-bosheth] His name was really Eshbaal (1 Ch 8 33) i.e. 'man of Baal.' The name Baal means 'lord,' and so could be used for Jehovah (Hos 2 16), but afterwards it was confused with the Canaanite Baal and altered to Bosheth, i.e. 'Shame': cp. Mephibosheth. Ish-bosheth was the fourth son of Saul, and now that his three elder brothers were slain (1 S 31 6), he became the heir to the throne: see on 5 20. **Mahanaim**] was David's capital during his flight from Absalom (17 24).

9. The Ashurites] This is doubtless a mistake for Asher. Abner first gained possession of eastern Palestine, then of Asher in the extreme north of western Palestine, next of the great central plain of Issachar, then of the hill-country of Ephraim and Benjamin.

By this time his master's dominions touched those of David, and before long a collision occurred (vv. 12, 13).

10. Forty years old] This number is probably wrong. David was 30 years old when he began to reign (5⁴), and Jonathan would be about the same age or a little younger. Ish-bosheth would be younger still. Probably we should read 20 for 40. In old Hebrew writing, the numbers would be much alike.

10, 11. Two years.. seven years and six months] Either it was five years and six months after the death of Ish-bosheth before the Israelites would accept David, or it took Abner that length of time to establish his master's son as king (v. 9).

13. The pool of Gibeon] Gibeon was a large and important town (Josh 10²), 5 m. N. of Jerusalem. The pool still exists. Robinson mentions it as an open pool 120 ft. long by 100 broad. **14. Play**] As this word is not used elsewhere of fighting, a preliminary contest to the serious battle must be intended.

16. Helkath-hazzurim] i.e. 'Field of sharp edges.' **23. The hinder end of the spear**] Abner did not wish to kill him. The spear had a sharp point by which it was stuck into the ground. **Stood still**] out of grief at the sight : cp. 20¹².

27. The AV and RV represent two different explanations : (a) If Abner had not spoken, the pursuit would have continued till the morning. (b) If Abner had not proposed the mimic fight, there would have been no battle at all. The former explanation seems preferable. **28. Neither fought they any more**] i.e. on that day, for see 3¹. **29. All that night**] for fear of pursuit. **The plain**] RV 'the Arabah,' i.e. the valley of the Jordan.

Bithron] the name of some ravine they passed through on their way. **32. All night**] i.e. all the night after the burial.

CHAPTER 3
ABNER IS TREACHEROUSLY MURDERED BY JOAB

3. Chileab] We read nothing more of him and he probably died as a child. In 1 Ch 3¹ he is called Daniel. **Geshur**] a kingdom on the border of Bashan, where Absalom afterwards took refuge (13³⁷). It must not be confused with the Geshur of 1 S 27⁸.

4. Adonijah] see 1 K 1.

7. Rizpah] see 21⁸⁻¹¹. **Gone in unto my father's concubine**] According to Eastern ideas this was equivalent to laying claim to the throne : see 12⁸ 16²² 1 K 2²². **8. Am I a dog's head, which against Judah ?**] RV 'Am I a dog's head that belongeth to Judah ?' i.e. a despised enemy. **Do shew kindness this day**] RV 'This day' (i.e. at the very time you bring this trivial charge) 'do I shew kindness' : see on v. 17. **This woman**] LXX 'a woman.' It was the question of a mere woman. **9. Except .. even so I do to him**] RV 'if .. I do not even so to him,' i.e. support David instead of Ish-bosheth. **12. On his behalf**] RM 'where he was.' **Whose *is* the land ? saying**] LXX omits. **13. Except thou first bring Michal**] see 1 S 25⁴⁴. **16. Bahurim**] in Benjamin, on the road from Jerusalem to the Jordan. It was probably the last town in the dominions of Ish-bosheth.

17. Ye sought for David] It would thus seem that even in northern Israel there was a strong party, who wished to make David king on the death of Saul. It was probably the personal influence of Abner that decided the day in favour of Ish-bosheth. The whole passage clearly shows how weak was the hereditary principle, and how completely the 'king' was still regarded merely as a military leader and 'judge.' The element of popular choice is more fully emphasised here than in Judges (except for the Abimelech episode).

19. Benjamin] as being Saul's fellow-tribesmen they would be specially attached to the royal house and need additional persuasion.

21. Make a league with thee] as they did with Saul (1 S 10²⁵) and as they tried to do with Rehoboam (1 K 12⁴). Before making him king, they wished to see their rights safe guarded. **22. From *pursuing* a troop**] RV 'from a foray.' David had probably arranged a time when Joab was absent. **24. Why *is* it *that* thou hast sent him away ?**] As a kinsman of Asahel, Joab thought that David should have avenged his death.

27. For the blood of Asahel his brother] According to Eastern ideas Joab was bound to avenge his brother's murder. Neither Judaism, Christianity, nor Mohammedanism has been able to eradicate this feeling. But the Law provided a remedy in the Cities of Refuge (see Nu 35¹¹ f.). In the case before us, Joab was probably influenced by the fear that Abner would interfere with his authority : see on 8¹⁷.

29. On all his father's house] According to Jewish ideas the family was involved in the fate of the ancestor : cp. 21⁶ 2 K 5²⁷. **Leaneth on a staff**] rather, 'that holdeth the spindle' : cp. Prov 31¹⁹. It was despicable work for a man. **31. Mourn before Abner**] i.e. precede the bier. This was all the punishment David was strong enough to inflict. **33. Died Abner as a fool dieth ?**] i.e. as one who runs into needless danger, or meets his death when engaged in a shameful conspiracy : see on 1 S 25²⁵.

35. Till the sun be down] The regular time for ending a fast, as it still is in Mohammedan countries. The Hebrew day was reckoned from sunset to sunset.

CHAPTER 4

The Murder of Ish-bosheth

2, 3. Beeroth was near Gibeon. The object of this note is to explain how the Beerothites came to be Benjamites. Properly they should have been Canaanites, for Beeroth was included in the treaty with Gibeon (Josh 9 17, 27). But owing to the persecution of Saul (21 1) the Canaanites of Beeroth fled to Gittaim, and the town passed into the possession of Benjamin. **Gittaim**] in Benjamin.

4. Mephibosheth] His name is given in 1 Ch 8 34 as 'Merib-baal': see on 2 8. **5. Who lay on a bed at noon**] rather, 'and he was taking his noon-tide rest,' or siesta.

6. The LXX has an altogether .different text for this v., 'and, behold, the woman who kept the door of the house was winnowing wheat, and she slumbered and slept ; and the brothers, Rechab and Baanah, escaped notice.' This explains how it was they were able to enter unperceived. **10. Who** *thought* that I would have given him] better, 'in order to give him.' **12.** Chronicles omits all mention of the reign of Ish-bosheth.

CHAPTER 5

David is anointed King, captures Jerusalem, and smites the Philistines

1. There was no longer any member of the house of Saul who could take the lead.

2. Feed] lit. 'act as shepherd to' (cp. 7 7). 'Shepherd' became a technical term for a ruler (Jer 3 15). The figure is developed in Ezk 34.

4. The capture of Jerusalem marks a most important point in the history of Israel. Hitherto, the national life had had no real centre ; the residence of a judge or a prophet or a king would be a temporary rallying place, such as the 'palm-tree of Deborah,' Shiloh (see on 1 S 7 1), Mizpah, Gibeah (of Saul), Nob or Hebron. From this time, the centre is fixed, and, at least for the southern kingdom, all the other cities grew less and less important in comparison with the new capital. Its position, however, in the midst of the rocky, barren ridge running down central Palestine, made it always more suitable for a fortress than a commercial and wealthy capital, such as Solomon tried to make it.

6. Except thou take away the blind and the lame] RM 'but the blind and the lame shall turn thee away.' The Jebusites considered their city so strong that it needed no other defenders.

7. The strong hold of Zion] called later on the 'city' (i.e. citadel) 'of David,' because he built and fortified it. It is to be noticed that the city of David does not mean the city of Jerusalem but the fort on Mt. Zion. David does not yet venture to live in Jerusalem itself, outside the fort.

The city of Jerusalem is built on high ground, which is shaped like a cloven tongue ; and it is probable that the 'city of David' occupied the eastern 'tip,' behind which rose in later times the Temple. Gradually the city spread to the western 'tip' of the tongue. 'Millo' appears to be the name of the part of the city which was not fortified ; its meaning is uncertain ; later on it also was included within the fortifications. The original 'city of David' is thus a triangle, two sides of which are naturally protected, and the third, probably at this time, as later, artificially. Below the height on which the fort is built is the Kidron valley.

8. LXX reads 'Whosoever smites the Jebusite, let him slay with the sword both the lame and the blind, and those who hate David's soul.' 1 Ch 11 6-9 reads, 'Whosoever smiteth the Jebusites first shall be chief and captain,' and adds, 'And Joab the son of Zeruiah went up first, and was made chief' (RV). **9. Millo**] see on v. 7 and Jg 9 6.

11. Hiram] If we accept the statements of Josephus, this Hiram was the father of Solomon's friend (1 K 5 1). **Tyre**] the leading city of Phœnicia. **They built**] For the skill of the Phœnicians in masonry and building see 1 K 5 7.

14–16. The list of David's sons is given also in 1 Ch 3 5 f. 14 4 f. The variations are interesting and instructive. **14. Nathan**] one of the ancestors of the Messiah (Lk 3 31).

17. This was a united and determined effort to crush David before he became too powerful. **The hold**] It is uncertain what place is meant. **18. The valley of Rephaim**] a valley SW. of Jerusalem, separated by a slight, rocky ridge from the valley of Hinnom.

20. Baal-perazim] Perazim means 'breaches.' Hence the play upon words. 'The LORD has made a breach .. like the breach .. he called the name .. Breaches.' It is common to find the names of places compounded with the name of the Baal to whom they were considered to belong : e.g. Baal-Peor, Baal-Gad, Baal-Perazim. Here the Baal is, of course, Jehovah. **21. Their images**] They had brought them into the battle to secure victory : cp. 1 S 4 3. **Burned them**] RV 'took them away,' i.e. as trophies.

23. Thou shalt not go up] LXX adds 'to meet them.' **24. The sound of a going**] RV 'the sound of marching.' It was the heavenly host marching to join in the attack on the Philistines.

25. Geba] LXX and Chronicles both have Gibeon, which is doubtless correct. This battle is apparently referred to in Isa 28 21, where also we have Gibeon.

CHAPTER 6

THE BRINGING OF THE ARK FROM KIRJATH-
JEARIM TO JERUSALEM

1. Again] This probably refers to the
previous assembling of the chosen men of
Israel to repel the Philistine invasion (5 22-25).
2. From Baale of Judah] should probably be
'to Baal of Judah' (1 Ch 13 6). The town was
also known as Kirjath-baal (City of Baal).
3. Out of the house of Abinadab] It had
been there ever since its removal from Beth-
shemesh (1 S 7 1). **In Gibeah**] RV 'in the hill.'
Kirjath-jearim was situated on high ground.
5. On all manner of *instruments made of* **fir
wood**] Read with Chronicles 'with all their
might, even with songs.'
7. He died] If this punishment seem severe,
we must remember that one great lesson the
Israelites had to learn was reverence and fear
of God. The whole symbolism of both
Tabernacle and Temple was intended to
impress upon them the holiness of God and
the fact that He could not be rashly approached
by sinful man. **10. Gittite**] The later tradition
(1 Ch 15 18) makes him a Levite. If this is
correct, he probably came from Gath-rimmon,
a Levitical city (Josh 21 25).
13. When they .. had gone six paces] They
offered sacrifices as soon as it was seen that
God permitted the removal of the ark.
17. The tabernacle] This translation, though
correct, is misleading. It was an ordinary
tent. The Tabernacle was at Gibeon. **Burnt
offerings**] represented the self-dedication of
the worshipper. **Peace offerings**] were sacrifices of thanksgiving. **19. A flagon** *of wine*]
RV 'a cake of raisins.'
23. David thus inflicted on Michal the
greatest disgrace which could befall an Eastern
woman. This condemnation seems to our
minds extreme ; but such sudden impulses
were characteristic of David.

CHAPTER 7

THE PROMISE OF GOD TO DAVID IN
REQUITAL OF HIS DESIRE TO BUILD THE
TEMPLE

This c. affords an excellent illustration of
the way in which prophecy has often two quite
distinct applications, one to the more immediate and the other to the more distant
future. The primary reference is to Solomon
(see especially vv. 12–14), but the prophecy
looks beyond him to a greater Son, of whom
he was only an emblem and type. We get a
somewhat similar instance in Isa 7 14-17 (see
especially v. 16). Chronologically this c.
should follow c. 8.
2. Nathan] The prophet is here mentioned
for the first time. He played an important
part in David's reign (chs. 7, 12, 1 K 1) and

afterwards wrote a history of it, and of part,
at least, of the reign of Solomon. **Curtains**]
i.e. a tent: see on 6 17. **3.** This v., when read
in connexion with vv. 4, 5 f., is important as
showing the difference between the prophet
as an ordinary man and the prophet as the
spokesman of God : cp. 1 Cor 7 6, 10, 12.
5. Shalt thou build] LXX ' Thou shalt not
build.' 'But his son shall' (v. 13). According
to 1 Ch 22 8 the prohibition was connected with
his having been a man of war. **6. Whereas**]
RV ' for.' This v. gives the reason why David
was not to build. **In a tent and in a tabernacle**]
The tent denotes the outer covering: the tabernacle the framework of boards and bars.
7. Tribes] Chronicles has preserved the
true reading 'judges' (1 Ch 17 6). **9. Have
made**] RV ' will make.' Nathan turns from
the past to the future. **11. Also the LORD
telleth thee**] The revelation turns to David's
posterity.
12. In Ac 2 30 this v. is directly referred to
the Messiah. **13. He shall build an house**]
fulfilled in the person of Solomon (1 K 8 16-20).
**I will stablish the throne of his kingdom
for ever**] On this is based the statement in
Lk 1 33. **14. I will be his father, and he shall
be my son**] In Heb 1 5 this is applied to Christ,
who was God's Son in a sense that Solomon
never was. **If he commit iniquity**] History
records many instances of the transgressions
and punishment of David's posterity. **The rod
of men**] Such chastisement as fathers inflict
on their sons. **16. Before thee**] LXX and
Chronicles ' before me.' **For ever**] The promise was conditional on conduct : but the kingdom of Messiah, David's greatest Son, is eternal.
19. *Is* **this the manner of man**] rather, 'this
is the law of (i.e. imposed on) man.' God has
made it a law regulating men's conduct, that
kind intentions should be recognised and requited. But it was a sign of condescension
that God should consider Himself bound to
reward David's zeal by such proofs of regard
and affection. **21. For thy word's sake**] i.e.
to perform the promise made to David through
Samuel.
23. To render this v. intelligible we must
do two things: (*a*) with LXX omit the words
' for you,' (*b*) with Chronicles change ' for thy
land' into 'drive out.' Render, therefore, 'and
to do great things and terrible, to drive out
nations and their gods before thy people,
which thou redeemedst to thee from Egypt.'

CHAPTER 8

DAVID'S VICTORIES, AND A LIST OF HIS
OFFICERS

This c. concludes this account of David's
reign. The remainder of the book is taken
from a different source.
1. Metheg-ammah] RV ' the bridle of the

mother city.' This is supposed to mean 'the authority of the capital,' namely, Gath (cp. 1 Ch 18¹). Many take it, however, as the name (perhaps corrupted) of a place which David took from the Philistines. RM retains Metheg-ammah.

2. Casting them down to the ground] RV 'making them to lie down on the ground.' David then slew two out of every three. The reason for this severity is not known. **Gifts**] Moab continued tributary till the death of Ahab (2 K 3⁵). **3. Hadadezer**] i.e. 'Hadad is a help': cp. Eliezer, Joezer, Azariah. Hadad was the supreme god of Syria. In 10¹⁶ his name is given more correctly as Hadarezer. **Zobah**] a Syrian kingdom, whose territory seems to have lain N. of Damascus and not far from the Euphrates. **To recover his border**] Chronicles reads 'to establish his dominion' (1 Ch 18³). **4. A thousand** *chariots*, **and seven hundred horsemen**] RV 'a thousand and seven hundred horsemen.'

5. Damascus] is situated 'in a plain of vast size and extreme fertility, which lies east of the great chain of Anti-Libanus, on the edge of the Desert.' It has always been one of the most important cities of Syria. It succeeded in throwing off the yoke of Israel in the reign of Solomon (1 K 11²⁴). Its history is related in the books of Kings. **6. Syria of Damascus**] The phrase indicates the small Aramæan states in the regions of Damascus.

8. Exceeding much brass] i.e. copper. It is said that the Egyptians of the 18th and 19th dynasties got so much copper from Syria that they gave up working the mines on Mt. Sinai. **9. Hamath**] on the Orontes. **10. Joram**] LXX 'Jeddoram,' Chronicles 'Hadoram.' A Jewish scribe has probably altered Hadoram to the more familiar Joram. **12, 13. Syria .. Syrians**] LXX and Chronicles (1 Ch 18¹²) rightly read 'Edom,' 'Edomites.'

15–18. These vv. are intended by the author to form the conclusion of his history of David's reign. Another list of officers is given in 20²³⁻²⁶. **17. Zadok .. and Ahimelech ..** *were* **the priests**] Zadok seems to have become chief priest under Saul: David had his own high priest, Abiathar. He solved the resulting difficulty by dividing the office between them. But for the prompt action of Joab, he would probably have divided the command of the army between Joab and Abner. **Ahimelech the son of Abiathar**] His name was really Abiathar, the son of Ahimelech (see 1 S 22²⁰ 2 S 15³⁵). But both in OT. and NT. the names are continually confused. **18. The Cherethites and the Pelethites**] see on 1 S 30¹⁴. They formed part of David's foreign bodyguard. **Chief rulers**] RV 'priests.' There can be no doubt that the translation of RV is correct, for the word has never any other

meaning than that of 'priests.' But it is far from clear what were the precise duties which they discharged. Zadok and Abiathar were the priests for the nation, while 20²⁶ and 1 K 4⁵ show that these 'priests' stood in some special relation to the king. Accordingly Ewald conjectures that they were his domestic priests. In Egypt, the king's confidential advisers are said to have been chosen from among the priests, and it is this view of their functions which is taken in Chronicles. 'The sons of David were chief about the king.' See Intro. § 5.

CHAPTER 9
DAVID AND MEPHIBOSHETH

Chs. 9–20 have apparently been taken from a single document, written not long after the events recorded, and with special and unique knowledge of the circumstances of David's court and its life.

1–6. As soon as his wars were over, David remembered his promise to his friend Jonathan, and sends for his son Mephibosheth (or Merib-baal).

7–13. David entertains Mephibosheth at his table, and bestows on him all the property that formerly belonged to Saul.

12. Mephibosheth had a young son] When Saul died, Mephibosheth was only five years old (4⁴), so that this brings us nearly to the middle of David's reign.

CHAPTER 10
THE WAR WITH AMMON AND SYRIA

2. His father shewed kindness unto me] Occasion not stated. **3. The city**] i.e. their capital, Rabbah. The Ammonites probably were thinking of the severity with which David had treated the neighbouring Moabites (8²).

4. Shaving the beard is the greatest insult that can be offered to an Oriental. The Arabs regard it as we should regard flogging or branding.

6. Hired] cp. 1 K 15¹⁸⁻²⁰. **Beth-rehob**] near Laish or Dan (Jg 18²⁸). **King Maacah**] RV 'the king of Maacah.' Maacah was a small Syrian kingdom on the border of eastern Manasseh. **Ish-tob**] RV 'the men of Tob.' See on Jg 11³. **8. Came out**] from Rabbah. *Were* **by themselves**] This implies distrust and disunion between the allies. **9.** Joab took advantage of the division of the enemy to attack them in detail. Abishai kept the Ammonites in check while Joab crushed the Syrians, and then the two brothers combined their forces and fell on the Ammonites. **14. So Joab returned**] The great strength of Rabbah rendered it hopeless to attempt to carry it by assault, and so Joab rested his army during the winter : see on 11¹. **16. The river**] i.e. the Euphrates. **Helam**] position unknown.

18. **Forty thousand horsemen**] 1 Ch 19 18 'forty thousand footmen.' 19. **All the kings** *that were* **servants to Hadarezer**] cp. 1 K 20 16.

CHAPTER 11
DAVID AND BATH-SHEBA

This narrative is of the greatest value. It shows the faithfulness and the high morality of the historian, who relates, without a single attempt at palliation, this scandalous chapter in the great king's history. Further, the position of the prophet, even in these early days, as the 'conscience' of the individual or the nation, is clearly described. What Nathan is to David, Elijah (with equal courage) is to Ahab. In other nations, even in much later times, such an act if committed by a powerful king would have gone unnoticed or unblamed.

1. **After the year was expired**] RV 'at the return of the year,' i.e. in the spring. **When kings go forth** *to battle*] In ancient times hostilities ceased during the winter and began again in the spring. **David tarried still at Jerusalem**] He was not required to be present during the lengthy operations of the siege.

2. **David arose from off his bed**] He had been resting during the heat of the day.

6 f. The subterfuges to which the sinner is compelled to stoop are described in pitiless detail. 8. **A mess** *of* meat **from the king**] This was regarded as a special mark of distinction. Cp. Gn 43 34 1 S 9 23. 9. It would seem that Uriah's suspicions had been aroused.

11. **The ark**] This accidental mention of the ark suggests that it was no unusual occurrence for it to be taken to the field of battle. 15. The only resource left was murder.

21. **Who smote Abimelech?**] see Jg 9 53. 23. **We were upon them**] i.e. we opposed them.

CHAPTER 12
DAVID'S REPENTANCE AND PARDON. THE CAPTURE OF RABBAH

4. **To dress for the wayfaring man**] We may notice Eastern ideas of hospitality: cp. Gn 18 3-5. 5. **Shall surely die**] David's impulsive temper breaks out again: cp. 1 S 25 22.

11. For the fulfilment of this threat, see 16 21, 22. David's repentance secured the forgiveness of God, but it did not avert the punishment of his sin. 13. **Thou shalt not die**] This was the punishment David himself had pronounced on the offender.

14. **Thou hast given great occasion to the enemies of the LORD to blaspheme**] There is little doubt that the original reading was, 'Thou hast blasphemed the LORD,' and that it was altered to avoid any appearance of irreverence.

23. **I shall go to him**] There is a suggestion here of belief in some form of continued existence beyond the grave.

24. **Solomon**] 'Peaceful.'

25. **Jedidiah**] 'Beloved of Jehovah.' It is curious that this name should have been laid aside in favour of his other name, Solomon.

27. **The city of waters**] i.e. the lower town of Rabbah, on the Jabbok. It received this name because of a perennial stream which rises within it and which still flows through it. 28. **Encamp against the city, and take it**] Now that the waters of the lower town were in the possession of the besiegers, the fate of the upper town, or citadel, was only a question of time.

30. **Their king's crown**] The reference is probably to Milcom, the god of the Ammonites (1 K 11 5). His name is merely an altered form of Melech, i.e. 'king.' The weight of the crown (a talent of gold) renders it certain that no living person could have worn it for long.

31. **Put** *them* **under saws, etc.**] The Heb. must be translated, 'put them to saws,' i.e. set them to work at saws, and harrows, and axes. For the forced labour of captives, cp. 1 K 9 15, 21. **Made them pass through the brick-kiln**] read, 'made them work at the brick-mould.'

CHAPTER 13
THE CRIME OF AMNON, AND ABSALOM'S VENGEANCE

This narrative and the history of Absalom's rebellion is omitted in Chronicles.

2. **Tamar** was in the women's apartments, and, therefore, safe. She was his half-sister and Absalom's sister: see 3 2, 3.

4. **Lean from day to day**] i.e. getting thinner and paler every morning. 5. **Make thyself sick**] RV 'feign thyself sick.' 13. **He will not withhold me**] Tamar said this as a last, desperate expedient, for such marriages were unlawful (Lv 18 9). 16. Amnon was adding insult to injury. 18. **Garment of divers colours**] RM 'a long garment with sleeves': cp. Gn 37 3. 20. **He** *is* **thy brother**] So Tamar could not reproach herself for having gone to see him.

23. **Ephraim**] an unknown town.

37. **Talmai**] Absalom escapes to his grandfather (3 3) to avoid the revenge of Amnon's relatives.

David **mourned**] His sin was finding him out, and he was tasting the first bitter fruits of it in the death of one son and the alienation of another.

CHAPTER 14
ABSALOM'S RETURN FROM GESHUR

After waiting for two years, Absalom forces Joab to use his influence to bring about a reconciliation between him and his father.

2. Tekoah] 6 m. S. of Bethlehem. It was the home of the prophet Amos (Am 1 ^{1}).

7. We will destroy] She purposely makes the case appear as bad as possible. **My coal**] The word means a glowing piece of wood. The surviving son is compared to a spark left when the rest of the fire has gone out. The passage casts an interesting light on the informal and almost casual administration of justice. According to Hebrew custom the youth had no claim to a reprieve; on the other hand, the extinction of a family was an admitted calamity.

9. The iniquity be **on me**] i.e. if the king is breaking the law of God, she is willing to bear the punishment: cp. Gn 9 ^{6}. **11. Let the king, etc.**] She wishes him to ratify his promise by an oath. **13. As one which is faulty**] The king's merciful disposition towards the son of a stranger condemned his severity to his own son.

14. We must needs die, etc.] Life may end at any time, and when ended cannot be recalled. Hence the regret that follows harsh judgment when the offender is dead. **Neither doth God, etc.**] RV 'neither doth God take away life, but deviseth means, that he that is banished be not an outcast from him.' God is so far from taking away life that He is anxious that the outcast should not be lost, but should be enabled to return. It is possible that the woman was hinting at the contrast between David's treatment of Absalom and God's treatment of David: see 12 ^{13}.

15. The people] i.e. her family. The woman still keeps to her fictitious tale. **20. To fetch about this form of speech**] RV 'to change the face of the matter'; i.e. the present position of Absalom.

25. His beauty] Absalom inherited the personal beauty of his father (1 S 16 ^{12}). The fact is also mentioned in the case of Tamar (13 ^{1}) and of Adonijah (1 K 1 ^{6}). **26. The king's weight**] We do not know the exact weight of the king's shekel, but probably 40 shekels were roughly equivalent to an English pound. This notice is inserted to distinguish it from the sacred shekel. **27. Three sons**] It would appear from 18 ^{18} that none of them lived to grow up. **29.** Joab had risked a good deal in sending the woman of Tekoah, and he did not choose to venture a second attempt.

CHAPTER 15
THE REBELLION OF ABSALOM

His party is so strong that David is obliged to flee from Jerusalem. He is joined by Ittai the Gittite, and by Zadok and Abiathar the priests, and by Hushai the Archite. The king, however, orders Zadok, Abiathar, and Hushai to return to Jerusalem.

1. Fifty men to run before him] Such runners have always formed part of royal state in the East: cp. 1 K 1 ^{5} 18 ^{46}. **2. Rose**] rather, 'used to rise,' and stand by the gate so as to meet all who went in or out.

7. Forty years] This is obviously a mistake. Some versions read 'four.' **8. I will serve the LORD**] i.e. by sacrifices and offerings (v. 12). Absalom may have remembered his father's device (1 S 20 ^{6}). **9. Went to Hebron**] Absalom probably hoped that the ancient capital, Hebron, would be jealous of Jerusalem. **11. Called**] i.e. invited to share in the festivities. They were probably men of influence and position.

12. While he offered sacrifices] This gave him an opportunity of conferring with Ahithophel without exciting remark: cp. 1 S 16 ^{2}.

14. Let us flee] LXX adds 'lest the people come upon us.' David is taken completely by surprise, and mistrusts his subjects and his household. **17. A place that was far off**] RV takes it as a proper name, 'Beth-merhak.' **18. Gittites**] see on 1 S 30 ^{14}. Ittai and his followers from Gath (Goliath's city) were now among David's staunchest followers.

19. With the king] i.e. with whoever chances to be king. As a foreigner Ittai had nothing to do with the internal quarrels of Israel. David generously suggests that he should keep them out of his own conflicts. **24. And Abiathar went up**] These words are probably out of place. They are omitted in some MSS of the LXX, and look like a scribe's insertion. **26.** In spite of all his anxiety and misery, David's resignation and piety never waver. **27.** *Art not* **thou a seer? return**] LXX 'see, thou shalt return.'

28. The plain of the wilderness] The locality is that described in 2 K 25 ^{5} as 'the plains of Jericho.' It was in the level plain of the Jordan valley and near the fords (17 ^{16}).

32. Where he worshipped God] RV 'where God was worshipped.' Olivet was a well-known high-place: cp. 1 K 11 $^{7,\,8}$. **The Archite**] i.e. an inhabitant of Erech, a town on the southern frontier of Ephraim, between Bethel and Beth-horon.

CHAPTER 16
ZIBA, SHIMEI, AND AHITHOPHEL

David, during his flight, is assisted by Ziba, but is cursed by Shimei. The cause of Absalom is promoted by the wise counsel of Ahithophel.

1. An hundred of summer fruits] a hundred cakes into which summer fruits were compressed. **2.** With true Oriental deference he does not venture to say they are for the king's own use. **8. All the blood of the house of Saul**] The reference is probably to the incident recorded in 21 $^{1-14}$.

11. The LORD hath bidden him] David recognised that all his misfortunes were the consequence of his sin. The Lord had punished him through his own son, whom he had forgiven and restored. Why not also through Shimei? **14 Came weary**] RM ' came to Ayephim.' **23. Enquired at the oracle of God**] i.e. consulted God by means of the Urim and Thummim.

CHAPTER 17
THE FALL OF AHITHOPHEL

Absalom follows the advice of Hushai rather than that of Ahithophel, who thereupon hangs himself. David retreats to Mahanaim.

3. The death of David would put an end to all resistance, and bring about peace. **7. At this time**] RV ' this time.' Hushai contrasts this suggestion of Ahithophel with his former advice (16 21), which was good. **8. A man of war**] Ahithophel's advice, though plausible, was not sound. David was too experienced a warrior to be caught unprepared.

16. Hushai was afraid that Absalom might change his mind and be guided by the advice of Ahithophel. **17. Went and told**] RV ' used to go and tell.' This v. describes how communication between Hushai and David was regularly carried on.

23. Ahithophel saw clearly that following the advice of Hushai meant the failure of the conspiracy.

24. Mahanaim] E. of Jordan, near the Jabbok. **25. Israelite**] more probably ' Ishmaelite ' (1 Ch 2 17). **Abigail** was a sister of David (1 Ch 2 15, 16), and consequently Amasa was his nephew : cp. 19 13.

CHAPTER 18
THE DEFEAT AND DEATH OF ABSALOM

1. Numbered] rather, ' mustered.' **3. Succour us out of the city**] David, holding Mahanaim with a sufficient force, would be of the greatest assistance to the fugitives, if his army were defeated. **5. The people heard**] This statement explains v. 12.

6. The wood of Ephraim] LXX reads ' Mahanaim ' here. **8. The battle was there scattered**] So Joab was able to destroy Absalom's forces in detail. **The wood devoured**, etc.] The thickness of the wood, its swamps, precipices, etc., militated against the fugitives, and increased the slaughter : cp. the manner of Absalom's death. **9. Met**] RV ' chanced to meet.' By misfortune, in his flight Absalom encountered some of the pursuers. **His head**] The tradition that Absalom was caught by his hair comes from Josephus. **13. Against** *me*] RV ' aloof.' Joab would have stood on one side and let his accomplice bear the brunt of the king's anger. **16. Joab held back the people**] Absalom was dead and the war ended.

17. A very great heap of stones] This might be simply to mark his burying-place. **18.** This v. is evidently parenthetical, and informs us that Absalom had a suitable permanent memorial, though the building now known as Absalom's tomb in the vicinity of Jerusalem is of much later date. Evidently Absalom's three sons (14 27) had died before him. **Place**] RV ' monument.'

21. Cushi] RV ' the Cushite.' He was probably a slave of Joab, who could be trusted to say exactly what he was told. **22. Thou hast no tidings ready**] RV ' thou wilt have no reward for the tidings.' His message would be a sad one. **23. By the way of the plain**] The direct way lay across the hills, but Ahimaaz, by choosing the level road along the Jordan valley, reached his goal first. **24. Between the two gates**] i.e. between the outer and the inner gate in the city wall. **25. If he** *be* **alone,** *there is* **tidings**] Had he been a fugitive, he would have been followed by others.

29. And *me*] RV ' even me.' **I knew not what** *it was*] This statement was untrue (v. 20). Probably Joab had commanded him to leave the announcement to the Cushite

CHAPTER 19
DAVID'S RETURN TO JERUSALEM

David's excessive grief for Absalom is rebuked by Joab. He punishes Joab for Absalom's death by making Amasa commander of the army. The details of his return to Jerusalem are given, with the strife it caused between the men of Israel and the men of Judah.

David has often been accused of ingratitude on account of his treatment of Joab. It has been urged that he would never have been secure with Absalom at liberty, and Joab knew how uncertain was his master's mind. On the other hand, it was a serious matter to murder the heir to the throne, for which deposition was probably a lenient punishment. **8. Then the king arose**] He recognised the truth of Joab's statements. **Sat in the gate**] where kings were wont to give audiences (15 2). **11.** The talk of the people of Israel about David's return had come to the king's knowledge, but so far the elders of Judah had not approached him on the subject. **16, 17.** Shimei tries to make his peace with David (see 16 5 f.) by bringing the tribe of Benjamin back to their allegiance. **20. The house of Joseph**] here stands for northern Israel. Ephraim was the most powerful tribe in the northern and central tribes, as Judah was in the south. **23. Sware unto him**] At first sight it appears as if David broke his oath by his last directions to Solomon (1 K 2 8, 9). But the way in which Solomon acted on those instructions suggests that he understood his father to be merely putting him on his guard against a dangerous man. He put Joab to death at once, but merely placed Shimei where he could do no mischief.

26. I will saddle] better, with LXX, 'saddle.' The command was given to Ziba, but, instead of obeying it, he drove off the asses to meet David. **29. I have said**] RV 'I say,' i.e. I declare that this is my intention. **Thou and Ziba**] see 16⁴.

41. Here again we may notice the jealousy between the powerful tribes of Judah and Ephraim : see on v. 20. **42. Hath he given us any gift?**] This was probably a hit at the Benjamites, who seem to have profited by their connection with Saul (1 S 22⁷). **43. That our advice should not first be had**] cp. the conduct of the men of Ephraim, narrated in Jg 8¹ 12¹, although they had more excuse (see on Jg 8¹).

CHAPTER 20
THE REBELLION OF SHEBA

Sheba takes advantage of the jealousy of the men of Israel to begin a rebellion, which, but for the prompt action of Joab, might have resulted in a disruption between Israel and Judah. During this expedition Amasa is murdered by Joab. The c. concludes with a list of David's officers.

This c. evidently continues the narrative of the concluding vv. of the preceding. During the period of the Judges, Ephraim had been the leading tribe and they could not brook to see their place taken by Judah. For the present their attempt failed, and the rule of Solomon was too strong for them to renew it. But on the accession of Rehoboam the old jealousy broke out again.

This c. ends the account which the editor took from the document he has been following since c. 9. The list with which it concludes is similar to that at the close of the earlier document (8¹⁶⁻¹⁸).

1. The son of Bichri] rather, 'a son of Bichri,' i.e. a member of that clan (1 Ch 7⁶⁻⁸). **We have no part .. Israel**] This was the very cry raised by the rebellious Israelites in the time of Rehoboam (1 K 12¹⁶). **3.** See 15¹⁶ 16²¹, ²².

5. He tarried] The reason is unknown. **6. Abishai**] When Amasa failed him, David, determined at all hazards to suspend Joab, turned to Abishai. Joab went with his brother in order to watch for his opportunity, which soon came. **8.** It would seem that Joab had two swords, and that Amasa, seeing one lying on the ground, did not suspect that he had another. **9. Took Amasa by the beard .. to kiss him**] This is said to be still an Arab custom. **14. Unto Abel, and to Beth-maachah**] read 'unto Abel of Beth-maachah.' **All the Berites**] read 'all the Bichrites' (see on v. 1). Sheba

went to the Bichrites (his kinsmen) and then proceeded to Abel-beth-maachah, in the extreme N. of Palestine, where he was besieged by Joab.

15. They cast up a bank against the city] cp. 2 K 19³². It enabled the besiegers to bring their battering-rams close up to the wall. **It stood in the trench**] RV 'it stood against the rampart.'

18. The wisdom of the inhabitants of Abel was so generally accepted, that their decision settled all disputed questions. The woman says this to give weight to her remonstrance.

19. A city and a mother] i.e. a mother-city, a metropolis. **20.** Joab was utterly unscrupulous, but never wantonly cruel : cp. 18¹⁶.

23–26. This list of officers concludes this part of the book. What follows is an appendix. When we compare it with the list given in 8¹⁶⁻¹⁸, we find the amount of variation which we should expect, if one list refers to the earlier and the other to the later part of the reign. The names of Joab, Benaiah, Jehoshaphat, Zadok, and Abiathar occur in both lists. Sheva replaces Seraiah, and Ira takes the place of David's sons, while the office of Adoram is new.

24. Adoram] He held the same office through the long reign of Solomon till the accession of Rehoboam (1 K 12¹⁸). It has, however, been supposed that the Adoram mentioned in Kings was the son and successor of the Adoram mentioned here.

CHAPTERS 21–24

These chapters contain six appendices, which have been placed at the end of the book in order not to interrupt the history of the reign. These appendices are (1) the account of a famine (21¹⁻¹⁴); (2) exploits against the Philistines (21¹⁵⁻²²); (3) a psalm of David (c. 22); (4) David's last words (23¹⁻⁷); (5) further exploits against the Philistines and a list of David's heroes (23⁸⁻²⁹); (6) the census of the people (c. 24). Of these six, the first and sixth are closely connected (24¹ refers to 21¹), while the account of exploits against the Philistines has been cut in two by two psalms. But these psalms, though placed side by side, have no connexion with one another. C. 22 is identical with Ps 18, and is best explained under that title.

CHAPTER 21
THE FAMINE AND SOME EXPLOITS AGAINST THE PHILISTINES

1. *It is* for Saul, and for *his* bloody house] rather, 'upon Saul and his house rests bloodshed.' **The Gibeonites**] The lives of the Gibeonites had been spared, through fear of God's anger being excited by any breach of the covenant made with them (Josh 9, especially v. 20). **2. Amorites**] Strictly speaking, the Gibeonites were Hivites (Josh 9 7), but ' Amorites ' was a general name for the Canaanites. **3. Wherewith shall I make the atonement ?**] i.e. what sum of money shall I pay as compensation ?

4. RV ' It is no matter of silver or gold between us and Saul, or his house; neither is it for us to put any man to death in Israel.' They would not accept compensation in money, nor did they wish that Israel, apart from Saul, should suffer. **6. Hang them up**] The method of execution is uncertain. *Whom* **the LORD did choose**] RV ' The chosen of the LORD.' **8. Michal**] Evidently a mistake for ' Merab.' It was Merab who married Adriel (1 S 18 19). **Brought up**] RV ' bore.' **9, 10.** Barley harvest is in April, and the early rain (**until water dropped**) in October.

15–22. The text in this section and also in its continuation (23 8-39) is very corrupt.

15, 16. Read, ' and his servants with him, and settled in Nob, and fought against the Philistines, and —— which was of the sons of the giant.' The giant's name has been lost.

19. Jaare-oregim] in 1 Ch 20 5 ' Jair.' **Elhanan .. slew** *the brother of* **Goliath**] AV represents the reading of Chronicles. RV represents the text of Samuel, as we now have it, ' Elhanan .. slew Goliath the Gittite.' If we adopt it, we must suppose that Elhanan was another name of David ; but see on 1 S 17.

CHAPTER 22
DAVID'S THANKSGIVING PSALM

This beautiful poem has also been preserved as the Eighteenth Psalm. It probably belongs to the earlier portion of David's reign, when his conquests and God's promise (2 S 7) were still fresh in his mind. See on Ps 18.

CHAPTER 23
DAVID'S LAST WORDS. THE EXPLOITS OF HIS HEROES

1–7. This psalm is not contained in the book of Psalms. It is called ' the last ' (rather, ' the latter ') ' words of David,' in contrast with the earlier psalm, which forms c. 22. We have no other means of determining its date.

2. By me] RM ' in me.' The idea is that God used the psalmist as His instrument and spokesman to repeat His words to the people : cp. 1 K 22 28 Hos 1 2.

4. *As* **the tender grass** *springing*] render, ' when the tender grass springs.' The righteous ruler is like a bright, sunny morning, when there are no clouds and the grass springs out of the earth. There are no clouds to darken the present or threaten the future, and the whole land is alive with gladness and life.

5. This v. is better taken as a question: ' For is not my house so with God, seeing He

hath made . for all my salvation and all my desire, shall He not make it to grow ?' David refers to the promise actually made in the past and looks forward with confidence to the future. **Everlasting covenant**] cp. 7 15, 16.

Ordered in all *things*] i.e. properly drawn up and arranged in every respect. **Grow**] i.e. continue and increase: cp. Isa 45 8.

6, 7. These vv. contrast the fate of the wicked. **Thorns** cannot be pulled up with the naked hand, but the man who wishes to cut them down must take in his hand a long staff with an iron weapon at the end.

8–39. This list of heroes originally contained the first three, then a second three, then the 30 : 36 names in all, or with Joab, 37 names. This is the number actually given in v. 39.

8–11. The first three, Ishbosheth, Eleazar, and Shammah. **8. The Tachmonite that sat in the seat**] read, ' Ishbosheth the Hachmonite.' **Chief among the captains**] read, ' the chief of the three ': cp. v. 19. **The same** *was* **Adino the Eznite**] Chronicles rightly reads ' he lifted up his spear.' **11. Into a troop**] read, ' to Lehi.' Lehi was the scene of Samson's exploit against the Philistines (Jg 15 9 f.).

13–16. We now get a great exploit, which promoted three other heroes to a place above the 30. **16. Poured it out unto the LORD**] as too precious for human use.

18–20. Two names only of the second three have been preserved : Abishai and Benaiah.

24–39. Chronicles reduces this list to the correct number of 30, by omitting the name of Elika (v. 25). But we know that Asahel died early in David's reign, and another may have been chosen in his place.

CHAPTER 24
THE NUMBERING OF THE PEOPLE, AND ITS PENALTY

In punishment for David's sin in numbering the people, God sends a pestilence, which slays 70,000 men. In gratitude for the stay of the plague, David erects an altar in the threshing-floor of Araunah the Jebusite.

1. Again] This refers to the former occasion mentioned in c. 21. **He moved**] Chronicles states that ' Satan .. provoked David.' The older account does not enter into the distinction between what God permits and what God causes. This distinction is the result of later reflection and more subtle theology.

5–8. Their course is easy to follow, though several of the names are corrupt. They started from the city of Aroer on the Arnon, and passed through eastern Palestine. They next crossed to Zidon, and traversed western Palestine to Beersheba in the extreme south. **5. On the right side** (i.e. on the south) **of the city that** *lieth* **in the midst of the river** (RV ' valley ')] Perhaps this city was Ar of Moab (Isa 15 1).

6. Tahtim-hodshi] Thenius conjectures that this is a mistake for 'Kadesh,' a town on the Orontes marking the extreme northern limit of Israel. **Dan-jaan**] read 'Dan.'

10. David's sin consisted in pride in his own strength and forgetfulness of his dependence on God. It was the very sin which ruined Saul.

13. Seven years] LXX and Chronicles read 'three years.' **15. From the morning even to the time appointed**] These words occasion some difficulty as the pestilence was stayed before the appointed time. They are omitted in Chronicles. **22. Instruments of the oxen**] i.e. the wooden yoke: cp. 1 K 19 21. **23.** This v. continues Araunah's speech : RV 'all this, O king, doth Araunah give.'

THE FIRST AND SECOND BOOKS OF KINGS

INTRODUCTION

1. Character and Contents. The books of Kings take up the account of the Jewish people at the point where it is left by 2 Samuel. The division into two books is not original, and seems to have been introduced from the LXX, where they are termed the 'Third and Fourth books of the Kingdoms,' the First and Second being 1 and 2 Sam. Their contents embrace the history of the period between the last years of David's reign (about 980 B.C.) and the Fall of Jerusalem in 586, closing with the release of Jehoiachin from prison by Evil-Merodach in 561 ; so that the space of time covered is rather more than 400 years. Their final completion must be later than the date last mentioned, and their composition is separated from many of the events related by a considerable interval ; so that for the bulk of the information which they comprise they are dependent upon earlier records. In the Talmud, the authorship is attributed to Jeremiah (perhaps on the strength of the general tone of the books, or of the recurrence in Jer 39–42 and 52 of parts of 2 K 24, 25), but the statement is improbable, so far at least as the present form of the books is concerned. Jeremiah, whose prophetic ministry began as early as the 13th year of Josiah [Jer 1 2], i.e. about 627, can scarcely have survived till after 561.

2. Sources. In the course of the narrative reference is made to three different sources as authorities for the history of the times described, viz. the Acts of Solomon (1 K 11 41), the Chronicles of the Kings of Israel (1 K 14 19, etc.), and the Chronicles of the Kings of Judah (1 K 14 29, etc.). The mention of a Recorder among the officials of many of the Kings (1 K 4 3 2 K 18 18) suggests that the several writings just named may have preserved information derived from the State archives, though the nature of some of the statements for which they are cited renders it probable that they were not themselves official documents (see 1 K 16 20 2 K 15 15 21 17). In certain instances they are referred to as supplying matter which the books of Kings do not furnish (see 1 K 14 19 22 39) ; but it seems likely that much that is included in Kings is really drawn from them. There is no explicit statement, however, to show in what way these or any other sources were utilised in the compilation of the work, though certain conclusions respecting the nature of some of the written documents that lie behind our books and the method followed in the composition of them may be obtained from an analysis of their structure, which consists of the following elements :—

(*a*) A detailed account of the last days of David (1 K 1, 2).

(*b*) Passages relating in detail the construction or repair of the Temple (1 K 6–9 2 K 12 4-16 16 10-16, etc.).

(*c*) Lengthy narratives dealing with the prophets Elijah and Elisha (1 K 17–19, 21, 2 K 1 2-17 2, 4–6 23, etc.).

(*d*) Passages relating at length certain political events (1 K 20 22 1-38 2 K 3 4-27 6 24–7 20 18 13–20 20, etc.).

(*e*) Succinct accounts of many of the kings, written in stereotyped phrases, beginning with the date of each king's accession, the length of his reign and his character (certain other particulars being added in the case of kings of Judah), and ending with a reference to the 'Book of the Chronicles' of the kingdom concerned, and a mention of the king's successor. Of these (*a*) probably comes from the same source as the narratives contained in 2 S 9–20, which it resembles in character ; (*b*) may be assumed to be based on records drawn up by the priesthood ; whilst (c) must have originated in prophetic circles (such as the communities of the 'Sons of the Prophets'). The passages classified under (d) and (e) may be derived from the annals to which reference is made. But the brevity and uniform phraseology characteristic of (e), which are in marked contrast to the picturesque and varied style of the longer sections, make it probable that these are epitomes constructed by the actual compiler of Kings out of his materials, whereas the other portions of his book are extracts made by him from the sources he used. As may be seen by a comparison of numerous passages in Chronicles with the parallels in Kings, Hebrew historians were in the habit of incorporating in their own compositions passages taken *verbatim* from other works ; and the differences in style and vocabulary between various sections of Kings, the abruptness with which personages not previously mentioned are introduced (e.g. 1 K 17¹), and certain discrepancies in the narratives, all indicate that the course which the writer of Chronicles has pursued towards the books of Kings the writer of the latter has followed in regard to still earlier productions.

For the sake of convenience the writer of these books has been spoken of in the singular, and the completion of his work has been fixed as later than 561 B.C., and therefore some time after the destruction of the kingdom of Judah. But in certain of the narratives phrases are used which imply that when they were written Judah existed as a state, and the Temple was still standing (see 1 K 8⁸ 12¹⁹ 19³ 2 K 8²² 14¹¹ 16⁶ 17¹⁸). Some of the phrases occur in sections which have probably been incorporated from previous writings (e.g. 1 K 19³), and consequently the use of them only shows that the sources from which the author of Kings borrowed were composed before the exile ; but there are others (e.g. 2 K 8²²) which are found in the short annalistic passages that have been assigned to the compiler. Consequently it is probable that the bulk of the book was composed before the exile ; but that subsequently additions were made to it by a writer who lived after the Fall of Jerusalem, and who appended chs. 24 and 25. In the earlier chapters also there are a few expressions which could only have been written in Babylonia after the overthrow of Judah, e.g. 1 K 4²⁴ (see note) 2 K 17¹⁹, ²⁰ ; so that the author of the supplementary chapters seems not only to have continued his predecessor's work, but to have introduced a few insertions into the body of it. But the spirit and style of the two writers are so much alike that except where specific allusions betray the date of the narrator, it is as unnecessary as it is difficult to distinguish between them.

3. Value. If the conclusions just stated respecting the probable sources of the narratives be correct, it will be apparent that Kings is a most valuable authority for the history of the times it deals with, especially in those parts which may reasonably be regarded as based upon the State and Temple records. Unfortunately the information respecting this period which is obtainable from other sources, such as the Egyptian and Assyrian monuments, is not as full as could be desired ; but in general, what has been learnt from these quarters harmonises with, or plausibly supplements, the biblical account, even where it does not actually confirm it. In order, however, to estimate fairly the good faith of the writer and his merits as an historian, it is important to bear in mind the conditions under which he wrote. Neither the means at his disposal, nor the methods of composition that then prevailed, were calculated to secure the accuracy and precision of statement which are now expected in historical works.

(a) The materials employed by Hebrew writers generally are not expressly named, but there are allusions in various passages of the OT. to tablets (probably of wood) and rolls (of skin or leather) : see Isa 8¹ 30⁸ Hab 2² Jer 36² Ezk 2⁹. Materials like these must have rendered it difficult for mistakes once made to be corrected ; and if the documents consulted by successive historians were of such a character, it is obvious that the process of verifying statements could not be an easy one. Moreover, the nature of the Hebrew writing, in which there were then no vowel signs, must have conduced to the production of various readings; and many of the differences between the Heb. original and the LXX version have arisen from this cause.

(b) The practice of reproducing the exact words of previous writers has led to the retention of many discrepancies and inconsistencies, which may have admitted of being harmonised by the compiler, through knowledge which he possessed, but of which the explanation is, in many instances, quite irrecoverable by us.

(c) In the absence of a fixed era an accurate system of chronology was almost impossible. In connexion with the kings of Israel and Judah, the accession of each king is generally marked by reference to the corresponding year in the reign of the contemporary sovereign ; but whereas, in most cases, fractions of a year are counted as a whole year (e.g. Nadab is said to have reigned *two* years, though he came to the throne in Asa's *second* year and was succeeded by Baasha in Asa's *third*, 1 K 15²⁵, ³³), in other cases this rule is not observed (e.g. Rehoboam is described as reigning only 17 years, though his successor Abijam came to the throne in the 18th year of Rehoboam's contemporary Jeroboam: 1 K 14 21 15 1). Owing to these different systems of reckoning or other causes, many of the chronological statements in Kings are inconsistent (as is pointed out in detail in the Commentary). The discrepancies apply to the totals as well as to individual figures, for whereas the sum of the reigns between Jeroboam and Jehoram of Israel, and between Rehoboam and Ahaziah of Judah, should be equal, the numbers are respectively 98 and 95 ; and similarly, whilst the years between Jehu and the Fall of Samaria, and between Athaliah and the 6th year of Hezekiah (when Samaria was taken), should be the same, they are respectively 143 years 7 months and 165 years. Moreover, the mention of certain Hebrew kings in the Assyrian inscriptions as being contemporary with particular events which are precisely dated shows that the length of some reigns is over-estimated by the Hebrew historian (e.g. those of Pekahiah, Pekah and Hoshea, which together seem to have amounted to 16 instead of 31 years).

But to regard the writer of Kings as a secular historian would be to mistake the purpose of his history. That his main object was not to chronicle political and social events is plain from two facts. (a) He treats with extreme brevity reigns which on his own showing were, from a secular point of view, of great importance, e.g. that of Jeroboam II (2 K 14 25) ; (b) he expressly refers his readers to other sources for further information respecting wars and other occurrences of interest (1 K 14 19 22 39). His principal aim was to set forth the religious lessons which the history of his countrymen afforded, to trace the ill consequences that followed upon disobedience to the divine laws, and the happy results of faith in, and loyalty to, the LORD. In pursuance of this aim, he selected from the narratives which his authorities supplied the incidents which illustrated the principles he sought to enforce. In particular, he gave prominence to the glory of Solomon, which confirmed the divine promises made to his father David, the misconduct of the same king and the chastisement that punished it, the words and works of the various prophets who appeared at intervals, and the final overthrow which overtook both branches of the house of Jacob for their sins. In the sections which he himself composed he briefly appraised the character of the several sovereigns according to their faithfulness or unfaithfulness to the Law ; and at certain crises of the national history he reviewed at length the causes of the catastrophes described.

4. Summary of the History. The political history contained in the books of Kings may be conveniently divided into four periods :— (a) The reign of Solomon over the united people ; (b) the period of about 200 years from the revolt of the Ten Tribes (about 937 B.C.) to the downfall of Jehu's dynasty in Israel and the reign of Uzziah in Judah ; (c) the century that elapsed between the close of the last-mentioned period and the reign of Josiah ; (d) the last fifty years of the kingdom of Judah, from about 630 B.C. to the Fall of Jerusalem in 586.

(a) The successful wars waged by David had secured for Israel control over many of the smaller Palestinian states, such as Moab, Ammon, and Edom ; and garrisons had been placed even in Damascus. The position thus established was maintained throughout the pacific rule of Solomon except that Damascus regained its independence ; but the interest of Solomon's reign centres not so much in the country's external relations, as in its internal development. It was marked by (i) the extension of foreign commerce through the help of Hiram of Tyre, (ii) the execution of great building schemes, intended partly to secure the safety of the kingdom against attack, and partly to foster religion and adorn the capital. The king's trade was conducted by sea with Ophir (probably S. Arabia) and perhaps Tarshish (Tartessus or Tarsus) ; and by land with Egypt, the Hittites, and the Syrians. It doubtless increased the wealth and advanced the culture of the nation ; but the people nevertheless suffered much in consequence of the contributions exacted for the support of the royal court, and the system of forced labour imposed to carry out the king's building projects. The discontent thus created was a principal cause of the revolt of the Ten Tribes against the authority of Solomon's son Rehoboam.

(b) The period that succeeded Solomon's death began with a conflict between Israel and Judah, owing to a natural desire on the part of the early Judæan kings to recover the lost provinces of their house ; but it was mainly occupied by a protracted war between Israel and Syria. Syria entered the war as an ally of Judah, but the hostility between the two Hebrew kingdoms subsequently gave place to better relations, and Judah became Israel's ally against the Syrians. The object which the latter people chiefly had in view in its struggle with Israel was the command of the roads, leading on the one hand to the Mediterranean coast and Egypt, and on the other hand to Arabia along the E. side of the Jordan and the Dead Sea. During this period the northern kingdom underwent many dynastic changes, but its foreign policy was not greatly affected in consequence, and the house of Jehu, no less than the house of Omri which it displaced, suffered from the attacks of its eastern neighbours. Another nation with which Israel at intervals had hostilities was Moab, which, after being severely handled by Omri (as the Moabite Stone declares) rebelled in the reign of Ahab and conquered several cities belonging to Reuben and Gad ; but was again subdued by Jeroboam II, who extended his rule to the 'brook of the Arabah.' During this period Judah, besides helping Israel against Syria, was also frequently engaged in maintaining by force its authority over Edom, or else in recovering it when lost.

(c) The third period, which may be regarded as beginning with the reigns of Shallum and Menahem in Israel, was marked by the ascendency of Assyria. Israel had previously come into contact with the Assyrians in the reign of Ahab (who fought against Shalmaneser II in defence of Hamath in 854), and of Jehu (who paid tribute to the same monarch) ; but it was Tiglath-pileser who first seriously interfered with the Hebrew states. The advance of Assyria produced counter movements on the side of Egypt (which had left its Hebrew neighbours undisturbed since the invasion of Shishak in the reign of Rehoboam), and there consequently arose both in Israel and Judah parties which relied for help on one or other of these two powers against its rival. Egypt, however, proved a broken reed, and constantly disappointed those who reposed confidence in it. The common danger threatening from Assyria finally drew Syria and Israel together, and they sought unsuccessfully to force Judah to join a coalition against their enemy. Eventually both the confederates succumbed before the Assyrian arms ; whilst Judah, which in the reign of Hezekiah, acting in conjunction with an anti-Assyrian faction in Philistia, revolted against Sennacherib. was only preserved by what was regarded as a signal interposition of divine providence. At a later date Egypt itself was successfully invaded by the Assyrian kings Esarhaddon and Asshurbanipal.

(d) The final period saw the downfall of the Assyrian power. This was accomplished by the Babylonians and Medes, who took Nineveh in 607. Egypt, which had regained its independence, attempted to assert claims to a share in the partition of the Assyrian possessions, and Nechoh, the Egyptian sovereign, advancing into Palestine, not only killed Josiah in battle but deposed his successor. He was, however, defeated at Carchemish by the Babylonians, who succeeded to the position previously occupied by Assyria. Disaffection on the part of Judah against Babylonian authority brought speedy retribution, and finally Jerusalem was captured and its population carried into captivity in 586.

Judah survived by nearly 150 years the sister kingdom of Israel, although the latter was the larger and more powerful of the two. From a secular point of view the chief reason for the earlier extinction of Israel is to be found in its position. The main roads leading from the Euphratene states (Syria and Assyria) to Phœnicia and Egypt passed through its territory and exposed it to the designs of its ambitious neighbours ; whereas Judah lay off the route between the eastern and western empires, and it was only because Jerusalem was too strong a fortress to leave on the flank of an army invading Egypt, that its conquest became desirable. A contributing factor likewise was the weakness introduced into the northern kingdom by dynastic rivalries, whilst, on the contrary, Judah was undisturbed by internal commotions, the house of David occupying the throne without a break for more than 400 years, except during the brief usurpation of Athaliah. But to one who, like the writer of Kings, traced in the fortunes of men the judgments of God, the ultimate cause must have appeared to be the greater corruption of religion which prevailed in Israel as compared with Judah, and which brought upon it a swifter and more irreversible punishment.

5. The Religion of the Period. The religious history of each of the two kingdoms was characterised by distinct features. In Israel there was no preëminent sanctuary like the Temple at Jerusalem to suggest any restriction upon the practice of worshipping at local shrines (' high places') ; and this practice prevailed as long as the kingdom stood. At certain of these shrines Jehovah was worshipped under the emblem of a calf or young bull ; and the use of these symbols was maintained by all those kings who upheld the ancestral Hebrew faith. The ' high places,' however, were not always devoted to the service of the LORD, for both the historian and certain contemporary prophets imply that the worship of the Canaanite Baalim was sometimes practised at them (Hos 2 13). And at two periods alien forms of religion were introduced from abroad and diffused through the influence of the reigning sovereign. The first was that of the Phœnician Baal, brought into Israel by the alliance of Ahab with Ethbaal, king of Zidon, and strenuously opposed by the prophets Elijah and Elisha. The second, imported at ' a later date, was due to connexion with Assyria, and consisted of planet- or star-worship, to the prevalence of which allusion is made by the prophet Amos (5 26).

In Judah the Temple built by Solomon naturally dwarfed the importance of all other sanctuaries, but the ' high places ' were nevertheless long maintained even under the rule of pious kings. But in the reign of Hezekiah an attempt was made to suppress them and to confine all national acts of religion to the Temple ; and a still more complete reform in this direction was effected by Josiah. The greater success that attended Josiah's efforts was largely due to the discovery of a copy of the book of Deuteronomy, in which the restriction of worship to a single locality is expressly enjoined. In Judah calf-worship never seems to have been practised ; and though the worship of the LORD was often corrupted, its supremacy was never seriously disputed by any other religion during the first half of the history, except in the reign of Athaliah, who was a votary of the Zidonian Baal. Subsequently, however, Assyrian forms of worship penetrated into Judah as they had into Israel. Ahaz was attracted by the rites which he saw at Damascus when summoned thither by Tiglath-pileser, whilst Manasseh is described as having worshipped the ' host of heaven.' After Assyria had fallen before Babylon, Babylonian cults began to be imitated ; and both Jeremiah and Ezekiel allude to the worship paid to the ' queen of heaven' (perhaps Ishtar) and to Tammuz, a deity adopted by the Greeks under the name of Adonis (see Jer 44¹⁸ Ezk 8¹⁴).

6. The Prophets who appeared at intervals in the course of the history fall into 3 groups : —(a) Those who were contemporary with the war against Syria, such as Elijah and Elisha ; (b) those who witnessed the rise and predominance of Assyria, viz. Amos, Hosea, Isaiah and Micah ; (c) those who lived during the decline of Assyria and the early years of Babylonian supremacy, viz. Nahum, Zephaniah, Habakkuk, Jeremiah, and Ezekiel. At all periods the prophets were statesmen no less than moral teachers, religion being viewed from a national rather than an individual standpoint.

But the prophetic ideals and methods varied in different ages, those of Elijah and Elisha, for instance, offering many features of contrast to those of later times. Thus Elijah was content to maintain the claims of Jehovah to be the God of Israel without explicitly affirming Him to be the only God, and he seems to have tolerated the unspiritual conception of religion involved in the worship of the golden calves ; whereas Hosea ridiculed such worship, and Isaiah expressly described by a term meaning ' nonentities ' the gods revered by foreign nations and disloyal Israelites. And similarly whilst Elisha sought to bring about a religious reformation by means of a political revolution, and presumably sympathised with Jehu's action in exterminating by violence the family of Ahab, the later prophets, in trying to direct the policy of their countrymen into right channels, confined themselves to peaceful methods, and Hosea even declared that the LORD would visit upon the house of Jehu the blood shed by him in Jezreel.

7. Chronological Table. As has been already said, it is difficult to construct an accurate scheme of chronology from the statements furnished by the Hebrew historians, partly because they did not fix events by any era which can be determined with precision, partly because they used inconsistent methods of reckoning the length of reigns, and partly in consequence of miscalculations or textual corruptions. But the mention of certain Hebrew kings in the Assyrian and other inscriptions enables us to bring the biblical history into relation with that of the surrounding nations ; and from a comparison of the figures given in the books of Kings with the dates obtained from the inscriptions, a table has been drawn up (see HDB. i. pp. 401–402), which may be taken as an approximation to the truth : see art. ' Chronology of the Bible.'

---

1 KINGS

CHAPTER 1

AN INTRIGUE FOR THE SUCCESSION

This c. relates Adonijah's attempt to obtain the succession, its defeat through the agency of Nathan, and the enthronement of Solomon. The history contained in it is omitted in 1 Ch, where, however, mention is made of Solomon's having been crowned not once only but twice (1 Ch 29²²). Probably the second occasion corresponds to what is related in 1 K 1³⁹ (cp. 1 Ch 29²⁴ with 1 K 1⁵³).

1. Now] better, ' and,' connecting this

book with the history contained in the preceding.

5. Adonijah] The fourth son of David (2 S 3⁴). Of his three elder brothers, two, Amnon and Absalom, were certainly by this time dead ; and the indulgence with which Adonijah was treated by his father (v. 6) makes it probable that he was the eldest surviving son. **6. His mother bare him after Absalom**] RV ' he was born after Absalom'; Adonijah and Absalom were sons of different mothers (2 S 3³,⁴).

7. Joab] David's nephew, and at this time

captain of the host or national militia (2 S 8 16).
His support of Adonijah was probably due to
the latter's being the eldest surviving son of
David, and to his active character. **Abiathar**]
son of Ahimelech the priest of Nob, who had
been put to death by Saul (1 S 22 20). He was
a descendant of Aaron's son Ithamar.

8. Zadok] a descendant of Aaron's son
Eleazar (1 Ch 6 4-8). It is not clear what were
the relative positions of Abiathar and Zadok
to one another. In 1 Ch 16 39 Zadok is stated
to have ministered at the sanctuary at Gibeon,
but in 2 S 15 24 both Abiathar and Zadok are
represented as being at Jerusalem. In the
LXX of 1 K 2 35 it is implied that Abiathar
was the first, or principal, priest, and Zadok
presumably the second. **Benaiah**] son of
Jehoiada (v. 36) and commander of the body-
guard of Cherethites, Pelethites and Gittites
(see further on v. 38). For his early exploits
see 2 S 23 20-23. **Nathan**] For other notices of
Nathan see 2 S 7 2 f. 12 1 f. **The mighty men**]
This was a body of distinguished warriors,
nominally 30 in number, who were perhaps
officers either of the bodyguard or of the host,
and whose names are given in 2 S 23 24-39 1 Ch
11 26-47.

9. Slew sheep and oxen] probably a sacrificial feast is meant, whereby Adonijah intended to solemnise his succession : cp. 2 S
15 12. **The stone of Zoheleth . . En-rogel**] En-
rogel is probably to be identified with the
modern Bîr-eyûb, a well (not a spring) situated
at the junction of the valley of Hinnom and
the gorge of the Kidron, S. of Jerusalem
(cp. Josh 15 8 18 16).

13. Didst not thou . . swear?] That this was
true is acknowledged by David in vv. 29, 30.

20. The eyes of all Israel *are* **upon thee**]
Though the right of the firstborn to succeed
was beginning to be recognised, the sovereign
still possessed the power of nominating his
successor.

33. Gihon] probably the modern Virgin's
Fountain. in the ravine of the Kidron, about
half-a-mile from En-rogel (Bîr-eyûb).

36. Amen] an expression of assent or concurrence : cp. Nu 5 22 Jer 28 6.

38. Cherethites] a bodyguard of foreign
extraction, like the Swiss guards of the French
kings or the Varangians of the Byzantine
sovereigns. The Cherethites came from the
S. of Philistia (1 S 30 14), the name being
generally supposed to be connected with
Crete, and the **Pelethites** were perhaps likewise
Philistines. David may have enrolled this force
after the conclusion of his Philistine wars.

39. The tabernacle] RV 'the Tent'; probably the tent erected by David to shelter the
ark (2 S 6 17). According to 1 Ch 16 39 the
Tabernacle made by Moses was at Gibeon.
For the anointing **oil** see Ex 30 22-33.

42. Valiant] RV 'worthy.' **46. Solomon
sitteth on the throne**] similarly Jotham ruled
during the lifetime of his father (2 K 15 5).

47. Bowed himself] i.e. in worship: cp. Gn
47 31.

50. The horns of the altar] The altar intended was probably one erected in or before
the tent that sheltered the ark : see on v. 39
and cp. 2 29 3 15. The horns were projections
at the four corners (Ex 27 2), to which the
victim to be sacrificed may have been attached
(Ps 118 27), and which were sometimes smeared
with its blood (Ex 29 12). It was customary
for homicides to seek refuge at the altar of
the LORD from the avengers of blood, but
deliberate murderers might be dragged from
it (Ex 21 14). A similar right of asylum belonged to heathen temples in classical times
and to Christian churches in the middle ages.

51. To day] RM 'first of all.'

CHAPTER 2
DAVID'S LAST WILL AND TESTAMENT

The recital of David's last charge to Solomon and his death is followed by an account
of the execution of Adonijah, Joab, and
Shimei.

3, 4. Cp. Dt 17 2 S 7.

5. Abner . . Amasa] For Abner see 1 Ch 9 36
1 S 14 50 2 S 2,3 ; for Amasa see 2 S 17 25 (cp.
1 Ch 2 17), 19 13 20 4-13. Joab's slaying of Abner
may be palliated, though not justified, in consideration of his kinship with Asahel, whom
Abner had killed ; but his assassination of
Amasa was due merely to the mortification he
had sustained when the latter displaced him in
the king's favour. He had thus been guilty
of murder, which, if unavenged, would bring
guilt on the land : cp. 2 S 21. David may also
have thought it expedient to remove Joab in
order to safeguard Solomon's throne, which
could never be secure so long as so capable
and unscrupulous an officer was alive. **The
blood of war . . girdle**] The LXX has 'innocent
blood,' which the sense requires.

6. The grave] Heb. *Sheol*, the abode of
departed spirits.

7. Barzillai] For his kindness to David see
2 S 19 31 f.

8. Shimei] For his offence against David
and David's oath to him see 2 S 16 5-13 19 18-23.

9. Hold him not guiltless] Personal resentment seems to have entered into David's feelings towards Shimei, but it is probable that
his injunctions respecting him were partly
dictated by political reasons, for Shimei was a
Benjamite who had reproached David with
supplanting Saul, and might be suspected of
hostility towards David's successor ; and who
was influential enough to be attended by a
thousand of his fellow-tribesmen when he met
the king after Absalom's defeat (2 S 19 17).

10. The city of David] i.e. the stronghold of Zion : see 2S5⁶⁻⁹. At this time Jerusalem probably occupied only the eastern of the two hills upon which the modern city stands.

David's reign was more important and critical than any other in the history of Israel, both from a secular and from a religious point of view. In the first place, he consolidated into a kingdom what had previously been an aggregate of jealous tribes, and so enabled his countrymen to take a place among the nations of the Eastern world ; and, in the second place, he strengthened his people's attachment to the LORD, alike by the zeal he showed for God's honour and worship, and by the obedience he rendered to the prophets who counselled or admonished him in the divine name. Consequently later times regarded the period of his rule as Israel's golden age, and the memories of it coloured the anticipations which were entertained respecting the coming of the Messiah. His character, indeed, was not free from reproach ; for, besides being guilty of adultery and murder, he was cruel in war (2S8² 12³¹) and negligent of justice at home (though in these respects he was doubtless no worse than his contemporaries). But if he sinned grievously, he repented sincerely ; and by his humility under reproof (2S12¹³), his resignation in adversity (2S15²⁵,²⁶), and his faith in the divine mercy (2S24¹⁴), he still affords an example for Christian people.

17. That he give me Abishag] Amongst Eastern nations the wives and concubines of a deceased or dethroned king were taken by his successor (see 2S12⁸ 16²¹,²²) ; and so Adonijah's request for Abishag was regarded as tantamount to a claim on the throne. **19. Rose up to meet her**] the queen-dowager occupied a very important position at the court of the kings of Israel : cp. 1K15¹³ Jer13¹⁸.

23. God do so, etc.] an expression implying a wish that God would avenge the failure to carry out what was promised or threatened.

24. Made me an house] see 2S7¹¹.

26. Anathoth] NNE. of Jerusalem. It was the home of the prophet Jeremiah (Jer1¹).

Barest the ark] perhaps referring to the transport of the ark from the house of Obededom to Jerusalem (1 Ch15), or to its removal from Jerusalem on the occasion of Absalom's rebellion (2S15²⁴,²⁹). **27. That he might .. the LORD**] see 1S 2³¹⁻³⁶. It is not meant that the fulfilment was designed by Solomon, but he was the unconscious agent of divine providence.

28. Horns of the altar] see on 1⁵⁰. **The tabernacle**] see on 1³⁹. **31. Bury him**] Denial of burial would have made Joab's fate more ignominious : see 2K9¹⁰,³⁴ Isa14¹⁹,²⁰. **Take away the innocent blood**] This, if not avenged, would have brought a judgment upon the

king and his people : see Nu35³³, and cp. 2S21¹⁻¹⁴. **32, 33.** In these vv. the futures are best rendered as wishes. **Captain of the host of Judah**] At this time there was no formal division between Israel and Judah, but Amasa had been specially connected with the latter : see 2S19¹¹⁻¹³ 20⁴. **34. Buried in his own house**] cp. 1S25¹ 2K21¹⁸. **In the wilderness**] i.e. of Judah, to which tribe Joab belonged. **35. Put .. Abiathar**] i.e. appointed him to be first priest, instead of Abiathar.

36. Build thee an house in Jerusalem] i.e. that he might be under surveillance. **37. The brook Kidron**] This would actually limit him only on the E., the quarter in which his former home, Bahurim, was situated ; but it was doubtless meant to designate the distance beyond which he was not to go in any direction : cp. v. 42. **39.** Shimei's visit to Achish might be construed as an intrigue with a foreign power. **43. The oath of the LORD**] i.e. the oath which the LORD witnessed.

CHAPTER 3
SOLOMON'S CHOICE

This c. relates how Solomon, out of various gifts offered to him by the Almighty, chose wisdom, and adds an illustration of the use he made of the gift with which he was endowed.

1. Pharaoh] probably one of the immediate predecessors of the Shishak (Sheshonk) mentioned in 11⁴⁰ is intended. **His own house .. LORD**] see chs. 7 and 6. Both of these buildings were outside the limits of the city of David.

2. High places] Both the Canaanites (see Nu33⁵² Dt12²) and the early Israelites (see 1S9¹² 2S15³⁰,³²) used to worship on hill-tops, possibly as being nearer heaven, the dwelling-place of the Deity, or perhaps (more probably) as being the best sites for burning the victims that were offered in sacrifice. In Dt12¹⁰ᶠ· the worship of the LORD is ordered to be restricted to a single sanctuary ; though the history shows that religious practices at the high places were permitted even by the best of kings (see 15¹⁴ 22⁴³) until the reign of Hezekiah (see 2K18⁴).

4. Gibeon] in the tribe of Benjamin (Josh 18²⁵). **To sacrifice there**] in 2Ch1³ it is stated that the Tabernacle of the congregation was at Gibeon ; if so, it must have been removed thither from Shiloh when the latter place was destroyed (Jer7¹²), or from Nob, to which it may have been conveyed from Shiloh. The ark which it had originally contained, was not restored to it when brought back by the Philistines (1S6), but put by David in a tent at Jerusalem.

7. I am but a little child] The words seem to imply that Solomon was quite youthful when he came to the throne ; but the politic measures by which he secured his crown, as described in c. 2, suggest that he had attained to full manhood, and according to 1 K 14 21 he left, after a reign of 40 years, a son who was 41 when his father died, and who therefore must have been born before his father became king (but see note there). Josephus gives Solomon's age at the beginning of his reign as 14. **Go out or come in**] i.e. pursue the active life of a man in his prime : cp. Nu 27 17 1 S 18 13 Dt 31 2.

9. Solomon's prayer exhibits (a) a strong sense of responsibility and a conviction that high position involves a corresponding duties ; (b) a consciousness that truth and falsehood, right and wrong, are not always easy to distinguish, and that to discern between them there are needed special gifts of the heart and understanding ; (c) that such gifts are derived from God, who bestows them in answer to prayer. **14. I will lengthen thy days**] The promise was made on conditions which Solomon did not observe : see 11 1-8.

15. **The ark of the covenant**] This had been placed by David in a tent at Jerusalem (2 S 6 12, 17). Solomon fitly inaugurated his reign by acts of religious worship at his capital as well as at Gibeon (v. 4). **Burnt offerings .. peace offerings**] see on Ex 18 12.

26. **Her bowels**] i.e. her heart. 27. **Give her the living child**] The pronoun refers not to the last speaker but to her rival (as LXX explains). 28. **The wisdom of God**] Solomon's wisdom was divine not only in its source but in its quality.

CHAPTER 4
SOLOMON'S OFFICERS AND COURT

2. **Azariah the son of Zadok**] he was really the grandson of Zadok (1 Ch 6 8, 9). 3. **Shisha**] also called Shavsha and Sheva. In David's reign he filled the same office now discharged by his sons (2 S 20 25). **Scribes**] i.e. the royal secretaries. **Jehoshaphat**] he had previously served David (2 S 8 16 20 24). **Recorder**] probably the keeper of the state archives (RM 'chronicler'), though some suppose that his function was to remind the king of state matters that required his attention. 4. **Abiathar**] Abiathar was priest during a very brief period of Solomon's reign : see 2 26, 27. 5. **The officers**] probably the officers named in vv. 7–19. **Principal officer**] RV 'priest.' The term is used in 2 S 8 18 of David's sons, and in 2 S 20 26 of Ira a Jainite, who perhaps belonged to the tribe of Manasseh—both being, to all appearance, instances of priests of other than Levitical descent. **The king's friend**] The same title is applied to Hushai in 2 S 15 37. 6. **Over the household**] i.e. steward or treasurer : cp. Isa 22 15. The position was one of sufficient dignity to be filled sometimes by the son of the sovereign (2 K 15 5). **Adoniram**] The name

appears in a shortened form as Adoram in 2 S 20 24 1 K 12 18. **Tribute**] RV 'levy.' This was a body of men subjected to forced labour and employed on Solomon's buildings (9 15). It corresponded to the French *corvée*. 8. **Mount Ephraim**] RV 'the hill country of Ephraim': and so elsewhere.

9-12. Of the localities mentioned in these vv. several (**Makaz, Elon-beth-hanan, Aruboth, Hepher**) are unknown. **Shaalbim** was in Dan ; **Beth-shemesh** (modern Ain shems) and **Sochoh** were in Judah ; **Dor** was on the coast, near Carmel ; **Taanach, Megiddo, Jezreel, Jokneam** (RV 'Jokmeam') were in or near the plain of Esdraelon ; **Beth-shean** (the modern Beisan), **Zartanah**, and **Abel-meholah** were in the Jordan valley. **13, 14.** The places named in these vv. were E. of Jordan. **Argob** is the Trachonitis of the NT., a volcanic district, now called the 'Leja,' lying S. of Damascus. **19.** *He was . . land*] The text is probably corrupt. It will be observed that in the division of the land between the several officers, the tribal boundaries were to some extent ignored, only five or six tribes being retained as departments. Possibly this was done to weaken tribal sentiment, which tended to disunion.

21. **The river**] the Euphrates. 22. **Measures**] Heb. *cors* (a cor = a homer, and contained over 80 gallons). 24. **On this side the river**] RM 'beyond' (i.e. W. of) 'the River' (Euphrates), i.e. Palestine and the neighbouring region as viewed from the standpoint of a resident in Babylon (E. of the Euphrates) where the book of Kings was probably completed. **Tiphsah**] Thapsacus, on the upper course of the Euphrates. **Azzah**] Gaza in Philistia.

26. **Forty thousand**] in 2 Ch 9 25 'four thousand,' which would be sufficient for the 1,400 chariots mentioned in 10 26. The possession of a large force of cavalry was a departure from the practice of David, who, like Joshua, destroyed the horses taken from his enemies.

27. **Those officers**] i.e. the officers described in v. 7 f. **They lacked nothing**] better, 'they let nothing be lacking.' 28. **Dromedaries**] RV 'swift steeds.' **Where** *the officers* **were**] RM (after LXX) 'where the king was'; RM 'where it' (the barley and straw) 'should be,' i.e. wherever it was required

29. **Largeness of heart**] i.e. great intellectual capacity : see on v. 3 9. 30. **Children of the east country**] The term is applied in Jer 39 28 to the Arab tribes dwelling at Kedar, and probably describes generally the inhabitants of the Syrian desert : cp. Gn 29 1 Jg 6 3. For Arab wisdom see Jer 39 7. 31. **Ethan, etc.**] The same four names (with the substitution of Dara for Darda) occur among the sons of Zerah the son of Judah in 1 Ch 2 6. If the allusion is to these, Mahol may be their father and Zerah a remote ancestor. The individuals

meant must have been ancient sages proverbial for their wisdom. **32. Proverbs**] Some are doubtless included in the extant book of Proverbs. **Songs**] The Song of Songs and two of the canonical psalms (72 and 127) bear Solomon's name. Certain so-called 'Psalms of Solomon' really belong to the age of Pompey. **33. He spake of trees**, etc.] This may mean both that he drew examples from the vegetable and animal kingdoms to illustrate his maxims (as in Prov 6 6), and that he investigated and described their properties (as in Prov 30 15, 29-31). **34. All people**] cp. the visit of the Queen of Sheba (c. 10).

CHAPTER 5
SOLOMON'S PREPARATIONS FOR BUILDING THE TEMPLE

1. Hiram] see 2 S 5 11 1 Ch 14 1. It has been questioned whether this Hiram, who was living as late as Solomon's twentieth year (1 K 9 10), is really identical with the Hiram mentioned in connexion with David (2 S 5 11 1 Ch 14 1), because, according to Josephus, his reign lasted only 34 years. But it is possible that David did not undertake the buildings in which Hiram assisted him until comparatively late in his life.

3. Could not build an house] see 1 Ch 22 8. Here the reason given why David could not build the Temple is the turmoil that filled his reign. **4. Occurrent**] i.e. occurrence. **5. As the LORD spake**] see 2 S 7 13.

7. Blessed be the LORD] Hiram, who, as king of Tyre, was a worshipper of Melkarth and Ashtoreth, would not regard the LORD (Jehovah) as the only God, but would acknowledge Him as the God of Israel. Jehovah's existence and power were similarly recognised by the Syrian Naaman, who was himself a worshipper of Rimmon (2 K 5 11) : cp. also the language of the Moabite king Balak (Nu 23 17 24 11). **9. Convey them**, etc.] RV 'make them into rafts to go by sea.' **The place**] Joppa (2 Ch 2 16). **To be discharged**] RV 'to be broken up.' **11. Measures**] Heb. *cors* (see on 4 22). For **twenty measures of pure oil** LXX has '20,000 baths of oil' (a 'bath' being one-tenth of a 'cor' : cp. 2 Ch 2 10. For the export of corn and other produce from Judah to Tyre cp. Ezk 27 17. The nearness of Lebanon must have prevented the Tyrians from obtaining much corn from their own soil. **13. Thirty thousand men**] These were probably taken from native Israelites (cp. the prediction in 1 S 8 11-18) ; whereas the 150,000 labourers mentioned in v. 15 were 'strangers that were in the land of Israel' (2 Ch 2 17 : cp. 1 K 9 20, 21). David seems to have imposed forced labour upon the latter only (1 Ch 22 2) ; and the different practice of his son caused the discontent that eventually rent the kingdom in

two (12 4). **14. By courses**] i.e. by turns or shifts. **Adoniram**] see 4 6, the Adoram of 12 18.

17. Great stones] Some of these perhaps still remain, for stones 30 ft. long and 7½ ft. high have been found (it is said) 'at the SW. angle of the wall of the Haram area in the modern Jerusalem.' **18. The stonesquarers**] RV 'Gebalites' : the inhabitants of Gebal or Byblus, a maritime town at the foot of Lebanon.

CHAPTER 6
THE CONSTRUCTION OF THE TEMPLE

In shape the Temple was a rectangular hall 60 × 20 × 30 cubits (a cubit being about 18 inches). On its E. face it had a porch (forming an entrance) which extended across the whole front and added 10 cubits to the length of the building (v. 3). The height of this is given in 2 Ch 3 4 as 120 cubits; but such a measurement is out of all proportion to the others, and is probably an error (one of the MSS. of the LXX substitutes 20 cubits). On three sides of the house were built a number of chambers (Josephus says 30) in three storeys (vv. 5, 10), intended for the accommodation of the priests and for storing things required for the Temple services : cp. 2 K 11 2, 3 Neh 13 4, 5 (of the Second Temple). The beams that supported the cielings of these storeys rested on ledges in the outer face of the Temple wall formed by successive reductions of its thickness (v. 6). Above the topmost row of chambers the Temple wall was pierced with **windows of narrow lights** (RV 'windows of fixed lattice work,' i.e. which could not be opened like most lattices), resembling the clerestory of a modern cathedral. In the interior, the building was divided by a partition (see v. 16) into two apartments, the larger (to the E.) being called the Holy Place, and the smaller (to the W.) being styled the Oracle or Most Holy Place, which bore to one another the same relation as the nave and chancel of our own churches.

Solomon's Temple resembled in general plan the Tabernacle as described in Ex 25–27, its length and breadth being exactly double. In idea, it was, like the Tabernacle, the dwelling-place of the God of Israel (see 1 K 8 13, and cp. Ex 25 8), wherein He received, and held communion with, His worshippers (2 K 19 14 f., cp. Ex 33 7). But it differed from most other sanctuaries of antiquity in containing no image ; so that though the conception of divine worship had not yet become independent of locality or material oblations (see Jn 4 21-24), the conception of the Deity Himself was purely spiritual.

In the Holy of Holies (the Presence chamber of the Divine King) there was nothing except the ark (containing the Decalogue), the cover of which was regarded as the throne of the LORD, who was thought of as seated between the cherubim that overshadowed it (2 K 19 15). In the Holy Place there were situated the Altar of Incense and the Table of Shewbread. In the court before the House stood the Altar of Burnt Offerings and the several vessels used by the priests in their ablutions (7 23 f.).

1. The four hundred and eightieth year] The sum of the periods mentioned or implied in the previous books since the exodus much exceeds this figure. The real length of the interval is uncertain, and the number of years here indicated is probably not based on historic records but is a conventional expression for twelve generations (a generation being reckoned at 40 years). Approximately the date of the commencement of the Temple may be put at 973 B.C. **The month Zif**] In early times the Hebrew year ended and began in the autumn (see Ex 23 16 34 22), but at a later period the beginning of the year was in the spring, and Zif, which corresponded to our April-May, became the second month. It was subsequently called Iyyar.

2. The house] The Temple was built on the N. of the hill upon which Zion, 'the city of David,' stood, there being an ascent from the latter to the former (see 8 1). Its site had originally been occupied by Araunah's threshing-floor (2 Ch 3 1). For its position relative to the rest of Solomon's buildings see on 7 9.

8. The middle chamber] LXX has 'the lowest chamber,' which the sense requires. **The right side**] the S. **9. Covered the house**] Roofed or cieled it. Whether the roof was flat or gable-shaped is uncertain, though, as houses were generally flat-topped, this was probably no exception.

12. *Concerning* **this house**, etc.] The erection of the Temple was an external and material indication of Solomon's allegiance to the LORD; but to obtain the Almighty's continued favour, it was necessary besides to submit his life and conduct to the control of God's moral laws. **Which I spake unto David**] see 2 S 7 13. God renewed to Solomon the promises made to his father on condition of his obedience.

15. Both the floor, etc.] mg. 'from the floor of the house unto the walls,' etc., i.e. from top to bottom. **16. He built .. on the sides, etc.**] RV 'he built .. on the hinder part,' etc. This, as appears from a comparison of the measurements given in vv. 2 and 17, does not mean that the Most Holy Place (or Oracle) was an additional structure built on the rear of the house, but that it was an apartment formed within the house (cp. v. 19) at its W. end by the erection of a partition made with boards of cedar. As its length, breadth and height were each 20 cubits (v. 20), its form internally was a perfect cube, though externally it was

perhaps of the same elevation as the rest of the buildings. **18. Knops**] i.e. knobs, and so in 7 24. RM has 'gourds,' implying that the ornaments intended, which were carved in relief, were globular in shape, resembling pumpkins. **20. The oracle in the forepart**] better, 'the oracle within.' **The altar**] i.e. the altar of incense : for its situation see v. 22.

21. Made a partition, etc.] RV 'drew chains of gold across before the oracle,' i.e. across the entrance that led from the Holy Place into the Most Holy. But 2 Ch 3 14 mentions a veil, and the translation should perhaps be 'drew a veil before the oracle by means of chains of gold.' **22. By the oracle**] The altar was not actually within the oracle but near it.

23. Cherubims] These were large winged figures of composite character, perhaps with four faces, those of a man, a lion, an ox, and an eagle (Ezk 1 10), or with the face of an ox only (to which the term 'cherub' seems to have strictly applied: cp. Ezk 10 14 with 1 10). They represented God's chariot (cp. Ps 18 10), and perhaps symbolised certain of the divine attributes (power, celerity, etc.). The original conception (as Ps 18 10-14 suggests) was probably derived from a storm-cloud: see on Ex 25 18.

27. The inner house] i.e. the Oracle or Most Holy Place. **29. Palm trees**] Figures of these are frequent on the Assyrian monuments. **Within and without**] i.e. within and without the dividing partition between the Holy and Most Holy Place, so that both chambers are meant.

31. The lintel] According to some 'the pilasters,' small pillars projecting from the surface of the side posts. **A fifth part**] mg. 'five-square,' i.e. the top of the door was pentagonal in form. The words 'of the wall' are not in the original. **32. The two doors**] i.e. two leaves, forming a single door. **33. A fourth part**] mg. 'four-square.' The head of the door was square: see on v. 31.

34. The two doors] The door of the Holy Place consisted of two halves, but each half had two leaves.

36. The inner court] This was the court before the house (8 64), open to the air, and was surrounded by a fence of stone surmounted by a row, or paling, of cedar beams. It was on a higher level than the 'great court' of 7 12, and is called in Jer 36 10 'the upper court.'

38. The month Bul] Corresponding to October-November. As this was the eighth month and the Temple was begun in the second, the time actually occupied in its construction was, in strictness, 7½ years.

CHAPTER 7
SOLOMON'S PALACE

This c., besides giving a description of

Solomon's palace, contains an account of the principal utensils belonging to the Temple.

1. Thirteen years] The Temple was of small extent compared with the royal palace, so that the time spent on the latter exceeded that required for the former. The various buildings mentioned in vv. 2–8 seem together to have constituted the house of v. 1.

2. He built also] RV 'for he built.' **The house of the forest of Lebanon**] so called from the quantity of cedar wood from Lebanon employed in its construction. It was a rectangular hall, 100 × 50 × 30 cubits, its roof being supported by cedar beams resting upon three rows (so LXX for **four rows**) of cedar pillars, numbering 45 in all ; and was used as an armoury (Isa 22 ⁸). **4. Light .. ranks**] The external walls were pierced with three rows of windows, so arranged that those in each side corresponded in position to those in the opposite side.

5. *Were* square, **with the windows**] RV 'were square in prospect': i.e. the doors were rectangular (not pointed or arched).

6. A porch of pillars] There was another building with numerous pillars, having a portico (**the porch** *was* **before them**), of which the **thick beam** was the threshold.

7. A porch for the throne] This was a third building which served as a court of justice. **From one side .. other**] better, 'from floor to cieling.'

8. Another court] i.e. behind the porch of judgment there was a court which enclosed the king's palace; this was probably the same as 'the middle court' of 2 K 20⁴ (if that is the right reading).

9. According to .. stones] RV 'even hewn stone, according to measure': and so in v. 11. **Within and without**] i.e. both the outer and inner surfaces. **The great court**] This was perhaps a large court enclosing *all* the preceding structures, including the Temple. It contained (in order from S. to N.), 1. certain public buildings, (*a*) the house of the forest of Lebanon, (*b*) the porch of pillars, (*c*) the porch of the throne ; 2. a second court, enclosing the royal residences, the king's house and the house of Pharaoh's daughter; 3. the 'inner court' (6³⁶), surrounding the Temple. **12. Both for .. and for**] RV 'like as .. and.' The meaning is that the great court, the inner (or Temple) court, and the court of the house (or palace) each had a fence of similar construction : cp. 6 ³⁶.

13. Hiram] also spelt 'Huram' and 'Hirom.' The Tyrian king and the Tyrian architect both seem to have borne the same name. **14. A widow's son .. Naphtali**] in 2 Ch 2¹⁴ his mother is called a daughter of Dan, the Danite settlement within Naphtali being perhaps meant.

15. Two pillars] These pillars, though placed at the porch (v. 21), probably did not support its roof but were detached from the building, and intended for symbolic purposes only. Two similar pillars are said to have stood in the temple of Melkarth at Tyre, one of gold and the other of emerald (or green glass) ; and the like are depicted on the coins of Paphos. Originally such pillars, whether natural obelisks or artificial columns, were regarded as the abode of the Deity, so that offerings were placed or poured upon them in order to be conveyed to the indwelling spirit (of which primitive notion the action of Jacob at Bethel shows a surviving trace, Gn 28¹⁸), but subsequently they became emblems merely, marking the spot where they stood as sacred: cp. Isa 19¹⁹. The details of the pillars erected before the Temple are obscure (the text in places being defective or disordered), but their general appearance is easily intelligible. They were hollow (Jer 52²¹) columns of brass, 12 cubits in circumference and 18 cubits high, surmounted by capitals (**chapiters**) five (in 25¹⁷ three) cubits high, globular in shape (v. 42) and decorated with tracery (v. 17). Around each capital ran two rows of pomegranates, and above each rose an ornament, 4 cubits high, shaped like the cup of a lily. **17. Seven .. seven**] probably a mistake for 'a network .. a network,' there being only two networks in all (see v. 41).

21. Jachin .. Boaz] i.e. 'He (God) will establish,' and 'In Him (God) is strength.'

23. A molten sea] i.e. a large vessel containing water. For its use see 2 Ch 4 ⁶.

26. An hand breadth] i.e. 3 inches. **With flowers of lilies**] RV 'like the flowers of a lily,' the rim curving outwards. **Two thousand baths**] A 'bath' was rather more than 8 gallons. To contain all this, the sides of the molten sea must have bulged considerably.

27. Bases] movable supports or carriages for the lavers of v. 38. The description is very obscure, but it has been in part elucidated by a bronze stand of Mycenæan workmanship recently found in Cyprus. Each base consisted of a hollow cube (4 × 4 × 3 cubits), the sides of which had panels (**borders**) between raised edges (**ledges**). At the lower corners there were legs (the **undersetters** of v. 30, 34), which rested on large wheels. Above rose a pedestal (the **base** of vv. 29, 31) with a capital (the **chapiter** of v. 32) which had a hollow (**mouth**) to receive the laver, which was further supported by stays (the **undersetters** under the laver of v. 30). **29. Additions made of thin work**] RV 'wreaths of hanging work,' i.e. festoons; so also in vv. 30, 36. **34.** *Were* of the very base itself] i.e. were cast with it and not subsequently attached. **36. According to the proportion**] RV 'according to the space of each': i.e. so far as the space permitted.

38. Ten lavers] for the purpose of these

see 2 Ch 4⁶. **Forty baths**] about 320 gallons.
39. Eastward .. south] i.e. at the SE. corner.

40. Lavers] LXX has 'pots' as in v. 45.
41. The bowls] i.e. the globular portions of the two capitals. **46. The plain of Jordan**] i.e. the Jordan valley. **Succoth and Zarthan**] Succoth was in Gad (Josh 13 ²⁷). Zarthan is probably the Zaretan of Josh 3 ¹⁶. **48. The altar of gold**] i.e. the altar of incense (6 ²²).

The table of gold] in 2 Ch 4 ⁸ mention is made of ten tables, but cp. 2 Ch 13 ¹¹ 29 ¹⁸. The Tabernacle had only one table for the shewbread (Ex 25 ²³).

49. The candlesticks] better, 'lampstands.' In the Tabernacle there was only one (Ex 25 ³¹).

50. Censers] RV 'firepans.' **51. Which David .. had dedicated**] see 2 S 8 ¹¹.

CHAPTER 8

THE DEDICATION OF THE TEMPLE. SOLOMON'S PRAYER

1. The chief of the fathers] i.e. heads of families. **Out of the city**] The Temple and Palace were built on the site of Araunah's threshing floor (2 Ch 3 ¹), which would naturally be outside the city walls and on higher ground : cp. 9 ²⁴. **2. Ethanim**] The later Tishri, corresponding to Sept.-Oct. The feast referred to was Tabernacles (Lv 23 ³⁴).

3. The priests] 2 Ch 5 ⁴ has 'the Levites,' certain of whom (the Kohathites) had, according to Nu 4 ¹⁵, the special duty of bearing the ark. But the priests are likewise represented as bearing the ark in Josh 3 ⁶, ¹³ 4 ⁹, etc.

4. Tabernacle of the congregation] RV 'tent of meeting' : i.e. the sanctuary in which the LORD used to commune with His worshippers (Ex 33 ⁹ Nu 11 ²⁵). This, which (according to 2 Ch 1 ³) was at Gibeon, may have been preserved for its sacred associations, for the ark had long been separated from it.

7. The staves] the poles, inserted in rings, by means of which the ark was carried : see Ex 25 ¹²⁻¹⁵. **8. They drew out the staves**] RV 'the staves were so long' : owing to their length they could be seen from the Holy Place, though not **without** (i.e. outside it).

Unto this day] The date implied is that of a narrator living before the destruction of the Temple, whose language the compiler (who lived after that event, cp. 2 K 25) has incorporated without alteration : cp. 9 ²¹.

9. *There was* .. stone] The writer of Hebrews (9 ⁴) mentions also the golden pot that contained manna, and Aaron's rod ; but, in strictness, these were placed before the ark (Ex 16 ³⁴ Nu 17 ¹⁰).

10. The cloud] cp. Ex 40 ³⁴, ³⁵ 33 ⁹ Nu 11 ²⁵ 12 ⁵. This was called by the later Jews the Shechinah. **11. Could not stand**] for the awe which the near Presence of the LORD inspired : cp. Ex 3 ⁶ Isa 6 ⁵ Ezk 1 ²⁸.

12. The thick darkness] cp. Lv 16 ². Hitherto the LORD had dwelt not in an habitation made by human hands, but in Nature's cloud-pavilions (Ps 18 ¹¹). **15. Which spake .. unto David**] through the prophet Nathan (2 S 7 ⁵⁻⁷).

22. The altar] The altar of burnt offering, in the court before the Temple.

23. And he said] The passage that follows is full of a sense of God's infinitude (v. 27), righteousness (v. 32), and omniscience (v. 39), whilst at the same time it manifests faith in His constancy and forgivingness (vv. 25, 29, 30, 34, etc.) ; and though it contemplates principally the needs of Israel, yet it embraces a petition for the stranger that is not of Israel (vv. 41–43). **25. So that**] i.e. provided that (as in 6 ¹²). **27. The heaven .. contain thee**] cp. Isa 66 ¹ Jer 23 ²⁴. **29. Make toward this place**] In later times the Jews, when praying in foreign lands, turned their faces toward Jerusalem (Dan 6 ¹⁰). **31. And the oath come**] RV 'And he come and swear.'

37. In the land of their cities] LXX 'in one of their cities.' **38. The plague of his own heart**] i.e. the plague or chastisement which each is conscious of suffering : cp. 2 ⁴⁴ Ex 9 ¹⁴.

41. Concerning a stranger, etc.] for the future worship of the LORD by the Gentiles, cp. Isa 2 ³ 56 ⁷ Zech 8 ²⁰⁻²². **43. Is called by thy name**] i.e. belongs to Thee : cp. 2 S 12 ²⁷, ²⁸.

50. Give them compassion .. captive] The prayer was fulfilled when Cyrus allowed the Jews, who were captives in Babylon, to return to their home (Ezr 1 ³). **51. Furnace of iron**] i.e. a furnace hot enough to melt iron. **53. O Lord GOD**] better, 'O Lord JEHOVAH.'

56. Hath given rest] cp. Ex 33 ¹⁴.

60. That all the people, etc.] Israel had a mission to discharge to the other nations of the world, partly by exhibiting conspicuously in its fortunes the moral principles on which God governed mankind (Josh 4 ²⁴ Isa 55 ⁵ Ps 67 ⁷) and partly through the agency of its spiritual teachers the prophets (Isa 42 ¹).

61. Perfect with] i.e. not divided between the LORD and other gods : see 9 ⁶ 11 ⁴.

63. Two and twenty thousand, etc.] The quantity seems enormous, but numbers in the OT., as in other ancient writings, cannot always be relied on, and profuse sacrifices were common in antiquity. **64. The middle of the court**] On what is believed to be the site of the Temple court there is a large slab of rock, which would form a natural altar. **Meat offerings**] RV 'meal offerings,' and so elsewhere. **65. A feast**] i.e. of Tabernacles (v. 2).

The entering in of Hamath] Hamath was situated on the Orontes, the approach to it from the S. being by the gorge between Lebanon and Hermon. **The river of Egypt**] the modern Wâdy el Arish, a stream flowing from the Sinaitic peninsula into the Mediterranean. **Seven days and seven days**] The seven days' feast of Tabernacles was preceded by a seven days' Dedication festival. **66. On the eighth day**] i.e. at the close of the seven days' feast of Tabernacles. **Unto their tents**] The phrase is a survival from the tent-life which prevailed before the settlement in Canaan.

CHAPTER 9

GOD'S RESPONSE TO SOLOMON'S PRAYER. SOLOMON AND HIRAM

1. When .. finished] The Temple does not seem to have been dedicated until all the king's buildings were completed, the Temple and Palace being probably included within a single wall and regarded as a unity. In vv. 3–9 is contained the divine response to the prayer offered by Solomon at the dedication festival.

3. Mine eyes .. perpetually] Though God's care extends over all His creation, yet those are nearest to His heart who render to Him the sincerest and worthiest service. At Jerusalem not only did the splendour of the Temple attest Israel's desire to pay honour to the LORD, but the worship conducted there was the most spiritual of contemporary forms of devotion, being free from the sensuous and often impure elements that entered into religious rites elsewhere.

8. At this house, *which* **is high**] The original has 'the house shall be high,' which may mean 'shall be conspicuous,' as a warning to others. But the Syriac has 'this house shall be a heap' (of ruins).

11. Twenty cities] As the payment for the supply of timber consisted of wheat and oil (5 9-11), the cities must have been in return for the supply of gold : see on 2 Ch 8 2. **Galilee**] The region thus designated is not defined in the OT., but the name seems to have been applied to a part of Zebulun and Naphtali, where the non-Israelite population was numerous enough to lead to its being called 'the Galilee (or Circuit) of the Gentiles' (Isa 9 1). In NT. times it extended from the Leontes in the N. to the ridge of Carmel in the S.

13. Cabul] There was a city called Cabul in Asher (Josh 19 27), and its name may have been taken to describe the district owing to its assonance with a Heb. phrase signifying 'as good as nothing.' **14. Sixscore talents**] weighing nearly 13,000 lb.

15. Millo] some part of the fortifications of Jerusalem is meant, perhaps a solid tower, but its place is not known. The LXX renders it by 'citadel,' and its importance is evidenced by its being so frequently rebuilt (11 27 2 Ch 32 5). **Hazor and Megiddo**] Hazor, near Lake Merom, guarded the northern frontier, whilst Megiddo protected the approach to the plain of Esdraelon from the SW. **Gezer**] on

the W. border of Ephraim, the modern Tell Jezer, 18 m. from Jerusalem. Gezer and Beth-horon (v. 17) protected the valley of Aijalon.

16. A present] RV 'a portion' (or dowry).

18. Baalath] a little N. of Beth-horon the nether. **Tadmor,** afterwards called Palmyra, in the Syrian desert, NE. of Damascus. Another reading has 'Tamar,' a place in the S. of Judah (Ezk 47 19), the same as Hazezor Tamar or Engedi (Gn 14 7 2 Ch 20 2). **In the land**] i.e. within the borders of Israel. This, as it stands, is only appropriate as a description of Tamar, but it is possible that some name (e.g. of 'Aram' or of 'Hamath'), descriptive of the locality of Tadmor, has been lost.

19. Desired to build] i.e. for his pleasure : cp. v. 1. **In Lebanon**] where residence would be desirable during the summer heats.

22. No bondmen] This apparently means that no native Israelites were permanently compelled to render forced service. But a considerable body of such was temporarily employed upon the construction of the Temple (5 13): cp. also 11 28 12 4. **23. Five hundred and fifty**] These were probably the officers who directed the labour of the 30,000 native Israelites : 2 Ch 8 10 has 250. **24. Unto her house**] see 7 8. For Millo see on v. 15. **25. Three times in a year**] see 2 Ch 8 13, and cp. Ex 23 14-17 34 23 Dt 16 1-17.

26. Ezion-geber .. Eloth] The two places were at the N. extremity of the gulf of Akaba. **28. Ophir**] variously identified with the Indian coast (near the mouth of the Indus), the E. coast of Africa (Abyssinia or Somaliland), and S. Arabia. In favour of the latter is the fact that in Gn 10 29 Ophir is represented as the son of Joktan, the ancestor of several Arabian tribes. **Four hundred and twenty talents**] For the weight of a talent see 9 14.

CHAPTER 10

SOLOMON AND THE QUEEN OF SHEBA

1. Sheba] the Sheba of Gn 10 28 (in Arabia), not of Gn 10 7 (in Africa). Arabia seems frequently to have been ruled by queens; more than one is mentioned in the Assyrian inscriptions. If Ophir was in Arabia (see on 9 28), it may have been through the traders at that port that the queen here alluded to had heard of Solomon.

Hard questions] These were probably of the nature of puzzles or riddles, the same word being used of Samson's riddle (Jg 14 12). Legend relates that one of the puzzles that Solomon was set to solve was how to distinguish between a bunch of natural and a bunch of artificial flowers without leaving his seat to examine them. The king ordered the windows of the room to be opened, and the bees, coming in, alighted on the former and ignored the latter.

5. His ascent, etc.] perhaps better, 'his burnt offering which he offered in.'

9. Blessed be the LORD] cp. the language of the Phœnician Hiram (5⁷).

11. Almug trees] conjectured to be sandal wood. 2 Ch 9¹⁰ has 'algum trees.' **12. Pillars**] RM 'a railing,' or balustrade for the staircase : cp. 2 Ch 9¹¹. **Harps . . psalteries**] The former probably had a square frame, with the sound-box at the base ; the latter may have been triangular in shape, with the sound-box forming one of the sides.

15. The kings of Arabia] RV 'kings of the mingled people,' i.e. the population of mixed descent which lived on the confines of the kingdom. The same word is used of the 'mixed multitude' that came up with Israel out of Egypt (Ex 12³⁸). **16. Targets**] large shields. *Shekels*] a shekel was 224 grains. The shields were probably overlaid with the gold, not made of it. **17. Pound**] Heb. *maneh*. This contained 50 shekels. **The house . . Lebanon**] see on 7². The shields here described were taken away by Shishak in the reign of Rehoboam (14²⁶). **19. The top of the throne**] perhaps a canopy over the throne, of which the stays were the arms.

22. A navy of Tharshish] better, 'Tharshish ship,' i.e. a stoutly-built vessel, such as was accustomed to voyage to Tartessus in Spain, or perhaps Tarsus in Cilicia, but which Solomon probably sent to Ophir (see 9²⁶⁻²⁸ 10¹¹), since Ezion-geber was his port.

27. Sycomore trees] not the English sycamore, but a kind of fig-tree. **In the vale**] RV 'in the lowland,' i.e. the downs between the hills of Judah and the coast.

28. Horses . . Egypt] The Jews depended upon Egypt for horses not only at this time, but also in the reign of Hezekiah (Isa 31¹ 36⁹), and at a still later date (Ezk 17¹⁵). **Linen yarn**] This should probably be rendered 'droves,' and connected with the following clause—'and in droves the king's merchants received them, each drove at a price.' But for 'in droves' the LXX has 'from Tekoa,' where there may have been a horse fair, whilst the Latin has 'from Coa' (i.e. Cilicia).

29. The Hittites] This people were probably of Mongolian race, and drew their origin from Cappadocia. They came in contact with Israel chiefly on its northern border (Jg 1²⁶).

By their means] Heb. 'in their hand,' i.e. with them. Solomon's merchants conducted the profitable traffic in horses between Egypt and the various states on the N. and NE. of Palestine.

CHAPTER 11
SOLOMON'S ERRORS AND THEIR CONSEQUENCES. HIS DEATH

This c. furnishes an account of Solomon's marriages with numerous foreign princesses, and traces the evil effect of such in the toleration of idolatry, which provoked the LORD's anger. This was manifested in the growth of opposition abroad and disaffection at home, so that an otherwise brilliant reign had a cloudy ending.

3. Seven hundred wives] The Persian king Darius Codomannus is said to have had, besides his own wife, 329 concubines. **4. Not perfect**] Solomon's heart was divided between the LORD and other gods. Without abandoning the service of Jehovah, he tolerated, and even took part in, the religious rites practised by his wives. His luxury and sensuality led to more serious errors still. **5. Ashtoreth**] the Phœnician name of the goddess worshipped by the Babylonians under the title of Ishtar, the goddess of love. **Milcom**] identical with the Molech of v. 7. **7. Build an high place**] i.e. construct an altar or sanctuary upon a height. **Chemosh**] The name of this god occurs on the inscription of Mesha, king of Moab, who was contemporary with Ahab. **Before Jerusalem**] i.e. E. of Jerusalem, the corresponding expression 'behind' being used to denote the W. (Josh 8⁴﹐⁹ Dt 11²⁴ RV). The hill here designated is the Mt. of Olives : cp. Ezk 11²³.

15. David . . Edom] see 2 S 8¹⁴. **Joab**] cp. Ps 60 (title). According to 1 Ch 18¹² the actual victory over the Edomites was gained by Abishai, the brother of Joab. **18. Midian . . Paran**] NE. and N of the Sinaitic peninsula.

19. Pharaoh] either the Egyptian king whose daughter Solomon had married, or his predecessor. **23. Zobah**] a small Syrian state lying eastward of Mt. Hermon. **24. Damascus**] According to 2 S 8⁶ David had placed garrisons in Damascus, which Rezon and his followers must have expelled.

26. Ephrathite] i.e. an Ephraimite (as in 1 S 1¹), not a Bethlehemite (as in Ruth 1²).

28. Made him . . charge] RV 'gave him charge over all the labour'; see 5¹³﹐¹⁴. As the system of forced labour introduced by Solomon had as its object the adornment of his capital, which was most closely connected with Judah and Benjamin, it would be the more resented by the other tribes : cp. 12⁴﹐¹⁶. Jeroboam's position enabled him to detect and work upon the discontent, which would be strongest in Ephraim, inasmuch as in the times of Joshua and the Judges it had enjoyed the preëminence which had now passed to Judah.

29. The Shilonite] i.e. a native of Shiloh (14²). **30. Rent it . . pieces**] The prophets frequently illustrated the meaning of their utterances by the use of impressive symbolic actions: see 22¹¹ Isa 20²ᶠ. Jer 19¹⁻¹³ Ezk 12 Zech 11⁷﹐¹⁰﹐¹⁴.

32. One tribe] in 12²¹﹐²³ Benjamin is reckoned with Judah, but see on 12²⁰. **36. A**

light] cp. Ps 132[17] and contrast Job 18[6]. The figure is drawn from the fire or lamp which is usually associated with a permanent habitation. **38. If thou wilt hearken**] the same condition as in 9[4]. **A sure house**] i.e. a long and unbroken line of descendants. As the condition imposed was not fulfilled, the promise was not carried out, and Jeroboam's house was extirpated in the second generation by Baasha.

39. Not for ever] in spite of the humiliation suffered by the house of David through Jeroboam's revolt, the Davidic dynasty in Judah outlasted the kingdom of the Ten Tribes; and though it finally lost all temporal power, it attained higher preëminence than ever when Christ was born of Mary, a descendant of David. **40. Sought . . to kill**] This implies that Jeroboam had excited the king's suspicions by some open act of disloyalty. **Shishak**] i.e. Sheshonk, the first king of the 22nd dynasty, of Libyan descent.

41. The book, etc.] probably a history based on the official documents kept by the ' recorder.'

The instructiveness of Solomon's history is twofold. (1) Outward zeal for the honour of the LORD, such as Solomon showed by building the Temple, is no proof of inward devotion. (2) Material blessings bestowed by God (like the wealth and honour conferred on Solomon) bring with them increased temptations, needing divine grace for their conquest.

CHAPTER 12
THE REVOLT OF THE TEN TRIBES. REHOBOAM AND JEROBOAM

The revolt of the Ten Tribes against the rule of Rehoboam had its origin partly in the discontent which the burdens laid on the people by Solomon had created and which Jeroboam (who knew of it, see 11[28]) had perhaps stimulated, and partly in the jealousy subsisting between the northern tribes and Judah, which had manifested itself previously in the separate kingdoms of Ish-bosheth and David, and the insurrections that disturbed David's reign over the whole people (2 S 20[1]); whilst the bond of union constituted by a common religious faith must have been weakened by Solomon's idolatry.

1. Shechem] The principal town of Ephraim (the modern Nâblûs): it had manifestly been restored after its destruction as related in Jg 9[45]. The choice of this city as the place of assembly was due partly to the importance of Ephraim as a tribe, and partly to its nearness to a sanctuary (that on Mt. Ebal, Josh 8[30]). It was a gathering place for the tribes in Joshua's days (Josh 24[1]). **For all Israel . . king**] The tribal spirit of independence was still sufficiently strong to make it necessary

for the Judæan Rehoboam to receive separately the homage of the other tribes. **2. Dwelt in Egypt**] LXX has 'returned from Egypt.'

3. Called him] This implies that Jeroboam was known to sympathise with the grievances under which the people laboured. **4. Made our yoke grievous**] i.e. by the forced labour imposed upon them (5[13]). **7. If thou wilt be a servant**] i.e. by making timely concessions to his people. **10. My little** *finger*] a figurative expression, explained by what follows.

11. Scorpions] a rod or lash used in scourging. **15. The cause . . LORD**] i.e. the turn of events was the means appointed by God's providence to bring about the punishment merited by Solomon's sin (11[11-13]).

16. What portion] for this signal of revolt cp. 2 S 20[1]. **Now see . . house**] a declaration of independence and a warning against further interference. **17. Children of Israel . . Judah**] probably, in the main, members of the tribe of Simeon: cp. 1 K 19[3] with Josh 15[28]. **18. Adoram**] cp. 2 S 20[24]. He is called Adoniram in 4[6]. **Tribute**] RV 'levy.' **Stoned him**] Stones were the usual weapons in outbreaks of popular fury: cp. Ex 17[4] 1 S 30[6]. **19. Unto this day**] This passage must originally have been written not only before the destruction of Jerusalem but of Samaria: cp. 8[8].

20. The tribe of Judah only] This accords with the words of Ahijah in 11[32]; and if the remaining tribes that fell to Jeroboam are reckoned as ten (11[31]) and not eleven, the explanation is to be found in the omission of Levi (as the priestly tribe) and in regarding Ephraim and Manasseh as constituting the single tribe of Joseph: cp. 11[28]. But in vv. 21, 23, Benjamin is joined with Judah as belonging to Rehoboam; and this, in large measure, was really the case, the frontier between the two kingdoms lying within that tribe. Simeon, too, by its position must have been practically absorbed by Judah.

22. Shemaiah] mentioned again in 2 Ch 12[5,7,15]. **23. The remnant of the people**] i.e. those belonging by lineage to the other tribes: cp. v. 17.

25. Built] i.e. fortified: cp. 9[17]. **Penuel**] in Gilead, E. of Jordan: cp. Jg 8[8].

26. Now shall . . David] Jeroboam feared that if his people still went to Jerusalem three times a year to keep the feasts, they would be tempted to return to their allegiance to Rehoboam. He had not sufficient faith in God's power to bring about His promises (11[38]), and so adopted measures to safeguard his newly-won throne which branded his name for ever with infamy (cp. 14[16]), and brought calamity both on his house and his people.

28. Two calves *of* **gold**] The calves were not intended as substitutes for the LORD (Jehovah) but as symbols of Him, as appears from the king's words to the people. It has been thought by some that such symbols were derived from Egypt where the living bull Apis was worshipped, and where Jeroboam had lived in exile. But the calves which he set up were probably imitations of the calf made in the wilderness by Aaron ; and it is scarcely likely that the Israelites, when escaping from Egypt, would, to represent their own God, borrow an emblem from their task-masters. It is more probable that a calf or young bull was chosen as a religious symbol because to an agricultural people the bull was a natural emblem of force and vigour. But though Jeroboam, in setting up the calves, did not break the first commandment of the Decalogue, he yet violated the second, and from motives of state policy (vv. 26, 27) corrupted the religious worship of his people, not only by making it sensuous instead of spiritual, but by employing symbols which represented merely Jehovah's power (whether displayed in creation or destruction) and altogether failed to suggest His highest attributes—those of righteousness, holiness, and love. That these coarse symbols long continued to be worshipped appears from Hos 8[5,6] 10[5]. **Thy gods**] The plural is used because there was more than one image, but the same God was represented by both.

29. Beth-el.. Dan] on the S. border of Ephraim and in the N. of Naphtali respectively, and so at the two extremities of the kingdom to meet the convenience of the people. Both places had previously been the seats of religious worship : see, for Bethel, Gn 28[1-22] 35[1,7] Jg 20[26] 1 S 10[3] ; and for Dan, Jg 18[30]. Jeroboam hoped to revive their ancient popularity. **30. Before the one**] The text is incomplete : RM 'before each of them.'

31. An house of high places] LXX 'made houses (i.e. sanctuaries) upon high places' : see on 3[2]. **Of the lowest of the people**] better, 'from all the people indiscriminately.' In Dt the priesthood is restricted to the Levites (see on 8[4]), and the narrator judges Jeroboam's conduct from the standpoint of the Deuteronomic law.

32. The feast] i.e. the Feast of Tabernacles or Ingathering, on the 15th day of the 7th month. The new feast instituted by Jeroboam was placed a month later, probably on account of the later date of the vintage in N. Palestine. **He placed in Beth-el**] Bethel appears to have been, at least in later times, the royal sanctuary (Am 7[13]). **33. Of his own heart**] For political and self-regarding reasons he disturbed the hallowed associations which had gathered round the month previously set apart for the Festival of Ingathering. **He offered upon the altar**] The king himself officiated as priest. The v. is closely connected with 13[1].

CHAPTER 13
THE DISOBEDIENT PROPHET

2. Josiah] for the fulfilment see 2 K 23[15-20]. Some 300 years separated the prediction from the event, and the mention by name of the king destined to accomplish it is unlike the methods of Hebrew prophecy in general. It is possible that the records upon which the present account is based were less precise, and that Josiah's name was introduced by the compiler of the book of Kings, who lived after Josiah's time and was familiar with what he had done. **Offer**] better, 'slaughter.' They would not be offered in sacrifice. **3. A sign**] The fulfilment of the prediction in v. 3 would be a warranty for the fulfilment of the prediction in v. 2 : cp. 1 S 2[34] Isa 38[7,8].

8. I will not .. thee] The prophet, who had come from Judah, was not to hold any friendly intercourse with the offending nation, or receive hospitality within its borders.

11. There dwelt .. Beth-el] The fact that the old prophet remained at Bethel and acquiesced without protest in the king's idolatry indicated that he was not loyal to the principles of spiritual religion. Being unfaithful himself he became the tempter of others (v. 18).

22. Shall not come .. fathers] This was esteemed a dishonour : cp. 2 Ch 21[20].

24. A lion] for lions in Palestine cp. Jg 14[5] 1 S 17[34] 2 S 23[20] 1 K 20[36] 2 K 17[25]. Their chief haunt would be the jungle in the Jordan valley.

28. The lion had not eaten] So strange an occurrence was calculated to attract attention to the prophet's fate **31. Lay my bones,** etc.] To prevent them from sharing the dishonour which the man of God had said would befall the graves at Bethel : see 2 K 23[17,18].

The moral conveyed by the fate of the prophet from Judah is that those who, like the old prophet of Bethel, are false to their own manifest duties (see on v. 11), are to be distrusted when they offer advice in matters of right and wrong.

33. Consecrated] see on Ex 28[41] 29[24].

CHAPTER 14
THE SINS OF JEROBOAM AND REHOBOAM AND THEIR PUNISHMENT

2. Shiloh] The modern Seilûn, N. of Bethel and E. of the road leading from Bethel to Shechem (Jg 21[19]). **3. Take with thee**] The gift proffered by the queen was a small one to suit her disguise : contrast 2 K 5[5]. **Cruse**] a flask or bottle (and so in 17[12]). **9. Above all that were before thee**] Solomon's idolatry was perhaps worse than Jeroboam's in being the worship of false gods, but it was at any rate not deliberately propagated among the people at large.

10. Shut up and left] A comprehensive phrase to describe all classes, but its precise signification is uncertain. It has been taken to mean (*a*) restrained by, and free from, ceremonial impurity (which prevented persons suffering from it from entering the Temple, cp. Jer 36⁵); (*b*) imprisoned and free (cp. Jer 33¹); (*c*) married and single; (*d*) under, and over, age. **Will . . remnant**] For the fulfilment of the prediction see 15²⁹. **13. He only . . grave**] Abijah, for his goodness, was taken away from the evil to come (cp. Isa 57¹), though it is possible that the reward of his piety is meant to be not a timely death, but an honourable burial. **14. But what? even now**] i.e. is not the predicted event happening even now?

15. The river] i.e. the Euphrates. **Groves**] RV ' Asherim ' (pl. of Asherah), and so in v. 23 and elsewhere. These were poles used as religious emblems (cp. Isa 17⁸), and were probably intended to imitate trees, which, from being endowed with life and growth, were in early ages thought to be the abodes of divine powers, and so were regarded as appropriate seats of worship : cp. v. 23. Though perhaps most commonly associated with Ashtoreth, the goddess of fertility and productiveness, they were not the exclusive symbols of any particular deity ; and the Israelites were inclined to adopt them even in connexion with the worship of their own God, as may be gathered from the prohibition against planting ' an Asherah of any kind of tree beside the altar of the LORD ' (Dt 16²¹ RV), and the fact that though Jehu restored in Israel the worship of the LORD, yet in the reign of his son Jehoahaz ' there remained the Asherah in Samaria ' (2 K 13⁶ RV). **17. Tirzah**] afterwards the capital, until Samaria was built by Omri (see 15³³ 16⁸,¹⁵,²³). It was NW. of Shechem, overlooking the Jordan valley. **19. The rest of the acts of Jeroboam**] see 2 Ch 13³⁻²⁰, which describes a severe defeat which he sustained at the hands of Abijah of Judah. **The book of the chronicles**] probably annals based on the state documents kept by the official recorder. A similar reference occurs in connexion with most of the following reigns. **21. Forty and one years old**] It is implied in 12⁸ 2 Ch 13³ that Rehoboam was young when he came to the throne ; and one MS of the LXX here substitutes ' sixteen years old.' **His mother's name**] the name of the mother of each succeeding king (see 15¹⁰ 22⁴² 2 K 8²⁵, etc.) is expressly mentioned because of the position which the queen dowager occupied : see on 2¹⁹. **23. Images**] RV ' pillars ' : for their significance see on 7¹⁵. **24. Sodomites**] Persons who dedicated themselves to the impure rites which were observed in honour of certain deities in the neighbourhood of their temples.

25. Shishak] see on 11⁴⁰. A list of towns taken by Shishak has been preserved in an inscription by the conqueror himself at Karnak in Egypt. Among them were Keilah, Socoh, Aijalon, Beth-horon. Gibeon and Makkedah in Judah, and Taanach, Shunem, and Mahanaim in N. Israel. The mention of Israelite as well as Judæan towns seems to imply that Shishak attacked both of the Hebrew sovereigns, unless the towns in Israel were in revolt against Jeroboam, and the Egyptians were helping him to reduce them. **31. Abijam**] called Abijah in LXX and in 2 Ch 12¹⁶. The latter is probably the correct form of the name.

CHAPTER 15
THE REIGNS OF ABIJAM AND ASA, NADAB AND BAASHA

2. Abishalom] i.e. Absalom. In 2 Ch 13² his mother is called Micaiah, the daughter of Uriel, and if this is correct, Absalom was probably her grandfather, and her mother the Tamar mentioned in 2 S 14²⁷. **4. A lamp**] see on 11³⁶. The divine promise made to David prevented Abijam's sins from being punished by the transfer of the throne to another line. **6. There was war . . life**] a repetition of 14³⁰. 2 Ch 13² has ' between Abijah and Jeroboam.' **7. The rest of the acts**] In 2 Ch 13³ᶠ· there is described a great battle between Judah and Israel. Before the engagement Abijah (Abijam) contrasted the worship of the calves and the expulsion of the Levitical priests by Jeroboam with the different practices followed by the kings of Judah. Jeroboam laid an ambush for the Judæans, but the latter called upon the LORD, who delivered them, and Israel was not only defeated but lost several cities. **10. Maachah**] If the Maachah of v. 2 is meant, mother must mean ' grandmother.' **13. From *being* queen**] i.e. from being queen dowager : see on 2¹⁹. **An idol in a grove**] better, ' an abominable image for Asherah.' The term Asherah here seems to mean not an emblem but a goddess : cp. 18¹⁹ 2 K 21⁷. **By the brook Kidron**] better, ' in the torrent valley of the Kidron,' i.e. the ravine E. of Jerusalem, between the city and the Mount of Olives (mod. Wâdy Sitti Maryam). **14. The high places were not removed**] The same condition of things continued until the reign of Hezekiah : see 1 K 22⁴³ 2 K 12³ 18⁴. **15. Brought in . . of the LORD**] to replace the losses sustained in the invasion of Shishak (14²⁶). **17. Ramah**] the modern er Râm, on the S. frontier of the kingdom, some 5 m. N. of Jerusalem, which it menaced. **18. Sent them to Ben-hadad**] Asa's appeal to Syria illustrates how far the Jewish kingdom had declined since

Solomon's time. Probably three kings of this name are mentioned in OT. : see 20 1 2 K 13 24.

19. *There is* **a league,** etc.] Asa, as the descendant of David, to whom the Syrians had submitted (2 S 8 6), urged that Syria's connexion with the royal house of Judah was of longer standing than its connexion with the house of Baasha ; but he ignored the revolt of Damascus in the reign of Solomon. **Break thy league**] As Israel cut Syria off from the sea, Benhadad would be the more willing to accept Asa's overtures. In 2 Ch 16 7-10 Asa's conduct is represented as being condemned by the seer Hanani. **20. Ijon, Dan,** etc.] localities in the neighbourhood of Lake Merom and the Sea of Galilee. **Cinneroth** is the Gennesaret of the NT. **21. Left off . . Ramah**] The invasion in the N. prevented further operations in the S. **Dwelt in Tirzah**] LXX has 'returned to Tirzah,' which suits the context better.

22. Geba . . Mizpah] fortresses N. of Jerusalem.

23. The rest of all the acts of Asa] see 2 Ch 14 9 f. The chief incidents added by Chronicles are the defeat of an invasion by the Ethiopian Zerah, the making of a national covenant with the LORD, the king's punishment of the seer Hanani for censuring his alliance with Syria, and his oppression of his people. **27. Gibbethon**] within the territory assigned to Dan (Josh 19 44). The Philistines, who had been crushed by David, now that the Hebrew kingdoms were in conflict, once more began to move. **29. The saying of the LORD**] see 14 7-11. The personal ambition of Baasha was the agency through which the LORD punished the house of Jeroboam for the sins of its founder. The decay of spiritual religion in N. Israel was accompanied by the weakening of moral restraints, and none of the dynasties that successively occupied the throne lasted longer than four generations.

CHAPTER 16

THE REIGNS OF ELAH, ZIMRI, AND OMRI

1. Jehu the son of Hanani] Hanani is mentioned in 2 Ch 16 7-10. Jehu's denunciation of Baasha is similar to Ahijah's denunciation of Jeroboam (14 7-11). **9. As he was . . drunk**] Elah's incapacity and dissoluteness doubtless tempted Zimri to aspire to the throne.

13. Vanities] i.e. idols, and so in v. 26. **15. Gibbethon**] see 15 27. The siege, begun in the reign of Nadab, had apparently not succeeded, and had been resumed. **18. Palace**] RV 'castle.' **19. For his sins,** etc.] The phrase is a stereotyped one, and so is applied to Zimri in spite of the fact that he only reigned seven days.

23. In the thirty and first year of Asa] probably an error : v. 27 gives 'in the twenty-seventh year of Asa.' **24. The hill Samaria**] This stood in the middle of a wide and fertile valley (cp. Isa 28 1), and was a place of great natural strength, as is evidenced by the protracted sieges sustained by the city that was built upon it (2 K 6 24 17 5). **Called the name . . Samaria**] Heb. *Shōmeron.*

27. The rest . . Omri] Omri seems to have engaged in war with the Syrians, but was so unsuccessful that he had to grant them the privilege of having 'streets' (i.e. trading quarters) in Samaria (20 34). Two additional facts respecting Omri's reign are furnished by certain inscriptions. (*a*) On the Moabite Stone it is stated by Mesha, the king of Moab, that Omri 'afflicted' that country. (*b*) On the Assyrian monuments Israel is regularly termed 'the land of Omri,' a designation which suggests that it was in his reign that the Assyrians came first into contact with Israel. It was probably in view of Assyrian aggression that Omri cemented an alliance with the king of Zidon and Tyre (Ethbaal) by a marriage between his own son Ahab and the Zidonian princess Jezebel (v. 31). According to Menander, Ethbaal (Gk. *Ithobalos*) was the great-grandfather of Dido, the founder of Carthage.

31. Served Baal] Baal was merely a title (meaning 'lord' or 'owner') and was applicable to a number of deities (hence the plural Baalim) who were described as the Baals of particular localities ('Baal Peor,' 'Baal Hermon'). The introduction into Israel of the worship of the Zidonian Baal was more dangerous than that of other Baals in proportion as it was more powerfully supported ; whilst Ahab's sin was worse than Jeroboam's, since the calves worshipped by the latter were at least symbols of the LORD.

34. Did . . build] i.e. fortified. Jericho, in the Jordan valley, a little N. of the Dead Sea, had been rebuilt since its destruction by Joshua, for it is mentioned in David's time (2 S 10 5). **In Abiram**] RV 'with the loss of Abiram.' **The word of the LORD**] see Josh 6 26. For the potency believed to attach to a curse see Nu 22 6 2 K 2 24. Possibly the mention of Hiel's conduct in fortifying Jericho in spite of the malediction of Joshua is intended to illustrate the prevalent lack of faith in Jehovah's power.

CHAPTER 17

ELIJAH AND THE WIDOW OF ZAREPHATH

The prophet Elijah, who occupies so large a space in the succeeding history, is, like his successor Elisha, conspicuous among the prophetic figures of the OT. as a worker of miracles ; and to him belongs the further distinction of having been removed from earth without dying. His prophecies differed from those of most later prophets in having in view only certain critical occasions of contemporary history, and in having no reference to the remote future or the Messianic age, though the moral and religious principles which they affirmed had, of course, a wide application.

1. Of the inhabitants of Gilead] RM 'according to LXX, of Tishbeh of Gilead.' **Said unto Ahab**] Nothing is related about the reason for the drought which the prophet predicted ; but the cause was doubtless Ahab's idolatry (16 31-33 : cp. Lv 26 19 Dt 11 17). Josephus quotes a Tyrian historian who states that a drought occurred during the reign of Ethbaal (the king of Tyre and Zidon named in 16 31), which lasted a year. **3. Hide thyself**] The prophets of the LORD were in danger from the anger of Jezebel : cp. 18 13.

Brook] strictly, a ravine or torrent-valley. **Before Jordan**] i.e. E. of Jordan, in the Gilead he was familiar with. **4. The ravens**] The original may possibly mean 'traffickers' (or merchants) or 'Arabians' : if this is the real meaning of the word, the command resembles that given in v. 9.

9. Zarephath] The 'Sarepta' of Lk 4 26. The modern Sarafend. It lay between Tyre and Zidon, and, from its nearness to these localities, might be a safe, because unsuspected, hiding-place. **12. As the LORD . . liveth**] Elijah was probably recognised by speech or dress as an Israelite. **May eat it, and die**] implying that the drought and consequent famine extended to Zarephath : see on v. 1.

16. The barrel, etc.] cp. the miracle of Elisha (2 K 4 42-44).

18. To call . . to remembrance] The presence with her of a prophet whom the divine care watched over might (she feared) attract God's attention to herself and to some past sin which seemed to have been overlooked. **19. A loft**] better, 'the upper chamber': cp. 2 K 4 10.

20. Hast thou . . evil] A like despondency is observable in the prophet's language in 19 4. Here he complains that evil dogs his steps wherever he turns and fastens even on those who befriend him. **21. Stretched himself**] As though to convey the warmth of life from his own frame to that of the dead child: cp. 2 K 4 34 Ac 20 10.

CHAPTER 18

JEHOVAH OR BAAL ?

1. In the third year] in Lk 4 25 Jas 5 17 the duration of the famine is given as 3 years and 6 months. **3. The governor of *his* house**] The same office as that alluded to in 4 6 16 9. **Feared the LORD greatly**] His name ('Servant of Jehovah ') was a true index of his character. **4. Cut off the prophets**] Nothing is related of this beyond what is implied in 19 10. **12. The Spirit . . thee**] cp.

2 K 2 16 : the prophet's movements being directed toward different and higher purposes than those of ordinary men, his friends would have no clue to guide them in tracing him.

17. *Art* thou he . . Israel ?] RV 'Is it thou, thou troubler of Israel ? ' : alluding to Elijah's prediction in 17 1. **18. Baalim**] RV ' the Baalim ' : i.e. the Baals : see on 16 31.

19. Carmel] The only promontory on the coast of Palestine, rising at the summit to nearly 1,800 ft. above the sea. **The prophets of the groves**] better, ' the prophets of Asherah ' (the term here apparently denoting a deity). These prophets are not mentioned in the sequel.

21. Halt] not in the sense of suspending judgment, but of pursuing a vacillating and irregular course, serving at one time Baal and at another time the LORD (Jehovah). The word literally means 'limping.' **And the people, etc.**] They were reluctant to break with either form of worship. **22. I, *even* I only**] The other prophets of the LORD, if not destroyed (see v. 4), were at any rate silenced.

24. Your gods] RV ' your god ' : and so in v. 25. **The LORD**] better, ' Jehovah,' and so in v. 39. **The God that . . fire**] For the consumption of sacrifices by fire from heaven, cp. Lv 9 24 1 Ch 21 26 2 Ch 7 1.

In the minds of the multitude the question to be decided doubtless was not whether Jehovah or Baal was the sole god, but which of them was the more powerful god, and, therefore, had the greater claim upon the nation's devotion. It was not until a later date that it was explicitly asserted by the prophets that Jehovah was the only Deity and that beside Him there was no other (Isa 44 6, 8 45 5, 6). Elijah, as his mocking language in v. 27 suggests, must have come near to holding the same belief, though the fact that he denounced Ahaziah for consulting a foreign, not an imaginary, god (2 K 1 6) seems to imply that he had not quite attained to it.

25. Dress *it* first] The contrast between Jehovah's power and Baal's impotence would thus be more impressive. **26. Leaped upon**] RV ' leaped about': lit. 'limped about': i.e. they performed an irregular and uncouth dance round the altar. **27. Talking**] RV ' musing ': i.e. lost in meditation. **Pursuing**] RV 'gone aside.' **28. Cut themselves**] Gashing the body was frequently practised by the votaries of heathen deities, probably for the purpose of making a ' blood covenant ' between themselves and the god they worshipped.

Lancets] should be 'lances.' **29. Prophesied**] i.e. gave utterance to fervid and ecstatic cries : cp. 1 S 10 5. **The *evening* sacrifice**] the same as ' the evening meat (i.e. meal) offering' of 2 K 16 15.

30. The altar . . down] Carmel had been a

' high place ' dedicated to the worship of Jehovah, but the spread of Baal worship had led to its neglect, and the altar on it had been overthrown (19 10). **31. Twelve stones]** In spite of the partition of the Hebrew tribes into two kingdoms, a sense of their original unity was continually present with the prophets, and certain of them looked forward to their reunion: see Hos 1 11 Jer 3 18 Ezk 37 15-22.

Israel .. thy name] see Gn 32 28 35 10.

32. Measures] Heb. *seahs*, a seah being $\frac{3}{10}$ of an ephah, about 2½ gallons. **33. Fill .. with water]** A well still exists a little below the summit of Carmel. **37. Thou** *art* **the LORD God]** better, ' Thou Jehovah art God.'

39. The LORD .. God] better, ' Jehovah, He (not Baal) is the God.'

40. The brook Kishon] a stream flowing into the Mediterranean at the foot of Carmel. **Slew them there]** in accord with the spirit of Dt 13 6-11 17 2-7. The prophet probably was not himself their executioner, but made the people give practical evidence of the sincerity of their conversion.

42. Cast himself down] in fervent prayer : cp. Jas 5 17. **43. Seven times]** used vaguely of a considerable number : cp. Ps 12 6 119 164.

44. Like a man's hand] i.e. in size.

45. There was a great rain] Solomon's prayer (in 8 35, 36) that if the people turned from their sin, the LORD would send rain upon the land was now granted. **46. The hand of the LORD .. Elijah]** i.e. the prophet acted under a divine impulse : cp. 2 K 3 15. **To the entrance of Jezreel]** between 15 and 20 m. from Carmel. Ahab had a palace there (21 1).

The contest on Mt. Carmel was of the greatest importance for the future of religion in Israel, for it determined whether Jehovah, whose character was moral and spiritual, was to command the exclusive allegiance of the people, or was to share their devotion with the god of Zidon, who, like other Baals, was a nature-god, and whose worship was associated with unspiritual ideas and immoral rites. But whilst it primarily relates to a particular crisis in the history of a single people, it is also typical of every conflict in which opposite principles of conduct meet, and in which the need of prompt decision must always be as urgent as in the days of Elijah.

CHAPTER 19
ELIJAH AT HOREB

2. Then Jezebel sent, etc.] Her religious feelings as a votary of Baal and her dignity as the queen had both been outraged by the prophet, and she at once sought revenge.

3. And when he saw *that*, etc.] In men of impetuous disposition displays of fiery courage often alternate with moods of despondency. Elijah's character resembled that of St. Peter,

who first struck a blow in defence of his Master and then denied Him (Jn 18 10, 15 f.).

Beer-sheba] within the territory of the tribe of Judah, but assigned to Simeon (Josh 15 28 19 2). It was a sanctuary in the time of Amos, and may have been the same in the time of Elijah.

4. Into the wilderness] Since the king of Judah was an ally of Ahab, the prophet did not consider himself safe from Jezebel's fury until he was beyond Judæan territory. **A juniper tree]** a kind of broom, with purplish white flowers, that grows to the height of 10 or 12 ft. **Requested .. might die]** The nervous tension caused by the scene on Carmel was now succeeded by reaction and exhaustion. Elijah felt that he had been no more successful in checking the nation's apostasy than the prophets who had been before him.

6. Coals] perhaps stones heated by a fire of wood, kindled with twigs of broom : cp. Ps 120 4.

8. Horeb] i.e. Sinai. The forty days and forty nights are not to be taken as a measure of the distance of Horeb from the prophet's starting-point (vv. 3, 4), for this (about 180 m.) could be traversed in a much shorter time, but are meant to associate Elijah with Moses (see Ex 24 18 Dt 9 11, 18). In solitary communion with God, such as Moses had enjoyed, the prophet would recover his fortitude. **The mount of God]** cp. Ex 3 1. Horeb had probably been a sanctuary even before Moses' time.

10. Thine altars .. thy prophets] cp. 18 30, 13.

11. The LORD passed by] All the experiences here described formed part of a single manifestation of the divine presence, but the earlier stages did not reveal God in the same degree as the last. Elsewhere in the OT. wind, fire, and earthquake are frequent accompaniments of a Theophany : see Ex 19 18 Ps 18 7-13 97 3-5 2 S 5 24 Job 38 1 Ezk 1 4.

12. A still small voice] cp. Job 4 16. The LXX renders, ' the sound of a gentle breeze.' The hurricane, the earthquake, the lightning, were all tokens and agencies of God, but none disclosed Him so convincingly as the peaceful calm that followed the tempest. It awakened, and blended with, the prophet's conscience ; and he thus came to realise the true value of patience and forbearance in the furtherance of the divine purposes, as compared with the violence which he himself had displayed in his conflict with idolatry (18 40).

13. He wrapped his face in his mantle] in awe at the near presence of God. Moses similarly hid his face when God addressed him out of the bush (Ex 3 6). **14. I have been very jealous]** The prophet, as yet unsubdued by the influences of the scene, returned the same indignant answer as before (v. 10).

15. The wilderness of Damascus] i.e. the

Syrian desert in which D. is situated. **Anoint**] not used in a strict sense, since neither Hazael nor Elisha is described as having been anointed, whilst Jehu was anointed not by Elijah but by a young prophet commissioned by Elisha (2 K 9). The lesson which the direction given to Elijah in this v. conveyed was that he still had work to do even though he might not see the issue of it. He was not to relinquish it as he had desired (v. 4), just because he was himself unsuccessful, but was to transmit it to others, and so pave the way for success in the distant future. **Hazael**] see 2 K 8⁸ᶠ.

16. Jehu the son of Nimshi] He was really son of Jehoshaphat and grandson of Nimshi (2 K 9²). **17. The sword of Hazael**] For the calamities brought on Israel by Hazael see 2 K 10³². **The sword of Jehu**] For the destruction of the house of Ahab by Jehu see 2 K 9 and 10. **Shall Elisha slay**] doubtless through the agency of others. The prophets are frequently described as effecting what they enjoin or announce (Hos 6⁵ Jer 1¹⁰).

18. I have left] better, 'I will leave.' Elijah was mistaken in thinking that he was the only survivor of the LORD's loyal servants. Jehovah's cause was not desperate because His prophet had fled from the field of conflict. **Kissed him**] For this as an act of devotion see Hos 13². In Job 31²⁶,²⁷ sun-worshippers are described as kissing their hand to the object of their adoration. **19.** *With* **twelve yoke**] Elijah himself guided only one 'yoke' (or pair), the remaining eleven being in charge of his servants. **His mantle**] A hairy mantle was the characteristic garb of the prophets (Zech 13⁴). **20. What have I done to thee?**] whatever sacrifice was involved in the prophetic call was to be made ungrudgingly. Elijah, like our Lord, would have no half-hearted service : cp. Lk 9⁵⁹⁻⁶². **21. The instruments of the oxen**] The wooden yoke and the framework of the plough served as fuel : cp. 2 S 24²².

CHAPTER 20
WAR BETWEEN ISRAEL AND SYRIA

The Syrians besiege Samaria, but a sally being made from the city by the direction of a prophet, they are driven off, and the next year are beaten at Aphek. Ahab, having spared Benhadad the Syrian king, is rebuked by a prophet in the name of the LORD.

1. Ben-hadad] probably the son of the Benhadad mentioned in 15¹⁸. In the Assyrian inscription he is termed Dad-idri, i.e. Hadadezer. The history here reverts to the Syrian attacks upon Israel made originally at the instigation of Judah (15²⁰). **Thirty and two kings**] probably vassal princes : cp. v. 24. **14. The young men .. provinces**] the servants (or esquires) of the Israelite chiefs who had been driven by the Syrian invasion from the pro-

vinces into the capital. **16. At noon**] a time when the beleaguering host would be resting during the heat of the day. **20. With the horsemen**] RV 'with horsemen' : i.e. with some mounted attendants. **21. Smote**] the LXX has 'took.' To aid his pursuit Ahab took the horses abandoned by the Syrians.

22. See what thou doest] i.e. consider what thou shouldest do, take the necessary precautions. **At the return of the year**] in the spring, when military operations would again be possible : cp. 2 S 11¹.

23. Their gods .. the hills] RV 'Their god is a god of the hills.' A national god was believed to exert his power chiefly within his own land, and the Syrians regarded Jehovah's power as confined to the hill-country in the neighbourhood of Samaria ; whereas in the plain (or plateau) E. of the Jordan, of which they doubtless considered themselves masters, they expected their own deity to prevail.

24. Take the kings away] The disaster recorded in v. 20 seems to have been in part attributed to the misconduct of the vassal kings, and their places (or posts) were now taken by Syrian officers, in whose loyalty and obedience more confidence could be placed.

26. Aphek] probably a city E. of the Sea of Galilee. **27. Were all present**] RV 'were victualled.' **30. A wall** (RV 'the wall') **fell**] either as a result of the Israelites' assault, or in consequence of an earthquake. Probably it was crowded with defenders.

33. Did diligently observe .. from him] RM 'took it' (i.e. the expression 'he is my brother') 'as an omen, and hasted to catch it from him' : i.e. they fastened on the kindly expression and repeated it to attract attention to it and make withdrawal difficult. **To come up .. chariot**] This was a mark of honour : cp. 2 K 10¹⁵. **34. The cities .. I will restore**] This promise was apparently not faithfully fulfilled : see 22³. **Make streets .. Damascus**] i.e. have certain parts of Damascus assigned for the use of Israelite traders (like the 'English quarters' in Shanghai and other Chinese towns).

35. A certain man] identified by Josephus with Micaiah (22⁸). **The sons of the prophets**] bodies of youths organised and trained by the prophets to serve as their ministers and envoys, and perhaps eventually to succeed them in their office. They were established at Bethel, Jericho, and Gilgal (2 K 2³,⁵ 4³⁸), and doubtless at other centres. **Smite me**] The wounds would support his story that he had been present in the battle (v. 30), and had received injury either from the enemy or from the man whose prisoner he suffered to escape.

38. With ashes, etc.] RV 'with his headband over his eyes' : to conceal his identity : so in v. 41. **40. Thyself hast decided** *it*] by his own confession he had neglected his charge.

42. Because thou hast let go] It is possible that Ahab's clemency towards Benhadad was due to the threatening attitude of the Assyrians, against whom it may have seemed expedient for Israel and Syria to unite. In any case, the Assyrian inscriptions record that Ahab and Benhadad both sent forces to aid Hamath, when it was attacked by Shalmaneser II in 854, and with their allies were defeated by the Assyrian king at Karkar (a city near the Orontes). The alliance between the two countries thus failed in its object ; and that the Syrians proved false to their engagement to restore the captured Israelite cities is probable from 22³. The prophet's censure of Ahab's conduct thus appears to have been justified by events.

CHAPTER 21
NABOTH'S VINEYARD

1. After these things] The LXX places this c. after c. 19, and so prevents the separation of chs. 20 and 22, which are closely connected. **Jezreel**] in the plain of Esdraelon. **3. The inheritance of my fathers**] cp. Lv 25²³ Nu 36⁷,⁸. **8. Unto the elders .. nobles**] The administration of justice rested with the chief men of each locality : cp. Dt 19¹² 21². **9. Proclaim a fast**] perhaps intended as a public act of humiliation for Naboth's alleged crime (cp. 1 S 7⁶), but in any case calculated to draw the people together. **Set Naboth on high**] perhaps equivalent to placing him at the bar of justice, but Josephus takes it to mean that he was given a position of honour as being of illustrious family. **10. Set two men**] The testimony of two witnesses is required by the law in Dt 17⁶. **Sons of Belial**] RM 'sons of worthlessness': cp. Dt 13¹³ 1 S 2¹². **Blaspheme**] RV 'curse': cp. Ex 22²⁸ Lv 24¹⁶. **Carry him out**] Jezebel had no doubt that the evidence of the perjured witnesses would be accepted.

15. Take possession] Presumably the property of one who was executed as a criminal passed to the crown. **18. Behold .. vineyard**] The details of the meeting between the king and the prophet are given somewhat differently in 2 K 9²⁶. **19. In the place, etc.**] Naboth must have been executed just outside Jezreel (v. 13), but the fulfilment of the prediction respecting Ahab took place at Samaria (22³⁸) ; on the other hand, the dead body of Ahab's son Jehoram was actually cast 'into the portion of the field of Naboth': see 2 K 9²⁵. **23. The dogs .. Jezebel**] For the fulfilment of the prediction see 2 K 9³⁶,³⁷. **The wall**] 2 K 9¹⁰ has 'the portion' (i.e. the district). **26. Amorites**]

here used for the heathen inhabitants of Canaan generally : see on Gn 10¹⁶ Josh 24¹⁸.

27. Went softly] i.e. went quietly, as one who was humbled and penitent. **29. I will not bring, etc.**] The judgment incurred by Solomon had been postponed (11¹²) for his father's sake. In Ahab's case the threatened penalty was mitigated in consideration of his repentance.

CHAPTER 22
AHAB AND MICAIAH. AHAB'S DEATH AT RAMOTH-GILEAD. REIGN OF JEHOSHAPHAT, KING OF JUDAH

1. Three years] probably calculated from the peace described in 20³⁴. **2. Jehoshaphat .. came down**] The earlier hostility between Judah and Israel (see 15¹⁶⁻²⁴) had by this time given place not only to peace but to friendship, which had been cemented (as appears from 2 K 8¹⁸) by a marriage between Jehoshaphat's son Jehoram and Ahab's daughter Athaliah. It is possible that the change in the relations of the two countries had been brought about by success on the part of the northern kingdom, and that Judah had become a vassal of its neighbour: at any rate, both on this occasion and on a later one (2 K 3⁷ᶠ.), the king of Judah is found aiding the king of Israel in a war which only promoted the interests of the latter. The cessation of hostilities between the two kingdoms was in many ways a benefit to both ; but for Judah the connexion with Israel was attended by serious drawbacks, for besides having to furnish assistance in war, it became infected with the Baal worship introduced by Ahab. Jehoshaphat's alliance with Ahab is explicitly condemned in 2 Ch 19². **3. Ramoth in Gilead**] situated a little N. of the Jabbok (the modern es Salt). The city had perhaps been amongst those which had been taken from Omri by Benhadad I, king of Syria, and which his son, Benhadad II, had agreed to restore (20³⁴). **5. Enquire .. of the LORD**] Jehoshaphat's piety led him to seek the divine guidance before starting on the proposed expedition. **To day**] better, 'first of all': cp. 1⁵¹ Gn 25³¹ (RM). **6. The prophets**] These must have been prophets of the LORD (vv. 5, 11), so that though the worship of the LORD (Jehovah) had ceased to be predominant in Israel, it was far from being extinguished, and the prophets had probably recovered some of their influence after the repentance of Ahab recorded in 21²⁷. But though the 400 were doubtless prophets of the true God, they were presumably in sympathy with the prevalent calf-worship, and escaped persecution by tolerating Baal worship.

7. A prophet of the LORD besides] i.e. is there not another prophet of the LORD beside these, one who dissociated himself from the prophets alluded to in note on v. 6. **8. He doth not .. good]** cp. on 20 35. **10. In the entrance of the gate]** the usual place for popular assemblages (cp. 2 S 19 8) and the dispensing of justice (2 S 15 2). **11. Made him .. iron]** For symbolic acts employed by prophets see on 11 31. **Horns** were natural emblems for weapons of offence (Dt 23 17).

15. Go, and prosper] Micaiah, as the king saw, was not speaking seriously, but repeated in mockery the words of the 400 prophets (v. 6), which had doubtless been reported to him (v. 13).

19. I saw the LORD] For similar prophetic visions see Isa 6 Ezk 1. **The host of heaven]** i.e. angelic spirits (cp. Ps 103 20, 21) constituting the court of heaven in attendance upon its king. **21. There came forth a spirit]** In several passages in the OT. infatuation is ascribed to the influence of an evil spirit from the LORD (see Jg 9 23 1 S 16 14 19 9), though the personal nature of such a spirit is not generally so clearly implied as here. The **lying spirit** is regarded as one of God's ministers, occasioning harm, indeed, but in subordination to the divine purposes : cp. Job 1 6 2 Th 2 11. The doctrine of an evil spirit antagonistic to God is not developed in the OT.

24. From me .. to thee] Zedekiah claimed to be inspired by the LORD (v. 11), and therefore challenged Micaiah to explain how he, likewise professing to speak in the name of the LORD, could utter a prophecy of such different tenor. **25. To hide thyself]** when the news arrived of Israel's defeat. **26. The king's son]** He was obviously placed in a position of authority. The sons of Jehoshaphat similarly had charge of 'fenced cities' (2 Ch 21 3).

27. Bread of affliction] i.e. prison fare.

29. Jehoshaphat .. went up] Jehoshaphat had consented to Ahab's proposal before

seeking counsel of the LORD, and in spite of Micaiah's warning found himself committed to the expedition. **30. I will disguise myself]** Ahab's action implies that Micaiah's words had made some impression upon him, though not sufficient to make him desist from his purpose. **Put thou on thy robes]** cp. 2 S 1 10.

31. Thirty and two captains] cp. 20 24. The command given to them is, of course, not to be understood literally. **32. Cried out]** Something in his cry, which was perhaps a prayer to the LORD (cp. 2 Ch 18 31), revealed that he was not the king of Israel. **34. At a venture]** Not without a definite aim, but in ignorance that his mark was the king of Israel (RM 'in his simplicity ').

39. The ivory house, etc.] For the use of ivory in building see Am 3 15 Ps 45 8. Though Ahab by his alliance with Zidon had corrupted the religion of the nation, he must have augmented its material prosperity.

41. And Jehoshaphat, etc.] This account of Jehoshaphat's reign follows on 15 24. **45. The rest of the acts, etc.]** see 2 Ch 17-20, which records (in addition to what is here related) the institution of a body of Levites to visit the various cities of Judah to teach the people the Law, the establishment of courts of justice both in Jerusalem and in the fenced cities, and the providential deliverance of the king and his army from a great host of Moabites, Ammonites, and Edomites.

47. A deputy *was* king] The royal house of Edom, which had recovered power in the time of Solomon, had been overthrown, and a viceroy, appointed by the king of Judah, now ruled the country. The subjugation of the Edomites probably followed upon the disaster sustained by them and their allies as described in 2 Ch 20.

48. Ships of Tharshish .. Ophir] The ships that sailed to Ophir (in Arabia or E. Africa, see on 9 28) were similar to those which traded to Tartessus or Tarsus (in the Mediterranean).

---

2 KINGS

CHAPTER 1

ELIJAH CALLS DOWN FIRE FROM HEAVEN

1. Moab .. Ahab] Moab had been conquered by David (2 S 8 2), and at the revolt of the Ten Tribes had passed under the authority of the northern kingdom. The revolt here alluded to took place, according to the inscription of Mesha, before the death of Ahab, whereas the present passage implies that it

happened later, in the reign of Ahaziah or Joram : cp. 3 6.

2. A lattice] lit. 'a network,'—perhaps a balustrade. **Baal-zebub]** supposed to mean 'lord of flies,' in the sense of being their controller and averter, since flies are one of the greatest plagues of Eastern countries : cp. the Gk. *Zeus Apomuios.* But in kindred names like Baal-Peor, Baal-Hermon, etc., the second element is the name of a place, which suggests that -zebub is likewise a local name. **Ekron**] One of the five confederate Philistine cities, lying nearest to the frontiers of Israel. **3.** *Is it* **not because,** etc.] RV 'Is it because there is no God in Israel ?' and so in vv. 6, 16. **8. An hairy man**] better, as in RM, 'a man with a garment of hair,' a characteristic dress of the prophets : cp. Zech 13⁴ Mk 1⁶. **9. A captain of fifty**] a recognised division of the Israelite army : cp. 1 S 8¹².

10. Let fire come down] The king in despatching soldiers to arrest the prophet dishonoured the LORD, whose servant Elijah was ; and the unity that subsisted between a king and his subjects (as between a father and his children) was so strongly felt in ancient times that there was little sense of the injustice involved in the death of so many innocent persons for the sin of another : see on 9²⁶. A consciousness of individual rights only asserted itself gradually in Israel (see Jer 31²⁹,³⁰ Ezk 18²⁻⁴) ; and a spirit akin to that of Elijah was manifested even by the Apostles, but met with rebuke from their Lord (Lk 9⁵⁵).

17. In the second year of Jehoram] The calculation here arrived at seems to follow upon what is stated in 1 K 16²³, where Omri begins to reign in Asa's thirty-first year (Omri's 12 + Ahab's 22 + Ahaziah's 2 + Jehoram's 1 = Asa's last 10 + Jehoshaphat's 25 + Jehoram's 2). A different reckoning is adopted in 3¹.

Had no son] Jehoram, who succeeded Ahaziah, was his brother.

CHAPTER 2
ELIJAH'S TRANSLATION TO HEAVEN

The great service rendered to Israel by the prophet whose life is here closed was the stand which he made for the religion of Jehovah when its supremacy was threatened by the worship of the Zidonian Baal introduced by Jezebel. In view of such a crisis, the degradation of Jehovah's worship by the association with it of the golden calves set up by Jeroboam could for a while be ignored, a superstitious form of the true faith being preferable to total apostasy ; though later, when the religion of Baal had been abolished by Jehu, the time came for a protest against the calf-worship, such as that which was made by Hosea (10⁵) and Amos (8¹⁴). The pre-eminence which Elijah, by his zeal and devotion in this struggle against Baal worship, won for himself among the prophets of the Old Testament is evidenced by the expectation subsequently entertained that he would come again : see Mal 4⁵,⁶, and cp. Mt 11¹⁴ 17¹¹ Lk 1¹⁷ Jn 1²¹. It is said that a chair is still placed for him by the Jews at the circumcision of every child, and that at the Paschal feast the door is set open for him to enter. At our Lord's Trans-

figuration he is recorded to have been present, together with Moses, and to have talked with Him (Mt 17³ Mk 9⁴).

1. When the LORD . . Elijah] The only parallel to this narrative in the OT. is the account of the translation of Enoch in Gn 5²⁴. The mention (in 2 Ch 21¹²) of a letter from Elijah in the reign of Jehoram has led some to think that the event related in this c. is placed out of its proper order. **Gilgal**] probably identical with the modern Jiljilia, a place between Bethel and Shechem in the hill-country of Ephraim.

2. Tarry here] Elijah may have wished to spare Elisha the awe-inspiring vision of his departure. **The sons of the prophets**] see on 1 K 20³⁵. **3. Knowest thou,** etc.] Knowledge of Elijah's impending departure seems to have prevailed both at Bethel and Jericho. **9. A double portion**] i.e. the share of the firstborn son (Dt 21¹⁷), twice as much as that of any of the other 'sons' of the prophet. Elisha wished to be, in spiritual power, the chief among Elijah's disciples and successors. **11. A chariot of fire**] cp. 2 K 6¹⁷.

12. The chariot of Israel] The words are probably a figure to describe the prophet, who in virtue of the supernatural powers that were at his service had been to Israel a greater protection than its military forces : cp. the similar expression used of Elisha in 13¹⁴. **Rent them**] a usual token of grief : cp. 5⁷ 6³⁰ Gn 37²⁹ 2 S 13¹⁹ Ezr 9³. **13. The mantle**] The symbol of prophetic authority : see 1⁸, and cp. 1 K 19¹⁹. **16. The Spirit of the LORD**] some strong impulse of divine origin : cp. 1 K 18¹². **17. Till he was ashamed**] i.e. to persist in further refusal.

19. This city] Jericho (v. 18). **The water**] not of the Jordan but of an affluent of it, the modern Ain es Sultân. **20. Salt**] a preservative and a symbol of wholesomeness and purity : cp. Mt 5¹³. **22. Unto this day**] see on 1 K 8⁸.

23. Little children] RM 'young lads.' Bethel, one of the seats of the calf-worship, was at a later date a royal chapel (Am 7¹³), and perhaps enjoyed the same distinction in Elijah's day ; and the prophet, by his zeal for the LORD, may have there incurred popular resentment, of which the mockery here described was a symptom. **Thou bald head**] a bald forehead might give rise to the suspicion and reproach of leprosy (Lv 13⁴²⁻⁴⁴).

24. Cursed them] see on 1 K 16³⁴. Elisha seems to have shared the fiery disposition of his master Elijah (1¹⁰), and the spirit he manifested on this occasion stands in impressive contrast with that enjoined and exemplified by our Lord (Mt 5⁴⁴ Lk 23³⁴). **She bears**] for the presence of bears in Palestine cp. 1 S 17³⁴⁻³⁶.

CHAPTER 3

JEHORAM AND ELISHA. VICTORY OVER MOAB

1. The eighteenth year of Jehoshaphat] according to 1[17], 'in the second year of Jehoram son of Jehoshaphat.'

2. The image of Baal] RV 'the pillar of Baal.' No mention is made of this in the account of Ahab's reign; but it is stated that Ahab erected an altar for Baal (1K16[32]), beside which the pillar here alluded to was doubtless raised. For the significance of such pillars see on 1K7[15]. That Jehoram's religious reformation was not very complete is plain from 10[19-28]: cp. c. 13.

4. Mesha] see on Nu21[29]. This king, in his inscription on the Moabite Stone, refers to the affliction which his country suffered from Israel, and to the war which put an end to it, though he places the latter in the time of Ahab. **Lambs..rams]** For a tribute, or present, of sheep from Moab cp. Isa16[1].

7. Sent to Jehoshaphat] see on 1K22[2]. Jehoshaphat himself had been attacked by the Moabites (2 Ch20[1]). **8. Which way shall we go?]** The usual route from Israel would be across the fords of the Jordan near Jericho, Moab being then invaded from the north. **Through the wilderness of Edom]** i.e. S. of the Dead Sea. Edom, though it had a king, was at this time under the control of Judah (1K22[47]), and additional forces could be obtained from thence in the course of the march.

9. Fetched a compass] RV 'made a circuit.' **11. Poured water on the hands of]** i.e. acted as his attendant. In the East water is still poured over the hands after eating, since the fingers generally serve as forks.

14. I would not look toward thee] Jehoram was not only the son of the idolatrous Ahab, but is described in v. 2 as having done evil in the sight of the LORD. At a later date, however, Elisha's attitude towards him changed: cp. c. 6.

15. Bring me a minstrel] For the connexion of music with prophecy cp. 1S10[5]. **The hand of the LORD]** cp. Ezk33[22].

16. Valley] The Heb. means a ravine or water-course which was then dry—possibly the Wâdy el Ahsa. **Ditches]** RV 'trenches': to retain the promised water for drinking purposes. **17. Neither shall ye see rain]** It is not implied that the water would be produced by any other means than rain, but the rain would fall at a distance: cp. v. 20. **20. When the meat offering was offered]** i.e. the daily morning sacrifice at Jerusalem: cp. 1K18[29].

22. As red as blood] Coloured by the red soil of Edom (Edom meaning 'red'), or reflecting the red tints of the morning sky.

25. Filled it] thereby rendering it useless for tillage or pasture. **Kir-haraseth]** probably the Kir of Isa15[1] and the Kir-heres of Jer48[31,36]. **26. The king of Edom]** probably in the hope that he, as a discontented vassal of Judah, would connive at his escape. **27. For a burnt offering]** presumably to Chemosh, the Moabite deity. Human sacrifices in ancient times prevailed amongst most Semitic nations; but the offering of a son or daughter must generally have been confined to occasions when some great offence had to be atoned for (cp. Mic6[7]) or some great calamity averted. Such sacrifices at one time were not unknown in Israel (Gn22 Jg11[30f.]); but the higher religious consciousness of the Hebrews led them to realise much earlier than other races how alien they were to the divine character. **There was great indignation]** RM 'there came great wrath upon Israel.' Probably the combined forces of the invaders met with some signal disaster which was attributed to divine anger against them, stimulated by the king's sacrifice. **From him]** i.e. from the king of Moab. On the Moabite Stone Mesha relates his capture of various towns (Nebo, Jahaz) and the fortifications of others (Baal-Meon, Kiriathaim, Bezer, Dibon, Medeba, Beth-diblathaim), which were all N. of the Arnon, and some of which are expressly enumerated in the Bible among the cities of Reuben and Gad; so not only must the Israelites have retired from Moab, but the Moabites must have made themselves masters of what had previously been Israelite territory.

CHAPTER 4

VARIOUS MIRACLES OF ELISHA

The miracles related of Elisha in this and the following chapters resemble many of those previously recounted of Elijah. Thus both prophets multiplied the sustenance of a woman in need (2K4[1-7] 1K17[8-16]); both restored a dead child to life (2K4[8-27] 1K17[17-24]); both came into conflict with their king on the occasion of a famine (2K6[24-33] 1K18); and both brought a violent death upon certain individuals who offended them (2K2[23,24] 2K1). But the habits of Elisha were seemingly more social, and his disposition less stern, than were those of his great predecessor: he was a frequenter of cities, was closely associated with the 'sons of the prophets,' and many of the miracles recorded of him are connected with private individuals and incidents of common life. The contrast in this respect which Elisha offered to the ascetic Elijah resembles that which subsisted between our LORD and St. John the Baptist: cp. Mt11[18,19].

The several stories here told of Elisha are somewhat disconnected, the indications of time that occur in them are vague (see 4[8,11,18]), and there are a few inconsistencies which are left unexplained by the historian : contrast 6²³ with 6²⁴ and 5²⁷ with 8¹⁻⁶.

1. To be bondmen] For the sale of an insolvent debtor and his family see Lv 25³⁹, and cp. Neh 5⁵.

8. A great woman] i.e. wealthy and influential : cp. 1 S 25² 2 S 19³². **10. A .. chamber .. on the wall**] probably an upper chamber, above the ordinary roof. **A stool**] better, a 'chair' or 'seat' (the same word being used of a royal throne). **Candlestick**] better, 'lampstand' : cp. Ex 25³¹.

13. He said unto him, etc.] in the East women were (and are) lightly esteemed, and direct communications were rarely held with them by persons who had a character for sanctity (cp. Jn 4²⁷) : see v. 27 and 5¹⁰. **What *is* to be done for thee?**] Elisha, who, unlike Elijah, seems to have attended the royal court (5³), offers to use his influence on her behalf.

I dwell .. people] i.e. I live among friends, and therefore do not need special protection against oppression. **16. According to the time of life**] RV 'when the time cometh round,' i.e. in the spring of the following year.

19. My head] He had perhaps sustained a sunstroke.

23. Neither new moon, nor sabbath] The Shunammite's husband did not connect his wife's proposed visit to the prophet with the death of his child, but with some religious duty. The new moon (i.e. the first day of the month) and the sabbath were feasts at which the prophets might be asked to preside, as Samuel did at the feast held at the high place of Ramah (1 S 9¹²,¹³).

24. Slack not *thy* riding] RV 'slacken me not the riding' : the servant probably ran on foot beside his mistress. **26. *It is* well**] The purpose of the answer was obviously not to deceive but to dismiss the questioner.

29. Gird up thy loins] The direction was necessary, for the garments were usually worn loose and flowing. **Salute him not**] To do so would waste time. **Lay my staff**] Elisha seems to have thought that as Elijah's mantle had been powerful in his own hand (2¹⁴), so his own staff would be equally potent in the hands of another. But the secret of miracles must be looked for in personalities, not in inanimate things.

35. He returned, etc.] The prophet showed the importunity which should mark all effort to obtain a divine blessing.

38. A dearth] Perhaps the famine related in 8¹⁻⁶. **39. A wild vine**] not a real vine, but a vine-like plant, usually identified with the bitter cucumber or colocynth, bearing a fruit resembling an orange, which is very bitter in taste. **42. Baal-shalisha**] Perhaps the same as the 'land of Shalisha' (1 S 9⁴) in the hill-country of Ephraim. **The firstfruits**] Elisha

probably dwelt at a sanctuary (perhaps Gilgal) where firstfruits were required to be presented (Ex 23¹⁹). **In the husk thereof**] RV 'in his sack.' **43. What, should .. men?**] cp. the like doubt raised by the disciples of our Lord (Jn 6⁹), and the similar, but even more impressive, sequel.

CHAPTER 5
The Healing of Naaman and the Punishment of Gehazi

1. The LORD .. Syria] Possibly the enemies from whom the Syrians had been saved were the Assyrians. Naaman, in delivering his countrymen from them, had been an unconscious instrument in the hands of Jehovah. **A leper**] see on Lv 13. Leprosy is of slow development, and as Naaman retained his military command, his malady cannot have reached a very advanced stage. It is not likely, in any case, that the Syrians observed the same strict rules regarding it as the Jews.

2. By companies] i.e. by raiding bands.

5. The king of Israel] probably Jehoram. **Ten talents**] A talent was a weight of 96 lb. *Pieces* **of gold**] probably shekels, and so in 6²⁵, a shekel being a weight of 224 grains. **Changes of raiment**] For such a present cp. Gn 45²². The expression implies costly robes.

6. That thou mayest recover] i.e. by using his influence with the prophet.

10. Sent a messenger] cp. 4¹³. **Seven times**] The figure probably stands for an indefinite number (cp. 1 K 18⁴³) ; but it is possible that it also had special religious associations (cp. Gn 21²⁸ Josh 6⁴). The prophet's direction to Naaman to wash in the Jordan did not imply any miraculous quality in the water of the river, but was intended to test the sufferer's faith.

11. Strike] better, 'wave,' for he would probably avoid actual contact.

12. Abana and Pharpar] These two rivers rise in Mt. Hermon and lose themselves in a marshy lake near Damascus. Though smaller, they are much clearer than the Jordan.

13. My father] a title of honour : cp. 2¹² 6²¹. **15. He returned**] The distance from the Jordan to Samaria was some 30 m.

A blessing] RV 'a present' : cp. Gn 33¹¹ Jg 1¹⁵. Naaman did well to seek to show his gratitude to the LORD by a gift to His prophet, but Elisha's refusal meant that for imparting a divine blessing which he was empowered from on high to bestow, he could receive no personal gain.

17. Two mules' burden of earth] It was believed that a national deity was intimately connected with the country he protected, so that Naaman, being desirous of worshipping the LORD (Jehovah) in Syria, wished to transport thither some of the soil of Israel as being associated with His presence and so most fitted for the construction of an altar to Him.

18. Rimmon] identical with the Assyrian storm-god Ramman.

19. Go in peace] Elisha, to avoid putting too severe a strain upon the incipient devotion of his foreign convert, did not demand consistency, though his predecessor Elijah, in the case of native Israelites, had protested against such divided allegiance (1 K 18²¹).

22. Mount Ephraim] RV 'the hill country of Ephraim.' Bethel and Gilgal, where there were bodies of 'sons of the prophets' (c. 2), were situated in this district. **23. Be content**] i.e. consent : cp. 6³. **24. The tower**] RV 'the hill' : probably an elevation near Samaria. Some take it to mean 'the citadel.'

26. Is it a time] The occasion had not been a suitable one for acquiring gain, but for rejoicing over the manifestation of the LORD'S power and graciousness, calculated as it was to awaken the wonder and gratitude of the foreigner, Naaman, which Gehazi's covetousness might now repress.

CHAPTER 6
ELISHA AND THE SIEGE OF SAMARIA

1. The place where we dwell] The mention of the Jordan (v. 2) suggests that these sons of the prophets dwelt near Jericho : cp. 2⁵. Probably Elisha did not permanently abide with them, but visited them occasionally for supervision and instruction. **6. The iron did swim**] The prophet's powers were exerted to help one who was honest enough to be the more concerned for his loss because the axe was not his own.

8. The king of Syria] perhaps the Benhadad of v. 24 and 1 K 20¹. **13. Dothan**] commanding a pass which crossed the ridge of Carmel (the mountain of v. 17).

17. Round about Elisha] cp. Ps 34⁷ 91⁴. God's servants often experience providential succour in times of danger, though they cannot confidently reckon upon protection from earthly peril. What alone is assured to them, if they continue loyal, is spiritual security.

22. Wouldest thou smite, etc.] If the king would not smite captives whom he had taken by his own valour, much less could he expect to be allowed to smite those who had been delivered into his hands by another. The prophet by preserving their lives, secured that information respecting his wonderful powers was conveyed to the Syrian king.

24. And it came to pass, etc.] This section obviously has no close connexion with the preceding, as the inconsistency between this v. and v. 23 shows, though Josephus explains that the king of Syria, out of fear of Elisha, abandoned his secret designs against the Israelites in favour of more open war.

25. An ass's head] The ass being an unclean animal, its flesh would not be eaten except in times of great scarcity. **Cab**] a little less than 2 quarts, so that a fourth part would be about a pint. **Dove's dung**] Though this is usually supposed to be a kind of pulse, yet pigeon's dung was eaten in a siege that took place in the year 1316 A.D., probably because of the seeds it contained. **29. Boiled my son**] The same kind of incident occurred in connexion with the siege of Jerusalem by Nebuchadnezzar, Lam 4¹⁰ : cp. also Lv 26²⁹ Dt 28⁵²⁻⁵⁵. **31. The head of Elisha**] Possibly the prophet had held out promises of relief which had not been realised. **32. This son of a murderer**] i.e. this murderer : cp. Isa 1⁴. **Hold .. door**] RV 'hold the door fast against him.' **Is not .. feet**] The king, after giving orders to execute Elisha, had changed his purpose, and was hastening after the messenger to countermand his directions.

33. And he said] These words are spoken by *the king*, which should be substituted for **the messenger** in the first part of the v. : cp. 7¹⁷. **Wait**] i.e. hold out in the hope of God's intervention.

CHAPTER 7
THE RELIEF OF SAMARIA

1. A measure] Heb. a *seah*, equal to 6 cabs, and rather less than 3 gallons. **In the gate of Samaria**] The open space at the gate of an Eastern city served as a market-place.

2. Windows in heaven] These were the outlets from which the rain came (Gn 7¹¹), and the officer asked scornfully whether the famine could be relieved even if rain fell immediately.

3. The gate] Lepers would be required to keep outside the city : cp. Lv 13⁴⁵, ⁴⁶. **5. The uttermost part**] RV 'the outermost part' : i.e. the outer limits of the camp on the side nearest to them.

6. The Hittites] see on 1 K 10²⁹. The Assyrians used their name to describe the whole of Palestine, which they called 'the land Khatti.' **The Egyptians**] Parts of Egypt were governed by petty kings who were vassals of the Pharaohs. A combination of Hittite and Egyptian forces, coming from the N. and S. respectively, would have entrapped the Syrians between them. But mention is made in the Assyrian inscriptions of a land called Musre adjoining the Hittite country, and it is possible that Mizraim (the Heb. for Egypt) is a mistake for this.

10. The porter] Perhaps used collectively (see v. 11) and hence the plur. pronoun 'them.'

13. They are as, etc.] i.e. they are in danger of starvation like the rest of us, and so have no more to fear, if they are captured by the enemy, than will befall them if they remain in the city : cp. v. 4. **15. Unto Jordan**] The Syrians in their retreat from Samaria would naturally make for the fords of the Jordan at Bethshan and Bethbarah.

17. The people trode, etc.] He was knocked down in the rush of famished citizens hastening to the Syrian camp, and trampled to death, thus fulfilling Elisha's prediction (v. 2).

CHAPTER 8

ELISHA AND THE SHUNAMMITE. ELISHA AND HAZAEL. REIGNS OF JEHORAM AND AHAZIAH OF JUDAH

1. Then spake Elisha] The occasion is not indicated, all the stories related of Elisha in this and the three preceding chs. being disconnected. **A famine**] Perhaps the same as that referred to in 4³⁸. **2. The land of the Philistines**] This was a corn-growing district, near the still more productive country of Egypt. **3. To cry unto the king**] Her property, being vacant during her absence, had seemingly passed to the crown : cp. v. 6.

7. To Damascus] It is possible that Elisha in thus visiting the Syrian capital was carrying out a commission of Elijah's (1 K 19¹⁵). For Ben-hadad see 6²⁴. **8. Hazael**] one of Ben-hadad's servants. **10. Say unto him**] Elisha presumably meant that the disease from which Benhadad was suffering was not a fatal one, but that he would die by other means. Some suppose that Elisha spoke ironically (like Micaiah in 1 K 22¹⁵). **11. Until he was ashamed**] Hazael became discomposed under the prophet's gaze, being conscious of a guilty purpose. **12. The evil**, etc.] described in 10³², 13³,²² Am 1³,⁴.

13. But what, etc.] RV 'but what is thy servant, which is but a dog,' the expression 'a dog' being a term of contempt (1 S 17⁴³ 24¹⁴). Hazael meant that he could scarcely credit that so great a destiny was in store for one so humble as himself.

16. Jehoshaphat *being* **then king of Judah**] an accidental repetition of the words 'Jehoshaphat king of Judah,' that follow.

18. He did evil .. LORD] This does not imply that he abandoned altogether the worship of the LORD, since he made offerings to the Temple (12¹⁸). **19. A light**] see 1 K 11³⁶ 15⁴. In consequence of the divine promises made to David, Jehoram's sins were not punished by the overthrow of his dynasty but by other means.

20. Edom revolted] in the reign of Jehoshaphat Edom had been subject to Judah and ruled by a viceroy (1 K 22⁴⁷). Its success in throwing off the yoke of Judah is alluded to in Gn 27⁴⁰. **21. Zair**] This place is only mentioned here, and the Vulgate reads Seir, another name for Edom. **The people .. tents**] The people referred to is the people of Judah.

Joram, when surrounded by the Edomites, cut his way through them and escaped, but his army was defeated and dispersed. The verse accounts for the successful revolt of Edom.

22. Yet] RV 'so': see 2 Ch 21¹⁰. **Unto this day**] The writer whose materials the author of Kings is here drawing upon must have lived before the destruction of the Judæan kingdom. **Libnah**] situated in the lowland. Its revolt was perhaps aided by the Philistines: cp. 2 Ch 21¹⁶,¹⁷. **23. The rest .. Joram**] see 2 Ch 21, which relates both the public and personal losses sustained by the king.

24. Ahaziah] in 2 Ch 21¹⁷ called Jehoahaz. **26. Two and twenty**] in 2 Ch 22² 'forty-two.' **Daughter of Omri**] strictly she was 'grand-daughter' of Omri. The terms 'son' and 'daughter' were used not only of remote descendants but even of successors who were not blood-relations ; e.g. Jehu in the Assyrian inscriptions is called ' the son of Omri.' **28. He went with Joram**] Ramoth Gilead at this time was in the hands of Israel, but threatened by Syria (9¹⁴). **29. Ramah**] i.e. Ramoth Gilead.

CHAPTER 9

JEHU AND HIS BLOODSHED

This c. relates the anointing of Jehu by order of Elisha ; and the death of Jehoram (of Israel), Ahaziah (of Judah), and Jezebel.

1. Box] RV 'vial.' For the use of oil in anointing sovereigns see 1 S 10¹ 16¹³. **Ramoth-gilead**] The Israelite army was on guard here (v. 14). **9. Like the house of Jeroboam .. of Baasha**] Both these families had been extirpated: 1 K 15²⁹ 16¹¹. **10. In .. Jezreel**] the scene of Ahab's murder of Naboth (1 K 21).

11. This mad *fellow*] The wild demeanour and excited utterances of the prophets (see 1 S 10⁵ᶠ 19²⁰ᶠ) particularly exposed them to this reproach : cp. Jer 29²⁶. **Ye know the man**] Probably the sons of the prophets, like the prophets themselves, could be distinguished by their dress: see on 1⁸. But Jehu's words possibly imply that he suspected his colleagues of having prompted the prophet's action.

13. Put *it* **under him**] either for a cushion (as an extemporised throne) or for a carpet. **On the top of the stairs**] RM ' on the bare steps '; these would be outside the house.

17. *Is it* **peace ?**] i.e 'is all well ?' (the same word as in v. 11 and in 5²¹). **18. Turn thee behind me**] The command had the same object as that in v. 15, viz. to prevent warning being given.

22. Whoredoms] i.e. the practice of idolatry: see Jg 2¹⁷ Hos 2²ᶠ. **Witchcrafts**] i.e. dealings with wizards and diviners (prohibited in Ex 22¹⁸ : cp. also Dt 18¹¹ Lv 20²⁷).

23. Turned his hands] i.e. to wheel his chariot about. **25. Rode together after Ahab**] i.e. behind him in the same chariot, as his

attendants. **Laid this burden upon him**] RM
'uttered this oracle against him.' The term
'burden' is similarly used of a prophetic utterance in Isa 13¹ 15¹ 17¹ Nah 1¹ Hab 1¹, etc.

26. The blood of his sons] The execution
of Naboth's sons has not previously been
mentioned ; but at this period a man's guilt
was held to attach to his children likewise
(the sense of individual responsibility being
only imperfectly developed), and his offence
was generally expiated by their punishment as
well as his own.

27. The garden house] better, 'Bethgan,' a
place on the direct road from Jezreel to the
S. **Ibleam**] about half-way between Samaria and Jezreel. A different account of
Ahaziah's death is given in 2 Ch 22⁹. **Megiddo**] on the ridge of Carmel.

29. Eleventh] in 8²⁵ 'twelfth.'

30. Painted her face] RV 'painted her
eyes' (eyelids), i.e. with a preparation of antimony, to make them appear larger and more
brilliant.

31. *Had* **Zimri peace, etc.**] RV 'is it peace,
thou Zimri, thy master's murderer': see 1 K
16⁹⁻¹⁹. Perhaps Jezebel, by reminding Jehu
of the fate of Zimri, wished to suggest to him
the wisdom of making overtures to her.

34. A king's daughter] She was daughter
of Ethbaal, king of Zidon (1 K 16³¹).

35. They found no more, etc.] The loss of
burial added further ignominy to her death :
see on 1 K 2³¹. **36. In the portion of Jezreel**]
see 1 K 21²³.

CHAPTER 10
JEHU'S EXTERMINATION OF BAAL WORSHIP

1. Ahab .. sons] These were probably his
grandchildren rather than his children. **Unto
the rulers of Jezreel**] LXX has 'unto the
rulers of Samaria,' which the sense requires.
2. A fenced city] i.e. Samaria. Ahab's
dynasty had obtained the throne by force of
arms (1 K 16²¹,²²), and Jehu implied that its
supporters must defend it by the same means.
4. Two kings] Jehoram of Israel and
Ahaziah of Judah. **5. Over the house .. over
the city**] These officials are also alluded to in
1 K 4⁵⁻²²²⁶ 2 K 18¹⁸ Isa 22¹⁵. **6. Take ye
the heads**] By slaying the young princes the
rulers and elders would be implicated in
Jehu's treason and would therefore in self-
defence have to support him.
9. Ye *be* **righteous**] Jehu appeals to the
people to judge between him and any that
might accuse him. The fact that the elders of
the city had put Jehoram's sons to death argued
that the overthrow of Ahab's dynasty was not
due solely to Jehu's private ambition but to
widespread disaffection against a guilty house.
But Jehu unfairly concealed his own communications with the elders (vv. 1–3).

10. The word of the LORD] see 1 K 21¹⁹,²⁹.
Though Ahab had repented of his murder of
Naboth, and the chastisement he had incurred
was for a time postponed, and though Jehoram
seems to have attempted some religious
reform (3²), yet the evil influence of Jezebel
had spread widely (see 10¹⁹ᶠ·), and eventually
brought judgment upon the impious family.
13. The king .. the queen] i.e. Joram and
Jezebel (the term 'queen' denoting the queen-
mother). **14. The pit**] i.e. the tank or pool
where the sheep were washed.
15. Jehonadab] Jehonadab was a Kenite
(1 Ch 2⁵⁵), the tribe of Arabian nomads to
which Jethro, Moses' father-in-law, belonged
(Jg 1¹⁶). **If it be**] spoken by Jehu (so the
LXX). **Give** *me* **thine hand**] i.e. as a pledge :
cp. Ezr 10¹⁹ Ezk 17¹⁸.
18. And Jehu, etc.] Jehu proceeded to use
the same crafty secrecy in the extirpation of
Baal worship as he had displayed in destroying
Ahab and his house (9¹⁶ᶠ· 10¹ᶠ·). **22. The
vestry**] Part of the Temple where the 'changes
of raiment,' usually worn on festal occasions,
were stored. **25. To the city of the house
of Baal**] This seems unintelligible, and the
word 'city' is probably a corruption of the
word 'oracle' (see 1 K 6⁵), the Hebrew being
somewhat similar. **26. The images**] RV
'the pillars' : and so in v. 27. They were
probably mere columns, not figures of the
human form. **27. Draught house**] equivalent
to a dunghill : cp. Ezr 6¹¹ Dan 2⁵. **Unto this
day**] see on 1 K 8⁸.
30. Of the fourth *generation*] see 15¹². The
four generations were Jehoahaz, Joash, Jeroboam II, and Zechariah. Jehu's dynasty sat
longer than any other on the throne of Israel.
31. Jehu took no heed .. heart] Jehu was a
worshipper of the LORD (Jehovah), and, in
his violent extirpation of the house of Ahab,
was doubtless actuated by religious zeal as
well as by motives of ambition, whilst his
desire to suppress the worship of Baal which
had been encouraged by Ahab and Jezebel
was reinforced by indignation at the tyranny
manifested by the reigning house in the matter
of Naboth : cp. 9²⁵,²⁶. But the combined
revolution and reformation which he effected
were accompanied by massacres which, at a
later date, excited the abhorrence of the prophet
Hosea (1⁴) ; and though the religion of
Jehovah was restored by him to its previous
supremacy, it retained the idolatrous character
which Jeroboam I had given it by representing the Deity under the figure of a young bull.
32. Coasts] i.e. borders. For Hazael's
barbarities in Gilead (v. 33) see Am 1³,⁴.
34. The rest of the acts of Jehu] An Assyrian
inscription (now in the British Museum)
records that Jehu paid tribute to Shalmaneser
II. That king in 842 B.C. defeated Hazael the

king of Syria ; and the injuries that the latter inflicted upon Israel (vv. 32, 33) would naturally lead Jehu to court the friendship of his conqueror. Among the gifts that formed part of Jehu's tribute were ' bars of silver, bars of gold, a golden ladle, golden goblets, golden pitchers, bars of lead, a staff for the hand of the king, shafts of spears' (Schrader, COT, i, 199).

CHAPTER 11
THE USURPATION OF ATHALIAH AND PRESERVATION OF JOASH

1. Athaliah] She was the daughter of Ahab and Jezebel (8 18, 26), possessed her mother's high courage, and, like her, was a devoted worshipper of Baal. Her position as queen-mother she would naturally lose on the accession of Ahaziah's son, the deceased monarch's wife becoming queen-mother in her stead. She, therefore, took measures to place herself on the throne by removing all rivals, and then proceeded to make the worship of Baal predominant in the land : see 2 Ch 24 7.

2. In the bedchamber] This was presumably one of the side-chambers of the Temple described in 1 K 6 5-10.

4. Jehoiada] He was the high priest and married to the princess Jehosheba (2 Ch 22 11). **Rulers**] For their names see 2 Ch 23 1. **Captains**] RV ' Carites ' (and so in v. 19). These were probably foreign mercenaries from Caria in Asia Minor (they are mentioned by Herodotus as employed by the Egyptian king Psammetichus), who formed the bodyguard of the Judæan sovereigns.

5. A third part of you, etc.] The precise arrangements are obscure, but it is probable that on the sabbath one-third of the royal guards were on duty at the palace and two-thirds at the Temple ; of these the former body, separated into three divisions (vv. 5, 6), was posted at different parts of the building to prevent Athaliah's personal supporters from leaving it (though she herself was allowed to do so), whilst the latter, and larger, body was assembled at the Temple to secure the safety of Joash (v. 7).

6. The gate of Sur] RV omits ' of.' In 2 Ch 23 5 it is called 'the gate of the foundation.' Position unknown. **That it be not broken down**] better, ' and be a barrier.' **8. Ranges**] RV ' ranks,' and so in v. 15. **11.** *Along* **by the altar**] i.e. the troops were posted in two columns converging towards the altar of burnt offering in the Temple court, so as to enclose a triangular space.

12. The testimony] i.e. a copy of the Law : cp. Ex 25 16, and see Dt 17 18. But the literal rendering is, ' they put upon him the crown and the testimony,' and the last word should perhaps be ' the bracelets ' which kings wore

as part of their insignia (2 S 1 10). (In the Heb there is only a difference of a single letter.)

14. By a pillar] perhaps better, ' on the platform,' from which the king used to address the people. **15. Without the ranges**] RV ' between the ranks,' so that she was surrounded by troops. **16. Laid hands on her**] So the LXX. RV has, ' made way for her ' (so that she might be got out of the Temple before she was slain).

18. The house of Baal] i.e. of the Zidonian Baal to whose worship Athaliah, as the daughter of Jezebel, adhered. According to Josephus this temple was built by Jehoram and Athaliah.

20. All . . rejoiced] The brief usurpation of Athaliah was the only interruption to the orderly succession of kings of the house of David throughout the history of Judah, a fact which testifies to the strong attachment which the people felt towards it, and forms a striking fulfilment of the promise made to David (2 S 7 15, 16).

CHAPTER 12
JOASH REPAIRS THE TEMPLE

2. All his days] According to 2 Ch 24 17f. Joash took to evil courses after the death of Jehoiada. **3. The high places**, etc.] The worship at the ' high places ' was first abolished by Hezekiah, and then, after its renewal by Manasseh, by Josiah.

4. The money . . is set at] RV ' the money of the persons for whom each man is rated.' The money devoted to the repair of the Temple was that received for (a) the supply of vessels dedicated to the Temple services ; (b) the redemption of vows (Lv 27 2-8) ; (c) free-will offerings. According to 2 Ch 24 6, 9 the chief source of the money was the half-shekel appointed by Moses to be paid by every Israelite for the maintenance of the Tent of the Testimony (Ex 30 11-16). *The account*] RM ' *the numbering.*'

9. The altar] i.e. the altar of burnt offering, outside the Temple building : cp. 2 Ch 24 8. The **door** would be the entrance into the Temple court. **11. Told**] RV ' weighed out.' **13. There were not made**] 2 Ch 24 14 has ' were made,' perhaps having in view the surplus remaining after the repairs of the Temple were completed. **16. The trespass money**, etc.] RV ' money for guilt offerings and money for sin offerings.' Some suppose that fines are meant, but the money may have been applied to the purchase of victims for sacrifices : see Lv 4, 5.

17. Gath] one of the five Philistine cities ; to reach it Hazael must have marched through the kingdom of Israel, and his invasion is probably to be connected with the attacks upon Jehu and Jehoahaz (10 32 13 3, 4). For the movement upon Jerusalem see 2 Ch 24 23, 24, where it is stated that Jehoash sustained a severe defeat before he surrendered his treasure.

19. The rest of the acts of Joash] see 2 Ch 24 17-27, which relates that after Jehoiada's death Joash departed from the LORD, and even killed Zechariah, the son of Jehoiada, who had rebuked him for his idolatry.

20. The house of Millo] If Millo was a fort in Jerusalem (see on 1 K 9 15) 'the house' was perhaps a palace attached to it. **21. Jozachar**] in 2 Ch 24 26 (where 'Jozachar' is corrupted into 'Zabad') the conspiracy is described as intended to avenge the death of Zechariah : see on v. 19.

CHAPTER 13
REIGNS OF JEHOAHAZ AND JOASH OF ISRAEL. THE LAST PREDICTION OF ELISHA

3. All *their* **days**] RV 'continually,' i.e. throughout the reign of Jehoahaz. **5. A saviour**] either Jehoash (v. 25) or Jeroboam II (14 25-27) is meant. **In their tents**] i.e. in their homes, the phrase being a survival from earlier times when the Israelites were a body of nomads roaming the desert. **6. The grove**] RV 'the Asherah' : see on 1 K 14 15. If Jehu had altogether abolished the worship of Baal (10 28), this Asherah must have been connected with the worship of the LORD, like the pillars before the Temple of Solomon (1 K 7 15 f.).

13. Jeroboam] usually designated as Jeroboam II.

14. Joash . . unto him] Both Elijah and Elisha, though strenuous antagonists to the religion of Baal, yet seem to have tolerated the worship of the LORD under the form of a calf, for both prophets had friendly relations with kings who retained that mode of worship. Corrupt in character as it was, it was nevertheless directed towards the true God. This passage is the first mention of Elisha since he sent a prophet to anoint Jehu (c. 9). **The chariot of Israel**] The reference is to Elisha, who had been Israel's greatest safeguard, a host in himself : cp. 3 15 f. 6 9.

16. Elisha put, etc.] in order to indicate that the king's destined success came from another source than from his own strength. **17. The arrow, etc.**] The shooting of the arrow eastward was symbolic of a victory in that direction, Syria lying NE. of Israel. **Aphek**] the Aphek of 1 K 20 26. **19. The man of God was wroth**] because the king displayed too little confidence in the God whose minister the prophet was.

20. The bands of the Moabites] If Elisha was buried either at Samaria or at his home of Abel-meholah, the Moabites must have crossed the Jordan. **21. Touched**] The corpse would not be placed in a coffin but swathed in grave-clothes ; and the tomb was probably an

excavation in the side of a hill, not a hole in the ground.

24. Ben-hadad] Probably the third of the name mentioned in the Bible : see 1 K 15 18 20 1.

25. Three times] in accordance with Elisha's prophecy (v. 19). The success of Israel over Syria was probably aided by the disasters which that country sustained from Assyria. The contemporary Assyrian king was Ramman-nirari, who in his inscriptions relates that he besieged Damascus and compelled its ruler to tender allegiance and pay tribute. The Syrian king is called 'Mari,' but this may be a title, not a proper name. Ramman-nirari also claims to have received tribute from ' the land of Omri,' i.e. Northern Israel ; so that Jehoash may have purchased the aid of the Assyrian king against Syria by sending presents to him.

CHAPTER 14
REIGNS OF AMAZIAH OF JUDAH AND JEROBOAM OF ISRAEL

1. In the second year of Joash . . king of Israel] Joash of Judah reigned 40 years, and as his thirty-seventh year corresponded to the first year of Joash of Israel (13 10) the accession of his son Amaziah could not coincide with the Israelite king's second year ; so that there is some slight error of calculation.

3. Not like David] He was not perfectly faithful to the LORD, for late in his reign he worshipped the gods of Edom (2 Ch 25 14).

6. The children . . he slew not] see Dt 24 16, and cp. Ezk 18 2-4. The contrast between Amaziah's conduct and the practice recorded in 2 S 21 6 2 K 9 26 shows that by this time a clearer conception had been acquired of the rights of individuals, which prevented the guilt of the parent from being held to extend to all his family.

7. Edom] see further in 2 Ch 25 5-16. **The valley of salt**] immediately S. of the Dead Sea. **Selah**] the later Petra, E. of the Arabah. **Joktheel**] said to mean 'subdued by God.' **Unto this day**] i.e. unto the time of the writer whose materials are here used by the historian. The date is probably early, for the Edomites practically recovered their independence in Ahaz' reign (16 6), and would naturally restore their capital's former name.

8. Let us . . face] i.e. meet face to face in battle. If Judah at this time was a vassal of the northern kingdom (see on 1 K 22 2), Amaziah's motive in courting a quarrel with his neighbour was probably a desire to free Judah from this position of subservience. His recent success over Edom doubtless encouraged him ; but he miscalculated the respective resources of himself and his opponent. His

9. The thistle] The thistle represents Amaziah and the cedar Jehoash, whilst the lion symbolises the ruin that humbled the arrogance of the former; but the fable does not quite suit the circumstances, as Amaziah was seeking, not a friendly alliance, but a quarrel. For the use of fables cp. Jg 9 8-15.

11. Bethshemesh] In the Lowland (Shephelah) of Judah, 15 m. W. of Jerusalem.

13. From the gate .. gate] The wall that was dismantled was on the N. side of the city, which was thus left defenceless to attacks from that direction, in case it gave further provocation. **19. Lachish**] on the Philistine border, but within the territory of Judah (Josh 15 39). It is usually identified with the modern Tell el Hesy.

21. Took Azariah] called in 15 13 (see note) and elsewhere Uzziah. The fact that though Amaziah was dethroned and put to death, his son was nevertheless made king in his room witnesses to the affection that continued to be felt for the dynasty of David.

The Assyrian king Tiglath-pileser mentions among the kings from whom he received tribute a certain Azriyahu of Jaudi, who has been thought by some scholars to represent Azariah of Judah, but the identity of the two names is now questioned.

22. Elath] see on 1 K 9 26, and for its eventual loss see 2 K 16 6. Its restoration to Judah implies the subjugation of Edom.

23. Jeroboam .. forty and one years] This is inconsistent with the figures given in 14 2 and 15 8, for Jeroboam's reign covered 15 years of Amaziah's and 37 of Azariah's, making 52 in all.

25. Restored the coast] i.e. extended the territory of Israel to its original boundaries when at the height of its prosperity: see on v. 28. **The entering of Hamath**] i.e. the gorge between Lebanon and Hermon. **The sea of the plain**] RV 'the sea of the Arabah': i.e. the Dead Sea, the Arabah being the long depression extending from the Sea of Galilee to the Gulf of Akaba. Jeroboam's conquests probably included Moab, and to his reign the invasion of that country described in Isa 15 1 to 16 12 may be most plausibly assigned. His success was facilitated by the inactivity of Assyria at the time. **Jonah**] The same prophet who is the subject of the book of that name. **Gath-hepher**] in Zebulun, a little to the N. of Nazareth.

Jonah was not the only prophet who was active in Israel during this reign, for both Hosea and Amos were his contemporaries. Of these Hosea belonged by birth to the northern kingdom, but Amos was a native of Judah. From the writings of Amos it was plain that though the prosperity of the kingdom had greatly increased during the reign of Jeroboam, its moral condition was sadly in need of reform. Social oppression (Am 2 6-8 5 11), commercial dishonesty (8 5, 6), and judicial corruption (5 7)

were rife in the land, and in consequence the prophet declared that the nation would be punished by captivity in a foreign land (5 27 6 7 7 9, 17). Amaziah the priest of Bethel denounced him to Jeroboam, and bade him flee back into Judah, counsel which the prophet requited by predicting that Amaziah would share the captivity of his countrymen and his family be destroyed by the sword.

26. Any shut up] see on 1 K 14 10.

28. Damascus and Hamath] Both these places had been included within the possessions of Solomon (1 K 4 21), but the former was lost to him by the success of Rezon related in 1 K 11 23-25. The re-conquest of the places here named could not have been long maintained, for Amos speaks of Damascus, the nearer of the two, as an independent state (Am 1 3).

CHAPTER 15
Sundry brief Annals

This c. relates the reigns of Azariah and Jotham of Judah, and of Zechariah, Shallum, Menahem, Pekahiah, and Pekah of Israel.

1. In the twenty and seventh year] Since Jeroboam came to the throne in the fifteenth year of Amaziah (14 23), and Amaziah only reigned 29 years (14 2), his son must have succeeded him in Jeroboam's fifteenth year. Azariah in vv. 13, 30 is called Uzziah.

5. The LORD smote the king] For the reason see 2 Ch 26 16-20. **A several house**] RM 'a lazar house,' in which he was secluded in accordance with the principle laid down in Lv 13 46. *Was over the house*] He held the same office as that alluded to in 1 K 4 6. **Judging the people**] i.e. acting as regent for his father.

6. The rest of the acts of Azariah] For details see 2 Ch 26 1-15. It was in the last year of Azariah (Uzziah) that the prophet Isaiah entered upon his ministry (Isa 6).

12. This *was* **the word of the LORD**] In spite of the ability and success of Jeroboam II the corruption of the people (which Amos and Hosea attest) bore its natural fruit, and the nation became the prey of faction, resulting in the downfall of Jehu's dynasty.

13. Uzziah] For the two names Uzziah and Azariah applied to the same individual see 1 Ch 6 24, 36; and the interchange of Azareel and Uzziel in 1 Ch 25 18, 4 mg. **14. Tirzah**] see on 1 K 14 17. Though it had ceased to be the capital, it was doubtless still an important place. **16. Tiphsah**] not the Tiphsah of 1 K 4 24, which represents Thapsacus, a far distant town on the Euphrates, but some unknown place in Israel itself. Some suggest that it is a mistake for Tappuah (Josh 17 8).

19. Pul] usually identified with the Tiglath-pileser named in v. 29, who was the successor, though not the son, of Asshur-nirari, his reign lasting from 745 to 728 B.C. The Assyrians had come in contact with Israel previous to this (see on 10 34) ; but it was only under Tiglath-pileser that they began seriously to endanger the independence of the northern kingdom, and the invasion here described is the first recorded of their many attacks upon the Hebrew states. **Menahem gave Pul**] cp. Hos 5 13. Tiglath-pileser himself in his inscriptions records that he received tribute from ' Menahem of Samaria.'

20. Exacted the money] The sovereigns of Judah usually bribed their foreign allies, or bought off foreign invaders by drawing upon the treasures stored in the Temple (1 K 15 18 2 K 12 18 16 8 18 15) ; though Jehoiakim followed the same course as Menahem, and taxed his subjects (23 35).

25. Pekah] Menahem and his son Pekahiah had depended for support upon the protection of Assyria ; but Pekah belonged to a faction which was opposed to Assyrian influences.

Palace] RV ' castle ' : cp. 1 K 16 18.

27. Twenty years] The Assyrian inscriptions show that no more than four years separated the close of Pekah's reign from that of Menahem, so that the latter here must be over-estimated.

29. Tiglath-pileser] see on v. 19. The invasion here described was connected with the attack made by Pekah and his ally Rezin of Damascus, upon Ahaz of Judah (16 5 f.). Of the places taken by Tiglath-pileser **Ijon** and **Abel-beth-Maachah** were near the sources of the Jordan, N. of Lake Merom ; **Kedesh** and **Hazor** lay to the W. of the same lake ; the site of **Janoah** is uncertain. **Carried them captive**] This deportation took place in 734 B.C. It is recorded by Tiglath-pileser himself in his own inscriptions, though he says exaggeratedly that he deported ' the whole of the inhabitants.' The purpose of such wholesale removals of the population of a conquered country was to destroy national sentiment and traditions, and so prevent all attempts to recover independence by killing the aspiration for it.

30. Hoshea . . conspiracy] Hoshea pursued a different policy to Pekah and sought Assyrian support by paying tribute (17 3). **In the twentieth year**] According to v. 33 Jotham reigned only 16 years, and Pekah's reign was contemporary with part of that of Ahaz (17 1).

35. He built, etc.] Other allusions to his buildings occur in 2 Ch 27 3.

36. The rest . . Jotham] see 2 Ch 27 2-8. The prosperity which Judah enjoyed during Uzziah's reign continued through that of his successor (if Isa 2 may be taken as descriptive of it) ; but the accumulation of wealth was accompanied by religious corruption : see Isa 2 6-8. **37. Rezin . . Pekah**] The war which broke out in the reign of Ahaz was threatening during the reign of Jotham (see on 16 5).

CHAPTER 16
AHAZ AND ASSYRIA

This c. describes the reign of Ahaz of Judah, his appeal to Assyria when attacked by Pekah of Israel and Rezin of Syria, and the overthrow of Damascus by the king of Assyria.

3. He walked, etc.] see 2 Ch 28 2 where he is described as making images for Baalim. **Made his son . . fire**] Children were sometimes actually sacrificed and burnt (see 17 31 3 27), and the same thing may be meant here, but some think that the rite here described was a kind of ceremonial purification by fire, the child being merely passed across, or over, the flame in the course of idolatrous worship. Ahaz is the first Judæan king who is said to have adopted this practice ; but he was followed in it by Manasseh (21 6), and frequent protests against it occur in the writings of successive prophets (Jer 7 31 19 5 Ezk 20 26, etc.).

5. Came up to Jerusalem] Pekah's policy was to oppose the Assyrians, and in conjunction with Rezin he sought to induce Ahaz to join a coalition against them. Failing to persuade him, they took up arms for the purpose of dethroning him, and replacing him by ' the son of Tabeal ' (Isa 7 6), who was either a creature of the two confederates, or Pekah himself (' Tabeal ' being a cypher for Remaliah, the name of Pekah's father). The successes of the invaders are described in 2 Ch 28 5-15, but though they inflicted much loss on Judah, they failed to take Jerusalem.

6. To Syria . . the Syrians] The context requires ' to Edom . . the Edomites ' (the latter correction being found in the LXX), since Elath had belonged to Edom and had been taken from it by Azariah (Uzziah, 14 22). According to 2 Ch 28 17 the Edomites took part in the war.

7. Sent . . Tiglath-pileser] This step was opposed by the prophet Isaiah, who counselled Ahaz to put his trust in the LORD, and asserted that the combination against him was not really formidable and would soon be overthrown (i.e. by Assyria, whom they had provoked). As a sign to reassure the king the prophet predicted the birth of a child whom his mother would call Immanuel (' God with us ') ; and declared that before he ceased to be an infant, both Israel and Syria would be deprived of their kings. Ahaz, however, disregarded Isaiah's counsel ; and the prophet accordingly predicted that the intervention of Assyria which he was inviting would be attended by calamities for Judah as well as for her enemies. See Isa 7.

8. Sent *it for* **a present**] Tiglath-pileser, in his inscriptions, records that he received tribute from ' Jehoahaz of Judah,' Jehoahaz being probably the full name of Ahaz.

9. Hearkened unto him] The adhesion of Judah would facilitate Assyria's operations against Egypt. **Damascus**] Damascus was taken and its people deported in 732 B.C., the event having been predicted by Amos (1⁵).

Kir] near the lower Euphrates, the original home of the Syrian people (Am 9⁷).

10. Went to Damascus] perhaps to do homage to the Assyrian king there. **Saw an altar**] probably of Assyrian pattern, since Ahaz would be more likely to introduce into his own land the religion of the victors than of the vanquished. **11. Urijah**] perhaps the Urijah of Isa 8². **13. Meat offering**] RV ' meal offering ' : and so in v. 15.

14. The brasen altar] i.e. the altar constructed by Solomon (1 K 8⁶⁴). This had hitherto occupied a central position in the court in front of the Temple ; but now, in order to make room for the new altar (the 'great altar' of v. 15), was placed between the latter and the N. side of the court.

15. To enquire *by*] i.e. to obtain indications of the divine will, possibly by the inspection of the victims that were offered upon it. But some render, 'shall be left for further consideration.' If this is correct, Ahaz was too busy with his new altar to decide what was to become of the other that was consecrated to the service of the LORD. **17. The borders**] RV ' the panels ' : i.e. of the stands of the ten lavers made for Solomon : see 1 K 7²⁷⁻³⁹.

The sea] i.e. the molten sea (1 K 7²³⁻²⁶). Ahaz probably removed these various works of art to conceal them from the cupidity of the Assyrians.

18. The covert] RV ' the covered way ' : not mentioned in the description of Solomon's Temple. **Turned he from**] RV ' he turned unto.' What is meant is obscure. **For**] RV ' because of ': probably the alterations described were intended to make the Temple appear less attractive, lest the Assyrian king should wish to dismantle it and appropriate its decorations.

19. The rest of the acts of Ahaz] see 2 Ch 28²⁴, ²⁵. In Isa 7 is an account of the interview between Ahaz and the prophet Isaiah alluded to in the note on v. 7.

CHAPTER 17

THE FALL OF SAMARIA

This c. relates the reign of Hoshea. He intrigued with Egypt and rebelled against Assyria ; and Samaria, in consequence, was taken and its people carried into captivity, their place being filled by a mixed population. **1. Hoshea**] Hoshea, unlike Pekah (16⁵), belonged to the faction in Samaria which relied on Assyrian support, and Tiglath-pileser, in his inscriptions, states that after he had slain Pekah, he ' appointed ' Hoshea to rule

over Israel, and received as tribute 10 talents of gold and 1,000 talents of silver.

3. Shalmaneser] succeeded Tiglath-pileser, his reign lasting from 727 to 723 B.C.

Gave him presents] i.e. rendered him tribute.

4. So] This king, whose name should perhaps be written Seve, is generally identified with Sabako, the first king of the 25th dynasty, though some authorities regard him as a petty prince who was vassal of the Pharaoh. The interference of Assyria with the Israelite kingdoms raised the fears of Egypt, which accordingly encouraged any disaffection which the Israelite sovereigns manifested towards their Assyrian over-lords. But the hopes which Hoshea entertained of Egyptian support proved as delusive to him as they did subsequently to Hezekiah and Zedekiah : cp. Isa 30³ 31¹ Jer 37⁷. **Shut him up, and bound him**] Possibly Hoshea was either captured, or surrendered before his capital was taken.

6. The king of Assyria] Not Shalmaneser (v. 3), who died before Samaria was captured, but his successor, Sargon (723–705). The fall of Samaria took place in 722 B.C. **Carried Israel away**] The numbers deported, as given in Sargon's own inscription, amounted to 27,280 ; so that a considerable population must have been left behind : cp. 2 Ch 34⁹. Of the localities where the captives were settled, **Halah** is not known. **In Habor** *by* **the river of Gozan**] should be 'on Habor' (the Chaboras, mod. Khabour), ' the river of Gozan' (part of Mesopotamia). **The cities** (LXX 'mountains') **of the Medes**] S. of the Caspian Sea.

8. The kings of Israel] especially Jeroboam, who introduced the calf-worship, and Ahab, who introduced Baal worship.

9. The tower of the watchmen] i.e. the watch towers erected for solitary guardians of the vineyards and flocks in lonely localities, the phrase **from the tower . . fenced city** thus embracing thinly and thickly populated places.

12. Ye shall not do this thing] cp. Dt 12³¹. Some of the pillars and Asherim (so read for ' images and groves' in v. 10) were probably, like the calves, erected in honour of the LORD, and the LXX after ' things ' adds ' unto the LORD.' If so they had an evil tendency, because they were associated with the corruptions of the old Canaanite worship.

13. By all the prophets] Among the prophets who laboured in Israel were Ahijah, Jehu (son of Hanani), Elijah, Elisha, Micaiah, Jonah, Oded, Amos, and Hosea ; whilst those who ministered in Judah included (up to the time here indicated) Shemaiah, Iddo, Azariah, Hanani, Jehu, Zechariah (son of Jehoiada), Micah, and Isaiah. Through such agents God exhorted and warned His people before sending upon them the punishments which their sins deserved.

15. Vanity] often applied to idols (1 K 16 13)

16. All the host of heaven] i.e. the stars. There is no previous reference in Kings to this form of idolatry in N. Israel, but an allusion to it occurs in Am 5 26, where the name 'Chiun' probably denotes the planet Saturn. Warnings against it are found in Dt 4 19 17 3.

19. Walked .. Israel] as when Athaliah, the daughter of Ahab, introduced Baal worship: cp. 8 18, 27 16 3. **20. All the seed**] The writer here anticipates the future, and refers to the destruction of Jerusalem, an event which he still has to relate.

24. Brought *men* **from**, etc.] Of the names that follow, **Babylon** was on the Euphrates; **Cuthah** was between the Euphrates and the Tigris; **Ava**, perhaps the Ivah of 18 34, is identified by some with the Ahava of Ezr 8 15; **Hamath** was on the Orontes; **Sepharvaim** ('the two Sippars') was in Babylonia. The conquest of some of these places is alluded to in 18 34. Sargon in one of his inscriptions mentions the transportation of some of the inhabitants of Babylon to 'the land Khatti,' which, though strictly designating the country of the Hittites, may be intended to denote Palestine generally; but according to another inscription the people settled in Samaria consisted of Arabian tribes.

25. Lions] These, which were common in the Jordan valley, would multiply in consequence of the depopulation of the country.

26. The manner] i.e. the ordinances of worship. **27. One of the priests**] The priests alone were acquainted with the proper ritual. **Let them**] i.e. the priest and his attendants.

30. Succoth-benoth] perhaps Zir-bânit, the wife of Merodach. **Nergal**] the Assyrian god of war. **31. Adrammelech and Anammelech**] probably the gods Adar and Anu, with the addition of the word 'melech' ('king').

32. Of the lowest of them] better, 'of all classes': cp. 1 K 12 31.

33. They feared the LORD and served, etc.] cp. v. 41. The religion that prevailed was a combination of the worship of the LORD (Jehovah), as the God of the land of Israel (v. 27), with that of the various deities adored by the different nations from which the settlers were drawn. The worship of the LORD was maintained among them as late as the return of the Jews under Zerubbabel (see Ezr 4 2, one reading); and they approached the latter with a request to be allowed to share in the restoration of the Temple. **Whom they carried away from thence**] RV 'from among whom they' (the settlers) 'had been carried away.'

34. They fear not the LORD] i.e. the worship of the LORD implied in v. 33 was not such as God desired.

41. Unto this day] i.e. as late as the time of the writer of the passage, though whether the statement proceeds from the compiler of the book, or from one of his authorities, is not certain.

The Israelite exiles, whose native land was thus occupied by strangers, lost their nationality in the country of their captivity, and never again formed a distinct community. When, however, the people of Judah were deported some 150 years later into Babylon by Nebuchadnezzar, individual members of the northern tribes joined themselves to them in the course of the Exile, and accompanied them back to Palestine when Cyrus the Persian permitted them to return to their homes. In 1 Ch 9 3 'children of Ephraim and Manasseh,' as well as of Judah and Benjamin, are mentioned as dwelling in Jerusalem after the Return; and Anna the prophetess was of the tribe of Asher (Lk 2 36): cp. also Tob 1 1 Judith 6 15. But in 2 Esdr 13 39-47 it is related that the Ten Tribes, after being carried into Assyria by Shalmaneser, decided to leave the heathen and go forth 'into a further country where never mankind dwelt, that they might there keep their statutes which they never kept in their own land'; and from thence their restoration is predicted. These Lost Tribes have been fancifully identified with various nations, including our own.

CHAPTER 18

HEZEKIAH AND SENNACHERIB

This c. describes the reign of Hezekiah of Judah, his religious reforms, and the invasion of Judah by Sennacherib, king of Assyria, who sent one of his officers to demand the surrender of Jerusalem.

1. Now it came to pass, etc.] The northern kingdom having been destroyed, the history is henceforward confined to the events connected with Judah only.

2. Twenty and five years old] Probably an error, for if Ahaz was only 36 at his death (16 2) his son could scarcely be 25.

4. He removed the high places] cp. v. 22. This was the first attempt to put an end to the provincial shrines which had co-existed with the Temple as seats of worship from the time of Solomon onward: see 1 K 14 23 15 14 22 43 2 K 12 3 14 4 15 4. Though dedicated to the service of the LORD, the rites conducted at them were peculiarly liable to corruption, and the interests of true religion were now seen to require their abolition. But the religious reform here described cannot have been very thorough, for the 'high places' built by Solomon for his foreign wives were not destroyed until the reign of Josiah (2 K 23 13); and Isaiah, in prophecies belonging to this reign, alludes to graven and molten images as being still objects of adoration (Isa 30 22 31 7). **The brasen serpent**] see Nu 21 9. Nothing is recorded of its history since the time of Moses. **Nehushtan**] It is not clear whether this was the name ('the Brasen') by which it was known when an object of worship, or a term of contempt ('a mere piece of brass') applied to it when marked for destruction.

5. None like him] The same praise is given to Josiah (23 25).

7. The LORD was with him] Though Hezekiah, in consequence of pursuing a mistaken policy, experienced great calamities in the course of his reign, yet his fidelity to the LORD had its reward in a signal overthrow of the same Assyrian power that within Hezekiah's lifetime had destroyed the much stronger kingdom of Israel.

He rebelled] It may be inferred from Isa 14 28-32 that Hezekiah at the beginning of his reign received from the Philistines a proposal urging him to join a movement against Assyria, but that Isaiah, confident that the LORD would protect Zion, sought to dissuade him from accepting it. Probably Isaiah's counsel prevailed, and the king continued for a time to be a vassal of Assyria. But when in 705 Sargon was succeeded by Sennacherib, several of the vassal states again attempted to regain their independence ; and with a view to obtaining Hezekiah's help, envoys were sent to Judah (about 703) by Merodach Baladan of Babylon (see 20 12 f.) and by the Ethiopians (Isa 18), the latter probably on behalf of the king of Egypt. At the Judæan court the hope of an Egyptian alliance exercised a strong attraction (see Isa 30, 31), but it was opposed by Isaiah, who continued to advocate confidence in the LORD, the promotion of social and religious reforms, and abstention from foreign entanglements. Eventually those who supported the alliance with Egypt prevailed ; and in 701 Hezekiah, in co-operation with a section of the Philistines, rebelled against Assyria.

8. Smote the Philistines] probably such as remained loyal to Assyria.

9. Shalmaneser .. came up] vv. 9–12 repeat in brief the account of the capture of Samaria already given in 17 5 f. **11. The cities of the Medes**] Media was the mountainous district S. of the Caspian.

13. In the fourteenth year] The Assyrian invasion here described took place in 701, and therefore according to this v. Hezekiah's accession was in 714 ; but v. 10 states that Samaria, which fell in 722, was captured in Hezekiah's 'sixth' year, which makes 727 the date of his accession. The section vv. 13, 17–37 recurs in Isa 36 1-22.

Sennacherib] succeeded Sargon in 705. The beginning of his reign was much disturbed, and his first campaign was against the Babylonian prince, Merodach Baladan, whom he drove from his capital. This was followed

by an invasion of the Cassi, a people of Elam ; and then in 701 he undertook the expedition against Judah and the other Palestinian states, which is described in the text.

Against all the fenced cities] Sennacherib in his inscriptions relates that he captured forty-six cities of Judah and deported more than 200,000 of the inhabitants. Hezekiah himself was besieged in his capital and compelled to tender submission, as recorded in v. 14.

14. Lachish] The place at this time was being besieged by Sennacherib (2 Ch 32 9). **Three hundred talents**] According to the inscriptions the fine was 800 talents of silver and 30 talents of gold, besides other treasures.

17. The king of Assyria sent] It is probable that the surrender, described in v. 14, was expected by the Jews to secure their city from further molestation ; but Sennacherib was moving towards Egypt, and doubtless thought it dangerous to leave so strong a fortress in other hands than his own. The consequent demand for its capitulation, here recorded, exposed Sennacherib to the charge of breaking his covenant : see Isa 33 8.

Tartan .. Rabsaris .. Rab-shakeh] the titles of military officers, meaning respectively 'commander-in-chief,' 'chief of the princes,' and 'chief of the captains.' **The conduit of the upper pool**] This pool has been identified by some with the modern Birket Mamilla, situated W. of the city ; but more probably it is the pool of Siloam, near the S. end of Mt. Zion, to which the conduit here mentioned carried water from the spring of Gihon in the Kidron valley (see on 1 K 1 33).

18. Shebna] Shebna, who, from his name, was probably a foreigner, had previously occupied the position now filled by Eliakim (Isa 22 15), and seems to have advocated reliance upon the support of Egypt, a policy which Isaiah had opposed. When Hezekiah was compelled to make submission to the Assyrian king, Shebna naturally fell into disgrace and was degraded to an inferior office, Eliakim being promoted in his room.

21. This bruised reed] For a similar contemptuous estimate of Egypt cp. Ezk 29 6.

Pharaoh] This was probably Shabako, the successor of So (17 3). The inability of Egypt to help those who trusted it, as shown in the case of Hoshea of Israel (see 17 4-6), was again displayed by the defeat of an Egyptian army at Eltekeh, which had come to relieve Ekron, one of the Philistine towns besieged by Sennacherib. It was this success which left the Assyrian king free to invade Judah, as described in v. 13. **22. Whose high places, etc.**] Rabshakeh thought that such sacrilege was calculated to provoke the anger of the LORD, whereas Hezekiah's action really conduced to religious purity : see on v. 4.

23. Give pledges] RM 'make a wager.'

24. Put thy trust .. horsemen] For reliance upon Egypt for a supply of horses see Isa 31 1-3. **25. Am I now come up without the LORD?]** He might have regarded his capture of the Judæan cities, described in v. 13, as an indication that the LORD had given them up into his hand because of Hezekiah's action in removing the high places.

26. The Syrian language] i.e. Aramean, a language which served as the principal medium of intercourse between the various nationalities in the East. This would be intelligible to the state officials both of Assyria and Judah, but unfamiliar to the bulk of the citizens of Jerusalem ; and so Eliakim, who desired to keep both the threats and promises of the Assyrian officer from the multitude, wished the conference to be conducted in it.

27. That they may eat, etc.] The garrison had taken up their position on the ramparts, with all the extremities of starvation before them ; and Rabshakeh now appealed from the king and his advisers to the rank and file of his army (in violation of all honourable usage).

31. Come out] i.e. capitulate, before incurring the further calamities of a protracted siege.

34. Hamath, etc.] For most of the towns here named see on 17 24. **Arpad** has been identified with some ruins NW. of Aleppo.

35. That the Lord should deliver, etc.] The Assyrian argued that the national god of a little state like Judah would not be able to defend His people more effectually than the deities of other nations, subdued by the Assyrians, had done. He had to learn that the God of the Jews was also the Lord of all the earth.

CHAPTER 19
THE DELIVERANCE OF JERUSALEM

2. Isaiah the prophet] This is the first mention of Isaiah in this book, but his own writings show that he had been an active teacher and statesman not only during the earlier years of Hezekiah himself, but also during the reign of Hezekiah's predecessor Ahaz : see on 16 7 18 7. The chapters in the prophet's writings which relate to the present occasion are 10 5-12 6 14 24-27 17 12-14 22, 29–33, 36, 37 (the last two of which substantially repeat 1 K 18, 19).

3. Blasphemy] RV 'contumely' : such as the nation was experiencing at the hands of the invader. **The children .. bring forth]** a figure for powerlessness in the time of peril.

4. Remnant] cp. v. 30, Isa 10 20. A large number of the Judæan cities had been captured (see on 18 13), so that the population of the capital might well be thus described. **7. Send**

a blast upon him] RV 'put a spirit in him' : i.e. an impulse of fear. **A rumour]** Ill tidings respecting his army, which was destined shortly to perish in its advance against Egypt.

8. Returned] to Sennacherib. **Libnah .. Lachish]** in southern Judah.

9. Tirhakah] an Ethiopian, who was at first the general and subsequently the successor of the Egyptian king Shabako (18 21). He was contemporary not only with Sennacherib, but with his two successors, Esarhaddon and Asshurbanipal.

12. Gozan, etc.] These places were all in the neighbourhood of the Euphrates. **Gozan** is mentioned in 17 6 ; **Haran** in Gn 11 31 ; **Eden** in Ezk 27 23. **13. Hamath]** see on 17 24. It had revolted against Sargon in 720 B.C., but the insurrection was crushed and its king Jahubidi slain.

15. Thou .. even thou alone] Whereas Sennacherib had counted the God of Israel among a number of deities all equally unable to withstand him (18 33-35), Hezekiah here asserts that the LORD (Jehovah) is the only God, and implies that whatever the Assyrian had accomplished had been done by His permission. **19. That all .. may know]** If a small kingdom like Judah successfully resisted Assyria, it could only be through the supremacy of its God.

21. The daughter of Zion] For the personification of a city as a woman cp. Mic 4 10 Isa 23 10, 12 47 1 f. **23. The lodgings, etc.]** RV 'his farthest lodging place, the forest of his fruitful field.'

24. I have digged .. waters] Sennacherib implies that the progress of his armies on foreign soil could not be hindered by the enemy stopping up the water-springs: he at once digs fresh wells. **Besieged places]** RV 'Egypt.' The numerous channels of the Nile were ordinarily a means of defence to Egypt (cp. Nah 3 8), but Sennacherib implies that they were inadequate to stay his advance.

25. Hast thou .. done it] This begins the LORD's response to Sennacherib's boastings. The Assyrian king had in reality only been an agent deputed to carry out the divine purposes: cp. Isa 10 12 f. 47 6 Zech 1 15.

28. My hook] cp. Ezk 38 4. The expression may be an allusion either to the method adopted for controlling wild animals (cp. Ezk 19 4), or to a practice employed by the Assyrians towards their captives : see 2 Ch 33 11 RM.

29. A sign unto thee] i.e. unto Hezekiah. The occurrence of the earlier and harsher part of the prophet's prediction would be a warranty for the fulfilment of the later and more cheerful portion of his message, viz. that the land should be free from invasion and cultivated in peace. **This year ..**

the third year] The reckoning is inclusive, 'this year' meaning the year of the invasion, and 'the third year' being the second year after it.

30. The remnant] cp. v. 3. The population, so sadly thinned by the war, would again recover its strength and numbers. **31. Out of Jerusalem, etc.**] The country folk that had been driven into the capital by the invasion would again return to their homes. **32. Cast a bank**] a mound of earth with an inclined surface, raised against the wall of a besieged city to enable the besiegers to reach the top.

34. Mine own sake] God's intentions towards His people could not be foiled altogether through the sins of the latter ; so that though the divine justice had demanded the chastisement of the nation, the divine faithfulness required that it should be preserved from complete destruction.

35. The angel of the LORD] cp. Ex 12 23. In 2 S 24 15, 16 the pestilence that punished David's numbering of the people is attributed to an angel ; and it is probable that it was a similar calamity that destroyed Sennacherib's army. It seems more likely that the disaster occurred in the low-lying ground on the Egyptian frontiers than in the neighbourhood of Jerusalem ; and the Greek historian, Herodotus, who gives a fanciful account of an overthrow sustained by the Assyrians in a campaign against Egypt, places it near Pelusium. But wherever and however it happened, it was a signal confirmation of Isaiah's faith in the LORD and a striking vindication of his prescience.

36. Nineveh] its ruins have been found opposite the modern Mosul.

37. His sons smote him] Sennacherib's death did not occur until some 20 years after the destruction of his army, as described in v. 35 ; but though he took part in several expeditions subsequent to his invasion of Judah, he never again molested the Hebrew state. **Esarhaddon**] reigned from 681 B.C. to 668.

CHAPTER 20
HEZEKIAH'S SICKNESS AND RECOVERY

1. In those days] The incidents related in this c. probably took place *before* Sennacherib's invasion, for (*a*) the deliverance from the Assyrians is still future (v. 6) ; (*b*) Hezekiah is in possession of great treasures (v. 13), which could scarcely have been the case after the surrender described in 18 14, 15 ; (*c*) Merodach Baladan, king of Babylon, was driven from his throne before Sennacherib attacked Judah. Chronologically, therefore, this c. should precede 18 7f. **Thou shalt die**] Prophetic predictions were generally conditional and not absolute ; a threatened judgment might be averted by repentance and a promised blessing forfeited by misconduct : see Jer 18 7-10 26 18, 19.

3. How I have walked, etc.] In the absence of any complete belief in a future life, this world was held to be the only sphere within which God's moral governance of mankind displayed itself, length of days being regarded as the reward of righteousness, and a short life being thought to imply great guilt. Hence Hezekiah, with the prospect of an untimely death before him, appealed to God to bear witness to his uprightness. **A perfect heart**] i.e. a heart not divided between devotion to the LORD and devotion to other gods : cp. 1 K 8 61 and contrast 1 K 11 4.

4. The middle court] RV 'the middle part of the city.'

7. A lump of figs] A plaster of figs is known from other sources to have been used as a remedy for boils, but since Hezekiah was 'sick unto death' (v. 1), his cure is doubtless regarded as miraculous.

8. What *shall be* **the sign, etc.**] vv. 8-11 ought to precede the statement of the king's recovery in v. 7.

9. Shall the shadow, etc.] better, as in RM, 'the shadow is gone forward ten steps, shall it go back ten steps ? '

11. The dial of Ahaz] Probably a platform surrounded by steps and surmounted by a pillar, the shadow of which fell upon a smaller or larger number of the steps according as the sun mounted or declined in the sky. It has been conjectured that a slight alteration of the length of the sun's shadow might be produced by a partial eclipse ; if so, the sign consisted in the event taking place in agreement with the prophet's prediction.

12. Berodach-baladan] Isa 39 1 has the more correct form 'Merodach-baladan.' This prince was a Chaldean who twice made himself master of Babylon and was twice expelled from it by the Assyrians. In 2 Ch 32 31 the motive of his embassy is said to have been a wish to enquire into the unusual occurrence described in v. 11 ; but it is probable that he likewise sought to obtain Hezekiah's aid against the Assyrians.

13. The house of his armour] Probably the house of the forest of Lebanon ; cp. 1 K 10 17 Isa 22 8.

14. Then came Isaiah] Isaiah opposed all political entanglements as involving reliance upon material resources instead of confidence in the LORD. Hezekiah had still to learn how powerless was his own strength or that of foreign allies to save him in the hour of his need.

17. Into Babylon] The prophet probably regarded Babylon as a province of Assyria, not as an independent power ; and it was to Babylon that an Assyrian king carried Manasseh the son of Hezekiah (according to 2 Ch 33 11).

19. Good *is* the word] Hezekiah showed the same submissiveness as Eli had manifested on a similar occasion (1 S 3 18).

20. The rest of the acts] Among other acts related in 2 Ch 29-31 are the purification of the Temple (desecrated by Ahaz), the celebration of a solemn passover, and the arrangement of the priestly courses. **A pool, and a conduit**] The 'pool' is probably the pool of Siloam, which was fed by a conduit from the spring of Gihon : cp. 2 Ch 32 30. The 'conduit' was perhaps at first a surface aqueduct, which Hezekiah replaced by a tunnel to secure the supply of water from being interrupted. Such a tunnel has been found, and an inscription describing its construction.

CHAPTER 21
The Reigns of Manasseh and Amon

3. The high places, etc.] Manasseh not only restored the country sanctuaries which had been destroyed by Hezekiah as seats of corruption (see 18 4, 22), and renewed the Baal worship practised by the house of Ahab (see 11 18, and cp. 1 K 16 31,32), but also introduced star worship, a form of religion previously unknown in Judah. **The host of heaven**] The worship of the stars, which was probably introduced from Assyria, was conducted on the flat roofs of the houses : see Jer 19 13 Zeph 1 5, and cp. 23 11,12.

5. In the two courts] If the view expressed in the note on 1 K 7 12 be correct, the two courts may be the inner (or upper) court immediately surrounding the Temple, and the court enclosing the Palace.

6. Pass through the fire] see on 16 3. For his son 2 Ch 33 6 has 'his children.' **Observed times**] RV 'practised augury' : by the observation of the clouds, etc. **Familiar spirits**] RV 'them that had familiar spirits' : such persons were believed to be animated by, or to have intercourse with, the spirits of the dead : cp. 1 S 28 7. One of the devices employed by them was probably ventriloquism, the spirit appearing to speak from the ground (Isa 8 19 29 4).

7. A graven image of the grove] better, 'a carved Asherah.' This was placed in the Temple itself, whence it was removed by Josiah (23 6).

9. Manasseh seduced them] The evil example of Manasseh and his court had a worse effect upon the people at large than that of any previous Judæan king, so that at a much later date the prophet Jeremiah declared that it was for what Manasseh did that the judgment announced by him was to come upon the nation (Jer 15 4).

11. The Amorites] The inhabitants of Canaan had been destroyed for the very iniquities which Manasseh was now surpassing : cp. Dt 9 5.

13. The line of Samaria] The judgment denounced against Judah would be carried out with the same precision and exactness as the judgment that overtook the northern kingdom and the dynasty of Ahab. **As *a man* wipeth a dish**] i.e. Jerusalem would be finished and done with. **14. The remnant**] see 19 2. Jerusalem had survived the calamities that had been inflicted on the rest of Judah by the Assyrians (18 13), but it would not be delivered from the enemies that awaited it in the future.

17. The rest of the acts] see 2 Ch 33 12-19, where it is related that Manasseh was taken captive by the king of Assyria to Babylon, repented there of his sins, was restored to his kingdom, and instituted a religious reformation.

19. Jotbah] cp. Dt 10 7 Nu 33 33.

CHAPTER 22
Josiah. The finding of a Book of the Law

1. Boscath] in Judah : cp. Josh 15 39.

4. That he may sum, etc.] Josiah was contemplating a restoration of the Temple similar to that carried out previously by Joash (12 4 f.), and a collection of money had been made for the purpose : see 2 Ch 34 9. **5. The doers of the work .. to the doers of the work**] The first were the overseers, the second were the labourers. **7. There was no reckoning**] cp. 12 15.

8. The book of the law] As the book found in the Temple was brief enough to be read at a single assembly (23 2), whereas the reading of the Law by Ezra occupied several days (Neh 8 18), it can scarcely have included the whole of the Pentateuch ; and the religious reforms that Josiah carried out after its discovery and perusal (23 4 f.) point to its being Deuteronomy only. Deuteronomy contains a record of Moses' farewell address to his countrymen, and reproduces much of the Mosaic legislation that is comprised in Ex 20-23, 34. But it does not profess to be written by Moses (indeed, in its present form it cannot proceed from him since it gives an account of his death, 34 5), and there are certain features in it which, when compared with other parts of the Pentateuch and with the history of the period between Moses and Joshua, have led many scholars to conclude that it was composed after the time of Moses out of materials of earlier date. Its concealment in the Temple was probably due to the persecution of the worshippers of the Lord by Manasseh, for it condemns in particular those idolatries which Manasseh practised.

13. Because our fathers, etc.] Whether Deuteronomy was actually written by Moses or at a later date, the bulk of its teaching had long been familiar to the people, since it contained the substance of the book of the covenant (Ex 24 7), embracing Ex 20-23.

14. Huldah] The only other prophetesses mentioned in the OT. are Miriam (Ex 15²⁰), Deborah (Jg 4⁴), and Noadiah (Neh 6¹⁴). **In the college]** RV 'in the second quarter,' a certain division of the city which in Zeph 1¹⁰ is associated with ' the fish gate,' a gate in the N. or NW. wall.

19. A curse] cp. Dt 28¹⁵. The condition of Jerusalem should be such that people desirous of cursing their enemies could wish them no worse a fate.

20. In peace] Josiah, though he fell in battle (23²⁹), yet was spared the pain of witnessing the calamities sustained by his country in the time of his successors. He was one of ' the righteous who were taken away from the evil to come ' (Isa 57¹).

CHAPTER 23
RELIGIOUS REFORM. JOSIAH'S DEATH

2. The prophets] Jeremiah, Habakkuk, and Zephaniah lived about this time. **Read in their ears]** cp. the similar proceeding related in Neh 8⁴ᶠ. **3. By a pillar]** or, ' upon a platform ' : cp. 11¹⁴.

4. The priests of the second order] probably to be corrected into ' the second priest ' (as in 25¹⁸), i.e. the high priest's deputy. **Grove]** see on 21⁷. **5. The planets]** or, ' the signs of the zodiac.' The word is said to mean ' mansions,' the stars being the abodes of gods.

6. Of the children of the people] RV ' of the common people ' : cp. Jer 26²³. The graves of the poorer classes were probably made in the ground, whereas the tombs of the wealthy were constructed in the rocks, and were not so available for the purpose here described—viz. the defilement of the idolatrous emblems : cp. v. 14. **7. Sodomites]** The suppression of such is directed in Dt 23¹⁷,¹⁸. **Hangings]** lit. ' houses,' i.e. tents which sheltered the Asherah (or emblem of Ashtoreth).

8. Defiled the high places] That some of these were dedicated to the worship of the LORD appears from the following v., which implies that the priests who served them were priests of the LORD. The destruction of these sanctuaries thus resulted in confining the public rites of worship to the Temple at Jerusalem (according to the law of Dt 12⁵⁻¹⁴), and the removal of the priests who had previously ministered at them. **From Geba to Beersheba]** the northern and southern borders of the kingdom. **Of the gates]** Probably an error for ' of the satyrs ' or ' he-goats,' which were objects of worship and called ' devils ' in Lv 17⁷ 2 Ch 11¹⁵. The Heb. words closely resemble one another.

9. Did eat . . bread] It is not clear whether they were maintained by the offerings of their kinsfolk in their several localities or whether they shared the offerings made to the priests

at Jerusalem, but were debarred from ministering in the Temple (as was the case with priests who were otherwise disqualified, Lv 21²¹⁻²³) : cp. Dt 18⁶⁻⁸. By **unleavened bread** is probably meant the priestly dues generally.

10. Topheth] The name literally means ' spittle ' or ' spitting,' and so designates the locality as a place of abhorrence. **The valley . . Hinnom]** usually identified with the valley that flanks the modern city of Jerusalem on the W. ; but if the ancient city occupied only the eastern of the two hills upon which the present city stands, the valley here mentioned may have been the depression between them (subsequently called the ' Tyropæon '). Topheth, however, was in any case situated in the broad space formed by the junction of the three valleys immediately S. of the city. It was from the sacrificial fires lighted there for human sacrifices, as well as from those that were afterwards kindled in the same place to destroy the refuse of the city deposited in it that the Heb. name *Ge Hinnom* in the form *Gehenna* came to be used to denote the place of punishment for the unrepentant after death. **Molech]** see 1 K 11⁷. The rite here referred to is prohibited in Dt 18¹⁰.

11. The horses] A chariot was similarly dedicated to the sun at Sippar in Babylonia ; and it is probable that it was connected in idea with the sun's course through the sky. **The kings of Judah]** presumably Manasseh and Amon : see 21³,⁵. **Of the house . . by the chamber]** better, ' from the house . . to the chamber,' marking the extent of the stables.

12. On the top of the upper chamber] These altars were probably connected with the worship of the host of heaven : see on 21³.

13. Before Jerusalem] i.e. E. of the city. It is surprising that these, dating from the time of Solomon (see 1 K 11¹⁻⁸), had not been destroyed by Hezekiah ; but see on 18⁴. **Mount of corruption]** i.e. the Mt. of Olives, the later 'mount of offence.' **14. The bones of men]** i.e. to desecrate them, since dead bodies communicated uncleanness : cp. Nu 19¹⁶. **15. The altar that** *was* **at Beth-el]** see 1 K 12³²,³³. **Burned the high place]** probably the shrine erected upon it, which elsewhere is styled a 'house of high places.'

16. In the mount] presumably some adjoining elevation. **According to the word of the LORD]** see 1 K 13². **17. Title]** RV 'monument' : marking the place of burial. **18. Samaria]** here used of the country rather than the city, since the prophet alluded to belonged to Bethel.

21. The passover] Of this passover details are given in 2 Ch 35¹⁻¹⁹. **22. There was not holden, etc.]** On this occasion not only were the injunctions of the Law more strictly followed than had been the case previously, but exceptionally large numbers took part in the festival.

24. Images] RV 'teraphim,' which were probably models of the human figure representing household deities and used in divination : see Gn 31 ¹⁹ 1 S 19 ¹³ Ezk 21 ²¹.

29. Pharaoh-nechoh] i.e. Nechoh II, a king of the 26th dynasty (610–595 B.C.), whose father Psammetichus, at one time a tributary of the Assyrians, had secured independence for Egypt in 664 B.C.

The king of Assyria] i.e. the king of Babylon. Nineveh, the capital of Assyria, fell in 607 before the united forces of the Median Cyaxares and the Babylonian Nabopolassar ; and it was to dispute the spoils of the fallen empire with Nabopolassar that Nechoh advanced northward through Palestine. The king of Babylon is here called by the name of Assyria, the country he had conquered (cp. Ezr 6 ²², where a Persian king is likewise styled 'king of Assyria,' the Persians having subdued and dispossessed the Babylonians).

Josiah went against him] Josiah's motives can only be conjectured, but it is probable that in the downfall of Assyria's power he hoped to extend his authority over what had once been the northern kingdom, and feared that his designs would be foiled by the Egyptian advance. **At Megiddo**] see on 9 ²⁷. Josiah took up his position here to dispute the passage across Carmel. The Greek historian Herodotus probably alludes to this battle when he states that Nechoh defeated the Syrians at Magdolus. **When he had seen him**] i.e. when he encountered him in battle : cp. 14 ⁸. For the sorrow occasioned by Josiah's death see 2 Ch 35 ²⁵ Ecclus 49 ^{2, 3}.

30. Jehoahaz] also called Shallum (Jer 22 ¹¹ 1 Ch 3 ¹⁵). He was the younger brother of Jehoiakim who succeeded him (v. 36).

33. Riblah] on the Orontes, between Damascus and Hamath. Nechoh, after his success at Megiddo, had marched northward to meet the Babylonians, who eventually defeated him at Carchemish (Jer 46 ²).

34. Made Eliakim . . king] Jehoahaz had been chosen by the people without the sanction of Nechoh, who therefore asserted his authority by deposing him, and substituting his brother. **In the room of Josiah**] Nechoh did not recognise Jehoahaz. **Turned his name to Jehoiakim**] The bestowal of a new name by Nechoh upon Eliakim indicated that the latter was a subject or vassal prince of the Egyptian king. For a similar change cp. 24 ¹⁷, and see Gn 41 ⁴⁵ Dan 1 ⁷ (where, however, the new names are foreign, not, as here, Hebrew).

CHAPTER 24

Jehoiachin and Nebuchadnezzar

This c. recounts the reigns of Jehoiakim

and Jehoiachin, the invasion of Judah by Nebuchadnezzar, king of Babylon (who carried into captivity Jehoiachin and numbers of the people), and the reign of Zedekiah.

1. Nebuchadnezzar] called more accurately in Jer 25 ⁹ and elsewhere ' Nebuchadrezzar.' He was the son of the Nabopolassar who conquered Nineveh (see on 23 ²⁹), and, as his father's general, defeated the Egyptians in 605 at Carchemish on the Euphrates (Jer 46 ²). This success left the countries lying between the two great powers of Babylon and Egypt at the mercy of the former (24 ⁷) ; and consequently when Nebuchadnezzar succeeded his father, Jehoiakim (as here related) submitted to him. Some inscriptions of Nebuchadnezzar have been discovered in various parts of Palestine, but such as are decipherable relate not to his campaigns but to his buildings.

Became his servant three years] It is rather difficult to harmonise the statements respecting Jehoiakim's reign contained in this c. with 2 Ch 36 ⁵⁻⁸ and in Dan 1 ². In 2 Ch 36 ⁶ Jehoiakim is said to have been bound in fetters by Nebuchadnezzar in order to be carried to Babylon, and in Daniel his capture is described as having taken place in his third year. He was, however, in his own capital in the 'fourth' year of his reign (Jer 36 ¹) ; so that if these passages are to be reconciled with Kings it must be assumed that he was restored to his throne by the Babylonian king, and that the events here related took place after his restoration.

2. The Chaldees] here used to designate the Babylonians. **Syrians . . Moabites . . Ammon**] For these as enemies of Judah at this period see Jer 35 ¹¹ 48 ²⁷ Ezk 25 ^{1 f}.

His servants the prophets] The most prominent of the prophets who denounced judgment against the offending nation at this time was Jeremiah : see especially Jer 25, 26, 35, 36, 45. Unlike his predecessor Isaiah, the prophet declared that Jerusalem would be totally destroyed if its inhabitants did not repent ; and for this he was adjudged worthy of death, though his life was preserved by the interference of certain elders. Another prophet named Urijah, who also prophesied against the city, fled to Egypt to escape destruction, but he was surrendered to Jehoiakim by the Egyptian king and put to death : see Jer 26.

5. The rest of the acts] The circumstances of Jehoiakim's death are uncertain. The predictions of Jeremiah (22 ^{18, 19} 36 ³⁰) suggest that he died a violent death and that his corpse was left unburied, and Josephus states that Nebuchadnezzar, to whom Jehoiakim had capitulated, broke his pledges and slew him. But v. 6 is rather opposed to this.

7. The river of Egypt] see on 1 K 8 ⁶⁵.

8. Jehoiachin] also called Coniah and Jeconiah (Jer 22 ²⁴ 24 ¹).

11. And .. besiege it] RV 'while his servants were besieging it,' implying that the city was invested before Nebuchadnezzar, who was engaged in besieging Tyre, appeared in person to conduct the war.

12. His mother] i.e. the queen-mother : see on 1 K 2 19. **In the eighth year**] i.e. of Nebuchadnezzar's reign. In Jer 52 28 mention is made of a capture of 3,023 persons in Nebuchadnezzar's seventh year, of which there is no record in Kings, while Jeremiah makes no allusion to the deportation of prisoners here related.

14. The poorest sort] They were as worthless in character as obscure in station : see Jer 24 1-8. Among the better class who were carried away on this occasion was the prophet Ezekiel.

16. Seven thousand .. a thousand] If these numbers are included in the 10,000 of v. 14, it must be assumed that the princes and their numerous retainers constituted the remaining 2,000.

17. Mattaniah] as Mattaniah was brother of Jehoiakim, he must have been uncle of Jehoiachin ; so that 2 Ch 36 10 in describing him as brother of the latter uses the term vaguely. In 1 Ch 3 16 he is called son of Jeconiah, in the sense of successor. **Changed his name**] see on 23 34.

18. Hamutal] Zedekiah was only half-brother of Jehoiakim but full brother of Jehoahaz (see 23 31), and as Jehoahaz was imprisoned by the king of Egypt, Nebuchadnezzar may have calculated that in his brother he would find a loyal vassal who would support Babylonian rather than Egyptian interests.

19. He did *that which was* **evil**] cp. Jer 37 2. Zedekiah seems to have been weak but not unmerciful, and he was unable to cope with the princes who were his advisers : cp. Jer 38 4, 5. When the latter put Jeremiah in prison on a charge of deserting to the enemy, Zedekiah delivered him (Jer 39 11-21) ; and on a second occasion, when he was flung into a foul dungeon, he was once more rescued with the king's consent (Jer 38 6 f.).

20. Rebelled] Zedekiah was bound by oath to Nebuchadnezzar (2 Ch 36 13 Ezk 17 13), but overtures from Edom, Moab, Tyre, and other countries drew him from his allegiance, in spite of the opposition of the prophet Jeremiah (Jer 27), and as hopes were entertained of Egyptian help rebellion was finally resolved on.

CHAPTER 25

THE FALL OF JERUSALEM

This c. relates the siege and destruction of Jerusalem, the capture of king Zedekiah, and the deportation of most of the Jewish people.

1. In the tenth *day*] The successive stages

in the overthrow of the city are carefully marked by the historian : cp. vv. 3, 8. **Forts**] perhaps movable towers for throwing troops upon the walls.

3. The famine] the sufferings of the besieged are described in Jer 21 7-9 Lam 4 8 f. 5 10 f.

4. The city was broken up] RV 'a breach was made in the city.' Before this happened an Egyptian force had advanced to the relief of Jerusalem, and the Babylonians in consequence retired (Jer 37 5-11), but the relief was only temporary (as Jeremiah had predicted) and the siege was resumed. **The king's garden**] S. of the city near the pool of Siloam (Neh 3 15). **The plain**] RV 'the Arabah' : i.e. the valley of the Jordan. The design of the fugitives was to cross the river by the fords of Jericho.

7. Put out the eyes] Zedekiah was taken to Babylon, but he did not *see* it, just as Ezekiel had predicted (12 13). An Assyrian king is represented on one of his monuments as blinding a captive with the point of his own spear.

11. The rest of the people] i.e. those that remained in the country after the deportation related in 24 14, 15. **Of the multitude**] better, 'of the artificers.' In addition to this deportation in Nebuchadnezzar's 19th year Jeremiah (52 29) mentions one that occurred in his 18th year and another in his 23rd year, though the first of these may be identical with the one here described.

13. The pillars of brass, etc.] see 1 K 7 15 f. Jer 52 17-23, where some of the details are given differently. **15.** *In* **gold ..** *in* **silver**] better, ' as so much gold .. as so much silver.'

18. The second priest] i.e. the high priest's deputy. For **Zephaniah** cp. Jer 29 25, 29. **Keepers of the door**] i.e. of the entrance of the Temple.

19. That .. presence] i.e. those of the king's ministers who enjoyed freedom of access to him. **The principal scribe, etc.**] RM 'the scribe of the captain of the host' : i.e. the official who superintended the conscription. Nebuchadnezzar, instead of consigning the citizens to indiscriminate massacre, selected for punishment only the most responsible personages.

21. So Judah was carried away] The destruction of Jerusalem and the final deportation of its chief inhabitants took place in 586 B.C. The kingdom of Judah, like the kingdom of the ten tribes, now came to an end, as Jeremiah (20 4) had predicted ; and its historian here brings his record to a close, only pausing to describe the arrangements made for the government of the desolated country and the treatment received from Nebuchadnezzar's successor by the captive Jehoiachin. The mention of the latter fact is probably due to the writer's desire to show that the divine mercy attended the house of David even in the time of its deepest humiliation.

22. The son of Ahikam] Ahikam had befriended Jeremiah when the people sought to put him to death (Jer 26 24).

23. And when all the captains, etc.] For a fuller account of the events recounted in vv. 23–26 see Jer 40 7–43 13, from which it appears that Ishmael was instigated by Baalis the king of Ammon, and murdered Gedaliah treacherously. **Mizpah**] perhaps Mizpah in Benjamin (1 K 15 22).

25. In the seventh month] subsequently observed as a fast (Zech 7 5).

26. Came to Egypt] In doing this the people acted in defiance of the counsel of Jeremiah, whom they took with them : see Jer 42, 43.

27. Evil-merodach] son of Nebuchadnezzar, succeeding to his throne in 561 B.C. It was in the first year of his reign that he manifested to Jehoiachin the leniency here recorded. **Did lift up the head**] i.e. showed favour to: cp. Gn 40 13.   **28. The kings that** *were* **with him**] possibly other captive sovereigns.

29. Did eat bread . . before him] i.e. was a guest at the royal table. For a like privilege see 2 S 19 3 1 K 2 7.

THE FIRST AND SECOND BOOKS OF
CHRONICLES

INTRODUCTION

1. Character and Contents. Chronicles at first not only formed a single book but probably constituted one continuous work with Ezra and Nehemiah. The English name is a tolerable equivalent of the Hebrew ; whilst the corresponding Greek rendering probably means 'supplement' (lit. 'things passed over,' i.e. by the preceding historical books). Its author is unknown ; but from the prominence which is given in the book to the Levitical order it has been conjectured that he was himself a Levite. Its contents comprise, (a) certain genealogies, (b) the history of David and Solomon, and (c) the history of Judah (the history of the northern kingdom being entirely omitted). Its date, in conjunction with that of Ezra and Nehemiah, may be approximately determined by the mention in 1 Ch 3 24 of the sixth generation after Zerubbabel (who was living in 520 B.C.), which implies a date subsequent to 340 ; and this is supported by the reference in Neh 12 11, 22 to Jaddua, who was high priest in the time of Darius Codomannus (335–330) and of Alexander the Great (336–323). It was thus probably composed not much before 300 B.C., and consequently separated by a much longer period than Kings from the events it records.

2. Sources. Among the sources of information referred to in the course of the narrative are (a) genealogical tables (1 Ch 5 17) ; (b) the book of the kings of Judah and Israel (2 Ch 16 11, the same work being probably meant by the slightly different titles in 27 7 33 18) ; and (c) the writings of certain prophets, Samuel, Nathan, Gad, Ahijah, Shemaiah, Iddo, Jehu, and Isaiah (1 Ch 29 29 2 Ch 9 29 12 15 13 22 20 34 26 22 32 32). But certain of the authorities included in (c) are expressly stated to have been inserted in the historical work mentioned in (b)—see 2 Ch 20 34 32 32 RV ; and it is possible that the others were also embodied in the same book, which will then be the immediate authority to which the writer is principally indebted. It will be obvious, however, from a comparison of the parallels between Chronicles and earlier books of the Bible, that large parts of the former are practically derived from Genesis, Samuel, and especially Kings, by a process of mere transcription ; so that at first sight it would seem that the canonical books of Kings constitute the work just alluded to. But as the latter is quoted as recording the prayer of Manasseh, which finds no place in our Kings (2 Ch 33 18), and as Chronicles also contains much matter (2 Ch 11 5-12 26 6-10 28 17, 18) which is likely to have come from an annalistic writing, but does not occur in Kings, it is probable that the book which is cited by name was different from, but based on, our Kings, and was the means through which the writer of Chronicles came to incorporate portions of the latter. The differences between Chronicles and Kings consist of omissions, additions, and minor modifications. The former, besides leaving out all the history of the Ten Tribes after the Separation, omits most of the sins and weaknesses of David and Solomon. Its principal additions comprise details of the Temple organisation and certain incidents in the history of the kings of Judah. For some statements of Kings it substitutes others, the alterations being most noticeable in connexion with numbers, those of Chronicles being generally the higher (cp. 1 Ch 21 5 with 2 S 24 9, 2 Ch 3 15 with 1 K 7 15, 2 Ch 4 5 with 1 K 7 26).

3. Value. In considering the historical value of Chronicles account need only be taken of those parts in which it differs from Kings. In view of its greater remoteness from the events described, it cannot be considered so good an authority as the latter, and in cases of discrepancy the statements of Kings deserve the preference. In regard to matters upon which it is the sole informant, earlier materials seem to have been utilised; but in many cases the numbers given in connexion with the different subjects are too large to be probable (see 1 Ch 29, 2 Ch 13, 14, 17, etc.), and later details appear to have been read into the description of the Temple arrangements as organised by David (1 Ch 23–26). On the other hand, the religious value of Chronicles is as manifest as that of Kings. In it, as in the latter, those events of the national history have been selected for treatment which most conspicuously illustrated the divine purpose and providence. The writer, even in a greater degree than his predecessor, points the moral of the events which he relates (2 Ch 12 12 25 20 27 6), both the judgments and mercies of God being shown to stand in intimate connexion with human conduct. Even if there are anachronisms in his account of the Temple services, light is thereby thrown on the state of the organisation of religion in his own time, and the spiritual instruction conveyed is not seriously affected. The interest manifested in the details of the Temple regulations calls attention to the care which the public worship of God ought at all times to claim. The music, to which such importance is attached, has its value in promoting unity of feeling amongst a number of individual worshippers, and in elevating and sustaining the religious emotions. The author of Chronicles, in dwelling at such length upon the external side of religion, was animated by the spirit of his age. But he is far from being exclusively concerned with the outward forms of worship. He devotes a great deal of space to the activities and teaching of the prophets; and those who have less sympathy than he with religious ceremonial can still derive edification from his work.

1 CHRONICLES

CHAPTER 1
GENEALOGIES

The writer begins his history with a series of genealogies, without introduction or heading, which embraces the descendants of Adam to Noah, the descendants of Noah through Japheth, Ham and Shem, the descendants of Abraham through Ishmael and the sons of Keturah, the descendants of Isaac through Esau and the rulers of Edom. These genealogies, which occupy the first nine chapters of this book, and occur frequently throughout the remaining chapters, relate to (*a*) peoples, (*b*) localities, (*c*) families. Those which refer to peoples (1 Ch 1 5 f.) and to localities (1 Ch 2 42, 43, 50 7 8) for the most part imply nearness of position, not blood relationship; it is only those which refer to families which are genealogies in the strict sense. Such became extremely important after the exile when descent from Aaron was rigorously required as a condition for the priesthood (Ezr 2 61, 62 Neh 7 63, 64), and when efforts were made to secure the purity of the Jewish race as a whole against contamination by prohibiting intermarriage with foreigners (Ezr 9, 10 Neh 13 23 f.). In certain places there are gaps in the lines of descent, some names having fallen out (e.g. 2 47 3 22 4 8, 9, etc.), whilst others have undergone textual corruption.

1 f. The names that are enumerated are taken, with a few unimportant variations, from various chs. of the book of Genesis: see Gn 5, 10, 11, 16, 21, 25, 36.

5. The sons of Japheth] Where several children of one father are mentioned, the descendants of the son through whom the main line of descent is transmitted are reserved until the collateral branches have been described and dismissed: cp. vv. 29, 32, 35.

38. The sons of Seir] These were aboriginal Horite families (Gn 36 20) who dwelt in Seir (Edom) before the descendants of Esau.

51. And the dukes of Edom were] better, 'and there arose dukes of Edom, to wit, duke Timnah,' etc. The writer implies that after Hadad's death, kings were replaced by dukes.

CHAPTER 2
GENEALOGIES (continued)

The genealogies in this c. comprise the descendants of Isaac through Israel (Jacob), and the descendants of Judah.

3. The sons of Judah] Some of the names that follow are given differently in the other books where they occur. **9. Chelubai**] the Caleb of vv. 18, 42. **15. David the seventh**] In 1 S 17 12 it is implied that Jesse had eight sons.

18. And of Jerioth] The passage is probably corrupt, and Jerioth may be the name of

Azubah's father. **21. The father of Gilead**]
i.e. the occupier and lord of Gilead: see
Nu 32 40. The term 'father' is used in the
same sense in vv. 24, 42, 45, 50, 51, etc.

22. Jair] apparently the Jair of Jg 10 3, 4.

23. And he took, etc.] RV 'and Geshur
and Aram took the towns of Jair from them.'
Geshur was a small Aramean (Syrian) state
on the border of the Manasseh settlements
E. of the Jordan (Dt 3 14), and the passage
implies that the Geshurites and other Aramean
peoples eventually deprived the tribe of
Manasseh (from whom Machir was descended)
of the cities here mentioned.

24. In Caleb-ephratah] The LXX suggests
that the true reading is 'Caleb went in unto
Ephrath, the wife of his father Hezron' (see
v. 19), 'who bare him Ashur,' etc. The union
here implied was not in early times held to
be incestuous, for an heir inherited his father's
wives like the rest of his property : cp.
2 S 16 21.

25. The sons of Jerahmeel] For the Jerahmeelites in Israelite history see 1 S 27 10 30 29.

35. To Jarha his servant] with the purpose
of making him his heir. For the inheritance
by a servant of his master's property cp.
Eliezer and Abraham : Gn 15 2 RV. **49. She
bare also Shaaph**] better, with the LXX,
'Shaaph' (v. 47) 'begat the father of Mad-
mannah.'

50. These were .. Caleb] This sentence
refers to the preceding vv. 42–49, and should
be followed by a full stop. **The son of Hur,**
etc.] This should be 'the sons of Hur the firstborn of Ephratah' (v. 19) 'were: Shobal,' etc.

55. Kenites] for the Kenites in Israelite
history see Jg 1 16 4 11 1 S 15 6 27 10. **Rechab**]
Allusions to the descendants of Rechab occur
in 2 K 10 15 Jer 35 2.

CHAPTER 3
GENEALOGIES (continued)

The genealogies here include the sons of
David, his successors on the throne of Judah,
and the descendants of Jeconiah (Jehoiachin).

1. The sons of David] Some of the names
that follow are given differently in the corresponding sections in 2 S 3 2-5 5 13-16 : cp. also
14 3-7. **5. Nathan**] According to St. Luke's
genealogy he was ancestor of our Lord, 3 31.
Bath-shua] i.e. Bathsheba. **15. Johanan**]
This son of Josiah was never king and presumably died before his father. **Shallum**]
probably the Jehoahaz of 2 K 23 30, since he
was younger than his brother and successor,
Jehoiakim : cp. also Jer 22 11.

16. Jeconiah] called also Jehoiachin
(2 K 24 6) and Coniah (Jer 22 24). **Zedekiah
his son**] The Zedekiah of this verse is probably
identical with the Zedekiah of v. 15, and consequently was brother (not son) of Jehoiakim

(2 K 24 17), and uncle of Jehoiachin (Jeconiah)
whom he succeeded.

17. Jeconiah ; Assir] RV 'Jeconiah the
captive.' **Salathiel**] the Shealtiel of Ezr 3 2.
He is called son of Jeconiah because he was
his heir, but he belonged to the line of Nathan,
a younger son of David. **18. Shenazar**]
possibly the Sheshbazzar of Ezr 1 8 : see note
there. **19. Zerubbabel**] here represented as
son of Pedaiah and nephew of Salathiel
(Shealtiel) ; but in Ezr 3 2 styled 'son of
Shealtiel' : see note there.

21. Pelatiah, etc.] It seems most likely that
this and the five names that follow all represent sons of Hananiah, constituting a single
generation, in which case the generations
reckoned after Zerubbabel amount to six.
Zerubbabel lived about 520 B.C., and if 30
years be reckoned as a generation, the sixth
generation would bring the last down to about
340 (the time of Alexander the Great).

CHAPTER 4
GENEALOGIES (continued)

This c. enumerates further descendants of
Judah, and the descendants of Simeon.

1. Sons] rather, 'descendants.' **Carmi**] probably an accidental substitution (from 5 3) for
Chelubai or Caleb : see 2 9,18. **2. Reaiah**]
the Haroeh of 2 52, whence the posterity of
Shobal is continued.

9. And his mother .. sorrow] better, 'though
his mother called his name Jabez, saying,
Because I bare him with sorrow' (Heb. *ozeb*).
The sorrow implied by his ominous name was
averted by his prayer.

17, 18. And she bare] It has been conjectured that the last clause of v. 18 (**And
these** *are* **.. Mered took**) should be inserted
before these words, **Bithiah** and **Jehudijah**
(or 'the Jewess') being the two wives of
Mered. **The daughter of Pharaoh**] If
Pharaoh here means the king of Egypt, Mered
must have been a person of distinction. The
name **Bithiah** (lit. 'daughter of Jehovah')
suggests that his Egyptian wife at her marriage adopted the religion of her husband.

19. *His* **wife Hodiah**] RV 'the wife of
Hodiah.' **22. Who had the dominion in Moab**]
better, 'who married in Moab' (like Mahlon
and Chilion, Ruth 1 1-4). **And Jashubi-lehem**]
The Vulgate suggests the reading, 'and
returned to Beth-lehem.' **23. And those ..
hedges**] RV 'and the inhabitants of Netaim
and Gederah.' **Dwelt with the king**] i.e. on
the royal estate as workmen.

24. The Simeonites are mentioned here
because they shared Judah's inheritance
(Josh 19 9).

31. Unto the reign of David] The writer
seems to be quoting from some account
belonging to the time of David, in whose

reign a census was taken of the people (2 S 24) : cp. 7². **41. These written by name**] probably those enumerated in vv. 34–37. **The habitations**] RV 'the Meunim' (who are the Maonites of Jg 10¹²). **43. The rest of the Amalekites**] In spite of Saul's destruction of them, as related in 1 S 15, a certain number survived : see 1 S 27⁸ 30¹ 2 S 8¹². **Unto this day**] The phrase, like the parallel expressions in Kings, refers to the date of the source which the writer is incorporating in his own work.

CHAPTER 5

GENEALOGIES (continued)

This c. gives lists of the descendants of Reuben, the families of Gad, and the families of the eastern division of Manasseh.

1. His birthright] This was a portion of the inheritance, twice as great as that given to each of the other sons. The two children of Joseph together received the share which, in right of birth, should have been Reuben's, each being placed on a level with their uncles, the sons of Jacob : cp. Gn 48⁵. **And the genealogy**] Joseph, though receiving Reuben's birthright, is not given precedence of him in the table of descent ; and so Reuben's sons are enumerated before Joseph's.

2. For Judah prevailed, etc.] This v. explains why Judah's descendants were described before those of his elder brother Reuben : he was the ancestor of the royal line. **6. Tilgath-pilneser**] i.e. Tiglath-pileser, whose invasion is described in 2 K 15 ²⁹.

7. *Were* **the chief, Jeiel, etc.**] better, 'were, Jeiel the chief,' etc. : cp. the expression in v. 12. **8. Aroer, etc.**] All the places named in this v. were E. of the Dead Sea. **9.** The Reubenites touched the Syrian desert between the Euphrates and Palestine.

10. Hagarites] Arabian tribes who traced their descent to Hagar through Ishmael : cp. v. 19 with 1³¹. **The east** *land* **of Gilead**] RV 'The *land* east of Gilead,' i.e. in the Syrian desert.

16. In Gilead in Bashan] perhaps, better, 'in Gilead, in Jabesh' (1 S 11¹). Bashan was given to Manasseh (Josh 13 ³⁰). **Suburbs**] better, 'pasture lands,' and so elsewhere.

17. Jeroboam] i.e. Jeroboam II, whose reign was contemporaneous with at least part of Jotham's reign.

22. The captivity] i.e. the deportation of the eastern tribes by Tiglath-pileser : cp. vv. 6, 26.

26. Pul .. and .. Tilgath-pilneser] The two names denote the same person, Pul being the proper name of a usurper who in 745 took possession of the Assyrian crown and assumed the title of Tiglath-pileser III (after an earlier sovereign). **Halah, etc.**] In 2 K 15²⁹ 17⁶ these

are the places to which the Israelites on the W. of Jordan were deported by Sargon in 722. **Habor** was the river Chaboras, **Halah** a city and **Gozan** a district near it, whilst **Hara**, if not a corruption, may represent Haran (Gn 11³¹) on the Euphrates. **The river Gozan**] RV 'the river of Gozan.'

CHAPTER 6

GENEALOGIES (continued)

This c. records the descendants of Levi, traces the line of the high priests to the captivity, and enumerates the cities of the Priests and Levites.

3. Nadab, and Abihu] see Lv 10¹,² 1 Ch 24². **Ithamar**] The descendants of Ithamar are not given here, but several occur in Samuel and Kings (Eli, Hophni and Phinehas, Ahimelech, Abiathar), and 'courses' of priests who traced their origin to him are enumerated in 1 Ch 24.

4. Eleazar begat, etc.] The section vv. 4–15 is a list of high priests from the death of Aaron to the captivity, but is incomplete, for between Ahitub and Zadok in v. 12 another name is inserted in 9¹¹, and several names are omitted which occur in the history of the monarchy, viz. Jehoiada (2 K 11¹⁵), Urijah (2 K 16¹⁷), and the Azariahs who were contemporary with Uzziah and Hezekiah (2 Ch 26¹⁷ 31¹⁰). In vv. 9 and 10 there is some confusion, for the chronology makes it probable that the Azariah of v. 9 (and not of v. 10) was the high priest in Solomon's reign.

22. Amminadab] the Izhar of v. 38 : Nu 16¹.

27. Elkanah his son] ought to be followed by 'Samuel his son.' **28. Samuel**] Samuel's father Elkanah is here regarded as a Levite, whereas in 1 S he is an Ephraimite.

Vashni] This is a corruption of the word for 'the second,' the name of the firstborn (Joel v. 33) being lost.

31–48. The genealogies of David's singers. Such names as **Heman, Asaph, Ethan** (or Jeduthun) are familiar to us from the Psalm titles. **39. His brother**] i.e. kinsman, or perhaps fellow-craftsman, both being singers.

54. Castles .. coasts] RV 'encampments .. borders.' **Their's was the lot**] RV 'theirs was the *first* lot' : Josh 21¹⁰. **61.** *Which were left*] i.e. other descendants of Kohath, exclusive of the sons of Aaron. *Out of* **the half** *tribe*] The names of Ephraim (v. 66) and Dan are accidentally omitted : see Josh 21⁵.

65. Which are .. names] RV 'which are mentioned by name' : vv. 57–60. **67. The cities of refuge**] In strictness Shechem alone of those mentioned in this and the following vv. was a city of refuge. **69. And Aijalon**] This and the following city belonged to Dan : Josh 21²³,²⁴. **77. The rest of the children of Merari**] RV 'the rest of *the Levites*, the sons of Merari.'

CHAPTER 7

GENEALOGIES (continued)

This c. traces the descendants of Issachar, Benjamin (Dan), Naphtali, Manasseh, Ephraim, and Asher.

2. Of Tola] The numbers given in this v. are those of Tola's descendants by his younger sons as contrasted with his descendants through his firstborn Uzzi : vv. 3, 4.

11. By the heads of their fathers] RV 'according to the heads of their fathers' *houses*' : and so elsewhere. They were divided into a number of patriarchal clans. **12. Sons of Aher**] better, 'the sons of another,' the 'other' being Dan, from whom Hushim was descended : Gn 46 23.

14. Whom she bare] The name of Asriel's mother is lost. **The Aramitess**] i.e. a Syrian woman. **15. The second**] i.e. the second son of Manasseh, Machir being the first.

21. Whom the men of Gath . . slew] The occurrence alluded to probably took place after Israel was settled in Canaan, the Ephraimites having descended from the hill-country to make a raid upon the Philistines in the maritime plain. In v. 22 **Ephraim** is a collective, not a personal, name. **23. Beriah . . evil**] Heb. *Beriah . . beraah*. **27. Non . . Jehoshuah**] i.e. Nun and Joshua. **28. Gaza**] not the Philistine Gaza, which, though it is assigned to Judah in Josh 15 47, can never have belonged to Ephraim.

40. The children of Asher] These close the historian's enumeration, the descendants of Zebulun being entirely omitted.

CHAPTER 8

GENEALOGIES (continued)

This c. contains a second account of the descendants of Benjamin, and traces the ancestors and descendants of Saul.

1. Now Benjamin, etc.] The names of Benjamin's descendants are repeated (with some variants) from 7 7 f., in order to lead up to the mention of Saul (v. 33), the predecessor of David (10 14), whose history forms the chief subject of this book.

3. And Abihud] perhaps to be corrected to 'father (Heb. *Abi*) of Ehud' : see v. 6 and Jg 3 15. **6. Removed**] RV 'carried them captive' : and so in v. 7. The occasion is not known. **8. After he had, etc.**] RM ' after he had sent away Hushim and Baara his wives.'

12. Ono and Lod] These towns elsewhere are mentioned only in post-exilic times (Ezr 2 33), so that the personal or family names in these vv. probably belong to that period. Benjamites are expressly mentioned in 9 3 Neh 11 4, as being among those who returned from the captivity. **29. The father of Gibeon**] the 'Jehiel' of 9 35.

33. Ner begat Kish] Ner and Kish were brothers (9 36), so that the text should be corrected to ' Ner begat Abner and Kish begat Saul': cp. 1 S 14 57. **Esh-baal**] the 'Ish-bosheth' of 2 S 2 8. The title ' Baal,' meaning 'lord' or 'possessor,' was at first used of Jehovah as well as of other deities (see Hos 2 16) and entered into several Hebrew names (' Eshbaal,' 'Merib-baal,' 'Beeliada'). But in consequence of the evil associations that gathered round it, it afterwards came to be disused in connexion with the LORD, and in the personal appellations of which it formed part the word *bosheth* ('shame') was often substituted to indicate abhorrence (' Ish-bosheth,' 'Mephibosheth').

34. Merib-baal] i.e. Mephibosheth : see on v. 33. **40. Archers**] for the skill of Benjamites with the bow see 2 Ch 14 8.

CHAPTER 9

GENEALOGIES (concluded)

This c. furnishes a record of the families and numbers of those who dwelt at Jerusalem after the captivity, and relates the ancestry and posterity of Saul.

1. In the book, etc.] RV 'in the book of the kings of Israel : and Judah was carried away . . to Babylon.'

2. Now the first inhabitants, etc.] This section (vv. 2–34) relates to the reoccupation of Jerusalem after the return from the exile, and appears to be a defective duplicate of Neh 11 3 with some variations in the names.

The Israelites] i.e. the lay population as contrasted with the ecclesiastical orders.

Nethinims] These were persons selected from the people, in the ratio of one for every fifty, and given to the Levites as their servants in the times of Moses and David (Nu 31 47 Ezr 8 20). From the mention of Mehunims among them (Ezr 2 50), who were doubtless descendants of the people of that name who were conquered by Uzziah (2 Ch 26 7), it has been inferred that they included foreigners who were either prisoners of war, or who surrendered as the Gibeonites did : Josh 9 27.

5. Shilonites] better, ' Shelanites,' the descendants of Judah's son Shelah : Nu 26 20.

11. The ruler of the house of God] applied in 2 Ch 31 10, 13 to the high priest, but in 35 8 to others besides.

18. The king's gate] In pre-exilic times this communicated between the Temple and the royal palace (2 K 16 18). **The companies**] RV ' the camp' : the phrase is transferred from the time of the wanderings, certain positions in the Temple corresponding to similar positions in the camp of the wilderness.

33. These *are* **the singers**] a list of names has fallen out. **Free**] i.e. were exempt from other duties. **35. And in Gibeon, etc.**] This account of Saul's ancestry and descendants **is**

repeated from 8 29-38 as an introduction to the narrative of his death given in c. 10.

CHAPTER 10
SAUL'S OVERTHROW AND DEATH

This c. is abbreviated from 1 S 31 1-13, but supplements it by statements that Saul's head was fastened in the temple of Dagon, and by a brief explanation of the causes of his overthrow.

6. All his house] This cannot mean 'all his family,' since Ish-bosheth and others of his children survived him (2 S 2 8 21 8), but must refer to those of his household who attended him at Gilboa.   **13. His transgression**] The writer refers to what is related in 1 S 13 13, 14 15 1-9 28 7.   **14. Enquired not of the LORD**] Saul at first enquired of the LORD (2 S 28 6), but on receiving no answer had recourse to the witch of Endor instead of being importunate in his supplications.

CHAPTER 11
DAVID'S CORONATION AT HEBRON AND HIS CAPTURE OF ZION

The writer, though mentioning David's crowning at Hebron, omits all description of his 7 years' reign there, and in this c. unites with some variations and additions two sections of 2 S, viz. 5 1-10 and 23 8-39.   **6. So Joab**, etc.] This is an addition to the account in 2 S 5 8.   **10. Strengthened themselves**] better, 'exerted themselves.'   **11. The chief of the captains**] another reading is 'chief of the thirty' : cp. v. 15.   **Three hundred**] 2 S 23 8 has 'eight hundred,' which is preferable as representing Jashobeam's prowess as greater than Abishai's: v. 20.   **12. The three mighties**] The third, not here mentioned, was Shammah (2 S 23 11), to whom vv. 13 (last-half) and 14 refer (where 'they,' 'themselves,' 'them' should be 'he,' 'himself,' 'him').   **18. The host of the Philistines**] i.e. the outpost at Bethlehem (v. 16), not the camp in the valley of Rephaim, which was N. of Bethlehem.   **20. Chief of the three**] It is difficult to make out the relations between this three, the 'three' of v. 12, and the 'thirty' of vv. 15 and 25 ; and there is probably some corruption.   **25. Honourable among**] RV 'more honourable than.'   **47. Mesobaite**] This should perhaps be corrected into 'from Zobah.'

It is noteworthy that this list of David's 'valiant men' contains several non-Israelites : vv. 39, 41, 46.

CHAPTER 12
VARIOUS STATISTICS

This c. is entirely supplementary to what is related in 2 S, and gives particulars respecting certain companies that joined David at various times, and the numbers that came to crown David at Hebron.

2. The right hand and the left] For this faculty in connexion with Benjamin cp. Jg 3 15 20 15, 16.   **Saul's brethren**] i.e. fellow-tribesmen : cp. v. 29.   **4. Among the thirty**] not included in the lists of 2 S 23 24 f. 1 Ch 11 26 f., and presumably belonging to the thirty at a different period.   **8. Buckler**] RV 'spear.'   **14. Was over**] RV 'was equal to': cp. Lv 26 8.   **15. The first month**] Nisan (= March-April), when the river was in flood after the melting of the snow.   **Put to flight, etc.**] Their endeavours to join David were opposed on both sides of the river, but unsuccessfully.   **17. If ye .. come peaceably**] The advances of a second body of deserters made David suspicious of treachery.   **18. The spirit came upon, etc.**] Amasai's decision to throw in his lot with David was due, like every other wise resolve, to the inspiration of the Divine Spirit.   **19. They**] i.e. David and his men : see on 1 S 28 1, 2 29.   **Upon advisement**] i.e. upon reflection : cp. 21 12.   **21. The band**] i.e. the Amalekites who attacked and burned Ziklag during David's absence with the Philistines (1 S 30).   **29. Kept the ward, etc.**] i.e. maintained their allegiance to Saul (2 S 2), a fact which accounted for so small a number assembling at Hebron.   **32. Had understanding, etc.**] possessed practical statesmanship : cp. Esth 1 13.   **All their brethren**] The rank and file were obedient to their chiefs. The full numbers of Issachar are not given.   **39. Eating and drinking**] A covenant was usually accompanied by a feast (see Gn 31 44, 46), and the passage doubtless has in view a compact made between the new sovereign and his people : cp. 1 K 1 9.   **40. They that were nigh**] i.e. relations.

The total numbers of those who assembled to crown David at Hebron, as enumerated in vv. 23-40, amount to 340,822, a military force (v. 23) which contrasts remarkably with the 30,000 (described as 'all the chosen men of Israel') of 2 S 6 1. It is noteworthy, too, that 128,600 come from the three northern and most distant tribes, Zebulun, Naphtali, and Asher ; 120,000 from the eastern tribes, Reuben, Gad, and half Manasseh ; and only 6,800 from Judah. Some corruption of the numbers may be suspected.

CHAPTER 13
THE REMOVAL OF THE ARK FROM KIRJATH-JEARIM

This c. merely expands 2 S 6 1-11, with some unimportant differences.

3. We enquired not at it] perhaps, better, 'we did not seek it,' i.e. to convey it to a place of honour : cp. 15 13.   **5. Shihor of Egypt**] usually employed to designate the Nile (Isa 23³ Jer 2¹⁸), but here applied to the 'brook of Egypt' (Josh 15⁴), the modern El Arish, a small stream on the borders of Egypt flowing into the Mediterranean. **The entering of Hemath**] i.e. the defile between Lebanon and Hermon, forming the approach to Hamath from the S.

6. Whose name is called *on it*] better, 'who is called by the Name,' this serving as a substitute for a more explicit mention of the divine name which is disguised in Jehovah.

11. Made a breach] RV 'had broken forth.' **Perez-uzza**] i.e. the Breach of Uzza.

CHAPTER 14

HIRAM AND DAVID. DAVID'S CHILDREN

This c. reproduces 2 S 5¹¹⁻²⁵ with some variations in the names of David's children, and the additional fact that David burnt the idols of the Philistines.

7. Beeliada] This name contains the title 'Baal,' which, as has been already implied (see on 8³³), had at first an innocent sense. When, later, it contracted evil associations, the names in which it occurred underwent alterations, and for Beeliada was substituted the form 'Eliada': 2 S 5¹⁶.

12. Left their gods] These had doubtless been carried into battle in the belief that they would bring success to the Philistine forces just as the Israelites carried the ark with them to the battle of Ebenezer: 1 S 4³. **16. Gibeon**] in 2 S 5²⁵ 'Geba,' both places being close together.

CHAPTER 15

THE TRANSPORT OF THE ARK TO JERUSALEM

This c. is parallel to 2 S 6¹²⁻²³, but contains much new matter respecting the Levites who bare the ark, and the singers.

1. Pitched for it a tent] According to 16³⁹ the Mosaic tabernacle still existed, but the ark, since its capture by the Philistines, had not rested in it, and a new tent was now substituted to contain it. **4. The children of Aaron**] i.e. the priests. **13. After the due order**] It is implied that the conveyance of the ark in the manner described in chapter 13 was irregular.

16. *To be* the singers] Singing had accompanied the ark on the first occasion (13⁸), but the musical arrangements were now committed exclusively to the Levites who subsequently had charge of the music of the Temple services: 23⁵ 2 Ch 5¹² 7⁶.

18. Ben] The word means 'son of,' and the name of Zechariah's father has probably been lost. The word does not occur in the corresponding lists in v. 20, 16⁵. **The porters**] This applies only to Obed-edom and Jeiel.

20, 21. Alamoth . . Sheminith to excel] see Pss 46 and 12 for meaning of these musical terms. **22. *Was* for song**] RM 'the carrying,' i.e. of the ark. **24. Trumpets**] made of metal and straight in shape, whereas the 'cornets' of v. 28 were of rams' horns and curved in shape. **Jehiah**] The Jeiel of v. 18.

26. When God helped] The fact that the ark was now moved without disaster indicated that God's favour was attending those who carried it. **27. The master of the song**] better, 'the chief for carrying' (the ark): cp. v. 22. The addition **with the singers** is probably an interpolation.

CHAPTER 16

THE CELEBRATION OF THE EVENT

Only the first three vv. and the last v. of this c. are derived from 2 S 6¹⁷⁻²⁰, the rest, describing the musical arrangements, being new.

7. Delivered first, etc.] RV 'did . . first ordain to give thanks unto the LORD, by the hand of': i.e. the appointment of Asaph and his brethren to have charge of the singing dated from the day when the ark was brought to Jerusalem. The psalm that follows consists of Pss 105¹⁻¹⁵ 96¹⁻¹³ 106¹, ⁴⁷, ⁴⁸. The last section (v. 35) seems to reflect the conditions of the exile.

22. Mine anointed] i.e. my chosen, the allusion being to the patriarchs : see Gn 12¹⁷ 20³⁻⁷. **29. The beauty of holiness**] RM 'in holy array': i.e. in sacred vestments. **35. And say ye**] a liturgical direction which does not occur in Ps 106⁴⁷.

38. With their brethren] probably the name of 'Hosah' has been lost after Obed-edom.

Also] better, 'even Obed-edom.' **39. The high place . . Gibeon**] This has been mentioned previously in 1 K 3⁴, but the presence there of the Tabernacle is here referred to for the first time.

40. The altar} This was the altar at Gibeon ; there was another before the ark at Jerusalem.

41. Jeduthun] perhaps the same as the 'Ethan' of 15¹⁷. Asaph seems to have attended upon the ark at Jerusalem (v. 37), whilst Heman and Jeduthun served at Gibeon.

CHAPTER 17

DAVID'S DESIRE TO BUILD THE TEMPLE DISALLOWED

This c. is almost identical with 2 S 7¹⁻²⁹.

17. Hast regarded me . . degree] i.e. hast treated me with great distinction.

CHAPTER 18

DAVID'S WARS AND OFFICERS OF STATE

This c. is closely parallel to 2 S 8¹⁻¹⁸, but with some variations in names and numbers.

1. Gath] probably meant to explain the difficult phrase 'Metheg-ammah' which occurs in 2 S 8¹. Gath was independent in the time of Solomon : 1 K 2 39. **3. Hadarezer**] 2 S 8 3 has ' Hadadezer,' which is more correct, 'Hadad' being the name of a Syrian god and ' Hadadezer' being a formation parallel to 'Eliezer.' **4. An hundred chariots**] RV ' for an hundred chariots.' **8. The pillars**] i.e. the two columns in front of the porch of the Temple. **12. Abishai**] In Ps 60 (title) this success is attributed to Joab, and the number of the slain is stated at 12,000.

16. Abimelech the son of Abiathar] This should be 'Abiathar the son of Abimelech ' : see on 1 S 22 20 2 S 15 29 20 25. **17. Chief about the king**] 2 S 8 18 AV has ' Chief rulers,' but the RV has ' Priests.' For the latter word the Chronicler substitutes a different expression, because the sons of David belonged not to the priestly tribe of Levi but to Judah.

CHAPTER 19

DAVID'S WARS WITH THE AMMONITES AND THE SYRIANS

This c. is parallel to 2 S 10 1-19 with some differences in certain names, and a few additions.

7. Thirty and two thousand chariots] The reading is probably corrupt : in 2 S 10 6 it is ' thirty two thousand footmen,' with a thousand more from Maachah (whose forces are not here numbered), no mention being made of chariots. **18. Seven thousand .. chariots .. forty thousand footmen**] 2 S 10 18 has ' seven hundred chariots and forty thousand horsemen.'

CHAPTER 20

THE SIEGE OF RABBAH. THE SLAUGHTER OF THREE PHILISTINE GIANTS

This c. corresponds, with some unimportant differences, to several distinct sections in 2 S, viz. 11 1 12 26-31 21 18-22.

2. David took, etc.] This implies David's presence at Rabbah, and as it stands here is inconsistent with the previous verse. In 2 S 12 the discrepancy is explained by a passage which Chronicles omits, relating that Joab summoned David to Rabbah and that the king went thither.

5. Elhanan the son of Jair, etc.] Both this passage and the parallel in 2 S 21 19 have undergone corruption, and the true text probably had ' Elhanan the son of Jair, a Bethlehemite, slew Goliath the Gittite.' As Goliath is said in 2 S 17 to have been killed by David, there seems to have been variant accounts of his death, unless there were two giants of the same name.

CHAPTER 21

DAVID'S NUMBERING OF THE PEOPLE AND HIS PUNISHMENT

This c. is parallel to 2 S 24, but includes a few additions : see vv. 6, 26.

1. Satan] In 2 S 24 1 the LORD is said to have been angry with Israel, and to have moved David to number the people ; for the Hebrews in early times did not hesitate to describe God as prompting to evil as well as to good, men being punished for one sin by being led to commit another. But in later ages the idea that God tempted men to wrong was felt to conflict with His absolute holiness ; and this created the belief that temptation was the work of a spirit of malevolent character, who, though subordinate to, and attendant upon, God, was yet an adversary (lit. the ' Satan') of men, and sought to bring about their ruin (see on 1 K 22 21, 22 Job 1 6 f, Zech 3 1). In Job and Zechariah the name is still only a title ; but in Chronicles it has become a proper name (being used without the article).

5. A thousand thousand, etc.] 2 S 24 9 represents Israel as 800,000 and Judah 500,000. According to 27 24 the numbers were not entered in the official records, and they have probably undergone corruption in the course of transmission. **6. But Levi, etc.**] This is not mentioned in 2 S. If the numbering of the people was due to a presumptuous reliance upon material resources, or some specific command connected with the taking of a census (e.g. Ex 30 11-16) had been neglected, the non-inclusion of two tribes by Joab was perhaps a device to prevent the full completion of the king's purpose, in the hope of averting the evil consequences that were feared.

12. Three years' famine] This harmonises better than the ' seven years ' of 2 S 24 13 with the three months and three days. **15. Ornan**] in 2 S 24 16 'Araunah' or 'Ornah.' **18. The angel .. Gad**] For divine communications made to prophets through angels cp. 1 K 13 18 19 5,7 Zech 1 11, etc. **23. Meat offering**] RV ' Meal offering ' : and so elsewhere. **25. Six hundred shekels of gold**] in 2 S 24 24 ' fifty shekels of silver.'

26. Answered .. by fire] Other instances of sacrifices consumed by fire from heaven occur in Lv 9 24 1 K 18 38 2 Ch 7 1. This fact is not recorded by the writer of Samuel, but is specially mentioned by the Chronicler because the acceptance of the sacrifice was taken by David to indicate where he was to build his intended Temple, the preparations for which are described in the next chapter.

30. He was afraid] In his alarm David was loath to leave the spot where God's favour had just been renewed to him.

CHAPTER 22

DAVID'S PREPARATIONS FOR THE BUILDING OF THE TEMPLE

This c. is supplementary to the narrative in the earlier books, its contents coming chronologically between 2 S 24 and 1 K 1.

1. This *is* **the house**] This v. connects with 21²⁸ (21²⁹,³⁰ being parenthetical). **2. The strangers**] i.e. the non-Israelite population, who were employed in forced labour upon his building projects : 2 Ch 2¹⁷.

9. Solomon . . peace] Heb. *Shelômôh . . Shalôm.* Peace was the ideal condition appropriate for the building of God's Temple as well as for the advent of Him who was greater than the Temple : Lk 2¹⁴.

14. In my trouble] Some render 'in spite of my trouble,' i.e. in spite of wars and other distractions. David, like other loyal servants of God, was content to pave the way for the accomplishment of a result which he himself would never witness. **An hundred thousand,** etc.] The weight of gold and silver is so enormous, amounting in intrinsic value to £1,025,000,000 sterling, that great exaggeration may be suspected. The gold that was received annually by Solomon was only 666 talents : 1 K 10¹⁴.

19. The holy vessels] e.g. the table of shewbread, the candlesticks (or lampstands), with their lamps and snuffers, the cups, basons, and spoons, etc.

CHAPTER 23

DAVID MAKES SOLOMON KING. PARTICULARS RELATING TO THE LEVITES

This and the following three chs. (supplementing the earlier history) describe the arrangements made by David for the organisation of the Temple service after Solomon had been appointed his successor. The incidents relating to this last event, which are recorded in 1 K 1, are omitted by the writer, who passes over all David's domestic troubles.

3. From the age of thirty years] This limit is given in Nu 4³, but 'twenty-five' is fixed in Nu 8²⁴, possibly having in view different and lighter duties. **By their polls**] i.e. by heads. **9. Shimei**] This was a fourth son of 'Laadan,' not the 'Shimei' of vv. 7, 10, who was Laadan's brother. **11. Zizah**] the 'Zina' of v. 10. **Jeush . . Beriah**] These together constituted a third 'course' belonging to the house of the elder Shimei, RV 'they became a fathers' house in one reckoning.'

14. His sons . . Levi] i.e. the sons of Moses were reckoned as Levites, not (like the sons of Aaron) as priests. **24. From the age of twenty years**] David, at the end of his reign (v. 27), seems to have lowered the limit of age (see v. 3) above which the Levites entered on their duties, and his regulations were observed in subsequent times : 2 Ch 31¹⁷ Ezr 3⁸. **27. By the last words**] better, 'in the Last Acts,' i.e. a history of the closing part of his reign. **29. For all . . size**] i.e. for dispensing the various quantities used for the different offerings (as in Ex 29⁴⁰).

31. The set feasts] These were the festivals of the Passover, Unleavened Bread, Weeks, and Tabernacles ; for the number of victims appointed for each occasion see Nu 28, 29.

CHAPTER 24

THE COURSES OF THE SONS OF AARON

1. Divisions . . Aaron] i.e. courses of the priests, corresponding to the course of the Levites described in 23⁶. **3. Ahimelech**] an error (through an accidental omission) for 'Abiathar son of Ahimelech,' and so in v. 31. **4. Chief men**] i.e. heads of families or clans (the 'principal households' of v. 6). **6. Ahimelech the son of Abiathar**] to be corrected into 'Abiathar son of Ahimelech.' **19. These** *were* **the orderings,** etc.] i.e. the order in which they succeeded one another in attendance at the Temple had been determined by Aaron. **20. And the rest of the sons of Levi,** etc.] The section vv. 20–30 gives the names of the representatives of the 'courses' of Levites enumerated in 23⁶ᶠ·, but with the omission of the 'courses' of the Gershonites : vv. 7–11. **26. Beno**] This is not a proper name, but means 'his son,' Jaaziah being a third son of Merari. **29. Kish**] another son of Mahli : see 23²¹. **31. Over against**] better, 'equally with.'

CHAPTER 25

PARTICULARS RESPECTING THE SINGERS

1. Separated to the service] RV 'separated for the service certain of the sons,' etc. **Jeduthun**] as in 16⁴¹, this name takes the place of 'Ethan' in other lists : 6⁴⁴ 15¹⁷. **Prophesy**] see on v. 5. **And the number . . was**] The sentence is interrupted, and continued in v. 7.

3. Six] only five names are given, but the LXX adds a sixth, 'Shimei' : cp. v. 17. **5. The king's seer**] Music and singing were often associated with prophecy (cp. 1 S 10⁵), and conversely the Temple singers are here accounted seers : cp. 'prophesy,' v. 5. **In the words of God**] better, 'in matters pertaining to God' : cp. 26³². **To lift up the horn**] i.e. the number of Heman's sons enhanced his dignity : cp. Ps 89¹⁷.

8. They cast lots, etc.] The wards of Asaph alternated with an equal number of wards of Jeduthun until they were exhausted ; then the rest of Jeduthun's wards alternated with an equal number of Heman's ; and finally the residue of Heman's followed in unbroken succession. **11. Izri**] Some of the names in vv. 9–31 differ slightly from those that occur in vv. 2–4, 'Izri' being the 'Zeri' of v. 3, 'Jesharelah' the 'Asarelah' of v. 2, and 'Azareel' the 'Uzziel' of v. 4.

CHAPTER 26

PARTICULARS RESPECTING VARIOUS TEMPLE OFFICIALS

1. The divisions of the porters] i.e. the courses of the gate-keepers or sentries who stood on guard at the entrances of the Temple. They were drawn from three families, Meshelemiah (the 'Shallum' of 9 19), Obed-edom, and Hosah. **Asaph**] the 'Ebiasaph' of 9 19. **5. For God blessed him**] see 13 14. The blessing consisted in the number of his children : cp. Gn 1 28 24 60.

13. For every gate] Though the Temple was not yet built, David is regarded as having settled the plan of it : see 28 11 f. **14. Shelemiah**] the 'Meshelemiah' of vv. 1, 2. **15. The house of Asuppim**] RV 'the storehouse,' and so in v. 17.

16. To Shuppim and] the name **Shuppim** is an accidental repetition of the previous 'Asuppim.' To each of the three families of porters were allotted the gates on one of the four sides of the house, the gates on the fourth side being assigned to the eldest son of Meshelemiah. **The gate Shallecheth** has not been identified. **The causeway**] some road leading up the Temple hill.

18. Parbar] RM 'the Precinct,' possibly a colonnade or portico. **25. His brethren**] i.e. his cousins. **27. Out of the spoils**] So in Joshua's time, the spoils of Jericho were put into the treasury of the LORD : Josh 6 24.

30. On this side Jordan westward] RV 'beyond Jordan westward' : an expression which indicates that the writer did not live in Palestine. **31. Jazer of Gilead**] a town in the territory of Gad : Josh 13 25 21 39.

CHAPTER 27

PARTICULARS RESPECTING VARIOUS MILITARY OFFICERS

This c., as distinguished from the four preceding chapters which describe David's ecclesiastical officials, relates to his secular officers.

1. Which came .. out] i.e. relieved each other in turn : cp. 2 Ch 23 8. For particulars concerning several of the officers mentioned in the following vv. see c. 11. **3. Of the children, etc.**] RV 'He was of the children of Perez, the chief of,' etc. **4. Dodai**] The words 'Eleazar son of' have been lost : cp. 11 12.

5. A chief priest] RV 'of Jehoiada the priest, chief.'

16. Over the tribes] In the following list Gad and Asher are omitted, and the Aaronites are distinguished from the Levites. **18. Elihu**] the 'Eliab' of 2 13 1 S 16 6. **23. From twenty years old and under**] In Nu 1 3 it is laid down that those required for military service should be above this age.

25. Over the king's treasures] The account implies that David had large private estates as well as considerable accumulations of treasure. Some of his possessions may have formed part of what the king could claim from the nation in virtue of his position (cp. 1 S 8 14, 15), or may have been given him freely by his subjects (cp. 1 S 10 27), but the bulk was doubtless derived from his successful wars (see 1 S 30 20 2 S 8 6-8). The lands in the low plains (v. 28) were probably in part taken from the Philistines. **Castles**] better, 'towers' to shelter the herdmen and serve as look-outs.

27. Over the increase, etc.] better, 'over the wine-cellars which were in the vineyards.'

28. The sycomore trees] not the English tree that goes by this name, but one that bears a fig-like fruit. **The low plains**] RV 'Lowland' : a name applied to the downs that extend from the central hills to the maritime plain.

32. David's uncle] better, 'David's nephew' : see 20 7. **34. Jehoiada the son of Benaiah**] probably to be corrected to 'Benaiah the son of Jehoiada' : cp. 18 17.

Some of the names mentioned in this c. belonged to periods much earlier than David's closing years, for Asahel (v. 7) was killed before David became king at Jerusalem (2 S 2 14 f.), and Ahithophel killed himself in the course of Absalom's rebellion : 2 S 17 23.

CHAPTER 28

DAVID'S LAST DIRECTIONS

2. The footstool of our God] i.e. the Mercy Seat : 2 S 6 2 Ps 132 7. **5. The throne of the kingdom of the LORD**] cp. 17 14 29 23. Israel's kings were the LORD'S vicegerents and representatives : He was their true ruler. **7. If he be constant**] The continuance of God's favour was conditional upon continued obedience, and the writer, living after the exile, knew how the condition had been violated.

11. The pattern] The pattern of the Tabernacle is similarly stated to have been communicated to Moses by God : Ex 25 9, 40. **The houses**] the Holy Place and the Most Holy Place : see 1 K 6. **Treasuries .. upper chambers**] probably the side-chambers, described in 1 K 6 5 f., of which there were three storeys.

Inner parlours] perhaps the lowest of the side-chambers.

12. By the spirit] i.e. by revelation. **The chambers round about**] perhaps detached buildings constructed round the courts that enclosed the Temple. **15. Candlesticks**] better 'lampstands,' and so elsewhere. Ten are mentioned in 1 K 7 49, but only one in 2 Ch 13 11. **16. The tables**] Ten are alluded to again in 2 Ch 4 8, but only a single table is mentioned in 1 K 7 48 2 Ch 13 11 29 18. **18. The chariot of the cherubims**] RV 'the chariot, even the cherubim' :

cp. Ps 18 10 Ezk 1, 10 8 f. **20. He will not fail thee**] A similar assurance of God's constant aid was given to Jacob and Joshua : Gn 28 15 Josh 1 5.

CHAPTER 29
DAVID'S OFFERINGS, THANKSGIVING, AND DEATH

1. The palace] The word in the original is more strictly applicable to the fortress which was attached to the Second Temple (Neh 2 8) and afterwards called the tower of Antonia, but here and in v. 19 is employed of Solomon's Temple.

3. Of mine own proper good] RV 'a treasure of mine own.' **4. Three thousand, etc.**] The weights here named, as in many other places in Chronicles, are incredibly large, amounting in value to £21,320,000 of our money.

7. Drams] The dram (Gk. *drachma*) was ½ shekel ; and the value (according to the early Hebrew weights) of all the gold mentioned in this v. would be about £30,760,000, and of the silver about £4,100,000.

10. And David said] David in his prayer recognised that it was not in his, or any man's, power to add to God's glory. The building of the Temple could only manifest his and his people's devotion and gratitude for the goodness which had bestowed such wealth upon them. **15. None abiding**] better, ' no hope of abiding.' **20. Worshipped the .. king**] cp. Ps 45 11. The same kind of prostrations were made both in divine worship and in paying respect to the sovereign.

22. The second time] The 'first time' is only described at length in 1 K 1 39, though the writer of Chronicles alludes to it in 23 1.

Zadok *to be* **priest**] This seems to anticipate the promotion which Zadok received when Solomon, after David's death, deposed Abiathar : 1 K 2 27. **30. The times that went over him**] i.e. the fortunes that befell him.

---

2 CHRONICLES

CHAPTER 1
SOLOMON'S CHOICE OF WISDOM. HIS WEALTH AND COMMERCE

This c., after the opening vv., repeats, with some modifications and additions, what is related in 1 K 3 5-14 and 10 26-29.

5. The brasen altar] This identification of the altar at Gibeon with the brazen altar of the Tabernacle is an addition made to 1 K 3 4.

CHAPTER 2
SOLOMON'S NEGOTIATIONS WITH HIRAM

This c. substantially reproduces 1 K 5, with some differences in numbers, names, and expressions.

1. An house for his kingdom] The description of this, which is given at length in 1 K 7, is omitted by the Chronicler.

5. *Is* great] i.e. in magnificence, but not in actual dimensions—the external length and breadth being only 120 × 45 ft., less than many parish churches. It was not intended to hold an assemblage of worshippers, but to be a sanctuary for the Deity, where He might receive the offerings of His servants : v. 6.

10. Beaten wheat] probably a corruption of ' wheat for food ' : cp. 1 K 5 11.

13. Of Huram my father's] RM ' even Huram my father': the term ' father ' being a title of honour : cp. Gn 45 8. But the whole expression may be a proper name, ' Huram

Abi '; and so in 4 16. **14. A woman .. of Dan**] see on 1 K 7 14, where she is termed a widow of Naphtali. **16. Joppa**] The modern Jaffa, some 35 m. from Jerusalem.

17. The strangers] Solomon in imposing forced labour upon his subjects did not, like his father, confine it to those who were of foreign origin, but extended it to native Israelites : 1 K 5 13. **18. In the mountain**] probably the hill-country of Judah.

CHAPTER 3
PARTICULARS RELATING TO THE TEMPLE

This and the following c. abbreviate what is recorded in 1 K 6, 7.

1. Moriah] Here the designation of the Temple hill, but in Gn 22 2 of the ' land ' in which was situated the hill where Isaac was to be sacrificed. **Where** *the* LORD **appeared unto**] better ' which was shown unto,' i.e. by the acceptance of the king's sacrifice (1 Ch 21 28 22 1).

3. These *are the things*, **etc.**] RV ' these are the foundations which Solomon laid ': the v. going on to give the ground plan. **After the first measure**] This implies that the length of the cubit had changed between the time of Solomon and that of the writer of Chronicles. Ezekiel (40 5) speaks of a cubit measuring a cubit and a hand-breadth, which, if the smaller cubit was equal to 6 hand-breadths (about 18 in.), must have been equivalent to 7 (about

21 in.). In estimating the size of the Temple, the cubit, for the sake of convenience, has been reckoned at 18 in. ; if the cubit of 21 in. was the one really employed, the dimensions must be modified accordingly.

4. An hundred and twenty] One MS of the LXX has 'twenty.' The figures given in the text are suitable only for a tower, not a porch.

5. The greater house] i.e. the Holy Place.

Cieled] The walls, as well as the roof, were lined with wood. **Chains**] i.e. festoons of chain work, carved in relief. **6. Parvaim**] unknown.

10. Of image work] LXX has 'wrought-in wood': cp. 1 K 6 23. **11. Twenty cubits**] This was the length of the four wings together.

13. Inward] RV 'toward the house': i.e. the Holy Place. **14. The vail**] This is not mentioned in Kings. **15. Thirty and five**] In 1 K 7 15 'eighteen': see also 2 K 25 17 Jer 52 21.

16. Chains, *as* in the oracle] The text is probably corrupt ; the **chains** must be 'the wreaths of chain work' of 1 K 7 17, which were carved on the capitals.

CHAPTER 4
The Contents of the Temple

1. An altar] This was in the Temple court. Though its construction is not described in Kings, it is mentioned in 1 K 8 64 2 K 16 14.

3. Oxen] rather, 'knops' (i.e. gourds) : see 1 K 7 24. **7. According to their form**] RV 'According to the ordinance concerning them.' **In the temple**] i.e. in the Holy Place.

9. The great court] The word here used differs from that employed for 'the court of the priests.' It was in the 'great court' that the scaffold mentioned in 6 13 was placed : see on 1 K 7 9. **10. The right side of the east end**] i.e. at the SE. corner. **12. Pommels**] RV 'bowls,' i.e. the globes of the capitals ; and so in v. 13. **14. He made .. made he**] probably an error for 'ten .. ten.' **16. Fleshhooks**] probably an error for 'basons,' v. 11 : cp. 1 K 7 45.

20. After the manner] RV 'according to the ordinance.' In the Law (Ex 27 21) it was required that a light should burn always before the veil. **22. The entry**] probably an error for 'the hinges,' 1 K 7 50.

CHAPTER 5
The removal of the Ark to the Temple

This c. is a repetition of 1 K 8 1-9, with additional particulars respecting the descent of the glory of the LORD.

4. The Levites .. the ark] The mention of 'the Levites' in this connexion is more in accordance with the requirements of the Law than the statement of 1 K 8 3 that the 'priests' took up the ark.

9. From the ark] better (as in the LXX) 'from the Holy Place': cp. 1 K 8 8. **Unto this day**] The Chronicler, like the compiler of Kings, retains the expression of the original writer, who lived before the destruction of the Temple.

11. Did not .. course] On this occasion all the priests (and not a single course only) had sanctified themselves to officiate. **12. At the east end**] i.e. facing westward, towards the Temple building.

CHAPTER 6
Solomon's Prayer

The first 39 vv. of this c. repeat 1 K 8 12-50, the conclusion of the prayer, as given in 8 51-61, being omitted and three additional vv. being substituted.

5. Neither chose I any man] Saul, though chosen, was subsequently rejected : 1 S 15 26.

13. For Solomon had made, etc.] This is not mentioned in 1 K 8.

41. Now therefore arise, etc.] The same words occur in Ps 132 8, 9. **Be clothed with .. goodness**] i.e. enjoy victory and prosperity.

42. Turn not away, etc.] i.e. do not reject his prayer and make him turn away in disappointment. For **anointed** cp. 1 S 12 3 24 6.

The mercies of David] i.e. the mercies promised and shown to David : cp. Ps 89 49.

CHAPTER 7
Solomon's Sacrifices, and the Lord's Promises

This c. reproduces with some additions portions of 1 K 8 62-66 and 9 1-9.

1. The fire came down] This, which marked the acceptance of Solomon's sacrifice (cp. 1 Ch 21 26), is not mentioned in 1 K 8.

21. Shall be an astonishment] i.e. a cause of astonishment.

CHAPTER 8
Solomon's Buildings. His Trade with Ophir

This c. reproduces the substance of 1 K 9 10-28 but describes some additional buildings.

2. Had restored] If the reference is to the cities which Solomon gave to Hiram, it seems best to assume that they had been merely pledged as security for money which Solomon borrowed and afterwards repaid : 1 K 9 14.

3. Hamath-zobah] Perhaps a Hamath in Zobah (a country E. of the Sea of Galilee, in the region of the modern Haurân).

4. Tadmor] the later Palmyra, a city 150 m. NE. of Damascus in the Syrian desert.

8. Them did Solomon, etc.] RV 'of them did Solomon raise a levy *of bondservants*.' **13. After a certain rate, etc.**] RV 'as the duty of every day required' : cp. v. 14. **16. Unto the day**] LXX has 'from the day.'

18. In 1 K 9 26-28 it is stated that Solomon 'made' a navy of ships at Eziongeber, and that Hiram sent him skilled mariners.

CHAPTER 9
The Visit of the Queen of Sheba.
Solomon's Splendour

This c. is a close repetition of 1 K 10 1-28 and 11 41-43.

8. On his throne] i.e. God's throne : see on 1 Ch 28 5.

10, 11. These vv. should follow v. 12.

11. Terraces] 1 K 10 12 has 'pillars' (or balustrades).

12. *That* which she had brought] 1 K 10 13 has 'beside that which Solomon gave her of his royal bounty.'

21. The king's ships went to Tarshish] If this is not a misunderstanding of the phrase 'ships of Tarshish' (1 K 10 22), which describes a particular kind of vessel, it must be assumed that Solomon's ships sailed from a Phœnician port, Tarshish (whether Tartessus or Tarsus) being on the Mediterranean.

29. In the book, etc.] The three works here referred to may possibly have been inserted in 'the book of the kings of Israel and Judah' (see 16 11, etc.), as was the case with the 'book of Jehu the son of Hanani' (20 34 RV).

CHAPTER 10
Reign of Rehoboam

This c. is a repetition of 1 K 12 1-19 with slight differences.

2. Returned out of Egypt] Preferable to 1 K 12 2, 'Jeroboam dwelt in Egypt.'

4. Thy father made, etc.] The passages in 1 K 5 13, 14 11 28, which throw light upon the oppressiveness of Solomon, are omitted by the Chronicler.

CHAPTER 11
Reign of Rehoboam (continued)

This c. repeats the substance of 1 K 12 21-24, and adds much information relating to Rehoboam's buildings, the withdrawal of the Levites from the kingdom of Jeroboam, and Rehoboam's marriages.

5. Built cities] Of the towns named in the following vv. **Beth-lehem, Tekoa, Beth-zur, Adoraim, Ziph,** and **Hebron,** were in the hill-country of Judah ; **Etam, Shoco, Adullam, Mareshah, Azekah, Zorah** and **Aijalon,** were in the lowlands, whilst **Gath** (a Philistine city, which in Solomon's reign was independent) and **Lachish** were in the maritime plain. The fortification of these places was intended to guard the Judæan frontier on the side of Egypt, with which country Jeroboam had had friendly relations : 10 2.

14. Cast them off] When Jeroboam made priests from all the tribes indifferently, the Levites lost their privileged position as the only legitimate priestly tribe.

15. Devils] lit. 'he-goats,' the deities that were worshipped being supposed to assume the forms of these animals, like the Greek Satyrs and the Roman Faunus.

18. Jerimoth] not included in the list in 1 Ch 3 1-9, so that he was probably the son of a concubine. *And* **Abihail**] RV '*and of* Abihail' : Abihail being the wife of **Jerimoth** and mother of **Mahalath. 20. Daughter**] probably 'granddaughter' : see 2 S 14 27 and 13 1. **Abijah**] The 'Abijam' of 1 K 15 1.

23. He dealt wisely] By acting as here described he sought to secure the tranquil succession of the son whom he had chosen as his heir : cp. 21 3. **Desired**] probably for his sons.

CHAPTER 12
Reign of Rehoboam (concluded)

This c. is parallel to 1 K 14 21-31, but supplies additional particulars respecting Shishak's army and the prophet Shemaiah.

3. The Lubims, the Sukkiims] The **Lubims** were probably Libyans ; the **Sukkiims,** who are not mentioned elsewhere, are called in LXX 'Troglodytes,' i.e. 'cave-dwellers.'

6. The princes of Israel] The term 'Israel' is often applied in Chronicles to the people of Judah, as more nearly realising the ideal of the true Israel than the sister kingdom : cp. 20 34 21 2, 4 23 2 24 5 28 19, 23.

12. Things went well] RV 'there were good things *found*' : cp. 19 3 1 K 14 13. The king's repentance was accompanied by a moral reformation on the part of the people.

15. The book of . . Iddo] The writings of **Iddo** are also mentioned in 9 29, 13 22.

CHAPTER 13
Reign of Abijah

This c. expands the account given of Abijah (Abijam) in 1 K 15 1-8 by giving details of his war with Jeroboam, which is there only briefly mentioned.

2. Michaiah] In 11 21 and 1 K 15 2 she is called 'Maachah,' and was probably daughter of Uriel and granddaughter of Absalom.

3. Four hundred thousand, etc.] These numbers (see also v. 17) are in keeping with the large figures that appear elsewhere in Chronicles : see 14 8, 9 17 14-18.

4. Zemaraim] Possibly a hill near the place of the same name in Benjamin : Josh 18 22.

5. A covenant of salt] cp. Nu 18 19. The use of salt in connexion with sacrifice (see Lv 2 13) probably arose from its association with a meal ; and 'there is salt between us' is said to be a phrase still employed to denote the bond which secures, for any one who has partaken of an Arab's hospitality, protection and (in case of need) assistance.

7. Children of Belial] i.e. worthless persons. **Young**] That Rehoboam was young when the Ten Tribes revolted is implied in 10 8, though in 12 13 his age is given as 41.

8. The kingdom of the LORD] The high prerogative that once belonged to all Israel (1 Ch 28 5 2 Ch 9 8) was now confined to Judah.

9. After the manner, etc.] The LXX has 'out of the people of all the land,' which agrees with the true sense of 1 K 12 31. **12. Sounding trumpets**] cp. Nu 10 9 31 6. **19. Jeshanah . . Ephraim**] The first is not known, the second is identified by some with the 'Ephraim' mentioned in Jn 11 54. **20.** The mention of Jeroboam's death here is chronologically out of place, since he outlived Abijah.

22. In the story] RV 'in the commentary.' The original term ('midrash') meant the didactic treatment of a subject or narrative; and in the 'midrash' of **Iddo** the reign of **Abijah** was presumably related with a view to moral instruction rather than historic accuracy. Possibly the account of Abijah's speech in vv. 4–12 has been taken from it : contrast 1 K 15 3.

CHAPTER 14
REIGN OF ASA

This c. adds to what is related of Asa in 1 K 15 9-24 an account of the invasion of the Ethiopian Zerah.

3. Took away . . the high places] In 15 17 (= 1 K 15 14) the opposite of this is stated ; if the two passages are to be reconciled, it must be supposed that Asa sought to effect a reform which was only imperfectly executed : cp. also 17 6 with 20 33.

7. The land *is* **yet before us**] i.e. free from the presence of an enemy.

9. Zerah] Zerah, if an Ethiopian (Heb. *Cushite*) or Egyptian, is probably to be identified with Osorkon II, an Egyptian king of the 22nd dynasty, who, on a monument recently found, declares that 'the upper and lower Rutennu' (i.e. the peoples of Palestine) had been thrown under his feet. But in v. 14 the cities spoiled by Asa after the defeat of the invaders are said to be near Gerar ; so that Zerah may have been the chief of an Arabian tribe, a view with which the description of the spoil taken by Asa (v. 15) agrees. **Mareshah**] in the lowland of Judah (Josh 15 44), where there are some ruins still called 'Mar'ash.' To the N. there is a Wâdy called 'Wâdy es Sufieh,' which may be **Zephathah.**

11. *It is* **nothing, etc.**] RV 'there is none beside thee to help, between the mighty and him that hath no strength' : i.e. to help the weak under unequal conditions. Asa's prayer 'breathes the true spirit of faith and trust in God.'

13. Gerar] 6 m. S. of Gaza and 25 m.

from Beersheba. **14. The fear of the LORD,** etc.] They were so panic-stricken that they could offer no resistance : cp. 17 10 20 29.

15. The tents of cattle] i.e. the tents of nomadic tribes with large possessions of flocks and cattle.

CHAPTER 15
REIGN OF ASA (continued)

An account of how Asa, moved by the prophet Azariah, made a covenant to seek the LORD. This c. is almost entirely supplementary to what is recorded of Asa in 1 K 15.

1. Azariah] not mentioned elsewhere.

3. For a long season] The writer seems to have principally in view the times of the Judges : see Jg 2 12 3 7 17 6 21 25. **A teaching priest**] For this function of the priesthood cp. Lv 10 11 Mal 2 7.

5. No peace . . came in] i.e. travelling was unsafe : cp. Jg 5 6 6 2. **The countries**] i.e. the different divisions of Israel : see Jg 12 4 20, 21.

8. The prophecy of Oded] The words ' Azariah son of ' have dropped out before **Oded :** the Vulgate has them. **The cities . . taken**] This seems to refer to the conquests of Abijah : 13 19.

9. The strangers] Those members of the Ten Tribes who removed to Judah on account of the calf - worship : 11 16. **Simeon**] The territory of Simeon must have practically belonged to Judah from the time of Jeroboam's revolt, but some Simeonites may have resided in the northern kingdom.

11. The spoil] i.e. the spoil taken from the Ethiopians : 14 13-15.

19. Five and thirtieth] This is inconsistent with the chronology given in 1 K, for Baasha died in the 26th year of **Asa** (1 K 16 8) ; but see on 16 1.

CHAPTER 16
REIGN OF ASA (concluded)

This c. reproduces with some verbal differences 1 K 15 17-24, but adds an account of a rebuke received by Asa from the seer Hanani.

1. Six and thirtieth] Since, according to 1 K 16 8, Baasha did not live until the 36th year of **Asa**. some have supposed that the **six and thirtieth year** is reckoned from the revolt of the Ten Tribes.

4. The store cities of Naphtali] LXX suggests that the true reading is 'the surrounding parts of Naphtali.'

7. Hanani] Nothing is known of him beyond what is here related, and the fact that he was the father of the prophet Jehu (19 2). **Because thou hast relied**] cp. the similar protests of Isaiah against reliance upon foreign support instead of upon the LORD (Isa 30 1 31 1). **The host of . . Syria**] The prophet seems to imply that Asa might have beaten both Israel and Syria, if he had trusted in the LORD.

8. Lubims] These were not amongst the forces of Zerah (14⁹), but those of Shishak (12³).

12. Sought not to the LORD] Contrast the conduct of Hezekiah in his sickness : see 2 K 20².

14. A very great burning] i.e. of the spices previously mentioned : cp. Jer 34⁵. The bodies of the dead were not ordinarily burnt but buried ; the burning of the bodies of Saul and Jonathan (1 S 31¹²) was exceptional.

CHAPTER 17
REIGN OF JEHOSHAPHAT

An account of a mission of Levites to teach the Law, and of the king's army.

The particulars of Jehoshaphat's reign here given are additional to those contained in 1 K 22⁴¹⁻⁵⁰.

1. Strengthened himself against Israel] Jehoshaphat came to the throne in the fourth year of Ahab, and it is probable that some interval elapsed before he made peace with him, as recorded in 1 K 22⁴⁴.

2. Which Asa .. taken] see 15⁸, and note.

3. His father David] LXX omits ' David,' so that his father means Asa, whose early actions (14²) are here contrasted with the oppressiveness and want of faith that he displayed in his later years (16⁷⁻¹⁰). **Baalim**] RV 'the Baalim' (and so elsewhere), i.e. the various false gods to each of whom the title ' Baal ' (= Lord), was applied.

4. The doings of Israel] an allusion either to the worship of the calves (13⁸,⁹) or to that of the Zidonian Baal, introduced into Israel by Jezebel, the wife of Jehoshaphat's contemporary, Ahab.

7. He sent to his princes] The princes were to organise the teaching which was carried out by the Levites named in the next v.

9. Went about] This is the only record in the historical books of the diffusion of a knowledge of the Law by means of a mission. In the reign of Josiah (2 K 23²) and after the return from the exile (Neh 8³⁻¹⁸) the Law was merely read before assemblies of the people at Jerusalem.

13. Much business] i.e. was busily employed on works of defence. **And the men of war .. were**] better, ' and he had men of war .. in Jerusalem.'

14-18. It is generally agreed that there must be some error in these enormous numbers.

CHAPTER 18
REIGN OF JEHOSHAPHAT (continued)

This c. reproduces 1 K 22¹⁻³⁵ with very slight differences.

31. The LORD helped him] This, which is

an addition to the narrative of Kings, seems to imply that the writer regarded Jehoshaphat's cry as a prayer for help, which God answered, as explained in the next v.

CHAPTER 19
REIGN OF JEHOSHAPHAT (continued)

The c. narrates how Jehoshaphat was reproved by the seer Jehu for helping Ahab, and how he instituted judges in the cities of Judah.

This c. is entirely supplementary to the account of Jehoshaphat as given in 1 K.

2. Jehu] previously only named in connexion with the northern kingdom in the reign of Baasha (1 K 16⁷). **Shouldest thou help the ungodly**] The peace with Israel, ratified by a marriage (2 K 8¹⁸), put an end to a war between two kindred peoples, yet brought evils in its train, since the Baal worship which polluted the northern kingdom was introduced into Judah by Athaliah, the daughter of Ahab and the daughter-in-law of Jehoshaphat : 24⁷.

5. He set judges] Local courts of justice may have existed before, but Jehoshaphat improved them, and likewise established a court in the capital, which seems also to have heard appeals : v. 10.

6. The LORD .. judgment] Judges were administrators of the divine justice, so that even the term ' God ' could be used to describe them in their official capacity : see Ex 21⁶ RV.

8. For the judgment of the LORD .. controversies] Perhaps the former means cases relating to religious obligations, and the latter ordinary civil and criminal trials. **When they returned**] RV 'and they returned,' the reference being to the king and his retinue.

10. Between blood and blood] e.g. the determination of what was murder and what was merely manslaughter : cp. Ex 21. **Between law and commandment**] i.e. the decision, where laws seemed to conflict, which of them applied to a particular case.

11. And, behold, etc.] The court at Jerusalem was divided into two sections, one (under Amariah) dealing with ecclesiastical causes, and the other (under Zebadiah) dealing with secular causes.

CHAPTER 20
REIGN OF JEHOSHAPHAT (concluded)

An account of how a host of Moabites and others invaded Judah ; how Jehoshaphat prayed to the LORD, and was directed by Jahaziel not to fear ; and how the enemy was overthrown by God.

The early part of this c. is additional to the narrative in 1 K : the latter part reproduces 1 K 22⁴¹⁻⁴⁹.

1. *Other* beside the Ammonites] better (with LXX), 'some of the Meunim' (or Maonites): cp. 26⁷ and Jg 10¹². They seem to have been the people from Mt. Seir mentioned in vv. 10, 23.

2. Beyond the sea] i.e. from the eastern side of the Dead Sea. **On this side Syria**] lit. 'from Syria,' but **Syria** is probably a mistake for 'Edom.' The Moabites and Ammonites had marched round the S. end of the Dead Sea, and passing through Edom (the 'Mount Seir' of v. 10) had been joined by some of the inhabitants. **En-gedi**] on the W. shore of the Dead Sea, the modern Ain-jidy.

5. Before the new court] probably 'the court of the priests' of 4⁹, which was distinct from the one in which Solomon prayed : 6¹³.

10. Wouldest not let, etc.] The Moabites, Ammonites, and Edomites were all spared on the ground of their kinship with Israel through Lot and Esau : Dt 2⁴, ⁹, ¹⁹.

16. Ziz] The word perhaps survives in the name El Husasah which attaches to a district near Tekoa : v. 20.

21. The beauty of holiness] Perhaps better, 'in holy apparel' : cp. 1 Ch 16²⁹.

22. Ambushments] RV 'liers in wait.' Apparently the enemy fell out among themselves.

25. Riches with the dead bodies] LXX points to another reading, 'riches and garments.'

26. Berachah] i.e. 'Blessing.' The place has been identified with the Wâdy Bereikût near Tekoa.

34. Who *is* **mentioned**] RV '(the book) which is inserted in.'

36. To go to Tarshish] 1 K 22⁴⁸ has 'ships of Tarshish' (i.e. large merchantmen) 'to go to Ophir' (in Arabia, or E. Africa), for which Ezion-geber was the natural port of departure.

CHAPTER 21
REIGN OF JEHORAM

This c. in part reproduces 2 K 8¹⁷⁻²² but adds several particulars respecting the judgments brought upon Jehoram.

2. Azariah . . Azariah] One of the names is probably an error, perhaps for 'Ahaziah' : cp. the mistake in 22⁶. **3. And their father**] cp. 11²³.

10. So the Edomites revolted] The writer omits the final sentence in 2 K 8²¹ which accounts for the successful revolt of the Edomites : see note there.

11. Fornication] A figure for religious infidelity.

12. A writing . . from Elijah] If this mention of Elijah as living in the reign of Jehoram is to be reconciled with 2 K 3¹¹, which relates that Elisha (Elijah's successor) prophesied in the reign of Jehoshaphat, it must be supposed that Elisha entered upon his ministry before Elijah was translated ; and that 2 K 2 is out of its proper chronological order. The incident here described is the only instance of Elijah having concerned himself with the affairs of Judah.

14. A great plague] i.e. the great blow inflicted by the invasion described in v. 16.

16. The LORD stirred up] The invaders, though pursuing designs of their own, were really agents of the divine judgment : cp. 1 Ch 5²⁶ Isa 10⁵⁻⁷ 37²⁴⁻²⁹. **The Arabians . . Ethiopians**] These Arabians came from the W. coast of Arabia, facing Ethiopia across the Red Sea.

17. In the king's house] better, 'belonging to the king's house.' It is not meant that the invaders assaulted Jerusalem, but that they carried off the royal property in the country districts. **Jehoahaz**] called in 22¹ 'Ahaziah.'

19. Made no burning, etc.] i.e. they did not use the same quantity of spices as were burnt at the funeral rites of former kings. **20. Departed . . desired**] i.e. he died unregretted. But some (following LXX) render 'he walked (i.e. lived) in an undesirable way.'

CHAPTER 22
REIGN OF AHAZIAH

This c. reproduces with some differences 2 K 8²⁴⁻²⁹ and 11¹⁻³ (the intervening chs. being omitted because they relate exclusively to Israel).

2. Forty and two] This must be an error, for his father was only 40 when he died (21²⁰). 2 K 8²⁶ has 'twenty-two.' **6. Azariah**] An error for 'Ahaziah,' which LXX has. **7. Had anointed**] see 2 K 9¹⁻¹⁰.

8. The sons of the brethren, etc.] i.e. of the elder sons of Jehoram who were killed by the Arabians (21¹⁷). If Jehoram was only 40 at his death (21²⁰), his grandsons at this time (v. 2) must have been quite young children.

9. He was hid in Samaria] 2 K 9²⁷ states that he was mortally wounded in his chariot when escaping from Jehu, and died at Megiddo. **They had slain . . they buried**] The first verb refers to the emissaries of Jehu, the second to the servants of the murdered Ahaziah. **To keep still**] i.e. to retain.

CHAPTER 23
REIGN OF JOASH

This c. repeats 2 K 11⁴⁻²⁰, but brings into prominence the ecclesiastical officials in place of the soldiers of the royal guard.

4. This *is* **the thing**, etc.] The arrangements differ from those described in 2 K 11 (see note there). Here there are three divisions which are posted (*a*) at the doors of the Temple, (*b*) at the palace, (*c*) at the gate of the foundation (which in 2 K is called the 'gate Sur' and connected with the palace). Here too only priests or Levites are allowed to enter the Temple, whilst the rest take up their position outside ; but in Kings the distinction is not observed.

16. Between him, etc.] RV 'between himself, and all the people, and the king.'

18. Appointed the offices, etc.] better, 'put

the offices .. into the hand of.' **The priests the Levites**] LXX has (preferably) 'the priests and the Levites,' the priests alone being authorised to offer sacrifice (according to Nu 18[7]).

CHAPTER 24
REIGN OF JOASH (concluded)

An account of the repair of the Temple, the idolatry of Joash after the death of Jehoiada, the murder of Jehoiada's son, and the king's violent death.

The early part of this c. reproduces 2 K 11[21]–12[16], with unimportant variations, but vv. 15–22 are entirely supplementary, and give a different account of the closing years of the reign of Joash from that contained in 2 K.

6. *According to* .. **Moses**] This refers to the half-shekel required to be paid by every Israelite as an atonement for his soul : Ex 30[13-16].

7. The sons of Athaliah] perhaps her adherents, rather than her children, who had been killed in the lifetime of their father Jehoram : 21[17].

15. An hundred and thirty] an age unprecedented since Joshua : Josh 24[29].

16. Among the kings] Jehoiada thus received an honour which was refused to Joash : v. 25.

20. The son of Jehoiada] called in Mt 23[35] 'the son of Barachias' by confusion with Zachariah the prophet. **Which stood above the people**] probably on a platform.

23. The host of Syria] Hazael, the king of Syria, was engaged in attacking Gath, and from thence made an incursion into Judah.

Destroyed all the princes] These were the instigators of the king's impiety : v. 17.

25. The sons of Jehoiada] better, as in LXX, 'the son of Jehoiada' (vv. 20, 21).

27. The burdens, etc.] better, 'the multitude of the oracles uttered against him' : see v. 19, and cp. 2 K 9[25]. **The story**] RV 'the commentary' : see on 13[22].

CHAPTER 25
REIGN OF AMAZIAH

This c. is derived in the main from 2 K 14[1-20], but with two insertions, vv. 5–10 and 13–16.

5. Made them captains, etc.] better, 'arranged them according to their fathers' houses under captains.' **From twenty years old**] Under this age military service was not required : Nu 1[3] 1 Ch 27[23].

7. *With* **all .. Ephraim**] added to explain the sense in which 'Israel' is used, since ordinarily in Chronicles it is equivalent to Judah : see on 12[6]. For the protest against an alliance with the northern kingdom cp. 19[2] 20[37].

8. But if thou wilt go] LXX has 'if thou

thinkest to prevail with these' (i.e. the forces from Ephraim) 'God shall make thee fall.'

11. The children of Seir] i.e. the Edomites.

13. From Samaria] i.e. from the frontier of the kingdom (not from its capital).

14. He brought the gods, etc.] Similarly the Philistines brought away the ark which the Israelites had carried with them into battle at Ebenezer : 1 S 4[11].

17. Come, let us, etc.] In connexion with the preceding narrative Amaziah's challenge might be explained as due to a desire to have satisfaction for the conduct of the Israelite forces as described in v. 13, but see on 2 K 14[8].

23. Jehoahaz] i.e. Ahaziah : 21[17].

24. With Obed-edom] i.e. with the descendants of Obed-edom, who were porters of the Temple : 1 Ch 26[4-8].

28. The city of Judah] LXX has 'the city of David,' as in 2 K 14[20] and 2 Ch 24[1] 16[14] 21[1,20], etc.

CHAPTER 26
REIGN OF UZZIAH

This c. adds largely to the parallel account of Uzziah's reign in 2 K 15[1-7], and furnishes information respecting his wars, his military defences, and the cause of his leprosy.

1. Uzziah] This is the usual form in Chronicles except in 1 Ch 3[12]; in Kings it is generally 'Azariah.'

6. Jabneh] between Joppa and Ashdod : afterwards called Jamnia.

7. The Mehunims] see on 20[1].

9. The valley gate] probably a gate leading into the valley of Hinnom, at the S. end of the W. hill.

10. In the desert, etc.] Uzziah's cattle were pastured in three different districts, (a) the desert (or wilderness) in the S. and SE. of Judah, which has some fertile spots ; (b) the low country (or lowland), consisting of the slopes that extend from the Judæan hills to the Mediterranean ; (c) the plains, or tableland, E. of the Dead Sea and the Jordan, where Uzziah may have secured rights of pasturage from the Ammonites (v. 8). **Carmel**] RV 'the fruitful fields' : or level garden-land, as distinct from the 'mountains' or hilly districts.

14. Habergeons] RV 'coats of mail.'

Slings *to cast* **stones**] RV 'stones for slinging' : which had to be supplied of a certain size and in sufficient quantity. **15. Engines**] These were machines of the nature of catapults.

16. To *his* **destruction**] RV 'so that he did corruptly.' **Into the temple**] The altar of incense was in the Holy Place. **18. To the priests, etc.**] The restriction to the sons of Aaron of the duty of offering incense is enforced in the Law by the history of Korah ·

Nu 16 40. **21. In a several house**] i.e. in a lazar house. For the seclusion of leprous persons from the community cp. Lv 13 46 Nu 5 2.

22. Isaiah] The prophet received his prophetic call in the year that Uzziah died (Isa 6 1).

23. In the field of the burial, etc.] i.e. in the royal burial ground, but not in the royal sepulchres.

CHAPTER 27
The Reign of Jotham

This c. repeats the substance of 2 K 15 32-38, but expands the account of Jotham's buildings, and relates a war with Ammon about which Kings is silent.

2. The people did .. corruptly] If Isa 2 is rightly assigned to this reign, it furnishes illustrations of the historian's statement, for it represents idolatry, sorcery, and arrogance, as prevalent amongst the people (Isa 2 6-8, 11 f.).

3. Ophel] the southern extremity of the Temple hill.

5. Measures] lit. 'cors': a 'cor' being rather more than 10 bushels, the whole quantity of each kind of grain was over 100,000 bushels. For such payments in kind cp. 17 11 2 K 3 4.

CHAPTER 28
The Reign of Ahaz

This c. recounts how the idolatry of Ahaz was punished by the attacks of Syria and Israel; how the captives taken by the Israelites were restored; and how Ahaz in his distress appealed to Assyria.

This c. corresponds to 2 K 16, but it omits many facts related there, whilst expanding the account of the war with Israel.

5. The king of Syria] i.e. Rezin, who, with Pekah of Israel, wished to depose Ahaz: see Isa 7.

7. Maaseiah, the king's son] perhaps a son of Jotham and brother of Ahaz, since Ahaz himself was only 20 at his accession and 36 at his death (v. 1). **Next to the king**] i.e. the principal counsellor of state: cp. Esth 10 3.

9. *That* **reacheth**, etc.] i.e. immoderate and excessive: cp. Ezr 9 6.

16. The kings] The LXX, more appropriately, has 'the king,' the allusion being to Tiglath-pileser (v. 20). But Chronicles frequently uses the plural where the singular would be more accurate: see v. 23, also c. 32 4, 31 30 6.

17. The Edomites] Rezin had previously captured Elath and returned it to the Edomites (2 K 16 6), and this doubtless encouraged them to retaliate upon the Judæans, who had withheld it from them for so long.

18. The Philistines] These had suffered at the hands of Judah during the reign of Uzziah (26 6, 7), and now took the opportunity to seek revenge.

19. Made Judah naked] RV 'dealt wantonly in Judah.'

20. Distressed him, etc.] The intervention of Assyria not only imposed the burden of tribute upon Judah, but also awoke the jealousy of Egypt, with evil results to the small kingdom placed between the two empires; yet for a time at least the Assyrians delivered Judah from Syria and Israel: 2 K 16 9 15 29.

23. Because the gods, etc.] i.e. as shown by the successes of Rezin (v. 5).

CHAPTER 29
The Reign of Hezekiah

This c. describes a cleansing of the Temple and a sacrifice for the sins of the people.

This and the following chs. 30–32, cover the same period as 2 K 18–20, but, for the most part, have in view a different side of Hezekiah's reign, Chronicles relating in great detail his religious reforms, whilst Kings is concerned mainly with the political events of the time.

3. Opened the doors] The Temple had been closed by Ahaz: 28 24. **4. The east street**] RV 'the broad place on the east,' perhaps one of the courts in front of the Temple: cp. Ezr 10 9 RV.

10. A covenant] The covenant between the nation and its God had been previously renewed in the time of Asa (15 12).

15. By the words of the LORD] The king was moved by a divine impulse, perhaps communicated through a prophet: cp. 30 12.

16. The inner part of the house] i.e. from the courts into the interior of the building. The Holy Place is meant (not the Holy of Holies, which the Levites might not enter). **17. The sixteenth day**] In the first period of 8 days the Temple itself was cleansed, in the second period the Temple court (where the altar of burnt offering was: v. 18).

21. Seven bullocks, etc.] It is possible that the bullocks, rams, and lambs constituted the burnt offerings mentioned in v. 27 (the victims for which are not otherwise named), and that the he-goats alone formed the sin offering (as v. 23 suggests). **For the kingdom**] i.e. for the king as distinguished from the people (Judah).

25. By his prophets] i.e. David's arrangements, as described in 1 Ch 23 5 25 1, were made under divine direction.

30. Of Asaph the seer] Twelve of the Psalms bear the name of Asaph.

31. Thank offerings] a form of peace offering (Lv 7 12), most of which was eaten by the worshipper. **Burnt offerings**] wholly consumed on the altar. **Of a free heart**] RV 'of a willing heart.'

34. *Were* **more upright .. than the priests**] Many of the priests had perhaps taken part in Ahaz's impieties as Urijah the high priest had done : 2 K 16 16.

36. Prepared the people] The zeal of the people was so remarkable that it could only be attributed to divine influence : cp. 30 12.

CHAPTER 30
REIGN OF HEZEKIAH (continued)

This c. relates how a passover was kept on the second month for Israel and Judah.

1. Should come . . at Jerusalem] This implies an endeavour to centralise the national worship by the abolition of the local sanctuaries (as described in 2 K 18 4).

2. In the second month] The Law allowed individuals to keep the Passover in the second month instead of the first, if they were prevented by some temporary hindrance (Nu 9 10, 11), and this permission Hezekiah thought might be extended to the whole community.

3. At that time] i.e. at the proper season, viz. the 14th day of the first month. The cleansing of the Temple was not completed till the 16th day of that month : 29 17.

5. Done it **of a long** time] RV 'kept it in great numbers.' According to Ex 12 6 the Passover was to be observed by 'the whole assembly of the congregation of Israel.'

6. The posts] lit. 'the couriers,' who were probably some of the royal guards. **You, that . . Assyria**] Since what is here related took place (according to 29 3) in Hezekiah's first year, the reference must be to the invasion of Tiglath-pileser : 2 K 15 29 1 Ch 5 26.

13. The feast of unleavened bread] This, though distinct from the Passover, was not separated from it by any interval, and the two came to be treated as one which could be described indifferently by either name : vv. 2, 13, 15. **14. The altars**] i.e. those erected by Ahaz : 28 24. **15. Were ashamed**] The zeal of the laity roused the priests, who had formerly been remiss (29 34), to a sense of their duty.

17. The passovers] i.e. the paschal lambs, which (according to Ex 12 6, 7) ought to have been killed by the head of each household.

18. Otherwise than it was written] As this Passover in the second month took the place of the one ordinarily held in the first month, there could be no supplementary passover for such as were unclean ; so Hezekiah preferred that the people should break the letter of the Law and eat without being sanctified than that they should be debarred from such an important festival and so be unfaithful to the spirit of the divine legislation.

20. Healed] i.e. did not send upon them the punishment which they had incurred : cp. Lv 15 31.

25. The strangers] i.e. proselytes of foreign descent, who either had come out of the northern kingdom or were settled in Judah.

CHAPTER 31
REIGN OF HEZEKIAH (continued)

This c. gives an account of Hezekiah's reorganisation of the Temple service.

2. Appointed the courses] The succession (see 1 Ch 23–26) had been suspended during the idolatry of the previous reigns, and required to be rearranged. **The tents of the LORD**] The phrase is borrowed from the conditions that prevailed in the wilderness.

3. The king's portion, etc.] The king set an example to his subjects by providing for the sacrifices named, for which see Nu 28, 29, whilst the people were required to support the priests (according to Nu 18).

6. That dwelt in the cities of Judah] The provincial population, as distinguished from the inhabitants of the capital. **The tithe of holy things**] The words **tithe of** have been accidentally repeated from the preceding ; they are omitted in v. 12. **11. Chambers**] i.e. some of the side chambers that surrounded the Temple. **14. Toward the east**] RV 'at the east gate': cp. 1 Ch 26 17.

15. To give to their brethren] The general sense of vv. 15–18 is that the officers named in v. 15 distributed to all the priests who dwelt in the priestly cities a share of the people's offerings, those alone being excluded from sharing, who, whilst in their courses at Jerusalem, were supported at the Temple itself : these, including priests, Levites and their families, are referred to in vv. 16–18.

16. Beside] i.e. excepting. **Genealogy**] i.e. list.

19. Also of the sons of Aaron, etc.] The meaning is that the six persons named in v. 15 furnished support to the priests and Levites who dwelt outside the cities, as well as to those who dwelt within them.

CHAPTER 32
REIGN OF HEZEKIAH (concluded)

This c. abbreviates the account of Sennacherib's invasion as related in 2 K 18 13–20 21, but supplements it by various particulars respecting Hezekiah's preparation to meet the attack.

3. To stop the waters, etc.] The chief spring which was thus stopped (or 'hidden') was the fountain of Gihon : see v. 30. **4. The brook**] lit. 'torrent-valley.' The Gihon spring was in the ravine of the Kidron.

6. The street of the gate] RV 'the broad place at the gate': where the people were wont to assemble.

9. After this] The Chronicler omits all account of the surrender of Hezekiah related in 2 K 18 14-16.

18. They cried] i.e. the 'servants' of v. 16. **In the Jews' speech**] see 2 K 18 26.

22. Guided them] LXX has 'gave them rest,' which suits the context better.

24. In those days] In vv. 24–26 the writer summarises very briefly what is related at length in 2 K 20 Isa 38.

30. Brought it, etc.] better, 'stopped the upper spring of the waters of Gihon and brought them straight down' (or, 'underground') 'westward to the city of David.' Gihon lay to the E. of Jerusalem, and Hezekiah conveyed its waters by a subterranean aqueduct to the pool of Siloam at the foot of the Temple hill.

31. The ambassadors] i.e. of Merodach-baladan, the king of Babylon : see 2 K 20[12 f.] Isa 39.

32. *And* **in the book of the kings,** etc.] The conjunction and should be omitted, the **vision of Isaiah** being incorporated in **the book of the kings of Judah and Israel,** like the 'book of Jehu the son of Hanani': 20[34].

33. In the chiefest] RV 'in the ascent': i.e. on the road that led up to the sepulchres.

CHAPTER 33
THE REIGN OF MANASSEH

This c. repeats, with certain omissions, 2 K 21 ; but the section v. 11–17, relating the captivity in Babylon, repentance, and release of Manasseh, is supplementary to the account in 2 K.

6. Observed times] RV 'practised augury': perhaps, as the original suggests, by watching the motions of clouds.

8. So that] RV 'if only': God's promises to Israel were conditional upon its obedience.

11. Among the thorns] RM 'with hooks': a monument still exists which shows the Assyrian king Esarhaddon leading two captives by hooks or rings put through their lips.

To Babylon] This city was for the most part subject to Assyria until the overthrow of the Assyrian power in 607 B.C. Shortly before 648 the brother of Asshurbanipal (who is probably the king of Assyria alluded to in this v.) revolted, and received support from some of the Palestinian states ; but the insurrection was suppressed, and if Manasseh had been among those who aided the insurgents, he may well have been punished in consequence. The Assyrian inscriptions, though they mention that Manasseh was a vassal of Assyria, do not refer to the events here related.

13. Brought him again, etc.] i.e. by prompting the Assyrian king to restore him to his throne. Such leniency on the part of Asshurbanipal finds a parallel in his conduct towards Necho, an Egyptian feudatory prince, who was taken captive for intriguing against his suzerain, but was subsequently restored to his country.

14. A wall without .. David] RV 'an outer wall to the city of David.' **The fish gate**] This was in the N. wall of the city ; through it fish is supposed to have entered from Tyre.

16. Commanded .. to serve the LORD] In spite of Manasseh's reformation here related, Jeremiah subsequently declared that his sins had not been expiated, and that the nation was doomed to destruction in consequence : Jer 15[4].

18. His prayer] What purports to be Manasseh's prayer is preserved in the Apocrypha, but is not considered genuine. **19. The sayings of the seers**] This follows the LXX. The Heb. has 'the sayings of Hozai.' **20. In his own house**] LXX has 'in the garden' (or 'park') 'of his own house': cp. 2 K 21[18].

CHAPTER 34
REIGN OF JOSIAH

The c. narrates how Josiah suppressed idolatry and repaired the Temple ; how a book of the Law, found in the Temple, was read to the king and the people ; and how the nation's covenant with the LORD was renewed.

This c. and the following are, in general, parallel to 2 K 22, 23[1-30], with some unimportant variants ; but the Chronicler gives more prominence than the writer of 2 Kings to the passover celebrated by Josiah.

3. In the twelfth year] In 2 K the abolition of the 'high places' is described as subsequent to the repair of the Temple, and the latter is assigned to Josiah's 'eighteenth' year : 2 K 22[3] 23[5, 8].

5. Burnt the bones] This was believed to afflict the souls of the dead priests, as well as to desecrate the shrines at which they had ministered. The condition of the spirit after death depended in a large measure upon the treatment sustained by the body. **6. With their mattocks**] A slight alteration gives 'in their ruins' (so RV), i.e. the desolate sites of the cities destroyed by the Assyrians.

9. And they returned to Jerusalem] Another reading is 'and of the inhabitants of Jerusalem.'

11. The houses] i.e. the Holy Place and the Holy of Holies : cp. 1 Ch 28[11] 29[4].

22. In the college] RV 'in the second quarter' (of the city). It has been suggested that this may have occupied the upper end of the Tyropœan valley, W. of the Temple.

CHAPTER 35
REIGN OF JOSIAH (concluded)

This c. contains an account of how Josiah celebrates the Passover, and how he provoked Necho the king of Egypt, and was slain at Megiddo.

1. On the fourteenth *day*] Josiah's passover, unlike Hezekiah's, was kept at the prescribed time.

3. Put the holy ark, etc.] The following words suggest that during the repair of the Temple, it had been removed and committed to the care of the Levites.

4. According to the writing, etc.] The reference is to the arrangements described in 1 Ch 23–26 2 Ch 8 14. **5. According to the divisions,** etc.] The sense is ' let there be for each family of the people a portion of a Levitical family to minister.' **6. Prepare your brethren**] RV ' prepare for,' etc. The killing of the passover victims by the Levites for the laity, which was exceptional in Hezekiah's time (30 17), had now become customary.

12. Removed] Perhaps they separated those parts (the fat, etc.) of the victims which were to be burnt. If so, these sacrifices were not strictly ' burnt offerings,' for in such, the whole of the victim was consumed by fire.

15. They might not depart] RV ' they needed not to depart.'

18. There was no passover, etc.] Hezekiah's passover had surpassed all that had preceded it (30 26), but Josiah's exceeded even that.

20. Against] better, ' at.' Necho's purpose was to share the spoils of the falling Assyrian empire. Nineveh was taken by the Babylonians about 607. **21. He sent ambassadors,** etc.] Necho's remonstrance to Josiah against interfering in the war between himself and the Babylonians, the conquerors of Assyria, is not recorded in 2 K.

22. Disguised himself] The same is related of Ahab in 18 29, but LXX has ' strengthened himself.' **From the mouth of God**] The writer regards Necho's words as a divinely-sent warning, which Josiah disregarded to his cost.

24. All Judah . . mourned] It is possible that this is the ' mourning of Hadadrimmon in the valley of Megiddo,' alluded to in Zech 12 11.

25. Made them] i.e. those in authority made such lamentations an **ordinance. In the lamentations**] probably not the book that bears this name, but a composition now lost.

CHAPTER 36
THE FALL OF JERUSALEM

This is a brief record of the reigns of Jehoahaz, Jehoiakim, Jehoiachin, and Zedekiah, and of the destruction of Jerusalem.

The first twenty vv. of this c. are abbreviated from 2 K 23 30–25 21, with some variations of statement.

6. Nebuchadnezzar] He was the son of Nabopolassar, the conqueror of Nineveh.

Bound him in fetters] This is not recorded in Kings. Perhaps this was the ' purpose' of the invasion described in 2 K 24 2, but Jehoiakim may have averted the threatened consequences by a timely surrender. The statement of Chronicles is followed in Dan 1 1, 2.

8. That which was found in him] i.e. his offences : cp. 1 K 1 52.

9. Eight] 2 K 24 8 has ' eighteen,' which, as he was married (2 K 24 15), is doubtless correct.

10. His brother] In reality Zedekiah was brother to Jehoiachin's father Jehoiakim, 1 Ch 3 15.

12. Jeremiah the prophet] For Zedekiah's disregard of Jeremiah's warnings see Jer 34 8 f. 37 2 38 17 f. Contrast the attitude of Ahab towards Elijah, as described in 1 K 21 27-29.

13. Made him swear] Ezekiel refers to this in 17 13.

14. Moreover, etc.] In vv. 14–16 the writer briefly explains the causes which led to the final destruction of Jerusalem and its inhabitants. For instances of the **abominations of the heathen** see 2 K 21 7, and what is implied in 1 K 15 12 22 46.

15. Rising up . . sending] In the OT. such expressive anthropomorphisms are common ; thus it is related that the LORD ' walked' in the garden of Eden (Gn 3 8), ' smelled' Noah's sacrifice (Gn 8 21), ' came down' to see Babel (Gn 11 5), etc. Yet nowhere is the infinite distance separating God from human limitations and frailty more forcibly asserted ; see Nu 23 19 Isa 55 9. **16. Mocked the messengers**] In the reign of Jehoiakim the prophet Urijah was put to death (Jer 26 20-23), and in the reign of Zedekiah, Jeremiah underwent much persecution (Jer 37, 38).

18. All the vessels, etc.] i.e. all that survived the spoliation described in v. 10.

20. The reign . . Persia] i.e. until the overthrow of Babylon by Cyrus in 538. **21. To fulfil threescore and ten years**] If the period of 70 years is reckoned from the time when Jeremiah's prophecy was uttered (Jehoiakim's 4th year, 605 B.C.) till the return of the Jews to their own land in 536, the prediction (for which see Jer 25 11 29 10) was almost exactly fulfilled. Between the final destruction of Jerusalem in 586 and the Return just 50 years elapsed.

22. Now in the first, etc.] vv. 22, 23 are identical with the opening words of Ezra (1 1-3), and end in the middle of a sentence. (For the notes see the passage in Ezra.)

EZRA and NEHEMIAH

GENERAL INTRODUCTION

1. The period of the Exile. The contents of Ezra and Nehemiah are separated from the last events in the previous historical writings by an interval of 50 years. The books of Chronicles, like the books of Kings, virtually close with the capture of Jerusalem by Nebuchadrezzar and the deportation of a large number of its inhabitants into Babylonia. There they were probably gathered into colonies or settlements at various places, such as Tel-abib (Ezk 3 15), Tel-melah, Tel-harsha (Ezr 2 59), Casiphia (Ezr 8 17), and others. So long as they remained quiet subjects they were not, as a rule, persecuted or enslaved. They were at liberty to cultivate the land and to acquire servants (Jer 29 5 Ezr 2 65); and, to judge from the value of the contributions made for religious purposes (Ezr 2 65, 69 Zech 6 10, 11), some must have accumulated considerable wealth. On the other hand, those who were disaffected and insubordinate brought upon themselves cruel punishments (Jer 29 22); and several passages in the prophets imply that many of the exiles were not unacquainted with harsh conditions of service (Isa 14 3 47 6).

Jewish religious life in the time of the Exile was distinguished from that of the pre-exilic period by the suspension of the sacrificial system. Not only was the Temple at Jerusalem destroyed—the place which the LORD had chosen to put His name there—but the captive Jews were withdrawn from the actual soil of Israel and were dwelling in an 'unclean land' (cp. Am 7 17), where acceptable sacrifices could not be offered. They maintained, however, such religious ordinances as the sabbath and circumcision; and the cessation of material oblations probably intensified rather than impaired the practice of prayer. Reflection upon the calamities sustained by their race must have deepened their sense of national sin; and the lessons of experience at last bore fruit in the gradual eradication of their propensity towards idolatry. The hope of a future restoration to their own country led to an increasing study of the ceremonial law which circumstances prevented them from carrying out in the present; and the loss of national independence enhanced the interest attaching to the records of their past greatness, some of the historical books (including the books of Kings) being completed during this period.

The Exile was brought to a close when the Babylonian empire fell before Cyrus, prince of Anshan or Elam. Cyrus, though an Elamite, was connected by descent with the Persian house of Achæmenes; and he not only became master of Media (in 549 B.C., through the deposition of Astyages), but subsequently of Persia likewise. In character he was courageous, magnanimous, and pious; and when he advanced to attack Babylon (then ruled by Nabunahid, or Nabonidus, a feeble prince), his career was watched with intense interest by the Jews, who regarded him as their destined deliverer. In 538 he took possession of Babylon, which surrendered peaceably; and when Nabonidus, who had fled, was captured, the Jews passed under the rule of a new lord. The way in which their expectations respecting Cyrus were fulfilled forms the subject of the opening narrative of the book of Ezra.

2. Political and Religious Conditions after the Return. When the Jewish people returned from exile their political condition was very unlike what it had been before the Fall of Jerusalem and the deportation of its inhabitants. With those events the national existence which they had enjoyed for many centuries came to an end; and though a number of them were restored to their country by Cyrus they remained subjects of the Persian empire. Jerusalem and the surrounding districts were under the control of a governor (Pehah or Tirshatha), who, though he might be occasionally a Jew, must often have been an alien. And whilst the Persian rule was probably in general not oppressive, various circumstances must have made the position of the Jewish community rather a hard one. They were surrounded by a hostile population, who seized every opportunity of bringing them into disfavour with the Persian authorities. They were for the most part poor (the richest men, according to Josephus, having remained in Babylon), and the land they cultivated, which was naturally not very fertile, had doubtless suffered from neglect; and yet they not only had to pay tribute, custom, and toll to the royal exchequer (Neh 5 4 Ezr 7 24), but had to contribute to the support of the local governor. And the pressure of external hardship was aggravated by internal friction. The poorer classes, to meet the payments required of them, had to borrow of their more prosperous neighbours at a high rate of interest, and the latter enforced to the full the rights which the Jewish laws conferred upon the creditor over an insolvent debtor. Many, to support themselves, had not only to part with their fields, but with their families, who were sold into bondage. The bitter feelings created by this situation might have had serious results, had it not been for the prudence and self-sacrifice of Nehemiah, who from 445 to 433 was Tirshatha. By his exhortation and example he succeeded in averting the social divisions that at one time threatened the people ; and though some of the measures he adopted to safeguard the religion of his countrymen did not conduce to friendly relations with their neighbours, his statesmanship ensured during the tenure of his authority not only the security but the contentment of the community

In religion the Jews enjoyed a degree of freedom denied them in civil affairs. When they returned to Jerusalem they were authorised by Cyrus to restore the Temple ; and though some years elapsed before the Temple was actually reconstructed, the altar of the LORD was set up as soon as they were once more settled in their own land, and the system of sacrificial worship, which had been suspended during the Exile, was re-organised. But though the religious life of the community again flowed in its old channels, its general tenor was in some respects unlike what it had previously been. Three points of difference may be noticed here. (a) The proneness to adopt alien religious rites, or to worship the LORD by means of material symbols, which was so common before the Exile, disappeared after the Return. The severe national judgment which they had sustained, and the experience of polytheism which they had acquired in Babylon, seem to have confirmed them finally in their allegiance to the God of their fathers and in the principles of spiritual religion ; and the protests against idolatry, so frequently required in earlier times, are henceforward seldom heard. (b) Prophecy, which in pre-exilic days had been so conspicuous a feature in their religious

history, now declined in importance ; and though several prophets did arise in the course of this period, they were more circumscribed in the range of their thoughts and less vigorous and original in the expression of them. In some respects the diffusion of a knowledge of the Law among the people at large rendered the need of such exceptional teachers less urgent, their places as moral and religious instructors being, in a measure, filled by the scribes. (c) Ritual was regarded differently by the leaders of religious thought before and after the Exile, in consequence, no doubt, of a difference in the needs of the times. When Israel enjoyed national independence, there was less need to emphasise the external features distinctive of Jewish worship, the prophets being chiefly concerned to insist upon the moral conditions demanded by the LORD of His worshippers. But after the Exile, when the nation had lost its independence, it was only by its ecclesiastical organisation and observances that its separateness as a community could be maintained, and therefore increased importance was attached to the ceremonial requirements of the Law.

LIST OF KINGS OF BABYLON AND PERSIA

		B.C.
Babylon—	Nebuchadnezzar	604
	Captures Jerusalem	586
	Evil Merodach	561
	Nergal Sharezer	560
	Labashi Merodach	556
	Nabunahid	555
	Fall of Babylon	538
Persia —	Cyrus, king of Babylon	538
	Cambyses	529
	Pseudo-Smerdis	522
	Darius Hystaspis	521
	Xerxes	485
	Artaxerxes Longimanus	464
	Sogdianus	424
	Darius Nothus	423
	Artaxerxes Mnemon	405
	Artaxerxes Ochus	358
	Arses	337
	Darius Codomannus	335–330

EZRA

INTRODUCTION

1. **Character and Contents.** The book of Ezra was combined by the Jews with the book of Nehemiah, the two being regarded as constituting a single work, of which Ezra himself was the reputed author. In the Hebrew Bible

they both precede Chronicles ; but it is probable that with the latter they form a consecutive history of which Chronicles is the first half. The close connexion between these three books is shown, not only by the way in which the closing verses of Chronicles are practically repeated in the opening verses of Ezra, but by (a) a common interest in statistics and genealogies ; (b) a common sympathy for the ecclesiastical side of Jewish life ; (c) a common use of certain phrases (e.g. 'father's house') which are comparatively rare elsewhere. If the three are all portions of one single work the composition of it cannot be earlier than the close of the 4th cent. ; for, as has been seen, Chronicles must be as late as 340 B.C., whilst Nehemiah contains a reference (12 11, 22) to the high priest Jaddua, who was contemporary with Alexander the Great (336–323). Consequently, since Ezra cannot have outlived the 5th cent. B.C., his authorship of the connected books is out of the question ; and the writer is really unknown.

The book of Ezra relates the history of the Jewish people from their return under Zerubbabel from Babylon to their own country in 536 to the arrival at Jerusalem of a second body of exiles under Ezra in 458, and includes an account of the building of the Second Temple. It thus covers a period of rather more than 78 years ; but of these the 15 years between 535 and 520 and the 58 years between 516 and 458 are practically a blank ; so that it is less a continuous record than a description of selected incidents.

2. Sources. The principal sources employed in the compilation of the book are (a) the actual memoirs of Ezra, distinguished by the use of the first person (7 27–9 15) ; (b) genealogies and registers (2, 10 18-44) ; (c) extracts derived from documents written not in Hebrew but in Aramaic (4 7–6 18 7 12-26).

3. Value. The historical importance of Ezra is very great, since it is the chief authority for the period of Jewish history with which it deals. Though the work of which it forms part is separated by a considerable interval from some of the events narrated, it makes use (as has been just shown) of earlier documents, and, for some portion of the time covered by it, it draws upon records composed by one of the principal actors in the incidents described. Nor is its religious value inferior to its secular interest. As a record of the past it recounts the fulfilment of one of the most remarkable predictions of Hebrew prophecy, namely, the restoration to their own land of the exiles who 50 years before had been carried into captivity ; it relates the establishment at Jerusalem of the community to which the world owes the preservation, arrangement, and completion of the Hebrew Scriptures ; and it marks the beginning and development of that intense attachment to the Mosaic Law which became so conspicuous a feature of Jewish religious life in after times. And as a means of conveying practical instruction the book is animated with a spirit of fervid patriot-

ism, of uncompromising adhesion to principle, and of loyal devotion to God. The character of Ezra in particular exhibits qualities deserving much admiration—deeply-rooted personal piety conjoined with a high regard for ecclesiastical order and the external rites of religion, and unwavering faith manifesting itself in, and through, active works.

CHAPTER 1
The Return of the Jews from Captivity

The c. narrates how Cyrus, king of Persia, permitted the Jews in Babylon to return to Jerusalem to rebuild the Temple there, and restored the vessels taken from it.

1. Now, etc.] The book of Ezra begins with the last words of 2 Ch ; vv. 1, 2 and the first half of v. 3 occurring in 2 Ch 36 22, 23. The three books, Chronicles, Ezra, and Nehemiah, were probably at first continuous, in this order ; but subsequently the arrangement in the Hebrew Bible was altered to Ezra, Nehemiah, and Chronicles, Ezra being placed first in order to form a sequel to the history contained in Kings. 2 Chronicles was then made to conclude with the same words that form the beginning of Ezra.

In the first year of Cyrus] i.e. of Cyrus' rule over Babylon, 538 B.C.

The word of the LORD . . Jeremiah] see Jer 29 10 25 11-13 ; cp. also Ezk 11 17 37 12. The period of the Captivity was described by Jeremiah as 70 years and by Ezekiel as 40 (4 6). Its actual duration, reckoned from the Fall of Jerusalem in 586, was about 50 years, but the interval between the destruction of the Temple and its restoration in 516 (Ezr 6 15) was almost exactly 70. The accordance of the event with predictions uttered so long before witnesses to the remarkable faculty of prevision possessed by the Hebrew prophets, inasmuch as there was nothing (so far as can be judged) within the political horizon at the time when the predictions were made to create such an expectation.

The LORD stirred up, etc.] Josephus states that the divine will respecting the Jews was made known to Cyrus by the prophecies of Isaiah (see Isa 44 28 45 1-4, where Cyrus is styled 'the LORD's servant' and 'the LORD's anointed'). Be this as it may, God's purposes were fulfilled, whatever may have been the motives by which the Persian king was consciously actuated. From the inscriptions it appears that Nabunahid (Nabonidus), the last king of Babylon, had caused great discontent by removing to his capital the gods of various cities, and that Cyrus sent them back to their respective sanctuaries ; and the restoration of the sacred vessels (v. 7) of the Jews, whose God was not represented by any image, was doubtless part of the same policy. The permission given to the

Jews themselves to return to Jerusalem to reconstruct the Temple there conciliated a number of people who might otherwise have been a source of danger to the empire. The old idea that Cyrus as a Zoroastrian had sympathy with the religion of the Jews is disproved by evidence from the monuments.

2. The LORD God . . hath given me] Cyrus showed great regard for the religious sentiments of his various subjects ; and just as in his inscriptions it is represented to the Babylonians that he had obtained his victories through Merodach their chief god, so here in a decree issued to the Jews his success is ascribed to the LORD. But it is possible that the Hebrew colouring of the decree is due to a Hebrew scribe, commissioned to make it intelligible to his countrymen, rather than to its royal author.

4. Whosoever remaineth] RV 'whosoever' (of the captive people) 'is left' (cp. Neh 1 2), there being an allusion to the remnant of Israel.

The men of his place] i.e. his Babylonian neighbours (v. 6).

5. Whose spirit, etc.] It was only a small proportion of the exiled Jews who were inspired with such zeal for their land and the sanctuary of their God as to exchange the comfort of Babylon for the desolation of Judæa. In this passage those who took advantage of Cyrus' decree are represented as belonging to Judah and Benjamin only, but there were also among them some from Ephraim and Manasseh : 1 Ch 9 3.

7. Had brought forth] see 2 K 24 13 2 Ch 36 7.

8. Sheshbazzar] It seems probable that this was the Persian or Babylonian name of Zerubbabel (2 2). In favour of the view that the same person is designated by the two names is the fact that the foundation of the Temple is ascribed to both (5 16 3 8), whilst the double name may be paralleled by the instances of Daniel, Hananiah, Mishael, Azariah (Dan 1 6,7), Eliakim, and Mattaniah (2 K 23 34 24 17). But some distinguish between the two (as is done in 1 Esdr 6 18), and either regard Sheshbazzar as identical with Shenazzar the uncle of Zerubbabel (2 Ch 3 18,19), or take him to be a Persian commissioner accompanying Zerubbabel (for although he is here called the prince of Judah, i.e. the representative of Judah's royal line, the LXX in 5 14 styles him 'the guardian over the treasure,' or 'treasury').

9. Chargers . . knives] The words probably mean different kinds of vessels.

CHAPTER 2

The Names and Number of those who
RETURNED

1. The province] i.e. the Persian province of Judæa (5 8). **Had carried away**] in 597 B.C. and 586 B.C. **Every one unto his city**] i.e. to the provincial towns. This process can only have taken place very gradually.

2. Zerubbabel] for his relation to Sheshbazzar see on 1 8 ; for his ancestry see on 3 2. The list of names that follows is repeated, with some variants, in Neh 7 7-73. **Jeshua**] the high priest, called by Haggai 'Joshua.' The names in this v. number 11, but in the corresponding passage in Neh (7 7) they amount to 12, and are probably intended to be symbolic of the 12 tribes of Israel (cp. 6 17), the number of which was recalled at a later date by the 12 he-goats offered as a sin-offering at the dedication of the restored Temple (6 17), and by the sacrifices described in 8 35 : cp. also the expression 'all Israel' in 2 70. **Nehemiah**] not the Nehemiah of Neh 1 1.

3–9. The names in these vv. are those of families. **16. Of Ater of Hezekiah**] i.e. the descendants of Ater through Hezekiah, one of his sons.

20–35. The names in these vv. are those of localities. **29. Nebo**] not the Nebo in Reuben, E. of the Jordan (Nu 32 38), but situated in Judah, identified by some with Nob (Isa 10 32), by others with the modern Nuba, S. of Jerusalem. **31. The other Elam**] in contrast to the Elam of v. 7.

36–39. Of the four priestly houses here named, one, **Pashur**, is not among the 24 enumerated in 1 Ch 24 7-18, but is probably a branch of the house of Malchijah (1 Ch 24 9): see Neh 11 12.

40. Seventy and four] The small number betrays a backwardness on the part of the Levites similar to that which they manifested on a subsequent occasion : see 8 15. **42. The porters**] they kept the Temple gates (1 Ch 9 17). **43. The Nethinims**] i.e. Temple servants : see Neh 8 17, and on 1 Ch 9 2. **55. The children of Solomon's servants**] probably descendants of the native Canaanites employed by Solomon on his buildings: see 1 K 9 21. **59. Tel-melah**, etc.] localities in Babylonia.

62. Sought their register, etc.] i.e. sought their entry among those who were enrolled as being Israelites of pure descent. **As polluted**] Only those were admitted to the priesthood who could prove their descent from Aaron, in accordance with Nu 3 10 16 40.

63. The Tirshatha] i.e. Zerubbabel, the title meaning 'governor,' perhaps one subordinate to a 'satrap.' **Eat of the most holy things**] the privilege of the priesthood only (Nu 18 8-19). **Till there stood up**, etc.] In early times the high priest used to enquire of the LORD by Urim and Thummim : see on Ex 28 30.

64. Forty and two thousand, etc.] The total number here given disagrees with the sum of the items, which only amounts to 29,818 (in Neh 7 66, 31,089, the difference perhaps being due to textual errors).

65. Singing men, etc.] These were minstrels employed on secular occasions (cp. Eccl 2[7,8]), distinct from the singers of v. 41, who were intended for the Temple.

69. Drams] The dram (Gk. *drachma*), like the pound (*maneh*), was a weight, equivalent to the Hebrew half-shekel. The pound contained 100 drams. Some authorities render the word translated ' dram ' by daric, a gold coin worth a guinea. A pound of silver was worth about £4.

70. Dwelt in their cities] i.e. occupied several of the provincial cities. Some scholars have held that only a few (if any) Jews returned to Jerusalem in the reign of Cyrus (whose decree in Ezr 6[3-5] only directs the construction of the Temple, not the restoration of any exiles), and that the Temple was not begun as related in c. 3, but built for the first time in the reign of Darius by the remnant of the people left in Judæa (Hag 1[12,14] Zech 8[6,11]). There seems, however, no adequate reason to question the substantial truth of Ezr 1–3.

CHAPTER 3
The Refounding of the Temple

1. The seventh month] i.e. Sept.-Oct. of (probably) 537 B.C.

2. Jeshua] called in Hag 1[1] ' Joshua.' His father Jozadak had been carried into exile by Nebuchadnezzar (1 Ch 6[15]). **Son of Shealtiel]** In 1 Ch 3[19] Zerubbabel is called the son of Pedaiah, the brother of Shealtiel (Salathiel). The discrepancy may be explained by the suppositions (*a*) that he was the real son of Pedaiah and the legal son of Shealtiel (Pedaiah having married Shealtiel's widow, according to the law of Dt 25[5f.]), (*b*) that he was grandson of Shealtiel and son of Pedaiah, (*c*) that he was grandson of both. But LXX of 1 Ch 3[19] makes him the son of Shealtiel (Salathiel), in agreement with the evidence of this passage and of Hag 1[1].

Builded the altar] Possibly an effort had for a time been made to continue the worship of the LORD on the site of the Temple after its destruction (see Jer 41[5]) ; but the altar erected had apparently been overthrown. The Jews now proceeded to restore it, in order to have the privilege of public worship whilst the Temple was in course of reconstruction. **As** *it is* **.. Moses]** Special sacrifices were enjoined for the 1st day of the 7th month (Nu 29[1-6]).

3. Fear] i.e. of interruption from the enemy. **4. The feast of tabernacles]** This began on the 15th day of the 7th month, and lasted 7 days, followed by a solemn assembly on the 8th day : Nu 29[12f.] **5. Both of]** better, ' and the offerings of ' : see Nu 28, 29. •

7. And meat and drink, etc.] cp. 1 K 5[6-11] regarding Solomon's Temple. **To the sea**

of Joppa] RV 'to the sea, unto Joppa ': cp. 2 Ch 2[16].

8. In the second year] probably 536 B.C. The second month would correspond to April-May.

9. Jeshua] not the ' Jeshua' of v. 8 (who was high priest), but a Levite (2[40]). **10. The ordinance of David]** This is set forth in 1 Ch 25[1f. 16][4-6]. **11. Together]** RV ' one to another': i.e. antiphonally.

12. Wept] Though the younger among the people were filled with hope, now that the house of the LORD was once more established in their midst, the older, who could remember the earlier Temple, destroyed about 50 years before, wept at the contrast to it which was presented by the meanness of the new building, and the inadequate resources available for its completion : cp. Hag 2[3] Zech 4[10].

Some scholars have questioned whether the foundations of the Temple were really laid by Zerubbabel in the second year after the Return, as related in vv. 8–10, on the ground that Haggai and Zechariah seem to imply that it was not begun until the 2nd year of Darius Hystaspis (520 B.C.) : see Hag 2[15] Zech 8[9]. But the language of the prophets is sufficiently explained if it is assumed that only a commencement was made in 536, that the progress of the work was very soon suspended, and that the renewal of it in 520 was practically a fresh start, as indeed the book of Ezra itself declares it to have been (5[2]).

CHAPTER 4
Feud between the Jews and Samaritans

This c. describes the desire of the Samaritans to take part in the rebuilding of the Temple, and their successful opposition to the Jews on their request being refused.

1. The adversaries] The term is here anticipatory of the opposition subsequently displayed. The people thus designated were the Samaritans, who, in the main, were the descendants of the immigrants who, to replace the Israelite population that had been deported after the fall of Samaria, had been introduced, first of all by Sargon, from Babylon, Cuthah, and other places (2 K 17[24]), and also at a later date by Esarhaddon and Asshurbanipal (vv. 2, 10). But there must likewise have been mingled with them a certain number of native Israelites, who had been left behind in the country by their Assyrian conquerors.

2. We seek your God] A priest had been brought back from captivity to teach them how to fear the LORD (2 K 17[28,32,33]). **We do sacrifice unto Him]** so one reading of the Heb., followed by the LXX, the clause expanding the plea of common worship. Another reading is ' yet we do no sacrifice,' the argument implying that they had hitherto had no opportunity of offering acceptable sacrifices, but now desired to do so at Jerusalem, the only lawful sanctuary. **Esar-haddon**] the successor of Sennacherib (681–668 B.C.). **Assur**] i.e. Assyria.

3. As king Cyrus, etc.] The fact that they were not authorised to extend to others the privileges conferred upon them by Cyrus was probably not the only motive that actuated the Jews. They no doubt felt that to admit to closer association such a hybrid community as the Samaritans, with their mixture of Hebrew and heathen rites of worship, would neutralise the impulse in the direction of purity of religion which they had derived from their experiences as exiles. **4. The people of the land**] i.e. the Samaritans and the other hostile neighbours of the Jews; the annoyances they caused are referred to in Zech 8 10.

5. The reign of Darius] i.e. Darius Hystaspis, the third in succession to Cyrus, who was followed on the throne by Cambyses, Gomates (who personated Smerdis, and is consequently often styled Pseudo-Smerdis), and Darius, in the order named. Darius reigned from 521–485, so that the rebuilding of the Temple was interrupted for fifteen or sixteen years (536–520).

6. Ahasuerus] i.e. Xerxes (485–464), the successor of Darius Hystaspis.

7. Artaxerxes] i.e. Artaxerxes Longimanus (464–424), the successor of Xerxes. Since both Xerxes and Artaxerxes lived after Darius Hystaspis, to whom v. 24 probably refers, and to whose reign the contents of c. 5 belong, the section, vv. 6–23, departs from the chronological succession of events either in consequence of some accidental misplacement, or because the writer has in view a comprehensive summary of the several occasions when opposition was offered to the Jews by their enemies. The charge made in this section against the Jews is not the building of the Temple (the subject of which is resumed in v. 24 and c. 5), but the fortification of Jerusalem (v. 12), either by Nehemiah (as related in the book of Neh) or by a body of Jews who came from Babylon before him, perhaps those who accompanied Ezra (see c. 7). Some, who consider the chronological sequence in this c. to be unbroken, identify the 'Darius' of v. 24 with Darius Nothus (423–405) ; whilst others, who take vv. 6–23 to be a detailed explanation of the opposition summarised in v. 5, identify Ahasuerus and Artaxerxes with Cambyses and Gomates, the two kings who came between Cyrus and Darius Hystaspis.

7. In the Syrian tongue, etc.] RV 'written in the Syrian (Aramean) *character*, and set forth in the Syrian (Aramean) *tongue*.' Aramean was the chief medium of communication between the different peoples of the East : cp. 2 K 18 26.

8. Rehum . . Shimshai] It is not clear whether vv. 7, 8 refer to more than one letter sent on different occasions by the enemies of the Jews, or to a single letter written by the persons named in v. 7 (who were presumably Samaritans) and communicated through the Persian officials named in v. 8.

9. Dinaites] The identification of most of the peoples mentioned in this v. is uncertain. The Susanchites were the natives of Shushan, the capital of Elam. **10. On this side**] RV 'beyond' (and so in vv. 11, 16, 5 3, 6 8 36), regarded from the point of view of the Persian court. **11. At such a time**] RV 'and so forth' (and so in vv. 11 and 17). **12. Joined the foundations**] RV 'repaired the foundations.'

13. *So* **thou shalt endamage**] RV 'in the end it will endamage.' **14. We have . . palace**] lit. ' we have salted the salt of the palace ' : cp. the term 'salary,' from *salarium*, 'money given to provide salt.'

15. The book of the records] For such see 6 2. **A rebellious city**] This, so far as it was true, applied to Jerusalem only under Babylonian rule (see 2 K 24 1, 20). But the circumstances of the time rendered the walling of the city suspicious, since Egypt, which lay so near, had recently been in revolt.

24. The second year . . Darius] 520 B.C., if, as is most probable, Darius Hystaspis is meant, as in v. 5 (the closing words of which are here repeated). But some suppose Darius Nothus (423–405) to be intended.

CHAPTER 5
THE BUILDING OF THE TEMPLE
RECOMMENCED

This c. gives an account of a renewed attempt to rebuild the Temple, and recites a letter from the Persian officials in Judæa to the Persian court to enquire whether the Jews had leave to proceed with the work.

1. Then the prophets] The hostility of their neighbours (4 4, 5), coupled with disastrous seasons (Hag 1 10, 11 2 17), had so discouraged the people that they said 'The time is not come for the LORD's house to be built' (Hag 1 2). Out of this despondency they were roused by two prophets, whose presence amongst them must of itself have convinced them that the Spirit of the LORD was once more with them.

Haggai] The prophecies of Haggai were all delivered in the second year of Darius. In them he upbraided the people for building substantial houses for themselves whilst neglecting the House of God ; attributed to such neglect the prevalent scarcity, which was God's judgment upon them ; and when the work was once again taken in hand by Zerubbabel, predicted that the glory of the second Temple would exceed that of the first.

Zechariah] The prophecies of Zechariah (who was really son of Berechiah and grandson of Iddo) were delivered at intervals between the second and fourth years of Darius. In them he consoled his countrymen for their afflictions, denounced God's wrath upon the nations who had oppressed Jerusalem, encouraged with hopes of a great future both Zerubbabel and Joshua in their work of rebuilding the Temple, and exhorted the people to truth, justice, and mercy.

In the name .. even unto them] RM 'in the name of the God of Israel which was upon them' : cp. Jer 14 9 (which is lit. 'thy name is called upon us ').

2. Began to build] It had really been begun sixteen years before (3 8 f.), but the work having been suspended, it had to be recommenced.

3. Tatnai] perhaps the satrap of all the Persian possessions W. of the Euphrates (the 'river ').   **4. Said we**] better, with the LXX, ' said they.'

5. They could not cause them to cease] Tatnai could not venture to arrest a work which was alleged to have the sanction of Cyrus (v. 13), though he cautiously sent to Persia to have the statement verified. **Till the matter came,** etc.] RV 'till the matter should come to Darius, and then answer should be returned.'

13. Cyrus the king of Babylon] The king of Persia included Babylon within his dominions : cp. Neh 13 6.   **14. Sheshbazzar**] i.e. Zerubbabel : see on 1 8.

CHAPTER 6
COMPLETION AND DEDICATION OF THE TEMPLE

This c. relates the authorisation of the construction of the Temple, and the completion of the work.

2. Achmetha] i.e. Ecbatana in Media.

3. Threescore cubits, etc.] The dimensions here given, which considerably exceed those of Solomon's Temple (1 K 6 2), perhaps marked the limits beyond which the builders were not to go. **4. With three rows,** etc.] cp. 1 K 6 36, which suggests that these materials were used in the construction of the Court, not of the edifice, of the Temple. **Out of the king's house**] i.e. from the king's resources : cp. 7 20. **6. Now** therefore, etc.] At this v. the decree of Darius begins. **7. The governor of the Jews**] i.e. Zerubbabel (Sheshbazzar), who was subordinate to Tatnai (5 3). **10. Sacrifices of sweet savours**] cp. Gn 8 21 Ex 29 18. **12. To alter**] i.e. the decree. **14. Artaxerxes**] The Temple was really completed in the reign of Darius (v. 15), but Artaxerxes (464–424 B.C.) bestowed treasure upon it (see c. 7).

15. Adar] February-March.

The sixth year] i.e. 516 B.C. The Temple, which was begun for the second time in the

second year of Darius, 520 B.C. (Hag 1 14, 15), had taken more than four years to finish. No complete description of it is forthcoming, but some information respecting it can be derived from allusions. If the measurements given in the decree of Cyrus (6 3) were actually adopted, it must have been larger than that of Solomon (1 K 6 2), but otherwise it was much inferior to it (3 12 Hag 2 3). Like the earlier structure, it consisted of a Holy of Holies and a Holy Place, before each of which hung a vail (1 Mac 4 51) ; whilst it had in front of it more than one court (1 Mac 4 38, 48). The Holy of Holies was empty (the ark being lost) ; but the Holy Place contained the golden altar of incense, the candlestick, and the table of shewbread, together with various vessels (1 Mac 1 22). In one of the courts was the altar of burntoffering, constructed of ' whole stones ' (1 Mac 4 47) ; and round the Temple building there were chambers, for the use of the priests and the storage of provisions (Ezr 8 29 10 6 Neh 10 34 13 5 1 Mac 4 38).

17. Twelve he goats] The number (see Nu 7 87) was representative of the twelve tribes of Israel, though only a few of them had returned from their exile and were present at the festival. **20. For the priests,** etc.] better, ' for the priests had purified themselves, and the Levites, as one man, were all of them pure.' **Killed the passover for all**] i.e. the Levites, who in Hezekiah's time killed the passover lambs only for such as were not clean, now killed them for all alike, both priests and laity.

21. All such as had separated, etc.] cp. 10 11 Neh 10 28. The allusion is to the Israelites left in the country when the flower of the population was removed by Nebuchadnezzar to Babylon, who had become contaminated by the surrounding heathen, but now detached themselves from them. **22. The king of Assyria**] i.e. Darius, whose predecessors had conquered Babylon, the mistress of Assyria.

CHAPTER 7
THE JOURNEY OF EZRA TO JERUSALEM

1. Now after .. Artaxerxes] The interval of time here implied amounted to more than fifty years, from the sixth year of Darius (516 B.C.) to the seventh year of Artaxerxes Longimanus (458 B.C.). Between the reign of Darius and Artaxerxes there intervened the reign of Xerxes (485–464 B.C.), to which belong the incidents related in the book of Esther. In the early years of his successor Artaxerxes an effort was made to surround Jerusalem, with a wall (see 4 12), though with no success. Probably to the same period should be assigned the ministry of the prophet Malachi. From his writings it may be gathered that the religious and moral condition of the Jewish community at Jerusalem was very unsatisfactory. The people were divided into two sections, the one scrupulous in their religious duties, the other sceptical and indifferent (Mal 3 13). The latter party had contracted marriages with heathen women (2 11); oppression and immorality were prevalent (3 5); the Temple services were neglected (1 6-14); and the maintenance of the priesthood stinted (3 8-10). Against the continuance of these evils the prophet raised a strong protest, denouncing divine judgment upon the offenders, but promising that God's blessing would attend them upon their reformation (3 10 4 1-3).

Ezra .. Seraiah] Ezra was a descendant of the Seraiah who was chief priest in the reign of the last king of Judah (2 K 25 18). His genealogy as given in vv. 1-5 is abbreviated by the omission not only of all the generations separating him from Seraiah, but also of many of those between Seraiah and Aaron: cp. 1 Ch 6 3-15.

6. This Ezra] Ezra, as his history shows, was a devout and zealous ecclesiastic, of passionate temperament, strong religious faith, and rigid principles, who, though he met with temporary failure, in the end permanently influenced the thoughts and habits of his countrymen. **A ready scribe**] Ezra belonged to the class of literary men who, being acquainted with the art of writing, had, in the time when the nation was independent, furnished its statesmen with their secretaries (2 S 8 17 1 K 4 3 2 K 18 18), but now that its political life had ceased, were students of the Law, which they copied, and interpreted (cp. Neh 8 7). **All his request**] The nature of this is implied in the letter of Artaxerxes (vv. 12-26).

9. Began he to go up] better (by a slight correction), 'he fixed the going up.' The actual journey was not begun till the twelfth day (8 31). **The first month**] i.e Nisan. (= Mar.-April). **The fifth month**] i.e. Ab (= July-August). The journey, which lasted some three months and a half, was probably made by way of the Euphrates to Carchemish, then across to Hamath, and so southward along the Orontes. The distance was about 900 m.

10. To teach in Israel] Ezra, though like Zerubbabel he led a body of settlers to Jerusalem, is never styled 'Tirshatha' (as Zerubbabel is in 2 63), and his mission appears to have had purely religious ends in view. The Jews who remained in Babylon, and who were surrounded by a population wholly heathen, were marked off from their neighbours by a much deeper line of cleavage than were the Jews of Palestine, and a higher standard of religious devotion prevailed amongst them : consequently when the religious laxity of the people of Jerusalem became known at Babylon, Ezra was sent to enquire into it (v. 14), to introduce reforms,

and, by authority of the Persian king, to enforce the observance of the Law by means of penalties (v. 26).

12. King of kings] The same title was used by the kings of Babylon (Ezk 26 7 Dan 2 37). **Perfect** *peace*, **and at such a time**] better, 'the whole' (of the usual heading) 'and so forth.'

13. His priests] RV 'their (i.e. Israel's) priests.' **14. His seven counsellors**] In Esth 1 14 mention is made of seven princes 'who saw the king's face and sat the first in his kingdom.' **16. Canst find**] i.e. obtain from the native Babylonians and Persians : cp. 1 4, 6.

22. Talents .. measures .. baths] The 'talent' used by the early Hebrews weighed 96 lb., the Persian talent was 66 lb. A 'measure' (Heb. *cor*) contained 83 gallons, a 'bath' a little more than 8 gallons. The wheat, wine, oil, and salt were required for the sacrificial offerings : see Ex 29 40 Lv 2 13. **23. Why should there be wrath, etc.**] The piety of the Persian kings led them to seek the favour of the deities worshipped by the different nationalities under their sway : cp. 6 10. **26. Banishment**] or exclusion from the congregation : cp. 10 8.

27. Blessed *be* **the LORD, etc.**] This introduces Ezra's thanksgiving for the king's letter. His gratitude to God is conspicuous throughout the passages in this book which proceed directly from him (e.g. 8 18, 22, 31), and is reflected in the account of the historian (7 6, 9, etc.).

CHAPTER 8
PARTICULARS OF EZRA'S COMPANY

1. Them that went up] The sum of the numbers given is 1,496. Only males are mentioned, and if no women accompanied them, the absence of such doubtless increased the tendency that the people manifested to intermarry with heathen families. **2. Hattush**] This should be connected closely with the following clause, Hattush being grandson of Shecaniah : 1 Ch 3 22. **3. Of the sons of Pharosh**] Most of the families in this list also appear (with some variations) in c. 2 and Neh 7 as having contributed members to the body of immigrants that accompanied Zerubbabel in the reign of Cyrus. **13. Of the last sons of Adonikam**] perhaps those who belonged to the youngest branch of Adonikam's house. **15. Ahava**] This was the name both of a town and of a river (v. 21) in Babylonia, on the road to Palestine. **None of the sons of Levi**] Only a small number of Levites had previously accompanied Zerubbabel (2 36). **17. Casiphia**] unidentified, but presumably near Babylon. *And* **to his brethren the Nethinims**] The text is defective, and should probably be corrected to 'and to his brethren (i.e. the Levites) and to the Nethinim.' **18. Of the sons of Mahli**] Either the name of the 'man of understanding' has dropped out of the text, or else this expression itself represents a proper name, Ish-sechel : so RM.

22. The enemy in the way] probably such marauders as were accustomed to attack defenceless travellers : cp. v. 31. **24. Shere-biah, Hashabiah**] These were Levites, not priests (Neh 12 24), so that the individuals selected were twenty-four in all, twelve priests and twelve Levites : cp. v. 30. **26. Six hundred and fifty talents**, etc.] The value of the offerings mentioned in this and the following v. is so great (approaching a million sterling), that exaggeration or textual corruption may be suspected.

30. Took . . silver] i.e. took the silver weighed out to them (v. 26). **33. By the hand of**] RV 'into the hand of' : the persons named being those with whom the silver brought from Babylon was deposited. **34. By number . . of every one**] RV 'the whole by number and by weight.' **36. The king's commissions**] i.e. the directions intended for the royal treasurers (7 21). **Lieutenants**] lit. 'satraps'

CHAPTER 9
EZRA'S INDIGNATION AT INTERMARRIAGES WITH THE HEATHEN

1. The Canaanites, etc.] In the Law it was only with the various Canaanite nations that marriage was altogether forbidden (Ex 34 12-16 Dt 7 1-3). David was descended from a union between an Israelite and a Moabitess (Ruth 1 4 4 17), and Solomon had married an Egyptian princess without reproach (1 K 3 1). But the principle which excluded alliances with certain nations was doubtless felt to be applicable to others also, and Solomon's marriages with women of the Moabites and Ammonites had certainly been attended with calamitous results (1 K 11 1, 2).

3. Plucked off the hair] Baldness artificially produced was a sign of mourning : Isa 15 2 22 12 Jer 16 6 Am 8 10 Job 1 20. **8. A nail**] a figure for security : cp. Isa 22 23. **In his holy place**] i.e. Jerusalem : cp. Ps 24 3 Isa 56 7 57 13.

9. We *were* bondmen] RV 'we are bond-men' : i.e. subjects of the Persians : cp. Neh 9 36. **A wall**] i.e. protection (RM 'a fence').

11. The filthiness of the people] The iniquity of the Canaanite peoples, whose land Israel had taken in possession, is alluded to in Gn 15 16 Dt 9 5 : cp. also 1 K 21 26.

13. *Such* deliverance] RV 'such a remnant.'

15. For we . . escaped] better, 'for we are left but a remnant that is escaped.' God's righteousness had been vindicated by the almost complete destruction of the guilty people ; but His mercy had been manifested in the survival of a few who were now imperilling themselves by fresh offences.

CHAPTER 10
THE FOREIGN WIVES ARE DIVORCED

3. According to the law] see Dt 24 1-2, which required a bill of divorcement. **5. The chief priests**] RV 'the chiefs of the priests': see 2 Ch 36 14.

6. Johanan] If the Eliashib meant is the contemporary of Nehemiah (13 4, 7) and Johanan was really his grandson (not his son, see Neh 12 22), he must have lived a long while after Ezra, and consequently the description of the chamber, here alluded to, as **the chamber of Johanan** applies not to the time of Ezra, but to that of the compiler of the book. But it is possible that another Johanan is intended.

8. Forfeited] lit. 'placed under the ban.' Goods that were 'banned' were brought into the treasury of the LORD (Josh 6 19). For the authority under which these proceedings were undertaken see 7 26. **9. The ninth month**] i.e. Chisleu (=Nov.-Dec.). In Palestine rain falls regularly in December, and on this occasion was perhaps heavier than usual. **13. We are many**, etc.] better, 'we have greatly transgressed.' **14. Let now our rulers . . stand**] i.e. as a committee to see into the question of the divorces. **15. Were employed about**] RV 'stood up against.' The opposition was not really strong. **16, 17. The tenth month . . the first**] i.e. Tebeth (= Dec.-Jan.) and Nisan (= Mar.-Apr.).

18. Of the guilty there were 17 priests, 10 Levites, singers and porters, and 86 laymen, making a total of 113. **25. Of Israel**] i.e. of the laity, as contrasted with the priests and Levites. **44.** *Some* **of them, etc.**] The text is obscure and perhaps corrupt : the LXX renders 'and had begotten children by them'; whilst 1 Esdr 9 36 has 'and they put them away with their children.'

The harsh measures here described were adopted by Ezra and his supporters owing to the necessity of preserving the distinctive faith of their race from being contaminated by, and finally lost in, the heathendom that surrounded it. A small and feeble community, deprived of national independence, was peculiarly exposed to external influences ; and Ezra might well fear that the proneness to idolatry from which his countrymen had been purified by the exile might revive, if marriage alliances were permitted with the neighbouring peoples, whose women, in the words of Malachi (2 11), were 'the daughters of a strange god.'

Nothing further is related of Ezra himself after this attempt to prevent mixed marriages until his reappearance in company with Nehemiah in 444 (Neh 8 1) ; and nothing is known for certain respecting the condition of affairs in Judæa between the last events here recorded and the arrival of Nehemiah at Jerusalem, as narrated in Neh 2. But one section of this book (4 6-23) shows that in the reign of Artaxerxes an endeavour was made to rebuild the fortifications of the city by a body of Jews who had recently arrived there (v. 12), and it is natural to connect this body with those who accompanied Ezra. The offence given to the peoples with whom intermarriage had lately been prohibited would render it desirable to secure the safety of the reforming party and it may well have been to them that the scheme for surrounding the place with a wall was due. As has been seen, it was frustrated through information being sent respecting it to the Persian authorities ; and if Ezra was in any way thought to be responsible for it, it is easily intelligible that his influence was in consequence impaired, and he himself forced into the obscurity in which the history leaves him.

NEHEMIAH

INTRODUCTION

1. Character and Contents. The book of Nehemiah, as has been already noted, probably forms part of a single work embracing Ezra, Nehemiah, and 1, 2 Chronicles, and its date, therefore, is that of the larger whole (perhaps about 330–320 B.C.). Its contents are separated from those of Ezra by an interval of thirteen years, so that the rule which the writer has previously observed of confining his history to an account of a few critical periods is again followed here. The record comprises Nehemiah's visit to Jerusalem in 445, his repair of the city walls, and the measures taken by him to secure obedience to the Law. The latest date in his life mentioned in the narrative is the thirty-second year of Artaxerxes, 433 B.C. (5 14).

2. Sources. The chief sources referred to, or implied, in the book are (a) the memoirs of Nehemiah (1 1–7 5 12 27-43 13 4-31) ; (b) genealogies and registers, partly incorporated in the memoirs just described, and partly reproduced by the compiler (3, 7 6-73 10 1-27 12 1-26).

3. Value. The book of Nehemiah carries the history of the Jewish people down to a later date than any other of the avowedly historical works in the canon of the OT. Its interest is manifold, since it describes not only the rebuilding of the walls of Jerusalem, but the reconstruction of the Jewish ecclesiastical organisation ; and as an authority for the events it relates, is first-rate, since it is largely based upon contemporary materials. And its value is augmented by its vivid portrayal of the noble character of Nehemiah himself. His career presents an exceptional combination of strong self-reliance with humble trust in God, of penetrating shrewdness with perfect simplicity of purpose, of persistent prayerfulness with the most energetic activity ; and for religious faith and practical sagacity he stands conspicuous among the illustrious personages of the Bible.

CHAPTER 1

ILL NEWS FROM JERUSALEM. NEHEMIAH'S PRAYER

1. The words] better, 'the history.' Some thirteen or fourteen years separate the visit of Nehemiah to Jerusalem, recorded in this book, from that of Ezra which is related in Ezr 7.

Nehemiah] Nehemiah, as stated in v. 11, occupied an important position at the Persian court, seems to have been a favourite with the king, and probably possessed considerable wealth (5 14 f.). Unlike Ezra (who was of priestly family and a student), he was a layman and a man of action. His career shows that he was self-reliant (2 12), energetic (chs. 3, 4), shrewd (c. 6), and masterful (c. 13) ; but his vigour and determination were directed not to the promotion of his own interests, but to the service of his countrymen, for whom he made great sacrifices. His religious faith was strong, and his prayerfulness is repeatedly illustrated in the narrative : see 1 4 2 4 4 4, 9, etc.

The month Chisleu] i.e. November-December. **In the twentieth year**] i.e. of Artaxerxes Longimanus, to whom reference is made in Ezr 4 7 7 1. The year intended is probably reckoned to begin with the month of his accession, not with the first calendar month Nisan, since the events that happened in Chisleu, the ninth month, are related before those that occurred in Nisan, 2 1. The date is 445. But some scholars regard **twentieth** in this c. as an error for 'nineteenth' (446 B.C.). **Shushan**] i.e. Susa, in Elam. The term **palace** is strictly 'fortress,' or 'castle.' **2. Which were left,** etc.] i.e. the Jews dwelling at Jerusalem.

3. The province] Judæa was now a province of the Persian empire (Ezr 5 8). **The wall .. broken down**] This is most naturally explained by the supposition that some recent attempt had been made to fortify Jerusalem, which had been forcibly stopped; and such an attempt seems described in Ezr 4 7-23. But some authorities suppose the allusion to be to the destruction of the walls by the Babylonians in 586, some 140 years before.

4. Prayed] Nehemiah's prayer consists of a confession of sin, an appeal to God's promises, and an entreaty for help in the undertaking he contemplated.

CHAPTER 2
NEHEMIAH'S RESOLVE TO REBUILD JERUSALEM

This c. gives an account of Nehemiah's request for leave to rebuild Jerusalem, his arrival there, and his survey of the ruined walls, which it was decided to restore. **1. Wine** *was* **before him**] LXX has 'wine was before me,' implying that it was Nehemiah's turn to act as cup-bearer (the king having several). This would explain why Artaxerxes had not observed his servant's sadness during the four months that had elapsed since the arrival of the news from Jerusalem. **2. Sore afraid**] i.e. for the success of his intended request. **6. I set him a time**] Nehemiah's absence seems to have lasted twelve years (5 14). **7. Convey me over**] RV 'let me pass through,' i.e. the Persian provinces between Shushan and Judæa. **8. The king's forest**] RM 'park,' identified by some with certain gardens at Etham, some 6 m. from Jerusalem, in which (according to Josephus) Solomon used to drive. **The palace**] RV 'the castle': and so in 7 2. This was situated on the N. of the Temple (**the house**), and subsequently called (by Herod) 'Antonia.' **9. Captains of the army**] Nehemiah as Tirshatha or governor (8 9 10 1) was invested with civil and not, like Ezra, ecclesiastical authority only; and consequently was attended by a body-guard: contrast Ezr 8 22. **10. The Horonite**] so named either from Beth-horon or Horonaim. Nothing is known of Sanballat beyond what is related in this book. **Heard** *of it*] Nehemiah on his way to Jerusalem had probably passed through the Samaritan colony of which Sanballat was leader (4 1-3). **12. At Jerusalem**] RV 'for Jerusalem.' **13. Viewed the walls of Jerusalem**] The topography of ancient Jerusalem is too obscure to admit of the various parts of its walls being identified with certainty, but 'the valley gate' from which Nehemiah issued on his survey was at the SW. corner of the SW. hill, and opened into the valley of Hinnom. From it he pursued his course first along the south wall, and next along the eastern wall, up the side of the 'brook' (v. 15), i.e. the Kidron. **14.** *There was* **no place**] The ground was so rough and encumbered with fallen masonry that he could not follow the line of wall

closely. **15. Turned back**] presumably along the N. wall, so as to make the circuit of the city. **19. Geshem**] called 'Gashmu' in 6 6; he was doubtless an Arab sheikh. **Will ye rebel?**] The same construction had been put upon the Jews' proceedings on a previous occasion: Ezr 4 13. **20. Ye have no portion**] Nehemiah's words had reference to the desire which the Samaritans once had to unite with the Jews (Ezr 4 1-5).

CHAPTER 3
PARTICULARS RESPECTING THE REBUILDING

1. Then, etc.] For the purposes of repair the wall was parcelled out between a number of working parties consisting of various important families, the inhabitants of certain towns, and different professional and trading bodies. The description of the several sections of the wall begins near the Temple at the **sheep-gate**, through which the flocks used to be driven for sacrifice. The writer's purpose in enumerating all who undertook to rebuild these sections is to put on record the names of those who devoted their labour and their substance to restoring the city which protected Jehovah's sanctuary, and to challenge the emulation of later generations.

5. Their Lord] better, 'their lord,' i.e. Nehemiah. **7. Unto the,** etc.] RV 'which *appertained* to the,' etc. Part of Mizpah was under the direct control of the Persian officer who governed the region W. of the Euphrates, whilst part was under Jewish rule (v. 15). **8. The son of** *one of* **the apothecaries**] better, 'one of the perfumers.' **They fortified**] RM 'they left,' meaning that the builders at this point left the fortifications untouched because they were in good repair, or that they departed in their reconstruction from the existing ground-plan. **9. Of the half part**] RV 'of half the district,' the ruler of the other half being the Shallum of v. 12. **11. The other piece**] RV 'another portion': and so in vv. 19, 20, 21, 24, 27, 30. **14. Part of**] RV 'the district of': and so in vv. 15, 16, 17, 18. **15. The pool of Siloah**] i.e. the pool of Siloam. **The stairs**] These were steps leading to the pool, perhaps from the Temple hill: cp. 12 37. **16. The sepulchres of David**] i.e. the tombs of David's descendants and successors: cp. 2 Ch 32 33. These were near the Temple (Ezk 43 7, 8), probably NW. of the city. **The pool that was made**] perhaps the pool alluded to in 2 K 20 20. **The house of the mighty**] perhaps the barracks of the soldiery. **17. In his part**] RV 'for (i.e. representing) his district' (of Keilah). **19. The armoury**] the site of 'the house of the forest of Lebanon' (1 K 10 17, 21 Isa 22 8). **22. The plain**] better, 'The Plain,' the specific name of part of the Jordan valley (Gn 13¹⁰).

23. After him .. After him] RV 'After them .. After them.'

26. Moreover] RV 'now,' the v. being parenthetical. **Ophel]** the southern extremity of the Temple hill. **The water gate]** leading to the spring of Gihon in the gorge of the Kidron. **28. The horse gate]** This, like the 'water gate,' faced eastward (Jer 31⁴⁰).

31. The goldsmith's son] better, 'a member of the body of goldsmiths.' **And of the merchants]** better, 'and (after him repaired) the merchants.' **32. The sheep gate]** The circuit of the walls ended with the original starting-point (v. 11).

CHAPTER 4
THE MACHINATIONS OF THE ENEMIES OF THE JEWS

1. Sanballat] His irritation at Nehemiah's arrival (2¹⁰) was increased by the work accomplished by the latter. **2. Fortify themselves]** The same word as that used in 3⁸, with a like uncertainty of meaning. Some render 'will they (the Persian authorities) let them alone ?' **Will they sacrifice ?]** i.e. in the hope of obtaining supernatural assistance. **4. In the land of captivity]** Nehemiah's desire for the confusion of his enemies not unnaturally took the form of a wish that they might experience the fate which he and his countrymen had undergone. **6. Was joined .. thereof]** The circuit of the wall was completed and raised to half the intended height.

7. The walls .. made up] RV 'the repairing of the walls .. went forward.' **9. We made our prayer .. a watch]** Nehemiah and his followers, whilst commending themselves in prayer to God, took every precaution within their power. **10. Judah]** i.e. the Jews.

12. From all places, etc.] perhaps, 'from all places, Ye must return to us,' this being an appeal from the Jews of the neighbouring towns to their fellow-citizens who had gone to work at Jerusalem, summoning them to return for their protection. But LXX has 'From all places they come up against us.'

13. On the higher places] RV 'in the open (i.e. exposed) places' : where they could be seen to be on guard. **15. We returned]** This implies that the enemy for a time abandoned the design described in v. 11. **16. Habergeons]** RV 'coats of mail.' **17. With those that laded]** RV 'laded themselves' : i.e. laboured vigorously. *Every one .. weapon]* This clause probably refers to the second of the two classes named in the beginning of the v., viz. those **that bare burdens.** These with one hand carried materials and with the other held a missile, The 'builders' (v. 18), on the

contrary, who had to use both hands for their work, only wore swords.

21. Half of them] This refers back to the servants mentioned in v. 16. **23. Men of the guard]** i.e. the Persian guard attached to Nehemiah as governor : cp. 2⁹. *Saving that .. washing]* RV renders, 'every one *went with* his weapon *to* the water' : whilst others suggest, 'every one sent for water' ; but the text is too defective to be translated with certainty : the LXX omits the clause.

CHAPTER 5
NEHEMIAH'S MEASURES IN ALLEVIATION OF POVERTY

1. The people] i.e. the commons (as contrasted with the nobles and rulers, v. 7). These had neglected their own interests to labour gratuitously on the fortifications, and now in the time of dearth were feeling the pinch of want. **2. Therefore we take up corn]** better, 'we must get corn.' The language is that of desperate men, compelled by necessity to accept the harsh conditions imposed by those to whom they had recourse for the corn they required.

4. The king's tribute] The common people were not exempted from paying taxes to the Persian king, like the priests and other ministers of the Temple (Ezr 7²⁴ Neh 9³⁷).

5. Our flesh, etc.] i.e. we are as much Jews as the creditors to whom we have sold our children. **Bondage]** The sale of children to defray a debt was recognised in the Mosaic Law : see Ex 21²·⁷ Dt 15¹²ᶠ· ; cp. also 2 K 4¹.

7. Ye exact usury] Usury was prohibited by the Law in connexion with loans made to fellow-Israelites (Ex 22²⁵ Dt 23¹⁹) ; but the Jews doubtless interpreted the prohibition with the same latitude as Christians have done the similar command in the Gospel (Lk 6³⁵). The Law probably had in view cases where money was borrowed under the pressure of misfortune, not as a help in commercial ventures ; and the like considerateness towards the necessitous is incumbent upon Christians. **8. Have redeemed .. heathen]** probably during Nehemiah's residence in Persia. **9. The reproach]** the humiliation they had undergone in consequence of their failure to walk in the fear of God.

10. Might exact] RV 'do lend .. on usury.' Nehemiah, to conciliate those whom he wished to persuade, admitted that he (probably in the persons of his relatives and dependents) had been guilty of the same conduct against which he was protesting. **11. Their lands, etc.]** These had been given in pledge, and, if unredeemed, were retained by the creditor. **The hundredth** *part]* usually regarded as one per cent. a month, and so equivalent to twelve per cent. a year. The expression **restore,** in connexion with the interest, probably means 'cease to require': cp. v. 12. **Corn, wine, oil**] i.e. interest paid in kind. **12. Took an oath of them**] i.e. took of the money-lenders an oath which the priests administered to them. **13. Shook my lap**] For similar symbolic acts cp. 1 K 22 11 Jer 27 2 28 10.

14. From the twentieth .. unto the two and thirtieth] i.e. from 445–433 B.C. The fact that Artaxerxes seems to have been unwilling to part with his cup-bearer for a long period, and stipulated for a date by which he was to return (2 6), makes it rather surprising that he should have thus been absent from court for twelve years ; but it is to be assumed that his leave of absence was extended by the king.

The bread of the governor] i.e. the supplies due to the Persian governor from the people. **16. Neither bought we**] better, 'neither got we' (by foreclosing mortgages). **All my servants**] He did not retain them to attend to himself or to his own interests. The whole conduct of Nehemiah was that of a warm-hearted, generous man.

CHAPTER 6
ATTEMPTS OF SANBALLAT TO HINDER THE COMPLETION OF THE WALLS

2. Ono] near Lod (Ezr 2 33), now Kefr 'Ana, some 25 m. from Jerusalem. **5. An open letter**] in order that its contents might reach and intimidate others. **6. According to these words**] better, 'and so forth' (and so in v. 7), the quotation from the letter in v. 6 ending with **king**.

10. Who *was* **shut up**] perhaps meaning 'ceremonially unclean': cp. Jer 36 5. Shemaiah probably hoped that Nehemiah would conclude that only for the most urgent reasons would he under such circumstances make the proposal described. **Within the temple**] i.e. to seek asylum there (as Joab fled to the tent of the LORD, 1 K 2 28). **11.** *Being* **as I** *am*] Only the priests might enter the Temple buildings. **15. Elul**] The 6th month (August-September) of 445 B.C. **18. Arah .. Meshullam**] see Ezr 2 5 Neh 3 4.

CHAPTER 7
A LIST OF THOSE WHO RETURNED FROM BABYLON WITH ZERUBBABEL

2. Hanani] after carrying information to Nehemiah respecting the condition of Jerusalem (1 2), he must have returned with him to Judæa. **3. Until the sun be hot**] By this time the mass of the citizens would be astir. **While they stand by**] RV 'while they (i.e. the sentries) stand *on guard*.' **4. The houses** *were* **not builded**] i.e. the area of the city was not yet fully occupied with buildings.

5. Reckoned by genealogy] It was proposed to take a census of all the persons of Jewish descent, with a view to transferring part of the country population to the capital. Particulars derived from such a census appear in 11 4 f. Here, however, the subject is for a time dropped, and the register that follows relates to the period of Zerubbabel (v. 7).

7–73. The names here enumerated are repeated, with certain small differences, from the list contained in Ezr 2. **70. Basons**] used in connexion with the sacrifices. **Five hundred and thirty priests' garments**] For this should perhaps be substituted 'five hundred pounds of silver and thirty priests' garments,' a change which would make the quantities named in vv. 70–72 approximate closely to those given in Ezr 2 69. **73. And when the seventh month came**] These words in RV are connected with the subject of c. 8, the seventh month (Tishri) being probably the one immediately following the sixth (Elul) mentioned in 6 15.

CHAPTER 8
THE READING OF THE LAW BY EZRA

1. The street] RV 'the broad place': and so in vv. 3, 16. **The water gate**] This probably led to the spring of Gihon (the Virgin's spring).

2. Ezra] It has been argued in the note on Ezr 10 44 that the effort to fortify Jerusalem described in Ezr 4 6-23 was made whilst Ezra was present there, and that the failure of it destroyed for a time his influence among his countrymen. The interval that elapsed between the destruction of the newly-built walls and Nehemiah's arrival was probably not long, and during it Ezra may have remained in retirement at Jerusalem. Some, however, have supposed that after effecting the reforms described in Ezr 9 and 10, he returned at once to Babylon, and only revisited Palestine after Nehemiah's arrival there. The absence of his name amongst those who helped to build the walls of Jerusalem (c. 3) has been urged in favour of this view ; but there would be little reason to distinguish his co-operation from that of the other priests (3 1). **To bring .. of Moses**] The teaching of the Law was the purpose of Ezra's journey to Jerusalem some fourteen years before.

2. The first day of the seventh month] This was one of the festivals (cp. v. 9) of the New Moon, termed in the Law the Feast of Trumpets, and kept with special rites : Lv 23 24, 25 Nu 29 1-6. **7. And the Levites**] omit **and**.

8. Gave the sense] i.e. with such additional explanation as was required for the people to understand what was read.

9. The Tirshatha] i.e. governor. The same title was borne by Zerubbabel (Ezr 2 63). **All the people wept**] from a consciousness of their transgressions which the reading of the Law had awakened. **11. Hold your peace**] in order to guard against uttering words ill-suited to a holy day.

14. Should dwell in booths] This command in connexion with the Feast of Tabernacles (kept on the fifteenth day of the seventh month) occurs only in Lv 23 42. **15. The mount**] better, 'the hill-country.' **Pine branches**] RV 'branches of wild olives' (or oleaster).

16. The roof of his house] This was flat, and available for walking or sleeping : cp. Dt 22 8 1 S 9 25 2 S 11 2 16 22. **The gate of Ephraim**] in the N. wall, facing the former kingdom of Ephraim.

17. Since the days of Jeshua] i.e. of Joshua. The exceptional feature in this observance of the ancient Feast of Tabernacles seems to have been the dwelling in 'booths,' though the dwelling in 'tents' had been previously practised (cp. Hos 12 9). Either the command of Lv 23 42 had been disregarded, or it was a modification of the older usage which had only recently been incorporated in the Law.

CHAPTER 9
THE RENEWAL OF THE COVENANT

4. Stairs] lit. 'ascent' : probably the pulpit of wood mentioned in 8 4. **Bani .. Bani**] One of the two names is probably an error for 'Binnui' : cp. 12 8.

6. Thou, etc.] Before this LXX inserts 'And Ezra said.' The prayer that follows first recalls God's early mercies to the nation, the unworthy return made for such, the divine forbearance, the people's renewed offences, and their consequent punishment ; it next acknowledges the justice of the chastisement undergone ; and it concludes with a solemn promise of future amendment. But though it is a confession of national sins and ends with a national covenant, the sequence of thought it presents might well be followed in private devotions. **All their host**] i.e. the stars : cp. Gn 1 2 Isa 40 26. **The host of heaven**] i.e. the angels : cp. 1 K 22 19.

7. Didst choose] The religious privileges enjoyed by Israel could only be ascribed to the free grace of God, and such privileges carried with them corresponding responsibilities. The same is true of the advantages, material or intellectual, possessed by other peoples. **8. Righteous**] i.e. faithful to Thy promises : cp. Ps 40 10. **16. They and our fathers**] better, 'they, even our fathers.'

22. Didst divide .. corners] RV 'which thou didst allot after their portions' : i.e. according to their several boundaries. **26. Slew thy prophets**] see, for instance, 1 K 18 4 19 10 2 Ch 24 20-22 Jer 26 20-23. **29. Withdrew the shoulder**] like a restive ox that refuses the yoke.

32. The kings of Assyria] The kings of Assyria that distressed Israel were Shalmaneser II (to whom Jehu paid tribute), Tig-

lath-pileser (2 K 15 29), Shalmeneser III and Sargon (2 K 17 5, 6), Sennacherib (2 K 18, 19), and perhaps Asshurbanipal (2 Ch 33 11). **Unto this day**] The rule over Israel exercised by Assyria had been succeeded by that of Babylon and Persia. **33. Done right**] RV 'dealt truly' : i.e. faithfully : cp. v. 8.

38. And because of all this] RV 'and yet for all this.' **We make a sure** *covenant*] The original covenant between Israel and the LORD made at Sinai (Ex 24) had been renewed by Hezekiah (2 Ch 15 12) and Josiah (2 Ch 34 30-33): cp. also Ezr 10 3. **Seal** *unto it*] lit. (and the names of) 'our princes, etc., are on the sealed writing.'

CHAPTER 10
LIST OF THOSE WHO PARTICIPATED IN
THE COVENANT

1. Now those that sealed *were*] The names that follow Zidkijah's are those of families whose living representatives sealed on behalf of their houses. Several of these family names occur in the list of those who accompanied Zerubbabel to Jerusalem (c. 12). **Zidkijah.**] The fact that his name is coupled with Nehemiah's suggests that he was a person of importance, but nothing is known of him.

29. To walk in God's law, etc.] The enactments of the Law which they more particularly undertook to carry out were those directing (a) abstention from marriage with aliens, (b) the observance of the sabbath and sabbatical year, (c) the provision of supplies for the Temple and its ministers. These enactments gained in importance from the circumstances of the times, for there was a persistent tendency on the part of many of the people both to form alliances with their heathen neighbours and to be indifferent to the external ordinances of religion (see Ezr 9 Neh 13). It was to counteract these evils that prominence was given to those regulations which were calculated to preserve the separateness of the Jewish race, and to accentuate the sacredness of their religious institutions. The stress thus laid upon the ceremonial law was not due to any relapse from the spiritual faith of the prophets to the more material and mechanical ideas of primitive times, but was intended to impress upon the people a sense of the transcendent sanctity of the God with whom they enjoyed such privileged relations.

31. Leave the seventh year] i.e. forego the produce of the land in that year. **32. The third part of a shekel**] In Ex 30 11-16 the amount named is 'a half shekel' (cp. Mt 17 24), the change being perhaps due to an alteration in the weight of the shekel. **34. The wood offering**] This is not specifically prescribed in the Pentateuch. Josephus speaks of it as a festival (the Xylophory). **38. The priest**] i.e.

some priest was to attend when the Levites took their tithes. **39. Forsake**] i.e. fail to provide for.

CHAPTER 11
MEASURES TO SUPPLEMENT THE POPULATION OF JERUSALEM

1. This v. resumes the subject of the paucity of population in Jerusalem: see 7⁴. The rulers were already residing in the capital, and means were now taken to transport thither a proportion of the commons that had made their homes in the country towns (v. 3). The city had received fortifications ; but these were useless unless they were manned.

3. The province] i.e. Judæa : Ezr 5⁸.

4. At Jerusalem, etc.] The list that follows apparently enumerates the provincial families that removed to Jerusalem. It likewise occurs, with some variations in the names and figures, in 1 Ch 9³ᶠ. **9. Second over the city**] presumably second to Joel : cp. v. 17. But some render, ' over the second quarter of the city ' : cp. 2 K 22¹⁴ Zeph 1¹⁰. **14. The son of** *one of* **the great men**] RV ' the son of Haggedolim.'

16. The outward business of] Perhaps the judicial administration described in 2 Ch 19⁸⁻¹⁰ 1 Ch 26²⁹. **17.** *Was* **the principal**, etc.] i.e. led the praises of the Temple singers after prayer had been made. **The second**] i.e. to **Mattaniah** : cp. v. 9.

20. This v. interrupts the account of the residents at Jerusalem : it should precede v. 25.

22. The overseer, etc.] RV ' The overseer .. the son of Micha, of the sons of Asaph, the singers, over the business,' etc. The words **over the business** are connected with **overseer**. The **business** meant is the conduct of the Temple services. **23. For** *it was*, etc.] RM ' for there was a commandment .. and a sure ordinance concerning the singers ' : **The king**] Artaxerxes : cp. Ezr 7²⁴. **24.** *Was* **at the king's hand**] Possibly Pethahiah was a royal officer, subordinate to Nehemiah, having charge of civil, as distinct from ecclesiastical, matters.

25. The villages, with their fields] better, ' the villages in their fields,' i.e. the unwalled towns (Lv 25³¹). Most of the names that follow occur in Josh 15¹³ᶠ. **31. From Geba** *dwelt*] RV ' *dwelt* from Geba *onward*.' **35. The valley of craftsmen**] RM ' Gehaharashim,' another locality. **36. And of the Levites**, etc.] RV ' and of the Levites, certain courses in Judah ' (i.e. formerly reckoned to Judah) ' *were joined* to Benjamin.'

CHAPTER 12
THE DEDICATION OF THE WALL OF JERUSALEM

1. The priests] The names in vv. 1–7 likewise appear with some variations in 10³⁻⁸ ;

see also Ezr 2³⁶⁻³⁹. **8. The Levites**] cp. 10⁹⁻¹⁴ Ezr 40⁴². **Over the thanksgiving**] RM ' over the choirs.'

10. Jeshua] The high priest who returned with Zerubbabel. The succession of high priests is carried down to Jaddua, who was contemporary with Alexander the Great, so that the six generations cover the period from 536 to about 340. Eliashib the grandson of Jeshua was contemporary with Nehemiah.

12–21. The names that are repeated in these vv. from vv. 1–7 present certain variations.

22. Johanan] probably the same as the ' Jonathan ' of v. 11. **Darius**] Since Jaddua was contemporary with Alexander the Great, the Darius here meant is probably Darius Codomannus, who was successively defeated by Alexander at the battles of the Granicus, Issus, and Arbela. **23. The book of the chronicles**] some official record, not the ' Chronicles ' of the OT. **24. Jeshua the son of Kadmiel**] to be corrected to ' Jeshua, Binnui, Kadmiel ': see v. 8, 10⁹. **Over against them**] i.e. in the choir, where the singing was antiphonal.

25. The thresholds] RV ' the storehouses.'

26. In the days of Nehemiah] a date subsequent to the days of Joiakim, for the high priest in Nehemiah's time was Eliashib, son of Joiakim.

27. The dedication of the wall] It is reasonable to suppose that the dedication of the wall followed closely upon its completion (related in 6¹⁵), so that the events described in chs. 8–10 may be later than those narrated in this c., which from the use of the first person (vv. 31, 38, 40) seems to be derived from Nehemiah's memoirs. **28. The plain country**] better, ' The Plain ' (lit. ' circle '), i.e. the S. end of the Jordan valley : cp. 3²². Others suppose the word to be used here in a general sense of the circuit of country round Jerusalem. **Netophathi**] RV ' the Netophathites.' **29. The house of Gilgal**] RV ' Beth-gilgal.'

31. Two great *companies*, etc.] RV ' two great companies that gave thanks and went in procession.' **Went on the right hand**] The two companies probably mustered on the W. side of the city, facing eastward : the company on the right under Ezra then moved southward, whilst the company on the left under Nehemiah moved northward ; and the two eventually reunited on the E. of the city near the Temple.

35. Zechariah] the overseer of the right-hand company, corresponding to Jezrahiah (v. 42) in the other. His descent from Asaph suggests that he was a Levite, not a priest, so that for ' *namely*, **Zechariah** ' should be substituted ' also Zechariah.' **37. And at the fountain gate**, etc.] better, ' and by the fountain gate and straight on.'

38. Went over against *them*] The words **over against them** should probably be altered, by an easy correction, to 'on the left hand' (cp. v. 31), and the whole should run, 'and the other company .. which went on the left hand, and I and half of the people after it (went) upon the wall above the tower of the furnaces .. and above the gate of Ephraim and by the old gate and by the fish gate,' etc. **39. The prison gate**] RV 'the gate of the guard.'

40. In the house] better, 'at the house.'

44. Out of the fields] RV 'according to the fields': alluding to certain arrangements for storing. **Portions of the law**] RV 'portions appointed by the law.' **45. The ward**] better, 'the charge': cp. 2 Ch 13 11. **46. In the days, etc.**] LXX has 'in the days of David Asaph was of old chief.' **47. Every day his portion**] RV 'as every day required.' **Sanctified** *them* **unto**] RV 'sanctified for': i.e. Israel set apart as holy certain portions for the Levites, and the latter for the priests.

CHAPTER 13
THE REFORM OF ABUSES

The reforms embraced the separation of Israel from the mixed multitude and the abolition of certain abuses that had arisen in connexion with the chambers of the Temple, the provision for the Levites, the observance of the sabbath, and mixed marriages.

1. On that day] the particular time intended is uncertain. **Was found written**] see Dt 23 3-6. **3. Separated**] see Ezr 9, 10. **All the mixed multitude**] cp. Ex 12 38 Nu 11 4. The term may be illustrated by Ezr 9 2, where 'mingled themselves with the peoples of *those* lands' is a kindred expression.

4. Eliashib] previously mentioned in 3 1 12 10. **Chamber**] RV 'chambers.' **6. The two and thirtieth year**] i.e. 433 B.C. **Obtained I leave**] i.e. to return to Palestine. **7. Understood of**]

better, 'perceived.' **10. For**] RV 'so that.' The Levites not receiving the support due to them had to work to maintain themselves.

11. Forsaken] i.e. unprovided for. **Gathered them**] i.e. the Levites.

17. What evil .. the sabbath] The protests made by the prophets and others against the profanation of the sabbath (see Ezk 20 12, 20 44 24 Isa 56 4, 6 58 13) eventually brought the Jews to observe it so strictly that they even allowed themselves to be massacred rather than desecrate it by defending themselves (1 Mac 2 32-38).

23. *That* **had married wives, etc.**] The same practice was condemned by Ezra (chs. 9, 10). **24. Their children spake half**] better, 'of their children half spake,' etc. **26. Outlandish**] i.e. foreign.

28. Chased him from me] i.e. expelled him from the Jewish community. According to Josephus (who, however, places the incident at a much later date) Joiada's son was named Manasseh, and when expelled by Nehemiah, was induced by his father-in-law Sanballat to join him at Samaria by the promise of being appointed high priest of a temple that was to be built on Mt. Gerizim. **29. Defiled the priesthood**] The actual high priest was prohibited from taking as his wife any but a virgin of his own people (Lv 21 14). **30. The wards of**] better, 'charges for.'

At this point the OT. record of Nehemiah closes ; but in 2 Mac 2 13 it is added that he collected together 'the books about the kings and prophets, and the books of David, and letters of kings about sacred gifts'—a statement the precise meaning of which it is unnecessary to discuss here. In Ecclus 49 13 he is eulogised for having 'raised up the walls that were fallen, and set up the gates and bars.'

ESTHER

INTRODUCTION

1. Character and Contents. The book of Esther is one of a group of writings known as the Five Rolls (the other four being the Song of Songs, Ruth, Lamentations, and Ecclesiastes). Its contents fall within the period embraced by the book of Ezra, namely, the reign of Xerxes (485–464 B.C.), when the Jews were under Persian rule, and when, though a large body had returned to Jerusalem under Zerubbabel, yet numbers of them were still scattered over the Persian empire. The events recounted

are put forward as those which led to the institution of the Jewish feast of 'Purim,' held on the fourteenth and fifteenth days of Adar (= February-March), and preceded by a fast on the thirteenth (called the Fast of Esther). The author is quite unknown, but his familiarity with Persian customs and Persian words makes it probable that he lived in Persia itself. He was not, however, contemporaneous with the events he relates, for Xerxes is described in language which implies that his reign was past ;

and his work is perhaps to be placed in the fourth century B.C. The book came to be held in very high esteem by the Jews; it was called *par excellence* 'the Roll'; it was read annually at the Feast of Purim; and Maimonides is reported to have said that in the days of the Messiah the only Scriptures left would be the Law and the Roll. In the Apocrypha there are certain additions to the book, called the 'Rest of Esther,' which are probably later in date than the original work, and are certainly different in style and spirit.

2. Sources. In the course of the narrative allusion is made to Persian state-records (2^{23} 6^1 10^2), as well as to documents written by Mordecai, upon which some of the facts related may be based.

3. Value. That the account contained in the book has some historical foundation is probable for several reasons. It offers an explanation of a well-established Jewish festival; reference is made in 2 Mac 15^{36} to the fourteenth day of Adar as being 'the day of Mordecai'; and acquaintance is shown throughout with Persian customs (see 1^{19} 3^{13}). A certain parallel to the destruction inflicted by the Jews upon their enemies, and the institution of a feast to commemorate it, is afforded by the slaughter of the Magi by the Persians and the festival by which it was celebrated. The extraordinary conduct of Xerxes in countenancing a general massacre of his subjects is in keeping with his irrational behaviour on more than one occasion, as described by Herodotus. And finally, the interval of time between the disgrace of Vashti in Xerxes' third year (1^3), and the elevation of Esther in his seventh year (2^{16}), agrees with his absence from Persia on his expedition against the Greeks, the battle of Salamis taking place in 480 B.C., after which engagement the king returned to Asia. On the other hand, certain features in the narrative suggest that the writer has sought to enhance the effectiveness of his recital by striking contrasts, embellished descriptions, and large figures. It is not likely that either Vashti or Esther was Xerxes' queen; according to Herodotus it was Amestris who held that position, and Vashti and Esther were probably nothing more than favourite concubines. The six months' feast (1^4), the ten thousand talents of silver (3^9), the gallows (or stake) 50 cubits high (5^{14}), and the 75,000 (LXX 15,000) slain (9^{16}), are probably all exaggerations. And there is some lack of plausibility in the statements that orders were issued for the slaughter of the Jews and of their enemies eleven and nine months respectively before the massacres were to be carried out ($3^{12,\,13}$ 8^9).

4. The moral instructiveness of the book centres in the character of Esther, who, as depicted in the narrative, appears as virtuous as she was fair, being dutiful to her foster-father, faithful to the king, loyal to her people, and pious towards her God. Her story breathes the spirit of truest patriotism, for she is represented as willing to face death to save her countrymen. It also illustrates the working of Divine Providence, for though the name of God does not appear in the book (at least in the original Hebrew, in the LXX it is introduced freely), the whole history implies the belief that it was as an instrument in His hand that Esther wrought her people's deliverance. And whilst prayer is likewise not actually mentioned in the book, yet the fast of Esther and her countrymen (described in 4^{16}) presumes the practice, and the sequel of the narrative is meant to attest its efficacy.

CHAPTER 1

THE DISOBEDIENCE AND DISGRACE OF QUEEN VASHTI

1. Ahasuerus] LXX has 'Artaxerxes,' but probably 'Xerxes,' the son of Darius Hystaspis, is meant, who succeeded his father in 485 B.C.

India . . Ethiopia] India here means not the peninsula of Hindostan, but the region near the Indus: **Ethiopia** is the modern Nubia.

2. Shushan] i.e. Susa in Elam, the country lying to the E. of the Persian Gulf. **The palace**] lit. 'the fortress,' as in Neh 1^1. **3. In the third year**] i.e. 483 B.C. **Thy power**] better, 'the forces': and so in 8^{11}.

6. White, green, and blue] Some take the second term to designate the 'material,' and render 'of white cotton and blue,' white and blue (or violet) being the Persian royal colours (8^{15}). **The beds**] RV 'the couches,' upon which the feasters reclined. **7. Royal wine**] LXX has 'wine which the king himself used to drink.' **The state**] RV 'the bounty.'

8. According to the law] i.e. according to the king's express command on this occasion; for it is implied that in general the drinking was regulated by the court officials, and the guests had to drink just as much or as little as they were bidden, not as they pleased.

9. Vashti] According to Herodotus, Xerxes' queen was called Amestris.

13. The wise men, which knew the times] probably experienced counsellors (cp. 1 Ch 12^{32}); but according to others, astrologers and diviners: cp. Isa 44^{25} Dan 5^{15}. **For so was the king's manner toward all**] better, 'for so was the king's business brought before all,' etc. The king was expected to consult 'those who knew law and judgment' in all matters before coming to a decision. **14. The next unto him**] i.e. nearest to the king in rank and importance.

18. *Likewise* **shall the ladies**, etc.] RV 'And this day shall the princesses of Persia and

Media which have heard of the deed of the queen say *the like* unto all the king's princes.'

19. That it be not altered] cp. Dan 6 8. Any command written in the king's name and sealed with his ring was similarly irrevocable.

20. For it is great] i.e. the decree is weighty and important.

22. According to the writing thereof] i.e. the letters sent to the several provinces were written in the characters and language that prevailed in each. Many of the extant inscriptions of the Persian kings are tri-lingual. **And that** *it* **should be published**, etc.] better (by a slight correction), 'and that he should speak all that seemed good to him,' i.e. should speak his mind freely, without regard to the feelings of his women-folk.

CHAPTER 2
The Choice of Esther to be Queen.
Mordecai's Service

1. He remembered, etc.] LXX has 'he thought no more of Vashti, remembering what,' etc. **3. The house of the women**] This was the house of the virgins, as contrasted with the house of the concubines (v. 14).

Their things for purification] Various perfumed oils and ointments (v. 12).

5. Mordecai] The name, though used by Jews (cp. Ezr 2 2 Neh 7 7), was derived from the Babylonian deity Merodach (Marduk).

Shimei . . Kish] probably Mordecai's grandfather and great grandfather (v. 6 applying to Kish). Others regard the genealogy as abbreviated, and take **Shimei** and **Kish** to be remoter ancestors, identifying them with the **Shimei** and **Kish** of 2 S 16 5 1 S 9 1 (in which case v. 6 must refer to Mordecai's family two or three generations back).

7. Hadassah] a Hebrew name meaning 'Myrtle.' **Esther**] connected by some with the Persian word for 'star'; according to others, the same as the Babylonian 'Ishtar,' the Canaanite 'Ashtoreth.' **9. Such things as belonged to her**] lit. 'her portions'; perhaps richer viands than ordinary : cp. Dan 1 5.

11. And Mordecai walked, etc.] He apparently occupied a position in the king's household (cp. 3 2), and in the apocryphal 'Rest of Esther' (11 3) he is expressly styled a servitor in the king's court. He would thus have opportunities of communicating with Esther.

12. After that she had been, etc.] RV 'after that it had been done to her according to the law for the women, twelve months.' **13. Whatsoever she desired**] i.e. for the adornment of her person. **14. Into the second house of the women**] so LXX. Some render, 'returned a second time '(i.e. back again) 'into the house of the women,' but at any rate into a different quarter of it, where they were under the charge of **Shaashgaz**, not of Hegai.

15. She required nothing, etc.] i.e. instead of selecting her articles of attire for herself like other maidens (v. 13), she left everything to the choice of Hegai. **16. Tebeth**] i.e. December-January. **The seventh year**] i.e. 479 B.C. Thus four years elapsed between the degradation of Vashti and the promotion of Esther (see 1 3). In the interval between 483 and 479 Xerxes' expedition into Greece took place, the battle of Salamis being fought in 480 B.C. **18. Made a release**] Either from taxation or military service. Some would render 'granted a holiday.' **According to the state**] RV 'according to the bounty of' : i.e. with regal generosity.

19. And when the virgins, etc.] Some connect this with v. 14, and take ' the virgins' to mean ' the young women.' Others render, ' now when virgins were gathered together a second time' (as on the earlier occasion described in v. 8). **Sat in the king's gate**] perhaps as the official who received applicants that desired to have audience with the king.

23. Hanged] or, 'impaled,' a form of punishment frequently inflicted by Persian sovereigns. **The book of the chronicles**] Herodotus relates instances of Xerxes' similarly recording the names of certain men who distinguished themselves in the war against Greece.

CHAPTER 3
Haman's Revengeful Design against the Jews

1. The Agagite] It has been suggested that the name is an epithet meant to recall the Amalekite Agag hewn in pieces by Samuel (1 S 15 33), and intended to indicate contempt and abhorrence.

2. Mordecai bowed not, etc.] In the apocryphal 'Rest of Esther' Mordecai explains in a prayer to the Almighty that he refused to bow down to Haman, ' that he might not prefer the glory of man above the glory of God.' Amongst many heathen peoples divine honours were paid to human beings.

7. Nisan] i.e. March-April. **The twelfth year** of Xerxes would be 474 B.C. **They cast Pur**, etc.] i.e. early in the first month they cast lots for every day of the year to find out which day would be the most favourable for the success of Haman's design. In the Assyrian calendars there are lucky and unlucky days; and the Persians doubtless entertained a like belief. *To* **the twelfth** *month*] The Heb. is probably defective, and the LXX gives a completer sense by adding, 'and the lot fell on the fourteenth '(an error for the 'thirteenth,' v. 13) 'day of the month, which is Adar.' Adar corresponded to February-March.

9. Ten thousand talents] The Persian talent weighed 66 lb. **That have the charge of the**

business] i.e. those whose business it is to receive money paid into the king's treasury.

10. Took his ring] For the significance of this see 8 8. **11. The silver**] The money which Haman had pledged himself to pay into the treasury the king confers upon him for his services in pointing out a serious danger to the kingdom (v. 8).

12. The thirteenth day of the first month] Eleven months were thus to elapse between the issue of the decree and its execution.

Lieutenants] lit. 'satraps,' of whom, according to Herodotus, there were twenty. **13. Posts**] Horsemen (cp. 8 10) were posted at regular intervals of a day's journey along the main roads to transmit in succession the messages they received until they reached their destination. **15. Was perplexed**] i.e. at the magnitude and arbitrary character of the contemplated massacre.

CHAPTER 4
Mordecai's Appeal to Esther to save her Countrymen

1. When Mordecai perceived] His position at the door of the palace (2 21) would enable him to obtain early intelligence. **2. Even before**] better, 'as far as before.' The LXX adds, 'and stopped. **6. The street**] RV 'the broad place': and so in 6 9, 11. **11. One law of his**] RV 'one law for him': i.e. who approached the king without leave given.

14. *Then* **shall there enlargement, etc.**] RV 'Then shall relief,' etc. Mordecai's speech, though no mention is made in it of God, nevertheless breathes a spirit of trust in His Providence, and expresses a conviction that help will come from some unperceived quarter.

But thou .. destroyed] Divine judgment would overtake her if she neglected her duty to her countrymen. **Whether .. as this**] i.e. who knows whether thou hast not been raised to the throne by God for the express purpose of averting the dangers threatening at the present crisis?

16. Fast ye for me] Fasting was an accompaniment of prayer (cp. Ezr 8 23 Neh 1 4), and Esther's request was for united prayer on her behalf. **If I perish, I perish**] Esther proceeded on her dangerous venture in a spirit of resignation.

CHAPTER 5
Esther's Petition to the King

An account of how Esther, being favourably received by the king, invited him, together with Haman, to a banquet whereat she promised to make known her petition, and how Haman prepared for the execution of Mordecai.

1. On the third day] This indicates that the fast of 4 16 is not to be regarded as extending over three whole days. **6. The banquet of**

wine] This presumably followed the dinner. Herodotus states that the Persians, though moderate at their meals, were much addicted to wine. **8. I will do .. hath said**] i.e. to make known to him her request. Esther hoped that by preparing a second banquet for the king before presenting her petition, she would render him more disposed to grant it.

9. In the king's gate] Since his hopes had been raised by Esther's undertaking to supplicate the king, he had laid aside his garb of mourning (4 2), and resumed his previous station (2 21). **11. The multitude of his children**] A Jew regarded a large family as a blessing (Gn 30 20), and, according to Herodotus, a Persian's strongest motive for pride, next to his personal bravery, was the number of his children. Haman had ten sons (9 10). **14. A gallows**] lit. 'a tree' (or 'stake').

CHAPTER 6
Mordecai is honoured

An account of how the king being reminded of Mordecai's services, and wishing to reward him, consulted Haman, and how Haman, thinking himself the object of the king's interest, counselled him, and was directed to render to Mordecai the honours he had advised.

1. The book .. chronicles] in which the chief occurrences of the king's reign, including any signal services done by his subjects (2 23), were recorded.

8. The royal apparel .. *useth* to wear] Not apparel similar to that which was worn by the king, but apparel which the king had actually used, just as the horse upon which the person to be honoured was mounted was that which the king had actually ridden (cp. 1 K 1 23). **The crown royal .. head**] RV 'and on the head of which' (i.e. of the horse) 'a crown royal is set.' The royal charger bore on its head a crown or coronet. **12. Having his head covered**] as a sign of humiliation and woe: cp. 2 S 15 30 19 4 Jer 14 4. **13. If Mordecai .. fall before him**] LXX adds, 'for the Living God is with him.'

CHAPTER 7
The Execution of Haman

4. We are sold] an allusion to Haman's tender of 10,000 talents (3 9). **Although the enemy, etc.**] The rendering is uncertain; RV 'although the adversary could not have compensated for the king's damage' (which would have resulted from the loss of so many of his subjects); RM 'for our affliction is not to be compared with the king's damage' (or 'annoyance' occasioned by Esther's complaint). Perhaps, 'although no enemy is comparable (to Haman) in doing damage to the king.'

8. The bed] RV 'the couch,' on which Esther was reclining at the table. **They**

covered Haman's face] preparatory to his execution. **9. One of the chamberlains . . the king**] better, 'one of the chamberlains that were before the king said.' Harbonah is mentioned in 1[10]. **Who had spoken good**] i.e. by the disclosure of the conspiracy described in 2[21, 22]. **Hang him thereon**] Haman suffered the retribution declared by the Psalmist to await the wicked : see Ps 7[15, 16].

CHAPTER 8
The Jews are saved

1. Did . . of Haman] The property of Haman, after his execution, was confiscated to the use of the king, to be disposed of as he thought fit. **2. Took off his ring, etc.**] The bestowal of the ring implied that Mordecai was appointed to be a minister of State, since the ring was used for giving authority to royal decrees (see v. 8) : cp. Gn 41[42].

4. Then the king held out] This seems to imply that Esther had approached the king unbidden : see 4[11].

7. Behold, I have given, etc.] The king mentions this to show that his denial of her request to reverse the letters of Haman (v. 5) was due not to lack of desire, but lack of ability to meet her wishes. **8. Write ye also**] The letters written by Haman and sealed with the king's ring could not be reversed as Esther had requested (v. 5), but she and Mordecai could be empowered, as Haman had previously been (3[11, 12]), to write such letters as they might think expedient to enable the Jews to stand on their defence. **9. The third month**] i.e. May-June. Rather more than two months had elapsed since Haman's letters had been despatched (3[12]). **10. Riders on mules, etc.**] RV 'riding on swift steeds that were used in the king's service, bred of the stud.'

15. In royal apparel] not the same as that described in 6[8], but a dress befitting the high office to which he had been appointed. His present magnificence was in striking contrast to his previous distress and humiliation (4[1]).

A great crown of gold] i.e. a circlet, indicative of high, though not royal, rank. In the Heb. a different word is used to describe the royal crown worn by the king and queen (1[11] 2[17]). **17. Became Jews**] i.e. proselytes.

CHAPTER 9
The Jews slay their Enemies. Institution of Purim

3. All the rulers, etc.] The great massacre described in v. 16 is thus represented as being in part the work of the Persian authorities with the forces at their disposal. **10. On the spoil, etc.**] In this respect they did not carry out the king's decree (8[11]); their vengeance was not sullied by sordid motives.

12. What have they done, etc.] An excla-

mation, not a question. **What** *is* **thy petition ?** etc.] The king was willing to gratify Esther further, perhaps to make amends for having been unable to grant her earlier request (8[5-8]).

13. Be hanged] i.e. let their dead bodies be exposed, such exposure being a mark of infamy.

16. Had rest] This anticipates what took place on the 'fourteenth' of Adar (v. 17).

Seventy and five thousand] LXX has 'fifteen thousand.' **19. The Jews of the villages**] better, 'the Jews of the country districts.'

Sending portions] i.e. to the poor among them : cp. Neh 8[10].

20. Mordecai wrote these things] This refers not to the existing book of Esther, but to an account contained in the letters sent to effect the purpose indicated in vv. 21, 22. This was the establishment as yearly festivals for all Jews throughout the empire both the fourteenth and fifteenth days of Adar ; and consequently involved a modification of the usage described in vv. 17, 18, according to which only a single day (in Susa the fifteenth, in the country districts the fourteenth) was so observed.

23. As they had begun . . written unto them] i.e. they undertook to celebrate both the day observed at first (vv. 17, 18) and also the additional day suggested by Mordecai. **25. When** *Esther* **came**] The name 'Esther' does not occur in the Heb., so that the correct rendering may be 'when it' (i.e. Haman's device) 'came before the king.' **26. For all**] RV 'because of all.' **This letter**] the 'letters' of v. 20.

27. Such as joined themselves unto them] i.e. religious proselytes : cp. 8[17]. **29. This second letter**] 'second' in relation to the letter mentioned in v. 20.

31. The matters of the fastings and their cry] Seemingly it was directed that there should be a commemoration not only of the deliverance granted to the Jews, but also of the distress that preceded it : see 4[3]. No account is here given of the day thus appointed for fasting and lamentation ; but in later times the thirteenth day of Adar, as being that which Haman had fixed for the destruction of the Jews (3[12]), was observed as a day of humiliation. **32. In the book**] probably a book, not now extant, dealing with the Purim festival ; but some authorities think that 'the book of the chronicles of the kings of Media and Persia' (10[2]) is meant.

CHAPTER 10
The Greatness of Mordecai

1. The isles of the sea] or, 'coast lands,' i.e. the countries bordering on the Mediterranean. The description of the king's dominion serves to enhance the glory of Mordecai, who was his minister. **3. Seeking the wealth**] i.e. seeking to promote their welfare : cp. Ezr 9[12].

JOB

INTRODUCTION

1. Theme and Contents. The book of Job, it may safely be said, is not known and read as it deserves to be. It is a fascinating book, and one of the most valuable in the OT. It deals with a theme which is as old as man and as wide as the world, viz. the reason of human suffering, the why and wherefore of those afflictions that fasten not merely upon the guilty, but, as it often appears, upon the righteous and the innocent. This immemorial problem, the crux of theology and the darkest mystery of human life, is the subject of this book, where it is treated in a most brilliant manner. In style the book of Job is a masterpiece of literature. It contains some of the deepest thought and the sublimest poetry that have come down from antiquity.

The difficulties that beset the ordinary reader are due not merely to the nature of the subject, but also to the fact that it is written in poetry, which is always more difficult than prose, and also to the too common practice of reading only short extracts. The work, being a discussion carried on at considerable length, must, if it is to be rightly understood, be read as a whole. It must, moreover, be read in the Revised Version, the meaning and sequence of thought being often much obscured in the Authorised Version.

The book is artistically constructed, and consists of three parts—a Prologue, the Poem, and an Epilogue. The Prologue is contained in the first two chapters, and the Epilogue in the last. These are written in prose, and form the setting of the Poem, which extends from c. 3–42⁶. The Prologue introduces the characters, and tells how they come together. The Poem contains the debate between Job and his three friends, followed by a speech from a bystander called Elihu, and concludes with an address by the Almighty and a penitent confession by Job. The Epilogue relates the further fortunes of Job, his restoration to prosperity, and his death.

The Prologue (chs. 1, 2) presents to us an Eastern chieftain called Job, who lives in the land of Uz, probably near Edom. He is a very pious man, 'perfect and upright, one that fears God and eschews evil,' and a very prosperous man. He is surrounded with what are commonly regarded as unmistakable tokens of the divine favour. He has a large family, possesses immense herds of camels, oxen,

asses, and sheep, and is described as 'the greatest of the children of the east.' He is as good as he is great.

In these circumstances a scene is opened in heaven. One of God's angels, called 'The Satan,' i.e. The Adversary, whose office seems to be to test the sincerity of men's characters, suggests that Job's piety is dependent upon his prosperity, that he does not 'serve God for nought,' that his religion is mere selfishness, and that if God were to withhold His blessings Job would withhold his worship and 'curse God to His face.' Satan obtains permission to put Job to the proof. From the height of his prosperity and happiness Job is suddenly plunged into the depths of misery. He loses all his property, and his children are cut off by violent death. Job is profoundly grieved, but he submits reverently to the will of God. So far he stands the test. In a second heavenly council Satan asserts that the test has not been severe enough, and receives permission to afflict Job's person. He smites him with a severe and loathsome disease, which makes him an outcast and an object of abhorrence to all. Still he is resigned. His faith remains unshaken. 'What?' he says, 'shall we receive good at the hand of God, and shall we not receive evil?' He makes no complaint against the Almighty.

Three friends now appear upon the scene: Eliphaz the Temanite, Bildad the Shuhite, and Zophar the Naamathite, who having heard of his great calamities come to condole with the ruined and childless man. They are appalled at the sight of his misery. Job is hardly recognisable. The words of consolation fail upon their lips, and they sit down beside him for seven days and seven nights, uttering never a word. Hitherto Job has been able to restrain himself, but now in the presence of his speechless friends a change comes over him. He is unmanned, and breaks down. He opens his mouth, and, in a passage of marvellous pathos and power, he curses the day that he was born and calls for death to come and put an end to his sufferings (c. 3).

With Job's first words begins the main portion of the book, which is continued for 39 chapters, and is written in poetry. It comprises a debate between Job and his three friends as to the reason of his sufferings. The debate is conducted in an orderly manner.

19

All three speak in turn, and Job answers each after he has spoken. This is repeated three times, except that according to the present arrangement of the book Zophar, who speaks last, fails in the third round of the debate to come forward. Perhaps this is due to some dislocation : see the introductory remarks to the third series of speeches. The theory with which all three begin is that suffering is a certain proof of previous transgression, and accordingly they all adopt a tone of rebuke towards Job on account of his supposed shortcomings, and urge him to repent of his sin, whatever it may be, saying that if he does so God will restore to him his prosperity. No doubt sympathy is more in place than argument in times of trouble, but the object of the book is not to show how to comfort sufferers, but how to account for the sufferings.

The Argument of the three friends is simple. God, they say, is always just. If a man suffers it must be because he deserves it. The righteous never suffer. Job, they conclude, must have been a great sinner to be afflicted thus. And they strive to get Job into a proper frame of mind. To this Job replies that the moral government of the world is not such a simple, uncomplicated thing as his friends suppose. Their theory may be true as a general rule, but there are exceptions. His own case is one. He protests that he is not conscious of any such great sin as they assume to be the cause of his present misery. His sufferings must have some other explanation. They are meanwhile a mystery to him. Nor is he the only exception to the rule of ' Be good and you will be prosperous.' It is a matter of universal experience that the innocent suffer as well as the guilty, and the wicked are frequently allowed to end their days in peace. In the debate this difficulty is put with great boldness, and Job is tempted occasionally to think and say hard things of God. With exquisite pathos he describes his bodily sufferings and mental perplexity, and his last speech concludes with a pathetic contrast between the former days, when the candle of the Lord shined upon his head, when the Almighty was with him and his children were about him, and he was honoured and respected by all, and his present state, when days of evil have laid hold upon him and wearisome nights and days are appointed unto him, when he is poor, and childless, and friendless, an abhorrence and a byword to young and old. To the end he protests his innocence and demands to be shown wherein he has transgressed. His great desire is to come face to face with his Maker. If he only knew where he might find Him, he is sure all would be explained. Meanwhile all is dark, a mystery he cannot fathom, a riddle he cannot explain, ' I go forward, but He is not

there ; and backward, but I cannot perceive Him ; on the left hand, where He doth work, but I cannot behold Him ; and on the right hand, but I cannot see Him ; but He knoweth the way that I take. His way have I kept, and not declined. Neither have I gone back from the commandment of his lips. When He hath tried me, I shall come forth as gold.' In a dim way he feels that though he is destined to die without learning the reason of his affliction, yet after death in another world the mystery will be solved. God will show Himself his friend and vindicate his innocence.

When the discussion between Job and his three friends is ended, and their explanation of his afflictions put aside as inadequate, a new speaker is suddenly introduced. A young man, called Elihu, has been listening to the debate, and he now comes forward as a critic of both sides. He is not satisfied with Job's assertions of self-righteousness, and he is disappointed with the three friends for bringing forward such poor arguments and allowing themselves to be silenced by Job. He hopes to set them all right, but one has a difficulty in discovering wherein he differs from the other three reprovers of Job. In great measure he repeats their arguments that God is just and deals out to every man exactly what he deserves. In two particulars, however, he seems to go beyond them, and so far approaches the right view of the question in the more explicit statements, (a) that chastisement may be the expression not of the divine indignation but of the divine goodness, and (b) that it may be designed as a warning, a restraint to keep men from falling into further sin ; in other words, that chastisement is discipline, a prevention as well as a cure, having a reference to the future as well as to the past.

This brings us to the last section of the Poem. Job had expressed an earnest desire to meet God face to face. In answer to this, ' the LORD answers Job out of the whirlwind ' (chs. 38–41). The striking thing about God's answer is that it is not at all what Job expected. He hoped that God, when He appeared, would give an explanation of His servant's sufferings. But this God does not do. He never alludes to Job's sufferings. What He does is simply to bid Job look around and observe the wonder and mystery of the world in which he is placed. In a series of splendid pictures God causes the panorama of nature to pass before the eyes of His human creature, and asks him if he could make any of these things, or even understand how they were created—the earth, the sea, the stars, the light, the rain, the snow and frost, the lightning, the variety of marvellous instincts and powers possessed by the animals. Could Job rule the world or even subdue any of its wonderful creatures ? If not, why should he presume to cavil at the ways of the Almighty or criticise His government of the world? From first to last the answer of God is simply a revelation of His omnipotence. It seems, therefore, to be irrelevant to the subject. It is no explanation of the mystery of human suffering. And yet Job is satisfied. It brings him face to face with God. He feels how presumptuous he has been in questioning the way of God to men, how ignorant and weak and vile he is in the presence of God's omniscience and omnipotence and perfect holiness. 'Behold, I am vile,' he says; 'I will lay mine hand upon my mouth. I have uttered what I understood not. Mine eye seeth thee; wherefore I abhor myself and repent in dust and ashes.' He has regained the old trust in God, but it is a deeper trust. Before his trial he had walked with God in the glad, unquestioning confidence of a child; now he has sounded the abyss of misery, but in the fullest knowledge of the world's pain, he is wholly assured of the righteousness of God. In the vision of God, which has replaced the old knowledge of God at second hand, even more than in the exhibition of God's omnipotence, he enters into peace. The answer to his problems is not simply the manifestation of God's power, it is God Himself. He does not understand, he is content to be humble and to trust. And with this attitude of humility and trust God is represented as well pleased.

In the Epilogue (c. 42 7-17) Job is restored to double his former prosperity and dies 'old and full of days.'

It is not easy to sum up the distinctive teaching of the book of Job. As a matter of fact, the problem which it states is insoluble. The book itself does not offer a solution. What it does is to show the true spirit in which the calamities of life should be met, a spirit of submission to the omnipotence and of trust in the wisdom of the Almighty. Incidentally, however, the following truths emerge in the book of Job, and have been noted by various commentators.

(a) Even a righteous man may suffer in this world from severe afflictions. (b) It is wrong, therefore, to make a man's sufferings a reproach to him, as though he were 'a sinner above all other men.' They may be permitted by God as a trial of his righteousness. (c) True religion is always disinterested. A truly righteous man will serve God and trust in Him in spite of all temptations to renounce Him arising from his sufferings. (d) It is presumption to accuse God of injustice on account of the sufferings that the good endure or the prosperity that the wicked are permitted to enjoy; man is unable fully to understand God's moral government of the world. (e) The true solution of all such moral perplexities is to be

sought in a fuller and larger sense of God's presence and power and wisdom.

It only remains to consider briefly how far we as Christians, living in the clearer light of Christ's life and teaching, have advanced in the knowledge of the purpose and meaning of suffering. Again, this may be summed up under a few separate heads:

(a) Christ Himself is the most conspicuous instance of innocent suffering. 'Though He were a Son yet learned He obedience by the things which He suffered.' 'He was made perfect through sufferings.' His words and example show that suffering may be innocently endured for the sake of others, or for the sake of righteousness, or in self-denial, or for the glory of God. (b) Christ has taught us that freedom from outward ills is not the greatest good. The highest good lies in the sphere of character and spirit. Jesus congratulated, not the rich and prosperous and those who never know what pain and sorrow are, but the poor, the meek, the mourning, the persecuted. In spite of all affliction a man may be truly blessed. In this Jesus reversed the common judgment of the world. As Bacon paradoxically puts it, 'Prosperity is the blessing of the Old Testament, adversity that of the New.' (c) Christ has taught us to call God our Father. He is not, therefore, a mere Judge dispensing abstract justice with indifference to the result upon the individual. God seeks to train and discipline His children so that they may be 'partakers of His holiness.' For their own sakes, therefore, it may be better, considering the end, that in some cases the innocent should 'endure grief' and the guilty be treated with long-suffering and leniency. Under a paternal government the treatment in each case will be accommodated to serve the best result. It will not always follow the rule of abstract justice. (d) Christ has revealed a future life. This Job and his friends, with the OT. saints in general, only dimly perceived or faintly hoped for. Having no certainty of the future life they naturally demanded that justice should be meted out in the present. Perceiving that this was not always done they were beset with many perplexities and doubts as to the justice of the divine government of the world. With the Christian revelation of a future life many of the embarrassments and anomalies of the present disappear. The end is not yet. The time of the final settlement of accounts is still future. There need be no fear that justice will not be done. Meanwhile the wicked flourish and the righteous suffer. But they may suffer in patience and hope. The afflictions of the present are 'light' and 'but for a moment.' 'They are not to be compared with the glory to be revealed.' 'Wherefore let them that suffer according to the will of God commit the keeping of their souls to Him in well-doing, as unto a faithful creator.'

2. Occasion, Authorship, and Date. It has always been a question whether the book of Job is to be regarded as history or parable. Among the Jews themselves the prevailing opinion was that it was strictly historical, though some of their Rabbis were inclined to think that the person of Job was created by the writer of this book in order to set forth his teaching on the problem that was vexing human thought. Rabbi Lakish, e.g., said 'Job existed not, nor was he created ; he is a parable.' The opinion of Luther is probably the correct one, viz. that a person called Job did really exist, but that his history has been treated poetically. The allusion to Job as a real person in Ezk 14 14 seems to show that there was a tradition connected with his name, and that he was famed for his piety. There may also have been a tradition that he suffered from a grievous reversal of fortune. On this historical foundation a later writer built up this dramatic poem, adopting Job as his hero and freely utilising his history to discuss a problem which was probably pressing with special weight upon men's minds at the time. It would not have served the writer's purpose so well to have created an altogether fictitious hero. But many things indicate that the traditional history of Job has been freely adapted, as, e.g., the elaborately constructed dialogues, the employment of symbolic numbers in the Prologue and Epilogue, the dramatic way in which the scene in the council chamber of heaven is depicted and in which the messengers bring to Job the tidings of his successive calamities, and, moreover, the very fact that the book is a 'poem' in which four men are represented as doing what men never do in real life, conversing with each other in measured strains of lofty and impassioned poetry.

To what writer we owe this poem, which Victor Hugo called 'perhaps the greatest masterpiece of the human mind,' and which has captivated the minds of men by no means prejudiced in favour of the literature of sacred Scripture, we shall never know with certainty. It belongs to the great class of anonymous masterpieces of which the literatures of all languages contain examples. Job himself, Moses, Solomon, Isaiah, Hezekiah, Baruch, have each been credited with its composition. Whoever he was, he was a poetic genius, an earnest philosopher, and a truly religious soul. He probably lived after the downfall of the kingdom of Judah, in any case not earlier than the time of Jeremiah. At that period the perplexing problems connected with the divine government seem to have pressed heavily on men's minds : cp. e.g. Jer 12 1 31 29 Ezk 18. Professor Davidson thinks that behind the author's time there probably lay some great public calamity which forced upon men's minds the questions of evil and the righteousness of God, and that such a calamity could be nothing short of deportation or exile. 'We may infer,' he says, 'that it was the design of the author to teach Israel, amidst its sorrows and the perplexities caused by them, that sufferings may be a trial of the righteous which if reverently borne will lift them up into fuller knowledge of God and therefore into more assured peace and felicity.' In view of the fact that national disaster would occupy men's thoughts before they felt the problem of individual suffering, there is much to be said for the view, held by many scholars, that the book of Job, which is concerned with the individual, not with the nation, and represents an advanced stage in the discussion of the problem, belongs to the period after the Return, perhaps about 400 B.C. This is also suggested by several other features in the book.

CHAPTER 1
THE PROLOGUE

Chs. 1 and 2, which form the Prologue to the book, describe (a) the prosperity and piety of Job ; (b) a scene in heaven in which the Satan questions the motives of his piety ; and (c) his subsequent trials, which are permitted by God in order to test and confirm His servant's righteousness, and to show to angels and men that a man may serve God for His own sake and not from self-interest. So far from being dependent on outside conditions the true servant of God will endure the severest trials which can befall human nature, and yet retain his faith and uprightness. It should be observed that whilst the author reveals to his readers the source and purpose of Job's trials these are unknown to Job and his friends. It is the mystery of his suffering which forms the problem of the book.

Chs. 1, 2 are in prose. The rest of the book, except 32 1-5 and 42 7-17, is in poetry. See on c. 3.

1-5. The prosperity and piety of Job.

1. The land of Uz] a district to the E. of Palestine, and near Arabia and Edom : cp. Jer 25 20 Lam 4 21. The word Uz occurs (a) as the name of a son of Aram (Gn 10 23) ; (b) as a descendant of Seir (Gn 36 28) ; (c) as a son of Nahor (Gn 22 21). The names ' Aram ' and ' Seir ' seem to point to the lands of Syria and Edom, but the exact position of Uz cannot be exactly defined. From various allusions in the book we must probably think of ' the red sandstones of Edom ' (the ' red ' land), ' and of the remote desert city in the hollow of the hills—Sela, afterwards Petra ; of the broad grey plain of the Arabah to the west ; of the dark rugged peaks rising high to the east, their summits white with snow in winter, and beyond this the high desert plateau with its great pilgrim and trading road to Arabia' (see on 6 15-20); ' a region with few springs, where the white broom grows' (see on 30⁴); 'and where the ostrich still runs and the wild ass scours the plain seeking the scanty green patches in spring' (39 5-8, 13-18). (Conder.)

Job] Meaning uncertain; either 'persecuted' or 'pious.' **Perfect**] Not sinless; rather, ' single-hearted,' blameless : cp. Noah (Gn 6⁹).

2. Seven .. three] sacred numbers indicating perfection. We are dealing with ideal history, as the rest of the numbers and other features here and in the Epilogue show.

3. Job was a prince of the desert. He possessed herds of **camels** yielding milk and food and hair for making tents; **asses** for riding, and fetching water; **cattle** and **sheep.** He even possessed **fields** (31 38). The description corresponds in each respect to the life of a free Arab chief E. of Jordan to-day. The term **men of the east** is applied to the tribes dwelling on the borders of Palestine, e.g. Syria and Arabia (cp. Gn 29¹ Jg 6³).

4. RV ' And his sons went and held a feast in the house of each one upon his day.' They took it in turns to entertain each other at their respective homes. **5. When the days .. were gone about**] i.e. when all seven sons had given their feast. It appears that it was Job's pious custom to gather together his children at stated intervals that atonement might be made for any neglect of God at their feasts. He **sanctified** them, i.e. prepared them by ablutions, etc., for taking part in the sacrifices he afterwards offered (cp. Gn 35² Ex 19 10 Lv 9⁷ 1 S 16⁵). Here we have an instance of the piety alluded to in v. 1. **Burnt offerings**] Observe that it was not the sin offering of the Mosaic Law which Job offered, but a burnt offering wholly given to God, which was common to many peoples (cp. Nu 23 Mic 6 5-8). As head of the family Job acted as priest : cp. Jethro (Ex 2 16 3¹). **Cursed**] RV ' renounced '; ' blasphemed ' or ' blamed ' may be better.

6–12. The first interview between God and Satan. The scene in heaven is based on the conceptions of the spirit world prevailing in the author's time (cp. 1 K 22 19-22 Zech 3 1, 2), and introduced by him to explain the origin and purpose of Job's trials. See last section of Intro.

6. Now there was a day] better, ' Now it was the day,' as if at a special season. **The sons of God**] i.e. the angels : cp. 38⁷. They come before God to give account of their ministry : cp. 1 K 22 19.

Satan] rather, ' the Satan,' lit. ' the adversary.' The word is in common use to-day among Orientals. The presence of the definite article shows that it is not used in this book as a proper name. The Satan is again spoken of in 1 Ch 21¹ and in Zech 3 1, 2 (see note). In the Adversary we have presented to us a spirit whose mission it is to try and test the lives of men and the motives of their acts : cp. 2³. He sees the bad side of life and therefore opposes man's standing with God. Naturally the constant discovery of evil motives underlying good actions has destroyed his faith in human nature. He is not represented as opposed to God, he is rather His loyal servant, who will not see His kindness abused, and zealously fulfils his duties by leaving no part of the earth unvisited. Malignant motives are, however, already attributed to him ; he seems to delight in opposing men, and tortures Job without compunction to justify his own cynicism. But he is not yet regarded as a fallen and evil being, opposed to God. The personality and character of the Devil had not yet been fully revealed.

9–12. In answer to God's challenge the Satan makes the slanderous suggestion that Job's religion is based on selfishness. He serves God for reward. The Satan obtains leave to put Job to the test.

9. The principles of Job's conduct are questioned. Perhaps his integrity is only skin deep. Will he continue his righteous life if he is called on to suffer ? **10. An hedge**] i.e. God's protecting care. **11. Curse thee to thy face**] see on v. 5.

12. God permits the Adversary to try Job in order to test his integrity and manifest his piety. Observe that Job's person is exempt from attack in this first trial. In view of the Satan's eagerness to prove his judgment of Job correct, God knows that this limitation of his power is necessary.

' Between vv. 12 and 13 there is an interval, an ominous stillness like that which precedes the storm. The poet has drawn aside the curtain to us, and we know what is impending. Job knows nothing' (Davidson).

13–22. The first trial of Job's integrity arising from the loss of his property and children. The way in which the messengers are introduced, and the similarity of their message, shows that we are not reading actual history, but a drama. The poet represents the catastrophe as falling on the day when the feast was at the eldest brother's house, because on the morning of that day the sacrifices had been offered for Job's children after the feast in the youngest brother's house on the day before. The death of the children cannot therefore be explained as due to their sin, for this had just been atoned for. Each catastrophe is worse than the previous one.

15. Sabeans] Arab tribes. Saba is the great S. Arabian kingdom of which inscriptions going back to an early date are preserved. The Bedouin Arabs still make raids on tribes at a distance, and also, when strong enough, on the settled population. **16. The fire of God**] i.e. lightning. **17. Chaldeans**] Heb. *Kasdim*, from the neighbourhood of the Euphrates and the Persian Gulf.

20. Rent his mantle] Tearing the robe has always been an Eastern sign of mourning, as was also shaving the head or pulling out the hair (see Jer 7 29 Mic 1 16). **Worshipped**] lit. 'prostrated himself': cp. Gn 18 2 Mt 8 2. The first act of worship is submission, humility.

21. Thither] i.e. to the womb of mother earth. This v. (but somewhat differently rendered, cp. 1 Tim 6 7) is used in the Burial Service. All is from God, and He has the right to do what He will with His own.

The LORD] It will be noticed as a rule the Hebrew author only uses in the dialogues such names for the Deity as were common to other peoples besides the Hebrews, e.g. 'God,' 'the Almighty.' The occurrence of the Heb. title 'Jehovah' here and in 12 9 is commonly explained on the supposition that it was a slip on his part. It is keenly disputed whether the name may not have been much older than the time of Moses, and known in Babylonia and Assyria. The evidence must at present be regarded as indecisive, though such a wide diffusion is not antecedently unlikely : see on Gn 2 4 Ex 3 13.

22. Charged God foolishly] lit. 'and did not offer (or, attribute) folly to God.' Thus Job successfully withstands the first test of the Adversary and remains loyal to God.

CHAPTER 2
THE PROLOGUE (continued)

Job's second trial. He refuses to renounce God when afflicted with an excruciating disease. Three friends come to comfort him.

3. Although thou movedst, etc.] or, 'so that it was in vain thou movedst me against him to destroy him.'

4, 5. Skin for skin, etc.] The precise meaning of the proverb is uncertain, but the general meaning seems to be that as long as a man does not suffer in his own person he will gladly bear the sacrifice of everything else ('skin for skin'). But it is a different matter when his life is endangered. Let Job suffer this last and greatest trial, then his integrity will fail him (so the Adversary insinuates) and he will renounce God. **His life** the Satan is not permitted to touch, short of that he has full liberty, and uses it.

7. Sore boils] lit. 'an evil inflammation.' The disease with which Job was afflicted is commonly taken to be elephantiasis, a terrible form of leprosy. It has also been identified with the 'Oriental sore,' also with ecthyma,

for which a plausible case has been made out.

8. A potsherd] A piece of earthenware to remove the scurf skin. **He sat down among the ashes**] Perhaps those of his camp fires. This was a sign of mourning. Tradition places him on a dunghill, like the 'Mizbeleh' or mound of refuse found outside an Eastern town or village where lepers and other outcasts sit, and men sometimes meet to talk.

9. Job's wife would have had him act as the Adversary expected him to do. ' You may as well renounce God's service since you benefit so little by it, and meet your fate at once instead of lingering in intolerable pain.'

10. Both good and evil are from God's hand, and must be taken in the same spirit. The words of Job are in notable contrast to those of his wife. **With his lips**] The reader must not be misled into thinking that the author means to suggest that Job nursed in his heart a rebellion he would not utter with his lips.

11. The three friends of Job now come upon the scene. They are represented as persons of importance like himself. **Temanite**] connected with Edom (Jer 49 7). **Shuhite**] Shuah was a son of Abraham by Keturah, who was sent ' to the East' (Gn 25 2, 6). **Naamathite**] unknown. The friends, like Job, were probably descendants of Abraham, but not of Israel (Jacob). **12. Knew him not**] so disfigured was he by his sickness and misery.

Sprinkled dust upon their heads] This was generally done when lying prostrate on the ground (cp. Lam 2 10), but the words 'toward heaven' suggest that they were standing. They throw dust in the air, which falls on their heads. **13. Seven days**] the time of mourning for the dead : cp. 1 S 31 13 Ezk 3 15

CHAPTER 3
JOB CURSES HIS DAY

Job curses the day of his birth. He asks why he did not die at birth : why should his wretched life be prolonged ?

We are now confronted with a striking change in Job's frame of mind from that presented in 2 10. Probably a considerable interval had elapsed before his friends arrived. He complains in the speeches which follow of the emaciated state into which he had fallen, and that from being the honoured of all he had become a byword to his neighbours : cp. 1 3 19 8-22 30 1-15. It is evident from this c. that he has been brooding over the miseries of his condition and the hopelessness of the future, and complaint has taken the place of resignation. The presence of his friends only provokes him to give vent to his anguish. In their silent amazement he sees as in a mirror the extent of his own misery. He casts himself confidently on their sympathetic comprehension, and freely utters the dark thoughts he has hitherto restrained. He knows that if left to himself he may lose the fear of the Almighty, and trusts that they will deliver him from this temptation. But an obsolete theology froze their power to help.

Chs. 3–42⁶ are poetical in form, not in exact metre as if for song, but rhythmical for reading. The parts of which the couplet or triplet forming the verse are composed show a marked parallelism, the thought in one half corresponding to or completing the thought in the other. C. 3 is a good example.

There is much similarity between this c. and Jer 20¹⁴⁻¹⁸, but the thoughts are those natural to the Hebrew mind, and we need not necessarily suppose them to be borrowed in either case.

3–10. Job curses the day of his birth. **1. His day**] the day of his birth. It was thought that the days of the year had an existence of their own, so that any given day would come round again in its turn. Hence Job is not cursing a day which long ago ceased to be, but one which year by year comes back to blight the happiness of others as it blighted his : see on v. 5. **3.** Observe the piled-up malediction. The power and pathos of the c. are remarkable. **5. Stain it**] RV 'claim it for their own.' **Blackness of,** etc.] RV 'all that maketh black the day'; e.g. eclipses and unusual darknesses. **6. Let it not be joined,** etc.] let it be blotted out of the calendar. The ancients believed in lucky and unlucky days. Let this day ruin no more lives, it has ruined enough. **7. Solitary**] RV 'barren.' **No joyful voice**] as on the occasion of a birth.

8. Let them curse it that curse the day] A reference to magicians who professed to be able to cast spells on a day and make it unlucky, apparently causing eclipses, as the next line suggests. **Who are ready to raise up their mourning**] RV 'Who are ready to raise up leviathan' (a mythical dragon). It was an ancient superstition that when an eclipse happened it was caused by a dragon which swallowed the sun or moon, or enfolded them in its coils, and so created darkness. A curious present-day confirmation of this idea occurs in the daily papers of Nov. 11, 1901. In a telegram from Peking it was reported that for the first time in history a few foreigners were invited to be present at the Chinese Board of Rites to witness 'the rescuing of the sun, which was suffering from the attacks of a dragon. The rescue was accomplished by means of prostrations, the burning of incense, and beating of drums and gongs.' **9. Dawning of the day**] lit. 'eyelids of the morning.'

11–19. Job asks why he did not die at birth ; a very fine passage expressive of great bitterness of soul.

12. Prevent me] RV 'receive me.' It was usual for the newborn child to be laid on its father's knees in token of ownership. If he suffered it to remain he pledged himself to bring it up. **14. Desolate places**] RM 'solitary piles': cp. the pyramids of Egypt, which were the royal burying-places.

15–19. In reading these verses, in spite of their great beauty, we cannot help contrasting the vague and cheerless ideas about the future state in these early days with the clearer knowledge and glorious hope of the Christian. Although believing that the soul retained its consciousness, men do not appear to have regarded death as but the beginning of a higher form of existence, in looking forward to which man learns to bear the trials of life with patience. They thought of Sheol as the dim and cheerless underworld, where the pale shades of the departed dragged on a colourless existence, dark and monotonous. Yet the gloom of Sheol is to Job a welcome refuge, where he would be at peace. How terrible must be the pain from which he would gladly escape to so wretched a home.

15. Perhaps an allusion to the valuables buried in ancient tombs. **18. Oppressor**] rather, 'taskmaster.'

20–26. Job asks why his wretched life should be prolonged.

22. There may be a connexion of thought here with the 'hid treasures' of v. 21. The idea is perhaps that of violating an ancient tomb. The entrance was usually hidden carefully. **23. Whose way is hid**] in perplexity and doubt. **24.** Translate, 'For my sighings are instead of my eating, and my groans are poured out like drink' : cp. Ps 42³.

25, 26. The verbs should all be in the present tense in these vv. Job's grief and sickness make him full of gloomy forebodings, which are constantly being realised.

The passionate complaints and longings for death in this c. testify to the agitation of Job's soul. There are signs of impatience and resentment at God's dealings, which shock his friends and evidently influence the tone of their language towards him in the debate which follows.

THE FIRST SERIES OF SPEECHES (Chs. 4–14)

CHAPTER 4

THE FIRST SPEECH OF ELIPHAZ (Chs. 4, 5)

Eliphaz is the principal and probably the oldest of the three friends : cp. 32⁶ᶠ. He is also the most considerate. But the complainings of Job in c. 3 had evidently deepened in him the bad impression which must have been created by Job's sufferings, and being ignorant of the true cause of his trials he draws false conclusions from them. Whilst admitting that Job is fundamentally a pious man, Eliphaz infers that his sufferings must be the punishment of some sin, and that therefore the correction which God is sending should be received with humility and the sin repented of. These premises, which are held by all the friends, are throughout denied and combated by Job.

1-11. Eliphaz gently rebukes Job for yielding to despair, since the godly do not perish under their affliction, but it is the wicked who reap the evil they have sown.

2. Note the courtesy of Eliphaz. He loses his temper in later speeches.

2-5. Eliphaz is greatly struck with the reverse in Job's fortunes. He who had been the great comforter of those in distress is now overcome by his own troubles. Observe that Eliphaz quite underrates their severity, and ignores the wonderful resignation Job has displayed. **4.** Cp. 29 12-17. **5. It is come**] i.e. calamity.

6. RV 'Is not thy fear (of God) thy confidence, *and* thy hope the integrity of thy ways?' Surely Job may reckon on the uprightness of his past life as a pledge of speedy deliverance! He must not despair. The v. is important as proving that the friends recognised Job's fundamental goodness, into whatever sins he may have suffered himself to be betrayed.

7-9. Whereas gross sinners are sure to be cut off, the righteous man, though he may have to suffer for his faults, has reason to hope that he will not perish. **10, 11.** The wicked, who are compared to lions, will certainly be destroyed: cp. Ps 22 13.

12-21. By way of awakening in Job a sense of sin Eliphaz describes a vision in which was revealed to him the perfect purity of God, and the imperfection in His sight of men and even of angels. We have here one of the most wonderful passages in literature. The secrecy, the hush, the sudden panic, the breath that passes over the face, the hair erect with horror, the shadowy figure whose form he cannot discern, the silence broken by the voice, all combine to produce the impression of terror, and terror not of the definitely known, but of the vague and mysterious, leaving the imagination full play to heighten it.

15. A spirit] rather, 'a breath.' **17.** RM 'Shall mortal man be just before' (i.e. in the eyes of) 'God? Shall a man be pure before his Maker?' **18. He put no trust**] because of their imperfections. **Servants**] attendant angels. **19. Houses of clay**] perishing bodies : cp. 2 Cor 5 1. If spiritual beings like the angels were imperfect, how much more men with material bodies. **Before**] RM 'like.' **20. From morning to evening**] i.e. in a day.

21. Doth not, etc.] rather, 'Is not their tent-cord (or tent-peg) pulled up in them?' The falling tent is a figure of collapse and death. **Even without wisdom**] i.e. without having learnt the great lessons of life.

CHAPTER 5

The First Speech of Eliphaz (concluded)

1-5. Eliphaz warns Job that to show a resentful temper at God's dispensations is folly, and that fools never prosper.

1. Call, etc.] i.e. 'make your complaint against God to the angels'; 'do you think they will help you?' **Saints**] RV 'holy ones,' i.e. the angels. **2. Wrath**] RV 'vexation.' **Envy**] RV 'jealousy.' Such rash conduct brings destruction.

3. Cursed] i.e. rejected as an accursed thing. At first Eliphaz was inclined to envy the prosperity of the wicked; but in a moment he sees there is no room for envy. He would not accept their position at any price, so sudden and sure was their downfall.

4. Crushed in the gate] the gate of the city, where justice was administered : cp. Ps 127 5. There are none to support their cause or to influence the judge. **5. The thorns**] the protecting thorn hedge.

6, 7. Affliction is not accidental, but is due to man's sinful nature. **Although**] RV 'for.'

8. I] RV 'As for me, I.' Eliphaz, instead of murmuring, would leave his case in the hands of One who is both great and wise. **11. To set**] RV 'so that he setteth,' i.e setteth men up by raising them from despair. **13. He taketh the wise in their own craftiness**] quoted by St. Paul in 1 Cor 3 19, the only quotation from Job in the NT. **Is carried headlong**] i.e. furthered to their hurt. **14.** The bewildered, haunted state into which the crooked devices of the wicked bring them. **15. From their mouth**] RV 'of their mouth.'

17-27. The blessedness of affliction if regarded as correction.

21. Scourge of the tongue] of false accusers and slanderers : cp. v. 15. **23. In league with the stones of the field**] His land will be free from stones ; a part of the general thought of being at peace with all creation : cp. Prov 16 7. For the idea of a sympathy between man and nature cp. Ro 8 19 f. **24. Tabernacle**] RV 'tent.' **Shalt not sin**] RV 'shalt miss nothing.'

CHAPTER 6

The First Speech of Job (Chs. 6, 7)

1-13. Job, smarting under the remarks of Eliphaz, which he feels are not appropriate to his case, renews and justifies his complaints. He bemoans the heaviness of God's hand, and wishes that He would slay him outright.

2, 3. Job admits that he was rash in his

remarks (in c. 3), but declares that his language was justified by his miserable condition.

3. Are swallowed up] RV 'have been rash.' **4.** It is because he feels that his troubles are due to God that he is almost beside himself, since he cannot understand their motive. In c. 3 he had not charged God with being the author of his sorrows.

5–7. Job continues to assert that he would not complain without good cause. **5.** The animals cease their cries when their wants are satisfied. **6. Unsavoury**] without flavour.

The white of an egg] Some prefer RM 'the juice of purslain.' **7.** RV 'My soul refuseth to touch *them;* They are as loathsome meat to me.' Vv. 6, 7 may mean that Job's afflictions are as intolerable to him as loathsome food.

8–10. Job longs for the stroke of death to descend and release him from his pain.

10. Yea, I would, etc.] RV 'Yea, I would exult in pain that spareth not : for I have not denied,' etc. Job fears not death, for he is unconscious of sin towards God. The passage is difficult, since Job does not expect retribution after death. The original text may not be correctly preserved.

11. Prolong my life] RV 'be patient.' Since there is nothing but death before him, how can he help being impatient for its arrival ? **12.** He is not made of stone or brass that he can bear such troubles. **13.** RV 'Is it not that I have no help in me, and sound wisdom is driven quite from me ?' He is exhausted and without resource.

14–30. Job complains of the lack of sympathy and false conclusions of the friends. They have bitterly disappointed the hopes he had set on them.

14. But he forsaketh] RV 'even to him that forsaketh.' Kind words from his friends might have helped Job to retain his trust in God, which he feared to lose.

15–20. Job likens the treatment of the friends to sudden torrents which fill the deep ravines or wadies of his land after storms. These flow abundantly in the winter, when they are least needed. In the parching heats of summer they dry up, and are sought in vain by wandering caravans which perish from thirst. So his friends fail him when most wanted.

16. In the winter the torrents are black and turbid with melting snow. There is plenty of ice in winter in the upper parts of Edom. **18.** RV 'The caravans *that travel* by the way of them turn aside' (in search of water). They go up into the waste, and perish.

19, 20. Troops] RV 'caravans.' **Tema . . Sheba**] in Arabia. The vv. describe the disappointment (**ashamed**) of the Arab caravans.

21. Ye are nothing] RM 'ye are like

thereto,' i.e. to the deceptive brooks. But it would be better to read 'so have ye been to me.' **And are afraid**] perhaps of showing sympathy, since they thought him guilty of sin. **22, 23.** All that Job looked for from them was sympathy. **25. Forcible**] perhaps 'irritating' would be better, a bitter sarcasm.

What doth your arguing reprove ?] At what sin are they aiming ? **26.** 'Are you finding fault with desperate words uttered in distress ?' **27.** Render, 'Would you sadden the bereaved and wound your friend ?'

28. Look upon me] i.e. in the face. **For it is evident,** etc.] RV 'For surely I shall not lie to your face.' **29.** Render, 'Reconsider my case ; do not do me such injustice.' Yes, reconsider it ; my cause is a righteous one !

Iniquity] RV 'injustice.' **30. Is there iniquity,** etc.] rather, 'Is my tongue perverted ?' **Cannot my taste,** etc.] 'Cannot I distinguish between right and wrong as well as you can ?'

CHAPTER 7

JOB'S FIRST SPEECH (concluded)

1–10. Job laments the hardship and misery of his destiny.

1. Man's life is a lot of hardship. **Appointed time**] RM 'time of service.' **2, 3.** As the labourer longs for the weary day to end and to receive his wages, so Job bemoans the length of his sufferings and sighs for death to end them. **3. Months of vanity**] so called because they were unsatisfactory, hopeless. 'Months' imply that Job's sufferings had lasted a considerable time. **5. Worms**] from the diseased flesh. **Clods of dust**] the crust of his sores. These symptoms are found in leprosy, though they are not peculiar to it.

6. Weaver's shuttle] the implement which carries the thread swiftly backwards and forwards in weaving. Job has just been longing for death, but yet he feels that length of days is desirable in itself if freed from so much misery. **Without hope**] of recovery. **7. Good**] i.e. happiness. **8. Thine eyes,** etc.] render, 'Thine (God's) eyes shall look for me, but I shall be no more.'

9. Grave] better, as RV, 'Sheol,' the place of the departed : see on 3$^{15-19}$. Note how hopeless is the outlook here and elsewhere towards the future.

11–21. He appeals to God, complaining of the undeserved severity of his treatment. He demands why God concerns Himself to interfere with so insignificant a being as man.

12. 'Am I so dangerous a character that I need such persistent persecution ?' **Whale**] rather, 'sea monster,' perhaps the personification of the sea, the mythical dragon of the ancients. The Babylonians told the myth of the dragon Tiâmat, who waged war against heaven and was slain by the God Marduk. (See art. 'Genesis and the Babylonian Inscriptions.') This myth is referred to here, but in a form which represented the monster, not as slain, but imprisoned and kept under strict observation. The sea needs to be held down lest it flood the earth or smite the sky (cp. 38 8-11), the dragon must be watched lest it bursts its bonds. Is Job as formidable as they that God should watch him as closely ?

14. Dreams] the bad dreams of the sick. **15. Strangling**] or, suffocation. Job longs for the arrival of this sign of approaching death. **My life**] RV '*these* my bones.' He was reduced to a skeleton. Possibly we should read 'my pains.' **16.** RV 'I loathe *my life :* I would not live alway.' **Vanity**] RM 'as a breath.'

17. Magnify] i.e. consider of such importance. **Set thine heart**] or 'fix thy thoughts.' The thought of vv. 17f. is 'Surely man is too insignificant for such constant persecution. Even his sins are hardly worth heeding.' Cp. Ps 8 4, 5, of which these vv. seem to be a bitter parody. **19. Till I swallow,** etc.] i.e. for a moment.

20. RV 'If I have sinned, what do I unto thee, O thou watcher of men ?' : i.e. granting that I have sinned (which Job does not), how can it affect Thee who art so great ? **Against thee**] RV 'for thee.' **21. In the morning**] RV 'diligently.' Job believes that one day God will turn to him once more in love, but then it will be too late. The faint hope expressed here gradually becomes a conviction : cp. 13 15-18 14 13-15 16 19-21 19 23-27.

The speech of Eliphaz, while considerate in tone, yet took Job's guilt for granted. This shows the sufferer that he can expect no sympathetic insight from the friends, and the shock of the disappointment drives him not simply to scornful attack on them, but to bitter accusation of God, whom he regards as the direct author of his troubles. He thinks of Him as petty and spiteful, yet he cannot forget the blessed communion of happier days, and ends with the thought that when His present anger is passed, He will desire a renewal of that fellowship.

CHAPTER 8

THE FIRST SPEECH OF BILDAD

Holding the same doctrine about sin and suffering as Eliphaz, Bildad supports the views of his friend by an appeal to the teaching of antiquity. He shows less sympathy and more narrowness of mind than Eliphaz.

1–7. Bildad maintains the justice of God's actions. Since Job's children have perished it must have been for their sins. As for Job, if he would but repent he would be restored to prosperity.

2. *Like* **a strong wind**] violent, headstrong. **3.** Can there be injustice with God as Job seems to think is possible ? Bildad thinks the All-powerful must in the nature of things be righteous. Job does not deny the omnipotence, but he questions the righteousness. **4. And he have cast,** etc.] RV 'he delivered them into the hand of their transgression,' i.e. abandoned them to the consequences of their sins. This conclusion about the death of Job's sons was quite unjustifiable (cp. Lk 13 4 Jn 9 2, 3), but is in accordance with the general views about retribution. The catastrophe had fallen on the very day on which their father had offered the sacrifice : see on 1 13. **6. Awake for thee**] LXX reads 'hearken unto thee.'

8–22. Bildad appeals to the experience of antiquity to show that God uproots the wicked, though they seem firmly established, and does not cast away the upright.

8. To the search of their fathers] RV 'to that which their fathers have searched out.' **9. We**] the men of his own day. **11–15.** As surely as a water-plant perishes without water so surely will the sinner perish when God turns from him. **11. The rush**] RM 'the papyrus,' a reed from which the Egyptians made paper, light boats, etc. **13. Hope**] of prosperity. **15. Hold it fast**] RV 'hold fast thereby.'

16–18. The sinner is compared to a fast-growing weed which flourishes under the heat of the sun, and whose roots plant themselves firmly in the earth (**seeth the place of stones**), but when destroyed it passes at once into oblivion. A slight correction of the Heb. would give for 17 b, 'It lives in a house of stones.' **17. Heap**] The Heb. also means 'fountain,' and possibly the sense may be that the plant lives in the stone erection over the fountain in the garden. **19. The joy of his way**] the short-lived prosperity of the sinner. **Others grow**] who fill his place.

21. Till he] RV 'He will yet.' Bildad, sharing the view of Eliphaz that while Job must have fallen into some heinous sin he was nevertheless a pious and upright man at heart, bases on this his prophecy that God will restore him. He must be chastened, but he cannot be cast away.

CHAPTER 9

JOB'S SECOND SPEECH (Chs. 9, 10)

Chs. 9, 10 are, perhaps, in their religious and moral aspects the most difficult in the book.

Driver in his 'Introduction to the Literature of the OT.' analyses them as follows :—'Job as well as his friends believes suffering to be a mark of God's displeasure for some grave sin. Job, however, is conscious that he has not so sinned. Hence the terrible dilemma in which he finds himself and which forces him to the conclusion that God, though He knows him to be innocent (10⁷), is determined to treat him as guilty, and that it is hopeless for him to attempt to clear himself.' Davidson characterises the leading features of the speech as 'awe before an Omnipotent Power, and moral terror and indignation, mixed with piteous despair at the indiscriminate severity with which it crushes men!'

The strange blending of conflicting emotions is one of the most striking features in this and some other of Job's speeches. With great skill and psychological insight the poet has shown us the rebellion which, springing from God's apparent cruelty, gives place for the moment to a softened mood as the sufferer recalls his former life in God's favour. Then this, in turn, is brushed aside to make way for a darker accusation than ever; God had deliberately led him on to believe in His love that He might make all the bitterer the revelation of His hate. Then the mood changes once more and he appeals to the pity of that God, whose pitilessness he has just asserted.

2-13. Job admits that it is impossible for him to maintain his righteousness before God. But this he implies is not due to his consciousness of guilt, but to the hopelessness of attempting to defend himself against God's irresistible power which is manifested throughout creation. **3. If he will]** RM 'If one should desire to.' **Contend]** argue his cause. **One of a thousand]** viz. charges against him, or questions with which he might be entrapped. **5. And they know not : which overturneth]** RV 'And they know it not when he overturneth.' The catastrophe is so sudden. **6.** The v. describes an earthquake. The roots of the mountains were thought of as pillars supporting the earth : cp. 26¹¹ Ps 75³. **7. It riseth not]** because of darkness or eclipse. **Sealeth up]** i.e. in the abode where the stars were thought to dwell, and where they were brought forth by night to shine in the sky (Isa 40²⁶). **8.** Cp. Isa 40²². The points of resemblance between the book of Job and the latter part of Isaiah are striking and frequent. **9. Arcturus]** RV 'the Bear.' The Heb. names in this v. are supposed to refer to three well-known constellations, the Bear, the Pleiades, and Orion. **Chambers of the south]** the southern heavens. So the Babylonians divided the sky into 'lunar mansions.' **11.** Job is baffled by the suddenness and mystery of God's actions. There is no escaping Him. **13.** RV 'God will not withdraw his anger ; the helpers of Rahab do stoop under him.' The word 'Rahab,' which means 'pride,' occurs again in 26¹² RV, and is there evidently applied to the raging sea. 'This stormy sea, assaulting heaven with its waves, was personi-

fied in ancient myth as a monster leading his helpers on to wage war with heaven' (Davidson). Rahab is the same as Tiâmat (see on 7¹²). The myth relates that she brought forth a brood of monsters to help her in her battle. To this the term 'helpers of Rahab' alludes. See also Isa 51⁹.

14-21. God, Job feels, is resolved to regard him as guilty. It is therefore vain to assert his innocence, yet while he can assert it he will. **15. Would I not]** i.e. 'would I not dare to.' **I would make supplication]** rather, 'I must ask mercy.' It would be useless to attempt to establish his innocence. **Judge]** rather, 'adversary-at-law.' **16.** 'If God allowed me to plead my cause, I cannot believe He would condescend to attend to me.' Job feels that God is indifferent to his cry for justice. **17, 18. Breaketh .. multiplieth .. will not suffer .. filleth]** rather, 'would break .. would multiply .. would not suffer .. would fill.' **19.** God is represented as speaking. 'If it be a question of strength, it is I who am strong ; if of judgment, who would dare appoint me a day ?' 'The words imply the irresponsibility and superiority to all law of the speaker' (Davidson). **20.** Job speaks. Render, 'Though I am innocent, a word may put me in the wrong ; though I am upright, He can pervert me.' It is therefore useless to plead. **21.** RV 'I am perfect ; I regard not myself ; I despise my life.' Job now boldly asserts that he is innocent, even though it may cost him his life.

22-24. Job boldly arraigns the morality of the divine government of the world. **22. This *is* one *thing*]** RV 'It is all one.' Apparently he means, 'It makes no difference whether I live or die.' God destroys indiscriminately both innocent and guilty. This directly controverts the friends' view (8²⁰). There is no such thing as a moral government of the world. **23. Scourge]** e.g. famine, etc. **Trial]** RM 'calamity.' **24. He covereth the faces,** etc.] so that they are blind to justice. **If not, where,** etc.] RV 'If *it be* not *he*, who then is it ?' To whom but God can this state of things be ascribed ?

25-31. Job's life speeds away ; God will make him out to be guilty however pure he may be. **25, 26.** Cp. Wisd 5⁹, ¹⁰, where two of the same metaphors are similarly used. **25. A post]** RM a 'runner' with messages. **26. Swift ships]** Heb. 'ships of reed,' light boats made from the papyrus reed, and very swift. **28.** Since God is determined to hold Job guilty, it is useless for him to try and establish his innocence. **I am afraid of all my sorrows]** because they seem to be evidences of God's anger. Apparently there were times when the pain was less acute, but the cheerfulness he might have felt was checked by the knowledge that it would come back again. **29.** *If I be wicked*] RV 'I shall be condemned.'

30. And make, etc.] RM 'And cleanse my hands with lye,' or potash. He means that he is really righteous, but God is determined to make him seem wicked.

32-35. Job is conscious that he cannot meet God on his own level and plead his cause on equal terms, nor is there any one to act as mediator.

33. Daysman] an Old English word meaning 'umpire,' or 'arbitrator'; one who mediates between two parties.

33-35. Translate (with Cox): 'There is no arbiter between us to lay his hand upon us both, who would remove His (God's) rod from me so that the dread of Him should not overawe me. If there were, I would speak and not fear Him.' Job laments that there is no being, having power with God and man, who would interpose and arbitrate between him and God, and make both parties yield to his decision.

This passage is the first occurrence of the idea of intervention on his behalf, which takes more definite shape in 16^{19} and 19$^{25-27}$. But in those passages Job advances to the thought that, since he has no umpire to vindicate him, God Himself will be his umpire, and vindicate Job even against Himself. This longing of pious men of old for some mediator who would bring about peace between them and God has been satisfied in the person of our Lord Jesus Christ, both God and man.

34. His fear] i.e. the fear He causes, as in Ex 23^{27}. **35. But** *it is* **not so with me**] RV 'For I am not so in myself,' i.e. In my own soul I am not guilty.

CHAPTER 10
Job's Second Speech (concluded)

1-7. Job seeks the reason of his trial, and protests against God's treatment as inconsistent with the natural relations between Creator and created, and with God's knowledge of his innocence and inability to escape Him.

1. I will leave, etc.] RV 'I will give free course to my complaint.' **3. The work of thine hands**] i.e. man, God's creature.

4-6. 'Is God's judgment liable to mistakes like that of frail man' (**eyes of flesh**), 'or is His time so short that He is in a hurry to find Job guilty and to punish him?' Observe that Job cannot altogether give up his conviction that God must be really just, although the reason of his suffering causes him the greatest perplexity. **7. Thou**] RV 'although thou.'

8-17. Job dwells on God's past goodness. Does he not owe to Him his existence and his preservation up to the present? Yet He had apparently purposed all along to destroy him in the end.

10, 11. The conception and growth of the infant. **Curdled me**] made him take solid form.

11. Fenced me] RV 'knit me together.'

12. Visitation] RM 'care.'

13. And these, etc.] RV 'Yet thou didst hide these things,' etc. **I know that this** *is* **with thee**] rather, 'I know that these things were with thee.' Job concludes that even from his childhood God had purposed to afflict him, making him happy so that his misery might be deeper by contrast.

14, 15. Whether guilty or innocent he would be condemned. **15.** *If* **I be righteous,** etc.] 'Were I righteous I must not lift up my head as an innocent man.' *I am* **full, etc.**] RV 'being filled with ignominy, and looking upon my affliction.' But a slight correction gives the very much better sense, 'drunken with affliction.' **16. Marvellous**] in his persecutions; a sorry sequel to the marvel of creation (chs. 38, 39). **17. Thy witnesses**] Job's afflictions, which seem to witness to his guilt. **Changes and war, etc.**] RM 'Host after host is against me.'

18-22. Job begs for a little respite before his death: cp. Ps 39^{13}. Observe how appeal follows hard on accusation. **21, 22.** Note the dreary, hopeless conception of the dim shadowland of death.

It should be observed that in spite of the rash and despairing utterances to which Job in his misery gives vent in chs. 9, 10, his position is one of religious perplexity, rather than of reasoned doubt. Calmer and more hopeful views soon appear, and the conviction that God will restore him to His favour and justify him comes out more and more clearly as we read on: cp. 14^{13} 16^{19} 19^{25} 27$^{1-6}$. 'Job never entirely gave up his faith in God, though, like Jacob, he wrestled with Him. And, as in that case, the issue shows that God was not displeased with such an unburdening of the soul that still kept close to the strict line of truth' (Bradley). 'Much of the interest of this drama of the soul lies in the growth of a consciousness in Job that God's present anger does not represent His inmost self. It is a mood that will pass, a dark cloud eclipsing His truest character. This thought does not, however, emerge as yet' (Peake).

CHAPTER 11
The First Speech of Zophar
The speech is short and unsympathetic.

1-6. Zophar rebukes Job for daring to assert his innocence.

3. Thy lies] RV 'thy boastings,' viz. Job's assertions of innocence (v. 4). **6. That** *they are* **double, etc.**] RV 'That it is manifold in effectual working.' **God exacteth, etc.**] RM 'God remitteth unto thee of thine iniquity';

He does not bring up all Job's guilt, which is greater than he is aware of. So far from the penalty being excessive, Job has not received all that he deserved.

7–12. God knows Job's sinfulness if he does not himself.

7. RM 'Canst thou find out the deep things of God ?' **8.** *It*] God's wisdom. **10. If he cut off,** etc.] rather, 'Should he pass by, imprison, arraign before an assembly ?' If God, with perfect knowledge of sinful man, visits him in various ways, who shall gainsay His actions ? **12.** Perhaps we may render, 'Thus vain man gets understanding, and a wild ass's colt is born a man.' The description of affliction brings wisdom to the foolish and transforms the most unpromising natures.

13–20. Repentance the way to restored prosperity.

14. Tabernacles] RV 'tents.' **15. Without spot**] of guilt. **16. Waters**] rather, 'floods.'
17. *Thine* **age**] RV '*thy* life.' **Thou shalt shine**] RV 'Though there be darkness, it shall be as the morning.' **18. Dig**] RV 'search,' viz. for danger, but find none. **20.** *As*] RV omits. There is nothing before the wicked but death. The statement is general, but Zophar, unlike the other friends, hints that Job may belong to the wicked.

CHAPTER 12
Job's Third Speech (Chs. 12–14)

The friends have said God is wise and mighty. Job replies, 'I know that as well as you. You infer that He is also righteous, but experience shows that His power and wisdom are directed to unrighteous ends.' But it is with God rather than with them that he wishes to argue, and come what may he will utter all he feels. He challenges God to name his sins, presses man's hopeless destiny as a reason for God's pity, longs that God might shelter him out of reach of His anger, till it has passed away, and then renew His communion with him, but closes again on the note of man's hopeless fate. The thought that God might take Job's part against Himself here comes to expression.

1–12. Job sarcastically praises the wisdom of the friends, which, however, is not greater than his own, or indeed than any one may learn from God's creation and government of the world. It is easy to mock one who is down: yet the prosperity of the wicked is a fact as patent as the wisdom and power of God.

2. A sarcastic allusion to the omniscience of the friends : Ye *are* the people ; the only wise ones. **4. Who calleth**] RV '*A man* that called.' Job complains that he, a servant of God, has become the subject of mockery.

5. RV 'In the thought of him that is at ease there is contempt for misfortune ; it is ready

for them whose foot slippeth.' An allusion to the way his friends treat him now that he is in trouble. How easy to despise the man who is down ! **6.** The wicked, on the other hand, seem to fare better than the good. **Into whose hand,** etc.] Another rendering is, 'Who bears (his) god in his hand' ; i.e. who regards his sword as his god : cp. Hab 1 [11-16].

7. Even the animals know the commonplaces that constitute the friends' stock of wisdom. **9. In all these**] among all these creatures. **The LORD**] see on 1 [21]. **Hath wrought this**] i.e. orders all things. **11, 12.** 'I test your arguments as the palate tests its food ; the aged are not necessarily wise.' **11. And the mouth,** etc.] RV 'Even as the palate tasteth its meat.' **12.** RM 'With aged men, *ye say*, is wisdom.' Job is not stating his own views.

13–25. With God are wisdom and might, no one can reverse His actions. The mightiest are overthrown by Him, and He takes away the understanding of the wise.

13. With him] viz. God. Absolute power and wisdom are inherent in God, not acquired by pains and years as man acquires such power and wisdom as he possesses. **14.** The impotence of man in the hands of the Almighty. **Shutteth up a man**] e.g. in prison. **16.** *Are* his] exist by His permission.

17. Perhaps the original text meant 'He sends mad counsellors.' **18.** God sets kings free, or imprisons them according to His will. **19. Princes**] RV 'priests.' Perhaps, 'He sends mad priests and perverts the mighty.'
22. 'The v. means that God through His wisdom sees into the profoundest and darkest deeps, and brings what is hidden to light' (Davidson). **23. Straiteneth them** *again*] RM 'leadeth them away into captivity.' **24. Wilderness**] The Heb. is used of the primeval chaos of Gn 1 [2].

CHAPTER 13
Job's Third Speech (continued)

1–12. Job claims to understand as much about God as the friends. He rejects their opinion as to the cause of his troubles, and regards it as an attempt to curry favour with God.

1. The v. is in close connexion with c. 12. **Eye** refers to 12 [7,8], **ear** to 12 [13 f.] : cp. 12 [11].
3. Surely] rather, 'but.' **4. Forgers**] better, 'plasterers,' i.e. they plaster their lies over God's misgovernment and hide its evils. **7, 8.** 'Does God require His actions to be defended by their untruths and servile flattery ?' The friends condemned Job unjustly in order to uphold God's justice. They were special pleaders for God, because they wanted to curry favour with Him.

8, 10. Accept] RV 'respect.' The phrase

is used of a judge who shows partiality. Considerations of self-interest lead them to give God their verdict and not Job. **9.** 'Do they think they can deceive God with their partiality? He penetrates their cowardly motives.'

10. Job believes that God will not approve of those who lie for Him, an assertion of God's righteousness in remarkable contrast to the assertions of His unrighteousness. **12.** RV 'Your memorable sayings *are* proverbs of ashes, your defences *are* defences of clay.' Job regards their view as worthless, and their arguments such as any one could refute.

13-22. He turns from man, and boldly pleads his cause with God.

14, 15. Render, with a slight alteration, 'I will take my flesh in my teeth and I will put my life in my hand (be daring). Lo, he will slay me : I have no hope, but I will maintain my words before him.' The meaning of the phrase 'to take the flesh in the teeth' is uncertain. Probably it signifies just the same as to 'put the life in the hand,' which means to dare the uttermost peril. Job is resolved to speak out, though he feels that God will kill him for doing it.

16. He] RV 'This.' The v. may mean that God would pardon his boldness but not a false confession of sin : see 42⁷. **18. Ordered** *my* **cause**] i.e. prepared his defence.

19. Plead with] RV 'contend with' : to prove him a sinner. **For now,** etc.] RV 'For now shall I hold my peace and give up the ghost' : i.e. if his innocence were disputed. Note how in prospect of his case coming into court Job's spirits rise. He is so certain of his innocence that he cannot believe that it can help being established. The axiom on which this rests is his conviction of God's righteousness, once more a strange contrast to his charges against Him. **20, 21.** Job begs that God will free him from the sense of terror which he naturally feels. **Thy dread**] i.e. dread of Thee.

23-28. He seeks to know his sins, and the reasons of God's treatment.

26. Possess] RV 'inherit.' Job thinks he must be suffering for his early follies.

27. Stocks] rather, 'clog,' to prevent slaves escaping. **Thou settest,** etc.] lit. 'Thou dost make a mark upon the roots of my feet,' perhaps, i.e. make them sore with the clog upon them. **28. And he,** etc.] RV 'Though I am like a rotten thing that consumeth'; an allusion to his miserable state.

CHAPTER 14

JOB's THIRD SPEECH (concluded)

1-6. Job pleads for God's forbearance on the grounds of man's shortness of life and sinful nature.

1, 2. The well-known Sentence in the

Burial Service. **3. Open thine eyes**] i.e. watch so vigilantly : cp. vv. 16, 17. **4.** Job pleads the innate sinfulness of man. **5, 6.** Let man spend his days in peace, seeing that his time is but short : cp. c. 7.

7-12. A tree has a chance of a second growth after it is cut down. Not so man. With him death is final. Job here reaches the depth of despair.

13-22. Despairing of any return to God's favour before death, Job is seized with a longing to remain in the place of the departed (Sheol) until God's wrath is past, when he should be forgiven and restored to His favour. Notice how Job assumes that God's hostility to him will not be permanent. He pictures God as conscious of this and as, in view of the future love He would feel for him, sheltering him in Sheol from His present anger. Yet though he dwells upon a possible return from Sheol to life in fellowship with God, he does not dream that it is more than an enchanting thought. If only a man might die and live again ! No, that is impossible. **14. Will I wait**] RV 'would I wait.' **Come**] RV 'should come.' **15.** RV 'Thou shouldest call and I would answer thee : Thou wouldest have a desire to the work of thine hands.'

16, 17. These vv. probably are not, as AV and RV take them, the present contrast to the glowing picture of the future that he has been wishing might be true, but a continuation of that picture. Render, 'For then Thou wouldest number my steps ; Thou wouldest not watch over my sin ; my transgression would be sealed up in a bag, and Thou wouldest cover over my iniquity.' God would number his steps in kindly care (cp. 'the very hairs of your head are all numbered'). He would no longer treasure up his sin against him, but hide it away out of sight. **18, 19. And**] render, 'But.' Under God's visitation the hopes of men come to nought, like undermined mountains or water-worn rocks.

20-22. A description of what happens after the death change passes over the face and the spirit goes away to Sheol. The dead have lost all knowledge, all interest in the things of earth, even in the fortunes of their own children (cp. Eccl 9⁵,⁶). In the grave the body passes through the painful process of decomposition, the pain of which is also felt by its shade in Sheol.

THE SECOND SERIES OF SPEECHES
(Chs. 15–21)

The rejection by Job of the opinions and advice of the friends, his sturdy maintenance of his innocence, and the fearlessness with which in his anguish he has arraigned the divine government of the world, have all alike deepened their conviction of his guilt.

Without actually charging Job with definite sin, for which indeed they have no ground, they now administer stern rebukes, and draw terrible pictures of the certain misery which awaits the godless, and this evidently with an eye to the sufferer. They no longer encourage him to repentance, or predict consequent prosperity.

Job, for his part, laments their harshness, and rejects anew their doctrine of retribution as contrary to experience, and as not applicable to his case. He feels himself to be abandoned by God and man ; he cries out for pity ; he reasserts his innocence, and is still troubled by the problem of evil. Yet in the very midst of his trouble he makes some advance towards the solution of the mystery. Already he has had dim visions of a mediator between himself and God (9 $^{32\,f.}$), and of the possibility of a restoration to the divine favour (14 $^{13\text{-}15}$). These were only momentary glimpses of a brighter day amidst the gloom, but now they develop into a stronger conviction that God must in the end restore the light of His countenance to His servant, and vindicate his innocence to the world, though it can only be after his death : see 16 ^{19} 19 $^{25\text{-}27}$. It is, however, no longer an umpire between himself and God that he desires. The conviction has come to him that since there is no umpire who can force his decision on God, God Himself will be the umpire to vindicate the righteousness of Job against the stigma of unrighteousness which He had Himself seemed to fasten upon him by his affliction.

CHAPTER 15
THE SECOND SPEECH OF ELIPHAZ

1–16. Eliphaz accuses Job of impiety and arrogance.

2. And fill, etc.] utter idle, empty remarks.

7. It was a popular idea that there was a primeval man endowed with perfect wisdom, corresponding to the figure of the Divine Wisdom in Prov 8. **8.** Render, ' Didst thou hearken in the council of God ? ' i.e. before the creation of the world. **10.** Eliphaz, perhaps, refers here to himself.

11. RV ' Are the consolations of God too small for thee, and the word *that dealeth* gently with thee ?' The 'consolations of God' are the comforting views about God's government and purposes which Eliphaz would have Job accept : cp. 5 $^{8\text{-}27}$. **12. What do thy eyes wink at ?**] render, ' why do thy eyes flash (in anger) ?' **14.** Eliphaz uses Job's own words (14 ^{4}) to convict him of his sinfulness.

15. He] i.e. God. **Saints**] RV 'holy ones' : the angels, cp. 4 ^{18}. **Heavens**] i.e. probably, 'heavenly beings.' **16. Drinketh**] thirsts after, is greedy for.

17–35. Eliphaz describes, doubtless as a

warning to Job, the troubled conscience and inevitable doom of the wicked.

18, 19. Eliphaz refers to a time when his ancestors had not mingled with other people, who would corrupt the purity of their wise sayings. His countrymen the Edomites, who were descended from Abraham, would have the same pride of race as their Hebrew cousins.

20–23. The haunting fears of the wicked oppressor. **20. And the number,** etc.] RV ' even the number of years that are laid up for the oppressor.' **22.** He loses hope of deliverance from misfortune. **23**^{a}. He imagines he is always coming to poverty. **24. Ready**] fully prepared. **25. For**] RV ' Because.'

26. Render, ' It (trouble) leaps at his throat, past the thickest boss of his shield.' The boss is the central knob of the buckler. **27.** A picture of sensual luxury : cp. Ps 73 ^{7}.

28. Illustrative of his daring impiety : he ventured to dwell in cities that lie under the curse : cp. Josh 6 ^{26}. **29. Neither shall he prolong,** etc.] RV ' neither shall their produce bend to the earth' ; a figure of fruitfulness.

30. By the breath, etc.] God's wrath will destroy him like a withering sirocco. **31.** RV ' Let him not trust in vanity, deceiving himself.' **Accomplished**] RM ' paid in full.' **His time**] the natural time of his death.

32, 33. The speedy end of the wicked. ' His branch prematurely withers ; he puts forth grapes, and cannot ripen them ; he flowers, but he fails of fruit ' (Davidson).

CHAPTER 16
JOB'S FOURTH SPEECH (Chs. 16, 17)

See introductory remarks on chs. 15–21.

1–5. Job retorts scornfully that he too could offer such empty ' comfort ' if he were in the friends' place.

2. The friends can do nothing but repeat their exasperating commonplaces. **3. Shall vain words,** etc.] i.e. ' will you never stop ? '

5. Job would have acted very differently (4 ^{3}, ^{4} 29), giving no mere lip-comfort.

6–17. Job enlarges on the wrath of God and the enmity of man. Neither speech nor silence brings him relief.

7–9. These vv. seem to refer to the hostility of God, v. 10 to that of man. In vv. 7–9 Job varies between complaint of God in the third person and direct address to Him.

7^b. Perhaps a reference to the loss of his family (1 ^{18}, ^{19}). **13. Archers**] RM ' arrows.' **Reins**] i.e. kidneys. **14. With breach upon breach**] with one blow after another, as a battering-ram makes breaches in a wall.

15. Sackcloth] the sign of mourning.

Horn] the emblem of pride and strength.

17. Not for *any* **injustice**] RV ' although there is no violence.' Cp. the suffering Servant of Jehovah in Is ^{r} 53 ^{9}.

18. Conscious of his innocence and yet of his impending death, which seems a token that he is condemned as guilty, Job invokes the earth not to conceal his blood, but to let it cry aloud for justice. The idea that the earth would not absorb innocent blood occurs also in Gn 4^{10} Ezk 24^{7,8}. **No place**] RV 'no *resting* place.' Let it be heard everywhere !

19-21. Rejected by men who count him guilty, Job is for a moment cheered with a bright vision of a 'witness in heaven,' one who will vouch for and testify to his innocence (v. 19). From vv. 20, 21 RV it is supposed that Job has an intuition that the God who now seems to be his enemy is after all the God of love, in communion with whom his past life has been spent, and to Him he turns :

> 'But thou giv'st leave, dear LORD, that we
>   Take shelter from Thyself in Thee ;
> And with the wings of Thine own Dove
> Fly to the sceptre of soft love.'
>   (Crashaw, quoted by Cheyne.)

We see here a development of the idea of a 'daysman' or mediator first mentioned in 9^{33}. There it appears as a longing impossible to be realised. In this c. it turns into a definite hope, and in 19$^{25-27}$ it rises to a certainty. It is evident from 16^{22} 17$^{1-3, 13-16}$ that Job does not expect this vindication before his death, which seems at hand.

19. Also now] RV 'Even now.' **My record**] RV 'he that voucheth for me.' **21.** RV 'O that he (God) would maintain the right of man with God, and of a son of man with his neighbour.' Some render the second half of the sentence, 'as a mortal man does for his neighbour.' **22.** Connected in subject with 17^{1,2}. Some by a slight correction read in the first line, 'For the mourning-women shall come.'

CHAPTER 17
JOB'S FOURTH SPEECH (concluded)

1-9. Job prays God to pledge Himself to vindicate his innocence in the future, for his friends have failed him, and he rejects their promises of restoration in the present life.

1. RV 'My spirit is consumed, my days are extinct, the grave is *ready* for me.' The v. is connected with 16^{22}. **2.** Job rejects the delusive hopes of restoration held out by the friends. **3.** RV 'Give now a pledge, be surety for me with thyself ; who is there that will strike hands with me ?' Job begs that God will promise to testify to his innocence after he is dead. There is no one else who will do this. To 'strike hands' was the Hebrew sign of becoming surety for another. **4.** The friends are too prejudiced against Job to speak on his behalf. **Not exalt them**] i.e. not let their views triumph. **5.** RV 'He

that denounceth his friends for a prey, even the eyes of his children shall fail.' **6. He hath made me**] Render, 'I am made.' **And aforetime**, etc.] RV 'And I am become an open abhorring.'

8, 9. The upright, astonished at Job's calamities, will rise against the ungodly, while the righteous holds on his way with increasing strength. This does not fit in well with Job's attitude, so that there is plausibility in the view of some scholars that the vv. are a misplaced fragment of Bildad's speech.

10. Job invites the friends to renew their arguments, although he expects nothing worth hearing from them. **11, 12. The thoughts,** etc.] Render, perhaps, 'The thoughts of my heart put night for day. Darkness is nearer than light.'

13-16. Job declares that it is vain to look for any restoration or justification (**my hope**) in this life. His hope will go to the grave with him. **13.** RM 'If I hope, Sheol is mine house.' **16. They**] RV 'it' (i.e. his hope). **Bars of the pit**] the gates of the world of the dead: cp. Isa 38^{10}. **When,** etc.] RV 'when once there is rest in the dust.'

Job moves forward in this speech to the great thought that after he is dead, God will clear his reputation of the stain placed upon it by his disasters, which seemed to the world to prove his guilt. He does not expect the old relations between God and himself to be renewed, but since he cannot bear the thought that he will be permanently branded as an evil-doer, he wins the conviction that he will ultimately be righted. And since God alone can or will clear his honour (for man cannot and will not) he is assured that God, who is now slaying him by slow torture, will at last vindicate him. God's present mood is not an index to His permanent character.

CHAPTER 18
BILDAD'S SECOND SPEECH

Bildad replies with a rebuke to Job and a reassertion of the miserable lot of the wicked already asserted by Eliphaz ; not so much, however, with covert reference to Job, to whose case the description is largely unsuitable, as in answer to his impeachment of God's moral government.

1-4. Bildad protests against Job's violent language.

2. RV 'How long will ye lay snares for words' ; i.e. hunt for arguments. **Mark**] RV 'consider (the matter).' **3.** Cp. 17$^{2, 4, 5, 10}$. **4**^{a}. RV 'Thou that tearest thyself in thine anger,' a rebuke to Job's rash utterance in 16^{9}. **Shall the earth,** etc.] Did Job imagine that God's universal law that sin must be followed by suffering would be reversed in his case, because of his expressions of indignation ?

5-21. He insists on the misery in the present life and the dishonour after death, which are the portion of sinners.

5, 6. The sinner's house shall be desolate. **Tabernacle**] RV 'tent.' **7^b.** His crafty plans shall be his ruin. **9. Gin**] i.e. trap. The word was originally 'grinne.' **9^b.** RV 'a snare shall lay hold on him.' **11. Drive him to his feet**] RV 'chase him at his heels.'

12. Hunger-bitten] exhausted by hunger.

13. Strength of his skin] RV 'members of his body.' **Firstborn of death**] i.e. a deadly disease. **14^a.** Render, 'He shall be rooted out of the tent he trusted was his own.' **King of terrors**] death.

15^a. RV 'There shall dwell in his tent that which is none of his,' i.e. his possessions will pass into the hands of strangers. Some read, 'Lilith shall dwell in his tent.' Lilith is a nocturnal demon, that plays the part of a vampire. **Brimstone shall be scattered**] a sign of God's wrath (cp. Gn 19²⁴ Ps 11⁶ Isa 34⁹).

17. No name in the street] he is quite forgotten. **19. Nephew**] RV 'son's son.'

20. Render, 'They of the west shall be astonished at his day (i.e. fate), and horror shall seize those on the east.' His name will be a byword throughout the world.

CHAPTER 19
Job's Fifth Speech

In this speech Job repeats his bitter complaints of God's injustice, and man's contemptuous abandonment of one formerly so loved and honoured. He appeals in broken utterances to his friends to pity him ; then from them he would fain appeal to posterity, wishing that he might engrave in the rock a declaration of his innocence, sure that those who read it in the after-time would feel the ring of sincerity and exonerate him of guilt. But, baffled by the callous unbelief of his friends and the impossibility of an appeal to generations unborn, he is driven, as he had been driven before, from man to God. Already he had uttered the conviction that God would vindicate him to the world. Now he reiterates the conviction and rises to a still loftier height in the assurance that he will be permitted to know of his vindication. He does not expect to be restored to life, nor yet to escape from Sheol, nor to renew the old fellowship with God. His deepest anxiety is that his honour should be cleared from stain, and the thought that this will be accomplished, and that he shall be allowed to see God reversing the verdict against him, fills him with overwhelming emotion.

1-22. After reproaching the friends for unfeeling conduct, Job again rejects their insinuations as to the reason of his calamities. He declares that God is treating him with unjustifiable severity, and that he has become estranged from all.

3. Ten times] i.e. continually : cp. Gn 31⁷ Nu 14²². **4. Mine error remaineth with myself**] i.e. 'is my own affair,' or, perhaps, 'injures myself alone.'

6. Job maintains, rightly, that his calamities were not due to his sins, but, wrongly, that they were the result of God's unjust action. As the reader knows from the Prologue, God permitted these trials in order to test and make manifest Job's uprightness. Job's ignorance of this explains and excuses much that otherwise might be deemed unpardonable.

7. Render, 'Behold, I shriek "Violence;" and am not answered. I clamour, and there is no justice.' **8.** Job's bewildered state : his mind sees no clear course. **9. Glory .. crown**] probably Job's righteousness, on which his sufferings seemed to throw doubt. **10. Mine hope**] viz. of recovery, or perhaps of happiness.

12. Troops] of afflictions : cp. 'battalions of sorrows' ('Hamlet,' IV, 5). **Raise up their way**] The figure is that of casting up a mound by which to attack a city. **15. They that dwell in mine house**] the servants or guests.

17. Render, 'My breath is offensive to my wife, and I am loathsome to the children of my (mother's) womb'; owing to his complaint. **18. I arose**, etc.] RV 'If I arise, they speak,' etc. ; i.e. the children mock him. **19. Inward**] i.e. intimate. **20^a.** The words describe his leanness. **I am escaped**, etc.] Some would substitute, 'And I am escaped with my flesh in my teeth' (cp. 13¹⁴). **22^b.** 'You cannot tear me to pieces enough !' An 'eater of flesh' is an Eastern expression for a slanderer.

23-27. Job had frequently expressed a hope that his righteousness would be proclaimed, as a reply to the insinuation of the friends that he was suffering for his sins (cp. 13¹⁵⁻¹⁹). We have also noted his longings, more or less definitely expressed, that he might find a mediator or vindicator who would do this office for him (cp. 9³²⁻³⁵ 17³). In this c. these longings, already turned into conviction in 16¹⁹⁻²¹, receive an even higher expression. He utters his belief (vv. 23-27) that God Himself will once more manifest Himself as his friend, and vindicate his character after his death, and that he shall be suffered to see God proclaiming his righteousness over his grave. It is unfortunate that the rendering 'Redeemer' and the traditional reference of the vindicator to Christ, together with the supposition that Job expects a resurrection of the body, have completely disguised the true meaning from most readers. The vindicator is God Himself, who is now his persecutor, and Job anticipates neither deliverance from death nor a resurrection of the body after death, nor even a deliverance from Sheol and renewed fellowship with

God, only the experience of one thrilling moment, when his shade will wake from its semi-conscious stupor to see God standing over his grave and declaring his innocence to the universe.

23, 24. Job longs to write down or, better still, to engrave upon a rock (a durable material to last into the future) his protestation of innocence. **Lead**] This may refer to the pouring of molten lead into the carved-out letters, though we have no other mention of such a practice.

23. Printed in a book] RV 'inscribed in a book'; but since a book quickly perishes, he substitutes the wish that his words might be graven in the imperishable rock.

25-27. Render, 'But as for me I know that my vindicator is alive (i.e. exists), and hereafter He will stand above the dust (either of Job or of his grave, as his vindicator). And after (the loss of) my skin, which has been destroyed (i.e. after my death) this shall be, I shall have vision of God, whom I shall gaze on as for me (i.e. as my friend), and mine eyes shall behold and not as a stranger.'

25. Redeemer] Heb. *Go'el*, from *ga'al*, 'to make a claim.' The *Go'el* was the next of kin whose duty it was to prevent land being sold out of the clan (Lv 25 25), and to avenge murder. See also Ruth 3, 4 and notes. Driver points out that the word means here the opposite to the Christian idea, viz. a deliverer, not from sin, but from affliction and wrong not due to sin. The best rendering here is 'Vindicator.'

26. In my flesh] rather, 'without' or 'apart from my flesh,' i.e. after death.

27. For myself] RM 'on my side.' **Not another**] or, 'not as another,' i.e. no longer estranged.

27b. RV 'my reins are consumed within me.' He faints with emotion at the thought of this vindication.

28. Probably with 'many ancient authorities' (RM) we should read 'him' instead of 'me' in the second line, and translate, 'If ye say, How we will persecute him, and find the root of the matter in him,' i.e. probe relentlessly till they find the secret sin which has led to Job's afflictions. Job proceeds in v. 29 to warn them of the vengeance that will overtake them.

CHAPTER 20
ZOPHAR'S SECOND SPEECH

Zophar ignores Job's conviction that God will one day establish his innocence, and proceeds to describe the short triumph of the wicked and his certain downfall and punishment at God's hand. Perhaps he wishes Job to apply the description to himself and take warning therefrom; though quite apart from that the speech is relevant to his argument

that the moral order of the world is not, as Job maintains, unrighteous.

3. The check of my reproach] RV 'the reproof which putteth me to shame.' He refers to Job's reproaches in c. 19. **10.** *Seek* **to please the poor**] i.e. seek in distress the favour of the humblest. For **his hands** Budde reads 'his offspring.' **Restore their goods**] which he had extorted from them in his prosperity. **11.** RV 'His bones are full of' (the vigour of) 'his youth, but it shall lie down with him in the dust.' **12, 13.** Like a sweetmeat which is retained in the mouth as long as possible, so the sinner revels in his sin.

14-16. The consequences of sin figuratively described: cp. Prov 23 29-32. **His meat**] better, 'this food of his,' i.e. sin. **Asps**] a species of serpent. **17. The floods, etc.**] RV 'the flowing streams of honey,' etc. : a figure of prosperity. **Surely he shall not feel quietness**] RM 'Because he knew no quietness in his greed.' His greed was never satisfied. **21.** RV 'There was nothing left that he devoured not ; therefore his prosperity shall not endure.'

22b. RV 'The hand of every one that is in misery shall come upon him'; i.e. all who have suffered at his hands.

23-29. The terrible death of the wicked.

24. Steel] better, 'bronze.' **25a.** RV 'He draweth it forth, and it cometh,' etc. **26.** RV 'All darkness is laid up for his treasures : a fire not blown *by man* shall devour him ; it shall consume that which is left in his tent.'

27. The v. seems to be Zophar's harsh retort (*a*) to Job's conviction of a vindicator from heaven of his innocence (16 19 19 25), and (*b*) to his appeal to the earth (see 16 18).

CHAPTER 21
JOB'S SIXTH SPEECH

Zophar, like the other friends, had insisted on the certain retribution for sin which befalls the wicked in this life. Now at length these views draw from Job a direct contradiction. It is his manner to wait till the three friends have spoken before he demolishes their case.

1-21. Job declares that as a matter of common observation bad men often go prosperously through life without any sign of God's displeasure.

4. To man] RM 'of man.' It is of God that Job complains. **And if, etc.**] RV 'And why should I not be impatient ?' **6.** Job trembles at the thought of the bold arraignment of God's government which he is about to make, or possibly at the remembrance of how unrighteous that government seems to him.

8. Unlike Job, who had lost all his children at a stroke. **12. Timbrel**] a small drum still used in Palestine. **Organ**] RV 'pipe.'

13. In a moment] without prolonged illness or pain, such as that from which he himself suffers. **14. Therefore**] better, 'though' or 'yet.'

16. Lo, their good, etc.] It may mean, They cannot control their fortunes : it must be God who has prospered them. **Is far**] rather, 'be far.' Job repudiates the devices of sinners. Possibly the whole v. is an objection uttered by the friends. **17, 18.** The vv. should be read as questions, the words 'How oft' being prefixed to each sentence. The answer implied is ', very seldom.'

19. RV '*Ye say*, God layeth up his iniquity for his children. Let him recompense it unto himself that he may know it.' The friends may argue that retribution may, at all events, fall upon the wicked man's children. To which Job replies that the sinner ought to suffer personally. Possibly, however, we should read in the first line, 'Let him not lay up iniquity for his children.' **21. Pleasure**] better, 'interest.'

22–26. It is presumptuous for the friends to settle what are the rules by which God decides the fate of men, God who judges even the angels. **24. Breasts**] mg. 'milk-pails.'

And his bones, etc.] RV 'And the marrow of his bones is moistened' : he is strengthened and refreshed.

27–34. Job says he knows that the friends' remarks are aimed at him. He is to take warning from the sure doom of the sinner. But experience does not justify their conclusions.

28. Prince] here probably means 'tyrant.'

29, 30. The meaning is : Have you not asked the traveller who has seen the world what are his conclusions on the subject ? Are you not familiar with the examples he quotes ? He would tell you that the wicked is spared in the day of destruction, and led away (safely) in the day of wrath. **31.** Who boldly rebukes or punishes the tyrant ? **32.** RM 'He is borne to the grave and keepeth watch over the tomb' ; i.e. he is buried with honours. Perhaps we should read, 'they keep watch.'

33. After his life of happiness he rests in the sweet-smelling earth. His career of successful wickedness draws many to imitate him, as indeed he had himself many to anticipate him.

34. Job concludes that the arguments of the friends are worthless, since he has shown that the wicked do not get their deserts.

So ends the second cycle of debate, the main theme of which is the assertion denied by Job, that trouble overtakes the evildoer. Job does not deal with this in his first and second speeches, which centre about his own calamities, and rise to the conviction that after his death God will reverse the verdict upon him, and that in Sheol he shall himself know of this vindication. In his third speech he

asserts against the friends the prosperity of the wicked.

The Third Series of Speeches
(Chs. 22–31)

Having failed to convince Job by the argument derived from God's greatness and wisdom, and to make good their assertion that it fared ill with the wicked, the friends have only one new line of argument left. This is a downright accusation of Job as a high-handed tyrant. Eliphaz adopts this, though he softens its severity by a fervent exhortation to Job, and a description of the felicity that awaits him if he will but make peace with God. The rest of the debate on his side is difficult to appreciate, owing to the uncertainty attaching to the distribution of the speeches. According to the present arrangement Bildad utters only a few sentences reasserting the greatness of God, and the impossibility that man should be pure in His sight. Zophar does not come forward at all. Several scholars infer from this that the poet means to suggest that the friends have exhausted their case. But since in other instances Bildad and Zophar substantially re peat what Eliphaz has said, the poet could very well have made them follow on the same lines here. Moreover, the symmetry is spoiled if Zophar does not speak. Since we have in 27 13-23 a description of the fate of the wicked exactly repeating the sentiments of the friends, it is a probable conjecture that this is part of Zophar's missing speech. In that case, however, there is plausibility in the view that Bildad's speech was originally longer than the few verses at present assigned to him. Several attempts at reconstruction have been made, the most recent (that in the Century Bible) assigns 25 2,3 26 5-14 to Bildad, 26 2-4 27 2-6, 11, 12 to Job, 27 13-23 (with possibly 27 7-10) to Zophar. 25 4-6 is regarded as a gloss based on 15 14-16, and it is supposed that the greater part of Job's reply to Bildad, which stood between 27 11 and 27 12, has been struck out on account of its boldness. If this or a similar view is correct, Bildad repeats the theme of the friends in the first cycle of debate, Zophar that in the second.

CHAPTER 22
The Last Speech of Eliphaz

1–11. Eliphaz ignoring Job's last speech, perhaps because he could not answer it, argues that God's treatment of man must be impartial, since He has nothing to gain or lose at his hands. Job can therefore only be suffering for his sins, and Eliphaz suggests those of which he has been guilty.

2b. RV 'Surely he that is wise is profitable to himself' : i.e. benefits himself only.

3. Pleasure] rather, 'advantage.' **4. RV**

'Is it for thy fear *of him* that he reproveth thee, that he entereth with thee into judgment?' Is it likely you are suffering as you do for your goodness?

5-9. The sins with which Eliphaz now definitely charges Job were the usual faults of Eastern rulers, such as oppression and injustice. There is no reason to suppose that there was any justification for these accusations, which indeed Job repudiates in chs. 29, 31. **6.** Cp. Ex 22 26 Dt 24 10-13, 17. **8. The honourable man]** RM 'Heb. he whose person is accepted.'

11ᵃ. LXX 'Thy light has become darkness.' **12-20.** The distance of God's abode and His majesty do not prevent Him from seeing men's deeds, as sinners thought in the days of the Flood. Let not Job follow in their steps. **14. In the circuit]** RM 'on the vault.' **15. Hast thou marked]** RV 'wilt thou keep.' **16. Out of time]** RV 'before their time.'

17. Do for them] RM 'do to us.' This and v. 18 are largely a repetition of parts of 21 14-16, and are regarded by some scholars as an insertion. **19. It]** the sinner's downfall. **20.** RV '*Saying*, Surely they that did rise up against us are cut off.' **The remnant of them]** RM 'that which remained to them.'

21-30. Eliphaz advises Job to make his peace with God, assuring him of restoration and prosperity. **22. The law]** RM 'instruction.' **23. Thou shalt put away]** RV 'if thou put away.' **24.** RV 'and lay thou *thy* treasure in the dust, and *the gold of* Ophir among the stones.' Fling thy earthly treasure away! **25.** Render, 'Yea, the Almighty shall be thy treasure and precious silver unto thee!' **27. Thou shalt pay thy vows]** Job should carry out the promises made to God in times of distress: cp. Ps 50 14.

28. When he has repented, all his desires will be granted. **29.** RM 'When they are made low,' i.e. Job's ways. If he should decline in prosperity he will assert with confidence that his ways will soon take an upward turn.

30. Render, 'He (God) shall even deliver him that is not innocent, (through Job's intercession). 'Yea, he shall be delivered through the cleanness of thy hands' (i.e. on account of Job's piety). This actually happens at the close of the book (42 8, 9).

CHAPTER 23

JOB'S SEVENTH SPEECH (Chs. 23, 24)

Job makes but slight reference to the remarks of Eliphaz, but continues to brood over the mysteries of God's dealings with himself (c. 23), and with mankind (c. 24). All seems to betoken a God that hideth Himself. Yet he is evidently calmer and more trustful in God's justice than in earlier speeches.

1-7. Job longs that he may find God and plead his cause before Him, confident that He will acquit him of guilt. **2ᵇ.** RM 'My hand is heavy upon my groaning,' i.e. I suppress it as much as I can. **6.** Render, 'Would He contend with me with great force? Nay, He would hear me!' A truer conception of God's character than e.g. in c. 9. **7ᵃ.** Lit. 'Then a righteous man would be pleading with him,' i.e. then it would appear that the man who pleads with Him is righteous (Davidson).

8, 9. The bright vision fades. God ever escapes his search. **8. Forward .. backward]** better, 'east' .. 'west.' **9. Left .. right]** better, 'north' .. 'south.' In ancient times the cardinal points were described by facing the east. **10ᵃ.** RM 'For he knoweth the way that is with me'; i.e. my innocence. **11. Declined]** RV 'turned aside.' **12ᵇ.** LXX better 'In my breast I have stored up his words.'

13-17. Job returns to the old tormenting idea that God must be resolved to hold him guilty, since he suffers so much in spite of his innocence. **14ᵇ.** Job is not the only victim of the inscrutable actions of Providence. **16. Soft]** RV 'faint.' **17.** RM 'For I am not dismayed because of the darkness, not because thick darkness covereth my face.' Job means that his sufferings do not distress him so much as the fact that it is God who so mysteriously sends them without just cause.

CHAPTER 24

JOB'S SEVENTH SPEECH (concluded)

1-25. Job continues to express his perplexity at the ways of Providence in the ordering of the world. The poor and the weak suffer; violence and wrong go unpunished. **1.** Render, 'Why are times not laid up' (i.e. set apart for doing justice) 'by the Almighty, and why do not those who know Him see His days?' The last clause means, Why do not the godly see signs of divine retribution?

2-12. Those who commit open violent crimes are left unpunished. **2. Remove the landmarks]** cp. Dt 19 14 27 17. **Feed *thereof*]** RV 'feed them': as if they were their own. **3. Pledge]** i.e. security for debt: cp. 22 6 1 S 12 3.

5-12. This passage depicts the misery of the homeless outcasts from society, driven into the rocks and mountains, unsheltered from the pitiless storms and hard put to it to save themselves and their children from starvation. The outcasts, lean with hunger like the wild ass in the desert, have to search diligently for the poor bits of food on which they keep body and soul together. **5ᶜ.** Render, 'The

Arabah' (the plain W. of Edom near Job's home) ' gives food to their young men.'

6. Merx reads, ' They reap by night in the field.' They are driven to theft to get food. ' Wicked ' should perhaps be ' rich.' **7.** RV ' They lie all night naked without clothing, and have no covering in the cold.'

9ᵃ. RV ' There are that pluck the fatherless from the breast.' The v. appears to introduce a new description. Since, however, vv. 10, 11 seem to continue v. 8, this v. is apparently out of place. **9ᵇ.** Perhaps we should read, ' And take the suckling of the poor in pledge.'

10. RV ' So that they go about naked without clothing, And being an-hungered they carry the sheaves.' Probably the outcasts are described as stealing the corn, and making oil and wine at the expense of the farmer.

12. Layeth not folly *to them*] render, ' regardeth not the wrong.'

13–17. Criminals who work at night. They hate (**rebel against**) the light of day, preferring darkness for their crimes.

13. They are of those] RV ' These are of them.' **14. With the light**] i.e. while it is still twilight. But with a very slight emendation we might read, ' when there is no light.'

16. Dig through houses] Walls of Eastern houses are often made of clay or sun-burnt bricks, which crumble easily : cp. Mt 6²⁰ RM. The robbers do not break in by the door since the threshold is sacred. **17.** If *one* **know**, etc.] RV ' For they know (are familiar with) the terrors.' **The shadow of death**] i.e. midnight. Light they shrink from, but midnight is their day.

18–21. These vv. cannot express the sentiments of Job, and we must either, with RM, prefix ' Ye say,' to indicate that Job is giving the views of the friends, or remove it from this speech either as an insertion or as part of a speech by one of the friends which has been displaced, or possibly as an interruption by one of them. RV renders v. 18, ' He is swift upon the face of the waters ; Their portion is cursed in the earth : He turneth not by the way of the vineyards.' The meaning is apparently that the doom of the wicked comes rapidly ; there is a curse upon his property ; he goes no more to gaze upon its prosperity. Vv. 19, 20 then describe the complete destruction of sinners. V. 21 render, ' Even he that evil entreated,' etc.

22–24. In these vv. we have Job's own view, viz. that (22) God continues the wicked in power, (23) His eyes watch over their welfare, and (24) when they die, it is in the maturity of old age like ripe ears of corn.

24. Tops of the ears of corn] Egyptian wall-paintings show that the ripe corn was cut just below the ears instead of near the ground as with us. The straw was ploughed in.

25. ' Who can dispute my contention ? '

CHAPTER 25
BILDAD'S LAST SPEECH

He ignores Job's questionings respecting the justice of God's rule, but declares His perfection and majesty, and the imperfection of all created things, repeating the theme of the first cycle.

2. With him] i.e. with God. **He maketh peace,** etc.] He keeps in order the hosts of heaven : cp. Isa 24²¹ Dan 10¹³. **3. Armies**] e.g. the angels and the elements. **4. Justified with God**] RM ' just before God ' ; a rebuke to Job's presumption : cp. 4¹⁷ 15¹⁴. **5ᵃ.** RV ' Behold, even the moon hath no brightness ' ; i.e. in the presence of God's glory.

With this c. the speeches of the three friends, according to their present allocation, come to an end, for it will be observed that Zophar, the third speaker, offers no reply. It is probable, however, that, as already pointed out, 27⁷⁻²³ are his concluding words. If the present arrangement is correct, we may perhaps infer that they came to the conclusion that they and Job regarded the whole question from different and irreconcilable standpoints, and that further argument was useless. Or the poet may intend to suggest by Bildad's brief speech and Zophar's silence that they felt their case to be exhausted. Indeed, (in 32¹) Elihu regards the friends as practically acknowledging themselves worsted in the debate.

CHAPTER 26
JOB'S EIGHTH SPEECH (Chs. 26, 27)

1–4. Job taunts Bildad with the worthlessness of his remarks as a solution of the problem.

2, 3, 4 are spoken ironically. **2.** *Him that is* **without power**] i.e. Job himself. **4. To whom hast thou uttered words ?**] i.e. surely not to Job who knows it already.

5–14. The manifestations of God's power and work in the world below, in earth and in heaven. Some scholars think these vv., which are quite in the tone of 25²,³, should be inserted after 25³ as a misplaced portion of Bildad's last speech, and that Job's remarks (26¹⁻⁴) are continued at 27².

5. The inhabitants] probably sea-monsters. The Babylonians believed in a judgment in Sheol under the ocean. **6.** RV ' Sheol ' (the place of the departed) ' is naked before him, and Abaddon ' (i.e. destruction, another name for Sheol, cp. Rev 9¹¹) ' hath no covering,' viz. from God. **7. The empty place**] RV ' empty space.' The writer seems to speak here of God stretching the vault of the northern heavens with their bright constellations above the atmosphere, and of the earth hanging unsupported, as instances of His power.

8. The retention of rain in the clouds as in a skin or bag : cp. 38 37. **9. He holdeth back**] RV 'He closeth in.' God veils His throne from men. **10.** Davidson renders, 'He hath drawn as a circle a bound upon the face of the waters (of the sea) at the confines of light and darkness' : i.e. God has marked out the horizon which forms to us the limit of vision. **11.** The mountains (see on 9 6) tremble in the earthquake. **12. Divideth**] RM 'stilleth.' The sea is a power hostile to God, that tosses its waves in impotent fury towards heaven.

Pride] RV 'Rahab,' i.e. the dragon of chaos, Tiâmat : cp. 7 12 9 13. **13.** Render, ' By His breath the heavens are bright (through the scattering of the storm clouds), and His hand pierceth the flying serpent,' or dragon, which was supposed to cause darkness or eclipse by swallowing the heavenly bodies : see on 3 8. **14.** Job (or Bildad), after thus depicting the marvels of God's working, declares that what he has said is but a faint whisper of His power.

CHAPTER 27
Job's Eighth Speech (concluded)

1–6. Job protests that he is innocent.

Vv. **1–6** are an enlargement of what Job had previously said (13 16) of his determination not to admit that he was being punished for his sins, since he felt that he was innocent of any great offence. This much is plain, but the rest of the c. (vv. 7–23) is puzzling ; inasmuch as the sentiments expressed regarding the fate of the wicked seem opposed to Job's views in the rest of the book when he enlarges on the prosperity of sinners in this life : see e.g. c. 21 and notes. It is therefore commonly considered that vv. 7–23 are really a misplaced speech of Zophar's corresponding with the final speeches of Eliphaz and Bildad (chs. 22, 25), and this view is strongly confirmed by the subject-matter. Vv. 11, 12 are Job's (see intro. to chs. 22–31).

1. Parable] i.e. discourse : cp. Nu 23 7. **2. My judgment**] RV 'my right.' God has not yet vindicated Job's uprightness, on which his sufferings throw doubt. **3**ᵃ. RV ' For my life is yet whole in me.' The v. is a parenthesis, explaining that Job is in full possession of all his faculties, when he makes this deliberate utterance. **Spirit of God**] cp. Gn 2 7. **4.** He will not acknowledge guilt of which he is unconscious. **5. I should justify you**] i.e. by admitting their contention that he was suffering for his sins. **6**ᵇ. RM ' My heart doth not reproach *me* for any of my days.'

7–23. The fate of the wicked. Here it would seem that Zophar speaks.

7. Hypocrite] RV ' godless.' **8. Though he hath gained**] RM ' when God cutteth him

off.' **15. Buried in death**] rather, ' buried by death.' ' Death' should here be rendered, ' pestilence' : cp. Jer 15 2 18 21. In such a case there would be only maimed funeral rites. **18. As a moth**] like the frail chrysalis or cocoon. **As a booth**] like the temporary shelter of the vineyard watchman.

19–23. The passage refers to the final fall of the wicked. In the Persian sacred books we read that the dead pious man is led by an angel created by his own good life to the ' bridge of the gatherer' leading to heaven, whilst a storm sweeps the wicked man to hell. The same idea seems to occur here. The sinner is not ' gathered,' but blown away into darkness.

CHAPTER 28
The Mystery of Divine Wisdom

In this famous chapter Job declares that Wisdom—that is, the principle of the divine government of the world—is a mystery not to be solved by man. Man's wisdom lies in fearing God, and in departing from evil. But this conclusion is quite at variance with the position taken by Job in the chs. before and after it. ' It might no doubt be supposed that Job has reached a calmer mood ; and abandoning the attempt to discover a speculative solution of the difficulties which distress him, finds man's wisdom to consist in the practical fulfilment of life (v. 28). But if Job has risen to this tranquil temper, how comes it that he falls back into complainings (30 20-23) and dissatisfaction at not having been justified by God (31 35) ? And, further, if he has reached by the unaided force of his own meditations this devout and submissive frame of mind, how is the ironical tone of the Divine speeches (chs. 38f.) to be accounted for ? If he is already resigned to the inscrutability of the divine ways, how does it need to be again pointed out to him ?' (Driver). These considerations have induced many scholars to regard the c. as a later insertion. Some have regarded it as a part of Zophar's third speech, but its quiet beauty and detachment in temper forbid this view. The c. constitutes an independent poem, which a reader may have inserted here to indicate that the discussion which has just closed deals with subjects too lofty for human understanding.

1–11. Man can discover precious metals by mining processes, but where can Wisdom be found ?

1. Surely] RM ' For.' Perhaps the question in vv. 12 and 20, ' Where shall Wisdom be found ?', ' Whence then cometh Wisdom ?' may be understood at the beginning of this verse. It has even been suggested that it once stood at the beginning and has been omitted by accident.

1. **Vein**] RV 'mine.' Remains of mines have been found in Edom a little N. of Petra, and it is well known that copper and turquoise mines were worked by the Egyptians in the Sinaitic Peninsula at least as early as the reign of Sa-nekht, the founder of the third Egyptian dynasty, i.e. according to Prof. Flinders Petrie about 4950 B.C. (see his 'Researches in Sinai'). *Where* **they fine** *it*] RV 'which they refine.' **2. Brass**] rather, 'copper.' **3.** Render, 'Man setteth an end to darkness, and searcheth out to the furthest bound the stones,' etc., a reference to mining operations.

4. RV 'He (the miner) breaketh open a shaft away from where men sojourn ; They (miners) are forgotten the foot *that passeth by* (overhead) ; They hang afar from men, they swing to and fro (i.e. by ropes).' The word rendered 'shaft' should be 'channel.' Ancient mines were often not vertical shafts, but sloping tunnels. A slight change would give 'He breaketh open a shaft away from light.'

5. As it were fire] RV 'as it were by fire,' a reference to mining operations. **7. A path**] the miner's tunnel. **9.** The miner's excavations. **10. Rivers**] RM 'passages.' **11ª.** RV 'He bindeth (with clay) the streams that they trickle not,' i.e. he prevents water from entering the mine.

12–28. Man can discover some things by his cleverness, but Wisdom, the mystery of the universe and its ordering, is beyond his ken. It is the secret of God who ordained its existence.

13. The price thereof] LXX reads, 'the way thereof.' **14. The depth**] the primeval abyss supposed to lie under the earth : cp. Gn 1². **15f.** Cp. Prov 3 14, 15 8 10, 11. **17. Crystal**] RV 'glass' : known to the ancients, but extremely costly. **18. No mention**] because there is no comparison. **Rubies**] RM 'pearls.' **22. Destruction**] Heb. *Abaddon*, the realm of the dead. The fame of Wisdom, but not the knowledge of it, has reached these gloomy regions.

23. See on **12–28.** Since God is the creator of the universe, and knows even its most secret recesses, He must know where Wisdom is to be found. Not only so, but the very work of creation and the adjustment of natural phenomena are indications of Wisdom, and prove not merely God's knowledge of Wisdom's abode, but his possession of Wisdom itself. **25.** RM 'When he maketh a weight for the wind : yea, he meteth out the waters by measure,' i.e. the regulation by God of the forces of nature. **26. A decree for the rain**] i.e. for its regulation. **27.** 'When God ordered creation, Wisdom was present to Him ; He declared it, gave it existence, and contemplated it in all its fulness with divine approval'

(Gibson). **28.** Man's wisdom is a distinct thing from the Divine Wisdom. It is that right conduct which accompanies reverence for a holy God.

The description of Wisdom in this c. closely connects the book of Job in this respect with the other Wisdom literature of the OT., viz. Proverbs and Ecclesiastes. The personification is, however, less distinct in Job. Wisdom here is only God's attribute. Prov 8 22-31 should be carefully compared with this c.

CHAPTERS 29–31

These chs. form a section by themselves, in which Job reviews his life. He first of all draws a picture of his past prosperous career, when he was happy and respected (c. 29). With this he contrasts his present condition, when men he once despised now hold him in contempt, and he is in pain and sorrow and disgrace (c. 30). Finally, he reasserts his innocence of wickedness in any form (c. 31).

CHAPTER 29
JOB'S PAST GREATNESS AND HAPPINESS

Job mournfully recalls the days of God's favour, and the prosperity and honour he once enjoyed. In this c. we have the picture of a great and worthy chieftain looked up to and respected by all. It confirms the description of Job's importance in c. 1.

3. Candle] RV 'lamp' ; a figure of God's favour. **4. Days of my youth**] RV 'ripeness of my days.' **Secret**] RM 'friendship.' **Tabernacle**] RV 'tent.' **6.** A figure of prosperity : cp. Dt 33 24.

7. Through the city] RV 'unto the city.' Job went with other elders to administer justice at the city gate. Observe that Job did not live in the city ; his usual abode was in his camp. But he was influential in the city, just as a great Arab prince is sometimes in our own times.

8. Hid themselves] because of the awe which Job inspired. **11. Gave witness to me**] i.e. to my goodness, which it saw. **14.** Lit. 'Justice clothed itself in me.' He was the very personification of justice. **Diadem**] RM 'turban.'

16. The cause *which* **I knew not**] RV 'the cause of him that I knew not.'

18. As the sand] RM 'as the phœnix.' This was a fabulous bird alluded to in Egyptian, Hebrew, and Arabian tradition. It was supposed to be immortal, burning itself in its nest every thousand years and renewing its life in the flames.

19, 20. The verbs should be read in the future tense. **19. By**] RV 'to' : cp. Ps 1 3.

Dew] cp. Prov 19 12 Dt 32 2. The dew was an emblem of prosperity in a land where rain was infrequent. **20ª.** The respect paid him would not fail him. **20**ᵇ. His physical powers should endure : cp. Gn 49²⁴, 'His bow abode in strength.'

21–25. These vv. would more naturally follow v. 10, and some think this was their original position. **22. Dropped upon them**] as refreshing rain : cp. Dt 32². **23. The latter rain**] the spring rains as contrasted with those of the autumn. **24.** *If* I laughed, etc.] RM 'I smiled on them when they had no confidence,' i.e. to encourage them. **24**ᵇ. They failed to remove his cheerfulness. **25.** Job speaks as if he used to be the natural guide and comfort of his fellow-men.

CHAPTER 30
Job's Present Misery

Job bitterly contrasts his present with his past condition, as described in c. 29. It must be borne in mind that Job was now outcast and beggared.

1–8. Job complains that he is insulted by abject outcasts, the class of broken men who are expelled from respectable tribes and live by thieving. They are common E. of Jordan in the nomadic regions.

2ᵇ. RV 'Men in whom ripe age' (or vigour) 'is perished.' **3. Solitary**] RV 'gaunt.'

Flying, etc.] render, 'Fugitives in the desert on the eve of want and ruin.' **4.** Render, 'They pluck salt-wort' (a plant sometimes eaten by the abjectly poor) 'among the bushes, and the roots of the white broom to warm them.' This broom is a distinctive shrub of the southern desert hills : cp. 1 K 19⁴ RM.

7. Render, 'They snore under bushes and huddle under thorny shrubs.' **8**ᵇ. RV 'They were scourged out of the land.'

9–14. A description of a poor old man mobbed and worried by the rabble. Or possibly 11–15 refers to God as assailing him with troops of afflictions. The Heb. is very obscure.

11. RV renders, 'For he hath loosed his cord, and afflicted me, and they have cast off the bridle before me.' RM gives another reading, 'my cord (or bowstring).' Perhaps 'loosed my bowstring' is the best of these alternatives : cp. 29²⁰. Conder suggests, 'For they spy the (tent) door and insult me, and stretch out a headstall before my face.' This was an insult and one which is still customary. The headstall means that the man is regarded as an ass.

12. Conder suggests, 'The brood (of boys) stand upon my right hand (an insult, for the place of honour was on the right hand). They trip up my feet and jostle me on the dangerous paths.' They no longer make room for him. The last clause is more usually regarded as a metaphor from a siege ; so RV 'And they cast up against me their ways of destruction.'

13. They have no helper] Perhaps we should read, 'There is none to check them.' **15. My soul**] RV 'my honour.'

16–31. Job laments his misery of mind and body, and the severity of God.

17. Are pierced] by acute pain. **Sinews**] render, 'gnawing pains.' **18. Changed**] lit. 'disfigured.' His complaint causes painful changes in his appearance. **20. Regardest me** *not*] rather, 'lookest at me,' with indifference to his sufferings. **22.** Figurative of the storm of God's anger. **Dissolvest my substance**] RV 'dissolvest me in the tempest.' **23. House appointed**] RM 'house of meeting.' Job is convinced that his sufferings can only end in death. **24.** Render, 'Doth not a sinking man stretch out his hand, and cry out in his calamity ?'

27ᵃ. Figurative of his agitated condition. **27**ᵇ. **Prevented me**] RV 'are come upon me.' **28**ᵃ. RM 'I go blackened, but not by the sun' ; the result perhaps of his disease : see v. 30. **28**ᵇ. RV 'I stand up in the assembly and cry for help.' **29. Dragons**] RV 'jackals.'

Owls] lit. 'daughters of screeching.' These are animals associated with desolate places : cp. Isa 13²¹, ²². **30**ᵃ. RV 'My skin is black, and *falleth* from me.' **31. Organ**] RV 'pipe.' Job's happiness is turned to sorrow.

CHAPTER 31
Job protests the Innocence of his past Life

Job's virtues are those of a great Arab prince, such as are admired still : namely, blameless family life, consideration for the poor and weak, charity, modesty, and generosity concerning wealth, pure religion (according to his creed), the absence of vindictive feelings, hospitality to strangers, fearless honesty and just dealings.

1–12. Sensual sins.

1. I made a covenant with mine eyes] Job resolved to keep a guard over them that they should not transgress. **Why then should I think ?**] RV 'How then should I look ?'

2ᵃ. RM 'What portion *should I have* of God ?' i.e. How would God visit such sin ? **3.** *Is* not] RV 'Is it not.'

6. Even balance] i.e. balances of justice. In the Egyptian Book of the Dead the soul is represented as being weighed in the balance before Osiris at the judgment. **10.** To grind at the mill is a menial task, the work of slaves.

12. The evil results of lust : cp. Prov 6²⁴⁻³⁵.

13–23. Sins of oppression.

14. Riseth up] i.e. to judge. **18. He**] the fatherless. **Her**] the widow. **21. When I saw my help in the gate**] Job could have counted on the judges supporting his side of the question. **Gate**] see on 29⁷. **22. Bone**] i.e. collar-bone. **23.** The thought of God's displeasure checked him, and a sense of His majesty kept him from sinning.

26-28. A reference to the worship of the heavenly bodies (cp. 2 K 21 3-5 Jer 44 17f. Ezk 8 16. **27. My mouth hath kissed my hand**] a form of idolatrous worship : cp. 1 K 19 18.

29f. The high moral tone is very significant: cp. Mt 5 44 Ro 12 19-21. **31.** Render, 'If the men in my tent have not said, Who can find one that hath not been satisfied with his flesh?' : i.e. Job had more than satisfied his servants. **33ᵃ.** Render, 'If I hid my fault like a common man' : i.e. as men usually do.

34. Did I fear] RV 'Because I feared.' Job declares that he had nothing to hide in his conduct and did not fear enquiry.

35-37. Job breaks off and does not complete the sentence begun in v. 33. For his whole soul is moved by the words he has just uttered, and with the proud assertion of his innocence he challenges God to answer him, to give him the writing which contained the charges against him. Proudly, even with God's stigma upon him, he would enter God's presence, the certainty of his rectitude changing the disgrace into distinction. Most scholars feel that the addition of vv. 38-40 spoils the effect of this splendid conclusion.

35. RV 'Oh that I had one to hear me ! (Lo, here is my signature, let the Almighty answer me !) And that I had the indictment which mine adversary hath written !' Job puts his signature to the declaration of his innocence. The **adversary** is God. **37.** Conscious of his integrity, Job would lay bare every act of his life to God.

38-40. The grand challenge thrown down by Job in vv. 35-37 seems to form such a suitable conclusion to his speeches that most scholars hold that vv. 38-40 stood originally in an earlier part of the c., e.g. after vv. 8 or 25.

40. Cockles] RM 'noisome weeds.' Job for the last time has maintained the integrity of his past life, and expressed his readiness to answer all charges of guilt brought against him. The third and final series of his speeches comes to an end. It cannot be said that any explanation of the ways of Providence has been put forward so far, but the popular theories that suffering must always imply previous sin, and that compensation according to conduct is invariably meted out to both good and bad in this world, have been refuted. Moreover, we see the noble spectacle of a good man in adversity clinging in spite of all his trials to his uprightness. Job has been able to find no foothold in the thought that God would revive him, or that the life beyond the grave will restore him to blessed fellowship with God. Nor has he gained any hope that the government of the world will become more righteous. But he has reached the assurance that God will vindicate his innocence, and that he shall be permitted to know of this vindication.

CHAPTERS 32–37
The Speeches of Elihu

It is the view of almost all scholars that the speeches of Elihu are a later addition. The grounds for this view are the following. His presence comes upon the reader with surprise, he is not mentioned with the other friends in the Prologue, and we have had no intimation that he has all the while been listening to the debate. It is still more remarkable that he is not mentioned at the close. Here God passes judgment on Job and the friends, and it is strange that Elihu is ignored. If the author intended Elihu to represent the true view, why did he not represent God as praising him, if not, why is he not condemned with the friends ? This silence is the more surprising in view of the contents of the speeches. Elihu blames the friends for the ineffectiveness of their attack, yet he adopts somewhat the same attitude and repeats their arguments, though passing, to some extent, beyond them. He elaborates the thought that suffering is discipline, and may actually be an expression of the goodness of God. He works out this vein of argument more fully than the three friends. Still it is difficult to think that, after the debate between Job and the friends had been exhausted, the poet should have introduced a new speaker unless he had something better to say, unless, in fact, he could sum up the case and decide between the disputants. Job could have met the arguments of Elihu as easily as those of the friends. We may be well assured that the author who made him triumph over them would never have let him be silenced by the similar contentions of Elihu. It is also noteworthy that Elihu in his description of celestial marvels to some extent anticipates the speech of God which is to follow, and thus robs it of some of its effect. The style of the speeches is throughout on a much lower level, they are prolix and hard to understand, and the language is more coloured by Aramaic influences. It is also noteworthy that the opening words in Jehovah's speech, 'Who is this that darkeneth counsel by words without knowledge ?', which refer to Job, do not well admit the view that another speaker has made a lengthy speech since Job finished speaking. There are minor arguments that need not be mentioned here.

A few scholars, however, still regard the speeches as part of the original poem. It is argued that the function of Elihu is to exhibit and correct the spiritual pride of Job, which he had himself failed to detect and overcome. Elihu brings home his fault to him, and shows how the discipline through which God has brought him was designed to purify him of his unsuspected sin and raise him to a loftier spiritual eminence. In spite of the subtle arguments urged in favour of this view it must be dismissed as very unlikely. The main lesson of the book on this theory nowhere finds clear expression, while the debate is largely irrelevant. The representation of the design of God does not harmonise with that in the Prologue, and the Divine speeches lose much of their significance. Moreover, according to the Prologue, which represents the author's view, Job is a truly blameless man, acknowledged as such by God Himself. With this Elihu does not agree, hence it was not the original author who introduced him into the book. Nor is it the fact that Elihu convicts Job, it is the vision of God that brings him to contrition.

The reasons for the insertion of these speeches lie on the surface. The author wished to reassert the doctrine held by the friends, but also to develop aspects of it which had not received due weight. He dwells on the value of affliction for discipline, and lays much stress on the goodness of God. He also wished to rebuke Job for his unbecoming words about God. And he seems to have dissented from the poet, to whom we owe the rest of the book, in his representation of Job's character before his trial, while he also thought it an impropriety to represent God as condescending to debate with Job.

CHAPTER 32

The Speeches of Elihu

Elihu explains his reasons for intervening in the debate.

2. Elihu] Heb. 'He is my God.' **Buzite**] In Gn 22 21 Buz is closely connected with Uz (RV), which was Job's country. To the Assyrians Huz and Buz ('Haza' and 'Baza') were known as places not far from Edom.

Ram] uncertain. It occurs again in Ruth 4 19 1 Ch 2 9, 10. **He justified himself rather than God**] Job, in asserting his own innocence so warmly, had charged God with injustice in treating him, as he thought, as if he were guilty. **3.** The friends had not succeeded in refuting Job's arguments, and they only asserted that he was wicked without proving it. **8. A spirit**] a divine impulse which moved him to speak.

13. RV 'Beware lest ye say, We have found wisdom; God may vanquish him, not man.' The friends must not excuse themselves for their failure on the score that Job was too clever for man to debate with. Job had not yet contended with Elihu, and the latter intended to use different arguments. The author criticises the poet for letting God intervene in the debate.

15. Elihu describes the discomfiture of the friends. **19. Belly**] We use 'heart' in the same way, of the emotions. **New bottles**] i.e. new wine-skins. If wine was put into new skins before it had finished fermenting it might cause them to burst : cp. Mt 9 17. **21, 22.** Elihu will show no partiality to either side in the remarks he is about to make. **22**ᵇ. RV '*Else* would my Maker soon take me away.'

CHAPTER 33

The Speeches of Elihu (continued)

1–13. Elihu blames Job for regarding himself as sinless, and complaining that God is his enemy and will not answer him.

4. Elihu feels that God is inspiring his mind to speak aright. **6.** RV 'Behold, I am toward God even as thou art.' Job need have no fear in facing a man like himself, such as he had felt about God : cp. 9 32 13 21. **9.** Cp. 9 21 RV 10 7 16 17 27 4-6. But Elihu exaggerates Job's protestation of innocence : cp. 7 21 13 26.

10, 11. Cp. 13 24, 27 19 11 30 21. **12**ᵇ. God is too great to have His actions questioned by mortals : to do so is presumptuous. **13. For**] i.e. 'because.' Why does Job complain because God does not explain His treatment of him ? God does answer man, as he proceeds to point out in two ways.

14–30. Elihu especially insists that the purposes of God's visitations are often to teach and to discipline ; vv. 15–18 represent one method of God's training, vv. 19–24 another. 'In the first Elihu probably had Eliphaz in his eyes, in the second it is all but certain he had Job' (Cox).

15. Cp. the vision of Eliphaz in c. 4. **16. Sealeth**] Impresses on the mind like a seal. **18. He keepeth back**] RM 'That he may keep back.' **22. The destroyers**] or, 'the slain.'

23, 24. An angel messenger, interpreting God's will, comes to the sufferer and shows him what right conduct is. Thereupon God declares that He has found a means of reconciliation (**ransom**), perhaps the man's repentance, and pardons him. Some regard the angel as a mediator who comes between man and God and pleads his cause. 'Jewish prayers show that the "interpreter" of this verse was always identified in their minds with the expected Redeemer of Israel' : thus, 'Raise up for us the righteous Interpreter, say, I have found a ransom' (Cook).

26. He will render, etc.] God restores to the penitent his righteousness, i.e. a position of acceptance with Him. **27.** Render, 'He (the penitent) singeth before men and saith, I have sinned and .. it was not requited to me.'

29, 30. Elihu has now shown Job the loving purposes of God in chastening man. Job himself had only advanced to the idea of **his**

own vindication after death. Elihu teaches the use of evil in this present life. **32. I desire to justify thee**] I am ready to admit you are right if you can prove it.

CHAPTER 34
THE SPEECHES OF ELIHU (continued)

1-9. Elihu appeals to his hearers to judge the matter. He protests against the complaints of Job that he was treated unjustly by God, and that it was no profit to be righteous.

3. Cp. 12 11. **4. Judgment**] RV 'that which is right.' **5. My judgment**] i.e. my right.

6. RV 'Notwithstanding my right I am *accounted* a liar : My wound is incurable, *though I am* without transgression.' **Right** = innocence. **7, 8.** Elihu implies that, in indulging in such reckless remarks, Job was linking himself with sinners. **7**b. Cp. 15 16. **9.** Cp. e.g. chs. 9 and 21.

10-37. Elihu meets Job's doubts. The omnipotent God cannot commit injustice : the idea is inconsistent with the conception of One who creates and sustains and governs all mankind. Instances are given of His judgments.

13. God has not been entrusted with His rule by a higher Power.

14a. RM 'If he cause his heart to return to himself,' i.e. if God ceased to concern Himself with the affairs of man, and only selfishly regarded Himself. If He acted thus He might withdraw from man the breath of life He had given him (14b), and then he would perish (15).

17. Render, 'Doth one hating right rule ?' The thought is the same as Abraham's, 'Shall not the Judge of all the earth do right ?' (Gn 18 25) : cp. also Ro 3 5. Of course this begs the very question in dispute. **19. Accepteth not**] RV 'respecteth not,' shows no undue partiality to. **20.** The impartiality of God's judgments. **Without hand**] i.e. without human agency.

23. RV 'For he needeth not further to consider a man, that he should go before God in judgment.' God at the same time sees and judges every act : there is no need to set apart a special time for trying man. **24. Without number**] RM 'without inquisition.' **25. He knoweth**] RV 'he taketh knowledge of.'

28. Oppression causes God's intervention.

29. Make trouble] RV 'condemn.'

30. RV 'That the godless man reign not, that there be none to ensnare the people.'

31. Render, 'For hath any said unto God, I have borne *chastisement* though I offend not ?'

32. 'Show me my sin, and I will give it up.' In vv. 31-33 Job is rebuked for presumption in criticising God's treatment of him.

33. RV 'Shall his recompence be as thou wilt, that thou refusest it ? For thou must choose and not I : Therefore speak what thou

knowest.' Elihu asks Job ironically if he is to lay down the law to God.

34. RV 'Men of understanding will say unto me, yea, every wise man that heareth me.'

36. Answers for] RV 'answering like.'

Elihu does not really advance on the position of the friends. Omnipotence cannot go wrong, the supreme tribunal cannot be unjust. This is just the point to be proved, and the proof derived from the fact that God gives and sustains man's life, while sound as far as it goes, does not go far enough. God may have His own ends to serve in this, rather than be prompted by benevolence, and the hard facts of human misery are left to suggest the darker interpretations of God.

CHAPTER 35
THE SPEECHES OF ELIHU (continued)

1-8. Elihu (34 9) had charged Job with saying that there was no advantage in being righteous. He now deals with this assertion.

2. Right] RV '*thy* right,' thy just cause.

3. *If I be cleansed* **from my sin**] RV 'more than if I had sinned.' **4. Thy companions**] those who held the same views.

5-8. Elihu points to the infinite distance between God and man, and shows that He cannot be injured by the evil or benefited by the good which we do. But a man's conduct is most important both to himself and to his fellows.

9-16. Coming to the problem why the cry of the oppressed seems often unanswered, Elihu replies it is because there is a lack of real prayer and trust in God. Hence Job must not expect to be heard so long as he murmurs at the way God treats him.

9. They make *the oppressed* **to cry**] rather, 'men cry out.' **10. Who giveth songs in the night**] i.e. who delivers in the night of trouble, and causes men to sing with joy. **12.** Render, 'They cry because of the pride of evil men, but none giveth answer ' ; i.e. because there is no humble, trustful appeal to God.

13. Vanity] or, unreality. **14. Shalt**] rather, 'dost.' Although Job thinks God is indifferent to his cause, it is not forgotten, only he must wait patiently. **15.** RV 'But now, because he hath not visited in his anger, neither doth he greatly regard arrogance ' ; i.e. because God does not seem to punish sin at once. **16. In vain**] i.e. with foolish views.

In this c. Elihu follows Eliphaz in explaining that righteousness is profitable to the upright, since God is too exalted to have any interest of His own to serve in perversion of justice. He urges further that the reason for God's silence when the wretched appeal to Him is that their cry is prompted by their selfishness. Both arguments are quite irrelevant to the case of Job.

CHAPTER 36

The Speeches of Elihu (continued)

1–15. Elihu maintains the wisdom and impartial justice of the rule of God. His purpose is to discipline and improve men, even by their afflictions.

3. From afar] from a review of the whole universe. **4. He**] RV 'one'; i.e. Elihu.

7b. RV 'But with kings upon the throne he setteth them for ever.' **9. Their work**] i.e. their faults. **Exceeded**] RV 'behaved themselves proudly.' **12. Without know-ledge**] without learning God's lessons.

13. Hypocrites] RV 'godless.' **Heap up wrath**] RV 'lay up anger'; they cherish rebellious feelings. **They cry not**] in submission. The way the godless take God's chastening is contrasted with that of the righteous, vv. 7 f. **14.** Is **among**] render, '*perisheth* like.'

15. RM 'He delivereth the afflicted by their afflictions, and openeth their ears by adversity.' Such are the effects of God's discipline when taken in the right spirit.

16–21. Elihu applies these remarks to Job, urging him to humble himself instead of remaining rebellious.

17. Hast fulfilled] RV 'art full of.' Job acts like the wicked under affliction : cp. v. 13. **18.** Render, 'For beware lest wrath lead thee away into mockery : neither let the greatness of the ransom (Job's sufferings) turn thee aside,' i.e. into rebellion.

19. Nothing but affliction can save him. **20. The night**] probably, of judgment. **People**] rather, 'nations.' **21. Iniquity**] i.e. rebelliousness.

22–37 24. The wonders of the heavens testify to the majesty and unsearchableness of God. Let Job refrain from judging Him. **22. Exalteth by**] RV 'doeth loftily in.' **Who teacheth like him**] This is Elihu's great point, that afflictions are intended to teach, to discipline, and to purify even the good.

23. Iniquity] RV 'unrighteousness.' **26–37 13.** Elihu illustrates the marvellous workings of God by a vivid description of a rising storm.

27. The formation of rain. RV 'He draweth up the drops of water which distil in rain from his vapour.' **29b.** RV 'The thunderings of his pavilion'; i.e. of the clouds. **30.** Render, 'Behold, He spreadeth His light around Him, and covereth it with the deeps' (lit. 'roots') 'of the sea' : see on 26 5 and cp. Ps 104 2, 3. Modern scholars generally correct the text ; some read with Duhm, 'Behold, He spreadeth His mist about Him, And He covereth the tops of the mountains.'

31. The people] rather, 'the peoples.' The purpose of storms may be either punishment or a bountiful provision. **32.** RV 'He covereth his hands with the lightning' (to conceal them) : 'and giveth it a charge that it strike the mark.'

33. The present text is difficult. The vowel-points should probably be somewhat altered, and the v. should run, 'The noise thereof telleth concerning Him as one that kindles His wrath against wickedness.'

CHAPTER 37

The Speeches of Elihu (concluded)

2. The thunder is frequently called the **voice** of God : cp. Ps 29. **Sound**] RM 'muttering.' **4. Them**] the flashes and thunderclaps. **6c.** RV 'And to the showers of his mighty rain.' **7b.** RV 'That all men whom he hath made may know *it*.' The suspension of work by storms shows men that they are subject to a higher Power.

9. Render, 'The whirlwind comes from its chamber, and cold from the scatterers,' i.e. from the winds (so RM), which scatter the clouds. But we should probably read, 'from its storehouses,' with a trifling change.

10. Straitened] RM 'congealed.' **11.** RV 'Yea, he ladeth the thick cloud with moisture : he spreadeth abroad the cloud of his lightning.' **12.** The lightning flashes and falls in obedience to the behest of God. **13.** Probably the first line should run, 'Whether it be for correction for his land.' The word translated ' or ' has been repeated by mistake.

14–24. A series of questions to Job, intended to produce submission and belief in God's providence.

15. Dost thou know ?] can you explain ? **16. The balancing of the clouds**] the way in which they are poised. **17.** Render, 'When thy clothes are hot, and the earth still by reason of the south wind.' Vv. 17, 18 refer to the sultry weather and sky of brass before the storm breaks. **18. Looking glass**] RV 'mirror' (of metal). **19–20.** Elihu shrinks from the presumptuous thought of contending with the Almighty, such as Job had uttered.

20b. RV 'Or should a man wish that he were swallowed up.'

21. RM 'And now men cannot look on the light when it is bright in the skies, when the wind hath passed and chased them.'

22. Fair weather is literally 'gold.' The author probably intended 'brightness,' for which he may have used a different word. The reference may be to the Northern Lights.

23, 24. Elihu concludes by summing up the character of God as He manifests Himself to man. Though His dealings may be beyond man's comprehension, yet He is just as well as mighty, and will not afflict unjustly. But He expects humility, not presumption from His creatures. **24. Respecteth**] RV 'regardeth.'

Wise of heart] i.e. confident in their own wisdom, as Job was in Elihu's opinion.

CHAPTERS 38–41
THE SPEECHES OF THE ALMIGHTY

When the human debate was over, and Job had proudly asserted his readiness to confront God, conscious of his innocence (31 35-37), there was nothing left, if the contest was to be decided, except a direct intervention of God. This Job had himself again and again demanded. He had challenged God to meet him and justify the treatment He accorded to him. He complains bitterly that God evades him, and lets him suffer, though He knows that he is innocent. Now at last God speaks. But not at all as Job had demanded. For he had implored God to remove His hand from him, in other words, to release him from pain that he might not be distracted by it, and not to make him afraid with His terror, since otherwise he might be driven, though innocent, to confess to guilt. God does not heal him, and He speaks out of the storm. Nor does the matter of His utterance conform to what Job had demanded, any more than the manner of it. For He does not deal with the question of Job's sin, or tell him the reason of his affliction. He puts question after question to him, challenging him to explain the mysteries of the universe. These he cannot comprehend ; with what right then does he criticise God's government of the world ?

It is a surprise to some that God should be represented by the poet as taking this line. Why should He speak with such irony, and why not offer the man who had suffered so deeply some explanation and comfort ? Partly because Job had brought deserved rebuke on himself for his attack on God's rule of the world. Partly because he needed to rise to a higher point of view from which he could see the complexity of the problem. Moreover, God does not explain to Job the cause of his suffering, since the supreme lesson of the book is that he becomes so sure of God that he knows his affliction to be in harmony with God's righteousness, though he is wholly incapable of reconciling the two intellectually. But after he has reached this position God restores him to health and prosperity.

The vital element in his experience is not the speech of God, but the vision of God. It is in a true relation to God, which is possible only to him to whom the divine vision is vouchsafed, that Job learns to trust God utterly. And as he looks back on the charges he has brought against Him, whom in this deep, mystical manner he has just come to know, he loathes the words he has uttered, and repents in dust and ashes. 'I had heard of thee by the hearing of the ear, but now mine eye seeth thee.'

CHAPTER 38
THE FIRST SPEECH OF THE ALMIGHTY
(Chs. 38, 39)

The marvels of creation, which witness to the infinite wisdom, power, and watchful care of the Creator, are presented to Job in such a way as to force from him a confession of ignorance and weakness, and of presumption in venturing to contend with God.

1–38. The wonders of earth and heaven. What does Job know of their nature and origin and ordering ?

1. Whirlwind] rather, 'storm.' Theophanies, or manifestations of God to man, are usually represented in OT. as accompanied by convulsions of nature : cp. Ex 19 16-20. There is no necessary reference to the storm in c. 37.

2. The question evidently refers to Job. 'God condemns Job for making dark the divine plan of the world. He had spoken as though it was all a tangled riddle. Really there is in it a beautiful luminous order' (Peake). But this makes Job the last speaker, not Elihu, and supports the view that the latter's speeches are an interpolation.

3. Job had expressed too boldly his desire to contend with God concerning his righteousness. But he has still to learn that he must trust where he cannot understand.

4–7. The creation of the earth.

5. Who hath laid] RV 'Who determined.'

7. Sons of God] the angels.

8–11. The sea.

8. When it brake forth] The ancients thought that the sea issued from the subterranean abyss, with which it was connected by springs in the bed of the ocean : cp. v. 16 and Gn 7 11. **10ᵃ.** Render, 'and prescribed for it its boundary.'

12–15. The dawn.

12. Since thy days] RV adds 'began.'

13. Deeds of darkness are checked by the coming of light : cp. Jn 3 20. **14.** RM 'It is changed as clay under the seal, and *all things* stand forth as in a garment.' Objects which have hitherto been obscure and shapeless take form and colour, as if wrapped in a clinging garment, when daylight comes. **15.** Darkness, which is the light of the wicked, disappears, and with it their power to harm is gone.

16, 17. The deep and the under-world. The deep lies beneath the bed of the sea.

16. Search of the depth] RV 'recesses of the deep.' **17. Opened**] RV 'revealed.' **Death**] Sheol, the place of the dead.

19–21. The abode of light and darkness.

19. Where] rather, 'whither.' **20. Take it to the bound thereof**] i.e. track it. **21. Knowest thou** *it*] RV '*Doubtless* thou knowest' : spoken ironically.

22–30. The secrets of snow and hail, rain and frost.

22. Treasures] RV 'treasuries'; storehouses. **22, 23.** Cp. passages such as Josh 10¹¹ Ps 18, where God is represented as intervening in the affairs of men through the elements of nature. **24ᵇ.** RV 'Or the east wind scattered upon the earth.'

25. 'Who has made a channel for the tropical rain to pour down from the heavens through the skies?' **26, 27.** God's providence neglects no part of His creation. Job had at the most thought of man, but mainly of himself. God reminds him of the vast animate and inanimate creation. **28ᵃ.** 'Does man beget the rain?' **30.** Render, 'The waters are congealed like stone.'

31ᵃ. Render, 'Canst thou group together the Pleiades?' **Sweet influences]** RV 'cluster.' **Pleiades]** see on 9⁹. **32.** Render, 'Canst thou lead forth the signs of the zodiac in the season?' i.e. Can you influence their appearing? The zodiacal signs were known 3,000 years B.C. (The zodiac was that part of the sky which includes the apparent paths of the sun, moon, and planets. The 'signs' are the divisions of 30 degrees into which, for astronomical and other purposes, it is divided.) **Arcturus with his sons]** or, 'the Bear over her sons,' i.e. the revolution of the Bear round the Pole and Little Bear.

33. The laws of the seasons and their influence on the earth. **36. Inward parts]** RM 'dark clouds.' **Heart]** RM 'meteor.' **37. In]** RV 'by.' **Stay]** RV 'pour out.' **Bottles of heaven]** i.e. rain-clouds.

37–41. These vv. are connected in subject with c. 39. **41. They wander]** RV 'and wander.'

CHAPTER 39

The First Speech of the Almighty (concluded)

Chs. 38³⁹⁻⁴¹ and 39 depict the wonders of animate creation, and the instincts with which animals are gifted by the providence of God. In view of His works Job must learn to trust Him and to believe in His goodness.

1–4. The wild goat or ibex. **1. Knowest thou?]** i.e. do you control? **3. Their sorrows]** their young, whose birth causes pain. **4. With corn]** rather, 'in the desert.'

5–8. The wild ass, which is still found in the deserts of N. Arabia and Syria. **6. Barren** *land]* RV 'salt land,' districts coated with this mineral, which is much sought after by cattle. **7.** Note the contrast between the life of the wild and the domestic ass. **Regardeth he the crying]** RV 'heareth he the shoutings.'

9–12. The wild ox.

9. Unicorn] RV 'wild-ox.' The word 'unicorn' is based on the LXX translation, and is incorrect. The nearest extant representative of the wild ox is the bison, which still lingers in the forests of Lithuania, the Caucasus and N. America. Its bones are found in Lebanon bone-caves. **10–12.** The untameable nature of the wild ox. **12. Believe]** i.e. confide in, trust. **Gather it into thy barn]** RV 'gather *the corn of* thy threshing floor.'

13–18. The ostrich.

13. There is nothing about peacocks in the Hebrew. Perhaps the sense is, 'The wing of ostriches is goodly. Is it a stork's wing for flight?' The ostrich cannot fly like a stork, which comes to Palestine in the spring on its way from Africa to Europe. **14. In the earth]** RV 'on the earth.' Dr. Tristram says: 'The ostrich is polygamous, and several hens deposit their eggs in one place, a hole in the sand. The eggs are then covered over and left during the heat of the day; but in the cold regions at any rate, as in the Sahara, the birds sit regularly during the night, and until the sun has full power.' **16. She is hardened against]** RM 'She deals hardly with.' If her nest is discovered the ostrich often destroys her young: cp. Lam 4³. **16ᵇ.** RV 'Though her labour' (of laying the eggs) 'be in vain, *she is* without fear,' i.e. acts still without due caution.

17. 'More stupid than an ostrich' is an Arab proverb. **18. Lifteth up herself on high]** RM 'rouseth herself up to flight.' **Scorneth the horse]** by outrunning him. Tristram puts the stride of an ostrich at full speed at from 22 to 28 ft.

19–25. The war-horse. **19ᵇ.** RV 'Hast thou clothed his neck with the quivering mane?' (lit. 'with shaking'). **20. Afraid as a grasshopper]** RV 'to leap as a locust.' **Nostrils]** RV 'snorting.' **23. Against]** rather, 'over.' **Shield]** RV 'javelin.' The horse probably is not being ridden here, but driven in a chariot, on which quiver, spear, and shield (or dart) are hung. He is not afraid of the noise they make, or, perhaps, of the enemy. **24. He swalloweth]** render, 'he digs' or 'paws.' **Neither believeth, etc.]** RM 'Neither standeth he still at.' **25ᵃ.** Render, 'at each trumpet he saith, Ha!' **25ᵇ.** The sense of smell in horses is very acute, and they are much discomposed by the odour of carrion.

26–30. The hawk and the eagle. **26.** The migratory hawk is intended, which leaves Palestine for the S. in winter. **27.** 'Eagle' is masculine throughout. **30.** Cp. Mt 24²⁸.

CHAPTER 40¹⁻⁵

A short dialogue between the Almighty and

Job, ending in the latter's confession and submission.

2. Cox renders, 'Is he who contended with the Almighty corrected ? Let him who disputed with God reply.' **4. Vile]** RV 'of small account.' Job confesses that in view of these marvellous works of God, it was presumption to think of criticising His actions.

CHAPTERS 40⁶–41³⁴
THE SECOND SPEECH OF THE ALMIGHTY

Job, we know, in his anxiety to prove his integrity had been led into casting doubts on the justice of God's government of the world. He is here ironically invited to take God's place as ruler of the universe, and to display a wisdom as great as that of God. If he proved himself competent to do this, then, and not till then, he may consider himself independent of God and criticise His actions.

8. Disannul my judgment] deny my righteousness. **13. In secret]** RV 'in the hidden *place* ' ; Sheol, the abode of the dead.

15–41³⁴. In this passage the mightiest beast of the earth and the one most dreaded in the water are portrayed to Job, and he is asked if he can subdue them. Many scholars regard these descriptions as a later insertion.

15–24. The Elephant or Hippopotamus.

15. Behemoth] the word means 'a large beast.' Most scholars consider that the hippopotamus is meant, but some regard the description as more applicable to the elephant. Buxtorf, the great Hebraist, renders 'elephas.' He has a 'nose,' i.e. a trunk, and swings a tail 'like a cedar.' Elephants were known on the Euphrates about 1550 B.C. Thothmes III of Egypt is represented as receiving one from Syria. **Which I made with thee]** i.e. it and Job are alike God's creatures. Or render, ' which is with thee,' i.e. you can see him.

16. Navel] RV 'muscles.' **17. Like a cedar]** it is so firm and strong. **17ᵇ.** RV ' The sinews of his thighs are knit together.'

19ᵇ. RM ' He that made him hath furnished him with his sword ' ; i.e. his tusks or teeth.

20. Mountains] Unlike the hippopotamus, the elephant is found in hill forests.

23. RV ' Behold, if a river overflow, he trembleth not : He is confident though Jordan swell even to his mouth.' **Jordan]** means a river as swift and strong as Jordan. **24.** RV ' Shall any take him when he is on the watch, or pierce through his nose (or, his trunk) with a snare ? '

CHAPTER 41
THE SECOND SPEECH OF THE ALMIGHTY
(concluded)

The second great creature, the Crocodile (with which the ' leviathan ' is generally iden-

tified) is now described. If Job cannot control the crocodile, dare he contend with Him who made it ? The crocodile is found in the Crocodile River under Carmel as well as in Egypt.

1. Hook] RV 'fishhook.' **1ᵇ.** RV ' Or press down his tongue with a cord.' This may be an allusion to the method of treating a refractory camel or mule by tying down its tongue with the head-rope. **2. Hook]** RM ' rope of rushes.' **Thorn]** RV ' hook.'

4. Wilt thou take] RV ' That thou shouldest take.' **6ᵃ.** RV ' Shall the bands *of fishermen* make traffic of him ? ' **Merchants]** lit. ' Canaanites ' or ' lowlanders ' on the trading route from Syria to Egypt, who were great merchants. Their name is sometimes used for merchants generally : cp. Prov 31²⁴ Isa 23⁸ Zech 14²¹. **8. Lay thine hand upon him]** i.e. if you dare. **Do no more]** or, ' do not repeat it.' **9. The hope of him]** i.e. of overcoming him.

10, 11. If the creature is so great, who can withstand the Creator ? **11. Prevented me]** RV ' first given unto me.' **12. His parts]** i.e. the crocodile's. **13.** RV ' Who can strip off his outer garment ? Who shall come within his double bridle ? ' **14. Doors of his face]** his mouth. **14ᵇ.** RV ' Round about his teeth is terror.'

18ᵃ. RV ' His neesings (i.e. sneezings or snortings) flash forth light.' This and the following vv. poetically describe the snorting and heated breath and spray thrown from the crocodile's mouth. **18ᵇ.** In the Egyptian hieroglyphs the dawn is expressed by crocodile's eyes. **20. Caldron]** The crocodile's breath is likened to vapour that rises from a steaming pot. **22ᵇ.** RV ' And terror danceth before him.'

25ᵇ. RV ' By reason of consternation they are beside themselves.' But the v. may perhaps, with a slight alteration of the text, be rendered : ' When he raiseth himself up the deer are afraid who slip (or stray) among the broken places on the banks of the river.' It is not the usual term for ' the mighty ' that is used here. Shebarim, ' broken places,' in Josh 7⁵, refers to the slope of a ravine.

26. Habergeon] RV ' pointed shaft.' An ordinary bullet will not pierce a crocodile's scales.

30. RV ' His underparts are *like* sharp potsherds : He spreadeth *as it were* a threshing wain upon the mire.' **31.** He lashes the water into foam. **Like a pot of ointment]** perhaps a reference to the strong musky smell of the crocodile.

34. The meaning is probably, ' Everything that is high feareth him : He is king over all the sons of pride,' i.e. the other great beasts (28⁸).

CHAPTER 42 1-6

JOB'S FINAL WITHDRAWAL

Job at last has learned his lesson. The convincing evidences of wisdom, power, and love which God has offered him, have led him to lay aside his pride of intellect and pride of innocence. He feels that he may safely trust, even though he may never fully understand, and with Abraham he may rest convinced that the Judge of all the earth must do right.

The difficulties of Job were the difficulties of the author and of the thoughtful men of his day. ' He had pondered the ethical and religious problem presented by the moral order of the world. With a flaming hatred of wrong and tender pity for the oppressed, he saw the triumph of the wicked and the misery of the just. He was familiar with the current doctrines, and knew how they ignored the most patent facts. A truly religious man, he had found his heart drawn to God by the irrepressible instinct for fellowship with Him, driven from Him by the apparent immorality of His government. He had known what it was to be baffled in his search for God and to feel himself slipping from the fear of the Almighty. An intellectual solution he had not been able to reach. But in humble submission to God's inscrutable wisdom, and in a profounder sense of fellowship with Him, he had escaped into the region of unclouded trust ' (Prof. A. S. Peake's ' Job').

2b. RV ' And that no purpose of thine can be restrained.' 3. Job soliloquises. ' Well might God say to him (38 2) : Who is this that hideth counsel without knowledge ? ' i.e. that misreads in his ignorance the real facts of divine providence. The point is that Job now agrees in God's estimate of himself.

4. Again he repeats God's words in 38 3 and 40 7.

5, 6. Job declares that he now understands God's relations towards man in a far deeper and truer sense than he had hitherto. At once he retracts and repents of all that he had said amiss. The sight of God, i.e. a clearer apprehension of His majesty and righteousness, humbles Job to the dust. 6. Abhor myself] RM ' loathe my words.'

THE EPILOGUE (42 7-17)

7-17. These vv. describe the happy ending to Job's trials and his restoration to prosperity. It is a sequel in full accord with the religious ideas of the Hebrews. With no clear idea of a future state, where compensation will be found for the ills of this world, long life and earthly happiness were regarded as the only evidence of God's favour and approval. The feeling that the happy ending spoils the effect is modern, but incorrect. For it would have made a very bad impression on the reader, if God had been represented as callously leaving Job to suffer, when the occasion for trial had passed away.

7-9. The friends receive the divine condemnation. ' The three friends had really inculpated the providence of God by their professed defence of it. By disingenuously covering up and ignoring its enigmas they had cast more discredit on it than Job, who honestly held them up to the light. Their denial of its apparent inequalities was more untrue and dishonouring to the divine administration as it is in fact conducted than Job's bold affirmation of them ' (W. H. Green's ' Argument of the Book of Job unfolded '). At the same time there is a strange contrast between the judgment on Job expressed here and that expressed in the speech out of the storm, which supports the view that the prose portions were borrowed by the writer from an older book.

11. A piece of money] Heb. *Kesitah*, a very early word occurring only in Gn 33 19 and Josh 24 32. It was probably an uncoined piece of silver representing the value of a lamb as the LXX and Vulgate translate it. This, with the rings, ' constituted, I suppose, the *nuzzur*, or present, such as Orientals still make on paying a visit of ceremony ' (Cox).

12. Note that the numbers are double those mentioned in 1 3, an indication of the ideal nature of this history of Job : see on 1 2. The prophets often allude to the double compensation in store for their afflicted people : Isa 61 7 Jer 16 14-18 Zech 9 12.

14. These names contain allusions to feminine charms. Jemima means ' dove ': cp. Song 1 15. Keziah probably means ' cassia ' or ' cinnamon,' a fragrant spice : cp. Ps 45 8. Keren-happuch means ' a horn of eye paint.' It was a dye made of antimony with which the eyelashes were tinged, and was considered by Orientals to enhance the beauty of the eye : cp. 2 K 9 30 Jer 4 30 Ezk 23 40. 15. Inheritance among their brethren] this was an unusual privilege to women : cp. Nu 27 1-11.

17. In LXX a postscript is added, ' It is written that he will rise again with those whom the Lord raises up.' This is probably an addition made by some reader, who felt the inadequacy of any material compensation or reward.

PSALMS

INTRODUCTION

1. Name. The book of the Psalms is the name given in our versions to the first of the books of the third division of the Hebrew Bible called *Kethubhim* or *Hagiographa*. It is followed in that division by Proverbs, Job, Song of Songs, Ruth, Lamentations, Ecclesiastes, Esther, Daniel, Ezra, Nehemiah, and Chronicles. The name of the book in Hebrew is *Tehillim*, i.e. 'Praises.' Our name, Psalms, is a transliteration of the Greek title of the book, and signifies 'songs accompanied by stringed instruments.' The title Psalter is from the Greek *psalterion*, 'a harp,' and is applied to the book of Psalms just as 'Lyre' or 'Harp' is sometimes used for a collection of hymns.

2. Hebrew Poetry. The history of Hebrew poetry, as evidenced in extant sacred literature, can only be sketched in briefest outline. It is predominantly lyric in character, i.e. it expresses, or refers to, the poet's own thoughts or emotions. Epic poetry, i.e. poetry narrating the achievements of heroes, is not represented. Some of the poetry is of a dramatic nature, as Job, and especially the Song of Songs, but there is no drama properly so called. Fragments of early songs of various kinds have been preserved, and are embedded in the literature of the OT. Examples of these are the 'Song of the Sword,' uttered by Lamech in Gn 4 23, 24 ; the 'Song of the Well,' recorded in Nu 21 17, 18 ; and the burden of the thanksgiving for the deliverance from Egypt in Ex 15 1, 21, the whole fine composition contained in vv. 2–18 being probably of later date. One of the very oldest portions of Hebrew literature is the Song of Deborah in Jg 5. Most critics consider the Song of Moses, recorded in Dt 32, to be of comparatively late date, and Hannah's Song in 1 S 2 can hardly be of contemporary authorship. Many of the poetic strains that have come down to us are laments in memory of the departed, one of the most notable examples being David's elegy on the death of Saul and Jonathan (2 S 1), and another the lament for Abner in 2 S 3 33. The 'last words of David,' recorded in 2 S 23, are cheerful in strain, forming a marked contrast to the dirge of Hezekiah in view of his approaching death (Isa 38). Traces of harvest and vintage songs, and songs for banquets, are discernible : see Am 6 5. Wedding songs are, perhaps, preserved in the book of Canticles.

Interspersed among the prophetic writings a few beautiful lyrics are to be found : see Isa 12, Jon 2, and Hab 3. A sublime and powerful *Mashal*, or Taunting Song, is preserved in Isa 14 4-27. It is notable for its bold symbolism, and its daring and bitter irony, rather than for its beauty.

Careful readers of the OT. will not fail to notice scattered references to collections of poems that have not been preserved. One of these is called in Nu 21 14 'The book of the Wars of Jehovah,' containing, presumably, martial songs ; and another, 'The book of Jashar,' i.e. the Upright, may well have consisted of verses in pious memory of departed saints and heroes. The titles of the Psalms, when closely examined, render their own evidence to the existence of other collections of Hebrew lyrics which have perished, as well as to some that have been taken up into that larger collection, which now forms one of the most precious possessions of the world.

The book of Lamentations may stand as an illustration of the elaborate versification of later days. Short as the book is, it consists of several parts distinguishable from one another by their various metres, one being styled the *Kinah* or Elegiac metre, and all displaying considerable artistic skill. The acrostics which have been preserved in the book of Psalms and in Lamentations are probably the product of a comparatively late period.

It remains only to mention the Gnomic verse (i.e. didactic poetry, dealing in maxims), of which the book of Proverbs furnishes such abundant illustration. Some of the Psalms, and parts of the book of Job, may perhaps be included under this heading, but the attempt accurately to classify under modern subdivisions the many-voiced poetry of the OT. is more than futile. It is clear that one marked type of poetical composition is recognisable in the sententious, regular, evenly-balanced clauses, such as constitute the main portion of Proverbs. In the Hebrew, however, there is no monotony. There is variety enough in the rhythm of the lines, in the kind of parallelism adopted, and in the various building up of lines and couplets into stanzas, to remove the feeling of sameness which an English reader experiences in reading Proverbs or the 119th Psalm. Hebrew poetry in all its parts pulsates with the spontaneity, the freedom, and the sparkling variety of full and vigorous life.

3. Hebrew Poetical Construction.

The distinction between poetry and prose in Hebrew does not depend upon the presence or absence of rhyme. Nor is metre—that is, arrangement in lines of a measured length, consisting of a definite number of syllables or 'feet'—characteristic of Hebrew poetry, though some approach to this is occasionally found. Poetical construction depends upon rhythm of thought and balance of sentences. Each psalm is made up of lines, arranged so as to produce a 'parallelism of members,' so that in two or more lines words and matter correspond to one another with a carefully-studied equality. In the simplest form, two such lines match one another in a couplet, e.g.—

'The heavens declare the glory of God
  And the firmament sheweth his handy work.'
'Enter into his gates with thanksgiving
  And into his courts with praise.'

In these examples, the second line repeats the general sense of the first and strengthens its emphasis. This is called synonymous parallelism. Sometimes the second line affirms the opposite of the former, in antithesis or contrast, e.g.—

'The wicked borroweth and payeth not again,
  But the righteous sheweth mercy and giveth.'
'The Lord knoweth the way of the righteous,
  But the way of the ungodly shall perish.'

Sometimes a triplet is found, as—

'I call to remembrance my song in the night,
  I commune with my own heart,
  And my spirit made diligent search.'

Four lines may be included in the scheme, and then the first and third may be called parallel, and the second and fourth ; or three of the lines may preserve a close parallelism, while one of them, either the first or the last, stands independent ; or two ordinary couplets may constitute a verse of four lines, e.g.—

' In my distress I called upon the Lord,
  And cried unto my God:
  He heard my voice out of his temple,
  And my cry before him came into his ears.'

Close examination will show that these distichs, tristichs, and tetrastichs, as they are called—i.e. verses of 2, 3 and 4 lines respectively—assume a great variety of forms in the Psalms, thus avoiding the sameness and monotony characteristic of the poetry of the Proverbs. Order can be discerned, but, like the symmetry in the life of nature, it manifests itself amidst endless variety, so that the charm of freshness and unexpectedness is never lost. (For examples, see the arrangement of the verses in RV.)

As two, three, or four lines make a verse, so a number of verses constitute a stanza, or strophe, corresponding to a paragraph in prose. The end of such a stanza is sometimes marked by a refrain, such as ' The Lord of hosts is with us, the God of Jacob is our refuge ' in the 46th Psalm, and ' Oh that men would praise the Lord for his goodness and for his wonderful works to the children of men,' which is found four times in the 107th Psalm. But the stanzas do not recur with strict regularity, and the writers of these marvellous sacred lyrics never allow themselves to be chained by any mechanical rules.

There is, however, one apparent exception to this rule. Though rhyme is not found in Hebrew poetry, alliteration and assonance—the repetition of a letter or of similar sound-endings—is not infrequent, and the alliteration sometimes takes the form of an acrostic. That is to say, a psalm may be composed so that each verse shall begin with a letter of the Hebrew alphabet, arranged in order from the first to the last—as we should say, from A to Z. This is practically the case in Pss 25, 34, 145. Or every other verse may thus follow on with consecutive letters, as in Ps 37 ; or every single line may begin with a fresh letter, as in Pss 111, 112. In the 119th Psalm, as is well known, there are twenty-two stanzas, each consisting of eight verses, and each verse in the stanza begins with the same letter, the letters of the whole alphabet being taken in regular succession. It is difficult to imitate this in English, and if it were done, an appearance of stiffness and artificiality would be produced. But, excepting perhaps in the elaborate scheme of the 119th Psalm, the mechanical arrangement does not seriously fetter the Hebrew poet, and the English reader would hardly guess how completely the alphabetical system is carried out. This is very marked in the 3rd chapter of Lamentations, a striking example of acrostic composition.

4. Hebrew Music.

Tradition places the introduction of musical instruments at a very early date. In Gn 4²¹ Jubal is described as ' the father of all such as handle the harp and pipe.' Amos (5²³) speaks of ' the melody of viols' as being heard in the services, and Isaiah (30²⁹,³²) similarly mentions pipe and tabret and harp. The nature of the music is more a matter of speculation than of knowledge : it was probably what we would consider harsh and discordant. The singing at the Temple services seems, from notices in the Psalms, to have been antiphonal, sometimes by the two divisions of the choir, sometimes by the choir and the people, the latter joining at intervals in a refrain (e.g. 136). The singing in later times, at any rate, was accompanied, in some cases if not always. by instrumental music. Pss 4, 6, 54, 55, 67, 76 are headed ' On Neginoth ' (RV ' upon stringed instruments ');

and Ps 5 has the direction 'Upon Nehiloth' (RM ' with the wind instruments'). Two stringed instruments are mentioned in the Bible, the *kinnor* (harp) and the *nebel* (psaltery). The former seems to have been a lyre, an instrument of a light and simple nature upon which the performer could play while walking ; the latter was probably more like our harp. The chief wind instruments are the *halil* (flute), *shophar* (horn), and *hazozerah* (trumpet). The flute was played in religious processions (1 S 10⁵ 1 K 1⁴⁰ Isa 30²⁹). The horn (made at first of a ram's horn, sometimes later of metal) was used to summon the people to worship, or as a signal, or for special purposes, as e.g. to proclaim the year of Jubilee. The trumpet was a long instrument of silver, blown on ceremonial occasions by the priests (Nu 10²⁻¹⁰). It is the instrument portrayed on the Arch of Titus at Rome. There were also percussion instruments used, the chief of which were the *toph* (a small hand drum, Gn 31²⁷ 'tabret,') and cymbals both flat and conical (Ps 150⁵ Zech 14²⁰).

5. The Titles of the Psalms. The titles, or short inscriptions, found at the beginning of many psalms, are not to be regarded as forming a part of the sacred text, but they were prefixed at a very early date, and are very instructive. The exact meaning of each will be explained where it occurs, but a few general remarks may here be made. Titles occur chiefly in the first three books, and only thirty-four psalms are without any. These the Jews called 'orphans.'

Some of the titles are musical directions, some suggest a historical setting for the psalm, and others indicate the authorship or the source from which it was taken. (The names Alamoth (46), Sheminith (6, 12), Neginoth (4), and Nehiloth (5), refer to the music ; the first two probably indicating pitch, and the last two enjoining the particular instrumental accompaniments.) Several psalms, e.g. 9, 22, 45, etc., have some words prefixed which seem to indicate the tune of some well-known song to which the psalm was set. Prefixed to thirteen psalms are notes suggesting a suitable historical occasion for the psalm. All of them refer to the history of David, the majority being placed in the period of his flight from the jealousy of Saul. Many of them, however, are irreconcilable with the words of the psalms themselves, and are therefore unreliable as sources of information. At the same time, they often provide apt historical illustrations of thoughts and principles dwelt upon by the psalmists.

Many of the titles give hints of authorship or source. Seventy-three psalms are headed 'Le David,' which is translated 'Of David' in our versions. It is more correct to translate the preposition 'Belonging to' ; and while many of the psalms bearing this title may be the productions of the shepherd king, all that is indicated by the title 'of David' is that the psalm to which it is prefixed was taken from an early collection called the Psalms of David or the Prayers of David (72²⁰). Similarly other psalms are distinguished as 'belonging to Asaph,' 'belonging to the Sons of Korah,' 'belonging to the Chief Musician,' these names being those of collections of sacred pieces which had been made at different times. The same preposition being used in all the cases, it is evident that it must be interpreted in the same sense of David and Asaph as of the Chief Musician and the Sons of Korah ; and if in the latter cases it does not refer to authorship in the strict sense of the word, it can scarcely do so in the former. The view is now generally accepted that the titles for the most part refer to collections which had come to be known by certain familiar names, without its being implied that every psalm in a collection was written by the person whose name it bears. In the case of David, it is easy to understand how his honoured name came to be given to all the psalms in a particular collection, though he only wrote some of them. The 72nd Psalm is entitled 'of Solomon,' yet it is included among those that are styled 'prayers of David, the son of Jesse.' It was a rule among the Jews that a psalm without an author's name attached to it was to be ascribed to the author of the one immediately preceding. This shows how the name 'David' came to be given to the whole Psalter, as in Heb 4⁷.

6. Date and Authorship. What then may we infer as to the date and authorship of the several psalms ? The belief that David wrote all the psalms to which his name is attached cannot now be maintained. Modern scholars differ widely in their estimate of the number of psalms which may safely be ascribed to him, some including over forty in the list, while others allow no more than three, and one or two admit none at all. While, however, it cannot be demonstrated that David wrote any of the psalms, the probability is that he wrote a number. The 18th Psalm is given at length in 2 S 22 as well as in the Psalter, and in both cases a note is prefixed, setting forth that the psalm was written by David to celebrate his deliverance from his enemies, and especially from Saul. If we might build upon this statement it would give us firm ground on which to rest arguments concerning David's style and mode of composition. Considerable weight, too, is due to tradition, which is too strong and too persistent to be lightly set aside. The very fact that so many psalms were handed down to the compilers of the Psalter under David's name, is a very strong argument in favour of his authorship of a considerable number. It may be, indeed, that many psalms composed by him were modified and altered in some respects by later editors, in order to fit them for use in public worship and apply them to the circumstances of a later age ; but tradition gives strong ground for believing that the 'sweet singer of Israel' was the author of songs of praise which are included in our book of Psalms. Critics of the moderate school ascribe to David Pss 3, 4, 7, 8, 15, 18, 23, 24, 32, as well as 19 1-6, with perhaps 101 and 110, and some others. It is possible, however, that most of those in the first book are Davidic in their original form. It is difficult on any other supposition to account for the facts that the earliest collection was called by his name, and that so many psalms were ascribed to him.

It is as impossible to fix the dates at which the various psalms were composed, as to settle the questions of authorship. Incidental allusions to place or circumstance will sometimes show the date earlier than which a particular psalm cannot have been written. References to the Temple (5 7 27 4 28 2 65 4, etc.) imply the existence of that centre of national worship ; and the mention of 'the hill of God' (15 1 24 3, etc.) seems to indicate that the worship on Zion had been established for some time. It is evident again that some psalms must be dated as late as the exile (e.g. 137), and that others (e.g. 126) are post-exilic. Some scholars hold that many of the psalms must be dated as late as the Maccabean age. But while it is possible that some psalms belong to that period (e.g. 44, 74, 79, 83), it is not likely that the number is very great.

Readers may be reminded that the spiritual benefit of these inspired lyrics is not lessened by their detachment from a particular name and occasion. The Psalms should be studied in the light of eternal truth, and the local significance should be lost in the universal. Pre-eminently among the books of the OT. they are intended not for one age but for all time.

7. The Compilation of the Psalter. The book of Psalms, as we know it, was not made —it grew. A long history, partly obscure, partly traceable, and directed throughout by the guidance of the Divine Spirit, lies behind the final collection of these hundred and fifty sacred lyrics into one Psalter, for the use of Israel and the spiritual benefit of the world. The RV follows a very ancient Jewish tradition in dividing the whole into five books— Pss 1–41, 42–72, 73–89, 90–106, 107–150. This division is supposed to have been made in imitation of the five books of the Pentateuch. Each book closes with a doxology. But this arrangement of the Psalms, though dating from the 2nd cent. B.C., does not represent the earliest grouping. Closer examination shows

that smaller collections existed in earlier times, and that these were gradually brought together and re-arranged on principles which we can only partially and with difficulty trace out. The note which closes the second book (72 20) shows that the psalms included in this collection were in some sense 'of David,' and that the writer of the note knew of no other Davidic psalms. We observe also that the same psalm occurs more than once in slightly differing forms : cp. Ps 14 with 53, 40 13-17 with 70, and 108 with 57 7-11 and 60 5-12. It will be seen that one feature of difference, in verses which are almost identical otherwise, is that different names of God are used. The sacred name Jehovah, the covenant name of Israel's God, is used in Book 1 272 times, while Elohim, a more general name for the Deity, occurs only 15 times. In Book 2 the proportion is reversed ; in it Jehovah is found only 30 times, while Elohim is employed 164 times. This cannot have happened by chance, and the names Jehovistic and Elohistic have been given to indicate the prevalence of the two names respectively. The reason of this peculiarity is not perfectly clear. It is probably due to different editions, and perhaps shows that the respective names were prevalent at different periods.

The Psalter seems to have been formed very much as modern hymn-books are formed. The earliest collection would be the Davidic, of which a large part is preserved in Book 1 ; later collections would be those of Asaph and the sons of Korah. The psalms described in their titles as *Mizmor* (AV 'A Psalm') may have formed a collection by themselves selected from the earlier Psalters with additions. Later still would come the collection made by the Chief Musician, probably for the Temple worship after the exile ; this again being selected from the earlier collections. Perhaps about the same time the Elohistic collection was made ; that it was formed from earlier sources is shown by the fact that Ps 53 = Ps 14, and Ps 70 = Ps 40 13-17 ; Jehovah, in the earlier version, being changed into Elohim in the later. Prof. Briggs thinks that the Psalter of the Chief Musician was formed in Palestine in the middle Greek period (3rd cent. B.C.), and that the Elohistic collection (partly preserved in Books 2 and 3) was made about the same time in Babylonia. Other groups of psalms of late date are the Songs of Ascents (Pss 120–134), a title which probably refers either to the 'going up' from Babylon to Jerusalem after the exile, or to the annual pilgrimage to the Temple to celebrate the feasts ; and the Hallelujah Psalms, 104–107, 111–117, 135–136, 146–150. The editor of our Psalter, taking the principal collections as his basis, and adding to them such other psalms as were suitable for the Temple service of praise, formed them into a complete Book of Praises probably in the Maccabean age—the 2nd cent. B.C.

It is sometimes argued that the Psalms express not personal but national feelings and aspirations ; that the 'I' of the Psalms represents not the writer but the Jewish nation. But while this may be the case in some psalms (e.g. 44, 76), especially those written in later times, it can scarcely be so in the great majority. These certainly express the desires and hopes of the faithful community, but it is because they first expressed the desires and hopes of individuals. They are natural and spontaneous, especially the Davidic Psalms. It is only later that the composition becomes more artificial, as in the case of the acrostic or alphabetical Psalms (e.g. 119, 145).

Allowing, then, for the measure of uncertainty surrounding the date and authorship of the Psalms, we may summarise the following conclusions : (1) The earliest date admissible for the composition of any psalm is the time of David, and in all probability some now extant may be ascribed to that king. (2) Additions to Hebrew psalmody were made during the period of the monarchy, several specimens of which are to be found in the Psalter : see Pss 2, 20, 21, 46, 48, etc. (3) A considerable part of the book of Psalms dates from the period immediately after the captivity, and about that time the process of collecting and arranging the Psalms was probably begun. (4) This process continued till the early part of the 2nd cent. B.C., when the Canon of the OT. was virtually complete.

8. Religious Ideas. The Psalms are the outpouring of the spirit of **devotion to God.** It is to God that the Psalmist's thoughts and hopes are directed, to whom he looks for deliverance, or whom he blesses for personal or national mercies. The Psalms are full of expressions of trust in God at all times, and they contain glowing testimonies to the perfection of God, to His love, His power, His faithfulness, His righteousness. They are specially valuable to us as a mirror and mould of devotion. They show us the human heart laid before God in all its moods and emotions ; in penitence, in desire for holiness, in doubt and perplexity, in danger, in desolation, or, again, in deliverance and triumph. The reader will always find something in the Psalms in sympathy with his own spiritual state. They are 'as comprehensive as the human soul and varied as human life ; .. they treat not life after the fashion of an age or people, but life in its rudiments.'

A problem frequently touched upon in the Psalms is the difficulty of reconciling the sufferings of the righteous and the prosper-

ity of the wicked with **God's moral government of the world:** cp. Intro. to Job. This problem is handled at length in Pss 37 and 73. In the former psalm the solution reached is the somewhat superficial one that the success of the wicked is but temporary, and that the righteous will soon come to his own. In the latter the writer goes deeper. His faith had been severely tried by his experiences, but when he cast his burden on the Lord, as he worshipped in the sanctuary, he received new light in his darkness, and was enabled to leave the issues of the future with God. The one unfailing truth which comforted the Psalmists was 'The Lord reigneth.' Evil may endure for a time, and the wicked may oppress the just, but 'He that sitteth in the heavens will laugh' at them, and wait His opportunity to deliver His servants. There is nothing more noticeable in the Psalms than this triumphant faith in God's overruling power—a faith which neither personal nor national misfortune was able to destroy.

This is one aspect of the Psalmists' doctrine of God: another aspect of it is found in **the divine relation to nature.** Everything in nature speaks of God's power and glory. 'The heavens declare the glory of God and the firmament sheweth His handiwork.' The Hebrew poets have no pleasure in nature for her own sake ; they value her only as she speaks of the invisible presence of God. If they regard the earth, they view it as the footstool of the Lord ; if they see the clouds gathering, they speak of them as the curtains for Jehovah's pavilion ; if they listen to the thunder rolling, they hear in it 'the voice of the Lord upon the waters' ; if they watch the lightning flashing, they think of it as 'the arrows of the most High.' It is, however, the transcendence rather than the immanence of God that is the thought of the Psalmists' minds: while He uses nature to make known His presence and power, He is high above it (cp. Pss 18, 19, 29, 93).

Another point that may be noticed is the attitude of the Psalmists to **ritual and sacrifice.** There are frequent references in the Psalms to the Temple worship and sacrifices. The Psalmists declare their intention of offering burnt offerings and paying their vows in the presence of all the people (e.g. 66 [13-15] 116 [14,17]). The spiritual aspect of the ritual is, however, the most prominent in the Psalmists' thoughts. They know that offerings are insufficient of themselves, and that they are only valuable in so far as they typify the 'living sacrifice' of self, which every true worshipper must offer. Indeed, if that sacrifice be offered, the material offering is unnecessary (cp. Ps 40 [6-8] 50 [7-15]). In Ps 51 the writer at one moment declares that sacrifice and burnt offering are not desired by God ; 'the sacrifices of God are a broken spirit' (51 16, 17); and immediately afterwards declares that only when the walls of Jerusalem are rebuilt can sacrifice be acceptable to Jehovah (51 18, 19). It is probable that the latter vv. are a later liturgical addition ; but, even so, the whole psalm was used without any sense of incongruity.

Another feature of the Psalms is their **intense patriotism.** Patriotism and religion were inseparably associated by the Hebrews. That God was good to Israel was the first article of their creed. The historical Psalms developed this idea, and illustrate it from the national history (e.g. Pss 104, 105, 106). His blessings were destined to teach them His ways, and make His mighty power known to them (106 8). Even His punishment was for their good, to renew them to repentance and bring them to realise the greatness of their privilege (106 43, 44, etc.). The purpose of God in choosing Israel was that they might extend His Kingdom. Sometimes, indeed, 'the heathen' or 'the nations' are regarded as God's enemies (2 1, etc.) ; but at other times they are looked upon as the witnesses of the Psalmists' praise (57 9), and even as God's people (47 9). God's mercy is given to Israel that they make His way known upon the earth, and His saving health among all nations (67 1, 7). But, above all, Israel is His peculiar people (73 1); their enemies are His enemies ; misfortunes to them are hindrances to His cause ; their success is His triumph.

In this lies the explanation of two features of this book which call for comment—the **self-righteousness of the Psalmists,** and their vindictive **resentment against their enemies.** Let us remember at the outset the distinction between the OT. and NT. standards in this matter. We must not expect to find in the OT. the humility arising from the deep sense of sin, or the meek, forgiving spirit, inculcated by the Lord Jesus Christ. To judge the Psalmists by these standards is unfair, and the attempt to explain away the plain meaning of their words, in order to palliate a moral fault, is unsound exegesis. None the less it is possible, within limits, to defend the position taken up in what are called the imprecatory Psalms (e.g. 58, 68, 69, 109) without doing violence to sound ethical standards. The Psalmist claimed to be 'holy' and 'perfect,' without implying all that we mean by those lofty words. He meant that he was striving to be upright, a man of integrity, mindful of the claims of God upon him according to the law, and to the best of his ability endeavouring to be faithful to duty. He was placed, however, in the midst of men animated by entirely different motives ; some

of them openly and violently opposed to the God of Israel and His worship, others nominally acknowledging Him, but in reality idolaters, or disloyal to Jehovah. The contrast between the faithful and the unfaithful was sharp and strong ; the former were always in a minority, they usually suffered cruel persecution, and were often in extremest peril. Under these circumstances it is easy to understand that the Psalmist felt entitled to identify himself with the cause of righteousness. He pleads for his own personal triumph, and the utter overthrow of his enemies, with a passionate earnestness, which is only warrantable in the light of the words, 'Do not I hate them, O Lord, that hate Thee ? and am not I grieved with those that rise up against Thee ? I hate them with perfect hatred, I count them mine enemies.' Not to hate the enemies of Jehovah is to be a traitor to His holy covenant.

The distinction familiar to us between hating the sin and being angry with the sinner, and the possibility of loving the offender with a desire to save him, were not present to the mind of the Psalmist. Evil and evil-doer were for him identical, and in this respect he stands upon a lower ethical plane than the Christian. Further, the forms of imprecation common in the Psalms belong to an earlier, a sterner, and more violent age than ours. Such horrible curses as are invoked in Ps 109 6-15 are, rightly, shocking in our ears. But this moral inferiority of the earlier dispensation once granted, no true Christian can afford in a Pharisaical spirit to look down upon these faithful men to whom the light of the gospel had not been granted. Rather should we ask ourselves what is to be learned from denunciations in which Christians are forbidden to indulge. Personal resentment is always unlawful to the man who takes the Sermon on the Mount as his guide ; but there is a stern hatred of evil manifest in the Psalms which is only too rare in later and more indulgent days. The Puritan strain in our national character is to some extent a reflexion of the spirit of whole-hearted and indignant righteousness which breathes in the denunciatory Psalms ; and, despite the hardness and narrowness too often associated with it, that spirit has proved of the utmost value in its uncompromising protest against prevalent evils in social and national life.

Another fact must be borne in mind, if we would fully understand the reasons for the strong denunciatory element found in the Psalms. To the Jew no clear revelation had been granted of a future life ; his horizon was, for the most part, limited by the present. The true Israelite did, in a sense, look to the future. He hoped for a numerous posterity as a mark of God's favour, he anticipated a better state of things for his nation and the world in the coming of the Messiah, and he certainly did not regard death as virtual annihilation. But he had no clear hope of immortality, no vision of a heaven as a state of future blessedness ; neither the law nor the prophets warranted any such outlook beyond the grave. It followed that the cause of truth and right must be vindicated here and now, or it could not, properly speaking, be vindicated at all. This at least was the attitude for the most part taken up by the orthodox Jew, and there was much to be said in its favour. It is easy for religious men of to-day, living in a land of freedom and amidst all the blessings of peace, and taught to expect a Day of Judgment in the future, when all earth's wrongs shall be completely redressed, to possess their souls in patience, and wait for the coming of the Day of God and the new earth wherein dwelleth righteousness. But the problems of life pressed much more grievously upon the saint of old time, crushed by brute force, oppressed under a cruel and relentless Oriental despotism, with no earthly hope of redress, and no clear prospect of a better life to come. No wonder if such men prayed with a certain fierce indignation of soul, 'Up, Lord, and let not man have the upper hand ; let the heathen be judged in thy sight, that the nations may know themselves to be but men.'

But, it will be asked, had the Jew then no **hope of immortality** for himself, and is not the 16th Psalm a prophecy of the resurrection of Christ, as it is more than once declared to be in the NT. ? The subject thus opened up cannot be adequately dealt with in a few sentences, and scholars have differed in their judgment upon it. The view taken by the present writer may be thus briefly expressed. No explicit revelation of a future life was given to the Jew, and no definite expectation of a future state of rewards and punishments entered into his ordinary view of life. But the truly devout Israelite possessed so clear and strong a sense of religion, so firm a hold by faith upon the living God, that he was enabled sometimes to transcend the conditions of his ordinary religious creed and reach a state of joyful personal confidence of a very lofty kind. These moments of insight and foresight were, however, comparatively few ; the glimpses thus gained were transient, they belonged to the individual only, and could not furnish a basis for definite dogmatic teaching. Thus Job believed that his Redeemer would at the last appear and vindicate his cause upon the earth, though he had no light upon the time and manner of such manifestation, and the confidence expressed in Job 19 25-27 is the expression of an exalted mood which subsequent chapters prove not to have been permanent.

Similarly it will be found that some passages in the Psalms, such as 6⁵ 30⁹ 88 10-12 are full of gloomy foreboding concerning the future state. They describe it as a condition of helplessness and forgetfulness, which hardly deserves the name of life at all. There are other passages, however, of which 16 9-11 17 15 49 15 73 24, 25 are examples, in which the Psalmist's assurance of the care and favour of God is such that he appears to triumph not only over the dangers and vicissitudes of the present life, but over the fear of death itself. It is quite true that these hopes are not very clearly expressed, and that some commentators have questioned whether they contain an assured belief in immortality. But St. Peter's quotation from the 16th Psalm on the day of Pentecost shows that the words suggested a hope of immortality which was fully realised in the Resurrection of Christ. We may well find in the 16th and 73rd Psalms another illustration of the argument which the Lord Jesus Christ drew from the phrase ' The God of Abraham, of Isaac and of Jacob.' He is not the God of the dead, but of the living ; and the Psalmists, who had God for their portion in this life, entertained a trust and confidence in God which at intervals blossomed into incipient hope that He who was not ashamed to be called their God would preserve them in life, in death and for ever.

The Messianic hope has been spoken of, and certain Psalms—2, 8, 16, 22, 45, 72, 110, and others—have been specifically styled **Messianic Psalms**. But here a distinction must be made. The word Messianic may be used either in the narrower sense of prophecies which contain a distinct reference to a personal Deliverer called the Messiah, or in a wider sense of predictions of great and glorious blessings to be enjoyed by the nation in a brighter and better age to come. Often without any reference to a personal Messiah, prophets and psalmists are found confidently anticipating a Day of God, when He shall appear in righteous judgment and shall manifest His glory among men. A little group of Psalms, of which 96–98 form the nucleus, may be described as Messianic, because they anticipate a theophany, a manifestation of God in the earth. They contemplate a period when in some sense God shall ' come and not keep silence,' when ' He cometh to judge the world with righteousness and the peoples with equity.' The mode in which this is to be carried out is left indefinite, but the hope is invincible and inextinguishable. In the 2nd and 72nd Psalms a righteous earthly ruler of the house and dynasty of David is celebrated ; in Ps 110 the advent of a Priest-King is heralded, and the author of the Psalm looks to the Anointed One who is to rule in Zion, not as his son, but as his Lord. It would be a mistake, however, to restrict the conception of the Messianic hope to passages in which a personal Messiah is foretold. The 22nd Psalm, for example, is in its earlier portion clearly descriptive of the sufferings of the persecuted but faithful servant of God, and its language is frequently quoted in NT. in reference to Christ. But it contains no reference to the personal triumph of the sufferer, whilst the latter part of the Psalm points unquestionably to a great victory over unrighteousness, which is to be gained after and by means of his patient fidelity. The promise is here repeated which elsewhere is given in noble and more explicit words, ' He shall see of the travail of his soul and shall be satisfied.'

The subject of **the relation of the Psalms to Christ,** and the fulfilment in the New Testament of hints and prophecies contained in the Old, is too large to be entered on here. It may suffice, however, to say that one simple key will open many otherwise difficult locks. Christ claimed in Lk 24 44 that many things were written ' in the psalms ' concerning Him.

St. Peter, in Ac 2, shows how this saying is to be understood. Words, which were true only in a secondary and imperfect sense of David as the writer of the 16th Psalm, received their complete and perfect illustration in the resurrection from the dead of David's greater Son. The testimony of Jesus is the spirit of prophecy. The writers of the Psalms, like their brethren who are specifically called prophets, were inspired to write words true, indeed, of themselves and their contemporaries, but perfectly fulfilled only in Him of whom Moses in the Law, and the prophets, did write, Jesus of Nazareth, Son of Man and Son of God, the hope of the Psalmists and the Saviour of the world.

The Prayer-Book version of the Psalms was taken in 1549 from the English version of the Bible called the ' great Bible,' which was issued in 1540, and set up to be read in churches. In 1661, when the Prayer Book was revised, other portions of Scripture in the Prayer Book were changed for the AV of 1611. But the Psalter was not altered. People were accustomed to its wording, and it was thought to be more suitable for singing.

BOOK 1 (Psalms 1–41)

The Pss. in this book are probably among the earliest in the Psalter, and include most of those generally regarded as Davidic. They seem to have existed separately as an early hymn-book, which, with some slight additions from the final editor, was used as the nucleus of the entire collection. They have two well-marked characteristics : (1) the constant use of the name Jehovah (rendered the Lord), and the comparative absence of the name God (Heb. *Elohim*) ; the former occurring 272 times, the latter only 15 times : and (2) the description of them all, with the exception of Pss 1, 2, 10, and 33, as ' of David ' (Heb. *Le David*), a fact which has been taken to indicate their derivation from a still earlier collection which bore David's name. The first two Pss. seem to have been prefixed to the others when the present Psalter was formed. Historical notices are attached to some of them, connecting them with the life of David, but these are of doubtful importance. Most of the Pss. contained in the book are spontaneous and unaffected in their style, but a few of them are of artificial construction, Pss 9, 10, 25, 34, and 37 being acrostics.

The contents are exceedingly varied, and the same Ps. sometimes expresses such diverse feelings as joy and sorrow, bitter disappointment and lofty aspiration. Usually, however, there is some great thought more or less prominent, which enables us to make the following rough classification of their subjects :—(a) the contrast between the righteous

and the wicked, 1, 5, 10, 37 ; (b) the cry of the righteous in presence of trouble, 3, 4, 6, 7, 12, 13, 22, 31. 38, 39, 40 ; (c) the glory of God in nature, 8, 19, 29 ; (d) the law, 1, 19 ; (e) the king, 2, 18, 20, 21 ; (f) the future life, 16. In addition, there is a reference to sacrifice in Ps 37, an allusion to the Temple services in Ps 24, and a foreshadowing of the Messianic hope in Pss 2, 20, 28, and 40. The following Pss. are either quoted from or distinctly referred to in NT. : 2, 4, 5, 8, 10, 14, 16, 18, 22, 24, 32, 34, 40, 41. In several instances the NT. writer finds the fulfilment of the OT. passage in Christ. Thus Ps 2, with its defence of Jehovah's righteous King, of whom He says, ' Thou art my Son, this day have I begotten Thee,' is regarded as descriptive of Christ in Ac 13 33 and Heb 1 5 5 5 ; and Ps 22, with its pathetic presentment of the suffering Servant of Jehovah, is reported to have been actually quoted by Christ upon the cross (Mt 27 44 Mk 15 34), and v. 18 is asserted in Jn 19 24 to have been literally fulfilled in one of the incidents of His crucifixion.

The moral teaching of this first book of Psalms is simple and emphatic. It rests upon an unswerving belief in the will and power of God to uphold the moral values of life, and mete out punishments and rewards according to personal desert. In whatever circumstances they may be placed, the writers never lose hold of their conviction of the ultimate prosperity of the righteous and destruction of the wicked. Appearances may seem to contradict their faith, but they cling to it all the more strenuously, and insist that in the long run the balance will be redressed. The ideal character portrayed by them is that of the good man, defamed, wronged, and oppressed by irreligious foes, but holding fast his faith in God, and trusting confidently that, in His own good time, He will deliver him. Sometimes there is a note of joy and thankfulness at the accomplishment of the deliverance ; and this leads on to the anticipation of a time when, throughout the whole world, the justice of God will be manifested, and His power felt.

PSALM 1

This Ps. forms an appropriate introduction to the whole Psalter. In some Hebrew MSS it is not numbered with the Psalms, but stands before them as a prologue, and in others it is combined with Ps 2. It is one of the 'orphan' psalms, and the want of a title indicates that it did not originally belong to the Davidic collection, 3–41. The subject of the Ps. is the blessedness of the righteous man who studies the Law of Jehovah, as contrasted with the unhappy end of the ungodly. It consists of two strophes, vv. 1–3 and vv. 4–6, the former describing the character and destiny of the righteous, and the latter the character and destiny of the wicked.

1. Blessed] RM 'happy.' The first of the Old Testament beatitudes. Walketh not] There seems a gradual progression intended in the three clauses of the v. : walk, stand, sit, and wicked, sinner, scoffer. 2. Law] the whole revelation of God's will as made known in the sacred writings, especially the Pentateuch.

Doth .. meditate] lit. 'crooneth over,' repeats again and again in a low tone.

3. And he shall be] better, 'for he becomes,' i.e. in consequence of his constant study of God's law. Like a tree, etc.] cp. Jer 17 7, 8, where the illustration is more fully developed, and the character of the wicked is similarly illustrated (17 5, 6) ; and Ezk 47 12. And whatsoever, etc.] The illustration is dropped at this stage, and the words apply to the righteous man. Shall prosper] the simple faith of the pious Israelite, which no adversity was able wholly to overcome : cp. Ps 112 and see Ps 37, where the problem of the suffering of the righteous perplexes another Psalmist.

4. Chaff] A common OT. type of the wicked : cp 35 5. Threshing-floors were usually on high ground, where the wind would easily catch the chaff when it was beaten from the corn and drive it away (Isa 17 13). Driveth away] PBV adds, 'from the face of the earth,' following LXX and Vulgate. 5. The judgment] every visitation of God's providence, or perhaps the final judgment. Congregation] the faithful people of Israel.

PSALM 2

The historical situation of this Ps. cannot now be recovered. It may refer to some threatened rebellion of subject kings in the early days of Solomon, or to some similar movement under one of the later kings ; but it is impossible to give it any precise date. This, however, is of the less importance, as the leading feature of the Ps. is its application to the Messianic King—the ideal ruler of Israel. Some writers deny that it had any historical setting, and hold that it refers exclusively to the ideal King, the viceroy of Jehovah. As one of the Messianic Pss. it is appropriately used on Easter Day. It is divided into four strophes or verses, and is a dramatic poem, different speakers being introduced. The divisions are, vv. 1–3, 4–6, 7–9, 10–12. In the first two strophes the Psalmist is the speaker ; in the last two the King. (1–3) The poet views the nations plotting against Jehovah and His representative, the Messianic King ; (4–6) but remembering the power and majesty of God, he sees a speedy end to their devices. (7–9) Then the King is introduced relating Jehovah's decree and promise of sovereignty over all nations, and (10–12) bidding the rebellious kinglets therefore be warned in time and repent.

1. The heathen] RV 'the nations,' i.e. the Gentile or non-Jewish peoples. Rage] better, 'plot together.' 2. Against the LORD] In rebelling against Jehovah's anointed King they were rebelling against Jehovah Himself.

3. Bands] The words of the kings are of course metaphorical ; they were seeking to cast off what was to them a foreign yoke.

4. The contrast between Jehovah in His majesty and the puny plotters is dramatically introduced. 5. Then] i.e. when the plot ripens into action. 6. Yet] lit. 'and.' Upon my holy hill of Zion] Zion is the eastern hill of ancient Jerusalem on which the 'city of David' with its stronghold was built ; it is used poetically for Jerusalem the holy city : cp. Isa 64 10.

7. The Messianic King now speaks, quoting the promise given to David, the father of the dynasty, through Nathan the prophet : see 2 S 7 4-17. Thou art my Son ; this day, etc.] on the day of his anointing, when he was set apart to his high office. But some refer it to the day of his birth. In any case the king was adopted as the son of God, reigning in His name over His people (cp. Ac 13 33 Heb 1 5 5 5). 9. A rod of iron] because they are rebels who can only be restrained by repressive methods.

10. Be wise] The obvious lesson from the truths stated in the preceding vv.

12. Kiss the Son] This is a difficult pas-

sage. The translation of the AV is only got by assuming that the Psalmist has chosen the Aramaic word for 'Son' instead of the Hebrew. LXX renders, 'Lay hold of instruction,' which is in harmony with the general drift of the passage, and is supported by the Targum. Others translate 'Kiss' (i.e. worship or serve) 'with sincerity.' The doubt does not affect the teaching of the Ps. as a whole. *From* the way] RV 'in the way.' **When his wrath**, etc.] better, 'For soon His wrath will burn.' **Blessed** *are* **all they**, etc.] This is either a pious reflexion of the Psalmist at the end of the words put into the mouth of the King ; or, as Prof. Briggs holds, a liturgical addition suitable when the Ps. was used in worship.

PSALM 3

This is the first of the 'Davidic' Psalms. It is a morning prayer as v. 6 suggests. The heading of the Ps. provides a historical setting for it in the revolt of Absalom, and it is the only Ps. specifically dated at that time. There are many features in that revolt (2S16–18) which suit the circumstances to which the Psalmist refers. He speaks of the increasing number of his enemies (cp. 2S17 11), of the contempt in which many held him (cp. 2S 16 7-10), of the danger in which he lay (cp. 2S 17 2), and of his preservation by Jehovah (cp. 2S17 14). The Ps. contains the Psalmist's description of his foes (1, 2); his inward assurance of God's help (3, 4); his statement of his present experience (5, 6); and his prayer for complete deliverance and national blessing (7, 8).

1. Increased] cp. 2S15 12, 13. **2. Of my soul**] i.e. of myself. **3. A shield**] a natural metaphor in days when kings were warriors : cp. 18 2 84 9, 11 115 9, etc. **4. Out of his holy hill**] i.e. Zion, the seat of Jehovah's worship, where in a special sense He was present. The Psalmist was probably at a distance from Jerusalem. **Selah**] This word is found 71 times in the Psalter. It occurs in 40 Pss., as well as three times in Hab3, which is also a Ps. Its meaning and use are both uncertain. Possibly it is derived from a root, meaning to 'lift up.' LXX translates it 'interlude,' while the Jewish tradition renders it 'for ever.' (1) Some think that it is an instruction to the musicians to 'strike up' with an interlude during an interval of the singing. (2) Prof. Briggs suggests that the LXX and Jewish renderings are really two aspects of the same thing : the former ('interlude') denoting the point where the benediction might be sung and the Ps. concluded for that service ; while the latter ('for ever') gives the last word of the benediction, which would indicate the same thing. (3) Taking

another derivation (from *sallem*, 'supplement'), others conjecture that the note may indicate the point at which the MS has to be, or has been, supplemented from another MS. It is best, perhaps, just to regard it generally as a 'musical interlude.'

5. I laid me down, etc.] His very sleep, natural as it was, was a proof of God's care, for he might have slept the sleep of death.

Sustained] RV 'sustaineth,' suggesting continual oversight. **7. Arise, O LORD**] The ancient marching-song of the Hebrew host began with these words (Nu 10 35). **8. Salvation** *belongeth* **unto the LORD**] A triumphant assertion of what the adversaries denied in v. 2. **Thy blessing** *is*] RV 'thy blessing be' upon the people as upon their leader. **Selah**] see on v. 4.

PSALM 4

This is an evening hymn, and though no occasion is mentioned it may perhaps be referred, like Ps3 (its natural companion), to the time of Absalom's revolt, but to a somewhat later stage in the course of events, when the peril had largely passed away. It contains David's appeal to God (v. 1), his appeal to his enemies (vv. 2–5), and his own resolve (vv. 6–8).

Title.—(RV) 'For the Chief Musician ; on stringed instruments (**Neginoth**).'

1. God of my righteousness] The God who is on the side of the Psalmist's righteous cause. **Enlarged me**] RV 'set me at large.'

2. Sons of men] in contrast with God, who is addressed in v. 1. **How long** *will ye turn*, etc.] RV 'how long shall my glory be turned,' etc. **Leasing**] RV 'falsehood.' **3. But know**] introduces the truth which the Psalmist's enemies ignored. **4. Stand in awe**] LXX renders, 'Be ye angry,' and is followed by St. Paul in Eph4 26. **Be still**] cease your striving after vanity. **Selah**] see on 3 4.

5. Sacrifices of righteousness] sacrifices accompanied by right conduct, offered in a right spirit, and so acceptable to God. Perhaps there may be a reference to the insincere sacrifices of 2S15 12.

6. *There be* **many**] possibly in allusion to the discontented people whom Absalom sought to win by fair promises (2S15 4). **LORD, lift thou up**] a striking transition from the vain quests of men to the one source of the chief good. **The light of thy countenance**] favour, such as earthly kings express by a smiling face : see Nu6 26 Ps80 3, 7, 19. **7. More than in the time**] RV 'more than they have when,' etc. 'They' seems to refer to the enemies of the writer. He in his hardships is happier than they in their plenty : the peace of God is better than the mirth of harvest. **8.** The note of evensong. Read, 'In peace will I both lay me down and sleep.' The whole night's rest is peaceful, because God, the only source of protection, is on the Psalmist's side.

PSALM 5

This is a morning prayer before going to the sanctuary. The chief difficulty in ascribing it to David lies in the reference (v. 7) to 'thy holy temple.' The word means a 'palace,' and is not strictly applicable to the tent which David provided for the ark (2 S 6 17). But it was used of the sanctuary at Shiloh (1 S 1 9), and may have been poetically transferred to David's humbler tent ; or it may be figuratively employed to denote the heavenly temple. The Psalmist appeals to God for hearing (vv. 1–3), contrasts the exclusion of the wicked from God's presence with his own access (vv. 4–7), asks for guidance in the midst of his enemies (vv. 8, 9), and prays for their overthrow and for the triumph of the righteous (vv. 10–12). This is one of the Pss. for Ash Wednesday.

Title.—Nehiloth] RM ' wind instruments.'
1. My meditation] the thoughtful desire of the heart which hardly finds expression in words. It is in contrast with the 'cry' of v. 2. 2. My King] If the writer is David he forgets his own royalty in the presence of the heavenly King. Will I pray] RV 'do I pray.' 3. In the morning] emphatic and twice repeated. Direct] RV ' order,' arrange, perhaps, as a sacrifice (Gn 22 9 Lv 1 7,8). But see Job 23 4 32 14 33 5 37 19. Look up] RV 'keep watch' for an answer.
4. Neither shall evil dwell] RM ' the evil man shall not sojourn.' 5. Foolish] RV 'arrogant.' Stand in thy sight] endure the holiness of thy presence. 6. Leasing] RV ' lies.' Will abhor the bloody] RV 'abhorreth the bloodthirsty.' 7. The two features of access to God are (1) God's grace, and (2) the worshipper's reverence. Toward] The worshipper in the Temple court prostrated himself towards the sanctuary. 8. Straight] RV 'plain,' level, easy to walk in. 9. The heart and the speech of the wicked are alike corrupt. See Ro 3 13, where this v. is quoted. The throat of the flatterer is compared to an open grave, ever clamouring for fresh victims—a very suggestive figure.
10. Destroy .. them] RV 'hold them guilty.' Against thee] The Psalmist identifies God's cause with his own. 11. Love thy name] thy revealed character. A name comes to be the equivalent of all that we know about the person who bears it : cp. 'Hallowed be Thy name.'

PSALM 6

This is the first of the Penitential Psalms, the others being Pss 32, 38, 51, 102, 130, 143. It is the prayer of a sufferer whose experience is like that of Job. He is prostrated by severe illness, and is even in danger of death, while the mockery of his enemies makes his trouble the harder to bear. He entreats earnestly that God may deliver him (vv. 1–7), and rises to a sudden confidence that his prayer has been heard and that his enemies will be put to shame (vv. 8–10).

. Title.—On Neginoth upon Sheminith] RV ' on stringed instruments, set to the Sheminith (lower octave).'

1. Rebuke .. chasten] the two aspects of affliction—the one being for punishment and the other for discipline ; the one proceeding from displeasure and the other from love. 2. Weak] RV 'withered away': see Ps 102 11. My bones] the innermost framework of my body. Vexed] used here of physical pain, and in the next v. of mental anguish : cp. Ps 2 5. 3. My soul .. also] The bodily pain has produced distress of spirit. There is an echo of these words in Jn 12 27. O LORD, how long?] The broken sentence is more expressive than if it had been completed : see Ps 90 13. 5. The grave] RV ' Sheol,' the shadowy abode of the dead. In the OT. time there was no clear expectation of immortality in the sense of a happy future life. 6. All the night] RV 'every night.' 7. Mine eye is consumed] The sunken eye is a sure token of bodily anguish or mental distress.
10. Read, 'All mine enemies shall be ashamed .. they shall turn back, they shall be ashamed suddenly.'

PSALM 7

This Ps. is an appeal to God as the righteous Judge against an ungrateful and vindictive enemy. Nothing is known of Cush the Benjamite, but the case of Shimei affords a parallel to the circumstances here referred to (2 S 18 21). The absence of any Scripture mention of Cush makes it all the more probable that the title of this Ps. is genuine, and not invented. The Psalmist asserts his own innocence (vv. 1–6), calls on God, the righteous Judge of all the earth, to exercise His power against evil-doers (vv. 7–13), and describes how the malice of the wicked works its own defeat (vv. 14–17).

Title.—Shiggaion] perhaps, ' a wandering (i.e. changeful) melody.'
3. If I have done this] with which Cush charged him. See further in v. 4. 4. The second clause may be read without the parenthesis, ' or despoiled him that without cause was mine adversary.' 5. Take] RV ' overtake.' Mine honour] RV 'my glory,' an equivalent for 'soul' and 'life' in the previous parallel clauses. Selah] see on 3 4. 6. Awake for me] a daring figure, as if God's delay had been due to sleep. To the judgment that, etc.] RV 'thou

hast commanded judgment,' i.e. exercised the justice of which Thou art the source.

7. So shall, etc.] RV 'and let,' etc. **People**] RV 'peoples.' So in v. 8. An assize of all the nations is pictured. **For their sakes, etc.**] RV 'over them return thou on high,' or 'sit thou above them,' i.e. in judgment. **8. Shall judge**] RV 'ministereth judgment to.' **9. Just**] RV 'righteous,' the same epithet which is applied to God. **The hearts and reins**] the whole inner life. The reins are the kidneys, and are spoken of like the heart, the bowels, and the internal organs generally, as the seat of thought and feeling.

11. Read, ' God is a righteous judge, yea, a God that hath indignation every day.' **12.** Read, 'If a man turn not He (God) will whet,' etc.

13. He ordaineth, etc.] RV 'He maketh his arrows fiery *shafts*.' The sense is parallel with the last clause of v. 12.

14. There is a transition at this point from God to the wicked man. **15. He made**] RV 'he hath made.' The evil he planned for others comes on himself. **16.** another figure for the same thing. Mischief is like a stone thrown up, which falls back upon the thrower's head. **Pate**] Old English for 'head.' **17.** All that has been said illustrates the righteousness of the Lord, which is accordingly the ground of this concluding ascription of praise.

PSALM 8

This Ps. is a poem of wondering praise, called forth by the thought of the supremacy and honour that God has given to man, who in himself holds such an insignificant place in the universe. The glory of the heavens and the variety of the works of nature combine to emphasise the marvel of this choice. The Ps. is based upon the story of creation (Gn 1 26-28), and sets forth the ideal dignity of man. V. 6 is applied in 1 Cor 15 27 Eph 1 22 to the exaltation of Christ, in whom alone the ideal is realised. In Heb 2 6-8 the same thought is expressed in another way, man's failure to attain to full dominion being contrasted with the supremacy Christ has won. The Ps. is used on Ascension Day.

Title.—**Upon Gittith**] RV 'set to the Gittith' (perhaps an instrument, or tune, of Gath).

1. O LORD our Lord] lit. 'Jehovah, our Lord.' So in v. 9. **Thy name**] see on Ps 5 11. **Above**] RV 'upon.' The glory of God is stamped or impressed on the visible universe.

2. Babes and sucklings] a figure for men in their weakness and ignorance. The words are quoted by our Lord in a more literal sense (Mt 21 16). **Ordained strength**] RV 'established strength,' laid a foundation for Thy great work. LXX has 'perfected praise,' and our Lord follows this version in the quotation just mentioned. **Because of thine enemies,**

etc.] God's use of feeble instruments to display His glory puts His adversaries to silence: see 1 Cor 1 27-29.

3. The work of thy fingers] The wisdom and skill of the Creator are thus poetically expressed. **The moon and the stars**] It is the glory of the sky by night which is before the writer's mind. The discoveries of astronomy only make the conceptions of the Ps. more impressive. **4. What is man**] The word rendered 'man' means 'frail man'—humanity in all its weakness and limitation. **The son of man**] the human race. The expression is a simple variant, and is exactly equivalent to 'man' in the former clause. **Visitest**] with loving care and remembrance.

5. A little lower than the angels] RV 'but a little lower than God.' 'A little less than divine' would represent the meaning. Man, the only creature made in God's image, stands nearest to Him in the ranks of the universe. Philosophy and science are at one with Scripture in placing man at the top of the scale of creation. **6. All *things* under his feet**] A reference to Gn 1 26-28: applied to Christ, 1 Cor 15 27 Heb 2 6-8.

PSALM 9

Pss 9 and 10 are combined in LXX, and there is certainly a real, though obscure, relationship between them. The two together form one 'acrostic,' the vv. beginning with the successive letters of the Hebrew alphabet, though in both Pss. there is a gap in the arrangement. The subject matter of the two Pss., however, does not suggest that we have in them the two halves of what was originally a single Ps. Ps 9 is distinctly national and Ps 10 as distinctly personal, and though both may be by the same author, the problem of their connexion must be left unsolved.

Ps 9 is the song of a king who has gained a victory over a foreign enemy, and finds in this a proof of God's righteous rule over the whole earth—a rule which he prays may be yet more fully displayed. Only in vv. 13, 14 is the note of personal affliction and need to be heard.

Title.—**Upon Muth-labben**] 'Muth-labben' means 'Death to the son,' and probably indicates some well-known song, to the tune of which the Ps. was directed to be sung.

3. They shall fall] RV 'they stumble.'
4. Judging right] RV 'judging righteously.'
5. Heathen] RV 'nations.' So in vv. 15, 19. **6.** RV 'The enemy are come to an end, they are desolate for ever: and the cities which thou hast overthrown, their very memorial is perished.' The words are still part of the prayer to Jehovah. Faith in God demands complete deliverance. **7. Shall endure**] RV 'sitteth as king.' The eternal rule of God contrasted with the passing powers of earth.

8. People] RV 'peoples.' **10. Thy name**] see on 5 11.

11. Which dwelleth in Zion] Jerusalem, and especially the hill of Zion, was regarded as the earthly throne of God, after David had placed the ark there : see 76 2 132 13. **12.** RV 'For he that maketh inquisition for blood remembereth them.' God is represented as the avenger of blood (Gn 9 5). **Humble**] RV 'poor' or meek. One of a group of words which in OT. have at first an outward and then a more spiritual sense, the chief sufferers from want and oppression being often God's true people.

13, 14. This personal cry of distress seems to break the connexion rather abruptly. Possibly we should read, 'The Lord has had mercy . . he has considered my trouble.' **The gates of death**] the extremity of affliction. **The gates of the daughter of Zion**] 'The daughter of Zion' is a figure for Jerusalem : see Isa 1 8 Lam 2 25 Ps 45 12 137 8. The gates of an Eastern city were its most public and busy spots. The throng of life is thus contrasted with the solitude and dreariness of ' the gates of death ' in v. 13.

16. RV ' The Lord hath made himself known, he hath executed judgment.' **Higgaion**] a musical term applied only here. It occurs in the text of 92 3, and probably means something like our *forte*. **Selah**] see on 3 4. ' Higgaion. Selah ' together may mean *fortissimo*. **17. Be turned into hell**] RV ' return to Sheol,' the place of the dead, not regarded specially as a place of torment. ' Return ' seems strictly to apply to the body, which goes back to the dust whence it was taken : cp. Gn 3 19 Ps 90 3 104 29.

18. Needy] Another of the group of words referred to in the note on v. 12. **Poor**] The same word as in v. 12. **19. Man**] The word means ' frail man,' as in 8 4.

PSALM 10

This Ps. has no title. Its relationship to Ps 9 has been discussed in intro. to that Ps. It reflects a time of great social disorder, in which wickedness and violence are rampant, and the righteous are sorely oppressed. It falls roughly into two parts. The wrongs which call for redress are described (vv. 1–11) and God's interposition is invoked (vv. 12–18).

1. God seems to be ignorant of what is taking place, or indifferent to it. The Psalmist, however, does not really believe this, or he would not appeal to God at all. **2** b. RM ' They (the poor) are taken in the devices that they (the wicked) have imagined.' **3. And blesseth the covetous**, etc.] RV ' And the covetous renounceth, yea, contemneth the Lord.' **4. Will not seek**, etc.] RV ' *saith*, He (God) will not require *it* ': see v. 13. **God is not**, etc.] RV ' all his thoughts are, There is no God.' **5. Always grievous**] RV ' firm at

all times.' He seems to prosper in all his plans. **Puffeth**] in scorn and contempt.

7. Fraud] RV ' oppression.' **Vanity**] RV ' iniquity.' Part of this v. is quoted in Ro 3 14 as a description of human depravity in general.

8. The brigand life here described has never been uncommon in Eastern lands, and the picture given is by no means metaphorical : see Prov 1 10-18. **Poor**] RV ' helpless,' RM ' hapless,' a word found only here and in vv. 10, 14.

10. RM ' And being crushed he (the poor) boweth down, and the helpless fall by his strong ones ' (by the wicked man's followers). **11.** Cp. vv. 1, 4. The blindness of God, which the Psalmist knows is only apparent, is what the wicked man really believes in.

14. Thou hast seen *it*] A direct contradiction of the wicked man's thought in v. 11.

15. Break . . the arm] destroy the power. **16.** The faith of the Psalmist here asserts itself. **The heathen**] RV ' the nations.' The past extermination of the Canaanites, or some repulse of foreign invaders, is regarded as a pledge that God will remove the present troublers of society. **18. The man of the earth**] RV ' the man which is of the earth.' The word is again ' frail man.' Foreign enemies and evil-doers at home must alike be made to feel their impotence against God.

PSALM 11

The Ps. is a song of confidence in God, and in the security of the righteous under His protection, notwithstanding the timid counsels of less trustful friends, and the evil devices of the wicked, who are doomed to destruction.

3. If the foundations be destroyed] if those in high places disregard the first principles of righteousness. This is an argument of unbelief and cowardice. It is suggested that wickedness may be so successful as to make resistance useless. **4.** God is the great Reality whom such pleadings leave out of account.

His holy temple] the heavenly sanctuary.

Try] test, as precious metals are tested.

5. Trieth] tries and approves. They stand the test.

6. Snares] Another reading is ' burning coals,' which fits the context better. **Fire and brimstone**] as in the destruction of Sodom : Gn 19 24. **An horrible tempest**] RV ' burning wind,' like the simoom of the desert. **Their cup**] a common Scripture figure for ' their destiny ' ; men's experiences in life being like a draught which they have to drink.

7. RV ' The Lord is righteous : he loveth righteousness.' God's dealings with men reflect His own character. **His countenance**, etc.] RV ' the upright shall behold His face,' shall be admitted to His favour, as worthy subjects are admitted to the presence of a king : cp. Mt 5 8.

PSALM 12

The same subject may be traced here as in Pss 9–11, viz. a time of persecution and oppression coupled with a conviction that God lives and will yet deliver.

Title as in Ps 6.

2. Vanity] empty and false words. **A double heart**] a figure for treachery and deceit. **4. Our lips** *are* **our own**] We have a right to say what we please, to gain our end. **5. Now will I arise**] God's time for interposition always arrives sooner or later. The Psalmist pictures the proper moment as having come. *From him that* **puffeth,** etc.] RV 'at whom they puff.' **6. The words of the LORD**] His promises of help to the righteous. They are reliable, in contrast to the deceitful words of the wicked in v. 2. **A furnace of earth**] RV 'a furnace on the earth.' The meaning is perhaps, ' silver tried in a furnace (and flowing out) on the earth.' **7.** This v. is the conclusion of the thought of the Ps., though v. 8 repeats the opening complaint.

PSALM 13

The prominence which the Ps. gives to one enemy (v. 2) among the writer's numerous adversaries (v. 4), suggests the circumstances of David's persecution by Saul (1 S 21–27). The Psalmist begins in agitation and despondency, and ends in tranquillity and faith.

1. PBV ' How long wilt thou forget me, O Lord, for ever ? ' A single question instead of the double one of AV. 'Forget for ever' means 'continue to forget.' The seemingly self-contradictory form of the question reflects the conflict of the writer's feelings, ' Hope despairs and yet despair hopes' (Luther). Note the four repetitions of ' how long ' in vv. 1, 2. **2. Take counsel in my soul**] be compelled to make vain plans for my own deliverance. **3. Lighten mine eyes**] give me new life and hope. ' Dying eyes are glazed : a sick man's are heavy and dull. Returning health brightens them ' : see 1 S 14 27, 29.

PSALM 14

This Ps., like Ps 12, gives a picture of a corrupt state of society in which God is ignored, and His people are oppressed. David's authorship is not absolutely disproved by v. 7, which some have regarded as a later addition, and where, in any case, ' bring back the captivity ' may only mean 'restore the fortunes.' Though God is denied (v. 1), He really sees (v. 2), speaks (v. 3), and acts (v. 4). The Ps. reappears with some variations as Ps 53. Vv. 1–3 are quoted in Ro 3 10–12.

1. The fool is a character who in Scripture is marked by wickedness as well as by what we call folly. His defect is moral as well as

mental. **In his heart**] His denial is a practical one, and he really acts upon it, whatever he may say or think that he believes. *There is no God*] cp. Ps 12 4, 11, 13.

2. The LORD looked down] cp. Gn 6 5 11 5 18 21, where similar figures describe God's perception of the wickedness of men in the primitive world.

3. Gone aside] from the true path.

4. God speaks in surprise at the folly of the wicked. **Eat up my people** *as* **they eat bread**] conduct at once rapacious and unconcerned. **Call not upon the LORD**] Such wickedness is naturally prayerless.

The Septuagint (LXX), Vulgate, and Syriac versions insert between vv. 4 and 5 four verses which are retained in the PBV q.v. They were probably inserted first as a marginal note in some codices, being quoted from Ro 3 10-18 as an illustration of this passage, and so ultimately found their way into the text of some MSS.

5. There were they in great fear] a sudden mention of God's interference. Some historical event, like the destruction of Pharaoh's host, seems to be in the writer's mind. **6.** RM ' Ye put to shame the counsel (i.e. the righteous thoughts) of the poor, but the LORD is his refuge.' ' The poor ' are the afflicted righteous : see 9 12.

7. Out of Zion] Zion is regarded as God's dwelling-place, from which He sends forth His help : see 3 4. **Bringeth back the captivity**] The phrase may have the general sense of ' restoring prosperity to,' and need not refer to the Babylonian exile : see Job 42 10. **Jacob,** like ' Israel,' is a name for the nation.

PSALM 15

In this Ps. we have a fine summary of the essentials of OT. piety. It sets forth the character and conduct required in the worshipper for acceptance with God. The occasion of its composition may have been the bringing of the ark to Jerusalem (2 S 6 17). Cp. with the whole Ps. Isa 33 14, 15. This is another of the Pss. for Ascension Day.

1. Abide] RV ' sojourn.' The worshipper is conceived as the guest of God. **Tabernacle**] lit. ' tent,' the kind of structure prepared by David for the ark. **Thy holy hill**] Mt. Zion, viewed as God's dwelling-place, and specially consecrated first by the presence of the ark, and afterwards by Solomon's Temple.

2. In his heart] Emphasis is laid on inward sincerity as well as on outward integrity.

3. Backbiteth] RV ' slandereth.' **Taketh up a reproach**] The phrase refers to receiving and repeating what is to another's discredit. **4.** *He that* **sweareth to** *his own* **hurt, and changeth not**] A truly upright man will keep his word even to his own disadvantage.

5. Usury] was forbidden by the Mosaic Law (Lv 25 36, 37 Dt 23 19, 20) as inconsistent with the kindly spirit of brotherhood among Israelites. Interest was allowed to be taken from foreigners. The absence of greed and exaction is what the Psalmist commends. Nor taketh reward against the innocent] Bribery has always been one of the greatest corruptions of society in the East. It was sternly forbidden in Israel (Ex 23 7, 8 Dt 27 25), and the worthy guest of Jehovah could not stoop to such a thing. Shall never be moved] an expressive way of summing up the strength and stability of a righteous life.

PSALM 16

The Ps. is the confident and joyous prayer of one whose highest satisfaction is in God and in good men (vv. 2, 3), who renounces all the ways of idolatry (v. 4), and who finds in God not only ample wealth and happiness for the present (vv. 5–7), but also a continuous prospect of the truest life (vv. 8–11). The Ps. is quoted in Ac 2 25 13 35 as a prophecy of the Resurrection of Christ. While this is not its primary reference, and while the language does not necessarily involve all that is read into it in the NT., it is true that the thought of the Ps. suggests the hope of immortality, and that the Resurrection of Christ affords the most striking illustration of its meaning.

Title.—Michtam of David] The meaning is uncertain. 'Michtam' may possibly be 'a golden Psalm,' or it may have some musical reference.

2. RV 'I have said unto the LORD (Jehovah), Thou art my Lord : I have no good beyond thee.' 3. RV 'As for the saints that are in the earth, They are the excellent in whom is all my delight.'

4. That hasten, etc.] RV 'that exchange the LORD for another god.' Drink offerings of blood] to be understood perhaps not literally, but in the sense of cruel and impure sacrifices. Their names] the names of the idols which are thus worshipped.

5, 6. There are two figures here, one contained in the words portion, lot, lines, heritage, suggested by the division of the land of Canaan among the tribes, and another contained in the word cup, which denotes the experiences of the Psalmist's life. In Nu 18 20 God is the only portion of the Levites, who received no earthly territory. The writer here claims the same goodly heritage.

7. My reins] or as we should say, 'my heart': see 7 9. God's inward voice heard in hours of quietness, is one of the chief blessings of His people. 8. I have set the LORD, etc.] the constant, deliberate, and conscious exercise of faith. 9. My glory] my soul: see Ps 7 5 108 1. Rest in hope] RV 'dwell in

safety.' The primary reference is not to the dead body in the grave, but to the continuance of bodily life on earth.

10. In hell] RV 'to Sheol.' The meaning is, 'Thou wilt not suffer me to die.' Thine Holy One] RV 'thine holy one'; RM 'thy godly (or beloved) one.' The allusion is primarily to the Psalmist himself, though the passage is used by St. Peter (Ac 2 25-28) to prove that the resurrection of Christ was in accordance with prophecy. Corruption] RM 'the pit,' the grave, the state of the dead.

11. The path of life] not specially of life after death, but of true life in the fellowship of God. In thy presence] the presence in which the Psalmist already lived (v. 8). At thy right hand] RV 'in thy right hand.' For evermore] The contrast which the Ps. draws is not, perhaps, so much between life here and life hereafter, as between life without God and life with Him. In its very nature, however, the latter life is enduring, and hence the Psalmist's words contain an anticipation (though it may be a dim and only semi-conscious one) of the immortality which Christ has brought to light.

PSALM 17

The Psalmist makes his appeal to the justice of God (vv. 1, 2), and supports his prayer by an assertion of his conscious innocence (vv. 3–5) and an account of the eager cruelty of his enemies (vv. 9–12). The concluding thought, that true satisfaction is found in God alone (vv. 14, 15), recalls the teaching of Ps 16, with which this Ps. presents other points of likeness.

1. Feigned] false, insincere. 2. My sentence] my judgment, in the favourable sense of 'vindication.' Let thine eyes, etc.] better, 'thine eyes look upon equity,' a confident assertion of God's justice. 3. Proved] tested. In the night] when man is alone with God, and conscience shows things in their true character. Shalt find, etc.] RM 'findest no evil purpose in me.' 4. Concerning] RV 'as for.' By the word of thy lips] the commandments of God. 5. RV 'My steps have held fast to thy paths, My feet have not slipped.'

8. The apple of the eye] The pupil of the eye, a specially important and delicate organ, with peculiarly sensitive arrangements for its protection : see Dt 32 10. Under the shadow of thy wings] as a mother-bird shelters her young. 10. They are inclosed in their own fat] better, 'they have shut up their heart,' a figure for arrogance. 11. Us] The Psalmist mentions his companions along with himself. Bowing down] RV 'to cast us down.' 12. Like as a lion] RV 'He is like a lion,' the chief enemy (perhaps Saul) being meant. 13. Disappoint] RV 'confront.' From the

wicked, *which is*, etc.] RV 'from the wicked by thy sword.' **14. From men** *which are*, etc.] RV 'from men by thy hand.' **From men of the world**, etc.] RM 'from men whose portion in life is of the world,' whose ideal is animal gratification, a numerous offspring, and wealth to leave behind them. **Full of children**] RV 'satisfied with children.'

15. The Psalmist's satisfaction, present and future, lies in the fellowship of God. **When I awake**] either 'after each night's rest,' or 'after the night of trouble is past.' The thought of life after death may not have been clearly in the writer's mind, but his conviction and experience that true life is life in God involve the foundation of the Christian hope. **With thy likeness**] cp. Nu 12 8 Ps 139 18. The Psalmist seeks continual fellowship with God.

PSALM 18

Of all the Pss. this is the one which can be ascribed with greatest confidence to David. It is found, with some variations, in 2 S 22, and the title is largely taken from 2 S 22 1. It consists of a series of triumphant thanksgivings to God, with which the writer connects a highly figurative account of his deliverance from danger (vv. 4–19), an assertion of his own uprightness (vv. 20–24), and a description of the victories he has won by God's assistance (vv. 29–48).

1. I will love thee] RV 'I love thee.' This v. is omitted in 2 S. It was perhaps inserted when the Ps. was adapted for use by the congregation in the Temple. **2.** Notice the succession of figures drawn from the experiences of a warrior's life in a country where natural strongholds as well as artificial fortresses were common. **Strength**] RV 'strong rock.' **Buckler**] RV 'shield.' So in v. 30. **Horn**] a symbol of irresistible strength. **4. Sorrows**] RV 'cords.' So in v. 5. **5. Hell**] RV 'Sheol,' the state of the dead. **Prevented**] RV 'came upon.' So in v. 18. Vv. 4, 5 mean that David felt himself in peril of death. **6. His temple**] in heaven.

7–16. In these vv. the manifestation of God's power to deliver is poetically described as the physical appearance of God Himself, accompanied by the most impressive natural phenomena, such as earthquake and thunderstorm. He is conceived as dwelling in the heart of the thunderstorm, surrounded by fires which break forth as lightning through the cloud.

10. A cherub] Cherubim are most familiar to readers of Scripture as symbolic figures appearing in the furniture and decoration of the tabernacle and the Temple. They also appear in Ezekiel's vision of the mystic chariot as the bearers of God's throne (Ezk 1, 10). Here the cherub seems to be a personification

of the storm cloud, as the parallel idea in the next clause shows.

12. Read, 'From the brightness before him there passed through his thick cloud hailstones and coals of fire.' **Coals of fire**] lightning. **13. His voice**] the thunder. **14. His arrows**] another figure for lightning. **15.** The drying up of the Red Sea is woven into the imagery of the storm. **16. Many waters**] the emblem of David's troubles. The whole sublime manifestation of God was on his behalf. **19. A large place**] the opposite of 'straits.'

24–26. David finds in his own case an illustration of the truth that God deals with all men according to their works, opposing those who oppose Him, as well as showing His perfections to those who are like Him.

27. High looks] RV 'the haughty eyes.' **28. My candle**] RV 'my lamp,' the symbol of David's prosperity : see Job 18 6. **29.** This v. may refer to the pursuit of the Amalekites (1 S 30) and the capture of Jerusalem (2 S 5 6-8).

33. Hinds' *feet*] agile, swift, and sure. **My high places**] The figure of the hind, climbing precipitous hills, is continued. **34. A bow of steel**, etc.] RV 'mine arms do bend a bow of brass' (i.e. copper or bronze), a harder task than to bend a wooden bow.

35. Gentleness] RM 'condescension.' For the thought cp. 113 6 Isa 57 15 : see also Ps 23. **36. Enlarged my steps**] given me freedom to move without obstruction. **40. Given me the necks of mine enemies**] RV 'made mine enemies turn their backs unto me.'

43. Heathen] RV 'nations.' So in v. 49. David subdued all the countries around Palestine (2 S 8). **Shall serve**] This and the following future tenses to the end of v. 45 are better rendered as past. **45. Be afraid**] RV 'come trembling.' **47. People**] RV 'peoples.'

PSALM 19

This Ps. falls into two well-marked divisions. Vv. 1–6 describe the glory of God (*El*) as seen in the heavenly bodies, especially the sun, and are thus parallel to Ps 8. Vv. 7–14 deal with the excellence of the revelation of God (*Jehovah*) in the Law—the subject which is expanded in Ps 119. It is possible that two independent Pss. are here combined, as in Ps 108, or that the second half was written as an addition to the first by another hand. The first part may quite well have been David's work. The second part may be divided into the praises of the Law (vv. 7–11), and the Psalmist's prayer for preservation from sin (vv. 12–14). This is one of the Pss. for Christmas Day.

1. The firmament] the sky, conceived of as a solid canopy: see Gn 1 6. **2. Days and nights** in unbroken succession testify to God's glory.

3. RV 'There is no speech nor language; Their voice cannot be heard.' Their witness is none the less impressive for its silence.

4. The silent testimony of the heavens is world-wide. **Their line]** the measuring line, marking off the region to which the message of the skies comes. LXX has 'their sound,' and is followed by St. Paul, who quotes this v. in Ro 10 18. **Tabernacle]** or tent : see Isa 40 22. The sun, as the most glorious of the heavenly bodies, is personified as a hero. 5. **As a bridegroom]** The comparison suggests the vigour and beauty of youth as well as the splendour of wedding attire. **A race]** RV 'his course' from E. to W., the two 'ends' of heaven mentioned in v. 6. 6. **There is nothing hid,** etc.] another way of putting the universal scope of the sun's testimony.

7-9. Here we have a sudden transition from nature to revelation. The word **law** (*torah*) means 'teaching' or 'instruction,' and describes not only the Law of Moses, but all the commandments of God. It is described as a **testimony** (see Ex 25 16, 21) or witness to God's character and requirements (v. 7), as **statutes** (RV 'precepts '), a **commandment** (v. 8), **judgments** or moral decisions (v. 9). Each term is connected with some practical benefit which the Law confers on men.

7. **Converting]** RV 'restoring.' 8. **Enlightening the eyes]** imparting refreshment and vigour to the soul : see on 13 3. 9. **The fear of the LORD]** another expression for the Law, which produces this fear in the heart. **Clean]** opposed to impurity of life. **Enduring for ever]** as the expression of God's eternal righteousness. 10. **The honeycomb]** rather, 'the droppings of the honeycomb,' the purest of the honey.

12. **Understand]** RV 'discern.' **Cleanse]** RV 'clear,' in the sense of 'acquit.' Unconscious sins could be atoned for (Nu 15 22-26), and for such sins forgiveness is asked here.

13. **Presumptuous** *sins*] those deliberately committed, in contrast to those of ignorance and inadvertence. For such transgressions the Law provided no atonement (Nu 15 30, 31), and the Psalmist prays to be restrained from committing them. **Innocent from the great transgression]** RV 'clear from great transgression.' 14. **Strength]** RV 'rock.'

PSALM 20

This and the following Ps. form a closely connected pair. The one is a prayer for a king going out to battle, and the other is a thanksgiving for his triumphant return. Both have the same title. There is nothing against the early date of the Pss., and David may be their subject, but it is hardly natural to regard him as their author. In Ps 20, vv. 1–5 are the prayer of the people, v. 6 is the confident

utterance of an individual (perhaps a priest or the king himself), and in vv. 7–9 the people again take up the strain.

1. **The name]** is equivalent to the God to whom it belongs. It expresses all that is known about Him. **Defend thee]** RV 'set thee up on high,' over all enemies. 2. **The sanctuary]** God's dwelling-place on Mt. Zion is here meant, as the next clause shows. But see v. 6. 3. **Remember .. accept]** The words refer to the sacrifices both of the past and of the present. Sacrifices were usual before going out to war : see 1 S 7 9, 10 13 9, 12.

4. **According to thine own heart]** RV 'thy heart's desire,' i.e. victory. **Counsel]** plan of campaign : see 2 S 17. 5. **Thy salvation]** the deliverance to be wrought by the king's success. **Set up** *our* **banners]** lift them up and wave them in triumph.

6. **Now]** A single person here takes up the song after the sacrifice has been offered. Faith is assured that the offering has been accepted and the king's prayers heard. **His anointed]** the king : see 2 2. **From his holy heaven]** God's real dwelling, of which Zion is but the type.

7. **Some]** refers to heathen enemies, like the Egyptians (Ex 14 Isa 31 1). **Remember]** RV 'make mention of,' as a watchword.

8. **Brought down]** RV 'bowed down.'

9. Read with LXX 'O Lord, save the king : and answer us when we call.'

PSALM 21

The title and authorship have been discussed under Ps 20, to which this forms a sequel. Its contents include a thanksgiving to God for His blessings to the king (vv. 1–7), an address to the king promising future victories over his enemies (vv. 8–12), and a closing ascription of praise to God (v. 13). The Ps. is used on Ascension Day.

1, 2. The prayers for victory in Ps 20 have been answered. 3. **Preventest him]** lit. 'goest to meet him.' **A crown]** the victory confirming his rule, like a second coronation.

4. In OT. times long life on earth was regarded as one of the greatest of blessings : see 1 K 3 11. The language here is ideal, but it was not unusual to speak so of kings (1 K 1 31 Neh 2 3). 5. **Thy salvation]** the victory bestowed by God, which reflects divine attributes—' glory,' ' honour and majesty'— upon the king. 6. **With thy countenance]** RV ' in thy presence.'

9. **Oven]** RV 'furnace,' as fuel for a furnace. 10. The king will destroy young and old among his enemies—the terrible custom of ancient conquerors. 11, 12. Read, ' For though they intend .. though they imagine .. they shall not prevail, for thou shalt make them turn .. thou shalt make ready,' etc.

PSALM 22

The Ps. has two sections, in the first of which (vv. 1–21) the writer earnestly seeks God's help in a time of extreme trouble, while in the second (vv. 22–31) he breaks into a song of thanksgiving and praise. The trouble is caused by strong and relentless enemies who scorn his trust in God, and persistently threaten his life. The thanksgiving is remarkable for its anticipation of the worldwide acknowledgment of God that is to follow the Psalmist's deliverance. The last-named fact has led some to the view that the Ps. describes a national rather than a personal experience, while the use made of it in the NT. has caused others to regard it as wholly prophetic of the sufferings of Christ. There seems to be a real personal element in the Ps., but at the same time the writer as a righteous sufferer has a representative character, and his words have a partial fulfilment in the experiences of the faithful remnant in Israel, and a complete fulfilment in those of Jesus Christ, which are the supreme type of righteous suffering leading to the establishment of a universal kingdom of God. The contents of the Ps. explain its use on Good Friday.

Title.—(RV) ' Set to Aijeleth hash-Shahar ' (the hind of the morning) ; probably the name of some well-known song, to the melody of which the Ps. was intended to be sung.

1. The opening words (in the Aramaic form) were quoted by our Lord on the Cross (Mt 27⁴⁶). It has been supposed that He repeated the whole Ps., and that the remainder was drowned in the tumult and jeers of the mob. **2. And am not silent]** RM ' but find no rest.' **3. The praises of Israel]** which have deservedly surrounded God in the past, and which He will not cease to deserve by ceasing to deliver His people. The thought is expanded in vv. 4, 5.

6. This v. describes the Psalmist's humiliation in terms similar to those used of the suffering Servant of the Lord in Isaiah (41¹⁴ 49⁷ 52¹⁴ 53²,³). **7. Shoot out the lip . . shake the head]** gestures of contempt and hatred. **8.** These very words were used by the priests in mockery of our Lord as He hung on the Cross (Mt 27⁴³). **12. Bulls . . strong** *bulls* **of Bashan]** suggesting the strength and aggressive rage of the Psalmist's enemies. Bashan was the N. part of the region E. of the Jordan, and was a rich pasture land. **15. The** parching effects of a fever supply another metaphor for the Psalmist's trouble.

16. Dogs] which haunt Eastern towns and villages in savage and cowardly packs—fit emblems of the Psalmist's fierce and yet contemptible foes. **They pierced my hands and**

my feet] The reference is still to the dogs, who snap at the exposed parts of those whom they attack. The singular coincidence between this v. and what was done at the Crucifixion is not noted in NT. **They pierced]** taken from LXX and Vulgate. Other versions read, ' they bound.' Heb. has, ' like a lion': see RM.

17. I may tell all my bones] i.e. count them all. They are visible through his emaciated flesh. The words may be either a literal or a figurative description of the writer's miserable state. **18.** The conduct of his enemies is that of robbers. The application of this v. in Jn 19²⁴ is well known. **20. My darling]** RM ' my only one,' my precious life. **From . . the dog]** cp. v. 16. **21. Thou hast heard me]** a sudden conviction of faith which gives a new tone to the rest of the Ps. **Unicorns]** RV ' wild-oxen.' In this and the preceding v. the figures of vv. 12, 13, 16 (bulls, lions, dogs) are repeated. **22.** These words are put into the mouth of Christ in Heb 2¹². **26. The meek]** the afflicted righteous, like the ' poor ' and the ' humble.' **Eat and be satisfied]** in the meal which accompanies their sacrifice (Lv 7¹⁶), or to which they may be invited by the Psalmist when he presents his thankoffering.

Your heart shall live] RV ' let your heart live,' the writer's prayer for his sacrificial guests.

27-30. These vv. extend the circle in which God is to be praised. It includes all the inhabitants and rulers of the earth, and all the generations to come.

29. *They that be* **fat,** etc.] RV ' the fat ones of the earth,' the mightiest rulers. **Eat and worship]** join in the sacrificial feast. Or perhaps the words mean ' shall worship Him alone.' **They that go down to the dust]** all mortal men, perhaps specially referring to the kings of the earth with their transient glory. **None can keep alive,** etc.] Read with LXX (joining this clause with the beginning of v. 30) ' and as for him that could not keep his soul alive, his seed shall serve Him ' (Jehovah). The weakest and most distressed will leave a posterity to praise God. **30. It shall be accounted,** etc.] RV ' It shall be told of the Lord unto the *next* generation.'

PSALM 23

This is a Ps. of simple and unclouded confidence in God, who is described first as a shepherd (vv. 1–4) and next as an host (vv. 5–6). The beautiful imagery of the first part would be natural on the lips of the king who was a shepherd in his youth. The reference to ' the house of the Lord ' in v. 6 may be a continuation of the figure of the host, and need not indicate a date after the building of the Temple.

3. Leadeth] RV ' guideth.' **An Eastern**

shepherd goes before his flock. **For his name's sake**] in consistency with the character which He has already made known.

4. Shadow of death] rather, 'deep darkness': see Jer 13[16] Am 5[8]. The **rod** was a short oaken club for defence ; the **staff** a longer pole for use in climbing, or for leaning upon. An Eastern shepherd still carries both.

5. In the presence of mine enemies] as when David enjoyed the hospitality of Barzillai (2 S 17[27-29]). **Anointest**] RV 'hast anointed,' as a host anoints an honoured guest : see Lk 7[46]. **Runneth over**] God's hospitality is lavish and generous. **6. Goodness** and **mercy**, like two angels, 'pursue' the Psalmist, determined, as it were, to run him down. **For ever**] lit. 'for length of days,' referring to prolonged earthly life rather than to life beyond the grave.

PSALM 24

This Ps. is generally, and very appropriately, connected with the occasion when David brought up the ark from the house of Obed-edom to the tent prepared for it on Mt. Zion. It declares the universal sovereignty of God the Creator (vv. 1, 2), and describes the character of those who may approach His earthly dwelling (vv. 3-6). Then there follows a twice-repeated scene, in which the gates of Jerusalem are summoned to open, that God, as represented by the ark, may enter ; while the warders ask who the approaching conqueror is, and the people reply that He is the Lord of hosts (vv. 7-10).

1. The fulness] all that fills it, all that is in it. **2.** This v. expresses the ancient idea of the structure of the universe, with 'waters under the earth' (Gn 7[11] Ex 20[4]). **4.** Cp. Ps 15. **5. Righteousness**] is a gift of God and a part of the salvation He bestows.

6. O Jacob] RV 'O *God of* Jacob.' **Şelah**] see on 3[4].

7. Lift up your heads] as if to make the entrance more roomy. **Everlasting**] RM 'ancient,' with an illimitable history behind them.

10. The LORD of hosts] one of the great OT. titles of God. The 'hosts' may include the armies of Israel, as well as the stars and angels who form 'the host of heaven.' **Selah**] see on 3[4].

PSALM 25

This is the second of the 'acrostic' or 'alphabetic' Pss. (cp. 9, 10). As it now stands there are a few irregularities in the arrangement, some of which appear again in Ps 34. The closing v. suggests the circumstances of the exile, but it is probably an addition, as the last letter of the alphabet is reached in v. 21. The rest of the Ps. contains nothing to indicate its date or authorship, and its value is independent of any view that may be taken as

to these. Some have supposed that the writer speaks in the name of the nation, but much of the Ps. has a distinctly personal character. It falls into three parts—a humble prayer for defence, instruction, and forgiveness (vv. 1-7); a meditation on the character and ways of God (vv. 8-14) ; and a further prayer for deliverance from trouble (vv. 15-21).

1. Aspiration reveals and determines character. The man who lifts up his soul to God stands contrasted with him who lifts up his soul to vanity (24[4]). **2. I trust in thee**] RV 'in thee have I trusted.' **5. Lead** (RV 'guide') **me in thy truth**] i.e. 'in thy faithfulness.'

6, 7. Note the threefold use of **remember**. God's remembrance is sought, *not* for the Psalmist's sins, but for His own changeless character of grace, and, in accordance with that character, for the Psalmist himself. It has been suggested that the writer, living late in Israel's history, colours his personal prayer with the thought of the nation's early sins and of God's past deliverances. **7. Mercy**] RV 'lovingkindness,' as in v. 6. So in v. 10.

8. Sinners] a truly evangelic thought. God's grace is not for those who have deserved it alone, but for all who seek it in penitence.

9. In judgment] in the principles of practical righteousness.

10. Covenant .. testimonies] God's law is viewed in the one case as the basis of His gracious contract with Israel, and in the other as a witness to His own character. **11. For thy name's sake .. pardon**] Forgiveness is asked because it is God's nature to forgive. **For it** *is* **great**] The plea appears strange, but it is the utterance of deep penitence, combined with strong faith in the forgiving grace which is characteristic of God. **12. Teach in the way** *that* **he shall choose**] God's instruction moulds the will, and directs it to right decisions and resolves. **13. Earth**] RV 'land.' The promise of temporal blessing to the good man and his posterity is in harmony with the general thought of the OT. **14. Secret**] RM 'counsel' or 'friendship'; confidential fellowship. The earthly blessing is crowned with a spiritual one. **15. The net**] the entanglements and perplexities of trouble and sin.

21. There is a seeming inconsistency between the plea of **integrity and uprightness** and the confessions of sin in vv. 7, 11. But what the Psalmist claims is not perfection, but a sincere love of goodness, and the humble dependence on God expressed in the words **I wait on thee.**

PSALM 26

This Ps. appears to belong to a later age than David's, when the Temple (v. 8), with its altar (v. 6), and its public assemblies for worship

(v. 12), was a familiar institution. The writer, conscious of his own uprightness, protests against the idea of being classed with the wicked, and sharing their untimely fate. He appeals at the outset to God's judgment, and at the close preaches the assurance that it will not fail him.

1. *Therefore* **I shall not slide**] RV 'without wavering.' **2. Reins**] see on 7⁹. **3.** The Psalmist's conscious integrity is not self-righteousness. His knowledge of God's character has made him what he is.

6. Wash mine hands] a figure perhaps taken from the practice of the priests (Ex 30¹⁷⁻²¹), or of the city elders (Dt 21⁶,⁷) : cp. Mt 27⁴.

Compass thine altar] as the worshippers in the Temple gathered to witness the sacrifices. **7. Publish**, etc.] RV 'make the voice of thanksgiving to be heard.' **8. Honour**] RV 'glory,' God's manifested Presence, associated with the ark and the mercy seat.

9. Gather not my soul] 'Do not cut it off.' Let me not share their fate. The persons described in vv. 9, 10 are evidently men in places of power, who use violence and have wealth to protect themselves by corrupting justice. **11. Redeem me**] Save me from being destroyed with the wicked. **12. An even place**] a symbol of comfort and safety.

PSALM 27

This Ps. falls naturally into two parts, vv. 1-6 and vv. 7-14, which are in such marked contrast as to make it probable that here, as in Ps 19, two independent poems have been combined. The one breathes a spirit of fearless and triumphant confidence in the face of hostile armies, while the other, though trustful, is the prayer of one in deep distress, orphaned and beset by false accusers. The warlike tone of vv. 1-6 is in favour of ascribing them to David, and vv. 5-6 do not necessarily imply a reference to the Temple, which would be inconsistent with this view.

1. Strength] in the sense of 'stronghold' : see 18². **2. To eat up my flesh**] like wild beasts of prey. **They stumbled and fell**] Past victories inspire present confidence : cp. David's words to Saul (1 S 17³⁴⁻³⁶). **3. In this**] RV 'even then.'

4. Dwell in the house of the LORD] as the guest of Jehovah : see 23⁶. The figure suggests constant fellowship with God.

Beauty] RM 'pleasantness,' the gracious aspect of the divine Host. **To enquire in his temple** (or palace)] to find out all that such intercourse with God can teach.

5. The abode of Jehovah, like the tent of a desert chieftain, affords protection as well as hospitality. The figure of vv. 4, 5 may have been based on the visible dwelling-place of Jehovah at Jerusalem, and if so the words

used need imply nothing more than the temporary structure erected by David.

8. The original is condensed, but the words in italics express the thought. This v. gives the essence of all divine revelation and of all human response to it. **Seek ye my face**] as a visitor seeks access to the presence of an Oriental king. The figure is continued in v. 9.

10. RV 'For my father and my mother have forsaken me, but,' etc. **11. A plain path**] not a path clearly marked, but one that is level and safe. **13.** *I had fainted*] is a phrase supplied to complete the sense of the abbreviated original. **The land of the living**] as opposed to Sheol, the state of the dead—an illustration of the value of the present life for OT. faith.

PSALM 28

This Ps. is in many respects similar to Ps 26, especially in the writer's prayer that he may be distinguished from the wicked, and may escape their fate ; and in the confidence which he reaches in the closing verses. In this Ps., however, the peril of death appears more acute (v. 1), and some have supposed that both Pss. were written in a time of pestilence.

1. The pit] the grave, or Sheol, the state of the dead. Unless his prayer is heard he looks for nothing less than death. **2. Thy holy oracle**] RM 'the innermost place of thy sanctuary,' the Holy of Holies, where God's Presence specially dwells. Here, as in Ps 26, the existence of the Temple seems to be indicated. **3. Draw me not away**] to punishment and destruction : cp. 26⁹. **4. Deeds**] RV 'work.' **Endeavours**] RV 'doings.'

Work] RV 'operation.' These changes bring out the intended contrast between this v. and the next. **5. Destroy**] RV 'break down,' in direct opposition to **build up.**

8. Their strength] RM 'a strength unto his people.' **The saving strength**] RV 'a stronghold of salvation.' **His anointed**] the king.

9. Feed them] as a shepherd. **Lift them up**] RV 'bear them up,' a beautiful continuation of the same figure : see Isa 40¹¹.

PSALM 29

This is a Nature-Psalm, calling on the angels to praise God (vv. 1, 2), describing the manifestation of His power in the thunderstorm (vv. 3-9) and the flood (v. 10), and ending with an assurance of His favour to His people.

1. Give] in the sense of 'ascribe.' **Mighty**] RV 'sons of the mighty.' The angels are meant. **2. The beauty of holiness**] RM 'holy array,' like the robes of the priests in an earthly sanctuary.

3. The voice of the LORD] the thunder. The phrase occurs seven times in the Ps. **The waters**] not of the sea, but of the storm-cloud :

see 18¹¹. **5. The cedars**] the strongest trees, yet riven in the thunderstorm.

6. Them] the mountains which the thunder shakes, besides breaking the trees that grow on them. **Sirion**] Hermon. Lebanon and Hermon are the highest mountains in Palestine. **Unicorn**] RV 'wild-ox.' **7. Divideth** (RV 'cleaveth,' RM 'heweth') **the flames of fire**] The reference is to the sharp, pointed lightning flashes which accompany the thunder.

8. The wilderness of Kadesh] in the extreme S. of Palestine, as Lebanon and Hermon are in the extreme N. **9. Maketh the hinds to calve**] an actual effect of terrifying thunderstorms; or perhaps the meaning is, 'whirleth the oaks.' **Discovereth**] RV 'strippeth bare,' by the wind, or the strokes of lightning. **His temple**] or palace, is not the great temple of Nature, but heaven itself, where the angels minister (vv. 1, 2). **Doth every one speak, etc.**] RV 'everything saith, Glory,' but better, 'every one,' i.e. of the angels. From the heavens they look down with wonder and delight upon the storm, in which they see the manifestation of the divine glory.

10. Sitteth upon the flood] RV 'sat *as king* at the Flood,' the great traditional convulsion of nature (Gn 7, 8), which revealed God's mercy as well as His power and wrath. The attributes then disclosed remain unchanged, and this is the ground of the assurance expressed in v. 11, which is a beautiful conclusion to a Ps. of sublime grandeur. **11. Give strength**] The power of this mighty God is given to His people as they need it : see Isa 40²⁹⁻³¹.

PSALM 30

Title.—(RV) 'A Psalm ; a Song at the Dedication of the House ; *a Psalm* of David.'

There is no obvious connexion between the contents of this Ps. and its title. It is a thanksgiving for recovery from an illness which had threatened to be fatal, and in itself may very well have been written by David. But it is difficult to find in his life an occasion corresponding to the title, though the dedication of David's own palace, or of the site of the Temple, has been suggested. It is more likely that the words, 'A Song at the Dedication of the House,' were inserted into the title at a later time, when the Ps. was adopted for use at the dedication of Solomon's Temple, or of the second Temple, or at the re-dedication of the latter after it had been polluted by Antiochus Epiphanes (the origin of the Feast of Dedication mentioned in Jn 10²². See Intro. to Daniel). The Ps. opens with praise for the writer's restoration (vv. 1–5), tells next of his troubles and his prayer (vv. 6–10), and concludes with another thanksgiving (vv. 11, 12).

1. Lifted .. up] RV 'raised up,' from sickness. **3. The grave**] RV 'Sheol,' which, like the pit, means the state of the dead. **4. At the remembrance of his holiness**] RV 'to his holy name.' For 'remembrance' or 'memorial' in the sense of 'name' see 9⁶. **5. In his favour** *is* life] better, 'his favour is for a lifetime,' in contrast to 'his anger .. a moment.' **Endure for a night**] RV 'tarry for the night' as a passing stranger. **7. Hast made**] RV 'hadst made,' referring to the time of health and prosperity. **My mountain**] would be a figure for stability, but the reading is doubtful. Possibly it should be, 'hadst made me to stand upon strong mountains.' **Thou didst hide thy face**] a sudden change of experience, by which the Psalmist was shaken out of his self-confidence, and taught his entire dependence on God. **9.** This v. shows how little the future life counted for in ordinary OT. thought. **The pit**] see v. 3. **The dust**] is the dead body. **11. Sackcloth**] the garb of sadness. **12.** *My* glory] my soul.

PSALM 31

The writer of this Ps. gratefully records God's past deliverances (vv. 1–8), appeals to God for help against the enemies who assail him in the present (vv. 9–18), and ends with fervent thankfulness and serene assurance (vv. 19–24). The language suggests a later age than David's, and has many parallels with the book of Jeremiah, the most evident being in the words 'terror on every side' (v. 13, Jer 20¹⁰). These parallels are mostly in the central section (vv. 9–18), and possibly this is an insertion in the middle of an earlier Davidic Ps. In the closing vv. there are several resemblances to Ps 27.

3. For thy name's sake] see 23². ³. **4. Strength**] RV 'stronghold.' **5.** The first clause of this v. formed one of the Sayings of our Lord on the Cross (Lk 23⁴⁶). The Psalmist's attitude in life was Christ's attitude in death. **God of truth**] i.e. of faithfulness, of changeless consistency of character. God is always true to Himself. **6. Have hated**] RV 'hate.' **Lying vanities**] idols : see Jer 8¹⁹ 10⁸. **7. Considered** (RV 'seen') **.. known**] with sympathy, followed by succour. **8. Large room**] RV 'large place,' the opposite of 'straits.'

9. Belly] RV 'body.' **10. Iniquity**] As it stands this clause traces the Psalmist's sufferings to his sin. But the LXX and some other versions read 'affliction,' which agrees better with the context. **11.** Cp. Jer 20⁷. ⁸. **12. A broken vessel**] a thing altogether neglected.

13. This whole verse is closely parallel to Jer 20¹⁰. **Fear** *was* **on every side**] cp. Jer 6²⁵ 20³ᵐᵍ. ¹⁰ 46⁵ 49²⁹ Lam 2²². **15. My times**] all the occasions of my life. **16. Make thy face to shine**] Smile upon me in Thy favour : see

Nu 6 25. **17.** This repetition of the prayer of v. 1 may suggest that after all the Ps. is a unity : cp. 25 2, 3 Jer 17 18. **The grave**] RV 'Sheol.'

19. Wrought .. before the sons of men] i.e. openly. **20.** The same thought as in 27 5. Even a desert tent may be a protection if its owner is powerful. **Secret**] RV 'covert.'

Pride] RV 'plottings.' **21.** A strong city] RM 'a fenced city.' A change of figure from the tent of v. 20. If literally understood the words might refer to Jeremiah's experiences during the siege of Jerusalem. **22.** Haste] RM 'alarm.' Fear is rebuked by God's answer to prayer.

PSALM 32

The subject of the Ps. is the happiness that follows the confession of sin and the experience of forgiveness. This is generally set forth at the beginning (vv. 1, 2). Then the Psalmist relates his own spiritual history of misery before confession (vv. 3, 4), and of relief after it (v. 5). He next commends the practice of prayer (v. 6), and expresses his own confidence in God (v. 7). In v. 8 God speaks in words of promise, and the closing vv. are devoted to counsel and exhortation (vv. 9–11). The period in David's life which best fits the references in the Ps. is the time of his impenitence after the murder of Uriah, followed by the rebuke of Nathan, and the king's acknowledgment of his sin (2 S 11 26–12 23). The Ps. is one of those for Ash Wednesday.

Title.—*A Psalm* of David, Maschil] The word **Maschil** has been generally explained as 'a didactic Psalm,' a Psalm of instruction. But few of the Pss. so designated have this special character, and the more probable meaning is 'a skilful Psalm' (see 47 7 RM), one set to more elaborate music than usual.

1, 2. Note the threefold description of wrongdoing as **transgression,** breaking beyond bounds ; **sin,** failure to reach the true aim of life ; and **iniquity,** moral deformity or perversity—also the threefold nature of pardon as 'forgiveness,' literally here the lifting of the burden of guilt ; 'covering,' in the sense of hiding the sin from the eye of the judge, or protecting the sinner from punishment ; and 'not imputing,' the cancelling of an obligation to pay the penalty. **2. No guile**] This may refer to the sincerity of repentance, or, more probably, to the changed character of the forgiven heart.

3, 4. These vv. may be taken as a description either of actual sickness, which brought sin home to the conscience, or of spiritual suffering represented in physical terms. **4.** Is turned into] RV 'was changed *as* with.'

5. Have I not hid] lit. 'covered,' as in v. 1. It is only when man does not cover his sin that God does cover it. **Selah**] see on 3 4.

6. Shall every one] RV 'let every one.' The Psalmist wishes others to take his experience as an example. **In a time when thou mayest be found**] Another possible rendering is, 'in the time of finding out sin' (RM). **In the floods, etc.**] RV 'when the great waters' (of trouble, and especially of God's wrath) 'overflow they shall not reach unto him.'

7. Songs of deliverance] possibly songs sung by others. God's grace to one brings joy to many. **Selah**] see on 3 4.

8. Guide thee with mine eye] RV 'counsel thee with mine eye upon thee.' God does not leave those whom He counsels to walk in their own strength, but watches over their way.

9. Lest they come near .. thee] RV '*Else* they will not come near .. thee.' The horse and mule are thought of not as dangerous, but only as obstinate and stupid—incapable of being brought where they are wanted except by force. Men ought to draw near to God in unconstrained obedience.

PSALM 33

This is an anonymous Ps. of national deliverance, called forth by some historical occasion which it is now impossible to fix with any certainty. From its central conception of God as the ruler of all the earth and all the nations, it appears to belong to the later prophetic age. The metrical structure is specially regular. The first three and the last three vv. form corresponding groups of 6 lines each, and vv. 4–19 consist of six groups of 4 lines each. The opening call to praise (vv. 1–3) is followed by a description of God's character (vv. 4, 5); of His rule over all the inhabitants of the earth, based on His creative power (vv. 6–9); of His rule over the nations, and of the special privilege of Israel as His people, whose defence is not in military power, but in Jehovah (vv. 10–19). The closing vv. (20–22) respond to the summons at the beginning of the Ps.

1. Ye righteous .. the upright] the Israelites who are genuine servants of God. **2.** The psaltery *and* an instrument of ten strings] RV 'the psaltery of ten strings.' The harp and the psaltery were both stringed instruments, the latter being the larger. **3. A new song**] to celebrate a new deliverance. The phrase occurs in several Pss., and has a special connexion with the deliverance from the Babylonian exile : see Isa 42 10.

4. Truth] RV 'faithfulness.' **5. Righteousness**] is the principle of God's character, **judgment**] its practical application to the government of the world. **Goodness**] RV 'lovingkindness.' **7. The depth** (RV 'deeps') in storehouses] The ancient idea of a reservoir of water beneath the earth : see Gn 7 11.

9. Read, 'He spake and it was : He commanded and it stood,' referring to the repeated 'it was so' of Gn 1. **10. The heathen**] RV 'the nations.' **The people**] RV 'the peoples.' **12.** Cp. Dt 33 29. **15.** RV 'he that fashioneth . . that considereth.' **Their hearts alike**] RV 'the hearts of them all.' **17. An horse**] The Israelites had no cavalry, and the chariots and horsemen of their enemies appeared specially formidable to them : see Dt 17 16 Ps 20 7 147 10 Prov 21 31 Isa 31 1.

PSALM 34

The reliability of this title (*A Psalm* of David ; when he feigned madness (RM) before Abimelech, who drove him away, and he departed) is doubtful, both because the Philistine king in question is called Achish and not Abimelech in 1 S 21 13, and because the contents of the Ps. are akin to the proverbial wisdom of a later age than David's. The Ps. is an alphabetic or acrostic one, with some of the same irregularities which are found in Ps 25. Vv. 10–16 are quoted in 1 Pet 3 10-12.

1. At all times . . continually] the utterance of a faith which can maintain gratitude in adversity as well as in prosperity. **2. Humble**] RV 'meek,' all patient and trustful souls. **5. They**] The Psalmist's individual experience is also a general one. **6. This poor man**] may refer to the Psalmist himself, but if so it is as a type of others. **7. The angel of the LORD**] a Being frequently mentioned in the OT. : see Ex 23 20 Isa 63 9. He is not merely an angelic messenger, but is in some sense identified with God Himself. He may be said to stand for God in His self-revealing character, and in His activity among men. **Encampeth**] cp. 2 K 6 17. **10. Young lions**] proverbially strong and courageous, and able to provide for themselves. **11. Come, ye children**] an address in the tone of the book of Proverbs : see Prov 4 1. **15. *Are* upon**] RV 'are toward,' not only in watchfulness, but in favour. See the contrast in the next v. **16. The remembrance of them**] their 'memorial' or 'name' : see on 9 6 30 4. **21. Evil shall slay the wicked**] Sin is self-destructive, and works out its own punishment. Or perhaps the words mean simply, 'a calamity shall slay the wicked.' **Desolate**] RV 'condemned.' So in v. 22.

PSALM 35

This is a prayer for the defeat and destruction of malignant enemies, whom the Psalmist has formerly befriended, and who now treat him with ungrateful cruelty. The circumstances are partly similar to those of David's persecution by Saul, but no prominent individual is mentioned as hostile, and David's attitude to Saul was more forgiving than that

of the Psalmist towards those of whom he complains. The Ps., like Ps 31, has many resemblances to the book of Jeremiah, and some ascribe it to that prophet's time. For a discussion of the vindictive tone of such Pss. see Intro. There are three sections—a prayer for the confusion of the writer's enemies (vv. 1–10), an account of their wickedness (vv. 11–18), and a further appeal for the vindication of the right (vv. 19–28).

1. Plead *my cause*] RV 'strive thou,' as in a court of law : see v. 23. **5, 6. The angel of the LORD**] see on 34 7.

13. My prayer returned] better, 'shall return.' The blessing, withheld from the unworthy, will come back to the Psalmist himself : cp. Lk 10 6. **15. Abjects**] the most worthless outcasts : see Job 30 1, 8. **And I knew *it* not**] RM 'and those whom I knew not.' **16. With hypocritical mockers, etc.**] RV 'like the profane mockers in feasts'—buffoons and parasites, who get a place at table in return for entertaining the guests with scurrilous jokes. **17. My darling**] equivalent to 'my soul' : see on 22 20. **18. In the great congregation**] The Psalmist looks for a public vindication of his cause.

19. Wink with the eye] here a sign of triumphant malice. **That hate me without a cause**] quoted by our Lord, and applied to Himself in Jn 15 25. **20.** *Them that are* quiet in the land] the same as the 'poor' or 'meek' —the humble and patient righteous. **21. Opened their mouth**] in contempt. **Hath seen** *it*] i.e. the fulfilment of their wicked desires. **23. My judgment**] the vindication of my just cause.

PSALM 36

This Ps. consists of two strongly contrasted pictures, one of the wickedness of the wicked man (vv. 1–4), and one of the goodness of God (vv. 5–9), followed by a prayer that the Psalmist may continue to enjoy God's blessing (vv. 10, 11), and by a confident assurance of the final overthrow of the wicked (v. 12). The Ps. seems to reflect the social conditions of a later age than David's.

1. The transgression of the wicked saith] Sin is personified as an oracle to whose voice the wicked man listens. **Within my heart**] A better reading is, 'within his heart.' *There is no fear of God, etc.*] quoted in Ro 3 18. **2. Until, etc.**] RV 'that his iniquity shall not be found out and be hated.' **3, 4.** A description of the character and conduct of the man who is deceived by sin.

5. There is an abrupt transition here to an infinitely nobler theme. **6. Great mountains**] RV 'mountains of God.' In these vv. all that is infinite, sublime, and unfathomable in nature is made emblematic of the perfections of Jehovah. **8.** God is host as well as protector. The figure is perhaps taken from the sacrificial meals eaten by the worshippers in the Temple (Lv 7[15]). **9.** A highly spiritual conception of the nature of man's fellowship with God, anticipating some of the loftiest teaching of the NT. **12. There**] The overthrow of the wicked is already a visible fact for the Psalmist's faith.

PSALM 37

This is an acrostic Ps., in which the alphabetic arrangement is carried without a break through 22 stanzas of varying length, to which the vv. of the English Bible do not correspond. The contents are closely akin to the maxims of the book of Proverbs, but they are touched with a fervour which elevates them into true poetry. The creed of the Psalmist is that sooner or later, even in this life, wickedness is punished, and righteousness vindicated. This is a theory which, of course, is too simple to cover all the facts of experience, but it is true as far as it goes, and its practical doctrine of 'trust in God and do the right' is sound at all times.

3. *So* **shalt thou dwell .. and .. be fed**] RV 'dwell in the land and follow after faithfulness.' Do not go to other lands: an utterance of patriotism. **8. In any wise to do evil**] RV '*it*' (fretfulness) '*tendeth* only to evil doing.' **9. The earth**] RV 'the land' of Canaan. So in vv. 11, 22. **10. It** *shall* **not** *be*] RV 'he shall not be.' **11.** See Mt 5[5]. **13. His day**] of retribution. **14. Conversation**] conduct, manner of life.

18. Knoweth the days] regards with favour and watchful care: cp. 1[6] 31[7]. **For ever**] from generation to generation. For OT. thought there was satisfaction in the blessings of one's posterity as well as in those of one's own life: see vv. 26, 27, 29. **20. Fat of lambs**] RV 'excellency of the pastures,' the grass and flowers which wither away—a figure distinct from that of the burning which follows.

23. Ordered] RV 'established.' **35. A green bay tree**] RV 'a green tree in its native soil.' **36. He passed by**] RV 'one passed by.' Perhaps we should read, 'I passed by.' **37. End**] RM 'future' or 'posterity.' **39. Strength**] RV 'strong hold.'

PSALM 38

This Ps. may be compared with Ps 6. It is the prayer of one who, like Job, is in great bodily suffering (vv. 1–10), and is also deserted by his friends (v. 11), and beset by treacherous enemies (vv. 12, 19, 20). He is conscious that his trouble is due to his sin (vv. 4, 18), and appeals trustfully to God for pardon, healing, and deliverance. The description of personal suffering is too minute for a purely national

Ps. It has been suggested that the author, if not David, may have been Jeremiah (see Jer 20). This is another of the Pss. for Ash Wednesday.

Title.—The phrase 'to bring to remembrance' probably indicates that the Ps. was used in connexion with the offering of the 'memorial' of incense (Isa 66[3 mg.]), or of the shewbread with incense (Lv 24[7]), or of the meat offering with incense (Lv 2[2]).

1. This v. repeats 6[1].

2. Arrows] represent God's judgments as sent from afar, while His **hand** suggests closer dealing. **3. Rest**] RV 'health.' **4.** Sin is compared first to a flood, and then to a burden.

7. Loathsome *disease*] RV 'burning,' inflammation. **14. No reproofs**] no arguments in his own defence. **15.** His silence before men is explained by his hope in God. **20.** While the Psalmist admits his own sin he is at the same time a sufferer for righteousness: see on 25[21].

PSALM 39

This is a Ps. of great pathos and beauty. The writer's sore sickness, accepted as the punishment of sin (vv. 9–11), has impressed him with the frailty and vanity of human life. He refrains at first from all complaint lest his words should be sinful and harmful (vv. 1, 2). When he does speak it is to utter without bitterness his conviction of life's brevity and nothingness (vv. 3–6). He concludes with a humble prayer that though he is but a pilgrim on earth God may grant him pardon and recovery before he passes from the world (vv. 7–13).

Title.—(RV) 'For the Chief Musician, for Jeduthun,' etc. Jeduthun was one of the directors of sacred music in David's time (1 Ch 16[41] 25[1]). If the Ps. be of later origin the phrase in the title may mean 'after the manner of Jeduthun,' as in Pss 62, 77.

1. While the wicked is before me] The visible prosperity of the wicked afforded the temptation to complain. **2.** *Even* **from good**] RM 'and had no comfort.' **3.** Complete silence proved impossible. Pent-up feeling found a safe relief in prayer. **5. Vanity**] or, 'a breath' (Heb.). **6. In a vain shew**] RM 'as a shadow,' like a phantom in a dream: the eager efforts of life are contrasted with the emptiness of their results.

7. What wait I for?] If life ends in vanity what is there to hope for? The answer is 'God,' and the meaning is not so much that God will be the soul's portion in the future life, as that God's presence here redeems life from its nothingness. **8. The foolish**] those who have mocked at his troubles. **9.** The characteristic tone of the whole Ps. is in these words. The writer accepts with reverent, resignation all the facts and experiences of life.

11. This is another v. summing up the philosophy of the Ps. **Makest his beauty,** etc.] RM 'consumest like a moth his delights': see Isa 50[7] Mt 6[19]. **12. Stranger .. sojourner**] The fact that life is transient becomes here a plea for favour. **13. Spare me**] lit. 'look away from me,' 'avert thy frown.' **Recover strength**] lit. 'brighten up.' The day of life may be short, but the Psalmist seeks for sunshine while it lasts.

PSALM 40

This Ps. falls into two well-marked divisions, which many think to have been originally separate Pss. In vv. 1–11 the writer recalls with thankfulness how God has heard his prayers and delivered him from trouble (vv. 1–4), declares the greatness of God's mercies (v. 5), presents himself as a living sacrifice (vv. 6–8), and desires the continuance of God's blessing on account of his fearless witness for righteousness (vv. 9–11). In vv. 12–17, on the other hand, the Psalmist is in distress, both from sin (v. 12) and from persecution (vv. 14, 15). He pleads for the speedy confusion of his enemies, and for the deliverance both of himself and of all who seek God (vv. 13–17). This part of the Ps. resembles Ps 35. Vv. 13–17 are reproduced with some variations as Ps 70. Vv. 6, 7 are applied to Christ in Heb 10[5-9]. The Ps. is probably a national Psalm. In it the nation, or the church, rather than the individual, is speaking. The horrible pit will then be the pit of exile, and the new song will be that sung for deliverance from exile and restitution to the home-land. This is one of the Pss. for Good Friday.

2. Pit .. clay] The combination of these figures for trouble is illustrated by the dungeon, with mire at the bottom, into which Jeremiah was cast (Jer 38[6]). **A rock**] a place of firmness and security. **3. A new song**] a song of praise for new mercies : see on 33[3].

6. Sacrifice and offering, etc.] a striking recognition that spiritual service, even in OT. times, is more than all forms of worship : see 1 S 15[22]. **Mine ears hast thou opened**] to understand the true requirements of the Law. The boring of the ears in token of perpetual servitude (Ex 21[6] Dt 15[7]) is not here referred to. LXX has, 'a body hast thou prepared me,' and is followed in the quotation in Heb 10[5].

7. RV 'Lo, I am come,' the Psalmist's personal consecration to God's service : see Isa 6[9]. **In the volume of the book** *it is* **written**

of me] rather, 'in the roll of the book it is prescribed to me.' The words are a parenthesis, and the reference is probably to Deuteronomy (see 2 K 22[8 f.]), with its spiritual and inward view of obedience. The writer to the Hebrews rightly recognises that Christ's obedience perfectly fulfilled this ideal of devoted surrender to God's will.

9. In the great congregation] among the people assembled at some festival. **10. Have not hid,** etc.] In a good sense God's law is hidden in his heart (v. 8, cp. 119[11]), but here he means that he has not concealed his convictions from cowardice.

PSALM 41

The Psalmist has been brought low by sickness, and pronounces a blessing on those who consider such sufferers as himself (vv. 1–3). His own experience has been of an opposite kind. His enemies have triumphantly anticipated his end, and their hypocritical sympathy has only been the guise of malice (vv. 5–8). One friend in particular has done his utmost to injure him (v. 9). He asks God to restore his health that he may requite all this unkindness, and finally expresses his confidence in God's favour and unchanging support (vv. 10–12). In Jn 13[18] the words of v. 9 are appropriately applied to Judas. V. 13 is not a part of the Ps., but forms the concluding doxology to Book 1 of the Psalter.

1. Poor] a different word from that so often used for the afflicted righteous. It means the 'weak' or 'sick.' **2. Blessed upon the earth**] rather, 'counted happy in the land.'

6. The visitor who comes in pretended sympathy only seeks information to be maliciously used outside. **8. An evil disease**] or, a result of wickedness ; lit. 'a thing of belial.'

9. Which did eat .. my bread] The ties of hospitality, which in the East are regarded as specially sacred, had been violated as well as those of friendship. **Lifted up** *his* **heel**] a figure for unfeeling violence and brutality.

10. That I may requite them] a touch of vindictiveness which Christians may not imitate : see Intro. **11.** Recovery has begun. The enemy has been disappointed of his triumph. This is already taken as a proof of God's favour. **12. Integrity**] The consciousness of an upright purpose is not inconsistent with the confession of sin in v. 4 : see on 25[21]. **Settest me before thy face for ever**] the opposite of the fate predicted by his enemies in vv. 5, 8. To be in God's presence is to enjoy true and unending life.

BOOK 2 (PSALMS 42–72)

The second and third Books of the Psalter (Pss 42–72 and 73–89) are but the two parts of a whole, the largest section of which (Pss 42–83) is called the Elohistic Psalter, because the name Elohim (God) is used almost exclusively instead of the name Jehovah (the LORD), which is predominant in the rest of the Psalms. It is evident from the contents of these two books that the Elohistic compiler gathered them from at least three earlier collections, for Pss 42–49 are Psalms of the Korahites (43 is part of 42), as are also Pss 84–89 (except 86); Pss 50 and 73–83 are Psalms of Asaph; while Pss 51–72, 86, are Psalms of David. Ps 72 originally ended a collection of Psalms attributed to David; and it is a plausible conjecture that Pss 42–50 once stood after Ps 72, the Davidic Psalms being thus together and the subscription (72 20) appropriate.

Taking Book 2 by itself, we may notice that in the Davidic collection Pss 66 and 67 did not originally belong to it, while Ps 72 is called 'a psalm of Solomon.' The great majority of these Pss. have the rendering in AV 'To the chief musician'; indicating (see Intro.) that they had been included in the collection of the Chief Musician as well as in that of the Elohistic collector, both of these editors working on previously existing collections. Ps 53 is an Elohistic form of Ps 14, and Ps 70 of Ps 40 13-17; while Pss 57 7-11 and 60 5-12 are combined in Ps 108. Several of the Davidic Psalms in this book are referred by their titles to incidents in David's life; these are of varying degrees of probability, and are discussed in their places.

It is difficult to classify the Pss. according to their subjects or references, but a rough division may be attempted. Thus, (a) Pss 42, 43, 51, 54, 55, 56, 57, 59, 61, 64, 69, 70, 71 are prayers for personal help and deliverance; (b) Pss 44, 46, 47, 48, 62 are thanksgivings, and breathe the spirit of confidence and triumph; (c) Ps 45 is a marriage ode; (d) Ps 49 is a didactic piece akin to the book of Proverbs; (e) Ps 65 is a thanksgiving in time of harvest. References to the Temple as the centre of worship are found in Pss 42, 43, 48, 50, 65. The following are quoted in the NT.: 44, 45, 48, 50, 55, 32, 67, 68, and 69. The writers of the Pss. in this Book evince the same perfect trust in God and confidence in His power to relieve them from their troubles, as are exhibited in the first Book.

Several of the Pss., such as the 51st, have an unmistakable personal tone; and there are not wanting indications of a highly spiritual **view** of religious worship and ritual. The desire of the true Israelite is not only for the Temple (42 4), but 'for God, for the living God.' Burnt offerings are of small account in the sight of Him to whom belongs 'the world and the fulness thereof' (50 7-14). 'The sacrifices of God are a broken spirit' (51 17).

In this Book the 45th and 72nd Pss. are usually classed as Messianic. They both describe the character of the ideal king, ruling in righteousness, watching over the poor and punishing the oppressor, having dominion over subject nations 'from sea to sea,' and being blessed by all nations, because they have been blessed by him. Probably they were written in connexion with definite historical events—in the one case the marriage of a king, in the other a king's accession to the throne; still they unite themselves with that Messianic hope which gradually took shape among the Jews, and came to fill a large place in their religious thought.

PSALM 42

This Ps. and the following one are closely connected, and it is practically certain that they were originally one. Ps 43 has no separate title, and its closing refrain occurs twice in Ps 42 (vv. 5, 11). Both Pss. belong to a time when the Temple worship was in full activity, and the writer is a Levite who is detained in the N. of Palestine (v. 6), and beset by enemies, apparently heathen (42 9 43 1, 2), who taunt him about his God (42 3, 10). He longs to return and take his part in the Temple service, and is confident that God will yet fulfil his desire.

Title.—Maschil] see on Ps 32. For (RV 'of') the sons of Korah] i.e. from a collection compiled by the Levitical guild bearing that name.

2. Appear before God] in the Temple at Jerusalem. 4. Read, 'These things would I remember as I pour out my soul within me.' AV and RV suggest that the Psalmist's memories of better days add to his sorrow; but the meaning is rather that they give him hope. For I had gone, etc.] RV 'how I went with the throng, and led them to the house of God.' Holyday] a sacred festival, the original meaning of 'holiday.' 5. For the help of his countenance] We should probably read, 'who is the health of my countenance and my God,' as in v. 11, Ps 43 5.

6. Land of Jordan .. Hermonites] RV 'land of Jordan and the Hermons,' the sources of the Jordan in the NE. of Palestine. The plural 'Hermons' refers to the separate peaks of the mountain. The hill Mizar] the 'little mountain,' some lower hill in the same locality.

7. At the noise of thy waterspouts] better, 'in the roar of thy cataracts,' the cascades that rush down Hermon when the snow melts in spring. **Thy waves and .. billows]** a figure for trouble, probably in this case suggested by the appearance of the Jordan in flood. **8.** *And my prayer]* RV '*even* a prayer.' **10.** *As with a sword in my bones]* better, 'as though they would crush my bones,' the whole framework of my being.

PSALM 43

1. An ungodly nation] RM 'an unmerciful nation,' a loveless, heathen people. **2.** Cp. 42⁹. **3. Thy holy hill]** the Temple on Mt. Zion. **Thy tabernacles]** or dwelling-place. **4. O God my God]** instead of 'O LORD my God '—showing that the Ps. is ' Elohistic.'

PSALM 44

This is a prayer for deliverance from national trouble which has not been deserved by any apostasy or idolatry. The strong assertions of national faithfulness are akin to the spirit of the Maccabean age, but the conditions indicated in the Ps. may be found also at an earlier date, such as the time of the invasion by Sennacherib in the reign of Hezekiah. God has helped His people in the days of old (vv. 1–3), and they are still confident in Him (vv. 4–8), yet He has allowed their enemies to bring them low (vv. 9–16). But they are still loyal to Him (vv. 17–22), and cry earnestly that He would remember them and save them (vv. 23–26).

Title.—See on Ps 42.

2. Heathen] RV 'nations.' **People]** RV 'peoples,' the inhabitants of Canaan. So in vv. 11, 14. **8. Selah]** see on 3⁴. **11, 12.** Some are slain, and others sold into captivity.

12. For nought, etc.] God does not gain by such transactions. His name and cause are rather discredited. **13, 14.** See the speech of Rabshakeh (2 K 18 ²⁷⁻³⁵). **19. Place of dragons]** RV ' place of jackals,' a desert, to which condition the country had been reduced. **Shadow of death]** deep darkness and gloom. **23. Why sleepest thou ?]** an expression of startling boldness, yet the prayer of v. 26 shows that its daring springs not from unbelief but from faith.

PSALM 45

The poem celebrates the marriage of a king. After the prelude (v. 1) come addresses to the royal bridegroom (vv. 2–9) and bride (vv. 10–12), a description of the bridal procession (vv. 13–15), and a final address to the king (vv. 16, 17). The marriage of Solomon to the Egyptian princess, of Ahab to Jezebel, of Jehoram to Athaliah, as well as later alliances, have all been suggested as the occasion in view. But while the Ps. had no doubt a historic reference, yet the language used of the king is of such a transcendent character that it could only be strictly true of the Messiah, or ideal King, and we find it quoted with a Messianic meaning in Heb 1 ⁸,⁹. The Ps. is consequently used on Christmas Day.

Title.—RV ' Set to Shoshannim.' **Shoshannim** (' lilies ') indicates the melody to which the Ps. is set, or possibly instruments shaped like lilies on which it was played ; and **A Song of loves** describes the nature of the poem. **1. Is inditing, etc.]** RV 'overfloweth with a goodly matter.' **I speak, etc.]** RM 'I speak : my work is for a king.' **3. With thy glory,** etc.] RV 'Thy glory and thy majesty.' These are the weapons with which the king girds himself. **4. Because of]** in the cause of. **5. In the heart, etc.]** RV 'The peoples fall under thee ; *they* ' (the arrows) '*are* in the heart of the king's enemies.'

6. Thy throne, O God, *is*] RM ' Thy throne *is the throne of* God.' This gives a good sense, and meets the difficulty that the human king who is addressed in the first instance could hardly be called ' God.' There are textual reasons for believing, however, that the original reading was simply, ' Thy throne *shall be* for ever.' **Right sceptre]** RV 'sceptre of equity.' **7. Oil of gladness]** the oil, not of the coronation, but of a festive occasion. **8. Myrrh .. aloes .. cassia]** These perfumes are not the substances now so named. **Ivory palaces]** palatial chambers ornamented with inlaid ivory work. Ahab had such a palace (1 K 22 ³⁹ : cp. Am 3 ¹⁵). **Whereby, etc.]** RV ' stringed instruments have made thee glad.' Their music greets the king as he enters. **9. Did** (RV ' doth ') **stand the queen]** the new consort, who takes the place of honour. **Gold of Ophir]** the finest gold. Ophir was either in Africa or in S. Asia. **11. Thy Lord]** rather, ' thy lord ' : see 1 Pet 3 ⁶. **Worship .. him]** rather, ' do him homage.' **12. The daughter of Tyre]** the city of Tyre, a personification like ' daughter of Zion,' ' daughter of Babylon.' Tyre was the wealthiest of Israel's neighbours, and was in alliance with David and Solomon. It would naturally grace a royal Israelite marriage with a gift, even if the bride were not, like Jezebel, herself a Tyrian princess. **The rich among the people]** better, ' the richest among the peoples.' **13.** *Is* **all glorious within]** RV 'within *the palace* is all glorious' : i.e. in the inner chamber from which she comes forth to meet the king. **Of wrought gold]** RV 'inwrought with gold.' **16. Instead of thy fathers, etc.]** A distinguished posterity is better than a long ancestry, which was lacking in Solomon's case. **Mayest make]** RV 'shalt make.' **In all the earth]** a world-wide dominion is promised for the king's children. **17. People]** RV 'peoples.'

PSALM 46

Pss 46–48 form a group which we may assign with little doubt to the reign of Hezekiah, when Sennacherib's army was suddenly destroyed (2 K 19 35). They all strike the same note of gratitude, confidence, and praise, which is found in Isaiah's references to the same event (Isa 29–31, 33, 37). Ps 46 is divided into three strophes, and the refrain of vv. 7, 11 probably stood also between v. 3 and v. 4.

Title.—RV ' Set to Alamoth.' **Alamoth** is generally understood to mean ' soprano ' (see 1 Ch 15 20).

1. **Our refuge and strength**] the original of Luther's famous *Ein' feste Burg*. 2, 3. The language is figurative of stress and trouble. 4. **A river**] the river of God's presence and favour : see v. 5, Isa 33 21 ; cp. Isa 8 6. **Shall make glad**] RV 'make glad.' 5. **Right early**] RM ' when the morning appeareth.' 6. **Heathen**] RV 'nations.' So in v. 10. 7. **LORD of hosts**] see on 24 10. 8. **Desolations**] rather, ' astonishments ' or ' wonders.' 10. **Be still**] Desist from your vain efforts : cp. 4 4.

PSALM 47

This Ps., though akin to Pss 46, 48, is less definitely historical, and simply summons the earth to join in a chorus of praise to God as the victorious King, not only of Israel, but of all the nations of the world.

1. **People**] RV 'peoples.' So in vv. 3, 9. 3. **Shall subdue . . shall choose**] RM ' subdueth . . chooseth . .' 4. **The excellency** (or ' pride ') **of Jacob**] the fair land of Israel. 5. **Gone up**] to heaven, in triumph after the battle : see 68 11. 7. **With understanding**] RM ' in a skilful psalm (Maschil).' 8. **Reigneth . . sitteth**] better, ' hath become king . . hath taken his seat.' 9. *Even* **the people**] RV ' *To be* the people ' —the Gentiles actually becoming the people of the true God. Possibly the right reading is, ' together with the people '—the Gentiles joining with the Jews in homage to Jehovah. **Shields of the earth**] the princes : see 89 18 Hos 4 18 (RM).

PSALM 48

This Ps. celebrates the safety and glory of Jerusalem, and the praise of her divine King. The deliverance He has wrought is vividly portrayed, and we can hardly fail to recognise that the overthrow of Sennacherib is in view. The Ps. is used on Whitsunday.

2. **For situation**] RV ' in elevation.' *On* **the sides of the north**] An obscure clause. ' The sides of the north ' may mean the Temple hill, as distinguished from the rest of the city :

or, as some think, there may be a comparison of Mt. Zion to the sacred mountain in the remote north on which Assyrian mythology placed the home of the gods : see Isa 14 13 Ezk 38 6 39 2 (RV).

3. **Is known**] RV 'hath made himself known.' 4. **Kings**] The vassal kings of Sennacherib (Isa 10 8). They gather and march in order till they see Jerusalem. Then they are amazed, and forced to turn back in confusion. 7. **Ships of Tarshish**] a general phrase for large sea-going vessels. Tarshish was somewhere in the western Mediterranean, perhaps in Spain. Sennacherib's army was like a wrecked navy. 8. **As we have heard, so have we seen**] History has repeated itself. 10. RV ' As is thy name . . so is thy praise.' God's name is His revealed character, which now receives due recognition and response from the whole world. 14. Probably the last v. originally ran : ' For such is Jehovah our God : He it is that shall guide us for ever and ever.'

PSALM 49

There is little to fix the date of this Ps. The writer moralises, in the fashion of the book of Proverbs, on the vanity of wealth and honour apart from understanding. The rich man cannot deliver his friends or himself from death, and his prosperity need cause no dismay to those who are less fortunate in this world The upright, among whom the Psalmist counts himself, will be received by God, and thus made superior to the power of death. Vv. 12, 20 form, by their similarity, a kind of refrain.

1. **People**] RV 'peoples,' explained by inhabitants of the world. 4. **Parable . . dark saying**] We might render, ' proverb . . riddle ' : see 78 2 Prov 1 6. 5. *When* **the iniquity of my heels, etc.**] RV ' When iniquity at my heels,' etc. RM gives a still better sense, connecting vv. 5, 6, ' When the iniquity of them that would supplant me compasseth me about, even of them that trust,' etc. 7. See Ex 21 30 (RV). **Redeem . . ransom**] Life that is forfeit to man may be bought back with money, but not life that is claimed by God. 8. This v. is a parenthesis, interrupting the connexion between vv. 7, 9. *Is* **precious, and it ceaseth**] RV 'is costly, and must be let alone.' 10. **Leave their wealth to others**] losing it for themselves. 11. LXX and other versions imply a slight change of reading which gives a better sense : ' Graves are their houses for ever, the dwelling-places for all generations of those who called their lands after their own name.' 12. *Being* **in honour abideth not**] RV ' abideth not in honour.' 13. **Their posterity**] RV 'after them men.' **Approve, etc.**] persist in the same foolish view of life. 14. **Like sheep, etc.**] RV ' They are

appointed as a flock for Sheol ; Death shall be their shepherd '—a grim and forcible figure.

In the **morning**] when God's day of reckoning dawns. **Shall consume, etc.**] R.V 'shall be for Sheol to consume, that there be no habitation for it.'

15. The grave] RV 'Sheol.' The hope expressed is not necessarily that of a definite resurrection after death, but may be that of deliverance from the premature ending of life in this world. But the words **he shall receive me** show that what the Psalmist values most is life with God as opposed to life without God, and this thought is the germ of the Christian doctrine of immortality : see on 16 10, 11.

18. Blessed his soul] congratulated himself on his wealth : cp. Lk 12 19. **19. They shall never see light**] shall abide for ever in the darkness of Sheol. **20. And understandeth not**] Those who perish like the beasts are not the rich as such, but the rich who do not know God.

PSALM 50

The title (**A Psalm of Asaph**) is discussed in Intro. to Book 3, where the other Pss. of Asaph are found. The present Ps. is one of solemn warning to those who attempt to serve God by formal sacrifices while their lives are full of wickedness. God will come to judge His people (vv. 1–6). He tells the formalists that He does not need animal sacrifices (vv. 7–13), and asks for praise, obedience, and prayer (vv. 14, 15). He reproves the hypocrites for their sins (vv. 16–20) and ends with a call to repentance (v. 21) and a promise of salvation to true worshippers (v. 22). The teaching of the Ps. is that of the great prophets of the 8th and 7th centuries B.C., and it is probably to be assigned to that period.

1. The mighty God, *even* **the LORD**] RV 'God, *even* God, the LORD.' **From the rising,** etc.] from the E. to the W., not from morning to evening. **2. Zion, the perfection of beauty**] see 48 2 Lam 2 15. **Shined**] RV 'shined forth,' from His earthly dwelling-place. **4. Heavens from above**] RV 'heavens above.'

5. Saints] the true Israel, whose worship is not hypocritical. **A covenant . . by sacrifice**] The covenant between Jehovah and Israel at Sinai was ratified in every act of sacrifice, as one to which the worshipper bound himself afresh. This shows that the Ps. recognises the true religious value of sacrifice, and only condemns the abuse of it.

7. Against thee] RV 'unto thee.' **8. Will not reprove**] because such offerings were not what God most regarded. **Or thy burnt offerings, etc.**] RV 'and thy burnt offerings are continually before me.' **13. Eat . . drink**] The primitive idea of sacrifice was that the god partook of the offerings in a physical sense. This view is rejected here. **14. Thanksgiving**]

RV 'the sacrifice of thanksgiving.' **21. Kept silence**] not in indifference, but in patience.

23. Conversation] RM 'way,' manner of life.

PSALM 51

Title.—(RV) 'For the Chief Musician. A Psalm of David : when Nathan the prophet came unto him, after he had gone in to Bath-sheba.'

It is impossible not to feel the general appropriateness of this Ps. to the occasion mentioned in the title, and there is no historic OT. figure except David to whom we can point as an illustration of the great sin and deep penitence which are the theme of the Ps. The theory that the speaker is the nation of Israel hardly accounts for the highly personal tone of the whole poem. At the same time, the affinity of the thought and language with the closing chapters of Isaiah (see especially on v. 11) favours the view that the writer lived during the exile, in which case he may well have chosen David's great transgression and its results as the subject of a 'dramatic lyric.' On any supposition as to authorship and date vv. 18, 19 are to be regarded as a liturgical addition appended to the Ps. when it came to be used in the Temple services. Part of v. 4 is quoted (from LXX) in Ro 3 4.

4. Against thee, thee only] David had sinned against Uriah and Bath-sheba as well as against God : but as all obligations to men have their foundation in God's law, so all sin against them is included and hidden in the one fact of offence against God. **That thou mightest be justified . . be clear**] that Thy justice and holiness might be clearly shown. **5. This v.** does not reflect any stain on the Psalmist's birth, but traces his sin to the inborn evil of his nature.

6. Truth in the inward parts] truth as opposed to self-deception or conscious hypocrisy, in the inward parts as opposed to mere superficial goodness. **Thou shalt make me to know**] God is willing to give what He desires men to have. **7. Hyssop**] employed in the OT. ceremonies of purification, a bunch of the herb being used to sprinkle blood (Lv 14 6. 7) or water (Nu 19 18) on the unclean. **Snow**] cp. Isa 1 18. **8. Bones** *which* **thou hast broken**] see on 42 10.

10. Create in me] RM 'create for me.'

Renew] better, 'make new.' What is sought is something that has never been in the Psalmist's life before. **A right spirit**] RM 'a stedfast spirit,' that will not yield to temptation. **11. Thy holy spirit**] The only other mention of this in the OT. is in Isa 63 10, 11.

12. *With thy* **free spirit**] RV 'with a free spirit,' a spirit of willing and unforced obedience. **16. Desirest not**] RV 'delightest not in.' **Delightest not**] RV 'hast no pleasure.'

17. Cp. 34 18.

18. This and the next v. form a prayer for the restoration of Jerusalem, written either during the exile or in the troublous times before Nehemiah's mission. 19. Be pleased with] RV 'delight in.' Burnt offering and whole burnt offering] two expressions for the same sacrifice, the one emphasising its being burnt, the other the completeness with which it was consumed. The conception of the essence of religion here is evidently very different from that of vv. 16, 17, which almost look like a criticism of—some even maintain, a protest against—animal sacrifice. In any case they assert that the sacrifice of the broken heart is that which God loves best.

PSALM 52

Title.—(RV) 'For the Chief Musician. Maschil of David : when Doeg the Edomite came and told Saul, and said unto him, David is come to the house of Ahimelech.'

In some respects Doeg (1 S 22 9) might stand for the original of the wicked man in this Ps., but the absence of all reference to the massacre of the priests at Nob (1 S 22 17-19) throws grave doubt upon the correctness of the title. The Ps. appears to reflect the social evils denounced by the prophets of later times (see Am 5 11 8 6 Mic 2 2 3 2,3 7 3), and to be directed against some prominent oppressor, whose character and fate are depicted in vv. 1–5, while vv. 6–9 describe the contrasted happiness of the righteous man.

1. Goodness] RV 'mercy.' God] is here 'El,' the Strong One, whose power is greater than that of the mightiest man. 'The goodness of God' is the fact that makes the boast of the strongest evil-doer to be vain. 6. Fear .. laugh] These two emotions are not inconsistent. The one is the solemn awe inspired by the suddenness of the tyrant's downfall, the other the gladness caused by the revelation of God's righteousness.

7–9. These vv. are put into the mouth of the righteous, and are introduced in RV by 'saying.' 7. Cp. Ps 49. 8. But I am] RV 'But as for me, I am.' A green olive tree] in contrast with the wicked who is rooted up like a weed (v. 5): cp. 92 13,14. 9. Before thy saints] RV 'in the presence of thy saints,' to be connected with I will wait. Possibly we should read, ' I will declare that thy name is good,' etc.

PSALM 53

This is a second version of Ps 14 with the important difference that God (Elohim) is everywhere substituted for the LORD (Jehovah). There are a few other variations and additions, especially in v. 5 (= 14 5,6). The changes are interesting chiefly as an illustration of the process of editing which was applied to many

Pss. and many portions of the OT., and in particular of the consistent preferences, on the part of separate writers, for one divine name rather than another.

Title.—Mahalath] variously interpreted : (1) as a corruption of Alamoth (see Ps 46), (2) as the first word of the song to the tune of which the Ps. was set, and (3) as an instrument such as the flute or cithern. For Maschil see on Ps 32.

5. God hath scattered the bones of him that encampeth against thee] This is the most important addition in the Ps., and seems to point to some definite historical occasion for which Ps 14 was adapted by the editor.

PSALM 54

Title.—(RV) 'For the Chief Musician; on stringed instruments. Maschil of David: when the Ziphites came and said to Saul, Doth not David hide himself with us ?'

Whatever be the value of the title there is nothing in the Ps. to make us reject it, unless it be the allusion in v. 3 to the Ziphites as 'strangers.' For the historical incident see 1 S 23 19 26 1. The Ps. consists of a prayer for deliverance from enemies (vv. 1–3), and an expression of confidence and praise (vv. 4–7). For Maschil see on Ps 32. The Ps. is used on Good Friday.

1. Judge me] Do justice to me. By thy strength] RV 'in thy might.' God's 'judgment ' is a practical vindication of His people's cause. 3. Strangers] In 86 14 this v. is repeated, with the substitution of ' the proud' for ' strangers,' and possibly we should read ' the proud ' here. The difference depends on the interchange of two very similar Heb. letters. 'Strangers,' if not applicable to the Ziphites, may refer to the men of Keilah, who were perhaps Canaanites. Oppressors seek] RV 'violent men have sought.'

4. The Lord] here 'Adonai,' not 'Jehovah.' 5. Reward evil] RV 'requite the evil ' that they have done. Thy truth] thy faithfulness, or righteous self-consistency. 6. Freely] RV ' with a freewill offering ' (Nu 15 3); LXX 'with free will.' O LORD] the one occurrence of ' Jehovah ' in this Elohistic Ps.

PSALM 55

The author of this Ps. can hardly be David, for he speaks as a citizen of a distracted city rather than as its king, and the friend of whom he complains is his equal and not his subject. There is really nothing to fix the date of the Ps., though some of the experiences of Jeremiah may illustrate it. It falls into three portions, which have been described as marked by despair (vv. 1–8), indignation (vv. 9–15), and trust (vv. 16–23).

3. Cast iniquity upon me] attack me with

wicked devices, as they might roll down stones on an enemy. **6. A dove**] the wild rock-dove, which can fly fast and far. **8. Hasten my escape**] RV 'haste me to a shelter.'

9. Divide their tongues] with a confusion like that of Babel. **13. Guide . . acquaintance**] RV 'companion . . familiar friend.' **14. Unto . . company**] RV 'in the house of God with the throng.' **15. Quick into hell**] RM 'alive into Sheol.' For the light in which we are to regard such imprecations see Intro.

18. From the battle *that was* **against me**] RM 'so that none came nigh me.' **There were many with me**] RV 'they were many *that strove* with me.' **19. Because,** etc.] RV (with comma after **old**) '*The men* who have no changes, and who fear not God.' By 'changes' we may understand ups and downs of fortune, or pauses in their wickedness. A slightly different reading would give, 'who have no faithfulness.' **23. Bloody**] RV 'blood-thirsty.'

PSALM 56

Title.—(RV) 'For the Chief Musician; set to Jonath elem rehokim. *A Psalm* of David: Michtam: when the Philistines took him in Gath.'

For **Michtam** see on Ps 16. **Jonath elem rehokim** ('the dove of the distant terebinths') indicates the song to the melody· of which the Ps. was to be sung. As in the case of Ps 34 the title hardly describes accurately the occasion which it mentions (1 S 21¹⁰), and consequently too much weight must not be attached to it. The Psalmist, with many enemies around him, casts himself on God's mercy, and his confidence utters itself in a twice-repeated refrain (vv. 4, 10).

1. Daily] RV 'all the day long.' So in v. 2. **2. Against me, O thou most High**] RV 'proudly against me.' **4. In God I will praise his word**] By God's help I will praise Him for the truth of His promises. **7. Shall they escape by iniquity?**] A slight change of reading would give, 'Requite them according to their iniquity.' **People**] RV 'peoples.' This prayer would become more intelligible if national rather than personal enemies were in view. **8. Tellest**] countest. **Put thou my tears**] or, 'my tears are put.' **Thy bottle**] or 'skin.' God treasures His servants' tears as if they were water or wine. St. Bernard says, 'the tears of penitents are the wine of angels.' **Thy book**] in which all things are recorded. **12. Thy vows,** etc.] The vows I have made to Thee bind me to Thy service. **13.** *Wilt* **not** *thou deliver?* etc.] RV '*hast thou* not *delivered,*' etc.—an affirmation in the form of a question. The meaning is, 'Yea, and my feet from falling.'

PSALM 57

Title.—(RV) 'For the Chief Musician; *set to* Al-tashheth. *A Psalm* of David: Michtam: when he fled from Saul, in the cave.'

This and the two following Pss. were set to the melody of the song beginning **Al-tashheth** ('Destroy not'), which was apparently a vintage song (Isa 65⁸). The occasion referred to in the title is either David's stay in the cave of Adullam (1 S 22¹), or the incident in the cave of Engedi (1 S 24³), but the Ps., has no relation either to the one or to the other. It is a companion to Ps 56. The general situation is the same, but the refrain in this case (vv. 5, 11) is even more triumphant. Vv. 4, 8 (see notes) mark the Ps. as an evening hymn. Vv. 7–11 form Ps 108¹⁻⁵. This is one of the Pss. for Easter.

1. Trusteth] RV 'taketh refuge.' **3.** *From* **the reproach,** etc.] RV 'when he that would swallow me up reproacheth,' i.e. reproacheth God, blasphemeth. **His truth**] his faithfulness.

4. *And* **I lie,** etc.] better, 'I will take my rest even among fiery foes '—an expression of the calm courage of faith. **6. My soul is bowed down**] LXX 'They have bowed down my soul '; but perhaps we should read, 'their soul is bowed down,' which makes the v. consist of two contrasts. **7. My heart is fixed**] is firm and steadfast in its courage. **8. My glory**] my soul, as in 7⁵ 16⁹ 30¹². **Psaltery and harp**] see on 33². **Will awake early**] RM 'will awake the dawn,' by singing even before the morning appears.

9. People] RV 'peoples': see on 56⁷.

PSALM 58

This Ps. denounces the wickedness of unjust and oppressive judges, and prays, in a series of powerful metaphors, for their destruction, in order that righteousness may be vindicated, and God exalted as the supreme Judge. It is uncertain whether the injustice complained of is exercised by Israelites or by foreigners, and so the Ps. has been variously placed before and after the exile. In any case it cannot be regarded as David's. For its subject it should be compared with Ps 82.

Title.—See on Ps 57.

1. O congregation] RV 'in silence.' Both are doubtful renderings of a word which occurs only here. The reading now generally accepted gives the meaning, 'O ye gods,' or 'mighty ones,' in the sense of 'judges': cp. 82¹. **Sons of men**] Judges are reminded that they are human, in spite of their high office: see 82⁷. **2. Weigh**] RV 'weigh out.' The 'scales of justice' are abused. **3. Estranged**] from God and righteousness. **4, 5.** The comparison with serpents is twofold, first as to venom, and second as to obstinate refusal to be influenced. **4. Adder**] RM ‘asp.’ **5. Will not hearken**, etc.] cp. Jer 8 17. The ancient art of snake-charming is still practised in the East.

6. Read with LXX ‘God shall break,’ etc., and in the following vv. ‘They shall melt .. shall be.’ This gives solemn prediction in the place of mere imprecation. **7. Cut in pieces**] RV ‘cut off,’ blunted. **8.** Read, ‘*They shall be* as a snail which melteth and passeth away.’ The idea is perhaps derived from the snail’s slimy track, or from the commonness of empty snail shells.

9. He shall take, etc.] Read, ‘While the flesh is still raw wrath shall sweep them away like a whirlwind.’ Flesh is about to be cooked in a pot, but almost before the fire has kindled a whirlwind scatters the whole arrangement. The figure suggests a judgment of startling suddenness. **10.** This v. breathes a spirit of ferocity not unnatural in the warlike days of the OT., but impossible to be reconciled with the spirit of Christ. **11. He is a God**] RV ‘there is a God.’

PSALM 59

Title.—(RV) ‘For the Chief Musician ; *set to* Al-tashheth. *A Psalm* of David : Michtam : when Saul sent, and they watched the house to kill him.’

For the first part of the title see on Ps 57. The second part, which alludes to 1 S 19 11, scarcely explains the contents of the Ps., which has foreign enemies in view throughout (vv. 5, 8, 13). ‘My people’ in v. 11 has been held to imply that the writer was a king, while David at the time in question was only a subject. It is probable that the Ps. should be assigned to the period of the later Jewish monarchy. Like many other Pss., it presents the three features of danger, prayer, and confidence.

2. Bloody] RV ‘bloodthirsty.’ **3. Not** *for* **my transgression**] This might express the Psalmist’s conscious innocence before God, but more probably it means that he had done nothing to provoke the hostility of his enemies. **4. Awake**] cp. 44 23. **5. God of Israel**] specially invoked because His people are being assailed by the heathen. **Selah**] see on 3 4.

6. The writer’s foes are compared to the savage dogs which infest Eastern cities and prowl round at night in search of garbage. Possibly there is a hint here that Jerusalem was actually besieged. **Make a noise**] ‘snarl.’

7. Swords *are* **in their lips**] Their speech is cutting and injurious. **Who**, *say they*, **doth hear ?**] They question whether there is a God. **9.** *Because of* **his strength**, etc.] RV ‘O my strength, I will wait,’ etc. **10. Shall prevent me**] i.e. shall come to meet me.

11. Slay them not] must be understood in

the light of v. 13. The prayer is that they may not be suddenly cut off, but may be allowed to perish gradually in their sin, in order that Israel may have a more memorable object-lesson in the righteousness of God.

13. Let them know, etc.] Read, ‘Let them know unto the ends of the earth that God ruleth in Jacob.’ Zeal for God’s glory is the one motive of the Psalmist’s prayer, however vindictive some of his requests may appear.

14. Almost a repetition of v. 6. It may mean that the contemptible attitude of the heathen described in v. 6 is all that is to be left them. **15. Grudge**] RV ‘tarry all night.’

15, 16, Read, ‘As for them they shall wander .. But I will sing.’ **16. In the morning**] Though his enemies prowl all the night it will be in vain.

PSALM 60

Title.—(RV) ‘For the Chief Musician ; set to Shushan Eduth : Michtam of David, to teach : when he strove with Aram-naharaim and with Aram-zobah, and Joab returned, and smote of Edom in the Valley of Salt twelve thousand.’

Shushan-eduth (‘the lily of the testimony’) denotes that this Ps. was set to the same melody as Pss 45, 69, 80. For ‘Michtam’ see Ps 16. The historical occasion in the title is described in 2 S 8 3-8, 13, 14 1 Ch 18 3-8, 12, 13, but in these passages Abishai is mentioned instead of Joab, and the number of the slain is given as 18,000. 1 Ch 8 12 is probably right in reading ‘Edom’ instead of ‘the Syrians’ (*Aram*) of 2 S 8 13. The Ps., however, is plainly written after a lost battle, not after a victory. It has been suggested that while David was engaged with the Syrians in the N. of Palestine, the Edomites may have gained a temporary success in the S. before they were routed by David’s generals, and that the Ps. may have been written under the shadow of this reverse. Others think that vv. 6–8, asserting God’s sovereignty over the whole territory ruled by David, are a Davidic fragment worked into a later poem of national distress. The last six verses form the second part of Ps 108. Vv. 1–4 describe the defeat of Israel. The prayer in v. 5 leads to a confident expectation of extensive conquests by God’s assistance (vv. 6–12).

1. Turn thyself to us] RV ‘restore us,’ not necessarily from captivity. **2. Earth**] RV ‘land.’ The imagery is that of an earthquake. **3. Wine of astonishment**] RV ‘wine of staggering,’ or reeling : see Isa 51 17, 22, where God’s wrath is similarly compared to stupefying wine. **4. That it may be displayed**, etc.] Read with LXX ‘that they may betake themselves to flight before the bow.’ Israel has raised the standard only to flee. **5. Thy beloved**] better, ‘thy beloved ones.’

6 f. The Psalmist gives the grounds of his confidence in God. All the nations are His, and He deals with them as He sees good.

6. Rejoice] exult as a victor. **Mete**] measure. **Shechem . . Succoth**] W. and E. of the Jordan respectively. Both places were connected with Jacob (Gn 33 17, 18). **7. Gilead . . Manasseh**] both E. of the Jordan, Gilead being N. of Manasseh. **Ephraim . . Judah**] both W. of the Jordan and again named from N. to S. They were the two most powerful Hebrew tribes, and became the heads of the separate kingdoms after Solomon's death. Hence they are distinguished, the one as the helmet (RV 'the defence of mine head'), the other as the 'sceptre' (RV) of God.

8. Moab . . Edom . . Philistia] Israel's neighbours on the E., SE., and W. respectively. They are all described as reduced to the lowest subjection. Moab is the vessel in which the conqueror's feet are washed, Edom the slave who cleans his sandals (reading 'unto Edom' with RM), or the corner into which the sandals are thrown when soiled (reading 'upon Edom' with RV). **Philistia, etc.**] Read, as in Ps 108 9, 'Over Philistia will I shout in triumph.' **9. The strong city**] Petra, the almost impregnable capital of Edom. It is the Psalmist who now speaks, asking how Edom is to be conquered. **10.** RV 'Hast not thou, O God, cast us off ? And thou goest not forth, O God, with our hosts.' **11. From trouble**] RV 'against the adversary.'

PSALM 61

This Ps. was written at a distance from Jerusalem, and is either the prayer of a king for himself, or the prayer of a subject for himself and the king. In the former case it would naturally be assigned to David, and to the time of his stay at Mahanaim beyond Jordan, during Absalom's rebellion. In the latter it might belong to any time before the exile. In present trouble the memory of past mercies inspires confidence for the future.

2. The end of the earth] or perhaps 'of the land.' Jerusalem is the centre, absence from which is banishment. **The rock** *that* **is higher than I**] 'a rock too high for me,' some inaccessible place of security. **4. Tabernacle**] tent. The word may be purely figurative (cp. Ps 23 7), or it may refer to the 'tabernacle' which David made for the ark. **Trust**] RV 'take refuge': see Ps 17 8.

5. Vows] here stand for the prayers which accompanied them. **Thou hast given** *me*, etc.] RM 'Thou hast given an heritage unto those that fear thy name.' This may mean that Absalom's rebellion has been crushed, and that the land is in the possession of loyal Israelites. **6.** If David is the writer he speaks of himself here in the third person: cp. Zede-

kiah's words in Jer 38 5. The v. is an assurance rather than a prayer. **7. Abide . . for ever**] in the continuance of his royal line : see 2 S 7 12, 13, 16. **Prepare**] or appoint. **Mercy** (RV 'lovingkindness') **and truth** are personified as guardian angels : see Ps 57 3.

PSALM 62

This is a Ps. of the strongest faith, in which the experience of hostility (vv. 3, 4) and the contemplation of life (vv. 9, 10) only provide the background against which a serene confidence in God displays itself. Its tone is not inconsistent with the character of David, who 'strengthened himself in the Lord his God' (1 S 30 6 RV). Vv. 1, 2 are practically repeated in vv. 5, 6.

Title.—**Jeduthun**] see on Ps 39.

1. Truly . . waiteth] RV 'my soul waiteth only.' The word rendered 'only' occurs six times in the Ps. **3. Ye shall be slain**] RV 'that ye may slay him,' or better still, 'battering him,' a figure continued in the next clause.

As a bowing wall *shall ye be*, etc.] RV 'like a bowing wall and like,' etc. The comparison applies not to the assailants but to the person assailed.

9. While God is all, men are nothing, whether they be high or low. **Vanity** or breath, and lie or illusion are the most that they can be called. **To be laid in the balance**] RV 'in the balances they will go up,' because of their lightness. **Altogether**] RV 'together,' both high and low combined. **11, 12. Power and mercy**] the two sides of the full-orbed character of God, both displayed in His unerring judgments of men.

PSALM 63

Title.—**A Psalm of David, when he was in the wilderness of Judah.**

The writer of this Ps. is a king (v. 11), who is at a distance from the sanctuary, and in danger from eager foes. If the title be correct it must refer, not to David's earlier experiences in the reign of Saul (1 S 22 5), but to the time when his flight from Absalom led him through the wilderness of Judah, between Jerusalem and the Jordan (2 S 15 23-28). His longing for God's presence (vv. 1, 2) passes into joyful confidence (vv. 3–8) and certain expectation of his enemies' overthrow.

1. O God, thou *art* **my God**] the 'Elohistic' equivalent of 'O Lord, thou art my God.' **Early**] RM 'earnestly.' **2.** RV 'So (or 'thus') have I looked upon thee in the sanctuary, To see thy power and thy glory.' The sanctuary may be the temporary abode of the ark at Jerusalem. It is the memory of communion with God there which inspires the Psalmist's present longing. **4. Thus**] better. 'therefore.' **Lift up my hands**] in prayer. In

thy name] trusting in the revealed character of God. **5.** Hunger is now substituted for thirst to describe the spiritual longing which God satisfies.

6. The *night* **watches**] were three in number —the first, the middle, and the morning watches. **8.** The clinging effort of the human soul and the upholding grasp of God are the two sides of the relationship of faith. **9.** The **lower parts of the earth**] the under-world of Sheol. **10. Foxes**] jackals. **11. By him**] by God : see Isa 65 16.

PSALM 64

This is a Ps. on a familiar theme. The Psalmist's life is in danger. He describes the injurious words and malicious plans of his enemies, and foretells how their overthrow will be a warning to all who see it, and a new ground for the righteous to rejoice in God. The same figure (shooting an arrow) is employed both for the assaults of the wicked and for their discomfiture by God.

4. In secret] RV 'in secret places.' **The perfect**] the upright man : cp. 37 37. **Fear not**] regard neither God nor man. **5. Matter**] RV 'purpose.' **They say, Who shall see them ?**] cp. 10 11. **6. They accomplish**, etc.] better, 'we have perfected, *say they*, a careful device.'

8. RV 'So shall they be made to stumble, their own tongue being against them,' their evil words coming back upon themselves. **See them**] 'see their desire upon them' : cp. 54 7. **Flee away**] RV 'wag the head,' in scorn : see 22 7 Jer 48 27. **9.** Note the contrast with 28 5.

PSALM 65

The allusions to the Temple worship show that this Ps. belongs to a later age than David's. As to its occasion we can gather that a national religious festival at Jerusalem was in view (vv. 1–4), that a striking national deliverance had produced a wide-spread impression of God's power (vv. 5–8), and that a favourable season gave promise of an abundant harvest (vv. 9–13). The presentation of the firstfruits at the Passover (Lv 23 10-14) would suit the first and last conditions, and the repulse of the Assyrian invasion in Hezekiah's reign would fulfil the second.

1. Waiteth] 'is silent,' an obscure expression. LXX has 'praise beseemeth thee.' **2. All flesh**] God is thought of as the God, not only of Israel, but of all the world : cp. 5 b. **3. Me .. our**] The Psalmist speaks, now for himself, now in the name of the nation. **4.** *Even* **of thy holy temple**] RV 'the holy place of thy temple.' **5.** *By* **terrible things**] by impressive deliverances. **In righteousness**] connected with 'thou wilt answer us' (RV). **7. People**] RV 'peoples.' **8. Thy tokens**] the manifestations of Thy power. **Outgoings**, etc.] the

gates of morning and evening, the E. and the W. **Rejoice**] shout for joy—the inhabitants of E. and W. are meant.

9. With the river, etc.] RV 'the river of God is full of water.' The rain is meant, or its source in the sky. **Thou preparest**, etc.] RV 'thou providest them corn when thou hast so prepared the earth,' i.e. by the plentiful early rain (Nov.-Feb.). **10. Ridges**] RV 'furrows.' **Settlest**] levellest. **Furrows**] RV 'ridges.' **11.** Read, 'Thou crownest the year of thy goodness' (RM). The prospect of a rich harvest was only the last gift in a year of many blessings and deliverances. **Thy paths drop fatness**] God is pictured as walking through the land, and causing fertilising showers to fall wherever He treads.

12. The wilderness] not a desert, but open pasture-land—a 'steppe' or 'veldt.' **The little hills**, etc.] RV 'the hills are girded with joy' —a fine poetic personification of nature which the next v. continues.

PSALM 66

This Ps. triumphantly celebrates a great national deliverance. The whole earth is summoned to join in the chorus of praise (vv. 1–4). The memories of the exodus are recalled (vv. 5–7), but only as an introduction to more recent trials and triumphs (vv. 8–12), and the Ps. ends with vows of lavish sacrifice (vv. 13–15), and with enthusiastic testimony to God's great goodness (vv. 16–20). The failure of Sennacherib's invasion, and the return from Babylon have each been suggested as the occasion of the Ps., and the former is the more probable. There is a striking change from 'we' and 'us' (vv. 1–12) to 'I' and 'me' (vv. 13–20), which is best explained by supposing that the Psalmist at first merges himself in the nation, and afterwards regards his people's deliverance in the light of a personal blessing, as it has been an answer to personal prayer.

3. *Art thou in* **thy works**] RV 'are thy works' : see 65 5. **6. The sea**] the Red Sea. **Flood**] RV 'river,' the Jordan. **There**] both at the Red Sea and at the Jordan.

8. People] RV 'peoples.' These foreign nations are to praise 'our God,' Israel's God. **9. Holdeth**] RM 'putteth,' or better, 'hath set.' There is a definite allusion to a recent deliverance from national ruin. **Suffereth not**] better, 'hath not suffered.'

10–12. The peril is described in a succession of figures, the refining furnace, the net, the burden, the prostration of the vanquished under the trampling of the victors' horses, fire, water.

11. Affliction] RV 'a sore burden.' **13. Pay .. my vows**] make the offerings I promised.

15. Incense of rams] not actual incense, but the 'sweet savour' of the burning flesh.

16. For my soul] for the deliverance of my life : see v. 9. **17. He was extolled,** etc.] RM 'high praise was under my tongue,' ready to break forth when prayer should be answered.

18. RM 'If I had regarded iniquity .. the Lord would not hear.' The answer of God was the proof that the prayer had been offered from an upright heart.

PSALM 67

This short and joyful Ps. is in the first place a harvest thanksgiving (v. 6), perhaps at the Feast of Tabernacles. God's goodness to Israel reveals Him also to the nations (v. 2), and calls forth their praise (vv. 3, 5), their submission (v. 4), and their worship (v. 7). There is a symmetrical parallelism on either side of the middle verse, v. 5 corresponding to v. 3, and vv. 6, 7 to vv. 1, 2.

1. This v. is partly taken from the priestly benediction (Nu 6²⁴), but with the change of ' the LORD' (*Jehovah*) into ' God' (*Elohim*). **2. Thy way**] of dealing with men. **Saving health**] salvation. **3. People**] RV 'peoples.' So in vv. 4, 5. **4. Righteously**] RV 'with equity.' **Govern**] RM 'lead,' as He led Israel. **6.** RV 'The earth hath yielded her increase.'

PSALM 68

This is one of the grandest of the Pss., but its origin and date are involved in much obscurity. It contains expressions borrowed from the Blessing of Moses (Dt 33) and the Song of Deborah (Jg 5), and presents several parallels with the exilic prophecy of Isa 40–66. It may be assigned with some probability to the close of the exile, in which case it is to be regarded as a triumphant anticipation of God's victory over His enemies in the restoration of His people from the Babylonian captivity. After an inspiring prelude (vv. 1–6) the Psalmist recalls some of God's triumphs in the past—at the exodus and in the wilderness (vv. 7–10), in the conquest of Canaan (vv. 11–14), and in the choice of Zion as His dwelling (vv. 15–18). God next appears as the present Saviour of His people and as the Vanquisher of their enemies (vv. 19–23). Then comes a picture of a triumphal procession of a reunited Israel in honour of His victory (vv. 24–27), and of heathen kings bringing tribute to Jerusalem (vv. 28–31). A magnificent doxology (vv. 32–35) closes the Ps., which is another of the Pss. for Whit Sunday.

1. Taken from the invocation of Moses at the moving of the ark (Nu 10³⁵), with the change of LORD (*Jehovah*) into God (*Elohim*).

2, 3. The wicked .. the righteous] the heathen and Israel respectively. **4. Extol .. heavens**] RV ' cast up a high way for him that rideth through the deserts' : cp. Isa 40³. **By**

his name JAH] RV 'his name is JAH,' an abbreviation of Jehovah, as in Hallelu-jah.

5. His holy habitation] heaven : see Dt. 26¹⁵. **6. In families**] RM ' in a house.' **Those .. chains**] RV 'the prisoners into prosperity' : cp. Isa 61¹ Ps 146⁷. **Dwell in a dry** (RV ' parched') *land*] like the rebellious Israelites who perished in the wilderness.

7, 8. A free quotation from the Song of Deborah (Jg 5⁴,⁵). Note again the substitution of 'God' for 'LORD.' **Selah**] see on 3⁴.

8. The heavens also dropped] in the rain which accompanied the thunderstorms of Sinai : see 77¹⁷. **9. A plentiful rain**] here a figure for all the blessings of the sojourn in the wilderness. Omit **whereby** with RV. **10. Hath dwelt**] RV ' dwelt.' **Therein**] in the wilderness. **Hast prepared**] RV ' didst prepare.' **The poor**] or afflicted, the needy wanderers in the desert.

11. Gave the word] secured the victory by his simple command. **Great** *was* **the company,** etc.] RV 'the women that publish the tidings are a great host.' In the East it is the women who celebrate victories with song and dance : see 1 S 18⁶,⁷. Vv. 12, 13 are the words of the women. **12.** Another echo of Deborah's Song (Jg 5³⁰). The kings are the kings of Canaan subdued by Joshua.

13. Among the pots] RV 'among the sheep-folds,' another phrase from Deborah's Song (Jg 5¹⁶), where it rebukes the inactivity of the Reubenites. RV reads, 'will ye lie .. sheep-folds, as the wings of a dove,' etc., in the same sense of reproof. But the best rendering is in RM, 'When ye lie among the sheepfolds' (i.e. when ye return to your homes) '*it is as* the wings,' etc., describing the brightness and peace of the prosperous time after the conquest of Canaan. Some understand the silver and gold to refer to the spoils of the victors. **14. It was** *white,* etc.] RV '*It was as when* it snoweth in Zalmon.' Zalmon was a wooded hill near Shechem (Jg 9⁴⁸). The scattered kings of Canaan were like the driven snowflakes seen against the dark green background.

15. RV 'A mountain of God' (i.e. a great mountain : see 36⁶), 'is the mountain of Bashan ; an high mountain is the mountain of Bashan.' Hermon, which bounds Bashan on the N., is probably meant. Though it is so lofty God has chosen Zion in preference to it (v. 16). **16.** RV 'Why look ye askance' (i.e. why are ye jealous), 'ye high mountains, at the mountain' (Zion), 'which God hath desired for his abode ?' **17. Thousands of angels**] RV 'thousands upon thousands.' God enters Zion in a great procession of His heavenly armies : cp. Dt 33². *As in* **Sinai,** etc.] RM ' Sinai *is* in the sanctuary.' The holy associations of Sinai are transferred to Zion.

18. Having taken possession of Zion God

has returned to His heavenly throne. **Captivity**] RV '*thy* captivity,' thy band of captives. See Deborah's Song (Jg 5 ^{12}). **For men** . . *for* **the rebellious**] RV 'among men . . *among* the rebellious.' God's conquered enemies pay Him tribute. St. Paul's quotation in Eph 4 ^{8} changes 'received' into 'gave.'

19. Loadeth us *with benefits*] RV 'beareth our burden.' **20.** RV 'God is unto us a God of deliverances : and unto JEHOVAH the Lord,' etc. **The issues from death**] the ways of escape from death, which God can provide.

21. Wound] RV 'smite through.' **The hairy scalp**] the long flowing locks which were the sign of the warrior's strength and of his devotion to his cause. See Dt 32 ^{42} RM, and the Song of Deborah (Jg 5 ^{2}), where we should read 'For that flowing locks were worn in Israel.'

22. Bring *my people*] RV 'bring *them*,' i.e. Israel's enemies, who will be gathered for vengeance from the most inaccessible hiding places. Bashan was a country of intricate and rocky retreats. **23.** RV 'That thou mayest dip thy foot in blood, that the tongue of thy dogs may have its portion from *thine* enemies.' God is still the speaker, and Israel is addressed. For the tone cp. 58 ^{10}.

24. In] RV 'into.' **26. From the fountain**] RV '*ye that are* of the fountain,' all the descendants of Jacob : cp. Dt 33 ^{28}. **27.** *With* **their ruler**] RV 'their ruler,' the tribe from which the first king was taken (1 S 9 ^{21}).

Council] 'company.' **Zebulon** and **Naphtali** (see Jg 5 ^{18}) represent the northern kingdom, **Benjamin** and **Judah** the southern.

28. Read, 'O God, command thy strength : be strong, O God, thou that hast wrought for us.' **30. The company of spearmen**] RV 'the wild beast of the reeds,' the hippopotamus, the symbol of Egypt. **Bulls, with the calves of the people** (RV 'peoples')] heathen kings and their subjects. *Till every one* **submit**, etc.] RV 'trampling under foot the pieces of silver.' God treats the tribute of the heathen with contempt. **31. Egypt**] as Israel's ancient enemy. **Ethiopia**] as one of the remotest of lands. **33, 34.** Cp. Dt 33 $^{26-27}$.

PSALM 69

This whole Ps. should be compared with Pss 22, 31, 35, 38, and 40. It is the prayer of one who is in deep distress, wrongfully persecuted by enemies, and conscious that, though he is sinful, his sufferings are due to his fidelity to God (vv. 1–12). He pleads for deliverance (vv. 13–20) and calls upon God to take the severest vengeance on his adversaries (vv. 21–28). The Ps. closes with a triumphant strain of praise (vv. 29–36). V. 35 points to a date long after the age of David—either during the exile, or, more probably, in the last years of the Jewish monarchy (see Jer 33 ^{10} 34 ^{7}).

The situation of the writer closely resembles that of Jeremiah, and the numerous parallels between the Ps. and his prophecies give colour to the conjecture that he may have been its author. This Ps. is more frequently quoted in the NT. than any other, except Ps 22.

Title.—**Shoshannim**] see on Ps 45.

1. Are come in unto *my* **soul**] threaten my very life. **2. Mire .. deep waters**] to be understood figuratively of danger and distress.

3. Weary of] RV 'weary with.' **4. I** re-**stored**, etc.] RM 'I had to restore,' etc., possibly a proverbial phrase for unjust treatment. **7.** Cp. Jer 15 ^{15}. **8.** Cp. Jer 12 ^{6}.

9. The zeal, etc.] The Psalmist was consumed by his devotion to God's cause. **Thine house**] either the actual Temple, profaned by idolatry, or the Jewish nation, fallen from its high ideal. For the latter sense, see Jer 11 ^{15} 12 ^{7} 23 ^{11}. The clause is quoted in Jn 2 ^{17}.

The reproaches, etc.] see Jer 6 ^{10} 20 ^{8}. The words are applied to Christ in Ro 15 ^{3}.

11. Sackcloth] the sign of mourning. **A proverb**] or byword. **12. The gate**] the open space beside the city gate where worthless loafers gathered.

13. *In* **an acceptable time**] lit. 'in a time of good pleasure,' i.e. at the time thou pleasest.

The truth of thy salvation] the faithfulness of Thy saving grace. **15. The pit**] may be, like the waters, a general metaphor for trouble, but it is more likely that the grave is meant. **18.** Cp. Jer 15 ^{21}. **19. Thou hast known**] RV 'thou knowest' : cp. Jer 12 ^{3} 15 ^{15} 18 ^{23}.

20. Hath broken my heart] cp. Jer 23 ^{9}.

21. Gall] some bitter and poisonous plant, perhaps the poppy. **Vinegar**] wine become sour and undrinkable. The language is figurative, and perhaps proverbial, for cruel mockery of one in trouble. In spite of the verbal coincidence in Mt 27 ^{34}, the treatment of Christ by the soldiers had not this character, but was intended to allay His sufferings ; and, except as to the fact of His thirst (Jn 19 ^{28}), there is no direct reference in the Gospels to this v.

22. And *that which* .. **welfare**] RV 'and when they are in peace.' This v. is quoted freely along with v. 23 in Ro 11 ^{9}. **23.** A prayer that blindness and paralysis may fall upon the Psalmist's enemies. **25.** This v. is quoted freely (from LXX) in Ac 1 ^{20}. **26. Talk to the grief**] RV 'tell of the sorrow.' LXX 'add to the sorrow.' **27. Add iniquity,** etc.] cause their guilt to be filled up, rather than forgiven. **Into thy righteousness**] into the salvation which God's righteousness secures for His people. **28. The book of the living**] RV 'of life,' the list of the righteous who are to be preserved alive. The reference is not to the future but to the present life.

31. Praise is the truest sacrifice : cp. 50 $^{13, 14}$. **Hath horns and hoofs**] is full grown as well as ceremonially clean (Lv 11³). **33. His prisoners**] perhaps an allusion to the victims of the first captivity (2 K 24¹⁰⁻¹⁶).

PSALM 70

This Ps. is simply a repetition of Ps 40¹³⁻¹⁷, with a few variations. 'LORD' (*Jehovah*) is changed into 'God' (*Elohim*) except in v. 1ᵇ. On the other hand, 'Elohim' is changed into 'Jehovah' in v. 5ᵇ. By a change of one letter in the Hebrew 'turned back' is substituted for 'desolate' in v. 3, and 'make haste unto me' appears instead of 'thinketh upon me' in v. 5. The five vv. composing the Ps. constitute a cry to God for help and deliverance.

Title : see on Ps 38.

PSALM 71

This Ps. of prayer (vv. 1–13) and praise (vv. 14–24) was apparently written by an old man (vv. 9, 18) and in the time of the exile. Some parts of it are undoubtedly national, but much of it expresses personal experience and desire and faith. It is largely made up of extracts from other Pss., yet it has a unity and a beauty of its own.

1–3. Practically taken from 31¹⁻³. **5, 6.** See 22⁹,¹⁰. **7. As a wonder unto many**] a striking example of God's mysterious chastisement of His own : see Isa 52¹⁴. **12.** See 22¹¹ 40¹³.

13. See 35⁴,²⁶ : cp. also v. 24.

15. I know not the numbers] cp. 40⁵. **16. Go in the strength**] RV 'come with the mighty acts,' bringing them as the subject of the song.

18. *This* **generation**] RV '*the next* genera- tion.' **20.** For me read 'us' all through this v. (RV). The Psalmist predicts a resurrection of his nation which is, as it were, dead and buried in its exile. **21. Thou shalt increase**] RV 'increase thou.' **Comfort me on every side**] RV 'turn again and comfort me.'

PSALM 72

Title.—*A Psalm* for (RV 'of') **Solomon.**
The title in AV suggests that David is the writer, and Solomon the subject, of this Ps., but, as RV shows, the authorship is really ascribed to Solomon. The Ps., however, ap- pears rather to be the prayer of a subject for the king. Some actual ruler—Solomon, Heze- kiah, or another—is no doubt in view, but, as in Ps 45, the royal figure is so idealised that the Ps. becomes truly Messianic, and applicable only to the perfect divine King, though it is nowhere expressly quoted in this sense in the NT. The justice and beneficence of the king's reign, the ,world-wide extent of his dominion, the prosperity of his country, and the perpetuity

of his fame, are successively described. Vv. 18, 19 are the closing doxology of Book 2 of the Psalter, and v. 20 is an instructive editorial note.

1. Judgments . . righteousness] the qualities of a great and upright ruler : see v. 2. **The king's son**] a parallel expression for the king. **2. Thy poor**] the class who suffered most from unjust and oppressive rulers. **3. By righteousness**] RV 'in righteousness.' Under a righteous government peace will be the fruit that grows on all the wooded slopes of the land : see Isa 32¹⁷. **5. They shall fear thee**] not the king, but God. LXX reads instead, 'He shall endure as long as the sun, and while the moon doth shine.' **6. Upon the mown grass**] to start the new growth. LXX and Vulg. render, 'upon a fleece' : cp. PBV 'into a fleece of wool.' **7.** The metaphor of v. 6 is continued. 'Righteousness' (LXX) and peace are the vegetation which springs up after the fertilising showers.

8–11. These vv. should be read as a prayer rather than as a prediction. 'May he have dominion . . May they bow,' etc. **8. From sea to sea**] from the Red Sea to the Mediter- ranean. **The river**] RV 'the River,' the Eu- phrates in the E. **The ends of the earth**] the extreme W. : see Ex 23³¹ 1 K 4²¹. **9. They that dwell in the wilderness**] the wandering desert tribes. **Lick the dust**] the attitude of abject submission. **10. Tarshish**] probably Tartessus in Spain : see on 48⁷. **The isles**] the coast-lands of the Mediterranean. **Sheba**] Saba in S. Arabia. **Seba**] an unknown locality, elsewhere connected with Ethiopia (Isa 43³ 45¹⁴).

12. The poor also, etc.] RV 'and the poor that hath no helper.' **14. Precious shall their blood be**] Human life will be protected, and not held cheap, as it is where tyranny flourishes.

15. He shall live] better, 'May he live, and may men give him . . may they pray,' etc. **For him**] PBV renders, 'prayer shall be made ever unto him': an indefensible translation, which has arisen from an exclusive reference of the Ps. to Christ.

16, 17. These vv. also are best read as a prayer. 'May there be . . may his name en- dure,' etc. **16. An handful**] RV 'abundance.'

In the earth] better, 'in the land.' **Shake like Lebanon**] wave or rustle like the cedars of Lebanon. *They* **of the city, etc.**] better, 'may men spring forth out of the city like grass of the earth.' **17. Be blessed**] RM 'bless themselves': see Gn 22¹⁸ 26⁴ (RM), and cp. Isa 65¹⁶.

20. See Intro. to Book 2.

BOOK 3 (PSALMS 73–89)

There are two groups of Pss. in this book, Pss 73–83 being Psalms of Asaph, and Pss 84–88 (except 86) Psalms of the Sons of Korah. The likeness of the title of Ps 89 to that of Ps 88 suggests that it belongs to the same group. The Sons of Asaph and the Sons of Korah were guilds of singers connected with the second Temple (2 Ch 20 19 Ezr 2 41 Neh 7 44), and these groups of Pss. belong to collections made by them for the Temple services.

The Psalms of Asaph, though of different dates, are of a similar character, having many features in common. They are national and historical Pss., setting forth God's working in history, expressing national wants, and suggesting lessons from the past for use in the future. These Pss. have a definite doctrine of God. On the one hand, He is the Shepherd of Israel (80 1), and the people are the sheep of His pasture (74 1 77 20 79 13). This idea is frequently suggested, and it is elaborated at length in Ps 78. On the other hand, God is the Judge (75 7), defending Israel against enemies (76 3-6), executing His judgments against the wicked (76 8, 9), and also administering justice to the poor and defending them from oppressors (82 2-4). Another feature of these Pss. is the way in which history is used for instruction, admonition, and encouragement. Ps 78 is a lesson of comfort and courage from the past experiences of the nation (cp. 77 11 80 8-10 81 7, 10 83 9, 11).

The Psalms of the Sons of Korah are largely devoted to the exaltation of the Temple worship. Those who dwell in its courts are blessed (84 4); a day spent there is better than a thousand elsewhere (84 10). Jerusalem is the favourite place of God (87 2); to be born there is a high privilege (87 5); and a special blessing attends those who have it (87 6).

The problem of the prosperity of the wicked presses upon all the Psalmists, and the author of Ps 73 dwells upon it. Only religion enables him to bear the burden that oppresses him (73 17); but when comforted by the thought of God's presence and healed by communion with Him, he is able to persevere in faith and hope. Ps 89 is frequently referred to in NT., e.g. Ac 13 22 (v. 20), 2 Th 1 10 (v. 7), Rev 1 5 (vv. 27 and 37); while Ps 78 2 is applied in Mt 13 35 to Christ's teaching by parables.

The Pss. of Asaph, like those of Book 2, are 'Elohistic': the Korahite Pss. are 'Jehovistic,' like those of Books 1, 4, and 5 (see Intro. to Book 2).

PSALM 73

This Ps., like Pss 37 and 49, and the book of Job, deals with the perplexing problem presented to thoughtful minds by the prosperity of the wicked and the sufferings of the righteous. The Psalmist has been deeply exercised by this question (vv. 2–14), and after struggling with doubt (vv. 15, 16) has learned in the sanctuary of God to understand the end of the wicked (vv. 17–20), and to repent of his own unbelieving thoughts (vv. 21, 22). He has found rest in the conviction that the only true and lasting blessedness lies in the fellowship of God—a fellowship which ensures present guidance and future welcome (vv. 23, 24), which is the object of his supreme desire (v. 25), and which is independent of all possible change (v. 26). Separation from God is destruction (v. 27). Nearness to God is happiness (v. 28). There is no indication in the Ps. as to its date, except the allusion in v. 17 to the existence of the Temple.

Title.—See Intro. to Book 3.

1. The conclusion reached by faith precedes the account of the struggle with doubt. **Of a clean heart**] a spiritual rather than a merely national conception of Israel. **3. Foolish**] RV 'arrogant.' **4.** Most scholars read, 'For they have no torments ; sound and stalwart is their body.' **6. Compasseth .. chain**] RV 'is as a chain about their neck,' in the sense of an ornament : see Prov 1 9. **7.** Render, 'Their iniquity cometh forth from the heart : the imaginations of their mind overflow.'

8. RV 'They scoff, and in wickedness utter oppression.' **9. Against**] RV 'in,' a description of pride. **10. His people**] the followers and imitators of the wicked man. **Return hither**] better, 'turn hither,' after the wicked man's example. **Wrung out to** (RV 'by') **them**] rather, 'are supped up by them.' They drink in the wicked man's principles, or share in his prosperity : see PBV.

12–14 are best understood as the utterance of the Psalmist's doubts. **15. Say**] RV 'had said.' **Should offend against**] RV 'had dealt treacherously with.' **Thy children**] God's true people, of whom the Psalmist was one, and to whom he felt that he dare not be disloyal. This thought is a practical refutation of doubt, even before the theoretical answer is found.

16. To know] RV 'how I might know.' **17.** *Then .. end*] RV 'and considered their latter end.' Difficulties are resolved and the soul strengthened against the temptations of doubt in the presence and communion of God, as enjoyed in His sanctuary. **20. When thou awakest**] better, 'when Thou stirrest up Thyself.' **Their image**] not themselves. The end of the wicked is nothingness. It is only a shadow of them that survives for God to contemplate.

22. Foolish] RV 'brutish.' **23. Thou hast holden,** etc.] Though the grasp of faith on God may waver, fellowship with Him depends most of all on His grasp of His people.

24. The experience of God's fellowship contains in itself a promise that it will continue and become closer. This thought plainly leads to belief in immortality. **26. My flesh and my heart**] both the outer and the inner man. Though both of these should perish, something would yet remain in eternal union with God. **27. Whoring**] a familiar OT. figure for departure from God.

PSALM 74

Pss 74 and 79 seem to reflect the same historical situation, and are usually ascribed to the same author. Both were written in a time of national calamity, when the Temple was profaned (Ps 74), and the Israelites ruthlessly slaughtered (Ps 79) by a heathen enemy. The occasion described must have been either the destruction of Jerusalem by Nebuchadrezzar's army (586 B.C., 2 K 24 2 Ch 37 11 f. Jer 39 1-8 52 1-14), or the persecution of the Jews by Antiochus Epiphanes (168–165 B.C.: see 1 Mac 1–4 and the Intro. to Daniel). V. 7 seems to point to the former, vv. 8, 9 to the latter period. After an opening appeal to God (vv. 1, 2) the Ps. describes the ravages of the enemy in the Temple (vv. 3–7), and the distressed condition of Israel (vv. 8, 9). A second appeal (vv. 10, 11) is followed by recollection of God's past mercies, especially in leading His people from Egypt to Canaan (vv. 12–15). Next comes an ascription of praise to God as the Ruler of Nature (vv. 16, 17), followed by a final prayer that He will vindicate His own glory, which the heathen have dishonoured (vv. 18–23).

Title.—**Maschil**] see on Ps 32. **1. Smoke**] Like a dark thunder-cloud threatening a flock : see 18 8. **2. The rod . . redeemed**] RV 'which thou hast redeemed to be the tribe of thine inheritance.' **3. Lift up thy feet unto**] Hasten to see. **4. Their ensigns**] either military standards or religious emblems : see 1 Mac 1 47, 54, 55, 59. **5. A man . . lifted up**] RV 'They seemed as men that lifted up.' **The thick trees**] RV 'a thicket of trees.'

8. Synagogues] The mention of these points to the later date for the Ps., as they only arose after the return from the Babylonian exile. **9. Our signs**] either God's miraculous interpositions, or Jewish religious customs such as sacrifice, circumcision, and sabbath-observance, all of which Antiochus Epiphanes forbade under the heaviest penalties : see 1 Mac 1 45, 48, 50. **No more any prophet,** etc.] This hardly applies to the Babylonian capture of Jerusalem, when both Jeremiah and Ezekiel were alive, and when

the former had foretold that the captivity would last 70 years. For the absence of prophets in the days of Antiochus Epiphanes see 1 Mac 4 46 9 27 14 41.

11. The last clause is condensed in the original. RV adds to the last clause, 'and consume *them*.'

13. The sea] the Red Sea : Ex 14 21. The **dragons**] 'sea monsters,' a figure for Egypt.

14. Leviathan] probably the crocodile, another figure for Egypt : cp. Ezk 29 3-5 32 1-5. **The people inhabiting the wilderness**] the wild beasts of the desert. **15. Cleave the fountain**] i.e. cleave the rock from which the fountain flowed : see Ex 17 6 Nu 20 8. **Rivers**] the Jordan : Josh 3 13 4 23. **16, 17.** The signs of God's presence in nature. **18. The foolish people**] RV 'a foolish people,' a heathen nation : see Dt 32 21. **20. Of the earth**] better, 'of the land,' the hiding-places to which the Israelites were pursued by their enemies : see 1 Mac 1 53 2 27-38. **23. Increaseth**] RV 'ascendeth.'

PSALM 75

In contrast with the plaintive strains of Ps 74 this is a Ps. of thanksgiving for some national deliverance (v. 1). It celebrates God as the Judge of all the earth, who interposes in His own time amid the confusions of men (vv. 2, 3). His enemies are warned against pride (vv. 4–8) by the certainty that His cup of punishment is prepared for the wicked (v. 8). The Ps. ends with an ascription of praise (v. 9), and a declaration of God's righteous purpose (v. 10). In vv. 2, 3, 10, God Himself is the speaker. There is nothing to indicate the date or occasion of the Ps., which presents some parallels with the Song of Hannah (1 S 2 1-10).

Title.—(RV) **Al-tashheth**] see on Ps 57. **1**b. RV 'for thy name is near : Men tell of thy wondrous works.' God's 'name' means His saving presence (Isa 30 27). **2.** God speaks. **Receive the congregation**] RV 'find the set time' for judgment. **3. Bear up**] RV 'have set up.' God's moral order stands sure even when it seems that 'the world is out of joint' : cp. 1 S 2 8. **Selah**] see on 3 4. **4. Fools**] RV 'arrogant' : cp. 1 S 2 4. **4, 5.** 'Lifting up the horn' and having 'a stiff neck' are figures for self-exaltation and obstinacy. **6. Read,** 'For neither from . . cometh judgment.' Foreign invasions of Israel generally came from the N., and deliverance might naturally be looked for from some of the other quarters mentioned.

7. Setteth up] RV 'lifteth up' : cp. 1 S 2 6, 7. **8. A cup**] The same figure for God's punishment is found in Isa 51 17 Jer 25 15 f. 48 26 49 12.

PSALM 76

Like the previous Ps. this is a song of national deliverance, which may have been called forth, as the title in LXX suggests, by the overthrow of Sennacherib's army (2 K 19 35 2 Ch 32 21 Isa 37 36). In vv. 1–6 God is described as returning to His dwelling-place in Zion from the mountains where He has overthrown His adversaries. In vv. 7–9 another figure is introduced which represents God as uttering sentence from heaven upon His enemies, while the earth is hushed in silence. V. 10 explains how God gains glory even from the rebelliousness of men, and vv. 11, 12 call the whole world to render Him the homage which is due to His terrible majesty.

Title.—**Neginoth**] see on Ps 4.

2. Salem] Jerusalem.   **3. Selah**] see on 3 4.

4. More glorious . . than] RV 'glorious . . from.' **Mountains of prey**] God comes back like a lion from hunting and slaying His foes.

8. Judgment] RV 'sentence.' **10ᵇ**. RV 'the residue . . gird upon thee.' The spent and powerless anger of men is worn as an ornament by God, or becomes His sword by which they are destroyed.

PSALM 77

The Ps. records the writer's experience of personal perplexity and darkness, which, however, has been caused by the contemplation of Israel's national distress. It may be dated appropriately in the time of the exile. Vv. 1–3 describe the Psalmist's trouble, in which even prayer has brought no comfort. Vv. 4–9 speak of his meditations on the brighter past, which lead to the question whether God has finally rejected His people. In vv. 10–20 he turns for comfort to the story of God's wonderful works of old, and dwells especially upon His deliverance of Israel from Egypt (v. 15), His sublime manifestation of power at the Red Sea (vv. 16–19), and His guidance of His people through the wilderness (v. 20). At this point the Ps. comes to an abrupt close.

Title.—**Jeduthun**] see on Ps 39.

1. Cried . . gave] RV 'will cry . . will give.'

2. My sore ran] RV 'my hand was stretched out,' in the attitude of prayer.   **3. Selah**] see on 3 4.   **4. Mine eyes waking**] rather, 'the guards of my eyes.' The eyelids are kept from closing.   **6. My song in the night**] a former time of happiness and praise : see Ps 42 8 Job 35 10.

10. This *is* my infirmity] The Psalmist here recognises that his doubts are due to his own weakness and not to any change in God. **10ᵇ**. RM reads, 'That the right hand of the Most High doth change,' which may be taken as an exclamation, mentioning the idea only to dismiss it as impossible. **11. Remember**] RV 'make mention of.' **12. Talk of**] RV 'muse on.'

13. In the sanctuary] RV 'in holiness.'

14. People] RV 'peoples.'

15. The sons of Jacob and Joseph] Jacob re-

presents the kingdom of Judah, and **Joseph** (father of Ephraim and Manasseh) the northern kingdom of Israel. The division of the nation is clearly hinted at : see on 80 1, 2.

16. The waters] the Red Sea : Ex 14 21-31.

17. Sound] thunder. **Arrows**] lightning.

18. Heaven] RV 'whirlwind.'   **19. *Is* . . are**] RV 'was . . were.' **Footsteps . . not known**] when the waters had returned to their place.

PSALM 78

This long historical Ps. may be compared with Pss 105, 106, and with Dt 32. It traces the course of God's relations with His people from the exodus down to the time of David, and dwells on the repeated manifestations of Israel's rebelliousness, on the chastisements by which they were visited, and on the patient mercy of God which continued to bless them in spite of all their sins. The Ps. does not follow a strict chronological order, but records first Israel's ingratitude for God's provision of food and drink in the wilderness (vv. 12–34), and afterwards the plagues of Egypt (vv. 43–51), the journey to Canaan (vv. 52–55), the defections of Israel in the days of the Judges (vv. 56–58), the calamities of the Philistine wars (vv. 56–64), and the establishment of David's kingdom (vv. 65–72). While the conduct of the whole nation is in view throughout the Ps. the tribe of Ephraim is singled out for special condemnation at the first (vv. 9–11), and emphasis is afterwards laid on its rejection in favour of Judah, and on the rejection of Shiloh in favour of Jerusalem as the national sanctuary (vv. 67–69). The date of the Ps. is subsequent to the building of the Temple (v. 69), but apparently before its destruction by the Babylonians. The phrase 'the Holy One of Israel' (v. 41) is characteristic of Isaiah's prophecies (Isa 6 13 10 17 29 23), and suggests that the Ps. was written in or after his time. The historical allusions are confined to the primitive narrative of the Pentateuch (JE), which was earlier than the exile. The references to Ephraim indicate a time after the disruption of the kingdom (1 K 12 2 Ch 10), but the object of the Ps. was probably not to rebuke Ephraim, but rather to warn the whole nation by recalling the lessons of the past.

1. Law] RM 'teaching.'   **2. Parable**] in the sense of 'didactic poem.' **Dark sayings**] lit. 'riddles.' The history of Israel is an enigma, requiring an explanation such as the Psalmist gives. These two words occur together in 49 4 Prov 1 6 Ezk 17 2. The v. is quoted in Mt 13 34, 35 with reference to Christ's method of teaching by parables. **3, 4.** The vv. are connected. Read, 'The things which we have heard . . we will not hide from their children' : cp. Dt 4 9 6 7 11 19.

9. This v. does not refer to a particular

incident, but is a general figurative description
of Ephraim's opportunity and failure, anticipating what is said in v. 67. Even before the
revolt of Jeroboam Ephraim had shown a
tendency to rivalry with Judah (2 S 19⁴¹–20²²).

12. Zoan] Tanis, a city in the Delta of the
Nile : see v. 43. **18, 21.** Cp. Ex 16, 17 Nu 11.
26. The wind that brought the quails (Nu
11³¹). **29. Their own desire**] RV 'that they
lusted after.' **36, 37.** There was no real
change of heart. **His covenant**] see Ex 24⁷.
40. Provoke] RV 'rebel against.'
41. Limited] RV 'provoked.'
43–51. The plagues in Egypt. **44. Floods**]
RV 'streams.' **45. Divers sorts**] RV 'swarms.'
47. Frost] RM 'great hailstones.' **48.** Hot
thunderbolts] lightning (Ex 9²⁴). **49. By sending evil angels** *among them*] RV 'a band of evil
angels,' the disasters being personified as messengers of God. **51. Tabernacles**] RV 'tents.'
Ham] or *Kem*, meaning 'black,' because of
the soil, was the Egyptian name for Egypt.
54. Sanctuary] the land of Canaan, as sacred
to God. **This mountain**] the mountain land
of Canaan : cp. Ex 15¹⁷. **55. Heathen**] RV
'nations.' **Divided .. an inheritance**] see Josh
13, etc.
56–64. The reference is to the days of the
Judges. **57. Unfaithfully**] RV 'treacherously.'
A deceitful bow] which causes the archer to
miss the mark (Hos 7¹⁶). **60.** Shiloh] see on
Jg 18³¹ 1 S 1³,²⁴ Jer 7¹²⁻¹⁴ 26⁶.
61. Strength .. glory] the ark : see 1 S 4.
64. Priests] see 1 S 4¹¹. **Made no lamentation**] In the perils of the time mourning rites
could not be observed : see Job 27¹⁵.
65. For this bold figure cp. Isa 42¹³,¹⁴.
66. In the hinder parts] RV 'backward.'
67. Joseph .. Ephraim] Joseph was the
father of Ephraim. Both names are used for
the northern kingdom as a whole. Shiloh,
where the ark had been, was in the territory
of Ephraim. Now it was taken to Zion.
69. High *palaces*] RV 'heights,' the heavens.
Like the earth] firm as the earth. **71. Great
with young**] RV 'that give suck,' as in Isa 40¹¹.

PSALM 79

For the occasion and date of this Ps. see
intro. to Ps 74. It gives a pathetic picture of
the calamities that have fallen upon God's
people (vv. 1–4), entreats God to withdraw His
anger from them, to forgive their sins, and to
avenge them on the heathen (vv. 5–12), that
they may give Him perpetual praise (v. 13).

1. Jerusalem on heaps] This is truer of the
Babylonian captivity than of the time of
Antiochus Epiphanes. **6.** Quoted from Jer
10²⁵. **8. Former iniquities**] RV 'the iniquities
of our forefathers,' which are regarded as justly
punished by the present calamities. **Prevent**]
in the Old English sense of 'go before,' antici-

pate our need. **9.** Here as in Ps 74 God's
regard for His own glory is the Psalmist's
chief plea.
10ᵇ. RV 'Let the revenging of the blood of
thy servants which is shed be known among
the heathen in our sight.' **11. The sighing of
the prisoner**] Some of the people had been
carried into captivity. **12.** The prayer for
vengeance expresses a moral sentiment less
advanced than that of the NT. It springs,
however, not from mere personal or national
vindictiveness, but from a sincere religious
indignation at the dishonour done to God's
name.

PSALM 80

This Ps. is an appeal to God to save His
people from the adversities that have come
upon them, and have made them the laughing
stock of their enemies (vv. 1–7). Their past
history is recalled under the figure of a vine,
once flourishing, but now wasted by wild beasts
and fire (vv. 8–16). Special prominence is
given to the tribes of Ephraim, Manasseh, and
Benjamin (v. 2). The Ps. was probably written
at least after the fall of the northern kingdom
(721 B.C., 2 K 17⁵,⁶ 18⁹⁻¹¹), if not during the
Babylonian exile. The Psalmist either belonged to that kingdom or had a special
sympathy with it in its misfortunes. After
the kingdom of Israel came to an end its
rivalry with Judah was largely forgotten, and
the later prophets cherished the hope of a
restoration which would embrace the whole
nation (Jer 3¹¹⁻¹⁵ 31¹⁻²⁰ Ezk 37¹⁵⁻²⁸).
Title.—Shoshannim-Eduth] see on Pss 45
and 60.
1. O Shepherd of Israel] a representation of
God characteristic of the Asaphic Pss. (see
Intro. to Book 3). **Joseph**] the father of Ephraim and Manasseh. The name is applied to
the kingdom of the Ten Tribes. **Dwellest**
between, etc.] RV 'sittest upon the cherubim' :
see Ex 25²⁰⁻²² Ezk 1²⁶ 10¹. **2. Ephraim .. Benjamin .. Manasseh**] These three tribes were
the descendants of Rachel. They encamped
together in the wilderness, and followed immediately after the tabernacle when Israel was
marching (Nu 2¹⁸⁻²⁴). The Psalmist prays that
they may be restored to their ancient place of
favour. **3.** This v. recurs as a refrain in vv.
7, 19. **Turn us again**] bring us back from
captivity. **Cause thy face to shine**] from
Nu 6²⁵.
8. For the vine as an emblem of Israel see
Isa 5¹⁻⁷ 27²⁻⁶ Jer 2²¹ Ezk 17¹⁻¹⁰. **11. The sea**]
the Mediterranean on the W. **The river**]
RV 'River' : the Euphrates on the E. These
were the ideal boundaries of Israel (Gn 15¹⁸
Ex 23³¹ Dt 11²⁴ Ps 72⁸), which were reached
for the time in the days of Solomon (1 K 4²⁴).
13. Boar .. wild beast (RV 'beasts')]

Israel's enemies, especially, perhaps, the Assyrians. **15. Vineyard**] RV 'stock'; another reading gives 'protect.' **16. They perish**] The figure of the vine is dropped here.

17. Let thy hand be upon] to protect. The **man of thy right hand**] the nation of Israel personified, with a special allusion to the name Benjamin, which means 'son of the right hand': see v. 15. **Son of man**] another expression for the nation in its human weakness : cp. the use of the phrase in Ezekiel (2¹, etc.).

18. Quicken] make alive, revive.

PSALM 81

After a summons to celebrate the Feast of Tabernacles (vv. 1–3) this Ps. recalls the meaning of Israel's national festivals as memorials of their deliverance from Egypt (vv. 4–7). From v. 6 onward God is the speaker. In vv. 8–10 He repeats His ancient command to Israel to worship Him alone, and in vv. 11, 12 He tells of their disobedience and its consequences. The concluding vv. express His desire that Israel may now prove more loyal than of old, that He may bless them with victory over their enemies, and with all outward prosperity (vv. 13–16). There is nothing to fix the date of the Ps., except that the allusion to the feast in vv. 1–3 shows that either the first or the second Temple was in existence when it was written, and that vv. 14, 15 point to a time when Israel was confronted by enemies. It was after the return from the exile that the Feast of Tabernacles came into greatest prominence (Ezr 3⁴ Neh 8¹³⁻¹⁷ Zech 14¹⁶⁻¹⁹).

Title.—**Gittith**] see on Ps 8.

3. In the time appointed] RV 'at the full moon.' The Feast of Tabernacles began on the 15th day of the seventh month (Lv 23³⁴), i.e. at full moon. The beginning of the same month (the new moon) was celebrated by the Feast of Trumpets (Lv 23²⁴). **5. He went out through**] RV 'he went over' (RM 'against') : cp. Ex 13, etc. 'He' refers to God. *Where* I **heard . . understood not**] rather, 'I heard the speech of one that I knew not,' i.e. of God. The Psalmist puts himself in the place of the ancient Israelites, and thus introduces the words of God which follow. Before the exodus God had been unknown to Israel by His name 'I Am,' or 'Jehovah' (Ex 3¹³,¹⁴ 6²⁻⁸).

6. Pots] RV 'basket.' Baskets for carrying bricks, etc., are often represented on the Egyptian monuments. **7. Secret place of thunder**] the pillar of cloud and fire : see Ex 14²⁴. **Meribah**] = 'Strife' : see Nu 20¹³.

Selah] see on 3⁴. **9.** is a quotation of the first commandment (Ex 20³ Dt 5⁷). **10. Open thy mouth,** etc.] So Orientals feast their favoured guests. **12.** *And* **they walked**] RV 'that they might walk.'

13–16. The verbs refer to the present— Would hearken . . would walk . subdue . . turn . . submit . . endure . . feed . . satisfy. **15. The haters of the LORD**] i.e. Israel's enemies.

Unto him] probably means 'unto Israel.'

PSALM 82

This Ps. is an impeachment of unjust judges, who are officially called 'gods.' It represents them as put upon their trial at God's tribunal (v. 1). God Himself denounces their wickedness (v. 2), and reminds them of their duties (vv. 3, 4). In v. 5 He declares that they are incorrigible, and in vv. 6, 7 pronounces sentence upon them. V. 8 is the Psalmist's own prayer that God may manifest His righteous judgment to all the nations. The date of the Ps. is quite uncertain. Oriental judges have been corrupt in all ages.

1. Of the mighty] RV 'of God' (*El*). A heavenly assembly is meant, as in Job 1⁶ 2¹ Zech 3. **The gods**] the judges of Israel, so called as the official representatives of God on earth. See Christ's explanation in Jn 10³⁴,³⁵. **2. Accept**] RV 'respect.' **3. Defend**] RV 'judge.' **5. They know not**] The judges are deaf to reproof. **Out of course**] RV 'moved.' Injustice leads to the wreck of society. **6.** See on v. 1. **7.** The v. contrasts the purely human fate of the unjust judges with the superhuman dignity of their calling.

PSALM 83

This Ps. describes a confederacy of God's enemies, the object of which is to attack and exterminate Israel (vv. 2–5). A list of the allies is given (vv. 6–8). The Psalmist appeals to God to interpose (v. 1), and to deal with these hostile nations as He dealt with the Midianites (Jg 6–8) and the Canaanites (Jg 4, 5) of old (vv. 9–12). Vv. 13–18 continue the prayer for their overthrow, in order that they may seek and acknowledge the true God. No historical occasion is known on which all the nations mentioned were leagued against Israel. The Ps. is connected by some with the invasion in the reign of Jehoshaphat (2 Ch 20), by others with the opponents of Nehemiah (Neh 4⁷,⁸), and by others still with the enemies of Judas Maccabæus (1 Mac 5).

3. Thy hidden ones] those in God's protection : cp. 27⁵ 31²⁰. **5. Are confederate**] RV 'make a covenant.' **6, 7. Edom . . Moab . . Ammon**] The neighbours of Israel on the SE. and E. **6. Tabernacles**] RV 'tents.'

Ishmaelites] wandering desert tribes.

Hagarenes] or Hagrites, a nomadic tribe in the region E. of Gilead (1 Ch 5¹⁰). **7. Amalek**] a tribe of the desert S. of Palestine.

Gebal] a district of Edom, S. of the Dead Sea. **The Philistines**] RV 'Philistia,' between Palestine and the Mediterranean on the SW.

Tyre] a city and kingdom on the NW. sea board of Palestine.

8. Assur] RV 'Assyria.' This empire did not come into close contact with Israel till after the time of Jehoshaphat. After the fall of Assyria the name was used generally for the region of the East, even under the Persian kings (Ezr 6 22). **The children of Lot**] the Moabites and Ammonites (Gn 19 36-38) already mentioned, and apparently the leaders of the hostile combination.

9. Sisera . . Jabin . . Kison] see Jg 4, 5.

10. En-dor] not mentioned in Jg 4, 5, but it was in the locality referred to in Jg 5 19 : see Josh 17 11. **11. Oreb, and . . Zeeb**] the princes of Midian (Jg 7 25). **Zebah, and . . Zalmunna**] named as kings of Midian in Jg 8 5-21. **13. A wheel**] RV 'the whirling dust.' **15. Persecute**] RV 'pursue.'

PSALM 84

This Ps. sets forth the attractiveness of the Temple and its worship (vv. 1–4), and the happiness of the pilgrims who gather to it from different parts of the land (vv. 5–7). After a prayer for God's favour (vv. 8, 9), it speaks of the privilege of the humblest office in the Temple (v. 10), and closes by describing the graciousness of God (v. 11), and the blessedness of trusting Him (v. 12). The Ps. belongs to a period when the Temple was standing, and when its services were regularly carried on. If v. 9 is a prayer for the king, it must be the first Temple that is in view. Pss 42, 43 have points of resemblance to this one, and may possibly be by the same author.

Title.—Gittith] see on Ps 8.

1. How amiable] RM 'how lovely,' and how lovable. **4. They that dwell in thy house**] the priests and other Temple officials. **5. The ways** *of them*] RV 'the high ways *to Zion.*' The reference is to Israelites whose hearts are set on the journey to Jerusalem. **6. Baca**] RM 'balsam trees,' which grow in dry situations. This fact gives the v. its point. The pilgrim heart finds refreshment even on thirsty ground. **A well**] RV 'a place of springs.' **The rain . . pools**] RV 'the early rain covereth it with blessings.' **7. From strength to strength**] The pilgrimage brings no weariness, but the opposite : see Isa 40 31, and cp. 'The Pilgrim's Progress.'

9. Our shield] This phrase may either refer to God (see v. 11) or to the king, in parallelism with 'thine anointed' in the following clause : see 89 18 RV. **Look upon the face**] regard with favour. **Thine anointed**] probably the king. Some suggest that the high priest or the nation as a whole may be meant.

10. Better than a thousand] spent elsewhere. **A doorkeeper**] This was the special duty

of the sons of Korah, who are mentioned in the title of the Ps. (1 Ch 9 19).

PSALM 85

This Ps. looks back upon the mercy which God has shown to His people in bringing them back from captivity (vv. 1–3), entreats Him to remove the displeasure that has again fallen on them, and to deliver them from present troubles (vv. 4–7), and ends with a hopeful picture of the blessings that will follow the answering of the prayer (vv. 8–13). It evidently belongs to a time soon after the return from the Babylonian exile—either the days of discouragement before the building of the second Temple (Ezr 4 4, 5, 24 Hag 1 Zech 1 12-21), or the period of Nehemiah (Neh 1 3). The Ps. is one of those for Christmas Day.

2. Selah] see on 3 4. **9. That glory may dwell**] The reference is to the Shechinah, the symbol of God's presence.

10, 11. Mercy . . truth, etc.] These characteristics, which are thus personified, are, first of all, attributes of God, but they are also to be reflected in the lives of His people. This is shown by the mention of earth as well as heaven in v. 11. **12. Material** prosperity will accompany spiritual blessings. **13. Set us . . steps**] RV 'make his footsteps a way to walk in.'

PSALM 86

This is a Ps. of general supplication for help in trouble, and breathes a devout spirit of gratitude and confidence towards God. Specially remarkable is the hope of v. 9 that God will be universally worshipped. The Ps. is made up of quotations from other Pss. and portions of the OT., and is to be dated after the return from the exile.

1. Hear] RV 'answer.' **Poor and needy**] see 40 17 70 5. **2. Preserve my soul,** etc.] see 25 20. **Holy**] RV 'godly'; rather, 'one whom thou favourest.' **3. Daily**] RV 'all the day long.' **4. See 25 1. 7. See 50 15. 8. See Ex 15 11 Dt 3 24. 9. See 22 27-31. 11. See 26 3 27 11. Unite my heart**] deliver me from divided purposes and affections.

13. The lowest hell] RM 'Sheol beneath,' the state of the dead : see 56 13. **14. See 54 3. Assemblies**] RV 'congregation' : see 22 16. **15. See Ex 34 6. 16. See 25 16. The son of thine handmaid**] another phrase for 'thy servant' : see 116 16.

PSALM 87

This Ps. expands the thought of Ps 86 9. Zion is the chosen dwelling of God (vv. 1–3), the spiritual birthplace of the other nations (vv. 4–6), and the source of joy to them all (v. 7). In v. 4 God is the speaker. The mention of Babylon as no longer an enemy of

Israel, but as receiving spiritual blessing from Zion, shows that the Ps. was written after the bitter experience of the captivity was over.

1. His foundation] i.e. God's. **The holy mountains**] the hills on which Jerusalem stood. **2. Zion**] Jerusalem. **The dwellings of Jacob**] other cities of Judah. **3. Selah**] see on 3⁴. **4. Rahab**] Egypt : see Isa 30⁷ 51⁹ Ps 89¹⁰.

To them that know me] RV 'as among them that know me.' **This** *man*] RV 'this one,' this nation. So in v. 6. **5. This and that man**] RV 'this one and that one.' This and that nation shall be converted to God.

6. People] RV 'peoples.' God is represented as making a register of the nations which have been born into His kingdom.

7ᵃ. RV 'They that sing as well as they that dance *shall say*.' The nations which have been born again will rejoice in their new connexion with Zion, and will address her accordingly. **7ᵇ. Springs**] RV 'fountains.'

PSALM 88

This is the saddest and most despairing of all the Pss. The writer is apparently the victim of some incurable disease like leprosy, with which he has been afflicted from his youth (v. 15), and which cuts him off from the society of men (vv. 8, 18). His life is already a living death (vv. 3–6), and beyond death he has no hope (vv. 10–12). He traces his trouble to God's displeasure (vv. 7, 14, 16), yet it is to God that he turns in pathetic appeal for relief (vv. 1, 2, 9, 13). Nothing is known as to his identity, or as to the date of the Ps.

Title.—Mahalath] see on Ps 53. **Leannoth**] may mean 'for singing.' **Heman**] see 1 K 4³¹. **3. The grave**] RV 'Sheol,' the under-world of the dead. **4 Strength**] RV 'help.' **5. Free**] RV 'cast off.' **6. Pit .. darkness** (RV 'dark places') .. **deeps**] expressions for Sheol. **9. Mourneth**] RV 'wasteth away.' **11. In destruction**] RV 'in Destruction.' The Heb. is *Abaddon*, used as a proper name for Sheol : see Job 26⁶ 28²² 31¹² Prov 15¹¹ 27²⁰ Rev 9¹¹. **13. Prevent**] RV 'come before.' **17. Daily**] RV 'all the day long.'

PSALM 89

We have here another national and historical Ps., written when the Jewish kingdom and its king had fallen very low before their enemies, contrasting the promises made to David with their seeming lack of fulfilment in the course of events, and appealing to God to vindicate His faithfulness. Vv. 1–4 are introductory, announcing the Psalmist's purpose of praising God, and recalling the covenant made with David. The following vv. celebrate God's glory among His heavenly hosts (vv. 5–7), in His victory over His enemies, especially Egypt (vv. 8–10), and in the world of nature (vv. 11,

12). Vv. 13, 14 declare His attributes of strength, righteousness, mercy, and truth, and vv. 15–18 speak of the blessedness of His people and their king. His promises to David are repeated at length (vv. 19–37), and the present humiliation of king and people are graphically described (vv. 38–45). The closing vv. are a prayer, in which the Psalmist pleads the shortness of his own life, and the reproaches of the heathen, as reasons for a speedy manifestation of God's faithfulness to His word (vv. 46–51). V. 52 is the closing doxology of Book 3 of the Psalter. The Ps. was probably written during the exile, and it has been supposed that the king of vv. 39–45 is Jehoiachin, who was deposed and carried away to Babylon in his youth, after a reign of three months (2 K 24⁸⁻¹² 2 Ch 36⁹⁻¹¹ Jer 24¹ 29²), and kept a prisoner there for thirty-seven years (2 K 25²⁷).

Title.—Maschil] see on Ps 32. **Ethan the Ezrahite**] mentioned in 1 K 4³¹ and 1 Ch 2⁶. **3, 4.** God is here the speaker : see on vv. 19–37. **Selah**] see on 3⁴. **5. Congregation of the saints**] RV 'assembly of the holy ones.' The angels are meant. **6. Sons of the mighty**] angels : see 29¹. **7. Assembly of the saints**] RV 'council of the holy ones,' as in v. 5. **Had in reverence of**] RV 'feared above.' **8. Or to thy faithfulness**] RV 'and thy faithfulness is.' **10. Rahab**] Egypt : see on 87⁴. **12. Tabor and Hermon**] the most prominent mountains of Palestine. **14. Justice**] RV 'righteousness.' **Habitation**] RV 'foundation.' **15. The joyful sound**] perhaps the sound of trumpets on the occasion of Israel's national and religious rejoicing. **17. Our horn**] see 75⁴,¹⁰. **18.** RV 'For our shield belongeth unto the LORD ; and our king to the Holy One of Israel.' The 'shield' is the same as the 'king,' who is under God's protecting care.

19. In vision] 2 S 7¹⁷. **Thy holy one**] RV 'thy saints,' the nation of Israel. **I have laid help, etc.**] I have given a brave man **My** aid to defend Israel.

19–37. are a poetical expansion of 2 S 7⁸⁻¹⁶. **22. Exact upon him**] RM 'do him violence.' **25. In .. in**] RV 'on .. on' : see on 80¹¹. **27.** *My* **firstborn**] The position formerly given to the nation (Ex 4²²) is here assigned to its king. **30 f.** The promises of the past are recalled in view of the sad present. Israel had suffered for his sins. Should he not be restored ? **37. And** *as* **the faithful witness,** etc.] The meaning is uncertain. The 'faithful witness' may be the moon, or we may read, 'and the witness in the sky (God) is faithful.'

38. Abhorred] RV 'rejected.' **Thine anointed**] Israel's king. A particular individual, probably Jehoiachin, seems to be in view in this and the following vv., though they may also be understood of the nation as a whole.

39. Made void] RV 'abhorred.' **40.** The thought passes from the king to the nation. For the figure cp. 80 12. **45. The days of his youth**] a phrase specially appropriate to Jehoiachin. **46. Shall**] RV 'how long shall.' **47. Wherefore .. in vain ?**] RV 'For what

vanity hast thou created all the children of men !' **48. Hand of the grave**] RV 'power of Sheol.' **50. People**] RV 'peoples,' the enemies of Israel.

52. The doxology marks the close of Book 3 : cp. 41 13 72 18, 19.

BOOK 4 (PSALMS 90–106)

The Pss. in this book, as in that which follows, are mostly of comparatively late date, and suitable for use in the worship of the sanctuary.

The two books seem to have been conjoined at one time, and to have formed the third great division of the Psalter. In the 17 Pss. of Book 4 several smaller groups or collections are to be distinguished. Pss 93, 95–100 are called the 'theocratic' Pss., because they celebrate God as King, finding in the restoration of Israel from Babylon the evidence of His rule over the world. These Pss. are probably to be dated soon after that event, when it was still the one thought in men's minds. Pss 90, 91, 94 and 102 probably belong to the exile, as their language suggests such a time of national humiliation and sorrow. Pss 103 and 104 go together, and are probably by one author, who belonged to the period of the return. Pss 105 and 106 form a pair of about the same date. The whole book is 'Jehovistic' in its use of the divine name.

The Pss. of the fourth book may be classified thus, the divisions necessarily overlapping one another : (*a*) Penitential Pss., 90, 91, 94, 102 ; (*b*) Pss. of Thanksgiving, 92, 93, 95–100, 103–106 ; (*c*) National Pss., 94, 97, 99, 102, 105, 106 ; (*d*) Historical Pss., 105, 106 ; (*e*) a Gnomic Ps., 101.

Most of the Pss. in this book are anonymous, but Pss 101 and 103 are ascribed by their titles to David. LXX, however, also gives as Davidic Pss 91, 93–99, 101, 103 and 104.

There are definite references to the Temple worship in several of these Pss., indicating that the sacred building was restored to permit of the sacrifices being offered and public worship performed. The musical service was rendered with instrumental accompaniments (98 5, 6) ; the people were called upon to join in praise (95 1 96 1 98 1, 4) and kneel in prayer (95 6) ; offerings were to be made in the courts of the Temple (96 8).

The Messianic hope appears in this book in the form of an expectation of Jehovah's coming in judgment. This was strengthened, if not wholly suggested, by the restoration from captivity, in which the pious Israelites saw the beginning of that coming. The people were led to look for a still greater day when their enemies would be finally overthrown, and

the faith of those who had trusted in God would be completely justified (see Pss 96–98).

PSALM 90

The title of this Ps. (**A Prayer of Moses the man of God**) ascribes it to Moses, but several considerations have been pointed out which suggest a later date for its composition. The average length of life in the time of Moses is supposed to have been greater than that mentioned in v. 10 (Dt 34 7 Josh 24 29). Israel's national life seems not to be just beginning, but to have lasted already for many generations (v. 1). The recent past has been a time of calamity rather than of deliverance (v. 15). The Ps. contains resemblances to the book of Deuteronomy, which is now generally regarded as much later than the time of Moses, and these resemblances may have suggested the title. At the same time, there is much in the Ps. which is consistent with the title, and some scholars still maintain its Mosaic authorship. If not written by Moses it may most probably be assigned to the exile. The Ps. contrasts the eternity of God with the transience of human life (vv. 1–6), traces the brevity and troublousness of man's existence to God's displeasure with sin (vv. 7–12), and ends with a prayer for God's forgiveness and favour (vv. 13–17). It is appropriately used in the Burial Service.

1. See Dt 32 7. **2. Mountains**] see Dt 33 15. **3. Return**] to dust (Gen 3 19). **4. A watch in the night**] of which the sleeper is unconscious. There were three night-watches among the Israelites (Lam 2 19 Jg 7 19 1 S 11 11).

5. They are *as* **a sleep**] or, ' they fall asleep' in death. **9. Spend**] RV ' bring to an end.' **As a tale** *that is told*] RM 'as a sigh,' a breath.

10. Their strength] RV ' their pride.' **11**b. RV ' and thy wrath according to the fear that is due unto thee ? ' Who understands Thine anger against sin so as to give Thee fitting and holy reverence ?

12. Apply .. wisdom] RV ' get us an heart of wisdom ' : see Dt 5 29 32 29. **13. Repent**] see Dt 32 36.

14. Early] RV 'in the morning.' **15. According to**] i.e. in proportion to. **17. The work of our hands**] The phrase occurs in Deuteronomy seven times.

PSALM 91

This Ps. describes the safety of those who trust in God, and may have a special reference to the nation of Israel at a time when other nations were involved in calamity. The dangers that threatened Babylon towards the end of the exile have been suggested as a probable occasion for it. The Psalmist sometimes speaks in the first person (vv. 1, 2, 9), and sometimes addresses his promises to the godly man, or to the nation, in the second person (vv. 3–8, 9–13). God Himself is the speaker in vv. 14–16.

1. Secret place] covert. **Shadow**] the shelter which a mother-bird gives her brood, as in v. 4: see 17 ^{8}. **3. And .. pestilence**] LXX 'from the destroying word,' the snare being explained as malicious speech: see 38 ^{12}. 'Pestilence' comes later, in v. 6. **5. The terror, etc.**] assaults by night, as compared with attacks by day. **6. Destruction**] plague. Pestilence and Plague are here personified : see 2 S 24 $^{16, 17}$ Isa 37 ^{36}. **9. Because .. refuge**] RV 'For thou, O LORD, art my refuge !' *Even . habitation*] RV 'Thou hast made the Most High thy habitation.' **11, 12.** These vv. are quoted in the accounts of our Lord's temptation (Mt 4 ^{6} Lk 4 ^{10}). **13. Dragon**] RV 'serpent.'

PSALM 92

This is a Ps. of praise, called forth by some special manifestation of God's lovingkindness. This general theme is set forth in vv. 1–4. Vv. 5–11 contain reflections on the meaning of God's works, a meaning which is hidden from the foolish (v. 6). The wicked seem to flourish only that they may be destroyed (v. 7). God is supreme, and His enemies must perish (vv. 8, 9). This has been proved in the experience of the Psalmist, or of the nation for which he speaks (vv. 10, 11). Vv. 12–15 describe the abiding prosperity and blessedness of the righteous. The Ps. contains no definite indication of date, but it may most probably be taken as a song of the return from exile.

4. Works] doings—a different word from 'work' in the same v. **7, 8.** refer to a definite event which the Psalmist has in view. Read, 'did spring .. did flourish .. it was that they might be,' etc. **10. Shalt .. exalt**] RV 'hast exalted.' **Unicorn**] RV 'wild-ox.' **Shall be**] RV 'am.' **11. Shall see .. shall hear**] RV 'hath seen .. have heard.'

13, 14. The righteous are compared to trees in the Temple courts. **14. Fat and flourishing**] RV 'full of sap and green.'

PSALM 93

This Ps., along with Pss 95–100, celebrates God as King. The thought which is common to this whole group seems to have been awakened by a national deliverance, which was probably the return from the Babylonian captivity. The present Ps. is brief, and speaks of God's sovereign rule, His majesty and strength (v. 1), the eternity and steadfastness of His royal throne (v. 2), His supremacy above the waves of the sea (vv. 3, 4), and the holiness of His Temple (v. 5).

1. The world .. is (or, 'shall be') **stablished**] see 75 ^{3} 82 ^{5}. God's rule is the security of all moral order in the world. **3, 4.** The floods and waves are emblems of the heathen nations. **4. Noise**] RV 'voices.'

PSALM 94

This is a national Ps., written at a time when Israel was oppressed by foreign enemies. It may be connected either with the days of the exile or with some later period of national distress. The opening vv. appeal to God to show Himself as judge of the earth (vv. 1, 2). The misdeeds of the oppressors are next described (vv. 3–7), and a rebuke is addressed to certain Israelites who were tempted to give up their faith in God (vv. 8–11). The next vv. speak of the blessings of adversity (vv. 12, 13), and the certainty that God will not forsake His people (vv. 14, 15). The Psalmist has found in God his only refuge and comfort (vv. 16–19), and concludes his Ps. with the conviction that He will overthrow the wicked (vv. 20–23).

1. Shew thyself] RV 'Shine forth.' **2. A reward**] RV 'their desert.' **4. *How long,* etc.**] RV 'They prate, they speak arrogantly,' etc. The v. is a statement, not a question.

7. The oppressors not only injure Israel, but despise Israel's God.

8. Understand] RV 'consider.' **Brutish .. fools**] These words refer to Israelites who are tempted to adopt the heathen point of view.

9, 10. These vv. form an argument for the knowledge and effectual government of God.

10. Heathen] RV 'nations.' *Shall not he know ?*] These words are supplied to complete the sense. The Psalmist breaks off his argument abruptly. **11.** This v. is quoted with some modification in 1 Cor 3 ^{20}. **14.** The first clause is quoted in Ro 11 ^{2}. **15. Return unto righteousness**] shall again be just. **17. Almost**] RV 'soon.' **Silence**] the grave, or Sheol.

PSALM 95

This Ps. (the 'Venite,' 'Invitatory Psalm') consists of a call to praise God as King, as the Creator of the world, and the Shepherd of His people (vv. 1–7), followed by a warning against unbelief, drawn from the fate of the rebellious Israelites in the wilderness (vv. 7–11). There is nothing to mark its date, but like the other Pss. of the same group it may be referred to the days of the return from Babylon.

4. **Strength of the hills**] RV 'heights of the mountains.' 7. **If ye will**] RV ' Oh that ye would.' 8. **In the provocation**] RV ' at Meribah' (Nu 20 13). **Temptation**] RV 'Massah' (Ex 17 7).

7-11. These vv. are quoted in Heb 3 7-11, and are the basis of the argument that follows.

PSALM 96

This is a triumphant song of praise to God (vv. 1–3), contrasting His power and glory with the nothingness of the heathen idols (vv. 4–6), calling all the earth to worship Him (vv. 7–9), exulting in His rule (v. 10), and calling all nations to rejoice in the prospect of His coming in judgment (vv. 11–13). The tone of the Ps. is closely akin to that of Isa 40–66, and was in all likelihood inspired by the deliverance from exile. The existence of the second Temple will then be implied in vv. 6, 8. This Ps. has been wrought into the composite poem of 1 Ch 16 8-36.

3. Heathen] RV 'nations.' So in v. 10. **People**] RV 'peoples' So in vv. 7, 10, 13. **9. The beauty of holiness**] RM 'holy array.' **13.** God's judgment is welcomed and not feared, for it means the deliverance of His people and the overthrow of their enemies.

PSALM 97

This is another ' theocratic' Ps., declaring how God has taken vengeance on His enemies in a way to which all nature responded (vv. 2–6), denouncing idols and their worshippers (v. 7), expressing the joy of the cities of Israel at His judgments (vv. 8, 9), calling His people to hate evil (v. 10) and to share the gladness which ought to be their portion (vv. 11, 12). The Ps. is a 'mosaic' of phrases from other Scriptures, and, like the preceding Pss., is probably to be referred to the end of the exile.

1. Isles] the coastlands beyond Palestine, an expression for the Gentile world. **2.** Whatever may be mysterious about God's rule, it is certainly founded on righteousness : see 89 14. **3.** See 18 8. **4.** See 77 16-18. **5.** See Jg 5 5. **8. Zion**] Jerusalem. **Daughters of Judah**] the other cities of the land : see 48 11. **9.** See 83 18. **11. Light is sown**] A more probable reading is, ' light hath arisen.' **12. At . . holiness**] RV ' to his holy name,' this being the true meaning of ' remembrance ' or ' memorial': see 32 11 30 4.

PSALM 98

This Ps. closely resembles Ps 96, especially in its beginning and ending, and is to be referred to the same occasion. It celebrates a deliverance which God has wrought for Israel in the sight of all the earth (vv. 1–3), summons all men (vv. 4–6), and all nature

(vv. 7–9) to praise Him. V. 6 proclaims Him as King, and v. 9 anticipates with gladness His coming to judge the world.

2. Heathen] RV 'nations.' **5. A psalm**] RV 'melody': see Isa 51 3. **9. People**] RV 'peoples': see 96 13.

PSALM 99

This Ps. is like the preceding ones in the prominence it gives to God's Kingship, and no doubt belongs to the same period with them. God's holiness, too, is emphasised in the refrain of vv. 3, 5, 9. The Ps. begins with a call to worship God with the awe and reverence which are due to Him (vv. 1–3). His righteous rule in Israel is a reason for repeating the summons (vv. 4, 5). The history of His dealings with His people from the days of Moses and Aaron to the time of Samuel is summed up (vv. 6–8). V. 9 is almost a repetition of v. 5, and implies that the Temple has been restored.

1. People] RV 'peoples.' So in v. 2. *Between* **the cherubims**] RV 'upon the cherubim ' : see on 80 1. **2. Zion**] The Temple at Jerusalem is God's dwelling and the seat of His rule. **3.** *For* it *is* **holy**] RV ' holy is he.' **4. The king**] God : see v. 1. **5. His footstool**] The ark is so called in 1 Ch 28 2, but if this Ps. was written after the exile the ark cannot be directly referred to here. The language may be a survival of an earlier usage. *For* he *is* holy] RV 'holy is he,' as in v. 3.

6–8. These vv. may be taken as an illustration from the past of the principle on which God still deals with His people, or they may be translated by present tenses, as referring to the intercessors in Israel whose prayers God has answered in the deliverance from captivity, and who are figuratively called ' A Moses . . a Samuel.' **8.** Both in the past and in the Psalmist's time God has shown at once His hatred of sin and His forgiving love to His people. **Inventions**] RV 'doings.'

PSALM 100

This famous Ps. (the ' Jubilate,' ' Old Hundredth ') does not give God the title of King, but its contents are otherwise so similar to those of the previous 'theocratic' Pss. that it is naturally grouped along with them both as to subject and date. It calls the world to worship God (vv. 1, 2), describes Him as the Creator and Shepherd of His people (v. 3), points to the second Temple as the seat of His service (v. 4), and closes with an ascription of praise which was often repeated in post-exilic worship (v. 5).

3. Us] refers specially to Israel, **ye** being addressed to the nations : see v. 1. **And not we ourselves**] RV ' and we are his.' **The sheep of his pasture**] see 95 7, and the

'Asaphic' Pss. (73–83). **5.** *Is* everlasting]
RV 'endureth for ever': see 1 Ch 16 34, 41
2 Ch 7 3-6 20 21 Ezr 3 11 Ps 106 1 107 1 118 1-4 136,
138 8, etc. The Chronicler evidently trans-
poses into earlier times Pss. which were written
after the exile, and the same thing appears to
be the case with this formula of praise.

PSALM 101

This Ps. is the prayer of a ruler, apparently
of a king. Many scholars believe that the
title which ascribes its authorship to David is
correct, and connect it with David's desire to
have the ark brought from the house of Obed-
edom to Jerusalem (2 S 6 6-19). Others suppose
it to have been written by Hezekiah, Josiah,
or one of the Maccabees. The writer first
utters his resolves as to his personal life and
conduct (vv. 1–4), and then announces his
purpose of choosing his servants only from
among the upright, and of discouraging and
exterminating all forms of wickedness (vv. 5–8).
2. When wilt thou come unto me ?] This
interjected phrase may refer to David's longing
for the presence of God, as symbolised by the
ark, in his capital. **4. Not know a wicked**
person] RV 'know no evil thing.' **7. Tarry
in my sight**] RV 'be established before mine
eyes.' **8. Early**] RV 'morning by morning.'

PSALM 102

This Ps. belongs to the closing days of the
exile, and utters the hope of Israel's restoration (vv. 13–22). The Psalmist has been
supposed by some to speak simply in the name
of the nation, but it is more probable that he
describes his personal distress, though this
was caused by the captivity and humiliation
of his people. In v. 14 he speaks of his
fellow-countrymen in the plural, and his
shrinking from premature death (vv. 11, 23,
24) breathes a distinctly personal note. He
is wasted away with lonely sorrow (vv. 1–7, 9),
mocked by enemies (v. 8), and conscious that
his affliction is a token of God's displeasure
(v. 10). But the eternity and changelessness
of God are the ground of his hope (vv. 12,
24–28) both for himself and for the whole of
God's people.
3. Like smoke] RM 'in smoke.' **An
hearth**] RV 'a firebrand.' **5. Skin**] RV
'flesh.' **6, 7.** describe figuratively the
Psalmist's mournful love of solitude.
6. Desert] RV 'waste places.' **8. Are
sworn against me**] RV 'do curse by me,' the
literal meaning of 'execrate.' **10. Lifted ..
up .. cast down**] RV 'taken .. up .. cast away.'
11. That declineth] that vanishes when the
sun sets. **12. Remembrance**] RV 'memorial,'
i.e. name : see Lam 5 19. **13. Favour**] RV
'have pity upon.' So in v. 14. **The set time**]
see Isa 40 2 61 2.

15. Heathen] RV 'nations.' **16, 17.** Shall
build .. appear .. regard .. despise] RV 'hath
built .. appeared .. regarded .. despised.'
18. The people] RV 'a people.' The
restored Israel will be a new nation.
19. His sanctuary] heaven, as the parallelism
shows. **21. To declare**] RV 'that men may
declare.' **22. People**] RV 'peoples.'
25–27. Quoted in Heb 1 10-12. **27, 28.** The
changelessness of God is a guarantee that
His kingdom will endure among men. This is
an argument for national rather than for personal immortality. For the higher Christian
truth see Jn 14 19.

PSALM 103

In this Ps. the hope of the previous one has
been fulfilled, and sorrow has given place to
thanksgiving. Its probable date is soon after
the return from exile. The Psalmist utters
his personal gratitude and praise (vv. 1–5), and
tells how God has shown to Israel in his own
day the same power and grace which He showed
in the days of Moses (vv. 6–12). Special
emphasis is laid on God's fatherly pity for His
people in their frailty, and on the eternity of
His mercy as shown to generation after generation (vv. 13–18). An ascription of praise to
God as the universal King, in which all His
angels and all His works are called to join,
closes the Ps. (vv. 19–22).
5. See Isa 40 31. The eagle's strength seemed
to indicate perpetual youth. **6. Righteousness
and judgment**] RV 'righteous acts and judgments,' i.e. deliverances. **17.** Expresses the
same assurance as 102 23-28. **19. Prepared**]
RV 'established.' **21. Ministers**] servants,
referring to the angels.

PSALM 104

This is a Ps. of Nature, celebrating God's
glory as seen in His works both inanimate and
animate. It is an expansion of the closing vv.
of Ps 103, and like that Ps. begins and ends
with the phrase, 'Bless the Lord, O my soul !'
The two Pss. are probably the work of the
same author. Ps 104 follows to some extent
the order of the creation-poem in Gn 1, and
may be compared also with Job 38–41. Vv.
5–9, 19 speak of the creation of the world,
but the greater part of the Ps. describes its
present condition and arrangements, which need
not be analysed in detail. The closing vv.
consist of an ascription of praise (vv. 31–34),
and a prayer for the destruction of the wicked
(v. 35).
3. Chambers] lit. 'upper chambers': see
Am 9 6. The waters referred to are those
above the firmament (Gn 1 7 Ps 148 4), which
are the source of rain : see v. 13. **Wings of
the wind**] see 18 10.
4. His angels spirits] read either, 'his angels

winds,' or 'winds his messengers' (RV). The former rendering is the more natural, is parallel to that of the next clause, and is adopted in Heb 1⁷, where the v. is quoted. The latter reading seems to give a simpler sense, but the other is quite intelligible also. As God manifests His own glory in the universe, so He manifests the power of His angels in the winds and the lightning. **7–9.** These vv. are parallel to Gn 1⁹, ¹⁰. God's command to the waters is conceived as having been uttered in thunder (v. 7). **16.** Full *of sap*] RV 'satisfied,' as in v. 13. **19.** See Gn 1¹⁴⁻¹⁸. **22. Gather themselves together**] RV 'get them away.'

25. *So is* this great and wide sea] RV 'Yonder is the sea, great and wide.' **Things creeping,** etc.] or, 'things moving,' etc.: see Gn 1²¹. **26. Leviathan**] see Job 41, where the crocodile is referred to. Here a sea-monster is meant. **31. The glory . . shall endure . . the** LORD **shall rejoice**] RV 'Let the glory . . endure . . let the LORD rejoice.' **34. My meditation of him shall be sweet**] RV 'Let my meditation be sweet unto him ': see 19¹⁴. **35.** The point of the Psalmist's prayer is that evil may be banished ⁻rom the world, though he identifies sin with sinners, and seems to include their destruction in his wish. **Praise ye the** LORD] This sentence should probably be read as the beginning of the next Ps.

PSALM 105

This Ps. and the following one form a closely connected pair, and may be looked on as by the same author. From the closing vv. of Ps 106 it appears that they were written after the first return from exile had taken place, but while many Israelites were still scattered among the heathen. Both Pss. are partly wrought into the composite poem in 1 Ch 16. Ps 105 is a song of thanksgiving, recalling with gratitude God's covenant with Abraham, Isaac, and Jacob (vv. 8–12), His guidance of Israel into Egypt, with special reference to the history of Joseph (vv. 13–23), His goodness to them there in the days of oppression (vv. 24, 25), His deliverance wrought through Moses and Aaron by means of the plagues (vv. 26–38),

His mercies in the wilderness (vv. 39–41), and finally His gift of Canaan to His people in fulfilment of His ancient promise (vv. 42–45). **1. People**] RV 'peoples.' So in vv. 20, 44. **14. Kings**] Pharaoh (Gn 12¹⁷), and Abimelech (Gn 20¹⁷, ¹⁸). **15. Anointed**] a phrase not literally applicable to the patriarchs, but used by the Psalmist because they were the heads of the nation, like the kings of later times. **Prophets**] Abraham is so called in Gn 20⁷. **19. His word**] Joseph's interpretation of the butler's and baker's dreams (Gn 40²⁰⁻²²). **28–36.** The ninth plague is placed first, the third and fourth are transposed, and the fifth and sixth are omitted. **31. Divers sorts**] RV 'swarms.' **Coasts**] RV 'borders.' So in v. 33. **44. Heathen**] RV 'nations.' **Inherited**] RV 'took in possession.' **45. Praise ye the** LORD] see on 104³⁵. Ps 105, like Ps 106, probably begins and ends with 'Hallelujah.'

PSALM 106

As Ps 105 gives thanks for God's goodness, so Ps 106 confesses Israel's sin and acknowledges God's mercy, both being illustrated in an historical retrospect from the deliverance from Egypt down to the return from captivity: cp. Ps 78 Ezk 20. **1.** See on 100⁵. **7. Provoked** *him*] RV 'were rebellious.' So in vv. 33, 43. **8. For his name's sake**] see Ezk 20¹⁴. **26. Lifted up his hand**] sware. **To overthrow**] RV 'that he would overthrow.' So in v. 27. **28.** See Nu 25² Hos 9¹⁰. **The dead**] the lifeless heathen gods. **29. Inventions**] RV 'doings.' So in v. 39. **32. Strife**] RV 'Meribah ': see 95⁸. **34. Nations**] RV 'peoples.' **Concerning whom**] RV 'as.' **35. Were mingled**] RV 'mingled themselves.' **Heathen**] RV 'nations.' So in vv. 41, 47. **37. Devils**] RV 'demons ': see Dt 32¹⁷. **46.** Implies the return from captivity.

48. This doxology concludes Book 4 of the Psalter, but appears at the same time to have been an original part of Ps 106. **Let all the people say,** etc.] A direction to guide the people in worship. 1 Ch 16³⁶ shows how it was carried out.

BOOK 5 (Psalms 107–150)

This book, which seems originally to have been joined with Book 4, contains forty-four Pss., the vast majority of which are of late date. The contents of these Pss. are a surer guide to the period to which they belong than is the case in the other books, as many of them give either direct references or unmistakable hints regarding experiences of the exile or the return. Thus Ps 107¹⁰⁻¹⁶ refers to the years of captivity, as does also Ps 137. Other Pss., such as 126, refer to the joy of the

return, and others still, e.g. 132, are prompted by the rebuilding of the Temple.

The feature of this book which is most marked is its liturgical character. Many (though not all) of the Pss. contained in it are not individualistic but congregational, and bear traces of having been composed for use in public worship. Pss 115⁹⁻¹⁸ 116¹²⁻¹⁹ 118, 135 and 136 may be cited as good illustrations. Many smaller groups have been incorporated in this book, and can be easily recognised. The principal are the Hallel Psalms (113–118), the Songs of Ascents or Pilgrim Psalms (120–134), and the Hallelujah group (145–150). Psalm 108 is composed of Pss 57 7-11 and 60 5-12, and was obviously compiled for liturgical purposes. Ps 136 is a chant with responses for choir or congregation after each verse.

Fifteen of the Pss. of this book bear the title 'Of David,' indicating that they were taken by the final editor from the earliest or Davidic psalter. One of these (Ps 142) has a historical note, which describes it as 'a prayer when he was in the cave'; but there is nothing in the Ps. to justify the reference. The book is Jehovistic in its choice of the divine name, Jehovah occurring 236 times and Elohim only 7 times.

PSALM 107

The Psalmist sings the lovingkindness of the Lord, giving examples from (a) Israel in the wilderness (vv. 4–9), (b) people in captivity (vv. 10–16), (c) people in sickness (vv. 17–22), (d) vicissitudes of sea-going men (vv. 23–32), (e) and a rescue from drought (33–42). The Ps. has a refrain at intervals (vv. 8, 15, 21, 31).

1. For his mercy *endureth* **for ever**] evidently a well-known refrain: cp. Ps 136. **Mercy**] better, 'lovingkindness.' **2. Redeemed**] perhaps from exile. **3. Lands**] i.e. foreign lands. **4.** The v. might refer to wanderings on the way from Egypt, but the reference to 'a city of habitation' (v. 7) points rather to a return from Babylon to Jerusalem. **10. Sit**] RV 'sat.' **Iron**] perhaps metaphorically: cp. 105 18. The reference is evidently to captivity, i.e. slavery. **11. The words of God**] as declared by His prophets. **14. Bands**] i.e. their state of subjection: cp. 2 3.

16. Cp. Isa 45 2. **17.** A new illustration. Read, probably, 'Sick men, because of the way of their transgression,' etc. **20. Sent**] RV 'sendeth.' The phrase is noteworthy as heralding, unconsciously perhaps, the Word (Jn 1 14). **23–30.** A striking description of mariners in a storm. **27. Are at their wit's end**] RM 'all their wisdom is swallowed up.' **30. Their desired haven**] RM 'the haven of their desire.' The word rendered 'haven' is an Assyrian loan-word, and properly means an 'emporium' or 'mart.' It is found here only.

33. General instances of God's kindness in various districts. Some suggest that this is a later addition to the Ps. It has great likenesses to Job and Isa 40–66. **34. Barrenness**] better, RV 'a salt desert'—perhaps thinking of Sodom: cp. Job 39 6. **35.** Cp. Isa 41 18.

39. Again] better, 'and when'; but the v. is abrupt and the connexion obscure.

40. Quoted from Job 12 21, 24. It interrupts the connexion, and by some is omitted. **41.** Cp. Job 21 11: 'He set the needy on high from

(above) affliction, and established (for him) families as a flock.' **43.** Cp. Hos 14 9, a closing admonition.

PSALM 108

This is a composite Ps. 1–5 is practically Ps 57 7-11, and 6–13 is the same as 60 5-12. For notes on individual vv. the reader is referred to these two Pss. Probably the two fragments were brought together in a separate collection from Book 2, and subsequent perhaps to the formation of that book. This Ps. preserves its Elohistic character. It bears the title, 'A Song, a Psalm of David.' It is one of the Pss. for Ascension Day.

PSALM 109

The strongest of the imprecatory Pss. (see Intro.). Probably it is just to regard the Psalmist as speaking in the name of the whole nation, vexed and harried by foreign enemies, e.g. Antiochus Epiphanes. The theory that the Psalmist recounts the curses used against him by his enemies is untenable. Calvin notes the awful use of this Ps. by certain monks, who hired themselves out to recite it against private enemies.

6. Satan] RV 'an adversary.' The word has both meanings in Hebrew. Satan was the accuser who blamed men before God: cp. Job 1, 2 Zech 3. **7. Let his prayer become sin**] truly a horrible curse: cp. Prov 15 8. **8. Let another take his office**] cp. the reference to Judas Iscariot (Ac 1 20). Hence this was known to the early Fathers as 'Psalmus Iscarioticus.'

10. Let them seek, etc.] better, 'let them be driven out far from their desolate homes.'

11. Spoil] better, 'make spoil of.' **23. I am tossed up and down**] better, 'I am shaken off like a locust.'

PSALM 110

A fragment of an ode of victory to a priest-king—'Worthy,' says Luther,'to be set in a frame of gold and diamonds.' A truly Messianic Ps., finding its fulfilment in the triumphs of Christ in the world, and quoted Mt 22 43 Mk 12 36 Lk 20 42 Ac 2 34 Heb 1 13 5 6 : see Intro.

1. Lit.' Oracle of Jehovah to my lord.' The Psalmist seems to hear God addressing the king, whom Jehovah invites to a seat at His right hand, the place of honour. Our Lord applies this v. in the Messianic sense in which it was evidently understood by His countrymen.

2. Send] better, 'stretch . . (saying), Rule thou,' etc. **3. Thy people**, etc.] better, 'Thy people offer themselves in the day of thy mustering,' i.e. of the army for battle. **In the beauties of holiness**] Many scholars, with slight change in Heb., render, 'on the mountains of holiness,' i.e. on the holy mountains. 'From the womb of the morning comes to thee the dew of thy youth,' i.e. thy young men gather to thy standard in the morning like the dew for vigour and freshness. **4.** The king is to be priest as well. This might be true of a Davidic prince : cp. 2 S 6 14, or of Simon Maccabæus, cp. 1 Mac 10 21. But it is ultimately most certainly Messianic : cp. Zech 6 11-13. ' After the manner (RM) of Melchizedek,' who was king and priest in Salem, i.e. Jerusalem : cp. Gn 14 18.

5. The LORD] i.e. Jehovah. The v. describes the victory of the king. **Shall strike**] RM ' hath stricken.' **6.** The Hebrew is difficult, but the meaning is clear. Dead bodies cover the field ; heads of men are smitten over a wide area (in the pursuit). **7.** The victor king stoops to drink of the brook by the way, and with renewed strength (head uplifted) continues the pursuit of the flying enemy.

PSALM 111

Pss 111, 112 are closely connected both in form and substance, and are apparently the work of one author. They are alphabetical (see Intro.). A liturgical introduction is prefixed to both, viz. ' Praise ye the Lord ' : in Hebrew ' Hallelujah.' The theme of Ps 111 is the refrain of Ps 107, ' Oh that men would praise the LORD for his goodness, and for his wonderful works to the children of men.' The Ps. is used on Easter Day.

1. Assembly] RV ' council ' ; the word means, ' a secret gathering.' **5. Meat**] i.e. food.

6. That he may give them] RV ' in giving them.' Probably the writer refers to the conquest by Joshua. **9. Redemption**] i.e. from Egypt. **He . . commanded**, etc.] i.e. He made a covenant, which was never to be violated. **10. The fear**, etc.] a very frequent saying among the sages of Israel : cp. Prov 1 7 9 10, etc. The meaning is that religion is the foundation of all wisdom.

PSALM 112

See on Ps 111. This also is an alphabetical Ps., every half-verse beginning with a successive letter of the Hebrew alphabet. The subject is specially the blessedness of the truly religious man.

5. A good man] RV ' Well is it with the man that.' **He will guide his affairs with discretion**] RV ' he shall maintain his cause in judgment,' i.e. in court of law. **9. His horn**] symbol of strength and power.

PSALM 113

This Ps. begins the group (113–118) known in the Jewish Church as the Hallel Psalms, or Hymns of Praise, from *hillel*, to praise. They are sung at the Passover Feast—Pss 113, 114 before the second cup, and 115–118 after the fourth cup ; formerly recited also at the other

two feasts, at the New Moons, and on the eight days of the Feast of Dedication (Cheyne). Ps 113 has been called the Magnificat of the Old Testament. Note the liturgical introduction and conclusion (' Hallelujah ' = ' Praise ye the LORD ') for use in the Temple service.

6. ' Who stoopeth down to look in heaven and on earth.' **9. The barren woman**] a grievous sorrow to a Jewish wife. There is here an echo of Hannah's song (1 S 2 1-10).

PSALM 114

This has been called ' one of the finest lyrics in literature.' Probably it is a post-exilic psalm wherein, under the figure of the old exodus from Egypt, the Psalmist chants the return from Babylon. In all ages of the Church it has been used to celebrate the release from the bondage of sin. Hence it is a hymn for Easter night.

1. Strange language] i.e. unintelligible speech—foreign. **2. Was**] RV ' became.' **3. Saw it**] i.e. the presence of God. The allusion is to the dividing of the Red Sea and of Jordan, the opening and closing events of the deliverance from Egypt. **4. Skipped**] i.e. trembled : cp. Sinai, Ex 19 18. **5. What ailed ?**] The answer is, the presence of God. **8.** Cp. Ex 17 6 Nu 20 11.

PSALM 115

In LXX 114, 115 are one Ps., while 116 is divided into two. Apparently Ps 115 was written to be sung antiphonally : cp. the responses in vv. 9, 10, 11—the first eight and the last three verses to be sung by the congregation. Probably it is a very late Ps. The writer proclaims the vanity of idols, and ascribes all help and blessing to Jehovah alone.

1. Israel is reviled by idolatrous foreigners, and appeals to God to vindicate His honour. **3.** God is the God of heaven, therefore He can save His people. **4.** This the idols cannot do. **9.** A Levite sings, ' O Israel, trust thou in the Lord.' The choir respond, ' He is their help and their shield ': so 10, 11. **12–15.** is sung by a different person.

16. ' The heavens are the heavens of Jehovah,' etc. : His peculiar dwelling as opposed to the earth, which is the habitation of men. **17. Silence**] i.e. Sheol, where there is no communion with God.

PSALM 116

Pss 115–118 were probably the hymns sung by our Lord and His disciples. Some modern scholars, however, deny this, on the ground that, in Christ's time, the Hallel was only in its beginning, and consisted simply of Ps 113, or, at most, also of Ps 114 : see Mt 26 30 Mk 14 26. Ps 116 is apparently a song of thanksgiving after severe illness, but the Ps. has been used by both churches and individuals in spiritual as well as temporal deliverances. The Psalmist's experiences pass through various stages, viz. suffering (v. 3), prayer (vv. 4, 5), deliverance (vv. 6–9), thanksgiving in public (vv. 12–19). At v. 10 LXX begins a new Ps.

3. Hell] RM 'the grave.' He was at the gates of death. **9.** His life will be preserved. **10, 11.** The sense is most obscure. Two meanings are proposed : (*a*) I believed even when I spoke, saying, I am greatly afflicted, even when I said in my haste, All men are liars ; (*b*) I believe (for I will speak) that I was greatly afflicted. In my alarm I said, All men are liars. **13.** The Psalmist intends to offer a sacrifice, and already anticipates the feast which follows when he would solemnly raise the cup to Jehovah in gratitude for deliverance ; hence he calls it the cup of salvation. **15. Precious**] i.e. of such consequence to God that He will require penalties for it.

PSALM 117

The shortest chapter in the Bible, and the middle chapter. It is a doxology, calling all peoples to praise Jehovah. It may have been appended to some Ps.

PSALM 118

This Ps. was evidently written for the Temple worship on the occasion of some great festival (v. 24), when it might be used as a processional hymn. It has been variously referred (*a*) to the time when Zerubbabel laid the foundation of the second Temple ; (*b*) to the time of Nehemiah ; (*c*) to the cleansing of the Temple by Judas Maccabæus. It is a noble song. Luther declared that he owed more to Ps 118 than to all the princes and friends who supported him.

Vv. 1–18, dealing with the subject of God's mercy, which has brought them out of trouble, are sung by the procession antiphonally in half-verses ; 19 is the request of the procession before the gates, and 20 the Levite reply ; 21–24 are sung antiphonally ; 26 is the cry of the Levite choir within ; while 29 is a closing liturgical chant for the whole congregation.

3. House of Aaron] lit. the *élite* of the nation. **5. In distress**] lit. 'in a strait place.' The **LORD**] RM 'Heb. *Jah*,' a contraction of Jehovah. **12. Are quenched**] but Bæthgen, with a slight change of Hebrew, renders, 'they flared forth like a fire of thorns,' and this makes admirable sense. Omit **for. 13–16.** The thought changes to the scene of the encounter. **14.** Quoted from Ex 15². **15. The right hand, etc.**] This and the following v. are what the **voice** says. **19. Gates of righteousness**] i.e. the gates of the Temple

whence God's righteousness streams forth, or it may mean the gates into which righteous men enter : cp. v. 20.

22. The stone] i.e. Israel primarily. **The builders**] the nations of the world. There is, however, a tradition that such a stone really existed in the building of the second Temple. The ultimate application to Jesus Christ is most fitting : cp. Mt 21⁴² Ac 4¹¹, etc. **24. The day**] a day of triumph.

25. Save now] Heb. *hoshêea na anna ;* hence, 'Hosanna,' which became a liturgical formula : cp. Mt 21⁹. **26. Cometh**] better, 'entereth' (the courts of the Lord). **27. Which hath shewed**] RV 'and He hath given.' **Bind, etc.**] The Hebrew is obscure. 'Bind the sacrificial victim with cords even till you come to the horns of the altar,' or, less likely, ' Bind the procession with festal garlands and approach the horns of the altar.' There is nothing about binding the sacrifice *to* the horns, etc.

PSALM 119

The longest Ps. and the best example of an alphabetical Ps. There are in it twenty-two stanzas ; each of the 8 vv. of each stanza commences with the same Hebrew letter. The subject is practically the same throughout, viz. the great help and guidance and comfort to be derived from studying continually the Law of the Lord. Much ingenuity is displayed in expressing the same thoughts under various forms.

Note in this connexion the following variety of terms—**Law,** or instruction (*torah*) ; **Testimonies,** or affirmations of God's will ; **Judgments,** or judicial pronouncements as to the Law ; **Statutes** (lit. ' inscriptions '), or published enactments ; **Commandments, Precepts,** or injunctions.

It is difficult to locate the Ps. in time or circumstances. Such devoted meditation on the Law is a feature of later Judaism which arose chiefly after the exile. This is also true of the mechanical arrangement of the Ps. If the writer records his own experiences they must have been very trying—trouble, sorrow, the hostility of powerful foes, and even captivity. But some scholars believe that the writer sometimes records his own experiences, sometimes the experiences of the pious remnant of Israel.

19. Stranger] or, 'sojourner,' passenger, with but a short time to learn God's will. **21. The proud**] perhaps Jews who had been influenced by foreign culture. **25. Quicken**] i.e. revive. **29. Way of lying**] i.e. faithlessness to God's law. **39. My reproach which I fear**] viz. of sinning against God. **43.** He prays never to be deprived of the power of testifying to God's truthfulness. **46. Before kings**] i.e. in exile.

54. 'Melodies have thy statutes been to me in the house of my sojourning,' i.e. in this brief life : cp. 39 12. **56.** 'This (comfort) I have that I have kept thy law.' **70. Fat as grease]** dull, gross : cp. Job 15 26, 27 Isa 6 10.

83. Bottle] RM 'wine skin.' Bottles were made of the untanned hide of an animal. In the smoke they would be dried up, shrivelled and useless. Such Israel seemed to be in captivity. **84. How many,** etc.] i.e. my days are few.

91. They] i.e. the heavens and the earth. **96.** The most perfect earthly things are finite and limited ; but God's law is for all needs and for all time. **109. My soul,** etc.] i.e. my life is ever in jeopardy. **118. Their deceit** *is* **falsehood]** better, 'their self-deception is a lie.' **123. Fail for]** fail through longing for. **130. The entrance]** RV 'the opening,' i.e. the unfolding. **132. Usest to do]** i.e. art wont to do. **140 Very pure]** i.e. true metal : cp. 18 30. **147. I prevented,** etc.] i.e. Before daybreak I cried. **148.** 'Mine eyes forestall the night-watches,' i.e. when each watch comes I am already awake. **161. Princes]** probably it was Israel, i.e. the Jewish nation, that was so persecuted.

164. Seven times] i.e. very often. **165. Nothing shall offend them]** RV 'they have none occasion of stumbling.' **176. Like a lost sheep]** probably refers to the Jews scattered in exile. The last clause of the v. precludes the idea of straying into sin.

PSALMS 120–134

These Pss. are similar in thought, style, and language. Each bears the heading **A Song of degrees,** RV 'A Song of Ascents.' Scholars now agree for the most part in interpreting this title 'A Song of Pilgrimages' (lit. 'goings up'), as indicating the use of these Pss. for pilgrims on their annual journeys to keep the various feasts at Jerusalem. Others explain the 'Ascent' as referring to the return of the exiles from Babylon. This section had doubtless been a separate Psalter with this title, 'Songs of Pilgrimages,' affixed. When these Pss. became a part of the greater collection 90–150, the title was affixed to each Ps. separately. There is also an indication in these titles that the Pss. are specially intended for vocal music. Exquisitely beautiful they are, well fitted for pilgrim songs, either for the Jew to Jerusalem, or for the Christian to that heavenly Zion whose builder and maker is God : see Intro.

PSALM 120

A cry for help to Jehovah in the midst of sore distress, evidently by an exile under foreign oppression.

4. 'Sharp arrows of a mighty man, with glowing coals of broom,' i.e. burning charcoal made of broom. Both expressions are figures for divine judgments : cp. 140 10.

5. Mesech] i.e. the Moschi, a tribe dwelling near the Euxine Sea : cp. Gn 10 2, also Herodotus 3.94. **Kedar]** tribes of N. Arabia famous for their black tents : cp. Song 1 5. Here the two names are probably taken as typical examples of the wild and inhospitable peoples among whom many of the Jews were exiled.

6. Long] the emphatic word 'all too long.' Turbulent tribes fond of war surround the writer.

PSALM 121

The song of the traveller, whose guide is Jehovah.

1. Hills] RV 'mountains.' The mountains suggest strength, and the Psalmist asks a question, 'Whence shall *my* help come ?' The answer is given in v. 2 : 'from Him who made the mountains and all else.' If this Ps. were sung going up to Jerusalem then the 'mountains' may be the hills around Jerusalem, or those on which that city is built.

5. Shade] i.e. shelter for defence.

6. A belief in the injurious influence of the moon is an almost universal superstition. If e.g. the moon shines on the face of a sleeper he may become blind : cp. 'moonstruck.'

PSALM 122

The writer recalls a journey tc Jerusalem and the many sacred memories associated with that much-loved city.

1. 'I rejoiced with them that said unto me.' **2. Shall stand]** rather, 'were standing,' i.e. came to be standing. **3. Jerusalem is builded]** RV 'Jerusalem that art built.' **Compact]** descriptive of the appearance of the rebuilt city, with the breaches restored and the walls complete, after the return from exile.

4. Go up] better, 'went up,' in days gone by. **Unto the testimony]** RV 'for a testimony' of God's relationship to Israel : cp. 81 5.

5. Thrones] i.e. tribunals. **House of David]** either the Davidic line of kings or the princes of the house of David.

6. They shall prosper] RM 'let them prosper.'

PSALM 123

The Psalmist looks up steadfastly to God, and expresses his confidence in Him.

4. The scorning of those, etc.] the mocking of them that are at ease—heathen oppressors living in careless security. The circumstances are similar to those in Ps 120.

PSALM 124

This Ps. is sung at the Feast of Purim to commemorate the deliverance from Haman. It is a gladsome lyric, thanking Jehovah for escape from heathen destruction, and may well have been composed under the impulse of deliverance from the Babylonian exile. In its formation it illustrates a particular rhythmic effect, viz. the ascending scale of a series of phrases.

1. Now may Israel say] what Israel says in vv. 1–5. **3. Quick**] RV 'alive,' as Assyria and Babylon did to many nations. **4. Stream**] better, 'torrent,' the winter torrent familiar in Palestine. **Over our soul**] overwhelming the very life of the nation.

PSALM 125

Jehovah is the bulwark of Israel, but evildoers shall perish. Evidently the nation is under foreign rule : cp. v. 3.

2. The mountains] Jerusalem is high, but the hills, such as the Mt. of Olives and the Hill of Evil Counsel, are higher. **3. The rod of the wicked**] RV 'the sceptre of wickedness,' i.e. heathen dominion shall be broken off lest in despair the righteous be tempted to turn aside to sinful practices. **5.** Those who hesitate between serving Jehovah and worldliness will be swept away with heathen idolaters.

PSALM 126

A song of those who have been redeemed (from exile), and a hopeful prayer for those who have not yet returned.

1. Turned again the captivity of Zion] either, brought back the exiles who returned to Zion, or, turned again the fortunes of Zion, i.e. perhaps, set her free from foreign yoke. **4. Turn again our captivity**] perhaps, 'bring back the exiles.' **As the streams in the south**] i.e. like the hill streams in the arid S. land of Judah (the Negeb), dry for a time in summer but becoming suddenly swollen torrents in the rains of autumn. **5.** A proverb—sow in tears, reap with ringing cries. The reference may be to the difficulties amid which the pioneers of the return from exile had to work : cp. Ezr and Neh. **6. Weepeth**] suggestive of the patient labour of the sower. **Bearing precious seed**] better, 'bearing a measure of seed.' The sower carried the seed in a cloth tied to his body—this cloth full is a 'measure.'

PSALM 127

A warning against over-anxiety in any work. Let it be left in the wise hands of Jehovah, who gives the best blessings without human aid. Perhaps the Ps. was addressed to some too-zealous workers in the restoration of Jerusalem. The title assigns it to Solomon, but probably it was written long after his day. Its proverbial philosophy may have led to its association with his name : cp. Prov 1 1. **2. Bread of sorrows**] RV 'bread of toil' :

cp. Prov 10 22. *For* **so he giveth his beloved sleep**] a difficult phrase. With a slight change in the Hebrew we may render, 'surely he giveth his beloved in sleep.' Others may toil and worry and vex themselves and make little progress. But to His loved ones God gives prosperity even while they sleep : cp. Mk 4 27. **3. Children**] according to Jewish belief one of God's greatest blessings, yet given without the laborious thought and care of men. **4.** Children of a man's youth would grow up and be able to help and protect him when he is old. **5. But**] RV 'when.' **In the gate**] Here the market was held and justice administered. The man with stalwart sons need not fear false accusers at the judgment-seat : cp. Job 5 4.

PSALM 128

The man who fears God will be blessed in his family life. The Ps. has been called the 'Home, Sweet Home' of Judaism.

3. By the sides of thine house] RV 'in the innermost parts of thine house,' i.e. in the women's apartment. **Olive plants**] a precious tree in Palestine. **5.** 'May the Lord bless thee out of Zion,' i.e. from His dwelling-place. **6.** The Psalmist closes with a note of patriotism : RV 'Peace be upon Israel.'

PSALM 129

A song of deliverance in trouble and the overthrow of the wicked.

3. Made long their furrows] Descriptive of the persecutions Israel had endured. **6. Afore it groweth up**] better, 'before it is plucked,' or, 'before it is unsheathed,' i.e. before it shoots into blossom. **8.** Cp. Ruth 2 4.

PSALM 130

The *De Profundis*—a song of redemption from trouble through faith in God. Probably a very late Ps. The Ps. is antiphonal. First voice (vv. 1, 2), Second voice (3, 4), First voice (5, 6), Chorus (7, 8).

1. Out of the depths] i.e. from sore trouble. **4. Feared**] Rather a startling statement. But the fear of God means true, earnest religion : cp. 19 10 Gn 20 11. **6.** RV 'more than watchmen look for the morning,' i.e. impatiently. **7. Plenteous redemption**] i.e. abundant means of effecting salvation for His people. **8. Redeem, etc.**] i.e. deliver not only from the consequences of sin, but from sin itself.

PSALM 131

A song of child-like resignation of one committing himself to God in time of trouble.

2. Behaved] RV 'stilled.' Children were weaned between two and three years of age. **Even**] better, 'within me,' or 'upon me,' referring to the child upon its mother's bosom.

PSALM 132

This is the most difficult of the Pilgrim Songs. According to accepted literary criticism it must be a post-exilic Ps. The Temple worship has been restored. The days of David are in the distant past. The circumstances of the time are such that God's promise to David of a perpetual dynasty is recalled as a ground of hope. Accordingly we must believe that the writer either incorporated a fragment from an earlier period, vv. 6–10, or represented Israel speaking, dramatically describing three periods, (1) vv. 6, 7, the time of David ; (2) 8, 9, the time of Solomon ; (3) 10, the writer's own age. In any case, the Ps. is one of great charm and delicacy, echoing and re-echoing the promise that Jehovah hath chosen Zion for His habitation.

1. 'Lord, remember unto David all his afflictions' (cp. 1 Ch 22 14), i.e. for good—to do him good in consequence : cp. 137 7. **David**] perhaps, here, 'the house of David,' or 'the representative of David.'

3–5. David's vow to find a permanent home for the ark : cp. 2 S 7 2. **6. We heard of it at**] i.e. the people heard the ark was at Ephratah, perhaps the district round Kirjath-jearim, where the ark stayed till a place was prepared for it in Mt. Zion : cp. 1 Ch 13 5. **Fields of the wood**] 'field of Jaar,' i.e. Kirjath-jearim, shortened for the sake of rhythm.

8–10. These vv. are found in 2 Ch 6 41,42, undoubtedly refer to the dedication of the Temple by Solomon. **8. Ark of thy strength**] the symbolical centre of Jehovah's power in Israel. The ark is mentioned only here in the Psalter. Unless, as suggested above, the whole passage is quoted from the very late book of Chronicles, it is difficult to account for its presence in this Ps. **9. Thy saints**] God's chosen people. **10. Turn not away the face**] owing to the rejection of his prayer. **Thine anointed**] means the king.

11, 12. Cp. 1 K 8 25. In vv. 11–18 we may trace the divine answer to the prayers of vv. 8–10. **13.** This is the keynote of the Ps. **14.** See 68 16. **15.** A Messianic promise against famine, very welcome in such a country as Palestine.

16. Salvation] here, 'health,' ' prosperity.'

17. The horn] which is generally a symbol of strength, is in Daniel the symbol of a king. **To bud**] sprout: see Jer 23 5 33 15 Zech 3 8, where the ' branch' or ' sprout' denotes the Messianic King : see also Lk 1 69. **Ordained**] RM ' prepared.' **A lamp**] symbol of undying prosperity in a house : cp. 1 K 11 36 Prov 20 20. **18. Flourish**] i.e. sparkle.

PSALM 133

An exquisite gem of song describing the blessings of unity—suitable for a pilgrim song, when rich and poor, priest and peasant, might fraternise with Zion in sight.

2. Precious ointment] better, ' goodly oil.' It is doubtful whether the second relative clause is parallel to the first referring to the oil, or whether it refers to Aaron's beard. The Heb., like the AV, can be interpreted either way. It is probably best to take it as referring to the oil. So LXX takes it. The idea is to emphasise the richness and fulness of life which friendship gives.

3. RV ' Like the dew of Hermon that cometh down on the mountains of Zion.' Hermon is the most conspicuous feature in Palestine, standing in the extreme N. away beyond the springs of Jordan, and over 9,000 ft. in height. The writer evidently thought that the dew came down from the distant Hermon cool and fresh, and settled on Zion. **For there**] i.e. in Zion. Peace and harmony are life to the nation.

PSALM 134

A night-greeting addressed to the priests and Levites in the Temple. V. 3 is their reply to the greeting.

PSALM 135

A Ps. of praise suitable for public worship, beginning and ending with the liturgical Hallelujah. It is full of rich mosaics illustrating Jehovah's greatness and the vanity of idols. Pss 134, 135 were sometimes taken as one by the Jews, Ps 135 being an expansion of 134, with certain elements from Ps 115.

4. Peculiar treasure] see on Ex 19 5. **7. For the rain**] i.e. to produce rain, as it was thought : cp. Zech 10 1 RV. **Treasuries**] storehouses, where, according to ancient belief, the winds were kept. **10, 11.** Cp. Nu 21 24. **13. Memorial**] that by which Jehovah is remembered.

14. Judge] i.e. do justice on behalf of : cp. Dt 32 36. **Repent himself**] i.e. pity, relent towards. **15, 18.** See 115 4-8. **21. Out of**] i.e. from out of.

PSALM 136

A song of praise to God ever merciful. It is sometimes known as the great Hallel, although the Talmud includes also Pss 120–135 under this title. It differs from all other Pss. in the Psalter in that each v. closes with a refrain. **6.** Cp. 24 2. **19–22.** Cp. 135 11, 12.

23. Low estate] i.e. condition of abasement, perhaps the exile or subjection to a foreign yoke.

PSALM 137

A lifelike memorial of the bitter experiences of exile concluding with (a) a strong expression of patriotism, and (b) an outburst of hatred against the enemies of Jerusalem. Probably written soon after the exile.

1. Rivers of Babylon] *The* river was the Euphrates, from which branched off a network of canals, on whose banks grew the willows here referred to. These were a species of poplar. **2. Harps**] the *Kinnor* was the most ancient kind of harp, properly a lyre. **3. A song**] lit. 'the words of a song.' **Sing us,** etc.] probably in mockery. Hebrew music would not be so good as Babylonian. **5. Forget** *her cunning*] i.e. her skill in playing on the harp. **7. The children of Edom in the day**] RV 'against the children of Edom the day,' i.e. the day of the destruction of Jerusalem by the Chaldeans (2 K 25 8 f.), when Edom rejoiced at its fall: see Obad vv. 10–12. **8. Who art to be destroyed**] i.e. doomed to destruction. **9. Stones**] RV 'rocks.' We cannot defend this terrible curse, but the cruelties of these Eastern oppressors were a provocation which fortunately we cannot now realise.

PSALM 138

Although the title ascribes this Ps. to David, it is generally considered to belong to the post-exilic period, of whose earnest piety it is one of the best examples. According to some scholars the speaker is Israel, but this is doubtful.

1. Before] i.e. in front of, in opposition to the (false) gods. **2. Thy name**] Thy character, as hitherto revealed. The present fulfilment of thy promise surpasses the renown of all thy former doings.

3. Strengthenedst me] RV 'Thou didst encourage me,' lit. 'madest me proud.'

6. Afar off] RV 'from afar.' They are not hidden from God's eye, or beyond the reach of God's justice. **8.** 'Jehovah accomplisheth (all things) for me.' **The works of thine own hands**] i.e. the Jewish nation, if Israel is the speaker.

PSALM 139

One of the very greatest of the Pss. No grander tribute has ever been paid to the omniscience and omnipresence of God. The Ps. is ascribed to David, but the Hebrew is decisive in favour of a date very long after David, being marked by Aramaisms.

1–6. God's omniscience. **7–12.** God's omnipresence. **13–18.** God's wonderful providence in human life. **19–22.** God's hatred of sin. **23, 24.** A prayer that the Psalmist may be cleansed from all evil.

3. Compassest] RM 'winnowest,' i.e. scrutinisest. **5. Beset**] surround, influence. **6. High**] the word means 'inaccessible': cp. Dt 2 36.

8. Hell] RV 'Sheol,' i.e. the under-world.

9. The wings of the morning] i.e. follow the first rays of dawn which stretch like outspread wings to the far horizon. **Uttermost parts of the sea**] i.e. the West—Mediterranean. **11. If**

I say] The text has, 'and I said.' **Cover**] some, with slight change, render 'screen me,' and this is evidently the thought of the Psalmist. **Even the night,** etc.] RV 'and the light about me shall be night'—a parallel to previous clause.

13. Possessed] rather, 'formed,' or 'created.' **Reins**] the kidneys, seat of thought, feeling, etc., according to Hebrew belief. **Covered me**] rather, 'woven me together,' like a piece of cloth, with bones, sinews, muscles, etc.: cp. Job 10 11. **15. In the lowest parts of the earth**] Probably the writer is speaking poetically of the mysterious origin of a human personality in the womb.

16. A most obscure verse. 'Thine eyes beheld my' (yet) 'unformed substance, and in thy book were they all written,' (even) 'the days which were preordained when as yet there was none of them.' The Psalmist himself, all his days, and all their happenings, were in the mind of God before he was born.

18. I am still with thee] either, 'my thoughts still go out to thee and thy wonders,' or, 'I am still in thy thought as an object of care and love.'

19. Surely thou wilt] RM 'O that thou wouldest.' **Bloody men**] RV 'bloodthirsty men.' **21.** The thought is evidently, 'hateful to all right-thinking persons must those be who rebel against such a wonder-working God.'

24. Wicked way] better, 'way leading to sorrow'; the idea is the same. **Way everlasting**] i.e. the enduring way—well expressed in Prov 12 28.

PSALM 140

A prayer for deliverance from enemies (perhaps national), ascribed to David probably because it consists mainly of quotations from, and adaptations of, earlier Pss.

2. 'Continually do they stir up wars': cp. Prov 15 18. **3. Selah**] see on 3 4. **7. Covered**] better, 'screened.' **11. Let not,** etc.] better, 'a slander shall not.'

PSALM 141

An evening prayer in time of trouble. The Psalmist prays that he may be strengthened to resist temptation, and so escape the fate of evil men.

2. Be set forth] lit. 'raise itself,' like the smoke of incense. **5.** Correction from friends is desirable. **An excellent oil,** *which* **shall not break my head**] RV 'as oil upon the head ; let not my head refuse it.' **For yet,** etc.] 'for still my prayer is against their wrong-doing.' **6.** An obscure verse. 'When their judges are flung headlong by the sides of the crag, then shall they hear my words that they are sweet.'

7. Also obscure; perhaps, 'Their bones will be scattered at the mouth of Sheol as when one cleaveth and breaketh up the earth,' referring to the judges. **8. But**] better, ' for.'

Leave not, etc.] RM ' Pour not out my soul,' i.e. let me not die : cp. Isa 53 12.

PSALM 142

A prayer of a hunted soul : ascribed to David ' in the cave,' but not likely to be by him.

3. ' When my spirit is faint within me' (then I remember) ' thou knowest my path.'

7. Prison] metaphorical : cp. 107 10. **Compass me about**] RM ' crown themselves because of me.' The meaning is, that they will rejoice with him in his rejoicing.

PSALM 143

A late Ps., though ascribed to David, consisting mainly of appropriate reminiscences from earlier Pss.

2. Shall no man living, etc.] perhaps, ' is no man living righteous.' **3. That have been long dead**] better, ' that are for ever dead' : cp. Lam 3 6. **4. Is . . overwhelmed**] better, ' faints.' **Is desolate**] better, ' is bewildered.'

6. Selah] see on 3 4. **7. Hear**] better, ' answer' : cp. 28 1. **10.** ' Let thy good spirit lead me in an even' (i.e. safe, peaceful) ' country' : cp. 27 11.

PSALM 144

This Ps. consists mainly of thoughts and quotations from earlier Pss., e.g. 8 and 18. Vv. 12–15 are, however, quite unlike anything else in the Psalter, and some suppose them to be a quotation from a lost Ps., possibly by David.

2. My goodness] lit. ' my lovingkindness,' but with the change of a single Hebrew letter we can render ' my castle,' which is much more suitable. **My people**] probably we should render, ' the peoples.' **3, 4.** Cp. 8 4 39 5.

7. Strange children] i.e. strangers. **9.** See 33 2.

12. The want of connexion seems to point to a new fragment. **Our daughters, etc.**] Two renderings are possible: (1) ' our daughters be draped in purple cloth like the hangings of a palace,' or (2) ' our daughters as corner stones carved after the similitude of a palace,' strong and graceful. For ' palace' PBV reads 'temple.'

14. Breaking in] invasion by an enemy. **Going out**] either into exile, or to surrender to an enemy. **Complaining**] RV ' outcry' : cp. Isa 24 11 Jer 14 2.

PSALM 145

This is an alphabetic Ps., but the v. with the letter *Nun*, which should come after v. 13, has been lost. It is a noble Ps., celebrating the praise of God as the bountiful Giver of all good things, used in the Jewish church at morning service, and worthy to be used in all the churches. It is the last Ps. ascribed to David in the Psalter.

5. RV ' of the glorious majesty of thine honour and of thy wondrous works will I meditate.' **13.** Here LXX adds the missing v., as follows : ' Jehovah is faithful in all his words and kind in all his works.'

PSALM 146

Here begins the final group, Pss 146–150, known as the ' Hallelujah ' Pss., because each begins and ends with that word, meaning, ' Praise ye the LORD.' They sum up the joy of the returned exiles, and form a fitting doxology to the Psalter. They are, of course, specially intended for use in the second Temple. Ps 146 praises God as the true Helper.

9. Turneth upside down] lit. ' causeth to turn aside ' (into the trackless desert, where it disappears).

PSALM 147

A song of praise in which the Psalmist recounts God's mercies (1) in restoring Jerusalem, (2) in helping those cast down, (3) in caring for the animal world, and (4) in the changing seasons.

2. Build up] i.e. rebuild, after the captivity.

7. Sing praise] better, ' make melody.'

10. Against self-reliance. **11. Hope in his mercy**] better, ' wait for His lovingkindness.'

17. Morsels] crumbs (of bread). Frost and snow at Jerusalem are comparatively rare. A change soon follows : cp. v. 18.

19, 20. The writer returns to God's doings for Israel. **Judgments**] better, ' ordinances,' revealed only to Israel.

PSALM 148

This is the ' Gloria in Excelsis ' of the Psalter, wherein all created things, animate and inanimate, are called upon to praise Jehovah.

1. From the heavens] i.e. angels and the heavenly bodies. **4. Waters that *be* above the heavens**] So God divided the waters : see Gn 1 6, 7. **6. Which shall not pass**] RM ' which none shall transgress.' **8. Vapours**] smoke or steam : cp. 119 83. **13. Excellent**] RV ' exalted.' **14.** RM ' a horn for his people, a praise for all his saints,' i.e. the giving victory to God's people ('exalting the horn') is a subject of praise.

PSALM 149

A song of praise to God who gives the victory, including vengeance on the enemies of Israel.

4. Salvation] RM ' victory.' **5. Upon their beds**] even in the night-season. **9. The judg-**

ment] probably referring to the prophecies and Pss. concerning the destruction of the heathen : cp. 18 30-43 83 10-13 Isa 45 14. **This honour, etc.**] better, 'This' (the overthrow of their enemies) 'shall be an honour for all his saints.'

PSALM 150

This is 'the grand Finale of the spiritual concert,' and worthily closes not only this little Hallelujah group, but the whole Psalter. **1. Firmament of his power**] the spreading roof of the sky which His power has made. **3. Trumpet**] i.e. *Shopher*, a kind of horn.

Psaltery] i.e. *Nebhel*, a species of harp, or guitar, or lyre, with a bulging resonance box at one end. **Harp**] i.e. *Kinnor*, the most ancient form of harp ; a lyre. **4. Timbrel**] i.e. *Toph*, a circlet of wood covered with skin and ornamented with brass bells ; tambourine. **Stringed instruments**] i.e. *Minnim*, properly, 'strings,' i.e. of a harp. **Organs**] RV 'the pipe,' i.e. *Ugabh*, perhaps a Pan's pipe : cp. Gn 4 21. **5. Cymbals**] i.e. *Tseltselim*, evidently of two kinds. **High sounding**] cp. 1 Cor 13 1.
6. The climax is reached. 'Let every thing that hath breath praise the LORD. Hallelujah.'

PROVERBS

INTRODUCTION

THE Hebrew word *Mashal* covers a much larger area than our 'Proverb.' The latter signifies a pithy, pointed saying, which, by its obvious correspondence with the facts of human nature and experience, wins popular acceptance. Of such brief, clear and sensible utterances there are abundant examples in the book before us. But it also contains other forms of composition. There are passages in which the subject is continued for several verses, especially in the earlier and some of the later chapters ; lengthy descriptions, such as that of the Bad Woman (c. 7) and the Excellent Woman (31 10-31) ; homilies and addresses (1 20-33 8). In other books of the Bible the *Mashal* has a still wider range of meaning : it is an allegory (Ezk 17 2) ; a figurative discourse (Nu 23 7, 18) ; a byword (Jer 24 9) ; a taunt (Isa 14 4) ; a lament (Mic 2 4) ; an argument (Job 29 1). The idea at its root is that of a similitude or parallelism, a comparison with some well-known object, and it is, as a rule, distinguished from the other parallelism with which we are familiar in the Bible, that of the Psalms, in that it is spoken, not intended to be sung.

The proverbs contained in the book which bears this name are not of the kind which spring unbidden to the lips of the people, the

'Bits of ancient observation by his fathers garnered, each
As a pebble worn and polished in the current of his speech.'

They show on their face that they were composed by thinkers, by the class of men who were known as 'the wise' (Job 15 18 Jer 18 18). In some cases this is distinctly stated (1 6 22 17 24 23). They arrange themselves in

five main divisions. The Introduction c. 1–9 ; 10 1–22 16 ; 22 17–24 ; 25–29 ; the Appendix, 31, 31. To the Introduction (1 1) and to two of the collections (10 1 25 1) the name of Solomon is prefixed. We are not, however, to understand that he was the author of all the sayings under these headings. He was traditionally regarded as the representative of all wisdom, and at 1 K 4 32 we read that he 'spoke three thousand proverbs.' The majority of the maxims and discourses preserved in our book belong to times and circumstances altogether unlike his, but we have no means of distinguishing with certainty any that may have originated with him. The collection probably contains many pre-exilic proverbs besides those of Solomon ; but it also contains others of a later date and cannot have been cast into its present form till some time after the exile.

Proverbs occupies an important place in what is known as the Wisdom Literature of the Jews. This consists of the Canonical Books, Job, Proverbs and Ecclesiastes, the apocryphal Ecclesiasticus and the Wisdom of Solomon. Job handles the serious problem of the relation between the sufferings of the righteous and the justice and goodness of God. Ecclesiastes discusses the value of life from a pessimistic standpoint. The Wisdom of Solomon seeks to demonstrate, both to the Gentiles and to those Jews who were tempted to apostasy, that there is no true wisdom apart from the faith in the One God. Proverbs and Ecclesiasticus are guides for daily life, not concerning themselves with intellectual difficulties or the controversy between monotheism and idolatry, but devoted to the promotion of uprightness and purity. It was said of Socrates that he brought philosophy down from heaven to earth. He turned men from speculations on the origin of the universe to their duties as individuals and members of the commonwealth. A somewhat similar remark might be made about this branch of the Wisdom Literature. Its chief concern is with the sane and prudent ordering of daily life. It looks on wisdom as the art of living well. It enforces virtue as the way by which the goal of happiness may be reached. It guards against stumblingblocks, pitfalls, and bypaths. It makes great use of prudential considerations. Yet it is religious at heart. The fear of the Lord is its beginning. God's law, revealed in Scripture and experience, or imparted by meditative and observant men, is never forgotten. His government is over all human affairs; His rewards and punishments take effect in this present life, and are sincerely believed in. But wisdom is not regarded as confined to these strictly practical matters. Agur (30³) uses the word almost in the sense of philosophy. And the wisdom which displays its excellence by guiding aright a young man's course is seen to be essentially one with that attribute of God which directed the creation of the world (c. 8).

The ideal of life here enjoined is by no means an unworthy one. Honesty, industry, chastity, considerateness for all, helpfulness towards the distressed; humanity, reverence, and trust towards God are urged unweariedly. There is no base or unworthy maxim, no sanction of the spirit of revenge, like the Italian, ' Wait time and place for thy revenge, for it is never well done in a hurry': no recommendation of fawning obsequiousness, like the Eastern, 'If the monkey reigns, dance before him.' In some respects it is even healthier in tone than its companion books. Compare, for instance, its view of woman (14¹ 18²² 19¹⁴ 31¹⁰⁻³¹) with Eccl 7²⁸ Ecclus 25¹⁶⁻²⁶. On the other hand, there are defects. Two weaknesses are especially to be noticed. First, the absence of all belief in a real life beyond the grave. This is a serious draw-

back. When men came to realise that rewards and punishments are not distributed on earth in accordance with conduct, the foundation was destroyed on which the proverb-writers built their recommendations of virtue. The Wisdom of Solomon, which owes much to its contact with Greek thought, marks a great advance in this particular (2²³ 3, 4²⁰ 5¹⁵ 6¹⁹); and in the teaching of Christ the prospect of a future dispensation of judgment occupied an important place. Secondly, there is no warm and inspiring hope of the reclamation of the foolish and sinful. If a man is on the wrong side of the line it is taken for granted that he will remain there, contrary to the charity and hopefulness of Him who ' came not to call the righteous, but sinners to repentance.'

As to the notes which follow, it should b₎ remembered that our limits of space preclude anything beyond a short explanation, illustration, or paraphrase of the more difficult ambiguous and interesting paragraphs. The reader is strongly recommended to have the Revised Version always before him. In concise sayings, where everything depends on the exact point being touched, the rendering of a single word makes all the difference. The RV or its margin often hit the mark which the AV has missed. For example, the latter uses the word ' wisdom' to represent several words of the original. It is always worth noting where the RV substitutes 'wise dealing,' 'prudence,' 'subtilty.' Again, the RV has sometimes availed itself of the help furnished by the LXX. This is of great importance. Passing from mouth to mouth, not deemed equally sacred with the utterances of the Law or even of the Prophets, these adages frequently failed to keep their original form. And the form presented by the Greek Version sometimes recommends itself as the correct one.

One other recommendation may be permitted. Ecclesiasticus is well worth reading along with Proverbs. Its tone is very similar, but it was written somewhat later (about 200 B.C.); it is an invaluable aid to the understanding of the Jewish mind.

PART 1 (Chs. 1–9)

CHAPTER 1

The c. falls into three principal divisions.

1–6. Title and Introduction explaining the object of the whole book, which is to instruct the inexperienced and add to the educated man's knowledge. It is assumed that good conduct is an art which can be taught. But the learner must be in sympathy with the subject; a right judgment concerning moral

truth is attainable only by those who hunger and thirst after righteousness. The method of instruction is by proverbs, figures, parables and vivid pictures, and is therefore substantially the same as that which our Lord adopted.

7–19. A Warning against Companionship with Robbers. We are at first astounded at finding such a warning necessary. Only in days of weak government, such as the 5th and 4th cent. B.C., when the rulers were mere representatives of a distant foreign monarch, was such a state of affairs possible.

20–33. Wisdom's Call and Threats. Wisdom is represented as a preacher, who goes out into the streets, the broad places near the city gates, the long gateways through which men enter or leave the town, the 'dusky lane and wrangling mart,' there to lift up her voice. As the prophets (Isa 20 2 Jer 5 1 Mic 1 8) went amongst their fellows, as Socrates was daily found in the marketplace conversing with all who would, as Jesus Himself ever taught in synagogues and in the Temple, where all the Jews come together (Jn 18 20), so Wisdom is not fastidious or exclusive; none can complain that they have been denied the opportunity of hearing. But the hour is now past. The simpletons, the unbelieving scoffers and the crassly stupid are threatened with swift and sudden punishment. For the Wisdom which here speaks is not of quite the same spirit as that of NT., which is peaceful, gentle, easy to be entreated, full of mercy (Jas 3 17) : there is more of Elijah than of Christ in it.

4. Read, 'to give prudence to the simple.' The simple, open to each new impression, believes anything. The prudent, or subtle, has learnt caution from experience. **6. Interpretation]** RV 'figure' (Hab 2 6). **Dark sayings]** RV 'riddles' (Jg 14 18 Nu 12 8 Ezk 17 2 Hab 2 6).

7. A motto for the whole book. True morality is based on a right relation to God. Fear is the keynote of OT. piety ; not slavish terror, but reverence and humility.

8. The teacher addresses the learner as ' My son' : parents will also give moral instruction.

9. Read, 'a chaplet of grace.' At banquets the heads of the guests were crowned with garlands. **Chains]** cp. Gn 41 42 Dan 5 29.

12. Grave] 'Sheol' (RV) and the **pit** are the cheerless under-world, away from God and all real life, which the dead were supposed to inhabit (2 18 23 14).

17. Warning is useless : they do not see that they are rushing to destruction.

23. Turn and listen whilst I declare my purpose.

31. Mediæval theologians taught that molten gold would be poured down the throats of the avaricious in hell and that other vices also would be punished in kind. 'That they might learn that by what things a man sinneth, by these he is punished ' (Wisd 11 16).

32. When simpletons turn away from instruction they shall suffer for it. 'He who will not be ruled by the rudder must be ruled by the rocks.' **Prosperity]** RM 'carelessness,' false security. 'Serious things to-morrow,' the Greek tyrant said, thrusting under the pillow of his couch the letter which would have saved him from assassination.

CHAPTER 2
THE SEARCH FOR WISDOM

1–4. The condition which must be fulfilled. Spinoza said, ' The effort to understand is the first and sole basis of virtue.'

1. Hide] i.e. as a treasure. **2. The heart** in OT. is the seat of the intellect. **4.** Wealth was hoarded in the shape of gold and jewels. In times of peril this was buried (Gn 43 23 Job 3 21 Jer 41 8 Mt 13 44). Hence the suspicion with which Orientals have often regarded modern explorers.

5–8. The result. It brings us into relation with Him who is the only source of wisdom and safety.

7. Sound wisdom] read, ' deliverances.'

8. His saints] read, 'His pious' or ' loving ones' ; those who love and are beloved by Him (Ps 12 1 30 4 31 23).

9–19. A further result. It saves from the seductions of bad men and women.

10. When] RV 'for.' It becomes part of his very mind.

16–18. The stress laid in these chs. on sensual vice proves that the evil was a flagrant one. The population was drawn to the great towns where such temptations are common. The **strange woman** (22 14) was not a foreigner but an adulteress or harlot, to whom the man was not related. In later ages Jewish pride entitled such a person 'an Aramæan,' as though no Jewess would stoop so low.

17. The ' friend of her youth' (RV) is her husband (Jer 3 2-5). **The covenant of her God]** Though there was perhaps no religious ceremony, the marriage relation was a religious one (Ex 20 14 Mal 2 14).

18. Read,

> ' For her house leads down unto Death,
> And her paths unto the Shades.'

She and her guests are on their way to that under-world which is tenanted by the Shades, the disembodied, shadow-like, hopeless dead (9 18). The ancient idea of a future existence, not worthy of the name of existence, prevails all through this book.

CHAPTER 3
THE BLESSINGS OF OBEDIENCE AND OF CHASTISEMENT

The first and third divisions, 1–10, 21–35, are exhortations to good conduct and promises of consequent blessing. The second, 11–20, declares the profitableness of divine chastening and the value of wisdom.

1. Law] or ' direction.' The teacher speaks as one having authority. **3. Mercy]** RM ' kindness.' He is to retain kindness and faithfulness, as he would the signet-ring which hangs from his neck by a cord (Gn 38 18 Song 8 6), or as the phylacteries on arm and forehead:

ₚp. Ex 13⁹ Dt 6⁸ 11¹⁸. **5.** We are easily misled by passion and sin. 'Thanks to our wisdom, we should, once for all, refrain from being clever.'

8. For **navel** read 'flesh,' as at 4²². This change only requires the addition of a single letter, and it gives us the pair, 'flesh and bones,' which in biblical language make up the body (Gn 29¹⁴ 2 S 5¹, etc.). The drying up of the bones is a figure of extreme distress (17²² Ps 32³,⁴): hence the word 'moistening' (RM) here. **9.** To **honour** is to pay the dues (Isa 43²³ Dan 11³⁸ 1 Tim 5⁷). **10. Presses**] i.e. 'vats.'

11, 12. Bp. Andrewes prayed: 'From Thine anger, and yet more from Thy ceasing to be angry, good Lord, deliver us.' **15. Rubies**] here, and at 20¹⁵ 31¹⁰, more probably, 'red coral.' The finest red coral has always been very costly. **18. A tree of life**] a figure derived from Gn 3 : see also Ezk 47¹² Prov 11³⁰ 13¹² 15⁴. **19.** It is an additional reason for esteeming her, that creation could not have been accomplished without her. **20. The depths,** etc.] i.e. the subterranean storehouses from which fountains and rivers were supposed to be derived.

24. Not affrighted by horrible dreams (Job 7¹⁴). **29. Securely**] i.e. without suspicion. **32. Secret**] 'counsel' or 'friendship' (RM): they belong to His 'Privy Council' (Gn 18¹⁷ Job 19¹⁹ 29⁴ Ps 25¹⁴ 55¹⁴ Am 3⁷). **35.** Joseph, Daniel, Ezra, Mordecai are examples.

CHAPTER 4
ANCESTRAL WISDOM. THE TWO PATHS

In vv. 1–9 the teacher lays stress on the fact that his instruction is a repetition of his father's. No teaching was thought valuable save that which was handed down from one generation to another. The best pupil was the one who was 'a cemented cistern which loses not a drop.' Vv. 10–19 might be called the doctrine of the two paths, the two ways of life. 20–27 enjoin strict attention to instruction and to conduct.

7. Lit. 'The beginning of wisdom is, get wisdom' (RM). When we feel our deficiency we should make a start. Socrates was the wisest of the Greeks because he felt that he was not wise. **And with all,** etc.] Read, 'Yea, with all thou hast gotten' (RV): cp. Mt 13⁴⁵,⁴⁶. **8. Exalt**] i.e. prize highly. **12.** His life is like a broad road in which are no obstacles to trip up the unwary. **16, 17.** There were many rapacious officials whose appetite for oppression grew with what it fed on. **18.** The prosperity of the righteous is 'as the light of the dawn' (RM), ever waxing. **23.** Watch over the inner life of thought and feeling; on it prosperity depends (1 S 16⁷

Mt 15¹⁹). **25.** Keep your eye fixed on the goal : let nothing turn you aside into the devious paths of wickedness. **26.** Make your way even and level : walk in the smooth, strait path of righteousness.

CHAPTER 5
UNHOLY PASSION. HALLOWED LOVE

A dissuasive from immorality addressed exclusively to men. The two leading thoughts are (1) the disastrous consequences of adultery ; loss of honour, property, life, opportunity of repentance, and (2) the sufficiency and desirableness of conjugal love.

6. Read, 'Lest she should ponder the path of life, her ways are unstable, and she knoweth not.' So far is she from entering on the level path which leads to life, her ways are unstable and she is reckless about it.

9–11. All the fruits of a man's labour are preyed on by the false-hearted woman and her confederates:

'Gaming, Women and Wine,
While they laugh, they make a man pine.'

14. He has only just escaped being brought before the assembly of the people, who would have sentenced him to death (Lv 20¹⁰ Dt 22²²). **15–17.** A man's pleasures should be sought at home. Read, with RV, 'Should thy springs be dispersed abroad, and rivers of waters in the streets ?' **18.** It is **blessed** when enjoyed legitimately. **19.** The opening words are an exclamation: 'Lovely hind ! Charming wild goat !' **22.** He has had the instruction, but took no heed of it. Now it is too late.

CHAPTER 6
DISSUASIVES FROM HURTFUL THINGS

Vv. 1–19 are inserted here from some other collection, and contain warnings against suretyships (1–5), sloth (6–11), falseness (12–15), evils which the LORD hates (16–19). At v. 20 the thread of c. 5 is resumed.

1. The surety appears to have taken the creditor's hand in the presence of witnesses : cp. 2 K 10¹⁵. **3.** Read, 'Seeing thou art come into the hand of thy neighbour, go, bestir thyself, and beset thy neighbour. Make haste to get out of his power ' (Mt 5²⁵). **7.** Ants really have an elaborately organised society : in some species there is a king and queen ; others keep slaves. **11. One that travelleth**] RV 'a robber.' The roads were insecure, as English ones were in the times when 'highwayman' meant 'robber.' **13.** Cp. the Arab's prayer: 'O God, pardon us the culpable winking of the eyes.' Here the winking, etc., are signals to confederates. **16. A proud look**] lit. 'haughty eyes' (RV) : see our word 'supercilious,' from *supercilium* = the eyebrow **25.** The beauty of an Eastern woman's eyes is enhanced by being painted round with kohl in the shape of an almond. **26.** A harlot brings him down to a loaf of bread, to extreme poverty ; an adulteress will involve him in utter ruin. **30.** The OT. never treats theft leniently. Read, 'Do not men despise,' etc. Yes ! and much more an adulterer. **31.** In divers cases twofold, fourfold, fivefold restitution was prescribed (Ex 22, etc.): **sevenfold** means very great (Gn 4 15).

CHAPTER 7
THE BAD WOMAN

A picture drawn from life of the enticing of a young man by a wicked woman.

2. The apple] lit. 'the little man' of the eye, so called because an image is reflected from the pupil of the eye. It is a figure for the most precious and delicate things (Dt 32 10 Ps 17 8). **3.** The Jews wear a long leather band twisted round the arm and fingers during prayer. Passages of Scripture written on parchment and enclosed in a small leather box are at the same time worn on the forehead.

4. My sister] the title by which bride and wife are addressed (Song 4 9).

6. The window is the opening; the **casement** is the lattice-work filling it, looking through which one may see and remain unseen.

9. Twilight ends suddenly, and is followed by dense darkness. **11. Stubborn**] or 'wilful'; an epithet applied to an unruly beast which has shaken off the yoke (Hos 4 16). **14.** Lv 7 16-18 shows that such sacrifices were followed by a feast : the blood and the fat of the intestines were offered to God ; the rest of the animal was consumed by the offerer, his family and guests. The woman is therefore inviting to a sumptuous feast.

19, 20. The husband is a merchant, who is absent on a long journey, as is evident from his having taken with him his purse. He will not be home till the 'full moon' (RV).

26. Read, 'Yea, many are those she has slain.' **27. The chambers of death** are the many diverse receptacles supposed to be in the under-world : cp. Jn 14 2.

CHAPTER 8
WISDOM'S CRY

Wisdom now reappears as a preacher, holding forth in all the places where men most do congregate. After expounding in varied ways the excellence of the gifts which she can bestow, she asserts that she was the first of all God's creatures, who stood at His side when He formed our world, and took part in His work as a master workman, whose delight has always been in the lives and affairs of men. In vv. 1–21 we find only the ordinary kind of personification, in which a quality is spoken of as though it were a living individual. In vv.

22–31, however, it is almost as though Wisdom were an actual person, distinct from God. No one can wonder that in the 4th cent. of our era theologians of diverse schools made considerable use of this c. in the controversies respecting the Second Person in the Holy Trinity. But there is no convincing force in the arguments which either side derived from this source. The object of the writer was to recommend that wisdom which is his constant theme, which manifests itself in the right conduct of life, by showing that it is exhibited and exemplified in the wonders of Nature and the Creation of the world. There is also a trace here of the idea which at a later time asserted itself very strongly, that a medium was required to bridge over the distance betwixt the Spiritual Creator and the material universe. Job 28, 38 Ecclus 1 1-21 24 Wisd 7 8– 8 21 should be read along with this c.

2. The high places are the walls and towers, vantage-points for a speaker. **5. Wisdom**] rather, 'prudence' or 'sagacity.' **12.** Read, 'I, Wisdom, have made prudence my dwelling,' i.e. I am complete master of it.

14-16. There is no genuine statesmanship apart from wisdom.

22-31. This account of creation reminds us of Gn 1 Job 38. God makes a vault, the firmament, which rests on the surrounding waters (v. 27). He settles the mountains (v. 25) on foundations which are at the level of the floor of the sea (Ps 104 8 Jon 2 6). He firmly encloses the fountains of the deep, so that they cannot break through (v. 28). **22.** Read, 'The LORD formed me as the beginning of his creation': cp. Col 1 15 Rev 3 14. **23. Or**] i.e. ere, before. **30.** *As* **one brought up** *with him*] as a nursling or foster-child ; RV 'as a master workman.' **I was daily** *his* **delight**] lit. 'I was delight daily day.' ; my whole existence was delight : cp. Ps 120 7, 'I am peace,' all peace, nothing else. **34.** A king or great man would every morning find a crowd of clients waiting to pay their court and receive his bounties. Happy the client at Wisdom's door. **36.** He who misses wisdom wrongs himself.

CHAPTER 9
THE RIVALS

Folly and Wisdom invite guests to their respective houses. The consequences of accepting either of the two invitations are described. We are reminded of the Greek parable, 'The choice of Hercules,' which related how the hero, at the beginning of his career, was accosted by two fair women, Virtue and Vice, who would have him tread, one the rough, the other the flowery way.

1-6. Wisdom's invitation.

1. The word **Wisdom** is in the plural, to

indicate her variety and perfection. She has a house, and therefore is always ready to entertain. The **seven pillars**—a complete number—are in the courtyard, supporting a gallery. **2.** The wine was mixed with spices (Isa 5 22). **3.** Messengers are sent when the meal is ready (Lk 14 17). **4. Simple**] i.e. inexperienced, easily led, capable of being turned either way. Hence Folly (v. 16) has equal hopes of influencing them. **5. Bread**] The name for food in general (v. 2). **6.** Read, 'Forsake folly.'

7–12 are out of their proper context.
7. He will insult and revile you. **10.** The

holy] RV 'the Holy One.' **12.** Cp. Ezk 18 4 Gal 6 5.

'From David's lips this word did roll,
'Tis true and living yet:
No man can save his brother's soul,
Nor pay his brother's debt.'

13–18. Folly is personified as a woman, the traits of whose character are drawn from the description already given of the lewd woman; and unchastity is looked on as the supreme exhibition of folly. **13.** She is 'loud' and ignorant. We speak of a 'loud,' meaning a vulgar woman. **17.** The forbidden is attractive.

PART 2 (Chs. 10 1–22 16)

Here we reach the first collection of what were supposed to be Solomon's proverbs. Most of them consist of two lines parallel to each other. The parallelism is one of contrast, or agreement, or explanation, or of different persons and objects. It is impossible to trace any principle underlying the order in which the proverbs stand. Several of them are more or less exactly repeated in chs. 25–29.

CHAPTER 10

The main subject, not treated continuously, but recurred to again and again, is the blessing which attends goodness and diligence, the penalty which follows sin and sloth.
2. Treasures of wickedness] acquired by wrong-doing (Am 3 10). In many synagogues this v. is inscribed over the alms-box. To the later Jews 'righteousness' meant almsgiving (Dan 4 27 Tob 4 10 12 9 Mt 6 1). **4.** To **deal** *with* **a slack hand** is to be lacking in energy. **5.** 'Make hay while the sun shines.'
7. 'Only the ashes of the just
     Smell sweet and blossom from the dust.'
10. Winketh with the eye] i.e. to stir up by malicious hints. In the LXX the second half of the v. runs: 'but he that openly rebuketh maketh peace.' **12.** Love hides them from sight.
14. Near destruction] destruction nigh at hand.
16. The wealth earned by a good man will be rightly employed and therefore will bring him lasting gain, but revenue spent in self-indulgence and sin brings nothing but loss in the end. **19.** Simeon, son of Gamaliel, said: 'All my days I have grown up among the wise, and I have found nought of better service than silence. . . Whoso is profuse of words causes sin.'
21. Feed] instruct. **24. The fear of the wicked**] that which he fears.
25. The storm carries him completely away (Ps 1 4).

CHAPTER 11

1. False weights were exceedingly common (16 11 20 10 Am 8 5). **6. Transgressors**] RV 'they that deal treacherously.' **10.** The **shouting** expresses exultation. **12.** Disparaging remarks concerning neighbours are foolish.
14. For **counsel** read 'statesmanship.'
16. A woman of gracious disposition and manners obtains honour. **18. Worketh a deceitful work**] RV 'earneth deceitful wages,' fairy gold, apples of Sodom.
21. Hands were struck in confirmation of a bargain. Hence the meaning here and at 16 5 is, 'My hand upon it!' 'Assuredly!' **22.** A gold ring was and still is worn by Oriental women, depending from the right nostril to the mouth. **24.** Wise and liberal expenditure is contrasted with ill-advised niggardly economy. **26.** Buying up corn to sell at famine prices was the evil in those days which corresponded to monopolies, trusts, and combines of later times. 'It is a wicked thing to make a dearth one's garner.' **29.** He throws his household into confusion by bad management, arbitrariness, etc.

CHAPTER 12

4. A crown, etc.] Possibly there may be a reference to the crown worn on their wedding-day by bride and bridegroom (Song 3 11 8 9). In Damascus the bridal crown consists of a silver hoop covered with a network of strings of corals. On this net are fastened strings of gold coins.
5. Two kinds of plans. **6.** Their very words are an ambush, meant to cause destruction.
9. Even a poor man in those days could afford to have a slave (cp. Ex 21 32), and such a man, although others might look down on him, would be happier than a person who maintained much state and show but was starving all the while.
11. Follow a regular business: to be occupied with 'vain things' (RM), speculations, and the

like, brings disaster. **12.** Read, 'Wickedness is the net of evil men.' Their own badness entraps them. **16.** A fool blurts out his annoyance : a wise man is in no hurry to publish the insult he has received. **18.** Thoughtless talk inflicts grievous wounds : if a wise man is present he heals them.

20. The counsellors of peace] Those who promote prosperity. **21. Mischief]** i.e. calamity (17 20 28 14). **23.** 'Still waters run deep.' 'Empty vessels make the most sound.'

24. Under tribute] forced to do taskwork (1 K 9 21). **26. More excellent than]** RV 'is a guide to.' **Seduceth them]** RV 'causeth them to err.' **27.** He is too lazy to look after his own food (19 24).

CHAPTER 13

2. Read, 'the desire of the treacherous is for violence' (RM). **3.** The times were out of joint : those alone were safe who said nothing. **4. Soul]** as in v. 2 and many other passages, means 'appetite.' **Made fat]** abundantly gratified. **5.** Read, 'but a wicked man behaves shamefully and abominably.'

7. One 'feigneth himself rich' (RM), to gain consideration ; another 'feigneth himself poor,' to avoid giving and paying. **8.** Providence equalises matters : wealth may buy one off from peril, but poverty saves us from fear of being robbed. **Not rebuke]** RV 'no threatening.' **9.** The extinction of the lamp is a sign of disaster : cp. 20 20 31 18 Job 18 6 Jer 25 10.

10. 'By pride cometh only contention' (RV) : willingness to be advised saves from this and many evils.

11. The proverb originally ran : 'Wealth gotten in haste, etc., but wealth gotten by degrees,' etc. 'Come lightly, go lightly.'

14. Such vv. as this indicate the existence of a definite class of wise men, whose teachings were highly esteemed. **15.** Read, 'A man of tact obtaineth favour, but the way of the treacherous is their destruction.'

21. Evil] i.e. misfortune. **Good]** i.e. prosperity. **23. Tillage]** RM 'tilled land.' **For want of judgment]** RV 'by reason of injustice.' The idea is that God blesses the labour of the righteous poor, but the unjust, though they may be rich, will not flourish.

24. Egyptian proverb : 'The ears of the young are placed on the back, and he hears when it is flogged.'

CHAPTER 14

1. The prosperity of the family depends on the wife (31 10-31). **3. Of pride]** RM 'for his pride.' **4.** Where there are no oxen men have not to labour at keeping the crib clean, but at the same time there is no profit. The men who unload coal in Calais harbour used to sing : The coal is black, but the money's white.'

8. The wise man's concern is how shall he act ; the foolish man's how shall he deceive others. **9.** Lit. 'the guilt-offering mocketh at fools.' This seems to mean that fools trust in its expiatory virtue, but that on their behalf it has no efficacy. **10.** Every one knows where his own shoe pinches (1 K 8 38). **11. Tabernacle]** or 'tent,' used for 'house' (1 K 12 16). **12.** He mistakenly thinks that the path of self-indulgence leads to lasting prosperity.

13. Men do not always wear their heart on their sleeve. Black Care sits behind the horseman.

14. We get our deserts. **The backslider in heart** is he who forsakes God. **15.** 'Quick believers need broad shoulders.' **16. Rageth]** RV 'behaveth himself insolently' ; will not be told, knows better than any one else.

17. Anger is temporary madness. **19.** Not always : see Lk 16 20. **22.** They wander from the way of safety and peace. **24.** Riches rightly used are a crown : but a rich fool has no crown, has nought but folly.

28. Let the king follow a policy which shall increase, not diminish, the number of his subjects. **29. Exalteth folly]** i.e. exhibits great folly. **30.** A 'tranquil' heart (RM) is contrasted with a jealous one. **32.** If we transpose two letters we get the following rendering : 'The wicked is thrust down through his evil-doing, but the righteous hath a refuge through his integrity.' In any case, it is hardly in keeping with the rest of Proverbs to find here a reference to the life beyond the grave.

CHAPTER 15

1. Grievous] i.e. annoying. 'If one pour in hot water let the other pour in cold.'

3. Beholding] RV 'keeping watch upon,' as watching over a city (Isa 52 8), or the prophets over the people (Ezk 3 17). **4.** Read, 'a soothing tongue .. a wound in the spirit.' **7.** *Doeth not so]* RM 'is not steadfast.' **8.** A costly offering from the one is unacceptable : the mere prayer of the other is accepted (Mk 12 42).

11. Hell and destruction] RV 'Sheol and Abaddon.' The latter means 'place of destruction' : cp. 27 20 Job 26 6 28 22 31 12 Ps 88 11. At Rev 9 11 Abaddon is the Angel of Destruction. Subsequently it became the name for the lowest part of Gehenna. **15.** 'Cheerful,' not **merry** : it is not the word rendered 'merry' in v. 13. **16.** Religion delivers from harassing care. **17. A stalled ox]** is one kept up and fattened for slaughter. **19.** The one sees imaginary hindrances : the other's course is a well-made level road.

21. RV 'maketh straight his going' : i.e. acts straightforwardly. **23.** Well-considered and opportune speech brings joy. **24.** Lit. 'The way of life upward is to the wise man' : he escapes the premature death of the wicked

26. RV 'pleasant words are pure' (in God's eyes). **27.** Bribery is one of the greatest curses of the East (Ex 18²¹ Ezk 22¹² Eccl 7⁷).

30. The light of the eyes] i.e. good fortune. **31.** He who does not wish to learn will be neither welcome nor happy among the wise.

CHAPTER 16

1–9. God's control of human life.

1. Read, ' the preparations of the heart belong to man, but the answer of the tongue is from the LORD.' Man prepares his plans, but the decisive, final word is suggested by God. ' There's a divinity that shapes our ends, roughhew them as we will.' **2.** Cp. 1 Cor 4⁴.

4. Read, ' The LORD hath made everything for its own end.' God is the absolute Sovereign (Am 3⁶). The wicked are created for punishment (Ex 9¹⁶ Ezk 38¹⁶ 39²¹ Ro 9¹⁷). The truth here pointed to would be expressed in milder terms to-day : we should say that nothing escapes the control and the judgment of God. **5.** *Though* hand, etc.] read, ' he will assuredly not go unpunished' (11²¹). **6.** Sin is expiated by kindness and faithfulness towards others (Isa 27⁹ 40² Dan 4²⁷ Hos 6⁶).

9. ' Man proposes, God disposes.'

10–15. The vv. relate chiefly to a king's powers and functions.

10. His sentence has the force of a divine oracle. **11.** Probably the word, the ' LORD,' is mistakenly inserted : the human king is meant. The merchant carried his (stone) **weights** about in a bag. Explorers have found in Palestine ancient weights of hæmatite, limestone, etc. **15.** The light of . . countenance] i.e. his friendly regard. The latter rain] is the spring rain, required to ripen the crops.

16–19. The advantages of a right spirit.

17. The road they travel does not lead to misfortune.

20–25. deal with wisdom and its results.

20. He that handleth, etc.] read, ' he that giveth heed to the word' (of God or of the teacher). **21.** The sweetness, etc.] Attractive speech disposes the listener to learn.

22. Instruction] RV 'correction' : their folly is their punishment.

26. Hunger prompts labour. It has been wittily said that every boy should pray that he may be born poor. **30.** Read, 'he that shutteth his eyes (as if pondering deeply) does it to devise froward things : he that (scornfully) compresses his lips has brought evil to pass.' Slanderers and backbiters are meant. **31.** RV ' It shall be found,' etc. The NT. does not teach that the righteous are always rewarded with long life.

> **32.** ' Yet he who reigns within himself, and rules
> Passions, desires and fears, is more a king ;
> And who attains not, ill aspires to rule
> Cities of men or headstrong multitudes.'

33. The lot was put in the folds of the garment and then shaken out (Jg 1³ Isa 34¹⁷, etc.).

CHAPTER 17

1. Lit. ' the sacrifices of strife.' There would be no pleasure in the festal meal which followed a sacrifice (7¹⁴) if it was accompanied with a quarrel. ' A little with quiet is the only diet.' **2.** The Israelite slave was a member of the family (Gn 24¹² Dt 5¹⁴, etc.), might become the heir (Gn 15², ³) or marry the daughter (1 Ch 2³⁴,³⁵). **4.** Naughty] injurious. **7.** The proverb writers show no hope of redeeming the lost. Their verdict is, ' He that is filthy let him be filthy still.'

8. He who gives a bribe regards it as a precious stone, a stone which brings favour ; whithersoever he turns he prospers. Philip of Macedon boasted that he had taken more towns with silver than with iron. **10.** A hundred strokes would be more than double the number allowed by the law (Dt 25³). **11.** The meaning is doubtful. Either, ' An evil man seeketh only rebellion,' or, ' Rebellion seeketh only mischief.' The rebellion may be against God or the king ; if the former, cp. Ps 78⁴⁹ for the cruel messenger.

14. Before it be meddled with] RV ' Before there be quarrelling.' The bursting of a dam begins with a small crack. ' Little strokes fell great oaks.' **16.** Money cannot buy it if the mind is indisposed to it. **19.** To ' exalt the gate ' may mean to set oneself above the neighbours, and so become a target for their envy. But the original probably ran : ' He that speaketh proud words.' **24.** The fool lacks the power of concentration. **27, 28.** ' I have found nought of better service than silence.' ' Silence is a fence to wisdom.'

CHAPTER 18

1. Lit. ' One who separates himself seeks desire, quarrels with all wisdom.' This would mean that a solitary recluse follows his own wishes and opposes everything reasonable. But LXX suggests, ' The alienated friend seeks an occasion of quarrel, seeks by all means to stir up strife.' **2.** He likes to talk about his own notions. **4.** The second half of the v. shows that it is a *wise* man who is in view ; his words are ' as deep waters,' i.e. are inexhaustible ; he is ever ready to give helpful answers.

8. Wounds] RV ' dainty morsels.' Malicious gossip finds ready acceptance (Jer 15¹⁶).

10. The name of Jehovah is Jehovah Himself as revealed to men, His manifested character (Ps 75¹). Orientals have always ascribed mysterious powers to the divine titles. Mohammedans repeat them one by one as they count the ninety-nine beads. One of the ancient Persian books declares that the recital of God's names is the best defence against all danger.

14. Bear] RM 'raise up.' **16.** A superior cannot be approached in the East without a present. **17.** 'Hear the other side.' **20.** A man's happiness depends on the way in which he governs and uses his tongue (Mt 12 36 15 11). **22.** A good wife (Eccl 7 28). **24.** RV 'He that maketh many friends *doeth it* to his own destruction ; but'

'The friend thou hast, and his adoption tried,
Grapple him to thy soul with hooks of steel.
But do not dull thy palm with entertainment
Of each new-hatched, unfledged comrade.'

CHAPTER 19

1. Fool] read, 'rich' (28 6). **2.** Read, 'Also, desire without knowledge,' etc. Desires must be controlled by knowledge. The hasty in action will miss his mark. 'While the discreet advise, the fool doth his business.' **3. Perverteth**] RV 'subverteth.' It is his own fault, yet he blames God for it. **6.** Great nobles and great donors are always sought after. **10. Delight**] RV 'delicate living.' He cannot appreciate refinement. Slaves have often risen to great power in the East : the danger is that they may become like the Felix of Ac 23, who was said to exercise royal power with a slave's disposition. **13.** The Arabic proverb is, 'Three things render a house uninhabitable —*tak* (rain leaking through), *nak* (a wife's nagging), and *bak* (bugs).'

> **17.** 'So much hast thou of thy hoard
> As thou gavest to thy Lord ;
> Only this will bring thee in
> Usance rich and free from sin :
> Send thy silver on before,
> Lending to His sick and poor.
> Every dirhem dropped in alms
> Touches Allah's open palms,
> Ere it falls into the hands
> Of thy brother.'

18. RV ' . . seeing there is hope, And set not thy heart on his destruction.' Not to discipline is to destroy. **19.** 'Attempt to soothe him, and he will rage the more. **22.** 'Words are as breath, and will is all.' Only the intention counts (23 6-8 Mk 12 42 2 Cor 8 12). **24.** RV 'The sluggard burieth his hand in the dish,' etc. : the allusion is to the large dish in the centre into which all dip (Mk 14 20). **28. Devoureth**] i.e. gulps down greedily.

CHAPTER 20

1. Raging] RV 'a brawler.' **Is deceived**] RM 'reeleth.' It makes a man sneer, quarrel and reel about. **2. Fear**] the 'terror' which he causes. **Soul**] RV 'life.' **4.** Read, 'In the autumn . . therefore when he seeketh,' etc. : the first season begins about October, the second about April. **5.** A clever cross-questioner elicits one's plans. **8. Scattereth away**] RM 'winnoweth' (1 K 3 28).

9. 'What mortal when he saw,
Life's voyage done, his heavenly Friend,
Could ever yet dare tell Him fearlessly :
"I have kept uninfring'd my nature's law ;
The inly-written chart Thou gavest me,
To guide me, I have steer'd by to the end" ? '

13. Open thine eyes] i.e. Wake up !
15. Read, 'There is gold and abundance of corals and precious vessels—wise lips are all these.'
16. 'Strangers,' not **a strange woman.** He does not deserve to escape the consequences of his folly. **19.** A 'chatterbox,' not a 'flatterer,' is meant.
25. RV 'It is a snare to a man rashly to say, It is holy,' etc. Reflect before vowing (Eccl 5 1 f. Mt 15 8). There is a Greek story of one who found a gold mine, and thereupon vowed a gold ram to Juno : soon he substituted a silver one ; then a small brass one ; eventually she got nothing. 'The river past and God forgotten.'
26. The wheel of the threshing-cart, crushing in its weight (Am 1 3). **27.** Conscience is a searchlight, piercing the depths of the heart (1 Cor 2 11). **28.** It is **the king's** goodness and reliableness that are meant. **30. The blueness,** etc.] RV 'Stripes that wound cleanse,' etc. (Ps 119 67).

CHAPTER 21

1. The 'watercourses' (RV) are the artificial irrigation channels of Egypt and Babylon (Isa 58 11). **4.** There is no connexion between the two halves of the v. RM 'The tillage of the wicked is sin,' i.e. the result of his labour is sin. **5.** One who is in a hurry to be rich hastens to want. **6.** By a very slight alteration of the Hebrew text we get the greatly improved rendering of RM, 'Is a vapour driven to and fro ; they are snares of death.'
9. A small room is often built on the flat roof of an Oriental house (1 K 17 19 2 K 4 10 Ps 102 7). 'A needle's eye is wide enough for two friends ; the whole world is too narrow for two foes.'
12. Read, 'The righteous considereth the house of the wicked ; he overturneth the wicked to ruin.' Perhaps **the righteous** means God.
14. Bribes are carried ready for use in a fold of the robe. **16.** He will come prematurely to his final resting-place amongst 'the Shades' (2 18).
17. The **oil** is that used at banquets for anointing (27 9 Dt 14 26 Neh 8 12 Am 6 6). **18.** Cp. 11 8.
22. Strength of the confidence thereof] the stronghold in which it trusted. **25.** He **desires** ease and self-indulgence. **27.** Read, 'When he bringeth it to atone for wickedness' (RM): cp. Lv 19 20-22. **28.** The man who actually heard what he swears to, will speak **constantly** or ' for ever '; his testimony will never be

shaken. **29.** A wicked man boldly maintains whatever suits him ; a wise man 'considereth his way' (RM).

CHAPTER 22 1-16

1. To be regarded with favour is better than silver and gold. This v. is inscribed in large letters on the walls of Manchester Exchange. Rabbi Simeon used to say : 'There are only three crowns ; the crown of the Law, the crown of priesthood, and the crown of kingdom ; but the crown of a good name excels them all.'

2. 'A man's a man for a' that.' **6.** 'As the twig is bent so the tree's inclined.' **In the way he should go**] i.e. according to the position and work to which he is destined. **8. The rod,** etc.] i.e. the power of his tyranny shall vanish.

12. Read, 'The eyes of the LORD are in him that keepeth knowledge.'

PART 3 (Chs. 22 17–24 34)

CHAPTER 22 17-29

These proverbs are very unlike the preceding in tone and style. The author's own personality is brought distinctly into view (22 17-21 23 15) ; he had a high opinion of the value of his maxims ; he arranges them in strophes, not in couplets.

18. Fitted] RV 'established together,' i.e. ready (1 Pet 3 15). **20. For excellent things** RM suggests 'heretofore.' Perhaps we should read 'triply': cp. Hos 8 12 RV. **21.** RM 'Them that send thee,' i.e. his parents. Perhaps it ought to be, 'them that ask thee' (1 Pet 3 15).

27. If the debtor has failed to meet his obligation and the unlucky surety has no money, the creditors will seize the poor man's scanty belongings, even to his bed. **28.** Landmarks were of extreme importance when there were no fences : see on Ruth 2 22. **29. Stand before**] i.e. serve (1 S 16 21 1 K 10 8).

CHAPTER 23

1. RV 'him that is before thee.' Do not excite his contempt. **2.** Restrain your appetite. **3.** He invites you for his own purposes. **4. Cease,** etc.] i.e. desist from the attempt to be rich.

6–8. Estimate the niggard according to his thoughts, rather than his words. Your pleasant conversation is wasted labour.

10, 11. Read, 'The landmark of the widow.' God Himself is the *Goel*, the **redeemer**, the next of kin, who protects widows and orphans (Ex 22 21-23 Lv 25 25 Nu 30 12 Ruth 4 3,4 Jer 50 34). **16. Reins**] lit. 'kidneys.' Heart and kidneys were considered to be the seat of mental and spiritual life (Job 19 27 Ps 16 7 Jer 10 20 20 12). **18. End**] lit. 'latter end,' crowning the life. **21.** The **drowsiness** follows nights of intemperance.

27. In Galilee there are scores of ancient cisterns, bottle-shaped, into which one may fall and find it impossible to climb out. **28.** The miserable duplicities and 'treacheries' (RV) of an unholy passion.

29. 'Complaining'—not babbling—arises amongst boon companions. **Redness of eyes**] is due to dissipation. **30. Seek**] RV 'seek out,' try it thoroughly. **Mixed wine**] see on 9 2. **31. Giveth his colour**] i.e. sparkles. **Moveth itself aright**] RV 'goeth down smoothly.' **34. The midst of the sea**] i.e. on the high seas (30 19 Ezk 27 25). With a slight change in the text we get, 'in a great storm,' instead of, **upon the top of** a mast. **35.** The sot is represented as saying that the blows which were showered on him when drunk have neither injured nor pained him, and as longing to be fully awake from his drunken sleep in order to return again to his carousing.

CHAPTER 24

5. Read, 'A wise man is better than a warrior, and a man of knowledge than a man of strength.' **7.** When put on his trial 'in the gate' of the city, where public business was usually transacted, he has nothing to say (Mt 22 12). **10.** Adversity is sent to bring out your strength : if you are slack and irresolute in the day of trial you are proved to be a weakling. **11, 12.** Do not seek to evade your responsibilities (Gn 4 9 Jas 4 17). **13, 14.** Wisdom is as sweet as honey.

16–18. Seven] an indefinite, but considerable number. The wrath will now fall on you.

20. Candle] RV 'lamp' (31 18). **21, 22.** Take no part in conspiracies and revolutions.

23–34. is a short collection of sayings, with the heading, 'These also are sayings of the wise.'

26. *Every man,* etc.] 'He kisseth the lips': i.e. behaves as a true friend. **27.** Before 'building the house' (i.e. getting married), make proper provision. **28.** This is in opposition to the ancient law of retaliation (Ex 21 23-25 Lv 24 17-21 Dt 19 21).

PART 4 (Chs. 25–29)

CHAPTER 25
COURTS. QUARRELS

1-7. relate to kings and courts. **1.** By the **men of Hezekiah** the author of this v. doubtless means literary men at the king's court. These, he says, transcribed the following proverbs from some other collection or collections. It will be noticed that many of them have appeared earlier in the book. **2.** The works of God in history and nature are beyond us (Dt 29 29 Job 11 7 15 8 Isa 45 15 Ro 11 33). A king should be conversant with all that is going on (1 K 3 16 Job 29 11).

4, 5. Finer] a contraction of 'refiner,' as 'fining pot' (17 3) is of 'refining pot.' But we learn from LXX that the original reading was, 'And it cometh forth perfectly pure.'

6-8. Forth] RV 'forward': cp. Lk 14 11. The last words of v. 7 belong to v. 8, 'What thine eyes have seen, go not forth hastily to dispute about. For what wilt thou do in the end, when,' etc. **9, 10.** To disclose the discreditable secret even of an adversary brings one an evil name. **11.** The words appear to mean, 'A word spoken in season is golden fruit in silver carvings.'

13. Snow is used in the East to cool a beverage, as we use ice. **14. Of a false gift**] RV 'of his gifts falsely.' 'Much cry and little wool.' **18.** A maul is a mace, club, or hammer. **20.** The first clause should probably be omitted, and the v. should begin thus: 'Vinegar on a wound,' etc. The Heb. words for **nitre** and 'wound' are almost identical. To sing songs for one who is of a heavy heart is almost as cruel as to pour vinegar on a wound.

22. Heap coals of fire, etc.] i.e. make him burn with shame: cp. Ro 12 20 f. **23. Driveth away**] RV 'bringeth forth.' **26.** The fountain is troubled by the feet of animals (Ezk 32 2 34 18).

27. LXX reads, 'It is not good,' etc.: 'Therefore be sparing in words of commendation.' Too much flattery is like too much honey. **28.** 'Man who man would be must rule the empire of himself.'

CHAPTER 26
FOOLS. SLUGGARDS. TALKERS

1-12. The vv. refer chiefly to fools. **1.** The Palestinian seasons were more regular than ours (1 S 12 17). **2.** This is a contradiction of the idea that the deity invoked in a curse was bound to inflict it (Gn 27 33 Jg 17 2). The undeserved curse is compared to the aimless movements of a bird. **4, 5.** Answer or not, according to circumstances (Mt 12 30

Mk 9 39). **6.** 'He that sends a fool means to follow him.'

7. A fool is no more qualified to use a proverb than a lame man his legs. **8.** This may be read, 'As he that bindeth,' etc. It should not be 'bound' there. Or, 'As a bag of gems,' etc. (RV). That is not the place for them. **10.** The proverb seems to be directed against employing fools and strangers, but it is impossible to be sure how the Hebrew words at the beginning of the v. originally ran. **17.** RM 'A passing dog,' which does not know you. **18-28.** The evil effects of much speaking. **18, 19.** Sport to them is death to others. **21.** For **coal** read 'bellows.' **23.** A potsherd covered with the lead oxide which remains after silver has been refined looks valuable, but is worthless; so are 'fervent lips and a wicked heart' (RV): cp. Lk 22 47.

CHAPTER 27
SUNDRY OBSERVATIONS. AGRICULTURE

4. Envy] a husband's jealousy is meant (Song 8 6). **5, 6.** Men 'hide' (RV) love when they refrain from telling a friend his faults. An enemy will be 'profuse' (RV) in deceitful kisses: Judas kissed Jesus *much* (Mt 26 49 RM). **7.** The Spartan king told the tyrant Dionysius that the broth was nothing without the seasoning of fatigue and hunger. **8.** 'East, West, hame's best.' **9.** Sweetness of disposition is desirable when it arises, not from mere emotion, but from a settled purpose of the soul. **14.** Early and loud demonstrativeness is not stable. 'Evening words are not like to morning.'

16. The RV makes this difficult v. mean that he is attempting the impossible. **17.** The solitary grows dull. 'The best mirror is an old friend.' The Greek proverb is, 'One man. no man.' **19.** Judge another by yourself.

21. Estimate him by the reputation he wins. The Russian proverb is, 'A man's reception is according to his coat; his dismissal according to his sense.' **22.** 'Heaven and earth fight in vain against a dunce.' 'Fools grow without watering.'

23-27. A homily in praise of careful attention to the flocks and herds. The writer is not disposed to depreciate agriculture, as some of the later Jewish proverb-makers were. One of these says, 'Lay out your money in trade, and you will have flesh and wine daily; lay it out in land, and you will have but a bare subsistence.' **24.** Riches and honour (**the crown**) are fleeting: attention to field and flock are profitable. **26.** Sell your stock, and with the proceeds buy clothing and land

CHAPTER 28

OBSERVATIONS RELATING CHIEFLY TO SOCIAL LIFE

2. Cp. the many changes of rulers during the unsatisfactory period described in 2 K 15. **3.** The addition of a single Hebrew letter gives 'wicked' instead of **poor**. **4.** See the account of Phinehas (Nu 25). But the **law** here means religious and moral teaching in general. **5.** Cp. 1 Jn 2 20.

8. Unjust gain] RV 'increase.' The OT. denounced usury and interest because it was assumed that the borrower was a person in distress (Ex 22 25 Dt 23 19 Ps 15 5). That is quite a different matter from the lending on interest, without which modern trade could not be carried on.

10. The **evil way** is the one which ends in calamity. **14** He **fears** to do wrong. **18.** For **at once**, read, 'into a pit.' **21.** RM 'For a piece of bread a man will transgress.' 'I was taken by a morsel, says the fish.' **22. Evil eye**] avaricious.

27. Hideth his eyes] He 'passes by on the other side' (Lk 10 31, 32).

CHAPTER 29

KINGS AND FATHERS

3. Cp. the prodigal son (Lk 15). **6. His transgression** is the snare which catches and ruins him. **9.** If a wise man has a lawsuit with a fool the latter will exhibit the most diverse moods, but one thing he will not do, and that is to listen quietly. **10.** RM 'But the upright care for his soul.' **12.** They argue that truth does not pay. **13.** To the poor and 'the oppressor' (RV), to all classes alike, God gives the light of life (Ps 13 3 38 10). **17.** 'Better the child weep than the father.'

18. The **vision** of the prophet (Isa 1 1) and the instruction of the **law** deterred the people from 'casting off restraint' (RV). Morality requires the safeguard of religion.

19. Ecclus 33 24-29 recommends blows.

21. LXX has, 'He who has been luxurious from a child will become a servant, and in the end will be wretched.' **24.** This does not mean a man who goes shares in the booty, but one who knows the thief, hears the adjuration to testify (Lv 5 1), and fails to respond.

27. 'Birds of a feather flock together.'

PART 5 (Chs. 30, 31)

CHAPTER 30

THE WORDS OF AGUR

The simplest way of treating the title is to read as follows: 'The words of Agur, son of Yakeh, of Massa.' Then we may proceed, with RM, 'The man saith, I have wearied myself, O God; I have wearied myself, O God, and am consumed; for I am too stupid to be a man.' Nothing is known of Agur or Yakeh, and we can only say of these proverbs that they are unlike any that have preceded, and are evidently of later date. The grouping of objects in twos, threes, and fours reminds us of Job 5 19 Ps 62 11 Am 1, 2, and of later Jewish books, such as 'The Ethics of the Fathers' and the Talmudic treatise 'Horajoth.'

1-4. He lays no claim to the wisdom of which some boast: he does not profess to understand the 'Holy One' (RV), or to be Master of Nature (Job 38). The **garment** is the clouds. **5, 6.** Men should attend to the **word** of revelation, which is pure as refined gold; they add to its teachings at their peril.

7-9. Two desirable things. **8.** Each household slave had an allotted portion of food (31 15): God is here the head of the family, weighing out to me 'the bread of my portion' (RM). **9.** When in great distress men often blaspheme (Isa 8 21 Rev 16 9). But the meaning may be that he dishonours the name of his God by stealing (Ezk 36 20).

11-14. Four classes of detestable people.

15, 16. Read, 'The leech hath two daughters—Give, Give.' There is an Indian proverb: 'Fire is not satiated with wood, nor the ocean with streams, nor death with all the living, nor woman with man.' **17.** The unburied corpse will be devoured by ravens of the wadi and by vultures (RM): **eagles** do not eat corpses.

18, 19. Four mysterious things: cp. Wisd 5 10, 11.

19. Maid] lit. 'young woman.' **20.** This woman is an animal, in whom conscience has never been developed.

21-23. Four intolerable things.

23. The **odious** woman is the one who has long been rejected, but she secures a husband at last. **A handmaid, etc.**] Either she inherits from, or she supplants, her mistress: if the latter is meant, cp. Sarah's jealousy of Hagar.

24-28. Four animals, small but wise. **26.** The creature improperly called **coney** here and at Lv 11 5 Dt 14 7 Ps 104 18 is the Syrian 'hyrax,' an animal about the size of a rabbit, which feeds on grass, and lives in companies in the clefts of the rocks. **27. By bands**] cp. Joel 2.

28. The 'lizard' (RV) is so small that 'you can grasp it with your hands' (RM).

29-31. Four creatures of stately gait. **31.** Instead of **greyhound** LXX has the 'cock.' The fourth creature can hardly be the **king**: the passage is corrupt. **33.** Retain the same word throughout: pressing milk, pressing the nose, pressing strife. The 'curd' (not butter), which is a favourite and refreshing drink in the East, is made by shaking the milk about in a vessel of skin.

CHAPTER 31

THE MOTHER OF LEMUEL. THE EXCELLENT WOMAN

1-9. An exhortation addressed to king Lemuel by his mother, urging him to avoid women and wine. The latter leads to slackness and unfairness in the administration of justice.

1. Read the title thus: 'The words of Lemuel, king of Massa, which his mother taught him.' It is possible that the Massa of Gn 25 14 is meant. 2. The repeated What? appears to point to an inclination towards these excesses. Son of my vows] see 1 S 1 11.

3. Read, 'Give not thy love to those who destroy kings.' 4. 'More are drowned in the wine-cup than in the ocean.'

6. Of heavy hearts] read, 'the bitter in soul.' The Talmud treats this verse as the foundation of the pious custom of the Jerusalem ladies, who provided medicated wine to dull the pain of those condemned to death (Mk 15 23).

10-31. A complete alphabetical poem, each of its 22 vv. beginning with a letter of the Hebrew alphabet. It describes the perfect housewife, the virtuous, or, as the word rather means, the 'excellent,' the 'capable' woman. Industrious herself, she sees to it that her servants are the same. She sells the products of their spinning and weaving, and buys lands with the money. She watches over the conduct of the entire household. She is kind to the poor and gentle to all. Husband and children pay her honour as the prime source of all their welfare. She is self-respecting and dignified. Religion lies at the root of her character.

The ideal is a worthy one, well adapted to life in one of the towns of antiquity, where the men were engaged in public business (v. 23) and the women were supposed to attend to all domestic and business affairs. No doubt we should need some additional features for the portrait of the highest type of womanhood. This lady is not in the fullest sense the help-meet for man. She is too much the toiler on his behalf, too little the partner of his thoughts and plans. Tennyson's 'Princess' strikes a note which we cannot afford to miss:

'Let her make herself her own
To give or keep, to live and learn and be
All that not harms distinctive womanhood.
. . . .
Till at the last she set herself to man,
Like perfect music unto noble words;
And so these twain, upon the skirts of Time,
Sit side by side, full-summed in all their powers,
Dispensing harvest, sowing the To-be,
Self-reverent each and reverencing each,
Distinct in individualities,
But like each other ev'n as those who love.'

11. Spoil here means gain. 13. Read, 'worketh at that which her hands delight in.'

15. The portion is either the proper quantity of food or the allotted quantity of material for work. 21. Scarlet dye being costly, the garments would be of good material, thick and warm. 22. Read, 'She maketh for herself coverings' (7 16). There is no justification for the addition, 'of tapestry.' 25. 'She laugheth at the time to come' (RV), because she is prepared for anything.

26. On an Egyptian tombstone is the inscription: 'Peace was in the words which came from his mouth, and the book of the wise Thoth' (the divine scribe of the gods) 'was on his tongue.' A later Jerusalem proverb was: 'Gentleness is the salt which preserves wealth from corruption.' 30. Favour] i.e. charm and attractiveness.

ECCLESIASTES

INTRODUCTION

1. Title. The title 'Ecclesiastes' has been adopted by the English Version through the Latin Vulgate from the Septuagint (the earliest translation of the OT. into Greek from the original Hebrew), which gives it as the rendering of the Hebrew title *Koheleth*. It is, however, uncertain whether that word (derived from a root meaning 'to collect') denotes (a) a member of a collective body, i.e. an assembly (Gk. *Ecclesia*, whence the title 'Ecclesiastes'), implying that the writer was one of a body of persons who thought and discoursed on the subjects engaging attention in the book, or (b) one who collects or convenes an assembly, 'the great orator' which RM substitutes for 'the Preacher' in 1 1.

2. Authorship and Date. Was Solomon the author of this book, as 1^1, if taken literally, implies ? We may safely reply, No, for (a) the original Hebrew throughout the book shows traces of verbal forms, idioms, and style later than Solomon's time ; (b) the writer says, 'I .. (not 'am,' but) was king' (1^{12}) ; (c) he refers apparently to a series of kings preceding him (1^{16}) ; (d) he tells us that he was king 'in Jerusalem,' thus pointing to a date later than the Disruption on Solomon's death, when there began to be kings outside Jerusalem ; (e) Solomon would not have drawn with his own hand a picture of moral evils (cp. 4^1 5^8 8^9 $10^{6,7,16}$), for which he would be held himself in large measure responsible ; (f) there is no reference to features characterising Israelitish history in Solomon's day. Besides all these reasons for placing the book later than Solomon's time, it bears distinct traces of the Greek culture established throughout the civilised world after the break up of the Empire of Alexander the Great (died 323 B.C.). Such traces, e.g. appear in (a) the writer's advice to enjoy the present life (2^{24} 3^{22} 5^{18} 9^7) ; (b) his comments on human weakness and disorder (5^8 $7^{7 8 9, 14}$ 9^{16} $10^{16 f.}$), on the vanity and brevity of life (e.g. 1^{2-17}), and on the common destiny of human and brute creation ($3^{18 f.}$) ; (c) his references to man's inventive capacity (7^{29}), and (d) his remarks on the phenomena of nature ($1^{5,6}$).

Thus the book is decidedly later than the days of Solomon. On the other hand, an acquaintance with its language seems to be shown in the apocryphal book called 'Ecclesiasticus,' written circ. 180 B.C. We may, therefore, with confidence place Ecclesiastes earlier, though probably not much earlier, than that date.

But if belief in the traditional authorship is on these grounds to be put aside, we need have no scruple in at once rejecting the notion that the writer, whoever he may have been, had the smallest intention of fraud or deceit in thus assuming Solomon's character for literary purposes. Such personation is nothing more than has been practised alike in ancient and modern times with perfectly straightforward motives. Plato's dialogues or the speeches in Thucydides (to take two of the best known cases in classical literature) are examples of language put into the mouths of great men, not as having been literally spoken by them, but as expressing the sentiments which in the writer's opinion under given circumstances might fairly be attributed to them.

We may notice that the claim to personate the great king, such as it is, is more conspicuous in the earlier than in the later part of the book. The thought of Solomon gradually fades from the writer's mind, and he proceeds to give us undisguisedly his own attitude towards life and its problems in words that do not even mean to suggest the Solomon of Israelitish history.

3. Design of the Book. The main purpose of the author is evidently to offer men counsel, the result of his own experience, as to the principles on which they shall order their lives. The Divine Creator, he is sure, carries on the world in accordance with a plan, but that plan is hidden from us. What rule, then, shall we follow ? Man, God's creature, by nature aims at happiness. How shall happiness be attained ? A glance around us shows that it does not go simply by merit ; for instances are patent where virtue suffers and vice is prosperous. What path, therefore, shall we follow to gain our quest ? Shall it be wisdom, or unrestrained pleasure, or devotion to business, or the pursuit of wealth ? None of these will avail. Our rule must be to alternate wholesome labour with reasonable relaxation, assured that, although the ways of God's judgments are obscure, all well-doing shall in the end be shown forth as approving itself to the Divine Judge.

Many a devout reader, turning over the pages of this book, has been conscious of a sort of uneasy wonder that it should form part of the Bible ; so different is its general tone from that of the sacred volume as a whole. For—

(a) Throughout the whole book the gaze is turned inwards. Existence is represented as a puzzle beyond our powers to solve. In other OT. books the writer feels that he is showing us God's hand in His dealing with individuals or with nations. But here God is a God who 'hides Himself,' and we must grope on in the dark in our endeavour to become acquainted even with 'parts of His ways.'

(b) Elsewhere, specially in the prophetical and devotional books, God is not only a King and moral Governor, a Creator and a Judge, but He is tender, willing to forgive the penitent, ready to succour and sustain. But to the writer of this book God is only the Judge, austere, needing care in approach, omnipotent, and righteous. The element of love in His character is hidden. That He is, in the full sense of the word, the Divine Father, is seen dimly or not at all. The book thus shows the low-water mark of the religious thoughts of God-fearing Jews in pre-Christian times.

(c) Human existence is looked at mainly on its darker side. It is at once monotonous and vain. There is nothing new anywhere. Its good things, even if attained, are fleeting. Close upon the enjoyment of them the 'days of darkness' follow, and they 'shall be many.' The book thus emphasises in a way not found in the rest of the OT. the lack of a clear vision of a future life which had not yet been brought to light by Christ.

But these very peculiarities, which have caused perplexity to devout readers, form, when rightly viewed, a signal part of the credentials of the book as a constituent part of the Divine Library,' which, through its various elements, historical, prophetical, devotional, ethical, was destined in God's providence to appeal to the needs of successive periods of man's existence. To the question characteristic of much of the thought of the present day, 'Is life worth living?' the book gives the best answer which a Jew, at once influenced by heathen philosophy, and placed amidst political and social miseries, could give. There is a wide-spread habit of mind, called by the convenient name of pessimism, which takes a gloomy view of human existence, either because of the miseries of the world in general, or because of the deficiencies to be found in man's nature. Now it is in Ecclesiastes, and Ecclesiastes alone, that this tendency is dealt with upon anything resembling the lines in which it expresses itself in the working of men's minds in our own generation.

It is, then, in a very real sense a present day question, which is here treated. If thoughtful people are now saddened by the sorrows and sufferings of the world, and by the evil that goes unpunished, so too was 'the Preacher.' But the point for us to notice here is that, unlike many now, he retained his reliance on God's justice, although devoid of our mainstay, viz. the Christian faith which was then unborn. The forms of philosophical culture familiar to him were not unlike some of our own, while one special form of argument which we can use was unavailable in his day. The steady growth of sympathy with every kind of suffering and need, the widening sense of human brotherhood—this practical result of the fuller realisation of the meaning of Christ's teaching and life constitutes for us a special form of argument on the side of the Christian faith. He had no such help to retain his hold upon the God of his fathers. Nevertheless, we mark that his faith, however imperilled at times, did not fail him. How much less, then, should ours fail to whom God has been revealed as a God of love through Christ Incarnate, and the Sacrifice for sin.

4. **Analysis of Contents.** Although the general aim of the book is clear, the connexion of thought is not always easy to follow. There are many breaks, repetitions, and deviations into side-issues. The following is an outline of the contents.

Introduction. Man's life is saddened by its brevity, and by the purposeless and monotonous repetition which meets him on all sides (1^{1-11}). Various methods may be tried in order to obtain relief, viz. the pursuit of wisdom (1^{12-18}), of enjoyments and of art (2^{1-11}). Of these wisdom is the noblest, and yet all of them are but vanity (2^{12-23}). The best course is to alternate toil with frugal enjoyment; though even this also is vanity (2^{24-26}). At least, however, we can see that God is a God of order (3^{1-8}); yet man's insight into God's plan is extremely limited. The best course, therefore, is to combine the enjoyment of God's gifts with uprightness of life (3^{9-15}). True, man and beast alike return to the ground; nevertheless, if not here, then hereafter wrongs shall be righted (3^{16-22}). The ills inseparable from both poverty and success cut men off from the helpful companionships of life (4^{1-12}). Wisdom prevails over the highest rank; but even so there is nought that is lasting (4^{13-16}). In religious life ignorance and hypocrisy prevail (5^{1-7}), in political and social matters cruelty and avarice (5^8). Greed of gain is unsatisfying and in the end futile (5^{9-17}). Let a man, avoiding these, make tranquil enjoyment his aim (5^{18-20}). Length of life only increases man's liabilities to suffering; yea, though he be possessed of all possible advantages (6^{1-6}). The only wise course is to use what we have, avoid all vain grasping at that which is beyond our reach, and accept the limitations which the very name man suggests (6^{7-12}). Advice for the conduct of life (7^{1-14}). Avoid extremes whether of asceticism or excess (7^{15-18}). Wisdom is rare, yet needed by all. Righteousness, seldom found among men, is absolutely unknown among women (7^{19-29}). Wisdom is needed by none more than those who have to do with kings' courts (8^{1-5}). Many as are the disorders and disappointments of life, it must still be that God will in the end show Himself a just Ruler. Make, therefore, a cheerful use of the good things of life, while convinced that His ways are 'past finding out' (8^{6-17}). Death is universal, and what lies beyond is in the darkest shadow (9^{1-6}); nevertheless, combine innocent enjoyment with diligent work (9^{7-10}). The wise, the strong, and the rich are all the puppets of chance. One foolish slip may bring about much havoc (9^{11}–10^1). There is practical wisdom in patient and quiet regard to duty (10^{2-7}). The incautious reformer brings untoward results to himself (10^{8-11}). The fool's talk, unlike that of the wise man, is wordy and wearisome, and also abortive (10^{12-15}). A boy-ruler is a disaster to the kingdom; but the prudent will submit in silence (10^{16-20}). Fulfil plain duties, even if success be dubious. While the powers of youth remain, let life, though fleeting, be as bright as may be (11^{1-10}). The service of God will not bear postponement to the winter of life (12^{1-7}). The outcome of the whole book is summed up (12^{8-14}).

CHAPTER 1
ALL IS VANITY

1–11. The writer describes himself. He declares that all things are transitory and without result, whether they be the works or the life of man, or the natural forces of heat, air, and water. Language cannot do justice to nature's wearisome sameness. The oblivion which overtakes all.

1. Preacher] see Intro. §§ 1, 2.

2. Vanity of vanities] lit. 'breath of breaths'; the form of expression being a Hebrew way of indicating the superlative degree. Of all fleeting things existence is the most fleeting. The same figure is used in Pss 62⁹ 144⁴ of the brevity of man's life. The word **vanity**, occurring thirty-eight times, strikes the keynote of the book. All things living and otherwise bear the stamp of the transitory.

3. What profit] Man toils ; but even granting that he gains some tangible result, he cannot retain. **4. The earth abideth**] Man is so far from being lord of the earth, that it survives ever fresh generations of its inhabitants, and so by contrast brings out more clearly the brevity of their existence. **5. Hasteth to his place**] The sun, on the supposition of his apparent motion across the heavens from E. to W. by day, returns eastward beneath the earth by night.

6. The wind, etc.] We may render more closely thus : 'Going toward the south, and circling toward the north ; circling, circling goeth the wind, and on its circlings returneth the wind.' The sameness involved in the constant renewal of its changes of direction is brought out by the wording. The 'circling, circling,' the changing, at once endless and monotonous, marks here too an emptiness of aim. **7. Unto the place**] The writer supposes that the salt water percolates by underground fissures, getting rid of its salt on the way, and so through hidden channels returns to the sources whence it had set out.

8. All things *are* **full of labour**] RM 'all words are' too 'feeble' to set forth the case, so vast is the subject. **9. The thing**] History has been repeating itself from all time, and will do so evermore.

10, 11. Is there] He calls on any one who may doubt his word to point to something which is really new. The only reason that events strike us as new is because that which has been is swept into oblivion. Previous generations have no existence for us, and we in like manner shall have no existence for those who come after us.

12–18. The writer, availing himself of his status, recounts how he had tested the various aspects of life in their aims and results, but all to no profit. Everything is perverse or de-

fective. Great as were his acquirements, the result is *nil*, nay, worse than nothing.

12. Was king] see Intro. § 2.

13. My heart] We should say my 'mind,' but the heart was considered by the Jews to be the seat of the intellectual powers as well as of the emotions. All *things*] the different ways that men work, and their hopes and fears in so doing ; their circumstances, pains, pleasures, feelings, aims. Perhaps, he says to himself, men of various trades, modes of life, surroundings, will enlighten me, or help me to bear my burden. **This sore travail, etc.**] Men who are endowed with any activity of mind cannot but be interested in all human endeavour ; and their researches and enquiries, unsatisfying though they be, are a part of God's order.

14. Vexation of spirit] RV 'striving after wind': cp. Hos 12¹. The satisfaction that might have been expected from these studies is not to be attained. Air itself is not more elusive to the grasp. **15. Crooked**] for the phrase here cp. Isa 40⁴. The world is disordered, and there is no cure discoverable.

Numbered] The required numbers are lacking, which were needed to make up the sum of human action, and no amount of skill in arithmetic can supply the deficiency.

16. Great estate] RV 'Lo, I have gotten me great wisdom above all,' etc. (omitting 'am come to great estate and '). He has had exceptional advantages in gaining wisdom, and has made the most of his opportunities. Yet even so he has failed. What hope, then, can there be that others will solve the problem that remains dark to him ? All *they*] see Intro. § 2. **Wisdom and knowledge**] knowledge, the possession of facts ; wisdom, skill in employing them. **17. And folly**] He tries whether the study of folly may perchance give him some grasp of its opposite, viz. wisdom. But this too only serves to confirm him in his general conclusion. **Vexation of spirit**] see on v. 14.

18. Much grief] Sir Isaac Newton spoke of himself as a child picking up a few pebbles on the shore of the wide sea of knowledge. So the more the veil is lifted, the wider is seen to be the extent of that which is still unknown. Bodily and mental exhaustion, sleepless and futile endeavour—this is the picture which concludes the writer's sketch of his quest after the highest good in the shape of wisdom.

CHAPTER 2
EPICUREANISM AND WISDOM ALIKE
PROFITLESS

1–3. The writer makes enjoyment his quest, while aware that it is folly, and avoiding excess in a philosophic spirit.

1. I will prove thee with mirth] Wisdom, whether sought in nature or in human things, having proved unsatisfying, he now makes a cast in another direction. Increase of knowledge is increase of sorrow; but what, if he were to try the fascination of enjoyment?

2. It *is* mad] He knows all the time that no solid comfort will be the issue. Mirth is a brief madness: cp. 7⁶. **3. To give myself unto**] RV 'to cheer my flesh with.' **Yet acquainting mine heart**] RV 'mine heart yet guiding me.' Whatever indulgences he may yield to, he is careful not to drift, and so vitiate his experiment. Through all he retains a prudent self-control.

4-6. He tries another method, viz. culture and art.

4. I made me great works] The occupation of mind and exercise of taste may help him in his quest. **Houses**] Personating Solomon, he thinks of the palaces built by that monarch (1 K 7¹⁻¹²): op. the cities mentioned in 2 Ch 8⁴⁻⁶. **5. Orchards**] pleasure ground; RV 'parks.' **6. Pools**] essential in a land where water is scarce, as well as pleasing in effect. **The wood that bringeth forth trees**] RV 'the forest where trees were reared.'

7-11. He acquires slaves, herds, and flocks, and precious metals, musicians, and inmates of the harem. Without being the slave of these delights he yet indulges in every desire of his heart, but, as before, all is vanity.

7. Got] RV 'bought.' **8. Silver and gold**] cp. 1 K 9²⁸ 10²,¹⁴,¹⁵,²⁷. **Peculiar treasure**] The specialities and rarities of each country found their way to him. **Of kings and of the provinces**] cp. 1 K 10¹⁵, where Solomon receives precious things as tribute from the kings of Arabia and the governors of the country. **Musical instruments, and that of all sorts**] RV 'concubines very many' (but RM agrees with AV). The meaning of the Heb. is obscure. Probably, however, the reference is to the grosser sort of sensual enjoyments: cp. 1 K 11¹⁻³.

9. I was great, and increased] now in splendour and luxury, as before in knowledge. In closing the account of this experiment he expresses himself as he did at the end of his endeavour to find satisfaction in wisdom (1¹⁶).

10. My portion of all my labour] At least he had the zest of joys obtained through toil or ingenuity. **11. Vexation of spirit**] cp. 1¹⁴. None of these could satisfy the cravings of his spirit.

12-17. Wisdom is to folly as light to darkness; yet the same end awaits both. Life, therefore, is nothing but a weariness. The cycle of experiments being completed, there is nothing to do but to hark back to the first of them, and to consider knowledge and its opposites.

12. What *can* the man *do*] None can hope to attain or approach to the favourable conditions under which Solomon carried on his quest

of the highest good. **After the king?** *even that which hath been already done*] RM 'after the king, even him whom they made king long ago?' the writer now letting go his personation of Solomon, and looking back at him as an historical personage.

13. Wisdom excelleth folly] for, at any rate, in seeking it there is no fear of self-reproach. **14. *Are* in his head**] Unlike the fool, the wise man can see what and where to choose. **15. Why was I then more wise?**] rather, 'what was the use of troubling myself to surpass others?' **16. *There is* no remembrance**] not meaning that no memories of famous men had survived them, but that such cases were too rare to be of any solace against the practical ills of life. **17. Vexation of spirit**] see 1¹⁴.

18-23. Besides, no one knows what his heir may do.

20. Went about] RV 'turned about,' i.e. looked back sadly at the absence of the permanent element in the labours of my life past. **21. Equity**] RV 'skilfulness.' **Hath not laboured**] The heir acquires good things without earning them. This too shows the dismal tangle of human affairs. **22. Vexation**] RV 'striving' (but RM as AV).

24-26. Whatever enjoyment there is in life is from God, and He thereby favours the righteous, not the sinner.

24. Eat and drink] enjoy in moderation the good things of life: cp. Jer 22¹⁵. **25. Hasten**] RV 'have enjoyment.' **More than I?**] RM 'apart from Him?' i.e. it is only through God's ordinance that simple bodily pleasures can change to joy the sadness which is the natural outcome of the pursuit of knowledge. This acknowledgment shows that the writer, after all, clings to the faith of his fathers. The rendering of AV (based on a slightly different rendering of the Heb.) would mean, 'Who is in a better position than I to testify that all good comes from God?'

26. *That he* may give] The sinner's possessions pass to the just man, to be used aright: cp. Job 27¹⁶,¹⁷ Prov 13²². **Vexation of spirit**] see on 1¹⁴. The sinner's toil and expectations are alike great; his joys *nil.*

CHAPTER 3

THE PRACTICAL IDEAL. ACCEPTANCE OF THE UNIVERSAL SCHEME

1-15. God is a God of order.

The problem which the writer has set himself is not yet solved. He has found that wisdom, culture, pleasure, are all good, though, even if we combine them, there is still something lacking, and they will not explain the mystery of existence. In continuing to seek for a rule of life that shall lead him to the highest good, he reminds himself that God is a God of order, and wisdom lies in adapting ourselves to that order. It is at a time appointed by the Creator that the individual life begins and ends, and the same is true for all the events intermediate between birth and death which make up the sum of human existence. All our undertakings are thus subject to His unchangeable decrees.

2. To plant .. to pluck up] i.e. to begin and end a career. **3. To kill**] perhaps, to make war or peace. **To break down**] e.g. to make a way for what shall better meet the needs, secular or spiritual, of a new generation.

5. To cast away stones] Probably the whole v. means peace and war, the former expressed by leisure to clear away stones from a vineyard (cp. Isa 5²), and to indulge in family joys, the latter by the action of a hostile force spreading stones over fertile lands (cp. 2 K 3¹⁹), and by the claims of military service. **6. To get .. to lose**] to add to, and to forego gains.

7. To rend .. to sew] to act in a way that involves the sundering of friendship .. to knit hearts together again.

9–14. Man's work, ignorant though he be, is fulfilling God's design. Let him aim at pleasure and uprightness, while the whole scheme of things from first to last is in the hands of God.

9. What profit] how can he be sure that he has found the right season?

11. The world] rather, as RM, 'eternity.' Though man's powers are bounded, he is capable of recognising the grand and immeasurable scope of God's ordering of all things. His mind reflects the universe. This is better than, taking AV, to explain it as referring to man's natural love of living in the world. **So that**] RV 'yet .. so that.'

12. No good .. a man] RV 'nothing better for them than.' **14. That men should fear**] God's unchanging ordinances are for the purpose of calling forth man's reverence. We must trust Him with our future. **15. Requireth**] RV 'seeketh again; bringeth back in an unchanging sequence: cp. 1⁹.

16–22. Men wrest judgment; but God shall right all wrongs, though how, is beyond our ken.

16, 17. The judges of his time troubled the writer. Yet in God's purposes, either here or in the future, unrighteous decisions shall be reversed.

18. Manifest] RV 'prove,' i.e. sift or test whether they will be upright, in spite of the knowledge that death comes to them no less than to the beasts. **Beasts**] RV 'but as beasts.'

19. That which befalleth .. them] RM 'The sons of men are a chance, and the beasts are a chance.' They are the sport of hazard alike in birth and in death. **20. All are of .. again**] 'Nature the womb and tomb of all' (Lucretius).

21. That goeth] RV 'whether it goeth upward .. downward,' thus neither denying nor affirming that there is an intrinsic difference in the soul of man. Christ had not yet come to bring 'life and immortality to light.' Yet contrast the brighter hope of 12⁷. **22. There is nothing better**] If man is no better off than a beast, let him at least learn, like them, to enjoy the present. **Bring him**] RV 'bring him *back*,' to see the results of his work.

CHAPTER 4

VICISSITUDES OF LIFE. 'OH, THE PITY OF IT!'

1–3. The mass of human suffering and the absence of pity are such that better off are the dead and still more the unborn.

It is not only through God's ordinance, but by reason of man's perversity, that he is disturbed and perplexed by the social disturbances around him. The world is full of trouble. The weak are oppressed by the strong.

4–6. Success involves envy. Better be secure and at peace. **4. Right**] RV 'skilful,' RM 'successful.' **For this .. neighbour**] RM 'it cometh of a man's rivalry with his neighbour.' Effort is stimulated by competition, but then what man has gained by toil is marred by the hostility of the less fortunate. **Vexation of spirit**] see on 1¹⁴. **5.** Even the fool who idly runs through his substance is for the time better off, for he is at peace.

7–12. Two more ills of life are covetousness and loneliness.

8. There is one *alone*] The avaricious has none to share his wealth or to succeed him; yet his toil is insatiable.

9–12. The advantages of companionship are shown by four illustrations, three of which are such as have special fitness in the mouth of an Oriental writer. Two companions in travel find their partnership of value, whether (*a*) they are walking upon a rough and steep path, or (*b*) sleeping at the end of the day in a narrow chamber with unglazed windows, or (*c*) in a sudden encounter with thieves, who have availed themselves of the darkness of the night to dig through the earthen walls in search of valuables. Lastly, (*d*) a threefold cord is strong to resist. **12.** RV 'And if a man prevail against him that is alone.'

13–16. A man may rise from the lowest to the highest station by wisdom; yet even so there is no permanence.

13. Child] RV 'youth.' **14. He cometh**] i.e. the poor and wise youth. **Whereas also .. poor**] RV 'yea, even in his kingdom he (the child) was born poor.' Thus in RV the subject of the whole v. is the youth, whereas in AV two persons are spoken of, viz. the prisoner who rises through wisdom to be a king, and the king who becomes a beggar.

These vv. have been taken to refer to actual events, perhaps in the writer's own day ; but no satisfactory reference for them has been found. Thus they had best be understood as a general statement. **15. With the second, etc.**] RV 'that they were with the youth, the second, that stood,' etc. **16.** *There is*] RV 'there was.' *Even* of **. . them**] RV 'even of all them over whom he was.' The sketch is continued ; there is an endless stream of those who crowd to pay court. **They also**] RV 'yet they,' etc. Oblivion will soon wipe out all.

CHAPTER 5

DISHEARTENING OUTLOOK ON LIFE

1–8. Disorders in the religious, in the political world. In the earlier part of this c. the writer turns from secular to religious matters. He points out the irreverence which belongs to worship offered without due thought. **1. Keep thy foot**] cp. Ps 119 101 Prov 1 15. Either be silent, or use thoughtfully framed words of prayer, as contrasted with hasty offerings combined with ungodliness of life. **And be more ready to hear**] RV 'for to draw nigh to hear is better.' **3. A dream cometh**] excessive distractions by day bring disordered visions at night. Even so excess in words shows folly in him who utters them. *Is known* by] RV ' with a.'

4. Defer not to pay it] A vow is not essential, but once made it is binding : cp. Dt 23 21-23. Vows had an important place in the religion of Israel, as we see from Gn 28 20 Nu 6 2 f. Jg 11 30 1 S 1 11 Mk 7 11 Ac 18 18 21 23 23 21. Cp. also the rule of the Pharisees (Mt 5 33), which, however, does not add the caution to think before speaking. **6. Suffer not, etc.**] i.e. suffer not your hasty vow to lead you into wrongdoing. **The angel**] either the angel who, according to Rabbinic belief, presided over the sacrifice (this is, however, somewhat out of harmony with the tone of the book), or the priest, to whom the person who makes the vow addressed himself. RM has ' messenger of God' (see Mal 2 7). **An error**] He has brought an offering of inferior value, or gives a frivolous excuse for the non-fulfilment of the vow. **And destroy**] Punishment will ensue. He here recognises that the world is no mere machine : there is a righteous Judge. **8. Violent perverting**] The cruelties of a satrap, or pasha, were part of a system extending through every grade. Each watches (regardeth) with jealousy those below him, and seeks his opportunity for plunder. *He that is* higher than the highest regardeth] For highest RV has ' high.' The supreme ruler is no exception. *There be* higher than they] those who in an Eastern court practically

bear rule over the nominal governors. The whole v., however, is obscure with perhaps an intentional ambiguity, and it is possible to explain it as meaning that there is a chance of getting justice by appeal from a lower to a higher tribunal, yea, even to the king himself.

9–17. The evil of avarice.

9. RM 'But the profit of a land every way is a king that maketh himself servant to the field ' ; because a ruler whose taste lies in that wholesome direction is unlikely to be given to amassing wealth : cp. 2 Ch 26 10. **10, 11.** Avarice is attended by two evils : (*a*) it is never content ; and (*b*) responsibility, trouble, and expenditure increase in the same proportion. **14.** *There is* **nothing in his hand**] Through a reverse of fortune the wealth, which should have descended to the son, has disappeared. The case is thus the converse misfortune to that of 4 8. There the riches were to be had, but the heir was lacking.

18–20. Riches are not inconsistent with happiness. **20. For he shall not much remember**] He will not be overtroubled by the knowledge that these pleasures are fleeting, and that life itself is uncertain.

CHAPTER 6

LIFE AN ENIGMA

1–6. Riches will not secure happiness **1. Common among**] RV 'heavy upon. **2. A stranger**] because he has no child to whom to leave it. The Easterns have a dread of being without a child, to keep the parents' name in remembrance : cp. Gn 15 2. **3. And his soul**] RV 'But his soul.' Misfortunes may render him miserable, though he has abundance of children and of years of life. Examples are Rehoboam (2 Ch 11 21) and Ahab (2 K 10 1). *That* **he have no burial**] The greatest importance was assigned to this tribute of respect : cp. Jer 22 19. **4. He**] RV 'it,' i.e. the untimely birth : so in v. 5. **6. Yet hath he seen**] RV 'and yet enjoy.' **To one place ?**] The grave embraces all alike.

7–12. The conditions of man's life are essentially uncertain. Man's aim is in the main directed to the satisfaction of his bodily desires. Yet at best this cannot be perfectly attained. The wise, no less than the fool, the poor equally with the rich, finds imperfect satisfaction in life.

8. That knoweth to walk before the living ?] In other words, that has the skill so to conduct himself as to earn respect in the eyes of his fellows. **9. Better is**] To enjoy what we have is better than yearning after things which elude our grasp. **Vexation of spirit**] see on 1 17.

10. That which hath been] RM 'Whatsoever he be.' **Is named already**] RV 'the name thereof was given long ago.' **Man**] RM 'Heb. *Adam*.' Thus the sense of the v. is, 'From the beginning man's nature has corresponded to his bodily frame. He is known as man (Adam), because he was made out of the earth (Heb. *Adamah*), and he must accept his position: cp. Isa 45 9 Ro 9 20.

11. Things] RM 'words,' perhaps the profitless discussions common in the philosophical schools (e.g. on fate and free-will).

12. Man can neither judge what is really for his happiness in life nor foresee the future fate of that in which he may be interested.

CHAPTER 7
PRACTICAL APHORISMS

1-6. Things useful to remember in life. The writer has just warned us that we cannot rely on either the present or the future. We can, however, guide ourselves in the conduct of life by bearing in mind useful truths. These he now proceeds to give.

1. Precious ointment] This was a much-prized luxury in the East (cp. Ps 45 8 Am 6 6 Mt 26 7 Lk 7 37), but to be held in esteem is still better. There is a play on words in the Heb. (*Shem*, 'a name,' and *Shemen*, 'ointment'), which can scarcely be reproduced in English. Plumptre suggests, 'A good *name* is better than good *nard*.' **The day of death**] Even in this respect, however, a man's life cannot be judged happy till its end is reached.

2. The living will lay *it* **to his heart**] Oriental mourning is elaborate and prolonged. Hence there is abundant opportunity for those who take life in earnest to obtain a hearing for their counsels.

6. As the crackling of thorns] Frivolity is like the fire which the wayfarer lights from the thorns that he has gathered, and which goes out as suddenly as it has sprung up, leaving only dead ashes: cp. Ps 58 9.

7-14. Ill-treatment may well provoke anger, yet pause and exercise control. Accept the present with submission. Wisdom and money are both valuable, but wisdom is the better of the two. All things are in the hands of God.

7. Oppression] RV 'extortion': sufferings inflicted on the weak by the strong. **Mad**] RV 'foolish.' **The heart**] RV 'the understanding.' To be condemned by one whose decision is determined by a bribe causes a man to lose all power of calm judgment. **8. Better** *is* **the end**] The connexion seems to be this: the danger of being warped in our view by outward circumstances is such a real one that we cannot pronounce an unqualified judgment upon anything till the end is reached. **10. Thou dost not enquire wisely**] We have not the materials for a just comparison.

11, 12. Some men through the attainment of wisdom or wealth have reached a vantage ground

in the battle of life. Of the two wisdom is to be preferred, as possessed of a quickening power which money cannot bestow.

11. Them that see the sun] i.e. the living. **12. A defence**] lit. a shadow: cp. Isa 30 2,3 32 2.

13. Who can make *that* **straight**, etc.] If trouble be God's will for us, we cannot change it. **14. Consider**] Ask yourself what you may learn from it. **Over against**] RV 'side by side with.' Both run through the course of human life. **To the end,** etc.] So that we cannot forecast the part which the one and the other will play in the future.

15. The anomalies of life.

15. A just man *that* **perisheth,** etc.] It was perplexing enough that there should be but one end to the righteous and the wicked (3 19). It is more so when we see the just man cut off by an untimely death and the evil-doer enjoying a green old age.

16-18. Extremes, whether of asceticism or of excess, are bad.

17. Over much wicked] The expression seems strange, as though moderate wickedness were allowable. But the sense is probably as follows: the author had just said, 'Be not righteous over much,' perhaps alluding to the over-scrupulousness of the Jews in observing ceremonies, etc.: cp. Mt 23. He may now be meeting the thought of those who would reply, 'There is no fear that we shall exceed in that direction,' and he warns them that there is an opposite kind of excess to which they are more prone. Excess in either direction, and folly, tend to disturb and shorten life.

18. From this] RV 'from that.' Whatever the nature of the experience to which God subjects you, take cognisance of the evil as well as of the good. That in using such language he is not condoning sin is clear from the last part of the v. If only he fear God, he shall come forth unscathed.

19-22. Be wise enough not to be over-sensitive to criticism, since you also indulge in it.

19. Wisdom strengtheneth] There is a power greater than brute force.

23-28. Wisdom eludes the grasp. Sweeping condemnation of the female sex.

24. That which is far off] RV 'That which is is far off.' 'That which is,' viz. God's world-plan, all the phenomena of the world and of human life, can only be realised by us in fragmentary form. **25. Madness**] As in 2 12, wickedness and madness are closely connected.

26-28. The writer gives us the general result of his experience of human character. Among men he has found but one true friend. The other sex he condemns without exception. We cannot tell why, ignorant as we are of the circumstances of his life. We must, however, remember that the position of women in the

East has always been favourable to the growth of habits of frivolity, cunning, and licentiousness; also that elsewhere (c. 9 : cp. perhaps also 4⁸) he modifies this judgment. It remained for Christianity to bring woman back to her rightful position as a helpmeet for man.

29. Many inventions] From the Fall in Eden there has been a continued display of manifold ingenuity to thwart God's benevolent purposes for man.

CHAPTER 8

KINGS' COURTS NEED WARY WALKING

1–17. Be discreet in relation with a ruler. God's purpose must be carried out. His rule must be righteous, though this is often not seen in actual life. God's ways are just, and past finding out.

The writer now enters on a subject which it would not have been wise to treat too plainly, viz. the need of showing tact in dealing with the arbitrary power of an absolute monarch. No part of the book is more decidedly at variance with the Solomonic authorship than this c.

1. Who *is*, etc.] Which of his readers has skill to see the meaning of his language, intentionally left obscure ? **Boldness**] RV 'hardness.' Skill of this kind refines the features.

2. Oath of God] Ptolemy Soter, king of Egypt (305–285 B.C.), having transplanted certain Jews from Palestine to Alexandria, caused them to swear allegiance to his successors. It is possible that the reference here may be to that event. If so, we have an indication of the place and time of writing.

3. Be not hasty] Do not rashly throw up office. **Stand, etc.**] RV 'persist.' Do not take sides with the ruler's open or covert enemies. The expression, however, in the Heb. is obscure, probably of set intention.

5. Whose keepeth, etc.] Submission is a practical guide in life. **Time and judgment**] The wise man will bide his time, hoping that justice will be done in the end.

6. To every purpose] God's purpose must eventually prevail, and retribution, if deserved, come even on the highest. **Therefore**] RV 'because.' **Misery**] RM 'evil.' Wickedness, like a lead, bears the bad man down to his doom.

8. Spirit] RM 'wind,' which it is God's prerogative to control. **No discharge**] Under the Jewish law exemption from service in war was granted in certain cases (Dt 20⁵⁻⁸). In the battle with death no such release may be had.

9, 10. These vv. are expressed in such guarded language that to us they are scarcely intelligible. The line of thought is probably as follows. Although death swallows up the wicked in the end, nevertheless the writer's wide experience ever brings back to his mind

cases where a man has exercised misrule to the hurt of his fellow-men. And then these evil men have received a stately burial, and been gathered to their fathers with all due observances. On the contrary, those who had lived virtuously have been dishonoured, expelled from the Temple and the Holy City, and dismissed from the minds even of the people among whom their good deeds had been done. Both honour and oblivion had been misplaced. **10. Who had come**] RV 'and they came' to the grave. **And gone .. so done**] RV 'and they that had done right went away from the holy place, and were forgotten in the city.'

12. I know that it shall be well] The writer, after all, is one of those who 'keep' (or at any rate revert) 'to the sunny side of doubt.' The rule of final justice, he says, must hold.

14, 15. But now it is often not so. Therefore temperate enjoyments, joined with labour, are the most abiding possession of man : cp. 2²⁻⁴, etc. **16, 17.** These problems are beyond man's power.

16. For also, etc.] RM 'how that neither by day nor by night do men see sleep with their eyes.'

CHAPTER 9

LIVE WORTHILY WHILE YOU MAY

1–3. The future is in God's hands. Good and bad alike must die.

1. Considered in] RV 'laid to.' **Declare**] RV 'explore.' **No man .. before them**] RV 'whether it be love or hatred, man knoweth it not ; all is before them.' Whether God's dealings with them shall be such as to suggest His favour or displeasure is unknown, because the part of life not yet traversed cannot be penetrated. **2.** There seems no discrimination in the lot of men.

4. A living dog] Life has at any rate one advantage over death. The miserable hope that either positive happiness, or at least better fortune than in the past, may lie before them. The saying receives its point from the contempt with which a dog is regarded in the East. **5. The living know**] A conscious recognition of the inevitable is better than the oblivion which belongs to death.

7–10. Couple enjoyment and work.

8. White] as symbolical of cheerfulness (2 Ch 5¹²), and perhaps here, as later (e.g. Rev 3⁴ᶠ.), of purity. White was constantly worn at feasts. **Ointment**] Sweet fragrant unguents for perfuming the person. **10.** Be not half-hearted in any duty. The present alone is yours : cp. 'in diligence not slothful' (Ro 12¹¹ RV). In St. Paul's day the darkness had been lighted up, and this precept consequently transformed in the words which close the great Resurrection chapter (1 Cor 15⁵⁸).

11–18. Results must be left to God. Wisdom is better than strength, yet it is despised.

17. Are heard in quiet] RV 'spoken in quiet are heard.' There are times when men's voices are hushed to listen to wise counsel. **18. One sinner, etc.**] One man's evil deed may bring to nought wide-reaching purposes of good.

CHAPTER 10
PRACTICAL ADVICE TOUCHING LIFE'S PUZZLES

1–8. Cultivate wisdom and tact, specially in the dangers that attend upon courts, but also in ordinary operations.

1. Dead flies, etc.] This v. really belongs to the end of c. 9. As a few of the poisonous flies abounding in hot countries would render valueless a whole jar of perfume, so a man by a slight admixture of error may render nugatory much of his own skilful or upright conduct.

2. At his right hand .. left] A wise man's mind directs him to appropriate conduct. A fool is sure to do the wrong thing. He is *gauche*. **3. Saith to every one**] He advertises his folly by his speech. **4.** The advice of 8³ is repeated. St. Peter (1 Pet 2²⁰⁻²³) is able to add to the same precept a new and inspiring motive. **Yielding pacifieth great offences**] RM 'gentleness leaveth great sins undone' : both sides will be saved from committing serious misdeeds. **6, 7.** He hints that through the ruler's error of judgment, as he gently puts it, the wrong people have received promotion.

8, 9. Prudence is needed in many applications. Otherwise you may dig a pit to entrap your enemy, and then fall into it yourself ; or, in pulling down a fence, if you are not heedful, one of the serpents lodging in the crannies may bite you. Similarly the quarrying of stones and the felling of timber call for watchfulness. **10.** If you are not wise enough to act with tactful sagacity, you must compensate for this by extra force.

11. RV 'If the serpent bite before it be charmed, then is there no advantage in the charmer.' The snake charmer, who has neglected to use his voice with proper skill in order to effect his object, will have cause in his own person to discover that the mere fact of his proficiency will not avail him.

12–15. Description of folly and its results.

12. *Are* **gracious**] there is beauty in his talk. **Will swallow up himself**] he often will have to eat his own words. **14.** A fool talks confidently and fluently of the future, as though it could be foreseen. **15.** He wearies himself with ineffectual attempts, because he is incapable of carrying on the most ordinary affairs of life.

16–20. Much depends on the ruler. Whatever he be, he must be reverenced.

16, 17. The case referred to can hardly be an imaginary one. Ptolemy Epiphanes succeeded his father Philopater as king of Egypt at the age of six years (205 B.C.), and during his minority there was much strife between the Syrian and Jewish factions in Egypt, and, on the part of some in high places, licentious indulgence all day and every day (**eat in the morning**). **18.** When the timber-work of a house is neglected, it gives way. So will it be also with the fabric of the state. **Droppeth through**] RV 'leaketh.' **19.** If a man is wealthy enough to pay his way, there need be but little stint to the pleasures, lawful or unlawful, in which he may recklessly indulge. But in proportion to the height of the position he occupies, will be the injury done. **But**] RV 'and.' **Answereth**] i.e. provides. **20.** Nevertheless silent submission to authority is the only safety for an ordinary person.

CHAPTER 11
LIFE AFTER ALL IS WORTH LIVING

1–3. Fulfil the duty of beneficence, knowing that results are in the hands of God.

1. Cast thy bread, etc.] show kindness, even where a return is least to be expected. A blessing in some sort, although it may be long delayed, will result. There is perhaps a reference to the sowing of seed on irrigated land. **2. Give a portion, etc.**] be not niggardly or calculating in the bestowal of favours. You know not when you may need them yourself. **3.** The fixed laws by which the world is governed. **Where the tree falleth, etc.**] There is no reference here to the state of man after death.

4–6. Man's knowledge is limited, while God's purposes are inscrutable. Winds, clouds, and the whole ordering of nature are His. Submit to His decrees, and do thy daily part, leaving the issue to Him.

7–9. Existence has its pleasures, but its span is brief. Youthful enjoyment is commended, provided it be such as need not dread God's judgment. **8.** RV 'Yea, if a man live many years, let him,' etc. The remembrance that life is brief is to be itself a motive for enjoyment while it is possible.

9. Rejoice, O young man] Youth is naturally cheerful. Be it so. But there must be present that which shall check excess, viz. the knowledge that the Divine Judge will mark and punish sinful indulgence ; not always in this life (for cp. 8¹⁴), but, if not, then beyond the grave. **10. Childhood and youth**] RV 'youth and the prime of life.' **Vanity**] i.e. fleeting.

CHAPTER 12

IN LIFE REMEMBER DEATH AND JUDGMENT

1. The Creator is to be remembered in youth. When the powers of mind and body are failing, it will be too late.

1-7. Commentators have differed much as to the interpretation of this passage. It has been taken by many as a description of the gradual failing of one bodily organ after another till death supervenes. In that case we may explain vv. 2 f. thus : The **light** grows dim to the aged sense, and reason is dulled and ceases to illuminate. The old man weeps in his distress, and the troubles that draw forth those tears ever recur (v. 2) The limbs tremble ; the arms, once **strong**, are become bent and feeble ; the **few** teeth that are left no longer do the work of mastication ; the eyes grow **darkened** (v. 3). The means by which the processes of nourishment and sensation have been carried on, in other words, the body's means of communication with the outer world, are **shut** ; the voice is **low** and feeble ; the slightest sound breaks in upon rest (or, 'the bird shall rise with a cry,' i.e. the voice assumes the piping treble of age), and music no longer gives pleasure (v. 4). Fancied terrors haunt the soul, and bar the path. The sleeplessness, of which the **almond tree** (the Heb. name for it meaning ' the early waker,' cp. Jer 1[11]) is a symbol, becomes the old man's lot ; the lightest weight is **a burden**, and nothing rouses the flagging appetite, because he is setting out on his journey to the tomb, and the hired **mourners** are already awaiting him ; even before the actual dissolution comes (v. 5), and **the golden bowl** of the lamp of life is **broken**, and **the silver cord**, by which it is suspended, **loosed** ; and **the pitcher**, which has gone so oft to draw at the fountain of life, is shattered, and so is **the wheel**, which works the rope and bucket to raise water from the deep-sunk well (v. 6). Some refer these last two clauses respectively to the action of the lungs and of the heart.

Others, however, have explained these vv. as setting forth a description of a storm and the alarm which it produces, under which figure are indicated the signs which accompany death. The following is a sketch of that interpretation of the passage which sees in it a description of the time specially fatal to aged persons in Palestine, that is to say, the last few days of winter, marked by a violent tempest ;

the picture being continued by a description of the spring time of nature, which, however, brings no returning vigour to those who are in the extreme winter of their days.

There comes on the storm of exceptional severity, which concludes the broken weather of winter (v. 2). Servants and masters are alike dismayed. The grinding women cease from their work, and the ladies of the harem, stricken with fear, no longer idly gaze from the lattices on the passers by (v. 3). Ordinary work has ceased, and the house is shut up. But soon the last and greatest storm of winter is over, and the advent of spring is welcomed by the bird-note, to imitate the sweetness of which is the despair of the professional daughters of song (v. 4). Nature is joyous, but the aged are full of suspicion that danger lurks about and above their path. And yet there is on every side evidence of renewed power. The almond tree blossoms ; the locust crawls out from its shelter ; but the aged are not in sympathy. They are beyond the influence of appetising stimulants ; for they are approaching the grave, and the hired mourners are near (v. 5). Then follow the figures of speech, already touched on, indicating bodily dissolution (v. 6).

8-13. Eulogy of the Preacher and his method. Summary of his teaching.

This is the Epilogue, and was probably added by a different hand. It answers to a commendatory preface in the case of a modern book.

10. Acceptable words] He feels that proverbs were a form of speech that will find favour.

11. The words of the wise, etc.] Leaders of thought in each age have the gift of fixing their words securely in the memories of their disciples (**goads . . nails**), a gift which comes to them from Him who is the supreme Guide and Disposer of the affairs of men (**one shepherd**). **Masters of assemblies**] RM ' collectors of sentences.'

12. Be admonished] Jewish teaching was largely oral. Gentile philosophers, on the other hand, committed their speculations to writing, sometimes, e.g. Epicurus, to the extent of many volumes. Among such it was easy to be bewildered and wearied.

13-14. The writer's conclusions. There is a moral Governor of the world. Here or hereafter there shall be a recompense, good or evil.

THE SONG OF SOLOMON

INTRODUCTION

1. Contents. Two points strike every careful reader of the poem : the extreme difficulty of determining its meaning as a whole and deciding as to the class of poetry in which it is to be placed ; and the fascinating beauty of its details. The former is evident on a mere glance at the attempts which have been and still are being made to define its scope and character. The Jews admitted it into the Canon on the supposition that it depicts the relations between Jehovah and His people. But for that interpretation the doubts which gathered round it and were not authoritatively discouraged till the Synod of Jamnia (90 A.D.), would never have been dispelled. The Christian Church followed the same general line, explaining the Song as an allegory of the love between Christ and the Church or Christ and the soul. In this sense St. Bernard wrote no fewer than eighty-six sermons on the first two chapters. The headings of chapters and pages in the English Bible express the same idea. In all ages, however, amongst both Jews and Christians, there were thinkers who perceived that the theme is not divine love but human. In course of time the poem came to be regarded by many as a drama. The adherents of this view were divided as to the plot. Some took it to be the story of Solomon's love for a country maiden, whom he raised to the rank of queen, himself for a while adopting a simpler mode of life, and although he eventually reverted to luxury and polygamy the poem remained as a protest against undue self-indulgence. The other and more plausible version of the dramatic theory is that the maiden was carried off to Solomon's harem and exposed to the blandishments of the monarch, who was seconded by the ladies of the court. But she continued faithful to her shepherd-lover, to whom, in the end, the king magnanimously restored her. Another opinion has recently been maintained with much confidence and has found considerable acceptance. According to it we have to do neither with drama, opera, nor unity of any kind, but with a collection of love-ditties, partly composed for, and all suitable for use at, marriage festivals. The title 'king' ($1^4, ^{12}$ 7^5) is explained by the fact that in Syria bride and bridegroom play the part of queen and king during 'the king's week,' the first week of married life. Seated on a throne which is erected on the village threshingfloor, they receive the homage of the whole country-side. Nuptial songs and dances are executed by the bridesmen, the chorus of male and female bystanders, and the wedded pair. A plausible account can thus be given of the abrupt transitions, the apparent lack of connexion between the parts of which Canticles is composed. But the whole of the facts are not quite explained. Amidst all the admitted inconcinnity there is an equally undeniable unity. The recurrence of certain expressions (2^7 3^5 8^4 : 2^{17} 4^6 8^{14}) is doubtless meant to mark breaks in what is conceived of as a single poem. The sentiments and style are too similar throughout to have sprung from divers writers. Nor is this to be met by the assertion that we have before us a collection of folk-songs which resemble each other because they all belong to the same period and locality. Canticles reads like the work of an author who composed amatory poems on various occasions and subsequently wove them into a garland of verse. Perhaps some of the shorter pieces have fallen out of the places which he assigned to them : this has been forcibly argued with reference to $8^{11f.}$ $8^{13f.}$ But when we remember the irrelevance, from our point of view, of the verses which are often sung in Eastern lands to-day we shall be slow to deny that the singers and hearers of the Song of Songs understood allusions and perceived a fitness which are hidden from us. We shall be compelled to admit that there is no definite line of advance, no initial simplicity, followed by complication, rounded off by a dramatic *dénouement*. Matters are as far advanced at 1^4 2^4 as at 8^4.

Yet the following brief **analysis** shows that the book falls into what may fairly be called seven cantos. Canto I, 1^2–2^7 : A rural bride declares her ardent affection for her husband, deprecates the townswomen's criticism of her beauty, desires to know where she may find her beloved. The lovers praise each other. Canto II, 2^8–2^{17} : She relates a visit he once paid her and the invitation he addressed to her. Canto III, 3^1–3^{11} : Her thoughts of him and search for him by night. An interlude. Canto IV, 4^1–5^1 : He depicts and eulogises her charms. He is ready to escort her through the most dangerous regions. Her invitation and his response. Canto V, 5^2–6^9 : A waking dream, with painful ending. She describes her lover. He has entered his garden. Once more he dilates on her loveliness, which surpasses that of the ladies belonging to the royal harem. Canto VI, 6 10–8 4 : A short dialogue betwixt these ladies and her. Again he praises her and she replies in terms of love and desire. Canto VII, 8 5–8 14 : An inquiry. The bride reminds her husband of their early experiences, celebrates the might and spontaneity of love, remembers how carefully her brothers guarded her. He sets forth her preciousness in figurative language. Then he begs her to sing. She closes the poem with a repetition of 2 17.

2. Value. At the first blush we are surprised to find in the Bible a poem on human love. But we must remember that the mutual attraction of the sexes is of God's ordaining. So far from being intrinsically evil, it contains for both parties an immeasurable possibility of blessing. And the love which is here sung is ordered, regulated, legitimate. The imagery is too suggestive, and the description of physical charms too minute, for our taste, but it was produced by an Oriental for Orientals. More reticence does not necessarily imply truer purity. No doubt we should have welcomed a clear recognition of the intellectual, ideal, and spiritual side of marriage, but it would be a mistake to argue that the poet was a stranger to this better part. And such love as 8 7 describes is based on broader foundations than those supplied by mere sensuous charms alone.

Again, whilst it is admitted that the poem was not meant to be understood either typically or allegorically, all true human love is, in the Apostle's sense of the word, a mystery (Eph 5 28-33) which carries the Christian's mind upward to the union of the soul with Christ. Sensuous thoughts and images are never to hold us prisoners. The earthly is a stepping-stone to the heavenly. Spenser tells us that, having in the green time of his youth composed two Hymns in praise of Love and Beauty, ' and finding that the same too much pleased those of the like age and disposition, which being too vehemently caried with that kind of affection, do rather sucke out poyson to their strong passion, then hony to their honest delight,' he afterwards resolved, ' by way of retractation, to reforme them, making, in stead of those two Hymnes of earthly or naturall love and beautie, two others of heavenly and celestiall.' In this he is a safe guide—

' All the glory and the grace of things,
Witchcraft of loveliness, wonder of flesh,
Fair symmetry of forms, deep harmonies
Of line and limb—are but as shadows cast
From hidden light of Beauty and of Love.'

It would be a dull eye that missed the beauty of the poem. Its author responded immediately to every charm of Nature or of Art. Above all was his soul attuned to Nature. He

carries us along with him into the open air, to the vineyards, the villages, the mountains. He awakes us at daybreak to catch the scent of the forest trees, to gather the apples and the pomegranates, to listen to the grateful plash of falling waters. How he loved the flocks of wild pigeons, the crocuses, the fields embroidered with lilies ! His verse is fragrant with the breath of spring. And the soul of artistry within him was moved by the pomp of the court, the magnificence of a royal litter, the glittering whiteness of an ivory tower, the proud display of warriors' shields, the ornaments and costly dress of women. No other poem in the Bible can be compared with this. It still merits the title, prefixed by the men who inserted it in the Canon, ' The Song of Songs,' the most beautiful, the one that most nearly corresponds with the ideal of its class.

3. Authorship. But whilst we admit that the title is a fitting one, we must remember that it has no authority to determine date or authorship (see v. 1). The internal evidence is conclusive against Canticles having been written by Solomon, and points to a date subsequent to the exile, not earlier than the 4th cent. B.C. The language alone suffices to prove these points : it is of the very latest strain of biblical Hebrew.

4. The following are improvements on the Authorised Version :—

CHAPTER 1

4. RV ' Make mention of,' for **remember.**
RV ' Rightly do they love Thee,' for **the upright,** etc.
6. RV ' Swarthy,' for **black.**
7. RM ' Wandereth,' for **turneth aside.**
9. RV ' A steed ' (better still, ' a mare '), for **a company of horses.**
13. RM ' Bag,' for **bundle.** ' That lieth,' for **he shall lie.**
14. RV ' Henna-flowers,' for **camphire.**

CHAPTER 2

1. RM ' Autumn crocus,' for **rose.**
4. Lit. ' House of wine,' for **banqueting house.**
5. RM ' Cakes of raisins,' for **flagons.**
7. RM ' Gazelles,' for **roes.**
RV ' Awaken love, until it please,' for **awake** *my* **love, till he please.**
9. The sense requires that she gaze forth at him, not he at her.
13. RV ' Ripeneth,' for **putteth forth.**
RV ' The vines are in blossom, they give forth their fragrance,' for **the vines** *with* **the tender grape give a** *good* **smell.**
14. RV ' Covert of the steep place,' for **secret** *places* **of the stairs.**
15. RV ' Vineyards are in blossom,' for **vines** *have* **tender grapes.**
16. RV ' Feedeth his flock,' for **feedeth.**

CHAPTER 3

6. ' What ' is better than **Who**.

7. RV ' It is the litter of Solomon,' for **his bed, which** *is* **Solomon's**.

9. RV ' Palanquin,' for **chariot**.

10. ' Inlaid with ebony from,' for **paved** *with* **love for**.

CHAPTER 4

1. RV ' Thine eyes are as doves behind thy veil,' for **Thou** *hast* **doves' eyes within thy locks**. RV ' Lie along,' for **appear**.

2. RV ' Ewes that are newly,' for *sheep that are even*. RM ' Are all of them in pairs,' for **every one bear twins**. RV ' Bereaved,' for **barren**.

3. RV ' Mouth . . behind thy veil,' for **speech . . within thy locks**.

4. RM ' With turrets,' for **for an armoury**.

6. RV ' Be cool,' for **break**.

9. RM ' One look from,' for **one of**.

12. RM ' Barred,' for **inclosed**. ' Garden,' for **spring**.

13. RM ' Paradise,' for **orchard**. RV ' Henna,' for **camphire**.

15. RV supplies ' Thou art.'

CHAPTER 5

1. RM ' Of love,' for **O beloved**.

2. RV ' I was asleep,' for **I sleep**.

3. ' Tunic,' for **coat**.

5. RV ' Bolt,' for **lock**.

7. ' Wrapper,' for **veil**.

12. RM ' Sitting by full streams,' for **fitly set**.

14. RM ' Topaz,' for **beryl**. ' Lapis lazuli,' for **sapphires**.

16. RM ' Speech,' for **mouth**.

CHAPTER 6

4. ' Awe-inspiring as bannered hosts,' for **terrible as an army with banners**.

10. RM ' Pure,' for **clear**.

11. RV ' Green plants,' for **fruits**. RV ' Budded,' for **flourished**.

12. RV ' Set me *among*,' for **made me** *like*.

13. RV ' The dance of Mahanaim,' for **the company of two armies**.

CHAPTER 7

1. RM ' Steps,' for **feet** ; ' in sandals,' for **with shoes**. ' The turnings ' or ' windings,' for **the joints**.

2. RV ' Mingled wine,' for **liquor**.

5. RV ' Held captive in the tresses thereof,' for **held in the galleries**.

8. RV ' Breath,' for **nose**.

12. RV ' Whether the vine hath budded, *and* its blossoms be open,' for **if the vine flourish,** *whether* **the tender grape appear**.

13. RV ' Doors,' for **gates**.

CHAPTER 8

1. RV ' And none would despise me,' for **Yea, I should not be despised**.

2. RV ' Spiced wine, Of,' for **spiced wine of**.

5. RV ' I awakened,' for **I raised**.

6. RM ' Hard,' for **cruel** ; ' Sheol,' for **the grave**. RV ' Flashes,' for **coals** ; ' a very flame of the LORD,' for **a most vehement flame**.

7. ' Would any man despise him,' for **it would utterly be contemned**.

9. RM ' Battlement,' for **palace**.

10. RV ' Peace,' for **favour**.

12. RV ' Shall,' for *must*.

13. RV ' For,' for **to**.

CHAPTERS 1 2–27

THE ARDENT AFFECTION OF THE LOVERS

2–7. Songs of the bride : her enquiry and his answers.

2. Love] The original has ' loves,' i.e. expressions of love, repeated kisses and embraces.

3. Ointments] Orientals have always been passionately fond of perfumes. The literatures of Egypt, Greece, and Rome abound in references to them : in the Bible see Ps 23[5] 45[7,8] Prov 7[17] 27[9] Lk7[46] Jn12[3]. A modern traveller writes : ' Arabs are delighted with perfumes ; the nomad housewives make treasure of any they have, with their medicines ; they often asked me, " Hast thou no perfumes to sell ? " ' The ' poured-out ' unguent gives forth its fragrance : even so is the beloved's name praised of many.

4. The king, i.e. the bridegroom, has brought the bride into his house, and she, freed from any taint of envy, nay, and with an ingenuous pride, mentions the love with which others ' rightly ' (RV) regard him. Some scholars prefer to read, ' Bring me, O king,' etc. **5.** In speaking of herself as **black** and ' swarthy ' (RV), she is acknowledging herself to be a country girl : in the current songs of Palestine town-girls are called ' the white ' ; those of the country ' the black.' For **Kedar** see Gn 25[13] Isa42[11] 60[7]. The Arab **tents** are often made of black goats' hair or black woven stuff. If our present text is correct the maiden claims a beauty of her own, comparable to that of the richly embroidered curtains in Solomon's palace. But possibly the reference may be to the Salamites, who followed the Kedar-enes in occupying the territory S. of Palestine. Her face has been bronzed by the sun's ' looking upon her,' as the prince of Morocco, in the ' Merchant of Venice,' speaks of his complexion :

' The shadow'd livery of the burnish'd sun,
To whom I am a neighbour, and near bred.'

6. Her mother's sons have made it impossible for her to avoid this, treating her with that arbitrary tyranny which male relatives so often display in the East. ' I have known an ill-natured child,' says Doughty, ' lay a stick on the back of his good cherishing mother ' : cp. 1 S 17[28]. **Her own vineyard,** her complexion, she was forced to leave uncared for. **7.** Running to her lover, she would fain spend the siesta hour, the hot midday, with him. Failing to find him, she would have to wander aimlessly (RM) beside the other shepherds, in whom she took no interest.

8. With kindly banter he bids her lead out her little **flock** of female **kids** and take her chance of finding him. **9–11.** It would not occur to us to compare a woman to a beautiful mare : but an Eastern at once appreciates the simile. In Damascus ' the mare comes before wife and child ' : she may be worth £40,000, and there really is no more beautiful creature. The Egyptian horse was once prized much as the Arab now is (2 Ch 9 28).

10. With the ' string of jewels ' (RV) compare a song which may be heard now in Syria :

> From above, Abu Tabba, from above, Abu Tabba,
> Put golden coins upon her, and under her neck a
> string of pearls.'

The necklace usually worn consists of three rows of pearls. Lady Burton says of a Samaritan woman : ' Upon her head she wore a coat of mail of gold, and literally covered with gold coins, of which a very large one dangled on her forehead. She wore diamond and enamelled earrings, and a string of pearls coquettishly arranged on one side of her head in a festoon.'

12–14. The **king**, i.e. the bridegroom, is reclining on his divan or couch, and the bride's presence is as delightful to him as the scent of the costly oil of the Indian nard (Mk 14 3). The odoriferous **myrrh** is a gum, which exudes from the bark of a spiny shrub growing in Arabia and India. Women wore little flasks of this on their breast. **14.** The henna (RV ' the flower of paradise ') has fragrant yellowish white flowers, growing in clusters like grapes. It is still found in the wadi of En-Gedi, the most delightful spot on the W. shore of the Dead Sea, an oasis of luxurious vegetation. The sentiment of these vv. is thus reproduced in a song still popular in Palestine :

> ' Make of me a silver necklace,
> And toss me about on thy breast.
> Make of me a golden earring,
> And hang me in thine ear.'

15. He compares her **eyes** to **doves.** Eastern women spend much pains on their eyes, painting them round with kohl to add to their apparent size and increase their expressiveness. And the comparison of maidens to doves is exceedingly common in the popular poetry :

> ' Lovely girls are there, like a flock of doves.'

16, 17. She looks forward to their union in the sweet rural district, amongst the **cedars** and the **firs**. It is as in the bower which Milton found in the earthly Paradise :

> ' The roof
> Of thickest covert was in woven shade,
> Laurel and myrtle, and what higher grew
> Of firm and fragrant leaf ; on either side
> Acanthus, and each odorous bushy shrub
> Fenc'd up the verdant wall ; . . . . . .
> Here in close recess,
> With flowers, garlands, and sweet-smelling herbs,
> Espoused Eve deckt first her nuptial bed.'

CHAPTER 2

1. She compares herself to a simple wild flower, the crocus (RM) of **Sharon**. The plain, which extended from Joppa to Cæsarea, was proverbial for its flowers (Isa 35 2), and travellers continue to revert to this feature : ' We constantly had reason to admire the faint harmonious colouring of the wild flowers on the untilled plain. Cæsarea was surrounded by fields of the yellow marigold. Other flowers were also conspicuous—the red pheasant's eye, in some cases as big as a poppy ; blue pimpernels, moon-daisies, the lovely phlox, gladioles, and high hollyhocks.'

2. He will not suffer her to depreciate her own value : compared with other women she is a **lily** among **thorns** (Prov 31 29). The Hûleh lily, in the north of the Holy Land, grows in the midst of thorns, which lacerate the hands of the flower-gatherers. The soil near Bethlehem, in the S., is enamelled with lilies and covered almost everywhere with dwarf thorns.

3–7. In this strife of mutual compliments she now likens him to the beautiful, flowering, fruit-bearing **apple tree,** which gives a welcome shade, gratifies the sense of taste, and is to Orientals a symbol of love. **4.** He has brought her to a ' house of wine ' (RM), a place of feasting and enjoyment, where the **banner** floating over them was not merely inscribed with the word Love, but was **Love** itself. The entire description is figurative, and if the language were not sufficient to indicate this we should be driven to the conclusion by the fact that it was not considered decorous for women to be present at banquets (Esth 1 12 Dan 5 10, 23). In Egypt the house where a marriage-festival is in progress is marked by rows of flags and streamers stretched across the street. **5.** She begs her friends to sustain her with cakes of pressed raisins (RV), such as were given to those who were fainting for hunger (1 S 25 18 30 12 2 S 6 19 Hos 3 1). **7.** And they are to leave her and her beloved for the present undisturbed by the festal dances and songs. The request is repeated 3 5 8 4, and on each occasion is evidently meant to mark one of the main divisions of the poem. The adjuration, **by the gazelles** (RM), **and by the hinds of the field,** is suggested by the beauty and the timidity of those graceful creatures.

CHAPTERS 2⁸–2¹⁷

A VISIT AND AN INVITATION

8-13. After an interval she relates one of his visits to her home. He comes swiftly and easily; **hills** and **mountains** are no obstacle. He stands behind the **wall** of her mother's house, and she gazes at him through the **lattice**, for she has seen his approach from afar. The unglazed, latticed windows of an Oriental house admits air and a softened light, allow those within to see out, and prevent their being observed from outside. **10.** He would have her accompany him to the open country. **11.** It is the right season. The **winter** and the **rains** are over, for in that climate there is a cloudless sky from the beginning of May to the end of October.

12. It is the time of **flowers:** 'Everywhere this day the earth was beautifully green, and carpeted with flowers. The air was fresh and balmy and laden with the sweet scents of spring... The sky was so blue, the mountains and plains looked so beautiful, the birds, insects, the wild flowers, the fresh balmy breeze, the sweet smells, and gentle sun, the black tents, all combined to make one glad to be alive.' 'Come here in spring, O traveller!' Lady Butler says, 'and not in the arid, dusty, burnt-up autumn.'

13. The early **figs** are growing spicy; the **vines** are all blossom and fragrance. It is the season when a young man's mind turns lightly to thoughts of love. Even in our cold England the poet sings—

'"Twas when the spousal time of May
  Hangs all the hedge with bridal wreaths,
And air 's so sweet the bosom gay
  Gives thanks for every breath it breathes;
When like to like is gladly moved,
  And each thing joins in Spring's refrain,
"Let those love now who never loved;
  Let those who have loved love again."'

14, 15. He begs her to lay aside her coyness, for she is concealing herself, like a dove in an inaccessible mountain gorge. Where there is no village pigeon-house the wild doves of Syria build in hollows of the steep **rocks.** At the monastery of St. Saba 'one sees, sailing on outstretched wings from out of those caverns, flights of the fair blue pigeons.' **15.** She sings him the little ditty concerning the **foxes** that ruin the vineyards: any song, on any theme, would have pleased him, and short poems that seem to have no special relevance to the occasion are still in common use amongst the peasants and the Bedouin.

16, 17. She declares their unchangeable, mutual devotion, and bids the shepherd, who pastures his flock in the fields bright with lilies, come to her.

17. At midday the heat is overpowering—

'All round the coast the languid air did swoon,
Breathing like one that hath a weary dream.'

But at sunset the day 'breathes' (RM); a cool breeze blows, and the shadows gradually disappear (Gn 3⁸ Job 14²). The gazelles (RM) descend at night to the plains to feed; they leap and run safely on **the mountains of Bether.** The meaning of the last word is not clear: it may be the name of a locality not mentioned elsewhere in Scripture; it may signify 'the cloven mountains'; it may be the same as the *bĕsamim* (= spices) of 8¹⁴, or, as RM suggests, the spice *malobathron*.

CHAPTER 3

NIGHT THOUGHTS AND AN INTERLUDE

1-4. There is a charming lightness of touch and quickness of movement in the story she tells, and it is all the more interesting for our having to supply the prosaic connecting links. 'The Unrest of Love' is an apt title. We can only understand it as a maiden's dream. **2.** The **broad ways** are what we should call the squares; wide, open spaces by the city gates and elsewhere. **4.** The '**mother's house**' is the women's apartments, into which a strange man dare not enter.

6-11. It is possible that this is a song of the bridegroom's companions on the morrow of the wedding, when the throne is set up for the bridal pair. But more probably it is a kind of interlude, intended to convey the sense of contrast between the simple, fearless life of the happy pair, and the luxurious but anxious state which the most magnificent of Hebrew kings had kept. The singer sees in imagination King Solomon's procession. He makes us hear the questions and remarks of the crowd, as in the last scene of Shakespeare's 'Henry the Fourth.' **6.** One man asks, 'What is this litter (RV) that is coming out of the wilderness, the uncultivated grazing land?' The **pillars of smoke** are caused by the burning of sweet perfumes. **Frankincense** was an aromatic gum-resin obtained from balsamic plants which grow in Arabia and Eastern Africa. The **powders of the merchant** are powdered perfumes. The question of v. 6 is answered in vv. 7, 8, and possibly we have a third speaker in 9, 10. In any case, another word is here used for 'litter' (RV), a word which came afterwards to be specially employed for the litter in which the bride was carried in procession.

9. King Solomon's palanquin (RV) is made of the costly woods of Lebanon, cedar and cyprus. **10.** The **pillars** supporting the canopy are of silver, the arms of gold, the seat (RV) covered with a costly **purple** fabric. And, as the Hebrew words for **love** and 'ebony' are very similar, the closing part of the description may originally have run, 'inlaid with ebony from the daughters of Jerusalem.' **11.** The women of the chorus are to fancy themselves meeting the procession and feasting their eyes with the sight of the king in all his glory. At a Jewish wedding both bride and groom wear **crowns**: in Syria, at the present day, the bride wears one; in Bulgaria she has a crown of alloyed silver.

CHAPTERS 4¹–5¹
DESCRIPTION OF HER CHARMS. HER INVITATION

1–7. This short poem belongs to the class which the Arabs call *wasf*, in which the bride's charms are described: they are sung while she is being dressed, or when she exhibits herself in her nuptial array, or on the day subsequent to the ceremony. Here is one that is still to be heard in Palestine:

'Oh, her eyes are like the line of ink drawn by the
   stylus,
And her hair, when she dyed it with henna, like
   birds' feathers ;
Her nose as the handle of a glittering Indian sword ;
Her teeth like hailstones, yea, even more lovely ;
Her cheeks like rosy apples of Damascus ;
And her breasts lovely pomegranates, hanging on
   the tree ;
Her neck like that of a scared antelope ;
And her arms staves of pure silver ;
And her fingers sharp-pointed pens of gold.'

1. The maiden's **eyes** are here compared to **doves**, peeping out from behind the veil (RV). As is usual with Syrian brides her **hair** is not braided, but hangs loosely down, like a **flock** of black **goats** which graze along the slope of a mountain, and look as though they were suspended from it (RV). **2.** Her **teeth** are white, regular, a perfect set. Her cheek resembles the rich colours of the pomegranate. She has a swan's **neck**, a graceful, slender **tower**, hung round with ornaments, as the **tower of David** —whatever that may have been—was hung with shields (1 K 10 ¹⁶, ¹⁷ 2 K 11 ¹⁰ Ezk 27 ¹¹ 1 Mac 4 ⁵⁷). For sweetness she may be compared to **mountains** on which odoriferous shrubs abound.

8. The idea conveyed by this abrupt and obscure v. seems to be that she will be perfectly safe, even in regions remote from home, and where many dangers lurk, if only her lover is at hand. His presence ensures happiness and security. The exclamation, 'Look,' etc., reminds us of a modern traveller's remark concerning the southern part of Lebanon : 'I have travelled in no part of the world where I have seen such a variety of glorious mountain scenes within so narrow a compass.' **Amana** may perhaps be the name of what is now called Jébel ez-Zebedâni, below which is the source of the river Amana or Abana (2 K 5 ¹²). On some inscriptions of the Assyrian kings the range of Anti-Libanus is called Ammana. Here, and at 1 Ch 5 ²³, **Shenir** is distinguished from **Hermon.** The highest point of Hermon,

Jébel el-Shêkh, 9,166 ft. high, is visible from the greater part of Palestine.

9–15. He praises her in ecstatic terms. In the ancient Egyptian love-songs the lovers call one another 'brother' and **sister.** One glance from her eyes, one pendant hanging from her **neck**, is enough to steal his heart, as it is said of Judith (16 ⁹), 'Her sandal ravished his eye.'

10. The smell of her garments is like the fresh and healthy odour of the cedars, or, as we in England should say, of the pinewoods: cp. Gn 27 ²⁷ Ps 45 ⁸.

11. **Honey and milk** are most highly prized amongst Orientals (Isa 7 ¹⁵).

12. She is as a **garden** barred (RM) to strangers.

13. Her charms are like the young plants in an **orchard of pomegranates,** protected from the depredations of wild beasts.

14. The **saffron** is the autumnal crocus, the dried flowers of which are employed in medicine, dyeing and perfumery. The thick, creeping rootstock of the **calamus** is pungent and aromatic. The resin of **aloes** is used in the preparation of incense. **15.** The 'flowing' (RV) **streams,** etc., reminds us of the many streams which run into the sea between Tyre and Beyrout.

16. Accepting his figurative description of her, she bids him welcome. The colder north wind and the warmer south are naturally mentioned : not the east, which brings drought, nor the west, which carries moisture from the sea.

C. 5. **1.** The bridegroom's reply. He bids his friends follow his example : 'Drink, yea, drink freely of the delights of love' (RV).

CHAPTERS 5²–6⁹
A DREAM. HIS BEAUTY AND HERS

2–7. Another dream of hers, with a painful ending. The accumulation (v. 2) of names of endearment reminds us of the frequent repetition, by a Palestinian bridegroom during the wedding dance, of *Yâ halâli, Yâ mâli,* 'O my property, O my possession !' **2.** Heavy dew falls, especially during spring and in the second half of the night. The Spanish poet whom Longfellow translated had in his mind our passage and Rev 3 ²⁰ :

' Lord, what am I, that, with unceasing care,
   Thou didst seek after me,—that thou didst wait,
   Wet with unhealthy dews before my gate,
And pass the gloomy nights of winter there ?

How oft my guardian angel gently cried,
   " Soul, from thy casement look, and thou shalt see
How he persists to knock and wait for thee."'

And our Lord's parable (Lk 11 ⁵⁻⁸) presents a parallel to v. 3. The tunic had been put off (Ex 22 ²⁶ Dt 24 ¹³). The feet, shod only with sandals, needed washing each night. **4.** A hole is still cut in the door of Syrian houses, through which the owner can insert his arm and the key. **5.** ' Myrrha stacta,' liquid **myrrh,** which flowed from the bark of the plant, was the finest and most costly. In two modern Egyptian poems we find : ' My love hath perfumed herself on the nights of the festival,' and ' O thou, with sweet hands ! '

7. The watchmen treat her as a mere night-wanderer : cp. the solicitude of Boaz for Ruth (Ruth 3 [14]). They tore off her wrapper (Mk 14 [51, 52]), a light garment which rested on the shoulders, or was thrown round the head as a **veil.**

9. The chorus prepares the way for her eulogy of her beloved.

10–16. Nuptial songs in praise of the bridegroom's beauty are at the present day comparatively rare in Palestine. His **head is the most fine gold,** an expression which recalls Shakespeare's ' Golden lads and girls.' His **eyes** are **doves,** building in a ravine through which a stream flows. Possibly the fact that these birds delight in clear water and frequently bathe in it may explain the ' sitting by full streams ' of the RV, or, ' sitting upon fulness,' which literally represents the original.

13. The ' banks of sweet herbs ' (RV) have also been rendered, ' towers of perfumes.' The **lips** are compared to red **lilies,** red being the dominant colour of the flora of that land.

14. The fingers are round and shapely ; the nails like topazes ; the body (RV) a plate of ivory encrusted with lapis lazuli, blue veins showing through the lighter skin. **15.** The **pillars of marble** remind us of a song still current in those regions : the singer avers that his dear one's foot is of white silver, which would be scratched if she walked even on cloth.

C. 6. **1–3.** The chorus enquire where he may be found, and she, in dreamy and indefinite language, informs them.

4–9. He again strikes in, celebrating her beauty. **Tirzah** is in a lofty and delightful situation, surrounded by olive groves : its name (= ' Delight ') implies its attractiveness. **Jerusalem** has always been lovely to an Israelite's eye (Ps 48 [2] 50 [2] Lam 2 [15], etc.). A pure and charming woman is ' awe-inspiring as bannered hosts ' (RM). Coventry Patmore speaks of ' her awful charm of grace and innocence sincere ' :

> ' And though her charms are a strong law
>   Compelling all men to admire,
> They go so clad with lowly awe
>   None but the noble dare desire.'

5. Her **eyes** have thrown him into confusion. **8.** She is far above all the **queens** and **concubines,** the ladies of the harem, who are just now at hand. **9.** She is her mother's **only,** i.e. dearest, **one** (Gn 22 [2]), and her pure one.

CHAPTERS 6 [10]–8 [4]

A DIALOGUE. HER LOVELINESS

10–13. A dialogue between these ladies and her. They compare her to the dawn, stooping down to look on the earth from the sky. It is still common in Arabic poems to address the beloved as ' Moon,' or ' Full moon ' !

11, 12. She tells of her visit to the **nut-garden,** where, ere she was aware of it, her soul, i.e. her desire, set her in **the chariots of Ammi-nadib.** The precise meaning of this expression cannot be determined. The general sense appears to be that she was sunk in reverie, carried away in a lover's dream, a flight of fancy. Aroused from this, she would shyly hasten away. **13.** But the chorus beg her to return and perform for them the ' Dance of Mahanaim ' (RV), a sword-dance, no doubt, such as the bride executes, sword in hand, on the evening of the marriage, amidst a half-circle of men and women, whilst a poem (*wasf* = ' description ') of the character of 7 [1-6] is being sung. The title **Shulamite** is derived from the town-name Shulem (otherwise spelled ' Shunem '), from which Abishag, the fairest maiden of her day, came (1 K 1 [4]) : obviously it is another way of calling her ' fairest among women ' (1 [8] 5 [9] 6 [1]).

CHAPTER 7

1–6. The *wasf* begins with a eulogy of her dancing : her steps in sandals (RV) are lovely, and the circling movements of her body are graceful as ornamental chains. In Eastern dancing the twisting and vibration of the body are of more consequence than the rapid movement of the feet. The title ' noble's daughter ' may be merely a conventional compliment, or it may point to the dignity of her character : cp. ' a daughter of Belial,' 1 S 1 [16]. **2.** The Talmud states that the proportions for mixed wine (RV) were two-thirds water, one-third wine. In Syria the colour of **wheat** is considered to be the most beautiful for a human body.

4. Her **neck** is like a **tower of ivory,** long, and dazzling white. But what about the swarthiness of 1 [5, 6] ? The answer is that the exactness and consistency of prose are not to be expected in an epithalamium. **Heshbon** lies five and a half hours E. of the N. point of the Dead Sea, in a fertile, well-watered region : there are several deep wells cut in the rock, and a large reservoir. **5. Carmel** was regarded as the ' Park ' of the land ; there alone were rocky dells, with deep jungles of copse. A ' king is held captive in the tresses ' (RV) of the bride's hair : cp. the Arab song :

> ' Oh, thy thick hair hangs down ;
>   Seven plaits of it take us captive.'

6–10. The bridegroom begins with a general assertion of the delightfulness of his beloved :

then, in like manner as the Greek poet Theocritus compares Helen to the straight cyprus tree, our poet likens the bride to the tall, straight palm, the loveliest of all trees in his eyes, 'man's sister,' as the Arabs call it. Something of the same feeling appears in the English poem :

> 'A daughter of the gods, divinely tall,
> And most divinely fair.'

One or two slight changes in the text, partly supported by the ancient versions, make of v. 9 an expression of desire that her mouth may be like the **best wine for** her **beloved,** 'gliding over his lips and teeth.' Syrian women cried out to an English lady : 'Go on ! when you speak Arabic, your words drop out of your mouth like sugar.'

10-14. Again she declares her affection. An intense delight in rural life breathes through these lines. **13.** For the effect ascribed to the **mandrake** see Gn 30 14-16. It is not a very common plant in the neighbourhood of Jerusalem, but grows freely in Galilee ; its reddishgolden apples, about an inch and a half in diameter, emit a somewhat sweet odour. On a shelf over the inner door (RV) of the house she has laid up some of the old fruits for him.

C. 8. 1 f. Obviously this is supposed to be spoken in the days of their first love, before others were aware of it. Amongst the Bedouin, brothers and cousins on the father's side are the only male relatives who may **kiss** a maiden. In place of the very difficult expression, **who would instruct me,** two ancient versions have a clause parallel to the preceding one, 'and to the chamber of her who conceived me.' In Persia **wine** is obtained from **pomegranates.**

CHAPTER 8 5-14
MEMORIES. THE CLOSE

5. The chorus enquire who this happy bride may be. And the bridegroom points her to the apple-tree where he had once found her asleep, and to the spot where she was born. These are lovers' reminiscences, sweet to them, trivial to others.

6, 7. Her passionate clinging to him, and her assertion of the irresistibleness, the indestructibleness, the unselfishness of genuine love.

6. She would fain be as inseparable from him as the **seal**-cylinder, which men wore on a cord round the neck, or the seal-ring on the right hand (Gn 38 18 Jer 22 24). Love is strong as resistless death. Jealousy can be hard as Sheol (RV), the place of the dead.

> 'Turning all love's delight to miserie,
> Through feare of loosing his felicitie.'

And this is especially true of Orientals : 'A son of the East cannot quietly enjoy his inward felicity, cannot love without being consumed with the suspicion that others will rob him of this sweet treasure ; and jealousy, the passion which gives birth to hatred and blood-feuds, establishes its way in his heart, growing apparently out of a morbid excess of sentiment.' Othello kills the person he most dearly loves. It is 'a very flame of the Lord' (RV), resistless, fierce, consuming (Gn 23 6 Ps 80 10 Jon 3 2 Ac 7 20).

7. Render, 'If a man were ready to give the whole substance of his house for love, could any one despise him ?' No. It is better worth the purchase than anything else on earth.

8, 9. The solicitude which the brothers once felt concerning their **sister.** If she repels all improper advances they will do her honour : if she is weak they will carefully guard her. When she **hath no breasts,** she is not of marriageable age. To be **spoken for** is to be asked in marriage.

10. Our heroine can proudly assert her purity, and her beloved honours her.

11, 12. In figurative speech he expresses his contentment. King Solomon has a fertile and profitable vineyard at **Baal-hamon** (perhaps the town mentioned in Josh 19 28). Any one would give for its produce a **thousand** shekels (about £130). Those to whom it is entrusted will not make less than **two hundred** shekels profit. But the happy lover is well satisfied that Solomon should have his thousand shekels and the keepers their two hundred, provided he may have his dear one. The Arab poet sings, 'Take away all roses ; one little garden is enough for me.' Solomon here is the typical wealthy king, the Crœsus of Hebrew fancy (1 K 10 21) : cp. also Eccl 2 5.

13. The bridegroom once more (see 2 14) begs her to sing. His **companions** are the young men (Jg 14 11) who attended him all through the festivities.

14. Her final word, of invitation to her husband, is a slightly modified repetition of the refrain 2 17.

ISAIAH

INTRODUCTION

WE know comparatively little of the personal life of Isaiah. He was the son of Amoz (1¹), and from his influence at court it has been inferred that he was of royal blood, a rabbinic tradition making him nephew to king Amaziah. He was married and had at least two sons to whom were given symbolic names, embodying the substance of his teaching (7³ 8³,¹⁸). Isaiah lived in Jerusalem, and there, in close connexion with the king and court and in the centre of the national life, he exercised his ministry. He received his call to be a prophet in the last year of Uzziah (740 B.C.), and his latest prophecies which can be dated with certainty are connected with Sennacherib's invasion of Judah (701 B.C.), so that his ministry extended over a period of at least 40 years. How long Isaiah survived the crisis of Sennacherib's invasion we know not, but according to a Jewish tradition, alluded to by Justin Martyr about 150 A.D. ('Dial. Trypho,' cap. cxx), he suffered martyrdom by being sawn asunder during the persecution of the true servants of Jehovah under king Manasseh. It is thought that the traditional manner of Isaiah's death may also be alluded to in Heb 11³⁷.

THE HISTORICAL SETTING OF ISAIAH'S PROPHECIES

Reign of Uzziah. In the last year of this king Isaiah received his call (740 B.C.), c. 6.

Reign of Jotham (740–736). It would seem that Isaiah's ministry was not immediately exercised, for no utterances have come down to us which can with certainty be assigned to this reign.

Reign of Ahaz (736–728). About 736 the prophet becomes a more prominent figure. Chs. 2–5 form a summary of his teaching at this period, and throw much light upon the internal condition of Judah during the reign of Jotham, and at the time of Ahaz's accession, while they exhibit Isaiah as an ardent religious and social reformer. The period of the prophet's youth had been an age of prosperity and material progress for Judah under Uzziah and Jotham. The relations of the kingdoms of Israel and Judah were on the whole harmonious, and both were free from aggression from without. Uzziah conducted successful campaigns against the tribes bordering on Palestine, reducing the Edomites and Ammonites to vassalage. He greatly strengthened the fortifications of Jerusalem and reorganised the army. He also did much to develop the resources of the country and to encourage commerce, the port of Elath (on the Red Sea) being rebuilt in his reign. Under Jotham a like policy was pursued, and the country enjoyed prosperity and peace. But though outwardly prosperous Judah was, at the time of Ahaz's accession, inwardly corrupt. The development of national wealth brought with it social evils ; the accumulation of large estates in the hands of a few holders (5⁸), oppression of the poor (3¹⁴,¹⁵), perversion of justice (5⁷,²³), luxury and wrongful indulgence (2⁷ 3¹⁶ᶠ· 5¹¹,¹²,²²). In religion there was a corresponding decay ; the land was full of idols (2⁸,²⁰), and the people, having lost their faith, were given to superstitions, magic and necromancy (2⁶ 3³), or had become callous, indifferent and sceptical (5¹⁹). Isaiah's teaching in view of this condition of affairs is outlined in the vision wherein he received his call. Jehovah is the all-Holy (6³), and as the Holy One of Israel (a characteristic title in this book) cannot let these things go unpunished, but is bound to vindicate His holiness (6¹¹ᵃ 2⁹ᵇ) ; this He will do by a searching judgment (6¹¹,¹² 2¹⁰⁻²² 3²⁴⁻⁴¹ 5²⁶⁻³⁰), which will not, however, destroy the nation, but a faithful remnant shall be left (6¹³ 4²⁻⁶) through which Israel will attain its glorious destiny.

The Syro-Ephraimite invasion. It is in connexion with this crisis in the history of Judah that Isaiah first comes forward as a statesman. Tiglath-pileser, the Assyrian monarch, had inaugurated a new epoch for that Empire by forming a great scheme of conquest which should unite all W. Asia under his sway. The smaller states naturally took alarm and sought by combination to keep off the common enemy. Rezin, king of Syria, and Pekah, king of Israel, thus made an alliance, and further endeavoured to compel Judah to throw in its lot with them. Towards the end of Jotham's reign they first assailed Judah (2 K 15³⁷), and before Ahaz had long been on the throne they made a determined attack with the object of overthrowing the Davidic dynasty, and setting on the throne of Ahaz a nominee of their own, probably a Syrian, who would follow their line of policy (7⁶). The invasion caused a panic in Judah, and Ahaz suffered serious losses. The passages bearing on the crisis are chs. 7^{1}–9^{4} 9^{8}–10^{4} 17^{1-11} (the last two being more especially concerned with the kingdom of Israel): cp. $2 K 16^{5-9}$ $2 Ch 28^{5f}$. Ahaz formed the project of calling in the aid of Tiglath-pileser ($2 K 16^{7}$ $2 Ch 28^{16}$), a course which Isaiah strongly opposed, foreseeing that it would bring calamity upon Judah (7^{17-20}); he urged that Judah had really nothing to fear from Rezin and Pekah, whose power was doomed to speedy overthrow (7^{4} 8^{4} $17^{1,3}$), and urged reliance in faith upon Jehovah (7^{9}) as the only way to secure the safety and prosperity of the kingdom. Ahaz, however, persisted in his policy of buying the support of Assyria, with the result that Judah became a dependency of that Empire, and was further committed to religious apostasy ($2 K 16^{7,8, 10-18}$). While the seeds of future trouble and disaster were thus sown, as Isaiah foresaw, Judah was saved from the danger of the moment, for the Assyrians overran Syria, captured Damascus (732 B.C.), slew Rezin, and deported the people ($2 K 16^{9}$); the kingdom of Israel was also at the same time reduced to a dependent condition and the people of its N. tribes taken captive to Assyria ($2 K 15^{29}$).

Reign of Hezekiah (727–699). This reign forms the third period of Isaiah's prophetic activity. Hezekiah was guided by the true prophets of Jehovah, and with the support of Isaiah and Micah (Jer $26^{18, 19}$) carried out a great reformation in religion, so that Isaiah's ministry was exercised under more favourable conditions than before. About the time of Hezekiah's accession, Tiglath-pileser was succeeded on the throne of Assyria by Shalmaneser IV. Egypt at this time was ruled by Shebek (Sabaco, or So) of the Æthiopian dynasty. Efforts were apparently made in the early years of Hezekiah's reign to unite the smaller states with Egypt in order to oppose the Assyrian advance westward. Hoshea, king of Israel, actually allied himself with So ($2 K 17^{4}$), and a strong party in Judah favoured a like course. This line of policy Isaiah consistently opposed. Earlier he had endeavoured to dissuade Ahaz from committing himself to Assyria and from entangling Judah politically, urging him to 'take heed and be quiet' (7^{4}). Now that Judah had become tributary to Assyria, he discouraged the project of attempting, in combination with neighbouring states and relying on Egyptian aid, to throw off allegiance, for he saw that prosperity for the future lay in accepting the situation, and that restless plotting against Assyria would involve disaster; 'in returning and rest shall ye be saved, in quietness and confidence shall be your strength' was the burden of his advice (30^{15}). Most

especially were his utterances directed against the politicians who looked upon Egypt for support against Assyria, exposing their scepticism, mistrust in Jehovah, and misplaced confidence in material power which could not avail them in the time of need (chs. 28–31). Shalmaneser led an army to Palestine to subdue the disaffected states; and, after a siege of three years, Samaria was captured (722 B.C.) by his successor Sargon, the Israelites were taken into exile, and the northern kingdom came to an end. Sargon then advanced against the Egyptians whom he completely overthrew in battle at Raphia (720 B.C.), thus justifying Isaiah's warnings as to the futility of trusting in the power of Egypt. Sargon was again in Palestine in 711 B.C., quelling revolts of some of the smaller states. To this period belong chs. 19, 20 (and perhaps 22^{1-14}), and at this time were probably delivered the utterances concerning the fate of some of the neighbouring nations and tribes in view of the Assyrian advance westward (15, 16, 18, 21^{11-17} 23). Sargon was succeeded by Sennacherib in 705 B.C. Again attempts were made to stir up revolt against Assyria on a large scale with the support of the Æthiopian Tirhakah, now king of Egypt (704 B.C.); in the negotiations a leading part was taken by Merodach-Baladan, king of Babylon (c. 39). Hezekiah at this time refused to be guided by Isaiah's counsel of submission to the suzerainty of Sennacherib and joined the rebellion. Sennacherib promptly set out to put down his vassals; Babylon was captured (21^{1-10}); Hezekiah was reduced to submission and made to pay a heavy fine ($2 K 18^{13-16}$), and the Assyrians advanced against Egypt. A little later, seeing the unwisdom of leaving so strong a fortress as Jerusalem intact in his rear, Sennacherib sent an embassy to demand its surrender, contemptuously defying Jehovah's power to defend it. The history of the crisis is told in chs. 36, 37, and the prophecies bearing on this great invasion of Sennacherib (701 B.C.) are contained in chs. 10^{5}–12^{6} 14^{24-27} 17^{12-14} 33 $37^{6,7, 21-35}$. The prophet taught that Jehovah is supreme over all, the Assyrian invader was but His instrument appointed to chastise His people for their sins; he could not therefore defy Jehovah with impunity; but when his work was finished would be punished for his arrogance; a sudden disaster should overtake the Assyrians, and Jehovah would preserve Jerusalem inviolate, a prophecy which received a remarkable fulfilment (37^{36}). This was the culminating point of Isaiah's ministry, and no prophecies of a later date which may be with certainty assigned to him have come down to us.

THE WORK OF ISAIAH AS A PROPHET

It was the work of a prophet, in the first

410

place, as a preacher of righteousness, to speak in the Name of Jehovah, and it is in this capacity that Isaiah appears about the time of Ahaz's accession, rebuking the idolatry, superstition and oppression that were rife in the nation, announcing the approaching divine judgment for these things, yet holding out hope of a golden age in the future, for a faithful remnant would be preserved to be the nucleus of a new people, true to its divine calling. This doctrine of the remnant is specially characteristic of Isaiah ; for, while we meet with it in other prophets (Amos, Zephaniah, Habakkuk), it forms the keynote of his teaching and is an essential and persistent element in it. The idea takes shape in his call to be a prophet (6¹³), it is embodied in the name of one of his sons (7³), and is referred to again and again in his discourses (4³ 10²¹ 30¹⁸ᶠ·). But Isaiah's position and influence at court gave a wide scope to his genius, so that he comes before us as a statesman, and adviser of kings ; both under Ahaz and under Hezekiah it was his work to endeavour to guide the counsels of the nation in accordance with the principles of true religion, and with the will of Jehovah as revealed to himself. Thus he attempted to dissuade Ahaz from buying Assyrian aid in the crisis of the Syro-Ephraimite invasion, and in Hezekiah's reign was the consistent opponent of the policy of alliance with Egypt. But it was also the characteristic function of a prophet to foretell the future, and in connexion with his work as a statesman Isaiah uttered some remarkable predictions which received speedy and striking fulfilment. During the panic caused by the invasion of Rezin and Pekah, Isaiah supported his exhortations to equanimity by foretelling the speedy ruin of the hostile kingdoms (7¹⁶ 8⁴), and the event proved him right. Again during the Assyrian invasions in Hezekiah's reign Isaiah consistently taught the inviolability of Jerusalem and repeatedly predicted sudden and unlooked-for disaster to the Assyrians in the moment of their apparent triumph (10¹⁶,³³ 14²⁵ 17¹²⁻¹⁴ 37⁶,⁷,²¹⁻³⁵), prophecies which received a remarkable fulfilment in the mysterious mortality in Sennacherib's army which obliged that monarch to abandon his designs against Jerusalem. These forecasts must have been quite beyond the range of a politician's calculation, and can only be adequately accounted for by the possession of prophetic insight. The future of Judah is, in Isaiah's view, bound up with the fortunes of the royal house, whose continuance he affirms (9⁷), though he anticipates for it dark days and apparent overthrow (10¹¹) in the near future. The deliverer of God's people from its foes, and from the Assyrian in particular, is to be a king of David's line whose reign is to introduce a golden age

for the whole world, being marked by righteousness and universal peace. While earlier prophets (Amos and Hosea) had merely foretold the permanence of David's line, Isaiah goes further, fixing his attention on an individual Messianic King, whose character and work he outlines (9⁶,⁷ 11¹⁻⁹). He is the agent of Jehovah, but He is more than this, for Isaiah calls Him by the Divine Name (9⁶) and pictures the spirit of Jehovah as resting upon Him in all its fulness (11²,³). Thus, according to Isaiah, Jehovah was to be fully present in the person of the Messianic King, who was to be His perfect manifestation as Ruler of His people. It is true that Isaiah connects the appearance of this glorious monarch with the defeat of the Assyrians, the last enemy of Judah on his horizon, his view of future times being foreshortened, and it may be doubted how far he understood the true import of the words that he spoke concerning the person and work of the King, seized as he was by overmastering inspiration and carried quite beyond himself ; but Christians can read his utterances in a larger, fuller light, and see how wonderfully they were fulfilled in the Person and work of Jesus Christ our Lord.

CHRONOLOGICAL TABLE

B.C.

745	Tiglath-pileser, king of Assyria
740	Call of Isaiah
735	Ahaz, king of Judah
734	Pekah, king of Israel, defeated and slain by the Assyrians
732	Rezin, king of Syria, slain, and Damascus taken by the Assyrians
727	Shalmaneser, king of Assyria
726	Hezekiah, king of Judah
722	Sargon, king of Assyria. Fall of Samaria and end of kingdom of Israel
711	Siege of Ashdod by the Assyrians
710	Defeat of Merodach-Baladan and capture of Babylon by Sargon
705	Sennacherib, king of Assyria
701	Great invasion of Judah by Sennacherib
607	Nineveh taken by the Babylonians. Rise of the Babylonian Empire under Nebuchadnezzar
586	Jerusalem taken by Nebuchadnezzar. End of kingdom of Judah
549	Beginning of Cyrus' victorious career
538	Capture of Babylon by Cyrus, followed by decree for the return of the Jewish exiles

NON-ISAIANIC SECTIONS

A careful study of the internal evidence (the contents, allusions, implied historical setting and literary style) has led the majority of modern scholars to the conclusion that some portions of this book as we now have it are not the work of Isaiah the son of Amoz, but were added to his prophecies at a later period, much in the same way as psalms by later writers were added to the original collection ascribed to David, and as prophecies of various dates by unknown authors were appended to the written works of Zechariah. The most considerable sections which have thus been separated by critical study from the works of Isaiah are :—

(1) Chs. 40–66, now assigned by quite a general consensus of opinion to an author (or possibly authors) who lived towards the close of the Babylonian exile.

(2) Chs. 13–14 23 (see notes).

(3) Chs. 24–27 (see notes).

(4) Chs. 34, 35 (see notes).

(5) Chs. 36–39, parallel, and in the main identical, with 2 K 18 13–20 19. An historical appendix added because of its bearing on Isaiah's prophetic activity in the reign of Hezekiah.

The reasons for separating chs. 40–66 from the acknowledged prophecies of Isaiah are :—

(a) The standpoint of the writer is that of the Babylonian exile, more than a century after Isaiah's death : he is living amongst, and speaking to, the Jews in exile. See e.g. 42 22 43 28 47 6 52 5. Jerusalem is no longer inviolate as in 1–39, but has been for some time deserted and in ruins (44 26 58 12 61 4 63 18 64 10, 11), and the return of the captives to their own land is anticipated in the immediate future (46 13 48 20). In Isaiah's time Assyria under Shalmaneser, Sargon, and Sennacherib was the dominant world power. But in 40–66 the Babylonian Empire, which under Nebuchadnezzar had succeeded to the power of Assyria, is tottering to its fall, and destined to be overthrown by Cyrus who has embarked on his victorious career. Isaiah's name and personality, again, so prominent in 1–39, are never alluded to in 40–66. Now, however far an OT. prophet may project his vision into the future, the standpoint from which he does so is always that of his own time, and his words are for the warning or encouragement of those of his own age. But on the supposition that Isaiah is the author of these chs. not only does he project his vision into the future, but first projects himself to a standpoint in the future, and, though living while the kingdom of Judah was still in existence and Jerusalem outwardly flourishing, addresses himself to the encouragement of the Jews of a future age, when they should be in exile, and their city and Temple a heap of ruins. But this would be a case without parallel in OT. prophecy, and it is therefore much more likely that these chs. are the work of one who actually lived towards the close of the exile.

(b) The argument in chs. 41, 45 seems to depend on the fact that Cyrus, the Persian conqueror, has begun his victorious career. The action of Cyrus is appealed to as a proof that Jehovah has not forgotten His people and will perform His promises. The passages concerning Cyrus are not prophecies of his coming (as is sometimes said), but rather triumphant appeals to the fact that he has come. His career is followed with anxious interest, and his successes are regarded as accumulating evidences of Jehovah's care for His people, and of the working out of His will in the course of human history. This points to a date shortly after the middle of the 6th century B.C.: for Cyrus, whom the Jews rightly anticipated as their deliverer, first appeared about 550 B.C., overthrew the Median empire in 549, and after other achievements captured Babylon in 538, and gave permission for the return of the captive Jews to their own country.

(c) When we look into chs. 40–66 we find that they differ considerably from the earlier part of the book both in language and style. This by itself is not a conclusive argument, because a man's style may alter a great deal at different periods in his life, being liable to modification from varying circumstances, age, or change of subject matter ; nevertheless it materially strengthens the case when taken in connexion with the other arguments noticed. Some of the more striking differences of style observable are :—

(1) Some words or expressions characteristic of 1–39 are absent from 40–66, such as : the title 'the Lord Jehovah of hosts' (1 24 3 1 10 16, 33 19 4) ; the word used for 'idols' (2 8, 18, 20 10 11 19 1, 3 31 7) ; the use of the figure of Jehovah's 'arising' or 'being exalted' (e.g. 2 11, 19 5 16 28 21 30 18) ; the expression 'glory' of a nation (e.g. 5 13 8 7 10 16, 18) ; the figure of Jehovah's 'hand stretched out' in judgment (e.g. 5 25 9 12, 17, 21 10 4 14 26, 27 23 11 31 3) ; a peculiar word for the 'blinding' of the eyes, variously rendered in AV 'shut' (6 10), 'closed' (29 10), 'dim' (32 3) ; a striking word 'stir up' (9 11), 'set up,' 'set' (19 2) ; the expression, 'head and tail, palm branch and rush,' figuratively used (9 14 19 15) ; the term 'fruitful field' (10 18 29 17 and other places) ; the very characteristic word 'remnant' (in the name Shear-jashub, 7 3 10 20, 21 11 11 and elsewhere) ; an unusual word for 'many' (16 14 17 12 28 2).

(2) On the other hand, noticeable words or expressions recur in 40–66, which are absent from undoubted prophecies of Isaiah, such as : 'all flesh' (40 5, 6 49 26 66 16, 23, 24) ; the expression 'as nothing' (40 17 41 11, 12) ; the exhortation to 'lift up the eyes' (40 26 49 18 51 6 60 4) ; the verb 'choose' in connexion with Jehovah's choice of His people (41 8, 9 43 10, 20 and frequently) ; the verb 'praise' and cognate noun (42 8, 10, 12 43 21 and often) ; a rare

expression for 'things to come' (41²³ 44⁷ 45¹¹); the verb rendered 'spring up' or 'spring forth' (e.g. 42⁹ 44⁴ 45⁸); an uncommon word for 'bow down' (44¹⁵,¹⁷,¹⁹ 46⁶); an unusual word meaning to 'break forth' into singing (44²³ 49¹³ and other places); the title 'Holy City' (48² 52¹); references to the 'mirage' (49¹⁰, also 35⁷ [non-Isaianic]); the phrase 'to clothe oneself,' or, 'be clothed with,' used figuratively (49¹⁸ 50³ and elsewhere); frequent reference to the 'sons of Zion' (49¹⁷,²²,²⁵ 51²⁰ and often); utterances of Jehovah beginning with the words 'I am' (45⁵,⁶,¹⁸ and very frequently).

Some of the most striking differences in phraseology have been noted by way of example, but much longer lists might be given. It is true that those who argue for unity of authorship are able to point to certain resemblances, such as the use of the characteristic title 'Holy One of Israel' and the recurrence of *Tohu* ('chaos,' Gn 1²); but the undoubted affinities between the two parts of the book may be explained, it is thought, by the influence of the prophecies of Isaiah upon the author of 40–66.

(*d*) As there is considerable divergence in phraseology between the two main divisions of the book, so the underlying ideas and doctrines are in some respects widely different, e.g.:

(1) The conception of the faithful remnant so characteristic of chs. 1–39, though it may be implied in a few places (59²⁰ 65⁸,⁹), has no important position in 40–66, and Isaiah's word 'remnant' (*Shear*) does not occur.

(2) The conception of Jehovah in chs. 40–66 shows an advance on that of the acknowledged prophecies of Isaiah. It is broader and fuller, bringing into prominence, not the transcendent greatness and holiness of God, but His infinite wisdom, knowledge, and power, as seen in the creation, sustaining, and government of the world.

(3) Chs. 40–66 are marked by the introduction of subjects that are new. The most remarkable of these is the wonderful conception of 'the servant of Jehovah.'

(4) Again, subjects that are not new in themselves receive in chs. 40–66 quite different treatment. Jerusalem in 1–39 is the capital and sanctuary, threatened yet secure in Jehovah's protection. In 40–66 the city is already ruined (61⁴), but destined to be gloriously restored, and the delineation of the glories of the new Jerusalem, with intimation of the part that the nations of the world shall take in its restoration, forms a remarkable feature of the later chapters of the book (see especially c. 60).

(5) Very remarkable is the change which comes over Messianic prophecy when we pass to chs. 40–66. In the utterances of Isaiah the hopes for the realisation of the ideal future are centred in a Scion of the House of David (9⁷ 11¹); but the promises so imperfectly realised during the period of the kingdom are in 40–66 transferred from the Messianic king to the nation as Jehovah's chosen servant; not, however, to the people considered in themselves, but in dependence on an individual, a personal representative of Jehovah, in whom as a perfect servant are summed up the ideal qualities of Israel.

Taking together the arguments thus briefly summarised, it is difficult to avoid the conclusion that chs. 40–66 are not the work of Isaiah, but of a prophet who exercised his ministry towards the end of the period of the Jewish exile in Babylon. There is no reason why the student of Holy Scripture should be disquieted by such a conclusion, for it does not follow that the trustworthiness and inspiration of chs. 40–66 must be given up. The author of these chs. does not claim to be Isaiah, and the name of that prophet is not even mentioned in them. Belief in the inspiration and divine authority of the OT. cannot fairly be held to bind us to a particular theory or to human traditions, as to the literary structure of the several books. This has to be investigated by the ordinary methods of literary research, because God's revelation has come down to us embodied in a literature which has not been exempted from the ordinary conditions of literary composition and transmission.

CHAPTER 1

JEHOVAH'S ARRAIGNMENT OF HIS PEOPLE

This c. is general in character, and much of it (e.g. vv. 10–17) might refer to almost any period. This general character of the prophecy renders it especially suitable as an introduction, and may account for its position at the beginning of the book. It gives us a picture of the internal condition of Judah in Isaiah's age, and not only brings out his characteristic teaching, but more than any other OT. passage indicates the general line of prophetic doctrine. Owing to the corrupt state of the nation Jehovah will avenge Himself by a judgment, through which, while it proves the destruction of sinners, the people will be purified, and its ideal character realised by the remnant that shall be left (vv. 24–26 : cp. v. 9). Some indication of date is afforded by vv. 7–9, where the prophet states that the land is wasted by foreign invaders and the capital cut off from outside help. The prophecy might accordingly be assigned to (1) the invasion by Rezin and Pekah in the reign of Ahaz (7¹), 735 B.C.; (2) an invasion by Sargon (20¹), 711 B.C.; or (3) the invasion by Sennacherib (chs. 36, 37) in Hezekiah's reign, 701 B.C. It is in favour of (1) that the prophecy occurs in connexion with others belonging to the reign of Ahaz (chs. 2–5), and perhaps the rebuke of formal worship suits this period best; the 'strangers' of v. 7 would then be Pekah's Syrian allies. Most recent commentators, however, assign the prophecy to date (3). There is a similar rebuke of formal religion in 29 13 (same period), though the tone of this c. is unlike that of those prophecies which undoubtedly refer to Sennacherib's invasion (e.g. chs. 29, 30).

2–9. Judah's unnatural conduct and its consequences. **10–17.** Sedulous worship of Jehovah is no defence, because a merely formal service is displeasing to Him. **18–23.** Jehovah offers reconciliation on condition of amendment. **24–31.** The gracious offer being refused, sentence is passed.

1. See Intro.

2. Children] Jehovah claimed Israel as His son at the exodus (Ex 4 22). **3.** The unnaturalness of Israel's conduct is similarly contrasted with the behaviour of the animal creation, in Jer 8 7. **4. Seed of evildoers**] i.e. consisting of evildoers (14 20). **Are corrupters**] RV 'deal corruptly.' **The Holy One of Israel**] The use of this title is characteristic of Isaiah, and traceable to the impression made by the vision wherein he received his call and heard the seraphic 'Ter-Sanctus.' See Intro.

5. RV 'Why will ye be still stricken, that ye revolt?' etc. Why expose yourselves to further punishment? Read, 'Every head .. every heart.' The noblest parts of the body stand for the rulers and counsellors of the body politic.

7. As overthrown by strangers] lit. 'as an overthrow of strangers,' i.e. (a) as an overthrow wrought by strangers, or (b) as when strangers (whom God cares not for) are overthrown.

8. Cottage .. lodge] solitary huts where watchmen lived : cp. Lam 2 6 RV. The figures express isolation. Owing to the occupation and devastation of the country by invaders the city is left helpless.

9. The cities of the plain had perished through lack of a righteous remnant (Gn 18 24-32). The possession of such a remnant had proved the salvation of Judah.

10. The rulers of Jerusalem are addressed as **rulers of Sodom,** and the nation as **people of Gomorrah.** Thus are emphasised both their wickedness and their peril : cp. Ezk 16 48-50.

The law of our God] referring not to the written law, but to the divine teaching which follows, delivered through the prophet : see 2 3 8 16.

11. I delight not] cp. Pss 40 6 51 16 Am 5 21, 22 Mic 6 7. **12. Tread**] RV 'trample'; like beasts without understanding. The worship was

merely formal. **13. Vain oblations**] Not the offerings in themselves, but their hypocritical character is reprobated. **Iniquity**] lit. 'nothingness,' 'worthlessness.' **14. New moons**] referring to the monthly festivals (Nu 28 11 1 S 20 5).

15. Your hands, etc.] The hands, uplifted in prayer, are stained with blood.

16, 17. Condition of acceptance with God. **17. Judgment**] i.e. justice. **Relieve the oppressed**] RM 'set right the oppressor.'

18. Let us reason] i.e. that the right may appear. Forgiveness will follow obedience and repentance.

21. An harlot] figuratively expressing the faithlessness, through its idolatry, of the nation which had been betrothed to God : cp. Ex 34 15 Dt 31 16. **Judgment**] i.e. justice, as in v. 17.

22. Mixed] read, 'weakened.' The images describe the degeneracy of the rulers; the best have become debased. **23. Companions of thieves**] i.e. conniving at miscarriage of justice : cp. Mic 7 3.

24. Mine adversaries] the evildoers in Jerusalem. God will purge the city of them.

25. Purely purge, etc.] RM 'purge away thy dross as with lye,' lye, or potash, being used as a flux in purifying metals. **Tin**] i.e. alloy. **27. With judgment .. with righteousness**] i.e. (a) through the manifestation of God's justice and righteousness, or (b) through the justice and righteousness which the regenerate people exhibit. **Her converts**] i.e. those of her who return (to Jehovah).

29. They shall be ashamed .. ye have desired] The subject in each clause is the same in thought, though the person of the verb is changed. Such abrupt change of person is not uncommon in Hebrew, especially in the prophets, e.g. Mic 7 19 Mal 2 15.

29. The oaks] mentioned as connected with idolatrous worship : cp. 2 K 16 4 17 10. Sacred trees were supposed to be inhabited by a deity, to whom the worship was offered. The prophet indicates that such nature-worship will disappoint its votaries. **The gardens**] referred to as the scene of heathen rites : cp. 65 3. **30.** The fate of the wicked described in imagery suggested by v. 29. **31.** Read, 'And the strong' (i.e. the wealthy and powerful man) 'shall be as tow, and his work' (i.e. the idolatrous image) 'as a spark.' The meaning is that his sin will be the cause of his ruin.

CHAPTERS 2–5

ISAIAH'S PREACHING EARLY IN THE REIGN OF AHAZ

Chs. 2–4 are closely connected, and c. 5 is generally thought to belong to the same period, though it probably represents discourses delivered rather later. There are two points which serve as indications of date : (a) The influx of foreign fashions, both in religion (2 6, 8) and in common life (3 16-23, where the difficulty of explaining the names for the various articles of female attire from the Hebrew suggests that the articles, like the names, were of foreign importation). (b) The weak and capricious character of the king and his advisers (3 12). These features point to the reign of Ahaz, who was an innovator in religion (2 K 16 2-4, 10), but in that case these chs. must be placed quite early in his reign, because we should gather from the mention of deep-sea ships (2 16) that Elath, the one seaport of the kingdom, was still in the possession of Judah, while we read in 2 K 16 6 that the Syrians captured it during the invasion by Rezin and Pekah.

C. 2. 2-4. Isaiah quotes a prophecy that the nations shall resort to Zion, and there learn true religion, with the result of universal peace. 5-9. Before this future can be realised, God's own people must trust in Him and forsake their idolatry. 10—22. The retributive judgment that is coming on the nation is described in detail.

C. 3. 1-15. The ruin of social order in Judah, traceable to the misconduct of the rulers, who shall be punished.

16-C. 4 1. The sin and punishment of the ladies of Jerusalem. 2-6. The day of the Lord, though a day of judgment for the wicked, will prove a day of salvation for the faithful remnant.

C. 5. 1-7. Judah compared in a parable to an unfruitful vineyard. 8-24. The charge of bringing forth evil fruit is proved in detail. [25-30. The coming invasion and dark prospect.]

CHAPTER 2

2-4. occur also with a few slight variations in Mic 4 1-4. The passage appears to be borrowed in Isaiah, because (a) it suits its context better in Micah, and (b) it is more complete in Micah, Mic 4 4 being a part of it. If Isaiah is quoting from Micah, the latter prophet must have spoken the words before the occasion referred to in Jer 26 18. Both prophets may be quoting from some ancient and well-known prediction regarding the future of Zion. 2. In the last days] RV 'in the latter days.' The phrase has the general meaning of 'future time' (Gn 49 1 Dt 4 30 Jer 23 20). Its use in the prophetic books makes the expression practically equivalent to 'Messianic times,' and the Apostles in NT. use the corresponding Gk. in the sense of 'the Christian dispensation' (Ac 2 17 1 Pet 1 20 1 Jn 2 18 Heb 1 1, 2). In the top of] RM 'at the head of.' Under the figure of a physical change is set forth the supremacy of Israel's religion : Zion will be recognised as the spiritual capital of the world.

3. People] RV 'peoples.' The law] RM 'teaching' or 'instruction,' such as was given by prophets and priests : see 8 16. 4. Among] RV 'between.' The nations will submit their disputes to the arbitration of Israel's God. The conviction of the universality of the religion of Israel is here plainly shown.

5. The prophet urges the people to repent, that they may fulfil their destiny.

6. Therefore] RV 'For.' Replenished from the east] alluding to the influx of settlers and foreign customs from that quarter. Soothsayers, etc.] Soothsayers are forbidden amongst the Israelites in Dt 18 10. We find an Israelite king sending to consult at the Philistine town of Ekron (2 K 1 2). Please themselves in] RV 'strike hands with': i.e. 'make compacts with' born heathen. The reference is to bargains and commercial undertakings (2 K 14 22 16 6).

7. The increase of wealth and military organisation here referred to were features of Uzziah's reign (2 Ch 26 1-15). 9. Boweth down .. humbleth himself] i.e. before the idols.

12. The day of the Lord of hosts shall be] RM 'the Lord of hosts hath a day.' 'Day' might mean (a) day of battle or victory, cp. Am 5 18-20, the earliest mention of the Day of the Lord, or (b) day of judgment. This became the usual meaning ; so regularly in NT. Cp. 1 Cor 4 3-5. 13-16. The proud will be humbled by the destruction of the things that minister to their pride. 15. Alluding to the works and fortifications of Uzziah and Jotham (2 Ch 26 9, 10 27 3, 4).

16. Ships of Tarshish] i.e. deep-sea ships used for foreign trade. Tarshish is supposed to have been in S. Spain, at the furthest limit of Phœnician commerce. Judah at this time possessed a mercantile fleet, the station of which was at Elath, on the Red Sea (2 K 16 6)

Pleasant pictures] The word rendered 'pictures' means something figured or with imagery upon it. A cognate word is used of idolatrous imagery (Nu 33 52) and of idolatrous images painted on walls (Ezk 8 12). Since the word here occurs in close connexion with ships, the reference may be to the sails, which were often embroidered with figures in ancient times. Some prefer the meaning 'watchtowers,' the root having in Aramaic the sense 'to look out.'

20. Cast his idols] in disgust at their inability to help. 21. Men will try to hide from God in terror. 22. Wanting in LXX, and perhaps a gloss.

CHAPTER 3

1. Stay and the staff] A prophecy of famine: cp. v. 7, as the clause following explains. But if the latter clause is a gloss then 'stay and staff' would refer to the classes upon which the stability of the life of the community depends.

'Staff' in the Heb. is the fem. form of 'stay.'

2. The prudent] RV 'the diviner,' at this time in high estimation (2^6). **The ancient**] RM 'the elder,' who held offices in villages and towns (Ruth $4^{2,4}$ 2K10^1). **3. Artificer**] cp. Jer 24^1; but RM 'charmer.' **Eloquent orator**] 'skilful enchanter.' **4. Children .. babes**] in character rather than in years.

6, 7. The meaning is, the state of society shall be such that a man who apparently has the bare necessaries of life shall be invited to be dictator, but in vain.

9. The shew of their countenance] i.e. their expression; the meaning being that their character may be read in their face. But RM has, 'Their respecting of persons doth witness,' etc. **12.** Cp. v. 4. **They which lead thee**] lit. 'they that set thee right,' i.e. they that should set thee aright. The reference is to king Ahaz and his counsellors, amongst whom the queen-mother was prominent. **13. People**] RV 'peoples.' **14. Ancients**] see v. 2. **For ye**] the pronoun is emphatic : RV 'It is ye that have eaten up.'

16 f. A protest against prevalent luxury as evidenced in the extravagant toilette of the ladies of Jerusalem.

16. Tinkling] caused by silver bells on the ankles. **18. Cauls**] RM 'networks.' **Round tires like the moon**] RV 'crescents'; mentioned as Midianitish ornaments (Jg$8^{21,26}$).

19. Chains] RV 'pendants,' or 'eardrops'; mentioned as Midianitish ornaments (Jg8^{26}).

20. Bonnets] RV 'headtires.' The same word is used of a bridegroom's headdress (61^{10}).

Ornaments of the legs] RV 'ankle-chains.' **Headbands**] RV 'sashes,' such as were worn by brides (49^{18} Jer2^{32}). **Tablets**] RV 'perfume boxes.' **Earrings**] RV 'amulets.'

21. Nose jewels] fastened to the nostril : see Gn24^{22}. **22. Changeable suits of apparel**] RV 'festival robes.' **Wimples**] RV 'shawls.' **Crisping pins**] RV 'satchels.'

23. Glasses] RV 'hand mirrors.' **Hoods**] RV 'turbans.'

24. Instead of, etc.] RV 'instead of sweet spices there shall be rottenness.' **Rent**] RV 'rope,' i.e. binding the captive. **Burning**] RV 'branding,' i.e. of a slave.

25, 26. Thy, her] the pronouns refer to Zion. **26. Sit upon the ground**] a posture of mourning : cp. Lam1^1.

CHAPTER 4

1. The women do not claim to be kept as the man's wives, but only pray that he will remove from them the reproach of being childless (cp. Gn30^{23}), so depopulated has the land become. The v. belongs to c. 3.

In that day] i.e. when the Day of God's judgment (2^{12} 3^{18}) is over.

2. Branch] not here a title of Messiah (the word is not the same in 11^1) but referring to the verdure of the land. Fertility of the soil is often a feature of the ideal future in the prophets (30^{23} Am9^{13} Zech$9^{16,17}$). For the expression 'branch of Jehovah' cp. 'cedars of God,' Ps80^{10}; 'trees of Jehovah,' Ps104^{16}.

Escaped] referring to the godly remnant (6^{13}). **3. Shall be called holy**] i.e. as actually being so : cp. 1^{26}. **Written**] i.e. enrolled as a citizen. **4. Spirit**] RM 'blast.' **5. Upon every dwelling place**] RV 'over the whole habitation.' **A cloud, etc.**] the sign of God's protecting presence ; the imagery is from the exodus (Ex$13^{21,22}$ $14^{19,20}$). **Upon all, etc.**] 'over all the glory shall be spread a canopy,' i.e. for shadow and refuge, as explained in the next v. **6. Tabernacle**] RV 'pavilion.'

CHAPTER 5

1-24. Judah, God's unfruitful vineyard, and the judgment upon it.

1. I] i.e. Isaiah. **To my**] rather, 'for my,' or 'of my.' The **beloved**, as appears later, is Jehovah : cp. our Lord's parable (Mt21^{33}). The allegory is rhythmical in form : cp. Song 8^{11-14}). **2. Tower**] watch-tower : see on 1^8.

3 f. God speaks.

7. Judgment] i.e. justice. **Oppression**] perhaps better, 'bloodshed.' **A cry**] i.e. of the oppressed.

8-10. Unjust seizure of land resulting in barrenness and want of population. **8. Place**] RV 'room.' **10. Bath**] about 8 gallons. **And the seed, etc.**] RV 'and a homer of seed shall yield but an ephah.' An ephah is the tenth part of a homer, which was 10 or 12 bushels (Ezk45^{11}).

11. That continue until night] RV 'that tarry late into the night.' **12. Regard not, etc.**] i.e. have no regard for the working of the LORD'S will in the events of history. **13. Are gone into captivity**] an example of the 'prophetic perfect.' The future is regarded as so certain that it is described as past. **14. Hell**] Heb. *Sheol*, i.e. the place of departed spirits, RM 'the grave' : cp. Gn37^{35}. **15.** Cp. $2^{9,17}$.

17. After their manner] RV 'as in their pasture.' So desolate will the cities be.

Strangers] RM 'wanderers.' The meaning is that nomad tribes wander over the land at pleasure.

18. The people have chained themselves to sin like beasts of burden. **19.** They scoff at the declared judgments of God. **20.** The perverting of all moral distinctions. **23.** Bribery and injustice.

25-30. The position of these vv. is doubtful. Very probably they should be connected with the prophecy, 9^8-10^4. In that section the closing words of v. 25 occur four times as a sort of refrain.

26. Lift up an ensign] i.e. as a signal to muster them : cp. 11 10 18 3 49 22 62 10. **Nations**] i.e. those under the dominion of the Assyrian king and serving in his army. **Hiss**] The metaphor is from collecting a swarm of bees (7 18). **30. They shall roar against them**] i.e. the enemies against God's people.

CHAPTER 6
THE PROPHET'S CALL

This c., which recounts the prophet's call and commission, would stand first in a chronological arrangement of the book. The opening words remind us of the vision of Micaiah (1 K 22 19), and we should compare the visions of Jeremiah and Ezekiel which inaugurated their prophetic activity. In St. John's vision (Rev 4) the same anthem, 'Holy, holy, holy,' is sung by the six-winged living creatures round about the throne. Isaiah's vision foreshadows such leading elements of his thought as, (1) the majesty of God, (2) the uncleanness of the people, (3) his conviction that he had a divine message for them, (4) their stubbornness and heedlessness, (5) the necessity of judgment, (6) the idea of the remnant.

1–4. Isaiah's vision of Jehovah enthroned and the worship of heaven. **5–7.** He confesses his sin and is absolved. **8–13.** He receives his prophetic commission.

1. The year that king Uzziah died] 740 B.C. See Intro. The prophet, when meditating perhaps on the condition of the nation and its gloomy prospects, is favoured with a vision of the glory of God. **Train**] i.e. the skirts (RM) of his royal robes.

2. Above it] RV 'above him.' **The seraphims**] here only in OT. the word denotes supernatural beings. It is derived from the verb 'to burn,' and may simply indicate the fiery or glowing appearance of Jehovah's attendant angels (Ezk 1 13, 14). Elsewhere, however, the same word stands for venomous serpents (Nu 21 6 Isa 14 29 30 6), and it may here be intended to convey the meaning that the guardians of Jehovah's throne are of serpentine form. This is scarcely borne out by the context (vv. 6, 7), though in Ezekiel's vision of heaven animal forms are introduced (Ezk 1 10.) **Covered his face**] in reverence.

3. Holy, holy, holy] The threefold repetition denotes emphasis or intensity (Jer 7 4). It is significant that the title of Jehovah most characteristic of Isaiah's prophecies is 'the Holy One of Israel.' In the light of later revelation Christians have not unnaturally seen here a foreshadowing of the Holy Trinity: cp. Rev 4 8. **4. The posts of the door moved**] RV 'the foundations of the thresholds were moved.' **Smoke**] a symbol of the divine presence, as in Ex 19 9, 18 1 K 8 10, 11.

5. Lips] the pure praises of the seraphim

made Isaiah think by contrast of his own sins of the lips. **For mine eyes have seen, etc.**] No man could see God and live (Ex 33 20). **6. Live coal**] Fire is the symbol of purification : cp. Mal 3 2 Mt 3 11. **8. For us**] the plural in the mouth of God as in Gn 1 26 3 22 11 7. Jehovah consults with the angels around His throne ; similarly in Micaiah's vision (1 K 22 19. 20 : cp. Ps 89 7).

10. The result of the prophet's preaching described as though it were the purpose. Most of his hearers will stubbornly reject his message, with the result that they will become dead to all impressions. **The heart**] regarded by the Hebrews as the seat of the understanding : cp. Hos 7 11. **Convert**] RV 'turn again.'

11, 12. Isaiah feels that such a state of things cannot be allowed to continue, and is assured that Jehovah will interpose with a terrible judgment of war and exile. **12. There be a great forsaking**] RV 'the forsaken places be many.'

13. RV 'And if there be yet a tenth in it, it shall again be eaten up : as a terebinth, and as an oak, whose stock remaineth, when they are felled ; so the holy seed is the stock thereof.' The meaning is that the coming judgment is not a single one but a series. Yet as when an evergreen tree is cut down the stump remains from which new shoots may grow, so there will be a faithful remnant of Israel left, to be the germ of a renewed people. This doctrine of the remnant is characteristic of Isaiah : cp. 4 3 7 3 10 20, 21.

CHAPTERS 7 1–9 7
THE SYRO-EPHRAIMITE INVASION

The group of prophecies contained in this section belongs to the reign of Ahaz, when Judah was threatened by the allied forces of Syria and Israel (7 1 2 K 15 37 16 5-9 2 Ch 28 5-15). With the reign of Tiglath-pileser, the Assyrian empire entered on a new epoch, that monarch aiming at bringing the whole of W. Asia under his sway. With a view to resisting the Assyrian advance and preserving their independence, Rezin, of Syria, and Pekah, of Israel, formed an alliance, and their war against Ahaz was apparently undertaken in order to force Judah to join the coalition, the immediate object of the invaders being to dethrone Ahaz and set over the kingdom one who would be willing to favour their projects (7 6). Isaiah foresaw that Syria and Israel were doomed to fall before the Assyrian power, and, therefore, exhorts to calmness and confidence in Jehovah (7 4, 8, 16 8 4). Ahaz, on the other hand, was set upon seeking aid from Tiglath-pileser, a policy which Isaiah reprobated as indicating want of trust in Jehovah, and as certain to lay Judah also open to disaster from Assyrian inroads (7 17-25).

C. 7. 1, 2. The occasion of the prophecies following. **3–9.** In view of the panic caused by the Syro-Israelite invasion, Isaiah is sent to the king with a message of encouragement (**10–16**), which is confirmed by the sign of Immanuel. **17–25.** The disastrous consequences of the policy of seeking aid from Assyria foretold.

C. 8. 1–4. The speedy ruin of Syria and Israel foretold by the sign of Maher-shalal-hash-baz. **5–8.** The Syrian invasion of Judah foretold. **9–15.** The nations' fear in the present crisis contrasted with the assurance that should spring from trust in Jehovah. **16–20.** Isaiah's own confidence in his message. **21–C. 9. 7.** The coming calamity and the bright future that lies beyond. Those parts of the land which first suffered from the Assyrian shall be correspondingly glorified, for the Messiah shall appear and the kingdom of David shall be established on an indestructible foundation.

CHAPTER 7

1–16. Isaiah assures Ahaz by a sign that Judah will be delivered from Syria and Israel.
1. See prefatory note to the section.
2. Ephraim] the popular name for the northern kingdom (9⁸,⁹). **His heart was moved**] i.e. the heart of king Ahaz, because of the formidable confederacy against him. Serious reverses suffered by Judah at this time are recorded in 2 Ch 28 ⁵⁻¹⁵.
3. Shear-jashub] i.e. 'a remnant shall return.' Already in the reign of Ahaz the prophet had summed up the characteristic feature of his teaching (see on 6¹³) in a symbolic name given to his son. Similarly he called another son Maher-shalal-hash-baz ('spoil speedeth, prey hasteth') that he might impressively indicate the speedy spoliation of Syria and Israel (8³,⁴). Thus the prophet and his family were for signs to the people (8¹⁸). There is a special significance in the presence of Shear-jashub at this meeting of Isaiah with king Ahaz. The prophet has to foretell invasion and spoliation of Judah by the Assyrians (v. 20), but the presence of Shear-jashub gives assurance that a remnant shall return. **The conduit**] The king's object doubtless was to stop the waters outside the walls of the city (2 Ch 32³), so that the enemy, in the siege that was imminent, might be without supply of water. **Upper pool**] probably the same as the upper watercourse of Gihon on the W. of Jerusalem (2 Ch 32³⁰). A lower pool is mentioned in 22⁹.
4. Neither be fainthearted, etc.] RV 'let not thine heart be faint because of these two tails of smoking firebrands.' The prophet regards them as no more than expiring torches.
6. Tabeal] the name is Syrian, not Hebrew: see prefatory note.

8. Within threescore, etc.] We should probably regard this prophecy as fulfilled when the power of the northern kingdom was finally broken by the importation of foreigners under Esarhaddon (Ezr 4²). On account of the manner in which this prediction interrupts the parallelism, some modern scholars regard it as an addition by a later editor.
9. The need of faith is emphasised; without it there is no security.
11. Ask thee a sign] to prove that he may trust in Jehovah's promise. Ahaz's choice should be unlimited, he might ask a sign in heaven or from the nether world.
12. Neither will I tempt, etc.] Ahaz gives utterance to a sound principle (Dt 6¹⁶). But Jehovah had offered a sign, and to refuse it showed distrust of God. Ahaz had already made up his mind to the Assyrian alliance and cloaks his self-will with the language of faith.
13. The prophet's indignation.
14. A virgin] The Hebrew word is not the distinctive one for virginity, but denotes rather one of maturing and marriageable age: cp. e.g. Gn 24⁴³ Ex 2⁸. In the first place, this prophecy must have been intended by Isaiah as a sign of encouragement to Ahaz—before a child, shortly to be born, could arrive at years of observation the enemies of Judah would be brought to nought. At the same time, it is evident that the child is no ordinary one, from the way in which the prophet refers to him as Lord of the land (8⁸), and from the titles given to him in 9⁶. The child is, in fact, the Messiah, whose advent Isaiah seems to have expected in the near future in connexion with the Assyrian invasion (9¹⁻⁷ 11¹⁻⁹). The prophet's anticipations were realised, but in a manner far surpassing his expectations, in the birth of our Lord.
Immanuel] i.e. 'God is with us' (8¹⁰). The child whom the prophet has in mind received this symbolic name as being a pledge of God's presence with His people. Christ, the true Son of David, is in the highest conceivable sense Immanuel. The sign given by Isaiah is not concerned with the manner of the child's birth, but rather connected with his name Immanuel. Accordingly in Mt 1²³ the emphasis is upon the name.
15. Butter (RM 'curds') **and honey**] i.e. simple pastoral products, not bread and meat, because the land has gone out of cultivation: the 'honey' was probably wild honey. That privation is implied is clear from the context (vv. 20–22). **That he may know**] so some ancient versions, but better, 'when he knoweth' (RV), or 'till he know.'
16. Though the child about to be born must in his early years endure privation, yet before he comes to years of discretion Judah's present enemies shall be brought to nought. **The**

land, etc.] RV 'the land whose two kings thou abhorrest' (i.e. 'fearest horribly') 'shall be forsaken.'

17-25. The disastrous consequences of any alliance between Judah and Assyria foretold.

17-19. Isaiah foresees that Judah will be involved in the struggle between Egypt and Assyria and will be invaded by both powers, their armies penetrating everywhere like swarms of insects.

17. Ephraim departed] alluding to the disruption of the kingdom in Rehoboam's reign. Since Ephraim was the most powerful of the seceding tribes the northern kingdom was called by its name (v. 2 ; 9 8,9).

18. Hiss] see 5 26.

19. Desolate] RV 'rugged.' **Bushes**] RV 'pastures.'

20. A razor that is hired] The reference is to Ahaz's policy of calling in the aid of Tiglath-pileser. Retribution would come through that very power on which Ahaz relied, and the land would be laid bare.

21-25. A pastoral life will be the only possible one, because the land is laid waste, and where vineyards once flourished men will hunt wild beasts in the thickets, or seek pasturage for their cattle.

22. The v. means there will be curds and wild honey, and nothing else.

23. Every place, etc.] RV 'every place, where there were a thousand vines at a thousand silverlings, shall even be for briers and thorns.' **Silverlings**] i.e. pieces of silver, shekels ; 1,000 shekels would be an average price.

25. RV 'And all the hills that were digged with the mattock, thou shalt not come thither for fear of briers and thorns.' Vines were usually grown on terraces on the hills of Palestine. **Lesser cattle**] RV 'sheep.'

CHAPTER 8

1. Take, etc.] read 'Take thee a great tablet, and write upon it with the pen of a man, Maher-shalal-hash-baz.' **A man's pen**] i.e. such as a common man would use for writing in large characters that all might undertsand the words. **Maher-shalal-hash-baz**] i.e. 'The spoil speedeth, the prey hasteth.' The inscription intimated the speedy spoliation of Syria and Israel (v. 4).

2. And I took] RV 'And I will take,' the speaker being Jehovah as in v. 1. **Witnesses**] who would be able when the fulfilment came to testify that the prophecy had been delivered.

3. The prophetess] i.e. the prophet's wife. **Call his name**] see on 7 3. **4.** This prophecy was fulfilled, Damascus being captured by the Assyrians in 732 B.C., and Samaria ten years later: cp. 10 9.

6. This people] i.e. the Ten Tribes (re-ferred to as 'this people' again in 9 16), who refused the mild rule of the House of David, and, having set up their own king, have allied themselves with Rezin. **The waters of Shiloah**] The gently-flowing stream that issued from Zion near the sanctuary (Ps 46 4) symbolises the divinely-appointed government of the House of David, and is contrasted in the next v. with the wide flood of Euphrates, symbolising the devastating power of Assyria, which within a short period overthrew the kingdoms of Israel and Syria (2 K 16 9 18 9,10), as Isaiah repeatedly foretold : cp. 7 8,16.

7. The river] i.e. as elsewhere, the Euphrates (Josh 24 2) ; denoted in RV by a capital R.

8. Pass through] RV 'sweep onward into.' **To the neck**] The head, therefore, will escape. So Isaiah regularly indicates the preservation of a remnant in the judgment, that are coming upon the nation. **The stretching out,** etc.] The image is suddenly changed from that of a devastating flood to that of a bird of prey swooping with wings outspread. **O Immanuel**] The country thus threatened is the land to which the divine pledge has been given and embodied in the child Immanuel (7 14-16). At the thought the prophet is filled with confidence in the protection of Jehovah; hence the triumphant strain of defiance in which he addresses the invaders in the vv. that follow.

9, 10. Alliances formed against God's people must end in disaster and hostile purposes must fail, for 'God is with us.' **9. People**] RV 'peoples.' **Gird yourselves**] i.e. for warfare.

10. God is with us] alluding to the significance of the name Immanuel (v. 8, cp. 7 14).

11, 12. The prophet has been divinely warned not to show the unreasoning fear of the Syro-Ephraimite alliance which the men of Judah exhibit.

11. With a strong hand] In Heb. phraseology the coming of prophetic inspiration is spoken of anthropomorphically as seizure by the hand of Jehovah (2 K 3 15 Ezk 1 3 3 22 8 1 37 1).

12. A confederacy] alluding to the alliance between Israel and Syria, which caused so much fear in Judah (7 2). The same word is, however, elsewhere rendered 'conspiracy' or 'treason' (2 K 17 4 2 Ch 23 13) : so RV 'conspiracy' here. In that case the allusion would be to the cry of 'Conspiracy !' which, as some suppose, was raised against Isaiah and his followers in Judah by those in Judah who opposed the line of policy he advocated, and favoured Ahaz's project of alliance with Assyria. Similarly, the political opponents of Jeremiah attempted to discredit his teaching by accusing him of treachery against his country (Jer 37 13).

13. The meaning is, 'recognise Jehovah in His true character as the all-holy One' (so He had revealed Himself to the prophet, 6³), 'and stand in awe of Him accordingly.'

14. Sanctuary] The secondary meaning of ' refuge ' is here the prominent one (1 K 1⁵⁰ 2²⁸).

Both the houses] i.e. the two kingdoms of Judah and Israel. Every revelation of God puts men on their trial and sifts them : to those who accept it in faith and turn to Him it means deliverance, but those who reject it bring judgment on themselves. This was seen in God's revelation of Himself in Christ ; to those who accepted Him He gave power to become sons of God (Jn 1¹²). He came to save the world (Jn 12⁴⁷) ; yet it may also be said that for judgment He came into the world (Jn 9³⁹), because those who received Him not brought judgment on themselves, and found Him to be a rock of offence. Thus Isaiah's words are quoted in NT. with a Christian application (Mt 21⁴⁴ Ro 9³³ 1 Pet 2⁷,⁸).

15. Many among them shall stumble] RV ' many shall stumble thereon.'

16. Bind up] i.e. tie up the parchment roll on which the prophet's teaching has been written, and lay it aside to be consulted later.

The testimony] i.e. the inspired admonition which the prophet has just delivered. **The law**] not referring to the written law of God, but used in the wide sense of ' instruction ' or ' teaching ' (RM) : the inspired teaching given by the prophet himself (cp. 1¹⁰ 5²⁴ 30⁹), which he commits to writing and delivers to his disciples.

18. The ground of the confidence just expressed. The prophet and his children are by their names Isaiah (salvation of Jehovah), Shear-jashub (a remnant shall return, 7³), and Maher-shalal-hash-baz (8³), pledges of a brighter future in fulfilment of the prophet's words. **Wonders**] i.e. omens : cp. Ezk 12⁶,¹¹ 24²⁴,²⁷ Zech 3⁸. This v. is quoted in NT., Heb 2¹³, without regard to its original context, but the writer simply uses it there that he may express in scriptural terms the truth of the community of nature between Christ and His people.

19. Seek unto] i.e. with a view of consulting as an oracle, despairing of other help. **Familiar spirits**] The forms of necromancy referred to are forbidden in Dt 18¹¹, and the nature of the practices reprobated is well illustrated by the famous example of the witch of Endor (1 S 28⁷ᶠ). **Peep**] i.e. ' chirp ' (RV) as a bird (10¹⁴) ; referring to the thin and feeble voice of ghosts from Sheol (29⁴). **For the living to the dead**] RV ' on behalf of the living should they seek unto the dead ? '

20. The law .. the testimony] i.e. Isaiah's own teaching, which, by his direction, had been written down and carefully preserved (v. 16).

If they speak not, etc.] The meaning seems to be, ' If they speak not according to this word ' (viz. ' to the law and to the testimony ') ' surely there is no morning for them ' (RV) : i.e. the only hope of a brighter dawn lies in being guided by Isaiah's teaching. But another rendering is possible, ' Surely according to this word shall they speak for whom there is no morning ' (RM), i.e. they will recognise too late the value of the principles inculcated by Isaiah.

21. Curse their king, etc.] RV ' curse by their king and by their God.' The expression is the same as in 1 S 17⁴³. **22. Dimness, etc.**] RV ' gloom of anguish ; and into thick darkness they shall be driven away.' Note the close connexion with c. 9, where a brighter future is predicted.

CHAPTER 9¹·

1. RV ' But there shall be no gloom to her that was in anguish. In the former time he brought into contempt the land of Zebulun and the land of Naphtali, but in the latter time hath he made it glorious, by the way of the sea, beyond Jordan, Galilee of the nations.' By the contempt brought upon the land of Zebulun and Naphtali the prophet signifies the spoiling of the country and deportation of the inhabitants by Tiglath-pileser (narrated 2 K 15²⁹). **Galilee of the nations**] lit. ' the circuit,' or ' district of the nations.' The region indicated lay in the extreme N. of Naphtali and received its name, probably, from the intermixture in that locality of Israelites with the former inhabitants. The term *Galil* later became the proper name Galilee.

2. Walked in darkness] as described in 8²¹,²². **Have seen**] The light of the new age to which the prophet looked forward was of course in the future, but to his vision it is so assured that he describes it as having already dawned. Such use of the past tense (prophetic perfect) is frequent in the prophetic writings. **Dwell**] RV ' dwelt ': the tense being parallel to ' walked ' in the preceding clause.

Vv. 1, 2 are referred to in Mt 4¹⁵,¹⁶ as fulfilled in our Lord's Galilean ministry. We need not suppose that Isaiah had this distinctly in mind. He only speaks in these verses in general terms of the light of the new and glorious age shining upon that district which should be the first to suffer the affliction of conquest and captivity. When Christ, the true Sun of Righteousness, illumined that very same district it was natural that the Evangelist should see the ultimate fulfilment of the prophecy which Isaiah, unconscious of the wonderful fulfilment which awaited his words, had uttered.

3. *And* not increased the joy] So Heb. written text, ancient Greek versions and Vulg. But Heb. traditional reading, Syr., and LXX give 'increased the joy to it,' RV 'increased their joy'; and this reading is demanded by the context, where figures are multiplied to indicate excessive joy. The past tenses (prophetic perfect, see v. 2) are again used to describe what is yet in the future. **Before thee**] appearing as worshippers before Jehovah in His sanctuary (Dt 12 12).

4. Staff of his shoulder] i.e. with which he is beaten by the taskmaster. The dominion of Assyria shall be broken. **As in the day of Midian**] referring to the memorable victory of Gideon (Jg 7, 8).

5. Read, 'For all the armour of the armed man in the tumult, and the garments rolled in blood, shall be for burning, for fuel of fire.' After the great victory over the oppressor the weapons of war are burnt (Ezk 39 9) as a prelude to the era of peace which is to follow.

6. From a general description of the future reign of peace the prophet goes on to picture the king upon whom it depends, and whom he apparently identifies with the child of 7 14. Then he proceeds to indicate the features of his rule by a series of majestic titles. **Wonderful, Counsellor**] RM 'Wonderful Counsellor,' or 'Wonder-Counsellor.' The title implies that the future king's rule shall be guided by a divinely-inspired wisdom (11 2-4) which shall command the awe with which men regard the counsel of God. The word 'wonderful' (with its cognates) is constantly used of the divine action (Ex 15 11 Jg 13 19 Ps 118 23), and is applied to the divine name (Jg 13 18). **The mighty God**] The word 'God' has been explained by some in the sense of 'ruler' or 'king.' The plural of the same word is sometimes so employed (Ex 21 6 Ps 82 1, 6). Isaiah, however, here uses the singular, and directly applies the very same title to Jehovah elsewhere (10 21; cp. Dt 10 17 Jer 32 18). It should be noted also, (1) that the significance of the word 'God' (*El*) as a title of Jehovah was at this time in the prophet's thoughts in the name Immanu-El; and (2) the titles that precede and follow this one seem to have a mysterious divine significance. For such direct ascription of a divine title to the Messianic King the nearest parallel is Ps 45 6 : cp. Zech 12 8 1 Ch 29 23. **The everlasting Father**] Father because of the protecting care exercised by him over his people. **Everlasting** because his kingdom is to be for ever (v. 7). **Prince of Peace**] peace being regarded as a prominent feature of that great future (2 2-4) which the Messiah is to inaugurate (Mic 5 5 Zech 9 10).

7. David] The mention of David implies that the ideal king is to be of the lineage of David. The v. might be explained as a promise that the dynasty of the great king whom the prophet has in mind should reign in undisputed possession of the kingdom, and should

not fail. The prophecy would in that case be parallel to those earlier ones which promise a lasting dominion to the House of David (2 S 7 12-16 Hos 3 5 Am 9 11); but the title, 'Everlasting Father,' which has just preceded, makes it more likely that the promise is one of personal sovereignty to the individual king of whom the prophet is thinking. **To order it, and to establish it**] RV ' to establish it, and to uphold it.'

Justice] RV 'righteousness.' **The zeal**, etc.] the jealous love of God for His people is a guarantee of this.

CHAPTERS 9 8–10 4
DIVINE JUDGMENTS ON THE KINGDOM OF ISRAEL

This section relates throughout to the kingdom of Israel. It belongs to the same period as the chs. immediately preceding, and treats of the ruin which Isaiah foresaw would shortly overtake the kingdom of the Ten Tribes : cp. 7 16 8 4. The prophet traces the fall of Israel to the moral and social condition of its people. His prophecy was speedily fulfilled in the conquest of Syria and Israel by the Assyrian armies. The prophecy falls into four parts, each closing with the refrain, 'For all this his anger is not turned away, but his hand is stretched out still.' As the same phrase occurs in 5 25, many commentators are of opinion that the short section 5 25-30 is connected in date and subject with this prophecy.

C. 9. 8–21. Because of its pride and self-confidence foes are stirred up against Israel on all hands, and sudden calamity shall overtake it, followed by internal anarchy.

C. 10. 1–4. The kingdom being hopelessly corrupt cannot stand when attacked.

CHAPTER 9 (continued)

8. Jacob .. Israel] Both names here stand for the northern kingdom, as is made clear by what follows in the next v. **9. Shall know**] i.e. shall be taught by experience (Nu 14 34).

10. If the language is to be understood literally, the allusion is to the way in which the people set themselves to repair, and more than make up for, the devastation caused by invasion. But it is more likely that the prophet refers in a figure to the frequent changes of dynasty in the N. kingdom ; no sooner is one dynasty overthrown than another rises up to take its place in vain self-confidence. This interpretation is suggested by the word 'we will change,' which literally signifies, ' we will make cedars to succeed.' The Arabic *Caliph*, meaning successor (of the prophet Mohammed), is from the same Semitic root.

11. The adversaries of Rezin] Perhaps we should read (with some Heb. MSS) 'the princes of Rezin'; the meaning would then be that

the Syrian allies of Israel (7 1, 2) will turn
against it. This suits the context, for we
read in the next v. **the Syrians before. Join his
enemies together**] RV ' stir up his enemies.'

12. Before] RM ' on the east.' **Behind**]
RM ' on the west.' The point is that Israel
is attacked on all hands.

14. Branch] RV ' palm branch ' : ' palm-
branch and rush '—a proverbial expression signifying high and low (19 15).

15. Explanatory of the metaphorical language in v. 14 : cp. vv. 20, 21.

18. Briers and thorns] figuratively put for
evil men (28 23 6). **19. Darkened**] RV
' burnt up.' **20. He shall**] RV ' one shall ' :
not to be taken literally as indicating the approach of famine, but a figurative prophecy of
the ruin of the nation through anarchy and
civil strife, as is made clear by the first part
of v. 21.

C. 10. 1. And that write, etc.] RV ' and to
the writers that write perverseness,' referring
to the registering of unjust and oppressive legal
decisions by the scribes. There is thus a
double reference (a) to unjust legislation, and (b)
to unjust administrations of the law. **3. Glory**]
i.e. wealth and possessions, in which the people
take pride. See the same word in the same
sense Gn 31 1.

4. Without me they shall bow down]
rather, RV ' except they bow down,' or
' they shall only bow down.' Ironical—men's
only safety will be with the wretched train
of captives, or beneath the corpses on the
battle-field.

CHAPTERS 10 5–12 6
THE ASSYRIAN INVASION AND ITS SEQUEL

This is one of the finest of Isaiah's prophecies. The subject is the advance against
Jerusalem of the arrogant Assyrian conqueror,
who meets with a sudden check and is foiled
when his triumph is apparently secure. Then
with Jehovah's interposition for the deliverance of Zion is connected a forecast of the
reign of the Messianic king (11 1–10). The
occasion to which the prophecy probably refers
is Sennacherib's famous invasion in the reign
of Hezekiah, 701 B.C. (36, 37 2 K 18 13–19 36),
but some scholars place it earlier, in the time
of the preceding Assyrian king, Sargon. The
cities referred to in 10 9 were captured between
740 and 717 B.C., so that the Assyrian king's
boast must at least be later than 717 B.C. It
may be true that the line of march which
Sennacherib followed was not identical with
that which the prophet represents the invader
as taking in 10 28-32 ; but Isaiah speaks before
the event, and naturally thinks of the Assyrians as approaching Jerusalem by the usual
route from the N.; he is drawing a vivid
imaginative picture of the threatening danger,

and expresses his confident expectation of
a wonderful deliverance through a sudden
discomfiture of the foe (10 16-19, 33, 34). The
same remarkable anticipation is a feature of
Isaiah's other utterances at this crisis (14 25
17 13, 14 33, 37 6, 7, 29-35), and it received a startling fulfilment (37 36, 37).

C. 10. 5–11. The Assyrian, though proud
of his conquests, is but the instrument of
divine punishment, **12–19.** and when God's
purposes have been accomplished through him
he shall be punished for his pride.

20–27. The faithful remnant of God's people,
therefore, need not fear. **28–34.** Though his
advance towards Jerusalem seems irresistible,
the Assyrian will meet with a sudden
discomfiture.

C. 11. 1–10. The future king of David's
line and the nature of his kingdom.

11–16. God's people shall be restored to
their own land and re-united.

C. 12. Two hymns of the redeemed. **1–3.** A
hymn of joy in the deliverance Jehovah has
wrought. **4–6.** A hymn of praise for God's
mighty deeds, which have manifested His glory
to all the world.

CHAPTER 10 5-34

5. And the staff in their hand] RV ' the
staff in whose hand ' : Jehovah speaks, declaring the Assyrian the minister of His wrath.

6. Hypocritical] RV ' profane.' **Nation . .
people**] not merely referring to Judah, but to
be understood generally : the Assyrian has
been commissioned in the divine providence to
punish godless nations. Similarly in later
history Christians recognised Attila as ' the
scourge of God.'

7–11. The spirit of the Assyrian is represented ; he has no idea of his mission, but
is fired by ambition and pride of conquest.

8. Altogether] RV ' all of them.' **9.** The
places named were all captured by the
Assyrians under Tiglath-pileser, Shalmaneser,
or Sargon ; **Calno** (a Chaldean city, cp. Gn 10 10)
in 738 B.C., **Carchemish** (on the W. bank of
the Euphrates) in 717 ; **Hamath** (on the
Orontes, in early times the Hivite capital) in
720 ; **Arpad** (near Hamath, with which it is
always coupled in OT.) in 740 ; **Samaria**
(capital of Israel) in 722 ; **Damascus** (capital
of Syria) in 732. The mention of the last
two cities amongst the Assyrian conquests
shows that at this time Isaiah's prophecy
in 8 4 had been fulfilled.

10, 11 The Assyrian's argument is—how
can Jerusalem, with fewer gods to protect it,
hope to hold out successfully ?

12. Work] i.e. of judgment, or punishment.

13. People] RV ' peoples.' **I have put down**]
RV ' I have brought down as a valiant man
them that sit *on thrones*.' **14.** The helplessness

of the world before the Assyrians is vividly imaged. **Left**] RV 'forsaken.' **Peeped**] RV 'chirped': cp. 8 19.

15. The prophet now speaks in indignant retort to the vain-glorious boasting of the Assyrian; how can he, being but an instrument of providence, exalt himself against Jehovah? **As if the rod,** etc.] RV 'as if a rod should shake them that lift it up, *or* as if a staff should lift up *him that is* not wood.'

16. The two figures of famine and fire are used to express the destruction of the Assyrian host. **17. The light of Israel**] i.e. Jehovah, who, while He gives light to His own people, at the same time consumes their enemies (29 6,7 30 27 33 14). **In one day**] Isaiah anticipates a sudden catastrophe for the Assyrians (vv. 32–34).

18. A standardbearer fainteth] RV 'a sick man pineth away.' **19. Rest**] RV 'remnant' (of the Assyrian armies).

20–23. The divine judgment will have a purifying effect on Judah; a remnant shall escape (1 9 6 13) who shall be truly devoted to Jehovah.

20. Upon him that smote them] i.e. the Assyrian, on whose help Ahaz relied (7 20).

21. Characteristic teaching of Isaiah, which he had embodied in the symbolic name Shear-jashub ('a remnant shall return'), given to his son (7 3). It is noteworthy that in this same verse there occurs also the divine title 'Mighty God,' which the prophet had ascribed to the Messianic king (9 6). **22.** *Yet* **a remnant**] RV 'only a remnant.' **The consumption,** etc.] RV 'a consumption' (i.e. judgment) 'is determined, overflowing with righteousness.'

24. He shall smite, etc.] RV 'though he smite,' etc. **After the manner,** etc.] alluding to the oppressive cruelty of Pharaoh.

25. Cease] RV 'be accomplished.' God's **indignation** against His people will be appeased after their punishment, and His **anger** will then turn to the **destruction** of their enemies. **26. Scourge for him**] i.e. for the Assyrian. **According to**] RV 'as in.' The slaughter of Midian is also referred to as a typical deliverance in 9 4. **His rod**] i.e. Jehovah's, contrasted with the Assyrian oppressor's rod (v. 24). As the Egyptian oppression was followed by the exodus, so the Assyrian oppression is to be succeeded by a similarly striking deliverance.

27. Because of the anointing] i.e. because of the anointed king of David's house to which God has promised a lasting kingdom. But RV 'by reason of fatness.' A new metaphor. Judah is compared to a bullock which grows so fat and strong that a yoke can no longer be imposed upon it. A conjectural emendation by Robertson Smith makes the last sentence of this v. read, 'There cometh up from the north the destroyer.'

28–32. The prophet reverts to the present.

The Assyrian advance and consequent panic vividly portrayed.

28. The towns mentioned are all to the N. of Jerusalem. **Passed to**] RV 'passed through.' **Hath laid up,** etc.] RV 'layeth up his baggage': cp. 1 S 17 20. **Carriage** is used in AV for 'things carried.' **29. Passage**] RV 'pass.'

30. Cause it to be heard, etc.] RV 'hearken, O Laishah,' viz. to the noise of the approaching armies. **O poor Anathoth**] RM 'Answer her, O Anathoth.' **31. Is removed**] RV 'is a fugitive.' **Gather themselves to flee**] rather, 'save their households by flight': cp. Ex 9 19.

32–34. Arrived within sight of Jerusalem, and threatening the city, the Assyrian meets with sudden disaster.

32. RV 'This very day shall he halt at Nob, he shaketh his hand at the mount,' etc. **33. Haughty,** etc.] RV 'lofty shall be brought low.' **34.** The figure is the same as in vv. 17–19. The Assyrians are to fall like a forest that is hewn down. Note close connexion with c. 11.

CHAPTER 11

1. Rod out of the stem] RV 'shoot out of the stock,' implying that the tree has been cut down. The Assyrians have been compared in the vv. preceding to cedars, which when felled throw out no fresh suckers; now the house of David is likened to an oak whose life remains in it after it has been cut down (6 13). From the royal family of Judah, though it may seem ruined, is to spring the ideal Ruler in the future. It has been already implied (9 7), and is here expressly stated, that the Messiah is to be of the house of David (Mic 5 2).

2. Leaving the figure Isaiah here indicates the character of the future Ruler. The gifts of the divine Spirit bestowed upon Him are arranged in three pairs, the first pair indicating perfection of intellectual endowment, the second pair full possession of a ruler's practical qualities, and the third referring to the religious spirit which is to crown and direct all other gifts.

3. Make him of quick understanding] RV 'his delight shall be in the fear of Jehovah,' i.e. when He sees it in others. **Not judge,** etc.] i.e. by appearances or hearsay. **4.** The ideal Ruler combines mercy and judgment (Ps 101 1). **With the rod of his mouth**] The power ascribed to the word of Messiah is a striking feature (49 2 Zech 9 10), and suggests a superhuman personality (Hos 6 5). **5. The girdle**] stands for readiness for action—He shall be always ready for righteousness and faithfulness.

6. From the person and character of the Ruler Isaiah now passes on to the effects of His rule. Evil having been eradicated from human society, there will be a corresponding regeneration of the rest of creation (65 25 Ro 8 19 f.). **8. Cockatrice**] RV 'basilisk,' or 'adder' (RM): probably the great yellow viper common in Palestine. **9. My holy mountain**] i.e. Zion wonderfully transformed according to the prophecy in 2 2 (Zech 14 10, 11).

10. RV 'And it shall come to pass in that day, that the root of Jesse, which standeth for an ensign of the people, unto him shall the nations seek.' **Root of Jesse**] the same as the shoot growing from the root (v. 1). The great scion of the house of David is not only to be king of Israel, but the nations of the world shall rally to him. **Seek**] i.e. resort, a word specially used of resorting for prayer (55 6) or of consulting oracles (8 19 19 3). **Rest**] i.e. resting-place : referring to Jerusalem, the seat of the royal house.

11. Next the prophet speaks of the restoration of the dispersed Israelites from their exile in the various kingdoms by which Judah was surrounded. **The second time**] The first time was at the Mosaic exodus. **Recover**] RM 'purchase' : cp. Ex 15 16. **Pathros**] upper, or southern, Egypt. **Cush**] Ethiopia, still further S. (18 1 37 9). **Elam**] the country at the head of the Persian Gulf. **Shinar**] i.e. Babylonia. **Hamath**] see on 10 9. **Islands of the sea**] a phrase found here only in chs. 1–39, but several times in chs. 40–66. It denotes the islands of, and lands bordering upon, the Mediterranean Sea, and sometimes stands for distant countries generally.

13. A further feature of Messiah's sign. The bitter feeling between the N. kingdom and Judah (9 21) shall cease. **The adversaries of**] RV 'they that vex.'

14. The reunited people will be victorious over their old enemies, the tribes immediately surrounding Palestine. **Shoulders**] 'shoulder,' i.e. side or border, as in Josh 15 8, 10, 11. **Them of the east**] lit. 'the children of the east,' i.e. the Bedouin Arabs : Jg 6 3 2 Ch 21 16.

15, 16. Isaiah pictures a miraculous deliverance of the exiles parallel to the former deliverance from Egypt. **The tongue**, etc.] i.e. the Gulf of Akaba. **Tongue** is used for an arm of the sea as in Josh 15 2 18 19. **The river**] i.e. Euphrates. **In the seven**] RV 'into seven.' **An highway**] i.e. a raised road such as Eastern monarchs made for the passage of their armies (19 23 49 11). **It was**] RV 'there was.'

CHAPTER 12

1. The thanksgiving that now follows is the counterpart of the hymn of praise sung after the passage of the Red Sea (Ex 15), and is partly based upon it. Some scholars doubt its Isaianic authorship and date it after the return from exile.

3. Draw water] Under a figure it is indicated that there shall be a continual supply of divine protection and deliverance. Or, if we follow the Talmud, there may be an allusion to the ceremonial of the Feast of Tabernacles, on the last day of which water was drawn from the pool of Siloam by the priests and poured at the altar of burnt-offering (see Jn 7 37). **5. He hath done excellent things**] from Ex 15 1, 'triumphed gloriously,' the same word. **This** *is* **known**] RV 'let this be known.'

CHAPTERS 13 1–14 23

THE JUDGMENT OF BABYLON AND ITS KING

This is the first of a series of prophecies dealing mainly with foreign nations. Its subject is Babylon, where the Jews are represented as undergoing exile, from which they are about to be delivered (14 1-3) owing to the capture of Babylon by the Medes (13 17). The historical setting of the prophecy is thus much later than the age of Isaiah, in whose time the Assyrians were the great enemies of God's people. On this ground most modern scholars regard this section as non-Isaianic, and date it during the Babylonian exile. As the Medes alone (not Cyrus and the Persians) are mentioned as the instruments used by God in the deliverance of His people, the prophecy must be dated before 549 B.C., the year in which Cyrus overthrew the Medes, who afterwards were united with him in the conquest of Babylon (538 B.C).

C. 13. **1.** Title prefixed to the section.

2–18. Hostile hosts are mustered to carry out Jehovah's purpose of judgment against Babylon, **19–22.** with the result that it shall be utterly desolate.

C. 14. **1–3.** The deliverance of captive Israel.

4–20. A song of triumph over the king of Babylon. 1st scene : Hades, where the spirit of the vain-glorious monarch is brought low (4–15). 2nd scene : The battle-field, where his dishonoured corpse lies with the slain (16–20). **21–23.** The completeness of Babylon's overthrow.

CHAPTER 13

1. Burden] The corresponding verb means 'to lift up' (*a*) a load, (*b*) the voice (cp. 3 7 42 2. 11), used of Balaam lifting up his voice in oracular utterance (Nu 24 3, 15, 23). Hence the noun signifies an utterance, or oracle (e.g. 2 K 9 25), and is often prefixed, as here, to prophetic utterances (Zech 9 1 12 1 Prov 31 1). Since it is often applied to threatening utterances, the meaning of 'burden' is also suitable. In Jer 23 33 there is a play on the two meanings of the word.

2. Banner] RV 'ensign,' i.e. a signal for the

mustering of distant armies (5 26). **High**] RV 'bare,' i.e. without trees; upon such a mountain the signal would be clearly seen. **Unto them**] i.e. the people whom the prophet has in mind, though they have not yet been mentioned.

Shake the hand] the threatening gesture of besiegers (10 32). 3. **Sanctified ones**] RV 'consecrated ones,' i.e. warriors. The thought may be that the war is a holy one, Babylon's destroyers being the ministers of Jehovah's vengeance.

4. The prophet hears the noise of the armies assembling at the signal (v. 2). **Of the battle**] RV 'for the battle.'

6. **The Almighty**] Heb. *Shaddai*, a name of God frequent in the Pentateuch, and belonging to the pre-Mosaic revelation (Ex 6 3); it is not often found in the prophets, and when it occurs the severe and awful aspect of the divine nature is the more prominent one (Joel 1 15 Ezk 1 24 10 5).

8. *As* **flames**] RV 'faces of flame,' i.e. flushed with agitation.

10. The day of Jehovah is accompanied by signs in the heavens as in Joel 2 10, 31 3 15 Zeph 1 14, 15. Such language need not be understood literally, but vividly expresses a time of terror and dismay. 12. **Precious**] RV 'rare'; the slaughter will be so great that few men will be left (24 6). **Golden wedge**] RV 'pure gold'; the gold of Ophir was most esteemed.

13. See a similar description Hag 2 6. The prophets are carried in thought beyond the particular political convulsion in view to the final overthrow of all that is hostile to God.

14. RV 'And it shall come to pass that as,' etc. **That no man taketh up**] i.e. without a shepherd. **They shall . . turn**] i.e. the settlers in Babylon, either taken captive from other countries, or resorting thither for trade (Jer 50 16), will, on the overthrow of the city, disperse to their own lands. 15. The reason for the hurried flight of v. 14; the fall of the city will be accompanied by indiscriminate slaughter.

Joined *unto them*] i.e. by colonisation. But RV 'taken,' not having been able to make good his escape. 16. The atrocities referred to frequently accompanied the sack of a city (2 K 8 12 Hos 10 14 13 16).

17. The invaders of Babylon are here first mentioned by name, though the prophet has had them in mind from v. 2. The **Medes** had settled in the district SW. of the Caspian Sea, and are mentioned in Assyrian annals from Sargon's time onwards (cp. 2 K 17 6 18 11): see intro. to this section. **Shall not regard**] i.e. they are not to be turned aside by bribes.

18. **Bows**] The Medes were noted archers (Jer 51 11). 19. **Excellency**] RV 'pride.'

20. **Make their fold**] RV 'make their flocks to lie down.' A more terrible desolation

awaits Babylon than that which had been foretold for Judah (7 21, 25).

21. **Doleful creatures**] probably owls. **Owls**] RV 'ostriches.' **Satyrs**] i.e. uncanny creatures, or demons (so Targum, LXX, and Syr.), such as were thought by the Jews to haunt ruins and desert places: cp. Lk 11 24. But as the other names in the context stand for animals many prefer to render, 'he-goats' (RM, Vulg.).

22. The **wild . . houses**] RV 'wolves shall cry in their castles.' **Dragons**] RV 'jackals.'

The anticipation of the utter ruin of Babylon has been literally fulfilled. In 538 B.C. it was captured by the Medes and Persians under Cyrus; and, though its glory lingered for a time, it died away before the beginning of the Christian era, and Babylon is now, and has long been, only a heap of ruins.

CHAPTER 14

1. **Strangers**] The thought of the voluntary adhesion of strangers is prominent in the later chapters of the book (44 5 55 5 60 5).

2. **People**] RV 'peoples.' Similar anticipations are found in 49 22 60 10 61 5: these were in some measure fulfilled in the time of Ezra: Ezr 1 1-4 6 7, 8.

4. **Proverb**] RV 'parable' (Hab 2 6), or 'taunting-song.' **The King**] Nabonidus was king of Babylon from 555 till its fall 549 B.C. **Golden city**] rather, RM, 'exactress,' or 'raging one.' 7. The nations rejoice in the peace which follows the fall of their oppressor.

9. The spirit of the dead king of Babylon is greeted by the shades in Hades. **The dead**] lit. 'feeble ones'; the word is used in Heb. for disembodied spirits (Ps 88 10). **It hath raised,** etc.] In Hades the dead monarchs are conceived as retaining some shadow of their former greatness: cp. Ezk 32 21. 11. **The grave**] RV 'hell,' as in v. 9; i.e. Hades.

12. The fall of the mighty king is compared, first, to the fall of the bright star of dawn from the sky, then, by a sudden change of figure, to the felling of a great tree. **Lucifer**] RV 'day-star.' **Weaken**] RV 'lay low.'

13. The arrogant self-deification here put into the mouth of the Babylonian king finds a parallel in some of the Assyrian inscriptions.

Mount, etc.] not Zion, as many ancient commentators explain, comparing Ps 48 2, but the mount in the far N. where the gods are imagined to reside—the Babylonian Olympus: cp. Ezk 28 12-14. **Sides**] RV 'uttermost parts,' and so in v. 15.

16. The scene now shifts to the battle-field, where men gaze upon the dishonoured corpse of the dead king. 18. **Lie**] RV 'sleep.' **In his own house**] i.e. in a tomb of his own.

19. **An abominable branch**] i.e. a blighted branch cut off from a tree and left to rot upon the ground. *And as* **the raiment . . slain**] RV

clothed with the slain.' The king's corpse lies under heaps of the slain on the field of defeat. **The stones of the pit**] referring to stones flung together in a hastily-made grave on the battle-field.

20. Shalt not be joined, etc.] To be excluded from burial was the extremest disgrace for a king: Jer 22 19 2 Ch 21 20 24 25. **With them**] i.e. the honourably buried kings (v. 18).

Shall . . renowned] RV 'shall not be named for ever'; a similar curse is pronounced on Jehoiachin (Jer 22 30). The taunt-song ends with this verse, and in vv. 21–23 the prophet speaks in his own person.

21. With cities] as emblems of their dominion. **22. Nephew**] RV 'son's son.'

23. Pools of water] The works of irrigation connected with the Euphrates being destroyed the land would become a morass. This, in fact, happened after the conquest of Babylon by Cyrus.

CHAPTER 14 24-27
The Destruction of the Power of Assyria

A short section belonging to the same period as 10 5–12 6 (cp. v. 25 with 10 27); the subject is the overthrow of the Assyrian invader, and the prophecy was literally fulfilled in the destruction of Sennacherib's army.

24-27. It is Jehovah's sworn and unalterable purpose to destroy the Assyrian power, that his burdensome rule over Judah and the nations may cease.

25. Upon my mountains] i.e. the mountains of Judah (49 11 65 9). **26. All the nations**] Jehovah's merciful purpose embraces not only His own people, but the nations generally.

CHAPTER 14 28-32
Warning to the Philistines

This prophecy is assigned, in the title prefixed to it, to the year that king Ahaz died (728 B.C.). The Philistines are represented as exulting over the death of their oppressor, but are warned that their joy is premature, for worse times are in store for them. The oppressor of Philistia referred to may be (1) Ahaz, whose death may have formed the occasion of the utterance, or, more probably, (2) Tiglath-pileser, whose ally Ahaz had been; in that case Sargon and Sennacherib are indicated by the cockatrice and fiery serpent (v. 29), each one proving more terrible and formidable to the nations of Western Asia than his predecessor. The joy of Philistia is premature, for, though apparently broken, the Assyrian power will recover and become more formidable than before (**v. 29**). While Judah escapes, Philistia will suffer from famine and sword (**30**), and the smoke on the horizon already marks the invader's approach (**31**). Philistine ambas-

sadors arrived in Judah to arrange a defensive alliance; the prophet's answer is an expression of confidence in Jehovah, who has promised safety to Zion (**32**).

29. Thou, whole Palestina] RV 'O Philistia, all of thee.' **Rod of him,** etc.] RV 'rod that smote.' The **rod** symbolises the Assyrian power, as in 10 24. **Serpent's root,** etc.] Each species mentioned is more deadly than the preceding, the fiery serpent being the worst of all (30 6 Nu 21 6); the serpent also symbolises Assyria in 27 1.

30. Firstborn of the poor] i.e. the very poor, those inheriting a double portion (Dt 21 17) of poverty. The reference is to the people of Judah, who, though afflicted, shall escape, whereas of the Philistines will be left no remnant to return. **31. Thou . . dissolved**] RV 'thou art melted away, O Philistia, all of thee.' **The north**] the way by which the invader would naturally approach. *Shall be* **alone in**] RV 'standeth aloof at.' The meaning is that no soldier is missing from the ranks of the enemy. **32. Trust**] RV 'take refuge.'

CHAPTERS 15, 16
Moab's Calamity and the Way of Escape

This section consists of two parts: (*a*) 15 1–16 12, a prophecy announcing that a great disaster is about to fall upon Moab, and (*b*) 16 13, 14, a short appendix in which Isaiah affirms the speedy fulfilment of the foregoing prophecy. The first part is not necessarily by Isaiah, and may have been uttered earlier than his time; much of it is also quoted by Jeremiah (48 1-47). Cp. 2 2-4, where there is reason to suppose that an earlier prophecy has been used by both Isaiah and Micah. The Moabites inhabited the elevated land E. of the Dead Sea, and though a people related by blood to Israel, the mutual relations of the two nations were hostile from the time of Saul onwards. Saul fought against them (1 S 14 47), and David overcame them (2 S 8 2). Ahab oppressed them and exacted tribute (2 K 3 4, confirmed by king Mesha of Moab in the inscription known as the Moabite Stone); but after his death the Moabites threw off the Israelite yoke (2 K 1 1 3 5, Moabite Stone), and Jehoram's efforts to maintain his authority over them were ineffectual (2 K 3 6-27). The exact date of the prophecy is uncertain, but the enemy who will inflict the coming calamity upon Moab is the Assyrian king, either Sargon or Sennacherib, referred to, perhaps, in 15 9 under the figure of a lion.

C. 15. 1-9. Calamity is imminent for Moab; the terror and flight of her people.

C. 16. 1-5. A condition of safety indicated. Let Moab acknowledge the suzerainty of Judah (vv. 1–3); Zion will shelter her fugitives (4), for to Zion the promise of the Messianic king has been given (5). **6-12.** Moab's proud spirit prevents her from accepting the condition. Desolation therefore awaits her land. **13, 14.** The above prophecy had been delivered at an earlier period. Isaiah affirms that it shall speedily be fulfilled.

CHAPTER 15

1. Burden] see on 13[1]. **Because .. night**] RV 'For in a night.' **Ar of Moab**] i.e. city of Moab. The capital (Nu 22[36] Josh 13[16]) is doubtless meant. The places referred to in the c. are in Moabite territory. **Silence**] RV 'nought.' **Kir**] probably Kerak, a fortress on the Dead Sea. **2. He is gone**, etc.] i.e. the Moabite people. **Bajith**] 'the house,' i.e. the temple of the Moabite deity, Chemosh. **Dibon**] here the Moabite Stone, with inscription by king Mesha (2 K 3[4]), was found in 1869. **Nebo**] not the mountain (Dt 34[1]), but a Moabite city in its vicinity, thought to be called after the deity of the same name. **Baldness**, etc.] in token of mourning. **Heshbon, Elealeh**] neighbouring hill-towns of Moab.

4. His life, etc.] RV 'his soul trembleth within him.'

5. Fugitives] RV 'her nobles.' **An heifer of three years old**] i.e. not broken in : implying that the place was hitherto impregnable. Places are thus sometimes compared to animals (Jer 46[20] Hos 4[16] 10[11]). Most modern scholars, however, understand the words as a proper name ' to Eglath-shelishiyah ' (RV). **Mounting up**] RV 'ascent': the prophet sees the ascent of Luhith crowded with weeping fugitives.

6. Shall be desolate] because they have been stopped at the source (2 K 3[19, 25]). **Hay .. grass**] RV 'grass .. tender grass.' **7. The brook of the willows**] Evidently mentioned as the boundary of the land and generally identified with the brook Zered (Nu 21[12] Dt 2[13]). The fugitives are pictured as carrying their possessions to the border for safety. **8. The cry**] i.e. of destruction (v. 5). No part of the land escapes. **9. The waters of Dimon**] i.e. the Arnon. **Dimon** is probably a symbolical variation for Dibon, adopted because the sound of it suggests blood (*dam*). **Lions**] perhaps to be understood literally (2 K 17[25]), or it may stand metaphorically for invading foes : Jer 4[7] 5[6].

CHAPTER 16

1. RV ' Send ye the lambs for the ruler of the land from Sela *which is* toward the wilderness,' etc. Mesha, king of Moab, had rendered to Israel tribute of lambs and rams (2 K 3[4]). The prophet here bids the Moabites send tribute to Judah and thus secure protection by renewing their allegiance to God's people ; or perhaps in this v. the Moabite chiefs are pictured as exhorting one another to this step. **From Sela**] in Edom, where the fugitive Moabites have taken refuge. **2.** Timid and

not knowing which way to take, the people are gathered at the Arnon preparatory to migrating. **3.** An appeal from the Moabites to Zion that she will interpose and shelter the fugitives. **Take counsel**] ' bring counsel,' i.e. give us advice. **Execute judgment**] ' make a decision,' by interposing between us and our oppressors.

4. The appeal to Zion continued. Read, ' Let mine outcasts dwell with thee (Zion) ; as for Moab, be thou (Judah) a covert,' etc. The reason follows why safety may be sought at Zion—because of the peace to be enjoyed there under the rule of the Messianic king (v. 5), the establishment of whose kingdom is, in the prophet's view, to follow upon the destruction of the Assyrians. **5. Hasting righteousness**] RV ' swift to do righteousness ' : cp. 11[4, 5].

6. The pride] which prevented Moab from accepting conditions : the same national failing is alluded to 25[11] (cp. Zeph 2[8]). *But* **his lies**, etc.] RV ' his boastings are nought.'

7. Foundations] RV ' raisin-cakes ' : cp. Hos 3[1]. The trade in these would cease through the desolation of the vineyards.

Kir-hareseth] named in 2 K 3[25] as a strong fortress.

8. The lords, etc.] RM ' her choice plants did break down the lords of nations,' alluding to the strength of the wine of Sibmah.

Principal] RV ' choice.' **Are come .. *through* .. are stretched out, they are gone over**] RV ' reached .. into .. were spread abroad, they passed.' The words describe the area over which the cultivation of the vine extended in Moab, but which is now desolate; or perhaps the language used in this v. may be used figuratively to express the wide extent of Moabite influence : cp. Ps 80[8 f.], etc.

9. With the weeping of Jazer] i.e. with sorrow as genuine as that of the Moabites themselves. **For the shouting**, etc.] RV ' for upon thy summer fruits and upon thy harvest the *battle* shout is fallen.' **11. My bowels**] regarded as the seat of the emotions (Jer 31[20]). The speaker is probably Jehovah, as in v. 10 (63[15]).

12. RV 'And it shall come to pass, when Moab presenteth himself, when he wearieth himself upon the high place, and shall come to his sanctuary to pray, that he shall not prevail.' The allusion is to the worship of the national deity, Chemosh.

13. Since that time] RV ' in time past.' The expression may denote a previous time in the speaker's life (2 S 15[34]), or a more distant past (44[8]).

14. The years of an hireling] i.e. definitely reckoned, with no grace allowed. **Feeble**] RV ' of no account.'

CHAPTER 17 [1-11]
JUDGMENT ON SYRIA AND ISRAEL

This section is headed, 'oracle concerning Damascus,' but its subject is in fact wider ; it treats of the impending ruin not only of Syria, but also of Ephraim, i.e. the kingdom of Israel (v. 3). This connexion of Ephraim with Syria is best explained by the alliance of the two kingdoms against Judah (7 [1,2]). Isaiah here teaches (as in 7 [16] 8 [4]) that they will both be completely overthrown, an anticipation which was literally fulfilled (10 [9] 2 K 15 [29] 16 [9]). The date of this prophecy would thus be subsequent to the formation of the Syro-Ephraimite alliance (i.e. the reign of Jotham in Judah, 2 K 15 [37]), and some time before the capture of Damascus by the Assyrians (732 B.C.).

1-3. The imminent ruin of Damascus, in which Israel also will be involved. **4-6.** The state to which Israel will be reduced figuratively set forth. **7, 8.** The spiritual effect of the chastisement. **9-11.** The cause of it—desertion of Jehovah for foreign deities, who cannot help in the day of calamity.

1. Burden] see on 13 [1]. **2. The cities of Aroer**] This Aroer is probably the one in Gad (Josh 13 [25]), and the reference is to the cities belonging to the kingdom of Israel on the E. of Jordan. Some ancient versions, however, read, ' the cities are forsaken for ever.' **3. And the remnant, etc.**] RM 'and the remnant of Syria shall be as,' etc. **As the glory**] explained in vv. 4–6, where it is shown that the glory of Israel shall pass away.

4-6. By three separate figures the gloomy prospects of Israel are set forth : (*a*) that of an emaciated body, v. 4 ; (*b*) that of a harvest field that is reaped, v. 5 ; (*c*) that of vines or olives when the fruit is gathered, v. 6. The teaching is characteristic of Isaiah, for the figures imply that for Israel, as for Judah (4 [3] 6 [13] 7 [3]) there shall be a remnant. **5. As he that gathereth**] RV 'as when one gleaneth.' **Valley of Rephaim**] SW. of Jerusalem (Josh 15 [8]).

8. Groves] Heb. *Asherim* (RV). These were symbols of the Canaanite goddess Asherah. The symbol seems to have been a pole, tree-trunk, or carved pillar (Dt 16 [21] 2 K 21 [7]), erected near an altar (Jg 6 [25]). **Images**] RV ' sun-images,' pillars dedicated to the sun-god. **9. As a forsaken, etc.**] RV ' as the forsaken places in the wood and on the mountain top, which were forsaken from before the children of Israel.' LXX, however, reads, 'forsaken places of the Amorites and the Hivites which were forsaken,' etc. The sense is that Israel shall be punished with a desolation like that which the former inhabitants experienced at the hands of the Israelites. **10. Rock**] a title of Jehovah (30 [29] Dt 32 [4]). **Shalt thou plant . .**

shalt set] RV 'plantest . . settest.' This is a metaphor of the foreign worships so carefully introduced.

CHAPTER 17 [12-14]
DISCOMFITURE OF THE ASSYRIANS

A short prophecy, in which Isaiah foretells sudden disaster for the Assyrian invaders ; it is parallel to 14 [24-27], and belongs to the same period.

12-13. The Assyrian hosts advance against Judah, but are suddenly dispersed in a single night.

12. Read, ' Ah, the uproar of many peoples, which roar like the roaring of the seas ; and the rushing,' etc. **Many people**] The Assyrian army was recruited from many nations. **13. Rolling thing**] RV ' whirling dust '; cp Ps 83 [13]. **14.** Specially fulfilled in the destruction of Sennacherib's army (37 [36]).

CHAPTER 18
ETHIOPIA REASSURED

Isaiah here addresses the Ethiopians, who, agitated at the advance of the Assyrians westward, were sending ambassadors to other states to organise resistance. He foretells the sudden overthrow of the Assyrians, as in 10 [28-34] 14 [24-27] 17 [12-14] ; and this prophecy should accordingly be grouped with those, as relating to Sennacherib's great invasion in the reign of Hezekiah, 701 B.C.

1-3. The Ethiopians need not be anxious, but are bidden, with all nations, to watch.

4-6. For Jehovah will interpose and utterly ruin the Assyrian plans. **7.** On witnessing the deliverance, Ethiopia will render homage to Jehovah.

1. RV ' Ah, the land of the rustling of wings,' probably alluding to the buzzing swarms of flies characteristic of **Ethiopia** (the land between the Upper Nile and the Red Sea and Arabian Gulf), but some see a reference to the disk with wings, which appears in ancient Egyptian paintings as a symbol of Ethiopian sovereignty. **2. Vessels of bulrushes**] i.e. made of papyrus, such as are still in use on the Nile. Omit *saying* and understand the exhortation **Go ye**, etc., as addressed by the prophet to the Ethiopian ambassadors, bidding them return home and prepare their nation, not for war, but to be spectators (v. 3) of what follows. **A nation scattered, etc.**] AV implies that the reference is to Judah ; but we should doubtless take it as referring to the Ethiopians, and read, ' a nation tall and smooth . . that meteth out and treadeth down, whose land the rivers divide ' (RV). Notice in all these short prophecies the familiarity of Isaiah, not only with the physical features of the different countries, but with their national characteristics : cp. 16 [6] 19.

4. The v. vividly depicts the calmness of Jehovah in contrast to the unrest amongst the nations. **Like . . herbs**] RM 'when there is clear heat in sunshine.' **5. When the bud . . flower**] RV 'when the blossom is over and the flower becometh a ripening grape.' The Assyrian plans are maturing (under apparently favourable conditions, v. 4), but just as they become ripe they are suddenly marred. The sudden overthrow of the Assyrians is similarly foretold, 10 17 14 25 17 13. **6.** Leaving the figure, the prophet refers to the corpses of the slain.

7. A people scattered] Correct the rendering as in v. 2.

CHAPTER 19
THE JUDGMENT ON EGYPT

A prophecy concerning Egypt, probably belonging to the same period as c. 18, and designed to show the speedy collapse of Egypt's power, on which a strong political party in Judah in Hezekiah's reign had placed their hopes (see Intro.). Sargon defeated the Egyptians at Raphia in 720 B.C., and the prophet in vv. 2, 3 may refer to the anarchy and confusion consequent upon that overthrow. At any rate, he shows a remarkable acquaintance both with the country and the people of Egypt.

1–10. The impending calamity of Egypt. **11–15.** Its helplessness at the crisis. **16–25.** The outcome of the judgment: (a) a state of terror (16, 17); (b) recognition of Jehovah (18–22); (c) followed by a call to share the blessings of God's chosen people (23–25). **1. Burden**] see on 13 1. **Rideth**] cp. Ps 18 9, 10. The strength of Egypt is broken at Jehovah's approach. **2.** Civil war rages between the petty princes of lower Egypt. **4.** The Assyrian monarch Sargon may be the cruel lord in the prophet's thoughts; he defeated the Egyptians more than once (720, 711, B.C.). **6.** RV 'And the rivers shall stink; the streams of Egypt shall be minished and dried up.' **7.** RV 'The meadows by the Nile, by the brink of the Nile,' etc. **8.** With the failure of the river the occupation of the fishermen will be gone. **Brooks**] RV 'Nile.' **9. Networks**] RV 'white cloth.' **10.** RV 'And her pillars shall be broken in pieces, all they that work for hire shall be grieved in soul.' **Pillars**] i.e. the foundations of society (Ps 11 3), or principal men (Gal 2 9). **11. Zoan**] or Tanis, in the Delta. **12.** The first proof of their folly; they cannot foresee the future. **13.** A second proof, by ill-judged counsel they have brought about disaster. **Noph**] i.e. Memphis, a chief city of Lower Egypt. **Stay**] RV 'corner stone': cp. Zech 10 4. **15. Branch**] RV 'palm branch': cp.

9 14; the expressions in the v. are figurative of all classes of society. **16. In that day**] the Day of God's judgment. **17.** Egypt is filled with terror at the mention of Judah, because of Judah's God.

18. Five] a small number. **Language of Canaan**] Hebrew. **Swear**] i.e. swear allegiance. **Shall be called**] as deserving the name (1 26). **City of destruction**] i.e. Heliopolis, the city of the sun (*Ir-hacheres*), but by a slight change in one letter (*Ir-haheres*), the prophet symbolically indicates its fate—the place where the sun was worshipped will be destroyed. Somewhat similarly Beth-El ('house of God') is written Beth-Aven ('house of nought'), Hos 4 15, and Bosheth ('shame') stands for Baal (Jer 11 13). **19.** There will be visible signs of Egypt's allegiance to Jehovah. **Pillar**] or obelisk, such as were common in Egypt; the mark of a holy place. **20–22.** Isaiah looks forward to a time when, instead of Egypt exercising an evil influence over the destiny of Judah, Judah shall be the means of spiritual blessing to Egypt. **23–25.** The prophet in rapt vision sees the historic and traditional enemies of his nation joined with it in membership of one holy people of God, where all share equal privilege. A like wonderful catholic and missionary spirit is shown in Ps 87.

Like Isaiah's other pictures of the ideal future, this prophecy (vv. 20–25) yet awaits its complete fulfilment. We may, however, trace partial and, as it were, preparatory fulfilments (a) in the influence of the Persian monarchy, which succeeded the Assyrian empire and did much for the spread of monotheism in the world. Cyrus himself, in his proclamations, recognised Jehovah as the God of heaven (Ezr 1 2); (b) the Jewish exiles in Egypt acted as leaven, and under the Ptolemies the Hebrew Scriptures were translated into Greek. Thus, in a wonderful manner was the way prepared for the extension of the gospel of Christ, and the bringing of the nations to the knowledge of the true God.

CHAPTER 20
EGYPT'S CAPTIVITY SYMBOLISED

This c. is assigned in the title to the time when Sargon besieged Ashdod (711 B.C.). The Philistine city was at that time the centre of revolt. Sargon interposed and set up a new king, but the people were dissatisfied and substituted another; the siege and capture of Ashdod by the Assyrians followed. It seems that the Palestinian peoples who revolted against Assyria relied upon the support of Egypt. Isaiah, by putting on captive's garb, and walking the streets of Jerusalem for three years, indicates in a striking manner the vanity of their expectations.

2-6. Isaiah's striking action intended to symbolise the captivity of Egypt and Ethiopia, which would confound those who looked to them for aid.

1. Tartan] rather, 'the Tartan': the official title of the Assyrian commander-in-chief (2 K 18 17). **Sargon**] The only known mention of this monarch until modern times. Inscriptions have now thrown much light on his reign. He followed Shalmaneser (2 K 18 9) 722 B.C. and reigned till 705, when he was succeeded by Sennacherib. **2. Sackcloth**] such as prophets sometimes wore (2 K 1 8 Zech 13 4). **Naked, etc.**] i.e. in the guise of a captive. Not only by word, but by action calculated to arrest attention, Isaiah strove to impress his message. Such symbolic actions were frequently performed by the prophets (1 K 11 30 Jer 19 1f. 27 2). **4.** The prophet's strange action explained. **6. Isle**] RV 'coast-land,' referring especially to Philistia, which had been foremost in the revolt against Assyria. **Flee**] RV 'fled.'

CHAPTER 21 1-10
VISION OF BABYLON'S FALL

The subject of this section is the siege of Babylon, and the dismay with which the prophet receives tidings of its fall. The siege referred to can scarcely be the one at the close of the exile, as is maintained by many scholars, because (*a*) the prophet is much depressed at the thought of Babylon's fall, which he foresees will involve calamity for Judah (vv. 2-4, 10); (*b*) distance from Babylon is presupposed (vv. 6-9); and (*c*) Assyrian researches have revealed three earlier sieges, in 710 by Sargon, and in 703 and 696 by Sennacherib. In 710 and 703 the king of Babylon was Merodach-Baladan, who sent an embassy to Hezekiah (39 1), and whose immediate interests were identical with those of Hezekiah with whom he desired an alliance. This would account for the depression in this prophecy; in the capture of Babylon by the Assyrians, Isaiah sees a warning of the fate that may overtake Judah (v. 10). The prophecy accordingly may be dated either after 710 or 703.

1-5. The prophet is filled with terror at a vision of the fall of Babylon. **6-9.** To the expectant prophet tidings of its fall is brought by a travelling caravan. **10.** His dismay because of the suffering involved for Judah.

1. Burden] see 13 1. **Desert of the sea**] i.e. Babylonia : **sea** refers to the Euphrates, the word being used in Hebrew of a large river, as in 19 5 of the Nile. **South**] the technical name for the S. of Judah, a region specially liable to tempests : Jer 4 11-13 Hos 13 15 Zech 9 14. **It cometh**] i.e. the tidings conveyed in the

prophet's vision. **2. Treacherous dealer**] i.e. the Assyrian (33 1). **Go up, etc.**] the command of the Assyrian to the tributaries serving in his army. **Sighing thereof**] i.e. caused by Babylon.

5. Prepare .. drink] read these verbs as present indicative, 'they prepare,' etc. ; the Babylonian feast is at its height when the cry to arms is raised. **Anoint the shield**] Leather shields were greased before going to battle that the weapons of the enemy might glide off. **6.** The prophet himself is the watchman. **7.** RV 'And when he seeth a troop, horsemen in pairs, a troop of asses, a troop of camels, he shall hearken,' etc. **8.** RV 'cried as a lion.' **9.** Just as he groans aloud in impatience, he sees a company approaching, and recognises that they are the bearers of the expected tidings.

10. Referring to Judah which has suffered much from the Assyrian invader already (10 5). The news of this fresh Assyrian victory over Babylon is distasteful, but the prophet must deliver his message.

CHAPTER 21 11,12
THE FATE OF EDOM

An oracle concerning Edom, here symbolically called Dumah ('silence'), because of the silence and desolation in store for it. The prophecy, like that which follows, refers to a time when the peoples concerned were in danger, probably from the Assyrians ; and, as Sargon was waging war in these districts both in 720 and 711 B.C., the two prophecies may be referred to either of these years.

11, 12. To the enquiring Edomites the prophet gives enigmatic answer—while the immediate future looks bright, calamity is impending.

11. Seir] another name for Edom (Gn 36 8 Dt 2 12). **12. If ye will, etc.**] suggesting the possibility of there being another answer at another time.

CHAPTER 21 13-17
JUDGMENT UPON ARABIA

This section concerns the N. Arabian tribes. For the occasion see prefatory note on 21 11,12.

13-17. Owing to the incursions of the Assyrians the Dedanite caravans must take to flight, and other Arabian tribes shall share their fate.

13. In the forest, etc.] The trading caravans must turn from their route and hide themselves because of the invasion. **Arabia**] in OT. denotes the N. part of what we call Arabia. **Dedanim**] a tribe dwelling near Edom (Ezk 27 15). **14.** The Edomites (**inhabitants of .. Tema**) succour the fugitives. **Prevented, etc.**] RV 'did meet the fugitives with their bread.' **16. According to the years, etc.**] see 16 14.

Kedar] a general name for the tribes of N. Arabia (Ps 120⁵).

17. The forecast was fulfilled in the victories over the Arabian tribes by Sargon and Sennacherib, as related in their inscriptions.

CHAPTER 22¹⁻¹⁴
JERUSALEM REBUKED

A severe rebuke of the conduct of the people of Jerusalem in a time of calamity. The crisis refered to cannot be certainly identified. The difficulty in assigning the passage to Sennacherib's invasion (701 B.C.) is that other prophecies relating to it are marked by encouragement, not, as here, by a tone of rebuke. Perhaps the present prophecy should be dated 711, the time of Sargon's invasion.

1–7. The unworthy behaviour of the people of Jerusalem when attack is imminent.

8–11. Every measure is taken for defence except to turn to Jehovah. 12–14. Instead of mourning, they give themselves to reckless revelry. Such conduct must bring destruction as its punishment.

1. **Valley of vision**] This expression in the title is evidently taken from v. 5. It is generally understood to signify Jerusalem.

Housetops] the natural place of concourse (Jg 16²⁷). The city is apparently *en fête* (v. 13). 2. The joy is the forced gaiety of despair (v. 13). **Slain**] It is implied that they have died through famine. 3. *Which . . far*] RV 'they fled afar off.' 4. **Daughter**] poetical personification of the people (10³²). 5. **By the Lord**] RV ' from the Lord.' **Valley of vision**] Jerusalem may be so designated as being the home of prophetic vision. 6. **Elam . . Kir**] peoples who furnished auxiliaries to the Assyrian army. **Uncovered**] took off its case in preparation for battle. 7. **Shall be . . shall set**] RV ' were . . set.'

8. **Discovered, etc.**] RV ' took away the covering,' which concealed the danger from the people's eyes. **Thou didst look**] The people of Judah are addressed. Instead of looking to Jehovah for help, they rely wholly on their material resources. **House of the forest**] i.e. the house of the forest of Lebanon (1 K 7² 10¹⁷), part of Solomon's palace, used as an armoury. 9. **Seen**] i.e. inspected. Vv. 9, 10 refer to hasty measures taken for defence. **Gathered together, etc.**] to secure a supply during the siege. 10. **Numbered**] to see what material could be spared for strengthening the fortifications. 11. **Ditch**] RV ' reservoir.' **The old pool**] probably the pool of Siloam. **The maker thereof**] RV ' him that hath done 'his,' i.e. God who has brought this trouble upon them.

12. **Weeping**] the outward tokens of national repentance. 13. The reckless enjoy-

ment of the despairing people, who urged the shortness of the time that remained to them as an excuse for their excesses. **Let us eat,** etc.] the argument of men who believed in no hereafter (1 Cor 15³²).

CHAPTER 22¹⁵⁻²⁵
DENUNCIATION OF SHEBNA

This section contains Isaiah's only invective against an individual. He denounces Shebna, the king's chief minister, who may have been a leader of the party which favoured alliance with Egypt. The prophecy was delivered before Sennacherib's invasion (701 B.C.), because at that time we read that Eliakim held the office Isaiah here promises him, while Shebna occupied a subordinate position (36³ 37²).

15–25. The deposition of Shebna. The elevation of Eliakim.

15. **Over the house**] i.e. steward of the royal palace, a very high office sometimes held by a king's son (2 Ch 26²¹). 16. **What hast**] RV ' what doest.' Shebna was apparently a foreigner, who ostentatiously presumed to treat Jerusalem as his native place. **A sepulchre**] Kings and great men in the East used to prepare their tombs in their life-time.

17. **Carry, etc.**] RV ' hurl thee away violently as a strong man, yea he will wrap thee up closely.' 18. **Large country**] i.e. a broad land, where it may roll on and on and not return. **There the chariots, etc.**] RV ' there shall be the chariots of thy glory, thou shame of thy lord's house.' The chariots are another feature of Shebna's ostentation. 19. **I will . . shall he**] Though the person is changed, the subject is the same (viz. Jehovah) in both clauses. Such changes of person are common in Hebrew (1²⁹ 10¹²).

22. **The key**] the symbol of the office. The v. shows the powerful influence exercised by this official. He had the right of admitting to, or excluding from, the king's presence. This is symbolically applied to Christ (Rev 3⁷).

23, 24. The office of Eliakim is to be firmly established. His family will rest upon him, and all kinds of dependents cluster round him. Eliakim means 'God establishes.' 25. **The burden, etc.**] i.e. the vessels hanging upon the nail; figuratively put for the dependents upon a great man.

25. Perhaps the prophet may revert in thought to the fall of Shebna, but the continuation of the figure of the nail seems to point to Eliakim, whose fall, if he abused his power, would involve the ruin of his dependents. Neither the promises nor the denunciations of the prophecy need be considered as absolute, but rather conditional. Eliakim did indeed succeed to Shebna's office (see prefatory note), but we do not know that Shebna

suffered the penalty of exile (v. 18); this may have been averted by repentance.

CHAPTER 23
THE DOOM OF TYRE

Tyre was a great mercantile centre of the ancient world, and at the time of the Hebrew monarchy chief state of Phœnicia, the parent of many colonies, and mistress of the Mediterranean. It is uncertain what siege of Tyre is here referred to ; but see on v. 13.

1–5. The news of the fall of Tyre is spread. **6–9.** Tyre must take refuge in her distant colonies, for her doom is purposed by Jehovah. **10–14.** But even her colonies will afford no refuge, for the power of Phœnicia will be altogether broken. The fate of Chaldea serves as a warning of coming desolation. **15–18.** After seventy years Tyre shall recover her commercial prosperity, but her gains shall be consecrated to Jehovah's service.

1. Homeward-bound ships are greeted at **Chittim** (Cyprus) with the news that Tyre has fallen. **Ships of Tarshish**] Tarshish is probably Tartessus, in Spain ; the expression denotes deep-sea ships. **2. Isle**] 'coastland,' i.e. of Phœnicia. **3. Sihor**] i.e 'black,' a name for the Nile (Jer 2 18). **River**] RV 'Nile.' Tyre reaped large revenues from Egypt by carrying her corn. *Is . . is*] RV 'was . . was.' **4. Strength**] stronghold, i.e Tyre. **Saying,** etc.] The once busy quays are deserted, and the prophet pictures the city as a bereaved mother mourning her children. **5.** RV 'When the report cometh to Egypt they shall be sorely pained.'

6. Tarshish] Tartessus, in Spain. The Tyrians are bidden to seek refuge in their western colonies on the shores of the Mediterranean. Of these Phœnician colonies Carthage was the most famous. **7. Her own**, etc.] RV 'whose feet carried her.' **8. Taken this counsel**] RV 'purposed this.' **Crowning** *city*] alluding to the many dependent kings in her colonies.

10. A river] RV 'the Nile.' *There . .* **strength**] 'There is no girdle about thee any more.' The Tyrian colonies, released from all restraint, throw off allegiance. **11. Against** *. . city*] RV 'concerning Canaan,' i.e. Phœnicia. **12. Oppressed**] or 'defiled.' Tyre was no longer a virgin citadel. **Pass over to Chittim**] Flight to Cyprus would not secure safety from Assyria.

13. This people, etc.] According to AV rendering, this v. describes the consolidation of the Chaldeans into a nation by the Assyrians. There is, however, no other record of this, and it is better to read, 'This people is no more ; the Assyrian hath appointed it for the beasts of the wilderness' (i.e. made it desolate): 'they set up their towers' (siege-towers), 'they overthrew the palaces thereof ; he made it a ruin' (RV). The fate of the Chaldeans at the hand of the Assyrians is quoted as a warning for Tyre. Babylon, the Chaldean capital, was taken by the Assyrians in 710 and 703 B.C. (see on 21 1-10). The present prophecy accordingly should be dated between one or other of those years and Sennacherib's invasion of W. Asia (701). **14. Strength**] RV 'stronghold.'

15. Seventy] perhaps a symbolic number for a long period. **According to,** etc.] i.e. without revolution or change. **16.** The v. is figurative of Tyre seeking to renew her commerce. **17.** Figurative of her restored traffic. **18.** The old occupation will be renewed, but purged of its worldliness.

CHAPTERS 24–27
THE COMING JUDGMENT AND ESTABLISHMENT OF JEHOVAH'S KINGDOM

The subject is the overthrow of a power hostile to God's people, with a description of the deliverance of the Jews and their future glory. The hostile power is not named, and the tone of the whole prophecy is so general that it is impossible to assign it to any occasion. With the anticipated overthrow of the enemy the prophet associates in thought Jehovah's final judgment of the world. Most modern scholars assign this whole section to a date later than the age of Isaiah, urging that (*a*) Isaiah's time does not afford a suitable occasion, (*b*) the literary style is unlike Isaiah's, and (*c*) some of the thoughts are characteristic of a later age, e.g. the conception of guardian spirits of earthly kingdoms (24 21), and the anticipation of a resurrection of God's people from the dead (26 19). In these particulars the section exhibits affinity with the book of Daniel (Dan 10 13 12 1, 2). The wide and general expressions used in these chs. make it easier to apply the important spiritual teaching contained in them to God's people in every age.

C. 24. 1–12. The imminent judgment caused by man's guilt. **13–15.** The result— the remnant praise Jehovah. **16–23.** The judgments that precede the establishment of Jehovah's kingdom.

C. 25. 1–5. The hymn of those delivered when Jehovah's kingdom is set up. **6–8.** The blessings of which Zion shall then be the centre. **9–12.** The thanksgiving of the redeemed for the fall of Moab.

C. 26. 1–4. Another hymn of the redeemed. **5, 6.** The ground of this thanksgiving, the overthrow of the hostile city. **7–14.** Jehovah's judgments teach the world righteousness and destroy oppression. **15–21.** The wonderful revival of God's people.

C. 27. 1–6. Jehovah's care for His people

7–11. Their sufferings are due to their own sin and folly. 12, 13. But restoration awaits them.

CHAPTER 24

2. All class distinctions are obliterated and confused. 5. Defiled] i.e. desecrated by bloodshed (Nu 35³³). Everlasting covenant] The phrase seems to allude to Gn 9¹⁶, the covenant with Noah and his sons. The bloodshed, upon which the great world-empires were founded, was a violation of this primitive covenant.

7–9. The meaning is that every form of enjoyment has ceased. 10. Confusion] or, 'chaos' (Gn 1²), so called because of the desolation awaiting it. No man, etc.] the entrance being blocked with ruins. 11. Crying for, etc.] i.e. 'because of' wine, the vintage having failed (Joel 1⁵).

13. When .. people] RV 'For .. peoples.' Omit 'there shall be.' 14. They] i.e. the escaped remnant, figuratively described in v. 13 : cp. 17⁶. The majesty] as shown in their deliverance. They shall cry .. from the sea] i.e. the dispersed remnant shall raise their cry of praise from the far West. The sea, as usual, denotes the Mediterranean.

15. Fires] RV 'east.' Songs of praise arise both in E. and W. (the isles).

16. Glory, etc.] i.e. splendid is the lot of the righteous. My leanness, etc.] RV 'I pine away, I pine away, woe is me !' Songs of joy are premature ; the barbarian has yet to complete the desolation. 17 f. The desolation yet to come. 18. Windows, etc.] a judgment like the deluge (Gn 7¹¹). 20. Removed, etc.] RV 'moved to and fro like a hut.'

21. Host, etc.] i.e. the guardian spirits of the nations (Dan 10¹³ 12¹), who are responsible for their respective nations, and whose fate is bound up with theirs. 22. Visited] i.e. favourably, and set free. 23. The prophet has passed in thought to the final convulsion of nature, and the manifestation of Jehovah's kingdom in all its glory.

CHAPTER 25

1. Thy counsels, etc.] RV 'even counsels of old' (i.e. formed of old) 'in faithfulness and truth.' 2. A city] viz. the one that oppressed God's people (24¹⁰). Strangers] aliens from God's covenant people (1⁷). 3. The hostile power is not utterly destroyed ; its remnant acknowledges Jehovah. 4. Strength] RV 'stronghold.' 5. As the heat] i.e. as heat is assuaged by the shadow of a cloud. Branch] RV 'song' ; viz. of triumph.

6. The temporal and spiritual blessings which the rule of Jehovah will bring to mankind. This mountain] i.e. Zion (2¹,²). Fat things] i.e. of flesh, offered in sacrifice. On the lees] left on the lees to heighten the

flavour. 7. Covering] Covering the face was a token of mourning for the dead (2 S 19⁴) ; the taking away of the veil or covering is symbolically put for the destruction of death (v. 8). 8. In victory] so some early Gk. versions and St. Paul in quoting this passage (1 Cor 15⁵⁴). Heb. text has 'for ever' (RV). Will wipe, etc.] quoted Rev 7¹⁷ 21⁴. Rebuke] RV 'reproach.'

10. Hand] protecting hand. Under him] RV 'in his place,' where he stands. Moab is here mentioned as being a proud (c. 16) and hostile power, a typical enemy. For the dunghill] RV 'in the waters of the dunghill.' 11. He shall spread] i.e. Moab, who vainly endeavours to save himself. He shall bring] i.e. Jehovah. Spoils] RV 'craft.'

CHAPTER 26

1. Salvation, etc.] the assurance of divine protection takes the place of material bulwarks.

4. Everlasting strength] RM 'a rock of ages.' Rock is applied as a title to God (30²⁹ Dt 32⁴). 5. Lofty city] the power hostile to God's people (24¹⁰).

7. Uprightness] 'straightness,' implying freedom from impediment. Weigh] RV 'direct.' 8. In the way of thy judgments] i.e. in the way which God, by His judgments or decrees, set out for His people to walk in. The context (v. 7) shows this to be the meaning. Thy name] i.e. the manifestation of thyself. The remembrance of thee] RV 'thy memorial,' a synonym for 'name' : Ex 3¹⁵. 9. Night] the season of meditation (Ps 4⁴).

10. Carries on the thought of v. 9. God's judgments are necessary, because His favour is ineffectual. 11. But they shall see, etc.] RV 'but they' (the adversaries) 'shall see thy zeal for the people' (Israel : cp. 63¹⁵ f.) 'and be ashamed ; yea, fire shall devour thine adversaries.'

12. In us] RV 'for us.' 13. Other lords] the oppressors of Israel. Perhaps the prophet also has in mind the deities in whose name they professed to act. Make mention, etc.] i.e. celebrate Thy name in praise. 14. They are dead] i.e. the oppressors. 15. The nation] i.e. Israel. Thou hadst, etc.] RV 'thou hast enlarged all the borders of the land.' 18. The fruitlessness of human effort. Fallen] i.e. been born.

19. Thy dead .. arise] RV 'Thy dead shall live ; my dead bodies shall arise.' The pronouns 'thy' and 'my' both refer to Israel. The passage seems to imply that for God's people, as opposed to the heathen (v. 14), the prophet expected a literal resurrection. Some think, however, that a national restoration, surpassing all expectation, is set forth under

the figure of resurrection from the dead, as in Hos 6 2 Ezk 37 1-10. **Herbs**] RM 'light': i.e. morning dew (Ps 110 3). **20.** Israel may retire and be secure, while the divine judgments pass by. **21. Disclose her blood**] so that it may cry for vengeance (Gn 4 10, 11).

CHAPTER 27

1. The powers hostile to God's people are here symbolically represented as monsters. **Leviathan the piercing** (RV 'swift') **serpent** perhaps stands for Assyria, watered by the rapid Tigris, and 'leviathan the crooked serpent' (RV) for Babylon, whose river was the winding Euphrates. **The dragon**] crocodile, i.e. Egypt, as in 51 9. **2. Sing ye**, etc.] RV 'a vineyard of wine, sing ye unto it.' The vineyard is God's people (c. 5); the song begins at v. 3. **4. Who would**, etc.] RV 'would that the briers and thorns were against me.' **Go through**] RV 'march upon.' God's anger against his vineyard has ceased, and He will now turn against their enemies, figuratively represented as briers and thorns (9 18 10 17). **5.** A gracious overture even to God's enemies. **6. He shall cause**] RV 'In days to come shall Jacob take root'; the image of the vineyard continued.

7. Hath Jehovah smitten Israel as he smote their oppressors? Is Israel slain according to the slaughter of those slain by Jehovah? The implied answer is No. **8. When**, etc.] RV 'when thou sendest her away thou dost contend with her; he hath removed her with his rough blast,' etc. Israel has been smitten but only in measure.

9. The sense is that Israel's sin will be purged on condition that it rejects all idolatry. **The fruit**] RV 'the fruit of taking away': i.e. the result or proof of contrition required as a condition of taking away. **Groves and images**] RV 'Asherim and sun-images': see 17 8. **Not stand up**] RV 'rise no more.' **10. Defenced city**] i.e. of the enemies (as in 25 2). Some, however, understand Jerusalem, which must for a season be desolate. **11. It**] i.e. Israel.

12. Beat off] RV 'beat off the fruit' as from olive trees (Dt 24 20). The ingathering of exiled Israel compared to a fruit harvest. **River**] RV 'River,' i.e. Euphrates. **Stream of Egypt**] the stream dividing Palestine from Egypt (1 K 8 65). **13. Trumpet**] summoning the sacred assembly (Nu 10 1-10).

CHAPTERS 28-33
WARNINGS TO JUDAH

These chs. refer to the state of affairs during the reign of Hezekiah, when Palestine was threatened by Assyria, and an influential party in Judah favoured resistance, relying on the support of Egypt; a line of policy consistently opposed by Isaiah.

CHAPTER 28

This c. must be assigned (v. 1) to a date prior to the capture of Samaria by the Assyrians (722 B.C.) and fall of the northern kingdom.

1-6. Samaria's luxury and self-indulgence pave the way to ruin. **7-10.** Judah likewise is given up to indulgence and heeds not the prophet's warning. **11-13.** Therefore Jehovah will teach the people by means of foreign invasion and disaster. **14-22.** Judah's safety lies not in faithless diplomacy, but in trust in Jehovah. **23-29.** A parable of Jehovah's way of working, drawn from the action of the husbandman, who conducts his operations in accordance with a wise plan.

1. RV 'Woe to the crown of pride of the drunkards of Ephraim, and to the fading flower of his glorious beauty which is on the head,' etc. The city of Samaria crowning its fair valley is destined to fade and pass away like the flower-garlands of her revellers. **2. A mighty . . one**] viz. the Assyrian, Jehovah's agent. **4. Hasty fruit**] RV 'first-ripe fig': a delicacy eagerly devoured. **5.** In place of the false glory destined to perish, Jehovah is to be a true glory for the faithful remnant. **6.** True administration of justice within, and strength to repel the invader. **Turn**, etc.] RV 'turn back the battle at the gate.'

7. They also] the men of Judah. **They err in vision**, etc.] They are drunk when engaged in the sacred duties of their office; the tables they have just left prove it (v. 8).

9. They mock the prophet; his teaching is only fit for babes! **10.** The people's mockery continued. *Must be*] RV 'is.' **Precept . . line**] The words in Heb. are monosyllables, such as would be used in teaching little children.

11. Isaiah's retort, Jehovah will teach them through a foreign invader. RV 'Nay, but by men of strange lips and with another tongue,' etc. **12. This is the rest**, etc.] cp. 30 15. Jehovah through His prophet had pointed out the way of peace and recovery for the nation that already under Ahaz had suffered much through foreign alliance. But the politicians of Judah were without patient trust in Jehovah, and were preparing further trouble by seeking alliance with Egypt. **13.** RV 'Therefore shall the word of the LORD be unto them,' etc. The teaching they refused will prove a burden and a stumblingblock.

15. Made a covenant] they thought that by their policy they had, as it were, bought off death and Hades—made themselves secure. **Lies**, etc.] Though the words are put into the mouth of the politicians, the point of view is the prophet's. **16. Zion**] as being Jehovah's foundation, shall stand firm. The imagery was suggested by the large stones of the Temple. **Shall not make haste**] i.e. hasten hither and thither to seek security by alliances (e.g. with Egypt), but may wait confidently on Jehovah. The Apostles saw the ultimate spiritual fulfilment of Isaiah's words in the person of Christ (Eph 2 20 1 Pet 2 6, 7).

17. RV 'Judgment also will I make the line and righteousness the plummet.' Righteousness is the standard by which Jehovah will try conduct. The sense of what follows is that the false refuges and alliances (v. 18), by which men seek to secure themselves, will be swept away. **19. From . . forth**] RV 'As often as it passeth through.' **A vexation,** etc.] RV 'nought but terror to understand the message,' which they before rejected (vv. 12, 13); it is now nothing but terrifying rumours. **20.** Depicts in an expressive figure the failure ending in restless discomfort and distress, towards which the policy of the dominant party is tending.

21. Perazim . . Gibeon] referring to David's victories over the Philistines (2 S 5 20 1 Ch 14 16). Then God interposed on behalf of His people, His **strange work** is His work of judgment against them. **22.** Their scornful attitude will only lead to heavier foreign oppression. **Lest your bands**] They are acting in such a way as to fix the Assyrian yoke more firmly upon Judah, and render it more galling. **Consumption**] RV 'consummation': see 10 22, 23.

24. The implied answer is No; he doth not do these things continually. **25. Fitches**] (i.e. fennel-seed) and **cummin** were the smallest and most delicate seeds. **Cast in,** etc.] RV 'put in the wheat in rows, and the barley in the appointed place, and the spelt in the border thereof.' **28.** 'Is bread *corn* crushed? Nay, he . . and though the wheel of his cart and his horses scatter it, he doth not grind it.'

29. Working] RV 'wisdom.' In vv. 24–29 the skill of the agriculturalist in varying his operations is treated as a reflexion and parable of the divine wisdom. Delicate grains are threshed but not crushed so heavily as to spoil them (vv. 27, 28); so Jehovah's judgments are not for destruction, but to prepare men for their great destiny.

CHAPTER 29

This c. and the three which follow and complete the section, evidently belong to the very eve of Sennacherib's invasion of Judah in 701 B.C.

1–8. Jerusalem is besieged and at the last extremity, but the enemy shall be suddenly discomfited. **9–24.** Judah's infatuation at this crisis, contrasted with the very different and teachable spirit that shall mark its future

1. RV 'Ho Ariel.' Ariel is a symbolic name for Jerusalem, meaning either (1) lion of God, i.e. hero (2 S 23 20), the lion being the symbol of Judah; or (2) altar-hearth of God.

Dwelt] RV 'encamped.' **Add ye,** etc.] The meaning is that when the new year succeeds that which is now running its course, and the cycle of feasts has been completed, Jehovah will bring distress upon Jerusalem. **Let them,** etc.] RV 'let the feasts come round.' **2. And it shall . . Ariel**] RM 'Yet it shall be,' etc. In spite of all, the name shall not be falsified. Jehovah will protect His sanctuary as indicated in vv. 6–8. **4. Out of the dust**] so deep will be her humiliation. **Thy voice,** etc.] cp. 8 19.

5–8. As in other prophecies of the same period, Isaiah foretells sudden and overwhelming disaster for the enemy (37 36). **5. Strangers**] RV 'foes.' **7. Multitude . . nations**] The Assyrian army was recruited from many nations. **Munition**] RV 'strong hold.'

9 f. Here the prophet sets out the sins which brought upon Judah the punishment of invasion. **Stay . . cry**] RM 'Be ye amazed and wonder; blind yourselves and be blind.'

10. Hath closed, etc.] RV 'hath closed your eyes, the prophets; and your heads, the seers, hath he covered.' Even the prophets, who ought to be the nation's watchmen (cp. 21 8), share the general infatuation.

13. The service of Jehovah is merely formal. **Their fear,** etc.] RM 'their fear of me is a commandment of men, learned by rote.'

14. Marvellous] because Jehovah acts contrary to expectation against His people (28 21).

15. The politicians who sought alliance with Egypt endeavoured to conceal their project.

16. Surely, your turning, etc.] RM 'O your perversity! Shall the potter be counted as clay?' The potter stands for Jehovah, whom the politicians of Judah ignored in their schemes.

17. The future change in the aspect of affairs is expressed under the figure of physical transformation. **18.** Reversal of vv. 10–12. **20. Terrible one**] the foe without. **The scorner**] within (28 14). **21. For a word**] RV 'in a cause': i.e. a case brought for judgment. **Reproveth**] pleadeth; the reference is to the corrupt rulers who attempt to silence those that plead for justice. **The gate**] the place of judgment. **23.** There are alternative interpretations: (1) when the nation sees fresh generations growing up under the divine favour, it will serve God more perfectly; (2) when his children see the work of My hands, etc.

CHAPTER 30

1–7. The Egyptian alliance is profitless. **8–11.** The perversity of Judah, **12–17.** and its disastrous consequences. **18–26.** There is a glorious prospect for the repentant people.

27–33. But first Jehovah will destroy the Assyrian.

1. Cover, etc.] seek pretence to conceal their designs (29 15). **4. Were .. came**] RV 'are .. come ' : the ambassadors of Judah go from place to place in Egypt seeking aid.

Zoan (Gk. Tanis) and **Hanes** (Gk. Heracleopolis) were both cities in the Delta of the Nile. **5. Were all**] RV 'shall all be.' **A people**] Egypt.

6. The burden .. south] a title prefixed to the short utterance, vv. 6, 7. **Burden**] see 13 1.

South] Negeb, i.e. the desert tract S. of Judah on the way to Egypt. The v. pictures the journey of the Judæan ambassadors through a district infested with dangerous beasts, their camels and asses laden with presents, wherewith they hope to purchase Egypt's aid.

7. This] i.e. Jerusalem (according to AV), who, instead of thus seeking foreign aid, ought to rest confident in Jehovah's protection (v. 15). But more probably the reference is to Egypt. ' Therefore have I called her Rahab that sitteth still ' (RV), i.e. is inactive in the day when help is expected from her (36 6). ' Rahab' (' pride') : a symbolic name for Egypt, as in 51 9.

8. Write it] i.e. the foregoing prophecy or the name Rahab (8 1). **Table**] RV 'tablet.' **9. The law**] i.e. oral instruction given through the prophet (8 16). **13. This iniquity**] i.e. disregard of Isaiah's admonition and reliance on Egypt is a symptom of ruin, like the bulging of a wall on the point of falling.

15. In returning, etc.] i.e. in giving up your restless trust in man and calmly relying upon Jehovah. **16.** It was the reputation of its cavalry especially that made Egypt so desirable an ally (36 9). **17. One thousand,** etc.] the words indicate the complete rout (Lv 26 8).

Beacon .. ensign] striking symbols of solitariness.

18. Wait] The above threatenings are conditional, Jehovah will wait to give them an opportunity of repentance. **Of judgment**] and therefore not unduly severe. **20. Removed .. corner**] RV 'hidden ' ; the prophets will not need to hide themselves but will be publicly recognised. **22.** The altered frame of mind manifested in destruction of idols. **Covering .. ornament**] RV 'overlaying .. plating.'

23–26. treat of the corresponding change in nature which shall mark the ideal future (4 2). **24. Clean**] 'salted.' Even the cattle shall not lack carefully prepared and seasoned provender. **25. Slaughter**] i.e. of the Assyrians.

Towers] siege-towers. **26. Breach**] RV 'hurt.'

27. Reverts to the more immediate future, the judgment on the Assyrians which is preparatory to the great future. **The name**] practically equivalent to ' the manifestation.'

And .. heavy] RV 'and in thick rising smoke,'

smoke being a symbol of anger. **28. With .. vanity**] i.e. the sifting will reduce them to nothingness. **29. Ye**] i.e. God's own people.

Mighty One] RV 'Rock' implies that Jehovah is the strength of His people. **30. Voice**] the thunder. Jehovah's wrath is figured as a storm. **Scattering**] RV 'a blast.'

31. Beaten down] RV 'broken in pieces.' *Which* **smote**] see 10 24. **32. And .. pass**] RM ' And every stroke of doom.' **With tabrets,** etc.] i.e. with songs of exultation on the part of God's people. **With it**] RV 'with them.'

33. The destruction of the Assyrian set forth under the image of a funeral pyre. **Tophet**] ' a Tophet,' i.e. a place of burning. The name was given to the valley of Hinnom, where, previous to Hezekiah's accession, sacrifices were offered by fire (2 K 16 3). **The breath,** etc.] It is here indicated as elsewhere (cp. 31 8) that the destruction of the Assyrians shall not be brought about by human agency.

CHAPTER 31

1–5. Judah should trust not in Egypt, but in Jehovah. **6–9.** The wonderful deliverance from the Assyrian.

1. See 30 16. **2.** Somewhat sarcastic ; Jehovah is wise, as well as the politicians of Judah. **Evil**] i.e. calamity. **5. Flying**] i.e. hovering over the nest to protect it. **Passing over**] an allusion to the Passover, the same word being used.

6. The children, etc.] RV 'ye have deeply revolted, O children of Israel.' **8.** The Assyrian's fall will be brought about by no human agency. For the fulfilment see 37 36. **Be discomfited**] RV 'become tributary.' **9. And he shall,** etc.] RV 'and his rock' (i.e. strength) ' shall pass away by reason of terror.' **Ensign**] the word denotes a standard, or signal, forming the rallying point of an army. In this context the signal is for the gathering of the foes of the Assyrian. **Whose fire**] see 10 16, 17. The presence of Jehovah is as a consuming fire to His enemies.

CHAPTER 32

1–8. Characteristics of the future age. **9–14.** A warning of coming desolation to the overconfident people. **15–20.** Afterwards shall be a peaceful and prosperous future.

1. The ideal future. **2.** Men will defend and protect their inferiors instead of oppressing them. **3.** Cp. 29 18. **5 f.** Moral confusion shall cease ; men shall be taken at their true value, their character being clearly seen in their actions. **6. Hypocrisy**] RV 'profaneness.'

8. By .. stand] RV ' in liberal things shall he continue.'

9–14. Cp. 3 16-26. **10. Many .. years**] RM ' Days above a year,' i.e. in little more than a year. **12. Lament .. teats**] RV ' smite upon the breasts,' a gesture of despairing lamentation over the desolated vineyards. **14.** Multitude .. city] RV 'populous city.'

15. A limit is set to the desolation. A bright future is in store, when the outward transformation of the country will correspond with the moral reformation (v. 16). This change alike in man and in nature is attributed to an outpouring of the divine and life-giving spirit. **19.** When] RV 'but': a judgment is to precede the time of peace just described.

Coming, etc.] RV 'in the downfall of the forest,' i.e. of the Assyrian. **The city]** Jerusalem too must be humbled. **20.** Refers to the bright future again, when the land shortly to be desolate (vv. 13, 14) shall be fully cultivated. **Beside all waters]** for the land will be everywhere irrigated (30 25).

CHAPTER 33

1–12. The deliverance of Jerusalem from the invader. **13–24.** The consequences of the interposition of Jehovah for those that dwell in the city.

1. The Assyrian is addressed. **That spoilest,** etc.] may mean, (1) that the Assyrian attacked Judah without provocation, or (2) that he has so far spoiled other nations unchecked.

2. Their arm] viz. Jerusalem's defenders'.

3. Disaster overtakes the enemy. **People .. nations]** refer to the various races subject to Sennacherib and serving in his army.

4. As .. upon them] RV 'as locusts leap shall they leap upon it': the people of Jerusalem seizing the spoil compared to insects devastating the fields.

6. Thy times .. his treasure] The pronoun in each clause refers to the people of Judah. In the last clause there may be an implied rebuke of the tendency of Hezekiah to trust in his material treasure (cp. 39 2, etc.).

7. Ambassadors of peace] i.e. sent to obtain peace. The reference is to Hezekiah's ineffectual embassy to Sennacherib at Lachish (2 K 18 14-16). **8, 9.** describe the country ravaged by the invader. **Broken the covenant]** cp. 2 K 18 14. **11, 12.** set forth figuratively the destruction of the Assyrian army.

14. Jehovah's interposition strikes terror to the unworthy in Zion. **Fire .. burnings]** i.e. God, who is a consuming fire (30 33 31 9).

15, 16. The righteous finds in the manifestation of Jehovah his protection. **17. The king]** i.e. the reigning king of Judah, Hezekiah. **In his beauty]** no longer in sackcloth (37 1). **The land .. off]** RV 'a far-stretching land,' no longer hemmed in by foes.

18. Meditate] i.e. muse upon it as something past. **Where .. receiver]** RV 'where is he that counted, where is he that weighed?' The Assyrian officials before whom the people had to appear with their tribute will be no more.

19. The common language of Syria and Assyria was Aramaic, which, though a Semitic tongue, was unintelligible to the ordinary Hebrew-speaking Israelite : cp. 28 11 36 11.

20. Zion likened to a tent which nothing can root up. **21.** The image is changed to that of a city encircled by a protecting stream : cp. Ps 46 4 Nah 3 8. **23.** Reverts to the present. Zion is like a shattered ship. Nevertheless the spoil from her foes will be so great that even cripples take their share.

CHAPTERS 34, 35
SENTENCE ON THE NATIONS. BLESSINGS IN STORE FOR GOD'S PEOPLE

These chs. are now generally considered non-Isaianic and referred to the period of the exile, on two grounds : (*a*) the literary style is unlike Isaiah's. (*b*) The strong feeling against Edom points to a date subsequent to the capture of Jerusalem by Nebuchadnezzar, when the Edomites exulted in the city's fall and sided against the Jews, conduct which provoked bitter resentment (Obad vv. 10–16 Lam 4 21, 22 Ps 137 7).

C. 34. 1–4. The judgment upon the nations, **5–17.** and upon Edom in particular.

C. 35. The blessings in store for God's redeemed people.

CHAPTER 34

4. Cp. 13 10. **5. Shall be bathed]** RV 'hath drunk its fill.' **Idumea]** RV 'Edom.'

6. Bozrah] a strongly fortified city of Edom (63 1 Am 1 12 Jer 49 13). See the same imagery Jer 46 10. The men slain by divine vengeance are compared to beasts offered in sacrifice.

7. Unicorns] RV 'wild-oxen.' **Come down]** i.e. to the shambles. **8. Controversy]** 'quarrel.' The calamity of Edom is a punishment from Jehovah for its hostility to Zion.

9, 10. Imagery suggested by the fate of Sodom and Gomorrah (Jer 49 18), and by the volcanic character of the land of Edom.

11–15. A graphic picture of a desolate land haunted by wild and uncanny creatures.

11. Cormorant .. bittern] RV 'pelican .. porcupine.' **Stones]** RV 'plummet,' implying that the work of destruction will be as thorough as that of building generally is. **Confusion .. emptiness]** The words are those of Gn 1 2, and suggest a return to primeval chaos.

13. Dragons .. owls] RV 'jackals .. ostriches': cp. 13 21, 22. **14. Wild .. islands]** RV 'wolves' (13 22). **Satyr]** see on 13 21. **Screech owl]** Heb. *Lilith,* the name of a night-demon or vampire ; RV 'night-monster.' **15. Great owl]** RV 'arrowsnake.' **16. Seek,** etc.] An invitation to future generations to compare the event with the prediction, and note its precise fulfilment. **Fail]** RV 'be missing.'

17. God, who assigns to nations their

territories (Ac 17²⁶), has allotted Edom to the desert creatures for ever.

CHAPTER 35

1. While Edom becomes a desert, for God's people, on the other hand, the desert places burst into bloom, the fairest parts of Palestine sharing their fertile beauty with the waste places (v. 2).

7. Parched ground] RM 'mirage': this which so often deceives travellers in the desert will become a real lake.

Dragons] RV 'jackals.' **8. An highway**] by which the exiles may return through the desert. **9.** Cp. 51¹¹.

CHAPTERS 36, 37

THE INVASION OF SENNACHERIB

An account of Sennacherib's invasion of Judah (701 B.C.) and its sudden termination. The narrative is closely parallel to that of 2 K 18¹³–19³⁷ (where see notes), from which it was probably taken, and added to this book by a compiler because of its bearing on the prophetic activity of Isaiah.

C. 36. 1–3. The mission of the Rabshakeh from Sennacherib to Jerusalem. **4–10.** The Rabshakeh's first speech—the folly of resistance, relying either upon Egypt, or upon Jehovah. **11–20.** The Rabshakeh's second speech—the fall of Jerusalem certain, favourable terms offered in case of surrender. **21, 22.** The Rabshakeh's words are reported to Hezekiah.

C. 37. 1–7. Hezekiah sends a deputation to Isaiah, who in reply foretells the retreat of the enemy. **8–13.** Sennacherib's second embassy to Jerusalem—trust in Jehovah will not avail to save the city. **14–20.** Hezekiah's prayer to Jehovah to vindicate Himself. **21–35.** The answer through Isaiah—the Assyrian is Jehovah's instrument, under His control, and shall be turned back from Jerusalem. **36–38.** The fulfilment of Isaiah's words.

CHAPTER 36

1. In the fourteenth year] The chronology is difficult. From 38¹ 39¹ we might conclude that Hezekiah's sickness and the Babylonian embassy followed Sennacherib's invasion, whereas chs. 38 and 39 chronologically must precede chs. 36, 37. Samaria fell in 722, Hezekiah's 6th year (2 K 18¹⁰); Sennacherib's invasion of Judah was in 701, which would therefore be Hezekiah's 27th year. The date 14th year here given must then be an error. Hezekiah reigned in all 29 years; 15 additional years were promised in his sickness (38⁵), which accordingly must have befallen him in his 14th year. It looks as though the note of time in this v. originally applied to c. 38, where it

would be accurate, but has by the compiler been transposed to the commencement of this historical appendix to Isaiah's prophecies.

2. Rabshakeh] is a title, 'the Rabshakeh,' i.e. chief officer, or cupbearer. **6. Broken**] RV 'bruised.' **Pharaoh**] This was Tirhakah, of the Ethiopian dynasty (37⁹). **7.** The allusion is to Hezekiah's reformation; the reduction of the number of shrines would seem to a heathen to dishonour the national god.

19. Cp. 10⁹⁻¹¹.

CHAPTER 37

7. Send .. him] RV 'put a spirit in him.' **22. Virgin**] the figure as in 23¹². **24. Sides**] RV 'innermost parts.' **The height .. Carmel**] RV 'his farthest height, the forest of his fruitful field.'

25. Digged] Deserts cannot impede his march, for he digs wells there. **Have I dried,** etc.] RV 'will I dry up all the rivers of Egypt': the Assyrian boasts that he will pass on to conquer Egypt. **26.** Jehovah is here the speaker. **Done .. formed it**] Referring to the ordering of events in the divine providence. **That thou,** etc.] The Assyrian is Jehovah's instrument. **28. Abode**] RV 'sitting down.' **29. My hook**] Assyrian sculptures represent both captives and beasts as led in this way. Jehovah will treat the Assyrian as His captive, or as a beast which must be tamed and restrained.

30. A sign given to the people of Judah that the Assyrian shall not return. This year, the year of the invasion, since the harvest has been destroyed they must eat the aftergrowth. Since they have not been able to sow this year, next year they must depend upon what grows of itself, but the year after they will be able to sow and reap freely, for the land will be free from enemies.

33–35. Another short utterance repeating the promise of deliverance. **36.** The striking fulfilment of Isaiah's words. **The angel**] The expression points to pestilence as the instrument of the Assyrians' overthrow (1 Ch 21¹⁴, ¹⁵ Ps 78⁴⁹, ⁵⁰). **38.** The death of Sennacherib took place in 681 B.C., so that it did not immediately follow the discomfiture of his army.

With the sword] in fulfilment of Isaiah's words (v. 7).

CHAPTER 38

SICKNESS AND RECOVERY OF HEZEKIAH

Continuation of the historical appendix to Isaiah's prophecies. The c. is parallel to 2 K 20¹⁻¹¹ (where see notes), but contains a considerable addition in the shape of Hezekiah's song of thanksgiving upon his recovery. Chronologically this c. precedes 36 and 37: see on 36¹.

1–8. To Hezekiah in his sickness Isaiah

promises 15 more years of life, and confirms the promise by a sign. **9–20.** Hezekiah's song of thanksgiving. **21, 22.** The remedy for the king's disease was suggested by Isaiah, and the sign was given at the king's request.

1. Thus saith, etc.] The passage affords a striking illustration of the conditional nature of prophetic utterance, for at Hezekiah's intercession the sentence was revoked. **5. Fifteen years**] Hezekiah's sickness therefore befell him in his 14th year (714) : see on 36[1]. Though some long time before Sennacherib's great invasion, danger was already apprehended from Assyria (v. 6). **8.** The account in 2 K 20[8-11] is fuller. **Degrees .. sun dial**] RV 'steps .. steps.' Some kind of clock is evidently indicated, probably a pillar standing upon steps and casting a shadow in such a way that a particular portion of time was represented by a step.

10. Cutting off] RV 'noontide.' **11. See the LORD**] Hezekiah is probably thinking of the Temple worship. The v. illustrates the gloomy conception of the Hebrews as to the state of man after death : cp. v. 18. **12. Cut off**] RV 'rolled up.' **With pining sickness**] RV 'from the loom.' **From day .. night**] i.e. in one day. The words refer to the swiftness with which the end comes, not to prolongation of suffering. **13. I reckoned .. lion**] RV 'I quieted myself until morning ; as a lion,' etc.

14. Mourn] i.e. moan, referring to the sound made by the dove. **Undertake for me**] RV ' be thou my surety ': Gn 43[9] 44[32].

15. Softly] RM 'as in solemn procession ' (Ps 42[4]). **In**] RV ' because of. **16. By these things**] i.e. the word of God and the action of His providence. The reference is to the first part of v. 15: cp. Dt 8[3] Mt 4[4]. **So wilt thou**] RV ' wherefore.' **17. Behold .. bitterness**] RV ' Behold it was for my peace that I had,' etc. He sees on looking back that the chastisement had been for his good. **My sins**] God's favour in restoration to health is viewed as a sign of forgiveness.

CHAPTER 39

ALLIANCE WITH BABYLON DENOUNCED

Conclusion of the historical appendix. The c. belongs to the period when Merodach-Baladan of Babylon was making efforts to bring the various peoples of W. Asia into alliance against the common enemy, the king of Assyria (at this time Sargon, 20[1]). The arrangement of such alliance with Hezekiah was, doubtless, the object of the embassy, and this explains Hezekiah's gladness and exhibition of his resources (v. 2). Congratulation to the king of Judah on his recovery, and enquiry into the astronomical marvel at Jerusalem (38[8]) formed pretexts for the embassy (v. 1 ; 2 K 20[12] 2 Ch 32[31]).

1, 2. The embassy from Babylon. **3–8.** Isaiah rebukes the king and foretells captivity in Babylon.

5 f. Isaiah consistently opposes reliance upon a human ally in place of trust in Jehovah. **6, 7.** A remarkable prophecy of captivity in Babylon, though the Assyrians were the foe which at this time threatened Judah.

7. Thy sons] fulfilled in the captivity of Manasseh (2 Ch 33[11]), and later in the fate of Jehoiachin (2 K 25[27]). **8. Truth**] i.e. stability (Jer 14[13]).

With words of pious resignation Hezekiah acquiesces in the will of Jehovah (cp. 1 S 3[18]), then in the words that follow—**For there shall be peace**, etc.—he expresses his thankfulness that the punishment has been postponed. The prediction of the captivity of the royal house must have been a great blow to Hezekiah, especially so since the Hebrews firmly held the principle of the solidarity of the forefather and his posterity. The postponement of the blow was a divine mercy and token of God's favour, for which Hezekiah did well to be thankful. It is quite unnecessary to read a tone of selfishness into his utterance ; on the contrary, his spirit at this time seemed rather to have been one of humble contrition (2 Ch 32[26]).

CHAPTERS 40–66
ISRAEL'S RESTORATION FROM EXILE IN BABYLON

On the authorship and date of these chs. see Intro. According to their subject matter, they fall naturally into three divisions of almost equal length (chs. 40–48, 49–57, and 58–66), the close of each division being marked by an intimation that the wicked shall not share in the blessings promised to God's people.

§ 1. CHAPTERS 40–48

The hope of return is grounded by the prophet upon the fact that Jehovah is the only God, the Creator and Ruler of all things, the Disposer of the fate of nations, who guides the course of history according to His will. The tone of this section is argumentative, the respective claims of Jehovah and of the heathen gods being discussed as in a court of justice. The object of the argument is to encourage the Jews in their exile by showing that, since Jehovah is thus supreme, no obstacles will be able to interfere with the restoration to their own land which He has promised. With fine irony the prophet exhibits the infatuation of idol-makers and idol-worshippers ; proving that, while the idols are senseless blocks and less than nothing (40[17]), Jehovah is Lord of the world and controls all things. The Israelites can testify to His power, because through His prophets He has told them of things before they came to pass. Jehovah is, therefore, set forth as the deliverer of His people. But in the carrying out of His purposes He employs agents : (*a*) Cyrus, who is commissioned as His shepherd (44 28), His anointed (45 1), to perform all His pleasure in the overthrow of Babylon and deliverance of the Israelites from their exile ; (*b*) the nation of Israel, which has its own work to do in the furthering of Jehovah's purposes. The title 'servant of Jehovah,' hitherto applied to individuals, is in these chs. (41 8 44 1, 2, 21 48 20) applied to the nation in its corporate capacity : perhaps also, though less directly, to the faithful Jews within the nation (42 1-7, 18 43 8, 10) on whom would devolve the fulfilment of God's will. The name implies, in the first place, the fact of the nation's election by Jehovah (48 8 f.), and further the truth that Israel has a mission in the world, viz. to bring the knowledge of true religion to the Gentiles, and be a means of universal blessing (42 1 f.).

CHAPTER 40
The Proclamation of Deliverance

1, 2. The theme of the prophecies following: the period of Zion's trouble and affliction is over. **3-26.** Celestial voices give the message of restoration to God's people, who are encouraged by the thought of His infinite power. **27-31.** Trust in Jehovah is, therefore, the source of true strength.

2. Warfare] RM ' time of service,' i.e. enforced service and hardship: cp. Job 7 1. **Double**] i.e. double (ample) penalty (Jer 17 18), in the sufferings of the exile.

3-5. A first voice enjoins preparation for the progress of the great King, who will bring back His people from exile. **3. Crieth, etc.**] RV ' crieth, Prepare ye in the wilderness.' The passage was understood by the Baptist as prophetic of his own mission (Jn 1 23), and is so taken by the Evangelists (Mt 3 3 and parallels). **4.** This imagery is from the practice of Eastern monarchs, who thus made roads for the passage of their armies. **5. Shall see**] shall see Jehovah's glorious deeds for His people, and acknowledge Him.

6-8. The message of the second voice. Human things must decay : Israel's oppressors are mortal, but Jehovah's promise is sure. **6. He said**] i.e. the prophet himself ; then in the words following, in reply to his question, a message is put into his mouth. **7. Spirit**] RV 'breath,' or wind.

9-11. The third voice—the good tidings brought to Zion that Jehovah is approaching in triumph, bringing back His people. **9.** Read, ' O thou that tellest good tidings to Zion . . O thou that tellest good tidings to Jerusalem.' 'Thou that tellest' is fem. in Heb. The prophet in spirit sees a maiden, or a company of women

(Ps 68 11), bringing the news. **10. His reward,** etc.] The figure is that of a conqueror bringing the spoils of war. **His work**] RV ' recompense,' his redeemed people regarded as the prize of war. **11.** The v. indicates in a figure the tender care with which God will support His people on their journey home. **Are with young**] RV ' give suck.'

12-26. The prophet's object is to show the power of Jehovah to deliver the people from captivity. He emphasises two thoughts : (*a*) the wonderful order and proportion in the universe show His infinite power and wisdom (vv. 12-17), and (*b*) no representation can be made of Him. How futile are the idols that men make ! (vv. 18-20).

20. RV 'He that is too impoverished for *such* an oblation,' etc. **24. Shall not**] read the tenses as past (RV). The v. expresses the transitory character of earthly powers in the sight of Jehovah. **26. Faileth**] is missing.

27. The foregoing argument is addressed to a people who had suffered so long, that they thought God had forgotten them, and were despondent.

CHAPTER 41
Cyrus God's Agent

1-7. Jehovah and the gods of the heathen compared as in a court of judgment. Jehovah has raised up Cyrus and given him victory, in order to carry out His good purposes, while the heathen gods are powerless to affect the course of events. **8-20.** A digression : the events which bring terror to the nations bring deliverance to Israel. **21-29.** Comparison of Jehovah with the gods of the heathen continued.

1. The heathen nations lately conquered by Cyrus are called to plead their case as in a law-court.

2-4. The evidence produced on Jehovah's side. It is He who has called Cyrus to his career of conquest in fulfilment of His own purpose. **2. Who raised up, etc.**] RV ' Who hath raised up one from the east, whom he calleth in righteousness to his foot,' i.e. to accompany Him. The one thus raised up is Cyrus : cp. 44 28 46 11. He is called in righteousness by Jehovah, i.e. in fidelity to His covenant promises, which are to be realised through Cyrus. See the same thought, 42 6 45 13.

5-7. The heathen, alarmed by Cyrus's successes, make alliances for mutual support, and attempt to avert disaster by manufacturing or repairing idols. **7. Saying, etc.**] RV 'saying of the soldering, It is good.'

8-10. Israel, on the other hand, descended from the patriarchs, God's chosen people, need have no fear.

8. Servant] with a special mission, as will hereafter appear. But here the emphasis is on what God does for Israel, not on what Israel does for God. **Friend**] cp. 2 Ch 20⁷ Jas 2²³. ' The friend of God ' is still the usual title of Abraham in the East. **9. Chief men**] RV ' corners.' **10. My righteousness**] i.e. faithfulness to My purpose as declared in My promises (see v. 2). **11–14.** It is impossible that the servant thus chosen and honoured can be cast off (oppressed for ever).

15–16. With Jehovah's aid Israel shall become terrible to its foes.

17–20. Jehovah will make easy their return through the desert, exchanging their misery and need for plenty and happiness, that man may acknowledge Him. **18. High places**] RV ' bare heights.' **19. Shittah**] RV ' acacia.'

21. The v. reverts to the scene of the court of judgment (v. 1). **22, 23.** A challenge to heathen gods to foretell the future, to do something or other to show that they exist.

24. The case is summed up against them.

25. Jehovah, on the other hand, has shown His power by raising up Cyrus. **The north .. the rising of the sun**] referring to the Medo-Persian empire. **Princes**] i.e. of Babylon, who hold Israel in bondage. **26, 27.** While the heathen oracles have been dumb, Jehovah has promised restoration to Zion. **26.** *He is* **righteous**] i.e. has been proved right by the fulfilment of His prophecy. **27.** RV ' I first *will say* unto Zion,' etc. **Behold them**] the returning exiles. **28, 29.** No reply is possible on the part of the heathen ; their gods are nought.

CHAPTER 42
The ideal Servant

1–9. The characteristics and functions of Israel as the ideal Servant of Jehovah. **10–17.** A song of praise to Jehovah. **18–25.** The deficiencies of the actual Israel, considered as Jehovah's Servant.

1. My servant] On the conception of these chs. see Intro. **Judgment**] or ' right.' The Servant's office is to teach the world true religion. **2, 3.** He will not be ostentatious nor unduly severe. How Christ corresponded to the ideal is noted in Mt 12¹⁷⁻²¹ **3. Smoking flax**] RM ' dimly-burning wick.' **Unto truth**] RV ' in truth.'

4. The v. implies that the Servant's work will be attended with difficulty, which he will face and overcome. **Set judgment**] established true religion.

6. Two purposes of the Servant's call indicated, (*a*) to be the embodiment of a new covenant with Israel (**the people**), (*b*) to be the instrument of a revelation to the Gentiles.

In righteousness] i.e. in faithfulness to My purpose as declared in My promises (41²,¹⁰ 45¹³). **7.** The thought of enlightenment continued, the imagery being suggested by the

condition of the Jews in exile. **8, 9.** A return to the thought of Jehovah's superiority to heathen gods. He shows His control of events by foretelling them. **11. Kedar**] the tribes of Arabia. **The rock**] RV ' Sela,' the rock-city of Edom.

13–17. The vv. refer to the coming deliverance : in vv. 14 f. the speaker is Jehovah.

13. Jealousy] on behalf of His people : cp. 9⁷. **14. Holden my peace**] leaving prayers unanswered (Ps 28 ¹ Hab 1¹³). **Refrained myself**] not interposing by miracles or mighty acts. During the period of the exile there had been no divine interposition on behalf of Israel. **Destroy and devour**] RV ' gasp and pant.' **15, 16.** The difficulties in the way of the returning exiles will disappear.

18–20. Israel, though called to be Jehovah's Servant, cannot comprehend His message given through the prophet. Note the contrast to the ideal Servant (vv. 1–4), which suggests that, in the end, the Servant will be an Israel within Israel. **19. Perfect**] RV ' at peace *with me*.' **20. Opening the ears**] RV ' his ears are open.' **21.** RV ' It pleased the LORD, for his righteousness' sake, to magnify,' etc. In accordance with His purpose, Jehovah had sent prophetic teachers : their teaching had been great and glorious, both in itself and in its fulfilment. **The law**] RM ' the teaching,' given through His prophets. Jehovah, on His part, graciously taught His people, but their insensibility (vv. 18–20) has brought them to their present condition of misery and exile (vv. 22–25). **23. Who among you**, etc.] i.e. who will learn the lesson of the past ?

CHAPTER 43
The Mission of Israel

1–21. The dispersed Israelites shall be ransomed and restored. They are witnesses before the world that Jehovah is the true God. A second and more wonderful exodus is in store for Israel. **22–28.** This deliverance is not a return for service rendered to God, but a free gift.

1. But now] In contrast to the wrath poured upon Israel (42²⁴,²⁵) God will manifest His redeeming love. **3. Egypt**, etc.] The meaning is that these nations shall take the place of Israel as vassals. Jehovah is willing to give the richest lands as ransom for His people. **4. Thou hast been**] RV ' and hast been.' **People**] RV ' peoples.' **5, 6.** Every nation where Israelites were dispersed must restore them to their home. **8. Blind**, etc.] see 42¹⁸. **9 f.** Another judgment scene, similar to 41²¹. **9.** The heathen are challenged to bring witnesses on behalf of their gods, that they can foretell the future. **10–13.** The Israelites themselves are Jehovah's witnesses, proving in their experience that He alone is the Eternal, the Almighty, who can save and foretell the future.

14. Babylon] Here for the first time the place of exile is named. **Have . . nobles**] RV 'will bring down all of them as fugitives, even the Chaldeans.' **Whose cry, etc.**] RV 'in the ships of their rejoicing.' Babylonia was famous for its shipping ; ships belonging to it and other cities on the Persian Gulf are referred to in the earliest Babylonian legends.

16, 17. The imagery for this second exodus is borrowed from the exodus from Egypt.

18, 19. The mighty works of the past shall be forgotten, in view of a still greater deliverance : cp. Jer 23 ^{7,8}. **20. Dragons . . owls**] RV 'jackals . . ostriches.'

22–24. Israel's service has not been such as to deserve Jehovah's interposition. **23. Small cattle**] Heb. 'lambs or kids' (mg.). **I have not caused, etc.**] i.e. I have not laid too heavy burdens on you. **24. Sweet cane**] from which anointing oil was prepared (Ex 30 ^{23}). **Thou hast made me to serve, etc.**] i.e. I have had to endure.

26. An invitation to produce any argument in defence of their conduct. **27, 28.** Nothing can be urged ; they have sinned from the beginning of their national existence ; hence the calamity of the exile, which has made them an object of scorn to the world. **27. First father**] Jacob: cp. v. 28. **28. Profaned, etc.**] i.e. treated the chief priests (cp. 1 Ch 24 ^{5}) as though they were ordinary unconsecrated men. During the exile their priestly functions were in abeyance.

CHAPTER 44
The Impotence of Idols

1–23. The reproach of God's people shall be entirely removed. Jehovah the Eternal, who rules the events of history, contrasted with the futile gods of the heathen. **24–28.** This great Jehovah pledges the restoration of His people through Cyrus. **2. Jesurun**] i.e. 'upright,' a symbolic name of Israel (Dt 32 ^{15}), indicating its ideal character. **Fear not**] i.e. on account of past failure and apparent inability to realise the future which God sets before you. **3.** Cp. 43 ^{20}.

5. The meaning is that the nations of the world will count it an honour to associate themselves with Israel and be reckoned as the LORD's people. **Subscribe, etc.**] i.e. sign himself as the LORD's. **Surname** *himself*] as with a title of honour.

6. Cp. 43 ^{11,13}. **His redeemer**] i.e. the deliverer of Israel. **7.** A challenge to others to foretell the future, as Jehovah does by His prophet (41 ^{22}). RM 'And who, as I, can proclaim ? let him declare it,' etc. **8. From that time**] RV 'of old.' **My witnesses**] see 43 ^{10,12}. **No God**] RV 'no Rock.' Rock, as a title of God (cp. 17 ^{10} Dt 32 ^{4,15,18}), expresses

the permanent strength and protection He affords.

8–20. The folly of idolaters exposed.

9. They *are* **their own, etc.**] RV 'their own witnesses see not,' i.e. the witnesses on behalf of the idols (the heathen), as opposed to Jehovah's witnesses (the Jews), v. 8. **11. All his fellows**] RM 'all that join themselves thereto.' **They** *are* **of men**] i.e. of human origin, and, therefore, cannot make God. Read, 'The smith sharpeneth *a tool* and worketh,' etc. (RM). **12.** Description of the making of a metal idol. The maker is frail man.

13, etc. Description of the making of a wooden idol. **A line**] RV 'a pencil.' **Fitteth**] RV 'shapeth.' **14.** The v. describes the choosing of the wood, and the planting of the tree, for making an idol. **Cypress . . ash**] RV 'holm tree . . fir.' **Strengtheneth**] i.e. carefully tends its growth, or chooses, selects. **15–17.** The uses to which the tree is put. Part is used for human purposes, part to make a god.

18–20. Idolaters are so infatuated that they do not see the contradiction involved in such conduct.

21–23. A contrast. Jehovah will show His power and graciousness in the deliverance of His people. **22. A cloud**] which soon disperses. **24.** He is supreme over all things. **By myself**] RV 'who is with me ?' implying that Jehovah alone does these things. **25.** He frustrates false prophets, but pledges Himself to fulfil the predictions of His own prophets as to the restoration of Jerusalem (vv. 26–28).

26. Servant] here a synonym for 'prophet': cp. 20 ^{3}. **Messengers**] the prophets generally. **27.** The allusion is to the drying up, (a) of the waters which would impede the returning exiles, or (b) of the waters which protected Babylon (Jer 50 ^{38} 51 ^{36}). Cyrus, in fact, entered Babylon by diverting the Euphrates from its usual channel and marching by the river bed.

28. As the Assyrian was Jehovah's appointed instrument for the chastisement of His people (10 $^{5f.}$), so Cyrus is singled out as His instrument for their restoration. **Even saying, etc.**] literally fulfilled in the decree of Cyrus (Ezr 1 $^{1f.}$ 2 Ch 36 ^{22,23}).

CHAPTER 45
The Meaning of the Conquests of Cyrus

1–13. The conquests of Cyrus are ordained by Jehovah for His purposes. Let not Israel criticise the manner of its deliverance. **14–17.** Great honour awaits Israel. **18–25.** All the world shall recognise Jehovah's righteousness and power.

1. His anointed] as being consecrated to carry out the purposes of Jehovah, i.e. to release Israel from Babylon. This is the only place where a non-Israelite king is so entitled. Somewhat similarly Nebuchadnezzar is called Jehovah's servant (Jer 27⁶ 43¹⁰).

Whose right hand I have holden] cp. 41¹³.

Loose the loins] lit. 'ungird,' i.e. disarm.

The two leaved gates] i.e. of the cities which Cyrus attacks.

2. Crooked . . straight] RV 'rugged . . plain.'

3. Treasures] referring primarily to the vast wealth of Babylon : cp. Jer 51¹³. Cyrus also captured Sardis with the riches of Crœsus (Herod. I, 84). **4. Surnamed]** i.e. given an honourable title, referring to 'Anointed' (v. 1), or to 'shepherd' (44²⁸). **5. Though thou hast]** better, 'when thou didst not know me,' i.e. before thy birth : cp. 49¹. Or it may mean, before thou didst acknowledge me: cp. Ezr 1¹,². **7. Evil]** not moral evil, but misfortune or calamity, the opposite of peace.

8. Righteousness] i.e. fidelity to promises : so also v. 13.

9 f. A possible objection is now met from Israelites dissatisfied, either with the nationality of the deliverer (a Gentile instead of a prince of the House of David), or with the tardy approach of the deliverance. *Let . . potsherd]* RV 'a potsherd among the potsherds of the earth !'

11. Ask, etc.] Read as interrogative, ' Will ye ask . . will ye command me ?' **13. Him]** i.e. Cyrus. Will Israel venture to dictate to Jehovah what He shall ordain for His people ?

14. The nations shall come to acknowledge the God of Israel. **15.** An exclamation of wonder on the prophet's part at the unsearchable ways of God. Some have understood the words as an expression of the wondering adoration of the nations. **Hidest]** refers to the period of the exile, when Jehovah seemed not to hear the prayers of His people nor to help them. **19. Not . . in secret]** Jehovah had plainly foretold the future, so that men might compare the prophecy with the event. **I said not . . Seek ye me in vain]** Israel's hopes will not be disappointed.

21. A challenge to the idolaters, Jehovah is the only God who can fulfil His prophecies ; therefore shall all the nations acknowledge Him (vv. 22, 23). **23.** The religion of Israel is to become the religion of the whole world. This anticipation finds its fulfilment in the Christian dispensation, and thus St. Paul applies the latter part of the v. to Christ in Phil 2¹⁰,¹¹. **24.** Read, 'Only in the LORD, shall one say unto me, is righteousness and strength.' **25. Be justified]** lit. 'be righteous.'

CHAPTER 46

THE CONTRAST BETWEEN JEHOVAH AND THE DEITIES OF BABYLON

1, 2. The idols of Babylon will be borne away by the conquerors amongst the spoil, the gods being powerless to save their images.

1. Bel] the chief Babylonian deity (Jer 50²).

Boweth . . stoopeth] before the conqueror. **Nebo]** son of Bel, the Babylonian Mercury. The name means 'revealer.' **Your carriages, etc.]** RV 'the things that ye carried about in processions are made a load,' of spoil for the conquerors: see on 10²⁸. **3, 4.** So far from being thus ignominiously carried about, Jehovah, on the other hand, carries His people.

5–7. The argument against idolatry renewed (40¹⁸f. 44⁹f.).

8 f. These vv. are addressed to those amongst the Jews who were inclined to object to God's manner of deliverance (cp. 45⁹) ; they are bidden to remember the things He has done for His people in the past (v. 9), and how He has shown by prophecy that He orders events according to His purpose (v. 10); they may accordingly rely on the fulfilment of the prophecies concerning Cyrus (v. 11). **11. A ravenous bird]** i.e. Cyrus. The conqueror is compared to a bird of prey as in Jer 49²² Ezk 17³. The image is the more appropriate, because the standard of Cyrus was a golden eagle. **12. Stouthearted]** i.e. stubborn.

CHAPTER 47

AN ODE ON THE HUMILIATION OF BABYLON

1–15. The coming calamity. The reason of Babylon's fall. Her helplessness to avert it. **2. Grind]** i.e. as a slave (Ex 11⁵).

Uncover, etc.] RV 'remove thy veil, strip off the train, uncover the leg.' The overthrow of the city is set forth under the figure of a maiden carried away into slavery. **Pass over]** on the way to exile. **3. Will not meet, etc.]** RV 'will accept no man,' i.e. none shall be spared.

6. Babylon is to be thus punished because, when the Jewish exiles were in her power, she had treated them cruelly (Zech 1¹⁵), and in her false security she acted as though irresponsible (vv. 7, 8). **Polluted]** i.e. treated as common, RV 'profaned.' **9. Perfection for]** 'full measure in spite of.' **Sorceries]** Babylon was renowned in the ancient world for astrology, and for the practice of all kinds of magic.

11. From whence it riseth] RM 'how to charm it away.' **12. Stand . . with]** i.e. persist in. **13.** See on v. 9. **14.** *There shall not be]* 'it shall not be,' i.e. it will not be like a fire on the hearth, but a devouring conflagration.

CHAPTER 48

LET THE EXILES TRUST IN JEHOVAH, AND COME OUT OF BABYLON

1–11. Jehovah's purpose will be executed, but not for Israel's merit. **12–22.** Let Israel recognise His leading in the course of history, and learn to obey Him.

1. The prophet here addresses those whose professions of allegiance to Jehovah are hollow

(46^8), and who in the land of exile had in their hearts apostatised: cp. 42^{17}. **Come .. waters**] i.e. are descended from Judah (Ps 68^{26}).

3–5. Events of their history had been foretold by Jehovah long before they happened, lest in their perversity they should attribute them to their false gods.

6–8. But now the things Jehovah purposes are declared on the eve of the event, lest in their presumption they should say that they knew them before.

6. I have shewed] RM 'I shew.' **7. Before,** etc.] RV 'and before this day thou heardest them not.' **8. Yea, from,** etc.] RV 'yea, from of old thine ear,' etc. **10.** Read, 'not as silver' (RV). So severe a refining (Ps 12^6) would have meant the destruction of Israel. **Chosen**] RM 'tried.' **11. Do** *it*] i.e. execute My purpose.

13. Spanned] RV 'stretched out.' **14.** A challenge to the heathen, as in 43^9. **14, 15. Loved him .. called him**] i.e. Cyrus: cp. 44^{28} 45^1.

16. Jehovah, unlike the idols (v. 14), declared the future unambiguously. **And now**] i.e. now that the crisis is at hand the LORD has sent His prophet with the message of deliverance.

18, 19. Hadst hearkened .. had been as] This is the literal rendering, but the passage may be a promise for the future, ' O that thou wouldst hearken .. shall be.' **19. Thy seed,** etc.] Old promises would have been realised (Gn 22^{17}). **20.** The exiles are bidden to prepare to leave Babylon. **21.** The imagery is from the former exodus from Egypt. **22.** Those who are unfaithful cannot share the promised peace. The words are repeated almost exactly at 57^{21}.

§ 2. CHAPTERS 49–57

This section is not so argumentative in tone as the last. Its distinguishing feature is the development of the prophet's teaching concerning the Servant of Jehovah. The conception seems to arise, as has been noted, with the nation considered collectively as a Servant of God ($41^{8,9}$ $44^{1,2,21}$ 45^4). So long as the attitude and work of God in relation to the nation are solely in view, there is no limitation of the idea ; but when the nation's work and attitude to Him and the fulfilment of His purposes come to be considered, the Servant of God seems to take on a narrower sense. The actual Israel, with its many shortcomings—its blindness to the truth, its deafness to God's message —gives way to those more select souls—a part only of the people—through whom the duties and destiny of the nation will be fulfilled. At the same time, it is clear that the idea passes on to an individual distinct from the nation ($49^{5,6}$), in whom are concentrated all the attributes of the ideal nation, and who shall realise all that Israel was intended to be. His character and office are thus delineated : (*a*) He is prepared by Jehovah from the womb for His life-

work ($49^{1,2}$) ; (*b*) He is endowed with the Divine Spirit (42^1) ; (*c*) He is not ostentatious or unduly severe ($42^{2,3}$); (*d*) He is to be the embodiment of a New Covenant between Jehovah and His people (42^6 49^8) ; (*e*) and to teach all nations true religion ($42^{1,6}$ 49^6) ; (*f*) but most remarkable of all, and especially characteristic of this division of the book, are the passages which intimate that this great work is only to be accomplished through humiliation, suffering, and death, issuing in a new and glorious life. The first hint that the Servant's work is to be carried on in face of difficulty and discouragement is found in 42^4. His exposure to insult and contumely in the exercise of His mission is expressly indicated in 50^6 ; then follows (52^{13}-53) a section entirely devoted to the subject, in which the prominent features are the Servant's gentleness and patience under affliction, the vicarious nature of His sufferings, which are not endured on His own account, but for the sins of His people, and the intimation that after pain and death there awaits Him new life full of joy in the contemplation of the success of His work. The correspondence, even in detail, with the Passion of Jesus Christ cannot fail to arrest attention. The way in which the Servant is despised and misunderstood by His contemporaries (53^3), His patience and silence before His accusers (53^7), and His association with malefactors in His death (53^9) : these read like a description of what happened in the case of our Lord. How far the prophet understood the meaning of his own words it is difficult to say. No doubt he was thinking at the outset of the faithful core of Israel as being Jehovah's Servant with a great mission to accomplish, and the experience of the exile showed him that this great work for the whole world was only to be wrought through contumely and suffering ; yet Jehovah sometimes spake 'with a strong hand' (Ezk 3^{14}), and we can scarcely doubt that the Divine Spirit in these wonderful passages through the prophet foreshadowed the things that should be suffered and accomplished by the perfect Servant of God, the embodiment of Israel's splendid ideal, our Lord Jesus Christ.

CHAPTERS 49, 50

The Servant of Jehovah

C. 49. 1–13. The Servant of Jehovah tells of His call and mission. Jehovah confirms the confidence of His servant. **14–26.** Objections arising from little faith answered : (*a*) it cannot be that Zion is forgotten by Jehovah, as she thought (vv. 14–23) ; (*b*) the grasp of the captors is not too strong for Jehovah to release His people (vv. 24–26).

C. 50. 1–11. The people's banishment is not by Jehovah's will, and He is able to deliver them. The Servant of Jehovah declares the conditions of his work. The prophet's comment on the Servant's words.

CHAPTER 49

1. The speaker is the Servant of Jehovah. **From the womb**] The thought is that of pre-destined creation, as in Jer 1⁵ Lk 1¹⁵ Gal 1¹⁵.
2. He is trained and protected by Jehovah.
3. Though here identified with Israel as fulfilling its ideal, the Servant is yet a Person distinct from the nation, or perhaps a personification of the pious core of the nation, who is to be the means of its restoration (v. 6).
4. Though for a moment discouraged, the thought that God will vindicate the right and reward him reassures him. **Work**] RV 'recompense.' **5. Though .. glorious**] RV 'and that Israel be gathered unto Him ; for I am honourable.' **6.** Cp. 42⁶. The Servant's mission is not limited to Israel. He is to proclaim a world-wide salvation.
7. A promise to the nation now despised and in bondage that the highest honour is yet in store for it. **And he shall choose**] RV 'who hath chosen.' **8. To establish,** etc.] RV 'to raise up the land, to make them inherit,' fulfilled in the first place in the work of Zerubbabel. **Give thee for a covenant,** etc.] see 42⁶. **9.** Cp. 42⁷. **High places**] RV 'bare heights.' **The prisoners**] i.e. in Babylon.
10, 11. The journey homeward shall be made easy for them. The language of v. 10 is borrowed in Rev 7¹⁶,¹⁷. **10. Heat**] properly, 'mirage' (35⁷). **12.** From all quarters the returning exiles will come. **Sinim** stands for distant lands generally ; in the opinion of most scholars it strictly signifies China.
16. Graven] refers to the custom of tattooing, by which devotees often indicated their consecration to a deity. According to the prophet's bold figure, Jehovah is devoted to Jerusalem, and cannot use His hands without being reminded of her. **17. Children**] LXX and Vulgate read, 'builders.'
19. The land of thy destruction] RV 'thy land that hath been destroyed.' **20. The children .. other**] RV 'the children of thy bereavement,' i.e. the children born in the days (of the exile) when Zion thought herself bereft of all her children.
22. Arms] RV 'bosom.' A particular fulfilment of vv. 22, 23 may be traced in the favour shown by Persian monarchs to Jerusalem after the return from the exile (Ezr 1¹⁻⁴ 6¹⁻¹⁵ 7¹¹ Neh 2¹⁻⁹) ; a higher and spiritual fulfilment in the way in which princes in all lands have shown themselves patrons of the Church.
24. An incredulous question on the part of despondent Israelites. **Lawful** (lit. 'righteous') captive] i.e. captive taken from the righteous, **or,** adopting a slight emendation, 'captive of

the terrible one ' (Vulg., Syr., RM). **26. Feed,** etc.] a figure expressing the destruction of Zion's enemies by mutual hostility (9²⁰).

CHAPTER 50

1. The children of Zion (49²⁰,²¹) are addressed. Their servitude is not irrevocable ; Jehovah has not formally repudiated Zion (Dt 24¹) ; nor, though they had to learn by discipline, can any creditors claim His people as slaves (2 K 4¹) : cp. Jer 24⁴⁻⁶ Ezk 37.
2, 3. The imagery is from the exodus from Egypt. **2. Wherefore .. answer**] These clauses emphasise the hopelessness of Israel's case from a human point of view. Only the divine power could effect the deliverance of the exiles.
4. The Servant of Jehovah is here the speaker (as in 49¹). He is taught by Jehovah, receiving the divine message each morning. **To speak,** etc.] RV 'to sustain with words him that is weary.' **5, 6.** The Servant does not shrink from his mission in spite of the suffering and humiliation involved.
7, 9. Being sustained by the strength of Jehovah, and therefore confident of victory, he is unflinching and challenges his adversaries.
10, 11. Words addressed by the prophet to the Israelites ; let the faithful ones amongst the exiles trust in Jehovah (v. 10) ; as for those who resist Him and arm themselves against His prophets, their weapons shall recoil upon themselves (v. 11). **10.** Read, ' .. servant ? he that walketh in darkness and hath no light, let him trust,' etc. (RV).
11. Sparks] RV 'firebrands.'

CHAPTERS 51–52¹²

THE HOPE OF SPEEDY RETURN FOR THE EXILES

C. 51. 1–16. Encouragement from consideration of the past. Jehovah's purpose for His people is sure. Prayer for deliverance (based on the deliverance of the exodus). Jehovah in response reassures His people. **17–23.** The divine wrath, which was upon Jerusalem, shall be turned against her oppressors.
C. 52. 1–6. The glorious change in Zion's fortune. **7–12.** The deliverance of the exiles imminent.

CHAPTER 51

1, 2. In the past God made Israel a great nation from a single ancestor, and that wonderful growth should be an encouragement to the righteous remnant now to believe in their restoration. **2. Alone**] RV 'when he was but one,' i.e. childless.
4. A law, etc.] through Israel, Jehovah purposes to reveal Himself to the nations (42¹). **4, 5. The people**] RV 'peoples.'
6. The v. contrasts the certainty of God's

purposes for His people with the transitory
character of the visible world. **8. My righteousness**] i.e. as shown in faithfulness to My
promises.

9–11. An appeal from Israel to Jehovah
that He will show His power as of old at the
exodus, that the exiles may return triumphantly to Zion. **9. Rahab**] a symbolic name
for Egypt, as in 30⁷ RV. **Dragon**] standing
for Egypt (Ps 74¹³).

12–16. God assures His people of their
speedy deliverance. **13. As if .. ready**] RV
'when he maketh ready.' **14.** Read, 'He that
is bowed down shall speedily be loosed, and
he shall not die in the pit, neither shall his
bread fail.'

15. Divided, etc.] RV 'stirreth up the sea,
that the waves thereof roar.' Jehovah rules
in the world, and therefore has power to perform His promise. **16.** While vv. 12f. are
spoken to the Jewish exiles, the parallel
between this passage and 49² suggests that
the ideal Israel—Jehovah's Servant—is here
addressed.

17. Hast drunk] The prostrate condition
of Jerusalem under the wrath of Jehovah is
set forth under the figure of one stupefied
and reeling owing to a deep draught. **19. By
whom**] RV 'how.' **20. A wild bull**] RV 'an
antelope': the figure denotes helplessness.

21–23. Jehovah's wrath is now to be turned
against Jerusalem's oppressors.

CHAPTER 52¹⁻¹²

1, 2. Zion invited to array herself as a
queen and sit enthroned, freed from the presence of heathen foes, and with her children
restored from captivity. **1. Thy strength**]
Strength returns to Zion when the Arm of
Jehovah works within her (51⁹). **3. Her**
captors paid no price, and therefore have no
claim upon her. **4. The Assyrian oppressed**]
alluding to the sufferings of God's people at
the hands of Sargon and Sennacherib.

5. What have I] RV 'what do I.' The
argument is that the Egyptian and Assyrian
oppressors were but temporary; is there any
reason why the Babylonian exile should be
permanent? **Make .. howl**] RV 'do howl.'
Every day] RV 'all the day.' **6. Shall
know my name**] Owing to the exile men had
doubted Jehovah's power (cp. v. 5, 'my
name .. is blasphemed'), but in the ensuing
deliverance He will vindicate Himself, and
His people shall know Him in His true
character.

7. Cp. 40⁹. This and the following vv.
refer to the return from the exile. **8. Watchmen**] may refer to prophets (cp. 21 ⁶,¹¹,¹² 56¹⁰),
or to heavenly spirits (cp. Dan 4¹³). **Eye to
eye**] i.e. as one looks into the eye of his
friend. **10. His holy arm**] cp. 51⁹.

11. No unclean *thing*] cp. v. 1. **That bear
the vessels, etc.**] i.e. the priests and Levites,
who are to carry back to Jerusalem for use in
the restored Temple the sacred utensils, which
Nebuchadnezzar had taken away to Babylon.
See the fulfilment of this recorded in Ezr
1⁷⁻¹¹. **12. With haste, etc.**] in contrast to
the exodus from Egypt (Ex 12³⁹).

Rereward] i.e. rearguard.

CHAPTER 52¹³–53¹²

THE SUFFERING OF JEHOVAH'S SERVANT:
ITS MEANING AND RESULTS

See introductory note to chs. 49–57.

C. 52. 13–15. The contrast between the
Servant's humiliation and exaltation; its
effect upon the world.

C. 53. 1–12. The import of the Servant's
suffering not understood. The vicarious nature
and triumphant issue of the Servant's suffering.

CHAPTER 52¹³⁻¹⁵

13. Deal prudently] RV 'wisely.' The word
implies success as the result of prudent plan;
it is used of David's behaviour (1 S 18¹⁴,¹⁵,³⁰).
Exalted, etc.] The idea is repeated for
emphasis.

14, 15. At the Servant's exaltation, following
upon his deep humiliation and suffering, the
nations and their rulers are dumb with awe,
and learn truth unknown before. This was
fulfilled in the effect upon the world of the
resurrection and exaltation of Christ following
upon His passion.

15. So corresponds to **as** (v. 14), the words
his visage .. men being a parenthesis. **Sprinkle**]
i.e. so as to cleanse (Pesh. 'he shall purify'):
or, read, 'startle' (RM).

CHAPTER 53

1–3. The tenses are past (prophetic perfect),
the future being viewed as already accomplished.

1. The questions are asked by the prophet,
and the implied answer is 'No one.' None or
few received the divine message, or recognised
the working of Jehovah's power in His Servant.
Arm] cp. 51⁹ 52¹⁰.

2. The people here speak. There was
nothing in the servant's appearance to attract
them. **Shall grow**] RV 'grew.' **Before him**]
i.e. before God. **Tender plant, etc.**] not like
a stately tree, but like a lowly plant, struggling
in arid soil. So the human life of the Messiah
was one of obscurity and humility.

3. Sorrows .. grief] lit. 'pains .. sickness.'
He was despised, etc.] literally fulfilled in
the attitude of His contemporaries generally
towards our Lord: cp. Jn 1¹⁰,¹¹ 8⁴⁸ 9²⁴ 10²⁰.

4–6. Though they thought him the object
of Jehovah's wrath, he was in truth afflicted
that they might be delivered; the penalty of
their sin fell on him, instead of recoiling upon

the transgressors. A remarkable prophecy of Christ, Himself sinless, suffering that men might be delivered from their sins and the penalty due to them.

5. Chastisement of our peace] i.e. resulting in our peace.

7. The v. expressively sets forth the meekness of the Messiah under persecution. See the literal fulfilment recorded in Mt 26 63 27 12, 14 and parallel passages.

8. Read, 'By oppression and judgment he was taken away ; and as for his generation, who *among them* considered that he was cut off,' etc. (RV) ; i.e. his persecution ended in death, but his contemporaries did not understand that this was for his people's transgressions, not for his own. The ignorance of those who crucified Christ (Ac 3 17 13 27 1 Cor 2 8) is here foreshadowed.

9. He made .. because] RV 'they made .. although.' Though himself guiltless, he was, in his end, associated with malefactors. **Rich** is parallel to **wicked**, and stands for the wrongfully rich (Ps 49 6 Prov 11 16). The words received their fulfilment in detail in the crucifixion of Christ between two robbers.

10. Yet it pleased] His sufferings were in accordance with the divine purpose (cp. Ac 2 23 4 28). **Offering for sin**] lit. 'trespass-offering' (Lv 5 14 f.). Sin is an infringement of God's honour and rights, and the life of the Servant is the satisfaction paid for it. This sacrifice of the Servant is the condition (*a*) of spiritual parentage, (*b*) of continued life after death, and (*c*) of the fulfilment of his divine mission (49 5, 6). The prophet here plainly teaches the atoning efficacy of the death of the Messiah, the accomplishment of His work through His sacrifice and His glorious after-life.

11. His knowledge] i.e. either (*a*) the knowledge which he possesses (cp. Jn 17 25), or (*b*) knowledge of him (cp. Jn 17 3). **Justify many**] RV 'make many righteous,' by delivering them from the guilt and consequences of their sins.

12. Jehovah gives him victory as a great ruler of mankind because of his willing self-sacrifice.

CHAPTERS 54 1–56 8

RENEWED PROMISES OF RESTORATION

C. 54. **1–6.** Zion addressed as a woman whose period of barrenness and affliction is over ; the desolation and reproach of the exile are to be things of the past. **7–10.** From His promise of mercy to Zion Jehovah will not go back. **11–17.** The re-establishment of the city. Its security from enemies.

C. 55. **1–7.** The prophet invites mankind to those blessings which Jehovah has covenanted ; and exhorts to put away obstacles to their enjoyment. **8–13.** Jehovah's promise is sure, and great joy and glory await His people.

C. 56. **1, 2.** They that do right shall be rewarded. **3–8.** In the restored Jerusalem the privileges of God's people shall be for all without distinction.

CHAPTER 54

1. Married wife] referring to the days of Jerusalem's prosperity. **2.** The figure is that of a tent which must be enlarged to take in increasing numbers (33 20). The ultimate fulfilment is seen in the extension of the religion of Zion so as to embrace the nations in the Christian dispensation. **3. Break forth**] RV 'spread abroad.' **Make the desolate cities, etc.**] (cp. 49 8 58 12 61 4) i.e. reoccupy cities which had suffered from Babylonian invasions.

4. Shame of thy youth] i.e. desertion of Jehovah for other gods in her earlier history. **Thy widowhood**] the period of the exile, when Jehovah seemed to have forsaken her. **5. Thine husband**] and therefore faithful, even though Israel may be faithless. **6. Called thee**] i.e. back again to take thy place as wife. **When .. refused**] RV 'when she is cast off.' **7. A small moment**] i.e. during the 70 years' exile in Babylon : cp. 26 20. **8. In a little wrath**] 'in overflowing wrath' (RV), i.e. in transient outburst. **9.** Referring to Gn 9 11. **10. Covenant .. peace**] RM 'covenant of peace.'

11. The restoration of Jerusalem. **Fair colours**] lit. 'antimony,' to set off their brilliancy : mentioned elsewhere as used for painting the eye-lids, to enhance the brilliancy of the eyes (2 K 9 30 RV). **12. Windows of agates**] RV 'pinnacles of rubies.' See similar symbolism in connexion with the new Jerusalem, Tob 13 16, 17 Rev 21 19, etc. **13.** The outward splendour is to be worthy of the citizens (Jer 31 34).

15. They shall surely] RV 'they may.' This refers to Zion's enemies. **Not by me**] i.e. not at Jehovah's bidding, as was the case with Sargon and Sennacherib, who were divinely appointed instruments of chastisement : cp. 10 5 37 26. **For thy sake**] RV 'because of thee.' **16. I have created, etc.**] and therefore they cannot work against My will. **17. This *is* the heritage**] viz. the discomfiture of their enemies. **Righteousness** i.e. justification in the eyes of the world through Jehovah's faithfulness to His promises.

CHAPTER 55

1. Waters .. wine .. milk] These stand figuratively, as the whole context shows, for spiritual blessings. **2. Wherefore, etc.**] refers to the assiduous practice of idolatry, which had been Israel's besetting sin. **3. Mercies**] loving-kindnesses. The meaning is that Jehovah will, without fail, fulfil for His people the promises of loving-kindness made to David (Ps 89 35). **4.** Read, 'I gave him,' i.e. David. **People**] RV 'peoples.' David's successes gave him a position which made his religion known in the world, and thus he witnessed for Jehovah. **5.** Israel shall similarly so testify that the nations shall turn to Jehovah. **6, 7.** The exhortation shows that the promises given are conditional. **8, 9.** These vv. are especially addressed to those of the Israelites who were incredulous as to the possibility of restoration to their own land. **10, 11.** As certainly as the elements fulfil their purposes, so will Jehovah fulfil His promise.

12. With joy .. peace] not in haste or flight, as from Egypt. The passage describes the exodus from Babylon. All nature rejoices with God's people. **13.** Cp. 35 1 41 19. **And it shall be**, etc.] These words form an assurance that the state of things foretold in the clauses preceding shall surely come to pass and shall be permanent.

CHAPTER 56 1-8

1, 2. Further conditions to be observed that men may share in the approaching deliverance. **1. Keep ye .. justice**] i.e. keep the law, and practise righteousness. **2. Layeth hold on**] RV 'holdeth fast by.' **Polluting**] RV 'profaning.'

3-7. The privileges of the people of God are open to all, even to those who think themselves excluded by race, or by physical disability (Dt 23 1). The sabbath appears to have been more strictly observed in the Babylonian period than it had been under the monarchy (Jer 17 19 f. Ezk 20 11 f. Neh 13 15 f.).

5. Place] RV 'memorial.' **7. People**] RV 'peoples.' The passage is referred to by our Lord at the cleansing of the Temple (Mt 21 13). **8. Beside those**, etc.] RV 'beside his own that are gathered.'

CHAPTERS 56 9–57 21
THE IDOLATRIES OF ISRAEL

It is difficult to determine the date of this section with certainty. Many scholars assign it, with the rest of chs. 40–66, to the period of the exile, or to a date after the return ; but some give it a pre-exilic date, on the following grounds : (*a*) The picture that is drawn of the self-indulgent and infatuated leaders of the nation (56 10-12) would, it is thought, apply more accurately to the period preceding the exile, than to the exile. (*b*) The idolatrous rites alluded to (57 5-9) are those practised in the later days of the Jewish monarchy. (*c*) 57 1 implies persecution of the true servants of Jehovah, such as marked the reign of Manasseh. (*d*) The natural features in 57 5, 6 are Palestinian. (*e*) The allusion in

57 9, 10 to seeking foreign alliances suits the days of the monarchy better than the exile period. Those who assign the section to the exile period maintain that the above reasoning is scarcely conclusive, because the writings of Jeremiah and Ezekiel show that heathen rites such as are here described prevailed right up to the exile, and the tendency to practise them no doubt was strong amongst the Jews generally during the exile : cp. 65 3-5, 11. Again, there were other and later persecutions than that under Manasseh ; and that the Jewish exiles were subject to persecution is shown by the case of Daniel and his friends. The Palestinian setting of the idolatrous sacrifices referred to may be accounted for by supposing that these are described as they had been practised by the nation in Palestine.

Chs. 56 9-12–57 2. Rebuke of the unworthy leaders of the nation. Israel is exposed to danger because the rulers are infatuated, self-seeking, self-indulgent, and careless of justice.

C. 57. 3-10. Rebuke of those given to idolatry. A picture of the idolatrous rites in which they have indulged. **11-14.** Jehovah will not endure this, but will interpose. **15-21.** He points the way of restoration through penitence.

CHAPTER 56 9

9. Israel pictured as a neglected and helpless flock, exposed to the attacks of wild beasts.

CHAPTER 57

2. The peace of the grave is better than the condition of unrest under their rulers (v. 1). **Shall enter .. shall rest**] RV 'entereth .. rest.'

3, 5. Sons, etc.] i.e. descendants, perpetuating the character of their ancestors. **Seed**, etc.] i.e. through your idolatry violating the mystical union between Jehovah and His people : cp. Ezk 16 44. **4. Sport yourselves**] implying that they find delight in the misfortune of the servants of Jehovah. **5. Enflaming**] The word describes the excitement attending the orgies which accompanied the celebration of heathen rites : cp. 1 K 18 26, 28. **Slaying**, etc.] referring to human sacrifices practised under Ahaz and Manasseh (2 Ch 28 3 2 K 21 6). **6.** An allusion to stone-worship (Jer 3 9). Large stones, such as those referred to, were fetiches of the Semitic races in early times, and were thought to be abodes of a deity : cp. the action of Jacob, Gn 28 11,18. **Thy lot**] whereas Jehovah was their true portion (Jer 10 16 Ps 16 5). **Should .. these ?**] RV 'shall I be appeased for these things ?' **7. Thy bed**] Idolatry is in OT. commonly figured as adultery (Ex 34 15 Dt 31 16) ; hence *bed* is put for the place of idol-worship. **8. Remembrance**] RV 'memorial,' i.e. idolatrous inscription, in place of the memorial of God's law (Dt 6⁹).

9. The figure is that of a woman trying to attract admirers. Judah had coquetted with foreign kings, especially with the king of Assyria (2 K 16⁷,¹⁰). Or perhaps for **the king** we should read 'Moloch'; the reference then is to idolatry, as in the preceding vv.

Messengers] RV 'ambassadors.' **Unto hell**] i.e. Hades, put for the lowest abasement.

10. In the greatness] RV 'with the length.' **Hast found .. hand**] RV 'didst find a quickening of thy strength,' i.e. Judah imagined her power increased by foreign alliances. **Grieved**] RV 'faint.' **11. Of whom**] i.e. heathen gods. **Lied**] in outwardly recognising Jehovah, while in heart faithless to Him. **Of old**] RV 'of long time.' **12.** Ironical. **And thy works,** etc.] RV 'and as for thy works, they shall not profit thee.'

13. Companies] RM 'rabble,' alluding to the numerous gods introduced. **Vanity,** etc.] RV 'a breath shall carry them away.' **14.** Let all barriers to the return be removed.

15. Jehovah remembers and will restore the faithful among the exiles. **16. For the spirit should fail**] i.e. mankind could not survive God's judgments. **17.** God hid His face and was angry, in order to turn His people from their sins. **Covetousness**] cp. Jer 6¹³ Am 8⁴. **18. His ways**] of repentance. **19. I create,** etc.] i.e. Jehovah gives men occasion to praise Him. **Far off .. near**] referring to the dispersed Israelites, those far off from Jerusalem, and those near to it : cp. Dan 9⁷.

§ 3. CHAPTERS 58–66
THE GLORIOUS FUTURE OF THE JEWISH RACE

This concluding group of chapters is chiefly distinguished by glowing pictures of the future of Jerusalem, when the Jews shall be restored to their land again. A glorious restoration is promised (60¹,² 61⁴,¹⁰,¹¹), all nations are to be members of the restored city (60³⁻⁵), the glories of which are vividly pictured (60⁶ᶠ.), the crowning glory being the holiness of the citizens (60²¹). The fulfilment of the prophet's utterances may be traced in the spiritual glories of the new Jerusalem above, which is the mother of us all.

C. 58. 1–7. Mere outward service of Jehovah is vain ; He desires mercy rather than sacrifice. 8–12. They who thus serve Him in a right spirit shall be wonderfully rewarded, and shall restore Jerusalem ; 13, 14. as also shall they who duly observe the sabbath.

C. 59. 1. But why is Jehovah's help so long delayed ? 2–8. Because of the depravity of the leaders of Israel, 9–15ᵃ. and because of the sins of the people, which they recognise and confess. 15ᵇ–21. No human aid can suffice to

right matters, but Jehovah will interpose to vindicate and deliver His oppressed people.

C. 60. 1–9. Then shall the dispersed Israelites be gloriously restored. 10–13. Jerusalem shall be rebuilt with splendour, and 14–22. her people shall be dominant and prosperous.

C. 61. 1–3. The prophet is commissioned to announce the restoration of exiled Israel. 4–9. The rebuilding of Jerusalem and the coming glory of her people. 10–12. Jerusalem's song of praise.

C. 62. 1–7. The great change that is imminent in the fortunes of Jerusalem, and 8–12. in the lot of her afflicted people.

CHAPTER 58

2. Did righteousness] i.e. kept the law. They are ready enough for the external requirements of religion. **3.** The questions express surprise that the fast is without effect. **Find pleasure,** etc.] render, 'carry on business and oppress all your labourers.' With all their professions of self-denial they are selfish. **4. For strife**] i.e. strife is the result of this formal fasting. **Ye shall not,** etc.] RV 'ye fast not this day so as to make your voice,' etc.

5–7. Literal fasting is not here excluded, but the prophet declares its uselessness when divorced from the spirit of love. Our Lord in the Sermon on the Mount closely connects fasting and almsgiving (Mt 6¹,¹⁶). **6. The heavy burdens**] RV 'the bands of the yoke.' **8. Health**] RV 'healing.' **Thy righteousness**] i.e. thy inward personal righteousness : cp. 1²⁷ ; or, perhaps, 'thy justification in the eyes of the world': cp. 54¹⁷. **Shall be thy rereward**] i.e. shall protect thee. The allusion is to the exodus, when the visible manifestation of Jehovah's presence was a defence to the Israelites from the Egyptians pursuing in the rear (Ex 14¹⁹). **Rereward**] i.e. rearguard. **9. Yoke**] i.e. of enforced or oppressive labour. **Putting .. finger**] i.e. in scorn. **Vanity**] RV 'wickedly.' **10. Draw out,** etc.] i.e. supply to the hungry such things as thou thyself desirest. **11. Fat**] RV 'strong.'

12. Primarily the prophet contemplates the restoration of the ruined buildings of Jerusalem, but the wider spiritual application of his words is obvious. The faithful soul is not only itself fruitful (v. 11), but a means of bringing help and blessing to others. **13. Turn away thy foot from the sabbath**] so as not to profane it. **14. Cause thee,** etc.] i.e. give thee triumphant possession of the land.

CHAPTER 59

1, 2. An answer to the implied objection that the promises of restoration have not yet been fulfilled. **3.** Cp. 1¹⁵. **4.** RV 'None sueth in righteousness .. in truth.' The allusion is to unjust prosecutions. **5. Cockatrice**]

RM 'adder.' **He that eateth,** etc.] i.e. the man who falls in with their plans is ruined thereby, and he who opposes them is confronted with a still greater danger. **6.** Their schemes cannot even benefit themselves. **9.** The prophet and the people confess their sins. **Light**] i.e. deliverance.

10. Grope .. wall] seeking guidance: cp. Dt 28²⁹. *We are .. dead men*] RV 'among them that are lusty we are as dead men.' **11. Mourn**] i.e. moan (38¹⁴). **12. With us**] i.e. present in our thoughts. **14. The street**] the open space in the city where business is done, and cases are brought before the judges.

15. Injustice arouses God's indignation. **Faileth**] RV 'is lacking.' **Judgment**] justice. **16 f.** Cp. 63⁵ᶠ· **17.** The attributes of Jehovah, which come out clearly in His interposition, are figured as His armour. St. Paul's imagery (Eph 6¹⁴ᶠ·) is based on this passage.

18. Islands] put for distant lands generally. The judgment affects the world at large as well as Israel. **19. When .. against him**] RV 'for he shall come as a rushing stream, which the breath of the LORD' (i.e. a strong wind) 'driveth.'

20. Redeemer] i.e. Jehovah, who is so called elsewhere: cp. 41¹⁴ 43¹. This was fulfilled at Christ's first coming, when He was accepted by the faithful few in Israel. But St. Paul (Ro 11²⁶) applies the promise to the time when Israel, which did not accept the gospel, shall be restored again to God's Church, so that its final fulfilment is yet in the future. **Zion**] i.e. the faithful remnant of the nation, as the next clause explains. **21. My spirit,** etc.] The faithful remnant is to be the inspired organ of Jehovah's revelation.

CHAPTER 60

1. The light of deliverance so long waited for (59⁹) is about to shine. This prophecy received its highest fulfilment at the coming of Christ, the true Light of the world, which was followed by a great ingathering of the nations to the Church of God (vv. 3, etc.). **2. People**] RV 'peoples.' **4.** Cp. 49¹⁸. **All they gather themselves**] i.e. the exiles who had been dispersed. **Nursed .. side**] i.e. carried on the hip, in the Eastern fashion. **5. Flow together**] RV 'be enlightened.' **Fear**] RV 'tremble,' with strong emotion. **Abundance of the sea**] the rich seafaring people. **Forces,** etc.] RV 'wealth of the nations.'

6 f. The nations are pictured as coming in a long train, to bring their riches for the service of the sanctuary. **Ephah**] a Midianite tribe (Gn 25⁴). **Sheba**] Ps 72¹⁰. **7. Kedar**] cp. 21¹⁷. **Nebaioth**] a tribe allied to Kedar, descended from Ishmael (Gn 25¹³). **8.** The ships with sails spread speed over the waters, like doves to their nest. **9. Isles**] the maritime

lands of the west (49¹). **Ships of Tarshish**] cp. 2¹⁶ 1 K 10²² 22⁴⁸. Deep-sea ships suitable for long voyages, such as that to Tarshish across the Mediterranean.

10. In my wrath] cp. 54⁷⁻⁸.

11. The **gates are open continually,** that the trains of caravans bearing gifts may enter.

And *that* **their kings,** etc.] RV 'and their kings led with them,' i.e. as captives. The rebuilding of the Temple is pictured in language recalling its erection in the days of Solomon. **13.** Cp. 35². **Place of my feet**] i.e. the Temple (Ps 99⁵ 132⁷).

15. The figure is that of a forsaken wife (54⁶), but is quickly changed to that of a desolate land. **16.** The thought is the same as in 49²³. **17.** The language suggests a return to the prosperity which marked Solomon's reign, with the great difference that the officers shall not be agents of oppression (1 K 12⁴). **Exactors**] RM 'taskmasters.' **18. Thy walls,** etc.] cp. 26¹. **19.** Cp. Rev 21²³ 22⁵. **21.** The people shall all fulfil the law, so that there will be no need of the discipline of exile: cp. 59¹³,¹⁴.

22. A little one] RV 'the little one,' i.e. the smallest; he who has no children, or few. **In his time**] RV 'in its time.'

CHAPTER 61

1. The speaker is the prophet, either in his own person, or in that of the Servant of Jehovah. The mission here spoken of is identical with the mission of the Servant as already indicated; e.g. to bind up, etc. (cp. 42³,⁷), and, again, proclaim liberty, etc. (cp. 42⁷ 49⁹). This phrase is taken from the law of the year of jubilee (Lv 25⁸⁻¹⁰). Our Lord applies the passage to His own work in Lk 4¹⁶ᶠ. **Anointed**] i.e. to prophetic office (1 K 19¹⁶). **2.** The period of God's favour (**acceptable year**) is contrasted with the short time that His wrath endures (**day of vengeance**). **3. Appoint**] assign to, provide. **Beauty**] RV 'a garland.'

4. The outcome of the mission recounted in v. 1 is the same as the issue of the Servant's work (49⁸). **5.** Other nations represented as filling menial offices. **6.** Israel will attain its original ideal (Ex 19⁶). **Riches .. Gentiles**] wealth of the nations. **In their glory,** etc.] RM 'to their glory shall ye succeed.' **7. Double**] i.e. by way of compensation or reward (40²).

8. Judgment] i.e. justice. **For burnt offering**] RV 'with iniquity.' The reference is to the spoliation of which Israel is the victim. **Direct their work**] RV 'give them their recompence.' **9. Known**] i.e. renowned.

10. Decketh .. ornaments] lit. 'decketh himself with a priestly head-dress.' The allusion is to the custom of the bridegroom wearing a special head-dress on the wedding day (Song 3¹¹). **11. As the earth,** etc.] i.e. as surely as the seasons come round. **Righteousness**] i.e. the justification of his people in the eyes of the world.

CHAPTER 62

1. The speaker is probably Jehovah Himself. **Hold my peace**] cp. 42 14. **The righteousness**] i.e. her vindication, the setting of her right in the eyes of the world (cp. 58 8). **Salvation**] i.e. deliverance. **2. New name**] as befits her new character (1 26 Jer 33 16) : see v. 4.

3. In the hand] so held for the admiration of the world.

4. The figure is again that of a bride (54 6) in whom her husband delights. **Hephzi-bah .. Beulah**] meaning, 'My delight is in her,' and 'Married.' **5.** The same image differently applied, the people being regarded as the bridegroom and their country as the bride.

6. Watchmen] These are angelic beings who report to Jehovah what happens on earth, and intercede for mercy to Zion (Zech 1 11, 12).

Ye that make, etc.] RV 'ye that are the LORD's remembrancers, take ye no rest.'

8, 9. The foe will no more rob them of their harvests, but the produce of the land shall be used for the service of the Temple. **Holiness**] RV 'sanctuary.' **10.** A command to prepare the way for the returning exiles (40 3 57 14).

For the people] RV 'for the peoples,' that they may escort the Israelites. **11. His reward**, etc.] see on 40 10. **Work**] RV 'recompence.' **12. Holy people**] Israel's ideal character realised (Ex 19 6 ; cp. Isa 61 6). **Sought out**] contrast Jer 30 17. **Not forsaken**] Cp. v. 4.

CHAPTER 63 1-6
THE DIVINE WARRIOR

1. The prophet asks who is this warrior coming from Edom ? The Warrior replies, He is the Divine Deliverer. **2** The prophet asks why is His raiment red ? **3-6.** The Warrior explains, He is returning from vengeance upon the enemies of His people.

1. Travelling] lit. 'bending,' denoting movement in marching (RV). **In righteousness**] i.e. in faithfulness to promises. **Speak**, etc.] cp. 45 19. **3.** The winepress is the symbol of slaughter in battle (Joel 3 13 Rev 14 18-20).

Alone, etc.] i.e. no human agent assisted. **People**] RV 'peoples.' **I will tread**, etc.] RV 'trod .. trampled .. is sprinkled .. have stained.'

4. *Is*] RV 'was.' **Year**] see 61 2. **5.** The absence of human aid (v. 3) further emphasised (50 2 59 16).

6. Will tread .. make] RV 'trod .. made.' **People**] RV 'peoples.' The divine vengeance falls upon the nations in general, but upon Edom in particular (v. 1), the prophet fixing his thoughts upon this nation because of the long-remembered hostility of Edom in the day of Jerusalem's calamity (see prefatory note to

c. 34). **Drunk**] a figure for stupefying disaster (51 17). **Will bring**, etc.] RV 'poured out their lifeblood on the earth.' The imagery of Christ's final triumph and judgment is taken from this passage (Rev 19 13), which is thus shown to be a prophecy that will receive its full fulfilment in the punishment of the enemies of God's Church at the last day. The Warrior, who in v. 3 is represented as treading the winepress alone, thus stands for the Son of God, to whom alone the Father has committed all judgment (Jn 5 22). The prophecy is also sometimes applied by analogy to Christ's victory over the powers of evil in His Passion (Jn 12 31, 32), wherein He contended alone (Mt 27 46).

CHAPTERS 63 7–64 12
PAST DELIVERANCES AND PRESENT NEEDS

C. 63. **7–14.** Commemoration of Jehovah's mercies to Israel in the past. **15.–C. 64. 5ᵃ.** Prayer that He will interpose to deliver His people from their present calamities.

C. 64. **5ᵇ–12.** Acknowledgment that these are due to their sins. Appeal to Jehovah that He will look upon the pitiable state of His people and sanctuary.

CHAPTER 63 7-19

8. Lie] RV 'deal falsely.' **9. He was afflicted**] so Heb. traditional reading, meaning that He felt His people's pains as His own (Jg 10 16). But Heb. written text 'he was no adversary' (RM), but, on the contrary, their deliverer. **The angel**] see Ex 23 20 32 34 33 2.

Bare them] see Dt 1 31 32 11.

10. Cp. Ps 78 40. **11. He (Israel) remembered**] The thought of past mercies evoked penitence (Ps 78 35). **Shepherd**] RV 'shepherds.' **Within him**] i.e. Israel, e.g. Ex 35 31 Nu 11 25. **12.** RV 'That caused his glorious arm to go at the right hand of Moses.' **Arm**] see 51 9 (also in connexion with the exodus).

13. In the wilderness] i.e. in a grassy plain. **14.** RV 'As the cattle that go down.' This refers to the settlement in Canaan.

15. Strength] RV 'mighty acts.' **Sounding of thy bowels**] stands for sympathetic pity (16 11). Read, 'the sounding .. and thy mercies toward me are restrained.' **16.** The patriarchs might disown their descendants, but Jehovah's love is sure. The thought is similar to 49 15. The passage is remarkable as one of the very few in OT. where God is addressed as Father (64 8). **17 f.** A bold expostulation. **Hardened**, etc.] Have their sins caused God to give them up and become their adversary, as in Pharaoh's case ? **18. A little while**] whereas Jehovah had promised them an everlasting inheritance !

19. RV 'We are become as they over whom thou never barest rule ; as they that were not called,' etc.

CHAPTER 64

1–3. The imagery is taken from the account of the divine manifestation at Sinai (Ex 19 18). **2.** RV 'As when fire kindleth the brushwood, *and* the fire causeth,' etc. **4. O God,** etc.] RV 'a God beside thee, which worketh for him that waiteth for Him.' St. Paul (1 Cor 2 9) alludes to this passage to emphasise the fact that human wisdom cannot fathom the working of God. **Meetest**] i.e. as a friend.

Art] RV 'wast.' **In those,** etc.] RV 'in them' (i.e. our sins) '*have we been* of long time, and shall we be saved ? ' **6. An unclean *thing***] RV 'one that is unclean.' **Filthy rags**] RV 'a polluted garment ': such as was ceremonially unclean. **8.** Cp. 63 16 Ro 9 20. An appeal to God that He will not abandon the work of His own hands.

10, 11. Another motive for Jehovah's interference—the present desolation of the land and sanctuary dedicated to Him. **10. Holy cities**] Elsewhere Jerusalem only is so called, but the attribute is here extended to the whole land (Zech 2 12). **11. Pleasant things**] the same word as 'goodly vessels,' 2 Ch 36 19.

12. Refrain thyself] i.e. refuse to give way to natural tenderness (Gn 45 1).

CHAPTERS 65, 66

The Punishment of Apostate and Reward of Faithful Israel

C. **65.** 1–10. Israel's obduracy to Jehovah's appeals, and persistent idolatry, which He will surely punish ; yet a faithful remnant shall be preserved. **11–25.** The fate in store for the unfaithful. The glories of the coming age for God's faithful people.

C. **66.** 1–4. The danger of trusting in externals ; a merely formal worship is an abomination to Jehovah. **5.** A message of comfort for the faithful who are persecuted. **6–14**a. The wonderful restoration of Israel. **14**b**–18**a. The divine judgment on the nations, and on all idolaters. **18**b**–24.** The recognition and worship of Jehovah by all nations.

CHAPTER 65

1. Render, ' I have offered answers to those who asked not ; I have been at hand to those who sought me not . . a nation that hath not called upon my name.' The v. refers to the Israelites who neglected Jehovah's appeals so often made. St. Paul (Ro 10 20) applies the passage by inference to the heathen world. **3. Gardens**] the scenes of idolatrous rites in the pre-exile period (1 29 57 5). **Upon altars,** etc.] RV 'upon bricks,' i.e. perhaps the tiled roofs of houses (2 K 23 12). **4. Monuments**] RV 'secret places.' The v. alludes to the custom of sleeping in sepulchres or vaults of idol temples to learn the future through

dreams. **Eat swine's flesh**] i.e. in sacrificial meals (66 17) ; it was forbidden by the Law as unclean (Lv 11 7 Dt 14 8). **Broth,** etc.] referring to a sacrificial feast of unclean food.

5. Which say, etc.] The words are uttered by those initiated into heathen mysteries, and who therefore considered themselves peculiarly sacred. **6.** *It* (i.e. their sin) *is* **written**] cp. Jer 17 1. **7. Upon the mountains**] cp. 57 7 Hos 4 13.

Therefore . . work] RV 'there will I first measure their work.' Jehovah must first of all punish these deeds.

8. The meaning is that as a few good grapes often save a cluster from being destroyed, so Israel shall be preserved through the faithful remnant. **10. Sharon**] the maritime plain on the W. of Palestine and **the valley of Achor** near Jericho on the E., are put for the whole land. **11. Ye *are* they that**] RV 'ye that.' **Prepare a table**] alluding to rites such as are described in Jer 7 18. **That troop**] Heb . *Gad*, i.e. 'Fortune ' (RV): cp. Josh 11 17. **Furnish,** etc.] ' fill up mingled wine unto Meni ' (i.e. ' destiny '). 'Meni' and 'Gad' in the clause preceding are names of heathen deities.

12. Number you] RV ' destine you.' **15. Ye shall leave,** etc.] So fearful will their fate be that their name will be used in imprecation. Jer 29 22 exactly illustrates what is meant.

16. The meaning is that men will recognise the faithfulness of Jehovah. **17.** The same language is in NT. applied to God's final interposition and restoration of all things (2 Pet 3 13 Rev 21 1). Nature itself will be transformed to be in harmony with regenerate Israel: cp. 11 6-9. **20.** The future, in the prophet's view, will be marked by a return to patriarchal longevity (Gn 5), the power of death being not altogether removed, but limited. Those who die at 100 will be reckoned as but children, or as prematurely cut off for their sins. **21, 22.** Reversal of the curse (Dt 28 30). **25.** Together with the coming golden age for humanity the prophet anticipates a transformation of the lower creation, as in 11 6 f. : cp. Ro 8 19 f. **Dust,** etc.] the serpent will be content with the food God assigned to it (Gn 3 14).

CHAPTER 66

1. Where, etc.] RV 'what manner of house . . what place shall be my rest.' The v. is a strong rebuke of such as, without a really religious spirit, idly trusted in the inviolability of Zion, and the protection they thought the sanctuary would afford. A like fault is rebuked in Jer 7 1-16. This passage is quoted by St. Stephen (Ac 7 49, 50). **2. Those *things***] i.e. the universe. **All . . have been**] RV ' so all these things came to be.' **3.** They who offer the due sacrifices, yet without a proper spirit, are no better than they who perform unclean or idolatrous acts. **4. Their delusions**] i.e. things to delude them. **5. Your brethren, etc.**] These are the apostate Israelites (also referred to 65⁵) who despise the true worshippers of Jehovah. **Let the LORD, etc.**] RV 'Let the LORD be glorified, that we may see your joy ; but they' (who so speak) 'shall be ashamed.' The apostate taunt the faithful with worshipping a God who does not help them.

6. The prophet seems to hear a sound as of one stirring in the Temple and preparing for vengeance.

7–9. The mother is Zion, the child regenerate Israel, and in v. 8 the normally slow processes of birth and growth are contrasted with the astonishing development of God's people. **8. Shall the earth . . bring forth**] RV 'Shall a land be born.' **9.** God will not delay, or leave unfinished, the work of restoration.

11. The figure of Zion as a mother is still continued. **12. Flowing**] RV 'overflowing.' **14. An herb**] RV 'the tender grass'; their youth will be renewed.

16. Plead] i.e. hold judgment. **17. Sanctify themselves**] referring (as in 65⁵) to the apostates who are initiated into some form of heathen mysteries. **Behind one**] i.e. (*a*) 'behind one Asherah,' i.e. idol tree-trunk (RM, cp. 17⁸) ; or, (*b*) 'behind one man,' as priest and leader of their worship. LXX omits the words. **Eating, etc.**] cp. 65⁴. **The mouse**]

unclean by the Law (Lv 11²⁹). **18. It shall come**] RV 'the time cometh.'

19. Those that escape the divine judgment on the nations opposed to Israel are represented as going as missionaries to the more distant peoples. **Tarshish**] in Spain ; put for the far West. **Pul** (i.e. Phut) **and Lud**] probably African peoples ; they are mentioned together as serving in the Egyptian army (Ezk 30⁵). **Tubal**] Scythian tribes near the Black Sea (Ezk 38²,³). **Javan**] Ionians, i.e. Greeks settled in Asia Minor. **20.** The remoter nations bring back the Israelites dispersed among them. **21. Take of them**] i.e. (*a*) of the nations who bring back the Jews ; or, (*b*) of the Jews themselves thus brought back ; all Israel shall be eligible for the priesthood. 61⁶ favours this latter interpretation. **22.** Cp. 65¹⁷.

24. The picture of restoration is completed with the thought of the judgment upon the wicked (similarly 48²² 57²¹), who are here thought of as having been slain in battle by Jehovah (vv. 15, 16). **Their worm, etc.**] These words may be intended to refer only to the literal destruction of their corpses, or may also include the torment of the spirits of the ungodly. Jewish interpretation adopted the latter view (Ecclus 7¹⁷ Judith 16¹⁷), and it appears also to have the sanction of our Lord's teaching (Mk 9⁴³⁻⁴⁸).

JEREMIAH

INTRODUCTION

1. Life and Times of Jeremiah. Jeremiah (the name probably meaning 'appointed by God') belonged to a priestly family living at a small town named Anathoth (now 'Anâta, consisting of about a dozen houses and the remains of a church) some two miles to the NE. of Jerusalem. The high priest Abiathar, of the line of Ithamar, had settled there in the days of David (1 K 2²⁶). The prophet's family had apparently been owners of land in that region ever since Abiathar's time, and their social status is further indicated by the fact that Jeremiah had for his scribe Baruch, whose brother was chief chamberlain to Zedekiah (51⁵⁹ : see also on 45¹). We may add that Hilkiah, the father of Jeremiah, is not to be identified with the reforming high priest of Josiah's day (2 K 22⁸), as the latter belonged to the line not of Ithamar but of Eleazar.

At an early period in Jeremiah's life (though

the expression 'child' in 1⁶ may partly at least refer to his sense of unfitness for such a task) he was moved to realise—probably in gradually increasing measure—the working of the divine spirit within him. In the thirteenth year of Josiah, 626 B.C., he received his call to be a prophet, and his prophetic life was continued under that king's four successors, viz. Jehoahaz, Jehoiakim, Jehoiachin, and Zedekiah. Eventually the danger which had long threatened the southern kingdom culminated in the overthrow of the Jewish monarchy by the Babylonian power, which had lately risen on the ruins of that of Assyria. Zedekiah and a large number of his subjects were carried captive to Babylon. The prophet, with unselfish patriotism, rejecting the conqueror's offer of honourable treatment in exile, remained in Judæa, carrying on his prophetic office during the turbulent times which ensued, until a body of his countrymen forced him to accompany them to Egypt (43 4 f.). There, according to a Christian tradition, he met a martyr's death at Tahpanhes, being stoned by the Jews who resented his faithful reproofs.

Thus Jeremiah has fitly been called ' the prophet of the decline and fall of the Jewish monarchy,' and the manner of his end seems to have been in close accord with the character of his life-work and sufferings. For, like Cassandra, it was his fate through life to gain but little credence for his warnings.

Jeremiah is one who reveals with frankness the workings of his mind. Hence his prophecies are charged with a large element of human interest. His countrymen as a whole— alike those who had, and those who had not, sympathised with Josiah's reforms (2 Ch 34)— refused to see that nothing short of a thorough amendment of life and morals would satisfy God's law and avert national disaster. The prophet's office then was to utter and reiterate a needed warning, emphasising it by fervour of language and variety of illustration, though sensible all the time that his appeals were probably in vain. The end was approaching, and at last, when princes and people alike proved faithless, he centred his hopes upon the few in whose case adversity and exile had had their chastening uses.

Belonging to the orders both of priest and prophet, and living at the very time when each had sunk to its lowest degree of degradation, he was compelled to submit to the buffeting which they each bestowed upon one who by his every word and deed was passing sentence upon them. Hostility, abuse, powerlessness to avert the coming ills, a solitary life and prohibition of marriage (16 2)—these were the conditions of life allotted to a man of shy and timid disposition and naturally despondent mind. No miracle was wrought for his benefit. His predictions were scorned. He failed to induce his compatriots to recognise the solidity of his claims to a hearing. At times he despaired even, as it seems, of life (20 14-18). And yet he could not be silent. The divine message must find its utterance (20 8, 9), and in fact the promise made to him at the time of his call (1 18), and renewed later (15 20), did not fail.

Reign of Josiah. During the reign of this king, commencing 639 B.C., the dangers arising to Judæa from its geographical position became painfully evident. It was the natural battleground between the rival powers of Assyria and Egypt. So small a kingdom could not cope with either of these dangerous neighbours without the support of the other, and therefore the problem which pressed for solution was with which of the two it was most prudent to throw in their lot. There was still, as earlier, in Isaiah's time (Isa 30 1-5 31 1-3), a strong party in the state favouring either. alternative. The extension of Josiah's work of reformation (to which we are about to refer), beyond the borders of his own kingdom northwards (to Geba, 2 K 23 8), showed that the power of Assyria, which just a hundred years earlier had overthrown the kingdom of the Ten Tribes, was on the wane. On the other hand, it by no means followed that Egypt was to be depended on, even though the Chaldean (Babylonian) power, soon to take the place of Assyria, was scarcely yet above Judæa's political horizon.

Notwithstanding this precarious position with regard to external politics, the inner life of the state did not lack certain hopeful features. The new king, unlike his idolatrous predecessors, Manasseh and Amon, was one whose ardour on the side of Jehovah, seconded as it was by wise counsellors, took the form of a vigorous campaign against the idol-worship and immorality which had polluted those two reigns. The altars erected to Baal, the worship of ' the host of heaven ' (2 K 17 16), the images of the horses and chariots of the sun within the very precincts of the Temple, the offering of human sacrifices in the valley of Hinnom (on the S. and W. of Jerusalem), the gross immoralities of Canaanitish worship— these were wide-spread indications of the religious corruptions which Josiah assailed. The great principle underlying his reforms was that Jehovah alone should be the object of worship, and that that worship should be centralised at Jerusalem. So far as this principle took effect, it had very important consequences on the religious life of the nation. This centralisation was a standing protest against the worship of a plurality of gods. Moreover, the limitation of sacrifice to the central sanctuary tended to throw into greater relief worship in its more spiritual aspect independent of any particular locality.

But, as Jeremiah clearly saw, the abuses were too deeply rooted for these reformers to penetrate much below the surface, and the mass of the people were supported in their adherence to the old ways by the priests of the local shrines ('high places') throughout the land, who naturally resisted a change that deposed them from their office and cut away an important source of subsistence (2 K 23 9). Accordingly, the picture which the prophet draws of the condition of society is a startling one. On every side among high and low there was dishonesty, false swearing, murder, and' open licentiousness. (For an account of the local Baal-worship see Intro. to Hosea.)

Many, doubtless, were the influences which culminated in what we term Jeremiah's call. The sight of abounding immorality and idolatry, the tradition of his house, and the hostility to reforms on the part of many of the natural guardians of religion, both priests and prophets, moved him to painful self-communing, and urged him to lift up his voice against the sins of the nation. A strong impetus no doubt was given to his prophetic ardour when, five years after his call, the Book of the Law came to light in the Temple (2 K 22⁸). That book contained at least a considerable portion of our book of Deuteronomy. Such graphic pictures of punishment for unfaithfulness to Jehovah, as are to be found in Dt 28, cannot but have served as an antidote to the shyness of his nature, and nerved him afresh for the task appointed him. He had to face, on the one hand, the immoral and idol worshippers, on the other, persons who maintained that, to secure the abiding favour of Jehovah, it was only necessary to offer more numerous and costly sacrifices and to increase the splendour of the Temple ritual. According to them, the Temple was in itself a charm which must render Jerusalem and its inhabitants secure (7⁴).

Shortly before the newly risen Chaldean power, by the capture of Nineveh, made good its claim as the successor to Assyria (607 B.C.), Josiah openly espoused its side (2 K 23²⁹), confronted Necho, king of Egypt, on his march against Chaldea, and was slain in battle at Megiddo (608 B.C.).

Reign of Jehoahaz (the Shallum of 22¹¹), 608 B.C. After a brief reign of three months this king was carried captive to Egypt by Necho, and the land made tributary (2 K 23³³). The prophet evidently felt that in Jehoahaz the nation had lost one who would have used his power for good (22¹⁰⁻¹²).

Reign of Jehoiakim, elder brother of Jehoahaz (2 Ch 36², ⁵). The king of Egypt placed him on the throne, and his reign lasted for eleven years (608–597 B.C.). His policy, the reverse of that of his father Josiah, was a disastrous one (2 K 24¹⁻⁴). Under him the hope of averting the ruin of the country soon faded away. In the worship of 'the high places' and in the bloodstained rites, either encouraged or at least connived at by him, men sought deliverance from the troubles of servitude to a foreign oppressor. The king was cruel, frivolous, eager for his own glorification, and regardless of the national religion (Jer 22¹³⁻¹⁷). Under his rule the faithful few were refined by adversity, and it was seen, as in the time of Manasseh, that faithfulness to God might easily lead to martyrdom. The priests and false prophets, exasperated by Jeremiah's rebukes and warnings, and encouraged by the king's murder of Urijah, even demanded that Jeremiah too should die, but were foiled in their purpose (26¹⁶).

Real and not pretended service is the great lesson which Jeremiah at this time enforced, and in so doing he excited the animosity of his foes by the very truth of the charges that he brought against them. In opposition to those who still advocated alliance with Egypt against Babylon, he declared that the latter would assuredly prevail, and illustrated his words by the symbol of the potter's clay and the breaking of the earthen vessel (chs. 18, 19).

The fourth year of Jehoiakim's reign (605 B.C.) gave noteworthy proof of Jeremiah's prescience. Nebuchadnezzar, king of Babylon, defeated the army of Necho at Carchemish on the Euphrates, and, advancing into Palestine, drove many, including the Rechabites (c. 35), to seek shelter within the walls of Jerusalem. The conqueror advanced to the capital and bore away both captives and sacred vessels to Babylon (2 Ch 36⁶, ⁷). The complete overthrow was deferred, only because of Nebuchadnezzar's hasty return home on the report of his father's illness, in order to secure his succession to the throne. From this time forth Jeremiah's forecasts assume an air of greater definiteness. He speaks no longer, as in 1¹⁴ 6¹, of an enemy from 'the north,' but declares plainly that the king of Babylon, as God's instrument of punishment, is destined to prevail, urges submission, and promises that those who abide by his counsel shall be left undisturbed in their land. The rest, though captivity for seventy years is to be their lot, shall in the end be restored. Probably it was soon after the battle of Carchemish that there occurred the scene of the king's burning of the prophet's roll and repudiation of his warnings (c. 36). From this time till the end of Jehoiakim's reign Jeremiah seems to have been absent from Jerusalem. The king received no more warnings. After three years' payment as vassal of the tribute which he yearned to spend upon self-indulgence, he rebelled, was attacked by bands of Chaldeans and others, and probably in an engagement with some of them, came to a violent end and a dishonoured burial (22¹⁸, ¹⁹).

Reign of Jehoiachin (the Jeconiah of 24¹, and the Coniah of 22²⁴, ²⁸), 597 B.C. He was the son of Jehoiakim, was set up by Nebuchadnezzar, and, like his uncle Jehoahaz, reigned but three months, when he and the flower of the community with him (the 'good figs' of c. 24) were deported to Babylon. After thirty-six years' imprisonment he was released by Nebuchadnezzar's son and successor, Evil-merodach (52³¹). To this period belongs c. 13, with its acted symbol of the linen girdle.

Reign of Zedekiah, 597–586 B.C. He was the youngest son of Josiah, well disposed, but utterly weak. He showed more disposition than his predecessors had done to consult with Jeremiah (37¹⁷⁻²¹ 38¹⁴⁻²⁸), and under his advice to submit to Babylon. On the other hand, he was devoid of any real zeal for religion, and yielded, now to the suggestions of the prophet, now to those of the princes, who advocated resistance, either single-handed or in alliance with Egypt. Thus he was virtually powerless against the strong wills and more vigorous leaders opposed to him ($38^{5,25}$). To the worthiest part of the nation, who were in captivity, Jeremiah writes a letter of comfort (c. 29), advising submission, and promising restoration in due time.

At the beginning of the ninth year of Zedekiah a Chaldean army laid siege to Jerusalem. Jeremiah had already from time to time worn a yoke upon his neck, symbolical of the coming servitude ($Jer 27^2$), and when the false prophet, Hananiah, who promised deliverance, had broken the yoke (28^{10}), he received the sentence of speedy death at the mouth of Jeremiah (28^{16}) because he had 'spoken rebellion against the Lord.' It was natural for self-reliant, irreligious men to be highly displeased with such acts and words as these, and much persecution, including imprisonment, fell to the prophet's lot in consequence, the king being too weak to give him any permanent support ($Jer 37^{11-21}$). In the eleventh year of Zedekiah, 586 B.C., the city was sacked and the Temple burnt. Zedekiah's eyes were put out, and he was brought to Babylon, and immured in a dungeon, apparently till his death.

Jeremiah was permitted to remain under Gedaliah, Nebuchadnezzar's new governor, who was of a family friendly to the prophet. But in two months' time Gedaliah was murdered by the irreconcilables among the remnant in the land. In the turbulent period that followed, the prophet, viewed by the people as a traitor, foretold the want and misery that would ensue, if, through fear of the vengeance of Nebuchadnezzar ($42^{7f.}$), they went down to Egypt. They only replied by compelling him to accompany them thither. From Tahpanhes, a town near the eastern border of Lower Egypt, we draw the last certain notice of him that we possess. He declares that the fate which had befallen Judæa shall also be that of Egypt, and that Nebuchadnezzar's throne shall be set up at the entrance to Pharaoh's house (43^{10}). He also makes a dying protest against the idolatrous worship practised by his countrymen (c. 44). We have no notice in the Bible of his death.

2. Jeremiah's Attitude towards the Ceremonial Law and the Sabbath. Jeremiah's unvarying theme is that in God's sight the moral always takes precedence of the ceremonial Law (although laxity in sabbath observance is sharply rebuked in 17^{19-27}). This principle he applies to the people's reverence for the ark (3^{16}) and the tables of the Law ($31^{31f.}$, cp. 32^{40}), to circumcision (4^4 6^{10}

9^{26}), to the Temple ($7^{4,10f.}$ 11^{15} 17^3 $26^{6,9,12}$ 27^{16}), to sacrifices (6^{20} $7^{21f.}$ 11^{15} 14^{12}). We may further note that in many of the passages where the 'Law' is mentioned, the prophet is describing the 'oral' teaching given by priests ($Dt 17^{11}$) and prophets to those who consulted them on points of ritual or practice : see 2^8 9^{13} 18^{18} $26^{4,5}$.

3. The Messianic Passages and the Nature of the Prophet's Hope for the Future. A characteristic of Jeremiah's style is to insert a bright thought among gloomy ones, so that at the most terrible period of his country's fortunes his Messianic hopes are clearest in their expression. These hopes are gathered round (a) the Davidic house, (b) Jerusalem.

The chief Messianic passages ($17^{25,26}$ 23^{5-8} $30^{9,21}$ 33^{14-18}) are deserving of close study, as indicating the gradually increasing clearness of the hope. The worthless rulers of the prophet's days should be succeeded by a king of David's line, who should reign in righteousness ; out of the ruins of Jerusalem should arise a new city, which should bear the name, 'The Lord is our righteousness' ; and the old covenant, which had proved itself unable either to cleanse from sin or to enforce obedience, should give place to a new covenant of grace, written not on tables of stone, but on fleshy tables of the heart. Then 'they shall all know me from the least of them even unto the greatest of them' (31^{34}). Such was the dim forecast, as revealed to Jeremiah, of the New Order which, in the fulness of time, was to arise out of the Jewish dispensation through the coming of the Saviour of the world. 'The New Covenant has been established in the spiritual dispensation of the gospel, in a law written by the Spirit in the hearts of men, and in the new revelation the means of pardon and of purification have been provided and made known to man' (Kirkpatrick, 'The Doctrine of the Prophets,' p. 324). Christ, both Priest and King, and heir of David's line, has come to dwell among men in a higher sense than it was given to Jeremiah to realise.

4. Arrangement of the Contents of the Book. The book of Jeremiah gives us interesting indications of what we may call the literary history of a prophetical collection. More than twenty years had elapsed since Jeremiah's call when Baruch was bidden, apparently for the first time, to take down prophecies from his dictation. And when the roll which thus came into existence was burnt, that which succeeded it contained the same, and, in addition, 'many like words' (36^{32}). From the nature of the case there must have been a certain amount of condensation, as the *ipsissima verba* of the prophet's utterances would not remain in his mind during so long a period, and much of what he said must have been from time to time substantially repeated in the course of the twenty years. We also find that while the arrangement of the prophecies preceding c. 36 is in the main the order of delivery, that order is occasionally broken, the prophet grouping with some particular deliverance other prophecies of kindred subject-matter. Moreover, the roll, we may perceive, can only have been in general agreement with the section of the book down to c. 36, for portions of that section are clearly later than the fifth year of Jehoiakim; while the prophecies against foreign nations, some of which were contained in the roll (c. 36²), are now all at the end of the book according to the Hebrew arrangement (see next section, 'The Septuagint Version of Jeremiah'). We can trace signs of a distinction between the methods in which the earlier and later parts of the book (those directly dictated to Baruch, and those which Baruch himself arranged, as editor) assumed their present shape. For such a formula as 'the word of the Lord came unto *me*' in the earlier part, we find later 'The word of the Lord came to *Jeremiah*.' In the same way the expression 'Jeremiah the prophet,' more likely to be used by Baruch when acting as editor than as amanuensis, is characteristic of the later chapters. In this way the earlier seem to give us the voice of the prophet himself, while in the later we have the scribe collecting the utterances of his master, arranging them as he deems best, and editing the records of his life. It follows from what we have said that the order of the groups of prophecies is not always that of time. Moreover, while it is in some cases clear, it is also often uncertain when they were delivered. The convulsions through which the nation was passing during the latter part of the period were far from favourable to any formal arrangement of the contents. But the very lack of order here and there observable serves a valuable end, in showing that we may consider ourselves to possess the words of Jeremiah put together in those same troublous times at which they were spoken, and not as they might afterwards have been remodelled and fitted to the notions of men of a later generation.

The following can only claim to be a rough approximation to a chronological arrangement.

CHS.		
1–12	.	Josiah
14–20	.	Jehoiakim
26	.	1st year of Jehoiakim
25	.	4th ,, ,,
46–49	.	,, ,, ,,
35, 36	.	,, ,, ,,
45	.	,, ,, ,,
13	.	Jehoiachin
29	.	(? 1st year of) Zedekiah
27	.	,, ,, ,,

CHS.		
50, 51	.	(? 4th year of) Zedekiah
28	.	4th ,, ,,
21–24	.	9th ,, ,,
34	.	,, ,, ,,
37	.	(9th or) 10th ,, ,,
30–33	.	10th ,, ,,
38	.	,, ,, ,,
52	.	11th ,, ,, or later
39–44	.	Period of exile

5. The Septuagint Version of Jeremiah. The LXX, as a whole, adheres with tolerable fidelity to the Hebrew as we now possess it. But the book of Jeremiah in the Greek presents in various places so startling an exception to this rule, that it has been questioned whether the Greek is not in this case at least the more correct text.

The two main points of difference in the two texts are (*a*) that the Greek version omits, at different points, words amounting in the whole to about one-eighth of the text as it stands in the Hebrew; (*b*) that in the Greek the prophecies against foreign nations, instead of coming near the end of the book (chs. 46–51), stand after 25¹³, their logical place, where in the Hebrew text there is merely a reference to them. Also their order of sequence among themselves varies from that of the Hebrew.

Space does not allow further treatment of the question here; but it may be said that while there seems good reason for thinking that the form of the book on which the Greek translators' work was based preserves purer readings in many passages, and that the Hebrew has in some passages glossed or expanded the text, 'on the whole the Massoretic text deserves the preference' (Driver).

6. Jeremiah's Relations to his Predecessors. The prophet to whom Jeremiah is most closely related in thought and teaching is Hosea. Just as Hosea found idolatry and licentiousness in the kingdom of Israel in the years before its fall, so Jeremiah found them in Judah in similar political circumstances. It is probable that Jeremiah was acquainted with the prophecies of his large-hearted predecessor. Both were men of the same type of mind; both were deeply religious and jealous for Jehovah's service; and certain passages in the book of Jeremiah suggest the influence of the prophet of the North: cp. Jer 2¹⁻⁶ with Hos 2¹⁻⁵, Jer 3¹,² with Hos 3¹, Jer 3²² with Hos 14⁴, Jer 5³¹ with Hos 4⁹, etc.

As already mentioned, in the early part of the prophet's career the 'book of the Law' (Deuteronomy) was found in the Temple. Its teaching supported him in his appeals to the people, and as the results of its discovery the reformation of worship was made by Josiah.

That Jeremiah was influenced by this book is seen, negatively, in the fact that we have no prophecies belonging to the latter part of Josiah's reign, the teaching of Deuteronomy and the adoption of its precepts having rendered his work unnecessary for the time; and positively in the frequent references to it which occur in his prophecies : cp. 2⁶ with Dt 32¹⁰, 5¹⁵ with Dt 28⁴⁹, 7³³ with Dt 28²⁶, 11³ with Dt 27²⁶, 11⁵ with Dt 7¹², ¹³, 24⁹ with 28²⁵, etc.

Jeremiah is concerned with the sin of the people as exhibited in their unfaithfulness to God. It was not enough that they should have a reform of worship ; the true reform was that of the human heart (4⁴) ; what they needed was a change of heart (24⁷ 31³¹). The importance of the individual in the sight of God is a prominent thought with our prophet. Men were to be punished for their own sins, he taught, not for those of their forefathers (31²⁹). Individual responsibility was to be the foundation of character and spiritual life. And consequently the new law was to be a spiritual bond between God and man, a law written in men's hearts, and obeyed in love and loyalty (31³¹). This teaching of the importance of the individual was the first step towards that faith in personal (as distinguished from racial) immortality, which from this time begins to be dimly sought after by Jewish thinkers.

CHAPTER 1

THE CALL OF JEREMIAH (13th year of Josiah). FIRST PROPHECY

1-3. See Introduction.

3. The fifth month] i.e. when Jerusalem was destroyed (2 K 25³, ⁸).

4-10. Jeremiah's call and first prophecy.

4. The word of the LORD came unto me] see art. 'Introduction to Hebrew Prophecy.' We cannot doubt that Jeremiah had long mourned over his people's sins, and yet perhaps hesitated to undertake the burden of witnessing against them. At length he became conscious of a divine call to the prophetic office, which was not to be restricted : cp. 20⁷.

5. I knew thee] approved, selected thee : cp. Gn 18¹⁹ Ps 1⁶ Nah 1⁷. **Sanctified**] consecrated : cp. John Baptist (Lk 1¹⁵⁻¹⁷) and St. Paul (Gal 1¹⁵,¹⁶). **Unto the nations**] This points out a distinction between the work of Jeremiah as a prophet and that of many of his predecessors, e.g. Elijah and Elisha. Their predictions were concerned with the Jews only. Those of Jeremiah, on the other hand, had to do with the heathen world as well, and also with the nations of subsequent ages, as he foretold the blessings that were to come on the earth through the Messiah. See Intro.

6. A child] not probably in years, but in fitness. 'Who is sufficient for these things?'

9. Touched my mouth] symbolic of divine grace and inspiration : cp. Isa 6⁶ Ezk 2⁹-3³.

10. Jeremiah's work was to be radical and destructive in denouncing the sins of his people and predicting their chastening, but also one of restoration and rebuilding through leading them to repentance.

11-19. Words of encouragement. Jeremiah is vouchsafed two visions. The first (11, 12) was the branch of an almond tree, which is extremely early in blossoming. This indicated that God would very soon execute His purposes and judgments. **12.** Since the days of Manasseh the Lord had not visited upon the people their sins. That period of rest was like the winter. The Lord is now rousing Himself ; yet not only to punish, but to save as well. Through Josiah's reforms and Jeremiah's ministry religion is to be kept alive in a remnant, viz. those carried to Babylon, and so the return shall at last be brought about.

13. The second vision was that of a seething pot with its mouth 'towards the south' (lit. 'from the face of the north'), and about to boil over. The meaning was as hinted in v. 14, that the great Babylonian power to the N. of Palestine, which had long been at strife with Elam and Media, would soon be directed against Judæa, the danger to which always depended upon the fact that it lay on the direct route of an army proceeding from the E. against Egypt.

15. Shall set every one his throne, etc.] This prediction was literally fulfilled (see 39³). The function of administering justice was exercised by the king in person, and the neighbourhood of the city gate was the ordinary place at which trials were held. Here then the rulers of the invader's army will sit in judgment on the conquered people.

17. Gird up thy loins] The shortening of the robe by drawing it up through the girdle was preparatory to active exertion : cp. Elijah 1 K 18⁴⁶. **18. I have made thee . . a defenced city, etc.**] God would endue Jeremiah with firmness and resolution to carry out his mission in spite of all opposition.

CHAPTERS 2-6

THE PROPHET SETS FORTH THE SIN OF THE NATION AND POINTS OUT THE INEVITABLE RESULT (Reign of Josiah, and probably before the reforms of that king : cp. 3⁶)

This section furnishes us with the gist of the prophet's testimony during the early years of his ministry, and doubtless represents the commencement of the roll written by Baruch at Jeremiah's dictation. In these five chs. he lays before his hearers the grossness of their conduct in deserting Jehovah, and urges repentance and amendment while yet the impending judgment is delayed. For the idolatrous and 'high place' worship of the period see Intro., and cp. Intro. to Hosea.

CHAPTER 2
JEREMIAH'S SECOND PROPHECY (2 1–3 5)

The prophet expostulates with Israel because of their unfaithfulness to Jehovah.

1–13. Under the figure of the marriage relation Jehovah reminds the people of His past favours, and charges them with faithlessness to their first love, as shown by their idolatry.

2. The kindness of thy youth, etc.] Israel's earliest devotion to Jehovah at Sinai (Ex 24 8).
3. Firstfruits of .. increase] i.e. the consecrated part. **All that devour, etc.**] The priest and his family alone were to eat of the first fruits (Lv 22 10, 16). If any unhallowed person took of them, he trespassed or 'offended.' In like manner if heathen nations meddle with Israel (the consecrated people), they will be guilty as those who eat the fruits.
5. Vanity] i.e. idols : cp. 10 15. **6. The shadow of death**] RV 'deep darkness,' as referring to a region where the supply of the necessaries of life was so precarious that the fear of death was always present.
8. The priests, the pastors (i.e. rulers) and the prophets were all alike in sympathy with the degraded worship of Jehovah at the high places, mingled as it was with the worship of the Baalim. The priests were more concerned with gain than with purity of worship ; and the prophetic guilds had also become corrupted by the general idolatry and immorality. It was the most degraded period of both these orders.
9. Plead] 'argue,' or 'contend.' **10. Chittim**] probably Citium in Cyprus. **Kedar**] As Chittim represented the parts to the westward of Palestine, so did Kedar (the NW. of Arabia) those to the east. **11.** None of the nations have forsaken their ancestral worship, false though it be. Israel has forsaken her ancient religion, though true.
13. God's blessing, under the figure of fresh water as supplied by a spring or rivulet, is contrasted with the vanity of serving idols, which is as devoid of profit as a cracked reservoir (dug to collect rain water) for that which it is intended to supply.
14–35. Not only by her idolatry, but by her quests for alliance, now with Egypt and now with Assyria, has Judah shown her faithlessness. For both these sins she will be punished.
14. Is Israel, etc.**] The meaning here probably is, How is it that Israel, the people of God, has become a slave to neighbouring powers? V. 17 gives the answer. **15. The young lions,** etc.**] the enemies of Israel. **16. Noph**] probably Memphis, the capital of northern (lower) Egypt. **Tahapanes**] the classic Daphnæ, an

Egyptian fortress on the E. frontier of Lower Egypt. It is again mentioned (43 7-10) as the future scene of the acknowledgment of Nebuchadnezzar's supremacy over Egypt. The sense of the v. is, Egypt is God's instrument for punishing Judah. **Have broken**] RM 'fed on,' so as to make it bald ; a disgrace.
18. Egypt] Some of Judah's politicians desired an alliance with Egypt ; others with Assyria, or rather with Babylonia, Assyria's successor in the command of the East. **Sihor**] here the Nile ; so in Isa 23 3. **Assyria**] The Assyrian power had passed to Babylonia, but the name had been familiar for generations and was still in use for the great Eastern power. **The river**] Euphrates.
20. See Intro. respecting worship in 'high places,' simultaneously with that of Jehovah, which they thought a lawful combination. **I have broken .. and burst, etc.**] RM 'thou hast broken,' etc., i.e. thou hast cast off allegiance to Me, thy Maker. **Transgress**] RV 'serve.'
When] RV 'for.' **Wanderest**] RV 'didst bow thyself,' in idolatry, thus dishonouring thy rightful spouse. **21. A noble vine**] a 'Sorek' vine, the word probably indicating the dark-purple colour of the fruit. **Strange vine**] cp. Isa 5 2, 4. **22. Nitre**] RV 'lye,' i.e. natron, or carbonate of soda.
23. Baalim] the Heb. plural of 'Baal' : cp. 'cherubim,' 'seraphim.' The Baalim were the images of the local Baals under the form of a bull at the various shrines. **The valley**] Most likely Hinnom (S. of Jerusalem), which was defiled by Josiah in order that the impure rites (viz. the worship of Moloch = Baal) here referred to might cease. **Traversing**] running quickly hither and thither in the eagerness of her passion. Vv. 23–25 are figurative of Israel's shameless love of idolatry. **24. At her pleasure**] RV 'in her desire.' **25. Withhold, etc.**] pursue not thy reckless wanton quest with parched throat and worn-out sandal.
30. Your prophets] Such as Isaiah (said to have been sawn asunder) and Zechariah son of Jehoiada (2 Ch 24 20), and those whom Jezebel (1 K 18 13) or Manasseh (2 K 21 16) slew : cp. Mt 23 29-39. **31. A wilderness**] i.e. fruitless, useless. **We are lords**] RV 'we are broken loose'; we are our own masters. **33.** Why art thou so careful in thy devotion to strange gods ? In so doing thou hast made wicked ways to be a second nature to thee (or, thou hast taught the wicked women thy ways).
34. Poor innocents] RV 'the innocent poor.' **By secret search**] RV 'at the place of breaking in.' The allusion is to the law (Ex 22 2) by which it was permissible to slay a thief caught in the act of breaking into a house. But those 'innocent poor' had committed no such crime, yet their blood had been wantonly shed : cp. the cruelties of Manasseh 2 K 21 16.

Upon all these] RM 'upon every oak,' or, perhaps, 'because of this,' i.e. your lust for idolatry.

35. Plead] RV 'enter into judgement.'

36. Ashamed of Egypt] literally fulfilled when the Egyptians in the reign of Zedekiah were expected to raise the siege of Jerusalem, but failed to do so: cp. 37⁵. **Ashamed of Assyria**] A conspicuous instance was in the reign of Ahaz (2 Ch 28²¹). **37. Thine hands upon thine head**] clasped in disgrace.

C. 3. 1. That land] an allusion to the law (Dt 24¹⁻⁴) that under such circumstances the reunion of husband and wife would pollute the land. **Yet return again, etc.**] RM 'and *thinkest thou* to return again.'

2. The Arabian] the Bedouin freebooters. As they are eager to despoil a passing caravan, so is Israel eager for the worship of false gods. **5. Behold, thou hast spoken, etc.**] RM 'Thou hast spoken *thus*, but hast done evil things.' **As thou couldest**] RV 'and hast had thy way.'

CHAPTERS 3⁶–4⁴

JEREMIAH'S THIRD PROPHECY. THE FATE OF THE TEN TRIBES A WARNING TO JUDAH

In this prophecy, as in the last, idolatry is denounced under the figure of unfaithfulness to the marriage vow. But as a marked distinction, God here invites to repentance, and on this there hinges pardon.

6–20. Israel and Judah have both forsaken their Divine Spouse, but forgiveness will follow repentance.

7–11. Samaria, the capital of the kingdom of the Ten Tribes, after a stubborn resistance had been captured by Sargon, king of Assyria, 722 B.C., and more than 27,000 of its inhabitants deported. The isolation and comparative poverty of Judah helped her to survive her northern sister for well over a hundred years. But failure to take advantage of the warning thus afforded her brought its inevitable results. Moreover, in spite of greater privileges, she had added to apostasy treachery, by hypocritically feigning still to pay homage to Jehovah under cover of idolatrous rites. She had rejected Josiah's reforms, and this rejection sealed her fate. 'It is not by the act of its government that a nation stands or falls; Ahaz and Manasseh lent the weight of their influence to the cause of idolatry; Hezekiah and Josiah to the cause of truth: but the nation had to determine which should prevail' (Speaker's Commentary).

8. I saw] some read, 'she saw.' **Bill of divorce**] i.e. exile.

11. Justified herself more] for Judah had even more warning than Israel.

12. Toward the north] to Assyria, the place of Israel's captivity.

14. One of .. two of, etc.] A 'city' might be a mere village. A 'family,' i.e. descendants of a common ancestor, suggested a larger number. There were, e.g., only four or five families in the whole tribe of Judah. The reference here is to the return from the exile to Palestine.

16. The blessings of repentance and obedience. Even the ark with the mercy seat on which the brightness which marked Jehovah's presence rested shall be forgotten, for Jehovah shall no longer be confined to one place or one people. All nations shall serve Him; His dominion centred in Jerusalem shall extend to the ends of the earth. **17. Imagination**] RV 'stubbornness.' **19.** The Lord tells of His affection for Israel. **But**] rather, 'and.' **How**] i.e. In what honourable position? **The children**] the nations of the earth, all of them God's children, as created by Him.

22–25. An acceptable prayer of repentance.

23. The multitude of mountains] RV 'the tumult' (RM 'the noisy throng') 'on the mountains': the orgies and clamorous supplications of idolatrous crowds at the high places.

24. Shame] RV 'the shameful thing,' i.e. the god Baal: cp. 11¹³. **Hath devoured**] hath consumed in the form of sacrifices the fruits of our toil.

C. 4. 1–4. The assurance of forgiveness.

1. Then shalt, etc.] RM 'and wilt not wander.'

3. Break up, etc.] As the farmer is careful to clear the soil of weeds before sowing his seed, so with Israel. The sowing of repentance must be serious and real.

4. Circumcise] Circumcision was a dedication of self to God's service, and a removal of imperfections.

CHAPTERS 4⁵–6³⁰

JEREMIAH'S FOURTH PROPHECY (OR GROUP OF PROPHECIES). GOD'S JUDGMENT UPON THE UNREPENTANT

When the check which Josiah's personal character and influence put upon idolatry was removed, Jeremiah foresaw that the condition of the nation would become well-nigh desperate.

CHAPTER 4⁵⁻³¹

5–10. Destruction approaches Jerusalem.

6. Set up the standard] to mark out the safest route to those who were seeking the shelter of the walls of Jerusalem. **Evil from the north**] The enemy (see v. 13) used chariots, and were therefore probably the Chaldeans, not (as some have supposed) Scythians. **7. The lion**] i.e. the enemy. **Of the Gentiles**] RV 'of nations.'

10. Jeremiah here struggles against the fate announced for the nation. After all its glorious history and the many promises of coming glory that prophets like Isaiah had made to it, was this to be the end ? The prophet was 'in a strait betwixt two,' sorrowing for the doom of the nation and anxious to avert it, and yet desirous to vindicate Jehovah's ways to them. Hence this exceeding bitter cry. Some, however, regard the v. as a reference to the mischief done by the false prophets, who had promised peace in the name of the Lord.

11-18. Description of the attack.

11. A dry wind] the Chaldean army coming like a sirocco from the E.   **15. Dan** was on the northern border of Palestine. **Mount Ephraim** was the range immediately N. of Judah, only about 10 m. from Jerusalem itself. Thus the enemy's approach is rapid.

16. The nations summoned to witness the vengeance on the chosen people. The **watchers** are the Chaldean besiegers. **17.** The besiegers' tents compared to the booths of shepherds or husbandmen.

19-31. The prophet expresses horror at the approaching calamity.

19. My bowels] supposed to be the seat of emotions. **21.** See v. 6. **22.** God's answer to the implied appeal to know why the invasion was permitted. It is not without cause, for, etc. **24. Lightly**] RV 'to and fro.'

27. Yet will I not make a full end] The destruction will not be complete : a remnant shall return : cp. Am 9⁸. **30. And** *when* **thou** *art* **spoiled**] better, 'and thou, spoiled one,' i.e. Jerusalem. **Rentest thy face with painting**] RV ' enlargest thine eyes with paint.' The Eastern custom was to paint black the border of the eyes, so as to give the effect of size and brilliancy. So Jezebel in 2 K 9³⁰.

CHAPTER 5

1-9. The universal corruption of the city prevents forgiveness.

2. Though they say, The LORD liveth] i.e. though they take the most solemn form of oath, as opposed to those held by the Jews to be of less obligation : cp. Mt 5³⁴, ³⁵. **3. The truth**] RM 'faithfulness.' It is this that God looks for. **4. These** *are* **poor**, etc.] i.e. the ignorant ones who know no better. **5. Yoke . . bonds**] i.e. restraints of God's law. **6. Lion**] i.e. the invader : cp. 4⁷. **Evenings**] RM 'deserts.'

7, 8. All idolatry was unfaithfulness to God, to whom Israel was espoused, but gross licentiousness was literally the common accompaniment of the worship of the reproductive powers of nature, such as was practised by the Canaanites.

8. In the morning] RM 'roaming at large.'

10-31. In spite of fancied security desolation is at hand in requital for rebellion and faithlessness.

10. Jerusalem is likened to a walled-in vineyard, and the Chaldean host is bidden to batter and trample it. Yet the overthrow shall not be complete, for Israel is, after all, a chosen nation. **Battlements**] RV 'branches,' so as to keep up the figure of the vine. Though the tendrils be cut away yet the stock shall be left.

12. *It is* **not he**] It is not God who sends these messages of woe. **13. The prophets,** etc.] These are still the words of the scoffing Jews. **15. A nation**] the Assyrian. **16.** *Is* as **an open sepulchre**] for it is filled with missiles dealing death.

19. Note the distinct prophecy of the captivity of Judah. **24.** Jeremiah reminds them of the providence of God, who sends the winter and spring rains, so needful for the crops, and maintains a dry season between Passover and Pentecost for harvesting.

25-28. A strong testimony to the deception, avarice, and oppression of the time. **28. Yet they prosper**] RV 'that they' (the orphans) ' should prosper.'

31. Prophets, priests, and people alike connived at and took part in these crimes. **By their means**] RM 'at their hands.' Formerly the prophetic guilds had borne witness for righteousness and withstood the priests : now they are become false prophets, abetting the priests in their idolatry and wickedness.

CHAPTER 6

1-8. The hostile army approaches.

1. Benjamin] Jerusalem was within the territory assigned to this tribe. **Tekoa**] 11 m. S. of Jerusalem, and in the line of flight for its inhabitants seeking to escape an enemy from the N. **A sign of fire**] a warning signal. **Beth-haccerem**] probably a hill between Jerusalem and Tekoa, and thus suitable for a beacon station. **2.** RV 'The comely and delicate one, the daughter of Zion will I cut off,' a tenderly worded lament over the ill-fated city. **Daughter**] is used for the inhabitants collectively. **3.** A figure of the devastating enemy. Flocks eating the herbage on every side are a figure to express devastation.

4, 5. The invaders propose a determined and continuous attack. **4. Prepare**] RM ' Heb. sanctify.' Entering on a war was accompanied by religious ceremonies : cp. Dt 20²ᶠ. **6. Hew ye down trees**] to clear the approaches to the city. **Cast a mount**] earth was carried in baskets and poured in a heap until it was on a level with the walls : cp. this method of assault in 2 K 19³² Isa 29³.

To be visited] with punishment. **7. Grief**] RV 'sickness.'

9-21. Retribution awaiting the guilty people.

9. Into the baskets] RM 'upon the shoots.' As the grape-gatherer goes back over the tendrils, lest he should have missed any of the fruit, so the people shall be subject to successive gleanings at the hand of their conquerors, who are here addressed. **10. Uncircumcised**] in the sense of 'imperfect': cp. Ex6^{12}. **11. Abroad**] RV 'in the street.'

14. They] the leaders, prophets, and priests. **The hurt**] the sins and shortcomings. They are like physicians who for their own ease assure their patients that all is well.

16. God's appeal. 'A national calamity is at hand. As prudent men ye will desire to avoid it. Make enquiries what paths led your ancestors to prosperity. Were they those of idolatry or of true religion and purity?'

17. Watchmen] the prophets sounding the alarm. **The trumpet**] warning of approaching danger. **18. What** *is* **among them**] i.e. what is the punishment impending over Judah.

20. Sheba] in the S. of Arabia. The general sense of the v. is, 'To obey is better than sacrifice' (1S15^{22}). **Cane**] i.e. calamus, a sweet-scented reed, used in making the anointing oil. **21. Stumblingblocks, etc.**] the enemy's invasion, which would, as it were, trip them up in their easy-going ways.

22–24. The approaching invader. These vv. are repeated with necessary changes in 50$^{41-43}$, where Babylon is the object of the threat.

22. The sides of the earth] an expression for the far distance.

23. The Assyrian monuments show us rows of impaled victims hanging round the walls of besieged towns, also men collecting in heaps hands cut off from the vanquished enemy.

25. Fear *is* **on every side**] a favourite expression with Jeremiah (20$^{3\,\mathrm{mg.}\,10}$ 46^5 49^{29}). **27-30.** The nation incapable of reform. Jehovah reassures Jeremiah of his divine commission. The prophet appears under the figure of one testing metal by smelting. The result of the process is that no precious metal is found. All is dross.

27. A tower] RM 'trier,' or tester. **A fortress**] He shall have God's protection in his task. **28.** *They are* **brass and iron**] They have none of the precious metal in them.

29. All the prophet's fervour is without effect. Nothing of value rewards the long assay. **Are burned**] RV 'blow fiercely.' **Plucked away**] i.e. eliminated from the good. **30. Reprobate**] RV 'refuse.'

CHAPTERS 7^1–10^{25}

JEREMIAH'S FIFTH PROPHECY (OR GROUP OF PROPHECIES). ADDRESS AT THE TEMPLE GATE (Reign of Josiah or beginning of that of Jehoiakim)

The prophet takes advantage of a solemn gathering of the people at Jerusalem to stand at one of the Temple gates as they pass in,

and warns them against their superstitious confidence that the possession of the Temple was itself a charm against danger from without. As immorality had already brought about the overthrow of an older sanctuary (Shiloh) as well as of the Ten Tribes, so shall it be with them. Punishment for the wickedness of leaders and people can only be averted by a speedy amendment of life.

It is possible that these chapters may be an expanded account of the prophecy closely resembling them, which is recorded in c. 26 as spoken at the commencement of Jehoiakim's reign. But it is more likely that the two occasions are distinct.

CHAPTER 7

1–20. Ceremonies and sacred places shall be no defence.

4. God, said the false prophets, will never allow His Temple to be overthrown: cp. Mic3^{11}. **The temple, etc.**] The threefold repetition suggests 'the energy of iteration that only belongs to Eastern fanatics' (Stanley, 'Jewish Church,' ii, 438).

5-7. Their tenure of the Temple is conditional on obedience to the covenant made by God with their fathers. **10. We are delivered**] By the discharge of this formality we are set free for a return to wickedness. **11. Den of robbers**] a place of retreat in the intervals between acts of violence: see Mt21^{13} and parallel passages.

12. Shiloh] a town of Ephraim, in a central position, chosen by Joshua as the resting-place of the ark and for the Tabernacle. It was a considerable place in the time of the Judges (Jg21$^{19,\,21}$). Its fall into idolatry was followed by loss of the ark (1S4) and subsequent capture and cruel treatment (Ps78$^{58\,f.}$). Thenceforward it became insignificant, so that Jeroboam, when setting up calves for his rival worship, passed it by. **15. Ephraim**] meaning, as often (e.g. Isa7^2), the ten northern tribes in captivity for nearly a century.

16. So in 14^7, when Jeremiah does intercede for them, the prayer is rejected. **18. Queen of heaven**] identified either with the moon or with the Assyrian Ishtar, the planet Venus. The Jewish women were specially given to that worship, offering incense and cakes stamped with a representation of the goddess: cp. 44^{17}. **19. Do they provoke me**] Their sin does not provoke God to a mere helpless anger, but to a wrath that is quick to punish and destroy them. **21-28.** The moral law has always taken precedence of the ceremonial.

21. Put your burnt offerings, etc.] Multiply your victims *ad libitum*. It will avail you nought.

22, 23. This need not be more than a forcible oratorical expression, not meaning that no ceremonial laws were given to Israel when brought out of Egypt, but that in the promulgation of the Ten Commandments on Sinai there was no direction concerning sacrifice. These were the only precepts which had the honour of being treasured up in the ark. Thus from the first they were shown to hold the chief place : cp. Isa 1 11-14. 'The law of obedience was the earliest law of all (Gn 2 16 f.), and the most important ; that of sacrifice was of secondary importance' (Deane). **24. Imagination**] see on 3 17. **27.** Jeremiah need not therefore expect that his words will be heeded.

29-34. Where they sinned there shall they be punished.

29. Cut off thine hair] in token of mourning, or as a Nazirite shaved his head after immediate contact with a dead body (Nu 6 9) to mark defilement. The hair was the mark of consecration of the High Priest (Ex 29 6) and of the Nazirite (Nu 6 5). Here it is the mark of Jerusalem as chief city of a consecrated people.

31. Valley of Hinnom] on the W. and S. sides of the city, Tophet being near the E. extremity of the S. reach. The valley had an evil name, (a) as the place of human sacrifices ; (b) as defiled by Josiah ; (c) as the receptacle of the offal and filth of the city. Hence it afterwards became with the Jewish Rabbis the visible emblem of the place of future punishment, Gehenna : cp. Mt 5 22. **To burn**, etc.] in honour of Moloch, often identified with Baal, the sun-god (see on Gn 22 2 K 16 3). **32. Till there be no place**] rather, 'for want of room' (elsewhere). The carnage of war shall extend far beyond the valley.

Some think that the immediate result of this discourse was the trial of the prophet, as recorded in 26 7-24, when the mob rose against him and he was saved with difficulty.

CHAPTER 8

1-3. The dead shall share in the universal punishment.

1. Shall bring out the bones] either from pure wantonness, or in the hope of finding treasure or ornaments of value. **2. Before the sun**] the heavenly bodies will not be prevented by all the offerings and devotions that they have received from using their influence to hasten the rotting of the carcases of their sometime worshippers.

3. Family] the whole nation : see on 3 14.

4-17. The people are hardened in sin.

4. They] RV 'men.' If a man stumble, he will naturally regain his footing : if he lose his way he will return to it. Not so with this people. **6. As the horse**, etc.] meaning, an eager plunge into wrongdoing.

7. The turtle and the crane and the swallow] rather, 'The turtle dove and the swift and the crane' : cp. Isa 1 3.

8. Lo, certainly in vain . . in vain] RV 'But, behold, the false pen of the scribes hath

wrought falsely,' i.e. they have used their knowledge of the Law to deceive others, persuading them that they may transgress with impunity. The scribes (frequently mentioned in NT.) were a class of persons who devoted themselves to the study and exposition of the Law. That they were a leading class as early as the time of Josiah (and Jeremiah's whole argument depends on this fact) is a strong argument in favour of the belief that the Book of the Law even at that time had well-grounded claims to antiquity.

10. Shall inherit *them*] shall take possession of them. The idea is forcible seizure by the invader. **11.** See on 6 14. **13. And** *the things* **. . from them**] RM 'I have appointed them those that shall pass over them' : viz. the Assyrians invading them as a flood.

14 f. The people address one another, while suffering under the troubles thus described. **Enter into the defenced cities**] i.e. out of villages for protection. **Water of gall**] bitterness is our portion. **16. His horses**] i.e. those of the Babylonian invader. **Strong ones**] war-horses. So in 47 3 50 11. **17. Cockatrices**] RV 'basilisks,' RM 'adders' : Jeremiah may have chosen the word because of its resemblance in sound in the Hebrew to the word *northern*, the invaders coming from that quarter. **Charmed**] so as to be harmless.

18-22. Jeremiah speaks. **18.** *When* I **would**] RV 'O that I could.' **19 f.** Jeremiah is in thought anticipating the captivity and the distressful cries of the exiles in the direction of their home. **20.** When the harvest was bad there was still hope of the yield from grapes, etc. But the people had lost one chance of deliverance after another, and might now despair. **Summer**] RM 'ingathering of summer fruits.' **21. Black**] RM 'mourning.' **22.** 'Is there no way of saving this people ?' **Gilead** was a mountainous part of Palestine E. of the Jordan. **Balm** (balsam) was found there, and naturally in the same place would be found those skilled in its use.

CHAPTER 9

1-22. The prophet continues his lament. The impending doom.

2. A lodging place, etc.] a caravanserai (khan), supplying a bare shelter, even the most desolate spot, if he may thereby escape the crimes of Jerusalem.

7. Melt . . try] i.e. remove the dross, and test whether the metal is now pure. **8. His wait**] RV 'wait for him.' **10. Habitations**] RV 'pastures.' **11. Dragons**] RV 'jackals' ; so in 49 33. **12. For what**, etc.] rather (with RV), a new question, 'Wherefore is ?' etc. Why this heavy chastisement ?

17. Mourning women] professionals, who

with dishevelled locks and bared breasts led the loud weeping. **Cunning**] skilful.

23, 24. The people have been trusting in worldly wisdom, power, and riches ; but the only sure trust is in knowing the will of God, who Himself acts righteously, and desires that men should do the same.

25. *Them which are* **circumcised with the uncircumcised**] RV ' Them which are circumcised in their uncircumcision.' They are circumcised in the flesh, but uncircumcised in spirit : cp. Dt 10 16 Ro 2 28, 29. Judah is become as the other nations which observe the outward rite, but have not the spirit of which it is the symbol. **26.** *That are* **in the utmost corners**] RV ' that have the corners *of their hair* polled ' : cp. Lv 19 27. The reference is to the tribes of Kedar : see 49 28, 32.

CHAPTER 10

1–16. The folly of idolatry.

This section of the prophecy is of doubtful authorship. For (*a*) it introduces a break in the sense ; (*b*) there is less smoothness between the parts than we generally find in Jeremiah's writings ; (*c*) its language differs considerably from his use elsewhere, and closely resembles that of Isaiah 40–44 ; (*d*) the writer emphasises the fact that false gods are incapable of hurting, while Jeremiah elsewhere speaks rather of them as powerless to aid ; (*e*) vv. 2, 4 read as though addressed to men who were contemplating the idolatry around them, rather than guilty of it themselves. For these reasons it is held by some to be a discourse addressed by an unknown author during the captivity to the exiles at Babylon : cp. the spurious letter ascribed to Jeremiah, which forms c. 6 of the (apocryphal) book of Baruch.

It should, however, be said, on the other hand, that the Septuagint version of this book, though omitting much that is found in the Hebrew (see Intro.), yet contains this chapter.

2. Signs of heaven] portents in the sky, such as comets and meteors. **3. People**] nations. **5. Upright as the palm tree**] RV ' like a palm tree, of turned work.' These idols are as stiff and lifeless. **7. To thee doth it appertain**] Thine is the supreme kingship. **8. The stock, etc.**] RV ' the instruction of idols, it is but a stock ' : an idol is wood, and can never get beyond it. **9. Tarshish**] probably Tartessus in Spain, or perhaps Tarsus in Cilicia. **Uphaz**] perhaps the same as Ophir, which was probably either in India or on the E. coast of Arabia. **Founder**] RV ' goldsmith ' : so in v. 14.

11. This v. is in the later Hebrew or Aramaic It may therefore have been originally a note on the margin of the manuscript,

afterwards copied into the text. **13.** The ascent of the vapours in clouds is spoken of poetically, as though it were the consequence of the thunder (**his voice**), because it is seen to follow it. **14. In** *his* **knowledge**] RV ' *and is* without knowledge.' **16. The portion of Jacob**] i.e. the true God, upon whom Israel has a claim. **Former**] Maker, Fashioner. **The rod**] RV ' tribe.' **17–25.** The coming troubles. This section seems to be closely connected with, and should probably be read after, 9 7-22.

17. Gather up, etc.] i.e. collect articles for a hasty flight, O thou who art in a besieged city ' ; i.e. prepare for exile. **18. Find** *it so*] RV ' feel *it*'. **19** f. The lament of Jerusalem. **20.** The spoiling and exile represented in figurative language. **Tabernacle**] RV ' tent.' **21.** The condemnation of the rulers. **22. The bruit**] RV ' a rumour.' **The north country**] see on 1 13. **Dragons**] see on 9 11. **23.** Jeremiah's prayer : the helplessness of man, and his dependence on God.

CHAPTERS 11, 12

JEREMIAH'S SIXTH PROPHECY (Reign of Josiah). THE BROKEN COVENANT ENTAILS A CURSE

These chs. form a connected prophecy. They probably belong to Josiah's time, for (*a*) ' the words of this covenant' (11 3) seem to refer to the reading of the newly discovered law mentioned in 2 K 23 3 ; (*b*) Jeremiah has not yet removed from Anathoth to Jerusalem (11 21), and (*c*) the apparent allusion (12 4) to a drought accords with similar references in prophecies belonging to Josiah's reign (3 3 5 24).

CHAPTER 11

1–14. Punishment must follow faithlessness. **3. Cursed,** etc.] cp. the language of the warnings in Deuteronomy (27 15-26), a book with which this passage has other features in common. **4. The iron furnace**] the brick-kilns of the bondage in Egypt (Ex 1 14) may have given rise to the figure as expressive of affliction. **6. The cities of Judah**] Jeremiah may have accompanied Josiah in the journey which he made to Bethel and to the cities of Samaria for the overthrow of idolatry (2 K 23 15, 19). **7. Rising early**] a frequent phrase with Jeremiah to denote earnestness, but not occurring in that sense elsewhere. **8. Imagination**] RV ' stubbornness.'

9. A conspiracy] The words seem to point to an actual secret combination against Josiah on account of his reforms. **10. The iniquities of their forefathers**] referring to the idolatry in the wilderness days. **They went after**] RV ' they are gone after,' viz. the Jews of the prophet's own day. The reformation had not taken hold of the hearts of the people, they had returned to their heathenism.

13. The worship of Baal was practised secretly or openly in all parts of the country and city. **Shameful thing]** i.e. Baal.

15-20. The people resent rebuke.

15. Faithless Judah's presence in the Temple is only an intrusion. **And the holy flesh is passed from thee]** better, perhaps, 'shall vows and holy flesh (i.e. sacrifices) take away thy wickedness?'

16. The fair promise and the punishment which apostasy brought about.

18. The prophet passes from the general to the particular, and charges his fellow-townsmen of Anathoth with conspiring to silence and even to kill him. The Lord had shown him their intentions.

19. Like a lamb or **an ox]** RV 'like a gentle lamb.' **The tree with the fruit thereof]** apparently a proverb. Not only is the tree to perish but there is to be no chance of reproduction by the sowing of its seed.

21-23. Anathoth shall be punished.

23. There shall be no remnant of them] viz. of the actual conspirators. Among those who return from exile are mentioned 'men of Anathoth' (Ezr 2 23).

CHAPTER 12

1-4. The prosperity of the wicked perplexes Jeremiah.

1. Wherefore, etc.] The question was one which much exercised men of pre-Christian times who had no clear view of any but temporal rewards and punishments. See Pss 37, 39, 49, 73, and Job (specially 21 7f.). The plots of his fellow-townsmen at Anathoth (see c. 11) were probably the occasion of this outburst of Jeremiah's. **2. Near in their mouth, etc.]** They honour God with their lips but their heart is far from Him. **4.** A drought has been sent in punishment. **He shall not see, etc.]** Jeremiah's denunciations are derided by his enemies.

5, 6. God's answer to the prophet's appeal. By two proverbial expressions He shows him that he must prepare to endure worse things than any he has yet been called upon to face. He has been in danger at Anathoth, but greater dangers await him at Jerusalem. Let him therefore be strong and play the man.

5. Swelling] RV 'pride,' referring to the luxuriant vegetation on the banks, which formed a source of danger, as a covert for wild beasts.

7-13. A lament over the desolate land. Some scholars think that this passage belongs to the time after the first siege and capture of Jerusalem, where Jehoiachin was led into captivity.

8. The v. indicates the hostile attitude of the people to God. **9.** The figures to represent the coming desolation are, first, that of

birds assembling round one of their own kind and maltreating it, because its plumage attracts their attention as unusual, and then that of hungry beasts of prey. **10. Pastors]** leaders of the invading armies : cp. 6 3, where they are called 'shepherds.'

12. High places through] RV 'the bare heights in' : no spot shall escape.

13. And they shall be ashamed] RV 'And ye shall,' etc. **Revenues]** RV 'fruits.'

14. Mine evil neighbours] Syrians, Edomites, Moabites and others who would feel that Judah's difficulty formed their opportunity. Both they and Judah shall be punished by exile ; but God will restore them in His mercy. If the heathen will but seek to serve God, they shall share in the blessings He has in store for Judah after they have suffered and repented.

CHAPTER 13

JEREMIAH'S SEVENTH PROPHECY (Reign of Jehoiachin). THE LINEN GIRDLE

The date of this prophecy is shown pretty clearly by the word 'queen' (v. 18), which means queen-mother, namely, Nehushta, mother of Jehoiachin. The queen-mother had always a high position, and in Jehoiachin's case this would be specially so, owing to his tender years.

1-11. The symbol of the linen girdle.

1. Go, etc.] It is doubtful whether this and the subsequent acts of the prophet were real or done only in symbol. As, however, Jeremiah appears to have been absent from Jerusalem during the most of the latter years of Jehoiachin, he may well be supposed during part of that time to have been in or near Babylon : cp. v. 4. This would account for the kindly feeling shown towards him afterwards by Nebuchadnezzar (39 11), which seems to point to an earlier acquaintance.

The girdle represents the people of Judah (vv. 9, 10). Jehovah chose them for His service and glory, but they turned away and served other gods. Therefore as the girdle lost its beauty, so will they lose their beauty and come to ruin beside the Euphrates.

10. Imagination] RV 'stubbornness.'

12-14. The symbol of the bottles. Under the figure of intoxication, through which the people shall be helpless to resist the enemy's attack, the prophet intimates God's punishment for headstrong continuance in sin : cp. 25 15 ; and for Israel under the figure of a bottle or jar, cp. 18 1-6. **Bottle]** RM 'jar' (of earthenware ; not the skin bottles of NT.). The bottle represents the people, and the wine the wrath of God. But the people failed to see the significance of the message.

15-27. Vain appeal to Judah.

16. Give glory] a Hebrew idiom, meaning,

confess your sins : cp. Josh 7[19] Jn 9[24]. Danger, difficulty, and gloom are near. **17. In secret places**] The prophet will mourn apart, as he did in Jehoiakim's reign. **18.** See note at head of c. The kings practised polygamy ; hence the high position taken by the queen-mother : cp. 1 K 15[13] 2 K 10[13]. **Principalities**] RV 'headtires,' diadems.

19. Cities of the south] i.e. of Judah.

Shall be] RV 'are.' **Shut up**] i.e. besieged, blockaded, by the Chaldeans.

20. The north] see on 1[13]. **Where** *is* **the flock?**] Where are the towns that once lay, like a fair flock of sheep, grouped around thee ?

21. RV ' What wilt thou say when he shall set thy friends over thee as head, seeing thou thyself hast instructed them against thee?' The reference is to Egypt and Babylon, the friendship and guidance of which countries Judah had alternatively courted, and thus was but preparing the way for subjection to them. **He is Jehovah**. **22. Made bare**] and thus subject to the roughness of the road as thou art led captive. **23.** They are incapable of repentance. **24. The wind of the wilderness**] see on 4[11]. **25. Of thy measures**] RV 'measured unto thee.' **Falsehood**] i.e. idolatry: cp. 10[14] 16[19]. **27. Made clean**] i.e. from infidelity and idolatry. **When** *shall it* once *be ?*] RV 'How long shall it yet be ?'

CHAPTERS 14, 15

JEREMIAH'S EIGHTH PROPHECY (Reign of Jehoiakim ?). THE IMPENDING DROUGHT AND OTHER WOES

Dialogue between the prophet and God. He intercedes ; but in vain, for the nation persists in sin. In this section we probably see the state of matters in the early part of Jehoiakim's reign. There is no historical allusion to the drought which formed the occasion of the prophecy.

CHAPTER 14

1–6. Description of the drought.

2. The gates thereof languish] Figurative of the people who collect there. **They are black unto**] RV 'They sit in black (mourning) upon.' **3. Covered their heads**] as a sign of grief or confusion: cp. David (2 S 19[4]) and Haman (Esth 6[12]). **6. They snuffed up the wind**] RV ' They pant for air.' **Dragons**] RV 'jackals.'

7–22. Jeremiah's pleadings and God's replies.

7. Do thou *it*] RV 'work thou.' **8. As a stranger**, etc.] one who has no interest in the people. **Turneth aside**] RM 'spreadeth *his* tent.' **9. Astonied**] hesitating, inactive. **13.** Jeremiah pleads that the false prophets have misled the people. **17. The virgin**

daughter of my people] i.e. Judah, whom God had hitherto protected. **19.** The prophet again intercedes. **21. The throne of thy glory**] Jerusalem, or, more particularly, the Temple.

22. A reference to the drought (v. 1). God alone can remove it.

CHAPTER 15

1–9. The coming woes described.

1. Moses (Ex 17[11] 32[11 f.] Nu 14[13-20]) and Samuel (1 S 7[9] 12[23]) were successful pleaders with God in time past : cp. Ps 99[6]. **2. To death**] meaning, by pestilence. **4. To be removed into**] RV 'to be tossed to and fro among.' For Manasseh's wickedness see 2 K 21[3 f.] **7.** They shall be dispersed and driven forth from the land by every way of exit. **8.** Even the mothers of warriors in the prime of youth shall have none to protect them. **At noonday**] taking them by surprise : see 6[4]. **I have caused** *him*, etc.] RV 'I have caused anguish and terrors to fall upon her' (the mother) 'suddenly.'

10–21. Jeremiah's lament and appeal. God's reply.

10. I have neither lent, etc.] The Jews were forbidden to take interest from one another (Dt 23[20]), and the money-lender accordingly was held in extreme disfavour. Jeremiah laments that his mission is constantly one of strife with his people. **11. It shall be well with thy remnant**] RV 'I will strengthen thee for good.' His enemies shall not only spare Jeremiah, but invoke his aid. This took place more than once : see 21[1 f.] 37[3] 42[2].

12. Judæa is not tough enough to withstand the Chaldean power. For **northern**, cp. 6[1]. **14. I will make** *thee* **to pass with**] Some authorities read, 'I will make thee to serve.' So it runs in the parallel passage, 17[4].

16. He describes the joyful acceptance with which he first received the divine commission.

17. The mockers] RV 'them that make merry.' There is no suggestion of wrong doing in the original word. **Because of thy hand**] meaning God's guidance, His inspiration. For this sense of 'hand' cp. Isa 8[11] and Ezk 1[3] 37[1]. **18. Liar**] RV 'deceitful *brook*.' *As* waters *that* fail] The figure is that of a watercourse, which being dried up belies the anticipations of the thirsty traveller : cp. Job 6[15 f.] Jeremiah laments that his message seems to have no effect.

19. Return] i.e. repent of his murmuring. **Stand before me**] as my servant : cp. for the phrase, 1 K 18[15] 2 K 3[14]. **Take forth the precious from the vile**] i.e. purge himself of his distrust. **Let them return**, etc.] Deliver your message, regardless of the people's favour. They must turn to God. **20.** See 1[18,19].

CHAPTERS 16, 17¹⁻¹⁸

JEREMIAH'S NINTH PROPHECY (Reign of Jehoiakim ?). PUNISHMENT OF JUDAH BY PESTILENCE AND EXILE

It is clear from 17¹⁵, in which the people challenge the prophet to point to a fulfilment of his prophecies of woe, that it is at any rate earlier than the capture of Jerusalem at the end of Jehoiachin's reign.

CHAPTER 16

1–13. Self-denial and an ascetic life are to be the prophet's lot.

6. Nor cut themselves] in token of mourning : cp. 47⁵. **7. Tear** *themselves* **for them**] RV 'break bread for them.' The reference here and in the rest of the v. is to the custom that the friends should urge the mourners to eat and drink : cp. 2 S 3³⁵ 12¹⁶ᶠ· Prov 31⁶.

12. Imagination] cp. 3¹⁷. **13. There shall ye serve other gods**] if you please. Spoken ironically.

14–21. The deliverance will be in proportion to the severity of the punishment.

14, 15. Yet the coming deliverance shall be one in comparison with which even the exodus from Egypt shall pale. For Jeremiah's custom of throwing in a bright thought among gloomy ones see 3¹⁴ 4²⁷ 5¹⁰,¹⁸ 27²² 30³ 32³⁷.

15. The land of the north] i.e. Babylon : a promise of restoration after the exile.

16. Many fishers] Judah's enemies. The people shall be hunted down with energy wherever they may be found.

19–21. God's power thus shown in the care of His people for evil and then for good, and witnessed by other nations, shall lead even the most distant of them to acknowledge Him.

CHAPTER 17¹⁻¹⁸

1–4. The sin of Judah is indelible. Hence the severity of the punishment.

2. Groves] RV 'Asherim,' wooden pillars, or monuments, set up in honour of Astoreth (Astarte), generally near altars (e.g. Jg 6²⁵). The Law ordered them to be pulled down (Ex 34¹³). **3. O my mountain in the field**] The hill on which Jerusalem is built rises high above the plain. On the other hand, it is lower than the surrounding mountains, hence can be spoken of as a 'valley' in 21¹³. **For sin**] i.e. because of sin.

5–8. God alone is worthy of trust.

6. The heath] RM 'a tamarisk.' The figure is that of a barren, profitless life. **7, 8.** Note the parallels to Ps 1. But which has been influenced by the other is a question more difficult than important. **8. See**] RV 'fear.' **Careful**] i.e. anxious.

9–11. God searches out and punishes evil.

11. RV 'As the partridge that gathereth

young which she hath not brought forth,' and which will soon fly away—a popular belief of which Jeremiah avails himself to illustrate the truth that riches unlawfully gotten are a precarious possession.

12–18. God is the Saviour of the faithful.

12, 13. Connected with the preceding v. The covetous man will be disappointed ; and all they who forsake Jehovah and His sanctuary shall not endure. **12. Place of our sanctuary**] i.e. Zion, where Jehovah's glory abode. **13. Shall be written in the earth**] i.e. shall disappear—a natural simile, a board covered with sand being used for writing lessons in Eastern schools to this day, owing to the scarcity of writing materials. **15.** See intro. to c. 16. **16. I have not hastened, etc.**] I have not sought to resign the office of assistant shepherd for Thy people. **The woeful day**] when his predictions would be fulfilled.

CHAPTER 17¹⁹⁻²⁷

JEREMIAH'S TENTH PROPHECY (Reign of Jehoiakim, or even Josiah, for it speaks of the possibility of the continuance of the Monarchy). THE SABBATH OBLIGATION

19. The children of the people] perhaps meaning the lay folk as opposed to the priests.

25. A promise of the continuance of the lineage of David. **26. The plain**] from the hill-country westward to the Mediterranean. **The mountains**] the central portion of the land running from N. to S. **Meat offerings**] RV 'oblations.' RM 'meal offerings.' They were made of flour and oil, with frankincense strewn on the top (Lv 2¹).

CHAPTERS 18¹⁻20¹⁸

JEREMIAH'S ELEVENTH PROPHECY (Reign of Jehoiakim). PROPHECIES ILLUSTRATED FROM THE WORK OF THE POTTER

C. 18 gives and explains the figure of the potter's clay, and tells of the effect upon the people. C. 19 gives and applies the figure of the potter's broken vessel, while c. 20 describes the consequent sufferings of Jeremiah and his complaints.

The outrage on the prophet committed by Pashur (20²) would certainly not have been permitted in Josiah's time. On the other hand, there seems from the language used to be still a chance for the people, and the calamity threatened had not yet arrived. Therefore we may date the symbolical actions early in Jehoiakim's reign.

CHAPTER 18

1–17. Figure of the potter's clay.

3. The potter's house] Clay from which pottery was made was found S. of Jerusalem : cp. Zech 11¹³ Mt 27¹⁰. The potter teaches

Jeremiah important lessons concerning the providential rule of the world. 'As I watched him shaping the pliant clay, remodelling the imperfect vessels until they conformed to his ideal, God revealed to me the manner in which He is able to mould at His will the nations. At the same time I realised that man may render God's work imperfect' (Sanders and Kent, 'Messages of the Earlier Prophets').

7-10. Predictions of good or evil were conditional on the moral state of those addressed.

11. Frame] the Hebrew word is the same as that for 'potter.'

14. Will *a man* **leave,** etc.] RV 'Shall the snow of Lebanon fail from,' etc. Understand the answer, 'No, it is perpetual.' **Shall the cold,** etc.] RV 'Shall the cold waters that flow down from afar' (mg. 'of strange land that flow down') 'be dried up?' Nature is constant in her operations, but God, the Rock of Israel, is forsaken by those who used to trust in Him.

15. Vanity] i.e. idols.

16. Hissing] not in contempt, but amazement.

17. I will shew them the back] God's countenance will be turned away.

18-23. Invocation of evil on the prophet's enemies.

18. The people's appeal against Jeremiah's words to the three classes of persons whom they thought to be in undoubted possession of the truth.

21-23. The stern spirit of the OT. dispensation, as shown in these imprecations, was connected with the comparative darkness in which a future existence was then shrouded. This would make righteous men more eager that God's glory should be vindicated and His people avenged in this life.

CHAPTER 19

In c. 18 the special lesson was the power of God to alter at any moment the destinies of a people. Here, on the other hand, it is taught that the time may come when the only alteration must take the form of a breaking or overthrow.

1-13. Figure of the broken vessel.

1. Ancients] RV 'elders.' **2. Valley of the son of Hinnom**] see on 7³¹. **East gate**] Hebrew is obscure. RM 'gate of potsherds,' perhaps because refuse of this sort was thrown there. **3. Kings**] the whole dynasty with their accumulated transgressions. **4. Estranged this place**] i.e. alienated it from the worship of God. **6. Tophet**] see on 7³¹. **8. An hissing**] see on 18¹⁶. **9.** This was fulfilled in the Chaldean siege of Jerusalem : see Lam 2²⁰ 4¹⁰. **11. Till** *there be* **no place to bury**] see on 7³². **13.** The flat roofs were easily used

as gathering places : see e.g. Jg 16²⁷ Neh 8¹⁶ Zeph 1⁵.

14. This v. as introducing another address should commence a new paragraph ending with 20⁶.

CHAPTER 20

1-6. Pashur's act and Jeremiah's reply.

2. Pashur] In c. 38¹ two Pashurs are mentioned. This one is perhaps the father of Gedaliah there spoken of, while Pashur the son of Malchiah of that v. is probably identical with the Pashur of 21¹. The houses represented by both men were strong in numbers amongst the few priestly courses that returned from Babylon (Ezr 2³⁶⁻³⁹).

3. Magor-missabib] i.e. 'fear is on every side' : see on 6²⁵. The name is symbolic of his coming fate, consisting in part, at least, of remorse at the ruin which he had brought upon his country by opposing the warnings of Jeremiah and perhaps claiming prophetic powers. For other cases of names given to symbolise and sum up a prophetic message, cp. Shear-jashub, 'a remnant' (only) 'shall return' (Isa 7³), and Maher-shalal-hash-baz, 'speedy spoliation' (Isa 8³ᶠ.).

7-13. The prophet's cry to God.

7. Deceived] RM 'enticed,' to undertake his mission. **8. For since I spake, I cried out**] RV 'for as often as I speak I cry out' (complain loudly). **9.** The prophet cannot refrain from delivering his message, though it entailed derision and mockery. **10. Report** *say they*, etc.] the words of two groups of his foes, the first arguing that his language should be brought under the notice of those in power, the second undertaking to do so.

14-18. For the vehemence of the imprecations cp. Job 3³ 10¹⁸, and David's address to Gilboa (2 S 1²¹). It is interesting to note that in later time, when the prophet had still more afflictions to endure, we no longer read of his trembling or bewailing the sufferings connected with his calling. **16. The cry .. the shouting**] of war and trouble.

CHAPTER 21¹⁻¹⁰

Jeremiah's Twelfth Prophecy (Reign of Zedekiah during the siege). Zedekiah's Roll

This c. commences a new division of the book extending to the end of c. 24. We pass from the time of Jehoiakim to that of the last king of Judah, when Jerusalem was attacked by the Chaldeans. The city must be taken, but surrender may still ensure safety.

1-10. The king's appeal to the prophet, and the reply.

1. Pashur] see on 20². **Zephaniah**] mentioned again 29²⁵ 37³ 52²⁴. In c. 52 he is spoken of as 'the second priest,' meaning next in rank to the high priest. Both men were for resisting Nebuchadnezzar. **2. Nebuchadrezzar**] meaning, 'O Nebo, defend the landmark.' It is a more correct spelling than 'Nebuchadnezzar' in 34¹. **4.** The defenders will be driven back into the city. **9. He that goeth out,** etc.] Many acted upon this suggestion: see 39⁹ 52¹⁵. **His life shall be unto him for a prey**] i.e. he shall snatch it from destruction. **10. He shall burn it with fire**] see 52¹³.

CHAPTERS 21¹¹—24¹⁰
JEREMIAH'S THIRTEENTH PROPHECY

A collection of short prophecies here forming one group, delivered, however, at various dates, and perhaps reissued with modifications from time to time to suit the needs of successive occasions.

Chs. 21¹¹–22³⁰ deal with the sins of successive kings, 23¹⁻⁸ give expression to Messianic hopes. 24¹⁻¹⁰ show by the figure of baskets of worthless figs the rottenness to which the state had been reduced under Zedekiah.

CHAPTER 21¹¹⁻¹⁴

11–14. Exhortation and warning to the royal house.

12. Execute judgment] An important part of the king's duties was to adjudicate cases of dispute in the open space at the gate of the city: cp. 2 S 15²ᶠ. **13. Valley**] see on 17³. **14. The forest**] referring to the houses of Jerusalem clustered together, or perhaps to the house of the forest of Lebanon (1 K 7²).

CHAPTER 22

1–9. Call to amendment of life.

1. Go down] The king's house was on lower ground than the Temple: cp. 36¹². **3.** The reference is to the special crimes of Jehoiakim more fully stated in vv. 13 f.: cp. 2 K 23³⁵. He oppressed his people in order that though paying tribute to Necho he might yet build himself sumptuous palaces. **Neither shed innocent blood**] For his sins in this respect cp. 26 ²⁰ᶠ. **4.** Cp. 17²⁵. **6. Gilead,** with its balm (8²²) and its flocks of goats (Song 4¹ 6⁵), and the forests crowning the highest parts of **Lebanon,** represent things that are most precious. **7. Prepare**] see on 6⁴. **Thy choice cedars**] either the house of the forest of Lebanon (see on v. 6), or figuratively for the chief men of the state.

10–12. Lament for the fate of Jehoahaz.

10. Weep ye not for the dead] viz. Josiah. The sense is that even his fate (as slain at Megiddo) is preferable to that of his son and successor Jehoahaz (Shallum) carried into hopeless captivity in Egypt: see 2 K 23²⁹⁻³⁴. Lamentations for Josiah came to be a fixed custom (2 Ch 35²⁵).

13–23. Jehoiakim's evil deeds and fate.

15. Closest *thyself*] RV 'strivest to excel,' rivalling Solomon with his cedar palaces instead of aiming at just rule. **Thy father**] Josiah. **18. Ah my brother ! or, Ah sister**] The reference may be to a chorus of mourners male and female addressing themselves antiphonally. **18, 19.** The capture and death of Jehoiakim are mentioned in 2 Ch 36⁶ 2 K 24⁶. **20. The passages**] RV 'Abarim,' a range of mountains in the SE. **Thy lovers**] Egypt and the other nations whose aid Judah hoped for : see 27³. **23. Inhabitant of Lebanon**] referring to the king and his nobles as dwelling in cedar houses. **How gracious**] RV 'how greatly to be pitied.'

24–30. Punishment of Jehoiachin.

24. Coniah] so in 37¹: called Jeconiah in 24¹, etc. The change of his name to Jehoiachin, as in the case of his uncle Jehoahaz (the Shallum of v. 11), was probably made on his accession to the throne. All three names mean, 'The LORD will establish.' **Signet**] emblem of royal authority. **26.** See 52³¹ᶠ.

28. A lament over Jehoiachin's fate. **Idol**] RV 'vessel,' a piece of earthenware cast out as useless. **29.** For the emphasis by threefold repetition cp. 7⁴.

30. Write ye, etc.] addressed to those who kept his family registers. They are bidden to enter the fact now instead of waiting for his death. Even though he had children (1 Ch 3¹⁷ᶠ.) they were not to succeed to the throne. 'Whether childless or not Jehoiachin was the last king of David's line. His uncle, indeed, actually reigned after him, but perished with his sons long before Jehoiachin's death (52¹⁰).'

CHAPTER 23

1–4. A remnant shall return.

1. The pastors] i.e. the rulers of Judah. **4. Shepherds**] e.g. Ezra, Nehemiah, etc.

5–8. Promise of the Messiah.

5. Branch] rather, 'sprout,' 'shoot,' that which is immediately connected with the root, and contains, as it were, the springs of life. So in 33¹⁵, and in later time Zech 3⁸ 6¹². On the other hand, the word in Isa 11¹ denotes 'branch,' properly so called. The v. predicts the coming of an ideal descendant of David, a king who shall reign in righteousness over the people. We see the fulfilment of the prophecy in the spiritual conquests of Christ. **And prosper**] RV 'and deal wisely,' as David did (1 S 18⁵⁻¹⁴). **6. THE LORD OUR RIGHTEOUSNESS**] RV 'The LORD is our righteousness.' The coming king shall be a righteous ruler, whose reign shall be marked by absolute justice ; He shall be called Jehovah-Tsidkenu ('The Lord is our righteousness') ; and His name shall be the sign that God will make His people righteous : cp. 33¹⁶. Cp. also 'Immanuel' ('God with us'), Isa 7¹⁴ 8¹⁰

7, 8. See on 16¹⁴ᶠ· The deliverance after the captivity will be even more wonderful than that from Egypt.

9–40. Rebuke of false prophets and priests. Their disgrace is foretold.

10. Swearing] RM ' the curse ' (of God). **Pleasant places**] RV ' pastures.' **Course**] manner of life. **Force**] exercise of power.

13. Samaria] the northern kingdom. **In Baal**] i.e. the name of Baal. **14.** The representatives of God encourage evil doers by their own misdeeds. **17.** These false prophets promised deliverance from Babylon. **18. For who hath stood**, etc.] meaning that at any rate these false prophets had not done so.

20. Consider] RV ' understand.' **21. Yet they ran**] as if appointed. **23.** Think you that My knowledge is subject to human limitations? These men do not deceive Me as they do the people. **25. I have dreamed**] By repeating this formula they caught the ear of the crowd.

28. The contrast between true and false prophecy. God's word contains nourishment and life. Other words are but as chaff, or, rather, straw. **29. Fire**] which consumes the dross. **30, 31.** The false prophets steal the phrases of the true, e.g. ' He saith.' **32. Lightness**] RV ' vain boasting.'

33. They ask jestingly of Jeremiah, What is thy latest message for us? what is the burdensome oracle of the LORD? ' Burden ' was often used in this sense : cp. Nah 1¹ Hab 1¹ Zech 9¹. **What . . burden**] LXX ' ye are the burden.'

34, 35. The misused phrase ' the burden of the LORD ' is to be used no more. Some other expression is to take its place. **36.** Every man's burden shall be his use of the word. For he who has jokingly enquired after the ' burden of the Lord ' shall find that those lightly spoken words of his are in very deed a load upon him. **Perverted**] used jestingly.

CHAPTER 24
THE TWO BASKETS OF FIGS

The evil figs were such of the people as had not been carried away with Jehoiachin to Babylon after the first siege of Jerusalem, 597 B.C., but had failed to draw any warning from the fate that had overtaken their brethren. Those who had been made captives, on the other hand, should yet be the subjects of God's love and grace. The ripening time for both baskets was over, but here the likeness between them ceased.

1. Carpenters] RV ' craftsmen,' the most valuable captives. **2. First ripe**] In the case of trees bearing twice in the year, the first crop, ripening in June, was considered a special delicacy. **Naughty**] RV ' bad.'

5. Acknowledge] RV ' regard.' **8. Egypt**]

cp. 22¹⁰,¹¹. **9. To be removed into**] RV ' to be tossed to and fro among.'

CHAPTER 25
JEREMIAH'S FOURTEENTH PROPHECY (Reign of Jehoiakim). THE WINE CUP OF GOD'S FURY

We have here the first closely dated prophecy, taking us back from Zedekiah's reign to the fourth year of Jehoiakim, between the news of the victory of Nebuchadnezzar over Pharaoh-Necho and the Egyptians at Carchemish (605 B.C.) and the arrival of the Chaldean army under the walls of Jerusalem. The prophet advises submission to Babylon as God's agent, but promises its overthrow at the end of the seventy years' captivity which impends. He announces the judgment that shall descend on the nations.

1–7. The people's prolonged waywardness.

3. The three and twentieth year] of Jeremiah's prophetic ministry. **7. The works of your hands**] i.e. your idols.

8–14. Babylon's victory and subsequent overthrow.

9. Families of the north] the races near the Tigris and Euphrates. **My servant**] God's agent in carrying out His purposes of chastisement.

11. Seventy years] for the definite number cp. 29¹⁰. The Jewish love for round numbers would lead them to consider the number seventy used in such a connexion as standing for any approximation to that amount. The captivity seems to have been, in fact, for somewhat less than seventy years.

Immediately upon v. 13 there come in the Septuagint (Greek) version of this book the prophecies against foreign nations, which in the English (following the Hebrew) stand at the end (chs. 46–51).

14. Of them] viz. of the Chaldeans. As they have done to the people of God, so shall it be done to them.

15–29. The wine cup of God's fury to be drunk by the nations.

15. Wine cup] representing disaster, so often in OT. : cp. 49¹² 51⁷. **16. Be moved**] RV ' reel to and fro.' **17. Then took I the cup**] not, however, in a literal sense, the cup being itself only figurative. **18. As** *it is* **this day**] a later insertion by Jeremiah or another as comment on the fulfilment. **20. The mingled people**] those who had attached themselves to a nation without being connected with it by blood. **Uz**] Job's country near Idumea (Lam 4²¹). **Ashkelon**, etc.] the chief cities of Philistia. **Azzah**] RV ' Gaza.' **22. Isles**] RV ' isle,' RM ' coastland,' a phrase denoting generally the region W. of Palestine, with special reference to the Grecian Archipelago. **23. For Dedan** see *on* 49⁸. **Tema and Buz**

(to which Elihu belonged, Job 32 2) were neighbouring Arabian tribes. **Utmost corners]** see on 9 26. **25. Zimri]** quite unknown.

26. Sheshach] Sheshach stands in all probability for Babel (or Babylon). The Jews had a species of cypher writing, the form of which consisted in substituting the last letter of the Hebrew alphabet for the first, the last but one for the second, and so on. Omitting vowels, we find that thus Sh, Sh, Ch will represent B, B, L : cp. 51 41, where Sheshach and Babylon stand in parallel clauses. Another instance of the cypher is in 51 1, where the Heb. for 'in the midst of them that rise up against me' becomes, when thus transmuted, 'Casdim,' i.e. Chaldeans.

30-38. Judgment shall come upon all the peoples of the earth.

30. Upon his habitation] RV 'against His fold,' i.e. His people. **31. Plead]** in a legal sense, judge. **32. Coasts]** RV 'uttermost parts.' **34. Shepherds]** i.e. rulers. **Like a pleasant vessel]** fair but fragile. **37. Habitations are cut down]** RV 'folds are brought to silence.'

38. As the lion] The LORD is gone forth in wrath to lay waste.

CHAPTER 26
JEREMIAH's FIFTEENTH PROPHECY (Early in the reign of Jehoiakim)

For vv. 1–8 see intro. to chs. 7–10. This c. gives us a sketch of the difficulties and dangers under which Jeremiah had spoken the preceding prophecies.

1-6. The prophet warns the people. **6. Like Shiloh]** see on 7 12. **A curse]** i.e. a subject of their cursing, as being contemptible. **8.** A prophet speaking without God's command was to be put to death (Dt 18 20). This was the charge against Jeremiah, and the alleged proof was that God could not permit such a calamity to fall on Jerusalem.

7-15. The charge against Jeremiah, and his defence. **10. The princes]** apparently heads of prominent houses, who had taken up their quarters in Jerusalem.

16-24. The princes and people, not being prejudiced against Jeremiah, as were the prophets and priests, gave a fair decision.

17. The elders] for their action in criminal procedure cp. Dt 21 2f. ; in civil, Ruth 4 2f.

18. Micah] the minor prophet : see Mic 3 12. The king and the people listened to his warnings. **20-23.** An instance of the ill-treatment of a prophet. This part of the narrative was probably introduced later. It would have been dangerous for any of those present to have made such an attack upon the reigning king.

24. Ahikam] father of Gedaliah, who, when appointed governor by Nebuchadnezzar, stood the prophet's friend (39 14 40 5).

CHAPTERS 27–29
JEREMIAH's SIXTEENTH PROPHECY (Reign of Zedekiah, earlier part). THE BABYLONIAN YOKE

Babylon had already shown its power. Jehoiakim and the chief of the people had been carried captive. Zedekiah was king only on sufferance. The neighbouring nations were under those circumstances willing to make common cause with the Jews against Nebuchadnezzar, many of whom, however, refused to realise the gravity of the danger. In these chs., therefore, Jeremiah sets himself to show that the power of Babylon would be permanent and irresistible. He addresses on this subject (27 1-11) the neighbouring nations, (vv. 12–15) Zedekiah, (vv. 16–22) the priests and prophets, (c. 28) the false prophets, (c. 29) the exiles in Babylon.

CHAPTER 27
1-29. Judah is warned to submit to Babylon. **1.** For **Jehoiakim** read ' Zedekiah ' : see vv. 3, 12, 20. The former word may be a copyist's accidental repetition of 26 1. **2.** It is plain from 28 10 that Jeremiah actually wore a yoke in public. **3. Messengers]** These ambassadors had come to Jerusalem probably with the view of forming an alliance against Babylon. This, however, was not accomplished, as Zedekiah was compelled to go to Babylon and swear allegiance to Nebuchadnezzar (51 59). **6. My servant]** see on 25 9. **7. Him, and his son, and his son's son]** meaning simply that there was to be no speedy riddance. In point of fact, Nebuchadnezzar had *three* successors, Evil-Merodach, Neriglissar, and Nabonidus, in whose seventeenth year Babylon was taken by Cyrus. **The very time]** the appointed end. **Great kings]** Persia and Media became masters of Babylon. **9-11.** Rebellion will entail exile. Therefore let them submit. **16. The vessels, etc.]** Some had been taken in Jehoiachin's reign (2 K 24 13). The rest were destined to follow (2 K 25 13). They were given back by Cyrus (Ezr 1 7). **19. The sea]** in which the priests washed their hands and feet before sacrificing (1 K 7 23 f.). **The bases]** the supports of the ten lavers (1 K 7 27f.).

CHAPTER 28
1-11. Opposition of Hananiah and the false prophets. **2. Thus speaketh the** LORD **of hosts, the God of Israel]** a formula of Jeremiah's, and hence, perhaps, assumed by Hananiah as implying an equal claim to inspiration. **6. Amen : the** LORD **do so]** i.e. would that it might be so. **7-9.** Hananiah's forecasts of peace being in

opposition to those of his predecessors, the presumption is against him, and can only be removed by the fulfilment of his predictions (the test laid down in Dt 18 22), which assuredly is not to take place. **10.** See on 27 2.

12-17. Hananiah rebuked and punished. **13.** Hananiah's act by inciting Zedekiah and his people to resistance only makes the servitude which they will have to undergo harsher. **17. The seventh month**] cp. v. 1.

CHAPTER 29

1-14. Jeremiah's letter to the exiles. Release after seventy years. **1. Prophets**] The exiles in Babylon had also false prophets, e.g. Ahab and Zedekiah (v. 21), and Shemaiah (of v. 24) among them. But they were on the whole of a better class (see 24 5-7), and the prophet might hope that his words would have more effect. **2. Carpenters**] RV 'craftsmen.' **4-7.** They are not to sit loose to the land of their exile, but to make homes for themselves there. Else they will soon dwindle away. **10. At Babylon**] RV 'for Babylon,' referring to the duration of its power : cp. 25 11. **11. An expected end**] RV 'hope in your latter end.'

15-23. The exiles reply :—The prophets here tell us that we shall be delivered speedily. Jeremiah answers that their teaching shall soon be disproved by the overthrow of Jerusalem, and they shall themselves die miserable deaths. **17. Vile figs**] cp. 24 2 f. The exiles would probably already know that prophecy.

24-32. On the arrival of Jeremiah's letter at Babylon, Shemaiah had written to Zephaniah, the acting high priest (52 24) at Jerusalem, to have the prophet silenced as a madman. Jeremiah, having seen the letter, writes again to denounce the writer, and foretell his punishment. **26. In prison, and in the stocks**] RV 'in the stocks and in shackles.'

CHAPTERS 30–33

JEREMIAH'S SEVENTEENTH PROPHECY (Reign of Zedekiah during the siege). ISRAEL'S HOPE

Hitherto the general character of Jeremiah's prophecies has been gloomy. The whole tone of this section, on the other hand, is one of hopefulness, which is the more remarkable inasmuch as it was delivered at a time when the prophet was subject to imprisonment, and famine and pestilence held possession of the city, and the prospects of the nation were at their lowest. It was under such circumstances then that it was announced through Jeremiah that the chosen people should not perish, that through them the Gentile nations should be led to a knowledge of the true God, that the Righteous Branch should yet arise from the house of David, and Zion 'shall be called, The LORD our righteousness': see on 33 16.

CHAPTER 30

1-9. When the gloom is deepest, deliverance shall come. **2. In a book**] Thus his words would bring abiding comfort in the approaching time of exile. **3. Bring**] RV 'turn.' **4. Concerning Israel . . Judah**] Both divisions of the kingdom of David are the subject of c. 31 : see above. **5. Of fear, and not of peace**] RM 'There is fear and no peace,' and the present circumstances are evil. There is nothing but fear and terror in the hearts and on the faces of men. **7. That day**] the day of Babylon's overthrow. **8. Serve themselves of him**] see on 25 14. **9. David their king**] the ideal king who, as coming of David's line, here receives his name. So in Ezk 34 23 f. 37 24. For David, meaning the line of kings of his house, see 1 K 12 16.

10-17. God will remember Israel in her affliction. **11. In measure, etc.**] RV 'with judgment, and will in no wise leave thee.' **12-15.** These vv. describe the present condition from which the nation shall be delivered. **13. Thy cause, that thou . . medicines**] rather, join 'that thou,' etc., with what follows. 'For the closing up of thy wound there is no healing, no plaister.' **14. Thy lovers**] the nations that sought to ally themselves with thee: see 27 3.

18-24. Jerusalem shall be restored to favour. **18. Bring**] see on v. 3. **Tents**] a name for dwellings generally, which was retained from nomadic times : cp. 4 20. **Remain**] RM 'be inhabited.' **After the manner thereof**] occupied by a king, and kept up suitably as aforetime. **21. Nobles**] RV 'prince,' a reference to the ideal king. **Of themselves**] no longer foreigners. **Engaged his heart**] RV 'hath had boldness.' The new king will have close access to Jehovah. He will do His will, and rule in righteousness. And is not this to know the Lord ? (22 16). **23, 24.** These vv. are nearly identical with 23 19. **24. Consider**] RV 'understand.'

CHAPTER 31

1-22. Jeremiah speaks of the restoration first of Israel (Ephraim, vv. 2-22), then of Judah (vv. 23 f.). Those who survive the sufferings of the captivity are promised a safe journey home. The words, 'found grace in the wilderness' (v. 2) are probably an allusion to the journey from Egypt under Moses, which was thus a prophecy to the captive Israelites of the return from Assyria. **3.** In this v. the people are the speakers. **4. Tabrets**] tambourines. **5. Shall eat** *them* **as common things**] RV 'shall enjoy *the fruit thereof*'

6. Watchmen] posted on heights to announce seasons of prayer and, according to Jewish tradition, the appearance of the new moon as determining the dates of festivals. In the present case they are posted on the hills of Ephraim that members of the northern kingdom may go up to keep the feasts in Jerusalem, thus betokening the reunion of the Twelve Tribes in worship. **8. The blind,** etc.] None, even the feeblest, shall be left behind. **Thither**] RV 'hither' to Palestine. **9. With weeping**] tears at once of contrition and joy. **Ephraim** *is* **my** firstborn] see 1 Ch 5¹. God will not forget the house of Joseph, the head of northern Israel.

10. The isles] see on 25²². **12. To the goodness of the LORD**] to receive from Him the blessings of a fruitful land. **For wheat,** etc.] RV 'to the corn, and to the wine.' **Sorrow**] rather, 'droop,' 'fade,' keeping up the image of a garden. **13. Both young men**] RV 'and the young men' (shall rejoice with the old). **14.** The sacrifices shall be so numerous that the priests and their families shall have abundance for their share : see Lv 7³¹ᶠ.

15. The mourning which took place at Ramah, whether on account of some unrecorded butchery there on the part of the Chaldean conquerors, or in reference to their general cruelty to the exiles there assembled for deportation to Babylon (see 40¹), is referred to by St. Matthew (2¹⁷ᶠ.) as a forecast of the wailing at the slaughter of the Innocents by Herod. **Rahel**] the appropriateness of calling upon Rachel to weep in Ramah consists in this, that she, the one of Jacob's wives who had so ardently longed for children and the mother of Joseph and so of Ephraim and of Manasseh (whose lot was with Judah), should lament the overthrow of her offspring in a conspicuous border town of the two kingdoms, with both of which she was thus immediately connected. **16. Thy work shall be rewarded**] Rachel by the death of her descendants had, as it were, been deprived of the reward for which she had laboured in bearing and bringing up children. Now by their restoration she shall at last receive her recompense. **17. In thine end**] RV 'for thy latter end.'

18. Ephraim] i.e. the northern kingdom, which for over 100 years had been devastated by the Assyrians, and its people exiled. **19. Instructed**] by punishment. **I smote,** etc.] in contrition. **The reproach of my youth**] the shame incurred through the sins of his youth. **20.** God is represented as addressing Himself even as a father might do, when dwelling upon the ingratitude and rebellion of a son, whom, nevertheless, he cannot but continue to love. **Pleasant**] i.e. beloved. **Bowels**] the supposed seat of the emotions. **21. High heaps**] RV 'guide-posts' for the returning exiles. **22. Compass**] i.e. as protector. In the peaceful future the women will be a sufficient guard against danger from without, while the men perform their daily tasks.

23-26. The LORD now turns from Israel (Ephraim) to Judah and promises her like blessings. **23. As yet**] RV 'yet again.' **Habitation of justice**] the same expression is used of the LORD in 50⁷. **Mountain of holiness**] Jerusalem, or in particular the Temple mount. **26.** The words of the prophet at the conclusion of his pleasant vision. **27. I will sow,** etc.] a figure to express prosperity and rapid increase. **28.** See on 1¹⁰. **29-34.** The new covenant between Jehovah and His people. **29, 30.** The proverb here quoted, which was common among the Jews, induced them to throw upon their predecessors the responsibility for their own misdeeds. Accordingly the prophet restates in an amended form the truth which it embodies. It was true that their fathers had sinned, but the children had repeated their sins and they were suffering the consequences of their own acts. The prophet emphasises individual responsibility for sin. **31-34.** The new covenant is to be of a spiritual, personal character, rather than external and national. It shall supersede that of the exodus, and shall differ from the older Law both in permanence and in the spring of action. Under it the sense of forgiveness (v. 34) ensures a willing service based on love, not on fear. 'God comes to man as giving and not as requiring' : so Bp. Westcott on Heb 8⁸⁻¹², which reproduces this passage, applying it to the Christian dispensation. **34.** The sense is not that there shall be no longer any need of instruction in religion, but that for both Jews and Gentiles there shall be directness of access to God. It was left for later times to reveal clearly Christ as the means of this approach. **35. Which divideth the sea when**] RV 'which stirreth up the sea, that.' **36.** Israel's national existence is as assured as the unchangeableness of the laws imposed by God on the universe, or as its limitless character. **38-40.** See on 7³¹. Jerusalem in her future extension is to enclose spaces hitherto considered unclean. **Tower of Hananeel**] at the NE. corner. **The gate of the corner**] at the NW. (see on 2 K 14¹³). **Gareb . . Goath**] not mentioned elsewhere. Gareb means 'leper's hill.'

CHAPTER 32

This c. forms the introduction to the most continuously historical part of the book, which describes incidents in the two years preceding the final destruction of Jerusalem, viz. chs.

34-43. The first of these incidents is here given, viz. Jeremiah's purchase with all legal formality of a field of which he had the right of redemption, in order to encourage the people while the Chaldeans were investing the city by showing thus his faith in the return which he foretells in these chs.

1-5. The general position. 2. Of the prison] RV 'of the guard,' i.e. of the palace sentries. For Jeremiah's imprisonment see chs. 37, 38.

6-15. Jeremiah's purchase at Anathoth. 6. An interesting example of legal proceedings in connexion with Hebrew land-customs : cp. Ruth 4 1-8. 7. If land was to be sold it was the duty of the nearest of kin to buy it, so that it should not pass from one family to another : see Lv 25 24 f. Ruth 4 6. 8. Jeremiah bought the estate as next heir by the right of preëmption. 10. The evidence] RV 'the deed,' and so in vv. 11, 12, 14, 44. Jeremiah made out two copies of the deed, one to be sealed, the other left open, the former to be referred to in case at any time it were suspected that the latter had been tampered with. 11. According to the law and custom] RM 'containing the terms and conditions.' 15. Possessed] RV 'bought.'

16-25. Jeremiah cannot reconcile the obvious sense of the transaction which he had just carried out at the LORD's command, with the overthrow which he had been so often bidden to announce to the guilty city. 24. Mounts] see on 6 6.

26-35. The first part of God's reply, viz. judgment.

36-44. The second part of God's reply, viz. mercy. 36. The words resume the thought of v. 27, 'Is there anything too hard for me ?' 44. The mountains .. the valley .. the south] The several parts of the land are specified, viz. the central (hilly) portion, the plains westward from it to the sea, and the thinly inhabited S. of Judah. Cause their captivity to return] i.e. restore them from captivity.

CHAPTER 33

1-13. Restoration and honour again promised. 1. See on 32 2. 2. The maker thereof] RV 'that doeth it' (viz. that which He hath purposed). 4. By the mounts, and by the sword] RV 'to make a defence against the mounts, and against the sword,' to make room for the besieged to erect defensive works. For 'mounts' see 6 6. 5. They] the besieged. The only result of their fighting is that they fill these houses with the slain. 11. Praise the LORD, etc.] Jeremiah quotes from the Temple liturgical forms : cp. 2 Ch 5 13 Ps 106 1.

13. Mountains, etc.] see on 32 44. Telleth] counteth.

14-18. Permanence of the kingly and priestly line.

15, 16. See on 23 5 f. 16. The LORD our righteousness] RV 'The LORD is our righteousness.' The name is here given to the city, as it was given in 23 6 to the king.

17, 18. In these vv. the prophet declares the permanence of the office of king in the Davidic line, and of the priesthood among the Levites. The prophecy is sometimes mystically interpreted of Christ. 18. Meat offerings] see on 17 26.

19-26. God's covenant is as sure as the ordinances of nature.

19 f. See on 31 36 for the argument. 21. For the covenant with David's line see 2 S 7 12 f., and for that with the Levites (in the person of Phinehas) Nu 25 13. 24. The people, seeing that both Israel and Judah (the two families) are being apparently cast off, despise their own nation, despair of any better days, and consider their national existence to be a thing of the past.

CHAPTER 34

JEREMIAH'S EIGHTEENTH PROPHECY (Reign of Zedekiah). THE FATE OF ZEDEKIAH. THE TREATMENT OF HEBREW SLAVES

Early in the campaign of Nebuchadnezzar, whose scheme of conquest included all the region as far as Egypt inclusive, the policy urged by Jeremiah was that Zedekiah should make the best terms he could. In this c. we seem to have a sort of abbreviated memorandum of the conditional promise, which in that case the prophet was commissioned to announce to Zedekiah, viz. peace followed by kingly obsequies. The condition, here omitted, is expressed in 38 17.

The laws as to the limitation of the length of servitude in the case of Hebrew slaves (Ex 21 2 Lv 25 39-55) had apparently fallen out of use with many Jews, especially in the country parts. Very possibly the arrival of many of the wealthier Jews at Jerusalem from the country to escape the invading army made the laxity on their part more conspicuous by contrast. The agreement here spoken of seems to have been brought about in view of the impending danger of invasion, in resisting which the slaves, if enfranchised, might be more willing to co-operate. But when the Babylonian army withdrew for a short time (37 5) to meet the Egyptian forces, which they believed to be threatening them, the masters basely cancelled their agreement.

1-7. Capture and burning of Jerusalem foretold.

3. Thine eyes shall behold .. the king, etc.] i.e. at Riblah, before being blinded and carried to Babylon : see 39 7 52 9, and cp. 32 4 Ezk 12 13.

5. Shall they burn *odours*] RV 'Shall they make a burning': see details in 2 Ch 16 14.

7. Against Lachish, and against Azekah] in SW. of Judah near the border of Egypt. Nebuchadnezzar would not venture to advance into that country on his career of conquest, leaving these fortresses untaken.

8–22. The masters of Hebrew slaves to be punished for their cruel treatment of them.

13. Out of the house of bondmen] The point is that Israel's position at the time when the covenant was made, as having themselves been delivered from Egyptian slavery, should have taught them better. **17.** The people shall no longer as hitherto be under God's protection as His servants, but be thrown by Him on their own resources, and so exposed to their perils. **18. Cut the calf in twain**] For such mode of ratifying a covenant see on Gn 15 8.

21. Which are gone up from you] i.e. which have raised the siege for the time.

CHAPTER 35

JEREMIAH'S NINETEENTH PROPHECY (Reign of Jehoiakim). THE OBEDIENCE OF THE RECHABITES

This and c. 36 form a break in the narrative, bringing us back from the tenth year of Zedekiah to the insecurity which followed upon Nebuchadnezzar's victory of Carchemish (fourth year of Jehoiakim), when predatory bands of Chaldeans and others had compelled many of the inhabitants of Palestine to take refuge within Jerusalem. Among these were the Rechabites, a nomadic tribe of Kenite descent. The prophet contrasts their obedience to the precepts of their leader Jonadab (who lived about two centuries and a half before this time, 2 K 10 15 f.) with the disobedience of Judah. Each shall receive its meet recompense.

1–11. The Rechabites' rule of life.

2. The Rechabites were descended from Hobab, brother-in-law of Moses, of the Kenite tribe. They migrated with the Israelites from the wilderness to Palestine : cp. Nu 10 29-32 Jg 1 16. **5. Pots**] RV 'bowls.' **6. Commanded us**, etc.] perhaps owing to the excess which he saw to be fostered by city life. For **Jonadab** see 2 K 10 15.

12–17. Application of the lesson to the Jews.

18, 19. The Rechabites' reward.

CHAPTER 36

EVENTS CONNECTED WITH THE COLLECTION OF JEREMIAH'S PROPHECIES INTO A VOLUME (4th and 5th years of Jehoiakim)

The prophecies concerning Israel and Judah are now ended, and we have here the record of the embodying in a permanent form by Jeremiah of the substance of these prophecies. For further remarks see Intro.

2. A roll of a book] Several skins were stitched together and attached to a roller of wood. The writing was arranged in columns parallel to the roller, so that as the parchment was gradually unfolded the successive columns could be read. **4. Baruch**] the prophet's companion and assistant already mentioned (32 12 f.). **5. Shut up**] not meaning imprisoned (with which v. 19 would be inconsistent), but hindered perhaps by the extreme unpopularity of his recent utterances.

9. In the ninth month] our December. It was thus a specially appointed fast, not that of the seventh month which alone was prescribed by the Law (Lv 16 29 23 27). **10. Gemariah**] he was brother of Ahikam (see 26 24), who was friendly to Jeremiah and distinct from Gemariah of 29 3.

11. When Michaiah . . had heard] As it was in the chamber of Michaiah's father that Baruch had been allowed to read the roll, Gemariah, who was engaged at a council of the leading men in another room, would naturally be desirous to learn as soon as might be what had occurred. **12. Went down**] see on 22 1. **Elnathan**] mentioned in 26 22.

15. Sit down] Baruch was invited to take the position ordinarily assumed by an Eastern teacher. This together with v. 19 shows that the princes were favourably disposed towards Jeremiah. **17. How didst thou write, etc.**] They desired to know how much was Baruch's own that they might be able to state to the king the amount of responsibility that rested upon each.

22. The winter-house] a separate portion of the palace, as appears from Am 3 15. **On the hearth**] RV 'in the brasier': so in v. 23. Braziers containing charcoal were placed in a depression in the middle of a room for warming purposes. **23. Leaves**] RM 'columns': see on v. 2. **He**] i.e. the king. **24. They were not afraid . .** *neither* **the king**, etc.] Contrast with this the conduct of the king's father Josiah when the newly discovered Book of the Law was read to him (2 K 22 11).

29. Shall certainly come, etc.] fulfilled in the time of Jehoiakim's son, Jehoiachin, and finally when Zedekiah was carried captive.

30. He shall have none to sit, etc.] for his son was carried captive in three months from his accession: cp. 22 30. **His dead body, etc.**] see on 22 19. **32.** The substance of the second roll is doubtless to a large extent preserved to us in this book.

CHAPTERS 37, 38

EVENTS DURING THE SIEGE OF JERUSALEM (Reign of Zedekiah)

Here after two parenthetical chapters (35, 36) concerning the time of Jehoiakim, we revert to the narrative (beginning in c. 32) of the last two years of Zedekiah.

CHAPTER 37

1–5. The general position.

1. Coniah] see on 22 24. **Whom**] referring to Zedekiah. **3. Zephaniah**] see on 21 1.

5. This refers to the temporary raising of the siege of Jerusalem by the Babylonians on the approach of an Egyptian army under Pharaoh-Hophra. He either retired or was defeated, for the siege was soon renewed.

6–10. The return of the Chaldeans foretold.

11–15. Jeremiah imprisoned.

12. To separate himself thence] RV 'to receive his portion there,' probably referring to an allotment of communal land at Anathoth.

In the midst of the people] there was naturally a rush to get out of the city on account of the confinement as well as the scarcity of provisions.

16–21. The king takes compassion on Jeremiah.

16. Cabins] RV 'cells.' **17. Secretly**] dreading in his weakness the interference of the princes. **21.** See on 32 2.

CHAPTER 38

1–3. The removal of Jeremiah from the prison was favourable to the publication of his message. Hence the alarm of the princes.

1. Pashur] see on 20 2.

2. He that goeth forth] i.e. submits: so v. 17.

6. Dungeon] RM 'pit,' or cistern. It is conjectured that Ps 69 may have been composed by Jeremiah on this occasion.

7–13. Jeremiah is rescued by Ebed-melech.

10. Thirty] possibly a copyist's error for 'three.' The two words resemble each other much more closely in Hebrew than in English.

14–28. The king again asks the prophet's advice. Result.

14. The third entry] Probably referring to some passage between the Temple and the palace. **15. Wilt thou not hearken unto me?**] RV 'Thou wilt not hearken unto me.' **18. The king of Babylon's princes**] Nebuchadnezzar was probably himself at Riblah: see 39 5.

19. And they mock me] for not surrendering sooner as they had done.

22. The women of the harem shall join in the reproaches, saying, Thy friends have persuaded thee against thy better judgment, and then deserted thee.

24–26. Zedekiah's weakness is again conspicuous. **28. And he was, etc.**] RV 'And it came to pass when Jerusalem was taken'; the words thus belonging not to what precedes, but to c. 39.

CHAPTERS 39–43 7

JEREMIAH'S HISTORY FROM THE FALL OF JERUSALEM TILL HE GOES DOWN TO EGYPT. See Introduction

CHAPTER 39

THE CAPTURE OF JERUSALEM (11th year of Zedekiah)

The narrative in this c., with some varieties in detail, coincides with that of c. 52 and with 2 K 25.

1–7. The city taken. Zedekiah's fate.

3. From the Eng. it would appear that there are six persons named. But **Rab-saris** (chief of the eunuchs) and **Rab-mag** (chief of the sorcerers) are only the titles of those whose names they follow. **4. The way of the plain**] so as to escape to the eastern bank of Jordan. **5. Riblah**] on the high road between Palestine and Babylon. **7.** See on 34 3. Putting out the eyes was a common punishment in the East.

8–10. Fate of the city. If we had only this narrative we should suppose that Nebuzaradan was present in person, but 52 12 shows that he did not arrive till a month after the taking of the city.

11–14. Nebuchadnezzar and the prophet.

12. Look well to him] for Jeremiah had always counselled submission to Babylon : cp. 40 1. **14. Gedaliah**] see on 26 24.

15–18. Message to Ebed-melech.

CHAPTER 40

GEDALIAH AS GOVERNOR (586 B.C.)

Chs. 40 7–43 6 are briefly summarised in 2 K 25 22-26. The account in the book of Kings mentions merely the accomplished results; while here the process by which these results were brought about are fully detailed. We learn here in particular that Ishmael ben-Nethaniah was prompted to assassinate Gedaliah by the Ammonite king, Baalis, and that Gedaliah was warned of the plot by Johanan, but that he refused to believe that Ishmael would do such a thing. Full details of the slaughter of the people at Mizpah are also given here, as well as an account of the pursuit of Ishmael by Johanan and the recovery of the captives. We are told here also what is omitted in Kings that when Johanan desired to go to Egypt for safety, Jeremiah sought to dissuade him, promising safety if the people remained in Judah, but destruction if they went to Egypt. Johanan, however, was incredulous, and took the remnant of Judah down to Tahpanhes in Egypt, and with them Jeremiah and Baruch.

1. The word that came] including the history which follows. No prophetic utterance comes till 42 9. To the Jews history and prophecy were intimately connected; e.g. they included most of the historical books of the Bible under the title of Prophets.

5. Reward] RV 'present.'

6. Mizpah] a city of Benjamin, NW. of

Jerusalem, and the chief scene of the events now to be described. **7. Forces which** *were* **in the fields**] keeping out of the way until the Babylonian army departed, and they should have learned the nature of the new government : cp. v. 13.

8. The Netophathite] Netophah was a village near Bethlehem (Neh 7 26).

10. Gather ye wine, etc.] Make provision for the winter.

12. Returned] reassured by the fact that the new governor was their own countryman.

14. Ishmael felt aggrieved that he, though of royal birth (see 41 1), had been set aside in favour of Gedaliah. The instigation by Baalis may have arisen through designs of conquest.

CHAPTER 41
PLOT AGAINST GEDALIAH AND ITS RESULTS
(586 B.C.)

1-10. Ishmael murders Gedaliah and others, and carries off captives.

1. And the princes] RV 'and *one of* the chief officers' ; a further description of Ishmael himself, not an addition to his band. **Even**] RV 'and.' **5. Having their beards shaven**, etc.] in mourning for the destruction of the Temple : see on 16 6. **6. Weeping all along**] feigning equal concern with them, so as to put them off their guard. **7. Pit**] RV 'cistern.' **8. Treasures**] RV 'stores hidden.' Dry cisterns, covered with a deep layer of earth, are commonly used for this purpose in the East. **9. Because of**] RV 'by the side of,' i.e. their bodies placed by his. **Asa .. Baasha**] see 1 K 15 22.

11-18. Johanan rescues the captives and they start for Egypt.

12. Gibeon] the modern El-jib, a city of the priests (Josh 18 25 21 17), in the tribe of Benjamin. **14. Cast about**] turned round.

15. These acts of treachery may well have been connected with woes predicted for Ammon in 49 1f. **17. The habitation of Chimham**] RM 'the lodging place' (i.e. inn or khan) of Chimham : see 2 S 19 37. It was natural that David as a mark of gratitude to the son of Barzillai should have given Chimham a piece of his patrimony.

CHAPTER 42
JEREMIAH'S MESSAGE FROM GOD TO
JOHANAN

1. Jezaniah] the Azariah of 43 2 (and probably not the Jezaniah of 40 8).

7-22. The people are forbidden to go down to Egypt. Jeremiah had always denounced connexion with Egypt (2 36 37 7).

15. And now] RV 'now.' **20. Ye dissembled in your hearts**] RV 'ye have dealt deceitfully against your own souls,' i.e. while persuading yourselves that you are prepared

to accept God's decision, all the while nothing but your own way would content you.

CHAPTER 43
THE FATE OF EGYPT

1-7. They disobey and go to Egypt.

7. Tahpanhes] see on 2 16.

Here ends the historical portion of the book, the remainder consisting of prophecies directed mainly against foreign nations.

8-13. Prophecy of the overthrow of Egypt.

9. In the clay in the brick-kiln] RV 'in mortar in the brickwork.' **11. Death**] by famine or pestilence. **12.** Nebuchadnezzar shall have no more difficulty in spoiling Egypt than has the shepherd in wrapping his outer garment about him after his labour.

13. Images] RV 'pillars,' RM 'obelisks.' **Beth-shemesh** (Gk. 'Heliopolis,' Egyptian 'On') was a city of obelisks, two of which stood before the Temple of the Sun. Its site is about 10 m. NE. of Cairo.

CHAPTER 44
JEREMIAH'S LATEST PROPHECY (after 586 B.C.). (The prophecies against the Gentile nations (chs. 46-51) were mostly uttered after the battle of Carchemish, 605 B.C.)

He denounces the unabated idolatry which still characterised the people now that they dwelt in Egypt. Their experience of suffering had taught them nothing.

1-10. Jeremiah's countrymen rebuked.

1. Migdol] on the northern boundary of Egypt. For Noph and Tahpanhes see on 2 16.

8. The works of your hands] i.e. your idols. **Might cut yourselves off**] RV 'may be cut off.'

11-14. Their punishment foretold.

15-19. They persist in their idolatry.

15. All the women that stood by] Probably the occasion was an idolatrous festival in which the women were taking a leading part. **All the people**, etc.] not, of course, to be taken literally, but meaning that they were very numerous and represented the whole.

17. Whatsoever thing goeth forth] RV 'every word that is gone forth.' They refer to their religious vows : cp. Nu 30 2 Dt 23 23.

Queen of heaven] see on 7 18. *Then* **had we plenty of victuals**] They perversely attribute the misfortunes which had befallen their country from the battle of Megiddo and death of Josiah onwards to the attack made upon idolatry (2 K 23) by that king, and not to the gradual degradation of the people through the medium of that idolatry during the reigns of Manasseh and Amon and the earlier part of that of Josiah. **19. Worship**] RM 'pourtray,' referring to the full moon, as represented either by the shape of the cake itself or by a figure upon it. **Men**] RV 'husbands.' A wife's vow was not binding unless with the consent of the husband : see Nu 30 6 f.

20–23. Jeremiah answers. It was, he says, owing to the idolatry, which had been so long rampant and which Josiah's reforms had scotched, not killed, that the overthrow at last came.

25. With your hand] RV 'with your hands,' pointing, perhaps, to the cakes which they were carrying. **Ye will surely,** etc.] RV 'Establish then .. and perform.' If ye persist, then be it so. **26.** As being faithless to their covenant with God, they shall lose the right of calling upon His name as such. **29.** The sign referred to, viz. Nebuchadnezzar's invasion of Egypt, did not take place till 586 B.C. For other instances of a sign not to take effect for a considerable time after its announcement cp. Ex 3 12 2 K 19 29.

It is not improbable that it was on this occasion that Jeremiah met with a martyr's death at the hands of his apostate countrymen, as tradition recounts.

CHAPTER 45
BARUCH'S APPENDIX TO THE ROLL OF c. 36

Baruch, a man of social position (see Intro.), seems to have expected either important office in the state or more probably the gift of prophecy. On the occasion of his writing of the roll at Jeremiah's dictation, the prophet warns him that his ambition is not to be gratified.

3. Sorrow] RV 'pain' at the sins of his countrymen. The added 'grief' was caused by the predictions of punishment. **5. But thy life,** etc.] Baruch's life should be preserved amidst all perils.

CHAPTERS 46–51
PROPHECIES CONCERNING THE NATIONS

The custom of placing in a group, as here, prophecies against heathen nations is illustrated by Isaiah (chs. 13–33), Ezekiel (chs. 25–32), and Amos (chs. 1, 2). For the position of the prophecies at the end of the book as compared with that which they hold in the LXX, see Intro. and on 25 11. We may divide them thus :—

(a) Chs. 46–49 (mostly of the fourth year of Jehoiakim). This section contains prophecies concerning Egypt and five other nations doubtless included in the roll of c. 36, with the exception of the second concerning Egypt (vv. 14–28 : see note on v. 13) and of the last against Elam (49 34-39 : first year of Zedekiah). These prophecies follow a natural order. Egypt is at the head as the nation whose overthrow by Nebuchadnezzar would be the signal to those others of a similar fate. We go thence to Philistia (including Tyre and Sidon); then (passing round to the E. of Palestine) to Moab,

Ammon, and Edom ; then to Damascus, as representing the kingdoms of the North ; to Kedar and Hazor, as indicating the kings mentioned in the summary of 25 24 ; while, lastly, the nations of the East are included under Elam.

(b) Chs. 50, 51 (of doubtful authorship). This prophecy concerning Babylon forms an appropriate conclusion to the series. The nations immediately bordering upon Palestine have had their fate foretold, and then the more remote. Now the empire which was to execute God's vengeance upon them is itself declared to be destined in its turn to fall. See further, in intro. to c. 50.

CHAPTER 46
AGAINST EGYPT

1. Against the Gentiles] RV 'concerning the nations' around. **2. Carchemish**] see Intro. and 2 Ch 35 20-24 ; also on 47 1.

3–6. A lively description of the preparation and advance, followed by the defeat at Carchemish. **4. Brigandines**] RV 'coats of mail.' **5. Seen them dismayed**] RV 'seen it ? They are dismayed.' **7. A flood**] RV 'the Nile,' their own sacred river in its overflow. So in v. 8. **9. The Ethiopians,** etc.] mercenary troops forming the chief part of the Egyptian armies. **10. A day of vengeance**] on the Egyptians. They are to be the **sacrifice,** because of their treachery to Judah. **11.** The medical science of Egypt was in high repute. **12. The land**] RV 'the earth.'

13. The second part of the prophecy concerning Egypt suggests by its tone a more intimate acquaintance, and is probably to be ascribed to the time of the prophet's residence in that country. **14.** See on 44 1 and 2 16. **16. They said**] the mercenaries : see on v. 9. **17. The time appointed**] the period of grace is over. **18.** Omit the second *is.* The v. means that Nebuchadnezzar shall resemble Tabor and Carmel, standing out conspicuous as compared with neighbouring rulers.

20. *Is like*] RV 'is.' This probably is an allusion to the sacred bull Apis, worshipped at Memphis. **Destruction**] RM 'the gadfly.' The **north**] i.e. Chaldea. **22. Like a serpent**] rustling as it escapes through the thick underwood. Such shall be the sound of Egypt as it flees away. **23. Her forest**] her beauty : cp. 21 14. **Grasshoppers**] RV 'locusts.' **25. The multitude of No**] RV 'Amon of No,' i.e. the god worshipped there. **No**] i.e. Thebes in Upper Egypt.

CHAPTER 47
AGAINST PHILISTIA

The Chaldean armed men with horses and

chariots shall carry terror and desolation into Philistia and its cities.

1. Before that Pharaoh smote Gaza] The main views as to the date of this prophecy are (*a*) that the 'Pharaoh' is Necho, and that he captured Gaza about the time of his defeat of Josiah's army at Megiddo (608 B.C.) ; (*b*) that the reference is to the same king, as having taken Gaza on his way back from his defeat at Carchemish (605 B.C.) ; (*c*) that the 'Pharaoh' is Hophra (588–570 B.C.), and that he captured Gaza in the course of an expedition against Tyre and Sidon.

2. Waters.. out of the north] i.e. the Chaldean army. **4. Caphtor**] the place of origin of the Philistines (see Dt 2 23 Am 9 7), probably to be identified with Crete. **5. Baldness**] in token of mourning : cp. 48 37. **Cut thyself**] see on 16 6.

6. The prayer of the Philistines. **7.** Jeremiah's reply.

CHAPTER 48
AGAINST MOAB

Moab, in recompense for its pride and security, and for its triumphing over Israel in the day of her calamity, shall itself be laid waste and taken captive : cp. the 'burden of Moab' in Isa 15, 16.

1. Nebo] not the mountain, but the Reubenite town (Nu 32 38), which had been annexed by Mesha, king of Moab (about 895 B.C.), according to the 'Moabite Stone' records. Several places mentioned in this c. have not been certainly identified. **2. Heshbon**] an Ammonite town on the border of Moab, where the Chaldean invaders would lay their final plans. **Madmen**] a place unknown. **5.** RV 'For by the ascent of Luhith with continual weeping shall they go up.' **6. The heath**] see on 17 6. **7. Chemosh**] the god of Moab's national worship. **8. The valley**] of Jordan, bounding part of Moab on the W. **10. Deceitfully**] RV 'negligently.' Moab's foe must not be slack in executing God's command.

11. Settled on his lees] i.e. like wine which has remained undisturbed and not lost its flavour. **Lees** means sediment. Moab had retained its strength, but it was not to last.

12. Wanderers, that shall cause him to wander] RV 'them that pour off, and they shall pour him off.' The figure of jars of wine is continued. They are emptied by being tilted on one side, an operation that was performed slowly and carefully, that the jars might be safe and the wine run off clear, while the sediment was left. This work, however, in the case of Moab, shall be done roughly. **13. Bethel**] the southern seat of the idolatrous worship introduced by Jeroboam (1 K 12 29).

15. And gone up *out of* **her cities**] RM 'and her cities are gone up *in smoke*.' **18. Come down**] Dibon stands on two hills. **25. Horn**] symbol of strength and pride. **27. Was he

found **among thieves**] that he merited such treatment. **Since**] RV ' as often as.' **30. But,** etc.] RV ' that it is nought ; his boastings have wrought nothing.'

32. Cp. Isa 16 8, 9. **With**] RV 'with more than.' **Plants**] RV ' branches.' Sibmah seems to have been famous for its vineyards. **Over the sea**] as far as the W. shore of the Dead Sea. **Jazer**] N. of Heshbon. Near its ruins are two large ponds. **33.** *Their* **shouting, etc.**] The vintage shout shall be changed to the cry of panic.

36. Pipes] They were used at funerals, so that the word is appropriate to express mourning. **37.** All shall have the usual emblems of mourning : cp. 47 5. **38. Vessel**] see on 22 28. **40. He shall fly**] i.e. the Chaldean power.

45. They that fled .. force] RV ' They that fled stand without strength under the shadow of Heshbon.' While the fugitives of Moab wait in hope of aid under the walls of the Ammonite city, there bursts forth from it a flame kindled by the Chaldean foe like that which in old days was kindled at the same place by Sihon, the Amorite conqueror (Nu 21 28). **Tumultuous ones**] the fugitives.

47. For the note of comfort at the end of the prophecy cp. 46 26 49 6, 39.

CHAPTER 49
AGAINST AMMON, EDOM, AND OTHER NATIONS

1–6. The territory of Ammon was N. of Moab, and the two peoples were connected by descent. The carrying away of the tribes on the E. of Jordan by Tiglath-pileser, king of Assyria (2 K 15 29), strengthened the hands of Ammon, and it is their occupation of the portion of Gad upon that occasion that forms the crime which is dwelt on in this prophecy, and which shall bring on them judgment.

1. Their king] RV 'Malcam,' or Moloch, the god of the Ammonites, and so in v. 3. So in 48 7 Chemosh is used for 'Moab.' **2, 3. Rabbah .. Heshbon .. Ai**] Ammonite towns. **Hedges**] fences, inclosures of vineyards.

4. Thy flowing valley] Ammon was full of valleys and streams running into Jordan.

7–22. Concerning Edom] The bitterness of the tone in which Edom is addressed in this prophecy is doubtless to be ascribed to the affinity between them and the Jews, which made the unnatural exultation of Edom over the fallen fortunes of their kinsmen the more offensive.

Much of the earlier part of this prophecy is almost verbally the same as Obad vv. 1–8, while in Obadiah the vv. come in more natural sequence. Obadiah seems to have written (see his v. 11) after the destruction of Jerusalem, whereas the prophecy in Jeremiah is connected by its grouping with the 4th year of Jehoiakim (see intro. to chs. 46–49). To meet this difficulty it has been suggested either (a) that the earlier part of Obadiah's prophecy was written before Nebuchadnezzar's overthrow of Jerusalem, and only the latter part after that event ; or, (b) that both prophets embodied in their writings an earlier prediction. Another suggested solution is that Obadiah is referring to an earlier overthrow, viz. in the time of Jehoram (2 Ch 21 17).

7. *Is* wisdom no more in Teman ?] Wisdom seems to have been a special characteristic of Edom : see v. 20, Obad v. 8, and cp. (apocryphal) book of Baruch 3 22 f. 8. Dedan] a tribe descended from Abraham by his wife Keturah (Gn 25 3), and dwelling SE. of Edom. They are bidden to keep well out of the way lest they should be involved in the overthrow of their neighbours : cp. v. 30. Esau] i.e. Edom.

9. Would they not leave *some ?*] RM 'they will leave no,' etc. In Obad v. 6 the words are interrogative, but probably not so here. The enemy, under the simile of grape-gatherers and of thieves, will bring about complete desolation. 10. Secret places] retreats and fastnesses. 11. The widows and orphans of the slain may, however, look to God's protection.

12. Whose judgment *was* not] RV ' to whom it pertained not.' If Israel itself has not escaped the cup of woe, how should Edom ? 16. Thy stern mountain fastnesses have persuaded thee thou art impregnable.

Rock] Heb. *Selah*, is probably an allusion to the precipice-protected town of that name (identical with Petra), the capital of Edom : see 2 K 14 7. 17. A desolation] RV ' an astonishment.'

19. He] the enemy of Edom. Like a lion from the swelling of Jordan] see on 12 5. Against the habitation of the strong] RM ' unto the permanent pastures,' as the spot where a lion would be most likely to find his prey. But I will suddenly, etc.] RM ' for I will suddenly drive them away,' i.e. the Edomites. And who *is* a chosen *man, that* I may, etc.] RV 'and whoso is chosen' (viz. my servant Nebuchadnezzar) ' him will I,' etc. The time] RV ' a time.' God identifies Himself with His human agent for punishment. The reference is to the right of the plaintiff in a suit to appoint the time of trial. Who shall dare to claim such a right here ? cp. Job 9 19. Who *is* that shepherd ?] What ruler will attempt to defend his flock against Me ? 20. The least, etc.] RV ' They shall drag them away, *even* the little ones of the flock.' Edom shall be as helpless before the foe as sheep. 21. Red sea] probably the Gulf of Akaba, to the S. of Edom, not the Gulf of Suez.

23–27. Concerning Damascus] The prophecy relates to Syria generally, of which this was the most important city.

23. On the sea] If with some Heb. MSS we read ' as ' for ' on ' it will refer to the hearts trouble-tossed by conquest. 25. How is . . not left] i.e. how sad it is that the inhabitants, paralysed with fear, have not saved themselves by fleeing in time ! 27. Ben-hadad] Three kings of Damascus bore this name (1 K 15 18 f. 20 1 f. 2 K 13 25).

28–33. Concerning Kedar. Kedar] see on 2 10. Hazor] perhaps in Arabia.

30. Dwell deep] see on v. 8. 31. Addressed to the invaders. Wealthy] RV ' that is at ease,' feeling secure against invasion. 32. Corners] see on 9 26. 33. Dragons] RV ' jackals.'

34–39. Against Elam] RV ' concerning Elam,' a country to the E. of Chaldea. For the date, as compared with the other prophecies, see intro. to chs. 46–49.

35. The bow] their chief weapon : cp. Isa 22 6. 36. The four winds] i.e. invasion from all sides. 39. See on 48 47.

CHAPTER 50
The Fall of Babylon and the Restoration of Israel

The prophecy concerning Babylon is ascribed to Jeremiah in 51 59. This, however, need not mean more than that it represents the tone of Jeremiah's utterances as expanded by a follower, e.g. Baruch, at a later date. The reasons for doubting Jeremiah's authorship are : (a) he elsewhere speaks in friendly terms of the Chaldeans ; here their overthrow is predicted ; (b) the style and words betray another writer ; (c) the knowledge displayed of Babylonian matters is greater than could be expected of the prophet ; (d) the Jews are in exile away from Jerusalem (50 4, 6, 17, 33). The prophecy was fulfilled when Babylon was taken by Cyrus or his general Gobryas (perhaps the Darius of Daniel) in 539 B.C., nearly 50 years after the fall of Jerusalem.

2. A standard] as the speediest way of calling attention to the news. Merodach] another name for Bel (Baal), the tutelary God of Babylon. 3. Out of the north] referring to the Medo-Persian power. Media was NW. of Babylon.

4. The overthrow of their captors shall free the Jews. 5. Thitherward] RM 'Heb. hitherward.'

8–16. The triumph of Babylon over Israel shall be avenged.

8. As the he goats] in joyful alacrity.

9. An assembly of great nations] see for some of them 51 27. Herodotus (vii. 61 f.) says there were twenty-two. 11. It is for exulting over Israel that Chaldea suffers. At grass] RV ' that treadeth out *the corn*.' The command in Dt 25 4 would have this effect. 12. The

hindermost, etc.] RV 'She (Babylon) shall be the hindermost,' etc. **15. Given her hand**] RV 'submitted herself,' surrendered. **Foundations**] RV 'bulwarks.' **Her walls are thrown down**] not done by Cyrus, but (according to Herod. iii. 159) at the later capture by Darius.

16. They shall turn, etc.] The captives of other nations as well as of the Jews shall be released.

17–32. Babylon and her empire are doomed, while Israel shall be forgiven.

17. The lions] The sculptured winged lions (Assyrian and Babylonian) give the image a special point. Assyria had devoured the Ten Tribes, and now Babylon was crushing the feeble remnant of the people. Assyria had paid the penalty; so too shall Babylon. **20. Reserve**] RV 'leave as a remnant.'

21. Merathaim .. Pekod] Proper names bearing the significant senses of 'double-rebellion' and 'visitation,' alluding to Babylon.

23. Hammer] Babylon: cp. 51 20. Individuals at other times have borne this title; Judas Maccabæus for his victories over Syria; Charles Martel, grandfather of Charles the Great (Charlemagne), who conquered the Saracens in a decisive battle at Tours, 732 A.D., and Edward I of England, on whose tomb at Westminster Abbey are the words, 'Scotorum Malleus,' or 'hammer of the Scots.'

27. Bullocks] i.e. her choice young warriors: cp. 48 15. **28. The vengeance of his temple**] the requital for having burnt it: cp. 51 11.

29. The Holy One of Israel] cp. 51 5, not elsewhere in this book, but characteristic of Isaiah.

33–40. Babylon shall be utterly laid waste.

34. Redeemer] Heb. *Goel*, the near kinsman, to whom belonged the duty of avenging a murder. So the LORD is about to avenge His people. **36. Liars**] rather, 'boasters.'

37. Mingled people] see on 25 20. **38. Her waters**] the many canals which drained and irrigated the country around Babylon: cp. 51 13.

Idols] Heb. 'terrors,' meaning their grotesque forms, such as winged bulls and human-headed lions. **39. The wild beasts of the islands**] RV 'the wolves,' Heb. 'howling creatures.' **Owls**] RV 'ostriches.'

41–46. The enemy approaches and fulfils God's behests.

41–43. See on 6 22 f.

44–46. Adapted from 49 19-21.

CHAPTER 51

1–14. The end of Babylon arrives.

1. See on 25 26. **1, 2.** The imagery is of the wind scattering the chaff on the threshing-floor. The **wind** and the **fanners** are the Medes (v. 11). **3.** *Him that* bendeth] i.e. his bow in defence of Babylon. **Brigandine**] coat of mail. **5.** See on 50 29. **7.** Babylon has

been God's instrument in His vengeance on the nations. **10. Hath brought forth our righteousness**] has judged that the Jews' idolatry has been sufficiently punished, and that they are again to be treated as righteous.

11. The kings of the Medes] the leaders of the various tribes which together formed the nation: cp. v. 28. **His temple**] see on 50 28.

12. Upon] RV 'against.' **13. Many waters**] see on 50 38. **Covetousness**] RM 'dishonest gain.' **14. Caterpillers**] RV 'the cankerworm.'

15–19. The Creator of all things is the only true God. See on 10 13 f.

20–58. The fate appointed for Babylon.

20. My battle ax] Many commentators think that Babylon is meant, but as Babylon is in this passage not the instrument but the object of God's vengeance (vv. 24–26), it seems more natural to regard Cyrus as indicated here. **Will I break**] rather, 'I break.'

25. O destroying mountain] The same phrase is used of the Mount of Olives (AV 'mount of corruption') in 2 K 23 13, as the scene of pernicious idolatry. Babylon here receives the title, as at once hurtful and conspicuous. **Burnt**] i.e. probably, burnt out, extinct.

27. Ararat, Minni, are districts of Armenia, and so probably was **Ashchenaz**. Minni is frequently mentioned in Assyrian inscriptions, the kings of Assyria having had to quell frequent revolts against their overlordship among its people. **28. Prepare**] lit. 'sanctify': so in 6 4 22 7. **His dominion**] referring to the king of Media, who is to gather to the attack his tribes with their leaders: cp. v. 11.

31. Post] running messenger. **At** *one* **end**] RV 'on every quarter.' **32. Passages**] with fords, or ferries. **Reeds**] RM 'marshes,' Heb. 'pools.' The reservoirs and pools around Babylon which prevented inundations shall disappear as completely as what is inflammable does by the action of fire. **33.** *It is* **time to thresh her**] RV 'at the time when it is trodden.'

34 f. Oppressed Israel speaks.

34. Dragon] here, 'sea-monster.' **Delicates**] dainties; here only used as a substantive in the Bible. **36. Sea**] a great lake, or reservoir, made by the Babylonish queen Nitocris. **Springs**] RV 'fountain,' referring to the net-work of canals dug for commerce and irrigation. **37. Dragons**] RV 'jackals.' **39.** While they are exulting and carousing, I will destroy them unawares. **In their heat**] when hot with wine.

41. Sheshach] see on 25 26. **42. The sea**] a figure for the invaders: cp. v. 55, 46 7 f.

44. Bel] see on 50 2. **That which he hath swallowed up**] the riches of the subjugated nations.

46. Lest] RV 'let not.' **Rumour**] the state

of unrest preceding the final catastrophe : cp. Mt 24 6, 7.

48. Shall sing for] RV 'shall sing for joy over.'

50. Ye that have escaped the sword] by being already in exile at Babylon. **Afar off**] RV 'from afar,' viz. Babylon.

51. The exiles have been scoffed at for worshipping a God who has not defended His Temple from sacrilege.

53. Allusion to the height of the walls or of the tower of Bel.

55. The great voice] the hum of the city's life. **When her waves**] RV 'and their waves,' the surging hosts that encompass the city : cp. v. 42.

58. Broad walls] They were 30 or 40 ft. wide: see Herod. i. 178.

And the people . . shall be weary] The labour expended on these splendid edifices will have been in vain.

59. Seraiah] brother of Baruch : see 32 12. **Went with Zedekiah**] Zedekiah's visit was probably an act of homage to Nebuchadnezzar, perhaps to allay suspicions caused by the communications between the former and neighbouring peoples : see on 27 3. Possibly, however, we should read ' from,' instead of ' with.'

A quiet prince] RV ' chief chamberlain,' mg. ' quarter-master,' who prepared for the king's reception at each halting-place on the journey.

61. And shalt see, and shalt read] RV ' then see that thou read,' so that the Jewish witnesses who heard could testify in after time to the prediction.

64. And they shall be weary] the last word (in Heb. but one) of the prophecy (see v. 58) with which the symbolic act is thus coupled.

Thus far, etc.] showing that c. 52 is by another hand.

CHAPTER 52

HISTORICAL APPENDIX (probably by the compiler of the book)

This c. is substantially the same as c. 39 (see notes there), but adds particulars relating to the Temple vessels (vv. 17 f.), while omitting Nebuchadnezzar's charge as to Jeremiah's safety (39 11 f.). Both accounts are probably based on that of 2 K 24 18–25 30.

1–11. Capture of the city. **12–27.** Subsequent severities. **28–30.** Nebuchadnezzar's deportations. **31–34.** Concluding notice of Jehoiachin. **4.** Nebuchadrezzar] see on 21 2.

6. Famine] described in detail in the 'Lamentations.' **7. Then the city was broken up**] RV ' Then a breach was made in the city.'

9. Riblah] see on 39 5. **11. He put out the eyes**] see on 39 7. **17 f.** See prefatory remarks.

18. Caldrons] RV ' pots,' for carrying away ashes after sacrificing. **22. A chapiter**] a capital. **24. Zephaniah**] see on 21 1.

25. The principal scribe of the host] RV 'the scribe of the captain of the host.'

28–30. This passage seems to have been taken by the compiler from a separate document. For **seventh** we should probably read ' seventeenth,' corresponding to Zedekiah's tenth year, while the siege was going on. Thus this captivity would consist chiefly of people from the country parts. The next, i.e. Nebuchadnezzar's **eighteenth** year, was that with which this chapter deals. Of the deportation of his **three and twentieth year** we have no other mention.

31. The seven and thirtieth year] 561 B.C. **Evil-merodach**] son of Nebuchadnezzar. **Lifted up the head**] released : cp. Gn 40 13, 20. **32. The kings**] captives kept at his court to commemorate his conquests.

33. He was admitted to the king's table.

THE LAMENTATIONS OF JEREMIAH

INTRODUCTION

1. Name, Place in Canon, and Subject. To the Hebrews this book is known by its initial word, *'Ekhah*, 'How' ; by the ancient Jews of Alexandria it was called *Threnoi*, ' Dirges' ; by St. Jerome, *Lamentationes*, whence our English title. Its position in the English and other versions is due to the influence of the Greek or LXX version, which placed it immediately after the prophecies of Jeremiah ; but in the Hebrew canon it is usually found among the *Hagiographa*, or ' Writings,' constituting, along with Canticles, Ruth, Ecclesiastes, and Esther, a small collection known as the five *Megilloth*, or ' Rolls.' The great theme of the book is the siege, capture, and destruction of Jerusalem by Nebuchadnezzar. Josephus, on the basis of 2 Ch 35 25, erroneously supposed that it was written as an elegy over the death of king Josiah. For vividness and pathos the book is unsurpassed in all literature.

2. Analysis.

C. 1. Zion's desolation and sorrow.

C. 2. Zion's sorrows due to Jehovah's anger.

C. 3. Zion's hope in God's mercy.

C. 4. Zion's former glory contrasted with her present humiliation.

C. 5. Zion's earnest petition for deliverance.

3. Structure. Of the five lyric poems of which the book consists, the first four, in Hebrew, are acrostics ; each poem consisting of 22 portions or verses, corresponding to the number of letters in the Hebrew alphabet, except the third, in which each letter is used thrice, and in which, consequently, there are 3 times 22, or 66 verses. The fifth poem, though not an acrostic, has 22 verses. The metre is known as Kinah rhythm or elegiac, sometimes spoken of as 'limping verse,' because the second line is usually considerably shorter than the first. No book shows greater art or more technical skill in composition. Isa 14 4-21 is written in the same metre.

4. Author. In the original these poems are anonymous, but tradition has long since ascribed them to Jeremiah. The LXX prefaces the book with these words : 'And it came to pass, after Israel had been carried into captivity and Jerusalem had been laid waste that Jeremiah sat weeping and lamented with this lamentation over Jerusalem and said' ; and this ancient tradition is confirmed by the Syriac, the Latin Vulgate, the Targum of Jonathan, the Talmud, and by modern Jews and Christians, who point to the very cave or grotto, near the Damascus gate on the N. side of the Holy City, in which Jeremiah is supposed to have written them. Various allusions in the poems themselves look in the same direction ; especially the vivid descriptions of Jerusalem in chs. 2 and 4, which are evidently the pen-pictures of an eye-witness ; likewise the strongly sympathetic temper and prophetic spirit of the poems throughout, as well as their style, phraseology, and thought, which are all so characteristic of Jeremiah.

On the other hand, it is possible, of course, that they were written by a contemporary of Jeremiah, perhaps Baruch ; for, as has been suggested by Professor McFadyen, being anonymous, it is easier to think that the traditional title has been added by the Greek version than that a genuine one has been lost from the Hebrew. Besides, the allusion to the prophets in 2 9, bearing the iniquities of the fathers in 5 7, and the expectation of help from Egypt in 4 17, are unlike Jeremiah. But notwithstanding all the objections to the contrary, the balance of evidence, both internal and external, is probably in favour of Jeremiah.

5. Unity and Date. As may be seen from the outline given above, the unity of the book is not logical, but emotional ; hence the question of its literary unity is largely dependent upon one's attitude toward its authorship and date. As to its date, it is very generally agreed that it was composed soon after the downfall of Jerusalem in 586 B.C. How soon, it is difficult to state : the author's vivid language points to a time immediately subsequent, whereas the highly artificial and acrostic character of the composition would indicate that the bitterness of the siege had passed, and that the poet had had time for calm reflection.

6. Permanent Religious Value. The richest portion of the book is doubtless the section contained in 3 19-39, in which vv. 22–27 are particularly precious. But the entire book is of value to teach not only patriotism, and patience, and prayer, and confession of sin, but the divine character of chastisement, the disciplinary value of yoke-bearing, how God pities those whom He is compelled to afflict ; and, what is deepest and most important of all, how ideal Zion, in suffering for the sins of the nation, is typical of the Messiah who 'bore our sins and carried our sorrows.' The book is also of liturgical value, being read by pious Israelites every Friday afternoon at the Jews' wailing place, within the city of Jerusalem, but just outside the Temple area, and in Jewish synagogues the world over on the 9th of Ab (August), the day on which the Temple was burned.

CHAPTER 1
Zion's Desolation and Sorrow

Though the five poems contained in the book have practically the same theme—the downfall of Jerusalem—yet each poem dwells on a different phase of the subject as intimated in the opening words of each c. This first one emphasises the desolation and misery of the city, describing it as 'solitary,' as 'a widow,' and as 'tributary,' i.e. Judah has lost her independence ; and there is 'no comforter,' vv. 2, 9, 17, 21. It falls naturally into three sub-divisions, as seen below. In structure it is strictly alphabetical : each v. being of triple construction.

1-11. The poet laments Zion's utter desolation.

1. How] a characteristic word for the commencement of an elegy : cp. 2 1 4 1, 2 Isa 14 4.

Sit solitary] in the sense of empty houses and deserted streets. **Provinces]** the neighbouring countries, such as Edom and Moab.

2. Lovers] synonymous with **friends,** viz. her allies Edom and Egypt (4 22).

3. Because of affliction and . . great servitude] i.e. Judah chose exile to escape the sufferings to which she was exposed in her own land (Jer 40 11). **Between the straits]** RV 'within the straits.' **4. The ways of Zion**

do mourn] The roads by which pilgrims came up to the feasts are now deserted (Jer 14 2).

Her virgins] those who took part in the festal occasions (Ps 68 25). **5. Are the chief**] RV 'are become the head': i.e. Judah has lost her leadership. **Before the enemy**] driven as slaves. **6. Her princes are become like harts**] referring to Zedekiah's flight with his sons (Jer 39 4-7).

7. Remembered] RV 'remembereth.' **Sabbaths**] RV 'desolations,' in the sense probably of ceasings: cp. the enforced sabbaths of Lv 26 34, 35. The Heb. word employed here is not found elsewhere in OT. **8. Is removed**] RV 'is become as an unclean thing.' **Her nakedness**] her sin and its punishment (4 21). **9. Her filthiness**] moral pollution, expressed by a bold but common Oriental figure (Jer 13 22). **She remembereth not**] RV 'she remembered not.' **10. Pleasant things**] primarily the vessels of the sanctuary (2 Ch 36 10, 19), but including all of Jerusalem's precious possessions.

12-19. Zion's comfortless condition due to Jehovah's righteousness.

12. Zion yearns for sympathy. **13. From above**] RV 'From on high.' **14. Is bound**] a bucolic figure, God being represented as binding Judah's sins upon his neck as a ploughman binds the yoke upon oxen (Jer 27 2). **He hath made my strength to fall**] rather, 'it (the yoke) hath caused my strength to stumble.' **The** LORD] in Heb. *Adonai*, used 14 times in Lamentations to express lordship; the name Jehovah conveys the covenant idea of redemption. **15. He hath called an assembly**] lit. 'an appointed time': i.e. a religious festival (Lev 23 4); not for Israel, however, but for the enemy, to celebrate the defeat of Zion's soldiers. **16. Mine eye, mine eye**] The emphatic repetition reminding one of Jeremiah's style (Jer 4 19 6 14). **17.** *That* his adversaries *should be* round about him] i.e. that his nearest neighbours should be his most hateful foes. In this v. the poet speaks. **19. Lovers**] see on v. 2. **My priests and mine elders**] Even the most honoured chiefs of the city died of starvation.

20-22. In distress Zion appeals to Jehovah for redress.

21. The day] i.e. the day of vengeance 'on Zion, long before announced (Jer 25 17-26).

22. Let all their wickedness come before thee] a not infrequent prayer of OT. saints for righteous retribution upon the enemy: cp. Pss 69, 109, 137 Jer 18 20-23; not altogether unjustifiable, for the Hebrew was conscious that wickedness must be punished, but far below the plane of the Sermon on the Mount.

CHAPTER 2

ZION'S SORROWS DUE TO JEHOVAH'S ANGER

In this second dirge, the cause of Zion's woe is dwelt upon. Jehovah has become angry with His people, therefore He has cast them off. Zion's miseries are the judgments of God, which have been sent because of Judah's sins. In structure the poem is an acrostic, each v. being of triple character, as in c. 1. The prophet speaks.

1-10. The agonies caused by Adonai's anger.

1. The beauty of Israel] the Temple (Isa 64 11), or possibly the heroes of Jerusalem (2 S 1 19). **His footstool**] the ark of the covenant (1 Ch 28 2), or possibly the sanctuary (Pss 99 5 132 7 Isa 60 13). **2. Swallowed up**] i.e. destroyed by earthquake. **Habitations**] open villages of the shepherds. **Strong holds**] fortified towns. **3. All the horn**] better 'every horn,' in the sense of self-protection or of resistance, the horn being a symbol of strength. **4. In the tabernacle of the daughter of Zion**] The division of the v. in AV is faulty. The colon after **Zion** should stand after **eye**, as in RV. **6. As** *if it were of* a garden] i.e. God has destroyed His Temple as easily as a man removes a vintage booth, which has served its purpose, from a garden (Isa 1 18).

8. He hath stretched out a line] Jehovah surveys, but to destroy: cp. Isa 34 11 Am 7 7.

9. Her gates are sunk into the ground] a metaphor expressing their total destruction, not a vestige being left above ground. **The law** *is* no *more*] including the national ritual and government. **Her prophets also find no vision**] because so hardened by sin.

10. The elders .. sit upon the ground] i.e. in banishment.

11-19. Zion's bitter sorrow and lamentation. **11.** The scene of Jerusalem's woes is to the poet heartrending. **My liver**] a phrase not found elsewhere in OT., but expressive of strong emotion: cp. our English use of 'spleen' and 'humorous.' **12.** The picture of helpless innocent children crying in vain for food is touching. **13. What thing shall I take to witness for thee?**] RV 'What shall I testify unto thee?' in the sense of attempting to comfort Jerusalem. **14. False burdens**] RM 'oracles of vanity' (Jer 23 33). **Causes of banishment**] The Heb. word employed here is not found elsewhere, but probably means things which draw aside and drive out (Jer 27 10, 15). **17. The** LORD **hath done**] The poet points to Jehovah as Zion's Destroyer, only later to show that He may become her Saviour. **18. O wall**] apostrophised as a human mourner (Isa 14 31). **No rest**] RV 'no respite.' **Apple of thine eye**] lit. 'daughter,' i.e. pupil of the eye: cp. Ps 17 8.

20-22. In bewilderment Zion appeals to Jehovah.

20. To whom thou hast done this] viz. to His own chosen people. **Children of a span**

long] RV 'the children that are dandled in the hands': cp. v. 22, Jer 19⁹. **22. My terrors round about**] as in Jer 6²⁵ 20³,¹⁰. Jehovah has now summoned His terrors (*Magor-missabib*), as at other times He had summoned His people to the festivals (**a solemn day**).

CHAPTER 3
ZION'S HOPE IN GOD'S MERCY

This third poem is the most elaborate in structure and the most sublime in thought of all. The poet speaks not only for himself, but for the nation. The order of thought is sorrow, confession, repentance, prayer. Though consisting of 66 vv. the poem is but a little longer than the others. Three consecutive vv. are built upon each letter of the Heb. alphabet : each triplet is usually closely associated in thought, and consequently grouped together as in the RV.

1–18. Zion bewails her calamities.

1–3. I *am* the man] The author is a representative sufferer, an eye-witness, and typical of Christ. **4–6. Gall**] bitterest sorrow (Jer 8¹⁴). **Travel**] RV 'travail,' which is the more modern spelling, in the sense here intended, of painful labour (Nu 20¹⁴). **He hath set me**] RV 'He hath made me to dwell' (Ps 143³). **Be dead of old**] RV 'have been long dead.' **7–9. He hath made my paths crooked**] in the sense that every avenue of advance is blocked. **10–12. He *was***] RV 'He is.' **As a bear .. as a lion**] God is even lying in wait to oppose him (Jer 4⁷ 5⁶).

Danger follows distress. **13–15. Arrows of his quiver**] RM 'sons of his quiver,' a poetical expression for the enemies' taunts (Jer 20⁸).

My reins] The English equivalent is heart, denoting the seat of the affections (Jer 12²).

To all my people] better, 'to all peoples,' as in many Heb. MSS and the Peshitto.

16–18. Broken my teeth with gravel stones] i.e. God has forced him to eat bread full of grit (Prov 20¹⁷). **He hath covered me with ashes**] or, 'He made me cower in the ashes.' Such dreadful thoughts about God are almost without a parallel in the OT.

19–39. Hope of relief through God's mercy. In this section we reach the highest point of trust to which the mourner attains.

19–21. Remembering] RV 'remember,' in the imperative sense (1⁷). **This I recall**] viz. what just precedes, his affliction. **25–27. The LORD *is* good**] 'good' is the initial word of each v. in this group. Goodness to the poet is an essential attribute of Jehovah and the basis of his hope. He is too good to keep them always in despair. **Should both hope and quietly wait**] lit. 'should wait and in silence'; quiet waiting being the pre-requisite of perceiving that God is good. **Yoke**] discipline, or work that is irksome, compulsory and

painful. These vv. have the ring of autobiography. **28–30.** The leading verbs in this triplet are to be taken hortatively, as RV 'Let him sit,' 'put,' 'give,' the argument being that yoke-bearing in order to be beneficial must be submitted to willingly. **Hath borne**] RV 'hath laid.' **Giveth *his* cheek**] the climax of patience is reached when suffering that comes through human agency is borne without murmuring.

31–33. Three grounds are given for resignation : (1) because chastisement is only temporary (Ps 77⁷ Jer 3⁵,¹²); (2) because by nature God is merciful, and therefore the distress sent will not exceed what is absolutely necessary (Isa 54⁸); (3) because all affliction is against His will, hence God cannot commit an injustice. **34–36.** In this triplet the order of thought is transposed to accommodate the alphabetic structure. The teaching is, the Lord **approveth not,** (1) of cruelty to prisoners in war, as Nebuchadnezzar to the inhabitants of Jerusalem ; (2) of perverting justice in court (Ex 23⁶) ; (3) of dishonesty in private business (Ex 22⁸,⁹). **37–39.** This group rounds out the thought of the section : each v. contains a separate interrogation : (1) **Who** can command and bring to pass except Adonai ? (Ps 33⁹). (2) Do not evil (i.e. suffering) and good alike proceed from God ? (Am 3⁶ Isa 45⁷). (3) Why should a man who still lives complain when he is only being punished for his sins? (Jer 45⁵). **A living man**] The word 'living' is emphatic. Life in itself is more than the sinner merits. Instead of having been overpaid, he is not even paid in full : for 'the wages of sin is death' (Rom 6²³). The poet is here championing the divine cause.

40–54. Exhortations to repent and confess.

40–42. Our heart with *our* hands] strictly, our heart to our palms, in the sense that the heart should actually follow in the direction in which our hands point (Jer 4³¹).

43–45. Zion's condition is dire because Jehovah will not hear the prayers of His miserable victims. **People**] RV 'peoples,' i.e. the foreign nations round about. **52–54.** These vv. are thought to point to Jeremiah as the author of the poems : cp. Jer 38. **Cast a stone upon me**] i.e. covered with a stone the pit into which they cast him. **Waters flowed over mine head**] There was no water, but mire, in Jeremiah's dungeon (Jer 38⁶). **I am cut off**] the sufferer is a type of Christ (Ps 88⁵ Isa 53⁸).

55–66. In despair Zion prays for vengeance upon the enemy.

55–57. I called upon thy name] i.e. upon the attributes of God ; referring possibly to Ps 69, supposed by some to have been composed by Jeremiah while in the dungeon.

Fear not] God's answer was brief, consisting of but two words, but enough since they came from him. **58–60. Pleaded**] as an advocate

(Jer 50³⁴). **All their imaginations**] RV 'all their devices' (Jer 11¹⁹ 18¹⁸). **63. Musick**] RV 'song.' **64-66.** AV by translating the imperfect tenses of the verbs in this triplet as imperatives, makes the language appear harsher than it really is; still it must be allowed that the poet prays for retribution upon the enemy (Jer 18²³ 2 Tim 4¹⁴). **Sorrow of heart**] RV 'hardness of heart.'

CHAPTER 4
ZION'S FORMER GLORY CONTRASTED WITH HER PRESENT HUMILIATION

In this fourth dirge the poet describes the miseries of the various classes in the sack of Jerusalem, concluding with a warning to Edom. In structure, each alphabetic v. is composed of two rather than of three sub-divisions, the ideas and phrases balancing as in ordinary Hebrew poetry. This is considered the finest poetry of the book. The mourner speaks throughout.

1-10. The terrible distress of the people and nobles.

1. How is the gold become dim] The three words used for gold, pure gold, and fine gold, in vv. 1, 2, all stand metaphorically for Jerusalem's most precious possessions, particularly her inhabitants. **The stones of the sanctuary**] the choicest portion of Zion's citizens (2¹⁹ Zech 9¹⁶). **2. Earthen pitchers, the work of the hands of the potter**] The contrast is not merely one of the materials, gold and clay, but of workmanship (Jer 18¹⁻⁶ 19¹⁻¹⁰). **3. The sea monsters**] RV 'the jackals' (Jer 9¹¹). The thought is that even wild beasts suckle their young, but the women of Jerusalem are become cruel and take no heed of their children's pitiful cries. **Like the ostriches**] here taken as the type of cruelty and heartlessness, because they forsake their young at the least alarm (Job 39¹³⁻¹⁷). **5. Delicately**] daintily (Prov 29²¹). **Brought up in scarlet**] lit. 'carried upon scarlet,' as infants. **Embrace dunghills**] lie upon dust heaps. The contrast is most vivid. From the highest luxury, the upper classes in Jerusalem have been reduced to the extremest poverty.

6. For the punishment of the iniquity] RV 'For the iniquity.' **As in a moment**] Sodom was overthrown suddenly; Jerusalem's sufferings were prolonged. Hence it is inferred that Jerusalem's sin was greater than Sodom's. Our Lord modified this ancient view of sin and punishment (Lk 13¹⁻⁵). **And no hands stayed on her**] RV 'and no hands were laid upon her,' i.e. Sodom's punishment was direct from God. **7. Nazarites**] RV 'nobles,' probably alluding to the Rechabites, famous at that time for their purity and temperance (Jer 35).

9. Better] i.e. better off. Death by the

sword, prior to the siege, is pronounced preferable to being gradually wasted by famine.

For *want of* **the fruits of the field**] lit. 'from the produce of the field,' famine being more cruel than the enemy (Ps 109²⁴). **10.** This v. describes a gruesome scene, alluded to in 2²⁰, and predicted in Jer 19⁹. **Pitiful women**] the daughters of an effete civilisation, who had been nursed in the lap of luxury.

11-16. The ignominious fate of the prophets and priests.

This section begins and ends with an account of the wrath of Jehovah. **11. Kindled a fire in Zion**] poetic for the glowing of Jehovah's anger (2 Ch 36¹⁹). **13. For the sins of**] RV 'It is because of the sins of.' Zion's prophets were really murderers (2 Ch 24²¹ Jer 26²³). **14. They have wandered**] reeled and staggered, reckless of their responsibilities as leaders. **15. They cried unto them**] the people applied to them what lepers were required to declare of themselves, viz. Unclean ! Unclean ! (Lv 13⁴⁵). Theirs was spiritual leprosy. **They said among the heathen**] When ostracised, people abroad said, They shall tarry here no longer. They were unwelcome everywhere; fugitives and vagabonds, with the mark of Cain upon them.

16. The anger of the LORD hath divided them] lit. 'the face of Jehovah hath scattered them.'

17-20. The vain hope of escape; even the king being captured. This short section is in the first person plural.

17. RV 'Our eyes do yet fail *in looking* for our vain help.' Egypt or some other expected ally disappoints (Jer 37⁷ Isa 36⁶). **19. Our persecutors**] RV 'our pursuers.' **20. The breath of our nostrils**] a rather strong expression to use of Zedekiah, yet he was Jerusalem's king, and though weak, 'the anointed of Jehovah.' **Under his shadow**] even as captives, they hoped to be allowed some sort of national organisation with Zedekiah as their head. The hope expressed is pathetic.

21, 22. The doom of Edom.

21. Rejoice and be glad] i.e. enjoy thy malicious but fleeting satisfaction (Jer 49⁷⁻²²). Edom is typical of the church's foes to-day.

Uz] the territory lying SE. of Palestine, extending probably into Arabia (Jer 25²⁰). **The cup**] the symbol of divine wrath (Jer 25¹⁷). **22. The punishment of thine iniquity is accomplished**] lit. 'ended.' For one brief moment the curtain of gloom is lifted, and a hope—in a sense a Messianic hope—is held out to Zion (Isa 40²). **He will discover thy sins**] i.e. he will punish thy sins; for, if to cover is to forgive, to discover must be to punish (Pss 32¹ 85²). Thus the poem closes with a contrast. Zion's sins shall be covered, Edom's discovered. Zion's captivity is past. Edom's yet to come. The Hebrews' debt is paid, the Edomites' is yet to be exacted.

CHAPTER 5

ZION'S EARNEST PETITION FOR DELIVERANCE

This final poem is not so much an elegy as a prayer or meditation. The tone is more calm and spiritual than the others, with no trace of vindictiveness. The poet, speaking for the people, 'will have God know everything.' Though divided into 22 vv., it is not an acrostic. Rhyme takes the place of the alphabetical structure, the poem having not less than 45 words ending in the sound *u* : cp. Ps 124. Like c. 4, each v. is composed of two members which are balanced with the greatest care, both as to form and thought. In the Vulgate this c. is given a separate title, 'Oratio Jeremiæ prophetæ.'

1–18. A pathetic review of Zion's condition. **1. Remember, O LORD]** Like the initial sentences of the other poems, the opening words strike the key of what follows. The poet is about to pray, so he secures first of all God's attention. **2. Our inheritance]** Canaan (Lv 20 24). **3. Our mothers** *are* **as widows]** i.e. without protection and support. **5. Our necks** *are* **under persecution]** RV 'our pursuers are upon our necks.' **6. To the Assyrians]** Babylonians of course are meant (Jer 2 18 2 K 23 29).

7. And we have borne their iniquities] not in contradiction to Jer 31 29 Ezk 18 2, nor that they were not themselves great sinners, for v. 16 shows that they acknowledged they were, but that the nation's guilt extended back into the past. Ideal Zion, like Christ, was to 'be made perfect through sufferings' (Heb 2 10). **8. Servants have ruled over us]** Babylonian satraps were often simply household favourites, promoted by the king to posts of honour, such as the headship of the wretched remnant of Judah (Jer 39 3). **9. We gat]** RV 'We got,' lit. 'we bring in.' **Because of the sword of the wilderness]** alluding to the

raids of the Bedouins, who may have fallen upon the remnant in their attempts to snatch a little food.

10. Black] RM 'hot.' **Terrible famine]** RV 'burning heat of famine.' **12. Hanged up by their hand]** The Assyrian custom was to impale bodies after death in order to expose them to the most utter contempt possible (Dt 21 23 1 S 31 10-12). **13. They took the young men to grind]** RV 'The young men bare the mill,' work usually done by women and slaves (Isa 47 2).

14. From the gate] corresponding to our public square or park (Jer 14 2).

16. The crown is fallen *from* **our head]** a figurative expression conveying the thought that Zion has lost her dignity of statehood.

Woe unto us, that we have sinned] a distinct confession on the part of the people, and the effect desired has been obtained. **17. For this . . for these** *things*] loss of nationality and present distress respectively.

19–22. A final appeal to Jehovah to remove Zion's reproach.

The book closes with a majestic apostrophe to Jehovah. **19. Remainest]** RV 'sittest,' as king. Jehovah had not abdicated, though Zedekiah had (Ps 45 6 102 12). **20. Wherefore . . so long time]** a hint may be contained in these last words as to the time of composition, at least of c. 5. **21. Turn thou us unto thee]** The poet realises that they cannot turn themselves. The doctrine clearly is that repentance is of grace. It is useless simply to resolve to turn (Jer 31 18).

22. But] RV 'unless,' which is better ; for that Jehovah has utterly rejected Zion is to the poet unthinkable. The tone of the v., however, is so melancholy that in some MSS v. 21 is repeated ; so that, in reading the roll in the synagogue, the book might end more hopefully. The Jews delighted in cheerful conclusions. Similar repetitions occur at the close of Ecclesiastes, Isaiah, and Malachi.

EZEKIEL

INTRODUCTION

1. History of Ezekiel's Times. Ezekiel was preëminently a prophet of the Captivity of Judah, but the allusions in his book go back over the last half-century of the existence of the Jewish kingdom.

Assyria, Babylon, and Egypt. The kings of Judah had long been vassals of Assyria, but in the latter half of the 7th cent. B.C. the power of that empire was declining. Soon after 630 B.C. Western Asia was invaded by the Scythians—hordes of northern barbarians who penetrated to the borders of Egypt. Their irruption is not directly mentioned in Scripture, but it made a strong and terrifying impression, of which traces are found in both Jeremiah and Ezekiel, and the possibility of its recurrence was long present to men's minds. About 625 B.C. Babylon, hitherto a tributary of Assyria, became independent under Nabopolassar, and about 607 B.C. Nineveh, the Assyrian capital, fell before Nabopolassar and his allies. The supremacy of the E. was thus transferred to Babylon. When Nineveh fell, Pharaoh-Necho of Egypt made himself temporarily master of Palestine, but in 605 B.C. he was defeated at Carchemish by Nebuchadrezzar, the son of Nabopolassar, who immediately succeeded his father as king of Babylon and ruler of all Western Asia.

The last kings of Judah. The reign of Josiah (639–608 B.C.) was signalised by the discovery of the Book of the Law in the Temple (621 B.C.), and by the great reformation that followed it. Josiah was slain in battle at Megiddo, when attempting to oppose the northward march of Pharaoh-Necho (608 B.C.). The people of Judah placed **Shallum** (generally known as Jehoahaz), Josiah's youngest son, on the throne, but their choice did not satisfy Pharaoh-Necho, who deposed **Shallum**, and carried him captive to Egypt, putting **Jehoiakim**, another son of Josiah, in his place. Jehoiakim reigned as a vassal of Egypt for four years, but Nebuchadrezzar's victory at Carchemish made him a subject of Babylon. For three years longer he was loyal to Nebuchadrezzar, but at last he began to intrigue again with Egypt. He died in 597 B.C. before Nebuchadrezzar could punish his unfaithfulness, but the blow fell on his son and successor, **Jehoiachin**, who was deposed after a reign of three months, and carried captive to Babylon, along with the flower of the nobility and the best of the craftsmen of the land.

This was the first captivity (597 B.C.). Nebuchadrezzar, however, spared the kingdom of Judah a little longer, and set **Zedekiah**, a third son of Josiah, on the throne. But Zedekiah proved a weak ruler, unable to resist the anti-Babylonian party in Judah. He too was led into intrigue with Egypt, and revolt against Babylon. Nebuchadrezzar sent an army against Jerusalem. The siege began on the tenth day of the tenth month of Zedekiah's ninth year; and after being temporarily raised owing to the approach of an Egyptian army, was resumed, and ended on the ninth day of the fourth month of Zedekiah's eleventh year. The king fled, but was captured, had his eyes put out, and was taken to Babylon. A month later Jerusalem was burnt, and the bulk of the people of Judah carried into exile. This was the second captivity (586 B.C.).

After the Second Captivity. Gedaliah, a Jewish noble, was made Babylonian Governor of Palestine, but after three months he was murdered, at the instigation of the king of Ammon, by a noble of the anti-Babylonian faction. The Jewish leaders of Gedaliah's party fled with their followers into Egypt. It was probably to avenge the murder of Gedaliah that a further deportation of Jews to Babylon took place five years later (Jer 52³⁰). This was the third captivity (581 B.C.).

Babylon, Tyre, and Egypt. Tyre as well as Judah revolted against Nebuchadrezzar, and was besieged by him for thirteen years from the seventh year of his reign (597–584 B.C.). In his thirty-seventh year (567 B.C.) Nebuchadrezzar was engaged in a campaign against Egypt.

2. Ezekiel's personal history. Ezekiel ('God strengthens,' or 'God is strong'), the son of Buzi, was a priest who was carried to Babylon at the first captivity (597 B.C.). This is the point from which the dates in his book are reckoned. Nothing is known of his age at the time of his transportation, or of his previous history. In the fifth year of his captivity (592 B.C.) he was called and consecrated to the work of a prophet by a remarkable vision with which the book opens, and he carried on his ministry at intervals for twenty-two years, the latest date in the book being the twenty-seventh year of the captivity (570 B.C.). Our knowledge of his personal career is very meagre. He lived in a house of his own, among a colony of his fellow exiles, who were settled at a place called Tel-abib. He was married, and his wife died suddenly on the very day when the siege of Jerusalem began.

3. Ezekiel's Audience. This consisted outwardly of the exiles at Tel-abib, who were an organised community with 'elders' at their head. They were at first opposed to Ezekiel, and were inclined to believe the false prophets who held out hopes of a speedy return to their own land (Jer 29 8, 9). This antagonism prevented him from speaking in public, but the elders visited him from time to time in his house. After the fulfilment of his earlier prophecies in the fall of Jerusalem, the attitude of the exiles to the prophet became more favourable. Though living in Babylonia Ezekiel's chief concern was with the fate of Jerusalem, and he took the deepest interest in all that was happening in Palestine. The prophecies spoken to the elders and other exiles at Tel-abib were really addressed to the whole people of Israel whom they represented. At times Ezekiel makes a distinction between the exiles and their brethren in Palestine, and in these cases his verdict is in favour of the former.

4. The Book of Ezekiel falls into three well-marked divisions. The first (chs. 1–24) predicts the fall of Jerusalem as the necessary consequence of Israel's sin. The second (chs. 25–32) deals with God's judgments on the surrounding nations. The third (chs. 33–48) describes the restoration of Israel and the establishment of the perfect kingdom of God. There is no doubt as to the unity and authenticity of the book, though a few passages here and there have been thought to be duplicates of the same prophecy. The Hebrew text, however, has become obscure in some places through the mistakes of transcribers, and the true sense has to be sought either in ancient translations like the LXX, which frequently give a better meaning, or in simple and obvious corrections. The prophecies of Ezekiel have a peculiar style and character, due to the prophet's special mental qualities. The most marked of these qualities was his powerful imagination, which not only displayed itself in strange and weird conceptions, but wrought these out with great minuteness of detail, akin to what we find in Dante. Three forms of prophecy are specially characteristic of Ezekiel. We have *symbolic actions*, in which the truths to be taught are practically illustrated ; *allegories*, which present the subjects in hand under elaborate figures ; and *visions*, in which material emblems stand out spontaneously before the prophet's mind. It is possible that some of the symbolic actions described were not actually performed. In 24 3 we see that the symbolic action and the allegory cannot be sharply distinguished. The visions, too, have been supposed by some to be merely allegories thrown into a peculiar literary form, but there is no reason to doubt that they were real experiences, though some of the details may have been worked out more fully when the visions were committed to writing.

5. Ezekiel and Jeremiah were contemporary prophets, though the latter was much the older of the two. Neither prophet mentions the other, but the book of Ezekiel contains many traces of Jeremiah's influence. During the eleven years of Zedekiah's reign both were engaged, the one in Jerusalem, and the other in Babylonia, in proclaiming practically the same truths—the guilt and coming punishment of Judah, the sin and folly of opposing Babylon and seeking help from Egypt, the certainty of the destruction of Jerusalem. After the captivity both foretold the ultimate restoration of the exiles. Jeremiah's prophecy of the New Covenant is closely paralleled in different parts of Ezekiel, but the latter left a larger place for ritual and external law than the former in his conception of the perfect kingdom of God.

6. Ezekiel's Leading Doctrines. The glory and holiness of God are very prominent in the book of Ezekiel. He is the God of Israel, and has chosen Israel as His people. His holiness has been outraged by Israel's sin, and the display of His glory is the great motive of all His dealings with them both in judgment and mercy. What He does is 'for His Name's sake.' The sin cannot be unpunished, and yet the choice of Israel cannot be finally revoked. God will restore and purify His people and dwell among them for ever. The result will be the manifestation of His true character to men. 'They shall know that I am the LORD' is the most frequent phrase in the book.

7. Ezekiel's Messianic Prophecies. The whole of the last part of the book pictures an ideal kingdom of God, and an ideal future king. The latter is symbolised by the twig taken from the top of the cedar (17 22, 23), is further hinted at in 21 27, and is clearly represented by the Davidic king of 34 23, 24 37 24, and the 'prince' of the concluding chs.

8. Fulfilment of Ezekiel's Prophecies. Those in the first part were accomplished in a general sense when Jerusalem fell. Those in the last part were partially realised in the return of the Jews from captivity and the rebuilding of the Temple ; and in their essence, though not in their literal form, they have been or are being fulfilled in the Church of Jesus Christ. Ezekiel conceived of the future kingdom of God as a national and Jewish one, and allowance must be made for this limitation of his view in dealing with the prophecies of the second part as well as with those of the third.

The future of the foreign nations is foretold with reference to their influence on God's kingdom, and as the latter did not preserve the national form which Ezekiel contemplated, the literal fulfilment of the prophecies about the former was not to be looked for either. These prophecies embody general truths about the overthrow of the powers of evil rather than precise anticipations of actual history.

9. Ezekiel and the Law. The last nine chapters of Ezekiel have an important bearing on the questions connected with the dates of the different parts of the Pentateuch. The ritual and legal details they contain show that such regulations were the subject of much thought during the exile, and their differences from the Pentateuch show that on particular points the Law was not absolutely fixed from the first, but allowed a certain elasticity in practice. The most important question is that connected with the relationship between the priests and the Levites. In Deuteronomy, which guided Josiah's reformation, the two classes are regarded as identical, while in the parts of the Pentateuch known as the Priests' Code they are distinct. Ezekiel (44 10-16) indicates that up to his time the priesthood had been common to all the tribe of Levi, but that in future it would be confined to the family of Zadok, and that the other Levites would be reduced to the rank of Temple servants. Ezekiel thus marks a transition from the arrangement of Deuteronomy to that

of the Priests' Code, and the inference is that the latter took its present form during or after the exile. With the part of the Priests' Code, however, known as the Law of Holiness (Lv 16–26), the book of Ezekiel has many points of correspondence. This portion of the Pentateuch, therefore, must have been in substance as early as his day.

10. Ezekiel and the New Testament. The language and thought of Ezekiel have had a considerable influence on the writers of the New Testament. His allegory of the Good Shepherd evidently suggested some part of our Lord's parables of the Lost Sheep and the Good Shepherd. The promise of the new heart of flesh is referred to in 2 Cor 3 3. The idea of judgment beginning at the house of God reappears in 1 Pet 4 17. The influence of Ezekiel is specially evident in Revelation, which reproduces the eating of the roll (Rev 10 9, 10), the invasion of Gog and Magog (20 7-9), the measuring of the Temple (11 1, 2), the life-giving river (22 1, 2), and the four-square city with its twelve gates (21 12-16). Many of the judgments on 'Babylon' in Rev 18 are taken from Ezekiel's chapters on Tyre.

11. The Permanent Message of Ezekiel. This book has an abiding value to the Christian because of its promise of the new heart, its doctrine of the individual's relation to God, and its assurance that God has no pleasure in the death of the wicked, but desires that all should turn to Him and live.

PART 1
SIN AND JUDGMENT. THE OLD ISRAEL AND ITS OVERTHROW (Chs. 1–24)

§ 1. EZEKIEL'S CALL AND CONSECRATION AS A PROPHET (chs. 1–3).

Date, June-July, 592 B.C.

Ezekiel's call and consecration to his prophetic work took place by means of a vision of God's glory (c. 1), and of a divine commission, or rather series of commissions, conveyed partly in speech and partly in symbol (chs. 2, 3).

CHAPTER 1
THE VISION OF GOD'S GLORY

This vision, unlike the inaugural visions of Isaiah and Jeremiah, came to Ezekiel not only at the beginning of his prophetic ministry, but also several times during the course of it. It was early repeated in connexion with his call and commission (3 23), and it appeared on two other occasions (chs. 8–11, 43 1-5). In c. 10 in particular the account in c. 1 is closely reproduced, with some additional details.

In a state of trance, or ecstasy, Ezekiel saw approaching from the north a glowing storm-cloud, which resolved itself into a remarkable group of four living creatures, arranged symmetrically in a square. Their general appear-

ance was human, and every one had four faces, a human face looking outwards, the face of a lion on the right, the face of an ox on the left, and the face of an eagle looking inwards to the centre of the square. Every one had also four wings, two of which were stretched out to meet those of the living creatures on either side, the points where the tips of the wings touched each other being the corners of the square. The other pairs of wings covered the bodies of the living creatures, and under these wings were human hands. The living creatures had straight, jointless limbs, and feet like the hoofs of a calf. The whole group was pervaded with glowing lambent fire, from which lightnings shot forth. It moved to and fro with lightning speed, and did so without turning, as its four sides were exactly alike, and any one of them could be the front for the time. Beside the living creatures were four vast wheels, the rims of which were full of eyes. These wheels also were so arranged that they could move in any direction without changing front. Though apparently unconnected with the living creatures they moved in perfect harmony with them, ascending and descending, going backwards and forwards, or from side to side, exactly as they did. The motion of this living chariot was accompanied by a majestic rushing sound. Above the heads of the living creatures there was a solid crystalline platform, supporting an enthroned human Figure, who was clothed in a fiery iridescent radiance. Overawed by the sight, Ezekiel fell upon his face, and as he lay he heard a divine voice addressing him.

The whole vision brought before Ezekiel's consciousness the presence and glory of God, but the part of it in which God Himself was more directly manifested is described with a reverent reserve. Ezekiel is careful not to identify the divine essence with the material emblems which he beheld. What he saw was 'the likeness of a throne,' and upon it 'a likeness as the appearance of a man.' The whole was 'the appearance of the likeness of the glory of Jehovah.' The details of the vision are concerned rather with the subordinate appearances by which the divine glory was accompanied and upborne.

We are not, of course, to understand that the living creatures and the wheels which Ezekiel saw were actually existing realities. They were only the forms in which certain aspects of God's glory were bodied forth before his mind's eye. And while the visionary combination of the symbols, and the impression which it produced, were the results of divine inspiration acting through a peculiar mental condition, it is permissible to seek the origin of the symbols themselves among objects which were familiar to Ezekiel's ordinary sight, and conceptions which were familiar to his ordinary thought. Composite animal figures, such as winged bulls and lions with human heads, and winged and eagle-headed men, were very common objects in the temples of Babylonia. There has even been found on an ancient Babylonian seal a representation of a god in a four-wheeled chariot drawn by a winged monster. Then Ezekiel tells us himself (10 20) that the living creatures were cherubim, like those which formed part of the furniture (Ex 25 18-20) and decoration (Ex 26 31) of the tabernacle, and of the Temple of Jerusalem (1 K 6 23-29). In Hebrew poetry, too, the cherubim were personifications of the storm-cloud on which Jehovah rode (Ps 18 10, also Pss 80 1 99 1 RV). In the winged attendants, the glowing fire, and the throne, Ezekiel's vision has points of resemblance to that of Isaiah (Isa 6), but while the imagery of Isaiah's vision was evidently that of the Temple at Jerusalem expanded and glorified, the scene of Ezekiel's was rather the great temple of nature, where Jehovah's throne is above the blue sky, and His chariot is the thunder-cloud, with lightnings flashing from its heart of fire.

The details of the vision are all suggestive of the attributes of God. The Figure on the throne is an emblem of His sovereign rule. The general human form and the various faces of the living creatures symbolise different aspects of divine majesty and strength. The imposing height of the wheels, and the sublime sound with which the whole living chariot moved, convey the same impression. The symmetrical arrangement of the living creatures and the wheels, and their swift movements in every direction, indicate the omnipresence of God. The eyes on the wheels denote His omniscient intelligence. The spontaneous and united motion of wheels and cherubim suggest the pervasive presence and universal working of God's Spirit, controlling things that seem to be independent. The fire is a symbol of divine purity and holiness. The rainbow colours add a touch of sublime beauty to the conception of the glory of God.

1. The thirtieth year] The reference of the number is uncertain. Suggested explanations are, (1) that Ezekiel's age is meant ; (2) that the reckoning is from some recent era, such as Josiah's reformation (621 B.C.), or the independence of Babylon under Nabopolassar (625 B.C., taking thirty as a round number), or the accession of Nebuchadrezzar (604 B.C., reading 'thirteenth' for 'thirtieth'), or some Babylonian epoch otherwise unknown to us ; (3) that 'the thirtieth year' is an insertion made with the object of harmonising the different periods assigned for the duration of the exile by Jeremiah (70 years, Jer 25 11 29 10) and Ezekiel (40 years, 4 6) respectively. Of these explanations (1) is improbable, and if (3) be not accepted we are shut up to some of the forms of (2). Among these 625 B.C. (Nabopolassar) seems a more likely starting-point for an epoch than 621 B.C. (Josiah's reformation), but, on the other hand, the latter date agrees more exactly with the number given. **The fourth month**] the month *Tammuz* = June-July: see on 8 14. **The river of Chebar**] the *nâr Kabari* (Great River, or 'Grand Canal') of the inscriptions. It was a large navigable canal branching off from the Euphrates, and passing near Nippur, SE. of Babylon. It is probably represented by the modern Shatt-en-Nîl, a canal 120 ft. wide, which divides the ruins of Nippur in two. **2. King Jehoiachin's captivity**] the first captivity, 597 B.C. : see Intro. **The fifth year**] 592 B.C. **3. The word of the LORD came**] the usual formula for prophetic inspiration. **Chaldeans**] Babylonians, **The hand of the LORD was .. upon him**] producing the trance in which he saw the vision.

4. Amber] RM 'electrum,' an alloy of gold and silver. **7. Feet**] rather, 'limbs.' **Straight**] kneeless, unjointed. The living creatures did not move by walking. **Like .. a calf's foot**

not projecting in one direction as a human foot does. **11. Stretched upward**] RV 'separate above.' **15. One wheel .. with his four faces**] RV 'one wheel .. for each of the four faces thereof,' four wheels in all.

16. A wheel in the middle of (RV 'within') **a wheel**] an obscure expression. One explanation is that every wheel had another joined to it at right angles, so that the compound wheel would appear thus + from above, and could revolve backwards and forwards on one rim, and from side to side on the other. Another theory places the four wheels symmetrically thus ⌐, in which arrangement, taking any side as the front, the back wheel would overlap the front one and could be seen through the spokes of the latter. A third suggestion is that every wheel was made up of two concentric circles, the outer rim having a smaller wheel within it, surrounding the axle, thus ⊗.

17. They turned not when they went] as in vv. 9, 12. The wheels of course revolved, but, like the living creatures, they could move in different directions without changing front. **18. Rings**] RM 'felloes.' **20, 21. Living creature**] The group of four is spoken of as one. **24. The voice of the Almighty**] the voice of Jehovah is a common OT. expression for thunder. **Voice of speech**] RV 'noise of tumult.' The articulate voice, as distinguished from the sound of the wheels, is not mentioned till afterwards. **26. A sapphire stone**] see the very similar vision of God's glory in Ex 24 10.

CHAPTERS 2, 3

EZEKIEL'S COMMISSION TO BE A PROPHET

Ezekiel's commission came to him by three stages, and on three distinct occasions. The first and principal occasion was the immediate sequel of the vision described in c. 1. The account of it occupies the whole of c. 2, and the first 13 vv. of c. 3. The second was seven days later, among the exiles at Tel-abib (3 14-21). The third was connected with a repetition of the vision, apparently in the neighbourhood of Tel-abib (3 22-27).

THE FIRST COMMISSION (2 1–3 13)

This consisted of two series of instructions (2 1-7 and 3 4-11) separated by a visionary symbol of prophetic inspiration (2 8–3 3), and was followed by the withdrawal of the vision for a time (3 12, 13). As Ezekiel's opening vision recalls that of Isaiah, so his first commission has much in common with that of Jeremiah, and indeed the contents of the two are closely parallel in order as well as in substance.

(a) **First Instructions** (2 1-7)

The voice which addresses Ezekiel bids him

stand on his feet, and when he has been raised from the ground by an unseen force he is told that God has given him a mission as a prophet to the children of Israel. He is warned of their rebelliousness and hardness of heart, and encouraged to deliver his message fearlessly no matter how they receive it. This exhortation corresponds to that in Jer 1 8.

1. Son of man] a term reminding Ezekiel of his human weakness, like the word 'mortal.' It occurs nearly 100 times in the book. **Stand, etc.**] God's call does not suppress human powers, but reinforces them and makes use of them at their best. **3. Nation**] RV 'nations,' the whole Hebrew people, both Judah and Israel. **Rebellious**] a frequently recurring description of Israel's character found very often in the phrase a 'rebellious house,' as in v. 5.

5. Hear, or .. forbear] The latter is chiefly expected. **They .. yet shall know,** etc.] the result which will keep the prophet's work from being in vain. His warnings may be fruitless at the time, but they will be fulfilled, and he will be recognised in the end as God's messenger. This will be very far from utter failure. The result thus indicated is the first of an ascending series which runs through the whole book. They are all introduced by the phrase 'they shall know,' and they describe the production in Israel's mind of convictions which increase in depth, and solemnity, and blessedness. The final conviction, which itself has various stages of growing significance, is 'they shall know that I am the LORD.' **6. Briers .. thorns .. scorpions**] figures for the opposition of the Israelites to Ezekiel and his divine message.

(b) **A Symbol of Inspiration** (2 8–3 3)

In Jeremiah's commission God says to him, 'Behold, I have put my words in thy mouth' (Jer 1 9), and Jeremiah himself says afterwards, 'Thy words were found, and I did eat them, and thy words were unto me a joy and the rejoicing of mine heart' (Jer 15 16 RV). The experience thus described metaphorically came to Ezekiel in his trance in a concrete, material way. God's words seemed to be set before him in the form of a book, which he ate at God's command, and found to be as sweet as honey. The truth underlying this visionary symbol was that Ezekiel was divinely inspired, in other words, that God had communicated to him a message which he was called to proclaim to men. This passage is the basis of Rev 10 9, 10.

9. A hand] This hand is not said to be that of the Figure on the throne. The vague expression is another instance of Ezekiel's reverent reserve. **A roll**] the usual form of Eastern books : see Jer 36 2. **10. Spread it before me**] Ezekiel had a view from the first of the whole nature of his message. **Within and without**] indicating the abundance of calamity which Ezekiel had to proclaim. Book rolls were usually written on the inner side alone : see Rev 5[1]. **Lamentations**, etc.] the character of Ezekiel's message.

C. 3. 3. As honey for sweetness] The privilege of being God's messenger brought a great joy, though the message itself was of the saddest.

(c) **Further Instructions** (3[4-11])

Having thus received his message Ezekiel is again told to speak it to his countrymen. He is warned in fresh terms of their indifference and obstinacy, and encouraged further by the assurance that he will be strengthened to withstand their utmost opposition. These vv. should be compared with Jer 1[17-19].

4. With my words] An advance upon the general instruction of 2[7], following the symbolical act just described. **6. People**] RV ' peoples.' Israel will be less responsive to Ezekiel's words than a foreign nation to whom his speech would be unintelligible. **7. Impudent**] RV ' of a stiff forehead.' This rendering gives greater point to ' thy forehead ' in vv. 8, 9. **9. Adamant**] diamond : see Jer 17[1]. **11. Them of the captivity**] a closer definition than in 2[3] of Ezekiel's immediate audience : see Intro.

(d) **The Vision withdrawn** (3[12,13])

The voice that has been speaking to Ezekiel has proceeded from the Figure enthroned above the living chariot of c. 1, which has therefore been present during all these instructions. Ezekiel now hears the sound of its movement as it departs. **12. Behind me**] Ezekiel's face is now turned away from the visionary chariot. As it appeared from the N. he is probably looking S., and Tel-abib may have lain in the latter direction from the Chebar. **Blessed** be **the glory,** etc.] A change of one letter in the Hebrew gives the much better sense, ' When the glory of the LORD went up from its place,' i.e. when the vision was withdrawn. **13. Noise of the wheels**] in addition to the noise of the wings of the living creatures. The latter sound alone is mentioned in 1[24].

THE SECOND COMMISSION (3[14-21])

Ezekiel, still under a strong, divinely produced excitement, came to the community of exiles at Tel-abib, near the Chebar, and after seven days of stupefaction he received a further commission from God. It was unaccompanied by any vision, and the manner in which he received it is undescribed, as is so often the case with the prophets. The new element in this second commission was the thought of Ezekiel's responsibility for the fate of his people, and it was set forth in the title of ' watchman,' now given to him for the first time. This responsibility was exhausted when he had warned them of their danger and duty. Only if he failed to do so would he be held accountable for their sin and doom.

14. The spirit lifted me] to be taken along with **I went**. Ezekiel was not miraculously transported to Tel-abib, but in his movement thither he was under the influence of God's Spirit, like Elijah in 1 K 18[46]. **15. Tel-abib**] a place near the Chebar, where a colony of Jewish exiles lived. The exact site is unknown. The name is usually explained to mean ' Hill of cornears ' or ' Corn-hill,' but some recent editors suggest that it is rather the same as *til-abûbi*, ' Hill of the deluge,' the Assyrian name for the numerous heaps of sand and *débris* formed by floods in Babylonia. **Astonished**] RV 'astonied,' in a stupor of reaction after the vision. **18. Die .. 21. Live**] not to be understood in the highest NT. sense. To die was to be cut off from the restored kingdom of God, foretold in the latter part of this book. To live was to survive and enjoy its blessedness. **20. I lay a stumblingblock before him**] This difficult phrase does not mean that God seeks to make the righteous fall, but that the temptations of the righteous are under God's providential control. Where there is a temptation He also sends a warning, and the two constitute a discipline by which the righteous man is tested, and under which he has an opportunity of moral growth. The case of a righteous man sinning and perishing in spite of warning is not contemplated at all.

THE THIRD COMMISSION (3[22-27])

In a plain or valley near Tel-abib the great vision of God's glory formerly seen by the Chebar again appeared to Ezekiel. The divine voice further explained the nature of his commission. His prophetic activity would be subject to a double limitation. He would be restrained from public speech by the opposition of the people, and God would impose silence upon him except when a divine message should be given him from time to time. This intermittent silence became permanent from 24[27] (January, 587 B.C.) onward, till the restraint on his speech was removed altogether three years later (33[21,22]). **22. Plain**] RM ' valley.' **25. They**] Ezekiel's fellow exiles. **Bands**] not literal but figurative. **26. Dumb**] as far as prophetic speech is concerned, as the following words **not .. a reprover** show.

§ 2. THE OVERTHROW OF THE JEWISH KINGDOM FORETOLD (chs. 4–7)

The great theme of the first part of Ezekiel's prophetic ministry was the certainty of the complete downfall of the Jewish state. Though Zedekiah had been set on the throne by Nebuchadrezzar after the first captivity, there was no hope for the kingdom. Zedekiah's reign was viewed by Ezekiel, as well as by Jeremiah, only as a temporary respite, to be followed by a second captivity which would bring the state to an end. Chs. 4–7 contain the first group of Ezekiel's prophecies to this effect. They are to be placed between the date of his prophetic call (June-July, 592 B.C.) and that of the next group of prophecies (August-September, 591 B.C.). The present group includes a series of symbolic prophecies of the siege and captivity of Jerusalem (chs. 4, 5), a prophecy against the mountains of Israel (c. 6), and a description, partly in the form of a poetic lament or dirge, of the final desolation of the land (c. 7).

CHAPTERS 4, 5

Symbolic actions representing Jerusalem's Siege and Captivity

Ezekiel is commanded to perform four remarkable actions setting forth the coming siege with its hardships, and the approaching captivity with its evils. It is uncertain whether these actions were literally performed or not. Symbolic methods of this kind were certainly used by various prophets, but some of those in c. 4 are so extraordinary that many suppose that they were not actually carried out, but only imagined and described. The explanation of the second and third symbols is given along with the account of the symbols themselves. The first and fourth are explained more fully in 5 5-17.

(a) A Symbol of the Siege (4 1-3)

Ezekiel was told to draw a representation of a city on a slab of clay, and to conduct a mimic siege of it. In this action the prophet played the part of the enemies of Jerusalem, and especially of God, who was now the great Adversary of the city.

1. A tile] or 'brick,' a slab of clay, such as the Babylonians used for inscriptions and sculptures in relief. **2. A mount**] an embankment raised in ancient warfare by besiegers to enable them to approach the top of a city wall.

3. Pan] RM 'flat plate,' such as was used for baking (Lv 6 21 7 9). This may be taken as a symbol either of the stubbornness of the defence or of the rigour of the siege. Or it may represent the hopeless barrier which now separated God from His people. **A sign to the house of Israel**] The symbol was intended to teach those who witnessed or heard of it that the stern reality which it represented was close at hand.

(b) Symbols of the duration of Siege and Captivity (4 4-8)

Ezekiel was directed to lie on his left side for a fixed number of days (390), and then on his right side for another fixed number (40). The whole time was supposed to represent the length of the siege of Jerusalem, and the two numbers of days were supposed to correspond to the years of the respective captivities of Israel and Judah. The constrained posture of the prophet was a symbol of the loss of freedom awaiting the people.

4. The house of Israel] used here and in v. 5 in the limited sense of the northern kingdom of the Ten Tribes.

5. Three hundred and ninety days] This is a difficult number. Ezekiel expected the captivities of Israel and Judah to end together (37 15 f.). As Israel's captivity was to be 350 years longer than Judah's, it must have begun 350 years sooner. The captivity of Judah may be dated (a) from the first captivity (597 B.C.), or (b) from the second captivity (586 B.C.). The latter was still in the future at the time of this prophecy, and would not be a fixed date for Ezekiel, who would therefore probably reckon from 597 B.C., which he elsewhere calls ' our captivity' (40 1). The captivity of Israel is most naturally reckoned (a1) from the fall of Samaria (721 B.C., 2 K 17 6); but it may possibly be calculated (b1) from the first ravages of Tiglath-pileser (734 B.C., 2 K 15 29). From (a1) to (a) gives 124 years, and from (b1) to (a) 137 years. Taking (b) instead of (a) for the captivity of Judah, these numbers become respectively 135 and 148. The LXX has 190 instead of 390, which would give 150 instead of 350 for the difference between the two captivities, and this would agree approximately with the actual dates, especially with (b1) to (b). The only way to reach anything like 350 years is to count Israel's captivity from the revolt of the Ten Tribes (939 B.C.). This was 342 years before (a) and 353 years before (b), but it is unlikely that Ezekiel should have given the time of Israel's sin and only the time of Judah's punishment. Another explanation is that since 390 + 40 = 430, Ezekiel represented the united captivities of the two kingdoms as equal in length to the bondage in Egypt (Ex 12 40), and that of Judah as equal to the period of wandering in the wilderness (Nu 14 34). The latter v. is certainly closely parallel to this passage, and possibly we have here an ideal and artificial scheme of numbers with no relation to actual historic dates. If a historic explanation be preferred, 350 (or 150) must be taken not as an exact, but as a round number.

6. Forty days] the years of Judah's captivity and of Babylon's supremacy (29 11-13). The return of the exiles took place about 538 B.C., fifty-nine years after the first and forty-eight years after the second captivity. If the number 40 is not taken from Nu 14 34 (see the note above), it is a round number, meaning 'more than a generation.' **7. The siege of Jerusalem**] the mimic siege described in vv. 1–3. The first and second symbolic actions were to be carried on together. **Thine arm . . uncovered**] a threatening gesture.

8. Bands] By some divine restraint Ezekiel would be prevented from turning. **The days of thy siege**] The number 430 represented the days of the siege of Jerusalem as well as the sum of the years of the two captivities. The actual siege lasted almost exactly a year and a half (2 K 25 1-3 Jer 39 1, 2).

(c) **Symbols of Scarcity during the Siege and of Defilement in Captivity** (4 9-17)

Ezekiel was commanded to prepare bread from a mixture of various kinds of grain, and to live on scanty rations of meat and drink while he lay upon his side. This was in token of the scarcity which the inhabitants of Jerusalem would suffer during the siege. The bread was to be baked with loathsome fuel, as a sign of the banishment of Israel to an unclean foreign land.

9. Wheat, etc.] a mixture of all sorts of grain, fine and coarse, symbolising the poor fare which would be used in Jerusalem during the siege.

10. Twenty shekels] eight or nine ounces. **11. The sixth part of an hin**] less than a quart. **12.** Bread thus baked would be unclean (Lv 5 3 7 21).

13. Eat their defiled bread] RV 'eat their bread unclean.' Foreign lands were regarded as unclean in themselves (Am 7 17), and, besides, all food eaten in them would be unclean, because it could not be consecrated by offering a portion to God in the Temple : see Hos 9 3, 4.

14. Ezekiel, as a priest, was peculiarly sensitive about ceremonial defilement. **15.** A partial mitigation of the symbol for the prophet's sake. The dung of domestic animals was often used as fuel, and does not seem to have defiled the food cooked upon it. Though the symbol was modified, it was not implied that the defilement of captivity, signified by the fuel first prescribed, would be any the less.

(d) **Symbols of Three Calamities awaiting Jerusalem** (5 1-4)

In the previous symbols Ezekiel himself personated both the besiegers and the besieged. Now the hair of his head and beard is made to represent the people of Jerusalem. He is bidden to shave it off and divide it into three parts. One of these he is to burn, as an emblem of those who will die of pestilence and famine ; another he is to smite around with a sword, as a symbol of those who will be slain ; while the third part he is to scatter to the wind, as representing those who will go into captivity. A few hairs are to be reserved as an emblem of

the pious remnant ; but even these are partly to be burned, in token of the trials the remnant will endure.

1. A sharp knife . . a barber's razor] RV 'a sharp sword, as a barber's razor.' **4.** *For* thereof] RV 'therefrom.' The clause thus introduced is obscure. The meaning seems to be that the punishment of Jerusalem will extend to the whole nation.

(e) **Explanation of the First and Fourth Symbols** (5 5-17)

The pictured city is Jerusalem, and God is her great Adversary (vv. 5–8). Her unparalleled sins deserve an unparalleled punishment. Famine and pestilence, the sword, and captivity await her people. Only thus can God's righteous wrath be appeased (vv. 9–17).

5. This] the city depicted on the tile (4 1-3). **In the midst of the nations**] God gave Jerusalem a great opportunity of displaying His righteousness and truth to the world. Her position, near the highway between Asia and Africa, was peculiarly central and conspicuous.

7. Multiplied] RV 'are turbulent.' **Neither . . my judgments . . the judgments** (RV 'ordinances') **of the nations**] Israel had been worse than the heathen, who had at least been faithful to their own gods : see Jer 2 10, 11. **8. In the sight of the nations**] Punishment must be as conspicuous as the lost opportunity.

11. Defiled my sanctuary] This charge is substantiated at length in c. 8. **13. Cause my fury to rest**] RV 'satisfy my fury.'

CHAPTER 6

A Prophecy against the Mountain Land of Israel

The coming judgment is here announced to the land of Israel, which is identified with the people. Vv. 8, 9, following up the hint in 5 3, 4, speak of a remnant of the nation which will be led to repentance in exile.

2, 3. The physical features of the land are described, not only because their variety was in strong contrast to the monotony of the Babylonian plains where Ezekiel lived, but also, and chiefly, because they were associated with different forms of idolatrous and impure worship. The mountains and hills were the sites of the 'high places'—shrines of Canaanite origin (Dt 12 2). The ravines and valleys were the scenes of Baal-worship (Jer 2 23) and of child-sacrifice (Isa 57 5) : see also v. 13.

4, 6. Images] RV 'sun-images,' probably obelisks representing the sun-god.

7. Ye shall know that I *am* **the LORD**] Ezekiel's favourite expression for the result of God's dealings with men in prophecy and in history. It means the recognition now of one, now of another, aspect of the character of the true God. Here it is the conviction that His warnings are not empty threats : see vv. 10, 14.

8. A remnant] already hinted at in 5 3.

9. Because I am broken with, etc.] RM 'how that' (better, 'when') 'I have broken their .. heart .. and their eyes.' The metaphor of breaking is extended to 'eyes,' though it strictly applies only to 'heart.' Idolatry was accompanied by licentiousness, and this is one reason why the prophets so often described it under the figure of a breach of the marriage vow : see especially chs. 16 and 23.

11. Smite (i.e. 'clap') .. **and stamp**] emphatic gestures of satisfaction in the calamities that are announced. Ezekiel was called to be in complete sympathy with God's attitude towards Israel : see 21 14, 17 25 6. **Alas !**] rather, 'Aha !' : see 25 3. **12. He that is far off,** etc.] The judgment would fall on idolatrous Israelites not only in Jerusalem, but wherever they might be. **14. More desolate than**] RV 'waste, from.' **The wilderness toward Diblath**] RV 'Diblah.' Diblath, or Diblathaim, was in Moab, beyond the Dead Sea (Nu 33 46 Jer 48 22). The phrase in AV would mean the wilderness of Judæa, which lay in that direction (eastwards) from Jerusalem. Another and more probable reading is 'Riblah' instead of 'Diblah.' Riblah was a city of Hamath in the far north (2 K 25 21). 'From the wilderness to Riblah' would mean 'from one end of the land to the other.'

CHAPTER 7

THE DESOLATION OF THE LAND OF ISRAEL

This is a final message of doom upon the whole land (v. 2). God's wrath against Israel's sin is relentless, and the judgment is inevitable and close at hand. Social relations will be broken up (v. 12); preparations for defence will be unavailing (v. 14); wealth, which has been an occasion of sin and an instrument of idolatry, will not avert calamity, but will become the spoil of the heathen (vv. 19–21); priests and prophets, king and nobles, will be helpless to deliver (vv. 26, 17); the Temple will be profaned (v. 22); the remnant will be overwhelmed with sorrow (v. 16). Vv. 5–7, 10–12 are in the poetic metre commonly used for laments or dirges.

7, 10. The morning is come] RV 'Thy doom is come.'

7. Not the sounding again of the mountains] RV 'not of joyful shouting upon the mountains.' The shouting of harvest or vintage is meant : see Isa 16 9, 10 Jer 48 33.

9. Ye shall know, etc.] another aspect of the result of God's judgment. He would be recognised as the God who punishes sin.

10, 11. The meaning here is rather obscure. If **the rod** in v. 10 is that of chastisement,

pride will mean the same thing. Babylon is called 'Pride' in Jer 50 31 (RM). But the **violence** in v. 11 seems to be that of Israel, and the **rod of wickedness** to be a figure for its developed form. Possibly 'the rod' and 'pride' in v. 10 may also refer to Israel's sin.

12. The same kind of social confusion as in Isa 24 2. **13. The seller,** etc.] This may mean, either that those of Ezekiel's fellow-exiles of the first captivity who had sold their possessions before leaving Jerusalem would not return to regain them, or that land which ought to have come back to its seller at the year of Jubilee would not do so, since the destruction of the city would obliterate this and all other social institutions. **The vision** *is* **touching,** etc.] A more probable reading is, 'wrath is upon,' etc., as in vv. 12, 14.

15. No safety either in Jerusalem or out of it : see 6 12.

18. Baldness] a sign of mourning.

19. Removed] RV 'as an unclean thing.' Similarly in v. 20.

20, 21. The rendering in AV and RV means that the Temple, profaned already by Israel's idolatry, would be further polluted by the heathen conquerors. Most scholars, however, take **the beauty of his** (the people's) **ornament** to refer to the silver and gold of v. 19, and render as in RM, 'they turned it to pride and they made the images .. thereof.' The wealth which had been turned to idolatrous uses would be defiled by passing into heathen hands.

22. Secret *place*] RM 'secret treasure.' Not the Holy of Holies specially, but Jerusalem and the Temple viewed as God's precious possession.

23. A chain] a figure for captivity. Violence must be punished by forcible restraint.

26. Prophets] were consulted for oracles as to God's will, **priests** for authoritative decisions as to the law, elders or **ancients** for general advice : see Jer 18 18.

§ 3. A VISION OF JERUSALEM'S SIN AND DOOM (chs. 8–11)

Date, August-September, 591 B.C.

A year and two months after his call to be a prophet, Ezekiel was visited in his house by the elders of the Jewish colony at Tel-abib, and in their presence he fell into a trance, during which he was transported in spirit to Jerusalem, and witnessed, as in a dream, a remarkable drama being enacted there. The glory of God was present during this vision in the same symbolic form, and accompanied by the same living chariot, as in c. 1, but with this difference, that it sometimes left the chariot and took up its position elsewhere. Ezekiel witnessed first the idolatries practised in the Temple (c. 8), then the slaughter of all the idolaters in Jerusalem (c. 9), and next the destruction of the city by the fire of God's holiness (c. 10). He then heard a parable of judgment pronounced against the leaders of Jerusalem's wicked policy, and a message of comfort addressed to the exiles who were despised by their countrymen at home. Finally he saw the glory of God departing from the Temple, and having come back in spirit to Babylonia he awoke from his trance and recounted his vision to the exiles there (c. 11). There is no reason to doubt that Ezekiel here describes an actual experience. He was not, of course, literally transported to Jerusalem, but only seemed to be taken thither, as one might in a dream. The idolatries he saw were those which he knew to be carried on in Jerusalem, and the persons mentioned in the vision were doubtless also known to him as prominent leaders in the sin of the city. Yet in his trance these persons and practices, and the whole scene, stood out before his mind's eye with a vividness and reality which enabled him to describe them as actually seen. The truths presented in the symbols, and expressed in the messages, of judgment were really communicated to him by God.

CHAPTER 8
The Idolatry of Jerusalem

Various forms of idolatry, increasing in heinousness and rising to a climax, were seen practised in the precincts of the Temple. First there was the 'image of jealousy'(vv. 3–6), next a species of secret animal-worship (vv. 7–12), then the lamentation of the women for Tammuz (vv. 13–15), and lastly the worship of the sun (vv. 16–18).

1. The sixth year .. the sixth *month*] August-September, 591 B.C. **Mine house**] to which Ezekiel's prophetic activity was confined (3 24). **The elders of Judah**] the leading men of the exiled community at Tel-abib. **The hand of the Lord GOD fell**] as in 1 3. The vision, with all its meaning, was the result of divine inspiration.

2. The same appearance as the enthroned Figure in c. 1. The living chariot is not mentioned here, but, as it appears afterwards without any special explanation, it was probably present in the vision from the first.

3. The form of an hand] the same reverent reserve as in 2 9. **In the visions of God**] Though Ezekiel's transference is described in physical terms he was not taken to Jerusalem in body, but only in spirit. **Inner gate**] RV 'gate of the inner court.' Solomon's Temple had two courts : the great or outer court (2 Ch 4 9), and the inner court or court of the priests (1 K 6 36 2 Ch 4 9). We know very little about the arrangement of the gates, but in Ezekiel's

time the inner court had probably three, one on every side except the W., and the outer court at least two, one on the N. and one on the E. The gate in this v. is the inner northern gate. We must distinguish between the **gate** or gateway, which was a block of buildings, and the **doors** by which the gateway was entered at either end. **The image of jealousy**] An idol figure, so called from the divine jealousy which it aroused. The reference is probably to the image set up by Manasseh (2 K 21 7) and removed by Josiah (2 K 23 6). **The seat** means the place where it had stood.

4. The glory .. *was* there] perhaps over the main Temple building, S. of the gate where Ezekiel was. In the next v. he turns and looks N. All the idolatries were thus enacted in God's very presence.

5. Northward at] RV 'northward of.' **Gate of the altar**] apparently still the northern inner gate. It is uncertain why it was so called. **This image of jealousy**] Ezekiel saw the image, which had not been there when he left Jerusalem, now restored to its old place. It was in the outer court, and Ezekiel, standing within the gateway, saw it through the entrance.

7. The door of the court] the opening of the gateway next the outer court. **8. A door**] leading into one of the chambers of the gateway. **10.** This animal-worship may have been borrowed from Egypt, where beetles, crocodiles, snakes, cats, jackals, and other animals were worshipped ; or it may have been a survival and revival of ancient superstitions native to Palestine. Some think that Babylon is as likely as Egypt to have been the source of the practices.

11. Jaazaniah the son of Shaphan] Shaphan was a famous scribe who took part in Josiah's reformation (2 K 22 8 f.). Two of his sons, Ahikam (Jer 26 24) and Gemariah (Jer 36 10, 25), were friendly to Jeremiah. If Jaazaniah was the son of this Shaphan he was of a different character from his father and brothers.

12. In the dark] Secrecy was a marked feature of this animal-worship. **The LORD seeth us not,** etc.] This was the excuse and perhaps the belief of these idolaters, though God's glorious presence was even then manifest to Ezekiel's eyes.

14. The door .. toward the north] probably the outer doorway of the outer northern gate. The women would thus be outside the Temple precincts altogether. **Tammuz**] a deity worshipped both in Babylonia and in Phœnicia— the same as the Greek Adonis. He appears to have been a god of the spring, and the myth regarding him told of his early death and of the descent of Istar his bride into the underworld in search of him. The death of Tammuz symbolised the destruction of the spring vegetation by the heat of summer, and it was celebrated annually by seven days of women's mourning in the 4th month (June-July), which was called Tammuz. This superstition had been introduced into Jerusalem.

16. Between the porch and the altar] The altar of burnt offering was probably in the centre of the inner court, and the main Temple building faced it on the W. The sun-worship now described was just in front of the sacred building : cp. Mt 23 [35] Lk 11 [51]. **With their backs,** etc.] This followed from their turning towards the rising sun. Their position implied the greatest contempt for the God of Israel, whose glory was at that moment visible to the prophet close to them. The worship of the sun and other heavenly bodies was introduced by the kings of Judah before Josiah's day, and abolished during his reformation (2 K 23 [5, 11]). Sun-images are mentioned as early as the days of Asa (2 Ch 14 [5] RV). Jeremiah describes the worship of the Queen of Heaven (probably the moon or the planet Venus) as prevalent in Jerusalem before the second captivity (Jer 44 [17]). **17. The branch to their nose]** usually explained as a ceremony connected with sun-worship. Persian sunworshippers held bunches of the twigs of certain trees before their mouths, that they might not contaminate the sun with their breath. Many scholars think we should read, 'they send a stench to my nostrils.'

CHAPTER 9
THE SLAUGHTER OF THE IDOLATERS IN JERUSALEM

The voice which has been speaking to Ezekiel now summons six supernatural beings armed with weapons of slaughter. They are attended by a seventh robed like a priest and equipped as a scribe. They come from the north, and take their stand by the brasen altar in the inner court. The 'glory of God' leaves the living chariot and stands at the threshold of the main Temple building. The man who acts as scribe is instructed to go through the city and set a mark on the foreheads of all those who mourn for the prevailing idolatries. The other six are instructed to follow him, to slay all those who are not thus marked, without respect to sex or age, and to begin at the Temple itself. The command is obeyed, and the sun-worshippers in the Temple are the first victims. Ezekiel, appalled at the fate of the citizens, falls on his face to plead that the whole nation may not be destroyed, but he is told that punishment must be sternly executed on those who have so fully deserved it. The scribe-angel reports that his work is done, and we are left to imagine that the work of slaughter was carried out too. This c. teaches that

while God visits sin with doom, He is perfectly just, and will not suffer the righteous to perish with the wicked.

2. The higher (RV 'upper') gate .. toward the north] the northern gate of the inner court, as in 8 [3, 5, 7]. **The brasen altar]** made by Solomon (2 Ch 4 [1]), and probably placed in the middle of the inner court. Ahaz made a new altar of stone, and removed Solomon's brasen altar to the N. side of it (2 K 16 [14]).

3. The cherub] mentioned without explanation. Throughout this vision 'cherub' is used for 'living creature' for the reason given in 10 [20]. The singular number is used here, as in 1 [20, 21], for the group of four. **The house]** the chief Temple building, which was on the W. side of the inner court, with its front facing E. **4. A mark]** lit. 'a *Tav*,' the last letter of the Hebrew alphabet. Its early form was like a cross, thus $+$. Rev 7 [3] is based on this passage.

6. The ancient men] the sun-worshippers in 8 [16]. The thought of this v. is taken up in 1 Pet 4 [17]. **7. Defile]** The presence of corpses would pollute the sanctuary. **8.** One of the few instances in which Ezekiel's love of his nation struggles with his approval of God's judgments upon them. He fears that all Israel may share Jerusalem's fate.

CHAPTER 10
THE DESTRUCTION OF JERUSALEM BY FIRE

In this c. the living chariot accompanying the vision of God's glory is the most prominent object. The living creatures are now recognised by Ezekiel as cherubim, and called so. Otherwise the description is largely a repetition of c. 1. The man with the inkhorn is directed to take coals of fire from the glowing interior of the chariot and to scatter them over the city. This part of the vision points forward to the burning of Jerusalem as the final stage of her punishment.

1. As the 'cherub' was mentioned without any introduction in 9 [3], the living chariot with all its parts now appears in the same way. It is not directly stated that the glorious Figure is on the throne. The 'glory' had left the chariot for the threshold of the Temple in 9 [3], and is in the same position in 10 [4]. It may or may not have returned to the chariot in the interval.

2. Wheels] RV 'whirling wheels,' and so in vv. 6, 13. The word is not the ordinary one for 'wheels.' **Cherub]** the singular denoting the group, as in 9 [3].

3. The right side] the S. side. The Hebrews described the points of the compass as for a spectator facing E. The S. side of the Temple building was the part of the precincts nearest to the city.

4. The house was filled with the cloud] a

comparison with 1 K 8 10, 11 shows that the 'glory' which Ezekiel saw in his visions was the same as that by which God's presence had been hitherto manifested in the Holy of Holies.

5. As the voice, etc.] like thunder.

6. Beside the wheels] RV 'beside a wheel.'

7. *One* **cherub**] RV 'the cherub,' the cherub next the particular wheel just mentioned. The scribe-angel did not actually go between the wheels himself, but stood beside the chariot and received the fire from one of the cherubim.

12. The cherubim, as well as the wheels, are now said to be full of eyes.

13. It was cried unto them .. O wheel] RV 'they were called .. the whirling wheels.'

14. The face of a (RV 'the') **cherub** here takes the place of the ox-face of 1 10. This seems at first sight to indicate that the cherubim already known to Ezekiel were ox-faced. But the cherubim in the decoration of Ezekiel's visionary temple (44 18, 19) had only the faces of a man and a lion. The substitution of 'cherub' for 'ox,' and the change in the order of the faces, may be explained by supposing that Ezekiel, still standing near the N. gate of the inner court, looked S. towards the chariot, which was about to move E. (v. 19). The cherub on the E. side of the chariot would be the leading one, and so might be called '*the* cherub.' Ezekiel would see the left, or ox-, face of this cherub, the front, or human, face of the cherub on the N. side of the chariot, the right, or lion-, face of the cherub on the W. side, and the back, or eagle-, face of the cherub on the S. side, thus :

18. The 'glory' now returns to its place above the chariot. **19.** *Every one*] RV 'they.' **The east gate**] the eastern gate of the outer court. The presence of God moves to the very verge of the Temple precincts, which it is about to leave altogether.

20. I knew that they *were* **the cherubims**] RV 'I knew that they were cherubim.' Ezekiel now recognised for the first time that the 'living creatures' were identical with the 'cherubim' of Hebrew poetry and sacred symbolism. He thus gives a clue to the source of the ideas which had unconsciously moulded his visionary conceptions from the beginning.

CHAPTER 11

THE DOOM OF THE LEADERS OF JERUSALEM'S WICKEDNESS. COMFORT FOR THE EXILES

The slaughter in c. 9 was only the visionary rehearsal of a judgment still in the future. The vision now takes another turn, and shows the wicked inhabitants still alive. Ezekiel is brought to the outer eastern gate of the Temple where he finds a group of the leaders of Jerusalem's sinful policy, two of whom are mentioned by name (vv. 1–2). A proverb by which they express their light-hearted security is turned into a parable of the doom that awaits them (vv. 3–12). The warning is ratified by the sudden death of one of the leaders (v. 13), after which a comforting message is spoken to the exiles whom the people of Jerusalem despised (vv. 14–21). The glorious symbol of God's presence then forsakes Jerusalem (vv. 22, 23). The vision ends, and Ezekiel finds himself again in Babylonia, where he describes to the exiles all that he has seen (vv. 24, 25).

1. The east gate] the outer eastern gate, to which the chariot with the 'glory' upon it had already moved. **At the door of the gate**] just outside the Temple precincts. **Jaazaniah .. and Pelatiah**] men of whom nothing further is known. Jaazaniah is not the same as the Jaazaniah of 8 11.

3. It is not near ; let us build, etc.] or, as in RM, 'Is not the time near to build?' etc. : an expression of security. **This** *city is* **the caldron,** etc.] The 'wicked counsel' of v. 2 is usually understood to mean proposals of revolt from Babylon, which would involve the prospect of war and siege. In that case the proverb about the caldron and the flesh would express the plotters' trust in the strong fortifications of Jerusalem, which they hoped would save them from the 'fire' of Nebuchadnezzar's armies. This would be a grimly humorous way of describing the desperate course they were meditating. They expected, as we might say, to be in the frying-pan, but thought that it would at least save them from the fire. Another explanation is that the saying is a boast over the exiles, who had been taken away from Jerusalem, as the useless 'broth' is poured out of a pot when the cooking is over, leaving the valuable 'flesh' behind. This is more in line with the latter part of the chapter.

6. The wicked counsellors, whatever their policy may have been, had already put many of their fellow citizens unjustly to death. **7.** The proverb would prove true in quite a different sense from that in which it was first used. The only flesh in the caldron would be that of the wicked leaders' victims. Those who thought they were the flesh would be taken out of the caldron and slain by strangers elsewhere. **10, 11. In the border of Israel**] Instead of being safe in Jerusalem they would meet their fate far away from it, on the very outskirts of the land. Over seventy of those taken at the second captivity, including twelve prominent officials, were put to death by Nebuchadrezzar at Riblah, in the extreme N. of Palestine (2 K 25 18-21 Jer 52 24-27).

13. The sudden death of Pelatiah may have been an actual occurrence, of which Ezekiel had heard, and which was reproduced in the vision. It may, however, have been an imaginary incident, symbolising the certainty and suddenness with which the prophecy of judgment on the wicked counsellors would be fulfilled. **Then fell I down,** etc.] As in 9 8 Ezekiel was dismayed at the speedy execution of God's threatening, and besought God that the whole nation might not be destroyed. This time he received a comforting assurance that the exiles should be spared and restored, while the people of Jerusalem who despised them should perish.

15. Thy brethren .. all the house of Israel] The exiles of the first captivity are identified with the true Israel. **Get you far from the LORD,** etc.] The people of Jerusalem claimed that God was only among them, and that the exiles were banished from His presence. This was a different sentiment from that expressed in 8 12. Unprincipled men can change their theology to suit their circumstances. **16. As a little sanctuary**] RV 'a sanctuary for a little while.' God's presence and the privileges of the Temple were not confined to Jerusalem. **17. People**] RV 'peoples.' **19.** A promise of an inward change, which Ezekiel afterwards repeats and expands (18 31 36 25-27).

22, 23. The emblem of God's presence now leaves the holy city, which is abandoned to its fate. What the idolaters had said in unbelief (8 12) became a terrible truth. **23. The mountain .. on the east**] the Mount of Olives. We cannot but think of Christ's words of doom, spoken from the same mountain, to the Jerusalem of His day (Lk 19 37, 41-44).

§ 4. FURTHER PROPHECIES OF ISRAEL'S GUILT AND APPROACHING PUNISHMENT (chs. 12–19)

This is a somewhat miscellaneous group of prophecies intermediate in date between the preceding (August-September, 591 B.C.) and succeeding (July-August, 590 B.C.) sections. It includes fresh symbols of exile, flight, and famine (12 1-20), a doctrine of prophecy, true and false (12 21-14 11), an explanation of God's exceptional treatment of Jerusalem in sparing a remnant (14 12-23), Ezekiel's parable of the Vine (c. 15), the parable of the Foundling Child (c. 16), a parable of Zedekiah's perfidy and its

punishment (c. 17), a vindication of God's equity (c. 18), and a lament over the royal house of Judah (c. 19).

CHAPTER 12 1-20
SYMBOLS OF EXILE, FLIGHT, AND FAMINE

Ezekiel's audience being blind to the meaning of the vision he has just described, he is commanded to give them, in new symbolic actions, a further representation of the coming fate of Jerusalem and its king and people. He is told to gather together such things as one leaving home would take with him, and to carry these out of his house by day. At night he is to dig a hole in a wall, and pass through it with his face covered and his baggage on his shoulder. When the people ask him next morning what these proceedings mean he is directed to tell them that the action of the day-time is a symbol of the captivity awaiting Jerusalem, and that the action of the evening foreshadows the secret flight which Zedekiah will attempt, and the punishment of blindness which will prevent him from seeing the land of his exile (vv. 1–16). Another symbolic action, resembling that of 4 9 f., is also commanded. Ezekiel is to eat and drink sparingly and with trembling, in token of the famine which the coming siege will cause in Jerusalem (vv. 17–20).

2. The story of the vision seems to have produced no impression. **5. The wall**] Some understand the town-wall of Tel-abib, or the wall of the courtyard of Ezekiel's house, but we cannot be sure that these walls existed. The house-wall itself may be meant, but in that case Ezekiel would have to carry his luggage indoors again. **6. Twilight**] RV 'dark,' and so in vv. 7, 12. **Cover thy face**] A natural emblem for disguise and secrecy, but with a special reference, as v. 13 shows, to Zedekiah's blindness. **7. Captivity**] RV 'removing,' as in v. 4.

10. The prince] Zedekiah, the last king of Judah : see Intro. That *are* **among them**] Changing one letter we may render, 'that are in it.' **The prince .. shall go forth**] Zedekiah attempted to escape from Jerusalem towards the end of the siege, but was captured and brought to Nebuchadrezzar at Riblah. There his eyes were put out, and he was then taken to Babylon (2 K 25 4-7 Jer 39 4-7 52 7-11). **12. That he see not**] RV 'because he shall not see.' **16. I will leave a few**] This is really an explanation of the symbol in 5 3.

CHAPTERS 12 21-14 11
ON PROPHECY, TRUE AND FALSE

After rebuking certain prevalent forms of contempt for prophecy (12 21-28), Ezekiel reproves the false prophets (13 1-16) and false prophetesses (13 17-23) of Israel. A visit from the elders next supplies the occasion for an announcement of the principles on which God deals both with false enquirers and with the prophets who answer them (14 1-11).

(a) Contempt of Prophecy Rebuked (12 21-28)

This contempt took two forms. On the one hand it had become a common saying that prophecy was no longer fulfilled at all (v. 22), and on the other hand it was supposed by many that Ezekiel's prophecies, though true, referred to a very distant future (v. 27). In answer to both of these false views God said that His word would be fulfilled, and that without delay.

22. Ezekiel's message frequently takes the shape of a criticism of current proverbs, as in 11 3 12 25 18 2 20 32. **24. Vain vision . . flattering divination**] Forms of false prophecy, more fully exposed in c. 13. These had been unfulfilled, and this had led to contempt for all prophecy. But God's true word would no longer be confounded with such things.

25. Prolonged] RV 'deferred,' and so in v. 28.

(b) False Prophets Reproved (13 1-16)

False prophecy accompanied true prophecy in Israel like its shadow. While the true prophets spoke in God's name a message which they had really received from Him, the false prophets used God's name to sanction messages which He had not given them (vv. 6 7), which were merely the product of their own heart and spirit, and not the result of inspired insight (vv. 2, 3). These messages were smooth and agreeable (vv. 10, 17), but they were also vain, false, and seductive (vv. 6–10). They did not deserve the name of prophecy, but were on the same level as heathen divination (vv. 6, 7, 9). Ezekiel compares the false prophets first to foxes that burrow in ruins and make them more ruinous (vv. 4, 5), and next to men who daub with untempered mortar (or whitewash) a slim and tottering wall; the wall symbolising the vain attempts of the people to defend Jerusalem, and the mortar or whitewash the futile encouragement which the false prophets lent to these efforts. Such prophets would be blotted out of Israel (v. 9). The wall would be destroyed by the storm of God's wrath, and the daubers would perish along with it (vv. 11–15).

4. Deserts] RV 'waste places,' ruins.

5. Gaps] RM 'breaches.' **Hedge**] RV 'fence.' The false prophets did nothing to repair or strengthen Israel's defences. **6. That they would confirm the word**] RV 'that the word should be confirmed.' **9.** The false prophets would have no share in the restoration of Israel which Ezekiel foretold.

10. A wall] RM 'a slight wall,' the vain

defences of Jerusalem. **And one built, etc.**] RV 'and when one' (the people) 'buildeth up a wall, behold they' (the false prophets) 'daub it,' etc. **Untempered** *morter*] or whitewash. The false prophets could only give the wall a specious appearance of strength.

(c) False Prophetesses Denounced (13 17-23)

True prophecy was represented by women like Deborah, Huldah, and Noadiah, as well as by men, and false prophecy was also practised by women in Ezekiel's day. In their hands it was accompanied by various superstitious rites and ceremonies (v. 18), and seems to have been a species of fortune-telling. As such it might be popular and seem harmless, but it was mercenary, ensnaring, and fatal to souls (vv. 18, 19). It discouraged the righteous and encouraged the wicked (v. 22). These women would find their occupation gone (vv. 20, 21, 23).

18. Pillows] probably 'amulets,' supposed to have magical virtues. They were worn by the false prophetesses themselves (v. 20).

Armholes] RV 'elbows,' RM 'joints of the hands.' The amulets were worn in some way on the arms or wrists. **Kerchiefs**] or 'fillets.' These were apparently veils put over the heads of those consulting the false prophetesses, and were of different sizes to suit persons of different stature. **19. Will ye pollute**] RV 'ye have profaned.' **Handfuls of barley, etc.**] The fees received by the false prophetesses. **Die and live**] see on 3 18. This whole passage should be read in the light of the description of the true prophet's duty in 3 16-21. **20. To make** *them* **fly**] RM 'as birds.' **22.** The truth of prophecy may be judged by its moral tendency. Whatever encourages sin betrays itself as false: see Jer 23 22. **By promising him life**] RV 'and be saved alive.'

(d) On Insincere Enquirers and those who answer them (14 1-11)

The Jewish elders of Tel-abib again came to consult Ezekiel, evidently with idolatrous leanings in their hearts. God commanded him to speak a warning to all such enquirers, calling them to forsake idolatry, and threatening that God Himself would answer them by destroying them if they persisted in their sin. The prophet who should answer such people according to their desire would share their fate.

3. The stumblingblock, etc.] idolatry: see 7 19. **Should I be enquired of ?**] Such enquiry was a mockery of God. **4. That I may take, etc.**] Sin hardens the heart and so leads on to destruction. This is a self-acting law of divine retribution, and so in a sense the result is God's doing. But God does not seek to ensnare men. On the contrary, He pleads with them to forsake their evil way (v. 6).

9. When he hath spoken a thing] RV 'and speaketh a word.' A true prophet will not answer insincere enquirers at all, but will leave it to God to answer them by destruction (vv. 7, 8). To give any answer is to be a false prophet, deceived if not consciously deceiving. **I . . have deceived that prophet**] the same idea as that of the 'lying spirit' from the LORD by which Ahab's false prophets were inspired (1 K 22 19-23 2 Ch 18 18-22). The meaning can only be that the deception is the penalty of previous disloyalty to truth. No man becomes a false prophet without blame on his own part. To lend oneself to the purposes of insincere enquirers reveals a certain share of their spirit, which leads naturally to increasing blindness. As this law is of God's appointment the deception is in a certain sense His work. The OT. writers emphasised God's supreme control of all events, and were not troubled by the questions which may be raised as to the bearing of the events on the moral character of God. Hence they were not careful to avoid expressions which appear startling to us. **10. The punishment of their iniquity**] RV 'their iniquity.' **Punishment . . punishment**] RV 'iniquity . . iniquity.'

CHAPTER 14 12-23
A DIVINE PRINCIPLE AND AN APPARENT EXCEPTION

As a rule when God punishes a land for its wickedness by such judgments as famine, wild beasts, sword, or pestilence, the presence in it of the most eminently righteous men will not save the wicked, not even the members of their own families. They will only escape themselves. Jerusalem will be a seeming exception to this principle, since a remnant of its wicked sons and daughters will be spared when the city is taken, and will escape into exile. But this is in order that the earlier exiles, seeing the abandoned conduct of the later, may realise how thoroughly Jerusalem has deserved its punishment, and may cease to regret its fate.

13. The land] RV 'a land.' Vv. 13–21 suppose a series of general cases. **Then will I stretch, etc.**] RV 'and I stretch . . and break . . and send . . and cut off.' All this is part of the supposition. **14, 20. Noah, Daniel, and Job**] Typical righteous men, like Moses and Samuel in Jer 15 1.

21, 22. It might be expected that none of the wicked in Jerusalem would be spared, yet, in apparent violation of the law just described, some of them would escape and go into exile. **22. Ye shall see . . and be comforted**] The exiles of the first captivity would be distressed at the fate of Jerusalem, but the conduct of the survivors would convince them that it had been well deserved, and was not to be regretted.

CHAPTER 15
EZEKIEL'S PARABLE OF THE VINE

Jerusalem and Israel are compared elsewhere in Scripture to a cultivated vine, bearing or expected to bear fruit. Ezekiel's similitude, however, is that of the wild vine (v. 2, RV), regarded simply as a tree. It is the most worthless of trees. Its wood is of no use for any purpose, being too weak even to make a peg of. A vine branch that happens to be half-burnt is even more worthless than it was before. Jerusalem is such a half-burnt vine, already charred by the first captivity. It is only fit for fuel, and will be wholly consumed.

2. *Or than* **a branch**] RV 'the vine branch.'
7. From *one* **fire, and** *another* **fire**] RV 'from the fire, but the fire.' Jerusalem has survived one captivity, but will be overtaken by a second and final disaster.

CHAPTER 16
THE FOUNDLING CHILD WHO BECAME AN UNFAITHFUL WIFE

From Hosea onwards the prophets spoke of idolatry under the figure of unchastity. God was the husband of Israel, but she proved unfaithful to Him. This thought has already been expressed by Ezekiel in 6 9, and it is now expanded into an elaborate historical allegory. The subject is nominally the city of Jerusalem, but really the whole nation of Israel. Jerusalem was a girl-child of heathen extraction, who was exposed in infancy to die (vv. 1–5). God saw her and saved her life, and she grew to maturity, though still in a poor and mean condition (vv. 6, 7). Then He took her to be His wife, loading her with every honour (vv. 8–14). But she was disloyal to Him, admitting idols as her lovers at the high places, and lavishing on them the gifts God had bestowed upon her (vv. 15–19). She even sacrificed to them her own children whom she had borne to God (vv. 20, 21). By borrowing the idolatries of the surrounding nations, Egypt, Assyria and Babylonia, she made them all her paramours, with every aggravation of guilt (vv. 23–34). Her sin had already brought reproach upon her from hostile neighbours like the Philistines (v. 27), but she had proved incorrigible and must now suffer utter humiliation and destruction (vv. 35–43). Men would speak of her as the true daughter of her parents, the true sister of Samaria and Sodom, whose guilt had been less than hers, though she had despised them in her pride (vv. 44–52). Her humiliation would be completed by her being put on a level with them, and sharing the mercy extended to them (vv. 53–59). Nevertheless God would not forget His love for her, but would pity and restore her, giving her Samaria and Sodom for daughters instead of sisters. Humbled, ashamed, and forgiven, she would know at last the true character of God (vv. 60–63).

3. Thy birth, etc.] Though the allegory deals with the history of Israel as a nation it begins by tracing the origin of Jerusalem. It was a Canaanite city, inhabited by Jebusites, long before it became the capital of God's kingdom. Josh 15 63 Jg 1 21 19 11 2 S 5 6-8.

Amorite] a general name for some of the tribes originally inhabiting Canaan : cp. Gn 15 16 Dt 20 17. **Hittite**] The Hittites, or children of Heth, were another portion of the original inhabitants of Canaan : cp. Gn 10 15 Nu 13 29. Another branch of the Hittites had a powerful empire to the N. of Palestine (Josh 1 4 Jg 1 26).

7. Thou hast increased, etc.] RV 'thou didst increase,' etc. The past tense should be read throughout the verse. **Whereas**] RV 'yet.'

8. A covenant] a marriage covenant, probably with reference to the covenant at Sinai.

10. Badgers' skin] RV 'sealskin,' probably the skin of the dugong, an herbivorous cetacean found in the Red Sea. **12. A jewel on thy forehead**] RV 'a ring upon thy nose' : see Isa 3 21.

16. High places] the seats of ancient Canaanite worship, retained by the Israelites for the worship of the true God, but perverted to their old uses : see 6 3, 6, 13. **20, 21.** Human sacrifice was not unknown in early Israel : see on Gn 22 1-14 Jg 11 30-40, and was introduced in later times by Ahaz (2 K 16 3 2 Ch 28 3) and Manasseh (2 K 21 6 2 Ch 33 6). It was also practised in the northern kingdom (2 K 17 17).

24, 25. Besides the high places throughout the land, idolatrous shrines were established in the streets of Jerusalem. **27.** Israel suffered from the Philistines both in the days of the Judges and the early kings, and in later times (2 Ch 28 18).

29. In the land of Canaan, etc.] RM 'unto the land of traffic,' etc. See 17 4.

38. As women .. are judged] see Lv 20 10 Dt 22 22 Jn 8 5. **41. Many women**] the neighbouring nations. **45. Your mother .. your father**] The plural pronoun refers to the three sisters. **46. Samaria**] the capital of the kingdom of the Ten Tribes, standing for the whole of that kingdom. **Left hand .. right hand** mean north and south respectively : see 10 3.

Elder .. younger] refer not to historical antiquity but to importance. **57. Syria**] Heb. 'Aram.' We may change one letter and read 'Edom.' The Edomites exulted over the fall of Jerusalem (Obad vv. 10–14 Ps 137 7). The Philistines seem to have done the same. Both nations are denounced in similar terms in 25 12-17.

61. Not by thy covenant] The new relation of Jerusalem to Samaria and Sodom would not depend on anything in the past, but would be a fresh arrangement of God's grace.

CHAPTER 17
Zedekiah's Perfidy and its Punishment

Zedekiah had been placed on the throne of Judah as a vassal of Babylon, but was led by his nobles to intrigue with Egypt and to throw off the Babylonian yoke. The revolt actually took place in 588 B.C., but it had been contemplated much earlier : see Jer 27 1-11, where 'Zedekiah' should be read for 'Jehoiakim' in v. 1. V. 15 of this c. refers to an embassy to Egypt, of which Ezekiel had heard in Babylonia. The prophet exposes this rebellious policy in an allegory, condemns it, and predicts its failure and punishment. The royal house of Judah is a cedar of Lebanon. Babylon (or Nebuchadrezzar) is an eagle, which crops off the highest twig of the cedar (Jehoiachin) and carries it to a land and city of commerce (Babylon). The eagle takes of the seed of the land (Zedekiah) and plants it so that it becomes a dwarf vine bending towards the eagle (subordinate to Babylon). There is another eagle (Egypt, or Pharaoh-Hophra) towards which the vine (Zedekiah) turns (seeking Egyptian instead of Babylonian overlordship). God will not allow such treachery to prosper. The vine will be uprooted. Egyptian help will fail. Zedekiah will be taken captive and will die in Babylon (vv. 1–21).

But God Himself will take another twig of the cedar, and will plant it on a high mountain of Israel, where it will become a great, spreading, and fruitful tree. All the trees (nations) will learn that God directs the destinies of every one of them (vv. 22–24). This is a prophecy of the restoration of the Jewish kingdom which was never literally fulfilled, but which contains a promise of the Messiah— the ideal future king.

5, 6. A willow .. a vine of low stature] indicating the dependent position of Zedekiah's kingdom : see v. 14. **12, 13.** These vv. describe the captivity of Jehoiachin (597 B.C.) and the appointment of Zedekiah as king under a solemn oath of allegiance to Babylon.

17. The Egyptians succeeded in raising the siege of Jerusalem (Jer 37 11), but the relief was only temporary, as Jeremiah foretold that it would be (37 6-10). **19.** Zedekiah had sworn allegiance to Nebuchadrezzar in God's name. His revolt against Babylon, therefore, did dishonour to God. For another example of Zedekiah's perfidy see Jer 34 8-11. **20, 21.** A repetition of 12 13, 14.

22–24. Ezekiel expected that the restored kingdom of God would have a prince (45 7, 8 46 1-18 47 21, 22). This was only fulfilled in a Messianic sense.

CHAPTER 18
GOD'S EQUITY VINDICATED

The popular view of Israel's calamities, as expressed in a current proverb, was that they were the punishment of the sins of former generations. Though there was a measure of truth in this, the proverb was used in a false and mischievous sense. It led the present generation to ignore their own sin, to doubt the justice of God's providence, to despair of escape from the working of a blind fate. Ezekiel, consequently, emphasised in the strongest way the truths of individual responsibility, and of God's impartiality in dealing with every man according to his own character (vv. 1–4). If a man is righteous he shall live (vv. 5–9). If a righteous man has a wicked son, the son will not be saved by his father's righteousness, but will die (vv. 10–13). If this wicked man, in turn, has a righteous son, the latter will not die for his father's sin, but will live (vv. 14–18). Further, a wicked man who repents and becomes righteous will live (vv. 21, 22, 27, 28), and a righteous man who becomes wicked will die (vv. 24, 26). All this is unquestionably just, and God does not wish any to die, but appeals to all to forsake sin and live (vv. 19, 20, 23, 25, 29–32). This c. recalls 3 17-21, and the teaching of both passages is repeated in 33 1-20.

2. The fathers, etc.] The same proverb is quoted and refuted in Jer 31 29, 30. **4. All souls are mine**] God deals directly with every one, and not with the son through the father.

It shall die] 'Die' and 'live' are used in the sense explained under 3 18. **6. Eaten upon the mountains**] shared in an idolatrous meal at a high place. **7. Restored .. his pledge**] see Ex 22 6 Dt 24 12. **22. Mentioned unto**] RV 'remembered against': so in v. 24.

24. Ezekiel does not raise the question whether a truly righteous man could thus fall away. He assumes that a man's final conduct expresses his real and final character.

CHAPTER 19
A LAMENT FOR THE ROYAL HOUSE OF JUDAH

This c. is a poem in which the measure used for a dirge or elegy is more or less traceable throughout. It describes first a lioness, two of whose whelps are successively caught and taken away from her (vv. 1–9), and next a vine with lofty branches, which is ruined by a fire proceeding from one of them (vv. 10–14). There is no doubt that the branch from which destruction spreads to the vine is Zedekiah. The vine itself may be the nation of Israel, or the royal house, or the mother of Zedekiah. There are two interpretations of the first allegory. The lioness is usually understood to be

the nation or the royal family in general, and the two whelps to be Shallum and Jehoiachin. But some take the lioness to be Hamutal, one of the wives of Josiah, and the whelps to be her two sons, Shallum and Zedekiah.

2. Thy mother] Hamutal, whom some suppose to be meant here, was one of the wives of Josiah, and the mother of Shallum (or Jehoahaz) and Zedekiah (2 K 23 31 24 18). Jehoiakim, the other son of Josiah who became king, had a different mother (2 K 23 36).

3, 4. One of her whelps, etc.] Jehoahaz, or Shallum, the youngest son of Josiah (1 Ch 3 15), was set on the throne by the people after his father's death, but after reigning three months he was deposed and carried away captive to Egypt by Pharaoh-Necho (2 K 23 30-34 2 Ch 36 1-4). His fate is lamented in Jer 22 10-12.

5–9. Another of her whelps, etc.] Either Jehoiachin or Zedekiah. Jehoiachin was a grandson of Josiah, who came to the throne as a youth and was carried captive to Babylon in 597 B.C. after a reign of three months (2 K 24 8-16 2 Ch 36 9, 10). Zedekiah, the last king of Judah, was a son of Josiah and Hamutal. He succeeded his nephew Jehoiachin, and was carried captive to Babylon in 586 B.C. : see Intro. The high terms in which the second whelp is spoken of do not agree well with Ezekiel's estimate of Zedekiah in c. 17.

9. In ward in chains] RV 'in a cage with hooks.' Lion cages are represented on the monuments. **10. Thy mother**] The language in this allegory is much more applicable to the nation than to Hamutal. **In thy blood**] a meaningless phrase. Perhaps we should read with RM 'in thy likeness.' **11. Strong rods for the sceptres**] a double figure. The rods represent both the kings and their sceptres.

12, 13. These vv. describe the final destruction and captivity of Judah. **14. Out of a rod,** etc.] Zedekiah's rebellion was the cause of the ruin of the nation.

§ 5. A FINAL SERIES OF PROPHECIES ON THE NECESSITY OF ISRAEL'S PUNISHMENT AND THE DESTRUCTION OF JERUSALEM (chs. 20–24) Date, Aug.-Sept. 590 B.C. to Jan.-Feb. 587 B.C.

This group includes a warning to the exiles against idolatry (20 1-44), a description of the sword of the Lord directed against Jerusalem (20 45–21 27), a short prophecy against the Ammonites, connected with the foregoing (21 28-32), an indictment of Jerusalem (c. 22), an allegorical history of the sins of Samaria and Jerusalem (c. 23), a fresh parable of the coming siege and destruction of Jerusalem (24 1-14), and an account of the death of Ezekiel's wife, and of his significant conduct in his bereavement (24 15-27).

CHAPTER 20 1-44

HISTORY REPEATING ITSELF

Some four years before the fall of Jerusalem the elders of Tel-abib again came to consult Ezekiel, who declared that God had no answer to give them. The reason was that their enquiry was insincere, and this passage is consequently an illustration of the principle of 14 3. The exiles were beginning to avow idolatrous tendencies (v. 32), with which the elders were in secret sympathy. Ezekiel recounted how God had dealt with Israel's idolatrous spirit in the past, and announced that He would deal in the same way with those who still cherished it.

Israel had been idolatrous in Egypt and yet had been brought forth (vv. 5-12). Successive generations had been idolatrous in the wilderness, and of these the first had been shut out of the Promised Land, while the second had been brought into it under a warning of exile and dispersion should they continue unfaithful (vv. 13-26). They had not heeded the warning, but had adopted the worship of the Canaanites, and God's threat had now been fulfilled (vv. 27-29). In all this course of mercy and judgment God had 'wrought for His name's sake,' that His character might be truly known to Israel and to the world.

The present exiles were no better than their fathers. They too were resolving to be like the heathen (vv. 30-32). But God would frustrate their purpose. He would bring them also into a wilderness, and would deal with them there as He had dealt with those who came out of Egypt (vv. 33-36). The persistent sinners among them would not enter the land of Israel, but the others would again be brought into a covenant with God, and restored to their own country, where they would worship God acceptably in humble penitence (vv. 37-43). In all this God would act from the same great motive as before (v. 44).

1. The seventh year .. the fifth *month*] July-August, 590 B.C.   **5. Lifted up mine hand**] i.e. sware, and so in vv. 6, 15, 23, 42.   **8.** Ezekiel speaks more definitely than any other OT. writer about the idolatry of the Israelites in Egypt: see 23 8.   **9. For my name's sake**] God's consistent motive was that His character should be known to the world. When He was patient with Israel it was because sudden judgment upon them would have been misunderstood by the heathen: see v. 22.   **11.** Referring to the Law given at Sinai.   **12. My sabbaths, to be a sign**] Though Ezekiel attached great importance to the sabbath, he regarded it not as one of the moral

ordinances, obedience to which brings life (v. 11), but rather as a special sign of God's covenant which Israel was bound to observe.

15. The first generation in the wilderness was shut out of Canaan (Nu 14 24-30 Ps 95 11).   **23.** The second generation was warned that unfaithfulness would be punished by captivity (Lv 26 33, 34).   **25. Statutes** *that were* **not good**] The reference (as v. 26 shows) is to the practice of child sacrifice, which might seem to be justified by such a law as that in Ex 22 29. The firstborn of men, however, were expressly excepted (Ex 13 12,13 Nu 3 46,47), and Jeremiah declared that human sacrifice had never been commanded by God (Jer 7 31 19 5). God did not impose sinful laws, but some of His laws could be perverted by sinful men and made an excuse for their wrongdoing. Both the ambiguity of the Law and the blindness which led to the misunderstanding of it were the penalty for previous sin.   **29.** A play upon words, 'What (*mah*) .. go (*ba*)?' **Bamah** is the Hebrew for 'high place,' and by this punning derivation of the word (not of course the true one) Ezekiel expresses his contempt for the thing itself.   **32.** God's zeal for His name is stronger even than the purpose of the human will to rebel.   **34. People**] RV 'peoples': so in vv. 35, 41.   **35. Wilderness of the people**] the desert between Babylon and Palestine, corresponding to the desert between Egypt and Palestine which had been the scene of Israel's former discipline.   **37. The rod**] the shepherd's rod, used in counting the flock (Lv 27 32). **The bond of the covenant**] The old covenant made at Sinai will be renewed. Ezekiel does not contemplate such a difference between the past and the future as is expressed in Jeremiah's prophecy of the New Covenant (Jer 31 32).   **38.** Obstinate transgressors will perish in the wilderness like the first generation who came out of Egypt. **39. Pollute ye .. no more**] RV 'My holy name shall ye profane no more.' Those who wished to choose idolatry might do so, but they would no longer have any connexion with God and His cause. **40. In the land, serve me**] RV 'serve me in the land,' a promise of restoration.

44. When God does not deal with men as they deserve, it is for the sake of His own glory. This really means that His mercy is the highest aspect of His character, and that which He is most desirous to display to the world.

CHAPTERS 20 45-49, 21

THE SWORD OF THE LORD AGAINST JERUSALEM (AND AMMON?)

C. 21 of the Hebrew Bible begins with 20 45 of the English. It is mainly concerned with Jerusalem (20 45-21 27), but has an appendix consisting of a short prophecy about Ammon, which has been interpreted in different ways (21 28-32).

(a) Against Jerusalem (20 45–21 27)

An enigmatic parable of a forest fire in the S. (20 45-49) is explained as referring to the land of Israel, against which God's sword is drawn (21 1-5). Ezekiel's distress at the announcement is a sign of the dismay which all will feel when it comes to pass (vv. 6, 7). A 'Song of the Sword' follows (vv. 8–17). Next comes a picture of Nebuchadrezzar halting on his march on Palestine, and consulting his oracles as to whether Jerusalem or Ammon should be attacked first. The omens decide for Jerusalem, which is doomed to capture, though its people make light of the heathen oracles (vv. 18–24). The prophecy ends with a denunciation of Zedekiah, and a hint of the future ideal king (vv. 25–27).

46, 47. Field .. forest of the south] Palestine lay almost due W. of Babylon, but the way between them took a circuit N. owing to the desert, and to one coming from Babylon, Palestine lay directly S. in the last stages of the journey.

CHAPTER 21

3, 4. The righteous and the wicked] corresponding to the green tree and the dry in the parable (20 47). In spite of his strict theory of retribution in c. 18, Ezekiel recognised the fact that good men as well as bad would perish in the siege of Jerusalem.

10. It contemneth, etc.] RV 'The rod of my son, it contemneth every tree.' These words are almost hopelessly obscure, and the text is probably corrupt. As it stands, the meaning may be (a) that the rod (the sword) with which God chastises His son (the king or people of Israel) is more severe than any mere rod of wood (any previous chastisement), or (b) that the king of Judah (the rod or sceptre of my son) despises all other powers (every other rod or tree).

12. Cry .. howl .. smite] tokens of Ezekiel's excited sympathy with God's justice. **Terrors .. upon my people]** RV 'they '(the princes) 'are delivered over to the sword with my people.'

13. What if *the sword* **contemn even the rod ?]** equally obscure with v. 10. RV 'what if even the rod that contemneth shall be no more ?' What if Judah in its pride shall be destroyed ?

14. Smite, etc.] another gesture of excited sympathy. **Doubled the third time]** rather, 'doubled and trebled ' in its destructive power. **Slain]** RV 'deadly wounded.' **The great** *men that are* **slain]** RV 'the great one that is deadly wounded'—Zedekiah. **15. Point]** RM 'consternation.' **Ruins]** RV 'stumblings.'

Wrapped up] RV 'pointed.' **17. I will also smite]** God also exults in His judgment.

His sternest justice is a true expression of Himself.

Cause .. to rest] RV 'satisfy.'

19. Choose thou (RV 'mark out') a place] rather, 'grave a hand,' i.e. a sign-post. Nebuchadrezzar is imagined as halting at some point where the roads to Jerusalem and Rabbah (the capital of Ammon) diverge, and as consulting his oracles as to which way he shall take.

20. In Jerusalem] rather, 'unto Jerusalem.' **21. He made** *his* **arrows bright]** RV 'He shook the arrows to and fro.' Two arrows, inscribed with the names of the two cities, were put into a bag and shaken, and then one was drawn out. **With images]** RV 'the teraphim,' the portable images of the gods whose advice was sought. **Looked in the liver]** another ceremony of divination. The liver would be that of the animal sacrificed on the occasion, and an omen would be drawn from its shape or colour.

22. At his right hand] RV 'In his right hand. Nebuchadrezzar drew the arrow marked 'Jerusalem.' **23. The people of Jerusalem would make light of Nebuchadrezzar's omens.

That have sworn oaths] This may refer to the broken oaths of allegiance to Babylon (see 17 13-16), or perhaps to the covenant to free their slaves which the people of Jerusalem made in Zedekiah's reign (34 8-10), and which may have led them into self-righteous confidence.

25. Profane wicked] RV 'O deadly wounded wicked one.' Zedekiah is addressed.

27. Until he come] the future ideal king.

(b) Concerning Ammon (vv. 28–32)

The Ammonites were a nation E. of the Jordan, and descended from Lot (Gn 19 38). They had joined in the league against Nebuchadrezzar (Jer 27 3), and had reason to fear his vengeance (v. 20 above). But they seem to have thought they would escape, and to have indulged in reproach, and even hostility, against Judah. Ezekiel foretells their certain punishment. For another prophecy against Ammon see 25 1-7.

28. The sword .. is drawn] most naturally understood to be the sword of the LORD against Ammon, as against Jerusalem in v. 9. But others take it to be the sword which Ammon drew against Jerusalem : see on v. 30.

29. They see vanity] The Ammonites were misled by false prophets. *Them that are* **slain, of the wicked]** RV 'The wicked that are deadly wounded '—the people of Jerusalem (v. 14).

30. Shall I cause *it*] RV 'cause it.' As it stands this is a command to Ammon to sheathe the sword, and hence the sword in v. 28 is generally understood to be theirs. But the prophecy is so closely parallel otherwise to the preceding one that it is probable that the text in v. 30 is corrupt, and that the sword in

v. 28 is the LORD'S. **31. Brutish men**] most naturally understood of the Babylonians, but see 25⁴.

CHAPTER 22

ANOTHER INDICTMENT OF JERUSALEM

The various religious and social evils that prevail in the city are recited (vv. 1–11). Their coming punishment is then predicted, first in direct terms (vv. 13–16), and next under the figure of a smelting furnace (vv. 17–22). Lastly, all classes in Jerusalem, prophets, priests, princes, and people, are included in the general condemnation (vv. 23–31).

2. The bloody city] referring to those unjustly put to death by the wicked rulers of Jerusalem : so in vv. 3, 6, 12, 27 ; see also 11⁶. **5. Much vexed**] RV ' full of tumult.'

6. To their power] RV 'according to his power.' **13. I have smitten mine hand**] God's gesture of indignation. **16. Take thine inheritance**] RV 'be profaned.' **18. Dross**] the baser metals from which silver has to be purified.

19–22. Jerusalem will be heated like a furnace for smelting silver, and all that it contains will be melted in the fire of God's wrath. Though silver is mentioned in vv. 20, 22, it is not suggested that any of the precious metal will be left after the refining process. The whole nation is ' dross.'

24. Not rained upon] not blessed with fertilising showers. **28, 3c.** The same figures as in 13⁵,¹⁰⁻¹⁵.

CHAPTER 23

THE UNCHASTE SISTERS, OHOLAH AND OHOLIBAH

The idolatries and foreign alliances of Jerusalem and Samaria are here described under the same strong figure which is used in c. 16. Oholah (Samaria) and Oholibah (Jerusalem) were two sisters, both seduced in Egypt in their youth (v. 3), both espoused by God (v. 4), and both unfaithful to Him. Samaria took as her lovers first the Assyrians (vv. 5–7), and then the Egyptians (v. 8), and was at length slain by the former (vv. 9, 10). Jerusalem, not warned by her sister's fate, made first the Assyrians and then the Babylonians her paramours (vv. 11–16). Being alienated from the latter she has turned to her early lovers of Egypt (vv. 17–21), but she will be destroyed, like her sister, by the lovers whom she has just forsaken (vv. 22–35). The sin and judgment of the two sisters are described afresh (vv. 36–49).

3. Another instance of Ezekiel's belief that Israel practised idolatry in Egypt : see 20⁸. Of course the distinction between the two branches of the nation does not really go back so far.

4. Aholah . Aholibah] RV 'Oholah .. Oho-

libah.' The words perhaps mean ' her tent' and ' my tent in her,' respectively. It was an Eastern custom to give similar names to members of the same family. **Samaria**] stands for the kingdom of the Ten Tribes, of which it was the capital. Oholah is called the elder sister, probably because the northern kingdom was the larger and stronger of the two. **Were mine**] RV ' became mine,' in marriage.

5. The Assyrians] In 2 K 15¹⁷⁻²⁰ we read that the northern kingdom became tributary to Assyria in the reign of Menahem. But the Assyrian monuments show that this subjection began as early as the reign of Jehu.

8. Egypt] The northern kingdom wavered for a time between an Assyrian and an Egyptian policy (Hos 7¹¹). Its last king, Hoshea, revolted against Assyria and allied himself with Egypt (2 K 17⁴). This was the cause of the destruction of his kingdom.

12. The Assyrians] The southern kingdom made alliance with Assyria in the days of Ahaz, who eagerly introduced foreign idolatries (2 K 16⁷ᶠ·). Except in the reign of Hezekiah the Assyrian overlordship continued till that of Babylon took its place. These political relations were accompanied by religious defections. **14. Images of the Chaldeans**] Such pictures were common on the walls of Babylonian palaces. Ezekiel imagines them as being seen in Jerusalem, and as awakening the nation's desire for these unknown lovers. **17. Her mind** (RV ' soul ') **was alienated**] Judah under Jehoiakim (2 K 24¹) and Zedekiah (2 K 24²⁰) became weary of Babylonian supremacy.

19. Egypt] Like Samaria, Jerusalem went back to her first seducers. Intrigues with Egypt were frequent from the days of Hezekiah onwards (Isa 30³¹), and it was trust in Egypt which led to Zedekiah's revolt and the nation's fall : see 17⁷.

23. Pekod .. Shoa .. Koa] Eastern peoples tributary to Babylon. They are all mentioned in the inscriptions. **The Assyrians**] These now formed part of the Babylonian Empire.

34. Pluck off] RV 'tear.'

39. Human sacrifice was combined with the forms of God's worship. This only aggravated its guilt. **42. Sabeans**] RV 'drunkards.'

45. The righteous men] The allegory carries out the forms of justice observed in an Israelite city, but we need not look for a counterpart to the righteous men in the actual history.

CHAPTER 24

THE ALLEGORY OF THE BOILING CALDRON. EZEKIEL'S BEREAVEMENT AND SIGNIFICANT SILENCE

This prophecy is dated on the day on which the siege of Jerusalem began. Ezekiel is commanded by God to note the date, and to speak to the exiles a final parable of the city's coming fate. Jerusalem is a rusty pot filled with water and meat and set upon a fire. The meat is well boiled, and brought out piece by piece at random. The empty pot is then set back on the fire that the rust may be burned away. The rust denotes Jerusalem's impurity and bloodshed. The boiling is the siege, and the emptying of the pot the captivity. The heating of the empty pot symbolises the burning of the city at the end of the siege (vv. 1–14).

Ezekiel spoke this message in the morning, and his wife died on the evening of the same day, but in obedience to a divine command he indulged in no sign of mourning. His silent sorrow was an emblem of the stupor into which the exiles would be cast when they should hear of the fall of Jerusalem. When the survivors of the siege should reach Babylonia, however, Ezekiel's silence would be at an end (vv. 15–27).

1. The ninth year .. the tenth month] January-February, 587 B.C. For the date see 2 K 25¹ Jer 39¹ 52⁴. **3.** Pot] RV 'caldron': so in v. 6. **5.** Burn

.. the bones, etc.] We must read either with RV 'pile .. the bones under it' (the flesh), or, 'burn .. the wood under it' (the caldron). The bones were in the pot, not below it. **6.** Scum] RV 'rust': so in vv. 11, 12. Let no lot fall] The meat was to be taken out indiscriminately. **7.** The top of a rock] RV 'the bare rock.' Jerusalem's bloodshed was open and unconcealed. **8.** I have set] What was mere shameless wickedness on Jerusalem's part was yet the working out of God's purpose of judgment. **10.** Kindle] RV 'make hot.' Consume] RV 'boil well.' Spice it well] RV 'make thick the broth.' Burned] not in the fire, but singed in the pot by the intense heat of the cooking. **12.** With lies, and] RV 'with toil, yet.' **13.** Caused .. to rest] RV 'satisfied.'

17. Loosening the head-dress, baring the feet, and covering the lips, were signs of mourning (Lv 10⁶ 2 S 15³⁰). **22.** The bread of men] probably food offered by sympathising friends. See Jer 16⁷ (RV). **23.** Pine .. mourn (RV 'moan')] The sorrow of the exiles for the fate of Jerusalem would be tearless and inarticulate, like Ezekiel's sorrow for his wife. **27.** See 33²².

PART 2 (Chs. 25–32)

PROPHECIES AGAINST FOREIGN NATIONS

These chs. come between those which deal with the overthrow of the Old Israel (1–24) and those which describe the establishment of the New Israel (33–48), and they form an introduction to the latter group. Their significance is well explained in 28²⁴⁻²⁶. The fall of Jerusalem seemed to be a victory of heathendom over the people of the true God, and it was needful to show that it was not so. The God of Israel who had visited His people with this punishment would send His judgments on the heathen nations also, and would convince them that He was the living God. The humiliation of these nations would clear the stage for the restoration of Israel, which would no longer be troubled by its formerly hostile neighbours. These prophecies fall into three groups : (1) against the lesser and nearer nations, Ammon, Moab, Edom, and the Philistines (c. 25), (2) against Tyre and Sidon (chs. 26–28), (3) against Egypt (chs. 29–32). With the exception of 29¹⁷⁻²¹, these prophecies are mostly dated in years either just before or just after the capture of Jerusalem.

§ 1. Ammon, Moab, Edom, and Philistia

CHAPTER 25

These four nations were the neighbours of Israel on the E., SE., and SW. respectively, and are dealt with in their geographical order.

Ammon and Moab are denounced for their exultation at the fall of Jerusalem, Edom and Philistia for their revengeful share in Israel's humiliation. All of them are threatened with destruction from God. The instruments of the judgment are to be the Bedouins of the desert in the case of Ammon and Moab, and Israel in the case of Edom. The destroyers of the Philistines are not indicated.

1–7. Ammon.
For the Ammonites see on 21²⁸. In addition it may be observed that the king of Ammon was a party to the plot against Gedaliah, the governor whom Nebuchadrezzar left in Palestine after the capture of Jerusalem (Jer 40¹⁴ 41¹⁰,¹⁵). See Intro. **3.** The destruction of Jerusalem has taken place. The Ammonites have rejoiced at Israel's calamity. V. 6 speaks of their gestures of triumph. **4.** Men of the east] the Bedouins of the desert : so in v. 10. Palaces] RV 'encampments.' **5.** Rabbah] the capital of Ammon.

8–11. Moab.
The Moabites, like the Ammonites, were descended from Lot (Gn 19³⁷). Their country lay E. of the Dead Sea, and S. of Ammon, the Arnon being the boundary. They were at times subject to Israel and at times independent, but always hostile. **8.** And Seir] These words should be omitted. Edom (Seir) is dealt with separately

below. **Behold,** etc.] The Moabites denied Israel's claim to be the people of the true God. **Heathen]** RV 'nations.' **9. Side]** RM 'shoulder,' i.e. frontier. **Beth-jeshimoth, Baal-meon, Kiriathaim]** three frontier cities of Moab : see Nu 33 49 Josh 12 3 13 17,19,20. The last two were in the territory of Reuben (Nu 32 37,38).

12-14. Edom.

The Edomites were descended from Esau (Gn 36 43). They showed a specially unbrotherly spirit when Jerusalem fell : see Ps 137 7 Lam 4 21,22 Obad vv. 11-16.

13. Teman] a grandson of Esau (Gn 36 11). Also a town or district of Edom (Jer 49 7,20 Am 1 11 Obad v. 9). **And they of Dedan]** RV 'even unto Dedan.' Dedan was a district of N. Arabia, and is mentioned here as the southern border of Edom, Teman being presumably the northern extremity : see Gn 10 7 25 3 Isa 21 13 Jer 25 23.

15-17. Philistia.

The Philistines dwelt on the coast, SW. of Palestine. They were oppressors of Israel in early times, but were vanquished by David. They sought every opportunity of annoying Israel afterwards (2 Ch 21 16 26 7 28 18), and they seem to have joined with Edom in embittering the fate of Jerusalem : see 16 57.

15. For the old hatred] RV 'with perpetual enmity.' **16. Cherethims]** RV 'Cherethites,' a Philistine tribe (1 S 30 14 Zeph 2 5) from which David's body-guard was partly drawn (2 S 8 18 15 18 20 7 1 K 1 38, etc.).

§ 2. TYRE (AND SIDON) (chs. 26-28)

Tyre was the capital of Phœnicia, the seaboard country on the NW. of Palestine. The Phœnicians were the great mariners of the ancient world, and Tyre was a famous seaport, renowned for its wealth and splendour. It joined in the league against Nebuchadrezzar, and was besieged by him for thirteen years (597-584 B.C.). See Intro. Ezekiel predicts its overthrow in three prophecies, one in general terms (c. 26), one describing Tyre under the figure of a gallant ship (c. 27), and one directed specially against the king of Tyre (28 1-19). Zidon (or Sidon) was another Phœnician sea-port, about 20 m. N. of Tyre, which was its younger rival. It also joined in the league against Babylon (Jer 27 3), and its downfall too is predicted by Ezekiel (28 20-26). Part of the language of these chs. is reproduced in Rev 18.

CHAPTER 26

THE FALL OF TYRE PREDICTED

The desolation of Tyre is announced (vv. 1-6), its siege by Nebuchadrezzar is vividly described (vv. 7-14), a lamentation for its fall is put into the mouths of the princes of the sea (vv. 15-18),

and God's threat of judgment is again repeated (vv. 19-21).

1. The eleventh year] 586 B.C. The month is not given, but the date must have been after the destruction of Jerusalem, in the fifth month of that year (2 K 25 8) : see v. 2. **2. Tyrus]** RV 'Tyre,' and so throughout chs. 26-28. **Aha,** etc.] Tyre had rejoiced because of the commercial advantage she would reap from the fall of Jerusalem. **Gates of the people]** RV 'gate of the peoples.' Jerusalem lay near the highway of traffic which led northward to Tyre, and its fall would remove a barrier to Tyrian trade.

4. Like the top of a rock] RV 'a bare rock' : so in v. 14. **6. Her daughters]** tributary states or cities. **15. Isles]** the maritime countries of the Mediterranean. **16. Princes of the sea]** the rulers of these sea-board lands. **20.** Tyre is personified, and represented as going down into the under-world of the dead : see 31 14-18 32 18-32. **And I shall set glory]** perhaps we should read, with LXX, 'nor arise.'

CHAPTER 27

THE WRECK OF THE GALLANT SHIP

Under the figure of a ship, splendidly equipped, fully manned, and richly laden, but steered into stormy waters and wrecked, Ezekiel describes the fall of Tyre. In vv. 10-20 the figure is partly dropped.

3. People] RV 'peoples'; and so everywhere. **5. Senir]** Mt. Hermon (Dt 3 9). **6. The company of the Ashurites .. ivory]** RV 'they have made thy benches of ivory inlaid in boxwood.' The 'teasshur' (mistaken in AV for **Ashurites** or Assyrians) was a species of tree (probably box or cypress) found in Lebanon, and mentioned in Isa 41 19 60 13. **Chittim]** Cyprus.

7. Elishah] mentioned in Gn 10 4 along with Javan (Ionia), was some Mediterranean country, perhaps the Peloponnesus (Morea), which was famous for purple dye. **8. Arvad]** a Canaanite city (Gn 10 18 1 Ch 1 16) built on an island (Ruwād) 2 m. off the Syrian coast and nearly 100 m. N. of Tyre.

9. Gebal] a coast town some 50 m. N. of Tyre, the classical Byblos : see Josh 13 5 1 K 5 18(RV). **Occupy]** RM 'exchange.' This is the old meaning of the word, which is regularly used in this sense in the Bible : see Lk 19 13.

10. Lud and .. Phut] Ludim appears in Gn 10 13 as the eldest son of Mizraim (Egypt), and Phut in Gn 10 6 as a son of Ham and brother of Mizraim. Both nations are mentioned as allies of Egypt in 30 5 (RV). They were probably N. African peoples. **11. Gammadim]** a word of unknown reference. **12. Tarshish]** either Tartessus in Spain, or the land of the Tyrsenians (Etruscans) in Italy. **13. Javan, Tubal, and Meshech]** these nations are named together in Gn 10 2. Javan is Ionia in Asia Minor. Tubal and Meshech are usually identified with the

Tibareni and Moschi, two tribes in the N. of
Asia Minor. For the slave trade of Javan
see Joel 3⁶. **14. Togarmah**] (Gn 10³) probably Armenia. **15. Dedan**] see on 25¹³.
17. Minnith] an Ammonite town (Jg 11³³).
For Ammonite wheat in Judah see 2 Ch 27⁵.
Pannag] a word of unknown meaning. RM
says, 'Perhaps a kind of confection.' **18. Hel-
bon**] a wine-growing district 13 m. N. of Damascus. **19. Dan also**] RV 'Vedan.' **Going to
and fro**] RM 'from Uzal.' Vedan and Uzal
are uncertain localities. **21. Kedar**] an Arabian
district (Gn 25¹³). **22. Sheba and Raamah**]
countries in S. Arabia (Gn 10⁷).
23. Haran] in Mesopotamia (Gn 11³¹).
Canneh] perhaps Calneh, a Babylonian city
(Gn 10¹⁰). **Eden**] either Beth-Eden, a state in
the W. of Mesopotamia, mentioned in the inscriptions and in 2 K 19¹² Isa 37¹² Am 1⁵ (RM),
or Aden in Arabia. **Asshur**] Assyria. **Chilmad**]
an unknown place. Perhaps instead of taking
it as a proper name we should read, 'Were as those
accustomed to be thy merchants.' **25. Ships
of Tarshish**] deep-sea vessels in general : see
1 K 22⁴⁸. **Did sing of thee in**] RV 'were thy
caravans for.'

CHAPTER 28 ¹⁻¹⁹
THE KING OF TYRE

The overweening pride of the prince of Tyre,
which has led him to claim to be a god, is rebuked, and his destruction by strangers is foretold (vv. 1–10). He is compared to an inmate
of Eden, the garden of God, who is cast out
for his sin (vv. 11–19). **2. The prince of Tyrus**] the king of Tyre at
this time was Ithobalus (Ethbaal) II. **3. Daniel**]
a type of wisdom here, as of righteousness in
14¹⁴, ²⁰. Ezekiel's references to Daniel suggest
a sage of ancient times rather than a youthful
contemporary in Babylonia. **7. Strangers**] the
Babylonians. **10. Deaths of the uncircumcised**]
a phrase for an ignominious end. So in 31¹⁸
32¹⁹, ²¹, ²⁵, ³².
12. Thou sealest, etc.] an obscure phrase,
alluding in some way to the wisdom of the king
of Tyre. **13. Thou hast been (RV 'wast ') in
Eden**, etc.] Ezekiel here evidently refers to a
legend similar to the story of the Fall in Gn 3.
His use of it seems to indicate that in his day
it had not been fixed in the biblical form.
Every precious stone] the stones mentioned
are the same as those in the first, second, and
fourth rows of stones on the high priest's
breastplate (Ex 28 ¹⁷⁻²⁰). **Gold.. tabrets.. pipes**]
rather, 'of gold was the workmanship of thy
sockets and grooves,' referring to the setting of
the precious stones. **14. Thou** *art* (RV 'wast')
the anointed cherub] more probably, 'thou
wast with the .. cherub.' **The holy mountain**]
another phrase for the garden of God.
16. I will destroy (RV 'have destroyed ')

thee, O covering cherub] more probably, 'the
covering cherub hath destroyed thee,' i.e. expelled thee. As it stands the passage describes
the fall of a cherub, but the alternative renderings in vv. 14–16 bring it more into line with
Gn 3, the cherub being the guardian of the garden, and the prince of Tyre a privileged inmate
of it, who is driven out for the sin of pride.

CHAPTER 28 ²⁰⁻²⁶
GOD'S JUDGMENT ON SIDON

Sidon, the partner of Tyre in opposing
Nebuchadrezzar, will be its partner in destruction (vv. 20–23). The overthrow of the
heathen nations will vindicate the supreme
power of the God of Israel, will prepare the
way for His people's restoration to their own
land, and will ensure their security and peace
in the future (vv. 24–26). These last vv. have
an important bearing on the significance of all
Ezekiel's prophecies against the nations.

§ 3. EGYPT (chs. 29–32)

The most of this series of prophecies
against Egypt are connected with dates during
the siege of Jerusalem, the time when Ezekiel
was silent as a prophet of Israel. They were
therefore probably written rather than spoken.
C. 32 is dated in the year after the fall of Je
rusalem, and 29¹⁷⁻²¹ belongs to a much later time.
In chronological order the series includes (1) the
destruction of the crocodile (29¹⁻¹⁶), (2) the
invasion of Egypt by Nebuchadrezzar (30¹⁻¹⁹),
(3) the breaking of Pharaoh's arms (30²⁰⁻²⁶),
(4) the fall of the great cedar (c. 31), (5) two
lamentations for Pharaoh and Egypt (c. 32),
(6) Egypt substituted for Tyre (29¹⁷⁻²¹).

CHAPTER 29 ¹⁻¹⁶
THE DESTRUCTION OF THE CROCODILE

Pharaoh is compared to the crocodile of the
Nile. God will drag him forth with hooks,
and cast him, with the fish that stick to his
scales, into the wilderness, as a punishment
for his deception of Israel (vv. 1–7). Egypt
will be desolate for forty years (vv. 8–12),
after which it will be restored, but not to its
former greatness (vv. 13–15). Israel will no
longer place a mistaken confidence in it (v. 16).
1. The tenth year .. the tenth *month*] January-February, 587 B.C., about seven months
before the fall of Jerusalem. **2. Pharaoh**]
The king of Egypt at this time was Pharaoh-
hophra (Apries) : see Jer 44³⁰. He reigned
from 588–569 B.C. **3. Dragon**] the crocodile.
His rivers] the Nile and its branches.
4. Fish] the subjects of Pharaoh. **6, 7.** This
was the constant character of Egypt in its relations with Israel. It incited Israel by promises of help to rebel against Assyria or
Babylon, and failed in the hour of need : see
2 K 18²¹ Isa 30⁷ 31³ Jer 37⁷. **10. From the**

tower of Syene] RM 'from Migdol to Syene,' and so in 30⁶. The places named represent the N. and S. extremities of the country. Migdol was a town in Lower Egypt. Syene is the modern Assouan, in Upper Egypt.

11, 12. Forty years] a round number, standing for a full generation, as in 4⁶. The period represented Ezekiel's forecast of the duration of Babylonian supremacy: see Jer 25⁹⁻¹¹, ¹⁹.

14. Pathros] Upper Egypt.

For vv. **17-21** see the end of the Section, after c. 32.

CHAPTER 30¹⁻¹⁹
THE INVASION OF EGYPT BY NEBUCHADREZZAR

No special enemy of Egypt has been mentioned in 29¹⁻¹⁶, but the king of Babylon is now pointed out as its conqueror.

5. Libya, and Lydia] RV 'Put and Lud': see on 27¹⁰. **Chub**] an unknown people. **The land that is in league**] perhaps we should read, 'the land of the Cherethites' (Philistia). **9. In ships**] ascending the Nile to Ethiopia. **13. Noph**] Memphis, the capital of Lower Egypt. **14. Zoan**] Tanis, an ancient Egyptian city (Nu 13²²). **No**] No-ammon, or Thebes, the capital of Upper Egypt. **15. Sin**] Pelusium, a frontier city at the NE. extremity of the Delta of the Nile. **17. Aven**] On, or Heliopolis: see Gn 41⁴⁵, ⁵⁰ 46²⁰. It lay on the E. edge of the Delta. **Pi-beseth**] Bubastis, a city of Lower Egypt. **18. Tehaphnehes** (or Tahpanhes)] Daphnæ, a city on the E. frontier of Lower Egypt: see Jer 43⁷ 44¹ 46¹⁴.

CHAPTER 30²⁰⁻²⁶
THE BREAKING OF PHARAOH'S ARMS

This prophecy appears to have been occasioned by some reverse sustained by Pharaoh shortly before the fall of Jerusalem. Probably the reference is to the failure of his attempt to raise the siege (Jer 37⁵⁻¹¹). The disaster is metaphorically described as the breaking of one of Pharaoh's arms. Ezekiel predicts that God will break the other arm also, so that Pharaoh will drop his sword. The king of Babylon's arms will be strengthened. God's sword will be put into his hand, that it may be stretched over Egypt. The Egyptians will be scattered in other lands.

20. The eleventh year . . the first *month*] March-April, 586 B.C., about four months before the fall of Jerusalem. **21. Roller**] bandage.

CHAPTER 31
THE FALL OF THE GREAT CEDAR

Egypt was a stately cedar, thick, lofty, and spreading; sheltering all the fowls and beasts (the nations) in its branches and under its shadow (vv. 1–6). It was the envy of all the trees (other great empires) in Eden, the garden of God (vv. 7–9). But because of its pride it is given into the hands of a mighty one (Nebuchadrezzar), who will cut it down. Those whom it sheltered will be scattered or will trample on it when it has fallen (vv. 10–13). This will be a warning to all trees (empires) against pride (v. 14). Egypt will go down to the nether world, and all the great nations already there will be comforted when it arrives.

1. The eleventh year . . the third *month*] May-June, 586 B.C., about two months before the fall of Jerusalem. **3. The Assyrian**] has evidently no connexion with the subject of the prophecy, which is Egypt. It has been supposed that the c. describes the downfall of Assyria, as a type of that of Egypt, but it is much more probable that instead of 'the Assyrian' we should read 'a teasshur' or box-tree, as in 27⁶. 'Behold a box-tree, a cedar,' etc. **4. Waters . . rivers**] the waters of the Nile. The allegory is not strictly consistent as to locality. The cedar is in Lebanon and also apparently in Eden. **11. I have therefore delivered**] RV 'I will even deliver.' **14. All that drink water**] all trees: so in v. 16. **Delivered unto death**] another instance of Ezekiel's conception of the nations as personified and surviving in the under-world: see Isa 14⁹⁻²⁰. **15. The deep . . the floods** (RV 'rivers') . . the waters] those referred to in v. 4. Ezekiel poetically says that the rivers of Egypt would cease to flow, in token of mourning for the nation's fall.

CHAPTER 32
TWO LAMENTATIONS FOR PHARAOH AND EGYPT

This c. consists of two prophecies, both dated more than a year and a half after the capture of Jerusalem, and separated from each other by a fortnight. In the first Pharaoh is likened, no longer to a young lion, but to a foul river monster, which will be caught, cast on the mountains, and devoured by birds and beasts of prey. At the monster's end the lights of heaven will be darkened, and the nations will be dismayed (vv. 1–10). The allegory is explained to mean the desolation of Egypt by the king of Babylon (vv. 11–16).

The second prophecy is a burial song over Pharaoh and his people (vv. 17–32). They go down to the under-world, which is weirdly conceived as a vast land of graves, the occupants of which, however, retain their consciousness and their speech. Two regions are distinguished in it. Sheol or 'hell' (vv. 21, 27) is the abode of the ancient heroes who have received honourable burial, while 'the pit' is a remoter region, reserved for the nations which have filled the earth with violence and terror, and whose people have died ingloriously in battle. Each of these nations has its own portion of 'the pit,' where the graves of its people are grouped around a central grave, occupied by the king or the personified genius of the nation. Pharaoh and his people will have a place among these dishonoured nations, and will be comforted to find that they are not alone in their humiliation.

1. The twelfth year.. the twelfth month] February-March, 584 B.C., almost a year and seven months after the fall of Jerusalem.

2. Thou art like.. and thou *art*] RV 'thou wast likened.. yet art thou,' a contrast between a noble and a base comparison. **Whale]** RV 'dragon': probably a crocodile or a hippopotamus is meant. **3. People]** RV 'peoples.'

6. With thy blood.. swimmest] probably 'the earth with the outflow of thy blood.'

7. Put.. out] RV 'extinguish.' Pharaoh is represented as a heavenly luminary, at the extinction of which the other heavenly bodies veil their light. Some suppose that there is a special reference to the constellation of the Dragon. **14. Deep]** RV 'clear.' Clear and smooth rivers betoken an uninhabited land: see v. 13.

17. The month is not mentioned, but it may be assumed to be the same as in v. 1. **18. Cast them down]** i.e. in the burial song. *Even* **her,** etc.] rather, 'thou and the daughters,' etc., following up the thought of v. 16. **19. Uncircumcised]** dishonourably buried: see on 28 10. The term is practically equivalent to 'slain by the sword': so in vv. 21, 24, 25, 26, 29, 30, 32. **20. Draw her]** RV 'draw her away,' to her burial-place in the under-world. **21. The strong among the mighty]** the ancient heroes, referred to also in v. 27. **Hell]** Sheol, the place of the honoured dead: so in v. 27.

They are gone down, etc.] the taunt uttered by the heroes against the Egyptians and their allies.

22. Asshur] Assyria. **His graves** *are* **about him]** The central grave is that of the king, or of the embodied genius of the nation ('her

grave,' v. 23, etc.). **23. Sides]** RV 'uttermost parts,' a remoter region of the under-world than that assigned to the heroes. **24. Elam]** a country E. of the Tigris, formerly a part of the Assyrian empire (Isa 22 6, where Elamite archers appear in Sennacherib's army). In Jer 49 34-39 Elam is an independent state, and is threatened with conquest by Nebuchadrezzar.

26. Meshech, Tubal] see on 27 13. These tribes may have taken part in the Scythian invasion : see Intro. and 38 2, 3. **27. The mighty of.. the uncircumcised]** A very slight change in the original gives the much better sense of the LXX, 'the mighty, the Nephilim of old time.' The violent nations would not be permitted to share the place of the heroes in the under-world. For the Nephilim see Gn 6 4 Nu 13 33 RV. **Their iniquities shall be]** rather, 'their shields are.' The heroes were buried honourably with their weapons and armour. **29. Edom]** see on 25 12. **30. Princes of the north.. Zidonians]** the states of Syria and Phœnicia. **32. I have caused my terror]** RV 'I have put his terror.' Pharaoh in his violence had been unconsciously carrying out God's purpose.

CHAPTER 29 17-21
Egypt as Nebuchadrezzar's Wages for the Siege of Tyre

This is the latest of Ezekiel's dated prophecies, and was uttered nearly sixteen years after the destruction of Jerusalem. Nebuchadrezzar's siege of Tyre was now over, and had not ended so successfully as Ezekiel prophesied in chs. 26–28. Ezekiel now proclaimed that Egypt would be substituted for Tyre as Nebuchadrezzar's reward, and concluded with a promise of revival to Israel.

17. The seven and twentieth year, the first *month*] March-April, 570 B.C. **20. They wrought for me]** Nebuchadrezzar and his army were God's instruments. **21. The** humiliation of Egypt would open the way for Israel's restoration, and the prophet would no longer be silenced by the incredulity of his people.

PART 3
The New Israel (Chs. 33–48)

So long as the Jewish kingdom remained in existence Ezekiel's prophecies (those in chs. 1–24) dealt almost exclusively with the nation's sin, and with the certainty of its overthrow. But when these prophecies were fulfilled by the fall of Jerusalem his message assumed a new and hopeful character. God's punishment of Israel's sin was not the end of His dealings with His people. The destruction of the old sinful Israel would be followed by the establishment of a perfect kingdom of God. The

humiliation of the foreign nations (described in chs. 25–32) would prepare the way for this, and would be succeeded by the restoration of the exiles. The new kingdom would be set up under new conditions of worship and fellowship with God. This concluding part of the book falls into two sections, the first dealing with the restoration from captivity (chs. 33–39), and the second with the new arrangements and laws of the future kingdom (chs. 40–48).

§ 1. THE RESTORATION (chs. 33–39)

After an introductory passage (33 1-20), and two short prophecies against the wicked survivors of Jerusalem and the careless exiles (33 21-33), this section describes the restoration in connexion with the Ruler, the Land and the People successively. As to the Ruler, God is pictured as the Shepherd of Israel (c. 34). As to the Land, a prophecy against Edom (c. 35) introduces a new address to the mountain land of Israel (c. 36). As to the People, the revival of the dead nation, and the reunion of the two kingdoms of Israel and Judah are allegorically set forth (c. 37). Finally, we have a description of the invasion and overthrow of Gog, the last enemy of God's people (chs. 38, 39). The beginning of the section is dated in December-January, 585-4 (or 586-5) B.C. See on 33 21.

CHAPTER 33 1-20
THE PROPHET AND THE INDIVIDUAL

This passage combines an expanded repetition of 3 17-21 with a condensed repetition of 18 5-29. The prophet is a watchman, responsible for warning his people of the consequences of sin. God deals with individual souls in strict justice, and desires that all should turn from their evil ways and live. These principles, already announced, became of special importance, and found their real application, after the fall of Jerusalem. As Ezekiel had foretold (24 23), that disaster stunned the exiles by its shock. They were overwhelmed by the judgment that had overtaken the nation for its sin. They pined away under it and felt that recovery was hopeless (v. 10). The nation being thus destroyed there was only a company of individuals left, and the religion of the individual came to have a new significance which has never passed away.

2. The sword] usually a symbol of impending calamity (see 14 17, c. 21), but here it is simply a detail in the figure of the watchman. The destruction of Jerusalem was past, and no further judgment was specially in view. **Of their coasts**] RV 'from among them.' The prophet's position is represented as due to the people's choice as well as to the call of God. This indicates that Ezekiel had now more recognition from the exiles than before.

5. But .. deliver] RV 'whereas if he had taken warning he should have delivered.'

10. If our transgressions .. be] RV 'our transgressions .. are.' **13. For**] RV 'in.' **For it**] RV 'therein.' **16. Mentioned unto**] RV 'remembered against.' **18. Thereby**] RV 'therein.'

CHAPTER 33 21-33
THE PROPHET, THE SURVIVORS, AND THE EXILES

In 24 27 it was announced to Ezekiel that the silence which began with his wife's death and the siege of Jerusalem would be ended when fugitives from the captured cities should arrive in Babylonia. This took place a year and five months (but see on v. 21) after Jerusalem fell, and Ezekiel began once more to receive and proclaim messages from God. This passage contains two of these. The first was directed against the wicked survivors who remained in the land of Israel and boasted that it would still be theirs. They were destined to perish, and the land to be utterly desolated, in order that God's wrath against their sin might be shown to the uttermost (vv. 23–29). The second describes the changed attitude of the exiles towards Ezekiel. They were now interested in his words, discussing them in their gatherings, and listening eagerly to what he had to say. Yet their interest had more of curiosity than of earnestness. Not till the final punishment of the wicked survivors took place would they recognise Ezekiel as a prophet indeed (vv. 30–33).

21. The twelfth year, the tenth *month*] December 585-January 584 B.C. The Syriac Bible reads 'the eleventh year.' Five months seem more likely than a year and five months as the time to be allowed for a journey from Palestine to Babylonia.

22. Was] RV 'had been.' Ezekiel had come under the power of divine inspiration the previous evening, when the truths in vv. 1–20 had shaped themselves in his mind. The prophecy against the wicked survivors (vv. 23–29) was probably called forth by information which the fugitives brought as to their attitude.

24. They that inhabit, etc.] the surviving wicked remnant in the land of Israel. Their wickedness is described in vv. 25, 26. For an historical account of the events in Palestine after the fall of Jerusalem see Jer 40–43. The survivors to whom Ezekiel refers are probably the anti-Babylonian party, led by Ishmael, the son of Nethaniah, who were responsible for the murder of Gedaliah : see Intro.

Abraham was one, etc.] These survivors reasoned—'If Abraham, who was only one man, obtained this land for his descendants, much more may we, who are many, hope to do so in spite of all that has happened.' For a sounder use of the same argument see Isa 51 2.

28. From Jer 52 30 we learn that there was a further deportation of 745 Jews to Babylonia five years after the fall of Jerusalem.

30. The children of thy people] the exiles of the first captivity. Still are talking against thee] RV 'talk of thee.' **32.** The exiles listened to Ezekiel's words as they would to music, which was entertaining but had no practical influence on their lives. **33. Whea**

this cometh to pass] the utter desolation of Palestine foretold in vv. 27, 28.

CHAPTER 34

The Good Shepherd of Israel

In this c. Israel is described as God's flock. Its former kings were evil shepherds who sought their own selfish ends and were careless what became of the sheep. The flock had become the prey of wild beasts (the heathen nations). God would judge the evil shepherds and deliver the sheep from them. He would Himself be the Shepherd of His people, gathering the scattered and lost, caring for the sick and wounded, feeding the flock in security (vv. 1–16). The flock, too, had been divided against itself. The fat and strong cattle (the upper classes) had tyrannised over the lean and weak (the common people). God would judge the overbearing cattle also. He would unite His flock under David as their shepherd (an ideal king of David's line), who would feed them in a peaceful and fertile land, untroubled by beasts of prey (vv. 17–31). This c. is the basis of our Lord's parables of the Lost Sheep (Mt 18 12, 13 Lk 15 3-6) and the Good Shepherd (Jn 10 1-16).

3. Fat] rather, 'milk.' Them that are fed] RV 'the fatlings.' Flock] RV 'sheep' : so in vv. 6, 8, 10, 15, 19, 31. 5. There is] RV 'there was.' 12. In the day .. scattered] better, 'in the day when all his sheep are scattered.' 13. People] RV 'peoples.' 16. With judgment] RV 'in judgment.'

17. Between cattle and cattle, etc.] rather, 'between sheep and sheep, even the rams and the he-goats.' The rams and he-goats are the second class of sheep, the weaker members of the flock being the first class. 18. Deep] RV 'clear.' 23. My servant David] David, the shepherd king, is introduced as a type of the ideal ruler of the future kingdom of God : see 37 24 Jer 30 9 Hos 3 5. 24. Prince] instead of king, is Ezekiel's usual designation of the ruler of the future : see chs. 45, 46. 25. A covenant of peace] see 37 26. Wilderness] means not 'desert,' but 'pasture-land' : see Ps 65 12.

26. Read with LXX 'I will set them round about my hill, and I will send you the rain (in its season), a rain of blessing.' There is a hint here of the place which the Temple is to have in the life of the new Israel : see c. 40.

27. Those that served themselves of them] the evil she herds. 28. Land] RV 'earth.' The wild beasts denote the heathen. 29. Plant of renown] RV 'plantation for renown.' The reference is not to the Messiah, who is already represented in the allegory by David, but to the fertility of the land. Other readings are, 'a plantation of peace,' or 'a fat plantation.'

30. The result of the restoration will be

that Israel will recognise not only the character of their God, but the fact that they are His people. 31. Omit are men, and read 'and ye are my flock,' etc.

CHAPTERS 35, 36

The Land of Israel in the Future

C. 35 is an introduction to c. 36, the connexion being shown by 36 5. The claim of Edom to the land having been repudiated (c. 35), its reoccupation by Israel is promised (36 1-15), and the reason of the restoration is explained (36 16-38).

(a) The Punishment of Edom's Presumption (c. 35)

Edom has already been included by Ezekiel among the nations whose humiliation would prepare the way for the restoration of Israel (25 12-14), and this new prophecy requires a special explanation, which is easily found. Before the land could be given to its true owners all false claimants had to be disposed of. The claim of the wicked survivors of Jerusalem has already been set aside (33 23-29), and the claim of the surrounding heathen has to be dealt with in the same way. Edom is introduced here as their representative (vv. 10, 12). Its former enmity and malice are recalled (v. 5), and the arrogance and blasphemy of its pretensions to possess the land of Israel are specially denounced. Ezekiel foretells that God will repay the Edomites in their own coin, making their land desolate, and compelling them to recognise Him as the true God.

2. Mount Seir] Edom : see on 25 12-14. 5. Time .. end] RV 'time of the iniquity of the end,' as in 21 25, 29. 9. Return] RV 'be inhabited.' 10. These two .. countries] the territories of Israel and Judah. The LORD was there] God might seem to abandon His Temple and forsake His people, but He never gave up His choice of them or His possession of their land. 14. When .. rejoiceth] rather, 'to the rejoicing of the whole earth.' 15. Idumea] RV 'Edom.'

(b) The Mountain Land of Israel re-peopled (36 1-15)

This prophecy is the counterpart of c. 6. The land, made desolate for the people's sin, as was foretold, and presumptuously claimed by Edom and the other surrounding nations, will again become fertile, fruitful, and populous. Israel will inhabit it once more, and will no longer suffer famine, or be oppressed by the heathen.

1. The mountains of Israel] the mountain land of Israel, as in 6 1, 2. 2. The ancient high places] the everlasting hills, with no reference to the idolatrous worship associated with them :

see Dt 33 15.   **5. Idumea**] RV 'Edom.' This v. makes clear the connexion of c. 35 with the present passage. **To cast it out**] better, perhaps, 'to possess it.'   **7. Have lifted up mine hand**] have sworn.

8. They are at hand to come] The restoration of Israel is viewed as close at hand.

13. Bereaved thy nations] RV 'been a bereaver of thy nation.' The famines to which the land of Israel had been subject had given rise to the reproach that it bereaved and devoured its inhabitants (Nu 13 32). This would be the case no longer.   **14. Nations**] RV 'nation': so in v. 15.   **15. Cause .. to fall**] rather, 'bereave,' as in v. 14.

(c) God's Reason for restoring Israel
(36 16-38)

God had justly sent Israel into exile for their sins (vv. 17–19), but the heathen had misunderstood this event, taking it as a sign of God's inability to save His people (v. 20). In this way the exiles had occasioned the profanation of God's name, and to vindicate His own honour He was compelled to restore them (vv. 21–24). This high argument passes into a promise of the moral renewal, as well as of the outward blessings, which would accompany the restoration (vv. 25–30). Yet the fact is reiterated that all this will be done, not because Israel has deserved it, but because God's glory has required it. It must minister not to pride, but to humility (vv. 31, 32). When the sinful nation has been purified, and the desolate land repeopled, the heathen will know that the whole is God's doing (vv. 33–36). The blessing, too, though undeserved, will be sent in response to Israel's prayers (vv. 37, 38).

20. Profaned] not now by actual wickedness, but indirectly, as the v. goes on to explain. **When they said to them**] RV 'in that men said of them.'   **23. Sanctify**] the exact opposite of 'profane.'

25–28. These vv. expand the promise in 11 19, 20. They include purification from guilt, inward renewal, the spirit of obedience, and the privileges of the people of God. In its essence this passage repeats Jeremiah's promise of the New Covenant (Jer 31 31-34).   **26. Heart of flesh**] see 2 Cor 3 3 (RV).   **31, 32.** Cp. 16 61 Jer 29 11-14.   **36. Build .. *and* plant**] RV 'have builded .. and planted.'   **37. I will yet *for* this**] RV 'for this moreover will I.'

38. Holy flock] RV 'flock for sacrifice,' the point of comparison being the great numbers : see 1 Ch 29 21 2 Ch 7 5 29 33 35 7-9. **Solemn**] RV 'appointed.'

CHAPTER 37
The Revival and Reunion of Israel

From the future of the land Ezekiel now turns to that of the nation, long ago divided by the revolt of the Ten Tribes, and now seemingly extinct. The exiles feel themselves to be but its scattered bones (v. 11). In a striking and beautiful vision, suggested no doubt by this current saying, Ezekiel predicts that the dead nation will come to life again (vv. 1–14), and by a symbolic action he represents the coming reunion of the rival kingdoms of Israel and Judah (vv. 15–28).

(a) The Revival (vv. 1–14)

Ezekiel is transported into a valley full of dry bones. As he prophesies to them they come together into complete skeletons, which become covered with sinews, flesh, and skin. Then the wind blows upon the inanimate bodies and they stand up alive. The prophecy does not refer to a literal resurrection of the Israelites actually dead, but to a revival of the dead nation, of which the exiles seemed to be the scattered remains.

1. Ezekiel saw this vision in a prophetic trance, under the influence of God's inspiration. At the same time its details were no doubt due to the peculiar working of his imaginative mind on the thought expressed by the exiles in v. 11.   **7. A shaking**] RV 'an earthquake.'   **8, 9. Wind .. breath**] The same Hebrew word means wind, breath, or spirit. The wind of the vision represents the Spirit of God in the actual process of the nation's revival : see v. 14.

11. Cut off for our parts] RV 'clean cut off.'

12, 13. Graves] The figure here is somewhat changed. Still the reference is not to the graves of those actually dead, but to the heathen world as the grave of the dead nation of Israel, compared to which their own land was the land of the living.   **14. My spirit**] see on vv. 8, 9.

(b) The Reunion (vv. 15–28)

Ezekiel is directed to take two pieces of wood, one having 'Judah' and the other 'Joseph' inscribed upon it, and to join them together (vv. 15–17). The explanation of the symbol is that the two divisions of the nation, so long separated, will be reunited in their former land, governed by one king of the house of David, under the same covenant with God, and worshipping at the same sanctuary (vv. 18–28).

16. Judah] the southern kingdom of the Two Tribes. **Joseph .. Ephraim**] the northern kingdom of the Ten Tribes ; Ephraim, one of the two tribes descended from Joseph, being the principal one of the ten. **Israel**] used here and in v. 19, as generally by Ezekiel, in the sense, not of the northern kingdom, but of the whole nation.

19. Him] RV 'it.' **Mine hand**] probably

rather, 'his' (Judah's) 'hand,' to correspond with 'the hand of Ephraim' already mentioned in the v. The united stick is placed in Judah's hand because the king is to belong to Judah's royal house. **23. Dwellingplaces**] RM 'backslidings.' **So shall they be my people,** etc.] another feature taken from Jeremiah's New Covenant (Jer 31 33) : see also vv. 26, 27.

24, 25. My servant David] in the same sense as in 34 23, 24.

26. A covenant of peace] as in 34 25.

26, 27. My sanctuary .. my tabernacle] Jeroboam had set up rival sanctuaries to Jerusalem at Dan and Bethel (1 K 12 28-32), but the reunited nation would have one centre of religious worship. God had forsaken the Temple at Jerusalem (11 23), but He would return, never to leave it again. The latter aspect of the promise is developed in chs. 40-48.

CHAPTERS 38, 39
GOD'S FINAL VICTORY OVER THE HEATHEN

Ezekiel's earlier group of prophecies against the nations (chs. 25-32) was concerned with Israel's nearer neighbours, which had interfered more or less in former times with her prosperity ; and their humiliation was regarded as a necessary condition of Israel's peaceful and happy future. Ezekiel, however, contemplated a wider extension of God's glory than these prophecies involved. This is described under the form of an invasion of the restored Israel by hordes of the remotest heathen, who will be destroyed by God without any fighting on Israel's part. His glory will thus be manifested to the very ends of the earth. Ezekiel is alone among the Old Testament prophets in expecting another crisis to arise after the restoration has been accomplished. His conception is reproduced in the New Testament in the book of Revelation (20 7-10), and the underlying idea in both cases is that what seems the triumph of God's kingdom may be followed by a fresh assault of the forces of evil, which, however, are destined to be overthrown at last. The picture of Gog may have been suggested partly by the memory of the great Scythian invasion (see Intro.), and partly by the ravages of Nebuchadrezzar's armies.

C. 38 describes Gog's allies (vv. 1-7), his nefarious plans (vv. 8-13), his great invasion (vv. 14-17), and God's turning of the forces of nature against him (vv. 18-23). C. 39 foretells that God will lead him on to destruction (vv. 1-7) ; his weapons will provide Israel with fuel for seven years (vv. 8-10) ; seven months will be required to bury the corpses of his host, which will fill a whole valley on the E. of the Dead Sea (vv. 11-13) ; when the seven months are over special officers will still be required to search out and bury

the dead bodies that remain (vv. 14-16) ; birds and beasts of prey will enjoy an enormous banquet (vv. 17-20) ; all the earth will recognise the power and glory of the true God, the heathen will understand at last the real meaning of Israel's exile, and Israel will learn the lessons of all God's dealings with them in judgment and in mercy (vv. 21-29).

CHAPTER 38

2. Gog, the land of Magog] RV 'Gog, of the land of Magog.' The exact reference of the names is unknown. Magog is the land ruled over by Gog. The conjecture that 'Magog' (Mgg = Ggm = Bbl) is a cryptogram for 'Babel' (Babylon) has no probability. Gog in any case is the representative of remote heathendom, and is located in the far N. (38 6, 15 39 2), while he has allies in the distant S. (38 5).

Chief prince of Meshech, etc.] RV 'Prince of Rosh, Meshech,' etc., and so in v. 3, 39 1. The land meant by 'Rosh' is unknown, but there can be no allusion to Russia. On Meshech and Tubal see on 27 13.

4. Turn thee back] RV 'turn thee about.' Perhaps we should read, 'lead thee,' and so in 39 2. God directs the movements even of the enemies of His kingdom. **5. Persia**] a doubtful rendering. **Ethiopia, and Libya**] RV 'Cush and Put' : see on 27 10 30 5. **6. Gomer**] (Gn 10 2), a people in the N. of Asia Minor, usually identified with the Cimmerians.

Togarmah] Armenia : see on 27 14. **The north quarters**] RV 'the uttermost parts of the north.' **Bands**] RV 'hordes,' and so throughout. **People**] RV 'peoples,' and so throughout, except in v. 12, and 39 13. **7. Be thou a guard unto them**] LXX reads, 'hold thyself in reserve for me.'

8. The latter years] The invasion of Gog is in the distant future. **The land** that is .. **gathered,** etc.] The sense requires 'the nation' to be supplied before 'that is gathered' : see v. 12. **11.** The peaceful state of the restored Israel is here described. **12. Midst of the land**] RV 'middle of the earth,' the supposed geographical position of Palestine. **13. Sheba .. Dedan .. Tarshish**] see on 22 23, 25 27 15, 20.

Young lions] does not give a clear sense. Other suggested readings are, 'Canaanites,' 'Cyprians,' or 'traffickers.' The nations mentioned were spectators of Gog's invasion, and inquired what commercial advantage they might reap from the disposal of the spoil.

15. North parts] RV 'uttermost parts of the north.' **17.** Certain older prophecies were understood by Ezekiel to refer, though not by name, to the coming invasion of Gog. Perhaps he had in view Zeph 1 14f. 38 Jer 3-6.

18. At the same time] RV 'in that day.' **In my face**] RV 'into my nostrils.'

19. Shaking] or, 'earthquake.'

CHAPTER 39

2. Leave but the sixth part of thee] RV 'lead thee on.' **6. Isles**] RM 'coast-lands.' God will not only destroy the army of Gog in Palestine, but will extend His judgments into the lands from which Gog and his allies have come. **8. It is come . . it is done**] RV 'it cometh . . it shall be done.' **9. Set on fire**] RV 'make fires of.' **Burn them with fire**] RV 'make fires of them': so in v. 10. **11. There of graves**] RV 'for burial.' **Valley of the passengers**] RV 'valley of them that pass through.' Others read, 'a valley of Abarim,' Abarim being the region E. of the Dead Sea. **The sea**] the Dead Sea. **Stop the** *noses*, etc.] RV 'stop them that pass through.' The valley, formerly a roadway, will be blocked by corpses. **Hamon-gog**] means 'the multitude of Gog.' **14. With the passengers**] should probably be omitted, and **bury** should perhaps be 'search out.' There were to be two classes of officials, the searchers and the buriers, and this v. deals with the former. The duties of both are described in v. 15. **Earth**] RV 'land.'

15. And the passengers, etc.] RV 'and they that pass through the land shall pass through.' When the searchers found any human remains they were to set up a mark to attract the attention of the buriers, who followed them. **16. And . . Hamonah**] RV 'and Hamonah shall also be the name of a city.' The reference seems to be to a city to be built near the valley of Hamon-gog, in commemoration of God's victory over Gog and his 'multitude.' **18. Bashan**] a district E. of the Jordan, famous for its cattle : see Dt 32 14 Ps 22 12. **24. Have I done**] RV 'did I.' **26. After that they have borne**] RV 'and they shall bear'; more probably, 'and they shall forget.' **Dwelt safely . . made** *them* **afraid**] RV 'shall dwell securely . . shall make them afraid.' **28. Have left**] RV 'I will leave.'

§ 2. THE ORDINANCES OF THE NEW ISRAEL (chs. 40–48)

This concluding section of the book is dated in the twenty-fifth year of Ezekiel's captivity, i.e. the fourteenth year after the fall of Jerusalem (572 B.C.). It is therefore thirteen years later than the previous section (chs. 33–39), and, with the exception of 29 17-21, forms the latest part of the book. It is in the form of a vision, which is the counterpart of that in chs. 8–11. There God forsook the old Temple which had been polluted by idolatry. Here we have a description of the Temple of the restored kingdom, of God's return to it, and of the various religious arrangements and institutions of the future. The vision is marked by great minuteness of detail, and no doubt Ezekiel

had brooded long and deeply over the particulars of the Temple and its ritual. Yet, as in former cases, there is no reason to doubt that this vision was an actual experience, in which the subjects of previous reflection stood out vividly before the prophet's mind. While the material details are so minute, some features of the vision are supernatural and miraculous. The whole forms an ideal picture, which was never actually to be realised, but which strikingly embodied the conception of the abiding presence of God with His people, and of their perfect fellowship with Him.

The Plans of Ezekiel's Temple, on p. 518, are by permission of the Cambridge University Press.

CHAPTERS 40–42
THE NEW TEMPLE

Ezekiel, transported in vision to Palestine, is set down on the N. side of the Temple mountain, and sees the Temple buildings extending to the S. like a city. A supernatural figure, like those in c. 9, appears, and measures the various parts of the Temple in Ezekiel's presence (40 1-4).

(a) The Outer Court and its Gateways
(40 5-27)

The Outer Eastern Gateway (vv. 5–16), Fig. 3, *E.* For the following details see Fig. 1. The outer boundary of the Temple was a wall 6 cubits thick and 6 cubits high (v. 5). Steps led up to the E. gateway, which had a threshold (*a*) 6 cubits broad (v. 6, *ef*), and 10 cubits wide (v. 11, *ee*, *ff*). Within the threshold were three guard-rooms (*b*) on either side (vv. 7, 10), each 6 cubits square, and separated by wall-spaces (posts) of 5 cubits (*gh*, *ik*). The inner threshold (*c*) had the same dimensions as the outer one (vv. 6, 7). Beyond it was a porch (*d*) 8 cubits wide (*mn*), the jambs (posts) of the doorway being 2 cubits broad (*no*, v. 9). The whole length of the gateway (*eo*) was 50 cubits (v. 15), and its breadth 25 cubits (v. 13). The guard-rooms and the porch were lit by windows, and there were also windows in the wall-spaces (posts) between the guard-rooms. These spaces, too, were decorated with palm trees (v. 16).

5. Cubit] Various sizes of cubit, from 18 in. to nearly 24 in. were employed in ancient measurements. Ezekiel's cubit was one of the larger forms—an ordinary cubit and a handbreadth. **6. The other threshold**] is that mentioned in v. 7 (*c*). **7. Within**] RV 'toward the house,' or Temple proper. **8. Should be omitted. It** contradicts v. 9, and is evidently a copyist's repetition. **9. Inward**] RV 'toward the house.' **11. The length of the gate, thirteen cubits**] an obscure statement, not reconcilable with the

FIG. 2. TEMPLE HOUSE.

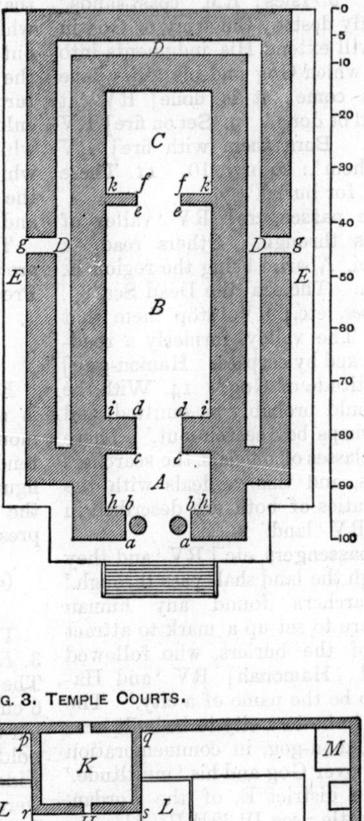

FIG. I. OUTER GATEWAY.

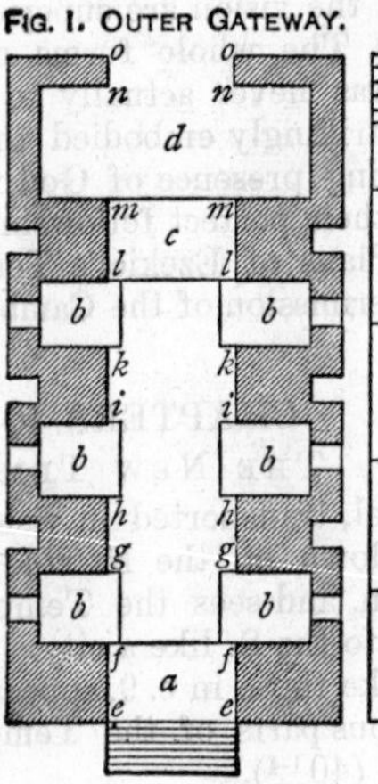

FIG. 3. TEMPLE COURTS.

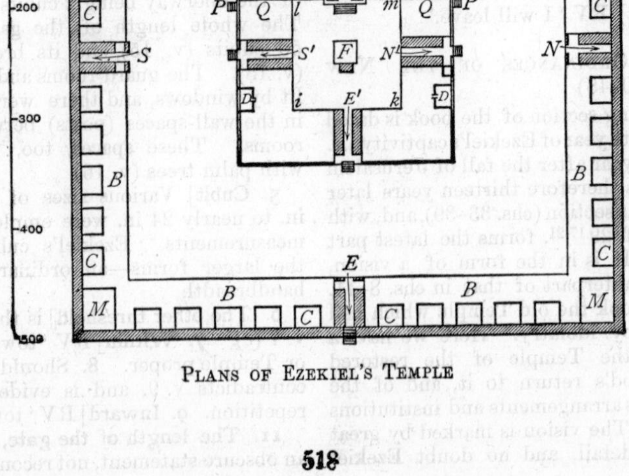

PLANS OF EZEKIEL'S TEMPLE

other measurements. If 'breadth' instead of 'length' were meant $13 + 6 + 6$ would make 25, but this would allow no space for the outer walls of the guard-rooms. **12. The space**] RV 'and a border,' probably a low parapet in front of each guard-room (fg, hi, kl) taking a cubit on either side off the width of the passage.

14. He made.. threescore cubits] read, with LXX, 'and he measured the porch (d) 20 cubits' (i.e. in length, the breadth being 8 cubits, v. 9). The latter half of the v. is obscure.

16. Arches] should be 'porch,' and so everywhere.

The Outer Court (40^{17-19}) had a pavement (Fig. 3, B) 50 cubits wide, corresponding to the length of the gateways. On this pavement were 30 chambers (C), the exact arrangement of which is unknown. From the inner opening of the outer gateways to the inner gateways was 100 cubits. The whole outer court including the pavement was therefore 150 cubits wide. **18. Over against**] RV 'answerable unto.'

The Outer Northern Gateway (vv. 20–23), Fig. 3, N. This was similar to the E. gateway. 'Porch' should be read for 'arches.' Seven steps led up to this gateway, and the breadth of the outer court was the same on the N. as on the E. side.

The Outer Southern Gateway (vv. 24–27), Fig. 3, S. This was similar to those already described. 'Porch' for 'arches' as before.

(b) The Inner Court and its Gateways
(40 28-47)

The Inner Southern Gateway (vv. 28–31), Fig. 3, S^1. This was reached from the outer court by 8 steps. It was exactly similar to the outer gateways, except that the porch (Fig. 1, d) was at the outer and not at the inner end. V. 30 should be omitted with LXX.

The Inner Eastern Gateway (vv. 32–34), Fig. 3, E^1, and **the Inner Northern Gateway** (vv. 35–37), Fig. 3, N^1, were similar to that on the S.

Arrangements for Preparing the Sacrifices (vv. 38–43). At one of the inner gateways (probably that on the N.) there were a chamber for washing the burnt offerings (v. 38) and a number of tables for slaying and preparing them (vv. 39–43). The exact position of the tables must remain uncertain.

38. The chambers and the entries] RV 'a chamber with the door.'

The Chambers for the Singers (vv. 44–47), Fig. 3, DD. These were two in number. One, by the N. gateway and looking toward the S., was for the priests. The other, by the S. gateway and looking toward the N., was for the Levites.

44. East] should obviously be S. : see RM.
Without the inner gate] means not 'in the

outer court,' but 'beyond the gateway, in the inner court.'

Dimensions of the Inner Court (v. 47). Excluding the space occupied by the gateways, this court formed a square (Fig. 3, $iklm$) of 100 cubits each way. The altar (F) was in the centre of the court.

(c) The Temple Proper (40 48–41 26)

The main Temple building was on the W. side of the inner court. The details that follow are illustrated in Fig. 2.

The Porch ($40^{48, 49}$), Fig. 2, A. This was 20 cubits long (hh) and 12 cubits broad. The posts or jambs (ab) of the doorway were 5 cubits across, and the side-walls (hb, bh) were of 3 cubits each. This left 14 cubits for the width of the entrance (aa, bb). Each jamb had a pillar beside it. The porch was approached by 10 steps.

48. Breadth of the gate] should be 'sides of the entrance,' as in 41^2.

49. Eleven] should be 'twelve,' as the LXX reads, and the other measurements require: see 41^{13}. **And he brought me.. whereby**] RM 'and by ten steps.'

CHAPTER 41

The Holy Place ($41^{1, 2}$), Fig. 2, B. This was the 'temple' strictly so called. The posts of its doorway were 6 cubits across (cd). The entrance was 10 cubits wide (cc, dd), and the side-walls (id, di) were of 5 cubits each. The apartment itself was 40 cubits long and 20 cubits broad.

1. Tabernacle] should probably be 'posts.'

The Holy of Holies ($41^{3, 4}$), Fig. 2, C. Ezekiel did not accompany the measurer into this sacred chamber. The posts of the entrance (ef) were two cubits across. The entrance itself was 6 cubits wide (ee, ff) and the side-walls (kf, fk) were of 7 cubits each. The chamber itself was a square of 20 cubits each way.

The Side Chambers (41^{5-7}). The Temple had a double wall, the inner being 6 cubits

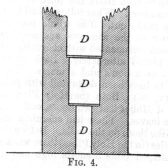

Fig. 4.

thick (v. 5), and the outer 5 cubits thick (v. 9). Between these was a space of 4 cubits (D), which was occupied by 30 chambers arranged in three stories. The chambers in each story were wider than those below, as the supporting beams were not let into the Temple wall, but rested on ledges, which took away successively from the thickness of the wall (Fig. 4).

6. Three] RV 'in three stories.' **They entered into**] should probably be 'there were rebatements in,' as in 1 K 6⁶, which in any case gives the key to the meaning here.

7. And *there was* **.. chambers**] RV 'and the side chambers were broader as they encompassed the house higher and higher.'

The Raised Platform and Surrounding Space (41⁸⁻¹¹). The Temple building and the side chambers stood on a basement which rose 6 cubits above the level of the inner court. This basement extended 5 cubits (the 'place that was left') beyond the outer wall on either side (Fig. 2, *E*), and from this space entry was gained to the side chambers on either side (Fig. 2, *gg*). Round the platform there was a clear space of 20 cubits (the 'separate place') on the N., W., and S. (Fig. 3, *H H H*).

8. The height of the house] RV 'that the house had a raised basement.'

The Western Building (41¹²), Fig. 3, *K*. This was on the W. of the Temple beyond the 'separate place' (*H*), and had walls 5 cubits thick. Its internal measurement was 90 cubits by 70, and its external one 100 cubits by 80.

General Measurements (41¹³⁻¹⁵ᵃ). The Temple was 100 cubits long, and the western space *H* (20 cubits) with the building *K* (70 cubits) and its walls (10 cubits) made up another 100 cubits (v. 13) from E. to W. The front of the Temple with the E. ends of the separate places *H H* on either side of it made up 100 cubits (*l m*) from S. to N. (v. 14). The building *K* with its 'galleries' (walls) was also 100 cubits (*p q, r s*) from S. to N. (v. 15).

The Interior Decorations of the Temple (41¹⁵ᵇ⁻²⁶). V. 15 should end with 'cubits.' The vv. that follow are somewhat obscure. The windows that lit the interior of the Temple must have been above the third storey of the side chambers. What follows is all that can be clearly made out. The whole interior from the floor to the windows was panelled with wood and ornamented with cherubim and palm trees, placed alternately. Each cherub had two faces, a lion's and a man's. The porch seems to have been decorated with palm trees only (v. 26). Both the Holy Place and the Holy of Holies had two doors, each consisting of two leaves. These had cherubim and palm trees like those on the walls. Before the Holy of Holies (in the Holy Place) there was a wooden altar-shaped table 3 cubits high and 2 cubits long.

15ᵇ, 16. should perhaps read, 'and the Temple, and the inner house, and its outer

porch were covered with a roof work, and they three had their closed windows and their galleries round about.' The 'galleries' may have been borders or dados. **21.** An obscure verse.

22. The second **length** should be 'base.'

25. Thick planks stands for a word of unknown meaning.

(*d*) **The Priests' Chambers** (42¹⁻¹⁴)

This is the most obscure part of Ezekiel's description. The following are the clearest points. On the N. side of the Temple, and separated from it by the space *H* (Fig. 3) was a group of buildings (*o u m w*) 100 cubits long and 50 cubits broad (v. 2). It consisted of a block (*G*), next the Temple, 100 cubits long, and another (*G¹*), next the outer court, 50 cubits long (v. 8). The remaining 50 cubits next the outer court was occupied by a wall (*v w*, v. 7), and between the blocks was a walk (*O*) 10 cubits wide and 100 cubits long (v. 4). This left 20 cubits as the width of each block. The chambers in these buildings were in three storeys, and were over against the space *H* on the one hand, and the pavement (*B*) of the outer court on the other (v. 3). The upper storeys were narrower than the lower, their breadth being diminished by galleries (vv. 3, 5) which faced each other across the walk *O* (Fig. 5). The doors of *G* were towards the N., opening on the walk *O* (vv. 2, 4). The entry (*P*) from the outer court was at the E. end of the whole group (v. 9). There was an exactly similar group of buildings on the S. of the Temple (vv. 10–12). All these chambers were to be used by the priests for eating the sacrificial flesh and for changing their garments (vv. 13, 14).

4. One cubit] RM 'a hundred cubits.'

5. Were higher than] RV 'took away from.' **Than the lower**] RV 'more than from.'

10. East should obviously be S.

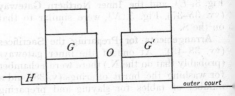

FIG. 5.

(*e*) **Dimensions of the Temple Area** (42¹⁵⁻²⁰)

The whole formed a square of 500 cubits each way. This follows from the measurements already given. 'Reeds' is a mistake for 'cubits,' arising from the fact that the reed was used in the measurement.

CHAPTERS 43, 44¹⁻³

THE RESTORATION OF THE TEMPLE WORSHIP

This c. describes God's return to the Temple

(43 1-12), and His directions as to the construction (43 13-17), and dedication (43 18-26) of the altar of burnt offering. When these directions were carried out God's sacrificial intercourse with Israel would be resumed (43 27). The outer eastern gateway, by which God's glory returned, was to be permanently shut (44 1-3).

(a) God's Return to the Temple (43 1-12)

Ezekiel, standing at the outer E. gate, saw the appearance of God's glory in the same form in which he had beheld it in previous visions. It came from the E., and entered the Temple by the gate on that side, the same by which it had formerly departed (10 19 11 22, 23). Ezekiel was then brought to the inner court, where he saw the glory filling the Temple as in 10 4. A voice from within the Temple announced that God would now dwell for ever in the midst of His people, and that His sanctuary would no longer be defiled as of old by the people's wickedness, or by the nearness of the royal palace and sepulchres. Ezekiel was further directed to make known the plan and ordinances of the new Temple to the people.

6. The man] RV 'a man,' the divine voice personified. **7. Whoredom]** a figure for idolatry : see 6 9 16, 23. **High places]** RM ' death.' **Carcases,** etc.] The royal sepulchres were in the vicinity of Solomon's Temple.

8. Solomon's palace and Temple were close together, and formed practically a single group of buildings. In Ezekiel's vision of the future the city stood far away from the Temple : see 48 15-17.

(b) Measurements of the Altar of Burnt Offering (43 13-18)

The altar (Fig. 3, P) was to have a base (a b s t, Fig. 6) a cubit high (a b, ts) and a cubit broad (b c, r s). This base was to have a border a span in height (b, s). Above this was to be

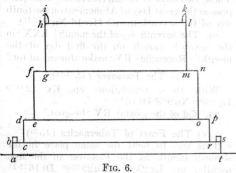

FIG. 6.
PLAN OF THE ALTAR OF BURNT OFFERING

the lower settle (c d p r), 2 cubits high (c d, r p) and a cubit broad (d e, o p). Next was to come the greater settle (e f n o), 4 cubits high (e f, o n) and a cubit broad (f g, m n). Highest of all was to be the upper altar (g h l m), 4 cubits high,

and having a square top 12 cubits each way (h l). There were to be horns (h i, k l) at the four corners. The upper settle would form a square 14 cubits each way (f n). The whole height of the altar, excluding the horns, would be 11 cubits (nearly 20 ft.), and the top of the altar was to be reached by stairs on the E. side.

13. Higher place] RV 'base.' **15. So the altar]** RV ' and the upper altar.' **From the altar]** RV 'from the altar hearth' : so in v. 16. **16. Squares]** RV ' sides ' : so in v. 17. **17. The border about it]** is probably not a border about the settle, but a border about the base described in v. 13. The three last clauses of v. 17 refer to the altar as a whole.

(c) The Consecration of the Altar (43 18-27)

Seven days would be required for this. Each day a he-goat was to be sacrificed as a sin-offering, and a ram and a young bullock were to be sacrificed as burnt offerings. On the first day a young bullock was to take the place of the he-goat. These vv. may be compared with Ex 29 36, 37 Lv 8 11 15 33. **20. Purge]** RV ' make atonement for' : so in v. 26.

22. Kid of the goats] RV ' he-goat.' **26. Themselves]** RV ' it.'

(d) The Closing of the Outer Eastern Gate (44 1-3)

This gateway, by which God's glory had returned to the Temple, was to be permanently shut thereafter. The prince, however, might use it for sacrificial meals, entering it by the porch (Fig. 1, d) from the outer court, and leaving it by the same way.

CHAPTER 44 4-31
THE PRIESTS AND THE LEVITES

Standing at the inner northern gate Ezekiel again saw the glory of God filling the Temple and was again addressed by the divine voice (vv. 4, 5). The Speaker first rebuked the custom which had prevailed in the old Temple, of having foreigners as servants in the sanctuary (vv. 6–8). He directed that in future their place should be taken by the Levites who were not of the family of Zadok. These had formerly shared the priestly office, but for their encouragement of Israel's idolatry they were to be deprived of this privilege, and to have humbler services assigned to them (vv. 9–14). The Levites of the family of Zadok alone were to exercise the priesthood in future (vv. 15, 16). No mention is made of the high priest. Various regulations follow as to the priests' clothing, marriage, public duties, defilement and purification, and sacrificial perquisites (vv. 17–31). This passage has an important bearing on the date of certain parts of the Pentateuch (see Intro.).

7. Strangers] In 2 K 11 we have an instance of

foreign mercenaries (' Carites,' v. 4, RV) being employed as guards in the Temple. The Nethinim (Ezr 8 20) were apparently captives employed as Temple slaves: see Zech 14 21.

They] RM ' ye.' **Because of**] RV ' to add unto.' **10. Are gone away**] RV ' went.' The reference is to the worship at the high places, abolished by Josiah (2 K 23 8, 9). **15. Zadok**] made priest by Solomon when Abiathar was deposed (1 K 2 26, 27, 35). **17, 18.** Cp. Ex 28 39-42 39 27-29 Lv 16 4. **19. The holy chambers**] those described in c. 42: see 42 13, 14.

20. Cp. Lv 21 5. **21.** Cp. Lv 10 9. **22.** Cp. Lv 21 14. **23.** Cp. Lv 10 10. **24.** Cp. Dt 17 8-13 19 17 21 5, where the priests are associated with secular judges. **25.** Cp. Lv 21 1-3. **26.** Cp. Nu 19 11. **28.** Cp. Nu 18 20. **29. Meat offering**] cp. Lv 2 3 7 9-11. **Sin.. and.. trespass offering**] cp. Lv 6 18 7 6, 7 Nu 18 9, 10. **Dedicated**] RV ' devoted': cp. Lv 27 28 Nu 18 14. **30. The firstfruits**] Cp. Ex 23 19 34 26 Nu 18 13 Dt 18 4.

Oblation] RM ' heave offering': cp. Nu 15 19-21 18 19. **31.** Cp. Ex 22 31 Lv 22 8.

CHAPTER 45 1-8

THE LANDS FOR THE PRIESTS, LEVITES, PRINCE, AND CITY

The division of the whole country is described in ch. 48, which includes the substance of the present passage, and shows the position of these lands in relation to those of the tribes. The holy portion (Fig. 7, $abgh$) was to be 25,000 cubits long (ab, gh) and 20,000 cubits broad (ag, bh). The sanctuary (s) was to occupy a square of 500 cubits each way, with a border on every side of 50 cubits more. The holy portion was to be subdivided into a portion ($efgh$) 25,000 by 10,000 cubits, containing the

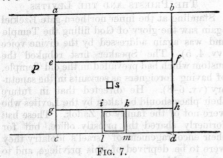

FIG. 7.

sanctuary, and allotted to the priests ; and a portion ($abef$) of the same size, allotted to the Levites. Alongside the priests' portion was to be a strip ($ghcd$) 25,000 by 5,000 cubits, for the city and the people. These three portions would form a square of 25,000 cubits each way, and E. and W. of this the possessions of the prince (P, P) were to extend to the boundaries of the land.

1. Ten thousand] RM ' twenty thousand.'

Reeds] should be ' cubits.' **3.** *And* the **most holy** *place*] RV ' which is most holy.'

5. The five and twenty.. the ten] omit **the** with RV. **For twenty chambers**] read with LXX, ' for cities to dwell in.' **6.** For details of this portion see 48 16-19. **7. The length.. portions**] RV ' in length answerable unto one of the portions,' i.e. the tribal portions on the N. and S. See Fig. 8 and 48 22.

CHAPTER 45 9-17

THE PRINCE'S DUES AND OBLIGATIONS

The oppressive exactions of the former rulers were to be unknown in the restored Israel. Weights and measures were to be just and correct. The prince was to receive from the people a sixtieth of their wheat and barley, a hundredth part of their oil, and one in two hundred of their flocks. Out of these supplies the prince was to provide all the regular sacrifices for the Temple.

10. The ephah (dry measure) and the **bath** (liquid measure) were each the tenth of an homer. **12. Twenty shekels.. maneh**] read with LXX, ' five (shekels) shall be five, and ten shekels ten, and fifty shekels shall be your maneh.' A shekel was 20 gerahs, and a maneh 50 shekels or 1,000 gerahs. **13.** 1 in 60: see v. 10. **14. Cor**] equivalent to ' homer.' The proportion is 1 in 100.

CHAPTERS 45 18-46 24

THE OFFERINGS AT THE SACRED SEASONS, etc.

(This whole passage should be compared with Nu 28, 29.)

(a) The Atonement for the Sanctuary (45 18-20)

This was to take place twice yearly, on the first days of the first and seventh months. These two days in Ezekiel serve the same purpose as the great Day of Atonement on the tenth day of the seventh month (Lv 16 Nu 29 7-11).

20. The seventh *day* **of the month**] LXX ' in the seventh month, on the first day of the month.' **Reconcile**] RV ' make atonement for.'

(b) The Passover (45 21-24)

With these regulations cp. Ex 12 18-20 Lv 23 5-8 Nu 9 2,3 Dt 16 1-8.

23. Kid of the goats] RV ' he-goat.'

(c) The Feast of Tabernacles (45 25)

This was to hold the same place in the seventh month as the Passover in the first month: cp. Lv 23 34-36 Nu 29 12-38 Dt 16 13-15. Ezekiel makes no mention of the Feast of Weeks (Pentecost).

(d) The Sabbaths and New Moons (46 1-8)

On these occasions the E. gateway of the inner court, which was shut at other times, was opened all day. The prince was allowed to enter the gateway by the porch, which was next the outer court (40 34), to prepare his offerings, and to worship at the (inner) threshold of the gateway, but not to enter the inner court. The people worshipped in the outer court, at the entrance of the same gateway : cp. with these vv. Nu 28 9-15.

5, 7. Meat offering] RV 'meal offering.'

7. His hand . . unto] RV 'he is able.'

(e) Various Regulations for Worship
(46 9-12)

No one was to leave the outer court by the gate by which he came in. If he entered by the N. gate he must go out by the S. and *vice versâ* (v. 9). The prince and the people were to enter and leave together (v. 10). The meat offering on all sacred occasions was to be the same as that on the new moon (v. 11 : cp. v. 7). When the prince wished to make a free-will offering the inner E. gate was to be opened for him as on the sabbaths and new moons (v. 12).

8. The prince in the midst of them . . shall go in] RV ' the prince . . shall go in in the midst of them.'

12. Voluntary] RV 'freewill offering, a.' **Voluntarily**] RV 'as a freewill offering.'

(f) The Daily Burnt Offering (46 13-15)

Cp. with this Ex 29 38-40 Nu 28 3-8. The proportions of Ezekiel's meal offering differ from those in Ex and Nu, and he says nothing about a drink offering or an evening sacrifice.

14. Temper with] RV 'moisten.' **Meat offering**] RV 'meal offering ': so in v. 15.

(g) Gifts of Land by the Prince (46 16-18)

Such gifts could only be made from the Prince's own possessions (Fig. 7, *P P*). If they were given to his sons they were made in perpetuity, but if to his servants, they returned to him in the year of jubilee : see Lv 25 10 27 24.

(h) The Kitchens of the Priests and the People (46 19-24)

On the W. of the holy chambers N. of the Temple (Fig. 3, *G G*[1]) Ezekiel was shown a place (*L*) where the priests cooked the parts of the sacrifice which they ate in the chambers (42 13). We may assume that there was a similar place (*L*) adjoining the holy chambers (*G G*[1]) on the S. of the Temple (vv. 19, 20). In every corner of the outer court there was a building (*M*) 40 cubits by 30, where the Temple servants (the Levites) cooked the sacrifices to be eaten by the people (vv. 21–24).

22. Joined of] RV 'inclosed.' **23. Places of them that boil**] RV ' boiling houses.'

CHAPTER 47 1-12
THE LIFE-GIVING STREAM

Ezekiel was now brought in his vision to the

door of the Temple proper. Here he saw a stream of water which came from beneath the threshold somewhat to the S. of the entrance, and ran eastwards, crossing the inner court on the S. of the altar, and leaving the outer court on the S. of the outer E. gate. It rapidly deepened till it became an unfordable river, with trees on both its banks. It traversed the barren region between Jerusalem and the Dead Sea, and entering the latter removed its bitterness, so that its waters, hitherto lifeless, were filled with fish. Only the salt marshes bordering the Dead Sea were unaffected by the river, as they were necessary for the supply of salt to the country. The trees on the banks of the river were evergreen and bore fruit every month. Their fruit was nourishing and their leaves medicinal. This picture probably had its origin in the fact that a small stream of water actually arose in the Temple hill, but everything in the account of Ezekiel's river points to the greatest possible change in the physical conditions of the coming age, a change that would involve the miraculous, as no natural stream could increase in volume without tributaries. To Ezekiel this river was not a mere symbol of spiritual refreshment. The perfect kingdom of God still presented itself to him in an earthly form, accompanied by outward fertility and other material blessings. This passage is the basis of Rev 22 1, 2. For a similar, yet differen⁺ picture of physical change in the future age see Zech 14 8.

1. Right side] i.e. S. : so in v. 2. **2.** Ezekiel was led from the inner court through the inner and outer N. gates, round to the outside of the outer E. gate. This was necessary, as both the inner and outer E. gates were shut. **8. East country**] the wilderness of Judæa, between Jerusalem and the Dead Sea. **Desert**] RV ' Arabah,' the great depression of the Jordan valley and Dead Sea. **9. Rivers**] should be 'river,' as in LXX. **10. En-gedi . . En-eglaim**] places on the shore of the Dead Sea. The situation of the latter is unknown. **The great sea**] the Mediterranean. **12. Be consumed**] RV 'fail.' **According to his months**] RV 'every month.' **Medicine**] RV 'healing.'

CHAPTER 47 13-23
THE BOUNDARIES OF THE LAND

This passage may be compared with Nu 34 1-12. The N. border started from a point on the Mediterranean, and ran eastward by Hamath and other places to Hazar-enon, between Damascus and the Hauran. The E. border ran southward from here, between Gilead and the land of Israel, and followed the Jordan, ending at Tamar, S. of the Dead Sea. From Tamar the S. border ran by Meriboth-kadesh to the brook of Egypt at the SE. corner of the Mediterranean. The W.

border is formed by the Mediterranean (vv. 13–21). Strangers born in the land were to share it with the Israelites (vv. 22, 23).

14. Lifted up mine hand] sware.

15, 16. Hethlon .. Zedad .. Berothah, Sibraim] are unknown localities. **As men go to Zedad ; Hamath]** RV 'unto the entering in of Zedad, Hamath.' Hamath and Zedad have probably changed places. 'The entering in of Hamath ' was a well-known pass between Lebanon and Anti-Lebanon.

17. Hazar-enan, the border, etc.] RV 'Hazar-enon at the border.' Hazar-enon and Hazar-hatticon (v. 16) are probably the same.

18. Ye shall measure] should possibly be ' from Hazar-enon ' (see v. 19). **From Hauran, and from Damascus]** must mean ' between Hauran and Damascus,' where Hazar-enon lay (vv. 16, 17). **Hauran** is a district E. of the Jordan and S. of Damascus. **From Gilead, and from the land of Israel]** means, 'between Gilead' (E. of the Jordan) 'and the land of Israel' (W. of it). **The east sea]** the Dead Sea. **19. Tamar]** unknown, but probably near the S. end of the Dead Sea.

Strife *in* **Kadesh]** RV 'Meriboth-kadesh,' Kadesh-barnea, in the wilderness on the S. of Palestine (Nu 20[13]). **The river]** RV 'the brook of Egypt,' the Rhinocolura or Wady-el-Arish, which enters the Mediterranean at its SE. corner.

CHAPTER 48
The Division of the Land and the Plan of the City

(*a*) **The Tribes** (vv. 1–7, 23–29)

These were twelve in number, as the two tribes descended from Joseph (47[13]) made up for the exclusion of Levi. From the N. border (v. 1) to the S. border (v. 28) the country was divided into 13 parallel zones, running across it from the E. to the W. boundary. Starting from the N., seven of these were assigned in order to the tribes of Dan, Asher, Naphtali, Manasseh, Ephraim, Reuben, and Judah. Passing over the eighth portion, the remaining five were allotted to the tribes of Benjamin, Simeon, Issachar, Zebulun, and Gad respectively (see Fig. 8).

1. To the coast of] RV 'beside.' **As one goeth to]** RV 'to the entering in of.' **For these are his sides]** RV 'and they shall have their sides.' **28.** See on 47[19].

(*b*) **The Sacred Territory** (vv. 8–22)

This has already been partly described in 45[1-8]. It formed a zone extending from the Mediterranean to the Jordan, between the portion of Judah on the N. and that of Benjamin on the S. (see Fig. 8). Its breadth was 25,000 cubits from N. to S. (v. 8). The central portion formed a square of 25,000 cubits each way, and included the domains of the Levites,

priests, and city, as described in 45[8-15] (see Fig. 7). The strip of 25,000 cubits by 5,000 (Fig. 7, *g h c d*), assigned to the city, consisted of a central square 5,000 cubits each way (*i k l m*), which contained the city proper, a square of 4,500 cubits each way (v 16), surrounded on all sides by a border (suburbs) 250 cubits across (v. 17). E. and W. of this square were two rectangles (*g i c l*, *k h m d*), each 10,000 cubits by 5,000, to be cultivated by the citizens for food (vv. 18, 19). On the E. and W. of the great square formed by the lands of the Levites, priests, and city, lay the possessions of the prince (Fig. 7, *P P*), extending to the Mediterranean on the W. and the Jordan on the E., as described in 45[7] (vv. 21, 22).

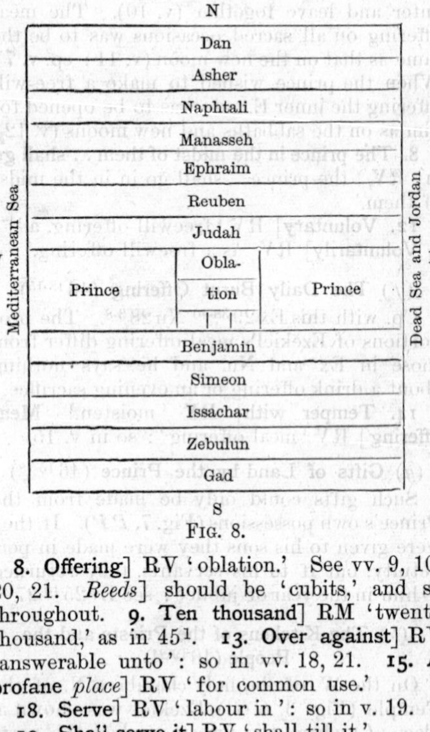

FIG. 8.

8. Offering] RV 'oblation.' See vv. 9, 10, 20, 21. *Reeds]* should be 'cubits,' and so throughout. **9. Ten thousand]** RM 'twenty thousand,' as in 45[1]. **13. Over against]** RV 'answerable unto': so in vv. 18, 21. **15. A profane** *place]* RV 'for common use.'

18. Serve] RV 'labour in ': so in v. 19. **19. Shall serve it]** RV 'shall till it.' **21. The portions]** The territories of Judah and Benjamin.

(*c*) **The Gates of the City** (vv. 30–35)

The city, excluding the suburbs, was a square of 4,500 cubits each way, or 18,000 cubits in circuit. It had twelve gates, three on each side, and called after the twelve tribes, Joseph being here one tribe. The name of the city, **Jehovah-Shammah**, expressed the abiding presence of God with His people. This passage is the basis of Rev 22[12, 13, 16].

30. Measures] means 'cubits': so in vv. 33 **35.** In vv. 32, 34 for **reeds** (RV) read ' cubits.

DANIEL

INTRODUCTION

THE book of Daniel occupies a place by itself in the OT., owing to the exceptional features which it presents and the peculiar difficulties with which it confronts the reader. It has been the subject of much discussion and controversy, especially in recent times, and most Christian scholars now hold views both of its interpretation and of its literary character, authorship, and date, different from those which were formerly accepted in the church. Before entering on the special questions at issue regarding it, it will be of advantage to take a general survey of its contents.

1. Contents. The book professes to be a history of Daniel, a Jewish exile who was carried away to Babylon before the fall of his native kingdom, lived at the court of Nebuchadnezzar, and survived till the days of Cyrus, the Persian conqueror of Babylon. It falls naturally into two parts : (a) chs. 1–6, containing narratives about Daniel and his companions, written in the third person, and (b) chs. 7–12, containing the visions of Daniel regarding the future, and written in the first person. One of the narratives—that of Nebuchadnezzar's Dream-Image in c. 2—is akin in subject to the latter section. From 2^4 to the close of c. 7 the book is written in Aramaic (known also as Chaldee, or Syriac, a kindred language to Hebrew), the rest of the book being in Hebrew. The division of language is not clearly connected with any division of subject, and has not yet been satisfactorily explained. The following table shows the contents of the book in outline :

Narratives.
C. 1. The training of Daniel and his companions.
C. 2. The Dream-Image (predictive).
C. 3. The Fiery Furnace.
C. 4. The Madness of Nebuchadnezzar.
C. 5. Belshazzar's Feast.
C. 6. The Den of Lions.

Visions.
C. 7. The Four Beasts.
C. 8. The Ram and the He-Goat.
C. 9. The Seventy Weeks.
C. 10–12. The Kings of the N. and S.

2. Historical Survey. While various points in the predictive portions of the book have received different interpretations, there are undoubted allusions to the course of events for several centuries following Daniel's time, and a brief outline of the period is therefore necessary at this stage.

The Babylonian Empire was founded by the father of Nebuchadnezzar, and became supreme in western Asia after Nebuchadnezzar's victory over the king of Egypt at Carchemish in 605 B.C. ($Jer 46^2$). It was under Nebuchadnezzar that the fall of the Jewish kingdom and the final captivity of the Jewish nation took place in 586 B.C. The Babylonian empire lasted through the reigns of several kings who succeeded Nebuchadnezzar, and came to an end in 539 B.C., when Babylon was conquered by Cyrus, king of Persia, who in his first year issued an edict permitting the captive Jews to return to Palestine to rebuild the Temple at Jerusalem ($Ezr 1^{1-4}$).

The Persian (or **Medo-Persian**) **Empire** lasted from 539 to 333 B.C., when its last king was conquered by Alexander the Great. Its first, fourth, fifth, and sixth kings, Darius Hystaspes, Xerxes (Ahasuerus), and Artaxerxes are mentioned in the OT. It was Xerxes who conducted the great invasion of Greece which was so gloriously repelled, and which has made the names of Thermopylæ and Salamis (480 B.C.) immortal in history.

The Greek Empire, founded by Alexander the Great, was of short duration in its undivided state. Alexander died in 322 B.C., and his dominions were broken up. After several years of conflict they were finally divided among four of his generals. Our attention in the book of Daniel is confined to two of these and their successors. **Seleucus** obtained the Babylonian and Syrian portions of Alexander's empire, and fixed his capital at Antioch. His descendants are known as the Seleucidæ, or Greek kings of Syria. **Ptolemy Lagi** got possession of Egypt, and assumed the surname of Soter. He was followed by a line of Lagidæ or Ptolemies, the Greek kings of Egypt. These two kingdoms of Syria and Egypt had a long history of rivalry, varied by fruitless attempts to establish alliance through royal marriages. Palestine formed a debateable ground between them, and many struggles took place for its possession. Speaking generally, it was at first under the power of Egypt, and afterwards passed into the hands of Syria. The eighth Syrian king, **Antiochus Epiphanes** (176–164 B.C.), is especially important in relation to the book of Daniel. He engaged in several wars with Egypt, and persecuted the Jews with great severity on account of their resistance to his attempts to introduce heathen religious observances among them. His profanations and oppressions led to the heroic and successful struggles of Judas Maccabæus and his brothers, which are recorded in the books of Maccabees in the Apocrypha.

3. The Visions of Daniel. The interpretation of the predictive portion of the book is quite distinct from the question of date and authorship, and may be treated separately. There are five outlines of the future which call for consideration—those in chs. 2, 7, 8, 9, and 10–12 respectively. Of these the third and the last are clearly explained in the book itself to refer to the events of which an outline has been given in the last paragraph. The vision of the Ram and the He-Goat (c. 8) describes the Medo-Persian empire (the two-horned Ram), its conquest by Alexander the Great (the He-Goat), the four successors of Alexander (the four horns of the Goat), and the career of Antiochus Epiphanes (who is universally recognised under the figure of the Little Horn). The concluding vision, of which c. 11 is the most important part, similarly describes the first kings of Persia, and alludes to the war of Xerxes against Greece. Then come Alexander's conquest of Persia, and the breaking up of his kingdom into four. The greater part of the vision is occupied with a minute account of the political relations between successive kings of Syria and Egypt, and at the end special prominence is given to the doings of a 'vile person,' in whom again all interpreters recognise Antiochus Epiphanes. With regard to the remaining predictions, the four parts of Nebuchadnezzar's Dream-Image (c. 2), and the Four Beasts of c. 7, have always been rightly regarded as parallel, and the interpretation of the one series therefore decides that of the other. In both of these visions four successive kingdoms are spoken of, which the older expositors identified as the Babylonian, Medo-Persian, Greek, and Roman. The chief ground for understanding the fourth kingdom to be the Roman is the statement in 2^{24}, 'In the days of those kings shall the God of heaven set up a kingdom which shall never be destroyed,' the supposed reference being to the Advent of Christ under the Romans. On this view the Ten Horns of the Fourth Beast in c. 7 have to be connected in some way with the Roman empire, while the Little Horn of the same chapter is identified with the Antichrist foretold in the NT. The Seventy Weeks of c. 9, too, have been supposed

to reach down to Christian times, and to include the Crucifixion of Christ, and the destruction of Jerusalem by the Romans in 70 A.D. This interpretation is mainly based on the references to 'Messiah the Prince' ($9^{25, 26}$), and on our Lord's quotation of the phrase 'the abomination of desolation' (9^{27}) in His discourse on the destruction of Jerusalem and the end of the world (Mt 24^{15} Mk 13^{14}). The more modern view of these visions, however, is that the fourth kingdom of chs. 2 and 7 is not the Roman but the Greek empire, that the Ten Horns of c. 7 are to be found among the successors of Alexander the Great, and that the Little Horn is Antiochus Epiphanes. The Seventy Weeks, too, are regarded as terminating with this king, the last 'week' covering the last seven years of his reign (171–164 B.C.).

The reasons in favour of the latter view may be briefly indicated. They arise mainly from a comparison of the different predictive outlines in the book. The more closely these outlines are studied side by side the more clearly does it appear that they are all parallel to one another, and have all the same termination in the days of Antiochus Epiphanes. Starting for example with c. 8, where the Little Horn (vv. 9–12, 23–25) is undoubtedly Antiochus Epiphanes, we may compare it with c. 7, where another Little Horn and its end are described in very similar terms (vv. 8, 24–26). Further, the period of 1,150 days (2,300 evenings and mornings) in 8^{14} is approximately the same as the 'time, times, and dividing of time' ($3\frac{1}{2}$ years) in 7^{25}. Or we may compare c. 8 with c. 9. In $8^{11, 12}$ the abolition of the daily sacrifice by Antiochus Epiphanes is described, and the 1,150 days already referred to represent the period during which the Temple was polluted in his reign. Now in 9^{27} we read of the cessation of the daily sacrifice for a similar time—the half ($3\frac{1}{2}$ years) of the seventieth 'week.' Or again we may start from the undisputed ground of the last vision. Here the abolition of the daily sacrifice and the setting up of the 'abomination of desolation' are ascribed to Antiochus Epiphanes (11^{31}), while the same events are in 9^{27} placed together at the end of the Seventy Weeks. C. 12 is the conclusion of the vision of which c. 11 forms the principal part, and further defines the 'time of the end' to which the outline in the latter chapter reaches. Here again we have the taking away of the daily sacrifice and the setting up of the 'abomination of desolation' (12^{11}). The duration of the persecution by Antiochus Epiphanes is described as 'a time, times, and a half' (12^{7}), while two other turning points in the history are indicated as happening a little later, at the end of 1,290 and 1,335 days respectively. The phrase the 'time of the end' ($8^{17, 19}$ 11^{40} $12^{4, 9}$) defined as the termination of the visions in these chapters.

is also the limiting horizon of Daniel's whole outlook upon the ordinary history of the future: see 7^{26} 9^{26}. These parallelisms are more clearly explained in the subjoined table.

c. 7	c. 8	c. 9	c. 11	c. 12
A little horn ($7^{8, 24-26}$)	The little horn. Antiochus Epiphanes ($8^{9-12, 23-25}$)			
	Daily sacrifice taken away by Antiochus ($8^{11, 12}$)	Daily sacrifice taken away (9^{27})	Daily sacrifice abolished by Antiochus (11^{31})	From abolition of daily sacrifice (12^{11}) and
	'Transgression of desolation' (8^{13})	'Abomination of desolation' set up (9^{27}) for	'Abomination of desolation' set up by Antiochus (11^{31})	Setting up of 'abomination of desolation' (12^{11})
Power of the little horn lasts till 'a time, times, and the dividing of time' (7^{25})	Temple cleansed after 1,150 days (8^{14})	Half a 'week' (3½ years) (9^{27})	. . . . . .	'A time, times, and a half' (12^7) 1,290 days 1,335 days to
'the end' (7^{26})	The 'time of the end' ($8^{17, 19}$)	'the end' (9^{26})	The 'time of the end' (11^{40})	the 'time of the end' ($12^{4,9}$)

It thus appears probable that Antiochus Epiphanes is the Little Horn, not only of c. 8, but also of c. 7; that the fourth kingdom in chs. 2 and 7 is consequently not the Roman but the Greek empire; that the last of the Seventy Weeks falls within the days of Antiochus; that all the references to the taking away of the daily sacrifice and the setting up of the 'abomination of desolation' are connected with his profanations of the Temple; and that the various expressions denoting exactly or approximately 3½ years refer to a part of his reign.

The reasons adduced in support of the older interpretation are easily met. The statement in 2^{44} about the establishment of the kingdom of God 'in the days of those kings' (the Greek kings of Egypt and Syria) is to be explained by the absence of perspective which is characteristic of OT. prophecy, and which is illustrated elsewhere in Daniel. Thus in 12^2 the resurrection of the dead seems to be placed immediately after the destruction of Antiochus Epiphanes and the deliverance of the Jews, and here even such a strenuous defender of the older interpretation as Dr. Pusey sees only an instance of 'that same foreshortening which we find throughout Holy Scripture, and in our Lord's own prediction, first of the destruction of Jerusalem, and then of His second coming to judge the world.' This 'foreshortening' is equally applicable to 2^{44}. As for the vision of the Seventy Weeks (c. 9), while the phrases 'Messiah the Prince' and 'Messiah' in the AV naturally suggest a direct reference to Christ, the true rendering in each case is much less definite, and can be most consistently explained from the historical events of earlier times (see RV and notes). Our Lord's reference to the 'abomination of desolation' is an instance of the frequent NT.

usage by which OT. words and phrases are quoted with an application different from that which they originally bore. That the 'abomination of desolation' was primarily connected with Antiochus Epiphanes is proved by 11^{31} and by 1 Mac 1^{54}, where this very phrase is used of the heathen altar set up by Antiochus at Jerusalem.

Assuming the fourth kingdom to be the Greek empire there is more than one way of identifying the other three: see notes on chs. 2, 7, and table on p. 539. If the Seventy Weeks end with the reign of Antiochus there are various schemes for reckoning the earlier 'weeks,' none of which is quite free from difficulty (see notes). But the difficulties of the older view in calculating the Seventy Weeks and in identifying the Ten Horns of the Fourth Beast, are much greater, and have given rise to the most varied, arbitrary and conjectural explanations. The newer interpretation of the visions is the result of reading the book of Daniel by its own light, and is supported by scholars like the late Bishop Westcott, who have not committed themselves to modern views of its authorship and date.

4. Literary Character, Date, and Authorship of Daniel. It has generally been supposed, and is still maintained by some, that the book of Daniel is the work either of Daniel himself, or of a contemporary who composed the narratives and joined to them Daniel's own account of his visions. On this view the narratives are literal history, and the predictive chapters describe revelations of the future actually made to Daniel during or immediately after the Babylonian exile.

In recent times, however, a different view of the origin of the book has met with increasing acceptance. It is one which, though startling at first sight to the ordinary reader, has very much to be said in its favour, and ought not to be dismissed until the grounds on which it rests, and the possibility of reconciling it with the divine inspiration of the book, have been fairly considered. The modern conception of the book of Daniel is briefly this, that it dates not from the age in which Daniel's career is placed, but from the close of the period to which its visions refer—in other words from the days of Antiochus Epiphanes; that its apparent outlines of the future are really past history thrown by the author into the guise of ancient prediction; that the narratives, though founded more or less on historical tradition, are to be regarded chiefly as stories with a practical moral, and are valuable mainly on this account; that the aim of the writer, both in the narratives and in the view of history presented in the visions, was to encourage the Jews to constancy under the religious persecutions of Antiochus Epiphanes; and that the true prophetic element of the book lies in its confident anticipations of the overthrow of God's enemies, the establishment of God's kingdom, the triumph of God's people, the resurrection of the dead, and the final reward of the righteous. The reasons for this view may be summarised as follows:—

(1) **The Contrast Between the Predictions in Daniel and other Old Testament Prophecies.** Prophecy was not merely, nor chiefly, prediction of the future. The prophets were preachers of righteousness to their own times. Their messages conveyed rebuke, or warning, or encouragement to those among whom they lived. In this work the prophets spoke in God's name, and claimed a special knowledge of His will and purpose. Hence they made use of an element of prediction, foretelling the consequences of evil-doing on the one hand, and the results of penitence and obedience on the other. But in so far as these predictions were definite, they related to the immediate future, dealing with the destinies of men and nations already existing, or with the issues of movements already in progress. Further, such predictions were always provisional. Their fulfilment depended upon certain moral circumstances and conditions. Threatened doom might be averted by repentance. Promised prosperity might be forfeited by disobedience. This principle, clearly stated in Jer 18 7-10, is of universal application. The prophets undoubtedly spoke of the distant future also, but their predictions regarding this were always of a more or less general nature, consisting not of minute anticipations of particular historic events, but of ideal pictures of the triumph of righteousness, of the universal sway of God's kingdom, and of the advent of a perfect King and Saviour. The last-mentioned features are not wanting in Daniel, but in all the other respects which have been referred to, this book

differs widely from those of the prophets properly so-called. Except in the solitary exhortation of 4 27, it contains no practical message for the age of the exile, in which Daniel is placed. Its teaching is expressly represented as sealed up for a future age (8 26 10 1-14 12 4, 9). The earliest period (as interpreters of all schools agree) in which it was fitted to convey instruction and encouragement, was that of Antiochus Epiphanes, 400 years after the captivity. Again, it appears to predict, not in the conditional manner of the prophets, but with absolute certainty, the leading particulars of the course of history during these intervening centuries, the successive empires which arose after the fall of the Babylonian power (chs. 2, 7), the Persian invasion of Greece (11 2), the conquests of Alexander the Great (8 5-7, 21 11 3), and the breaking up of his empire (8 8, 22 11 4), the minute details of the relations between the later kings of Syria and Egypt (11 5-20), and finally the character and career of Antiochus Epiphanes (8 9-12, 23-25 11 21-45). The contents of c. 11 in particular are altogether unique in this respect, and have no resemblance to the predictions of OT. prophecy in general. So obvious is the contrast that some recent scholars, while seeking to maintain the earlier authorship of the book as a whole, have been constrained to regard c. 11 as an addition, composed after the events which it describes. But the exceptional features which appear so strikingly in this c. are more or less characteristic of all the visions in the book, and point to the same conclusion with regard to them all.

(2) **The Resemblance of Daniel to the so-called 'Apocalyptic' Books.** At first sight the only alternative to the older view of the book of Daniel appears to be that it is a mere forgery which can have no right to a place in the Scriptures. But a closer acquaintance with the Jewish literature of the centuries before and after the beginning of the Christian era shows that this assumption is by no means necessary. There is a well-defined class of works, known as 'apocalyptic,' which, though unfamiliar in modern and Western literature, was largely represented during the period in question. The most important of them have only come to light during the last hundred years, and the study of them has shown that the very features which distinguish the book of Daniel from ordinary prophecy serve to connect it closely with this other class of writings. The most accessible example of 'apocalyptic' literature is the Second book of Esdras in the Apocrypha. The principal work of the kind, however, is the book of Enoch, and in addition to it there may be mentioned the book of the Secrets of Enoch, the Assumption of Moses, the Ascension of Isaiah, the Apocalypse of Baruch,

the Testaments of the Twelve Patriarchs, the Psalms of Solomon, and the Sibylline Oracles. Many of these in their present form are composite works, and embody Christian as well as Jewish elements. But in so far as the original groundwork can be separated from the later additions, it may be said in general that these 'apocalyptic' books were written in times when the Jewish religion seemed in danger of being overthrown by heathen oppressors. Their authors preferred (perhaps from prudential motives) to conceal their own personalities and to put their messages to their contemporaries into the mouths of great figures in the past, such as Enoch, Noah, Moses, or Ezra. They based what they had to say about the present and the future upon a view of the world's history as providentially guided and controlled by God, and hence they frequently presented more or less extended surveys of the past under the form of predictions uttered by the great men of earlier times. It was also common for the history, thus disguised as prophecy, to be further wrapped up in symbolic visions. Thus, in the Second book of Esdras, which is to be dated shortly before or after 100 A.D., there is a veiled, yet quite recognisable, description of the Roman emperors of the first Christian century, which is said to have been given in answer to the fastings and prayers of Ezra in Babylon. In the earliest portion of the book of Enoch (dating from the second century B.C.) a prediction of the Deluge is attributed to the patriarch whose name it bears. The Assumption of Moses (written about the beginning of the Christian era) tells how Moses addressed to Joshua a long account of the future history of the Israelites, including the destruction of Jerusalem by Nebuchadnezzar, the restoration of the Jews from captivity, the oppression of Antiochus Epiphanes, the rule of the descendants of the Maccabees, and that of Herod the Great. Now the predictive portions of Daniel have the closest resemblance to this kind of veiled history, and this analogy of itself suggests that the book may be reasonably regarded as a specimen of the 'apocalyptic' class of literature, that it was written not earlier than the time of Antiochus Epiphanes, and that the writer chose Daniel, a great sage whom he placed in the time of the Babylonian captivity, as the mouthpiece of his teaching. This view of the book of Daniel is borne out by its striking resemblance in several other respects to the 'apocalyptic' writings. In common with them it makes a large and peculiar use of vision and symbol. These, indeed, are found to a certain extent in some of the regular prophets, especially in Ezekiel and Zechariah, but it is only in Daniel and the 'apocalyptic' books that they are employed to represent the prolonged course of

history. In Second Esdras, and the Apocalypse of Baruch, as well as in Daniel, the visions are granted after fasting and prayer. The 70 'weeks' of Daniel mark out the course of time according to an artificial scheme, which finds parallels in the 10 'weeks' of the book of Enoch, the 250 'times' of the Assumption of Moses, and the 12 epochs of world-history in Second Esdras. Finally, Daniel is the only OT. book in which angels have names given to them (Gabriel, Michael), and special nations assigned to their care (8^{16} 9^{21} $10^{13, 21}$ 12^1). This is a feature which is still further developed in the other 'apocalyptic' books, where additional angelic names (Raphael, Phanuel, Uriel, etc.) appear. While these resemblances between Daniel and the 'apocalyptic' writings are undeniable, it has been supposed by the supporters of the older view of the book that Daniel is a work containing genuine predictions of detailed history, and has simply provided the model after which the spurious predictions of later 'apocalypses' were composed. But this leaves the special features of Daniel without any real parallel either in Scripture or outside of it, and it seems to be a more reasonable deduction from the facts that Daniel not only has supplied the pattern of the other 'apocalyptic' writings, but is actually a member, though the earliest and greatest one, of the same class of literature to which they belong.

(3) **The Absence of External Evidence for the Earlier Date of Daniel.** Along with the foregoing considerations there must be taken the important fact that there is nothing to show that the book of Daniel existed before the age of Antiochus Epiphanes. The mention of Daniel's name in Ezekiel ($14^{14, 20}$ 28^3) has no bearing upon the date of the book, since these prophecies of Ezekiel were uttered, the one before, and the other immediately after the fall of Jerusalem in 586 B.C., while the book of Daniel, at the earliest, cannot have been composed before the third year of Cyrus (536 B.C.) to which its narrative comes down (11^1). Then, though in the English Bible Daniel appears among the prophetical books, it is not classed among them in the Hebrew Bible, but belongs to the miscellaneous group of 'Writings,' which forms the third division of the Jewish Canon. Now the Jewish Canon of the Prophets was not closed till after the date of Malachi (about 450 B.C.), and if the book of Daniel was in existence then it is not easy to understand why it should not have been included in this collection. It is probable, indeed, that 'the books' (9^2), among which Jeremiah was included, are to be understood of the Canon of the Prophets as already complete when the book of Daniel was written. Again, the book of Ecclesiasticus in the Apocrypha, written about 200 B.C.

contains (chs. 44–50) a list of the worthies of Israel, in which Daniel is not found, though Isaiah, Jeremiah, Ezekiel, the Twelve Minor Prophets, Zerubbabel and Joshua (from Ezra), and Nehemiah, are all mentioned. The earliest references to the contents of the book of Daniel are those in the Sibylline Oracles, an 'apocalyptic' work written about 140 B.C., and in 1 Maccabees, a book of the Apocrypha, composed about 100 B.C. This silence about Daniel, previous to the age of Antiochus Epiphanes (176–164 B.C.), is significant. Though the mere absence of allusions to the book before that time does not by itself prove that the book was not then in existence, it nevertheless lends an additional emphasis to the arguments for the 'apocalyptic' character and later date of the work, which have been already given.

(4) **Historical Difficulties in Daniel.** The book of Daniel seems to contain certain historical inaccuracies regarding the earlier period with which it deals, which present grave objections to the view that it was written by the Daniel of the exile, or by one of his contemporaries. These features, however, present no difficulty on the other view, and in no way diminish the value of the book of Daniel as an 'apocalyptic' work. It is not surprising that an 'apocalyptic' writer, casting into the form of prediction a series of past events, should be more accurate in describing those which are more recent than in his account of those which are more remote. Thus in Second Esdras the author confounds Ezra with Zerubbabel, calling him the son of Salathiel, and placing his vision in the 30th year of the captivity, about a century before Ezra's real time. The Apocalypse of Baruch, again, is dated in 'the twenty-fifth year of Jeconiah, king of Judah,' though Jeconiah (Jehoiachin) only reigned 3 months and 10 days. In the same way while the visions of Daniel describe accurately and minutely the events of the age of Antiochus Epiphanes and his predecessors, the book is rather meagre and vague with regard to the history of Daniel's own time, and in particular its statements about the supposed date of Daniel's captivity, the position of Belshazzar and his relationship to Nebuchadnezzar, and the reign of Darius the Mede, are difficult to reconcile with our knowledge of the period derived from other reliable sources.

(5) **Peculiarities in the Language of Daniel.** The name of the Babylonian conqueror of Jerusalem is always spelt in Daniel as Nebuchadnezzar, while contemporary writers like Jeremiah and Ezekiel generally give the correct form Nebuchadrezzar (*Nabû-kudurri-utsur*), which is found on the monuments. The 'Chaldeans,' who in Jeremiah and Ezekiel are the same as the Babylonians in general, appear in Daniel as a special class of Babylonian wise

men. This usage is found elsewhere only in the later classical writers. It points to a time when the Babylonian empire had passed away, and when the name formerly borne by all its people was confined to the sages or magicians who were the only survivors of its lost civilisation. Lastly, in addition to the Aramaic section of the book, there are in Daniel certain Persian and Greek words, and the evidence of date furnished by the language has thus been summed up by Professor Driver : 'The Persian words presuppose a period after the Persian empire had been well established : the Greek words *demand*, the Hebrew *supports*, and the Aramaic *permits* a date *after the conquest of Palestine by Alexander the Great* (B.C. 332).'

All these lines of enquiry lead to the same general conclusion, that the book of Daniel belongs, as to its literary character, to the extensive class of 'apocalyptic' writings, and that its author lived not earlier than the age of Antiochus Epiphanes. The references to the setting up of the 'abomination of desolation' show that it was written after Antiochus had set up his heathen altar in the Temple at Jerusalem in 168 B.C., while on the other hand the general terms in which the death of Antiochus (164 B.C.) is spoken of indicate that the writer was not acquainted with the exact circumstances in which it took place. If the modern view of the character of the book be accepted its composition may be placed with certainty between these two dates.

5. **The Narratives of Daniel.** On the 'apocalyptic' view of the book it is not necessary to regard these as literal history throughout. They are to be viewed primarily as stories with an instructive moral for the writer's own time. At the same time it is probable that they were, partly at least, founded on fact. The mention of Belshazzar, who is not named elsewhere in OT., shows that the writer had access to some independent sources of information about Babylonian history, and the picture given of the achievements and the character of Nebuchadnezzar is in perfect keeping with what is known of that monarch from his own inscriptions. As to Daniel himself, there is no doubt that his name was a famous one in Jewish history (Ezk 14 [14, 20] 28 [3]), but it is not so clear from these references that he was a fellow-exile of Ezekiel. The name Daniel occurs in the list of exiles who returned with Ezra (Ezr 8 [2]), and it is possible that this person may have come to be identified with the great Daniel of Ezekiel, and may have been placed by tradition in Babylon in the century before Ezra's day. It seems likely that many stories about Daniel had been handed down to the age of Antiochus Epiphanes, and that the writer of our book selected and combined those which were best

fitted to stir up his oppressed and persecuted countrymen to courage and faithfulness to God. Examples of other stories about Daniel and his companions are found in the additions to the book contained in the LXX and the English Apocrypha. They include 'The Song of the Three Holy Children,' 'The History of Susanna,' and 'Bel and the Dragon.'

6. The Right of an 'Apocalyptic' Book to a place in Scripture. It is perhaps natural that the modern view of the book of Daniel should at first sight present difficulties to reverent Christian minds. It seems to involve a degree of fiction, if not of fraud, inconsistent with the divine inspiration which we attach to the books of Scripture, and especially inconsistent with the way in which the book has been used by our Lord. But it is coming to be more and more clearly recognised that the inspiration of the Bible, which guarantees the truth of its spiritual teaching, is compatible with the greatest variety of literary form, that God has used many kinds of human writing to convey His revelation to men, and that each kind must be judged and interpreted according to its own ordinary rules —history as history, poetry as poetry, parable as parable, etc. And if we find that the book of Daniel belongs to a class of literature comparatively unfamiliar to us, but quite common at a certain period in the past, we must not assume that inspiration could not attach itself to such a form of composition, or that divine revelation could not be conveyed by it. We must rather seek to interpret it according to its own nature, when this has been understood, and learn to place its real value in the special religious truths in which it stands apart from, and above, other writings of the same kind. The objection of fraud would only have weight if the writer were supposed to have desired to deceive his readers. But when we read in 'Paradise Lost' (Books 11, 12) the long account of the future history of the world which the angel Michael is represented as setting before Adam, we feel that Milton is only using a literary device which is as transparent to his readers as to himself—a device which had been used by poets like Virgil and Dante long before. And there is every reason to believe that the authors of the 'apocalyptic' books meant their writings to be understood in the same way. Reference has already been made to the supposed predictions contained in the book of Enoch and the Assumption of Moses. Now both of these works are quoted in NT. (2 Pet 2 11 Jude vv. 9, 14, 15), but this does not compel us to take the story of their predictions as literally true. It is but a single step from these cases to the book of Daniel. If 'apocalyptic' writings like those just

mentioned can be quoted by NT. writers, there is no reason why a work of the same kind should be unworthy of a place in the OT. itself. The term 'prophet' used by our Lord is not inapplicable to the writer of Daniel, and there is nothing in His reference to the book committing us to any view of its literary character which we are not compelled to adopt with regard to the book of Enoch and the Assumption of Moses.

It is true that the character and claims of the book of Daniel must have been very early misunderstood. The age of Antiochus Epiphanes, in which it appeared, was a time when the real nature of OT. prophecy was largely forgotten, and when there was a growing tendency to confound prophetic revelation with that mere prognostication of the future which formed the heathen conception of inspired oracles. Not only the book of Daniel, but the other 'apocalyptic' writings as well, soon came to be regarded by the Jews as the actual utterances of the men whose names they bore, and the fact that Daniel was included in the OT. Canon caused this view of it to be taken over and long maintained in the Christian church. But the mere length of time during which such a tradition is accepted without question is no guarantee of its correctness. Many errors, more serious than this, survived in the church for centuries before the progress of knowledge dispelled them. And in the new light which has been thrown on the book of Daniel in modern times it is right to acknowledge the guidance of the Holy Spirit, whose progressive work it is to lead the church of Christ into all truth. If the book of Daniel, when interpreted in the same way as other 'apocalyptic' writings, is found 'profitable for teaching, for reproof, for correction, for instruction in righteousness,' its inspiration is not less real than on the older view which regarded its narratives as contemporary history, and its apparent predictions as unique and miraculous disclosures of the remote future. Tried by this test the book, viewed as an 'apocalyptic' work, appears well worthy of a place in Scripture. While it formed the model on which later books of the same kind were framed, it stands far above them all in simplicity, clearness, dignity, and freedom from tedious digressions and extravagant conceptions. It teaches in an incomparably superior way the truths which they only feebly echo and obscurely reflect. Beneath its artificial literary form we can read the great lessons that God presides over the history of the world ; that the Gentile nations as well as the Jews have always been under His control ; that the succession of human empires is ordained by Him ; that He permits the pride and fury of oppressors for a time, but humbles them in the end, and saves His own ; that His kingdom will come at length, and will endure for ever ; that faithfulness and constancy to Him lead to a life beyond death, and to an eternal reward of glory.

7. Influence of Daniel on the New Testament Writers. Besides the reference to the 'abomination of desolation,' a few other sayings of our Lord are based on the language of the book of Daniel, as, for example, the description of the great tree in the Parable of the Mustard Seed (Mt 13 32 Mk 4 32 Lk 13 19), the pictures of the Son of Man coming in the clouds of heaven (Mt 24 30 26 64 Mk 13 26 14 62), and other expressions in the great discourse on the Last Things (Mt 24 Mk 13 Lk 21). The angel Gabriel appears again in Lk 1 19, 26. St. Paul's description of the Man of Sin in 2 Th 2 includes features derived from the portraits of Antiochus Epiphanes in Daniel. But it is in Revelation, itself an ' apocalyptic ' book, that the influence of Daniel is most manifest. The coincidences in language and imagery are too numerous to mention. We may notice, however, the description of the appearance of the Son of Man (Rev 1 13-15) ; His coming in the clouds to judge the world (Rev 14 14) ; the composite form, and especially the Ten Horns, of the Dragon (Rev 12 3), and the Beast (Rev 17 3) ; the part played by the archangel Michael (Rev 12 7), and the repeated mention of the period of 3½ years (' a time, times, and half a time,' Rev 12 14 ; ' forty and two months,' Rev 11 2 13 5 ; ' 1,260 days,' Rev 11 3 12 6). In contrast with Dan 8 26 12 9 we have the command in Rev 22 10 not to seal up the prophecy, since the time is at hand.

CHAPTER 1
INTRODUCTORY. THE ABSTINENCE OF DANIEL AND HIS FRIENDS FROM UNCLEAN FOOD

Daniel is introduced as one of a band of Jews taken captive to Babylon by Nebuchadnezzar in the third year of Jehoiakim (vv. 1, 2). Along with three of his youthful countrymen he is chosen to be trained during three years for personal attendance on the king (vv. 3-7). As the food and drink provided for those in this position are ceremonially unclean Daniel resolves not to partake of them. After an unsuccessful appeal to the chief official in charge, he persuades a subordinate official to give himself and his friends vegetable food and water for ten days. The results of the experiment are favourable, and the four Jewish youths continue to live on this fare during the three years of their training (vv. 8-16). At the end of this time they are found superior to their fellow-students both physically and intellectually, and indeed wiser than all the learned men of Babylon. They

are accordingly appointed to attend upon the king (vv. 17-20). Special emphasis is laid upon Daniel's understanding of visions and dreams, and the superiority of the Jewish youths is traced, not to their heathen training but to God (v. 17). A biographical note about Daniel is added in v. 21.

Teaching. This c. emphasises the duty of abstaining from food contaminated by idolatry, or otherwise unclean, and teaches that firmness in this respect will bring its own reward from God. These lessons bore very plainly on the position of the Jews in the days of Antiochus Epiphanes (see 1 Mac 1 48, 62, 63 2 Mac 6 18-31 7 1-41), and were of practical importance also in the early days of Christianity : see Ro 14 1 Cor 10 20, 27-29. The wider moral as to the grandeur of fidelity to principle is one for all time.

1. The third year . . of Jehoiakim] presents a historical difficulty at the outset. Nebuchadnezzar's supremacy over Palestine dated from the battle of Carchemish (605 B.C.). This battle took place in the fourth year of Jehoiakim (Jer 46 2), which is also called the first year of Nebuchadnezzar (Jer 25 1). The first question is how Nebuchadnezzar could be king of Babylon in the third year of Jehoiakim. The monumental evidence, however, makes it probable that the first year of Nebuchadnezzar coincided partly with the third and partly with the fourth year of Jehoiakim, so that the statements of v. 1 and Jer 25 1 may both be correct. The second and more serious difficulty is as to a siege of Jerusalem by Nebuchadnezzar in Jehoiakim's third year. The chastisement of Jehoiakim by ' bands of the Chaldeans ' (2 K 24 1, 2) took place when he revolted after serving Nebuchadnezzar for three years, i.e. not earlier than his seventh year. It is said in 2 Ch 36 5-6 that Nebuchadnezzar bound Jehoiakim in fetters to carry him to Babylon, and also took away the vessels of the house of the Lord, but there is no indication of the date of these events, while it appears from Jer 25 9 36 9, 29, that in the fourth, and even in the fifth year of Jehoiakim a siege of Jerusalem by Nebuchadnezzar was still a thing of the future. It has been thought possible that Nebuchadnezzar may have followed up his victory at Carchemish by a rapid excursion southwards, during which Jehoiakim may have averted attack by a timely submission, and a gift of captives and sacred vessels, and that this may be referred to in the words ' Nebuchadnezzar came up' (2 K 24 1). This, however, is very doubtful. It is much more probable that the writer of Daniel mistook the three years of Jehoiakim's submission to Babylon (2 K 24 1) for the first three years of his reign, and placed the invasion of 2 Ch 36 5, 6 in the last of the three.

Nebuchadnezzar] For the spelling see Intro.

2. His god] The patron deity of Babylon was Marduk (Merodach, Jer 50 ²). **Shinar**] the old name of Babylonia (Gn 10 ¹⁰).

3. Master of his eunuchs] T. Heb. is *rab sarisim*, the same title as 'Rabsaris' in 2 K 18 ¹⁷.

The king's seed . . the princes] It is uncertain whether Israelites or Babylonians are meant. **4. Children**] RV 'youths,' and so in vv. 10, 13, 15, 17. **Blemish**] in a physical sense. **Cunning**] intelligent. **Science**] knowledge, so rendered in v. 17. **Learning**] lit. 'book,' literature : so in v. 17. **Chaldeans**] not the Babylonians in general, but a special class of learned men. **5. Meat**] RM 'dainties.' A Persian word occurring nowhere in OT. save in Daniel. **Stand before the king**] as court attendants.

6. Children of Judah] Daniel and his friends belonged to the royal tribe. **Daniel**] The name means 'God is my judge.' **Hananiah**] 'Jehovah is gracious.' **Mishael**] 'Who is what God is?' **Azariah**] 'Jehovah has helped.' All these names are found elsewhere in OT.: see especially Neh 3 ⁸, ²³, ³⁰ 8 ⁴. **7.** The changes of name have a parallel in the case of Joseph (Gn 41 ⁴⁵). The new names had no reference to the God of Israel, and perhaps contained the names of Babylonian deities.

Belteshazzar] *Balatsu-utzur*, 'Protect his life.' Not to be confounded with Belshazzar. **Shadrach**] Perhaps *Shudur-Aku*, ' the command of Aku,' the Moon-god. **Meshach**] of uncertain meaning. One suggestion is *Mi-sha-Aku*, 'Who is what Aku is?' **Abed-nego**] Probably a corruption of *Abed-Nebo*, 'Servant of Nebo.'

8. Defile himself] The king's food might consist of the flesh of unclean animals, or might not be freed from blood, or part of it might have been offered in sacrifice to idols. Part of the wine would have been poured out as a libation to the gods. **10. Your sort**] RV 'your own age.' **11. Melzar**] RV 'the steward': so in v. 16. **12. Pulse**] RM 'herbs': so in v. 16.

17. Daniel had understanding, etc.] A special statement by way of introduction to what follows in the book. **20. Magicians**] A word used only in Daniel, and of the Egyptian magicians in Gn 41 ⁸, ²⁴ Ex 7 ¹¹, ²² 8 ⁷ 9 ¹¹. **Astrologers**] RV 'enchanters.' The Babylonians had an elaborate system of magic, the fame and practice of which survived long after the Babylonian empire had ceased to exist.

21. The first year of king Cyrus] 538 B.C., some 66 years after the third year of Jehoiakim.

CHAPTER 2

Nebuchadnezzar's Dream-Image

Nebuchadnezzar in his second year had a

dream, which he required the wise men of his court to describe and interpret on pain of death. They said this was beyond their power, but professed their readiness to explain the dream if the king would tell them its nature. Nebuchadnezzar persisted in his first demand, and as the wise men could not satisfy him he gave orders that they should be slain (vv. 1–13). Daniel, however, interposed and asked that the execution of the penalty should be delayed. In answer to his prayers and those of his three companions God revealed the dream and its meaning to Daniel, who gave thanks and praise for this favour (vv. 14–23). Daniel was then brought before Nebuchadnezzar, and after explaining the true source of his knowledge proceeded to describe and interpret the dream (vv. 24–31). What Nebuchadnezzar had seen was a great image with a head of gold, a breast and arms of silver, a belly and thighs of brass, legs of iron, and feet of iron mingled with clay. A stone fell on the feet and broke them in pieces, and the whole image crumbled into fragments, and was carried away by the wind. The stone then became a great mountain, which filled the whole earth (vv. 31–35). The head of gold represented Nebuchadnezzar's empire (vv. 36–38). The parts of the image made of silver, brass, and iron represented three other kingdoms that should arise, with characteristics corresponding to their various materials (vv. 39–43). In the days of the last of these God would set up a universal and everlasting kingdom (vv. 44, 45). On hearing the interpretation of the dream Nebuchadnezzar acknowledged the greatness of the true God, and made Daniel governor of the province of Babylon, and chief of the wise men (vv. 46–48). At Daniel's request his three companions also received posts of honour and authority (v. 49).

Teaching. On any interpretation of this c. its central truth lies in the prophecy of the divine kingdom, which is to supersede all human empires—a prophecy which in NT. times is receiving an ever-increasing fulfilment. The reasons for regarding the fourth kingdom as the Greek empire have been given in the Intro. The first three are usually taken to be the Babylonian, the Median (represented by 'Darius the Mede,' whom the writer of Daniel places before Cyrus), and the Persian. Another interpretation supposes that Nebuchadnezzar and Belshazzar were the only Babylonian kings known to the author (see on 5 ⁷), and makes the first two kingdoms to be those of Nebuchadnezzar and Belshazzar, followed by the Medo-Persian empire as the third.

1. The second year] seems inconsistent

with the statement in 1⁵, that Daniel and his companions were under training during three years of Nebuchadnezzar's reign. But it appears from the monuments that the Babylonian kings counted the year after their accession as their first year. The 'second' year might therefore be really the third, while the 'three' years of 1⁵ might include, by another mode of reckoning, the year of accession, the following year, and part of the next. The 'three' years might, therefore, be over before the end of the 'second' year.

2. Sorcerers] another class of wise men. **Astrologers . . Chaldeans**] see on 1⁴,²⁰. **3. Was troubled**] RV 'is troubled.' **4. In Syriack**] RM 'in Aramaic.' The Aramaic portion of the book begins with the words 'O king.' The phrase 'in Aramaic' should probably be regarded as a parenthesis indicating that at this point a change of language takes place: see Intro. **5. The thing is gone**] RM 'the word is gone forth.' Nebuchadnezzar had not actually forgotten the dream, but he was resolved to test the wise men's power by insisting that they should describe as well as interpret it: so in v. 8. **Made a dunghill**] cp. Ezr 6¹¹. **8. Gain the time**] RV 'gain time.' **9. Till the time be ⸃hanged**] till something should divert the king's ⸃pose. **10. Therefore there is**] RV 'foras⸃h as.'

⸃Arioch] *Eri-Aku*, 'servant of Aku,' an ⸃bylonian name (Gn 14¹). **16. Give** ⸃] RV 'appoint him a time.' Daniel's ⸃as very different from the temporis⸃wise men in v. 9. **27. Soothsayers**] ⸃ class of Babylonian wise men. ⸃th known] RV 'he hath made ⸃ in v. 29. **29.** The dream was ⸃o Nebuchadnezzar's waking ⸃For *their* sakes that shall make ⸃oretation] RV 'to the intent ⸃tion may be made known.' ⸃s (RV 'the ') head of gold] ⸃y be identified either with ⸃npire which Nebuchadnezzar ⸃, or with Nebuchadnezzar person⸃ The latter is the more natural inter⸃pretation.

39. Another kingdom inferior] either the Median rule of Darius, which the writer of Daniel mistakenly supposed to come before that of Cyrus the Persian (see on 8²⁰), or the kingdom of Belshazzar, who is contrasted with Nebuchadnezzar in c. 5. **Another third kingdom**] either the Persian empire, beginning with Cyrus, or the Medo-Persian empire, which is represented by a single animal (the ram) in c. 8. **40. The fourth kingdom**] is the Greek empire, founded by the conquests of Alexander the Great. **41. The feet and toes**] represent Alexander's empire as broken up

after his death. **Miry clay**] RM 'earthenware.' There were elements both of strength and weakness in the rival kingdoms of the Seleucidæ and Ptolemies. **43. They shall mingle themselves with the seed of men**] referring to the royal marriages by which these kingdoms sought to establish alliance: see 11⁶,¹⁷.

44. The Messianic kingdom of God will overpower and succeed the kingdoms of Syria and Egypt. **And the kingdom . . other people**] RV 'nor shall the sovereignty thereof be left to another people.' The Messianic kingdom will be in the hands, not of foreigners, but of the Jews. Both the national limitation and the foreshortening of view in this v. are characteristic of OT. prophecy, and do not affect the value of the central truth which is taught. **45. The dream *is* certain, and the interpretation thereof sure**] Note the absoluteness of the prediction, so unlike the conditional utterances of the prophets in general: see Intro.

46. Nebuchadnezzar worshipped Daniel, but it is plain that, though Daniel is not said to have prevented him, the king really meant to give the glory to God. **47. Of a truth, etc.**] RV 'of a truth your God is the God of gods and the Lord of kings.' On the view that this narrative is literal history it is difficult to account for Nebuchadnezzar's conduct in c. 3.

48. Chief of the governors] RV 'chief governor.' **49. *Sat*]** RV 'was.' **In the gate of the king**] RM 'at the king's court': see Esth 2¹⁹,²¹ 3².

CHAPTER 3

THE GOLDEN IMAGE AND THE FIERY FURNACE

Nebuchadnezzar sets up a colossal golden image, and summons to its dedication all the officials of his empire, who are commanded to fall down and worship the image at a given musical signal, on pain of being cast into a furnace (vv. 1–6). They all do so, with the exception of Daniel's three friends, whose refusal is reported to Nebuchadnezzar (vv. 7–12). They are summoned before the king, and persist in their refusal (vv. 13–18). Nebuchadnezzar commands the furnace to be heated seven times hotter than usual, and the three Jewish youths are bound and cast into it, the flames slaying their executioners (vv. 19–22). The king sees them walking in the fire unbound and accompanied by a divine figure (vv. 23–25). He summons them forth, finds them unharmed, magnifies their God, decrees that He be held in universal reverence, and gives them further promotion (vv. 26–30).

Teaching. This story of religious constancy and its reward was specially fitted to instruct and encourage the Jews in the days of

Antiochus Epiphanes. There is a similar legend about Abraham and Nimrod.

1. Of gold] not necessarily solid, but perhaps overlaid. **Threescore cubits .. six cubits**] 90 feet by 9, or rather more. **Dura** is represented by the mounds of Dura, some 12 m. SSE. of Babylon. **2. Princes .. governors .. captains**] RV 'satraps .. deputies .. governors': so in vv. 3, 27. 'Satraps' is a distinctly Persian term. **Judges**] RM 'chief soothsayers.' **Sheriffs**] RM 'lawyers.'

4. People] RV 'peoples.' **5. Sackbut**] properly *trigon*, a stringed instrument with a triangular frame: so in vv. 7, 10, 15.

Psaltery] *psanterin* = Gk. *psalterion*—a stringed instrument. **Dulcimer**] RM 'bagpipe': so in vv. 7, 10, 15. **6. Burning fiery furnace**] a form of death penalty mentioned in Jer 29 22 as inflicted by Nebuchadnezzar.

8. Chaldeans] a special official class, moved by jealousy. **12.** See 2 49. **14.** *Is it* **true .. do not ye serve**] RV 'Is it of purpose .. that ye serve not.' Nebuchadnezzar is willing to put a favourable construction on their first refusal, and to give them another opportunity of obeying. **16.** *Are* **not careful**] RV 'have no need.' **17. If it be** *so*, etc.] read, 'If our God .. is able .. he will deliver us.' The words do not really question God's power, but mean rather, 'If our God sees fit,' etc. **18. But if not**] The refusal is absolute, come what will. **20. The most mighty men**] RV 'certain mighty men.' **21. Coats .. hosen .. hats**] RV 'hosen .. tunics' (RM 'turbans') .. 'mantles.' **23.** In LXX the 'Song of the Three Holy Children' is inserted after this v.

25. The Son of God] RV 'a son of the gods,' a heavenly being, called an angel in v. 28. Nebuchadnezzar could not have used the expression in the definite Christian sense suggested by AV. **29. Made a dunghill**] see on 2 5.

CHAPTER 4
NEBUCHADNEZZAR'S DREAM AND ITS FULFILMENT

In the form of a proclamation Nebuchadnezzar records his experience of the power of the Most High God (vv. 1–3). He had a dream which none of his wise men could interpret (vv. 4–7). He then called Daniel, and told him the dream, in which he had seen a lofty and spreading tree, which at the bidding of an angel had been cut down, its stump being bound among the grass for seven 'times' (vv. 8–18). Daniel explained that the tree was Nebuchadnezzar in his greatness, that he would lose his reason and live a beast's life for seven years, after which he would be restored to his throne (vv. 19–27). All this has come to pass (vv. 28–33), and Nebuchad-

nezzar now magnifies the King of heaven who is able to abase the proud (vv. 34–37).

The picture here given of Nebuchadnezzar's pride is in keeping with the evidence of his own boastful inscriptions. The form of madness attributed to him is not an uncommon one, and is generally known as 'lycanthropy.' No historical record of such an event in his life has come to light. There is, however, a tradition, quoted by the church historian Eusebius from Abydenus, a Greek writer of the 2nd cent. A.D., which, though quite different as a whole from the story in this c., has one or two points of contact with it.

Teaching. The example of pride brought low which this c. contains would afford a significant lesson to the Jews under the tyranny of Antiochus. It is suggestive also that the conduct of Antiochus led some to substitute for the title Epiphanes ('the illustrious') that of Epimanes ('the madman ').

1. People] RV 'peoples.' **2. High**] RV 'Most High.' **7. Astrologers**] RV 'enchanters.' **8. According to the name of my god**] This is merely an assonance, not a strict derivation. The chief god of Nebuchadnezzar was Marduk (Merodach). The word Belteshazzar does not contain the name of the god Bel : see on 1 7. **9. Master of the magicians**] see on 2 48. **13. A watcher and an holy one**] Both terms refer to the same being. The name 'watcher' is first used for 'angel' in Daniel, and is common in the later apocalyptic books. **16.** In this v. the figure of the tree is dropped. **Times**] years. **17. Matter**] RV 'sentence.' The angels are represented as entrusted with the power of deciding the destinies of men. **19. One hour**] RV 'a while.' The dream *be*] i.e. be fulfilled on. **27. If it may be**] RV 'if there may be.'

28–33. In these vv. the narrative, which has hitherto been in the terms of Nebuchadnezzar's proclamation, passes into the third person. The first person is resumed in v. 34. **30. House of the kingdom**] RV 'royal dwelling place.'

CHAPTER 5
BELSHAZZAR'S FEAST

Belshazzar, king of Babylon, holds a great feast, at which he profanely uses the sacred vessels taken by Nebuchadnezzar from the Temple at Jerusalem (vv. 1–4). He is terrified at seeing part of a human hand writing mysterious words on the wall of the banqueting room, and vainly offers great rewards to the wise men of Babylon if they can read and explain the writing (vv. 5–9). The queen tells him of Daniel, and of his fame for wisdom, acquired in Nebuchadnezzar's days. Daniel is accordingly sent for, and Belshazzar repeats to him his request and his promises (vv. 10–16).

Declining the offered reward Daniel rebukes Belshazzar for neglecting the lessons of humility taught by Nebuchadnezzar's history, and interprets the writing as a message of doom (vv. 17–29). That night Belshazzar is slain and Darius the Median receives the kingdom (vv. 30, 31).

Teaching. The profanations of Belshazzar were very similar to those of Antiochus Epiphanes (1 Mac 1 20-24 2 Mac 5 15-17), and Belshazzar's fate would encourage the Jews in the time of Antiochus to hope that their oppressor would be similarly cut off.

1. Belshazzar the king] These words raise another historical difficulty. We learn from the inscriptions that Belshazzar was the son of Nabuna'id (Nabonidus), the last king of Babylon, and never occupied the throne himself. As Nabuna'id, however, was much occupied with antiquarian pursuits Belshazzar was practically 'prince-regent.' See on 7 1 8 1.

2. Vessels] see 1 2. **His father Nebuchadnezzar**] another historical difficulty. Nabuna'id was the father of Belshazzar, and was a usurper, who did not belong to the same family as Nebuchadnezzar. It is possible that he may have married a daughter of Nebuchadnezzar, but of this nothing is known. In that case 'father' would have the general sense of 'forefather' which it often bears in OT. But the emphasis laid on 'father' (vv. 11, 13, 18) and 'son' (v. 19) seems to indicate that the writer had the literal relationship in view, and regarded Belshazzar as the actual son and immediate successor of Nebuchadnezzar.

7. Scarlet] RV 'purple': so in vv. 16, 29. **Be the third ruler**] RM 'rule as one of three': so in vv. 16, 29. The meaning is illustrated by the arrangement described in 6 2.

12. Hard] RV 'dark.' **13. Jewry**] RV 'Judah.' **19. People**] RV 'peoples.'

25. The words are names of weights. The U in Upharsin stands for 'and,' and P(h)arsin is the plural of Peres (v. 28). The literal meaning of the writing was 'a mina, a mina, a shekel, and half minas.' **26–28.** The interpretation given by Daniel is connected with the derivation of two of the terms. Mene signifies 'numbered'; Tekel (= shekel) suggests the process of weighing; and Peres is doubly explained, first by its etymology ('division'), and second by its assonance with 'Persian.'

30. Chaldeans] here used in the national sense, as equivalent to 'Babylonians.'

Was Belshazzar .. slain] The traditions about the capture of Babylon by Cyrus, which classical historians have preserved, are now known from the inscriptions of Cyrus himself to be incorrect. The army of Cyrus occupied Babylon without fighting, and Nabuna'id was captured. Cyrus himself afterwards entered the city in peace. A little later, however, there was a night assault made by Gobryas, the governor under Cyrus, in which 'the king's son' was slain.

31. Darius the Median (RV 'Mede')] presents the greatest historical difficulty in the book. In this v. he receives the kingdom of Babylon upon the death of Belshazzar. In 6 1, 2, 25, 26 he acts and speaks as a supreme sovereign ; in 6 28 he appears as a predecessor of Cyrus the Persian ; in 9 1 he is called 'Darius the son of Ahasuerus, of the seed of the Medes, who was made king over the realm of the Chaldeans.' No such person, however, is mentioned in any other historical source, and the inscriptions leave no room for an independent king of Babylon between Nabuna'id and Cyrus. Cyrus had conquered Media before invading Babylon, and his army comprised both Medes and Persians. Gobryas, the general of Cyrus, who acted under him as governor of Babylon, was probably a Mede, and the author of Daniel has apparently mistaken his subordinate office for an independent monarchy, and has confounded his name with that of Darius Hystaspes (the Darius of the book of Ezra), who was the father, and not the son, of Ahasuerus (Xerxes).

Took] RV 'received.'

CHAPTER 6
THE DEN OF LIONS

Darius the Mede divides his kingdom into 120 satrapies, the whole being superintended by three higher officials, of whom Daniel was one (vv. 1, 2). Daniel is in special favour, and Darius meditates giving him a still higher office (v. 3). This rouses the jealousy of his colleagues, who plot his ruin (vv. 4, 5). They persuade Darius to make a decree that no one shall ask anything for 30 days from God or man, save from the king, on pain of being cast into the den of lions (vv. 6–9). Daniel, as his enemies expect, disregards this rule, and being accused he is found guilty, and is cast, much against the king's will, into the den of lions (vv. 10–17). After a sleepless night Darius comes to enquire for Daniel, and finds him alive and unhurt (vv. 18–22). Daniel is taken out of the den, and his accusers, with all their families, are thrown to the lions and instantly slain (vv. 23, 24). Darius then makes a decree to all the world in honour of Daniel's God (vv. 25–27). A biographical note is added in v. 28.

Teaching. Apart from the question about Darius the Mede (see on 5 31) this c. presents other difficulties if taken as literal history. The decree of Darius seems one which even a heathen king would not be likely to make. If, however, the writer's purpose was to construct a situation for Daniel similar to the circumstances of the pious Jews under

Antiochus Epiphanes, and to read them an encouraging lesson by this imaginative use of the past, the c. well fulfils this object : see especially 1 Mac 1 50.

1. Princes] RV 'satraps' : so in vv. 2, 3, 4, 6, 7. The division of the Persian empire into 20 satrapies was actually made by Darius Hystaspes. Gobryas, however (see on 5 31), is said in the inscriptions to have appointed governors in Babylon, and this may have led to the confusion between him and Darius. Cp. the 127 provinces of Esth 1¹ 8 9.

2. *Was* first] RV 'was one.' This was the arrangement contemplated by Belshazzar (5 7,16,29).

7. Governors . . captains] RV 'deputies . governors.' **Decree**] RV 'interdict' : so in vv. 8, 9, 12, 13, 15. **God**] RV 'god' : so in v. 12. **8. Medes and Persians**] see on 5 31. **Which altereth not**] cp. Esth 1 19 8 8. **10. Toward Jerusalem**] cp. 1 K 8 35 Ps 5 7 28 2. The Talmud says that the Jews in foreign lands turn in prayer towards the land of Israel, those in the land of Israel towards Jerusalem, and those in Jerusalem towards the Temple. The Mohammedans turn in the same way towards Mecca. **11. Praying**] RV 'making petition.' **12. Ask** *a petition* **of**] RV 'make petition unto.' This exact rendering brings Daniel's conduct into sharp opposition against the interdict in v. 7. **14. Displeased with himself**] RV 'displeased.' **17. That the purpose might not be changed**] RV 'that nothing might be changed.' **18. Instruments of music**] RM 'dancing girls.' **23. Believed**] RV 'had trusted.' **25. People**] RV 'peoples.' **26. Every dominion**] RV 'all the dominion.'

CHAPTER 7

THE VISION OF THE FOUR BEASTS

In the first year of Belshazzar Daniel sees in a dream four beasts rising out of the sea (vv. 1–3). The first is like a lion, with eagle's wings (v. 4), the second like a bear (v. 5), the third like a leopard (v. 6), while the fourth is a unique and ferocious monster with ten horns (v. 7). Among the horns of the fourth beast there comes up a little horn with human eyes, which displaces three of the other ten, and carries itself proudly (v. 8). God then appears sitting on His throne of judgment (vv. 9, 10). The fourth beast is slain (v. 11). A human figure appears in the heavens, and receives an everlasting kingdom (vv. 13, 14).

At Daniel's request an angel explains the vision (vv. 15, 16). The four beasts represent four kings (or kingdoms : see on v. 17) which are to appear in succession, and are to be followed by the kingdom of the people of God (v. 18). Daniel's interest centres specially in the fourth beast and the conclusion of the vision (vv. 19–22). The fourth beast is ex-

plained as a conquering kingdom (v. 23), the ten horns are ten of its kings, and the little horn is an eleventh king who shall put down three of the former ten (v. 24), and shall blasphemously persecute the saints for 'a time, times, and half a time' (v. 25). In the day of God's judgment the little horn will lose his dominion (v. 26) and the everlasting kingdom of the saints will follow (v. 27).

Interpretation. The four kingdoms in this c. are presumably the same as those in c. 2. The reasons for regarding the fourth as the Greek (rather than the Roman) empire are given in Intro. See also on c. 2.

Teaching. This c. contains a prophecy of the Messianic kingdom of God. It is expected to appear after the overthrow of Antiochus Epiphanes, and to be in the hands of the Jewish people.

1. Belshazzar king of Babylon] For the historical difficulty see on 5¹. Belshazzar is clearly regarded as actual king, since the years of his reign are reckoned by both here and in 8¹.

2. Strove] RV 'brake forth.' **The great sea**] the Mediterranean. **3.** The imagery recalls the figures, so often found on Babylonian bas-reliefs, of winged lions and other monsters. The sea symbolises the confused welter of nations before the Babylonian empire arose. **4. The first**] beast is either the Babylonian empire, or more probably Nebuchadnezzar himself (see on 2 38), the changing of the beast from the brute to the human condition referring possibly to Nebuchadnezzar's improvement under God's discipline (c. 4). **The feet**] RV 'two feet.' **5.** The second beast may be either the alleged Median empire of Darius (the three ribs in its mouth being perhaps three nations conquered by it before the taking of Babylon), or Belshazzar (the picture of the bear describing his sluggish and sensual nature): see on 2 39. **6.** The third beast is either the Persian empire founded by Cyrus, as distinguished from the Median rule attributed in this book to Darius, or the Medo-Persian empire regarded as one. The four heads are perhaps the four Persian kings who are mentioned in OT.—Cyrus, Darius (Hystaspes), Xerxes (Ahasuerus), and Artaxerxes. **7. A fourth beast**] the conquering Greek empire of Alexander the Great. **Ten horns**] see on v. 24. **8. Another little horn**] Antiochus Epiphanes. The description of this horn is continued in vv. 24, 25. **Three of the first horns**] see on v. 24.

9, 10. The judgment scene is presented in the form of a material spectacle, which is first found in Daniel, though it is common in other apocalyptic books and in the NT. **Cast down**] RV 'placed.' **His wheels**] RV 'the wheels thereof' (of the throne). **Ancient of days**] An expression for God peculiar to Daniel. The book of Enoch has, 'The Head of Days.'

12. The rest of the beasts] the former kingdoms, survived as nations, but without power.

13. *One* **like the Son of man**] RV 'one like unto a son of man'—a human figure as opposed to the four brute figures, and coming from heaven as opposed to their coming from the sea. This figure denotes, not the Messiah as an individual, but the kingdom of God as the successor of the kingdoms of this world.

14. People] RV 'peoples.'

17. Four kings] This statement must be taken loosely. The fourth beast is not strictly a king, but a kingdom with various kings (vv. 23, 24). **18. Take**] RV 'receive.'

19–22. A recapitulation of vv. 9–14.

23. The fourth kingdom] RV 'a fourth kingdom,' the Greek empire of Alexander the Great.

24. The ten horns] are to be sought among Alexander and his successors. The following table of the Greek kings of Syria and Egypt may be useful here :

SYRIA.	B.C.	EGYPT.	B.C.
Seleucus I (Nicator)	312–280	Ptolemy I (Soter)	305–285
Antiochus I (Soter)	280–261	Ptolemy II (Philadelphus)	285–247
Antiochus II (Theos)	261–246		
Seleucus II (Callinicus)	246–226	Ptolemy III (Euergetes)	247–222
Seleucus III (Ceraunus)	226–223	Ptolemy IV (Philopator)	222–205
Antiochus III (the Great)	223–187	Ptolemy V (Epiphanes)	205–181
Seleucus IV (Philopator)	187–176	Ptolemy VI (Philometor)	181–146
Antiochus IV (Epiphanes)	176–164		

Antiochus Epiphanes was the son of Antiochus the Great, and the younger brother of Seleucus IV, whom he succeeded on the throne. Seleucus IV was murdered by a usurper named Heliodorus ; but Antiochus speedily drove out the latter. The real heir to the throne was Demetrius, the son of Seleucus IV, but he only obtained the kingdom after the death of Antiochus. Another rival of Antiochus is said to have been Ptolemy VI, of Egypt, whose mother, Cleopatra, was a daughter of Antiochus the Great. These relationships are shown in the accompanying table :

ANTIOCHUS THE GREAT

Seleucus IV	Antiochus Epiphanes	Cleopatra, m. Ptolemy V
Demetrius		Ptolemy VI

The ten horns are variously reckoned as including or excluding Alexander the Great, and as comprising only Syrian, or both Syrian and Egyptian kings. Including Alexander, the first seven may be Alexander the Great, Seleucus I, Antiochus I, Antiochus II, Seleucus II, Seleucus III, Antiochus III, and the last three Seleucus IV (whose murder may have been instigated by Antiochus Epiphanes), Heliodorus, and Demetrius. If Alexander be omitted, the first seven will include Seleucus IV ; while the last three may be Heliodorus, Demetrius, and Ptolemy VI. The number ten may be a round one, and the exact interpretation of

the ten horns is of less consequence than the recognition of the little horn as Antiochus Epiphanes.

25. The v. exactly describes the conduct of Antiochus (1 Mac 1[41-50]). **Laws**] RV 'the law.' **A time, times, and the dividing of** (RV 'half a') **time**] Three years and a half appears all through the book of Daniel as the period appointed for the tyranny of Antiochus. It is to be regarded as a round period (the half of seven years), denoting a short and incomplete interval of time. **27. Of the kingdom**] RV 'of the kingdoms.' **People of the saints**] Here and in v. 18 these are spoken of as the rulers of the future kingdom of God. The 'Son of man' is not a personal king, but a symbolic figure for God's kingdom in its superiority to the other kingdoms symbolised by the four beasts. **28. Hitherto**] RV 'here.'

The table on next page sums up the general interpretation of chs. 2, 7 adopted in the notes.

CHAPTER 8

THE VISION OF THE RAM AND THE HE-GOAT

In the third year of Belshazzar Daniel has a vision in which he seems to stand by the river Ulai, near Susa (vv. 1, 2). He sees a two-horned ram which behaves aggressively for a time (vv. 3, 4), but is attacked and overthrown by a he-goat which comes rapidly from the W. (vv. 5–7). The he-goat has a notable horn (v. 5), which is presently broken, and instead of which four others come up (v. 8). From one of these there springs a little horn, which

Identification	c. 2	c. 7	Compare c. 8
The Babylonian empire, or Nebuchadnezzar himself	The head of gold	The lion	
The 'Median' empire, or Belshazzar	The breast and arms of silver	The bear	
The Persian, or the Medo-Persian empire	The belly and thighs of brass	The leopard	The ram (the Medo-Persian empire)
The Greek empire of Alexander and his successors	The legs of iron and the feet of iron and clay	The beast with 10 horns	The he-goat
The Messianic kingdom	The stone cut from the mountain.	The human figure 'a son of man'	

prospers greatly, and behaves arrogantly and wickedly, especially against the sanctuary and the continual burnt offering (vv. 9–12). An angel proclaims that its oppressions will last for 2,300 evenings and mornings (vv. 13, 14). The angel Gabriel then explains the vision to Daniel (vv. 15, 16). It relates to ' the time of the end ' (vv. 17–19). The ram is the Medo-Persian empire (v. 20), and the he-goat the Greek empire (v. 21). The notable horn is the first Greek king (Alexander the Great), and the four horns which succeed it are the rulers of the four divisions of his empire (vv. 20, 21). The little horn is a king of one of these divisions, and the description plainly points to Antiochus Epiphanes. Gabriel foretells his various acts of oppression and blasphemy and his sudden overthrow (vv. 23–25). The last two vv. contain Gabriel's parting message to Daniel, and describe the effect of the vision on the latter (vv. 26, 27).

2. A vision] RV ' the vision.' **Shushan .. the palace**] Susa, the capital of the Persian kings (Neh 1 1 Esth 1 2). **Elam**] a region NW. of Persia proper, frequently mentioned in OT. (Gn 10 22 Isa 11 11 Jer 49 34, etc.). **Ulai**] the Eulæus, a large canal in the vicinity of Susa : cp. the ' Chebar ' in Ezekiel's vision (Ezk 1 3), and the 'Hiddekel' (10 4). **8.** For it] RV ' instead of it.' **9.** Pleasant (RV ' glorious') land] Palestine.

10. The host of heaven] the stars, symbolising in Daniel the righteous Israelites (12 3), some of whom were slain by Antiochus : see v. 24 1 Mac 1 24, 30, 57, 63). **11.** The prince of the host] God. And by him, etc.] RV ' And it took away from him ' (God) ' the continual burnt offering ' : see 11 31 1 Mac 1 45, 59. The place of his sanctuary was cast down] see 1 Mac 1 21-23, 39 3 45 4 38. **12.** The rendering of this v. is uncertain. RV ' And the host ' (of the Israelites) ' was given over to it ' (the little horn), ' through transgression ' (the apostasy of the heathen party in Jerusalem, 1 Mac 1 11-15). Practised] RV ' did its pleasure.' Similarly in v. 24. **13.** Saint] RV

' holy one,' angel : see 4 13. Transgression of desolation] see 9 27 11 31 12 11 1 Mac 1 54, 59.

14. Days] RV ' evenings and mornings,' 1,150 days. The period between 1 Mac 1 54 and 1 Mac 4 52, 53, when the Temple was cleansed, was 3 years and 10 days. The 1,150 days may be reckoned from a slightly earlier starting-point in the profane career of Antiochus. **16.** Gabriel] the first mention in Scripture of an angelic name. **17.** At the time of the end, etc.] RV ' The vision belongeth to the time of the end.' This defines the limit of Daniel's outlook upon the future. The termination of this vision is therefore that of all the visions in the book. **18.** Was in] RV ' fell into ' : see Ezk 2 1, 2. **19.** Last end] RV ' latter time.' Indignation] the troubles of Israel are tokens of God's displeasure : see 11 36 1 Mac 1 64. At the time appointed, etc.] RV ' It belongeth to the appointed time of the end.' **20.** Kings of Media and Persia] The Medo-Persian empire is symbolised here by one animal, but its two portions are distinguished, and the Persian rule is regarded as succeeding the Median, since the higher of the two horns comes up last (v. 3). **21.** The king of Grecia (RV ' Greece ')] ' King ' is evidently used loosely for ' kingdom ' (as in 7 17), since the kings are particularised as horns in what follows. The first king] Alexander the Great. **22.** Four kingdoms] those of Alexander's four generals—Macedonia, Thrace, Egypt, and Syria : see Intro. In his power] RV ' with his power.' These kingdoms were severally inferior to Alexander's empire. **23.** A king of fierce countenance] Antiochus Epiphanes. Understanding dark sentences] skilled in deceitful intrigues. **24.** Not by his own power] This rendering may mean ' by God's permission,' or, ' by craft rather than force.' But RM has, ' not with his ' (Alexander's) ' power,' as in v. 22. Mighty] RV ' mighty ones.' **25.** By peace] RV ' in their security.' Some of the worst outrages of Antiochus upon the Jews had this treacherous character : see 11 21, 24 1 Mac 1 29, 30 The

Prince of princes] God. **Broken without hand**] destroyed by God's power : cp. 2 34, 35.

26. Evening . . morning] RV 'evenings . . mornings.' The reference is to v. 14.

Wherefore] RV 'but.' *Shall be* **for many days**] RV 'belongeth to many days to come,' to a future remote from Daniel's time.

CHAPTER 9
THE SEVENTY WEEKS

In the first year of Darius the Mede, Daniel, studying the prophetical books, finds that Jeremiah has predicted that the desolation of Jerusalem will last for seventy years (vv. 1, 2). He prays, confessing the great sin of Israel, and entreating God to have mercy on His people (vv. 3–19). Thereupon the angel Gabriel explains to him (vv. 20–24) that Jeremiah's seventy years are seventy 'weeks,' or 'sevens,' of years (=490 years), which are to be made up of (7 + 62 + 1) 'weeks.' The seven 'weeks' begin with 'the going forth of the commandment to restore and to build Jerusalem,' and end with 'the anointed one, the prince,' and the sixty-two 'weeks' include the building of the city in troublous times (v. 25). The events of the last 'week' are more minutely described. An anointed one is cut off, and a hostile prince destroys the city and the sanctuary (v. 26). He makes a covenant with many for the one 'week'; for the half of the 'week' he makes the sacrifice and oblation to cease, an ' abomination of desolation' appears, and finally the desolator comes to a sudden end (v. 27).

Interpretation. The interpretation of this c. is not without difficulty on any view of the book. Its explanation of the 70 years (Jer 25 11, 12 29 10) is of course an artificial one. Jeremiah meant that the dominion of Babylon over all the nations of Western Asia would last for 70 years from the fourth year of Jehoiakim (605 B.C.) (Jer 25 1, 11), 70 years being a round number for two generations : cp. the 40 years of Ezk 4 6 29 11, 13. In this c. the meaning is extended so as to refer to the humiliation of Jerusalem under a long succession of heathen powers. There are two main interpretations to be considered. The first places the beginning of the last 'week' in the time of Christ, and starts in its reckoning of the 70 'weeks ' from the mission of Ezra (458 B.C.) or that of Nehemiah (444 B.C.). But though the end of the 70 'weeks' is to be placed 490 instead of 70 years after Jeremiah's time, yet the beginning of this period ought to coincide more closely with the beginning of Jeremiah's 70 years. And apart from other difficulties this view fails to give any clear explanation of the different events of the last 'week.' The death of Christ abolished the OT. sacrifices not merely for ' half a week '

but for ever, while the destruction of Jerusalem (70 A.D.) was much more than seven years (one ' week ') after the crucifixion. The second interpretation finds in the events of the last 'week' another picture of the last seven years of Antiochus Epiphanes, and in the first seven 'weeks' the time (49 years) between the captivity (586 B.C.) and the edict of Cyrus (538 B.C.). That the Jews already reckoned Jeremiah's 70 years from the date of the final captivity is shown by 2 Ch 36 20, 21. The difficulty of this view relates to the 62 'weeks.' The time from the edict of Cyrus (538 B.C.) to the beginning of the last seven years of Antiochus Epiphanes (171 B.C.) is only 367 years, which is less than 62 'weeks' (434 years) by 67 years. To this it may be replied either that the 62 'weeks' are merely a broken period, not to be reckoned exactly, or that the writer of Daniel was not in a position to know the precise length of this interval. Josephus and other writers make similar errors in the chronology of that time.

1. Darius] see on 5 31. **Chaldeans**] Here in the national sense. **2. Books**] RV ' the books,' evidently referring to a collection of sacred writings. The Canon of the Prophets was not completed at the time assigned to Daniel.

4–19. The prayer of Daniel contains many expressions found elsewhere in the OT., which may be traced by the aid of a reference Bible. **21. Being caused to fly swiftly**] RM ' being sore wearied.' For Gabriel see 8 16.

24. Seventy weeks] or, 'sevens'—490 years. The expressions that follow certainly form a true description of the results of the sacrifice of Christ, but their terms are general, and they contain nothing that is not included in the pictures of the Messianic salvation which all the prophets connected with the restoration of the Jews to God's favour : see Isa 4 3 32 16, 17 45 17 60 21. **To finish the transgression, and to make an end of sins**] to bring Israel's time of guilt and punishment to an end. **To bring in everlasting righteousness**] to introduce a new era of obedience. **To seal up the vision and prophecy**] read, ' to seal ' (ratify) ' vision and prophecy,' to fulfil the anticipations of all the prophetic books. **To anoint the most Holy** (RV ' holy ')] to consecrate a most holy thing, an altar or a sanctuary.

25. The going forth of the commandment, etc.] Jeremiah's prophecy of restoration (Jer 29 10-14 31 38-40), viewed as delivered at the time of the captivity. **The Messiah, the Prince**] RV ' the anointed one, the prince.' Probably Cyrus, who is called God's anointed in Isa 45 1. Possibly Joshua the high priest, or Zerubbabel (Ezr 3 2 Hag 2 20-23 Zech 3 1-10 6 9-15). **Seven weeks, and threescore and two weeks**] read, ' seven weeks ; and for threescore and two weeks, etc. The 7 weeks' refer to what precedes, the 62 'weeks' to what follows. **The street.. times**] RV 'it' (the city) 'shall be built again, with street and moat, even in troublous times' (the days of Ezra and Nehemiah).

26. After threescore, etc.] RV 'after the threescore,' etc. **Messiah**] RV 'the' (better, 'an') 'anointed one.' A different person from the 'anointed one' of v. 25 is evidently meant. The one appears at the end of 7, and the other at the end of 69 'weeks.' The reference is probably to the high priest Onias III, who was deposed by Antiochus in 175 B.C., and murdered by a rival in 171 B.C. (2 Mac 4 7-9, 23-27, 32-35). **But not for himself**] RV 'and shall have nothing,' an obscure phrase, meaning perhaps, 'shall have no legitimate successor.' **The prince that shall come**] Antiochus Epiphanes. See on 8 11.

The end thereof] RV 'his end.' **Unto the end of the war**] RV 'Even unto the end' (see 8 17, 19) 'shall be war.'

27. Confirm the covenant] RV 'make a firm covenant.' There was a party among the Jews which supported the heathenising policy of Antiochus : see 1 Mac 1 11-15. **One week**] The last seven years of the reign of Antiochus (171–164 B.C.). **In the midst** (RV 'for the half') **of the week**] The same period of 3½ years elsewhere assigned to the profanations of Antiochus : see 7 25 8 14 12 7. **Sacrifice and .. oblation**] see on 8 11, and cp. 11 31 12 11. **For the overspreading of abominations, etc.**] A slight change in the Heb. gives the clearer sense 'and in its place shall be the abomination that maketh desolate' : see on 8 13, and cp.11 31 12 11. **Desolate**] RV 'desolator,' Antiochus.

CHAPTERS 10–12
THE FINAL VISION

These chs. form a connected whole, with three sub-divisions. Chs. 10 1–11 1 are introductory ; chs. 11 2–12 4 contain a detailed account of future events down to the 'time of the end.' This time is further defined in the concluding section, c. 12 5-13.

(a) Introduction (chs. 10 1–11 1)

In the third year of Cyrus, after three weeks of mourning and fasting, Daniel has a vision by the river Hiddekel of a glorious angelic being (vv. 1–10), who addresses him in encouraging words (vv. 11, 12). This angel has been delayed by a conflict with the guardian angel of Persia, in which he has been helped by Michael, the guardian angel of the Jews. He is about to return to the conflict, and will afterwards have to oppose the guardian angel of Greece (vv. 13–21). Michael has formerly been indebted to the speaker for help (11 1).

This conception of guardian or patron angels of the different nations is not found elsewhere

in the OT., but is prominent in the book of Enoch (chs. 6–15).

1. The third year of Cyrus] 536 B.C., the latest date mentioned in Daniel's life. **But the time appointed** *was* **long**] RV 'Even a great warfare.' **4. Hiddekel**] the Tigris (Gn 2 14) : see on 8 2. **7.** Cp. Ac 9 7. **9.** See 8 18. **11.** Cp. Ezk 2 1. **12. For thy words**] RV 'for thy words' sake.'

13. Prince] guardian angel : cp. vv. 20, 21, 12 1. **One and twenty days**] the period of Daniel's fasting (v. 2). The conflict with the angel of Persia explains the speaker's delay.

Michael] a second angelic name. In Daniel Michael is the guardian angel of the Jews (v. 21, 12 1). **One of the chief princes**] a distinction in rank among the angels is here recognised, which other apocalyptic books carry out in great detail. In Jude v. 9 (in a quotation from the Assumption of Moses) Michael is called an 'archangel,' and in Rev 12 7 he appears as a leader among the angels.

Remained] RM 'was not needed.' The arrival of Michael enabled the speaker to come to Daniel.

20. Grecia] RV 'Greece.' The interests of the Jews would have to be maintained against the Persian and Greek powers in succession. **21. Scripture**] RV 'writing,' the book of destiny. **In these things**] RV 'against these' (the 'princes' of Persia and Greece)

C. 11. 1. Darius the Mede] see on 5 31. **Him**] Michael.

(b) History of Persia, Greece, Syria, and Egypt (chs. 11 2–12 4)

The angel describes the reigns of the first Persian kings up to the Greek wars of Xerxes I (11 2). Then he passes to the conquests of Alexander the Great (v. 3) and the subdivision of his empire (v. 4). Next follows a very minute account of various episodes in the history of the Greek kingdoms of Syria and Egypt (the kings of the N. and S. respectively, vv. 5–20). Finally we have a full description of the career and fate of Antiochus Epiphanes (vv. 21–45), and a picture of the troubles which will follow his death and will usher in the resurrection and the reward of the righteous (12 1-4).

It has been supposed by some that vv. 36–45, on account of their resemblance to 7 25 9 26, 27, refer not to Antiochus, but to Antichrist, but this view does violence to the plain continuity of the sense. The resemblances only go to prove that the other passages allude not to Antichrist but to Antiochus.

2. Yet three kings] in succession to Cyrus who is already reigning (10 1). The three are Cambyses, Darius I (Hystaspes), and Xerxes I (Ahasuerus). **The fourth**] including Cyrus I, is Xerxes I, who was a king of vast wealth, and prepared a great army and navy for the invasion of Greece (Herod. vii, 20–29). The expedition was an utter failure, and the battles of Thermopylæ and Salamis (480 B.C.) and those of Platæa and Mycale (489 B.C.) are among the most glorious events in Greek history. **3. A mighty king**] Alexander the Great (333–322 B.C.). **4.** The partition of Alexander's empire is described : see c. 8 8, 22.

5–20. Along with the notes on these vv. the table of Syrian and Egyptian kings on p. 538 should be consulted.

5. The king of the south] Ptolemy I (Soter), the first Egyptian king. *One* **of his princes**] Seleucus I (Nicator), the first Syrian king, was originally an officer under Ptolemy I. **He**] Seleucus. **Above him**] above Ptolemy.

6. The king's daughter of the south] Berenice, the daughter of Ptolemy II (Philadelphus) was given in marriage to Antiochus II (Theos), **the king of the north**, who divorced his former wife Laodice. On the death of Ptolemy II Antiochus divorced Berenice and took Laodice back. Laodice poisoned Antiochus, and their son Seleucus (afterwards Callinicus) murdered Berenice and her child. **She shall not retain . . she shall be given up**] allusions to the fate of Berenice. **Neither shall he stand**] referring to the murder of Antiochus by Laodice. **He that begat her, and he,** etc.] read, 'he that begat her and strengthened her.' Ptolemy II is meant.

7, 8. Ptolemy III (Euergetes), the brother of Berenice, in revenge for his sister's death, invaded Syria (then ruled by Seleucus II, Callinicus), captured Seleucia, and returned to Egypt with much spoil. **7.** A branch of her (Berenice's) **roots**] her brother Ptolemy III. **In his estate** (RV 'place')] in place of Ptolemy II. **The fortress**] Seleucia. **8. Continue** *more* **years than**] RV 'refrain some years from.' **9.** Seleucus II (Callinicus) invaded Egypt in 242 B.C., but had to retreat. **So the king of the south,** etc.] RV 'And he' (Seleucus II) 'shall come into the realm of the king of the south' (Ptolemy III).

10–12. Seleucus II (Callinicus) was succeeded by his two sons, Seleucus III (Ceraunus) and Antiochus III (the Great). The war described was really conducted by the latter. After some preliminary campaigns, Antiochus III was defeated by Ptolemy IV (Philopator) at Raphia (217 B.C.). **10. But his sons**] Seleucus III and Antiochus III, the sons of Seleucus II. **And** *one*] RV 'which.' **Then shall he**] RV 'and they shall.' **His** (Ptolemy's) **fortress**] probably Gaza. **11.** And he (Antiochus) **shall set forth . . into his** (Ptolemy's) **hand**] alluding to the battle of Raphia. **12.** Refers to Ptolemy IV. **13, 14.** Twelve years later Antiochus joined with Philip, king of Macedon, in an attack on Ptolemy V (Epiphanes), the son of Ptolemy IV.

13. After certain years] The actual interval was 12 years. **14. Many**] referring to the Macedonian and other allies of Antiochus III. **The robbers,** etc.] RV 'the children of the violent among thy people.' The allusion seems to be to some faction among the Jews, which took the side of Syria, and thus helped indirectly to 'fulfil the vision' by establishing the power afterwards abused by Antiochus Epiphanes.

15, 16. Scopas, a general of Ptolemy V, was shut up by Antiochus III in Sidon, and compelled to surrender after a siege (198 B.C.) Antiochus then overran Palestine and menaced Egypt. **15. The most fenced cities**] RV 'a well-fenced city,' Sidon.

16. He that cometh] Antiochus III. **Against him**] against Ptolemy V. **The glorious land**] Palestine : see 8 9. So in v. 41. **Which .. consumed**] RV 'and in his hand shall be destruction.'

17. Antiochus III now gave his daughter Cleopatra in marriage to Ptolemy V. **And upright ones with him ; thus shall he do**] read, with LXX, 'but shall make an agreement with him' (Ptolemy V). **Corrupting her**] better, 'to destroy it.' Antiochus in this alliance aimed at the ultimate conquest of Egypt.

18, 19. Antiochus III next overran Asia Minor and invaded Greece. This brought him into contact with the Romans, by whose general, Lucius Cornelius Scipio, he was defeated at Magnesia in Asia Minor. Three years later he was slain in Persia (187 B.C.). **18. The isles**] RM 'coastlands,' the countries on the shore of the Ægean Sea. **A prince for his own behalf**] RM 'a captain,' the Roman general Scipio. **Without his own reproach,** etc.] RV 'Yea, moreover, he' (Scipio) 'shall cause his reproach' (the insults of Antiochus to the Romans) 'to turn upon him.'

19. Fort (RV 'fortresses') **of his own land**] After his defeat at Magnesia Antiochus withdrew to Syria.

20. Antiochus III was succeeded by Seleucus IV (Philopator), who sent his chief minister Heliodorus to take possession of the Temple treasures at Jerusalem (2 Mac 3). Heliodorus murdered Seleucus IV and attempted to usurp the kingdom, but was dispossessed by Antiochus IV (Epiphanes), the brother of Seleucus. **Estate**] RV 'place'—in place of Antiochus III. **A raiser of taxes** *in*] RV 'one' (Seleucus IV) 'that shall cause an exactor' (Heliodorus) 'to pass through.' **The glory of the** (Syrian) **kingdom**] Palestine: see v. 16.

21–45. Antiochus IV (Epiphanes) (176–164 B.C.).

21–24. A general account of Antiochus, describing his accession, his deceitful policy, his hostility to the Jewish religion, his prosperity and his ambitious plans.

21. Vile] RV 'contemptible.' **Shall not give**] RV 'had not given.' Though Antiochus seized the kingdom, the real heir was Demetrius, the son of Seleucus IV: see on 7 24.

Peaceably] RV 'in time of security'; so in v. 24 : cp. 8 25. **22. They**] the opponents of Antiochus. **The prince of the covenant**] the high priest Onias III, deposed by Antiochus in 175 B.C. : see on 9 26.

25–27. The first campaigns of Antiochus in Egypt. The king of Egypt was now Ptolemy VI (Philometor), the son of Ptolemy V and Cleopatra (see on v. 17), and thus the nephew of Antiochus. In 170 B.C. Ptolemy was preparing to recover Palestine, but was attacked by Antiochus, who defeated and captured him. Physcon, the brother of Ptolemy VI, was proclaimed king by the Egyptians, and Antiochus in 169 B.C. again made war on Egypt, pretending to act in the interest of Ptolemy VI, whose friend he now appeared to be. **26.** The defeat of Ptolemy VI in 170 B.C. is traced to the treachery of his subjects.

Overflow] rather, 'be swept away.' **27.** Describes the friendship which was afterwards professed between Antiochus and Ptolemy, but which was insincere on both sides.

28. Returning from Egypt after his first campaign Antiochus heard of disturbances at Jerusalem, due to the struggles of two rivals for the office of high priest. He came to the city, slew many of the Jews, entered the Temple, and carried away the greater part of its sacred vessels and other treasures to Antioch (1 Mac 1 20-28 2 Mac 5 11-16).

29, 30ᵃ. Another Egyptian campaign of Antiochus. This was caused by the news that Ptolemy VI and his brother Physcon had been reconciled. The Romans, however, interfered. Their legate Q. Popilius Lænas met Antiochus four miles from Alexandria and demanded the recall of his forces. When Antiochus said that he would take time to consider, the Roman legate drew a circle round him in the sand with his staff, and insisted on his replying before he should leave the spot. Antiochus then yielded and withdrew (168 B.C.).

29. As the former, etc.] RV 'in the latter time as it was in the former.' **30. Ships of Chittim**] the Roman fleet. **Chittim is Cyprus.**

30ᵇ–35. The persecution of the Jews by Antiochus. After the failure of his Egyptian campaign he vented his disappointment and anger on the Jews, who resisted his attempts to introduce heathen worship among them (1 Mac 1 29-64). In particular he abolished the Temple sacrifices (1 Mac 1 45), and on the 15th of Chisleu (December), 168 B.C., he caused a small heathen altar to be set up on the

great altar of burnt offering (1 Mac 1 54). This altar was used for sacrifice on the 25th of the same month (1 Mac 1 59). The severest measures were taken against those who adhered to the practices of the Jewish religion.

30. Intelligence with] RV 'regard unto.' Antiochus favoured the apostate Jews who supported his policy : see 9 27. **31.** See 8 11, 13 9 27. **32. The people, etc.**] referring to the heroic resistance of the Jews, even to death (1 Mac 1 62-64). **33. Understand**] RV 'be wise.' Similarly in v. 35 : see 12 3, 10.

34. A little help] the Maccabæan revolt (1 Mac 2–4). **Many .. flatteries**] The strict Jewish party had insincere adherents of its own. **35.** The martyrs included leaders whose death tested and developed the faithfulness of their followers. **The time of the end**] see 8 17, 19 9 26.

36–39. The blasphemous pride of Antiochus.

36. According to his will] like Alexander the Great (8 4 11 3) and Antiochus the Great (11 16). **And magnify himself, etc.**] Antiochus IV called himself on his coins *Basileus Antiochus Theos Epiphanes* (' King Antiochus, God Manifest'). **The indignation**] of God against Israel : see 8 19. **That that** (RV 'which') **is determined**] see 9 27. **37. The God** (RV 'gods') **of his fathers**] All the Greek kings of Syria were heathens, but Antiochus honoured the Greek Zeus (Jupiter) more than the Syrian deities of his forefathers. **The desire of women**] probably the Syrian god Thammuz, who was specially worshipped by women (Ezk 8 14) **38. In his estate** (RV 'place')] instead of Thammuz. **The God** (RV 'god') **of forces** (RV 'fortresses')] probably Zeus (Jupiter), to whom Antiochus built a temple at Daphne near Antioch. **39. Whom he shall acknowledge, etc.**] RV 'Whosoever acknowledgeth him he will increase.' **Gain**] RV 'a price.' Offices were disposed of for bribery.

40–43. A final Egyptian campaign of Antiochus. He invades Egypt with a great army and navy. Palestine is overrun and many countries are overthrown, but Edom, Moab, and Ammon escape. The treasures of Egypt are seized, and the conquest extends westwards to Libya and southwards to Ethiopia. Nothing is known of this expedition from contemporary historians.

40. At the time of the end] This expedition introduces the historical crisis which terminates Daniel's prospect of the future.

44, 45. The sudden end of Antiochus. He is recalled from Egypt by tidings of trouble in his Asiatic dominions, returns in anger and encamps between the Mediterranean and Jerusalem, and perishes helplessly. The death of Antiochus actually took place at Tabæ in Persia (164 B.C.). The vague account of his end is in striking contrast with the minute historical description of the rest of his reign, and suggests that the author is here writing of the future and not of the past. For the bearing of this on the date of the book see Intro.

45. Seas in] RV 'sea and.'

C. 12. 1-4. These vv. describe the final tribulation of Israel which follows the death of Antiochus Epiphanes, the deliverance of the faithful Jews, the subsequent resurrection of the dead, both good and evil, and the glorious reward of the righteous, especially of their eminent leaders. The last-mentioned ideals are part of the Christian faith, but, in accordance with the limited view of all OT. prophecy, they are presented in connexion with the Jewish race, and without reference to their distance from the prophet's horizon.

1. Michael] see on 10 13. His intervention at this point indicates a special crisis in the fortunes of the Jews. **The book]** cp. 7 10.

2. Many] The resurrection contemplated is not universal, though it will include both the righteous and the wicked. **3. They that be wise]** see 11 33, 35. **4. Knowledge]** better, with LXX, 'evils.' The last half of the v.

sums up the confusions and calamities of the long period which has been described, between Daniel's days and the 'time of the end.'

(c) Concluding Explanations (12 5-13)

The angel who has spoken throughout the vision has now two companions, one on either side of the river. In reply to one of these he states that 'a time, times, and an half' shall elapse before the end to which the vision points. In answer to Daniel he explains that from the taking away of the daily sacrifice and the setting up of the abomination of desolation 1,290 days are first to be reckoned, and then 45 days more, making in all 1,335 days. The 1,290 days seem to correspond to the general distress under Antiochus Epiphanes, and the 45 days to the further period of tribulation spoken of in v. 1. As the author is here writing of the actual future no exact correspondence of these numbers with historical dates is to be looked for.

9. repeats v. 4, and **10.** repeats 11 35.

10. The wise] RV 'they that be wise,' as in 11 33, 35 12 3. **11.** See 8 11, 13 9 27 11 31.

HOSEA

INTRODUCTION

1. The Man and his Message. The book of Hosea is for several reasons one of exceptional interest. With that of Amos, his older contemporary, it marks the beginning of literary, as distinct from purely oral, prophecy. By this is not meant that Hosea was a composer in the sense that the word would be applied to a Macaulay or a Bishop Butler; but that his discourses, some or all of them at first delivered orally, were afterwards written down in a collected form, together with such incidents of his life as had a direct bearing upon his teaching. This fact is of great importance. We know that Elijah and Elisha exercised a great influence upon the religious history of their time; but we can only to a small extent gauge that influence, because we can form only a crude notion of what their teaching was really like. It is their acts, rather than their words, which claim the reader's interest. With Hosea it is very different. It is impossible not to see that he was a living force; and if his actual influence was not great, that was due to no weakness or omission on his part, but to the fatuity and moral degradation of the people.

Like Amos Hosea was a prophet *to* the northern kingdom, but unlike him he was also a prophet *of* the north. His sympathy was unquestionably with Israel: the fortunes of Judah have only a subordinate interest for him. His mission was to check, if possible, the growing corruption of morals, religion, and politics; and to rouse the nation to repentance, in order to ward off the impending catastrophe. The nation had acquired great prosperity and wealth under Jeroboam II; but these, without moral character and religious purity, only tended to disruption and decline.

What gives quite a unique and pathetic interest to the book is the personal history of the prophet, and its influence on the form which his early and, to some extent, all his teaching took. Other prophets performed various symbolical acts to explain or enforce their teaching (see e.g. Isa 20 2, 3 Jer 13 1 f. Ezk 4), but Hosea's domestic life was itself an acted parable. Sweet and noble as that life was, its importance, as the prophet understood it, lay not in itself, but in the religious truth which it symbolically expressed. In early life he married a woman who proved a faithless wife, and he seems to have made many fruitless efforts to reclaim her (1 2, 3).

After bearing him three children, to whom he gave symbolic names, she deserted him for her lovers (2 2). So forbearing was he, however, that he redeemed her for the price of a slave (3 1), and tried to win her back to purity and love by gentle restraint (3 3).

As Hosea looked abroad on the idolatry and wickedness of his time, he realised that ' the state was the individual writ large,' and that here was being repeated on a larger scale his own domestic tragedy. In Gomer's unfaithfulness to him, he saw a parable of Israel's unfaithfulness to God ; in his own love and tenderness, he saw the reflection of God's love to Israel ; and in his own forgiveness and continued efforts for his wife's salvation, he saw a parallel to Jehovah's loving-kindness and tender mercy towards the faithless nation (3 3-5). Israel, the paramour of heathen gods, had been wooed and wedded by Jehovah, but had proved faithless, going back again to idols, and coquetting with foreign powers. But ever and again, and now most of all, Jehovah was seeking to win the nation back ; even though, as with Gomer, a painful discipline might be necessary (4 1-4).

Tenderness may, in fact, be described as the keynote of Hosea's prophecy. It was a necessary attribute of God, without which He would not be true to Himself. Those who imagine that the God of the Old Testament is only a God of justice and wrath might well study this book attentively.

Though we find no such definite Messianic pictures as those of Isaiah, more than once the prophet foretells the restoration of Israel from captivity, the union of Israel and Judah in one kingdom under a Davidic king, and the establishment of a purer worship and a fuller knowledge of God, as constituting a glorious hope. This hope appears sometimes as imminent, as succeeding a short period of captivity, or even as an alternative to it ; sometimes as belonging to a far-off, or possibly ideal, future : see especially 1 10, 11 3 5 6 1-3 14 4-8. St. Paul explains some of Hosea's prophecies as fulfilled in the Christian church : see Ro 9 25, 26 1 Cor 15 55.

The style of the book is very terse and difficult, and marked by rapid changes of thought and feeling. In some cases it may be conjectured that we have before us fragments of teaching, rather than complete discourses. In many verses the meaning is so obscure that the explanations offered must be regarded as far from certain. In some few no really satisfactory explanation has been yet given, and that partly because our knowledge of many of the events alluded to is very meagre.

2. The Historical Situation. Hosea lived and prophesied in the last period of the northern kingdom of Israel, and probably witnessed, perhaps even shared, the captivity. His work began in the closing years of Jeroboam II (782–741), and was continued under his successors : see 1 1. In Jeroboam's hands the government was firm and stable, and the northern kingdom extended its boundaries as far as the borders of Hamath (2 K 14 25) on the north, and to the Dead Sea and ' the brook of the wilderness ' (Am 6 14) on the south. The death of Jeroboam was followed by a period of anarchy and terror, which was only ended by the Assyrian captivity. Zechariah, the son of Jeroboam, reigned for only six months, when his career was closed by assassination at the hands of Shallum, an adventurer, who mounted the throne only to be slain and succeeded a month later by Menahem, the general commanding the troops at Tirzah (2 K 15 10-14 Hos 7 3-7). In order to strengthen his position, Menahem seems to have asked assistance from Tiglath-pileser III, king of Assyria (the Pul of 2 K 15 19), who took advantage of the weakness of the king's position to claim a tribute. Menahem's reign extended only over four or five years. He was succeeded by his son Pekahiah (2 K 15 23), who reigned two years when Pekah, one of his generals, murdered him in his palace and seized the throne. Pekah was probably the leader of the party in the state that was opposed to Menahem's alliance with Assyria, and preferred to seek the aid of Assyria's rival Egypt (Hos 7 11). In 735 Pekah joined with Rezin of Damascus in an expedition against Ahaz, king of Judah (2 K 16 5 Isa 7 1-9). Ahaz invoked Assyrian aid, and Tiglath-pileser came to his assistance, ravaging Galilee and Gilead (2 K 15 29), and taking the inhabitants into captivity. Pekah, who had reigned for about three years, fell a victim to a conspiracy headed by Hoshea, whom the Assyrian ruler recognised as king. Hoshea ruled quietly for nine years (731–722) ; but, on the death of Tiglath-pileser, he entered into a conspiracy with Seve or So, king of Egypt, and ceased his tribute to Assyria. Shalmaneser, the new king of Assyria, thereupon invaded his territory, and laid siege to Samaria, which fell to his successor Sargon (722), when the kingdom of Israel came to an end.

3. Politics and Religion. There seem to have been two political parties in the kingdom of Israel in the latter years of the nation, just as there were in the kingdom of Judah, one of which favoured alliance with Assyria, the other alliance with Egypt and resistance to Assyria (Hos 7 11). Sometimes one of these was in the ascendant and sometimes the other, but the prophets looked upon the policies of both parties as unfaithfulness to God (Hos 8 9). Isaiah told the people of Judah that their true policy was to trust in Jehovah, and not entangle themselves in foreign bonds. The prophets of Israel took up a similar attitude, and maintained that every movement after outside help was a movement away from God, who would watch over them and preserve them, if they repented and put their trust in Him.

The religious condition was also extremely corrupt. Worship was offered to Jehovah at many high places throughout the land. These were probably in many cases the old Canaanite shrines, and it was but natural that when the Israelites first came into possession of the land they should worship Jehovah at the places where the Canaanites had worshipped their gods. In Hosea's day Jehovah was worshipped at these high places. He was symbolised by the figure of a bull—the natural symbol to an agricultural people of life and power. Jeroboam I set up two such symbols, one at Bethel and one at Dan, where he established the northern kingdom ; and in all probability similar symbols were erected at other holy places : cp. Am 4 4 5 5 Hos 4 15 5 10-15 12 11. The temptation to combine the worship of Jehovah with elements borrowed from the worship of the Canaanite nature-gods was too strong for the Israelites, who had adopted many of the old religious festivals in celebration of the agricultural seasons.

Their familiarity with the worship of the Canaanite local deities or Baalim (Hos 2 17) made the lapse into idolatry easy for them, especially as the Israelites were in the habit of addressing Jehovah as Baali (my Lord) (2 16), a title innocent and proper enough in itself, but improper and dangerous in view of its heathen application. It was no great step from worshipping Jehovah symbolised by a bull to worshipping the bull-image as a symbol of the local Baal : consequently they came to identify Jehovah with the local deity, and assimilated the worship of God to the worship of the Baalim in such a way that the former was practically lost sight of, and they became to all intents and purposes idolaters (2 5). 'For they served idols, whereof the LORD said unto them, Ye shall not do this thing' (2 K 17 12). This worship of the bull-images (or 'calves,' as AV renders) is the idolatry which Hosea so vehemently denounces (4 12,17 8 5 9 10 10 1,2 11 2 13 1,2,8).

The religious condition of the people was reflected in their moral state. The sanctuaries were scenes not only of idolatry, but of gross immorality. The whoredom and adultery of which Hosea speaks (4 10-15 5 3,4, etc.) are not only figurative of the departure of Israel from the service of God ; they are also descriptive of actual moral degradation. The priests were

men of no principle (4 6) ; they let the people destroy themselves for lack of teaching (4 6) ; they rejoiced at the sin of the people, because they benefited by their sin-offerings (4 8) ; and they provided temptations to induce them to evil (5 1). And so it came to pass, as the proverb has it, 'like people, like priest' (4 9). The worshippers were only too ready to abandon themselves to the sensual rites of debasing worship, and thus degradation and decay spread through the nation. ' The heathenish, secular worship and heathen immorality overpowered it, and brought about the premature dissolution of the state.'

4. Contents. The book falls into two parts.

1. Chs. 1–3 describe in different ways and at different stages the domestic tragedy of Hosea's life and its symbolical interpretation.

2. Chs. 4–14 contain separate prophecies dealing with Israel's moral, religious, and political faults, the impending calamity, and the possibility of averting it by repentance or recovering from it after punishment has done its work.

The first part belongs to the time of Jeroboam II (see 1 1), when the judgment had not yet overtaken the dynasty of Jehu (1 4) ; the second, for the most part at least, to that of his immediate successors, but especially Menahem. There are passages which imply a change of dynasty effected by violence (cp. 8 4 and 7 5-7), a state of general disorder such as is naturally associated with a weak government (4 10,18 6 8-10, etc.) and the heavy taxation exacted under Menaham (7 9-11 8 10).

CHAPTERS 1–2 1

HOSEA'S MARRIAGE AND ITS LESSONS

1. A general heading. **2–9.** The prophet's marriage with Gomer, the birth of her three children, and the symbolical meaning attached to them. **10–C. 2 1.** The future material and religious prosperity of the people.

1. A general heading, perhaps the work of a late Judæan editor. Chs. 1–3 probably belong to the time of Jeroboam II ; but it is extremely improbable that any of the prophecies belong to so late a date as the days of Hezekiah, when the punishment foretold at the hands of Tiglath-pileser (Pul) had already been partially fulfilled on Israel (2 K 15 29). That Hosea wrote the book is clear from 3 1.

2. The beginning .. LORD] RV ' When the LORD spake at the first by Hosea.' **A wife of whoredoms]** Hosea is probably speaking in the light of his later experiences. His wife was probably innocent of this evil when he married her—or if not the prophet was ignorant of her true character.

4. For the giving of names for a prophetic purpose cp. Isa 7 3-14 8 1-4. The name **Jezreel** (' God will sow ') signified, (1) the town which was the capital of Israel during Jehu's dynasty, and the scene of the murders by which he established his rule (2 K 9) ; (2) the resowing of the restored Israel (v. 11). The name was given to the child as a reminder of the punishment due for the massacre. **I will avenge the blood]** This prophecy was fulfilled by the overthrow of the ruling dynasty when Jeroboam's son, Zechariah, had reigned six months : see 2 K 15 10, and cp. Am 7 9. Hosea looks at Jehu's murders from a different point of view from that of Elisha and the editors of the book of Kings : see especially 2 K 10 30. They regarded chiefly his outward religious policy and his probably genuine detestation of Baal-worship. Hosea sees mainly the motives of personal ambition and lust of cruelty which underlay his actions. Time had shown that neither Jehu nor his descendants had justified his zeal by any high religious principle. **Will cause to cease]** This and v. 5 extend the prophecy to the final destruction of the kingdom at the hands of the Assyrians : see 2 K 17 6. The valley of Jezreel was the battlefield of Palestine, and nothing would seem more probable to the prophet than that the final overthrow would take place there.

6. Lo-ruhamah] i.e. 'not pitied.' **But.. away]** RV 'that I should in any wise pardon them.' **7.** The verdict on the kingdom of Judah is in the earlier portions of the book more favourable than in the later : cp. 5 10, 14, etc. This prophecy was fulfilled by the destruction of Sennacherib's army (2 K 19 35).

9. Lo-ammi] i.e. 'not my people.' By their sin and perfidy Israel had ceased to act as God's people. They had refused the responsibilities of their calling, and could not expect its privileges.

10. Here, as elsewhere, Hosea cannot bear to dwell upon God's punishments without looking beyond them to His greater mercies. Here he evidently contemplates a restored people, fulfilling the promise of earthly greatness made to Abraham (Gn 32 12), and brought into even closer relation to God, that of sonship : cp. Ro 9 26. **Living God]** i.e. God manifesting His power in action. **11.** As with many other prophecies, the vision of the future includes the union once more of **Israel** and **Judah** in one people (cp. Isa 11 13 Ezk 37 19), a prophecy unfulfilled except so far as the church is symbolised by the whole of Israel. **The day of Jezreel]** The union of Israel and Judah is to be marked by a prosperity which shall take away the reproach from Jezreel (see on v 4). This is more fully explained in 2 23.

C. 2. 1. Ammi.. Ruhamah] This v. is closely connected with 1 10, 11, and must be read along with them. As Jezreel is to become a name of honour in the predicted future, so also the old names of the other two

children will have become quite inappropriate. The **not** will have to be omitted, and they will become 'My people,' 'Pitied.'

CHAPTER 2 2-23
The Discipline and Restoration of Faithless Israel

The unfaithful conduct of Gomer and the prophet's gentle treatment of her are regarded as an analogue of the nation's faithlessness and God's gentle correction, a proof of the love which will triumph in the end. But the acted parable and its interpretation are so blended that they cannot always be separated ; and frequently the prophet's personal experience is overshadowed by the larger thought of God's dealings with His people.

2. Plead] addressed to Gomer's sons. The people Israel in this acted allegory are sometimes the sons, as in 2 1, but more generally the wife. When as here distinguished we may suppose that the prophet is appealing to those willing to hear to remonstrate with the faithless majority. There is a somewhat similar mixture of figure in Isa 62 5. **She is not my wife]** The people by their idolatry had put themselves into a false relation with Jehovah. He was no longer their God, nor they His people : cp. 1 9.

3, 4. As a punishment for her faithlessness, the country would be made desolate by an invading enemy, and the inhabitants slain with the sword. So would she be put to shame. **Children of whoredoms]** By their idolatries the people had proved themselves to be children of other gods, the **lovers** of v. 5.

5. They worshipped the gods of the land— the local deities who were supposed to give abundant crops if propitiated. See Intro. They did not ascribe the fertility of the land to Jehovah, but to the local Baalim, who were personifications of the reproductive powers of nature, and in whose worship they had practically merged the worship of Jehovah.

6, 7. Through the disasters brought by a foreign enemy, including the siege of their cities, the people would discover the impotence of their idols, and seek Jehovah in earnest : cp. 14 8, etc. **Make a wall]** RV 'make a fence against her.' **7. Lovers]** i.e. the Baalim.

8. They prepared for Baal] RM 'made into the *image of* Baal.' How absurd and how insulting to use God's gift in this way !

9. Will I.. take away] RV 'will I take back.' **In the time thereof]** i.e. when it should be ripe, the crop would fail. God would thus punish them for the abuse of His gift.

10. Her lovers] The idols would be ashamed, unable to help their devotees, when the land was laid waste. **11.** Jehovah would put an end to her religious **feasts** of all kinds. **New moons** and **sabbaths** were the most distinctive feasts in connexion with the worship of Jehovah in the N. ($1 S 20^5$ $2 K 4^{23}$).

12. Rewards] RV 'hire': the bribe for which Israel had worshipped the idols (**lovers**) under the mistaken belief that *they* gave them these things : see on v. 5.

13. Baalim] RV 'the Baalim,' i.e. the images of Baal : cp. v. 8. The allusion here is to heathen or heathenish festivals looked upon as acts of faithlessness to Jehovah. They are spoken of as past in relation to the future judgment which Hosea has in mind, or because idolatry had from the first been the besetting sin of the northern kingdom.

14. Therefore, etc.] 'This being her miserable condition, I will entice her to repent by gentle discipline.' The key to such expressions lies in the tenderness felt by Hosea for his sinning wife (see Intro.). **The wilderness**] either the land of captivity in which she realises her sin and turns to God, or the land wasted by the enemy. Men **allure** to destruction : God allures to punishment, to make the outpouring of love possible. **Comfortably**] Heb. 'to her heart,' as in $Isa 40^1$, etc. **15. I will give**] The vineyards destroyed by the enemy (v. 12) would be restored. **Achor**] i.e. trouble. Achor was the valley where Achan was stoned for his sin ($Josh 7^{26}$). It was on this account called the valley of Achor, or trouble. What is meant by its use here is that, while the Israelites would find that as of old sin would be followed by punishment, the punishment was meant to purify and discipline, and the 'trouble' was thus the 'door of hope.' Though Israel had been again unfaithful, God was still 'plenteous in mercy.' **Sing**] RV 'make answer,' i.e. listen to the call of God. **16. Ishi .. Baali**] Both words were used by a wife to her husband. The first, 'my man,' implied a relation of intimacy : the second, 'my lord,' that of servitude, or at least ownership. But the passage seems to imply that Baal, a common name for all heathen gods, had in common practice been used also of Jehovah. This would account for its appearing in several place-names, such as Baal-Hamon, Baal-Shalisha. **17. Baalim**] RV 'the Baalim.' Whether they represented Jehovah or heathen gods, the names with their debasing associations would be utterly discarded.

18. Make a covenant] Jehovah is here represented poetically as making an agreement with, or laying a command upon, noxious animals, that they will not, it may be supposed, hurt either man or the fruits of his labours : cp. $Isa 11^9$. **Break the bow, etc.**] destroy the weapons of warfare no longer needed in a land of security : cp. $Isa 9^5$ (RV).

19, 20. The idols had hired Israel's love with gifts of worldly prosperity, and even these they could not really give (v. 12). Jehovah would woo Israel in the first place with much higher gifts, righteousness, judgment, etc.

21, 22. I will hear, etc.] The natural order of thought is reversed, because Jehovah (through the prophet) is speaking of His work. The whole thought is highly poetical. **Jezreel** ('God-soweth,' used for Israel, for the sake of the play on the word) cries for the corn and wine and oil. These cry to the earth to produce them. The earth in its turn cries to the heaven for rain, and the rain cries to Jehovah to send it. Jehovah hears the cry, and so the heart's desire of the people is granted, even without their expressly asking Jehovah for it.

23. I will sow] With reference to the name Jezreel see on 1^4. Jehovah promises the renewed increase of the population : cp. $Jer 31^{27}$.

I will have mercy] a repetition of the promises of 1^{10} 2^1.

CHAPTER 3

The Attempts to reclaim the erring Wife

In an episode in the life of Hosea and his relations with Gomer (cp. 2^{14}) the prophet finds a parable of Jehovah's punishment of Israel. Having bought back his erring wife, as though she were a slave, he subjects her to gentle restraint, depriving her for a time of conjugal rights, in hope of securing her love (1–3). So Israel, deprived in exile of forms of government and of outward worship, would be ready to receive her true king and spouse (4, 5).

1. *Her* **friend**] rather, 'neighbour,' i.e. a guilty lover. To refer it to Hosea involves a clumsy tautology. **Yet, etc.**] RV 'and an adulteress, even as the LORD loveth.' The love of the prophet for his adulterous wife, here as before spoken of as a direct inspiration of God, is a symbol of the love of Jehovah for Israel, who nevertheless coquets with idols. **Flagons of wine**] RV 'cakes of raisins,' such as were offered to idols. **2. Bought her**] She appears to have become the voluntary slave-concubine of her paramour. **Fifteen .. silver**] presumably the ordinary price for a female slave. Joseph was sold for twenty ($Gn 37^{28}$). **3. For me**] i.e. as my property. **For** *another* **man**] RV 'any man's wife.' For awhile Gomer was to live as though unmarried.

4. Gomer's isolation is the symbol of that of exiled Israel, deprived of political organisation and religious services. **Sacrifice, etc.**] cp. 2^{11}. All forms of religious symbolism are included in this v. **Image**] RV 'pillar.' A religious symbol, probably borrowed from the Canaanites. **Ephod**] The word is most frequently used of the high priest's dress, but in $Jg 8^{27}$ of a golden or gold-plated image set up by Gideon, and that would appear to be the meaning here. **Teraphim**] small household images, probably something like Roman Lares: see Gn 31 , Jer 17⁵, etc. Their use was probably general in early times. Even David did not discard them in his early life (1 S 19¹³ᶠ·), and they were in use at the time of Josiah's reformation in Judah (2 K 23²⁴). **5. Return**] often used of a new line of action or change of life : cp. 14⁷. **David their king**] The idolatrous worship of Israel was closely connected with their political schism : see 1 K 12²⁷⁻²⁹. Hosea contemplates once more a united kingdom under the Davidic monarchy. It is quite possible, however, that by **David** is here meant the Messiah ; cp. Jer 30⁹ Ezk 34²⁴ 37²⁴. **In the latter days**] lit. 'In the after part of the days,' i.e. at the end of time, used of the Messianic age : cp. Isa 2² Mic 4¹.

CHAPTER 4
CONDEMNATION OF THE PRIESTHOOD

An arraignment against Israel as a whole, because of all manner of wickedness against God and man. Prophet and priest, who ought to have taught them better, are only too like them in character, and must share their doom. In vv. 15–17 there is an appeal to Judah not to follow the idolatrous practices of Israel.

1. Controversy] i.e. a lawsuit : cp. Isa 3¹³,¹⁴. **2. By swearing**] RV 'There is nought but swearing.' **Break out**] commit acts of violence. **Blood toucheth blood**] The whole land is covered with the blood of the murdered, a strong expression to denote the frequency of murder : cp. Isa 28⁸. **3.** The whole land (with its animal and vegetable life) is polluted by their sin, and must share their punishment : cp. Jer 4²³, etc. **4. Thy people, etc.**] The reading here seems corrupt. We should probably read, 'thy people are as they that strive with Me. O priest, thou shalt stumble,' etc., vv. 5, 6 being addressed to the priest.

5. The prophet] i.e. the class of prophets who said what they knew would please their hearers : cp. 1 K 22¹¹,¹² Isa 30¹⁰ Jer 5³¹.

Mother] i.e. the nation : see on 2².

6. Lack of knowledge] The priests should have instructed the people in God's law (i.e. His moral teaching), and were therefore responsible for their ignorance. Instead of that they had wilfully refused even to learn themselves. **Thy children**] i.e. the whole body of priests, who only sinned worse as they increased in number. **8. They eat up**] RV 'they feed on.' The priests enriched themselves with the sin-offerings, and with this aim encouraged instead of checking sin : cp. Ezk 34. **Set their heart**] i.e. took delight in, because it paid so well. **9. Like..priest**] Priest and people had sinned alike, and would be punished alike. **10. Eat..enough, etc.**] Greed and lust were both violations of God's

natural laws, and would therefore have an unnatural result. **11. Heart**] here probably as the seat of 'the understanding' (RV).

12. Cp. Jer 11²⁷. Idols were frequently made out of stumps and stems of trees, and were not only worshipped, but sometimes used for oracular purposes. Such a thing proved how senseless the people had become.

Whoredom is here faithlessness to Jehovah ; but as such rites as those referred to were characterised by gross licentiousness, the metaphor is especially appropriate. **13.** The summits of hills were the most frequent situations for sanctuaries in primitive times ; hence the 'high places.' **Elms**] RV 'terebinths.' Trees were often connected with sacred rites : cp. Isa 1²⁹ 57⁵. **Therefore**] Such faithlessness towards Jehovah would be punished by the faithlessness of their daughters. **14. I will not punish**] They have no right to ask Jehovah to punish sins in their daughters or their brides, which in another form they commit themselves in their impure rites.

15. Let..offend] Hosea appeals to Judah not to imitate Israel's sins. **Gilgal** (that of Benjamin : cp. 1 S 13⁸ᶠ·) and **Bethel** ('house of God,' here contemptuously called **Beth-aven**, 'house of vanity,' i.e. idolatry) were two of the most important Israelitish sanctuaries: see Am 4⁴,⁵. The latter had been a sanctuary since the days of Jacob (Gn 28²² 35¹⁻⁸ Jg 21²). **Nor swear..liveth**] Hosea is here condemning the use of Jehovah's name in oaths, because that name has been so profaned by its association with idolatrous symbols. **16. Slideth back.. heifer**] RV 'hath behaved himself stubbornly like a stubborn heifer,' as yet not fully trained to bear the yoke, which jibs instead of going obediently forward. **Now the LORD will feed them, etc.**] better, 'now would the LORD feed them,' etc. He would gladly have treated them as docile lambs, not as stubborn heifers. Others understand it as an exclamation: 'Israel is stubborn and self-willed. How then can the Lord feed them as a lamb in a wide pasture!'

A large place] always in Scripture used as a symbol of safety (Ps 18¹⁹ 118⁵). **17. Ephraim**] i.e. Israel. **Let him alone**] a general exhortation to any who might seek to meddle with idolatrous Israel.

18. Their drink is sour] RM 'their carouse is over.' Hosea is referring to some idolatrous festival. **With shame..Give ye**] RV 'dearly love shame,' with reference probably to licentious practices connected with idolatrous feasts.

19. Wings] RM 'skirts': a curious metaphor to express the completeness of their punishment. They would be carried off without reprieve by the wind of judgment. **They.. sacrifices**] RM 'Their altars shall be put to shame,' i.e. by being destroyed.

CHAPTER 5

PREDICTIONS OF PUNISHMENT

The priests, the people, and the royal dynasty have alike sinned, and will alike be punished. Their coquetting with Assyria will prove utterly futile. Judah has also sinned, and will receive their punishment. But there is ever yet hope in the future, if they will but repent.

1. Toward you] RV 'unto you.' Judgment belongs to you by right, and having abused your privilege you deserve greater punishment.

Mizpah and **Tabor** are both spoken of as ancient sanctuaries : cp Jg 21 1, 8 1 S 7 5-10, and see on 4 13. The assemblies for religious and political purposes had been made occasions for robbing the people by unjust judgments and perhaps by extortionate demands for sacrifices : see on 4 8. **2. Are profound .. slaughter**] lit. 'have gone deep to slaughter,' i.e. have committed horrible slaughter. It refers probably to the violence of political factions: cp. 7 7.

Though I *have been*] RV 'but I am.' Their violence will not escape punishment. **Them all**] priests, people, and rulers (v. 1). **3. I know .. from me**] Israel and Ephraim are in this book synonymous. The people had corrupted themselves by sins of impurity, but Jehovah had seen it and would punish : cp. Ps 10 14. **4. They .. doings**] RV 'Their doings will not suffer them.' To repent would mean to give up their cherished vices. **5. The pride .. face**] Worse still ; they were actually proud of themselves and their doings. Their vaunting of their wickedness was its most obvious proof. **6.** The time would come when they would in vain offer sacrifices to Jehovah.

7. Strange children] Some see here an allusion to intermarriage with the Canaanites: cp. Ezr 9, 10. But it may be merely metaphorical. The result of their faithless union with heathen gods was a race of people who were not true Israelites, acknowledged and loved of Jehovah. **A month**] RV 'the new-moon.' The profanation of their festivals would be punished by the enemy destroying them and their land. **Portions**] RV 'fields.'

8. With this begins what is probably a new prophecy. Hosea ironically bids the herald call the people to arms to defend themselves against an invading foe. **Gibeah** ('a hill') and **Ramah** ('a high place') would both be suitable spots for sounding an alarm. **Beth-aven**] see on 4 15. **After thee .. Benjamin**] RV 'behind thee,' etc. From Jg 5 14 it is supposed that this was the battle cry of the Benjamites, used by the soldiers in following their leaders. It would have been a summons to the Benjamites to battle. **9.** But such preparations would be quite useless. The judgment was surely coming.

10. The princes .. bound (RV 'landmark')]

They had abused their power to oppress and rob the people. The prophet here includes Judah in his denunciations and threats of consequent punishment. The Assyrians who demolished the northern kingdom crippled Judah in the days of Hezekiah. The deliverance of Judah, temporary as it in fact proved, was a later revelation of prophecy. **11. Broken in judgment**] i.e. defeated in his suit and condemned. **After the commandment**] RM 'after vanity,' i.e. idolatry.

13. Assyrian .. Jareb] cp. 10 6. This refers probably to Menahem paying voluntary tribute to Tiglath-pileser (Pul, 2 K 15 19). The name Jareb ('adversary') is coined by Hosea to point out the absurdity of their seeking help from such a source. In the words, **when Judah** *saw* **his wound**, Hosea seems to hint at a similar policy on the part of Judah, which was afterwards pursued by both Ahaz and Hezekiah (2 K 16 7, 8 18 14-16). **14.** See on v. 10. **15.** The prophet still hopes that these calamities will produce repentance and the remission of the full calamity. Meanwhile Jehovah will leave them to the discipline of His punishment.

CHAPTER 6

THE SHALLOWNESS OF ISRAEL'S REPENTANCE

Hosea now represents the people as counselling one another to repentance in presence of the impending danger ; and goes on to point out the futility of a hurried repentance, and the greatness of their sin.

2. After two days] This is probably a proverbial expression for a very short time.

3. Then .. know, etc.] RV 'And let us know, let us follow on.' **His going forth**] Just as the morning will dawn after the darkest night, so God will arise bringing brightness and hope. **As the rain**] The land of Palestine was absolutely dependent on its winter rains : the former rain beginning about the end of October with fair intervals which permitted the seed to be sown, becoming heavier about the end of December and continuing at intervals during the winter ; the latter rain coming in showers in March and April refreshing the ripening crops.

4. The thought of the possible future stands in deep contrast to the gloomy present, and the note of joy passes into a note of wailing. **Morning cloud**] As the morning cloud and the dew rapidly disappear, so the efforts of Israel after real goodness (especially 'kindness,' RM) lack endurance. **5. Hewed .. slain them**] The prophets are here spoken of as themselves doing what their language threatened. **Thy judgments .. forth**] It is better to read with LXX, 'My judgment goeth forth as the light.' The reference is to the clear manifestation of the judgment.

6. God cared more for goodness and piety —the knowledge and doing of His will—than for formal offerings and sacrifice, and nothing at all for religious observances that were insincere and corrupt : cp. Isa 1 13-15 1 S 15 22. Our Lord twice quotes the first clause in justification of doing good on the sabbath day : cp. Mt 9 13 12 7. **7. Like men]** RV 'like Adam.' In regarding mere sacrifice as a substitute for goodness which God had made the condition of His covenant they had broken it as much as Adam had done by his disobedience : cp. Gn 2 16,17 Ex 20 21–24 11. **There]** in the land given them on condition of a good and holy life.

8. Gilead] cp. 12 11. Probably Ramoth-Gilead. Being a city of refuge it was doubtless the place of an early sanctuary. But holy cities were now become notorious for their wickedness. **9. In the way by consent]** RV 'in the way toward Shechem.' At Shechem also, as we know from Josh 24 1, there was an ancient sanctuary. In the time of Jeroboam I it was the capital of the northern kingdom. Hosea here appears to refer to some definite act of robbery and murder in which some priests were actually implicated. **11. He hath set]** RV 'there is appointed.' **When I returned]** RV 'when I bring again.' This v. is often understood of the harvest of judgment (cp. Joel 3 13), but the phrase 'to turn, or bring again, a nation's captivity,' means its restoration. The words, however, should probably be taken with what follows.

CHAPTER 7
CORRUPTION OF THE COURT

In this c. the tone again becomes despondent. How can Israel be saved when her iniquity is so deep, so glaring, so obstinate ? Samaria is especially instanced as the centre of a wicked and corrupt government sustained by a lawless people and false teachers. Hosea dwells chiefly on some plot which ended in regicide and the reliance on foreign powers which meant want of faith in God.

2. They fail to realise how patent in God's sight their iniquity is, while they attempt to combine a profession of religion with sins of the worst type. Now they are 'holden with the cords of their sins' (Prov 5 22). **3.** They induced their rulers not only to connive at, but to take part with delight in their wicked practices. **4.** The fire of lust is likened to a baker's **oven.** But the simile seems also to include the passion of anger which worked in the heart and produced acts of violence, such as regicide.

5-7. A scene from the palace. The king carouses with his courtiers, who have formed a plot against him, and wait the fitting moment

to rise and put him to death. It would appear that Hosea has in his mind the assassination of a king at a feast, or just after a feast, in the early morning. The case is perhaps that of Zechariah, son of Jeroboam II (see Intro.).

5. The day .. king] some royal feast, probably the king's birthday. **Have .. wine]** RV 'made themselves sick with the heat of wine.' By their drunken carouse they heaped up fuel on the fire of their malicious hate. **He stretched out]** i.e. in hospitality. The hand is stretched out by the host to offer the cup to his guests. **Scorners]** those who in their heart despise the king and are ever plotting his death. **6. Their baker]** Perhaps we should follow the LXX, etc., and read, 'their anger.' Their anger sleeping would mean that they manage to control it, until it can work with effect. If we keep the reading 'baker,' it will mean that just as the baker sleeps when once he has made up his fire and heated his oven ready for use in the morning, so they wait for the morning to execute their purpose.

7. Judges .. kings] whatever definite event the prophet has in his mind this describes the general character of the northern kingdom, a restless disloyalty to kings and rulers. The only dynasties of any duration were those of Omri and Jehu. **None .. calleth unto me]** Irreligion lay at the root of this constant disloyalty.

8. Ephraim, he hath mixed himself among the people] RV 'the peoples' or nations. Another fault, and another evidence of a want of patriotism, the tendency to court foreign alliances and foreign influences, such as was seen in the policy of Menahem with reference to Tiglath-pileser (2 K 15 19). **A cake not turned]** which is therefore burnt on one side, and half raw on the other, and so spoilt. **9. Strangers .. strength]** the natural consequence of seeking help from a foreign alliance, which meant the exaction of what was practically tribute, and consequently heavy taxation (2 K 15 20). Israel did not realise that these signified the beginning of national decrepitude, just as grey hairs here and there are the first signs of old age.

10. The pride .. face] see on 5 5. He is so besotted with pride that he recognises neither the evil itself nor its true remedy.

11. A silly dove] As the dove flies helplessly one way and another, so Israel turns to one power after another, only eventually to make enemies of both. The only recorded alliance with Egypt was that of Hoshea (2 K 17 4); but it was a common policy of Judah, and is frequently condemned by the prophets. There was a natural temptation to play off Egypt against Assyria, and such an alliance may have been already projected by those opposed to Menahem's action. **Heart**] RV 'understanding,' as in 4¹¹. **12. They shall go**] i.e. for help. This courting of alliances will inevitably, by God's providence, end in their destruction. The metaphor of the dove suggests that of the fowler. Jehovah will through their own folly lure them to their ruin. **As their congregation hath heard**] Hosea had warned them beforehand of what was to befall.

14. Howled .. beds] Their prayers do not proceed from any reverential fear of God. They are like the howling of an animal from pain. They cry out because they are in trouble, but their prayers are for material blessings, and they are still rebellious at heart: cp. Job 35⁹ᶠ. **They assemble themselves**] i.e. meet in religious exercises, but RM has 'cut themselves,' referring to heathen practices in time of tribulation: cp. 1 K 18²⁸.

15. Bound] RV 'taught,' by chastisement. **16. They return**, etc.] Their turning is ever farther away from God. **Their princes shall fall**] As a punishment for their insolence they would perish amidst the derision of the very people whose aid they had sought: see v. 11.

CHAPTER 8

THE LONG-MERITED RETRIBUTION

The enemy is coming immediately to destroy their temples and palaces and desolate the land, and as a punishment for their idolatry and disloyalty to God. In vain will they appeal to Jehovah.

1. RM 'The trumpet to thy mouth! As an eagle against the house of the LORD.' **2.** RV 'They shall cry unto me, My God, we Israel know thee.' They use the name Israel with its sacred associations, as an inducement to God to help them. **3. Israel**] Hosea answers their appeal by saying that the name is worthless without the character which God requires. **4.** In the constant changes of dynasty there was no thought for the religious character of the king, nor counsel asked of God's prophets. Revolution and idolatry had all along been the besetting sin of Israel. **That .. off**] Had self-destruction been their object, they could not have achieved it more effectually.

5. Thy calf .. off] RV 'He hath cast off thy calf, O Samaria'; meaning that the calf would be taken off by the enemy, Samaria, the capital, being put for the whole people. The allusion is, of course, to the golden bull at Bethel, under which symbol they worshipped God. **6. From Israel**] The idol was the mere creation of Israel. **Therefore .. God**] RV 'and it is no God.' It has no real existence: cp. 1 Cor 8⁴. **7. The wind**] i.e. idolatry. **It .. stalk**] RV 'he hath no standing corn,' as the result of his sowing. **The bud**] RV 'The

blade.' **If so be .. up**] Again Hosea formally modifies his previous statement, only to hint more plainly at the fate of the nation.

8, 9. The condition of Israel in the land of captivity is here described. **A vessel wherein is no pleasure**] i.e. a cheap and worthless piece of pottery. **9. Hired lovers**] with reference to the tribute paid to Tiglath-pileser by Menahem (cp. 7⁹⁻¹¹), and the attempts made by others to coquet with Egypt. **10.** This courting of foreign princes will be of no avail. Very soon the people will be gathered for judgment by God and taken into a strange land.

They shall .. little] They already begin to feel the oppressive tribute exacted by Tiglath-pileser: see on 7⁹⁻¹¹. **King of princes**] perhaps with reference to the many small dependencies under the Assyrian sway: cp. Isa 10⁸. **11.** The multiplication of altars and sacrifices only led to increased wickedness.

12. I have written .. law] RV 'Though I write for him my law in ten thousand *precepts*.' It mattered not how emphatically God's teaching should be made known to Israel; they would ignore it. **13.** The sacrifices to Jehovah are a merely formal act, only killing and eating. Such sacrifices without repentance are not acceptable to Him, and will not induce Him to forget or overlook their sins: cp. Isa 1¹². **They .. Egypt**] The prophet in God's name here threatens to undo the greatest act that God had ever done for His people: cp. 7¹⁶. Hosea evidently contemplated the possibility of the punishment which he foresaw coming from Egypt. More frequently he speaks of Assyria as the instrument of God's vengeance.

14. Temples] RV 'palaces.' The building of fenced cities by Israel and Judah implied a want of faith in God's power to save.

CHAPTER 9

EXILE IS AT HAND

This prophecy appears to have been written in a time of rejoicing over a good harvest and vintage. Israel need not rejoice, says the prophet, with the wild joy of the heathen. Their praises to the local Baals are insults to Jehovah, whom they have denied. Their rejoicing will end in disaster, culminating in captivity either in Egypt or Assyria.

1, 2. People] RV 'peoples,' i.e. the heathen nations around. The allusion is probably to the orgies of the heathen festival. The sins of the people called rather for sorrow and contrition. **Reward**] RV 'hire,' the bounteous crops being regarded as due to the favour of the idols in return for Israel's worship. As a punishment the corn and wine would fail. **3.** See on 8¹³. Egypt and Assyria were the nations which assailed them on either side. By one of them they would be taken captive. 'Unclean food' (RV), in contrast to the fertile products of their own land : cp. 2 K 18 27.31 Ezk 4 12,13.

4. Bread of mourners] Instead of being joyous festivals they would be like funeral feasts. **For their bread**, etc.] RV 'for their bread shall be for their appetite : it shall not come,' etc. A further step in their misery. They would only have enough bread to satisfy the pangs of hunger, and have none left to offer to God. The reference here appears to be to the horrors of a siege. **5.** The feast days come, but no one is ready or able to observe them. Their only concern is to escape destruction. **6. Egypt .. up**] Their efforts to escape are useless. They would be captured and brought to Egypt, with only death and burial to look forward to : see on 8 13. **The pleasant .. silver**] RV 'their pleasant things of silver.' While they die in captivity, all their treasures are laid waste and overgrown with weeds : cp. Isa 34 13. **Tabernacles**] RV 'tents.'

7. Israel shall know .. it] The people have refused to believe the prophet's threats ; they would realise the truth very soon, when the calamities came upon them. **The prophet** *is* **a fool**] The meaning is doubtful. Some interpret thus : 'Into such excesses have they fallen that their prophets have gone mad, so that they utter no clear message, but only the incoherent muttering of frenzy.' In this case the prophet would refer to the false prophets. Or it may mean that their iniquity and enmity had hitherto made them ignorant of the real character of the true prophet, who appeared to them a mad fool. **The spiritual man**] lit. 'the man of the spirit,' an unusual synonym for prophet. **8. The watchman**] 'Watchman' is similarly used metaphorically of a prophet in Isa 21 6,11. The meaning is very uncertain. *Was* **with my God**] perhaps, 'is with my God,' i.e. is in the keeping of my God. **A snare of a fowler .. ways**] Wherever he goes he is in danger of being trapped. **Hatred in .. God**] The enmity of the people dogs him in his most sacred duties.

9. Gibeah] The reference is to the glaring sin of the Gibeonites described in Jg 19 : cp. 10 9.

10. Grapes in the wilderness] the last place to find grapes. But God had found these poor tribes in the wilderness, and made them His people. **Time**] RV 'season.' The first ripe fruit is eaten with peculiar relish, all the more so if it be the first crop of the figs : cp. Isa 28 4. Israel was the first nation which God had chosen. **Baal-peor**] see on Nu 25. God's love even at the beginning did not hinder them from acts of idolatry and gross impurity. **Separated .. shame**] RV 'consecrated themselves unto the shameful thing,' i.e. the idol and the licentiousness which its worship involved.

11–13. The prophet threatens them with

barrenness as the punishment for immorality : cp. 4 10. Even if children should be born, they would fall by the sword of the enemy. **13. As I saw Tyrus**] i.e. like Tyre. **Pleasant place**] perhaps **fold**, as in Jer 23 3, the reference being to security rather than natural beauty.

14. The prophet here appeals to God's justice to carry out the punishment foretold. The prophet has his moods ; at one time an earnest hope for the nation's repentance, at another a disgust at their hopeless irreligion and immoralities. Even here the language implies a struggle of different feelings. He seems to begin with a prayer and to end with something like a curse. **15. Gilgal**] cp. 4 15. Gilgal was the home of idolatry and its accompanying iniquity. There Israel called forth the wrath of God. **Mine house**] These words show that the worship at Gilgal was at least in theory paid to Jehovah.

CHAPTER 10

DENUNCIATIONS AND ENTREATIES

This prophecy appears to have been uttered at a later date than the last. There is no longer any mention of Egypt, but the calamity from Assyria seems imminent. Again Hosea urges them to repent while there is time, and again gives way to despair.

1. Empty] RV 'luxuriant,' with reference to the prosperity of Israel. The more he prospered, the more he multiplied his heathenish altars and symbols. **Fruit unto himself**] RV 'his fruit.' **Images**] RV 'pillars' : see on 3 4.

2. Their .. divided] It is no simple worship of Jehovah, but a confused heathenish worship, which God will altogether destroy : see Intro.

3. What .. us] RV 'and the king, what can he do for us ?' They have no king, because they have not submitted themselves to their natural king, Jehovah ; and they realise too late the impotence of him who is a king only in name (i.e. probably Hoshea). **4. They .. covenant**] They have spoken words, i.e. mere words not followed by deeds, and sworn falsely to agreements which they have not kept. The reference is probably to their commercial dealings with each other as in 4 2. **Hemlock .. field**] Judgment will come upon them like the rank growth of a noxious weed. **5. Samaria**] as in 8 5f., for the whole people. **Calves of Beth-aven**] see on 4 15. They will be terribly afraid lest their God be taken away. Priests and people alike will mourn for sorrow. **6. King Jareb**] see on 5 13. There is a fine touch of irony in the suggestion that a god is sent off as a present to a king. **7.** Samaria is doomed, and her king disappears, like a foam-bubble bursting on the water. **8.** A picture of the desolation and terror following invasion. **Aven**] for Beth-aven : see on 4 15. **They .. us**] In their despair they would welcome the most violent death. The words are quoted by our Lord in His prophecy of the destruction of Jerusalem (Lk 23 30): see also Rev 6 16.

9. From the days] RM 'more than in the days.' **Gibeah**] see on 9 9 **The battle**] RV 'that the battle.' Hosea finds a parallel between the battle of vengeance against the Benjamites in Gibeah (Jg 20) and the judgment that is coming against Israel. They remain impenitent, hoping that a similar calamity may not overtake them. **10.** *It . . should*] RV 'when it is my desire, I will,' etc. There may be some delay, but, when God wills, the punishment must come. **When . . furrows**] RV 'when they are bound' (RM 'yoked') 'to their two transgressions,' usually explained of the two 'calves.' For a somewhat similar figure cp Isa 5 18. But translation and interpretation are both very uncertain.

11. See on 5 3. Ephraim is like a heifer accustomed only to the light work of threshing; but both she and Judah must now bear the yoke of a foreign oppressor. **I passed . . neck**] a rather curious but forcible way of saying, 'I have put the yoke upon her neck.' It is an instance of the prophetic past, describing as done an event only determined by God. The images which follow express the same general thought, the dominion of a foreign power. **Jacob**] instead of Israel or Ephraim.

12, 13. The metaphor of ploughing leads to that of sowing and reaping. Hosea uses it to make another appeal for repentance. In the past they had devoted themselves to iniquity, and were beginning to reap the consequences. Let them now devote themselves to righteousness, and they will receive mercy. **Rain righteousness**] RM 'teach you righteousness.'

Trust . . way] i.e. you chose your own path instead of allowing yourselves to be directed by God. Another reading is, 'in thy chariots,' which is a better parallel to the next clause.

14. Among] RM 'against.' Their confidence would be found misplaced. The fortresses manned by their mighty men would be destroyed by the enemy. **Shalman . . battle**] Nothing is known of this event, and neither the man nor the place can be identified with certainty; but the sack of **Beth-arbel** had evidently created a terrible impression of the horrors of war.

15. So shall Beth-el do] RM 'so shall it be done unto you at Beth-el.'

CHAPTER 11 1-11
The Ingratitude of Israel

Jehovah had been like a tender father and a kind master to Israel from the first, yet had they ever rejected Him and turned to idols. He cannot bear the thought of punishing them, but punish them He must. Yet punishment will be tempered with mercy, and lead at last to repentance and deliverance. The tenderness of the whole passage and the changing phases of feeling are very characteristic.

1. The allusion, of course, is to the deliverance out of the bondage of Egypt, a proof of God's fatherly love to Israel. St. Matthew refers the last clause to the recall of the Infant Jesus from Egypt : see on Mt 2 15. **2.** *As them*] An interesting example of the terse style of Hosea. It is God who calls, but He calls by the instrumentality of others, Moses and the prophets. The call is the call out of bondage to the service of God. **3. I**] RV 'Yet I.' Jehovah is here compared to a father teaching his child to walk, and carrying it when tired. **Taking . . arms**] RM 'He took them,' etc. The prophet sometimes speaks as the mouthpiece of God in the first person ; less frequently he speaks of God in the third. **4. Cords . . man**] not with cords used in drawing a beast which is being broken in, but something more gentle, the kindly discipline needful for winning a man's allegiance. **And I was . . unto them**] In the evening, when work is over, the kind master takes off the yoke, gently passing it over the animal's face, and then gives it food.

5. Kindness has failed to lead them to repentance ; therefore they must be purified by punishment. Not to Egypt, however, shall they go, but the Assyrians shall conquer and carry them away. **Not . . into . . Egypt**] In 8 13 9 6 the prophet spoke of Egypt as a possible place of captivity ; but now, at this later date, it was evident that Assyria was to be the instrument of God's vengeance **6.** The mention of apostasy produces a severer tone of threatening. **Abide on**] RV 'fall upon.' **His branches**] RV 'his bars,' i.e. his defences, meaning either his strong cities or his nobles, on whom he depended for safety. But their evil counsellors (if we take it in the latter sense) would prove their ruin. **7. Though . .** *him*] Though they formally called on God, they do not really exalt Him in their hearts.

8. Hosea's feeling again turns to tenderness. How can the loving Father bear to chastise His people as they deserve ! **Admah . . Zeboim**] with reference to the destruction of the cities of the plain : cp. Dt 29 23. **My repentings**] RV 'my compassions.' **9.** Jehovah's feelings grow stronger still. He will not punish His people. **I** *am* **God**] therefore more long-suffering and less vindictive than man : cp. Ps 130 4 and Collect, 'Who declarest Thy almighty power most chiefly in showing mercy and pity.' **Enter into the city**] RM 'come in wrath.' **10.** Hosea is confident that the people will make themselves deserving of Jehovah's love and follow Him. **Roar . . lion**] In Am 3 8 the same figure is used of God's threatening through the prophet. Here it is used of His calling for His people out of captivity, the point of comparison being the earnest longing on God's part, reverential awe on man's. **Shall tremble**] RV 'shall come trembling.' **West**] i.e. Egypt, as distinctly stated in the next v. **11. They .. Egypt**] Taken literally, it is in contradiction to v. 5 ; taken together, they may be paraphrased thus : They shall not go into Egypt ; and even should they go, thence will I bring them—a form of thought similar to that in 9 11, 12, etc. **Dove**] The timidity of the dove is what is probably thought of. For another use of the simile see 7 11.

CHAPTERS 11 12–12 14
A REPROOF OF COMMERCIAL DISHONESTY

The Hebrew text divides the c. more correctly at this v. The prophet returns to the subject of the unfaithfulness both of Israel and of Judah. They have sought help where it was not to be found, and neglected God, the only source of help, in forgetfulness of the example of their ancestor Jacob.
12. Judah .. saints] RM better, ' and Judah is yet unstedfast with God, and with the Holy One who is faithful.'
C. 12. 1. Ephraim .. east wind] an attack on Israel's foreign policy and cunning commercial dealings with foreign powers. The **wind** stands for what is useless and unsatisfying. The east wind was noted for its violence and destructiveness : cp. Ps 48 7. They seek eagerly to obtain what in the end will destroy them.
Oil .. Egypt] Oil was one of the richest products of Palestine : see Dt 8 8 2 K 18 32.
2. Jacob] as before used to introduce the personal history of the Patriarch, from which Hosea seeks to draw an analogous lesson for the people. Jacob had begun life by cunningly supplanting his brother, but afterwards had made a covenant with God. Israel is now exhorted to do likewise. **3. By his strength**] RV ' in his manhood.' It refers to Jacob's wrestling with the angel at Penuel (Gn 32 24-30). **4. He wept**] Not mentioned in Gn 32 25. **He found him**] the subject is Jehovah. **In Beth-el**] The reference is probably to Jacob's dream (Gn 28 10-22). **With us**] Hosea here regards God's promises to Jacob as made to the people Israel, whom in fact they chiefly concerned. **5.** Lit. ' And Jehovah is the God of armies. Jehovah is His memorial.' The thoughts emphasised are, (1) the protective power of God ; (2) His faithfulness. Hosea has probably in his mind Ex 3 15. Jehovah was the God of the Patriarchs, who would keep the promises which He had made to them. **Memorial**] that by which a person is known, his name : see Ex 3 15.
7-14. Israel, too, is unjust and unmerciful. In the pursuit of gain they are no better than the heathen, though they pride themselves on their honesty. Jehovah has long warned them : now He will punish them : their sanctuaries will be utterly destroyed.

7. He is a merchant] RM 'as for Canaan the balances,' etc. **Balances of deceit**] cp. Am 8 5. **8. And Ephraim**] The Israelites had only too readily learnt the tricks of cheating from the Canaanites. **Yet**] RV ' surely.' It is the natural consequence of his unjust dealing. **In all .. sin**] Israel is nevertheless perfectly self-satisfied and has no pangs of conscience. **9. And**] RV ' But.' In spite of all this I will not leave you to your evil ways.
Tabernacles] RV 'tents.' Israel had learned nothing since the days in the wilderness. In religion and morality they were still like those who came out of Egypt. Therefore they would have to go back to captivity and begin their discipline anew. **Solemn feast**] i.e. the Feast of booths (Tabernacles). **10.** The moral degradation of the people was not from want of warning. **Visions and similitudes**] two of the commonest modes of prophetic utterance. We have instances of the first in the vision of Micaiah (1 K 22 19-22), the basket of summer fruit (Am 8 1), etc. ; of the latter in the simile of the baker in Hos 7. A definitely acted parable became a common feature of later prophecy, e.g. Ezk 4.
11. Gilead .. Gilgal] both sanctuaries : see 4 15 6 8. *Is there iniquity*, etc.] RV ' Is Gilead iniquity ?' The question is only a rhetorical way of stating an astounding fact. **12.** The idolatry of Israel implies a forgetfulness of God, by whose providence Jacob was rescued from servitude. The reference is to Jacob's servitude under Laban in order to win Rachel (Gn 29, 30). **13.** The rescue of Jacob was repeated in the deliverance of Israel out of Egypt by Moses, and their preservation in the wilderness. Moses, as Israel's first inspired teacher, was their first **prophet** : cp. Dt 18 15 f. 34 10. **14. Ephraim .. bitterly**] In spite of all this kindness Ephraim had provoked God to great anger. **His blood**] plural, meaning ' bloodshed.' The blood which he has shed shall not be wiped off, but remain in God's eye, a witness of his crime. For a somewhat similar idea cp. Gn 4 10. **His reproach**] God will punish him for his reproach, i.e. for his scornful contempt of God : cp. 2 K 19 4, 22.

CHAPTER 13
ISRAEL'S IDOLATRY AND ITS CONSEQUENCES

The main thought of this c., which is a continuation of the last (cp. 12 9 13 4), is the folly of Israel incurring the enmity of God, who had shown Himself such a loving friend, but might become so terrible an enemy. The sudden change of tone in v. 14 is highly characteristic.
1. When .. trembling] RV 'When Ephraim spake, there was trembling.' Ephraim was a strong and powerful tribe, which could command obedience, as especially in the days of

Joshua. **He died**] Baal-worship was the cause of the national decay and its final doom.

2. Kiss] as an act of worship. For **men that sacrifice** RM has 'sacrificers of men.' Murder is combined with sacrifice: cp. Isa 1¹⁵. **4. Yet . . Egypt**] see on 12⁹. **5, 6. I . . thee**] In the wilderness Jehovah became their friend. He knew them, and bade them know Him. But when they prospered in a land of fertility, they became proud and forgot Him. **10. I . . king**] RV 'Where now is thy king?' What use would the king and princes whom they had so clamoured for be in their trouble? **11. I . . anger**] This has often been referred to Saul, but the Hebrew tenses suggest repeated action, and the allusion may, therefore, be to the frequent changes of dynasty in the northern kingdom. **12. Hid**] RV 'laid up in store.' The sin of Israel is kept stored in God's remembrance, and will surely bring about its own punishment. **13. He** *is* **an unwise son,** etc.] Ephraim is like a foolish child that delays his own birth by staying in the passage from the womb. In other words, he has not the wisdom to rouse himself in this great crisis.

14. With a startling transition of thought, Hosea contemplates the power of Jehovah to save, even from death itself: cp. Isa 26¹⁹. If it is too much to regard it as a definite prophecy of the resurrection, it is at least an example of faith in the unbounded mercies of God, and His power to trample even upon death and Hades.

O death . . destruction] RV 'O death, where are thy plagues? O grave' (RM 'Sheol'), 'where is thy destruction?' Cp. v. 10, where the same negative answer to the rhetorical question is intended. See 1 Cor 15⁵⁵, where St. Paul, quoting freely from LXX, gives a better rendering than AV. Sheol is the place of departed spirits, Hades, as in Isa 14⁹, etc.

Repentance . . eyes] i.e. I will not relent in my purpose.

15. Suddenly again the hope vanishes. Ephraim in his prosperity is compared to a fertile country suddenly dried up by the east wind from the desert, and the failure of water. **Wind . . LORD**] RV 'breath of the LORD,' the wind being poetically conceived of as God's breath, just as the thunder was His

voice: cp. Gn 1². **He shall spoil**] i.e. the east wind, or rather the enemy whom it typifies.

16. Shall become desolate] RV 'shall bear her guilt,' i.e. be punished for her sin. **Their . . up**] Ephraim would have to bear the cruelties inflicted by a merciless foe in a barbarous age.

CHAPTER 14

ISRAEL WILL SURELY REPENT AND BE FORGIVEN

Hosea makes a touching final appeal for repentance. He assures Israel of God's mercy, and closes with a description of the blessings that will follow the renewal of His favour.

2. Take . . words] go to Him, prepared to confess your sins. **Receive** *us* **graciously**] RV 'accept that which is good,' i.e. what is good in us, in contrast to the iniquity which God is asked to take away. **Render**] i.e. offer. **The calves . . lips**] better, 'our lips as bullocks'— that sacrifice of penitence which is outwardly expressed not in the sacrifice of animals, but in confession of sin: cp. Ps 51¹⁷. **3.** Israel would no longer depend upon the help either of foreign powers or of the idols, but trust in Jehovah, the helper of the fatherless.

5. Dew] a frequent metaphor to express spiritual blessing: cp. Dt 32². The paucity of rain made the land dependent on frequent and heavy dews: cp. 1 K 17¹. **Grow**] RV 'blossom.' **6. Olive**] the emblem of fatness and fertility.

8. This v. passes into a sort of dialogue between Ephraim and God. Thus:

Ephraim. **What have I to do any more with idols?** i.e. I will in future have nothing more to do with them.

Jehovah. (RV) 'I have answered, and will regard him,' i.e. I have heard his prayer, and will answer it.

Ephraim. **I** *am* **like a green fir tree**] I am strong and prosperous.

Jehovah. **From me is thy fruit found,** i.e. do not in prosperity once more forget that it comes from Me: cp. Jn 15⁴.

9. A general reflection on the teaching of the book, which cannot be understood except by the wise and prudent, but in the end will be found to be true wisdom: cp. Ps 107⁴³. This epilogue may have been added at a later date, to point the moral of the whole book.

JOEL

INTRODUCTION

1. Author. Nothing is mentioned concerning the personality of the prophet Joel beyond the name of his father, Pethuel (1¹) ; but he clearly lived in Jerusalem, since the Temple appears ever present before him (1⁹, ¹³, ¹⁴, ¹⁶ 2¹⁷), and the sound of alarm is given from Zion (2¹), and the people are summoned thither for a solemn assembly (2¹⁷). He also does not notice the northern kingdom, but speaks of Judah and Jerusalem having suffered from their enemies (3¹, ⁶), and promises to them a recompense (3⁸, ¹⁷ᶠ. ²⁰).

2. Date. The date of the book of Joel is determined alone by internal evidence. A *terminus a quo* is fixed by the dispersion and wrongs mentioned in 3¹⁻⁶. Many have seen in these a reference to the sacking of Jerusalem during the reign of Jehoram (about 850 B.C.) by the Philistines and Arabians, recorded in 2 Ch 21¹⁶ᶠ. In that case the book would probably be one of the earliest of the prophetic writings, a formerly prevalent view, suggested by its position in the Canon after Hosea. Agreeable to this early date have been pointed out, (1) that the condemnation of Egypt and Edom for having shed innocent blood (3¹⁹) may refer to the invasion of Shishak during the reign of Rehoboam (1 K 14²⁵), and to the revolt of Edom under Jehoram (2 K 8²⁰) ; (2) that the mention of the valley of Jehoshaphat preserves a lively recollection of that king's victory at the valley of Berachah (2 Ch 20²⁶) ; (3) that the simplicity of the teaching of Joel indicates an early period of written prophecy ; (4) especially as fixing the date of his book in the early part of the reign of Joash (837–801 B.C.), that it is silent concerning the king—then in his minority ; (5) that idolatry and Baal worship are not mentioned, since they did not flourish when the king was under the influence of Jehoiada the priest (2 K 12² 2 Ch 24¹⁷ᶠ.) ; (6) that the priests and the worship of Jehovah are made prominent (1¹³ 2¹⁷), something also to be expected at the same time through the influence of Jehoiada ; and, finally, (7) that the failure to mention the Syrians, Assyrians, or Chaldeans as enemies of Judah, is also agreeable to this date, since only late in the reign of Joash did the Syrians, through Hazael, threaten Judah (2 K 12¹⁷ᶠ.).

But, in spite of this apparent accumulation of evidence, it is doubtful whether the dispersion and wrongs of 3¹⁻⁶, where the partition of the land is definitely stated (3²), can refer to any other event than the Chaldean conquest of Judah, and the following considerations also are in favour of a post-exilic date. (1) The words of Joel stand in strong contrast to those of the early prophets, Amos, Hosea, Isaiah, Micah, and Jeremiah, who emphasised the defection of Israel from Jehovah through deeds of violence and oppression, political alliances and idolatry, and based almost wholly upon these their calls for repentance or forebodings of divine judgment. But these features are entirely wanting in the book of Joel. Human agencies, also, are not found as instruments of divine judgments, as in the earlier prophets, except in the slightest degree, but supernatural manifestations take their place, and thus the book is of the nature of an apocalypse, a kind of writing prevalent from the captivity and onward. One feature of the apocalyptic literature is the use made of parallels from earlier writings, and these are frequent in the book of Joel. (2) The stress laid upon sacrifices and the prominence given to the priests (1⁹, ¹³, 2¹⁷) reflect a highly developed ecclesiastical community, which the Jews became after the exile. (3) The mention of the Grecians in connexion with the slave trade (3⁶) points strongly to the post-exilic period when Syrian slaves were in request in Greece. (4) The silence concerning the northern kingdom and the Syrians, Assyrians and Chaldeans, and a king in Judah, already mentioned, favour a post-exilic date. (5) The references to Edom and Egypt can also readily be explained from the post-exilic point of view, since bitter feeling then continued toward Edom, and Egypt might be mentioned typically : see 3¹⁹. And, finally, (6) the language favours a post-exilic writer. Hence the more prevailing view among scholars now is that the book of Joel belongs to the post-exilic period, and was written circ. 500 B.C., though possibly considerably later.

3. Subject and Occasion. The general subject of Joel is divine judgment, or the Day of Jehovah. This is depicted in 1–2¹⁷ under the form of a locust plague, which undoubtedly was the occasion of the prophecy. So vivid is the description of the locusts, especially under the figure of an army (2⁶⁻¹¹), that some have supposed the language figurative and have taken the account as presaging a future invasion or experience of Israel after the analogy of that of the hosts of Gog and Magog described in Ezk 38, 39. But the prophet is rather speaking of literal locusts, addressing his contemporaries in view of present distress. His description of the advent of these insects as a Day of Jehovah and as a destruction from the Almighty (1 15) with terrifying natural phenomena (2 10) is none too strong to express the feeling awakened by the presence of real locusts. The fearfulness of their devastations has been attested again and again by travellers and scientific observers. Locusts darken the sky, their sound is like that of a rushing wind or falling water; nothing can break their ranks or turn them back; neither fire nor water as ordinarily applied stays their progress; they devour all vegetation; they penetrate into houses; and finally, when their work is accomplished, driven by the wind into the sea their dead bodies have been cast up in heaps to putrefy the atmosphere and produce disease. Thus the interpretation that finds literal locusts is justified, and yet, doubtless, in the prophet's mind the scourge itself was a figure of a great and final day of judgment, and that thought intensified his language and made it somewhat ideal.

After a two-fold description of this day of judgment through locusts, with calls for fasting and prayer (1 2–2 17), it is said, 'Jehovah had pity on his people' (2 18 RV), implying that the people had fasted and prayed and that their intercession had availed. Then the promises are given of the removal of the locusts and the restoration of the fruitfulness of the land (2 19-27), and of the bestowal of the divine spirit of knowledge (2 28-32). In connexion with this latter promise a glimpse of the already suggested terrible day of final judgment is given (2 30-32), and this becomes the direct theme of the remainder of the book in two different forms: first, a judgment restricted to the immediate neighbours of Israel (3 1-8); and then, secondly, one embracing all nations (3 9-21).

4. Teaching. The book of Joel addresses the Christian Church under visitations of evil with a call for humility and intercession both through outward form and ceremony and through the inward motions of the heart, with the assurance that God hears and answers prayer, turning the day of calamity into one of prosperity. It heralds Jehovah as the judge of all mankind to right wrongs, giving temporal and spiritual blessings unto His faithful people without distinction, and punishing evildoers. Thus it appeals to our innate sense of justice and becomes a source of hope and strength when the righteous are tried. A final blissful salvation is assured to the people

of God. But, at the same time, the book has limitations in fostering a spirit of retaliation (3 8), in presenting no salvation for the heathen (cp. in contrast Isa 2 2-4 19 18-25), and, while doubtless the assumption is that the saved Israelites are righteous and the other nations are wicked, yet the distinction between the saved and unsaved is racial rather than spiritual and moral, and the narrow feeling of the Jews, which the book of Jonah was written to counteract, is reflected, and its universal judgment scene (3 9-21) needs to be supplemented by that of Mt 25 31-46, even as its promise of the outpouring of the Spirit (2 28 f.) finds fulfilment in spiritual gifts to the Church which are far wider than those of the single day of Pentecost (Ac 2 14 f.).

CHAPTER 1
The Coming of the Locusts a Harbinger of the Day of the Lord

After the title (v. 1), the prophet announces an unheard of and long to be remembered ruin, wrought by locusts (vv. 2–4), and summons the users of wine to bewail the destruction of vineyards (vv. 5–7). He calls for lamentation, like that of a widowed bride, over the loss of sacrificial offerings, and wasted fields and orchards (vv. 8–12). He commands the priests to lament and to appoint a fast and a meeting for prayer (vv. 13, 14), and then he vividly describes the failure of crops and distress of cattle (vv. 16–20).

1. Joel] see Intro. **Pethuel**] entirely unknown.

4. The **palmerworm, cankerworm, caterpiller,** and **locust**, are not different insects, but in the original four different names of the locust, possibly representing it in different stages of growth; yet here in a climactic description, i.e. 'swarm upon swarm.' The use of synonyms for a common object is characteristic of Hebrew.

5. New wine] RV 'sweet wine,' primarily the freshly pressed juice of the grape or other fruit. **6. A nation**] figurative of the locusts: cp. similar figure for ants and conies in Prov 30 25 f. **My land**] i.e. of Jehovah since the prophet gives His message. **The teeth of a lion**] in destructiveness. **The cheek teeth**] RV 'The jaw teeth.' The lion was common in ancient Palestine.

7. Locusts consume not only plants and vegetables, but also small branches and tender bark, thus exposing the white wood. **Cast** *it* **away**] i.e. the unedible fragments of bark and wood which fall to the ground.

8. A general address to the people. The simile may contain an underlying reference to the abandonment of the people by Jehovah, since the union between them was often typified by the marriage relation, and the disaster of the locust plague implied that

Jehovah had forsaken the land. **9. The meat offering** (RV 'meal offering') **and the drink offering**] Two daily offerings which went with the morning and evening sacrifice of a lamb, the one consisting of fine flour mingled with oil and the other of a libation of wine : cp. Ex 29 38-42 Nu 28 1-8 Lv 2 1-16. **Is cut off**] i.e. cannot be provided. **10. The land mourneth**] Nature is represented in the OT. with the same feelings as those of man. Cp. for mourning Isa 33 9 Jer 12 4, 11 23 10 Am 1 2.

Corn, wine, and **oil,** the three principal products of the soil of Palestine, frequently mentioned together as from Jehovah (2 19 Dt 7 13 11 14 28 51 Jer 31 12 Hos 2 8, 28). The **corn** (ARV 'grain') was principally wheat, barley, and spelt or vetch. Rye and oats were not grown. The **oil** was that of the olive. **11. Be ye ashamed,** etc.] RM 'The husbandmen are ashamed, the vinedressers howl.' **12. Palm tree**] Symbol of glory or beauty (Ps 92 12 Song 7 7f. Jer 10 5), but here mentioned as a fruit tree. Its dates are very valuable. **The apple**] sometimes rendered 'apricot,' although apples are found in Palestine: cp. Prov 25 11 Song 2 3, 5 7 9. **13. Gird yourselves**] i.e. with sackcloth : cp. Isa 32 11. **Lie all night**] cp. David (2 S 12 16), Ahab (1 K 21 27). Nothing was more terrible to the Jewish mind than the failure of the daily sacrifice.

14. Sanctify .. a fast] i.e. keep a holy fast unto Jehovah. As feasting is a natural expression of joy so fasting is of grief, and fasts were observed in times of distress along with confession of sin and prayer for divine favour (Jg 20 26 1 S 7 6 2 S 12 16 1 K 21 27 Ps 69 10 f. Ezr 10 6 Neh 9 1 Jon 3 5-9 Dan 9 3), and entered also regularly into the Jewish calendar (Lv 16 29 Zech 7 3, 5 8 19). **Gather the elders,** etc.] better, 'Gather, O elders, all the inhabitants,' or omit ' elders.'

15. The day of the LORD] early in popular thought a time when Jehovah granted victory unto Israel (Am 5 18), but in prophetic discourse a time of signal divine manifestation in judgment (as here in the locust plague, 2 1, 11, cp. Isa 2 12 13 6 Am 5 18 Zeph 1 7, 14 Mal 4 5), and especially in connexion with the final consummation of Jehovah's plan for Israel, and thus a day of salvation (2 31 f. 3 14 f. Mal 4 5 f.). **16. Meat**] i.e. food. Many of the celebrations at the Temple were occasions of rejoicing over abundant harvests and the like (Dt 16 10 f. 13-15 12 6, 7 26 1 f. 10 f.). **17.** RM 'The seeds shrivel,' from the drought, which seems to have accompanied the locust plague. **19. Fire .. flame**] figurative of the drought.

CHAPTER 2

REPENTANCE FOLLOWED BY RESTORATION

Vv. 1–17 are another description of the locust plague. An alarm is sounded as though the Day of Jehovah had come (vv. 1–3). The advance of the locusts into the city is described under the figure of an invading army (vv. 4–11). A message to the penitent is given from Jehovah (vv. 12–14), and a call is issued for a fast of supplication (vv. 15–17). Then follow the announcements that Jehovah has had pity on His people, and that He will remove the locusts (vv. 18–20), and restore abundantly the prosperity of the land (vv. 21–27), and afterward pour out His spirit and grant deliverance in His great day (vv. 28–32).

1. The blown **trumpet** was a signal of danger (Jer 6 1 Ezk 33 3 f. Am 3 6). **Day of the LORD**] cp. 1 15. **2. Darkness,** etc.] caused either by the clouds of locusts, or a figure of calamity : cp. Am 5 18 Zeph 1 5. **3.** The devastation wrought by the locusts was as though the country had been swept by a fire. **Garden of Eden**] Gn 2 8 f.; called also ' garden of Jehovah,' Gn 13 10 : cp. Ezk 28 13 36 35. **4.** The head of a locust resembles somewhat that of a horse, hence the German name *heupferd* and Italian *cavalletta*. **So shall they run**] RV ' so do they run.' The description in this and the following vv. is not of a future but a present catastrophe, hence the verbs are to be rendered in the present, as in RV. **5. Shall they leap**] RV ' do they leap.' The rustling noise of locusts has been likened by travellers to the sounds ' of the dashing of waters by the mill wheel,' and ' of a great cataract,' and their feeding to the noise ' of the crackling of a prairie fire.' **6.** RV 'At their presence the peoples are in anguish : all faces are waxed pale.' **7.** RV ' They run .. they climb .. they march .. they break not.' **8.** RV ' Neither doth one thrust another ; they march every one in his path : and they burst through the weapons, and break not off *their course.*' Thus compact is the march of locusts. No weapons avail to stem their approach. **9.** RV ' They leap upon the city ; they run upon the wall ; they climb up into the houses; they enter.' **10.** ' The earth quaketh .. heavens tremble .. are darkened .. stars withdraw.' The advent of the locusts is idealised as though with them came also the earthquake and the eclipse. The Hebrews conceived of the heavens as solid, and hence spoke of their trembling. **11.** RV ' uttereth.' The voice of Jehovah is thunder (Ps 29), hence the thought is that of a great storm accompanying the locusts.

12. With all your heart] cp Dt 6 5. **13. Rend your heart**] even as the Psalmist speaks of a broken heart (Ps 51 17). **14.** The divine will is neither arbitrary nor fixed, but is deeply affected by human intercessions and conditions, and hence a purpose of destruction may be changed (Jer 18 18 42 10 Am 7 3, 6). **15.** Cp.v. 1,1 14. **16. Closet**] The same, of course, as the chamber of the bridegroom. The Heb. word means ' canopy' or ' pavilion,' and its usage comes from the primitive nuptial tent provided for the wedded pair. **17.** **The porch of the Temple,** in front of which stood the **altar** in the court of the priests. **That the heathen,** etc.] RM ' that the nations should use a by-word against them,' i.e. that they should become a byword through their wretched abandonment by God. RV 'among the peoples.' On the taunt, cp. Ps 42 10 79 10 115 2. **18.** ARV ' Then was Jehovah jealous for his land and had pity on his people.' It is implied that the fast and solemn assembly were held, and that Jehovah responded to the cry of His people with the promises of vv. 19–32. **19.** RV 'and the LORD answered and said unto his people.'

20. The northern *army*] or, ' the northerner,' i.e. the locusts, which might possibly have come from the N., although usually in Palestine from the S. or SE. Probably they are idealised as typical of the enemies of Israel, who are frequently spoken of as coming from the N. (Jer 1 14 4 6 10 22 Ezk 38 6, 15 39 2). **Land barren and desolate**] the deserts S. and SE. of Judah. **With his face**] RV ' his forepart.' **The east sea**] i.e. the Dead Sea. **The utmost sea**] RV ' the western sea,' i.e. the Mediterranean.

And his stink, etc.] See Intro. **Hath done,** etc.] i.e. in destruction. The same phrase is used of the beneficent acts of Jehovah in v. 21. **21.** Introduces the promise of renewed prosperity. **22. Be not afraid**] of famine. **Do spring**] i.e. are renewed with fresh grass : cp. 1 7, 12, 18 f., where the desolation is described.

23. Moderately] RV ' in just measure.' **The former .. and the latter rain**] the rains at seedtime in early winter and before the harvest in early spring. **In the first** *month*] RM ' at (= as at) the first,' i.e. before the calamity of drought and locusts. **25.** Cp. 1 4 2 11.

26. And my people, etc.] probably by copyist error from next v. **27.** The rain and the harvests are evidences of Jehovah's presence. **Israel**] the Jewish community so called after the exile. **None else**] an assertion of monotheism : cp. Dt 4 35, 39 1 K 8 60 Isa 45 5, 6, 18.

And my people, etc.] The glorious climax. Under the figure of the locust plague and the promised years of plenty, the prophet saw the final judgment and felicity of Israel, and thus he is naturally led to the thought of vv. 28–32.

28. Afterward] The prophets saw the future purposes of God realised one after the other without fixed intervals of time. Material blessings imply spiritual ones : both nature and man are to be renewed. **My spirit**] of knowledge or divine revelation, since it results in prophecy, dreams, and visions : a spirit of obedience is presupposed : cp. Jer 24 7 31 33 f. 32 29 Ezk 11 19 36 27 39 29 Isa 32 15 44 3. All

flesh] all classes of society, as the context shows. **Your daughters**] Women frequently had the prophetic gift in Israel. Under prophecy we may understand an utterance, through divine ecstasy or compulsion (1 S 10 10 f. Am 3 8 Isa 8 11 Jer 17 f. 20 9). Dreams, although belittled by Jeremiah (23 28), and visions were frequent means of divine revelation : cp. Dreams, Gn 20 3 28 12 37 5, 9 ; Visions, Isa 6 1 Am 7 1, 4, 7 8 1 Jer 1 11 Ezk 1 1 f., etc. Since young men are dreamers and old men seers, it may be implied that youth shall have the knowledge of age and age the enthusiasm of youth. **29.** All persons, even menials, receive the spirit. **30.** Great events, according to the thought of the ancient world, were accompanied with striking historical and natural phenomena ; hence the great Day of Jehovah, which involved the destruction of His enemies and the redemption of His people, would be heralded with wonders. **Blood, and fire, and pillars of smoke**] indications of warfare are the **wonders in** the earth. **31.** Eclipses are the **wonders in** the heavens : cp. Am 8 9 Isa 13 10 Ezk 32 7 Mt 24 29 Lk 21 10 f. **32.** RV ' In Jerusalem shall be those that escape as Jehovah hath said, and among the remnant those whom Jehovah doth call.' In the general destruction the condition of escape is calling on Jehovah, and the saved remnant of Israel is at Jerusalem, and among them are those whom Jehovah has called from elsewhere, i.e. the Jews of the dispersion : cp. Isa 27 12 f. 66 19. Vv. 28–32 are applied in Ac 2 16 f. to the day of Pentecost. This application shows that this OT. prophecy is fulfilled in facts of divine manifestations rather than in an identity of form.

CHAPTER 3
THE JUDGMENT OF THE HEATHEN AND THE GLORY OF ISRAEL

A general judgment of all nations, for their mistreatment of Israel, is announced in the valley of Jehoshaphat (vv. 1–4). Tyre, Zidon, and Philistia, immediate neighbours of Israel, are arraigned for robbery and slave trade, and sentenced according to the *lex talionis* (vv. 5–8). All nations are then summoned as though to a tryst of arms before Jehovah (vv. 9–13), whose terrible Day is described (vv. 14–17), ending with the blessing of Judah through the fertility of its land, and with the doom of desolation for Egypt and Edom (vv. 18–21).

1. In those days, etc.] i.e. the period of the Day of Jehovah just mentioned. **Bring again the captivity**] restore the prosperity, a technical phrase for an epoch-making change, cp. Am 9 14 Ps 14 7 Job 42 10 Ezk 16 53.

2. Valley of Jehoshaphat] an ideal valley in the neighbourhood of Jerusalem, called **Jehoshaphat** from the meaning of the name,

'Jehovah judges.' This prophecy probably occasioned the name (not traced earlier than 300 A.D.) of the modern valley of Jehoshaphat, S. of Jerusalem. **3.** Captives of ancient warfare were distributed by lot (Obad 11 Nah 3 10) and bartered in connexion with carousals.

4. Coasts of Palestine] RV 'regions of Philistia ? ' The question implies a protest against punishment by Tyre, etc. **Will ye render,** etc.] RM ' Will ye repay a deed of mine, or will ye do aught unto me ? swiftly,' etc. Do you think to repay me a wrong which I have done you ? or will you wrong me ? In either case vengeance will be speedily executed upon you.

5. My silver, etc.] not necessarily from the Temple, but the property of the people was reckoned as Jehovah's. **Temples**] i.e. palaces, the dwellings of the rich. **6.** The Phœnicians (Tyre and Zidon) were famous as slave traders (Ezk 27 13 Am 1 9). **Grecians**] Heb *Jevanim,* i.e. ' Ionians,' the name by which the Greeks were commonly known amongst the Hebrews : cp. Gn 10 2-4 Ezk 27 13 Isa 66 19 Zech 9 13. **That ye might,** etc.] and thus increase your gain ; since the further a slave from home, the greater his value, owing to his less opportunity to escape. Vv. 5, 6 do not necessarily refer directly to any specific events, but to a long course of conduct whereby these peoples profited by every disaster that befell Judah. **7, 8.** The captives are to be returned ; the enemies in turn are to be taken captive and sold by the Jews to the far distant **Sabeans** in Arabia, a people famous for traffic in spices and gold (Isa 60 6 Jer 6 20 Ezk 27 22 Job 6 19) : cp. for story of their queen 1 K 10.

9. The theme of the general judgment announced in vv. 1, 2 is resumed. Heralds are to summon the nations as though to a trial of arms with the hosts of Jehovah (vv. 9–11). **Gentiles**] RV 'nations.' **Prepare**] RM 'sanctify' with sacrifices or other religious ceremonies (1 S 7 8 f. Jer 6 4 Mic 3 5). **10.** Instruments of peace are to be made those of war, the reverse of the promise of Isa 2 4 Mic 4 3. **11. Assemble yourselves**] RV 'Haste ye.' Jehovah also is to bring His heavenly hosts (Ps 68 17 103 20 Zech 14 5).

12. Jehovah now speaks announcing His advent for judgment. According to the NT. the advent of Jehovah is fulfilled in the first and second advents of Christ : cp. Mt 25 31 f., and see below. **13.** The heavenly host is

addressed. The harvest, ordinary symbol of joy and bounty (Ps 4 7), is here one of terror (Isa 63 1 f. Rev 14 15) : cp. also Mt 13 30, 39.

14. The valley of decision] determination, judgment: the valley of Jehoshaphat (vv. 2, 12). **15.** Cp. 2 10, 31. **16. Roar**] suggests the lion. **His voice**] the thunder : cp. Ps 29. The figure is of a great tempest with the cry of the beast and thunder combined. **Shake**] cp. 2 10.

The hope . . the strength] RV 'a refuge . . a stronghold' : cp. Ps 14 6 27 1 31 4 43 2 46 1. The very sounds announcing the doom of the nations will herald a place of safety for Israel.

17. The prophet knew of no heavenly Jerusalem, and he thought of the final consummation of the people of God in Palestine. **Holy**] inviolable. No enemy should again pass through Jerusalem.

18. Judah shall be wonderfully productive : cp. Am 9 13. The perennial spring of the Temple mountain, which Isaiah (8 6) and the author of Ps 46 had mentioned as a symbol of Jehovah's presence, Joel saw, after the manner of Ezekiel (47 1 f.), issuing as a stream to water the dry and desert portion of the land symbolised under **the valley of Shittim,** or, RM, 'Acacias' (which is the meaning of Shittim), since the acacia grows in very dry places. A Shittim E. of the Jordan is mentioned (Nu 25 1 33 49 Josh 2 1), but it is not probably referred to here. **19.** As a foil to the fertility of Judah is the desolation of **Egypt** and **Edom,** probably mentioned as typical examples of the countries hostile to Judah, and from which Israel had suffered the cruelties of warfare and massacre from the outset of their history. Edom, after the exile, was the object of bitter feeling for recent hostilities. Egypt, it may have been thought, had never adequately suffered for its treatment of Israel when in bondage, since it had escaped the overthrows of Assyria and Chaldea.

20. In their felicity, as described in vv. 17 f.

21. For I will cleanse, etc.] Either the city will be cleansed from all bloodguiltiness, cp. Ezk 22 3 f. Isa 4 4 Mal 3 3 ; or, more probably, we must render, with RM, ' and I will hold as innocent their blood which I have not held as innocent,' i.e. the blood of Israel will be held to have been shed innocently, and hence will be avenged upon their enemies. The guarantee is, **For the LORD dwelleth in Zion** : cp. v. 17. 'Joel, in his little book, passes from the City of Destruction to the City Celestial.'

AMOS

INTRODUCTION

1. The Man. We have but one trustworthy source of information concerning Amos, viz. the book which bears his name. Happily it is so written as to convey a sufficiently full and clear impression of the man and his career. He was born in the land of Judah, of unnamed and unimportant parents, during the first half of the 8th cent. B.C. His possessions consisted of a few sycomore trees, and a small flock of sheep which belonged to a peculiar breed, ugly and short-footed, but valuable for the excellence of their wool. These he pastured in the neighbourhood of Tekoa, in the wilderness of Judah. Although his means were but meagre, his position was independent, and when he wished to leave his flock he was able to do so, entrusting them perhaps to some lad, like that son of Jesse who in the same neighbourhood had followed the ewes great with young.

2. His Call. Three causes combined to turn the shepherd into a prophet. First, his knowledge of the deplorable state of affairs in the northern kingdom. The victories won by Jeroboam II (2 K 14) had brought wealth and power to the ruling classes in Israel. But luxury, impurity and intemperance were rife amongst them ($2^{7,8}$ 6^{4-6}). And as to the poor, their case could hardly have been worse. They groaned under the most oppressive exactions; they were totally unable to get justice; they were treated as chattels, not as men (8^{4-6}). And the warnings sent by Providence—drought, locusts, famine, pestilence—were not understood by the well-to-do oppressors of the poor ($4^{6f.}$). There is nothing to wonder at in the fact that Amos, a subject of Uzziah of Judah, knew all this. And the shepherd's soul was stirred with deep indignation, like Nehemiah's at a later day (Neh 5). Secondly, he had heard of the campaigns against Western nations, waged by the great kings of Assyria; he could not help foreboding that God would use this mighty instrument for chastising the crying sins of Israel (5^{27} 6). Thirdly, and most important of all, God's spirit communed with him and impelled him to speak. Amos was as conscious of a direct call from heaven as St. Paul was (7^{15} Gal 1^1). He knew himself to be in possession of the divine counsel; he could not refuse to declare it (3^8).

3. The Prophet's Work. It is impossible to state precisely when the call came. If we

could determine the date of the earthquake (1^1 Zech 14^5). there would be no difficulty. We must be content to know that it lay within the period when Jeroboam II and Uzziah occupied contemporaneously the thrones of Israel and Judah, about 775–750 B.C. It was at Bethel, the religious centre of the former kingdom, that his voice was heard. But Amaziah, chief priest of that famous sanctuary, soon intervened, sending a message to the king to accuse the uncourtly prophet of treason, and trying meanwhile to frighten away the preacher (Am 7^{10-17}). Jeroboam does not seem to have taken any notice. Probably he cared as little for Amos as Leo X did for Martin Luther. And the prophet was not to be frightened. He explained his position, completed his message, turned upon the worldly-minded priest with a threat of divine retribution, and then withdrew unmolested. An unreliable Christian tradition of the 6th cent. asserts that Amaziah's son struck him on the forehead with a club, and that he died from the effects of the blow soon after reaching home.

4. The Book. One thing is certain. On his return to Judah he reduced to writing the substance of his speeches at Bethel; not, indeed, giving us a verbatim report of each several address, not indicating precisely where one ends and another begins, but furnishing, rather, copious notes of these weighty discourses. And the exclamation, 'Oracle of Jehovah' (see on 2^{16}), is the *Nota Bene* of the writer, calling attention to peculiarly grave words. Besides writing out his message he added to it. He had preached against the crimes of Israel; he writes of the sins and punishments of surrounding nations (1^3–2^{16}).

Remembering that the book of Amos is in all probability the earliest of the prophetic writings, it helps our comprehension of him and his successors to keep four points in view.

(a) **His Idea of God.** His faith in the Unity of God was not won by reasoning. He had a deep sense of the nearness, greatness, righteousness of One Holy Being; there was no room for another. The One God is all-powerful in Heaven and Hades, Carmel and the depths of the sea, Caphtor and Kir, Edom and Tyre. His mightiness appears in the control of human history, especially in His direction of the fortunes of Israel. It directs all that happens;

there is no such thing as chance ; calamity, equally with prosperity, is of His ordering. This implies dominion over Nature ; drought, dearth, mildew, pestilence, locusts obey His orders. He is not a mere Power, however great ; but a distinctly Personal Being, who can be spoken of as rising up against the wicked, sword in hand, or as moved by pity to change His purpose.

(*b*) **The Relation between Jehovah and His People.** In common with all other Hebrews, the prophets believed that Jehovah was in a peculiar sense their God. But in their eyes the bond was a natural and indissoluble one, so that if they paid His dues in the form of sacrifices, He was under an obligation to protect and bless them. Amos, on the contrary, insisted that the tie was a moral one, inevitably dissolved by unrighteousness (3^2 9^7). Here his splendid originality comes out. Ceremonial worship has no intrinsic value (4^4 5^{21}). Justice and righteousness form the true service of God (5^{24}) : if His worshippers are immoral and oppressive, He shrinks from contact with them as a defilement (2^7) ; inhumanity and unbrotherliness are hateful to Him, whether displayed by heathen or Hebrew (chs. 1, 2). To Amos, Jehovah is above all else the God of Righteousness.

(*c*) **The Coming Judgment.** This is the first Scripture in which ' the Day of Jehovah ' is mentioned. Not but what it had already become a current phrase. The Israelites thought that when the Lord should arise in judgment it would be to their advantage—their sufferings would terminate, their dominion would be extended. Now they were told that this ' Day ' would be one of judgment upon themselves, and that its advent was nigh ($5^{18, 19}$). Repentance would have averted destruction, but they have put it off too long.

(*d*) **The Picture of a Happier Future** (9^{8-15}). This is quite unlike the general tenor of the prophecy. Israel has been the almost exclusive subject of the prophet's thought. Here Judah comes into the foreground, or, if Israel is in view, it is only as reunited to Judah. The Davidic kingdom is to be restored, but no stress is laid on the person or the character of the monarch. The ancient bounds of the empire will be reëstablished, Edom and other foreigners being reduced to subjection. The restored exiles rebuild the wasted cities. Agriculture and kindred pursuits flourish to a miraculous degree on an extraordinarily fertile soil. And the people will never be dispossessed from this earthly paradise. Whether this appendix was added by Amos himself or by a later patriot need not be discussed here.

' The style is the man.' It is so in this case. When the shepherd from the south of Judah interfered in the social and religious life of Israel, he displayed extreme boldness. His style is a bold one. His language is clear, vigorous, direct. The imagery, as might have been expected, is drawn from rural affairs— threshing-sledges, wagons, harvests, cattle, birds, lions, fishing. But the Oriental shepherd, though he be not familiar with books, is not necessarily uncultivated. The poetic structure of c. 4 is quite perfect : the refrain, ' Yet have ye not returned unto me, saith Jehovah ' ($4^{6, 8, 9, 10, 11}$), is used with great effect ; the technical arrangement of the dirge is perfectly understood (5^2 8^{10}), and Amos knows how to work up to a climax.

5. Contents. We have already shown what is the substance of the prophet's teaching, but it will interest some readers if we roughly trace the order of his ideas as they appear in the book. It opens with a denunciation of the cruel wrongs done by the surrounding nations to each other and to Israel. All of these shall have their due recompense of reward (1^3–2^3). Judah's turn comes next : her offence is more directly against God, but her punishment is no less certain ($2^{4, 5}$). When Israel is reached, the note is struck which resounds all through the book : it is the oppression of the poor, unchastity, a wrong idea of the character and requirements of Jehovah which will bring down chastisement (2^{6-8}). These sins are due to ingratitude for God's mercies, and are aggravated by attempts to silence the voice of truth. They will bring on an attack and utter defeat at the hands of an enemy (2^{9-16}). The next section teaches that the closeness of the relation between Jehovah and Israel itself involves the punishment of the people (3^{1-8}). The neighbouring nations are summoned to witness the oppressions which are going on : the doom of palaces and altars is pronounced (3^{9-15}). The rich women are rebuked and threatened (4^{1-3}) ; the futility of superstitious worship is proclaimed ($4^{4, 5}$) ; the failure of God's attempt to reform Israel is bewailed (4^{6-12}). A bitter lament over Israel is followed by some account of the injustice practised by the powerful ; then the fond hopes cherished respecting the ' Day of the Lord ' are shattered, and the elaborate ritual with which it was sought to please Him is sternly rejected (c. 5). The luxury of the higher classes is the main theme of the next address, which ends with an intimation of Assyrian invasion (c. 6). Three visions set forth in pictorial form the speedy end of the nation (7^{1-9}). Amaziah, the priest of Bethel, attempts to drive Amos out of the country (7^{10-17}). Another vision is described, and the common theme of dishonesty and injustice is again taken up : from the penalty thus provoked there will be no deliverance either in man or God (c. 8). None shall escape (9^{1-6}). Jehovah repudiates a special interest in Israel (9⁷). The final paragraph rejoices in the hope of a happier future, a restoration of the kingdom in the line of David, a fertile land, an undisturbed security of tenure (9¹¹⁻¹⁵).

CHAPTERS 1–2⁵

THE SINS OF ISRAEL'S NEIGHBOURS AND THE PUNISHMENTS WHICH SHOULD FOLLOW

1. We may paraphrase the main part of the sentence thus : 'The words of Amos, describing what he saw in prophetic vision.' **Herdmen**] or rather, 'keepers of a peculiar breed of sheep called *naqad*.' There must have been a number of these sheepowners in and near Tekoa. Mesha, king of Moab, is called by the same name *noqed* (2 K 3⁴), where our English Bible uses the word 'sheepmaster.' **Tekoa**] 5 m. S. of Bethlehem, on a hill 2,788 ft. high, was at the border of the 'wilderness of Tekoa' (2 Ch 20²⁰ 1 Mac 19³³), which was fit only for pasturage and largely used for this. Palestine has always been subject to **earthquakes,** but the one here referred to, which occurred in the reign of Uzziah (Zech 14⁵), seems to have been of exceptional violence. The language of many passages in the poetical and prophetical books is derived from the alarming movements of the earth-shaken ground (Ps 46²,⁶ 60² Isa 24¹⁹, etc.).

2. The threatening character of this v. gives notice beforehand of the tone of the whole prophecy. **Zion** and **Jerusalem** are God's abode, from which His voice is heard like a lion's roar. The burning wind is His voice. A modern traveller speaks of the simoom ' caressing you like a lion with flaming breath.' **Habitations**] RV 'pastures,' i.e. the sheep, which mourn because the grass is parched (Joel 1¹⁸,²⁰ Isa 3²⁶). The summit of **Carmel** is usually wet with heavy dews ; even it becomes withered.

3. Amos was sent to preach to Israel, but he here (1³–2⁵) prefixes to his records of that preaching a section which shows that Jehovah is the Guardian of Righteousness, the Avenger of wrong and cruelty, amongst all the neighbouring races as well, Syria, Philistia, Tyre, Edom, Ammon, Moab.

For] i.e. because of. **Three transgressions .. and .. four**] an indefinite and considerable number (Job 5¹⁹). For the attacks made by **Damascus** see 2 K 8¹² 10³² 13²². **Gilead,** being the nearest Israelite district, bore the first brunt. The threshing-sledge, a thick wooden board with pointed pieces of iron or of basalt on the under side, and a heavy weight or a driver above, is the figure for the harshest severity.

5. The **bar** is that by which the city gate was secured. The plain (RV 'valley') **of Aven**] the plain of Cœle-Syria, in which Heliopolis (since called Baalbek), the great seat of sun-worship, was situated. **Beth-Eden (the house of Eden)** was in Syria, but its precise locality is uncertain, and we can only say of **Kir** that it must have been not far from Elam in the distant east (Isa 22⁶) : cp. 2 K 16⁹ Am 9⁷.

6–8. During the troubles with Syria the Philistines doubtless made raids, carrying off **the whole captivity,** i.e. the whole of the population of the district, at one swoop. The captives were sold to their bitterest enemies, the Edomites. **Gaza**] richest and strongest city of Philistia, on the caravan route to Petra, the capital of Edom. The expression **the remnant of the Philistines** indicates that a portion of them had already been destroyed. In 2 Ch 26⁶ Uzziah's victories over them are enumerated.

9, 10. Tyre became the leading city in Phœnicia about 900 B.C. The Phœnicians were the great slave-dealers of antiquity : see 1 Mac 3⁴¹ 2 Mac 8²⁵. The 'covenant of brethren' (RM), or **brotherly covenant** (AV), is the friendly agreement which always subsisted between Tyre and the Hebrews (2 S 5¹¹ 1 K 5¹ 9¹¹,¹⁴, etc.), and doubtless had occasionally been cemented by formal treaty. We never read of wars waged by the Israelites against Tyre or Sidon.

11, 12. Edom's crimes were hostility against a kindred nation, his **brother** (Mal 1²) ; the **casting off all pity,** or, as RM has it, ' the corrupting his compassions' (cp. Ezk 28¹⁷), i.e the doing violence to his own better, kinder nature ; the tearing his prey continually, like an infuriated beast (1 K 13²⁸ Job 16⁹) ; the insatiableness of his revenge. We know that in later times Israel had no more relentless foe (Obad 10–14 Ps 137⁷).

12. Teman was the name of a city and district of Edom, 15 m. from Petra. The ruins of **Bozrah** are 4 m. SE. of the Dead Sea.

13. Jg 11 and Jer 49¹ show how eager the **Ammonites** were to 'enlarge their border.' Such barbarities as are here mentioned were quite common in Oriental warfare (2 K 8¹² Hos 14¹), but the OT. seems to represent the Ammonites in a peculiarly unfavourable light (1 S 11² 2 S 10). **14. Rabbah**] on the banks of the Upper Jabbok (2 S 11, 12). The **shouting** means the war-cry. **15.** Some of the ancient translations, with which Jer 49³ (see RV) agrees, understand this v. as referring, not to the king, but to the Ammonite god Malcam, with his priests and his princes. This involves no alteration in the consonants of the principal word, which in either case is *Malcam*.

C. 2. 1–3. Jehovah will punish the wrongs which these petty nations do each other, as well as their outrages upon Israel.

1. Burning the king's bones into lime was a gross indignity (Josh 7²⁵ 2 K 23¹⁶,¹⁸). Their thorough destruction prevented the man's being 'gathered to his fathers.' And there may have been a belief that the spirit suffered when the corpse was abused (Job 14 22 Isa 66 24). Jewish tradition looked on this cremation as an act of vengeance for the part taken by Edom in the campaign described 2 K 3. **Kirioth**] RV 'Kerioth.' Perhaps to be identified with Ar, the capital of Moab : when one of these is named the other is omitted. It is mentioned in the famous inscription of Mesha, who was king of Moab in Ahab's time, and seems to have been a sanctuary. His words are, 'before Chemosh in Keriyyoth.' **3. Judge, sceptre-holder** (1 5-8), **king** (1 15), are all practically identical in meaning.

4, 5. The surrounding nations are charged with violations of the law written in the heart, **Judah** with offences against a law set forth in positive commandments. **Their lies**] the unreal, imaginary deities, the Baalim and Ashtaroth, who have no existence save in the mind of the worshipper, and therefore are sure to disappoint his hopes.

CHAPTER 2 6-16
ISRAEL'S SINS AND INGRATITUDE

6-8. Israel is now threatened in the same form as the rest, but vv. 6–16 were not spoken by Amos at Bethel ; they form the conclusion of the preface which he wrote after his return home.

6. The unrighteous judges condemn the innocent for the sake of a bribe. **A pair of shoes** would have been too paltry a present, but for the fact that the shoe was a symbol of property (Ruth 4 7 Ps 60 10). To hand over the shoes was equivalent to our delivery of title-deeds.

7. They begrudge the very **dust**, a sign of mourning, which a poor man has sprinkled on his head : they hinder the man who is in a lowly position from attaining his modest purpose. **To profane . . name**] The religion of many of the nations of antiquity sanctioned unchastity and even adopted it as part of the worship of the gods, but if Jehovah's worshippers are morally unclean they pollute His Holy Name. **8.** The poor in the East sleep in their day-clothes. Garments taken in pledge should therefore be restored ere nightfall (Ex 22 25 Dt 24 12) ; but these creditors, undeterred by their supposed nearness to their god, treat the needy man's clothes as if they belonged to themselves. Possibly, however, Amos wrote, 'And they stretch out beside every altar clothes taken in pledge,' meaning that they hung them up as a votive offering in honour of their god.

They drink the wine of the condemned *in* **the house of their god**] that is to say, at their sacrificial banquets they drank wine obtained by unjust fines, and whilst they imagined themselves to be worshipping the God of Israel He disclaimed them : they were really worshipping an idol of their own imagination.

9-16. The ingratitude thus evinced and the judgment which it provokes.

9. We may exhibit the emphasis designed by Amos by rendering thus : 'Yet it was *I* who destroyed . . and it was *I* who brought you up,' etc. **The Amorite** here is a name for all the earlier inhabitants of the Holy Land. Instead of **fruit from above**, etc., we say ' root and branch.' But the Canaanites were not utterly extirpated (Josh 13 13 16 10 Jg 1 19-36 2 S 5 7). **11.** The accounts we have of Samuel, Elijah, Elisha, and the ' schools of the prophets,' show that **prophets**, declaring God's will by word of mouth, had been more numerous in the northern than in the southern kingdom. The 'Nazirites' (RV) showed their obedience to His will by self-control, austerities, renunciations of pleasant things (Nu 6). God's most precious gift to His people consisted in true men, and, above all, in inspired prophets. **12.** It was exceedingly base to tempt the Nazirite to break his vow. For the silencing of the prophets see 1 K 22 Isa 30 10, 11 Mic 2 6, 11.

13. The v. may be understood in two ways. First, as in AV, which represents Israel as a burden on God (Isa 1 14 7 13 etc.). Secondly, and better, as in RV, ' Behold, I will press you in your place, as a cart presseth that is full of sheaves.' As the ground reels under the loaded wagon so shall they under God's heavy hand (Ps 32 4 Job 33 2). **16.** The stress lies on the word **naked**. In headlong flight the long, outer garment would be cast away as a hindrance.

Here, and at 3 13, 15 4 3, 5, 6, 8, 9, 10, 11 6 8 8 11 9 7, 8, 12, 13, the expression rendered **saith the LORD** is a kind of exclamation, thrown in parenthetically to call attention to the gravity of what is said. Utterance of Jehovah ! the prophet cries.

CHAPTER 3
THE FIRST ADDRESS

1-8. A call to attention. **9, 10.** The oppressions practised by the powerful. **11-15.** The disasters which should overtake them, their sanctuary and their palaces.

1. ' Race ' would be a more correct word than **family**. Judah is included in the appeal, but immediately drops out of sight again.

2. In the Bible to **know** frequently means to care for, to be deeply interested in (Gn 18 19 Hos 13 5 Nah 1 7 Job 22 13 Ps 1 6 73 11 Prov 2 1c Gal 4 9): at Jer 1 5 and here it has the allied sense ' to choose.' Jehovah chose Israel alone to be His people. And they argued as Dr Arnold did when he was a child : 'I could not make out how, if my mother loved me more than strange children, she should find fault with me and not with them.'

3. Be agreed] RV 'have agreed,' have made

an appointment. If two people were seen walking together in the desolate regions with which Amos was familiar it might be assumed that they had not met by chance. Nothing happens by chance. There is a reason and cause for Israel's calamities. **4.** 'Thicket' is preferable to **forest** : wild and broken country is in view. Amos intimates that a prophet's threats are not idle sound, any more than a lion's roar is. **5. Shall** *one* **take up a snare from the earth?** etc.] RV ' Shall a snare spring up from the ground?' etc. The **snare** is the bird-trap as a whole : the **gin** (the word is a contraction of 'engine') is the mechanism by which the trap acts. But the trap does not go off till the bird starts it. The thought is that when the time of misfortune arrives Israel will be caught in it as the bird in the trap. **6.** Israel cannot plead lack of warning (Ezk 33 4, 5). All things are ordered by God, and therefore His prophets are able to give such warning. **Evil** here means disaster.

7. His secret is the purpose He has formed : cp. Gn 18 17. **8.** Luther said, at the Diet of Worms : ' Here I stand : I can do no other.'

9. In the palaces] RM 'upon ' ; the proclamation is made from the flat roof : cp. Lk 12 3 Those who dwell in palaces are to be judged by their peers. Possibly Amos wrote, 'Asshur and Egypt,' the two great nations, Assyria and Egypt, the hammer and anvil, between which Israel lay. **The mountain of Samaria** (the capital of Israel) is surrounded by loftier ones, on which the spectators are supposed to stand. **The oppressed**] RV ' oppressions.'

10. They have lost the power to do equity. Their eyes gloat over treasures of gold and silver in their palaces : a prophet's eye sees only stores of **violence and robbery** (Ro 2 5 Jas 5 1-4).

12. Even the wealthiest will escape with nothing but bare life. ' They sit in Samaria in the corner of a couch, and on the silken cushions of a bed ' (RV). These cushions formed the divan, which is often the sole article of furniture in an Oriental reception room : the corner seat is the place of honour. The shepherd prophet loathed these modern luxuries.

14. Beth-el had been a sanctuary prior to the Israelite occupation of the land. In the days of Amos it was the undisputed religious capital of the northern kingdom (7 13), whose subjects gathered there for seasons of special worship (4 1). No doubt the sacred pillar and post which we read of so often in connexion with the high places stood near the altar. The idol to which devotion was paid as the representative of Jehovah was the golden calf set up by Jeroboam I (1 K 12 29). Burnt offerings, thank offerings and meal offerings were presented on the altars (5 22), and the

service was made more attractive by singing and the music of the viol. But all this was vitiated by two faults. First, the god whom the worshippers adored was not the Holy One who alone is worthy, but a mere nature-god, dispenser of corn and wine and oil, of water, flax and wool (Hos 2 5 9 1). And, secondly, the worship was not of a kind to make men better, it was closely associated with immorality and with luxurious eating and drinking (Am 2 7, 8) ; it did not promote either justice or generosity to others (Am 2 8 5 24). **The horns** were the most sacred part of the altar : to cut them off was to desecrate it thoroughly.

15. Winter and **summer house** were in some cases distinct buildings, but in others were parts of the same structure differently situated (Jg 3 20 Jer 3 22). The **houses of ivory** remind us of Nero's ' Golden House ' at Rome : ' The interior was decorated in the most lavish way, with gold, precious stones and ivory. . . The supper rooms had panelled ceilings, overlaid with ivory.' It was a valuable commodity. Sennacherib, on one of the inscriptions which have come down to us, states that Hezekiah gave him 'a couch of ivory, thrones of ivory, an elephant's tusk.'

CHAPTER 4
THE SECOND ADDRESS

1–3. The heartless luxury of the rich women. **4, 5.** The elaborate sacrifices and pilgrimages. **6–12.** The failure of God's chastisements to produce amendment.

1. These pampered women are compared to cows grown fat through feeding in the rich pastures of Bashan (Nu 32 1-5 Dt 32 14 Mic 7 14).

Masters] RV 'lords,' i.e. husbands (1 Pet 3 6). **2. He**] RV 'they,' i.e. the conquerors. **Your posterity**] RV ' your residue.' Those farthest removed from danger will be dragged out of their retreats like fish from the water.

3. Like excited cattle each woman would make for the nearest breach in the city wall and endeavour to escape through it. The second half of the v. is corrupt. Possibly it may have run : ' And ye shall be cast out of your palaces ' (Mic 2 9).

4. This v. shows that the pilgrimage to a holy place was then, as it has been in almost all times and lands, one of the popular forms of devotion. The pious Jew delighted in the annual visit to Jerusalem for the Feasts of Passover or of Tabernacles. Jeroboam I set apart Bethel and Dan as the two sanctuaries to be visited by his subjects (1 K 12 29-32) for the same purpose. Other places were venerated in like fashion. Amos mentions Beersheba (8 14) and Gilgal. The latter place, which was situated between Jericho and the Jordan, derived its name, ' a circle,' from the circle of sacred stones which existed there from time immemorial. Josh 4 and 5 speak of it as the site of the first camp of the Hebrews in western Palestine and the scene of the circumcision of the great mass of the people.

The prophet asserts that these journeys to the holy places, for the purpose of worship, failed to win the favour of God : the more zealously they were engaged in the greater the guilt of the pilgrims. The reason was that men substituted such devotions in place of good morals. There is an Arabic proverb concerning the ceremonies performed by pilgrims to Mecca : ' Circumambulate, and run, and commit the seven deadly sins !' Another plays thus on words : *Al-harám f'il Haramayn*= 'Unholiness dwelleth in the two holy cities.'

Every morning .. after three years] 'in the morning .. on the third day,' seems preferable. On the morning after arrival the pilgrims brought an oblation : on the next day—the third, according to Heb. reckoning—they paid the tithes. In the great Mohammedan pilgrimage to Mecca the observances due on each day are strictly defined. **5.** According to the Levitical legislation **leaven** might not be burned as part of a sacrifice (Ex 23 18 Lv 2 12) ; but even in those laws there are traces of some degree of freedom (Lv 7 13 23 17). And in northern Israel it would seem that leavened cakes were consumed on the altar as a praise or thank offering. **This liketh you**] i.e. this is what you like.

6. Doughty speaks of an Arab who ' would often show that he had nothing left to eat .. in crackling the thumb nail from the backward upon the upper front teeth.' **Yet have ye not returned unto me**] a pathetic refrain, expressing His disappointment and His appealing love. All warnings have been in vain. **7.** In the plains harvest comes at the end of April ; a month later in the hills. Heavy rains are necessary from Nov. to Jan. to soften the ground sufficiently for ploughing and sowing. **One piece was rained upon,** etc.] cp. Gideon's fleece (Jg 6 37-40). **8. Cities**] i.e. the inhabitants. **9. Blasting**] the effect produced on grain by the burning wind from the desert (Gn 41 6).

Palmerworm] or locust. **10. After the manner of Egypt**] ' Life and death march in "double companies" through Egypt. All epidemics revel here.' 2 K 13 7 is an illustration of the loss of horses. We are to think of the people as shut up in a fetid camp, with decaying bodies of men and horses, and all the other foul odours of the East. **11.** The overthrow of these cities had become a type of utter destruction (Dt 29 23 Isa 1 7, 8 13 19 Jer 49 18 50 40). The **brand plucked out of the burning** is a figure for grievous damage.

12. Thus] but we are not told how Imagination is to fill up the blank, and the partial overthrow already inflicted is enough to

indicate what the final and total ruin will be. They must **meet** God as a foe (Josh 5 13).

13. This verse, 5 8, 9, and 9 6, were probably written on the margin by an admirer of Job 9 4-10. **His thought**] i.e. the determination He has arrived at. He darkens the heavens with storms and eclipses. He marches majestically over the mountains in clouds and thunder (Dt 33 13 Mic 1 3 Hab 3 19 Job 9 8).

CHAPTER 5
THE THIRD ADDRESS

1-6. A lament, a warning, and an invitation. **7, 10-20.** Denunciation of injustice and oppression, with threats of pestilence and judgment. **21-27.** A repudiation of their attempt to please God by mere ritual.

1, 2. Lamentation] a technical term for mournful poetry consisting of short lines of unequal length : here, for instance (v. 2), the dirge consists of four lines, the first and third having three accents, the second and fourth two. **Virgin**] because, though often defeated, Israel had not yet been thoroughly conquered.

5. Pass not to Beer-sheba] People living in the northern kingdom would have to 'pass,' to cross over, the territory of Judah to reach the famous sanctuary in the extreme S. of the land. In the reference to **Gilgal** there is one of those plays on sound which are so common in impassioned speech : ' Hag-Gilgāl galōh yigleh.' And in that to **Beth-el** a play on ideas : Bethel (' House of God ') shall become Aven (' Nothing '). Hosea actually calls it **Beth Aven,** ' House of Nothing ' (4 15 5 8 10 5), and also **Aven** (10 8). Bethel is now called Beit-in. **6.** The better reading would be : ' Lest he send forth fire ' (cp. 1 4, 7, 10, 12 2 2, 5) ' upon the house of Joseph and there be none to quench it for Bethel.' Israel is entitled **the house of Joseph,** because Ephraim, the descendant of Joseph, is the chief tribe in the northern kingdom.

7. Instead of justice there is injustice, bitter as wormwood.

8, 9. Cp. 4 13, and see Job 38 31 Isa 13 10 25 2, 12. **8. The seven stars**] RV ' the Pleiades,' lit. ' the heap.' **The shadow of death**] RM ' deep darkness,' is better.

10. The subject of v. 7 is now resumed : they who turn justice into wormwood, etc., hate in the gate the man who reproves injustice. The **gate** is the broad, open space before the city wall, where all business is discussed and justice is supposed to be administered : cp. v. 12.

11. Burdens of wheat] RV ' exactions of wheat.' These remind us of the way in which the French nobility used to ' grind down the peasantry to the utmost farthing to extort money to spend in debauchery and riot in Paris ' : cp. also 2 S 12 3. Houses of hewn stone were a mark of great wealth (Isa 9 10).

12. RV 'For I know how manifold are your transgressions and how mighty are your sins ; ye that afflict the just, that take a bribe, and that turn aside the needy,' etc. **Bribe**] The word means 'ransom' (see Ex 21 ^{30} Nu 25 ^{31} Prov 6 ^{35}) ; on many occasions it would defeat the ends of justice if a ransom was accepted.

13. What is the use of talking? As a modern writer says :

'For what avail'd it, all the noise
And outcry of the former men ?'

14. As ye have spoken] RV 'as ye say,' i.e. as ye say He is, as ye flatter yourselves He is. **15. The remnant**] At best a mere fraction will escape. **16, 17. Streets**] RV 'broad ways' : what we call squares and open spaces. The **wailing** is the tremulous, high-pitched lament for the dead. The most necessary occupations are suspended because of the great number of deaths. Where the merry shout of the grape-gatherers had been common, sounds of woe may now be heard. The **skilful of lamentation** are the professional mourners (Mt 9 ^{23} : cp. 2 S 3 ^{31} Jer 34 ^{5} Ezk 26 ^{17} 27 ^{32}).

I will pass through, etc.] as the destroying angel passed through Egypt (Ex 12).

18–20. Day of the LORD] see Intro., and cp. Isa 5 ^{30} 8 ^{22} Joel 2 ^{2} Obad v. 15.

21. Festivals such as Tabernacles (1 K 12 ^{33}) are meant. **I will not smell**] RV 'I will take no delight.' The original words refer to the smelling the pleasant odour of the sacrifice (Gn 8 ^{21} Lv 26 ^{31}). **22.** The burnt offering was the costliest of sacrifices, and in early times was not often presented by private individuals.

Meat offerings] RV 'meal offerings' : flour, or flour mingled with salt, oil, and incense.

Peace offerings] The 'thank offerings' of RM is better. These were partly eaten by the worshippers. Fat beasts were, of course, a costly sacrifice. **23, 24.** Vocal and instrumental music was employed in the Temple service at Bethel, but was utterly distasteful to God because of the unrighteousness of the singers and the people generally : cp. Isa 1 ^{13} Ezk 26 ^{13}.

Viols] a kind of lute or guitar, with ten or twelve strings and a sounding-board. **Mighty stream**] RM 'ever-flowing.'

25. Have ye offered?] RV 'Did ye bring ?' The answer is 'No.' So far is God from being influenced by sacrifices that all the time when His Providential care over them was most marked they were in the habit of presenting Him no oblations at all : cp. Josh 5 $^{5-7}$ 1 S 15 ^{22} Jer 7 $^{22, 23}$. **26, 27.** Render, 'And ye shall take up *Sikkuth* your king, and *Kēwān* your images, the star of your god which ye made for yourselves. And I will cause,' etc. *Kēwān* is the name of one of the Babylonian planetary deities who has been variously identified with Saturn or Mars. Another title of the same god, *Tsalme*, is probably concealed under the

words rendered 'your images.' It is at present uncertain who is meant by *Sikkuth*. The idolaters will have to carry their idols into exile, beyond Damascus, i.e. into Assyria, which is thus vaguely indicated.

CHAPTER 6
THE FOURTH ADDRESS

1–3. False security of Judah and Israel. **4–6.** Carelessness and luxury. **7–11.** Captivity, siege, death, ruin. **12, 13.** Preposterous errors. **14.** The coming of the avenger.

1, 2. Render, 'Woe to the easy-going in Zion and to the secure in the mountain of Samaria ! Make the round of the foremost nations and come to them, O house of Israel. Pass over to Calneh and see, and from thence go to Hamath Rabbah : then, etc. Are you better than these kingdoms ? or is your border,' etc., that you should be so favoured. The site of **Calneh** is uncertain. **Hamath** is the well known city on the Orontes. **3.** They refused to think of the coming retribution ; they enthroned violence in their midst.

4. Reclining at meals was a custom introduced from the farther East : contrast 1 S 20 ^{24}. The grandees now 'stretched themselves,' etc. : cp. Spenser's 'Poured out in loosnesse on the grassy ground' ; luxury and idleness are implied. **Eat the lambs**, etc.] To a frugal shepherd the feeding up of beasts for food seemed shameful extravagance : 'Seldom the nomads eat other flesh than the meat of their sacrifices ; but it be some beast that will not thrive, or is likely to die on their hands' (Doughty).

5. Chant] RV 'sing idle songs' is an improvement. The musicians were lazy triflers.

Invent to themselves, etc.] In the psalm which closes the Greek Psalter, David is made to assert : 'My hands fashioned an instrument, and my fingers fitted together a psaltery' : see also 2 Ch 29 $^{26, 27}$. **6.** The goblet is not enough, they must have **bowls** to drink out of, bowls of costly material such as were generally used in divine service (Zech 9 ^{15} 14 ^{20}). The threatened ruin of the nation did not move these unpatriotic feasters to dispense with costly unguents, as men in trouble were usually ready to do (2 S 14 ^{2}).

7. First in sin, first in punishment. **The banquet**, etc.] RV 'The revelry of them that stretched themselves shall pass away.' A play on sounds : *Sar mirzach seruchim*. **8. Excellency**] i.e. the excellent things of which the nation was proud. **9.** The city is besieged, and if there is a house in which the pestilence has left ten men alive their turn shall come.

10. And a man's uncle, etc.] RV is a little different : 'And when a man's uncle' (RM 'kinsman') 'shall take him up, even he that burneth him, to bring out the bones out of the house, and shall say unto him that is in the innermost parts of the house, Is there yet any with thee ? and he shall say, No ; then,' etc. Taking this difficult v. as it here stands, we must remember that it was the duty of the next of kin to see to the disposal of the body, and that, whilst interment was the almost universal rule, cremation might be resorted to in special circumstances (1 S 31 12). The plague-stricken man in the inner rooms of the house must not defile the LORD's name by uttering it in the immediate presence of death, as a Mohammedan may not say his prayers in an unclean spot. A simpler form of the v., suggested in part by LXX, would be : ' A remnant shall be left' (in the plague-swept house), ' and when men break through to bring out the bones from the house it shall be said to him who is in the recesses of the house, Is there yet any with thee ? and he shall say, None.'

12. Read, ' Shall horses run upon the cliff ? Will a man plough the sea with oxen ? ' No ! but in moral and religious matters they will do things as absurd as these. 13. No alteration of the original is required to obtain the following : ' Ye which rejoice in Lo-Debar, which say, Have we not taken for us Karnaim by our own strength ? ' For Lo-Debar see 2 S 9 4 17 27, and for Karnaim Gn 14 5 Dt 1 4 Josh 21 27 1 Mac 5 26 : both towns lay E. of the Jordan and may have been taken by Jeroboam II.

A great change had come over the fortunes of Israel during the reigns of Joash of Israel and his son, Jeroboam II. Israel had been reduced to a very low ebb in the time of Jehoahaz by the repeated and successful assaults of the Syrians (2 K 13 7, 22). With the advent of Joash all this was altered. He recovered ten cities which Hazael had taken, and gained three victories (2 K 13 25). Jeroboam II carried these successes still further. ' He restored the border of Israel from the entering in of Hamath unto the sea of the Arabah ' (RV) and appears to have been uniformly victorious. This was largely due to the fact that he never came into collision with Assyria, whereas the power of Syria had been greatly reduced by the campaigns of Shalmaneser III and Assurdan.

Such a collision was, however, inevitable (v. 14). The earliest contact between Israel and Assyria of which we have any record was when Ahab, as an ally of Hadadezer of Damascus, shared in the disastrous defeat inflicted on the Syrian king by Shalmaneser II at the battle of Karkar, 854 B.C. On the famous obelisk of black basalt, now in the British Museum, ambassadors from Jehu are represented bringing tribute to the same Assyrian monarch at Hamath, 842 B.C. Tiglath-pileser III, called in the Bible ' Pul,' marched against Northern Syria in 738 B.C. and Menahem gave the king a thousand talents of silver, ' that his hand might be with him to confirm the kingdom in his hand '

(2 K 15 19). In 732 B.C. Tiglath-pileser III invaded Israel, took a number of towns, including the whole district of Naphtali (2 K 15 29), and compelled Pekah, king of Israel, to pay a considerable tribute. The kingdom of Israel was destroyed in the year 722 B.C., when Samaria was taken by Sargon in the first month of his reign, after a siege which was begun by his predecessor, Shalmaneser IV, and had lasted three years.

14. The entering in of Hemath] the ideal northern boundary of the Holy Land (Nu 13 21 2 K 14 25-28) : it is the great depression between the N. end of Lebanon and the Nusariyeh mountains. The river of the wilderness] RV ' the brook of the Arabah,' the Wādī-el-Ahsih, the southern boundary.

CHAPTER 7
THREE VISIONS AND AN INTERRUPTION

1–9. The visions. 10–17. The interruption.

There are two senses in which the word ' Vision ' may be used of one of the forms of Hebrew prophecy. In the first sense a state of mind closely akin to that of a dreamer is intended : ' I the LORD will make myself known unto him in a vision, I will speak with him in a dream ' (Nu 12 6). The prophet falls into a kind of ecstasy, and has no control over the pictures which pass before his mind. Every one will remember the language ascribed to Balaam : ' He saith .. which seeth the vision of the Almighty, falling down, and having his eyes open ' (Nu 24 4, 16). In the second sense of the word it is meant that the subject-matter of the preaching was divinely inspired, but the prophet's own mind and will played an important part in throwing this matter into the form of a picture. The visions of Amos belong to the latter class. God's Spirit made the coming destruction of Israel certain to this man. Amos drew, and then explained, the pictures which were emblems of that destruction, the locusts, the devouring flame, the measurement with a plumb-line, the basket of summer fruit, the fall of temple and column.

1. Grasshoppers] RV ' Locusts.' The latter growth may possibly mean the grass which springs in Palestine after the late rains in March-April. We cannot be quite certain whether the king's mowings or 'shearings' are here mentioned. Sheep-shearing in N. Palestine takes place about April. The king's mowings would be a portion of the crops taken to feed his horses. 2. Render, ' And as they were about to make an end of eating .. Who shall raise up Jacob ? ' The question is equivalent to an exclamation : ' Oh that Jacob might be raised up ! '

4. He would not conduct His controversy with words, but with a consuming fire (Isa 66 16). The great deep] the abyss on which the earth

was supposed to rest (Gn 7¹¹ Ps 24²). **A part]** RV 'the land,' the portion appointed to Israel: this, also, the fire was about to consume.

7, 8. Upon a wall] RV 'beside a wall.' The testing of the wall is a symbol of the searching investigation into the people's conduct, which would be followed by a strictly just recompense (2 S 8² 2 K 21¹³ Isa 34¹¹ Jer 1¹¹,¹² Lam 2⁸). **9. The high places of Isaac]** i.e. Beer-sheba (5⁵), which was especially associated with Isaac (Gn 27²³ 28¹⁰).

10, 11. Amaziah, being a royal official, intervenes as soon as the king's name is brought in (v. 9). He sends a message to Jeroboam II at Samaria (2 K 14²³), charging the prophet with stirring up sedition at the very centre of the national life. And he exaggerates. Amos had not said that the king himself should be killed. **12, 13.** How contemptuous Amaziah is! His words literally are: 'Seer, go, flee thee away,' etc. There is a proverbial saying, 'Eat your pudding, slave, and hold your tongue.'

The king's chapel] RV 'The king's sanctuary': his 'Chapel Royal.' **The king's court]** RV 'a royal house': one of his residences (Dan 4³⁰).

14. We catch the emphasis if we render: 'No prophet am I, and no son of a prophet am I.' The latter expression may mean that he had not been trained in one of the schools for prophets (1 S 19²⁴ 2 K 4³⁸ 9¹), but it is better to understand it as referring to the Oriental custom of the son following his father's occupation. **A gatherer of sycomore fruit]** RV 'A dresser of sycomore trees.' The sycomore fig required pinching or scraping to bring it to ripeness. It was not thought much of in Palestine. **15.** Cp. 2 S 7⁸ 1 K 19¹⁹ Ps 78⁷⁰,⁷¹ Gal 1¹. **16. Thou sayest]** in opposition to what **the LORD** said (v. 17). **Drop not** *thy word]* don't let it drip, drip, drip, in imbecile and wearisome fashion (Mic 2⁶,¹¹ Ezk 21²,⁷).

17. An harlot] violated by the victorious soldiers. The greatest disaster that can befall an Eastern is to leave no son to continue his name. The ample domain of the wealthy priest would be divided into small properties for the new settlers (Jer 6² Mic 2⁴). **A polluted land]** or, 'a land that is unclean' (RV), is one where Jehovah, not being its recognised lord, could not be legitimately worshipped (1 S 26¹⁹ 2 K 5¹⁷ Hos 9³⁻⁵ Ezk 4¹³).

CHAPTER 8
THE VISION OF THE RIPE FRUIT, FOLLOWED BY A FIFTH ADDRESS

1–3. The vision. **4–14.** The address, denouncing dishonest traders (vv. 4–6), threatening earthquakes, eclipse, mourning, a painful sense of abandonment by God, an utter destruction of the superstitious (vv. 7–14).

1–3. Notwithstanding the interference of

Amaziah, the prophet finishes the recital of his visions.

1, 2. Another play on words—*qayits* is the word for ripe fruit, and *qêts* for end. We might represent it by, 'A basket of *ripe* fruit. My people are *ripe* for judgment.' **3.** The literal translation of this picturesque v. is, 'And the songs of the Temple shall howl in that day— utterance of the Lord Jehovah! Many the corpses! In every place they cast forth! Hush!' **Temple]** RM 'palace.' The building is regarded as the palace of the Great King; the word came to the Hebrews from Babylonia, and literally signifies 'Great House.' The pestilence is so fatal that men have no time either to burn or bury the dead, and no inclination to talk.

4. To make the poor of the land to fail] i.e. to exterminate those who are in lowly circumstances. 'They make a solitude and call it peace.' **5.** The **new moon** was originally a more important festival than the **sabbath.** For points in its observance see 1 S 20⁶ 2 K 4²³ Isa 1¹³ Hos 2¹³, and cp. the Levitical ritual in Nu 28¹¹. **The ephah]** the measure by which they sold, was fraudulently small; the weight by which they tested the money paid them was as dishonestly great. Money was not coined, but was weighed on every business occasion (Gn 23¹⁶). The ephah contained about 65 Imp. pts.; the **shekel** of 252 grs. would be worth about £2 1s. of our money.

7. Jehovah Himself is the **Excellency**, the Pride and Boast of His people.

8. The movements of the land shaken by the earthquake, or whatever other calamity was divinely inflicted, are compared to those of the Nile: 'Yea, it shall rise up wholly like the River; and it shall be troubled and sink again, like the River of Egypt' (RV). The word for 'river' is regularly employed of the Nile.

9. The eclipse of June 15th, 763 B.C., may have impressed his imagination powerfully.

10. Feasts] religious, not secular. The cloth of camel's or goat's hair was bound round the loins with a cord. Shaving the head was a sign of mourning (Lv 21⁵ Isa 4²⁴ 22¹²). This day would end as badly as it began.

11. The **word** which they craved was not one of spiritual instruction, but of guidance out of trouble: cp. 1 S 3¹. **12. From sea to sea]** i.e. from the Mediterranean to the Dead Sea.

14. The **sin,** or, rather, the 'guilt' of Samaria, is the idolatrous object worshipped by the Samaritans, either the calf at Bethel (1 K 12²⁹ Hos 8¹⁵ 10⁵), or the Asherah at Samaria (2 K 13⁶). **The manner]** RV 'the way of Beer-sheba' may perhaps mean the pilgrimage thither. Mohammedans swear by the pilgrimage to Mecca. But Amos not improbably wrote, 'By the life of the deity of Beer-sheba.'

CHAPTER 9
THE CONCLUDING VISION AND A DISCOURSE.
COMFORTABLE WORDS

1. The vision. **2–10.** The discourse, declaring that none shall evade God's judgments (vv. 2–6); that Israel stands in no peculiar relationship to Jehovah (v. 7); that all the sinners amongst them shall perish (vv. 8–10). **11–15.** Comfortable words, predicting the restoration of the Davidic kingdom in all its former extent (vv. 11, 12); the exuberant fertility of the land (v. 13); the complete and final establishment of the nation on it (v. 15).

1. Read, ' I saw Jehovah standing beside the altar ; and he said, " Smite the capitals of the pillars, so that the thresholds may shake, and break them in pieces on the head of all of them .. there shall not one of them flee away, and there shall not one of them escape." ' The **altar** is that at Bethel, the chief sanctuary of the kingdom (1 K 12 33 Am 7 13); assembled there for worship, the great mass of the people meet with destruction, like the Philistines in the house of their god (Jg 16 29, 30). The blow from heaven shakes the building throughout, and its loftier parts come crashing down on the worshippers. **2. Hell**] Heb. *Sheol*, the abode of the departed. **3. Carmel's** lofty, rough, wooded summit would be an ideal place to hide in. Fugitives had the right of asylum on this sacred mountain. The reference to the **serpent** reminds us of the Babylonian myth in which the dragon of chaos is vanquished by Merodach : cp. also Isa 51 9 Ps 74 13. **5, 6.** This may have been a note written on the margin, suggested by 5 8 8 8. **6.** RV 'It is He that buildeth His chambers in the heaven, and hath founded His vault upon the earth.' The vault of the sky appears to rest on the ground. **7.** At 3 2 Amos admits that there is a special

bond between Israel and the LORD ; here, with splendid boldness, he repudiates it. Their conduct has dissolved the connexion. Not only so : Providence has guided other races as well as the Hebrews : cp. Mt 3 9 Jn 8 33 Ac 17 26). The **Ethiopians** inhabited that part of the Nile Valley which stretches from Assouan southwards. **Caphtor**] probably the island of Crete (cp. Ezk 25 16); but some authorities identify it with the coast of the Egyptian Delta.

8–10. The qualifications at the end of vv. 8, 9 rob the threat of much of its force, and are not quite in the manner of Amos. At all events, we have three stern messages here : the kingdom is to be utterly destroyed, the people are to be wanderers amongst all nations, the sword is to slay all the sinners.

11. The dominion exercised by David's descendants is spoken of as **the tabernacle of David**, and is figured as a small, dilapidated house, part of which has fallen in, the rest being full of gaps : cp. 1 K 12 16 Ezk 34 23, 24 37 24. **12.** The **remnant of Edom** is an expression which implies that this people has been much weakened ; the victories of Amaziah greatly reduced its power (2 K 14 7-22). Over other nations, also, Jehovah's **name** had been proclaimed as victor and owner : cp. Dt 28 10 2 S 12 28 Isa 63 19 2 Ch 6 33. **13.** Vintage comes in the dry months of autumn, and is soon over. In the happy future the **grapes** will be so plentiful that this work will last till the rainy season, when the grain is sown. **Sweet wine**] the newly expressed juice of the grape. **14.** To **bring again the captivity** is an expression which does not necessarily imply exile. It often means a favourable change in one's fortunes. But the mention of the waste cities, and the land gone out of cultivation, agrees with the idea of a real captivity, and the promise in the closing v. suggests that Israel had been ' plucked up out of their land.'

OBADIAH

INTRODUCTION

1. Contents. The book of Obadiah, as the title in v. 1 states, is a prophecy against Edom. The main divisions are as follows :—Vv. 1–9, Edom is about to be driven out of its land by a confederacy of nations ; vv. 10–14, this is in punishment for its participation in the capture of Jerusalem ; vv. 15, 16, a day of judgment is coming upon all nations ; vv. 17–21, in that

day Judah and Israel shall escape, and shall regain the lands that the Edomites and other enemies have taken from them.

2. Composition. All criticism of this book must set out from the remarkable correspondence between it and parts of Jer 49. The parallelism is as follows :—Obad 1a = Jer 7a, Obad 1b 2 = Jer 14, 15, Obad 3, 4 = Jer 16, Obad

5ᵃ = Jer 9ᵇ, Obad 5ᵇ = Jer 9ᵃ, Obad 6 = Jer 10, Obad 8 resembles Jer 7ᵇ slightly, Obad 9 resembles Jer 22 slightly.

(*a*) The theory that this parallelism is due to quotation of Obadiah by Jeremiah is open to a number of formidable objections. (1) Obad 10–14 seems to refer to the capture of Jerusalem by Nebuchadrezzar in 586 B.C., but Jer 49 is commonly supposed to have been composed immediately after the battle of Carchemish in 605 B.C. In that case Jeremiah wrote before Obadiah, and therefore cannot have quoted him. The words of Obadiah cannot be referred to the capture of Jerusalem by Shishak (1 K 14²⁵⁻²⁸), nor by the Philistines and Arabians (2 Ch 21¹⁶ᶠ.), nor by Israel (2 K 14¹³ᶠ.), for in none of these cases is there any record of a participation of Edomites. The pre-exilic prophets never accuse the Edomites of assisting in the sack of Jerusalem : cp. Amos 1⁹⁻¹² Jer 9²⁶ 25²¹ 49⁷ᶠ. Only in the post-exilic prophets is this charged: cp. Ezk 35 Ps 137 Lam 4²¹ᶠ. It seems impossible, therefore, to refer Obad 10–14 to anything else than the capture of Jerusalem by Nebuchadrezzar. (2) Obad 7 states that the allies of Edom have expelled him from his land. This event is anticipated in Ezk 25¹⁰,¹²,¹⁴, and it is an accomplished fact in Mal 1³. There is no event before the exile to which these words can be referred ; consequently Obadiah cannot be earlier than Jeremiah. The view that Jer 49 is a late post-exilic interpolation in the book of Jeremiah is inconsistent with the fact that Obad 7, 10–14 and all other allusions to late events in the book of Obadiah are absent from the parallel in Jer 49. (*b*) The reading of Jer 49¹⁵ᵇ is preferable to Obad 2. Jer 49⁹ lacks the clumsy addition found in Obad 5. Jer 49¹⁰ is a more natural sequel to Obad 5 than is Obad 6. These facts indicate that in several particulars the text of Jer 49 is more primitive than that of Obadiah.

(*d*) The theory that Jeremiah is quoted by Obadiah is also untenable. (1) Because the order of the vv. is more primitive in Obadiah than in Jeremiah. Obad 1 is evidently the beginning of the oracle, and this is logically followed by vv. 3–6, 8, 9. The different order of the vv. in Jer 49 is unnatural and cannot be primitive. (2) The text of Obad 1, 3, 5, 8 is more primitive than the parallel vv. in Jeremiah. (3) The form of the prophecy in Obadiah is much briefer than that in Jeremiah, and is therefore probably more primitive. Moreover, the vv. in Jer 49 that are not found in Obadiah show the characteristic language of Jeremiah.

(*c*) In view of these facts the only possible theory of the relation of Obadiah to Jer 49 is that both prophets quote a third earlier prophet. The vv. that are found both in Jeremiah and Obad 1–6, 8, 9, are the only ones that can be ascribed with certainty to the older prophecy.

3. Date. How long before Jeremiah the prophet lived who wrote Obad 1–6, 8, 9 and the parallels in Jeremiah can only be conjectured. Some regard him as a contemporary of Isaiah, and refer the disaster threatened in these vv. to the humiliation of Edom by Amaziah (2 K 14⁷). It seems, however, that the enemies of Edom in this passage are not Israelites but Gentiles, and it is perhaps better to understand the danger as the Arabian invasion mentioned in 2 Ch 26⁷. The same disaster apparently threatened Moab according to Isa 15–16¹². The second half of the book of Obadiah (vv. 10–21) was written during the exile, while the memory of Edom's wrong was still fresh.

4. Value. The purpose of the book of Obadiah is to express Judah's hatred of Edom and its confidence that Edom will ultimately be destroyed. This conviction rests upon a recognition of the fundamental difference between the national characters of the two nations. The Edomites were famous for their secular wisdom, but no allusion to their religion is ever made in the OT. Esau figures in Hebrew tradition as a profane person, destitute of spiritual instincts. The confidence that Edom shall not ultimately triumph over Israel is, therefore, no mere expression of Jewish patriotism, but is a spiritual conviction that the religion of Jehovah cannot be extinguished by the forces of evil. As an expression of this conviction the book of Obadiah has permanent value.

1–9. The question has been much discussed whether vv. 1–9 are prediction or description. V. 7 is clearly description, and on the strength of this some seek to explain the whole passage as descriptive ; but, as we have just seen, v. 7 is not found in Jer 49, and is, therefore, no part of the old prophecy that Obadiah quotes. It is to be attached to v. 10, and is part of Obadiah's addition to the original oracle. Apart from this v. there is no reason for regarding vv. 1–6, 8, 9 as predictive. The expression 'we have heard' (v. 1ᵇ) does not indicate that the disaster of Edom is past, but only that the news that it is impending has just reached the speakers. 'I have made' (v. 2) also does not indicate that the disaster is accomplished, but merely that it is determined in the divine purpose. V. 3 clearly implies that Edom it still dwelling in his rocky strongholds, and does not believe that he can ever be expelled from them, and in v. 4 the words 'I will bring thee down from thence' show that the catastrophe still lies in the future. To understand these words as a purpose of God uttered in the past is very unnatural. Accordingly, we conclude that the ruin of Edom predicted in vv. 1–6, 8, 9 lies in the future but that knowledge that it is impending has already reached Israel.

1. Vision of Obadiah] A title added by the collector of the Minor Prophets. Who Obadiah was is unknown. The name means 'Servant of Jehovah.' **Thus saith the Lord GOD concerning Edom**] a remark by the author of Obad 7, 10–21 designed to introduce his quotation from the older prophet. **We have heard**] a better reading than 'I have heard' (Jer 49 14). This sentence is not a natural continuation of the introductory formula in v. 1a, and it shows that the passage quoted was not originally an oracle spoken by the Lord, but a report heard by the Israelites. **Rumour**] a correct translation of the original. This word is never used in the sense of 'oracle.' This meaning is rendered certain by the parallelism of the next clause, **an ambassador is sent among the heathen.** The added words, **from the Lord,** do not indicate that the 'rumour' is an utterance of the Lord, but only that the coming disaster is caused by Him. The 'rumour' is news of the impending attack of the nations upon Edom. In v. 1b the language of Obad. is more original than that of its parallel Jer 49 14. **Heathen**] better, RV 'nations.' The allusion is probably to Arabian tribes that menaced Palestine in the time of Uzziah (2 Ch 26 7). The names of the kings of Edom in the Assyrian inscriptions in comparison with the list of Gn 36 31-39 show that a new Arabian population entered the land of Edom by the middle of the 8th cent. B.C. To this impending migration the author of this ancient prophecy probably refers.

2. Behold, I have made thee small] does not refer to an accomplished overthrow of Edom, since in v. 1b the nations are summoned to come against him, and since in vv. 3, 4 he still feels secure in his strongholds ; but it refers to a divine determination already made. The parallel in Jer 49 15 omits 'thou,' thus making it more clear that the whole v. refers to the divine purpose. **Small** and **despised** refer to the condition in which Edom will be left after the conquest by the nations. The word **greatly** is a textual corruption of 'among men' that is preserved in Jer 49 15.

3. The confidence of Edom that he cannot be dislodged from his rock-dwellings and fortresses. The land of Edom was full of caves, artificially enlarged and fortified, whose remains are still to be seen in great numbers at Petra and elsewhere throughout the land.

4. The divine determination to dislodge Edom from his land in spite of the inaccessibility of his strongholds.

5. States that even thieves leave something behind them, and that grape-gatherers leave a few grapes. The thought is the contrast in the condition of Edom after it has been invaded. The nomads of the desert will leave nothing behind when once they have overrun the land. In Obad. the thought is expressed in the form of a question expecting an affirmative answer, but in Jer 49 9 rm it is expressed as an affirmative statement. The form in Obad. is obviously the more poetic and original. The words 'how art thou cut off' are not found in the parallel in Jer., and are a weak addition made by the writer of the second half of the book or by a later scribe.

6. Things] RV 'treasures.' After v. 5 we naturally expect a statement of the contrast between the treatment of Edom and the conduct of thieves and grape-gatherers in leaving a remnant, but this is not found in the v. This leads some to reject it as a gloss and to regard v. 7 as the original continuation of v. 5 ; but, as we have seen, v. 7 is not found in Jer 49 and refers to an event after the fall of Jerusalem, so that it is unquestionably an addition made by the writer of the second half of the book. The best solution of the difficulty is to regard Jer 49 10, which is parallel to v. 6, as the original continuation of v. 5. This v. is much more perfect than the parallel in Obad., and contains a statement of the complete destruction of Edom that the context requires. Obad 6 is apparently merely a broken-down form of the text in Jer 49 10.

7. Brought thee] RM 'driven thee out.' The v. refers to the complete expulsion of Edom from his territory by the Nabatæan Arabs at some time during the exile of Israel. The event is spoken of in the past tense, and shows that the writer lived after the fall of Jerusalem. This v. is not found in Jer 49 and must come from the hand of the author of Obad 10–21. It joins on naturally to v. 10. The word translated in AV 'they that eat thy bread' is omitted by LXX. It is a dittograph of the last letters of the preceding word.

8, 9. Some reject these vv. as glosses because the verbs are in the future, instead of the past tense, as in v. 7 ; but, as we have seen, v. 7 is not part of the original prophecy, and vv. 1–6 regard the fall of Edom as still future. These vv. join on logically to v. 6. Jer 49 7 b, 22 contain slight resemblances to these vv. The text of Obad. appears to be more original on account of the use of the first person and the expression 'saith the Lord.' The worldly wisdom of the Edomites was proverbial among the Hebrews: cp. Jer 49 7.

10-14. The vv. describe the co-operation of the Edomites in Nebuchadrezzar's destruction of Jerusalem and state that the foregoing prediction of destruction is due to this unbrotherly conduct. These vv. together with v. 7 and vv. 15–21 come from the hand of the later writer. It is clear that he is ignorant of the original meaning of the ancient prophecy in vv. 1–6 and 8, 9, and regards it as a still unfulfilled prediction of the destruction of Edom. The last word of v. 9 is to be attached to the beginning of v. 10, translating 'because of the slaughter, because of the violence.'

10. The imperfects in Hebrew describe the present condition of Edom, and should be rendered 'shame covers thee, thou art cut off for ever.' The allusion is the same as in v. 7 to the recent Nabatæan migration through which Edom has been dispossessed.

11. This is a clear reference to the destruction of Jerusalem by Nebuchadrezzar. The Edomites are blamed for assisting in the work of destruction. The past tenses show that we are dealing with description, not with prediction. **Thou stoodest on the other side,** in a hostile sense (RM 'aloof') as in Ps 38 11. **Forces]** RV 'substance,' i.e. wealth.

12–14. These vv. describe poetically in the form of a warning what Edom has actually done. **12. Looked on,** with the sense of gloating over misfortune as in Mic 7 10b. **The day** is evidently the day of the fall of Jerusalem. The details of the hostility of Edom supplied by this v. are the same that are emphasised in Ezk, Lam, Pss, and other writings of the post-exilic period. This v. is partly identical with v. 14, and belongs logically after 13. It is, therefore, open to suspicion of being an editorial insertion. **14.** The word translated **crossway** by RV and AV is of unknown meaning. In LXX 'a mountain pass.'

15, 16. These vv. describe an impending day of judgment upon all the heathen. The expression **day of the LORD** is the technical term used by all the prophets for a turning-point in history when the new era of blessing for Israel shall be inaugurated. In the older prophets this day is ushered in by the assault of Assyria, Babylon, or one of the other foreign nations, upon Israel. In Ezk and the prophets that follow him it is a day of judgment upon the heathen. This is the conception of this passage and shows that it cannot be earlier than Ezk. In v. 15b Edom is addressed in the second person singular, as in the preceding vv., and is told that he shall be included in the general catastrophe of the nations. V. 16 is not to be understood of the Edomites, as is generally done, since the address is in the second person plural, and since the Edomites are included in **all the heathen** of the preceding v. The Jews are addressed 'who have drunk of the cup of the wrath of Jehovah,' and they are told that all the heathen shall be forced to drink the cup that they have drunk of. Instead of **swallow down,** a slight textual emendation will give

'stagger,' which is more consistent with the context.

17–21. These vv. describe the happy destiny of Israel. **17. Deliverance]** RV 'those that escape,' i.e. in the coming day of judgment, and regain the land that they have lost at the time of the exile. This suggests that they are still in captivity. **18. Jacob** is a designation of the kingdom of Judah, **Joseph** is a designation of the kingdom of Israel. Israel had certainly not returned at the time when this prophecy was written, and there is no more reason to think that Judah had returned. The thought of the reunion of the divided kingdoms of Judah and Israel is common in the prophets from the days of Amos onward. The closing words of the v., **for the LORD hath spoken it,** seem to be a reference to the ancient prophecy in vv. 1–6, 8, 9, which the author regards as still unfulfilled.

The text of vv. 19, 20 is very corrupt, and neither the AV nor the RV gives a satisfactory sense. The LXX allows us to restore the text and translate as follows :

'The Negeb (i.e. south Judah) shall possess Mount Esau (i.e. Edom), and the Shephelah (i.e. the inhabitants of the maritime plain of Judah) shall possess the Philistines, and the Mountain (i.e. the people of the mountain district of Judah) shall possess Ephraim and the open country of Samaria, and Benjamin shall possess Gilead. And the exiles of this host of the sons of Israel shall possess the land of the Canaanites unto Sarephath, and the exiles of Jerusalem who are in Sepharad shall inherit the cities of the Negeb (i.e. south Judah).'

20. Sepharad was probably the name of a district in the north of Asia Minor.

The historical situation here assumed is that Edom has been expelled from its own land, and has occupied the S. of Judah left vacant by the captivity. The maritime plain has been seized by the Philistines, the Samaritans have occupied the land of Judah, and the Arabs from E. of the Jordan have seized the territory of Benjamin. This condition of things shall be reversed in the good time coming. The invaders shall be expelled from the lands that they have unjustly seized, and the tribes of Israel shall occupy their ancient territory.

21. This v. describes the glory of Israel after Edom and all the other nations have fallen. **Saviours** refers to the monarchs that are to be raised up to rule the restored nation. The closing words, **the kingdom shall be the LORD'S,** show that the author's confidence of the fall of Edom and the triumph of Israel is based upon the conviction that the religion of Israel cannot perish.

JONAH

INTRODUCTION

1. The Book and its Hero. This little book stands alone amongst the writings of the prophets with which it is grouped. It does not contain any prophecies, except the message of Jonah to the Ninevites, yet it is placed with the books of Amos and Micah, which contain hardly anything else. It is written in prose, except the Psalm in c. 2, and appears at first sight to be a simple narrative of fact, yet it is separated from both the groups of books to which the histories of the OT., Samuel and Kings, Chronicles and Ezra, belong.

The hero of the story lived in the reign of Jeroboam II, king of Israel, in whose time Amos's work was accomplished. According to 2K 14 25, he prophesied the recovery from Syria of the lost border possessions of Israel. That fixes the date of his activity, as there recorded, in the first half of the 8th cent. B.C. He is said to have belonged to Gath-hepher, a town of Zebulon, and his grave is still shown in the vicinity of Nazareth.

2. The Author of the Book. But the author of the book before us cannot have been the hero of the story. That is proved, (1) by 3 3. 'Nineveh was an exceeding great city.' The Hebrew makes it plain that the writer is looking back on a time already past, writing to those who are no longer familiar with the greatness of Nineveh. But as Nineveh was the metropolis of the world till its fall in 607 B.C., this book must have been written after that date. Further, no writer of the time when Assyria was the greatest of the world-powers would have described its ruler as 'the king of Nineveh,' any more than Napoleon at the height of his power could have been called king of Paris. (2) As is shown in the notes, the Psalm in c. 2 is full of allusions to various Psalms. Most of these are certainly later than the 8th cent. (3) The language of the book contains words and phrases which were unknown before the captivity. Hence it is generally agreed that the book was not written earlier than the 5th or 4th cent. B.C., in the period following the reforms of Ezra and Nehemiah, three centuries after Jonah's day.

3. Character of the Book. Many Christian and Jewish expositors formerly considered the whole book a literal narrative of actual facts. At the present time nearly all scholars judge it to be an OT. parable, or instructive story, made to convey in pictorial form great spiritual truths. Against the strictly historical view of the book may be urged, (1) the complete silence both of the OT. and of other history as to any such conversion of the Ninevites as that described in c. 3. On the contrary, they are uniformly described as idolaters, and threatened with the direst punishment: cp. especially the whole prophecy of Nahum, or Isaiah, chs. 10, 37, etc. (2) The book breaks off most abruptly, giving no account at all of the future fortunes either of Jonah or of the repentant people. From the literary point of view this is one of the beauties of the book (see on 4 11), but it seems to show that the design of the writer was not the writing of history. (3) To many readers the whole book suggests inevitably that we are in the world of parable, as surely as does the 'Pilgrim's Progress' or the 'Holy War.'

A modern reader may find difficulty in understanding how in such a parable an incident like that of the great fish could be introduced; to him its very strangeness might suggest that it was not mere invention. But to a Jew of the 4th or 5th cent. no such difficulty would appear. In Jer 51 34-44 (the whole passage should be carefully considered) the Babylonian captivity had already been compared to the swallowing of the nation by a huge dragon, and the deliverance from the exile to being cast out alive from the devourer's maw. Other OT. passages, such as Job 7 12 26 12 (RV) Ps 74 13, show how familiar was the thought and the dread of the monsters of the deep. To represent a great disaster occurring to a man who ran away from duty by such an image, was as natural as was the picture of the Slough of Despond to a man who lived in a marshy and ill-drained locality. Against this view devout Christian thinkers used to urge the references of our Lord in Mt 12 39-41 16 4 Lk 11 29, 30, which they supposed compelled us to accept the narrative as historical. It must be carefully observed that those who hold the position advocated here, do not challenge the authority of our Lord, but only the justness of this method of interpreting His words. It may fairly be said that He is using an illustration which is equally forcible whether it is drawn from fact or from poetry. Just as we refer to the Prodigal Son, or the Good Samaritan, in precisely the same terms we should use were their adventures historical facts, so may Christ have done here. On the whole, then, we conclude with confidence that though it is possible that a historical tradition of the mission of Jonah to Nineveh suggested the writing of the book, its author has freely worked on this material, and has subordinated everything to the conveying of spiritual truths. So in the parable of the pounds (Lk 19 11-27), our Lord starts from the well-known incidents of the visits of Herod the Great and Archelaus to Rome, ' to receive a kingdom,' and from that point develops the story with its urgent lessons. So in his historical plays Shakespeare uses the old Chroniclers. But the historical parts of Macbeth or Richard the Second are of little interest to us, compared with the analysis of motive and the insight into character that are of such abiding value. It is of great interest to observe that in the OT. as in the NT. the natural human love for a story is so often appealed to, so that ' truth embodied in a tale may enter in at lowly doors.'

4. Aim and Teaching of the Book. The one pervading aim of the book is to exhibit the true relationship between man and God, only realised by understanding what men are, and what God is. In opposition to the teaching of later Judaism, with its bitter contempt and hatred of the heathen world, and its belief that God regarded it in the same way, the author is eager to show how kindness of heart and readiness to repent of sin may be found everywhere amongst men, and are always acceptable to God. So in the story of the voyage the heathen sailors shrink from the thought of violent or unjust dealings with Jonah, and both they and the people of Nineveh reverently own the power of Jehovah, so soon as His claims are put before them. With this may be compared our Lord's words in Mt 11 20-24 Lk 11 31, 32, and His choice of the Good Samaritan as the type of brotherly kindness, in contrast with the priest and the Levite.

From such teaching about mankind follows naturally the teaching about God. He is revealed as full of infinite compassion, looking pitifully upon the thousands of innocent little children and helpless cattle in the great city, swift to hear and receive the cry of penitence. It is in accordance with this general view that God's individual dealings with His disobedient servant are set forth. He may punish, but is always at hand to deliver. He is willing to reason with His messengers as He does with Jonah in c. 4. Again, we compare our Lord's picture of the pleading of the father with the elder brother (Lk 15 28-32).

One other truth is brought out with great beauty in c. 4, where Jonah's pity for the gourd is made an image of God's pity for Nineveh. We are taught that man may trust his nobler instincts as being true revelations of God, and from his own compassion argue upwards to find such qualities in perfection there.

'Though He is so bright, and we so dim,
 We are made in His image to witness Him.'

Nowhere else in the OT. is there so close an approximation to the great saying of 1 Jn 4 7, ' For love is of God, and every one that loveth is begotten of God and knoweth God.'

We see, then, that in this little book of 48 vv. we reach the high-water mark of OT. teaching. It is of priceless value, and will remain so as long as men need to learn what God thinks of the teeming masses in the world's great cities, what we ought to think of them, and how God judges us by our judgment of them.

5. It should be noted that many scholars give a more particular application to the story than has just been set forth. To them it is an allegory, teaching the meaning of the history of the nation. Jonah stands for Israel, intended from the first by God to be the missionary people to the rest of mankind, but refusing to recognise its destiny. The swallowing by the fish represents the captivity, the deliverance the return from exile. Read thus, the book is at once a reproof and an appeal to those who, like the community in Jerusalem, even after their marvellous restoration, were still narrow and bigoted, hating the nations round them, not able even yet to understand the breadth of God's love. ' Who is blind, but my servant, or deaf as my messenger that I send ?'

It is claimed that this permits a closer application of the vv. quoted from Jer 51. Against this, however, must be set the significant fact that the rest of that passage breathes the old bitter spirit of hatred against the heathen world. Further, the perfection of the allegory is certainly spoilt if both the great fish and the great city have to represent, in different connexions, the same thing.

Doubtless national implications are not excluded. But one is disposed to think that the real appeal of the book is to the common conscience of the people, perhaps also to some who claimed to be prophets, but could do nothing but repeat the harsh and cruel denunciations of days that ought to have been left behind for ever.

CHAPTER 1
THE DISOBEDIENCE OF JONAH

2. Nineveh] the world-famous capital of Assyria, on the Tigris. For its wickedness cp. Nah 3. **3.** Jonah seeks to escape from the unwelcome task, both because he hates the Ninevites, and because he fears that, after all, God may spare them. **Tarshish]** Tartessus in SW. Spain, probably an old Phœnician colony. It would be in the opposite direction to Nineveh. **Joppa**] Jaffa, the only port of any size on the Palestinian coast. **5.** The ship's crew is composed of a blend of nationalities. Each man appeals to his own god. Jonah, however, declares his God to be the Creator of all things (v. 9). For the story of the sleeper in the storm cp. Mk 4. 'Jonah was peaceful because he thought he was far from God's hand, Jesus was confident because He knew He was hidden in God's hand' (Marti). **6.** The captain thinks that the deity of their passenger might deliver them.

11. Wrought, and was tempestuous] RV 'grew more and more tempestuous.'

14-16. The natural piety of the heathen sailors is strikingly shown. Compelled to believe, by the rising of the storm, the impossibility of reaching land, and the falling of the lot, that Jonah is guilty, they make a last appeal to be held innocent if a mistake has been made. Then, convinced of the power of Jehovah, they at once offer sacrifices on the deck, and vow further offerings if they arrive safely from their voyage. For the vow cp. Gn 28 20 1 S 1 11, etc.

17. A great fish] Nothing is said of the species of the fish ; either a giant shark or a cachalot whale could swallow a man. But the Intro. shows that it is needless to argue whether the miracle of Jonah's remaining alive has ever been paralleled. We have given reasons for our view that the author never meant or expected his story to be regarded as anything but a parable. If that is so, it is useless for us to bring in a difficulty which never even occurred to him.

CHAPTER 2

His Prayer of Thanksgiving

This beautiful song of deliverance shows clearly the familiarity of the writer with earlier Psalms. It reflects very plainly the horror inspired by the sea in the minds of an inland people. It is not necessary, on the interpretation adopted, to argue whether or not it is suitable to Jonah's position. Advocates of the national view of the book think it specially suitable to describe the sorrows of the people when drowning in the deep gulf of exile. If so, the references to 'thy holy temple' are not happy. On the whole, a personal application suits best the quotations from the Psalms, especially v. 4 = Ps 31 22, v. 9 = 42 4 50 14.

2. Out of the belly of hell] hell = Sheol, the realm of the dead, thought of here as a devouring monster. The phrase is purely pictorial : cp. 'from the jaws of death.'

3. Both parts of this v. are echoes from Pss 88 6, 7 42 7. **4.** Cp. Ps 31 22. **Toward thy holy temple**] cp. 1 K 8 35-38, and for the longing for

the Temple Ps 84, etc. **5.** *Even* **to the soul**] cp. Ps 69 1. The meaning is that the waters so press in that life itself is threatened. **The weeds**] Floating sea-weed entangles him as he sinks. **6. The bottoms of the mountains**] their roots or foundations lying deep in the heart of the sea : cp. Milton, 'Hymn on the Nativity' : 'While the Creator great . . Cast the dark foundations deep.' *Was* **about**] RV 'closed upon.' The thought is that as he sinks he goes far from the earth, the home of the living, and its doors are closed and barred against him for ever. No return to the light and sunshine seems possible. **Corruption**] RV 'the pit,' i.e. of Sheol, as in v. 2. **7.** Cp. Pss 107 5 142 3 mg. 18 6. **8. Lying vanities**] cp. Dt 32 21 = idol gods. 'Vanity,' lit. 'a breath,' means something evanescent and worthless.

Their own mercy] This is used as a name for Jehovah. In Ps 144 2 the same word is rendered 'my goodness,' RV 'loving-kindness.' It is here a pregnant use describing Jehovah as the sum and source of mercy. **9.** Cp. Pss 42 4 50 14-23. For **vowed** cp. also 1 16.

CHAPTER 3

Repentance and Pardon of the Ninevites

3. An exceeding great city] lit. 'great unto God,' i.e. regarded as great by God: cp. Gn 10 1. **Of three days' journey**] i.e. in breadth.

8. Even the cattle join in the mourning. Neglected by their owners, they fill the air with their groanings. Cp. Joel 1 20, 'The beasts of the field pant unto thee,' and for an interesting parallel, Judith 4 9-15. The Persians are said, by Herodotus, to have clipped the hair of the horses and baggage animals that they might seem to share in the mourning for a general. **10.** For the term 'repentance' = 'change of purpose,' as applied to God, cp Jer 18 8, and for the action Ex 32 14.

CHAPTER 4

Jonah's Jealousy contrasted with Jehovah's Compassion

1. Jonah's anger has a double cause, wounded pride that his words are proved false, and indignation that the God of Israel should pity heathen, only fit to be fuel for fire. **3.** A striking parallel to the dejection and disappointment of Elijah (1 K 19).

4. Doest thou well to be angry?] RM 'Art thou greatly angry?' A kindly remonstrance to awake better feelings. Jonah makes no reply yet, but goes and sits in his booth to watch whether, after all, God will not change His mind again. **5.** The **booth**, like those used at the Feast of Booths, or Tabernacles, would be a rough structure made of poles and leaves. **6. Gourd**] most likely the bottle-gourd, often planted to grow over trellis-work whose broad leaves would form a good protection against the sun. **8. Vehement]** RV 'sultry' = the sirocco. **9.** See on v. 4. Jonah transfers his pity for himself, as an ill-used prophet, to the gourd which likewise has been hardly treated. A wonderfully true touch of human nature.

10. The argument is very fine. Jonah's feeling of pity for the gourd is just enough, a withered tree is always a sad sight. Yet on this gourd, 'child of night' (so the Heb.), he had spent neither labour nor strength. How

much more should God, of whose goodness man's highest virtue is but the faintest shadow, pity and spare the helpless and ignorant works of His own hands, who now fill the streets of Nineveh with pathetic appeals for forgiveness!

11. That cannot discern] i.e. little children. There is no finer close in literature than this ending. The divine question, 'Shall not I have pity?' remains unanswered. Its echoes are heard still in every crowded haunt of men. Above the stir and din and wickedness the Infinite Compassion is still brooding.

MICAH

INTRODUCTION

1. Date and Period. Micah the prophet was a younger contemporary of Isaiah. His work began, according to 1¹, in the days of Jotham, and may have lasted right through the reign of Hezekiah (726–697 B.C.), into the time of Manasseh his successor. This date is confirmed by the historical reference in Jer 26 ¹⁷⁻¹⁹, where the prophecy of 3 ¹² is quoted in defence of Jeremiah, and is said to have been spoken in the days of Hezekiah (see notes). The period of Hezekiah was marked by great outward changes. Northern Israel was finally overthrown when Samaria was captured by Sargon of Assyria. During Sargon's reign and the early part of that of Sennacherib his successor (705–680 B.C.) Judah also was constantly threatened by Assyria. Then came the great deliverance of Jerusalem (701), which formed the crowning triumph of Isaiah's life (see notes *in loco*). Micah must have lived through this, if, as seems probable, the last two chapters of the book come from him.

As it stands, the book consists of a number of short oracles which were uttered separately and brought together later. Unless the reader remembers this, he will be bewildered by the abrupt transitions. There are two main divisions, widely separated in time. The earlier, chs. 1–5, belong to the period of Jotham and Hezekiah; the later, chs. 6, 7, probably to that of Manasseh.

2. Social Condition of Judah. The inward changes in the social conditions of the people of Judah during this period were as great as the outward. Judah had been forced out of its isolation. Trade relations had sprung up with the neighbouring peoples. The best intelligence and energy left the country for the capital, where the opportunities of advancement

were greatest. Increased trade made the rich and clever richer, the poor relatively poorer. Power became centralised in Jerusalem. It was the seat of the Temple, which had won a new importance through Hezekiah's reforms, the heart of the national defence against Assyria, and the chief centre of the new wealth. The country districts and the city had lost touch with each other. Besides, whether Judah succeeded in maintaining a precarious independence, or became a vassal state to Assyria, its condition under Hezekiah required money, either to pay tribute or maintain its fortresses and army; and these charges fell specially on the peasantry.

3. Personality and Teaching of Micah. His Relation to Isaiah. Micah belonged to the country. He was a native of Moresheth-gath, a village among the low hills between the highlands of Judah and the Philistine plain. Prophesying at the same time as Isaiah, he speaks from a different standpoint. Isaiah was one of the ruling class in the capital; Micah was one of the oppressed peasantry. The vices of the city he selects are almost the same as Isaiah scourges, avarice (2 ²), oppression of the poor (2 ⁹), and luxury (2 ¹¹). But Micah is specially severe on the religious leaders (3 ⁵⁻¹¹). Evidently, when Hezekiah made the Temple the centre of the national religion, he unintentionally made the religious teachers more dependent on the ruling class.

Isaiah preached, however, the security of Jerusalem. God will intervene to deliver His city from Assyria. Micah found men misunderstanding this promise, and believing that God would not destroy city and Temple, no matter what they did. He told them the only reason why the city was to be preserved was that it might become the centre of a better morality and a purer faith. Samaria and Jerusalem, the centres of the nation, ought to be the centres of justice and true religion. Instead they were the centres of irreligion (1^5 $2^{1\text{-}11}$ $3^{1\text{-}10}$). Therefore Samaria has fallen (1^6) and Jerusalem shall fall (3^{12}).

But this does not mean that Judah shall pass away. Judah's mission does not depend, like that of Assyria, on money and arms. There was a time when Jerusalem was a mere hill fort, when the 'glory of Israel' could house in the cave of Adullam (1^{15}), when Bethlehem, an open village, was a king's birthplace. This 'former kingdom' could not compete with the other nations in chariots, fortresses, and a wealthy capital, but it was rich in a great ideal, the ideal of a king who shepherded his people, and received their willing obedience. Though this time should come back, and the pomp of the capital disappear, the result will be to show the nation their true mission of teaching religion to the world ($4^{6\text{-}10}$ $5^{10\text{-}15}$). God is not casting away His people, though He destroy Jerusalem. There shall arise One from the old stock to represent the divine ideal. Messiah cannot arise in the soil of Jerusalem, full of vulgar ideals of vain glory, but in Bethlehem, where power is turned to unselfish uses and the eternal because divine hopes can be cherished ($5^{2\text{-}5}$).

Then Israel will have a mission to the world. So long as she tries to compete with it in chariots ($5^{10\text{-}15}$), she is doomed to failure, and has nothing which Assyria cannot give better. But, when she stands for true religion, she offers what the world needs, and becomes the source of Messiah and the world's light ($4^{1\text{-}5}$).

It should be added that Micah seems to vary in his prophecy of the result of Israel's mission. This is due, (a) to the idea he has of true religion, as no mere observance of a ritual, but as implying a moral claim ($6^{5\text{-}8}$), in this showing a striking resemblance to the strong ethical teaching of Amos ; (b) to his view of the nations as free agents, who determine their own attitude to religion. Hence he now sees the peoples joyously accepting Israel's God, and sharing in Israel's peace and blessedness ($4^{1\text{-}5}$) ; again he sees them pursuing their own ideals and coming to ruin ($4^{11\text{-}13}$). But, because these truths are divine, they cannot fail of their effect, either in curse or in blessing ($5^{7\text{-}9}$).

4. Micah's Later Ministry. Chs. 6, 7 date from the time of Manasseh (690–641 B.C.), but the exact dates are very uncertain (cp. $2\,\text{K}\,21$). Sennacherib retreated from Jerusalem, but Asarhaddon — his successor — returned, subdued Phœnicia in 678, Tyre in 671, and made Judah tributary in 676. The old misery and uncertainty continued in Jerusalem. Men turned against the faith which seemed to have promised more than it could give. There was a reaction against Hezekiah's reforms. Men were not irreligious, only they doubted the supremacy of Jehovah. Their nation's impotence against Assyria seemed to prove the existence of other gods, whom it were wise also to propitiate (6^{16}). Their worship of Jehovah took on darker elements. They construed their misfortunes as the evidence of His anger, and, like their heathen neighbours, offered their children to propitiate this anger (6^7). The gloomy terror led them to persecute those who worshipped Jehovah only (7^2). Against this Micah raised his noble and simple definition of true religion (6^8). He rebuked anew their inhumanity to one another ($6^{9\text{-}15}$ $7^{3\text{-}6}$). He insisted on the historic facts which proved the grace of God ($6^{1\text{-}5}$).

The prophet speaks, however, like a man who is almost alone in his faith in Jehovah's supremacy. The basis on which a new Israel can be built is almost gone ($7^{1\text{-}6}$), since the faithful are so few and dispirited. But Micah rallies on his trust in God. God's purpose for and through Israel cannot fail ($7^{7\text{-}13}$). And the prophecy closes with prayer and a confident doxology. Though he has none save God, he will lean the more on God ($7^{14\text{-}20}$).

CHAPTER 1

JUDGMENT ON SAMARIA AND JUDAH

Sargon destroyed Samaria, the capital of North Israel, 722 or 721. Micah, about 720 B.C., declaring (v. 6) that Samaria's fall has been due to its sin, announces a like fate for Jerusalem, guilty of a like sin (v. 9). To the prophet this ruin of the people is not like that of the other nations Assyria has destroyed. Since God is manifesting Himself in it, Micah summons the nations to witness the event (vv. 2–4). The scourge will fall most heavily on the capitals, because the sin of the people has centred there (v. 5).

Micah sees the route of the invaders through Philistia and SW. Judah, and as he was a native of the district, he laments the fate of the villages he has known (vv. 10–16). Sargon may have marched along this route to attack Egypt at Raphia, 720 or 719 B.C.

1. Micah] A shortened form of Micaiah, 'who is like Jehovah.' **Morasthite**] native of Moresheth-gath : cp. v. 14. **Which he saw**] The revelation was made to his inward eye : cp. $1\,\text{S}\,9^9$.

2. All ye people] RV 'ye peoples, all of you.' **His holy temple**] i.e. heaven, as in Hab 2^{20} Isa 63^{15}. Israel's ruin is to be an object-lesson to the nations. **4.** God's judgments in figures taken from earthquake, storm, and lightning. **5.** The first **Jacob** must mean the whole nation, the second the ten tribes. **High**

places of Judah] LXX and Syr. read, 'sin of the house of Judah.' The capitals, **Samaria** and **Jerusalem**, were the centres of moral and religious corruption. **6, 7.** The verbs should be read as presents, 'I am making,' etc.

6. Plantings of a vineyard] Samaria is to become heaps of stones, like the stoneheaps over which vines were trained. **Into the valley**] Samaria stood on a hill (1 K 16 24).

7. The hires thereof] the offerings at the idol shrines. **For she gathered, etc.**] The wealth of the offerings and plating on the idols, part of which has been gathered through the unchasteness of their women at the idol shrines (cp. Dt 23 17,18), will be carried to foreign lands, and dedicated to similar idolatries and similar foul rites.

8. Stripped and naked] i.e. without the outer garment (cp. 1 S 19 24); here used as a sign of mourning. **Dragons**] RV 'jackals.' **Owls**] RV 'ostriches.' As a patriot Micah laments the calamities he predicts. **9. He is come**] RV 'it' (i.e. the wound) 'reacheth.' The **gate** was the seat of the old men, the scene of justice. Jerusalem is called the gate of the people, as the centre of its wisdom and justice.

10-16. The vv. contain a series of word-plays on the names of villages in SW. Judah. The text is often obscure, and the point of some of the references depends on local allusions which we have lost. The district may have suffered when Sargon marched by this route to attack Egypt at Raphia, and when he captured Ashdod in 711 B.C.

10. At Gath] cp. 2 S 1 20. In both cases the meaning is, 'Let us in our defeat be spared the malicious glee of our foes.' There is a word-play in the Hebrew here which may be imitated by saying, 'Tell it not in Tell-Town.' The Heb. for 'tell' and for 'Gath' being somewhat similar in sound. **Weep ye not at all**] read, 'in Akko (or Bokim) weep ye not.' 'Bokim' means 'weeping.' **House of Aphrah**] or, Beth le Aphrah. **Aphrah** and **dust** (Heb. *aphar*) are very similar. 'In House of Dust, roll thyself in dust.'

11. Saphir] 'beauty-town' with its beauty shamed. **Zaanan**] in sound like the Heb. for 'outgoing.' The town of outgoings shall be straitly shut up. **In the mourning, etc.**] RV 'the wailing of Beth-ezel shall take from you the stay thereof.' Beth-ezel may mean 'the house of stay.' Beth-ezel shall be so busy lamenting its own fate that it cannot support any one. **12. For the inhabitant, etc.**] RM 'for the inhabitant of Maroth is in travail (labour) for good, because evil is come down.' This fresh bitterness gives a new justification to the name of Maroth = 'bitternesses' when good was so much desired. **13. Bind the chariot to the swift beast**] i.e. 'you shall need your swiftest beasts for your flight.' Lachish

suggested by similarity of sound, the Heb. *reckesh*, i.e. 'swift beast.' We have not the key to the allusion in the end of this verse. It may mean that Israel's idolatry made its first entry into Judah through Lachish.

14. Presents] RV 'a parting gift,' the marriage portion of a bride: cp. 1 K 9 16. Judah shall be obliged to relinquish Moresheth-gath ('the possession of Gath'), once her possession, to the conqueror. **The houses of Achzib**] shall be *achzab*, 'deceitful,' i.e. the kings of Judah shall no longer be able to rely on their support. **15. Mareshah**] which may mean possession. 'I will bring to the possession a new possessor,' i.e. the king of Assyria. **He shall come, etc.**] read, 'the glory of Israel shall come even unto Adullam.' David, the glory of Israel, had already found shelter there (1 S 22 1). If those who are the glory of Israel return thither for refuge, it may be to rise with new vigour as David did. The threat is also a promise. **16. Make thee bald**] artificial baldness was a sign of mourning (Lv 19 27 Dt 14 1). **Eagle**] probably griffon vulture. Judah is here addressed as a woman mourning over the loss of her children.

CHAPTER 2
The Sins that bring Ruin

Chs. 2 and 3, as dealing with the same subject, should be read together.

Micah now enumerates the sins which must bring punishment on Judah. He inveighs bitterly against the rapacity of the rich towards their poorer neighbours. The leaders in the capital, judges, prophets, and priests alike are destitute of the religion which makes a man interpret his power as a means of helping men and so glorifying God. Instead they regard it as a means to win money and position to themselves. The national institutions have been degraded into a means by which selfish men aggrandise themselves (2 1, 2, 8, 9 3 1-5, 9, 10). Therefore these shall not continue (2 3-5), and even Jerusalem shall be plowed as a field (3 12). The leaders reproach Micah as no patriot since he utters such things against his people, and no prophet since he forgets that God must save His chosen nation (2 6, 7). Micah replies that God will keep His nation, but that Jerusalem is not essential to God's purpose. When the capital is ruined, the nation may only be made more fit to fulfil its true ends in the world (2 12, 13).

2. Cp. 1 K 21 for the Israelite's attachment to his heritage. **3. This family**] cp. 'The whole family which I brought up out of the land of Egypt' (Am 3 1). **I devise**] as contrasted with their devising (v. 1). **4. Turning away**] RV 'to the rebellious,' i.e. God divides the ill-gotten fields to heathen and idolaters. **5. This** may mean that the oppressor nobles shall have none to cast the measuring line on an allotment, when the periodical redistribution of the land took place, and some respect was had to old family rights. Their line is to fail.

The text of vv. 4 and 5 is uncertain, but the sense is clear. It shall be rendered to them as they have rendered to others.

6. Cp. Isa 30 9-11. Translate : 'prattle not, thus they (the nobles) prattle. They (the prophets) should not prattle of these things ; their scoldings are unceasing.' The nobles turn on Micah. Prophets have no right to meddle with social and political questions, but should leave them to men whose business it is to deal with them. We are weary of this eternal scolding. **7.** The first part of the v. probably continues the speech of the nobles: 'Shall it be said, O house of Jacob, is the spirit of the Lord straitened ? are these His doings ?' Can we, a nation whom God called the house of Jacob, endure to hear a prophet foretell its ruin ? Micah replies abruptly, 'Your sins are blinding you. My words are good to men who bring a conscience to their appreciation.'

8. Even] RV 'but.' **With the garment**] RV 'from off the garment.' The **robe** is a mantle, the **garment** what is usually called the upper garment. **Men averse from war**] quiet, peaceful people. Micah seems to refer to some merciless treatment meted out by creditors to their debtors: cp. Ex 22 26, 27.

9. My glory] i.e. their inheritance in the holy land. The prophet implies that women and children are being sold into foreign captivity. **10. Because it is polluted**, etc.] better, 'because of uncleanness ye shall be destroyed with a sore destruction.' They shall be driven from the land from which they have driven others. Their guilt makes the land no resting-place for them. **11. In the spirit and falsehood**] better, 'after wind and lies.' What promises material benefits alone appeals to them.

12, 13. An oracle of restoration, which has been inserted between the two denunciations, when the separate oracles were collected in writing. Micah promises restoration, when the judgment has done its work. The expulsion from the land (v. 10) shall not be permanent. **12. The sheep of Bozrah**, etc.] better, 'as sheep into a fold, as a flock into the midst of the pasture.' The **great noise** is the noise of the joy at return. **13.** Read the verbs throughout as perfect. The writer speaks as though what he promises had already taken place. **The breaker**] or, 'deliverer': they have been shut up as in a prison. One will come to open their way.

CHAPTER 3
WICKEDNESS IN HIGH PLACES
Micah returns to his indictment against the people's leaders. Their power was given for the sake of justice, and they have abused it for extortion (vv. 1–3). Their time shall be short (v. 4). The prophets have abused their trust in order, by flattery of the rich, to make a good living for themselves. To them Micah prophesies judicial darkness (vv. 5–7). He declares his own ideal of the prophetic office (v. 8). Finally, he accuses all the leaders of the nation of having followed their own appetites and trusted in their being necessary to God. God will prove by the ruin of Jerusalem that He loves righteousness more than Jerusalem (vv. 9–12).

1. *Is* it not for you, etc.] i.e. is it not the reason for your holding power, to declare right to the people ? **2. From off them**] i.e. the common people. **4.** When God comes to judgment, they will find no mercy. **5. That bite with their teeth, and cry, Peace**] i.e. any one who fills the prophet's mouth secures his silence about his patron's sins. **6.** Judicial darkness shall fall on these prophets. When men play fast and loose with principle for the sake of money, they lose all sense of principle. Right and duty become empty words.

7. Cover their lips] a sign of mourning : cp. Lv 13 45 Ezk 24 17, 22.

8. Micah's ideal of the prophet's function, viz. to call sin by its right name. **10.** i.e. they make the common people sweat blood to build their mansions in the capital. **11.** *Is* not the LORD among us?] the same mechanical faith in the presence of the Temple as in Jer 7 4: cp. 1 S 4 3.

12. Cp. Jer 26 17-19. The people of Jeremiah's time, angered by his prophecies of disaster, wished to put him to death. Some of the elders reminded them that, when Micah denounced a like judgment, Hezekiah, instead of killing him, repented at his words, and so averted the disaster. This implies that the religious minds of that time recognised how true prophecy is always conditional, and how the fulfilment of its predictions is conditional on the attitude men take to them. **High places of the forest**] better, 'heights in a wood.' The slopes of the ravines shall be overgrown with brushwood, out of which the bare scalp of the Temple-hill will rise.

CHAPTERS 4, 5
BRIGHT VISIONS OF THE FUTURE
Micah's view of Israel's future, especially in relation to the nations. He believes that God chose Israel to maintain and teach true religion, and that in this lies Israel's greatness. The people have forgotten this and have tried to emulate the other nations in wealth and pride and armed strength. Such a contest was hopeless, and God will prove its hopelessness by bringing ruin on Jerusalem, where these pomps were gathered. But, when the chastisement

has done its work, the nation will return to its divinely-given task. It will have a mission to the nations.

The chs. appear to contradict each other as to the result on the nations' fate. This is because Micah regards the peoples as free agents, and the religion Israel teaches as no mere ceremonial observances. The nations may recognise Israel's message, and, submitting to God's will, receive the blessing He gives (4 1-5). They may refuse it. But, if they obstinately oppose it, they shall be overthrown (4 11-13). For, since the truths Israel represents are divine in their origin, these must be a blessing or a curse, according as men accept or refuse them (5 7-9).

CHAPTER 4
Zion the Spiritual Centre of the Earth

1-10. Here purified Israel is the light to the nations, which joyously acknowledge the supremacy of its God. The Temple shall be glorified, because known as the source of a help which all men need. When men grow eager for this, their wars shall cease (vv. 1-4). Because Israel is holding its faith as a trust for all men, Micah bids his people hold it more resolutely (v. 5). Though their very national existence is threatened (vv. 9, 10), let them not despair, God can restore them. Their being driven out of their own land may be His means for making them see themselves as bearers of His religion (vv. 6-8, 10). The oracle may have been uttered when Sennacherib was threatening Judah, 701.

1-3. Cp. Isa 2 2-4. The great Messianic prophecy of the OT. which has been fulfilled since Jesus Christ of the stem of Jesse became the Light of the world. Some think that this *locus classicus* of Messianic prophecy was taken by both Micah and Isaiah from an older prophet. Professor Cheyne thinks that it is a post-exilic utterance, and was inserted by compilers or editors into the works of these prophets. **1. In the top**] RM 'at the head.' The kingdom of God will be supreme. **People**] RV 'peoples': Micah means the heathen nations. **3. Judge among**] RV 'between.' God shall be the arbiter of their quarrels, and so war will cease. The nations shall be more eager for justice than aggrandisement. **4.** This v. is not in Isaiah. Isaiah belonged to the city, Micah to the country.

5. Translate : 'because all the peoples walk, every one in the name of his god, let us (or, we will) walk in the name of the Lord.' Micah drops back into the present. Since Israel's faith is to enlighten the world, let them be the more diligent to keep the faith.

6. In that day] the latter days of v. 1.

7. Here and in 2 12 Micah expects the return from the Assyrian captivity, not of all Israel, but of the remnant who, remaining faithful to their religion, shall become the stock from which the Messianic future will spring: cp. Isa 6 13 10 20 f. 11 11 f. 24 13. **8. Tower of the flock**, etc.] i.e. Jerusalem. **Unto thee**, etc.] RV 'unto thee shall it come ; yea, the former dominion shall come, the kingdom of the daughter of Jerusalem.' When the people have repented of the sins which brought their ruin, God will restore them as wide a dominion as in the days of David.

9. The captivity which seems to destroy the kingdom with its king and counsellors will be the birthpangs of a better state. **10.** Probably **Thou shalt go** *even* **to Babylon** was added to explain the prophet's meaning, by one who saw the Babylonian exile. Essentially he was right. But the enemy in Micah's time was, not Babylon, but Assyria. And what Micah means is that his people shall be cast out of Jerusalem, and, when they are compelled to **dwell in the field**, i.e. without a capital and a court, they shall learn that God's ideal of a kingdom can be realised without these.

11-13. But Assyria is about to besiege Jerusalem : cp. Isa 36. Their aim is to destroy Jerusalem (v. 11). But they are only the instruments in God's hand (v. 12). Their proud self-confidence shall bring them to shame before Israel (v. 13).

11. Many nations] the polyglot hordes of Assyria : cp. Isa 33 3. **12. He shall gather**] RV 'He hath gathered.' God has brought them to their ruin. **13. Hoofs**] oxen were used to tread out corn (Dt 25 4). **I will consecrate**] RV 'thou shalt devote' : cp. Lv 27 28.

The nations, which try to destroy Israel, shall be destroyed by Israel in the interest of the truth Israel represents.

CHAPTER 5
The Birth of the Messiah

1-5ª. Jerusalem is besieged, its ruler insulted by the invader (v. 1). Micah proclaims not only deliverance, but a deliverer. He will arise from Bethlehem, David's birthplace (v. 2). God raised up thence a ruler who shepherded his people instead of fleecing them, and who represented God's eternal ideal of a ruler, not his own interests. He will send us in our new need another like the first. And this man shall be our peace (v. 5). It is Micah's prophecy of Messiah. Jesus Christ has taken away its temporary and local allusions, and made it greater than Micah knew.

1. Now gather thyself] better, 'now thou mayest gather thyself in troops, thou daughter of troops.' The reference is to Assyria. Micah sees the armies gather against Jerusalem, and foresees the possible overthrow of the dynasty (the judge of Israel). But Judah's future does not depend on Jerusalem. God can raise up from a village a deliverer.

2. Thousands] or, families : cp. Nu 1 16 10 4 Josh 22 14, 21. Several such families made up a tribe. **Unto me**] or, 'for me,' i.e. to fulfil my will. The true ruler represents God's will in Israel. Since God's will has been the same from everlasting and must be manifested, the **goings forth** of one who lives to manifest it are equally from everlasting. When Israel's rulers fail Him, He raises up another. **Bethlehem**] cp. 1 15 4 10. When Saul failed Him, God chose David from following the sheep, and set him to shepherd Israel. When the rulers of Jerusalem have failed Him, God will raise up even an obscure villager to represent His ideal of righteous government.

3. Will he give them up] better, ' He is giving them up.' **She which travaileth, etc.**] the reference is to Isaiah's prophecy of Immanuel (Isa 7 14). **Then the remnant, etc.**] better, ' and until the remnant of His, i.e. Messiah's brethren shall return unto the children of Israel.'

As Messiah was to arise from Judah, this means ' until the tribes are reunited.' The reference is to Isaiah's name for his son, Shear-jashub, 'a remnant shall return' (Isa 7 3). Probably the v. is a gloss from the exile : cp. 4 10. Some one explained that Micah's promise of a deliverer from Bethlehem was delayed, and God was still giving His people to captivity, until Isaiah's prophecies had been fulfilled.

4. Feed] not himself, but his flock. The figure of the shepherd-king is continued.

5. Connect the first clause with the preceding, and put a full stop after **peace.**

5, 6. The power of Assyria, which rests on brute force and has no sympathy with the mission of Israel, can only last till God raises up a stronger than itself. It fell, as a matter of fact, before Babylon.

5. Eight principal men] Seven was sufficiency, eight is super-abundance. ' We shall not want for leaders.' **6. Land of Nimrod**] cp. Gn 10 11.

7–9. Israel's dual mission. Its message has been trusted to it by God, and cannot remain without effect. To those who receive this truth gladly, it will come like refreshing dew. To those who oppose it, it will come like a ravening beast.

7. People] RV ' peoples.' The influence of Messiah is not to be confined to Israel. **Tarrieth not for man**] the mysterious dewfall, inexplicable by man, is meant. **9.** Better read as a prayer : ' let thine hand be lifted up upon thine adversaries, and let all thine enemies be cut off.'

10–15. Since war and pomp have driven

any higher national ideal from their minds, God will strip them of the things in which they have trusted. Micah puts chariots and idols on the same level and under the same condemnation.

11. As the centres of the oppression described in chs. 2, 3. **13. Standing images**] the stone pillars of Lv 26 1 Isa 19 19, etc.

14. Groves] RV 'asherim ' : cp. Jg 3 17 : emblems of idol-worship. **15. Such as they have not heard**] RV ' which hearkened not.' God will judge the nations according to their attitude to Messiah and Israel's faith.

CHAPTERS 6, 7

GOD'S GREAT CONTROVERSY WITH ISRAEL

Note the change in the prophet's attitude. He speaks no longer to a united nation, but to parties. Now he speaks to a party, pious but discouraged (6 1-8) ; again, he testifies against men who have turned their backs on the Law (6 9-16). Persecution for religion's sake has appeared, and taught men to distrust each other (7 2-6). Probably the chs. date from the time of Manasseh. Sennacherib recoiled baffled from Jerusalem, but Assyria was not exhausted. Esarhaddon succeeded in making Manasseh tributary in 676 B.C. Their religion had not brought Judah all the relief men expected. The heathen elements in the nation, repressed by Isaiah's and Hezekiah's influence, reasserted themselves. A reaction set in and found a leader in Manasseh : cp. 2 K 21. Especially men remembered that in his reign persecution for religion's sake was practised : cp. 2 K 21 16.

CHAPTER 6

GOD'S ARRAIGNMENT OF HIS PEOPLE

1–8. Micah's message to the discouraged believers. They have lost heart because of the apparent contradiction between the promises of their prophets and the hard facts of their history. They have lost faith in God's grace, and are trying to propitiate His favour by such sacrifices as the heathen offered to their gods. Micah appeals to nature, to history, and to the reasonable service God requires. He calls on the hills to witness what God has done (vv. 1, 2). He appeals to the great deeds of God's redemption for His people (vv. 3–5). He insists on the simplicities of God's requirements (vv. 6–8).

2. Strong] RV 'enduring.' The mountains have outlived so many generations of disobedience and unwearied mercy : cp. Isa 1 2.

3. Wearied] God's demands are so simple (v. 8). **5. From Shittim unto Gilgal, etc.**] RV ' Remember from Shittim unto Gilgal, that ye may know the righteous acts of the Lord.' Shittim was the last station of the desert-wanderings, Gilgal the first in Palestine itself. The prophet reminds them how in their national history God has proved His compassion.

6, 7. The people are represented as asking what more God requires from them. **6. Calves of a year old**] a choice gift: cp. Lv 9³.

7. Human sacrifice was practised (2 K 21⁶ Jer 7³¹ 9⁵), especially in times of great national danger (2 K 3²⁷).

8. Micah brings forward to a generation which is seeking fantastic ways of propitiating its God, the grave and tender simplicities of His requirements. He does not want their wine and oil and children: He wants their obedience. The other things are only valuable to Him as the evidence of their willing obedience. Compare how, when Abraham has shown himself willing to surrender his son, Isaac is not required from him.

9. The text is uncertain but the sense is clear. 'When God speaks in warning, it is the part of a wise man to fear (RM) and to seek to discover the reason why God uplifts His rod.' The reasons in this case follow in the succeeding questions. **10. The scant measure**] cp. Dt 24¹⁴f. Am 8⁵. **11. Shall I count** *them* **pure**] RV 'shall I be pure,' i.e. can any man be pure? **13.** RV 'Therefore I also have smitten thee with a grievous wound.'

14. Thy casting down, etc.] RM 'thy emptiness shall be in the midst of thee,' i.e. thy famine shall continue, because thou shalt have food but not sufficient. **Thou shalt take hold,** etc.] RV 'thou shalt remove but shalt not carry away safe,' i.e. thou shalt fail in the effort to remove thy people from the enemy's power. **15. Sweet wine**] RV 'vintage.' 'Thou shalt tread the grapes, but shalt not drink the wine made from them.'

16. The statutes of Omri and the works of Ahab's house are the worship of Baal: cp. 1 K 16³¹⁻³³. Manasseh has gone back to the sins of the northern kingdom, though its fate might have warned him: cp. 2 K 21¹³. **The reproach of my people**] better, with LXX, 'the reproach of the Gentiles,' which Ahab's house, through the captivity which was the punishment for its idolatry, is bearing.

CHAPTER 7
CONFESSION AND CONTRITION BRING BACK HOPE

1-6. Jerusalem laments her estate. The righteous among her children are taken from her by violence (vv. 1, 2). The rulers misuse their position for their selfish ends (vv. 3, 4). Worst of all, the trust of a man in his neighbour's honour, which makes the cement of all society, is gone. Even the ties of nature are disowned (vv. 5, 6).

1. Desired the firstripe fruit] RV 'desireth

the firstripe fig,' which, now the harvest is past, is gone. The righteous (the early figs) have been gleaned out of the city. **2.** Cp. Isa 57¹ Both passages speak of a scourge which has specially fallen on the righteous, and so point to a period of persecution. **3.** The probable sense is: 'their hands are busy in evil, the prince asks the judge to do some knavery, the judge is ready to do it at a price, the great man needs but utter his bad desire to find ready instruments: so they weave together a web of fraud and violence.' **4. The day of thy watchmen and thy visitation**] the day of God's visitation foretold by the prophets: cp. Isa 21⁶. It will confound such men, since its principles are the opposite of theirs. **5. Guide**] RM 'familiar friend.' **6.** The final proof of social corruption is the death of men's trust in each other. See our Lord's adoption of these words (Mt 10³⁶).

7-20. Everything seems lost but God: therefore Micah looks more to God (vv. 7, 8). His chastisements are tolerable, because they have meaning (v. 9). Their end will be that through her sufferings Israel shall rise glorious and purified (vv. 10-13). God who called them will restore them and work through them (vv. 14-17). Micah closes with a doxology. Even Israel's sin cannot weary God's faithfulness and compassion (vv. 18-20).

7. Therefore] RV 'but as for me.' In such evil days the true man finds refuge in God.

8. When I fall] calamity, not sin, is meant.

11. Decree] RM 'boundary,' i.e. when God restores the nation and permits the walls to be rebuilt, He will give ample room: cp. Isa 33¹⁷ ʳᵐ. **12.** RV 'In that day shall they come unto thee, from Assyria and the cities of Egypt, and from Egypt even to the River,' i.e. Euphrates. **From sea to sea** is not meant of any specific sea: rather the exiles from West to East and from East to West shall return home. **13. The land**] Canaan. Before this return must come chastisement.

14. The prophet passes abruptly to prayer. **Solitarily**] Israel was always separated from the nations as the flock of God: cp. Nu 23⁹. **Carmel .. Bashan .. Gilead**] perhaps chosen because they were districts devoted to pasture, as contrasted with the cities and their vices.

15. According to] RV 'as in the days of.' God in answer points back to His past mercy.

16. Confounded] RV 'ashamed' to see how impotent is their might. **17.** RV 'they shall come trembling out of their close places' (their useless fortresses); 'they shall come with fear unto the LORD our God.' **18. Who is,** etc.] Micah's name means 'Who is like the Lord?' The prophet concludes with an outburst of praise.

NAHUM

INTRODUCTION

1. The Man. All that we can learn concerning the prophet must be gathered from the brief superscription and from the contents of this small book; the traditions relating to his dwelling-place are late, uncertain, and contradictory. The name Nahum (probably = 'Comforter,' same root as in 3⁷) occurs only twice in the Bible, here and in Lk 3²⁵. 'Elkoshite' means belonging to Elkosh (cp. Mic 1¹), but the identification of the place is quite uncertain. The suggestion that Nahum was an Israelite, dwelling near Nineveh, a descendant of one of the families that had been carried off to that region by the Assyrians, is interesting but unreliable. The same may be said of the attempts to find a home for the prophet in Galilee. Although the writer is wholly concerned with the fate of Nineveh and the idea of Jehovah as an avenger upon the outside oppressor, it is still probable from the subject of the book and the sympathies of the prophet that he was a resident of Judæa.

2. The Date. The superscription gives us no help, and the date must be inferred from the contents of chs. 1 and 2. Here we have two fixed points, the destruction of No-Amon (Thebes) about 664 B.C. by Assurbanipal, king of Assyria (3⁸), and the fall of Nineveh about 606 B.C. The capture of No-Amon lies behind the prophet, how far we cannot tell, while the destruction of Nineveh, or some great disaster to that city, was immediately in front of him. It is likely that the fall of the Egyptian fortress would long be remembered by the Jews, as many of them looked to that nation for help against Assyria. In that case, Assyria was the conqueror: and the prophet saw in the disaster to Egypt the hand of the same living God, the God of Judah and the world, who was now about to mete out to the proud conqueror a similar fate. Hence it seems probable that these strong, stirring words were uttered not long before the final struggle which transferred the supremacy from Nineveh to Babylon.

3. Historical Situation. This was an important period in the small kingdom of Judah. It was the period before the destruction of Jerusalem; the Babylonian empire which became supreme for a while after the fall of Nineveh was destined to crush the kingdom of Judah and carry the people into captivity, but this lies beyond the ken of our prophet. It is probable that in his day Josiah, the good king, had attempted a religious reformation, and that Jeremiah was calling the people to a deeper life and a more spiritual service. But there is no echo of this in the book; its patriotic passion, its cry for vengeance, is all concentrated on the one hateful oppressor.

4. The Book. Though the book is small it has been subjected to keen investigation, and the text has given rise to much critical discussion. The attempts at detailed analysis cannot be considered here. Many scholars regard 1²⁻¹⁵ 2² as an eschatological psalm from later Judaism, describing Jehovah's judgment upon oppressors, and giving promise of salvation to Judah. Those who take this view have worked over this c. and discovered in it an alphabetic poem, but as a matter of fact, in the present state of the text, this alphabetic arrangement can only be discovered at the beginning. However, there is one thing clear, the c. is of similar spirit to the rest of the book; it gives a graphic poetic description of the coming of Jehovah to judgment, while the other part pictures in forcible language, a particular instance of such judgment, in the case of Nineveh. In chs. 2 and 3 there is a vivid description of the siege and a passionate denunciation of the blood-stained city.

5. The Spiritual Significance of Nahum. This short prophecy may be looked upon as one permanent expression of the cry of humanity for justice. It is not mere Hebrew patriotism that expresses itself here, though that gives form and colour to the message; this sharp cry might have come from any of the small nations of Palestine and Syria that had been trampled underfoot by the ruthless armies of Assyria. It is the cry of outraged human nature in the face of brutal oppression; it is a cry that God will not allow violence to rule unchecked, that He will not look calmly on when the earth is drenched with innocent blood. If the answer to the pathetic cry of the saints 'Lord, how long?' could be 'for ever,' then faith would be driven to despair, both piety and patriotism would wither at the roots. The preacher to-day may need to warn the people against a spurious patriotism, a patriotism which counts only material success and selfish glory, but behind all this preaching there must lie the great belief which Nahum grasped with such intensity, that God does arise and come to judgment, that He does vindicate the struggling few who love truth and righteousness ; that with all our lofty Christian sentiment we must sometimes stand face to face with the sterner majesty of the law, and prepare to meet the God who comes in the terror of judgment.

CHAPTER 1

GOD'S VENGEANCE ON HIS PEOPLE'S ENEMIES. DELIVERANCE FOR JUDAH

1, 2. Superscription : 'Oracle concerning Nineveh. The book of the vision or prophesying of Nahum the Elkoshite.' A theological introduction describing a theophany or a coming of Jehovah to judgment. Cp. the brief statements in a similar spirit, Am 1² Mic 1³,⁴. The whole should be printed as verse :

A jealous and avenging God is Jehovah ;
Jehovah is avenging and wrathful ;
Jehovah taketh vengeance on His adversaries,
And He reserveth wrath for His enemies.

3-6. The prophet sketches the character of Jehovah in terms suitable to his general theme ; it is the vengeance of God upon Israel's enemies, who are also His enemies, that we are here invited to consider : cp. Ex 20⁵ 34¹⁴ Dt 4²⁴ᶠ. Note the terrible manner of His appearance when He comes to judgment. **3.** He is **slow to anger, and great in power,** yet He will not absolve the guilty, etc.

The LORD *hath* **his way**] ' The meaning is not so much that Jehovah uses the whirlwind and storm as the vehicle of His movement as that these commotions and terrors in nature are created by His presence. The splendid feet, **clouds** *are* **the dust of his feet,** like the others, " the earth is His footstool," need to be conceived not explained ' (A. B. Davidson). The doings of God in history (Ps 114) and His appearances in nature's most awful moods are mingled in this sublime description of His irresistible strength and impetuous fury. **7-15.** Jehovah will completely destroy the enemies of His people.

7. Read, 'Jehovah is good towards those who hope in Him. A stronghold in the time of need.' An everlasting truth, but particularly appropriate in times of great shaking : cp. Pss 25³ 37⁹. In the following vv. the text is difficult ; if we follow AV we must find a reference to Nineveh. **8. The place thereof**] If this poem is an original part of the book we expect such references, though it comes abruptly here : cp. v. 14. On this view, the line of thought is the opposition of Jehovah to the proud oppressor and his favour towards judgment, with emphasis laid on the radical nature of the judgment. **9, 10.** ' Not twice does He take vengeance on His enemies ; He

makes a full end of them for ever.' You cannot easily set fire to the damp, closely packed thorns, but the fire of His vengeance will burn them up as dry stubble.

13-15. These vv., along with 2², must be grouped together. Read the last of these four vv., as in RV, 'For Jehovah bringeth again the excellency of Jacob,' etc. In these four vv. we have evidently an address to Judah ; she is called upon to rejoice over her ancient foe, to keep the feasts and carry out the vows made in the days of sorrowful oppression : cp. Isa 52⁷. V. 14 is a denunciation of the Assyrian.

The whole c. is difficult from the linguistic point of view ; the technical problems have called forth much ingenuity, but the main outline is clear. Jehovah is coming to judgment ; this coming means a day of terror and darkness for the proud oppressors, but the lowly believers shall find new hope. When freed from narrow patriotism and sectarian bitterness this is a great and abiding truth ; behind it there lies a keen faith in the true meaning of history and a righteous order of the world.

CHAPTER 2

ATTACK AND CONQUEST OF NINEVEH

1. Description of the attack begins, and Nineveh is called upon to face the invader.

' He that breaketh in pieces is come up
    against thee ;
Guard the watch, look out upon the way,
Gird up the loins, gather together thy
    strength.'

V. 2 seems misplaced, as it interrupts the sense. It should perhaps come after 1¹⁵.

3-10. Poetic picture of the sack of the city. It dwells upon, (1) The approach of the hostile army in brilliant, terrible splendour, with flashing shields, furious horses and onrush of chariots. The general impression is vivid, though some of the details have become indistinct. (**3.** *Shall be* **with flaming torches**] RV ' flash with steel.' **Fir trees**] RV ' spears.') (2) The attack upon the city. Here again individual features are uncertain : e.g. we are not sure whether v. 5 refers to the besiegers or the besieged. **Recount his worthies**] i.e. call up his bravest warriors. **Defence**] (RV 'mantelet') is a word difficult of interpretation ; it may refer to the movable roof which protected the battering-ram. It is not easy to give a precise explanation of the phrase, ' The gates of the river are opened,' but it is clear that the great city is attacked and its inhabitants thrown into confusion. The actual siege was spread over a long period : here it is sketched with a few sharp strokes and represented in a few memorable scenes. (3) The carrying away captive of the queen and her maidens ; the flight of the people and the spoiling of the city. (a) Huzzab is obscure ; we must take it to mean the queen of the city, or amend the text. RM has ' It is decreed : she is uncovered,' etc. **Tabering**] i.e. beating, lit. ' drumming.' A taber was a small drum. (b) **8.** The phrase translated **of old** is very awkward in the original. It may have arisen through dittography ; in that case we interpret ' Nineveh is like a pool of water,' whose waters rush away where the dam is broken down : thus do the inhabitants of the conquered city flee away.

9, 10. Then all its rich treasures and its magnificent adornments are given to the spoil. All who had any hope or interest in the doomed city are confounded and put to shame. **11.** The prophet exults over the downfall of Nineveh. In this stern ironical question the prophet implies that Nineveh has vanished completely ; it is vain to seek for it. Thus does he express his full confidence in its utter destruction. **12.** This destruction is justified by pointing to the selfish, cruel career of the Assyrian empire. **13.** An oracle of Jehovah containing a strong assurance of the judgment that is due and cannot be escaped.

CHAPTER 3
The Doom of Nineveh

1–7. Another threat against Nineveh, showing that disaster has come upon her on account of her sins. The keynote of the whole c. is the fierce cry, **Woe to the bloody city !** it *is* all full of lies, etc. In ancient states the capital was virtually the kingdom, and to Nineveh are here ascribed all the characteristics of the Assyrian monarchy. The cruelties perpetrated

by the Assyrians were shocking. Captive princes who had offered resistance in defence of their country were shut up in cages and exposed to the gaze of the populace ; the heads of those already executed were hung round the necks of those still living, and others were flayed alive. The Assyrians appear to have been the most ruthless people of antiquity (see Camb. Bible). **2, 3.** Picture of the attack made by the enemy's cavalry and chariots, these instruments of the divine vengeance. **4–7.** The reason for this doom, the evil influence which this great empire has exerted among the nations. Jehovah assumes responsibility for the execution of this judgment ; He will carry it out to the last extremity. **8–10.** Nations and cities quite as proud and strong have fallen when the hour of divine judgment has sounded. **Populous No**] RV ' No-Amon,' i.e. Thebes. See Intro. **Rivers**] RM ' canals.' **The sea**] i.e. the Nile. **Her wall,** etc.] The Nile was her protection. All the provinces of Egypt helped her (v. 9). **11. Strength**] RV ' a stronghold.' **12–15.** The outer defences have fallen ; it is the beginning of the end. **14. Go into clay,** etc.] make bricks to strengthen the walls. **15–17. Cankerworm . . grasshopper**] species of locusts.

16–19. Prosperity and pride have been ' the cankerworm that spoileth,' so that in the great crisis there is no power of resistance ; it is a mortal wound.

18. Thy shepherds slumber] Thy great rulers have passed away. **Thy nobles,** etc.] RV ' thy worthies are at rest.'

19. No healing of thy bruise] RV ' No assuaging of thy hurt.' **Bruit of thee**] i.e. the report of thy downfall.

HABAKKUK

INTRODUCTION

1. Author. Nothing whatever is known of Habakkuk other than what may be inferred from his book. The inference, based on the subscription ' on my stringed instruments' (3¹⁹), that he was a singer or player in the Temple choir is altogether precarious, if not untenable ; partly because there is no certainty that this c. is Habakkuk's own (see on 3¹⁷) ; partly because the text is probably faulty, the true reading being simply ' on stringed instruments ' ; and still more, because this subscription is in all probability no part of the original poem which forms c. 3. All that we know of

the person of Habakkuk is that he was a great prophet who has left us one of the noblest and most penetrating words in the history of religion (2⁴ᵇ).

2. Summary of Contents. (1¹⁻⁴) The prophet begins with a complaint to Jehovah touching the prevalent violence, oppression, and perversion of the law. ' How long,' he cries, ' and why ?' For answer (1⁵⁻¹¹) comes the divine word that the Chaldeans are to be raised up in chastisement, and the work which they will do is such as to be almost incredible. Then follows a graphic description of their terrible army, with their swift horses, their keen cavalry, their cruel and brazen faces. They laugh at all authority, and at every attempt to stop their advance. They worship might, not right. But in the next section (1 12-17) the prophet's attitude towards this people (if it is the same people as in vv. 5–11) has changed. He shudders at their impiety, and is confounded by it. They have overstepped the limits of their commission ; how can Jehovah reconcile with His own holiness and purity the barbarities perpetrated by the conqueror ?

(2 1-4) The divine answer to the prophet's perplexity comes when he climbs his tower (the tower of faith) and looks abroad. The answer is that the proud shall perish and the righteous shall ultimately live. It may not be obvious now : the visible solution may tarry a long time ; but faith sees it already. 'The just shall live by his faithfulness.' The next section (2 5-20) consists of five 'woes,' which elaborate the thought of 2 4a—the sure destruction of the proud. Woes are denounced upon the cruel rapacity of the conquerors, the unjust accumulations of treasure, the passion for building, the unfeeling treatment of the land, beasts, and people, and finally the idolatry. In contrast to the impotent gods worshipped by the oppressor, is the great Jehovah whose Temple is in the heavens, and before whom all the earth must be silent (2 20). He comes, and His coming is described in c. 3 in rich and varied imagery ; and this 'prayer' concludes with the expression of unbounded confidence and joy in Jehovah, even when all visible signs of His love may fail.

3. Occasion calling forth the Prophecy. The prophecy of Habakkuk may be dated approximately about the year 600 B.C. The last twenty-five years had been a time of great significance for Western Asia in general and for Judah in particular. At the beginning of that period Assyria had been the great world power ; but from the year 625 B.C., when Nabopolassar succeeded in establishing an independent Babylonian monarchy, the Assyrian empire had rapidly declined, till at length, in 607 B.C., Nineveh, the capital, was taken, and by the battle of Carchemish, in which Egypt, the great competing power in the West, was defeated, Babylonian supremacy was assured. Judah naturally became a vassal of Babylon, and about the year 601–600 was invaded because of the rebellion of king Jehoiakim.

Within Judah herself, much that was of first-rate importance both for history and religion had happened. Zephaniah and Nahum had prophesied, and Jeremiah was in the middle of his great career. In 621 B.C., on the basis of the newly-discovered book of Deuteronomy, king Josiah had inaugurated a reformation which had raised the hopes of good

men ; but its influence, as we learn from Jeremiah, had been, upon the whole, but brief and shallow. The death of Josiah upon the battlefield in 608 B.C. aggravated a situation already difficult enough. His son Jehoahaz, who reigned but three months, was succeeded by Jehoiakim, a man of extravagant tastes and contemptible character—the very last man to guide the state through the perplexities and perils of the time.

It was in his reign, apparently, that Habakkuk delivered his message. Through his words we can clearly read the prevalent disregard of law and order, and the abounding political confusion and religious perplexity occasioned by the supremacy of the Chaldeans. The precise interpretation and occasion of the book, however, are unusually hard to determine. We shall very briefly indicate the difficulties and the solution which seems the most probable. In 1 1-4 it is not clear who the oppressors are, whether foreigners or the ruling classes within Judah itself. As in 1 5-11, the Chaldeans (i.e. the Babylonians) appear to be raised up to chastise them, it is more natural to suppose that the oppressors are natives of Judah. But in 1 12-17 the Chaldeans themselves seem to be the oppressors—though this is not expressly said— as they are described in terms very similar to the description in 1 5-11 ; and they bring fresh perplexity to the prophet by 'swallowing up the man that is more righteous than' they (v. 13). The 'righteous' would in this case be Judah, and that description of Judah, coming after such a picture of anarchy as we have in 1 1-4, would be somewhat strange.

The difficulties may be partly met by assuming that the various sections were written at different times, 1 12-17, in which Judah is relatively righteous in comparison with the Chaldeans, being later than 1 1-4. The only real clue to the historical occasion of the prophecy is the mention of the Chaldeans in 1 5-11. Their appearance and their military methods are apparently well known, and this circumstance implies a date shortly before, or more probably shortly after, the great battle of Carchemish in 605 B.C., in which the Babylonian army under Nebuchadrezzar defeated the Egyptians, and established a supremacy, which lasted about seventy years, over Western Asia. The prophet welcomes the advent of the Chaldeans (vv. 5–11) as the divinely-appointed scourge of the evils among Jehovah's people in Judah (1 1-4); but this solution only heightens the horror of his problem, as he becomes better acquainted with the cruel and aggressive pride of the Chaldeans (1 12-17); and he must find a deeper solution. He finds it finally, upon his watchtower, in the assurance that somehow, despite all seeming, the purpose of God is hasting on to its fulfilment, and that the moral constitution of the world is such as to spell the ultimate ruin of cruelty and pride, and the ultimate triumph of righteousness (2¹⁻⁴). His faith was historically justified by the fall of the Babylonian empire in 538 B.C.

4. Religious Ideas of the Book. The dominant ideas of the book shine most clearly out of the great vision which Habakkuk saw from his watchtower (2¹⁻⁴). Briefly, they are Patience and Faith (2³,⁴). The prophet had expected an adequate solution to his doubts to arrive in his own day (cp. 1⁵, 'in *your* days'); and he welcomes the Chaldeans as divine avengers of sin. But Habakkuk is an independent and progressive thinker, and the more he watches the Chaldeans, the more he feels sure that the solution they bring is utterly inadequate. Then he lifts his sorrowful heart to God, and he is soothed and strengthened by a larger vision of the divine purpose and its inevitable triumph. He does not now know, as once he thought he did, by what human and historical means that triumph is to be secured ; but he knows that it is certain. 'It is sure to come, it will not lag behind.' That is faith, and the obverse of faith is patience. It is so sure that he can afford to 'wait for it, though it tarry,' and though it come not in his own day. It is 'trust' in God that will carry the 'righteous' across his doubts and fears, and sustain his 'life' even when he seems to perish (2⁴). 'The righteous shall live by his faithfulness.' This is also the great lesson of the closing vv. of c. 3, that God may be trusted, even when all visible signs of His presence fail ; and this trust is not resignation, but joy unspeakable (3¹⁷⁻¹⁹).

CHAPTER 1
The Prophet's Burden. The Answer of Jehovah

1. Burden] RM 'oracle': see on Isa 13¹.

2, 3. How long?.. Why?] Even a prophet (v. 1) can ask such questions. He never denies the existence of God, but he cannot understand His seeming failure to interpose in human affairs. In the end, however, the despondency merges into a faith which can believe where it cannot see (2³ 3¹⁷ᶠ.).

5. Behold ye among the heathen] For this we ought to read, 'Behold, ye treacherous' (as in the quotation in Ac 13⁴¹, 'ye despisers'). The despisers are those in 1¹⁻⁴ who trample upon moral and social law, thinking Jehovah will never intervene. **In your days**] The profounder solution in 2³ contemplates the possibility of a long postponement of the issue. **6. The Chaldeans**] possibly written after the battle of Carchemish, in 605 B.C., with reference to Nebuchadrezzar and his army, so graphically described in vv. 6–10.

7. The last clause means that the Chaldean recognises no master or judge : he is a law to himself. **9.** RM 'Their faces are set eagerly forwards, and they gather captives as the sand.' **10. They shall heap dust**] i.e. they shall throw up an enlargement of earth, to take the fortress. **11.** The correct translation should probably be : Then he sweeps by as a wind, and passes on and makes his might his God—an admirable climax to the description of the Chaldeans.

12–17. A new riddle.

12. Habakkuk's faith is staggered by the conduct of the Chaldeans. He had welcomed them as ministers of the divine judgment, and lo ! they had shown themselves to be cruel and haughty, working out not God's will, but their own. How was this consistent with the holiness of God ?

13. The cry of a perplexed heart : Thou art too pure to look upon evil, why then dost Thou look upon it ? God looks on in silence : He does nothing, says nothing ! The wicked (i.e. the Chaldean) swallows up one who is more righteous than himself (i.e. Judah).

14. And makest] probably this should be 'and makes.' It is, as vv. 15, 16 show, the Chaldean who makes men like fish, sweeping them into his net. **16. He sacrifices to his net**] i.e. to his weapons of destruction, as to a god : for was not might his god ? cp. v. 11.

17. This v. should probably read, 'Will he draw the sword for ever, slaying nations mercilessly evermore ?'

CHAPTER 2
Faith Triumphant

1–4. The view from the watchtower.

1. The prophet climbs his tower, for he must reach a vantage point, if he is to contemplate with real understanding and insight the confusion about his feet, i.e. occasioned by Chaldean aggressiveness and indifference to right. The tower is not, of course, a literal tower—some high and lonely place to which the prophet may retire ; it simply suggests the inner light of revelation, by the aid of which he contemplates the perplexing situation. The last clause should read, 'and what answer He will make to my complaint.'

2. The answer which he expects is given, and he is instructed to write it down on tablets, because it is of permanent value, and to write it plainly so that any one might be able to read it fluently. **Run**] i.e. in his reading, read easily.

3. The ultimate moral issue is clear, though it may be far away. If it is slow, it is sure. It may not come 'in your days' (1⁵), but 'it is sure to come, it will not be late : and if it tarry, wait for it,' for in 'your patience ye shall win your souls.' When the kingdom will come is not clear, but come it will ; for some day 'the earth shall be filled with the knowledge of the glory of Jehovah, as the waters cover the sea' (2¹⁴). That is the inevitable goal of history.

4. The first few words of this vision, which is regarded as so important and reassuring, are very obscure, but the two clauses of the v. appear to contrast the destinies of the good and the bad respectively; and the meaning probably is, 'As for the wicked, his soul is not straight, or is faint and feeble, within him,' that is, is doomed to death; 'but the righteous shall live by his fidelity,' i.e. his faithfulness, his firm trust of Jehovah. In the long march of history, the nations of men that trust in their power and resources and defy morality, are doomed, they do not live. It is the righteous that live, those who regard right and God. However much they suffer, and even when they seem to die, they live; and they live by their faithfulness, i.e. by leaning firmly upon the God who lives for ever, and whose life is a guarantee of theirs. This in one of the profoundest utterances of the Old Testament.

5–20. Woe to the oppressor.

This section is an expansion of 2⁴ᵃ: it describes the oppressor—no doubt the Chaldean—and thereby justifies the doom pronounced upon him. The section takes the form of a series of woes, dramatically pronounced by the nations which the Chaldeans had crushed.

5–8. Woe unto the lust of conquest! V. 5, which has nothing to do with wine, should probably read, 'Woe to the proud and the faithless, the haughty man who is never satisfied.'

6, 7. Woe to him who takes upon himself a heavy burden of debt—referring to the property of which the Chaldeans had plundered the nations. Instead of heavy 'pledges' (RV), AV (by dividing the single Heb. word into two) reads **thick clay.** Doubtless both senses are intended : the Hebrews were fond of such plays upon words. Suddenly will thy creditors arise. The 'biters' are the creditors (the words are alike in the Hebrew), and the Chaldeans will in their turn be bitten, i.e. they will be punished in kind; the plunderers will be themselves plundered (vv. 7, 8). **8. Of the land, of the city,** etc.] RV 'done to the land, to the city,' etc. **The city**] perhaps Jerusalem.

9–11. The third woe. 9. RV 'Woe to him that getteth an evil gain for his house.' The plunder was stored for security in great high buildings, but the very stone and timber cried out against the rapacity which had accumulated it. Their silent tongues were eloquent; accusing voices were everywhere. Considering the range of v. 10, however, it is possible, if not probable, that the whole passage has a larger meaning : for in v. 10 it seems best to interpret the house not as a literal house, but—as often in Hebrew—of the dynasty. In that case, the ruin of the Chaldean dynasty is predicted as the consequence of their cruel and unscrupulous ambitions. **10. Consulted**] i.e. contrived : cp. Mic 6⁵.

12–14. The fourth woe. Every fabric reared upon iniquity is doomed to destruction. The triumph of the kingdom of God, and of that alone, is sure. The world-conqueror is not Nebuchadrezzar, but Jehovah. **13. The people shall labour in the very fire**] RV 'The peoples labour for the fire' : i.e. their cities, built with blood, will be consigned to the flames. The parallel clause (v. 13ᵇ) shows that the meaning is, their efforts are spent in vain.

15–17. The fifth woe. The references in vv. 15, 16 to intoxication must, as v. 17 shows, be taken figuratively. The meaning is that the Chaldeans have dealt with other nations in a spirit of contemptuous cruelty, depriving them of their strength, and doing with them what they would. They will, therefore, be punished, as before, in kind, being compelled by Jehovah to drink the cup they had held to the lips of others. A specimen of their highhandedness is given in v. 17 : they had robbed the land and the beasts of their rights—for they, too, have rights—by destroying the cedars of Lebanon to secure material for their own palatial buildings.

18, 19. The sixth woe. The real explanation of the immorality of the Chaldeans is to be found in their foolish conception of God (cp. 1¹¹). They worshipped idols, gorgeous indeed, but stupid, impotent, dumb, and lifeless.

19. **Arise, it shall teach !**] RV 'Arise ! Shall this teach ?' The parallelism shows that **Arise** corresponds to **Awake,** and that, therefore, with the next words a new sentence begins. It is best to read this sentence interrogatively as RV, 'Shall this teach ?' 'This'—pointing with scorn to the motionless image—'what power has this to give the needed instruction or help ?'

20. What a contrast to these idols is the majestic God of Israel, the God of all the earth, whose Temple is in the heavens ! He is about to appear (c. 3); hush ! before Him, all the earth.

CHAPTER 3
JEHOVAH COMES TO JUDGMENT

This is one of the most brilliant poems in the OT. It was written by a man of imagination as well as of faith. It is not quite certain whether 3 ³⁻¹⁵ are intended to refer to a past or future manifestation of Jehovah : in any case, there is the hope, or rather prayer, that history may repeat itself (v. 2). The poem rests upon older theophanies : cp. Jg 5 Dt 33. Long ago at the exodus Jehovah had shown His power to interpose in history against all hope. He had come in the terrors of judgment and taken vengeance on the enemies of

Israel : and what he did then, the Psalmist prays that He will do again. The power which He revealed on Israel's behalf at the dawn of her history, He can make known again in the midst of the years.

1. Upon Shigionoth] RV 'Set to Shigionoth.' This very obscure phrase (cp. Ps 7) has been supposed to mean 'in a wandering, ecstatic manner,' implying that the poem that follows is a sort of dithyramb. Probably, as the LXX suggests, the original word simply meant, ' to the accompaniment of stringed instruments.'

3. The storm which accompanies Jehovah's coming begins in Sinai, His ancient home, and sweeps northward. **Teman**] a district in the NW. of Edom. **Paran**] the mountain range between Sinai and Seir. **4. Horns** *coming out of his hand*] RV ' Rays *coming forth* from his hand.' This clause some take with the next one, so that the meaning would be ' the rays at His side He makes the veil of His power,' that is, the brightness is so blinding that His real and essential majesty cannot be seen.

5–8. Accompanied by His dread attendants, He takes His stand upon the earth, which reels and rocks beneath Him, and the nomad tribes are in terror. **5. Burning coals**] RV 'fiery bolts.' **7. Cushan**] Some identify this with Cush, i.e. Ethiopia. The parallelism suggests, however, that it may indicate some district in the neighbourhood of Sinai.

8–11. Wherefore such wrath ? Why did Jehovah so confound the sea—perhaps the Red Sea — by means of His storm ? **9**ᵃᵇ probably ought to read, ' Thou didst bare Thy bow, and fill Thy quiver with shafts '—an allusion to the thunder and the lightning. Fear kept sun and moon from shining (v. 11).

12–15. It is to save His people that He comes. **13**ᵇ. **Thou woundedst the head out of the house of the wicked, by discovering** (RV 'laying bare ')**the foundation unto the neck.** There seems to be here a confusion of metaphor—' foundation ' suggesting a building and ' neck ' a man. The situation may be partially saved by reading ' rock ' instead of ' neck ' ; but even so, it is not quite clear whether **head** in the first clause refers to a building, as the second clause suggests, or to a man, as the same word is used unambiguously of a man in the very next v. (14ᵃ). In any case, the reference appears to be to the overthrow of Pharaoh.

14ᵃ. Probably we should read, ' Thou didst pierce with Thy staves the head of his warriors.' In the next line the word **me** shows that the description is passing into the present : they come storming on to scatter me.

16–19. The triumph of faith. It is difficult, if not impossible, to translate v. 16 ; provisionally we may accept the following, ' I will wait for the day of distress which cometh over the people that distresses us.' But the v. seems to indicate the terror with which the Psalmist (or prophet) listens to the dying notes of the storm. He had prayed for God to reveal Himself : and He had come in His terrible majesty—come, however, to save : and though the poet trembles, his faith is radiant and glad.

17. The connexion between this v. and the previous part of the poem is no doubt such as has just been suggested ; but it may be doubted whether it is an integral part of the original poem. With its flocks and fields and trees, it seems to presuppose a different situation from vv. 2–16 ; but, however that may be, the v., together with vv. 18, 19, expresses the same kind of faith as that of the poem, and indeed of the book at large, a faith which is independent of material evidences and supports (2³,⁴). It teaches that God is better than His gifts, and that the possession of Him, even without them, makes the heart strong and glad. In its independence of things material, the OT. never uttered a grander or more emancipating word than these concluding vv. of Habakkuk.

It is not certain that this poem was composed by the prophet. The title and musical directions seem to indicate that it was taken from a collection of Psalms : there are no references in it to the special circumstances of the age in which Habakkuk lived : while in vv. 14, 18, 19 the community rather than an individual is the speaker. The conclusion suggested by these features is that this poem belongs to a later date : it may be a Psalm composed for the post-exilic church in a time of distress. But, on the other hand, the ascription of it to Habakkuk is confirmed by the fact that it is wholly in conformity with his spirit in the other chs. of this book : and it is appropriately placed in its present position, as it shares with the prophecy a pure faith in God and in the certainty of His coming.

ZEPHANIAH

INTRODUCTION

1. The Prophet and his Message. Zephaniah, like his young contemporary, Jeremiah, was one of the first to break the long silence of more than half-a-century which followed the death of the great Isaiah. During the reactionary reign of Manasseh the Canaanitish Baal cults and the Assyrian star-worship and the other heathen institutions, to which the prophet alludes in his opening words, had been tolerated without rebuke in Jerusalem and Judah (2 K 21³⁻⁶). King and people had repudiated the teachings of the earlier prophets and reverted to the old heathenism, or else adopted the religion and customs of their Assyrian conquerors, although they still, as a nation, continued to worship the Jehovah of their popular belief.

At last, however, the Assyrian empire, which for centuries had stood as the embodiment of heathen might, began to show unmistakable signs of weakness and disintegration. The more thoughtful in Judah also commenced to weary of the crimes and excesses which followed in the train of popular idolatry. Probably a small group of disciples had never ceased to cherish in secret the noble ideals and principles of the earlier prophets, and to work for their ultimate acceptance by the nation. When Isaiah recognised that his teachings were rejected by the princes and people, he had turned with confidence to his disciples and expressed the hope that they would treasure up his doctrine (Isa 8¹⁶). This expectation was fully realised, and the eternal principle illustrated that truth, clearly and courageously proclaimed, can never be permanently put down, but will in time surely become a powerful factor in the life of mankind.

Silenced in public, the followers of the true prophets appear to have devoted themselves to revising the primitive laws of their race, incorporating the lofty principles laid down by Amos and Hosea and Isaiah, and adapting them to the new conditions presented by the reign of Manasseh. Many hold that in the book of Deuteronomy, which is a prophetic reformulation of the laws of Moses, designed to meet the needs of a new age, we have the supreme product of their activity. Later this became the basis of Josiah's great reformation in 621 B.C.

Before there could be any effective reform, it was necessary to educate the people and to secure the support of Judah's rulers. It is a surprising fact that Josiah, the son of Amon, and grandson of the reactionary Manasseh, should later become the leader in the great prophetic reformation. The records are silent, but there can be little doubt that the boy king, who was raised to the throne at the age of eight, early came under the influence of the prophetic party. The indications point strongly to Zephaniah as the one who was most prominent in exerting that influence, for the superscription affixed to his prophecy traces his ancestry back for four generations to Hezekiah, who was in all probability the king under whom Isaiah prophesied. If so, Zephaniah himself belonged to the royal line. This inference is confirmed by the boldness and assurance with which he proclaims the guilt of the princes and members of the royal family (1⁸). It is also significant that he says nothing about the sins of the king himself, but rather places all the responsibility upon his advisers (1⁹). The most satisfactory explanation of the omission is that Josiah was still a young man, and already known to be amenable to the counsel of true prophets like Zephaniah. If these inferences be correct, the prophet commands our interest, because he stood very near both by birth and influence to the great reformer-king, and because he was the pioneer in the religious movement which culminated in 621 B.C. Like Josiah and his prophetic colleague, Jeremiah, who calls himself a boy (Jer 1⁶), Zephaniah was probably still a young man when he first raised his voice in public. Youthful courage and undaunted zeal for righteousness ring through his brief prophecy. With the eye of faith he sees the speedy passing of the heathen practices, which for half-a-century had stood in the way of the general adoption of the noble ideals proclaimed by Hosea and Isaiah.

2. Occasion. The immediate occasion of his preaching appears to have been the advance of an enemy which threatened Judah and its neighbours with sudden and complete destruction. Evidently the dreaded foe is not their old masters, the Assyrians, nor their allies, the Egyptians, but the barbarous Scythians, who had already disturbed the politics of south-western Asia: cp. Herod. i. 105, Ezk 38⁸,¹⁷. A detachment of these ruthless foes, who worshipped their swords and gloried only in murder and plunder, was evidently already sweeping down the eastern shore of the Mediterranean.

The prophet had his text, and his audience good reason to listen. Their old complacency was shaken. The awakened national conscience found expression on the lips of the royal prophet. Rising above the terror of the moment, he announced that these pitiless destroyers were Jehovah's instrument of punishment, and the catastrophe that threatened His day of judgment. The horror and mystery that were inspired by the Scythians colour the prophet's picture of that day. It explains why the mediæval church and Thomas of Celano, in his *Dies Iræ, Dies Illa*, drew from Zephaniah the imagery of the last great Judgment Day. It was the influence of this same powerful prophecy that doubtless led the early Jewish and Christian writers to transform the original conception of the Day of Jehovah as a gradual process, working out in the life of nations, into the dramatic picture of one definite judgment scene, projected into the distant future.

3. **Teaching.** Zephaniah, like all the true prophets, aimed to arouse the moral sense of his contemporaries, and thus to render unnecessary the fulfilment of his grim predictions. Unlike most of his colleagues, he soon saw the fruits of his efforts ; and yet through all his utterances rings the knell of seemingly irrevocable doom. In its original form it is the most uncompromising of all the OT. prophecies. Like the passages from the Deuteronomic school of writers, who, in their version of the conquest, picture the wholesale slaughter of the heathen, it reveals the intense moral earnestness and zeal of the reformers who rallied about the young Josiah. As a chapter in the religious history of Judah, the prophecy is of great value.

Fortunately, it is also possible to date it with unusual exactness. It was probably delivered only a few days before the Scythian hordes, in 626 B.C., swept down the Mediterranean coast plain, devastating the Philistine cities. There is no evidence that they undertook the more difficult and less promising task of invading Judah itself ; but a deep impression had been made upon the popular consciousness, and Zephaniah's stern message of warning remained to remind Judahites of the doom that had impended.

4. **Contents.** The book of Zephanian contains two distinct themes : the one (1 2–3 13) is that of universal judgment upon guilty Judah (c. 1) ; upon her neighbours the Philistines, the Moabites, and the Ammonites ; upon her allies, the Ethiopians, and upon her old oppressors the Assyrians (c. 2) ; and upon Jerusalem's corrupt rulers (3 1-13). The last judgment is represented as culminating in the purification of the surviving remnant. This introduces the second theme, which is the song of rejoicing over redeemed and restored Zion (3 14-20). Thus

the book in its present form is a complete literary unit with its cycle of judgment, purification, redemption, and restoration. In striking contrast to the dark thunderclouds of Jehovah's wrath with which it opens is the brilliant sunshine of divine forgiveness and favour with which the book closes. This completeness is, however, probably due to a later prophet who appreciated both sides of the divine character. The original prophecy appears to have begun and ended with the same solemn message of warning, and to have included simply 1 2–2 2, 4-7b, 12-15 3 1-7 11-13. The rest assumes the point of view and very different conditions of the Babylonian exile, and voices the hopes of restoration which kept alive the faith of the scattered remnants of the Jewish race. Its language and vocabulary are also those of the later age. Like many other books of the OT. the prophecy of Zephaniah reflects the exceedingly diverse and yet significant religious experiences which came to the Israelitish race at various periods in their history. Each section, studied in the light of its historical setting, reveals certain important aspects of the divine character and purpose.

In the older portion of the prophecy the influence of Isaiah's brilliant figures of speech, as well as ideas, can frequently be recognised. Through Zephaniah the message of the great prophet again found fervent expression. The language is highly poetical. In several sections, especially those which predict the punishment and ruin of Judah, Moab, Ammon, Ethiopia, and Assyria, the lamentation metre, a line with three followed by a line with two beats, appears. Unfortunately the text of the first part of the prophecy has suffered considerably in transmission. In some cases the Gk. versions facilitate the restoration of the original.

CHAPTER 1

The Day of Jehovah a Day of Judgment for guilty Judah

The prophecy opens with the declaration of universal destruction for all living things. In this way the prophet impresses upon his hearers the completeness and appalling nature of the impending judgment. In the succeeding vv. he defines in detail the character of the punishment and the guilty classes in Judah upon which it will especially fall. It is in keeping with the genius of the Semitic mind thus to pass from the general to the specific. The Hebrews, for example, began with God and then turned to note the evidence of His work in history and nature ; while the Aryan mind first gathered the evidence from life and a study of the universe, and then from these ultimately rose to the conception of a deity.

3. **Stumblingblocks**] or, slightly correcting

the text to bring it into harmony with the rest of the v., 'I will destroy the wicked.'

4. I will also stretch out mine hand] cp. the similar powerful refrain in Isa 5 25 9 12, 17, 21. All traces of Baalism, together with the 'Chemarim' (RV), the black-robed priests of Baal are first to be destroyed, as well as the wicked priests of Jehovah, who degraded His worship.

5, 6. The sweeping judgment and reformation will also affect those who follow the example of their Assyrian masters and worship the stars upon the housetops (cp. 2 K 23 5, 12 Ezk 8 16), those who bow down before the moon (Heb. *Jehovah*, but cp. Jer 8 2 Dt 17 3, and the parallelism), those who swear fealty to the Ammonite god, Milcom, and all those apostates who have ceased to worship Jehovah.

7. Jehovah's Day is here conceived of as a day of judgment, as in Am 5 18, and is likened to a great sacrificial feast: cp. 1 S 9 13, and the guests are Judah's enemies: cp. for the same figure of speech, Isa 13 3.

8. The chief crime of the princes in the prophet's eyes is the introduction of foreign customs : see Isa 2 6-8.

9. Leap on the threshold] Evidently here also the crime is that of the members of the court, perhaps a foreign religious custom : cp. 1 S 5 5. But as there is no reference to religious customs in the context, the words may simply refer to the retainers of the king, who were in constant attendance at his doors, and who used their influence to enrich themselves at the cost of others. **Fill their masters' houses** (Heb. 'house ') **with violence and deceit**] i.e. by their acts of oppression and injustice.

10. The reference is to the advance of the enemy against Jerusalem from the N. **The fish gate** was at the northern end of the Tyropœan valley (cp. Neh 3 3 12 39), and opened into the second or new quarter : cp. 2 K 22 14 RV.

11. Maktesh] or, 'the mortar' : the local designation of the merchants' quarter, which probably lay in the Tyropœan valley, W. of the Temple area.

12. Search .. with candles] i.e. thoroughly, as was required in the poorly-lighted houses of Palestine : cp. Lk 15 8. **Settled on their lees**] i.e. have received no infusion of new and noble teachings, but retain the old fallacies : cp. Jer 48 11, 12. **13.** Cp. Am 5 11 Mic 6 15. **14, 15.** Jehovah's judgment day is compared with a fierce tempest rapidly advancing toward Judah. The figure was suggested by the swift approach of the hordes of Scythian invaders.

CHAPTER 2

JEHOVAH'S IMPENDING JUDGMENT UPON JUDAH'S NEIGHBOURS AND FOES

The universal note which is struck in 1 2, 3 is now further amplified. Jehovah's agents of punishment, the Scythians, shall carry desola-

tion along the Philistine plain to Egypt (as they actually did), and to the nations E. of the Jordan and Dead Sea, and even to distant Assyria, which in 605 B.C. fell before them.

1–3. Exhortation to repentance. The Heb. text is exceedingly doubtful. It is also not clear whether or not vv. 1–3 should go with the preceding or following section. If the latter, Philistia is the nation addressed : RV 'O nation that hath no shame.' **2.** *Before* **the day,** etc.] The parallelism suggests that the original read, 'before you become like the passing chaff.' **3.** The earnest exhortation in this v. must primarily have been addressed to the people of Judah, whether it comes from Zephaniah or from a later editor of his prophecy. In doing the will and winning the favour of God is man's only sure way of escape from all the dangers of life.

4. As in Am 1 6-8 their chief cities represent the Philistines as a whole. Each name suggests the fate awaiting it. To reproduce the assonance in exact English is impossible : ' Gaza shall be a ghastly ruin ; Ashkelon a deserted ash-heap.' The measure is elegiac, so that the literary form powerfully aided in conveying the prophet's message. **5. Cherethites**] a synonym of Philistines, as in 1 S 30 14 Ezk 25 16. **6, 7.** The Philistine coast plain shall be desolate and given up to shepherds and their flocks.

8. The nations of Moab and Ammon were hereditary enemies of the Israelites whom they treated with contempt on every possible occasion. Their hatred was returned by Israel, whose attitude is well expressed in their accepted view of the origin of these nations (Gn 19 30-38). **The reproach of Moab, and the revilings of . . Ammon** were the taunts and curses they had uttered from time to time, especially when Israel was in danger from other foes : cp. Isa 16 6 Jer 48 26, 27, 29, 30, 42. Cp. also for the same attitude at a later date Ezk 25 1-11. **11. Famish**] i.e. 'starve '; hence it means ' weaken,' ' cause to fail.' **12. Ethiopians**] lit. ' Cushites,' i.e. the Egyptians who at this time were ruled by Ethiopian rulers. Ethiopia was the part of Egypt S. of the first cataract of the Nile.

13-15. Assyria with its capital city, Nineveh, will also be destroyed. **The cormorant and the bittern**] RV 'the pelican and the porcupine' (i.e. the hedgehog), both of them being signs of desolation, as they avoid the presence of man: cp. Isa 34 11. **Upper lintels**] RV 'chapiters,' i.e. the capitals of the pillars, now lying with the other stones in heaps on the ground as they have fallen. *Their* **voice shall sing**] better, ' the little owl shall sing,' as many scholars read. For **desolation** read ' the raven.'

For he shall uncover] RV ' for he hath laid bare.'

CHAPTER 3

THE JUDGMENT UPON THE EVIL RULERS OF JERUSALEM, AND ITS ULTIMATE PURIFICATION AND RESTORATION

Like Amos and Micah, the prophet sternly denounces the crimes of the ruling classes in Jerusalem, points out their ingratitude to Jehovah, and announces the doom that is inevitable. The gloom of the opening vv. is dispelled, however, by the hopes of restoration which appear to reflect a later age. Vv. 9, 10, 14–20 have the exultant ring of Isa 40–55.

1. Her that is filthy and polluted] evidently Jerusalem. The cause is the crimes of her civil and religious leaders. **3. They gnaw not the bones till the morrow**] LXX is more in accord with the context and the habits of wolves, 'they leave nothing over till morning.'

6. Towers] i.e. the fortified towers at the corners of the walls. **7. So their dwelling . . punished them**] LXX renders, 'And nothing that I have enjoined her will be cut off from her sight.'

9. Pure language] cp. Isa 6⁵ Hos 2¹⁶,¹⁷. They will no more call upon the names of the heathen gods: cp. 1⁵. **10.** RM reads, 'From beyond the rivers of Ethiopia shall they bring my suppliants, even the daughter of my dispersed, for an offering unto me.'

14–20. A Messianic hymn, in which not the Messiah but Jehovah Himself is the promised King and Deliverer (vv. 17, 18). **18ᵇ.** RM 'which hast borne the burden of reproach.'

19. Her that halteth, and . . was driven out] i.e. the exiled Jewish race : cp. Mic 4⁶,⁷ Jer 33⁹ Isa 42⁷.

20. When I bring again (RV) your captivity] i.e. when I restore your captives : cp. Ps 53⁶ 126¹,².

HAGGAI

INTRODUCTION

1. The Prophet. Very little is known concerning Haggai. He was a contemporary (Ezr 6¹⁴) and colleague of Zechariah. His reference to the first Temple (2³) has been made the basis for a not improbable inference that he was a very old man at the time of his public prophesying, one who had outlasted the Babylonian exile. But, like many others through whom God has spoken, we know Haggai only through the messages he delivered.

2. The Date of the Prophecies. The book of Haggai is one of the few sections of Scripture which can be dated with great accuracy. Its messages were delivered in the course of four months, during the second year of the reign of Darius Hystaspes, 520 B.C., nineteen years after Cyrus had proclaimed the freedom of the Jewish exiles to return to their homes in Palestine. On at least five occasions during this short period, the prophet appealed to the people on behalf of what seemed to him to be the great and immediate need of the day. He was determined to carry it to completion.

3. The occasion of writing. The prophet had before him a very practical aim, the awakening of a popular enthusiasm among his fellow-countrymen for erecting or completing the second Temple. According to Ezra (chs. 1–3) there had been an immediate return of exiles from Babylonia to Judah after the permissive decree of Cyrus in 538 B.C. These exiles had promptly begun to build a new Temple on the hallowed site of the old one, now in ruins. They had been checked by Samaritan opposition, and for sixteen years the work of rebuilding had been neglected. At best the work accomplished had been slight, and, as a whole, was still to be achieved.

The prophet clearly addresses a people who need to be roused into activity. The hopes created by the generosity and friendliness of Cyrus had been crushed by the pressure of Samaritan jealousy in Palestine, and by the neglect of the successor of Cyrus. They had experienced a series of barren seasons, and were desperately poor. As a community they had lost heart, and needed some impelling power to give them renewed enthusiasm and hopefulness.

The voice of Haggai was uplifted at just the right moment. Whether old or young, whether he had bided his time all these years, or was seized by his first inspiration for leadership, he was the man of the hour. He saw in a political crisis his people's opportunity to go forward with the enterprise which would be of supreme spiritual significance for them, the building of the Temple.

The political crisis of which he took such instant advantage was the assumption of the throne of Persia by Darius Hystaspes, or Darius the Great. Darius had no indisputable claim to the throne ; and found himself at the outset compelled to exhibit his ability to subdue and rule the far-reaching provinces of his empire. The outcome was for some time in doubt. There was a 'shaking of the nations' on every side, and meanwhile the loyal peoples of Syria were left very much to their own devices. It was a crisis which seemed likely to become an opportunity. Darius was likely to prove a friend to the returned exiles, and to secure their friendship by withdrawing the prohibition of the work issued by his predecessor (Ezr 4 5, 24), and Haggai seized the opportunity to rouse the dormant energies and ambitions of the people.

4. The Prophecies. The book of Haggai contains four exhortations by the prophet. Three of these relate directly to the building of the Temple, and the last of all concerns Zerubbabel, the governor. These messages are direct and practical. They sound a fine ethical note, recalling the people to their manifest and immediate duty toward God. The first section (c. 1) is a summons to build the house of God, and its sequel ; the second (2 1-9), an encouraging word; the third (2 10-19), an acted parable of explanation ; and the fourth (2 20-23), a prediction regarding Zerubbabel. There is a unity of meaning from the beginning to the end, in harmony with the claims of the book that it represents the utterances of a brief period.

5. Characteristic Features of the Book. There is much vigour and individuality in Haggai's addresses. His words are those of a leader who perceives a great opportunity and seeks to meet it. He does not enlarge our inheritance of truth, nor give us new visions of God in His universe. He rather rendered a special service to his people at a time of need. He aroused them to their duty, dispelled their faintheartedness, sustained their flagging energies, gave the achievement its true significance as the next step which God called upon them to take, and kept alive their loyalty to the great hopes which his famous predecessors had kindled in their hearts. Altogether Haggai was an important link in the prophetic succession. He just precedes Zechariah, whose first preserved prophecy (Zech 1 1-6) belongs chronologically to the time between the utterance of Haggai in 2 1-9 and that in 2 10-19.

That the prophet's style differs from that of Isaiah or Jeremiah is not strange. His style fits the situation. A plain, insistent message of practical duty was what was needed. Spiritual life, hope for the future, loyalty to God and to national traditions—all these supreme aims waited on the erection of the Temple. That Haggai saw this was an undoubted proof of his prophetic quality.

CHAPTER 1

A CALL TO BEGIN BUILDING THE TEMPLE

1-11. Haggai repeatedly urges the leaders of Judah and the people to bend their energies to the rebuilding of the ruined Temple (August, 520 B.C.).

1. Darius the king] This was unquestionably Hystaspes, who was raised to the Persian throne after the death of the impostor, Smerdis.

Sixth month] the 6th of the Jewish year, i.e. the month Elul (August-September).

Zerubbabel] A prince of the royal line of Judah, and the accepted civil leader of the people, just as Joshua was the religious leader. He ruled Judah as a Persian province.

2. This people] Haggai, like other prophets, did not need to create a sense of wrongdoing, but only to awaken conscience. He challenged their idle excuses. **The time is not come**] Evidently this was no sincere desire to await some specified date, but a wilful delaying of duty. In the interests of religion it demanded attention. **4. Time for you, O ye**] lit. 'for you, you,' the repeated pronoun being very emphatic, so as to make a sharp contrast between them and the God they dishonoured. **Cieled houses**] houses panelled with costly cedar planks. They could seem to afford luxuries for themselves, but were indifferent to the ruined state of the Temple.

5. Consider your ways] lit. 'Set your heart on your ways,' i.e. consider thoughtfully the situation in which you find yourselves. An appeal made four times by the prophet. **6. Ye eat, but ye have not enough**] lit. 'but not to satisfy.' This v. formulates a series of vigorous comparisons, indicating that their labour had been ill rewarded. They had experienced failures of crops, continuous poverty, and lessening of physical vigour. **Bag with holes**] No one gets ahead, but seems to lose his money as fast as he accumulates it. A vivid picture of alluring hopes and baffling disappointments.

8. Go up to the mountain] They were to act at once. The prophet was in earnest. The **mountain** would be 'the hill-country of Judah,' the mountainous neighbourhood. Compare Neh 2 8 and 8 15. **Bring wood**] i.e. timber suitable for building. **The house**] the Temple of Jehovah, which had been lying in ruins since being destroyed at the command of Nebuchadrezzar (2 K 25 9). **And I will be glorified**] better, 'and that I may display my glory.' Here the prophet first interprets these calamities as being due to God's anger at their selfishness. The two following vv. emphasise this explanation. The people were zealous enough over their own affairs, but wholly neglectful of their obligations to God.

12-15. The leaders and people, their consciences awakened, encouraged by Haggai, begin work upon the Temple (September, 520 B.C.).

12. The remnant of the people] i.e. the rest of the people ; those who had returned from Babylon were but a fraction of the once numerous nation. **Did fear**] It was a real religious change that came over them. They obeyed, not because of terror, but from a new sense of reverence for God. **13. The LORD'S messenger**] This v. is rejected by many scholars as superfluous. They also question this title as needless. It is the only instance in Scripture where a prophet uses such a title concerning himself. Nevertheless, it is not incongruous. **I** *am* **with .you**] This encouraging word assured the people that they were acting as God would have them do. **14. Stirred up the spirit**] The first result of Haggai's unsparing sermon was a spiritual change in the hearts of his hearers. A zealous purpose was once more kindled. The second result was practical. Within three weeks from the date of his first appeal the work upon the Temple had begun, with unanimity and heartiness. What more searching test could a preacher have or what more convincing proof of his power ?

CHAPTER 2
WORDS OF ENCOURAGEMENT. THE GLORY
OF THE SECOND TEMPLE

1-9. An encouraging message in counteraction of disparaging comments upon the Temple structure, setting forth the significance and glory of the new Temple.

1. Seventh *month*] i.e. Tishri, September–October. This message was delivered just four weeks after the beginning of the work. So heartily had every one united in it that the general outline and character of the new edifice had become apparent. The Feast of Tabernacles was in progress. Haggai spoke to the people on the last day of this feast, when all were gathered in one great assembly. **3. Who** *is* **left among you**] More than 66 years had passed since the destruction of the first Temple, but it was quite possible that there were some who could describe that glorious structure as they had known it. These elders referred to the newer Temple with disparagement, to the dejection and dismay of the people. Gold and silver and rare woods made Solomon's Temple splendid ; the edifice now rising was of rough stone. No wonder the elders became reminiscent. **First**] better, ' former.' **4. Be strong**] or, ' have courage.' **And work**] keep at your task : cp. David's words to Solomon, 1 Ch 28 20. **5. My spirit remaineth**] RM ' abideth,' is standing in your presence. What a basis for continuing courage ! cp. Zech 4 6. Jehovah was in their midst, as He had always been in

times of need. Moreover, they would soon have adequate proof of His presence. **6. Yet once, it** *is* **a little while**] This is literal, but it evidently means ' But a little while.' It seems to refer to the shaking, which might be soon expected.

7. Shake all nations] This clearly refers to political overturnings. The prophet expected that the great empire, all aflame with rebellion, would be broken up, and that the Jewish community would have its coveted opportunity. His language, probably figurative, implies corresponding convulsions of nature. The general idea is that God will soon take hold of the situation and deal with it. **The desire of all nations shall come**] Through Jerome and the Vulgate the old Rabbinical Messianic interpretation of this phrase was given to the Christian church, as if it referred directly to Christ, but the verb ' shall come ' is a plural. More likely the meaning in Haggai's mind was (as RV), ' And the desirable things of all nations shall come.' These were under Jehovah's control. As the nations came to know Him and to render obedience, they would bring with joy to His Temple their choicest gifts. **With glory**] The Temple then would seem glorious enough.

9. The glory of this latter house] RV ' The latter glory of this house . than the former,' a prediction involving courage and foresight. It was spoken to a community politically insignificant, without resources, tributary to the powerful monarch of Persia, engaged in erecting a simple build ng for religious purposes. It was a triumph of religious idealism. As a permanent promise it beautifully phrases the assurance of the supremacy of Christ and the church in the world. **Will I give peace**] Where God is established, there is a peace which cannot be disturbed (Jn 16 33).

10-19. A symbolical message emphasising the significance of the long-continued neglect of God by the community and promising blessings for obedience.

10. Ninth *month*] i.e. Chislev, or Nov.-Dec. The work on the Temple had now been under way for three months. **11. Ask now the priests . . the law**] better, ' ask of the priests a thorah,' or deliverance. In the absence of a definite statement in the written Law covering a case it was the custom to submit a question of usage to the priests (Dt 17 8-13). Their reply was a ' thorah ' or law. The passage in the written Law most resembling the judgment here rendered is Lv 6 27, 28. **12. Holy flesh**] flesh that has been offered in sacrifice and is being taken home to be consumed. **Shall it be holy ?**] i.e. is the garment in which such holy food is being carried capable of giving holiness to other food ? The priests replied that holiness could not be communicated in that way.

13. Unclean by a dead body] A corpse was

regarded as making every one who came in contact with it ceremonially unclean. The priests declared that this pollution would extend to whatever these infected persons touched. Uncleanness, then, could be propagated readily ; holiness could not.

14. That which they offer there] An effective application of these decisions to the situation. The restoration of the ritual service, as described in Ezr 3, was good in its way but insufficient to make them holy as a people, while their actual neglect of the Temple was enough to pollute everything they did. In God's sight they could only be regarded as unclean and worthy of punishment.

15. From this day and upward] better, 'and onward.' He then bids them think of their past sufferings and resumes the thought here begun in v. 18. There should be a full stop after **upward. From before**, etc.] A better translation is that of Nowack, ' Before a stone was laid upon a stone in the Temple of the Lord, how did ye fare ? When one came to a heap of twenty,' etc. **16. Twenty** *measures*] Realisations were but half the expectations. **Pressfat**] winevat. **Fifty** *vessels*] rather, 'measures.' **18. And upward**] better, ' onwards.'

The day that the foundation of the LORD'S temple was laid] Probably the day on which he was speaking. Haggai refers to their bitter experience up to the day of active work.

19. Is the seed yet in the barn ?] Evidently he means to draw out a negative reply Yet his word is encouraging. God is going to bless them. It takes time to recover from the ill effects of selfishness, but a brighter future was before them.

20–23. An inspiring declaration to Zerubbabel that in him rested the ancient hopes of Israel.

20. Four and twentieth *day*] the same great festal day. **22. The throne of kingdoms**] LXX ' thrones.' Haggai looked forward to a disruption of the great Persian empire into its tributary nations and to struggles between them, which would give Israel its opportunity. **23. In that day**] The day of general political convulsion, would be the day of Messianic advance, and of the establishment of Jehovah's kingdom. The forwarding of Israel's spiritual hopes seemed to Haggai, as to earlier prophets, to necessitate the opening of political freedom. **Make thee as a signet**] the sign of authority. So far as we know Zerubbabel never exercised any real, independent power. He served, however, to embody and keep alive the Hope which gave permanence and power to Israel's ideals.

Haggai contributed but little to the volume of prophecy, but that little was of great value. At a critical moment in Israel's history he said the timely, vigorous, ethical word, and put into apprehensible form the great ideal

ZECHARIAH

INTRODUCTION

1. Historical Background. Zechariah was the grandson of Iddo, who is mentioned in Neh 12 4, 16 as the head of one of the priestly families that returned from the exile. The Jews had been carried captive to Babylon in 597 and 586 B.C. ; but Cyrus the Great, soon after the capture of Babylon in 538, promulgated a decree permitting them to return to their native land and restore Jerusalem, under the governorship of Sheshbazzar (called also Sanabassar), probably a prince of their own royal line (Ezr 1 1-11 2 Ch 36 22, 23 Isa 44 28 45 13). It is uncertain how many of the Jews took advantage of the liberty granted them, as the number given in the book of Ezra may be taken from a census of Judæa made at some time subsequent to the return. Certainly the returned exiles included some of the best Jewish families, and among them Zechariah,

then only a boy, probably accompanied his grandfather.

The religious and patriotic spirit of the exiles had been stirred by Ezekiel (11 17-20 16 60-63 34 11-31 36 22-38 37 21-28) and by such writings as Isa 48 20 49 8-17 52 7-12, etc. ; but in the difficulties of the return, and the weary task of rebuilding their ruined homes, their enthusiasm soon died away. Their efforts were watched and hindered by enemies (Ezr 4 5, 6), who tried to prejudice them at the Court of Babylon by reporting that they were plotting to obtain political freedom (Ezr 4 9-16). The years slipped past. Cyrus, the Jews' best friend, died in 529 B.C. His son Cambyses, who succeeded him, did nothing to help them ; and when Darius, his successor, ascended the throne in 521, the Jews at Jerusalem had altogether lost heart. Through the misrepresentations of their enemies they had been forbidden to rebuild the city walls. Their Temple, which had been burned in 586 by the Assyrian general, still lay a blackened ruin (although some maintain that the foundation-stone was laid as early as 537); nor did they see how it could be restored. At this critical moment God sent them a message which marvellously encouraged and uplifted them. The prophets Haggai and Zechariah were the bearers of this message.

These two prophets were contemporaries, and their prophecies were delivered almost simultaneously. They are mentioned together in Ezr 5 1 6 14, as having been raised up by God to encourage the Jews to rebuild the Temple. Haggai appeared first, and in August 520 B.C. charged the Jews with neglecting the building of God's House : cp. Hag 1. This appeal had immediate results. Within a month the foundation of the Temple was laid. Soon after, Zechariah uttered his first prophecy (Zech 1 1-6). Towards the close of the year 520, Haggai in two oracles finished his recorded prophecies ; and early in 521 Zechariah delivered the famous series, comprising eight symbolical visions, which appears in Zech 1 7–6 8, with an appendix, 6 9-15. Two years afterwards chs. 7, 8 were spoken in response to an enquiry by the men of Bethel, or perhaps a deputation from Babylon, as to the observance of a fast ; and these are now regarded in most quarters as completing the prophecies of Zechariah, as chs. 9–14 can hardly be ascribed to him.

2. Zechariah's Method. Haggai was a layman, Zechariah was of priestly descent. These facts, to a certain extent, explain the different methods of the two. Haggai is practical, plain, clear, in unfolding his message : Zechariah is equally practical, but his method is not so plain. He clothes his message in the language of symbol. It is true that in the opening passage (Zech 1 1-6) his language is simple and direct. He brings before his hearers the practical teaching of the earlier prophets, especially of Amos and Micah, and urges his own generation not to repeat the mistakes of their fathers. But from 1 7 to 6 8 he unfolds his message in a series of visions, the rich imagery of which would make a powerful appeal to the Oriental mind. This change from the direct method (the 'Thus saith the Lord') of the earlier prophets is characteristic of most of the post-exilic prophecies. From the time of Ezekiel onwards to the 2nd cent. of the Christian era, the symbolic method of writing occupied a leading place in Jewish religious literature The residence in Babylon would be responsible to some extent for the rise of this kind of prophecy. There the exiles would be subjected to the influences of a highly-developed art ; and their situation was such as naturally

to induce a visional or symbolic style of thought. To some extent also the change may be ascribed to the fact that Ezekiel, who initiated it, and Zechariah, who followed successfully in his steps, were priests, accustomed to read divine messages through the symbols of religious ritual. In any case, the method was abundantly justified by its results. Their symbolic messages touched the imagination of their hearers in much the same way as the parables of our Lord, in a later age, appealed to the Galilean multitudes. Zechariah's immediate aim was to raise the drooping spirits of his countrymen, and encourage them to proceed at once with the rebuilding of the Temple. In this he was entirely successful, the Temple being completed and dedicated in 516 B.C.

3. Zechariah's Teaching. In chs. 1–8, which are all that can with confidence be ascribed to Zechariah, the Messianic ideas are local and national for the most part. Sin is to be eradicated (5 1-11), the priesthood purified (3 1-5), Jerusalem made glorious (2 1-12), and a prince of the house of David (probably Zerubbabel) set up as ruler (3 6-10). These thoughts are repeated and re-enforced in the appendix to the series of visions (6 9-15). The idea that God dwells far away, and sends messages by angels, etc., appears in 1 9-11 4 1, etc. This is generally regarded as a feature of later Judaism, influenced by contact with Persia ; though, in view of recent discoveries, it is now admitted that points of resemblance between the religion of Assyria and the religion of Israel existed from the beginning. In 3 1,2 is the first mention of Satan in Hebrew literature. The idea is more fully developed in the (later) book of Job. The personification of wickedness (5 5-11) as a woman is a peculiar feature of Zechariah, and indicates that tendency to regard evil as an independent power warring against the power of good, which characterises the religion of Persia.

Zechariah is a prophet not only to his own time, but to every age. He teaches that repentance—' heart sorrow and a clear life ensuing '—is the first duty of a nation. He finds in the past guidance for men in the present, and seeks to impress upon them that 'the fear of the Lord is the beginning of wisdom.' Like all the prophets he is a patriot, anxious for the welfare and prosperity of his nation, but sure that only 'righteousness exalteth a nation,' and that God will dwell only with those who are willing to do His will. He sees that outward advantages are of no avail without the purified heart, and that there can be no real happiness until sin is removed from the national life. He realises too that the forms of religion are useless without the spirit, and proclaims that 'to obey is better than to sacrifice,' and that fasting is no substitute for truth and justice. Also he showed that Israel's priesthood, imperfect though it was, represented an ideal of holiness, and had its place in preparing the way for the ideal Priest—the Messiah.

4. Origin and Teaching of chs. 9–14. When we pass from c. 8 to c. 9 we come into a different atmosphere. In chs. 1–8 the situation is quite clear—dates are given, practical difficulties are discussed, well-known leaders are mentioned by name, and the people are engaged in a specific work, to which Zechariah encourages them. In chs. 9–14 all these guiding lines have disappeared. There is no mention of temple-building, or of Joshua or Zerubbabel, or even of Babylon : instead, we find cities and countries not mentioned hitherto —Hamath, Damascus, Egypt, Greece. In 1^{11} we read, 'all the earth sitteth still and is at rest' ; but in chs. 9–14 there is war, destruction, trouble, mourning. In chs. 1–8 there is a series of well-arranged oracles, with dates, and for the most part the same superscription, 'I lifted up mine eyes' : in chs. 9–14 the very period is a subject of conjecture, the various oracles are difficult to disentangle, and both thought and style are much changed. These are some of the reasons why most modern scholars agree that chs. 9–14 were not written by Zechariah. Who the real author was, and what were the date and purpose of his writing, it is not so easy to determine. According to one view, chs. 9–14 are composed of two distinct prophecies—(a) 9–11, 13^{7-9} ; (b) 12–14 (with the exception of 13^{7-9}). (a) is considered a very early prophecy, written in the time of Amos or Hosea about the year 740 B.C., on the following amongst other grounds : (1) Ephraim is mentioned (for Israel) with Judah (9^{10-13} $10^{6,7}$), which is hardly likely to have been the case after the northern kingdom came to an end in 722 ; (2) Assyria occurs along with Egypt as a world-power ($10^{10,11}$), whereas, long before the time of Zechariah, the empire of Assyria had passed away ; and (3) the three shepherds (c. 11) seem to represent Zechariah, Shallum, and a third person now unknown— kings of Israel who died a violent death.

These reasons, however, are not conclusive. Ephraim may be explained as referring to the exiles of the northern kingdom ; and Assyria seems to have continued in use as a territorial name to designate the rulers of that country, whether Persian, Greek, or Seleucid. With regard to the three shepherds of c. 11, the application to Zechariah, Shallum, and an unnamed king is mere conjecture.

In the same way, (b) (chs. 12–14) is dated in the pre-exilic age. The attacks on idolatry and prophesying ($13^{2,3}$) are thought to be consistent with the religious decay of the 7th cent. B.C., while the mourning (12^{10-14}) is

referred to the death of Josiah at Megiddo in 608 B.C. Neither here, however, nor in (a), is there anything which corresponds with the style of such pre-exilic writers as Amos and Hosea. The prophetic ideals embodied in chs. 9–14, and especially the visions of the last things (9^{14-16} 14^{1-15}, etc.), are consistent only with that well-known phase of Jewish thought which had its beginning not earlier than the time of Ezekiel. Nor is it likely that any pre-exilic writer would picture a state of things such as we find in 13^{1-6}, where prophecy is utterly discredited and abandoned. Apparently also there is no king even in Jerusalem : the king is yet to come (9^9). Besides, the reference to Greece (9^{13}), as a world-power over which Zion must win the victory, seems incomprehensible at any pre-exilic date.

Some writers find in chs. 9–11 a reference to the invasion of Asia by Alexander the Great in 334 B.C., and date this portion of the book accordingly ; but the most recent tendency is to assign the whole of the prophecies in chs. 9–14 to the 2nd cent. B.C. According to this view chs. 9–11, 13^{7-9} and 12–14 are two groups, each falling into two parts. The first two are 9^1–11^3, and 11^{4-17}–13^{7-9}, written in the first quarter of the 2nd cent. The Greeks (9^{13}) are the world-power against which Judaism must strive for supremacy. Assyria is the Seleucid kingdom founded in 312 B.C. by Seleucus, a general of Alexander the Great. It included at first nearly the whole of Syria and Babylonia—certainly all the places mentioned in $9^{1,2}$. When Antiochus the Great, one of the Seleucid kings, came to the throne in 223 B.C., Palestine was under the rule of the Ptolemies, kings of Egypt. In 198, however, Antiochus defeated the Egyptians, and Palestine passed into his hands. Hence the preëminence given to Assyria (10^{11}). Hence also the sheep are the Jews whose 'possessors' (the Seleucid sovereigns) 'slay them' (11^5). 'Their own shepherds' (11^5) may be the high priests and ethnarchs (in Jerusalem) of foreign sympathies, who 'pity them not.' In that age there was much intrigue and unrest in Palestine—murder and outrage even in high places were not uncommon ; so that the cutting off of three shepherds in one month would be no unlikely event.

In like manner chs. 12–14 are regarded as consisting of two prophecies (12, 13^{1-6} and 14), both belonging to the Maccabæan age. They may have been written soon after the accession of Antiochus Epiphanes, 175 B.C. The contrast of Judæa with Jerusalem (12^5), and the fact that help to the city comes from the country (12^6), are a likely reflexion of the situation in that age (see Jos. 'Ant.' bk. 12). On the whole, it can hardly be said that modern scholarship has reached a decisive conclusion on this part of Zechariah, though the view that assigns it to a late post-exilic age seems most in accord with the facts of the case.

5. General Characteristics. These chs. (9–14) witness, on the one hand, to a wider contact with the outside heathen world (9^{1-7} 10^{11} 9^{13}, etc.), which tends to universalism (9^1 14^9), and, on the other hand, to an intensely narrow patriotism, whose ideals can only be fulfilled by the direct interposition of God ($12^{3,6,7,9}$) Besides, we find in them the most primitive Messianic hopes—judgment of the nations (9^{1-7} $14^{3,12}$, etc.), advent of Messiah (9^9), deliverance ($9^{11,12}$ 10^{10}), conflict with the heathen ($9^{8,15}$ $14^{3,4}$), final victory over, and conversion of the heathen (14^{13-17}), ceremonial purity ($14^{20,21}$), and God's reign of peace ($14^{5,9}$). Only the true Messiah, our Lord and Saviour Jesus Christ, could have sifted these elements, and brought them into harmony with His great work.

6. Contents of chs. 9–14. 9^1–11^3. God will visit the nations in judgment and His people in mercy. Judah and Ephraim will be restored, and Assyria and Egypt discomfited. 11^{4-17} and 13^{7-9}. The parable of the good shepherds and the foolish shepherd. 12^1–13^6. The deliverance and the coming glory of Jerusalem. **14.** The destruction of the enemies of Jerusalem, and her exaltation as the centre of worship for the world.

CHAPTER 1

LESSONS FROM THE PAST. THE FIRST AND SECOND VISIONS

1–6. The Prophet's message. He calls the people to repentance. **8–17.** The First Vision: The Divine Messengers ever watching over the affairs of the nations. **18–21.** The Second Vision: Hostile nations subdued by divinely-appointed agents.

1. The eighth month] the month Bul (see $1 K 6^{38}$), corresponding to part of October-November. **The second year of Darius**] i.e. 520 B.C. This was the first Darius, son of Hystaspes, who had just succeeded to the Persian throne. Babylonia formed part of his dominions. He found the old decree of Cyrus in the archives of Babylon, permitting the Jews to return and build the Second Temple, and renewed it ($Ezr 6^1$). **The son of Iddo the prophet**] There should be a comma after Iddo. Zechariah was the prophet.

2–6. The people are warned to repent by the fate of their fathers, who suffered exile because they refused to listen to God's word by the earlier prophets.

3. Unto them] i.e. the people. **The LORD of hosts**] a frequent phrase in Zechariah. Probably the original idea was of Jehovah as the leader of Israel's armies, then of sun, moon, and stars, the hosts of heaven, then of angelic

hosts. The title expresses God's supreme power and majesty. **4.** Zechariah evidently knows the works of the earlier prophets: cp. Amos *passim*, Jer 26^5 35^{15}, etc. **5, 6.** Prophets and people alike die, but the Word of God lives anew in every generation, and from the experience of the past appeals to men to shun those errors of their fathers which brought such dire punishment. **Take hold of**] RV 'overtake.'

8–17. THE FIRST VISION: The horseman among the myrtles. The seven visions have one date, viz. the twenty-fourth day of the month **Sebat**, RV 'Shebat' (the name is Babylonish), i.e. part of January and February, 519 B.C. The occasion of the visions is the growing impatience of the returned exiles. They could perceive no sign of God's presence, or of His interest in their labours and difficulties. Haggai had assured them that in 'a little while' God would 'shake the kingdoms' and fill His house with glory ($2^{6,7}$). But time passed and there was no sign of this. The people began to lose faith in God. These visions of Zechariah thus came at a most important crisis. To his countrymen they were a bright panorama of hope, revealing the marvellous providence of God, and His love for His people.

The first vision assures them that God knows every detail of their circumstances. His messengers are ever on the alert, bringing tidings to their King from all parts of the earth.

8. Myrtle trees] rare in Palestine to-day, but once common around Jerusalem: cp. Neh 8^{15}. They have no special significance in the vision. **Bottom**] RM 'shady place.' **Red horses, speckled, and white**] RV horses, 'red, sorrel, and white.' Some take the colours to indicate various countries whence the messenger came, but this is unlikely. **9. O my lord**] addressing the angel of the LORD, who has not yet been mentioned. **10.** The figure is military and suggests horsemen hovering on the flanks of an army—the scouts of God's great host.

11. At rest] probably a lull in the wars of Darius, and so all the more remarkable.

12. One angel speaks from among the myrtle trees, another from beside the prophet. The second asks why in this universal peace Jerusalem alone is unvisited of God. To the nations He sends peace as a sign, to Jerusalem He seems to give no sign. **Threescore and ten years**] in round numbers: cp. Jer 25^{11} 29^{10}. The first captivity took place in 597 B.C.; the final destruction of Jerusalem in 586; Cyrus' decree for return in 537; this prophecy in 519. **14, 15.** Outward condition may be no indication of God's favour. Though the nations are at rest, God is angry with them. They have exceeded their commission in punishing Judah so severely. Though Jerusalem is troubled, yet God is returning with mercies for her. **16. A line**] the measuring line which the builders would use in restoring her ruined streets. **17. Shall yet be spread abroad**] better, 'shall yet overflow with prosperity' (RM), i.e. the cities of Judah: see v. 12. **Zion**] a synonym for Jerusalem; properly the higher of the two spurs on which Jerusalem was built.

18–21. THE SECOND VISION: The four horns and the four smiths. This vision forms a fitting supplement to the first, and describes the destruction of those enemies of Israel (the four horns) who, having been too zealous in punishing her for her sins, are now themselves worthy of punishment.

18. Four horns] Vain efforts have been made to identify these with four nations or races, who at one time or another were Israel's oppressors, e.g. Egypt, Assyria, Babylon, Persia. A more likely suggestion is that 'four' may indicate the whole of Israel's enemies from the four quarters of the globe. But even this seems arbitrary. On 'horns,' as a symbol of military power, see 1 K 22 11.

20. Four carpenters (RV 'smiths')] lit. 'workers' (sc. in iron), as in Isa 44 12. Probably one to deal with each horn. The language is symbolic, and does not necessarily imply the sending of four deliverers. **21. No man did lift up his head**] In the events culminating in the captivity, the people were utterly crushed. **Fray**] an obsolete word meaning 'terrify': cp. Dt 28 26. The root is seen in 'afraid,' i.e. affrayed. But the reading in LXX suggests a Hebrew word meaning 'file down,' which certainly gives a better sense to the whole passage. **Cast out**] RV 'cast down.'

Gentiles] RV 'nations,' and so throughout. The imagery of this vision is somewhat difficult, but the meaning is quite plain, viz. the judgment of those nations who had harried God's people.

CHAPTER 2
THE THIRD VISION

1–5. A young man with a measuring line goes forth to measure Jerusalem preparatory to rebuilding the walls. But an angel is sent to stop him. The population will so increase as to exceed all human expectations, and God will be the city's best defence. **6–9.** The Jews are summoned to leave Babylon, for judgment is to fall upon that city. **10–12.** God's gracious promise to dwell in Jerusalem, to which the nations will come.

1. A man with a measuring line] The vision is probably connected with what, at the time, was really under discussion, viz. the rebuilding of the walls. The Jews felt that they were few in number, and without proper defences. **3, 4.** The interpreting angel stands near the prophet. He goes forth to meet another angel, who asks him to stop this young man in a useless task. The city is destined to have an overflowing population. No walls will be able to contain it. It will stretch forth its houses far out into the surrounding country and seem, not like a walled city, but like a series of country towns packed together.

5. In addition to this reason, the prophet has no faith in warlike fortifications (cp. the subsequent disastrous sieges of Jerusalem by the Syrians and Romans: Jos. 'Wars of Jews,' 1. 6, etc.). God is her best protection. **A wall of fire**] a figure suggested by the watchfires, built round a desert caravan when camping at night, to scare away wild beasts: cp. 1 S 25 16.

6–13. This section forms a poetical prophecy, addressed to the Jews still remaining in Babylon.

6. Land of the north] Babylon. **Spread**] scattered in exile. **7. Deliver thyself, O Zion**] better, 'Ho, escape to Zion.' **8. After the glory**] better, 'after glory,' i.e. to win glory, by bringing judgment on the Babylonians who spoiled Israel. **Me**] the angel is still speaking. **Apple of his eye**] here lit. 'the door of his eye'; elsewhere, 'the daughter,' i.e. the pupil of the eye, which, from its position, importance, and surroundings, is used as an emblem of what is exceedingly precious: cp. Dt 32 10 Ps 17 8, etc. **10.** This prophecy was fulfilled when the Temple was completed and consecrated by Zerubbabel in 516 B.C.

11. Many nations shall be joined to the LORD] better, 'shall join themselves.' This was fulfilled after the coming of Jesus Christ, who also fulfilled the words, 'I will dwell in the midst of thee.' **12. His portion in the holy land**] better, 'his portion shall be upon holy ground,' i.e. in Zion. **13. Be silent**] lit. 'hush!' cp. Hab 2 20. **Is raised up**] better, 'hath roused himself'—said of God when He is about to execute some great purpose. **His holy habitation**] i.e. heaven.

CHAPTER 3
THE FOURTH VISION

Joshua, better known under the later form Jeshua (Ezr 2 2 3 2 Neh 12 7, 8, 10, etc.), was the son of Jehozadak, a member of the priestly order. He returned with the Jews from exile, and was prominently associated with Zerubbabel in the erection of the Second Temple. In 1 Esdras and Ecclus. the name appears simply as 'Jesus.'

1–7. Joshua, the high priest, is seen in a vision standing before the angel of God, accused by the adversary of being unworthy, as the sinful representative of a sinful nation, to stand before God in the holy office of high priest. He is, however, acquitted, purified, and given charge of the Temple. **8–10.** The promise of Messiah and of peace.

1. And he] the interpreting angel.

Satan] The word in the original Hebrew has the definite article, and is thus correctly rendered by RM 'The Adversary.' In OT. it is used first of a human adversary: see 1 S 29⁴ 1 K 11¹⁴. Compare also the angel who appears 'as an adversary' to Balaam (Nu 22³²). Then, in Zechariah and Job, it is used presumably of an angel, who is permitted to accuse men in God's presence. How far this 'adversary' is sanctioned by God, or works in God's service as one jealous for the right, it is difficult to say. In this c. he is reproved by God Himself for showing himself too eager to emphasise the sinful nature of Joshua, the high priest and representative of the nation. In 1 Ch 21¹ the word 'Satan' appears as a proper name, and he is represented as the Tempter, cunning, malicious, and opposed to God.

In this passage of Zechariah the motive we assign to Satan is not of much importance. This is a vision. Its purpose is to encourage the desponding Jews. How could they build and consecrate the Temple of God ? So feeble and sinful they seemed to themselves ; even their best men were polluted: cp. Ezk 22²⁶. By this vision the prophet assures them that their sin is removed, and that Joshua's priesthood is recognised.

At his right hand] the position of a plaintiff in Jewish law courts : see Ps 109⁶. **To resist him**] RV 'to be his adversary,' or accuser—the same word as in Hebrew expresses the noun 'Satan.'

2. Satan is reproved. He would induce God to cast off His people. **A brand plucked out of the fire**] i.e. something precious rescued from destruction : cp. Am 4¹¹. Joshua is the representative of the people who have just been rescued from exile. **3. Filthy garments**] symbolical of sin and unfitness for the pure service of God. Probably the sin here signified was the nation's past idolatry and neglect of the worship of God. **4.** God (and He alone can) changes all this. Israel's sin is taken away : her negligence changed to glorious service. **5. I said**] Here the prophet himself seems to intervene in the vision. But a more probable reading is 'he said.' **A fair mitre**] lit. 'a clean turban.' The root of the word indicates that it was made of a long piece of fine linen wound round and round : see Ex 28³⁶. **7.** God's solemn charge to Joshua. **Judge my house**] i.e. regulate the Temple and its services. **Places to walk**] RV 'a place of access,' probably to intercede with God for the people: Joshua is to have the right of *entrée* at the heavenly court. **Among these that stand by**] the attendant angels.

8. A great Messianic promise. Joshua and his fellow-priests are a sign of God's favour, which will culminate in the appearance of the Branch or Sprout, i.e. the Messiah King. So also on the **stone** (v. 9) with its seven eyes or facets—the stone prepared to be the headstone of the Temple—God will engrave the name of His Messiah, as a token of national sin forgiven. **Men wondered at**] men of omen : or perhaps the meaning is that being priests they could interpret symbols or omens ; consequently they would know what the Branch signified. **Branch**] better, 'Sprout.' The word has no article in Heb. It was well known as a symbol of the Messiah : cp. Isa 4² 11¹ Jer 23⁵ 33¹⁵. The new sprout was to grow from the nearly dead (extinct) stem of David. **9. Seven eyes**] symbolising God's watchful care over His people (see 4¹⁰), guarding them against their enemies. **10. In that day**] perhaps the day of dedicating the new Temple. Then shall there be peace and prosperity. **Call**] invite.

CHAPTER 4

The Fifth Vision

The prophet's thoughts now turn to the civil ruler Zerubbabel. The purpose of the fifth vision is to encourage him in the difficult task of rebuilding the Temple.

1–5, 11–14. The golden candlestick (i.e. the returned exiles) receives its supply of oil (i.e. the divine grace) through two channels ('pipes,' v. 12), viz. the spiritual and the temporal leaders, Joshua and Zerubbabel, through whose united efforts the prosperity of the nation would be accomplished. These are the two olive trees. **6–10** is an encouraging address to Zerubbabel ; weak though he is, yet by the help of God's Holy Spirit he will finish the great work.

1. And waked me] The visions evidently occurred in the night, but so vivid were they that Zechariah seemed to awake. **2. A candlestick all** *of* **gold**] In the first Temple ten candles gave light (1 K 7⁴⁹, but see Ex 25³¹).

Bowl] holding the main supply of oil. From it a pipe flowed to each lamp. RV reads, 'seven pipes to each of the lamps,' but LXX and Vulgate reading, followed in AV, is probably correct. **3.** The lamps are supplied from a perennial and inexhaustible source, viz. **two olive trees.**

6. Zerubbabel] son of Shealtiel, but called in 1 Ch 3¹⁹ son of Pedaiah, was governor ('pehah,' as Haggai calls him) of Judah in the time of Haggai and Zechariah. Shealtiel was a son of Jehoiachin, king of Judah, so that Zerubbabel was of royal blood. He returned from exile, probably in 538 B.C., along with his uncle Sheshbazzar, who was the first governor of Judah after the return. He probably succeeded his uncle as governor some time in 522–520 B.C. He is recognised by Zechariah as the civil head of Jerusalem, and as such is encouraged to proceed with the work of rebuilding the Temple. Of his ultimate fate nothing is known.

6. It is clear that v. 6 does not give the answer to the question asked in v. 4; consequently most modern scholars place the section 10ᵇ–14 after 6ᵃ, thus: 'Then he answered and spoke unto me saying, Those seven, they are the eyes,' etc. This makes a most excellent connexion. The seven lamps are symbols of the eyes of the Lord watching continually. And the question concerning the two olive trees follows naturally.

12. The v. seems to be simply an unnecessary repetition of v. 11, and modern scholars omit it. **14. The two anointed ones**] lit. 'two sons of oil.' These are Joshua and Zerubbabel, priest and king, both anointed, both receiving all their grace and power from God.

6ᵇ–10ᵃ. These vv. come naturally at the end of the completed vision: so scholars place the section after v. 14, and read: 'This *is* the word of the LORD unto Zerubbabel, saying, Not by might, nor by power, but by my Spirit, saith the LORD of hosts,' etc. God's Spirit is sufficient; obstacles apparently insurmountable will disappear. Zerubbabel will bring forth the copestone, and complete the Temple amid joyful acclamations. **7. Grace unto it**] i.e. May God bless it. **10ᵃ.** Scornful doubters shall, by this success, be put to shame. They shall see Zerubbabel moving the plumb-line to test the completed walls.

CHAPTER 5
The Sixth and Seventh Visions

1–4. A flying roll inscribed with curses comes down upon the earth. The previous visions had promised many blessings to the people; and the sixth and seventh teach that wickedness will be removed from the land; for if evil still remained, the blessings would be worthless. The first part of this process consists in the punishment of evildoers. The flying roll signifies the sin of the evildoer coming home to roost.

5–11. The Seventh Vision: A woman (typifying the besetting sins of Israel) is shut up in an ephah-measure, and carried off to the land of Shinar, the detested and sinful place, where she finds a fitting abode.

1. A flying roll] Rolls were of skin or parchment, on which all writing was inscribed. The document was rolled up much in the same way as a wall-map is rolled now. This roll was evidently unfolded, flying like a bird of prey, and seemed of enormous size (v. 2).

2. He] the attendant angel who is God's immediate messenger to Zechariah. **Twenty cubits**] over 30 ft.

3. Earth] RV 'land,' i.e. Palestine. For **every one that stealeth,** etc.] better, perhaps, 'for every thief shall be swept away from hence.' But the expressions are difficult. The exact meaning of the phrase 'on the one side according to it . . on the other side according to it' (RV) is most obscure. LXX renders, 'For every thief shall suffer death.' Some scholars refer the phrases to the roll, which does not seem likely. Others, by a very slight change in the Heb., render, 'For every thief has been too long unpunished, and every (false) swearer has been too long unpunished.' It is probable that there is a reference to certain people who did not subscribe to the rebuilding of the Temple, swearing (falsely) that they had no money.

4. Shall remain] RV 'shall abide,' but better, 'shall roost.' The idea is still of this roll as a huge bird of prey, descending upon the home of the evildoer and utterly consuming it. Zechariah's aim is still to encourage his desponding countrymen. Never again will the nation, as a whole, suffer for sin; only the sinner and his house shall perish.

6. Ephah] the greatest measure among the Jews, a round vessel holding about 7 gals. This vision describes the fulfilment of the promise given in 3⁹. **Resemblance**] A very slight change of one Heb. letter gives the reading, 'This is their transgression in all the land.' This makes much better sense. The prophet is referring to the deep consciousness of sin which weighs upon the people from the high priest downward.

7. A talent of lead] lit. 'a circle or round piece of lead,' the heavy lid of the ephah. The later use of the word is 'talent,' a Jewish weight somewhat over 1 cwt. When the lid was lifted, the woman was disclosed in the ephah. **8. Cast it into**] RV, 'cast her down into.' The woman, typifying the sin of the nation, is thrust down into the ephah and covered with the lid. **9. The wind** was **in their wings**] bore them along like long-winged birds ('storks') on a windy day.

11. Shinar] i.e. Babylonia: see Gn 10¹⁰ 11² Isa 11¹¹. Here regarded as the counterpart of Zion and the proper home of all that is evil, especially of sins such as fraud and false swearing. The vision is remarkable. God not only forgives the sins of His people, but carries them altogether away from their land, that they may deceive them no more. Sin is typified by the figure of a woman; but it is worthy of note that it is through women that the land is purified from its sin.

CHAPTER 6
The Eighth Vision. The Symbolic Crowning

1–8. Four war-chariots, with variously coloured horses, go forth to execute God's judgments against the enemies of oppressed Israel in different parts of the earth. Two, in particular, go northwards, to 'quiet His spirit' (i.e. to satisfy His anger) upon Babylon. **9–15.** Zechariah is commanded to take gold and silver from the Temple offerings, and make a crown for Joshua the high priest. At the same time, the Messiah ('Branch') is again promised. Under Him the Temple will be completed with the help of people from afar, probably returned exiles.

1. It is noteworthy that the first vision showed God's universal providence in mercy (messengers coming from all parts of the earth), the last vision reveals God's universal providence in judgment (war chariots going forth in all directions). **And I turned, and lifted]** RV 'Then again I lifted.' In Heb. to 'turn' and do something is to do it 'again.' **Chariots]** used for military purposes, and also on state occasions, therefore symbolical of power and majesty. They are **four** because they go to the four quarters of the earth.

3. Grisled and bay] lit. 'spotted, vigorous.' It is difficult to explain the two adjectives. The first etymologically means 'spotted as with a hailstorm'; and those who see a significance in the colours of the horses connect hail with the judgment which the fourth chariot carries: cp. Rev 8 [7] 16 [21]. The second adjective has, in reality, no reference to colour (see RM), and some scholars omit it. **Grisled]** = 'grizzled,' 'grey.'

5. The four spirits of the heavens] RV 'winds' (the word for 'wind' in Heb. means also 'spirit,' i.e. breath); but would the prophet speak of winds 'standing before the Lord'? The addition of a single letter in the Heb. gives the following reading: 'These (i.e. the chariots and horses) go forth to the four winds of heaven after they have presented themselves before the Lord.' **6. North country]** Babylonia. **South country]** Egypt. Egypt, like Babylon, was at this time part of the Persian empire, Cambyses having overcome the Egyptians in the battle of Pelusium in 527 B.C. Two of the chariots go **north**, a double doom on Babylon. But some scholars consider that the Heb. words for 'behind them' (RV 'after them') are a corruption for words meaning 'to the east.'

7. Through the earth] as a reserve force to go wherever they may be required, but some scholars read 'to the west.' **Bay]** or 'strong.' Some read 'red,' see RM.

The reading of the vision is somewhat complicated, but its meaning is clear. Jehovah will defend Judah against her enemies, and especially He will deprive Babylon of the power to do her harm.

8. Quieted my spirit in] lit. 'caused my spirit to rest in.' The meaning may be either,

(1) 'brought peace to,' or (2) 'sated my fury by stirring up trouble in.' The historical situation supports the second interpretation. Even while Cambyses was yet alive (in 522 B.C.) the magician Gautama, who pretended to be Smerdis, the brother of Cambyses, had been proclaimed king. Cambyses died of an accidental wound on his way to fight Gautama. The latter was in turn slain by Darius, who ascended the Persian throne in 521. Immediately revolts broke out in all parts of the empire, which were not subdued finally till 514.

9–15. A party of Jews had just come from Babylon. Zechariah is instructed to take part of the silver and gold which they have brought for the Temple, and to make a set of circlets for Joshua, the high priest. Thus he will more fully be a type of One to come, who is both Priest and King to His people.

11. Then take silver] RV 'yea, take of them silver.' **Crowns]** some read 'a crown.'

12, 13. These vv. are somewhat difficult. The simplest way out of the difficulty is to suppose that, after the word **head** in v. 11, the words 'of Zerubbabel and' have accidentally fallen out. This explains the use of the plural 'crowns' in vv. 11, 14, but it does not explain why only one of these rulers is addressed in vv. 12, 13. Many scholars hold that the crown is really for Zerubbabel, the civil ruler, whose name, for political reasons, has been suppressed, and that vv. 12, 13 refer to him, as fulfilling the prophecy of the Branch (see Isa 11 [1]) and completing the Temple. However this may be, the ultimate fulfilment of the prophecy is in Him, through whom we have the far more glorious Temple, 'not made with hands, eternal in the heavens.'

13. And he shall be a priest] RM 'there shall be a priest.' If the preceding clauses refer to Zerubbabel, this would refer to Joshua. We should then have a clear meaning for the following sentence, 'and the counsel of peace shall be between them both,' i.e. these two (Joshua and Zerubbabel) would rule together in harmony. Thus these vv. give the same thought as the vision of the golden candlestick. **14. The crowns** (RV 'crown') are to be laid up in the Temple, as a memorial of the generosity of the deputation which brought the silver and gold. **Helem** should probably be 'Heldai'; **Hen** seems to be a corruption of 'Josiah': see v. 10. **15.** As a sign of the fulfilment of Zechariah's word, more people will come (from Babylon) to assist in completing the Temple. **And this shall come to pass, if]** better, 'and it shall come to pass that if.' The v. breaks off unfinished.

CHAPTER 7

Warnings from the Past

Chs. 7 and 8 go together, and were spoken

on a date (fourth day of the ninth month in the fourth year of Darius) two years later than the series of visions described above, viz. in 518 B.C. (On contemporary events see on 6 8.) They are Zechariah's answer to a question put to him by certain visitors to Jerusalem, who asked whether the fast observed by the Jews in the fifth month, in memory of the destruction of Jerusalem by Nebuchadnezzar, should still be kept. Zechariah says, 'No ; God demands not fasts, but observance of moral laws, by neglecting which your forefathers suffered punishment.' C. 8. God has assuredly come to dwell with His people. The Messianic age is at hand. Fast days will soon become joyful feast days ; and even the heathen will desire to worship with the Jews.

1. In the fourth year of king Darius] 518 B.C. **Chisleu]** or 'Chislev,' corresponds very nearly to December. **2. When they had sent unto the house of God Sherezer]** RV 'now *they* of Beth-el had sent Sherezer.' The v. is difficult. Some scholars suggest the translation : 'Now Bethel, Sharezer, and Regemmelech . . had sent'; or, 'Now Bel-Sharezer sent Regem-melech . . and his men.' This latter is the reading favoured by those who think the deputation came from Babylon. But from what follows it is evident that the deputation was a local one—from Bethel rather than from Babylon. **To pray before the LORD]** RV 'to entreat the favour of God.'

3. Separating myself] The word is the root whence the term 'Nazirite' is derived. The fast involved abstinence from other things besides food and drink: see Lv 16 29, 31.

5. Fifth and seventh *month*] The fasts were four (see 8 19), viz. in the fourth month commemorating the fall of Jerusalem (Jer 39 2 52 6, 7), in the seventh month for the murder of Gedaliah (2 K 25 25), in the tenth month for the commencement of the siege of Jerusalem (Jer 39 1), and specially in the fifth month when the Temple was burned (Jer 52 12-14). But these fasts seemed now out of place. The form remained, but the spirit was gone.

7. Rather than lay stress on these mechanical devices of religious faith, they should study the words spoken by the old prophets, such as Amos and Hosea, before the exile, before the south land was denuded of its inhabitants. **8.** Most scholars omit v. 8 : the sense is preserved. V. 9 tells us what the former prophets said. **9, 10.** Cp. Hos 6 6 Isa 1 16-20 Mic 6 6-8 Jer 5 21-23.

11. Pulled away the shoulder] like an obstinate man refusing to listen to good advice, turning away quickly when a hand is laid upon his shoulder : cp. 'to give the cold shoulder.' **12. Hath sent]** better, 'had sent.' **14.** The prophet wishes to emphasise the truth, that to obey God's word is the supreme

demand of religious life : cp. 1 S 15 22. The rejection of God's message in days gone by brought desolation and exile. The true fast is to abstain from sin, and to listen to the voice of God.

CHAPTER 8
REITERATION OF GOD'S PROMISES CONCERNING JERUSALEM

The whole c. is made up of ten short oracles each introduced by the formula, 'Thus saith the LORD of hosts' (except v. 3). God has come to dwell with His people. Happiness and prosperity are in store for Jerusalem if it will do His will. All nations will seek to join in worshipping God in Jerusalem.

1. Again] RV 'and ' : there is no break in thought between the two chs. **2. I was jealous]** better, 'I am jealous.' The word indicates strong emotion either for or against some object. In this case the context shows it is on behalf of Zion : 'I burn with zeal for the cause of Zion.' **3. A city of truth]** RV 'The city of truth,' i.e. the faithful city : cp. Isa 1 26.

4, 5. A beautiful picture of a peaceful time. Amid so many wars and privations, old men and children had been comparatively rare in the ranks of the returned exiles, and even in the homes of Judæa. **6. If it be]** Although it may seem incredible to the people, it is not impossible to God : cp. Pss 118 23 126 1, 2. **8.** 'They shall be to me for a people ' : cp. Hos 2 23.

9. Prophets] i.e. Haggai and Zechariah, and perhaps others now unknown. The wording of the v. is difficult. What the prophets had said is given at the end, viz. 'The Temple must be rebuilt.' The rebuilding of the Temple has progressed steadily in the two years. The prophet encourages the workers to go on : cp. Hag 2 15-19. **10, 11.** The strife and poverty of the early days, when the building of the Temple was neglected, are contrasted with the peace and prosperity that are to come. **10. Hire]** i.e. wages. **The affliction]** RV 'the adversary,' probably the Samaritans and Ammonites, who plundered the helpless Jews : cp. Ezr 8 22. **12.** Nature also will contribute to the glory of the Messianic age—a frequent feature of Messianic prophecy : cp. Isa 35 1 55 12, 13. **The seed** *shall be* **prosperous]** RV 'there shall be the seed of peace.'

13. A curse among the heathen] a subject of reproach, something of which they spoke evil : see Jer 24 9. **14, 15.** God's promises of punishment were fulfilled ; so surely also will be His promises of blessing.

16, 19. In these vv. the prophet once more answers the question concerning fasts. 'Let them alone,' he says, ' and follow the principles of truth and righteousness, and God shall turn your fast-days into feast-days.' **16. In your**

gates] The gate was the market-place where all business transactions took place : see Ruth 4 1-11. **Execute the judgment of truth and peace**] be fair-minded and peaceable.

20, 23. The gathering in of the nations was never adequately fulfilled in regard to Jerusalem or the Temple then approaching completion ; but the prophecy foretells most strikingly the success of the kingdom of Christ. It was the dream of all Hebrew prophecy : cp. Mic 4 2 Isa 2 3.

23. Ten men] used for a large number : cp. Gn 31 7 Lv 26 26 Neh 4 12. **Take hold of the skirt**] the involuntary action of one who wishes to be listened to : cp. 1 S 15 27 Isa 4 1. How earnestly have men sought salvation ! They find it in Him—a member of the Jewish race—who is the Saviour of the world.

CHAPTER 9
JUDGMENTS ON THE NATIONS. THE PRINCE OF PEACE

1-8. A judgment is about to fall on Damascus, Hamath, Tyre, Sidon, and the cities of the Philistines. A remnant from Philistia will acknowledge God. God will encamp around His sanctuary. **9, 10.** The coming of Messiah and His kingdom of peace. **11-17.** Hope for Israel. God will enable her to contend successfully with Greece. He will aid and bless her.

1. Burden] oracle, or prophecy: see Jer 23 33-40. **In the land**] RV 'upon the land.'

Hadrach] not mentioned elsewhere in the Bible. On the Assyrian tablets it is associated with Damascus, and must have been somewhere in that quarter, in the valley of the Orontes. The various places mentioned follow the course pursued by Alexander the Great in his campaign in 332 B.C., viz. through Syria, Phœnicia, and Philistia. **The rest thereof**] RV 'its' (the prophecy's) 'resting-place.' **When the eyes of man**, etc.] better, 'for the Lord hath an eye upon man (i.e. the heathen) and all the tribes of Israel.' If the prophecy belongs to the beginning of the 2nd cent. B.C. (see Intro.), then the reference is to the kingdom of the Seleucidæ, in whose territories lay all the places mentioned.

2. Hamath] a city in the valley of the Orontes, in Upper Syria. It was renamed Epiphaneia by Antiochus Epiphanes. **Shall border thereby**] RV 'which bordereth thereon.' Tyre (Tyrus) and Sidon were famous cites on the coast of Syria, inhabited by the Phœnicians, who were renowned, like their descendants the Carthaginians, for their cunning. **Though it be very wise**] RV 'she is very wise.' This false wisdom of the world God will visit in judgment. **4. In the sea**] i.e destroy her commerce. **5. Ashkelon**, etc.] cities of the Philistines. After taking Tyre, Alexander marched

down the coast to these cities. He captured Gaza after a two months' siege. **For her expectation shall be ashamed**] i.e. her pride will be humbled.

6. A bastard] probably a son of a mixed race. The idea evidently is that the city would be depopulated by war, and aliens would be installed by the conquerors. **7.** This mixed race will be purified from their idolatry. The second half of this v. might be rendered as follows : 'But there shall be a remnant (i.e. of the Philistines) for our God, and one shall be as a chief in Judah, and Ekron (shall be) as a Jebusite.' **Jebusite**] The Jebusites were the ancient inhabitants of Jerusalem. The word is used for 'a native of Jerusalem.' **8. Because of the army**] RM 'for a guard or garrison.' **Because of him**, etc.] RV 'that none pass through or return.' **Oppressor**] better, perhaps, 'invader' ; the reference is either to Alexander or some similar conqueror. **Have I seen with mine eyes**] viz. the iniquity of the oppressing heathen.

9. The advent of the Prince of Peace, a striking contrast to a ravaging warrior like Alexander the Great, who visited the surrounding nations with fire and sword. **Just, and having salvation**] better, '(declared to be) righteous and victorious.' **Riding upon an ass**] the symbol, not of lowliness, but of peace, as the horse was of war : cp. Mt 21, etc.

10. The chariot .. the horse .. the battle bow] These too-familiar objects will have no place in Messiah's kingdom. He shall speak peace unto the nations. **From sea** *even* **to sea**] from the Dead Sea to the Mediterranean **From the river**] the Euphrates.

11. To the Jews in exile specially does the message of peace come. By that well-known relationship (covenant) with God, sealed by the blood of sacrifices, making them His own adopted people, He will restore them all to their own city (Jerusalem). **By the blood of thy covenant**] the blood sprinkled in the sacrifices whereby the covenant was ratified : cp. Ex 24 8. **Pit**] an empty cistern : cp. Gn 37 22.

12. Strong hold] probably Jerusalem. **Prisoners of hope**] i.e. the Jews, who by their covenant with God had a sure hope of deliverance. **Double**] cp. Isa 61 7 ; evidently a reference to restoration from exile.

13. The prophet again plunges into a vision of war. The vision is figurative ; God is to use Judah as a bow, and fit Ephraim as an arrow to the bow. Some who assign this prophecy to an early date believe that the words **against thy sons, O Greece**, may be a gloss of a later scribe.

Greece] Heb. *Javan*, so called from Javan, a son of Japheth, the supposed ancestor of the Europeans : cp. Gn 10 2, 4. According to Sayce, the word 'Javan' (to indicate 'Greeks') is found in various forms on the monuments both of Egypt and Assyria from a very early date, and is the same word as 'Ionian' (Ιαον). The thought of Greece as a power hostile to Judaism would hardly be possible prior to the Macedonian invasion of Alexander in the 4th cent. B.C. From that age onward, even in Jerusalem itself, the great struggle went on between Judaism and the invading influence of Greek culture. This struggle was specially keen, at the beginning of the 2nd cent. B.C. From a Jewish standpoint the Maccabæan wars were really between Jews and Greeks : cp. Jer 51 20.

14, 15. And subdue with sling stones] RV 'and shall tread down the sling stones'; but the text is obscure. It is a vision of war as a storm in which God is the moving Power : cp. Hab 3 Ps 29. **15**b. By a slight change in the Heb. text we might render, 'And they shall drink blood like wine, and they shall be filled (with it) like bowls, and as the corners of the altar (are filled with the blood of the sacrifices).' **16, 17.** God will save Israel in honour and prosperity. **His goodness**] RM 'prosperity.' The pronoun is uncertain, but the reference is to Israel.

CHAPTER 10
Restoration of God's People

1, 2. A warning to trust in God and not in sorcerers. **3–7.** The Lord will cast out the evil guides of the people, and under new leaders Ephraim and Judah will be victorious. **8–12.** Ephraim will be gathered, but Egypt and Assyria will be humbled.

1. The connexion with 9 17 is very slight, fertility demanding the necessary rain. Some believe that the passage is entirely independent. **The time of the latter rain**] The early rain was in October, when the ground would be broken up for sowing ; the latter rain was in Feb.-March, after the crops had sprung up, and was necessary for an abundant harvest. Even in the season it is wise to ask God for rain. **Bright clouds**] RV 'lightnings.'

2. Idols] 'teraphim,' household images, probably in human form : cp. 1 S 13 16. They were used for purposes of divination, and were probably connected originally with ancestor worship. **They went their way**] RV 'they' (i.e. the people) 'go their way,' as sheep when the pasture fails in one place go on to another.

3–12. The whole passage is difficult. A good conjecture summarises it as follows : God will visit Judah, in whom will arise brave and wise leaders. By their means the lost Ten Tribes (Joseph .. Ephraim, vv. 6, 7), who are still in exile, will have a glorious restoration to Gilead and Lebanon.

3. Shepherds] probably religious teachers are here meant : see Intro. **Punished the**

goats] RV 'will punish the he-goats,' i.e. the false guides of the people : cp. Jer 50 8. **Hath made**] RV 'shall make.' Evidently the word **shepherd**, closing v. 2, suggests an attack on the worthless shepherds, religious teachers, perhaps, of foreign extraction or of foreign sympathies. The he-goats may be ethnarchs or civil rulers in Jerusalem. **4. Out of him**] better, 'from him,' i.e. from Judah. **Came**] better, 'shall come.' **Corner**] i.e. cornerstone. **Nail**] rather, 'tent-peg' : something that will hold firm. **Oppressor**] RV 'ruler,' i.e. one who keeps guard over workmen.

6. House of Joseph] i.e. Israel, as represented by Ephraim and Manasseh, the two leading tribes. **Bring them again**] may refer to the many Israelites in exile in Egypt (v. 10) and elsewhere.

8. I will hiss for them] i.e. whistle to attract them : cp. Isa 5 26. God will bring back Israel to their own land. **9. I will sow them**] As it stands this seems to contradict what follows as well as what goes before. With a slight change of Heb. it is possible to render : 'I scattered them among the nations, but in far countries they remember me. And they will bring up their children and come back.' **10. Assyria**] Asshur might here be used of the Seleucid dominions in Syria and Persia ; see Intro. **11. He**] i.e. Israel. There will be a new exodus for God's people. **Sea with affliction**] better, perhaps, 'the narrow sea,' i.e. the arm of the Red Sea through which, once before, they passed. **The river**] i.e. Nile. **Assyria** and **Egypt** are chosen as representing the great world forces which harassed God's people. **12. Them**] i.e. Israel, to whose glorious restoration the thoughts of the prophet return. **Shall walk up and down in his** (i.e. the LORD's) **name**] LXX renders, 'In His name shall they boast themselves.'

CHAPTER 11
The Parable of the Shepherds

The perplexing nature of the prophecies in this c. renders exposition difficult, especially as we cannot be sure of the circumstances. Apparently, however, the passage deals with misrule in Jerusalem, either of worthless high priests, or of cruel foreign rulers, or of both, who are spoken of as shepherds : see Intro.

1–3. Another storm of war bursts apparently over northern Israel. **4–14.** The people reject their good ruler, and the prophet acts the part of a good shepherd tending the flock and defending it, but is held in contempt by the people. **15–17.** The prophet at God's command assumes the garb and insignia of a worthless shepherd, to signify that God will give them into the hand of a cruel and careless ruler. To this most scholars add, as a continuation, 13 7-9. The bad ruler will speedily perish. Two-thirds or the people will die, but a remnant will be saved.

1. Open thy doors, O Lebanon] Make way for the invaders. **2. Forest of the vintage**] better, 'the impenetrable forest.' **Mighty**] RV 'goodly ones,' i.e. nobles ; but the phrase is doubtful and spoils the whole thought of the passage. Some omit it. **3. The pride of Jordan**] the rank undergrowth where lions had their home : cp. Jer 49 19, where 'swelling' is really 'thickets.'

4. Flock of the slaughter] RV 'flock of slaughter.' i.e. destined or reared for slaughter. This might point to the cruel oppressions and martyrdoms in the times of the Maccabees.

5, 6. According to some views the **possessors** (RM 'buyers') are those ethnarchs and high priests in Jerusalem who were merely puppets of the Seleucid sovereigns. The latter farmed out the high offices to the highest bidder, who in turn oppressed the people by fraud and extortion.

7. The prophet takes up the office of shepherd (cp. Jer 25 1 Ezk 3, 4), but finds his task too difficult. He pities the poor oppressed people, but feels, at the same time, that they are so ignorant of their own good as to be unable to appreciate a beneficent ruler. But see 12 21. **Beauty**] better, ' Favour,' a symbol of God's protecting care. **Bands**] i.e. 'unity,' a symbol of His desire to make peace among the people. **8.** This is an allusion to some event of the time, of which nothing is now known. **9.** The good shepherd leaves the flock. According to a recent view the good shepherd, who in despair abandoned the flock, was Hyrcanus, the son of Joseph (see Jos. 'Ant.' 12. 4), who may have been paid to leave Jerusalem (vv. 12, 13), but at a price so small that he threw it into the treasury in disgust.

10. The prophet declares that God has broken His covenant of mercy with Israel.

People] better, 'nation,' i.e. Israel regarded as tribes. **11. The poor of the flock**] those wretched ones whom the prophet had been trying specially to instruct and help. But perhaps we should read, 'the dealers in the sheep.'

12. The prophet, personating a hired shepherd, asks for his wages, in order to see what value they put upon his services. His hearers insult him by offering him the price of a slave (Ex 21 32). **13. Unto the potter**] better, 'into the treasury' (see RM), by the change of one letter in the Heb. **A goodly price that I was prised at of them**] a sarcastic parenthesis. St. Matthew applies the incident to the case of Judas Iscariot (see Mt 27 9), but refers it to Jeremiah. **14.** The last hope of uniting broken and distracted Israel vanishes. The prophet abandons his task in despair.

15. Instead he will personate a worthless

ruler who will tear and destroy the sheep. According to some this worthless shepherd was Menelaus, a high priest whose rivalry with Jason, also a claimant for the priesthood, brought about the great oppression of the Jews by Antiochus Epiphanes, 171 B.C. In that case the good shepherd in 13 7-9 may refer in the first instance to Jason, who represented the patriotic, as Menelaus represented the foreign, party. Jason, however, was in sympathy with foreign fashions, and he ultimately died in exile. On the other hand, Hyrcanus may be intended. **16. Claws**] RV 'hoofs.' The idea is the cracking of the hoofs of the sheep by being overdriven. **17. Idol**] RV 'worthless.' The word is used of idols, because of their worthlessness : cp. Jn 10 12, 13.

C. 13. **7-9. My fellow**] one who has the same interests. **Smite the shepherd**] cp. 1 K 22 17, and the most fitting application of the words to our Lord (Mt 26 31). The whole section (chs. 11, 13 7-9) would most fittingly apply to the year 171 B.C., when Menelaus, with the aid of Antiochus Epiphanes, king of Syria, usurped the high priesthood in Jerusalem and Jason was expelled. Feuds and bloodshed followed, culminating in a terrible massacre, and the deportation of thousands of Jews by Antiochus. **The third**] i.e. a remnant.

CHAPTER 12
THE DELIVERANCE OF JERUSALEM

Many scholars believe that in chs. 12-14 (omitting 13 7-9) we have a third separate prophecy, the oldest in the book of Zechariah, written subsequent to the death of king Josiah, 609 B.C. (cp. the mourning in the valley of Megiddon, 12 11) but prior to the fall of the kingdom of Judah, 586 B.C. For this view there are some strong arguments—(a) frequent references to the House of David (12 7, 8, 10, 12 13 1) ; (b) Judah and Jerusalem represent the whole nation ; (c) idolatry is rampant (13 2); (d) prophets are in evil repute (13 2-6; cp. Jer 23 9-40) ; (e) Jerusalem is besieged (12 2 14 2; cp. 2 K 24 10 25 1).

Others produce arguments, perhaps more conclusive, in favour of a much later date. On the applicability of the chs. to the times of the Maccabees see Intro.

1-9. The natives gather to the siege of Jerusalem, but are miraculously smitten by the Lord, who comes to her help. Judah, at first taking part with the nations, perceives that God is fighting for Jerusalem, takes the side of the latter, and shares her salvation. **10-14.** A national mourning.

1. Burden] see 9 1. God's omnipotence is the guarantee that this prophecy will be fulfilled. **2. Trembling**] RV 'reeling.' The nations assailing Jerusalem would stagger like a drunken man. The figure is common: cp. Isa 51 17 24 20 Jer 51 7. **Against Judah and against Jerusalem**] This does not make sense; and most scholars, omitting two letters, render, 'Even Judah shall be at the siege of Jerusalem.' But, as no time is known when Judah was actively opposed to Jerusalem, it is simpler to read: 'And there shall be a siege against Jerusalem.' **3.** Those nations that take in hand to capture and rule Jerusalem will find it difficult. Probably the idea is that of raising and carrying a boulder that is too heavy for a man's strength. **4. Every horse of the people**] RV 'peoples,' i.e. nations attacking Jerusalem. The eyes of the Lord will be opened to look favourably upon His people, but their enemies will be blinded.

5, 6. The mutual reliance and helpfulness of Judah and Jerusalem. The victory is to be with Jerusalem, so that Judah may not boast over Jerusalem. The contrast between these two points to a post-exilic date, when the social and economic ideals of the city differed from those of the peasant population.

Jerusalem shall be inhabited again] 100,000 Jews were deported from Jerusalem by Ptolemy, king of Egypt, in 321 B.C.; 80,000 were either killed or carried away captive by Antiochus in 167 B.C. **6, 7.** These vv. would refer more fittingly to the latter period, and the subsequent uprising of the Maccabees: cp. 1 Mac. On the Maccabæan revolt and the causes which led to it see Jos. 'Ant.' 12. 5, 6, and 1 Mac. Judas Maccabæus drove the Syrians from the surrounding country of Judah before attempting to relieve Jerusalem.

8. The angel of the LORD] that led Israel in the wilderness: cp. Ex 23 20.

10. Even repentance comes of the grace of God. **Upon me**] better, 'unto me.' The text is obscure. Some read 'him,' when the reference would be to some unknown martyr in the cause of Jerusalem. **11.** The mourning is likened to some great national lamentation. Some connect it with the worship of Adonis (Tammuz, Ezk 8 14), taking Hadadrimmon as one of the titles of Adonis. Others refer it to a mourning over Ramman, the Assyrian thunder god; others ascribe the mourning to the sacrifice of children to this god; and many take it as the mourning at the death of Josiah, who was slain at Megiddo in the plain of Esdraelon. In any case, the ultimate application of the prophecy to the sufferings and death of Christ is most appropriate.

Megiddon] Elsewhere Megiddo—in central Palestine, the battlefield of Israel. Here fought Barak, Joshua, Saul, and Josiah; here the Jews believed would be the final battlefield of the nations—the Har-Magedon of Rev 16 16. Such a place where so many had been slain might well be a place of mourning.

12-14. Every family apart] indicating the deep personal significance of the mourning. Such had doubtless been the mourning for Josiah, whose death was one of the greatest calamities that could have befallen the Jewish nation. The depth and reality of the mourning is shown by the singling out of certain leading families. **Nathan**] a son of David and Bathsheba. **Levi**] a son of Jacob, and progenitor of the priestly tribe which bears his name. **Shimei**] son of Gershon (Ex 6 17 Nu 3 11). LXX reads, 'the family of Simeon.'

CHAPTER 13
PURIFICATION OF JERUSALEM

Important results follow this great act of national sorrow. **1.** The land is purged of sin; **2ª**, of idols; **2ᵇ–6**, of prophets, who as a class have fallen into disrepute, and who henceforth will be ashamed of their office.

1. The idea of water as a symbol of spiritual cleansing was familiar in Jewish thought: cp. Ezk 36 25 47 1. The Messianic reference is obvious. **2. Idols**] Idolatry was never rampant in Israel after the exile. Those who maintain a post-exilic date for this prophecy refer to the Maccabæan age, when Greek customs and Greek idolatry were common even in Jerusalem (1 Mac 1 54). **The unclean spirit**] which led men to sin. **3.** The office of prophet will be so hateful as to be a dangerous occupation. Prophecy had become utterly distrusted, because it had been degraded by men who spoke smooth things rather than truth.

4. Rough garment] RV 'hairy mantle,' either an untanned sheep-skin, or a cloak of camel's hair, such as the Baptist wore. **5. Man taught me to keep cattle**] better, with slight change in the Heb., 'the ground has been my possession.' I am so occupied with manual labour, I do not cultivate prophecy: cp. Am 7 14. **6. In thine hands**] Heb. 'between thine hands,' probably referring to self-mutilation practised in idolatrous rites: cp. Jer 48 37 1 K 18 28. These wounds, says the accused person, I received when frolicking with my companions.

On vv. 7–9 see at the end of c. 11.

CHAPTER 14
THE JUDGMENT OF THE HEATHEN. EXALTATION OF JERUSALEM

This c. has the appearance of a late work. It has all the general characteristics of the style of literature known to students in the book of Enoch, and popular in the Jewish church about the beginning of the Christian era. The terrible punishment of the heathen (v. 12), and the ceremonial purity of Jerusalem (vv. 20, 21), are typical of the narrower phases of late Judaism.

1, 2. Jerusalem again assaulted and taken.

3-7. The Lord descends to the help of Jerusalem, and strange phenomena follow. 8-21.
Then comes the Messianic age ; the face of
nature is changed ; the heathen are subdued ;
Jerusalem, restored, becomes the centre of
worship, and all therein are consecrated to the
Lord.

1. Lo i a day is coming by the instrumentality
of the LORD, i.e. a judgment day. Thy spoil] The
city is taken and sacked. 2. Cp. Josh 3 2. 3. Shall
the LORD go forth] An apocalyptic vision,
common to later Jewish literature. 4. An
earthquake heralds the presence of the Lord,
cleaving the Mount of Olives in two parts :
cp. Isa 29 6 Ezk 38 19, 20. 5. To the valley of
the mountains] RV 'by the valley of my
mountains.' This text is obscure. Would
.ney flee if God came to help them ? Azal]
RV 'Azel,' has been identified with Beth-ezel
(Mic 1 11), but this is doubtful. Others make
the word an adverb, 'very near.' The earth-
quake] not mentioned in the historical books,
but in Am 1 1. Josephus describes some of its
results ('Ant.' 9. 10. 4). 6. The light shall
not be clear, nor dark] i.e. a murky day. Cp.
the effect of modern volcanic eruptions.
Others render, 'in that day there shall be
neither heat nor cold nor frost.' 7. One day]
i.e. a unique day. At evening time] When
one would expect the deep darkness to settle
down, it will grow clear. The calamities will
have an end.

8. Now begin the blessings of the Messianic
kingdom. Living waters] flowing perennially,
an inestimable blessing in parched Eastern
lands : cp. Isa 35 7 Rev 22 1. Former . . hinder]
RV 'eastern . . western,' i.e. Dead Sea . . Mediterranean. 9. The universality of Messiah's
kingdom : 'the LORD shall be one, and his
name one' (RV). 10. As a plain] RV 'as the
Arabah,' i.e. the great plain which stretched
from the borders of Palestine to the Red
Sea.

Geba] marked the limit of northern Judah
(2 K 23 8). Rimmon] a city in the extreme S.
on the borders of Edom. And it] RV 'and
sne,' i.e. Jerusalem. Inhabited] RV 'shall
dwell.' The idea is that even the surrounding
country would be depressed in order that
Jerusalem might be more conspicuous. Benjamin's gate] on the NW. of the city The
first gate (some render the 'oldest' gate) and

the corner gate were probably in the E. The
tower of Hananeel] RV 'Hananel,' was part of
the Temple castle in the extreme NE. The
site of the king's winepresses is unknown.

11. Utter destruction] RV 'curse,' or 'ban.'
Jerusalem had hitherto seemed under a curse.
Now all this would pass away.

12. The ban in most awful form would turn
rather upon the nations who assail Jerusalem.
Such hatred of the heathen is characteristic of
Jewish apocalypse, and arose in great measure
from the cruelties and indignities suffered by
the Jews in post-exilic times. 13, 14. A
panic will fall on the enemies of Jerusalem,
and all their spoil will be left a prey to the
Jews. But many think that these two vv
should stand nearer the beginning of the c.
If we take v. 15 after v. 12 a much better
sense is secured.

16. Some take this v. as pointing to a late
date, when the Jews of the dispersion went up
to the feasts : cp. the Pilgrim Psalms, especially Ps 122. The feast of tabernacles] was
especially a thanksgiving for the harvest. So
the nations which do not keep that feast at
Jerusalem will be punished by lack of rain
(v. 17), and consequent failure of harvest.

18. That have no rain] RV 'neither shall
it be upon them.' Both phrases are unintelligible. They are due to an attempt w
account for the word not, which is omitted in
LXX. Omitting it the v. runs simply : 'and
if the family of Egypt go not up and come
not, on them shall be the plague,' etc. Egypt
is not dependent on rain. Her punishment
will therefore be plague.

20. Bells] here only in OT. HOLINESS]
RV 'HOLY.' Pots] This seems to refer to
the ash-pans used for receiving the ashes off
the altar : cp. Ex 27 3 38 3 1 K 7 40, 45. These
will be as holy as the bowls, probably the
golden basins used to hold the sacred blood
of the sacrifices in the Temple : cp. Neh 7 70
1 K 7 50 Jer 52 19. 21. Everything in Jerusalem
will be specially consecrated to the Lord.
The idea of ceremonial and outward holiness
is usually considered a feature of later Juda' n.
On the abuse of this idea, cp. Mt 23 25.

The Canaanite] RV 'a Canaanite,' RM
'trafficker,' i.e. any person who is there
simply to make money by trading rather
than to worship : cp. Mt 21 12-14.

MALACHI

INTRODUCTION

1. Author. Of the author of this book nothing is known apart from the book itself. Even the name 'Malachi' is not in reality a proper name at all, but a common noun with the possessive pronoun of the first pers. sing. appended, signifying 'My Messenger.' It has indeed been supposed that the word is a contraction of *Malachijah* ('Messenger of Jehovah'), but it is improbable that any man ever bore such a name. The oldest Jewish tradition, though without adequate reason, identifies the author of this book with 'Ezra the Scribe,' understanding the word 'Malachi' as an honourable title conferred by Jehovah upon His prophet: cp. Hag 1 13 Mal 2 7.

The headings of the various sections of the prophetical books generally bear evidence of being the work of later editors, and it is probable that Mal 1 1 is from the same hand as Zech 9 1 12 1. Since the most striking prophecy in this book is that in 3 1 (cp. Mt 11 10 Mk 1 2 Lk 1 76), it is not improbable that the book, being anonymous, came to be known as 'The prophecy of "My Messenger" (*Malachi*),' whence the idea arose that 'Malachi' was a proper name.

2. Date. The date of this book may be partly inferred from the fact that the head of the Jewish state is termed 'governor' (1 8, cp. Hag 1 1 Neh 2 7, 9), the title 'King' being used of Jehovah (1 14), as in the post-exilic Psalms. The only political event referred to is the devastation of Edom, the enemy of Israel (1 3, 4), which is adduced as a proof of Jehovah's love for His people. There is reason to suppose that 'the day of Jerusalem' (Ps 137 7) is not the destruction of Jerusalem by Nebuchadnezzar, but the disaster referred to in Neh 1 3, when, the jealousy of the neighbouring peoples having been aroused by an attempt to rebuild the walls of Jerusalem, an attack had been made on the city (Ezr 4 23), in which the Edomites had particularly displayed their animosity. Malachi (as we may call the prophet) would thus be a contemporary of Nehemiah's, an inference which is confirmed by the substance of his book, which is directed against the same evils that Nehemiah tried to reform.

It is probable that the law-book of Malachi comprised only Deuteronomy and the combined work of the Jehovist and Elohist, the Priestly Code having not yet been published in Palestine. From this it may be inferred that Malachi prophesied before the second visit of Nehemiah in 433 B.C. In this case the general depression which he represents as due to the apparent failure of Jehovah to vindicate the right may be easily accounted for by the disappointment which the godly in Jerusalem experienced when the first reforms of Nehemiah and Ezra proved abortive.

3. Form and Style. Although the book of Malachi evidently had originally a literary form, it is, to Western ideas at least, faulty in arrangement, and it has not improbably suffered somewhat in transmission. The prophet seems to state ideas as they occur to him, paying little or no attention to their logical sequence. Thus we should have expected that the section 3 7-12 would follow 1 14, while 3 13-4 3 is parallel to 2 17-3 6. In its style the book is peculiar. It is more argumentative than any other book of the OT., the arguments being developed by a series of imaginary objections brought against the prophet's assertion.

4. Readers. The people addressed throughout the book are professedly religious people, who, it would seem, are divided into two classes : (1) the sincerely religious, who have lost heart through the prevailing wickedness, and are beginning to question Jehovah's goodness ; (2) the worldly and covetous, who are religious only in name.

5. Contents. The argument of the book may be briefly stated as follows : Jehovah, in punishing the malicious enemy of Israel, has vindicated His claim to be the lover of Israel (1 2-5) ; but He is not treated by Israel with the respect due either to a father or to a master (1 6). In particular, the priests perform their ministrations with slovenly indifference ; the victims offered are a disgrace to the altar ; and it would be better to omit the sacrifices altogether (1 6-10) ; Jehovah does not need the ministrations of Israel, for even among the Gentiles throughout the world He has those who serve Him (1 11) ; let it be recognised that Jehovah is a great King, and will not accept a paltry offering (1 12-14) ; the priests must repent, or punishment will overtake them (2 1-3) ; Jehovah has made a covenant with Levi, and appointed him His messenger to the people (2 4-7) ; but Levi has abused his privilege, and distorted Jehovah's teaching, and lost the respect of the people (2 8, 9) ; the laity, too, have sinned in that they show lack of brotherly love (2 10), and are contaminated by the heathen (2 11), for which sin they will be punished (2 12) ; their prayers are vain, for they come to the altar with the sin of divorce upon them (2 13-16) ; Jehovah has, moreover, been wronged by the people's lack of faith (2 17) ; He has not forgotten, and will come as the prophets have said (3 1) ; but the day of His coming will be a time of crisis, and will overwhelm the sinners (3 2-6) ; let the people show their repentance by the payment of their tithes, and they will at once find a blessing (3 7-12) ; Jehovah has been charged with faithlessness, but He has not forgotten, and His Day will make manifest the difference between those who obey Him and those who disregard Him (3 13-4 2), when the former shall triumph over the latter (4 3) ; let the Law of Moses be had in remembrance (4 4), and let heed be given to the prophet who will come in this crisis as Elijah came of old (4 5) ; thus will the divisions which now break up families be healed, otherwise a curse will come upon the land (4 6).

6. Teaching. There is no Messianic prophecy in Malachi in the ordinary meaning of the word. Malachi does not look for a king upon the throne of David to deliver Israel, but for the restoration of that communion with Jehovah which existed when Jehovah led His people in a pillar of cloud by day and of fire by night.

In his theology Malachi is one of the most advanced thinkers of the OT., albeit he does not entirely free himself from OT. limitations. He not only recognises Jehovah as universal God, but recognises that the worship which the heathen perform, so far as it is sincere, is the worship of Jehovah. He lays stress also upon personal religion, and represents Jehovah not only as Father of the nation (2 10). but as showing in a special sense a fatherly care of the righteous (3 17). He is convinced that 'God is His own Interpreter, and He will make it plain.' He develops the teaching of Deuteronomy in a striking way, dwelling upon the necessity alike of the written Scripture and the spoken word, taking Moses as typical of the one, and Elijah of the other.

It is characteristic of Malachi's teaching as a whole, that it lays stress on the weightier matters of the law, judgment and mercy and faith, coupled with due reverence and devotion in the external expression of religion. It finds therefore its fulfilment, its completion, in the teaching of the greatest Prophet since the world began, who said, 'These ought ye to have done, and not to leave the other undone.'

CHAPTER 1
JEHOVAH'S LOVE AND HIS PEOPLE'S INGRATITUDE

1. Burden] RM 'oracle' ; properly, 'that which is lifted up,' hence in this connexion 'utterance' ; but with play on other meaning 'burden' in Jer 23 33 (RM). **2. Wherein hast thou loved us ?**] i.e. 'Wherein hast thou shewn thy love ?' So in v. 3, **I hated Esau** means 'I have shewn myself hostile to Esau.' 'Esau' and 'Jacob' here stand for the nations Edom and Israel, not for the patriarchs. **3.** The desolation of Edom here referred to had been already adduced by an unknown prophet (Isa 63) as a proof of Jehovah's care for Israel. Edom was devastated by an invasion of Arabs who for more than a century had been pressing into Palestine : cp. Ezk 25 4, 5, 10. **Dragons**] RV 'jackals.' **4. We are impoverished**] RV 'we are beaten down.' The text is somewhat uncertain : cp. Isa 9 10. **Thus saith the LORD**] In Heb. 'to think' is often represented by the verb 'to say.' A Hebrew does not hesitate to represent what he believes to be true, and therefore the 'thought' of Jehovah, as 'spoken' by Jehovah. In such a phrase there is no idea of a revelation by vision. **5. The LORD will be** (RV 'be') **magnified**] The Heb. may express either a prayer, as in Ps 40 16, or a statement. Here the meaning is probably that Jehovah habitually manifests His greatness.

From (more literally 'above') **the border**] Jehovah's activity is not confined to Jerusalem.

6. The priests especially stand to Jehovah in the relation of sons and servants.

7. Polluted] i.e. not actually unclean, but worthless, common : cp. Ezr 2 62. **Bread**] sacrificial offerings generally : cp. Lv 21 6. **Table**] the altar, not merely the table of shewbread.

8. Cp. Dt 15 21 17 1 Lv 22 20 f. **Blind . . lame . . sick**] i.e. animals unlawful for sacrifice.

It is **not evil ?**] RV 'it is no evil !' **Governor**] Heb. *Peḥā*. The term is applied to Zerubbabel (Hag 1 1, 14). It is impossible to say whether Malachi has a Jewish or Persian governor in view. **Accept thy person**] more correctly, 'favour thee.' **9. This hath been,** etc.] Translate the latter part of this verse partly corrected from LXX : 'When this hath been done by you, shall I accept,' etc.

10. RV 'Oh that there were one among you that would shut the doors, that ye might not kindle *fire on* mine altar in vain !' i.e. Sacrifices so offered are worthless ; better to let the altar fire go out and abstain from sacrifice.

11. *Shall be* (RV 'is') **great**] Jehovah does not need the worthless worship of lip-serving Jews, for even among the Gentiles, who are accounted heathen, He has those who worship Him : cp. Ac 10 34, 35. **Incense** *shall be* (RV 'is') **offered**] The sacrifices of the Gentiles when offered with sincere devotion, are offered to Jehovah's 'name': cp. Ac 17 23. **14.** Cp. Lv 22 19, 20. The title 'King' is applied to Jehovah in post-exilic writings composed when the Jews had not an earthly king.

Dreadful] RV 'terrible'; better, 'had in reverence.'

CHAPTER 2

THE DEGENERACY OF THE PRIESTHOOD

1. A reminder to the priests that they are to blame for the laxity denounced in 1 13, 14. They are responsible for the offering of fit victims, which in some cases it was their duty to provide.

3. I will corrupt your seed] RV 'I will rebuke the seed for your sake'; but the threat of a curse on the *crops* does not appear to be specially applicable to the *priests*. A very slight change in the Heb. which has been suggested, gives the admirable sense, 'I will cut off your arm' (cp. 1 S 2 31); i.e. I will make you powerless: cp. Ps 37 17.

The dung of your solemn feasts (RV 'sacrifices')] the offal of the animals slain for sacrifices, which at the three great feasts of the year would be very numerous, and a source of great gain to the priests.

The words rendered **upon your faces** do not necessarily mean more than 'in your presence.' To scatter offal and filth in a person's presence would be an insult to him: cp. Dt 23 14. Malachi seems to mean that the fastidious priests, who now hold aloof while the Temple servants clear away the offal of the sacrifices, will no longer meet with outward respect from the people who even now despise them (2 9), and who will treat them with less reverence than the humblest of Temple servants. The last words of the v. are obscure and possibly corrupt. They perhaps mean, 'You shall be taken away from your place of honour in the Temple to the place where the offal is taken.'

4. Cp. v. 1. This charge is given to the priests that they may repent, and that so the covenant with Levi may be confirmed to them. **5.** Lit. 'My covenant was with him; the life and the peace I gave unto him; fear and he feared me.' **6.** Cp. the ideal priesthood described in Dt 33 8-11. **7.** To Malachi, as to Haggai (2 11), the **law** is not yet completely crystallised into a book, but means the priests' decisions on points submitted to them. **Messenger**] cp. Hag 1 13. **8. Ye have caused many to stumble**] i.e. by giving unjust decisions the priests have brought many to ruin. With the charge of partiality in v. 9 contrast the ideal of Dt 33 9, where it is represented as a priest's duty to give his decisions without regard to his nearest relatives: cp. Mt 10 37. **9.** Cp. the whole section, 1 S 2 28-36, which was probably written about this period.

10. Malachi seems to have in view mainly such evils as are described in Neh 5. His argument here seems somewhat inconsistent with his argument in 1 2 f., since one God had created both Esau and Jacob; but it is an inconsistency natural enough in the as yet undeveloped teaching. A man must learn to love his brother before he can love his enemy.

11. The mention of **Israel** is quite out of place in this v. The word has probably arisen by a scribe's blunder from **Jerusalem**, which it somewhat resembles in Hebrew. **The daughter of a strange god** must mean either a foreign nation with which Judah has entered into some compact, whether political or religious (by which some alliance or understanding with the Samaritans might be intended); or the text must be corrected by the insertion of one letter, so that for 'daughter' we should read 'daughters.' In either case Malachi denounces the tendency of his people to fuse with the neighbouring nations. **12. The master and the scholar**] RV 'him that waketh and him that answereth.' A very slight change in the Hebrew gives the better antithesis, 'plaintiff and defendant;' two opposites being frequently used in Hebrew to denote all. Cp. 'going out and coming in,' etc. **Tabernacles**] better, 'homes.' **13. Insomuch that he regardeth**] better, 'because he regardeth.' The people are regarded as covering the altar with their tears in the intensity of their desire for the favours He is withholding.

14. The wife of thy youth] i.e. the wife married in youth. The evil here denounced is the divorce of an old wife in favour of a younger woman. **The wife of thy covenant**] The thought that there is a solemn compact between husband and wife is stated definitely here only in the OT.; but it is the natural inference from the representation of Israel as Jehovah's wife, for though Israel was false to Jehovah, He remained faithful. **15.** The text, as it stands, is unintelligible. A simple correction has been suggested, which gives the following sense: 'Did not one (God) make and continue life to us? And what does the one (God) seek? A sacred seed. Therefore take heed to your life, and deal not treacherously against the wife of thy youth': i.e. **One God** (cp. 2 10) has created a life to which He has given continuance through marriage. The object of marriage—God's object in its institution—is to obtain children, 'seed of God.' When children are born, the object of marriage is attained. Therefore let not a man put away his wife, because she has grown old and lost her attraction. **16. Putting away**] i.e. divorce. **Covereth violence with his garment**] The reference is probably to the illtreatment of the wife; but the Hebrew is obscure.

17. An address to those who are losing faith through their inability to solve the riddle of the prosperity of the ungodly: cp. Pss 37, 73.

CHAPTER 3
The Speedy Judgment

1. This v. is closely connected with the preceding. It is the answer to the question, 'Where is the God of judgment?' The **messenger** is evidently a prophet or a succession of prophets: cp. Dt 18 9-22. The phrase **he shall prepare the way before me** is probably borrowed from Isa 40 3-5, where the thought is that a highway must be prepared on which 'the Glory of the Lord' may lead Israel to the land of Canaan. Zechariah (8 3) had promised that Jehovah would come to His Temple. The promise in Malachi's days had not yet been fulfilled, but Jehovah would 'hasten it in its time.' **2.** Malachi shows himself here a true son of the older prophets. Jehovah cannot ignore sin; **the day of his coming** must therefore be a day of judgment: cp. Am 5 18-20 Isa 33 14-16. **3. He shall purify the sons of Levi**] The judgment will begin at the house of God. **4.** Malachi, like other late OT. writers, here idealises the past: cp. 2 5 1 K 4 20, 21.

6. I change not] better, 'I have not changed.' The **therefore** in the following clause is wrong: the Heb. has 'but you' (emphatic) 'are not consumed.' As this yields no antithesis, it is not improbable that there is a corruption in the text. The argument seems to be, 'I have not changed, but you have not kept your part of the covenant; you have not performed my words.' **7.** Cp. Zech 1 2 f.

9. Cp. Neh 13 10 f.

11. The devourer] i.e. locusts: cp. Joel 1 4 Am 4 2.

13. The godly are here addressed, and in their lack of faith are reminded that 'the Lord is mindful of His own.' **14.** Cp. Ps 73 13 Isa 58 3. **16.** The change from direct address to narrative utterly spoils the connexion. LXX gives, 'This' (i.e. the complaint of vv. 14, 15) 'have they spoken who fear the Lord; and the Lord hath hearkened, and heard it, and a book of remembrance hath been written before Him concerning those that fear the Lord,' etc.

17. In that day when I make up my jewels] RV 'in the day that I do make, even a peculiar treasure': better, 'in the day that I shew myself active' (so in 4 3), 'even a peculiar possession.' For the last words cp. Dt 7 6 14 2 26 18.

18. Malachi here treats the prosperity of the ungodly with more freedom than some of the OT. writers. He does not deny it, nor does he affirm that it is illusory or transitory, but that it cannot abide the crisis of 'the Day of the Lord.' **Ye**] the murmurers; those who were disturbed by the prosperity of the wicked (2 17).

CHAPTER 4
The New Elijah

1. The comparison is to an oven heated by a fire lighted within it: cp. Mt 6 30. This passage is closely connected with the preceding. **Stubble**] rather, 'straw.'

2. 'The day of the Lord is darkness and not light' (Am 5 20), but when the night of judgment is over, day dawns for the righteous.

The Sun of righteousness] 'Righteousness' is here almost equivalent to 'blessing,' as in Ps 24 5.

With healing in his wings] Since the dawn spreads with rapidity from the E. over the world (Job 38 12-14), it is said poetically to have wings (Ps 139 9). With the dawn of the new era there will be **healing**. It will be a 'time of restoration of all things.' **Grow up** (RV 'gambol') **as calves of the stall**] better, 'trample down like stall-fed oxen,' i.e. the most heavily treading animals with which Malachi was acquainted. **3.** The men of Malachi's generation have not yet been taught to pray for those that despitefully use them and persecute them. **They shall be ashes**] i.e. the righteous shall trample on the ungodly as on the ash-heaps outside their homes.

5. The history of Israel has already, to a great extent, become Scripture, and Elijah is a type for all time. Malachi's meaning would be clearer if we were to translate, with a slight concession to English idiom, 'I will send you a prophet Elijah': cp. 'a Daniel come to judgment.' It is in this sense that our Lord understood it: cp. Mt 11 14 17 11, 12, and also Lk 1 17. The fact that our Lord declared John the Baptist to be a fulfilment of this prophecy would alone be sufficient to entitle Malachi to a place among the goodly fellowship of the prophets. But Malachi's claim to Christian reverence is not exhausted by this one fulfilment of his words. Though John the Baptist was the last and greatest Elijah before that great 'Day of the Lord,' when 'the Word was made flesh,' there had been other fulfilments of Malachi's words before his time, as there have been since. Whenever 'the old order changes, giving place to new,' God sends the world an Elijah. The Old Testament is not made obsolete by the New, for the gospel is the continuation and the interpretation of prophecy.

6. A time of reform is a time of dissension: cp. Lk 12 51-53. The dissensions can only be healed by giving heed to God's teaching.

ST. MATTHEW

INTRODUCTION

1. The word Gospel. ' Gospel ' (lit. ' God story,' i.e. story about God) is the usual English translation of *euaggelion*, lit. ' good tidings,' which in the NT. always means the good tidings of salvation as preached by our Lord Himself (Mt 4 23 9 35), or by the apostles and other Christian teachers (e.g. 24 14 26 13 Ac 15 7, also Ro 2 16, where ' my gospel ' means ' the gospel message as preached by me '). Not till the 2nd cent., apparently, did it come to mean a written biography of Christ, though the way for this use had already been prepared by the title of St. Mark's Gospel, ' The beginning of the Gospel of Jesus Christ [the Son of God] ' (Mk 1 1).

2. The Gospels in general. Only four Gospels having any claim to historical authority have been transmitted to us, those of SS. Matthew, Mark, Luke, and John. There were numerous earlier ones (Lk 1 1) of which our evangelists have made full use, but the appearance of their far superior narratives rendered the earlier efforts comparatively useless, and they soon ceased to be copied. All that is known or can be probably conjectured about them is stated in the special article, ' The Synoptic Problem.' Numerous Gospels, generally called ' apocryphal,' were written later than the canonical four, but of these even the earliest, such as ' the Gospel according to the Hebrews ' (circ. 100 A.D.), and ' the Gospel of Peter ' (circ. 100–150 A.D.), are so obviously contaminated by fiction, that it is impossible to feel sure that any of the facts or sayings therein recorded (except those borrowed from our Gospels) are authentic.

The first three canonical Gospels (Mt, Mk, Lk) are generally called ' synoptic,' and their authors ' synoptists,' because they all present the same general view of our Lord's ministry. For the most part they record the same incidents, in the same order, in the same (or closely similar) words, and from the same point of view. To all of them Jesus is the promised Messiah of the Jews, and also the Saviour and Redeemer of all mankind ; He is true man, but He is also the superhuman Son of God, who perfectly knows and reveals the Father, who atones for sin by His death, and by His resurrection is exalted to almighty power over the universe. But the main interest of the writers is biographical, not theological. Their aim is to place before the reader a vivid picture of the historical Jesus of Nazareth ' in fashion as He lived,' going about doing good, teaching, healing, comforting, advising, guiding, rebuking, blessing, and drawing all men to Himself by the strong cords of admiration and love. Special objects in writing each evangelist doubtless had. St. Matthew, writing for the Jews, though not perhaps exclusively for them, presents our Lord's claims to the throne of David, and expounds fully His attitude towards the Law ; St. Mark, writing for the Romans, carefully explains for their benefit the Jewish customs and observances which were so unintelligible to Gentiles ; St. Luke, writing as St. Paul's interpreter, desires particularly to make it plain that in Christ there is neither Jew nor Greek, bond nor free, male nor female, that the poorest and humblest most easily enter God's kingdom, that the good Creator desires to save every soul which He has made, and that accordingly there is hope for the most careless of prodigals and the most abandoned of sinners. But the main aim of each synoptic writer is just the simple one of placing before the reader vividly the gracious personality of Jesus Christ, and letting it make its own appeal to the heart and understanding.

The aim of the fourth evangelist is different. Writing after the rise of heresy, he aims definitely at establishing the true doctrine of the person of Christ. Sayings and incidents are selected not for their biographical interest, but for their doctrinal importance as illustrating various aspects of the Incarnation of the Divine Son of God. The Gospel is, in fact, a sermon on the text ' And the Word was made flesh, and dwelt among us ' (Jn 1 14). Unlike the synoptists St. John is an allegorist, and expects the reader to detect a hidden spiritual meaning beneath the letter of his narrative. Assuming the synoptists to be well known, he omits for the most part the events and sayings which they record, and thus his Gospel forms a supplement—and one of priceless worth—to the synoptic record. Taken all together, the four Gospels give an adequate and harmonious picture of the God-Man, the synoptists delineating mainly His Humanity, and St. John His Deity. As an old writer (St. Irenæus, 177 A.D.) well says : ' The Word, who was manifested to men, has given us the gospel under four aspects, but bound together by one Spirit.'

3. Life of St. Matthew.

St. Matthew, the reputed author of the first Gospel, was a customs house officer. His business was to collect the tolls levied on the merchandise that passed through the dominions of Herod Antipas, tetrarch of Galilee and Perea. He was stationed at Capernaum, on an important caravan route leading to Damascus. Though probably not in the employ of the hated Romans, but of Herod Antipas, he belonged to a despised class. 'Publicans,' that is, collectors of taxes or tolls, were ostracised socially, and though not exactly excommunicated by the synagogue, were treated as 'sinners,' i.e. abandoned and irreligious persons. It required no small courage on the part of the new Teacher to choose as one of His inner circle of disciples a despised publican. Our Lord's object was probably to obtain influence among the class of religious and social outcasts. The call of Matthew was fully justified by its results. It brought Jesus into direct and fruitful contact with a class of persons for whose spiritual welfare none of the orthodox religious authorities had the least concern. The feast which St. Matthew made to celebrate his call was attended by a great multitude of publicans and sinners, and gave Jesus an opportunity of speaking to them of the things pertaining to the kingdom of God (Lk 5 29 f.).

St. Matthew's profession was a comparatively lucrative one (cp. Lk 19 2), so that it cost him something to 'forsake all' and follow Jesus (Lk 5 28). When the call took place, he had probably been a disciple for some time, as was the case with the other apostles. His original name was Levi, and to this, on the occasion of his call, was added the surname Matthew, i.e. 'gift of God,' by which he was generally known in Christian circles : cp. Mk 2 14 and Lk 5 27 with Mt 9 9.

According to the oldest traditions, he preached for fifteen years in Judæa and then visited Ethiopia, Persia, Media, and Parthia. His death seems to have been natural, though later authorities make him a martyr. He is commemorated by the church on Sept. 21st.

4. Composition and Authorship of the Gospel.

The first Gospel, though compiled from various sources, is a literary unity, the work of a single writer. This is shown by the occurrence of various characteristic phrases, not in certain sections only. but throughout the work. Thus the phrase 'the kingdom of heaven,' which is found in St. Matthew alone, occurs 14 times in sections which are peculiar to St. Matthew, and 18 times in sections which are common to him and St. Luke or St. Mark. Also the peculiar phrase 'that it might be fulfilled which was spoken by the prophet,' which occurs nowhere else in the NT., occurs in nearly every part of the first Gospel : see

1 22 2 15, 17, 23 4 14 8 17 12 17 13 35 21 4, [26 56] [27 9] [27 35]. It is plain, therefore, that the same compiler has worked over the whole of the book, and given it such unity as it possesses.

The author's sources were somewhat numerous, and several of them can still be clearly distinguished. His principal authority for narrative was St. Mark's Gospel, which he probably possessed in its complete form, in which it contained an account of an appearance of the risen Lord in Galilee : see Mk 16 7. He evidently wrote with this Gospel before him, making it the basis of his work, and inserting his additional matter, gained from other sources, at appropriate intervals, but very seldom departing from its order. In transcribing St. Mark, he reproduced his words with considerable exactness, but usually abridged them, generally only slightly, but sometimes very considerably. For example, St. Mark's account of the Gadarene demoniac runs to 20 vv., while St. Matthew's has only 7 vv. He seldom adds anything of importance to St. Mark's narrative. The chief exceptions are the account of the Temptation, where he adds important details from another source (4 1-11), that of the walking on the sea, where he adds the incident of Peter descending from the ship (14 22-33), and that of the confession of Peter at Cæsarea Philippi, which is described much more fully (16 13 f.). Altogether, St. Matthew has about 470 vv. out of a total of 1,068 vv. parallel to St. Mark, that is, he borrows nearly half his Gospel from St. Mark.

Another source (or sources) is indicated by the large amount of matter which St. Matthew has in common with St. Luke. A complete list of these correspondences, amounting in all to about 200 vv., or nearly one-fifth of the Gospel, has already been given (see art. 'The Synoptic Problem'), and the reader is requested to refer to it. He will find that in at least two-thirds of the cases, the subject-matter (which consists mainly of discourses and sayings) has been placed differently by the two evangelists, and that the variations of phraseology are also very considerable. This suggests that not more than one-third (if so much) of the correspondences between St. Matthew and St. Luke are due to the use of a common document, and that, for the most part, they used different sources. Our evangelist's main source for discourses seems to have been a document (called 'the Logia') in which our Lord's sayings were collected in masses according to subject-matter ; but the sources of the discourses in St. Luke seem to have been documents in which our Lord's sayings were preserved in their proper historical connexion. There is no sufficient evidence to show that our evangelist grouped together in his Gospel sayings that were separate in his sources, but rather the contrary, for he several times expresses his conviction that the great groups of sayings, which St. Luke separates, were delivered at one time and place, and this he would hardly have done if his sources had recorded them in widely-separated contexts: see especially 7 28 11 1 13 53 19 1 26 1.

A third group of sources is indicated by the matter peculiar to St. Matthew. This amounts to about 400 vv., and consists of the following sections :—

1 1-17.	Genealogy of Jesus.
1 18-25.	The Nativity.
2 1-18.	The Magi ; the massacre of the Innocents.
2 19-23.	Flight into Egypt.
3 14, 15.	St. John's scruple about baptising Jesus.
4 12-16.	Isaiah's prophecy fulfilled (Isa 9 1, 2).
4 23, 24.	Tours in Galilee.
5, 6, 7.	Much of the Sermon on the Mount.
9 27.	The two blind men.
10.	About 8 vv. of the charge to the Twelve.
11 28-30.	' Come unto me, all ye that labour.'
12 5.	The priests profane the sabbath and are blameless.
12 17-23.	Isaiah 42 1 fulfilled.
12 36, 37.	Every idle word.
13 14, 15.	Fulfilment of Isa 6 9.
13 24-30.	Parable of the tares.
13 35.	Fulfilment of Ps 78 2.
13 36-43.	Interpretation of the parable of the tares.
13 44.	Parable of the hid treasure.
13 45, 46.	Parable of the pearl-merchant.
13 47-51.	Parable of the net.
13 52, 53.	' Every scribe which is instructed.'
14 28-33.	Peter walks on the waves.
15 12-15 (in part).	' Every plant which my heavenly Father.'
15 23-25.	' I am not sent but unto the lost sheep.'
15 28-31.	Many are healed.
16 11, 12.	The leaven of the Pharisees and Sadducees (but cp. Mk 8 15).
16 17-19.	' Blessed art thou, Simon Barjona.'
17 24-27.	The stater found in the fish's mouth.
18 4, 7, 10, 11, 14.	Sayings about children.
18 15-20.	' If thy brother shall trespass.'
18 21-35.	' Lord, how oft shall my brother sin against me ?'
19 10-12.	Celibacy for the kingdom of heaven's sake.
20 1-16.	Parable of labourers in the vineyard.
21 4, 5.	Fulfilment of Isa 62 11 Zech 9 9.
21 10, 11.	Astonishment of Jerusalem at the triumphal entry.
21 14.	The blind and lame healed in the Temple.
21 15, 16.	The children cry ' Hosanna ' in the Temple.
21 28-32.	Parable of the two sons.
21 43.	' The kingdom of God shall be taken from you.'
22 1-14.	Parable of the marriage of the king's son (the wedding garment).
23 1-5, 8-10, 14-22, 24-33.	Woes pronounced on scribes and Pharisees.
24 11.	' Many false prophets shall rise.'
24 12.	' The love of many shall wax cold.'
24 30.	The sign of the Son of Man in heaven.
25 1-13.	Parable of the ten virgins.
25 14-30.	Parable of the talents (yet cp. St. Luke's parable of the pounds, Lk 19 12-27).
25 31-46.	Parable of the sheep and the goats.
26 25.	Judas asks, ' Master, is it I ?'
26 52.	' Put up again thy sword.'
26 53, 54.	' Thinkest thou that I cannot now pray to my Father ?'
27 3-10.	Remorse, suicide, and burial of Judas.
27 19.	Pilate's wife.
27 24, 25.	Pilate washes his hands.
27 51-53.	Earthquake, opening of tombs, and resurrection of saints.
27 62-66.	The tomb sealed, and a watch set.
28 2-4.	A great earthquake. An angel bright as lightning rolls away the stone, and terrifies the guards.
28 9-10.	Jesus appears to the women.
28 11-15.	The guards report to the chief priests, who spread a false report.
28 16-20.	Appearance on a mountain in Galilee.

Of this peculiar matter we may assign to the ' logia ' most of the discourses and sayings, which include parts of the Sermon on the Mount, of the charge to the Twelve, of the denunciations of the Pharisees ; also the parables of the tares, the hid treasure, the pearl-merchant, the net, the labourers in the vineyard, the two sons, the wedding garment, the ten virgins, the talents, and the sheep and the goats. Certain incidents similar in character to the common synoptic tradition, such as the Baptist's scruple (3 14), the tours in Galilee (4 23), the healing of the two blind men (9 27), the healing of the blind and lame in the Temple (21 14), the children's cry of Hosanna (21 15), the question of Judas (26 25), the remorse of Judas (27 3), perhaps also the appearance to the women (28 9), and to the eleven in Galilee (28 16), seem to point to the use of an authentic narrative source somewhat resembling St. Mark's Gospel. Very little of the Gospel seems due to oral, as distinguished from written, tradition—perhaps only the Nativity (which is confirmed in its essential features by the independent narrative of St. Luke), the visit of the Magi (which fits well into secular history, and is thoroughly credible), the incident of the temple-tribute, and certain details in the narrative of the resurrection, such as the resurrection of the saints, and the setting of a watch. On these the notes should be consulted.

From what has been said, it will be evident that direct authorship of this Gospel by the apostle Matthew is improbable. If St. Matthew had been the author, he would probably have given his own account of the transactions, and not have laboriously occupied himself with collecting and transcribing 'sources.' At the same time a connexion with the apostle Matthew is probable. The name of so obscure an apostle would hardly have been connected with the Gospel without some good reason. Ancient tradition (first in Papias, 130 A.D.) credits St. Matthew with the composition of a book of 'logia' or 'oracles,' written in Hebrew (Aramaic), which may have been a brief Gospel, but was more probably a collection of discourses classified (as we have already suggested) according to subject-matter. Of a Greek translation of these 'logia' our author seems to have made such liberal use, that he acknowledged his obligations to the apostle by calling his work 'according to Matthew.' St. Matthew, therefore, is responsible for the discourses, but probably not for the history.

The author was undoubtedly a Jewish Christian, familiar with Hebrew, and trained in rabbinical methods. His quotations from the OT. (when they are not copied from St. Mark) generally follow the Hebrew rather than the Greek. He arranges his book on the arithmetical principles so common in rabbinical writings, and shows a particular fondness for the numbers 7, 5, 3, 10. Thus there are seven beatitudes, seven petitions in the Lord's prayer (not five, as in St. Luke), seven woes denounced against the Pharisees; also the names in the genealogy are arranged in multiples of seven (7×2); there are five chief collections of our Lord's discourses, three temptations, three chief duties of religion (6^{1-18}), three prayers in Gethsemane; also between the first and second discourses of Jesus the evangelist inserts ten miracles (chs. 8, 9). Seven is, of course, the number of the sabbath day, five of the books of Moses, three of the priestly blessing, and ten of the plagues of Egypt. The author also shows his Jewish predilections in his affectionate references to Jerusalem as 'the holy city,' and 'the holy place' (4^5 24^{15} 27^{53}).

5. Date. The date of the Gospel is rather before than after 70 A.D. The reason for thinking this is that the author has so arranged our Lord's sayings about the fall of Jerusalem and His Second Advent as to leave the impression that these events would be coincident. Had he written later, he would have made it evident that they would be separated by an interval, as St. Luke has actually done (see Lk 21^{24}, and contrast Mt 24 ^{29,30}). But the Gospel cannot have been written much before 70, because it uses sources, some of which are probably not very early, and embodies traditions which in some cases are apparently not in their earliest form.

6. General Characteristics. This Gospel is one of the most attractive books ever written, and in modern times has exercised a wide influence even beyond the pale of Christianity. One of the most influential of modern Indian converts was brought to Christ simply by reading it. The effect of the book is partly due to its excellent arrangement. The author arranges his material not, like St. Luke, chronologically, but according to subject-matter. Material of the same kind is collected into great masses, which being read uninterruptedly, produce a cumulative impression upon the reader. Good instances of the author's method are the great collection of sayings known as the Sermon on the Mount (5–7); the great group of miracles intended to illustrate and confirm it (8, 9); the charge to the Twelve, apparently composed of sayings delivered at various times (10); the cluster of seven parables (13), the collection of denunciations of the Pharisees (23), and the sublime group of parables illustrating the end of the world (25). The great glory of this Gospel is the discourses. These are from the pen of the apostle Matthew himself, who evidently had a special gift of remembering and recording accurately the very words of the Master. In almost all cases where there is any difference, St. Matthew's version is superior to St. Luke's. This is specially the case in the Sermon on the Mount. In no Gospel, not even in St. Luke, are the unapproachable majesty and splendour of Christ's utterances so apparent. St. Matthew's Gospel is particularly helpful in its treatment of OT. prophecy, showing how completely and comprehensively Christ fulfilled the ideals and aspirations of the OT. saints. Sometimes his exegesis, following (like St. Paul's) rabbinical models, is of a kind more calculated to appeal to his original readers than to us, but, after making all deductions, it is not too much to say, that of all the remains of Christian antiquity dealing with the subject of Messianic prophecy, St. Matthew's Gospel is the most fruitful.

We have now to speak of the more special peculiarities of St. Matthew's Gospel, some of which are very definitely marked.

(1) The Gospel is predominantly Jewish-Christian. It reflects the tone of the church of Jerusalem before it was fully realised that the

Ceremonial Law had been abolished. Sayings are reported which (literally understood) teach that every letter of the Mosaic Law is binding in perpetuity (5 18), that its permission to divorce still holds good (5 32 19 9), that not the Levitical distinctions of meats, but only the Pharisaic glosses thereon have been abolished (15 20), and that the sabbath day, with all its Mosaic restrictions, will permanently be observed by Christians (24 20). The first place in the kingdom of God seems often to be assigned to the Jews (19 28), the Gentiles being obliged to content themselves with a subordinate position. Christ's mission is apparently restricted to the chosen people (15 24). As for the apostles, they seem expressly forbidden to go into the way of the Gentiles, or to enter into any city of the Samaritans (10 5).

But though the writer's sympathies are predominantly Jewish-Christian, he is a perfectly honest witness, and does not attempt to suppress facts or sayings which are of a broader or even of an opposite tendency. He introduces Gentiles as the first worshippers of the infant Messiah (2 1). He records the praise of the Roman centurion, and our Lord's striking words, 'Many shall come from the east and the west, and shall sit down with Abraham and Isaac and Jacob in the kingdom of heaven' (8 11), words which affirm not only the admission of the Gentiles to the kingdom, but their admission on equal terms. Other instances of sayings favourable to the Gentiles are, 12 18, 21 ('in his name shall the Gentiles trust'), 12 41 (the men of Nineveh), 13 38 ('the field is the world'), 13 47 (the net gathering of every kind), 15 30-39 (feeding of 4,000 believing Gentiles), 24 14 (the gospel to be preached in all the world for a witness unto all nations), 25 32 (Jews and Gentiles on an equality at the judgment day), 28 19 (all nations to be baptised). St. Matthew even records such anti-Jewish sayings as, 'the children of the kingdom shall be cast into outer darkness' (8 12), and 'the kingdom of God shall be taken from you, and given to a nation bringing forth the fruits thereof' (21 43).

That the evangelist expected to have Gentile as well as Jewish readers is shown by his occasional, though rare, explanations of Jewish words and customs (cp. 1 23 'Emmanuel'; 27 46 'Eli, Eli,' etc.).

(2) In accordance with the Jewish-Christian character of this Gospel, the apostle Peter, the acknowledged head of 'the circumcision,' is brought into special prominence. St. Matthew alone records the remarkable tradition of his attempt to walk upon the water (14 28), and the promise that upon him, as upon a foundation, the Christian church should be built, and that whatsoever he should bind on earth should be bound in heaven.

(3) As a Jew, the author is particularly interested in the correspondence between the two testaments. In his view the new dispensation grows out of the old by a process so natural and inevitable, that it can hardly be called new. The Law, the Prophets, and the Psalms are not abolished; they are fulfilled in Christ. To Him alone they pointed, in Him alone they find their true significance. The germs of Christian truth were planted of old by inspired men, and have so vitally influenced the subsequent development of religion, that the author can even speak of the events of Christ's life as taking place to fulfil the ancient prophecies. Thus Christ is born of a virgin at Bethlehem, is named Jesus, sojourns in Egypt, resides at Nazareth, migrates to Capernaum, heals the sick, speaks in parables, enters Jerusalem riding an ass, is deserted by the disciples, is betrayed, and put to death, 'that it might be fulfilled which was spoken by the Lord through the prophet' (so with slight variations of phrase 1 22 2 15, 23 8 17 12 17 13 35 21 4 26 54; cp. 2 5 13 14, 15 26 31 27 9). This conception is not found in the other synoptists, except perhaps in one or two isolated phrases (see, e.g. Lk 24 26, 44), but it is familiar to the fourth evangelist, and forms an important point of contact between the first and fourth Gospels (see Jn 12 39 17 12 19 24, 36 20 9). St. Matthew alludes to no less than 65 OT. passages, of which 43 are verbally quoted. St. Luke's allusions to the OT. number only 43, and of these only 19 are direct quotations.

(4) As a predominantly Judaic work, this Gospel portrays Jesus as the Messiah of the Jews. His genealogy is traced back only to Abraham, and not, as in St. Luke, to Adam. Stress is laid upon His descent from David (1 1, 20 9 27 12 23 15 22 20 30, 31 21 9, 15 22 42, 43, 45), and the genealogy is an elaborate attempt to prove His right to David's throne. The descent is, of course, traced through the legal father Joseph ('the son of David,' 1 20), and exhibits not so much physical descent, as the legal transmission of the right to occupy the throne, and be 'king of the Jews' (2 2). But Jesus also satisfies the other and more sublime OT. anticipations with regard to the Messiah. His miraculous conception by the Holy Ghost of a virgin mother is evidence that He is in a unique sense the Son of God. He is, in fact, divine (11 27), and consequently may rightly claim the title 'Emmanuel,' 'God with us.' He is the supernatural Son of man whose coming was predicted by the prophet Daniel, and at the end of His glory to judge the human race (16 27 24 30 26 64, etc.). Hence He is not only David's son, but David's Lord (22 44).

(5) The Messiah's kingdom is the most frequent topic in this Gospel. Its title is almost

always the rabbinical one, 'the kingdom of the heavens'; hardly ever, as in the other synoptists, 'the kingdom of God' (only in 12^{28} $21^{31,43}$). The rule over it has been committed by God to the Messiah, who sits on the throne of it as King ($25^{34,40}$). The author generally regards this kingdom as eschatological, i.e. beginning at the end of the world, which he expected would happen in his own time (24^{34}). Then there would be a 'regeneration,' i.e. a transformation or new birth of the whole creation, when the Son of man would sit on the throne of His glory and the apostles would sit upon twelve thrones judging (i.e. ruling) the twelve tribes of Israel, and the righteous would shine forth as the sun in the kingdom of their Father (19^{28} 13^{43}). Other passages illustrating the futurity of the kingdom are 6^{10} 7^{21} 8^{11} 16^{28} 18^3 $20^{1f.,21}$ $25^{1,34}$ 26^{29}. But the author's conception of the kingdom is many-sided, and he seems often to regard it (though this is disputed) as something present, like 'eternal life' in St. John. Thus the subjects of the beatitudes are already within the kingdom (5^3), and so are Christ's disciples (11^{11}), even young children (19^{14}), and great is the sin of those who hinder others from entering (23^{13}). Sometimes the kingdom means the spirit of Christ working secretly and silently in the world like the leaven (13^{33}); sometimes it is the visible Church ($16^{18,19}$), gathering of every kind like a net (13^{47}), and spreading abroad like the branches of a mustard-tree (13^{31}); sometimes, again, it is the Christian's secret communion with God through Christ, as symbolised by the hid treasure, and the pearl of great price ($13^{44,45}$). The conception is a broad and fluid one, and the attempt to define it too rigidly and exclusively is probably a mistake.

(6) Another feature of the Gospel is its anti-Pharisaic character. The pointed condemnations of Pharisaism in the Sermon on the Mount (5^{20} $6^{1,5,16}$) are peculiar to St. Matthew, and in c. 23 he has 35 vv. of denunciation as against 3 vv. in Mk and 3 vv. in Lk.

(7) An apologetic purpose may also be detected. The author refutes the Jewish calumny that the disciples stole the body of Jesus (28^{15}). To the objection to our Lord's Messiahship based on His Nazarene origin (see $Jn 1^{46}$ $7^{41,52}$ $Mt 2^5$), he replies that His birth took place at Bethlehem, in strict accordance with Micah's prophecy (2^1), and that if He afterwards went to live at Nazareth, this was to fulfil another prophecy (2^{23}). That He ministered in Galilee and Capernaum rather than in Judæa was not a real difficulty, for this had been prophesied by Isaiah (4^{13}). To the current calumny that He had visited Egypt to take lessons from a conjurer (see on 12^{22-37}), the author replies that Jesus was

never in Egypt except once, when He was an infant, and that this visit was necessitated by a prophecy of Hosea (2^{15}).

7. Analysis of the Gospel.

(a) The lineage and birth of the Messianic king (c. 1, 2).

(b) His solemn anointing to His Messianic office, and His preliminary temptation by Satan ($3-4^{11}$).

(c) The proclamation and inauguration of the Messianic kingdom on earth: its laws, principles, and officers ($4^{12}-13^{52}$).

(d) The Messiah and His kingdom accepted and rejected ($13^{53}-16^{20}$): accepted by the disciples (14^{33}), by the woman of Canaan (15^{22}), by great multitudes (15^{30}), by St. Peter (16^{16}); rejected by the Nazarenes (13^{57}), by the Pharisees and their sympathisers (15^{12} 16^4).

(e) The sufferings and death of the Messiah announced ($16^{21}-20^{34}$).

First clear announcement (16^{21}).

Second clear announcement (17^{22}).

Third clear announcement (20^{17}).

(f) The Messiah glorified by Death and Resurrection (chs. 21–28). The triumphal entry (c. 21); final denunciation of the Pharisees, Sadducees, and Scribes (chs. 22, 23); great prophetic discourses (chs. 24, 25); betrayal and death (chs. 26, 27); the resurrection, and the exaltation of the Messiah to the throne of the universe (c. 28).

CHAPTER 1

GENEALOGY AND BIRTH OF JESUS

1–17. Genealogy of Jesus: cp. $Lk 3^{23}$. The two genealogies of Jesus, which are constructed on quite different principles, require careful comparison and study, if their purpose and significance are to be understood. In both, the descent of Jesus is traced through Joseph, not Mary, partly because the claim of Jesus to the throne of David could only be established through His foster-father Joseph; partly because, in genealogies, the Jews took no account of female descent. The genealogies are not inspired documents. They are the work of Jewish pedigree-makers who did their best to fill the gaps of records which were frequently fragmentary. They are inserted by the evangelists as honest attempts to ascertain the truth. Their accuracy or inaccuracy does not affect the main point at issue, our Lord's descent, through His legal father Joseph, from David. Joseph's family certainly claimed descent from David, and even the enemies of Jesus admitted the claim (see 9^{27} 12^{23} 15^{22} 20^{30} 21^9 22^{42} and parallels). As Jewish families were particularly tenacious of family traditions, and were accustomed to preserve genealogical records, our Lord's Davidic descent through Joseph may be regarded as established. His Davidic descent through Mary is **more**

doubtful, but, on the whole, probable. Lk 1 36, taken alone, might suggest that she belonged to the tribe of Levi, but Lk 1 32 and 1 69 lose much of their point, unless it be supposed that Mary herself was descended from David. The OT. prophecies and the Apostolic Church regarded Christ as descended from David according to the flesh (Ro 1 3 Ps 132 11 Isa 11 1 Jer 23 5), and if Jesus were born of a virgin, His actual descent could only be upon the mother's side.

Both genealogies reflect current rabbinical ideas about the Messiah's descent. It was disputed, for instance, whether He would be descended from David through Solomon, or whether, owing to the curse on this line (Jer 22 28 36 30), through another son, Nathan (1 Ch 3 5). Accordingly St. Matthew's genealogy traces our Lord's descent through Solomon, St. Luke's through Nathan. Other rabbinical features are the omission of links in the genealogies, especially in St. Matthew, and the artificial arrangement of the names in numerical groups, probably as an aid to the memory. St. Luke's source probably grouped the names in multiples of ten (20 generations from David to the captivity, 20 from the captivity to Christ). This was the commonest method. St. Matthew employs multiples of seven (14 generations from Abraham to David, 14 from David to the captivity, 14 from the captivity to Christ). St. Matthew's list is a genealogy only in appearance. It is really an early Jewish-Christian attempt to construct a list of successive heirs to the throne of David, and so to exhibit Joseph, the legal father of Jesus, as the rightful king of Israel. Thus Shealtiel (Salathiel), v. 12, was not the actual son of Jechoniah, who was childless (Jer 22 28), but the next heir to the crown, and probably for that reason adopted by Jechoniah : see 1 Ch 3 17. According to St. Luke, Shealtiel's real father was Neri.

St. Luke's list, on the other hand, aims at being a true genealogy, and that not of Mary, as a few authorities still maintain, but of Joseph : see on Lk 3 23. We are thus faced with the serious difficulty that Joseph's father is called by St. Matthew ' Jacob,' and by St. Luke ' Heli.' Have we here an error made by one or both evangelists ? It is, of course, possible, but hardly likely, this being only the second step of the genealogy. Assuming both genealogies to be in this point correct, and taking into account the special character of St. Matthew's list, the statements are best harmonised by supposing that Jacob, the true heir to the throne, being, like Jechoniah, childless, adopted the next male heir Heli, who belonged to the other branch of the family, that, namely, which descended from Nathan. A less probable supposition is that Heli and Jacob were brothers, and that, one of them

dying childless, the other took his wife and raised up seed to him by what is called a Levirate marriage : see Dt 25 5 Mt 22 23. The point in favour of this view is that the fathers of Heli and Jacob, Matthat and Matthan, have nearly the same name. The point against it is that Matthat and Matthan have different fathers, and so were different persons, unless we again make use of the expedient of a Levirate marriage, or something similar.

1. The book of the generation] RM ' of the genealogy.' The phrase is from Gn 5 1, and is meant as a title not of the whole Gospel, nor even of the Nativity, but only of the genealogy (1 1-17), which the evangelist probably did not compose himself (though this is possible), but derived from an earlier source. **Of Jesus Christ**] ' Jesus ' is the Gk. form of the Heb. ' Joshua,' or ' Jeshua,' meaning ' Jehovah is salvation.' ' Christ ' (Christos) is properly the Gk. equivalent of the Aramaic ' Messiah,' lit. ' anointed one,' but here used as a proper name. The use of ' Christ ' as a proper name began soon after the Ascension, and is common in the Epistles. In the Gospels it occurs only in Mt 1 1, 16, 17, 18 Mk 1 1 Jn 1 17 and possibly 17 3. In all other places in the Gospels it should be rendered ' the Christ,' or ' the Messiah.' The use of the word in the sense of ' the Messiah ' is unquestionably the earlier one, and the fidelity of the Gospels in preserving it is no small evidence of their trustworthiness. **The son of David**] a standing title of the Messiah among the rabbis. E.g. it was said, ' The son of David cometh not until that wicked empire (Rome) hath extended itself over the whole earth.' ' If the Israelites shall keep the sabbath even for a single day as they ought, the son of David will come ': see Ps 132 Isa 11 1 Jer 23 5. The poverty of Joseph and Mary is no evidence against their Davidic descent. The great rabbi Hillel, another descendant of David, was even poorer. The Davidic descent of our Lord's family was never questioned in His lifetime even by His enemies, and was so notorious that the descendants of Jude, the Lord's brother, incurred the jealousy of the tyrant Domitian. **The son of Abraham**] St. Matthew, writing primarily for Jews, carries the genealogy to Abraham and no further. He wishes to show that Jesus is the Messiah of the Jews, born in accordance with the promise made by God to the ancestor of the race (Gn 12 3, etc.). St. Luke, writing for Gentiles, and emphasising St. Paul's principle that in Christ there is neither Jew nor Gentile, carries the genealogy back to Adam.

3. Of Thamar] RV ' Tamar.' Contrary to Jewish custom St. Matthew introduces into his genealogy four women, Tamar, Rahab, Ruth, and Bathsheba. Of these, two (Rahab and Ruth) were Gentiles, and three were guilty of gross sins. Their insertion is intended to teach certain spiritual lessons : (1) That Gentiles as well as Jews have their rights in the Messiah, seeing that two of His ancestors were of Gentile blood. (2) That Jewish Christians instead of regarding Gentile converts with contempt, should be proud of them, as their ancestors were of Rahab and Ruth, who, on becoming proselytes, were accounted mothers in Israel. Of Rahab the rabbis said, 'Ten priests, who were also prophets, sprang from her' ; and of Ruth, 'It is spoken in prophecy that the six most righteous men of the whole world will spring from her, David, Daniel and his companions, and King Messiah.' (3) That remission of sins, complete restoration to God's favour, and a high and privileged position in the kingdom of grace, are possible for the worst offenders. (4) That Christ did not shrink from the closest contact with sinful humanity. He touched and raised the very nature which had fallen He assumed our sin-stained flesh, and in assuming cleansed it, and made it the instrument of human redemption.

8. After **Joram** St. Matthew omits three names, Ahaziah, Joash, Amaziah (see 1 Ch 3 11,12), some think on account of their descent from the idolatrous Jezebel, but more probably simply to reduce the number of generations to fourteen. **11.** After **Josias** St. Matthew omits Eliakim (2 K 23 34). The **brethren of Jechoniah** (Jehoiachin) are really his uncles, Jehoahaz and Zedekiah. Zedekiah, the last king of Judah, though really the uncle of Jehoiachin (2 K 24 17 Jer 37 1), is called his 'brother' even in OT. (2 Ch 36 10). **12. Jechoniah** (Jehoiachin) was probably childless (yet see on Jer 22 30), and adopted **Salathiel** (Shealtiel) as his heir (see 1 Ch 3 17). Shealtiel seems also to have been childless, for although both here and in Ezr 3 2 Neh 12 1 Hag 1 1, etc., he is said to have had a son **Zorobabel** (Zerubbabel), this Zerubbabel seems to have been really the son of Shealtiel's brother Pedaiah (1 Ch 3 19), who may have married his childless brother's widow according to the Law.

16. Little importance attaches to the reading of the Sinai-Syriac version, 'Joseph begat Jesus,' which is certainly not original, lacking, as it does, all MS authority, and contradicting the plain statements of the evangelist (vv.18–25). Probably the reading comes from an Ebionite version of this Gospel. The Ebionites were an early sect, who, while admitting our Lord's Messiahship, denied His divinity and supernatural birth. Or the error may be due to the mechanical repetition by some scribe of the word 'begat,' which he had already written thirty-eight times.

17. As there are only thirteen generations from the captivity to Christ, probably a name has dropped out.

18–25. Circumstances of the Conception and Birth of Jesus: cp. Lk 1 26-56 2 1-20. The order of events is (a) Conception of John by Elisabeth, Lk 1 24, (b) Annunciation to Mary at Nazareth six months afterwards, Lk 1 26, (c) Visit of Mary to Elisabeth lasting three months, Lk 1 39, (d) Return of Mary to Nazareth, Lk 1 56, (e) Birth of John, Lk 1 57, (f) Mary is found to be with child, Mt 1 18, (g) An angel appears to Joseph, Mt 1 20, (h) Journey to Bethlehem, Lk 2 4, (i) Birth of Jesus, Mt 1 25 Lk 2 7.

Significance of Christ's Infancy. At first sight it seems unworthy of the Son of God to be conceived and born, and to pass through the stages of human growth. But in truth the interval between God and man is so infinitely great, that the minute difference between infancy and manhood is of no consequence. The marvel is that the Son of God should consent to become man at all ; it is no additional marvel that He should become an infant. If it was expedient for the human race which He came to redeem, that He should pass through all the stages of a truly human experience, then the same infinite loving condescension which caused Him to become man would cause Him to be conceived and born. It is a fact admitted by the most sceptical that the human birth of Jesus Christ has appealed to the imagination of mankind, more perhaps than any other event of His life, and has produced permanent effects of the utmost importance (Lk 1 51). (a) It has abolished the once common crime of infanticide by teaching that infant life is sacred. (b) It has raised the dignity of women, and produced in men the feeling of chivalry towards them, which is essentially Christian and was unknown to the ancient world. (c) It has sanctified motherhood and family life. (d) It has placed chastity both in men and women in the forefront of Christian virtues. (e) It has given a new importance to childhood, so that kindness to children and a willingness to conform to the ideal character of childhood, are marks of a true Christian. The human birth of Jesus is thus justified both by its results and by its adaptation to human needs. 'Jesus · Christ,' says Irenæus, 'came to save all by means of Himself. He therefore passed through every age, becoming an infant for infants, a child for children, a youth for youths, an elderly man for elderly men, that He might be a perfect Master for all.'

The Incarnation and the Virgin Birth. A difficulty has been felt in our days in accepting the miracle associated with the conception of our Lord. This arises chiefly from the facts that the two Gospels which record it differ to some extent in their accounts, and that the nature of the miracle itself precludes absolute demonstration.

It may be candidly admitted that the miraculous conception of Jesus has not the same evidence for it as the other miracles, and that if it were affirmed of any ordinary man it could not be believed. But Jesus was not an ordinary man. He was one who, according to credible testimony, worked many miracles, including the raising of the dead, and concluded an absolutely unexampled career by rising from the dead and ascending into heaven. The miraculous manner in which Jesus left this earth thus removes all theoretical difficulty from the miracle by which He is said to have entered it. The main question to be considered is: Do the existing narratives show signs of having proceeded from the only two persons who can have known anything about the matter, viz. Joseph and Mary? Certainly they do. St. Matthew's Gospel regards the matter entirely from Joseph's point of view. It is Joseph who discovers the condition of Mary (1 18), and is doubtful what course to pursue (1 19). It is to Joseph that the angel appears to announce the miraculous conception of Jesus (1 20), and again to bid him flee into Egypt (2 13), and to return (2 19). St. Luke's narrative, on the other hand, reflects entirely the point of view of Mary. It is to Mary that Gabriel appears (Lk 1 26). A full account is given of her visit to Elisabeth (1 39). The mother's memory appears in the mention of the swaddling clothes and of the manger (2 ⁷), and in the words, 'But Mary kept all these sayings and pondered them in her heart' (2 19), and again, 'Yea, a sword shall pierce through thy own soul also' (2 35). St. Luke's account is much fuller than St. Matthew's, and this is easily accounted for. When St. Luke was collecting his materials in Palestine, Mary was probably still alive, whereas Joseph (St. Matthew's authority) had long been dead, and his account had probably passed through several hands before it reached the evangelist. The historical character of both narratives is shown by their freedom from the extravagant features which mark the apocryphal Gospels, and by their essential agreement, in spite of the fact that they are absolutely independent. It is true that St. Matthew seems to represent Bethlehem rather than Nazareth as the original home of Joseph and Mary, though he does not actually say so. On the other hand, St. Luke seems ignorant of the flight into Egypt, and passes straight from the presentation in the Temple to the return to Nazareth. But these are only instances of one imperfect account supplementing another, not of radical inconsistencies. Both accounts agree as to the two main points, Christ's birth of a virgin and His birth at Bethlehem.

Granting the fact of a real Incarnation, the Virgin Birth would seem to be the most reverent and fitting way of bringing it about. Since natural generation invariably gives rise to a new person, it was plainly unsuitable to the case of Jesus, at whose conception no new person came into existence, but the already existing Son of God entered upon a new human experience. Moreover, natural generation having been generally associated, especially by the Jews, with sin, it was not desirable that the moral miracle of a sinless human nature should be marked by the physical miracle of a miraculous conception. The last appeal, and perhaps to many minds the only possible appeal, is that of the argument derived from 'cause and effect.' Look at the stupendous fact— Jesus. The miracle of the NT., the miracle of the ages is not the Resurrection, but Jesus Himself. The phenomena of His life and character, the incomprehensibility of His person, seem to demand uniqueness and mystery in His birth. To abandon the Virgin Birth because of the difficulties of a few would be to throw greater difficulties in the way of the many. The doctrine has always been regarded as an integral part of the faith. It appears in the earliest form of the Apostles' Creed (100 A.D.).

18. Was espoused] RV 'had been betrothed.' Betrothal was almost equivalent to marriage, and could not be broken off without a formal divorce: cp. on Jn 8 3 and Dt 22 23, 24. **She was found]** viz. by her husband. **Of the Holy Ghost]** Both here and in Lk 1 35 the miracle of the conception is ascribed emphatically to the 'Holy' Spirit, to mark the fact that Jesus was conceived sinless, and in a manner the most sacred imaginable. 'The Holy Spirit sanctified the flesh which it united with the Word. Not only was the "new departure in human life" which began with the birth of the Second Adam fitly preceded by a directly creative act, but the new humanity was consecrated at the moment of its conception by the overshadowing of the Divine Spirit' (Swete). The expression 'Holy Ghost' is especially characteristic of the NT., where it occurs over 80 times. In the Gk. OT. (LXX) it occurs only twice. The Jews did not regard the Spirit as personal, hence Mary must have understood the words of the angel, 'The Holy Ghost shall come upon thee,' as identical in meaning with, 'The power of the Highest shall overshadow thee.' Not so the evangelists, to whom 'the Holy Ghost' had become practically a proper name, and as such was used without the article.

19. A just *man]* i.e. a good or righteous man: here, in particular, a kind or humane man, because although he felt bound to divorce her, he wished to do so as privately as possible, and without assigning any reason. A Jewish husband could divorce his wife if she did not please him, simply by giving her a bill of divorce in the presence of witnesses, without specifying the true cause. The legal penalty for Mary's supposed fault was stoning (Jn 8 5).

20. The angel] RV 'an angel.' In St. Luke the angel who appears to Zachariah and Mary is named (Lk 1 [19, 26]), and the same angel (Gabriel) is to be understood here. In other passages of the NT. angels appear and speak : at the Resurrection, Mt 28 [5] ; at the Ascension, Ac 1 [11] ; to Peter in prison, 5 [19] 12 [7] ; to Philip, 8 [26] ; to Cornelius, 10 [3]. There is no real reason to question the actual existence of angels. Why should man be the highest being in the universe ?

21. JESUS] see on v. 1. **For he shall save**] more exactly, 'for it is He that shall save.' 'Saving from sin' includes two processes : (1) atonement for sin, and (2) sanctification. Both are works of Christ. The natural atonement for sin is penitence ; but inasmuch as human penitence is imperfect, and our very repentance requires to be repented of, the aid of a Divine Helper is required. Christ bears the weight of our sins, sorrows for them with a sorrow that is adequate, and gives us grace to repent of them in a manner acceptable to God. As we live the life of faith in Christ our penitence continually becomes deeper, and one day it will be perfect, and God will accept it as adequate. In the meantime God pardons us by anticipation. Sanctification, i.e. the putting away of sin and growth in virtue and holiness, is another most important work of redemption, and no one can safely assure himself of the divine pardon unless he is advancing in the Christian virtues. The faith which does not manifest itself in works is no true faith in Christ. **His people**] primarily, of course, the Jews ; but the Gentiles are also Israel, 'the Israel of God' (Gal 6 [16]).

22. That it might be fulfilled, etc.] It is characteristic of St. Matthew, though not, of course, peculiar to him, to regard the events of Christ's life as taking place in order to fulfil God's gracious promises in the OT. made through the prophets. This particular phrase occurs 10 times in St. Matthew, and nowhere else in the NT. : see Intro.

23. Behold, a virgin] RV 'the virgin' : see on Isa 7 [14]. It does not appear that the Jews regarded the passage as Messianic ; but St. Matthew, writing for Christians, applies it to the Messiah, in accordance with the rabbinical maxim, 'All the prophets prophesied only of the days of the Messiah.' St. Matthew quotes the passage as a prophecy not of the Virgin Birth, but of the giving to our Lord of a name expressing His divinity. He was called 'Jesus' (i.e. 'God is Salvation') to fulfil the prophecy which assigned to Him the name 'Emmanuel' ('God with us'). There is no indication that the evangelist, who was acquainted with Hebrew, attached importance to the word 'virgin' in this passage. In the Heb. it is 'almah, i.e. 'a young woman,' not necessarily a virgin. The LXX, however, renders it parthenos, i.e. 'virgin,' and hence many have incorrectly supposed that Isaiah prophesied the Virgin Birth.

Emmanuel] i.e. 'God with us.' This is a descriptive title rather than a name. It was never borne by our Lord, but He received instead a name ('Jesus') which expressed its meaning, and thus the prophecy was fulfilled. In the mind of Isaiah the title Emmanuel indicated that the bearer of it would deliver Israel from all their enemies. In the mind of the evangelist, who believed in the Incarnation (see especially 27 [19]), it meant that in Jesus God assumed human nature to save the children of men, and to dwell with and in them for ever (27 [20]). **25. And knew her not till**] Some have thought that the evangelist means to imply that after the birth of Jesus, Joseph and Mary lived together as man and wife, and that children were born to them. This may have been the case, but the words of the evangelist here are not meant to imply it. They simply affirm in the strongest manner that Joseph had nothing whatever to do with the conception and birth of Jesus, and are not intended to give information as to what happened afterwards. For the probable relationship to our Lord of His 'brethren,' see on 12 [50].

Her firstborn son] RV 'a son.' 'Firstborn' is interpolated from Lk 2 [7], q.v.

CHAPTER 2
THE WISE MEN

1-12. The star in the east and the visit of the Magi (peculiar to St. Matthew). The incident fits well into secular history. About the time when the star appeared (7 or 6 B.C.), Herod the Great, being alarmed by a prophecy that the royal power was about to pass away from him and his line, put the authors of it to death. It is evident, therefore, that the announcement by the wise men that Herod's supplanter in the kingdom had actually been born, would drive him to violent measures. The slaughter of the infants by Herod seems confirmed by the independent account of the heathen historian Macrobius (400 A.D.), who says that when news was brought to Augustus that Herod had ordered children under two years old in Syria to be slain, and that among them was a son of Herod, the emperor remarked, that it was better to be Herod's pig (hun) than Herod's son (huion).

That the Magi should be familiar with and sympathise with Jewish expectations about the Messiah, is not a difficulty. Synagogues existed throughout the East, and exercised a wide influence. At Damascus nearly all the women were proselytes (Jos. 'Wars,' ii. 20. 2 : cp. also 23 [15] Ac 2 [9] 13 [43], etc.). Belief that the appearance of the Messiah was imminent—

a belief widely cherished in Jewish circles, see Lk 2 25, 26, 38—joined to belief in the appearance of signs in the heavens at the birth of great men, would sufficiently account for the journey of these astrologers, even if they were ignorant of the more definite expectation, which, according to Edersheim, was entertained at this time by the Jews, that two years before the birth of the Messiah His star would appear in the East. The existence of Messianic expectations throughout the East at a somewhat later period is expressly affirmed not only by Josephus, but also by the heathen historians Tacitus and Suetonius. As to the nature of the star, the most probable view is Kepler's. He calculated that in 7 B.C. there occurred three times a most remarkable conjunction of the planets Jupiter and Saturn in the constellation Pisces, which was next year reinforced by Mars. This triple conjunction was followed by the appearance of a remarkably coloured evanescent star, which was the true star of the Magi. If this view be correct, our Lord's birth occurred about 6 B.C. (i.e. six years before the vulgar era of the nativity), and the visit of the Magi followed soon afterwards.

The spiritual significance of the story lies on the surface. Whereas Herod and the Jews were ignorant of the birth of the Messiah among them, and, when informed of it, manifested the most malignant hatred against Him, strangers from afar knew of it before then, and hastened to pay Him reverence. The incident is thus a prophecy of the history of the succeeding centuries, in which the chosen people have persistently rejected the Messiah, and the Gentiles have accepted Him. The incident also illustrates the true relations between science and religion. In the persons of the Magi, science paid homage to religion. The Magi were the men of science of the period, and their science brought them to Christ. And so it is now. The science of yesterday was (according to not a few of its exponents) hostile to faith, proudly boasting that it could solve the mystery of the universe. The science of to-day is more humble, acknowledging that the deepest natural knowledge only touches the outer fringe of things, and that so-called scientific 'explanations' of the universe are not explanations at all, but only descriptions. Religion and science move on differen' planes. There is and can be no real antagonism between them, and their natural relationship is one of mutual respect, and cordial coöperation.

1. Bethlehem] or Ephrathah, the city of David, is 5 m. S. of Jerusalem : see Gn 35 16, 19 48 7 1 S 16 4 2 S 2 32 23 14-16 1 Ch 11 16, 26 Ezr 2 21 Neh 7 26. The supposed site of the nativity is a rock-hewn cave, measuring 38 ft. by

11 ft., at one end of which is inscribed 'Hic de virgine Maria Jesus Christus natus est.' Above it stands perhaps the oldest Christian church in the world, the basilica built by Helena, mother of Constantine the Great, about 330 A.D. **Herod**] i.e. Herod the Great, who reigned from 37 to 4 B.C. As Christ was born at least two years before Herod's death (see 2 16), the date of the nativity cannot be later than 6 B.C. See art. 'The Dynasty of the Herods.' **Wise men**] lit. 'Magi,' a sacerdotal class among the Persians, Babylonians, and other Eastern nations, who occupied themselves with a knowledge of the secrets of nature, divination, astrology, and medicine. The Babylonian Magi are mentioned in Jer 39 3. Daniel was made chief of them owing to his skill in interpreting dreams (Dan 2 48). Here the word is used in its strict meaning, and in a good sense. Elsewhere in the NT. it means a juggler or cheat (Ac 13 6,8). Since astronomy was chiefly practised in Babylonia, and Jewish influence was particularly strong there, it may be conjectured that these Magi were Babylonians. But they may have come from Arabia. There is no warrant for the tradition that they were kings. **To Jerusalem**] The Magi came because they expected to obtain full information at the capital. **2. In the east**] better, 'at its rising.' **Worship**] see on v. 11.

3. And all Jerusalem] They had good reason to be troubled. Only two years before, in a similar fit of jealous fear, Herod had slaughtered all the leading Pharisees (Jos. 'Antiq.' 17. 2).

4. Herod summons not the Sanhedrin, which he had reduced to a shadow. having slain its members wholesale, but a national assembly of theologians learned in the Law. **Chief priests**] The name includes the high priest, the ex-high priests, and members of those families from which the high priest was generally chosen. **Scribes**] i.e. professional students, copiers, and expounders of the Law of Moses, who rose into prominence after the captivity (Neh 8 1, etc.), and were enrolled as members of the Sanhedrin. Called also 'lawyers' (Lk 10 25) and 'doctors of the law' (Lk 5 17). **Christ**] RV 'the Christ,' i.e. the Messiah.

5. In Bethlehem] cp. Jn 7 42.

6. See Mic 5 2. St. Matthew follows neither the Heb. nor the Gk., but gives a free paraphrase. He 'reproduces the prophetic utterance of Micah, exactly as such quotations were popularly made at that time. Hebrew being a dead language, the Holy Scriptures were always translated (in the synagogue) into the popular dialect (Aramaic) by a Methurgeman, or interpreter, and these interpretations, or Targums. were neither literal versions nor yet paraphrases, but something between them, a sort of interpreting translation. It is needless.

to remark that the NT. writers would "targum" as Christians' (Edersheim abridged).

9. The star . . went before them, etc.] a poetical way of saying that the star guided the wise men to Jesus.

11. The house] There is no mention of the stable (Lk 2 7). As soon as the enrolling was at an end, there would be no difficulty in obtaining accommodation. **Fell down, and worshipped him**] The customary method of doing homage to a monarch. But in their homage was mingled something also of religious worship, because they understood at least this, that the Child before whom they knelt was the Messiah, the religious head of the human race, standing in a unique relation to God, and destined to establish the kingdom of God on earth.

Gifts] It was, and is, the Eastern custom not to approach monarchs and princes without a gift : Gn 43 11 1 S 10 27 1 K 10 2. The Magi brought to Jesus the most costly products of the countries in which they lived, as if to show that nothing is too precious to be used in the service of God. It is a mistake to think that spiritual worship is necessarily a bare worship, or that religion is purest when it is most divorced from art. Art and the love of beauty are among God's greatest gifts to man, and it is right that man in worshipping should render of his best to God. The mystical interpretation of the gifts (gold, symbolising Christ's Royalty ; frankincense, or incense, His Divinity ; myrrh, His Passion, cp. Jn 19 39) is questionable. The Magi would not know that He was actually divine, still less that He would suffer.

12. In a dream] As the Magi were interpreters of dreams, this method of divine revelation was especially appropriate. It is part of God's loving condescension to mankind to make His revelations to different ages, races, and individuals by those channels through which they are accustomed to expect them.

13-15. Flight into Egypt (peculiar to St. Matthew). Egypt was the only place of refuge easily reached from Bethlehem. It was outside the dominions of Herod, under Roman government, and contained a population of at least a million Jews, who were more wealthy and enlightened than those of Palestine. It was notorious for its superstition and gross idolatry, and legend has represented the idols of Egypt as falling flat on their faces before the Holy Child.

15. Until the death of Herod] Herod died probably 4 B.C., possibly 3 B.C., so that the sojourn in Egypt was short, perhaps only a few months.

Out of Egypt] Hos 11 1. It is impossible that the flight into Egypt was invented to fulfil this prophecy, which in Hosea is simply an historical allusion to the deliverance of Israel from Egypt. **My son**] in the original passage is the nation, not the Messiah, and so the LXX understood it. St. Matthew, however, saw in the history of Israel a typical foreshadowing of the life of our Lord, and so, in accordance with rabbinical methods of interpretation, applied it to Jesus. Here St. Matthew quotes directly from the Heb. The LXX has 'Out of Egypt did I call his (Israel's) children.'

16-18. Massacre of the Innocents (peculiar to St. Matthew). The incident is fully in accordance with what is known of Herod's character, and could not have been suggested by the prophecy in v. 18, which really refers to the Babylonian captivity. It is a true instinct, born of the new significance which Christianity has given to child-life, which has led the Church to enroll the Innocents in 'the noble army of martyrs,' and to commemorate them in the Christmas festival (Dec. 28). 'Not in speaking, but in dying,' says the old collect, 'did they confess Christ.'

16. All the male (RV) children] 'Considering the population of Bethlehem, their number could only have been small—probably twenty at most.' The massacre is not mentioned by Josephus, but 'the murder of a few infants in an insignificant village might appear scarcely worth notice in a reign stained by so much bloodshed. Besides, he had perhaps a special motive for this silence. Josephus always carefully suppresses, so far as possible, all that refers to the Christ' (Edersheim).

18. Was . . a voice heard] Jer 31 15. Rachel was buried at Ramah (cp. Gn 35 19 1 S 10 2), and when Jerusalem was captured by Nebuchadnezzar, trains of Jewish captives were led by her tomb on their way to exile. Jeremiah poetically represents Rachel as coming out of her tomb, and weeping piteously over her dead and exiled descendants, and St. Matthew applies the prophecy to the circumstances of the slaughter of the Innocents.

19-23. Return to Palestine. Settlement at Nazareth. It is implied that Joseph had settled at Bethlehem and intended to remain there as the most suitable place for bringing up the future Messiah. But God judged that the despised Galilee was a better training-school for the future Saviour of the world.

22. Archelaus] see art. 'The Dynasty of the Herods.' **Did reign**] RV 'was reigning.' Properly speaking Archelaus was only an 'ethnarch,' but ethnarchs and tetrarchs were popularly called 'kings.' Augustus had promised Archelaus the title of king, if he should deserve it by ruling well. Joseph feared to go back to Judæa, because Archelaus was as suspicious and cruel as his father. The pleasure-loving Antipas who ruled in Galilee, was known to be more humane. **23. Nazareth**] or Nazara, was a town of lower Galilee, in the tribe of Zebulon. It lay in a lofty valley among the limestone hills to the N. of the plain of Esdraelon, or Megiddo. It was quite unimportant (Jn 1⁴⁶), and is not mentioned in OT. or Josephus.

A Nazarene] A thoroughly Jewish play upon words. In the OT. and in Jewish writings the Messiah is often called *Tsemach* (Jer 23⁵), or *Netser* (Isa 11¹), i.e. the Branch, so that 'Jesus the Nazarene' would sound very much like 'Jesus the Branch,' i.e. the Messiah. Edersheim says, 'We admit that this is a Jewish view, but then this Gospel *is* the Jewish view of the Jewish Messiah.'

CHAPTER 3
APPEARANCE OF THE BAPTIST. BAPTISM OF JESUS

1–12. John the Baptist's ministry. The circumstances of John's birth are detailed in Lk 1 (see notes there). He was sanctified from birth to be the forerunner of the Messiah (Lk 1 ¹³⁻¹⁷, ⁷⁶ f.), and received a special revelation to enable him to recognise the Expected One when He appeared (Jn 1³³). His mother Elisabeth was a cousin of the Virgin, and he was born about six months before Jesus. Knowing what his work in life was to be, he devoted himself from his earliest years to a life of strict asceticism. 'He was in the deserts till the day of his showing unto Israel,' imitating the austerities of the OT. prophets, especially Elijah, whom he greatly resembled. Some earnest Jews seem to have followed his example, and adopted the hermit life. For instance, one of the instructors of Josephus, a man called Banus, 'lived in the desert, and had no other food than that which grew of its own accord, and bathed himself in cold water frequently both by night and day.' Josephus adopted his practices and stayed with him three years. The ascetic and unsocial life of John contrasted strangely with the genial and social habits of Jesus, who came 'eating and drinking,' and mingling freely with people of all classes. Yet our Lord had the greatest esteem for John, and spoke of him as greater than the greatest of the prophets (11 ⁷⁻¹⁹).

The public appearance of the Baptist marked a new era. He came forward in the twofold capacity of a prophet and the forerunner of the Messiah. As prophecy had been silent for 400 years, and all patriotic Jews were longing for the coming of the Messiah to deliver them from the Roman yoke, it is not surprising that he was welcomed with enthusiasm, and that those who ventured to doubt his mission found it expedient to dissemble (21 ²⁶). He might undoubtedly have claimed the allegiance of Israel as their promised king (Lk 3 ¹⁵), but, true

to his mission, he declared himself only the forerunner of that greater One, whose ministry was about to begin. The testimony of John to the Messiahship of Jesus is undoubtedly a historical fact, and an important one. To it our Lord owed His first and most capable followers (Jn 1 ³⁵ f.), and much of His early success.

The teaching of John was confined within the limits of OT. ideas, and his aim was to make his converts pious Jews of the orthodox type. At the same time, his views were of a far more spiritual kind than those generally current. In his teaching he laid the main stress not upon the ceremonial law, but upon righteousness. He did not regard the Messiah's kingdom as—in its main aspect, at any rate— a temporal monarchy. It was a kingdom not of this world, a kingdom of righteousness. Not descent from Abraham, but righteousness entitled a man to be a member of it. Hence above all things repentance and amendment of life were necessary. Those who repented and received the Messiah, would be admitted into the kingdom, to whatever nation they might belong, but Israelites who refused to repent and believe would be rejected. John foresaw the difficulties with which Jesus would have to contend, and even predicted for Him a death like his own (Jn 1 ³⁶ f.). In his preaching John appealed largely to the emotion of fear He declared that the Messianic age would be ushered in by a terrible act of judgment. The Messiah would hew down every unfruitful tree with the axe of retribution. With the fan of judgment he would winnow the wheat, casting the useless chaff into unquenchable fire. Let hypocrites, especially Pharisees and Sadducees, beware, for only by true repentance could they flee from the wrath to come. Let all men practise charity, sharing their goods with their neighbours. Let publicans collect no more than the taxes due. Let soldiers avoid all violence, and be content with their wages. So and so only could they enter into the kingdom : see Lk 3 ¹⁰⁻¹⁴. Josephus alludes to John, but in a brief and guarded manner, as 'a good man, who commanded the Jews to exercise virtue both as to righteousness towards one another, and piety towards God, and so to come to baptism.'

St. Matthew and St. Luke both supplement St. Mark's brief account of John from other sources.

1. In those days] i.e. 26 A.D. **The wilderness of Judæa**] a desert tract about 10 m. wide to the W. of the Dead Sea, including also the W. bank of the Jordan near its mouth. The chief towns in it were Engedi and Tekoa.

2. Repent ye] Repentance is not mere sorrow for sin, but a real change of life. It includes, (1) contrition, i.e. sorrow for sin regarded as an offence against God ; (2) confession of sin, always to God, and, where man has been injured, also to man ; (3) amendment of life. **The kingdom of heaven**] St. Matthew nearly always employs this rabbinical phrase instead of 'the kingdom of God.' 'Heaven' so used is a reverential substitute for 'God.' 'The kingdom of heaven' is, of course, the kingdom of Christ, which the Baptist certainly regarded as spiritual. On the precise meaning of the phrase in this Gospel see the Intro., also the notes on the Sermon on the Mount (chs. 5–7), and on the parables.

3. For this is he, etc.] words of the evangelist, not of the Baptist. Isa 40³ is quoted according to LXX. In Isaiah the words are a summons to make level the roads before Jehovah, who is leading home His people from the Babylonian captivity. St. Matthew typically applies them to the entry of Israel, after their long period of waiting, into the Messianic kingdom.

4. Camel's hair] i.e. either a camel's skin, or cloth woven from camel's hair. John's dress was a protest against the luxurious robes of soft wool, which were fashionable at the time. **Locusts**] They are still eaten in the East, especially by the poor. After being thrown into boiling water their wings and legs are torn off ; they are then sprinkled with salt, and either boiled or roasted. Sometimes they are fried in butter or oil. **Wild honey**] still plentiful in the wilderness, where it flows from combs built in the crevices of the rocks. Certain trees also exude a juice called tree-manna, or honey, and some suppose that this is meant.

6. Were baptized] The Baptism of John was specifically a baptism of repentance, of which public confession was the pledge and evidence. Its significance can be best described in the words of Isaiah : 'Wash you, make you clean ; put away the evil of your doings from before mine eyes ; cease to do evil ; learn to do well ; seek judgment' (justice), 'relieve the oppressed, judge the fatherless, plead for the widow' (Isa 1¹⁶ ; cp. Zech 13¹). It has points of contact with the baptism of proselytes or converts from heathenism. John required circumcised Jews of the seed of Abraham to submit to his baptism, and thereby to declare themselves outside the Messianic kingdom, and unfit to enter into it without a moral purification. This was distasteful to the pride of the Pharisees, who took offence at being treated as proselytes (Lk 7³⁰). From Jn 1²⁵ it may be gathered that there was a general expectation that the Messiah and those closely associated with Him would baptise, so that John's action was in accordance with Jewish ideas. John's Baptism differed from that of Jesus in being of a

preparatory character. It did not confer the Spirit, and was not recognised as equivalent to Christian baptism (Ac 18²⁵ 19³). **Confessing their sins**] The Gk. word generally, but not always, means a public confession, and that seems to be the sense here. For an example of public confession and repudiation of past sins in connexion with Christian baptism, see Ac 19¹⁸.

7. Pharisees and Sadducees] The Pharisees were the strictest, the most active, and the most influential of the Jewish parties or sects. They were zealously attached to the Law, and still more to 'the traditions of the elders.' By the length of their prayers, the frequency of their fasts, and their devotion to ceremonialism, they sought to win honour with men and merit with God. They were hostile to foreign rule, intensely national and patriotic in spirit, and ready to suffer persecution even unto death for their religion. They believed in angels and spirits (also in revelations made by them), in eternal retribution in the next world, and in the resurrection of the dead. They also cherished with especial fervour the Messianic hope. They were closely allied with the scribes or lawyers, with whom they formed practically one party.

The views of the Sadducees were in most respects the opposite of those of the Pharisees. They made no special pretensions to piety. They acknowledged the Law of Moses as alone authoritative, and rejected the traditions of the elders. They were hostile to the aspirations of the national party, and leaned for support on Rome. Sceptical, or semi-sceptical, in their religious views, they rejected the popular beliefs in angels and spirits, in a future life, and in the resurrection of the dead. They were a worldly, wealthy, and selfishly ambitious party, and their adherents were chiefly found among the chief priests. Their opinions were so unpopular, that they often hesitated to express them publicly. In the Sanhedrin, although the leading Sadducees had seats, Pharisaic views were decidedly in the ascendant.

Come to his baptism] In consequence of John's severe denunciation of their conduct, most of the Pharisees and Sadducees who had come for baptism departed without it : see Lk 7³⁰. **Generation** (RV 'offspring') **of vipers**] This peculiar term of condemnation is also applied by Christ to the scribes and Pharisees (12³⁴ 23³³). Probably the allusion is to their poisonous opinions and corrupt influence : see Ps 58⁴ Isa 14²⁹. **Who hath warned you**] Are you, too, conscious of your danger ? **To flee**] The picture is that of vipers fleeing before the flames when the stubble in the fields is set on fire. **The wrath to come**] the great judgment with which it was generally believed that the age of the Messiah would open. The Jews regarded it mainly as a judgment upon the Gentiles, but John declared that it would be a judgment upon every hypocritical Jew.

8. Fruits meet for repentance] RV 'fruit worthy of repentance.' Fruit is a frequent metaphor for works, and a very suitable one. Fruit is not loosely attached to a tree, but is part of it. It derives its character from the tree on which it grows. So a man's works, i.e. his words and actions, are part of him, and express his true character.

9. We have Abraham to (for) *our* **father**] cp. Jn 8 33, 39, 53. This insolent spirit is best illustrated by a quotation from the rabbis : 'The fire of hell (Gehenna) has no power to consume even the sinners of Israel, but they go down only to be frightened and slightly singed for their bad actions. Then comes Abraham, who kept all the precepts of the Law, and through his own merit brings them up again.' **Of these stones**] a hint, not an express statement of the calling of the Gentiles: cp. Ro 4 9 6 Gal 4 28 Jn 8 39. **10. Ax**] a frequent and expressive type of imminent judgment (7 19 Lk 13 7 : cp. Ro 11 17). **The trees**] i.e. individual Jews, not the nation, though, as a matter of fact, judgment overtook the nation also for its rejection of Christ : cp. 7 19. **The fire**] see on v. 12.

11, 12. Here is emphatic testimony of John to the Messiahship of Jesus. Jesus is so great that John is unworthy to perform for Him the function of the meanest slave. Jesus is the dispenser of divine sanctification (**the Holy Ghost**). Jesus is the absolute judge of the human race, with power to reward the good in heaven and to punish the guilty in hell (v. 12). Nothing of importance is really added to this testimony in the Fourth Gospel. There, indeed, the Baptist calls Jesus the Lamb of God and the Son of God, and is aware of His preëxistence ; but these things follow naturally from the tremendous prerogatives which even in the Synoptics John assigns to Him. If it be remembered that the synoptic testimony is given before, and the testimony in the Fourth Gospel after Christ's Baptism, all difficulty disappears : see Jn 1 6, 15, 19 3 27.

11. Whose shoes, etc.] the office of the meanest slave. 'A slave unlooses his master's shoe, and carries it after him ; does what he needs for the bath, undresses, washes, anoints, rubs, re-dresses him, and puts on his shoes.' **With the Holy Ghost, and** *with* **fire**] St. Mark omits 'and with fire.' John says, in effect, 'I can bring you to repentance, but no further. My baptism gives no grace. It only symbolises the greater baptism which Jesus will give. His baptism will give you "the Holy Ghost," i.e. new spiritual life, and in-

ward sanctification, and "Fire," i.e. holy fervour and zeal in God's service' : cp. Ac 2 3. John here refers directly to Christian Baptism, the spiritual efficacy of which he contrasts with the inefficacy of his own.

12. St. Mark omits this v. **Whose fan** (or, 'shovel')] Jesus holds in His hand the winnowing fan of judgment, for He is the judge of quick and dead. Here John passes far beyond Jewish ideas about the Messiah. **His floor**] RV 'threshing-floor' : not merely Palestine, but the universe. **His wheat**] i.e. good persons. **The garner**] heaven. **The chaff**] the wicked. **Unquenchable fire**] i.e. Gehenna, hell.

13–17. Baptism of Jesus (Mk 1 9 Lk 3 21 Jn 1 32). The Baptism of Jesus has more than one aspect and significance. To John it was with its miraculous accompaniments a sign that Jesus was the promised Messiah and the Son of God (Jn 1 32-34). To Israel it was 'the showing to the people' of the promised monarch, and His consecration by the unction of the Holy Spirit to the threefold office of prophet, priest, and king. To the Christian Church it is the type and first example of all true baptism—the baptism, that is, of water and the Spirit. So far all is clear. But when we come to speak of its significance to Jesus Himself we are in a region of mystery, and both prudence and reverence teach us not to dogmatise. Yet we may venture to say this, that the vision at the Baptism was intended primarily for Jesus Himself, and neither for John nor for the multitudes who were present. It was Jesus to whom the heavens were opened, Jesus who saw the Spirit descending as a dove, and Jesus to whom the momentous words were spoken, 'This is My beloved Son, in whom I am well pleased.' This is expressly testified by St. Matthew and St. Mark, and is not contradicted by St. Luke and St. John, although the last states what St. Luke perhaps also implies in the words 'in a bodily form,' that the vision was also intended for the Baptist. If we take the most natural and obvious interpretation of the incident, we shall hold that our Lord's baptism marked the point in His career when there first awoke in Him the complete consciousness of His divine sonship, and of all the tremendous consequences which this unique relationship to God and man involved. There must have been a time when this consciousness first became fully explicit. He cannot have had it in unconscious infancy, or as a young child. Even as a boy (we are speaking, of course, of His *human* knowledge) He cannot have possessed it complete. He grew in knowledge of things human and divine (Lk 2 40-52), and one of the things in knowledge of which He grew was the awful mystery of His own Divine-Human Personality. He must, of course, have been always conscious, after attaining the use of reason, of the difference between Himself and other men, of the unique character of His communion with God, and of the greatness of the mission which lay before Him, but He need not have known *all*. It is possible that full self-knowledge might have hindered rather than helped Him during the thirty years of obscurity which preceded His public ministry. But however that may be, before the ministry began the veil that concealed the mystery of His nature was drawn aside by an inward revelation, and soon the outward testimony of miracles confirmed what the inward voice had declared.

14. I have need] not inconsistent with Jn 1 33 ('I knew him not'). As Jesus approaches, a prophetic presentiment passes through the mind of John that this is the Messiah. The descent of the Spirit makes it a certainty. It is possible, even likely, that as John and Jesus were cousins, they were already acquainted, although John 'knew him not' as the Messiah. As John's baptism was unto remission of sins, it seemed to him strange that Jesus should have consented to such a baptism. But, though sinless, Jesus came to identify himself with sinners. He would be 'under the law that he might redeem those that were under the law' (Gal 4 4, 5).

15. To fulfil all righteousness] i.e. to fulfil all the ordinances of the old covenant among which our Lord reckoned John's baptism.

16, 17. One of the leading Trinitarian passages in the NT. The voice of the Father is heard proclaiming the essential divinity of the Son, and upon the Son, as He rises from the baptismal waters, the Holy Ghost, the living bond of love and unity in the Godhead, descends. The appearance of the Holy Ghost in the form of a dove was a symbolical vision, and, as spiritual things are spiritually discerned, the vision was probably seen only by our Lord and the Baptist. The dove is a type of the Spirit, because of its innocence, gentleness, and affection ; cp. 10 16, ' Be ye therefore wise as serpents, and harmless as doves.' The voice from heaven may be paralleled by the voice at Sinai (Ex 20), to Nebuchadnezzar (Dan 4 31), at the Transfiguration (Mt 17 5), before the Passion (Jn 12 28), to St. Paul (Ac 9 4), and to St. Peter (Ac 11 7). The idea that a revelation might be communicated by a supernatural voice, was familiar to the Jews of our Lord's time. The rabbis taught that after the cessation of prophecy, God continued to make revelations to His people by means of the Bath-kol, or heavenly voice. At Jericho, for example, the Bath-kol declared the Rabbi Hillel to be worthy to have the Spirit of God abide upon him, and at Jamnia decided the dispute between the schools of Hillel and Shammai in favour of the former.

16. And he saw] i.e. Jesus saw, though John saw it also.

17. This is] This represents the form in which the Baptist heard the words. 'Thou art' (Mk, Lk) represent the form in which Jesus heard them. **My beloved Son**] cp. 17 5. The highest sense is to be given to these words. The Father bears witness, not only to Christ's Messiahship, but to His eternal and divine Sonship, in virtue of which He is from all eternity ' in the bosom of the Father,' loving and beloved. **In whom I am well pleased**] cp. Isa 42 1 Mt 12 18. Lest the Baptism of Christ should be thought to indicate that He was a sinner like ourselves, the Father was pleased to pronounce Him absolutely sinless. The tense of the Gk. is difficult. The Revisers (also Plummer) regard it as a timeless aorist. But it may be an ordinary historical aorist, and thus point to Christ's preëxistence—' in whom I *was* well pleased,' viz. before the Incarnation and before the creation of the world. The words are also a message full of grace to mankind. As the Son is ever well pleasing and acceptable to the Father, so also are all those who are found in Him.

CHAPTER 4
THE TEMPTATION

1–11. The temptation (Mk 1 12 Lk 4 1). The narrative, which can only have come from our Lord's own lips, describes an actual historical fact, the great temptation which He underwent at the very beginning of His ministry. He was tempted at other times (Lk 4 13), perhaps at all times (Heb 2 18), during His earthly life, but the two great seasons of trial were now, and immediately before the Passion Lk 22 42 Mt 26 39. Our Lord records His experience in symbolical language partly because the inward operations of the mind could hardly be represented to men of that age except as visible transactions, but more particularly because the story of Adam's temptation in Gn 3 1 is also told symbolically. Jesus here appears as the second Adam, victorious in the conflict in which the first Adam failed. He wins the victory as man, not as God, so that here the human race in the person of its Head begins to retrieve its defeat and to bruise the Serpent's head, receiving thereby an assurance of final victory. The temptation of the first Adam took place in a garden, i.e. in a universe as yet unspoilt by sin. The temptation of the second Adam took place in a wilderness, i.e. in a world rendered desolate by Adam's fall, and the ultimate effect of His victory will be to make it a garden again. In this connexion should be taken St. Mark's statement that ' He was with the wild beasts.' The wild beasts did not hurt Jesus, because He regained for man the empire over the beasts which Adam lost: 'The wolf also shall dwell with the lamb, and the leopard shall lie down with the kid... They shall not hurt nor destroy in all my holy mountain' (Isa 11 ^{6}).

The details of three temptations are recorded: (a) The first (vv. 3, 4) was a temptation to abuse His miraculous powers. If, as seems probable, Jesus first received authority to work miracles at His Baptism, the very freshness and greatness of the gift would suggest to the devil the most appropriate form of attack. Jesus was hungry, he also had an unlimited power of working miracles. Why should He remain hungry, when He had the power of making bread? 'Why,' suggested the devil, 'is it right to feed others, and wrong to feed thyself? If thou be the Son of God, command that these stones be made bread.' So the tempter suggested, but Jesus replied, 'Man shall not live by bread alone but by every word' (i.e. command) 'that proceedeth out of the mouth of God.' These words, taken from Dt 8 ^{3}, refer to Israel in the wilderness. There they, like Jesus, had no bread, yet they were fed by the word of God's mouth, for God commanded manna to fall from heaven. In effect Jesus said to the tempter, 'It is true that I have no bread, but, since I am here by God's command, He will keep me alive without bread. He has but to utter a word, and I shall be providentially fed, as the Israelites were of old.' If it be asked why it was wrong for Jesus to make bread for His own use, the answer is that in God's working in the world there is in general a strict economy of miraculous power. In the life of Jesus there is not a single example of a miracle worked for His own advantage. In every case His miraculous power was used for the good of others, to remove the ravages of disease and sin, and to advance the kingdom of God, and for these purposes alone was it entrusted to Him. The devil's suggestion was, therefore, a temptation to disobedience, like that of our first parents. Satan would have had our Lord act independently, setting up His will against God's, instead of conforming it to His in filial obedience.

(b) The next temptation (vv. 5–7) was more subtle. The devil took Him in spirit to the lofty platform (not **pinnacle**) overlooking the courts of the Temple, from which a great multitude could be conveniently addressed. It was from this platform or pulpit that James the Lord's brother delivered the public address which was the immediate occasion of His martyrdom (Euseb. 2. 23). Satan suggested that our Lord should address the assembled multitudes of Israel from this giddy height, and then prove His Messianic claims beyond all question by flying through the air, and descending to the ground unharmed. Stripped of its symbolical form, this was a temptation

to take a short and easy road to recognition as the Messiah by giving 'a sign from heaven' which even the most incredulous and unspiritual would be compelled to accept. This short and easy method Jesus decisively rejected. He determined to appeal to the spiritual apprehension of mankind, that they might believe on Him, not because they were astounded by His miracles, and could not resist their evidence, but because they were attracted by the holiness and graciousness of His character, by the loftiness of His teaching, and by the love of God to man which was manifested in all His words and actions. He intended His miracles to be secondary, an aid to the faith of those who on other grounds were inclined to believe, but not portents to extort the adhesion of those who had no sympathy with Himself or His aims.

(c) Then the devil made his last effort (vv. 8–10). He offered Jesus all that he had, 'all the kingdoms of the earth and the glory of them,' if He would but worship him, i.e. acknowledge his usurped authority, and do evil that good might come. The statement of the devil that all the kingdoms of the earth are at his disposal is a difficult one, but it is in harmony with the NT. view that wealth and power are dangerous snares, which are better avoided, and that religious safety lies in poverty and obscurity. It also harmonises with the familiar experience that the devil often tempts men most severely by making them rich and great. Yet the statement is an exaggeration. The devil's power to dispose of the honour and glory of the world is subject to the permission and overruling providence of God, who continually brings good out of evil. Moreover, since the Ascension of our Blessed Lord, the devil's power over the kingdoms of the earth has, at least in Christian lands, been greatly reduced.

1. Of the spirit] i.e. of the Holy Spirit God Himself ordained that Jesus should be tempted or tried, because only through temptation can human nature attain to perfection. Even the angels had to pass through a similar trial. **Into the wilderness**] Since Jesus was 'returning' towards Galilee (Lk), the traditional scene of the temptation, Mount Quarantania, near Jericho, is a suitable one. **The devil**] The word literally means 'slanderer' or 'accuser.' See special note below.

2. Fasted forty days] It was God's will that before beginning His work Jesus should retire from the world and give Himself entirely to fasting and prayer, with meditation upon His future plan of action. We may suppose that He was so absorbed in contemplation of His Messianic work, that He was not conscious of physical need. For parallels see Ex 34 ^{28} 1 K 19 ^{8} Lk 1 ^{80} Gal 1 ^{17}.

3. **If tnou be**] Probably Satan expressed doubt in order to tempt Jesus to prove Himself the Son of God by a miracle. **4.** See prefatory remarks. **5. The holy city**] This phrase, peculiar to this Gospel, marks a thoroughly Jewish affection for Jerusalem: see 27⁵³, and cp. 5³⁵. A (RV 'the') **pinnacle**] see prefatory remarks.

6. The devil is a good theologian, and can quote Scripture to his purpose. Here he quotes Ps 91¹¹,¹², omitting one line. The general nature of this temptation is indicated in prefatory remarks. It was, besides, an incitement to tempt God presumptuously by deliberately incurring unnecessary danger.

7. See Dt 6¹⁶. Deuteronomy was one of Jesus' favourite books. **8.** See prefatory remarks. **10.** See Dt 6¹³, and 10²⁰. **11. Ministered unto him**] i.e. perhaps with spiritual refreshment. Cp. Lk 22⁴³.

Note. (1) St. Matthew and St. Luke for the Temptation have access to some other authority than St. Mark, who is here very brief. The order of St. Matthew seems superior to that of St. Luke. (2) If the Temptation of Jesus was a reality (and we can scarcely doubt that it was), the Tempter must have been met and conquered by Him in the strength of His human nature, assisted by divine grace. As God, He could not be tempted at all.

12–17. Beginning of the Galilean ministry (Mk 1¹⁴,¹⁵ Lk 4¹⁴,¹⁵,³¹). It might be thought from the synoptic account that Jesus began His Galilean ministry immediately after His Baptism and Temptation. But from the Fourth Gospel it is clear that this was not so. Jesus was baptised late in 26 A.D. He then remained for a time in the neighbourhood of the Baptist, five of whose followers, Andrew, John, Philip, Peter, and Bartholomew, attached themselves to Him, and followed Him back to Galilee. Then in April 27 A.D. He went up to Jerusalem to keep the Passover (the first passover of the ministry) and cleansed the Temple for the first time. He then baptised in the country districts of Judæa with great success (Jn 2, 3). The length of this Judæan ministry is disputed. Prof. Sanday thinks that it lasted only 3 or 4 weeks, but most authorities assign to it 8 months: see on Jn 4³⁵. The Galilean ministry begins, therefore, either in May, 27 A.D., or more probably in December of the same year: see Jn 1¹⁹–4⁴⁵.

12. **Departed into Galilee**] i.e. from Judæa, where He was baptising (Jn 3²³). He took the route through Samaria (Jn 4⁴), staying at Sychar two days to preach to the Samaritans. Jesus had probably intended to make Jerusalem and Judæa the chief scene of His ministry, but changed His policy owing to the hostility of the Pharisees (Jn 4¹). In many respects Galilee was better suited to His

purpose than Judæa. The Galileans were more tolerant, less conservative, and less under the power of the priests and Pharisees than the Judæans. There was a large Gentile population in Galilee, and much of the trade between Egypt and Damascus passed through the country. The people were more industrious, prosperous, and enterprising than the Judæans, who were jealous of them, and affected to despise them.

13. **And leaving Nazareth**] He went, as was natural, first to Nazareth, but on account of His unfavourable reception there (Lk 4¹⁶), migrated to Capernaum, which is on the NW. coast of the Sea of Galilee. Capernaum is generally identified with the modern Tell Hum. It is in the tribe of Naphtali, but the borders of Zebulun are near. Capernaum was a busy place. Two caravan routes passed through the town. It had a custom-house, and a Roman garrison.

14. The quotation (from Isa 9¹) is, in view of Christ's ministry in Galilee, a singularly apt one, even according to modern ideas. Isaiah prophesies that the northern parts of Israel which have suffered most from the incursions of the Syrians and the Assyrians (2 K 15²⁹) will be the first to be restored to prosperity by the Messiah, who will win a great victory in these regions over the enemies of Israel, and establish an eternal kingdom. The quotation is made from memory, and reproduces the original somewhat freely.

15. **By the way of the sea**] RV 'towards the sea,' i.e. the Sea of Galilee. **Beyond Jordan**] must be taken to mean 'also the district beyond Jordan.' The other side of the lake was easily reached by boat, and was more than once visited by Jesus (8²³ 14¹³). The district S. of this, E. of the Jordan, was called Peræa, and was the scene of the last stages of our Lord's ministry (Jn 10⁴⁰). **Galilee of the Gentiles**] In Isaiah the expression means 'district of the Gentiles,' and refers not to the whole of Galilee, but to its northern borders, which were largely inhabited by Gentiles.

16. The **darkness** means in Isaiah the despair caused by the ravages of the Assyrians; in St. Matthew the spiritual darkness which Jesus came to dispel. **17. The kingdom of heaven**] see on 3².

18–22. Call of Simon, Andrew, James, and John (Mk 1¹⁶; cp. Lk 5¹). Simon, Andrew, and John had already been disciples for some time, and so probably had James: see Jn 1³⁵. The call was therefore not so sudden and unexpected as it appears to be in the synoptic narrative. In Lk 5¹ a very similar call is recorded in connexion with a miraculous draught of fishes, and many suppose the two incidents to be the same. If they are distinct, and this seems the preferable view (see on Lk

5¹), the order of events is as follows. Immediately after His migration to Capernaum Jesus called the four fishermen, who were already disciples, to be apostles. They did not, however, while Jesus remained in Capernaum, entirely leave their trade, but waited for a final summons. This soon came. When about to leave Capernaum for a tour through Galilee, Jesus appeared to them again, and after working a symbolical miracle (Lk 5¹), called them finally to accompany Him. He called them while actually at their work, as He called Matthew (9⁹), in order to show that no idle or useless person can be a Christian.

19. Fishers of men] 'The fisherman Peter did not lay aside his nets but changed them' (Aug.). **21.** According to Lk the four fishermen were partners. **22.** St. Mark mentions that there were hired servants in Zebedee's boat, which indicates that the family was not poor. St. John was known to the high priest, and probably had a house in Jerusalem (Jn 18 ¹⁶ 19 ²⁷). St. Matthew was rich. It cannot be shown that any of the apostles were specially poor or of a mean social position. 'Unlearned and ignorant men' (Ac 4 ¹³), simply means that they had not been trained in the schools of the rabbis. Manual labour was honourable among the Jews, and even the sons of the wealthy were taught trades.

23-25. Journeys of Jesus through Galilee: preaching and healing the sick. St. Matthew interrupts his narrative of what took place at Capernaum to give a general sketch of the early period of the Galilean ministry. After the sermon on the mount he returns to what happened at Capernaum (8¹).

23. All Galilee] A preaching expeditior. of so comprehensive a character must have lasted several months.

In their synagogues] Synagogues had their origin during the captivity, and rapidly became a general institution after the return. In the time of Christ there was a synagogue not only in every town, but in every village large enough to afford a congregation of ten adult men. The synagogue was primarily a place of worship, but it was also a centre of government, ts members forming a local self-governing ʝody. The governing body of a synagogue were called 'elders.' At their head was a 'ruler of the synagogue,' who maintained order during public worship (Lk 13 ¹⁴), and decided who was to conduct the service (Ac 13 ¹⁵). The ruler was not a scribe, but ranked immediately after the scribes. Each synagogue had an attendant (*Hazzan*) (Lk 4 ²⁰). He was a scribe, but ranked lowest in the scribal body. He had charge of the building, gave the rolls to the readers, called upon the priests to pronounce the benediction at the proper time, and also on week-days acted as schoolmaster. It was he

who carried out the judicial sentences of the elders. Many synagogues had an interpreter (*methurgeman*), who, after the Scripture had been read in Hebrew, gave the Targum, i.e. translated it into Aramaic, which was the vulgar tongue.

The elders of the synagogue were the rulers of the local community both in civil and religious matters. They had power to excommunicate (Lk 6 ²²), and to scourge (Mt 10 ¹⁷) with forty stripes save one (Dt 25 ³ 2 Cor 11 ²⁴). Unlike the Temple-worship the worship of the synagogue was under the control of the laity. A priest as such had no privilege but to give the blessing. The four chief parts of synagogue worship were, (1) the reading of the Law, (2) of the prophets, (3) the sermon, (4) the prayers. The prayers and lessons were read and the sermon delivered by members of the congregation selected by the ruler. This will explain how it was that Jesus, and afterwards St. Paul, were able to use the synagogues as centres for diffusing Christian truth : cp. Lk 4 ¹⁶ Ac 13 ¹⁵. On week-days the synagogues were used as schools for children.

24. All Syria] i.e. the Roman province of Syria. **Possessed with devils]** See special note below. **Lunatick]** (lit. 'moonstruck') RV 'epileptic.' Such sufferers were supposed to be influenced by changes of the moon.

He healed them] Great prominence is given in the Gospels to miracles of healing, and our Lord plainly regarded practical work of this kind as an integral part of His work of salvation. Briefly expressed, the teaching of the miracles of healing is as follows : (1) That the preservation of life and health by all the means in our power is a Christian duty. The Christian will seek 'a sound mind in a sound body' for himself and for others. In practice this leads to the establishment of hospitals, efficient sanitation, and factory legislation calculated to protect life and limb and health. (2) That the soul can often be reached through the body. Christ touched the souls of those whom He healed, and the early Church made as many converts by its works of mercy as by its preaching. Missionary societies are well aware of this, and send out many medical missionaries. (3) That pain, disease, and death are no part of God's will for man. Like sin they came into the world against His will, and they are part of those 'works of the devil,' which the Son of God was manifested to destroy. God permits disease, as He permits moral evil, He even overrules it for good, so that sickness may become a visitation from God full of spiritual blessings ; nevertheless, disease is no part of His original plan of creation, it is not natural but against nature, and it can have no part in the perfected kingdom of God.

25. Decapolis] i.e. 'ten towns,' a region beyond Jordan, containing originally ten allied or federated cities, among which were Gadara, Pella, Gerasa, and Damascus. It was part of Peræa, and its inhabitants were mainly Greeks.

Note on Diabolical Possession

In the NT. disease, except when it is a special visitation from God (Heb 12⁶), is regarded as the work of Satan (Mt 9³² 12²² Lk 11¹⁴ 13¹⁶ Ac 10³⁸, etc.). In particular, nervous diseases and insanity are represented as due to diabolical possession. This was the universal belief of the time, and our Lord, in using language which implies it, need not be regarded as teaching dogmatically that there is such a thing as possession. There were strong reasons why He should seek to 'accommodate' His language to the popular theory. (1) The insane persons whom He wished to heal, were firmly convinced that they were possessed by devils. This was the form assumed by the insane delusion, and to argue against it was useless. The only wise course was to assume that the unclean spirit was there, and to command it to come forth. (2) It was our Lord's method not rashly or unnecessarily to interfere with the settled beliefs of His time, or to anticipate the discoveries of modern science. The belief in demonic possession, though probably erroneous, was so near the truth, that for most purposes of practical religion it might be regarded as true. He, therefore, did not think fit to disturb it. Believing, as He did, that most of the evil in the universe, including disease, though permitted by God, is the work of Satan, He tolerated a belief which had the merit of emphasising this fundamental truth, and left it to the advance of knowledge in future ages to correct the extravagances connected with it. See also on Mt 8²⁸⁻³⁴, Mk 1²¹⁻²⁸.

Note on Satan

Although from the earliest times the Hebrews believed in various kinds of evil spirits, it was not till the time of the captivity that the idea of a supreme evil spirit, exercising lordship over all orders of demons, emerged into prominence. In the OT. Satan appears only in the prologue to Job (chs. 1, 2), where he ranks with the angels or 'sons of God'; in Zech 3¹, where he is the adversary of Joshua the high priest; and in 1 Ch 21¹, where he tempts David to number Israel. All these passages are subsequent to the captivity. In the NT. Satan is a much more prominent character. His influence is represented as all-pervading. He disposes of earthly kingdoms as he wills. He has an organised kingdom of darkness which cannot be overthrown even by the Christ without a fearful struggle, in which the conqueror tastes the bitterness of death. Physical evil is mainly due to him, for he and his ministers are the direct authors of pain, sorrow, disease, and death. The NT. writers indeed recognise that pain and disease are sometimes inflicted by God Himself for disciplinary purposes, but, upon the whole, they ascribe the universal prevalence of physical evil to the malignant activity of Satan The moral evil of the world is also ascribed in the main to him. He goes about the world like a roaring lion, seeking whom he may devour, and never ceases from his insidious attempts to detach mankind from their allegiance to their Creator.

That our Lord many times expressed belief in Satan as a personal being, is admitted on all hands. The only question is whether He may not in this matter have accommodated His language to the beliefs of His contemporaries, or perhaps have personified evil in order to express more vividly its pervasive activity. Both suppositions are, on the whole, improbable. The allusions to Satan and his angels as persons are too frequent and emphatic, to make it easy to suppose that our Lord did not believe in their personality; and, moreover, belief in an impersonal devil presents greater difficulties to faith than belief in a personal one. That evil should exist at all in a world created and governed by a good and all-powerful Being, is a serious moral and intellectual difficulty. But that difficulty is reduced to a minimum if we suppose that it is due to the activity of a hostile personality. Opposition to God's will on the part of a personal self-determining agent, though mysterious, is conceivable. Opposition to it on the part of any impersonal evil influence or physical force is (to most modern minds) inconceivable.

CHAPTER 5
The Sermon on the Mount

5¹⁻7²⁹. The Sermon on the Mount : see Lk 6²⁰f. This sermon is so similar to the sermon reported by St. Luke (Lk 6²⁰), that it is best to regard them as identically the same. It is true that it has been plausibly suggested that our Lord during His preaching tours often repeated nearly the same sermon to different audiences, and that St. Matthew has given us the sermon as delivered at one place and St. Luke as delivered at another, but the resemblances are so extremely close, and the divergencies for the most part so naturally accounted for, that to regard them as identical is more natural. St. Luke's version is much shorter than St. Matthew's (30 vv. against 107), and it contains nothing that is not in St. Matthew except the four woes (Lk 6²⁴⁻²⁶). There are, however, striking parallels to St. Matthew's sermon in other parts of St. Luke's Gospel. No less than 34 vv. scattered through his later cns. correspond to utterances in St. Matthew's sermon, so that altogether the two Gospels contain about 61 parallel vv. The natural inference from this is that, upon the whole, St. Luke gives the sermon as our Lord actually delivered it, and that St. Matthew (or, rather, his authority) has inserted at appropriate places in the sermon other utterances of our Lord dealing with the same or similar subjects. In a literal sense, therefore, St. Luke's report is, speaking generally, the more trustworthy, but St. Matthew's is the more valuable as containing numerous authoritative explanations of its meaning. The discourse was probably what we should call an ordination sermon, delivered, as St. Luke states, immediately after the choice of the twelve apostles (Lk 6 20). St. Matthew, however, inserts it appropriately enough at the beginning of the Galilean ministry, in order to give the reader a general idea of the Master's teaching at this period.

The great interest of the sermon is that it is a more or less full revelation of Christ's own character, a kind of autobiography. Every syllable of it He had already written down in deeds ; He had only to translate His life into language. With it we may compare the wonderful self-revelation in Jn 17, but there is an important difference. There we have His self-revelation as Son of God, holding communion with the Father in a manner impossible to us ; here we have Him pictured in His perfect humanity as Son of man, offering us an example, to which, if we cannot in this life completely attain, we can at least approximate through union with Him. In this sermon Christ is very near to us. The blessedness which He offers to the humble and meek, the merciful, the pure in heart, the peacemakers, the seekers after righteousness, and the persecuted for righteousness' sake, He first experienced Himself, and then commended to others. And the power by which He lived this life is the very power by which we also must live it—the power of secret prayer (6 5 f.). St. Luke tells us that the night before this sermon was delivered was spent entirely in private prayer (Lk 6 12).

The sermon is very important for a right understanding of Christ's conception of ' the kingdom.' It is ' the kingdom of the heavens.' It exists most perfectly in heaven itself, where angels and glorified saints live the ideal life of love and service, finding their whole pleasure in doing God's will and imitating His adorable perfections. This blessed life of sinless perfection Christ brings down to earth in His own person, and makes available for man. Every baptised Christian is taught to pray, ' Thy kingdom come,' and that is interpreted to mean, Let Thy will be done by men on earth as it is done by angels and saints in heaven. The kingdom, then, is just the heavenly life brought down to earth, and its aim and standard is nothing short of the perfection of God Himself, ' Be ye therefore perfect—especially be ye perfect in love— even as your Father which is in heaven is perfect' (5 48). Of this kingdom God the Father is King (cp. the phrase ' kingdom of God,' used by the other evangelists, and the ancient Doxology to the Lord's prayer), but Jesus Himself exercises the immediate sovereignty, being the Father's full representative and endowed with all His powers. He is expressly called King only in Mt 25 34-40, but His regal authority is sufficiently implied in the Sermon on the Mount, where He appears in the character of a divine legislator (5 21 f.), as the judge of quick and dead (7 21-23), and as the sole revealer of absolute truth (7 24-26).

The inward and spiritual view of the kingdom, which is prominent in the Sermon on the Mount, is not inconsistent with its identification elsewhere with the visible Church of Christ (16 18, 19), which includes both worthy and unworthy members (13 47). Our Lord identifies His Church with the kingdom of heaven (16 18, 19), because it is the divinely appointed means of establishing it. To it is entrusted the awful responsibility of implanting and nourishing the spiritual life of God's children. As to unworthy members of the Church, although they are ' in ' the kingdom, they are not ' of ' it.

The profound impression which the Sermon made at the time has been surpassed by the impression which it made on subsequent generations. The Mount of Beatitudes has become to all the chief nations of the world what Sinai was to Israel, the place where an authoritative moral code, and what is more than a code, an authoritative moral ideal, was promulgated. Not even the most sceptical deny that it shows originality and genius of the highest order, and reveals a character of unequalled moral sublimity. The many parallels and resemblances to this sermon adduced from rabbinical writings, some of which are quoted in the commentary, rather enhance than detract from its unique character. Its use of current rabbinical phraseology only throws into greater prominence its matchless originality and independence. But what struck the hearers even more than its moral splendour and originality, was the tone of authority with which it was delivered (7 29). Jesus spoke, not as a scribe dependent on tradition, nor even as a prophet prefacing His words with a ' Thus saith the Lord,' but as one possessed of an inherent and personal claim upon the allegiance and obedience of His hearers. In His own name and by His own authority He revised the Decalogue spoken by

God Himself on Sinai, and declared Himself the Lord and Judge of the human race, before whom, in the last great day, every child of man will stand suppliant-wise to receive his eternal recompense. It is sometimes said that the Sermon on the Mount contains little Theology and no Christology. In reality it expresses or implies every claim to supernatural dignity which Jesus ever made for Himself, or His followers have ever made for Him.

Analysis of the Sermon.

I. **The Beatitudes.** What kind of persons are really blessed or happy (5^{3-12}).

II. **The relation of Christ's disciples to the world as its salt and light** (5^{13-16}).

III. **The relation of the New Teaching to the Law and the prophets as their fulfilment.** It repeals ancient ordinances which were imperfect and transitory, expands the moral and spiritual principles of the OT. to their full development, and in so doing enables Judaism to become the religion of the human race (5^{17-48}).

IV. **Practical instructions in righteousness for the citizens of the kingdom, forming a striking contrast to the ideas of righteousness current among the Scribes and Pharisees.** Alms, prayer, forgiveness, fasting, wealth, freedom from anxiety, rash judgments, reserve in communicating sacred knowledge, persistence in prayer, the two ways, the necessity of good works, stability of character (6^1–7^{27}).

1. **The multitudes**] viz. those mentioned in 4^{25}. **A** (RV 'the') **mountain**] The traditional site is the Horns of Hattîn, or Mount of Beatitudes, a low, square-shaped hill with two summits, about 7 m. SW. of Capernaum. St. Luke says that the sermon (if indeed he is speaking of the same one) was delivered 'in the plain' (AV), or 'on a level place' (RV). If we wish to harmonise, we can say that 'the level place' was half-way down the mountain. **Was set**] The usual attitude of Jewish rabbis in teaching, indicating authority. So in the early church the preacher sat, and the congregation (including the emperor) stood. **His disciples**] i.e. not only the Twelve, as would be the probable meaning in the Fourth Gospel,

but Christ's followers in general. The Twelve had already been chosen, although St. Matthew places the event later (10^{2-4}), and this sermon was their ordination address : see Lk 6^{13}.

1–12. The Beatitudes. Properly speaking, the beatitudes are seven in number, vv. 10, 11, 12, forming an appendix. These three vv. being counted in, the number of beatitudes is raised, according to different methods of division, to eight, or nine, or ten, the last corresponding to the number of the ten commandments. St. Luke has only four, the first, fourth, second and eighth, in that order. As recorded in St. Luke the beatitudes are more paradoxical and startling. They appear to bless actual poverty, hunger, and mourning, and are followed by four woes upon the wealthy and those who receive their consolation in this life. In form St. Luke's beatitudes are possibly more original than St. Matthew's—they are certainly more difficult—but the sense is best expressed by St. Matthew. The beatitudes express, (1) the qualifications necessary for admission into Christ's kingdom ; (2) the blessedness or happiness of those who possess those qualifications ; (3) in St. Luke expressly, and in St. Matthew by implication, the misery of those who do not. Observe that the qualifications of the citizens of the kingdom are not the performance of certain legal acts, but the possession of a certain character, and that the 'sanctions' or promised rewards, unlike those of the Decalogue, are of a spiritual nature. The beatitudes must have been a painful disillusionment to those who believed that the coming kingdom of the Messiah would be a temporal empire like that of Solomon, only differing from it in its universal extension and unending duration. The virtues here regarded as essential, humility, meekness, poverty of spirit, are the very opposite of those ambitions, self-assertive qualities, which the carnal multitude admired. We cannot doubt that Jesus intended the beatitudes, and indeed the sermon generally, to act like Gideon's test, and to sift out those who had no real sympathy with His aims. Somewhat later He carried the sifting process still further, and some who had stood this test, 'went back, and walked no more with Him' (Jn 6^{66}).

Scheme of the Beatitudes (after 'The Teacher's Commentary '):—

I. THE POOR IN SPIRIT
(From this fundamental condition the other virtues mentioned grow.)

(The inner life towards God)		(Its outward manifestation towards man)
II. THEY THAT MOURN	answering to	III. THE MEEK
IV. THEY THAT HUNGER AFTER RIGHTEOUSNESS	" "	V. THE MERCIFUL
VI. THE PURE IN HEART . . .	" "	VII. THE PEACEMAKERS
(supplemental)		VIII. THE PATIENT IN PERSECUTIONS

First Beatitude

3. Blessed] The beatitude type of utterance, like the parable, is not without example in the OT. (Pss 1[1] 41[1] 65[4] 84[5-7] 89[15] 119[1,2] 128[1,2], etc.), but Christ has made both types peculiarly His own. Beatitudes express the essential spirit of the New Covenant, in contrast to the Old, which was prodigal of denunciations (Dt 27, 28, 29, etc.). The thunders of Sinai proclaiming the Decalogue form a striking contrast to the gentle voice of the Son of man on the Mount of Beatitudes proclaiming the religion of love. Blessedness is higher than happiness. Happiness comes from without, and is dependent on circumstances; blessedness is an inward fountain of joy in the soul itself, which no outward circumstances can seriously affect. Blessedness consists in standing in a right relation to God, and so realising the true law of a man's being. According to Christ, the blessed life can be enjoyed even by those who are unhappy, a paradox which the ancient world, with the exception perhaps of the Stoics, did not understand. The Greeks thought that the blessed life was possible only for a very few. It was impossible for slaves, for the diseased, for the poor, and for those who die young. Christ taught that it is possible for all mankind, for the meanest slave, and the most wretched invalid, as well as for the wealthy, the prosperous, and the great. He went even beyond the Stoics. They taught that the wise man is blessed. Jesus opened the blessed life to the simple and uneducated.

The poor in spirit] St. Luke, ' Blessed are ye poor.' The expression is difficult, and is interpreted in two ways. (1) ' The poor in spirit' are those who feel themselves spiritually poor, and in need of all things, and so approach God as penitents and suppliants, beseeching Him to supply their needs, clothe their nakedness, and enrich their poverty. Poverty of spirit is the opposite of pride, self-righteousness, and self-conceit ; the spirit of the publican rather than of the Pharisee ; the spirit of those who wish to learn rather than to teach, to obey rather than to command, and are willing to become as little children in order to enter into the kingdom of heaven. (2) Others, following St. Luke's version, see in the saying a more definite reference to actual riches and poverty. They understand our Lord to mean that a Christian, whether rich or poor, must have the spirit of poverty, i.e. he must possess his wealth as if he possessed it not, and be willing to resign it at any moment without regret, and to say with Job, ' The LORD gave, and the LORD hath taken away ; blessed be the name of the LORD.' This interpretation makes a spirit of detachment from the world and all its allurements, of which wealth is for most men the chief, the first condition of the blessed life.

For theirs is the kingdom of heaven] not only ' shall be theirs hereafter,' but ' is theirs now.' The kingdom is here regarded, like eternal life in the Fourth Gospel, as a present possession. Usually it is regarded in this Gospel as something future, manifested only at the end of the world. On ' the kingdom' see prefatory note and Intro.

The rabbinical parallel to this beatitude is chiefly interesting by way of contrast. It runs, ' Ever be more and more lowly in spirit, since the expectancy of man is to become the food of worms.'

Second Beatitude

4. They that mourn] St. Luke (following a different recension of the Sayings) has, ' Blessed are ye that weep now, for ye shall laugh.' That sorrow of the acutest kind (and that is what the Gk. indicates) can minister to blessedness, is a paradox which the world cannot understand, but which is profoundly true in the experience of believers. (1) The sorrows that God sends or permits, if received with humility and submission, ever refine and ennoble the character, and elevate it into closer union with the Father of spirits. Hence the apostle can even ' glory in tribulations also : knowing that tribulation worketh patience ; and patience, experience' (i.e. tried and proved character) ; ' and experience, hope' (Ro 5[3,4]) ; and a follower of his can write, ' Now no chastening for the present seemeth to be joyous, but grievous : nevertheless afterward it yieldeth the peaceable fruit of righteousness unto them that have been exercised thereby' (Heb 12[11]). (2) Those who mourn for the sorrows of others out of Christian sympathy, are rewarded by the very exercise of that sweet act of compassion, and find many comforters in their own real sorrows. (3) Those who mourn for sin with a godly sorrow, saying with the publican, ' God be merciful to me a sinner,' are comforted by the removal of the burden of sin, and the forgiveness of its guilt. (4) Those who mourn for the sins of others, who pray earnestly for their conversion, are often comforted by the success of their prayers.

Comforted] the word implies strengthening as well as consolation. The faculty which is exercised by the true mourner is strengthened by use. Those who bear their sorrows patiently grow in patience ; those who sorrow for others grow in sympathy ; those who sorrow for their own sin deepen their penitence ; those who intercede for the sins of the world grow in the likeness of the great Sin-bearer and Intercessor. The comfort comes from the exercise of the spiritual faculty, and from the consciousness of growing more like God ; but there is also that final comfort in the world to come, when 'God shall wipe away all tears from their eyes ' (Rev 7[17]).

THIRD BEATITUDE (not in St. Luke)

5. The meek] A quotation from Ps 37[11]. The 'earth' is not only the new earth spoken of 2 Pet 3[13] Rev 21[1], but refers also to the present world. The words are a prophecy that meekness will prove a greater power in the world than pride. This was revolutionary doctrine. Judaism meant pride of race and privilege ; Rabbinism, pride of learning ; Roman imperialism, pride of power ; Greek culture, either pride of intellect or pride of external magnificence. All agreed that the meek man was a poor creature, and the worldly world thinks so still. Nevertheless, meekness is irresistibly attractive, and exercises a wider spiritual influence than any other type of character. ' He hath put down the mighty from their seat, and hath exalted the humble and meek.' See further on 18[4].

Meekness is a virtue which can be exercised both towards God and towards man ; and inasmuch as it involves self-control, it is not a weak but an heroic quality. ' He that is slow to anger is better than the mighty ; and he that ruleth his spirit than he that taketh a city ' (Prov 16[32]). A meek man is one who is not easily provoked or irritated, and forbearing under injury or annoyance.

FOURTH BEATITUDE

6. That hunger and thirst after righteousness] St. Luke, ' ye that hunger now.' Righteousness here is goodness or Christian perfection in its widest sense : cp. v. 48 Ps 42[1, 2].

Filled] i.e. shall attain completely to the character at which they aim.

FIFTH BEATITUDE (not in St. Luke)

7. The merciful] Our salvation is made dependent upon our showing mercy to every creature that can feel. Every kind of cruel amusement, or cruel punishment, as well as every wanton act of cruelty, is strictly forbidden. It should be remembered that cruel speeches no less than cruel acts are forbidden by this commandment. Words can lacerate more deeply than stripes. By the ancient Greeks and Romans the emotion of pity was generally regarded as a fault, or at least as a weakness. The Stoics were in practice humane men, but they regarded pity in the abstract as a vice. ' The wise man,' they said, ' succours, but does not pity.'

SIXTH BEATITUDE

8. The pure in heart] The ' heart,' both in the OT. and NT., stands for a man's inmost

soul, and so the purity here required is not the ceremonial cleanness of the Levitical law, nor even the blamelessness of outwardly correct conduct, but complete purity of inward thought and desire. A thing is pure when it contains no admixture of other substances. Benevolence is pure when it contains no admixture of self-seeking ; justice is pure when it contains no admixture of partiality ; love is pure when it contains no admixture of lust. A man's heart is pure when it loves only the good, when all its motives are right, and when all its aspirations are after the noble and true. Purity here is not synonymous with chastity, but includes it. **See God**] Just as the liar does not understand truthfulness, and does not recognise it when he encounters it, so the unholy person does not understand sanctity, and cannot understand the all-holy God. But those who cleanse their hearts understand God in proportion to their purity, and one day, when they are cleansed from all sin, will see Him face to face (Heb 12[14] 1 Jn 3[2,3] Rev 22[4]).

SEVENTH BEATITUDE (not in St. Luke)

9. The peacemakers] Peacemakers are, (1) those who reconcile men at variance, whether individuals, or classes of men (e.g. employers and employed), or nations ; (2) those who work earnestly to prevent disputes arising or to settle them peaceably (e.g. by arbitration) ; (3) those who strive to reconcile men to God, and so to bring peace to their souls. **They shall be called the children (RV ' sons ') of God**] Because in this aspect they are especially like their heavenly Father, who has sent peace and goodwill down to earth in the person of His dear Son, who is charged with a message of reconciliation.

EIGHTH BEATITUDE

10. Which are persecuted] RV 'that have been persecuted.' The reference is not to past persecutions of OT. saints, but to those of the disciples, which Jesus sees to be inevitable, and graphically represents as already begun.

12. The prophets which were before you] By ranking His disciples with the OT. prophets, Jesus seems to imply that they also are prophets. It is this possession of prophetical gifts by the first disciples which justifies the Church in regarding the NT. as the inspired Word of God : see Ac 11[27] 13[1] 15[32] 21[10] 1 Cor 12[28] 14[1] Eph 2[20] 3[5] 4[11], etc.

13-16. The relation of Christ's disciples to the world. Nothing corresponding to this section is found in St. Luke's sermon, but parallels occur in Lk 14[34, 35] and 11[33]. The section is well placed by St. Matthew. The connexion of thought is clear and natural. Having spoken of their persecutions, Jesus proceeds to encourage His disciples by speaking of the greatness of their mission in the world. They are to be the **salt** of society. Salt preserves food from corruption, and seasons it, making it wholesome and acceptable. So the disciples are to purify the society in which they move, setting a good example and counteracting every corrupt tendency. For this purpose their Christianity must be genuine. Men must feel that they are different from the world, and have a savour of their own. **T**he salt which has **lost his savour** is the Christianity which is only worldliness under another name. Again, the disciples are to be **the light of the world,** being the representatives of Him who is the world's true Light (Jn 8 12). They are to enlighten it as its teachers, and also by the examples of their lives. They are also to be as **a city set on a hill,** which cannot be hid. In this figure they are contemplated not as individuals but as a visible society, or Church. The old city set on a hill was Jerusalem (Ps 48 2). This was shortly to be trodden under the foot of men as having lost its savour, and the new society was to take its place. Christ here solemnly warns us that the standard of living in the Church must be visibly higher than the standard of living in the world. A Church which tolerates a corrupt ministry, or laxity of life among its communicants, is not bearing its witness before the world.

13. Wherewith, etc.] i.e. either, ' Wherewith shall the world be salted ? ' or ' Wherewith shall the salt ' (i.e. the disciples) ' be salted ? ' cp. Mk 9 50 Lk 14 34. Salt in Palestine, being gathered in an impure state, often undergoes chemical changes by which its flavour is destroyed while its appearance remains.

15. A candle] RV ' a lamp ': see Mk 4 21 Lk 8 16 11 33. **A bushel** (Lat. *modius*)] RV ' the bushel,' i.e. the one which is kept in the house for measuring the corn or meal for the daily provision of bread. The *modius* here is probably the Heb. *seah* = 1½ pecks.

16. Let your light] This is not inconsistent with the command to be **humble** and to do good by stealth, especially as the collective good works of the Christian brotherhood as a whole are chiefly spoken of. ' Our light is to shine forth though we conceal it,' says St. Hilary. Origen and other writers testify that the good works of Christians did more to convert the world than miracles or preaching.

17–20. Christianity as the fulfilment of the Law and the Prophets. This section is especially appropriate in St. Matthew's Jewish Gospel. St. Luke's sermon, being for Gentile readers, has nothing similar, and in his whole Gospel there is only one parallel v. (Lk 16 17). In one aspect Christ's attitude to the Law was conservative. He regarded Christianity as continuous with, and in a true sense identical with, the religion of the Law and the Prophets. He could even repeat the current teaching of the rabbis that the Law was eternal, and that not a jot or tittle could be taken from it. He severely rebuked such of His disciples as should presume to despise or undervalue the smallest part of the OT. They should not indeed be excluded from His kingdom, but they should be the least in it (v. 19). On the other hand, He made it clear that this eternal validity did not belong to the Law as Moses left it, but to the Law as ' fulfilled,' i.e. developed, or completed by Himself. He superseded the Law and the Prophets by fulfilling them, and He fulfilled them in all their parts. The spiritual and moral teaching of the Law and of the Prophets He freed from all lower elements and carried forward to their ideal perfection. The political teaching of the Law He completed by laying down the principles of the perfect state. Even the ceremonial law He fulfilled. The Law of Sacrifice was fulfilled in His sacrificial death, and in the spiritual sacrifices of prayer and praise and thanksgiving in which His precious death is pleaded. Circumcision became ' the circumcision made without hands,' i.e. Holy Baptism. The Passover became the Lord's Supper. The sanctification which the Law gave to one day in seven, was extended by Christ to every day in the week, and even the sabbath itself was, in a certain sense, perpetuated and continued by Him as the Christian ' Lord's Day.' Even such minor matters as ceremonial ablutions and the distinction of meats received their due fulfilment when Christ made possible the inward holiness which these outward observances symbolised.

Above all, the prophets were fulfilled by Christ in a most comprehensive way. He was not content simply to carry out their idea of the Messiah, wonderful as it was. He improved upon it, or, in His own words, ' fulfilled it.' No careful student of the OT. can fail to see how infinitely the actual NT. fulfilment exceeded the expectation of even the most enlightened OT. prophets. This, and not the mere literal fulfilment of their predictions, is what Jesus meant by ' fulfilling the prophets.'

18. One jot (Gk. *iota*)] stands for *Yod,* the smallest letter in the Heb. alphabet. **Tittle** (lit. ' little horn ')] is one of those minute projections by which otherwise similar Heb. letters are distinguished : cp. Lk 16 17. The rabbis taught, ' Not a letter shall perish from the Law for ever.' ' Everything has its end : the heaven and the earth have their end ; there is only one thing excepted which has no end, and that is the Law.' ' The Law shall remain eternally, world without end.' Christ uses the rabbinical language in a new meaning of His own (see above).

19. A warning against the disparagement of the OT., now so common. **20.** The sense is, I mention doing as well as teaching, for unless you practise what you preach, you will be unable, like the Scribes and Pharisees, to enter into the kingdom of heaven.'

21–26. Revision of the Law of Murder (not in St. Luke's sermon, but a parallel to vv. 25, 26 occurs in Lk 12 58,59). Christ now shows by a few illustrative examples how the Law is to be understood and practised by His disciples ; in other words, how it is to be ' fulfilled.' The old law punished only the act of murder. The Law of Christ condemns the emotion of anger in its very beginnings. Unreasonable anger is declared a crime in itself, to be punished as such by the local tribunal (**the judgment**). Its mildest expression in word (**Raca**) is to be considered a capital offence, to be dealt with by the supreme Sanhedrin (**the council**). Its more abusive expression (**thou fool**) is worthy of hell-fire. Murder itself is not mentioned as being an impossible act for a disciple of Christ. The language is, of course, rhetorical. Its intention is to mark the immense gulf that separates the morality of the Law from the morality of the Gospel.

The passage is interesting as being the first clear reference in the NT. to Christianity as a Church or Organised Society. The Church is spoken of under Jewish terms (' the judgment,' ' the council,' ' the gift brought to the altar '), but a Christian sense is certainly to be read into them. It is implied that the Church will exercise moral discipline over its members, and that its public worship will be in a certain sense sacrificial : cp. Heb 13 10. If it be asked whether the graduated punishments mentioned are temporal or eternal, ecclesiastical or divine, the answer is ' both ' ; for, according to Christ's promise, the discipline of the Church on earth, when rightly exercised, will be ratified in heaven (Mt 16 19 18 18 ; cp. Jn 20 23).

21. It was said by them of old time] RV ' to them of old time.' It was said by God Himself. Hence Christ, in adding to it by His own authority ('But *I* say unto you '), claims to be equal to God. So also in vv. 28, 32, 34, 39, 43 : see Ex 20 13. **The judgment**] i.e. the local tribunals of seven men appointed in every village (Dt 16 18 2 Ch 19 5, Jos. 'Antiq.' 4.8.14). They appear to have had the power of the sword. **22. Brother**] either a fellow-Christian or a fellow-man. **Without a cause**] RV omits. **Raca** (Aramaic)] i.e. ' Empty-head ' : cp. Jg 9 4 11 3. **The council**] i.e. the supreme Sanhedrin of seventy-one members at Jerusalem having cognisance of the most serious offences, such as blasphemy. **Thou fool**] i.e. ' thou wicked and godless man ' : see Ps 14 1. Some

think that the word here (*more*) is not Gk. but Heb. (=*moreh*, rebel). **Hell fire**] RV ' the hell of fire,' lit.' the Gehenna of fire.' 'Gehenna,' i.e. the valley of Hinnom (an unknown person), was the place in or near Jerusalem where children were made to pass through the fire to Moloch, and, according to Jewish tradition, where the bodies of criminals were burnt. Hence Gehenna became a synonym for hell, the place of final punishment.

25. Thine adversary] The injured brother of v. 22 is now represented under the figure of a creditor who has power to bring the debtor before the judge, and to cause him to be cast into prison. **Prison**] i.e. divine punishment in general, whether in this world or beyond the grave in the intermediate state (Hades), from which release was regarded as possible (12 32). Not, however, in hell (Gehenna), from which there is no release (18 8). The idea is that God will exact the full penalty for all offences against the law of love. In 1 Pet 3 19 ' prison ' refers exclusively to punishment in the intermediate state : cp. Jude v. 6. **26. Farthing** (Lat. *quadrans*)] about half-a-farthing. Lk (12 59) has *lepton*, i.e. about a quarter of a farthing.

27-30. Revision of the Law of Adultery. Jesus expands the Mosaic prohibition of adultery into a law of inward purity of the strictest kind, and gives important counsel to the tempted. **27. By them of old time**] RV omits : see Ex 20 14. **29-30.** This saying is found in Mk 9 43, but in a less natural connexion. It is repeated Mt 18 8. Its meaning is that those who are seriously tempted should discipline themselves with the greatest severity, depriving themselves even of lawful pleasures. Thus certain amusements and certain kinds of reading, in themselves harmless, are to some occasions of sin. Such persons ought to avoid them altogether. Others find drink such a temptation that they ought to be teetotalers. Others find friendships that they value so dangerous that they ought to give them up. This giving up of what is pleasant and lawful, because to us personally it is a spiritual peril, is what our Lord means by plucking out the right eye and cutting off the right hand. Asceticism of this kind is different from the asceticism of those Eastern religions which regard the body as evil. Its principle is that it is better to live a sinless than a complete life. **29. Hell**] i.e. Gehenna, the place of final punishment.

31, 32. Revision of the Law of Divorce. Christ restrained the excessive licence of divorce which existed at the time, and declared marriage to be (with possibly a single exception) absolutely indissoluble. Since St. Matthew alone mentions the exception, and all other NT. passages speak of Christian marriage as absolutely indissoluble (Mk 10 2 Lk

16 18 Ro 7 3 1 Cor 7 10, 11), it is maintained by very many, probably the majority, of recent critics, that the words ' except for fornication ' both here and in 19 9 are an interpolation, introduced by Jewish Christians to modify the excessive strictness of the original utterance, and that Christ Himself forbade divorce altogether. On the principles of criticism now generally accepted, this view is highly probable.

If we accept the words ' except for fornication ' as authentic, it is best to understand them as meaning ' except for adultery,' and thus to bring our Lord's teaching into line with that of Shammai, who, in opposition to the laxer view of Hillel, who allowed divorce for any, even the most trivial cause, permitted it only for adultery. The other view that ' fornication ' here means prenuptial sin, for which, when discovered, a Jewish husband was allowed to repudiate his newly-married bride (see Dt 22 13 f.), is not so probable, though it is, of course, possible. The question of remarriage after divorce presents considerable difficulty. The remarriage of the guilty party is condemned by our Lord in strong terms : ' Whosoever shall marry her when she is put away ' (or, ' whosoever shall marry a divorced woman ') ' committeth adultery.' Whether the innocent party is permitted after a divorce to marry again is a disputed point among Christians. The Eastern Church permits it ; the Western Church, upon the whole, forbids it. The stricter rule, though it sometimes inflicts hardships upon individuals, seems the more desirable from the point of view of public policy, seeing that it best maintains the stability of the family, the sanctity and indissolubility of marriage, and the possibility of repentance and reconciliation after sin.

31. See Dt 24 1, and on Mt 19 3 f.

32. Shall marry her that is divorced] i.e. for adultery ; or, ' shall marry a divorced woman.'

33–37. Revision of the Law of Oaths. The prohibition ' Swear not at all ' is to be taken in its widest sense, and not simply as forbidding the common oaths of conversation. Christ looks forward to a time when truthfulness will be so binding a duty that oaths will no longer be necessary even in courts of justice. This is one of those ideal commands which cannot be fully carried out in the present state of society. Our Lord Himself at His trial allowed Himself to be put on oath (26 63). But one day there will come a time when a man's word will be as good as his oath.

33. By them] RV ' to them ' : see Nu 30 2 Dt 23 21, etc.

34. Oaths that did not expressly invoke the name of God were considered less binding than those that did. Jesus cuts at the root of the practice by showing that the oaths ' by heaven,' etc., were really in essence, if not in form, oaths by God.

37. Quoted by St. James (5 12). **Of evil**] RV ' of the evil one,' i.e. the devil : cp. 6 13.

38–42. Abolition of the Law of Retaliation : cp. Lk 6 29, 30. It is a difficulty to some that God should ever have sanctioned the barbarous principle of ' an eye for an eye and a tooth for a tooth ' (Ex 21 24). They do not reflect that in its own age this principle represented a far-reaching moral reform. The thirst for vengeance is not naturally satisfied with an eye for an eye ; it goes on to demand a life. Hence when Moses allowed the injured man to exact an eye and no more, he was imposing a salutary check on private vengeance. Our Lord goes further, and forbids private vengeance altogether. It is true that vengeance contains a good element, viz. righteous anger against wrong, but this is so bound up with personal vindictiveness, and so certain, if gratified, to let loose a man's worst passions, that our Lord forbids it altogether. Christians are not to resent injuries, they are not to attempt to retaliate, they are, in our Lord's figurative language, to turn the cheek to the smiter. Does this forbid us on fitting occasions to expostulate with a wrong-doer, or to bring him to punishment ? By no means. There are occasions when in the interests of society, and in the interest of the criminal himself, it is necessary to resist evil and to bring the wrong-doer to justice. Our Lord elsewhere fully recognises this (18 15).

38. See Ex 21 24 Lv 24 20 Dt 19 21. **39. Resist not evil**] RV ' Resist not him that is evil,' i.e. the person that would injure you. **Right cheek**] This is only a figurative illustration of the general principle : cp. vv. 40, 41, 42.

40. Thy coat (Gk. *chiton*)] ' Vest ' or ' shirt ' would be better. The **cloke** (*himation*) is the outer garment, used also as a covering by night : see on Jn 19 23.

41. Shall compel] RM ' impress.' When Roman troops passed through a district, the inhabitants were compelled to carry their baggage. This compulsory transport was a recognised form of taxation, and is probably what is alluded to here. Translated into modern language, the saying means that Christians ought to pay their taxes and undertake other public burdens cheerfully and willingly. The word translated ' compel ' is Persian, and had reference originally to the royal couriers of the Persian empire, who had power to impress men and beasts for the king's service. In Mt 27 32 it is used of Simon of Cyrene, who was compelled to bear our Lord's cross.

42. Give to him, etc.] Not an exhortation to indiscriminate charity, but to that brotherly love which Christians ought to feel even towards the improvident and wicked. It is right to give to him that asks, but not always right to give him what he asks. The best form of giving or lending is that which helps people to help themselves.

43-48. Hatred of enemies forbidden, love enjoined (Lk 6 27-36). The maxim ' Thou shalt love thy neighbour' is found in Lv 19 18. The words ' Thou shalt hate thine enemy' are nowhere found in the Pentateuch, which indeed contains isolated texts of an opposite tendency, e.g. Ex 23 4. Nevertheless, our Lord's words are a fair general description of a code which allowed the law of retaliation, and preserved the rights of the avenger of blood. Even in the Psalms, which represent a later revelation, personal hatred for enemies is openly expressed (e.g. Ps 109). The law of love here proclaimed by our Lord in its most comprehensive sense is the most characteristic feature of Christian morality. In the NT. God is revealed as Love, as a Father who loves his children with impartial affection. And as His supreme perfection consists in Love, so those who would be perfect must love their fellow-men, even their enemies, as He loves them (v. 45).

44. Love your enemies] The word for ' love' is carefully chosen. It is not demanded that we should love our enemies with a natural and spontaneous affection (*philein*), but with the supernatural Christian love that comes by grace (*agapan*). **Pray for them,** etc.] Jesus fulfilled His own injunction when He prayed for those who crucified Him (Lk 23 34) : see also Ac 7 60 1 Cor 6 12.

46-48. ' The love Christ enjoins is not to be confused with the good feeling and even affection that may exist between members of the same class, the love that is found even among despised tax-gatherers. But " ye shall be perfect " in the obligation of universal love.'

46. Publicans] In classical literature ' publicans' are wealthy Romans who bought from the Roman government the right of collecting the taxes in a certain district. The publicans of the NT. are the actual tax-collectors. In NT. times only duties on exports, not direct taxes, were collected by publicans. Publicans bore a bad reputation among the Jews, partly for their dishonesty and extortion, and partly for their unpatriotic conduct in collecting taxes for a foreign power. The rabbis ranked publicans with cutthroats and robbers. **48. Perfect**] Glorious words ! The perfection spoken of is the perfection of Love, the supreme virtue both of God and man (1 Cor 13 13 1 Jn 4 16).

CHAPTER 6
The Sermon on the Mount (continued)

1. God's approval, not man's, to be sought

in all our actions. Jesus does not say that we are to do good expecting no reward of any kind, but that we are to look for our reward to God alone : see on v. 4. **That ye do not your alms**] RV ' your righteousness.' The same Heb. word (*tsedakah*) means both righteousness in general and almsgiving in particular. Our Lord probably used it in the former sense in v. 1, and in the latter sense in v. 2 ; hence the evangelist translates it differently.

2-4. Ostentation in almsgiving reproved.

2. A trumpet] There was a trumpet in every synagogue, which was sounded on various occasions (e.g. at the beginning of the sabbath and at excommunications), not, however, so far as we know, at the collection of alms. The expression is, therefore, probably a metaphor for ' ostentation.' **Hypocrites**] In classical Gk. the word means ' an actor.' In the Bible it generally means one who acts a false part in life, i.e. one who pretends to be religious and is not, as here. But sometimes it simply means a wicked person without any idea of hypocrisy, e.g. 24 51, and several times in OT., e.g. Job 34 30. **In the synagogues and in the streets**] In a Jewish community alms were given publicly in three ways. (1) Every day three men went round with a basket collecting alms for ' the poor of the world,' i.e. Jews and Gentiles alike. (2) Two synagogue officials went from house to house collecting alms for ' the poor man's chest.' This was for Jews alone. (3) On the sabbath day alms were collected in the synagogue itself : cp. 1 Cor 16 2. The abuse which our Lord here attacks is probably that of publishing the amounts given, which would naturally lead to ostentatious rivalry. **They have their reward**] in the praise of men.

3. Let not thy left hand] A metaphor for secrecy. Yet alms need not on all occasions be secret (cp. 5 16, ' Let your light so shine before men,' etc.), provided that ostentation be avoided. The best Jewish thought strongly approved of alms done in secret. In the Temple was ' the treasury of the silent' for the support of poor children, to which religious men brought their alms in silence and privacy, and it was strikingly said by one of the rabbis that ' he that doeth alms in secret is greater than our master Moses himself.' **4. Reward thee openly**] RV omits **openly.** The reward will take place at the Day of Judgment, when the secrets of all hearts shall be disclosed. Yet even in this life there is the reward of a good conscience, and of God's approval.

5-15. Maxims for prayer, and the Lord's Prayer. Perhaps the most significant v. of this section is v. 8, ' Your Father knoweth what things ye have need of, before ye ask him.' Christians, therefore, are not to pray mainly with the object of bringing their needs before God who knows them already, but because they love Him and delight to be in His presence, and to open their hearts to Him, and to receive from Him those holy inspirations and aspirations which He gives to those who pray aright. Those who thus understand what prayer is, will not pray like the **hypocrites** (v. 5), or like the **heathen** (v. 7). They will pray in secret, as well as in public, from the mere delight of praying. The section concludes with the Lord's Prayer, which is given as the perfect model of all prayer.

5. To pray standing] Standing was the usual Jewish attitude in prayer, as kneeling is with us. In prayer a Jew usually (1) stood, (2) turned towards Jerusalem, (3) covered his head, (4) fixed his eyes downwards. The ancient Church prayed standing on Sundays and festivals, but kneeling on fast-days, and the Eastern Church still observes this rule.

In the synagogues and in the corners of the streets] During the synagogue services those who wished to be thought devout did not follow the public prayers, but said private self-righteous prayers of their own, loud enough to be heard and to attract the attention of the congregation. In the streets the same people would sometimes stand for three hours at a time in the attitude of prayer. The prayers of the phylacteries (see on Mt 23⁵) were required to be said at a fixed time with great parade and ceremony. When the time came, the workman put down his tools, the rider descended from his ass, the teacher suspended his lecture, to say them. The ostentatious were careful to be overtaken by the prayer-hour in a public place, and to remain longer praying than any one else.

6. Into thy closet] RV 'into thine inner chamber': cp. Isa 26²⁰ 2 K 4³³. There is no disparagement here of public worship, which our Lord elsewhere emphatically commends by precept and practice. But private prayer affords a test of sincerity which public worship does not. **Shall reward thee openly**] RV 'shall recompense thee.'

7. Use not vain repetitions] Our Lord reproves not repetitions, but *vain* repetitions. In the agony in the garden He Himself prayed three times in the same words. Vain repetition reaches its culminating point in Thibet, where there are mechanical prayer-wheels worked by the wind to spread out written petitions before the Almighty. Good examples of heathen repetitions are found in 1 K 18²⁶ and in Ac 19³⁴. The idea that prayers prevail by their number rather than by their earnestness is pagan, and whenever it appears in Christianity is a corruption.

8. Prayer is not to inform God of our needs, as the heathen think, but that we may have conscious communion with Him as His children.

9. After this manner therefore pray ye] Our Lord is not giving simply an illustration of the manner in which Christians ought to pray, but a set form of words to be learnt by heart and habitually used. This is clear from Lk 11¹, 'Lord, teach us to pray, as John also taught his disciples.' Every Jew was required to recite daily eighteen set prayers of considerable length, or, if hindered by press of business, a summary of them. The rabbis also taught their pupils an additional form of prayer composed by themselves, to be added to these eighteen prayers. Our Lord's disciples would therefore understand that they were to recite the Lord's Prayer every day at the end of their ordinary prayers. That this was done there can be little doubt, for 'The Teaching of the Twelve Apostles,' which probably dates from the 1st cent. A.D., directs the Lord's Prayer to be said three times a day by all Christians.

Our Lord's followers would further regard the prayer as a badge of discipleship, something intended to distinguish the disciples of Jesus from all other men. For this reason among others it has always been regarded as the prayer of the Church, not of the world. So jealously was its secrecy guarded in early times, that, like the Creed, it was only taught to catechumens just before their baptism, and was never used in those portions of public worship to which the heathen were admitted. It was always used at Holy Communion, where it formed the conclusion of the canon or prayer of consecration.

The Doxology ('for thine is the kingdom,' etc.), which is based on Jewish models, is no original part of the prayer. It was added as early as the 1st cent. in the Public Liturgy, and thence passed into the text of St. Matthew's Gospel, where it is found in many MSS.

The prayer is given by St. Luke (11²⁻⁴) in a shorter form (the petitions 'thy will be done' and 'deliver us from evil' being omitted, see RV) and in a different historical connexion. Many account for this by supposing that the prayer was given twice, once complete and once abridged, but it is more probable that it was given only once, viz. on the occasion mentioned by St. Luke, and that St. Matthew has purposely placed it earlier, inserting it in our Lord's first recorded sermon in order to set before the reader at once a comprehensive view of His teaching about prayer. As to the form of the prayer, St. Matthew's version is, without doubt, to be preferred. It is not only fuller, but contains distinct marks of greater closeness to the original Aramaic.

The originality of the Lord's Prayer has sometimes been called in question, but without reason. The parallels adduced from rabbinical prayers are for the most part superficial, and prove no more than that our Lord availed Himself of current Jewish forms of expression

The Lord's Prayer is generally divided into seven petitions, by some, however, into only six, the last two being reckoned as one. It falls into two distinct portions. The first portion, i.e. the first three petitions, is concerned chiefly with the glory of God ; the second portion, i.e. the four latter petitions, with our own needs. Even those needs are mainly of a spiritual character. Bodily wants are mentioned in only one petition, and even that has been generally interpreted of spiritual as well as bodily needs.

9. Our Father which art in heaven] Christians are taught to say ' Our Father ' not ' My Father ' because they are brethren, and may not selfishly pray for themselves without praying for others. Every time they use this prayer they are reminded that they are a brotherhood, a society, a Holy Church, a family, of which the members are mutually responsible for one another's welfare, and cannot say, as Cain, ' Am I my brother's keeper ? ' This was also, though in a lower way, a principle of Judaism. The rabbis said, ' He that prays ought always, when he prays, to join with the Church ' (i.e. to say ' we ' instead of ' I '). God is never addressed as Father in the OT., and references to His Fatherhood are rare. Where they occur (Dt 32⁶ Isa 63¹⁶, etc.) He is spoken of as the Father of the nation, not of individual men. In the Apocrypha individuals begin to speak of God as their Father (Wisd 2¹⁶ 14³ Ecclus 23¹,⁴ 51¹⁰), and ' Our Father ' becomes a fairly common form of address in later rabbinical prayers. Jesus first made the fatherhood of God the basis of religion, and gave it its full meaning. Since the Lord's Prayer is a distinctively Christian prayer, the prayer of the Church, not of humanity, ' Our Father ' must be understood in its full Christian sense. In a certain sense God is the Father of all men. He is their Father because He created them, and because, in spite of sin, they are spiritually like Him, being made in His image. But He is the Father of Christians in an altogether new sense. They are His sons by adoption, reconciled to Him by the death of Christ ; and, as a continual testimony that they are sons, He sends forth the Spirit of His Son into their hearts, crying, ' Abba,' i.e. ' Father.' Hence none but a Christian, i.e. one who by baptism ' has put on Christ,' and become ' a member of Christ, the child of God and an inheritor of the kingdom of heaven,' can rightly use the Lord's Prayer.

Which art in heaven] lit. ' in the heavens.' We are reminded that He who is called Father on earth, is also called Father in the heavens, by the hosts of angels who worship before His throne, and by the spirits of just men made perfect. Heaven is generally plural in NT. (as always in OT.) to indicate that there are various states of glory and blessedness assigned to different persons or to different celestial natures. The expression ' Our Father which art in heaven ' is found in Jewish prayers.

Hallowed be thy name] i.e. let Thy Name be regarded as holy by all creatures both in heaven and earth. God's name is His revealed nature, i.e. practically God Himself. Observe that the glory of God, not human needs, is here put first. ' Hallowed be Thy Name ' is a prayer that God may be rightly worshipped, and its utterance is in itself an act of worship.

The prayer begins with worship, because worship is the highest spiritual activity of man. It is higher than petition. An unspiritual man can ask for benefits, but no one can worship who does not in his inmost soul apprehend what God is. To worship is to give God His due, to be penetrated with a sense of His perfections, His infinity, His majesty, His holiness, His love, and to prostrate body and soul before Him. In the worship of God is included also due reverence towards all that is God's, or comes from God. We ' hallow His Name,' when we reverence His holy Word, His day, His Sacraments, His Church, His ministers, His saints, and the revelation which He makes to us outwardly through nature, and inwardly in our own souls through the voice of reason and conscience.

10. Thy kingdom come] A glorious prayer of infinite scope, known also, yet not in its full sense, to the Jews, who held it for a maxim that ' That prayer, wherein is not mentioned the kingdom of God is no prayer at all.' ' Thy kingdom come ' means, May justice triumph over injustice, truth over error, kindness over cruelty, purity over lust, peace over enmity. It is a prayer for the peace and unity of the Church, for the growth in grace of its members, and for the conversion of the world. But chiefly it is a prayer ' that it may please Thee, of Thy gracious goodness, shortly to accomplish the number of Thine elect, and to hasten Thy kingdom ; that we, with all those who are departed in the true faith of Thy holy Name, may have our perfect consummation and bliss, both in body and soul, in Thy eternal and everlasting glory.'

Thy will be done in earth, as *it is* **in heaven**] RV ' as in heaven so on earth.' (Lk in RV omits the whole petition.) The nearest Jewish parallel is, ' Do Thy will in heaven, and give quietness of spirit to those who dwell beneath.' ' Thy will be done ' is a prayer for grace to conform our wills to the will of God, and for diligence to carry out that will in action. It is also a prayer for the grace of patience. Sometimes God wills that we should suffer pain and sorrow, therefore we pray that we may suffer patiently. In the words ' as in heaven so on earth,' our Lord sets before us the example of the holy angels, who in heaven do God's will perfectly.

11. Give us this day our daily bread] We are not taught to pray for bread for many days, but for one day, God thereby reminding us of our continual dependence upon Him. Nor are we taught to pray for luxuries, but for bread, i.e. for necessary food, shelter, clothing, and health. We pray also for bread for our souls, i.e. the grace to confess our sins and to receive God's pardon, and to persevere, and to know God. But chiefly we pray that we may feed daily by faith on Jesus Christ, who is our true daily bread, and may be worthy partakers of the bread of blessing which makes us one with Him, and Him one with us, and which was to the first Christians literally their daily bread (Ac 2 46).

The Gk. word here translated 'daily' occurs nowhere else in Gk. literature, and its meaning is entirely unknown. The most likely meanings are, (1) daily bread, (2) to-morrow's bread, (3) heavenly bread. Probably the second is the true one, because the ancient Hebrew gospel of the Ebionites so understood it, perhaps preserving the original Heb. word used by Christ (*Mahar*).

12. And forgive us our debts as we forgive our debtors] RV 'as we also have forgiven our debtors.' No one who has not forgiven his enemies can pray the Lord's Prayer, which is another proof that it is meant for Christians alone. To forgive one's enemies is the act of a Christian, and the very opposite of the way of the world. Even for Christians it is so hard that our Lord thinks it needful to remind us of its urgent necessity every day when we say our prayers. Unless we forgive, we cannot be forgiven; unless we put away all malice and bitterness and hatred and revengeful feeling from our hearts, we are yet in our sins. Sin is here called a debt, i.e. it is regarded as 'an act by which we have robbed God of His rights, and incurred an obligation or debt which we cannot satisfy, and in regard to which we can only appeal to the divine pity.' For **debts** St. Luke substitutes 'sins.' St. Matthew's expression, being the more difficult, is the nearer to the original.

This petition, occurring as it does in a prayer intended for Christians only, is conclusive proof that our Lord did not expect His followers to attain sinless perfection in this life. The belief that a converted Christian lives a perfectly sinless life, is directly contrary to the NT.: see 1 Jn 1 8.

13. And lead (RV 'bring') us not into temptation] God does not Himself tempt (Jas 1 13), but He allows us to be tempted, and what God permits is often spoken of in Scripture as His act. The temptations here spoken of are not only the direct assaults of the evil

one, but the trials and sorrows of life by which our souls are purified and refined, as gold and silver are purged from their dross in a furnace. We pray here that we may not be tempted 'above that we are able,' but that with the temptation God may also make 'a way to escape,' that we may be able to bear it (1 Cor 10 13).

But deliver us from evil] RV 'from the evil one' (omitted by Lk in RV). This is a prayer that God may keep us 'from all sin and wickedness, and from our ghostly enemy, and from everlasting death.' The translation 'evil one' in this passage is adopted by nearly all modern commentators: cp. 13 19, 38 Jn 17 15 Eph 6 16 2 Th 3 3 (RV), especially 1 Jn 2 13, 14 3 12 5 18, 19.

For thine is the kingdom] RV rightly omits the Doxology, which is a liturgical addition, dating, however, from an early age, for it is found in 'The Teaching of the Twelve Apostles' (circ. 80–160 A.D., but probably before 100). It is Jewish in origin. In the Temple services the people did not respond 'Amen' to the prayers as they did in the synagogues, but 'Blessed be the name of the glory of His kingdom for ever.' **14, 15.** Repeated in Mk 11 25: cp. Eph 4 32 Col 3 13. One of the weightiest precepts and warnings of the Christian religion, and one of the most neglected.

16–18. Precepts for private fasts (not in St. Luke). Our Lord says nothing of public fasts, because when every one else is fasting there is little temptation to vainglory. In our Lord's time there were not more than five (or six) public fasts (see below), but the strict Jews, especially the Pharisees, were accustomed to fast also on Thursday (the day when Moses ascended Mount Sinai), and on Monday (the day when he came down): see Lk 18 12. Vainglorious persons fasted more frequently even than this, and were careful to advertise the fact. A faster did not wash, or bathe, or anoint the body, or shave the head, or wear sandals, but placed ashes on his head, thereby 'disfiguring his face.' It was said of a certain Rabbi Joshua, that 'all the days of his life his face was black by reason of his fastings.' Christians are directed by our Lord when fasting privately, to conceal the fact, lest they should be guilty of ostentation. This command does not apply to public fasts ordered by lawful authority. On such occasions Christians should fast publicly, both as an outward expression of obedience, and for the encouragement of others who are afraid of ridicule. All excessive fasting which would injure the body or interfere with the due discharge of social duties is contrary to Christianity. People who are strictly abstemious or temperate can fast very little with regard to the quantity of food, but it is open to them to fast with regard to its quality. To fast is also to abstain from usual and lawful indulgences and amusements, so far as can be done in charity and without attracting undue attention. The time saved can be given to prayer, meditation, visiting the sick, etc. Money saved by fasting should of course be spent in charity. The object of Christian fasting is, (1) to subdue the flesh to the spirit, and (2) to fit the mind for devotion. A fast which is not joined with prayer and devotion is no Christian fast. See further 9 14-17 Ac 13 2 14 23 2 Cor 6 5 11 27.

What fasts were observed in our Lord's time is not quite certain. Only one fast (the Day of Atonement) was prescribed in the Law. During the exile arose the custom of observing four yearly fasts to commemorate the calamities of Jerusalem. That of the fourth month commemorated the capture of Jerusalem (Jer 52 6 f.), that of the fifth the destruction of the city and Temple (Jer 52 12), that of the seventh the murder of Gedaliah (Jer 41 1), that of the tenth the beginning of the siege (Jer 52 4). Of much later origin was the fast on the 13th of Adar, supposed to commemorate the advice of Haman to massacre the Jews. To what extent, if at all, these fasts were observed in Palestine in our Lord's time, is a disputed question.

16. Disfigure their faces] viz. with ashes, or perhaps, 'conceal their faces with a veil': see 2 S 15 30 Esth 6 12. **17. Anoint**] This may mean 'Anoint thy head as for a banquet,' but anointing was a common practice at all times.

18. Shall reward thee openly] RV 'shall recompense thee.'

19-34. These vv. are not very closely connected, but they form a kind of unity, and are printed as a single paragraph in RV. They deal with excessive care for earthly things : (a) wealth, vv. 19-24 ; (b) food and raiment, vv. 25-34. For purposes of exposition they may be conveniently divided into three sections.

19-21. The earthly treasure and the heavenly treasure. When do we lay up 'treasure in heaven'? Whenever we give alms (v. 2), or pray (v. 5), or fast (v. 16), to please God rather than man. But these three examples are only introduced to prepare the way for the wider principle that in every action of our lives, and not only in almsgiving, prayer, and fasting, it is possible to lay up treasure in heaven. Not only by the right use of wealth, but by the right use of any faculty, talent, or opportunity with which God has entrusted us, heavenly treasure is laid up. Even when we are doing nothing actively for God, but are only patiently suffering what He wills that we should bear, we are laying up treasure in heaven. Every act, however small, which is done purely for the glory of God, and for no lower motive, will receive its reward.

19. Moth and rust] Wealth in Eastern lands is largely stored and hoarded. Much of it con-

sists of costly changes of raiment, which are liable to the attacks of moths. **Break through**] lit. 'dig through,' viz. the wall of the house, which was often only built of clay. **21. For where your treasure is**, etc.] see Lk 12 34. The heavenly treasure is the approval of our heavenly Father, which is represented as wealth stored up in heaven, ready to be enjoyed hereafter. The earthly treasure is not only wealth (though that is its most striking exemplification), but everything lower than God Himself on which men set their hearts,—honour, fame, pleasure, ease, power, excitement, luxury, animal enjoyment.

22-24. Singlemindedness in God's service, and how it is to be attained (Lk 11 34-36 16 13). The connexion of thought is—How can we be sure that we are laying up treasure in heaven, and acting simply and purely for the glory of God? Our Lord replies : By paying attention to our consciences, and keeping them in a healthy state. We are too much inclined to believe that our consciences are sure to lead us right, forgetting that the conscience itself may be darkened by sin. Conscience is like the eye. When the eye is in a healthy state the whole body is full of light (v. 22). Every object is seen in its true colours, true proportions, and accurate position. But if there is a cataract in the eye, or malformation of the lens, or colour-blindness, then the whole body is full of darkness, or distorted light (v. 23). So it may be with conscience, and therefore we are warned against blindly trusting our consciences, which may, through past sin or from lack of moral education, be seeing things in a false light, or may even be thoroughly corrupt, giving us moral darkness instead of light. We are to put our consciences to school with Jesus Christ, and to be quite sure before we trust them, that they give the same moral judgments and are as sensitive as those of the best Christians. When our consciences are sound, and our souls are full of light, we shall be able to discern whether we are serving God or mammon. If our consciences are unsound, we may go on serving mammon all our lives without knowing it.

22. The light] RV 'the lamp.' **The body**] In the parable the 'body' stands for the soul of man. **Thine eye**] i.e. thy conscience.

Single] i.e. seeing things in their true light.

24. Two masters] It is a common idea that virtue shades off into vice by imperceptible gradations, and that the majority of men are neither bad nor good. Our Lord pronounces absolutely that in the last resort there are only two classes of men, those who are serving God, and those who are serving the world. **Mammon**] RV 'mammon.' Not a proper name as readers of Milton would naturally suppose, but an Aramaic word for 'riches' (Lk 16 9, 11). Here it stands for 'worldliness,' which finds its chief expression in the love of money.

25-34. The Christian's freedom from care and anxiety (Lk 12 22-34). The worldly man is oppressed with care. He is always in fear that his deep-laid plans for the future will miscarry, that some object that he loves will be torn from his grasp, that his wealth will vanish, or that his health will fail so that he can enjoy life no longer. The actual failure of his earthly prospects makes him the most miserable of men, for those prospects were his all, and however little he may confess it to himself, he in truth loves nothing else. He seemed, perhaps, to be serving God much, and mammon a little, but he was in reality serving mammon with undivided devotion.

The Christian also pays attention to worldly things. He is diligent in his trade or profession. He makes all reasonable provision for the future. Often he prospers in business just because he is a Christian, and does honest work where a less scrupulous man would not. But his heart is not set on these things, nor is he anxious about them. He does his best, and leaves the issue to God : cp. Ps 37 25. Observe that the promise of sufficient maintenance is made not to the idle, the improvident, and the vicious, but to the righteous, who seek first the kingdom of God and His righteousness (v. 33). Those who do this can never be idle or improvident : cp. 1 Tim 5 8.

25. Take no thought] RV 'be not anxious': cp. 1 Pet 5 7. **26. They sow not**] God provides for the birds without labour on their part, because labour is not natural to birds. But labour is natural to men, therefore God provides for men by blessing their labour. There is a close rabbinical parallel to this saying : 'Have you ever seen beast or fowl that had a workshop ? and yet they are fed without trouble of mind.'

27. By taking thought] RV 'by being anxious.' **One cubit unto his stature**] Since no one would literally desire to have a cubit (a foot and a half) added to his stature, and the word translated 'stature' generally means 'age' (see RM), it is better to translate, 'Which of you .. can add one span to his age ?'

28. Take ye thought] RV 'are ye anxious.' **30. Into the oven**] Dried grass is used in the East for heating the baking ovens, which are holes in the ground rather more than 3 ft. deep and 2½ ft. wide, shaped like a jar. The walls are cemented to resist the action of fire. Grass is burnt in the ovens, until they are thoroughly hot. Then dough rolled out into thin sheets is spread on the sides of the oven, where it is baked in a few minutes, and is taken out in the form of wafer-cakes.

34. Take no thought] RV 'Be not anxious.' Our Lord regarded cheerfulness and joy, and the absence of care and anxiety, as the mark of a true Christian who puts his trust in God.

Similarly the rabbis said, 'There is enough of trouble in the very moment.'

CHAPTER 7

THE SERMON ON THE MOUNT (concluded)

The connexion of thought in this c. is less close than in the earlier part of the sermon, and the whole c. bears the appearance of an appendix of miscellaneous practical maxims, many of which, however, may have really formed part of the sermon. The words about rash judgment, and about a tree being known by its fruit, as well as the striking conclusion, are found also in St. Luke's sermon.

1-5. On the habit of criticising others (Lk 6 37-42). St. Luke's account is here the fuller, and he places the section in a more satisfactory relation to what goes before. Our Lord condemns all forms of censoriousness. He calls censorious persons hypocrites, and says that they are worse than the people they criticise. They are worse because they lack love. As love is the highest, and indeed in the last resort the only Christian virtue, so the lack of it absolutely excludes from the kingdom where all is love. Such persons are also blind. They see their brother's faults, but have no eyes for his virtues, and they neither see nor wish to see their own far greater faults.

1. Judge not] cp. Ro 2 1. Unkind and frivolous criticism is what is meant. Judgment as a serious and solemn act is not forbidden by Christ. It is indeed often the Christian's duty to judge and severely to condemn things which the world never thinks of judging : cp. 18 15 1 Cor 5 12 2 Tim 4 2.

2. With what measure ye mete (i.e. 'measure')] A Jewish proverb. The rabbis said, 'In the measure that a man measureth, others measure to him.'

3. Mote] lit. 'a small dry twig or stalk.' Here it stands for a relatively small fault.

The beam] i.e. the great roof-beam of a house, something a thousand times larger than the eye itself. Here it stands for 'want of love,' the most monstrous, under Christ's law, of all vices. Here Christ again adopts a Jewish proverb. It is said that when one Jewish judge criticised another and said, 'Cast out the mote out of thine eye,' the other replied, 'Cast you out the beam out of your own eye.'

6. That the most holy things ought not to be offered indiscriminately to all persons. The earliest comment on this v. is in the 'Teaching' (Didache) : 'And let no one eat or drink of your Eucharist, except those who have been baptised in the name of the Lord. For it is concerning this that the Lord hath said, Give not that which is holy unto the dogs.' This correctly apprehends the principle, which is, of course, capable of wider application. Gore well says, 'We are not to shriek the highest truths of religion at a street corner. We are to wait till people show a desire for the deepest things before we offer them religion. Such was the method of the early Church. It went out into the world. It let all the world see the beauty of its life... But it did not teach them the secrets of its life—its Creed, its Eucharist, its Prayers—till they were ready for them, and showed their readiness at least by enquiry.'

6. That which is holy] in its literal sense the flesh of the sacrifices. Metaphorically it stands for all that is most holy in Christ's religion, like **the pearls** below. **Dogs.. swine**] i.e. unclean and ferocious persons. They will trample on (i.e. revile and profane) what you offer them, and assail you with ridicule and blasphemy. While they are in this frame of mind, nothing can be done with them.

7–11. On urgency in prayer, and how God rewards it (Lk 11 9-13). God always answers urgent prayer. Every asker receives, every seeker finds. Yet not every asker receives what he asks, nor every seeker finds what he seeks. As an earthly father gives good gifts to his children, so God gives good things to those that ask Him, not always what they ask, for they often ask amiss, but something far better, even, as St. Luke's version has it, 'the Holy Spirit.' Those who would obtain exactly what they ask, must conform their wills to God's, and ask for things which they know that He is willing to grant. St. Luke connects this section with the Lord's Prayer, and illustrates it further by the parable of the Friend at Midnight. The connexion in St. Luke is much more natural and suitable.

7. Ask.. seek.. knock] A climax of increasing urgency. We are to wrestle with God in prayer, as Jacob wrestled with the angel (perhaps with God Himself), and said, 'I will not let thee go, except thou bless me' (Gn 32 26). The lesson is, 'That men ought always to pray and not to faint' (Lk 18 1).

9, 10. Bread.. stone.. fish.. serpent] A stone is like a loaf, and a serpent is like a fish, especially some fishes. The idea is that God will not mock an earnest suppliant, by appearing to answer his prayer, and giving him something which, though apparently good, is really noxious. **11. Being evil**] Christ took no roseate view of the characters of men, even after their profession of faith in Him.

12. THE GOLDEN RULE (Lk 6 31). This v. ought to form a distinct paragraph. Our Lord looks back to what He has been saying in c. 5 about the fulfilling of the Law, and sums up His teaching on the whole subject with this important practical maxim. As originally spoken, it probably formed part of our Lord's utterances upon the Law, as it still does in St.

Luke, who brings it into connexion with the command, 'Love your enemies': see 5 44. There are certain parallels to this saying. Once a would-be proselyte went to Rabbi Hillel and demanded to be taught the whole Law while he stood upon one leg. The good rabbi made him a proselyte, saying, 'What is hateful to thyself, that do not thou to another. This is the whole law, the rest is commentary. Go, thou art perfect.' The pious Tobias thus instructs his son Tobit (Tob 4 15), 'What thou thyself hatest, do thou to no man.' The Chinese sage Confucius is reported to have said, 'Do not to others what you would not wish done to yourself.' All these are noble sayings, but they fall far short of Christ's golden rule, which means, 'Not only avoid injuring your neighbour, but do him all the good you can.' They simply forbid injuries: Christ commands active benevolence.

A saying ascribed to the Gk. philosopher Aristotle is closer in form to the Golden Rule than any other, but it applies only to friends. Aristotle was once asked how we should act towards our friends, and replied, 'As we would that they should act towards us.'

12. Therefore all things] The 'therefore' looks back to Christ's teaching about the Law. The sense is, 'Because ye are my disciples, and bound to understand the OT. in its higher and more spiritual sense, *therefore* do unto others all that you would they should do unto you, for this is the true meaning of the Law and the Prophets.'

13, 14. The broad way and the narrow way (Lk 13 24-27). Although it is a blessed thing to be a Christian, it is not easy. The Christian journeys along the narrow way of self-denial discipline and mortification, perhaps of contempt and persecution, but the end of it is life. Much easier is the broad way of self-indulgence, avarice, pride and ambition, but the end of it is death. How many choose death, rather than life! St. Luke speaks only of the narrow 'door,' not of the narrow way, and describes the terrible condition at the last day of those who have not entered it. There is a fine heathen parallel in the allegory called 'the Tablet,' by Cebes, a disciple of Socrates: 'Seest thou not a certain small door, and a pathway before the door, in no way crowded, for only a very few travel that way, since it seems to lead through a pathless, rugged, and stony tract? That is the way that leadeth to true discipline.' There is another in the philosopher Maximus of Tyre (150 B.C.): 'There are many deceitful bypaths, most of which lead to precipices and pits, and there is a single narrow straight and rugged path, and few indeed are they who can travel by it.'

13. The strait gate] RV 'the narrow gate.' St. Matthew's word means a city gate, St.

Luke's a small gate or door. Even city gates are exceedingly narrow in the East. **For wide** *is* **the gate**] Several modern editors omit the words ' is the gate.' **14. Strait**] RV ' narrow.' **Narrow**] RV ' straitened.' **Few there be that find it**] lit. ' few be they who are finding it.' In St. Luke the disciples definitely ask, ' Lord, are they few that be saved ?' but Jesus avoids a direct answer, bidding them look to themselves, and take care that they themselves enter by the narrow door. So here Jesus does not solve the mystery of the ultimate destiny of human souls. He refuses to say what proportion of mankind will be finally lost or saved, but he does say that the majority of men do not, in this world at least, choose the narrow way that leads to life. Whether after this life God will interpose to save them from their doom, and will apply to them some chastening discipline which may bring them to a better mind is not revealed. It may be so. Holy Scripture contains certain hints in this direction (1 Pet 3 19 4 6), but nowhere gives any clear hope, lest men should be encouraged to neglect their opportunities of repentance in this life : see on 12 32.

15-20. How to detect false prophets and hypocrites in general (Lk 6 43-45). The gift of prophecy was widely diffused in the Apostolic Church, so that the warning against false prophets was needed, but the word is intended to include hypocritical Christian teachers of all kinds. How can they be known ? Not always by their doctrine, which, when it suits their purpose, is orthodox, but by their works, especially by their covetousness, which is the unfailing characteristic of false prophets.

The ' Didache ' has some interesting remarks about the false prophets of the sub-apostolic age. ' Let every apostle (itinerant missionary) that comes to you, be received as the Lord. He will remain one day, and if necessary, two. If he remains three days, he is a false prophet. And when the apostle goes forth from you, let him receive nothing but bread for his day's journey. If he asks money, he is a false prophet. . . A prophet who in the Spirit orders a table to be laid, shall not eat of it himself. If he does, he is a false prophet.' The modern representative of the false prophet is the minister or teacher who works for hire or popularity.

15. False prophets] Not the Pharisees, but Christian false prophets and teachers, as is clear from v. 22 : cp. also 24 11, 24 1 Jn 4 1.

Sheep's clothing] Not the official rough garb of prophets, as in Heb 11 37, but the disguise of those who wish to pass for sheep, i.e. for Christians. The sheep's clothing is the hypocritical professions and the outward ordination of the false teacher. **16. Fruits**] Not doctrines, but works, or moral character, as always in

NT. **17-19.** Our Lord echoes and reinforces the Baptist's teaching : see on 3 1-12.

21-23. The punishment of false prophets, and of all hypocrites. Our Lord carries us forward in thought to the day of judgment. Even then the false prophets will pretend to be sheep. They will say, ' Lord, Lord,' and plead their successful ministerial labours. But our Lord will say, **I never knew you : depart from me, ye that work iniquity.**

21. Lord, Lord] During His earthly ministry Jesus was generally addressed as ' Rabbi,' Teacher. Here He claims the higher title of ' Lord,' but in what sense ? Clearly as implying sovereignty over the universe, which was the sense in which it was applied to Jesus in the Apostolic Church : Act 10 36 1 Cor 12 3 Phil 2 11.

Kingdom of heaven] Here used of the final bliss of heaven. **He that doeth**] Everywhere in NT. it is said that men will be judged according to their works, not according to their faith or profession (16 27 25 35 Ro 2 6 1 Cor 3 8 2 Cor 5 10 1 Pet 1 17 Rev 2 23 22 12, etc.). If faith is to justify, it must be a living faith which issues in good works. **22. Cast out devils . . wonderful works**] There is no reason to suppose that this claim to successful ministerial work is unfounded. It is a fact that God does sometimes, for the sake of the flock, condescend to bless the work of evil shepherds, whose lives are not openly scandalous, and in general, we may say that ' the unworthiness of the ministers hinders not the effect of the sacraments.' Of course the best and truest work cannot be done by such men. **23. I never knew you**] i.e. as true disciples : cp. Lk 13 27. The divinity of Christ appears not only from His office of judge, but from His power to read the heart. He claims that the most secret thoughts of the millions of the human race are naked and open before Him, and this is in effect, a claim to be divine.

24-27. The true foundation for all permanent spiritual building (Lk 6 46-49). The great sermon concludes with a parable. Two men built houses near a watercourse. One dug deep and reached the rock, the other built upon the sand (i.e. the alluvial deposit of the watercourse). In the winter there was a flood, and the house built on the sand collapsed. The rock is Christ's own person and teaching, the only foundation for stable, spiritual and social building. Whatever is built upon that rock, lasts. Personal character built up on Christ, i.e. on faith in Him and loyal obedience to His commands, is stable. Men can count upon it, for they feel its strength as well as its gentleness. Societies or states, based on the supremacy of Christ's moral law, last. They have in them the elements of stability, prosperity, and progress. The Christian Church itself is the greatest example of this permanence and progress. Established originally by men who had dug down to the rock and based themselves on faith in Christ's divinity and absolute self-surrender to His service (see 16 18), it became a spiritual fabric which has outlasted the fall of empires, has spread to the most distant lands, and bids fair to fulfil the promise of its Founder that the gates of hell (i.e. of death or destruction) shall not prevail against it.

24. Doeth] Again the stress upon 'doing': see Jas 1 22. **25. Floods**] There are hardly any rivers in Palestine except the Jordan, but there are many watercourses or winter-torrents (Heb. *naḥal*, AV 'brook,' Arab. *wâdy*). These are mostly quite dry in the summer, but in the winter are full of muddy torrent-water, which descends with great violence, and often overflows its banks: cp. Job 6 15f. The foolish man in the parable had built his house either in or close by the channel of one of these wâdys, without thought of the winter rains.

28, 29. Effect of the sermon.

29. Not as the scribes] RV 'not as their scribes': see prefatory remarks to c. 5. The scribe relied entirely on tradition. Hence he was compared to a cemented cistern which held every drop of water put into it. So enamoured were the Jews of tradition, that they would hear nothing else even from a man so great as Hillel. It is said that though Hillel discoursed of a matter all day long, yet his hearers received not his doctrine, till at last he said, 'So I heard from Shemaiah and Abtalion.'

CHAPTER 8

The Leper Cleansed. The Centurion's Servant Healed. Healing of Peter's Wife's Mother and many others. Stilling of the Tempest. Healing of the Gadarene Demoniacs

1–4. Cleansing of the leper (Mk 1 40 Lk 5 12). No natural explanation of this miracle is possible. Leprosy has always been, and is still, one of the most intractable diseases. Under the Mosiac Law lepers were regarded as unclean and excluded entirely from human society: see Lv 13 and 14, and notes. Considered as a parable this miracle represents the cleansing of the human race by the Redeemer from the leprosy of sin.

1. When he was come down] Only St. Matthew mentions the historical connexion of this miracle, though both St. Mark and St. Luke agree that it took place during one of the early preaching tours in Galilee. St. Luke says that it was done in a city. The miracle comes appropriately after the sermon. Having said, 'I came not to destroy (the Law),' He now says, 'Offer the gift that Moses commanded.' Having taught with authority,

He now heals with authority, 'I will, be thou clean.' **2. Worshipped him**] Lk says, 'fell on his face.' The act of reverence that was paid to kings. Perhaps the leper already regarded Jesus as the Messiah, the rightful king of Israel. He certainly had full faith in His miraculous powers. He only doubted His willingness ('if thou wilt') to heal so miserable an outcast. Often men find it easier to believe in God's power than in His mercy and love.

Lord] Here a title of human respect, as in 8 25 16 22 Lk 9 54 10 17, 40 11 1, etc. **Make me clean**] 'Cleanse as well as heal me,' because leprosy was a Levitical defilement. **3. Touched him**] No one was allowed to touch or even to salute a leper. If he even put his head into a place it became unclean. No less a distance than 4 cubits (6 ft.) had to be kept from the leper, or if the wind came from that direction, 100 cubits were scarcely sufficient. By thus touching the leper, Christ also showed His superiority to the Law of Moses. So far from being Himself defiled, His touch imparted cleansing.

4. See thou tell no man] According to St. Mark He dismissed the man abruptly, almost violently, with an urgent command to be silent. Only one explanation of this is at all probable. He feared, as in Jn 6 15, that the people would proclaim Him Messiah, and force Him to be the leader of a revolution. **Offer the gift**] i.e. a sacrifice of two he-lambs without blemish, and one ewe-lamb of the first year without blemish. For the details see Lv 14. **For a testimony unto them**] i.e. a proof of the genuineness of his cure. The priests, after examining him, could not refuse his gift, and their acceptance of it would be valid testimony that he had really been cured of his leprosy. In face of the injunction to tell no man, we cannot imagine that Christ intended him to notify the priests of the manner of his healing, and so challenge them to examine His claims. The man seems, however, to have disobeyed the injunction (Mk 1 45), so that this miracle helped to arouse the opposition which Christ soon afterwards encountered (9 3, 11, 34).

5–13. Healing of the centurion's servant (Lk 7 1, not, however, Jn 4 47, q. v.). The accounts in St. Matthew and St. Luke are partly drawn from independent sources, which, though agreeing in essentials, differ considerably in details. In St. Matthew the centurion himself comes to Jesus. In St. Luke he first sends certain Jewish elders to plead for him, then some of his friends, and apparently does not see Jesus at all. St. Luke's narrative is the fuller and more original. The discrepancy with St. Matthew is not a serious one. It is quite common to represent a person as doing himself what he really does through others. St. Matthew alone records Christ's remarkable utterance as to the rejection of Israel and the call of the Gentiles, vv. 11, 12. St. Luke, however, has nearly the same words in another connexion (Lk 13 28).

5. A centurion] A Roman legionary officer commanding a century (i.e. from 50 to 100 men, the hundredth part of a legion), and occupying the social position of a modern sergeant or non-commissioned officer. Whether this centurion was directly under Roman authority, or was in the employ of Herod Antipas, in whose kingdom he served, is not certain. He was a heathen, and though favourably impressed by Judaism, it is probable from the language of v. 8 that he was not a proselyte. Several centurions appear in the NT., all in a very favourable light : 27 54 Ac 10, 27, and 28. 'Probably,' says Trench, 'in the general wreck of the moral institutions of the heathen world, the Roman army was one of the few in which some of the old virtues survived.' The troops of Palestine were recruited locally from the heathen of Samaria and Cæsarea, and were auxiliaries. The legionary soldiers proper were required to be Roman citizens. The centurion, being an officer, was probably a Roman. According to St. Luke, he did not venture to come himself, but sent certain Jewish elders, who said, ' He is worthy that thou shouldest do this for him, for he loveth our nation, and himself built us our synagogue.'

6. My servant] The expression might mean ' my little son,' but it is plain from St. Luke that it was a favourite slave who was ill.

8. Lord, I am not worthy] Both the centurion and the elders judged Jesus by Jewish standards. That Jesus should heal a Gentile at all, except for some very special reason, was thought impossible. Still more unlikely was it that He would enter a Gentile house, which was regarded as defiled, and defiling those who entered it (Jn 18 28). **Speak the word only**] lit. ' speak with a word.' In believing that Jesus could heal at a distance, the centurion showed remarkable faith. Perhaps his faith was assisted by the similar miracle worked shortly before in the same city upon the son of a certain ' nobleman ' (Jn 4 46).

9. For I am a man under authority] The sense is : I am myself only a servant of others, and yet I have soldiers under me whom I can send where I please to carry out my will. How much more canst Thou, who art Lord of the powers of nature, speak the word and be obeyed. The centurion expresses his faith that angels and spirits and diseases are as obedient to Jesus as his soldiers are to him.

11. Shall sit down (lit. ' recline at table ') **with Abraham, and Isaac, and Jacob**] The rabbis taught that the Messianic age would be ushered in by a great feast. All Israel, with its patriarchs, prophets, and heroes, would be

there. The Gentiles would be excluded, and would have the mortification of seeing all the sumptuous preparations. Every (clean) animal that exists, and many that do not, would be eaten at that feast, e.g. the Leviathan, Behemoth, the gigantic bird Bar Jochani, and certain fabulous fatted geese. The wine of the feast would have been kept in the grapes from the creation of the world. King David would return thanks according to Ps 116 13. Very startling, therefore, was the declaration of Jesus that Gentiles from all nations would be admitted to this Messianic feast, and many circumcised Jews (' sons of the kingdom ') excluded. In the NT., the figure of a banquet or marriage feast is several times used (as here) to represent participation in Christ's Kingdom, both in this world and the next : see 22 2 25 10 Rev 19 7. The present passage is a double prophecy (inserted most suitably in a Gospel meant for Jewish readers), (1) of the admission of the Gentiles on equal terms with the Jews into the Christian Church, and of the exclusion of many of the latter ; (2) the final salvation of many Gentiles, and of the reprobation of merely nominal Jews.

12. The children (RV ' sons ') **of the kingdom**] i.e. the Jews. **Outer darkness, etc.**] a rhetorical description of the sorrow and disappointment of those who are excluded. The **gnashing of teeth** represents anger and disappointment, not torture : see Ps 112 10 Ac 7 54.

14–17 Healing of Peter's mother-in-law, and of many sick and possessed persons (Mk 1 29 Lk 4 38). According to St. Mark and St. Luke these miracles took place on the sabbath, after the synagogue service at which Jesus preached and healed a demoniac.

14. Peter's house] Peter was a married man (1 Cor 9 5). He had a house in Capernaum, which he shared with his brother Andrew, and apparently with his wife's mother. **15. Ministered**] i.e. ' waited at table.' The fever had left no weakness. **16. Possessed**] According to St. Luke the devils cried out, ' Thou art the Son of God,' and recognised Him as the Christ. **17.** Isa 53 4, quoted from the Hebrew. This application of the passage to the miracles of healing does not conflict with its deeper fulfilment in Christ's atoning work on the Cross (Jn 1 29 1 Pet 2 24).

18–22. Sayings to a scribe and another disciple (Lk 9 57). St. Luke introduces these sayings much later in our Lord's ministry. Both evangelists apparently borrowed from a common source, which did not specify the occasion of the utterances.

19, 20. The offer of a recognised rabbi (scribe) to become a follower of Jesus was an attractive one, especially as no influential person had yet become a disciple. Jesus, however, did not hastily accept the offer. To test the sincerity of the new convert, he required him to count the cost. He must give up all to follow Christ—home-comforts, wealth, honour, and all prospects of advancement. Like his Master, he must have no place to lay his head. Probably the scribe, like the rich young ruler, found the conditions too hard.

19. Master] i.e. Rabbi, a title of respect properly belonging only to scribes. It was sometimes accorded by courtesy to our Lord, as here.

20. The Son of man] This title of Christ is found only in the Gospels and Ac 7 56, and (except in Ac 7 56) is found only in the mouth of our Lord Himself. It corresponds in Aramaic, which our Lord habitually spoke, either to *barnasha*, which may mean either 'the man,' or (but this is not so certain) 'the son of man,' or else to *b'reh d'nasha*, which means definite'y and emphatically 'the son of man' (lit. 'his son, that of man'). That our Lord, who was probably bilingual, occasionally used the Gk. title as found in the Gospels, is also very possible. The title was used by our Lord throughout His ministry, and not, as is sometimes erroneously supposed, only from the time of St. Peter's confession (16 13). This fact must be taken account of in ascertaining its probable meaning. It follows from this that it cannot have been, as is sometimes maintained, a definite and well-understood designation of the Messiah. Our Lord concealed His Messiahship from the multitude until the close of His ministry, and did not expressly reveal it even to the Twelve until the confession of Peter. That it was not understood by the multitudes to be a Messianic title is evident from Jn 12 34.

The title probably designates our Lord as the ideal or representative man, '*the* man in whom human nature was most fully and deeply realised, and who was the most complete exponent of its capacities, warm and broad in His sympathies, ready to minister and suffer for others, sharing to the full the needs and deprivations which are the common lot of humanity, but conscious at the same time of the dignity and greatness of human nature, and destined ultimately to exalt it to unexampled majesty and glory.' At the close of His life He invested it with a more definitely Messianic meaning by identifying Himself with the 'one like unto a son of man' of Dan 7 13, who was generally understood to be the Messiah : see Mt 26 63, 64. The expression was used by our Lord of Himself on at least forty different occasions, and in very diverse contexts. Thus he uses it in connexion with His authority to forgive sins (9 6), His lordship over the sabbath (12 8), His Second Advent in glory (10 23 13 41 16 27, 28 19 28 24 27, 30, 37, 44 25 31 26 64), His familiar intercourse with men in daily life (11 19), His poverty (8 20),

His preaching (13 37), His sufferings and resurrection (Mt 17 9, 12, 22 20 18 26 24 Mk 8 31), His giving His life as a ransom (20 28), and His seeking and saving that which was lost (Lk 19 10). St. Stephen uses it of our Lord as glorified in heaven. The title occurs twelve times in St. John's Gospel, for the most part in passages which clearly imply His divinity. The Son of man exists in heaven before His Incarnation, and descends to earth to become man (Jn 6 62); He gives His flesh and blood to believers to eat and drink, who are thus incorporated with Him and receive eternal life (Jn 6 27 f.); He holds unbroken communion with the Father during His earthly life (Jn 1 51); He is the object of divine and saving faith (Jn 3 15); His death on the cross is not a degradation but a glorification (Jn 12 23 13 31), and He ends His earthly course by a triumphant ascension (Jn 6 62).

The title 'Son of man' is used of the Messiah in a part of the book of Enoch (chs. 37–70), which is probably, but not certainly, pre-Christian. It is just possible that our Lord may have derived it from this source. But in any case the title was very little known, and was not popularly understood to mean the Messiah. Some have thought that the source of the title is Ps 8 (see especially v. 4).

22. Follow me ; and let the dead, etc.] This difficult saying is variously interpreted : (1) My claim comes before all other claims. It is better that the dead should remain unburied, than that thou shouldest delay to enter upon the solemn ministry to which I have called thee. (N.B. The funeral and subsequent mourning would cause a delay of several weeks.) (2) Let the dead (i.e. thy unbelieving relations who are spiritually dead through lack of faith in Me) bury thy father for thee, and come thou, follow Me at once.

The man's father was probably either dead or at the point of death, although some think that he was only aged, and that the disciple asked to remain at home till death occurred, thus indefinitely postponing his obedience to Christ's call.

23–27. The stilling of the tempest (Mk 4 35 Lk 8 22). St. Mark and St. Luke both place the incident after the series of parables which St. Matthew records in c. 13. This is at once one of the best-attested miracles, and one of the most incomprehensible to those who desire to limit our Lord's miracles to those of healing. It is perhaps possible to regard the cessation of the storm as a fortunate coincidence, but it is certain that Jesus Himself did not take this view of it. He rebuked the wind and sea, showing that He regarded Himself as the Lord of physical nature as well as of the spiritual world. By stilling the storm Christ showed that, behind the inexorable and **awful**

manifestations of nature, storm, pestilence, volcanic eruptions, and sudden death, which seem to treat man's sufferings with indifference, there is the loving hand of divine providence. In the last resort nature is subject to God's holy and righteous will.

The miracle is also a parable, setting forth Christ as a giver of peace and safety, both to individuals and to His Church. St. Augustine (400 A.D.) says, ' We are sailing in this life as through a sea, and the wind rises, and storms of temptation are not wanting. Whence is this, save because Jesus is sleeping in thee, i.e. thy faith in Jesus is slumbering in thy heart ? Rouse Him and say, Master, we perish. He will awaken, that is, thy faith will return to thee, and the danger will be over.' Tertullian (200 A.D.) says, ' But that little ship presented a figure of the Church, in that she is disquieted in the sea, i.e. in the world, by the waves, i.e. by persecutions and temptations, the Lord patiently sleeping, as it were until roused at last by the prayers of the saints He checks the world, and restores tranquillity to His own.'

24. Tempest] lit. 'shaking.' The word generally means 'earthquake.' ' To understand the causes of these sudden and violent tempests, we must remember that the lake lies low, six hundred feet lower than the Mediterranean Sea, that the vast and naked plateaus of Jaulan (the district E. of the lake) rise to a great height, spreading backward to the wilds of Hauran, and upwards to the snowy Hermon ; that the watercourses have cut out profound ravines and wild gorges, converging to the head of the lake, and that these act like gigantic funnels to draw down the winds from the mountains ' (Thompson).

27. What manner of man] The disciples already begin to think that Jesus is more than a mere man.

28-34. The healing of the Gadarene demoniacs (Mk 5 1 Lk 8 26). There are real difficulties in connexion with this narrative, but that upon which Professor Huxley laid so much stress in his controversy with Mr. Gladstone, 1889-91, is assuredly the least. Speaking of the destruction of the swine he said, 'Everything that I know of law and justice convinces me that the wanton destruction of other people's property is a misdemeanour of evil example,' as if He, who gives life and health and all things to all men, cannot take back His own gifts when He will. More serious is the difficulty presented by the transference of the devils from the men into the swine (vv. 31, 32). It may, perhaps, be sufficient to remark that it is not certain that this is the true interpretation of the incident. The transference itself could not from the nature of the case have been observed. It was an inference from the request of the devils

and the subsequent behaviour of the swine. The word **Go** used by Jesus may mean ' Go into the swine,' but it may also mean simply, ' Begone,' without implying any such permission. In the latter case the destruction of the swine may have been a natural occurrence, the herd taking fright at the paroxysms and cries of the demoniacs, which became more violent at the moment of their recovery : cp. Mk 1 26 9 26 Lk 9 42. If the former interpretation is correct, Jesus probably destroyed the swine to convince the insane men that the devils had really left them. The healing itself was certainly a miracle of the most striking kind, whether the men be regarded as really possessed by devils, or as maniacs under that delusion. St. Matthew in recording this miracle made use of another source besides that represented by St. Mark and St. Luke. He speaks of two demoniacs, they only of one.

28. The country of the Gergesenes (RV ' Gadarenes ')] Gadara was an important Gentile town, the capital of Peræa, situated at least 6 m. from the lake in a south-easterly direction, and separated from it by a broad plain and the gorge of the river Hieromax, a tributary of the Jordan. St. Matthew mentions Gadara as the nearest well-known town. St. Mark and St. Luke state more precisely that the incident took place at Gerasa, to be identified with the ruins of Kersa or Gersa on the E. side of the lake. There are ancient tombs in the vicinity of this place, and about 1 m. S. of it is a steep, even slope, which may be the ' steep place ' by which the swine rushed down into the sea. There was another Gerasa in Peræa, but it was fully 35 m. from the lake, and cannot possibly be the one meant.

Out of the tombs] Maniacs are still to be found among the tombs in the East. Warburton writes, ' On descending from these heights (of Lebanon), I found myself in a cemetery. The silence of the night was now broken by fierce yells and howlings, which I discovered proceeded from a naked maniac, who was fighting with some wild dogs for a bone. The moment he perceived me, he left his canine comrades, and bounding along with rapid strides, seized my horse's bridle, and almost forced him backward over the cliff.'

29. Thou Son of God] The demons similarly acknowledge Jesus in Mk 3 11 Lk 4 41. **To torment us before the time]** viz. of the Last Judgment, when the demons will be consigned to hell. The demoniacs identify themselves with the demons and speak in their names.

31. In St. Luke the demons beg not to be sent into the ' abyss,' i.e. into hell.

34. They besought him that he would depart] The drowning of 2,000 swine represented a considerable monetary loss, and they feared further losses if Jesus remained in their neighbourhood. It is not clear whether the owners of the swine were Jews or Gentiles. The population of Decapolis was mainly, but by no means exclusively, Gentile. If the owners were Jews, their loss might be regarded as a punishment for keeping swine contrary to the Law. The rabbis said, 'Cursed be he who keeps hogs, and cursed be he who teacheth his son the wisdom of the Greeks'; and again, 'It is forbidden to trade in anything that is unclean.' 'Keeper of hogs' was a Jewish term of abuse. **Coasts**] RV 'borders.' St. Mark and St. Luke add that our Lord, departing from His usual custom, bade the demoniac proclaim his cure publicly. As the population was Gentile, there was no danger of a Messianic outbreak.

We have adopted the now widely-accepted view (see note 'Possession' at 4 24), that the demoniacs of the NT. were insane persons under the delusion that they were possessed with devils, but their recognition of Jesus as the Son of God, and in a less degree the phenomenon of double consciousness exhibited in this and other instances, are plausible arguments for the older view that the possession was real : see on Mk 5 1-20.

CHAPTER 9

The Sick of the Palsy. Call of Matthew. Raising of Jairus' Daughter

1-8. The paralytic healed and his sins forgiven (Mk 2 1 Lk 5 17). The peculiarity of this miracle is that it was worked to prove a doctrine, and that in the face of opposition. There were present certain scribes and Pharisees, some of whom had doubtless come from Jerusalem expressly to oppose Jesus. Jesus at once threw them a challenge by saying to the man, 'Son, thy sins are forgiven thee.' The scribes understood this to mean that He claimed to forgive sins as God only can do. Instead of repudiating this suggestion, as a mere man would have done, Jesus accepted it, and proceeded to prove His claim by a miracle. 'Whether is easier,' said He, 'to say, Thy sins are forgiven ; or to say, Arise, and walk ?' The former, of course, is easier. Any impostor can say, 'Thy sins are forgiven,' because it is impossible for men to know whether the words have taken effect or not. But not every one can say, 'Arise, and walk,' because if such words are spoken without authority, the speaker is at once convicted of imposture.

This miracle, like the resurrection, may be regarded as a vindication by God Himself of the character of Jesus. No man could make the claims that Jesus did, without rendering himself liable to the most serious imputations upon his character. Either He was the Son of God, or, as the scribes rightly said from their point of view, a blasphemer. Hence in this miracle Jesus deliberately appealed to the judgment of God, and God by working the miracle vindicated the character of Jesus.

1. His own city] i.e. Capernaum.

2. They brought to him] According to the fuller accounts in St. Mark and St. Luke the bed of the paralytic was carried by four men, who, unable to approach Jesus for the crowd, ascended to the roof of the house by the outside stairs with which most Eastern houses are furnished, and making a hole in the flat roof ('the tiling,' Luke), let down the bed by cords in front of Jesus, who was addressing a great multitude. Where was Jesus at the time ? Some say in the upper chamber of the house, but this would hardly have held so many. More satisfactory is the suggestion of Edersheim that Jesus was preaching in the covered gallery or verandah of the house, and that the hole was made, not in the roof of the house, but in the roof of the verandah. The house was probably Peter's, and one of considerable size, as befitted a man of some means. It was built, as the better class of Eastern houses generally are, like an English college. A single gate or door opened into a large square courtyard, planted with trees. Round it were the various apartments of the house, opening directly into the courtyard. There was also a roofed verandah running round the court. Jesus was sitting in the verandah, addressing the crowds that filled the courtyard and the doorway and the street beyond, when the men unroofed the verandah from above and let the sick man down.

2. Son, be of good cheer] Words of encouragement and comfort to the man, who, we may conclude, knew that his disease was the result of past sin, and was therefore ashamed of himself. Not only drunkenness, but various other sins of self-indulgence produce paralysis. Jesus, who knew at a glance the whole history of the case (cp. Jn 5 14), first removed the sick man's spiritual trouble, and then healed him. The absolution was given for the man's own sake, but it was also a challenge to the Pharisees, who were present as enemies. Their hostility had been roused not only by the cleansing of the leper (8 1), but by the very similar miracle worked shortly before at Jerusalem (Jn 5 2), in connexion with which also Jesus had incurred the charge of blasphemy ('He called God His own father, making Himself equal with God,' Jn 5 18).

6. The Son of man] i.e. the Son of God in the humiliation of His life on earth. **Hath power** (RM 'authority') **on earth to forgive sins**] What is the force of **on earth** ? Bengel rightly says, 'This speech hints at His celestial origin.' Christ's design is to prove that His Incarnation has not emptied Him of His divine prerogatives. Though humbled on earth, the divine power of pardon was still His. By becoming man He had not ceased to be God.

8. Which had given such power (RM 'authority') **unto men**] The saying is a striking one. Although one man alone had exercised the power, the people rightly perceived that there had been established the principle that the divine forgiveness can be committed to man. Christ afterwards gave such power unto men when He committed to His Church the power to forgive sins (Jn 20 23). A strong distinction must, however, be drawn between Christ's own power to forgive, which is original and absolute, and the ministerial power of absolution which is delegated and conditional : see on Jn 20 23.

9–13. Call of Matthew (Mk 2 14 Lk 5 27 : see Intro.). The call of a publican was another challenge to the Pharisaic party. Considering the low estimation in which publicans were held (see on 5 46), it was an act of extraordinary boldness, and, if human success was aimed at, a most unwise one. But Jesus had a mission to the despised and outcast, whom He regarded as in many respects nearer the kingdom of God than the respectable Pharisees. The most obvious way to win their confidence and to acquire influence over them, was to call one of their number to the apostolate. He did so, and followed up the step by holding a great feast, at which He and His disciples publicly ate and drank with publicans and sinners. The incident has a double significance. (1) It is a protest by Jesus against the practice of social ostracism. If publicans are treated as if they were thieves, they are likely to become so. If actors are regarded as disreputable people, disreputable they will be. But if men are treated with respect, they are thereby taught to respect themselves, and to try to deserve the good opinion of others. (2) It is an intimation that the Church has a mission to the poor, the outcast, and the criminal, as well as to the respectable classes. Many signs show that this duty is now much more appreciated than it was. Parochial missions to the poor, street preaching, the police-court missionaries, the missions in prisons, are all imitations of our Lord's feast to publicans and sinners.

9. Matthew] The other Gospels call him 'Levi.' Matthew ('gift of Jehovah') was the name by which he was known among Christians. He may have adopted it at his call.

The receipt of custom] RV 'the place of toll.' Custom, or toll (Gk. *telos*), was a tax levied on goods imported or exported from one district to another, as distinguished from tribute (Gk. *censos*, or *phoros*), an annual tax on houses, lands, and persons. As customs generally went to the native government, Matthew was probably in the employ of Herod Antipas, not of the Romans. J. Lightfoot

thinks that the toll was levied on vessels plying on the lake. More probably it was levied on the caravans trading between Egypt and Damascus, most of which passed through Capernaum. **Follow me**] St. Luke says that St. Matthew 'left all' and followed Jesus. Probably he had been a disciple for some time and expected the call.

10. As Jesus sat at meat (lit. 'reclined') **in the house**] From St. Matthew and St. Mark it might be supposed that the meal took place in the house of Jesus, i.e. of Peter ; but it is clear from St. Luke that it was in the house of Matthew, who made a great feast for his Master. This feast is not to be regarded as a mere farewell banquet given by him to his old associates, but as part of a definite design on the part of Jesus to reach the despised and outcast classes. There being so great a multitude of guests, it is probable that the feast was held not in the upper-room, but in the great courtyard of the house. For the attitude of sitting (reclining) at meat, see on Lk 7 38 Jn 13 23.

11. When the Pharisees saw *it*] The Pharisees were not invited, but they walked in to see what was happening. In the East a banquet is a public affair, and any casual wayfarer may enter as a spectator. **Why eateth your master with publicans and sinners ?**] The Pharisees spoke to the disciples to seduce them from their allegiance to their Master. Publicans were social outcasts, and religiously half-excommunicate It was said, 'A religious man who becomes a publican, is to be driven out of the society of religion.' 'It is not lawful to use the riches of such men, of whom it is presumed that all their wealth was gotten by rapine, and that all their business was the business of extortioners, such as publicans and robbers are.' Publicans were forbidden to be judges or to give evidence : see on 5 46. Some think that 'sinners' is a mere Pharisaic term of abuse for publicans.

12. They that be whole, i.e. the Pharisees, **have no need of a physician**, i.e. of Christ, **but they that are sick**, i.e. the publicans and sinners. The saying is spoken in irony, for the Pharisees, wanting charity, wanted a physician even more than the publicans.

13. I will have mercy, and not sacrifice] i.e. I would rather see love and charity towards fellowmen than ritual observances. Ritual without love is an abomination. Quoted from Hos 6 6, and again in 12 7. **The righteous**] i.e. those who think themselves such, viz. the Pharisees. Ironically spoken. Of course Christ did come to call the Pharisees, but they refused to be called.

14–17. Controversy with the disciples of John and with the Pharisees on fasting (Mk 2 18 Lk 5 33). Matthew's feast probably took place on a Monday or a Thursday, days which were observed by the Pharisees and John's disciples as fasts: see Mk, 'The disciples of John and the Pharisees were fasting.' The jealousy of the disciples of John had showed itself even before John had been cast into prison (Jn 3 26). Now that John was in prison, they readily became the tools of the Pharisees, who instigated them to come forward and say, 'Why do we and the Pharisees fast oft, but thy disciples fast not?' The question had two purposes. (1) It was intended to hold up to public odium the laxity of the religious practices of Jesus as compared with the strictness of those of the Pharisees and of John. (2) It was intended to produce a breach between John and Jesus. The reputation of Jesus had been established very largely by the witness which John had borne to His Messiahship. If Jesus could be induced to condemn John (and it seemed impossible that He could defend His own disciples without doing so), John would perhaps disown Jesus, whose reputation would thereby be seriously diminished.

Jesus disappointed them by an answer at least as diplomatic as the famous one about the tribute-money. Addressing the disciples of John, He reminded them that their own master had called Him the Bridegroom, and added that at a wedding not even the Pharisees would desire the guests to fast. When the wedding-feast was over, or rather when the bridegroom was taken from them by a violent death, they would mourn and fast. Then in three parables (the last of which is in St. Luke only) He showed that the disciples of John were as right from their point of view as His own disciples were from theirs. In the first parable He compared the religious practices of John to an old garment, and His own to a new garment. John, He said, was not so foolish as to tear a piece of cloth from the new garment of Christianity in order to patch with it his own Jewish garment. He could not, for instance, consistently borrow from Christ the dispensation from fasting, and teach it to his disciples, without making a complete breach in his system. Let the disciples of John continue to fast until they came to Jesus, when they would adopt different practices altogether.

Having defended John, Jesus, in a second parable, defended Himself. John's wine was old, and was contained in bottles which suited it. His own was new, and required new bottles. In other words, the two different types of piety required different outward methods of expression. John's preparatory ministry of repentance was rightly accompanied by fasting and mourning, but now the fulness of joy was come, the time of feasting and rejoicing had begun.

In a third parable, given only by St. Luke, Jesus again defends the disciples of John.

'No one,' He says, 'having drunk old wine, desires new, for he says, The old is good enough.' In other words, the disciples of John, having tasted John's wine and found it to be good, are not to be blamed if they are not over anxious to taste new wine, i.e. to adopt the new and to them untried practices of Christ's disciples (Lk 5 39).

14. Fast oft] Some ancient authorities omit 'oft.'

15. The children (RV 'sons') of the bride-chamber] i.e. the friends of the bridegroom, who, amid singing and playing of instruments, conducted the bride, accompanied by her companions, to the house of the bridegroom and to the bridechamber, and remained to take part in the wedding-feast, which usually lasted seven days. Here the 'sons of the bridechamber' are the disciples of Christ. Christ was first called the Bridegroom by the Baptist himself (Jn 3 29). **Shall be taken from them]** The first prediction in St. Matthew of the Passion. **And then shall they fast]** The first reference is to the sorrow of Christ's disciples after His death. The words, however, may be taken to suggest for fasting a permanent place in the Christian system of devotion, but a less prominent one than in the austere system of John and the formal self-righteous one of Pharisaic Judaism: see on 6 16.

16. A piece of new cloth] lit. 'undressed cloth.' According to St. Luke the piece of new cloth is taken from the new garment of Christianity. It signifies the bright and joyous character of the religion of Christ, which cannot be successfully grafted upon the austere and joyless system of the Baptist.

Taketh from the garment] i.e. parts, or separates itself from the garment. **And the rent is made worse]** RV 'a worse rent is made.'

17. Old bottles] The most usual Eastern bottles are simply goat-skins drawn off the animal entire. The neck of the animal forms the neck of the bottle. Those used for wine are tanned with oak-bark and seasoned in smoke, which gives a flavour to the wine that is much appreciated. New wine is liable to a certain amount of after-fermentation, so that it cannot safely be stored in old bottles. Our Lord's saying about the old and the new bottles applies properly to the Baptist's teaching, but it may also be applied to Judaism in general. So taken, it means that the forms of Judaism are inadequate to express the spirit of Christianity, and that those who, like the Judaising Christians in the Acts, try to combine the Law with the Gospel and to enforce the Mosaic ritual, are trying to put new wine into old bottles.

18-26. The raising of Jairus' daughter, and the healing of the woman with an issue of blood (Mk 5 21 Lk 8 40). The most important point in the raising of Jairus' daughter is the reality of the death. This has been denied on account of our Lord's words, ' The maid is not dead, but sleepeth.' It is perfectly true that the mourners understood them in this sense, ' for they laughed him to scorn, knowing that she was dead' (Lk), but inasmuch as the narrative comes from Peter himself, who was present, and is told as a miracle, it must be held that she was really dead, and that Jesus spoke of her as sleeping, because He was about to wake her. He used the same words of Lazarus, and on that occasion explained them (Jn 11¹¹).

Some who are able to credit the miracles of healing, find difficulties in crediting the miracles of resurrection. There is, however, no more real difficulty in believing the resurrection of Jairus' daughter than in believing that of Jesus Himself. The former illustrates the latter, and is rendered probable by it. It should be observed in this connexion, (1) That miracles of healing, important as they are as proofs of God's benevolence, are entirely inadequate to illustrate the cardinal doctrine of a future life (2) That Jesus Himself regarded raising the dead as part of His ordinary ministerial work (11⁵ Lk 7²²), and, according to St. Matthew, delegated the power to the Apostles (10⁸), in accordance with which St. Peter afterwards raised Tabitha (Ac 9⁴⁰).

Christ's three miracles of resurrection form a graduated series. In the case of Jairus' daughter the spirit had hardly fled. The widow's son (Lk 7¹²) had been dead longer, but not more than twenty-four hours. Lazarus (Jn 11) had been dead four days, and decomposition had probably begun. Yet we are not to suppose that one miracle was more difficult than another to Him who is the Resurrection and the Life.

The **healing of the woman with the issue** is an example of the way in which Jesus accepted imperfect faith in order to render it perfect. The woman was superstitious. She thought that a kind of magical virtue resided in our Lord's body, ready to flow out to heal without any act of will on His part, or any act of faith on hers. All that she had to do was to touch, and in doing so she was careful to touch (v. 20) that portion of His garment which to a Jew was holiest, viz. the tassel, which, in accordance with Nu 15³⁷, every Jew was required to wear on the four corners of his cloak to remind him of Jehovah's commands. But since there was real faith mingled with her superstition, Jesus allowed her to be healed, only calling her back afterwards to make her faith perfect. By saying ' Who touched me?' and insisting on a full confession, He made it clear to the woman and to others that He had healed her by His own

deliberate act, and was fully aware of all the circumstances of the case. By saying ' Thy faith hath saved thee,' He reproved her super stition. Not the touch, nor the holy tassel, nor the supposed magic virtue had healed her, but her faith.

18. While he spake] According to this Gospel the ruler came to Jesus as He was sitting at meat with Matthew the publican. The other Gospels record the incident immediately after the return from the country of the Gadarenes (Gerasenes).

Is even now dead] According to the fuller narrative of St. Mark and St. Luke, Jairus says that his daughter is at the point of death. Afterwards a messenger arrives announcing that she is dead.

20. A woman] Eusebius (Church Historian, Bishop of Cæsarea in the 4th cent. A.D.) says that she was a heathen, residing at Paneas (Cæsarea Philippi), near the sources of the Jordan. ' Her house is shown in the city, and the wonderful monuments of our Saviour's benefit to her are still remaining. At the gates of her house, on an elevated stone, stands a brazen statue of a woman on her bended knee, with her hands stretched out before her like one entreating. Opposite to this is another statue of a man, erect, of the same materials, decently clad in a mantle, and stretching out his hand to the woman. This statue they said was a likeness of Jesus Christ.' It may, however, have been a statue of Æsculapius, the god of healing, who was in great favour at the beginning of the Christian era. **Touched the hem** (RV ' border,' or, rather, ' tassel ') **of His garment**] see prefatory remarks on vv. 18–26.

23. According to St. Mark and St. Luke only Peter, James, and John, and the parents witnessed the miracle. **The minstrels**] RV ' the flute-players.' The rabbis said, ' Even the poorest among the Israelites (his wife being dead) will afford her two flutes (i.e. two male flute-players to play at the funeral procession), and one woman to make lamentation.' The multitude of hired mourners marks the wealth and position of Jairus. **25.** St. Mark gives our Lord's actual Aramaic words, *Talitha cumi*, i.e. ' Maid, arise.' **26.** St. Mark and St Luke add that our Lord commanded the parents to be silent about the miracle. Some think that this was only a warning against religious gossip. More probably, since the house was surrounded by an excited crowd, His design was to prevent a tumult.

27–31. Healing of two blind men in the house (peculiar to St. Matthew). Blindness, chiefly as the result of ophthalmia, is exceedingly common in the East, and several miracles of restoring sight to the blind are recorded in the Gospels : 12²² 20³⁰ 21¹⁴ Jn 9. In this case Christ elicited a definite act of faith from the men before healing them. The act of touching their eyes was probably intended to aid their faith. Their addressing Him as Son of David need not imply that they believed Him to be the Messiah. **30. Straitly charged**] i.e. sternly (see RV) charged them, because He foresaw that they would disobey : cp. 12 16, etc.

32–34. Healing of a dumb man (Lk 11 14). This miracle is given by St. Luke in another connexion, and is there followed by a reply by Jesus to the criticisms of the Pharisees.

32. A dumb man] The Gk. word may either mean deaf or dumb, or both. **33. It was never so seen**] Their wonder was excited not merely by this miracle, but by a long series of miracles worked in succession, of which this was the last. **34. The prince of the devils**] St. Luke ' by Beelzebub ': see on 12 24.

35–38. Tours of Jesus in Galilee (peculiar to St. Matthew, but cp. Mk 6 6, 34 Lk 10 2). The early tours of Jesus in Galilee enabled Him to gain a comprehensive view of the actual spiritual condition of the people. It was a very unfavourable one, yet He was not moved to anger, but to pity, for the fault was not in them, but in their guides. ' They were distressed and scattered as sheep not having a shepherd.' True they had the scribes and Pharisees, but these were no true shepherds, but blind leaders of the blind. Yet the situation was hopeful. The people had received Him gladly, and were eager to be taught. ' The harvest truly is plenteous, but the labourers are few.' What was wanted was more missionaries to assist Him in His work. Hence the mission of the Twelve.

36. Cp. Mk 6 34. **37, 38.** St. Luke introduces this saying in connexion with the mission of the Seventy (Lk 10 2).

CHAPTER 10
MISSION OF THE TWELVE

1. Mission of the Twelve (Mk 6 7 Lk 9 1). This mission was intended partly to prepare the way for visits from Jesus Himself, and partly to train the apostles for their future ministry. He sent them out ' two and two ' (Mk), for the sake of mutual encouragement. That is the true method of undertaking missionary work, as the experience of St. Paul shows. The apostles were to preach a little, but not much, since they were beginners. They were to prepare the way for Jesus, saying, ' The kingdom of heaven is at hand.' All accounts agree that they were to work miracles on a great scale (' power over all the devils,' Lk ; ' to heal every disease, and every infirmity,' Mt). They healed by anointing with oil (Mk) : cp. Jas 5 14. Their power extended even to cleansing the lepers and raising the dead (Mt).

This mission began about five weeks before the second Passover of the ministry (Jn 6 4), and lasted about a month. Having dismissed the apostles, Jesus went up to Jerusalem to keep the feast of Jn 5 1, probably Purim, at the beginning of March. He then rejoined the Twelve shortly before Passover : see on Jn 6 1.

2–4. The names of the Twelve (Mk 3 13 Lk 6 12 Ac 1 13). At an early period in His Galilean ministry, Jesus selected Twelve from among the disciples already called (Mk, Lk), after spending a night in prayer in ' the mountain ' (Lk), as befitted so solemn and important an act. The ' Sermon on the Mount ' constituted their ordination address (Lk). St. Matthew assumes these facts to be known, and introduces the Twelve abruptly, **Now the names of the twelve apostles are these**, without mentioning how they were called together. The chief significance of the appointment of the Twelve is that it indicates the design of Jesus to provide His society with an ordained ministry, and to give it a thoroughly efficient organisation to cope with its world-wide mission. The number twelve was suggested by the number of the Jewish patriarchs. The apostles were to be the patriarchs or spiritual ancestors of the new Israel.

The names of the apostles are always given in three groups of four names, of which the leaders (Peter, Philip, James of Alphæus) are mentioned first in all the lists. The names are always kept in their own groups, but vary in order, except that the leader is always placed first.

2. Apostles] An ' apostle ' (lit. ' one sent ') is more than a messenger ; he is a messenger who represents the person who sends him, an ' ambassador ' (2 Cor 5 20). The name is here introduced because this mission was the first occasion on which the Twelve began to act as apostles or ambassadors of Jesus. The name, though specially applied to the Twelve, was extended to embrace St. Paul, St. Barnabas, and other apostolic men (Ac 14 4, 14, etc.).

Apostle is used without technical meaning Jn 13 16 (RM) 2 Cor 8 23 (RM). The Jews had ' apostles ' who were sent abroad from Jerusalem to collect the Temple-money. The Greek Church calls missionaries ' apostles,' and the Nestorian Christians apply the same term to the delegates of the Archbishop of Canterbury.

Simon, who is called Peter] in Aramaic *Kephas* (a ' rock ' or ' stone '). He received the name at his first call (Jn 1 43). The career of Peter can be constructed from these references : Mt 4 18 8 14 14 28 15 15 16 18 16 22 17 1 17 24 18 21 19 27 26 33, 37, 58, 69 Lk 8 45, 51 22 8, 61 24 12 Jn 1 43 6 68 13 6, 24, 36 18 10, 16 20 2 21 2 f Ac 1 13, 15 2 14 3 1 4 8 5 3, 15, 29 8 14 9 32 10 5 11 2 12 3 15 7 1 Cor 1 12 3 22 9 5 15 5 Gal 1 18 2 7 1 Pet 1 1 2 Pet 1 1. He had Mark for his ' interpreter ' (1 Pet 5 13).

The tradition of his Roman residence and martyrdom, though highly probable, is not quite certain. He is first in all lists of the apostles. For his position in the Church, see on Mt 16 18.

Andrew] 4 18 Mk 1 19 13 3 Jn 1 41 6 8 12 22.

James *the son* **of Zebedee**] sometimes called 'the great': Mk 1 19 3 17 10 37 Lk 5 1 9 53 Ac 12 1. The first apostle to be martyred.

John] 4 21 17 1 Mk 1 29 9 38 10 35 13 3 14 33 Lk 22 8 Jn 1 35 13 23 18 15 19 26, 35 20 2 21 7 Ac 1 13 3 1 4 13 8 14 Gal 2 9 Rev 1 1. See Intro. to St. John.

3. Philip] Jn 1 44 6 5 12 21 14 8.

Bartholomew] i.e. Nathanael of Cana of Galilee : see Jn 1 45 21 2.

Thomas] see Jn 11 16 14 5 20 24 21 2. There is a tradition that his real name was 'Judas.'

Matthew the publican] see Intro. and on 9 9. St. Mark calls him 'Levi.'

James *the son* **of Alphæus**] lit. 'James of Alphæus.' Called James 'the less,' or rather 'the little,' Mk 15 40. His mother was named Mary. He is not to be identified with James the Lord's 'brother,' who became head of the Church of Jerusalem, nor is his father Alphæus with Clopas (Jn 19 25), nor His mother Mary with the Virgin's sister (Jn 19 25) : see further on 12 46-50 Jn 19 25.

Lebbæus, whose surname was Thaddæus] He is the same as the 'Judas of James' (Lk 6 16), and the 'Judas not Iscariot' (Jn 14 22). Thaddæus is perhaps a form of 'Theudas,' and is, therefore, Greek. Lebbæus is Aramaic, but its meaning is unknown. Some regard it is a form of 'Levi.'

Although Westcott and Hort reject Lebbæus from the text of this passage, it is supported by excellent authorities, and it is hard to account for its insertion, if it is not genuine.

4. Simon the Canaanite] RV 'the Cananæan,' RM 'the zealot.' 'The Zealots were a sect founded by Judas of Gamala (or of Galilee, Ac 5 37), who headed the opposition to the census of Quirinius 6 or 7 A.D. They bitterly resented the domination of Rome, and would fain have hastened with the sword the fulfilment of the Messianic hope. During the great rebellion and the siege of Jerusalem their fanaticism made them terrible opponents, not only to the Romans, but to other factions among their own countrymen' (HDB.).

Judas Iscariot] Both Judas and his father Simon were called Iscariot, lit. 'man of Kerioth,' because they were natives of Kerioth, a village of S. Judah, near Hebron (Jn 15 25). He was the only Judæan apostle : see 26 14, 25, 47 27 3 Lk 22 3 Jn 6 71 12 4 13 2, 26, 29 18 2 Ac 1 16, 25.

5–42. Charge to the Twelve (Mk 6 7 Lk 9 1 : cp. also Lk 10 2, charge to the Seventy). The first eleven vv. of this great charge (vv. 5–15) represent Christ's words actually spoken to the Twelve on the occasion of this mission.

The rest of the charge (vv. 16–42), with the exception of the last three vv., represents instructions given by Christ at other times to His apostles with reference to their missionary work after His ascension. St. Matthew adds them to the charge in accordance with his custom of grouping our Lord's sayings of a similar character together. Specially to be noticed are, (1) the limitation of the mission to Israel, and (2) the extraordinary authority over the whole human race which Christ claims for Himself throughout the charge.

The charge to the Seventy (Lk 10 2) is almost the same as the charge to the Twelve. Our Lord probably repeated to the Seventy much of what He had said to the Twelve, because their missions were so similar.

5–15. The charge delivered on the occasion of the mission.

5. Way of the Gentiles] i.e. a road which leads to a Gentile district or city. The restriction to the Jews was part of the divine purpose that the gospel should be offered to the Jew first, and afterwards to the Gentile. It was also a condescension to the inexperience of the apostles, who would find their work easier among Jews than among hostile Samaritans or contemptuous Greeks. Only when their training was complete could they hope to face a hostile world with success. On account of the ease of their mission, and their certainty of a warm welcome, they were to take no money or food, or any staff to defend themselves with (vv. 9, 10). Yet if they were accustomed to use a staff they might take one (Mk). Afterwards, when Christ spoke of their future mission to an unbelieving and a hostile world, He said exactly the opposite (Lk 22 36).

7. They were also to preach 'that men should repent' (Mk). **8. Raise the dead**] to be taken literally. The clause is accepted by all recent editors. It is omitted by a few MSS, perhaps because there is no mention of raising the dead on this occasion. For the fulfilment see Ac 9 40 20 10. **Freely ye have received the** gift of working miracles, **freely** exercise it.

9. Purses] i.e. 'girdles,' in which money was carried. **10. Scrip**] RV 'wallet,' i.e. provision-basket. **Two coats**] i.e. two shirts or undergarments. **Shoes**] were forbidden as too luxurious. The apostles were to wear only sandals. 'Shoes,' said Lightfoot, 'were of more delicate use. A shoe was of softer leather, a sandal of harder.' **The workman is worthy of his meat**] or, 'of his hire' (Lk). Our Lord lays great stress on the principle that the clergy are to be supported by the Church, and not to be obliged to work at a secular calling : see 1 Cor 9 14 1 Tim 5 17, 18.

11. Worthy] of the honour of receiving you. **12. Salute it**] i.e. by saying 'Peace be to this house.' **13. If the house be worthy**] or, as St. Luke expresses it, 'if the owner be a son of peace,' i.e. a peaceful man, worthy of the blessing. **14. Shake off the dust**] The rabbis taught that the dust of heathen lands defiled. They said, 'The dust of Syria defiles, as well as the dust of other heathen countries.' The act of the apostles, therefore, signified that the city that rejected them was no better than heathen : see on Ac 13 51. **15.** Why was the sin of Sodom less ? Because the men of Sodom sinned largely in ignorance, but rejecters of the gospel sin against light.

16–39. Later charges of Jesus, referring to work after the Ascension. Vv. 16–22 were probably spoken in Holy Week : see Mk 13 9 Lk 21 12.

16. As sheep (Lk 'lambs') **in the midst of wolves**] This can only refer to the later persecutions of the apostles. According to a very early writer, Peter proceeded to ask, 'What, then, if the wolves rend the sheep ?' Jesus replied that after death the lambs need not fear the wolves, for the wolves have no power to slay the soul. **Wise as serpents, and harmless as doves**] cp. a saying of the rabbis, 'The holy and blessed God said to the Israelites, Towards Me the Israelites are uncorrupt like the doves, but towards the Gentiles they are as cunning as serpents.' Jesus meant that the apostles were to use every human device to protect themselves from persecution, as St. Paul did when he pleaded his Roman citizenship.

17. But beware of men] better, 'beware of the men,' viz. those wolves of whom I have been speaking. **Councils**] i.e. courts of justice generally. **Scourge you in their synagogues**] A synagogue was also a court of justice in which three Jewish elders sat to judge both secular and religious cases. 'Scourging,' said the rabbis, 'was by the bench of three' : cp. Ac 22 19 26 11 2 Cor 11 24. Wetstein quotes an interesting account of a modern Jewish scourging. It was done publicly in the synagogue in the presence of a large congregation of men and women. The man was bared to the waist. The porter tied his hands to a pillar. Then the 'precentor' approached, and scourged him with thirty-nine strokes, a Psalm being sung during the ordeal.

18. Before governors and kings] 'Governors' were the Roman governors of the provinces, viz. propraetors, proconsuls, and procurators : cp. Paul before Felix and Festus (Ac 24 1 25 6). 'Kings' were, (1) the emperor, who was generally so called in the East ; (2) subject kings, tetrarchs, and ethnarchs, such as the Herods and Aretas ; (3) independent kings, as of the Parthians, Arabians, and Indians.

For a testimony against them] RV 'to them,' i.e. to the Jews. The meaning is, that when the Jews should deliver up the apostles to

governors and kings, the speeches of the apostles in their own defence would be a powerful testimony of the truth of Christianity both to Jews and Gentiles. This really happened. The persecutions greatly contributed to spread the gospel, partly by the publicity which they gave to it, and partly through the inspired testimony which the martyrs gave to Christ. When the aged Polycarp (160 A.D.) was brought before the Proconsul in the amphitheatre of Smyrna and urged to revile Christ, 'he looked with a grave face at all the multitude of lawless heathen in the arena .. and said, Eighty and six years have I served Him, and in nothing hath He wronged me ; and how then can I blaspheme my King that saved me ?'

19, 20. Cp. Lk 12 11, 12 in addition.

19. Take no thought] RV 'be not anxious.' **It shall be given you**] cp. the courage of Peter and John (Ac 4 13) before the Sanhedrin.

21. The brother shall deliver up, etc.] Actual examples of Christians being delivered up by their nearest relatives are found in the Martyrologies, but the saying is to be taken more generally to refer to the rupture of all ties of kindred and affection on account of the gospel.

22. Hated of all *men*] cp. Tacitus the Roman historian : '(Nero) inflicted the most cruel punishments upon a sect of people who were holden in abhorrence for their crimes, and called by the vulgar "Christians." The founder of that name was Christ, who suffered death in the reign of Tiberius, under his procurator Pontius Pilate... This pernicious superstition, thus checked for a while, broke out again ; and spread not only over Judæa where the evil originated, but through Rome also, whither everything bad upon earth finds its way and is practised... A vast multitude were apprehended who were convicted, not so much of the crime of burning Rome, as of hatred to mankind... They were criminals, deserving the severest punishments': cp. also Ac 7 54. **To the end**] viz. of the trials and persecutions.

23. Flee ye into another] The apostles are forbidden to court martyrdom, and the wisest leaders of the later Church, e.g. Polycarp and Cyprian, gave the same advice. It was often found that those who rushed eagerly forward to claim martyrdom contrary to our Lord's command, were denied the grace to attain the martyr's crown. 'Flee ye into another' (RV 'the next'), 'for owing to the time wasted in going from city to city to avoid persecution, ye shall not have gone over the cities of Israel, till the Son of man be come, and the Jewish nation and dispensation destroyed.' The meaning, as interpreted in the light of events, is that until the destruction of Jerusalem the Twelve were to confine themselves mainly to evangelising the Jews, a task which would even then be incomplete, owing to the hindrances which would arise.

Our Lord here referred to His coming to destroy Jerusalem. The apostles understood Him to refer to His final coming. This accounts for the general expectation of the early Christians that the end of the world would come in the lifetime of the first believers (1 Th 4 15) : see on Mt 24 Mk 13 32.

24. The disciple, etc.] A favourite saying of Jesus used in several different connexions. Here it means that the apostles are not to expect better treatment than their Master. In Lk 6 40 it means that the disciples of blind spiritual guides are as blind as their teachers. In Jn 13 16 it means that since Jesus washes other men's feet, the disciples must do so too. In Jn 15 20 it means, as in St. Matthew, that the apostles are to expect the same persecutions which have befallen their Master.

25. Beelzebub] cp. 12 24 Jn 8 48, 52. The true form here is *Beelzeboul*, which is altered from *Baalzebub* (2 K 1 2) 'Baalzebub' means 'Lord of flies,' and appears in OT. as a god of Ekron who gave oracles. 'Beelzeboul' in NT. is the devil. The NT. form perhaps means 'master of the house' (of the demons). J. Lightfoot regards it as meaning 'lord of dung' : see on 12 22 f.

26-33. These vv. are found in quite another connexion in Lk 12 2-9.

26. Fear them not therefore] for the whole effect of their persecutions will be to publish abroad the gospel, which but for their action would have remained obscure : cp. Mk 4 22 Lk 8 17 12 2,3.

27. What I tell you in darkness] A prophecy that the labours of the apostles will be more successful than those of Jesus Himself. He taught with indifferent success in the obscurity of an insignificant and remote province. They will teach successfully in the publicity of the great cities of the empire, Antioch, Ephesus, Corinth, Alexandria, Rome. **What ye hear in the ear]** In the Jewish schools the rabbi sat in his chair, and whispered in Hebrew into the ear of his interpreter, who then proclaimed aloud in the vulgar tongue what the rabbi had said. So the apostles were to proclaim to the wide world what Christ had whispered to them in the retirement of Galilee. **Upon the housetops]** Proclamations are still made in the East from the flat roofs of houses. E.g. the sabbath is proclaimed by the 'attendant' of the synagogue, who ascends to a lofty housetop, and blows there three times with the synagogue-trumpet.

28. Him which is able] i.e. God, not, as some strangely take it, the devil. **In hell]** i.e. Gehenna, the place of final punishment : see 5 22.

29. Sparrows] At the present day, in the markets of Jerusalem and Jaffa, long strings of little birds, sparrows and larks, are offered for sale, trussed on wooden skewers. **Farthing]** (Lat. *assarius*) i.e. about a farthing and a third.

32, 33. The sense is that in the day of judgment men's fate will depend upon their attitude to Christ, and upon Christ's attitude to them, another proof of Christ's divinity.

34-36. These vv. occur in a somewhat different form and in a different connexion, Lk 12 51-53.

34. Think not, etc.] Christ could not expect that His claim to absolute dominion over the soul of man and all human institutions, would be accepted without a bitter struggle. But knowing such a struggle to be necessary for the establishment of peace with God and of permanent peace on earth, He deliberately willed it. 'The sword' stands for persecution, and for all kinds of social and domestic dissensions.

37. He that loveth father, etc.] This explains the stronger expression in Lk 14 26 about 'hating' father and mother. Observe here, again, the tremendous stress upon personal loyalty to Christ. **38. Taketh not his cross]** i.e. he that is not willing to follow Me to martyrdom is not worthy of Me. The 'cross' stands here, not for trouble in general (though this is included), but for actual crucifixion, the most painful and degrading form of martyrdom. The condemned criminal was forced to 'take' or carry his cross to the place of execution. Christ here indicates that He knew beforehand not only the fact of His death, but its manner. **39.** Cp. Lk 17 33, where the context is different. **He that findeth his life]** i.e. saves his life in time of persecution by denying Me, **shall lose it** in the next world. **He that loseth his life,** i.e. by martyrdom, **for my sake shall find it** in the next world, i.e. shall enjoy immortal life. The passage may also be applied to self-denial in general, by which man loses his life of self-centred worldliness, to find it again enlarged and purified.

40-42. These vv. form the conclusion of the charge to the Twelve, and are not to be referred to a later date. In St. Luke the substance of them forms the conclusion of the charge to the Seventy

40. Cp. Lk 10 16. **He that receiveth you]** Those who receive Christ's representatives, the apostles, and after them His ministers (i.e. those who believe their message spoken in His name), receive Him, and with Him His Father. **41. He that receiveth a prophet, etc.]** The meaning is that those who receive the apostles, because they recognise them to be prophets and righteous men and disciples, will receive the same reward as they, eternal life.

In the name of a prophet] i.e. simply because he is a prophet (a Hebraism). **42. These little**

ones] a tender name for the apostles themselves. Even those who only help on their mission by offering them a cup of cold water as they journey, will be rewarded : cp. Mk 9⁴¹. Some think that 'little ones' was a standing title for pupils of the rabbis, but clear proof is wanting.

CHAPTER 11
THE DISCIPLES OF THE BAPTIST

1. **Tours of Jesus after dismissing His apostles.** The apostles started on their mission about five weeks before the second Passover of the ministry (28 A.D.) and were away about a month. Jesus spent the interval partly in Galilee and partly in Jerusalem, whither he went to keep the Feast of Purim at the beginning of March (Jn 5¹). He rejoined the Twelve shortly before the Passover (Jn 6⁴), and immediately afterwards fed the five thousand (Mk 6³⁰ Lk 9¹⁰). St. Matthew does not mention the return of the Twelve, nor does he adhere to the chronological order of events.

2–6. **Deputation from the Baptist** (Lk 7¹⁸). John, knowing that his end was near, and that many of his disciples were jealous of the success of the new teacher, and disbelieved His claims, sent certain of them to Jesus, that by seeing His works and hearing His words they might be convinced of His Messiahship. The objections which the disciples of John brought against Jesus (besides the want of strictness in His life), were (1) that He did not openly proclaim Himself the Messiah, (2) that He did not work the mighty signs and wonders which were generally expected of the Messiah. The importance of the occasion, and the obvious sincerity of the enquirers, induced Jesus to depart somewhat from His ordinary policy of reticence. By a reference to Isa 6¹, He declared plainly enough, and yet not too plainly, that He was the Messiah, He worked a number of miracles in their presence in proof of His Messianic claims (Lk 7²¹), and finally sent them back to John with a message in which He expressly mentioned His miracles, and promised a blessing to those who should attach themselves to Him. The spectacle of Christ's miracles must have been particularly impressive to the disciples of John, who worked no miracles (Jn 10⁴¹).

It is very generally held by recent writers that John himself, as well as his disciples, was doubtful about our Lord's Messiahship. This is not impossible. The ideals of Jesus diverged so widely from those of John, that the Baptist, hearing of them only by report, would have a difficulty in understanding them. We must allow, moreover, for the depressing effect of a long and rigorous imprisonment. On the other hand, it must be remembered that the NT. always represents not John himself, but his disciples, as doubtful about the claims of Jesus, and that Jesus makes this deputation the occasion of one of the strongest eulogies upon John that the NT. contains.

2. **Sent two of his disciples**] RV 'sent by his disciples.' Only St. Luke gives the number.

5. See Isa 61¹ and 35⁵. **The dead are raised up**] This implies a larger number of such miracles than the three mentioned in the Gospels. St. Luke appropriately places the deputation immediately after the raising of the widow's son. **The poor have the gospel,** etc.] Some translate this ' the poor preach,' as if Christ alluded to the poverty of the apostles. 6. Blessed is he who, in spite of all hindrances, shall find himself able to believe in me as the Messiah.

7–19. **The praise of John the Baptist** (Lk 7²⁴). Lest the purpose of the question of John, ' Art thou he that should come ? ' should be misunderstood, Jesus hastens to assure the people that John is no **reed shaken by the wind,** who does not know his own mind, but a prophet, and more than a prophet. He then deplores the blindness of ' this generation,' i.e. the party of the scribes and Pharisees, who can discern the greatness neither of John nor of Himself. 8. John was no sycophant or flatterer, making friends with the great and wealthy for the sake of sharing their luxury and ostentation. 9. RV 'But wherefore went ye out ? To see a prophet ?' **More than a prophet**] John was more than a prophet, (1) because of his personal relation to Jesus as His Forerunner ; (2) because he actually pointed out and baptised Jesus ; (3) because his teaching was a nearer approach to the teaching of Jesus than that of any of the prophets.

10. **Before thy face**] In the original of Mal 3¹, from which these words are taken, Jehovah Himself speaks of His own coming, ' Behold, 1 will send my messenger, and he shall prepare the way before *me*.' All the evangelists change this into an address of Jehovah to the Messiah, 'shall prepare thy way before *thee*' (Mk 1² Lk 1⁷⁶, 7²⁷), which shows that they borrowed it not directly from Malachi, but from some common source in which the change or paraphrase had already been made.

11. **He that is least**] Jesus means that the meanest and least endowed Christian is greater in privilege than the greatest men of the Old Dispensation. The Baptist, though so near the kingdom, was not within it.

12, 13. St. Luke introduces these vv. in a quite different connexion : see Lk 16¹⁶ (a rebuke to the Pharisees). 12. **From the days of John**] Jesus gives John the credit for the multitudes of repentant sinners who are now crowding into the kingdom, and in their eagerness to enter may be compared to soldiers attempting to storm a town. **13.** The preparatory dispensation of the Law and the Prophets lasted till John. John first announced the kingdom as something present.

14. Jesus states, as again in 17^{12} (cp. Lk 1^{17}), that John was the Elijah whom the Jews expected in accordance with Mal 4^5. He hints that they may be unwilling to believe it, partly because of the position in which John now is, but more particularly because they expected a personal return of Elijah himself, and not another prophet with similar authority: see on 17^{10}.

15. He that hath ears] A frequent observation of Jesus, indicating that only those whose hearts are prepared can receive spiritual truth (13^9 Lk 8^8 Rev 2^7, etc.).

16-18. Jesus rebukes 'this generation,' i.e. the Pharisees and scribes (see Lk), who are pleased with neither John nor Himself, by comparing them to children in the streets playing at weddings and funerals, and falling out over their play. Like the children the Pharisees are only playing—playing at religion with empty ceremonies which no earnest man can take seriously. Like the children they are also peevish and irritable, unable to agree as to what they really do want from a religious leader. The asceticism of John, which corresponds to the wailing in the game, did not please them, nor does the joyous, full, human life of Jesus, which corresponds to the piping for the dance. Since they are not in earnest themselves, nothing that is really earnest can please them.

19. But wisdom is (or, ' was ') **justified of her children]** i.e. the superiority of the religion of the Baptist and of Jesus is proved by the lives of their disciples, which show more signs of genuine piety than those of the Pharisees. 'Wisdom' is here the religion of John and of Christ. 'Her children' are their disciples, who have been mentioned (v. 12) as crowding into the Kingdom of Heaven, while the Pharisees remained outside. (See Lk.) RV reads, 'Wisdom is justified by her works,' but the meaning is the same. 'Her works' are the holy lives of Christ's and John's disciples.

20-24. The woes upon Chorazin, Bethsaida, and Capernaum (Lk 10^{12}; cp. Mt 10^{15}). These were the cities in which 'most of His mighty works were done,' and yet nothing is said in the Gospels of any ministry at Chorazin, and of Bethsaida we only know that the five thousand were fed there. Chorazin lay 4 m. NE. of Capernaum, inland, but not far from the lake. There are said to have been two Bethsaidas, one E. of Jordan near the head of the lake, where the five thousand were fed, generally called Bethsaida Julias, the

other near Capernaum, W. of the lake. The latter is mentioned Mk 6^{45} (cp. Jn 6^{17}), and probably in Jn 1^{44} 12^{21}.

23. And thou, Capernaum] Jesus adapts to Capernaum the prophecy of Isaiah (Isa 14^{13}) upon Babylon and its king. **Shalt be brought down to hell]** (lit. ' Hades '). In themselves the words might simply mean that Capernaum shall cease to be a city and become desolate, as it is at present ; but the context suggests that the condemnation of its unbelieving inhabitants in the Day of Judgment is also alluded to. **24.** See on 10^{15}.

25-30. Christ's relation to the Father and to mankind (Lk 10^{21}). A sublime utterance, this 'pearl of the sayings of Jesus' (Keim), 'one of the purest and most genuine,' 'one of Johannean splendour' (Meyer), 'an aërolite from the Johannean heaven' (Hase). As a rule in the synoptists the relation of Jesus to mankind is the theme of the discourses, but here the divine Sonship of Jesus is affirmed in terms which cover the whole doctrine of the Fourth Gospel. 'This passage,' says Prof. Sanday, 'is one of the best authenticated in the Synoptic Gospels. It is .. part of that "collection of discourses," in all probability the composition of the apostle St. Matthew, which many critics believe to be the oldest of all the Evangelical documents. And yet once grant the authenticity of this passage, and there is nothing in the Johannean Christology that it does not cover. Even the doctrine of preëxistence seems to be implicitly contained in it.'

25. At that time] Since St. Luke connects this utterance with the return of the Seventy, which he alone records, it is probable that St. Matthew intends to connect it with the return of the Twelve, which, however, he does not mention. Yet he implies it, for at the beginning of the next c. the Twelve are again introduced.

Hast hid (RV 'didst hide') **these things]** Jesus thanks God that the simple gospel which the Twelve have preached has been understood and gladly received by the simple and unlearned people (**babes**) of the villages and towns through which they had passed, but has been misunderstood and rejected by the ' wise and prudent ' (RV ' wise and understanding '), i.e. by the scribes and Pharisees who think themselves such. Jesus is glad that the scribes and Pharisees have not declared themselves disciples. He does not wish to enrol them among His followers until they have given up their arrogance, and become as babes.

27. All things are (or ' were,' or ' have been ') **delivered unto me of my Father]** Having just called the Father ' Lord of heaven and earth ' (v. 25), He now declares that the same authority belongs to Himself, because all created things have been committed to Him by God. This supreme authority over the universe which was committed to Him at the creation, was exercised by Him in some degree even during the humiliation of His life on earth (Jn 3 ^{35} 13 ^{3} 17 ^{2}), and was fully restored at His resurrection (28 ^{18}) with all the glory pertaining to it. Such power could not be committed to a creature, and the possession of it by Christ can only be explained by assuming that He is, as the Fourth Gospel and the Epistles represent Him as being, the creator and sustainer of the universe.

No man (RV 'no one') **knoweth the Son, but** (RV 'save') **the Father**] lit. 'fully knoweth.' Men can know other men, but only God Himself can know Jesus. 'None but the Almighty Father has full, entire possession of the mystery of the Person and Office of the Son: it is a depth hidden from all being but His, whose purposes are evolved in and by it' (Alford).

Harnack in his 'What is Christianity?' says: 'Here two observations are to be made : Jesus is convinced that he knows God in a way in which no one ever knew Him before, and he knows that it is his vocation to communicate this knowledge of God to others by word and by deed—and with it the knowledge that men are God's children.'

Neither (fully) **knoweth any man** (RV 'any one') **the Father, save the Son**] Not only does Jesus alone fully know the Father, but He alone can reveal Him : cp. Jn 1 ^{18} 3 ^{46} 10 ^{15}.

28-30. Jesus invites to Himself all who feel the burden of sin, and who find their lives and even their religion a toil to them. He will release them from the yoke of mechanical religion, make them humble and meek like Himself, and give them pardon and peace.

28. Come unto me] He does not say 'unto God,' but 'unto Me,' making Himself the dispenser of grace and the centre of Christian devotion. **That labour**] that find life a toil to them. **Are heavy laden**] with the burden of sin, from which they can find no relief in the unspiritual and burdensome ordinances of Judaism and Pharisaism: cp. Ac 13 ^{39} Ro 3 ^{28} 8 ^{4} Heb 7 ^{19}. **I will give you rest**] Again not 'God,' but 'I' will give you rest—rest in this world and in the next—rest that comes from peace with God and pardon for sin, which I am empowered to give (9 ^{6}).

29. Take my yoke upon you] My yoke does not consist of a multitude of burdensome ordinances like that of the Law and of the Pharisees. It can hardly be called a yoke at all, it is so light. True, there are certain ordinances which every Christian must observe, **but** they are few and simple. The essence of

My religion is that men should be humble, and meek and loving and tender-hearted as I am, not hard and proud like the Pharisees. Practise these things, and you will find your lives easy, your religion a joy, and your souls at rest.

The ' Yoke of the Law ' was a common phrase among the rabbis to express the burdensome nature of its ordinances : cp. Ac 15 ^{10}. 'Why tempt ye God, that ye should put a yoke upon the neck of the disciples, which neither our fathers nor we were able to bear ?'

I am meek] Jesus says this while making Himself the object of the religious devotion of the whole human race. Obviously, therefore, His claim to be meek and lowly can only be justified, if He be truly divine.

CHAPTER 12

PLUCKING CORN ON THE SABBATH. BLAS-
PHEMY AGAINST THE HOLY GHOST

1-8. Plucking the corn on the sabbath (Mk 2 ^{23} Lk 6 ^{1}). This c. begins the period of active conflict with the Pharisees. It is characteristic of the pedantry of the Pharisees that their opposition turned more upon minute points of legal observance than upon broad principles. The Fourth Gospel agrees with the synoptists in making the sabbath controversy of leading importance in the development of hostility to Christ (Jn 5 ^{9} 7 ^{22} 9 ^{14}). St. Matthew's account of this incident is the fullest.

1. At that time] RV 'season.' This is one of the few events that can be accurately dated. The corn is in the ear, but not yet quite ripe for reaping. The time is therefore about May (perhaps April), and St. Matthew is therefore correct in placing the event soon after the return of the Twelve at Passover-time : see on 11 $^{1, 25}$. But there is no attempt at strict chronological order ; e.g. all the synoptists place this event before the feeding of the five thousand, which really preceded it. **On the sabbath day**] Lk ' on the second sabbath after the first ': see on Lk 6 ^{1}. **Were an hungered**] Why ? Some think they had been engaged with Jesus in some arduous spiritual labours. More probably they were coming home from a long synagogue service tired and hungry. Jewish custom allowed no food whatever to be eaten on the sabbath (except by the sick) until after morning service. **2. That which is not lawful**] Maimonides says: ' He that reaps on the sabbath, though never so little, is guilty. And to pluck the ears of corn is a kind of reaping.'

3. Have ye not read] Jesus might have defended His disciples on purely technical grounds, maintaining that they had broken not the Law, but the interpretation which certain rabbis placed upon it. But instead of this, He laid down the principle that even the Divine

Law itself, so far as it is purely ceremonial, is subservient to human needs, and can be broken without sin, for adequate cause. He took first the case of David, who together with his companions ate the shewbread. David's act, which was sanctioned by the high priest, who at the time was the authorised interpreter of the Law, involved three distinct breaches of the divine Law, (1) the entering into the holy place, (2) the eating of the shewbread, (3) the breach of the sabbath, for such the day seems to have been.

Our Lord's statement of the case shows careful study of the OT. narrative (1 S 21¹): e.g. it is not said in the OT. that David entered into the tabernacle, but it is inferred from v. 7, where he is seen by Doeg, who was 'detained before the Lord.' It is not said that David's attendants ate the shewbread, but it is inferred from v. 5. Nor is it said that the day was the sabbath. This is inferred from it being the day for the changing of the loaves (v. 6), which was the sabbath (Lv 24 ⁸). As to the name of the high priest at this time (a well-known difficulty), see on Mk 2 ²⁶.

5. Or have ye not read?] see Nu 28 ⁹. They had read it, but not understood the principle which it implied. Our Lord alluded to a recognised Jewish practice. The rabbis said, 'There is no keeping of the sabbath in the temple.' 'The servile work which is done in the holy things is not servile.' **6.** *One* **greater than the temple**] lit. 'a greater thing.' He means Himself. If the servants of the Temple, doing the Temple's work, may break the sabbath, much more may the servants of Christ, who is greater and holier than the Temple.

7. I will have mercy] Hos 6 ⁶, quoted also Mt 9 ¹³. Here the meaning is that God is satisfied if men keep the sabbath in the right spirit, i.e. as a day of holy rest. He does not demand obedience to an irksome code of sabbath observance. 'The sabbath was made for man, not man for the sabbath' (Mk 2 ²⁷). **8.** The authority of **the Son of man** (the Messiah) extends to the abrogation of the whole Law, and therefore of the Law of the sabbath. Observe that Jesus rests the final vindication of His disciples upon His own inherent authority, which extends to the abrogation even of the divine Law : cp. 5 ²¹ 9 ⁶.

Some understand the 'son of man' here to be not Jesus, but a personification of the human race, so that the meaning is, 'The human race may adapt the sabbath day to its needs.' This sense would suit the context, but it lacks authority, there being no clear and unambiguous passage where the phrase 'the son of man' means anything but our Lord.

9–21. Another sabbath controversy. The man with the withered hand (Mk 3 ¹ Lk 6 ⁶). The sequence is the same in all the evangelists.

St. Luke mentions that this took place on another sabbath.

10. A man] In the so-called Gospel of the Hebrews (65–100 A.D.) the man with the withered hand is described as a mason, who begged help from Jesus, saying, 'I was a mason earning my living with my hands. I pray Thee, Jesus, restore me my health, that I may not disgracefully beg my bread.'

Is it lawful] Only malice could call healing by a word, without labour or medicine, a breach of the sabbath. Even the use of medical assistance was not forbidden in all cases on the sabbath. The rabbis said, 'All danger of life or limb abrogates the sabbath,' and this was interpreted to mean even possible danger. **11. If it fall into a pit**] The schools of Hillel and Shammai differed on this point, but it is clear from our Lord's way of referring to the practice that it was generally allowed.

12. How much then] a striking saying on the value of human life and health. The literal meaning does not exclude the more spiritual interpretation that a man is of more value than a sheep as possessing an immortal soul.

14. Held a council] RV 'took counsel.' St. Mark adds, 'with the Herodians.'

15–17. Cp. Mk 3 ⁷⁻¹², where a fuller account is given. St. Mark mentions that the multitudes came from Idumæa, and from beyond Jordan, and from Tyre and Sidon. This explains the references to the Gentiles (vv. 18, 21), who were probably among those who were healed. **16. Charged them**] In St. Mark He charges the unclean spirits. The design of Jesus was to repress the dangerous popular enthusiasm which might lead to an outbreak.

17. Esaias] i.e. Isaiah. The quotation is from Isa 42 ¹⁻⁴. It is a free translation from the Heb., with occasional correspondences with the LXX. It curiously omits the words, 'He shall not fail nor be discouraged, till He have set judgment in the earth,' which would have been very applicable to our Lord in connexion with the discouragements which had just begun. **18. My servant**] i.e. 'the Messiah.' Jesus is so called frequently in the Acts (Ac 3 ¹³, ²⁶ RV, 4 ²⁷, ³⁰ RV), also in the 'Didache.' He is hardly ever so called in later writings.

19. He shall not court popularity.

20. The **bruised reed** and the **smoking flax** (or, rather, 'dimly burning wick') in this connexion are the persons weak in body whom Jesus healed, and those weak in faith, whose faith He strengthened. The idea is that Jesus is tender and loving, not harsh, towards human weakness. **Judgment** is here the Christian religion.

22–37. The Pharisees accuse Jesus of being in league with Beelzebub (Mk 3 ²² ; cp. Lk 11 ¹⁷⁻²³ Mt 9 ³²⁻³⁴). The ridiculous charge of

the Pharisees is strong evidence of the genuineness of Christ's miracles. They would have
denied them if they could (see Jn 9 18), but
this was impossible, so numerous and notorious
were they. So they started the flimsy theory
that Christ was in league with the devil, not
really believing it, but out of malice.

The later Jews said that Jesus learnt how
to work His miracles from an Egyptian juggler,
and the heathen Celsus (170 A.D.) repeated
their calumny with some improvements of his
own. The Jewish Talmudists said, 'The son
of the adulteress' (i.e. of the Virgin Mary)
'brought magic out of Egypt, by cuttings
which he had made in his flesh.' 'Jesus
practised magic and deceived, and drove Israel
to idolatry.' It is interesting to notice that
Mahomet indignantly repudiated these Jewish
calumnies.

23. The Son of David] the popular title of
the Messiah : 9 27 15 22 20 30 21 9 22 42 Jn 7 42.
See on Mt 1 1. **24. By Beelzebub**] see on 10 25.

26. Satan] The original Heb. word of which
diabolos ('devil') is the Gk. translation. It
means 'accuser,' 'calumniator,' 'adversary.'

27. Your children] i.e. 'your disciples.'
Famous rabbis and their disciples professed
to cast out devils by magic and exorcism, and
their success was attributed to the power of
God. Why then, asked Jesus, are My miracles,
which are much more striking than theirs, and
are not worked by magic, but by a mere word,
not regarded as coming from God, and why do
I not receive from you the same honour as
your own exorcists ? Josephus (born 37 A.D.)
writes : 'I have seen a certain man of my own
country, whose name was Eleazar, releasing
people that were demoniacal in the presence
of Vespasian and his sons and his captains.
He put a ring to the nostrils of the demoniac,
and drew out the demon through his nostrils
.. making mention of Solomon and reciting
the incantations which he composed.' See
also Ac 19 13 Tob 8 2.

28. By the Spirit of God] Lk 11 20, 'by the
finger of God.' **Then the kingdom of God is
come unto you**] This is shown not by the mere
fact of Jesus working miracles (the exorcists
were supposed to work them too), but by the
extraordinary character, number, and variety
of His miracles, which fully fulfilled what the
prophets had spoken of the wonders of the
Messianic age : see on 11 2-6.

29. The argument is, 'No man can carry
away the furniture from a strong man's house
until he has overpowered and bound the strong
man. So I could not remove the inferior
devils out of the bodies of men, unless I had
first conquered and bound their master, Satan
himself.'

30. He that is not with me is against me]
Jesus refers to the Pharisees. Since they do

not take His side in His warfare against Satan,
they are on Satan's side. Since they do not
help Him to gather the sheaves of the spiritual
harvest, they scatter them and prevent them
from being gathered into God's garner : see
3 12.

Some think that 'he that is not with me'
and 'that gathereth not with me' is Satan.
This also makes good sense.

31. The blasphemy against the Holy Ghost
(Mk 3 28-30 Lk 12 10). What this sin was is not
really doubtful. St. Matthew intimates that
the Pharisees had come very near to committing it. St. Mark states exactly what their
sin was. It lay in their malignant slander
that Jesus was possessed by an unclean spirit.
They regarded the spirit of holiness, which
showed itself in the acts and miracles of Jesus,
as diabolical. They called good evil and evil
good, having become like Satan himself, dead
to every impression of true holiness, and unable to recognise it when they saw it. The
sin is not a sin against the Holy Spirit considered as a divine person, but against the
Spirit, as manifested in the perfect life of
Christ, whose acts so evidently reflected God's
own benevolence and holiness, that to ascribe
them to the devil, was a sin of the most deadly
character. This, and not blasphemy against
Christ in general, or denial of His claims, or
active opposition to Him, or even putting Him
to death, is the unpardonable sin.

It is a significant fact that even the most
exacting modern critics of Christ repudiate
the Pharisaic position. Men like Renan and
Strauss, who reject His divine claims, and find
many faults with His career, yet recognise
Him as one in whom the Spirit of God dwelt,
and as one of the greatest religious heroes of
mankind. And those who think thus are not
far from the kingdom of God : cp. Lk 12 10 ;
see further on Heb 6 4 10 26 1 Jn 5 16.

32. The *world* to come] This phrase has
two meanings among the Jews, (1) the age of
the Messiah which begins with the resurrection
of the dead, (2) the state of souls after death.
E.g. they say, 'The world to come is, when a
man is departed out of this world.' The second
meaning is to be adopted. Jesus declares the
sin against the Spirit to be unpardonable either
before or after death. The punishment is
eternal, because, as St. Mark says, the sin itself
is eternal, a token of a nature so far gone in
depravity that repentance is impossible, and
recovery hopeless. It is this hardened and
vitiated character, not the isolated sin, that
God punishes.

This passage has frequently been regarded
as containing a hint of the possibility of pardon
beyond the grave. St. Augustine says, 'For
it would not be truly affirmed of certain persons that they are not pardoned in this world

or the next, unless there were some who though not pardoned in this, yet are pardoned in the world to come.' Plumptre says, ' If one sin only is thus excluded from forgiveness in that " coming age," other sins cannot stand on the same level, and the darkness behind the veil is lit up with at least a gleam of hope.' Stier speaks of ' the demonstrable inference that other sins are forgiven also in the world to come.' Olshausen infers ' that all other sins can be forgiven in the world to come, of course under the general presuppositions of repentance and faith.'

The view that pardon beyond the grave is impossible, is learnedly maintained by J. Lightfoot, who is followed by A. B. Bruce. Many commentators leave the question open, but there is a tendency in modern times to admit the possibility. With this question is closely connected that of prayer for the dead. Both the belief in the terminable nature of future punishment and the practice of prayer for the dead were familiar to our Lord's contemporaries.

33–36. Cp. Lk 6⁴³⁻⁴⁵.

33. ' Pharisees, be logical. You say that to cast out devils is good, but that I who do it, am corrupt. That is as if you said, The fruit of this tree is good, but the tree itself is corrupt. Make up your minds which way you will have it. Either say that My works are good, and therefore that I am good also, or else that My works are corrupt, and that therefore I am corrupt also. You cannot separate a tree from its fruit, for a tree is known by its fruit. Nor can you separate a man from his works, for he is known by them.'

34. ' The same argument applies to words. A man is known by his words. " Out of the abundance of the heart the mouth speaketh." Your evil and venomous words, declaring that I have an evil spirit, and work My miracles by Beelzebub, prove you to be really the " off-spring of vipers," as John has already rightly called you (3⁷). Such men as you cannot, even if you would, speak good words.'

36. Every idle word] i.e. every idle word that expresses the true inward character of the man. These will pronounce judgment upon him.

38–45. A sign demanded. Astounding impudence after they had just ascribed His miracles to Beelzebub, and declared Him possessed with an unclean spirit. It was the practice of Jesus to work signs for those who sought them in a right spirit. He worked many for the disciples of John (11⁴). He raised Lazarus ' that they may believe that Thou didst send Me ' (Jn 11⁴²). Signs, however, were for honest enquirers, not for malignant enemies like the Pharisees. Moreover, the sign which they asked was not of the

kind which Christ was willing to work. They wanted a mere portent which appealed to the sense of wonder, and had no spiritual or moral significance. Such signs Jesus always refused. Yet in refusing, He promised a future sign so remarkable as to startle believers and unbelievers alike, His own Resurrection.

38. Lk 11¹⁶ : cp. Mt 16¹ Mk 8¹¹. **A sign**] Lk ' a sign from heaven' : something startling, unlike the healing of the sick to which they were accustomed. Let Him repeat the miracle of Moses, and call down manna from the skies, as the Messiah was expected to do (Jn 6³⁰).

39–42. Lk 11²⁹⁻³⁶.

39. Adulterous] True religion was represented by the prophets as marriage with Jehovah, so that apostasy from Him was called adultery or fornication (Isa 57³, etc.).

The sign of the prophet Jonas] RV ' Jonah.' ' The sign of the prophet Jonah,' which is mentioned here and in 16⁴ as the only sign to be vouchsafed to unbelievers, is understood by some to be our Lord's Resurrection, and by others His preaching. The question turns upon the authenticity of 12⁴⁰. If this is authentic, the sign is certainly the Resurrection ; if it is not authentic, the sign is probably our Lord's preaching, which is expressly compared to Jonah's preaching to the Ninevites (12⁴¹ Lk 11³²). The question is a difficult one. Against the authenticity of the v. may be pleaded its omission by St. Luke and the nature of the context, which speaks of the preaching of Solomon and Jonah. In favour of the authenticity may be pleaded the fact that the v. shows clear traces of an Aramaic origin, and therefore presumably formed part of Matthew's Hebrew ' logia'; also that it contains an historic difficulty (the statement that our Lord's body lay for three nights in the grave) which would easily account for its omission by St. Luke. The present writer holds 12⁴⁰ to be an authentic part of the Matthæan 'logia,' and therefore ' the sign of Jonah ' to be the Resurrection : cp. 27⁶³ Jn 2¹⁹.

40. Three days and three nights] The difficulty is that our Lord only lay in the grave *two* nights. The expression resembles the Jewish inclusive way of reckoning (' on the third day,' etc.), but goes beyond it. The most plausible explanation is that of J. Lightfoot. He supposes that Jesus, speaking in Aramaic, said, ' The son of man shall be three *'onahs* in the heart of the earth.' *'Onah* meant a day and a night, and a part of an *'onah* was reckoned as a whole, so that the Gk. translator not quite accurately rendered the expression, ' three days and three nights.' **The heart** (i.e. ' centre ') **of the earth**] Not the grave, which is on the surface, but Hades, which popular imagination placed in the centre of the earth.

Our Lord's use of the story of Jonah and the whale, to illustrate His Resurrection, need not imply that He regarded it as literal history. The book of Jonah is probably a symbolical or allegorical narrative (see Intro. to Jonah). **42. The queen**] see on 1 K 10 1.

43-45. The return of the unclean spirit (Lk 11 24-26). The connexion in St. Matthew is preferable.

The expulsion of the evil spirit represents the submission of the nation to the baptism of John, which was a baptism of repentance. The sweeping and garnishing of the house represents the superficial but fairly general acceptance of Christ's teaching during the early part of His ministry, to which the Gospels bear witness. The return of the evil spirit with seven other spirits more wicked than himself represents the obstinate and final rejection of Christ by the nation, which was soon to follow, and of which the blasphemy of the Pharisees and their unbelieving demand for a sign were already an earnest.

According to the primary meaning of the parable, the possessed man represents the Jewish nation. But the Christian preacher is quite within his rights when he proceeds to apply it to the individual soul, and to urge the necessity of full and complete repentance, the deceitfulness of merely formal religion, and the danger of relapse. The details of the habits of demons are not to be pressed. Christ adopts the popular phraseology about them as part of the machinery of the parable, without necessarily endorsing it in all respects.

43. A man] i.e. the Jewish nation. **Dry places**] or deserts, were supposed to be the favourite abode of demons (Tob 8 3 Baruch 4 35 Isa 13 21 34 14). These pictorial details must not be pressed as if they were dogmatic statements.

44. My house] i.e. the man himself ; here, the nation. **Empty**] Though the evil has been temporarily expelled, nothing good has been put in its place, so that the demon can return. If our Lord had been admitted, the return would have been impossible. The 'sweeping' and 'garnishing' is that empty show of faith and repentance and good works, which only invites a more terrible fall.

45. Seven] Symbolical for completeness. As many as the house will hold. Mary of Magdala had seven devils (Mk 16 9 Lk 8 2).

46-50. His mother and brethren (Mk 3 31 Lk 8 19). Jesus here, as on other occasions, declares Himself independent of family ties, and united by spiritual kinship to all who do God's will.

The Brethren of Jesus

Our Lord had four 'brethren,' James, Joseph (Joses), Simon, Judas ; and at least three sisters (13 55). What their exact relationship to Him was, is not certain. There are three main views—(1) that of St. Jerome, hence called the Hieronymian view, that they were our Lord's cousins, being sons of Mary the Virgin's sister and of Clopas (see Jn 19 25 RV). Most supporters of this view think that three of the brethren were apostles. Jerome's theory, until recently the predominant one in England, is now held by very few. (2) The Epiphanian view, so called from its advocacy by St. Epiphanius, that they were sons of Joseph by a former wife. This is the theory of the Eastern Church, and has been learnedly supported in England by Lightfoot. (3) The Helvidian view, advocated in ancient times by Helvidius, that they were children of Joseph and Mary born after Jesus. Prof. Mayor is the chief recent exponent of this view.

The arguments for the last two views are nearly evenly balanced, and it is difficult to decide which is right.

The following points seem certain from the NT. :—

(1) That the 'brethren' did not live with 'Mary of Clopas,' but with the Virgin Mary, and were regarded as members of her family (12 46 13 55 Jn 2 12 7 3).

(2) That they were jealous of Jesus, and up to the Resurrection disbelieved His claims (Mk 3 21 6 4 Jn 7 5 f.).

(3) And that consequently none of the brethren were included among the Twelve Apostles.

(4) That they were converted after the Resurrection by the appearance to James (1 Cor 15 7), and henceforth associated themselves with the disciples (Ac 1 14).

The chief arguments in favour of the Epiphanian view are :—

(1) That it represents the most ancient tradition, being already current in Palestine in the 2nd century.

(2) That if the Virgin had had a large family, some of the members of which, like James the bishop of Jerusalem, attained to prominent positions in the Church, the (practically) unanimous tradition that she remained always a virgin, could never have arisen.

(3) That it is more reverent to suppose that our Lord's mother never had any other children.

(4) That Lk 1 26-38 implies that already before the birth of Jesus, she had devoted herself (with her betrothed's consent) to a life of virginity.

(5) That our Lord upon the cross would not have committed the care of His mother to St. John, if she had had four living sons to support her.

The chief arguments in favour of the Helvidian view are :—

(1) That the high esteem for virginity generally prevalent in the early Church made Christians unwilling to think of Mary as the mother of other children, and consequently the Epiphanian theory was invented.

(2) That Lk 2⁷ implies that Mary had other children.

(3) That Mt 1 18-25 imply that the connubial relations of Joseph and Mary after the birth of Jesus were of the usual kind.

(4) That 'brother,' when used without further explanation, naturally means a full brother, and not a half brother, or foster brother. In the opinion of the present writer the arguments for the Epiphanian view slightly preponderate.

CHAPTER 13
A DAY OF PARABLES

1-3ᵃ. Teaching by parables begun (Mk 4 1 Lk 8 4). This c. introduces a new type of teaching, that by parables. St. Matthew gives us a group of seven, the first four of which (the Sower, the Tares, the Mustard Seed, the Leaven) were addressed to the multitudes, and the last three (the Hid Treasure, the Pearl, and the Draw-net) to the disciples. St. Mark gives only four parables on this occasion, St. Luke only two. St. Matthew's group of seven forms ' a great whole, setting forth the mystery of the kingdom in its method of establishment, its corruption, its outward and inward growth, the conditions of entrance into it, and its final purification.'

St. Matthew and St. Mark both agree that Jesus did not begin to teach regularly in parables until opposition to His teaching had developed, and the people under the influence of the Pharisees and scribes had begun to harden themselves against His influence, and to criticise His doctrine (vv. 10–16 Mk 4 11, 12 : cp. also Lk 8 10). One purpose of His parabolic teaching was to conceal His doctrine from the unfit (see on vv. 10–16) as a punishment for their wilful blindness and spiritual unreceptiveness. But the parables also served to reveal the truth in suggestive and stimulating forms to the fit. They arrested the attention, remained in the memory, and could not fail in a reflective and devout mind to unfold gradually somewhat of their meaning. They acted as a test. They repelled those who were unreceptive and lacking in industry and earnestness, but they attracted the earnest disciples who knew that precious treasure was concealed beneath the surface, and were willing to dig deep until they found it.

The method of teaching by parables was not new. There are several good examples in the OT. (see e.g. 2 S 12 1-4 14 5 f. 1 K 20 39 f. Isa 5 1-6 28 24-28). It was also known to the rabbis : e.g. it was said of Rabbi Meir that a third part

of his discourses was tradition, a third allegory, a third parable ; but Christ made the parable form so completely His own that few since His time have ventured to imitate Him. Neither the Apostles nor any of the Christian fathers (except Hermas) are known to us as authors of parables.

There is some doubt as to the exact extent to which the details of our Lord's parables are intended to be interpreted. Many recent writers maintain that each parable is intended to enforce a single idea, and that none of the details are significant. This seems going beyond the evidence, and even against it. All the synoptic evangelists represent Jesus as interpreting the details of the parable of the Sower (13 18 Mk 4 13 Lk 8 11), and St. Matthew represents Him as giving a minute and detailed explanation of the parable of the Tares (13 36). It may be admitted that details are not always significant, and that interpreters of the allegorical school have often erred in making too much of unimportant features, but the evidence seems to suggest that Christ's parables are carefully constructed and finished works of art, of which the parts as well as the wholes are often intended to be interpreted.

1. The house] i.e. Simon and Andrew's at Capernaum (Mk 1 29, etc.).

3. Parables] In the NT. the word *parabole* is almost confined to the Synoptic Gospels, the only exceptions being Heb 9 9 11 19 (RV), where it is used of the OT. types of NT. realities. In the Gospels it occasionally means a maxim or proverb (15 15 Lk 4 23 (RV) 5 36 6 39), but nearly always a parable, that is (so far as our Lord's parables are concerned) 'a narrative, fictitious, but agreeable to the laws and usages of human life, by which either the duties of men or the things of God, particularly the nature and history of God's kingdom, are figuratively portrayed.' A parable is to be distinguished from a fable. The former is probable and might be true, the latter introduces impossibilities, such as trees talking ; the former teaches important spiritual truths, the latter does not advance beyond homely lessons of worldly prudence. The parable is also to be distinguished from an allegory. The parable is a story complete in itself, quite apart from its interpretation, whereas an allegory has no meaning at all apart from its interpretation. The parable differs still more from the myth, in which allegory and fact are so mixed that the allegory is taken for fact. No parables occur in the Fourth Gospel: their place is taken by *paroimiai*, ' allegories,' of which the most complete are those of the Fold (Jn 10 1), the Good Shepherd (10 7), and the Vine and the Branches (15 1): cp. Jn 10 6 (RM).

3ᵇ-9. The Sower (Mk 4 3-9 Lk 8 5-8). For the meaning of the parable, see on vv. 18-23.

Our Lord probably took as His text an actual field and an actual sower within view at the time. Stanley, who visited the probable spot, writes, 'There was the undulating cornfield descending to the water's edge. There was the trodden pathway running through the midst of it, with no fence or hedge to prevent the seed from falling here or there on either side of it or upon it ; itself hard with the constant tramp of horse, mule, and human feet. There was the good rich soil ; there was the rocky ground of the hillside protruding here and there through the cornfields ; there were the large bushes of thorn—the *nabk*, that kind of which tradition says the crown of thorns was woven—springing up, like the fruit-trees of the more inland parts, in the very midst of the waving wheat.'

9. **Who hath ears**] cp. 11[15] 13[43] Lk 8[8] 14[35] Rev 2[7] : see on vv. 10[f].

10-17. **The reason for speaking in parables** (Mk 4[10-12] Lk 8[9,10]). Because Christ's prejudiced hearers (see prefatory remarks) will not receive plain teaching, such as the Sermon on the Mount, they shall be punished by having the truth withdrawn from them, according to our Lord's own precept (7[6]), 'Give not that which is holy unto the dogs, neither cast ye your pearls before swine, lest they trample them under their feet, and turn again and rend you.' But those hearers who are worthy, i.e. those who are of the household of faith, and already 'have' religious truth, shall understand.

11. **Unto you**] i.e. not only to the Apostles, but to all spiritually receptive persons—to 'those who are within,' as opposed to 'those who are without' (Mk). Cp. the rabbinical saying, 'God entrusts not His mysteries save to the just.' **The mysteries**] The deeper things of Christ's kingdom can only be understood by the initiated and spiritually enlightened, hence they are rightly called 'mysteries.' Although the parables are said to be concerned with the 'mysteries of the kingdom,' they are, in fact, largely concerned with the person of Christ Himself. This is because He is the King of the Kingdom, and only by acknowledging His sovereignty can men enter into it. In NT. usage 'the mystery' of God generally means His plan of salvation for all mankind, concealed or dimly adumbrated under the old covenant, but manifested to the elect since the coming of Christ. This seems to be the principal meaning here.

Some think that the Christian use of the word is derived from the Greek religious mysteries ; others that it is a metaphor taken from Eastern courts, in which the king's counsels and designs are spoken of as his 'secrets' or 'mysteries,' because they are communicated to none but his most intimate friends.

12. 'You who are spiritually minded, who already "have" religious truth, shall learn more and more by My parables, until you become spiritually rich. But those who " have not," and do not desire to have spiritual knowledge, so far from learning more from My parables, will have even the poor confused notions of truth which they have (" seem to have," Lk) bewildered and darkened.' In 25[29] Jesus applies the proverb not merely, as here, to the use of the talent of spiritual understanding, but to all the talents or faculties of man.

14. **Esaias**] RV 'Isaiah.' The quotation is from LXX version of Isa 6[9]. The prominence of this passage in the NT. is remarkable: see Jn 12[40] Ac 28[26] Ro 11[7,8,25] 2 Cor 3[14]. The Christians found in it a reason for the surprising fact that God's own people refused to accept His promised salvation: see on vv. 1-3[a], 10, 12.

17. *Those things*] i.e. the mysteries of the kingdom of God, not merely Christ's earthly life and miracles in their outward aspect.

18-23. **The Parable of the Sower interpreted** (Mk 4[13] Lk 8[11]). The sower is, of course, Christ, and Christian teachers generally, but is not a prominent figure in the parable. The seed aptly stands for Christian truth, 'the word of the kingdom,' or 'word of God,' because when implanted in the heart and conscience, it grows, develops, and brings forth spiritual fruit. The sower scatters the seed not only on the good ground, but on the bad, as an example to Christian preachers not to neglect the unreceptive and the wicked in their ministrations. The seed falling by the wayside, or rather on a hard, beaten track across the field, is the case of those whose assiduous attention to business, social calls, and worldly affairs, renders them unreceptive to spiritual truth. Even while the sermon is being preached their minds are full of their own affairs, and when it is finished their first contact with the world sweeps all recollection of it away—'Satan cometh immediately, and taketh away the word that was sown in their hearts' (Mk). The seed falling upon the rocky places, where there is a thin layer of soil above and hard rock beneath, is the case of those who are susceptible—quickly and readily susceptible—to religious influences, but on whom, owing to their want of spiritual stamina, no permanent impression can be made. They are generally of an enthusiastic and excitable temperament, who when brought under strong religious influences 'run well' for a time, but soon tire, and fall away. The seed falling among thorns is the case of those who have every capacity for developing the highest spiritual gifts, but who fail because they deliberately attempt to serve two masters, God and mammon, which is impossible. The seed falling on good ground is the case of good and receptive Christians, who respond to the teaching of Christ in proportion to the spiritual capacity with which God has endowed them.

24-30. Parable of the Tares (peculiar to St. Matthew). One of the greatest, most characteristic, and most fruitful of the parables. In it Christ looked from the present into the distant future. He foresaw that scandals and offences would soon arise, which would cause great searchings of heart ; the denial of Peter, the treachery of Judas, the deceit of Ananias, the quarrels among the Apostles, the parties in the Church, the sensuality of the Corinthians, the treachery of false brethren and false teachers, the falling away of some, the love of others waxing cold ; and looking further over the later history of His Church, He saw a saddening picture of low morality, low ideals, avarice, ambition, disunion, and seeming failure. And therefore he warned His disciples beforehand that thus it must be, that ' in the visible Church the evil must be ever mingled with the good,' and that earnest men must not lose heart nor be impatient because they cannot make the Church as pure as they would have it.

The parable is interesting from the light it throws upon our Lord's person. He is the chief character throughout, and is endowed with divine attributes. He is the householder, the sower of the seed, the antagonist of Satan, the Lord of the world. The angels are His ministers and do His bidding. In the kingdom of heaven He is the King, and has the power to doom to heaven and hell. Christ Himself interprets the parable (vv. 37-43).

24. The kingdom of heaven] in this parable, as often, is identified with the Church on earth, regarded as a visible society embracing good and evil. **25. While men slept**] This detail may indicate the subtlety of the evil one in introducing evil into the Church in ways that cannot be traced. **His enemy**] By no more striking expression could the greatness of the power of Satan be indicated than by this, that he is described as the antagonist of Christ Himself. Nothing in the NT. lends colour to the modern tendency to minimise evil, or to regard it as another form of good. **Tares**] or 'bastard wheat' : so much like true wheat, that until the corn is in the ear the two cannot be distinguished. Hence any attempt to root up the tares would result in rooting up the wheat also. So in the Church any attempt to distinguish between true and false Christians is doomed to failure.

27. The servants] i.e. the apostles and those in authority or having influence in the Church.

31, 32. Parable of the Mustard Seed (Mk 4 30 Lk 13 18). This parable, and that which immediately follows, the leaven, are more hope-

ful and cheerful in tone than those that went before, in which most of the seed sown failed to bear fruit, and tares sprang up among the wheat. Both parables describe an enormous extension of the Kingdom of God from small beginnings, but there is this difference. In the parable of the mustard seed the growth of the Kingdom as a visible and powerful organisation is described, in that of the leaven its hidden and secret influence, spreading wider and wider until the whole of society is leavened with Christian ideas.

31. Christ takes the **grain of mustard seed**, by which is to be understood Christianity both as a doctrine and as an organised society, and plants it in His field, which is the world. **Mustard seed**] The vegetable or herb, not the so-called mustard tree, is meant. In hot countries it sometimes grows to a great size. The Jerusalem Talmud says, 'There was a stalk of mustard in Sichin from which sprang out three boughs, of which one was broken off, and covered the tent of a potter, and produced three *cabs* (12 pints) of mustard.' Rabbi Simeon said, ' A stalk of mustard was in my field, into which I was wont to climb as men are wont to climb into a fig-tree.' Although the mustard seed is not really the smallest of all seeds, it was so in popular estimation. The rabbis called the smallest possible quantity ' the quantity of a grain of mustard,' and Mahomet uses the same expression in the Koran.

32. Insignificant in its beginnings, founded by a supposed criminal in an obscure province, directed by twelve Galileans of little wealth or education, the Christian movement rapidly expanded into a world-wide Church, so powerful as a bond of union, that the Roman empire itself sought to strengthen itself by its alliance, so strong to succour the oppressed, that the poor and lowly took refuge under its protection, so majestic in its ordered stability that the rude barbarians who conquered Rome submitted to its sway. Its growth in modern times has been still more striking. From the year 1700 to 1800 it is estimated that the Christian population of the globe advanced from 155 millions to 200 millions. From 1800 to 1900 the progress has been from 200 millions to more than 500 millions, so that the disciples of Christ now equal, if they do not exceed, a third of the human race.

33. Parable of the Leaven (Lk 13 20-21). The leaven (or ' yeast ') is here the Spirit of Christianity working secretly in the world until the whole is leavened. Devotionally the parable may be applied to individual souls. St. Ambrose says, ' May the Holy Church, who is figured under the type of this woman in the Gospel, whose meal are we, hide the Lord Jesus in the innermost places of our hearts, till the warmth of the divine wisdom penetrate into the most secret recesses of our souls.'

33. Leaven] i.e. the influence of Christ, the power of Christianity. The figure is taken from the power of leaven (' yeast ') to make the dough light and wholesome, and to spread through an enormous mass of it with great rapidity. Generally leaven is used as a figure for wickedness (16⁶, etc.), and some wrongly so regard it here, taking the woman for the apostate Church, and the leaven as the 'mystery of iniquity' with which she corrupts the purity of the gospel.

Three measures] lit. ' three *seahs*,' a *seah* containing 1½ pecks. Since this was the usual quantity to be baked at once (Gn 18⁶: cp. also Jg 6¹⁹ 1 S 1²⁴, where the equivalent amount, an *ephah*, is mentioned), no special significance attaches to the number ' three.' The **meal** is mankind, as uninfluenced by the gospel. **Took**] i.e. from elsewhere, for Christianity is not of this world, but introduced from without. **Till . . was**] The past tense is a prophetic way of speaking of the certainty of the result.

34, 35. Christ's parabolic teaching (Mk 4 ³³,³⁴).
35. By the prophet] i.e. Asaph the seer, the author of Ps 78, from which the quotation (v. 2) is taken.

36–43. The Tares interpreted. See on v. 24.
The field is called the world as well as the Kingdom of God or the Church, because the Church is charged with a mission to the whole human race, and is destined to be universal.

The children of the kingdom] true Christians. **The children of the wicked** *one*] false Christians. **41. His kingdom**] His Church.

All things that offend] RV 'that cause stumbling.' **42. Gnashing**] indicating rage and disappointment, not pain. Their punishment continues because their sin continues: cp. 8¹², etc. **43. In the kingdom**] in the final bliss of heaven: cp. Dan 12³.

44–46. The Hidden Treasure and the Pearl of Great Price (peculiar to St. Matthew). These two parables were addressed to the disciples in the house on the subject of personal religion. Their teaching is that it is not enough to be outwardly a Christian or to be under Christian influences. The true Christian must be inwardly convinced that his religion is the most precious of all things. He must know Christ as a personal Saviour, and feel in his heart the spirit of sonship, crying, Abba, Father. In comparison with this he must despise all other things. But there is also a point of difference. The first parable (the hidden treasure) describes the case of a man who finds a treasure without looking for it. By some accidental circumstance he becomes aware that a treasure is buried in his neighbour's field, and immediately sells all that he has to buy it. This is the

case of a man who has long been possessed of the outward form of Christianity, but has been entirely unacquainted with its power. Then suddenly it is revealed to him what a surpassing treasure it is to love God and to know Christ. He sells all that he has, i.e. gives up all that can hinder him in his quest, and enters on possession of the treasure. The second parable, that of the merchant seeking goodly pearls, describes a man who all his life long has been in the pursuit of truth and at last finds it. Such a one was the philosopher Justin, who, dissatisfied with all the schools of pagan philosophy, found rest for his soul in Christ.

44. Treasure] Christ Himself and all that Christ brings with Him to the believing soul. **A field**] the outward forms of Christianity, as distinguished from their spirit. **He hideth**] i.e. throws the earth over it again, so that no one else may discover it, until he has effected the purchase. **Selleth all that he hath**] i.e. gives up every sin or self-indulgence which hinders him from giving himself wholeheartedly to Christ. **Buyeth**] In itself an immoral transaction, for the seller did not know that the treasure was there. But this is not the point which is proposed for imitation.

47–50. The Net (peculiar to St. Matthew). At first sight the teaching of this parable is the same as that of the parable of the tares. There is the same identification of the Kingdom of Heaven with the earthly Church, and the same idea that it will embrace the evil as well as the good. But whereas in that, the stress was laid upon matters pertaining to this life, in this the stress is laid upon what will happen in the next. In that the rulers of the Church were warned not to anticipate by too rigid a discipline the final separation between good and evil, in this they are taught that the process of separation will one day be performed, and that effectually, by the unerring judgment of Him who can read the heart of man. Then, and then only, will there be an absolutely pure Church, not having spot or wrinkle or any such thing.

47. A net] lit. ' drag-net,' i.e. an oblong net of immense length, employed near the shore. The bottom edge was weighted with lead, and swept the bottom of the sea. The upper edge floated on the surface of the sea, supported by corks. Escape from it was impossible, and when it was dragged to shore, it contained every fish in the area of sea which it had swept. The net is the Church, and the fishermen, on whom, however, no stress is laid in the parable, are the apostles and their successors. **The sea**] the nations of the world, as often in Scripture : Ps 65⁷ Isa 8⁷ Rev 17¹⁵. **Of every kind**] not merely of bad and good, but of every nation, kingdom, and tongue. A prophecy that the Church will be Catholic, or universal.

48. Shore] i.e. the end of this dispensation, or world. **Sat down]** In the parable those who drag the net, are not the same as those who sort the fish. The latter are the angels, the ministers of judgment. **Vessels]** i.e. the heavenly habitations, the final reward of the just. **50.** On gnashing of teeth, see v. 42.

51, 52. Concluding remarks to the parables (peculiar to St. Matthew). **52. Every scribe** *which is* **instructed** (RV 'who hath been made a disciple') **unto the kingdom of heaven]** Jesus is pleased with their answer, and speaks of them as the future scribes or teachers of His Church. **A man** *that is* **an householder]** i.e. Christ Himself the master of the house (the Church). Afterwards the apostles themselves will become 'householders,' exercising Christ's authority committed to them. **His treasure]** i.e. the chest where money and jewels are kept. The 'treasure' of the Christian preacher is the Holy Scripture, and His own inward experience of what true religion is. *Things* **new and old]** the old truths which God had long made known to the Jews, as well as the new truth declared by Christ. It is also an exhortation to the preacher to adapt his discourse to his hearers, to put milk before babes, and strong meat before men.

53–58. Second visit to Nazareth and its neighbourhood (Mk 6 1). The first is described Lk 4 16, where He received similar treatment and used the same proverb.

55. The carpenter's son] St. Mark has 'the carpenter.' **His brethren]** see on 12 46-50.

57. Were offended] lit. 'were caused to stumble,' i.e. were hindered from believing. **A prophet]** see on Lk 4 24 Jn 4 44. **58. Did not many]** St. Mark has 'could not do.'

CHAPTER 14
Death of the Baptist. Feeding the Five Thousand. Walking on the Sea

1, 2. Herod's opinion of Jesus (Mk 6 14 Lk 9 7).

1. Herod the tetrarch] son of Herod the Great, received by his father's will the government (tetrarchy) of Galilee and Peræa. His first wife was the daughter of the Arabian prince Aretas, called in 2 Cor 11 32 king of Damascus. During a visit to his half-brother, Herod Philip (not the tetrarch), who lived as a private citizen in Rome, he became enamoured of his wife, Herodias, and persuaded her to leave her husband. He at once divorced his own wife, and married her. The marriage gave the greatest offence to devout Jews, for (1) it was unlawful to take a brother's wife after his death, much less while he was alive (Lv 18 16 20 21). The only exception was when the brother died without an heir (Dt 25 5-10). (2) Herodias was the niece of her new husband : see art. 'Dynasty of the Herods.'

2. This is John the Baptist] The belief was the effect of a guilty conscience working upon a superstitious mind.

3–5. Arrest of John (Mk 6 17 Lk 3 19). The manner in which St. Matthew and St. Mark insert the arrest of John at this point, instead of in its proper historical place, the beginning of the Galilean ministry, is conclusive proof that their narratives are not independent. Either they borrow from one another, or from some common source : see art. 'The Synoptic Gospels.'

5. When he would have put him to death] This agrees with Josephus, who says that John was arrested for political reasons. 'Herod, who feared lest the great influence John had over the people might put it into his power and inclination to raise a rebellion, thought it best by putting him to death to prevent any mischief that he might cause.' St. Mark, on the other hand, represents Herod as friendly to John. 'Herod feared John, knowing him to be a just and holy man, and he kept him safe. And when he heard him, he was much perplexed and heard him gladly.'

The truth seems to be that Herod was really friendly to John, and favourably impressed by his preaching, but that John's denunciation of his new marriage rendered it difficult for that prince to protect him. He therefore yielded, though reluctantly, to the influence of Herodias, and first had John arrested, and then executed. But since it would have been impolitic to disclose the true reason of these proceedings, it was given out that John was suspected of treasonable practices.

6–12. Execution of the Baptist (Mk 6 21). The dramatic circumstances of the death of John are recorded only in the Gospels. Josephus simply says, 'Accordingly he was sent a prisoner, out of Herod's suspicious temper, to Machærus, the castle I before mentioned, and was there put to death.'

6. Birthday] One of the Greek customs introduced by the Herods. The Hebrews regarded the keeping of birthdays as a part of idolatrous worship. **The daughter]** Her name was Salome. She soon afterwards married her uncle, Philip the tetrarch. **Danced]** Another instance of Greek manners. It was the custom of the Greeks after a banquet to witness the performances of professional female dancers, which were of a mimetic and licentious character. For a woman of Salome's rank and position to play such a part was an outrage on decency. J. Lightfoot, however, takes a more favourable view of Salome's conduct—'she danced according to the custom of the nation, viz. to express joy, and to celebrate the day.'

7. With an oath] cp. the rash vow of Jephthah, Jg 11 31. In the OT. Ahasuerus makes exactly the same promise to Esther (Esth 5 3). **Whatsoever she would ask]** St. Mark adds, 'even to the half of my kingdom,' a rhetorical expression for a very great reward. The incident is in accordance with Eastern manners. 'Shah Abbas (Shah of Persia) being one day drunk, gave a woman who danced much to his satisfaction the fairest khan in all Ispahan, which yielded a great revenue to the shah (to whom it belonged) in chamber-rents. The vizier having put him in mind of it next morning, took the liberty to tell him that it was unjustifiable prodigality, so the shah ordered her to be given a hundred "tomans," with which she was forced to be content' (Thevenot).

8. Being before instructed] RV 'being put forward.' **A charger**] i.e. a dish. **10. He sent**] Josephus says that John was imprisoned at Machærus, a fortress 5 m. E. of the Dead Sea.

11. She brought it] The judgment of God fell upon Antipas and Herodias for their crime. Their country suffered severely in the disastrous war with Aretas, and when the guilty pair visited Rome to demand from Caligula the title of king, they were banished to Lyons, in Gaul, on a charge of misgovernment.

13–21. Feeding the five thousand (Mk 6 30 Lk 9 10 Jn 6 1). The only miracle recorded by the four evangelists, and also one of the most wonderful. It cannot be accounted for, as some of the miracles of healing possibly can, as the powerful effect of mind over mind, or of mind over body, but is distinctly a physical miracle incapable of natural explanation.

Some critics still accept Paulus's rationalising explanation of the miracle, viz. that the generosity of Jesus and His apostles in sharing their few loaves and fishes with others induced many more, who had brought food with them, to distribute it, and so enough was found for all. But Paulus's theory does not explain, (1) how St. Mark (i.e. Peter) came to describe it as a miracle ; (2) how St. John, who was also present, came to describe it as a miracle ; (3) why our Lord, if it was not a miracle, described it as such, and that in the oldest tradition (Mk 8 19 = Mt 16 9) ; (4) why the multitudes, who must have known the facts, were stirred to such enthusiasm by this 'sign' that they were convinced that He was the Messiah, and sought to make Him king by force (Jn 6 14, 15).

Considered as a parable the miracle teaches, (1) Christ's creative power and lordship over nature ; (2) His benevolence and bounty, giving His people enough and more than enough ; (3) that He is the spiritual food of mankind, the bread of life, sustaining the souls of those who believe on Him. In particular the miracle is a figure of the Lord's Supper, in which, through the agency of His ministers, He feeds the multitudes with 'the spiritual food of His most precious Body and Blood' : see on Jn 6. St Mark's account is

the fullest, and (except St. John's) the most graphic.

13. Heard of it] On hearing of the death of John, Jesus thought it better to retire from the kingdom of Antipas, until it was clear whether the designs of Antipas were directed against Him also. He therefore retired across the lake to Bethsaida Julias, in the dominion of Philip. His speedy return may be accounted for by the receipt of news that he had nothing to fear.

St. Mark gives another reason for the retirement. The Twelve had just returned from their mission, and Jesus wished to give them a little rest. His intention, however, was frustrated by the presence of the multitudes. This period (just before the second Passover) marks the culminating point of Jesus' popularity. But the tide was about to turn. His refusal to be made king (Jn 6 14, 15) displeased His more enthusiastic followers, and the Pharisaic opposition, already begun, became more active and effective.

15. His disciples] In St. John the initiative comes from our Lord Himself, and what is here put into the mouth of the disciples is said by Philip. **The time**] RV 'the hour,' i.e. the hour at which Jesus usually concluded His religious instructions. **17. We have here**] According to St. John a boy had them for sale. The disciples could be said to have what they could so readily obtain. **19. To sit down**] lit. 'to recline.' St. Mark says that the people sat down in separate companies, which he compares to the beds in a garden.

He blessed, etc.] A close resemblance to the consecration in the Lord's Supper. The miracle is to be regarded as taking place at this moment. **The disciples**] As Jesus did not baptise, so He did not personally feed the multitudes, but used the ministry of the Apostles, thus preparing them for their future ministry. They had just been engaged in the ministry of the Word. Now they are entrusted (in type and figure) with the ministry of the Sacraments. **20. Twelve baskets**] *Kophinoi* were large baskets such as were frequently carried by Jews. Each of the apostles had one. The gathering up of the fragments for future use was a lesson in economy, a protest against waste.

22–33. The walking on the sea (Mk 6 45 Jn 6 15). Another physical miracle, also belonging to the oldest tradition. As it is attested by actual eyewitnesses, it cannot be resolved into a legend or allegory, but must be accepted as an historic fact. Symbolically interpreted, it represents the struggles of the soul and of the Church with the troubles of the world, and the succour which Christ gives in the darkest hour of temptation and adversity.

The attempts to translate ' walking upon

the sea' in v. 25 and v. 26 by 'walking towards the sea,' or 'walking above the sea' (i.e. on the shore), scarcely require refutation. They are inconsistent with the general tenor of the narrative, which places the ship in the middle of the sea, and lays stress upon the fear of the disciples at so astounding a spectacle.

22. Constrained] The apostles were most unwilling to be sent away. St. John explains the reason. The people were desirous to make Jesus king by force, and the apostles thoroughly sympathised with the popular enthusiasm. **23. A mountain]** RV 'the mountain,' i.e. the mountainous country surrounding the lake.

The evening] But it was evening some time earlier (v. 15), before the multitudes were fed. The explanation is that the Jews reckoned two evenings, the first corresponding very much to our afternoon (St. Luke, 9 12, defines it as 'when the day began to decline'); the second extending from twilight to darkness. Here the second evening is meant. **25. The fourth watch]** This is Roman reckoning. The fourth or last watch was from 3 to 6 A.M. The Jews reckoned only three watches, beginning at 6 P.M. **26. A spirit]** RV 'an apparition.' St. Mark adds that 'He would have passed by them,' doubtless to test their faith, or to draw from them some expression of their need of Him : cp. Lk 24 37 f.

28. Peter] The incident is only in St. Matthew. It is thoroughly in keeping with St. Peter's character, confident and enthusiastic, and unconscious of his own weakness. 'So faith in the Lord's strengthening and upholding power conducts us securely over the agitated sea of a sinful life, but assuredly it too often happens that the weakness of this faith sinks down into the waters' (Olshausen). Well is it for us if we cry with Peter, 'Lord, save me.'

32. Into the ship] Not inconsistent with St. John's statement, 'they were willing to receive him into the ship.' They were willing and did so. **33. They that were in the ship]** the apostles and the crew. **The Son of God]** The first time, in the Synoptic Gospels, that the title is applied to Jesus by men.

34-36. Healings in the land of Gennesaret (Mk 6 53). Enthusiasm is still at its height. **34. The land of Gennesaret]** A fertile plain on the W. side of the lake towards its N. end, extending southwards from Capernaum.

Josephus says of it, 'Such is the fertility of the soil that it rejects no plant, and accordingly all are here cultivated by the husbandmen, for so genial is the air, that it suits every variety. Nature here nourishes fruits of opposite climes and maintains a continual supply of them. Thus she produces the most royal of all, the grape and the fig, during ten months without intermission, while the other varieties ripen the year round.' The

rabbis called it 'a paradise,' and 'a garden of princes.'

36. The hem] RV ' border ': see on 9 20. **As many]** Multitudes healed. No failures. Most of Christ's miracles unrecorded.

CHAPTER 15

The Traditions of the Elders. The Canaanitish Woman. Feeding the Four Thousand

1-20. Unwashed hands and the traditions of the elders (Mk 7 1). In this important controversy Jesus defined His position, (1) towards rabbinical traditions about the Law; (2) towards the Law itself. The first part of our Lord's discourse (vv. 3-9) is addressed to the Pharisees. In it He admits (or at least does not dispute) the binding character of the Law itself, but denies the authority of rabbinical tradition, and that on two grounds : (1) that it had no divine authority; (2) that instead of forming 'a hedge round the Law,' and assisting its observance, as it professed to do, it really abrogated it, by affording pretexts for its evasion. The second part of the discourse (vv. 10-20), addressed to the disciples and the multitude, carries the argument a step farther. Our Lord lays down the principle (Mk 7 15) that 'there is nothing from without a man, which entering in can defile him; but the things which come out of him, those are they that defile the man'; that is to say, that the whole ceremonial Law, with its distinctions of meats, its ablutions, its sacrifices, and its round of external observances, is no longer binding, and is about to be vabolished. At the time our Lord's line of argument was probably as distasteful to His own disciples as to the Pharisees. Long after this (Ac 10 14) St. Peter was so far from accepting it that he resisted the divine voice that bade him eat 'unclean' food, and hold familiar intercourse with Gentiles. But the lesson was learnt at last. In the second Gospel there is a note, due either to Peter or to his secretary Mark, which correctly glosses our Lord's words : 'This he said, making all meats clean' (Mk 7 19 RV.).

St. Mark's account of this incident is fuller than St. Matthew's, and contains notes upon such Jewish usages as would not be understood by Gentile readers. St. Matthew's account, however, though shorter, usefully supplements St. Mark's in several important particulars.

1. Were of Jerusalem] RV 'come from Jerusalem.' The active hostility of the hierarchy, strikingly manifested by the sending of these emissaries, is explained by the fact (known to us only from the Fourth Gospel) that Jesus had already preached in Jerusalem, and defied the authorities there.

2. The tradition of the elders] The 'elders' are mainly the scribes, but include also the old heroes of the nation, Moses, Joshua, and the prophets, to whom certain of the rabbinical ordinances were ascribed. The scribes regarded their traditions as equal or superior in authority to the Law of God. For instance, they said, 'The words of the scribes are lovely, above the words of the Law; for the words of the Law are weighty and light, but the words of the scribes are all weighty.'.. 'The words of the elders are weightier than the words of the prophets.'.. 'He that shall say, There are no phylacteries, transgressing the words of the Law, is not guilty. But he that shall say, There are five divisions in a phylactery, adding to the words of the scribes, is guilty': see on 23⁵.

They wash not their hands] The penalty for this neglect was excommunication by the Sanhedrin. Rabbi Eleazar ben Hazar was excommunicated, 'because he undervalued the washing of hands,' and dying unreconciled, was carried to the grave with a stone laid upon his bier, 'whence you may learn (say they) that the Sanhedrin stones the very coffin of every excommunicate person that dies in his excommunication.' The intricate details of the rabbinical ablutions are not worth describing, but a quotation from the Talmud will show the spirit in which they were performed: 'Whosoever hath his dwelling-place in the land of Israel, and eateth his common food in cleanness (i.e. with washed hands), and speaks the holy language (i.e. Hebrew), and recites his phylacteries morning and evening, let him be confident that he shall obtain the life of the world to come.' There was a special devil (Shibta), who was said to torment those who ate with unwashed hands. **4.** See Ex 20¹² Dt 5¹⁶.

5. But ye say, etc.] RV 'But ye say, Whoever shall say to his father or his mother, That wherewith thou mightest have been profited by me is given *to God; he* shall not honour his father (or, his mother).' *It is* **a gift**] Mk 'it is Corban.' 'Corban,' meaning originally a sacrifice or a gift to God, was used in NT. times as a mere word of vowing, without implying that the thing vowed would actually be offered or given to God. Thus a man would say, 'Corban to me is wine for such a time,' meaning that he took a vow to abstain from wine. Or a man would say to a friend, 'Corban to me for such a time is whatsoever I might be profited by thee,' meaning that for such a time he vowed that he would receive neither hospitality nor any other benefit from his friend. Similarly, if a son said to his father or mother, 'Corban is whatsoever thou mightest have profited by me,' he took a vow not to assist his father or mother in any way, however much they might require it. A vow of this kind was held by the scribes to excuse a man from the

duty of supporting his parents, and thus by their tradition they made void the word of God.

6. Honour not his father] RV 'shall not honour his father,' i.e. shall not be obliged to support his father.

8. See Isa 29¹³. The passage, which is paraphrased rather than quoted, appears in the same form in St. Mark. **11.** See vv. 17–20, and prefatory remarks. **14. They be blind leaders**] referring to the scribes and Pharisees. It is a proverbial expression occurring again Lk 6³⁹.

15. Peter] as usual he is spokesman of the Twelve. St. Mark (i.e. Peter), perhaps from modesty, does not mention Peter here.

17–20. Purity is to be sought in the soul, not in externals. See prefatory remarks.

21–28. The Canaanitish woman (Mk 7²⁴). The two accounts are, however, independent.

21. Departed] RV 'withdrew.' The withdrawal was due to the hostility of the Pharisees, and the alienation of friends caused by the speech in the synagogue of Capernaum (Jn 6⁶⁶). Celsus (the heathen opponent of Christianity, 170 A.D.) blamed Christ's policy of withdrawal from danger as cowardly. Origen well replied that it was part of Christ's education of the disciples, 'teaching them not at random, or unseasonably, or without sufficient object, to encounter dangers.'

Into the coasts (RV 'parts') **of Tyre and Sidon**] According to St. Mark (7²⁴, ³¹), Jesus made a long sojourn on heathen soil, passing near Tyre, then along the coast to Sidon, through which He passed, then across country to the sources of the Jordan, then through Decapolis to the E. shore of the lake.

22. A woman of Canaan] RV 'a Canaanitish woman.' She was one of that nation which the Jews had been bidden to exterminate, and was therefore more hateful than an ordinary heathen. St. Mark calls her 'a Greek, a Syrophœnician by race'; i.e. she spoke Greek, but belonged by race to those Syrians who dwelt in Phœnicia. The Phœnicians were of Canaanite descent. *Thou* **Son of David**] How did she know that Jesus was descended from David? Not because she was a proselyte, for below she is called 'a dog,' i.e. a heathen. Probably because the fame of Jesus, and the popular title by which He was known, had spread far beyond the confines of Galilee: see on 1¹ 12²³.

23. Send her away] viz. by granting her request and healing her daughter.

26. The **children** are the Jews; the **dogs** are the Gentiles. Christ here speaks as a Jew, not yet revealing His true sentiments towards the Gentiles, for which see 8¹¹ Jn 4²³ Ac 10²⁸, etc. The rabbis often spoke of the Gentiles as dogs, e.g. 'He who eats with an idolater is like one who eats with a dog, for as a dog is uncircumcised, so also is an idolater.' 'The

nations of the world are compared to dogs.'
'The holy convocation belongs to you, to you,
not to the dogs, to you, not to them that
are without.'

Yet Jesus, in adopting the contemptuous
expression, slightly softens it. He says not
'dogs,' but 'little dogs,' i.e. household, favourite dogs, and the woman cleverly catches
at the expression, arguing that if the Gentiles
are household dogs, then it is only right that
they should be fed with the crumbs that fall
from their masters' table.

27. Truth, Lord ; yet the dogs (RV 'Yea,
Lord : for even the dogs') **eat the crumbs,**
etc.] The ancients sometimes used, instead of
a napkin, soft pieces of bread to wipe their
hands upon. These fragments were then
thrown to the dogs. **Masters'**] i.e. the Jews.
The woman is humble. She is willing to be
called a dog, and to acknowledge the Jews as
masters.

28. O woman, great *is* **thy faith,** etc.]
Why did Jesus speak to her so harshly, and
wait so long before granting her request ?
(1) To test the strength of her faith ; (2) to
teach her the lesson that persistence and importunity in prayer will finally meet their
reward ; (3) to teach the disciples that greater
faith was often to be found among the heathen
than in Israel.

The miracle is interesting as one of the
rare cases in which the ministrations of
Christ were extended to a pure heathen. It
is one of the few 'preludes of the larger
mercy which was in store, first drops of that
gracious shower which should one day water
the whole earth.' In St. Mark's version our
Lord gives a clear intimation of the future
call of the Gentiles, by saying, 'Let the children *first* be filled.'

29-31. Various healings (Mk 7 31-37). St.
Mark here inserts the healing of a deaf man
with an impediment in his speech.

29. Unto the sea] According to St. Mark,
to the E. side of it, where the population was
mainly heathen. **A mountain**] RV 'the
mountain.' **31. The God of Israel**] implying
that the multitudes were mainly heathen.

32-39. Feeding the four thousand (Mk 8 1).
The multitudes in this case being heathen (see
v. 31), the miracle is no bare repetition of the
feeding of the five thousand (14 13). That
symbolised the communication of Christ to
Israel, but this symbolised His communication
to the Gentile world.

Several recent commentators regard this
miracle as only another version of the feeding
of the five thousand. They argue, (1) that
Jesus would not have repeated a miracle ; (2)
that the apostles would not have said, 'Whence
should we have so many loaves in a desert
place, as to fill so great a multitude ? ' if Jesus

had worked a similar miracle before. These
arguments would be weighty if the two miracles occurred in different Gospels, or were
derived from different sources. But this is not
the case. The two miracles occur both in St.
Matthew and St. Mark, the common matter of
which Gospels is by general consent assigned
to Peter himself. Peter's narrative also contains a saying of Jesus in which the two
miracles are expressly distinguished : see 16 9
Mk 8 19.

37. Seven baskets (Gk. *spurides*) **full**] In the
other miracle there were 'twelve baskets (Gk
kophinoi) full.' The difference in the baskets
is perhaps to be accounted for by the different
nationality of the multitudes. The 'kophinos'
was well known as the provision-basket of the
Jews. Juvenal, the Roman poet (100-130
A.D.), speaks of the Jews going about in heathen
countries carrying a 'kophinos' to hold their
food, and a bundle of hay for their bed, to
avoid the pollution of Gentile food and bedding. The capacity of the 'kophinos' was
about two gallons. The 'spuris' was probably larger. In a 'spuris' St. Paul was let
down from the wall of Damascus (Ac 9 25),
though St. Paul himself uses a different word
(2 Cor 11 33).

39. Magdala] RV 'Magadan.' St. Mark
says 'Dalmanutha.' Neither of these places
can be located with certainty. According to
Eusebius (4th cent.), Magadan was near Gerasa, i.e. on the E. side of the lake, and not,
as might have been expected, on the W.

CHAPTER 16
St. Peter's great Confession

1-4. A sign from heaven demanded (Mk 8 11 ;
cp. Lk 11 16 : see on Mt 12 38). **1. Pharisees..
Sadducees**] An unnatural and unholy alliance of
men whose only bond of union was hatred of
Jesus. The Sadducees had probably been sent
from Jerusalem by the chief priests, but some
regard them as the same as the Herodians mentioned by St. Mark, and, therefore, Galileans.

From heaven] Jewish superstition held that
the demons could work signs on earth, but
that only God could work them in heaven.

2, 3. They professed to be able to forecast
the weather, but shut their eyes to the signs
of the times which denoted the speedy fulfilment of the prophecies respecting the coming
of the Messiah.

The second half of v. 2 (' When it is evening,' etc.) and all v. 3 are omitted by some
important ancient authorities, but the evidence
in their favour, both internal and external, is
so strong that it is hazardous to reject them.
J. Lightfoot says, 'The Jews were very curious
in observing the seasons of the heavens, and
the temper of the air,' and gives examples of
their weatherwise saws.

4. But the sign of the prophet Jonas] RV 'the sign of Jonah.' St. Mark omits these words: see on 12³⁹ᶠ.

5-12. The leaven of the Pharisees and Sadducees (Mk 8¹⁴). But the narratives are independent. This incident could only be derived from an eyewitness and an apostle. The discreditable light in which it places the Apostles goes to confirm its authenticity.

5. To the other side] i.e. the E. side. This favours the view that Magadan (Dalmanutha) was on the W. side.

6. The leaven of the Pharisees and of the Sadducees] St. Mark says, ' of the Pharisees and of Herod.' Herod may have been a Sadducee in spite of his superstitious belief in John's resurrection, but, even if he was not, he exactly represented the secular, irreligious, worldly spirit of Sadduceeism. The leaven of the Pharisees is hypocrisy, ostentation, pride, formalism, scrupulosity, and the tendency to place the letter before the spirit. The leaven of the Sadducees is worldliness, and the temper of irreligious scepticism.

The disciples took Jesus' words literally as a command to lay in a fresh stock of bread, taking special precautions to avoid all bread made with leaven from the house of a Pharisee or a Sadducee. The misunderstanding is not so absurd, if it be remembered that Gentile food and Gentile leaven were regarded by the stricter Jews as unclean. Since Jesus had pronounced the Pharisees worse than the heathen, it was quite natural (from the strictly Jewish point of view) that He should proceed to pronounce their houses, food, and, therefore, their leaven unclean. Jewish writings contain subtle discussions as to when, why, and under what circumstances heathen, Samaritan, and Christian leaven is to be regarded as unclean.

9, 10. See on 15³². **12.** Cp. Lk 12¹, and see on v. 6.

13-20. St. Peter's confession (Mk 8²⁷ Lk 9¹⁸). Jesus now undertook another distant excursion, partly to escape the hostility of the Pharisees (v. 4), but chiefly to hold private converse with His disciples, and to lead them on to the recognition of His Messiahship and divine Sonship, which was the supreme object of His ministry so far as the Twelve were concerned. What was the significance of this confession, which clearly marked a great epoch in Christ's ministry? According to some its significance lay in the fact that He was now for the first time recognised as the Messiah. But is this so? Already He had been called the ' Son of God,' i.e. the Messiah, by the Apostles (14³³). He had been so designated by the Baptist (3¹¹,¹²) and by popular acclamation (' Son of David '=the Messiah, 9²⁷ 12²³ 15²²). So also in the Fourth Gospel the apostles regard Him

as the Messiah from the first (' We have found the Messiah,' Jn 1⁴¹; 'Rabbi, thou art the Son of God, thou art the king of Israel,' Jn 1⁴⁹). The significance of Peter's representative confession, therefore, lies in this, that what they had before received on the authority of the Baptist, and as a mere working hypothesis, which might or might not be proved by events to be true, they now deliberately ratified as their own conviction, based on their personal experience of what Jesus had shown Himself to be. Here then at last was the solid rock on which Jesus could build, not the shifting sand of possibilities and surmises, nor the weak faith which consists in mere submission to authority, but the strong conviction of earnest souls who know what they believe and why they believe it, and are willing to live by the truth they have apprehended, and, if need be, die for it.

13. Cæsarea Philippi] i.e. the Cæsarea built by Philip the Tetrarch (see art. ' the Herods '), was situated at the sources of the Jordan, near the foot of Mt. Hermon (9,000 ft.), in the midst of magnificent scenery. It was a Gentile city, and was often called Paneas (now Banias), because the god Pan was worshipped there. The other Cæsarea on the sea-coast was called, for distinction, Cæsarea Palestina.

14. Cp. 14². Why do not the apostles mention the belief that Jesus was really the Messiah, among the current opinions? Because this belief no longer existed. Those who held it, had abandoned it because of His continued refusal to declare Himself (Jn 6¹⁵), and to do what was expected of the Messiah, viz. deliver the oppressed nation from its enemies. Though the people could not deny His miracles or His greatness, they felt that He had disappointed them, and His popularity had already begun to ebb. **Elias**] RV 'Elijah': see on 17¹⁰. **Jeremias**] Jewish legend represented Jeremiah as well as Elijah, as preparing the way for the Messiah. He was said to have hidden the ark when Jerusalem was captured by the Babylonians, and to have called Abraham, Isaac, Jacob, and Moses from their tombs to assist him in mourning for the destruction of the Temple. In the days of the Messiah it was said that he and Elijah would dig up the ark from the cave on Mt. Nebo in which it was concealed, and replace it in the Holy of Holies.

16. The Christ] i.e. 'the Messiah.' So also St. Mark; but St. Luke has ' the Christ of God.' **The Son of the living God**] These words, together with the next three vv., are peculiar to St. Matthew, but are nevertheless authentic. They suit the context admirably, and are so thoroughly Hebraic in spirit, that their significance can only be apprehended by going behind the Greek to the Aramaic original. Their absence from St. Mark is readily explained. In confessing that Jesus was the Christ, Peter did no more than express the general sense of the apostolic circle. But in confessing that He was the 'Son of the living God,' he was going beyond what the others at that time believed. He, therefore, modestly suppressed his own personal confession and the special commendation with which Jesus greeted it.

'Son of God' here is no mere equivalent of 'the Messiah,' but a confession of Christ's unique filial relation to God. This is shown, (1) by the deep emotion with which the speaker makes, and Jesus receives, the confession ; (2) by the fact that the confession is perfectly satisfactory to Jesus, and is forthwith made the dogmatic foundation of Christianity ('Upon this rock I will build my Church ').

17. Simon Bar-jona] i.e. Simon, son of Jonah. The full name harmonises with the solemnity of the occasion and the emotion of the speaker. In Jn 1 [42] Peter's father is called 'Joanes' (John), of which Jonah is probably a contraction. **Flesh and blood**] corresponds exactly to the English expression 'mortal man,' and is often found in that sense in rabbinical writings.

18. Thou art Peter] Gk. *Petros;* Aramaic, *Kephas.* Jesus had given Peter this name at their first interview (Jn 1 [42]). Peter had now realised his character, and Jesus solemnly confirmed the honourable title. **And upon this rock**] Gk. *petra.* As the Gk. word here is different, most ancient commentators deny that Peter is the rock. The Roman Catholic Launoy reckons that seventeen Fathers regard Peter as the rock ; forty-four regard Peter's confession as the rock ; sixteen regard Christ Himself as the rock ; while eight are of opinion that the Church is built on all the apostles. Assuming, however, with the majority of modern commentators that Peter is the rock, the interpretation still remains nearly the same, because it is upon Peter, as confessing faith in Christ's divinity, that the Church is founded.

The next question is, 'Was the promise made to Peter exclusively, or did Christ address Peter as the representative of the Twelve, intending to give to all the same powers that He gave to Peter ? ' The answer can hardly be doubtful. The whole text speaks of the future. Christ says not 'I build,' but 'I will build'; not 'I give,' but 'I will give,' referring to the future for the explanation. The rest of the NT. shows in what sense the words of Christ are to be understood. On the evening of Easter Day He fulfilled His promise to Peter, by giving to all the Apostles present even greater powers than those which are here promised—'As my Father hath sent me, even

so send I you. And .. he breathed on them, and saith unto them, Receive ye the Holy Ghost : Whosesoever sins ye remit, they are remitted unto them ; and whosesoever sins ye retain, they are retained ' (Jn 20 [22, 23]). No power of any kind was then given to Peter which was not given equally to all the Apostles, and in harmony with this all the Apostles are jointly regarded in the NT. as the foundation on which the Church is built (19 [28] Eph 2 [20] Rev 21 [14]).

The position of Peter in the Apostolic Church was entirely unlike that of a modern Pope. In Ac 11 [2] he is sharply criticised for his conduct in the matter of Cornelius and makes his defence before the Church. At the council of Jerusalem (Ac 15) he plays quite a subordinate part. It is James who presides and pronounces the decision, and the decree runs in the name of the apostles and elders. St. Paul claims an authority equal to and independent of Peter's. He reckons himself 'not a whit behind the very chiefest apostles ' (2 Cor 11 [5]), and on a celebrated occasion resists Peter and rebukes him to his face (Gal 2 [11]). Moreover, the tone of St. Peter's first and certainly genuine epistle is thoroughly unpapal. ' The elders therefore among you, I exhort, who am a fellow elder,' etc.

What then was the nature of the primacy which Peter possessed ? It was a primacy of personal character and ability. He excelled the other apostles not in office, but in zeal, courage, promptness of action, and firmness of faith. He was their leader, because he was most fitted to lead. He boldly ventured, where others hesitated. And this explains the peculiarity of the present passage, that the promise was made, in form at least, to Peter alone. The other apostles had by this time attained to the conviction that Jesus was the Messiah (see the parallel narratives), but only Peter had made the great venture of faith which is implied in the acknowledgment of the divinity of Christ.

My church, with emphasis on the *My*, signifying that the Church is not a human but a divine institution. In this passage the Church is identified with the Kingdom of Heaven.

The gates of hell] i.e. the gates of Hades, Heb. *Sheol*, the abode of the dead. As the Church is often represented as a city, so here its great adversary Death is poetically represented as a fortified city with walls and gates.

Two distinct promises are here made : (1) that the Church as an organisation shall be indestructible. No persecutions, or assaults of Satan from within or without shall destroy it, because the life which is in it is Christ's ; (2) that individual members of the Church, united to Christ and sharing in His indestructible life, shall not be held by the power of death, nor overcome by judgment, but be made 'partakers of the inheritance of the saints in light.'

19. The keys of the kingdom of heaven] i.e. the keys of the earthly Church, not of heaven itself. Peter is not here compared to the porter of a house, who has only the key of the gate, but, since he possesses *all* the keys, to a house-steward exercising full authority over the house and all its inmates, in the master's name : cp. Isa 22 15-25. The power of the keys is, (1) the power to govern the Church ; (2) the power to exercise discipline in it ; (3) the power to decide who shall be admitted into it, and on what conditions (subject, of course, to the Law of Christ) ; (4) and indirectly, since the steward provides food for all the household, the ministry of the Word and Sacraments. Government and discipline, however, and not ministry, are the main ideas. The narrower interpretations of the power of the keys, as that it is the power to admit into the Church by the preaching of the gospel, are not so much erroneous as insufficient. The figure in Lk 11 52 (' the key of knowledge') is different. The best NT. parallel is Rev 3 7.

Bind . . loose] These words, unintelligible in Greek and English, become full of meaning when traced back to the original Aramaic. Every rabbi or scribe received at his ordination, which was, like that of the Christian Church, by the laying on of hands, the power to bind and to loose, i.e. to decide with authority what was lawful and unlawful to be done, or orthodox and unorthodox to be believed. To bind was to declare unlawful, to loose was to declare lawful. We read, for example, that 'Rabbi Meir loosed (i.e. permitted) the mixing of wine and oil, and the anointing of a sick man on the sabbath' ; that Rabbi Jochanan said, 'They necessarily loose (i.e. permit) saluting on the sabbath,' and 'Concerning gathering wood on a feast day, the school of Shammai binds (i.e. forbids) it,—the school of Hillel looses (i.e. permits) it.' The power, therefore, which Christ here promised to Peter and the other apostles was the power to decide with authority questions of faith and morals in the Christian Church,—the power to fix the moral standard and to determine the Christian creed. In the exercise of this authority the apostles 'loosed' the prohibitions of the Mosaic Law first to the Gentiles (Ac 15), and finally to the Jews (Mk 7 19 RV, see on Mt 15 1-20), decided what standard of morality should be enforced in the society, and pronounced with authority in controversies of faith.

When the Jewish rabbis differed upon an important matter of doctrine or practice, a conference was held, and the judgment of the majority was held to be authoritative. Similarly the apostolic power of 'binding and loosing' was intended to be exercised collect-

ively, and great deference was paid both in the apostolic and in subsequent ages to the decisions of synods (Ac 15).

In heaven] It is promised that God Himself will ratify the 'binding and loosing' of the earthly Church, when these powers are duly and legitimately exercised. 'Binding and loosing' is different from the power of remitting and retaining sins, for which see Jn 20 23.

21-23. Peter rebuked.

21. Began Jesus] There had been intimations of his death before (9 15 12 40 Jn 2 19 3 14 6 51), but now they began to be more distinct. St. Mark says expressly, 'and He was speaking the word openly.' **22. Be it far,** etc.] lit. 'God have mercy on thee.'

23. Satan] The sharpness of the words indicates a strong and intense emotion. The chief of the Apostles was addressed in the self-same terms as those which had been spoken to the tempter. St. Peter's suggestion was indeed something like a renewal of the same temptation. 'In this suggestion that He might obtain the crown without the cross . . Christ saw the recurrence of the temptation which had offered Him the glory of those kingdoms on condition of His drawing back from the path which the Father had appointed for Him.' **An offence**] lit. 'stumbling-block.' A play on the word Peter, 'A stone in my path, not a foundation stone of my Church.' **Savourest**] RV 'mindest.'

24-28. Exhortations to steadfastness and self-denial in prospect of Christ's return.

24. See on 10 38. By the **cross** Jesus means primarily martyrdom, either in will or act, and not merely self-denial, though this is included.

25. Whosoever will save his life (in this world in time of persecution by denying Me) **shall lose it. 26. Lose his own soul**] RV 'forfeit his life.' **27.** This v. refers to the Last Judgment.

28. The most probable interpretation of this v. refers it to Christ's coming to overthrow the old dispensation by the destruction of Jerusalem, 70 A.D. The decisive phrase is, 'There be some standing here, which shall not taste of death.' This obviously excludes the Last Judgment, and, hardly less obviously, Christ's Resurrection, for it would be a truism to say that some of the disciples present would live to see an event which happened only a few months later. Whether the Transfiguration is referred to is not so clear. It was witnessed by only some of those present, but, on the other hand, it can hardly be described as the kingdom of God coming 'with power' (Mk). Nevertheless it is not by an accident that the Transfiguration immediately followed the saying. The Transfiguration was an earnest of the greater manifestation of power shown at the destruction of Jerusalem, just as that event itself was an earnest and, as it were, a rehearsal of the final act of judgment : see further on c. 24.

Taste of death] a common rabbinical expression for 'to die.' Not in OT. **The Son of man**, etc.] St. Mark 'the kingdom of God come in power' ; St. Luke 'the kingdom of God.'

CHAPTER 17
THE TRANSFIGURATION

1–8. The Transfiguration (Mk 9 2 Lk 9 28).

St. Leo rightly apprehended the historical situation when he said that in the Transfiguration the principal object aimed at was that in the hearts of the disciples the scandal of the cross might be removed, and that throughout the terrible and humiliating events which were shortly to happen they might be sustained by the remembrance of the revelation which they had been vouchsafed.

The Transfiguration revealed Christ in His divine glory as Son of God. If, as is generally supposed, it took place at night (see Lk 9 37), the spectacle of the face of Christ, shining like the sun in its strength, must have been inexpressibly glorious. His form shone, not like that of Moses with borrowed light, but with a glory which came from within, and was His own. 'We were eye-witnesses of His majesty,' said one of the witnesses (if 2 Peter is authentic). 'And we beheld His glory,' said another, 'the glory as of the only begotten of the Father, full of grace and truth': 2 Pet 1 16-18 Jn 1 14.

Moses and Elijah appeared, the former as representing the Law, and the latter the prophets, and Christ was seen in the midst of them as greater than both. 'The unity of the Old and New Covenant is wonderfully attested by this apparition of the princes of the Old in solemn yet familiar intercourse with the Lord of the New ; and not the unity only, but with this unity the subordination of the Old to the New, that "Christ is the end of the Law" (Ro 10 4), and the object to which all prophecy pointed (Lk 24 44 Ac 10 13 28 23 Ro 3 21), that therefore the great purpose of these had now been fulfilled ; all which was declared in the fact that, after their testimony thus given, Moses and Elias disappear, while Christ only remains' (Trench).

Whether the Transfiguration was a vision seen in trance, or a waking reality, has often been discussed. In favour of the former view it is urged that their eyes were 'heavy with sleep,' but St. Luke, who alone mentions this fact, is careful to add that 'they remained awake throughout,' or at least (for the expression is somewhat ambiguous) that they were thoroughly awake at the actual time of the vision. That it was a real object-

ive occurrence, and not a mere illusion, is shown, (1) by its appearing simultaneously to the three apostles ; (2) by the conversation between Christ and the visitors. The appearance of Christ with two of His saints apparently in glorified bodies is an earnest of the time of the 'redemption of the body,' when the Lord Jesus Christ 'shall fashion anew the body of our humiliation, that it may be conformed to the body of His glory.'

The narrative in St. Matthew and St. Mark is derived from St. Peter. That in St. Luke is largely independent, and may be in part derived from St. John, the only other surviving witness when St. Luke wrote.

1. After six days] Lk 'after about eight days,' either an independent calculation or another way of reckoning. **An high mountain**] not Mt. Tabor, the top of which was occupied by a fortress, but more probably Hermon, which is near Cæsarea Philippi, and is an 'exceeding high mountain' (9,000 ft.), which Tabor is not (1,800 ft.). **2. Transfigured**] lit. 'metamorphosed.' The glory of the Godhead burst through the veil of flesh. St. Luke alone mentions that the change took place while Jesus was praying. **3. Moses** and **Elijah** were recognised through the supernatural power of insight which enabled them to be seen.

4. Three tabernacles] or, 'booths.' Peter wished to prolong the stay of the heavenly visitants, and offered to build them temporary houses on the mountain for their accommodation. He felt that it was good to be there in such glorious surroundings, and by no means wished to descend to earth again, to begin the fatal journey to Jerusalem of which Moses and Elijah were speaking (St. Luke). St. Mark adds : 'He wist not what to answer, for they were sore afraid.' **5. A bright cloud**] i.e. the visible glory which, according to Jewish ideas, manifested the divine presence. It is the same as the pillar of cloud and fire in the wilderness, the cloud that filled Solomon's Temple, and the visible glory which, according to the rabbis, rested upon the ark, and was called the 'Shechinah.' **This is my beloved Son**] Lk 'This is my Son, my chosen.' These words, in which the Father Himself testified to Christ's divine Sonship, are similar to those spoken at the Baptism ; but whereas those were spoken in part at least to Christ Himself, these were spoken entirely to the disciples. They contain a striking confirmation of Peter's late confession, and further teach what the Apostles found it so hard to learn, that the old dispensation was to be entirely superseded by the new. 'Hear,' said the voice of the Father, 'not Moses and Elias, but my beloved Son.'

9-13. Elijah and the Baptist (Mk 9¹¹).

9. The vision] lit. 'the thing seen.' The word does not imply the unreality of the occurrence. **To no man**] Not to the multitudes, lest they should be carried away by political enthusiasm ; nor to the other disciples, because they were not yet in a fit state to receive the lesson that it taught. To be witnesses of the Transfiguration was a special reward of the Three for their greater faith and greater spiritual receptiveness. 'To him that hath shall be given.' **Risen again**] Another clear prophecy of the Resurrection.

10. Why then say the scribes?] Jesus, by forbidding the incident to be spoken of (v. 9), seemed to attach little importance to the present appearance of Elijah. 'Why then,' ask the disciples, 'do the scribes attach so much importance to it? And why are we forbidden to reply to their leading objection to your Messiahship, by saying that Elijah has come, and that we have seen him.' **Elias must first come**] The Jews expected a personal return of Elijah to prepare the way for the Messiah, not another prophet like him : see on Lk 1¹⁷. It was supposed that his peculiar activity would consist in settling ceremonial and ritual questions, doubts and difficulties, and that he would restore to Israel, (1) the golden pot of manna, (2) the vessel containing the anointing oil, (3) the vessel containing the waters of purification, (4) Aaron's rod that budded and bore fruit. **11. Elias truly**, etc.] RV 'Elijah indeed cometh, and shall restore all things.' The future 'shall restore' is best explained as a quotation of the exact words of the scribes, and not as a prophecy that Elijah will come in person to prepare the way for Christ's Second Advent, though some understood it to mean this. **Restore all things**] see Mal 4⁶ Ac 3²¹. The Baptist, to whom Jesus alluded, did not in fact 'restore all things,' nor bring about the perfect moral purification anticipated by the prophet Malachi, but that was the fault of his hearers. The possibility of the Baptist's failure was distinctly contemplated by Malachi, for he adds, 'lest I come and smite the earth with a curse.' Malachi spoke of, and Christ understood by his words, a moral restoration of the nation. The scribes looked for the restoration of the pot of manna, stricter ceremonies, and similar frivolities. **12. But have done**] Herod, not the scribes, actually killed John, but Herod only did what the scribes would have been glad to do : cp. Lk 7³⁰, ³³.

14-20. Healing of the lunatic (epileptic) (Mk 9¹⁴ Lk 9³⁷). St. Mark's account is much the fullest. Christ descends from the mount to resume His works of benevolence. He who had communed with God and His prophets in the very atmosphere of heaven, now mingles in the common life of men, and concerns Himself with their troubles. He was full of grace as well as truth. Raphael brings this out in his great picture, which depicts the Transfiguration and the healing of the epileptic boy upon the same canvas.

The scribes had taken advantage of Christ's absence to undermine His influence with the multitude, and their designs had been assisted by the failure of His disciples to heal a peculiarly severe case of epilepsy (Mk). The return of Jesus discomfited the scribes. The epileptic was healed, 'and they were all astonished at the majesty of God' (Lk). J. Lightfoot remarks, 'It was very usual with the Jews to attribute the more grievous diseases to evil spirits, especially those wherein either the body was distorted, or the mind disturbed or tossed with a frenzy.' The demon of epilepsy, in the case of infants, was called 'Shibta,' in the case of adults, 'Cordicus.' How far the language of Christ about demons is an accommodation to the ideas of the time is discussed at end of c. 4.

15. Lunatick] i.e. epileptic, because epileptics were supposed to be affected by the changes of the moon (*luna*). **17. O faithless**] The rebuke is addressed not only to the disciples, but also to the father of the lad and the multitude. **20. Unbelief**] RV 'little faith.' **Faith as a grain of mustard**] i.e. the smallest amount : see on 13³¹. **Ye shall say unto this mountain**, etc.] a proverbial expression : see on 21²¹. **21.** The RV and Westcott and Hort omit the whole v., but it is too strongly attested to be lightly rejected. The parallel in Mk (RV) omits 'and fasting' : see on Mk 9²⁹.

22, 23. Jesus predicts His passion (Mk 9³⁰ Lk 9⁴³).

22. Abode] RV 'were gathering themselves together.' **Galilee**] mentioned because the last miracle had taken place beyond its borders, near Cæsarea Philippi. **23. Sorry**] They thought only of the Passion, not of the Resurrection, the allusion to which they did not in the least understand. St. Mark says, 'But they understood not the saying, and were afraid to ask him.'

24-27. The half-shekel or Temple tribute (peculiar to St. Matthew). Jesus is asked to pay the usual tax towards the maintenance of the Temple services. As Son of God He claims exemption, yet pays, lest He should be thought to despise the Temple. A significant indication of Christ's consciousness of a special relationship to God, unlike that of other men.

24. They that received tribute *money*] RV 'the half-shekel' (Gk. *didrachma*). Every male Israelite above the age of twenty was required by the Law (Ex 30¹¹⁻¹⁶ 38²⁵, ²⁶) to pay half a shekel annually (i.e. about eighteen pence) towards the maintenance of the Temple worship, as 'a ransom for his soul unto the Lord.' It was usually paid between the fifteenth and twenty-fifth of Adar (March), i.e. about Passover time, so that the money was now considerably overdue. **25. Custom**] i.e. taxes on merchandise. **Tribute**] i.e. taxes on persons and property. **26. Then are the children** (RV 'the sons') **free**] Therefore Jesus, being the Son of the Heavenly King, is free from the Temple tax. 'Children' (sons) is not meant to include the apostles or Christians generally. The plural is only part of the simile. **27. Lest we should offend them**] i.e. 'lest we give the collectors, who do not know that I am the Son of God, the false impression that I dishonour the Temple, and so hinder their conversion, go thou,' etc. **Offend**] RV 'cause to stumble.' **A piece of money**] lit. 'a stater.' A silver stater was exactly four drachmæ or denarii, i.e. a shekel, enough to pay for two. **For me and thee**] not 'for us.' The two cases were different. In our Lord's case the payment was a condescension, in Peter's a debt.

There are many authentic historical instances of valuables being found inside fish. Polycrates, tyrant of Samos (6th cent. B.C.), threw into the sea an emerald signet set with gold, the work of the Samian artist Theodorus. A few days later his cook found the signet inside a large fish, which a fisherman had presented to the monarch.

Although the supernatural element in this miracle is not greater than in the other physical miracles, yet its dramatic character, and the absence of the motive of benevolence which so generally characterises our Lord's miracles, suggest to some critics that we have here not strict history, but a mixture of history and tradition, the nucleus of historic fact being that our Lord sent St. Peter to catch a fish, and that this fish, when sold, realised a shekel. This explanation of the incident is quite possible.

CHAPTER 18
Offending the Little Ones. The Unmerciful Servant

1-14. Ambition reproved, and humility taught by the example of a little child (Mk 9 33-37 Lk 9 46-48).

1. Who is the greatest ?] RV 'Who then is greatest ?' The 'then' is explained from St. Mark's statement that on the way to Capernaum the disciples had been disputing who was the greatest. The Transfiguration had revived the hopes of the three leading apostles that the Kingdom of Christ was about to be established, and the Twelve were divided into three parties advocating the rival claims of Peter, James, and John to the office of

prime minister. Others were perhaps jealous of all three, and favoured other candidates. They, therefore, came to Christ. 'Who then,' said they ('since we cannot settle it ourselves), is the greatest in the Kingdom of Heaven ?' According to St. Mark and St. Luke, when they came into Christ's presence, they were ashamed to speak, but Jesus understood the question they desired to ask: cp. 20 20 Lk 22 24. The incident is well placed by St. Matthew after the incident of the half-shekel in which Jesus had shown His own humility by paying the tax. **The kingdom of heaven**] here the Kingdom of the Messiah wrongly conceived of as an earthly empire. **2. A little child**] Perhaps, as He was in Peter's house, one of Peter's children. Tradition, however, says that it was Ignatius, the martyr, afterwards bishop of Antioch.

3. Except ye be converted] RV 'Except ye turn.' A sharp rebuke. The disciples were disputing their rank and precedence in the Kingdom. Jesus denies that they are in it at all. They have turned their backs on it altogether. Only by reversing their course and embracing humility, can they hope even to enter it. Here Jesus uses the 'Kingdom of Heaven' to express the inward character of the true members of His Church.

4. Shall humble himself as this little child] A little child has no pride, knows nothing of worldly rank or position, and is simple, teachable, and loving. In using such an object-lesson, Jesus showed His greatness as a teacher. According to St. Mark, He took the little child in His arms to teach the lesson of love that follows. St. Bernard's definition of humility is true and deep. 'It is the virtue by which a man from the most true knowledge of himself is vile (i.e. of little worth) in his own eyes ; the esteeming of ourselves small, inasmuch as we are so, the thinking truly, and because truly, therefore lowlily, of ourselves' : see also on 5 5.

5. Shall receive] i.e. with affection, honour, and respect, and with the design of learning from them the special lesson, which they have to teach, viz. humility: cp. 10 40, where 'receiveth you' means 'receiveth your teaching.' **One such little child**] Not a literal child, but a child-like, humble person of any age. This is the meaning even in St. Luke, who writes, 'this little child,' because the child is taken as representing a class. **In my name**] i.e. for my sake. **Receiveth me**] Christ is honoured when His saints are honoured for their likeness to Him. St. Mark (cp. also St. Luke) adds, 'and whosoever receiveth me, receiveth not me, but him that sent me.'

Between vv. 5 and 6 St. Mark and St. Luke insert a saying of John's about a man who was casting out devils in Christ's name.

6-9. Mk 9 $^{42-4b}$. cp. also Lk 17 $^{1-2}$.

6. But whoso shall offend (RV 'shall cause to stumble') **one of these little ones**] i.e. whosoever shall bring about the ruin of the soul of a true believer, by depriving him of the child-like characteristics of humility and love.

It were better for him] RV 'it is profitable for him.' Why better ? Because the penalty for ruining the soul of another is eternal death, and it is better to suffer the worst earthly penalty, than to do anything which will incur that awful doom.

A millstone] lit. 'a millstone turned by an ass,' as opposed to one turned by hand, i.e. 'a great millstone ' (RV). **Were hanged . . were drowned**] more exactly, 'had been hanged . . had been drowned,' viz. before he did the deed. Drowning was a Roman and Greek punishment, reserved for crimes of peculiar enormity. It is not known to have been practised by the Jews.

7-9. A short digression. Jesus passes from the case of 'these little ones,' to temptations to sin in the world at large (v. 7), and in individual cases (vv. 8, 9).

7. Woe unto the world] Jesus has been dealing with 'offences,' i.e. temptations to sin, within the Church. He now applies the same principle to the world at large. It is in every case, He says, a greater sin to lead others into sin than to be led. There is a greater punishment, or 'woe,' for the tempter than for the tempted. **It must needs be**] A broad statement of the results of human experience, not a definition of the doctrine of fatalism or determinism. God does not compel men to sin, any more than He compels them to be virtuous. Perhaps Jesus had in His mind the case of His own death. The death of Jesus was (the religious state of the nation being what it was) practically certain, yet the human agent, Judas, through whom the offence came, acted freely, and was held responsible for his act. **8, 9.** How each man is to deal with his own individual temptations : see on 5 $^{29, 30}$.

10-14. Two reasons are given why we are not to despise 'one of these little ones,' i.e. any humble Christian. One is, that God Himself shows them honour, by appointing angels to be their guardians. The other is, that He cares so much for them, that He has sent His own Son to redeem them (v. 11).

10. Their angels] Though the general ministry of angels to those who are heirs of salvation is generally assumed in the NT. (Heb 1 ^{14}, etc.), only this passage and Ac 12 ^{15} teach that a special guardian angel is assigned to each individual. It is implied that the angels entrusted with this ministry are of the highest rank, because in an Oriental court only the highest officials see the king's face : cp. 2 K 25 ^{19}.

11. The RV, following many ancient authorities, omits this v. It is, however, difficult to account for its insertion, if it is not genuine. It is certainly not inserted from Lk 19 ^{10}.

12-14. Parable of the Lost Sheep, 'which is intended to show that it would be in direct opposition to God's desire for human salvation to lead astray one of those little ones, and to cause him to be lost, like a strayed sheep. Lk 15 ^{4} records the same beautiful parable, though in a different connexion ' (see the notes there). The practical lesson is that we must not only be kind to, and honour Christ's little ones (i.e. members of His Church), but, if they go astray, must show our love by seeking to reclaim them, like the Good Shepherd.

15-20. Treatment of an erring brother (peculiar to St. Matthew). The connexion with what precedes is as follows : ' Despise not one of the "little ones" (vv. 10-14) ; if, however, one "offends against thee," then proceed thus.' The subject changes from that of doing injury to the 'little ones,' against which Jesus has been warning (vv. 10-14), to that of suffering injury, in view of which He prescribes the proper method of brotherly visitation. A 'little one' is now defined as a Christian brother in general. Previously he was not only a Christian, but a humble Christian.

15. If thy brother shall trespass against thee] so RV. Westcott and Hort, however, omit ' against thee,' considerably altering the sense of the passage, which then applies to sin in general. **Hast gained thy brother**] viz. ' back to God, and to thyself.' While he was in his sin, he was lost to both.

17. Tell *it* **unto the church**] i.e. the Christian Church, as in 16 ^{18}, not the Jewish synagogue, as some have supposed. Jesus uses Jewish expressions, because those only were then intelligible, but He is plainly legislating for His own society. In dealing with offenders the Church is to use, (1) admonition, (2) if that be unsuccessful, excommunication. This was also the Jewish method of procedure. **As an heathen man** (RV 'gentile') **and a publican**] Social intercourse with the sinner, while unrepentant, is forbidden. But Jesus does not authorise the more severe forms of excommunication in use among the Jews, which involved cursing and anathematising. The discipline of His Church is to be mild and gentle. **18. Bind . . loose**] see on 16 ^{19}. Here the binding and loosing refer specially to judicial decisions, which Jesus says will be ratified in heaven.

19. Again I say] Having promised the ratification in heaven of the judicial decisions of the Church, Jesus proceeds to say the same thing about the prayers of Christians. He lays stress on united prayer. The way to obtain a request, is to call in the aid of a Christian brother and to pray with him. Still more, therefore, will the united prayer of the whole Church prove effectual. **20. For where two or three]** Christ proceeds to give the reason why God will grant such prayers. It is that He Himself, the great Intercessor, is personally present in every worshipful assembly of Christians, and presents their prayers to the Father. The passage applies to private prayer-meetings, but is particularly true of assemblies of the Church. The small numbers (two or three) are mentioned to encourage the Christians of the first ages, who would often consist of a mere handful in the midst of a great heathen population. A convincing proof of Christ's divinity may be drawn from this promise, which is rendered all the more evident by a comparison with the Jewish sayings from which it is adapted, e.g. ' Whence is it certain that the Holy and Blessed God is present in the synagogue?' (From Ps 82¹.) 'Whence is it certain that when ten persons are praying, the Divine Majesty is present ?' (From the same passage.) ' Whence is it certain that the Divine Majesty is present when two are sitting and studying the law ? ' (From Mal 3¹⁶.)

21, 22. How often a brother is to be forgiven. A favourite subject for discussion among the rabbis. They taught generally that three offences were to be pardoned.

21. Seven times] Peter thought himself more than twice as liberal as the rabbis. Our Lord's reply (v. 22) teaches that there must be no limit to human pardon, as there is none to God's : see on 6¹²,¹⁴,¹⁵, and cp. Lk 17³.

23–35. The unmerciful servant (peculiar to St. Matthew). The lesson is that, inasmuch as God has forgiven us the great and unpayable debt which as sinners we owe to Him, so we also must forgive our brethren the comparatively trifling debts which they have incurred by sinning against us. The parable concerns the Kingdom of Heaven, i.e. it illustrates God's dealing with Christians, not with the world.

23. A certain king] i.e. God. **Which would take account]** RV ' would make a reckoning with his servants.' ' We are the servants with whom He takes account. This account, as is plain, is not the final reckoning, but rather such as that of Lk 16². To this He brings us by the preaching of the law—by the setting of our sins before our face—by awakening and alarming our conscience that was asleep before—by bringing us into adversities—by casting us into sore sicknesses, into perils of death. Thus David was summoned before God by the word of Nathan the prophet ; thus the Ninevites by the preaching of Jonah ; thus the Jews by John the Baptist ' (Trench).

24. Ten thousand talents] An enormous sum (£2,500,000 of our money, if the Attic silver talent of £240 is meant, and still more if the Hebrew silver talent of £410, or gold talent of £6,150, is meant), indicating the absolute impossibility of a man making atonement for his own sin. Only Christ Himself could pay the ransom price of man's redemption and set the debtor free. For sin regarded as a debt, see on 6¹².

25. To be sold] The Mosaic Law allowed the sale of a debtor with his wife and children, these being regarded as his property (Lv 25³⁹ 2 K 4¹), but the rabbis disapproved this severity, except in the case of a thief. The reference is to Gentile customs, probably to the Roman law. Spiritually the selling is ' the expression of God's right and power altogether to alienate from Himself, reject, and deliver into bondage all those who have come short of His glory.'

26. Worshipped] i.e. prostrated himself. **I will pay thee all]** a sign that his repentance was very superficial, as indeed his subsequent conduct showed. Yet the merciful God accepted even this imperfect repentance, hoping for better things in the future. ' The slave,' says Euthymius, ' asked not for full remission but for time, but the lovingkindness of God granted full remission of the debt. Learn from this that God gives more even than we ask.' **28. An hundred pence]** (*denarii*), i.e. about £2 15s. 0d., an insignificant sum, representing the trifling character of offences against man, compared with those against God. **34. To the tormentors]** Torture was not a Jewish or Roman punishment for debtors, but it would naturally be applied by an Eastern despot to make the debtor disclose where he had hidden his treasures.

Till he should pay all that was due] ' i.e. (says St. Chrysostom) for ever ; for he can never possibly pay.' Others more plausibly see in the 'till,' a hope, or at least a possibility, of final release : see on 12³². **35.** See 6¹⁵.

CHAPTER 19

THE QUESTION OF DIVORCE. THE RICH YOUNG MAN

1, 2. End of the Galilean ministry. The Peræan ministry begins (Mk 10¹ Lk 9⁵¹ ; cp. Lk 17¹¹). The time was now late summer of 28 A.D. The Passion was less than six months distant. Jesus finally left Galilee, and entered upon what is generally called the ' Peræan ministry,' the scene of which was partly Peræa beyond Jordan, a district extending, roughly, from the Sea of Galilee to the Dead Sea, and partly Jerusalem and Judæa. To this period must be assigned a visit to Jerusalem at the Feast of Tabernacles (September), Jn 7² ; another at the Feast of Dedication (December),

Jn 10²³; also the mission of the Seventy, and many of the incidents in the great section peculiar to St. Luke's Gospel (9⁵¹–19²⁸).

1. Into the coasts (RV 'borders') **of Judæa beyond Jordan**] i.e. into the southern part of Peræa, opposite to Judæa.

3–9. The question of divorce (Mk 10²; see on 5³²). The Pharisees probably intended to entrap Jesus into some contradiction of the Law of Moses, which might form the basis of a charge before the Sanhedrin. Some, however, think that, as Peræa was in the territory of Herod Antipas, they wished to inveigle Him into speaking against that monarch's divorce of the daughter of Aretas: see on 14³. St. Matthew's narrative is fuller and perhaps more original than St. Mark's.

3. For every cause] In St. Mark the question simply is, 'Is it lawful for a man to put away his wife?' Jesus was asked to decide the point debated between the school of Hillel, who allowed divorce for every cause, and that of Shammai, who allowed it only for adultery. Rabbi Akiba (a Hillelite) said, 'If a man sees a woman handsomer than his own wife, he may put her away, because it is said, "If she find not favour in his eyes."' The school of Hillel said, 'If the wife cook her husband's food ill, by over-salting or over-roasting it, she is to be put away.' On the other hand, Rabbi Jochanan (a Shammaite) said, 'The putting away of a wife is odious.' Both schools agreed that a divorced wife could not be taken back.

Both schools objected to (though perhaps they did not forbid) the divorce of a *first* wife, with regard to which the dictum of Rabbi Eliezer, 'For the divorcing of a first wife, even the altar itself sheds tears,' was generally approved.

4. Male and female] i.e. one for one.

5. And said] Our Lord regards the words alluded to (see Gn 2²⁴) as spoken by divine inspiration. **His wife**] Ancient and modern interpreters find in the singular a prohibition of polygamy. The rabbis allowed three or four wives. 'It is lawful' (they said) 'to have many wives together, even as many as you will, but our wise men have decreed that no man have above four wives.'

6. What therefore God hath joined together] Our Lord takes up higher ground than either school. He goes behind the Law of Moses, which was in many cases a concession to Jewish infirmities and prejudices, to God's original intention at the creation of the human race, and declares this to be more venerable than the written Law, which the Jewish schools idolised. See further on 5³¹,³².

7. A writing of divorcement] see Dt 24¹. Jewish divorces were always from the bond of marriage, so that both parties could marry

again, unless the husband specially restrained the wife's liberty in that respect. Divorces were thus worded: 'I N. have put away, dismissed, and expelled thee N., who heretofore wast my wife. But now I have dismissed thee, so that thou art free, and in thy own power, to marry whosoever shall please thee; and let no man hinder thee. And let this be to thee a bill of rejection from me according to the Law of Moses and Israel.

'*Reuben*, the son of Jacob, witness.

'*Eliezer*, the son of Gilead, witness' (from J. Lightfoot).

8. Because of the hardness of your hearts] The rabbis regarded the liberty of divorce as a special privilege conferred by God upon the chosen people. Rabbi Chananiah said, 'God has not subscribed His name to divorces, except among Israelites, as if He said, I have conceded to the Israelites the right of dismissing their wives; but to the Gentiles I have not conceded it.' Jesus retorts that it is not the privilege, but the infamy and reproach of Israel, that Moses found it necessary to tolerate divorce. Moses allowed it only for the 'hardness of your hearts,' i.e. your unwillingness to accept God's will in the matter of marriage, or, as others explain it, for your brutality towards your wives, which would lead you to maltreat them, unless you had the privilege of divorcing them.

9. See on 5³². The exact text of this v. is very uncertain. **Whosoever**] Some ancient authorities read, 'Whosoever shall put away his wife, except for fornication, maketh her an adulteress,' omitting the rest of the verse.

10–12. Conversation ('in the house,' Mk) **on marriage and celibacy** (Mk 10¹⁰⁻¹²). The words of Jesus with regard to celibacy must be neither exaggerated nor minimised. They recognise and honour, along with marriage, the vocation of celibacy, when it is embraced for the Kingdom of Heaven's sake. The qualification is important. The Essenes of our Lord's time were celibates because they regarded marriage as unholy. The Christian hermits of later times adopted celibacy simply as a means towards attaining their own individual perfection. Many adopt it now because they will not face the responsibilities and anxieties of married life. The celibacy which Christ approves is that which is adopted for the sake of doing good to others in active works of religion and mercy, as in the case of the great sisterhoods and missionary brotherhoods. Any attempt to enforce celibacy upon whole classes of persons, as, for instance, upon the clergy in general, is forbidden by Christ ('He that is able to receive it, let him receive it'), and is also inexpedient.

10. If the case of the man] 'They mean that, if the tie of marriage is so strict that there is no separation except for adultery, it is inexpedient to marry. For how can a husband bear all the other faults of an abandoned woman?' (Euthymius). **11. This saying**] viz. 'that it is not expedient to marry.' The disciples had spoken of a worldly and prudential celibacy. This, Jesus warns them, is unnatural and perilous. The only celibacy which is safe and acceptable to God is that which is embraced for religious reasons in consequence of a divine call (' to whom it is given,' viz. ' by God '). **12. For the kingdom of heaven's sake**] i.e. who have embraced celibacy not merely for their own personal sanctification, but in order to undertake work for the advancement of Christ's kingdom on earth.

13–15. Christ and little children (Mk 10 13 Lk 18 15). A touching incident teaching the same lesson as the birth and infancy of Jesus Himself, viz. the sanctity of childhood. The disciples thought that children were not important enough to claim the Master's attention, and this aroused His just anger (St. Mark). We may learn from this that catechising and other ministrations to children are not to be despised, even by the most intellectual.

Most Christians find in this passage the leading principles upon which infant baptism is based. These are, (1) that children, however young, are capable of receiving divine grace. This is made clear by the fact that Christ *blessed* them (Mk 10 16). (2) Christ commands infants to be brought to Him, and we know of no way of bringing them except by baptism. (3) He declares infants to be specially fitted—more fitted even than adults —for admission into His kingdom (Lk 18 16, 17 Mk 10 14, 15), but the only covenanted admission into that kingdom is by baptism (Jn 3 5).

The chief objection to infant baptism is that it is not expressly commanded in the NT. But if the principle upon which it is based is found, that suffices. The NT. was not intended to be a code of law, like the Pentateuch. Moreover, the idea that infants could be brought into covenant with God during unconscious infancy was already familiar. Every male Israelite was circumcised on the eighth day after birth (Gn 17 12 Lv 12 3), and the apostles certainly regarded baptism as, equally with circumcision, a federal or covenanting rite (Col 2 11, 12). It is also worthy of note that baptism as an initiatory rite is older than the time of Christ. When a Gentile was converted to Judaism, he was admitted into covenant with God by three rites—baptism, circumcision, and sacrifice, and his infant children were baptised with him. This is expressly testified by the oldest rabbinical code, the Mishna. When, therefore, the apostles baptised the ' households ' of their converts (Ac

16 15, 33 18 8 1 Cor 1 16), they were only conforming to the usual Jewish practice in the case of converts. It is no valid objection to infant baptism that infants cannot have repentance and faith, because they are taught to exhibit these as soon as they reach the age of reason.

16–22. The rich young man (Mk 10 17 Lk 18 18). St. Luke calls him a 'ruler,' i.e. either a member of the Sanhedrin, or a ruler of a synagogue. The incident is a striking example of the seductive power of wealth. The young man was so good, and so near to the Kingdom of God, that Jesus 'looked upon him and loved him' (Mk); and yet he failed, because though he loved the Kingdom much, he loved money more.

16. Good Master] RV omits ' good.'

17. Why callest thou me good? etc.] RV ' Why askest thou me concerning that which is good? One there is who is good ' (see on Mk 10 18). **18.** All the commandments selected are those which test a man's love to his neighbour. Love of one's neighbour is a better test of inward religion than ceremonial piety. **20. All these things,** etc.] The answer showed how little the young man knew his own heart, but he was only repeating the vainglorious boasting of his teachers. The Talmud represents God as speaking of ' My sanctified ones, who have kept the whole law from Aleph to Taw.' Moses, Aaron, and Samuel were said to have kept the whole Law. It is said that when Rabbi Chanina lay upon his deathbed, he said to the angel of death, ' Bring hither the book of the Law, and see whether there is anything in it which I have not observed.' **21. If thou wilt** (RV ' wouldest ') **be perfect**] Jesus, who knew what is in man, knew that love of wealth was this man's besetting sin. He therefore urged him to abandon it, according to the precept, ' If thine eye offend thee, pluck it out.' Jesus was dealing with a case of covetousness, and, therefore, prescribed a proper remedy for covetousness, without recommending its general and indiscriminate adoption. **Treasure in heaven**] see on 6 1-20.

23–26. Conversation with the disciples on the perils of riches (Mk 10 23 Lk 18 24).

24. It is easier for a camel] Jesus rhetorically calls that impossible which is very difficult, or impossible without special grace. Such proverbs occur in most Eastern languages. We are told that Rabbi Sheshith said to Rabbi Amram, ' Perhaps thou art one of those of Pombeditha, who can make an elephant pass through a needle's eye.' The Greeks said, ' It is easier to hide five elephants under one's arm ' ; the Latins, ' More easily would a locust bring forth an elephant.' Some have thought (but it seems without sufficient authority) that 'the eye of a needle' is a term applied to a small gate for foot-passengers, situated at the side of the large city gate through which a camel would naturally pass.

The Gk. word *kamēlos* (or, with one letter altered, *kamilos*) also means 'rope,' and some interpreters give it this meaning here.

27–30. The reward of those who forsake all to follow Christ (Mk 10 28 Lk 18 28).

28. These words may refer to the position to be accorded the Apostles in the Church, after the resurrection, personally during their lives, afterwards through their writings and teaching : or they may have a real Eschatological sense, that is, they may refer to the new conditions after the final consummation.

In the regeneration] cp. Lk 22 28-30. The word occurs only once again in the NT., viz. Tit 3 5, where it is used of the grace of baptism. Here it is an open question whether by the Regeneration Jesus means His own resurrection, or the general resurrection at the last day, accompanied by the renewal of all created things.

Dalman says, 'The unusual expression " regeneration " is distinctly Greek, and cannot be translated literally into Hebrew or Aramaic.' The idea, however, is Hebrew, for it was believed that the Messiah would restore the world to its primitive perfection. There are also many analogies for the use of Regeneration in the sense of a personal resurrection. Josephus speaks of the resurrection as ' being born a second time.' St. Paul speaks of Christ's resurrection as His birth or begetting into a new and glorious life (Ac 13 33). Among the Greeks, too, Regeneration was the usual term for the transmigration of a man's soul into another body to begin a new life, which would be a kind of resurrection.

Judging] may also mean ' ruling.'

The twelve tribes of Israel] i.e. not the unbelieving Jews who would reject the apostles' preaching, but the Universal Church, the tribes of the New Israel of God. See Rev 7, where the twelve tribes of Israel (vv. 4–8) are identical with ' the great multitude which no man could number, of all nations and kindred and people and tongues ' (v. 9). The apostles at the time (perhaps even the evangelist when he wrote) understood it of Israel after the flesh, but in this case, as in so many others, enlightenment was to come later (see Intro.). **29. An hundredfold**] referring to spiritual compensations in this life : see on Mk.

30. See the following parable, especially 20 16.

CHAPTER 20

The Labourers in the Vineyard. The Journey to Jerusalem

1–16. Parable of the labourers in the vine- yard (peculiar to St. Matthew). This difficult parable is closely linked with what goes before, and can only be understood in connexion with it. It rebukes the spirit of Peter's enquiry (19 27), ' We have left all and followed thee ; what then shall we have ? ' The Twelve through Peter had demanded a superlatively great reward, because they had been called first and had laboured longest. Such a reward had been promised them, should they prove worthy of it (19 28), though at the same time it was darkly hinted, that some outside the apostolic circle would prove in the end more worthy than some of the apostles (19 30). Then follows the parable. It is a sermon on the text, ' But many shall be last that are first, and first that are last,' which opens (19 30) and closes it (20 16). It is addressed primarily to the apostles. It teaches them that great as their merit and their reward undoubtedly are, there will perhaps be others whose merit and reward will be equal or even greater. Thus St. Stephen (not an apostle) was the first to gain the martyr's crown, St. Paul laboured ' more abundantly than they all,' Barnabas and James the Lord's brother ranked with the leading apostles, and many great names in the subsequent history of the Church—Athanasius, Augustine, Jerome, Charlemagne, Alfred the Great, St. Louis— have completely eclipsed the fame of the more obscure apostles. The apostles are warned not to be jealous of the attainments and rewards of other followers of Christ, but to do their own work single-heartedly, and to leave the recompense to God. Another important lesson is taught by the identity of the recompense paid to the various groups of labourers. They all receive the same coin, a denarius, which at this time was regarded as a liberal, but not unusual day's pay (Tob 5 14). This does not necessarily signify that there will be no degrees of rank or blessedness in heaven, but it does signify that such degrees, if they exist, will be relatively unimportant. The supreme reward of all, to see God as He is in His unveiled splendour, will be enjoyed by all who are faithful to the end, and those who have this will care little what else they have or have not.

(*a*) Among the numerous conflicting interpretations of this parable, the following are the most noteworthy. (1) Calvin : a warning not to be over-confident because we have begun our Christian course well. (2) St. Irenæus : the various bands of labourers are the OT. saints ; those last called are the apostles. (3) Greswell : the labourers first called are the Jews ; those last called, the Gentiles. (4) St. Chrysostom : it refers to the periods of men's lives at which they begin to serve God. Some begin in infancy, others in youth, others in manhood, others in old age. It en* courages those who have entered late on God's service, to labour heartily. (b) The following interesting parallel is taken from the Talmud. 'To what was Rabbi Bon like ? He was like to a king who hired many labourers, among whom there was one who performed his work extraordinarily well. So the king took him aside, and walked with him to and fro. And when evening was come, those labourers came, and he gave him a complete hire with the rest. And the labourers murmured saying, "We have laboured hard all day, and this man only two hours, yet he hath received as much wages as we." But the king said to them, "He hath laboured more in those two hours than you in the whole day." So Rabbi Bon plied the Law more in twenty-eight years, than another in one hundred years.'

15. Is thine eye evil ?] i.e. Art thou jealous, because I am generous ? **16. For many be called, but few chosen]** These words are omitted by the RV, probably rightly. If retained, they are very difficult to interpret in such a way as to harmonise with the parable.

17-19. Another prediction of the Passion (Mk 10 ^{32} Lk 18 ^{31}). A prophecy remarkable for its detailed character. It mentions Christ's delivery to the Romans ('Gentiles'), His mocking, scourging, and crucifixion, and His resurrection on the third day. St. Luke adds, 'And they perceived not what was said' : cp. 16 ^{21} 17 ^{22}.

20-28. The ambition of the sons of Zebedee (Mk 10 ^{35}). The special promise to Peter (16 ^{18}) had aroused the jealousy of the other two most intimate disciples, who now came to claim the two most prominent of the twelve thrones promised in 19 ^{28}, making no mention whatever of Peter. The incident is a painful one, coming as it does immediately after the warning in the parable, and the prediction of the Passion.

20. The mother] Her name was Salome (27 ^{56} compared with Mk 15 ^{40}), and it is generally supposed that she was sister to the Virgin, and therefore our Lord's aunt : see on Jn 19 ^{25}.

21. The right hand was the first place of honour, the left the second : cp. the saying of Rabbi Acha, 'The Holy and Blessed God will cause King Messiah to sit at his right hand, and Abraham at his left.' **22. Ye know not what ye ask]** The mere fact that you ask for such a thing, shows that you are at present worthy not of the highest but of the lowest place in the kingdom : see vv. 16, 26. **To drink of the cup]** 'Cup,' a metaphor for 'lot in life,' is here used of Christ's rejection, persecution, and death : cp. Isa 51 ^{17} ('the cup of fury'), Jer 49 ^{12} 25 ^{15} Ezk 23 ^{33}. **To be baptized . . baptized with]** Interpolated from Mk ; omitted by RV. The 'baptism' has the same meaning as the 'cup.' **23. Ye shall drink**

indeed of my cup. James was martyred (Ac 12 ^{2}). According to tradition, John had many strange experiences ; such as, exile in Patmos, immersion in boiling oil, poison ; but survived these ordeals, and died a natural death.

Is not mine to give] i.e. in this way, as a piece of favouritism. Euthymius well says, 'Why is He, who is all powerful, unable to give this ? Not from want of power, but from regard to justice. This eminence is reserved for those who are worthy to attain it. For it is not only participation in a death like mine which wins the first seat, but undisputed pre-eminence in all good qualities.'

25-27. See on Lk 22 $^{25, 26}$. **26. Minister]** RM 'servant.' **27. Servant]** RM 'bondservant.'

28. A ransom for many] lit. 'a ransom instead of many.' An important doctrinal passage showing the importance which Jesus attached to His own death. He regards it as a redemption price, which, since men cannot pay it for themselves, He pays for them, and so releases them from the bondage of sin and death. In the OT. it is the ransom price paid for slaves (Lv 19 ^{20}), for captives (Isa 45 ^{13}), and for the ransom of a life (Ex 21 ^{30} Nu 35 ^{31}).

Many] either indicates all mankind, laying stress upon their multitude, or else those who actually accept redemption, as distinguished from those for whom the redemption price is paid : see 26 ^{28}.

After v. 28 the Codex Bezæ introduces an interesting saying of Jesus which may possibly be authentic : ' But do you seek to become greater from what is less, and less from what is greater ? Accordingly when ye have been invited to supper, and enter the house, recline not in the chief places, lest haply one more honourable than thou enter afterwards, and the host (or master of the feast) come and say to thee, "Go down yet lower," and thou be shamed. But if thou recline in the inferior place, and one inferior to thee comes in, the host will say to thee, "Eat thy supper higher up," and this shall be profitable to thee.' Cp. Lk 14 ^{8}.

29-34. Two blind men at Jericho (Mk 10 ^{46} Lk 18 ^{35}). Two apparent discrepancies call for notice : (1) St. Mark and St. Luke mention only one blind man ; (2) St. Luke says that the man was healed as Jesus was entering Jericho, not as he was leaving it. Euthymius says, 'Some say that one of these blind men, Bartimæus, was the more distinguished of the two, and so was mentioned by St. Mark and St. Luke, while the other was passed over as being his attendant, as in the case of the two demoniacs (8 ^{28}). But my own conjecture is, that one of these blind men is to be identified with St. Mark's and the other with St. Luke's, for St. Luke's blind man was apparently healed when Christ was entering into Jericho, and not when he was leaving it.' A more modern reconciliation is that the miracle took place between the old town of Jericho and the new city called Phasaelis, built by Herod the Great. The miracle might, therefore, be described with equal propriety as performed when leaving the old town, or when approaching the new.

30. Son of David] i.e. the Messiah : see 9 27.

31. Rebuked them] not because they disbelieved that Jesus was the Messiah, 'but out of honour to Jesus lest He should be disturbed.' **They cried the more**] a lesson in persistence in prayer, and its answer.

34. Followed him] not only in the way, but in the *Way* (Ac 19 9).

CHAPTER 21

The Triumphal Entry. Cleansing of the Temple

Chronology of the Last Week of Christ's Life, commonly called Holy Week (chiefly after Hastings' 'Dictionary of Christ and the Gospels ').

Sabbath, Nisan 8. Arrival at Bethany (Jn 12 1). Supper in the evening (Jn 12 2-8 Mt 26 6-13, where see notes).

Palm Sunday, Nisan 9. Triumphal entry into Jerusalem (21 1). The children's Hosannas, and healings in the Temple (21 14-16). Return to Bethany (21 17).

Monday, Nisan 10. Return from Bethany (21 18). Blasting of the fig tree (21 19). Cleansing of the Temple (21 12, where see notes). Retires to Bethany (Mk 11 19). Conspiracy of His enemies (Lk 19 47).

Tuesday, Nisan 11. Returning early He finds fig tree withered (Mk 11 20). His authority to teach questioned. The tribute money. The brother's wife. The first commandment of all. 'What think ye of Christ ?' (chs. 21, 22). Woes on the Pharisees (c. 23). Jesus in the Treasury. The widow's mite (Mk 12 41). Visit of the Greeks (Jn 12 20). Christ finally rejected (Jn 12 37). Lament over Jerusalem (23 37-39). Great prophecy of the fall of Jerusalem, and the Second Advent of the Son of man, followed by parables concerning the judgment (chs. 24, 25). Counsel of Caiaphas (26 3).

Wednesday, Nisan 12. This day was probably spent in retirement at Bethany (cp. Jn 12 36). On the evening of this day some place the supper at Bethany at which Jesus was anointed (Mk 14 1-9 Mt 26 6-13), but see above, Nisan 8. The bargain of Judas (26 14).

Thursday, Nisan 13. In the afternoon preparations for the last supper (26 17). In the evening, the last supper with the Twelve in the upper room (26 20). The feet-washing (Jn 13 2). Departure of Judas. Institution of the Holy Communion (26 26). Discourses in the upper room (Jn 13 31–14 31). Departure from the upper room (Jn 14 31). Allegory of the Vine (Jn 15 1). The Comforter promised (Jn 16). Christ's high-priestly prayer (Jn 17). Gethsemane (26 37). The agony lasts 'one hour' (Mk 14 37).

Good Friday, Nisan 14. About midnight Jesus is arrested (26 47). Preliminary trial before Annas (Jn 18 13). Peter's denials, about 3 A.M. (Jn 18 27). Jesus sent to Caiaphas (Jn 18 24). Trial before the Sanhedrin at daybreak, about 4 A.M. (27 1). Sent to Pilate, about 6 A.M. (27 2), from Pilate to Herod (Lk 23 7), and back to Pilate (Lk 23 11). Delivered to be crucified (Jn 19 16). Jesus crucified, 9 A.M. (see Mk 15 25, but contrast Jn 19 14, ' about the sixth hour '). Darkness from 12 noon to 3 P.M. (27 45). Death of Jesus, 3 P.M. (27 50). (The paschal lambs were being sacrificed in the Temple at the time of Christ's death, cp. Jn 19 36. In the evening was the Jewish Passover. Our Lord, knowing that His death was imminent, had eaten it the night before.) Burial of Jesus (27 57).

Easter Eve, Nisan 15. The first day of unleavened bread and the sabbath (Jn 19 31). The sepulchre sealed (27 62).

Easter Day, Nisan 16. The resurrection very early (Mk 16 9, etc.). Visit of the women to the sepulchre (28 1). Visit of Peter and John to the sepulchre (Jn 20 3). Appearance to Mary Magdalene (Jn 20 11-18). In the afternoon appearances to the two disciples (Lk 24 13), and to Peter (Lk 24 34). In the evening appearance to the apostles, Thomas being absent (Lk 24 36 Jn 20 19).

1-11. Solemn entry into Jerusalem (Mk 11 1 Lk 19 29 Jn 12 12). More than a third of the entire Gospel narrative is occupied with the last week of Christ's life, commonly called Holy Week. The cause of this is to be sought, partly in the special importance which the Apostolic Church attached to the death of Jesus, partly in the indelible impression which the words and acts of that solemn time made upon the disciples, and partly in the extreme activity of Jesus at this period, which crowded the last days of His life with striking events and sayings. All the evangelists lay stress on the voluntary character of the death of Jesus. They represent Him as coming up to Jerusalem deliberately to encounter it, as being the designed aim and end of His ministry (20 28 21 39 26 2, 12, 28, 39, 54, etc.). In view of His approaching death, which might appear to be a complete abnegation of His claim to be the Messiah, He judged it expedient to make the claim openly, and accordingly made arrangements for a formal entry into Jerusalem riding on an ass, as the Messiah was expected to do, and no longer restrained the enthusiasm of His followers, who were allowed openly to salute Him as the Son of David, i.e. the Messiah. The motives of political prudence which had previously restrained Him from an open avowal, had now ceased to operate. He knew that He had alienated the bulk of the Galileans, and that Jerusalem, in spite of certain appearances to the contrary, was thoroughly hostile. He therefore feared no political consequences from the superficial revival of popularity with which His change of policy would be greeted, the more so as He was about to raise the expectations of His adherents only for a moment, in order effectually to quench them.

The entry into Jerusalem is the one gleam of light in the dark days that closed our Lord's ministry. Its success was due to several causes : (1) The crowd was composed largely of Galileans, many of whom still remained faithful to Jesus. (2) His bold change of policy won back for a moment many who had left Him for His procrastination. (3) The extraordinary enthusiasm with which He was received in Jerusalem itself is to be explained by the recent raising of Lazarus, which had made a deep impression in the capital (Jn 11 45-48 12 9, 17).

Peculiar to St. Matthew is the mention of the two animals ; to St. Luke the complaint of the Pharisees, and the weeping over the city ; to St. John the mention of the palm-branches, and of the fact that natives of Jerusalem went out to welcome Jesus.

1. **When they drew nigh**] The synoptists make no break in the journey from Jericho to Jerusalem (20 m. of bad uphill travelling), but St. John says that Jesus came to Bethany six days before the Passover (i.e. on Friday or Saturday), and stayed there until the triumphal entry, which was probably on Sunday (Jn 12 1).

Bethphage] lit. 'House of Figs.' There was perhaps a village of this name, but in the Talmud Bethphage is the name of an extensive district stretching from the base of Olivet to the walls of Jerusalem, and perhaps all round the city. 'Whatever is in the exterior circuit of Jerusalem is called Bethphage.' 'What is meant by "outside the wall"? Rabbi Johanan said, Outside the wall is Bethphage.'

Mount of Olives] i.e. the range of hills facing Jerusalem on the E. and lying round about from NE. to SE., and separated from the Holy City by the Valley of Jehoshaphat or Kidron. It contains four summits : (1) Galilee or

Scopus, due NE. of the Temple site, and about a mile distant ; (2) the Ascension, due E. of the Temple site, and distant about ¾ m., 2,600 ft. high, and commanding a fine view of the city, the Olivet of the Gospels ; (3) the Prophets, the S. spur of this ; (4) the Mt. of Offence, ¾ m. SE. of the Temple site.

The traditional Gethsemane is at the foot of the Ascension towards Jerusalem. Stanley says that Jesus did not pass over the summit of the Ascension, but took the road which passes between the Prophets and the Mt. of Offence, 'because it is, and must always have been, the usual approach for horsemen and for large caravans.'

2. An ass tied, and a colt] The two animals are mentioned only by St. Matthew. An unused animal was preferred for an occasion like the present (see Mk 11 2 1 S 6 7). **3. The Lord**] i.e. Jesus. The ready way in which the owner parted with the animals proves that he was a disciple, and this is an argument for an earlier ministry of Jesus in Jerusalem.

5. A combination of Isa 62 11 with Zech 9 9. The rendering is free, partly following the Heb. and partly the Septuagint. According to St. John, the disciples did not at the time perceive that Jesus was fulfilling this prophecy.

And a colt] i.e. 'even a colt.' Zechariah makes no reference to two animals.

7. And put on them their clothes] either because they were uncertain which one He intended to mount, or in order gaily to caparison both animals for the procession. Eastern garments are brightly coloured. **And they set** *him* (RV 'he sat') **thereon**] i.e. on the clothes placed upon the colt, not, as some take it, that He rode upon both animals alternately.

By riding upon the ass Jesus deliberately fulfilled the prophecy of Zechariah, and so claimed to be the Messiah. The ass was chosen rather than the horse, because the ass was a symbol of peace, the horse of war ; the ass of humility, the horse of pride. The Jews fully accepted the Messianic reference of Zech 9 9. Rabbi Salomo said, 'This cannot be interpreted except of King Messiah.'

8. Spread their garments] An extraordinary token of respect, such as was paid to kings and great conquerors (2 K 9 13).

Plutarch says of Cato the younger that 'he was escorted, not with prayers which are common, nor with praises, but with tears and embraces which could not be satisfied, the people spreading their garments under his feet, and kissing his hands.'

It is said of Rabbi Nicodemus, son of Gorion, that, 'whenever he went into the school to lecture, his pupils spread garments of wool under his feet.' In quite recent times the inhabitants of Bethlehem spread their garments on the road under the feet of the horse of the

English Consul of Damascus, whose assistance they were anxious to obtain.

9. That went before] These were the multitudes mentioned by St. John, who went out from Jerusalem to meet Jesus. Those who followed behind were the Galileans. **Hosanna to the son of David**] This can only mean, 'Glory and honour to the Son of David,' just as St. Mark's phrase, 'Hosanna in the highest,' is translated by St. Luke, 'Glory in the highest (heaven).' How 'Hosanna' comes to have this meaning, is disputed. It is taken from Ps 118 25, where it is addressed to God, and means 'Save (us) now.' Probably it had become a mere exclamation of praise, 'a kind of holy hurrah,' the consciousness of its grammatical meaning being lost, as in the case of 'Alleluia.' This is clearly the case in the 'Didache,' which has the phrase, 'Hosanna to the God of David' (Did. 10).

The exclamation 'Hosanna' was used chiefly at the Feast of Tabernacles. The seventh day of that feast was called 'Hosanna Day,' and the branches carried by the worshippers were called 'Hosannas.' The events of Palm Sunday are thus an imitation of the ritual of that festival.

It is sometimes said that the well-known classical custom of carrying palms in token of victory was unknown to the Jews of our Lord's time ; but certainly the palms carried Rev 7 9 seem to be symbols of victory.

12–17. Cleansing of the Temple. Hosannas of the Children (Mk 11 15 Lk 19 45). In St. Matthew this event seems to take place on Palm Sunday, but Mk 11 11 makes it clear that it did not occur till next day. On reaching Jerusalem, Jesus went into the Temple, and 'looked round about on all things,' but, the hour being late, retired to Bethany.

This cleansing of the Temple is probably not the same as that described Jn 2 13 (see notes there), but a distinct event. For, (1) both events are definitely dated by the evangelists ; (2) the repetition of the act is natural, the abuses, during a period of two years, having had time to recur ; (3) the omission of the former event by the synoptists, and of the latter by St. John, are explained by the general design of the synoptists to record only the Galilean ministry, and of St. John to supplement rather than duplicate the synoptic narratives. The cleansing of the Temple and of its worship, and of the priesthood, were among the expected activities of the Messiah, according to Mal 3 1-3.

The incident of the children in the Temple is peculiar to St. Matthew.

12. The tables of the moneychangers] According to Edersheim the Temple-market was what is called in the Talmud 'the booths of the sons of Annas.' The bulk of the enormous

profits went to increase the wealth of Annas, his family, and adherents. The Talmud frequently speaks in strong language of the iniquities of this traffic, which was swept away by a strong explosion of popular feeling three years before the destruction of Jerusalem.

The money-changers sat in the Temple-court, (1) to receive the half-shekel which was due from every male Israelite at this period (see on 17 24), and could be paid either at home or in Jerusalem ; (2) to change foreign money into Jewish currency, with which alone the half-shekel could be paid, or animals for sacrifice be bought. The money-changers' commission was called *Kollubos*, hence the money-changers were called *Kollubistæ*. They probably paid a large percentage of their profits to Annas.

Plumptre compares with this incident 'the state of the great cathedral of London, as painted in the literature of Elizabeth and James, when mules and horses laden with market produce were led through St. Paul's as a matter of every-day occurrence, and bargains were struck there, and burglaries planned, and servants hired.'

13. Isa 56 7 Jer 7 11.

14–16. Peculiar to St. Matthew. 14. The blind and the lame] who were begging at the Temple gates (Ac 3 2). **15. Sore displeased**] because even children were calling Jesus 'son of David,' i.e. 'Messiah.' Boys under fourteen are meant.

17. Bethany] He probably lodged with Lazarus and his sisters. Bethany was on the further side of the Mt. of Olives, about 15 furlongs distant (Jn 11 18), on the road to Jericho.

18–22. Cursing of the fig tree (Mk 11 12-14 and 11 20-25). St. Mark makes it clear that the fig tree was cursed on Monday morning as they left Bethany, but that the effect of the curse was not noticed till Tuesday morning.

This, the only miracle of wrath worked by Jesus, is also a revelation of God's mercy, for whereas the countless miracles of mercy were all wrought upon men, this one was wrought upon a tree. 'He parches the tree' (says Theophylact), 'that He may teach men wisdom.' 'He exercises His power' (says Euthymius), 'not on a man, because He is a lover of men, but on a plant.' The whole incident is an acted parable. There is no reason to suppose that Jesus was really hungry, or expected to find figs. St. Mark says expressly that the time of figs was not yet. Probably His words and actions were entirely symbolic, like those of the prophets (Jer 13 1 27 2 1 K 22 11, etc.).

The one fig tree, standing apart from all other trees, is the Jewish nation, and whereas it alone had leaves, while the other trees were bare, it signifies that whereas Israel made great professions of righteousness and of the service of God, the other nations of the earth made none. Both Jew and Gentile were, indeed, equally unfruitful, but the Jew added to his unfruitfulness the appearance of fruit, for it is the peculiarity of the fig tree that its fruit appears and is well developed before there is any sign of leaves. When, therefore, leaves appear on a fig tree, ripe fruit may justly be expected. The fault of the fig tree, therefore, was not that it had no fruit, which was not to be expected at that season, but that it pretended to have it, and had not.

The curse of perpetual barrenness pronounced by Jesus upon the fig tree, i.e. upon Israel, has received a signal fulfilment. In the time of Christ it was an active missionary religion, making thousands of proselytes in every province of the empire, and leavening religious thought far beyond its own borders. Now it enrolls no proselytes.

20. How soon] RV 'How did the fig tree immediately wither away ?' The disciples, instead of asking the meaning of the miracle, ask how it was done ? Jesus did not explain its symbolical meaning, but made it an object-lesson in the power of believing prayer.

21. Cp. 17 20 Lk 17 6 1 Cor 13 2. **Be thou removed]** a proverbial expression for something very difficult. The rabbis, who could solve questions of great difficulty, were called 'rooters up of mountains,' and it was said of a skilful teacher that 'he plucked up mountains and ground them one upon another.'

22. All things] Not all things absolutely, but all things of which the petitioners are worthy.

23–27. Christ's authority to teach challenged (Mk 11 27 Lk 20 1).

23. The chief priests] A deputation from the Sanhedrin, seeking some excuse to excommunicate Him. **By what authority?]** Jesus had not received rabbinical ordination, and had no authority therefore to teach as a rabbi. **Doest thou these things]** referring not only to His teaching, but to His cleansing of the Temple, His miracles, His triumphal entry into the city, and His ministry in general. **27. We cannot tell]** To be forced to admit their ignorance, was more damaging to their reputation than a definite answer would have been, for one of the most important duties of the Sanhedrin, according to the Mishna, was to judge between true and false prophets, and to inflict exemplary punishment upon the latter. **Neither tell I]** By implication Jesus claimed the authority of a prophet, or an even higher authority.

28–32. Parable of the Two Sons (peculiar to St. Matthew). The 'certain man' is God, and He is represented as a father, to set forth His impartial love to all mankind, righteous and sinful alike. The son who said 'I go,

sir,' and went not, is the chief priests, scribes, and Pharisees, who 'rejected for themselves the counsel of God, not having been baptised of John' (Lk 7 30). The other son, who at first insolently refused to go, and then repented and went, is the publicans and harlots, who 'believed John, and were baptised by him.' More generally the first class embraces those who are satisfied with the outward form of godliness and with the avoidance of open sin ; the second class those who, though sinners, know that they are such, and so are more easily brought to repentance. **31. Before you]** Graciously intimating that the door of repentance was still open to them. **32. In the way of righteousness]** i.e. of legal righteousness. The Pharisees had no excuse for neglecting the preaching of John, for it was based on the Law which they idolised, and ran counter to none of their cherished convictions. The preaching of Christ was different, and could not easily be received by strict Jews, unless they had first passed through the preliminary baptism of John.

33–46. The Wicked Husbandmen (Mk 12 1 Lk 20 9). The doctrinal importance of this parable, which belongs to the oldest tradition, is great. In it Christ claims to be in a unique sense the Son of God. He calls Moses and the prophets slaves and bondservants, and places Himself at an immense elevation above them as the beloved Son of the Householder, and the sole heir of His possessions. The parable contains a remarkable prophecy of the destruction of Jerusalem by the Romans (v. 41).

33. 'The householder is God, who on account of His tender love is called a man. The vineyard is the people of the Jews planted by God in the land of promise. The hedge is the Law, which hindered them from mingling with the nations, the winepress the altar of sacrifice, the tower the Temple, the husbandmen, the teachers of the people, i.e. the Pharisees and scribes. And the householder (God) departed, when He no longer spoke to them in the pillar of cloud, or perhaps the departure of God is His longsuffering ; for God seems to sleep and to be in a far country, when He is longsuffering, and does not call men to account for their sins the moment that they are committed' (Theophylact). **Tower]** i.e. a watchtower for the keepers who were set to guard the vineyard when the grapes were nearly ripe (Job 27 18 Song 1 6 Isa 1 8).

34. Time of the fruit] 'In the history of souls and of nations, there are seasons which even more than all other are times of fruit ; when God requires such with more than usual earnestness, when it will fare ill with a soul or a nation, if these be not found' (Trench). 'And the fruits of the vineyard are the keeping of the commandments of the Law, and the practice of the virtues ; and the servants are the prophets who when sent to demand from Israel obedience to the Law and a virtuous life, were variously maltreated ' (Euthymius).

35. Killed] According to tradition Isaiah was sawn asunder, and Jeremiah stoned : see also 2 Ch 24 20-22 and cp. Heb 11. **37. They will reverence my son**] ' This He said, not as if they would do so, for He knew they would not, but pointing out what they ought to do ' (Euthymius). ' When God is said to doubt about the future, it is that human free-will may be preserved ' (Jerome).

41. They say] Jesus extorts their condemnation from their own lips. Otherwise in St. Mark and St. Luke. **He will**, etc.] RV ' He will miserably destroy those miserable men.' The allusion is to the destruction of Jerusalem 70 A.D., and the end of the Jewish dispensation.

Other husbandmen] i.e. the ministers of the Christian Church, many of them Gentiles, who succeeded to the charge which the scribes and Pharisees neglected.

42. The stone, etc.] Ps 118 22 Ac 4 11. The ' stone,' of course, is Christ. The ' builders ' are the Jews. The ' head of the corner ' is the most important position in a building, so that Christ represents Himself as the foundation upon which the Kingdom of God was to be built up in spite of His rejection by the Jews. In the Ps. the ' stone ' is the Jewish nation, rejected and despised by the Gentiles during the captivity, but after the return restored to a place of honour among the nations of the earth. But on the principle that what is said of Israel applies especially to the Messiah, the rabbis interpreted the passage Messianically, e.g. Rabbi Salomo on Mic 5 1 said, ' It is the Messiah the Son of David, of whom it is written, The stone which the builders rejected,' etc.

43. The favour of God will be withdrawn from a nation that obeys not His will, and bestowed on one that does. **The kingdom** = the privileges of the kingdom. **44.** Wetstein well says, ' He who falls upon a great stone, is bruised indeed, but can be healed, but he upon whom a great stone falls, is ground as it were to dust, like the chaff that is scattered to the winds.' Spiritually interpreted, those who fell upon the stone, are those who stumbled at the humiliation of Christ, but were to be recovered by His glorious Resurrection. Those upon whom the stone fell, are those who did not suffer themselves to be recovered even by that miracle, and so were involved in the common destruction of the Jewish nation. Euthymius says, ' Christ is called the corner-stone, because as the corner-stone unites in itself two walls, so also Christ unites in Himself two peoples, the Gentiles and the Jews, and by faith makes them one.'

CHAPTER 22

PARABLES OF THE MARRIAGE OF THE KING'S SON AND THE WEDDING GARMENT

1-14. Marriage of the King's Son (peculiar to St. Matthew). Jesus concludes His discourse by reiterating in still clearer and stronger language the teaching of the last parable, viz. His Divine Sonship, the impending destruction of Jerusalem, the rejection of the Jews, and the call of the Gentiles. He concludes with a warning to the Gentiles not to abuse the mercy about to be extended to them, by appearing at the feast (i.e. becoming Christians) without the garment of repentance and pureness of living.

This parable is probably quite distinct from that of the Great Supper (Lk 14 16). The latter says nothing of the wedding garment, of the fall of Jerusalem, or of the Sonship of Christ. Its occasion, moreover, was entirely different, and, from its contents, it was obviously spoken before the hostility between Christ and the Pharisees had reached its height. **1. And Jesus answered**] viz. their attempt to seize Him, 21 46, by another parable. **2. A certain king**] i.e. God. **A marriage**] RV ' a marriage feast,' which would last seven or fourteen days (Gn 29 27 Jg 14 12 Tob 8 19). The marriage is between Christ and His Church (Rev 21 2 2 Cor 11 2 Isa 54 5, etc.), which begins here, but is perfected in the world to come. For Jewish ideas as to the Messiah's great feast, see on 8 11. **3. His servants**] i.e. Moses and the prophets, and especially the Baptist, the last and greatest prophet of the old dispensation. **Them that were bidden**] i.e. the Jews.

4. Other servants] i.e. the Apostles. The repetition of the invitation was a Jewish custom ' What ' (said the rabbis) ' was the boast of the men of Jerusalem ? Not one of them went to a banquet, unless he were twice invited.' **6. The remnant**] are the chief priests, scribes, and Pharisees, who were the chief persecutors of the apostles (Ac 5 40 7 58 12 2 14 5, etc.), as distinguished from the nation generally, which only ' made light of ' the Apostles' message. **7. His armies**] ' The armies of the Romans, who, under Vespasian and Titus, slew these murderers, and burnt their city, Jerusalem.'

8. Then saith he] Not indicating that no Gentile converts were to be made before that date, but that from that time ' the fulness of the Gentiles ' would begin (Ro 11 25). **9. Into the highways**] RV ' the partings of the highways.' More probably it means the places where the roads from the country enter a city, and so by metaphor, Gentile territory (Grimm). So also Euthymius : ' He calls the cities and villages of the Gentiles the outlets of the highways, signifying the forlorn state of the Gentiles.'

To feast the poor was quite common. The Talmud says, 'It was a custom among rich men to invite poor travellers to feasts.'

10. Both bad and good] Signifying, as in the parable of the net, that the Church is to consist of good and evil, and that the entrance into it is not to be denied to any but scandalous sinners.

11. To see (RV 'behold') **the guests**] The scene changes to the last judgment, when the fitness of the guests to be there will be the subject of a solemn scrutiny. Theophylact well says, 'The entrance to the marriage feast is without scrutiny, for by grace alone were we all called, both good and bad. But the subsequent life of those who have entered in, will not be without scrutiny, but the King will make a most exact scrutiny of those who after their entry into the faith, shall be found with filthy garments. Let us therefore tremble, reflecting that unless a man live a pure life, faith by itself is of no avail, for not only is he cast out of the marriage feast, but is cast into the fire.' **A wedding garment**] Eastern etiquette is strict, and to appear without the festive garment that custom prescribes, would be a serious offence. Since the judgment is according to works, the wedding garment is not faith, or imputed righteousness, but a holy life.

13. The servants] RM 'ministers,' i.e. the angels.

14. Cp. 20 16. Some think that this indicates that only a few of all mankind will be finally saved, but Theophylact is probably right in saying that it refers to the Jews of our Lord's time, all of whom were called, but few were chosen, because few accepted the invitation. The 'calling' must be carefully distinguished from the 'choosing.' The calling is the act of God, and does not depend on human will; but whether a man is finally chosen or not, depends upon his own conduct after his call.

15–22. The tribute money (Mk 12 13 Lk 20 20). The Sanhedrin, not having the power of life and death, tried to entrap Jesus into an answer which might be made an excuse for handing Him over to Pilate on a charge of rebellion and treason. The Pharisees, who concocted the plot, did not appear in it openly, but sent their disciples, and the Herodians, who, from hostility to Jesus, were quite willing to join in the attempt to destroy Him.

16. Herodians] i.e. partisans of the dynasty of the Herods. They supported the Roman domination.

17. Is it lawful?] The party of the Zealots, founded by Judas of Galilee, held that, Israel being a theocracy, and God the only King, it was unlawful to pay tribute to any foreign power. The Pharisees asked whether Christ

agreed with Judas. The hypocrisy of the question appears in this, that the Pharisees at heart agreed with Judas, yet they were plotting to put Jesus to death on a charge of supporting his policy. **Tribute**] see on 17 25.

19. A penny] see on 18 28. It was a Roman coin, and the Jewish schools held it for a maxim that he whose coin was in circulation was king. The rabbis said, 'Wheresoever the money of any king is current, there the inhabitants acknowledge that king for their lord.' So in the Talmud, Abigail refuses to recognise David as king, saying, 'The money of our Lord Saul as yet is current.'

20. Whose.. image?] The rabbis objected to human figures on coins as savouring of idolatry. Edersheim says, 'Neither Herod nor Herod Antipas had any image on their coins. This must therefore have been either a foreign one (Roman), or else one of the Tetrarch Philip, who exceptionally had the image of Tiberius on his coins.' See Edersheim, 'Life,' App. II.

21. Render therefore unto Cæsar] A pregnant saying, destroying the basis of Jewish nationalism, and defining the relation of Church and State for all time. A brief exposition must suffice. Christ showed, (1) His sympathy with imperialism, as opposed to national and racial particularism. Intending Himself to found a universal Church, He openly showed His sympathy with the great and beneficent empire which broke down the barriers of national hatred and prejudice, established universal peace, and ensured the diffusion of culture, knowledge, and useful arts; (2) that submission and loyalty to civil power is a duty binding on the conscience. Christ says not only 'Give,' but 'Render,' signifying that submission is due : (3) that nevertheless there are limits to the obedience due to the civil power. When Cæsar asks not for tribute, but for worship, as actually happened at this time, he is to be resisted ; if the State prescribes the religious worship of its subjects, obedience is not due ; (4) that consequently Church and State are not one thing, but two, each with its peculiar powers given by God, and that all attempts to amalgamate them, or to subject the one to the other, are wrong ; (5) that religious persecution is unlawful. The State has no authority to enforce any particular religion within its borders, and the Church has no authority to use the sword of the magistrate in its behalf.

23–33. The Sadducees and the Resurrection (Mk 12 18 Lk 20 27). A less dangerous interview than the preceding. The Sadducees sought to bring Jesus into contempt and ridicule with the multitude by asking Him a question which they thought He could not answer.

23. Sadducees] see on 3 7. **24. Shall marry his wife**] see Dt 25 5. The Levirate marriage was falling into disuse at this time. The Mishna (200 A.D.) recommends that the custom should no longer be observed. **28. Whose wife shall she be?**] Two errors underlay the question : (1) That in the resurrection men will rise to a natural life ; (2) that the Law will continue in force. The sceptical Sadducees naturally represented the doctrine of the Resurrection in its most ridiculous form.

There was some division of opinion among the rabbis as to whether resurrection would be to a natural or to a supernatural (spiritual) life. A few took the spiritual view, e.g. Rabbi Raf is reported to have often said, ' In the world to come they shall neither eat, nor drink, nor beget children, nor trade. There is neither envy nor strife, but the just shall sit with crowns on their heads, and shall enjoy the splendour of the Divine Majesty.' But the majority inclined to a materialistic view of the resurrection. The pre-Christian book of Enoch says that the righteous after the resurrection shall live so long that they shall beget thousands. The received doctrine is laid down by Rabbi Saadia, who says, ' As the son of the widow of Sarepton, and the son of the Shunamite, ate and drank, and doubtless married wives, so shall it be in the resurrection ' ; and by Maimonides, who says, ' Men after the resurrection will use meat and drink, and will beget children, because since the Wise Architect makes nothing in vain, it follows of necessity that the members of the body are not useless, but fulfil their functions.' The point raised by the Sadducees was often debated by the Jewish doctors, who decided that ' a woman who married two husbands in this world is restored to the first in the next.'

30. The angels] Jesus takes the opportunity of rebuking the Sadducees' disbelief in angels (Ac 23⁸).

32. I am the God of Abraham] Ex 3⁶. The proof of the resurrection is taken from the Law, not because the Sadducees rejected the Prophets and Hagiographa, of which there is no certain proof, but because to every Jew the Law was of higher authority than any other part of the canon. Theophylact says, ' He said not "I was," but "I am the God of Abraham, Isaac, and Jacob." For though they are dead, yet they live through the hope of the resurrection. Here the Lord opposes the heresy of the Sadducees, saying, "God is not the God of the dead, i.e. of men who have altogether perished, but of the living, i.e. of those who have immortal souls, and though they are now dead will rise again."'

Strictly speaking, the argument of Jesus is an argument for human immortality, but to Jewish minds the idea of immortality necessarily carried with it the idea of a resurrection.

34–40. The great commandment of the

Law (Mk 12²⁸). Considering that this question was asked by an individual Pharisee, that there is nothing ensnaring in it, and that Jesus commended His questioner, saying, ' Thou art not far from the Kingdom of God ' (Mk), it is probable that this was not a temptation, but a test, an honest appeal for information on the part of one who had heard His last answer with admiration. St. Luke records a somewhat similar incident in another connexion (Lk 10²⁵). Some regard it as another version of this incident.

35. A lawyer] i.e. a scribe, or rabbi.

Tempting him] i.e. proving Him, testing His penetration and knowledge of the Law by a hard question.

36. Which *is* the great commandment?] A question debated by the Jewish schools. The best Jewish opinion coincided with our Lord's. Philo, our Lord's contemporary, says, ' To speak briefly, of the innumerable detailed exhortations and commandments, the two which in the most general manner sum up the whole, are the duties of piety and holiness towards God, and of lovingkindness and justice towards man. Each of these is subdivided into various special duties, all of them praiseworthy ' : see on 7¹². The first commandment is Dt 6⁵, the second Lv 19¹⁸. The former formed part of the prayers of the phylacteries, daily recited by every Jew : see on 23⁵. Both are somewhat freely quoted according to the LXX. **37. Heart . . soul . . mind**] i.e. all one's powers. ' Heart ' in Hebrew is the inward man, sometimes the understanding ; ' soul ' is life, often, but not always, physical life ; ' mind ' is nearly the same as reason, or rational soul. It must here be understood as embracing spirit, i.e. the religious faculty.

41–46. The title Son of David (Mk 12³⁵ Lk 20⁴¹). A saying of Jesus from the oldest tradition, of great doctrinal importance. He declares Himself dissatisfied with the honourable title of Son of David, because He is in reality also David's Lord. By applying Ps 110 to Himself He claims, (1) a seat at God's right hand ; (2) lordship over all the human race ; (3) an eternal priesthood and empire : ' Thou art a priest for ever after the order of Melchizedek.'

41. Jesus asked them] Having repelled the attack of the Pharisees, Jesus takes the offensive, and demonstrates that they are wrong to regard the Messiah as a mere man. **43. David**] The question has been raised whether our Lord here definitely decides the Davidic authorship of Ps 110. Probably not. His object is to show that the Pharisees' low view of the Messiah is inconsistent with their own premises, not to teach the true authorship of the Psalm.

44. The LORD (i.e. God) **said unto my Lord**] i.e. to David's Lord, the Messiah, Ps 110[1]. The Jews fully accepted the Messianic interpretation of this Psalm. Rabbi Joden said, 'In the time to come the Holy and Blessed God will place King Messiah at His right hand, according to Ps 110.'

CHAPTER 23

DENUNCIATION OF THE PHARISEES

1-36. Final denunciation of the Scribes and Pharisees. The other synoptists insert in this place a brief utterance directed against the scribes (Mk 12 [38-40] Lk 20 [45-47]), but the discourse as it stands is peculiar to St. Matthew. A portion of it, however, is inserted by St. Luke at an earlier period, on the occasion of a dinner at a Pharisee's house (Lk 11 [37-52]), and this suggests that we have here a collection of sayings against the scribes and Pharisees really spoken on various occasions. The scene is the Temple. In the foreground are Jesus and His disciples; a little farther off the multitudes; in the background are the discomfited Pharisees, who, instead of attacking, are now attacked. Christ addresses first the multitudes (vv. 1-7), then the disciples (vv. 8-12), finally the scribes and Pharisees (vv. 13-36).

2. Sit in Moses' seat] The scribes (who were ordained with the laying-on of hands) claimed to have received their authority through an unbroken succession from Moses. The 'sitting' refers to the judicial power, and the authority to teach, which all scribes or rabbis possessed, and which was centred in the Great Sanhedrin. In rabbinical writings one who succeeds a rabbi at the head of his school is described as 'sitting on his seat,' because the rabbis taught sitting on a raised seat. **Sit**] or, 'sat,' i.e. succeeded to Moses' authority. **3. All therefore whatsoever**] In spite of the wickedness and hypocrisy of the scribes, they were to be obeyed and respected on account of their office, to which they had a legitimate right, until their place was taken by the Apostles. Similarly a duly ordained Christian minister, however much he may deserve to be despised as a man, is yet to be tolerated as Christ's representative till he be deposed by lawful authority.

4. Lk 11 [46]. Bind heavy burdens] a metaphor from overloading a beast of burden. The 'burdens,' which they 'bind into bundles,' are the intricate and troublesome observances which the scribes had added to the written Law, and had declared to be more binding than the Law itself : see on 15 [2]. The one good point about the Sadducees was that they rejected these human traditions. **Will not move them** (Lk 'touch them') **with one of their fingers**] much less bear them upon their shoulders. They require their disciples to keep onerous rules, which they themselves will not observe, or (as others interpret it) they will not stretch out a finger to adjust these legal burdens to the backs of others, so that they may comfortably bear them.

5. Make broad their phylacteries] Every male Jew above the age of thirteen was required to say both morning and evening, except on sabbaths and feasts, when the synagogue services took their place, ' the prayers of the phylacteries.' The phylacteries themselves were cubical boxes (size from ½ in. to 1½ in.), made of the skin of a clean animal, and attached to a broad strip of material, by which they were bound to the body at prayertime. Two were worn. The head-phylactery was so fastened to the brow that the prayer-box came between the eyes. This was the one which the Pharisees made broad, i.e. as large and conspicuous as possible. The arm-phylactery was tied round the left arm on the inside, so as to be near the heart, and during use was invisible, being covered by the sleeve. The head-phylactery was divided into four compartments, containing on little rolls these four portions of scripture : Ex 13 [1-10] 13 [11-16] Dt 4 [4-9] 11 [13-21]. The arm-phylactery contained the same passages written on a single roll. The rabbis held these phylacteries, or *tephillin*, in the highest veneration. They were to be kissed when put on or off, they were holier than the frontal of the high priest's mitre, they were a preservative against demons, whence their name phylacteries, i.e. amulets (from a Gk. word meaning 'to guard'). They were sworn by, by touching them. God Himself was said to wear them, and to swear by them when He swore by 'His holy arm.' Orthodox Jews find the wearing of the phylacteries commanded in the Law (Ex 13 [9,16] Dt 6 [8] 11 [18]), but the Karaite Jews dispute the interpretation and do not wear them. The phylacterial prayers being said at stated times, the Pharisees would arrange to be seen saying them in public, at the 'corners of the streets' : see on 6 [5]. **The borders**] or, rather, 'holy tassels' : see on 9 [20]. In our Lord's time they were worn publicly on the four corners of the outer garment. Modern Jews wear them secretly on an under garment called a *tallith*, for fear of ridicule. In the synagogue a second and larger *tallith* is worn during the prayers to cover the head and neck. This *tallith*, or prayer-veil, was perhaps in use in our Lord's time.

6. Lk 11 [43] Mk 12 [38]. The chief seats in the synagogues were the semicircular bench round the ark facing the congregation. See further on 20 [28] Mk 12 [39] Lk 14 [7].

7. Rabbi] (Aramaic) lit. ' my master,' a title of respect applied to a scribe duly ordained in Palestine (cp. our 'Reverend'). Our

Lord, though unordained, received the title by courtesy.

9. Father (Aramaic *abba*) and **masters** (v. 10) are also titles of the scribes, the former being chiefly used as a prefix to the name, e.g. Abba Shaul. Some Christians take these prohibitions literally, and say that it is antichristian to use such titles of respect as 'Reverend,' 'Father in God,' 'Venerable,' and the like, which correspond to the titles of the scribes. But what Jesus condemned was not the titles themselves, so much as the presumptuous claims which the titles implied. The rabbis really did put themselves in the place of God, and almost on an equality with Him. Their traditions were more binding than the Law, and were regarded as in a sense binding upon God. One rabbi went the length of being buried in white garments to show that he was worthy to appear before his Maker. Another is said to have been summoned to heaven by God to settle a point of the law of ceremonial purification : see on 15 2.

13-36. The Seven Woes on the Scribes and Pharisees. Jesus, knowing that His death was at hand, and that the conversion of His enemies was hopeless, poured upon them a torrent of righteous indignation, in the manner of the prophets of old. These woes apply equally to the ministers of the gospel, who having the cure of souls, abuse it as did the Scribes.

13. Lk 11 52. **Shut up,** etc.] i.e. prevent the nation from being converted. The **Kingdom of Heaven** is here the Church. **14.** The omission of this v., which has been wrongly inserted from Mk 12 40 Lk 20 47, reduces the eight woes to seven : see on Mk. **15. To make one proselyte**] The Ethiopic version has the interesting reading 'to baptise one proselyte.' As, however, there is no evidence that the Pharisees were particularly anxious to make proselytes to Judaism, it is perhaps more probable that our Lord alludes to their zeal in making proselytes from among the Jews to their own sect. **Child of hell**] lit. 'a son of Gehenna,' i.e. one fit to go thither : see on 5 22. Why **two-fold more ?** Because the vices of teachers appear in an accentuated form, and without any redeeming features, in scholars. Others say, 'Because out of a bad heathen they made a worse Jew.' Others suggest a different translation altogether, viz. 'You make him a more deceitful child of hell than yourselves.'

16-22. On dishonest casuistry. The lax moralists of that time invented ways of evading the obligation of truthfulness, by saying that certain forms of swearing were binding and others not. Thus an oath by the Temple or the altar might be broken without sin, but not an oath by the gold of the Temple, or by the gift on the altar. Such refinements were a direct encouragement to dishonesty and un-

truthfulness, and our Lord denounced them with terrible severity, declaring that a man's word or oath, in whatever words expressed, is absolutely binding. The lesson here taught is truthfulness and honesty in general, as well as the sanctity of oaths. Christ's teaching here is not inconsistent with 5 34, where from a higher ideal standpoint He forbids oaths altogether. **16. It is nothing**] i.e. it is not binding. **The gold of the temple**] J. Lightfoot is probably right in regarding this gold, together with the 'gift on the altar' (v. 18), as dedicated to God, i.e. as *Corban*. An oath in which the word Corban was mentioned was held to be specially binding : see on 15 5, 6. **A debtor**] i.e. bound by his oath.

23. Lk 11 42. J. Lightfoot remarks, 'The tithing of herbs is from the rabbins. This tithing was added by the scribes, and yet approved of by our Saviour, when He saith. "Ye ought not to leave these undone."' The more scrupulous rabbis tithed not only the seeds but the leaves and stalks of these herbs. **Cummin**] used in cooking as a condiment. **The weightier** *matters*] Alluding to but not adopting the rabbinical distinction between the 'heavy' and 'light' precepts of the Law. Among the 'heavy' precepts were the sabbath, circumcision, and the prohibition to profane the Divine Name. Hillel and Shammai differed somewhat in their classification of the 613 precepts which the Law was supposed to contain. **Judgment**] stands here, by a Hebraism, for 'righteousness.' **Faith**] honesty, truthfulness, trustworthiness. **These ought ye**] i.e. Ye ought to have observed judgment, mercy and faith, and also to have tithed mint, anise and cummin.

24. A proverb meaning that the scribes scrupulously avoid insignificant breaches of the Law, while continually breaking its great commandments. **Strain at a gnat**] RV 'strain out a gnat,' viz. out of the wine that you are about to drink. The 'gnat' here is probably a minute animal bred from the fermentation of wine, and regarded by the rabbis as unclean. The camel was also unclean (Lv 11 4).

25. Lk 11 39. **Ye make clean**] see Mk 7 4. **But within they**] (i.e. the cups and dishes) are full of food and drink which has been obtained by extortion and excess.

26. Cleanse first that] i.e. first earn your meat and drink by honest labour, not by extortion, then your cups and dishes will be clean in God's sight.

27. Whited sepulchres] Contact with sepulchres defiled, so that the Jews smeared them with limewash yearly on the 15th day of Adar lest travellers touching them unawares should be made unclean. In Lk 11 44 Jesus compares the Pharisees to unmarked, here to marked, sepulchres, because they defiled those who came into close contact with them.

28. Alexander Jannæus, the Maccabean king of the Jews (c. 104–78 B.C.), gave utterance to a very similar sentiment. On his deathbed he warned his wife to 'take heed of painted men, pretending to be Pharisees, whose works are the works of Zimri, and yet they expect the reward of Phineas.' 'Painted men' are explained to mean 'men whose outward show doth not answer to their nature.'

29–31. Lk 11⁴⁷,⁴⁸. **29. Tombs of the prophets,** etc.] It is natural to suppose that Jesus alluded to some actual building operations then going on, or recently completed near Jerusalem. Herod the Great appears to have built or adorned the tombs and cenotaphs of many Jewish worthies. Calvin well remarks, 'It is customary with hypocrites thus to honour after their death good teachers and holy ministers of God, whom they cannot endure while they are alive. It is a hypocrisy which costs little to profess a warm regard for those who are now silent.' **31. Unto yourselves**] or, 'against yourselves.' The v. is an ironical commentary on the statement of the Pharisees (v. 30), 'If we had been in the days of our fathers,' etc. Jesus retorts, 'You witness to yourselves by your words that you are the literal sons of those who killed the prophets. You witness against yourselves by your actions that you are also their sons spiritually, for you, like them, reject the words of the prophets who are among you, viz. the Baptist and Myself.' **32. Fill ye up then**] i.e. 'Carry out your wickedness to the full, as your fathers did, by putting Me to death. You desire to do so, and I shall not hinder you.' **33.** See 3⁷ 12³⁴.

34–36. Lk 11⁴⁹⁻⁵¹. **34. I send unto you**] The parallel in St. Luke (which see) has 'Therefore also said the wisdom of God, I will send unto them prophets,' etc. The prophets, etc., are the apostles, prophets, teachers, evangelists, and other ministers of the Apostolic Church. Observe that here, as in 13⁵², our Lord speaks of Christian ministers under Jewish titles as 'wise men' (i.e. **rabbis**) and **scribes.**

35. That upon you] 'The scribes and Pharisees are regarded as the representatives of the people, for whom, as their leaders, they are held responsible' (Meyer). **The righteous blood**] i.e. the penalty for shedding it.

Zacharias son of Barachias] Jesus probably said 'Zachariah,' as in St. Luke, without mentioning the father's name, but the evangelist or one of the earliest copyists, who thought it necessary to distinguish among the twenty-nine Zachariahs of the OT., and understood the canonical prophet to be meant, added the words 'son of Barachias.' There can be no real doubt that the person meant is Zechariah, son of Jehoiada (see 2 Ch 24²¹), concerning whom there was a Jewish tradition, that his

blood could not be removed by washing, but remained bubbling on the ground where it had been shed. In the Jewish arrangement of the books of the sacred Canon, Chronicles stands last, so that Jesus chose His examples from the first and last books of the Jewish Bible.

37–39. Pathetic lament over Jerusalem (Lk 13³⁴,³⁵). St. Luke places these words in another, and much less suitable connexion. As they occur in St. Matthew they form a worthy close to our Lord's ministry in Jerusalem.

37. How often] 'It is fair to assume that Christ's exclamation over Jerusalem presupposes that the capital had repeatedly been the scene of His ministrations, which coincides with the visits on festival occasions recorded by John : cp. Ac 10³⁹' (Meyer). **Under her wings**] see 2 Esdras 1³⁰. **38. Your house**] i.e. either, (1) the city itself, (2) the Temple, or, (3) the Jewish dispensation. **39. Till ye shall say, Blessed is He,** etc.] i.e. either, (1) till the Second Advent, when they will see Christ as judge, and will unwillingly say 'Blessed is He that cometh,' or, (2) till the conversion of Israel (see Ro 11), when true believers will see Christ by faith and willingly say, 'Blessed is He that cometh,' etc.

CHAPTER 24
The Destruction of Jerusalem and the End of the World foretold

1. Jesus went out] RV 'Jesus went out from the temple, and was going on his way, and his disciples,' etc.

The buildings] The magnificent buildings, a mass of marble and gold, were not yet finished (see Jn 2²⁰). The rabbis said, 'He who has not seen the temple of Herod, has never seen a beautiful building. The sanctuary was made of green and white marble... Herod intended to have the building covered with gold, but the rabbis dissuaded him, saying that it was sufficiently beautiful as it was, for it appeared like the waves of the sea.' Josephus says, 'The front of the temple was covered all over with plates of gold of great weight, and at the first rising of the sun reflected back a fiery splendour, etc... The temple appeared to strangers, when they were at a distance, like a mountain covered with snow, for those parts of it which were not gilt were exceedingly white. Of its stones some were 45 cubits in length, 5 in height, and 6 in breadth.' (A cubit = 18 in.)

2. One stone] Josephus, an eyewitness, says 'Cæsar (i.e. Titus) now gave orders to demolish the whole city and temple, except the highest towers and the west wall. All the rest was so thoroughly laid even with the ground by those that dug it up to the foundation, that there was left nothing to make those who came thither believe that it had ever been inhabited.'

The Talmud says, ' On the ninth day of Ab (July-Aug.) the city of Jerusalem was ploughed up.'

3–51. Great prophecy of the destruction of Jerusalem, and the end of the world (Mk 13³ Lk 21⁷). Many of the most serious difficulties of this great discourse disappear when it is realised that our Lord referred in it not to one event but to two, and that the first was typical of the second. This is especially clear in St. Matthew's Gospel. The disciples ask Jesus (v. 3) for information on two subjects : (1) the date of the approaching destruction of the Temple, (2) the sign that will precede His second coming at the end of the world. That these two events were clearly distinguished in the mind of Christ Himself, and, therefore, in this discourse as He delivered it, admits of demonstration. Lk 21²⁴ especially, which speaks of 'the times of the Gentiles,' during which Jerusalem shall be trodden down by the heathen, and the Jews dispersed into all lands ' till the times of the Gentiles be fulfilled,' places an indefinite interval between the fall of Jerusalem and the end of the world. Similarly in St. Matthew and St. Mark, Jesus declares that He is ignorant of, or is not allowed to reveal, the date of the end of the world (24³⁶ Mk 13³²), but expressly says that the fall of Jerusalem will take place within the lifetime of the Apostles (10²³). Again the statement that the end will not come till the gospel has been preached to all nations (24¹⁴) postpones the end indefinitely : cp. also 22¹⁻¹⁴. The reasons why the two events are not equally distinguished in the discourse as we have it, are mainly four : (1) Our Lord's words, as in other cases, are condensed. We have not a full report of the speech, but its most striking passages, which being isolated from their context, are naturally somewhat difficult to interpret. (2) At the time when the speech was committed to writing, the apostles believed that Christ's second coming would occur in their lifetime, and that the fall of Jerusalem and the Last Judgment would be coincident : see on 1 Th 4¹⁵. This belief would affect, if not the faithfulness of their report, at any rate the arrangement of it. It would cause the evangelists to group together, as if referring to the same event, sayings which really referred to events widely sundered in time. (3) The discourse perhaps contains some sayings not spoken at this time, but inserted here because believed to refer to the same events. The hypothesis of extensive additions cannot indeed be admitted. Nevertheless, it is quite in the manner of the evangelists, and especially of St. Matthew, to group together in a single discourse utterances delivered at different times. (4) Our Lord for devotional reasons desired His disciples always to regard His coming as

if it were near. The time of it was purposely not revealed, in order that Christians might live in a state of continual watchfulness, looking for their Lord's coming. Such continual exhortations to watchfulness were easily understood to imply that the Second Coming was near.

Other views of the scope of the discourse are, (1) that it refers entirely to the destruction of Jerusalem ; (2) or entirely to the Last Judgment ; (3) or that ' the coming ' of Christ is a continuous process lasting from the fall of Jerusalem to the Second Advent ; (4) or that Christ's ' coming ' represents the extension of His kingdom which followed the Resurrection, or Pentecost, or the fall of Jerusalem ; (5) or that His coming refers to the coming of the Comforter, in whom Christ Himself returns to earth.

Some suppose (but without sufficient warrant) that the sections Mk 13 ⁷⁻⁹ᵃ, ¹⁴⁻²⁰, ²⁴,²⁷, ³⁰⁻³¹, were not spoken by Christ, but formed part of a short Christian apocalypse composed shortly before the fall of Jerusalem.

3. Olives] A magnificent view of the site of the Temple is obtained from this hill. **The disciples**] viz. Peter, James, John, Andrew (Mk). **These things**] i.e. the overthrow of the Temple. **The end of the world**] i.e. the Last Judgment. But those who refer the discourse entirely to the destruction of Jerusalem, understand by it the end of the Jewish dispensation.

4–14. Ebrard regards this section as referring to the last judgment, but in the opinion of most it refers to the fall of Jerusalem, with the possible exception of verse 14, q.v.

5. I am Christ] RV ' I am the Christ,' i.e. the Messiah. The false Messiahs who appeared before the fall of Jerusalem were Simon Magus, Menander, Dositheus, and perhaps Theudas, who raised a rebellion in 45 or 46 A.D.

6. Wars, etc.] There were three threats of war against the Jews by Caligula, Claudius, and Nero, as to the first of which Josephus remarks that the death of Caligula ' happened most happily for our nation in particular, which would have almost utterly perished, if he had not been suddenly slain.' There was also a war between Bardanes king of Parthia and Izates king of Adiabene, and between the same Izates and Bardanes' successor, Vologases. War was also continually threatened between Rome and Parthia. **The end**] according to the ordinary view is the end of the troubles, i.e. the fall of Jerusalem, not the end of the world.

7. Nation shall rise] i.e. there will be massacres and civil tumults. One fearful massacre happened at Seleucia on the Tigris, where dwelt three hostile nations, Greeks, Syrians, and Jews. The Greeks and Syrians joined together against their common enemies the Jews, and slew about 50,000 of them. Similarly at Cæsarea, in one hour's time about 20,000 Jews were massacred. **Famines**] Ac 11 28. The whole reign of Claudius (41–54 A.D.) was a time of great scarcity. Josephus mentions a famine in Palestine about 46 A.D. in which many died of starvation.

Pestilences] omitted by R.V. **Earthquakes**] There was an unexampled number at this period devastating the provinces of Asia, Achaia, Syria, Macedonia, Campania, etc. Josephus mentions one in Palestine accompanied by 'amazing concussions and bellowings of the earth—a manifest indication that some destruction was coming upon men.'

8. Beginning of sorrows] RV 'of travail.' Jewish writers speak frequently of the so-called 'sorrows of the Messiah,' which are to last nine months, and to be the birth-pangs of the coming age. They would be a period of internal corruption, and outward distress, famine, and war, of which Palestine was to be the scene, and Israel the chief sufferers. Some of these sorrows would fall upon the Messiah Himself (Edersheim).

9, 10. See on 10 17-23.

11. False prophets] see on v. 5. Josephus speaks of 'a body of wicked men, who deceived and deluded the people under pretence of divine inspiration, who prevailed with the multitude to act like madmen, and went before them into the wilderness, pretending that God would there show them the signals of victory': see also 2 Pet 2 1 1 Jn 2 18 4 1. **12.** Cp. Heb 10 25 Rev 2 4. **13. Shall endure**] i.e. shall resist the enticements of false prophets, stand firm in persecution, and not suffer his love of Christ to grow cold. **Unto the end**] viz. of the tribulation ; but it may mean unto the uttermost, or, unto death. **Shall be saved**] i.e. either literally by flight to Pella (v. 16), or, more probably, saved spiritually.

14. Since the gospel had not been preached to the whole world, or even to the whole Roman world by 70 A.D., as indeed Christ Himself indicated (10 23), many suppose that ' the end' here is the last judgment. Those who understand it to refer to the fall of Jerusalem, point out that by that time the gospel had been preached not only in the East, but at Rome, and perhaps in Spain and Gaul (Ro 15 24, 28).

15-28. The flight of the Christians before the fall of Jerusalem.

15. The abomination of desolation] i.e. the abomination which makes the Temple desolate, by causing God to forsake it (Dan 9 27). Some definite event is meant, because it is the signal of instant flight (vv. 16-20). It is to happen before the fall of Jerusalem, and in ·the holy place,' i.e. in that part of the Temple, which only the priests could enter. The only

event which answers this description is the capture of the Temple by the Zealots, or Assassins, 66 or 67 A.D., and the abominations which then ensued. The Zealots turned the Temple into a camp, defiled it with blood, made a creature of their own high priest, and finally caused the daily sacrifices to cease.

St. Luke's version, ' when ye see Jerusalem encompassed by armies,' is not an interpretation of 'the abomination of desolation,' but another sign outside Jerusalem, which took place at the same time as the desolation within. Jerusalem was encompassed with armies, (1) in 66 A.D. by the troops of Cestius Gallus ; (2) in 68 A.D. by those of Vespasian ; (3) in 70 A.D. by those of Titus. The first investment is St. Luke's signal for flight. Soon after this the Zealots seized the Temple and the city, guarded the gates, and prevented all escape. The prophecy in Daniel originally referred to the profanation of the Temple by Antiochus Epiphanes, 169–168 B.C., but its application to the events of 66–70 A.D. is very suitable.

Other views of the nature of the ' abomination of desolation ' worthy of notice are that it is, (1) the Roman eagles, or standards ; (2) a statue of Titus erected on the site of the Temple ; (3) the appearance of Antichrist at the end of the world : cp. 2 Th 2 4.

Whoso readeth, let him understand] not 'let him that readeth the prophet Daniel understand,' for the reference to Daniel is absent from St. Mark (see RV), but ' let him that readeth this prophecy of Christ's understand.' The occurrence in both evangelists is a proof that the common authority used by St. Matthew and St. Mark was not oral tradition, but a written document.

16. Flee into the mountains] Eusebius says, ' But the members of the Church in Jerusalem, having been commanded before the war in accordance with a certain oracle given by revelation to the men of repute there, to depart from Jerusalem, and to inhabit a certain city of Peræa called Pella, all the believers in Christ in Jerusalem went thither, and when now the saints had abandoned both the royal metropolis itself and the whole land of Judæa, the vengeance of God finally overtook the lawless persecutors of Christ and His Apostles.'

17. Not come down] but escape by the outside staircase, or over the roofs of the houses : see on 9 2.

20. On the sabbath day (peculiar to St Matthew, the Jewish evangelist). Alford says, ' That they were not said as any sanction of observance of the Jewish sabbath is most certain ; but merely as referring to positive impediments which might meet them on that day, the shutting of the gates of cities, etc., and their own scruples about travelling further than the ordinary sabbath day's journey (about a mile English) ; for the Jewish Christians adhered to the Law till the destruction of Jerusalem' (see Intro. § 6).

21. See Dan 12 1. Josephus says, 'The multitude of those that perished exceeded all the destructions that either men or God ever brought upon the world.' 'The number of those that perished during the whole siege was 1,100,000.' **22. Those days**] i.e. of the siege of Jerusalem, which occupied less than five months. **No flesh**] i.e. no inhabitants of the theatre of war, Palestine. **Be saved**] i.e. be left alive. **The elect**] i.e. the Christians.

23–26. Chrysostom and others, translating **then** 'afterwards' (which it may mean), refer these vv. to the Last Judgment, but it is better to suppose that the fall of Jerusalem is still spoken of. **24. False Christs, and false prophets**] see on vv. 5, 11. **Signs and wonders**] J. Lightfoot illustrates from the Talmud the magical practices of the Jews. 'The senior who is chosen into the council, ought to be skilled in the arts of astrologers, jugglers, diviners, sorcerers,' etc. 'The chamber of Happarva (in the Temple) was built by a certain magician by art magic.' 'Rabbi Joshua outdoes a magician in magic and drowns him in the sea.' **26.** (Lk 17 23.) **If they**] i.e. they who are deluded by false Messiahs. **Behold, he**] viz. the Messiah. **In the desert**] Some of the false prophets did actually lead out their dupes to the desert. **In the secret** (RV 'inner ') **chambers**] a poetical expression for ' in hiding.'

27, 28. Whether these vv. describe Christ's coming to destroy Jerusalem, or His second coming to judge the world, or both, is doubtful. The context suggests that the destruction of Jerusalem is meant, but it is just the context which is doubtful, for St. Mark omits both vv., and St. Luke gives them in quite a different connexion. As originally spoken, they probably referred to Christ's second coming. **27.** (Lk 17 24.) The second advent of the Son of man will be confined to no one locality, but will be manifested instantaneously to the whole universe. But if the reference is to the destruction of Jerusalem, this v. describes the conspicuous and world-renowned nature of the event.

28. A parable or proverb (Lk 17 37). Just as, wherever a carcase may happen to be, eagles or vultures will invariably be found ; so at Christ's second coming, wherever a man dead in trespasses and sins is found, there also will Christ be revealed as an avenging judge. Thus ' the carcase ' represents the wicked, and ' the eagles,' Christ and His avenging angels of judgment. Those who suppose the fall of Jerusalem to be meant, understand by ' the carcase,' the Jews, and by ' the eagles,' the Roman armies.

29–42. Most commentators refer these vv. (in the main) to the Second Advent, though some think that the fall of Jerusalem is still meant.

29. Immediately] RV 'But immediately.' This discourse, in the form in which it has come down to us, seems to place the Second Advent immediately after the fall of Jerusalem. Solutions of the difficulty : (1) Plumptre considers ' the boldest answer as the truest and most reverential,' and finds the explanation in Christ's ignorance of ' that day and hour' (Mk 13 32). But although Christ was ignorant, as man, of the *exact* day and hour of His Second Advent, He at least knew that it was separated from the fall of Jerusalem by an immense interval (see intro. to this discourse) Even if we assume, with Plumptre, His complete ignorance of the date, we are no nearer a solution ; for if He did not know the date, He would not attempt to fix it. (2) Stier maintains the theory of ' prophetic perspective.' As men gazing from a distance on two distant mountain peaks, one behind the other, see them in close proximity, so Christ saw the two events ' in close proximity, overlooking the wide intervening space.' A legitimate hypothesis, but inconsistent with the fact that Christ was fully aware of the ' wide intervening space.' (3) That ' immediately ' is to be interpreted with prophetic latitude, and may mean after an interval of thousands of years, as when our Lord says, ' And behold I come quickly ' (Rev 22 20 : see 2 Pet 3 8, 9). This is the best explanation of the passage *as it stands*. (4) That ' immediately after' means immediately after the premonitory signs of Christ's second coming, which have been omitted in the evangelists' report of the speech, which is doubtless condensed. **The sun, etc.**] prophetic imagery for the fall of earthly empires, thrones, and powers, and human pride (Isa 13 10).

30. The sign of the Son of man] As Christ does not explain this sign, it is useless to guess what it will be. In tradition it is the Cross. ' Then shall appear the Cross in the sky, shining more brightly than the sun, to convict the Jews ' (Theophylact). This interpretation is already found in the ' Didache.'

Mourn] lamenting their unbelief and disobedience : cp. Zech 12 12 Dan 7 13 Rev 1 7.

31. Usually explained of the gathering of believers into heaven at the last day. Those who think that the fall of Jerusalem is meant, explain it of the gathering of the heathen into the Church from all quarters of the world after that event, or of the flight of the Christians from all quarters of Palestine to Pella.

34. This generation] i.e. Jerusalem will be destroyed within the lifetime of men now living. This literal meaning is not to be evaded, as, for example, by regarding ' this generation' as the human race, or the Jewish nation, or the Christian Church, or the universe.

36. But of that day] i.e. the Day of Judgment. **Not the angels of heaven**] RV adds, 'neither the Son,' which, however, RM omits: see on Mk 13 32.

40, 41. The general idea is that, though to human eyes the righteous and the wicked will appear exactly the same, the angels in the judgment will be able to distinguish.

40. One shall be taken] viz. into glory, by the angels. **The other left**] viz. for reprobation, or punishment. But if the fall of Jerusalem is meant, the 'taking' means the successful flight from Judæa and Jerusalem; the being 'left' means failure to flee.

43-51. An exhortation to faithfulness and watchfulness addressed specially to the Apostles and other chief ministers of the Church (Lk 12 39-46). It appropriately closes the discourse, but whether it really belongs here may be doubted. St. Luke introduces it in a quite different connexion.

43. The goodman (RV 'master') **of the house**] i.e. in the application of the parable, the Apostles, and their successors in posts of authority in the Church. **The thief**] i.e. on account of the suddenness and unexpectedness of His coming, our Lord : see 1 Th 5 2 Rev 16 15. Although the second coming is chiefly in view, it must be remembered that Christ comes in judgment to the individual soul at death.

Broken up] RV 'broken through' : see 6 19.

45. A faithful and wise servant (RM 'bondservant')] though referring primarily to the Apostles and ministers of the Church, may be extended to all who have the care of the souls of others, or exercise spiritual influence over others (the 'household'). **46. When he cometh**] viz. at the Second Advent, or at the servant's death. **47. Make him ruler**] RV 'set him over all that he hath,' i.e. make him great in the future Kingdom of Heaven, and sharer of His own throne. Our Lord implies that in heaven there will be various degrees of authority : cp. Lk 19 11-27. **49. To smite**] a metaphor for the abuse of authority : cp. Ac 20 29 1 Pet 5 3.

51. Cut him asunder] RM 'severely scourge him,' i.e. consign him to the place of final punishment.

CHAPTER 25

The Ten Virgins. The Talents. The Sheep and the Goats

The whole of this c., which is entirely concerned with the Second Advent, and contains some of the most striking of all Christ's sayings, is peculiar to St. Matthew.

1-13. Parable of the Ten Virgins. Professing Christians, who alone are addressed here, are warned of the absolute need of sufficient oil, i.e. of sufficient depth and

reality in the spiritual life, if they are to be admitted into Christ's kingdom hereafter Unless the life of the soul is continually nourished by secret prayer, devout meditation upon God's Word, and reverent use of the Sacraments, there is extreme danger that the lamp of piety will flicker out, that even the outward show of conformity to Christ's Law will cease to be, and that death or the Second Advent will find the soul not ready.

1. Then] i.e. in the period immediately before the Second Advent. **The kingdom of heaven**] i.e. the Church on earth. **Unto ten virgins**] The ten virgins are not simply Christians, but good Christians ; not all the baptised, but those who make some attempt to act up to their Christian profession. The number ten represents the whole number of those who are apparently good Christians. It is chosen because among the Jews it was a complete number. Ten Jews constituted a congregation. **Which took their lamps**] RM 'torches,' i.e. their Christian profession. The 'lamps' are all that is outward in the life of professing Christians, as the oil is all that is inward. **To meet the bridegroom**] All Christian life is a going out to meet the bridegroom, i.e. a preparation for the second coming of Christ.

In the parable the wedding is supposed to take place at night. The bridegroom, accompanied by his friends, goes in procession to the bride's house to fetch her home to his. On the return journey the virgins, the friends of the bride, are supposed to join the procession, and to enter with her into the bridegroom's house, where, in accordance with Jewish custom, the wedding feast was held. The customs of the Jews with regard to weddings differed little from those of the Greeks and Romans, or of modern Oriental nations, who invariably celebrate weddings at night. The marriage of Christ with His Church is represented in the parable as taking place in the world to come, the betrothal having taken place in this world.

2. And five of them were wise and five were foolish] The foolish virgins are not identical with the wicked, or the hypocrites. There is nothing insincere about them, they are only foolish and shallow. They have some oil, that is, some genuine religion, but not enough. They are like those in the parable of the sower who have no depth of earth. They endure for a time, but cannot carry through what they have begun. Their stock of perseverance and patience is soon exhausted, and their lamps go out.

3. Took no oil with them] Oil is the symbol of the Holy Spirit, and of inward sanctification (Ac 10 38 Heb 1 9 1 Jn 2 20,27). Here it stands for all that is earnest and sincere in the Christian life : secret prayer, faith, humility, charity, and good works.

4. Oil in their vessels] The foolish virgins took some oil, but not enough. The wise virgins took an extra supply, in case the bridegroom delayed his coming.

5. Tarried] A hint (but it is no more) that Christ would not come as soon as the first Christians expected. **Slumbered and slept**] If a definite meaning is to be given to this detail it represents the repose of faith, the serene confidence in God, which those who have found Christ, and have ordered their lives after His word, have a right to feel. The confidence of the foolish virgins, however, was misplaced.

6. At midnight] i.e. the time of the Second Advent and the resurrection of the dead.

8. Are gone out] RV 'are going out.'

9. *Not so; lest*] RV 'Peradventure there will not be enough.' Jerome says: 'This answer they make not from avarice, but from fear. For each individual soul will receive the reward for his own deeds, nor in the day of judgment can the virtues of one make amends for the vices of another.' **To them that sell**] Clearly the bridegroom, though on the point of coming, had not yet come. If this detail is to be pressed, 'they that sell' are the teachers and ministers of the Church (Origen). **10. And the door was shut**] viz. the door of heaven.

12. I know you not] i.e. because in the true sense you have never known Me : cp. Jn 10¹⁴.

14–30. Parable of the Talents (distinct from, though similar to, that of the Pounds, Lk 19¹¹⁻²⁷, q.v.). The parable is intended for all Christians, warning even those of the meanest ability to use to the best advantage the talents with which God has entrusted them, if they would share in the future kingdom of Christ. It suitably follows and supplements the parable of the virgins ; for whereas that represented Christ's servants as *waiting* for Him, this represents them as *working* for Him ; and whereas that laid stress on their inward spiritual life, this lays stress on the outward activities in which the spiritual life shows itself. It differs from the parable of the pounds in being addressed to the disciples alone, in its simpler structure, and in its not inculcating the doctrine of diversities of rewards in the world to come. 'This parable shines clearest in the light of the circumstances. Jesus and His disciples are still on Olivet overlooking Jerusalem and the temple in all their glory. Jesus had foretold their destruction. What was the cause of that ruin ? Because the nation had buried the talent God had entrusted to them, instead of using it for Him.'

14. A man] i.e. Jesus Christ. **Travelling into a far country**] viz. when He ascended into heaven. An ancient writer beautifully says : 'He calls His going to the Father a journey

into a far country out of love to the saints whom He left on the earth, for He was more truly in a far country when He was on earth. Theophylact says : 'He is said to go into a far country, because He is long-suffering, and does not immediately demand the fruit of men's works, but waits.' **His own servants**] lit. 'slaves.' In ancient times slaves practised trades and professions, kept shops, carried on businesses, paying the whole, or a certain percentage, of their profits to their masters.

15. Talents] see on 18²⁴. 'It seems better to explain the five (talents) more extensively of all the gifts of God, whether called those of nature, or of grace, of condition, or opportunities, or sacraments. One receives five talents and another two ; one has a deeper insight into God's word, or has constitutionally a more kind or liberal disposition than another, or is trained up with more abundant means of grace, and with opportunities of turning the same to good account, or with a higher station in God's Church than another' (Isaac Williams).

According to his several ability] God gives men spiritual gifts according to their natural capacities ; e.g. a man with a natural gift of eloquence becomes by God's grace a good preacher ; a man of natural piety, a spiritual guide ; a wealthy man, a philanthropist ; a profound philosopher, a theologian ; a man of high social position, a powerful influence by virtue of his example, etc.

16. Traded] Christians are said to trade with their talents, when they employ them to the profit of their own souls and the benefit of others. **Other five talents**] The talents made in trade are the good which Christians do to themselves and others by the due use of the talents with which God has entrusted them. The talents gained by the apostles were human souls converted by them. **18. Digged in the earth**] The man who hides his talent, is he who neither employs his abilities for his own spiritual advantage, nor for that of others.

19. After a long time] Another hint that the Advent may be delayed. **Reckoneth with them**] viz. at the Judgment.

21. Well done] In this parable the servants having been equally faithful and diligent, receive, despite the difference of the talents entrusted to them, an equal reward. It is different in the parable of the pounds, where the servants, having shown different degrees of diligence, receive different rewards. The lesson of both parables is that not ability but faithful diligence is rewarded. **Over many things**] 'Here again, as in 24⁴⁷, we have a glimpse given us into the future that lies behind the veil. We see that the reward of faithful work lies, not in rest only, but in enlarged activity. The world to come is thus connected by a law of continuity with that in which we live ; and those who have so used their " talents " as to turn many to righteousness, may find new spheres of action, beyond all our dreams, in that world in which the ties of brotherhood that have been formed on earth, are not extinguished, but, so we may reverently believe, multiplied and strengthened ' (Plumptre). **The joy**] viz. of eternal blessedness (v. 34).

24. The one talent] ' Very instructive is the fact that it is the recipient of the one talent who proves the defaulter here. Henceforward none may excuse his sloth on a plea like this. So little is committed to my charge that it cannot matter how I administer that little. It is so little I can do for God, what signifies that little whether it be done or left undone ? ' (Trench). **I knew thee that thou art an hard man**] ' The churl accounted his lord churlish, esteeming him such a one as himself. He did not believe in his lord's forgiving love, and in his gracious acceptance of that work with all its shortcomings, which was done for him out of a true heart, and with a sincere desire to please him ' (Trench).

27. To the exchangers] RV ' bankers.' ' We cannot regard these words as a perfectly idle sentence, for they furnish an appropriate thought. These timid natures who are not adapted for independent labour on behalf of the kingdom of God, are now advised at least to associate themselves with persons of greater strength, under whose guidance they may apply their gifts to the service of the Church ' (Olshausen). **With usury**] i.e. ' with interest.'

29. For unto every one] see 13 12. It is a law of the natural as well as of the spiritual world, that the disuse of a faculty finally leads to its complete loss, whereas the due use of it leads to its development and increase.

30. Weeping] RV ' the weeping.' The penalty is not merely exclusion, as in the case of the foolish virgins, but punishment, in addition.

31–46. The last judgment described (peculiar to St. Matthew). Christ here speaks of the judgment of Christians alone, because that was the question which most concerned the Apostles and their future converts. That the persons to be judged are described in v. 32 as ' all the nations,' is in no way inconsistent with this. Jesus foresaw, and frequently prophesied, that His religion would become universal (8 11, etc.), and therefore appropriately described the Christians who at the Last Day will rise to be judged, as all the nations of the earth. A common interpretation, however, is that the judgment of all mankind is meant. Against this is to be set not so much the title ' Lord,' which even His enemies will then give to Christ, as the statement that all the persons

judged had regarded Christ as their Master during their lifetime, and had recognised the duty of serving Him.

32. All the nations] see above.

Sheep . . goats (or, ' kids ')] The sheep are the righteous ; the goats, from their comparative worthlessness, the wicked.

33. His right hand . . the left] These expressions have the same significance in most languages. In Plato's ' Republic ' Er the Pamphylian is allowed to see the judgment after death executed by the judges of the underworld. The judges sit between two gaps, one leading to heaven, the other to hell. ' After passing sentence, the judges commanded the just to take the road to the right upwards through the heaven, and fastened in front of them some symbol of the judgment which had been given ; while the unjust were ordered to take the road downward to the left, and also carried behind them evidence of all their evil deeds.' Similarly the rabbis said, ' Those on the right hand are the just, who study the Law, which is at the right hand of God (Dt 33 2) ; those on the left are the wicked, who study riches (Prov 3 16).' ' In those on the right hand righteousness, in those on the left hand guilt, preponderates.'

34. The King] i.e. Christ Himself, appearing in the glory of His kingdom : cp. Rev 19 16.

Inherit] i.e. receive by right of sonship.

35. For I was an hungered, and ye gave me meat] Faith in Christ being presumed (for the persons judged are professing Christians), the Judgment proceeds according to works, by which a living is distinguished from a dead faith (Jas 2 14-26). The absolute Lordship of Christ over the human race is expressed in a very simple yet most emphatic way when it is said that every good deed done to a fellow-creature is a good deed done to Christ, and that at the Last Day all men will be judged according to their attitude to Him.

The rabbis also have some great sayings on charity that deserve to be remembered. ' Whoever exercises hospitality willingly, to him belongs Paradise.' ' To entertain a traveller is a greater thing than to receive a manifestation of the Divine Majesty.' ' Whoever gives a crust to a just person, is as if he had observed the five books of the Law.' ' Whoever visits the sick, shall be free from the judgment of Gehenna.' ' Imitate the deeds of God. God clothes the naked (Gn 3 21) ; do thou also clothe the naked. God visits the sick (Gn 18 1), do thou also visit the sick. He consoles mourners (Gn 25 11), do thou also console mourners.'

41. Ye cursed] but not of My Father. Ye are the authors of your own ruin. **Prepared**] not for men, but for **the devil and his angels**.

46. Everlasting] RV 'eternal,' as also in v. 41. 'Woe to all sinners, and especially to those who have no pity. It is the man who had no pity who is banished to the fire, for instead of love he put in his heart hatred. This is the sum of all vices, and its chief manifestation is inhumanity' (Euthymius).

In the view of the present writer, the eternity of future punishment, as of future reward, is a necessary deduction from the doctrine of the immortality of the soul, and is expressly affirmed in this passage. The nature of it seems by no means so certain. Probably an essential part of it will be the loss of free-will, the abuse of this faculty being punished by its loss. Future punishment will in any case exhibit God's mercy and benevolence, as well as His justice.

CHAPTER 26

THE BETRAYAL. THE LAST SUPPER. AR-
REST OF JESUS, AND TRIAL BEFORE THE
HIGH PRIEST

1-5. A Council is held against Jesus (Mk 14¹ Lk 22¹: cp. Jn 13¹).

2. After two days] This fixes the date as Tuesday, if the Passover was on Thursday night ; or Wednesday, if, as is more probable, it was on Friday night. **Is betrayed]** This clear prediction is peculiar to St. Matthew.

3. And the scribes] RV omits. **The palace]** RV 'the court,' i.e. the central quadrangle, the house being built round a square plot of ground, like a college. From the place of meeting it may be inferred, but not with certainty, that this was not a formal meeting of the Sanhedrin. **Caiaphas]** in full, Joseph Caiaphas, son-in-law to Annas, was appointed high priest by the Roman procurator Vale-rius Gratus (Pilate's predecessor), and there-fore before 26 A.D. He was deposed by Vitellius 37 A.D. **5. Not on the feast** *day]* RV 'Not during the feast.' This strongly favours the view that the Jewish Passover that year took place on Friday night. If the Passover took place on Thursday night, as many maintain, Jesus was crucified on the feast day itself, which extended from the Passover evening till sunset the next day.

6-13. Jesus is anointed in the House of Simon the Leper (Mk 14³ Jn 12¹: see further on Jn). This incident seems in St. Matthew and St. Mark to take place on Tuesday or Wednesday evening, but the true chronology is probably given by St. John, who places it six days before the Passover. It is inserted here probably from the light it throws upon the character of Judas (see St. John's narra-tive), whose treachery immediately follows in the synoptists. For a similar, but quite dis-tinct incident, see Lk 7³⁶.

Some authorities (but without good reason) distinguish between this anointing and that of Jn 12¹, making altogether three anointings.

6. Simon the leper] His leprosy must have been healed, or he could not have entertained guests. The incurable character of leprosy renders it a sure conjecture that he owed his healing to Jesus. It is probably no more than a coincidence, yet it is a very singular one, that in the very similar incident in Lk 7³⁶, the name of the host is also Simon. This Simon was probably a near relation of the family of Lazarus.

7. A woman] i.e. Mary, sister of Lazarus (Jn). A quite untrustworthy but widely-spread tradition identifies her with the 'sinner' of Lk 7³⁷, who is (also without any sufficient reason) often identified with Mary Magdalene.

Alabaster box .. poured it on his head] see on Lk 7³⁷, ³⁸. **His head]** St. John says 'his feet.' Anointing was customary both in Jew-ish and Gentile feasts. The Talmud says, 'The school of Shammai saith, He holds sweet oil in his right hand and a cup of wine in his left. He says grace first over the oil, and then over the wine. He blesseth the sweet oil and anoints the head of him that serves.' Here, however, it is one who sits at meat who is anointed.

8. His disciples] St. John mentions espe-cially Judas. **9. For much]** for 300 denarii (Mk, Jn). **11. Ye have the poor]** cp. Dt 15¹¹ Mk 14⁷. **12. My burial]** Another prediction of His death, followed in the next v. by a re-markable prophecy of the universal extension of His religion.

14-16. Judas betrays Jesus (Mk 14¹⁰ Lk 22³). The exact date cannot be fixed. It may have been as early as Sunday night, or Mon-day. V. 16 implies a considerable interval between the betrayal and the arrest. The paltry sum for which Jesus was betrayed (the price of a slave, Ex 21³²) has raised the ques-tion whether avarice was really the main mo-tive of Judas. There have even been attempts to place his conduct in a favourable light, as if his desire was to bring about a rising of the people at the time of the feast, and so to con-strain 'the dilatory Messiah to establish His kingdom by means of popular violence' (Paulus), or by the exercise of His super-natural power. This is possible, but not prob-able. Judas was thoroughly alienated from Jesus. He found his Master's ideals diverging more and more widely from his own. Instead of an earthly kingdom, in which Judas hoped to hold a lucrative position, Christ seemed to be aiming at an impracticable ideal, which might, perhaps, be very beautiful, but which certainly did not seem to be a practical way of making money. He had already embezzled money from the common purse, and he could not be ignorant that he was suspected and disliked by his colleagues, and that his true character had long been discerned by his Master. His former love and trust were now turned to hatred and contempt, and in a frenzy of disappointed ambition he betrayed Jesus. Yet, when the fatal deed was done, there came a revulsion of feeling, and he would fain have undone it.

15. They covenanted with him] RV 'they weighed unto him,' in accordance with ancient custom (Gn 23 16), but money was probably at this period always coin, not bullion.

17–30. The Last Supper (Mk 14 12 Lk 22 7 Jn 13 1). For the order of events see on Jn, and intro. to c. 21. The question whether the Last Supper was the Jewish Passover or not, is discussed in a note on Jn 18 28, where it is argued that Jesus, knowing that He would be crucified on Friday, celebrated the Passover on Thursday evening, a day before the legal time. That the Jewish Passover did not take place till Friday evening (after the crucifixion) is abundantly plain from the Fourth Gospel (see especially Jn 18 28), and even in the Synoptic Gospels, which at first sight give an opposite impression, there are sufficiently clear indications that this was the case. The chief are, (1) The purpose of the priests not to take and execute Jesus during the festival, lest a tumult should arise (26 5 RV). (2) It was contrary to custom to hold trials and execute criminals on the first and holiest day of the feast, which was kept as a sabbath. (3) The feast day would not be called simply 'Preparation,' i.e. Friday. (4) The officers and the disciples would not have carried arms on the feast day. (5) Joseph of Arimathea would not have bought a linen cloth, or the women have prepared spices on that day (Mk 15 46 Lk 23 56).

17. The first *day* **of .. unleavened bread**] As, according to St. Mark and St. Luke, this was the day on which the Passover lambs were slaughtered, it must mean the day before the Passover (Jewish reckoning), i.e. from sunset on Thursday to sunset on Friday. The last supper was held on Thursday evening, and the lambs were killed at 3 P.M. on Friday, but that would be on the same day, according to Jewish ideas.

In strict usage 'the first day of unleavened bread' meant the first day of the Passover festival, which began with the paschal supper. But it is possible that the day before this, when the paschal lambs were sacrificed, and all leaven was expelled from the houses, was *popularly* spoken of as 'the first day of unleavened bread.'

The disciples came to Jesus] at or after sunset on Thursday, and within an hour or two the necessary preparations for the supper were complete. **Where wilt thou that we prepare**] 'For they might anywhere ; since the houses

at Jerusalem were not to be hired, but during the time of the feast, they were of common right' (J. Lightfoot). The rabbis say, 'It is a tradition that houses were not let for hire at Jerusalem, because they were not privately owned, nor were beds, but the householder received from his guests as a recompense, the skins of the animals sacrificed.' **To eat the Passover**] The Last Supper is here called 'the Passover,' because in many respects it resembled it. It is not, however, certain that there was a lamb. Jesus Himself was the Lamb, and, as He intended to supersede the type by the reality, it was not absolutely necessary for the type to be present.

The paschal lamb was slain in the court of the Temple on the afternoon of the 14th Nisan, and was eaten the same evening after sunset, when the 15th Nisan had already begun : see Ex 12, etc.

18. The Master saith] It is clear that the man was a disciple, so that here is another synoptic proof of a previous ministry of Jesus at Jerusalem. St. Mark and St. Luke here add additional details to the narrative, implying a miraculous gift of foresight on our Lord's part. **My time is at hand**] The disciple would doubtless be surprised at the proposal of Jesus to keep the Passover a day before the legal time. The apostles were therefore instructed to give the reason : 'My time is at hand,' i.e. My death will happen before the legal time of the Passover arrives.

20. He sat down] RV 'He was sitting at meat,' or, rather, 'reclining.' For the attitude at table, see on Jn 13 23. The Law (Ex 12 11) required the Passover to be eaten standing, but this was no longer observed. The Talmud says, 'It is the custom of slaves to eat standing, but now let them eat reclining, that it may be discerned that at the exodus they went out from slavery into freedom.'

23. He that dippeth] RV 'He that dipped' (Ps 41 9). St. John describes this incident in much fuller detail.

24. It had been good] A popular expression. The rabbis said, 'Whoever knows the Law and does it not, it were better for him never to have been born.' 'If a man does not attend to the honour of his Creator, it were better if he had not come into the world.'

The justice of Judas's punishment, seeing that the betrayal of Jesus was predestined, has been much discussed. The solution probably is that the betrayal by Judas was *not* predestined. It was morally certain that in a state of society like that in Palestine in our Lord's time, a teacher like Jesus would be betrayed by *some one*, but that some one need not have been Judas. Judas was rightly punished because he freely took the evil business upon himself. For the probable reasons why Jesus chose Judas to be an Apostle, see on Jn 6 71.

25. Master] RV 'Rabbi.' **Thou hast said**] i.e. Yes: a rabbinical idiom never found in the OT.

After v. 25 the evangelist probably (though not certainly) intenas it to be understood that Judas at once withdrew (see v. 47), thus agreeing with St. John, who also represents the traitor as leaving before the institution of the Holy Sacrament. In St. Luke Judas appears to be present and to receive the Sacrament, but that is probably because the third Gospel does not relate the events in order : see on Lk and on Jn 13 30.

26-30. Institution of the Lord's Supper (Mk 14 22 Lk 22 19 1 Cor 11 23). It is not certain how far Jesus at the Last Supper followed the customary Passover ritual, but it is clear that He did so to some extent. The following gives the usual order of proceedings, omitting a few details :

(1) The first cup was blessed and drunk. (2) The hands were washed while a blessing was said. (3) Bitter herbs, emblematic of the sojourn in Egypt, were partaken of, dipped in sour broth made of vinegar and bruised fruit. (4) The son of the house asked his father to explain the origin of the observance. (5) The lamb and the flesh of the thank offerings (*chagigah*) were placed on the table, and the first part of the Hallel sung (Pss 113, 114). (6) The second cup was blessed and drunk. (7) Unleavened bread was blessed and broken, a fragment of it was eaten, then a fragment of the thank offerings, then a fragment of the lamb. (8) Preliminaries being thus ended, the feast proceeded at leisure till all was consumed. (9) The lamb being quite finished, the third cup, the cup of blessing, was blessed and drunk. (10) The fourth cup was drunk, and meanwhile the second part of the Hallel (Pss 115–118) was sung.

Those who partook of the Passover were required to be ceremonially clean, and to have been fasting from the time of the evening sacrifice, which on this day was offered early, about 1.30 P.M. All male Israelites above the age of fourteen were required to partake of it.

26. As they were eating, Jesus took bread] This may correspond with No. 7, but it seems more probable that both the bread and the wine were consecrated together at the close of the meal, the bread when it was almost, and the cup when it was quite, finished.

The Jewish ritual of breaking the Passover bread was as follows: 'Then washing his hands, and taking two loaves, he breaks one, and lays the broken loaf upon the whole one, saying, "Blessed be He who causeth bread to grow out of the earth." Then, putting a piece of bread and some bitter herbs together, he dips them in the sour broth, saying this blessing: "Blessed be Thou, O Lord God, our eternal King, He who hath sanctified us by His precepts, and commanded us to eat." Then he eats the unleavened bread and bitter herbs together.' But it is unlikely that Jesus, who was founding a new rite, followed the Jewish ritual in every detail.

This is my body] see on v. 30.

27. The cup] RV 'a cup.' Since it was taken after supper (St. Luke and St. Paul), and is expressly called by the latter the 'cup of blessing' (1 Cor 10 16), it was clearly the third cup of the paschal supper, called by the rabbis the 'cup of blessing' (No. 9). The ritual was as follows : (1) It was washed and cleansed ; (2) the wine in it was mingled with water, and it was blessed ; (3) it was crowned, i.e. the worshippers stood round it in a ring ; (4) the householder veiled his head and sat down ; (5) he drank it, holding it with both hands.

That the cup of the Christian sacrament was also mingled with water, was indicated by Jesus Himself, when He called it 'this fruit of the vine.' The Talmud says, 'The rabbis have a tradition. Over wine which hath not water mingled with it they do not say the blessing, "Blessed be He that created the fruit of the vine," but, "Blessed be He that created the fruit of the tree."' And it is added, 'The wise agree with Rabbi Eleazar, that one ought not to bless over the cup of blessing till water be mingled with it.'

28. My blood of the New Testament] RV 'my blood of the covenant.' This is a clear proof that Jesus regarded His death as an atoning sacrifice for the sins of the world, and, therefore, as altering the relation of the whole human race to God. As Moses had once made a covenant with God by the blood of victims sprinkled on the people (Ex 24 8), so now Jesus by His own blood made a new and better covenant.

Shed for many] i.e. probably 'for mankind,' stress being laid on their multitude.

29. I will not drink henceforth, etc.] (Mk 14 25 Lk 22 18). These mysterious and beautiful words are a well-known 'crux' of interpreters. It seems clear, however, that they are to be taken as referring to the whole rite of the Lord's Supper, and not simply to the 'fruit of the vine,' or cup. This is evident from Lk 22 16, 'I will not any more eat thereof' (viz. of the Christian Passover or Supper) 'until it be fulfilled in the kingdom of God.' Interpretations fall into two main classes, according as 'the kingdom of God' ('My Father's kingdom') is understood to refer to the period after the Resurrection, or to the period after the Judgment. According to the first interpretation, the sacred rite which Jesus now institutes, and which He will not again celebrate until He has triumphed over death and sat down a conqueror on the throne of His Father's kingdom, will, after the Ascension, and especially after the descent of the Spirit, be to the disciples a new thing. No longer will the shadow of disappointment and seeming failure hang over their meetings. The sin of the world will have been atoned for, death will have been conquered, the Spirit will have been given, and Jesus will be present at the feast, not, as now, in the body of His humiliation, but in the power of His risen and glorious life. According to the other interpretation, the Lord's Supper is regarded as a type and prophecy of the eternal marriage supper of the Lamb (Rev 19⁹). These two views do not exclude one another. The title 'this fruit of the vine' which Jesus applies to the sacred cup even after consecration, would seem to exclude the mediæval doctrine of Transubstantiation.

30. Sung an hymn] i.e. the second part of the Hallel (Pss 115–118) which accompanied the fourth Passover-cup : see No. 10 above.

ADDITIONAL NOTES ON THE LAST SUPPER

(a) **Its theological and apologetic importance.** On the night of the Last Supper the fortunes of Jesus were at their lowest ebb. There was treason in His own camp. The triumph of His enemies was at hand, and He looked forward with certainty on the morrow to the degrading death of a common malefactor. Yet He chose this moment to ordain a rite in which His death should be commemorated by His followers to the end of time, showing that He foresaw His resurrection and the future triumph of His cause. Such conduct under such circumstances shows a strictly supernatural gift of faith and insight. Moreover He chose this moment of deepest depression and seeming failure, for the most studied declaration of His true Divinity. For what less than divine can He be said to be, whose death atones for the sins of the whole world, and reconciles the human race to God ? And how can He be other than the Author of Life Himself, who declares that His Body and Blood are the spiritual food and drink of mankind ? If all the records of Christianity had perished, and only the rite of the Holy Communion remained, it would still remain certain that One had appeared on earth who claimed to be the Divine Saviour of the world, and whose death was believed to have been followed by a glorious Resurrection and Ascension.

(b) **The doctrine of the Lord's Supper.** Space does not permit us to give an adequate account even of the best-known interpretations of our Lord's words in instituting this holy rite. All that can be done here is to indicate a few leading points which the reader may find devotionally helpful.

(1) Although some earnest believers have seen in the Lord's Supper nothing but a bare commemoration of the Lord's death, yet the great majority of Christians in all ages have believed that, attached to devout and reverent participation in the rite, is a special covenanted blessing, which cannot (ordinarily at least) be obtained in any other way, and which is necessary for the nourishment and growth of the spiritual life. Such a view seems clearly to underlie the statement of St. Paul (1 Cor 10¹⁶), that 'the cup of blessing which we bless' is to the faithful communicant 'the communion,' i.e. the partaking in common with others, 'of the blood of Christ,' and 'the bread which we break,' 'the communion of the body of Christ.'

(2) The covenanted blessing is generally conceived as a special realisation of the union between the believer and his Saviour, as suggested by our Lord's own allegory of the Vine and the Branches (Jn 15) spoken immediately after the institution, and by that of the Bread of Life (Jn 6), which was intended to prepare the way for it. It is specially true at the Table that 'Christ dwells in our hearts by faith,' 'we are one with Christ and Christ with us,' 'we dwell in him and he in us,' and He is in us the fountain of life, sanctification, and cleansing.

(3) The primary reference of the rite is to the death of Christ. The 'broken body' and 'shed blood' symbolise the atoning death upon the cross. It is implied that those who with faith and due thankfulness approach the Table, 'obtain remission of their sins, and all other benefits of his passion.'

(4) At the same time the reference is not exclusively to Christ's death. He does not say 'Do this in remembrance of my death,' but 'Do this in remembrance of me,' i.e. of all that I am to Christians ;—of My incarnation, resurrection, and ascension, as well as of My death. To the early Christians the rite was very largely a memorial of the Resurrection, and as such was regularly celebrated on the first day of the week (Ac 20⁷).

(5) Accordingly in the Supper it is with the ascended and glorified Lord that the Christian holds communion. While commemorating the tragedy of Calvary he communes with Him who 'is alive for evermore, and has the keys of hell and of death' (Rev 1¹⁸). He joins in the heavenly worship of 'the Lamb as it had been slain,' who, in recompense for His humiliation, is now endowed with almighty power (Rev 5⁶).

(6) There is some difference of view among believing Christians as to how the scriptural expressions, eating and drinking Christ's flesh and blood (Jn 6⁵³), or Christ's body and blood (1 Cor 10¹⁶), are to be understood. Many think

that Christ is present in the ordinance only according to His divine nature, and that He communicates to believers not His actual body and blood, but only the benefits which the offering of these upon the Cross procured for mankind. Others, however, interpreting our Lord's mysterious words in a more literal sense, are of opinion that Christ is present in the ordinance not only in His Deity, but also in His glorified humanity, and that in some spiritual and ineffable, but still most real manner, He imparts to believers not only His Godhead, but also His Manhood, making them partakers, not in figure only, but verily and indeed, of His sacred body and blood. We are here in the presence of very deep mysteries, of which we should speak with awe and reverence, remembering how very limited our faculties are.

(7) The Supper is a memorial rite, 'this do in *remembrance* of me,' more literally, 'as my memorial' (Lk 22 19 1 Cor 11 24). Some have regarded it as a memorial before man only, but the prevailing opinion among Christians is that it is a memorial also before God, a pleading before the Father of the merits of the precious death of His Son. The word used (*anamnesis*) is a rare one, and in biblical Greek means uniformly a memorial before God, both in the OT. (see e.g. Lv 24 7 LXX), and in the NT. (Heb 10 3). There is good reason, therefore, for thinking that this may be the meaning here.

Note. At this point must be inserted Jn 14–17.

31–35. Jesus predicts His Death, the scattering of the disciples, the fall of Peter, and His own Resurrection (Mk 14 27 Lk 22 31 Jn 13 38).

31. I will smite] freely adapted from Zech 13 7, a strictly Messianic passage. The quotation is intended to alleviate the scandal of the disciples' conduct, by showing that it was foretold. **33. Peter answered**] 'He ought rather to have besought Christ, and begged for aid (against the coming temptation). But he sinned in three ways at once : (1) in contradicting the Prophet and the Christ, (2) in placing himself above the rest, (3) in trusting in himself alone, and not in the help of God. Wherefore also he was permitted to fall, that he might be humbled, and might learn not to trust too much in himself, and that others also might learn the same. Also he was allowed to fall that he might learn to love more. For he to whom more is forgiven, loves more' (Euthymius). **34. Before the cock crow**] i.e. before the day begins to dawn. There is practically no difference of meaning between this and 'before the cock crow twice' (Mk), for when the cock once begins to crow in the morning, he does so at frequent intervals. The rabbis say, 'They do not keep cocks at

Jerusalem on account of the holy things (which they might pollute) ; nor do the priests keep them throughout all the land of Israel.' But this law was clearly not enforced.

36–46. The Agony in the Garden (Mk 14 32 Lk 22 40). The peculiar intensity of Christ's agony at Gethsemane presents a difficult problem. It cannot have been due to fear of death, for He came to Jerusalem expressly to die, and never faltered in His resolve, nor is the foreseen flight of the disciples, the treachery of Judas, the denial of Peter, and the sin of the Jewish nation in rejecting and crucifying Him, sufficient to account for it. Perhaps the explanation is to be found in the mystery of the Atonement. He was to bear the sins of the whole world, and the thought of that awful burden oppressed Him. 'The Lord felt the bitterness of death, He tasted it as the wages of sin ; and this alone is the bitterness of death—not His own, but so much the profounder and keener as the sin of the whole world' (Dale).

The best commentary on Gethsemane is Heb 5 7. Important additional details are found in St. Luke's Gospel (Western text).

36. Gethsemane] lit. 'oil-press.' On the W. slope of Olivet, near the foot. 'It is now' (says Sir C. W. Wilson) 'a small enclosure surrounded by a high wall. The ground is laid out in flower-beds, which are carefully tended by a Franciscan monk ; but the most interesting objects are the venerable olive-trees, which are said to date from the time of Christ, and which may in truth be direct descendants of trees which grew in the same place at the time of the crucifixion.' The gardens of Jerusalem were outside the city, because it was forbidden to plant a garden within the walls.

37. Peter, etc.] In this hour of agony He clung to the companionship of His closest friends, to whom also, as spectators of the glory of the Transfiguration, His present humiliation would be less of a stumbling-block. **And very heavy**] RV 'and sore troubled.'

39. Let this cup] i.e. not merely His death, but all that was implied in bearing the sins of the world in His own body on the tree : cp. 20 22. The prayer, 'Let this cup pass,' was not sinful, because it was accompanied by the resolution to submit to the divine will, whatever it was. **Not as I will**] As Christ was God and man, there were in Him two wills, a human will and a divine will, and the former did not always conform itself to the latter without an inward struggle : cp. Jn 5 30 6 38.

40. Asleep] 'You promised to die with me, and could you not watch with me one hour ?' (Euthymius). **41. Temptation**] i.e. the temptation to forsake and deny Christ. **44. The**

third time] not a 'vain repetition,' but a repetition of intense earnestness. In great agony men do not frame many words, but say the same words many times. **45. Sleep on now**] spoken with reproachful irony, 'You have slept through My agony. Sleep also through My betrayal and capture.' **46. Let us be going**] i.e. not to escape, but to meet the betrayer.

47-56. Jesus is taken (Mk 14 43 Lk 22 47 Jn 18 2) : see further on Jn.

47. From the chief priests] These were the Temple guard of Levites, sent by the Sanhedrin. St. John mentions that Roman soldiers were also present. **48. Kiss**] 'It was not unusual for a master to kiss his disciple ; but for a disciple to kiss his master was more rare' (J. Lightfoot).

49. Hail, master] RV 'Hail, Rabbi.' **Kissed**] a different word : 'Kissed and embraced him effusively.' Jesus received the kiss, (1) to soften the heart of Judas by His gentleness, if that were possible ; (2) in the words of St. Hilary, 'to teach us to love our enemies, and those whom we know to be bitter against us.'

50. Friend, wherefore art thou come ?] RV 'Friend, do that for which thou art come.' Lk adds, 'Betrayest thou the Son of man with a kiss ?' Here follows in St. John a dialogue between Jesus and those who came to seize Him ; after which they all fell to the ground. **51. One of them**] The synoptic tradition suppresses the name, probably to ensure the safety of Peter. St. John alone mentions that it was Peter, with whose character the act fully accords. **His sword**] see Lk 22 38. **A servant**] RV 'the servant' ('slave'). His name was Malchus (Jn). St. Luke alone mentions that Christ healed him. **52. All they that take the sword, etc.**] cp. Rev 13 10. This incident is a practical commentary on the third Beatitude (5 5). It discourages resort to violence on the part of Christ's followers, and recommends instead the meek endurance of injuries. Peace, not war, is their mission. Another interpretation has been given, 'All they that take the sword,' i.e. rashly and on their own authority, 'shall perish by the sword,' i.e. are worthy to perish by the sword, i.e. the sword of the magistrate. So that Christ here renews the precept given to Noah, 'Whoso sheddeth man's blood, by man shall his blood be shed' (Gn 9 6). **55. I sat daily**] This cannot merely refer to the two, or at most three days' ministry during Holy Week, but indicates a more extended ministry at Jerusalem at an earlier period, as the Fourth Gospel relates. **57-68. Trial before Caiaphas** (Mk 14 53 Lk 22 54). The synoptists omit the preliminary examination before Annas recorded by Jn,

because it led to nothing. St. John omits the trial before Caiaphas, because it had already been recorded. From St. Matthew and St. Mark it might be thought that the trial took place immediately after the arrest, but St. Luke, whose narrative is here independent, makes it clear that there was a considerable interval, during which the rest of the members of the Sanhedrin were summoned. The chief enemies of Jesus had not gone to bed, and were already assembled. It was necessary to wait for the morning (Lk 22 66), because it was unlawful to try capital offences at night. There was, however, very little attempt on the part of the Jewish authorities to preserve even the forms of a legal trial. The time of the trial would be about 4 A.M.

The following account of the judicial procedure of the Sanhedrin in capital cases is abridged from Schürer, who follows the Mishna. The members of the court sat in a semi-circle. A quorum of 23 was required. In front of them stood the two clerks of the court, of whom the one on the right hand recorded the votes for acquittal, and the one on the left hand the votes for condemnation. The 'disciples of the wise' (pupils of the scribes) occupied three additional rows in front. It was required to hear the reasons for acquittal first (a regulation violated in the case of Jesus) and afterwards the reasons for condemnation. The 'disciples of the wise' could speak, but only in favour of the prisoner. Acquittal could be pronounced on the day of the trial, but condemnation not till the following day (this regulation also was violated, though some suppose that there were two meetings, one on Thursday night, the other on Friday morning to render the proceedings technically legal). Each member stood to give his vote, and voting began with the youngest member. For acquittal a simple majority sufficed ; for condemnation a majority of two was necessary.

Was the assembly which condemned Jesus a regular and formal meeting of the Sanhedrin? Edersheim denies it, because 'All Jewish order and law would have been grossly infringed in almost every particular, if this had been a formal meeting of the Sanhedrin.' But the case of Stephen shows how little the Sanhedrin cared for order and law, when it was really angry. A stronger argument is drawn from the place of meeting, which was apparently the high priest's palace, though none of the evangelists expressly say so, and Lk 22 66 possibly suggests the contrary. This was certainly not the proper place for the Sanhedrin to meet, but we are not in a position to say that at this time such a meeting-place was impossible or even unlikely. The legal place of meeting was the Hall Gazith (lit.

'Hall of Hewn Stones') which was on the Temple mount, and probably within the Temple enclosure. But the Mishna says that forty years before the fall of Jerusalem the Sanhedrin removed to the 'booths,' or 'shops.' Whether these booths were in the Temple, or in Jerusalem, or on the Mt. of Olives, is uncertain, but if such an irregularity as meeting in the 'booths' was possible, so also was that of meeting in the high priest's house.

58. Unto the .. palace] RV 'unto the court' (i.e. quadrangle) 'of the high priest': see on v. 3. **The servants**] RV 'the officers.'

59. Sought false witness] That the judges sought witnesses at all, much less false witnesses, is enough to condemn them to perpetual infamy.

61. I am able to destroy] At the worst this was a boastful remark, and could not be made the basis of a capital charge. This incident strikingly confirms the accuracy of the discourses recorded in the Fourth Gospel, which alone records this saying of Christ (Jn 2 19). The false witnesses distorted the saying. Christ did not say 'I am able to destroy,' but 'Destroy this temple,' i.e. 'If you destroy this temple.'

63. I adjure thee by the living God] Jesus consents to be put on His oath, thus declaring oaths before a magistrate to be lawful. **The Christ, the Son of God**] The high priest asks not merely whether He is the Messiah, but whether He is a *divine* Messiah. To claim to be the Messiah whom all good Israelites were expecting, was no crime, but to claim to be the Son of God, in the sense of God's equal, was blasphemy. Here the synoptists again strongly confirm the peculiar features of the Fourth Gospel, for how did the high priest know or suspect that Jesus claimed to be divine, unless Jesus had publicly said so at Jerusalem, as related in the Fourth Gospel? (Jn 5 17-47 8 56-59 10 33).

64. Thou hast said] Christ's exact words which St. Mark and St. Luke render by 'I am' (see 26 25). **Nevertheless**] better, 'moreover.' **Hereafter** (RV 'Henceforth') **ye shall see, etc.**] Jesus here makes two distinct statements: (1) That henceforth, i.e. from the Ascension onwards, His enemies will behold Him sitting on the right hand of God, and causing His Kingdom mightily to prevail over the earth, in spite of all their efforts to prevent it. (2) That they will also see Him one day coming to judgment seated on the clouds of heaven. The reference is to Dan 7 13, which was then interpreted of the Messiah.

65. Rent his clothes] The Jewish law was: 'They that judge a blasphemer first ask the witness, and bid him speak out plainly what he hath heard; and when he speaks it, the judges, standing on their feet, rend their garments and do not sew them up again.'

66. He is guilty (RV 'worthy') **of death.** To condemn Jesus at once, was contrary to the law, which was, 'Judgment in capital causes is passed the same day if it be for acquitting; but if it be for condemning, it is passed the day after.' The reason is, 'He delays his judgment, and lets it rest all night, that he may sift out the truth.' But Edersheim remarks, 'It seems, however, at least doubtful, whether in case of profanation of the divine name, judgment was not immediately executed.' The trial was further illegal, as being held on the eve of the Passover, for 'Let them not judge on the eve of the sabbath, or on the eve of a feast day.' After passing sentence of death the judges were bound to taste nothing the whole day. The punishment for blasphemy was stoning.

67. Fulfilment of Isa 50 6.

68. Prophesy] Christ was blindfolded at the time. The mockery was carried out by the 'officers' of the Sanhedrin.

ADDITIONAL NOTE ON THE TRIAL

The synoptists all agree that Jesus was condemned for blasphemy, i.e. for claiming more than human powers and attributes. This is inconsistent with the contention of those who maintain that Jesus merely professed to be a mere human teacher, or at most a prophet. The trial itself is enough to show that there is essential unity between the synoptists and the Fourth Gospel in their doctrine of Christ's person. The Christ of the synoptists at the last great crisis of His life makes the same tremendous claims as the Christ of St. John, and is put to death for making them.

69–75. Peter's Denials (Mk 14 66 Lk 22 54 Jn 18 15-18, 25 27). The accounts agree in all main features, but the details are difficult to harmonise exactly. All agree that Peter was three times charged with being a disciple, and three times denied it; also that a cock crew at the time of the third denial, reminding Peter of the words of Jesus. St. Luke and St. John represent Peter in a somewhat more favourable light than St. Matthew and St. Mark, for they say nothing of his cursing and swearing. St. Luke alone mentions the look of Jesus which went to the heart of Peter. St. John represents the denials as taking place in the court of Annas, the synoptists in that of Caiaphas, but perhaps both had apartments in the same building. In any case the account of St. John, who was an actual eyewitness, is to be preferred: see on Jn.

69. In the palace] RV 'in the court,' i.e. in the quadrangle.

75. Wept bitterly] 'Thou hast seen Peter's sin, see also his repentance. For to this very end were the sins and the repentances of the saints written, that whenever we sin, we may imitate their repentance. And Peter was allowed to fall not only for the reasons mentioned before, but also that he might learn to make allowances for those that stumble, knowing from his own experience what human weakness is ' (Euthymius).

CHAPTER 27

Before Pilate. The Crucifixion

1, 2. Jesus delivered to Pilate (Mk 15 1 Lk 23 1 Jn 18 28 : see on Jn).

1. When the morning] Since according to St. Luke, who follows an excellent and independent authority, the trial itself did not take place ' until it was day ' (Lk 22 66), this second meeting must be placed some time later in the morning, considerably after cock-crowing (26 74). The object of the meeting, which was evidently largely attended, was simply to consider how to induce Pilate to carry out the sentence, and not as some think to pronounce sentence of death, and so technically to comply with the law which forbade the death sentence to be pronounced on the day of the trial.

2. Pilate] the fifth Roman procurator of Judæa, was appointed in 26 A.D., and held office for ten years. He was then summoned to Rome to answer certain charges made against him, and was banished to Vienna in Gaul, where he is said to have committed suicide. The Roman governor resided generally at Cæsarea, but came to Jerusalem at Passover time to keep order. The Sanhedrin could not lawfully execute Jesus without the consent of Pilate (Jn 18 31), and Pilate was not likely to regard seriously the purely religious charge upon which Jesus had been condemned. They, therefore, altered the charge to one of treason (v. 11).

3-10. End of Judas (see Ac 1 18). The divergences of the two accounts of the end of Judas are well known. In St. Matthew he hangs himself; in Acts he is killed by a fall. In St. Matthew the priests buy a field with the blood-money to bury strangers in ; in Acts Judas himself buys a field, presumably for his own purposes. It is possible by various ingenious conjectures to harmonise the accounts, but the truth of the matter probably is that the Apostles did not care to investigate at the time so hateful a subject as the fate of the traitor, and that when the Gospels came to be written the exact circumstances could no longer be ascertained.

3. When he saw that he was condemned] This somewhat favours the view that Judas did not intend by betraying Jesus to cause His death. But it is more probable that the meek demeanour of the Sufferer at His arrest and during His trial, brought about a revulsion of

feeling in Judas, who now detested himself for what he had done. ' This is the way of the devil. Before we sin, he suffers us not to see the evil of it, lest we should repent. But after the sin is done, he suffers us to see it, to cause us remorse, and to drive us to despair ' (Euthymius). **Repented himself**] Yet his sorrow was not of a godly nature (2 Cor 7 9), for it led to despair, and further sin. **4. What is that ?**] His wicked companions in crime desert him when the crime is done. **5. In the temple**] RV ' into the sanctuary,' i.e. into the holy place. Judas in his recklessness and despair penetrated where no one but the priests had a right to enter, or, it may be, standing outside the holy place, flung the money violently through the door. **6. It is not lawful**] An argument from Dt 23 18. **The treasury**] lit. ' the Corbanas,' so called because what was placed in it was ' Corban,' i.e. given to God : see Jn 8 20.

7. Bought] In Acts Judas buys the field. **The potter's field**] The potter probably used to obtain clay from it. **8. The field of blood** (Heb. *Aceldama*)] In Acts it receives its name from the death of Judas in it.

9. By Jeremy the prophet] This quotation, really from Zech 11 12, 13 (q.v.), is ascribed to Jeremiah, because Jeremiah stood first in the book of the Prophets, from which it was taken ; the order being Jeremiah, Ezechiel, Isaiah, the Twelve Minor Prophets. The passage is paraphrased rather than quoted.

This explanation is due to J. Lightfoot, who quotes ' a tradition of the rabbis.' ' This is the order of the prophets. The book of Joshua, Judges, Samuel, Kings (former prophets), Jeremiah, Ezechiel, Isaiah, the Twelve (latter prophets).' Other explanations are, a lapse of the evangelist's memory ; the word Jeremiah due not to the evangelist but to the first transcriber, who was thinking of Jer 18 2 ; an oral or traditional utterance ascribed to Jeremiah ; a quotation from a lost work of Jeremiah.

And they took] or, ' I took.' **Whom they**] RV 'whom certain,' RM ' or, whom they priced on the part of the sons of Israel.'

10. And gave] RM 'and I gave.'

11-26. Trial before Pilate (Mk 15 2 Lk 23 1-7 13-25 Jn 18 28-19 16). St. Matthew and St. Mark give practically the same account. St. Luke and St. John are independent of one another and of the others. All give a substantially harmonious account of the trial. Peculiar to St. Matthew was the dream of Pilate's wife, the washing of Pilate's hands, and the cry of the people, ' His blood be on us and on our children.' Peculiar to St. Luke are the exact formulation of the political charges (viz. stirring up rebellion against Cæsar, refusing to pay tribute to Cæsar, and professing to be Christ or king), and the trial before Herod.

The peculiarities of St. John are many (see on Jn). The chief are the conversations between Pilate and Jesus, Pilate's merciful purpose in scourging Jesus, and the final cry which overcame Pilate's resistance, ' If thou let this man go, thou art not Cæsar's friend.'

Pilate does not appear at the trial in an altogether unfavourable light. He is not without a rude sense of justice. He shrinks from the guilt of innocent blood, and finally yields only to the fear of being accused at Rome of disloyalty if he exasperates too much the Jewish leaders. Pilate shows his truly Roman contempt for the Jews, his superstition, and, what often goes with superstition, his shallow scepticism. He was, however, genuinely impressed with Jesus, which shows that he was not without religious susceptibility.

11. Thou sayest] i.e. ' I am.' But Jesus explained to Pilate privately that His kingdom was not of this world (Jn). Here, as so often, the Fourth Gospel alone renders the narrative clearly intelligible. **15. At that feast**] This is the only evidence of such a custom, which is, however, appropriate to the season of the Passover, which commemorates a deliverance.

17. Barabbas] Some ancient authorities have here the interesting reading ' Jesus Barabbas,' which may really have been the man's full name. The people may have preferred him to Christ because he had led a rebellion against Rome, whereas Christ had said, ' Render to Cæsar the things that are Cæsar's.' The two thieves probably belonged to his company.

19. His wife] In tradition her name is given as Procla, or Claudia Procula, and she is said to have been inclined to Judaism, or even to have been a proselyte, and afterwards to have become a Christian. In the Greek Church she is canonised. From the time of Augustus the wives of provincial governors commonly accompanied their husbands.

20. The multitudes were not unfriendly, until the chief priests used their influence against Jesus.

24. Washed *his* **hands**] A piece of Jewish symbolism (see Dt 21⁶) adopted by Pilate to make himself intelligible to the multitude.

I am innocent] It was customary for Gentile judges to protest ' before the sun ' that they were innocent of the blood of the person about to be condemned.

25. His blood *be* **on us**] A cry of blind and vindictive rage. They care not who bears the blame, so that Jesus be put to death. There is tragic irony in this unconscious prophecy, which was fulfilled in two ways. (1) As a curse upon the unbelieving part of the nation, on whom the blood of Jesus was avenged at the destruction of Jerusalem. (2) As a blessing upon believers, on whom the blood of Jesus

came for sanctification, and the remission of sins : cp. Jn 11⁵⁰.

26. Scourged] in accordance with the Roman custom before crucifixion. The culprit was stripped and tied in a bending posture to a pillar, or stretched on a frame, and the punishment was inflicted with a scourge made of leathern thongs, weighted with sharp pieces of bone or lead. Criminals sometimes died under it. According to St. John, Pilate scourged Jesus to move the Jews to pity.

27-30. Jesus is mocked by the Roman soldiers (Mk 15¹⁶ Jn 19¹).

27. Common hall] RV ' palace ' : see on Jn 18²⁸. But the expression may mean ' barracks.' **The whole band**] RM ' cohort ' : about 600 men : see on Jn 18³,¹². **28. Stripped him**] RM ' Some ancient authorities read, clothed Him.' The latter is probably right. He had been stripped previously for scourging. **A scarlet** (*or* purple) **robe**] an emblem of royalty. The **reed** was to represent a sceptre.

31-34. He is led to the Cross (Mk 15²⁰ Lk 23²⁶ Jn 19¹⁶). The cross was regarded as the most horrible and most degrading form of punishment, fit only for slaves. ' It is an outrage for a Roman citizen to be bound ; a crime for him to be scourged. It is almost parricide to have him put to death. What can I call having him crucified ? No word can be found adequate to describe so monstrous a proceeding' (Cicero). Crucifixion was not a Jewish punishment. It originated among the Phœnicians, from whom it passed to the Greeks and Romans. Alexander the Great once crucified 2,000 Tyrians. After the death of Herod the Great, Varus crucified 2,000 rioters. The crucifixion of Jesus was unconsciously avenged by the Romans, who, after the fall of Jerusalem, crucified so many Jews that there was neither wood for the crosses nor room to set them up. The cross consisted of two parts, a strong stake or pole 8 or 9 ft. high, which was fixed in the ground, and a movable cross-piece (*patibulum*), which was carried by the criminal to the place of execution. Sometimes the *patibulum* was a single beam of wood, but more often it consisted of two parallel beams fastened together, between which the neck of the criminal was inserted. Before him went a herald bearing a tablet on which the offence was inscribed, or the criminal himself bore it suspended by a cord round his neck. At the place of execution the criminal was stripped and laid on his back, and his hands were nailed to the *patibulum*. The *patibulum*, with the criminal hanging from it, was then hoisted into position and fastened by nails or ropes to the upright pole. The victim's body was supported not only by the nails through the hands, but by a small piece of wood projecting at right angles (*sedile*), on which he sat as on a saddle. Sometimes there was also a support for the feet, to which the feet were nailed. The protracted agony of crucifixion sometimes lasted for days, death being caused by pain, hunger, and thirst. Jesus was crucified on a cross with four arms (*crux immissa*), as is proved by a title being placed over His head.

THE SEVEN WORDS FROM THE CROSS

(1) 'Father, forgive them ; for they know not what they do' (Lk 23³⁴).

(2) 'Verily I say unto thee, To day shalt thou be with me in paradise' (Lk 23⁴³).

(3) 'Woman, behold thy son! Behold thy mother!' (Jn 19²⁶, ²⁷).

(4) 'My God, my God, why hast thou forsaken me?' (Mt 27⁴⁶ Ps 22¹).

(5) 'I thirst' (Jn 19²⁸).

(6) 'It is finished' (Jn 19³⁰).

(7) 'Father, into thy hands I commend my spirit' (Lk 23⁴⁶ Ps 31⁵).

32. As they came out] viz. of the city, executions being forbidden within the walls (Nu 15³⁵ 1K 21¹³ Ac 7⁵⁸ Heb 13¹²). Up to this point Jesus had carried His own cross (*patibulum*) : see Jn 19¹⁷. The tradition that Jesus fainted under the cross is probably true : see Mk 15²². He had been greatly weakened by the scourging. **Simon**] If Simon was coming home from working in the fields (see Mk, Lk), this is another indication that the Feast of the Passover had not yet begun. He was probably a Jew resident in Jerusalem, but born at Cyrene in Libya (N. Africa) where there were many Jews. The Cyrenians had a synagogue in Jerusalem (Ac 6⁹). Simon afterwards became a Christian (Mk 15²¹ : cp. Ro 16¹³).

Compelled] see on 5⁴¹. Here is to be inserted Christ's address to the daughters of Jerusalem (Lk 23²⁸), among whom, tradition says, was Berenice, or Veronica, a pious woman of Jerusalem, who gave Him her kerchief, or napkin, that He might wipe the drops of agony from His brow. The Lord accepted her offering, and, after using it, handed it back to her, bearing the image of His face miraculously impressed upon it. This napkin, it is alleged, is now in St. Peter's at Rome, but possession of it is claimed also by Milan, and Jaen in Spain. The legend of Veronica is unhistorical, but interesting from its wide diffusion.

33. Golgotha (Aramaic), or *Calvaria* (Latin), means 'a skull.' It received its name either from being the place of execution, or from being an eminence shaped like a skull. It was certainly not a 'mountain,' as it has been popularly called since the 5th cent. Calvary was close by the garden in which Jesus was buried (Jn), and there is no reason

why the traditional site (which lies within the Church of the Holy Sepulchre) should not be the true one. 'The traditional site, the Church of the Holy Sepulchre, has lately been proved to lie beyond the second wall, which was the outside wall at the date of the Crucifixion, and several rock tombs have been found about it. It was near a road. It may therefore have been the site' (Dr. G. A. Smith). Similarly Sir C. Warren.

34. Vinegar (RV 'wine').. **mingled with gall**] Mk 'wine mingled with myrrh': see Ps 69²¹. Pious women of Jerusalem were accustomed to offer to condemned criminals a draught of wine and myrrh just before their execution, to stupefy them. The editor of the Gk. Matthew, not understanding the custom, and thinking that the myrrh was added to make the cup bitter and distasteful to Jesus, has rendered it 'gall,' seeing in the incident a fulfilment of Ps 69²¹. **Tasted**] Jesus tasted it, in acknowledgment of the kindness of the women who offered it, but would not drink it, because He would die for the sins of the world with all His faculties of mind unimpaired.

35. Crucified him] It is important to notice, as bearing upon the question of the reality of Christ's death and resurrection, that the feet were nailed as well as the hands. Even if Christ was not quite dead, the nailing of the feet would effectually prevent His leaving the tomb to appear to the apostles : see Lk 24⁴⁰. The time of the crucifixion was the third hour according to St. Mark, but after the sixth hour according to St. John : see on Jn 19¹⁴.

Parted his garments] At this time the criminals' clothes were the perquisites of the executioners. **That it might be fulfilled**] This reference to Ps 22¹⁸ is omitted by RV : see on Jn 19²³, ²⁴.

37. The variations of the inscription on the cross are unimportant. St. John alone states that it was written in Greek, Latin, and Hebrew. **38. Thieves**] RV 'robbers,' i.e. brigands, as distinguished from thieves : see on Lk. **39. Passed by**] The reference to the passengers along the roads is another indication that this was a working day, not the Passover. **40. Thou that destroyest the temple** (RV 'sanctuary')] They called upon Him to perform what He was actually about to do, for 'the temple' was His body : see Jn 2²¹. **43. He trusted in God**] Ps 22⁸. The action of the judges in jeering at the sufferings of the man they had condemned to death, is indecent and brutal. Their misuse of the words of Scripture is blasphemous. **45. From the sixth hour** (noon)] Jesus had now been about three hours on the cross (Mk 15²⁵).

Darkness over all the land (or, 'earth')] The chief, if not the only, historical objection to this darkness, is the silence of Josephus.

But Josephus is silent, not only as to this, but as to almost every event connected with Christianity. Whether as a coincidence, or as a miracle, the fact of the darkness must be received, for the oldest tradition is unanimous on the point. The theory of an eclipse is impossible, as the moon was at the full. The apocryphal Gospel of Peter says, 'And it was midday, and darkness covered all the land of Judæa. And many went about with lamps thinking that it was night, and they fell. Then the sun shone out, and it was found to be the ninth hour.'

46. Eli, Eli, etc.] Ps 22¹. It is not certain whether Jesus spoke in Hebrew or Aramaic, for most MSS contain a mixture of both.

These words are a cry of the human nature of Jesus, which alone could suffer desertion, when He experienced the bitterness of death. They may serve to comfort Christian men and women when they experience the greatest of all trials, the temporary withdrawal of the consciousness of God's presence. But a deeper meaning is also to be sought. Upon the cross Jesus was making atonement for the sins of the world, 'bearing our sins in his own body on the tree,' for upon Him was laid 'the iniquity of us all.' He was so closely identified with the race which He came to save, that He felt the burden of its sin, and cried as the Representative of Humanity, 'My God, my God, why hast thou forsaken me ?'

'The Lord was forsaken, that we might not be forsaken ; He was forsaken that we might be delivered from our sins and from eternal death ; He was forsaken that He might show His love to us, and manifest to us His justice and His pity ; that He might attract to Himself our love, in short that He might exhibit to us a pattern of patience. The way to heaven lies open, but it is steep and difficult. He willed to go before us with an example full of wonder, that the way might not alarm us, but that the stupendous example of a suffering God might incite us ' (St. Cyprian).

47. Calleth for Elias] RV 'calleth Elijah.' 'No Jew could have mistaken *Eli* for the name of Elijah, nor yet misinterpreted a quotation of Ps 22¹ as a call for the prophet ' (Edersheim). 'The Jews said this in mockery, having many stories of appearances of Elijah to rescue men from peril of death ' (Wetstein).

48. Vinegar] i.e. *posca*, the sour common wine drunk by the Roman soldiers. Whatever may have been the sentiments of the bystanders, the motive of the man who offered the vinegar was compassion. The Fourth Gospel alone gives the reason of the act. It was our Lord's fifth word, 'I thirst ' (Jn 19²⁸).

49. Here many ancient authorities insert an account of the spear-thrust mentioned

Jn 19³⁴. It is remarkable that the interpolation (if such it is) mentions the spear-thrust before the death of Jesus, and not after it, as in St. John.

50. Cried again] with a loud voice in triumph, 'It is finished' (Jn 19³⁰), adding immediately, 'Father, into thy hands,' etc. (Lk 23⁴⁶). **50. Yielded up**] He died voluntarily (Jn 10¹⁸).

51. The veil of the temple] Two veils, a cubit apart, hung before the Holy of Holies. They are said to have been 40 cubits (60 ft.) long, 20 wide, and of the thickness of the palm of the hand. Both were rent. Josephus, for obvious reasons, does not record this event.

The significance of the rending of the veil is variously understood. Some see in it a sign that the old covenant was at an end, the sacrifices abolished, and the divine presence withdrawn from the Temple, even the Holy of Holies being now made common ground, open to the feet of all. Others who regard the Holy of Holies as a type of heaven, and the rest of the Temple as a type of earth, see in the rending of the veil the removing of the barrier between heaven and earth, the reconciling of God and man through the death of Christ : cp. Heb 10¹⁹, ²⁰.

The earth did quake] Probably to be connected with the rending of the veil. 'In the Gospel (according to the Hebrews) we read that the lintel of the Temple of infinite size was broken and divided. Josephus also relates that the angelic powers, who once presided over the Temple, then together cried out, Let us depart from these abodes ' (Jerome). The statement of Josephus, however, refers to a later period. **Rocks rent**] 'It would not be right altogether to reject the testimony of travellers to the fact of extraordinary rents and fissures in the rocks near the spot ' (Alford). 'To this day Golgotha is a proof of it, where the rocks were rent on account of Christ ' (St. Cyril of Jerusalem, 315–386 A.D.).

52. The graves were opened] i.e. by the shock of the earthquake. **And many bodies of the saints, etc.**] i.e. they rose, not immediately, but with Christ at His Resurrection.

This incident seems to be a pictorial setting forth of the truth that in the Resurrection of Christ is involved the resurrection of all His saints, so that on Easter Day all Christians may be said in a certain sense to have risen with Him.

54. The Son of God] RM 'a son of God,' i.e. a hero or demi-god, which is more suitable in the mouth of a heathen soldier. St. Luke, 'Truly this man was righteous.'

55. Ministering] It was the custom of Jewish women to contribute to the support of famous rabbis : see on Lk 8¹⁻³.

56. Mary Magdalene] Most authorities

regard 'Magdalene' as equivalent to 'of Magdala,' a town near Tiberias. There is no ground for the common identification of this Mary with the sister of Lazarus, or with the 'sinner' who anointed our Lord's feet (Lk 7 37).

Mary the mother of James and Joses] St. Mark calls this James, 'James the little': see on Jn 19 25. **The mother of Zebedee's children**] i.e. Salome (Mk). The synoptists omit all mention of the presence of the Virgin, either because she had been already led away by St. John, or because she was not one of the ministering women.

57-61. Burial of Jesus (Mk 15 42 Lk 23 51 Jn 19 38 : see on Jn). The burial of Jesus in the tomb of a wealthy and influential man was a literal fulfilment of Isa 53 9 : 'with the rich in his death.'

57. Arimathæa] unidentified. Perhaps Ramathaim Zophim in the hill-country of Ephraim.

Joseph] According to St. Luke he was a member of the Sanhedrin, who had not consented to the death of Jesus. According to St. John he was assisted by Nicodemus. **58. Begged the body**] According to St. Mark, Pilate assured himself that Jesus was really dead before surrendering the body. It was not lawful to suffer a man to hang all night upon a tree, Dt 21 23. Strictly speaking, Jesus had no legal right to honourable burial. The Jewish law was, 'They that were put to death by the council were not to be buried in the sepulchres of their fathers, but two burial places were appointed by the council.' **60. He had hewn**] Only St. Matthew mentions that the tomb belonged to Joseph. **61. The other Mary**] i.e. Mary the mother of James and Joses.

62-66. The sepulchre is guarded (peculiar to St. Matthew). It is sometimes argued that this incident is unauthentic, because the enemies of Christ would not be likely to remember obscure prophecies of the Resurrection, which even the disciples failed to understand. This view is possible. But they remembered the obscure saying, 'Destroy this temple,' etc., two years after it had been spoken, and there was a still more recent and clearer prediction addressed to the Pharisees (12 40).

62. Now the next day] RV 'Now on the morrow, which is the day after the Preparation.' The 'Preparation' is the usual word for Friday. **63. After three days**] Jn 2 19 Mt 12 40, etc. **65. Ye have**] RM 'Take a guard,' viz. of Roman soldiers. **66. And setting a watch**] RV 'the guard being with them.'

CHAPTER 28

THE RESURRECTION

For the Resurrection see special article.

1-10. The Resurrection and appearance to the women (Mk 16 1 Lk 24 1 Jn 20 1). If it be remembered that a considerable number of

women visited the tomb—Mary Magdalene, Mary mother of James, Salome (Mk), Joanna (Lk), and 'the other women with them' (Lk)— the fragmentary accounts of the evangelists are not very difficult to arrange in order. (1) Mary Magdalene and the other women visit the tomb immediately after the resurrection, and see one angel (Mt, Mk), or two (Lk). (2) She runs at once to Peter and John, who were probably alone at Peter's house, and thus misses the appearance of Christ to the women recorded by St. Matthew. (3) The other women returning more leisurely are met by Christ Himself (Mt), and report what they have seen to the other apostles. (4) Mary returns to the tomb, and after the departure of Peter and John, sees Jesus in the garden (Jn). Other arrangements of the events are also possible.

1. In the end of the sabbath] RV 'late on the sabbath.' Strictly speaking, the Jewish sabbath closed at sunset, but here St. Matthew, adopting the popular method of reckoning, regards the sabbath as lasting till dawn on Sunday morning. 'Late on the sabbath' is, therefore, between midnight and dawn on Sunday, as indeed is expressly stated. **The other Mary**] i.e. Mary, the mother of James. The women had come with ointment and spices (Mk, Lk) to anoint and embalm the body, either not knowing what Joseph and Nicodemus had done, or supposing that the work had been too hastily performed owing to the approach of the sabbath, which was also the feast day.

2-4. The descent of the angel, the earthquake, and the consternation of the watchers, which accompanied the resurrection, are peculiar to St. Matthew. He does not, however, state that the resurrection itself was visible, as do many of the later authorities.

5. The angel] Mk 'a young man'; Lk 'two men.' In Mk and Lk the angel (or angels) appears inside the tomb. Such slight discrepancies harmonise well with the excited feelings which such a vision would be likely to produce. Minute and detailed agreement in independent narratives under such circumstances would be suspicious. **Fear not ye**] The words of the angel are nearly the same in St. Matthew and St. Mark, but considerably different in St. Luke, who follows an independent tradition. St. Luke, who records no Galilean appearances, naturally omits the reference to Galilee.

7. He goeth before you into Galilee] as, indeed, Jesus Himself had already promised (26 32).

9. Jesus met them] This appearance is peculiar to St. Matthew. **All hail**] A common Jewish salutation. 'How do they salute an Israelite? "All hail."'

Held him by the feet] viz. to kiss them. This was not uncommon. 'As Rabbi Jann and Rabbi Jonathan were sitting together, a certain man came and kissed the feet of Rabbi Jonathan.' 'When Rabbi Akiba's wife came to him, she fell at his feet and kissed them.' Cp. 2 K 4 27. **Worshipped him**] now with more than merely human reverence. It is noticeable that Jesus never repelled any mark of reverence shown to Him, however profound.

10. Into Galilee] again emphasising the importance of this meeting.

The appearance to the women is not regarded by recent critics as belonging certainly to the oldest form of the tradition.

11–15. Bribery of the guards (peculiar to St. Matthew). The report of the soldiers may have had something to do with the conversion of so many priests described in Ac 6 7.

11. Chief priests] These were Sadducees, hostile to any idea of a resurrection. **12. Assembled**] This was a packed, informal meeting of the Sanhedrin. **13. His disciples**, etc.] A somewhat inconsistent statement, since if they were asleep, they could not know that the disciples had stolen the body. It is important, however, to notice that this fiction of the chief priests demonstrates that the tomb was empty, and that, therefore, the resurrection of Jesus was a bodily resurrection. **14. And secure you**] The ordinary punishment for an offence of this kind was death (Ac 12 19), but Pilate would hardly trouble himself about what the soldiers had done while under the orders of the chief priests.

16–20. Appearance on a mountain in Galilee (peculiar to St. Matthew, but there can be little doubt that the original ending of St. Mark, which is unfortunately lost, recorded the same appearance : see Mk 16 7). It is highly probable (see on v. 16), but is incapable of strict proof, that this appearance is identical with that to five hundred brethren at once mentioned by St. Paul (1 Cor 15 6). At any rate, it is a meeting of great importance, being mentioned once by the angel and twice by our Lord (26 32 28 10). If there were five hundred living persons who could give a particular account of this incident, the rapid way in which the evangelist passes over it is in part accounted for.

16. The eleven disciples] This does not of necessity imply that no others were present, but only that the words of Jesus were mainly addressed to them. **Where Jesus had appointed them**] St. Matthew does not say when Jesus made this appointment, thus indicating that he does not profess to give a full account of the appearances after the resurrection. That the meeting was by appointment renders it probable that all the disciples who could possibly be brought together were present.

17. They worshipped him] Certainly with divine worship : see Jn 20 28. **But some**

doubted] or, as the Gk. may perhaps be more correctly translated, 'but *others* doubted,' i.e. not the Eleven, but others who were present.

The doubt may have arisen from the change which had passed over our Lord's now glorified body (Mk 16 13 Lk 24 16 Jn 21 4), but more probably from the reason which Paley gives : 'Christ appeared first at a distance ; the greater part of the company, the moment that they saw Him, worshipped, but some as yet, i.e. upon this first distant view of His person, doubted ; whereupon Christ came up to them (v. 18) and spake to them, etc.' : the doubt, therefore, was a doubt only at first, for a moment, and upon His being seen at a distance, and was afterwards dispelled by His nearer approach, and by His entering into conversation with them.

18. And Jesus came] RV 'came to them,' viz. to resolve their doubt by giving them a close view of His person. It is worthy of notice that in all the appearances after the resurrection, our Lord allowed the disciples either to touch or to come into very close proximity to His risen body. His anxiety to remove all reasonable doubts as to the cardinal fact of His bodily resurrection, is especially evident in Lk 24 39 Jn 20 20, 27.

All power (authority) **is given**] lit. 'was given,' viz. at My resurrection. 'There was given Me, says Jesus, as man, the power which I before possessed as God' (Euthymius) : cp. Eph 1 20-22. 'Human nature, which was before condemned, now sits in heaven personally united to the Divine Word, and is adored by angels. For in truth human nature which was before enslaved, now in Christ rules the Universe' (Theophylact).

The view, which dates the glorification of Christ, not from the Ascension, but from the Resurrection, is safely grounded on this passage. It is the view of St. Augustine, of most of the fathers, of Albertus Magnus, of the schoolmen, and of many modern authorities. Von Gerlach correctly says, 'The Resurrection of Jesus, and not His Ascension, was His entrance into the new eternal, divine, and heavenly life, as in it all power in heaven and upon earth was already given to Him.' Similarly Milligan, 'The glorification of Jesus began at His Resurrection, not at His Ascension' ; and Westcott, 'After the Resurrection our Lord belongs already to another realm, so that the Ascension only ratifies and presents in a final form the lessons of the forty days in which it is included.'

The only really doubtful point is the locality of Christ's body during the forty days ; whether it was in heaven at God's right hand (Theophylact, Milligan, Rothe, etc.), or on earth (Aquinas). In either case, the heavenly reign and glory of Christ had begun.

19. And teach (RV ' make disciples of') **all nations, baptising them** (*or* 'by baptising them ')] In the clearest possible language Christ expresses His intention of founding a universal religion. It has sometimes been argued that these words cannot be authentic, because of the subsequent unwillingness of the Church of Jerusalem, and even of Peter, to receive Gentile converts. But the question in the Acts was not whether Gentile converts should be received, but whether they should first be circumcised.

The argument against infant baptism drawn from this passage (that infants cannot be 'taught,' and therefore should not be baptised, disappears in the RV, which says that the apostles are 'to make disciples of all nations by baptising them.' To Jewish hearers such words would naturally suggest infant baptism, because the idea of infant disciples or proselytes was familiar to Judaism : see on 19 [13-15].

In the name (RV 'into the name') **of the Father,** etc.] One of the leading dogmatic texts in the NT., being the nucleus around which the Apostles' Creed subsequently grew. It teaches, (1) the divinity of Christ, for no mere man could thus insert his name between those of the Father and of the Holy Spirit. (2) The unity of the Godhead, for one ' name,' or divine nature, belongs to the three. (3) The Trinity of persons, for since the former two are persons, so also is the third. (4) The subordination of the coequal persons to one another, viz. the Son to the Father, and the Spirit to both. ' Let therefore Arius and Sabellius be put to shame, Arius because Christ said not " Into the names (pl.)," but " Into the name (sing.)," and the name, or deity, of the Three is one. Wherefore the Three are but one God. Sabellius, because the Lord made mention also of the three persons, not of one person having three names, sometimes being called the Father, sometimes the Son, and sometimes the Spirit, as Sabellius ignorantly affirmed' (Theophylact).

The RV changes ' in the name ' to ' into the name.' If the difference is to be pressed (which is not certain), it implies that baptism is a change of religious condition. The baptised person passes *from* a state of alienation from God *into* a state of union and reconciliation with Him. This passage does not record the first institution of Baptism, which had been in use from the beginning of the ministry, but its solemn promulgation as a rite of universal, perpetual, and necessary observance see Jn 3 [22] 4 [1].

Although the Trinitarian formula in this passage is found in all MSS and versions, some recent critics regard it as an interpolation, or at least as an unauthentic utterance of Jesus. They argue that all the baptisms described in the NT. are into the name of Jesus, not into the name of the Trinity (Ac 2 [38] 8 [16] 10 [48] 19 [5]), and that so definite, and, as it were, stereotyped, a formulation of Trinitarian doctrine, must be later than the apostolic age. These arguments are not without weight, nevertheless there are important considerations on the other side. For the formula, whether spoken by Jesus or not, dates certainly from the apostolic age. It was clearly known to Clement of Rome (90 A.D.), who has three Trinitarian statements, mentioning Father, Son, and Holy Spirit thrice in that order ; it forms the basis of the earliest form of the Apostles' Creed (circ. 100 A.D.); it is expressly quoted in the 'Didache' (c. 100 A.D.); and is definitely alluded to by Justin Martyr (150 A.D.). It may be doubted whether any other single text of the NT. has such early and satisfactory attestation. Nor is it easy to say, with such a definite Trinitarian formula before us as 2 Cor 13 [14], that the baptismal formula must necessarily be later. Trinitarian doctrine and approximations to it, are diffused through the whole NT. literature, and the prevalence of such a type of teaching is most naturally accounted for by supposing that it has behind it some such pregnant utterance of our Lord as the present, the meaning of which was gradually unfolded subsequently under the guidance of the Spirit. The argument from the baptisms 'into the name of Jesus' or of ' the Lord Jesus ' in Acts is more plausible than strong. In no case is the actual formula given, and we cannot be sure that the author means more than that the baptisms in question were Christian baptisms. The 'Didache' (c. 100 A.D.), like Acts, speaks of Christian baptism as being into the name of the Lord Jesus, but when it comes to describe the rite in detail, prescribes the Trinitarian formula, and that only.

20. Teaching them] 'Next because it is not sufficient merely to be baptised, but it is necessary also to do good works after baptism, He saith, " Teaching them to observe all things whatever I commanded you," not one or two only, but all my commandments. Let us tremble therefore, brethren, reflecting that if one thing be lacking in us, we are not perfect servants of Christ, for we are required to keep all ' (Theophylact).

Lo, I am with you] This presence of Christ by His Spirit may be taken in the most comprehensive sense:—in His Church, to guide it into all the truth ; in the assemblies of the faithful, to receive their worship, and to present their petitions to the Father ; in the official acts of His ministers, as being the true High Priest and Pastor of His Church ; and in the hearts of the faithful, as the source of their spiritual life and growth. The omnipresence of Christ implies His divinity.

ST. MARK

INTRODUCTION

1. Life of St. Mark. Mark, i.e. Marcus, a common Roman prænomen, was the name by which the evangelist was usually known in Gentile and Christian circles. His original Jewish name was John (Ac 12 12). As St. Mark was the cousin of St. Barnabas, it is plausibly suggested that, like him, he was a Levite, settled in Cyprus (Col 4 10). An ancient tradition states that ' he ministered in the priesthood in Israel, being according to the flesh a Levite ' ; and that 'after his conversion, he amputated his finger that he might be rejected from the priesthood.' Certainly in early times he bore the title of *Kolobodactylus*, i.e. 'maimed in the finger,' but it is possible that the loss of his finger was due to accident or congenital malformation.

According to an unnamed ancient presbyter who lived in the apostolic age, St. Mark was not a follower of Jesus, but a convert of St. Peter. The presbyter's account is confirmed by certain indications in the NT. It is clear from the Acts that the mother of St. Mark, whose name was Mary, was living in Jerusalem not long after the crucifixion (12 12). She was a woman of some wealth, occupying her own house, and employing several servants or slaves. St. Peter probably lodged with her (12 12) ; at any rate, her house was used as a church, and formed an important Christian centre. St. Peter, being thus an inmate of the same house with St. Mark, was enabled to convert him, and afterwards spoke of him as ' Mark my son,' i.e. my convert (1 Pet 5 13) : cp. 1 Cor 4 15.

At the time of the crucifixion St. Mark, though not a convert, was probably already an enquirer. In Mk 14 51 mention is made of a certain young man who was so much interested in the fate of Jesus, that when the arrest took place, he hastily rose at midnight and followed the procession. This picturesque but unimportant incident is recorded by no other evangelist, and since the name is suppressed, it is at least probable that the young man was St. Mark himself. If this is correct, it would appear that St. Mark, though not technically a ' hearer ' of Jesus, was at least a witness of some of the events of Holy Week.

It is probable that St. Mark, as a convert of St. Peter, sympathised more with the Jewish party led by that Apostle than with the Gentile party of St. Paul. This probably gives the true explanation of the distressing incident related in Ac 13 13. Barnabas and Paul had brought Mark from Jerusalem to Antioch (Ac 12 25), and had chosen him to act as their ' minister ' (i.e. ministerial assistant for such work as catechising and baptising converts, which was not ordinarily done by the Apostles in person, 1 Cor 1 14-17) on their first missionary journey (Ac 13 5). But after passing through Cyprus, Mark left them and returned to Jerusalem (Ac 13 13). The causes of this action were partly personal. St. Mark, it seems probable, resented the growing ascendency of St. Paul over his cousin St. Barnabas, but most of all he disliked St. Paul's treatment of uncircumcised Gentiles as the equals of circumcised Jews. He therefore preferred to return to the thoroughly Hebrew Church of Jerusalem. The breach was not healed even by the Council of Jerusalem, which occurred some three or four years later. Soon after that event, when Barnabas proposed to Paul to take Mark on another missionary journey, St. Paul refused, and a warm dispute parted the two friends, St. Mark accompanying St. Barnabas to Cyprus (Ac 15 37). Ultimately, however, the breach between St. Mark and St. Paul was healed. St. Paul, writing from his prison in Rome (61 A.D.), speaks of him in affectionate terms as a companion and fellow-labourer (Philemon v. 24 Col 4 10). A few years later, writing shortly before his death (66 A.D.), he speaks of him as ' profitable to me for the ministry,' or, rather, ' profitable to me for ministering,' and bids Timothy bring him with him (2 Tim 4 11).

But it is as the companion of St. Peter that St. Mark is best known to ecclesiastical tradition. According to the apostolic presbyter before referred to, St. Mark became the ' interpreter ' of St. Peter, probably after the release of St. Paul from his first imprisonment. St. Peter, in all probability, was not a very good Greek or Latin scholar. Preaching in Aramaic, he required the services of an interpreter to translate his sermons clause by clause into Greek or Latin, as the case might be, and also to conduct his correspondence. The relation of St. Mark to St. Peter as his ' interpreter ' is confirmed by 1 Peter, written from Rome, where St. Peter says, ' The church that is at Babylon (i.e. Rome), elected together with you, saluteth you ; and so doth Marcus my son ' (1 Pet 5 13).

722

After the martyrdom of St. Peter (circ 67 A.D.) little is known of the life of St. Mark. Tradition makes him the founder and first bishop of the important Church of Alexandria. He is not spoken of as a martyr by any writer earlier than the 5th cent. He is commemorated by the Church on April 25th.

2. Authorship of St. Mark's Gospel. The direct authorship of the second Gospel by St. Mark has never been disputed in the Church, and even modern negative criticism is disposed to regard him as the author of at least the nucleus of the present Gospel. In ancient times it was sometimes alluded to as the 'memoirs of Peter,' or 'Peter's Gospel,' it being the common opinion that St. Mark did no more than reproduce the substance of St. Peter's preaching. The most ancient witness, the apostolic presbyter whose sayings are recorded by Papias about 130 A.D., gives the following important testimony : 'Mark having become (or, having been) Peter's interpreter, wrote all that he remembered (or all that Peter related) ; though he did not [record] in order that which was said or done by Christ. For he neither heard the Lord nor followed Him ; but subsequently, as I said, [attached himself] to Peter, who used to frame his teaching to meet the [immediate] wants [of his hearers] ; and not as making a connected narrative of the Lord's discourses. So Mark committed no error, as he wrote down some particulars just as he recalled them to mind. For he took heed to one thing—to omit none of the facts that he heard, and to state nothing falsely in [his narrative of] them.' From this it appears that the presbyter, while satisfied with St. Mark's general care and accuracy, was for some reason or other dissatisfied with his 'order,' preferring probably either that of St. Luke, who was specially careful to write 'in order,' or that of St. John, who gives a distinct chronology. The presbyter's statement that St. Mark's Gospel depends on St. Peter is confirmed by internal evidence. It records three events—the raising of Jairus' daughter, the Transfiguration, and the Agony—at which only Peter, James, and John were present. James was soon martyred (Ac 12 2). John wrote an independent Gospel. Peter alone remains as St. Mark's authority for these events.

3. Its Literary History. St. Mark's Gospel, having been used by St. Matthew and St. Luke, must be earlier than either. Its exact date depends upon the date assigned to the latter Gospel. If St. Luke's Gospel was written, as many suppose, during St. Paul's imprisonment in Rome about 61 A.D., St. Mark's Gospel must be dated about 60 A.D., or earlier. But the date of the third Gospel is quite uncertain, hence many authorities date

St. Mark as late as 66–70 A.D., relying mainly on Mk 13 14, on which see the notes. Ancient testimony is divided as to whether the Gospel was written before or after St. Peter's martyrdom (64 or 67 A.D.). The oldest witness, Irenæus (177 A.D.), says, 'After the decease of [Peter and Paul] Mark, the disciple and interpreter of Peter, himself also delivered to us in writing the substance of Peter's preaching.' But a witness nearly as ancient, Clement of Alexandria, says, 'When Peter had preached the Word publicly in Rome, and by the Spirit had declared the gospel, his hearers, who were numerous, exhorted Mark, as one who had followed him a long time, and remembered what was said, to write down his words. Accordingly Mark composed the Gospel and circulated it among those who asked him to write it. When Peter heard of it he neither hindered nor encouraged the work.'

That the Gospel was published at Rome is attested by nearly all the ancient authorities, and is the general verdict of modern criticism. The only passage which seems to suggest a Palestinian origin is 13 14. In this v. the evangelist shows his special affection and solicitude for the Churches of Jerusalem by inserting a special warning to them to watch for the sign of the desecration of the Temple, and immediately upon its occurrence to flee to a place of safety. But it does not follow that the evangelist, at the time of writing, was actually in Palestine. In distant Rome his thoughts would often turn to his old home at Jerusalem and his relations and friends in the neighbourhood, and nothing is more natural than that he should insert such an affectionate warning as this verse contains.

For the history of the Gospel after publication, the probable loss of its original ending, and the authorship of the present appendix, see on 16 9-20.

St. Mark certainly wrote in Greek. The recent attempts to prove an Aramaic original have failed to carry conviction.

4. Contents and Character of the Gospel. The second Gospel is addressed to Gentile Christians, primarily those of Rome. This is shown by its careful explanations of Jewish customs, localities, etc., washings (7 3), Passover (14 12), Preparation (15 42) ; and especially of Aramaic words, 'Boanerges' (3 17), 'Talitha cumi' (5 41), 'Corban' (7 11), 'Ephphatha' (7 34), 'Bartimæus' (10 46), 'Abba' (14 36), 'Eloi,' etc. (15 34): also by its numerous Latinisms, 'denarius' (6 37), 'census' (12 14), 'centurio' (15 39), 'quadrans' (12 42), 'legio' (5 9), 'sextarius' (7 4), 'speculator' (6 27), 'satis facere' (15 12). Significant also in this connexion is the fact that it contains no direct mention of 'the Law,' and hardly a single quotation from the OT., except in reports of our Lord's speeches. The Gospel has little, if any, theological or party tendency. It contains few of our Lord's numerous discourses, probably because extensive collections of them already existed. Of the numerous parables it records only four : the Sower (4³), the Seed growing secretly (4²⁶), the Mustard Seed (4³⁰), and the Wicked Husbandmen (12¹); of the great discourses only one, the prophecy of the fall of Jerusalem (13⁵). Its aim is to present a graphic picture of the events of the ministry as St. Peter knew them, from the baptism to the resurrection. It deals almost entirely with the objective facts, especially the miracles of healing, which it describes with great fulness.

As compared with the parallel narratives of St. Matthew and St. Luke, St. Mark's narrative is characterised by a vividness, fulness, and wealth of detail, which seem due to the testimony of an actual eye-witness. He notices our Lord's looks and emotions, His compassion (1⁴¹) ; His anger (3⁵) ; His turning about in the throng (5³⁰) ; His sighing and looking up to heaven (7³⁴) ; His leading the blind man, spitting, and putting His hands on his eyes (8²³) ; His sitting down and calling the Twelve (9³⁵) ; His putting His hands on little children (10¹⁶) ; His love of the young ruler (10²¹). He mentions graphic details neglected by the other evangelists : the two thousand swine (5¹³) ; the sitting down in ranks by hundreds and by fifties (6⁴⁰) ; the crucifixion at 'the third hour' (15²⁵) ; the sitting in the sea (4¹) ; the sleeping on a pillow (4³⁸) ; the sitting over against the treasury (12⁴¹). His accounts of the healing of demoniacs are particularly full. He evidently regarded these miracles as a special proof of Christ's Messianic dignity.

5. Matter Peculiar to this Gospel. The second Gospel contains only about 30 vv. peculiar to itself. These include the parable of the seed growing secretly (4²⁶), the healing of the blind man at Bethsaida (8²²), and the story of the young man who fled from his pursuers (14⁵¹).

6. Analysis of the Gospel.
(1) The Forerunner of Jesus (1¹⁻⁸).
(2) The baptism and temptation (1⁹⁻¹³).
(3) The ministry in and near Capernaum (1¹⁴–4³⁴).
(4) The ministry on both sides of the Sea of Galilee (4³⁵–7²³).
(5) In the neighbourhood of Tyre and Sidon (7²⁴⁻³⁰).
(6) On the eastern side of the lake (7³¹–8²¹).
(7) At Bethsaida (8²²⁻²⁶).
(8) Journey to Cæsarea Philippi (8²⁷–9²⁹).
(9) The last journey to Jerusalem (9³⁰–10⁵²).

(10) Holy Week (11¹–15⁴⁷).
(11) The Resurrection (16).

7. Relation to the other Synoptic Gospels. Since St. Mark contains hardly any matter not also contained in St. Matthew and St. Luke, he has until recent times been comparatively neglected. By the ancients he was regarded as an abbreviator of St. Matthew, and a few modern authorities have held the same view. But at present the superior originality of St. Mark is conceded on all hands, and it is generally admitted that the first and third evangelists derived from him all those incidents which they record in common with him.

Some critics have argued from the admitted 'priority' of St. Mark, that he alone is trustworthy, but this is a precarious inference. There is not the least evidence that the 'logia,' or collections of discourses used by St. Matthew and St. Luke are either less trustworthy or less ancient than the Second Gospel. For further information on this subject the reader is referred to art. 'The Synoptic Problem.'

8. St. Mark and the Miraculous Birth of Jesus. It is sometimes argued that, because St. Mark did not mention our Lord's birth of a virgin, he disbelieved it. But his silence is sufficiently explained by his design of recording only those facts about our Lord's life, of which St. Peter had personal experience. St. Peter's knowledge of Jesus began at His baptism, so that St. Mark naturally began his narrative at this point. Some think that St. Mark wrote before the miracle of our Lord's conception was generally known ; others that he shows his knowledge of it in 6³.

9. The last Twelve Verses : see on 16⁹⁻²⁰.
(The commentary on St. Mark in a work of this kind is necessarily a skeleton, because nearly the whole subject-matter has already been dealt with in the commentary on St. Matthew. By referring, as directed, to the parallel passages in St. Matthew [and occasionally in St. Luke], the student will be able to supply whatever is deficient in the commentary on St. Mark.)

CHAPTER 1

BAPTISM OF JESUS. BEGINNING OF THE MINISTRY

1–8. Appearance of John the Baptist (Mt 3¹ Lk 3¹). See on Mt and Lk. St. Mark's Gospel, being based on the reminiscences of Peter, begins with the public ministry of Jesus, or, rather, with His connexion with the Baptist, through which Peter and other apostles first became acquainted with Him. It, therefore, omits the birth narratives, although it is possible that St. Mark was acquainted with them (see on 6³).

1. The beginning] It is clear that at first

the elementary preaching of the gospel by the apostles began with the baptism of Jesus by John, and that it was only subsequently, and to the initiated alone, that the secret of our Lord's miraculous birth was disclosed. The reasons for this prudential reserve during the Virgin's lifetime are obvious. **The Son of God**] These words are omitted by Westcott and Hort, practically on the authority of a single MS. They are rightly retained by the RV, and by Swete. **2. In the prophets**] RV 'in Isaiah the prophet.' The quotation, however, is not entirely taken from Isaiah, but partly from Mal 3[1] and partly from Isa 40[3]. The quotation from Malachi does not occur in the parallels. **Before thy face**] In the Heb. 'before *my* face.' This was clearly a Christian adaptation of the passage : see on Mt 11[10].

9–11. Baptism of Jesus (Mt 3[13] Lk 3[21]). See on Mt.

12, 13. The temptation (Mt 4[1] Lk 4[1]). See on Mt. St. Mark alone has the graphic touch that He was 'with the wild beasts.'

14, 15. Arrest of John and beginning of the Galilean ministry (Mt 4[12] Lk 4[14] Jn 4[1-3]). See on Mt.

16–20. Call of Simon, Andrew, James, and John (Mt 4[18], cp. Lk 5[1]). See on Mt.

21–28. A demoniac healed in the synagogue at Capernaum (Lk 4[31]). A striking point in this miracle is the testimony of the demon to Christ's Messiahship, which, however, He refused to accept. If the possession was real, the demon's confession of Christ as 'the Holy One of God' was probably extorted by fear. If the possession was not real, but imagined by the insane man, the confession was probably due to the man's instinctive sense that a person with supernatural powers was present, ready to heal him.

22. Taught] To teach with authority, as distinguished from mere exhortation, was only allowed to those who had received rabbinical ordination. Christ was probably allowed to teach, like John, as a prophet, not as a rabbi.

24. What have we, etc.] The plural is generally understood to prove the actual existence of the indwelling evil spirit. At the same time, it is a well-known fact that if an insane person is the victim of a delusion, he adapts all his words and actions to accord with it. If the insane person believed that he was possessed by a devil, he would be likely to speak in the plural. **The Holy One of God**] see Jn 6[69].

25. It was not expedient that Christ or the apostles should receive what was generally supposed to be diabolical testimony (Mt 10[25] 12[24]). **26. Torn**] better, 'convulsed.' **27. What new doctrine**] RV 'A new teaching.'

29–34. Healing of Simon's wife's mother and others (Mt 8[14] Lk 4[38]). See on Mt. Ob-

serve St. Mark's graphic touch, **And all the city was gathered together at the door.**

35–39. Tours through Galilee (Lk 4[42]). See on Mt 4[23].

35. Prayed] To spend a night, or a great part of a night, in prayer, was our Lord's way of preparing for preaching (v. 38), for working miracles (9[29]), and for other important actions, such as the choice of the Twelve (Lk 6[12]).

40–45. The leper cleansed (Mt 8[1] Lk 5[12]). See on Mt.

45. (Peculiar to Mk.) It explains the reason why Jesus so often enjoined secrecy on those who were healed. He was afraid that the popular enthusiasm would lead to political complications.

CHAPTER 2
The Sick of the Palsy

1–12. Healing of the palsied man (Mt 9[1] Lk 5[17]). See on Mt.

13–17. Call of Levi (Mt 9[9] Lk 5[27]). See on Mt. **16. The scribes and Pharisees**] RV 'the scribes of the Pharisees' : implying that some scribes were Sadducees, though this was rare.

18–22. The controversy on fasting (Mt 9[14] Lk 5[33]). See on Mt. **21. New cloth**] RV 'undressed cloth.' **Else the new piece**] RV 'else that which should fill it up, taketh from it, the new from the old, and a worse rent is made.' **22. Old bottles**] RV 'old wine-skins.' **And the wine is spilled**] RV 'and the wine perisheth and the skins : but they put new wine into fresh wine-skins.'

23–28. Plucking the ears of corn on the sabbath (Mt 12[1] Lk 6[1]). See on Mt. **26. In the days of Abiathar the high priest**] RV 'when Abiathar was high priest.' A well-known difficulty, for Ahimelech seems to have been the high priest at this time. 'The whole expression, which occurs neither in Mt nor Lk, is omitted by a very important group of authorities, and may be an editorial note' (Swete). If it be retained, it is not to be regarded as a mere blunder, but as a deliberate inference from the somewhat conflicting data of the OT. For whereas in 1 S 21[1] Ahimelech appears as high priest, and is shortly afterwards slain by Saul for his friendship with David (1 S 22[16]), in 2 S 8[17] 1 Ch 18[16] 24[6] he appears long after his supposed death, officiating in the priesthood together with Zadok, and is represented as the son, not the father of Abiathar. St. Mark's expression is, therefore, quite in harmony with *one* of the two conflicting OT. accounts. Such confusions of proper names are not uncommon in the OT.

CHAPTER 3
Choice of the Twelve

1–6. The withered hand (Mt 12[9] Lk 6[6]). See on Mt. **6. Herodians**] see on Mt 22[16].

7-12. Withdrawal of Jesus. Multitudes healed. See on Mt 12¹⁵⁻¹⁷. St. Mark's account is much fuller. Observe here (a) the extraordinary sensation made by the appearance of Jesus, as shown by the great distances from which the multitudes were drawn; (b) the enormous number of cures, without any allusion to failures. Clearly the miracles recorded are only a very small proportion of the miracles performed.

8. Idumæa] The district S. of Judæa and the Dead Sea. **Beyond Jordan]** This district, like Tyre and Sidon, was mainly Gentile, and it is possible that among those healed were some Gentiles.

10. Plagues] lit. 'scourges,' diseases being regarded as a divine chastisement. **11. Thou art the Son of God]** i.e. 'the Messiah.' See on 1²¹⁻²⁸.

13-19ᵃ. Choice of the Twelve (Mt 10² Lk 6¹²). See on Mt.

17. Boanerges] The sons of Zebedee are so named from their vehement character, and perhaps also from their powerful eloquence (cp. 9³⁸ 10³⁷ Lk 9⁵³⁻⁵⁶). So Virgil speaks of 'the twin Scipiadæ, those two thunder-bolts of war.' The form *Boanerges* is corrupt and its derivation doubtful. Probably it stands for the Heb. *B'ne regesh*, 'sons of tumult.' *Regesh* means 'thunder' in Arabic, and it may have done so (though there is no clear evidence that it did) in Hebrew and Aramaic.

18. The Canaanite] RV 'the Cananæan' or 'zealot': see on Mt 10⁴.

19ᵇ-30. Christ is accused of dealings with Beelzebub (Mt 12²²). See on Mt.

19. An house] perhaps Simon's. **20.** A graphic touch derived from the personal reminiscences of Peter. **21. His friends]** From v. 31 they appear to have been His mother and brethren. 'There is both a logical and chronological relation between this attitude of our Lord's family and this new phase of the opposition of the scribes. The logical relation is found in the language of the two. His family said "He is beside Himself"; the scribes said, "He is possessed by the devil himself." It is not, however, implied at all that His family was in sympathy with the scribes, their apprehension being simply that His mind was unsettled, and that He needed to be put under restraint. This lack of human sympathy with Him led Jesus to point out the higher reality of spiritual relationship and association' (Gould). The Fourth Gospel agrees with the synoptists in representing the 'brethren' as unbelievers and altogether unsympathetic (Jn 7⁵). Only their anxiety, not their unbelief, is to be attributed to the Virgin mother: see Jn 2³.

31-35. His mother and His brethren (Mt 12⁴⁶ Lk 8¹⁹). See on Mt, and on v. 21.

CHAPTER 4
PARABLE OF THE SOWER. STILLING THE TEMPEST

1-9. Parable of the Sower (Mt 13¹ Lk 8⁴). See on Mt.

10-20. The parable interpreted (Mt 13¹⁰ Lk 8⁹). See on Mt.

21-25. Further remarks upon teaching by parables (Lk 8¹⁶⁻¹⁸). Omitted by Mt, who introduces these sayings in other connexions, viz. Mt 5¹⁵ 7² 10²⁶, which see.

21. A candle] RV 'the lamp.' **A bushel]** RV 'the bushel.' **A bed]** RV 'the bed.' **A candlestick]** RV 'the stand.' St. Matthew introduces this saying into the Sermon on the Mount (Mt 5¹⁵). There it bids the disciples give to the world the light of a good example. Here it bids them enlighten the world by their teaching. **22. For there is nothing hid]** 'Our Lord corrects a false impression which might have arisen from the mention of a mystery (v. 11). If the gospel was for a moment treated as a secret, it was so only because this temporary secrecy was essential to its successful proclamation after the Ascension. Those to whom the secret was now confided were charged with the responsibility of publishing it then' (Swete). See further on Mt 10²⁶, where the saying recurs. **23.** See on Mt 11¹⁵. **24. Take heed what ye hear** (AV, RV). The context, however, requires that this should be rendered 'Understand (weigh well the meaning of) what ye hear,' a quite possible rendering. **With what measure ye mete]** i.e. 'ye measure.' 'In that measure in which you measure your attention to My teaching, in the same measure will spiritual understanding be measured unto you' (Euthymius). This proverb occurs in several connexions (Mt 7² Lk 6³⁸ q.v.). **25.** To the diligent student of divine truth more of divine truth shall be revealed. The slothful student shall not only learn no more, but shall even forget what he already knows. In Mt 13¹² 25¹⁹, the context being different, these words have a different meaning.

26-29. The seed growing secretly (the only parable peculiar to Mk). Tatian in his 'Diatessaron' places it immediately before the Tares. Such a position for it is suitable, but it is wrong to regard it, with Weiss, as only an imperfect and mutilated version of that parable.

The point of the parable is not so much the secret invisible energy of the seed, or divine Word, as that of the earth into which the seed falls, i.e. the moral and spiritual nature of man. The seed of Christianity will grow, because the soil into which it will fall is suitable to nourish it. The human soul is 'naturally Christian' (Tertullian), and Christianity is the 'natural religion.' Christianity can, therefore, propagate itself without human effort, and often does so.

26. A man] i.e. the apostles and other preachers of the gospel. **Cast seed**] i.e. preach the gospel by word or example. **The ground**] i.e. the souls of men.

27. Sleep, and rise] i.e. ministers of the gospel having preached the word are to pursue their ordinary employments without undue anxiety. Visible results may be slow, but the seed is sure to germinate, because the soul of man is specially fitted by God to receive it, and will by its own spiritual activity cause it at last to bear fruit. Christ does not, however, discourage due pastoral care. Though the earth brings forth of herself, 'this does not exclude due cultivation, and rain from heaven, and sunshine' (Bengel).

28. First the blade, etc.] Therefore missionaries who have no results to show, are not to be discouraged. In India at present, few converts are made, but the seed is being sown, and the time of the harvest will come.

29. The harvest] is an earthly harvest. It is gathered in Christian lands, when a faithful pastor, after long waiting, gathers in a harvest of true penitents and genuine servants of Christ. It is gathered in heathen lands, when the hindrances to the gospel are at last removed, and the people ask for baptism. Many, however, regard 'the harvest' here as that at the end of the world.

30–32. The grain of mustard seed (Mt 13 31 Lk 13 18). See on Mt.

33, 34. Mt 13 34, 35. See on Mt 13 10-17.

35–41. Stilling the storm (Mt 8 18, 23-27 Lk 8 22). See on Mt. St. Mark's graphic details should be noticed—'the other boats with Him,' v. 36, and 'the pillow (cushion) in the stern,' v. 38.

CHAPTER 5

THE GADARENE DEMONIAC. JAIRUS' DAUGHTER

1–20. The Gadarene (Gerasene) demoniac (Mt 8 28 Lk 8 26). See on Mt; Mk's account is much the fullest.

1. Gadarenes] RV 'Gerasenes.' **9.** Mk and Lk (not Mt) state that the man called himself 'Legion,' because he believed himself to be possessed by numerous devils.

18–20. Our Lord thought the quiet of home life better for the man than the excitement of going about with Him. He told him to proclaim the miracle, because in this mainly Gentile district there was no danger of popular excitement. **20. Decapolis**] see on Mt 4 25.

21–43. The woman with the issue, and Jairus' daughter (Mt 9 18 Lk 8 40). See on Mt.

30. Knowing that virtue (peculiar to Mk and Lk). **37.** Mk and Lk (not Mt) mention that Peter, James and John witnessed this

miracle. These three were also privileged to be present at the Transfiguration and the Agony in Gethsemane.

41. Talitha cumi] (peculiar to Mk). St. Mark heard from St. Peter's lips the exact Aramaic words spoken by Jesus.

CHAPTER 6

VISIT TO NAZARETH. MISSION OF THE TWELVE. EXECUTION OF THE BAPTIST. FEEDING OF THE FIVE THOUSAND. WALKING ON THE SEA

1–6. Visit to Nazareth (Mt 13 54).

3. Is not this the carpenter ?] Mt 'Is not this the carpenter's son ?' Baur, Bleek, Renan, and Hilgenfeld regard St. Mark's version of this expression as a proof that he was acquainted with the Virgin Birth. 'Mark tolerates not the paternity of Joseph even in the mouth of Nazarenes' (Hilgenfeld). Most scholars dispute the inference.

It is not quite certain whether Jesus was a carpenter or a smith. The Greek word may mean either. According to an ancient tradition He made ploughs and yokes.

Celsus (160 A.D.) derides the mean and servile occupation of Jesus, but manual work was honoured among the Jews. 'It is incumbent,' said the rabbis, 'on the father to circumcise his son, to redeem him, to teach him the Law, and to teach him some occupation.' Rabbi Judah said, 'Whosoever teacheth not his son to do some work, is as if he taught robbery.' Rabbi Meir said, 'Let a man always endeavour to teach his son an honest trade.'

5. He could there do] This expression, as presenting an apparent difficulty to faith, is more original than St. Matthew's 'He did not there many mighty works.' Of course the inability was moral. Jesus required faith in those who were to be healed, or in persons connected with them, and only in a very few cases waived this requirement (Jn 5 13).

7–13. Mission of the Twelve (Mt 10 1 Lk 9 1). See on Mt. **13. Anointed**] cp. Jas 5 14.

14–29. Herod and Jesus. Execution of the Baptist (Mt 14 1). See on Mt: cp. Lk 9 7.

20. Observed him] RV 'kept him safe.'

He did many things] RV 'he was much perplexed.' Herod's conscience was uneasy.

21. High captains] RM 'or, military tribunes, Gr. *chiliarchs*.' **Chief** *estates*] RV 'the chief men.' **22. The daughter of . . Herodias**] Hort, relying upon only five MSS, alters this into 'his daughter Herodias,' a reading which is clearly the blunder of some scribe, since it violates, as Weiss says, 'all history, all grammar, and the context.' **27. An executioner**] AVmg. 'one of his guard.' The word is Latin, corresponding either to *speculator*, 'a watcher,' a soldier of the bodyguard, or *spiculator*, 'one armed with a javelin,' and so an executioner.

The word often occurs in rabbinical Hebrew in the sense of an executioner.

30–44. Return of the apostles. Feeding the five thousand (Mt 14 13 Lk 9 10 Jn 6 1). See on Mt and Jn. The graphic touches in Mk should be noticed : ' Come ye yourselves apart,' etc.; ' no leisure so much as to eat ' ; ' as sheep not having a shepherd ' ; ' the green grass ' ; ' like garden beds.' These are reminiscences of the eyewitness Peter.

40. Ranks] i.e. groups, lit. ' garden-beds.'

45–52. Walking on the sea (Mt 14 22 Jn 6 15). See on Mt and Jn.

53–56. Miracles in the land of Gennesaret (Mt 14 34). See on Mt.

CHAPTER 7

EATING WITH UNWASHED HANDS. THE SYROPHŒNICIAN WOMAN. HEALING OF A DEAF MAN

1–23. Eating with unwashed hands (Mt 15 1). See on Mt.

3, 4. A note added by St. Mark for the benefit of his Gentile readers, who would not be familiar with Jewish customs. St. Matthew's Jewish readers needed no such explanation. **3. Wash** *their* **hands oft**] lit. ' wash their hands with the fist.' The Jewish custom was to wash the hands up to the wrist, and that is probably the meaning here, although it is hard to extract it from the present (perhaps corrupt) Gk. text. Wetstein thinks that ' a fist ' is the minimum quantity of water ($\frac{1}{4}$ of a *hin*, or pint), which was allowed for washing the hands. ' A quarter of a hin of water is the quantity appointed for one man's hands.' The AV, amending the text, reads, ' Except they wash their hands *oft*.' RV gives ' diligently,' a possible conjecture.

4. Except they wash] lit. ' baptise themselves.' The Jews carefully distinguished ' washing ' the hands, i.e. pouring water over them, from ' baptising ' or dipping them. In v. 3 pouring water over them is meant ; but here, after a visit to the market-place, in which all kinds of defilement would be met with, dipping them is regarded as necessary. Dipping the hands was performed before meals, washing at meal-times. **Washing of cups,** etc.] The details are too intricate to be given here. In some cases the articles were washed, in others only sprinkled. The ' cup ' is the Lat. *sextarius* = 1 pint. **And of tables**] rather, ' of beds,' or, couches for reclining at dinner.

11. Corban] see on Mt 15 5.

19. Purging all meats] RV ' *This he said, making all meats clean* ' : see on Mt 15 1-20.

24–30. The Syrophœnician woman (Mt 15 21). See on Mt.

31–37. The deaf man with an impediment in his speech (peculiar to Mk). This miracle is selected by Mk for its unusual character.

Usually our Lord healed instantaneously, here by stages : usually by a word, here by material means. The reason for the difference of treatment must be sought in the spiritual state of the sufferer. The miracle was done privately that the man, in the absence of the multitude, might be able to concentrate his attention. Jesus made use of the language of signs, because the man was deaf. He put his fingers in His ears, indicating that He would pierce through the obstruction. He touched His tongue, indicating that He would remove the impediment in his speech. Having thus produced faith in the man, He worked the miracle. Edersheim thinks that our Lord used this elaborate process because the man was a Gentile, and, therefore, was with more difficulty brought to believe and to understand.

31. Tyre] see on Mt 15 21.

33. Spit] RV ' spat ' : see Jn 9 6. ' He spat on his tongue, using a means of healing accepted in popular opinion of Jew and Gentile. The use of saliva for cures is universally recognised by the rabbis ' (Edersheim).

34. Sighed] moved by the afflictions of humanity. **Ephphatha**] Here, as often, St. Mark, following St. Peter, preserves the actual Aramaic expression of our Lord : cp. 5 41.

The ceremony of ' opening the ears,' i.e. touching them with saliva and saying ' *Ephphatha*, Be opened,' was introduced into the Baptismal service probably in the 4th cent.

CHAPTER 8

FEEDING THE FOUR THOUSAND. THE SIGN FROM HEAVEN. HEALING OF A BLIND MAN. CONFESSION OF PETER

1–10. Feeding the four thousand (Mt 15 32). See on Mt.

11–13. A sign from heaven sought (Mt 16 1). See on Mt.

14–21. A warning against the leaven of the Pharisees and of Herod (Mt 16 4). See on Mt.

22–26. A blind man healed at Bethsaida (peculiar to Mk, and selected, like the healing in 7 32, for its unusual features). The man was healed in stages, probably because his faith was imperfect. Jesus first strengthened his faith by partly healing him, and then, when his faith was adequate, completed the cure.

22. Bethsaida] see on Jn 1 49. **23. Spit**] see on 7 33. **Put his hands**] cp. 9 18 19 13.

24. I see, etc.] RV ' I see men ; for I behold them as trees walking.' Medical testimony agrees with the process here described. Cheselden says of a patient of his who, having been born blind, recovered his sight, ' When he first saw, he knew not the shape of anything, nor any one thing from another, however different in shape or magnitude.'

26. Neither go, etc.] RV ' Do not even enter into the village.'

27-C. 9¹. Confession of Peter (Mt 16¹³ Lk 9¹⁸). See on Mt.

CHAPTER 9

THE TRANSFIGURATION. AN EPILEPTIC HEALED. PREDICTION OF HIS DEATH

2-8. The Transfiguration (Mt 17¹ Lk 9²⁸). See on Mt.

9-13. A question about Elijah. See on Mt 17⁹⁻¹³.

14-29. An epileptic healed (Mt 17¹⁴ Lk 9³⁷). See on Mt.

23. If thou canst believe] RV 'If thou canst ! All things,' etc. **29. By prayer and fasting]** RV omits 'and fasting,' but the evidence for it is strong.

30-32. Prediction of the Passion (Mt 17²² Lk 9⁴³). See on Mt.

33-37. The controversy as to which should be greatest (Mt 18¹ Lk 9⁴⁶). See on Mt.

38-40. The man casting out devils in Christ's name (Lk 9⁴⁹). The apostles report that a private Christian, who had not been called to the apostolic office ('he followeth not *with* us,' Lk), and had received no definite commission from Christ to work miracles, as the apostles had (3¹⁵), was nevertheless casting out devils in Christ's name. Jealous for the privileges of their newly acquired office, they forbade him, but Christ says that they ought to have welcomed his help. Cp. the history of Eldad and Medad (Nu 11²⁶), where Moses rebukes Joshua for the same jealous attitude. The lesson is that the spiritual gifts of the laity ought to be fully developed and utilised for the good of the Church, and that the clergy ought to welcome and not be jealous of their help.

38. John] The name only in Mark. The fiery temperament of Boanerges here comes out.

39. That can lightly speak evil of me] RV 'and be able quickly to speak evil of me.' The success of the man's ministry proved the genuineness of his faith. If he had been an enemy of Jesus, he could not have worked the miracles : see Ac 19¹³. **40. For he that is not against us is on our part]** Much to be preferred is the more pointed version of Lk, which is also strongly attested here : 'For he that is not against you is for you' (Lk RV). The meaning is, The man, though without your apostolic commission, was doing, and doing successfully, the very same benevolent work that you were doing. You ought, therefore, to have esteemed him a friend and a helper, not an enemy. A jealous and exclusive spirit is unworthy of the ministers of Christ.

41-50. On offences (Mt 18⁶ Lk 17¹). See on Mt. **41.** See on Mt 10⁴². **44, 46.** These vv. (which are identical with v. 48) are omitted by the best modern authorities.

48. Where their worm dieth not] Isa 66²⁴.

Literally, the worm is the maggot bred in putrefying substances (Ex 16²⁰ Isa 14¹¹ Ac 12²³). Figuratively it stands for the moral corruption and degradation which follow upon a long course of wilful sin, and ultimately issue in eternal death. The lost soul, being at length hopelessly corrupt, and loathsome even to itself, has its own hell within it.

49. For every one shall be salted with fire] The conclusion of this v. (and every sacrifice shall be salted with salt) is omitted by the RV, but is too strongly attested to be safely rejected. The saying is a most difficult one, and there are about twenty different interpretations. The probable meaning is, Every believer shall be 'salted,' i.e. purified and prepared for eternity, by the 'fire' of discipline, i.e. by the struggles with the flesh (v. 43), and other afflictions and temptations of this life ; and 'every sacrifice,' i.e. every person, who presents himself, his soul, and body, to be a reasonable, holy, and living sacrifice to God, shall be 'salted,' i.e. purified and prepared for eternity, by the salt of divine grace. The 'salt' here is the salt of the new covenant, i.e. the grace which is given to believers in Christ : see Lv 2¹³.

50. Salt *is* good] 'Divine grace is good, but if the divine grace given to you as Christians dies, owing to your neglect to use it, how will you revive it ? Preserve and make due use of the divine grace given to you, especially the grace of charity, and thus you will be at peace with one another.' In Mt 5¹³, by an easy transference, the apostles themselves are called 'salt,' as possessing divine grace. Among the ancients salt was an emblem of wisdom and of friendship. To the latter signification our Lord alludes when He says, 'Have peace one with another.'

CHAPTER 10

THE QUESTION OF DIVORCE. THE RICH YOUNG MAN. BLIND BARTIMÆUS

1-12. The question of divorce (Mt 19³). See on that passage, and on Mt 5³². St. Mark represents our Lord as prohibiting divorce absolutely, without mentioning any exception.

1. See on Mt 19¹ : cp. Lk 17¹¹.

13-16. The blessing of little children (Mt 19¹³ Lk 18¹⁵). See on Mt.

17-22. The rich young man (Mt 19¹⁶ Lk 18⁸). See on Mt.

17. Good Master] Mk and Lk represent the young man as saying, 'Good Master, what shall I do that I may inherit eternal life ?' and Jesus as replying, 'Why callest thou me good ?' etc. ; whereas Mt represents the young man as saying, 'Master, what good thing shall I do, that I may have eternal life ?' and Jesus as replying, 'Why askest thou me concerning that which is good ?'

etc. (RV). The true version is clearly that of Mk and Lk. The author of Mt (or perhaps an early scribe, for there is considerable reason for thinking that the original text of Mt agreed with Mk and Lk) altered the text slightly, to prevent the reader from supposing that Christ denied that He was good.

18. Why callest, etc.] RV 'Why callest thou me good? None is good save one, even God.' Since Jesus declares Himself, and is repeatedly declared by others to be sinless (Jn 6 61 8 46 14 30 1 Pet 2 22 1 Jn 3 5, etc.), this cannot mean that He was not good, but that for some reason or other on the present occasion He refused the title. (1) According to some He refused it, because in the sense in which it was offered, it was unequal to His merits and His claims. The young man, they think, called Him good, in the sense in which he would have called any eminent Rabbi good, whereupon our Lord pointedly remarked that only God is good, meaning, 'If you call me good in the same sense in which God is good, I am willing to accept it, but if you call me good in a merely human sense I reject it as insufficient.' (2) The other view is that the human nature of Christ, although 'sinless' during the whole of His earthly life, was not 'good' in the absolute sense. He advanced in 'goodness.' Passing through the different stages of a truly human experience, He acquired by conscious effort the virtues proper to each. He learned obedience (Heb 5 8), and was perfected through sufferings (Heb 2 10). He was truly tempted as we are, yet without sin (Heb 2 18 4 15), and maintained His virtue by prayer and constant watchfulness (Heb 5 7 Mt 14 23 f.). God, however, is 'good' absolutely. He can neither be tempted of evil nor advance in goodness. It is only as God, not as man, that Christ is 'good' in the absolute sense.

23-31. The perils of riches. The reward of those who despise them (Mt 19 24 Lk 18 24). See on Mt.

30. For their temporal losses they will have a hundredfold return in spiritual blessings, including holy fellowship with saints and angels. 'Houses' and 'lands' perhaps stand for rich spiritual possessions. If their literal meaning is to be pressed, our Lord indicates that, owing to the prevailing spirit of brotherly love, which issued in the apostolic communism, Christians would enjoy their houses and lands in common, as members of one family.

Persecutions] A startling word in the midst of a shower of blessings. Yet persecutions are often, to a Christian, the greatest blessing of all.

32-34. The passion predicted (Mt 20 17 Lk 18 31). See on Mt.

35-45. The ambition of James and John (Mt 20 20). See on Mt.

46-52. Blind Bartimæus (Mt 20 29 Lk 18 35). See on Mt. The name of the blind man (Bartimæus lit. 'son of Timæus') is given only by Mk.

CHAPTER 11

JESUS RIDES INTO JERUSALEM. THE FIG TREE. CLEANSING THE TEMPLE. CHRIST'S AUTHORITY CHALLENGED

1-11. The entry into Jerusalem (Mt 21 1 Lk 19 29 Jn 12 12). See on Mt and Jn.

10. Blessed be **the kingdom of our father David**] These words, peculiar to Mk, show that the people expected Him to set up an earthly kingdom like David's, and that immediately.

12-14. Cursing of the fig tree (Mt 21 18). See on Mt.

15-19. Cleansing of the temple (Mt 21 12 Lk 19 45). See on Mt and on Jn 2 13.

16. Any **vessel**] This prohibition is peculiar to Mk. The people make a thoroughfare through the Temple, carrying with them baskets, household utensils, etc. **17. Of all nations**] These words, though found in Isa 56 7, are recorded only by Mk. They show that our Lord distinctly contemplated the call of the Gentiles.

20-26. The withering of the fig tree. The power of faith (Mt 21 20). See on Mt.

25. This v. does not occur in the parallel passage in Mt, but there is something similar in the Sermon on the Mount (Mt 6 14).

Stand] The customary attitude of prayer: see on Mt 6 5 f.

26. This v. is omitted by many modern critics; but there is considerable evidence for its retention: cp. Mt 6 15 18 35.

27-33. Christ's authority to teach (Mt 21 23 Lk 20 1). See on Mt.

CHAPTER 12

VARIOUS INCIDENTS AND DISCOURSES IN THE TEMPLE

1-12. The wicked husbandmen (Mt 21 33 Lk 20 9). See on Mt.

13-17. The tribute money (Mt 22 15 Lk 20 20). See on Mt.

18-27. The Sadducees and the Resurrection (Mt 22 23 Lk 20 27). See on Mt. **26. In the bush**] RV 'in the place' (i.e. passage) 'concerning the bush.'

28-34. The great commandment (Mt 22 34). See on Mt.

35-37. Is Christ the son of David (Mt 22 41 Lk 20 41). See on Mt.

38-40. Warning against the scribes (Lk 20 45). Mt inserts at this point a long and severe discourse against the scribes and Pharisees (Mt 23 1).

38. Cp. Mt 23 6 (23 14). **Long clothing**] (lit. 'stoles'). The word is used in LXX for priestly and royal robes, and in NT. for dress worn on festive occasions. Not the use, but the ostentatious use, of dignified costume is condemned by Christ. **Salutations**] see on Mt 23 [7]. **39. Uppermost rooms, etc.**] RV 'chief places at feasts.' If there were three on a couch, the chief guest lay in the middle. If there were two on a couch, he lay on the right side. **40. Devour widows' houses**] Devout women were accustomed to contribute to the support of famous rabbis (15 [41] Lk 8 [2]), and our Lord probably here refers to the abuse of such generosity. But inasmuch as the scribes and Pharisees were the rulers and judges of the nation, He may refer to their corruption and rapacity in the administration of justice, whereby they oppressed the poor.

41–44. The widows' mite (Lk 21 [1]).

41. The treasury] According to the Talmud there were in the Court of the Women thirteen chests for offerings called 'Trumpets,' from which three times in the year, before the three chief feasts, the money was transferred to the treasury called *Corbanas*. Each was marked with the object to which the offerings it received were to be devoted, e.g. temple expenses, sacrifices, oil, wine, incense, sacred vessels, etc. Cp. Jn 8 [20]. **Money**] lit. 'brass.' Perhaps small copper coins, such as the *as* and *quadrans*, are meant (Mt 5 [26] 10 [29]).

42. A (lit. 'one') **poor widow**] cp. Mt 21 [19]: 'one fig tree.'

42. Two mites] lit. 'two *lepta*, which make a quadrans.' The *lepton* was a Greek coin, the smallest in circulation, equivalent to $\frac{1}{80}$ of a *denarius*, or $\frac{1}{8}$ of a farthing. The widow offered two, because the rabbis forbade a single *lepton* to be placed in the almschest.

43. Hath cast more in] i.e. more in proportion to her means, and so has pleased God more. 'A certain woman offered a handful of wheat meal, and the high priest despised her, saying, How worthless this is to eat, how worthless to offer. But in a dream it was revealed to him. Despise her not, for it is the same as if she had offered her soul (or, life)' (The Talmud). 'Liberality is estimated according to a man's substance' (Aristotle).

CHAPTER 13
GREAT PROPHECY OF THE FALL OF JERUSALEM AND OF THE END OF THE WORLD

1–37. Christ's great prophecy (Mt 24 [1] Lk 21 [5]). See on Mt.

14. Spoken of by Daniel the prophet] RV rightly omits these words. **Let him that readeth understand**] Words of the evangelist, not of Jesus, intended to warn Palestinian readers to watch carefully for the fulfilment of this sign, and immediately afterwards to flee for their lives. They do not necessarily indicate, as some think, that the fulfilment was already imminent, and that therefore the

date of the Gospel is as late as 66–70 A.D. See on Mt 24 [15].

32. Neither the Son] This is the true reading not only here, but in Mt 24 [36], where it has been altered in many MSS, probably as being a difficulty to faith. Rightly to understand it, we must remember that Jesus possessed two complete and perfect natures, the divine and the human. In His divine nature He knew all things whatsoever, but in His human nature He knew only such things as He willed to know. And since it was not expedient that we should know the day and the hour of the Last Judgment, He willed to be ignorant of it. This avowed ignorance implies no limitation of Christ's divine nature. Christ had no will but His Father's. When the Father willed to withhold from Him any of His designs, His will was to be ignorant.

The Arians taught that the Son was ignorant even in His divine nature, but Athanasius replied, 'But lovers of Christ recognise that the Word did not say, "I know not," as being the Word, for He knew; but He thus indicated His humanity, showing that ignorance is part of human nature.'

CHAPTER 14
THE LAST SUPPER. ARREST AND TRIAL OF JESUS

1, 2. A council of the Priests against Jesus (Mt 26 [1] Lk 22 [1]). See on Mt.

3–9. The anointing at Bethany (Mt 26 [6] Jn 12 [1]). See on Mt and Jn.

10, 11. Judas betrays Jesus (Mt 26 [14] Lk 22 [3]). See on Mt.

12–16. Preparations for the Last Supper (Mt 26 [17] Lk 22 [7]). See on Mt.

17–26. The Last Supper (Mt 26 [20] Lk 22 [14] Jn 13–17 1 Cor 11 [23]). See on Mt, Lk, Jn, 1 Cor.

24. The new testament] RV 'the covenant.' RM 'Some ancient authorities insert *new.*'

27–31. Jesus foretells Peter's denial. See on Mt 26 [31], where the other references are given.

30. Before the cock crow twice] 'Twice' is omitted by important ancient authorities, and is open to some doubt. The other three evangelists speak of only one crowing of the cock.

32–42. Agony in Gethsemane (Mt 26 [36] Lk 22 [40]: cp. Jn 18 [1]). See on Mt.

36. Abba] Aramaic for 'father.' Peculiar to Mk.

43–50. Arrest of Jesus (Mt 26 [47] Lk 22 [47] Jn 18 [2]). See on Mt and Jn.

51, 52. The young man who followed. The incident being peculiar to St. Mark, and a quite unimportant one, it is often supposed by modern commentators that the young man was the evangelist himself. Mark's mother certainly lived in Jerusalem (Ac 12 [12]). Other conjectures are St. John, James the Lord's brother, or a resident in the house where the last supper had been eaten.

51. A linen cloth] probably a night-dress, but J. Lightfoot thinks that it was a *tallith* (i.e. the large or synagogue *tallith*: see on Mt 23 [5]), which the young man, for ascetic purposes, wore as his only garment.

53-65. Trial of Jesus (Mt 26 [57] Lk 22 [54, 66]). See on Mt and Jn 18 [12].

58. I will destroy] Clearly the accusation was that Jesus had plotted to burn or otherwise destroy the Temple. Much less satisfactory is St. Matthew's version, ' I am *able* to destroy the Temple.' The words, ' that is made without hands,' and ' another made without hands,' are peculiar to Mk. Westcott and Hort give in their margin the remarkable reading, ' but in three days I will effect the resurrection of another (Temple) made without hands.' See on Mt 26 [61] Jn 2 [19].

66-72. Peter denies Jesus (Mt 26 [69] Lk 22 [55] Jn 18 [15, 25]). See on Mt and Jn.

68. And the cock crew] Omitted by important ancient authorities, and rejected as an interpolation by Westcott and Hort and RM. See on v. 30. **72. The second time**] Omitted by important ancient authorities ; bracketed by Swete : see on v. 30.

When he thought thereon] An expression of uncertain meaning, but the AV is probably right. Other interpretations :—' having covered his head ' (Theophylact, Field), ' he began to weep ' ; ' he wept vehemently ' ; ' when he had set his eyes on Jesus, he wept ' ; ' when he had rushed outside, he wept.'

CHAPTER 15
The Trial before Pilate. The Crucifixion

1-15. Trial before Pilate (Mt 27 [1, 11] Lk 23 [1, 13] Jn 18 [28]). See on Mt and Jn. For the trial before Herod see on Lk 23 [6].

16-20. The mockery (Mt 27 [27]). See on Mt. **16. Prætorium**] see on Jn 18 [28].

21-41. The Crucifixion (Mt 27 [31] Lk 23 [26] Jn 19 [16]). See on Mt, Lk, Jn.

21. Alexander and Rufus] These names occur only in Mk. They were clearly Christians of eminence, well known in the Roman Church for which this Gospel was composed. Rufus is probably the Rufus of Ro 16 [13], where he is called ' chosen in the Lord.' Who Alexander was, is unknown. It is unlikely that he is identical with any of the other Alexanders mentioned in NT. (Ac 19 [33] 1 Tim 1 [20] 2 Tim 4 [14]).

28. Nearly all modern editors omit this v. It is generally regarded as interpolated from Lk 22 [37], which, however, is not parallel.

31. Himself he cannot save] RM ' Can he not save himself ? ' **40. The less**] i.e. the little, generally identified with the son of Alphæus (Mt 10 [3]).

42-47. Burial of Jesus (Mt 27 [57] Lk 23 [50] Jn 19 [38]). See on Mt and Jn.

43. Waited for the kingdom of God] cp. Lk 2 [25, 38]. This, which is also St. Luke's expression, answers to St. Matthew's, ' who also himself was Jesus' disciple.' Joseph had discovered the King of the Kingdom for which he waited.

44. Whether, etc.] RM ' Whether he were already dead.'

47. Mary *the mother* **of Joses**] lit. ' Mary of Joses ' (or ' of Joseph,' for that spelling is also strongly supported). Who was this Mary ? She can hardly be the same as the ' Mary of James ' in 16 [1], for the evangelist (even if drawing from different sources) would hardly describe the same woman as ' of Joses ' and ' of James ' in two consecutive verses Nor is it easy to identify her with Mary the mother of James and Joses (15 [40]). She is not called ' Mary the mother of James and Joses,' or even ' Mary of James and Joses.' but simply ' Mary of Joses ' (or ' Joseph '). Hence it is most natural to translate, ' Mary the *daughter* of Joses ' (Joseph), and to regard her as the daughter (or just possibly the wife) of Joseph of Arimathæa, or of some unknown Joses (Joseph).

CHAPTER 16
The Resurrection

1-8. The women at the tomb, and the angel (Mt 28 [1] Lk 24 [1] Jn 20 [1]). See on Mt and Jn

1. Mary *the mother* **of James**] lit. ' Mary of James,' i.e. probably ' Mary daughter of James,' or just possibly ' Mary wife of James.' She is perhaps the same as Mary the mother of James and Joses, 15 [40].

9-20. Conclusion of the Gospel. One uncial MS gives a second termination to the Gospel as follows : ' And they reported all the things that had been commanded them briefly (or immediately) to the companions of Peter. And after this Jesus Himself also sent forth by them from the east even unto the west the holy and incorruptible preaching of eternal salvation.'

Internal evidence points definitely to the conclusion that the last twelve vv. are not by St. Mark. For, (1) the true conclusion certainly contained a Galilean appearance (Mk 16 [7], cp. 14 [28]), and this does not. (2) The style is that of a bare catalogue of facts, and quite unlike St. Mark's usual wealth of graphic detail. (3) The section contains numerous words and expressions never used by St. Mark. (4) Mk 16 [9] makes an abrupt fresh start, and is not continuous with the preceding narrative. (5) Mary Magdalene is spoken of (16 [9]) as if she had not been mentioned before, although she has just been alluded to twice (15 [47] 16 [1]). (6) The section seems to represent not a primary tradition, such as Peter's, but quite a secondary one, and in particular to be dependent upon the conclusion of St. Matthew, and upon Lk 24 13 f.

On the other hand, the section is no casual or unauthorised addition to the Gospel. From the 2nd cent. onwards, in nearly all manuscripts, versions, and other authorities, it forms an integral part of the Gospel, and it can be shown to have existed, if not in the apostolic, at least in the sub-apostolic age. A certain amount of evidence against it there is (though very little can be shown to be independent of Eusebius the Church historian, 265–340 A.D.), but certainly not enough to justify its rejection, were it not that internal evidence clearly demonstrates that it cannot have proceeded from the hand of St. Mark.

The most probable account of the literary history of the section seems to be the following. The Gospel of St. Mark, being the first extensive and authoritative account of our Lord's life as distinguished from His discourses, attained at its first publication (55–60 A.D.) a considerable circulation, first in the W. and afterwards in the E. At that time it concluded with an account of the Galilean appearance, which is now only to be found in St. Matthew (Mt 28 16). The subsequent publication of the First and Third Gospels, which incorporated practically its whole subject-matter, and were far more interesting as containing discourses, practically drove it out of circulation. When at the close of the apostolic age an attempt was made (probably in Rome) to collect the authentic memorials of the Apostles and their companions, a copy of the neglected Second Gospel was not easily found. The one that was actually discovered, and was used to multiply copies, had lost its last leaf, and so a fitting termination (the present appendix) was added by another hand. A recently discovered Armenian MS (1891) definitely ascribes the appendix to Ariston, i.e. probably Aristion, 'a disciple of the Lord' mentioned by Papias (130 A.D.).

Some think that the Gospel originally concluded at 16 8 ('for they were afraid'), but this is unlikely. Such a conclusion would be unaccountably abrupt—more so in the Greek than in the English ; and 16 7 14 28 prepare the way for and anticipate a Galilean appearance.

9–11. Appearance to Mary Magdalene. See on Jn 20 14.

9. Seven devils] cp. Lk 8 2.

10. She went] cp. Lk 24 10 Jn 20 18. **As they mourned and wept**] cp. Lk 24 17. The author of the 'Gospel of Peter' (150 A.D., or earlier) must probably be added to the early witnesses to these twelve vv., for he writes, 'And upon all these things we fasted and sat mourning and weeping night and day until the sabbath. . . But we, the twelve disciples of the Lord, wept and were grieved.' **11. Believed not**]

This appendix lays great stress on the slowness of the apostles to believe (vv. 13, 14). Cp. Mt 28 17 Lk 24 11, 25, 37 Jn 20 25, 27.

12, 13. Appearance to two disciples. They were walking to Emmaus : see Lk 24 13.

12. In another form] This is an explanation of the fact that Christ was not at first recognised. It differs somewhat from that of St. Luke, 'Their eyes were holden, that they should not know him' (Lk 24 16). **13. Neither believed they them**] Another slight discrepancy with St. Luke, who says (Lk 24 34) that when the two disciples reached Jerusalem they were greeted with the words, 'The Lord is risen indeed, and hath appeared to Simon.'

14–18. Appearance to the eleven. This is variously identified with the appearance on the evening of the resurrection day (Lk 24 36 Jn 20 19), and with the final interview (Ac 1 6). But Swete is probably right in thinking that after an allusion to the first appearance to the Eleven on Easter Day, the writer passes on to give a summary of the words of Jesus spoken on various occasions during the forty days.

14. Upbraided them] According to certain ancient MSS mentioned by Jerome (340–420 A.D.), the apostles thus replied to our Lord's reproaches : 'This age is the very essence of iniquity and incredulity, and on account of unclean spirits permits not the true virtue of God to be apprehended. Do Thou, therefore, now at this time reveal Thy justice (or, righteousness).'

15. Go ye into all the world] This seems part of the same charge as that mentioned Mt 28 18. **To every creature**] RV 'to the whole creation.' A rabbinical expression for mankind in general.

16. Baptism is here declared necessary to salvation only for those who have heard the gospel message. It is not declared necessary for unevangelised heathen, or for those who have not attained the age of reason. Not the want of baptism, but contempt of it condemns a man. (For infant baptism, see on Mt 19 13-15.) **Damned**] i.e. condemned.

17. New tongues] Some MSS omit 'new' : see on Ac 2 4. The gift of miracles was given in order to assist the diffusion of the gospel at the very first. When Christianity was firmly planted, the gift of miracles was withdrawn.

18. Serpents] cp. Lk 10 19 Ac 28 3. **Drink any deadly thing**] There is no example in the NT., but St. John and Barsabas (Ac 1 23) are said in early tradition to have drunk a cup of poison unharmed. **Lay hands on the sick**] doubtless at the same time anointing them with oil (6 13 Jas 5 14).

19, 20. The Ascension (Lk 24 50 Ac 1 9, which see). **19. On the right hand**] the place of highest honour and power. **20. Signs following**] viz. the miracles mentioned in vv. 17, 18

ST. LUKE

INTRODUCTION

1. Life of St. Luke. The word 'Luke' (*Loukas*) is a contraction of the Latin name *Lucanus*, often found in inscriptions.

St. Luke was a Gentile, or, as others think, a proselyte, of Antioch in Syria, where he followed the profession of a physician (Col 4 14). His connexion with Antioch which tradition affirms, is confirmed by the 'Western' reading of Ac 11 28, which implies that St. Luke was present when the prophet Agabus delivered his famous prophecy before the Church of Antioch. The same passage proves that he was not a convert of St. Paul, but one of the earliest members of the Church of Antioch, which apparently had from the beginning baptised Gentiles as well as Jews (see on Ac 11 20, where the true reading is 'Greeks').

He became a follower of St. Paul, and his companion in his missionary journeys. Many facts about his travels with St. Paul can be gathered from the Acts, because, though he does not name himself, he generally speaks of the Apostle's party as 'we' when he was present, and 'they' when he was absent. It thus appears that he joined the apostle at Troas on the Second Missionary journey (about 50 A.D.), and accompanied him to Philippi (Ac 16 10). Here St. Paul left him (17 1). After this for several years we cannot trace his movements, but he was probably engaged in missionary work in the district, for when St. Paul returned to Philippi some seven years later on his third missionary journey, St. Luke was still there (Ac 20 5). He then accompanied St. Paul on the rest of his travels until they reached Rome about 59 or 60 A.D.

During St. Paul's first imprisonment St. Luke was with him, though perhaps not continuously (Col 4 14 Philemon v. 24). He was also a companion of St. Paul during his second imprisonment (about 67 A.D.), when the Apostle was expecting martyrdom (2 Tim 4 11).

Nothing certain is known of St. Luke's subsequent life. A third-century authority says, 'Luke, by nation a Syrian of Antioch, a disciple of the apostles, and afterwards a follower of St. Paul, served his master blamelessly till his confession (martyrdom ?). For having neither wife nor children he died in Bithynia at the age of 74, filled with the Holy Ghost.'

2. Authorship of the Gospel. The canonical authority and authenticity of St. Luke's Gospel have never been questioned until quite recent times, and the following considerations seem to set the question beyond doubt.

It is admitted on all hands that Luke and Acts are by the same author. The reference in Acts to the 'former treatise,' the description of which exactly suits the Gospel (Ac 1 1), the common dedication to Theophilus (1 3 Ac 1 1), the general similarity of style, and the definitely Pauline conception of Christianity which both exhibit, are sufficient proofs of identity of authorship. That this author was St. Luke is proved at length in the Intro. to Acts (q.v.).

St. Luke's Gospel was used (and abused) by the heretic Marcion, 140 A.D. ; copiously quoted by Justin Martyr, 150 A.D. ; included by Tatian in his harmony of the four Gospels (*Diatessaron*), 160 A.D. ; used without doubt of its authenticity by Irenæus, 177 A.D. ; Theophilus of Antioch, 180 A.D. ; Tertullian, 200 A.D. ; and included in the Muratorian Canon of Scripture, 200 A.D.

3. Date, etc. The date of composition cannot be certainly determined. It is later than Mark, of which it appears to make use, and earlier than Acts, to which it forms an introduction. If, as seems probable, Acts was written at Rome about 62 A.D., Luke may be assigned to the preceding year, i.e. to the early part of St. Paul's imprisonment at Rome. Some suppose it to have been written earlier, about 57 A.D., at Cæsarea, and others considerably later, about 74, or even as late as 80 A.D.

4. Sources. When St. Luke wrote, a large number of written accounts of our Lord's life and work already existed (1 1), and it is to be supposed that he made diligent use of them. But since during the two years and more of St. Paul's imprisonment at Cæsarea (Ac 24 27) St. Luke was in Palestine, it is more than likely that he made good use of his opportunities of consulting the eyewitnesses themselves. Of written sources he almost certainly used St. Mark's Gospel. He is also said by some to have used St. Matthew's 'Logia,' i.e. a collection of our Lord's discourses written by St. Matthew, and now incorporated in the First Gospel But the differences of wording and arrangement in the sayings of our Lord common to the First and Third Gospels render this supposition some-

734

what hazardous. For a full discussion of this difficult question, the reader is referred to the article, 'The Synoptic Problem.'

Critics rightly argue from the presence in St. Luke's Gospel of a long section (9⁵¹–19²⁸), almost entirely peculiar to himself, that St. Luke must have used some 'special' source, i.e. some circle of traditions unconnected with those mainly Galilean traditions which underlie Mt and Mk. The materials for this section were either collected in Judæa, or more probably in Peræa, where most of the incidents are located. The birth narratives must also be assigned to a special source, which has been thought, from the nature of the information, to have been the Virgin mother herself. It is quite possible that she was still living when St. Luke was in Palestine. Since St. Luke is well informed about Herod, it is possible that one of his informants was Joanna, wife of Chuza, Herod's steward (8³).

Relation to St. John. There are some curiously close parallels between St. Luke's Gospel and St. John's. Both allude to the ministry in Judæa (4⁴⁴ 13³⁴). Both mention the visit of Peter to the sepulchre (24¹²), the sisters Martha and Mary (10³⁸), the appearance on Easter Eve (24³⁶). Both place the prediction of Peter's denial at the last supper (22³⁴), and the denial itself before the trial (22⁵⁴). Yet St. John's Gospel is probably quite independent of St. Luke's.

Relation to St. Paul. Ancient tradition exaggerated the influence of St. Paul upon St. Luke's Gospel. St. Paul's expression, 'according to my gospel' (Ro 16²⁵), was understood to mean 'according to St. Luke's Gospel.' Irenæus says, 'Luke, the companion of Paul, put down in a book the gospel preached by him (Paul),' whereas St. Luke himself says that he compiled his Gospel from the narratives of eyewitnesses. Yet the Pauline influence is real. Religious universalism is a more marked feature of this than of the other synoptic Gospels, and so is the doctrine of salvation by faith. The account of the Lord's Supper (at least in the usual text) is nearer to St. Paul's than to the synoptic account.

Relation to Marcion. The heretic Marcion issued about 140 A.D., an edition of St. Luke which began with Christ's teaching at Capernaum, and omitted many important passages. Some modern critics, at the risk of discrediting the authority of the Third Gospel, have maintained that Marcion's version of it is the only genuine one. It is, however, now generally recognised that the existing version of St. Luke is the older, and that Marcion altered it to suit his peculiar doctrinal views.

5. Style. Although not written in pure Attic Greek, St. Luke's Gospel and Acts have greater pretensions to style than any other NT. documents. St. Jerome says, 'his style is more polished, and savours of secular eloquence.' This is specially true of his preface, which follows classical models. But St. Luke varies his style to suit his subject-matter. Sometimes, as in the chs. describing the Nativity, he is intensely Hebraic, imitating the LXX. Sometimes, especially when describing our Lord's actions and words, he falls into the common unadorned style of the synoptic evangelists. But everywhere his style has its own distinctive marks, by which it can be readily recognised. He shows a considerable knowledge of the technical vocabulary of the Greek physicians, which harmonises with St. Paul's statement that he was a medical man (Col 4¹⁴).

6. Aim and Character. The Gospel is intended primarily for the edification of a single individual, Theophilus, a man of high position living at Rome, and apparently a convert of St. Luke. Yet there can be no doubt that it was intended to reach a large circle of Gentile readers. St. Luke claims for his narrative fulness, accuracy, order, and exhaustive research. In pursuance of his plan of writing 'in order,' he attempts to fix the chronology, and to place the gospel history in its true connexion with contemporary secular events. It is clear, that, like St. Paul, his sympathies were cosmopolitan, and that he was interested in the wider life and culture of the great empire. Of special dogmatic or party purpose the Gospel shows little trace. The writer is frankly a Paulinist, laying stress on the universal character of Christianity, but there is scarcely a trace of bias against the Twelve, or Jewish Christianity. This is especially clear in the Acts, where the exploits of Peter are as sympathetically recorded as those of Paul. St. Luke's universalism is shown by the pedigree from Adam (3²³), by the praise accorded to Samaritans (10³³), by the rebuke of Jewish intolerance against that people (9⁵²ᶠ· 17¹¹ᶠ·), and by the appointment of the 70 disciples whose mission was to carry the gospel to the Gentiles (c. 10). Universalism characterises our Lord's first-recorded discourse (4²⁴ᶠ·), and is emphasised in the discourses after the Resurrection (24⁴⁷ Ac 1⁸). Equally characteristic is the idea of free grace, not by the works of the Law, but by faith. St. Luke is full of the spirit of the Christian missionary, and delights in those words and acts of Jesus which offer salvation to the poor, the outcast, and the abandoned criminal. This sentiment is also found in Mt, who has the parable of the Lost Sheep, and the saying, 'the Son of Man came to seek and to save that which was lost'; but in St. Luke it is much more prominent. He alone records the touching parable of the Prodigal

Son, and the conversion of the penitent thief.

Some critics detect in St. Luke an Ebionite, i.e. a socialistic or communistic tendency. He certainly shows a special sympathy with the poor (4^{18} 14^{13} 19^8 21^3), and records many warnings of our Lord against wealth (6^{24}, etc.). He even regards community of goods as preferable to private property (Ac 2^{44}, etc.), but it must be remembered that the apostolic communism was voluntary (Ac 5^4). Other examples of this tendency are the parables of Dives and Lazarus, of the Rich Fool, and of the Unjust Steward. Another possible example is the beatitude, 'Blessed are ye poor' (6^{20}), where St. Matthew has 'poor in spirit.'

In speaking of our Lord, St. Luke, like St. John, is careful to notice the effect of His words and works on those who witnessed them : 'He was glorified of all' (4^{15}); 'they were all astonished at the majesty of God' (9^{43}); 'and all the people, when they saw it, gave praise unto God' (18^{43}). He also records carefully our Lord's prayers, being alone in mentioning that our Lord prayed on six distinct and memorable occasions: (1) At His baptism, 3^{21}; (2) after cleansing the leper, 5^{16}; (3) before calling the Twelve apostles, 6^{12}; (4) at His Transfiguration, 9^{29}; (5) on the cross for His murderers, 23^{34}; (6) with His last breath, 23^{46}. St. Luke, like St. Matthew, is specially interested in our Lord's discourses. He preserves more often than St. Matthew, a record of the circumstances in which the words were actually spoken, whereas St. Matthew collects and arranges them according to subject-matter. Hence St. Luke seems to scatter what St. Matthew has collected.

7. Matter peculiar to St. Luke. A proof of St. Luke's diligence in collecting materials is that about half of his Gospel consists of matter peculiar to himself. He alone mentions the parables of the Two Debtors (7^{41}), of the Good Samaritan (10^{30}), of the Friend at Midnight (11^5), of the Rich Fool (12^{16}), of the Barren Fig Tree (13^6), of the Lost Coin (15^8), of the Prodigal Son (15^{11}), of the Unjust Steward (16^1), of Dives and Lazarus (16^{19}), of the Unjust Judge (18^1), of the Pharisee and Publican (18^9); also the following miracles: the miraculous draught of fishes (5^1), the raising of the widow's son (7^{11}), the cure of a woman with a spirit of infirmity (13^{10}), of a dropsical man (14^1), of ten lepers (17^{11}), of Malchus's ear (22^{51}).

Besides these, much other important matter is peculiar to him, e.g. the first two chs., the questions put to John the Baptist by the people ($3^{10,14}$), the topic of conversation at the Transfiguration (9^{31}), the conversion of Zacheus (19^1), the weeping over Jerusalem (19^{41}), the promise to Simon that his faith

should not fail (22^{31}), the bloody sweat (22^{44}), the trial before Herod (23^7), the words addressed to the women of Jerusalem (23^{27}), the incident of the penitent thief (23^{40}); the words on the Cross, 'Father, forgive them for they know not what they do,' and 'Father, into thy hands I commend my spirit' ($23^{34,46}$); the walk to Emmaus (24^{12}), and most of the details of the appearance on the evening of Easter Day (24^{36}). It should be observed that almost the whole of the long section (9^{51}–19^{28}) consists of matter peculiar to St. Luke. Some of the sayings in it are found also in Mt, but generally in a different connexion.

8. Analysis of the Gospel.
(1) The preface, 1^{1-4}.
(2) The infancy and boyhood, 1^5–2^{52}.
(3) Ministry of the Forerunner, 3^{1-20}.
(4) The preparation for the ministry, Christ's baptism, pedigree, and temptation, 3^{21}–4^{13}.
(5) The Galilean ministry, 4^{14}–9^{50}.
(6) The later ministry, mainly in Peræa, 9^{51}–19^{28}. Many of the incidents recorded in this section really belong to other periods of the ministry. Marks of locality and date are vague and rare.
(7) The last visit to Jerusalem and the Passion, 19^{29}–23.
(8) The Resurrection (and Ascension?) c. 24.

9. The Text. Besides the two ordinary types of text, viz. that used by the Authorised Version and that used by the Revisers, there is another interesting type of text, generally called 'Western,' of very great antiquity. It is characterised by omissions, additions, and sometimes by changes. Some chief omissions are in 10^{41} 12^{39} 23^{34} $24^{36,40,51}$. The chief addition is after 6^4. The most interesting change of text is in the account of the institution of the Lord's Supper, which, in its 'Western' form, has no affinity with St. Paul's account of that event. Several of the 'Western' readings are discussed in the commentary, and as they are now regarded as of considerable importance, the student is recommended to make himself acquainted with them. In the Acts the 'Western' text is a still more important and interesting problem.

CHAPTER 1

Birth of John. The Annunciation

1–4. Preface. To write a preface to a history is not a Jewish, but a classical custom, and by following it St. Luke shows himself a true Gentile, trained in Greek culture and imitating classical models. Here he affects classical elegance and correctness of expression, but in the course of his Gospel he generally imitates tne simpler synoptic style.

This Preface contains all that is really

known as distinguished from what is guessed about the sources of the Synoptic Gospels. Its main statements are, (1) that already, when St. Luke was compiling his Gospel (56–58 A.D.), many earlier Gospels existed ; (2) that these Gospels were based upon the evidence of the eyewitnesses ; (3) that these eyewitnesses were the apostles and official Christian teachers ; (4) that the eyewitnesses 'delivered' their testimony in the form of a more or less definitely fixed tradition, which may have been either oral or written ; (5) that Christians were definitely instructed and catechised in the contents of this tradition.

St. Luke claims for his Gospel, (1) diligence in collecting all available materials, (2) fulness, (3) careful investigation especially of the earliest period (our Lord's birth and infancy), (4) orderly arrangement, (5) accuracy.

1. Surely believed] RV 'fulfilled.' **2. Even as**] i.e. these narratives were in exact accordance with the evidence of the eyewitnesses. **Eyewitnesses**] i.e. mainly the Apostles themselves, perhaps also the seventy disciples.

3. In order] may refer either to chronological order, or to orderly arrangement according to subjects.

Most excellent Theophilus] Some think that Theophilus is not a real person, but an ideal name for a Christian reader ('beloved of God'). More probably Theophilus was a distinguished Roman citizen resident in Rome. The epithet 'most excellent' was under the empire peculiarly appropriated to Romans of high rank, and became in the 2nd cent. a technical title indicating equestrian rank. This is probably its sense here. Both Felix and Festus, addressed by this title in Ac 23 26 24 3 26 25, were 'knights' (*equites*). Acts is also dedicated to Theophilus.

4. Instructed] lit. 'catechised,' i.e. taught by means of question and answer. At a very early period, probably in the apostolic age, candidates for baptism ('catechumens') were required to go through a preliminary course of training in Christian doctrine and morality, of which catechising formed a prominent part. Theophilus was probably one of St. Luke's own converts, who had with other catechumens attended regular catechising on the life of our Lord.

5–25. Conception of John the Baptist. The rise of Christianity was preceded by a long period of four hundred years, during which prophecy was silent, and the religious guidance of the nation passed to the rabbis and the scribes, who made void the Law of God by their traditions. The advent of Christ was heralded by a great revival of prophecy, and by the restoration of direct communications from God to man through supernatural agency, as in the cases of Zacharias, Joseph, Mary, Elisabeth, Simeon, Anna, the shepherds, the Magi, and,

in particular, John the Baptist, who, though he left no written prophecies, and worked no miracle, was declared by our Lord to be the greatest of the prophets, yea, and more than a prophet.

5. The classical style of the preface now changes abruptly to one which is deeply tinged with Hebraisms. This Hebraic style continues to the end of c. 2. Some scholars explain it by supposing that St. Luke is here using a Hebrew document. **Herod**] see Mt 2 1.

The course of Abia (Abijah)] David divided the priests into twenty-four 'courses' or groups, each of which in rotation was responsible for the Temple services for a week. Each course, therefore, officiated twice a year, at an interval of six months. The course of Abijah was the eighth. After the Captivity only four courses returned, but these were subdivided into twenty-four courses under the old names. The course of Abijah is said to have officiated in April and October : see 1 Ch 24 3 Neh 12 1.

6. Righteous] i.e. according to the OT standard. They were good, pious Jews, strict and careful observers of the Mosaic Law, but not, of course, sinless. **9. Lot**] To avoid disputes the various functions were decided by lot. **To burn incense**] This was done daily, morning and evening (Ex 30 6-8). The daily sacrifice of the lamb was offered on the great altar of burnt offering outside the Temple proper, in front of the porch. The incense was offered inside the Temple on the golden altar of incense which stood before the veil of the Holy of Holies. The officiating priest was alone within the Temple while offering the incense, and the other priests and the people were outside worshipping in the various Temple courts. Only once in a lifetime could a man enjoy this privilege, and he was ever afterwards called 'rich.' It was the 'highest mediatorial act,' 'the most solemn part of the day's service, symbolising Israel's accepted prayers.'

11. An angel] It was said of the high priest Simon the Just (died 320 B.C.) that 'for those forty years wherein he had served as high priest, he had seen an angel clothed in white coming into the Holy Place on the Day of Atonement and going out again.' St. Luke gives special prominence to the ministry of angels, and the appearances which he records are particularly difficult to account for as subjective phenomena : see 1 26 2 9,13,21 12 8 15 10 16 22 22 43 24 4,23, and often in Acts.

12. Was troubled] cp. 2 9 Jg 6 22 13 22, etc.

13. My prayer] Probably not for offspring, but for the coming of the kingdom of God, and of the Messianic salvation, the only suitable prayer for so solemn an occasion. It was a maxim of the rabbis that 'a **prayer in**

which there is no mention of the kingdom of God is no prayer at all.' **John**] lit. 'Jehovah is gracious.'

15. John was a Nazirite, i.e. one of a class of men in Israel who consecrated themselves to God by abstaining from all intoxicants, by avoiding with scrupulous care all ceremonial defilement, and by wearing the hair long, Nu 6 1-21. Usually men made the Nazirite vow for a definite time, not less than thirty days, but John, like Samson, Samuel, and the Rechabites in the OT., was a Nazirite for life. There are some examples of the Nazirite vow even among Christians (Ac 18 18 21 26). James the Lord's brother is said by Hegesippus to have been a life-long Nazirite.

John, the Nazirite and dweller in the wilderness (probably also a celibate), represents the austere and ascetic type of piety which few can imitate. Jesus, purposing in His life to offer an example to all mankind, came eating and drinking, and sharing the joys and sorrows and even the recreations of ordinary society. Both these types of piety, the ascetic and the social, have their place in the Kingdom of God.

Filled with the Holy Ghost] As Jesus was conceived without sin, so his forerunner was sanctified in the womb, though the reference is less to personal sanctification than to consecration to the prophetic office : see Jer 1 5 Gal 1 15. **17. Go before him**] RV 'go before his face,' i.e. before the face of Jehovah. **Elias**] RV 'Elijah' : see Mal 4 5,6 and on Mt 17 10. **To turn the hearts**, etc.] Malachi's exact words are, 'He shall turn the heart of the fathers to the children, and the heart of the children to their fathers.' 'The fathers' are the patriarchs and prophets of Israel, 'the children' are their degenerate descendants who have alienated the heart of 'their fathers' by their disobedience to their godly precepts. The preaching of John will turn the heart of the children to imitate their just (i.e. pious) ancestors, and thus the heart of their ancestors, now alienated, will be turned to them in love and approbation.

18. With the unbelief of Zacharias compare the laughter of Abraham, Gn 17 17, and of Sarah, Gn 18 12. To ask for a sign was not in itself wrong. Abraham, Gideon, and Hezekiah had done so without rebuke. But the appearance of the angel ought itself to have been a sufficient sign to Zacharias.

19. I am Gabriel, etc.] cp. Tob 12 15, 'I am Raphael, one of the seven holy angels which present the prayers of the saints, and go in before the glory of the Holy One.' Two angels only are named in the canonical Scriptures, Gabriel (lit. 'the mighty man of God'), Dan 8 16 9 21, and Michael (lit. 'Who is like God?'), Dan 10 13,21 12 1 Jude v. 9 Rev 12 7. In the Apocrypha, Raphael and Uriel are also named.

The rabbis say that the Jews learnt the names of the angels in Babylon.

The apparent sanction given here to current Jewish angelology is a good instance of the accommodation to human ideas which is so common in both Testaments. God's messenger reveals himself by the name of Gabriel, because that was the name by which he was commonly known among the Jews. The Jews themselves did not suppose that they knew the real names of the angels. According to the rabbis the names of the angels represented their mission, and were changed as their mission was changed.

21. Marvelled that he tarried] RV 'Marvelled while he tarried.' The people were afraid that the officiating priest might be struck dead for omitting some formality (Lv 16 13), hence the custom was for the priest to finish his ministry as quickly as possible. Once when Simon the Just delayed too long, the people became so anxious that they almost broke into the Holy Place. Afterwards they reproached him for his want of consideration for them.

22. Came out] His duty was now to pronounce the priestly benediction (Nu 6 24), but this he was unable to do. **23. The days**] i.e. the week of the course of Abijah. **24. Hid herself five months**] She desired to devote herself entirely to prayer and thanksgiving for so signal a mercy. The **reproach** of childlessness was deeply felt : see Gn 30 23 1 S 1 6, etc.

26–38. The Annunciation (see on Mt 1). Wonder and awe and adoring praise are the emotions with which Christians have ever regarded the unspeakable condescension of Him who, 'when He took upon Him human nature to deliver it, did not abhor the Virgin's womb.' That Mary fully understood who her child was to be, cannot be supposed. The thought of such a condescension of the Author of nature as is implied in the words of the Creed 'conceived by the Holy Ghost, born of the Virgin Mary,' is overwhelming even to us ; to Mary it would have been so appalling that she could not possibly have performed the duties of a mother. Hence the angel was only permitted to reveal to her, that her son would be the Messiah, and the 'Son of God' in some specially exalted yet human sense. The whole narrative moves within the circle of Jewish OT. ideas, and this is a proof of its truth, for an invented story would certainly show marks of a Christian origin. The grace modest reticence, and inimitable simplicity of the narrative, are in marked contrast to the vulgar details of the Apocryphal Gospels. The festival of the Annunciation (the day on which our Lord became man) is kept on March 25th.

26. The sixth month] i.e. from the conception of John, v. 24. **Nazareth**] see on Mt 2 23.

28. Came in] Local tradition states that Gabriel appeared to her as she was drawing water at the fountain of the Virgin outside Nazareth, where the Church of the Annunciaton now stands. But, as the angel ' came in ' to her, she must have been in the house, perhaps engaged in prayer, as painters are fond of representing her. Two well-known devotions have been founded on this incident : (1) the ' Ave Maria ' (' Hail, Mary ! ') ; (2) the ' Angelus.'

Highly favoured] or, rather, ' endued with grace ' (RM), not, as the Vulgate has it, ' full of grace.' She is addressed not as the mother of grace, but as the daughter of it (Bengel). The angel recognised in Mary a holiness of an entirely special kind, which God had given her to fit her to be the mother of the Holy One. Sinless in the absolute sense she probably was not (see on Jn 2⁴), yet we may reverently believe that no one approached the perfection of holiness and purity so nearly as she. **Blessed** *art* **thou among women**] These words are omitted by many good authorities : see on v. 42. **32. His father David**] This seems to imply the Davidic descent of Mary : cp. v. 27, which is ambiguous, and v. 69.

34. How shall this be, seeing I know not a man ?] The traditional view of this passage, which sees in it a proof of the perpetual virginity of our Lord's mother, is perhaps correct. Unless Mary had resolved to remain a virgin after her marriage with Joseph, and had obtained her husband's consent to do so, she would not, as a betrothed woman, regard it as impossible that she should have a child · see on Mt 1²⁵ 12⁵⁰.

35. The Holy Ghost, etc.] Mary would doubtless understand ' the Holy Ghost ' impersonally, as the creative power of God, but St. Luke's readers would understand it personally, as frequently in the Acts. The Holy Ghost, (1) miraculously forms and hallows our Lord's human body and soul at His conception ; (2) descends upon Him with an abiding unction at His baptism, consecrating Him to the Messianic office and preparing Him for His ministry ; (3) brings about the mystical union of the ascended Christ with His people.

Overshadow] like the Shekinah in the Temple, or the cloud of glory at the Transfiguration, which symbolised the divine presence. We have here ' a new, immediate and divine act of creation, and thus the transmission of sinfulness from the sinful race to him is excluded.' **That holy thing,** etc.] RV 'that which is to be born shall be called holy, the Son of God.' Mary would probably understand from this that her Child was to be sinless, but not that He would be divine, because the Son of God was an accepted title of the Messiah.

36. Unasked, the angel gives Mary a sign. He who has caused Elisabeth to conceive contrary to nature can make good His word to Mary also. **Thy cousin**] RV 'thy kinswoman.' It does not follow from this that Mary belonged, like Elisabeth, to the tribe of Levi. Male descent alone determined the tribe, and Mary may have been related to Elisabeth on her mother's side.

38. Behold the handmaid (lit. ' the slave ') **of the Lord**] In these words of humble submission Mary accepts her great destiny. She does so freely, with full understanding of the difficulty of her position. The future she leaves in God's hand. **Be it unto me according to thy word**] This sacred moment, which marks the beginning of our Lord's incarnate life, should be contrasted with Gn 3⁶. There the disobedience of a woman brought sin and death into the world. Here the obedience of a woman brought salvation, reversing the effect of the Fall.

39-56. Mary's visit to Elisabeth. The Magnificat. This beautiful narrative must be derived from Mary herself, probably directly. It is told as vividly and minutely after a lapse of half-a-century as if it were an event of yesterday. Clearly it was one of those things which the Virgin mother kept and pondered in her heart.

39. Into a city of Judah] or, ' into a city called Judah ' (i.e. possibly Juttah, a priestly city near Hebron).

41. The babe leaped] The Jews believed that children were intelligent before birth : cp. Gn 25²². **42. Blessed** *art* **thou among women**] A Hebraism for ' Thou art the most blessed of all women ' : see on v. 48.

43. The mother of my Lord] The aged Elisabeth acknowledges that the young maiden is greater and more highly favoured than she, because she is ' the mother of my Lord,' i.e. of the Messiah. **44.** See on v. 41. **45. For there shall be a performance**] RM 'that there shall be,' etc.

46-55. The Magnificat. This glorious song of praise, which has been used in the services of the Church from early times, tells us more than anything else in the NT. of the character of our Lord's mother, and of her spiritual fitness for her exalted destiny. She was one who diligently searched the Scriptures, and was able in spite of her youth to enter into their deepest spiritual meaning. Not that she had risen as yet beyond the standpoint of Judaism. She still regarded the coming of the Kingdom as an overthrow of Herod's dynasty and a restoration of Jewish nationalism (vv. 52, 54). But her thoughts were fixed on its ethical character. It meant to her the setting up of the ideal of humility, gentleness, and charity, in place of the pride of temporal greatness, a thought which her Son carried further when He said, ' Except ye be converted, and become as little children, ye shall not enter into the kingdom of heaven.' In the Magnificat Mary appears as a prophetess, like Hannah, whom she closely imitates, but greatly excels in spiritual elevation : see 1 S 2¹. The genuineness of the Magnificat is manifest from its thoroughly Jewish character. It contains no trace of definitely Christian ideas. These may be read into it, and were intended by the Holy Spirit to be ultimately read into it, but they are not there in such a form as to be apprehended by those who are not already Christians. The Magnificat is conveniently divided into two parts : (1) vv. 46–49, (2) vv. 50–55. The first part is personal in character, expressing the exultant praise of the holy mother for the signal favour which God has shown her, and foretelling that all future generations will call her blessed. The second part sets forth the character of the Kingdom as a moral revolution, and a reversal of all existing standards of goodness and greatness.

46. In the Gospels (not in the Pauline Epistles) 'soul' and 'spirit' are synonymous.

47. In God my Saviour] In Mary's idea of 'salvation' was doubtless included deliverance from foreign power as well as spiritual deliverance. 'God my Saviour' is, of course, in accordance with OT. ideas, God the Father. Not till much later did she come to regard her Son in this aspect. **48. The low estate**] cp. 1 S 1¹¹. Mary, though descended from David, was in humble circumstances.

All generations shall call me blessed] Prophetically spoken. She has become the pattern of womanhood and motherhood to the whole Christian world, and her song has been enshrined in the Liturgy of every Christian Church. Reverence for our Lord's mother, even in its abuses, has not been without its elevating effect on humanity. 'It is remarkable,' says a judicious writer, 'that one of whom we know nothing except her gentleness and her sorrow, should have exercised a magnetic power upon the world incomparably greater than was exercised by the most majestic female patriots of Paganism. Whatever may be thought of its theological propriety, there can be little doubt that the Catholic reverence for the Virgin has done much to elevate and purify the ideal of woman, and to soften the manners of men. It supplied in a great measure the redeeming and ennobling element in that strange amalgam of religious, licentious, and military feeling which was formed round women in the age of chivalry, and which no succeeding change of habit or belief has wholly destroyed' (Lecky).

49. Cp. Ps 111⁹. **50.** Cp. Ps 103¹⁷. **51.** Cp. Ps 89¹⁰. With prophetic certainty Mary regards the putting down of pride, and the establishment of meekness as already achieved.

52. Cp. Job 5¹¹ 12¹⁹ 1 S 2⁷. **The mighty**] RV 'princes,' include Herod and his dynasty, but the main idea is that a kingdom based on humility and love has entered into the world, more powerful than all earthly kingdoms, and destined to revolutionise them. **53.** Cp. Pss 107⁹ 34¹⁰ 1 S 2⁵. In true OT. style spiritual and temporal blessings are conceived of as united in the Messianic age. The temporal needs of the poor and lowly are to be cared for and their wrongs redressed. All things needful both for their souls and bodies will be bountifully supplied. **54.** Cp. Ps 98³. **55.** Cp. Mic 7²⁰. The national feeling is pronounced. The Gentiles are not mentioned, except indirectly in the allusion to the promise to Abraham. The true translation of vv. 54, 55 is (see RV) ' He hath helped Israel his servant, that he might remember mercy towards Abraham and his seed for ever, as he spake to our fathers.' **56.** Joseph's discovery of Mary's condition (Mt 1¹⁸) must have been subsequent to her return to Nazareth.

57–80. Birth and childhood of the Baptist. The Benedictus.

59. The eighth day] Circumcision took place on the eighth day, even though it was the sabbath : see Jn 7²². At the circumcision of a child the circumciser said, ' Blessed be the Lord our God, who hath sanctified us by his precepts and hath given us the law of circumcision.' The father replied, ' Who hath sanctified us by his precepts and hath commanded us to enter the child into the covenant of Abraham our father.' **63. Writing table**] i.e. a tablet covered with wax for writing upon.

68–79. The Benedictus. ' This song, which was composed in the priest's mind during the time of his silence, broke solemnly from his lips the moment speech was restored to him, as the metal flows from the crucible in which it has been melted the moment that an outlet is made for it' (Godet). It consists of five *strophes*, each of three vv., but is most conveniently divided into two portions : (1) vv. 68–75, (2) vv. 76–79. In the first portion Zacharias praises God for having now fulfilled His promises to Israel by raising up the Messiah in David's house, to save Israel from foreign oppression, and to establish peace, true religion, and righteousness. In the second portion Zacharias directly addresses his son as the destined forerunner of the Messiah, and the preacher of repentance to Israel. The song closes with a beautiful description of the salvation which the Messiah will bring to His people.

This song, like the Magnificat, is purely Jewish in tone. It does not even mention the Gentiles, and it is only in the light of subsequent events that a Christian sense can be read into it.

68. Hath visited] The past tense may express Zacharias' certainty that the Messiah will come, but more probably it implies prophetic knowledge that the conception of Jesus has already taken place. **Redeemed**] To Zacharias this would mean political redemption from foreign rule as well as spiritual redemption.

69. An horn of salvation] The power of the Messianic King is likened to the strength of a bull, or wild-ox (AV 'unicorn'), which is represented by his horns : cp. 1 S 2 10 2 S 22 3 Ps 75 10, etc. **David**] The expression implies that Mary was descended from David.

70. Since the world began] may be taken literally, Adam being regarded as the first prophet. More probably it is used vaguely for 'in olden times.'

71. Enemies] i.e. Herod and the Romans, but when Christians sing this hymn, they mean Satan and all the enemies of Christ. **72. To perform the mercy promised to our fathers**] RV 'To shew mercy towards our fathers.' The RV implies that the patriarchs, though dead, still exist, and take an interest in the fortunes of their posterity, a doctrine affirmed with authority by Christ (Mt 22 32).

Covenant] The 'covenant' and 'the oath' (v. 73) are identical, though the irregular grammatical construction conceals this : see Gn 22 16-18. **76. Of the Lord**] Zacharias understood it of Jehovah ; Christians understand it of Christ. **77.** This v. well describes the character of John's ministry, which joined the announcement of the Kingdom with the preaching of repentance. Translate, 'To give unto his people knowledge of salvation—salvation which consists in the remission of sins.'

78. The dayspring] The Gk. word here (*anatole*) is ambiguous. It may either mean the rising of a heavenly body, and hence the heavenly body itself, so that the Messiah is virtually called 'the Sun' or 'Star of Israel,' or it may mean 'the Branch,' a title applied to the Messiah (Jer 23 5 33 15 Zech 3 8 6 12).

79. Peace] not successful war is Zacharias' ideal for the Messianic period, and not only earthly peace, but 'peace with God.'

CHAPTER 2
BIRTH AND CHILDHOOD OF JESUS

1–5. The census of Quirinius. There are two historical difficulties in connexion with St. Luke's mention of the census of Quirinius : (1) There is no direct evidence, except St. Luke's statement, that Augustus (31 B.C.–14 A.D.) ever held a census of the whole Roman empire. (2) Quirinius was not governor of Syria at the time of our Lord's birth (about 7 or 6 B.C.), but either Sentius Saturninus (9–6 B.C.), or Quinctilius Varus (6–4 B.C.).

As to (1), the absence of direct confirmatory evidence ought not to be sufficient to discredit a statement which is made as a result of careful enquiry, by a nearly contemporary author who is honestly striving to be accurate (1 3, 4), and which is in itself credible, and in accordance with Augustus's character and methods of administration. In 8 B.C. he carried out a census of Roman citizens throughout the empire, and it is quite possible that he also planned a general census, which, however, owing to administrative difficulties, was not completely executed, in every part of the empire. (2) Although Quirinius was not governor of Syria in 7, 6 B.C., he may have been there as 'legatus Cæsaris' to conduct the census, or more probably to carry on the war with the troublesome tribe of the Homonadenses. It was not unusual, when a province was in a disturbed state, for the civil and military administration to be placed in different hands. It is probable, therefore, that, when our Lord was born, Saturninus or Varus was at the head of the civil, and Quirinius of the military, administration of Syria. Quirinius was civil governor of Syria some twelve years later (6 A.D.), when he carried out the well-known census of Ac 5 37, mentioned also by Josephus ('Ant.' xviii. 1. 1, 2. 1). It is known, however, from an inscription discovered at Tivoli, in 1764, that he held office in Syria at an earlier date, when he subdued the Homonadenses, and for this exploit was honoured by two 'supplicationes' (solemn thanksgivings to the gods), and the decorations of a triumphing general. We may conjecture, therefore, that this was in 7, 6 B.C., at the time when, according to St. Luke, the earlier and less-known census took place.

1. Augustus] The first Roman emperor. His actual reign dated from the battle of Actium 31 B.C. to his death in 14 A.D. **Taxed**] RV 'enrolled.' This enrolment was perhaps simply a census or numbering of the inhabitants. The second enrolment under Quirinius in 7 A.D. was for purposes of taxation, and excited a rebellion (Ac 5 37).

2. Cyrenius] RV 'Quirinius.'

3. Into his own city] It was a fixed principle of Roman government to respect the feelings and even the prejudices of subject peoples, and Herod, being a foreigner whose rule was barely tolerated by patriotic Jews, had every reason not to give offence. He enrolled his pagan subjects, therefore, in the Roman manner, but allowed the Jews the privilege of being enrolled in their place of origin according to their family and tribe.

5. His espoused wife] RV 'who was betrothed to him.' Yet they were probably married, because it was contrary to Jewish custom for betrothed persons to live together, and Joseph would wish to protect Mary by making her his wife as soon as possible.

6, 7. The Nativity. See on Mt 2[1]. There is an inward fitness that He, who for our sake emptied Himself of His glory, should be born in a stable and laid in a manger, but assuredly it would never have occurred to any one, Jew or Christian, to invent such a story, which accordingly may be accepted as authentic history. By the manner of His birth Jesus showed His sympathy with the hard lot of the poor, and His contempt for human splendour. He also gave a foretaste of His future manner of life, when He was despised and rejected of men, and had no place to lay His head.

7. Firstborn] A technical term among the Jews, signifying 'that which openeth the womb' (Ex 34[19f.]), and not implying the birth of other offspring. That St. Luke uses it in this technical sense is clear from 2[22, 23]. **No room**] It is clear from Mt 2[11] that as soon as the enrolment was over, and the crowds attending it had dispersed, Joseph and Mary obtained a house in Bethlehem, intending to settle there permanently, since it was the most fitting place for the residence of the Messiah.

8–20. Announcement to the shepherds, who visit the Holy Family. As Jesus was born in a stable, so His birth was first announced to peasants, in token that the gospel was meant for the poor and ignorant, as well as for the rich and learned.

8. Shepherds] David himself had been a shepherd at Bethlehem (1 S 16[11]). The flocks at Bethlehem were destined for the Temple sacrifices, and the shepherds who kept them occupied a higher social position than other shepherds, who were considered outcasts by the scribes because of their necessary isolation from religious ordinances. There was a Jewish tradition that the birth of the Messiah would be proclaimed from the 'Migdol Eder,' 'the tower of the flock,' which lay near Bethlehem on the road to Jerusalem (Edersheim).

10. To all people] RV 'to all the people' (of Israel). There is here no express mention of the Gentiles. **11. A Saviour**] The spiritual sense is certainly prominent here—'a Saviour from sin and death.' This title of Jesus is rare in the Gospels, being found only here and in Jn 4[42]; several times in Titus and 2 Peter.

Christ the Lord] RM ' Anointed Lord.'

12. *Shall be* **a sign**] RV ' is the sign.' The unusual sight of an infant in a manger would be a sign that the angel had spoken the truth.

14. The 'Gloria in excelsis' (**Glory . . in the highest**), in which the hosts of heaven praised God for His wondrous love to mankind shown in the Incarnation, was expanded into a morning hymn as early as the 2nd cent., and has been sung in the Communion service of the Western Church for many ages. Taking the old reading of the AV, the hymn, which

consists of two lines, may be thus paraphrased: (1) The angels are praising God in highest heaven for Christ's Nativity. (2) On earth men enjoy peace with God, and peace and goodwill with one another. But the reading of the RV ('men of good pleasure') is preferable, and the meaning is, (1) The angels are praising God in highest heaven for Christ's Nativity. (2) There is peace on earth (peace with God and peace with one another) among men to whom God shows His favour by this wondrous birth.

The hymn goes beyond the words of the angel, in declaring that God's favour in Christ is extended to all mankind.

19. Mary's was a quiet and reflective nature: cp. v. 51. These two vv. suggest that it was from her the information contained in these chapters was derived.

21. The Circumcision. Although our Lord was sinless, He was subjected to a rite which symbolised the putting off of the sinful lusts of the flesh. Although He was the Son of God, it behoved Him to be made a child of God through the covenant of Abraham. Now first His redeeming blood was shed, and the pain of the Circumcision was a foretaste of Calvary: cp. Mt 3[15] Ro 8[3] Heb 2[17] Gal 4[4]. Under the new covenant the sacrament of Holy Baptism (the circumcision made without hands, Col 2[11], has 'fulfilled,' and taken the place of circumcision.

22–38. The Purification and Presentation in the Temple. Women after childbirth were unclean, for a boy forty days, for a girl eighty days. They were then bound to present an offering for Purification, viz. a lamb for a burnt offering and a pigeon for a sin offering. Poor women might offer two pigeons, as the mother of Jesus did: see Lv 12[2]. A firstborn son was presented to God and redeemed with five shekels of the sanctuary (10 or 12 shillings), Ex 13[2] Nu 8[16] 18[15]. Neither of these ceremonies necessitated personal attendance of the mother in the Temple. A woman could offer her sacrifices of purification by proxy, and a firstborn son could be presented, and his redemption price paid to a priest anywhere. Joseph and Mary went to the Temple because they were near, and because they loved the house of God.

22. Her purification] RV 'their purification,' i.e. either, (1) the Jews' purification, or (2) the purification of mother and child. Strictly speaking, however, only the mother (not the child) was ceremonially unclean.

25–35. Simeon and the Nunc Dimittis] Simeon belonged, like Zacharias and Anna, to the class of humble and devout Jews who 'looked for the redemption of Jerusalem,' and whose type of piety was very different from that of the scribes: see vv. 37, 38. To such persons the sacrificial system of the Old Covenant and the spiritual teaching of the prophets had been a true preparation for Christ, and consequently God shed abroad among them the gift of prophecy, and revealed to them truths to which the doctors of the Law were blind.

25. Devout] more exactly 'God-fearing.' The word is peculiar to St. Luke (Ac 2⁵ 8² 22¹²). **The consolation of Israel]** a common expression among the rabbis for the Messianic age. 'So may I see the consolation' was a usual form of oath. **26. The Lord's Christ]** the same as 'the Christ of God' (9²⁰), i.e. 'H'm whom God has sent as the Messiah.'

29-32. This beautiful hymn (usually called the 'Nunc Dimittis'), which has been used in the evening service of the Church since the 4th or 5th century, is in thorough harmony with the spirit of this Gospel. It expressly includes the Gentiles in Christ's Kingdom, in accordance with the OT. prophecies.

29. The meaning is, 'My master and owner, now thou givest freedom to thy slave by a peaceful death, according to the prophetic word that thou spakest' (v. 26). Simeon regards his release from the toils and troubles of life as an enfranchisement from slavery, a change to a state of freedom and rest. In **peace** means 'in a state of peace with God.'

30. Thy salvation] is practically personal, meaning the Messiah.

31. All people] RV 'all peoples,' i.e. all the nations of the earth. **32. A light, etc.]** RV 'A light for revelation to the Gentiles,' i.e. the Messiah is the Light of the Gentiles, sent by God to reveal His truth to the heathen world. He is also the glory of the chosen people, because all nations in glorifying the Messiah will glorify the nation from whom the Messiah springs. ' In those days ten men of all languages of the nations shall take hold of the skirt of him that is a Jew, saying we will go with you, for we have heard that God is with you' (Zech 8²³).

33. Joseph and his mother] RV 'his father and his mother.' Since Joseph filled the place of a father to Jesus, he was naturally called his father : cp. v. 27, 'the parents.'

34, 35. These vv. contain the first hint in the NT. of the sufferings of the Messiah, and of His holy mother.

34. Behold this child, etc.] This child will divide Israel into two opposite camps. Some will reject His claims. To such He will be 'a stone of stumbling and a rock of offence' (Isa 8¹⁴), i.e. the occasion of their spiritual ruin. Others will accept His claims. Such He will raise through their faith to a higher spiritual life, which may be rightly called a resurrection (**rising again**) from death to life.

35. Yea, a sword] This prophecy was fulfilled when Mary saw her Son rejected, condemned, insulted, scourged, and crucified.

That the thoughts] i.e. that the true character of men (as shown in their reception or rejection of Jesus) may be made manifest.

36-38. Anna the prophetess also recognises Jesus as the Messiah, and speaks of Him as such among those who 'looked for the redemption of Jerusalem.' Her manner of life is described in detail, because she is a type of the 'widows indeed' of the Christian Church (1 Tim 5⁵), who did not marry again, but devoted themselves to works of charity and piety.

36. Prophetess] The title shows that Anna was known as a prophetess before this incident. Other instances of prophetesses are Miriam, Deborah, Hannah, Huldah, and the daughters of Philip. **Aser]** RV 'Asher.' It is clear that members of other tribes than Judah and Levi returned from the Captivity.

37. If she was married at 12, which is possible in the East, she must have been 103 years old. **Departed not]** i.e. was unfailing in her attendance. **38. All them that looked, etc.]** see on vv. 25-35.

39. Return to Nazareth. St. Luke represents the Holy Family as returning to Nazareth immediately after the Purification, without any allusion to the visit of the Magi, or the flight into Egypt. This seems to indicate that he did not use St. Matthew's Gospel.

40. Growth and spiritual development of Jesus. The information may have been gained from the mother herself. **Waxed strong in spirit]** RV omits 'in spirit.'

Filled with wisdom] lit. 'becoming full of wisdom' : cp. v. 52. 'increased in wisdom.' As Jesus was perfect God and perfect man so He possessed completely the attributes of both natures. As God He knew all things, but as man He 'waxed strong (in spirit), becoming filled with wisdom,' and 'increased in wisdom and stature, and in favour with God and man.' As an infant He possessed the knowledge proper to an infant ; as a boy, that proper to a boy ; as a man, that proper to a man ; as the anointed Messiah (3²²), that proper to one commissioned to establish the Kingdom of God on earth ; and as the ascended and glorified Redeemer, that proper to one who, as man, and not simply as God, rules the entire universe (Mt 28¹⁸). What this means we may not be able to say, but we may rest assured He still feels for man, and understands his needs. Although it was always possible for Him who was God as well as man, to draw, if the needs of His mission required it, upon the inexhaustible stores of His divine knowledge (cp. Jn 1⁴⁸), yet it was His usual custom to obtain His information through human channels and from human sources, and, even as a teacher, to use chiefly the ample stores of His supernaturally enlightened human knowledge. This supernatural enlightenment far exceeded both in range and in penetration that granted to the greatest of the prophets—it was the knowledge which was granted to the Incarnate Son for the purpose of communicating to man the Father's perfect and final revelation ; but it was limited in accordance with its object, and did not embrace matters which it was inexpedient for man to know, and therefore for the Incarnate Son to reveal : see on Mk 13 32, and cp. Ac 1 7.

40-52. The boy Jesus in the Temple. We know nothing directly of the childhood of Jesus except this one incident, which is recorded entirely for the sake of the remarkable utterance in v. 49.

41. As women were not obliged to attend, Mary's regular keeping of the feasts is a mark of special piety : cp. v. 22.

42. Twelve years] Jesus accompanied His parents for the first time, because He was approaching his thirteenth year, in which He would become, by Jewish custom, 'a son of the Law,' i.e. subject to its obligations.

43. Tarried behind] Jesus was probably staying with friends, and thought that His parents would remain in Jerusalem for the whole Passover week. Instead of this they seem to have left after two days, as was often done.

46. After three days] They spent one day looking for Him in the caravan, one day in the return journey to Jerusalem, and found Him on the third day. **Doctors**] i.e. scribes or rabbis. Among the famous men who may possibly have been present were the aged Hillel and Shammai, Rabban Simeon, Gamaliel, Annas, Joseph of Arimathæa, Nicodemus, Johanan ben-Zacchai, Caiaphas. It is said (but it is not certain) that there was a synagogue within the Temple enclosure, where members of the Sanhedrin gave public instruction on sabbaths and festivals. **Hearing them**] not teaching them, as the Apocryphal Gospels say.

49. How is it] 'Not a reproof, but an expression of surprise. He is not surprised at their coming back for Him, but at their not knowing where to find Him.' **About my Father's business**] This translation is possible, but that of the RV, 'in my Father's house,' is more probable. The words mean : ' There is only one place in Jerusalem where I, the Son of God, might be expected to be found, and that is in my Father's house.' The utterance shows that even at this early age Jesus was conscious that His true father was not Joseph (as His mother's words seemed to imply, v. 48), but God.

50. Understood not] The lapse of twelve years during which no miracle had occurred, had partly obliterated the impression made by the remarkable circumstances of the Nativity This and the next v. furnish another indication that St. Luke's information was obtained from St. Mary. **51. Was subject**] The evangelist guards against the possible supposition that Christ's words in v. 49 were intended as a repudiation of His parents' authority over Him. **52.** See on v. 40.

CHAPTER 3

JOHN'S MINISTRY. BAPTISM AND GENEALOGY OF JESUS

1-14. Preliminary Ministry of the Baptist (Mt 3 1 Mk 1 1). See on Mt.

1. In the fifteenth year] If the years of Tiberius are reckoned from the death of Augustus, who died 14 A.D., the date is 28, 29 A.D. Most authorities, however, suppose that the years of Tiberius are here reckoned from 11 A.D., when he was made the colleague of Augustus in the empire, with equal authority over all the provinces and armies. This gives the date 25, 26 A.D. for the beginning of the ministry of John. Jesus, who appeared soon afterwards, was, therefore, probably baptised 26 A.D., and kept the first Passover of His ministry (Jn 2 13) 27 A.D. Allowing three Passovers to the ministry, the crucifixion took place in 29 A.D.

Pilate] see on Mt 27 2.

Herod being tetrarch] see art. 'Dynasty of the Herods.'

Philip] the tetrarch, is to be carefully distinguished from his brother Herod Philip, who was of private station. He was the son of Herod the Great by a woman of Jerusalem named Cleopatra. He ruled for 38 years without reproach, and was favourably distinguished from the other sons of Herod by his gentleness and want of ambition. Josephus says of him : 'He was moderate, and peaceful in his rule, and spent his whole life in his country. He went out with only a small retinue, always taking with him the throne on which he might sit and judge. Whenever he met any one who had need of him, he made no delay, but set down the throne wherever he might be, and heard the case.' See, further, art. 'Dynasty of the Herods.'

Lysanias] The only Lysanias mentioned in profane history as ruling over Abilene was executed 36 B.C. by the triumvir Mark Antony, at the instigation of Cleopatra, queen of Egypt. He governed not only Abilene, but also Ituræa and other extensive districts. The Lysanias of St. Luke is probably his grandson.

Abilene] the territory round Abila, a town of some importance, situated on the River Abana, in a gorge of Mt. Antilibanus, 18 Roman m. from Damascus on the way to Heliopolis or Baalbec. There are still to be seen there an ancient temple, ancient aqueducts, and a Roman road.

2. Annas, etc.] RV 'in the high priesthood of Annas and Caiaphas.' A peculiar expression to indicate a peculiar state of things. Annas held office from 7–14 A.D., when he was deposed by Pilate's predecessor, Valerius Gratus. But inasmuch as his successors were either his relations, or entirely devoted to his interests, he retained supreme power, and was probably regarded by orthodox Jews as the rightful high priest. Ex-high priests retained their title, and Annas is called high priest again, Jn 18¹⁹ Ac 4⁶ : see on Jn 18¹³ and Mt 21¹². **Caiaphas**] see on Mt 26³ Jn 11⁴⁹ 18¹³. **The word of God came**] John received a definite call to his ministry, like Isaiah (Isa 6) and Jeremiah (Jer 1). **4.** See on Isa 40³.

5, 6. (Peculiar to Lk.) 'Spiritually interpreted, the **valleys** would represent unbelief and all sins of omission which must be filled up by the diligent adding of grace to grace (2 Pt 1⁵⁻⁷). The **mountains** would mean pride and haughtiness and self-will and obstinacy, which must be humbled and cast down. The **crooked places** would signify all sorts of deceit and guile and hypocrisy and untruthfulness. The **rough ways** would picture anger, strife, envy, hatred, malice, and all uncharitableness.'

10–14. See on Mt 3.

15–17. John's witness to Jesus (Mt 3¹¹ Mk 1⁷). See on Mt.

18–20. John is imprisoned by Herod (Mt 14³ Mk 6¹⁷). See on Mt.

21, 22. Baptism of Jesus (Mt 3¹³ Mk 1⁹). See on Mt.

23–38. Genealogy of Jesus. See on Mt 1¹.

23. Thirty years] The legal age for the Levites to begin their ministry (Nu 4³,⁴⁷).

38. Son of Adam] see on Mt 1¹.

CHAPTER 4

THE TEMPTATION. NAZARETH. CAPERNAUM

1–13. The Temptation (Mt 4¹ Mk 1¹²). See on Mt.

5. Lk inverts 2nd and 3rd Temptations.

13. For a season] 'These words signify "until a favourable time." The conflict foretold so precisely, can be none other than that of Gethsemane. "This is your hour and the power of darkness," said Jesus at this very time (22⁵³), and a few moments before He had said, "The prince of this world cometh" (Jn 14³⁰)' (Godet).

14, 15. Return to Galilee. Beginning of the Ministry proper (Mt 4¹² Mk 1¹⁴ Jn 4¹,⁴³). See on Mt and Jn.

14. In the power of the Spirit] Christ's miracles and preaching in Judæa (Jn 1²⁹–4⁴²) had already made Him famous, so that when He was come unto Galilee, the Galileans received

Him, having seen all the things that He did at Jerusalem at the feast (Jn 4⁴⁵).

16–30. Visit to Nazareth. See Mt 13⁵³ Mk 6¹. It must remain doubtful whether this visit to Nazareth, which Lk places at the beginning of the Galilean ministry, is identical with that placed considerably later by Mt and Mk. In any case, Lk here makes use of an important independent source. On synagogues see on Mt 4²³.

16. As his custom was] When living at Nazareth, Jesus had been accustomed to read the lessons as an ordinary member of the congregation. Even boys under age were allowed to do this. **Stood up for to read**] The Law and the Prophets, but not the Hagiographa, were read standing. The rabbis said : 'They do not read the law otherwise than standing up. Nay, it is unlawful for him that readeth to lean upon anything.' 'A man may read out of the book of Esther either standing or sitting, but not so out of the Law.' Jesus having stood to read, sat to expound. As He read in Hebrew, the Methurgeman, or Interpreter, translated into the vernacular Aramaic. See on Mt 2⁶.

17. There was delivered .. the book (or 'a roll')] The rolls were in the charge of the hazzan, or attendant (v. 20), who handed them to the reader, and received them back when read. Sometimes the prophets formed a single roll, sometimes (as here) they were divided into books.

18. From Isa 61¹,², with one clause 'to set at liberty them that are bruised' inserted from Isa 58⁶, LXX. This passage, in which the prophet declares to the exiles in Babylon their approaching deliverance, is now read in Jewish synagogues on the Day of Atonement, and may so have been read even at that time. The reading was very short (two verses only), because a sermon was to follow. When there was no sermon, the reading was made considerably longer.

The Spirit of the Lord, etc.] In Isaiah this is a soliloquy of the Righteous Servant of Jehovah, whom our Lord identifies with Himself. The Jews generally regarded it as a soliloquy of the prophet himself. **He hath anointed me**] viz. at My baptism. **He hath sent me to heal the brokenhearted**] RV omits.

To preach deliverance] RV 'to proclaim release to the captives.' The original words have reference to the release of the Jewish captives from Babylon. Jesus applies them to the release of sinners from the guilt and bondage of sin, through His ministry. **The blind**] Spiritual blindness is here chiefly in view. **To set at liberty them that are bruised**] From Isa 58⁶. Our Lord purposely inserted these words in the passage read according to a common custom. The rabbis said, 'The reader of the prophet may skip from one text to another, but he may not skip from prophet to prophet, but in the twelve (minor) prophets it is lawful.' **19. To preach the acceptable year of the Lord**] In Isaiah this is the year of the return, but Jesus applies it to His earthly ministry. It is not to be inferred from this that Christ's ministry lasted only a year.

21. This day is this scripture, etc.] With the emphatic self-assertion of this sermon, cp. the Sermon on the Mount (Mt 5–7). **22. Bare him witness**] i.e. declared that the report of His power as a preacher was not exaggerated.

And they said] or, rather, '*but* they said,' according to the Heb. idiom, which has only one word for 'and' and 'but.' **Is not this Joseph's son?**] and, therefore, not the Messiah, or a prophet, or any one great.

23. Physician, heal thyself] The defect or malady from which, in the opinion of the Nazarenes, Christ was suffering, was want of consideration among those who knew Him best, especially his fellow-townsmen. Let Him remove that defect by working such miracles as would convince them that He was a teacher sent from God, and He would then be more successful in 'healing,' i.e. converting, others. The Nazarenes were jealous because Jesus had worked miracles at Capernaum and other places before He worked any at Nazareth. The proverb occurs frequently in rabbinical writings, 'Physician, heal thine own lameness.' 'In a sad state is the city whose physician has the gout, and whose steward has one eye.'

24. No prophet is accepted] RV 'acceptable.' The truth is a familiar one. We often think lightly of what is very familiar. The blessings at our doors are those we value least. Here and in Mt 13 57, Christ's 'own country' is Nazareth, where He was brought up. In Jn 4 44 it is perhaps Judæa, where He was born. There is a curious parallel in the life of 'the heathen Christ,' Apollonius of Tyana, who is represented as saying, 'What wonder is it, if, when I am esteemed by the rest of mankind as like a god, and by some even as a god, my own country alone until now refuses to recognise me ?' Plutarch says, 'You will find that few of the most prudent and wisest of mankind have been appreciated in their own country.' Another ancient writer says, 'All the philosophers seem to have had a hard life in their own country.'

25–27. The vv. contain a refusal to work miracles in Nazareth. St. Matthew (13 58) gives the reason : 'because of their unbelief.' **25. Elias**] RV 'Elijah.' Our Lord gives two instances of prophets, who, being dishonoured in their own country, went and conferred great blessings upon foreigners. **Three years and six months**] So also in Jas 5 17. This

does not agree with the OT., which says that the rain returned in the third year (1 K 17 1 18 1), but it agrees with Jewish traditional usage, which frequently introduced the number three and a half, as being half of the mystical number seven. 'Ever since the persecution under Antiochus Epiphanes, three years and a half (= 42 months = 1,260 days) had become the traditional duration of times of great calamity (Dan 7 25 12 7 Rev 11 2,3 12 6,14 13 5)' (Plummer).

27. Eliseus] RV 'Elisha.'

28. They are angry with Jesus for venturing to compare Himself with the old prophets, and for rebuking them for their want of faith in Him.

29. That they might cast him down] perhaps as a preliminary to stoning Him as a blasphemer—'The place of execution was twice a man's height. One of the witnesses throws him down,' etc. As the local synagogues with their 'bench of three' could not condemn to death, Plummer conjectures that this was what the Jews call the 'rebel's beating.' This was administered by the people without trial and on the spot, when any one was caught in what seemed to be a flagrant violation of some law or tradition (Jn 8 59 10 31 Ac 21 31, 32).

30. Went his way] A mysterious restraint upon the power of His enemies is implied as in Jn 18 6.

31. Migration to Capernaum. See on Mt 4 13.

31 b–37. Demoniac healed in the synagogue. Mk 1 23. See on Mk 1 21 f.

38–41. Healing of Simon's wife's mother and others (Mt 8 14 Mk 1 29). See on Mt.

42–44. Retirement to a desert place. Preaching tours (Mk 1 35). See on Mt 4 23-25.

44. The synagogues of Galilee] The best critics read, 'the synagogues of Judæa.' This is the only express mention by the synoptists of the Judæan ministry, but see on Mt 23 37

CHAPTER 5
MIRACULOUS DRAUGHT OF FISHES.
THE PALSIED MAN

1–11. First miraculous draught of fishes (peculiar to Lk). Many critics identify this incident with that recorded in Mt 4 18 and Mk 1 16. But there are important considerations on the other side : (1) the persons are different (there four disciples, here Peter is addressed); (2) the words used, though similar in sense, are very different in form ; (3) the disciples are not said to have 'left all' in Mt, but only to have left their father in the ship. Moreover, in Mt and Mk the disciples are fishing, here they are washing their nets before putting them away. Besides, if Mt and Mk really describe the same event, why do they omit the most striking incident of all, the miraculous draught of fishes ? See on Mt 4 18.

The incident was probably a miracle, but it is possible to give a plausible natural explanation of it. Tristram says : 'The thickness of the shoals of fish in the Lake of Gennesareth is almost incredible to any one who has not witnessed them. They often cover an area of more than an acre; and when the fish move slowly forward in a mass, and are rising out of the water, they are packed so close together, that it appears as if a heavy rain was beating down on the surface of the water.' Fish so closely packed as this could not easily escape.

5. Master] implying that he was already a disciple. This particular word is peculiar to St. Luke.

8. Depart from me] 'Peter perceived that His command was effectual beyond expectation, and that He was a divine and supernatural man, and, therefore, feeling himself unworthy, begged Him to depart' (Euthymius). It is natural for the sinful soul to shrink from the presence of the all-holy God. The nearness of God had been brought home to St. Peter by the miracle which he had just witnessed : cp. Ex 20 18, 19.

10. Catch men] lit. 'catch them alive.' The apostles are to catch men for life, not for death, by means of their preaching. In the works of Clement of Alexandria, 200 A.D., there is a beautiful hymn to Christ as the fisher :

> 'Fisher of mortal men,
> Even of those that are being saved,
> Ever the holy fish
> From the wild ocean
> Of the world's sea of sin
> By thy sweet life thou enticest away.'

12-16. The leper cleansed (Mt 8 1 Mk 1 40). See on Mt.

16. And prayed] Peculiar to Lk, who more often than any other evangelist mentions our Lord's prayers.

17-26. The Paralytic (Mt 9 1 Mk 2 1). See on Mt.

27-39. Call of Levi, and the controversy as to fasting (Mt 9 9 Mk 2 13). See on Mt.

39. (Peculiar to Lk.) Christ means that He cannot expect the disciples of John and of the Pharisees, who have tasted the old wine of the Law, and found it good, to receive at once and without difficulty the new teaching.

The old is better] So AV and RM; but RV 'the old is good.'

CHAPTER 6
Choice of the Twelve. Sermon in the Plain

1-5. Plucking the ears of corn (Mt 12 1 Mk 2 23). See on Mt and Mk.

1. On the second sabbath after the first] Gk. *deuteroprōton*, lit. 'second-first.' There is considerable ground for omitting this obscure expression as interpolated, and reading simply,

'on a sabbath,' with the RV. If, however, it is genuine, it probably means, 'on the second sabbath after the waving of the sheaf on the second day of the Passover festival' (see Lv 23 1-15). It was the custom to number the sabbaths from Passover to Pentecost from this day. Of the numerous other interpretations the best are, 'the second chief sabbath of the year' (i.e. Pentecost), and 'the first sabbath of the second month of the year.' The 'Jewish Encycl.' conjectures that the disciples were blamed for plucking the ears before the sheaf was waved, which was forbidden (Lv 23 15).

5. In one important MS, the Codex Bezæ, this v. is placed after v. 10, and in its place is inserted this remarkable incident and saying of Jesus : 'On the same day He saw a man working on the sabbath, and said to him : "O man, if thou knowest what thou doest, blessed art thou. But if thou knowest not, cursed art thou, and a transgressor of the law."' The utterance is perhaps authentic. 'In substance it certainly bears the mark of genius. I regard it as an interpolated fragment of a true tradition' (Meyer). 'We may believe that this traditional story is true' (Plummer). 'Its form and contents speak for its originality, and, I am disposed to believe, its authenticity' (Alford). On the contrary, Godet says, 'This can only be an invention or a perversion.'

6-11. The man with the withered hand (Mt 12 9 Mk 3 1). See on Mt.

12-19. Choice of the Twelve (Mt 10 2 Mk 3 13). See on Mt and Mk.

16. Judas *the brother* **of James**] So AV and RM. But RV 'Judas the son of James.'

17. In the plain] RV 'on a level place.' This may have been a plateau, high up the mountains, but see on Mt 5 1.

20-49. Great sermon to the disciples and in part to the multitudes. It forms here the ordination address of the Twelve. In what sense it is identical with the Sermon on the Mount is explained on Mt 5 1. That it is for all practical purposes the same sermon, but abridged, is shown by the fact that it contains only five verses (vv. 24–26, 39, 40) which are not in St. Matthew's version, and that it follows St. Matthew's order.

ANALYSIS : (1) Four beatitudes, on the poor, the hungry, weepers, and the hated (vv. 20–23).

(2) Four woes, on the rich, the full, laughers, and the well spoken of (vv. 24–26).

(3) Exhortation to love, as shown in returning good for evil, not resisting evil, loving enemies, not judging rashly (vv. 27–38).

(4) Exhortation to stringent self-examination on the part of those who presume to guide others, lest they be found to be hypocrites (vv. 39–45).

(5) Exhortation to obedience. The strong foundation upon which obedient Christians build (vv. 46–49).

St. Luke's sermon is much less striking than St. Matthew's. It omits the whole question of the relation of the Gospel to the Law, and all those passages in which Christ claims to be the supreme Legislator, Judge, and Ruler of the human race ; it has only four beatitudes instead of eight, and in general gives the impression of an abridged and imperfect report, in which some of the sayings, owing to extensive omissions, do not appear in their true context. Some, but not all, of St. Luke's omissions can be accounted for by the fact that his Gospel was intended for Gentiles.

Some critics profess to find in St. Luke's sermon an Ebionitic, or as we should now say, a socialistic or communistic tendency. Probably wrongly, for by ' the poor ' and 'the hungry,' St. Luke does not mean the literally such, any more than St. Matthew, who expressly speaks of ' the poor in spirit,' and of those who ' hunger and thirst after righteousness.' So also St. Luke's rich, well-fed, and prosperous persons, are not simply the well-to-do, but those who have the vices of their station. Our Lord never approves poverty or condemns riches simply as such. See on Mt.

20–23. Four Beatitudes. See on Mt 5 3-12.

22. Separate you] viz. by excommunication. The usual sentence was for thirty days, during which the excommunicated might not come within four cubits of any one.

24–26. Four woes (peculiar to Lk). The ' woes ' refer chiefly to future punishment in the world to come, but not exclusively, for in the siege of Jerusalem they received a literal fulfilment.

24. You that are rich] i.e. those who, possessing wealth, trust in it (Mk 10 24), or spend it in selfish luxury like Dives (Lk 16 19), and despise the poor (Jas 2 6), and oppress them (Jas 5 4). **Ye have received your consolation]** cp. Abraham's words to Dives (16 25), ' Son, remember that thou in thy lifetime receivedst (in full) thy good things.' **25. You that are full]** and careless of your poorer brethren's needs, like the rich man ' who fared sumptuously every day ' (16 19). **Shall hunger]** Spiritual destitution is meant, in this world and the next. **That laugh]** The godless, contemptuous laughter of the wicked (Ecclus 19 30) is meant. Innocent mirth is approved by Christ (Lk 15 24). **Mourn and weep]** viz. in the world to come.

26. A warning to all Christian ministers and teachers not to court popularity by speaking smooth words, and saying ' Peace, when there is no peace.' Plutarch relates of Phocion the Athenian, ' Once while he was delivering a public speech and making a good impression,

and saw that all his hearers were equally pleased with what he said, he turned to his friends and said, " Surely I must have forgotten myself, and said something wrong." Similarly Diogenes Laertius relates of a certain philosopher, that when some one announced to him that all men were praising him, he replied, ' Why, what evil have I done ?'

The false prophets] cp. Jer 5 31 6 14 8 11 Ezk 13 10.

27–38. Exhortations to love, forgiveness of injuries, and avoiding of rash judgments.

27–30. See on Mt 5 39-42.

31. See on Mt 7 12.

32–36. See on Mt 5 42-48.

37, 38. See on Mt 7 1, 2.

39. St. Matthew gives this saying in a much more suitable connexion (Mt 15 14), where it is applied to the Pharisees. Here it appears to mean that before judging others we must judge ourselves, otherwise we shall be blind leaders of the blind. **The ditch]** RV 'a pit.' Palestine is full of unfenced wells, quarries, etc.

40. Another saying which occurs in a more natural context in Mt 10 24, q.v.

41–45. Exhortation to stringent self-examination on the part of religious guides.

41, 42. See on Mt 7 3-5.

43–45. See on Mt 7 16-20, and Mt 12 33, 35.

46–49. Obedient hearing. See on Mt 7 21-27.

CHAPTER 7

RAISING OF THE WIDOW'S SON. THE
WOMAN WHO WAS A SINNER

1–10. Healing of the centurion's servant. See on Mt 8 5.

11–17. The raising of the widow's son (peculiar to Lk). On the credibility and significance of Christ's miracles of resurrection, consult Mt 9 18 Jn 11 1.

11. Nain] 25 m. SW. of Capernaum on the hill ' little Hermon ' as it slopes down to the plain of Esdraelon : now a squalid collection of mud-hovels. **Much people]** RV 'a great multitude.' Lazarus also was raised in the presence of a multitude of witnesses.

12. Carried out] Jewish tombs were always outside the walls, and burials were required to be performed within 24 hours. **Only son]** see Jer 6 26 Zech 12 10 Am 8 10. **14. The bier]** a mere pallet, not a coffin.

I say unto thee] Elijah and Elisha raised the dead with difficulty, and after strong wrestlings with God in prayer (1 K 17 20, 21 2 K 4 33, 34), Christ without effort, by a single word of power : cp. Jn 11 43. **16. A great prophet]** or, ' even the prophet ' (Dt 18 15), for only the very greatest prophets had raised the dead.

18–23. A deputation from John the Baptist. See on Mt 11 2.

24–35. Christ's opinion of John. See on Mt 11 7.

29, 30. Peculiar to Lk.

30. Rejected] RV 'rejected for themselves the counsel of God.' God's 'counsel,' or design, was that they should be prepared for the coming of Christ by receiving John's baptism.

36–50. Christ anointed at the house of Simon the Pharisee (peculiar to Lk). Placed here as an illustration of how 'Wisdom' (i.e. the Gospel) is justified by the changed life of one of 'her children' (this sinful woman). 'We are still in that epoch of transition when the rupture between our Lord and the Pharisees, although already far advanced, was not yet complete. A Pharisee could still invite Him without difficulty. It has been supposed that this invitation was given with a hostile intention. But this Pharisee's own reflection, v. 39, shows his moral state. He was hesitating between the holy impression which Jesus made upon him, and the antipathy which his caste felt against Him' (Godet). The woman at the time of the incident was no longer a 'sinner'; she had been converted by Jesus, but the Pharisee did not know this.

This anointing is probably quite distinct from that at Bethany (Mt 26⁶ Jn 12²), and the woman is not to be identified either with Mary Magdalene, or with Mary of Bethany, who were clearly women of good position and character (see on Mt 26⁶ Jn 12²).

36. Sat down] or, rather, 'lay down,' 'reclined.'

37. A sinner] i.e. a woman of ill fame, or, rather, one who had been such. She would have no difficulty in entering the house, as banquets in the East are generally public functions. **An alabaster box** (RV 'cruse')] 'We have evidence that perfumed oils—notably oil of roses, and of the iris plant, but chiefly the mixture known in antiquity as *foliatum*—were largely manufactured and used in Palestine. A flask with this perfume was worn by women round the neck' (see on Song 1¹³). **38.** As Jesus was reclining (not sitting) with His head towards the table and His feet stretched out behind Him, the woman could easily act as indicated. **Tears]** She was overwhelmed by penitent recollections of her past life, and gratitude to Him who had saved her from it. **Hairs]** To appreciate this act we must remember that it was one of the greatest humiliations for a woman to be seen with her hair dishevelled. Similar acts of respect were sometimes, but rarely, paid to rabbis. A man once came to kiss the feet of Rabbi Jonathan, because he had induced filial reverence in his son. Anointing the feet was common among the Jews, the Romans, and the Greeks, especially at banquets.

39. This man, if he were a prophet] One good MS reads 'the prophet.'

40. Jesus answering] The Pharisee thought that Jesus did not know the woman's history. Jesus shows the Pharisee that He can discern even the thoughts of his own heart. **Simon]** the same as Simeon, or Symeon. It is a mere coincidence that the other anointing took place at the house of a man of the same name. There are eleven Simons in the OT., nine in the NT., and twenty in Josephus. **41. Pence]** i.e. *denarii*. According to weight a *denarius* was about 8*d.*, but according to purchasing power 2*s.* or more. The two debts were, therefore, about £50 and £5.

44. No water] cp. Gn 18⁴ Jg 19²¹ 1 S 25⁴¹, and see on Jn 13⁵. **46. Oil]** which was cheap, as opposed to **ointment**, which was dear.

47. 'Thou canst see that she is a reformed character and that her many sins have been forgiven, because of the love she bears to Me, who have saved her from her sinful life.' It should be carefully observed that the woman loved because she was forgiven, not forgiven because she loved.

To whom little is forgiven] i.e. 'Thou, Simon, like this woman, hast also been My disciple, but it is plain from the little love thou showest Me that, unlike her, thou hast not been brought to repentance through My ministry.'

48. Thy sins are forgiven] Christ had forgiven her before, when she turned from her old life. He now for her greater comfort renews the absolution. For the bearing of Christ's absolving power upon His divinity, see on Mt 9¹⁻⁸. **49. Sins also]** RV 'even sins.'

CHAPTER 8
PARABLE OF THE SOWER. THE DEMONIAC OF GADARA

1–3. Tours through Galilee. The ministering women (peculiar to Lk).

2. Mary called Magdalene] see on Mt 27⁵⁶. **Seven devils]** Mk 16⁹. The 'seven' indicates the greatness of her disease, not of her previous wickedness. There is no evidence that the persons possessed with devils in the NT. were specially wicked, or that Mary Magdalene had ever been a woman of evil life.

3. Joanna] see 24¹⁰. Our Lord did not, like the Pharisees, 'devour widows' houses.' Those who contributed to His support were women of wealth and position. **Chuza]** probably the steward of Herod Antipas, who as such managed his house and estates. From Joanna St. Luke probably obtained much of his special information. **Susanna]** Of her nothing is known.

Ministered unto him] This illustrates our Lord's precept (1 Cor 9¹⁴) that they which preach the gospel should live of the gospel.

4–15. Parable of the Sower (Mt 13¹ Mk 4¹). See on Mt.

16–18. Further remarks on teaching by parables (Mk 4 21-25). See on Mk.

19–21. His mother and brethren (Mt 12 46 Mk 3 31). See on Mt.

22–25. Stilling the storm (Mt 8 23 Mk 4 35). See on Mt, Mk.

26–39. The demoniac in the country of the Gadarenes (RV 'Gerasenes') (Mt 8 28 Mk 5 1). See on Mt, Mk.

40–56. Jairus' daughter. The woman with an issue (Mt 9 18 Mk 5 21). See on Mt.

CHAPTER 9

FEEDING THE FIVE THOUSAND. PETER'S CONFESSION. THE TRANSFIGURATION

1–6. Mission of the Twelve (Mt 10 1, 5-15 Mk 6 7-13). See on Mt.

7–9. Herod thinks that John is risen again (Mt 14 1 Mk 6 14). See on Mt.

10–17. Feeding of the five thousand (Mt 14 13 Mk 6 30 Jn 6 1). See on Mt and Jn.

18–27. Confession of Peter (Mt 16 13 Mk 8 27). See on Mt. St. Luke's account is the most imperfect. Why he omits to mention the locality (Cæsarea Philippi), and Christ's rebuke to Peter, which were certainly in his source, does not appear. He alone mentions that Christ was 'praying alone' (v. 18).

28–36. The Transfiguration (Mt 17 1 Mk 9 2). See on Mt.

31. Lk alone mentions the subject of the conversation, Christ's death.

37–43. The epileptic healed (Mt 17 14 Mk 9 14). See on Mt and Mk.

43b–45. He predicts His Passion (Mt 17 22 Mk 9 30). See on Mt. It is not clear why St. Luke omits the prophecy of the resurrection, which certainly was in the source used by the synoptists. See Mt and Mk.

46–48. Who should be greatest (Mt 18 1 Mk 9 33). See on Mt.

49, 50. The man casting out devils in Christ's name. See on Mk 9 38-41.

Chs. 9 51–19 28. The Peræan Ministry. Here begins a long and important section consisting of ten chapters (9 51–19 28) peculiar to the third Gospel, and called generally the 'Peræan section.' (For 'Peræa' see on Mt 19 1.) From the narratives of Mt and Mk, who devote but a chapter to it (Mt 19 Mk 10), it would be supposed that the final journey of Jesus to Jerusalem occupied not more than a week or two, but in St. Luke it is so crowded with incidents, that several months must be assigned to it. It need not, however, be supposed that all the incidents and discourses which St. Luke places in this period really belong to it. Marks of time are infrequent and vague, and lead to the conclusion that many of the incidents came into the evangelist's hands with no indications of date, and were, therefore, grouped together in this appendix to the Galilean ministry. All

the Gospels agree in bringing our Lord to Peræa shortly before the Passion.

Some think that St. Luke describes not one, but three journeys to Jerusalem : (1) 9 51 = Jn 7 1–10 39 (Feast of Tabernacles and of Dedication ; (2) 13 22 = Jn 11 (raising of Lazarus) ; (3) 17 11 = Jn 11 55 (journey from Ephraim to Jerusalem). But it is better to hold that St. Luke describes only one journey, which partook largely of the nature of an extended missionary tour.

51–56. James and John desire to call down fire upon a Samaritan village (peculiar to Lk). Though James and John did not gain their title 'Boanerges' (Mk 3 17) from this incident, yet it undoubtedly illustrates the character of the 'Sons of Thunder' on its weaker side. Their desire for vengeance was a fault, but a generous one. They resented, not a personal slight, but an insult to the Master whom they had now come to regard as greater than Moses or Elijah or any OT. saint. They were right to be angry. but they were wrong in their anger to forget mercy, and to desire to destroy rather than to save sinners.

51. When the time was come (RV 'when the days were well nigh come') **that he should be received up]** lit. 'for His Ascension,' St. Luke thus indicating that His painful death would have a glorious issue. **Set his face]** see Isa 50 7. St. Mark states that Jesus went before, and the disciples followed in amazement and apprehension (Mk 10 32).

52. Samaritans] see on Jn 4 4, 8, 9, 20. **To make ready]** viz. a lodging and a meal.

53. As though he would go to Jerusalem] The Samaritans expected a Messiah, but the fact that Jesus was going to Jerusalem to worship, rather than to their own holy mountain Gerizim, was a sufficient proof to them that Jesus was not he. The Jews often passed through Samaria, but they seldom availed themselves of Samaritan hospitality, though according to the rabbis 'their land was clean, their waters were clean, their dwellings were clean, and their roads were clean.'

54. Even as Elias (Elijah) **did]** 2 K 1 10. Omitted by RV. **55. Ye know not what manner of spirit ye are of]** (omitted by important ancient authorities, see RV), i.e. either, (1) ye know not that the spirit of the new covenant is one of forbearance and forgiveness ; or, (2) ye know not that the spirit which you exhibit comes from Satan not from God.

56. For the Son . . save *them*] These beautiful words are wanting in many ancient authorities, but are in any case an authentic utterance of Jesus, appropriately inserted here.

57–62. Jesus is joined by new disciples. See on Mt 8 19-22.

61, 62. Peculiar to Lk.

61. Bid them farewell] Our Lord probably

does not forbid the man to take leave of his relations, but only indicates in a striking and figurative way that those who aspire to be followers of Him, especially in the work of the ministry, must disentangle themselves from family ties, and give themselves wholeheartedly to the work.

CHAPTER 10
The Seventy. The Good Samaritan. Martha and Mary

1–16. Choice and mission of the Seventy (peculiar to Lk). Another step in the organisation of the Church. The Seventy receive a subordinate commission, similar to that of the apostles, to preach and to cast out devils (vv. 9, 17). Two motives may be discerned in the sending forth of so numerous a body of missionaries. (1) The time before His Passion was now short, and Jesus wished the message of salvation to reach as many Israelites as possible. (2) He wished to train His followers to act alone after His departure. Probably the Twelve did not accompany the Seventy. Jesus kept them with Him for special personal training.

The number 70 is significant. It was the number of the Sanhedrin. As Jesus had already set up twelve new Patriarchs of the New Israel, so now He establishes a new Sanhedrin. The Jews deduced this number from the seventy elders of Nu 11 16, 24. Or the number may symbolise the nations of the earth. The Jews held, agreeably to Gn 10, that the human race was made up of 70 peoples, 14 descended from Japhet, 30 from Ham, and 26 from Shem. If, as is not unlikely, the appointment of the Seventy took place about the Feast of Tabernacles, the ritual of the feast may have had something to do with the number, for then 70 bullocks were offered on behalf of the Gentile nations. The rabbis said, 'They offer seventy bullocks for the seventy nations, to make atonement for them, that the rain may fall upon the fields of all the world.'

The charge to the Seventy reads like an abridged report of St. Matthew's charge to the Twelve. It contains only one v., and that an unimportant one (v. 8), which is not in St. Matthew. St. Luke, however, is not dependent upon St. Matthew, for he arranges the sayings in quite a different order. The close similarity of the two charges is best accounted for by supposing that Christ gave nearly the same directions to the Seventy as to the Twelve. It should be observed, however, that He does not confine their mission to the Israelites. In Peræa the Gentiles were numerous.

1. Seventy] Many ancient authorities read 'seventy-two' here and in v. 17. **6. The son**

of peace] RV 'a son of peace,' i.e. one inclined to peace. A Hebrew idiom. **8.** Peculiar to Luke. The ministers of the gospel are not to be dainty or luxurious.

13–15. See on Mt 11 21-24, where the words occur in quite a different connexion.

17–20. Return of the Seventy (peculiar to Lk). **18. I beheld Satan**] Our Lord poetically compares Satan's discomfiture at the successful mission of the Seventy to his original fall from heaven. The only other allusion to the fall of Satan in the Gospels, and perhaps in the Bible, is Jn 8 44. **19. Serpents and scorpions**] Victory over spiritual foes is meant, rather than immunity from bodily injury, yet cp. Mk 16 18 Ac 28 3-5. **The enemy** is Satan (Mt 13 25). **20.** Jesus bids the disciples rejoice not, as they are doing, because they have miraculous powers, but because their names are enrolled as citizens of heaven in the book of life (Isa 4 3 Dan 12 1 Ex 32 32 Rev 3 5, etc.).

21–24. The revelation to babes (Mt 11 25-27). See on Mt.

21. In spirit] RV 'in the Holy Spirit.' One of St. Luke's characteristic references to the Holy Spirit. Christ's acts and emotions, as well as His words were inspired.

23, 24. See on Mt 13 16, 17.

25–37. Parable of the Good Samaritan (peculiar to Lk). This lawyer is not to be identified with that of Mt 22 35 Mk 12 28.

25–28. See on Mt 22 35-40.

29. Who is my neighbour ?] The 'lawyer' intended to justify himself by showing that, even upon a liberal interpretation of the word 'neighbour,' he had done his duty. He expected Christ to say that a neighbour was a friend or at least an Israelite. The idea that a 'neighbour' might be a foreigner had never occurred to him. The rabbis said, 'He excepts all Gentiles when he saith His neighbour.' 'An Israelite killing a stranger-inhabitant doth not die for it by the Sanhedrin, because it is said, If any one lifts up himself against his neighbour.' 'We are not to contrive the death of the Gentiles, but if they are in any danger of death we are not bound to deliver them, e.g. if any of them fall into the sea you need not take him out, for such a one is not thy neighbour.'

In answer Christ appealed to the man's conscience, not to his reason. If Christ had said 'a heathen is thy neighbour,' the man would have argued the point with learned subtlety. Instead of this Jesus told him a story in which a man treated a foreigner as a neighbour, and the lawyer was bound to confess that this was in accordance with the mind of God.

30–37. A sufficient motive for this parable is provided, if it be understood as simply inculcating the duty of benevolence to persons of all kinds with whom we are brought in contact, enemies as well as friends, foreigners as well as fellow-countrymen, because 'God has made of one (blood) all nations of men for to dwell on all the face of the earth' (Ac 17 26 10 28). The traditional allegorical interpretation, however, is too interesting to be entirely passed over. We give it in the words of Euthymius : 'The man is Adam and his off-spring, the descent from Jerusalem to Jericho is the Fall. The thieves are the demons who beset our path, and strip us of the garments of virtue and the fear of God, and wound us spiritually by causing us to sin. Man was made half dead, in that he remained immortal in the soul, but mortal in the body. The Priest is the Law given by Moses, the Levite is the teaching of the prophets, and the good Samaritan is Christ Himself. The inn is the Church which receives every kind of man. The innkeeper is every ruler of the Church, i.e. every bishop and successor of the apostles. And the two pence are the Old and the New Testaments, which minister healing to the sick.'

30. Jericho] see on Mt 20 29. A city of the priests. The road to Jerusalem is still extremely dangerous, being infested by brigands.

33. Samaritan] see on Jn 4 5 f. **34. Oil and wine**] used as remedies for wounds in the East. **35. Pence**] see on Mt 18 28.

38-42. Jesus at the house of Martha and Mary (peculiar to Lk). It is a striking confirmation of the historic truth of the Fourth Gospel, that the characters of the two sisters—the busy, active, hospitable Martha, the quiet, contemplative, teachable Mary—are the same there as here.

38. Village] i.e. Bethany (Jn 11 1). St. Luke was probably ignorant of the name. **Martha** (lit. 'mistress')] Sometimes supposed to be wife of Simon the Leper. She is a scriptural example of the virtue of hospitality.

39. Mary] Not identical with Mary Magdalene, or the 'sinner' (7 37).

At Jesus' (RV 'the Lord's) **feet**] Jesus was reclining on a couch for the meal, with His head towards the table and His feet stretched out behind him. Martha and Mary were both waiting at table, but whereas Martha occupied herself with offering dish after dish, and so was 'cumbered about much serving,' Mary spent most of her time sitting behind Jesus, and listening to what He was saying. When Martha complained that Mary allowed her to do all the work, Jesus said that He was quite contented with a single dish, and that both sisters would honour Him more by attending to what He said, than by giving Him an elaborate dinner.

42. But one thing is needful] 'There is no need of an elaborate meal. A few dishes or even one would suffice. Indeed, only one por-

tion is really necessary, that which Mary has chosen, to listen to Me.' Our Lord gently hints to Martha that He would rather have a quiet talk with her on heavenly things, than receive all these hospitable attentions at her hands.

CHAPTER 11

THE LORD'S PRAYER. THE SIGN OF JONAH

1-4. The Lord's Prayer (Mt 6 9-15). See on Mt. If the Lord's Prayer was given only once, St. Luke is probably right as to the occasion. His version, however (as in the case of the Beatitudes), is manifestly inferior to St. Matthew's. Of the seven petitions he omits two—the third (' Thy will be done,' etc.), and the seventh (' but deliver us from the evil one' : see the RV). In place of Mt's beautiful opening, 'Our Father in the heavens,' he has simply, 'Father,' and for the expressive metaphor 'debts' he substitutes 'sins.' He manifestly had not access to the original and authentic 'logia' of the apostle Matthew, of which the first evangelist makes such large and fruitful use.

2. Our Father which art in heaven] The true reading here is simply 'Father.' **Thy will be done, as in heaven, so on earth**] Modern editors omit this clause. **4. But deliver us from evil** (' the evil one')] Modern editors omit this clause also.

5-8. The friend at midnight (peculiar to Lk). The connexion with what goes before is suitable and natural. Having given the disciples a form of intercessory prayer, Jesus encourages them to persevere in its use, and also in the use of other prayers formed on its model, by a homely parable, the lesson of which is, If a churlish man can be forced by importunity to give against his will, how much more can persevering prayer bring down from the bountiful Father in heaven all good things.

8. Importunity] better, 'shamelessness.'

9-13. Prayer and the answer to prayer (Mt 7 7-11, Sermon on the Mount). See on Mt.

11, 12. In answer to prayer God gives neither what is useless (**a stone**) nor what is harmful (**a serpent**, or scorpion). The **scorpion** (10 19 Dt 8 15 Ezk 2 6 Rev 9 3, 5, 10) is a small poisonous crab-like animal, which, when at rest, is round like an egg. V. 12 is peculiar to Lk.

14, 15. A dumb devil cast out (Mt 9 32-34). See on Mt.

16. A sign from heaven demanded. See on Mt 12 38 16 1, and see on verses 29 f.

17-23. Christ and Beelzebub. See on Mt 12 25-30.

21, 22. Lk is here fuller and more picturesque than Mt and Mk. The imagery seems derived from Isa 49 24-26. **21. A strong man**] RV 'the strong man fully armed,' i.e.

Satan. His **palace** (RV 'own court') is the world, so far as it is under his usurped dominion. His **goods** are the souls which he holds captive. His **armour** is his crafty devices for keeping them in captivity and separating them from all good influences. The **stronger** is Christ, who, by casting out devils and preaching the gospel, rescues souls from Satan's power. The **spoils** are the rescued souls, which Christ 'divides' by setting them to work at various employments in His own service. **23.** In this contest between Christ and Satan no one can be neutral. **Gathereth .. scattereth**] He who does not help Me to gather and marshal My army, is working for its defeat and rout.

24–26. The peril of the vacant soul (Mt 12 43-45). See on Mt.

27, 28. A woman calls our Lord's mother blessed (peculiar to Lk). Mk and Mt insert at this point the incident of our Lord's mother and brethren wishing to see Him (Mt 12 46 Mk 3 31), which St. Luke has already recorded in a quite different connexion (8 19).

27. As he spake] What our Lord had just said about the danger of a relapse after a superficial repentance (v. 26) struck the woman as so true to life (probably through some unfortunate experience in her own family), that she was moved to express her appreciation of His teaching openly. **Blessed, etc.**] Edersheim quotes a good rabbinical parallel: 'Blessed is the hour in which the Messiah was created; blessed the womb whence He issued; blessed the generation that sees Him; blessed the eye that is worthy to behold Him.' **28.** Christ does not deny that His mother is blessed, but declares that to hear His words and obey them, and so to be brought into spiritual fellowship with God, is blessing infinitely greater.

29–32. The sign of Jonah (Mt 12 38-42). See on Mt.

33–36. Inward light and darkness. Christ is still rebuking those who refused to believe in Him without a special sign from heaven. In St. Matthew these vv. form part of the Sermon on the Mount.

33. A favourite saying of Christ's occurring in various connexions (8 16 Mt 5 15 Mk 4 21). Here it means that Christ by His public preaching and miracles has made Himself so conspicuous and public a 'sign' to this generation, that they ought to ask for no other.

34–36. (Mt 6 22, 23, q.v.) If they will only regard His work and teaching without prejudice, then their own consciences will testify that He has a real mission from God.

37–54. Christ is entertained by a Pharisee. He denounces Pharisaic formalism and hypocrisy. For the relation of this discourse to Mt 23 1-36, see on Mt 23 1.

38. Washed] lit. 'baptised': see on Mk 7 1-5.

39–41. See on Mt 23 25, 26. 'What is the use of you Pharisees cleansing the outward appearance of your conduct (symbolised by the outside of the cup and the platter), if your souls within are full of greed and wickedness? God, who made both the outside and the inside of man, expects both to be made clean. Only give what is within the cup and platter as alms to the poor, and in general practice generosity instead of greed, and all your vessels will become clean to you without ceremonial cleansing.

41. Give alms of such things as ye have] A possible, but unlikely translation. Better, 'Give as alms what is within (the cup and platter).' Others render, 'Give your hearts to almsgiving.' **All things**] i.e. all your vessels.

42. See on Mt 23 23. **43.** See on Mt 23 6. **44.** See on Mt 23 27. **46.** See on Mt 23 4. **47, 48.** See on Mt 23 29-31. **49–51.** See on Mt 23 34-36. **49. Therefore also said the wisdom of God**] In Mt 23 34 the words are an utterance of Christ Himself. Christ's knowledge of the divine counsels is so complete that His utterances are also utterances of the Wisdom of God. **52.** See on Mt 23 13. **The key of knowledge**] i.e. the key which opens the door to knowledge of the things concerning the kingdom of God.

CHAPTER 12

THE LEAVEN OF THE PHARISEES. THE RICH FOOL

1–12. Jesus warns His followers against Pharisaic hypocrisy, and exhorts them to be courageous in face of opposition. This speech is not unsuitable to the context in St. Luke, but the whole of the sayings are found also in St. Matthew's Gospel, generally in a more natural connexion (mostly in the charge to the Twelve, 10 5-42). Perhaps St. Luke here groups together sayings spoken at different times.

1. When there were] RV 'when the many thousands of the multitude were gathered together.' They were attracted by the dispute between our Lord and the Pharisees recorded in the last c. Since our Lord begins by addressing His disciples, and warns them of coming persecutions, it may be inferred that the multitude was at first inclined to side with the Pharisees; yet see v. 13, where the authority of Jesus is plainly recognised. **The leaven**] see on Mt 16 6, 11, 12.

2–9. See on Mt 10 26-33.

2, 3. These vv. have a different connexion and meaning in Mt.

2. Hypocrisy, like that of the Pharisees, is useless and foolish, for in the Judgment Day there will be a merciless exposure of it.

3. For in that day the most secret words and thoughts of hypocrites will be proclaimed to the whole creation. **Therefore** (RV 'Wherefore ')] is better translated 'for,' 'because' (cp. 1 20 19 44 Ac 12 23).

10. See on Mt 12 31, 32. **11, 12.** See on Mt 10 17-20.

13–21. Parable of the rich fool (peculiar to Lk). The parable teaches that since death and judgment are inevitable, men ought to devote their attention to laying up treasure in heaven, not on earth.

13. Divide the inheritance] Such questions were decided by the 'bench of three' of the local synagogues. Christ, as usual, refuses to be drawn into any political or semi-political action. The unseasonable request of the man (he appears to have interrupted our Lord's discourse to make it), showed that his mind was too much set upon worldly things. **14. Who made me?**] Cp. Ex 2 14. **15. For a man's life**] The Gk. is difficult and the translation doubtful, but the sense seems to be that neither a man's physical nor his spiritual life is dependent upon great possessions. A healthy and happy human life can be lived in a state of comparative poverty, and spiritual life is rather hindered than aided by great possessions. Others understand it to mean that a man's life is not like a possession, but infinitely more valuable. Cp. below (v. 23), 'the life is more than meat, and the body is more than raiment.'

16. Brought forth] The man's wealth was honestly and justly acquired. His fault was not injustice, but covetousness. **17. I have no room**] 'Thou *hast* barns, the mouths of the poor which can hold much ; barns which can never be pulled down or destroyed, for they are heavenly and divine, if indeed it be true that he who feeds the poor, feeds God ' (Theophylact).

19. To my soul] The fool speaks as if earthly wealth could supply the needs of an immortal soul. **20. This night, etc.**] lit. 'this night do they (i.e. the angels of vengeance) require thy soul of thee.' The righteous man willingly and joyfully commits his soul to God ; but from the wicked man it is exacted with stern terror. **21. Rich toward God**] On laying up treasure in heaven, which is here meant, see on Mt 6 19-21.

There is an interesting rabbinical parallel to this parable : 'Once Rabbi Simeon went to a certain circumcision and there feasted. The father gave them old wine, seven years old, to drink, saying, "With this wine will I grow old, rejoicing in my son." They feasted together till midnight. At midnight Rabbi Simeon, trusting to his own virtue, went out to go into the city, and on the way met the angel of death, who, he perceived, was very sad. He asked therefore, "Why art thou so sad ?" He replied, "I am sad for the speeches of those who say, I will do this or that ere long, though they know not how quickly they may be called away by death. The man who just boasted,

'With this wine I will grow old, rejoicing in my son,' behold his time draws near. Within thirty days he must be snatched away." The rabbi said to him, "Do thou let me know *my* time." The angel answered, "Over thee and such as thou art, we have no power ; for God, being delighted with good works, prolongeth your lives." '

22–34. Against anxiety about wealth and worldly things. Almost the whole of this section occurs in St. Matthew's Sermon on the Mount. The present context, however, is very suitable, and is perhaps correct.

22–31. See on Mt 6 25-33.

29. Neither be ye of doubtful mind] or, 'neither be ye high-minded.'

32. Fear not, little flock] A beautiful and tender saying peculiar to Lk, intended to encourage the disciples who would be for so long in so hopeless a minority. The sense is, 'If God is willing to give you the kingdom, much more will He give you food and raiment, therefore you need not be afraid (v. 33) to sell that ye have and give alms.' **33.** See on Mt 19 21 6 20. **Sell that ye have, etc.**] Christ addresses not all the disciples, but those who, like the apostles, had received a call to leave all, and devote themselves to the work of the ministry.

Bags (RV 'purses') **which wax not old**] The purses which will keep your money safely are not your own, but those of the poor on whom you bestow your charity. Placed in those purses, your earthly treasure will become 'treasure in the heavens that faileth not.'

34. See on Mt 6 21.

35–48. Exhortation to vigilance. The greater part of it appears also (and most appropriately) in Mt 24. The apostles and other ministers of the word are chiefly addressed, though there is a lesson for all (v. 41 f.). The question of Peter (v. 41) is peculiar to Lk.

35, 36. A little parable peculiar to Luke, warning the apostles to be ready for Christ's second coming, which will be sudden. The apostles are compared to slaves left to watch the house (the Church) while the master (Christ) goes to a wedding feast (i.e. ascends into heaven). Their loins are girded because they have housework to do (preaching the gospel and ruling the Church), and they have lighted lamps, because their task is to enlighten a dark and sinful world by their shining example. Christ's return from the marriage feast is His Second Advent, or it may mean His judgment of each individual soul at death. The 'marriage feast' here is not the final joy of the blessed, as in the parable of the Ten Virgins, but Christ's session at the right hand of God between the Ascension and Second Advent.

The parable, though primarily intended for the rulers of the Church, is applicable to all Christians, for all have received some kind of commission from Christ.

37, 38. See on Mt 24 46. These vv. continue the parable. Those whom Christ shall find watching at His Second Coming, He will invite to share in the final feast (the joy of heaven) ; when He Himself will serve them, supplying them with all blessedness, and wiping away all tears from their eyes. The **second** and **third watches** are the second and third of the Roman four watches (Mt 14 25). They thus represent the dead of night, and by metaphor the unexpectedness of the Second Advent. The Jews reckoned only three night watches.

39, 40. See on Mt 24 43, 44. Another parable in which, by a curious inversion, the goodman (master) of the house means the apostles, and the thief Christ. Christ is so called from the secrecy and unexpectedness of His coming.

41. (Peculiar to Lk.) Christ does not answer Peter's question directly, but His answer shows that He is speaking mainly of the apostles and those in authority.

42-46. See on Mt 24 45-50.

47, 48. (Peculiar to Lk.) Christ here seems to assert (cp. 10 12, 14) that there will be degrees of future punishment.

48. He that knew not] 'The reference is to the future pastors of the Church. "He that knew not," will still be punished, for he could have known ; but not punished so much as the other, for the other was presumptuous, but this one was slothful ; and presumption is a greater sin than sloth ' (Euthymius). **They will ask the more**] Christ through His angels will demand 'His own with usury,' i.e. will demand that the talents entrusted to each man shall have been improved, and turned to good use. In the case of the Apostles He will demand what souls they have gained besides their own.

49-53. The strife that the gospel will produce. In different connexions in Mt.

49. A paradox. The Prince of Peace comes to bring strife and bloodshed, fire and sword, into the world, because only through war can lasting peace be attained. Some, however, understand by **fire**, the fire of Christian love. **What will I,** etc.] i.e. 'how much I wish that it were already kindled !' (Theophylact). Other translations : 'What more have I to desire, if it be already kindled ?' (Plummer). 'What do I desire ? Would that it were already kindled !' (Origen).

50. See on Mt 20 22 = Mk 10 38. **A baptism**] i.e. Christ's Passion. **Straitened**] i.e. afflicted, oppressed.

51-53. See on Mt 10 34-36.

54-59. Ignorance of the signs of the times.

54-56. See on Mt 16 1-3.

57. Peculiar to Lk. Of yourselves] Why, even without signs, do you not judge rightly of Me and My doctrine (by the natural light of reason and conscience ?

58, 59. See on Mt 5 25, 26.

CHAPTER 13

The Galileans killed by Pilate. The Unfruitful Fig Tree. Lament over Jerusalem

1-9. Three exhortations to repentance, of which the former two are based on recent events, and the third is a parable. All are peculiar to Lk.

1. Whose blood Pilate] These men had evidently been killed in the courts of the Temple for some real or suspected sedition while they were slaying their victims, an act which was performed not by the priests, but by the offerers, or their servants. Nothing is known of this particular act of atrocity, but Philo, a contemporary writer, speaks of Pilate's repeated massacres of persons uncondemned, and insatiable and most grievous ferocity. It was perhaps either the cause or the consequence of the enmity between Herod and Pilate mentioned 23 12. **2. Were sinners**] see on Jn 9 3.

3. Shall all likewise perish] This was literally fulfilled at the destruction of Jerusalem, but probably Jesus means, 'as these have suffered literal death, so you shall all suffer spiritual death.' **4. Tower in Siloam fell**] Another unknown incident. It is plausibly conjectured that this tower was part of the waterworks and aqueduct which Pilate built with the sacred money of the Temple treasury (*Korbanas*), to the great scandal of pious Jews. The persons killed were probably workmen, whose death was regarded as a judgment for their impiety. For 'Siloam' see on Jn 9 7.

The idea was very common among the Jews that great calamities are a proof of great sin. This was the view of Job's friends, who were convinced that his great misfortunes argued him a great sinner (Job 4 7 8 2-14, 20 22 5). Our Lord on several occasions strongly opposed this view (see Jn 9 2). Sometimes, no doubt, suffering is a direct punishment for sin, but not always, perhaps not generally. In the case of the righteous it often arises from the sin of others, or is permitted as a trial of faith, or as a means of refining and purifying the character. A righteous man's sufferings may even be directly due to his righteousness, as in the case of our Lord, the apostles, Socrates, and numerous missionaries and reformers in all ages and countries.

6-9. The Barren Fig Tree. This parable illustrates the warning (vv. 3, 5), 'Except ye repent, ye shall all likewise perish.' A certain man (God) had a fig tree (the Jewish nation)

in his vineyard (the world), and he came (at various crises of their history) seeking fruit (good works and pure religion) and found none. And he said to the vine-dresser (the Son of God), Behold these three years (under the Law, under the Prophets, and under the Scribes) I come seeking fruit. Cut it down. Why, besides being unfruitful, doth it also cumber the ground (prevent the conversion of the world)? And the vine-dresser (Christ) answered, Lord, let it alone this year also (for a further time of grace), till I dig about it and dung it (i.e. preach the gospel, show signs and wonders, send down the Spirit, do all things for its conversion), and if it bear fruit thenceforth, well; but if not, thou shalt cut it down (i.e. shalt destroy the nation with its city and Temple): cp. Mt 21¹⁹. The parable is also capable of a more general application to the individual soul.

10-17. The woman with a spirit of infirmity (peculiar to Lk). The story is told not so much for the sake of the miracle, as for the light it throws upon the question of sabbath observance. It is the only case of Christ's preaching in a synagogue recorded in the latter part of the ministry.

12. He called her] An unasked-for cure.

14. Said unto the people] The ruler durst not openly rebuke Jesus, but indirectly censured Him by censuring the people.

15. Loose his ox] The rabbis, while permitting attention to beasts on the sabbath, did so grudgingly: 'It is not only permitted to lead a beast to the water on the sabbath, but also to draw water for it, yet so that the beast draw near and drink, without the water being carried to it and set down by it.'

16. Satan hath bound] The Jews attributed such ills to Satan. It is not implied that the woman was of evil life.

18-21. The Mustard Seed and the Leaven (Mt 13³¹⁻³³ Mk 4³⁰). See on Mt.

22-30. Are they few that be saved? Jesus does not directly reply to the question, but warns His hearers of the difficulty of obtaining salvation, of the danger of delaying repentance, and of the probable rejection of many unbelieving descendants of Abraham, and of the salvation of many believing Gentiles. There are close parallels in St. Matthew.

23, 24. See on Mt 7¹³,¹⁴. **Gate**] i.e. 'door.'

25. The master] i.e. our Lord. The 'shutting the door' takes place at Christ's second coming, or perhaps at the death of each individual. **Lord, open**] see on Mt 25¹⁰⁻¹², also Mt 7²³. **26.** This v. specially applies to the Jews. **27. Depart**] see on Mt 25⁴¹.

28, 29. See on Mt 8¹¹,¹². **30.** See on Mt 20¹⁻¹⁶.

31-35. Message to Herod Antipas, and lament over Jerusalem. This threat of Herod is peculiar to Lk.

31. Certain of the Pharisees] Probably they wished to frighten Jesus out of the dominions of Herod, where He was tolerably safe, into Judæa, where He would be in the power of the Sanhedrin: cp. Amaziah's attempt to frighten Amos (Am 7¹⁰⁻¹⁷). **Herod**] For his biography see on Mt 14¹⁻¹¹. **Will**] RV 'would fain kill thee.' Herod may have used threatening words, or there may have been a rumour to that effect, but it is certain that he did not seriously seek our Lord's death: cp. 23¹¹. **32. That fox**] The fox is an emblem of cunning, not of cruelty. **Behold**] i.e. 'I perform My ministry to-day and to-morrow (i.e. for the time appointed), and on the third day (i.e. when My hour is come) I shall be perfected by death. No threats of Herod can shorten My ministry, or hasten the hour of My death.' **Perfected**] He calls His death His 'perfecting,' because by it He perfected His work by atoning for the sins of the world, also because it was followed by His glorious resurrection and ascension, whereby His human nature was 'perfected' or glorified. **33. Nevertheless, etc.**] i.e. 'Yet although My death is so near, I must labour for the time appointed. Herod cannot prevent Me. He cannot destroy Me here in remote Galilee, for it is only in Jerusalem that a prophet can die.' **Walk**] RV 'go on my way.' **Out of Jerusalem**] 'The saying is severely ironical, and that in two ways: (1) According to overwhelming precedent, Jerusalem is the place in which a prophet ought to be put to death; for *it had obtained by usage the right to slay the prophets* (Grotius). (2) It is not Herod that will be the murderer. It is at *your* hands, in *your* capital that I shall die' (Plummer).

34, 35. Mt 23³⁷⁻³⁹. See on Mt.

CHAPTER 14

THE DROPSICAL MAN. THE GREAT SUPPER.
DIVERS SAYINGS AND PARABLES

1-6. The sabbath question again. The man with the dropsy healed (peculiar to Lk).

1. To eat bread] So far from being abstemious on the sabbath, the Jews carried the pleasures of the table to excess. 'The Hebrews honour the sabbath chiefly by inviting each other to drinking and intoxication' (Plutarch). 'Rabbah Abba bought flesh of thirteen butchers that he might be sure to taste the best, and paid them at the very gate, that he might hasten dinner, and all this in honour of the sabbath' (Talmud).

2. There was.. before him] Spectators often enter the house to witness an Eastern banquet. **3. Is it lawful to heal?**] See on Mt 12¹⁰. **5. An ass**] Nearly all modern editors read 'a son.' The rabbis allowed 'an ox or an ass, a son or a daughter, a man-servant or a maid-servant' to be drawn out of a well on the sabbath. Thus they allowed to themselves breaches of the sabbath day which they denied to Christ.

7–11. On places of honour at feasts (peculiar to Lk, but a similar discourse occurs in the 'Western' text of St. Matthew, 20 28, q.v.). It is probable that the dropsical man was healed before the dinner began, and that there then ensued an unseemly struggle for places, which gave occasion for the 'parable' following.

7. A parable] An elastic word. Here it means a piece of advice, inculcating humility.

Chose.. the chief rooms] RV 'seats,' i.e. places on the couches : see on Mk 12 39. A good illustration of the pride of the rabbis is the conduct of Rabbi Simeon ben Shetah, who when invited to dinner by king Jannæus (104–79 B.C.), placed himself between the king and queen, saying, 'Exalt wisdom and she shall exalt thee, and make thee to sit among princes.' But such conduct was not universally approved, and with the advice which our Lord here gives may be compared the more spiritual teaching of other rabbis. Rabbi Akiba said, 'Yield up thy place, and go down two or three seats, and sit down, until they say to thee, Go up higher. Go not higher of thyself, lest they say to thee, Go down lower, for it is better that they should say to thee, Go higher, than Go lower. Thus the son of Hillel used to say, 'My humiliation is my exaltation, and my exaltation is my humiliation.' **11.** Cp. Mt 23 12 ; repeated Lk 18 14.

12–14. On entertaining the poor (peculiar to Lk, whose Gospel is full of sympathy with the poor). **12. Thy friends, etc.]** A man is not in the true sense hospitable, who entertains only those who can entertain again. Such interested hospitality is not wrong, but there is no merit in it, and it does not lay up treasure in heaven. **14. At the resurrection of the just]** i.e. at the glorious resurrection to life eternal which the righteous only will enjoy, with which is contrasted 'the resurrection of condemnation' which awaits the unrighteous (Jn 5 29). 'The resurrection of the just' here answers exactly to 'the resurrection *from* the dead,' viz. of righteous persons only (Phil 3 11 RV), as distinguished from 'the resurrection *of* the dead,' which includes all mankind (Ac 17 32). Our Lord's words give no real sanction to the Jewish belief in two distinct resurrections, the first of the righteous the second of the unrighteous, traces of which some expositors find in 1 Cor 15 23 1 Th 4 16, and especially in Rev 20 5, 6.

15–24. The great supper (peculiar to Lk, although Mt 22 1-14 presents many points of similarity : see on that passage). Here the 'certain man' is God, the many bidden are the rulers of the Jews, the servant who invites them is Jesus Christ. When the

rulers refuse the invitation to the feast (i.e. to enter into Christ's Kingdom), the poor, the maimed, the blind, and the lame (i.e. the despised classes of the Jewish nation) are invited. They joyfully obey, and yet there is room, because the kingdom of Christ is meant to embrace all mankind (v. 22). Then Christ, through His Apostles, goes out into the highways and hedges (i.e. into heathen lands), and compels the Gentiles to come in. **15. Eat bread in the kingdom of God]** The mention of the 'resurrection of the just,' with which, according to Jewish ideas, the reign of the Messiah would begin, reminds this Jew of the great feast, which the Messiah would then hold : see on Mt 8 11. **18.** The excuses show careless unconcern, not hardened wickedness. Business occupations, family ties, and various distractions, are pleaded as excuses for not taking God's summons seriously. **23. Compel *them* to come in]** Our Lord does not here (as has often been supposed) sanction religious persecution. 'He said "Compel them," not commanding force to be used, but indicating that in the case of Gentiles a more urgent and persistent kind of preaching must be used, seeing that they were under the power of demons, and sleeping in the deep darkness of error' (Euthymius). **24. For I say]** Here Christ drops the parabolic form and speaks in His own person. 'For I (Christ) say unto you, that none of the Jewish rulers who have rejected My invitation shall taste of My supper, i.e. of the blessedness in store for the saints of God.'

25–35. That we must give up all to follow Christ, and count the cost before we do so. The two parables of the Rash Builder (vv. 28–30) and the Rash King (vv. 31–33) are peculiar to Lk. The multitude who follow Jesus (v. 25) are inclined to believe that He is the Messiah, and expect great temporal benefits from their discipleship. Jesus warns them that, instead of this, they must expect persecution and even death (v. 27), and that those who cannot make a complete sacrifice of earthly affections (v. 26), and ambition (v. 33), had better turn back while there is yet time.

26, 27. See on Mt 10 37,38. **26. Hate]** 'This does not imply the *feeling* of hatred, but a readiness to *act* as if one hated. The nearest and dearest must be forsaken, and opposed, and offended, if need be, to follow Christ.'

28–33. None of the details of these two parables or similes are significant. The parables simply enforce the one idea that it is folly to undertake a serious business (here, becoming a disciple of Christ), without counting the cost.

33. Forsaketh not all] Only the Apostles (and the Seventy) were required to do this in act, but every disciple is required to do it in will, i.e. to subordinate all earthly interests and claims to Christ's, when the two are incompatible.

34, 35. Salt] i.e. 'discipleship.' In Mt 5 13 (q.v.) it means the pure and unselfish lives of Christians. 'The salt which has lost its savour' is here the discipleship which refuses to make the sacrifices which Christ demands (vv. 26, 27, 33).

35. The land .. the dunghill] These have no special meaning. The sense is that the discipleship which makes no sacrifices is valueless for any purpose

CHAPTER 15

PARABLES OF THE LOST SHEEP, OF THE LOST COIN, OF THE PRODIGAL SON

1–7. Parable of the Lost Sheep. See on Mt 18 12-13. The first of a series of three parables for the encouragement of penitents. It shows the love of our Saviour for the outcast, the despised, and the criminal classes generally. It rebukes the Pharisees, who professed to be shepherds, for their neglect of that part of the flock that most needed their help, and lastly it indicates that the Pharisees are in many respects worse than the sinners they despise. The owner of the flock is our Lord Himself, the Good Shepherd (Jn 10 14) ; the flock is His Church, embracing men of all kinds ; the ninety and nine are those who seem to be righteous, like the Pharisees ; the one sheep that is lost and is found, is all truly penitent sinners. These are represented as one sheep not because they are few in number compared with the others, but to show Christ's love for each individual soul. The seeking and laying the lost sheep upon His shoulders, are Christ's work of love in pleading with the sinner, and finally after due repentance bringing him back to a state of grace. The friends and neighbours who rejoice with Him are the angels. 'On no image did the early Church dwell with more fondness than this, as witness the many gems, seals, fragments of glass, and other relics which have reached us, on which Christ is thus portrayed. It is frequent also in bas-reliefs, on sarcophagi, and paintings in the catacombs. Sometimes other sheep are at His feet, generally two, looking up with pleasure at Him and His burden. This representation always occupies the place of honour, the centre of the vault or tomb ' (Trench). The rabbis have a story that Moses, while tending Jethro's flocks, went after a kid (or lamb) which had gone astray. As he thought that it must be weary, he gently raised it and carried it on his shoulders. God was pleased and said, 'Since thou hast shown pity in bringing back a man's beast, thou shalt be the shepherd of my flock Israel all thy life long.'

1. Publicans and sinners] see on Mt 5 46 9 11.

7. Which need no repentance] i.e. which think they need no repentance, but really need it more than the publicans and sinners whom they despise. The rabbis divided the just or righteous into two classes, (1) the 'perfectly just,' or 'men of works,' who had never in all their lives committed a single sin, and (2) the 'penitents,' who, having once been wicked, had repented. The Pharisees considered themselves to belong to the former class, as also, perhaps, did the young ruler who said 'All these have I kept from my youth' (Mk 10 20). How external the Pharisaic standard of righteousness was, may be gathered from the story of the 'holy man,' who 'never committed one trespass all the days of his life, except this one misfortune which befell him, that one day he put on his head-phylactery before his arm-phylactery.' For 'phylactery,' see on Mt 23 5.

8–10. The Lost Coin (peculiar to Lk). The last parable set forth the work of Christ in seeking and reclaiming the lost, this one sets forth that of the Church. The woman is the Church ; the ten pieces of silver are the human souls in her keeping ; the lost piece is a soul that has fallen from grace through her negligence. Eager to atone for her neglect, and full of love for her erring member, she lights a candle, i.e. vigorously exercises the ministry of the Word, and by preaching the gospel and by loving pastoral intercourse brings back the lost soul to a state of grace. The sweeping of the house is the vehemence with which she sets about her task, thereby incurring the charge of 'turning the world upside down' (Ac 17 6). Having found the lost coin, she calls upon her friends and neighbours, i.e. not only her faithful members, but also the angels, to join in her joy. **8. Pieces**] Gk. *drachma*, a coin equivalent in value to the Roman *denarius* (Mt 18 28). **9. Friends**] lit. female friends and neighbours.

11–32. The Prodigal Son (peculiar to Lk). 'This parable, like the two preceding, is intended to show what joy there is in heaven at the conversion of sinners, and, therefore, how wrong the Pharisees were to murmur, because Christ consorted with sinners to convert them ' (Cornelius a Lapide). The father is God ; the elder son is just persons, or rather those who think themselves and are thought by others to be such, here, in particular, the Pharisees who 'trusted in themselves that they were righteous, and despised others.' The younger son is all penitent sinners, here, in particular, the publicans and sinners of vv. 1, 2. The portion of goods (v. 12) is the whole of a man's faculties and powers, which he ought to exercise and enjoy in his father's house, i.e. in dependence upon God and in His service, but which the prodigal son demands to have under his own control, to use according to his own will and pleasure. The lack of love and apostasy of heart shown in this demand is soon followed by apostasy of life, for not many days after (v. 13), he gathers all together, i.e. deliberately resolves to devote his whole fortune and all his powers to the pursuit of pleasure, and journeys into a far country, i.e. into the world of sin where God is not, or rather where He is forgotten, and wastes his substance in riotous living, i.e. throws off even the semblance of piety and respectability, and ruins not only his soul, but his health and fortune in extravagance and debauchery. Presently there arises a mighty famine in the land, i.e. his pleasures pall, his friends prove false, his animal indulgences fail to satisfy him. In his distress he goes and joins himself to a citizen of that country, i.e. at first he seeks relief by plunging deeper into sin, selling himself to Satan to kill regret. But he finds no relief. Satan is now his master, and shows his contempt for him by using him as a drudge and a slave. Finding now no pleasure or satisfaction in his sin, and the hunger of his soul remaining still unappeased, he determines to return to his father and to say 'Father, I have sinned .. Make me as one of thy hired servants,' i.e. place me lowest in thy kingdom. His father sees him a great way off, and goes to meet him, for God meets, nay, almost anticipates, the first efforts of sinners to return. He falls on his neck and kisses him, the kiss signifying the reconciliation between God and man brought about by Christ. The son makes his confession of sin, but does not add ' Make me as one of thy hired servants,' because he now sees that God wishes to restore him to his full privileges. Then the father says to his servants (the ministers of His Church), Bring forth the former robe, and put it on him (i.e. restore him to his former privileges as a Christian by the ministry of reconciliation), and put a ring on his hand (a symbol of rank and honour), and shoes on his feet (symbolising spiritual freedom, for slaves went barefoot), and bring the fatted calf and kill it (signifying the joy there is in earth and heaven over a repentant sinner, perhaps also the spiritual nourishment which the hungry soul will find in the ordinances of religion which have been so long neglected) ; for this my son was dead (in sin) and is alive again (by repentance). And they begin to be merry, i.e. to rejoice over the penitent, and to treat him with as much honour as if he had never sinned. The conclusion of the parable graphically traces the character of the elder brother, who represents the Pharisees and persons of their spirit. He is busied in the field (v. 25), i.e. in a round of regular, but loveless, religious observances. He shows anger and jealousy, and that in spite of the affectionate entreaties of his father, who in-

vites him to the festivities, and shows him equal honour and love (v. 28). He shows himself, like the Pharisees, quite unconscious of his own failings, and arrogantly boasts, 'I have never transgressed a commandment of thine' (v. 29) : see on v. 7. He puts the worst construction on his brother's past sins, perhaps exaggerating them (v. 30), and shows himself incapable of forgiveness (v. 30).

The parable may be suitably applied to illustrate the relations of Jew and Gentile (the Jew being the elder, the Gentile the younger son), but this is not its primary meaning.

12. Give me the portion] according to Jewish law, one-half of what the eldest received (Dt 21 ^{17}). He *may* have had a right to demand his property before his father's death. ' We have here perhaps a survival of that condition of society in which testaments " took effect immediately on execution, were not secret, and were not revocable," and in which it was customary for a father, when his powers were failing, to abdicate and surrender his property to his sons : cp. Ecclus 33 $^{19-23}$.'

15. To a citizen] i.e. Satan, or some companion more wicked than himself. **16. He would fain have filled**] i.e. and did so. **Husks**] i.e. the pods of the carob-tree, eaten only by the very poorest people. **And no man gave unto him**] food of any kind.

19. Hired servants] i.e. imperfect Christians, who perform their duties to God in the spirit of hirelings rather than of sons.

22. The best robe] or, rather, ' the former robe,' i.e. the state of grace in which he was before his sin. In its Christian application the robe of baptismal innocence, because in baptism we ' put on Christ ' as a garment (Gal 3 ^{27}).

CHAPTER 16
THE UNJUST STEWARD. THE RICH MAN AND LAZARUS

1–13. Parable of the Unjust Steward (peculiar to Lk). The details of this somewhat difficult parable are probably not significant. It is intended to illustrate the proper use of wealth. Christians should use it so well here on earth, by expending it not selfishly on their own pleasures, but unselfishly for the good of others, and for the advancement of God's kingdom, that instead of hindering them from reaching heaven, it will help them to enter there. The prudence (foresight) of the steward is commended in this parable, not his dishonesty.

5–7. Tenants in the East pay their rent in kind, not in money. The landlord provides them with seed, and they return him at harvest-time a certain proportion of the yield.

6. An hundred measures] lit. ' baths,' the ' bath ' being a Heb. liquid measure = 9 gallons.

759

Bill] RV 'bond.' **7. Measures**] lit. *cors*,
the *cor* being a Heb. dry measure = 11 bushels.
8. And the lord] RV 'his lord,' i.e. his
master. Many readers wrongly imagine that
Jesus is the speaker here. **Because he had
done wisely**] i.e. 'prudently.' The master
praised not the morality of the transaction,
but its far-sighted prudence, and it is just this
that Jesus holds up for imitation. **For the
children (sons) of this world** (i.e. worldly
people) **are in their generation** (i.e. in dealing
with other worldly people) **wiser** (i.e. more
prudent and far-seeing) **than the children of
light** (i.e. than the spiritually enlightened are in
making provision for their heavenly welfare).
9. Make to yourselves] i.e. make to yourselves friends in heaven by means of a prudent
use of your wealth (viz. by hospitality, almsdeeds, etc.), that when ye **fail**, i.e. die (or,
according to the RV, when 'it,' i.e. your
wealth, 'fail'), the angels may receive you
into the eternal habitations. **Of**] RV 'by
means of.' **Friends**] i.e. either 'the poor,'
who by their prayers obtain your admission
to heaven, or, more probably, 'the angels,'
who become the friends of those who give
alms, and at the last carry their souls to
heaven. **The mammon of unrighteousness**]
A common rabbinical expression. It occurs
in the pre-Christian book of Enoch. It does
not here mean wealth unrighteously acquired, but simply 'deceitful wealth.' So we
speak of 'filthy lucre,' not meaning unjust
gain, but gain in general : see Mt 6 24. So
rightly Calvin : 'By giving this name to
riches, he intends to render them an object of
our suspicion, because for the most part they
involve their possessors in unrighteousness.'
10, 11. V. 11 explains v. 10. If you are
unfaithful in such an unimportant matter as
money (i.e. if you do not spend your incomes
to the glory of God), God will not entrust you
with those spiritual gifts, graces, and virtues
which are much more important. **12.** If you
do not spend your money rightly, you will
not inherit the kingdom of heaven. Money is
here called **that which is another's**, because
Christians are to regard it not as their own,
but as a trust for which they must one day
give account. **That which is your own** is the
joy of heaven, 'the kingdom prepared for you
from the foundation of the world.' **13.** See
on Mt 6 24.
**14–18. The Pharisees mock Jesus. His
reply.** The connexion of vv. 16, 17, 18 is
difficult, and it may be that they do not properly belong here, but it is also possible that
our Lord's discourse is abridged, the connecting links being left out. **14. Covetous**] RV
'lovers of money' ; see on Mk 12 40.
15, 16. See on Mt 11 12, 13. The connexion
(if such is to be sought) is this : Before Christ

began to preach, it was comparatively easy for
the Pharisees to justify themselves before men,
but now that the deeper morality of the Gospel
is widely accepted, men are beginning to find
out the deficiencies of the Pharisees.
17, 18. See on Mt 5 18. Here the sense is :
The Pharisees, however, object to be tried by
the standard of the Gospel, and demand to be
tried by the standard of the Law. But even
according to this (which is still in force in its
spiritual sense), they are found to be deficient,
for, while observing it in trivial matters, they
break it in matters of weight, e.g. (v. 18),
whereas the Law forbids divorce except for
adultery, the Pharisees, or most of them, allow
it for every cause : see on Mt 5 32.
19–31. The rich man and Lazarus: peculiar
to Lk, and full of that sympathy with the
poor which characterises his Gospel. It does
not, however, as Strauss maintains, assert that
the mere possession of wealth is wrong, or
that mere poverty justifies. On the contrary,
the rich man is condemned, not because
he was rich, but because he was callous,
and Lazarus justified, not because he was
poor, but because he was poor in spirit. The
callousness of the rich man was due to his
scepticism. He consumed his wealth in selfish luxury, sparing none of it for the poor,
because he did not really believe in God or a
future life. If he had so believed, he would
have acted differently. The parable may
perhaps be directed against the Pharisees, who
were 'lovers of money' (v. 14) ; but inasmuch
as their covetousness did not take the form of
sumptuous living, it seems better to regard it
as a warning addressed to Christians generally
against luxury, worldliness, selfishness, and
unbelief.
19. Rich man] conveniently called 'Dives'
(Lat.). He represents all those who in the
enjoyment of wealth forget God and the world
to come, and neglect all acts of charity and
love. **Purple**] i.e. a rich material dyed with
the liquid obtained from the shellfish 'murex,'
formed the rich man's upper garment, and **fine
linen** his under garment, or shirt ; both were
exceedingly costly. **20. Lazarus**] = *Eleazar*,
i.e. 'He who has God for his help.' His
name expresses his character. From Lazarus
is derived *lazar* = leper. **Desiring**] but not
obtaining his desire. **21. The dogs**] Since the
dog was in the East an unclean animal, the
licking was an aggravation of the poor man's
misery. **22. By the angels**] The rabbis said :
'None can enter Paradise but the just, whose
souls are carried thither by angels.' 'When
an Israelite departs to his eternal home, the
angel in charge of the garden of Eden, who
receives every circumcised son of Israel, introduces him into the garden of Eden.' 'When
the just depart from the world three com-

panies of angels go before them in peace. The first says, "Let him come in peace"; the second says, "Let them rest in their beds"; the third accompanies him.' **Abraham's bosom**] A Jewish name, not of heaven, but of the intermediate state of bliss, in which the souls of the just await the resurrection. E.g. ' Ada bar Ahavah sits to-day in Abraham's bosom': cp. 4 Mac13 17. ' When we have thus suffered, Abraham, Isaac, and Jacob will receive us.' Other equivalent names are 'Paradise,' 'the garden of Eden,' and ' under the throne of glory.' **23. In hell**] RV 'in Hades.' Hades is here used in a wide sense for the intermediate state of all souls, just and unjust, between death and judgment. In this sense both Dives and Lazarus were in ' Hades,' though the one was comforted and the other tormented. This usage of the word is quite common. ' Hades, in which the souls both of just and unjust are detained' (Hippolytus). ' In the lower world are both torment and refreshment. There a soul is either punished or tenderly cherished, as a foretaste or rehearsal of the final judgment' (Tertullian). The rich man was not in 'hell' (*Gehenna*), because no one is sent there until after the Last Judgment.

In torments] Spiritual torment or punishment must be meant, for Dives was now a disembodied spirit. **Seeth Abraham**] The rabbis placed Paradise in sight of the place of torment, and were familiar with the idea of conversations among the dead : see on v. 26. There is a rabbinical story not unlike this parable : ' There were two partners in crime in this world, one of whom repented before his death, but the other did not. After death the one was carried away and placed in the company of the just; the other in the company of the wicked. The latter saw the former, and said, " Woe is me, for there is respect of persons in this matter. He and I robbed together and murdered together, and now he stands in the congregation of the just, and I in the congregation of the wicked." They answered him, " Thou fool, it was in thy power also to have repented, but thou didst not." He said to them, " Let me go now, and become a penitent." But they said, " Thou most foolish of men, dost thou not know that this world in which thou art is like the sabbath, and the world from which thou camest, like the eve of the sabbath ? If thou providest nothing on the sabbath-eve, what wilt thou eat on the sabbath ? " And he gnashed his teeth and gnawed his own flesh.'

In his bosom] The figure is not taken from reclining at a banquet (Jn 13 23), because the great banquet would not take place, according to Jewish ideas, till the coming of the Messiah (Mt8 11), but from children quietly resting in their parents' lap or bosom.

24. Father Abraham] He spoke as a Jew thinking that Abraham had power over the fires of Hades, and would help his own descendants. The rabbis said, ' The fire of Gehenna has no power over the sinners of Israel, for Abraham descends and rescues them from it.' **25. Thy good things**] i.e. thy wealth and pleasures. Dives was punished, not for his wealth, but for his abuse of it. Lazarus was justified, not for his poverty, but for his patience and humility. **26. Beside all this**] better, ' in all these regions of the dead.' **A great gulf fixed**] Somewhat different from the representations of the rabbis, who said (see Eccl 7 14), ' God hath set the one against the other, i.e. Hell and Paradise. How far are they distant ? A hand's breadth. Rabbi Jochanan saith, A wall is between. But the rabbis say, They are so even with one another, that you may see out of one into the other': cp. Rev 14 10. **29. Moses and the prophets**] These would give them sufficient light and guidance.

30, 31. Our Lord disbelieved the power of signs and wonders to produce repentance, and here declares that even the sign of His own Resurrection will leave many hard hearts unmoved.

The pains of Dives being those of Hades, not of Gehenna, many recent commentators regard his release from them as possible, and see in his new-born anxiety for the welfare of others (v. 27) an indication that his punishment is producing its intended purifying effect : see on Mt 12 32.

ADDITIONAL NOTE

The chief interest of this parable to modern readers is the light that it throws, or seems to throw, upon the state of departed souls between death and judgment. As to its significance in this respect, expositors are not entirely at one. Some regard all its statements on the subject as teaching definite doctrines binding on Christians, others regard them as only the poetic framework of the parable, embodying conventional Jewish ideas, and therefore as having no significance for Christians. Both extremes are to be avoided. On the one hand, the parable is plainly intended to inculcate, as against the unbelief of worldly and sensual men, the doctrine of future rewards and punishments beginning immediately after death, and to be so far a serious doctrinal statement. On the other hand, the thoroughly Jewish cast of the phraseology warns us against taking its details too literally. The essence of the teaching is thus expressed by Luckock : ' The souls of the departed in the intermediate state are possessed of consciousness, memory, and sensibility to pain and pleasure ; the life of all men, whether good or bad, is continued without interruption after the separation of soul and body; and retribution commences between death and judgment. These conclusions are in direct antagonism to the theory that the soul falls asleep when the body dies, and will not wake again till the resurrection of the dead.'

CHAPTER 17
OCCASIONS OF OFFENCE. THE TEN LEPERS.
THE SECOND ADVENT

1, 2. On causing others to sin. See on Mt 18 6, 7.

2. One of these little ones] An affectionate designation of the disciples, especially such as were beginners and easily led astray. Perhaps the converted publicans and sinners of 15 1, 2 are specially meant.

3, 4. The duty of forgiveness. We are to forgive an unlimited number of times, yet we may rebuke in love : cp. Lv 19 17. See on Mt 18 15, 21. **3. Trespass against thee**] RV 'sin.'

5, 6. On faith and its effects. See on Mt 17 20 21 21.

5. Increase our faith] Others render, ' Give us faith in addition,' i.e. add it to the gifts already promised. Whether the ' faith ' mentioned is faith in general, or the faith which enables to forgive a brother seven times, is not clear.

6. Sycamine] This word means sometimes the ' mulberry tree,' sometimes the ' sycomore.'

7–10. That works do not justify. ' Our Lord having exhorted His disciples to good works, now proceeds to rebuke the vainglory which so often accompanies them, showing that as a master is under no obligation to a slave who performs his appointed tasks, so neither is God to us. But since God is gracious, He treats those who are slaves, as if they were free hired labourers, and recompenses their labours with a reward, and receives their service which is strictly due, as if it were meritorious, and gives a requital out of all proportion to the toil. Thus the goodness of God is stronger than His justice ' (Euthymius). **7. A servant**] lit. ' a slave.'

11–19. Ten lepers cleansed (peculiar to Lk). For leprosy see on Mt 8 1-4. The healing of a Samaritan, and the stress laid upon his greater gratitude, is in keeping with the character of this Gentile Gospel.

11. Through the midst of (or, rather, ' between ') **Samaria and Galilee**] ' The caravans of Galilee took either the Samaritan route or the Peræan. Jesus follows neither, but travels along the boundary between Samaria and Galilee. He directed His steps from W. to E. towards the Jordan, which He must cross to enter Peræa ' (Godet). ' He seems to have crossed the Jordan at Scythopolis, where there was a bridge, and to have descended along the bank of Jordan in Peræa, until He crossed again near Jericho ' (Wetstein).

14. Unto the priests] The Jews probably went to Jerusalem, because of the necessary sacrifices ; the Samaritan to Mt. Gerizim, unless we are to suppose that he became a Jewish proselyte. **As they went**] The healing was delayed to test their faith. **19. Thy faith hath made thee whole** (or, ' saved thee ')] i.e. not only has it healed thy body, but also thy soul. It was otherwise with the other nine lepers. Their ingratitude imperilled their continuance in that state of salvation in which their faith had placed them.

20, 21. When and how the Kingdom of God appears (peculiar to Lk). The question of the Pharisees was probably a mocking one— ' When is this Kingdom of God of which thou sayest so much, and of which thou claimest to be King, visibly to appear ? '

20. Cometh not with observation] i.e. cannot be observed by the senses, is not manifested by outward signs or political changes. **21. Is within you**] i.e. within your hearts. But since Jesus would hardly say that the Kingdom of God is within the hearts of the Pharisees, the better translation is, ' The Kingdom of God is among you,' but ye do not perceive it.

22–37. On the coming of the Son of man. The Pharisees having now withdrawn, Jesus proceeds to speak more unreservedly to the disciples of the final and glorious coming of His Kingdom, which will be heralded by visible signs, which yet will be hard to interpret, so that in the end the Son of man will appear unexpectedly. St. Matthew inserts many of these sayings in the great discourse on the end of the world, and the fall of Jerusalem (Mt 24), where they are equally suitable to the context.

22. To see one of the days] i.e. ' In your future tribulations and persecutions you will desire to see one of the days of bliss and glory, which will follow the Second Coming of the Son of man. You will desire a glimpse of heaven to comfort you in your calamities.' Plummer ingeniously translates: ' You will desire to see *the first* of the days of the Son of man,' i.e. the day of the Second Advent. The ordinary interpretation, ' You will look back with regret on the peaceful and happy days of My earthly ministry, and long to see even one of them again,' does not suit the context.

And ye shall not see *it*] not because it will not come, but because it will not come in those days of your longing for it.

23. See on Mt 24 23. **See here**] is the Son of man, etc. **24.** See on Mt 24 27. **In his day**] Westcott and Hort (but not RV) omit these words. **25.** Cp. Mk 8 31.

26, 27. See on Mt 24 37-39. **26. Also in the days**] i.e. in the days when the Son of man will return. We should have expected ' in the *day* of the Son of man,' as in v. 30.

28–30. Peculiar to Lk. See Gn 19.

31. In Mt 24 17, q.v., these words are advice to the Christians of Jerusalem with regard to their hasty flight from the city just before its fall. Here they refer to Christ's Second Coming, and warn Christians, when that day is imminent, to be completely detached from worldly affairs and worldly interests. The language is parabolic, and must be spiritually interpreted.

32. Remember Lot's wife] who was not detached from worldly things, but looked back with longing towards Sodom, and the wealth and luxury which she had left there.

33. In Mt 10 39 16 25, where the same words occur, the reference is to willingness to suffer martyrdom. Here the idea is more general : ' He who sets too much value on his earthly life, shall lose his eternal life.'

34, 35. See on Mt 24 40, 41. **36.** Omitted by RV and the best authorities.

37. See on Mt 24 28 (first interpretation).

CHAPTER 18
The Unjust Judge. The Pharisee and the Publican. The Rich Ruler

1–8. The Unjust Judge (peculiar to Lk).

There is a close connexion with what precedes. The mention of the Second Advent leads Christ to speak of the need of prayer and watchfulness in view of it. The main lessons of the parable are : (1) The duty of continual prayer ; (2) the certain answer to prayer, if it be only persistent enough ; (3) the certainty that in the end God will maintain the cause of His elect against their adversaries ; (4) a warning against failure of faith in times of seeming abandonment by God.

The moral difficulty that in this parable God seems to be compared to an unjust judge, is best met by saying that in reality God is not so much compared as contrasted with him. The argument is, If justice can be obtained by persistence even from an unjust judge, how much more can it be obtained from the Author of all justice. It is true that God is said, like the unjust judge, to delay justice. But His motive is entirely different. His delay is due to love, love of the saints, whose faith He designs to purify and strengthen by much waiting, and love of their adversaries, to whom He gives a space for repentance before the day of vengeance comes.

1. Perhaps this is our Lord's own comment on the parable. **Always** *to* **pray**] On the other hand, the rabbis taught that God must not be fatigued by too frequent prayer. Three times a day was enough. ' If a man comes to address you every hour, you say that he holds you cheap : the same is true of God, whom no

man ought to fatigue by praying every hour.' The words are to be taken literally, because even purely secular acts, when done to God's glory, are acts of devotion. The whole lives of the faithful should be, in Origen's words, ' one great connected prayer.' **Faint**] i.e. become weary.

2. A judge] Probably a heathen judge, because, (1) The local Jewish tribunals consisted of three judges, and (2) Jewish judges (at least in NT. times) had no such evil reputation. They were required to have this sevenfold qualification, ' prudence, gentleness, piety, hatred of mammon, love of truth, that they be beloved, and of good report.' Yet see on Mk 12 40.

3. Avenge me] better, ' Give me justice against my adversary.' Her ' adversary ' was probably a rich neighbour, who, taking advantage of the death of her husband, had stolen her land. The offence of violently appropriating the property of widows and orphans is often alluded to in the OT., and forbidden with threats of divine vengeance (Ex 22 22-24, etc.).

5. Weary me] lit. ' give me a black eye.'

7. Avenge his own elect] i.e. the members of His Church. Christ comforts His disciples who are discouraged by the persecutions which are even now threatening, by promising that God will visit their persecutors (the Jews and afterwards the heathen) with condign punishment. This was literally fulfilled in the calamities which overtook the Jews and the chief heathen persecutors of the Christians. **Though he bear long with them**] better, ' though he is slow to act for them,' i.e. though His coming seem to be delayed.

8. Speedily] cp. Rev 22 20 2 Pet 3 8-10. Christ's coming, though it may seem to be long delayed, will be as speedy as the scheme of God's providence, which takes account of the needs of the whole world, will permit. It will not be delayed an instant longer than is necessary. **Nevertheless, etc.**] The sense is, ' Nevertheless, in spite of the warning and encouragement I am giving you, the faith of many will have waxed cold at the time of My return.' Christ does not mean that the elect will have lost their faith altogether, but that on account of the trials and disappointments which will precede the Second Advent, and also on account of its unexpected delay, they will be discouraged. **Faith**] or, rather, ' the faith,' i.e. the unshaken confidence in the certainty of My Second Coming, which I hope to find.

9–14. The Pharisee and the Publican at Prayer (peculiar to Lk). This parable is apparently addressed not to the Pharisees themselves, but to certain of the disciples of Jesus who were proud of their spiritual attainments, and lacking in the virtues of humility and penitence.

10. Into the temple] Probably into the second court, 'The Court of the Women,' at one of the stated hours of prayer. The Temple, like modern Christian churches, was used for private as well as public prayer.

Publican] see on Mt 5 46. **11. Stood]** i.e. placed himself conspicuously in the attitude of prayer : see on Mt 6 5. **God, I thank thee]** The words of the Pharisee can hardly be called a prayer. He asks for nothing, and feels his need of nothing. The Pharisee did, indeed, acknowledge that his virtues were derived from God, but he took all the merit of them to himself, and boasted of them before God and man.

12. Twice in the week] viz. on Mondays and Thursdays : see on Mt 6 16-18. **Of all that I possess]** RV 'of all that I get.' The Pharisee prided himself on his works of supererogation, i.e. works done over and above what God required : see on 17 7-10. The Law commanded only one fast in the whole year (viz. Day of Atonement, Lv 16 29). The Pharisee fasted twice a week. The Law tithed only the fruits of the field and the increase of cattle. The Pharisee tithed mint and cummin (Mt 23 23), and indeed his whole income (cp. Tob 1 7, 8).

13. Afar off] viz. from the Pharisee, whom, in his humility, he thought far more righteous than himself. **Would not lift up]** Since the rabbis forbade the eyes to be raised to heaven during prayer (see Mt 6 5), it is necessary to suppose that there was some special indication of humility in the publican's attitude. **Be merciful, etc.]** lit. 'be propitiated to me the sinner.' 'As the Pharisee had singled himself out as the one holy in the world, so the publican singles himself out as the chief of sinners, the man in whom all sins have met— a characteristic trait ! for who, when first truly convinced of sin, thinks any man's sins can equal his own (1 Tim 1 15) ?' (Trench).

14. Justified] A favourite word of St. Paul's, employed in St. Paul's sense, as is natural in the Pauline Gospel. 'Justify' in the NT. means always 'to regard as just,' not 'to render just,' or 'sanctify.' *Rather* **than the other]** This probably means that the publican was justified, and that the Pharisee was not ; not that the Pharisee was regarded as righteous, and the publican as more than righteous.

For every one] Mt 23 12 Lk 14 11.

15-17. Jesus and the children (Mt 19 13 Mk 10 13). See on Mt.

18-30. The rich young ruler. The reward of those who forsake all (Mt 19 16 Mk 10 17). See on Mt.

31-34. The passion and resurrection predicted (Mt 20 17 Mk 10 32). See on Mt.

35-43. The blind man at Jericho (Mt 20 29 Mk 10 46). See on Mt.

CHAPTER 19

ZACCHÆUS. THE POUNDS. CHRIST'S TRIUMPHAL ENTRY INTO JERUSALEM. HE CLEANSES THE TEMPLE

1-10. Zacchæus (peculiar to Lk). The narrative shows that our Lord's familiar intercourse with publicans and sinners was justified by its results. Zacchæus became a convert, surrendered half of his great wealth to the poor, and made restitution for his past misdeeds.

2. The chief] RV 'a chief publican.' 'There must have been at Jericho one of the principal custom-houses, both on account of the exportation of the balm which grew in that oasis, and which was sold in all countries of the world, and on account of the considerable traffic which took place on this road, by which lay the route from Peræa to Judæa and Egypt. Zacchæus was at the head of this office' (Godet). It is unlikely that Zacchæus belonged to the highest class of publicani, who collected the taxes of whole provinces or kingdoms, though occasionally Jews filled such an office. Zacchæus has a Hebrew name, and is clearly a Jew : see on Mt 5 46 9 9-13.

3. To see, etc.] RV 'to see who Jesus was,' i.e. to distinguish Him in the dense crowd which surrounded Him. **4. A sycomore]** not the English sycamore, but a tree which receives its name from the fact that its fruit is like a fig, and its leaves like those of the mulberry : cp. 17 6 and Am 7 14. Sycamores are not now very common in Palestine.

5. At thy house] Jericho was a priestly city, and according to the Talmud contained as many priests as Jerusalem. Specially significant, therefore, was Christ's resolution to lodge with a publican. **8. And Zacchæus stood]** Probably after the feast, or on the next day. The effect of our Lord's conversation was the complete conversion of Zacchæus, which immediately showed itself in act. **I give]** viz. at this moment. Up to the time of his conversion Zacchæus had given little in charity. He now atones for his past neglect by surrendering one-half of his capital. **If I have taken, etc.]** RV 'wrongfully exacted ought.' He proposes to examine into his past transactions, and if he has wronged any one, to make restitution out of the half of his capital which he still retains. **Fourfold]** The Law only required this from a detected thief (Ex 22 1). **9. To this house]** Because with Zacchæus his family and household servants were converted.

A son of Abraham] both in descent and character. This the Pharisees would have denied, for they ranked publicans with the heathen : see on Mt 5 46. **10.** Cp. Mt 18 11.

11-27. Parable of the Pounds (peculiar to

Lk, but similar to the Parable of the Talents, Mt 25 14, q.v.). It differs from that parable, (1) in the introduction of the rebellious citizens, vv. 14, 27; (2) in its graduation of the rewards and punishments of the next world; (3) in representing future bliss as a state of social activity in a perfect community.

The nobleman (v. 12) is Christ Himself, who goes into a far country (heaven), to receive for Himself a kingdom (almighty power over the universe), and to return (at the Second Advent). He calls His ten servants (all the members of His Church), and entrusts them with a pound each (i.e. all their bodily, mental, and spiritual capacities). The citizens who hate Him are all the enemies of Christ. They are called His citizens, because even the wicked are by right His subjects, seeing that He has created and redeemed them. On His return (to judge the world), He summons the ten servants (such Christians as appear to have been faithful to their trust), and enquires what use they have made of the capacities and opportunities entrusted to them. Some have made great use, others little, others none at all; and are accordingly recompensed, some by being placed over ten cities (a great reward), others over five cities (a less reward), others by being entirely excluded from all the rewards of the future kingdom. The taking of the pound from the man who did not use it, signifies that faculties which are not used, are finally lost; and the giving of the pound to him who had ten already, signifies that those faculties which are rightly used are capable of indefinite increase. The ten cities and the five cities indicate the different kinds of employment assigned in heaven to persons of different spiritual capacity. They also, perhaps, indicate different states of blessedness assigned to the saved in accordance with their behaviour in the previous state of probation on earth. In the corresponding parable in Mt the teaching is different. There all the faithful servants show the same diligence, and receive the same reward. The slaying of the rebellious citizens (v. 27) represents the judgment of the wicked at the Last Day. This parable, like so many others, assigns to Jesus the position of King and Judge of the human race. It may, therefore, be fairly used to prove His Divinity.

11. **Because they thought**] The multitudes thought that Jesus was going to Jerusalem to set up the Messianic kingdom at once. Jesus therefore explained by a parable that the kingdom would not be established till His Second Coming, and that even then not all the children of Abraham, but only the spiritually fit, would be admitted into it. This was the chief lesson to the multitudes, who expected that all Israelites would share in the future glory. To the disciples the lesson was that even among the saved there would be differences, and that, therefore, those who wished a great reward in the future kingdom of heaven must labour with all diligence in their various vocations on earth. **13. Servants**] lit. 'slaves.' **Pounds**] lit. *minæ*. The *mina* was the sixtieth part of a talent, i.e. 100 *denarii*, or £4.

14. We will not, etc.] This v. may have a special reference to Christ's rejection by the Jews after His Resurrection and Ascension. For the historical fact which perhaps suggested this incident in the parable, see art. 'Dynasty of the Herods' (Archelaus).

24, 25. This complete misapprehension of Christ's character shows that he had never really 'known' Christ with saving knowledge. **27.** Although this v. describes the final punishment of those who reject Christ, it may also have reference to the temporal destruction of those Jews who rejected Christ at the fall of Jerusalem.

28-40. The triumphal entry into Jerusalem (Mt 21 1 Mk 11 1 Jn 12 12). See on Mt and Jn. **37. The descent**] There was a magnificent view of Jerusalem and the Temple from this point, and at the sight of the capital of the new kingdom the multitudes broke into a shout of triumph. **38. Peace in heaven**] i.e. There is peace for man (i.e. favour with God) in heaven. By sending the Messiah, God shows that He regards His people with favour. The expression is peculiar to Lk: cp. 2 14. **41-44. Christ weeps over Jerusalem** (peculiar to Lk). 'The path mounts again; it climbs a rugged ascent; it reaches a ledge of smooth rock, and in an instant the whole city bursts into view. As now the dome of the Mosque El-Aksa rises like a ghost from the earth before the traveller stands on the ledge, so then must have risen the Temple-tower; as now the vast enclosure of the Mussulman sanctuary, so then must have spread the Temple-courts; as now the grey town on its broken hills, so then the magnificent city, with its background—long since vanished away—of gardens and suburbs on the W. plateau behind. Immediately below was the valley of the Kedron, here seen in its greatest depth as it joins the Valley of Hinnom, and thus giving full effect to the great peculiarity of Jerusalem seen from its E. side—its situation as of a city rising out of a deep abyss. It is hardly possible to doubt that this rise and turn of the road, this rocky ledge, was the exact point where the multitude paused again, and "He, when He beheld the city, wept over it"' (Stanley). Cp. Mt 23 37.

42. If thou hadst known] i.e. O that thou hadst known! This implies previous visits of Christ to Jerusalem. **This thy day**] i.e. the time of Christ's earthly ministry.

43. Enemies] i.e. the Romans. **A trench**] lit. ' a palisade.' The Romans actually raised a palisade round Jerusalem. The Jews burnt it, and the Romans replaced it by a wall.

44. Thy children] i.e. thy inhabitants.

The time of thy visitation] i.e. the time of Christ's ministry.

45, 46. Second cleansing of the Temple (Mt 21 12 Mk 11 15). See on Mt.

47, 48. Jesus teaches daily. Cp. Mk 11 18.

48. Were very attentive] RV ' hung upon him, listening.'

CHAPTER 20
VARIOUS INCIDENTS OF THE LAST WEEK

1–8. The authority of Jesus challenged (Mt 21 23 Mk 11 27). See on Mt.

9–18. The wicked husbandmen (Mt 21 33 Mk 12 1). See on Mt.

19–26. The tribute money (Mt 22 15 Mk 12 13). See on Mt.

27–40. The Sadducees and the Resurrection (Mt 22 23 Mk 12 18). See on Mt.

36. Neither can they die] This is perhaps given as a reason why after the Resurrection there is no more marriage.

37. At the bush] RV ' in the place concerning the Bush ' : cp. Ex 3.

41–44. Is the Christ David's son ? (Mt 22 41 Mk 12 35). See on Mt.

45–47. Jesus denounces the scribes (Mt 23 1 Mk 12 38). See on Mt.

47. Devour widows' houses] see on Mk 12 40.

CHAPTER 21
THE WIDOW'S MITE. PROPHECY OF THE FALL OF JERUSALEM AND THE SECOND ADVENT

1–4. The widow's mite (Mk 12 41). See on Mk.

5–36. Great prophecy of the Fall of Jerusalem and the Second Advent (Mt 24 1 Mk 13 1). See on Mt. St. Luke distinguishes these two events more clearly than the other evangelists (v. 24). He also describes Jerusalem as being ' surrounded by armies.' This greater definiteness is held by some to indicate that St. Luke wrote after the fall of Jerusalem, and added certain interpretative notes to our Lord's utterances. But there is no real reason why Christ should not have spoken exactly as St. Luke records. See on Mt.

9. Not by and by] i.e. not at once. **13. Testimony**] It shall be an opportunity for you to bear witness to Me. **15. Mouth**] i.e. eloquence.

18, 19. Peculiar to Lk. **19.** By patient continuance in well-doing and in suffering ye shall **possess** (i.e. keep safe the inward life of) your souls. **24.** The times of the **Gentiles**] i.e. the time of the rejection of Israel, and of Gentile predominance both in the affairs of the world and in the Kingdom of God. The times of the Gentiles will come to an end, when Israel is converted (Ro 11 25).

37, 38. Christ's daily teaching. He lodges at the Mount of Olives (Mt 21 17 Mk 11 19). See on Mt.

CHAPTER 22
TREASON OF JUDAS. THE LAST SUPPER. THE AGONY IN THE GARDEN. ARREST OF JESUS. THE JEWISH TRIAL

1–6. Conspiracy of the chief priests. Treachery of Judas (Mt 26 1-5, 14-16 Mk 14 1, 2, 10, 11). See on Mt. St. Luke omits the anointing at Bethany, because he has already recorded a similar incident (7 37).

4. Captains] i.e. the Levitical guard or police of the Temple, not the Roman garrison of Jerusalem.

7–13. Preparations for the Last Supper (Mt 26 17 Mk 14 12). See on Mt.

12. Furnished] arrayed for the Passover.

14–23. Institution of the Lord's Supper. Denunciation of the Traitor (Mt 26 20-29 Mk 14 17-25 1 Cor 11 23). See on Mt. St. Luke's account most resembles that in 1 Cor 11 23, which is only natural, seeing that he was a disciple of St. Paul. The most striking peculiarity of his account is that he mentions two cups, one before and one after the blessing of the bread. The latter is without doubt the cup of the Holy Communion, or Eucharist, which, as has been shown on St. Matthew, corresponded to the ' Cup of Blessing' or ' third cup' of the Passover Supper. The earlier cup of St. Luke may therefore have been the ' second cup ' of the Passover, which was drunk after the lamb was placed on the table (see on Mt). The mention of two cups by St. Luke was early felt to be a difficulty, and accordingly a few ancient MSS reduce the cups to one, some by omitting the former cup, others by omitting the latter. The latter omission, which has the support of only one Greek and five Latin MSS, has met with some support from recent critics. If it be accepted, St. Luke's first cup must be that of the Eucharist, and in that case he represents the Eucharistic cup as consecrated before the bread.

17. Took the cup] RV ' received a cup.'

18. I will not drink, etc.] If these words are in their true position they seem to show that Jesus did not Himself drink of the cup of the Eucharist. Mt and Mk, however, place them *after* the blessing of the Eucharistic cup, instead of before it. **19. In remembrance of me**] lit. ' for My memorial.' This command for the continual repetition of the ordinance is mentioned only by St. Luke and St. Paul. The word translated ' remembrance ' is a rare one, and in biblical Greek means always a memorial before God, e.g. Lv 24⁷ : 'Thou shalt put pure frankincense upon each row (of shewbread), that it may be on the bread for a memorial, even an offering made by fire unto the Lord.' So also in NT. (Heb 10³). Accordingly the rite is intended, not so much to remind men of the death of Christ, as to remind God of it, to plead before God the merits of Christ's sacrifice, as the only ground for mercy and favour. **20.** This cup *is* **the new testament** (RV 'covenant') **in my blood**] The meaning, according to 1 Cor 10¹⁶, seems to be : 'This cup conveys to those who with true and lively faith partake of it, the benefits of the new covenant, which the shedding of my blood procures for mankind' (i.e. remission of sins, eternal life, spiritual sustenance, etc.). Mt and Mk have, 'This is my blood of the new covenant.' There is no reason why our Lord should not have used both expressions in explaining to His disciples the spiritual effect of the rite. **21.** This v. is a strong support of the view that Judas received the sacrament, but it is not conclusive : see on Mt, and Jn 13³⁰.

24–30. A contention which should be the greatest (peculiar to Lk). This contention is probably to be placed at the very beginning of the supper, before the feet-washing : see on Jn 13¹⁻²⁰. Our Lord had previously rebuked a very similar contention provoked by the ambition of the sons of Zebedee : see Mt 20²⁵⁻²⁸, where almost the same words are used. **28. Temptations**] i.e. trials.

29, 30. See on Mt 19²⁷⁻³⁰.

31–34. Peter's fall foretold (common to all the evangelists). See on Mt 26³¹⁻³⁵. St. Luke agrees with St. John that Jesus made the prediction in the supper-room.

31, 32. These two vv. are peculiar to St. Luke. **Satan hath desired**] i.e. Satan hath procured that all of you should be surrendered to him to be severely tried, like Job. **Sift**] The violent motion of the sieve corresponds to the violent trial that the apostles were to experience when Christ was arrested. **32. For thee**] Christ prayed specially for Peter, because he was the leader of the Apostles, and so much depended on him. His primacy was personal, not official, being derived from the special faculty of faith from which he derived his name, and which, after his fall, he conspicuously displayed.

35–38. Jesus directs His disciples to make provision for a time of persecution (peculiar to Lk). 'The meaning of our Lord in this much controverted passage appears to be to forewarn the apostles of the outward dangers which will await them henceforward in their mission —unlike the time when He sent them forth without earthly appliances, they must now make use of common resources for sustenance,

yea and even of the sword itself **for defence**' (Alford).

35. When I sent you] see 9³, and cp. 10⁴.

36. He that hath a purse] Although under ordinary circumstances those who preach the gospel are to live of the gospel and not con cern themselves with worldly affairs, yet under exceptional circumstances, e.g. amid hostile surroundings, or in a heathen land, or in a church extremely poor, ministers of the gospel may engage in trade, or in other ways provide for their maintenance, as St. Paul did (Ac 18³).

Scrip] i.e. provision-basket.

And he that hath no sword] The better translation is, 'And he that hath no money and no scrip, let him sell his cloak and buy a sword.' The meaning is that the danger will be so great, that self-defence will be of primary importance. The best course for a man who has no money, will be to sell his cloak to buy a sword to defend himself. **Sword** stands here for all lawful means of self-defence. When St. Paul pleaded before Nero, he doubtless employed counsel to defend him. This was 'buying a sword' in the sense which Jesus intended.

37. The things concerning me] i.e. the prophecies of My death. **End**] i.e. fulfilment.

38. Here *are* **two swords**] The disciples thought that Jesus advised them to buy swords to protect Him from arrest. They pointed out, therefore, that they had two already, with which they were prepared to defend Him. Seeing Himself misunderstood, Jesus abruptly closed the conversation with the words, It is enough, i.e. 'Enough of this trifling!' He had intended the disciples to 'buy swords' (i.e. take measures) for their own safety, not for His. He Himself was resolved to die, but He wished their lives to be preserved.

39–46. The Agony in the Garden (Mt 26³⁶ Mk 14³²). See on Mt, and on Lk 4¹³.

43, 44. These vv., which contain the exquisitely human features of the bloody sweat, and the appearance of the angel to strengthen Jesus, are peculiar to Lk. They exhibit our Lord as true man, subject to all the weaknesses and trials of humanity, and requiring the same comfort and support in His agony as other men. Although omitted by a few ancient authorities, these vv. obviously describe an authentic incident : cp. Mt 4¹¹.

44. Drops of blood] Great mental agony has been known to produce this phenomenon.

47–53. Arrest of Jesus (Mt 26⁴⁷ Mk 14⁴³ Jn 18³). See on Mt and Jn.

51. Suffer ye thus far] i.e. Suffer My enemies to do even this, viz. arrest Me. Make no further resistance. **Healed him**] This healing is peculiar to Lk.

53. This is your hour] i.e. the hour in

which God permits you to do your wicked work, and Satan apparently to triumph.

54–62. Peter denies Jesus (Mt 26 57,58, 69-75). See Mt and references there. All the evangelists record the incident.

63–65. Jesus mocked by the high priest's servants (Mt 26 67 Mk 14 65). See on Mt.

66–71. The Jewish trial (Mt 26 59 Mk 14 55 : cp. Jn 18 19). See on Mt and Jn.

CHAPTER 23
TRIAL BEFORE PILATE AND HEROD. THE CRUCIFIXION AND BURIAL

1–5. The trial before Pilate begins (Mt 27 1, 2, 11-14 Mk 15 1-5 Jn 18 28-38). See on Mt and Jn.

6–12. Trial before Herod (peculiar to Lk). ' By sending Jesus to Herod the clever Roman gained two ends at once. First, he got rid of the business which was imposed on him, and then he took the first step towards a reconciliation with Herod (v. 12). The cause of their quarrel had probably been some conflict of jurisdiction. In that case, was not the best means of soldering up the quarrel to concede to him a right of jurisdiction within the very city of Jerusalem ?' (Godet).

7. Herod's jurisdiction This extended over Galilee and Peræa.

Was at Jerusalem] i.e. in order to keep the Passover.

13–25. Trial before Pilate resumed. Jesus is condemned (Mt 27 15-26 Mk 15 6-20 Jn 18 38—19 16). See on Mt and Jn.

26–32. The procession to the Cross (Mt 27 32 Mk 15 21, 22 Jn 19 17). See on Mt. The beautiful address to the women of Jerusalem is peculiar to Lk. These women are not the same as the Galilean sympathisers (8 1-3), but residents in Jerusalem. The warm feeling with which all classes of women regarded Jesus is especially marked in this ' the Gospel of womanhood.'

28. Weep not for me] You are not wrong in weeping for Me, nevertheless something is about to befall, for which you will weep with far greater reason, the destruction of your city and the overthrow of your nation.

30. Cp. Isa 2 19 Rev 6 16. **31.** If they do these **things**, etc.] i.e. ' If the Romans so cruelly treat Me whom they know to be innocent, how much more severely will they treat your children whom they will regard as rebellious and guilty ?' Or, ' If the inhabitants of Jerusalem are so guilty now in slaying Me, to what further stages of wickedness will they afterwards advance ?'

33–49. Crucifixion and Death of Jesus (Mt 27 33-56 Mk 15 23-41 Jn 19 18-37). See on Mt and Jn. Peculiar to Lk are three of the Seven Words from the Cross, and the incident of the Converted Thief.

34. Father, forgive them, etc.] (peculiar to

Lk). This, the first Word from the Cross, is omitted by a few early authorities, but is unquestionably authentic. Jesus here puts into practice His own teaching about loving enemies and forgiving them.

39. One of the malefactors] At first both malefactors reviled Jesus (Mt 27 47), then one of them, moved by the gentleness and majesty of the Sufferer, was ashamed, and rebuked his fellow. From shame he passed to penitence and faith.

42. Lord, remember me, etc.] RV ' Jesus, remember me when thou comest in thy kingdom.' The thief here acknowledges Jesus to be the Messiah, a stupendous act of faith under the circumstances. ' He was rejected by the Jews who saw Him raising the dead. He was not rejected by the thief who saw Him hanging with him on the Cross ' (St. Augustine). The thief apparently expected Christ to rise again and establish His kingdom.

43. To-day, etc.] (peculiar to Lk). ' The grace granted is more abundant than the prayer. For his prayer was that the Lord would be mindful of him when He should have come into His kingdom. But the Lord said unto him, " Verily I say unto thee, To-day shalt thou be with me in paradise." Where Christ is there is life, there is the Kingdom ' (St. Ambrose). On ' Paradise ' see Lk 16 22, 23. This incident teaches us not to despise even deathbed repentances.

44. In the RV the darkness is said to be due to ' the sun's light failing.'

46. Father, etc.] (peculiar to Lk). This ' word ' is a quotation from Ps 31 5. **Spirit**] i.e. Christ's human spirit. ' Spirit ' and ' soul ' are identical in the Gospels. Christ is said to have both (Mt 26 38 27 50 Jn 12 27 13 21 19 30).

50–56. The burial (Mt 27 57-61 Mk 15 42-47 Jn 19 38-42). See on Mt, Mk and Jn.

CHAPTER 24
THE RESURRECTION AND THE ASCENSION

1–11. Two angels appear to the women at the sepulchre (Mt 28 1-8 Mk 16 1-8 : cp. Jn 20 1, 2). See on Mt and Jn.

12. Peter visits the sepulchre. See on Jn 20 3-10. This v. is wanting in some ancient authorities.

13–35. The journey to Emmaus (Mk 16 12, 13). Though alluded to in Mk, this beautiful narrative is peculiar to Lk. The conjecture of Theophylact that one of the two disciples was St. Luke still finds supporters, but is unlikely.

13. Emmaus] Josephus speaks of an Emmaus 60 furlongs from Jerusalem, the habitation of a colony of Titus's soldiers. This may be the modern Kulônieh (lit. ' colony '), 7 m. W. of Jerusalem.

16. Their eyes were hoiden] Mk gives a

slightly different explanation ('He appeared in another form'). St. Luke implies that our Lord prevented their recognition of Him by an act of will. But apart from this a certain change seems to have passed over His body at the Resurrection: cp. Jn 21 4. **17. As ye walk, and are sad**] RV 'And they stood still, looking sad,' but the 'Western' text is nearly as AV.

18. Cleopas] a person otherwise unknown. The obscurity of the persons concerned is a pledge of the authenticity of the narrative.

Art thou] RV 'Dost thou alone sojourn in Jerusalem and not know the things,' etc.

21. Redeemed Israel] perhaps they were only thinking of redemption from Roman rule (Ac 1 6). **Third day**] Possibly they remembered Christ's prophecy (18 33). **26. Ought not Christ**] More exactly, 'Ought not the Messiah' (in consequence of the prophecies) 'to have suffered these things and to have entered into His glory?' This passage supports the view that Jesus entered into glory not at the Ascension, but at the Resurrection. The Gk. implies that the entering into glory was already past, and the phrase 'His glory' implies that the glory was complete. Probably our Lord was in heaven during the Forty Days, descending to earth for occasional interviews.

30. He took bread] RV 'the bread.' Although so similar to the institution of the Holy Supper, this was probably not a celebration of it, but an act resembling the blessing and breaking of the bread at the feeding of the 5,000, at which probably the two disciples had been present.

31. He vanished] Our Lord's risen body was a perfect organ of spirit, and could manifest itself in whatever place, or under whatever sensible conditions He willed. After disappearing at Emmaus He seems to have transported Himself instantaneously to Jerusalem, and there to have appeared to Simon, v. 34: cp. our Lord's mysterious appearance when 'the doors were shut,' Jn 20 19.

34. The Lord is risen] Apparently inconsistent with Mk 16 13, q.v. **To Simon**] see 1 Cor 15 5.

36–43. Appearance on Easter Evening (Jn 20 19-25 : cp. Mk 16 14). See on Jn. At first sight there appears to be no break in the narrative till the end of the Gospel, and the Ascension (v. 51) seems to take place on the very day of the Resurrection. But since it is unlikely that so careful an historian as St. Luke would contradict himself on so important a point of chronology (see Ac 1 3), it seems safer to hold that the conclusion of St. Luke from v. 44 is a summary of the whole events of the 40 days, and not simply of those of Easter Day. It is, however, just possible that v. 51 does not describe the Ascension. In this case there is no difficulty in assigning the whole of the events of this chapter to Easter Day.

39. And my feet] Probably the feet also were pierced. **Handle me**] A proof of a corporeal resurrection. Our Lord's body was now spiritual, but it was manifested by Him on this occasion under sensible conditions to show that it was the same body which was crucified. **Flesh and bones**] are mentioned as representing the solid and tangible framework of the body. Blood is not mentioned, but this is no proof that our Lord's body did not possess it: see 1 Cor 10 16.

42. And of an honeycomb] Some ancient authorities omit these words. Our Lord ate, not as needing food, but to afford a sign. The Apostles laid great stress on His eating and drinking with them as proof of the reality of the Resurrection, Ac 10 41 : cp. Ac 1 4 RM.

44–49. Summary of instructions given during the Forty Days. 44. The law . . the prophets . . the psalms stand for the three divisions of the OT. Canon recognised by the Jews. The 'Prophets' include the historical books except Chronicles and Ruth. 'Psalms' stand for 'the Writings,' i.e. the third division of the Canon, of which it is the principal book.

47. Among all nations] RV 'unto all the nations'; a proof that Jesus contemplated a universal Church. **49. The promise**] i.e. the Holy Spirit, Ac 1 4 : cp. Jn 15 26.

50–53. The Ascension (Ac 1 9 Mk 16 19). See on Ac. **51. And carried up into heaven**] A few ancient authorities omit these words. If they are omitted, it is possible to regard this event, not as the Ascension, but as a miraculous disappearance of Jesus at the end of the interview begun in v. 36. **52. And they worshipped him**] A few ancient authorities omit these words.

ST. JOHN

INTRODUCTION

1. General characteristics. Few books have exercised so wide an influence as this. Not only has it a message for believers, for whose edification it was primarily intended, but it casts a mysterious spell even over readers whose religious standpoint is furthest removed from its own. There is nothing like it in literature except the three Epistles attributed to the same source. The attempt to analyse the effect produced by a unique work of genius like the present is never successful—the effect is the product of the author's personality, and personality is unanalysable—but, without attempting this, it may be possible to draw attention in a helpful way, at the outset, to two of its leading characteristics.

(a) The writer possesses the unusual gift of clothing the profoundest ideas in language of childlike simplicity. His ideas are far deeper than St. Paul's, but are much more simply expressed. Take, for example, his descriptions of the nature of God : ' God is [a] spirit, and they that worship him must worship him in spirit and in truth ' ; ' He that loveth not, knoweth not God, for God is love ' ; or of the preëxistence and divinity of the Word, ' In the beginning was the Word, and the Word was with God, and the Word was God ' ; or of His oneness with the eternal Father, ' I and the Father are one ' ; ' Before Abraham was, I AM ' ; or of the Incarnation, ' And the Word was made flesh, and dwelt among us (and we beheld his glory, the glory as of the only begotten of the Father) full of grace and truth ' ; or of Christ as the Life, ' I am the Resurrection and the Life : he that believeth in Me, though he were dead, yet shall he live, and whosoever liveth and believeth in Me shall never die ' ; or of true faith, ' Blessed are they that have not seen, and yet have believed.' In these and many other passages the peculiar union of simplicity and profundity produces the effect of sublimity, a characteristic often noted by the ancients, who expressed it by the figure of a soaring eagle, which became the accepted symbol, even as early as the second century, of the Fourth Evangelist.

(b) The Gospel is not only a history, but an allegory. It is the work of a mystic, trained in the allegorical method of interpreting the Scriptures, and expecting his own work to be interpreted in a like manner. ' John,' says Clement of Alexandria (200 A.D.), ' having

observed that the bodily things [i.e. the bare historic facts] had been sufficiently set forth by the [earlier] Gospels, .. produced a spiritual [i.e. an allegorical] Gospel ' (Euseb. ' H. E.' vi. 14). We must not, however, press the idea of allegory too far. We are not to suppose, with Origen, that some of the incidents in the Gospel are not history at all, but only allegory. But we may assume that the author's choice of materials is dominated by an allegorical or didactic purpose. He sits down to write, not a biography, but an interpretation of the life of Christ, and since his method is that of allegory, we are justified in seeking a mystical meaning not only in every saying and in every incident, but even in minute details which at first sight seem trivial. This persistent symbolism gives to the Fourth Gospel much of its mysterious charm. It produces an effect on the mind not unlike that of one of Holman Hunt's pictures. Even the uninitiated feel that far more is suggested than is expressed on the surface. Specially clear and striking examples of the author's symbolism occur in 1^{51} (the open heavens), 2^{1-11} (the good wine of the gospel), 2^{21} (the temple of Christ's body), 3^5 (water and the Spirit), 3^{14} (the uplifted serpent), 4^{10} (the living water), 4^{35} (the fields white for harvest), 6^{31} (the true manna and the bread from heaven), 7, 8 (the symbolism of the feast of tabernacles), 9^{1-8} (the opening of the eyes of the man born blind, symbolising Christ as the Light of the world), $10^{9,11}$ (Christ as the Door of the sheep and the Good Shepherd), 11^{25} (the raising of Lazarus, symbolising Christ as the Resurrection and the Life), 11^{51} (the mystical meaning of the high priest's utterance), 12^7 (the anointing, symbolising Christ's death and burial), 12^{24} (the corn of wheat), 13^{15} (the symbolical feet-washing), 13^{30} (' and it was night '), 14^6 (Christ ' the Way '), 15^5 (the Vine and the branches), 16^{25} (Christ's words are ' in proverbs,' i.e. allegorical), $19^{34, 35}$ (the symbolism of the blood and water : cp. $1 Jn 5^{6, 8}$), 19^{36} (' a bone of him shall not be broken '), 20^5 (the symbolism of the grave clothes), 20^{17} (' Touch me not,' etc.), 21^{5-14} (symbolism of the draught of fishes and of the meal), 20^{18} (the ' girding ' of Peter).

2. Date and Authorship.

(1) *External evidence.* That the Gospel, by

whomsoever written, probably falls within the first cent. A.D., appears from the following quotations or references to it by early writers.

St. Ignatius, 110 A.D., reproduces 3[8] almost verbatim, 'He knoweth whence he cometh and whither he goeth.' He speaks of the Lord's Supper as Christ's 'flesh' (not 'body') and blood (cp. c. 6). He calls Christ the 'Logos' ('Word') of God, the Door of the Father, and the Living Water. He calls Satan 'the prince of this world.' All these phrases are peculiar to St. John.

St. Polycarp, 110 A.D. (a personal disciple of St. John), quotes St. John's First Epistle, a work most closely connected with the Gospel, and almost certainly by the same hand.

Basilides, the Gnostic, 120 A.D. 'And this is what is meant in the Gospels, "There was the true light which lighteth every man coming into the world"' (see 1[9]).

'That everything has its own proper seasons is sufficiently proved by the words of the Saviour, "Mine hour is not yet come"' (see 2[4]).

Aristides, the Apologist, circ. 130 A.D., uses the characteristic expression, 'came down from heaven,' in connexion with the Incarnation (see 3[13] 6[33f.]), and calls our Lord's sinless human nature 'flesh' (cp. c. 6).

Papias, 130 A.D., according to very ancient evidence, named John as the author of this Gospel. He certainly used the First Epistle of John, for which see above.

Valentinus, 140 A.D., quotes 10[8], 'All that have come before me are thieves and robbers.'

The Gospel of Peter, 150 A.D., or earlier, uses all four Gospels.

St. Justin Martyr, 150 A.D. 'As many as are persuaded and believe that what we teach and say is true, are brought by us where there is water, and are regenerated in the same manner in which we were ourselves regenerated. For in the name of God the Father and Lord of the universe, and of our Saviour Jesus Christ, and of the Holy Spirit, they then receive the washing with water. For Christ also said, "Except ye be born again, ye shall not enter into the kingdom of heaven." Now that it is impossible for those who have been once born to enter into their mothers' wombs, is manifest to all' (cp. 3[4,5]). He also often speaks of the Word becoming flesh in language evidently suggested by the Fourth Gospel.

Tatian, 160 A.D., compiled a harmony of the Four Gospels called *Diatessaron*.

Theophilus of Antioch, 180 A.D. 'And hence the holy writings teach us, and all the spirit-bearing men, one of whom, John, says, "In the beginning was the Word, and the Word was with God," showing that at first God was alone, and the Word in Him' (see 1[1]).

St. Irenæus, 177 A.D., a disciple of Polycarp, a disciple of John, speaks of this Gospel as St. John's again and again, and even argues that there *can* be only four Gospels, viz. those that we at present possess.

The Muratorian Fragment, 200 A.D. 'The author of the Fourth Gospel is John, one of the disciples.'

Clement of Alexandria, 200 A.D., **Tertullian,** 200 A.D., and **Origen,** 220 A.D., speak of the apostolic authorship as undoubted.

Eusebius, the Church historian, 330 A.D., classes it without hesitation among the 'undisputed' writings.

So far as is known, its authenticity was denied by no one, orthodox or unorthodox, in ancient times, except the obscure sect of the Alogi. Even these acknowledged its antiquity, for they ascribed it to St. John's leading opponent at Ephesus, Cerinthus.

(2) *Internal evidence.* It is a characteristic of writings which are forged, or issued without fraudulent intent under another name (pseudepigraphical), to indicate the supposed author prominently and clearly (Eccl 1 · Esdr 1[1-4] Tob 1[1] Wisd 7–9 Bar 1[1], so also Gospel of Peter, Apostolic Constitutions, etc.), and had this been the character of the Fourth Gospel, St. John's name would without question have been unmistakably prominent. As a matter of fact, the author has so carefully concealed his identity, that it requires considerable research and reflection to discover who he was. A careful reader, however, will discern, (1) that he was a Jew. His accurate acquaintance with Jewish laws, customs, and opinions, is enough to establish this (1[21] 4[25] 6[14f.] 7[40f.] 12[34] 4[27] 7[15,35] 4[9] 7[49] 7[22] 18[28] 7[37] 18[31]). Moreover, the author's style and syntax are rather Hebraic than Greek, and he occasionally shows knowledge of the original Hebrew of the OT. (6[45] 13[18] 19[37]). (2) That he was a Jew of Palestine. This is shown by his knowledge of unimportant Palestinian localities such as 'Cana of Galilee' (2[1,11]), 'Bethany beyond Jordan' (1[28]), Ephraim 'near the wilderness' (11[54]), 'Ænon near to Salim' (3[23]), Sychar (4[5]). (3) That he lived before the destruction of Jerusalem. This is clear from his accurate acquaintance with the topography of Jerusalem, and especially of the Temple. He knows, for example, the intermittent spring of Bethesda with its five porches near the sheep-gate, Solomon's porch, the distance from Jerusalem to Bethany, Kidron, the pool of Siloam, Gethsemane, the treasury, the pavement called Gabbatha, Golgotha 'nigh to the city where there was a garden.' He is well acquainted with the current views about the Messiah among the Samaritans and Jews of the period. He shows an exact knowledge of the ritual of the

feasts—e.g. Passover, Dedication, Tabernacles, and of other religious customs, e.g. ablutions before meals, and purifications before the Passover. He is familiar with the relations between the Jews and the Samaritans, with rabbinical ideas about being 'born in sins,' with the impropriety of a rabbi addressing a woman in a public place, with Jewish reluctance to enter a Gentile house, or to let dead bodies remain unburied on the sabbath, and altogether invests his narrative with a verisimilitude which can hardly be accounted for except on the supposition that he was a contemporary. (4) That he was an apostle and an eyewitness. That he was an eyewitness is three times stated : 1 14 'we beheld his glory' ; 19 35 'and he that hath seen hath borne witness, and his witness is true, and he knoweth that he saith true, that ye also may believe' ; 21 24 (appendix) 'this is the disciple which beareth witness of these things and wrote these things, and we know that his witness is true' (cp. also 1 Jn 1 1, written by the same author). In 21 20, 24 the writer is expressly identified with the disciple whom Jesus loved, the son of Zebedee (21 2), who was present at the Last Supper leaning on Jesus' breast (13 23), stood by the cross (19 26), received into his house the Blessed Virgin (19 27), ran with Peter to the tomb (20 2), and was present at the sea of Tiberias (21 7). He was not James the son of Zebedee, for James was martyred 44 A.D. (Ac 12 2). Tradition, therefore, seems to be right in asserting that he was John. It is a confirmation of this view, that the writer shows a closer acquaintance with the inner life and sentiments of the apostolic circle than any other evangelist (see e.g. 2 11, 22 4 27 6 66 f. 9 2 11 8 f. 12 16 chs. 13–17 18 2 20 19 f. c. 21).

3. Difficulties. We can only briefly allude to the chief objections which have been brought against the Johannine authorship of the Fourth Gospel.

Objection 1. The Synoptic Gospels, which mention only one Passover, obviously limit the ministry to one year, while the Fourth Gospel which mentions three (2 13 6 4 12 1), and perhaps four (5 1), extends it to three or four. *Reply.* The Synoptists nowhere state or even hin ; (not even in Lk 4 19, q.v.) that the ministry was confined to a single year.

Objection 2. The Synoptists confine the ministry to Galilee and Peræa, but the Fourth Gospel locates a large portion of it in Judæa. *Reply.* The Synoptic Gospels (for whatever reason) are written from an exclusively Galilean point of view, but even they hint at a ministry in Judæa (Mt 23 37 Lk 13 34 4 44 RV).

Objection 3. The Synoptists date the last Passover on Thursday evening, but the Fourth Gospel on Friday evening. *Reply.* The discrepancy is perhaps only apparent, but if it is

real, the account of the Fourth Evangelist is the more credible (see on Jn 18 28).

Objection 4. The style of the Gospel differs in such a marked degree from the style of the Revelation, that the same writer cannot have written both. *Reply.* If this is so, the Johannine authorship of the Revelation, which is a much more disputable book than the Gospel, may require to be given up. We may suppose, however, that the Revelation was written in the reign of Nero, and the Gospel a quarter of a century later, in which case the difference of style can be sufficiently accounted for (see Intro. to Revelation).

Objection 5. Our Lord's discourses in the Fourth Gospel differ altogether in style and subject-matter from those in the Synoptics, and therefore cannot be authentic. *Reply.* The Fourth Gospel does not profess to represent the general tenor and style of Christ's teaching. It is a didactic work, intended mainly to produce and enhance faith in our Lord's Divine Sonship (20 31). The author, therefore, purposely collects and records mainly those sayings of Christ which illustrate the Divinity of His Person.

4. Date and Place of Composition. According to all ancient authorities, this Gospel was written by St. John in his old age at Ephesus, i.e. about 90 A.D., or a little earlier.

5. The Writer's Purpose and Theological Position. (1) The main object of the Gospel is to produce faith in Jesus as the Messiah and the Son of God (20 31), and in general to promote those views of our Lord's person and work, which in the later Church were generally designated 'orthodox.' As against humanitarian (Ebionite) tendencies, whether within or without the Church, the author lays the utmost stress upon our Lord's true Deity (see especially 1 1 f. 18 (WH) 5 20 f. 8 58 10 30 17 5), and concludes his Gospel (for c. 21 is a later appendix) with St. Thomas's great confession, 'My Lord and my God' (20 28). On the other hand, as against Docetism, which, while confessing our Lord's Deity, denied that He was truly man, great stress is laid on our Lord's true humanity. The Word became 'flesh' (1 14), and that flesh could be handled (20 20, 27). The Incarnate Saviour possessed a true human soul (10 11, 17 12 27), and a human spirit (11 33 13 21), and was subject to painful human experiences, e.g. He was weary (4 6), wept (11 35), groaned and was troubled (11 33). Further, as against Cerinthus, the Apostle's opponent at Ephesus, who taught that Jesus was a mere man upon whom the heavenly Son of God descended at His baptism, St. John emphasises the unity of Christ's person, and the unbroken stream of His consciousness reaching back beyond the Incarnation into eternity (1 1 f. 3 13 6 33, 38, 41, 42, 50, 51, 58 8 58 17 5).

(2) Among the leading religious ideas of this Gospel, most of which are peculiar to, or at least characteristic of, St. John, are 'eternal life' regarded as a present as well as a future possession ; 'judgment' as a present act effecting a present separation between the friends and the enemies of God ; 'abiding in' (in a spiritual sense) 'flesh' in the sense of human nature without the connotation of sinfulness ; eating and drinking Christ's 'flesh and blood' ; the eternal predestination of events by God ($6^{37, 39, 44}$ 10^{28}, 12^{39} $17^{9\,12}$), which, however, is not identical with determinism or fatalism, because salvation is offered to *all men* (4^{42} 12^{32}) ; 'living water,' by which the grace of the Holy Spirit is typified ($4^{10f.}$) ; the 'new birth,' or 'birth from above' of water and the Spirit ($3^{3f.}$) ; 'truth' in the sense not only of veracity and correct belief, but also of that holiness which ought to follow from correct belief (8^{44} 16^{13} 17^{17} 18^{37} ; cp. especially the phrase 'to do the truth,' 3^{21} 1 Jn 1^6) ; 'the world' in the sense of the *wicked* world, alienated from God, and under the dominion of Satan, 'the prince of this world' (7^7 8^{23} 13^1 $14^{17, 27, 30}$ 15^{18} 16^{11} 17^{14}, etc.) ; 'light' and 'darkness' in a moral and spiritual sense (1^5 3^{20} 8^{12} 11^{10} $12^{35, 36}$, etc.); 'witness' and 'witnessing' to religious truth, affirmed of the Father ($5^{32, 37}$ 8^{18}), of the Son (3^{11} 4^{44} 8^{14}, etc.), of the Holy Ghost (15^{26}), of Moses and the prophets (5^{46}, etc.), of the Baptist ($1^{7f.}$ $1^{32f.}$ etc.), of the Apostles (15^{27}), of the words and miracles of Jesus (5^{36} 10^{25}).

(3) Among the titles of Christ peculiar to this Gospel or to the Johannine literature are, 'the Word,' or 'Logos' $1^{1, 14}$ (elsewhere only in 1 Jn 1^1 Rev 19^{13}) ; the 'Saviour of the world' (4^{42} 1 Jn 4^{14}) ; the 'Light of the world,' or 'of men' (1^4 8^{12} 9^5) ; the 'Manna,' or 'Living Bread' ($6^{31f.}$) ; the 'Door' (10^7) ; the 'Good Shepherd' (10^{11}) ; the 'Way, the Truth, and the Life' (14^6) ; the 'Resurrection and the Life' (11^{25}) ; 'the True Vine' (15^1) ; 'the Holy One of God' (6^{69} RV). The idea of Christ as the Paschal Lamb (19^{36}, perhaps also $1^{29, 36}$) is shared with St. Paul (1 Cor 5^7), but the application of the OT. types of Jacob's ladder (1^{51}) and of the brazen serpent (3^{14}) to Christ is peculiar to this Gospel. Peculiar also is the combination of Christ's Passion, Resurrection, and Ascension into one complex conception of which the leading characteristic is 'glory' ($13^{31, 32}$, etc.). The Passion is never contemplated in its native horror in and by itself, but always as interpreted and glorified by the Resurrection and the Ascension.

The doctrine of the Holy Spirit receives far more development in this Gospel than in the Synoptics. His personality is clearly implied by the masculine pronoun ($14^{16f.}$), by the personal title 'Advocate' peculiar to St. John ($14^{16, 26}$ 15^{26} 16^7), and by His functions ($16^{8, 13, 14}$).

6. Relation to the Synoptists. The author omits much of the matter in the Synoptics, and in a few cases seems to correct them or inferences drawn from them. He represents John the Baptist as giving more explicit testimony to the Messiahship of Jesus, and Jesus Himself as less reluctant to publish it. His attitude to miracles is also different. He records not a single example of the most frequent synoptic type of miracle, the casting out of devils, nor does he employ the synoptic term 'mighty works.' To him Christ's miracles, of which he records the mystic number seven, are 'signs,' or 'works.' They are recorded, not so much for their miraculous character, as for the sake of the doctrine or spiritual principle which they illustrate.

7. Relation to the Revelation. The Revelation may perhaps be by a different author from this Gospel, but, in any case, it belongs to the same theological school. The following are the chief words and ideas common to the two books—Christ as the Logos and as the Lamb, the Deity of Christ, and the duty of worshipping Him with the same worship as is due to the Father ; the prominence of Satan ; the idea of 'keeping the commandments,' and the emphasis laid on 'witness' and 'truth.'

8. Analysis of the Gospel (after Archdeacon Watkins).

  (1) The prologue (1^{1-18}).
  (2) Early manifestation of Jesus (1^{19}–4^{54}).
    (*a*) Witness of the Baptist (1^{19-40}).
    (*b*) Manifestation to individuals (1^{41}–2^{11}).
    (*c*) Manifestation in public (2^{12}–4^{54}).
  (3) The fuller revelation : growth of unbelief among the Jews (5^1–12^{50}).
    (*a*) Life (5^1–6^{71}).
    (*b*) Truth, light, love (7^1–10^{42}).
    (*c*) Fuller revelation of life, truth, light, love : more hostile unbelief of the Jews (11^1–12^{50}).
  (4) The fuller revelation : growth of faith among the disciples (13^1–17^{26}).
    (*a*) Love in humiliation (13^{1-34}).
    (*b*) Last words of love to the faithful (13^{35}–16^{33}).
    (*c*) Love in the intercessory prayer (17^{1-26}).
  (5) Climax of unbelief : surrender, and crucifixion (18^1–19^{42}).
  (6) Climax of faith : resurrection and proofs (c. 20).
  (7) Appendix (c. 21).

CHAPTER 1

THE DIVINITY AND INCARNATION OF THE WORD. WITNESS OF JOHN. THE FIRST DISCIPLES.

1-18. Preface, declaring (1) that the Word was God, (2) that He was made man, (3) that He revealed the Father.

This sublime preface is intended to commend 'the truth as it is in Jesus,' both to Jewish and Gentile minds. It describes our Lord's person and office by a term familiar to both, that of the Logos or Word of God. 'Logos' has two meanings in Greek : (1) reason or intelligence, as it exists inwardly in the mind, and (2) reason or intelligence, as it is expressed outwardly in speech. Both these meanings are to be understood when Christ is called 'the Word of God.' He is the inward Word of God, because He exists from all eternity ' in the bosom of the Father,' as much one with Him as reason is one with the reasoning mind. Nothing is so close to a man as his own thought. It is within him, and is in a very real sense himself. So nothing is so close to God as His own eternal Word. It is within Him, it is one with Him, and it is divine like Him (vv. 1, 2, 18). Christ is also God's outward Word. He expresses and explains and reveals to the world what God is. It was He who created the world (v. 3), making its order and beauty an outward expression of God's hidden nature. In spite of the Fall, He remained in the world, revealing to sinful man, through reason, through conscience, and through prophecy, the nature of the Father. He was the True Light that shineth in darkness, and lighteth every man that cometh into the world (v. 4 f.). In the fulness of time He revealed God still more perfectly, by becoming man, and living a perfect and sinless human life (v. 14 f.). So perfectly did Christ's wonderful life reveal the innermost character of God, that though 'no man hath seen God at any time' (1^{18}), those who have seen Christ may be said in a very real sense to have seen the Father also (14^9). The human life of Christ not only reveals what God is, it also helps man to become like God. The incarnate Christ is 'full of grace and truth' ($1^{14,16,17}$), and gives believers the power to put away their sinful nature, and to be born again as sons of God ($1^{12,13}$).

(1) The Hebrew-speaking Jews were familiar with the idea that God reveals Himself to the world through His *Memra*, or Word, which they distinguished from Himself as His organ of revelation. The Targums of the OT. speak, not of Jehovah, but of the *Memra* of Jehovah, as being manifested to Abraham, Hagar, Isaac, Jacob, and to Moses at the bush. St. John's preface, therefore, proclaimed to the Hebrew, 'That *Memra* of Jehovah, which appeared to the patriarchs and prophets, was no other than Christ before His Incarnation.' (2) The educated Greek-speaking Jews (Hellenists) were familiar with the writings of the Jewish philosopher, Philo of Alexandria (circ. 15 B.C.–50 A.D.). He believed that God does not act upon the world directly, but mediately through his Logos or Reason. To the Hellenist, therefore, St. John's Gospel said, 'That Logos, through which you say God acts upon the world and reveals himself in it, is no other than Christ.' (3) Educated heathens also believed in a divine Logos or Reason, diffused through the world, and disposing all things in a rational order. First Heraclitus, then Plato, and finally the Stoics developed this doctrine, until, in the apostolic age, it was the explanation of the universe commonly accepted by educated persons. To the heathen, therefore, St. John's preface said, 'That divine Logos, which inspired your philosophers, so far as they have spoken truly, and whose existence is admitted by all educated men, has finally manifested Himself in the life of Jesus of Nazareth. Read the account that follows of His wonderful life and sayings, and you will acknowledge that this is true.' St. John's doctrine of the Logos differs from the Jewish and the heathen doctrine mainly in these two points : (1) That the Logos is personal, and (2) that He became flesh.

1. In the beginning] not as in Gn 1^1, 'in the beginning of creation,' but 'in the beginning of eternity,' i.e. from all eternity : cp. 8^{58} 17^5. **Was the Word**] i.e. the Word existed. 'The Word' as a title of our Lord is only found in the Johannine writings (1^{14} 1 Jn 1^1 Rev 19^{13}). On its meaning, see above. **Was with God**] lit. 'was directed towards God,' the attitude of loving and intimate intercourse : cp. 'in the bosom of the Father' (v. 18). **Was God**] i.e. was divine, and is therefore to be worshipped with the same worship as is due to the Father. Jesus is again called God in express terms in v. 18 (RM) 20^{28} 1 Jn 5^{20} Ro 9^5 Tit 2^{13} (RV) Ac 20^{28} Heb 1^8 2 Pet 1^1 (RV). **3. Made by Him**] i.e. 'through' Him, as the Father's agent. That Christ is the creator of the universe is stated Col $1^{16,17}$ 1 Cor 8^6 Heb 1^2 1^{10} Rev 3^{14}, but not in any Gospel except this.

3, 4. The Word is not only the Creator of the world, but is also its **Life** ; i.e. He sustains it in existence, supplies life to all living organisms, and guides all the operations of nature. To rational beings like men, He is also their **Light**, or Instructor. He was this even before His Incarnation, instructing them through reason, through conscience, and through prophecy. (For another punctuation see RV.)

5. This instruction by the Word was hindered

by the Fall, which involved the world in moral and spiritual darkness. **And the darkness comprehended (RV 'apprehended') it not**] i.e. the people whose minds were darkened by sin did not understand or obey the instructions of the Word. Prejudice prevented them. Another translation is 'and the darkness overcame it not.'

6–8. Parenthesis : The mission of Christ's forerunner, John the Baptist. Perhaps this section is directed against those followers of the Baptist who maintained that he was the Messiah. The evangelist makes it clear, (1) that the Baptist had a true mission from God, and (2) that he was not the Light. His mission was to bear witness to it, and to reflect it.

9. The preface resumed. The true Light, Christ our Lord, existed even before His Incarnation, and enlightened every man, whether Jew or Gentile, born into the world. This important text teaches us that the light of revelation shines among all races, and that there is some truth, however distorted by error, in all religions. The best translation is, 'Already the true Light existed, which lighteth every man as he cometh into the world.' For other translations see the RV. **10. He was in the world**] viz. before His Incarnation. **11. He came,** viz. at the Incarnation, **unto his own** (home), viz. the Holy Land ; **and his own,** i.e. the Jews, **received,** i.e. believed, **Him not.**

12. Power] rather, 'the right,' or 'privilege.' Those who 'believed on His name,' i.e. accepted Him as the divine Son of God, and the Saviour of the world, received the privilege of becoming true sons of God. **13.** This sonship conferred on men depended not on human descent from Abraham (**blood**), nor upon the sexual relations of their parents (**the will of the flesh**), nor could it be had for willing or wishing it, i.e. human effort (**the will of man**). It was a free and supernatural gift from God, inward and spiritual, implanted by the Holy Ghost, and dependent for its maintenance on union with Christ : see on 3 3, 5.

14. The Word was made (RV 'became') flesh] a plain statement of the wondrous fact of the Incarnation, the central mystery of our religion. God became man to atone for sin, and to make us partakers of the divine nature. 'Flesh' in St. John means human nature (body, soul, and spirit) without the added idea of sinfulness, which attaches to it in St. Paul (see especially 6 51 f.). Our text affirms, therefore, that the Redeemer is ' perfect God and perfect man, of a reasonable soul and human flesh subsisting ; equal to the Father, as touching His Godhead, and inferior to the Father, as touching His manhood. Who although He be God and man, yet He is not two, but one Christ.'

Dwelt among us] lit. ' dwelt in a tabernacle among us,' the tabernacle being His body (see

2 19, and cp. 2 Cor 5 1, 4 2 Pet 1 13, 14). The allusion is to the 'Shekinah,' which the rabbis identified with 'the Word of Jehovah.' As the 'Shekinah,' or visible glory of God, dwelt in the tabernacle of old, so, when Christ was born into the world, His divine nature dwelt in His body as in a temple. **We beheld his glory**] i.e. not merely the visible glory of the Transfiguration and the Ascension, but the moral and spiritual splendour of His unique life, which revealed the nature of the invisible Father. The evangelist here claims to have been an eyewitness, as in 19 35. **The only begotten of (RV 'from) the Father**] The glory of Christ's life was not a reflected glory, as would have been the case had He been a mere human saint or prophet, but it was the glory of God's only begotten Son, and therefore God's own glory, for Christ and His Father are one. 'Only begotten' as a title of Christ is peculiar to St. John (1 18 3 16-18 1 Jn 4 9). It indicates that no man or even angel is God's son in the sense in which Christ is. A 'son' in the full sense of the word is of the same nature as his father, and hence Christ, being God's Son, is divine. **Full of grace and truth**] 'grace' is the divine favour and loving-kindness ; 'truth,' as often in St. John, is not simply veracity, but holiness in general (cp. 1 17 3 21 4 23 8 44 1 Jn 1 6). Christ was full of grace and holiness, not that He might keep them to Himself, but that He might bestow them upon men.

15. Another parenthesis, introducing further testimony of the Baptist, which the evangelist indicates as of permanent importance (' beareth,' ' crieth,' RV, not **bare, cried,** AV).

He that cometh after me] i.e. He who begins his work later than myself. **Is become (RV) before me**] viz. in honour. **For he was before me**] i.e. He existed before my birth, and even before His own birth, as the eternal Son of God. The Baptist learnt that Christ was God's Son by a special revelation, and by the voice of the Father at Christ's baptism : see vv. 32–34.

16–18. The preface concluded. The ' we ' of v. 16 shows that these vv. are not words of the Baptist, but that they express the spiritual experience of Christ's disciples, in whose name the evangelist speaks. **16. Of his fulness**] ' Fulness ' (*pleroma*) was a word much used (and abused) by the Gnostics against whom St. John contended. Here it means, (1) the fulness of the divine attributes which dwelt in Christ (Eph 1 23 Col 1 19 2 9), and (2) the fulness of the human virtues which He displayed. Both these ' fulnesses ' Christ imparts in some measure to true believers, as the evangelist testifies from personal experience. **Grace for grace**] i.e. grace succeeding grace, one act of love after another, ever increasing in proportion as we deserve it or require it. **17.** Moses set before us mere commands, without changing our nature, or giving us the power to obey them. Jesus Christ came to change our nature. He offers us ' grace,' whereby we are born again as children of God, and become heirs of everlasting life ; also ' truth,' i.e. Christian holiness, which becomes possible to those who abide in Christ: cp. Ro 5 21. **By Moses.. by Jesus**] lit. 'through' Moses, 'through' Jesus.

18. God the Father never reveals Himself to men directly, but always by and through His only-begotten Son. This was the case even before the Incarnation. It was God the Son who manifested Himself to the patriarchs, gave the Law to Moses, inspired the prophets, and enlightened the sages of the Gentiles. But now by His Incarnation He has revealed God more perfectly. So completely does ' the Word made flesh' represent the invisible Father, that ' he that hath seen me hath seen the Father' (14 9): cp. 5 37 6 46 Ex 33 20 Col 1 15 1 Tim 6 16 1 Jn 4 12, 20. **The only begotten Son**] Many very ancient authorities read, ' (the) only begotten God,' a striking statement of our Lord's Deity. **In the bosom**] i.e. in eternal, intimate, loving union with the Father : cp. the expression 'in Abraham's bosom' (Lk 16 22), and Jn 13 23. This v. explains how it is that God is love, not only since the creation, when He created objects for His love, but from eternity : cp. 17 24.

1 19–4 42. Preliminary ministry of our Lord. All the events recorded by St. John from 1 19 to 4 42 (the testimony of the Baptist ; the preliminary call of John, Andrew, Peter, Philip, and Nathanael ; the marriage at Cana ; the visit to Capernaum ; the first cleansing of the Temple ; the interview with Nicodemus ; the interview with the Samaritan woman) may be regarded as a preliminary ministry, for they took place before the Baptist was cast into prison (see Mt 4 12). The ministry proper begins with the imprisonment of the Baptist, upon news of which Jesus withdrew into Galilee (Mt 4 12 Jn 4 43, 46).

19–28. Public testimony of the Baptist to Jesus in reply to a deputation from the Sanhedrin. The independence and fulness of the account of the Baptist in this Gospel renders it highly probable that the evangelist had once been the Baptist's disciple. He knows, for example, the exact places where John baptised (1 28 3 23) ; the exact day and even hour when certain things were said (1 29, 35, 39) ; the contemporary disputes with the Jews about purifying (3 25) ; the relations, not always friendly, between the disciples of John and those of Christ (3 26) ; the exact time when John was cast into prison (3 24). His account of the Baptist's testimony agrees with that of

the Synoptists, but he adds to it important particulars. He mentions, for instance, that John actually saw the dove descending upon Jesus, and was thus enabled to recognise Him (1 32), that he applied to Him the titles Lamb of God (1 29, 36) and Son of God (1 34 3 36), the latter clearly in a superhuman sense, for he declares His preëxistence (1 15, 30), and says that to believe in Him is to have eternal life (3 36). For the historical difficulties, see on these passages and on Mt 11 2. The Synoptists record the Baptist's testimony *before* our Lord's baptism, and St. John his testimony *afterwards*, when the descent of the Spirit upon Jesus, and the voice of the Father, had convinced the Baptist that Jesus was truly the Son of God.

19. The Jews] In this Gospel ' the Jews' has the following special senses : (1) the inhabitants of Judæa, (2) members of the Sanhedrin (the meaning here), and (3) the enemies of Jesus. **Sent**] One function of the Sanhedrin was to judge false prophets, hence they now desired to judge the claims of John. **Priests and Levites**] the proper parties to enquire into a new religious movement. The priests performed the services of the Temple, offered the sacrifices, and burnt the incense. The Levites waited upon the priests in their ministry, and discharged subordinate duties.

20. Not the Christ] Some already believed that he was, Lk 3 15. **21. Elias**] i.e. Elijah, whose personal return to prepare the way of the Messiah was expected by many (Mal 4 5 Mk 6 15; see especially on Mt 16 14 17 10). John denied that he was literally Elijah, though his coming fulfilled Malachi's prophecy (Mt 11 14 17 12 Lk 1 17). **That prophet**] RV 'the prophet,' viz. the prophet mentioned Dt 18 15, and regarded by the deputation not as the Messiah, but as one of his forerunners. John, however, regarded the prophet of Dt 18 15 as actually the Messiah (cp. Ac 3 22), and therefore denied that he was ' that prophet.' **23.** The words in Isaiah (Isa 40 3) refer to the preparation for the return from Babylon of the exiled Jews : the Baptist applies them to himself, as descriptive of his work : see on Mt 3 3.

24. And they] RV 'and they had been sent from the Pharisees.' **25. Why baptizest thou ?**] Baptism was ordinarily administered only to proselytes. The meaning of the challenge seems, therefore, to be, ' What right hast thou, who art neither the Messiah, nor his forerunner " that Prophet," to treat Israelites as if they were proselytes ? ' It is implied that the Messiah, who came to inaugurate an entirely new covenant, might possibly be expected to baptise even Jews. **26. With water**] John's baptism was outward, symbolising repentance and remission of sin : Christ's was inward, conveying the gift of the Spirit, and the power to lead a new life. **28. Bethabara**] lit. 'house of passing over,' RV 'Bethany,' RM 'Bethabarah,' or 'Betharabah'; probably the same as the Beth-barah of Jg 7 24. A ford on the Jordan, NE. of Bethshean, is still called 'Abarah,' lit. ' passing over.'

29. The Lamb of God] The reference is perhaps not to the Paschal lamb, but to the Suffering Servant of Isa 53, who is 'brought as a lamb to the slaughter,' and whose death atones for sin. Contrast this description of the Messiah with the prevalent idea of a conqueror who would restore the kingdom to Israel. The Jews generally regarded the Messiah not as 'the Lamb of God,' but as 'the Lion of the tribe of Judah.' **The sin of the world**] The idea of atonement for the sins of *Israel* is found in Isa 53 : the further idea that the Messiah will atone for the sins of *the world*, follows naturally from the numerous utterances of the OT. prophets which speak of the participation of the Gentiles in the Messianic kingdom (Ps 87, etc.).

30. See v. 15. **31. I knew him not**] But in Mt 3 14 he seems to know Him, for he says, 'I have need to be baptized of thee.' The discrepancy, however, is only apparent. John is looking for the promised sign. Jesus presents Himself for Baptism. His majestic appearance strikes John with awe. Through prophetic insight (or perhaps as the result of a personal interview before the Baptism) he surmises that He is the true Messiah (' I have need,' etc.). The sign that follows makes the surmise a certainty. **34. The Son of God**] The chief difficulty as to the use of this term by the Baptist is removed by the statement that he first learnt that Jesus was ' the Son of God' at the Baptism. In the OT. it was a title of the Davidic king, and of the Messiah (2 S 7 14 Ps 89 27, etc.), and did not necessarily imply (though see Ps 2, and cp. Ps 110) superhuman dignity.

35–51. Preliminary call of five Apostles, Andrew, John, Peter, Philip, and Bartholomew (peculiar to Jn). This account, so far from conflicting with the (later) call described Mt 4 18 Mk 1 15 (cp. Lk 5 1), really removes a difficulty, for it shows how the Apostles came to obey the final call to follow Jesus so readily. After their preliminary call, described here, the Apostles loosely attached themselves to Jesus as learners, but did not leave their homes and occupations. Afterwards when further intercourse had strengthened their hope that He was really the Messiah, they left all and followed Him.

35. Two] One was Andrew, the other (who characteristically suppresses his name) was John himself (see v. 40). The Baptist points out Jesus, thus suggesting that henceforth they should be His disciples. **39. The tenth**

hour] i.e. by Jewish reckoning, about 4 P.M. But some think that at Ephesus, where this Gospel was written, hours were numbered as with us, in which case the time would be 10 A.M. (see 4 6 19 14). **42. Jona**] RV 'John'; see Mt 16 17. **Cephas**] At the very first interview our Lord reads Peter's character : see on Mt 16 18.

43. It would appear that Jesus Himself was acquainted with Philip. **45. Nathanael**] is probably an apostle, and is hence to be identified with Bartholomew, whose name also appears coupled with Philip's in Mt 10 3. 'Bartholomew ' means ' son of Tolmai ' : cp. Barjona, Barabbas, Bartimæus, Barjesus. **The son of Joseph**] This does not indicate the evangelist's own belief, but what was generally believed at this time. **46. Nazareth**] an obscure place not even mentioned in OT., which indicated Bethlehem as the birthplace of the Messiah (Mic 5 2). **47. No guile**] 'guile' or deceitfulness was the special failing of Jacob (Israel),' and of Israelites generally. Again our Lord discerns the heart of man. **48. I saw thee**] implies supernatural knowledge. Perhaps Jesus alludes to some recent prayer or resolution which Nathanael made under the figtree.

49. The Son of God] A title of the Messiah even in the OT. : see on v. 34. **51.** See Gn 28 12. As Jacob saw in his dream a vision of angels ascending and descending the ladder, so the disciples would see in Christ the link and connexion between heaven and earth. Through Christ the locked-up heavens were again to be opened, and communion between heaven and earth restored. The title ' Son of man' indicates Christ as completely partaking of human nature, and realising its original ideal : see especially the full note on Mt 8 20.

CHAPTER 2
THE WEDDING AT CANA. THE TEMPLE
CLEANSED

1–11. The marriage at Cana. This miracle is not recorded by the synoptists because it occurred before the beginning of the ministry proper. St. John records it, because, spiritually interpreted, it forms a suitable introduction to our Lord's ministerial work. It teaches, (1) the superiority of the Gospel to the Law. Christ changes the water of Judaism into the good wine of the Gospel. This is not a fanciful interpretation, but an entirely natural one, if it be granted (as is abundantly shown in the Intro.) that the ancients were right in regarding this Gospel as a 'spiritual' or allegorical one. (2) Being a physical or creative miracle, it manifests Christ as the Lord of matter as well as of spirit. (3) It sanctifies marriage, and gives Christ's approval to innocent mirth and gladness. (4)

It reveals God's goodness and overwhelming bounty. In recording it, St. John doubtless had in view the Gnostic false teachers, who regarded matter as evil, and practised a rigid asceticism, rejecting all bodily pleasures, and abstaining from flesh and wine, and even from marriage. Such teaching was very prevalent in Ephesus, where this Gospel was written (see 1 Tim 4 1-6), and tradition tells us that St. John vehemently opposed it.

1. The third day] It was a three-days' journey from Judæa to Galilee. **Cana**] now Kana-el-Jelil, a village 9 m. NW. of Nazareth, called 'of Galilee' to distinguish it from Cana (Kanah) in Asher (Josh 19 28). **3. They have no wine**] The deficiency happened towards the close of the festivities, which usually lasted seven or fourteen days (Jg 14 15 Tob 9 19). It was perhaps caused by the presence of so many (five or six) of the disciples of Jesus, and hence our Lord had a natural motive for working the miracle. **4. Woman**] A very gentle rebuke, but still a rebuke. Now that His ministry has actually begun, not even His mother may presume to suggest or control His course of action : cp. Mt 12 46 Lk 11 27. 'Woman,' or, rather, 'Lady,' is in Greek a title of respect, used even in addressing queens.

Mine hour (i.e. for putting forth My miraculous power) **is not yet come**] Yet it came a few minutes later, when the Father, by an inward revelation, had manifested His will to Jesus. 'Hour,' in the sense of 'appointed time,' is common in this Gospel (7 30 8 20 12 23,27 13 1 17 1). **6. Purifying**] Washing the hands before dinner (Lk 11 38) is meant : cp. Mk 7 3, and see the full notes on Mt 15 1-20.

Firkins] Gk. *metretes*, about 9 gallons.

9. Ruler] an honoured guest, who presided at the entertainment. **10. Well drunk**] RV 'drunk freely.' The expression is proverbial, and need not be literally interpreted of the present company.

11. Beginning of miracles] lit. 'signs.' Clearly Christ wrought no miracles in His childhood, as the Apocryphal Gospels assert. St. John calls our Lord's miracles 'signs,' because they indicate something beyond themselves. They are no mere marvels, but reveal God's character, Christ's divine nature, and the mysteries of the gospel dispensation. All the miracles in this Gospel are also parables : see Intro. **Manifested**] To 'manifest' is to display something which before was hidden ; here, the glory of His Messiahship, faith in which, already begun among the disciples (1 41), was confirmed by this miracle.

12. Short visit to Capernaum. This unimportant event seems recorded for some personal reason. Perhaps it was the occasion of the first visit of Jesus to the evangelist's own

house. **Brethren**] These are variously regarded as sons of Joseph by a former wife, sons of Joseph and Mary, and as cousins of Jesus : see special note on Mt 12 46-50.

13-17. First Passover and First Cleansing of the Temple. For a full commentary, see on Mt 21 12. By a striking sign our Lord at the very outset of His ministry brought His claims before the whole nation. The rulers at once took up an attitude of hostility, although a few, like Nicodemus, were favourably impressed. The people, upon the whole, approved our Lord's action. Many believed, but their faith, based on miracles, was superficial, and Jesus would not trust them. The disciples were confirmed in their faith by seeing Jesus fulfil OT. prophecies. By this act Jesus claimed to be, not merely a prophet, but the Messiah, as is shown by the expression 'My Father's house,' which asserts His right to the Messianic title 'the Son of God.' The Jews considered that the Temple court in which this sign took place (the Court of the Gentiles) was profane ; but Jesus by cleansing it showed that it was holy, and vindicated for the Gentiles a rightful place in the true Temple of God.

17. The zeal] Cited from Ps 69 9. This Ps. is elsewhere quoted as Messianic, Jn 15 25 19 28 Ac 1 20 Ro 11 9,10 15 3, and is ascribed to David. The Psalmist complains that his zeal for God's house and for true religion has brought upon him bitter persecution and unnumbered calamities. This was also the case with our Lord.

18-22. The Jews seek a sign. First prophecy of the Resurrection.

19. Destroy this temple (or, rather, 'sanctuary')] These words made a deep impression, and were quoted against Jesus, in a maliciously altered form, at His trial (Mt 26 61). The evangelist understood them (v. 21) to apply to the Resurrection, and this interpretation is confirmed by the fact that our Lord on other occasions also pointed to His Resurrection as a sign for His opponents (Mt 12 39,40, where consult the notes). Many critics, however, think that our Lord's real meaning was, 'When this old dispensation of the Ceremonial Law is destroyed, I will quickly raise up in its place a new and spiritual religion.'

20. Three temples have stood on Mt. Moriah : (1) Solomon's Temple, (2) Zerubbabel's Temple, (3) Herod's Temple. This last, however, some regard not as a new Temple, but as Zerubbabel's Temple repaired and enlarged. Herod the Great began to build it 20 B.C., and at this time, apparently, building operations had ceased. They were soon resumed, however, and the Temple was finally completed by Herod Agrippa, 64 A.D. Reckoning from 20 B.C. the date of our Lord's cleansing of the Temple would be about 26 A.D., but strict accuracy is not attainable.

23-25. Many believe on Jesus, but with imperfect faith.

23. In the feast *day*] RV 'during the feast,' which lasted a week. **24. Did not commit** (RV 'trust') himself unto them] because of their carnal conceptions of His person and work. They were impressed by His miracles, and thought that He would prove a militant and victorious Messiah.

CHAPTER 3

THE NEW BIRTH. JOHN'S TESTIMONY TO JESUS

1-15. Conversation with Nicodemus. The ministry at Jerusalem, though disappointing, was not fruitless. Christ's miracles and teaching had made an impression, not only on Nicodemus, but as Nicodemus himself says (v. 2, cp. 12 42), on other members of the Sanhedrin. This interview took place by night, on account of the timidity of Nicodemus (cp. 7 50), and probably in St. John's house at Jerusalem, the evangelist himself being present. Nicodemus may possibly be the Nicodemus, son of Gorion, mentioned in the Talmud. **1. A ruler**] i.e. a member of the Sanhedrin.

2, 3. Nicodemus had asked no question, but Jesus knew what he wished to ask, viz. 'If Thou art the Messiah, as some of us are inclined to believe, tell us how we must enter that Kingdom of God, which Thou hast come to establish, and of which Thou hast said so much.' Our Lord answers that a new birth, i.e. a new heart and a new nature, are necessary, according to the testimony of the OT. prophets: 'I will put my Law in their inward parts and write it in their hearts' (see Jer 31 31 f. Ezk 37 26, etc.). As evidence of the 'new birth,' our Lord would require *humility*, humble trust in God for salvation through Christ, not a vainglorious boasting in descent from Abraham, or in the punctilious fulfilment of legal ceremonies; also *repentance*, i.e. sincere abhorrence of sin, and not merely of ceremonial defilement; and, lastly, *love*, and that not only of one's friends, but also of one's enemies; not only of the righteous, but of publicans and sinners; not only of the Jew, but of the Samaritan and the Gentile—a love, moreover, manifesting itself not in word only, but in works of mercy, such as feeding the hungry, clothing the naked, and instructing the ignorant.

4. How can a man] Nicodemus is unwilling to believe that he, an orthodox and pious Jew, and withal a ruler and a Pharisee, must undergo so radical a change, before he can enter Christ's Kingdom. He therefore affects to misunderstand Christ's words: cp. 6 52.

5. Of water and *of* **the Spirit**] Our Lord again insists that a new birth is necessary, and explains that it must be an inward and spiritual one. It must not be only of 'water,' i.e. the reception of the outward rite of baptism without proper appreciation of what membership of Christ's Kingdom involves, but also of 'the Spirit,' i.e. Nicodemus must approach Christ's baptism with such sincerity of repentance and faith, and such earnest resolution to live up to the ideals of the new Kingdom, that in his case the outward rite will be accompanied by an effusion of the Spirit, that will make his baptism a real 'new birth of water and of the Spirit.'

Baptism is again spoken of as a 'new birth' by St. Paul—'according to his mercy he saved us by (RV 'through') the washing (RM 'laver,' i.e. bath) of regeneration (*or* 'new birth') and renewing of the Holy Ghost' (Tit 3 5). Christ's baptism is often distinguished from John's, as a baptism of the Spirit (Mt 3 11 Jn 1 33 Ac 1 5 19 4, etc.). It confers (on those who receive it rightly) spiritual graces which could not be fully given until Jesus had been glorified (7 39). We learn from 3 26 that already Jesus was admitting disciples into His Kingdom by the rite of baptism, and this explains the allusion to 'water' here.

JEWISH AND CHRISTIAN BAPTISM

(1) The phrase 'new birth' or 'regeneration' here applied by our Lord to Christian baptism was not a new one. The rabbis were accustomed to admit proselytes to Judaism by three rites, all of which they regarded as essential— (a) baptism (always by complete immersion) in the presence of witnesses who answered to the Christian 'sponsors' or 'godparents'; (b) in the case of males, circumcision; (c) sacrifice. The rabbis frequently spoke of this proselyte baptism as a 'regeneration,' i.e. a new birth from heathenism, in which the proselytes had been under the dominion of Satan, into the family of God, in which they enjoyed the privileges of the covenant of Abraham. Our Lord, therefore, might fairly expect Nicodemus, a rabbi and a sanhedrist, to understand Him when He spoke of His own baptism as a new birth from the ceremonies and shadows of the Law to the spiritual reality and power of the New Dispensation.

(2) The context of this v., in which much more is said about 'spirit' than about 'water,' warns us not to rely unduly upon the saving efficacy of baptism regarded as a merely external ordinance. Baptism is not a charm like the purifications of the heathen, nor a mere symbol of purity like those of the Jewish Law, but a *sacrament*, i.e. a moral means of grace, the full efficacy and effect of which depend upon the response in the soul of the baptised person to the covenanted grace proffered in the ordinance.

(3) No argument against infant baptism can be drawn from the words 'Except a man,' etc. The Greek is quite indefinite, 'Except any

one.' In the case of infants the conscious response of the soul to the proffered grace of the ordinance takes place when the age of reason is reached. On infant baptism, see on Mt 19 13-15.

(4) On this passage, together with Mt 28 19 (cp. Mk 16 16), is founded the prevailing opinion that baptism ('where it may be had') is indispensably necessary for admission into the Christian covenant.

6. The nature we inherit from our parents is corrupt ; the new nature which comes with the new birth is holy and spiritual. **8.** As none can trace the source or aim of the wind, yet all can hear and feel it, so is it with those who have experienced the new birth. There is something in the inner life not to be explained, but which reveals itself in its operations, and can be known only by experience.

10. ' You a teacher in Israel, and this, without which all religion is a dead thing, not known to you !' **11. We**] Probably St. John and a few other disciples were present.

12. Earthly things] i.e. religious facts and experiences (e.g. repentance, faith, the new birth, etc.), which happen upon this earth, and which are, therefore, comparatively easy to apprehend. **Heavenly things**] i.e. the hidden and unfathomable counsels of God for human salvation, e.g. the Incarnation, and the Atonement (vv. 13, 14, 15). **13. Ascended**] This word is not to be taken quite literally. Our Lord only means that He had been in heaven before His Incarnation, and hence could speak of heavenly things (i.e. the Father's most secret counsels) from personal experience. **Which is in heaven**] Some important authorities omit these words, which, if genuine, affirm that our Lord was at the same time on earth and in heaven, in a state of humiliation, and in a state of glory.

14. See Nu 21 6-9. As the children of Israel, bitten by the fiery serpents, were cured by looking at the brazen serpent, so sinners may receive remission of sins and eternal life by looking with faith at Jesus, who was ' lifted up,' first upon the cross, and afterwards into heaven : cp. 8 28 12 32, 34. **15.** RV ' that whosoever believeth may in Him have eternal life.' **Eternal life**] This expression, though found in the other Gospels (Mt 19 16, etc.) and in the Pauline Epistles (Ro 2 7, etc.), is specially characteristic of St. John. It is that state of blissful communion with God, which is enjoyed by the believer who is reconciled to God through faith in Christ. The NT. generally speaks of it as a future possession, but St. John often regards it as possessed already to some extent in this world. ' Eternal,' lit. ' æonian,' means not simply ' endless,' but ' belonging to the world to come,' and so ' supernatural,' ' spiritual,' ' heavenly.'

16-21. are probably words of Jesus, though some regard them as reflections of the evangelist. They state the broad saving truths of the gospel in direct opposition to the narrow Pharisaism in which Nicodemus had been reared. Whereas the Pharisees confined salvation to a single race, and believed that the Messiah would judge the Gentiles with extreme severity, our Lord declares that God has sent His Son to save the whole world, and not to judge or condemn any part of it. ' Whosoever will,' may believe and be saved.

17. Condemn] lit. ' judge ' (RV), but the context shows that an unfavourable judgment is meant. **18. Is condemned** (lit. ' hath been judged ') **already**] God's judgment upon men's actions is a present fact ; He judges men here and now. The publication of His judgment, however, will not take place until the Last Day.

18. The name] i.e. (practically) the Person.

19. This is the condemnation (RV ' judgment ')] i.e. the condemnation is based upon this, that the Light is come into the world, etc. It is implied that men whose deeds are really good, are irresistibly attracted by Christ's words and works, so that they become believers. **21.** To ' do the truth,' means to live the Christian life, for Christian truth is more than a belief, it is a way of life. The phrase is peculiar to St. John : cp. 1 Jn 1 6.

22-36. Jesus leaves Jerusalem and baptises in the country districts of Judæa, where He probably spent most of the time from the Passover, 27 A.D., to the late harvest (December) of the same year : see on 4 35. His great success rouses the jealousy of John's disciples (v. 26), but the Baptist, so far from regarding Christ's disciples as too many, laments that they are too few (v. 32), and again testifies his belief in Christ's Messiahship. **22. Baptized**] Our Lord baptised only through the ministry of His disciples (4 2). The synoptists represent Christian baptism as not ordained till after the Resurrection (Mt 28 19 Mk 16 16) ; but here it is said to have been practised from the beginning of the ministry. The two accounts are not really inconsistent. What had been Christ's practice during His ministry was raised to the dignity of a perpetual ordinance after the Resurrection. Some regard this preliminary baptism of Christ as a mere baptism of repentance like John's, but it is apparently called a birth ' of water and the Spirit ' (3 5), and consequently must have been specifically Christian baptism, although doubtless the fulness of the Spirit could not be given till after the Ascension (7 39). That the Spirit could be given in some measure before the Ascension, 20 22 is evidence. **23. Ænon**] lit. ' full of springs,' is generally located 8 m. S. of Scythopolis, near Salim (Salumias) and the Jordan. **24.** This **v.** corrects the impression which the synoptic narrative produces, that John was imprisoned immediately after our Lord's baptism. As a matter of fact, the two ministries overlapped by several months, perhaps by a whole year.

25. The Jews] RV 'a Jew.' Perhaps the Jew was a disciple of Jesus, and the dispute was about the comparative cleansing power of John's baptism and Christ's. **27.** 'Do not wonder at the success of Jesus. No man can usurp what heaven has not granted him.'

29. By Jewish custom 'the friend of the bridegroom' arranged the marriage contract between the bridegroom and the bride, and presided at the wedding feast. This John did for Jesus, by preparing the Jewish people (the bride) to receive our Lord's teaching.

31–36. Not, as some think, a reflection of the evangelist, but a continuation of the testimony of the Baptist. The Baptist places Christ (**he that cometh from above**) at an infinite elevation above himself (**he that is of the earth**) (v. 31). He declares that Christ came down from heaven, and so can testify to what He has seen there (v. 32). He alone can give the Spirit without measure (v. 34). He is God's Son; to Him all power is committed; and through faith in Him eternal life is offered. To disobey Him is to incur God's wrath (vv. 35, 36).

31. Christ's teaching is as superior to John's as the heavens are higher than the earth.

32. No man] a rhetorical overstatement. John deplores that the number of Christ's followers, though great, is as nothing compared with what it ought to be. **33. That God is true** (lit. 'truthful')] To believe the Messiah is to believe God, for the Messiah is God's ambassador and interpreter (see the next v.).

34. For God (RV 'he') **giveth**] This may either mean 'for Christ giveth not the Spirit by measure (to believers),' or, 'for God giveth not the Spirit by measure (to Christ).'

36. Believeth not] RV 'obeyeth not.'

CHAPTER 4
The Samaritan Woman

1–42. Christ in Samaria. The ministry in Samaria is recorded because it is the author's design to exhibit Christ as the Saviour, not only of Israel, but of the world (4 42).

The Samaritans were mainly an alien race, descended from the colonists planted in the land by the Assyrians (2 K 17 6, 24, 26, 29 Ezr 4 1, 9, 10). They boasted, however, of being Israelites, and with some degree of justification, for there was probably a considerable Jewish element in the population. Their worship, originally a compromise with heathenism, was now purely Jewish. They kept the sabbath, and the Jewish feasts, and observed circumcision and other traditional ordinances. Of the OT. they accepted only the Pentateuch, which they inter-

preted as commanding the erection of a Temple on Mt. Gerizim. That Christ should have preached in Samaria is somewhat surprising in view of such passages as Mt 15 24 and 10 5, but it must be remembered that He did not enter Samaria for this purpose, but simply to reach Galilee (v. 3).

1. The Pharisees had been hostile to John's ministry; they were likely to be more so to the more successful ministry of Jesus. Our Lord, therefore, left Judæa, the chief centre of Pharisaism, to avoid a rupture. **2.** Our Lord did not baptise, because it was His work to baptise with the Holy Ghost (1 33), and He could not do this (fully at least) till after His Ascension (see on 3 5 3 22). **4. Must needs go through**] Jesus had just heard that Herod Antipas had cast John into prison (Mt 4 12). To escape this fate, He avoided Peræa, the seat of Herod's power, and passed through Samaria. **5. Sychar**] now 'Askar, near Shechem. Jacob's well still retains its name. **The parcel of ground, etc.**] This is a Samaritan tradition, not expressly authorised by the OT., but based on a comparison of Gn 33 19 with Gn 48 22. **6. Thus**] i.e. wearied as He was. For Christ's subjection to human infirmity, see also 11 35, 38 19 28.

The sixth hour] i.e. either noon or 6 P.M. The number of events which happened subsequently seems to require the earlier hour, but see on 1 39.

8. The later rabbis declared that to partake of Samaritan bread was like eating swine's flesh, but in our Lord's time Samaritan food was accounted clean. **9. The Jews have no dealings**, etc.] Some ancient authorities omit this statement, which must be taken to refer only to intimate dealings. Our Lord had broken down the barrier by asking a favour. He wished to encourage her to ask a favour of Him, and so to give Him an opportunity of leading her to the truth. **10. The gift of God**] i.e. all the blessings offered to us in Christ, especially the gift of eternal life (see vv. 13, 14). **Living water**] As Christ does not identify Himself with the 'water,' as He does with the 'bread' in c. 6, the 'water' must be 'the grace and truth' of which He is full (1 14), and which are communicated to believers through the Spirit (7 39). Both the thirst and the hunger of the soul (and these are felt even by such outcasts as the Samaritan woman) are satisfied by Christ.. **11.** The woman takes 'living water' literally, as meaning the running water of a spring or stream as distinguished from the stagnant water of a cistern or well (Gn 26 19 Lv 14 5, etc.). **12.** In spite of their mainly heathen origin, the Samaritans claimed Israelitish descent. **14. Shall never thirst**] 'Every spiritual desire and aspiration of the soul shall be completely satisfied, and for ever, for the life which I give is eternal.' **15.** These mocking words show that the woman was still unimpressed.

16. Finding her impervious to gentleness, our Lord uses stronger measures. He reveals Himself to her as a prophet, and with a prophet's authority reveals and rebukes her sin: cp. 2 S 12. **18.** Although this woman had apparently been divorced by five husbands for unfaithfulness, and was now living in sin, our Lord did not deal with her harshly. For other examples of His considerate treatment of fallen women, see 8 1-11 and Lk 7 36-50.

20. The woman is ashamed, and seeks to change the conversation. Our Lord kindly permits it, knowing that the words He has spoken will bear fruit. She asks Him, since He is a prophet, to pronounce upon the main point in dispute between the Jews and the Samaritans. The Samaritans argued from Dt 27 4 that Gerizim was the one divinely appointed place of sacrifice, because there God had commanded an altar to be raised and the Law inscribed. The Samaritan text reads Gerizim in this passage instead of Ebal.

21-24. Speaking as a prophet, our Lord draws a sublime picture of the religion of the future. All that is transitory, national, local, and ceremonial about the religion of Jerusalem and Gerizim is to pass away, and God will accept for the future only the worship of the spirit and the heart. In the meantime, however, Jerusalem, not Gerizim, is the true centre of worship, there Jehovah has placed His name, there the Redeemer is to suffer, and there His religion is to be first established.

22. 'We Jews understand the nature of the God we worship: you Samaritans do not. We have the Psalmists and Prophets to teach us the meaning of spiritual religion: you reject all but the ceremonial Law of Moses. Moreover, you show your ignorance of God by setting up an unauthorised worship in a place which He has not chosen.' **Salvation is of the Jews**] alluding to the promises to Abraham (Gn 12), and to David (2 S 7 11-13, 16 Pss 89 3, 4 132 11), and to the historic fact that the gospel was to be preached to all nations 'beginning at Jerusalem' (Lk 24 47).

23. In spirit] i.e. with true inward reverence, as distinguished from mere outward observance. In truth] i.e. with true holiness of life. 'Truth,' in St. John, is not only correct belief, but also practical piety: see on 3 21.

24. God *is* a Spirit] or, rather, 'God is spirit' (RM). 'Spirit' is the name, in the NT., of the highest and most god-like faculties of the soul. Our Lord means, therefore, that God is the supreme understanding, knowledge, reason, will, love, holiness, etc., and hence must be worshipped with the corresponding faculties of the human soul, which is also 'spirit,' as made in His image.

25. Messias cometh] An excuse for delay. There is no need (says the woman) to trouble about a more spiritual worship until that distant day when the Messiah comes. **26.** The Samaritan idea of the Messiah was religious, not political, and hence Jesus could here proclaim Himself as the Messiah without causing a political ferment: contrast His action among the Jews (6 15 10 24, etc.).

Our Lord's teaching about worship in spirit and in truth (v. 24), though general in form, had special reference to the woman's needs. Her religion was an external one of forms and ceremonies, and this accounted for her evil life. If she could but be taught that religion is the attitude of the heart towards God, all would be changed.

27. With the woman] RV 'with a woman.' In His high estimate of womanhood Jesus rose far above the ideas of His time, and taught lessons which are only now being learned (see on Mt 1 18-25). The contemporary rabbis refused to teach religion to women, and would not even speak to a woman in a public place.

34. My meat, etc.] Jesus meant that in the joy of seeking to save a sinful soul His fatigue and hunger had vanished, and He no longer needed the food which the disciples had brought. **35. Four months**] Harvest began in April, so the date would be December, A.D. 27. The ministry in Jerusalem and Judæa (2 13-4 3) must accordingly have lasted eight months. **Lift up**] At this moment Jesus sees the Samaritans coming through the cornfields.

They are white already] The literal harvest is four months distant, but the spiritual harvest of the souls of these Samaritans is ripe, and will be reaped this very day.

36, 37. Christ had sowed alone in converting the Samaritan woman, but the Apostles would share in reaping the harvest of Samaritan converts (cp. Ac 8). And this was a type of the future conversion of the world. Christ would sow the seed, but the Apostles would reap the harvest. The **wages** are simply the unselfish joy of saving souls. **38. Other men**] In spite of the plural this means Christ Himself. **42. The Saviour of the world**] They accepted Him as the world's Saviour, because they had experienced His saving power in their own case. It is an instance of the argument from Christian experience: see 1 29 3 16, 17 6 33 12 47 1 Jn 4 14.

43-54. Beginning of the ministry proper in Galilee, December, 27 A.D. Healing of the nobleman's son.

44. Our Lord's **own country** here is probably Judæa, where He was born, and which the ancient prophecies indicated as His true home. Others suppose that it is Galilee, and that He deliberately went there to suffer dishonour and rejection. In Mt 13⁵⁷ our Lord applies the same proverb to Nazareth, where He was brought up.

46–54. This miracle cannot be the same as that recorded Mt 8⁵ Lk 7² ; the differences are too great. We have here a king's officer, there a centurion ; here a father and son, there a master and servant ; here a Jew (see v. 48), there a Gentile ; here a fever, there a palsy ; here weak faith which is blamed (v. 48), there strong faith which is commended ; here Jesus is asked to come, there He is begged not to come ; here He does not go, there apparently He does ; here the healing words are spoken at Cana, there at Capernaum.

46. Nobleman] The word means ' one of the king's officials.' The ' king ' is Herod Antipas, who was, strictly speaking, only a tetrarch, but was called king by courtesy.

48. Except ye see signs] Not too much must be made of this rebuke. Our Lord was trying his faith, as in the case of the Canaan-itish woman (Mk 7²⁷). It answered the test, and was rewarded by the healing of his son. For ' signs and wonders,' see on Mt 12³⁸ᶠ.

54. Translate, ' This again as a second sign did Jesus, after He had come out of Judæa into Galilee.' It thus clearly preceded all the Galilean miracles recorded by the synoptists.

The evangelist probably records this miracle to show that the effects of faith may extend beyond the person who exercises it ; perhaps also to show that our Lord's power to heal could be exercised at a distance.

CHAPTER 5

BETHESDA. CHRIST AND THE SABBATH

1–47. A miracle at the Pool of Bethesda on the Sabbath Day, and a controversy arising therefrom. This miracle may be regarded as a parable illustrating the deadly effects of sin, and the power of the Saviour to deal with the most hopeless cases. This poor man in his youth had shattered his nervous system by a life of sensual indulgence (v. 14), and had lain for thirty-eight years a hopeless paralytic (v. 5). This being an extreme case, the usual order of Christ's miracles is reversed. In-stead of being wrought as a reward of faith (see v. 13), the miracle is wrought to produce faith. The man was too much broken down in mind and body to believe, until some signal mercy had been vouchsafed to him. The mercy was vouchsafed, and repentance and faith followed (v. 14).

This visit to Jerusalem took place in March, 28 A.D., consequently the Galilean ministry mentioned 4⁵⁴ lasted three or four months. Among its most notable incidents were the appointment of the Twelve and the Sermon on the Mount. Desiring to visit Jerusalem without interrupting the Galilean work, our Lord sent the apostles on a preaching tour through the country (Mk 6⁷), and then went up to the capital, either alone, or more prob-ably accompanied by St. John, who acted as His host. Having stayed there about a week, He rejoined the Twelve in Galilee, shortly before the Passover, 28 A.D. (Mk 6³⁰: cp. Jn 6⁴).

1. A feast] i.e. the Feast of Purim, which occurs in March (Adar 14, 15), about a month before the Passover. Its origin is doubtful, though the Jews commemorated in it the triumph over Haman, who proposed to ex terminate the Jews in the Persian empire on a particular day (13th Adar, 473 B.C.), chosen by lot (*pur*, Esth 3⁷). The feast was mainly of a convivial and charitable character, but in the synagogues the book of Esther was read, and the congregation applauded the name of Mordecai, and cursed that of Haman. (An inferior but strongly supported reading here is ' the feast,' which would probably mean the Passover. Those who adopt it are compelled to add a whole year to Christ's ministry.)

2. Sheep *market*] RV ' sheep gate ' : cp. Neh 3¹ 12³⁹. **Bethesda**] i.e. ' house of mercy,' or, possibly, ' house of the stream,' is perhaps the Virgin's pool, SE. of the Temple, the only natural spring in Jerusalem. It is an intermittent spring, and when ' the troubling of the waters ' occurs, the Jews still bathe in it for medicinal purposes. Variant spellings are ' Bethzatha ' and ' Bethsaida.' **3, 4.** The best authorities omit the words waiting for . . whatsoever disease he had, which describe the troubling of the water by an angel. The troubling of the waters was a natural phe-nomenon, which popular superstition ascribed to supernatural agency. **8. Thy bed**] i.e. mat. **10.** The man's act was not unlawful, even from the OT. standpoint. Jer 17²¹ and Neh 13¹⁹ only forbid the bearing of burdens on the sabbath in connexion with labour and trade. **15. And told the Jews**] doubtless to win honour for Jesus as a prophet and worker of miracles.

17. RV ' My Father worketh even unto now, and I work.' (1) These words enunciate a new ideal of the sabbath. The ' rest ' of God after the creation, which the sabbath typifies, is not mere inertia, but activity in doing good. So man's true sabbath rest is not inactivity, but leisure for work of a higher character, e.g. the worship of God, and works of mercy. (2) The words also imply our Lord's Deity, for (a) He claims that God is His Father in a unique sense (' My Father,' not ' our Father '), and (b) He coördinates His own work with God's.

19–29. An important doctrinal section. Our Lord, while affirming His filial subordination to the Father (' the Son can do nothing of

Himself,' v. 19), and the derivation of His own Being from His (v. 26) ; yet declares that He exercises the Father's whole power and authority (v. 20) ;—the power to quicken those dead in sins (v. 25), the power to raise men from literal death at the Last Day (v. 28), and the power to judge the world (v. 22). He accordingly demands ' that all men should honour the Son, even as they honour the Father.'

20. Loveth the Son] Hence God is love (1 Jn 4⁸) from eternity. **Greater works**] something greater than miracles, the giving of new life to those dead in sins (see vv. 21, 24, 25).

21. This v. speaks both of spiritual and literal death. **24. Heareth**] and obeyeth.

25. The dead] i.e. the spiritually dead. They are raised from the death of trespasses and sins to a new life by the preaching of the gospel. **26.** The Father is the fountain of life even within the Godhead. From Him the Son is begotten, and the Spirit proceeds.

27. Because he is the Son of man] rather, ' because He is *man*,' lit. ' a son of man.' As man He can sympathise with the nature which he shares : cp. Heb 4¹⁵. **28.** The literal resurrection at the last day is meant.

29. Damnation] i.e. condemnation, lit. ' judgment.'

30–36. Our Lord mentions four ' witnesses' through which men may be brought to believe in Him : (1) the witness of the Baptist, good, but insufficient ; (2) the witness of the Father, which Christ's hearers are not willing to receive ; (3) the witness of Moses and the prophets, which they also reject ; and (4) the witness of Christ's own ' works,' the character of which is sufficient evidence that the Father has sent Him.

30. As I hear] viz. from the Father.

31. Christ's witness to Himself could not be received according to the principles of Jewish law : see 8¹³. and cp. Nu 35³⁰ Dt 17⁶.

32. Another] i.e. the Father, not the Baptist.

34. ' I attach little importance to John's testimony, for he, though a prophet, was but a man. Nevertheless, since *you* attach importance to it, I will use it, for I wish, in whatever way, to bring you to believe in Me, and so to be saved.' **35.** ' John is only a lamp or lantern, shining feebly by borrowed light ; I am the True Light which he feebly reflects.' **Ye were willing**] John's ministry was plainly past.

36. The works] include the miracles, but should not be confined to them. The gracious character, and redemptive purpose of Christ's acts, prove that they come from God.

37. The witness of the Father is given (1) in the OT. Scriptures, (2) in the response of all that is good in the heart of man to the teaching of Christ. The divine element in man, which the Father planted there, recog-

nises and welcomes the divine in Christ : cp. 3²¹. **38. His word**] is not here the Scripture, but the Divine Voice speaking through the conscience and spiritual nature of man.

39. Search] rather, ' Ye search ' (RV).

43. If another] ' A false Messiah, adapting his views to your carnal ideas, you will receive.' Our Lord's words were literally fulfilled a century later, when the bulk of the nation accepted the claims of the impostor Barcochba. **46. He wrote of me**] in type and figure as well as in direct prophecy.

CHAPTER 6
The Bread of Life

6 ¹–7 ¹. Feeding the five thousand. Walking upon the sea. Discourse upon the bread of life. Defection of many disciples. The Apostles stand firm.

Returning from Jerusalem, our Lord met the Apostles somewhere on the W. of the lake (perhaps at Capernaum), and heard their report of their mission (Lk 9¹⁰). He then spent about a fortnight preaching and healing the sick (6²), and afterwards, seeking retirement, sailed with them to a desert place on the NE. coast belonging to a city called Bethsaida (Mk 6³² Lk 9¹⁰ ; cp. Jn 6¹). The multitudes followed on foot, and Jesus took compassion on them and fed them (6²ᶠ.). The time was just before the Passover, 28 A.D. (6⁴), and immediately after the death of the Baptist (Mt 14¹³). For a full commentary on this miracle, which alone is recorded by all the evangelists (Mt 14¹⁵ Mk 6³⁵ Lk 9¹²), see on Mt 14¹⁵.

1. Tiberias] a Gentile city on the lake, built by Herod Antipas during our Lord's lifetime, and named after the emperor Tiberius. **3. A mountain**] RV ' the mountain.'

4. The passover] the second of the ministry. The nearness of the Passover accounts for the crowds seen approaching (v. 5). They were Galileans going up to Jerusalem to keep the Passover. Probably our Lord did not go up to Jerusalem for this feast, as there were plots against His life (7¹).

10. Make the men] RV ' the people.'

So the men] i.e. the males. **11. Given thanks**] The other Gospels say, ' blessed.' The usual benediction was, ' Blessed art Thou, Jehovah our God, King of the world, who causest bread to come forth from the earth.'

14, 15. This miracle marks a crisis in our Lord's ministry. His popularity was at its height. The people were convinced that He was the Messiah. They demanded that He should be crowned king of Israel, and should lead them against their enemies. By rejecting their overtures, and by showing, in His subsequent address at Capernaum, that His aims were of an entirely different character,

He forfeited His popularity, and never regained it (see 6 66).

Although this miracle had been recorded by the three synoptists, St. John (contrary to his usual practice) relates it again, because it forms a suitable introduction to the important discourse upon the bread of life which follows (vv. 26 f.), and which, in St. John's view, is an unfolding of its symbolical meaning. 'The miracle illustrates the mode of Christ's working in all ages ; both in temporal and in spiritual things, the spirit that proceeds from Him makes the greatest results possible to the smallest means ; that which appears, as to quantity, most trifling, multiplies itself, by His divine power, so as to supply the wants of thousands. The physical miracle is for us a type of the spiritual one which the power of His words works in the life of mankind in all time' (Neander).

16–21. The **miracle of walking on the sea** is recorded also by Mt (14 22) and Mk (6 45) : see on Mt. St. John records it, perhaps because of its close connexion with the miracle of feeding ; more probably because of the mystical signification which he discerns in it, for which see on Mt.

18, 19. The disciples were not to cross the lake, but to coast along it, and to take Jesus on board at an appointed place (see v. 17). A violent wind blew them out into the middle of the lake, so that Jesus was obliged to walk upon the water to reach them.

22–25. The multitudes which had been fed remained on the spot all night. In the morning they were surprised to find Jesus gone. They knew that He had not embarked with the disciples, who had taken away the only boat. How then had He departed ? Soon a fleet of boats arrived (perhaps to sell provisions), and they made use of these to cross the lake in search of Jesus.

26–59. Discourse on the Bread of Life. As in c. 4 Jesus is the giver of 'living water,' so here He is the 'living bread' or 'manna' of the soul. Such language had been to some extent prepared for by OT. references to the spiritual feast to which 'Wisdom' invites her children, 'Come eat ye of my bread, and drink of the wine which I have mingled' (Prov 9 5, etc.) ; and by the current view that the 'manna' of the OT. is to be spiritually interpreted (Philo identifies it with the 'Logos' or 'Word' of God ; St. Paul calls it 'spiritual meat,' 1 Cor 10 3 ; the Psalmist calls it 'angels' food,' Ps 78 25). There are also OT. references to the banquet of the Messiah (Isa 25 6, etc.), which are frequently echoed in the NT. (Mt 8 11 22 2 f. 25 10 26 29 Lk 14 15 Rev 19 9). But such passages do not lead up to, or explain our Lord's language about eating His flesh, and drinking His blood. The nearest parallel to this is the Passover. Our Lord's hearers were about to go up to Jerusalem to eat the Passover (6 4). Some of them, perhaps, had heard the Baptist call Him ' the Lamb of God that taketh away the sin of the world' (1 29, 36). Our Lord, accordingly, set before them His Person as the sacred reality of which the Passover lamb was a type. As the blood of the Paschal lamb had protected the Israelites of old from the sword of the destroying angel, so the death of the Lamb of God would give spiritual life to the whole world (v. 51). As in the Paschal meal the Israelites ate the flesh of a literal lamb, so in the feast which He came to prepare, they would spiritually eat the flesh and drink the blood of the True Lamb. By the 'flesh' of Christ is to be understood His human nature (see 1 14), and by His blood, His atoning blood, shed for the sins of the world. There is reference, therefore, both to the Incarnation, and to the Atonement. The eating and drinking of Christ's flesh and blood is spiritual (6 63), and can only take place through the medium of faith (vv. 35, 40, 47). It is not, however, identical with faith, but rather is the reward of faith. Those who have lively faith in Christ as the Son of God and the Redeemer of the world, are so incorporated with Him, that they dwell in Him and He in them (v. 56) ; He is in them a principle of spiritual life (v. 57), and of resurrection (v. 54) ; and He strengthens and refreshes their souls, so that they neither hunger nor thirst (vv. 35, 55), until they attain everlasting life (vv. 50, 51, 54, 58). This vital union between Christ and the believer is elsewhere illustrated by the parable of the True Vine (15 1 f.), and by St. Paul's metaphor of the body and the members (1 Cor 12 12 f.).

This discourse is regarded by nearly all commentators as intended to prepare the way for the institution of the Lord's Supper, by explaining the fundamental idea and principle of that holy rite, viz. the union of the believer with Christ's human nature through faith. The Supper was ordained (see on Mt 26 26-30) as the ordinary and covenanted means of feeding upon Christ—of 'eating his flesh and drinking his blood,' i.e. of appropriating spiritually and by faith His glorified humanity and sharing in the benefits of His passion. This, the original apostolic doctrine, which guarded both the reality of the reception by the believing soul of Christ's true humanity, and also the absolute need of a lively faith if this blessed result was to be achieved, was endangered in St. John's time by two opposite tendencies, that of Gnosticism, which, while confessing Christ's Godhead, denied His Incarnation and Atonement, and that of a false ecclesiasticism, which, while confessing both, imagined that union with the Incarnate Redeemer could be attained mechanically through the sacraments, without a living faith. As against the former the evangelist emphasises the reality of Christ's 'flesh,' or human nature, and of His ' blood ' or atoning sacrifice ; and as against the latter the need of a living faith, as the only means through which Christ's flesh and blood can be savingly appropriated, and become the food of the soul. The ' flesh ' of Christ, which is received by faith, is, of course, His glorified humanity, as it now is at the right hand of God, and as it is communicated to believers through the Spirit (vv. 62, 63). At the institution of the Supper, however, our Lord spoke not of His 'flesh,' but of His ' body,' and for this there was a reason. Both words denote Christ's human nature, but whereas to eat Christ's 'flesh' indicates only the union of the individual believer with his Saviour, to eat Christ's ' body ' indicates also his union with other believers, a fundamental idea of the sacrament of love, which was intended to be the centre of Christian unity (1 Cor 10 16, 17).

27. 'Do not earnestly strive to obtain food and raiment and luxuries for your bodies, but spiritual food for your souls. I am indeed the Messiah, but the Messiah's work is not to give temporal prosperity as you imagine, but everlasting life.' **Sealed**] ' By this miracle God the Father has " sealed " (i.e. publicly proclaimed) Me, not as the giver of temporal prosperity, as you carnally suppose, but as the giver of immortality.' **28. The works of God**] i.e. works well-pleasing to God. **29.** For the plural ' works,' i.e. a multitude of supposed meritorious acts, Jesus substitutes one single work, faith in Himself. Faith in Jesus is called a ' work,' because it is a definite act of the will. It is the one work required, because it is the solemn dedication of the whole life to God, and virtually includes in itself all other works, and renders them acceptable.

30, 31. Jesus having practically (in v. 29) claimed to be the Messiah, the people now require Him to repeat Moses' miracle of the manna. This was regarded as the greatest of the OT. miracles, and it was expected that the Messiah would repeat it.

32. Moses' manna, though it came from heaven, was not heavenly bread, and could not sustain spiritual life. **33. He which cometh**] RV ' that which cometh.' **35.** What bread and water are to the body, that Christ is to the soul. Every aspiration after God and holiness He is able to satisfy. **36.** The idea is contained in v. 26, but perhaps Christ is referring to some unrecorded words. **37.** Those whom the Father ' gives ' to Christ, are those who actually come. The Father desires the salvation of every man, and draws all men to

Christ (3 16 12 32), but some refuse to come (5 40). The Father foresees what men will come, and, as a result of His foreknowledge, ' gives ' them to Christ.

39. Raise it up] Jesus shows that He has come to abolish not natural, but spiritual death. Believers will die, but their death will be followed by a glorious resurrection. Here, as usually in the NT., ' resurrection ' means the resurrection of the righteous, not also of the wicked. **42.** The Jews argue that since Jesus has a human parentage, He cannot have existed before His birth, and so have come down from heaven. **Joseph**] see 1 45.

44. ' Your murmuring and unbelief are caused by your resistance to the " drawing " of the Father, who bids you believe on Me. You have hardened your heart, and closed your ears to His teaching, so that now you cannot believe.' **45.** A free quotation from Isa 54 13 : cp. also Joel 2 28 f. **46.** Only our Lord is ' taught of God ' in the fullest sense. **48.** ' I am the reality typified by the manna.'

51. Which I will give] an allusion to our Lord's atoning death, as is made evident by the mention of His blood in v. 53. **The world**] Salvation is offered to all mankind. **53.** Eating and drinking Christ's flesh and blood is not the same thing as faith, though faith is the means of it. It is an actual and vital union with Christ's human nature, whereby the believer dwells in Christ and Christ in him, and all the benefits of Christ's passion are communicated to him : see above. **55. Meat indeed**] lit. ' true meat . . true drink,' i.e. true nourishment for the soul. **57.** The life-imparting union between the Father and the Son, is a figure of the life-imparting union between Christ and the believer.

59. If Tell Hum is the ancient Capernaum, its synagogue has been excavated. We can still trace its dimensions, observe its fallen pillars, and discover over the lintel of its entrance the device of a pot of manna ornamented with vine-leaves and bunches of grapes.

62. ' After My Ascension, when I shall no longer possess a natural body, you will understand that My words about eating My flesh and drinking My blood, which now offend you, are to be spiritually interpreted.' **63.** ' What imparts the power of everlasting life to those who feed upon My flesh, is not the flesh as such, but the Spirit which pervades it. The flesh without the Spirit profits nothing : the flesh with the Spirit profits much. In heaven I shall be a quickening Spirit, and My body will be spiritual. After the Ascension the Holy Spirit will make you partakers of My flesh, and you will receive it spiritually by faith.' **The words that I speak** (RV ' have spoken ')] ' These words of Mine about eating and drinking My flesh and blood, about My

Ascension, and about the gift of the Spirit, contain the very essence of the gospel. Those who believe them and obey them, will be made partakers of My Spirit, and of eternal life.'

65. See vv. 44, 45.

66–71. Effects of the discourse. Many disciples forsake Jesus, but the Twelve stand firm, and their faith is strengthened.

69. That.. Christ, the Son of the living God] RV 'the Holy One of God,' which emphasises Christ's sinlessness. Not till later does St. Peter confess that He is the Son of the living God (Mt 16 16). **71. Judas]** RV 'Judas, the son of Simon Iscariot.' 'Iscariot' means an inhabitant of Kerioth, a town in Judæa. Judas was thus the only Judæan apostle.

CHAPTER 7
THE FEAST OF TABERNACLES

7 1–10 21. Jesus at the Feast of Tabernacles, October, 28 A.D.

After the discourse of c. 6, delivered just before Passover 28 A.D., Jesus did not go up to Jerusalem (7 1), but devoted Himself for five or six months to active work in various parts of Galilee, of which St. John says nothing. At the close of this period He visited the country of Tyre and Sidon (Mk 7 24), made a tour through Decapolis, where He fed the 4,000 (Mk 8 1), retired to Cæsarea Philippi, where St. Peter made his great confession (Mk 8 27 f.), and subsequently, at a place not specified, was transfigured. To this period belong the gradual falling away of the people, the widening of the breach with the Pharisees, the deepening of the faith of the apostles, who are led to acknowledge Him as the Son of God, and the prophecies of Death and Resurrection which followed the Transfiguration. When, in October, Jesus went up to Jerusalem to keep the Feast of Tabernacles, His Galilean ministry was over, and He knew that His death was impending.

The account of our Lord's teaching at the Feast of Tabernacles is remarkably vivid, and bears all the marks of historic accuracy (see especially the graphic details in 7 11-15, 25-27, 31,32, 40-52, and in c. 9). He sets His claims before the inhabitants of Jerusalem with great urgency, knowing that His time on earth is short. His hearers will die in their sins unless they believe that He is the Messiah (8 24). He is more than the Messiah ; He is the Son of God, self-existent and eternal (8 58), the Living Water (7 37), the Light of the world (8 12 9 5), the Good Shepherd who lays down His life for His sheep (10 14,15), and the giver of true freedom (8 36). He works only one miracle, but it is an important one, enforcing His claim to be the Light of the world (c. 9).

1. To kill] see 5 18.

2. Feast of tabernacles] or, 'feast of ingathering,' or, 'of harvest,' held in October, marked the completion of the harvest of fruit, oil, and wine. For eight days the people lived in booths, in memory of the wanderings in the wilderness. Numerous sacrifices were offered. Among the notable ceremonies were the procession to Siloam to fetch water, and its pouring out at the altar (cp. 7 37), the singing of the Hallel (Pss 113–118), the daily processions round the altar, and the lighting of the four great golden candlesticks in the Court of the Women (cp. 8 12).

3. Thy disciples] Only a few disciples followed Jesus in His Galilean tours. At the great Feast of Tabernacles they would be gathered together in great numbers. **5.** The unbelief of the brethren was removed after the resurrection by the appearance to James (1 Cor 15 7 Ac 1 14). Being unbelievers, they were evidently not of the number of the Twelve. For an account of them see on Mt 12 50. **6. My time]** as indicated by God's will. **Your time]** They, having no special commission from God, were bound by no such considerations as He. Moreover, they were in no danger : the world looked upon them as its own. **8. I go not up yet]** Many ancient authorities omit 'yet,' but in any case it is to be understood.

14. Finding that He had a strong party on His side, Jesus came forth from His retirement and taught. **15. Letters]** i.e. rabbinical learning. **Having never learned]** i.e. having never been the pupil of a recognised rabbi or scribe, as Paul was of Gamaliel. **16, 17.** 'My teaching, like that of the prophets of old, is a direct inspiration from God, and not, like that of the scribes, a tradition of men. It appeals to the heart, not to the head. Not the learned, but those who apply themselves earnestly to do God's will, will perceive that it comes from God. **19.** You are not keeping the Law. Moses commanded you not to shed innocent blood, and yet you seek to slay Me, an innocent man.' **20.** His opponents hypocritically try to make Him think them innocent.

21 f. I did one work (eight months ago when I healed the impotent man at the pool of Bethesda), **and ye are still marvelling** (because I did it on the sabbath day). 'Moses would not have marvelled. Moses recognised that works of piety and charity may be done on the sabbath day. In fact, he commanded circumcision to be performed on the sabbath day as on other days, and you obey his command. How, then, can you object to My miracle of healing ? To heal a man is as much a work of piety and charity as to circumcise him.' **22. Not because]** RV 'not that.'

27. Jewish ideas as to the Messiah were not

very consistent. One view was that His birth-place and lineage would be notorious (cp. Mt 2); others held that His manifestation would be shrouded in mystery.

33, 34. A call to decision, and a reproach for rejecting their deliverer. **34.** Hereafter, when misfortunes come upon you, you shall seek My help, and shall not find it. **35. The dispersed** (RV 'the Dispersion') **among the Gentiles** (RV 'the Greeks')] i.e. the Jews living in heathen lands. The Jews, not seriously but mockingly, attribute to our Lord the design which St. Paul afterwards carried out, of abandoning the Holy Land, and making the Jewish synagogues through-out the Empire centres for diffusing the gospel among proselytes and other Gentiles.

37. The last day] The feast proper closed on the seventh day, but the eighth day, which is probably here meant, was kept as a sabbath with a holy convocation to commemorate the entrance into Canaan (Lv 23 36). **If any man thirst**] Here, as to the woman of Samaria, Christ declares Himself the giver of 'the living water.' This declaration is connected with the ritual of the feast. On every day of the feast except the last, a golden pitcher of water was fetched (in literal fulfilment of Isa 12 3) from the pool of Siloam by a priest, and poured together with wine on the W. side of the altar at the time of the morning sacri-fice, amid the singing of psalms and hymns. This water was held to symbolise the mira-culous water which supplied the Israelites in the wilderness, and also the outpouring of the Spirit promised in the days of the Messiah. On the eighth day, when the water was not poured out, Jesus came forward declaring Himself the giver of the true water which that water typified, viz. the Holy Spirit.

38. The scripture] Our Lord combines the sense of several OT. passages, e.g. Isa 44 3 58 11 Ezk 47 1. **Belly**] here, by a Hebraism, for a man's inmost soul : cp. the use of *beten* ('belly') in Prov 18 8 20 27,30 22 18 26 22 Job 15 2,35 32 18,19. Christ compares Himself with the Temple. As the fountain of Siloam poured forth its waters from the Temple mountain, so a stream of heavenly life issues from the Redeemer, and from all who have become like Him. We have here a striking expres-sion of the power of Christian influence.

39. The Holy Ghost was not yet *given*] Under Christianity, the Holy Spirit, though personally distinct from Christ, is still the Spirit of Jesus, i.e. the Spirit of the Saviour. He could not, however, become this until the saving work of Christ was complete, until Christ had died for our sins upon the cross, risen again for our justification, and ascended into heaven to plead the merits of His sacrifice with the eternal Father. Hence the Com-forter could not be given *as* the Comforter, until Jesus had been glorified : cp. 16 7f.

40. The Prophet] i.e. the prophet of Dt 18 15, regarded not as the Messiah, but as a fore-runner of the Messiah. **42. Bethlehem**] St. John was not ignorant of the birthplace of Jesus. He is here only reporting the words of others.

49. Cursed] RV 'accursed,' viz. because of their ignorance. The contempt of the Phari-sees for those who have not received a rabbinical training is a touch true to life.

50, 51. Nicodemus has made some advance in boldness. He ventures, though timidly, to plead for justice for our Lord. He was certainly right on the point of law : see Ex 23 1 Dt 1 16 19 15. **52.** The Pharisees were wrong not only in their law, but in their facts, for Jonah at least was a Galilean. In any case the saying would not apply to our Lord, who was a Judæan. The narrative, interrupted by the interpolation 7 53–8 11, is resumed 8 12.

CHAPTER 8

The Feast of Tabernacles continued.
Christ the Light of the World

7 53–8 11. The woman taken in adultery. All modern critics agree that this section is no original part of the Fourth Gospel. It is not in the author's style ; it breaks the sequence of our Lord's discourses, and is omitted by most of the ancient authorities. Probably it is an authentic apostolic tradition inserted here to illustrate the principle of 8 15. Some MSS place it at the end of the Gospel. The incident probably took place in Holy Week, and is therefore appropriately inserted by some MSS after Lk 21 38.

3. In adultery] The woman was only betrothed, not married, otherwise her punish-ment would have been stoning, but strangulation, for so the rabbis interpreted Lv 20 10 Dt 22 22. But inasmuch as among the Jews betrothal was almost equivalent to marriage (see on Mt 1 18), the sin of a betrothed woman was regarded as a species of adultery.

6. Punishment of death for this offence was obsolescent, and some think that they wished to make Jesus unpopular with the people by inducing Him to advocate its revival. More probably they wished to embroil Him with the Roman authorities, who would not allow a death-sentence to be executed without their permission. The displeasure of Jesus was largely due to the officiousness of the accusers. It was not their business to accuse and judge the woman, but that of the husband and the judges. They had neither a legal nor a moral right to interfere. **Wrote**] Christ was always reluctant to interfere in civil disputes : see Mt 22 21 Lk 12 13-15 Jn 18 36. Writing on the ground was a symbolical action well known in antiquity, signifying unwillingness to deal with the matter in hand.

7. Without sin] Christ read their hearts, and under His searching glance all felt themselves sinners, if not against the letter, yet against the spirit of the seventh commandment : cp. Mt 5 28. They could not condemn her without condemning themselves. **A stone**] The principal witnesses cast the first stone (Dt 17 7 Ac 7 58). **9. In the midst**] viz. of the disciples who alone were left. Augustine says strikingly, 'the *misera* before the *Misericordia.*' **11. Neither do I condemn thee**] i.e. to judicial punishment, such as your accusers demand. Our Lord's gentle dealing with the woman was due to His desire not to break the bruised reed. She had already suffered much, and (we may suppose) was bowed down under the burden of sin. He perceived that in her case a warning to sin no more would suffice : cp. Lk 7 36-50.

8 12–10 21. The narrative of the Feast of Tabernacles (interrupted by the interpolated section 7 52–8 11) **is resumed.** The scene is the Temple (8 20), the time the last day of the feast (7 37).

12. The light of the world] The idea of the Messiah as 'the Light' was familiar to the Jews (see Lk 1 78, 79 2 32), and was especially appropriate at the Feast of Tabernacles, during which (or perhaps on the first day only) the two colossal golden candlesticks in the Court of the Women were lighted. Christ as 'the Light of the world' dissipates the darkness of ignorance and sin. **The light of life**] i.e. My guidance which leads to life eternal. **13.** See on v. 17. **14.** 'The law as to witnesses applies only to human witnesses. It does not apply to Me, who am more than man, seeing that I know that I came down from heaven, and shall return thither.' **15.** 'You judge only by outward appearance, and hence cannot discern the Divine in Me.' **17.** Cp. Dt 17 6 19 15.

17, 18. If the testimony of two men is true, how much more true is the testimony of two witnesses who are divine ! **18.** See on 5 36, 37. **20. In the treasury**] or, rather, 'by the treasury.' The 'treasury' consisted of thirteen brazen trumpet-shaped chests, in which were placed the Temple tribute and the people's voluntary offerings. They stood in the Court of the Women.

21–30. Another discourse of Jesus, delivered probably on the same day (some think a few days later). Jesus speaks of His return to the Father, which is misunderstood by the Jews and explained by Him. He also seeks to convince them of sin, and to show them their need of a Saviour.

21. I go my way (by death), **and ye shall seek me** (vainly in your misfortunes as your

deliverer), **and shall die in your sins** (RV 'sin') (because you refuse to believe on Me as your Saviour) : cp. 7 34. **22. Will he kill himself ?**] and thereby enter Gehenna, the punishment awarded to suicide? (Jos. 'Wars,' iii. 8, 5). In that case we shall certainly not care to follow Him ! The mockery is more bitter than in 7 35, q.v. **23.** Their earthly hearts are without the higher wisdom and divine life of those who are born of God. **24. I am he**] viz. the Messiah, and the Saviour. He alone can say, ' Thy sins be forgiven thee.'

25. Even *the same*] viz. the Messiah. This rendering alone suits the context. Another translation is, 'Why do I even speak to you at all ?' **26.** 'I have much fault to find with you, but I refrain. I am not sent to judge you, but to teach you ; and I teach you the absolute truth about God, which I learnt from Him before I came into the world.' **28. When ye have lifted up the Son of man** (upon the cross), **then shall ye know that I am he**] (i.e. the Messiah), because My death will be followed by My Resurrection, which will be a token from God that My words are true.

31–59. V. 31 begins another speech, delivered on the same day to those Jews who were inclined to regard Him as the Messiah. When these half-believers find that Jesus demands an entire change of heart, a breach with orthodox Judaism, and faith in Himself as the eternal Son of God, their feeling towards Him is changed to violent hatred.

31. Believed on him] RV 'believed him.' They had believed His statement (vv. 24–26) that He was the Messiah, but they had not believed 'on' Him with religious faith as the Light and Life of men. **31, 32.** Christ's words exasperated these Pharisaic believers, because He implied (1) that they would have to amend their lives in order to abide in His word, whereas they considered their conduct perfect ; (2) that they were ignorant of saving truth, whereas they regarded themselves in complete possession of it ; (3) that they were not spiritually free, because superstitiously attached to the letter of the imperfect Mosaic Law. **33.** They pretend to think that Jesus is alluding to their political bondage to the Romans. They indignantly deny the imputation of bondage. They declare themselves the superiors of their oppressors. **35.** A slave, unlike a son, formed no part of the family. He could be sold or expelled at will. So these Jews, slaves of sin and of the letter of the Law, were no true members of the Messiah's kingdom, and would be expelled from it. **The Son**] RV 'the son.'

37. Their desire to kill Christ, the promised seed of Abraham, proved that they were not children of Abraham, but of Satan. **Hath no place**] RV ' hath not free

course.' They had received Christ's word
for a moment, and then contemptuously rejected it. 41. Fornication] i.e. impure or
superstitious worship, as often in the OT.
The Jews claim to be the true spiritual, as
well as the natural, descendants of Abraham.
Inheriting his covenant and faith, they have
' one Father, even God.' 43. They misunderstood his expressions (speech), because the
subject-matter of His discourse (word) was
altogether above them. He was speaking of
spiritual things which are spiritually discerned. 44. He was a murderer from the
beginning] viz. of the human race, when he
sought to destroy our first parents, and abode
(RV ' stood ') not in the truth, i.e. in that
state of innocence in which he was created.
This is the only certain allusion in the Gospels to the fall of Satan (Lk 10 18 is doubtful).

46. Christ argues from His sinlessness to
His veracity. Since His enemies can find no
fault with His life, they ought to believe His
words. Christ's sinlessness is affirmed not
only by Himself, but by His most intimate
disciples : cp. 6 61 1 Pet 2 22 1 Jn 3 5. 48. To
Jesus' declaration that His hearers are ' not
of God,' i.e. not true Israelites, they retort
that He Himself is ' a Samaritan,' i.e. a heretic.

Hast a devil] They cannot deny Christ's miracles or the power of Christ's words, so they
ascribe them to diabolical agency : cp. Mt 12 24.

49. Christ's works cannot proceed from the
devil, because they are designed to honour,
not Satan, nor Himself, but God.

50. And (RV ' but ') I seek not mine own
glory : there is one (i.e. God) that seeketh it
for Me, and judgeth those who withhold it
from Me, and so dishonour Me.

51. By dishonouring Jesus the Jews have
incurred the judgment of the Father (v. 50),
i.e. the penalty of eternal death. But this judgment is not irrevocable. If even now they
will obey Christ's word, they may escape
eternal death. 52. The Jews understand our
Lord to speak of natural death, and so to
claim to be immortal, and the giver of immortality. Such a claim, implying superiority
to all the prophets of the OT., seems to them
the effect of frenzy or diabolical possession.

53, 54. ' The Son ' (says Westcott) ' makes
Himself to be nothing. He is and declares
Himself to be that which the Father, so to
speak, makes Him.' 56. ' I am greater than
your Father Abraham, for Abraham looked
forward with exultation to the manifestation
of one greater than himself, one in whom all
the nations of the earth should be blessed.'

He saw it] either in prophetic vision, or, as
some think, from Paradise. 57. The Jews
understand, or pretend to understand, our
Lord to mean that He was alive in the time
of Abraham ! 58. Before Abraham, etc.] lit.

' Before Abraham was born, 1 AM.' Christ
seems here to declare Himself to be the
Jehovah, or I AM of the OT., the eternal,
self-existent Creator : cp. Ex 3 14. 59. Going
through the midst of them, and so passed by]
RV omits these words.

CHAPTER 9
THE MAN BORN BLIND

1-12. The healing of the man born blind.
This miracle occurred on the same day as the
events of the last c., i.e. probably on the last
day of the Feast of Tabernacles. It is intended
to illustrate the truth that Christ is ' the Light
of the world' (8 12 9 5). Christ proves His
power to open the eyes of the soul by opening
the eyes of the body. The miracle, being
wrought on the sabbath day, intensified the
hostility of the rulers, which had already been
violently inflamed by the discourses of c. 8 :
see 8 59.

2. The disciples thought that possibly the
man had sinned, either in a previous state of
existence (in accordance with the doctrine of
the transmigration of souls), or more probably
as an infant before birth. To the Jews who
attributed intelligence to unborn children
(Gn 25 22-26 Lk 1 41) this last was a natural idea.

3. As in Lk 13 1-5, Jesus rebukes the hasty
inference, common among the Jews (see e.g.
Job 4 7), that misfortunes are always the direct result of sin. As a matter of fact diseases
often come as part of the present order of
nature, and not as special judgments : cp.
Lk 13 4. A great moral difficulty is involved
in such a state of things, but Jesus does not
discuss it.

4. Jesus saw that His death was impending,
and that His time for doing works of mercy
was short. 6. In two other miracles (Mk 7 33
and 8 23) Jesus heals by a gradual process, and
uses visible means. In this case the application of saliva and clay to the man's eyes
was an aid to faith (saliva being a recognised
remedy for eye-diseases), and his being sent
to bathe in the water was a test of faith
as it was in the case of Naaman (2 K 5 10).

7. Siloam] The evangelist regards this
pool of healing water as a type of Christ,
who is ' sent ' by the Father to heal the diseases of the soul. The OT. forms of the word
are Shiloah, Isa 8 6, and Shelah, Neh 3 15. It is
now called Birket Silwán. It is fed by an
underground conduit from the Virgin's Fountain. 8. Blind] RV ' a beggar.'

13-34. This whole section illustrates the
incredible blindness of the Pharisees (vv. 40,
41), who can see nothing in this unique sign,
except the technical breach of the sabbath, of
which they suppose Jesus to have been guilty.

14. The conduct of Jesus was illegal in two
ways : (1) It was forbidden to render medical

aid on the sabbath, unless there was imminent danger of death ; (2) there was a special provision against applying saliva to the eyes on the sabbath day. **17. He is a prophet**] This view, if accepted, would remove the difficulty about the sabbath day, for it was generally supposed that prophets had authority over the sabbath law. **22. Put out of the synagogue**] i.e. excommunicated. **24. Give God the praise**] RV ' Give glory to God,' a Hebrew idiom for ' Confess your error,' Josh 7 19 1 S 6 5 1 Esdr 9 8.

34. Born in sins] This gives the clue to v. 2. The Pharisees assume that the man had been born blind as a punishment for exceptional wickedness, which began even before birth.

Cast him out] i.e. excommunicated him.

35. When the door of the synagogue was shut, the door of the Kingdom of Heaven was opened. **The Son of God**] Christ so seldom uses this title of Himself, that it has been corrected in many copies into the more usual ' the Son of man.' Whichever title was used, the man rightly understood Jesus to claim superhuman dignity, and accordingly worshipped Him (v. 38).

39. For judgment I am come] This does not contradict 3 17, for the ' judgment' meant here is not the judicial act of rewarding and punishing, which Christ will exercise at the Last Day, but the present separation of mankind into two opposite camps, which is the inevitable result of His manifestation in the flesh. **That they which see not** (but are conscious of their ignorance) **might see : and that they which see** (or, rather, think they see) **might be made blind :** cp. Mt 13 11-17. **40. Are we blind also ?**] Christ's Pharisaic disciples rightly perceive that His words are directed against them. **41.** If the Pharisees were simply ignorant, but confessed their ignorance and were willing to learn, they would not be guilty. What makes them so guilty is that, though ignorant, they esteem themselves wise, and refuse to learn the way of life. They are still seeking the righteousness of the Law, rather than the righteousness of God.

CHAPTER 10

The Good Shepherd. The Feast of the Dedication

1-18. Allegories of the Fold and of the Good Shepherd. This c. continues Christ's discourse to His Pharisaic disciples begun at 9 39. His words take the form of an allegory which is intended partly to rebuke the Pharisees, partly to comfort the blind man, and partly to instruct the Church as to the duties of Christian pastors. The blind man, unjustly expelled from the fold of Judaism by false shepherds (the Pharisees), finds refuge in the flock of the True Shepherd, i.e. in the Christian Church, the mild discipline of which is con-

trasted with the cruel severity of the synagogue. The allegory is based entirely on OT. figures : see Ps 23 Ezk 34 Jer 23 1-4 Zech 11 4-17.

1. The thieves and robbers mentioned here are primarily the Pharisees who have unjustly excommunicated the blind man, and secondarily and prophetically false pastors in the Christian Church. Christ is the rightful owner of the flock, and those who would exercise the office of shepherd must ' enter by the door,' i.e. receive their authority from Him, and exercise it in His spirit. This the Pharisees have not done. **2.** To understand the imagery, it must be remembered that Eastern folds are large open enclosures into which several flocks are driven at the approach of night. There is only one door, which a single shepherd guards, while the others go home to rest. In the morning the shepherds return, are recognised by the doorkeeper, call their flocks round them, and lead them forth to pasture. **3. By name**] A beautiful picture of pastoral converse. The true pastor knows every member of his congregation individually.

4. Goeth before them] The false pastor, loving popularity, follows his flock. The true pastor leads them. He leads them, (1) by his teaching. He gives his people not what they want, but what they ought to want ; (2) by his good example, his holy life being an ensample to the flock (1 Pet 5 3).

7. I am the door of the sheep] i.e. ' I alone can endue pastors and teachers with spiritual authority over the flock of God.' In v. 9 Christ calls Himself ' the door ' in a wider sense. **8.** ' All who have taught Israel from the cessation of prophecy to My own coming have been false and unauthorised teachers.' Our Lord is alluding, of course, not to the OT. prophets, but to the scribes who had dominated the religious life of Israel for 400 years, but whose teaching had nevertheless been rejected by many spiritually-minded men, e.g. by the author of the book of Jonah, who earnestly protested against it, and by many of the later Psalmists, whose writings breathe a spirit the very opposite of that of the scribes and Pharisees. **9. I am the door**] ' Through faith in Me both shepherds and sheep enter into the Kingdom of God, and find all their spiritual needs supplied.' **Pasture**] i.e. the means of grace.

11. The good shepherd] The Gk. signifies the Perfect or Ideal Shepherd. This beautiful figure is often found in the OT. applied to Jehovah (Pss 23, 80 Isa 40 11) ; only in Ezekiel does it become a title of the Messiah (Ezk 34 23 37 24). **Giveth** (RV ' layeth down ') **his life for the sheep**] Another distinct prophecy of His death. Eastern shepherds are always armed, and are sometimes killed in defending their flocks against the wolves, leopards, and panthers, which infest the wilderness (Gn 31 39 1 S 17 34). The expression 'layeth down his life' is peculiar to St. John (see 13 37). **12. Seeth the wolf coming .. and fleeth**] The wolf (Satan) may come in various ways, as an open persecution, as a popular heresy, as a tendency to lax morality. The hireling shepherd is the cowardly compromiser who gives way to, instead of resisting, the evil tendencies of his age. **14, 15.** RV 'I know mine own, and mine own know me, even as the Father knoweth me, and I know the Father.' **16.** The Gentiles also are God's children. The gospel is for them also, and Jew and Gentile shall form one Church under one shepherd (Christ).

One fold] RV 'one flock.'

17. As usual in this Gospel, the death and resurrection of Christ are united in one idea.

18. Christ's death is the result, neither of a compulsory decree of the Father, nor of the power of the Evil One, but of a voluntary impulse springing from Christ's love for lost mankind.

22–39. Jesus at the Feast of the Dedication. As there is no statement that Jesus went up to Jerusalem, it is fair to infer that Jesus spent the two months between the Feast of Tabernacles and that of the Dedication in or near Jerusalem. Less probable is the view that these months were spent in Galilee, Samaria, and Peræa, and that the mission of the Seventy, and many other incidents recorded in Lk 9 51–19 27, belong to this period. **22.** The Feast of the Dedication (lit. 'the Renewal') was instituted by Judas Maccabæus, 164 B.C., to commemorate the purification of the Temple, which had been profaned by the idolatrous king Antiochus Epiphanes. It was held on the 25th of Kislev (about the middle of December), and on account of the brilliant illuminations was also called 'the Lights.'

23. Porch] i.e. portico, or, cloister. This portico was on the E. side of the Temple buildings, and, according to Josephus, was a portion of Solomon's Temple, which had been left standing by Nebuchadnezzar.

25. I told you] viz. in those discourses in which I claimed to be the Son of God (5 17-47 7 14-39 8 12-59), and the Good Shepherd (10 1-18). These were Messianic titles. **26. As I said unto you**] see 10 1 f. **28.** No power of the world or of Satan can pluck believers out of Christ's hand ; only their own unfaithfulness to grace received can do this. **29.** The Father is superior to all hostile powers, and therefore believers can never be lost through the power of the enemy. There is another reading, 'That which the Father hath given unto me is greater than all' (so RM). This means that believers, through grace, are superior to all their enemies, and can never be lost except

through their own fault. **30. I and** *my* **Father** (RV 'the Father') **are one**] lit. 'one thing,' i.e. one essence or substance. The Greek indicates that the Father and the Son are two Persons but one God.

31. Again] see 8 59.

34–36. If the fallible and sinful judges of Israel were rightly called 'gods,' much more may I, who am one with the Father and free from sin, claim the title of 'the Son of God.'

34. Your law] i.e. the OT., which you acknowledge. 'The Law' not infrequently stands for the whole OT. : see 12 34 15 25 1 Cor 14 21. The quotation here is from Ps 32 6. **Gods**] Judges, as God's representatives, are several times called 'gods' in the OT. (Ex 21 6 22 7, 8, 28 ; cp. also 1 S 28 13). **35.** The word of God 'came' to the judges when He appointed them to their office. **36. Sanctified**] consecrated to the office of Messiah and Redeemer of the world. **38. The Father** *is* **in me**] A commentary upon v. 30. Human personality differs from divine personality. Human persons exclude one another. The Divine Persons mutually contain, pervade, and include one another. They are absolutely one in knowledge, sympathy, will, and act.

40–42. The Peræan ministry. These vv. cover a period of about three months, which is generally spoken of as the Peræan ministry (see Mt 19 1 Mk 10 1, and cp. Lk 9 51). Its chief incidents were the mission of the Seventy (Lk 10 1), the question of divorce (Mt 19 3), the blessing of little children (Mk 10 13), the question of the rich young ruler (Mk 10 17), and Christ's message to Herod Antipas (Lk 13 31). The whole section, Lk 9 51–18 34, appears to belong to this period, but many of the incidents are not chronologically arranged.

40. The place was Bethany beyond Jordan, 1 28. **41.** The remark that John did no miracle shows that there was little inclination at this period to invest popular teachers with miraculous powers. **42.** Although John was dead, his influence was still strong in this district, and the people were ready to believe that He to whom John had borne witness was the true Messiah.

CHAPTER 11

CHRIST THE RESURRECTION AND THE LIFE

1–44. The raising of Lazarus. The last and greatest of the seven 'signs' recorded in this Gospel is related with such photographic minuteness of detail, that it is clear that the evangelist was present. Three points about it are specially noteworthy : (1) that it was a physical miracle, which no ingenuity can reduce to a case of faith-healing ; (2) that it was definitely worked to produce faith in Christ (v. 42) ; (3) that more than any other miracle it was performed under test conditions ;—the object of it was really dead (v. 39), and hostile witnesses were present (v. 42). Its spiritual meaning is given in v. 25, 'I am the resurrection, and the life.' The raising of Lazarus to corporeal life is to the evangelist a token and pledge that the worker of it can raise the dead soul to spiritual life, and endue it with a blessed immortality. The publicity and notoriety of this miracle explain the warm welcome which Jesus received from the inhabitants of Jerusalem at His triumphal entry on Palm Sunday. The synoptists mention the welcome (Mt 21 8-11 ||), but say nothing of its cause. Various reasons are alleged for the omission of this miracle by the synoptists. Some say that when they wrote, Lazarus and his family were still alive, and did not desire to be made the objects of public curiosity. More probably it was omitted as belonging to the Judæan ministry, which (for whatever reason) the synoptists did not undertake to record.

1. Lazarus] i.e. Eleazar, ' God is my help,' a man of good social position, probably a son or near relative of Simon the Leper (Mt 26 6) ; not to be identified with the beggar Lazarus of the parable. **Bethany**] a village at the Mount of Olives, a little less than 2 m. from Jerusalem, now called El 'Azerîyeh, 'the place of Lazarus.' **Mary . . Martha**] St. John supposes that they are known to his readers from St. Luke's narrative (Lk 10 38). The circumstances of the family, and the characters of the sisters in the two Gospels are quite in agreement. **2.** St. John assumes that the fact of the anointing is already known in a general way from the synoptists (see Mt 26 6 Mk 14 3, and cp. Lk 7 36), but since their narratives are somewhat obscure and confusing, he intends to give later on (12 1 f.) a more accurate account. **3. Lovest**] The love which Christ bore to the whole human race did not prevent Him from forming special friendships. **4. Not unto death**] i.e. not unto *permanent* death. **But for the glory of God, etc.**] Lazarus was allowed to die that God might be glorified by his resurrection. So the blind man was born blind that God might be glorified by his eyes being miraculously opened (9 3).

6. Two days] Our Lord waited two days, (1) that the death of Lazarus might be an indisputable fact : cp. v. 39 ; (2) that there might be time for a competent number of witnesses to assemble : cp. v. 42. There is a seeming want of tenderness in the sisters in allowing Lazarus to die, and then making them wait four days for the miracle ; but wider interests than those of a single family were involved. Moreover, the delay was the means of testing and strengthening the sisters' faith : cp. vv, 22, 27, 32. **9, 10.** Our Lord's allegorical answer means, ' The allotted time of My ministry is not yet finished, therefore I

shall be safe in Judæa, and so will you. But when My allotted time has elapsed, then I shall be in danger of death, and you also.' **9. The light**] i.e. the sun. **11. Sleepeth**] because Lazarus was soon to be awakened as from sleep : cp. Mk 5 39. **15.** A secondary object of the miracle was the strengthening of the disciples' faith.

16. Didymus] i.e. ' twin,' is the correct translation of the Aramaic ' Thomas.' Perhaps he was twin brother of Matthew with whom he is coupled (Mt 10 3 Mk 3 18 Lk 6 15). He here figures as the pessimist of the apostolic circle ; in c. 20 as the sceptic. Yet his love and devotion to our Lord are undoubted. **Die**] because of the danger in Judæa.

17. The grave] RV ' the tomb.' In Palestine burial took place on the day of death. The possession of a private tomb by the family of Lazarus is an indication of wealth. The poor were buried in cemeteries (2 K 23 6).

19. Visits of condolence were paid with great ceremony for seven days after a death. **20. Sat** *still*] RV ' still sat.' Sitting was the attitude of grief. ' After the body is carried out of the house, all chairs and couches are reversed, and the mourners sit on the ground on a low stool.' **22. Even now**] marvellous faith under the circumstances. She believes that Jesus can raise Lazarus, but dare not express the hope that He will.

24. A belief in a future resurrection was at this period professed by all pious Jews, and was not peculiar to the Pharisees. The expression ' the Last Day ' is peculiar to St. John. **25. I am the resurrection, and the life**] These solemn words, which are used most appropriately in the Burial Service, not only refer to the raising of Lazarus to a natural life, but indicate that Christ is also the author of the resurrection to eternal life. **He that believeth**] The words apply primarily to Lazarus. Lazarus was a believer in Christ. Lazarus was dead. And because Lazarus was a believer, he was about to be raised from the dead. His resurrection was a token and pledge of the resurrection of all believers. **26. Shall never die**] because death to Christians is not really death. Death did not break the living union between the soul of Lazarus and His Redeemer, nor will it break that of other believers. ' The souls of the righteous are in the hand of God ; there shall no torment touch them.' **27. The Son of God**] When used, as here, as a popular title of the Messiah, this expression implies a special nearness to God, but not necessarily actual divinity. **Which should come**] RV 'even he that cometh.' ' He that cometh ' was a common title of the Messiah : cp. 6 14 Mt 11 3.

31. For three days the mourners used to visit the grave, believing that the soul hovered round, fain to re-enter and reanimate its fleshly tenement. On the fourth day, it was thought, the soul departed and decomposition began.

33. He groaned] i.e. He sorrowed in sympathy with the mourners. But RM 'He was moved with indignation,' i.e. at the havoc wrought by death in thus cutting off a young life. Our Lord regarded not only sin, but also disease and death, as part of that kingdom of Satan which He came to destroy. Their dominion over the human race filled Him with acute distress. **In the spirit**] i.e. in His human spirit. The Gospels assign to Jesus, as perfect man, both 'soul' and 'spirit.' **And was troubled**] The RM more correctly renders 'and troubled Himself.' Christ was not subject to human emotions, as we are, against His will. Out of sympathy with mankind He condescended to feel them.

35. Jesus wept] An exquisitely human touch, showing that the evangelist, with all his insistence upon Christ's divinity, has a firm grasp of His true humanity. Contrast with the sympathetic tears of Jesus the Stoic ideal of indifference to human emotion. In Jesus the strength of a man was united to the tenderness of a woman. Men may learn from this that there is nothing unmanly in tears. Some think that Jesus wept because He was about to summon back a soul from the felicity of Paradise to the strife and sorrow of this mortal state.

37. Could not this man] Probably a hostile criticism, imputing to Jesus lack of love or lack of power. **38. A stone lay upon it**] which implies that it was an underground vault, or, 'a stone lay against it' (RV), which implies that it was a cavern hewn in the side of a hill. The tomb now called that of Lazarus 'is a deep vault like a cellar, excavated in the limestone rock in the middle of the village, to which there is a descent by 26 steps.' **39.** Martha thinks that Jesus wishes to take a last look at His friend, and she seeks to dissuade Him, fearing that, putrefaction having already begun, the corpse will present a fearful spectacle. The apparent failure, for the moment, of her half-formed faith is true to life.

41, 42. This prayer of Jesus is remarkable, for, (1) He thanks God beforehand for the miracle, as if it had already been performed ; (2) contrary to His usual practice, He offers the miracle as a proof of His divine mission, and that to unbelievers. **41. Hast heard me**] RV 'heardest me,' viz. four days ago in Peræa, when I prayed that Lazarus might be raised to life. **42. I said it**] viz. that Thou didst hear My prayer that Lazarus might be raised.

44. Came forth] doubtless with difficulty, his legs being bound together by graveclothes. Hence the command 'Loose him.' It is possible, however, that the legs of Lazarus were swathed separately after the Egyptian manner. **45, 46.** The Gk., interpreted strictly,

means that *all* the Jews who were present believed, and that some of them went, apparently in good faith, to the Pharisees, hoping to convince them. Perhaps they expected that such a miracle would receive favourable consideration from those who were the special champions of the doctrine of the Resurrection. They certainly reported the miracle as a *fact :* see v. 47.

47–53. A meeting of the Sanhedrin against Jesus. As in the synoptics, the chief priests, i.e. the Sadducees, take a more prominent part than the Pharisees in compassing the death of Jesus. Similarly in the Acts it is mainly the Sadducees who are hostile to the infant Church. The hostility of the Sadducees was due not so much to dislike of the doctrine of the Resurrection, as to selfish and political motives : see v. 48.

47. What do we ?] i.e. Why are we doing nothing ? **48. The Romans shall come**] They feared that Jesus would be proclaimed king by the people, and that the Romans would thereupon inflict summary judgment upon the nation. **Our place and nation**] i.e. our position in the State, and the very existence of the nation. Others understand 'our place' to be Jerusalem (cp. 2 Mac 3 18-30), or the Temple (cp. Ac 6 14 2 Mac 5 19). **49. Caiaphas**] In full Joseph C., a Sadducee. See on Mt 26 3. **That same year**] i.e. high priest in that memorable year in which Jesus was crucified. The expression does not imply that the high-priesthood was an annual office. **Ye know nothing**] see 18 14. Caiaphas speaks somewhat contemptuously of the Pharisees—' You Pharisees have no policy to offer. We Sadducees have a very definite one. Jesus must die, in our interests, and yours, and in the interests of the national existence.' **51, 52.** Of old the high priest had declared the divine will by Urim and Thummim (Ex 28 30, etc.). The prophetic power, long withdrawn, is restored for a moment, just as the Levitical priesthood was about to be abolished by the one offering of Christ upon the cross. **Die for** (i.e. on behalf of) **that nation**] The high priest unwittingly proclaimed Jesus as the true paschal lamb, whose blood would atone for the sins of the world. By sacrificing Jesus he brought about a blessing of which he never dreamed (the remission of sins), and compassed for the nation the very evil which he sought to avert (the loss of national existence). **52. In** (RV 'into') **one**] i.e. into one Church. **The children of God**] i.e. the Gentiles. **Scattered abroad**] The unity of the human race has been destroyed by sin. The death of Christ, by abolishing sin, reëstablishes its unity.

54–57. Retirement to Ephraim. Attitude of the multitudes at Jerusalem. Suppressed excitement.

54. To avoid the snares of His enemies, and to secure a short season of undisturbed communion with His disciples, Jesus retires to Ephraim, perhaps Ephrain or Ephron (2 Ch 13 19), or Ophrah (1 S 13 17). 55. To purify themselves] No man could eat the Passover while ceremonially unclean (see 18 28 Nu 9 10 2 Ch 30 17), hence the Passover pilgrims assembled in Jerusalem some time beforehand to purify themselves by ablutions, shaving the head, and sacrifice. In some cases the process lasted a week. 57. Jesus was still too popular to be taken publicly.

CHAPTER 12
The Triumphal Entry. Close of the Public Ministry

1-11. Supper at Bethany (see on Mt 26 6 and Mk 14 3, which record the same incident). The event in Lk 7 36 f. is different. The supper was at the house of Simon the leper, a near relation, perhaps the father, of Lazarus and the sisters. St. John alone mentions the name of the woman who anointed Jesus, the quantity of the unguent (1 litre = 12 oz.), and the author of the mean speech, 'Why was not this ointment sold for three hundred pence, and given to the poor?' He also states that the supper was held six days (not two days, as St. Mark) before the Passover. Mary probably anointed Jesus in gratitude for the restoration of her brother Lazarus to life.

1. Six days] Since the Passover, according to this Gospel, took place on Friday, Jesus apparently arrived on Saturday (the sabbath), and the supper must have taken place the same evening. 5. Three hundred pence (denarii)] about £9. 6. The bag (or, box)] The apostles had one purse, because they realised that those who have spiritual things in common, ought (ideally, at least) to have temporal things in common also. But though communism is the ultimate Christian ideal, and has always been regarded as such (see Ac 2 44), it does not, therefore, follow that it is practicable or good in the existing state of the world. Bare] RV 'took away,' i.e. stole.

7. Let her alone: against the day of my burying hath she kept this] i.e. She has done quite right not to sell the ointment. She has kept it for to-day, making to-day as it were My burial day, by performing the prophetic act of anointing and embalming My body. But a better reading is, 'Suffer her to keep it against the day of My burying'; i.e. She has only used a portion of the ointment in anointing My feet. Do not insist on her giving the rest to the poor. Rather let her keep it for anointing My body for burial after the death which I perceive to be impending. 9. Much people] RV 'the common people.' They came] doubtless into the house to watch the banquet. In the East a feast is a public ceremony, and there is a continual succession of sightseers. 11. Went away] i.e. apostasised.

12-19. The triumphal entry (see on Mt 21 1 Mk 11 1 Lk 19 29.) The purpose of our Lord's public entry was to testify to the nation and to mankind that He was actually the Messiah promised by the OT. prophets, and the person by whom the kingdom of God was to be established. St. John writes briefly, supplementing the synoptic account, a knowledge of which he assumes. The synoptists seem to regard the entry as a purely Galilean demonstration, and give no explanation of our Lord's favourable reception in Jerusalem. St. John represents the procession as consisting not only of Galileans (v. 12), but also of inhabitants of Jerusalem, who had seen Lazarus raised from the dead, and whose testimony to the truth of the miracle caused the extraordinary sensation in Jerusalem (vv. 17, 18).

12. The next day] This is now generally called Palm Sunday. Much people] evidently Galileans. 13. Palm trees] Among the Hebrews, as among the Greeks, palms were carried as symbols of victory and rejoicing (1 Mac 13 51 Rev 7 9). 16. Observe the author's intimate knowledge of the sentiments of the disciples.

20-22. Jesus and the Greeks. A dominant idea of this Gospel is universalism. Christ dies for all men, Gentiles as well as Jews, and is, therefore, the Saviour of the world (4 22 1 Jn 4 14). Appropriately, therefore, the evangelist notices that the last public utterance of Jesus was on the Gentile question. St. John sees in the request of these Greeks for an interview (which we are to presume was granted) a foreshadowing of the calling of the Gentiles.

20. Greeks] i.e. Gentiles, probably from Galilee or Decapolis, where there was a large Gentile population. Their presence at the feast shows that they sympathised—as so many devout Gentiles did—with the monotheistic faith of Israel.

23-26. Last public discourse of Jesus. The voice from heaven. The time is probably Wednesday afternoon, the place the Temple : cp. Mt 21 23. Jesus resigns Himself to death, comforting Himself by contemplating its glorious issues.

23. The humble request of these Greeks for an interview brings vividly before Christ's mind His approaching death, through which alone salvation can be offered to the Gentiles. Should be glorified] viz. by death, which in the case of Jesus was not a humiliation, but a triumph over the powers of evil. 24. As a grain of corn must rot in the ground before it can bring forth fruit, so must the Son of man

die and be buried before the harvest of the world can ripen and be reaped. The divine life, so long as Jesus remained on earth in the body of His humiliation, was confined to Himself. But when by His death and resurrection the earthly shell was cast off, the way was open for the diffusion of the divine life among all mankind. Our Lord's mysterious words would probably be understood by the Greeks, who, if they had been initiated in the mysteries of Eleusis, had seen the immortality of the soul represented under the figure of a grain of wheat buried in the earth that it might germinate and spring up into new life.

25, 26. Our Lord's followers also, if their labours for the conversion of the world are to be fruitful, must, like Him, 'love not their lives unto death.' Only by self-denial, self-sacrifice, self-mortification, and, if need be, by a martyr's death, can the faith be spread, and life given to a dying world. They are to expect no reward in this world, but in the world to come they shall have eternal life, and their heavenly Father will delight to honour them. **26. Where I am**] i.e. where I am soon to be, viz. in heaven.

27. Deeply pathetic are these words, and deeply comforting to all who feel their load of sorrow too heavy for them to bear. Even Jesus could not face His hour of agony without a struggle. The horror of His approaching death filled Him with anguish. His soul was troubled. For a moment He almost prayed to be spared the bitter cup. Then His purpose victoriously reasserted itself. It was to die that He came into the world, and by dying willingly He will glorify His Father. The intensely human struggle described here exactly corresponds to the agony in the garden recorded by the synoptists (Mt 26 39 ||), and is evidence that St. John, no less than they, realised our Lord's true humanity, and its subjection to human conditions. **Father, save me from this hour**] or, perhaps better, ' Shall I say, Father, save me from this hour ? ' **For this cause**] i.e. to die.

28. Father, glorify thy name] viz. by accepting My willing sacrifice upon the Cross. **A voice**] The voices from heaven in the NT. are objective in the sense that all present hear them and are startled by them, but only those for whom they are intended understand their meaning. Thus at the Baptism the heavenly voice was understood by Christ and the Baptist, at the Transfiguration by Christ and the chosen three, here by Christ and the apostles, perhaps by Christ alone. Similarly at St. Paul's conversion only St. Paul himself distinguished the words spoken from heaven, though all heard the voice. **I have both glorified** *it*] viz. by accepting the offering of Thy life's work, crowned as it is by Thy willing submission to suffer

death upon the cross, and **will glorify** *it* **again** by raising Thee from the dead, and placing Thee in glory at My right hand.

31. Now (i.e. within a few days) **is the judgment** (or, a judgment) **of this world**] i.e. of the persons in it. Christ's death followed by His Resurrection is a ' judgment,' because it is a deliberate challenge to mankind to accept Him as the Divine Redeemer of the world. Henceforth men must take sides for and against Christ. To accept Him is to accept eternal life : to reject Him is to be self-condemned. **Now shall the prince of this world** (i.e. Satan) **be cast out**] i.e. deposed by the power of Christ's Death and Resurrection from his usurped dominion over the human race. ' The prince of the world' (i.e. of the Gentile world) was a recognised rabbinical title of Satan.

32. And I, if I be lifted up (viz. upon the cross). **. will** (after My Resurrection and Ascension) **draw all** *men* **unto me** (RV 'myself')] St. John regards the crucifixion of Jesus as a symbol. His elevation upon the cross is an emblem of His being set up as the ensign (Isa 11 10) around which the nations are to rally. The attractive power of the cross lies largely in the fact that sorrow and suffering are universal, and that the sympathy for which all suffering souls crave is only to be found in the love of the Crucified. **All** *men*] The offer of salvation is made to all. **34.** The people understand Christ's allusion to His death, and find this difficult to reconcile with ' the Law,' i.e. the OT. (see 10 34), which teaches that the reign of the Messiah will be eternal (Pss 45 6 110 4 Isa 9 6,7 Dan 7 14). Can, therefore, Jesus be the Messiah ? Has He even claimed to be He ? He has only (v. 23) claimed to be the Son of man. Is this Son of man, whom He claims to be, the Messiah or not ? They press for an answer.

35, 36. Jesus gives no direct answer, though He implies that He is the Messiah by calling Himself the Light : see 8 12. Avoiding all controversy, He bids them believe on Him, while they have Him with them, and warns them of their danger if they do not.

36. Children (RV ' sons ') **of light**] i.e. enlightened persons. The phrase occurs Lk 16 8 Eph 5 8 1 Th 5 5. **Did hide himself**] lit. ' was hidden.' This was Christ's final retirement from His public ministry, and corresponds with Mt 24 1, where Christ leaves the Temple for the last time. He went, probably, to Bethany (Mt 21 17).

37–43. Cause of the unbelief of the Jews. At first they could believe, but refused. By and by they became incapable of it. In this too common experience St. John sees the judgment of God : cp. Ro 9–11. **38. Lord, who**, etc.] quoted exactly from LXX of Isa 53 1. **40. He hath blinded**, etc.]

A very free quotation from Isa 6¹⁰. **41. These things said Esaias** (Isaiah)] Strictly speaking, God said them to Isaiah about Isaiah's own contemporaries, but St. John sees in the passage a typical prophecy of the unbelief of the Jews in the time of Christ. **When he saw his glory**] i.e. Christ's glory. The words were spoken at Isaiah's call when he 'saw the Lord' (whom the evangelist identifies with Christ) 'upon a throne high and lifted up' (Isa 6⁵). **43.** They loved to be honoured by men, more than to be honoured by God.

44–50. Judgment of Jesus upon their unbelief. He refuses to condemn them formally (v. 47), because His First Coming was not to judge, but to save. Yet He adds that in the Last Day they will be self-condemned. His words, which they rejected, will rise up against them in judgment. These vv. are neither a public address, which Jesus came out of his retirement to deliver, nor a private exhortation to the Greeks, but rather a collection of striking sayings of Jesus on the subject of faith and unbelief, appropriately inserted by the evangelist in this place.

45. Cp. 14⁹. **46.** Cp. 8¹² 9⁵,³⁹, etc.
47. And believe not] RV 'and keep them not.' **I judge him not**] cp. 5⁴⁵ 8¹⁵,²⁶. **I came not**] cp. 3¹⁷. **48.** In the last day Jesus will but ratify the verdict of their own consciences.
50. 'The gospel message which the Father has committed to Me conveys to those who accept and obey it eternal life.'

CHAPTER 13
THE LAST SUPPER

1–17. The Supper and the Feet-washing. This supper is identified by almost all modern authorities with the Last Supper, which took place on Thursday night at Jerusalem (Mt 26²⁰ Mk 14¹⁷ Lk 22¹⁴). Writing to supplement the synoptists, St. John omits practically all that they have recorded, and this accounts for his omission of the institution of the Holy Communion. The points peculiar to St. John are the feet-washing, the incident of the sop, the details about the beloved disciple, and the wonderful discourses, of which the synoptists give no hint.

1. Before the feast] St. John corrects the impression, which many have derived from the synoptic narratives, that the Last Supper was the actual Jewish Passover. It was, in fact, a *Christian* Passover, held the day before the Jewish feast (18²⁸), and probably not conformed in all respects to the Jewish ritual. There is, for example, no mention of a lamb, though it is possible that there may have been one. **Unto the end**] or, 'to the uttermost.'
2. Supper being ended] or, 'during supper' (RV). But inasmuch as feet-washing took

place at the beginning of a meal, much is to be said for the rendering, 'supper having been served.' **The devil**] Judas had so often yielded to Satan's evil suggestions that now he made no resistance. **Heart** stands here as often for the soul, or inner man.

4. Riseth] The disciples had been disputing (Lk 22²⁴) which of them should be accounted greatest, and, as we gather from Christ's rebuke (Lk 22²⁷), not one of them would serve at supper, for fear of being thought inferior to the others. Jesus, therefore, after waiting a little for one of them to offer, rose Himself. Not content with waiting at table, which might upon occasion be done by a person of good position (12²), He washed their feet, the function of a slave. Feet-washing took place before a banquet, and was occasionally omitted, though its absence might be remarked (Lk 7⁴⁴). St. John's account supplements St. Luke's by recording the symbolical act by which our Lord enforced His words, 'I am among you as he that serveth' (Lk 22²⁷).

8. If I wash thee not] Besides the literal, the evangelist sees in these words a symbolical meaning : 'Unless I wash thee from thy sins, thou hast no part with Me' : see v. 10. **10. He that is washed** (i.e. has bathed his whole body) **needeth not save to wash** *his* **feet**] This is a parable of things spiritual. The complete bathing or immersion stands for the full and complete forgiveness which Christ offers to His disciples in Holy Baptism, and which cannot be repeated : the washing of the feet symbolises the daily forgiveness of sins committed after Baptism by repentance and prayer.
Not all] The apostles had repented of their pride and ambition, and had received forgiveness from our Lord (15³), except Judas, who could not be forgiven, because he cherished his sin.

12. Set down] rather, 'reclined at table' : see v. 23. **14–17.** Our Lord now draws from the incident the more obvious lessons of humility and willing service to others, as in St. Luke (Lk 22²⁴⁻³⁰). **14.** This precept was obeyed literally by many ancient Churches on Maundy Thursday, and still is by the Roman and Eastern Churches.

18–30. Jesus indicates the Traitor.
18. I do not call you all happy (blessed), for I know that among you is a traitor. But My choice even of the traitor is in accordance with the prophecy of Scripture. **The scripture**] The quotation is a free one from Ps 41⁹. The speaker is David, but since David is a type of Christ, the words are treated as a typical prophecy of Christ's betrayal. **19. That I am** *he*] i.e. the Messiah ; or, 'that I AM' (see 8⁵⁸).
20. Lest the knowledge that there is a traitor among them should weaken their confidence in one another, and in their divine call

to the apostolate, Jesus hastens to assure them that they will receive the fullest divine powers from Himself and His Father for the work of the ministry.

21-30. Cp. the parallel accounts in Mt 26²¹ Mk 14¹⁸ Lk 22²¹. St. John's main point is that the designation of the traitor was private, not public. It was made in a whisper to St. John only, and even to him the name was not mentioned. St. John's account is altogether probable. Had Jesus denounced the traitor clearly and openly, Judas would never have left the room alive.

23. Leaning on (RV 'reclining in') **Jesus' bosom**] The guests lay on their left sides, on separate but adjacent couches, each supporting his head upon his left hand, with his left elbow resting upon a cushion. The first place of honour (behind Jesus) was probably occupied by St. Peter ; the second place of honour (in front of Jesus) was occupied by St. John. St. John, therefore, could easily lean back on Jesus' bosom. **26. Answered**] evidently in a whisper, so that St. Peter could not hear. **A sop**] RV 'the sop.' The sop handed to another was a pledge of good will, like our old custom of taking wine with a person. At the Passover the sop consisted of three things wrapped together, the flesh of the paschal lamb, a piece of unleavened bread, and bitter herbs. **27.** The sop was the last appeal of divine love to Judas. He rejected it, and straightway at that moment the devil obtained full possession of his soul.

30. Went immediately out] St. John represents Judas as departing before the institution of the Holy Communion (see v. 34). The synoptists (or, at least, St. Luke) seem to represent him as remaining and communicating. St. John's account is altogether more probable.

Night] The word has tragic emphasis. It was night literally, a time appropriate for deeds of darkness ; also it was night spiritually in the soul of Judas, in which the light of God's Spirit had been for ever quenched.

13³¹-17²⁶. The Last Discourses of Jesus to His disciples. We come now to what is perhaps the most precious part of the whole evangelical history, those wonderful discourses, delivered by our Lord in the upper room just after the institution of the Lord's Supper. St. John alone records them. Like a consecrated priest, the evangelist conducts us into the Holy of Holies, revealing the inmost thoughts, desires, and aspirations of our divine Redeemer.

31-35. The Lord's Supper (Holy Communion) **and the New Commandment of Love.** Relieved of the traitor's presence, our Lord institutes the rite of Holy Communion, which is to take the place of the Passover, and proceeds to explain its significance as a pledge and bond of love among the disciples

(vv. 34, 35), and afterwards as a means of union and communion with Himself (15¹ᵗ·).

31. Now is the Son of man glorified] viz. by death. His death was already virtually accomplished, when the traitor went forth to arrange for His arrest. **32. God shall also glorify him**] viz. by raising Him from the dead, and exalting Him to His right hand in heaven. **In himself**] i.e. in the Father's peculiar glory, which the Son of God resigned at His Incarnation : cp. 17⁵ Phil 2⁸⁻¹¹.

33. Little children] This touching designation is almost, if not altogether, peculiar to St. John (1 Jn 2¹,¹²,²⁸ 3 7,¹⁸ 4⁴ 5²¹). In extreme old age, when too feeble to preach, he used to be carried into Church, and simply to say to the people, 'Little children, love one another.'

Ye shall seek me] 'You will be left here on earth for a time ; but, unlike the Jews, you will seek Me and will find Me, for if you love one another, I will answer your prayers, and reveal Myself to you.' **Ye cannot come**] not at once, but hereafter, for 'I go to prepare a place for you' (14²). **34. A new commandment**] Love is the fulfilling of the Law. The old commandment to love one another (Lv 19¹⁸), which our Lord regarded as the essential feature of the Law, is now reënacted in a higher sense, and grounded on a new motive, viz. the Love of Christ for all mankind, as shown in His Atoning Death. The feast which commemorates this death is to be the great bond of love and union among Christians.

36-38. Peter's denial foretold] Parallel with Lk 22³¹⁻³⁴, and similar in character to Mt 26³¹ Mk 14²⁷, q.v.

36. Thou shalt follow] a prophecy not only of Peter's martyrdom, but, as the event showed, of the manner of his martyrdom (crucifixion) : see 21¹⁸,¹⁹.

CHAPTER 14
The Comforter

1-31. The mansions in heaven. The mission of the Comforter. This great discourse, which is not easily susceptible of formal subdivision, deals with five main subjects : (1) the heavenly mansions ; (2) Christ as the Way to the Father ; (3) the mutual indwelling of the Father in the Son, and of the Son in the Father ; (4) the efficacy of prayer through Christ ; (5) the mission of the Comforter.

Some scholars think that a displacement has occurred in the farewell discourses, and particularly that this c., which seems to conclude Christ's words to His disciples, originally stood between chs. 16 and 17.

1. 'Be not disquieted at My departure (see 13³⁶). Have faith that I have the power to fulfil the promises that I now make to you.' **2. My Father's house**] i.e. heaven. **Many**

mansions] RM 'abiding-places.' There are various degrees of glory in heaven, and various employments, suitable to the desert and capacity of each (Lk 19 16-26, etc.). The word used, which sometimes denotes a place of refreshment for travellers, is thought by Westcott to suggest that heaven is a state of continual progress, but this is unlikely. **3. I will come again**] viz. at the end of the world.

4. 'You know whither I go, viz. to My Father in heaven ; and you know how you also may follow Me, viz. by believing in Me.' But the RV has simply, 'And whither I go, ye know the way.'

5. Thomas] For the character of Thomas see 11 16 20 25. Thomas expected an immediate manifestation of the Messianic kingdom on earth, and this prevented him from understanding Jesus. **6, 7.** 'The Kingdom which I have come to reveal is not an earthly one ; the mansions of which I have spoken are in heaven, not on earth. To share in My Kingdom, is to share that state of exalted and blissful communion with the Father, which is not possible on earth. I depart to heaven, to enter into that state of bliss ; and you may follow and enjoy it too, if you will have faith in Me as the one mediator between God and man (**the Way**), the one teacher authorised to reveal the things of God (**the Truth**), and the one author of spiritual as of natural life (**the Life**).' **6. No man**] It is important to remember that pious heathen, who have never heard of Christ, may and do find acceptance with God, through Him, whom, if they had known, they would have accepted as their Redeemer (Ro 2 14-16). **7. Have seen him**] not in His absolute nature, which is invisible (1 18), but in His character, which is revealed in My Person : see 6 46, and v. 9 below.

8. Philip desired to see the eternal invisible Father as a distinct being beside the Son. He wished for a visible Theophany : cp. Ex 24 10. **10.** See on 10 38. **11.** Cp. 10 38 15 24.

12. Greater *works*] The Apostles' work was more effectual than that of Christ Himself, because they were inspired by the Spirit of the Risen and Ascended Lord. Not till Christ had departed to the Father could the Spirit be fully given. **13.** Not only is Christian prayer to be offered in the name of (i.e. invoking the mediation of) the Son, but even answers to prayer are given through the Son, that the same honour may be accorded to the Son as to the Father. **Whatsoever**] cp. 15 16 16 23, 24. The limitations to be understood are that the petitioner must ask in faith (Mt 21 22), be in charity with his neighbours (Mt 6 14), and habitually keep God's commandments (1 Jn 3 22). **14.** Here, according to the reading of the RV, Christ teaches the disciples to pray directly to Himself, as well as to the Father

in His Name. Examples of prayer to Christ are Ac 7 59 9 14, 21 1 Cor 1 2.

16. Another Comforter] RM 'Advocate,' or, 'Helper.' Attractive, and suitable to the context, as the rendering 'Comforter' is, there can be little doubt that the true meaning of the Gk. *Paracletos* is 'Advocate.' The Holy Spirit is represented as Christ's Representative on earth, carrying on His work, and inspiring and strengthening His disciples to fulfil their vocation. As Christ's 'Advocate' he pleads Christ's cause in the hearts of the disciples, and appeals also to the better conscience of 'the world,' convicting the world of sin, of righteousness, and of judgment (16 8). He inspires believers with the spirit of prayer, and, when they pray, 'Himself maketh intercession for us with groanings which cannot be uttered' (Ro 8 26, 27). To His guidance the disciples are to resign themselves with implicit confidence, for He is the Spirit of Truth. He guides, not so much as an external authority, as an inward light shining in the heart—an interior monitor regulating the secret springs of character. In His coming, Christ also returns to earth, to dwell in the hearts of believers by faith ; but yet He must not be altogether identified with Christ, for He is 'another' Comforter. The functions of the Comforter sufficiently attest His divinity.

17. Spirit of truth] He inspires what is good and true in conduct, and reveals what is good and true in doctrine. **The world, etc.**] The experience of the Spirit is inward and spiritual: this the world cannot grasp. **Dwelleth with you**] viz. externally, by His presence in the Church. **And shall be in you**] as an inward principle, sanctifying, inspiring, guiding, and filling you with peace and joy. **18. Comfortless**] lit. 'orphans.' **I will come to you**] invisibly and spiritually in the coming of the Spirit. **19. But ye see me**] i.e. shall see Me, literally during the forty days, spiritually after Pentecost, when you shall enjoy communion with Me so deep and satisfying, that it will be better than sight. **Because I live**] 'because I live' for evermore, 'and ye shall live' (RM) spiritually in Me. **20. At that day** (i.e. after Pentecost) **ye shall know** by spiritual experience **that I** *am* **in my Father, and ye in me**] So close is the spiritual union between Christ and believers, that He compares it with the mutual indwelling of the Father and the Son.

22. Judas] called Thaddæus or Lebbæus (Mt 10 3), is not the same as Jude the Lord's brother. He thought that Jesus was about to establish an earthly kingdom, and therefore to manifest Himself to the **world**. **23.** Jesus, by adding that the Father also will come to believers, shows more clearly that it is a spiritual manifestation of which He is speaking, and that only to those who love Jesus, can the manifestation be made. **We will come**] Where the Son is, there of necessity is the Father also, as well as the Spirit, for the Three are One, being different forms of the subsistence and manifestation of the same Divine Being. This passage illustrates the doctrine that the Persons of the Holy Trinity are inseparable. and contain one another. The technical word is *perichorēsis* (Gk.), or ' *circumincessio* ' (*circuminsessio*), Lat. See on 10 38.

26. In my name] i.e. as My full Representative, endowed with all My powers, and with a mission to promote My cause in the world.

He (masculine, to show the Spirit's personality) **shall teach you all things**] i.e. all saving truth, which it is necessary for you and your successors to know. Those who would confine the Christian religion to the words of Christ recorded in the Gospels, are here reproved.

Bring all things] The Spirit would awaken the words of Christ which lay like slumbering germs in the minds of the disciples, and cause them to germinate and bear fruit after many days. Of this process St. John's Gospel itself is the most striking example.

27. Peace] more exactly defined as ' My Peace,' is the peace of reconciliation with God through the Death of Christ. **Not as the world giveth**] This peace is not mere earthly joy and prosperity: it is a removal of all elements of discord from the soul. **28. And come** *again*] i.e. in the coming of the Spirit.

For my Father is greater than I] ' Rejoice that I go to My Father, for it is good both for Me and for you. He will exalt Me to supreme authority over the universe, enable Me to dispense the Holy Spirit, and cause My work to prosper in your hands.' When Christ said ' My Father is greater than I,' He was probably thinking of the humiliation of His earthly life, and of His created human nature (' equal to the Father as touching His Godhead, and inferior to the Father as touching His manhood ') ; yet there is a sense in which even the eternal Son, as being begotten, is inferior to the Father.

30. Hereafter, etc.] rather, ' No longer will I speak much with you,' because time will not allow it. **The prince**] i.e. Satan, who, through the powers that be, works his will on Jesus : cp. 12 31. **Hath nothing in me**] i.e. hath no power over the Sinless One. **31. But I go** forth to meet My death **that the world may know**, etc. **Arise, let us go hence**] On account of these words, some plausibly (but without sufficient authority), wish to place this c. after c. 16. The discourses which follow (chs. 15, 16, 17) were delivered either (1) standing at the table before departing, or (2) in the Temple, or (3) in some retired place in Jerusalem, or (4) on the way to the Mount of

Olives. The last view seems to be the most plausible.

CHAPTER 15

1–17. The allegory of the True Vine and its interpretation. The metaphor of ' the vine ' was suggested by ' the fruit of the vine ' which had just been consecrated in the Holy Supper (Mt 26 29), and the allegory was intended to illustrate the main idea underlying that holy rite, viz. union with Christ. It sets forth Christ as the sole source of spiritual life, and of Christian sanctity. As long as the spiritual union between Christ and the believer, which (ideally and normally, at any rate) begins with Baptism, is maintained by faith love and prayer, the believer's soul is nourished by constant supplies of grace, just as truly as the branches of a vine are nourished by the sap that flows into them from the stem. Nourished by the life of Christ, the believer's soul is cleansed, sanctified, and made fruitful in all good works. Neglect of prayer, the holy sacraments and the other means of grace is punished by interruption of this union, and, finally, by its complete severance, resulting in spiritual death, and inability to perform works acceptable to God.

1. The true vine] i.e. the ideally perfect vine. ' The vine was the symbol of Israel, not in their national but in the'r church capacity ' (Edersheim): cp. Ps 80 8 Isa 5 1 Jer 2 21 Hos 10 1. It was also a symbol of the Messiah (Delitzsch). Accordingly Christ here affirms, (1) that He is the true Messiah ; (2) that His Church is the true Israel of God, and His followers the true Israelites (cp. 1 Cor 10 18 Gal 6 16 1 Pet 2 9 Rev 2 9 3 9, etc.) ; but, above all, (3) that He is the one fountain of spiritual life, supplying all needful grace to believers. The figure of the vine and the branches corresponds to that of the body and the members, used first by Christ at the institution of the Holy Supper (Mt 26 26) and often afterwards by St. Paul, to express the mysterious, but real and vital union which subsists between Christ and individual believers, and between Christ and His Church (Ro 12 5 1 Cor 10 17 12 12-31 Eph 1 23 3 6 4 4-16 5 30 Col 1 18-24 2 19 3 15). As the vine sends sap into every branch, causing the grapes to grow and ripen, so Christ communicates spiritual life and grace to every soul that is effectively ' in Him,' causing it to bring forth ' the fruits of the Spirit ' (Gal 5 22), to be ' fruitful in every good work ' (Col 1 10), and—greatest gift of all—to be ' partaker of the divine nature ' (2 Pet 1 4). Union with Christ is normally begun in Baptism (1 Cor 12 13 Gal 3 27 Ro 6 3, etc.), and maintained by constant faith (Eph 3 17), obedience (Jn 14 23 Rev 3 20), love (1 Jn 4 12), Holy Communion

(Jn 6 56 1 Cor 10 16). **The husbandman**] cp. Mk 12 1 Lk 13 6.

2. Every branch] refers primarily to individual Christians ; yet what is said applies also to Churches (Rev 2 5 3 16). **Taketh away**] yet not finally till the Last Judgment. **Purgeth**] RV 'cleanseth,' or, still better, 'pruneth.' The reference is (1) to the discipline of sorrow, disappointment, temptation, and trial, by which the saints are perfected (Heb 12 6 Rev 3 19 ; cp. Heb 5 8) ; (2) to the cutting off of the superfluities, ambitions, luxuries, and worldly pleasures and lusts, which hinder the Christian life (Gal 5 24 6 14 Jas 1 21). **3. Through the word**] The 'word' is the whole training of the Twelve, including the admonitions and severe rebukes with which He strove to correct their faults, and make them 'clean,' i.e. 'pruned,' and in a fruit-bearing state. 4. 'See that ye abide in Me by diligently using the means of grace, and I will abide in you.'

6. As a branch] i.e. as a useless branch. **Men** (RV ' they ') **gather them**] The angels gather the useless branches (i.e. persons who are not in Christ), and cast them into the fire (of future punishment in Hades or Gehenna), and they are burned (punished).

11, 12. The Saviour now resolves His commands into perfect self-forgetting love.

11. My joy] i.e. the joy which I have in loving the Father, and being loved by Him (v. 10). This joy Christ imparts to the disciples, thereby fulfilling (i.e. perfecting) their imperfect joy : cp. 16 24 17 13 1 Jn 1 4 2 Jn 1 12. **12.** See 13 34. **13. Lay down**] see 10 11, and cp. 1 Jn 3 16. The Saviour regards the offering up of life, and that for friends, as the highest expression of love, and expects the disciples to prove themselves capable of similar self-sacrifice. **15. All things**] This apparently contradicts 16 12 (cp. 14 26), but only apparently. Christ's teaching during His ministry was complete in the sense that it set forth all the principles of Christianity. Yet there was required the subsequent illumination of the Spirit, (1) to interpret the deeper meaning of those principles, and (2) to apply them practically to the needs of the Church. **16. Ordained**] RV ' appointed.' **Bring forth fruit**] This mainly refers to the conversion of the world, which was the fruit of the spiritual labours of the Apostles. **Should remain**] Their work has lasted nearly 2,000 years, and the vitality of Christian missionary work is still unimpaired. **Whatsoever**] see on 14 13. **In my name**] 'in accordance with My spirit and character. **17.** I command you to abide in Me, that by so doing you may have the power to love one another.'

18–25. The world's hatred] cp. the similar predictions, Mt 10 16-28 24 9 Lk 21 12,16 ; cp. also 1 Pet 4 12,13.

18. Cp. 1 Jn 3 13. The **world** is mankind regarded as alienated from God. **20. The word**] see Mt 10 24. The reference is not to Jn 13 16.

25. Their law] i.e. their Scriptures (see 10 34). The passage alluded to is Ps 69 4 : cp. Ps 35 11. David is the person hated, but David's case is typical of Christ's.

26, 27. The Witness of the Holy Spirit and of the Apostles to Christ.

26. The Comforter] see on 14 16. **Whom I will send**] According to 14 17,26, it is the Father who sends the Spirit ; now it is Christ Himself, showing clearly that ' what things soever the Father doeth, these also doeth the Son likewise ' (5 19). Cp. Lk 24 49 Ac 2 33, and see on 16 7. **Which proceedeth from the Father**] The Eastern Church uses this text to prove the eternal procession of the Holy Ghost from the Father alone, but the preposition used shows that not the eternal origin, but the temporal mission of the Comforter is meant. **He** (the masculine pronoun emphasises the Spirit's personality : cp. 14 26) **shall testify of me**] by His whole working in the Church from Pentecost onward : see on 16 8.

CHAPTER 16

The Resurrection and Ascension of Christ will prove the Disciples' comfort in time of Persecution.

1–6. The Persecution of the Apostles predicted. This section repeats many of the ideas of the previous c. (see 15 18-24). The reason of the anticipated persecution is ' because they (the persecutors) have not known the Father nor Me' (v. 3) ; i.e. because they have mistaken the character of the service which the Father requires of them. They think that He requires strict observance of the Ceremonial Law ; what He really requires is worship in spirit and in truth, according to My teaching.

1. Offended] i.e. that your faith should not be shaken (RV ' made to stumble '). **2. Out of the synagogues**] i.e. excommunicate you : see 9 22, 34 12 42, and cp. Mt 10 17. **Doeth God service**] more precisely, ' offereth sacrifice to God.' There was a Jewish saying, ' Every one that sheddeth the blood of the wicked, is as he that offereth a sacrifice.' **4. The time**] RV ' their hour,' i.e. the hour of your enemies' apparent triumph. **Ye may remember**] The Apostles' persecutions would be easier to bear, if it was clearly understood that they were foreordained by God and foretold by Christ : cp. 13 19 14 29. **I said not unto you at** (RV ' from ') **the beginning**] Some intimations of the coming persecutions had been given in the earlier charge to the Twelve (Mt 10 16), but only now does our Lord bring the matter prominently forward. **Because I was with you**] While Christ was with the Apostles, they were in no danger of persecution, and therefore there was no need to speak to them about it. But since persecution was to begin after His death, and His death was now impending, it was necessary for Him to begin to speak to them about it. **5. None of you asketh me**] The Apostles were so much disturbed by the thought of Christ's imminent death, and their own approaching persecutions, that they had no heart to enquire about the glorious abode to which Christ was going, and to which they also would one day go.

7–15. The work of the Comforter in the world and in the Church.

7. It was better for them that Christ's personal presence should be withdrawn, in order that His spiritual presence might be nearer to them than ever, or, rather, might for the first time truly begin. This would be effected by the coming of the Holy Ghost, when He who was now 'with' them, would be ever 'in' them. **If I go not away**] The glorification of Christ's humanity through the indwelling Spirit was not complete till the Resurrection and Ascension, hence not till after the Ascension could the Spirit of the glorified Christ be given. **Comforter**] see on 14 16.

8. Reprove] RV 'convict.' The Gk. word, which also occurs 3 20 8 9 (AV) 8 46, means to prove a person in the wrong, hence to convict. The Holy Ghost will 'convince' or 'convict' the world, by placing before it the claims of Christ with a force and clearness that cannot be evaded. The result will be twofold. Some will be 'convicted by their own consciences' (8 9), or 'pricked to the heart' (Ac 2 37), and so repent and believe (Ac 2 38). Others will be hardened in their sin and unbelief (Ro 11 8), and be 'convicted' of wilful blindness in the sight of God and good men.

9–11. The Holy Ghost, through the apostolic preaching, and through the new power of holiness manifested in the lives of believers, will convince mankind, (1) of their sin and folly in rejecting Christ ; (2) that Christ is a sincere and righteous teacher, and not, as they had thought, an impostor, as will be clearly demonstrated when the Father has raised Him from the dead and set Him at His right hand in heaven ; (3) that the unspiritual system of religion which they have hitherto professed, and which has led them to reject Christ, is of the devil and not of God, that God Himself has condemned it, and that therefore they must condemn it too.

This passage is an extremely difficult one, and various other interpretations of it are given. **11. Judgment**] i.e. condemnation. **The prince**] i.e. Satan : see 12 31 14 30. The Resurrection is the proof that Satan and the world (i.e. the opponents of Jesus) are condemned by God.

12, 13. This promise of divine guidance to the Apostles as teachers, justifies us in accepting their writings as specially inspired. The promise, however, is not exclusively to them, for in all time (and not least in our own) the Holy Spirit is guiding the Church into all truth. **13. Into all truth**] RV 'all the truth,' i.e. all that is necessary to the salvation of souls and to the well-being of the Church. It should be noticed that the Church's apprehension of truth is regarded as progressive.

Things to come] Here the prediction of events is regarded as one of the functions of true prophecy.

14, 15. One of the leading Trinitarian passages in the NT. In it (1) the three Persons are clearly distinguished ; (2) their relative subordination is clearly taught, the Father giving His all to the Son, and the Son communicating His all to the Spirit ; (3) their equality of nature is distinctly affirmed, for the Son receives from the Father 'all things whatsoever the Father hath' (see RV), i.e. His whole nature and attributes, and communicates them to the Spirit. **14.** The Spirit would **glorify** Christ, by progressively revealing the full sense of what Christ had taught them.

16–24. The Apostles' Sorrow turned into Joy.

16. Ye shall see me] (1) with bodily sight during the forty days ; (2) with spiritual vision after Pentecost (see on 14 18, 19). **20. But the world shall rejoice**] 'My enemies will rejoice at My death, and the apparent failure of My designs.' **22. I will see you again**] The reference is both to the Resurrection and to the coming of the Spirit. **23. In that day**] i.e. the time beginning at Pentecost. **Ye shall ask me nothing**] RM is preferable, 'Ye shall ask me no question,' i.e. about the true meaning of My words, for all will then be clear to you. **He will give** it **you**] RV adds 'in my name,' i.e. for My sake. **24. Hitherto . . name**] because prayer in the name of Christ presupposes His glorification.

25–33. Last Words. Temporary defeat in the present will be followed by final victory.

25. In proverbs] RM 'in parables.' Very many of our Lord's discourses were dark and enigmatical to the Apostles, until the coming of the Holy Spirit furnished the key to their meaning. Mere words can only hint at, not fully express, the things of God. It requires the inward teaching of the Holy Spirit to bring home to the soul God's message of salvation. **The time**] i.e. the dispensation of the Spirit beginning at Pentecost. **26. I say not . . that I will pray the Father for you**] 'After Pentecost you will have direct access to the Father. You will ask directly for what you need in My name, and no longer will it be needful for you, as it is at present, first to come to Me, and to ask Me to bring your needs before the Father.' This text does not deny Christ's heavenly intercession (Ro 8 34 Heb 7 25 1 Jn 2 1), but only such a view of it as would make it a barrier between the Father and the prayers of His children.

30. Needest not that any man should ask thee] Thou didst answer our questions before we asked them, for Thou didst know what questions were in our minds.

30, 31. Jesus shows that He can read the thoughts of their hearts in a deeper sense than they imagined. He knows precisely what their faith is worth, and prophesies their immediate desertion of Him. In Mt 26 31 = Mk 14 27 this prophecy is said to have been delivered at the Mount of Olives, or at least on the way thither. This favours the view that the discourses vv. 15–17 were delivered on the way to the Mount of Olives.

32. To his own] i.e. to his own house ; see 1 11 16 32 19 27 Lk 18 28 Ac 21 6. **Yet I am not alone**] Only for a few awful moments upon the cross (Mt 27 46) was our Lord's conscious communion with His Father interrupted.

33. I have overcome the world] See the sublime vision in the Revelation, where Christ goes forth 'conquering and to conquer' (Rev 6 2). The victory of Christ over the world, and the victory of believers through that victory, are favourite themes of the fourth evangelist (see 1 Jn 2 13, 14 4 4 5 4 Rev 2 7, 11, 17, 26 3 5, 12, 21 12 11 15 2 17 14 21 7).

CHAPTER 17
CHRIST'S HIGH-PRIESTLY PRAYER

1–26. Christ's Great Intercession for Himself, for the Apostles, and for the World. This prayer is often, and suitably called Christ's ' High-priestly prayer,' because in it He solemnly consecrates Himself to be priest and victim in the approaching sacrifice. The veil is drawn back for a moment from the inner sanctuary of His mind, and we are enabled to contemplate with awe and reverence the nature of that close communion which He habitually maintained with His heavenly Father.

Christ prays (1) *for Himself* (vv. 1–5), that as He has glorified the Father by His life on earth, so He may also glorify Him by His death, and after death may receive again that glory which for our sakes He resigned at His Incarnation. (2) *For the Apostles* (vv. 6–19), that they may be kept from sin, and from unfaithfulness in the midst of a wicked and hostile world, that they may be perfectly united in affection and will, and that they may be consecrated, even as He is consecrated, for the solemn mission which they are to undertake. (3) *For the world* (vv. 20–26), that it may be converted (v. 21), for believers that they may have perfect union and communion,

visible and invisible, with one another, in virtue of their union with the one God through the one Christ ; and that finally all may attain to everlasting salvation, and see Christ enthroned in that glory which He had with the Father before the world was.

1. The hour] viz. of My glorification through death. **Glorify thy Son**] Christ asks the Father to glorify Him by accepting the sacrifice of His death, and by raising Him from the dead. When this is done, the Son will glorify the Father by converting the world. **2. Power**] RV 'authority.' At the Incarnation the Father gave the Son authority to die for the sins of the whole world, and to proclaim the Father's gracious offer of salvation to all mankind. **As many as thou hast given him**] RV ' whatsoever thou hast given him.' Those whom the Father ' gives ' to Christ, are those who freely accept the offer of salvation which is freely made to all. **3. Eternal life** consists in a knowledge of God, and of Jesus as the Messiah sent from God, i.e. as a preëxistent, divine being. ' Knowledge' here is not intellectual knowledge, but knowledge based on the religious experience of the devout Christian soul. **4.** Our Lord's sinlessness and moral perfection are implied. **5.** The memory of Jesus extends beyond His birth, and beyond the creation of the world, back to eternity, when He was ' in the form of God,' and ' equal to God' (Phil 2 6) ; cp. v. 24. **With thine own self**] i.e. at Thy side.

6. Thy name] i.e. Thy nature. **The men**] i.e. the Apostles. **Kept thy word**] an expression especially characteristic of St. John's Gospel, 1st Ep., and Rev. (Jn 8 51 14 23 1 Jn 2 5, etc.).

9. I pray not for the world] rather, ' I am not now praying for the world.' Jesus prays for the world in vv. 20-26, especially in v. 21, and enjoins others to do so, Mt 5 44, etc. That Christ prays for the world is proved by the entire nature of His work, the object of which is the salvation of the world (Jn 4 42, etc.).

10. All mine, etc.] RV ' all things that are mine are thine, and thine are mine.' All the attributes which belong to the Son belong to the Father ; and all the attributes which belong to the Father (omniscience, omnipotence, etc.) belong to the Son. **11. Keep through thine own name**] RV ' keep them in thy name which thou hast given me,' i.e. keep them in a state of grace defended by that almighty power, which, by Thy gift, I share with Thee. God's ' name' here is practically His divine nature and omnipotence. **One**] How close must be that union and fellowship, which is compared with the unity of Persons in the Godhead itself !

12. The son of perdition] i.e. him who is destined to perdition, viz. Judas Iscariot. In 2 Th 2 3 the expression is used of Antichrist.

The phrase is a Hebraism : cp. Mt 23 15, 'a son of Gehenna.' **The scripture**] in accordance with 13 18, is Ps 41 9.

13. My joy] i.e. the joy which I derive from loving communion with the Father, as in 15 11 : see 1 Jn 1 4.   **14. Thy word**] i.e. Thy whole revelation of Thyself as disclosed in My life.   **Hath hated them**] i.e. will hate them, the past tense expressing the certainty of the hatred, already so clearly foretold, 16 2.

15. I pray not, etc.] Because, if the Apostles were taken out of the world, they would not be able to convert it.   **From the evil**] more correctly rendered by the RV, 'from the evil one.'   St. John habitually conceives of evil as personal : see 1 Jn 3 10, 12 5 18, 19.

17. Sanctify them (RM 'consecrate them') **through thy truth** (RV 'in the truth')] Consecrate them to their apostolic office, endowing them also with divine illumination and wisdom for their work : cp. Ex 28 41.   Our Lord also was 'consecrated' for His work when He entered the world : see 10 36.   **18.** 'As Thou didst not send Me into the world without first consecrating Me (see 10 36), so now I consecrate My Apostles before sending them forth.'   **19.** 'Now once more I consecrate Myself, not this time as a mere teacher, but as priest and victim in the approaching sacrifice. The blood of the new covenant, which My death will initiate and ratify, will consecrate My Apostles to their office and work.'   For 'sanctify' in the sense of offering a victim in sacrifice, see Ex 13 2 Dt 15 19 : cp. 2 S 8 11.   **Through the truth**] RV 'in truth,' i.e. truly.

21. That they all may be one] A leading passage on the unity of the Church. The centre of unity is not on earth but in heaven. Christians are 'one,' because they are spiritually united to the Father and the Son, whose divine life and blessed union they share through the faith that gives eternal life (3 16, etc.), and through believing participation in the sacraments (3 5 6 56 1 Cor 10 16, 17 12 13).   In this, its deepest sense, the unity of the Church cannot be broken by outward divisions.   But inward unity ought to show itself in visible outward unity, 'that the world may know that Thou hast sent Me.'   Hence every Christian is bound to pray and work for the reunion of Christendom.   **22. The glory**] i.e. according to the context, mainly the glory of unity and love.   **23. That the world may know**] The whole world will be converted when the Church of Christ presents the spectacle of perfect love and visible unity.   Divisions hinder the work of Christ, unity advances it.   **26. Thy name**] i.e. Thy nature.

CHAPTER 18
CHRIST BEFORE ANNAS, CAIAPHAS, AND PILATE
1-14. Christ's arrest and trial before Annas

(cp. Mt 26 30 = Mk 14 26 = Lk 22 39).   The narrative is now parallel with the synoptic account, with which, though obviously independent, it closely agrees.   Our Lord's agony in the garden is omitted as well known, but it is alluded to (v. 11), and the evangelist elsewhere uses language quite as definite as that of the synoptists in speaking of His agony of mind at the prospect of death (12 27 13 21).   In this Gospel, as in the others, the sufferer, though divine, is 'a man of sorrows, and acquainted with grief.'

1. The brook Cedron] RV 'Kidron,' a deep, precipitous ravine to the E. of Jerusalem, dividing it from the Mount of Olives, and now called the Valley of Jehoshaphat.   Both Jews and Moslems hold that the Last Judgment will take place there (see Joel 3 2, 12).   It is mentioned several times in the OT. (2 S 15 23 1 K 2 37 Jer 31 40, etc.), but in the NT. only here.   'Brook' should be 'valley' or 'ravine,' lit. 'winter-torrent' (RM).   **A garden**] i.e. Gethsemane: see on Mt 26 36.   **2. Ofttimes resorted**] cp. Lk 22 39.   A statement like this must rest on apostolic testimony.   **3. A band** *of men*] RV 'the band of soldiers,' viz. the Roman garrison which was always stationed in the fortress Antonia, near the Temple.   A 'band' or 'cohort' numbered about 600 men.   **And officers**] These were either officers of the Sanhedrin, or the band of Levitical police who kept order in the Temple.   **6. Fell to the ground**] To show that He could not be arrested against His will (see 10 18), Jesus, before giving Himself up, showed His preternatural power ; or perhaps the falling was an effect of superstitious fear.   **9. That the saying might be fulfilled**] see 17 2.   St. John here gives the sense, not the exact words.

Have I lost none] The original saying referred to spiritual loss ; and, perhaps, the meaning is not different here.   Jesus desired the Apostles to escape, lest, if they were arrested, they might be tempted to apostasy, which would involve the loss of their souls.

10. Simon Peter] Peter's and Malchus's names are mentioned only by St. John.   **Right ear**] This detail, a mark of intimate knowledge, is also in Lk, who further mentions that our Lord healed the servant's ear.

11. The cup] This is proof that St. John knew of the agony in the garden : see Mt 26 39 Mk 14 36 Lk 22 42.   **12. The band**] i.e. the Roman cohort.   **The captain**] i.e. the military tribune (Gk. *chiliarch*), was the officer in chief command of the Roman garrison : see Ac 21 31.   His presence in person marks the importance and probable danger of the arrest.   **13. To Annas first**] i.e. before He was taken to Caiaphas.   This, though not mentioned in the other Gospels, is intrinsically probable.   The authority of Annas was so great that it over shadowed that of the actual high priest Caiaphas. He is mentioned before Caiaphas, Lk 3² Ac 4⁶. He absolutely controlled the Sanhedrin, which at this period, according to the Talmud, transferred its place of meeting from ' the Hall of Hewn Stones ' in the Temple to the head-quarters of his party, ' the Bazaars of the sons of Annas.' He was high priest from 7 to 14 A.D., and even after his deposition by the Romans, retained the office in his family, no less than five of his sons being appointed high priests. For his character see on Mt 21¹². **Father in law]** This fact, in itself probable, is known only from St. John. **14. Caiaphas]** see 11⁴⁹⁻⁵².

15-18. St. John introduces St. Peter into the Palace. First denial. For the interesting but unimportant variations of the four accounts of St. Peter's denials, see on Mt 26⁵⁸ Mk 14⁵⁴ Lk 22⁵⁴.

15. Another disciple] clearly the same as the unnamed disciple of 13²³, who is the apostle John. **Known unto the high priest]** a fact by no means improbable, considering the comparatively good position occupied by St. John's family (Mk 1²⁰ ; see on 19²⁷). The high priest is Annas : see on v. 19. **The palace]** RV ' the court,' i.e. the inner quadrangle : see on Mt 26³,⁵⁸. **Of the high priest]** viz. Annas. Probably Annas and his son-in-law lived in the same large building. **18. Coals]** i.e. charcoal.

19-24. Preliminary examination before Annas (peculiar to this Gospel). The object of Annas's examination, which was irregular and informal, was obviously to induce Jesus to incriminate Himself in view of the approaching trial, the available evidence against Him being weak (Mt 26⁵⁹). It is passed over by the synoptists, because it achieved no result ; but the narrative of St. Luke allows ample time for it before the formal trial (Lk 22⁵⁴⁻⁶⁵).

19. The high priest] i.e. Annas : see v. 24. **20, 21.** Annas tried to entrap Jesus into the admission that He had founded a secret society. Jesus repudiated the suggestion, and refused to be drawn into making any statements likely to incriminate His disciples (cp. v. 8). **22. Struck Jesus]** This is corroborated by Lk 22⁶³, which agrees chronologically with St. John. **24. Now Annas had sent him]** The correct translation is, ' Annas, therefore, sent Him bound unto Caiaphas.' Our Lord was led out into the courtyard, and there, as he passed by on His way to the apartments of Caiaphas, which probably lay on the other side of the quadrangular court, ' He turned and looked upon Peter ' (Lk 22⁶¹). The subsequent trial before Caiaphas is omitted, as being well known.

25-27. St. Peter's second and third denials.

26. The knowledge that the servant was a kinsman of Malchus bears out the statement (v. 15) that ' the disciple ' was known to the high priest. **27. Crew]** This fixes the time as about 3 A.M.

28-32. Jesus is led to Pilate (Mt 27¹ Mk 15¹ Lk 23¹). See especially on St. Matthew. The pathos of this tragic spectacle of the rulers of the chosen people leading their promised Messiah to a Gentile ruler to be put to death, and thereby forfeiting their place in the Kingdom of God and their national existence, is by no evangelist so touchingly portrayed as by St. John. Yet even this great sin did not frustrate the divine purpose, but rather was the means of effecting it (11⁴⁹⁻⁵³). While St. John's account of the civil trial is by far the fullest and the most informing, he omits several important incidents ; the dream of Pilate's wife (Mt), the washing of Pilate's hands (Mt), the trial before Herod (Lk), and the prophetic cry of the people, ' His blood be on us and on our children' (Mt).

28. The hall of judgment] RV ' the palace,' lit. ' the prætorium,' here indicates the official residence of Pilate, which was either the castle of Antonia or a palace built by Herod on the W. hill of Jerusalem : see Mt 27²⁷. Pilate's judgment-seat was in the open air, but he more than once entered the building to confer with Jesus privately (Jn 18³³ 19⁹).

That they might not be defiled (RV)] A Gentile house would not have been purged from the presence of leaven in prospect of the Passover, and therefore by entering it they would have defiled themselves. St. John, who had already eaten the Passover with Jesus, was apparently not so scrupulous : he entered, and hence was able to report the conversations between our Lord and Pilate (vv. 33-38 c. 19⁹⁻¹¹).

But .. might eat the passover] It is obvious that St. John places the Jewish Passover, not on Thursday evening, as the synoptists seem to do, but on Friday evening, and regards the Last Supper on Thursday night as an anticipated Passover—a Passover eaten before the legal date, because Jesus knew that He was to suffer on the morrow. Some critics, however, following the *primâ facie* meaning of the synoptists, date the Jewish Passover on Thursday evening, and understand the expression here (' but might eat the Passover ') to refer not to the Passover proper, but to the ' chagigah,' a sacrifice offered on the morning after the paschal meal : see on Mt 26¹⁷.

30. According to Lk 23², they accused Him of sedition, of withholding tribute from Cæsar, and of assuming the royal title. The charge of blasphemy, on which the Sanhedrin condemned Him, would have no weight with

Pilate. **31. It is not lawful, etc.**] This apparently conflicts with $Jn 8^{5, 59}$ $Ac 5^{33}$ 7^{57} 21^{27}. It would seem, (1) that the Sanhedrin could sentence to death, (2) but could not execute the sentence without permission, and (3) that the governor sometimes permitted them to exceed their powers. The Talmud says that the power of life and death was lost 40 years before the destruction of Jerusalem.

32. Jesus had prophesied not only His death, but His crucifixion, and this could only be fulfilled by His being delivered to the Romans, for the Jewish penalty for blasphemy was stoning (8^{59} 10^{31} $Ac 7^{59}$).

33–38ª. Within the Prætorium. Pilate and Christ. With the exception of Pilate's first question, all is peculiar to St. John. With Roman directness Pilate goes straight to the point : Has Jesus any political designs ? His words, 'Am I a Jew ?' show his contempt for the Jews, and his question, 'What is truth ?' echoes the flippant (but perhaps only superficial) scepticism of polite circles in Rome.

37. Thou sayest that I am a king] RM 'Thou sayest it, because I am a king.' Probably the words are a surprised question : 'Dost thou, a heathen, say that I am a king !' Pilate was impressed with our Lord's personality, and was willing to confess that there was something kingly about Him. **To this end**] The only kingdom which Christ claims for Himself is absolute empire over 'the Truth' (14^6, etc.). **Every one, etc.**] All who are earnestly doing their duty according to the light vouchsafed to them, are ready to receive Christ's Gospel, when it is presented to them. **38. What is truth?**] Rome was infested with a horde of Greek sophists and juggling Oriental theosophists, who all claimed a monopoly of 'the truth,' and hence Pilate had learned to scoff at all mention of the search for it.

38ᵇ–40. Outside the Prætorium. Barabbas is preferred to Jesus (see $Mt 27^{15-26}$ $Mk 15^{6-15}$ $Lk 23^{18-25}$). All is in essential agreement with the synoptists.

CHAPTER 19
The Crucifixion. The Burial

1–3. Inside the Prætorium. Scourging and mockery by the soldiers ($Mt 27^{26}$ $Mk 15^{15}$). It might be supposed from Mt and Mk that the scourging was only the ordinary preliminary to a Roman execution, but $Lk 23^{16}$ suggests that it was an act of mercy to Jesus intended to save His life. This the Fourth Gospel fully confirms, showing how Pilate tried to work upon the compassion of the multitude. The present narrative elucidates, without in any way contradicting, the synoptic account.

4–7. Outside the Prætorium. 'Behold the man.' 'Crucify Him.'

5. Behold the man !] Lat. *Ecce homo.* The words are gently and sympathetically spoken, and are intended to move compassion : 'This meek and suffering form cannot be the usurper of a throne.' **6. Take ye him**] Pilate attempts to put the responsibility of shedding innocent blood upon the Jews. **7. We have a law**] This confirms the evidence of the synoptists that Jesus was condemned by the Sanhedrin, not simply for claiming to be the Messiah, but for claiming to be divine, and so blaspheming God ($Mt 26^{64}$ $Mk 14^{62}$ $Lk 22^{69}$).

7–11. Inside the Prætorium. Jesus refuses to satisfy Pilate's curiosity as to His origin.

8. The more afraid] viz. of allowing Jesus to be unjustly executed. In spite of superficial scepticism (19^{38}), Pilate was superstitious, and thought that Jesus might be some demigod or hero, some son of Jupiter, appearing in human form : cp. $Ac 14^{11}$. **9. Whence art thou ?**] Art thou a man or a demigod ?

11. Caiaphas was more guilty than Pilate. Pilate had lawful authority over Jesus, which, as ordained by God, was acquiesced in by Jesus Himself. Caiaphas had no such authority, for Caiaphas was only high priest, and Jesus was the Messiah. Again, Pilate was only Caiaphas's tool ; he knew not the issues at stake in the rejection and condemnation of Jesus, but Caiaphas did know, or ought to have known.

From above] i.e. from God (cp. $Ro 13^1$), though some think that it means from the high priest Caiaphas. **He that delivered me**] i.e. not Judas, but Caiaphas.

12–16. Outside the Prætorium. Pilate yields to the clamour.

12. Thou art not Cæsar's (i.e. Tiberius's) **friend**] The Jews now appeal to Pilate's selfish fears. They threaten to accuse him of disloyalty to the emperor, a charge which the cruel and suspicious Tiberius was only too willing to receive. St. John alone brings out the leading motive which induced Pilate to yield. **13. Sat down**] or, possibly, 'caused Jesus to sit down.' **The Pavement**] In front of a Roman judgment seat there was usually, at this period, a mosaic or tesselated pavement. **Hebrew**] i.e. Aramaic. **Gabbatha**] 'Gabbath or Gabbetha means a rounded height' (Edersheim).

14. St. John sees prophetic significance in Pilate's words, 'Behold your king,' and therefore times them precisely. Pilate, the representative of the Gentile world, sees in Jesus, whom Israel rejects, the true king of Israel. The Passover is mentioned, because, in the evangelist's view, Jesus is the true Paschal lamb.

The preparation] i.e. the day before the Passover, extending from sunset on Thursday to sunset on Friday. Those, however, who think that the Passover took place on Thursday, translate, 'And it was the Friday in Passover week,' a possible, but improbable rendering : see 18 28.

About the sixth hour] i.e. about noon. St. Mark says 'the third hour,' i.e. 9 A.M. (Mk 15 25). There is a discrepancy here of about 3 hours, which cannot be satisfactorily accounted for. However, Eastern ideas of time are vague, and if the actual time of crucifixion lay midway between 9 and 12, the discrepancy is not a very large one, and may possibly be explained by the complete absorption of the disciples in the dramatic incidents of our Lord's trial and execution, which rendered them unobservant of the flight of time. The discrepancy is not satisfactorily explained, by supposing (as some do) that St. John counts his hours from midnight, for this would throw back the crucifixion to 6 A.M., still leaving a three-hours' discrepancy.

16. Unto them] viz. to the chief priests, so that the crucifixion might appear their act, rather than Pilate's, who was heartily ashamed of it.

17–22. Jesus is crucified (cp. Mt 27 31 Mk 15 20 Lk 23 26). St. John, who is in thorough agreement with the synoptists, omits the incident of Simon of Cyrene (Mt, Mk, Lk), and the first 'word' on the cross (Lk), but adds the characteristic interview between the chief priests and Pilate.

19. Title] According to Roman custom an inferior officer bore before the condemned a block of white wood upon which was engraved the crime for which he suffered. The chief priests regarded Pilate's title as intended to insult the Jews by insinuating that the fitting ruler for such a nation was a condemned criminal. **20. Was nigh**] a local detail, peculiar to this Gospel. **Hebrew**, *and* **Greek**, *and* **Latin**] It was written in three languages, so that it could be read by every one, including foreigners. The evangelist records the fact as symbolising the universality of the gospel.

22. What I have written] A touch true to life. Pilate, though morally a coward, was obstinate—'by nature obstinate and stubborn'; 'at once self-willed, and implacable' (Philo).

23, 24. The Parting of the Garments (Mt 27 35 Mk 15 24 Lk 23 34). St. John alone sees in this incident a fulfilment of Scripture, and this accounts for his minute description of it. The dress of a Jew consisted of, (1) the head-dress, (2) the shoes, (3) the outer garment, (4) the girdle, (5) the inner garment. There were four soldiers (cp. Ac 12 4), who each took one part. There remained the seamless inner garment. For this they cast lots, fulfilling Ps 22 18, a Davidic psalm, from which the fourth 'Word' on the cross was taken. St. John quotes it from the LXX version. The garments of criminals were a perquisite of the executioners.

25–27. Jesus and His mother. This beautiful episode is peculiar to St. John. Its grace and naturalness, and withal its reticence, speak powerfully for its truth. It took place before the darkness, which St. John does not record.

25. His mother, etc.] According to the AV and RV, only *three* women are named, but most modern critics hold that four are intended. Translate, therefore, 'His mother, and His mother's sister' (i.e. Salome, the mother of the evangelist); '*and* Mary the daughter of Clopas, and Mary of Magdala': see further on Mt 27 56. **The wife of Cleophas** (RV 'Clopas')] A more probable rendering is, 'the daughter of Clopas.' Nothing is known of this Clopas, who (for reasons which cannot be fully given here, but which are accepted by most recent critics) is not to be identified with the Alphæus of Mt 10 3, or with the Cleopas of Lk 24 18. Clopas is a contraction of Cleopatros. For the view, now generally abandoned, that 'Mary of Clopas' was the mother of our Lord's 'brethren,' see the detached note on Mt 12 46-50. **26. Woman, behold,** etc.] Although bearing the sins of the whole world, Jesus was not forgetful of human ties, and solemnly commended his mother to the care of the beloved disciple, St. John. St. John was comparatively wealthy, and was, moreover, the Virgin's nephew, so that the arrangement was in every way suitable. She was not commended to our Lord's 'brethren,' probably because they were not her own children, and were not believers: see on Mt 12 46-50. It is clear that St. Joseph was by this time dead. **Unto his own** *home*] This implies that St. John had a separate establishment at Jerusalem. This would help to explain his acquaintance with Annas (18 15), and his special information about our Lord's ministry at Jerusalem. When our Lord visited Jerusalem, St. John was probably His host.

28–30. Death of Jesus (Mt 27 45-55 ‖). The sayings 'I thirst' and 'It is finished' are peculiar to St. John. The former explains, what the synoptics do not, why 'one of them ran and took a sponge, and filled it with vinegar,' etc. (Mt 27 48 Mk 15 35).

28. That the scripture, etc.] i.e. Ps 69 21: cp. Ps 22 15. Although Jesus mainly based His Messianic claim on His fulfilment of the OT Scriptures in their widest and most general sense (Lk 24 27 Ac 10 43), yet He attached some importance (though less than the disciples did) to their literal and detailed fulfilment. **I thirst**] the fifth 'Word.' These words of human anguish, attesting Christ's true humanity, are significantly absent from the Docetic 'Gospel of Peter,' which says that on the cross He felt no pain. **A vessel**] The Roman soldiers often drank a sour wine, or vinegar, called *posca*. Ulpian says, 'Our soldiers are wont to drink wine and vinegar, one day wine, another day vinegar.' **Hyssop**] i.e. the reed mentioned by the synoptists. But Post (in HDB.) takes it to be a plant like peppermint, added to the wine to make it quench thirst better. **30. It is finished**] (the sixth word). All My earthly work, including the world's redemption, is finished. The three synoptists mention Christ's loud cry, but only St. John mentions what He said. St. Luke alone adds the seventh word, which immediately followed. **Gave up**] The death was voluntary—'No man taketh it from me, but I lay it down of myself' (10 18).

31-37. The sign of the pierced side. A section peculiar to St. John, and claiming expressly to be the testimony of an eyewitness. The knowledge of Jewish and Roman custom displayed in it speaks for its historical truth.

31. The preparation] i.e. the day before the sabbath (Friday). The sabbath began at sunset on Friday: see on v. 14. **That the bodies**] An accurate account of the Jewish practice, as opposed to that of the Romans, who left corpses to rot on their crosses. The letter of the Law (Dt 21 22) required the removal of the bodies in all cases before night; much more was it necessary in this case for the bodies to be removed, seeing that the morrow was a sabbath and a high festival. **An high day**] It was at once the sabbath and the first day of unleavened bread. **That their legs**] A specially Roman practice. The criminal's legs were broken with heavy mallets to accelerate death.

34. Pierced his side] This was done to make sure of His death, and was a common practice at executions. The act was providentially ordered, that it might be made evident that the Resurrection was a resuscitation after a real death, not a mere recovery from a death-like stupor. **Blood and water**] No satisfactory medical explanation of this phenomenon has been given, though it has been suggested that the death of Christ was due to rupture of the heart consequent upon acute mental sufferings, and that thereupon the cavities of the heart became filled with a watery serum, which flowed out when Christ's side was pierced. The evangelist himself seems to have regarded the strange phenomenon as a miracle; he certainly saw in it a deep mystical significance, for which see on 1 Jn 5 6. **35.** The eyewitness claims to be the actual author of the Gospel, in spite of the third person: see 21 24. **36. A bone of him**] In the evangelist's view, Christ's legs were not broken, that it might be thereby made evident that He was the true paschal lamb. The Jews were specially forbidden to break the bones of the Paschal Lamb: see Ex 12 46. **37. They shall look**] St. John quotes directly from the Heb. **of Zech 12 10**, which the LXX has mistrans-

lated. We have here a point of contact with Rev 1 7.

38-42. The burial (see Mt 27 57 Mk 15 42 Lk 23 50). All is in agreement with the synoptists, but there are three additional particulars : (1) That Nicodemus assisted Joseph of Arimathæa; (2) that the tomb was in a garden close by; (3) that the body was embalmed after the Jewish manner with 100 lb. weight of spices. These details imply special knowledge.

39. Myrrh and aloes] The myrrh and the aloe wood were reduced to powder, and inserted between the bandages, which were wound fold upon fold round the body. The enormous quantity (about 75 lb. avoirdupois) of spices, though surprising, is credible as the offering of two wealthy men. According to Jewish and general Eastern custom, the neck and face of the corpse were doubtless left bare : see on 20 8. **42. The Jews' preparation**] see on v. 14.

CHAPTER 20
THE RESURRECTION

1-10. The Resurrection. Visits of Mary Magdalene, and of Peter and John to the tomb of Jesus. (For the Resurrection appearances see on the synoptics, especially on St. Matthew; for the visit of Mary Magdalene see Mt 28 1 Mk 16 1 Lk 24 1, 10; for that of St. Peter see Lk 24 12.) This section, peculiar to the Fourth Gospel, is marked by specially vivid features. The race to the tomb in which John, the younger man, outruns Peter; the impetuous nature of Peter, who enters first; the more reflective character of John, who reads the meaning of the sign of the graveclothes and believes first; the details of the scene inside the sepulchre; the state of mind of the disciples, who had not yet learnt to expect a resurrection ;—all these, as if caught on the plate of a photographic camera, the memory of the aged Apostle faithfully retained. Here is either absolute truth, or artistic realism of a kind unexampled in ancient literature.

2. We know not] Observe the plural, which corroborates the synoptic representation that other women, besides Mary Magdalene, visited the tomb (Mt 28 1 Mk 16 1 Lk 24 1). For the details see on Mt.

8. And he saw and believed] Why did John believe ? Probably because the body of Jesus had miraculously passed through the thick folds of the graveclothes, leaving them unmoved and untouched, just as, on the evening of the same day, the risen Lord appeared in the midst of the disciples, when the doors were shut. It was clear from the position of the clothes, which had not been unwound, that no human hands had removed the Lord's body, and further, since His body had passed unimpeded through solid matter, that it was now a spiritual and glorious body, not bound by the laws of terrestrial matter. Jesus had risen, therefore, not to an earthly but to a heavenly life.

11–18. The appearance to Mary Magdalene. This is different from that of Mt 28 9, but identical with that of Mk 16 9.

12. Two angels] as in Lk. Mt and Mk mention only one. St. John notices their exact attitude and position. **15. Supposing him to be the gardener**] Many did not recognise our Lord at first, because His appearance had undergone a certain change (Mt 28 17 Mk 16 12 Lk 24 16, 37 Jn 21 4). **16. Rabboni**] Edersheim regards this as the Galilean form of 'Rabbi.'

17. Touch me not, etc.] 'I have not come to renew the old intimacy, but am on the point of returning home to My Father. When I am enthroned in heaven, you shall touch Me once more, not however with the physical touch of your hands, but with the spiritual touch of a living faith.' **I ascend**] viz. after forty days. But many recent writers maintain that our Lord ascended immediately after the Resurrection, that He was in heaven during the forty days of earthly manifestation, and that the event called 'the Ascension' (Ac 1 9) was only His final farewell to the disciples, not His entry into glory. **My Father, and your Father**] Observe that Jesus never says 'Our Father,' or 'Our God,' as if He stood in the same relation to God as other men. The Lord's prayer is no exception, for it is a prayer of the disciples, not of Jesus Himself.

19–23. Jesus appears in the evening to the disciples: see Lk 24 36 (Mk 16 14). According to St. Mark, Jesus appeared ' to the eleven as they sat at meat.' St. John is more precise, noting the absence of Thomas. St. Luke says that Jesus appeared 'to the eleven and them that were with them.' By this time our Lord had appeared, not only to Mary Magdalene and the women, but also to the two disciples walking to Emmaus, and to Peter.

19. The doors were shut] A clear indication that our Lord's body had become a spiritual body, and was no longer subject to the ordinary laws of matter, or the conditions of space: cp. v. 26 Lk 24 31, 36 and Lk 24 51 RM. Yet there is no suggestion of an unreal or phantom (Docetic) body, for He offers it to be handled (Lk 24 39 Jn 20 27); and even eats before them (Lk 24 42 Ac 1 4 (RM) 10 41). It is to be presumed that Jesus closed the interview by mysteriously vanishing. **Peace**] The usual Jewish greeting, but how full of meaning now that the Cross had made peace between man and God!

21. Sent.. send] The Gk. words are different: cp. 17 18.

22. Breathed on *them*] The word for 'breath' and 'spirit' is the same in Gk. By this action

our Lord showed how closely the Holy Spirit is connected with His person, being in fact ' the spirit of Jesus.' The Church has never ventured to imitate this action, but has substituted in ordination the laying-on of hands.

Receive ye the Holy Ghost] i.e. for the purpose of consecration to the ministerial office. The Spirit was undoubtedly given at this time, and yet, we must suppose, not in its full power till Pentecost: see 7 39 16 7. **23. Whosoever sins ye remit**] This includes all the means by which, through the ministry of the Word, souls are reconciled to God ; e.g. baptism, the preaching of repentance, and moral discipline, as well as absolution (see on Mt 18 18).

As others were present besides the Apostles (Lk 24 33), it has been suggested that the ministerial powers here mentioned were conferred not upon the Apostles only, but upon the whole Church. St. John, however, who alone mentions the communication of ministerial powers, mentions the Apostles only as receiving them. It is possible indeed that our Lord's commission to baptise and teach, etc., was given to the corporate body of believers (see Mt 28 16-20), but it was clearly intended to be normally exercised through an authorised ministry.

Christians of different communions and schools of thought are not entirely at one as to the precise meaning of this verse, and their explanations of it differ very considerably, at least in detail. A full account of the numerous interpretations cannot be given here. It must suffice to indicate very briefly, for the information of the reader, the two main views which are taken of the nature of the power to 'remit' and 'retain' sins, which the risen Lord here communicates to His Apostles, and through them to His Church. (1) Many believers see in it nothing but the power to exercise ecclesiastical discipline. They regard sins as 'retained,' when a notorious offender is excommunicated, i.e. deprived for a time of the sacraments and other ministrations of the Church, and 'remitted,' when, as a penitent, he is restored once more to full communion. On this view, the forgiveness which the Church is empowered to bestow, is only a *human* forgiveness,—the forgiveness of the injured and justly offended Christian brotherhood. (2) Other believers hold that something more is intended. Impressed with the mysterious solemnity of the words themselves, of their occasion, and of the symbolical act which accompanied them, remembering also that our Lord more than once promised that the discipline of the earthly Church, when rightly exercised, should be ratified in heaven (Mt 16 19 18 18 : cp. 1 Cor 5 5 2 Cor 2 10), they believe the meaning to be that God Himself (normally and usually) ratifies in heaven the remitting and retaining of sins by the earthly Church, though He still, of course, retains in His own hands the power to remedy all injustice, and to grant pardon (where penitence is deep and real), even beyond the covenanted channel.

When the important and far-reaching qualifications with which the second view is now generally held are duly considered, it will probably appear to many readers that the two views are not so much fundamentally opposed, as expressive of two different aspects of truth. At any rate there is at present a strong tendency among theologians representing the two points of view to come to a better understanding by frank mutual explanations.

25, 26. The doubts of Thomas. Thomas in a sense represents the spirit of our age. He will be satisfied with nothing less than the evidence of the senses.

25. The print of the nails] It is clear that Thomas had witnessed the crucifixion.

26–29. Second appearance to the Apostles. Climax of the Gospel in the Confession of Thomas.

26. After eight days] i.e. on the next Sunday, both Sundays being counted in. Here we have the beginning of the observance of the Lord's Day, as the weekly memorial of the Resurrection. The other NT. references are Ac 20⁷ 1 Cor 16² Rev 1¹⁰. **Within**] viz. in the same upper room in Jerusalem ; not, as some think, in Galilee. **Thomas with them**] His presence shows a willingness to be convinced. **The doors being shut**] see on v. 19. **27.** Probably Thomas did not avail himself of our Lord's invitation. **28. My Lord and my God**] The climax of the gospel. The unbelief of Thomas passes into faith in Christ's true Deity. Observe that Jesus accepts and approves the confession of Thomas. **29.** It is better to be convinced by moral and spiritual evidence than by the evidence of the senses.

30, 31. Conclusion of the Gospel.

30. Many other signs] probably refers to signs done after the Resurrection. Those done before the Resurrection were done in the presence of the people. **31.** The author's purpose in writing is to produce faith in Jesus as the Messiah, and as the Son of God, i.e. as divine : see v. 28. **Life**] i.e. eternal life.

Through his name] i.e. through union with Him as the incarnate Son of God. His 'name' is His nature as the God-Man.

Here the Gospel originally closed.

CHAPTER 21

SUPPLEMENTARY

1–25. Appendix. The Gospel is brought to a definite close, its contents are reviewed, and its purpose stated in 20³⁰, ³¹. The present c. is therefore probably an appendix added at a later time, but (since all MSS and versions contain it) before the Gospel had been exten-

sively copied, or had passed into general circulation. There is good reason for supposing that it is by the same author as the Gospel. For (1) the style is identical. For example, there is a fondness for the same connecting particles, and for sentences beginning abruptly without any conjunction at all. The favourite Johannine words are used, such as ' manifest,' ' glorify,' ' witness,' ' love,' ' disciples ' (in the sense of ' apostles '). Everywhere too is displayed that peculiar and inimitable simplicity which characterises the Johannine writings generally. (2) There are also important correspondences with the narrative of the Fourth Gospel. The Sea of Tiberias and Cana of Galilee are mentioned only in that Gospel and in this appendix. Didymus and Nathanael, as actual characters and under these names, appear only in St. John. Common to this Gospel and this appendix, and to them only, is the mention of ' the disciple whom Jesus loved,' and of his leaning upon the Master's breast at supper, and the insistence upon the truth of his testimony : cp. 19³⁵. Characteristic also is the peculiar expression ' signifying by what manner of death he should glorify God ' : cp. 12³³ 18³². The only really doubtful vv. are the last two (vv. 24, 25), which may possibly have been added by the Ephesian elders, who first put the Gospel in circulation after the death of the Apostle, and who wished to testify to its genuineness and trustworthiness. The main object of the appendix is to correct a popular belief that the beloved disciple would not die before our Lord's Second Advent (v. 23).

1–14. Manifestation of the risen Lord to seven disciples at the Sea of Tiberias. The Fourth Gospel confirms the synoptic tradition that there were appearances in Galilee as well as in Judæa. The date of this appearance cannot be fixed.

1. Shewed (RV ' manifested ') **himself**] see on 2¹¹. **2. Of Cana**] A later writer would not have been likely to possess this additional information. **The** *sons* **of Zebedee**] i.e. James (called ' the Great '), and St. John the Evangelist. **Two others**] The ' Gospel of Peter ' seems to identify them with Andrew and Levi (Matthew). **3. I go a fishing**] The period of waiting had doubtless tried the Apostles severely, and it was more as a distraction, than as a means of livelihood that St. Peter returned to his nets. **That night**] At night it is easy to catch fish, because then they cannot see the nets. In daylight it is much more difficult. The successful draught (v. 6) was made in daylight, and is therefore probably to be regarded as miraculous. **4. Knew not**] A certain change had passed over our Lord's body : see on 20¹⁵. **5. Children**] cp. 13³³. From our Lord, St. John learnt to call his own converts by this affectionate title : see on 13³³. The exact word is in 1 Jn 2¹³,¹⁸, a similar one in 13³³, 1 Jn 2¹,¹²,²⁸ 3 7,¹⁸ 4 4 5²¹.

7. That disciple] As at the visit to the tomb, so here, the beloved disciple is the first to draw the true inference. This undesigned coincidence speaks for genuineness. **8. As it were two hundred cubits**] i.e. 300 ft. **9. Coals**] i.e. charcoal. **Fish**] or a fish. **Bread**] or a loaf

How Jesus prepared this meal is a mystery, but why He did so is plain. He wished, after the Resurrection, as well as before it, to set Himself forth as the bread of life, or the spiritual food of mankind, and He did so, as in c. 6, by a symbolical act. There is probably a reference to the Holy Communion, as was perceived already in the 2nd cent. The recently discovered inscription on the tomb of Abercius, bishop of Hierapolis in Phrygia in the reign of Marcus Aurelius (161–180 A.D.), contains the words, 'Everywhere faith led the way, and set before me for food the fish from the fountain, mighty and stainless, which a pure virgin grasped, and gave this to friends to eat always, having good wine, and giving the mixed cup with bread.' Here the fish is Christ, the fountain baptism, the pure virgin the Church (see Lightfoot, 'Apost. Fathers,' pt. 2, vol. 1, p. 480). In the catacombs at Rome also, in the cemetery of St. Lucina, is a fresco representing a fish (i.e. Christ) bearing upon its back a basket full of sacramental bread.

Yet was not the net broken] The earlier draught of fishes with the breaking net symbolised the Church on earth, imperfect in its organisation and methods, and allowing many souls to escape from its meshes. This draught, in which the net is unbroken and every fish is brought safe to shore, symbolises the Church triumphant in heaven, freed at last from all earthly imperfections, and embracing in its membership all genuine servants of God whose salvation is now for ever assured.

14. The third time] i.e. the third appearance to any considerable number of Apostles collectively. The appearances, private or semiprivate, to Mary Magdalene, the women, the two disciples, Peter, and James, are not reckoned. The appearances on the mountain in Galilee, and to the five hundred, had apparently not yet taken place.

This being a 'spiritual' Gospel, the allegorical interpretation of this incident is to be firmly maintained. So interpreted, it constitutes a renewed call by the risen Lord to the Apostles to become 'fishers of men,' and a renewed promise to be with them in their work. The details also, the unbroken net, the fish and the bread, probably even the number of the fishes,

are to be mystically interpreted, but the meaning of the last is uncertain. The other chief Johannine book, the Apocalypse, abounds in the mysticism of numbers.

15–17. Restoration of St. Peter to his apostolic office. By his threefold denial Peter had forfeited his position among the apostles. Hence, before restoring him, Jesus required from him a threefold confession of love. Quite baseless is the papal interpretation that St. Peter is here endowed with supreme ecclesiastical jurisdiction over the other apostles. All that is done is to restore him to his old position.

15. Simon, *son* **of Jonas**] RV 'son of John': see 1⁴². Observe that in this, as in the other Gospels, our Lord does not call him Peter. Lk 22³⁴ is the only exception. **Lovest thou me** (*agapās*) **more than these?**] i.e. more than these thy brethren love Me ? Once (Mt 26³³ Jn 13³⁷) Peter had boasted of a love and constancy greater than that of others. Now he is more humble. In his reply he will not say that he loves Jesus 'more than these.' He will not even say that he loves Jesus at all in the full sense of Christian love (*agapān, agapē*). All he will say is that he loves Jesus with the warmth of personal affection (*philein, philia*). Twice Jesus asks him, 'Lovest thou Me ?' (*agapān*). The third time He adopts Peter's own word, *philein*. **Feed my lambs**] lit. 'give food to them,' i.e. by the ministry of the Word and Sacraments. The 'lambs' here are probably neither Christian children nor recent converts, but, like the 'sheep' in vv. 16, 17, Christians in general, the name being one of affection : cp. 1 Pet 5²,³. **16. Feed** (RV 'tend') **my sheep**] Here the Gk. word indicates authority, so that the meaning is, Exercise discipline and authority over the flock : so Ac 20²⁸ 1 Pet 5² Rev 2²⁷ 7¹⁷, and often in OT. **17. Thou knowest**] or, rather, 'perceivest' (RV).

18–20. Prophecy of Peter's Martyrdom.

18. Thou shalt stretch forth thy hands (upon the arms of the cross), **and another** (i.e. the executioner) **shall gird thee** (viz. with the loincloth, the only garment allowed to criminals at their execution) **and carry** *thee* **whither thou wouldest not** (viz. to execution). St. John here assumes the manner of St. Peter's death to be known to his readers. According to the probably true tradition, St. Peter and St. Paul were martyred at Rome about 68 A.D., the former being crucified, the latter beheaded.

19. Follow me] i.e. by dying the death of crucifixion. 'Follow' here is metaphorical.

20–23. The misunderstood saying about the beloved disciple.

20. Following] viz. in a literal sense. Our Lord, during His conversation with Peter, had walked to a little distance from the others. Peter, happening to turn round, sees John fol lowing. **21. What** *shall* **this man** *do?*] i.e. Shall he also die a glorious martyr's death? Seeing that our Lord rebukes the question, there was probably in it some latent jealousy, or, at least, presumption. **22. Tarry**] i.e. remain alive. **Till I come**] The reference is not to the destruction of Jerusalem, but to the Last Judgment: cp. 14³. **23. Should not die**] In spite of this appendix, the opinion still persisted. One story was that he was translated like Elijah, another that he still breathed in his grave, a fable which even St. Augustine was inclined to believe.

24, 25. Conclusion. V. 24 is full of St.

Additional Note.

According to the generally received tradition, which dates from at least the former half of the second century, the Apostle John, the son of Zebedee, after the martyrdom of St. Paul, 67 A.D., or more probably after the fall of Jerusalem, 70 A.D., migrated from Jerusalem to Ephesus, and there ruled the Churches of Asia Minor for more than a quarter of a century, and finally died a natural death in the reign of Trajan (about 100 A.D.), having first composed and published the Fourth Gospel, and the First Epistle of John, perhaps also the Second and Third Epistles and the Revelation. As the trustworthiness of this tradition has lately been challenged, it will be convenient to place before the reader a summary of the early evidence.

St. Justin Martyr (150 A.D.) attributes the Revelation to the Apostle John, and since that book is in the form of a pastoral letter to ' the seven churches which are in Asia ' (1⁴), Justin must have believed in the Asiatic sojourn of the Apostle.

St. Irenæus, who wrote in Gaul 177 A.D., but whose youth was spent in Asia, where he had been a hearer of St. Polycarp, a personal disciple of St. John, says :

' Thus all the elders testify, who were conversant in Asia with John the disciple of the Lord. And he remained among them up to the times of Trajan ' (98-117 A.D).

' Afterwards John, the disciple of the Lord, who also had leaned upon His breast, himself published a Gospel during his residence at Ephesus in Asia.'

'While I was yet a boy, I saw thee (Florinus) in Lower Asia with Polycarp. I can even describe the place where the blessed Polycarp used to sit and discourse, and how he would speak of his familiar intercourse with John, and with the rest of those who had seen the Lord.'

Polycrates (who as bishop of Ephesus had

John's own phrases and mannerisms, and, therefore, in spite of the plural ' we know,' is probably by the Apostle himself. Nor is there any absolutely cogent reason for rejecting v. 25, which is absent from only one ancient MS.

We know] The apostle associates himself with the members of the Ephesian Church, who knew him well, and were convinced of his truthfulness. Some, however, think that the ' we ' are the Ephesian elders, who published the Gospel, and thus declared it authentic. **25.** The author apologises for the incompleteness and fragmentary character of his work.

John at Ephesus

special opportunities for knowing the truth) in a letter written to Victor, bishop of Rome, about 193 A.D., speaks of ' John who was both a witness and a teacher, who reclined upon the bosom of the Lord, and, being a priest, wore the sacerdotal plate. He fell asleep at Ephesus.'

Tertullian, 200 A.D., and **Clement of Alexandria,** 200 A.D., give similar evidence.

There are two main difficulties, which are held by some to throw a considerable doubt upon the truth of this tradition. (1) The ninth-century Chronicle of Georgius Hamartolos says, ' Papias, bishop of Hierapolis, declares in the second book of the Oracles of the Lord that John was put to death by the Jews.' Of course if Papias (130 A.D.) did say this, and if the execution of John took place in Palestine, the Ephesian ministry of the Apostle is excluded. But it is significant that the earlier ecclesiastical writers, most of whom, like Irenæus and Eusebius, were diligent students of Papias, seem to know nothing of this supposed Palestinian martyrdom of John, and, on the contrary, represent him as surviving all the other Apostles, and dying a natural death in extreme old age at Ephesus. Probably Georgius has misinterpreted some obscure statement of Papias, whose style is always slovenly, and often ambiguous. (2) Among the personal disciples of Jesus, according to Papias, were two Johns, John the Apostle and John the Presbyter (or Elder). It is suggested by some that the John who settled at Ephesus and was the instructor of Polycarp, was not the Apostle but the Presbyter. This view does not seem very probable. We are not told that the Presbyter had any connexion with Asia, and it hardly seems credible that Irenæus, who was a hearer of Polycarp, can have so completely misunderstood hi Master's references to John. as to suppose that he meant the Apostle when he really meant the Presbyter.

THE ACTS OF THE APOSTLES

INTRODUCTION

1. Plan and Purpose. (1) Acts represents the exact religious standpoint of St. Paul. Its theme, the expansion of Christianity from a Jewish sect into a world-wide religion, is in fact St. Paul's own ideal, in pursuit of which he broke every hindering tie, and strained every faculty of mind and body for upwards of thirty years. The keynote of the book is struck at once in 1⁸, 'Ye shall be witnesses unto Me both in Jerusalem and in Samaria, and unto the uttermost part of the earth.' These words, uttered by the risen Lord, fell at the time upon dull and inattentive ears. At first the Twelve realised only their mission to the house of Israel. It required a special revelation to procure the baptism of the Ethiopian eunuch, and a thrice-repeated vision to induce the reluctant Peter to baptise Cornelius. Even when these important steps had been taken, the Twelve showed such hesitation to undertake aggressive work among the Gentiles, that the Lord of the Church raised up a thirteenth apostle to champion Gentile rights, and to inaugurate a more liberal policy. This 'chosen vessel,' converted by a special miracle, and endowed with an authority independent of the Twelve, broke through the old prejudices which still hampered the original disciples, founded flourishing Gentile Churches, in which the Law was no longer observed, in the most important eastern provinces of the Empire, and, at the date when the book closes (about 61 A.D.), was proclaiming the gospel in the great western capital itself.

The book is thus a defence of Gentile Christianity, and of its great originator and advocate, St. Paul, of whom the author was a companion and enthusiastic admirer. What Boswell was to Johnson, that this unnamed writer was to St. Paul. Just as Johnson owes the affectionate regard of posterity in no small measure to the labours of his faithful and admiring biographer Boswell, so St. Paul owes his place of esteem in the minds of subsequent generations as the ideal Christian hero and missionary very largely to the author of Acts. The Pauline Epistles may teach us more of the Apostle's inner life, but it is Acts which gives us those outward facts which make him live before us as an actual character on the scene of history.

(2) But the writer of Acts has still a further purpose. He recognises in a manner quite remarkable for so thoroughgoing a supporter of St. Paul, the immense value and importance of the work of St. Peter and the earlier Apostles. It is probable that when he wrote (about 61 A.D.), there still lingered in Gentile Churches some suspicion of the opinions and methods of the Twelve, and in the Judaic Churches of Palestine some dislike and distrust of the Apostle of the Gentiles. This the writer deliberately determined to remove. He therefore divided his book into two distinct sections, chs. 1–12, in which the chief hero is St. Peter, and chs. 13–28 in which the chief hero is St. Paul. He intended his Gentile readers by a perusal of chs. 1–12 to be brought to understand and to admire St. Peter, and his Jewish Christian readers by a perusal of the rest of the book to be brought to understand St. Paul. True to his purpose of acting as a peacemaker, he places both his heroes in the most attractive possible light, passes lightly over the past differences and misunderstandings (e.g. he omits the serious dispute between Peter and Paul at Antioch, Gal 2¹¹ᶠ·, altogether), and dwells far more upon the points of agreement than upon the points of difference between two great Christian parties.

(3) There are reasons for thinking that the author intended his work to be also a kind of apology for Christianity addressed to the heathen world. Without going to the length of supposing, as some do, that it was intended to be produced and read at St. Paul's trial as a formal vindication of the Apostle and his religion against the misrepresentations of his accusers, we may still discern in almost every chapter a desire to influence favourably Gentile readers, especially those belonging to the cultured and official classes. The author is well equipped for his task. He writes as an educated man to educated men. He opens his book with a short preface and dedication in the approved classical manner. He writes in a style which, if not the purest Attic Greek, is still graceful, easy, refined, and forcible. It is not only superior to any other Greek in the NT., but it compares favourably with that of many of the best profane authors of the age, and is far superior to the Greek of the early patristic writers, such as St. Clement of Rome, the author of the so-called Second Epistle of Clement, the author of the Epistle to Diognetus, and even to that of such

professional scholars as Aristides and St. Justin Martyr. An educated pagan, happening to peruse Acts, could not fail to recognise that some at least of the despised Galileans were persons of culture and refinement. Our author is in close sympathy with the best side of heathen life and religion, recognising that even the worshippers of the false gods of pagan Greece and Rome were feeling after the true God if haply they might find Him, and that He had not left Himself entirely without witness even in the gross darkness of degrading superstition (14 [15] [17] [27]; cp.Ro1 [20]). He attempts to conciliate the official and power-holding classes, in whose hands was the actual administration of the Empire, by representing St. Paul as a peaceable and law-abiding subject, proud of his Roman citizenship, and, so far from cherishing disloyal designs against the Imperial Government, continually and successfully appealing to its aid against the hostile machinations of the turbulent Jews (18 [14] 19 [31-41] 21 [32] 22 [29] 23 [29] 24 [26] 25 [16-20, 25-27] 26 [32] 27 [3, 43] 28 [7, 10, 16, 30]).

2. Value of the Book. To modern readers the chief value of Acts is that it is the only authentic record which we possess of the first thirty-five years of the history of the Christian Church. With the exception of a few meagre hints in St. Paul's Epistles, Acts is absolutely our only first-century authority for the momentous events which followed the Resurrection and Ascension of our Lord. Even from the purely secular point of view, the process by which an obscure Jewish sect expanded into a world-wide Church, is a subject full of interest; but for Christians, who believe that the process was part of God's gracious purpose for the salvation and regeneration of the world, the subject possesses an interest and attractiveness altogether unique.

3. Trustworthiness and Historical Character of the Narrative. Modern scholars apply tests of great stringency to ancient historical writings which profess to embody the evidence of eyewitnesses or contemporaries. Every statement made in such writings which can possibly be tested, is scrutinised and compared with the statements of other ancient writings of undoubted authority, also with the now very voluminous and valuable evidence of inscriptions, monuments, and coins. If the writer's statements which can be tested are found upon the whole to be accurate and reliable, credit is also given to his statements which cannot be tested, and his work is pronounced to be a valuable authority for the events therein recorded. If, however, his statements which can be tested are found to be frequently false or inaccurate, his work is pronounced unauthentic and unreliable.

These tests have been applied with great and increasing rigour during the last half century to the remains of Christian antiquity, especially to those of a narrative character, like Acts. Tried by these tests, the various apocryphal Acts, e.g. the Acts of Andrew, the Acts of John, the Acts of Paul, the Acts of Peter, the Acts of Thomas, the Acts of Paul and Thecla, and the Preaching of Peter, have been demonstrated to be forgeries. But the canonical Acts of the Apostles has emerged from the ordeal with its reputation established. The book is full of geographical and political notices which admit of definite proof or disproof, and in practically every case (the statement about Theudas, 5 [36], is a possible exception) the author has been proved to be right. Thus he knows that Cyprus was at this time governed by a proconsul (AV 'deputy'), whose name is correctly given as Sergius Paulus (see 13 [7]); that Philippi was a Roman colony, having magistrates called 'prætors' (AV 'magistrates'), attended by 'lictors' (AV 'sergeants') (16 [20], [35]); that the magistrates of Thessalonica were called 'politarchs' (AV 'rulers') (17 [6]); that the ruler of Malta was called 'primus' (AV 'chief man') (28 [7]); that there were officers of the province of Asia called 'Asiarchs' (AV 'the chief of Asia') (19 [31]), with whose functions he is also familiar; that at Athens questions of religion were under the supervision of the 'Areopagus' (17 [19]); that Derbe and Lystra, but not Iconium, were cities of Lycaonia (14 [6]); that Ephesus was 'neocoros' (AV 'a worshipper,' RV 'temple-keeper') to the temple of Artemis, and that political power was exercised by the 'demos' ('people') meeting in 'the lawful assembly,' presided over by an influential officer called the 'secretary' (AV 'town clerk'); that the inhabitants of Ephesus were addicted to magic (19 [13 f.]), etc. He thoroughly understands the Jewish Sanhedrin, its functions and its parties; the position of the chief priests, of the Temple guard, of the Roman garrison in the fortress Antonia, and of the Herodian princes at Jerusalem. He is, moreover, familiar with Roman law, the procedure of Roman tribunals, and the rights and privileges of Roman citizens, e.g. freedom from binding and scourging, and the right of appealing to the Emperor. He seems also to be correct (though further evidence is desirable) in his allusions to the Italic and Augustan 'cohorts' (AV 'bands') at Cæsarea (10 [1] 27 [1]), and to the imperial troops called 'frumentarii,' whose head-quarters were on the Cælian Hill at Rome. He is well acquainted with navigation, and his account of the voyage to Rome has been shown to be true in every detail by professional navigators who have sailed over the course with the express purpose of investigating its accuracy. We may add that the author's allusion to the popular belief at Lystra that Zeus and Hermes (Jupiter and Mercurius) were accustomed to visit the earth in human form, and his descriptions of the temple and priest of 'Zeus propolis' and of the attempted sacrifice to the Apostles, are thoroughly true to life, and have every appearance of historical truth (14 8).

The natural inference from these facts is that either the author himself was a contemporary and an eyewitness, or that his book is based upon and closely follows the evidence of contemporaries and eyewitnesses.

4. Authorship. (1) *Internal evidence.* The book is anonymous, but from internal evidence it is possible to gain much information about, and perhaps to identify, the author.

Certain sections (16 10-17 20 5-15 21 1-18 27 1-28 16 ; also, in the D text, 11 28) are written in the first person plural, and are hence called 'the we-sections.' From them we learn that the author was a native of Antioch, and one of the earliest converts in that place (11 28 D text) ; also that he became a companion of St. Paul during the Second Missionary Journey. Joining the Apostle at Troas (16 10), he accompanied him to Philippi, where he was left behind, seemingly in pastoral charge of the newly-established Church (17 1). There he remained some years, probably engaged in evangelising the district, until St. Paul revisited Philippi on his Third Missionary Journey. He then accompanied the Apostle to Cæsarea, and Jerusalem (20 6 21 1-18), and finally to Rome (c. 27).

Who was this companion ? He cannot have been Silas (Silvanus), who was present at the Council of Jerusalem (15 22), and would therefore have used the first person in describing it ; nor Timothy, who is spoken of in the third person (17 14) ; nor Titus, who was a companion of the Apostle before the we-sections begin (Gal 2 3), and therefore, had he been the author, would have begun the we-sections earlier. There remains Luke, who, in harmony with the indications of Acts, appears as a companion of St. Paul only in the later Epistles (Col 4 14 Philemon v. 24 2 Tim 4 11), and who was certainly, as Acts indicates, with St. Paul at Rome (Col 4 14 Philemon v. 24). In Col 4 14, Luke is called the 'beloved physician,' and this again suits the author of Acts, who has an unusual (probably a professional) knowledge of medicine, and shows considerable acquaintance with the technical terms of the Greek medical writers (for instances see 3 7 9 18 12 23 13 11 28 8, etc.). Internal evidence, therefore, points with certainty to a companion of St. Paul, and with considerable probability to St. Luke, as the author.

(2) *External evidence.* The internal evidence is decisively confirmed by the external. Thus (a) the author of Acts is certainly also the author of the Third Gospel. The common dedication to Theophilus, the reference to a 'former treatise' of a scope and character exactly answering to the Gospel, the absolute identity of style spirit and Pauline standpoint, and, we may add, the common exhibition of unusual medical knowledge, point decisively to common authorship, and since the Gospel is ascribed by very ancient tradition to St. Luke, Acts must also be his. (b) Acts was received by all ancient authorities as the unquestioned work of Luke, the companion of Paul. Tertullian, Clement of Alexandria, and the Muratorian fragment (circ. 200 A.D.) all ascribe it to Luke. A little earlier Irenæus (177 A.D.) transcribes long passages from it into his work, 'Against Heresies.' There are also practically certain references to it in the works of Clement of Rome (95 A.D.), Polycarp (110 A.D.), and in the Epistle of the Churches of Gaul (177 A.D.). This strong combination of internal and external evidence raises the Lucan authorship to a practical certainty.

The suggestion of certain critics that only the 'we-sections' are the work of a companion of St. Paul, and that the rest of the book is by another and much later writer, cannot be taken very seriously. A uniform and easily recognisable style pervades the whole book, so that if any of it is by a companion of St Paul, the whole is.

It is probably unnecessary to say much about the theory of F. C. Baur and the Tübingen school that Acts is an unauthentic romance of the middle of the second century. Recent research has tended so strongly to confirm the antiquity and credibility of Acts, that the theory in question has been generally abandoned even in the circle in which it originated.

5. Date. The most natural date to assign to Acts is towards the close of the first Roman imprisonment (circ. 61 A.D.). It is hard to believe that if St. Paul's trial had actually taken place when the book was written, the author would have failed to mention the result.

So early a date, however, involves some difficulties. It throws back the date of St. Luke's Gospel to 60, perhaps to 56 or 57, and St. Mark's (which St. Luke used) still further. To many critics these dates seem altogether too early. Holding as they do, that St. Luke's Gospel contains indications (see on Lk 21) that it was not composed till after the fall of Jerusalem, 70 A.D., they date the Gospel shortly after 70, and Acts towards the close of the decade 70–80. We may fairly leave the question open, with a preference for the former view.

6. The Text. The codex Bezæ (D) and

certain other authorities, generally called 'western,' exhibit a text so different from that either of the RV or the AV, that it may almost be said to constitute a different edition of the book. The chief 'western' variations are at 8^{37} $11^{27, 28}$ 12^{10} $14^{3, 5, 6}$ 15^{2} 15^{26} 16^{35} $19^{9, 14, 25, 28}$ 20^{15} $21^{1, 6}$, where the notes should be consulted. The Bezan variations give additional particulars, which in nearly all cases seem to be authentic. We attribute them, therefore, if not to St. Luke himself, at any rate to some well-informed writer of the apostolic or sub-apostolic age.

7. Sources. For the early history of the Church of Jerusalem, there was available the testimony of St. Mark, who was certainly with St. Luke at Rome (Col $4^{10, 14}$); also the testimony of Philip, with whom St. Luke stayed 'many days' at Cæsarea (21^{10}). During the long waiting at Cæsarea, St. Luke doubtless visited Jerusalem, and obtained additional information from James, John, Peter, and others. His knowledge of St. Paul's career was of course obtained from St. Paul himself, and from his own experiences as his companion.

8. Theology of Acts. The extremely primitive and simple character of the theology of Acts is a strong proof of the authenticity of the record. The great dogmatic Epistles of St. Paul had already appeared when Acts was written, but hardly the faintest trace of their characteristic expressions occurs in the author's narrative.

(1) **Christology.** The Apostles insist that Jesus is the expected Messiah. His Messiahship is proved partly from prophecy and partly from the fact of the Resurrection. In general it is declared that 'to Him give all the prophets witness'; and again, 'yea, and all the prophets from Samuel, and them that followed after as many as have spoken, they also told of these days.' In particular Moses (Dt 18^{15}) is quoted as to our Lord's prophetic office, and Joel (2^{28}) as to the outpouring of the Spirit in the age of the Messiah. But most of the quotations are from the Psalms. Ps 16^{10} is quoted both by St. Peter and St. Paul as a proof of the Resurrection; and Ps 2^{7} by St. Paul in the same sense (see Ac 13^{33}). Ps 132^{11} is quoted to prove the Davidic descent of the Messiah, and Ps 110^{1} to illustrate the Ascension. Ps 118^{22} ('the stone which the builders rejected') is also applied to Jesus as in the Gospels. But the great proof of the Messiahship of Jesus is the crowning miracle of His Resurrection, which is appealed to on every occasion with the greatest confidence. In the house of Cornelius Peter claims to have eaten and drunk with Jesus after He rose from the dead (10^{41}). On the day of Pentecost Peter says, 'This Jesus did God raise up, whereof

we all are witnesses' (2^{32}), and in general the history declares, 'with great power gave the Apostles their witness to the Resurrection of the Lord Jesus.' (4^{33}).

But faith in our Lord's Messiahship was intended by the Apostles to lead on (as it had in their own case) to faith in our Lord's Divinity. The indications that Jesus was already regarded as a Divine Person are neither few nor insignificant. Such titles as 'the prince of life,' 'Lord of all,' 'Judge of quick and dead,' and 'Saviour,' are only really applicable to one who is divine. More significant still is the practice of prayer to Christ. The dying Stephen invoked not God, but Jesus, to forgive his murderers and to receive his spirit (7^{59} RV). The Christians even received their name from their practice of praying to Jesus (9^{14} 9^{21} 22^{16}). In that age, among a people trained to regard God as the only lawful object of religious devotion, and to guard His unique prerogatives with the utmost jealousy, prayer to Jesus clearly implied that He was within the Godhead. Another significant indication of what was believed about Jesus within the Church is contained in the confidential address of St. Paul to the elders of Ephesus (20^{28}). There, according to the best reading (see RV), St. Paul said to the elders, 'Feed the Church of God, which He purchased with His own blood,' thus expressly assigning the divine name to Jesus. It is somewhat remarkable that the title 'the Son (*huios*) of God,' so common in the Gospels and Epistles, never occurs in the early speeches in Acts. Its place is taken by another word, *pais* ($3^{13, 26}$ $4^{25, 27, 30}$), which the AV also translates 'Son,' but the RV 'servant.' Both translations are supported by good modern authorities. The Gospel title, 'Son of God' (*huios*), occurs only in the (probably genuine) confession of the eunuch (8^{37}), and in the preaching of St. Paul (9^{20} 13^{33}).

Characteristic of Acts is the stress laid upon the continued activity of the Ascended Lord, who is regarded as still carrying on from heaven the work which He began on earth.

(2) **The Doctrine of the Holy Spirit.** Much prominence is given to the activity of the Holy Spirit, who is regarded mainly as the Spirit of the Ascended Christ. Although He is a 'gift' of Christ to believers ($2^{3, 38}$), His will and personality are strongly marked ($8^{29, 39}$ 10^{19} 11^{12} 13^{2} $16^{6, 7}$ 20^{23} 21^{11} 28^{25}), as also is His Divinity ($5^{3 f.}$). The doctrines of the personality and divinity of the Spirit, however, are not as yet thrown into definite theological language.

(3) **Universalism.** The writer strongly sympathises with St. Paul's view that the obligation of the Ceremonial Law had been abrogated by Christ, and that Gentiles ought to be

admitted to the Church without being circumcised. At the same time, he is perfectly fair to St. Paul's opponents, and never uses bitter language against them. The tone of his book is generous and conciliatory. He does full justice to St. Peter and St. James and the other apostles of the circumcision : see § 1.

(4) **Petrine and Pauline Theology.** It is a proof of the accuracy of the writer that the speeches of Peter and Paul reflect the characteristic ideas of the speakers ; but yet so naturally and unobtrusively that it is obvious that the writer has not copied their Epistles. The speeches of St. Peter have many points of contact with 1 Peter (see on 2^{14}), and those of St. Paul have recognisable, though by no means close, coincidences with the Pauline Epistles.

9. Contents, Chronology, and connexion with the Epistles.

I. THE CHURCH IN JERUSALEM, 1^1–8^3. 29–35 A.D.

The Ascension, Pentecost. First conflicts with the Sanhedrin. Stephen's speech and martyrdom.

II. THE CHURCH IN JUDÆA AND SAMARIA, 8^4–11^{18}. 35, 36 A.D.

Philip in Samaria. Conversion of Saul (probably 35 or 36 A.D., though some place it as early as 30 A.D., shortly after the Ascension). Baptism of Cornelius, and important discussion thereupon.

III. THE CHURCH OF THE WORLD, 11^{18}–28^{31}. 35–61 A.D.

(1) **The Church in Antioch,** 11^{19}–13^3. 35–47 A.D.

Mission of Paul and Barnabas to Jerusalem. Persecution by Herod Agrippa I (44 A.D.). Barnabas and Saul sent forth from Antioch.

(2) **First Missionary Journey of Paul and Barnabas,** 13^4–15^{35}. 47 A.D.

Cyprus, Pisidia, Antioch, Iconium, Lystra, Derbe. Return to Syrian Antioch.

Possible date for the Epistle to the Galatians, beginning of 49 A.D.

Council of Jerusalem, Pentecost, 49 (?) A.D.

(3) **Second Missionary Journey of Paul,** 15^{36}–18^{22}. 49–52 A.D.

Galatia revisited, Europe, Philippi, Thessalonica, Berœa, Athens.

Corinth, 18^{1-18}. 1 and 2 Thessalonians written from Corinth, 50–52 A.D.

Possible date of St. Matthew's Hebrew 'Logia' or Gospel, about 45–50 A.D.

Visit to Jerusalem, and return to Syrian Antioch.

(4) **Third Missionary Journey of Paul,** 18^{23}–21^{16}. Aug. 52 A.D. to Pentecost, 56 A.D.

Galatia revisited, Apollos at Ephesus, Paul at Ephesus, 19^{1-41} (53–55 A.D.).

1 Corinthians written early in 55 A.D.

Paul in Macedonia and Greece (Corinth), 20^{1-6} (55, 56 A.D.).

2 Corinthians and (according to usual view) Galatians, written from Macedonia, and Romans from Corinth.

Possible date of St. Mark's Gospel.

Troas, 20^{7-12}. Voyage to Jerusalem, 20^{13}–21^{16}.

(5) **Paul in Jerusalem and Cæsarea,** 21^{17}–28^{16}.

Pentecost, 56–59 A.D.

Paul's arrest. Cæsarea. Paul before Felix, Festus, Agrippa. Possible date for St. Luke's Gospel, 57, 58 A.D. Voyage to Rome.

(6) **Paul in Rome,** 28^{17-31}. From 59 A.D.

Epistles to the Philippians, Colossians, Ephesians, and Philemon.

Probable date of Acts, 61 A.D.

———

St. Paul's trial before Nero, and acquittal, 61 A.D.

Labours in Spain, Crete, Asia Minor, Macedonia, Achæa. Epistles to Titus and 1 Timothy written, 65 (?) A.D.

Second imprisonment at Rome. The Second Epistle to Timothy written, 67 A.D.

Second trial, condemnation and martyrdom of St. Paul (probably of St. Peter also), 67 A.D.

[Some authorities place the martyrdom of SS. Peter and Paul earlier, in 64 A.D.]

PART 1

THE ESTABLISHMENT AND PROGRESS OF THE CHURCH AT JERUSALEM (Chs. 1–8^3)

The Acts of the Apostles] A more adequate title would be 'The Acts of Peter and Paul,' the Acts of Peter extending from c. 1 to c. 12, and the Acts of Paul from c. 13 to c. 28.

CHAPTER 1

THE ASCENSION. ELECTION OF MATTHIAS

1–5. St. Luke's Introduction. He recapitulates the general contents of his Gospel, adding, however, this additional information, (1) that the appearances of the risen Lord were numerous, and (2) that forty days elapsed between the Resurrection and the Ascension. If we possessed St. Luke's Gospel only, we might possibly conclude that the risen Lord appeared only three times, and that He ascended on the very day of His Resurrection.

1. The former treatise] i.e. St. Luke's Gospel : see Intro. **Theophilus**] see on Lk 1^3.

Began] The Gospel records the work that Jesus began to do. Acts records its accomplishment. The chief agent in this book is the Ascended Christ Himself, operating through His Spirit, and performing works which were not possible while He was still in the flesh (Jn 14 12). **2. Through the Holy Ghost**] St. Luke represents all the actions of Christ's ministry as performed by the power of the Holy Spirit, which He received at His Baptism to consecrate Him to His office of Messiah : see 10 38. **Commandments**] viz. to preach repentance and remission of sins to all nations beginning at Jerusalem, and to tarry in the city until they should be endued with power from on high (Lk 24 47 f.).

3. Many infallible proofs] RV omits 'infallible,' but the Gk. implies that they were reliable and convincing. The 'many' is important, for St. Luke records only four appearances, all in Judæa : see art. 'The Resurrection.'

Forty days] i.e. at intervals during forty days. **The kingdom of God**] Sometimes 'the Kingdom of God' denotes the inward and spiritual aspects of Christianity, sometimes Christianity as organised into a visible Kingdom or Church. Both meanings are here blended. The departing Lord doubtless wished to give the Apostles spiritual instructions to prepare them to receive the Holy Spirit, and also special directions for the future government of His Church : see intro. to Mt, § 6 (5), and prefatory remarks to Mt 5. **4. And, being assembled**] rather, 'and while sitting at meat with them' : see RM and cp. Mk 16 14. The fact of the risen Lord's eating is attested also by Lk 24 42, where Jesus eats 'before' the disciples ; and the sitting at table by Ac 10 41.

The promise of the Father] i.e. the promised gift of the Holy Ghost which was to be bestowed at Pentecost : see Lk 24 49.

5. Baptized with the Holy Ghost] There can be little doubt that the Apostles had already received baptism, not only from John, but also from Jesus Himself : see Jn 3 22, 26 4 1, 2. But Christian Baptism was not yet, in the full sense, a Baptism 'with the Holy Ghost and with fire,' because, Jesus being not yet glorified, the Holy Ghost could not yet be fully given (Jn 7 39).

6–11. The Ascension. Belief in the Ascension of Jesus follows necessarily from belief in His Resurrection. If Jesus rose from the dead not with a natural, but with a spiritual body (and this is undoubtedly the doctrine of Holy Scripture), then it was impossible for Him to remain permanently on earth. The translation of His body to that sphere of existence to which it now properly belonged, was both natural and necessary. The Ascension is only described in detail in the present passage. The allusion to it in Lk 24 51, though probable, is not certain, and that in Mk 16 19 is not by the writer of the Second Gospel. The paucity of allusions to the Ascension in the **NT.** is probably due to the fact that it was

not accompanied by any change in the condition of Jesus. It was on the first day of His Resurrection, not on the fortieth, that Jesus was glorified and invested with all authority in heaven and on earth (Mt 28 18) ; hence the event of Ac 1 9 was regarded by the Apostles as of secondary importance. In the Ascension, as in the Resurrection, Christ is the firstfruits of the human race, opening the Kingdom of heaven to all believers. He is also, as ascended, the high priest and intercessor of humanity, pleading on man's behalf, before the eternal Father, His completed sacrifice (Heb 7, 8).

6. They therefore] These words imply that at the common meal which the risen Lord shared with His Apostles (v. 4), He made an appointment with them to meet Him on the day of His Ascension. The Galilean meeting described by St. Matthew (28 16 f.), and mentioned by St. Mark, was also by appointment.

Restore . . the kingdom] i.e. make the Jewish nation independent of Rome, and dominant, politically and religiously, over all the nations of the earth. This was the current Messianic expectation of the Jews, and the fact that the author represents the Apostles as still entertaining it, is a mark of the historical truth of his narrative. It needed the Pentecostal outpouring of the Holy Spirit to teach the Apostles that the Christ's Kingdom is not of this world. The answer of Jesus implies that He *will* restore the Kingdom to Israel ; not, however, to 'Israel after the flesh,' as the Apostles imagined, but to 'the Israel of God,' i.e. to Christian believers of every nation, by making Christianity the dominant religion throughout the world.

7. It is not for you] The Apostles were to be not so much prophets of the future, as witnesses of the past. **Hath put in his own power**] see on Mk 13 32. There is another possible translation of these words : 'which the Father appointed by His own power.' **8. Samaria, etc.**] Jesus here revokes the temporary limitation of the mission of the Apostles to the Jews (Mt 10 5, 6). This passage is one of the many proofs that Jesus intended to found a universal religion.

9. A cloud received him] The visible and corporal Ascension does not necessarily imply that heaven is a place situated above the clouds. The object of the Ascension was not to indicate where or what heaven is, but to assure the Apostles by an unmistakable sign that Jesus had entered it. It is possible that heaven is not, strictly speaking, a place, but a condition. **10. Two men**] certainly angels, as in Lk 24 4.

11. Why stand] It is fruitless to gaze. Go rather and labour, that when He comes again in judgment He may approve your work. In

like manner] i.e. in glory, and in His human nature : cp. ' this Jesus ' above.

12–14. The waiting Church.

12. Olivet] lit. ' the olive-orchard ' ; called usually The Mount of Olives. This, the scene of Christ's agony and betrayal, is now made the scene of His triumph. **A sabbath day's journey**] i.e. 2,000 cubits, or 6 furlongs.

13. An upper room] RV 'the upper chamber,' probably that in which the Last Supper had been eaten ; not, as some have argued from Lk 24 53, a chamber in the Temple. It may have been in the house of Mary the mother of Mark . see 12 12. **Peter, etc.**] see on Mt 10 2 f. *The brother* of **James**] RV correctly, ' the son of James.'

14. With one accord] Unanimity and common action distinguish the Christian community in Acts. This characteristic expression (Gk. *homothumadon*) occurs again 2 46 4 24 5 12 7 57 8 6 12 20 15 25 18 12 19 29, and nowhere else in the NT. except in Ro 15 6. **In prayer**] add (from Lk 24 53) 'and praise'. **The women**] viz. those which had accompanied Jesus in Galilee, and ministered to Him of their substance. Among them probably were Mary of Magdala, Joanna, and Susanna (Lk 8 2, 3) ; Mary the mother of James and Joses, and Salome the wife of Zebedee (Mk 15 40) ; possibly Martha and Mary of Bethany ; and almost certainly Mary the mother of Mark (12 12), who, perhaps, was hostess. **Mary the mother of Jesus**] The last mention of the Blessed Virgin in the sacred history. Of her subsequent life nothing certain is known. **His brethren**] see on Mt 12 46-50.

15–26. The election of Matthias. As the Church was about to be established on a durable and permanent basis, it was necessary that the twelve foundations on which it was to rest (Eph 2 20 Rev 21 14) should be made complete. Matthias, therefore, was chosen to fill the place of the traitor Judas ; the twelfth Patriarch of the new Israel of God.

15. Peter] Peter, having been restored by Jesus to the office forfeited by his triple apostasy (Jn 21 15 f.), resumes his old rank as leader of the Apostles. This leadership was probably personal, not official : see on Mt 16 18.

16. Must needs] RV ' It was needful that the scripture should be fulfilled.' Just as the scandal and stumbling-block of the death of Jesus was diminished by the discovery that it was foretold in the OT., and was part of the determinate counsel of God (Lk 24 26, 46 Ac 2 23 3 17, 18, etc.), so the scandal of the fall of an Apostle was relieved by the discovery that David had foretold it in the Psalms : cp. Jn 13 18 Mt 26 24. Peter quotes Pss 69 25 and 109 8. David really spoke of his own enemies, perhaps (in Ps 109) of Ahithophel, but Peter regards the words as a typical prophecy of the treachery of Judas. **17. Part**] RV 'his portion ' (lit. ' lot,' Gk. *klēros*). In Patristic Greek the word designates the clergy.

18, 19. These vv. are, of course, a note by St. Luke, not a part of St. Peter's speech. For the historical difficulties see on Mt 27 3-10.

20. Bishopric] RV ' office ' (Pss 69 25 109 8).

21, 22. St. Peter names two qualifications of an Apostle, (1) to have followed Jesus from the day of His Baptism by John to the day of His Ascension ; (2) to have been a witness of His Resurrection. The former of St. Peter's requirements excludes St. Paul, who had some difficulty on this account in establishing his claim to be an Apostle. **23.** The Apostles might doubtless have added Matthias to their number on their own authority, but instead of doing so they consulted the brethren, thus introducing a popular element into the polity of the Church : see on 6 3-6. **Two**] The disciples (probably because the Holy Spirit had not yet been received) did not venture to make a final choice, but left the decision to God. **Joseph called Barsabas**] RV ' Barsabbas,' i.e. Joseph, son of Sabba, is probably brother of the Judas Barsabbas mentioned in 15 22. His surname ' Justus ' is Roman, and was assumed in accordance with a not uncommon practice of the Jews at this time : cp. ' Marcus ' (12 12), ' Niger ' (13 1), ' Paulus ' (13 9). According to Papias, this Joseph drank a draught of poison without receiving injury.

Matthias] lit. ' gift of Jehovah.' This apostle is not again mentioned in the NT.

24. They prayed] This, the first recorded Christian prayer, is probably addressed to Jesus Himself. For, (1) prayer to Jesus was no exceptional thing, but a usual practice of the Apostolic Church (see 9 14) ; and (2) it was appropriate that He who had chosen eleven of the apostles should be invoked to choose the twelfth. **25. His own place**] St. Peter speaks with merciful reserve, but probably means Hell (' Gehenna '). The same euphemism is found in rabbinical writings. **26. Gave forth their lots**] RV ' gave lots for them ' ; RM ' gave lots unto them.' The two names were probably written on tablets, and shaken in a vessel until one of them dropped out. The use of the sacred lot (*Urim*) was common from the age of Moses to that of David, but afterwards it fell into disuse. This solitary example of its revival, occurring, as it did, before the descent of the Holy Spirit, is not to be regarded as a precedent.

CHAPTER 2

THE DAY OF PENTECOST

1–13. Pentecost. On this day the risen Lord fulfilled His promise to send another Comforter (or Advocate) ' that He may abide with you for ever ; even the Spirit of Truth, whom the world cannot receive ; for it beholdeth Him not, neither knoweth Him ; but ye know Him ; for He abideth with you, and shall be in you ' (Jn 14 17). Primarily, Pentecost is to be regarded as the Consecration of the Church for its work of evangelising the world. The fiery tongues which lighted upon the Apostles symbolised the gift of ' boldness with fervent zeal constantly to preach the gospel unto all nations ; whereby we have been brought out of darkness and error unto the clear light and true knowledge of Thee, and of Thy Son Jesus Christ.' To assist in the work of evangelising the world, the gift of prophecy (i.e. of inspired preaching) was given, nor was this gift confined to the Apostles, for ' I will pour out of my Spirit upon all flesh ; and your sons and your daughters shall prophesy, and your young men shall see visions, and your old men shall dream dreams.' The books of the NT. remain to testify that this gift of prophecy was a real one. We must also believe (although St. Luke does not allude to the fact) that on the day of Pentecost the Holy Spirit was given as a principle of inward spiritual life. The Lord Jesus had definitely promised this at the Last Supper. He said that the Holy Spirit would come to dwell with them and within them for ever, and that He Himself would return with the coming of the Spirit to dwell in their hearts by faith. This Spirit was to be their Advocate with the Father, to teach them all things, to bring to their remembrance all things that Jesus had told them, and to guide them into all the truth. The Spirit was also to have a mission to those without. Through the earnest utterances of believers, He would ' convict the world of sin, and of righteousness, and of judgment,' and a beginning of this process was seen, when the hearers of St. Peter's first sermon ' were pricked in their heart, and said unto Peter and the rest of the Apostles, Brethren, what shall we do ? '

At Pentecost a new spirit entered the world, and began to transform it. That spirit is still at work, and the most sceptical cannot deny its presence or its power. Men may attempt to account for it by natural causes, but it is there, and history teaches us that it comes to us from Jesus of Nazareth, who, as Dr. Lecky says, ' has not only been the highest pattern of virtue, but the highest incentive to its practice, and has exerted so deep an influence that it may be truly said that the simple record of three short years of active life has done more to regenerate and to soften mankind, than all the disquisitions of philosophers, and than all the exhortations of moralists.'

1. Pentecost] so called because it was the fiftieth day from the first day of the Passover. It was also called ' the Feast of Weeks,' because it occurred a week of weeks (i.e. seven weeks) after the Passover. It marked the completion of the corn harvest, and according to the later Jews it commemorated the giving of the Law on Sinai. The characteristic ritual of this feast was the offering and waving of two leavened loaves of wheaten flour, together with a sin offering, burnt offerings, and peace offerings (Lv 23 15-20). Appropriately, therefore, on this day the gospel harvest began : and the old Law of ordinances was superseded by the new Law of love.

2. A sound] The miraculous accompaniments of the outpouring of the Spirit were intended partly to strengthen the faith of the Apostles in the reality of the gift, and partly to arrest the attention of the inhabitants of Jerusalem.

3. Cloven tongues] RV 'tongues parting asunder, like as of fire.' St. Luke means that the tongues or flames of fire appeared first in one mass over the assembled Church, and then divided, one flame or tongue settling upon the head of each disciple. The mighty wind symbolised the power and energy of the Spirit, and the tongues of fire the fervour with which the disciples were empowered to proclaim the gospel.

4. To speak with other tongues] We should not gather from the references to the gift of tongues in St. Paul (1 Cor 12–14) and in the appendix to St. Mark (16 17), that the gift in question was the power of speaking foreign languages. Nor do foreign languages appear to have been spoken when Cornelius and his companions spoke with tongues and magnified God (Ac 10 46), nor when the twelve men at Ephesus, upon whom St. Paul had laid hands, ' spake with tongues and prophesied' (19 6). Many, therefore, are of opinion— especially since St. Peter compares the case of Cornelius and his companions with the event at Pentecost (11 15)—that in this passage also the speaking with tongues is not to be understood as a speaking in foreign languages, but as some kind of ecstatic utterance of praise, not fully under the control of the speaker. This view is plausible, but difficult to reconcile with the *primâ facie* meaning of the present passage. In v. 6 it is said that the multitude were confounded, ' because that every man heard them speak in his own language.' Again in v. 7 the multitude ask, ' Behold, are not all these which speak Galilæans ? And how hear we every man in our own tongue, wherein we were born ?' (see also v. 11). The meaning surely must be that the disciples either spoke, or that they seemed to their hearers to speak, foreign languages. This being so, we are constrained to believe, either that St. Luke has misunderstood the nature of the event, or that this Pentecostal miracle was of a higher

and more extraordinary character than the later 'speaking with tongues.' Among modern parallels the most suggestive is the case of St. Vincent Ferrer, who, when preaching in Spanish, is said to have been understood by English, Flemish, French, and Italian hearers (see further on 1 Cor 12–14). We may see in this event, which seemed to obliterate the barriers of nationality and language, a reversal of the separation and confusion of tongues (Gn 11).

5. Were dwelling] i.e. were dwelling permanently. Their love of Jerusalem and the Temple had attracted them from all lands to take up their abode in the Holy City. **6. The multitude**] comprising not only these 'dwellers' in Jerusalem, but those who had come to keep the feast. Pentecost was one of the three festivals at which every Israelite was expected to appear before the Lord.

9. Parthians, and Medes, and Elamites] are nations beyond the empire and influence of Rome. Here were settled the Ten Tribes of the first captivity (2 K 17⁶). **Mesopotamia**] The chief Jewish centre here was Babylon, which, ever since the captivity of Judah, was famed for its rabbinical schools, and was for that reason regarded as part of the Holy Land.

Judæa] Judæa, as distinguished from Galilee, to which the Apostles belonged. **Cappadocia .. Pamphylia**] Jews were scattered throughout Asia Minor as far as Pontus, and even crossed the Euxine to the Crimea. They enjoyed everywhere full civic rights.

10. Egypt] According to Philo there were a million Jews in Egypt. They formed a large part of the population of Alexandria, where Judaism allied itself with the Platonic philosophy, and attempted to appropriate the best elements of Hellenic culture. **Cyrene**] A Greek city in N. Africa, founded 631 B.C. A quarter of its great population consisted of Jews, who possessed full rights of citizenship. See Mt 27³² Ac 6⁹ 11²⁰ 13¹.

Strangers of Rome] RV 'sojourners from Rome.' They probably possessed the Roman citizenship, like St. Paul. Jewish prisoners were brought to Rome by Pompey, but they soon regained their freedom, and settled, with full civic rights, in a district beyond the Tiber. In 19 A.D. they were banished, but, after the fall of Sejanus, were allowed to return.

14–41. St. Peter's sermon and its effects. Peter's sermon falls into four divisions :

(1) vv. 14–21. Explanation of the phenomenon of speaking with tongues as a manifestation of the outpouring of the Spirit foretold by the prophet Joel, Jl 2²⁸. (2) vv. 22–28. St. Peter shows that the outpouring of the Spirit is connected with the life and work of Jesus of Nazareth, whom, after His crucifixion by lawless men, God raised from the dead, accord-

ing to the prophecy of David in the Psalms (Ps 16⁸⁻¹¹). (3) vv. 29–36. St. Peter proves that Ps 16⁸⁻¹¹ refers to the Resurrection not of David but of Jesus, and adds the personal testimony of the Apostles that Jesus had really been raised. He then affirms the Ascension of Jesus, and declares that it is He who has sent down from heaven the gift of the Holy Spirit. From the Ascension which he illustrates by Ps 110¹, he further concludes that Jesus is the Messianic King so long expected by the Jews. (4) vv. 37–40. St. Peter concludes with a practical exhortation to his hearers to repent and be baptised, that they and their children may receive the gift of the Holy Ghost.

The genuineness of this speech is vouched for by the simplicity of its theology, and by its resemblances to 1 Peter (e.g. 'foreknowledge,' 1 Pet 1²; 'to call upon' (God), 1¹⁷; 'rejoicing,' 1⁶,⁸ 4¹³; 'the right hand of God,' 3²²; 'exalt,' 5⁶; 'the house' (= Israel), 2⁵ 4¹⁷, etc.).

15. *But* **the third hour**] On festival days the Jews tasted nothing until the morning synagogue service, held at the third hour (9 A.M.), was finished.

16. Joel] see Joel 2²⁸⁻³². The only important variation is that Peter changes Joel's 'afterward' into the more definite 'in the last days.' The 'last days' are the Christian dispensation. **19. Wonders in heaven, etc.**] A metaphorical description of the calamities which will happen on earth before Christ's Second Coming, which St. Peter probably regarded as near : cp. Mt 24²⁹. **20. That great and notable day**] i.e. either the destruction of Jerusalem, or Christ's Second Advent. **23. By wicked hands**] lit. 'by the hand of lawless men' (i.e. the Romans). **24. The pains of death**] lit. 'the birth-pangs of death.' Death being personified as a woman in travail, and receiving relief when the dead are 'born again' by resurrection. But it is more probable that St. Peter really spoke of the 'snares' of death, the word for 'snare' (*ḥēbel*) and that for 'birth-pang' (*ḥēbel*) being practically identical. **25.** See Ps 16⁸ᶠ. **26. Rest in hope**] lit. 'pitch its tent upon hope.' **27. Hell**] i.e. Hades, the abode of disembodied spirits waiting for the resurrection (Heb. *Sheol*). A proof text of the reality of Christ's descent into 'hell' (i.e. Hades). **33. By the right hand**] or, 'to the right hand.' **The promise of**] i.e. the promised Holy Ghost.

37. Were pricked in their heart] (1) because they had crucified Jesus; (2) because they had not acknowledged Him as the Messiah, and had thus deprived themselves of the hope of salvation. **38. In the name of Jesus Christ**] see on Mt 28¹⁹. **The remission of sins**] one of the principal benefits of Holy Baptism, when the ordinance is rightly received (22^{16}; cp. $10^{43,47}$ 13^{38} Heb 10^{22}; also 1 Cor 6^{11} Eph $5^{25,26}$). **The gift of the Holy Ghost**] It is to be inferred from 8^{15-17} 19^6, cp. Heb 6^2, that the Holy Ghost was given by the laying on of the Apostles' hands.

42–47. The life and worship of the first converts. The converts were still earnest Jews, attending the services in the Temple daily (v. 46), but they already formed a Church within a Church: for (1) they continued stedfastly in the Apostles' doctrine (v. 42), i.e. they no longer regarded the chief priests, scribes, and Pharisees as their accredited teachers, but rather the Apostles. Thus the breach with Judaism had already begun in principle. (2) They continued stedfastly in the Apostles' fellowship. (3) They continued stedfastly in the breaking of bread, i.e. in celebrating the sacrament of the Lord's Supper, or Holy Communion. At first the Lord's Supper was celebrated daily (v. 46), but afterwards every Lord's Day at least (20^7). (4) They continued stedfastly in the prayers, i.e. in the prayers offered at the celebration of the Lord's Supper, and at the other services of the Church (so the RV). The AV, however, translates 'in prayers,' which would include private prayers also.

42. In prayers] lit. 'in the prayers,' i.e. the public prayers of the Church. These would probably be partly liturgical, after the example of the Temple and the Synagogue (cp. the liturgical addition to the Lord's Prayer, Mt 6^{13} AV), and partly extempore. Extempore prayer was allowed to be offered at the celebration of the Lord's Supper by the Christian prophets (see the 'Didache'), and was apparently still in use in the age of Justin Martyr (150 A.D.), but shortly after this the public prayers of the Church became exclusively liturgical.

44. Were together] probably they had common meals. **Had all things common**] This arrangement was not exactly what we call communism, for, (1) the sale of property was voluntary, the result of a spontaneous outflowing of Christian love (5^4); and (2) even when property had been sold, the money usually remained in the hands of the vendor, to be distributed to the poorer saints from time to time 'as every man had need' (v. 45). The cases of Barnabas and of Ananias and Sapphira, who not only sold property, but even laid the money at the Apostles' feet, were exceptional, and because exceptional are specially noted by the evangelist. **46. Breaking bread from house to house**] RV 'breaking bread at home,' probably in the 'upper room' where the Sacrament had been instituted, and the Holy Ghost had descended. The reference is probably to the Lord's Supper, and not to an

ordinary meal; but it must be remembered that at this period the Lord's Supper was usually celebrated at the close of a sacred meal, called the *agapé* or love-feast: see below. **47. And the Lord**] RV 'And the Lord added to them' (RM 'together') 'day by day those that were being saved,' i.e. conscious of sin and seeking salvation.

THE LOVE-FEAST

It is clear from v. 46, and 1 Cor $11^{20f.}$, that Holy Communion was at first celebrated in connexion with a common meal called *agapé*, i.e. 'love-feast,' or 'feast of charity' (Jude v. 12). Our Lord had instituted the Sacrament at the close of a sacred banquet, and the Apostolic Church at first naturally followed His example. The feast was an afternoon or evening meal, at which rich and poor met together in the church, the food and drink being provided mainly by the rich. Prayers and benedictions, similar to those of the Jews, were said over each dish or course, and 'the kiss of charity' (1 Pet 5^{14}) probably concluded the meal. Then hands were washed, and there followed prayer and sacred psalmody under the leadership of a prophet or other minister. 'The breaking of bread,' or Holy Communion, seems to have followed (not preceded) the *agapé* (1 Cor $11^{21,25}$), and the *agapé* and the Holy Communion were regarded as forming one service, called 'the Lord's Supper' (1 Cor 11^{20}). The abuses to which this arrangement gave rise (see 1 Cor 11), led, somewhat late in the apostolic age, to the gradual separation of the two rites. Already in the time of Pliny (115 A.D.) the Holy Communion was celebrated in the morning, and the *agapé* in the evening; and Justin Martyr (150 A.D.), in describing the Holy Communion, makes no allusion to the *agapé*, which was by that time an entirely separate ordinance.

CHAPTER 3
THE LAME MAN HEALED

1–26. Healing of the lame man. Speech of Peter. St. Luke here singles out from the multitude of 'wonders and signs done by the Apostles' (2^{43}), the one which led to the first persecution.

1. The ninth *hour*] The hours of prayer were the third (2^{15}), when the morning sacrifice was offered; the sixth (noon); and the ninth, the time of the evening sacrifice.

2. Beautiful] This gate was of Corinthian brass. It faced the E., and its proper name was the Gate of Nicanor. 'Its height was fifty cubits, and its doors were forty cubits, and it was adorned in a more costly manner, having much richer and thicker plates of silver and gold than the others' (Josephus). **6. In the name**] i.e. by the power of Jesus Christ. It is significant that, whereas Jesus worked miracles in His own name, the Apostles only did so in dependence on Him. **11. Solomon's**] see on Jn 10 23, and cp. Ac 5 12.

12-26. Peter's Speech. Peter affirms that the miracle has been performed through faith in Jesus, who, though crucified, was truly the Messiah, as was shown by His Resurrection. The Apostle takes a lenient view of the conduct of the Jews in the crucifixion of Jesus, attributing it to ignorance; and he calls them to repentance, stating that the gospel must first be preached to them, before it is carried to the rest of mankind.

13. Hath glorified] viz. by raising Him from the dead, seating Him at His right hand, and enduing Him with almighty power, of which the miracle upon the lame man is a proof.

His Son] or, 'Child.' But many recent authorities render, 'His Servant,' supposing that Jesus is here identified with the 'Servant of Jehovah' in Isa 40–66. **14. The Holy One and the Just**] a strong affirmation of the sinlessness of Jesus: cp. Jn 6 69 (RV), 'We have believed and know that thou art the Holy One of God.' **15. The Prince of life**] i.e. the Author of eternal life: cp. Jn 3 16 11 25. The word translated 'Prince' occurs again, 5 31, 'a Prince and a Saviour'; Heb 2 10, 'the Captain of their salvation'; Heb 12 2, 'the Author of our faith.' The divinity of Jesus is implied in the fact that He is the author of life: cp. Jn 1 4 11 25 1 Jn 1 2. **16. His name**] virtually His Power. **18. Should suffer**] see especially Ps 22 Isa 50 6 and 53 5 Dan 9 26. Our Lord Himself found intimations of His sufferings in the OT., Lk 24 26 Jn 13 18, etc.

19. When the times of refreshing] RV 'that so there may come seasons of refreshing from the presence of the Lord, and that he may send the Christ who hath been appointed for you, even Jesus.' The idea that the Second Coming of Christ may be hastened or retarded by the conduct of the chosen people or of the Church, is also expressed in 2 Pet 3 12 (RM). The Jews believed that just before the coming of the Messiah Israel would be involved in terrible sufferings, and that from these the Messiah would relieve them, thus bringing 'seasons of refreshing from the presence of the Lord.'

21. Whom the heaven must receive] i.e. retain. This rendering is better than the alternative one, 'who must hold the heaven in possession.' **Restitution of all things**] In Mt 17 11 a restitution of all things by Elijah is mentioned, in preparation for the first coming of Christ. The restitution here spoken of is the restoration of the whole universe to its original and intended perfection, which will take place when Christ comes again. It is the same as 'the regeneration' of creation spoken

of by Christ, Mt 19 28; as 'the new heavens and new earth' of 2 Pet 3 13 Rev 21 1; and as 'the redemption' of the body and of the physical creation of Ro 8 18-23. **Since the world began**] The first such prophecy is Gn 3 15, immediately after the Fall; and St. Peter not unfairly assumes that all the prophets, even those whose utterances have not been transmitted to us, looked forward to the coming of a Redeemer, and the final restoration of all things. **22. Moses**] see Dt 18 15-19; and cp. 7 37. In Dt the prophet is to be understood collectively of the line of great prophets which began with Samuel. But it received its chief fulfilment in Jesus Christ; and to Him alone do the words 'like unto me,' and 'every soul which will not hear that prophet shall be destroyed,' strictly apply. **25. Unto Abraham**] see Gn 12 3 18 18 22 18 26 4 28 14 Gal 3 8. **26. Unto you first**] and afterwards to the Gentiles (Lk 24 47 Ac 1 8). St. Peter, as these words show, already contemplated the conversion of the Gentiles. **Son**] or 'Servant': see v. 13.

CHAPTER 4
ARREST OF PETER AND JOHN

1-22. Arrest of Peter and John. Peter's speech before the Sanhedrin. The proceedings of the Apostles displeased the authorities, (1) because they taught the people (v. 2) without having received the education and ordination of rabbis (cp. v. 13); (2) because they preached the Resurrection, a doctrine particularly distasteful to the Sadducees, the dominant party among the influential members of the priesthood; (3) because they feared that the people would become inflamed with enthusiasm, and that this would lead to collisions with the Romans. It is a mark of historic truth that the chief opposition to the Apostles is here assigned to the Sadducees, who denied the Resurrection. The Pharisees, who affirmed it, were comparatively friendly (5 34 23 6), and not a few of them became Christians (15 5).

1. As they spake] Clearly John also addressed the people. **The captain of the temple**] a priest next in dignity to the high priest, having under him a body of priests and Levites, who maintained order in the Temple.

The Sadducees] Most of the chief priests belonged to this party. They denied the oral traditions of the elders, the existence of angels and spirits, predestination and fate, the immortality of the soul, and the resurrection of the body: see Mt 3 7 16 1f. 22 23 Ac 5 17 23 6f.

5. Their rulers] A full and important meeting of the Sanhedrin was summoned. 'Rulers' = chief priest; 'scribes' = rabbis or 'lawyers,' professional teachers of the Law. Most of the scribes were Pharisees. 'Elders' = such members of the Sanhedrin as were neither chief priests nor scribes. **6. Annas the high priest**] see on Jn 18 13. **John**] An unknown person. But D reads 'Jonathan.' This is probably correct, for Jonathan was son of Annas, and succeeded Caiaphas. **Alexander**] is unknown.

8. Filled with the Holy Ghost] in fulfilment of the promise Lk 12 11. **11. This is the stone**] In Ps 118 22 the stone is Israel, which the heathen builders of the world's great empires reject and despise, but which nevertheless is destined to play the chief part in the world's history. In the NT. the stone is interpreted as the Messiah, and the builders as the rulers of the Jews : see Mt 21 42 ; cp. also Eph 2 19-22 1 Pet 2 4-8. **12. Neither is there salvation in any other**] Though salvation is offered to men through Jesus, and Jesus alone, it does not follow that those who are ignorant of His name are lost. God can save, through Christ, those who have never heard the gospel, if they respond to the degree of grace and enlightenment vouchsafed to them. **13. Unlearned and ignorant men**] This rendering gives a false impression. What is meant is that the Apostles had not received the training of rabbis, and were consequently unskilled in rabbinical traditions, and had no authority to teach. 'Ignorant' should be translated 'private persons,' or, 'laymen.'

23-31. Prayer of the Apostles on their release. 24. With one accord] The prayer was probably led by St. Peter, the others repeating the words after him. **25. Who by the mouth**] RV 'who by the Holy Ghost, by the mouth of our father David, didst say,' etc. **Why did the heathen rage?** etc.] verbatim from Ps 2 1 (LXX). This Ps. is directly Messianic, though it may have been suggested by the historical circumstances of some actual Davidic king, e.g. Solomon. **The people**] RV 'the peoples,' i.e. the Jews, regarded either as consisting of twelve tribes, or as dispersed in different nations. **Vain things**] vain, because, though the enemies of Jesus seemed to triumph at His Crucifixion, God raised Him from the dead, and placed Him at His right hand in heaven. **27. Child**] or, 'servant': see on 3 13. **Were gathered together**] add 'in this city' (RV). **28. Thy counsel**] There is a theological difficulty here. God is said to have foreordained the iniquitous proceedings of the scribes and Pharisees who condemned Jesus. The explanation is that God is said to foreordain what he foresees and permits. God permitted the death of Jesus, intending by it to redeem the world, and to destroy the works of the devil : cp. 2 23 3 18. **29. That with all boldness they may speak thy word**] rather, 'that with all boldness we may speak thy word'

30. By stretching] RV 'while thou stretchest forth thy hand to heal.' **31. The place was shaken**, etc.] The physical phenomena of Pentecost (see 2 3) were partly reproduced. **They spake the word**] They continued their public preaching to the people, and their private exhortations to the disciples, in spite of the opposition of the Jewish authorities.

32—C. 5 16. The communism of the Church of Jerusalem. Barnabas, Ananias, and Sapphira.

32. Neither said any *of them*] This expression shows that the Church of Jerusalem recognised the principle of private property. A disciple's property really was his own, but he did not *say* that it was his own ; he treated it as if it were common property. The Anabaptist principle that private property is unlawful, finds no real support in the Acts. The communism was voluntary. **33. With great power**] The expression suggests that the preaching was supported by miracles. **36. Joses**] RV 'Joseph.' **Barnabas**] lit. 'the Son of Prophecy.' We learn from 13 1 that he was a prophet ; and he probably gained his name 'Barnabas' from some specially comforting or consoling prophecy which he delivered to the Church of Jerusalem, soon after his conversion. **A Levite**] By the Mosaic Law Levites were forbidden to hold land in Palestine, but the regulation had been long in abeyance. **Cyprus**] from the time of Alexander the Great many Jews had settled in this fertile island. It is likely that Barnabas had been educated at the neighbouring university of Tarsus, and had there made the acquaintaince of St. Paul : cp. 9 27.

CHAPTER 5
THE APOSTLES AGAIN IMPRISONED

1-16. The sin of Ananias and Sapphira was not keeping back part of the price, which they had a perfect right to do (v. 4), but pretending that the money which they offered to the Apostles was the whole price of the possession sold, which was not the case. Their motive was vanity and ambition. They wished to have a greater reputation for liberality than they were entitled to.

1. Ananias] i.e. 'Jehovah hath been gracious.' **Sapphira**] If the word is Greek it means 'sapphire' ; if Aramaic, 'beautiful.' **3.** The death of Ananias and Sapphira is to be regarded as an act of God, not of Peter, like the blinding of Elymas (13 9). Peter acts, not on his own authority, but under the direct inspiration of the Holy Ghost, who informs him of the secret sin, and authorises him to execute the divine vengeance. Similarly St. Paul is inspired to pronounce sentence against Elymas. **4. Was it not thine own ?**] Clear proof that the apostolic communism was voluntary. **Unto God**] Ananias *had* lied unto men, but the sin against man was so insignificant, compared with the sin against God, that St. Peter rhetorically calls it no sin at all. **6. Wound him up**] others render, ' composed his limbs.'

The truth of the narrative of Ananias and Sapphira is guaranteed by its painful character. No historian would have gone out of his way to invent it. The punishment of death seems severe, but it must be remembered that our Lord's most severe denunciations were against hypocrisy. To brand religious hypocrisy for all time as infamous, seems to be the object of this miracle. It is not necessary to suppose that Ananias and Sapphira were eternally lost. After this terrible punishment, they may have been forgiven.

12. In Solomon's porch] see 3 11. Solomon's portico was practically abandoned to the Christians, who made it their place of daily assembly, the Apostles teaching and working miracles there. **13. Of the rest**] i.e. of the non-Christians. **15. The shadow**] With this should be compared the faith of the Corinthians in the efficacy of the cloths that had touched St. Paul's body (19 12). Something of superstition probably mingled with this faith, but true faith predominated, and God accepted it.

17–42. Second imprisonment of Peter and John. Speech of Gamaliel.

17. The Sadducees] see on Mt 3 7 Ac 4 1. **20. Words of this life**] i.e. the new life in God which the Death, Resurrection and Ascension of our Lord had made possible for man. **28. To bring this man's blood upon us**] viz. by causing the people to rise up and avenge the murder of Jesus by slaying us. **29–32.** Peter's speech is practically an epitome of previous speeches; see 4 19 3 13, 15 2 33, 36 3 15 3 26 2 4. **33.** **Were cut**] lit. 'were sawn asunder.' **Took counsel**] RV ' were minded.' **34. Gamaliel**] St. Paul's teacher (22 3), grandson of Hillel and son of Rabbi Simeon, was by far the most influential rabbi of the time. He was the first of the seven teachers who received the title *Rabban* (higher than Rab or Rabbi). Gamaliel's moderation on this occasion is to be explained, (1) by his hostility to the Sadducees, whom he would not allow to win a decisive triumph over a sect which had much in common with the Pharisees ; (2) by the favourable impression which the Apostles' preaching and miracles had made upon him. He was not a convert, but thought that something was to be said for the new teaching. Subsequent developments, particularly the preaching of Stephen, probably alienated him, as it did the other Pharisees. **36. Theudas**] The mention of this name is the greatest

historical difficulty in the Acts. Gamaliel's speech was delivered 36 A.D. or earlier, but the insurrection of Theudas, according to Josephus, did not take place till some 10 years later (about 46 A.D.) : see ' Antiq.' xx. 5, 1. Perhaps St. Luke alludes to an early Theudas, of whom we know nothing. **37. Judas of Galilee**] raised an important rebellion in the days of the taxing, or 'enrolment' by Quirinius (6, 7 A.D.). **40. Beaten** *them*] Probably with 'forty stripes save one,' a penalty inflicted upon St. Paul five times (2 Cor 11 24). They were punished for disobedience : see 4 18. **42. In every house**] RV 'at home,' i.e. in the private Christian assemblies, held in ' the upper room ' or elsewhere.

CHAPTER 6

STEPHEN AND THE SEVEN

1–7. The Hebrew-speaking Jews, who were in a majority in the Church of Jerusalem, were inclined to despise and neglect the minority who spoke Greek. In particular, the Greek-speaking widows received less food than their Hebrew-speaking sisters. This led to complaints, and the impartiality of the Apostles was called in question. The Apostles, finding the distribution of charity too great a burden for them, summoned a meeting of the Church, and called upon the brethren to elect seven men to undertake this business. The office to which they were appointed was in later times called the diaconate (Phil 1 1 1 Tim 3 8, 12) ; but the name had not yet come into use, and St. Luke consequently avoids it.

1. Grecians] i.e. Hellenists, or Greek-speaking Jews. **Hebrews**] i.e. Hebrew-speaking Jews. Hebrew was spoken mainly in Jerusalem and Judæa. **Ministration**] i.e. distribution of food (v. 2). **2. It is not reason**] rather, ' It does not please us.' **Serve tables**] i.e. attend to the distribution of food. Others think that the tables of bankers are meant, and that the Apostles complain that they cannot keep the accounts, or manage the finances of so large a community. **3. Full of the Holy Ghost**] All Church work requires to be performed in the power of the Spirit, and not least the management of charity and finance.

Wisdom] i.e. the practical discernment and tact so necessary in the distribution of charity.

5. The names are all Greek, which suggests that some at least of them were Greek-speaking Jews. That all were Hellenists is not probable. Greek names were quite common even among the Hebrews (cp. Nicodemus, Philip, and Andrew). One, Nicolas, was a proselyte, i.e. doubtless a full circumcised proselyte. Of two only, Stephen and Philip, have we any further account. The appointment of the Seven marks the first stage in the growth of liberal ideas within the Church.

The differences between the Hellenistic (Grecian) Jews and the Hebrews are noteworthy. The Hellenists used the Gk. OT. (Septuagint); were educated more or less in the Greek manner; studied (though to a limited extent) Greek literature and philosophy, and adopted a more liberal attitude towards the Gentile world than the Hebrews. The typical representative of Hellenism is Philo, who makes Moses and the prophets speak the language of philosophy. Josephus also (in spite of his knowledge of Hebrew) has pronounced Hellenistic tendencies.

6. The essential element in ordination is prayer, and the laying on of hands by the chief ministers of the Church. The laying on of hands in making appointments is ancient. Thus 'Joshua was full of the spirit of wisdom because Moses had laid his hands upon him' (Nu 27 18-23 Dt 34 9).

8-15. The preaching, miracles, and arrest of Stephen.

The reason why the preaching of Stephen gave so much greater offence than that of the Twelve probably was that he saw that the coming of Christ virtually abrogated the Ceremonial Law, and that its abandonment was only a question of time. He thus anticipated St. Paul, perhaps even went beyond him at least in theory (see on v. 14). But as his speech gives no clear indications of such views, not even in 7 48, some suppose that he attacked the authority, not of the Law of Moses itself, but only of those traditional additions to it which the scribes held to be of equal or greater authority. Stephen was probably a Hellenist, and his opponents in the synagogues (v. 9) were also Hellenists.

8. Of faith] RV 'of grace.'

9. There are said to have been no less than 480 synagogues in Jerusalem, and the Cyrenians and Alexandrians, at any rate, would have been sufficiently numerous to have synagogues of their own. **Libertines**] lit. 'freedmen.' These were descendants of those Jews who, having been carried by the Romans, particularly by Pompey, to Rome as prisoners of war, had afterwards been emancipated from slavery. **Cyrenians**] A fourth part of the inhabitants of Cyrene, the capital of Upper Libya, consisted of Jews. **Alexandrians**] At Alexandria (founded by Alexander the Great, 332 B.C.) two of the five parts into which the city was divided were inhabited by Jews, who were ruled over by a Jewish officer called an *alabarch*. At Alexandria the OT. had been translated into Greek. Here flourished a Jewish-Greek philosophy of which Philo is the chief exponent. Apollos was an Alexandrian (18 24). Tradition makes St. Mark the first

bishop of Alexandria. **Cilicia**] To this synagogue St. Paul probably belonged. **Asia**] The Roman province, not the continent. It embraced Lydia, Mysia, Caria, part of Phrygia. Its three chief towns were Ephesus, Smyrna, and Pergamos.

11. Suborned men] The success of these tactics against Jesus encouraged them to repeat them. **13. This holy place**] i.e. the Temple.

14. Destroy this place, etc.] What St. Stephen had probably said was that the Law would pass away as having been fulfilled in Christ, and that if the Jews persistently refused to acknowledge Jesus as the Messiah, their city and Temple would be destroyed, as Jesus had prophesied (Mt 24, etc.). Although the charge was malicious and false, there was some truth in it. Stephen's teaching was clearly more advanced and liberal than that of the Twelve. **15. The face of an angel**] This description is probably due to St. Paul, who was doubtless present : cp. 7 58.

CHAPTER 7

DEFENCE AND MARTYRDOM OF STEPHEN

1-53. Speech of Stephen. There is every reason to believe that this speech was really delivered by St. Stephen, and not composed by St. Luke ; for, (1) the speech does not (in any direct manner) answer the charges alleged (6 14), as a speech composed by the historian himself would have done ; (2) there are several erroneous references to the OT. (not all due to the use of LXX), natural enough in a speech delivered impromptu, but not natural in a speech composed deliberately. St. Paul who heard the speech probably reported it to St. Luke.

The exact point of the speech, and how it is intended to be an answer to the charges (6 14), is disputed. It would appear, however, that the great length at which the history of the Jews is related, is intended to show that Stephen was not a blasphemer of God but as firm a believer in the OT. as his accusers. He gives a particular account of Moses (vv. 20–44), and declares his firm belief in the divine authority of the Law delivered by him (' the lively oracles,' v. 38). He points out, however, that Moses himself predicted the coming of a prophet greater than himself, and that to hear this prophet (whom he identifies with Jesus, v. 52) is commanded by the Law itself. Stephen, therefore, who obeys this command of Moses to hear Jesus, is keeping the Law, while his adversaries, who disobey this command, are breaking the Law (v. 53). The prophets also predicted the coming of Jesus, and Stephen, who follows Jesus, obeys the prophets, while his adversaries are rebels against them, as their fathers were (vv. 51, 52). The speech contains no reply to the charge of predicting the destruction of the Temple. If the speech had been allowed to be finished, it is probable that it would have closed with a solemn warning that unless his adversaries accepted Jesus as the Messiah, in accordance with the teaching of Moses and the prophets, their city and Temple would be destroyed. The Apology of Stephen may be compared with the Apology of Socrates. Both were delivered, not with the object of gaining an acquittal, but of testifying openly to the truth, and of denouncing the blindness and injustice of the judges.

2. Men, etc.] RV 'Brethren and fathers'; i.e. Israelites, and Sanhedrists. **In Mesopotamia**] Genesis says nothing of an appearance in Mesopotamia, but such an appearance is implied, Josh 24 2,3 Neh 9 7 (cp. Gn 15 7), and affirmed by Philo. **3.** See Gn 12 1, which is mistranslated by the AV, to harmonise with this passage. **4. Charran**] i.e. Haran, or Carrhæ, an ancient city of N. Mesopotamia. Here Crassus, the Roman general, was disastrously defeated by the Parthians 53 B.C. See Gn 11 31 12 4,5.

When his father was dead] According to Genesis (see Gn 11 26,32 12 4), Terah lived 60 years after his son's migration into Canaan. Stephen's statement is not a mere blunder, but a divergent tradition, found also in Philo, and apparently intended to shield the patriarch from the charge of unfilial conduct, in thus abandoning his aged father. **5.** See Gn 12 7 13 15, etc.

6. See Gn 15 13,16. **Four hundred years**] so Gn 15 13; more precisely 430 years, Ex 12 40. But there was another tradition which made the 430 years of Ex 12 40 refer to the sojourn of the patriarchs in Palestine and Egypt. This is found in some MSS of the LXX (Ex 12 40); in Josephus, and in Gal 3 17. **7. In this place**] in Canaan, not Sinai, as is the case in Ex 3 12.

8. Circumcision] Gn 17 9f. **9.** See Gn 37 4f.

Envy] Stephen sees in Joseph a type of Jesus, and in the envy of his brethren, a type of the envy of the chief priests and scribes which caused the death of Jesus.

14. Threescore and fifteen souls] Stephen follows LXX of Gn 46 27 Ex 1 5. The Hebrew makes the number seventy. **16.** There are two errors in this v.: (1) Jacob was not buried at Sychem (Shechem), but at Hebron, in the cave of Machpelah (Gn 50 13). (2) It was not Abraham, but Jacob, who bought a sepulchre at Shechem, from the sons of Emmor (Hamor), Gn 33 19 Josh 24 32. Either St. Stephen is following a divergent tradition, or, as is more probable, the errors are due to a lapse of memory natural enough under the disturbing circumstances of the speech. *The father* **of Sychem**] The true rendering is the 'son' of Sychem, which would be another discrepancy with Gn 33 19. But the RV adopts another reading, 'in Sychem (Shechem).'

18. Knew not Joseph] i.e. knew not the history of Joseph and of his great services to his adopted country. **19. So that**] rather, ' that they might cast out their babes,' etc.

20. Was exceeding fair] lit. 'fair unto God,' i.e. fair even in the eyes of God: cp. Gn 10 9, ' a mighty hunter before Jehovah.'

22. Learned] i.e. taught. Undoubtedly true, though not mentioned in the OT. ' The wisdom of the Egyptians' consisted of natural science, magic, astronomy, medicine, and mathematics, and was mainly in the hands of the priesthood. **Mighty in words**] not inconsistent with Ex 4 10, for Moses' eloquence was acquired subsequently. **23. Forty years old**] His age is derived from tradition.

30. Forty years] Another tradition. The rabbis said, 'Moses lived in Pharaoh's palace 40 years, in Midian 40 years, and ministered to Israel 40 years.' **An angel**] in Ex 3 2 ' the angel of Jehovah,' who is afterwards identified with Jehovah Himself. **34. I will send**] rather, ' let me send.' **35. A ruler and a deliverer**] lit. ' a ruler and redeemer.' Moses' 'redemption' of the people from the bondage of Egypt was a type of Christ's greater redemption of them from the bondage of sin and Satan.

37. A prophet] The importance of Moses, according to Stephen, is that he is the type and forerunner of a greater than himself, whose coming he foretold: see Dt 18 15,18; and cp. Ac 3 22. Christ is the second and greater Moses, and, like him, a redeemer (v. 35), lawgiver (v. 38), and prophet (v. 37). Loyalty to Moses, therefore, necessarily implies loyalty to Christ.

38. In the church] i.e. in the congregation or assembly of all Israel at Mt. Sinai when the Law was given and the Covenant made and ratified. On this occasion Moses again typified Christ by acting as Mediator. He was with God (or God's angel) on Mt. Sinai holding converse with Him: he was also with the people below holding converse with them, and thus being intimately associated with both, made a covenant between them. **With the angel**] The idea that Moses did not receive the Law directly from God, but from an angel or angels, is contrary to the OT., but was current among the Jews at this period: see Jos. 'Ant.' 15.5,3, ' We have learnt the most holy part of our Law by angels.' The Fathers identify the angel who spoke to Moses with the Logos, or second person of the Holy Trinity. **Lively oracles**] An oracle is an inspired utterance, hence the term is suitably applied to the Scriptures. The oracles are lively, or living, because they have the power of God in them, and the promises which they contain are effectual.

39. Israel's rebellion against Moses is a type of their later rebellion against Jesus. **Egypt**] i.e. the Egyptian way of life, especially Egypt tian idolatry (bull-worship). In Egypt Apis was worshipped at Memphis, and Mnevis at Heliopolis under the form of a bull : see Ex 32 1.

42. The book of the prophets] The twelve minor prophets formed one roll or book. **O ye house,** etc.] freely quoted from LXX of Amos 5 25, 26. Stephen, following LXX, supposes that the worship of Moloch and of the stars took place **in the wilderness.** This is not expressly mentioned in the Pentateuch, but is not improbable, for the worship of Moloch is forbidden Lv 18 21, etc. **Have ye offered ?**] The answer is 'No.' In appearance sacrifices had been offered to God, but inasmuch as they were offered by worshippers polluted by idolatry, they were no true sacrifices.

43. Ye took up] viz. to carry in a religious procession, or, to carry from one halting-place to another. **The tabernacle of Moloch**] a profane imitation of the tabernacle of Jehovah. Moloch (Molech, or Milcom) was an idol of the Ammonites to whom children were offered. His image is said to have been hollow, heated from below, with the head of an ox, and outstretched arms in which children were laid, their cries of agony being stifled by the beating of drums. The Heb., however, should probably be translated not 'the tabernacle of Moloch' (LXX and AV), but 'Siccuth, your king' (another false god). **The star of your god Remphan**] i.e. his star-emblem. The Heb. has *Chiun* (not Remphan), i.e. the planet Saturn. **Beyond Babylon**] Amos says, 'beyond Damascus.' Stephen has adapted the prophecy (according to the rabbinical fashion) to later events.

44. Stephen's reference to the movable tabernacle in the wilderness is probably intended to show that the worship of God is not necessarily confined to one place (Jerusalem), and that for adequate cause (e.g. the persistent rejection of Christ by the Jews) the privilege of Jerusalem may be taken away. **The tabernacle of .witness**] Thus LXX translates the phrase, which really means 'the tent of meeting,' i.e. the tent where God met His worshippers. But the phrase is nevertheless an apt one, for the tent contained the ark, which was a witness of the covenant, and the two tables on which the fundamental law of the covenant (the Decalogue) was written. **The fashion**] see Ex 25 40 26 30 Heb 8 5.

45. RV 'Which also our fathers, in their turn, brought in with Joshua when they entered on the possession of the nations,' etc. Note **Jesus** = 'Joshua,' as in Heb 4 8.

48. Stephen's words do not indicate that the building of Solomon's Temple was a mistake, but they do indicate that God's worship is not necessarily tied to one place, and that the divine choice of Jerusalem as a place of wor-

ship is not irreversible. Solomon himself recognised this truth, 1 K 8 27. **49, 50.** See Isa 66 1, 2.

51–53. Stephen, not careful of life, and willing to be a martyr, now denounces his judges. **52. Have slain**] referring especially to Isaiah and Jeremiah, who both, according to tradition, suffered martyrdom. **The Just One**] i.e. Jesus : see 3 14. **53. By the disposition of angels**] RV 'as it was ordained by angels '; RM 'as the ordinance of angels.' The precise meaning is uncertain, but some kind of mediation of angels in the giving of the Law is probably meant: see Gal 3 19 Heb 2 2.

54–C. 8 3. Martyrdom of Stephen. Saul's persecution of the Church.

54. Were cut] lit. ' were sawn asunder ': see 5 33. **55. Standing**] Jesus rises from the throne on which He is represented as eternally sitting (Mt 26 64 Mk 16 19, etc.) to succour the martyr in his extremity, and to welcome his soul into bliss. **56. The Son of man**] Here only is this title applied to Jesus by any one except Himself. It indicates that Stephen saw Him in human form: see on Mt 8 20. **57. Stopped their ears**] because they regarded his words as blasphemous.

58. Out of the city] see 1 K 21 13 Lv 24 14-16. **And stoned** *him*] 'After a man has been condemned to be stoned, they bring him good strong wine, and give him to drink, that he may not feel too great horror of a violent death. Then come the witnesses, and bind his hands and feet, and lead him to the place of stoning. Then the witnesses take a great stone, large enough to cause death, and lay it upon his heart all together, lest one should act before another, according to Dt 17 7, "The hand of the witnesses shall be first against him": then all the Israelites can overwhelm him with stones' (Talmud). The execution of Stephen was tumultuous and illegal, for, (1) there was no formal sentence pronounced by the court, (2) the Roman authorities were not consulted about the death sentence : see Jn 18 31.

Saul] A young Jew of Tarsus in Cilicia, born a Roman citizen, a tent-maker by trade, of well-to-do parents, trained at Jerusalem in the rabbinical school of Gamaliel the Pharisee, and accustomed to speak Hebrew (21 39 f. etc.). His other name, Paul, first occurs 13 9.

59. Calling upon *God*] RV 'calling upon the Lord' (i.e. Jesus). **Receive my spirit**] A direct prayer to Jesus, and, therefore, a proof that the doctrine of the divinity of Jesus was already established in the Church. It is not a prayer to a mere saintly intercessor ('Jesus, pray for me '), but a direct prayer offered in the firm belief that Jesus can really grant what is asked, viz. the salvation of the soul. Prayer to Jesus was universal in the Christian

Church (9 14 etc.). **60.** Like his Master, Stephen dies praying for his enemies : cp. Lk 23 34.

C. 8. 1. At that time] RV 'on that day.'

Except the apostles] The apostles still wished to achieve the conversion of Jerusalem. Besides, as leaders of the flock, they disdained flight.

PART 2

THE EXTENSION OF THE CHURCH TO JUDÆA AND SAMARIA (Chs. 8 4–11 18)

The Christians, scattered by persecution, preach everywhere through Judæa and Samaria. The places specially mentioned are Samaria, Azotus, Cæsarea, Lydda, the Sharon valley, and Joppa.

CHAPTER 8

PHILIP IN SAMARIA. SIMON MAGUS

The graphic details of the ministry of Philip which follow, were doubtless obtained from Philip himself. St. Luke stayed at his house at Cæsarea, and made the acquaintance of his four virgin daughters, prophetesses (21 8). During St. Paul's three years' imprisonment at Cæsarea, St. Luke doubtless had much intercourse with Philip, with whose liberal views he was in sympathy. The historical character of the following narratives stands upon a firm basis. In later years Philip migrated with his daughters to Tralles, in Asia Minor, of which he became the first bishop. Philip the Deacon and Evangelist is confused by some early writers with Philip the Apostle, who in his later years migrated to Hierapolis, and who also had daughters.

5. Philip] The deacon and evangelist, not the Apostle (see vv. 1 and 14). **The city of Samaria**] doubtless the capital, called (like the district) Samaria, and also (since the time of Herod the Great) Sebaste, in honour of Augustus (Sebastos). **7. Unclean spirits**] Whether the NT. demoniacs were really possessed, or were insane persons whose delusion took the form of a belief that they were possessed, is an open question. In either case the miracles of healing performed on them are remarkable (see on Mt 4 24, 25).

9. Simon] Justin Martyr (150 A.D.), himself a Samaritan, says that Simon belonged to the Samaritan village of Gitto. He is regarded as the father of heresy, and is the reputed author of a Gnostic work called 'The Great Revelation,' of which fragments remain. **Bewitched**] 'astounded' (also v. 11). **10. The great power of God**] RV 'that power of God which is called Great,' i.e. the chief emanation from the Deity, and so entitled to divine worship. According to Justin, he went even further, claiming to be the first or supreme God.

13. Believed] i.e. believed in the genuineness of Philip's miracles, but did not believe in God with a spiritual and saving faith. Simon as a sorcerer and conjurer was an excellent judge of alleged miracles.

14. By sending Peter and John the apostles formally sanctioned the reception of the Samaritans into the Church. The Samaritans, though observing the Law, were almost entirely heathen in origin, so that the incident marks an important step towards admitting pure Gentiles.

15–17. This is the fullest account of the apostolic laying on of hands after baptism, which is more briefly described, 19 6, and alluded to, Heb 6 2. In later times the ordinance was administered by bishops, and was called Confirmation, the Seal, and the Chrism. The author of Hebrews speaks of it as one of the first principles of the doctrine of Christ (Heb 6 2).

18. Saw] It is probable that many upon whom the Apostles laid hands received miraculous gifts. That Simon, who made his living by working lying wonders, should have desired the power of working genuine ones, was natural enough.

26–40. Philip and the Ethiopian eunuch. The eunuch, though a believer in the God of Israel, was a Gentile. Luke the universalist delights to record his admission into that wider communion in which all races and all conditions stand on an equality. This is the first example of a Gentile baptism. That it did not lead to the same disputes as the baptism of Cornelius, is due to the fact that it was private.

26. Toward the south] or, about mid-day.

Gaza] The town is called **desert**, or deserted, because it had been destroyed, 96 B.C.

27. Candace] The Ethiopian kingdom of Meroë lay to the S. of Egypt, and was governed by queens, whose dynastic title was 'Candace.'

32. See Isa 53 7, 8 (LXX). Isaiah is speaking of the suffering Servant of Jehovah, whom the Apostolic Church rightly identified with Jesus the Messiah. **33. In his humiliation his judgment was taken away**] i.e. in the humiliation of His Passion, justice was denied Him by the Sanhedrin and by Pilate. **And who shall declare his generation?**] i.e. and what language is adequate to describe the wickedness of His contemporaries who unjustly crucified Him ? **For his life is taken from the earth**] This refers not to the Ascension of Jesus (as some have thought), but to His violent death.

36. Baptized] 'Preaching Jesus' had clearly included instruction upon the nature and necessity of the Christian sacraments.

37. which the RV omits, is a very early and trustworthy marginal addition, which was ultimately incorporated into the text. The simplicity of the baptismal confession is a proof of its genuineness. 1 Pet 3 21 alludes to the baptismal profession of faith. **38.** The eunuch was probably baptised by immersion, the usual practice of the early Church, though not held to be absolutely essential.

39. Caught away Philip] Probably the Holy Spirit prompted Philip to depart abruptly for Azotus (Ashdod). **Rejoicing**] According to Eusebius, the eunuch, on his arrival home, evangelised his countrymen. In his conversion was fulfilled Ps 68 31, 'Princes shall come out of Egypt ; Ethiopia shall soon stretch out her hands unto God.' **40. Was found at Azotus**] Azotus or Ashdod was one of the five Philistine cities, whose inhabitants were enemies of the Jews after the captivity (Neh 4 7). It was distant over 20 m. (northwards) from Gaza.

All the cities] These would include Jamnia, Joppa and Lydda. **Cæsarea**] see on 10 1.

CHAPTER 9
SAUL BECOMES A CHRISTIAN

1–30. The Conversion of Saul is to regarded as a miraculous event. The way for it may have been prepared by Stephen's speech, by the spectacle of the constancy of the Christian martyrs, and by Saul's own consciousness of the imperfections of the Law (Ro 7 7–8 11). Yet there is no indication that he was anything but a violent enemy of Christianity until the moment of his conversion. His own language on this point is quite clear (1 Cor 15 9 Gal 1 12-16 1 Tim 1 13). St. Paul always maintained that the appearance of the risen Christ to him which brought about his conversion, was as objective and real as the appearances to the other Apostles. He regarded it as the turning-point of his life, and the beginning of his new vocation. He claimed to be an Apostle of equal rank and authority with the other Apostles (2 Cor 11 5 Gal 2 8, etc.), (1) because Christ had appeared to him as to the others (1 Cor 15 8 9 1), and (2) because Christ had appointed him an Apostle just as He had appointed the others (Ac 22 21, etc.). For confirmation of the truth of this he appealed to ' the signs of an apostle ' (miracles, conversions, etc.) which accompanied his ministry (2 Cor 12 12).

Saul's conversion at once gave Christianity a higher social status. He was an educated man, of good family, a rabbi, and (probably) a member of the Sanhedrin. It could no longer be objected to the teachers of the new faith that they were all ignorant and unlettered men.

The conversion of Saul is a turning-point in the history of Christianity. By conversion he became not merely a Christian, but an enlightened Christian. He perceived that the ceremonial Law was no longer binding, and his perception of this fact enabled him to preach Christianity as a universal religion. The Twelve already held this view in principle, but to Saul belongs the credit of acting upon it with energy, and of carrying it out to its logical results.

1. The high priest] The Romans allowed the Sanhedrin to exercise civil and criminal jurisdiction (except in capital cases) over the whole Jewish community, even outside Palestine. **2. Synagogues**] clearly the Christians had not yet separated from the Jewish synagogues. **This way**] ' Way,' thus used absolutely for Christianity, is peculiar to Acts : see 16 17 18 25, 26 19 9, 23 22 4 24 14, 22.

3. A light] according to 1 Cor 9 1, Paul saw, within the light, Jesus Himself, in His risen and glorified body.

5. *It is* **hard for thee to kick against the pricks**] These words, which the RV omits as an interpolation from 26 14, mean that the *rôle* of a persecutor is impossible to Paul. Paul is really in the position of a plough-ox. Jesus is his driver, and holds the goad. Paul can no more resist Jesus than the plough-ox can resist his driver. There is probably no allusion to stings of conscience, as some have supposed.

6. According to 26 16, Jesus also told Paul that his mission would be to preach to the Gentiles. **7. Stood speechless**] According to 26 14, they fell to the earth. **Hearing a voice**] RV ' hearing the voice.' Yet in 22 9 Paul says, ' they heard not the voice of him that spake to me.' The latter account, being Paul's own, is to be preferred. Those who wish to harmonise the two accounts translate here 'hearing the sound' (RM). But it is not necessary to harmonise. The variations in unimportant details only accentuate the general harmony.

8. Saw no man] RV ' saw nothing.'
9. Saul fasted to show his penitence.

10. Ananias] probably the head of the Christian body at Damascus. Late tradition makes him one of the Seven, consecrated bishop of Damascus by Peter and Andrew, and a martyr. **15. A chosen vessel**] i.e. a chosen instrument : cp. 13 2 Gal 1 15, etc. **The Gentiles**] cp. 22 21 26 17 Ro 1 5 11 13 Gal 2 7, 8. **And the children of Israel**] Though Paul's mission was mainly to the Gentiles, it was his custom to preach the gospel first to the Jews : see 13 14, etc. **16. I will shew him**] see 20 23 21 11 2 Cor 11 23. **18. And was baptized**] It is added (22 16) that St. Paul received at his baptism the remission of his former sins.

The three accounts of St. Paul's conversion (chs. 9, 22, 26) present some not very important variations. Thus, St. Paul alone fell to the earth (c. 9), but in c. 26 *all* fell to the earth.

The men heard a voice (c. 9), but in c. 22 they heard *not* the voice. These men 'saw no man' (c. 9), but in c. 22 they 'saw indeed the light.' In c. 26 it is the Lord who declares that St. Paul is to be 'a minister and witness' to the Gentiles ; in c. 9 and c. 22 it is Ananias. In c. 26 no allusion is made to the Apostle becoming blind, or to Ananias, but it is noted that the Lord spoke in Hebrew.

19. Certain days] St. Luke makes no mention of the Arabian sojourn of St. Paul, which, according to Gal 1 17, took place immediately after the conversion. Either St. Luke did not know of it, or thought it unimportant for his purpose. By 'Arabia' is probably meant the territory of the Nabatæans, which in the period of their greatest prosperity extended from the Euphrates to the Red Sea. To this race belonged king Aretas, whose ethnarch in Damascus endeavoured to arrest St. Paul (2 Cor 11 32).

20. Christ] RV 'Jesus.' **The Son of God**] Whatever may be the meaning of this term in the Synoptic Gospels, in the Pauline theology it undoubtedly means a preëxistent divine being, consubstantial with the Father, and His agent in the Creation and Redemption of the world. **23. After many days**] according to Gal 1 18, after 'three years.' **The Jews**] These must have persuaded the governor of king Aretas to persecute Paul : see 2 Cor 11 32.

25. The disciples] RV 'his disciples.' **26. It** is strange that after this arduous work at Damascus the Church of Jerusalem should still doubt the fact of Paul's conversion. **27. To the apostles**] according to Gal 1, Paul stayed in Jerusalem fifteen days, and of the Apostles saw only Peter and James the Lord's brother. **29. Grecians**] i.e. Greek-speaking Jews. **30.** The reason why Paul was willing to leave Jerusalem is given in 22 18 (a vision of Jesus in the Temple).

31. Extension of the Church in Judæa, Galilee, and Samaria.
The churches] RV 'the Church.' The local churches formed one organic whole.

32-43. Activity of Peter at Lydda and Joppa.
32. Throughout all *quarters*] or, 'throughout all the saints.' **Lydda**] in the plain of Sharon, about 10 m. SE. of Joppa, on the way to Jerusalem.

33. Æneas] the name is different from that of the hero of Virgil's poem (Æněas).

34. The Apostle healed 'in the name of Jesus.' Jesus healed in His own name, as being Himself the author of the cure.

35. Saron] or, Sharon, is a very fruitful plain extending along the coast of the Mediterranean from Joppa to Carmel (1 Ch 27 29 Song 2 1, etc.). **36. Joppa**] now Jaffa, the port of Jerusalem, and the only seaport ever possessed by the Jews. **Dorcas**] i.e. 'gazelle.'

CHAPTER 10
Peter and the Gentiles

1-48. Conversion of Cornelius. The baptism of Cornelius was an event of far-reaching importance, and is, therefore, described by St. Luke in great detail. If it was not the first actual baptism of a Gentile (see 8 38), it was, at any rate, the first such baptism which was publicly acknowledged. The historical character of the incident has been called in question because St. Peter in Galatians is represented as opposing St. Paul on the Gentile question (Gal 2 11 f.). But, (1) Galatians represents Peter as in complete agreement with Paul on all essential points (Gal 2 6, 12) ; and (2) the Jewish prejudices of Peter are fully recognised in the narrative in Acts. Indeed, it required a thrice-repeated vision to remove them (10 9 f.).

1. Cæsarea] built by Herod the Great on the site of an insignificant town called Strato's Tower, and renamed Cæsarea Augusta in honour of his patron Augustus. There was a theatre, an amphitheatre, a royal palace, and a temple containing images of Augustus and of Rome. The majority of the inhabitants were Greek, but Jews enjoyed equal rights. At this time Cæsarea was the capital of the Roman province, and the residence of the governor.

Cornelius, a centurion] A legion consisted of about 6,000 men, and was divided into ten cohorts, each commanded by a tribune (or chiliarch, see 21 31). A cohort was divided into six centuries, each commanded by a centurion. Centurions were men who had risen from the ranks, and were therefore, as a rule, men of capacity and good character : cp. Lk 7 5.

The Italian *band*] rather, 'cohort.' In the smaller provinces legions were not stationed, and therefore St. Luke is doubtless right in saying that there was only a cohort of Roman soldiers at Cæsarea. The men were recruited in Italy, and were probably Roman citizens.

2. One that feared God] i.e. a believer in the one true God, but not a circumcised proselyte. The baptism of Cornelius would not have been an innovation if he had been circumcised : see 6 5. Cornelius was diligent in the three recognised religious duties of prayer, fasting (v. 30), and almsdeeds ; he kept the Jewish hours of prayer (v. 3).

3. Ninth hour] i.e. 3 P.M. **4. A memorial**] Acts of genuine piety cause God to remember us for good. Cornelius, by using well the grace already vouchsafed him, was thought worthy to receive greater grace. **8. To Joppa**] A distance of about 40 m.

9. The sixth hour] see on 3 1. The flat housetop of Oriental houses is used for prayer, meditation, recreation, and sleeping (2 K 23 12

Neh 8¹⁶ 1 S9 ²⁵,²⁶ (RV) 2 S11². **10. Trance]**
Trance, ecstasy, or waking vision, is only one
of the modes of divine revelation, and that by
no means the most frequent or most important.
For examples see Isa 6 Dan 7, 8, 9²¹ 2 Cor 12²
Rev 1¹⁰. Visions play a somewhat important
part in the history of Acts (9¹⁰ 16⁹ 18⁹ 22¹⁷ :
cp. 27²³ 2¹⁷). **16. Thrice]** the vision was
repeated to confirm and establish the lesson
taught by it (Gn 41³²).

The question of the distinction of meats
was important, because, so long as it was
observed, the Church (like the Jews) was
cut off from all real social intercourse with
Gentiles, who placed 'unclean' food on their
tables. A special revelation was accordingly
made to the chief of the Apostles announcing
that the distinction of meats was abrogated,
and that henceforth Jew and Gentile were to
associate and eat together, on terms of equality
(v. 28). Jesus had already laid down this
principle (Mk 7¹⁹ RV), but St. Peter had not
understood it.

28. An unlawful thing] cp. Jn 4⁹ 18²⁸ Ac
11³ Gal 2¹²,¹⁴. **30. Four days, etc.]** RV
' Four days ago, until this hour, I was keeping
the ninth hour of prayer in my house.' The
reference to fasting, omitted by the RV, has
considerable ancient attestation.

36–38. The construction is confused, reflecting St. Peter's deep emotion. Adopting the
reading of the RM, we may freely translate
thus : ' He sent the word unto the children
of Israel, preaching peace (for all mankind)
through Jesus Christ (He is Lord of all men).
Ye know the things that were done throughout
the whole of Judæa, beginning from Galilee,
after the baptism which John preached, (even
the deeds of) Jesus of Nazareth, how God
anointed Him with the Holy Ghost and with
power, who went about doing good,' etc.

41. Eat and drink] see on 1⁴. **42. Quick]**
i.e. living : see 2 Tim 4¹ 1 Pet 4⁵ ; cp. Ro 14⁹.
43. All the prophets] cp. 3²⁴ 26²². **44.** As
a rule, the Holy Spirit was given after baptism,

with the laying on of the Apostles' hands (2³⁸
8¹⁷ 19⁶). In this particular case the Holy
Spirit was given before baptism, as a miraculous
assurance that the Gentiles were not to be
excluded from the gift of the Holy Spirit,
but were to be baptised. **46. Speak with
tongues]** see on 2⁴. **47. Water]** the water,
viz. of Baptism. **48. In the name of the
Lord]** RV ' in the name of Jesus Christ ' : see
on Mt 28¹⁹.

CHAPTER 11
THE FIRST GENTILE CHURCH

**1–18. The baptism of Cornelius discussed
and approved at Jerusalem.** Those Christians
who maintained the need of observing the
Ceremonial Law did not attack the baptism
itself because, although they disliked it, our
Lord's command to baptise all nations was too
definite to be questioned. They attacked,
therefore, St. Peter's undoubted breach of
Jewish law and custom : ' Thou wentest in to
men uncircumcised, and didst eat with them '
(v. 3). What they apparently desired was,
that if Gentiles were baptised at all, they should
be regarded as an inferior class, and not allowed
to eat at the same table with their Jewish
superiors : cp. Gal 2¹²f. Peter did not discuss
the general principle, but defended himself
on the ground that he had received a special
revelation authorising, and indeed commanding, him to act as he did in this particular case.

2. They that were of the circumcision] This
may either mean the whole Church of Jerusalem
in contrast with Cornelius and his friends, or the
Judaising party in that Church which, perhaps,
already existed, as it certainly did some years
later (15¹,⁵).

18. The Church of Jerusalem unanimously
endorsed Peter's action, doubtless because the
case was an exceptional one, and was not likely
to become a precedent. When St. Paul made
a practice of doing what St. Peter had only
done as a rare exception, the controversy was
revived (c. 15).

PART 3
THE CHURCH IN ANTIOCH, 35–47 A.D. (Chs. 11¹⁹–13³)

**19–26. Extension of the Church to Antioch.
Admission of Gentile members.** Antioch in
N. Syria ranked next to Alexandria, as the
third city in the Roman empire. It was beautifully situated on the Orontes, about 15 m.
from the sea. Its port was Seleucia. The bulk
of the population was Syrian by race, but the
language and culture were Greek. There were
also numerous Jews, who had gathered round
their synagogues a remarkable number of
proselytes. Antioch was the capital of the
province of Syria, and the seat of the Roman
governor, so that here Christianity came into

contact for the first time with Greek and
Roman civilisation. Antioch remained a great
Christian centre : among its honoured names
were Ignatius and Chrysostom : its school of
theology and exegesis was famous, and its
bishop was one of the four patriarchs. Here
Christianity was first preached on any large
scale to Gentiles (see on v. 20). It is probable,
however, that most of them were, like Cornelius,
in some way attached to the synagogue. St.
Paul seems to have been the first to appeal to
Gentiles pure and simple : see 14²⁷.

19. The narrative goes back to 8¹, to trace

the chain of causation which led to the foundation of the first great Gentile Church. Christianity, it will be seen, spread along the great trade routes both by land and sea. **Phenice**] i.e. Phœnicia. **20. Men of Cyprus and Cyrene**] these would be Hellenists (Greek-speaking Jews), and therefore presumably more liberal in their views than Hebrews. To these unnamed Cyprians and Cyrenians belongs the credit of first preaching systematically to Gentiles. **Spake unto the Grecians**] i.e. to the Greek-speaking Jews. So the AV. But the context plainly requires 'spake unto the Greeks' (i.e. unto the Gentiles), and this reading is adopted by the RV.

22. The Church of Jerusalem on hearing the news acted with commendable self-restraint. They did not hastily condemn the new departure, little as they liked it, but sent a trustworthy person, Barnabas, to examine into the circumstances upon the spot, and to report.

23. Barnabas, after carefully observing the results of the policy, approved it (**was glad**), and **exhorted them all** (i.e. both Jews and Gentiles) to persevere in their profession of faith, and to form one united Church. Barnabas thus anticipated Paul in sanctioning the principle of Gentile equality, which involved eating with Gentiles (Gal 2 12), and it was because Paul was likely to be in sympathy with such a policy, that Barnabas summoned him to Antioch.

26. Christians] The giving of this name marked the recognition of the fact that 'the Way' was something more than a new Jewish sect. The inclusion of numerous Gentiles within the Church, and that without their becoming Jews, and the preaching of Jesus as one whose authority was superior to that of Moses, gave complete justification to those who saw in Christianity a new religion. The form of the word is Latin, so that it may have originated in the Latin-speaking court of the Roman governor. At any rate, the name was not invented by the Jews, who did not admit that Jesus was 'the Christ' (Messiah). In 64 A.D. Tacitus mentions that the name was in use among the common people at Rome. In the 2nd cent. a corrupted form, 'Chrestians,' lit. 'the good people,' was sometimes used.

27–30. The Church of Antioch succours the Church of Jerusalem in time of famine.

27. Friendly relations clearly prevailed between Jerusalem and Antioch, the former Church sending accredited prophets and teachers to Antioch to assist in the work of evangelisation. **Prophets**] The gift of prophecy specially distinguished the apostolic from the subapostolic and later ages. It was widely diffused, being exercised by private Christians, and even by women in the Church assemblies (1 Cor 14 1). Generally it took the form of inspired exhortation or instruction, but was sometimes predictive. The official prophets, who were recognised as possessing the gift to the fullest extent (e.g. Agabus, Barnabas, Symeon called Niger, Lucius of Cyrene, Manaën, Judas, and Silas, see 13 1 15 32 21 10) ranked next to the Apostles, and were regarded with them as the foundation upon which the Church was built (Eph 2 20). The chief product of Christian prophecy is the inspired NT.

Unto Antioch] The Bezan text here adds : ' And there was much gladness. And when we were gathered together, one of them named Agabus spake [and signified, etc.].' This reading, which seems trustworthy, confirms the tradition that St. Luke belonged to Antioch, and was one of the early converts there.

28. Agabus] see 21 10. **Great dearth throughout all the world**] There was a severe famine in the fourth year of Claudius, 45 A.D., which affected both Judæa and Greece. To this St. Luke probably refers. **Claudius**] reigned from 41–54 A.D. The prophecy of Agabus was perhaps delivered in 44 A.D.

30. The elders] lit. 'presbyters.' These officers are here mentioned for the first time. All the Apostolic Churches were governed by presbyters (14 23), or, as they were sometimes called at first, bishops (20 28 : cp. Phil 1 1). The presbyters ranked next to the apostles and above the deacons. On them devolved (under the apostles) the government and pastoral care of the Church. They visited and anointed the sick, and entertained strangers (see Jas 5 14). The more learned of them laboured in the word and teaching, and such were held worthy of double honour (1 Tim 5 18). They did not exercise what is now called episcopal authority. This was reserved to the apostles and apostolic men. They were essentially local officers. There were several in one Church, and they formed one body or 'college' (the presbytery, 1 Tim 4 14). Government by presbyters was adopted by the Church from the Synagogue. Jewish synagogues were governed by a body of presbyters at the head of whom was an officer called 'the ruler of the synagogue.' Many think that in Christian Churches also the leading presbyter had from the first a special position, similar to that of St. James at Jerusalem, and that towards the close of the apostolic age the title 'bishop,' at first applied to all presbyters indiscriminately, began to be restricted to him (see Intro. to Pastoral Epistles, notes on 1 Tim 3 2 Tit 1 7).

The usual view is that this visit of St. Paul to Jerusalem is nowhere else alluded to, being passed over in silence in the Epistle to the Galatians. But the writer's own view is that this visit is that mentioned Gal 2 1-10. See on c. 15.

CHAPTER 12

IMPRISONMENT OF PETER. DEATH OF HEROD

1-19. Persecution of the Church at Jerusalem by Herod. Martyrdom of James the son of Zebedee. Peter's imprisonment and miraculous release. The Church was persecuted (1) by the Sadducees and chief priests, 4 ¹ 5 ¹⁷; (2) afterwards by the Pharisees, 6 ¹¹ ᶠ. ; and now (3) by the king of the Jews. Not till later was persecution to come from the Romans.

1. About that time] viz. when relief was sent to the Church of Jerusalem (11 ²⁹, ³⁰). The death of Herod (v. 23) fixes the date as 44 A.D. **Herod the king]** i.e. Herod Agrippa I, son of Aristobulus (Herod the Great's son) and Bernice ; born 10 B.C. See art. 'The Dynasty of the Herods.'

2. James] i.e. James the Great, son of Zebedee. **4. Four quaternions]** four parties of four soldiers each, relieving one another at intervals. **Easter]** i.e. the Passover. **5. Without ceasing]** RV 'earnestly.' **7. The prison]** RV 'the cell.' **10. The second ward]** i.e the second guard of soldiers. **And they went out]** D adds, 'and went down the seven steps' (probably an authentic detail).

12. Mary] This Mary, mother of Mark, and aunt of Barnabas, was a widow of considerable wealth, as her style of living testifies. Her house had a gateway into the courtyard (not a 'door,' as AV), which was kept by a portress. There was room within for the Church to worship (12 ¹²). Many suppose that her house was the scene of the Last Supper, and of the descent of the Holy Ghost. **John .. Mark]** the evangelist: see Intro. to Mk.

13, 14. The gate] i.e. the gateway or vestibule. **15. His angel]** They thought that Peter's guardian angel had assumed his voice and appearance : see on Mt 18 ¹⁰. **17. Unto James, and to the brethren]** The meeting in Mary's house was clearly an unofficial one. Observe that Peter recognises James (i.e. the Lord's brother) as the head of the local Church of Jerusalem.

20-24. Death of Herod Agrippa I, 44 A.D. Josephus's account of Herod's death, which is quite independent, confirms St. Luke's (see 'Ant.' 19. 8).

20. Tyre and Sidon obtained their corn and provisions from Palestine. Hence when a dispute arose (perhaps over some commercial or tariff question), Herod forbade the exportation of corn to Tyre and Sidon. Famine prices prevailed, and the cities were obliged to come to terms. They 'persuaded' Blastus (AV 'made him their friend'), probably by a bribe, and desired 'peace,' i.e. a cessation of the tariff war.

23. The angel] RV 'an angel.' This is, of course, the Christian interpretation of the incident. No angelic appearance is to be assumed. **24.** So signal a judgment upon a persecutor was an indication of the righteousness of the Christian cause. It is a remarkable fact that most of the early persecutors perished miserably.

C. 12 ²⁵–13 ³. Separation of Barnabas and Saul for missionary work, 47 A.D.

25. Returned from Jerusalem] the best reading is 'returned to Jerusalem,' i.e. to fetch Mark to Antioch.

CHAPTER 13

ST. PAUL AS A MISSIONARY

1. Prophets] see on 11 ²⁷. **Simeon that was called Niger]** Niger was a Roman cognomen. **Lucius of Cyrene]** doubtless one of those Cyrenians who first preached at Antioch (11 ²⁰). **Manaen]** the OT. form is 'Menahem.' **Which had been brought up with Herod the tetrarch]** Two meanings are possible. Either, (1) Menahem's mother had been Herod's wet-nurse ; or (2) Menahem had been brought up with Herod as his foster-brother. The **tetrarch** (Herod Antipas) was the son of Herod the Great, by Malthace, and received (after his father's death) Galilee and Peræa. In 39 A.D. he was banished to Gaul, where he died. **2. As they ministered to the Lord]** i.e. celebrated divine worship. From the Gk. word used is derived our word 'liturgy.' **And fasted]** see on Mt 6 ¹⁶. **The Holy Ghost said]** an expression vividly suggesting the personality of the Holy Ghost, and His office as the Guide of the Church. Acts is so full of such expressions (10 ¹⁹ 8 ²⁹, ³⁹ 11 ¹² 13 ⁴ 16 ⁶), that it has even been called 'the Gospel of the Holy Ghost.' In this case the Holy Ghost probably spoke by one of the prophets. **Separate me Barnabas and Saul]** Some regard this incident as the ordination of Paul and Barnabas ; others as their solemn setting apart for missionary work. Henceforth they are called 'apostles' by St. Luke (14 ⁴, ¹⁴). **3.** This was the apostolic custom to fast at ordinations : see 14 ²³.

PART 4

THE CHURCH OF THE WORLD, 47-61 A.D. (Chs. 13 ⁴-28 ³¹)

13 ⁴-15 ³⁵. First Missionary Journey and Council of Jerusalem. During this journey St. Paul conclusively established his right to the title of Apostle, (1) by the success of his labours, 13 ⁴⁹ 14 ¹, ²¹ ; (2) by signs and wonders, 13 ¹¹ 14 ³, ¹⁰ ; and (3) by the foundation and organisation of churches, 14 23. It will be noticed that St. Paul takes the lead, and soon becomes a more prominent figure than Barnabas. Although upon a mission to the Gentiles, St. Paul always addresses the Jews first (13 46).

C. 13. 4-13. Cyprus. This island was familiar ground to Barnabas (4 36). It contained a large Jewish population, to which the apostles mainly confined their attention (v. 5). The principal town was Salamis, but the seat of government was Paphos (see v. 6). Cyprus was at this time a senatorial province, and the governor is therefore correctly described as proconsul (v. 7). The principal exports of Cyprus were copper and timber. The deity chiefly worshipped was Aphrodite (Venus). Paphos, the centre of her worship, had an evil reputation for laxity of morals.

5. *Their* **minister**] Possibly for the administration of baptism, which St. Paul usually performed by deputy (1 Cor 1 14-17). **6. A . . sorcerer**] lit. 'a magus.' Here in a bad sense: see on Mt 2 1. **7. Deputy**] Gk. *anthupatos*, i.e. ' proconsul,' the correct title of the governor of a senatorial province. **Sergius Paulus**] a member of the ancient patrician gens of the Sergii. An inscription has been discovered in Cyprus, which speaks of the proconsulship of this Paulus. **8. Elymas**] The name is Arabic, meaning ' the wise,' an equivalent of the Gk. *magus*. **9. Paul**] Saul, as a Roman citizen, had the well-known Roman name Paul. It is here introduced, because the apostle, for the first time, comes into intimate contact with the Roman world. The name Saul in Gk. has the ridiculous sense of ' waddling.' Observe that from this point Paul becomes a more prominent figure than Barnabas. **Filled with the Holy Ghost**] This miracle of wrath was justified by a special revelation.

13. John departing from them] Mark may have objected to the conversion of so many Gentiles. Others suggest personal resentment against St. Paul, whose reputation was now eclipsing that of St. Barnabas, Mark's cousin. Failure of courage or of perseverance is also possible.

14-52. Antioch of Pisidia. St. Paul's Sermon in the Synagogue.
The cities which the apostles now proceeded to evangelise (Pisidian Antioch, Iconium, Lystra, and Derbe) were situated in the southern part of the Roman province of Galatia, and it is now very generally supposed that the Epistle to the Galatians was addressed to the churches in these cities. If so, we can use that Epistle to illustrate this narrative. The other view that the Galatian Churches were situated in N. Galatia is less probable, because no missionary journey in N. Galatia is mentioned in Acts.

14. Perga] An important city, the capital of Pamphylia. **Antioch in Pisidia**] rather, ' Pisidian Antioch.' This Antioch was really in Phrygia, but from its position was called ' Antiochia ad Pisidiam,' ' Antioch bordering on Pisidia.' It was the centre of military and civil administration for S. Galatia, and commanded the great high-road from Syria to Ephesus and the West. We gather from Gal 4 13 that St. Paul preached in Galatia on account of an illness which overtook him on his travels. Prof. Ramsay supposes that having caught malarial fever at the low-lying Perga, he determined to try the effect of the mountain air of Antioch. **The Synagogue**] The sabbath service of the synagogue consisted then as now of, (1) the recitation of the Shema (i.e. of Dt 6 4-9 11 13-21 Nu 15 37-41); (2) fixed prayers and benedictions ; (3) a lesson from the Law ; (4) a lesson from the Prophets, intended to illustrate the law ; (5) a sermon or instruction. The ruler of the synagogue (at Antioch there appears to have been more than one) decided who was to read or preach.

16-41. St. Paul's sermon falls into three parts : (1) the historical introduction (vv. 16-25) ; (2) the preaching of salvation through the Incarnation, the Death and the Resurrection of Jesus, who is God's Son, to whom the prophets bore witness (vv. 26-37) ; (3) the practical application and appeal (vv. 38-41). The introduction reminds us of Stephen's apology, but whereas Stephen laid the main stress upon Moses, St. Paul lays it upon David. The description of our Lord's rejection by the rulers, and of His death and resurrection reminds us strongly of St. Peter's earlier speeches at Jerusalem, but St. Paul adds the further claim that Jesus is God's Son (v. 33). The Pauline doctrine of justification by faith, and not by the works of the Law, finds expression in v. 39 : cp. Gal 2 16 3 2 f., etc., which show that this doctrine was actually preached to the Galatians.

18. Suffered he their manners] Both here and in Dt 1 31 the true reading probably is ' bare he them as a nursing father.' **19. By lot**] RV ' for an inheritance.' **20. Judges about the space of four hundred and fifty years**] This period for the judges (more precisely 443 years) is also adopted by Josephus, but is inconsistent with 1 K 6 1. Another reading, adopted by the RV, makes the period of 450 years extend from the death of Joshua to the reign of David. **22.** See Ps 89 20 1 S 13 14. **24. His coming**] i.e. His entry upon the Messianic office (to be dated from His Baptism). **26. To you**] RV ' to us.'

33. In the second psalm] There is another reading ' in the first psalm,' which may be correct, as there is evidence that the first two psalms were sometimes counted as one. In the passage referred to (Ps 2 7) the Messiah is declared to be begotten as the Son of God on the day when Jehovah scatters His enemies before Him. So at the Resurrection, when the enemies of Jesus were confounded, He was 'declared to be the Son of God with power,' and made 'the first begotten of the dead' (Col 1 18 Rev 1 5).

34. I will give you the sure mercies of David] RV 'I will give you the holy and sure blessings of David.' See Isa 55 3. But how does this text prove the Resurrection of Jesus, and His unending life? Because unless Jesus had risen to unending life and power, the Messianic promises made to David could never have been fulfilled. **35.** See Ps 16 10, and cp. St. Peter's use of the passage, 2 31.

40. In the prophets] The particular prophecy quoted is Hab 1 5. Habakkuk had threatened the Jews with destruction by the Chaldæans (Babylonians). The passage, as applied by St. Paul, looks forward to the destruction of Jerusalem by the Romans.

42. RV 'And as they went out, they besought,' etc. The request for another sermon (according to the RV) was general and not confined to the Gentiles. **45.** What irritated the Jews was not the substance of the gospel message, but the fact that it was proclaimed to the heathen as well as to themselves.

46. Lo, we turn to the Gentiles] This momentous decision to appeal to the Gentiles directly, and not through the instrumentality of the Synagogue, required courage in the face of current prejudice. See further 18 6 28 28.

47. See Isa 42 6 49 6 Lk 2 32. **48.** As many as were ordained to eternal life believed] This expresses the Pauline and Apostolic doctrine of predestination, according to which God desires the salvation of all men (1 Tim 2 4 4 10, etc.), but inasmuch as He foresees that some (in the exercise of their free will) will actually repent and believe, while others will refuse to do so, He ordains the former to eternal life, and the latter to eternal death (Ro 8 28-30, etc.).

50. Devout and honourable women] i.e. proselytes to Judaism, and (probably) wives to the chief men of the city. Coasts] i.e. borders. **51.** Shook off the dust] see Mt 10 14 Mk 6 11 Lk 9 5, and cp. 18 6. Iconium] a Phrygian city of considerable importance situated in a most beautiful and fertile plain 80 m. SE. of Antioch. It is now called Konia.

52. In spite of the (apparently) successful persecution, and the departure of the apostles, the new converts stood firm, and were filled with joy and with the Holy Ghost: cp. 2 46 4 31.

CHAPTER 14

FIRST MISSIONARY JOURNEY (continued)

1-7. Paul and Barnabas at Iconium. The gospel meets with great success among both Jews and Gentiles in this populous city, and miracles are wrought in confirmation of the faith.

2. The first persecution at Iconium, which probably took the form of arraigning the apostles before the magistrates, failed. Accordingly the second persecution (v. 5) took the form of a popular tumult. V. 2 reads thus in D, 'But the rulers of the synagogue of the Jews raised a persecution against the righteous (i.e. the Christians), and exasperated the souls of the heathen against the brethren, but the Lord quickly gave peace.'

3. For the importance of miracles as a sign of apostleship, see 2 Cor 12 12 Ro 15 18. **4.** The apostles] The name is here first given to Paul and Barnabas: see on 13 1-3. **6.** Lystra and Derbe, cities of Lycaonia] Lystra (like Antioch) was a Roman colony, founded by Augustus, 6 B.C. Its official language was Latin. It lay 18 m. SSW. of Iconium. Derbe lay about 30 m. SE. of Lystra. Lystra and Derbe are correctly described as Lycaonian cities, in distinction from Antioch, which was Phrygian.

The curious second-century romance, 'The Acts of Paul and Thecla,' gives many additional particulars of St. Paul's proceedings at Iconium, some of which, perhaps, are authentic. Thecla, who belonged to one of the chief families of Iconium, overheard from a window the preaching of the apostle. She was at that time engaged to a young man named Thamyris, but on hearing St. Paul's words she became so enamoured of virginity that she broke off her engagement. For this interference with family life, and for impiety, St. Paul was scourged and expelled from the city, and Thecla was condemned to be burnt alive. A fall of rain extinguished the fire, and she escaped and followed Paul to Antioch. Here again she was persecuted, but was rescued by Tryphæna, a lady of great influence. The presbyter who composed this romance (though it was probably founded on fact) was deposed from his office.

8-20. Lystra. Here was a typical heathen population, but little affected by Judaism, as there was no synagogue. The people were grossly superstitious, and easily led into any kind of extravagance. Though Latin was the official language, the common people spoke their own uncouth Lycaonian dialect (v. 11). which was unintelligible to the apostles. While at Lystra the apostles probably lodged with the parents of Timothy: see on 16 1.

8. A cripple] Probably this man had learnt from the Jews the worship of the true God (D says that he was 'in the fear of God'), and consequently he had received some preparation for the gospel message. The circumstances and effect of this miracle are like those of the miracle worked by Peter and John, 3¹. **11. In the speech of Lycaonia**] This explains why the apostles did not protest against the proposals at the time. They appear to have gone home in entire ignorance of the construction which the people had placed upon the miracle. **The gods are come down**] The less educated or more credulous heathen at this time still believed that the gods were in the habit of visiting the earth in human form. It was in the neighbouring country of Phrygia that Jupiter and Mercury were said to have paid a visit to the virtuous peasants Baucis and Philemon, and to have been entertained by them. Even in Athens, in the age of Pisistratus, a visit of Athene (Minerva) in human form was believed possible. **12.** The majestic appearance of Barnabas caused him to be identified with the chief god (Zeus) corresponding to the Roman Jupiter. The insignificant stature of Paul (2 Cor 10¹⁰), and his gift of eloquence, suggested his identification with Hermes (the Roman Mercury). Hermes was the god of eloquence, and the attendant, messenger, and spokesman of Zeus.

13. Which was before their city] i.e. whose temple was before the city. **Unto the gates**] or 'porches.' It is difficult to decide where the sacrifice took place, whether at the porch of the apostles' house, or at the gates of the city, or at the gates of the temple. Perhaps the first is favoured by the statement (v. 14) that they 'sprang out' among the people.

14. Rent their clothes] in horror at the blasphemy: cp. Mt 26⁶⁵. **Ran in**] RV 'sprang forth.' **15. Of like passions**] i.e. of like nature. **Vanities**] i.e. vain gods. **17. Gave us rain**] RV 'gave you rains.' There was great scarcity of water in Lycaonia, owing to a deficient rainfall. **19. Persuaded the people**] The fickleness of the Lycaonians is reflected on by more than one Greek author, and perhaps St. Paul alludes to it in the Epistle to the Galatians (1⁶ 3¹ 4¹⁵, etc.). **20.** There is no reason to suppose a miracle here: cp. 20¹⁰.

Having at Lystra to deal with pure heathens, and not as usual with persons influenced by Judaism, St. Paul bases his teaching upon Natural Religion. The three main truths of Natural Religion according to him are, (1) God's Unity, (2) His creative power, and, (3) His benevolence. The main difficulty to which St. Paul addresses himself is, Why then has God permitted the nations to remain so long in ignorance? and the answer is that this ignorance is only for a time (v. 16); and that even in the time of ignorance God did not leave Himself entirely without witness (v. 17). The whole speech should be compared with that delivered at Athens, also to a purely heathen audience (17²²⁻³¹).

21–28. Visit to Derbe, and return journey to Antioch of Syria. Derbe, or Claudio-Derbe, where the work of the apostles seems to have been very successful, was a small Lycaonian town on the extreme boundary of the Roman province of Galatia. A convert of this city named Gaius is mentioned (20⁴).

21. To Lystra] thus showing remarkable perseverance and courage. **22. Confirming**] exhorting to steadfastness, so much needed by the fickle Galatians.

23. Elders] lit. 'presbyters.' We have a right to infer from this passage that wherever the apostles established a church, they established also a definite ministry. Presbyters only are mentioned, but it is to be presumed that there were also deacons to assist them. It is somewhat remarkable that St. Paul's Epistles (except the Pastorals) contain no allusion to presbyters. Bishops, however, probably in the sense of presbyters, are mentioned (Phil 1¹): see on Ac 11³⁰.

25. Attalia] the port of Perga. **26. Antioch**] They had been absent about 18 months.

27. furnishes the first example of a missionary meeting. It was a meeting of the whole Church, not of a few enthusiasts.

CHAPTER 15
The Question of Circumcision

1–35. The Council of Jerusalem, 49 A.D.

The usual view is that Gal 2¹⁻¹⁰ describes the visit of St. Paul to Jerusalem on the occasion of this Council. Adopting this, the following was the course of events. The baptism of Gentiles by St. Paul on his First Missionary Journey, without requiring them to be circumcised or to keep the Law, was keenly criticised at Jerusalem by the Pharisaic party within the Church. Some of these malcontents even came to Antioch, teaching that 'except ye be circumcised after the manner of Moses, ye cannot be saved' (Ac 15¹). They falsely professed to have the support of Peter and James, and St. Paul indignantly refers to them as 'false brethren privily brought in, who came in privily to spy out our liberty which we have in Christ Jesus' (Gal 2⁴). They demanded that Paul and Barnabas should go up to Jerusalem, and submit the matter to the superior authority of the Twelve. At first St. Paul refused to go, regarding himself as possessing an independent and equal authority. But on receiving a special revelation (Gal 2²) that the result would be favourable to his views, and would tend to the furtherance of the gospel, he consented to go, taking with him Barnabas, and Titus, one of his Gentile converts. Before the Council, private conferences were held between St. Paul and the heads of the Church of Jerusalem, with the object of reaching a settlement. As a step towards this, the circumcision of Titus was vehemently demanded by the Judaisers, and apparently recommended by the Twelve. As Titus was intended to be a fellow-worker of St. Paul, and would accordingly be brought into frequent close contact with Jews, much was to be said for this course. What happened is not quite clear. Most think that Titus was not circumcised; others that St. Paul, receiving an assurance that the main question, that of Gentile freedom, would be decided in his favour, gave way on the minor point, and circumcised Titus, not under compulsion, but as a spontaneous act of Christian charity (compare his conduct in the case of Timothy, 16³). Before the Conference a complete settlement was reached. The Twelve acknowledged Paul's teaching as orthodox, recognised him as the Apostle of the Gentiles, conceded his demand that the Gentiles should be free from the observance of the Law, and gave him the right hand of fellowship. After this the result of the Council was a foregone conclusion.

Some scholars take an entirely different view of the historical situation. They think that the visit to Jerusalem described in Gal 2 1-10 is not that of Ac 15 at all, but that of Ac 11 29,30. They regard the Epistle to the Galatians as written before the Council, during the heat of the circumcision controversy, and they place Peter's visit to Antioch (Gal 2 11f.) also before the Council. Much can be said in favour of this view, and the present writer is inclined to favour it.

1. Certain men] They falsely claimed to have been sent by James (see v. 24, Gal 2 12).
2. Barnabas] St. Luke passes over Peter's visit to Antioch, and Barnabas's temporary 'dissimulation' (Gal 2 12). **3.** The journey to Jerusalem partook somewhat of the character of a triumphant progress, or demonstration in favour of Paul and Barnabas. Outside Jerusalem the Pauline party was clearly in the ascendant. **4.** Even at Jerusalem the officials of the church, and its members as a whole, were favourably disposed towards St. Paul. The Judaisers were in a minority. **5. Pharisees**] The only express mention of converted Pharisees. What attracted the Pharisees in Christianity was (1) the fulfilment in Christ of the Messianic hope which the devout Pharisees cherished, and (2) the doctrine of the Resurrection.
7-11. The speech of St. Peter endorses the opinions of St. Paul in every particular. He speaks of the Law as a yoke 'which neither we nor our fathers were able to bear' (cp. Gal 5¹, where St. Paul bids the Galatians not to be entangled again with the yoke of bondage), and emphasises the Pauline doctrine of salva-

tion by grace and faith, and not by the works of the law: cp. Ro 3 24 Gal 2 16 3 6, etc. There is nothing incredible in this. It is plain from Galatians that Peter and even James were in complete agreement in principle with St. Paul (Gal 2 6 f.), and 1 Pet makes it evident that St. Peter was much attracted and influenced by St. Paul's theology.

13. James] James, the Lord's brother, presided at the Council, doubtless in the capacity of chief ruler of the local Church of Jerusalem. We should have expected Peter to preside.
14-21. St. James' speech proves him as decided an adherent of Gentile liberty as St. Peter. He approves St. Peter's conduct in baptising Cornelius, and quotes prophecies showing that the Messianic Church will embrace all nations. The Jews are to continue to keep the Law, but the Gentiles are only to be required to abstain from certain practices offensive to Jews.
14. Simeon] RV 'Symeon.' St. James uses the ancient Hebrew form of Peter's name, instead of the more usual 'Simon.' **For his name**] i.e. 'that his name might be glorified in them.'
16-18. St. James cites from memory, and not quite accurately, Am 9 11,12 (LXX), of which nevertheless he preserves the true sense.
16. After this I will return] Amos simply has 'In that day,' i.e. in the day of the Messiah. **The tabernacle of David**] i.e. the royal family descended from David. David's family is compared to a fallen tent, because, when Amos wrote, the southern kingdom was quite insignificant compared with the northern.
17, 18. Who doeth all these things. Known unto God are all his works from the beginning of the world] There is nothing in Amos corresponding to these words. RV reads, 'who maketh these things known from the beginning of the world.' RM reads, 'who doeth these things which were known from the beginning of the world.'
20. St. James mentions four prohibitions : (1) pollutions of idols, (2) fornication, (3) eating the flesh of strangled animals, (4) eating blood. The object of these prohibitions was to render social intercourse between Jews and Gentiles, and particularly common meals, less difficult. **Pollutions of idols**] No Christian would directly worship an idol, but Gentile Christians might easily incur pollution according to Jewish ideas, (1) by buying flesh in a heathen market, (2) by attending a feast in a heathen house. In both cases there would be a danger of eating flesh offered in sacrifice to idols. **Fornication**] Most interpret this of ordinary fornication, but seeing this was already forbidden to all Christians, there is much to be said for J. Lightfoot's view, that what

is really meant is marriage within the degrees forbidden in the book of Leviticus. Such marriages, common among the heathen, would be most distasteful to the Jews, and would be regarded by them as fornication : cp. 1 Cor 5[1].

Things strangled] This refers to Lv 17[13,14] Dt 12[16,23], according to which the blood was to be drained out of all animals before they were eaten. This prohibition, however, is entirely omitted by D and other ancient authorities both here and in v. 29. *From* **blood**] see Lv 3[17] 7[26] 17[10] 19[26] Dt 12[16,23] 15[23]. D and other authorities add here this injunction : ' And that they should not do to others what they would not have done to themselves.'

21. Here St. James recognises that Jewish Christians are still to attend the synagogue services and to keep the Law. **22.** This v. is evidence that the whole Church, and not merely the clergy, were consulted in matters of public policy. **Judas surnamed Barsabas (Barsabbas)**] probably the brother of the Joseph Barsabbas who was a candidate for the apostolate (1[23]). He was clearly a Hebrew. **Silas,** on the other hand, was probably a Hellenist, as his Latin name (' Silas ' = ' Silvanus ') indicates. He appears again, 15[40] 16[19] 17[4,10,14] 18[5] 2 Cor 1[19], as a companion of St. Paul. Later he was an associate of St. Peter (1 Pet 5[12]). Apparently he possessed the Roman citizenship (16[37]). **23. The apostles and elders and brethren**] Recent editors read, ' the apostles and presbyters, brethren.' Apparently the apostles and presbyters describe themselves as ' brethren ' to give the letter a fraternal and affectionate character. But the text is probably corrupt.

25. Being assembled with one accord] rather, ' having come to one accord.' **28.** Observe the claim to inspiration. **34.** This v. is omitted as an interpolation by many modern editors. It is contained in D, which adds, ' and Judas went alone.'

35. In Antioch] Here should be placed, according to the usual view, Peter's visit to Antioch, mentioned Gal 2[11f]. At first Peter ate publicly with the Gentiles, but on the arrival of ' certain from James,' he ' separated himself, fearing them that were of the circumcision.' The rest of the Jews, and even Barnabas, ' dissembled ' with him. St. Paul then publicly rebuked him, and apparently St. Peter confessed himself in the wrong. According to the other view, which the present writer favours, Peter's visit to Antioch took place before the Council. It is easier to understand the refusal to eat with the Gentiles *before* than after the Council.

St Paul's Second Missionary Journey, 49, 50 A.D. (Chs 15[36]–18[22])

Having secured the formal recognition by the Twelve of Gentile Christianity, St. Paul was free to resume his missionary labours. He first revisited the Churches founded on the First Journey, and then carried the gospel to Europe, preaching at Philippi, Thessalonica, Berœa, Athens, and Corinth. He then returned to the Syrian Antioch, and visited Jerusalem.

15[36]–16[5]. The Galatian and other Churches revisited.

C. 15. 36–41. St. Paul's grievance against Barnabas was that the latter insisted on taking with them an unsuitable assistant simply because he was a relation. The Church of Antioch seems to have sympathised with St. Paul (see v. 40). St. Paul was subsequently reconciled with Barnabas (1 Cor 9[6]) and also with Mark (2 Tim 4[11] Col 4[10]). **41. Confirming the churches**] see 16[5], and cp. 14[22].

CHAPTER 16
St. Paul in Europe

1. Timotheus] was probably of Lystra, not Derbe. His mother Eunice was perhaps a widow, and she, together with his grandmother Lois, educated the lad in the religion of Israel, though he was not circumcised (see 2 Tim 1[5]). The whole family had been converted at St. Paul's first visit. **3.** See Preface to c. 15. **4, 5.** Here we have evidence that the decrees of the Council were actually promulgated in the Galatian Churches, and that they were well received.

6–40. Journey into Europe, Philippi.

6. RV 'And they went through the region of Phrygia and Galatia, having been forbidden of the Holy Ghost to speak the word in Asia.' At Lystra (v. 6) they received a divine intimation that they were not to carry out their purpose (probably their main purpose in this journey) of preaching in the Roman province of Asia. Accordingly they passed through that part of the ancient Phrygia which belonged to the Roman province of Galatia, and in which were situated Iconium and Antioch, which they doubtless revisited.

Those who, like Lightfoot, hold that the churches to which the Epistle to the Galatians is addressed, were situated in *North* Galatia, understand ' the region of Phrygia and Galatia ' here to mean the district in N. Galatia once inhabited by Phrygians, but at this time by Gauls. Here they suppose that St. Paul was delayed by illness (Gal 4[13]), and seized the opportunity of preaching and founding numerous Celtic or Gallic churches which are nowhere mentioned in Acts.

7. RV 'And when they were come over against Mysia, they assayed to go into Bithynia, and the Spirit of Jesus suffered them not.' Leaving Antioch, St. Paul journeyed northward through the province of Asia till he came to the borders of Mysia (the north-western part of the province). He then attempted to strike westward into Bithynia, but was forbidden by 'the Spirit of Jesus.' This remarkable expression, which makes the Holy Spirit the Spirit not only of the Father, but also of the Son, is an evidence that the true divinity of Jesus was firmly held when St. Luke wrote.

8. And they passing by Mysia (i.e. passing through it without preaching) **came down to Troas**] Troas, the chief port of Mysia, was made a Roman colony by Augustus, and received many privileges, because of the supposed Trojan origin of the Roman people. Similar privileges were given to the neighbouring city of Ilion.

9. The **man of Macedonia** has sometimes been supposed to be St. Luke, or even the guardian angel of Macedonia (Dan 10 12). The man was recognised as Macedonian by his speech, or by his dress. The introduction of Christianity into that continent, where it was destined to win its chief triumphs, is fitly prepared for by a special revelation.

10. The **we** indicates that St. Luke was now a member of the party. Whether he joined it at Troas, or had accompanied it all along is not clear.

11. Samothracia] an island half-way between Troas and Neapolis. **Neapolis**] the port of Philippi.

12. Philippi] RV 'Philippi, which is a city of Macedonia, the first of the district, a Roman colony.' At Philippi, founded by Philip, father of Alexander the Great, Octavius and Antony had defeated the republican leaders, Brutus and Cassius, and the city, in honour of the victory, had been made a Roman colony with Latin rights. It lay on the great Egnatian way which united Italy and Asia, and was of great commercial importance. **The chief city**] lit. 'the first.' Some think that the meaning is that this was the first city reached by the Apostle in Macedonia, or in Europe.

13. Where prayer was wont to be made] RV 'where we supposed there was a place of prayer' (Gk. *proseuche*). Where the Jews were too few to build a synagogue, they were wont to assemble in open-air places of prayer (*proseuchæ*), by the seaside, or on a river's bank, for convenience of purification.

14. Lydia] She came from Thyatira in Lydia, a district where there were many dyers. She was a proselyte to Judaism, and a woman of some wealth and position. As she is not mentioned in the Epistle to the Philippians, she was probably then dead, or had left the city. Renan has the strange fancy that she was St. Paul's wife. **15. Her household**] the expression includes servants and slaves as well as children. Other examples

of the baptism of households are 16 33 18 8 1 Cor 1 16: see on Mt 19 13-15. **6. To prayer**] rather, 'to the place of prayer.'

A spirit of divination] The girl belonged to the class of 'clairvoyants' or 'mediums,' and really believed herself to be possessed by a spirit. Her recognition of the divine mission of St. Paul indicates a considerable degree of spiritual discernment. The expulsion of the 'spirit' need not have been a miracle. The girl recognised in St. Paul a minister of 'the supreme God,' supreme, therefore, over the spirit which possessed her. Hence the command to the spirit to come forth was (in her belief) authoritative, and consequently effectual.

18. Being grieved] Although the testimony of the girl was true, St. Paul would not receive it, because it emanated, as he supposed, from an evil spirit. Similarly Jesus would not receive the testimony of demons to His Divine Sonship and Messiahship (Mk 1 25, etc.).

20. Magistrates] At Philippi there were two magistrates (*duumvirs*) corresponding to the consuls at Rome. Provincial *duumvirs* often claimed and received the courtesy title of *prætors*, which is the title by which St. Luke calls them here. **Jews**] Christianity was not yet clearly distinguished from Judaism. Judaism was a lawful religion for Jews, but not for Roman citizens. **22.** Paul and Silas probably protested that they were Romans, but in the tumult their protest passed unheeded.

27. By Roman custom a gaoler who allowed a prisoner to escape suffered the same penalty as the prisoner. If the charge was a capital one he suffered death. The non-escape of the prisoners was due to terror and amazement. **30. What must I do to be saved?**] The gaoler, to have asked such a question, must have been a hearer of Paul and Barnabas, and have been impressed by their teaching. The strange events of the night and the kindness shown him by Paul now bring matters to a crisis. **35.** According to D, the motive of St. Paul's release was alarm at the earthquake. **The serjeants**] Gk. 'the lictors,' officers who attended the magistrates, carrying axes and rods, symbols of the power to punish.

37. Being Romans] i.e. Roman citizens. In his speech against Verres Cicero says : 'to fetter a Roman citizen is a crime, to scourge him a scandal, to slay him parricide.'

Roman citizenship could be acquired (1) by birth, if both parents were Romans ; (2) by grant to certain cities or districts ; (3) by grant to individuals for political or military services, e.g. long service in the army ; (4) by purchase (22 28). As Tarsus did not come under (2), and Paul was born free, his father and mother must have been Roman citizens. The chief privileges of citizenship at this time were, (1) the right to appeal to the Emperor, (2) freedom from degrading punishments, such as bonds, scourging, and crucifixion.

39. Desired *them* **to depart**] representing that in the excited state of the city it was impossible to protect them. **40. Comforted**] exhorted. **And departed**] Silas and Timothy accompanied St. Paul, but (since the ' we ' is now dropped) St. Luke was probably left behind to take charge of the Philippian Church (see 17[1]). He seems to have made Philippi his headquarters for several years, rejoining St. Paul at Troas during the Third Missionary Journey (20[5]).

CHAPTER 17
SECOND MISSIONARY JOURNEY (continued)
1-15. Thessalonica and Berœa.
1. Amphipolis] 32 m. W. of Philippi.
Apollonia] 30 m. W. of Amphipolis.
Thessalonica] now Saloniki, was the capital of the province of Macedonia, and an important commercial centre. St. Paul's plan was first to evangelise the seats of government and the trade centres, knowing that if Christianity was once established in these places it would spread through the Empire. **3. Christ**] RV 'the Christ,' i.e. the Messiah. **4. Devout Greeks**] Not necessarily proselytes, but persons who had given up idolatry, attended the synagogue services, and worshipped the God of the Jews. **5. Lewd fellows**] lit. 'certain evil men of the idlers in the marketplace.' **Jason**] probably identical with the Jason of Ro 16[21], and therefore a Jew. His correct name was probably Jesus or Joshua. **6. The rulers**] The Gk. word used here (*politarchai*, a rare and peculiar one) is proved to be correct by an inscription on an arch, which also contains the names Sosipater, Gaius, and Secundus. **9. Taken security**] The immediate departure of Paul and Silas renders it probable that Jason gave security that St. Paul would leave the city, and that the Apostle assented to this undertaking, and was thus prevented from revisiting the Thessalonians : see 1 Th 2[18].
The Epistles to the Thessalonians, who are represented as mainly a Gentile Church (1 Th 1[9] 2[14]), imply a much longer residence at Thessalonica than three weeks. V. 2, therefore, must be understood to mean that he worked for three weeks among the Jews, and afterwards turned to the Gentiles, among whom he laboured for three or four months.
10. Berea (Berœa)] a Macedonian town of some importance, 50 m. SW. of Thessalonica. To this 'out of the way' place (Cicero) St. Paul retreated, probably for rest and quiet.
14. As it were to the sea] i.e. they pretended to go to the sea (to elude pursuit), and then

turned off and went by land to Athens. Others translate simply ' to the sea,' and suppose that St. Paul embarked at Dium and went by sea to Athens. **15. Unto Athens**] D adds : ' But he passed by (i.e. did not preach in) Thessaly, for he was prevented from preaching the word to them.'
It appears from 1 Th 3[1] that Timothy and Silas did actually join St. Paul at Athens according to his instructions, but the Apostle being filled with anxiety about the state of the Macedonian Churches which he had just founded, sent them back again to confirm them, and to bring him accurate tidings concerning them. Timothy was sent to Thessalonica, Silas (apparently) to Philippi, so that St. Paul was left alone in Athens. On returning from their mission, Timothy and Silas found that St. Paul had gone on to Corinth, and there they rejoined him (18[5]).
16-34. Athens.
After leaving Berœa, St. Paul entered the Roman province of Achaia, which was at this time a senatorian province, governed by a proconsul, and of which the capital was Corinth. He first visited Athens. Athens, though fallen from its former glory, was still the artistic and philosophic, and, in many ways, the religious, capital of the world. The city was full of temples and altars, and the people so devoted to religious ceremonies and mysteries that they merited the title (whether in a good or bad sense) of 'superstitious' (v. 22). Athens, on account of its illustrious history, was held in honour by the Romans. It was allowed to retain its ancient institutions, but the democracy had long lost all real power, and the affairs of the city were administered by the aristocratic court of the Areopagus (v. 19). Athens was famed for its university, the most renowned in the world, at which a large number of students from all parts of the empire were always in residence. As the original home of philosophy, Athens was the headquarters of all the chief philosophic schools. Among its sacred spots were the Academy of Plato, the Lyceum of Aristotle, the Porch of Zeno, and the Garden of Epicurus. The only two philosophies, however, which at this time exercised an important influence upon politics and social life, were Stoicism and Epicureanism, which, for this reason, are singled out by St. Luke for especial mention.
16. Wholly given to idolatry] Xenophon calls Athens 'one altar, one sacrifice and offering to the gods.' St. Paul, as a Jew, would have no sympathy with the artistic beauty of the Athenian statues and temples, but only horror at the superstition which they represented.
17. In the market daily] So Socrates used to

sit every day and all day in the market-place of Athens, discussing philosophy with all comers. The market-place, or *agora*, of Athens afforded a glorious architectural spectacle. ' Here the eye fell on portico after portico, painted by the brush of famous artists, and adorned with the noblest statues. But St. Paul would not have admired these so much as the tower and water-clock of Andronicus, telling out to him the hours of his solitary waiting. This still stands to-day. The Agora was dominated on its S. side by the abrupt hill of Mars, and the still more impressive heights of the Acropolis. In the Stoa Pœcile he met with the successors of Zeno, the Stoics with whom, as with the Epicureans, he, like a second Socrates, disputed daily ' (F. C. Conybeare).

18. Epicureans and Stoics. At this time Stoicism was the philosophy of the majority of serious-minded people, Epicureanism that of the frivolous and irreligious. The Stoics, so called from the Porch (Stoa Pœcile) at Athens, in which their founder, Zeno of Citium, lectured (about 278 B.C.), had many points of contact with Judaism, especially with Pharisaism. Josephus speaks of the tenets of the Stoics and of the Pharisees as being very similar. The spirit of both was somewhat narrow and austere. Both rejected compromise, believing that a man should suffer persecution and even death rather than depart in the least degree from the path of piety and virtue. Both were devoted to Law, the Pharisees to the Law of Moses, the Stoics to the Law of Nature, which they regarded as an actual code imposed on mankind by the Creator. The Stoics were strong fatalists, denying the freedom of the will ; the Pharisees were strong predestinarians. Both believed in Providence, or the rational ordering of the world by an intelligent being, a doctrine denied by the Epicureans. The Pharisees were monotheists ; the Stoics approximated to monotheism. They believed in a Divine Reason, or Logos, pervading all things and ordering all things, though (being Pantheists) they regarded it as the soul of the world, rather than as a distinct and transcendent personal Being. They also believed in a future life for man, though not in actual immortality. St. Paul, therefore, decidedly sympathised with the Stoics as against the Epicureans, whose doctrine that the end of life is pleasure, was, of course, highly distasteful to him. Epicureanism was reprobated both by Jews and by serious pagans. Josephus says : ' The Epicureans cast providence out of life, and deny that God takes care of human affairs, and hold that the universe is not directed with a view to tne continuance of the whole by the blessed and incorruptible Being, but that it is carried along automatically and heedlessly.'

18. Babbler] lit. 'a picker up of seeds' (like a bird) ; hence a shallow talker who picks up scraps of information, and retails them at secondhand. **And the resurrection**] better, 'and Anastasis.' The Athenians, either in jest or in earnest, seem to have understood Anastasis (the Resurrection) to be a female deity, the wife of Jesus.

19. And they took him, etc.] Some translate, 'And they arrested him and brought him before the court of the Areopagus.' But there is no indication in St. Paul's speech that he was on his trial, or that any judgment was passed upon him (v. 32). We prefer, therefore, the rendering, ' And they took him by the hand, and brought him to the Hill of Ares ' (Mars' Hill). The Hill of Ares, or Areopagus, is an eminence situated nearly due W. of the Acropolis. Here, from early times, the Court of the Areopagus met in the open air. The court was not sitting, so that the place was available for a quiet lecture and discussion.

22–32. Paul's speech. It is discreet and to the point. It deals not with the OT., with which his hearers were unacquainted, but with the truths of natural religion, many of which were understood (though only partially) by the Athenian philosophers (cp. the speech at Lystra, 14 15 f.).

22. Too superstitious] rather, ' more religious ' (than other men). Both senses are possible, but the tactful apostle would be more likely to begin his speech with a compliment than with a reproach. **23. Your devotions**] RV ' the objects of your worship.' **TO THE UNKNOWN GOD**] RV 'TO AN UNKNOWN GOD.' Several ancient writers mention such altars. Pausanias speaks of 'altars of known (lit. ' named ') and unknown gods and heroes.' Philostratus says, ' It is more prudent to speak well of all gods, especially at Athens, where altars are erected even to unknown gods.' At Athens during a plague Epimenides let loose at the Areopagus black and white sheep, and commanded the Athenians to sacrifice ' to the proper god,' wherever the sheep lay down. Often ' the proper god ' could not be clearly ascertained, and so an altar was raised to an unknown god. The inscription (as St. Paul probably knew) had a purely pagan meaning ; but the phrase was a fine one ; it was capable of a higher sense, and in this higher sense St. Paul made it the text of his sermon.

24. Creation was altogether denied by the Epicureans, who regarded the atoms of matter as eternal ; and only imperfectly recognised by the Stoics, who were pantheists, and did not regard the Divine Person which shaped the world as distinct from it. The doctrine of creation, as preached by St. Paul, was consequently a strange one at Athens.

26. The Apostle rebukes the narrow pride

of the Greeks, who divided mankind into Greeks and barbarians, the latter being of no account. The Stoics, who believed in the spiritual equality of all men, would have agreed with St. Paul in this.

28. A quotation from the 'Phænomena' of Aratus, a Cilician poet. Almost the same words occur in the 'Hymn to Zeus' of Cleanthes. Both these poets were Stoics. St. Paul quotes the Gk. poets again, 1 Cor 15 33 and Tit 1 12 ; but it is not safe to assume that he had any wide acquaintance with Greek classical literature. His Pharisaic training would have made him indisposed to devote serious study to profane literature.

29. The argument probably is : Since we are the offspring of God, in that our souls are immaterial and immortal, we ought to regard the author of our souls as an immaterial and immortal spirit, and not like silver or gold or any material object. The Stoics would have sympathised with this sentiment. Seneca says, 'Thou shalt not form God of silver and gold, a true likeness of Him cannot be moulded of this material.' .. 'God is near thee, He is with thee, He is within.'

30. Times of this ignorance] cp. 14 16. **Repent**] i.e. turn from idolatry. Idolatry was pardonable in the times of ignorance, but now that the True Light has appeared, it is a heinous sin. **31.** St. Paul was accustomed, in preaching to the heathen, to lead up to the idea of a judgment to come (24 25). **Hath given assurance**] viz. that He will be the Judge. The Resurrection of Jesus is the evidence that He will be the future Judge of the world. **34. Dionysius the Areopagite**] i.e. a member of the Court of Areopagus. As all members of the Areopagus had passed through the office of Archon, Dionysius must have been of high social position. Tradition makes him bishop of Athens, and a martyr. The work 'On the heavenly hierarchy' attributed to him is spurious.

According to this passage Dionysius and Damaris were the first converts made in Achaia (Greece), but, according to 1 Cor 16 15, 17, a Corinthian named Stephanas, who must have been converted later. The explanation probably is that St. Paul regards Athens as a free and independent city, not as part of the Roman province of Achaia.

CHAPTER 18

SECOND MISSIONARY JOURNEY (concluded)

1–18. St. Paul at Corinth. Corinth was the capital of the Roman province of Achaia. The ancient town had been entirely destroyed in 146 B.C. by the Roman general Mummius, but it had been refounded as a Roman colony in 46 B.C. by Julius Cæsar. Situated on the Corinthian isthmus, it had two ports, Cenchreæ

on the Ægean, and Lechæum on the Gulf of Lepanto. The traffic between Italy and Asia chiefly passed through Corinth, which rapidly became a populous and wealthy trading centre. The morals of the Corinthians, who were devoted to pleasure and the worship of Venus (Aphrodite), were such as to outrage even pagan sentiment. Allusions to the prevailing sensuality of the city, which was encouraged by its religion, are to be found in the Epistles to the Corinthians. Here Paul stayed a year and six months, but St. Luke (for whatever reason) gives us few particulars of his work. From Corinth St. Paul indited his two Epistles to the Thessalonians.

2. Aquila .. Priscilla] As Aquila and Priscilla (Prisca) are not said to have been converted by Paul, they were probably already Christians. The edict of the emperor Claudius (about 52 A.D.) which expelled the Jews from Rome, was caused by tumults which arose in the Jewish quarter, when the faith of Christ was preached there. This at least is the probable inference to be drawn from the words of Suetonius, 'He expelled the Jews from Rome, because they were in a state of continual tumult at the instigation of one Chrestus' (Chrestus is probably 'Christus,' or Christ). Aquila and Priscilla were St. Paul's hosts at Corinth. Deporting from Corinth with St. Paul (v. 18), they remained at Ephesus, where they were instrumental in converting Apollos (v. 26). The church at Ephesus met in their house (1 Cor 16 19). They then revisited Rome, perhaps to prepare for the Apostle's visit, and there also their house was the Church's meeting-place (Ro 16 3-5). After St. Paul's trial they returned to Ephesus (2 Tim 4 19), which is our last notice of them. **Pontus**] with Bithynia formed a Roman province occupying the S. coast of the Euxine (Black Sea).

3. Tentmakers] All Jews, however wealthy, were taught a trade.

5. Silas and Timotheus] see 17 15. They brought money with them, so that Paul no longer worked with his hands, but gave himself entirely to preaching (2 Cor 11 9 Phil 4 15). **Was pressed in the spirit**,' RV 'was constrained by the word,' i.e. devoted himself continually to preaching. **6. Blasphemed**] They said 'Jesus is anathema' (1 Cor 12 3).

7. Justus] RV 'Titus Justus.' Probably a Roman colonist of the Roman colony Corinth. **8. Crispus**] St. Paul baptised this important convert with his own hands, as also Gaius, and the household of Stephanas (1 Cor 1 16). From 1 Cor 16 15, 17 we learn that Stephanas was the first convert made in Achaia.

12. Gallio] the brother of Nero's tutor Seneca, and uncle of the poet Lucan, was a well-educated, amiable, and accomplished man, who, having filled the office of consul, was sent out as proconsul of Achaia about 52 A.D.

17. The Greeks hated and despised the Jews, and seeing that their contempt was shared by Gallio, they ventured to insult the Jews in his presence by assaulting Sosthenes. **Gallio cared,** etc.] This may either mean that Gallio pretended not to see the assault on Sosthenes, or else that he cared nothing about the religious questions involved.

18. A vow] After delivery from danger or recovery from sickness, the Jews were accustomed to take upon themselves a modified form of the Nazirite vow (see Nu 6). As the special consecration of this state forbade intercourse with Gentiles, St. Paul deferred it till his work at Corinth was finished. The essential ceremony was the presentation of the hair grown during the period of separation at the altar at Jerusalem together with certain specified sacrifices ; hence the head was shaved both at the beginning and at the end of the period of separation. See further 21 26. It is not necessary to suppose that St. Paul took this vow to conciliate the Jews or the Jewish Christians. He simply adopted the usual Jewish way of thanking God for a great deliverance.

Many additional particulars about the Corinthian ministry of St. Paul can be learnt from 1 and 2 Cor. See the commentary on those Epistles.

19-22. Visit to Jerusalem. Paul probably sailed in a ship specially chartered to convey Jews to Palestine to keep the Passover.

19. Ephesus] The prohibition to preach the word in Asia (16 6) had now apparently been removed. Aquila and Priscilla were left in Ephesus to prepare the way for the great missionary effort that he desired to make in this important centre.

21. This feast] i.e. Pentecost (or possibly Passover) 52 A.D. Clearly St. Paul had vowed to make his Nazirite offering at this feast. The RV omits the words referring to the feast altogether, but they are strongly attested.

22. And gone up] viz. to Jerusalem. We may suppose that St. Paul spent some time at Jerusalem, before going to Antioch.

THIRD MISSIONARY JOURNEY, Aug. 52 A.D. to Pentecost 56 A.D. (Chs.18 23–21 16)

23. Visit to Galatia. St. Paul revisits Antioch in Syria and the Churches of Galatia and Phrygia, founded in the First Missionary Journey (i.e. Antioch in Pisidia, Iconium, Lystra, Derbe).

24-28. Apollos at Ephesus.

24. Apollos] The name is a contraction of Apollonius. He is mentioned again 19 1 1 Cor 1 12 3 4 f. 4 6 16 12 Tit 3 13 He had been instructed and baptised by the disciples of the

Baptist, and therefore regarded Jesus as the Messiah (Mk 1 7, etc.), perhaps even as 'the Son of God,' and 'the Lamb of God that taketh away the sin of the world' (Jn 1 29, 34). His knowledge was accurate as far as it went, and his faith was sincere. That he received Christian baptism (probably from Aquila) is a certain inference from v 25 compared with 19 1-7.

Eloquent] RV 'learned.' Both meanings may be included. Probably Apollos was acquainted with the philosophy of the Alexandrian Jew Philo, and his speculations about the Divine Logos ('Reason' or 'Word').

26. The synagogue] We infer that Priscilla and Aquila, though Christians, still attended the synagogue. **27. Wrote .. the disciples**] Christians travelling received 'letters of commendation' to other Christian Churches, which secured them hospitality and admission to communion (cp 2 Cor 3 1). **Helped them much**] RM 'helped much through grace them which had believed.' Apollos was so popular at Corinth, that his admirers soon formed a faction or party in the Church (1 Cor 1 12 3 4).

28. Convinced] RV 'confuted.'

CHAPTER 19

EPHESUS

1-41. Paul at Ephesus. Opposition of the manufacturers of idols. St. Paul, leaving Antioch in S. Galatia (see 18 23), approached Ephesus not by the usual level route leading through Colossæ and Laodicea (see Col 2 1), but through the northern and more mountainous route leading down the Cayster valley (see 19 1, 'the upper coasts,' RV 'the upper country '). He stayed at Ephesus over two years and three months, see vv. 8, 10, 22 (in 20 31 the Apostle calls it three years), and making the city his centre, evangelised the whole of the province of Asia. According to D he did not originally intend to preach in Ephesus, but the Holy Spirit constrained him (contrast 16 6) We hear little here of opposition from the Jews. The craftsmen and the uneducated classes were hostile, but the magistrates of the city (v 35) and of the province (v 31) were not unfriendly.

1. Ephesus] the capital of the Roman province of Asia, and the most important seaport of Asia Minor, was especially renowned for its great temple of Diana (Artemis), which was one of the wonders of the world. St. Paul chose it for a prolonged stay because (like Corinth) it was on the main line of communication between E. and W., and also because it was a great centre of religious pilgrimage: cp. v. 27

Certain disciples] They must have arrived since Apollos's departure, otherwise Apollos would have instructed them more perfectly.

2. Have ye received] RV ' did ye receive

the Holy Ghost when ye believed?' Of course they had heard of the Holy Ghost, but St. Paul means, had they experienced that new power of holiness, that peace and love and joy which the ascended Messiah had first given at Pentecost, and was still ready to bestow on all believers. **Whether there be, etc.**] RV 'whether the Holy Ghost was given.'

3. Unto (RV 'into') **what then were ye baptized?**] St. Paul assumes that if these men had received Christian baptism they must have heard of the Holy Ghost. It is probable, therefore, that the Trinitarian formula was used (see Mt 28 [19]). **4.** John's baptism was only preparatory, and did not confer the special gift of the Spirit. **6. Laid** *his* **hands**] As in c. 8, the Holy Spirit was conferred, not at the actual immersion, but at the laying on of hands which followed. **Spake with tongues**] see on 2 [4f]. **And prophesied**] cp. 10 [46]. Inspired and fervent utterances of praise are meant.

9. That way] i.e. Christianity, see on 9 [2].

The school] Tyrannus was probably a Gentile, who made his living by keeping a 'school' of philosophy. Paul no doubt appeared to the Ephesians as one of those wandering sophists' or professors of philosophy, who were so numerous under the early Empire. D adds that St. Paul disputed 'from the fifth hour to the tenth,' a probably authentic detail.

10. To this period is to be referred the foundation of the Seven Churches of Asia, Ephesus, Smyrna, Pergamum, Tyatira, Sardis, Philadelphia, Laodicea (Rev 1 [11]), and of Colossæ, Hierapolis, Troas.

11, 12. God condescended to work miracles through these handkerchiefs, having regard to the genuine faith of those who thus used them, and not to their superstition. It is not said that St. Paul approved the practice.

13. The exorcism of these vagabond Jews was simply the uttering of magical formulæ. They thought that the mere words 'in the name of Jesus' would produce the required effect. **15, 16.** There are two historical difficulties in this narrative : (1) It seems strange that sons of so distinguished a person as a Jewish chief priest should be strolling exorcists. The reading of D, 'Sceva, a [heathen?] priest,' removes this difficulty. (2) Seven sons are mentioned in v. 14, and only two in v. 16 ('mastered both of them,' RV). It may be supposed that only two took part in this particular incident.

18, 19. The incident led to a reformation within the Church. Many converts had continued their magical practices after their baptism. They now came forward and publicly renounced them, proving their sincerity by burning their books of spells. **Fifty thousand**

pieces **of silver**] 50,000 *drachmæ* = £1,700, or, in actual purchasing power, much more.

21. Rome] There is evidence that Paul planned the evangelisation of the Western Empire many years before he actually undertook it : cp. Ro 1 [10, 13] 15 [22-24]. **22.** Timothy and Erastus (not the Erastus of Ro 16 [23]) were sent, partly to remind the Churches of Europe of the teaching and example of St. Paul, and partly to collect money for the poor saints at Jerusalem (24 [17] 1 Cor 16 [1, 10]). Shortly after this 1 Corinthians was written.

23f. St. Luke mentions no persecutions or trials until the close of the Ephesian ministry, yet we know that though 'a great door and effectual' was opened to the Apostle, yet there were 'many adversaries' (1 Cor 16 [9]) ; that he was in daily danger of death (15 [30, 31]) ; that Prisca and Aquila to save his life 'laid down their own necks' (Ro 16 [3]) ; and that he 'fought with beasts,' i.e. savage enemies (1 Cor 15 [32]).

23. That way] i.e. Christianity (9 [2], etc.).

24. Shrines] Many small terra-cotta and marble shrines of Artemis, containing a figure of the goddess, have been found near Ephesus. They were either dedicated in the Temple, or taken home by devout worshippers as memorials of their pilgrimage.

Diana] Really a native Asiatic deity, a personification of the reproductive and nutritive powers of nature. From certain quite superficial resemblances the Greeks identified her with their own Artemis, but her worship always remained Asian in type. The Temple had been burnt down 356 B.C., and rebuilt on a scale of sumptuous magnificence. **26. All Asia**] The Temple had been built by contributions from the whole of Asia.

28. Were full of wrath] D adds, and 'running into the street' cried out, etc. **Great** *is* **Diana**] D has, 'Great Diana of the Ephesians!' an invocation of the goddess. This reading may be correct. **29. The theatre**] would hold over 24,000 people. **31. The chief of Asia**] Gk. the 'Asiarchs.' They were officials, not of the city of Ephesus, but of the province of Asia, and were specially connected with the worship of the Roman emperor.

33. Since Alexander was a Jew, it seems probable that the Jews put him forward to explain to the angry mob that they had no sympathy whatever with St. Paul's proceedings. The Jews' contempt for idols was well known, and therefore there was imminent danger that they would be involved in a massacre directed against enemies of idolatry.

And they drew Alexander, etc.] or, 'and some of the multitude instructed Alexander.' The reading is doubtful and the sense obscure.

35. The townclerk] This important official drafted the decrees of the senate and people, and sealed them when they were passed. He presided at the lawful assemblies of the people.

A worshipper] RV 'temple-keeper,' Gk. *neokoros*, lit. 'temple-sweeper.' A second-cent. inscription speaks of Ephesus as 'doubly temple-keeper of the Emperors, and temple-keeper of Artemis.' **From Jupiter**] or, 'from heaven.' The 'image' (the word is not expressed in the Gk.) was probably not an idol, but a meteoric stone, in which the goddess was supposed to dwell.

37. Blasphemers] It is clear that St. Paul had expressed his views with gentleness and moderation. **38. The law**, etc.] rather, 'the courts are open,' or, 'court days are kept.'

Deputies] rather, 'proconsuls,' the correct title of the Roman governor in a senatorial province like Asia. There was, of course, only one proconsul in Asia. The plural is colloquial, 'there are such things as law courts and proconsuls.' **Implead**] RV 'accuse.'

CHAPTER 20

THIRD MISSIONARY JOURNEY (continued)

1–6. Paul in Macedonia and Greece. St. Paul waited at Ephesus until the return of Timothy and Erastus, and left Ephesus shortly after Pentecost, 55 A.D. (1 Cor 16 8-12). We learn from Ro 15 19 that he spent some time in Macedonia, and extended his missionary labours (which were marked by signal miracles) as far as Illyricum. From Macedonia he wrote the second Corinthian Epistle, and (according to a widely held opinion) the Epistle to the Galatians. In Corinth he spent the three winter months of 55, 56 A.D., and there he wrote the Epistle to the Romans.

3. The plot was to kill Paul on board the Jewish pilgrim ship in which he had taken his passage.

4, 5. The men mentioned here were delegates bearing the contributions of St. Paul's Gentile churches to the afflicted mother church of Jerusalem. **Gaius**] to be distinguished from Gaius the Macedonian of 19 29, and the Gaius of 3 Jn. He was a neighbour, and, perhaps, a friend of Timothy, and had probably been converted, like Timothy, during St. Paul's first missionary journey. **Tychicus**] He was with St. Paul at Rome during his first imprisonment, and was the bearer of Ephesians (Eph 6 21, 22) and Colossians (Col 4 7, 8). He is mentioned again 2 Tim 4 12 Tit 3 12. **Trophimus**] a Gentile convert of Ephesus, whom St. Paul was accused of introducing into the Temple at Jerusalem (21 28 f.). He is mentioned again 2 Tim 4 12. **These**] i.e. probably Tychicus and Trophimus only, not the whole party.

6. We] St. Paul found St. Luke at Philippi, where he had left him in charge of the Church (c. 16), and, after celebrating the Passover with the local Christians, took him with him to Troas.

7–12. Troas.

7. The first clear reference to the keeping of the Lord's Day, with which may be compared 1 Cor 16 2. The expression 'Lord's Day' first occurs Rev 1 10. **The disciples**] RV 'we,' indicating the presence of St. Luke. **To break bread**] i.e. to celebrate the Lord's Supper. This was now clearly the stated Christian service on the Lord's Day. As the Jewish days began at sunset, probably the Christians assembled on Saturday evening, as we should call it : see further on 2 46, 47.

10. His life is in him] It has been argued both here and at Mt 9 24 that the death was only apparent ; but St. Luke, who was a medical man, and was present, says expressly that Eutychus was dead. We have here, therefore, probably a miracle of resurrection.

11. Broken bread] RV 'broken the bread,' viz. of the Eucharist. **And eaten**] probably of the *agapé*, which here apparently followed the Communion : see 2 46, 47.

13. Assos] A Greek (Æolic) colony on the S. coast of the Troad. By walking thither St. Paul avoided the tedious voyage round Cape Lectum. **14. Mitylene**] the capital of the isle of Lesbos. **15. Chios**] A large island forming part of the province of Asia. **Trogyllium**] is opposite Samos. **Miletus**] the most famous and important of the Ionian colonies. It was a seaport situated on the Carian coast.

18–35. St. Paul's Speech to the Elders of Ephesus. He reminds them of his ministry among them (vv. 18–21). And now that the Spirit draws him to Jerusalem, to face the unknown future, he entrusts the Ephesian church to the charge of the elders to guard her against the heresies and enemies which he foresees (vv. 22–31). He concludes by recommending them in touching words to the protection of the Almighty (vv. 32–35).

19. Temptations] trials or misfortunes. **Lying in wait**] RV 'plots.' **25. Shall see my face no more**] St. Paul is not here speaking as a prophet, but is merely giving utterance to an overpowering presentiment that the time of his death is near. As a matter of fact, his life was preserved many years, and he subsequently revisited Miletus (2 Tim 4 20), Ephesus (1 Tim 1 3 3 14), and other places in Asia.

28. We have here a very decided testimony that though Christian ministers may be elected by the people, their authority comes from God, whose ambassadors they are. **Overseers**] a literal translation of the Gk. word *episcopos* (Lat. *episcopus*, E. 'bishop'). At this time the title 'bishop' (i.e. overseer) was freely applied to the Christian *presbyters* ('elders') (Phil 1 1). By the beginning of the second cent. (perhaps already in the Pastoral Epistles) the term was generally restricted, as now, to the chief ruler of a church.

His own blood] The blood of Christ is here called 'God's blood,' a striking expression affirming with great emphasis the Deity of Christ. There is an inferior reading, 'Feed the Church of the Lord' (RM), which probably originated in a desire to eliminate the unusual expression 'the blood of God.' Westcott and Hort think that the original reading may have been 'the blood of His own Son.'

30. The heretics, Hymenæus and Alexander (1 Tim 1 20), also Diotrephes (3 Jn 9), were presbyters of Ephesus. From the Epistles of St. John, which were written at Ephesus, we learn that the Ephesian heresies were of the Gnostic and Docetic types. St. John's chief opponent at Ephesus was Cerinthus, who taught a Jewish form of Gnosticism.

34. Cp. 18 3 1 Cor 4 12 1 Th 2 9 2 Th 3 8.

35. Ye ought to support the weak] 'The weak' are here, probably, the poor and the sick. The presbyters are exhorted to work with their hands (like St. Paul), that with their earnings they may support the sick and the poor. **It is more blessed,** etc.] It is strange that this beautiful saying is found in no Gospel. Similarly Aristotle says, 'It belongs to virtue rather to confer than to receive a benefit.' On the contrary, Athenæus says, 'A giver is foolish : a receiver is fortunate.'

36–38. A striking example of the intense affection which the apostle's converts felt for him. If he had bitter enemies, he had also staunch friends.

CHAPTER 21

St. Paul arrested at Jerusalem

1. Were gotten] rather, 'had torn ourselves.' **Coos**] or Cos, a fertile island off the Carian coast, producing silks, ointments, wheat, and wines. **Rhodes**] a city, and large island, situated S. of Caria. The famous colossus was a statue of the sun-god, 105 ft. high, which stood at the harbour entrance. Erected 280 B.C., it stood for 56 years, when it was overthrown by an earthquake. Its fragments remained where they fell till 656 A.D. **Patara**] an important Lycian seaport. After Patara, D adds 'and Myra,' an accurate geographical touch : see 27 5.

3. Tyre] The greatest maritime city of the ancient world, claiming to have been founded as early as 2750 B.C. It produced glass and purple dye, but its chief wealth came from the fact that it almost monopolised the carrying-trade of the world. The Tyrian mariners were so skilled in astronomy, and constructed such accurate charts, that they sailed by night as well as by day, and made long voyages out of sight of land. They are known to have circumnavigated Africa—an extraordinary feat

for the small ships of the ancients. **4. Disciples**] RV 'the disciples.'

7. Ptolemais] Originally called Acco, its name was changed to Ptolemaïs by Ptolemy Philadelphus, when, after the death of Alexander the Great, it came into his possession. It is situated on the coast a few miles to the N. of the promontory of Carmel, and is now called Acre.

8. Philip] see 6 5 and c. 8. **The Evangelist**] Evangelists were itinerant officers, whose duty it was to break new ground, and establish new churches. They ranked below the prophets, and above the presbyters or pastors. Philip, originally a 'deacon,' has now, through the success of his missionary work, been advanced to a higher dignity. The NT. never uses 'evangelist' in the sense of a writer of a Gospel. **9. Prophesy**] There were female prophets under the OT.: Miriam, Ex 15 20 ; Deborah, Jg 4 4 ; Noadiah, Neh 6 14 ; Huldah, 2 K 22 14 ; cp. Isa 8 3. See Joel 2 28 Ac 2 17.

10. Agabus] see 11 28. For his symbolic action, cp. 1 K 22 11 Isa 20 2 Jer 13 1 Ezk 4, 5. For the fulfilment, see v. 27 f. **15. Took up our carriages**] rather, 'packed up our baggage.' **16. Brought with them one Mnason**] A more probable translation is, 'brought us to Mnason,' etc. Mnason's house was probably half-way between Cæsarea and Jerusalem. D (Latin) reads, 'and when they had come to a certain town, we lodged with Mnason, an old disciple of Cyprus, and leaving there we came to Jerusalem.'

St. Paul in Jerusalem (Chs 21 17–28 16)

17–40. Disturbances in the Temple. St. Paul arrested.

18. James] The Lord's 'brother,' the acknowledged head of the Church of Jerusalem : cp. 15 13, etc. **19. Particularly**] i.e. in minute detail. **20. The Lord** (i.e. Jesus)] RV 'God.'

23, 24. The four men were Nazirites (see Nu 6), and St. Paul was advised to pay for their sacrifices, and to associate himself with their Nazirite vow during the week that it had still to run (see v. 27). By thus becoming a Nazirite, and defraying the sacrificial expenses of these poorer Nazirites (the latter a most meritorious work, according to contemporary opinion ; see Jos. 'Ant.' 19. 16. 1), St. Paul would prove himself a good Jew as well as a good Christian.

The Jewish Christians were suspicious of St. Paul, not because he refused to circumcise his Gentile converts (this point had already been settled at the Council of Jerusalem), but because it was reported that he advised even Jews to neglect the observance of the Law (v. 21). The charge was false in point of fact, but it had this amount of truth in it, that St. Paul's principle that a man is saved by faith in Christ and not by the works of the Law, would naturally lead to the abandonment of the ceremonial Law even by Jews.

25. See c. 15.

26. Entered, etc.] We may freely translate this difficult passage thus : ' He entered into the Temple, informing the priests that within seven days (see v. 27) the days of their purification would be accomplished ; and he purposed to remain with them in the Temple for a whole week, until the legal sacrifice had been offered for each one of them.'

27 f. The outer court of the Temple was called ' the Court of the Gentiles.' Within this was ' the Court of Israel,' separated from it by a high wall with doors (see v. 30). Inscriptions upon the barrier denounced the penalty of death upon all Gentile intruders. One of these has been preserved, and runs : ' No alien is to pass within the fence and enclosure round the Temple. Whosoever shall be taken shall be responsible to himself alone for the death which will ensue.' See also Jos. ' Ant.' 15. 11. 5.

29. Trophimus] see on 20⁴.

30. They drew him and all his companions ' out of the Temple,' i.e. out of the Court of Israel, and closed the doors of this court, ostensibly to prevent any more Gentiles from entering. **31. Went about to]** i.e. were seeking to. **The chief captain of the band]** rather, ' the tribune of the Roman cohort,' which was stationed in the fortress Antonia, adjoining the Temple. **34. Castle]** lit. ' encampment.' The fortress Antonia is meant. **36. Away with him]** i.e. Slay him.

38. Art not thou] rather, ' Thou art not then the Egyptian,' etc. **Four thousand men]** rather, the four thousand men of the Sicarii. The Sicarii (i.e. assassins) were the extreme members of the ' zealot ' party. They carried out their ' national ' policy by openly assassinating influential Jews supposed to be friendly to Rome. Josephus says, ' But an Egyptian false prophet did the Jews more mischief still. He got together 30,000 deluded men, whom he led round from the wilderness to the Mount of Olives, and intended to break into Jerusalem by force from that place. He said that at his command the walls of Jerusalem would fall down ' (' War,' 2. 13. 5 ; ' Ant.' 20. 8. 6). Felix dispersed them, but the Egyptian escaped.

39. St. Paul was not without civic pride. Tarsus was the seat of a famous university, and had produced several of the most eminent Stoic philosophers. On its coins it proudly boasted itself ' Self-Governing Metropolis.' Citizenship of Tarsus was confined to a select few of the inhabitants, so that its possession was proof of respectability and social standing.

CHAPTER 22
St. Paul's Defence

1-21. St. Paul's Speech to the People. St. Paul was accused of (1) hostility to the Jews, (2) contempt for the Jewish Law, and (3) the desecration of the Temple. He answers all these charges by showing, (1) that he was a Jew by birth, trained by Gamaliel, and so zealous for the Law, that he had been a persecutor of the Christian faith ; (2) that his conversion to Christianity was the result of a direct divine revelation, made first at Damascus, and confirmed by a subsequent revelation to Ananias ; (3) that even after his conversion he continued to honour the Temple, and to worship there, and saw a vision there ; (4) that his preaching to the Gentiles was the result of a divine command, consequent upon the unbelief of the Jews.

1. Fathers] i.e. the Sanhedrists and rabbis. **3. Gamaliel]** see on 5³⁴. **4. This way]** i.e. Christianity : see 9². **5. The estate,** etc.] i.e. the Sanhedrin. **6 f.** See on 9³, and cp. 26¹². **9. And were afraid]** RV omits these words. **Heard not]** i.e. did not distinguish the words, or understand the meaning of the voice : cp. Jn 12²⁹. **13. Looked up]** or, ' received my sight again and looked.' **14. That Just One]** see 3¹⁴ 7⁵². **17. A trance]** Some identify this trance with that mentioned 2 Cor 12² ; but this is (for chronological reasons) unlikely.

22-C. 23¹¹. Paul before the Sanhedrin.

23. Cast off] or, ' shook.' **24. Chief captain]** i.e. tribune. **The castle]** i.e. the fortress of Antonia : see 21³⁴. **25. Bound him with thongs]** The correct reading probably means, ' And when they had stretched him out ready for the scourging.' **A Roman]** see 16³⁷. **27. Chief captain]** i.e. tribune.

28. See on 16³⁷. It is evident that the chief captain had not bought the citizenship under Claudius (41–54 A.D.), who sold it for a merely nominal sum.

CHAPTER 23
St. Paul sent to Cæsarea

1. St. Paul often asserts his good conscience before God and man : see 22³ 24¹⁶.

2. Ananias] is not the same as Annas (4⁶). He was the son of Nebedæus, and held the high priesthood from 47–59 A.D. His rapacity and violence were notorious. **To smite him]** because, being a prisoner, he spoke without being asked : cp. Jn 18²². **3. God shall smite thee]** St. Paul's angry retort has often been contrasted with our Lord's mild words on a similar occasion (Jn 18²³). But St. Paul's rebuke was well deserved. *Thou* **whited wall]** i.e. ' thou hypocrite.' The allusion is to the practice of limewashing dirty walls to conceal the filth : cp. Mt 23 27 Lk 11 44. **Contrary to the law**] see Jn 7 51, and cp. Dt 19 15, etc.

5. As the high priest, when present, presided over the Sanhedrin, it is somewhat strange that St. Paul should not have known who Ananias was. A possible explanation is that St. Paul was somewhat short-sighted. **Thou shalt not speak evil**] see Ex 22 28.

6 f. The Sadducees, who disbelieved a future life or a resurrection, derided the supposed appearance of the risen Jesus ; but the Pharisees, who believed both, heard St. Paul's story with considerable sympathy. St. Paul then, seeing how matters stood, declared himself a Pharisee of the Pharisees. He declared that, like the Pharisees, he looked for the coming (i.e. the Second Coming) of the Messiah ('the hope' of Israel), and for the future resurrection of the dead, and claimed Pharisaic sympathy against his Sadducean enemies. **11.** The appearance was vouchsafed to Paul to assure him that his life would not be cut short before the great desire of his life was attained.

12-35. St. Paul is sent to Cæsarea.

12. The men who plotted against St. Paul were probably Sicarii or Assassins (see on 21 38), whom we know that the high priest Ananias did not scruple to employ to remove his enemies. **16.** St. Paul's nephew was perhaps a rabbinical student at Jerusalem, as St. Paul himself had been.

26-30. Lysias presents his action in the most favourable light. He makes no mention of his illegal order to scourge the prisoner, and takes credit to himself for his zeal in succouring a Roman citizen, whereas, as a matter of fact, he had no idea at the time that St. Paul was a Roman citizen. **27. An army**] RV 'the soldiers.' **31. Antipatris**] founded by Herod the Great, now Râs-el-'Ain.

33. The governor] i.e. Antonius Felix, procurator of Judæa, circ. 52–58 A.D. His ferocious repression of the Zealots called into being a new and still more pernicious class of enthusiasts, the Sicarii, or Assassins : see on 21 38. His folly and cruelty goaded the nation into disaffection and rebellion. **34. Of Cilicia**] Cilicia and Judæa were at this time minor provinces, attached to the superior province of Syria. Hence Felix could have sent Paul for trial to the governor of Syria, if he had wished. **35. Herod's judgment hall**] the palace built by Herod the Great at Cæsarea, where the Roman procurator resided. It was also a fortress, and would contain a guard-room.

CHAPTER 24

St. Paul before Felix

1–27. St. Paul and Felix.

1. Tertullus] in spite of his Roman name may have been a Greek or even a Jew (cp. 'our Law,' AV v. 6). **2. Great quietness**] Felix really deserved some credit for his vigorous action against the brigands and zealots, when he first entered office, and for his suppression of the Egyptian false prophet. **And would have judged . . his accusers to come unto thee**] These words, though absent from many ancient authorities, seem from internal evidence to be genuine and authentic. They probably belong to the D text, but D is here deficient. **8. Of whom**] i.e. of Paul, if the above words are omitted ; but of Lysias, if they are retained. **9. Assented**] RV 'joined in the charge.'

10-22. St. Paul's Defence. St. Paul answered the charges as follows. (1) He had no seditious intentions, for he was found purified in the Temple 'neither with multitude, nor with tumult' (v. 18). (2) The sect of the Nazarenes, to whicn he belonged, was a perfectly orthodox and lawful combination of Jewish believers, accepting 'all things which are written in the law and the prophets,' accepting also the orthodox doctrine of the resurrection and the judgment, which some of his accusers (being Sadducees) denied (v. 14). (3) No evidence was produced of an intended pollution of the Temple (v. 19).

14. Heresy] RV 'a sect.' Tertullus had applied the word to the Christians in a bad sense.

15. Allow] rather, 'look for.' **16. Herein**] i.e. relying on this hope. But others understand it to mean 'during this earthly life.' **I**] RV 'I also,' i.e. 'I as well as they.' **17. Many years**] or, 'some years.' **18. Whereupon**] RV 'Amidst which.' **21. By you**] RV 'before you.' **22. That** (the) **way**] i.e. Christianity.

I will know the uttermost of] rather, 'I will determine.' **23. Liberty**] rather, 'indulgence.'

24. Drusilla] The youngest of the three daughters of Agrippa I (the Herod of 12 1). She deserted her husband, Azizus, king of Emesa, to marry Felix.

25. Felix trembled] Instead of simply stating what the Christian faith was, St. Paul, after the manner of the Baptist and the ancient prophets, boldly called his august hearers to repentance. He reasoned of **righteousness** (condemning Felix's receipt of bribes and evil government : cp. v. 26) ; of **temperance,** or, rather, 'continence' (with special reference to the adulterous union of Drusilla and Felix), and of the future **judgment,** which will be without respect of persons. The result was that Felix **trembled,** but delayed his repentance ; and that Drusilla was made an irreconcilable enemy.

27. Porcius Festus] succeeded Felix as procurator of Judæa about 58 A.D. He died after a short tenure of office, having governed, upon the whole, well. He is credited with having (for a time) suppressed the Sicarii or Assassins.

And Felix .. Paul bound] For these words the Bezan text substitutes, 'but Felix left Paul in prison for the sake of Drusilla' (a very probable statement).

Remark. St. Paul spent two whole years in prison at Cæsarea. How was the time occupied? Some critics suppose that he wrote the third group of his Epistles (Philippians, Colossians, Ephesians, Philemon). Much can be said for this view. E.g. in Phil 1 13 he says, 'my bonds in Christ are manifest in all the prætorium (or palace),' and we know from Ac 23 35 that he was confined in the prætorium (palace) of Herod. But upon the whole it seems more probable that all four were written at Rome (e.g. 'they of Cæsar's household,' Phil 4 22, naturally, though not necessarily, suggests Rome). St. Luke was doubtless busy collecting materials for his Gospel and Acts, transcribing his own notes, etc. He probably obtained much information from Philip the Evangelist who resided at Cæsarea; from James the Lord's 'brother,' and from Mary the Virgin, or from some intimate female friend of hers.

CHAPTER 25
St. Paul before Festus

1 f. St. Paul and Festus.

2. The high priest] RV 'the chief priests.'

3. Favour] They desired from the judge partiality, not justice; and probably offered him money. **5. Able**] rather, 'influential.'

6. More than, etc.] RV 'not more than eight or ten days.'

9. Provincial governors were generally anxious to be on good terms with their subjects, because, when their term of office was over, the provincials had the right to complain of them to the Emperor. **Before me**] The proposal was that Paul should be tried by the Sanhedrin, and that Festus should be present to see fair play.

10, 11. The appeal was forced upon him because, (1) trial by the Sanhedrin (even with Festus present as moderator) meant certain condemnation; and (2) there seemed no prospect of release without appeal. Festus was too just to pronounce his condemnation; but he was also too timid to incur the odium of pronouncing him innocent. **10. I stand**] RV (correctly) 'I am (now) standing before Cæsar's judgment-seat' (i.e. thy judgment-seat, O Festus); 'where I ought to be judged' (and not before a Jewish court, like the Sanhedrin). **12. The council**] i.e. the governor's legal advisers.

13. King Agrippa and Bernice] Agrippa II (Marcus Julius Agrippa) was the son of Agrippa I and Cypros. See art. 'Dynasty of the Herods.' His sister Bernice, with whom at this time he was living on terms of criminal intimacy, was an attractive but dissolute woman. At thirteen she was married to her uncle, Herod, king of Chalcis, to whom she bore two sons. After his death she became wife of Polemo, king of Cilicia, and mistress of Vespasian and Titus. **To salute**] RV 'and saluted.' On the arrival of the Roman governor, the inferior rulers naturally made haste to show him respect.

19. Superstition] RV 'religion.'

20. Doubted] RV '(was) perplexed how to inquire concerning these things.'

21. Augustus] lit. 'the Augustus.' 'Augustus,' originally a family name, had now become an official title of the Emperor.

23. Chief captains] i.e. tribunes.

26. As Agrippa was expert in all matters of the Jewish law, Festus hoped that he would help him to compose a letter to the Emperor. which would make it clear what the charges against Paul really were.

CHAPTER 26
Defence before Agrippa

1-32. St. Paul before Agrippa. This speech, though in form a defence to the Jews, is really intended by St. Luke to be St. Paul's defence to the world—an apology for his whole life and work.

Analysis. Opening compliment to Agrippa (vv. 2, 3); the Apostle's orthodox Pharisaic education (vv. 4, 5); he is really called in question because he believes in the hope of all orthodox Jews, the coming of the Messiah, and the Resurrection (vv. 6–8); his persecution of the Church in the time of his ignorance (vv. 9–11); his conversion and divine commission to preach to the Gentiles (vv. 12–18); his subsequent conduct the result of a direct divine command (v. 19); his labours among Jews and Gentiles (v. 20); the hostility of the Jews (v. 21); the conclusion, emphasising the fact that Christianity is nothing but orthodox Judaism properly understood. Moses and the prophets taught, (1) that the Messiah should come; (2) that He should suffer; (3) that He should rise again from the dead, the first-fruits of them that sleep; (4) that in the Messiah's days the religion of Israel would be taught to the Gentiles. This is precisely what St. Paul preaches, and therefore he claims acquittal from Agrippa, and from all orthodox Jews (vv. 22, 23, 27).

5. See 22 3 23 6 Phil 3 5. **6. The promise**] viz. of the Messiah, made to Abraham, Gn 22 18; also of the Resurrection, for it was believed by the Pharisees and orthodox Jews that all Jews would be raised to life to share in the Messianic kingdom. **7. Instantly**] RV 'earnestly.' **9, 10.** 'I once found the same difficulty in believing that God does actually raise the dead; and therefore I bitterly persecuted those who proclaimed the Resurrection of Jesus, just as you are now persecuting me.'

9. Contrary to the name] i.e. in order to suppress the confession and invocation of it.

10. My voice] RV 'my vote.' The Gk. means 'the vote of a judge,' and establishes the fact that at the time of the death of Stephen, Paul, though so young a man, was a member of the Sanhedrin.

12–18. See on 9³ 22⁶.

16–18. It appears from 9⁶ 22¹⁰ that all the directions that Jesus gave to Paul at the moment of his conversion were, 'Arise, and go into the city, and it shall be told thee what thou must do.' The command to preach to the Gentiles was apparently given through Ananias (22¹⁵), and more definitely in a subsequent vision at Jerusalem (22²¹). It seems reasonable, therefore, to suppose that St. Paul here summarises the contents of more than one revelation.

23. That Christ should suffer] RV 'how that the Christ must suffer'; RM 'if the Christ must suffer,' or, 'whether the Christ must suffer': see Lk24²⁶,⁴⁶ and Isa53. **The first**] see 1 Cor15²⁰, 'the firstfruits of them that slept'; Col1¹⁸, 'the firstborn from the dead'; Rev1⁵, 'the first begotten of the dead.' **Light**] see Lk2³² Isa9² 42⁶ 49⁶ 60¹⁻³. **The people**] i.e. the Jewish nation, 'the people of God.'

24. The exclamation of Festus shows impatience and perhaps anger at the idea that an uneducated peasant like Jesus (one, moreover, who had been crucified) could have anything to teach a Roman like himself. **Much learning**] lit. 'the numerous writings,' probably the writings of Moses and the prophets, quoted by St. Paul in his speech. Or the reference may be a general one to the Apostle's well-known studious habits. **25.** Observe the good temper and courtesy of St. Paul's retort.

Most noble] see Lk1³, 'most excellent Theophilus' (same word).

28. Almost thou persuadest me to be a Christian] This translation is now given up. The best rendering seems to be, 'Too easily art thou persuading thyself that thou canst make me a Christian !'

32. Agrippa, speaking as a Jew, pronounces St. Paul's views orthodox, or at least not heretical. There is nothing in them, he thinks, contrary to the OT., though, of course he does not accept them as true.

CHAPTER 27

THE VOYAGE AND SHIPWRECK

27¹–28¹⁶. The Journey to Rome.

This narrative is the most detailed account of an ancient voyage which we possess, and is our principal source of knowledge of the art of navigation as practised by the ancients. St. Luke describes the voyage at length, because it exhibits his hero in a very favourable light.

The details of the voyage are clearly authentic (see Intro.).

1. Julius] a person otherwise unknown. The narrative reveals him as courteous and humane, open to religious impressions, and able to appreciate a great character. **Augustus' band**] rather, 'the Augustan cohort.' This cohort has been generally regarded as one of the five cohorts which, Josephus tells us, were stationed at Cæsarea. Prof. Mommsen, however, thinks that it belonged to a body of troops called *frumentarii* (lit. 'victuallers'), whose headquarters were at Rome on the Cœlian hill. They not only superintended the provisioning of the imperial armies, but were continually going to and fro on the Emperor's business.

2. A ship of Adramyttium] i.e. a ship owned at Adramyttium, which was about to undertake its homeward voyage. Adramyttium was an important seaport of Mysia. **We launched, meaning to sail by the coasts of Asia**] RV 'which was about to sail unto the places on the coast of Asia, we put to sea.' **Aristarchus**] see 19²⁹ 20⁴. **3. Sidon**] an important seaport situated about 20 m. N. of its great commercial rival, Tyre. **To refresh himself**] rather, 'to receive attention.' **4. Under Cyprus**] RV 'under the lee of Cyprus'; i.e. to the E. of the island, as was usual with ships westward bound, to avoid the prevalent W. winds. **5. Myra**] see 21¹. This town was important as one of the great harbours in the corn trade between Egypt and Rome.

6. A ship of Alexandria] At this time Rome was almost entirely dependent upon foreign corn, obtained mainly from Egypt. This vessel was one of the great corn-ships (v. 38) employed to convey wheat from Alexandria to Puteoli or Ostia. The arrival of these corn-ships in Italy was a signal for great rejoicings. **7. Scarce**] i.e. with difficulty. **Cnidus**] a seaport of Caria. **Not suffering us**] viz. to pursue a direct course to Italy S. of Cape Malea. **Under Crete**] i.e. under the lee of Crete (to the E. and S. of it). **Salmone**] the NE. promontory of Crete. Upon it stood a temple of Athena. **8. Fair havens**] where St. Paul waited for a considerable time (v. 9), still preserves its ancient name. It is a small bay situated about 6 m. E. of Cape Litino. It is secure only against N. and NW. winds, whereas the harbour of Phœnix (v. 12) is secure against all winds. **Lasea**] has been identified by its ruins. It is mentioned by no other ancient writer.

9. The fast] i.e. the Day of Atonement, falling about the autumnal equinox. Ancient mariners reckoned the dangerous season of navigation from September 14th to November 11th. From November 11th till March 5th all navigation was suspended. **10. No revela-**

tion is to be assumed here. **12. Phenice**] RV 'Phœnix,' i.e. either the modern Loutro, or the neighbouring town of Phineka. **Toward the south west and north west**] i.e. the bay or harbour formed a semicircle, of which one half looked SW. and the other half NW.

14. Translate, 'But after no long time there beat down from it' (i.e. from Crete) 'a tempestuous wind which is called Euraquilo.' **Euroclydon**] The best reading is 'Euraquilo,' i.e. an E.N.E. wind.

16. RV 'and running under the lee of a small island, called Cauda, we were able, with difficulty, to secure the boat.' **Clauda**] or (RV) 'Cauda' (now Gavdo or Gozzo), is 23 m. S. of Phœnix. **To come by the boat**] RV 'to secure the boat.' This was a small rowing-boat towed from the stern of the ship. The storm having come on suddenly, there had been no time to haul it aboard. This was now done, but with difficulty, for it was full of water.

17. Helps] i.e. means of protection against foundering. **Undergirding**] Broad girths were passed under the ship, and strained tight, to hold the timbers together. Modern seamen sometimes resort to the practice, which is called 'frapping.' **Lest they should fall into the quicksands**] RV 'lest they should be cast upon the Syrtis.' The 'Greater Syrtis,' 'the Goodwin Sands of the Mediterranean' (Farrar), lay to the SW. of Cauda. **Strake sail**] better, 'reduced sail.' They probably lowered the mainsail more than half-way, but left the small 'artemon' or stormsail extended.

18. Lightened the ship] by throwing part of the cargo overboard. **19. We .. our**] RV 'they .. their.' **The tackling**] i.e. spars, ropes, etc. But a better translation is 'the ship's furniture,' i.e. beds, tables, benches, cooking utensils, chests, boxes, etc.

23. The angel] rather, 'an angel.' For other visions of Paul see 18 9 22 18 23 11.

26. St. Paul here speaks as a prophet, and accurately predicts the future. **27. The fourteenth night**] viz. from their departure from Fair Havens. **In Adria**] RV 'in the sea of Adria,' which lay between Malta, Italy, Greece and Crete. **28. They sounded**] 'J. Smith shows how exactly the geographical details in the traditional St. Paul's Bay (on the NE. coast of Malta) correspond with the description here' (Knowling).

34. For your health] RV 'for your safety.' Unless they were strengthened by food they might be drowned in the attempt to get ashore.

35. All pious Jews gave thanks to God before taking food. **37.** The number of persons on board is large, but not unusually so. The vessel on which Josephus was wrecked carried about 600 persons. **39. To thrust in the ship**] rather, 'to run the ship aground.'

40. RV 'and casting off the anchors, they left them in the sea, at the same time loosing the bands of the rudders ; and hoisting up the foresail to the wind, they made for the beach.'
Rudder bands] RV 'the rudders.' Ancient vessels had two rudders (in the form of a huge oar or paddle), one on each quarter. While drifting, the sailors had raised the blades of the rudders out of the water, to prevent them from being broken. Now that steering had to be done, they unlashed the rudders, and let them down into the water.

41. A place where two seas met] This may either mean, (1) a strait (i.e., in this case, the narrow strait which separates Selmun Island from the mainland) ; or, (2) a tongue of land (or spit of sand) washed on both sides by the sea. **42. To kill the prisoners**] cp. 12 19 16 27.

CHAPTER 28
St. Paul a Prisoner at Rome

1. They .. they] RV 'we .. we.' **Melita**] RM 'Melitene.' Melita is certainly Malta, and not (as has been erroneously supposed) Meleda off the Illyrian coast. Tradition correctly locates the shipwreck in St. Paul's Bay, about 8 m. NW. of Valetta. **2. The barbarous people**] RV 'the barbarians.' The Gk. word does not imply that they were uncivilised, but only that they were neither Greeks nor Romans.

3. Cp. Mk 16 18. As St. Paul was arranging the faggot on the fire, the viper, feeling the heat, glided out of the faggot and bit the Apostle's hand. There are now no vipers in Malta, but the clearing of the ancient forests, and the great density of the population, are sufficient to account for their disappearance.

4. Vengeance] rather, 'Justice' (personified as a goddess). **A god**] cp. the events at Lystra (14 11), which also illustrate the popular levity of judgment.

7. The chief man] lit. 'the first man.' Inscriptions show that this title is technically correct. Malta was part of the province of Sicily, and Publius was a subordinate of the prætor of Sicily. Tradition places his house at Città-Vecchia. **8. Bloody flux**] RV 'dysentery.' Observe in this v. the technical medical language. **9. Others**] We have here the first-hand evidence of a competent medical witness to the reality of St. Paul's miraculous cures.

11. After three months] i.e. probably somewhat early in February, before the usual time of navigation. **Castor and Pollux**] (lit. 'the Dioscuri'), the twin sons of Jupiter, and tutelary deities of sailors. **12. Landing**] RV 'touching.' **Syracuse**] 100 m. N. of Malta, the capital of Sicily, and a Roman colony.

13. Fetched a compass] i.e. made a circuit. **Rhegium**] an ancient Gk. colony situated on the Italian side of the Straits of Messina, near the dreaded rock of Scylla, and the whirlpool of Charybdis. **Puteoli**] also called Dicæarchia, was (with Ostia) the great corn mart of Italy, where the Alexandrian corn-ships discharged their cargoes. It lay on the N. shore of the Bay of Naples, and contained a certain number of Jews. **15. Appii forum**] RV 'the Market of Appius,' was 43 Roman m. S. of Rome on the great Appian Road, the main line of communication between Rome and the East. **The Three Taverns**] 10 Roman miles from the capital.

ST. PAUL IN ROME (28 16-31)

16. The captain of the guard] either the captain of the prætorian guard (*præfectus prætorio*), or, more probably, the captain of the troops called *frumentarii*, whose camp was on the Cœlian hill: see on 27[1]. **To dwell by himself**] This exceptional treatment was due to the favourable report of Festus and the goodwill of the centurion.

17. Called the chief of the Jews together] or, 'called together the Jewish community first,' in accordance with his usual plan of preaching to the Jews before he preached to the Gentiles. **21.** It is somewhat strange that the chief priests did not write. Perhaps

they did, but the letter was delayed, or mis-carried. **22.** The Jews profess no first-hand knowledge of the Christians, hence it is evident that at Rome the Church and the Synagogue were already definitely separated. The expulsion of the Jews from Rome by Claudius is probably the cause of this. There being no Jewish community, the infant Church started as a mainly non-Jewish body.

25. See Isa 6[9]. **Our fathers**] RV 'your fathers.' St. Paul renounces fellowship with the unbelieving Jews. **29.** This v. is omitted by important ancient authorities, but much is to be said for its genuineness.

30. Two whole years] Such delays of justice were not unusual. In this case the delay was apparently caused, (1) by the loss of the official papers in the wreck, (2) by the non-appearance of the accusers, (3) by the difficulty of getting together the witnesses. During this imprisonment St. Paul wrote the Epistles to the Philippians, Colossians, Ephesians, and Philemon. At his first trial he was acquitted, and released. A few years later he was again arrested, brought to trial at Rome, condemned, and executed.

On Rome and the Roman Church, see the Intro. to the Epistle to the Romans.

ROMANS

INTRODUCTION

1. Place in Scripture. This letter, though it is not the earliest nor the simplest of the noble group ascribed to St. Paul, and though equally with the rest it was prompted by special local needs, fitly comes first in the series. The book of Acts, with its prophecy in 23 11 concerning St. Paul, 'so must thou bear witness also at Rome,' ends with a vivid picture of him a prisoner in Rome. The first of the Epistles dramatically follows with its disclosure of his mind as in freedom he had looked forward to a purposed visit to that city. It is the greatest of his writings in importance as in length, the most characteristic and comprehensive, the letter best suited to form an introduction to his teaching, and an epitome of his thought. It was fitting that the chief letter of the Apostle to the Gentiles should be a letter to the Church in the capital of the Gentile world, and that it should have precedence in the final order of his published writings.

2. Place in the Life and Writings of St. Paul. It is not possible to date the events in his life with absolute precision, but the narrative in Acts, together with information contained in his own writings, enables us to arrange their sequence. If we accept the chronology of C. H. Turner, which approximates to that of Ramsay very closely, and forms a mean between those of Harnack and Lightfoot, the conversion of St. Paul took place 36 A.D., six years after the crucifixion; the first missionary journey, 47 A.D.; the Council at Jerusalem, 49 A.D.; the second journey, 49–52 A.D.; the third journey, 52–56 A.D.; the arrest in Jerusalem, 56 A.D.; the imprisonment in Cæsarea, 56–58 A.D.; the arrival in Rome, 59 A.D.; and the martyrdom there, 65 A.D.

Arranged in chronological order, the thirteen Epistles of St. Paul fall into four groups :

I. 1 and 2 Thessalonians, during the second journey, 51 A.D.

II. 1 and 2 Corinthians, Galatians, and Romans, during the third journey, 52–56 A.D.

III. Philippians, Ephesians, Colossians, and Philemon, during the Roman imprisonment, 59–61 A.D.

IV. 1 and 2 Timothy, and Titus, after his release.

In point of doctrine, as of time, there is a marked distinction between these four groups,

due in part to differences in the spiritual attainments and requirements of the recipients; in part, also, to the unresting activity of the writer's own reflections upon the meaning of the faith he proclaimed. In the first group the doctrinal statements are brief, simple, and practical; the second coming of Christ receiving special attention. In the second group the truth of God's salvation in Christ is presented as a whole, defined, through questioning and controversy and through opposition to Jewish legalism, as a universal scheme of grace, and its main principles are stated and applied. In the third group the ripened thoughts of the Apostle concerning the exaltation of Christ's person, and the true nature of the Church as His body, are gathered and set forth contemplatively. In the fourth group there is no continuous exposition of doctrine, but, instead, pastoral suggestions of practical details in Church life.

The Epistle to the Romans is thus at the very heart of the Apostle's teaching, the greatest literary product of his life's most strenuous period and of his highest powers. Repulsed by Jerusalem, towards which in pride of birth and education his face had formerly been set, he has turned to imperial Rome, whose people are in truth the world in miniature, the seed of Adam, if not of Abraham, not without law or conscience though beyond the pale of Jewish law, in their own way responsible to God and under condemnation. Behind and beyond the Christians in Rome he sees in thought the countless millions of the Gentile world unsaved. Equally with Israel they know and own a moral law, and recognise their inability to keep it. Towards them, also, he would fain fulfil his apostleship.

3. Date and Place of Composition. Comparison of the Epistle with Acts points to Corinth as the place, and to 56 A.D. as the date, towards the close of the third great journey, when he was about to return to Jerusalem with the alms of the Greek Churches. After the three years spent in Ephesus he 'purposed in the spirit, when he had passed through Macedonia and Achaia, to go to Jerusalem, saying, After I have been there I must also see Rome' (Ac 19 21); and when he reached Jerusalem he was the bearer of Greek alms to the distressed Church in that city (Ac 1 17). In the letter itself he states that it has oftentimes been his purpose to preach in Rome (1^{13} 15^{23}), but his sense of prior duty to other Gentiles who had not received the gospel has hindered him, and restricted his journeys hitherto to a circuit from Jerusalem to Illyricum (Ro $15^{19\text{-}22}$). 'But now I go unto Jerusalem ministering unto the saints ; for it hath been the good pleasure of Macedonia and Achaia to make a certain contribution for the poor among the saints that are at Jerusalem . . . When I have accomplished this, I will go on by you unto Spain' ($15^{25\text{-}28}$). It is therefore the winter of 55–56 A.D. He is in Achaia—in fact, in Corinth ; for Gaius, his host, whose house is the local church (16^{23}), had been baptised by him there (1 Cor 1^{14}). Erastus, who sends greeting, is treasurer of that city (16^{23}, cp. 2 Tim 4^{20}), and Phœbe, the bearer of the letter, is a 'deaconess of the church that is at Cenchreæ,' the port of Corinth (16^1).

It is a solemn moment in the Apostle's life, and his spirit is moved as he looks back upon his mission to the Gentiles in Greece and Asia Minor. Bitter opposition and controversy and misrepresentation (2 Cor, Gal) have been his portion, as well as wonderful success. Jewish pride, prejudice, and legalism have pursued him and stirred up enmity against him. His apostolate to the Gentiles, though it has put alms for the Jewish Church into his hands, has enlarged his thought and preaching beyond Jewish limits, and brought suspicion on his fidelity to Hebrew scripture and tradition. He has deepened his Roman citizenship and his grasp of human nature. The Western as well as the Eastern Empire must receive Christ. There is already a Church in Rome ; he will strengthen it, and pass on westwards, even to Spain. In this Epistle a heroic spirit, a universal outlook, a note of triumph over controversy and misrepresentation, an imperialistic instinct, and a profound insight into human nature, have united to inspire its intense passion and its unique power.

4. Occasion and Purpose. Like the other Epistles by St. Paul it is a true letter, not an epistolary treatise. It owes its massiveness and comprehensiveness to the greatness and impressiveness of the situation which called for it and of the subject with which it deals. Jerusalem and Rome are both in his thoughts, Jewish and Gentile unrest of spirit and need of a Saviour arise before him as he writes, and in response to them the divine scheme of redemption through Christ takes shape as never before in his mind. Thinking of them he lives over again the spiritual anguish of the crisis of his own life (chs. 7, 8). His experience of deliverance, himself a Pharisee of the Pharisees, a citizen of Rome, and a son of cultured Tarsus, must and will be repeated by proud Rome. There, in Jewish synagogue

and in Gentile church, the law will yield its forbidding sovereignty to the gospel of God's grace in Jesus Christ, as once it has done in his own experience upon the way to Damascus.

The letter finds its formal occasion in the approach of the long-expected opportunity to visit Rome. It is primarily a letter of self-introduction to an unvisited Church, to prepare its members for his coming. He has many friends among them. He has heard much of them, their faith, their obedience, their divisions, their difficulties, and their temptations (1^8 12–16) ; and it may be that they, like others, have received an evil report of his teaching. In any case, he does not mean to reside with them for long, but to make Rome his base for further evangelisation in the West, his work being ended for the present in the East. They will strengthen him, as he hopes to stablish them 'in the fulness of the blessing of Christ' (1^{12} 15^{29}).

But it has a larger purpose, reflected by its doctrinal outpouring. It is as though he foresaw in Rome the mingling of all the influences against which his own life-conflict, within and without, had had to be waged, for sooner or later all living things converged on Rome. With characteristic imagination he anticipates his arrival ; the floodgates of his soul are flung open, and the pent-up thoughts which he would then have voiced refuse to be restrained. The letter is an earnest, a foretaste, of the promised 'spiritual gift to the end ye may be established' (1^{11}), of the gospel which he is 'ready to preach to you that are in Rome' (1^{15}). The Roman Christians are themselves able to admonish one another (15^{14}) ; his object is but to put them again in remembrance (15^{15}) as a 'minister of Christ Jesus unto the Gentiles.' Though he is a stranger and they are Gentiles, he has an apostolate to Gentiles. His letter is more than a controversial contribution, or a personal apologetic, or a treatise ; it is an apostolic, and, therefore, authoritative utterance directed to meet their known and their presumptive needs. From the lips of an apostle not less than a Gospel was looked for, and such the Epistle came to be as it took shape.

5. Destination. As it stands, the letter plainly is addressed 'to all that are in Rome, beloved of God, called to be saints' ($1^{7,15}$ 15^{28}), 'called to be Jesus Christ's' (1^6). Are they Jews or Gentiles ? The presumption is that if it is for *all* Christians, both are included (cp. 9^{24}, '*us* whom he also called not from the Jews only, but also from the Gentiles'). Many passages refer to, or are applicable to, Gentiles only (e.g. 'among all the *nations* .. among whom are ye also,' $1^{5,6}$; 'fruit in you also, even as in the rest of the Gentiles,' 1^{13} ; 'I speak to you that are Gentiles,' 11^{13} ; 'I write unto you because of the grace given me that I should be a minister unto the Gentiles,' 15[15,16]: the argument in chs. 9–11 is for Gentiles exclusively, and in it the Jews ('my kinsmen,' not 'your' or even 'our') are spoken of as an outside body, while many of the sins against which warning is given are such as Gentiles rather than Jews were addicted to (6[12,13,17]13[13]). On the other hand, familiarity and sympathy with the Jewish standpoint is assumed both in writer and readers. In c. 2 under the general apostrophe addressed to all mankind ('thou art without excuse, O man, whosoever thou art,' 2[1]), the Jew is naturally addressed in the second person ('if thou bearest the name of a Jew,' 2[17-27]), but immediately thereafter the Jews are spoken of in the third person (2[28f.] 3[1f.]); the reference in 4[1] to 'Abraham *our* forefather' (cp. 3[9] 9[10]) betrays no more than the unfailing remembrance of the Apostle to the Gentiles that he is himself a Hebrew (cp. 9[3] 10[1], etc.), while in 7[1], 'I speak to men that know law,' the reference need not be to Jewish law at all, but simply to universal moral law (cp. 1[19,32]), and even if it were to Jewish law, they might have been Gentile proselytes to Judaism before conversion to Christianity, or, if they were converts to Christianity directly, the Old Testament was still the Christian Bible. In 9[1f.], and again in 10[1] especially, where Jewish privilege is dwelt upon wistfully, the Apostle gives no hint that any of his readers are Jews : his 'brethren and kinsmen according to the flesh' are referred to in the third person as if over against his readers in a separate camp. Several of the persons greeted in the letter bear Jewish names, but most have Gentile names, Greek for the most part, as was natural. It is noteworthy that, unlike the Thessalonians, Corinthians, and Galatians, they are not addressed collectively as 'a church.' In 16[5] the 'church' in the house of Prisca and Aquila is marked off from the rest. Presumably in Rome there would be a number of Christian circles and meeting-places. As a whole the evidence is convincing that the Roman Christians addressed are a loose-knit body, composed almost wholly of Gentiles, conversant, either as Jewish proselytes or as Christian converts, with the Old Testament religion, and concerned as Christians to adjust their ceremonial, moral, and spiritual relationship to it rightly.

6. History of Christianity in Rome.

(*a*) **Jewish preparation.** Between Jerusalem and Rome there had long been direct and easy communication. If the military heel of Rome was planted firmly on Jewish soil, the softer tread of Jewish commerce and religion was simultaneously heard upon the pavements of the Roman capital. As conquered Greece soon took her captor captive by the force of her literature, art, and culture, conquered Israel was already advancing towards a like success by means of its lofty ethics and religion, which were also enshrined in an imperishable literature. At least as early as the 2nd cent. B.C. Jews found their way to Rome on embassies, and in 63 B.C. the capture of Jerusalem by Pompey brought many against their will to settle as slaves or freedmen in the city. They formed a synagogue and a 'Ghetto,' and found protection and favour under the first emperors, numbering many thousands, and making many proselytes without effort. Tiberius and Caligula withdrew the imperial favour. Under Claudius many of them were temporarily expelled (52 A.D.), among them Aquila and Prisca (Ac 18[2]), on account, it appears, of disorders which broke out upon the preaching of Christ among them. Under Nero hitherto they had prospered.

(*b*) **The Christian Church.** There is evidence, as well as probability, that news was brought to Rome of Jesus' career and claims very soon after His death. To the Roman Jews all that passed in Jerusalem was deeply interesting (cp. Ac 2[10]), and the life-work and teaching of the Prophet of Nazareth, with the resurrection-faith of His followers and the conversion of Saul for sequels, formed an episode in Jewish history which could neither be suppressed nor ignored. The expulsion under Claudius of Aquila and Prisca, St. Paul's informants concerning Rome, and his fellow-workers in Corinth Ephesus and Rome, suggests that the gospel met with strenuous opposition, first from the Jewish, and later, as a cause of civil tumult, from the Imperial authorities. The account of St. Paul's arrival in Acts (28[15-28]) suggests that he was met and welcomed by *Gentile* 'brethren,' and proves that the Jewish authorities were not ignorant of the new 'sect everywhere spoken against,' but as a body had stood aloof, and with some exceptions persisted in their attitude. In Rome as elsewhere it had proved easier for Gentile proselytes than for born Jews to receive the new Teaching. To them St. Paul, as if in anticipation of Jewish coldness, chiefly appeals in his letter.

(*c*) **Connexion of Roman Christianity with** (1) **St. Paul and** (2) **St. Peter.**

(1) Plainly St. Paul has had no part in the introduction of Christianity into Rome, yet he knows its existing position intimately, and knows not a few of its Jewish and Gentile professors there.

(2) The late tradition that St. Peter was the founder is incompatible with the absence of any reference to him in c. 15 ; nor, had he been then the head of the Roman Church, could a personal greeting to him have been

absent. There is no indication of any apostolic origin. The foundation has been laid, Christ is there named (15 20), house-churches exist (16 5), but strictly speaking there is no united Church. Such apostolic basis as it was to have was first afforded by this letter. It is like a consecrating breath of the Apostle's presence. Though Christianity had long preceded him in Rome, its people, Jew and Gentile, were not fused into a single Church until the genius of St. Paul, who read the hearts of both, by letter and by word supplied the sacred fire.

7. The Epistle as a whole.

(*a*) **Authenticity and Integrity.** That it is the work of St. Paul admits of no serious question. The evidence, internal and external, is overwhelming. It is the supreme self-revelation of the Apostle. That the Epistle as we have it is a coherent unity has been doubted on substantial though inconclusive grounds. The doxology which marks the close of the Epistle after 16 24 in most of the best manuscript authorities, is found elsewhere, after 14 23, or in both places, in others. Moreover, apart from this massive and impressive doxology, there are other passages, benedictory in form, between 14 23 and 16 24, which look like endings, e.g. 15 33 16 20 and 16 24 ; in one important manuscript Rome is not mentioned, and some of the persons named in c. 16 are known to have been connected with Ephesus, which has suggested Ephesus as the original destination of that chapter. It is not impossible that in shortened or lengthened form the Epistle to the Romans may at some time have circulated among several groups of readers, but the unity of the Epistle in its present form cannot be disproved or seriously shaken. In any case its teaching remains unimpaired.

(*b*) **Style.** Like St. Paul's other letters, it was dictated to an amanuensis (16 22), a fact which helps to explain the irregularities of the language and the thought as it flowed on in a rushing broken torrent from the passionate soul of the Apostle. The tentmaker and the organiser of the Churches had scant leisure to polish his sentences and ponder his phrases. It may be that his hand was nimbler with the needle than the pen. His style is a mirror of himself. Not the letter, but the spirit ; not the seen and the superficial, but the unseen and the underlying ; not the part, but the whole ; not the nice details of argument, but the broad sweep of truth, is his concern. Doubtless these dictated letters preserve for us, even better than his reported speeches in the book of Acts, the form and manner of his preaching, as well as the vehemence of its intellectual, moral, and spiritual power.

(*c*) **Use and Interpretation of the Old Testament.** Familiarity with every portion of the Old Testament is assumed in the readers as well as exhibited by the writer. Its law, history, psalmody, and prophecy are all requisitioned in the argument in a manner strongly reminiscent of the rabbinical school, kindred snatches of Scripture being run together, allegory and type being traced in narratives, yet also with a masterly insight into the prophetic spirit of the book, and with a Christian's sense of its completion and fulfilment in Jesus Christ (cp. 3 10-18 9 25-33 10 16-21 ; also cp. chs. 4, 10, and 11). By some threescore quotations the universal reign of sin and need of grace, the saving power of faith, the sovereignty of the divine will, the judgment of unbelieving Israel, and the summons to the Gentiles, are confirmed by way of preparation for the universal truth in Christ. In legal language, and by scriptural thought, the legal is transcended, and way is made for grace. The stricken conscience of the Hebrew under law is healed by the hope of Israel realised in Jesus Christ.

(*d*) **Relation to Christ's Teaching.** As a teacher the Apostle, though wielding authority, differs vastly from the Master, who taught ' not as the Scribes.' The form and manner of his general teaching could scarcely differ more from His ; but it is impossible to read chs. 12–14 without discerning the ethical identity of the ideals enjoined by both. It is the same Christian life and character that each would fain see realised. Nor can it be gainsaid that the Apostle at bottom shares his Master's characteristic attitude to the burdens of the Pharisaic law, and extends the same invitation to weary and heavy-laden bearers of the yoke to come to Him for rest. Between the teaching of Jesus and that of Paul the two great facts of atoning death and triumphant resurrection have intervened, the facts which in succession cast Paul down and lifted him up, blinded him and gave him new sight, caused him to die and to live again. Of necessity Paul's own relation to the Cross as a Pharisaic persecutor in the name of law, and his experience as a convert of its regenerating power, suffuse his whole conception of Christ's gospel. Though Jesus in the Gospels might assure men of God's forgiveness apart from any reference to His death, Paul had no experience of any such unmediated forgiveness. The death and reappearance of the Lord alone had sufficed to bring home to him at once the full enormity of his guilty enmity to good and the irresistible sufficiency of the will of God to pardon and to save through Christ. If in the recorded words of our Lord we would find anticipations of the Pauline gospel, it is not to the parable of the Prodigal Son alone, but also to the institution of the Sacramental Supper on the eve of the Saviour's sacrifice that we must turn. Can it be seriously said that Paul's conception of the bond between the Saviour and the saved is any other than the Saviour's own ? All that we can say is that, while it was the simple comprehensive truth of God as it was in Christ Jesus that he saw and proclaimed, while it was a borrowed, not an original gospel, that he preached, he saw the truth with his own eyes unflinchingly, and declared it in his own language. None of the apostolic band could view the truth in Christ from so detached a standpoint as he, with his birth in the dispersion, his education as a rabbi, his Roman citizenship, and his Græco-Cilician home. It was a necessary consequence of this very detachment which enabled St. Paul to see the truth in Christ's life and Person so independently, so universally, and in such clear perspective, that his manner of teaching, his vocabulary, and his mode of thought should seem to be at utter variance with his Master's. But the more we study his teaching as a whole, and the more patiently we compare its burden and its spirit with that of Jesus, the more we realise the justice of that verdict of Christendom which has judged him to be the greatest and truest of Christians, and the justice of his own favourite self-description as a 'bondservant of Jesus Christ.'

(*e*) **The Contents.** (For detailed outline see p. 864 below, and for running exposition see the commentary.)

As has been said, the Epistle is a true letter, personal in testimony and in exhortation throughout. C. 1$^{1-17}$ contains the address and preamble. Chs. 1^{18}–11^{36} contain a foretaste of the 'spiritual gift' which it is the Apostle's longing to impart to the Roman Christians (1^{11}), a reasoned vindication of 'the gospel' which he is 'ready to preach' to them, of which he is not ashamed, which is 'the power of God unto salvation to every one that believeth,' and in which 'is revealed a righteousness of God from faith unto faith.' Though full of profound thought, the teaching in this section is not a treatise, it is personal instruction addressed again and again to 'brethren,' abounding in vivacious uses of 'I,' 'you,' 'we,' in true letter form. Chs. 12^1–15^{13} contain practical exhortations suggested naturally by the Apostle's presentation of the truth in Christ,—exhortations universally applicable to Christian people (chs. 12, 13), and exhortations specially addressed to the circle of his readers (chs. 14, 15). Chs. 15^{14}–16^{27} contain a variety of personal details : the Apostle's motive in writing (15$^{14-21}$), plans of travel, introduction of Phœbe, personal greetings, admonition against authors of error and dispeace, conveyance of greetings from his friends, and solemn final doxology.

8. The Teaching of the Epistle.

The following is an outline of the thought embodied in the Epistle, particularly in chs. 1–11, which, while rather a vindication than an exposition of his gospel, contain the substance of his whole message. To constitute a comprehensive summary of his teaching as a whole, it must be supplemented by the reader in many important details from the other Pauline Epistles, for a mind like the Apostle's was in continual movement, expanding, enriching, and maturing its convictions, and each of his letters has its own distinctive contributions to the sum of Christian truth. If we would complete our account of his teaching, e.g. on the Person of Christ and His relationship to the Christian, on the Church, the Ministry, the Sacraments, not to mention other themes, we must make use of the other Epistles. This outline, however, of the thought in the greatest of his writings may serve as a useful introduction to, and foreglimpse of, his teaching as a whole.

The Preamble (1$^{1-17}$). St. Paul writes not only as a servant of Jesus, the Christ, but also as a messenger of long-expected good news from God. The promised Son of David's race according to the flesh has at last been born and lived His life ; by resurrection from the dead He has been supernaturally shown to be the Son of God according to the Spirit. 'The mystery kept in silence through times eternal is now manifested' (16^{25}). This good news it is a sacred duty to tell both to Greeks and to the rest of the world. It is a gospel to be proud of ; for every man, be he Jew or Greek, who accepts it in faith receives from God not a theory of salvation but a saving power. It reveals a new righteousness, not human but divine, issuing from living faith.

(*A*) **The Need of the World.**

Of such good news, and such faith-righteousness leading to salvation, mankind is universally in sore need. Gentile and Jew alike are deservedly under the wrath of God, who has revealed His anger against all unrighteousness and irreligion. All have sinned. All are without excuse. God has suffered all to become in some measure hardened and reprobate through sinful habit.

(*a*) Think, first, of the Gentile world. Though less favoured than Israel, the Gentiles have not been without revelation. They have been able to discern from the open face of nature the everlasting power and divinity of the invisible God. In their minds they have had knowledge of God, the self-manifesting. But everywhere they have lapsed. They have trampled on the truth, reasoned foolishly, and fallen into all manner of idolatry, worshipping and serving the creature rather than the Creator. Their wisdom, their philosophy, has ended in failure. They have been ungrateful, and have not glorified God. Before Him they are without excuse. Deservedly He has given them up to the indulgence of their impure lusts, to abuse their bodies, to dishonour sex, to cherish a reprobate mind. By act and by consent they have been guilty of every form of social, domestic, and personal sin against God and man. They have known the divine ordinance, that they who practise such things are worthy of death, but they have chosen to ignore God. They are self-condemned, for they are ready to judge one another, knowing well when they are wronged that sin is sin, and their just judgment upon others recoils upon themselves. How is it that men are blind to this, abusing God's forbearance, which should prompt them to repentance, and aggravating their guilt? God will assuredly render to every man according to his works. To those who by patience in well-doing seek for glory and honour and eternal life He will grant the objects of their quest, to the factious and disobedient, anguish under His indignation (1 18–2 16).

(b) Are the Jews in better case? They are involved in the self-same judgment. Indeed, as first in privilege, they are first in condemnation. God has no partiality: His justice is even-handed. If the Gentile who has never enjoyed the privilege of Jewish law and revelation is condemned for his sins against his own more limited light, God cannot permit the privileged Jew to sin with impunity. The same justice that metes out stern punishment to the Gentile who is outside the pale of Jewish law and revelation because he sins against the unwritten law within the heart, demands an even sterner sentence upon the Jew who breaks his higher Law. There are Gentiles who do by nature the things of the Law, though they know not Moses and the Prophets: these become as it were their own law, in that they show the work of the Law written in their hearts, their conscience bearing witness therewith, and their reflections one with another accusing or else acquitting them —such men put many a Jew to shame.

It is indeed a great thing to belong to the Hebrew race, to be heir to the oracles of God, to the Law, the Promises, the sacred ordinances and rites of God's chosen and adopted people, to have the blood of Abraham in one's veins, to be of one flesh with the Christ who should come (2 17–3 2 9 3-5). But to be born a Jew, to be circumcised a Jew, to receive a Jewish name, is not enough. To God a man's heart is more than his flesh and blood, his conduct than his ceremonial. 'He is not a true Jew who is one outwardly: neither is that true circumcision which is outward in the flesh: but he is a Jew who is one inwardly, and circumcision is that of the heart, in the spirit not in the letter.' 'They are not all Israel who are of Israel: neither because they are Abraham's seed are they all children. . . It is not the children of the flesh that are children of God.' Hebrew history and Scripture are full of evidence that mere possession of the Law has never secured obedience to it; each of the commandments has been dishonoured daily; and instead of being the glory of God, Israel has too often been a reproach to Him among the nations. It is not more true that the Law is the pride of Israel as a nation among the nations, than that the Law is the condemnation of the individual Jew (2 17–3 8, also chs. 9–11).

Thus it appears that as the Greek or other Gentile is convicted by his unwritten law of conscience, so the Jew is convicted by his recorded law. All are under sin. There is none righteous, none whose works fulfil the demands of the divine Law under which he lives. Every mouth is stopped. Were law to have the final word, the doom of all were sealed (3 9-20).

(B) **The Inadequacy of Law to save** (c. 7).
The persistence of sin under the rule of Gentile conscience and Hebrew law is proof that law has been unable to save, though it is able to condemn: it can teach, threaten, and admonish, but it cannot inspire and empower. Indeed, in man's fallen condition, law seems but to aggravate the evil it denounces. But for it we should not know sin—our lives were innocent as those of babes or beasts. Obedience, the essence of duty, presupposes a command or prohibition, the essence of law. The insistence of law is a standing provocation and temptation to disobedience. The very words 'thou shalt not' suggest to man's wayward sense of freedom 'why not?' 'shall I not?' Apart from law sin is dead, lifeless, or unborn: through law sin finds its opportunity and enters the heart of man on its fatal errand.

Is law sinful, then, because it thus opens the way for sin? No: the sin is not in law, but in us who respond so perversely to its just demands. The law is in itself a thing of righteousness; it is the voice of God, whether the whisper of conscience or the peal of Sinai; it is good throughout. It is in fact the great instrument for showing up sin in its true character, in its naked ugliness. Sin is seen at its worst as man's enemy when it thus subverts the very law of God for its baleful uses. Law would fain guide us to life: 'obey and ye shall live' is its burden; but sin seduces us into the way of death. By pointing out the way of life law must, however unwillingly, disclose to us implicitly other ways which lead to death. Sin, when we have thus become familiar with the way to death, casts its spell over our eyes and invests the fatal way with a seductive glamour. But sin is not in law, is not in God; it can only be in us.

There is in us a principle of evil, our carnal nature, a kind of lower law. The mind of the flesh is enmity against God and rebellion against His law: it is death (8⁶˒⁷). In our moral life we are aware of division and discord within us. After the inward man we delight in the law of God, we hate evil, we desire to obey and do good, yet we do not succeed. The good which we would, we do not; the evil which we would not, that we habitually do. It becomes as it were a law of our life to sin. We are sin-possessed. *Another*, a *lower* law in our members, in our flesh, wages war against the law of our mind, and enslaves us. In the agony of despair the soul of man cries out, 'O wretched man that I am! who shall deliver me from this living death, from this sin-dominated, death-bringing bodily existence?'

(*C*) **A New Way of Salvation needed and foreshadowed.**

History and experience thus combine to attest man's need of deliverance. Man as man must be liberated from sin, from condemnation, from the law of his lower self, even in a sense from the grim grasp of the Revealed Law of Israel's Covenant-God. In himself man has proved powerless to achieve salvation even when guided by explicit law and encouraged by special providences and uplifting promises. Can it be that he is now without hope and lost? Gentile wisdom and Jewish privilege stand self-condemned and humbled. Unless God intervenes salvation is for ever beyond reach, and the divine end of creation frustrated.

With true prophetic insight St. Paul discerns a divine purpose in this humiliation of mankind. Thus humbled, man is prepared to look above for deliverance, and to remain humble should God deign to save him. And man's utmost need is God's utmost opportunity ('where sin abounded, grace did abound more exceedingly,' 5²⁰). Conscience and law are seen not only to be inadequate for man's complete salvation, but also by reason of their incompleteness to deepen man's sense of need and to point forward to the coming in God's providence of a higher law and a fuller revelation. To say with the Jew that either the law must save or we are lost, is to fetter and cramp the goodness of God, to make the law greater than its Giver. There may have been, nay, there has been, waiting in the secret counsel of God a way of salvation destined, not to discredit or set aside law, but to transcend the old method of attempting to satisfy conscience and law and to achieve work-righteousness. Gentile and Jew were right, were bound, to seek salvation by honouring their conscience and their law, and cherishing their light, and they have not been without their reward; but they were wrong to shut their eyes and their hearts to the limitation and the partiality of the old-time method and the pitiful inadequacy of its results: their failures ought to have led them to turn with increased humility and hope to God, from whom alone so great a boon as their soul's salvation could come. Man's unbelief cannot annul God's faithfulness.

The new way is not without some foreshadowing in the Old Dispensation (cp. c. 4). The children of Abraham might have remembered that the justice of God was never mechanical: that His favours were not always bought or earned, but might be freely given, and often descended on unexpected quarters. Who could say that Israel's position as God's peculiar people had always, had ever, been deserved? (cp. chs. 9–11). The history of Abraham, the Father of the Faithful, proves that God's dealings with him were based on other grounds than simple legal justice. God's recompense of good is far more than legally proportioned to man's desert. It was something more than virtuous acts that commended Abraham to God and gave value to his life: 'not through the law was the promise to Abraham or to his seed that he should be heir of the world.' The supreme merit of Abraham was his faith in God: it was his firm faith that enabled him alike to obey the call to leave home and kindred and to yield up his only son, and to believe that, in spite of his own old age and the barrenness of Sarah, God would give him a son and fulfil the promise that he would become the father of many nations. Abraham's true seed and heirs are those who cherish his faith in God: he will become the father of many nations when the Gentiles enter into that faith. It is circumcision of the heart, trustful self-surrender to God, that is the mark of the true child of Abraham, the true heir of that faith which was in Abraham's bosom before his flesh was circumcised, and of those promises which were out of all proportion to his actual deeds.

The prophets in their day looked beyond human actions and Hebrew merit for the salvation of Israel, and taught that God's eye is ever on the heart which moves the hand. The heart must be right, must be fixed on God, must look to Him for power to raise and wisdom to guide the hand that works. Did not the very hope and promise of Messiah, a Saviour from the right hand of God, imply that man was powerless to save himself? The Messianic hope was therefore the harbinger of a new righteousness not resting on works done by men, but instead resting on God's grace and enabling good works to be done—a righteousness of the heart, a conscience cleared not by human merit but by divine forgiveness and renewal.

This means that a new view must henceforth be taken of Israel's history, privilege and vocation, its sacraments and its Messiah, its righteous God who judges not as man judges, but looks upon the heart and reads its secrets. Pride of race, presumption upon God's favour, must for ever be laid aside. God's aim is not Israel's aggrandisement, but man's universal sanctification and attachment to Himself. The election of Israel is that all the nations may share the blessing. The coming of Messiah therefore could have no other purpose than the coming of God's universal and eternal kingdom of holiness, the highest good of the greatest number. Conscience, law, and Messiah have righteousness on earth as their common aim. Conscience and law are the world's schoolmasters to educate it up to Christ. His actual and attested coming is the fulfilment and therefore also the vindication of both (3^{31}), the achievement of righteousness by a new means which was beyond their reach. God is now fully disclosed in His true character, not as an arbitrary sovereign grasping at sovereignty for its own sake, nor as a stern judge administering a grim law over which He has no control, but as a Holy and Loving Father, jealously requiring righteousness in His children for their own sake, and putting forth every effort to realise their highest good. ' For the earnest expectation of the creation waiteth for the revealing of the sons of God .. for the whole creation groaneth and travaileth in pain together until now... For the creation was subjected to vanity, not of its own will simply, but of God's who subjected it, in hope that the creation itself also shall be delivered from the bondage of corruption into the liberty of the glory of the children of God ' (8^{19-22}). Of free grace His beneficent hand equips both men and nations with their several talents at the outset of their stewardship, while as yet of merit they can have none, and rewards them at the close of their day according to, yet far above, their works. Of free grace He bestows on some a larger stewardship than on others. Of free grace likewise He bestows His supreme gift of righteousness unto salvation which men can neither achieve nor earn, but which they must prepare themselves to receive through humble penitence for sin committed, and through heart-yearning and heart-trust, in a word, through faith in God who alone saves. ' O the depth of the riches both of the wisdom and of the knowledge of God ! how unsearchable are his judgments, and his ways past tracing out ! For who hath known the mind of the Lord, or who hath been his counsellor ? or who hath first given to him, and it shall be recompensed unto him again ? For of him, and through him, and unto him are all things ' (11^{33-36}).

(D) God's Salvation in Jesus His Christ (3^{19-31} 5, 8).

What conscience and law could not do in that they were weak through the flesh, God has accomplished, sending His own Son in the likeness of our human, sin-ridden flesh. He has set men free from their bondage to fleshly lust, to sin, and to the law which can condemn to death but cannot save unto life, through the higher law or principle of the Spirit of Life in Christ Jesus. This deliverance is not simply revealed but mediated and effected through Jesus, for He purifies and renews the heart as well as opens the eyes.

Jesus is the Christ, the promised Saviour from sin. He is God's true, unique, ' own ' Son, His representative on earth, doing His work, wielding His power, revealing His mind, sharing His Spirit, reconciling men to His Father as veritable sons. His coming was ' for sin.' His life and death were a condemnation of sin, as showing that human life could rise above it in the power of the Divine Spirit : they are also the destruction of sin, breaking its power over men, revealing its hatefulness and deadliness, and reconciling us to the Heavenly Father from whom it has estranged us. Jesus the Christ was a man (5^{15}), human as Adam : His work of grace will prove as far-reaching in its consequences for good as Adam's transgression has proved for evil. He is the second Adam (5^{12-21}), undoer of the mischief of the first. Through Adam's fall, his one trespass, sin and death entered the world and reigned over men, ' even over them that had not sinned after the likeness of Adam's transgression, and through the one man's disobedience the many were made sinners.' In like manner through Jesus' one life-comprehending act of obedience, His self-surrender in death the righteous for the unrighteous, His lifting-up, grace shall reign, the many shall be made righteous even though of themselves they shall not achieve the same obedience. Sin, condemnation, death formed our portion as Adam's heirs through the flesh : through Christ holiness, justification, and life are ours, a free portion given to us as partakers of His Spirit, joint-heirs of God with Him. According to the old *régime* a man must die to expiate his sin : ' he that hath died is justified from sin ' (6^7). In Christ a higher than forensic justification is accomplished without the necessity of physical death. If a man becomes by the grace of God one with Christ, knit to Him in spirit, he passes spiritually through the Saviour's experience of death and resurrection. He dies to the old life, to sin, with Christ. In spirit he is crucified with the Lord. The carnal in him falls away, as flesh falls away from spirit in death : mortality and sin are laid aside as in a grave : and the spirit, the true self, God's child in him, rises with the risen Christ to the new life, dead only to sin, alive unto God in Christ Jesus.

The life and work of Jesus as the Christ of God is thus not only the instrument of deliverance and a final revelation to man of God and of man's own self, but also an all-embracing cosmic fact. It is far more than a type or object-lesson of the Christian's experience, for it is also a supreme instrument in its own reproduction. It thus gathers up within itself all individual spiritual experience of salvation. Through the Cross and the open sepulchre every soul must find its exodus from bondage to liberty. It is the appointed way. Every soul has a death to die and a resurrection to receive : a life to withdraw from the world and yield up to God, and to receive back with the seal of acceptance and renewal upon it. We not only know this now through Christ and see it in Him, but we experience it in and with Him. He dies and lives again in us, or we die and live again in Him. We are one with Him in the Spirit. And if with the apostle we know Christ crucified and raised from the dead, that is self-yielded unto death for our sins, and God-accepted for our assurance and our justification through the faith which rests on His resurrection regarded as a proof of God's acceptance of His death for others, we know Christ fully. His death and resurrection are a summary and consummation of His whole life. To know Him in them is to know Him completely, and not only Him but the love of God disclosed in Him, for it was love that prompted God to send Him to us : ' God commendeth his own love toward us in that, while we were yet sinners, Christ died for us ' ; and it is the same divine love that is ' shed abroad in our hearts through the Holy Spirit which was given unto us.' Through Christ it has come about that our knowledge of God as the righteous vindicator of stern law is all but merged to vanishing in our knowledge of His tender love, the self-same love unto death which Jesus cherished towards us on earth, and still cherishes at the right hand of God as our constant intercessor, a love from which ' neither death, nor life, nor angels, nor principalities, nor things present, nor things to come, nor powers, nor height, nor depth, nor any other creature shall be able to separate us.'

Surveying this divine work of salvation, the Apostle clearly distinguishes certain activities on the part of God, whose succession need not be thought of as strictly temporal in the eternal will. The redeeming purpose of divine love involves the following *sequence of grace*. God *foreknows* His individual children ; *fore-ordains* them ' to be conformed to the image of his Son that he may be the firstborn among many brethren ' ; *calls* them to fulfil their destiny ; *justifies* them, i.e forgives their sin and imputes to them new righteousness when in faith they respond to His call ; and *glorifies* them, i.e. through sanctification brings them to the consummation of their life-purpose and the realisation of their true selves (8 29, 30). In each stage of the process the ' image of his Son' is present ; in each the eternal Christ participates ; our election, our vocation, our justification, our adoption, our sanctification, and our glorification are inseparable from Him.

(*E*) **The New Righteousness : Life in the Spirit** (chs. 5, 6, 8, 12–15).

With singular fulness and insight St. Paul describes the substance and the secret of salvation as an experience of the human soul. The Epistle is a revelation of the spiritual riches of his own experience, as well as a masterly delineation of a universal ideal. His touch is never firmer, his grasp never stronger, than when he lays bare in swift heart-searching sentences the meaning, the joys, the hopes, and the responsibilities of the new life in Christ. Whatever view be taken of the fidelity of other elements in his teaching to the letter of the explicit words of his Master, no one can seriously allege that the Apostle's conception of the regenerate life, or, for that matter, his practical embodiment of it, differs in any material respect from that which is enshrined in the Sermon on the Mount and in the Gospels as a whole. The words may be different ; the manner of the teacher may not be the same ; but beyond question the self-same spirit breathes through both, the same vision arises at the bidding of each.

(1) **In relation to God** the Christian lives a filial life. All that a son should be in thought, word, and deed, it is for him to be towards God. Perfect freedom of access to the Father, unbroken communion, childlike trust, unfailing hope, self-yielding love, are his. Intercourse with Him and service are his chief joy ; growth in likeness to Him is his chief reward. Gratefully he acknowledges his utter dependence upon the Father for forgiveness and reconciliation and new righteousness, and for every good gift. To glorify Him is the sum of duty and the summit of ambition. The Christian is a son and therefore an heir of God, joint-heir with Christ the Elder Brother and the First-born of many sons. Bondage and fear towards God are done away : ' Abba, Father ! ' is his cry.

(2) **In relation to Christ.** No words can exaggerate the intimacy of the bond between the believer and Christ. He belongs to his Lord ; in life and death his face is towards Him who died for him (14 8). From His love he is inseparable (8 35). He is *in Christ Jesus;* baptised into Him, into His death,—crucified,

dead, buried, and risen with Him. It is not simply the man Jesus, good, obedient, pure, and true till death, but Jesus the Eternal Christ of God—Christ in spite of crucifixion, Christ because raised from the dead, enthroned with the Father, and alive for evermore. 'The Lord is the Spirit' (2 Cor 3 17), known no longer after the flesh, visible only to the eye of faith. It is not so much the deliberate imitation or following of Jesus as a man, for that may mean but self-reliance after all, as faith in Him the Son of God, that is first demanded, for it is by faith that we are enabled to follow,—faith must precede, even where we cannot see. We are to 'put on the Lord Jesus.' Serving Him we please God, and are approved of men (15 18); receiving Him we have an earnest of the satisfaction of all our needs (13 14).

According to St. Paul, then, faith is the link that unites us to Christ in the unseen and eternal world, the principle that links our life to His so that we are one with Him, even as He is one with the Father in spiritual fellowship. Faith is our response to the advances of God's redeeming love. St. Paul is not content with St. John to dwell on love to God as our response to His love; doubtless he takes that answering love for granted, for he was no stranger to the power of love, and on occasion could hymn its praise as greater even than faith, and he speaks of the love of God as shed abroad in our hearts (5 5). Probably he had been constrained to believe in Jesus as Christ upon the way to Damascus even before he was conscious of passionate love towards Him, and therefore lays stress upon the priority of faith. He loved Him because he saw in Him the suffering and triumphant Christ of God; it was not simply because he loved Him that he believed Him to be the Christ. Love followed faith and crowned it. He fastens upon faith, a living trust in a living God, a personal reliance upon a Saviour Christ, as the root-principle of the Christian life, the instrument of Christian progress. Through this vital attachment, self is forgotten, the world recedes, the body is reduced to its true position, the higher life nourished and supported. Like love, faith lays hold of the whole man and transforms him; it is not blind or unintelligent: it trusts because it knows and has experience; it holds the key to obedience; such is its power over the springs of moral action, that 'whatsoever is not of faith is sin' (14 23). Christianity is the life of faith.

(3) **In relation to the Spirit.** If the Christian life upon its human side is a life of faith, on its divine side it is life in the Spirit of God, in the Spirit of Christ, in the same Holy Spirit who of old spake in prophecy, in Scripture, and in conscience. The Spirit is the motive-power of the Christian life, quickening its perceptions and faculties, flooding the heart with the love of God, identifying Himself with the believer's spirit, and witnessing with it that it is the true child of God the Father, helping us to pray, pleading with the Father, bringing Christ into the soul to mingle with it. ' As many as are led by the Spirit of God, these are sons of God ' (8 14). ' If any man hath not the Spirit of Christ, he is none of His ' (8 9). The higher instincts of men belong to the Spirit, and are divine; the kingdom of God on earth 'is not eating and drinking, but righteousness and peace and joy in the Holy Spirit' (14 17). Christian virtues are fruits of the indwelling Spirit. The work of grace is its unresting activity.

(4) **In relation to Society.** In chs. 12–15 the Apostle pours out from the treasury of his experience and reflection, ethical precepts and exhortations which glance like jewels in their spiritual brilliancy. Every aspect of the Christian character, every phase of the life in Christ, is here reflected. In the power of the Spirit, in the righteousness which is through faith, the Christian is to be modest, humble, sincere, patient, cheerful, sympathetic, merciful, generous, hospitable (c. 12). Remembering the death of his Lord for all, he will not live for himself, but sacrifice himself for others, deny himself innocent pleasures and lawful rights rather than lead a weak brother into temptation, or set a stumbling-block in his path (c. 14). He will not succumb to evil, not try to overcome evil with evil. He will eschew anger and revenge, will bless his persecutors, and feed his enemy (c. 12). As a citizen he will loyally recognise the lawful and divinely appointed authority of the ruling powers which restrain evil-doers, and encourage well-doing ; he will not withhold from them taxes, customs, fear, and honour (13 1-7). As a member of the Church, the one body in Christ, he will play his part diligently, in a fervent spirit serving the Lord; he will exercise his own spiritual gifts, and respect the varying gifts of others, whether prophecy, ministering, teaching, exhortation, ruling, or contributing to the temporal needs of the Church (12 6-8); he will by every means in his power help on his brethren, love them for Christ's sake, and encourage them in the Christian life, bear their infirmities (15 1), be slow to judge them (14 10-13), live in peace and harmony with them, avoid causes of stumbling and division in doctrine and practice (16 17).

(5) **In relation to Oneself.** The Christian will honour himself and keep himself pure. Remembering that Christ died for him and for sin, he will present his body a living sacrifice, holy, acceptable to God, in reasonable service (12 1). He will restrain his fleshly nature watchfully; keep the commandments ; culti-

vate the spiritual side of his nature resolutely, even at the expense of the bodily ; enter into the life of Christ, abhorring evil, cleaving to good. He will strive not to be fashioned according to this world, but to be transformed by the renewing of his mind into the image of God's Son, so proving God's good and perfect will (12²). As one who shall stand before the judgment-seat of God (14¹⁰), and who knows that the consummation of God's saving work draws nearer (13¹¹), and that the night

preceding the great day is far spent, he will put slumber far from him, and cast off the works of darkness, and put on the armour of light (13¹¹⁻¹⁴). Under difficulties he will be of good courage, assured that to those who love God all things work together for good (8²⁸). He is Christ's ; he has the Spirit dwelling in him ; he is the child of the Father in heaven. These things he cannot forget—his personal life is shaped by them, guided by the One Spirit.

Summary of the Epistle

The subject of the Epistle is the meaning and power of the gospel, i.e. God's message to man of salvation through faith in Jesus Christ, for Jew and Gentile alike.

I. Chs. 1–8. The Divine Way of Acceptance with God.

1¹⁻¹⁷. After an introduction fitted to engage the attention and sympathy of the Roman Christians (1¹⁻¹⁵), St. Paul sets down the subject of the Epistle. It is the gospel which works a moral miracle among men by proclaiming a state of acceptance with God, offered to all as a free gift, on the sole condition of faith (1¹⁶ᶠ·).

1¹⁸⁻3²⁰. St. Paul shows that all men need salvation. Both Gentile and Jew have sinned, though God has given each a law of life ; and each will be judged by the law he has (1¹⁸⁻2²⁹). In spite of his privileges, the Jew needs salvation as much as the Gentile, as his moral condition shows (3¹⁻²⁰).

3²¹⁻²⁶. The need of sinful man has been met by the love of God. Christ has shed His blood as an offering to God for man's redemption. Thereby God's holy displeasure against sin has been manifested, and all who join in that offering by self-surrendering faith in Christ are received by God into a state of acceptance.

4¹⁻5²¹. Reasons why men should welcome this way of salvation. (1) It is in harmony with God's dealings in the past. Acceptance with God has always been on account of faith (4¹⁻²⁵). (2) It brings to men peace and joy and everlasting security (5¹⁻¹¹). (3) By transferring us into relationship with Christ, it more than abolishes the evil effects of sin and death which we have derived from our former relationship with Adam (5¹²⁻²¹).

6¹⁻8³⁰. The power of the gospel. It does not merely provide against the consequences of sin. By his faith in Christ a believer is changed. He becomes so vitally united with Christ in His death and life that the man he used to be is dead, and his heart is joined with Christ in communion with God (6¹⁻²³).

Nothing else would do this. So evil is man's nature that even the holy law only emphasises the fact of his slavery to sin (7¹⁻²³). But the man who has faith in Christ is freed from slavery by a greater power than himself. The Spirit of Christ has entered into him, and the Spirit within overpowers the sin in his flesh, will deliver his body from the grave, and makes him God's son and heir of God's glory. Thus, in all his troubles, the Christian is secure in the divine love of Christ (8¹⁻³⁹).

II. Chs. 9–11. God's Way of Acceptance vindicated. St. Paul feels that some might object— The Messiah, and the blessings of His kingdom, were promised by God to Israel. But Israel as a whole has rejected Jesus, and is outside His kingdom. Therefore, if Jesus be the Messiah, God has broken His word to Israel ; which cannot be thought of.

He answers—God never bound Himself to Israel as a race. He has always claimed the right to select some descendants of Abraham to be His instruments, and to reject others (9¹⁻²¹). Yet He has been merciful to Israel, who have fallen by their wilfulness (9²²⁻10²¹). However, Israel's fall is partial and temporary, the disobedience of both Gentiles and Jews was reckoned with in God's purpose, and He will bring the Jews, finally, into His kingdom (11¹⁻³⁶).

III. Chs. 12–16. The Practical Life acceptable to God. In chs. 12 f. St. Paul points out the life of love and obedience which is the Christian's true sacrifice, and which would commend Christianity to the people of Rome and to the rulers of the empire.

In chs. 14 f. he enjoins love and tolerance between the Jewish and Gentile sections of the Roman Church (14¹⁻15¹³). He hopes to visit Rome after a visit to Jerusalem undertaken in the furtherance of unity (15¹⁴⁻²⁹), for which he asks their prayers (15³⁰⁻³³).

C. 16. In the midst of personal greetings occurs a warning (16¹⁷⁻²⁰) against hostile teachers, probably Jewish, whose appearance at Rome he expected.

CHAPTER 1

THE POWER OF THE GOSPEL AND THE NEED OF THE WORLD. THE GUILT OF THE HEATHEN

In his salutation the apostle emphasises his commission, and the greatness of the Person whose servant he is and who is the centre of his message (vv. 1–7). After expressing his desire to visit the Romans (vv. 8–15), he states the subject of his Epistle, viz. acceptance with God through faith in Jesus Christ (vv. 16, 17), and proceeds to develop it by showing that none have been able to merit acceptance with God. He begins by proving this of the Gentiles (vv. 18–32).

1–7. The Salutation.

Paraphrase. '(1) I, Paul, who write am a bondservant of Christ, set apart by God as an apostle to proclaim that message of good news (2) which was promised by His prophets. (3) The subject of the message is His Son, of David's lineage by human descent, (4) but, as regards His spiritual being, shown to be Son of God by the divine power exercised in His Resurrection. (5) Since, through Christ, I was brought into God's favour, and commissioned to be apostle to the Gentiles, (6) and that you at Rome, whom Christ has chosen, are Gentiles ; (7) therefore I write to you, praying that God may grant you His blessings.'

1. Servant] A title used in the OT. of those devoted to a special work for God : cp. Josh 24 29 Ps 36 (title) Jer 7 25 Dan 9 11 Zech 3 8. St. Paul claims a similar place in the New Covenant. **Servant of Jesus Christ**] cp. OT. expression 'servant of God' ; one of many undesigned testimonies to the Apostle's belief in the divinity of Christ : cp. 9 5 10 12.

Called] i.e. chosen by Christ. He emphasises this, because a party of Judaising Christians, who opposed the doctrine of salvation by faith, and held that circumcision was of perpetual obligation, denied his apostleship : cp. 1 Cor 9 1 f. Gal 1 1 : see Intro. Gal. **Apostle**] see on 16 7. **Separated**] cp. Ac 13 2 Gal 1 15.

3. David] Thus fulfilling prophecies, as Isa 11 1, and the expectation of the Jews (cp. Mk 12 35 Jn 7 42) that the Messiah would be descended from David : cp. Mt 1 1-17 Lk 3 23-32.

4. Declared] cp. Ac 13 33. **Son of God**] For St. Paul's teaching on the person of Christ cp. 8 3, 32 9 5 2 Cor 4 4 8 9 Phil 2 6 Col 1 15 f. 2 9.

With power] i.e. by a display of divine power. The Resurrection was a miracle : cp. 2 Cor 13 4 Eph 1 19 f. **According to**] i.e. as regards. **Spirit of holiness**] Not the Holy Spirit, but Christ's human spirit ' in which the Divinity or Divine Personality resided ' (Sanday and Headlam). **By the resurrection**] As His words and works marked Him out as more than mere man (cp. Mt 16 16), so did the

Resurrection. Notice the confidence and the emphasis with which the apostles proclaimed the Resurrection of Christ as being a certain fact, and as proving the truth of the gospel : see on 4 25 Ac 1 22 2 24 f. 17 18, 31, etc.

5. Grace] In Acts and Epistles this word usually means the unmerited favour of God, shown (1) in forgiveness and salvation, cp. 3 24 Eph 1 7 ; as opposed to debt, cp. 4 4, to works, cp. 11 6 Eph 2 8 f., and to law, cp. Gal 2 21 ; (2) in the call of the Gentiles, cp. Eph 3 2 f. ; (3) in special gifts of calling to and fitness for Christian work, cp. 12 6 15 15 1 Cor 3 10 Gal 2 9 Eph 4 7 f. Here 'grace' means the Christian standing generally, to which is added in Paul's case the distinctive gift of apostleship. **For obedience to the faith**] RV 'unto obedience of faith,' i.e. to win that obedience which is connected with faith : cp. 16 26. **Nations**] RV 'the nations,' i.e. Gentiles : cp. v. 13, Gal 1 16 2 7 f. **Name**] RV 'name's sake,' i.e. the Apostle works for the sake of Christ, and to promote His glory. The name of God is what God has revealed about Himself : cp. Ex 34 5 f. Mt 28 19.

7. Called to be **saints**] lit. 'summoned saints.' 'Saint' means 'consecrated to God' : cp. Ex 22 31. In this sense all Christians are saints : cp. 1 Pet 2 9.

8–15. The Apostle greatly desires to visit Rome.

Paraphrase. '(8) I thank God that your faith is so well known. (9) I constantly pray about you, (10) asking that God may permit me soon to visit you. (11) For I long to impart to you some spiritual benefit, (12) in fact that we may be mutually helped by each other's faith. (13) I have often planned a visit, although I have been prevented, for (14) all Gentiles, of whatever race, lie within the sphere of my duty. (15) Therefore, so far as the decision rests with me, I am eager to preach the gospel to you.'

9. Serve] The Gk. word is used of the worship of God by people or priest. St. Paul's work of preaching the gospel was a priestly service, in which he offered the Gentiles as a sacrifice to God : cp. 15 16. **With**] RV 'in.' **10. Have a prosperous journey**] RV 'be prospered.' He knew his journey to Jerusalem would be dangerous, cp. 15 30, but did not foresee that he would visit Rome as a prisoner : cp. Ac 27 24. **11. Spiritual gift**] The term is sometimes used of the special endowments which accompanied the reception of the Holy Spirit : cp. 1 Cor 12–14. The meaning here is that St. Paul hopes the Romans may increase in faith and love through his teaching and influence. **Established**] i.e. strengthened in faith and other virtues. **12.** The Apostle will not assume superiority. **13. Let**] RV 'hindered,' i.e. by more pressing calls : cp.

15 22 f. **14. Greeks**] The Roman Christians
were Greek-speaking for 250 years. To the
Greek and Roman, all the rest of the world
was barbarian. **15. In me**] Emphasis on 'me';
God might will otherwise. St. Paul was going
to Jerusalem, and felt that his life would be
in danger : cp. 15 25 f. Ac 20 22 f.

16, 17. The main subject of the Epistle—
Righteousness by Faith.

Paraphrase. '(16) I am not ashamed to
preach the message of Christ even in great
Rome, for it is the divine power whereby
God brings salvation to all who have faith in
Christ. (17) For in it is revealed that God
accepts men as righteous solely on the condition of faith, as is shown in the OT.'

16. Ashamed] cp. 1 Cor 1 23 f. **Salvation**] i.e.
deliverance from dangers or enemies. So it
signified the deliverance which the Messiah
would bring : cp. Lk 1 69-71. Here it is such as
belongs to a spiritual kingdom ; and is from
'sin,' cp. Mt 1 21 Lk 1 77 ; from ' wrath,' cp. 5 9;
from 'the grave,' cp. 13 11; and to 'eternal
life,' cp. Jn 3 15 f. As regards conversion and
baptism, Christians ' were ' or ' are saved,' cp.
8 24 (RV), Eph 2 5, 8 2 Tim 1 9 ; as recipients of
God's favour and blessing, Christians are
'being saved,' cp. Ac 2 47 (RV), 1 Cor 1 18 (RV);
as regards future glory, Christians ' will be
saved,' cp. 13 11 Mt 10 22. **Believeth**] i.e. who
devotes and entrusts himself to Christ as his
Lord and Saviour. **The Jew first**] to whom
the Messiah was promised and from whom He
came. **Greek**] i.e. any one not a Jew = Gentile. **17. The righteousness of God**] RV 'a
righteousness of God.' A state of righteousness, or acceptance with God, to which man
could not attain by his own efforts, but which
God bestows upon him of His free grace.

From faith to faith] RV 'by faith unto
faith,' i.e. given, on condition of faith, to those
who have faith : cp. 3 22. **Just**] RV 'righteous.' The quotation is from Hab 2 4, which
referred to preservation from the calamities of
the Chaldean invasion. The principle is that
it is faith which gains God's approval.

18-32. The Apostle has briefly stated God's
offer of righteousness in the Christian message. He now proceeds to show that all men
have failed to attain acceptance with God
by other means. First he speaks of the Gentiles. They lie under God's wrath on account
of their unrighteousness (v. 18). They might
have had a knowledge of God (vv. 19, 20),
but have turned away to idolatry (vv. 21–23),
and are sunk, in consequence, in moral corruption (vv. 24–32).

Paraphrase. '(18) The need of such a method
of salvation is evident when we consider how
mankind has always suppressed the truth within
and lived in wickedness. For them wrath, not
righteousness, is revealed. (19) For instance,

God has made Himself known to the Gentiles ;
(20) for His power and divinity are so clearly
impressed upon the visible creation that they
cannot plead ignorance. (21) They had a
revelation of God, but instead of worshipping
Him aright, they became so involved in useless
speculations about His nature, that they lost
the sense of truth and right. (22) Their
conceit led to such idolatrous folly (23), that
they regarded an image of man or beast as
a fitting representation of the majesty of
God. (24–27) Therefore God gave them over
to the degradation which was the result of their
apostasy. (28–31) Their rejection of the
true idea of God was followed, as a penal
consequence, by depravity and every kind of
sin. (32) So great is their wickedness, that
although they know the guilt of such sins, they
not only commit them, but approve of them
in others.'

18. Wrath] i.e. the steadfast indignation of
God against sin. God 'would not love good
unless He hated evil, the two being inseparable' (Trench). **Revealed**] by the state to
which sin had brought the Gentile world, and
by God's revelation of a coming day of wrath
cp. 2 5. **Hold**] RV 'hold down,' i.e. suppress. **19. Known . . in them**] i.e. nature
teaches a knowledge of God, and man has the
faculty of receiving the teaching. **20. From**]
RV 'since.' **By**] RV 'through.' **Godhead**]
RV 'divinity.'

21. Vain] i.e. foolish, empty. **Imaginations**] RV 'reasonings,' i.e. about God.

23. Changed] i.e. exchanged. **Glory**] i.e.
the manifested power and goodness of God.
Into] RV 'for.' **Man**] as in Greece and
Rome, where even immorality was ascribed
to the gods. **Birds, etc.**] as in Egypt.

24. Gave them up] Those who forsake God,
forsake Him who restrains evil and inspires
good. Further, one sin leads to another, by
natural consequence which is God's law : cp.
Ps 81 12 Ac 7 42. So the idolatry of success,
money, pleasure, and luxury, often leads to
gambling, dishonesty, and vice.

25. Who] RV 'for that they.' **Changed**]
RV 'exchanged.' **Truth of God**] i.e. the true
idea of God. **Into a lie**] RV 'for a lie,' i.e.
for an idol, a false conception of God. **More**]
RV 'rather.'

26. Affections] RV 'passions.'

28. Convenient] RV 'fitting.'

29. Debate] RV 'strife.' **Whisperers**] i.e.
secret slanderers.

30. Despiteful] RV 'insolent.' **Proud**] RV
'haughty.'

32. Knowing] i.e. by conscience. **Judgment**] RV 'ordinance.' **Have pleasure in**]
RV 'consent with.' A sign of ' complete victory
over conscience, and complete callousness to
the moral ruin of others' (Moule).

CHAPTER 2

THE FAILURE OF THE JEWS

In c. 1 St. Paul showed that the Gentiles were under God's judgment on account of sin. Now he is about to turn to the Jews. He asserts first, that God's judgment will fall impartially upon all sinners (vv. 1–11). Each man will be judged by the light which he has (vv. 12–16). The privileges and knowledge of the Jews only aggravated the guilt of their flagrant disobedience (vv. 17–24) ; and circumcision would not protect them, for God looks at the heart and life (vv. 25–29).

1–11. The Jew would agree in condemning the sins mentioned in c. 1, yet he himself was equally guilty, and must be judged, like the Gentiles, by his deeds, whether good or bad.

Note. There is no contradiction here to the doctrine of justification by faith, for (1) St. Paul is speaking of men apart from the gospel ; (2) 'faith is present in a more or less rudimentary state in every upward effort or aspiration of man' (Hort, quoted by Gore); (3) good works are the fruit and evidence of faith.

Paraphrase. '(1) Perhaps you condemn such sinners. In doing so, you condemn yourself, for you too are guilty. (2) We all know that God's judgment against evildoers is unerring and impartial. (3) Do you think you are different from others, and exempt from judgment ? (4) or do you think God is too kind to punish you, not understanding that His kindness is meant to move you to repent ? (5) Seeing that you do not repent, you are daily incurring a heavier judgment. (6) For God will judge every man by his deeds, (7–10) whether he be Jew or Gentile, giving eternal life to those who do good, while there will be wrath for all who persist in evil ; (11) for God judges impartially.'

1. Inexcusable] RV ' without excuse ' : cp. 1²⁰. **Judges]** cp. Gal 2¹⁵. **The same things]** of the same kind, if not so glaring. **2. Are sure]** RV ' know,' i.e. by reason and revelation. **5. After]** i.e. in accordance with. **Against]** RV ' in.' **8. Contentions]** RV ' factions,' i.e. upholding their ideas and traditions against God's voice : cp. Jn 5⁴⁴.

Indignation] RV ' shall be indignation.' **9. Jew first]** privilege increases responsibility. **11. Respect of persons]** i.e. regard for the outward circumstances of a man instead of his real character ; here of the partiality of an unjust judge : cp. Ac 10³⁴ Gal 2⁶ Eph 6⁹ Col 3²⁵ Jas 2¹.

12–16. All men are under a law of some kind, whether revealed law or the light of nature ; and by the law that they have they will be judged.

Paraphrase. '(12) I say God is impartial, for He will punish every man who sins against the light, whether, as with Gentiles, it be the light of conscience, or, as in the case of the Jews, the light of law. (13) It is not because a man has a law, but because he keeps it that he will be justified. (14) This applies to Gentiles as well as Jews. For Gentiles have an inner law of nature, as is shown by their good deeds, (15) which testify to a sense of right and wrong ; their conscience shows the same thing ; and so does the fact that they blame or praise one another's actions. (16) By this law they will be judged at the last.'

12. Without law] i.e. without a revealed law of right and wrong. **In the law]** RV ' under law.' **By the law]** RV ' by law.' The expression ' the law ' means the Law of Moses : 'law,' without the article, means law in general, ' the will of God for man's conduct.' St. Paul regards the pre-Messianic period as essentially a period of law, both for Jew and for Gentile ' (Sanday and Headlam). **13. The law]** RV ' a law.' **Justified]** i.e. declared righteous at the Judgment. **14. Not the law]** RV ' no law.' **By nature]** i.e. without a revelation.

15. Which] RV ' in that they.' **The work of the law]** i.e. the effect of the law in marking what is right from what is wrong.

Conscience] the faculty by which we reflect upon the character of our actions. It may be more or less enlightened, cp. 1 Cor 8⁷,¹⁰ᶠ·; it may become corrupt through sin, cp. Tit 1¹⁵, and give no light, cp. Mt 6²³. Therefore a man's appeal to conscience is not decisive, unless he has taken pains to inform it and keep it pure. **16. My gospel]** i.e. the message I am commissioned to preach : cp. 16²⁵ 2 Tim 2⁸. Judgment by Christ is a distinctive doctrine of the gospel : cp. Mt 25³¹ᶠ· Ac 17³¹ 1 Cor 4⁵ 2 Cor 5¹⁰.

17–24. Here, first, the Jew is expressly addressed. He relied upon God's favour and his knowledge of God's will. Yet his wickedness was a matter of common knowledge. (St. Paul is speaking generally ; there were bright exceptions.)

Paraphrase. '(17) I turn to the Jew, proud of his religious superiority, (18) and of the knowledge of God's will and the high ideal of conduct which he derives from the Law of Moses, (19, 20) thinking that he is in the light and all other peoples in darkness. (21–23) How shameful, then, is the conduct which is so contrary to his profession, (24) and which brings such dishonour upon the name of God among the heathen !'

17. Jew] the national name. **Restest in]** RV ' restest upon,' i.e. feeling secure of God's favour from the mere possession of the Law. **Of God]** i.e. as peculiarly bound to the Jew. **18. Approvest, etc.]** i.e. able to distinguish delicately between the more and the less good.

20. Form] i.e. perfect embodiment.
21. Cp. Mt3 7 Mk12 40 Jn8 7.   **22. Commit sacrilege**] RV 'rob temples': cp. Ac19 37.
24. Cp. Isa52 5 Ezk36 21 f.

25-29. The Jew thought that because he was circumcised, i.e. a member of the covenant people, he was sure of God's favour. But circumcision implied a surrendered life, which is the only thing acceptable to God.

Paraphrase. '(25) You trust in circumcision, and it is good to be a Jew; but if you are not obedient to God's Law, you are no better than an uncircumcised heathen, (26) while a heathen who, according to his lights, does what your law requires will be accepted by God although he is uncircumcised, (27) and will be in a superior position to you, seeing that you break the Law in spite of your advantages. (28) For the true people of God are those who are so, not by race or profession only, (29) but by obedience of heart and life. They may not be called Jews, but they are praised by God.'

25. Profiteth] cp. 3 1 f. 9 1 f. **Keep**] i.e. as a habit, opposed to habitual transgression.
26. The uncircumcision] i.e. the uncircumcised man. **Righteousness**] RV 'ordinances': cp. Ac10 35. **27. Judge**] cp. v. 1. **By the letter**] RV 'with the letter,' i.e. with written law. **28.** Cp. 9 6 f. Phil 3 3. **29. Heart**] cp. Dt10 16 Ac7 51. **Letter**] i.e. outward conformity to the literal command, contrasted with the spiritual change which it represented.
Praise] The word 'Jew' is derived from 'Judah,' which means 'praised': cp. Gn29 35.

CHAPTER 3
The New Way of Acceptance with God

In chs. 1 and 2 St. Paul has shown that both Gentile and Jew have sinned wilfully, and are under God's condemnation. He now digresses to Jewish objections against the gospel, which he had, no doubt, heard urged in synagogues (vv. 1–8). Returning to the main subject, he clinches his indictment of the Jew out of the Scriptures, and concludes that all the world is 'under the judgment of God' (vv. 9–20).

Having thus shown that man is sinful and lost, he now proceeds to set forth the gospel. God has provided a way by which acceptance, springing from God's love, and secured by the redemptive work of Christ, is granted to all who have faith in Christ (vv. 21–26). Thus acceptance depends upon faith, not upon human merit (vv. 27, 28), and is open to all (vv. 29, 30). At the same time, faith leads to true obedience (v. 31).

1-8. Jewish objections answered.
Paraphrase. '(1) You may say: If those only are God's people who are so inwardly and spiritually, what advantage is it to be a Jew? (2) I reply: Much; to begin with, God's Word with its precious promises was entrusted to them. (3) And since that is so, will God break His word because some have shown their want of faith by rejecting Christ? (4) Impossible! Whoever be false, God will be found true, His promises will be justified and His conduct vindicated. (5) You may say: If this be so, our sin in rejecting Christ has made God's faithfulness to His promises clear, and it is unjust of Him (humanly speaking) to punish us. (6) I reply: Horrible! On your grounds no sin would be punished. (7) If you plead: This is an exceptional case. My sin has glorified God by showing how He keeps His word: (8) why should I not be accepted by Him equally with the Christians who say, as I say, let us do evil that good may come? I can only reply: Such a principle is to be condemned, and to impute it to us is slanderous.'

2. Much] cp. 9 4 f. **Oracles**] i.e. the utterances of God in the OT. **3. Did not believe**] RV 'were without faith.' **Unbelief**] RV 'want of faith.' **Faith**] RV 'faithfulness.' **4. God forbid**] lit. 'let it not be.' **Written**] Ps51 4. **Art judged**] RV 'comest into judgment.'
5. Taketh vengeance] RV 'visiteth with wrath.' **As a man**] RV 'after the manner of men,' i.e. speaking of the dealings of God as if they were the dealings of men: cp. Gal3 15.
7. For] RV 'but.' **8. Evil**] St. Paul said, 'We are not justified because of what we do.' His adversaries represented him as saying, 'It does not matter what we do': cp. v. 31, 6 1, 15. **Whose, etc.**] i.e. those who hold such a principle as 'let us do evil,' etc., will be condemned, and that justly. **Damnation**] RV 'condemnation.'

9-20. Jewish Scriptures testify to Jewish sin.
Paraphrase. '(9) What follows then? We Jews have advantages over the Gentiles, but are we better than they? By no means. The charge I laid was against Jew as well as Gentile, that both are under the power of sin. (10–18) The Scriptures make the same charge, Psalmist and Prophet alike speak of universal corruption. (19) Such passages exclude self-justification on the part of the Jews, and prove the guilt of mankind against God. (20) This must always be so; weak, sinful man can never attain to acceptance with God through obedience to law; law, since it is never kept, cannot secure righteousness, it can only convict of sin.'

9. Proved] RV 'laid to the charge.'
10-18. From Pss5 9 10 7 14 1 f. 36 1 140 3 Isa59 7 f.
19. Them who are under the law] i.e. the Jews. **Become guilty before**] RV 'be brought under the judgment of.'

20. Therefore] RV 'because.' **The deeds of the law]** RM 'works of law,' i.e. done to merit salvation by fulfilling an appointed task: cp. 7⁷ᶠ. Gal 3¹⁹,²¹. 'Law is a factor in the moral life fitted to acquaint the intellect with the divine standard of conduct, but incapable of bringing the life of man into harmony with its precepts' (Robertson, HDB.). **No flesh]** cp. Ps 143².

21-26. The way of acceptance declared in the Christian message is independent of law (v. 21), a free gift from God through faith in Christ (vv. 22–24), and made possible because Christ's death was propitiatory (vv. 25, 26).

Paraphrase. '(21) We have seen that by obedience to law none can enter into acceptance with God because none have rendered it. Now a way of acceptance has been revealed which has nothing to do with law, to which both Law and Prophets bear witness. (22) God accepts all, without distinction, who have devoted their hearts to Jesus Christ. (23) I say all, and the want is universal. All alike have sinned, and feel far off from God. (24) But God's gracious favour is such, that He accepts them without question of merit, through the deliverance from sin and its penalty which Christ purchased, and which we receive by union with Him. (25) For on the Cross He offered up His life, to restore to the favour of God all who by faith appropriate that offering. In that awful spectacle God manifested His righteous displeasure against sin, forbidding us to attribute to indifference the forbearance by which He passed over, without adequate punishment, sins committed before Christ came. (26) In the death of Christ He so then displayed, I say, His judgment against sin, that now the perfect holiness of His character is vindicated, and He can also accept those who have faith in Jesus.'

21. Now] i.e. under the gospel. **The righteousness, etc.]** RV 'apart from the law a righteousness of God hath been manifested': cp. 1¹⁷. 'A righteousness of God,' i.e. a way of acceptance which God has provided. **Manifested]** i.e. in the Person and work of Christ: cp. 2 Tim 1¹⁰. **Witnessed]** i.e. by types and promises. **22. Faith of]** RV 'faith in': cp. Gal 2¹⁶. This further defines the 'righteousness' spoken of. The means by which it is received is faith in Christ, and it is given to all who have such faith. Faith is 'man's trustful acceptance of God's gift, rising to absolute self-surrender, culminating in personal union with Christ, working within .. as a spirit of new life' (Farrar, 'St. Paul,' p. 473). **Difference]** RV 'distinction.'

23. Come short] The Gk. word, which means 'to feel one's need,' is that used in Lk 15¹⁴ of the Prodigal. **Glory of God]** i.e. the divine perfection, which is manifested in Christ

(cp. 2 Cor 4⁶), and which shines upon man and transfigures him into the likeness of Christ. partially now, and completely hereafter: cp 8¹⁸ 2 Cor 3¹⁸ 1 Jn 3².

24. Justified] i.e. declared or accounted righteous, as by a judge; accepted: refers to 'them that believe,' v. 22. God can justly declare a sinner righteous who has faith in Christ because his face is turned to the light; he is in sympathy with Christ, and desires to follow His example. **Grace]** see on 1⁵. **Redemption]** 'Redemption' means, (1) deliverance from bondage by payment of ransom: cp. Lv 25⁴⁸; (2) deliverance in general, as of Israel from Egypt: cp. Ex 6⁶. Christ redeemed us from sin and its penalties: cp. 8²³ Eph 1⁷ Col 1¹⁴. The ransom was His life, not considered as paid to any one, but as the price which it cost Him to procure our deliverance (cp. Mk 10⁴⁵ 1 Tim 2⁶) and to restore us to God: cp. 1 Cor 6²⁰ 7²²ᶠ. **In Christ Jesus]** see paraphrase. The form 'Christ Jesus' (not 'Jesus Christ') always refers to the glorified Christ.

25. Propitiation] i.e. that which makes it possible for God to be propitious, or favourable to man. **In his blood]** RV 'by his blood,' i.e. Christ became a propitiation by shedding His blood. **Declare]** RV 'shew,' for, otherwise, it might have been doubted. **For the remission, etc.]** RV 'because of the passing over of the sins done aforetime': cp. Ac 17³⁰. 'Passing over,' i.e. temporary suspension of punishment (Sanday and Headlam). **Forbearance]** i.e. temporary suspension of anger.

27-31. Since salvation is by faith, it follows that no claim can be made on the ground of human merit (vv. 27, 28), that Jew and Gentile are on the same footing (vv. 29, 30), and that law becomes fulfilled at last (v. 31).

Paraphrase. '(27) It is plain that the gospel way of salvation by faith leaves no room for reliance upon privilege or merits, (28) for man is accepted through reliance upon his Saviour, not upon himself. (29) It is also plain that Jew and Gentile are on the same footing before God, (30) for there is one God for all, and He accepts all men on the same condition, viz. faith. (31) Some say that by preaching salvation through faith alone we abolish law. On the contrary, we set the principle that God's will must be done on a firmer basis.'

27. Boasting] cp. 2¹, ²³. **The law]** RV 'a law,' i.e. system. **28. Therefore]** RM 'for.' **Without]** RV 'apart from.' **30. Circumcision]** i.e. Jews. **Uncircumcision]** i.e. Gentiles.

By .. through] The Judaistic Christians seem to have held that they were justified on account of ('by') circumcision and obedience to the Law, if they had faith ('through faith'); but that Gentiles were justified on account of ('by') faith, if, in addition, they were circumcised and obeyed the Law ('through law'). St. Paul rejoins that justification depends on faith alone ; Jew and Gentile alike are justified both 'by' and 'through' faith : cp. v. 28, Gal 2 16. **31. The law**] RM 'law.' God's will is brought out more fully in the gospel (cp. Mt 5 17 f.), and the believer is enabled to fulfil it : cp. 6, 8 4 Gal 2 19 f.

CHAPTER 4
ACCEPTANCE BY FAITH FORESHADOWED IN THE OLD DISPENSATION

In 3 21 f. St. Paul set forth the great truth of acceptance by faith. A Jew might object that it was new, and therefore not true. In 3 31 St. Paul answered that in the Law and in faith there is the same moral and religious ideal, which is more completely developed and more perfectly fulfilled by faith. Now he turns to the past, to show that acceptance by faith is not a new idea. It was faith for which Abraham was accepted, not works (vv. 1–8), nor circumcision (vv. 9–12), nor on account of obedience to the Law (vv. 13–17). The history shows the nature of the faith which God accepts (vv. 18–22), in our case as well as in Abraham's.

1–8. It was faith, not works, for which Abraham was accepted.

Paraphrase. '(1) Take, e.g., the case of Abraham. His descendants should readily admit the force of his case, which shows that acceptance by faith is no new principle. (2) If he had been accepted on account of his deeds, he would have had something to be proud of in man's sight. And we men do honour him, and rightly. Yet even then he could not claim merit before God. (3) For the Scripture says that it was on account of his faith that he was reckoned as righteous. (4) Now reward for work would not be so spoken of. There is no favour in paying wages that are due. (5) Such an expression as "his faith is reckoned for righteousness" is only properly used of one who makes no claim for work done, but simply puts faith in God. (6–8) Notice, too, how David pronounced a man happy, although he had sinned deeply, simply because God forgave him and reckoned him as righteous.'

1. What .. then] refers to 3 27 f. **That**] RM 'of.' **As pertaining to the flesh**] i.e. by natural descent. The question is put in the mouth of a Jew. Therefore it does not follow that the Roman Christians were chiefly Jews. Cp. also 1 Cor 10 1, 'our fathers,' though the Corinthian Christians were mostly Gentile.

Hath found] RM omits.

2. Abraham] St. James also refers to Gn 15 6, but concludes 'that by works a man is justified, and not by faith only,' Jas 2 23 f. St. James wrote of mere intellectual belief: cp.

Jas 2 19. St. Paul meant by 'faith' a complete change of relation towards God, which would affect the believer's actions: cp. c. 6. Gn 15 6 was a common text for discussion among the Jews. Possibly St. James was thinking of perversions of St. Paul's teaching. **Glory**] cp. 3 27.

3, 5. Counted] RV 'reckoned.' **4. Worketh**] i.e. a workman in daily life. **5. Worketh not**] i.e. as ground of acceptance. **Ungodly**] not meant of Abraham ; the extreme case is put : cp. 5 6. **6. Describeth, etc.**] RV 'pronounceth blessing upon.' **Imputeth**] RV 'reckoneth.' **Without**] RV 'apart from.'

7. Blessed] i.e. happy ; from Ps 32 1 f.

9–12. The blessing was not dependent upon circumcision, to which as signifying admission to covenant with God, the Jews attach such importance.

Paraphrase. '(9) Again. The blessing was irrespective of circumcision. (10) For at the time that Abraham's faith was reckoned for righteousness, he was uncircumcised. (11) His circumcision was but a token, by which God sealed that acceptance which was his as a believing man. Hence, all Gentiles who believe are his spiritual children, and have righteousness reckoned to them. (12) And those Jews are his children who are not merely circumcised, but believe as he believed.'

9. *Cometh*] RV 'Is this blessing then pronounced.' **10.** Abraham's faith preceded circumcision by many years : cp. Gn 15 6 17 10, 24. **11. Sign**] cp. Gn 17 11, 'a token of the covenant.' **Seal**] ratifying his acceptance. **Imputed**] RV 'reckoned.'

13–17. The promise was independent of any system of law.

Paraphrase. '(13) Again. The promise to Abraham of world-wide inheritance was not to take effect by obedience to law. (14) For if the inheritance be for those who keep a law, then faith has lost its value, and the promise has been nullified. (15) For the effect of law, which reveals the requirements of a righteous God, is to bring about, not blessing, but consciousness of sin and expectation of God's wrath ; transgression cannot exist without some law to be broken. (16) Therefore acceptance was made to depend upon faith, that it might proceed from God's bounty not our merit, and that all Abraham's descendants might be certain of obtaining the promise. And by his descendants I mean, not Jews only, but all those who have the faith which he had. (17) For in spite of his old age, he fully believed God who promised him seed, and God has made him the father of all who believe in Jesus Christ.'

13. Heir of the world] i.e. by the universality of the reign of Christ: cp. Gn 12 2 f. 22 17 f.

14. Void] because an opposite condition would have been brought in : cp. Gal 3 18.
15. Cp. 3 20. **For where]** RV ' but where.'
16. By grace] RV ' according to grace,' i e. on the principle of free gift. **Sure]** because, (1) not depending on the fulfilment of a law which would certainly be broken, and (2) admitting Jew and Gentile by the same gate of faith. **Of the law]** i.e. believing Jews. **Abraham]** who was not under the Law. **Us all]** i.e. Christians, from 'many nations.'
17. Father] cp. Gn 17 5. **Before . . God]** i.e. God regards Abraham as father of all believers. **Quickeneth]** i.e. makes alive. When God promised Isaac, Abraham, and Sarah were as though dead : cp. v. 19. **Calleth]** i.e. summons. **Which be not]** i.e. the promised seed.
18–22. It was because Abraham's faith was so unwavering, that it was reckoned unto him for righteousness.
Paraphrase. '(18) His confident faith, when it was against human probability that God's promise of a son should be realised, led to the fulfilment of the promise. (19) His faith did not fail at the apparent impossibility. (20) Fixing his eye on God's promise, he received fresh youth, acknowledging God's power and truth (21) with complete certainty. (22) And because his faith was unwavering, God accepted it as though it were righteousness.'
18. Believed in hope] i.e. had confident faith. **That he might]** RV ' to the end that he might.' **So]** i.e. as the stars : cp. Gn 15 5.
19. Being not weak] RV ' without being weakened.' **Considered not]** RV ' considered,' i.e. he realised his weakness, but still believed. **Dead]** RV ' as good as dead.' **20.** RV ' yea, looking unto the promise of God, he wavered not through unbelief, but waxed strong through faith.' **21. Persuaded]** RV ' assured.'
22. Imputed] RV ' reckoned.'
23–25. Abraham's faith is the pattern of ours.
Paraphrase. '(23) Thus the history of Abraham's justification teaches us the principle on which God proceeds. (24) As Abraham trusted in God to bring Isaac as it were from death to fulfil His promise, so, if we believe on Him who raised up Jesus to fulfil His purpose, our faith will be accepted. (25) For Christ, who died because we had offended, was raised to bring about our acceptance.'
23, 24. Imputed] RV ' reckoned.' **24. Us]** RV ' our sake' : cp. 15 4 1 Cor 9 10. **If we believe]** RV ' who believe.' **25. Delivered]** RV ' delivered up,' i.e. by the Father : cp. 8 32 ; equally by Himself : cp. Gal 2 20 Eph 5 2. **Our justification]** The Resurrection brings about our justification, because (1) it shows the divinity of Christ, and therefore the value of His death : cp. 1 Cor 15 17 ; (2) through the Resurrection, faith in the Atonement became

possible, for it showed that the Atonement was complete : cp. 3 25 f. 6 10 ; (3) Christ risen becomes the source of new life to us by our union with Him : cp. 6 11.

CHAPTER 5
GOD'S SALVATION AND THE RESULTS OF ITS ACCEPTANCE

St. Paul completes his exposition of acceptance by faith by pointing to its blessed effects (vv. 1–11). In the following vv. he compares sin and acceptance, as to which he has shown that all men have sinned, while acceptance is open to all, and declares the cause of this universality. Sin is universal, because all men derive their being from Adam. But, over against Adam, Christ has entered into our race as its new head ; and from Him, all who become His derive righteousness and life, which overpower sin and death (vv. 12–21).

1–11. Acceptance brings about triumphant hope of glory, which is guaranteed by our assurance of the love of God.
Paraphrase. '(1) Blessed effects follow upon acceptance, and we should realise them. Such are reconciliation to God, (2) and admission to His gracious favour, with triumphant expectation of future glory. (3) Beyond this, we should triumph even in tribulations, because their bracing effect upon the character (4) strengthens our expectation of glory, (5) and this expectation is confirmed by a sense of God's love implanted by the Holy Ghost. (6) We are right in trusting utterly to such love as God revealed by the death of Christ. (7) Its like has never been known among men, for we were not good, (8) but sinful, when Christ died for us. (9) In view of this, we may trust Him to save us to the end. (10) For if God sacrificed His Son for His enemies, He will surely save His friends. (11) Reconciled, therefore, to God, we triumph continually in His abiding love.'
1. Therefore] cp. 4 24 f. **Justified]** i.e. accepted. **We have]** RV ' let us have.' **2. We have access]** RV ' we have had our access,' as into a king's palace : cp. Gal 5 4. **Rejoice]** RV ' let us rejoice.' **Glory]** i.e. the future and everlasting presence of God : see on 3 23.
3. We glory, etc.] RV ' let us also rejoice in our tribulations ' : cp. Ac 14 22. **Worketh]** i.e. brings about. **Patience]** i.e. bearing up under great trials without losing heart.
4. Experience] RV ' probation,' i.e. a test : here the character of one who has come through the test of suffering strong and ready for all things. **5. Maketh not ashamed]** RV ' putteth not to shame,' i.e. by proving mistaken. **Love of God]** i.e. to us. **Is given]** RV ' was given,' i.e. at a definite time : cp. Ac 10 44 19 2. St. Paul takes it for granted that all Christians have had a definite gift of the Holy Spirit,

ROMANS

which followed their acceptance of Christ (cp. Gal 3 2), one effect of which was to fill their hearts with a sense of God's love to them : cp. 8 15 f.

6. Without strength] RV 'weak,' i.e. morally. **In due time]** i.e. when the need was greatest.

7. Righteous] i.e. just, contrasted with the more lovable 'good man.' **8. Commendeth]** i.e. shows its excellence : cp. 3 5. **9. Wrath]** RV 'the wrath of God' : see on 1 18.

10. Enemies] i.e. opposing God's truth and will : cp. 8 7 Col 1 21. **Reconciled]** cp. 2 Cor 5 18 f. **Saved by his life]** RM 'in his life,' i.e. saved from the power of sin now, and from death and God's wrath hereafter, through our union with the life of the risen Christ : cp. 6 8 f. 8 10 f. **11. Joy]** RV 'rejoice,' referring to vv. 2 f. **In God]** i.e. in His love and fatherhood. **Now]** i.e. under the gospel. **Atonement]** i.e. at-one-ment ; RV 'reconciliation.'

12–14. Thus Christ is the head and representative of humanity, and we derive acceptance and life from Christ, as the OT. shows that we derive sin and death from Adam.

Paraphrase. '(12) Thus there are two heads, from whom the human race derives inheritance. From Adam all inherited a sinful tendency, which became active, so that all died. (13) When there is no law to be broken, there can be no guilt, yet even before the Law came, (14) death was universal, and those who had not broken any express command nevertheless died. Therefore sin and death are derived from Adam ; and in this respect Christ, from whom, by union with Him, we derive righteousness and life, is Adam's counterpart.'

12. Wherefore] refers to vv. 9–11. **As . . by sin]** sentence broken off ; would continue, 'so by one man righteousness and life entered.' **By one man]** cp. 1 Cor 15 21 f. 45. **Death]** i.e. physical. **Upon]** RV 'unto.' **For that]** i.e. because. **Have sinned]** RV 'sinned.'

13. Was in the world] as proved by human history. **Not imputed]** i.e. as guilty of wilful transgression of law : cp. 4. **14. After the similitude]** RV 'likeness,' i.e. by consciously breaking law.

15–21. But our inheritance from Christ more than repairs the ruin of the Fall.

Paraphrase. '(15) But the inheritances from Adam and from Christ differ in degree and in kind. For if Adam's Fall was so powerful for harm, God's favour, shown through Christ, is much more powerful for good. (16) Again, sin is so terrible, that one sin led to man's condemnation. But God's favour is still mightier. for it offers pardon to all sins. (17) So mighty is it that, while we know that Adam's sin brought death, it is much more easy to conceive that those who welcome God's bounty will attain to life and glory through Christ. (18) To sum up ; one sin

brought condemnation to all, but, over against this, one verdict of acquittal has brought acceptance and life within the reach of all. (19) For the obedience of the second head of humanity reverses the effect of the disobedience of the first. (20) The Law has a subordinate place ; it was meant to convert the unconscious sin of the world into definite transgression, that men might learn how far they are from doing God's will. But God's favour was so stupendously manifested as to overwhelm even this multiplied sin, (21) that the power of His gracious favour might prevail over that of sin, and bring man, through the work of Christ, to acceptance and to eternal life.'

15. Offence] RV 'trespass.' The Gk. word means a 'fall.' **Free gift]** i.e. of acceptance.

One] RV 'the one,' i.e. Adam. **Many]** RV 'the many,' i.e. mankind. **Be dead]** RV 'died,' i.e. became liable to death through sin. **Grace]** see on 1 5. **By grace, etc.]** RV 'by the grace of the one man.' **Abounded]** i.e. in power for good. **16. As** *it was* **by one]** RV 'as through one.' **To condemnation]** i.e. leading to condemnation. **Offences]** RV 'trespasses.' **Unto justification]** i.e. leading to a sentence of acquittal. **17. By one]** RV 'through the one.' **Abundance]** refers to 'abounded,' v. 15. **Righteousness]** i.e. acceptance. **Reign]** i.e. enjoy glory, and liberty from sin and death. **Life]** i.e. heavenly life. **18. By the offence of one]** RV 'through one trespass.' **To condemnation]** i.e. leading to condemnation. **Righteousness of one]** better, 'one sentence of acquittal,' passed by God in consequence of Christ's obedience : cp. v. 19. **Unto justification of life]** i.e. leading to acceptance which results in life. **19. One]** RV 'the one.'

Many] RV 'the many.' **Were made sinners]** in the sense of vv. 12–14. **Shall many be made]** i.e. as generation after generation arises. **20. Entered]** RV 'came in beside' : cp. Gal 3 19. **Offence]** RV 'trespass,' i.e. Adam's. **Abound]** i.e. multiply : cp. 3 20 7 13. **Much more abound]** overpowering the sin.

21. Sin, etc.] RV 'sin reigned in death,' i.e. sin had power which was death-bringing : cp. Isa 32 1. **Unto . . life]** i.e. resulting in . . life.

CHAPTERS 6–8

St. Paul has finished his exposition of Justification (3 19–5 21), and now passes to Sanctification. In other words, having shown how the believer is delivered from the guilt of sin, he goes on to show how he is delivered from its power.

C. 6 shows the Christian abiding in living union with the risen Christ by the power of faith. C. 7 describes the failure of the most earnest life apart from Christ. C. 8 shows

Christ abiding in the Christian by the power of the spirit : cp. Jn 15⁴.

CHAPTER 6
The New Righteousness in Union with Christ

St. Paul's begins by repeating an objection he must often have heard from Jewish adversaries (cp. 3⁸), and suggested here by 5²⁰— 'Does not this teaching of pardon by God's free favour practically encourage sin ?' The objection is stated in two forms (vv. 1, 15). The Apostle not only answers his opponents : he is still more concerned to build up his readers in a holy life. He opposes to the objection the fact of the believer's union with Christ. Faith in Christ means devotion to Christ's Person. The Christian is so vitally joined to Christ that he is dead with Him to sin, and risen with Him to a new state in which sin has no place (vv. 1–14). The Apostle then presents the same truth in a form more easily grasped. In coming to Christ, the Christian has experienced a change of service ; he is freed from Sin and bound to serve Righteousness (vv. 15–23).

1–14. The Christian life should be like Christ's risen life, i.e. it should be lived in God's loving Presence. Sin belonged to the old state, to which the Christian died in baptism. **Paraphrase.** '(1) It is objected that by "Justification by Faith" men are encouraged to continue in sin, since the greater the sin, the greater the opportunity that is afforded for the manifestation of God's pardoning love to sinners. (2) But our baptism implied such a breaking-away from the old sinful life as may be compared to death. Therefore, to say that a Christian may live in sin is a contradiction. (3) For our baptism signified an identification of our hearts and wills with Christ which amounted to a real union with Him, so that, while we look to His death as the ground of our acceptance, we also identify ourselves with that alienation from the sin of the world which crucified Him, of which His death was the final stage. (4) Therefore, our immersion beneath the waters of baptism signified death and burial with Christ from the sinful life of the world. But it is not only His death that is ours. We came up out of the water, as He rose from the dead, that we might begin to live in a new condition animated by His risen life. (5) This necessarily follows. For if we are united with Him in dying, we must be united with Him in new life, morally and spiritually now, and physically hereafter. (6) Make no mistake : by His death, Christ finally sealed His life-long refusal of sin, and showed that His followers must do the same. We, therefore, being like-minded with Him through our faith

in Him, also repudiated sin at our baptism, slaying our old sinful selves. Therefore, we should realise that the rule of sin over our earthly natures is ended ; (7) just as a master's rule over a dead slave is ended. (8) If so, then life with Christ follows, (9) because we are one with Him, and He lives a life in which death cannot touch Him any more. (10) This is certain, for His death ended that earthly state in which He had contact with sin, and His life is now one of unbroken communion with God. (11) Do you, then, look upon yourselves also as dead in regard to sin, but alive to God's presence and love and claims by your union with Christ. (12) Therefore, treat even your bodies as redeemed from sin, and do not yield to the lusts (13) which would use the parts and powers of your body to conquer you again for sin. Rather devote yourselves to God once for all, as if you had risen from the dead, and let all the powers of your bodies be weapons for the good fight in God's service. (14) Do not fear failure. The power which sin has over those who are under law cannot exist in the life-giving atmosphere of the redeeming love of God in which you live.'

2. Are dead] rather, 'died,' i.e. in baptism. Those addressed had been adult converts. Their baptism had been a definite act of attachment to Christ and of detachment from the sinful world. Although to crucify sinful and selfish desires is painful, it is done even joyfully by those who are inspired to the imitation of Christ by the perfect beauty and goodness of His sacrifice, for they have ' that mind ' in them 'which was also in Christ Jesus.' This, which is part of the inner meaning of baptism, is the spirit in which the true Christian will live his life.

3. Cp. Gal 3²⁷. **So many of us as]** RV 'all we who.' **4. Are buried]** rather, ' were buried' : cp. Col 2¹². **Into death]** i.e. into a state of death as regards sin. **Glory]** i.e. manifestation of love and power : cp. Jn 11⁴⁰. **Newness of life]** i.e. a newness consisting in life : cp. Jn 3³⁶ 10¹⁰ 17³ Ro 8² Col 3³ᶠ.

5. Been planted, etc.] RM 'become united with the likeness .. with the likeness,' as a slip is united with the tree to which it is grafted. **6. Is crucified]** rather, 'was crucified,' i.e. potentially, when Christ was crucified ; actually, in faith and baptism : cp. Mt 18⁸ᶠ. Gal 2²⁰. **Body of sin]** i.e. the body as the servant of sin : cp. Col 2¹¹ᶠ. **Destroyed]** i.e. as regards sin.

7. Is freed from sin] As a dead slave has completely escaped from his master's power, so one who has so believed in Christ as to be joined with Him in His death to the sin of the world, should remember that sin has no more, legitimately, to do with him. So far as its appeal to him is concerned, he should be dead. **8. Be dead**] rather, 'died.' **10. In that he died,** etc.] RV 'the death that he died .. the life that he liveth.' **Once**] RM 'once for all.' **11. Through Jesus Christ our Lord**] RV 'in Christ Jesus,' a phrase by which St. Paul often expresses our union with the glorified Christ. **12. Obey .. lusts**] RV 'obey the lusts.' **13. Yield**] RV 'present.'

Instruments] RM 'weapons.' **14. Under the law**] RV 'under law.' A code of precepts gives no power of fulfilment. It only (1) shows what is right, (2) reveals man's sinfulness, (3) stimulates him to opposition : cp. c. 7 1 Cor 15⁵⁶ Gal 4⁵. 'To be "under the law," in St. Paul's language, means to avoid sin from fear of penalties attached to sin by the law. This principle of fear is not strong enough to keep men in the path of duty. Union with Christ can alone give man the mastery over sin' (Conybeare and Howson).

15–23. The Christian is to regard sin as a master from whom death has freed him. He is now the bondservant of righteousness. **Paraphrase.** '(15) Some assert that if they are no longer under law they may indulge in sin. (16) Impossible ! You belong either to sin or to God ; you cannot belong to both. (17) And although you were the servants of sin once, you have now taken the Christian teaching as your rule of life, (18) thus exchanging the service of Sin for the service of Righteousness. (19) The illustration is inadequate, for you are better than slaves, you are God's children. But I want you to see that you must now devote your bodies to righteousness and sanctification as unreservedly as once you devoted them to impurity and licence. (20) Formerly, you served sin only, (21) and the only reward you had to look for was eternal death. (22) Now you serve God only, a service leading to sanctification, with everlasting life in prospect. (23) Make no mistake. Those who serve sin receive the death they have deserved. But God gives to His servants what they could never earn, even everlasting life in union with Christ.'

15. The law] RV 'law' : cp. Gal 5¹³.

16. Cp. Mt 6²⁴. **Unto**] i.e. resulting in.

Obedience] personified ; the mark of the lives both of the Redeemer and of the redeemed : cp. Phil 2⁸ Heb 5⁸ᶠ· 10⁷ᶠ.

17. That form, etc.] RV 'that form of teaching whereunto ye were delivered,' i.e. simple instruction in Christian truth and morality : cp. Ac 2⁴². **19. After the manner of men**] i.e. I use an illustration drawn from human affairs, because you have not had that deep spiritual experience to which I might appeal differently : cp. 3⁵. **Flesh**] i.e. unspiritual human nature. **Have yielded**] RV 'presented.' **Iniquity**] lit. 'lawlessness.' **Unto**

iniquity] i.e. iniquity leading to iniquity with the result of a lawless life. **Yield**] RV 'present.' **Holiness**] RV 'sanctification,' i.e. growth in holiness. **20. From**] RV 'in regard of.' **22. Holiness**] RV 'sanctification.'

Everlasting life] i.e. future bliss. **23. Gift**] RV 'free gift.' **Through**] RV 'in' : cp. v. 11, 1 Jn 5¹¹ᶠ.

CHAPTER 7
THE INADEQUACY OF THE LAW TO SAVE

1–6. St. Paul had spoken of the Law in a way which would offend an earnest Jew : cp. 3²⁰, ²¹ 4¹⁵ 5²⁰. In this c. (vv. 7–25) he shows that the Law is divine in its character and beneficent in its work, but unable to free a man from the power of sin. Indeed, though not the cause, it is the occasion of sin. But first, in vv. 1–6, the statement in 6¹⁴, that Christians are not under law, is enforced and explained. Law which governs one state of life is often not applicable to another. Of this the marriage law is an example. And the Christian, by the death of his old self, has passed into another state, one in which the Law no longer has force.

Paraphrase. '(1) Does any one hesitate at my statement (6¹⁴) that we " are not under law " ? Let me remind him that the power of any law over a man ends at his death. And we have died with Christ to the old state of sin in which law applies, and risen with Him to a new life. (2) Or the change in our condition may be compared to the remarriage of a woman after the death of her husband. By his death, the legal ties which bound her to him were annulled ; (3) for now the Law has no power to condemn the woman, although it condemned a second union while the husband lived. (4) In like manner, the Law which applied to us when we were wedded to our old self, had no more to do with us when our old self was crucified with Christ. So we were free to wed the risen Christ, that through union with Him we might bring forth fruit for God our Master. (5) The state in which our fleshly nature ruled was not of such a character that we should desire to return to it. For the sinful passions which the Law revealed, and by revealing stimulated, caused us to bring forth fruit for Death as our master. (6) But, as it is, the Law has ceased to affect us. This does not mean that we are free to sin, but that now we serve God from inward impulse, instead of because we are told to do so by a law.'

1. Know the law] lit. 'know law,' i.e. probably law in general : all know that law ceases to be concerned with people when they are dead. **2. Loosed**] RV 'discharged' : cp. v. 6. **Law of _her_ husband**] i.e. the marriage law. **4. By the body of Christ**] i.e. through your union with Christ crucified. **5. Motions**

of sins] RV 'sinful passions.' 'Passions' = passive feelings, e.g. hunger ; sinful, when they control the will. **By the law**] cp. vv. 7–25, 5²⁰, and on 6¹⁴. **6. Delivered**] RV 'discharged.' **That being dead**] RV 'having died to that,' i.e. to the Law. **Spirit**] RV 'the spirit.' In the new state, the spiritual part of the man has been emancipated, and has become the predominant part of him. He lives, as it were, in a spiritual world, and has become a spiritual person ; and therefore desires to carry out God's will freely and fully. In the old state, his obedience was constrained, and therefore limited, by a written code.

7–13. Although, in order that we might truly serve God, it was necessary that we should be set free from the Law (vv. 1–6), yet the Law is not evil. On the contrary, it does God's work, for it detects the sinfulness hidden in the soul, and exposes it in its true nature.

Paraphrase. '(7) Are we to infer (e.g. from v. 5) that the Law is evil ? Not so : the Law brings sin to light. For example, the tenth commandment made me conscious of the sin of coveting. (8) Not only so, but my sin became active when there was a commandment to resist, so that I coveted all the more because coveting is forbidden. Without law, sin is dormant. (9) So it was with me ; my conscience was untroubled until I realised the commandment, then sin sprang to life, and I knew myself to be dead before God. (10) How startling a consequence of a commandment which pointed the way to spiritual life ! (11) But it was the fault of sin within, which persuaded me to love that which I knew the commandment forbade, not the fault of the commandment, (12) which is holy and righteous and beneficent. (13) Thus I realised the exceeding wickedness of the sin within me, for it not only brought me to death, but did so by preventing the beneficent commandment from having any other effect than that of awakening my resistance.'

7. Lust] RV 'coveting.' St. Paul instances the most searching and comprehensive commandment of the second table. **8. Taking occasion**] RV 'finding occasion.' **By the commandment, etc.**] RV 'wrought in me through the commandment all manner of coveting.' **Without**] RV 'apart from.' **9. I was alive**] 'I' emphatic. **10. Ordained**] RV omits. **11. Deceived**] RV 'beguiled': cp. Gn 3¹³. 'All sin is committed under a deception, momentary at least, as to (1) the satisfaction to be found in it, (2) the excuse to be made for it, (3) the probability of its punishment' (Vaughan). **13. But sin**] Understand 'became death unto me.' **Working**] RV 'by working.'

14–25. St. Paul, taking his own case as typical, shows that spiritual death (vv. 11–13) is due, not to the Law, nor to the free choice of his true self, which approves the Law (vv. 14–16, 22), but to the power of sin within (vv. 17, 20 f.). In doing so, he draws a picture of conflict, in which he does evil unwillingly, and is unable to do the good he wishes (vv. 15–20). His personality includes two parts— 'flesh' (the lower animal nature) and 'mind' or 'inward man' (i.e. the part which thinks and reasons). The 'mind' reverences God's Law, but is conquered by the 'flesh,' which sin controls. He needs a deliverer (vv. 21–25).

The state described is that of one who has been awakened to the claim of God's Law and to hate sin, but is not under the power of the Spirit of Christ (c. 8). It probably describes St. Paul's experience for some length of time before his conversion.

Paraphrase. '(14) The Law appeals to man's spiritual nature, and that is why I cannot keep it, for the fleshly nature, over which sin rules, predominates in me. (15) I am like a slave, who works out his master's thoughts without sharing them. I do not what I wish, but what I hate, (16) thus acknowledging the moral excellence of the Law even while I break it. (17) It follows that the sin which dwells within me is the real agent of my wrong-doing. (18) For I know that no good dwells in my fleshly nature, because my good wishes are ineffectual, (19) and I do the evil I wish to avoid. (20) But if I do it against my will, the sin which dwells within me is the real agent. (21) Thus I am not free. Although I wish to do the good, sin says, "Thou shalt not do good, thou shalt do evil," and I am obliged to obey. (22) My reason and conscience delight in the Law of God, (23) but the law of sin (v. 21), which rules my body, wars against the dictates of my reason and conscience and robs me of my liberty. (24) I need a deliverer from this reign of sin in my body' (cp. 6⁶ 'body of sin '), '(25) whom I find in Christ. The sum of the matter is that, left to myself, I am divided, serving a law of God with my reason and conscience, but a law of sin with my fleshly nature.'

15. Allow] RV 'know.'

24. The body of this death] Sin and death go together. The body which is under the power of sin is also given over to death.

CHAPTER 8

The New Life in Christ in relation to God and the Spirit

It was shown in 5¹²ᶠ· that condemnation for the *guilt* of sin is done away by justification through faith in Christ. The question as to the *power* of sin then arose, answered by the doctrine of sanctification in chs. 6–8. In c. 6

it is asserted that the union of the Christian with Christ is a new condition, which involves death with Him to sin and resurrection to newness of life. In c. 7 it is made clear that there is no force in the Law to break the power of sin. Now, in c. 8, St. Paul brings forward the truth of the indwelling of the Holy Spirit, which accompanies union with Christ, conquering sin and death in the Christian (vv. 1–11), and bearing witness that he is child and heir of God (vv. 12–17). Hence the Christian has such hope of glory that he can bear his sufferings (vv. 18–25), in which the Spirit helps him by intercession (vv. 26, 27), and which are bringing about God's purpose of good (vv. 28–30). In the security of that purpose he triumphs (vv. 31–39).

1–11. The Christian is sanctified as well as justified. In Christ he receives the Spirit, who frees him from the power of sin and of death (vv. 1, 2). The object of the death of Christ was not only to win pardon for man, but also to produce right character and conduct (vv. 3, 4). This is essential, and is brought about by the indwelling of the Spirit (vv. 5–9). The change means life, of spirit now and of body hereafter (vv. 10, 11).

Paraphrase. '(1) The deliverance spoken of (cp. 7 25) for those who are united to Christ (2) is brought about by the power of the life-giving Spirit, whom they received by union with Christ, which freed them from the power of sin and death. (3) The Law could not overcome sin, because man's fleshly nature could not respond to its demands. But God, by the incarnation and atonement of His Son, sealed the death-warrant of sin in the flesh, (4) with the object of producing in us that character and conduct which the Law requires, by enabling us to live by the rule of the renewed spiritual nature. (5) There are two states of life, the difference between which is wide. According as the fleshly or the spiritual nature is the ruling power, so are men engrossed either with fleshly or with spiritual things ; (6) either they are in a state of separation from God, which ends in death both of soul and body, or they have joyful communion with God and a happy sense of reconciliation with Him. (7) Death must be the portion of the mind set on fleshly things, because such a mind is in a state of hostility to God, being rebellious against His Law. (8) They, therefore over whom the fleshly nature rules cannot be acceptable to God. (9) But you, who are in Christ, are not so. Not the fleshly, but the spiritual nature rules over you, if the Spirit of God dwells in you. And unless you have Him you are not Christ's, for it is by the Spirit that Christ comes to you. (10) But if Christ does dwell in you, although your body must die because of the curse of sin, your spirit has

already risen into new life because you are accepted in Christ. (11) And the Spirit within you is a pledge that God will cause your bodies also to participate in Christ's Resurrection.'

1. Who walk, etc.] RV omits : probably borrowed from v. 4. **2. Law of sin,** etc.] cp. 7 23, 24. **3. Likeness of,** etc.] Christ took real 'flesh,' i.e. human nature, cp. Jn 1 14, but without its sinfulness, cp. Heb 4 15. **For sin]** RV ' as an offering for sin.' **Condemned sin in the flesh]** (1) Christ proved, by a sinless human life, that sin is not necessary to human nature ; (2) Christ made expiation for sin on our behalf ; (3) Christ made it possible for us to die with Him to sin and rise with Him to newness of life, by union in love with Him, and by the power of the Spirit. **4. Righteousness]** RV ' ordinance.' **5. Things of the flesh]** i.e. things merely human : cp. Mt 16 23 ; merely earthly : cp. Mk 4 19 Phil 3 19 ; or absolutely sinful : cp. Gal 5 19 f. **6. To be carnally minded .. spiritually minded]** RV ' the mind of the flesh .. the mind of the spirit.' **7. Carnal mind]** RV ' mind of the flesh.' **8. In the flesh]** cp. 7 5. **Please God]** cp. Mal 3 4. **9. Dwell]** cp. Jn 14 17. **Spirit of Christ]** The Spirit of God is the Spirit of Christ, because He comes from the Son as well as from the Father. Also His Presence is in effect the Presence of Christ : cp. v. 10 Jn 14 16 f. Gal 4 6.

12–17. Let us live in accordance with the high position which the Spirit testifies is ours, namely, that we are God's sons and heirs with Christ of glory.

Paraphrase. '(12) Such a destiny involves the duty (13) of putting to death the impulses of the fleshly nature, by submitting yourself to your renewed spiritual nature. If you do so, you will live eternally, (14) an amazing destiny, but yours as sons of God. For you are shown to be sons of God by your following the guidance of God's Spirit, (15) and by the testimony of your own spirits, which, when you became Christians, no longer regarded God with the slavish fear the Law produced, but received such a consciousness of sonship that the prayer of our hearts is " our Father." (16) And this consciousness is caused by the Holy Spirit Himself, who thus unites with our own spirits in bearing witness that we are children of God. (17) Well, then, if we are God's children, we are heirs of His glory, and shall share it with Christ hereafter if we share in Christ's sufferings now.'

13. Shall die] RV ' must die,' i.e. spiritually. **Deeds of the body]** i.e. so far as the body is not under the dominion of the spirit.

14. Sons] cp. v. 16, ' children.' ' Children ' denotes ' community of nature,' ' sons ' denotes ' dignity of heirship ' (Westcott) : cp. Jn 1 12 Gal 3 24 f. 4 1 f. The privilege of sonship must be appropriated by faithful obedience to become actual. **15. Adoption**] cp. Gal 4 5, 6. **Abba, Father**] cp. Mk 14 36 Gal 4 6. ' Abba' is an Aramaic word, meaning ' Father.' Probably Christ used it in the Lord's Prayer, and perhaps it came to be used as a divine name, ' Father Abba.' **17. Heirs**] Under Roman law, ' a will that left the property away from the children was invalid' (Ramsay). **If so be,** etc.] cp. 2 Tim 2 11 f., and Mk 8 34 f. Col 1 24 1 Pet 4 13. Christ is ' the Way ' ; the main features of His life must be reproduced in the lives of His people.

18–25. The glory to come will far outweigh the sufferings we must bear now. All creation is moving on through the mystery of pain to full redemption, our hope of which is so sure that we can wait in patience.

Paraphrase. ' (18) I said we must suffer with Christ. Suffering belongs to this passing season, but it is not worth a thought in view of the coming glory (19) in which the sons of God will stand revealed. Even nature, animate and inanimate, eagerly expects that blessed future. (20) Although God subjected her to imperfection and decay, to further His purposes, it was not to be for ever. He gave her a sure hope (21) of future deliverance from the law of decay, and of sharing the freedom from all evil which God's children will have in glory. (22) She groans, indeed, but in the birth-throes of a better order of things. (23) And even we Christians, though we have the Spirit as a foretaste of blessedness, groan under the weakness and imperfections of our bodies ; but we await the full dignity of our sonship, when our bodies shall be delivered from death. (24) When we became Christ's we looked to the future for perfect happiness ; we cannot expect to have it now. (25) But we have certain hope of it, and, therefore, wait and endure.'

18. In us] RV ' to usward.' **19, 20, 21. Creature**] RV ' creation,' i.e. the irrational creation : cp. Gn 3 17 f. St. Paul represents nature poetically, as feeling that dissatisfaction with its pain and failure which exists in man's mind. There was a general expectation among the Jews, based on such passages as Isa 65 17 f., that the Messianic times would usher in a renovation of nature. This expectation is taken up in the NT. : cp. Ac 3 19 f. Col 1 20 2 Pet 3 13 Rev 21 1. In what way it will be fulfilled is beyond our knowledge. **19. Manifestation**] RV ' revealing' : cp. 1 Cor 15 51 f. 1 Th 4 16 f. **20. Vanity**] i.e. transitoriness, frustration : cp. Eccl 1 2. **Him**] i.e. God : cp. Gn 3 17. **20, 21. Hath subjected,** etc.] RV ' subjected it, in hope that the creation,' etc.

21. Glorious liberty] RV ' liberty of the glory.' **23. Firstfruits**] cp. Lv 23 10 2 Cor 1 22 Eph 1 13 f. **Groan**] cp. 2 Cor 5 2 f. **24. We are**

saved] RV ' by hope were we saved' ; better, ' in hope,' etc. : see on 1 16. **Hope that is seen**] here ' hope' means that which is hoped for.

For what, etc.] RV ' for who hopeth for that which he seeth ?' **25. Patience**] i.e. patient endurance.

26–30. While the Christian endures his sufferings in hope, the Spirit within is praying for him, better than he can pray himself (vv. 26, 27). Meanwhile he knows that his sufferings are helping to bring about that great and good purpose, in fulfilment of which God has brought him into a state of salvation (vv. 28–30).

Paraphrase. ' (26) Thus we both groan and hope. We cannot pray definitely for the removal of our sufferings, because we do not know what is best. But the Spirit prays within us in inexpressible longings, (27) which God understands, and which are (as our words might not be) in accordance with His will. (28) And this we do know, that all things, even our sufferings, are helping to fulfil a plan by which God is bringing about good to them that love Him. We know this, because it was in pursuance of His purpose that He called them to become Christians ; (29) and the whole course of their salvation is due to His purpose ; by which in eternity He regarded them with favour, and appointed them to attain to the likeness of His Son, that He might be the eldest in a glorious family, (30) then called them to be His, accepted them as righteous, and brought them to glory.'

26. Infirmities] RV ' infirmity,' i.e. ' our ignorance in asking.' **What . . for**] RV ' how we should pray' : cp. Phil 1 22 f. **Itself**] RV ' himself'; spoken of as a Person and distinct from the Father.

27. Because] RM ' that.' **Saints**] i.e. God's people : see on 1 7.

28. Called] see on 1 6. **According to his purpose**] cp. 9 11.

St. Paul does not say that God's purpose is to save some and reject others, but ' that he might have mercy upon all ' (11 32). In pursuance of this purpose first the Jews, and then Christians, specially Gentile Christians, were called to hold and spread the divine knowledge. Among those who had been called were those to whom the Epistle was addressed. St. Paul encourages them in their trials by the thought that God would not forsake those who had been so called by Him, and that, as to His favour, they were safe. On the other hand, he does not say that they could not rebel against God or forsake Him. On the contrary, he warns them against such presumptuous thoughts (11 20 f.).

29. Foreknow] For paraphrase cp. Ps 1 6 Am 3 2 Mt 7 28. **Did predestinate**] RV ' foreordained' : cp. Ac 4 28 1 Cor 2 7 Eph 1 5, 11.

Conformed] i.e. in essential type : cp. Phil 2⁶. **Image**] cp. 1 Cor 15⁴⁹ 2 Cor 3¹⁸ Phil 3²¹ 1 Jn 3². **Brethren**] cp. Heb 2¹⁰ᶠ.

30. Did predestinate] RV 'foreordained.'

Glorified] That which to us is future, is already complete in God's mind: cp. Eph 2⁴ᶠ.

31–39. Since the Christian is the object of the divine love and work spoken of in the last section, he need fear no evil.

Paraphrase. '(31) We may, therefore, face the future triumphantly, for God is on our side, (32) and the love which sacrificed His own Son will withhold from us nothing. (33) God's chosen need fear no accuser. Since He has acquitted, (34) none can condemn them. Since Christ, in His death and life and glory, has proved His love for them, (35) neither suffering nor death can part us from that love. (36) Even though we be martyred, like the faithful few of old, (37) His love will make martyrdom a surpassing victory. (38, 39) In short, no power in the universe will be able to part us from the divine love Christ has for us.'

32. Spared] allusion to Gn 22¹⁶, where LXX has the same word. **33. Elect**] i.e. chosen, practically = 'called.' *It is* **God**] cp. Isa 50⁸ᶠ. **34. Intercession**] cp. Heb 7²⁵ 1 Tim 2¹. **36.** Quotation from Ps 44²². **38. Principalities, powers**] Jewish titles of angels, here evil angels : cp. Eph 6¹² 1 Pet 3²².

39. In Christ] Christ's love is a manifestation of God's love.

CHAPTERS 9–11

It was obvious that the Church of Christ was coming to be almost entirely a Gentile Church, and that the Jews as a whole were refusing to accept Jesus as their Messiah. The Jew argued from this fact that Christianity could not be true. For if the Christian Church were really the fulfilment of the promised Messianic kingdom, and if the Jews were shut out from it, then God's promises to the Jews in the OT. would have been broken, which could not be imagined.

In chs. 9–11, St. Paul grapples with this objection :—

(1) He points out that in previous epochs God had narrowed His choice, making a fresh selection out of those already selected ; and He may be acting so again (9¹⁻¹³).

(2) God is supreme. He may choose His instruments as He will, and we have no right to criticise (9¹⁴⁻³³).

(3) If the Jews have failed, it is because of their unbelief (c. 10).

(4) After all, there may be more faithful Jews than is supposed, as in the time of Elijah (11¹⁻¹⁰).

(5) Seeing the reception of the Gentiles, the Jews themselves may be stirred up to accept Christ. God has forgotten neither them nor

His promises, and His gracious purpose will not fail (11¹¹⁻³⁶).

It should be noted that these chs. mainly treat of the selection by God of nations and Churches to spiritual functions and responsibilities. They have nothing to do with the predestination of individuals to salvation or condemnation, and the argument closes with the statement that what God has done has been with the purpose of having mercy upon all (11³²). While these chs. assume that God chooses His instruments for reasons which we cannot fathom, and which are independent of human merit and of birth or nationality, at the same time there are conditions which must be fulfilled on man's part. Those who have been chosen or elected, are free to fall away ; they have done so in the case of the Jewish nation —they may do so in the case of the Gentile Church. They can only retain their position by 'faith,' i.e. here, by submitting themselves to God's purpose (10²⁰ᶠ.).

CHAPTER 9

The Rejection of Israel no Disparagement or Disproof of the Gospel

The Apostle sorrows over the exclusion of Israel (vv. 1–5), but their exclusion does not involve any breach of God's promises, for He always made a selection, even among the members of the chosen family (vv. 6–13). This cannot be unjust, for God has stated it to be His method (vv. 14–18). We should have no right to cavil, even if God seemed to use us sternly (vv. 19–21). But He has acted with mercy (vv. 22–29), and Israel has fallen through want of faith (vv. 30–33).

1–5. It is with the deepest sorrow that St. Paul sees the Jews outside the kingdom, for he loves them as brethren and remembers their privileges.

Paraphrase. '(1) It is the solemn truth (2) that my heart aches (3) over my brethren of Israel, so that I could wish to give my soul for their salvation. (4) How terrible is the fall of those who had such privileges from God, (5) who are descended from the patriarchs, and from whom, on the human side, has come the Messiah, He who is almighty and divine !'

1. In Christ] see on 6¹¹ Col 3⁹. **In the Holy Ghost**] i.e. under His influence. **3. I could wish**] i.e. if it were lawful and possible.

Accursed] RV 'anathema,' reproducing the Gk. : cp. 1 Cor 12³ 16²² Gal 1⁸ᶠ. The word is used in LXX of that which is devoted to God, either as an offering (cp. Lv 27²⁸ᶠ.), or for destruction as evil : cp. Josh 6¹⁷ᶠ.

4. Israelites] 'Israel' being the name given by God to Jacob, 'Israelite' described the Jew as the inheritor of God's promises : cp. 11¹ 2 Cor 11²². **Adoption**] i.e. of Israel by

God as first-born son among other nations : cp. Ex 4 ^{22}. **Glory**] i.e. the light by which God's presence was manifested : cp. Ex 16 ^{10} 40 $^{34\,f.}$. **Covenants**] with Abraham, Isaac, and Jacob. **Service**] i.e. of Tabernacle and Temple. **Promises**] i.e. of the Messiah.

5. Of whom, etc.] RV ' of whom is Christ as concerning the flesh.' **God**] cp. Jn 1 ^{1} 10 ^{30} Col 2 ^{9}.

6–13. Jewish opponents argued that the privileges enumerated in the last section were guaranteed to them as a nation, unless God broke His word. St. Paul replies that God is not bound to the whole nation. There had been from the first a process of selection, by which some had been rejected. The same process of selection and rejection might be expected now.

Paraphrase. ' (6) Yet it does not follow that God's promises have failed because some have rejected them. Heirship of the promise does not belong to mere natural descent from Jacob. (7) For consider the case of Abraham. Ishmael was his elder son, yet Isaac was selected to be the father of the chosen race ; (8) which shows that a position of privilege with God is a matter not of accident of birth, but of special promise and choice ; (9) in fact, Isaac was born on purpose to inherit the promise. (10) Take a plainer example. Esau and Jacob had the same parents and were twins ; (11) yet in their case also God showed that He carries out His purpose by selecting whom He chooses, for before their birth (12) He destined Jacob's line for privilege, (13) as Malachi recognises.'

6. RV ' But *it is* not as though the word of God hath come to nought.' **Israel**] in the sense of inheritors of the promise. **Of Israel**] i.e. by physical descent from Jacob.

7. Seed of Abraham] i.e. by natural descent. **Children**] i.e. inheriting privilege. **In Isaac,** etc.] from Gn 21 ^{12}. **8. Children of the flesh**] i.e. those born into the family in the course of nature. **Children of God**] i.e. partaking of the ' adoption' to special privilege spoken of in v. 4. **Of the promise**] i.e. born in fulfilment of a promise : cp. Gal 4 ^{23}.

9. The word] RV ' a word.' **At this time**] i.e. at this season next year (Gn 18 ^{10}).

11. The purpose] i.e. the purpose of salvation which existed in God's mind before creation : cp. Ro 8 ^{28} Eph 1 $^{9\,f.}$ 2 Tim 1 ^{9}. **According to election**] i.e. the method by which God carries out His purpose is the selection of individuals and nations to be its instruments. So the Jews were selected to preserve the knowledge of God in the world, and to prepare for the call of the Gentiles. The selection is not to assured salvation, but to the privilege of helping to carry out God's plan of salvation for the world. **Not of works**] a

further thought. God's choice proceeds from unmerited bounty. **12.** From Gn 25 ^{23}.

13. Loved . . hated] cp. Mal 1 $^{2\,f.}$, which refers to the nations of Israel and Edom, and expresses the historical fact that Israel had privileges which were denied to Edom. ' Hated' implies decided rejection, but not vindictiveness : cp. Lk 14 ^{26} with Mt 10 ^{37}. There is no reference to eternal salvation or rejection.

14–18. It is objected that the freedom of choice, which St. Paul attributes to God, would be unjust. This cannot be, for in the OT. God claims the same freedom. And, if then, so also now.

Paraphrase. ' (14) The objector argues that such apparently arbitrary selection would be unjust. Far from it. (15) The Jew admits that all God does is just ; here, then, are two passages in which God claims this freedom of choice. First, He told Moses, leader of the chosen people, that not even he could lay claim as a right to the favour about to be shown. (16) Therefore, human desire and striving are not the cause of God's choice of any, but His sovereign will and mercy alone. (17) Secondly, the words addressed to Pharaoh show that God did not punish him because he was an Egyptian, but for special reasons. (18) So, then, God is seen to show mercy or to harden according to His own will.'

15. From Ex 33 ^{19}. **16. Runneth**] i.e. as a racer strives. **17.** From Ex 9 ^{16}. **Raised thee up**] i.e. as king. St. Paul quotes Scripture to show that it was simply due to God's choice that Pharaoh, not some one else, was to be a world-wide example of God's power in punishment. It was not because of Pharaoh's nationality. The Apostle confines himself, here, to one point. It is that a Jew must admit that what God is shown, in the OT., to have done, cannot be unjust. He is not speaking, here, of eternal life or death. And he says nothing of Pharaoh's deserts or conduct, because that is not his point here. Presently he will assert (1) that those whom God has rejected have been rejected by their own fault after long forbearance ; and (2) that it is God's will to have mercy upon all men.

18. Hardeneth] cp. Ex 4 ^{21}. God is said to harden, because He has made man so that, by the constitution of his nature, hardening follows persistent disobedience.

19–29. It is now objected that if God's will is irresistible, He ought not to blame the Jews. The answer is that, first, it is presumptuous of man to criticise his Maker ; and, secondly, that God has been longsuffering with the Jews, as well as merciful to the Gentiles.

Paraphrase. ' (19) Another objection. If those who resist God's will, do so because He has hardened them, and so fulfil His purpose, how can they be guilty? (20) The answer is twofold. First, we are not competent to criticise our Maker. (21) It is His right to mould each nation of mankind for whatever purpose He chooses. (22) But secondly, as a matter of fact, God has not been arbitrary. Although He is determined to punish sin, yet when the Jews have proved unfit for high purposes, He has borne long with them; (23) not only for their sakes, but that by their means He might be able to show mercy upon those prepared from the beginning, (24) even upon us, called—such is His mercy—from Gentiles as well as Jews. (25, 26) His word confirms this again: the call of the Gentiles was foretold by Hosea, (27–29) and the fact that only a remnant of Israel would enter the kingdom was prophesied by Isaiah.'

20. Shall the thing] cp. Isa 29 16 45 9.

21. Power] RV 'a right': cp. Isa 64 8 Jer 18 6. **Honour . . dishonour**] not referring to final salvation or condemnation, but to the inequalities of life. Nations as well as individuals are called to duties and positions of greater or less honour: cp. 2 Tim 2 20.

22. Longsuffering] cp. 2 4. **Vessels**] the metaphor of the potter continued. **Of wrath**] i.e. deserving wrath. **Fitted**] St. Paul does not say, 'God had made them fit for destruction' (contrast 'afore prepared,' v. 23). They had become 'fitted for destruction,' because, being intractable under the moulder's hand, they were of no use for His purpose.

23. Might make known] cp. 11 11 f. **Of mercy**] i.e. experiencing mercy. **Prepared**] cp. 8 28 f. **25, 26.** From Hos 1 10 2 23, passages used freely and typically; originally speaking of the restoration of the Ten Tribes, who had become like those who were not God's people. **27, 28, 29.** From Isa 1 9 10 22 f.

27. A remnant] RV 'it is the remnant that shall be saved.' **28.** RV 'for the Lord will execute his word' (i.e. sentence) 'upon the earth, finishing it and cutting it short,' i.e. making it conclusive and brief.

30–33. The Jews have been rejected because they sought acceptance with God in their own way by meritorious works. They had not that faith which would make them attentive to hear and do God's will, and so could not fulfil His purpose (see v. 22 paraphrase). Stereotyped in a conventional religion, they were unable, for want of living faith, to receive the Messiah.

Paraphrase. '(30) We conclude that Gentiles, who were not seeking acceptance with God, won acceptance given to those who have faith, (31) while Israel, who was seeking to be accepted because of meritorious works, has failed. (32) The reason is that instead of living by faith in God, i.e. instead of waiting

on God to learn what His will for them was, they fixed their attention on observances. Hence they refused the Messiah, fulfilling Isaiah's prophecy that the stone, the strength of those who should have faith in Him, would cause the fall of the unbeliever.

30. Followed . . attained] as a runner in a race: cp. Phil 3 12. **31. The law**] RV 'a law.' **32. By the works of the law**] RV 'by works.' **For**] RV omits. **Stumbling stone**] cp. 1 Cor 1 23. **33.** A combination of two passages. In Isa 28 16 the prophet spoke of a foundation stone which God was laying, and which would give a sense of security to those who trusted His promise. In Isa 8 14 the prophet spoke of Jehovah as being a stumbling-block to the unbeliever. St. Paul combines the two passages to show that Christ, who is strength and support to those who trust in Him, has been a stumbling-block to the faithless Jews. The 'stone' of Ps 118 22 was interpreted by Christ of Himself, Mt 21 42, etc., and from this, probably, the 'stone' of other passages was interpreted of Him. 'The stone' may have been a Jewish title for the Messiah.

CHAPTER 10

ISRAEL REJECTED THROUGH LACK OF FAITH

In c. 9 St. Paul, defending the gospel against objections founded upon the fact that it had been rejected by the Jews as a whole, showed that God had never bound Himself to the Israelitish race, but had always kept Himself free to choose His own instruments. In c. 10 he declares that Israel have caused their rejection by failure to recognise God's methods, and by obstinate rebellion in spite of the patience of His love.

1–15. The zeal of the Jews is useless, because they follow their own way instead of God's (vv. 1–4), although God's way of salvation is so easy (vv. 5–11), and open to all (vv. 12, 13), and made known to all (vv. 14, 15).

Paraphrase. '(1) I pray for the salvation of my people, (2) for they still are zealous for God, though with such lack of insight (3) that they are blind to His free offer of salvation, and vainly seek to win acceptance by their merits, (4) whereas faith in Christ has taken the place of obedience to law as the motive and inspiration of life and the condition of acceptance with God. (5) The old system of works called for an obedience beyond human power to give. (6) But acceptance by faith in Christ makes no impracticable demand. Christ has brought Himself within our reach by His Incarnation which made Him man among men, (7) and by His Resurrection which restored Him to us for ever; (8) so that the faith the gospel asks for is a simple thing, (9) only to acknowledge publicly that Jesus is Lord and really to believe in His Resurrection. (10)

All that is required can be done by human hearts and human lips, (11) even as Isaiah promises complete security to every one who has faith in the Christ. (12) The promise is for all, for Christ's Lordship extends over all races of men, and He has love enough for all who worship Him (13) as Joel testifies ; (14, 15) and God has made His offer known by commissioned preachers, so that the Jews have no excuse for unbelief.'

1. Might] RV 'may.' **2. Zeal**] which St. Paul had shared : cp. Gal 1 14 Phil 3 6. **Of**] RV 'for.' **Knowledge**] i.e. insight into God's will : cp. Col 1 9. **3. God's righteousness**] i.e. His gift of free acceptance on condition of faith. **Going about**] RV 'seeking.' **4. End**] i.e. termination. Law, as the means of winning favour with God by its fulfilment, has been brought to an end now Christ has come : cp. Gal 3 10, 13 Col 2 14. **For**] RV 'unto,' i.e. so that every one who has faith may be accepted. **5.** RV 'For Moses writeth that the man that doeth the righteousness .. of the law,' i.e. all the Law requires, 'shall live thereby' : from Lv 18 5. **6. Speaketh**] The words that follow are selected from Dt 30 11 f., where they refer to the accessibility of the Law. St. Paul applies them to the gospel, as opposed to the Law, not as formal quotation of Scripture, but as adapting familiar language. Yet the passage is one of several which show that holy men under the Law looked forward to the spirit of the gospel : cp. Ps 51 16 f. Hos 6 6 Mic 6 8. **7. Deep**] RV 'abyss,' i.e. Hades, the abode of the dead : cp. Ac 2 27 1 Pet 3 19 4 6. **8. The word of faith**] i.e. which announces faith as the method of salvation. **9. Confess**] i.e. at baptism ; in daily life ; and in persecution : cp. Mt 10 32. **The Lord Jesus**] RV 'Jesus as Lord,' i.e. as King and God : see on v. 12, and Jn 20 28 1 Cor 12 3 2 Cor 4 5. **Raised**] cp. 4 24 f. The Resurrection is spoken of as the object of faith, because, if not risen, Christ would be no Lord and no Saviour, and union with Him would be impossible. **10. Unto**] i.e. resulting in. **Salvation**] i.e. final salvation. 'Confession' represents the whole life of devotion to Christ which springs from faith.

11. From Isa 28 16: cp. Ro 9 33. **12. Difference**] RV 'distinction' : cp. 3 22. **Greek**] i.e. Gentile. **The same Lord**] i.e. Christ : cp. Ac 10 36 Ro 9 5. **Over all**] RV 'is Lord of all.' **Rich**] cp. Eph 3 8. **Call upon him**] i.e. as His worshippers : cp. 1 Cor 1 2. From the custom of beginning prayer with the name of the deity, the expression ' to call upon the name of ' came to signify ' to be a worshipper of.' Hence, this verse implies the Divinity of Christ. In the next verse, the name ' Jehovah ' (' Lord ') is applied to Him : cp. Jn 12 41. **13.** From Joel 2 32. **14. Not heard?**] supply, ' but they have

heard.' **Without a preacher?**] supply, ' but there are preachers.' **15. Sent**] The Gk. word is that from which ' Apostle ' is derived. Supply, ' but apostles have been sent.' **How beautiful**] from Isa 52 7.

16–21. The Jews have had every opportunity, and their fall is due to their own obstinate wilfulness.

Paraphrase. '(16) It is no argument against the message to say it has only partially succeeded, for Isaiah lamented that the Jews would not listen to it, (17) in words which imply that there would be a Divine message about Christ meant to call forth faith. (18) Nor can any one say that the Jews have not heard the message, for it has been preached everywhere. (19) Nor can it be said that the nation which had received the Scriptures did not know that the Gentiles were to be included in God's favour. Even so far back as Moses they were warned that it would be so ; (20) and Isaiah uses the plainest language. (21) No excuse can be made for them. Their fall is due to the same stubborn rejection of God's unwearied love which Isaiah saw in his day.'

16. Lord, etc.] From Isa 53 1. **17. Hearing**] The same Gk. word as that translated ' report ' in v. 16. **18. Their sound, etc.**] from Ps 19 4, i.e. the gospel message was diffused as widely as the declaration by the heavens of the glory of God. Not literally so, but probably every considerable Jewish colony had heard the gospel : cp. Col 1 6, 23. **19. I will provoke, etc.**] From Dt 32 21. **20.** From Isa 65 1. **21.** From Isa 65 2. **Gainsaying**] i.e. contradicting.

CHAPTER 11
Israel's Rejection not final. A Warning to the Gentiles

In this c. St. Paul brings to an end his great exposition of God's dealings with the Jews. He has shown in c. 9 that God is free to choose or reject individuals or nations as the instruments of His purpose ; and, in c. 10, that the Jews have deserved their rejection. Now he declares that, in spite of all this, God has not cast off His ancient people. He has seen fit, in His mercy, to preserve a portion of them faithful to His will, and the remainder are still loved by Him. Their having fallen away for a time has given an opportunity for the conversion of the Gentiles. When the Gentiles have been gathered into His kingdom, the Jews will be stirred up by their example and return to God.

1–12. God did not utterly reject the Jews as a nation (vv. 1, 2). Their failure is partial (vv. 2–10), and, as in former days, there is a faithful remnant ; their failure is used by God for good, and is temporary (vv. 11, 12).

Paraphrase. '(1) Does it follow that God has finally rejected those He made His own people ? I, who am proud to be one of them, cannot believe it. (2) And it is impossible, for from all eternity He marked them to be His instruments, and He is unchanging. They are no more rejected than they were in Elijah's day, (3) when, although Israel was rebellious, (4) God preserved a faithful remnant. (5) So also now there is such a remnant, selected out of the mass by God's undeserved favour, (6) not for any merit of their own. (7) Thus, a select portion of Israel, having minds open to God's will and believing in Christ, has obtained acceptance, which the rest, by seeking it in self-righteousness, have lost, incurring instead that hardening which follows self-will, (8) that heavy deafness and blindness toward God which Isaiah perceived, (9) that ruin caused by misuse of blessings (10) of which David spoke. (11) But although the majority have stumbled, even they have not fallen for ever. Their refusal of Christ has occasioned an earlier preaching to the Gentiles, and so has been the means of bringing salvation to them, and this, in turn, is meant to stir the Jews up to accept Christ, and thus regain their old privilege. (12) Thus they still are used by God, for their failure has been a means of blessing to the world, and much greater blessing will result from their complete conversion.'

1. Cast away] cp. Ps 94 14 1 S 12 22. Benjamin] the tribe which, with Judah, followed the house of David, and in whose territory Jerusalem stood. 2. People] i.e. the nation as a whole. Foreknew] see on 8 29 and v. 29. Wot] i.e. know. Of Elias] lit. 'in Elijah'; i.e. in the section of the Scriptures concerning Elijah : cp. Mk 12 26 (RV). 3. Lord, etc.] from 1 K 19 10. 4. Reserved to] RV 'left for.' To the image of Baal] RV 'to Baal.' 6. But if it be of works, etc.] RV omits this latter half of the v. 7. Election] i.e. the chosen remnant who have believed in Christ. Blinded] RV 'hardened,' i.e. by God, in punishment : see next v. Those who will not, at last cannot.

8. From Dt 29 4 Isa 29 10. The spirit of slumber] RV 'a spirit of stupor.' Unto this day] part of the quotation from Deuteronomy. 9. From Ps 69 22 f. 10. Bow down their back] i.e. in weakness and dejection.

11. Stumbled] cp. 9 32. Fall] i.e. so as not to rise again. Come unto the Gentiles] It was only when the Jews rejected the gospel that the Apostle turned to the Gentiles : cp. Ac 13 45 f. 28 28. A Church nationally Jewish would probably have been a hindrance to the complete evangelisation of the Gentiles. 12. Diminishing] RV 'loss.' As a defeated army suffers loss in battle, so the majority of the Jews had fallen away into unbelief. St. Paul anticipates great blessing to the world when the ' fulness,' i.e. the entire nation, of the Jews believes.

13-24. St. Paul now addresses the Gentiles.

They should hope for the restoration of Israel, because of the blessing it will bring the world, and because Israel still bears God's name (vv. 13-16). They should not despise Israel (vv. 17, 18), nor boast of preference (vv. 19, 20), for, if unfaithful, they too will fall (vv. 21, 22), whereas the Jews will be restored if they give up their unbelief (vv. 23, 24).

Paraphrase. ' (13) In this which I write, I am not disregarding my mission to you Gentiles. And you know my heart is in my work among you Gentiles. (14) If, then, I am always hoping that your conversion may stir up the Jews to yearn after their lost privileges, it is not only because I am a Jew, (15) but also because I am sure that as their rejection brought you to God, so their restoration will fill the nations of the earth with spiritual life. (16) And their restoration may certainly be expected, for the nation still retains the consecration it received in the patriarchs. (17) Again, although you have taken the place of some of them in God's kingdom, (18) do not think yourselves superior to them. Remember that you have been admitted into their kingdom, not they into yours. (19) If God rejected them for you, it was not because He preferred you. (20) Unbelief lost them their place, and faith alone preserves you. (21) The facts do not warrant self-satisfaction in you, but warn you against it. (22) Thus we see manifested both God's goodness and His severity. His goodness is upon you, but only so long as you are faithful. His severity is upon the Jews, (23) yet, if they give up their unbelief, He will receive them again. And their restoration is quite possible, (24) for they have more in common with the kingdom than you had as heathen.'

13. RV 'But I speak to you that are Gentiles. Inasmuch then as I am an apostle of Gentiles, I glorify my ministry.' As the Jews have been spoken of in the third person, we infer that the Roman Christians were chiefly Gentiles.

14. Emulation] RV 'jealousy' : cp. v. 11, 10 19. 15. Reconciling of the world] In the bringing in of the Gentiles, the world began to enjoy that reconciliation which Christ gained for it by dying for all mankind : cp. 2 Cor 5 19 Eph 2 13 f. 16. Firstfruit] metaphor from Nu 15 19 f. The 'firstfruit' and 'root' represent the patriarchs : cp. v. 28, 9 5. Holy] i.e. separated as God's people for His purposes. No reference to the salvation of individuals : cp. Mt 3 9.

17. The Church of God, both before and after Christ, regarded by St. Paul as one and the same, is here likened to an olive tree : cp. Jer 11 16 Hos 14 6. Graffed in] The usual practice would be to graft the cultivated olive upon the wild stock. St. Paul reverses the process in his allegory, to enforce the lesson that the Jews were the original Church, and

honourable. **18. Boast .. boast**] RV 'glory .. gloriest.' **19.** See on vv. 11, 12, 15. **24. How much more**] We may see indications of the purpose of God for the Jews in the permanence of their race and in their devoted adherence to the God of their fathers.

25–36. That Israel will be converted has been directly revealed by God (vv. 25–27). God's purpose of favour to them has not changed (vv. 28, 29). Their disobedience is reckoned with in God's plan of mercy for both Jew and Gentile (vv. 30–32). This view of God's dealings calls forth wonder and praise (vv. 33–36).

Paraphrase. '(25) Learn, then, in humble silence, God's revealed will. A partial and temporary hardening of Israel has been permitted. But when the Gentiles as a whole have entered the kingdom, (26) Israel, too, will accept the Messiah. So Isaiah foretold that the Redeemer would remove their ungodliness, (27) and that their sins would be forgiven, and thus God's covenant with them would be carried out. (28) Although they are shut out from the blessings of the gospel, that the gospel may come to you, yet they are still beloved by God for the sake of the patriarchs whom He chose, (29) for God, who granted them His favour, has not changed His mind, (30) but, having first used their disobedience as the means of bringing you from disobedience to mercy, (31) He intends them so to be stirred up by the mercy you have obtained, as to give up their disobedience and find mercy in their turn. (32) Thus one cannot boast over the other. By giving Gentile and Jew, respectively, the laws of conscience and of revelation, God compelled the sinful nature of both to show itself in disobedience, that both might receive His mercy as the sole cause of their salvation. (33) So we are forced to wonder at God's profound love and wisdom, and the mystery of His working. (34) Into His thoughts no one can enter, no one share the shaping of His plans. (35) His bounty is unmerited. (36) He is source and guide and goal of all things.'

25. Mystery] Among the Greeks, a 'mystery' meant a secret of religion revealed only to the initiated. St. Paul uses the word to express a truth once hidden, but now revealed by God: cp. 16²⁵ 1 Cor 2⁷,¹⁰ Eph 1⁹ 3⁴. **Blindness**] RV 'a hardening': cp. v. 7. **In part**] i.e. not affecting the 'remnant' who have accepted Christ.

Fulness] i.e. the full number: cp. v. 12.

26. All Israel] i.e. the Jewish race will enter the Christian Church. **There shall come, etc.**] from Isa 59²⁰. **27.** From Isa 27⁹.

29. Calling] cp. 1⁶ᶠ· 8³⁰. **Without repentance**] i.e. God's promises are changeless, because He could never do that for which afterwards He was sorry. He is sometimes said, in OT., to 'repent,' e.g. Gn 6⁶ Joel 2¹³. What is meant

in such passages is, not that He changes His purposes or principles, but that, because His principles are changeless, therefore His action or methods alter as men alter. Such OT. language is figurative, belonging to the simplicity of less-developed religion. Because, with men, change of action is caused by change of mind, therefore, in OT., when God changes His action, He is *said* to change His mind.

30. Have not believed] RV 'were disobedient to.' **Unbelief**] RV 'disobedience.' **31. Not believed**] RV 'been disobedient.' **Your mercy**] RV 'the mercy shewn to you.' **32. Concluded**] RV 'shut up,' i.e. without power of escape: cp. Gal 3²². **In unbelief**] RV 'unto disobedience': cp. chs. 2, 7. **Upon all**] i.e. who do not reject His mercy. **34.** From Isa 40¹³. **35.** From Job 41¹¹. **36. To him**] RV 'unto him'; i.e. all things are created to serve and praise God.

CHAPTER 12
The Consecrated Life. The Law of Love

The doctrinal part of the Epistle being finished, St. Paul now turns to practical exhortation. God's mercy, shown in the gospel set forth in the previous chapters, calls for the sacrifice of ourselves to do His will (vv. 1, 2), by the humble and devoted use of God's spiritual gifts (vv. 3–8), and in love (vv. 9–21).

1–21. Paraphrase. '(1) God's redeeming love should be answered by the true sacrifice and spiritual ritual service of a life of purity and self-denial and work for God. (2) Do not follow the fashions and customs of the worldly society around you, but let your ways of thinking be so changed by the Holy Spirit that you look for and recognise God's will, and love to do it. (3) So, although the world does not value humility, as God's Apostle I charge every one of you to be contented to do that work in the Church for which God has fitted him. (4, 5) The Christian Society is like a body; each individual has his particular function; while the welfare of the whole depends upon how he performs it. (6) Let us all learn, then, from our different gifts, what it is God's will that we should do. If your gift is prophecy, speak what God Himself has taught you; (7, 8) and whatever your gift, use it to the best of your power. (9) As to other matters of conduct; let your love be sincere; have strong moral principles; (10) as one family in Christ be affectionate to one another; let each regard others as more fit for honours than himself; (11) be diligent, fervent, devoted to the Lord's work, (12) joyfully expectant of future glory, brave in affliction, unflagging in prayer, (13) generous and hospitable. (14) Bless your persecutors; (15) be sympathising; (16) enter into one another's desires and aims ; do not aim at high place or honour for yourself, but be content with the humble duties that come in your way. (17) Never retaliate. Avoid even the appearance of dishonourable conduct. (18) Live at peace with every one, so far as peace is in your own power. (19) If any man wrong you, leave it to God to punish him. (20) Do him good, and you will make him ashamed of his enmity. (21) Do not let the wickedness of others provoke evil passions in you, but conquer their wickedness by doing them good.'

1. Living sacrifice] as opposed to the sacrifice of a slain beast : cp. 6 13. **Reasonable**] i.e. an act of the reason. **2. Conformed to**] RV 'fashioned according to.' 'Fashion' implies external resemblance, 'form,' essential nature: cp. Phil 2 6. **World**] lit. ' Æon,' or 'age.' The Jews called the Messianic age 'the age to come,' as contrasted with 'this age' : cp. Mt 12 32 Lk 20 34 Eph 1 21. At present, considered as the kingdoms of Christ and of the world, the two ages co-exist. **3. Grace**] cp. 1 5. **Faith**] Faith is God's gift, and is of differing power and character, carrying with it differing 'gifts' (v. 6), i.e. capacities of Christian service. **5. One body**] cp. 1 Cor 12 12 f. Eph 4 15 f. Col 1 18.

6. Gifts] see on 1 13. **Is**] RV 'was,' i.e. when the Holy Spirit was received. **Prophecy**] i.e. inspired speaking, whether foretelling the future, or unfolding spiritual truth: cp. Ac 11 28 1 Cor 12 28 14 1 Eph 2 20 3 5 4 11. **Proportion of faith**] RV 'proportion of our faith,' i.e. in proportion to the revelation the prophet's faith has received. **7. Ministry**] i.e. the service of others : cp. Mk 10 45 ; sometimes any Christian office: cp. 11 13 ; sometimes, as here, attendance on temporal wants: cp. Ac 6 1 1 Cor 16 15 2 Cor 8 4. **8. Simplicity**] i.e. without selfish aim ; RV 'liberality.' **Ruleth**] lit. 'presideth,' i.e. in the Church or the family : cp. 1 Th 5 12 1 Tim 3 4 f. 5 17.

9. Dissimulation] RV 'hypocrisy. **10.** RV 'In love of the brethren be tenderly affectioned one to another.' **11.** RV 'In diligence not slothful' ; 'diligence ' = zeal, moral earnestness, not merely in temporal affairs. **12. Instant**] RV 'stedfastly.' **13. Distributing**] RV 'communicating,' i.e. sharing your goods : cp. Ac 2 42. **Saints**] RV ' the saints,' i.e. Christians, God's people. **Hospitality**] The various Churches were linked by the visits of accredited messengers : cp. Heb 13 2 1 Tim 3 2 1 Pet 4 9 2 Jn 10 3 Jn 5 f. **14.** Cp. Mt 5 44. **16. Men of low estate**] RV 'things that are lowly.' **17. Provide**] RV 'take thought for.' **Honest**] RV 'honourable.' **19. Give place unto wrath**] i.e. leave room for God's wrath to execute the vengeance deserved. Do not usurp the prerogative of God. **Wrath**] i.e. the wrath of God : cp. 5 9. **Written**] Dt 32 35. **20. From** Prov 25 21.

Coals of fire] i.e. melt him into shame, as a furnace melts metals.

CHAPTER 13

The Christian's Duty to the State and to his Neighbour

St. Paul now passes to the duties of Christians to the State. In 12 19 he had condemned revenge ; but he asserts here that the State may rightly punish, as God's agent in temporal affairs. He enforces obedience to government, i.e. to social order, not to any special form of government. He gives no directions as to what is to be done when there is a conflict of civil authority (vv. 1–7). Our behaviour to men in general is to be regulated by love (vv. 8–10). The nearness of Christ's coming is a motive for holiness of life (vv. 11–14).

1–14. Paraphrase. ' (1) Obey civil rulers, for they are divinely ordained, (2) and therefore God will punish disobedience. (3, 4) They do God's work, rewarding the good and punishing the evil. (5) Therefore obey, not only for fear of punishment, but because it is right, (6) as is implied by our rule that Christians are to pay taxes. (7) To sum up, give all authorities their due. (8) Owe no debt but that of love, which you can never adequately discharge, (9) for love sums up and includes all the commandments, (10) and, by loving, you fulfil them. (11) Let the thought of Christ's coming awaken you to these duties. (12, 13) Let us put off all evil ways, and conduct ourselves as those who belong to the kingdom of light. (14) Provide for your spiritual nature by clothing yourselves with the likeness and power of Christ, but pay no attention to the wrong desires of your fleshly nature.'

1. Of God] i.e. having its source in God. **2. Damnation**] RV 'judgment.' **4. Revenger**] RV 'avenger.' **Wrath**] i.e. God's anger against evil-doing. **5. For wrath**] RV 'because of the wrath.' **6. Tribute**] i.e. taxes paid by subject races. The Christians obeyed Christ's direction, Lk 20 20 f. **7. Custom**] i.e. ordinary taxes. **Fear**] i.e. scrupulous obedience. **8. Another**] RV ' his neighbour.' **Hath fulfilled**] i.e. hath fully met its requirements : cp. Mt 22 40. For the Christian, faith and love have taken the place of law. **9.** The Ninth Commandment is omitted in the best texts.

Thou shalt love] cp. Lv 19 18 Lk 10 27 Jas 2 8.

10. Worketh no ill] cp. 1 Cor 13 4 f. No one who truly loves his fellow-man will injure him.

11. And that] RV ' and this,' i.e. and do this : cp. 1 Cor 6 6, 8. **Time**] RV ' season.' **Salvation**] i.e. complete salvation. **Nearer**] However long Christ tarry, death brings Him near to each. But the first Christians evidently expected His return in their own time. Sanday and Headlam point out that this belief proved beneficial, by quickening the zeal of the Church for its difficult task, and by preventing the apostles from laying down minute regulations for the future. **Believed**] RV ' first believed.'

12. The day] i.e. of Christ's appearing. **Armour of light**] cp. Eph 6 13 f. **13. Walk**] i.e. along the path of daily life. **Honestly**] or, ' becomingly.' **Envying**] RV ' jealousy.'

14. Put ye on] Christ is put on in baptism, cp. 6 3 Gal 3 27 ; but the union must be realised.

The reading of these last vv. marked the turning-point in St. Augustine's life : see his ' Confessions,' bk. 8, c. 12.

CHAPTER 14

The Duty of Sympathy and Toleration

In c. 13 12 f. St. Paul urged his readers, by their expectation of Christ's coming, to avoid the licence and immorality of the heathen. Now he turns to the opposite extreme, and deals with the ascetic scrupulousness of certain Christians.

Under the Jewish Law there was a distinction between clean and unclean meats. This distinction, which perpetuated the separation between Jew and Gentile, Christ abolished (Mk 7 19 RV), as was afterwards revealed to Peter (Ac 10 28), and decided by the Council of Jerusalem (Ac 15 28 f.). The Council, however, directed the Gentile Christians in Antioch, Syria, and Cilicia to abstain from meat which had been offered to idols, or which had not been killed in the Jewish manner, out of consideration for the feelings of the Jewish Christians and to preserve unity. Afterwards the question arose at Corinth how far the Gentile Christians could join with their heathen acquaintances in meals when the meat had been offered to idols. St. Paul decided that as the meat was God's gift it might be eaten, but that when it was avowedly connected with idolatrous worship, it should be abstained from, for the sake of the consciences of those who thought it wrong to eat such meat.

It would seem that at Rome a minority of the Christians scrupled to partake of meat or wine in any form. They were probably Jewish Christians, for such ascetic practices were held by certain religious Jews. St. Paul did not approve of their scruples. He called such Christians ' weak in faith,' i.e. without that strong and clear conviction of Christian liberty which he held to be in accordance with the truth. But such brethren were to be welcomed and allowed to follow their convictions ; and if there were any danger of wounding their consciences, the ' strong ' brethren were to abstain themselves for the sake of Christian love.

Although the Apostle so urged toleration, yet, when a vital principle was at stake, he allowed no compromise : cp. 1 Cor 5, 11 16 15 12 f. Gal 1 8.

1-12. The ' strong' and the ' weak' are lovingly to tolerate one another, remembering that Christ is master of each, and that each will be judged by God. **13-23.** It would be better that the strong should forego his right, if its exercise would injure his brother.

Paraphrase. '(1) Some Christians have not grasped the principle that acceptance by God depends upon faith alone, and are in consequence scrupulous about unessential observances. Admit them to Christian fellowship, and abstain from criticising their scruples. (2) For example, one man is confident that he may eat any kind of food, while another refrains from meat. (3) Let not him who eats meat despise the other as superstitious. And let not the other condemn him who eats as unspiritual and worldly, for God imposed no rule about food upon him. (4) It is not for you to say that what Christ allows His servants is dangerous for them : their Master will keep them safe. (5) Again, one man observes the Jewish distinctions of days, while another does not. Let each man be faithful to his own conscience, (6) and recognise that the aim of men of both opinions is to please Christ. (7, 8) For His will is our law, in this life and in the world of death, (9) as is right, seeing that He is Master in both states of existence. (10, 11) It does not befit those who must all stand before God's judgment seat, to pass judgment upon one another. (12) The account that each will have to give of himself is enough for each to think of. (13) Therefore, instead of judging one another, determine not to hinder your brother in his Christian life. (14) For while in itself no food is sinful, it is sinful to those whose consciences forbid it, (15) and therefore to insist upon your right might injure your brother, which would be a breach of love. If Christ gave up His life for your brother, can you not give up some particular food ? (16) Do not bring reproach upon the truth you hold, (17) by making it seem that you regard a well-spread table as more important than spiritual graces and unity, (18) for it is the practice of such graces which makes the service of Christ approved by God and man. (19) Let it be our aim to bring about peace and the welfare of the Christian community. (20) It would be monstrous to destroy God's Church for the sake of food. To eat any particular food is not in itself wrong ; but it becomes wrong if by doing so you harm your brother ; (21) while it is a noble thing to give up your own right for his sake. (22) Cherish your own convictions, but do not seek to impose them upon every one else. You have the great blessing of an undoubting conscience, be satisfied with that.

(23) and do not tempt another to eat, when the fact that he is not sure whether he is doing right condemns him; for it is always sinful for a man to do what his conscience does not approve.'

1. The faith] RV 'faith.' **To doubtful disputations]** RM 'for decisions of doubts.'

2. Believeth that he may] RV 'hath faith to'; i.e. has such a grasp of the gospel of Christ that he recognises the indifference of these matters. **3. Despise]** cp. Mt 5 22. **Hath received]** i.e. into the Church. **4. God]** RV 'the Lord,' i.e. Christ.

5. One day above another] The reference is, no doubt, to Jewish observances: cp. Gal 4 10 Col 2 16. The principle is that salvation does not depend upon the observance of special days and seasons. These are indifferent in themselves, although to set apart special days may be practically useful. St. Paul would probably have included in this the keeping of Sunday. But he would have said that Sunday is no different from other days, because all days should be holy, not because all days are common. The six days should approximate as far as possible to Sunday, not Sunday to the six days. Hence the inestimable value of Sunday to maintain the level of spiritual life, quite apart from the benefit of its rest. **Persuaded]** RV 'assured.' **6. And he that regardeth not the day, to the Lord he doth not regard it]** RV omits. **Eateth]** i.e. eateth flesh. **Thanks]** cp. Mt 15 36 Ac 27 35 1 Cor 10 30 11 24 1 Tim 4 4f.

9. RV 'For to this end Christ died, and lived again.' 'He who, to save them, had dwelt in both worlds, was their Master in both' (Moule). **10.** RV 'But thou, why dost thou judge thy brother? or thou, again, why dost thou,' etc. **All]** emphatic. **Christ]** RV 'God.' 'It is important to notice how easily St. Paul passes from "Christ" to "God"' (Sanday and Headlam). **11.** From Isa 45 23. **Confess]** i.e. God's sovereignty. **12. Himself]** emphatic. **13. Stumblingblock]** cp. Mt 18 6f. 1 Cor 8 9f. **14. By the Lord]** RV 'in the Lord,' i.e. in communion with Christ. **Unclean]** lit. 'common': cp. Ac 10 14, 28. **But]** RV 'save that.' 'Mistaken conscience calls for correction by better light, but never for violation. To follow conscience is, by itself, no security that we are doing what is in itself right; but to violate conscience, which is our actual view of right and wrong, is always wrong' (Moule).

17. Kingdom of God] i.e. the Messianic kingdom, expected by the Jews as an earthly kingdom, but really the reign of Christ over man, whether in grace or glory: cp. 1 Cor 4 20. **Righteousness]** i.e. here, right dealing in relation to others. **Peace]** i.e. with one another. **Joy]** i.e. of the united Christian brotherhood. **In the Holy Ghost]** i.e. through

His indwelling. **18. In these things]** RV 'herein'; i.e. in the exercise of such a life of Christian love. **19. Edify]** i.e. build up the Christian society, which is called in the next v. 'the work of God.' **20.** RV 'overthrow not for meat's sake. **Pure]** RV 'clean': cp. 1 Cor 10 23. **With offence]** i.e. to others.

21. Nor *any thing*] RV 'nor to do anything': cp. 1 Cor 8 13. **Or is offended, or is made weak]** RV omits.

22. Hast thou faith?] RV 'The faith which thou hast.' **Have** *it* **to thyself]** i.e. do not force it upon others; respect the scruples of the weak. **Condemneth]** RV 'judgeth.' **Alloweth]** RV 'approveth.' **23. Damned]** RV 'condemned.' **Faith]** here = strong conviction. 'The words do not apply to those who are not Christians, nor to the works of those who are Christians done before they became such, but to the conduct of believing Christians; and faith is used somewhat in the way we should speak of a "good conscience"; everything which is not done with a clear conscience is sin' (Sanday and Headlam).

CHAPTER 15
JEW AND GENTILE ALIKE THE OBJECT OF GOD'S LOVE. THE APOSTLE'S PLANS

1-13. The subject of c. 14 is continued. 'Strength' should be displayed in helping the 'weak' after Christ's example (vv. 1-4). Let both sections be united in God's praise, welcoming one another as Christ welcomed them (vv. 5-7). As the divergence of views originated in the difference between Jew and Gentile, let both remember that Christ became a Jew for the salvation of both (vv. 8-13).

Paraphrase. '(1) Since the weak are thus in danger, the strong should be patient with their scruples, and not indulge their own liberty. (2) Each should be tender to his neighbour's feelings, and seek to promote his good, (3) following the example of Christ, depicted in the OT., (4) which we should read to learn lessons of endurance and to receive encouragement which will help us confidently to look to future glory. (5) May God teach you these lessons, enabling you to bear with one another, and to be so united in aims and hopes and feelings, after the pattern of Christ, (6) that you may join as one body in the praise of God. (7) Therefore let both sections welcome one another, as Christ welcomed both. A Church so united in brotherhood will redound to the glory of God. (8) Let the Gentile especially remember that Christ became a Jew, to secure to the Jews the fulfilment of God's promises, (9) and to welcome the Gentiles through God's pure mercy, (10, 11, 12) that Jew and Gentile might unite in His praise, as Psalmist and Prophet foretold. (13) May God grant that your believing in Christ may fill you with such joy and peace that you may look for Christ in glory with the triumphant confidence of those who are possessed by the might of the Holy Spirit.'

1. Bear] cp. Gal 6 2. **2. To edification**] The words define the kind of good to be sought, i.e. the building-up of the Church, not of any particular member. The individual is to be willing to sacrifice himself for the good of the whole body : cp. 14 19 1 Cor 10 33. Contr. Gal 1 10, where 'pleasing' would not be for edification. **3.** From Ps 69 9 : cp. 2 Cor 8 9 Phil 2 6. The Psalm describes the sufferings at the hands of the wicked of the righteous man. The words, therefore, are applicable to Christ above all. **4. Learning**] i.e. 'instruction' : cp. 2 Tim 3 16. **5. Consolation**] RV 'comfort.' **Likeminded**] RV 'of the same mind.' **Towards**] RV 'with.' **6.** RV 'that with one accord ye may with one mouth glorify the God and Father,' etc. **7. Us**] RV 'you.'

8. Now] RV 'for,' introducing proof of v. 7 b. **Was**] RV 'hath been made.' **Minister of the circumcision**] i.e. Christ lived and worked under the Old Covenant marked by circumcision : cp. Gal 4 4 f. 2 Cor 3 6.

9. Quotation from Ps 18 49. **Confess**] RV 'give praise.' **10.** From Dt 32 43. **11.** From Ps 117 1. **12.** From Isa 11 10. **In**] RV 'on.' **Trust**] RV 'hope.' **13. Through**] RV 'in.'

14–33. The Apostle approaches the end of the Epistle with personal references.

14–21. His tone of authority is warranted by his commission as apostle to the Gentiles, and by the way in which Christ has owned and blessed his work.

Paraphrase. '(14) Do not suppose I think you lacking either in goodness or in grasp of Christian principles. (15) But I have reminded you of these things somewhat boldly, because God appointed me (16) apostle of the Gentiles to bring them to Him. (17) I speak with authority, therefore, not because of myself, but because I am Christ's minister, (18) and because He has worked through me (19) with miracles and spiritual power, so that I have preached the gospel widely ; (20, 21) always seeking the honour of preaching only where Christ has not yet been preached.'

14. Ye also] RV 'ye yourselves.' **Goodness**] i.e. goodness of heart toward others. **15. In some sort**] better, 'in part' (of the Epistle), e.g. 6 12 f. 11 17 f. 14. **Is given**] RV 'was given' : cp. 1 5.

16. The minister] RV 'a minister.' The Gk. word, the original of the word 'liturgy,' is used in LXX of priests and Levites, and denotes one who ministers in sacred things. **Ministering**] RM 'ministering in sacrifice.' He was called to offer the Gentiles as a sacrifice to God. He did this by preaching the gospel. **Offering**] cp. Isa 66 19 f. **17. Where-**

of I may glory] RV 'my glorying.' **18.** The only thing he will boast of is the work Christ has done through him for the conversion of the Gentiles. **Obedient**] i.e. in faith : cp. 1 5 16 26.

19. Through mighty signs] RV 'in the power of signs,' i.e. the power which miracles have upon those who behold them : cp. 2 Cor 12 12. He speaks of his miracles as well known and indubitable. **Round about**] He had evangelised on either side of the route from Jerusalem to Illyricum. **Illyricum**] On the E. coast of the Adriatic, and NW. of Macedonia. It was approached, and may have been visited, in the journey mentioned Ac 20 1, 2. **Fully preached**] i.e. in the chief centres, founding Churches which might carry on the work.

20. RV 'yea, making it my aim, so to preach,' etc. **Lest I should build**] cp. 2 Cor 10 12 f. **21.** From Isa 52 15.

22–33. He hopes, after a journey to Jerusalem, to visit Rome on his way to Spain (vv. 22–29). He desires their prayers (vv. 30–33).

Paraphrase. '(22) My work has often prevented me from coming to you, (23) but now that my work here is finished, (24) I hope to visit you on my way to Spain. (25) Meanwhile I am starting for Jerusalem, (26) to convey to the Christian poor there a contribution from Macedonia and Achaia, (27) which is an acknowledgment of the debt the Gentiles owe to the Jews in spiritual things. (28) Afterwards I will travel by you into Spain, (29) and I feel sure that visit will be the occasion of much blessing. (30) Wrestle in prayer, (31) that I may be delivered from the Jews, and that the Jewish Christians may accept the peace offering which I bring, (32) that I may come joyfully to you and find repose. (33) May God bless you with His peace !'

22. RV 'Wherefore also I was hindered these many times' : cp. 1 10, 13. **24. Brought on my way**] cp. Ac 15 3 28 15 1 Cor 16 6. **25.** Cp. Ac 19 21 20 3.

26. Poor saints] RV 'poor among the saints.' There was much poverty among the Christians at Jerusalem, increased, perhaps, by the ill-will of the rich Sadducees. St. Paul had been intreated to 'remember the poor' (Gal 2 10). At the same time there was mistrust at Jerusalem of him and his work. Therefore he had instituted a collection among the Gentile Churches, which, he hoped, would draw together the Gentile and Jewish Christians : cp. Ac 24 17 1 Cor 16 1 f. 2 Cor 8, 9. **27. Minister**] same Gk. word as 'minister' in v. 16.

Carnal] i.e. belonging to this earthly life : no bad association here.

28. Sealed] i.e. marked it as their property ; made it over to them. **To them**] i.e. the

Jerusalem Christians. **Fruit**] i.e. the contribution would be evidence to the Jewish Christians of the real faith and love of the Gentiles.

Into Spain] St. Paul may have visited Spain after he was released from Rome, though there is no evidence of his having done so. Clement of Rome (about 96 A.D.) says he went 'to the extremity of the West.'

29. Though St. Paul did not come to Rome in the way he anticipated, his coming was brought about by God's Providence for 'the furtherance of the gospel': cp. 1 $^{11f.}$ Phil 1 ^{13}.

30. Of the Spirit] i.e. awakened by the Spirit: cp. Gal 5 ^{22}.

CHAPTER 16
GREETINGS AND WARNINGS

1–16. Commendation and greetings. Observe the number of women to whom the Apostle sends greeting. The fact is indicative of the change wrought in the position of women by the gospel, and of the honourable place taken by them in the Christian Church. Observe also the difference of nationality indicated by the names. St. Paul, a Hebrew, sends salutation to Greeks, Romans, and perhaps Asiatics, many of them probably slaves—marking the universality of the gospel: cp. Gal 3 ^{28} Col 3 ^{11}.

1. Commend] i.e. introduce: cp. 12 ^{13} 2 Cor 3 ^{1}. Apparently, Phœbe was the bearer of the Epistle. **Servant**] lit. 'deacon', RM 'deaconess': translated 'deacon' in Phil 1 ^{1}, etc., but 'minister' in Eph 3 ^{7} 6 ^{21}, etc. Either Phœbe had been definitely appointed to minister to women (cp. 1 Tim 5 $^{3f.}$), or she is called 'minister' because she voluntarily devoted herself to good works. **Cenchrea**] the eastern port of Corinth. **2. Succourer**] or, 'patroness.' The Gk. word is used for an influential friend or protector. **3. Priscilla**] RV 'Prisca.' For the history of Aquila and Prisca cp. Ac 18, 1 Cor 16 ^{19} 2 Tim 4 ^{19}. **4. Laid down, etc.**] Perhaps they risked their lives at Ephesus: cp. Ac 19. **5. In their house**] i.e. meeting in their house: cp. Ac 12 ^{12} 1 Cor 16 ^{19} Col 4 ^{15} Philemon v. 2.

Firstfruits] i.e. an early convert. **Achaia**] RV 'Asia,' i.e. the Roman province of which Ephesus was the chief city.

7. Junia] RV 'Junias.' **Kinsmen**] i.e. Jews belonging to the same 'Tribe' of citizens of Tarsus as St. Paul. **Of note among the apostles**] i.e. distinguished apostles. 'Apostle' means 'one sent on a mission and representing the sender.' 'Apostles of Churches,' cp. 2 Cor 8 ^{23} (RM) Phil 2 ^{25} (RM), were men sent on special missions by particular Churches.

But, specially, 'apostles' means 'apostles of Christ,' cp. 1 Th 2 ^{6}, i.e. men sent to be Christ's witnesses everywhere. Such were the Twelve; Paul and Barnabas, cp. Ac 14 ^{14}; James, 1 Cor 15 ^{7} Gal 1 ^{19}; and Andronicus and Junias. 'Apostles of Christ' must have seen the Lord, cp. Lk 24 ^{48} Ac 1 $^{8, 22}$ 1 Cor 9 ^{1}; have shown spiritual power, cp. 1 Cor 9 ^{2} 2 Cor 12 ^{12}; and have received a call from God, cp. 1 Cor 12 ^{28} Eph 4 ^{11}.

9. Urbane] RV 'Urbanus.'

12. Persis] the name of a woman.

13. Rufus] cp. Mk 15 ^{21}. St. Mark probably wrote his Gospel at Rome.

Mine] i.e. St. Paul felt for her the affection of a son.

17–20. Warning against false teachers, probably Judaistic, whose doctrines St. Paul has dealt with in the Epistle. They may not have appeared at Rome as yet: cp. Phil 1 $^{15f.}$ (written from Rome).

17. Offences] RV 'occasions of stumbling. **Avoid**] RV 'turn away from.' **18. Their own belly**] i.e. they seek their own interests, and their religious ideas are low and materialistic: cp. Phil 3 $^{17f.}$ Col 2 $^{20f.}$

19. For] i.e. 'But they ought not to deceive you, for,' etc. **Simple**] i.e. harmless: cp. Mt 10 ^{16}. **20. Bruise Satan**] by defeating the false teaching: cp. 2 Cor 11 $^{12f.}$

21–23. Greetings from St. Paul's companions.

21. Lucius] cp. Ac 13 ^{1}. **Jason**] cp. Ac 17 $^{5f.}$ **Sosipater**] cp. Ac 20 ^{11}. **Kinsmen**] cp. v. 7. **22. Wrote**] RV 'write.' St. Paul's habit was to dictate his letters: cp. 1 Cor 16 ^{21} Col 4 ^{18} 2 Th 3 ^{17} Gal 6 ^{11}. **23. Gaius**] cp. 1 Cor 1 ^{14}. **Of the whole church**] i.e. the meetings were held in his house. **A brother**] RV 'the brother,' i.e. the Christian. **24.** RV omits: see Intro.

25–27. Concluding doxology, summing up the main points of the Epistle.

25. My gospel] i.e. his special teaching of acceptance by faith for Jew and Gentile. **Of Jesus Christ**] i.e. the object of his preaching was to bring about faith in Jesus the Messiah: cp. 10 $^{8f.}$ **According to the revelation, etc.**] i.e. the preaching of Jesus Christ explains God's purpose, which had been hidden: cp. chs. 9–11, 1 Cor 2 $^{6f.}$

Secret] RV 'in silence.' **Since the world began**] RV 'through times eternal.' **26. By the scriptures**] cp. 1 $^{1f.}$ 3 ^{21}. **For the**] RV 'unto,' i.e. leading to the obedience which faith implies: cp. 1 ^{5}.

Subscription. The subscriptions to the Epistles are said to have been the work of Euthalius, a bishop of the 5th cent.

1 CORINTHIANS

INTRODUCTION

ᴛ. The Corinthian Church.

(*a*) 'Corinth was in many respects the most important city in Greece under the Roman Empire. Whereas Athens was the educational centre, the seat of the greatest university in the world at that time, and the city to which the memories of Greek freedom and older history clung most persistently, Corinth was the capital of the Roman province, the centre of government and commerce, of actual life and development in the country' (HDB).

It was situated on the narrow isthmus which connected Macedonia and Achaia, and possessed two great harbours, Lechæum looking towards the Adriatic Sea and Italy, and Cenchreæ (Ac 18¹⁸ Ro 16¹) looking towards the Ægean and Asia. Though it lay a little inland it had all the advantages of a seaport, and, occupying as it did a central position on the lines of communication between Rome and the East, it was a great commercial clearing-house. Small ships were hauled across the isthmus by a prepared way to avoid the voyage round the Cape, and travellers from Italy to the East landed at Lechæum and re-embarked at Cenchreæ. It was thus a place where traders and officials were constantly coming and going. Its population was composed of Greeks and Romans, Jews and Orientals. Merchants and sailors were its most frequent visitors, staying for short periods on their voyages, and bringing to it the civilisation and the customs of many lands.

Corinth in St. Paul's day was a Roman colony. Two centuries earlier the famous Greek city on the same site had been destroyed by the Roman armies; but after lying in ruins for a hundred years it had been refounded by Julius Cæsar in 46 B.C., and had speedily regained more than its former greatness.

Besides its commercial importance Corinth was famous as the scene of the great Isthmian games, which every second year attracted a multitude of people to the city; and it was noted as the centre of the abominable worship of the goddess Aphrodite, in whose worship virgins sacrificed their chastity. The Corinthians were notorious even in the world of that time for their drunkenness and sensuality. They were also much given to faction and strife, being always anxious to discuss philosophical and moral problems, and to debate the qualifications and drawbacks of their public teachers.

It is a significant commentary on their way of life that a man of Corinth was usually introduced on the stage in a state of intoxication, and that 'to live like a Corinthian' had become a proverb to express a life of luxury and licence.

(*b*) **The Founding of the Church.** St. Paul's first visit to Corinth was made in the course of his second missionary journey, and lasted eighteen months (Ac 18). After his failure to make any deep impression at Athens, the Apostle passed on to Corinth; probably in the autumn of 50 A.D., but possibly a year or two later, as the dates are uncertain. On his arrival he met with Aquila and his wife Priscilla, Jews lately expelled from Rome on account of their race and religion. They were tentmakers, like himself, so he wrought with them and stayed in their house. At first, according to his custom (cp. Ac 13⁵,¹⁴ 14¹ 17²), he preached in the synagogue, and endeavoured to persuade the Jews and the Greek proselytes that Jesus was the Christ. The arrival of Silas and Timothy reinforced him, and the work was not without effect, for several Jews believed, among them being Crispus, the ruler of the synagogue, and Titius Justus, one of their proselytes. The majority, however, remained obdurate, and the Apostle had to withdraw from the synagogue. Eventually the wrath of the Jews culminated in an attempt to convict him before Gallio, the governor of the province, of teaching an illegal religion. The governor, however, dismissed the case, because the Apostle had not broken any Roman law, and the Greeks who were present gave a rough approval of his decision by beating Sosthenes, the new ruler of the synagogue, in sight of the judgment-seat. Thus protected by the law, St. Paul continued his work until the spring of 52 A.D., when he sailed for Ephesus and Jerusalem, to celebrate the Passover.

After his departure from Ephesus, Apollos, a learned Jew of Alexandria, who had embraced Christianity, arrived there, and made himself known to the Church. His knowledge of Christ was somewhat imperfect, but having been instructed more fully by Aquila and Priscilla, who had accompanied St. Paul to Ephesus, he became of great assistance in the work of the Lord. It was his desire to go to Corinth, and after a time the brethren in Ephesus commended him to the community across the sea (Ac 18 27 2 Cor 3 1). In Corinth his preaching was very successful (Ac 18 27), and his arguments proved attractive to many of the Corinthians, who preferred a more philosophical style to the plain words of St. Paul.

(c) **Composition of the Church.** The Church at Corinth was composed to some extent of Jews (Ac 18 8 1 Cor 7 18 10 32 2 Cor 11 22), but chiefly of Gentiles (Ac 18 7 1 Cor 12 2). The members were of all classes. Gaius, 'the host of the whole Church,' and Erastus, 'the chamberlain of the city' (Ro 16 23—the Epistle to the Romans was written from Corinth), were among the better class, as was, perhaps, also Stephanas, 'the firstfruits of Achaia' (16 15). But others were poor (1 26-28), and others were slaves (7 22). It is certain that here as elsewhere 'not many wise men after the flesh, not many mighty, not many noble' were called (1 26). The majority seem to have been of humble station (1 27, 28), and had to work hard for their living. Some of these Christian converts being of Jewish origin attached importance to Jewish rites (9 20), others prided themselves on their liberal views (8 8, 9 10 25, 27) ; many had been redeemed from vicious habits (6 9-11), and had to keep strict watch over their lives (6 12, 13, 20).

(d) **The Rise of Parties in the Church.** In order to understand the situation referred to in our Epistle, it is necessary to give a brief account of the factions which arose in the Church after the Apostle's departure (1 12).

Four parties are there named—called by the names of the leaders they had adopted—a party of Paul, a party of Apollos, a party of Cephas, and a party of Christ. The followers of Paul were those who had remained faithful to the teaching of the founder of the Church, and probably included the earliest converts who had felt the power of his personal influence ; but they made the mistake of opposing him to other teachers, and, perhaps, especially at first to Apollos, hence they received a special rebuke (1 13).

The party of Apollos evidently consisted of those who admired that eloquent speaker's ability in the use of argument and language. Apollos seems to have captivated a number of the converts by his skill in harmonising the teaching of the OT. with the current philosophy, and his ingenuity in using the allegorical method of interpretation in applying the Hebrew Scriptures to prove that Jesus was the Messiah. St. Paul may be contrasting the methods of Apollos with his own simpler style of teaching the Corinthians when he speaks of 'wisdom' and 'foolishness' in 1 17-31 2 1-13. The nucleus of the party of Apollos would be composed of those whom he himself had converted ; others would be attracted to it

who were easily impressed by a flowing style and a philosophic presentation of the truth. The differences between the parties of Paul and Apollos arose half-unconsciously, hence their hostility would not be very pronounced.

The other two parties had a different origin. It would appear that, some time after St. Paul's departure, representatives of that party in the Church at Jerusalem which maintained that acceptance of Christianity involved acceptance of circumcision and other Jewish rites, also came to Corinth. These Judaisers, as they are called, were always hostile to the wider developments of Christianity. They found fault with St. Peter for his liberal views and his attitude to the Gentiles (Ac 11 2) at an early period of the Church's history   St. Paul, however, was the principal object of their aversion and ill-will   It is possible that they had never forgiven his persecution of the Christians in his unconverted days, and certainly from the date of his return to Antioch, after his first mission to Galatia, they opposed his admission of uncircumcised heathen to the fellowship of the Church (Ac 15 1 Gal 2 4). We find them sending emissaries in his track to alienate the Jewish converts from allegiance to him and bring the Gentile brethren into bondage to the Mosaic Law (Gal 1 7 2 12, 13 3 1 5 2 6 12 Phil 3 2). Some of these Jewish Christians had brought letters of commendation (2 Cor 3 1) to Corinth, and had been received by the Church. They took occasion to exalt St. Peter (Cephas) as the chief of the Apostles, and tried to undermine the authority of St. Paul, insisting that he was not an Apostle, and that he lacked the qualification of having seen Jesus (9 1).

Thus was formed the party of Cephas, consisting, probably, of some of the Jews who had joined the Church, and, perhaps, of some of the proselytes, who, having first adopted the Jewish religion and rites, would be the more easily persuaded.

The party of Christ may have arisen as a protest against these three sections, whose members adopted the names of Apostles as party watchwords, or even as a separate and stricter Jewish party, maintaining the duty of all disciples of Christ to follow Him in His fulfilment of the rites of the Law (Lk 2 27 Jn 5 1, etc.). Its members seem to have become more extreme and fanatical as the strife went on, and to have maintained the strictest Judaistic principles : see further remarks in Intro. to 2 Cor, 1 (b). We find in the Second Epistle that some of its members withstood St. Paul's authority and denied his right to interfere in the discipline of the Church, and that it was with great difficulty that the Apostle asserted his position and regained his influence (2 Cor 10 7 11 13-15, 21, 22, etc.).

2. The First Epistle.

(a) Circumstances of its Origin, and Date.

Our First Epistle to the Corinthians is one, and that not the first, of a series of letters written by St. Paul to the Corinthian Church, in view of the party quarrels which rent it, and the difficulties of belief and conduct which perplexed its members. In the interval between St. Paul's departure from Corinth, after founding the Church, and the date of this letter, he had revisited the Churches of Galatia and Phrygia (Ac 18 23), and from there had come to Ephesus (Ac 19 1). At Ephesus he remained for more than two years (Ac 19 8-10), reaching the city perhaps in 53 or 54 A.D., and leaving it late in 56 or 57 A.D. During his residence there he seems to have received tidings from Corinth that some of the Christians had fallen back into immoral habits, and he wrote a letter to the Church, in which he directed the members to exercise discipline upon the offenders. To this letter (which is not now extant) he refers in 5 9, 'I wrote unto you in my epistle to have no company with fornicators' (RV). This letter was not well received by the Corinthians. Some of them, misunderstanding the counsel, declared that it was impossible to follow it without going out of the world (5 10), and others flatly denied his right to interfere at all (4 15, 18, 19). In reply they wrote a letter, frequently alluded to and even quoted from in the canonical First Epistle (5 10 7 1 8 1-10 10 25 11 2), in which they temporised in regard to the cases of immorality, asking for further information, and submitted a number of problems on which they requested his opinion. This letter was probably brought by three of their number, Stephanas and Fortunatus and Achaicus (16 17).

Meanwhile, however, St. Paul had also heard of the factions in the Church. The news had been brought by servants of Chloe (1 11), a lady evidently well known to the Corinthians, though whether she was herself a Christian does not appear. The tidings caused the Apostle much pain and anxiety. He sent Timothy to Corinth by way of Macedonia (Ac 19 22 1 Cor 4 17) to 'bring them into remembrance of his ways in Christ.' About the same time he wrote the First Epistle and sent it—perhaps by the hands of Titus and the brother mentioned in 2 Cor 12 18—by the shorter sea route, that it might arrive before his young comrade, whom he commends to their care (16 10). The letter contains first of all a remonstrance regarding their divisions and an exhortation to unity, and secondly detailed answers to the problems and questions submitted in the Epistle from the Church. It was probably written and despatched early in 55 or 56 A.D.

(b) Synopsis of Contents.

Introduction 1 1-9. Greeting and thanksgiving.

I. 1 10–6 20. Problems suggested by the reports of Chloe's people.

(a) 1 10–4 21. Parties and party spirit in the Church.

(b) 5 1-13. The case of immorality.

(c) 6 1-11. Christians and litigation.

(d) 6 12-20. The obligation of purity.

II. 7 1–16 4. Problems submitted in the letter from Corinth.

(a) 7 1-40. Marriage, divorce, and celibacy.

(b) 8 1–11 1. Food offered to idols:

   (i) 8 1-13. The principle of self-denial;

   (ii) 9 1-27. St. Paul's own example;

   (iii) 10 1–11 1. Historical illustrations and practical advice.

(c) 11 2-16. The veiling of women in Church.

(d) 11 17-34. The proper observance of the Lord's Supper.

(e) 12 1–14 40. Spiritual gifts:

   (i) 12 1-31. Their nature and relations;

   (ii) 13 1-13. The most excellent gift of charity;

   (iii) 14 1-40. The gift of tongues subordinate to prophecy.

(f) 15 1-58. The fact and the doctrine of the Resurrection.

(g) 16 1-4. The collection for the poor Christians in Jerusalem.

(h) 16 5-24. Personal messages and conclusion.

(c) Outline of the Epistle.

After saluting the Church and giving thanks for their Christian graces (1 1-9) the Apostle deals with the evils of which he has heard. First of all (1 10–4 31) he points out the scandal and danger of party spirit in the Church, reminding them that Christ is the only Master, the Apostles being only preachers of Christ. He shows them that the preaching of the Cross is powerful to accomplish their salvation, and that it is the only true wisdom to those who have understanding. The Corinthians, however, are still carnal, and do not know the truth, as is shown by their partisanship. Let them realise that Christian teachers are fellow-workers with God, servants of Christ, and let them give up this strife and rancour. The Apostle then passes on (c. 5) to deal with the case of incestuous marriage, and bids the Church put out of its membership the man who has caused the scandal. Litigation before heathen judges is forbidden (6 1-9) because it is both foolish and morally wrong, exhibiting the spirit of their uncon verted past, rather than the new spirit of love and peace, and then the Apostle urges them again (6 10-20) to purity of life.

The rest of the Epistle seems to deal with problems of Church life suggested by questions in a letter from the Corinthians to St. Paul. The subject of marriage is dealt with first (c. 7), the Apostle commending the married state to all who prefer it, and forbidding divorce on grounds of difference in religion. Meats offered to idols formed a cause of scandal to many, and the Apostle (c. 8) points out that while a man might well enough eat such meat with a pure conscience, his action might give offence to another who regarded the eating of such food as sin, in which case it was far better to avoid it. This suggests a reference to his own example (c. 9) of self-denial. He has the right to look for material aid from the Church, but he refuses to exercise it, and practises the same self-denial in this respect as in respect of his bodily appetites. He then (c. 10) returns to the subject of idolatry, showing its dangers by reference to Jewish history, and urging his converts to keep from its degrading influence.

The next subject taken up (11 2-16) is the place of women in the worship of the Church, after which the Apostle deals with the observance of the Lord's Supper (11 17-34), reproving the abuses which disfigure their sacred feast, reminding them of the manner of its institution by the Lord Jesus, and exhorting them to reverence in its use. The use and abuse of such spiritual gifts as prophesying and speaking with tongues is dealt with in its turn (chs. 12–14), and the Apostle, while commending the moderate and careful use of all the gifts, bids them cultivate above all (c. 13) the most excellent gift of charity. Then follows his teaching as to the fact and the doctrine of the Resurrection, in which he shows how intimately belief in the Resurrection of Christ (and consequently of the dead, of whom He is the first-fruits) is bound up with their Christian faith and new obedience, and how all their Christian practices and actions and aspirations were inseparably connected with it. Turning next to the manner of the Resurrection, he points out that as it is with the seed sown and the wheat reaped, so is it with the mortal body and the spiritual body. Through the grave man's body passes into a new and higher form, and then ' when this corruptible has put on incorruption, and this mortal has put on immortality, then shall be brought to pass the saying that is written, Death is swallowed up in victory.' The letter concludes (c. 16) with directions about a collection for the poor in Jerusalem, the Mother-Church, and with personal messages to various friends of the writer.

(d) **Authenticity.** This Epistle is accepted as St. Paul's by almost all schools of biblical criticism, including those often regarded as sceptical and extreme. The internal and the external evidences are both exceptionally good. The Epistle accords with the circumstances under which it is presumed to have been written, and presents a true picture of the nature and habits of the Corinthians. Its tone is real, its exhortations and counsels arise naturally out of the circumstances, and it reveals the Apostle in many characteristic moods. As regards the witness borne to this letter in early Church history, it is sufficient to say that Clement of Rome, writing to this same Church of Corinth about 97 A.D., quotes from it and bids them read it again for their guidance.

(e) **The Master-thought of this Epistle** and of the Second Epistle is the union of Christ and the Christian. 'I am crucified with Christ,' he says (Gal 2 20) : 'nevertheless I live ; yet not I, but Christ liveth in me : and the life which I now live in the flesh I live by the faith of the Son of God, who loved me, and gave himself for me.' Christ and the Apostle are so united in mind and spirit that the very life of Christ, so to speak, pulsates in Him. He has yielded Himself so completely to Christ's influence, and drunk so deeply of His spirit, that he acts, speaks, thinks, and suffers ' in Christ.' The sense of personal union with Christ sustains him in all his efforts, and he desires to realise Christ's presence abiding with him in increasing degree.

' Flow on my soul, thou Spirit, and renew me,
    Fill with Thyself, and let the rest be far ' (Myers).

What he has thus experienced in his own life, he assumes that his converts have in some degree experienced also (6 15 8 12 2 Cor 1 21 5 17). He realises indeed that their union with Christ is but imperfect and dimly realised by themselves ; he can treat them only as ' babes in Christ' (3 1). But though they do not comprehend this fact of their spiritual life, he is assured that Christ is indeed already dwelling in them (2 Cor 13 5) ; and he desires that they may receive more and more of the influence of Christ, until they live in complete and conscious union with Him. From this controlling thought of the union of Christ and the Christian the Apostle deduces the two dominant ideas—the necessity of union with one another, and the necessity of purity of life (see paraph. 2 Cor 4 13-15).

(f) **Special Teaching of the Epistle.** There are many points of Christian belief and practice which this Epistle sets in a unique light. (a) One most important feature is the independent witness it bears to the facts of Christ's life and death and resurrection. Especially does the Apostle dwell upon the Crucifixion and the Resurrection (2 2 5 7

6²⁰ 8¹¹ 15³⁻⁸,²⁰,²³,⁵⁷, etc.). The letter was written before our Gospels, within about twenty-five years of the death of Christ, and in all matters of fact it confirms the statements of the Gospels.

We learn from it too that the sacraments were duly celebrated, although some disorder was mingled with the observance of the Lord's Supper. Baptism was administered to those who confessed their faith in Christ (1¹²⁻¹⁶ 6¹¹ 12¹³), and the Lord's Supper was observed by the breaking of the bread and the giving of the cup, and was to be prepared for by self-examination (11²³⁻²⁹). Associated with the Holy Communion and prior to its celebration was the *agapé* or common meal, at which the members of the Church shared the food which each had brought, and ate together in token of their unity as members of one family. It was in connexion with the *agapé* that the abuses had arisen which St. Paul condemns in c. 11.

The doctrines of Christianity are not set forth here in a formal way, but are brought forward incidentally as they bear on Christian life and practice. Belief in God the Father (8⁶), in the Lord Jesus Christ (8⁶ 11¹), and in the Holy Spirit (12³), is the foundation of the faith. Christ crucified is the great subject of preaching (1²³). Christ has ransomed man (6¹⁹,²⁰); He has died for their sins according to prophecy (15³); He is the perfect example for them to follow (11¹), and the chief object of their love (16²²). Christ's death is the power of God unto salvation (1²⁴), and the great motive to holiness of life (5⁷,⁸). His Resurrection is the basis of belief in the resurrection of the dead (15¹⁶); the ground of the hope of immortality (15¹⁸); and the pledge of the forgiveness of sins (15¹⁷).

The Epistle bears witness also to the ideal unity of the Church of Christ (1²,¹³ 3¹¹ 11¹⁸), to the fact of forgiveness bestowed by Christ (15³), to the great Christian doctrines of the resurrection of the body (15⁴²⁻⁴⁴), and of the life everlasting (15⁵³⁻⁵⁷). Closely connected with doctrine is duty; and the Christian virtues of self-denial (8¹³), unity (1¹⁰), love (c. 13), and purity (3¹⁶,¹⁷), are inculcated in many passages, of which those indicated are mere specimens. What is insisted upon throughout is that the whole purpose of the death of Christ was to produce the life of the Spirit in the souls of men (1³⁰ 2²⁻⁵ 6²⁰ 7²³, etc.).

The public worship described is spontaneous and unrestrained. Each one prayed or sang or exhorted as the Spirit moved him, sometimes in a sort of raptured utterance which was unintelligible to the others (14¹²⁻¹⁷). We can understand that while such worship was often hearty and helpful and productive of deep impressions (14²⁵), it was liable to much abuse, and was in fact frequently spoiled by rivalry and disorder, and even by blasphemy (12³ 14¹¹,¹⁶,²³,³⁰). The Apostle lays down strict rules for its proper conduct on the principle that all things should be done unto edifying (14²⁶⁻⁴⁰). There seems to have been little or no organisation in the Corinthian Church at that early stage. Had there been responsible heads of the Church some of the causes of disorder could not have been present. Perhaps we may see an attempt on the Apostle's part to get such recognised 'elders' or 'bishops' appointed (cp. Phil 1¹), in his advice to the Corinthians to submit themselves to such as the house of Stephanas (16¹⁵,¹⁶). The principle of discipline was recognised in the Church, and the penalty for gross sin was expulsion by a solemn service (5³⁻⁵,¹¹). But there seems to have been some difference of opinion as to the authority by which the sentence was to be pronounced when the case arose: this caused delay, and the Apostle had to assert his right to exercise discipline when the Church as a whole was lax.

It is mainly the dark side of the Church life which is disclosed in this Epistle; but there was also a bright side. There was life in the Church; its members possessed the gifts of the spirit; they were growing in grace and in the knowledge of God (1⁴⁻⁹), and the Apostle could give thanks in spite of all drawbacks for the many aspirations and efforts and achievements which gave promise of better things to come (1⁴,⁸).

CHAPTER 1

GREETING AND THANKSGIVING. PARTISAN-
SHIP IN THE CHURCH

St. Paul, after greeting the Church and giving thanks for its spiritual gifts, rebukes the preference for various teachers which was prevalent among them; such a spirit lost sight of Christ crucified, the one subject of all Christian teachers.

1-9. Greeting and Thanksgiving.

1. Called *to be* **an apostle**] chosen by God, not self-appointed: see Ac 22¹⁷⁻²¹. **Sosthenes**] This may be the ruler of the synagogue of Ac 18¹⁷, converted since that time.

2. Sanctified in Christ Jesus] consecrated to God through faith in Christ, having Christ living in them and His influence moulding them. **Called** *to be* **saints**] lit. 'called saints'; because consecrated to Christ. They bore the name and should also show the nature of saints. The holiness of the Church is continually suggested in this Epistle. **With all that in every place call**] The greeting is extended to include all Christians in the neighbourhood. There was a branch of the Church at Cenchreæ, the eastern port of Corinth

(2 Cor 1¹ Ro 16¹). **Call upon the name**] Prayer was offered to Christ by all Christians from the time of the Ascension, and this is one of the clearest proofs that He was regarded as truly divine (Ac 7⁵⁹ 9²¹). **3. Grace** *be* **unto you, and peace**] St. Paul's invariable greeting to the Churches. **Grace** is the favour of God, and **peace** the result of the enjoyment of that favour.

4-9. Paraphrase. 'I praise God continually because through your spiritual union with Christ you have received the gifts of His grace. (5) I am especially thankful because your knowledge of the truth and your ability to give it expression have increased (6) with the increasing response of your spirits to the gospel of Christ. (7) You are thus on an equality with other Churches in respect of spiritual gifts; and you wait and watch for the coming of the Lord, (8) who will keep you faithful, so that none shall reproach you.'

4. I thank my God] St. Paul regarded the Corinthian Church, in spite of its sins and faults, as a true and living Church. **5. Are enriched**] RV 'were enriched.' **In all utterance, and** *in* **all knowledge**] The fact that they abused these gifts (12³ 13¹,² 14²⁻¹³) did not lead the Apostle to undervalue them. **6. The testimony of Christ**] The Apostle's witness to Christ's person and power and saving work was verified by its effects upon the Corinthians.

7. The coming of our Lord] cp. 4⁵ 7²⁹ 15⁵¹ 1 Th 4¹⁵ 2 Pet 3⁴,¹⁴. **8. Confirm you**] keep you steadfast. **9. The fellowship of his Son**] i.e. union with Him. This is the keynote of the Epistle, and leads to the thought suggested in the next paragraph, that they who are united to Christ should be united to one another.

DIVISION I. 1¹⁰–6²⁰. PROBLEMS SUGGESTED BY THE REPORT OF CHLOE'S PEOPLE

(a) 1¹⁰–4²¹. PARTIES AND PARTY SPIRIT IN THE CHURCH

10-17. Paraphrase. 'Brethren, I implore you by the Holy Name of Jesus to abstain from strife and party spirit. I have heard of your disputes and of your use of the names of Apostles and even of Christ's Holy Name as party watchwords. (13–16) Can Christ be claimed as the property of a faction! And are you putting my name on a level with His Sacred Name? I am thankful that I baptised so very few of you that none can say I baptised in my own name. (17) Preaching was my work, not baptism—the preaching of salvation through the Cross of Christ.'

10. By the name of our Lord] The Apostle appeals to them by the Holy Name of Jesus, which itself should remind them of their oneness as His followers, since they had all been baptised into it. **Speak the same thing**] i.e.

agree in calling Christ your only leader. **Perfectly joined, etc.**] lit. 'adjusted in the same mind and in the same view.' They should be reconciled, and try to be of the same spirit.

11. Chloe] We know nothing of her but her name. 'Those of her house' may have been sons or brothers or servants. **Contentions**] The 'divisions' of v. 10 had produced disputes probably at the meetings for worship.

12. This I say] The Corinthian Christians were divided into parties (see Intro.), each professing to follow the teaching and example of a favourite teacher. These parties had not yet separated into opposing sects, but their existence deprived the Church of the power of united action arising from united feeling.

13. Is Christ divided, etc.] see paraphrase St. Paul reminds the Corinthians indirectly but emphatically of the crucifixion of Christ for them and of their baptism into His name. By the one they had been redeemed from sin; by the other they had been dedicated to Christ's service, and had entered into communion with Him. How then could they put others side by side with their crucified Lord?

Baptized in (RV 'into') **the name of Paul**] Their baptism did not dedicate them to *Paul's* service. **14. Crispus**] the ruler of the synagogue (Ac 18⁸). **Gaius**] see Ro 16²³.

15. Lest any should say] This does not mean that the Apostle refrained from baptising because he had this danger in view, but only that because of the fact that a party had been formed in his name, it was well that he had not baptised, and so laid himself open to misrepresentation. **16. Stephanas**] was now with St. Paul (16¹⁷). He had been the first Corinthian convert (16¹⁵). **17. Not to baptize**] The Apostle reserved himself as far as possible for the work of preaching, and left baptism for the most part to his companions. **Not with wisdom of words**] i.e. paying attention, not to the manner of presenting the truth, but to the substance of the truth itself.

18-25. The gospel of the crucified Christ is no foolishness to those who know its power. The wisdom of the world has been shown to be mere folly by the wisdom of God in Christ. Men in their wisdom wandered away from God, and it is by this so-called folly of preaching that those who believe, both Jews and Greeks, have been saved.

18. Foolishness] Christ's self-sacrificing death produces no response in some hearts: cp. 2 Cor 2¹⁵,¹⁶ 4³⁴. **Perish . . are saved**] RV 'are perishing . . are being saved.' Salvation is here spoken of as present and progressive. The Apostle is thinking of the work of Christ in sanctifying those who believe. **The power of God**] Because the lives of those who receive it are transformed by the influence of Christ dwelling in them by His Spirit and moulding them to His will.

19, 20. Paraphrase. 'For God still works in the same way as when overruling the course of history He confounded those who in their boasted wisdom doubted His protection, and sought alliance with Egypt against Assyria. (20) Has He not confounded the wise, both learned Jew and keen-witted Greek, by revealing how little their learning and eloquence have done to save men from sin ?'

19. It is written] Quoted from the LXX version of Isa 29 14. **21. By wisdom]** The Greeks learned nothing of His character from nature or speculation, and the Jews failed to recognise the truth taught in their history and in their law (cp. Ro 1, 2). **The foolishness of preaching]** St. Paul, of course, is writing sarcastically. Yes ! you call it folly ; but it is wiser than all your wisdom !

22-24. Paraphrase. 'And this is true, as the facts declare. The Jews will not believe unless a miracle is wrought before their eyes ; the Greeks will accept no truth that is not commended by philosophical speculation ; (23) but the subject of our preaching is salvation through the crucified Christ—who has by His death set us free from the bondage and from the power of sin—a doctrine which moves the Jews to anger and the Greeks to mirth, (24) but which is true wisdom to us, because we have been delivered from sin and brought to God by the transforming power of Christ.'

23. A stumblingblock] The idea of a crucified Messiah was repugnant to the Jews. **Foolishness]** The Greeks made a jest of such a religion. As an illustration the raillery of Lucian in a later age may be cited. **24. Them which are called]** those whom the message has found responsive. **Christ the power . . and the wisdom of God]** He is the power of God because He enables the sinner to overcome his sin ; and the wisdom of God because He reveals the mind of God and the practicable way of salvation. **25. The foolishness of God]** This method of salvation by the Cross of Christ in point of fact saved men from their sins. And thus the so-called foolishness of God was proved in practice to be wiser than the wise methods of men.

26-31. Paraphrase. 'Look at the state of matters in your own Church. There are few among you eminent in the eyes of the world. (27-29) But it is just what is weak and lowly and of no account according to worldly standards that God has chosen to shame what is strong and lofty and worldly-wise ; that no man may boast or compare his work with God's. (30) And you Corinthians are the evidences of the work of God in Christ who has saved you from your sins ; (31) and so the word of prophecy has been fulfilled that if any one wishes to

boast let him boast of what God has wrought for him.'

26. Ye see your calling] RV 'Behold your calling.' **Calling]** Not 'worldly station,' but God's invitation given through Christ. **Not many wise, etc.]** The Corinthian Church was composed chiefly of people who from the worldly standpoint were of little account. There were probably many freedmen and slaves in the Church, the former being chiefly engaged in trade. Prof. Ramsay says that the names Fortunatus, Achaicus (16 17), Gaius (1 14 Ro 16 23), Tertius (Ro 16 22), and Quartus (Ro 16 23), were those of freedmen, i.e. former slaves, who had been set free or redeemed. 'Gaius was probably a rich freedman to whom the honourable duty of entertaining the guests of the Church was assigned.' **Noble]** i.e. of noble birth.

28. Base] i.e. of low birth. **Things which are not]** i.e. mere nonentities : cp. Mt 11 5, 25.

Hath God chosen] Thrice emphatically repeated, to mark the fact that all is due to God. **29. That no flesh should glory]** because God's call is not given on account of any earthly position or advantage.

30. Who of God is made unto us wisdom, and righteousness, etc.] RM 'Who was made unto us wisdom from God, both righteousness and sanctification and redemption,' etc. There are only three co-ordinate terms in the sentence. Righteousness, sanctification and redemption are subordinate to wisdom and descriptive or explanatory of it. Christ is the true wisdom of God, the expression of His desire for our salvation and of His power in accomplishing it. That wisdom is shown in Christ as He first forgives our sins and accepts us as righteous, then goes on to make us pure and holy by His indwelling influence, and finally promises to give us ultimate victory over sin and death, and to raise us to life eternal. **31. He that glorieth]** There was nothing of which human wisdom could boast. Philosophy had helped a few intellectual minds, but had never touched the ordinary man. But the Cross made its appeal to the lowly as well as to the noble, and 'the foolishness of God' transformed human lives, delivering them from the bondage of sin and making them 'new creatures' in Christ. Therefore let them glory in God alone.

CHAPTER 2

THE NATURE OF ST. PAUL'S PREACHING

1-5. Paraphrase. 'When I visited you in Corinth I made no attempt to reconcile my message with your Greek philosophy, (2) but kept to the proclamation of the facts of Christ's life and death upon the Cross. (3) It was with much anxiety and self-distrust that I preached the gospel to you ; (4) and the success I obtained was due not to my way of commending the truth, but solely to the spirit and power which animated me ; (5) and so God's purpose was fulfilled, that your faith should be based not upon the eloquence of man, but upon the grace of God.'

1. When I came] i.e. on his first visit some five years before (Ac 18 1-11). **Not with excellency of speech or of wisdom]** St. Paul did not try to win the Corinthians to the gospel either by the eloquence of his speech in presenting it, or by his adroitness in showing its connexion with some of the philosophical ideas which were popular at the time. **Testimony]** i.e. which God sent me to give about Christ. RV, following another reading, has 'mystery,' i.e. the hidden counsel and will of God revealed in Christ : cp. Ro 16 25, 26.

2. Save Jesus Christ, etc.] The Apostle relied for their conversion upon his witness to the great facts of Christ's life and death. The Crucifixion he dwelt upon all the more emphatically that he knew it must be an unattractive doctrine to many. **3. In weakness]** His first visit was paid at a time when he was either sick in body from his recurrent malady (2 Cor 12 7), or sick at heart from his failure at Athens (Ac 17 32), and dreading lest he were again to fail among these argumentative Greeks. **Fear and .. much trembling]** The Apostle frequently uses this expression to indicate an overpowering anxiety for the performance of duty, culminating in a supreme effort: cp. 2 Cor 7 15 Eph 6 5 Phil 2 12.

4. The success of the Apostle's preaching was the result of his own possession of the divine Spirit, and the power that resided in his message to arrest and convince the hearer.

6-16. Paraphrase. ' There is indeed a wisdom with which the facts of the gospel are in harmony and which we declare to those who are ripe to receive it. (7, 8) It is not the wisdom of this world, for that led its possessors to crucify the Lord ; but the wisdom which God has long kept secret (9) as the Scriptures confirm. (10) This secret wisdom God has revealed to us by His Spirit ; (11) for just as man's spirit alone knows his secret thoughts, so only the Spirit of God knows God's deep designs. (12) And that Spirit of God has revealed these designs to us, (13) and we preach them in words suited to convey their spiritual message. (14) Now to the man who has not been enlightened by the Spirit of God these truths make no appeal ; (15) but he whose mind has been thus enlightened is able to estimate them rightly, and he himself in his turn cannot be understood by the unspiritual. (16) For no one can know the mind of the Lord so as to instruct Him ; but we are in sympathy with the mind of Christ, and so can understand these spiritual truths which are revealed in Him.'

6. Wisdom] Christianity has a wisdom of its own. While it is centred in a Person, it is capable of being expressed in the terms of philosophy, and is in harmony with all that is best in human reasoning and speculation.

Perfect] St. Paul divides Christians into two classes, the beginners and the advanced. The former must be taught the simple truths of the gospel and grounded in its facts : the latter are able to receive teaching regarding God's plan in redemption and His purpose as it is revealed in Christ and illustrated in the history of the world. ' Perfect' means 'mature,' 'full-grown,' and is applied to Christians of ripe experience and character. It is often used in this sense in the Epistle to the Hebrews : cp. Eph 4 13 Col 1 28 Heb 2 10 5 9, 14 9 9 10 1, etc.

The princes of this world] ' The men of light and leading ' (Dods). They showed utter ignorance of God's mind : cp. v. 8.

7. In a mystery] Mystery means something formerly hidden in the counsels of God, but now revealed. The ' mystery' here is the reasoned account of the redemption brought by Christ. Theology is necessary if we are to understand our religion. **Unto our glory]** cp. Mt 25 34. **8. The Lord of glory]** The glory is His ; and He came to bestow it upon us, to bring us to the perfection of our nature. **9. Eye hath not seen]** A free quotation, perhaps from memory, of Isa 64 4 ; with the addition of ' neither have entered into the heart of man,' in order to emphasise the fact that man has had no share in the discovery. **The things which God hath prepared]** The spiritual blessings and comforts and enlightenment revealed in Christ. **10. Searcheth]** i.e. explores, fathoms : Ps 139 1 Ro 8 27. **The deep things]** lit. ' the depths of God': i.e. His counsels. **11. The spirit of man .. the Spirit of God]** The two expressions are exactly parallel. The spirit of man is man's conscious self in thought : and the Spirit of God is His conscious Self in thought.

12, 13. Render, ' Now when we accepted the salvation of the gospel our minds were enlightened not by any worldly wisdom, but by the wisdom which God's Spirit bestows upon the spiritually-minded and which enables us to understand and appreciate the blessings given us through Christ. (13) And these blessings we explain to you in terms suggested by no human philosophy, but by God's Spirit, interpreting spiritual truths in spiritual language.'

12. The spirit of the world] i.e. the wisdom falsely so called, which brought men no blessing. **The spirit which is of God]** i.e. true spiritual insight, which God gives by bestowing upon us a portion of His own Spirit, sending forth into our minds His light and truth (Ps 43 3). **The things that are freely given]**

The spiritual blessings brought by Christ, forgiveness, sanctification, redemption (1 30).

13. We speak] Our language no less than our truths are the result of the spiritual insight with which God has enlightened our minds. **Comparing spiritual things with spiritual**] The phrase should be translated either, (1) 'interpreting spiritual truths in spiritual language,' or, (2) as in RM, 'interpreting spiritual things to spiritual men.' The former connects it with the context of this v., the latter with v. 14. With the former also cp. v. 4.

14. The natural man] i.e. man as he is by nature before he has come under the influence of God's grace. He may have all the intellectual qualities necessary to comprehend the wisdom of man, but he cannot understand the wisdom of God without the spiritual qualities which come only from acceptance of the gospel, e.g. humility, purity of heart, and submission to the influence of Christ. **15. Is judged of no man**] The unregenerate man cannot estimate the spiritual man's experiences and aspirations : he is only bewildered when he hears these things mentioned. **16. Who hath known**] adapted from Isa 40 13. No man untouched by God's Spirit can know anything of His mind. His truth is only revealed to those in sympathy with the spirit and character of Christ.

CHAPTER 3
The Fault of Party Spirit

The immaturity of the Corinthian converts and their unfitness for anything but elementary instruction in the faith is proved by their mutual jealousies and their disagreements about their teachers.

1–9. Paraphrase. ' Ye yourselves, brethren, are an illustration of what I say. (2) I have treated you as beginners and given you elementary Christian teaching, for hitherto you have been unfit for any other. (3, 4) You are still but immature Christians, as the strife and division about your teachers show. (5–7) We apostles are but instruments in the hands of God to secure your salvation; we are powerless of ourselves. (8, 9) Both of us are alike in this respect, and all we are concerned with is the faithfulness of our work. For we co-operate to carry out God's purpose in tilling the field of your spiritual life, or, as we may put it, in contributing to the building of your Christian character.'

1. Not .. as unto spiritual] The hidden wisdom of which the Apostle has been writing is not for them. **Carnal**] The Gk. means ' fleshy,' and points to the fact that they were mere infants, so to speak. It is interpreted by the words which follow. **2. Milk**] the rudiments of the gospel ; the alphabet of

Christianity. We find samples of it in Paul's preaching (Ac 13 14-43 17 2,3 18 22-31 19 2-4).

Meat] more advanced teaching regarding the purpose of Christ's coming and the faith and hope of Christians, such as is presented in the Epistles to the Romans, Colossians, and Ephesians. **3. Carnal**] The Gk. here is different from that in v. 1, and means ' fleshly,' i.e. walking in the lusts of the flesh.

4. Carnal] The Gk. is again different from vv. 1 and 3, and means, as RV, ' men.'

5. Ministers] i.e. servants who ministered to your needs. **Even as the Lord gave**] i.e. according to the ability given by God. **6. I have planted**] St. Paul founded the Church at Corinth (Ac 18 1-18). **Apollos watered**] Ac 18 27. **8. One**] lit. ' one thing,' i.e. having a common aim. **9. Labourers together with God**] RV ' God's fellow-workers.' Perhaps, better, ' fellow-workers for God,' the emphasis all through being on God's power and work. The Apostles were fellow-workers with one another, but not fellow-workers with God in quite the same sense. **Husbandry**] i.e. tilled field. **Building**] The Apostle in the next few vv. develops the illustration taken from building, with which as a frequenter of cities he was more familiar. For this metaphor cp. Eph 2 20-22 Col 2 7.

10–15. Paraphrase. ' Let me remind you that by the favour of God I was the founder of your Church. Those who followed me took up my work. (11) The foundation I laid was faith in Jesus Christ. (12) No one can lay any other ; but every builder is responsible for what he builds upon it. (13) The tests applied to the spiritual life and character of the Church will prove his faithfulness or his unworthiness in the day when the Lord returns in judgment. (14, 15) If the spiritual life of his converts be healthy and their growth in goodness evident, he will be rewarded ; but if not, he will lose his reward and barely secure his own salvation.'

10. Another buildeth] Apollos and others carried on the work begun by St. Paul. **How he buildeth**] The Apostle indicates the great responsibilities of Christian ministers and teachers. **11, 12. Other foundation**] Faith in Christ as Saviour and willing submission to His influence are the foundation on which Christian character must be built. If these are set aside, the character is not based on Christ, and all teaching which does not begin from the statement of these principles and retain them as its basis is not in any true sense Christian.

13. The day] i.e. the day of judgment or the day of the Lord. The imagery of fire testing the building is both natural and suggested by the OT. accounts of the manifestations of Jehovah. **15. Saved**] because

of his own Christian life. **Yet so as by fire**]
As the builder may escape with his life while
the flames destroy the building on which he is
engaged, so the Christian teacher may be saved
himself, though his teaching be proved worthless for edification. 'Sincerity does not verify
doctrine, but it saves the man' (F. W. Robertson).

16, 17. Woe to the teacher who by pernicious teaching or example injures or destroys
the spiritual life of members of the Church of
Christ : God shall do even so to him. **If any
man defile**] A worse case than v. 15. There
the merely unprofitable teacher himself escapes ;
here the positively hurtful is punished. **Holy**]
i.e. sacred, not to be injured with impunity.
Which *temple* **ye are**] RV 'and such are ye,'
i.e. holy.

18-23. Paraphrase. 'Do not deceive yourselves ; but if there be any of you priding
himself on his worldly wisdom let him quickly
unlearn it, that he may learn the true wisdom.
(19, 20) For as Holy Scripture teaches, worldly
wisdom is but folly in God's sight. (21-23)
Do not, therefore, use the names of your
teachers as party watchwords, boasting about
your devotion to this or that one. Learn
what is good from them all, for they all alike
belong to you. And not only do they belong
to you, but all things belong to you ; and you
belong to Christ ; and Christ Himself belongs
to God.'

19. The wisdom of this world] The conceit
and vanity of men are folly with God. The
results of this folly in Christian teachers
are indicated in vv. 15, 17. **It is written**]
Job 5¹³.

20. And again] Ps 94¹¹. **21. Glory in men**]
boast of their preference for this, or that
teacher, as they had been doing (1¹²).

21. All things are yours] To him who is
united to Christ all things belong, contributing
to the growth of his Christian character and
the increasing perfection of his spiritual life.
He learns from all teachers ; the **world** provides him with the means of growth in grace,
for all his experiences in its possessions and
work influence his spiritual life ; **life** is full of
divine meaning and purpose ; **death** is revealed
to him as the gate of life ; he is delivered
from any danger to his spirit arising from the
perplexities of the **present** or the problems
of the future (**things to come**). **23. Ye are
Christ's**] i.e. you belong to Christ, not to Paul
or Apollos or Cephas. **And Christ** *is* **God's**]
i.e. God is over all ; even Christ belongs to
Him. And as we are Christ's, we belong to
God. Theodoret remarks, 'Christ belongs to
God, not as God's creature, but as God's
Son.' Perhaps the Apostle simply desires to
assert that God is supreme over all : cp. 15²⁴
Jn 4³⁴.

CHAPTER 4

CHRISTIAN TEACHERS ONLY THE INSTRU-
MENTS OF GOD

The folly and sin of quarrelling about
different teachers who are but servants of
Christ and responsible to Him.

1-5. Paraphrase. 'You have been engaged
in strife about the merits and position of your
teachers. Consider for a moment what they
are. They have no authority of their own ;
they only bear Christ's messages. (2-4) Servants are responsible to their master ; and so
I am responsible not to you or to any man,
but to Christ. (5) Have patience until Christ
comes, when every man will be rewarded as
he has deserved.'

1. Ministers] rather, subordinates.
Stewards] dispensing the truths entrusted
to them, not giving of their own. **Mysteries
of God**] the spiritual truths revealed by Christ,
and by His Spirit in Christian experience (Jn
16¹², ¹³). **2. Required in stewards**] cp. Mt
24⁴⁵⁻⁵¹ Lk 16¹, ². **4. I know nothing by myself**]
RV 'against myself.' The idea is the same
as in Ac 24¹⁶. **5. Before the time**] i.e. of
Christ's return. St. Paul evidently expected
the advent of Christ within the lifetime of
himself and his converts, though the exact
time was uncertain : cp. 15⁵¹.
The hidden things of darkness] the things
that are at present unknown. There is no
suggestion of evil in the phrase. Along with
the counsels of the hearts it denotes all the
materials for forming a just judgment.

6-13. Paraphrase. 'In speaking of the folly
of these divisions I have used only the names
of Apollos and myself ; but the same principles apply to your attitude to all your teachers.
(7) Why do some of you pride yourselves on
being better than others ? None of you has
anything that he did not receive. (8) You
boast as if you had all possible wisdom.
Would that it were so, that we might share it.
(9) It looks as if we who are Apostles were the
least worthy of all God's servants, a spectacle
for men and angels. (10) You are wise and
honourable ; we are foolish and contemptible.
(11-13) We suffer and toil, returning blessing
for cursing ; and are looked upon as outcasts
to this day.'

6. Not to think *of* *men* **above that which is
written**] RV 'not to go beyond the things
which are written.' The expression is ambiguous to us : it may refer either to what St.
Paul has already written or to the general
teaching of the OT. Perhaps it was a familiar
quotation, 'Do nothing beyond the injunctions
of Holy Writ.' **Be puffed up for one against
another**] lit. 'Be puffed up the one in favour
of one (say, Paul) against the other (say,
Apollos).' **7. Who maketh thee to differ**]

better, 'who maketh thee (who art puffed up) superior ?' **That thou didst not receive**] i.e. from us (whom ye now despise), as is shown by v. 8. **8. Now ye are full**] The Apostle now returns to the use of sarcasm, the weapon he has already wielded with effect. The several sentences are either interrogative or exclamatory, and should have marks of interrogation or exclamation. He expresses with bitter irony their own estimate of themselves as having reached perfection, 'come into their kingdom,' so to speak, and needing to learn nothing more. **Would to God you did reign**] How little they knew their true spiritual position : cp. Rev 3 17. **9.** The Corinthians' fancied position is contrasted with the Apostle's actual position. **Last, as it were appointed to death**] RV 'last of all, as men doomed to death.' He likens the Apostles to criminals condemned to fight to the death in the arena. For the metaphor cp. 15 32. A few years later Christians were often so put to death. **Spectacle**] Gk. 'theatre.' **10.** The sarcasm is continued. **We are fools**] in preaching the foolishness of the Cross. **Ye are wise**] i.e. shrewd, clever.

12. Working with our own hands] St. Paul's constant practice : cp. Ac 18 3 20 34 1 Cor 9 15 1 Th 2 9 2 Th 3 8.

14–21. Paraphrase. 'I write not to shame you, but to admonish you ; and I have the right to do so, for I am your spiritual father. (16, 17) Follow my example, therefore ; and attend to the instructions of Timothy whom I sent to remind you of my teaching and practice. (18) Some of you have been pluming yourselves on your attainments, and posing as authorities, as if I were never to return to you. (19, 20) Do not deceive yourselves. I shall soon be with you to test not the words of these authorities, but their power : for the kingdom of God is advanced not by empty words, but by spiritual power. (21) The spirit in which I shall come depends upon yourselves. If you continue in your evil courses I shall act with severity : if you repent I shall be gentle and encouraging.'

15. Instructers] RV 'tutors' : those who succeeded St. Paul at Corinth. **Begotten you through the gospel**] St. Paul had been the means of their conversion. He had given them the new life.

17. Timothy. See Intro. **My ways which be in Christ**] i.e. my manner and conduct as a teacher in Christ's service. **In every church**] He constantly appeals to the practice of other Churches as a check to the spirit of individualism and separation so prevalent at Corinth : cp. 7 17 11 16 14 33, 36. **18. Puffed up**] Some of the Corinthian converts conceived themselves so 'wise' as to be able to despise St. Paul's authority. Their opposition developed later on, and drew from St. Paul the 'severe' letter

which we have in 2 Cor 10–13. See Intro. 2 Cor. **As though I would not come**] RV 'as though I were not coming.' They seem to have thought that as he had remained so long in Ephesus he would not return to Corinth.

19. Shortly] cp 16 5. For his plans and their ultimate fulfilment see Intro. 2 Cor.

20. Not in word, but in power] The extension of God's kingdom is promoted not by eloquence of speech but by spiritual influence proceeding from Christ's followers, and becoming a power in men's lives : cp. Ro 14 17.

CHAPTER 5

(b) 5 1-13. THE CASE OF IMMORALITY

The Apostle had written (4 21) of coming to exercise authority. Here was a case in which it was needed. A man had created a scandal by marrying his stepmother, and the Corinthians had done nothing. They had allowed him to retain his membership in the Church. St. Paul instructs them to excommunicate the offender, and keep the Church pure.

1–8. Paraphrase. 'A rumour has reached me that unchastity exists among you, and that one of your number has taken his stepmother as his wife, an act which the very heathen abhor. (2) How can you maintain your attitude of self-satisfaction in presence of this scandal ? Why do you not rather humiliate yourselves and remove the sinner from your fellowship ? (3) For I who am at a distance feel the disgrace as though I were among you, and have already decided what must be done, as if I were in your assembly. (4, 5) When you are gathered together, I being present with you in spirit, proceed to pass sentence of excommunication on this man, delivering him solemnly to Satan in the name of Jesus our Lord, that his soul may be saved even if his body perish. (6) How senseless is your self-conceit in presence of this impurity. Do ye not realise that you are all in danger of being degraded by it ? (7) Put away this leaven of unholiness, then, and remain free from it. Remember how at the Passover all leaven was put away ; and now that our Paschal Lamb Christ Jesus has been sacrificed, and our feast of unleavened bread begun, (8) let us celebrate our Passover by putting away the leaven of vice and sin and using only the unleavened bread of purity and truth.'

1. It is reported commonly] RV 'It is actually reported.' **His father's wife**] The father may have been dead or separated from his wife : the stepson had then married her. The Corinthian Church was evidently unconscious that there was anything sinful in such a union. Had the man and woman been living in sin without marriage the Church could scarcely have made even a show of defending their conduct. The persons referred to in 2 Cor 7 12 have no connexion with this incident: see notes there. **2. Puffed up**] This is probably to be taken generally as referring to their boastfulness about their spiritual privileges and attainments: cp. 4 6-12. The Apostle expresses surprise that the scandal among them did not humble their pride. **3. Have judged already**] taking their concurrence for granted; or giving them a suggestion trusting that they would follow it at once. He here asserts his authority to guide them in matters of discipline; and it was over this question of authority, and not over that of the offender's conduct, that the dispute between St. Paul and the Church arose. **4. In the name of our Lord Jesus**] Placed emphatically at the beginning, to indicate the Church's final authority for taking this step to enforce discipline: cp. Mt 18 18, 20. **When ye are gathered together, etc.**] St. Paul did not take discipline out of the hands of the Church. He stepped in when the Church had failed in duty, pointing out the duty and leaving the Church to perform it. **My spirit**] They were to think of him as present in spirit, and to let his influence mould their deliberations. **5. To deliver .. unto Satan**] The offender was to be solemnly excommunicated and handed over to Satan, who had power to cause disease, in the belief that sufferings of body would assail him and work repentance and salvation in him, even if they ended in bodily death: cp. Lk 13 16 2 Cor 12 7. **6. Your glorying**] see on v. 2. **A little leaven**] Leaven is here used of corrupting influences as elsewhere in the NT., except in our Lord's parable of the leaven: cp. Mt 13 6, 12 Mk 8 15 Lk 12 1 Gal 5 9. A low ideal of conduct even in one case has far-reaching effects upon the whole community. **7. The old leaven**] Not (or, at any rate, not only) the unchaste sinner, but the spirit in the Church which is indifferent to the sin. **Christ our Passover**] The mention of leaven, which was associated with the Passover, causes the Apostle to think of that institution; and leads him to speak of Christ in allegorical fashion as the Christian Church's Passover. As Christ has been sacrificed the days of the spiritual feast of unleavened bread have begun; and consequently every vestige of impurity and malice and sin must be rigorously excluded.

9-13. Paraphrase. ' This is just what I wrote to you in my former letter—that you were to have no connexion with men of impure life. (10) I did not mean that you were to have nothing to do with the heathen, who are greedy and covetous and idolaters, in matters of business and such like, for that is impossible. (11) But I meant that if any professing Christian were guilty of such wickedness as impurity or drunkenness or evil speaking or greed, you were to have no fellowship with him. (12, 13)

I have nothing to do, so far as judgment is concerned, with the world at large. We have to judge those in the Church; whereas the judgment of the world we leave to God. Therefore, excommunicate that wicked man.'

9. In an epistle] This clearly refers to a previous letter no longer extant and prior to any of our Epistles to the Corinthians. See Intro. **11. But now I have written**] RM 'As it is, I wrote.' The meaning is, 'What I wrote was,' etc. The Corinthians probably asked St. Paul in their letter in reply to his first one, what they were to do when they met non-Christians in business and society. **Not to eat**] They might be compelled to meet with such men and to have some business or social relations with them, but they were not to have any association with them but what was absolutely unavoidable. **12. Them .. that are without**] i.e. the heathen generally; all outside the Church.

Do not ye] They exercised discipline in some cases though they had not recognised its necessity in this one.

CHAPTER 6

(c) 6 1-11. CHRISTIANS AND LITIGATION

St. Paul reproves the Corinthians for referring their disputes about ordinary affairs to heathen judges. The subject was suggested by rumours he had heard; and the mention of 'judgment' in v. 13 of the previous c. prompted its treatment at this stage.

1-6. Paraphrase. ' How is it that when you quarrel with one another you go before heathen judges and do not let some of the brethren decide your matter? (2) You spoke of the saints judging the world, why not allow them to settle these trifles? (3) You spoke of Christians as looking to sit in judgment on angels; why not then let them deal with the ordinary affairs of life? (4) And if you must have these things settled formally, make umpires of unimportant Church members rather than heathen. (5) I write thus to make you ashamed. Is there really no wise man among you who can be trusted to judge between his brethren, (6) and to prevent this unseemly practice of calling in unbelievers to settle your disputes?'

1. Dare any of you] Such action was antagonistic to the Christian spirit. **The unjust**] RV 'the unrighteous,' i.e. the heathen. The name is used in irony for ' unbelievers ' (v. 6). ' Do you call the heathen unjust, and yet dare to go to them alone for justice?' **Saints**] i.e. Christians.

2. That the saints shall judge the world] This v. and the two following vv. are written sarcastically. They appeal to the 'knowledge' of the Corinthians, and it is probable that they were suggested by expressions in the letter sent by the Corinthians to St. Paul. **They**

were puffed up with spiritual pride (5²), and in their conceit and vanity had spoken of their hope to judge both men (5¹² 6²) and angels (6³). If this be their expectation, says the Apostle, surely they are capable, even the meanest of them, of judging in matters of daily life. To take these expressions, about the saints judging the world and angels, seriously, is to miss the point of the Apostle's argument. Besides, he has already said that the Christians (both he and they) had nothing to do with judging the world, which was God's part (5¹², ¹³). (See Ramsay, 'Hist. Com. on Corinthians,' in 'Expositor,' VI. 4, p. 278.)

6. Before the unbelievers] The Corinthian converts referred their disputes about matters of daily life, such as 'prices and ownership' (Ramsay), to heathen judges or arbitrators. St. Paul urges them, if quarrel they must, to choose arbitrators from among the brethren.

7–11. Paraphrase. ' But the fault lies deeper than this, for you should have no such disputes at all. Far better be wronged and defrauded (8) than wrong and defraud your brethren. (9, 10) After all, in the end the unrighteous shall not inherit the kingdom of God. And who are the unrighteous but the unchaste, the greedy, the drunken, and the extortionate, none of whom have any part in that kingdom? (11) Such indeed were some of you Corinthians; but since your baptism you have professed that you are seeking to become pure and holy through the influence of Christ and the working of the Holy Spirit.'

7. There is utterly a fault] RV 'Already it is altogether a defect in you.' St. Paul here ceases to employ raillery, the weapon he has used so effectively in the previous vv., and remonstrates with them in the most serious fashion. The real fault was not in going to heathen judges to get their disputes arranged, but in having occasion to call in any one at all.

9. Shall not inherit the kingdom] i.e. have no share in its present privileges and future blessings. The kingdom of God is a spiritual kingdom (Jn 18³⁶); its blessings and privileges are spiritual; how then could such unspiritual men as those enumerated, whose conduct tended to harden the heart and dull the spiritual insight, have any part in it? cp. Ac 8²¹.

11. Ye are washed] RM 'ye washed yourselves,' i.e. submitted to baptism as the sign of the washing away of your sin.

Sanctified] set apart, dedicated to God's service. **Justified**] accepted as righteous.

In the name of the Lord] i.e. through spiritual union with Him and continual submission to His influence.

(d) **6**¹²⁻²⁰. The Obligation of Purity

The Corinthians seemed to have claimed that they were free to satisfy all bodily desires now that the gospel had set them free from the association of eating with idolatry.

St. Paul points out, first, that there are qualifications of this freedom even in things that are morally indifferent, and then that fornication is not one of these things. The subject arises naturally out of what he has said in vv. 9, 10.

12–20. Paraphrase. 'It is true as you suggest that "all things are lawful"; but this is not an absolute but a relative principle. You must not argue that the existence of appetites proves the lawfulness of their gratification: you must take care that what is lawful is also wise, and that appetite does not make you its slave. (13, 14) Both food and the organ which digests it are perishable. But the body has an eternal element, and unchastity harms that eternal element, designed as it is for the service of Christ and participation in the Resurrection. (15–17) You know that your bodies partake in the mystic union that exists between Christ and His people. How shameful is it, therefore, to violate this union by acts of immorality. Such acts cause a carnal union between those who participate in them, just as Scripture speaks of husband and wife being "one flesh": whereas the Christian is united to Christ in a spiritual union. And the immoral union is destructive of the spiritual union. (18, 19) Therefore keep yourselves unspotted by this sin; for there is none that defiles the body like this and makes it unfit for the dwelling-place of the Holy Spirit. (20) Remember that you are not your own possession; you have been purchased by Christ who has given His life for you; therefore, see that you honour Him by consecrating your very bodies to His service.'

12. All things are lawful] cp. 10²³. St. Paul seems to have stated this as a principle in regard to the use of certain kinds of food (e.g. meats offered to idols, 10²⁵, ²⁷), and the Corinthians had applied it generally to sensual indulgences. The Apostles, therefore, while still asserting the principle, points out two qualifications of it; (*a*) that what is lawful should also be beneficial, and (*b*) that no one should become a slave even to a lawful habit. We shall best understand the principle and its application if we think of it in relation to some such modern practice as, e.g., the use of strong drink. **13. Meats**] An instance of things indifferent: cp. chs. 8–10, where this matter is treated at length. St. Paul grants liberty in respect of meats; but the liberty does not excuse violating another man's conscience or becoming a slave to gluttony. **Now the body *is* not**, etc.] The Corinthians regarded the use of food and fornication as exactly on the same level, as both satisfying appetites:

they held that the existence of bodily appetites justified their gratification. St. Paul, on the contrary, draws a sharp line of distinction between these two things.

14. Will also raise up us] St. Paul's argument in the whole passage is based on his view of the Resurrection which he explained in c. 15 : see esp. vv. 35–53. Man's body is eternal ; death and the grave do not destroy but purify and change it, as the earth removes the husk and glorifies the corn cast into it. **16. Saith he**] i.e. God in Scripture (Gn 2 24). **One flesh**] The words spoken first of marriage are applied here to an unholy union. St. Paul does not place the two on the same plane, but only points out that in this one respect they are similar. **17. One spirit**] i.e. he shares in the life of the Lord : cp. Jn 15 4, 5. **18. Without the body**] i.e. outside it ; do not affect its spiritual nature and destiny in the same way as this sin. **Sinneth against his own body**] see on v. 14. **19. The temple**] i.e. the shrine wherein He dwells : cp. 3 16 2 Cor 6 16.

Ye are not your own] The best of all reasons for not defiling the body. **20. Bought with a price**] Christ has given Himself for you, and you are His ; yea, God has given Christ for you, and you belong to God through Him.

Glorify God in your body] RV omits the rest. St. Paul is dwelling on the necessity of bodily purity, and appropriately concludes with this appeal.

DIVISION II. 7 1–16 4. PROBLEMS SUBMITTED IN THE LETTER FROM CORINTH

CHAPTER 7

(a) ANSWER TO QUESTIONS ABOUT MARRIAGE

The Corinthians had in their letter (7 1) asked St. Paul's opinion on several points connected with marriage. His language in reply is guarded ; he speaks with some diffidence ; he constantly admits exceptions and lays down restrictions. This makes his meaning sometimes obscure ; but the general drift is that celibacy, though a good thing in itself, is not suited to the needs of many, especially in circumstances like theirs ; and marriage, though not obligatory, is not only sinless, but good in itself ; and those married, even to heathen spouses, should not separate without necessity.

1–7. Celibacy is good, but marriage is usually advisable ; only let it be real and complete.

Paraphrase. '(1) In answer to your questions—Celibacy is a good thing. (2) But because of the profligacy around you, it is well that each should marry. (3, 4) But the marriage must be a real one, each giving the other conjugal rights. (5) Let there be separation only by mutual consent, for a given time, for purposes of devotion. (6) But I say all this as a concession to your circumstances, not

as a command. (7) I should like all to be like myself. But all have not the same gifts from God.'

1. The things whereof ye wrote] Probably most of the rest of the Epistle is taken up with answers to these questions, and considerations arising out of them. It is not clear whether the letter from the Corinthians suggested that celibacy ought to be universal, or deprecated it as unnatural, or asked, as Ramsay thinks, whether it was incumbent on Christians to marry, as the Jews and Roman law maintained.' **Good**] i.e. celibacy is an excellent thing (the reasons for this are given, vv. 26, 32), but marriage is often the safer course. **2. To avoid fornication**] which was very prevalent at Corinth. St. Paul treats of the higher aspect of marriage elsewhere (Eph 5 25, 33). **Every** (RV 'each').. **his own**] Concubinage and polygamy are forbidden. **3. Due benevolence**] RV 'her due' ; i.e. primarily, cohabitation.

5. To fasting and prayer] RV 'unto prayer,' omitting 'fasting' on the authority of the best MSS. So Mk 9 29. **For your incontinency**] i.e. through your lack of self-control. **6. This**] Perhaps v. 5 ; more probably, all he has said in recommendation of marriage from v. 2 onwards. **7. Even as I myself**] i.e. able through self-control to lead a celibate life.

His proper gift] He to whom God has denied this ability, has received some other gift from Him. St. Paul must have been unmarried, or, just possibly, a widower.

8–16. Consequent advice or commands. (a) 8, 9. To the unmarried and widows—to remain so, unless they have an overmastering desire. (b) 10, 11. To the married Christians. The Lord's command is against separation ; if such take place, the separated party is to remain unmarried. (c) 12–14. In cases of mixed marriages St. Paul's opinion is that the two should continue to live together if the heathen partner is willing ; for the fact that the one is a Christian brings the other also into the Christian sphere, as is the case with the children. 15, 16. But if the heathen partner wants to separate, he or she may do so, and the Christian is then set free. But domestic peace is what God desires ; the heathen partner may possibly be converted.

8. Even as I] i.e. unmarried and without desire for marriage. **10. Not I, but the Lord**] This exhortation is confirmed by the Lord's own authority (Mt 5 32 19 4-9) which forbids divorce. This is one of the passages which show St. Paul's acquaintance with Christ's teaching, and the supreme authority he attached to it : cp. 1 Tim 6 3. **12. I, not the Lord**] Christ had said nothing about mixed marriages ; the Apostle is left to his own judgment : cp. v. 40. He does not encourage mixed marriages (2 Cor 6 14), but is thinking of cases where husband or wife has been converted since marriage. **14. Is sanctified**] i.e. brought into the Christian sphere, under Christian influences. **Now are they holy**] i.e. regarded as Christian children ; as are still more evidently the children of two Christian parents. This phrase 'enunciates the principles which leads to the thought of infant baptism, viz. that the child of Christian parents shall be counted as a Christian' (J. Lightfoot). **15. A brother or a sister**] the Christian partner. **Not under bondage**]i.e. is not bound to continue with the other.

15, 16. God hath called us to (RV 'in') **peace .. save** *thy* **wife**] v. 16 either (a) continues the thought of v. 15—God's aim for us is peace, which will here be best secured by separation ; and the possibility of saving the heathen partner by remaining is, after all, uncertain—but more probably, (b) it continues the main thought of vv. 12–14, v. 15 being parenthetical, 'But God desires that the married should live in peace together, and this may result in the conversion of the heathen partner.'

17–24. The general principle ; let each remain as he was when God called him (vv. 17, 20, 24). This holds good, (a) of circumcision and uncircumcision. Let each keep as he is ; the one important thing is to keep God's commandments. (b) Of slavery and freedom. A slave should not mind his position (though he may avail himself of an opportunity to become free). The Christian slave is Christ's freedman ; the Christian freeman, Christ's bondservant, owing service to Him, not to men. **17. But**] RV 'only' ; I only lay down the general rule. **Hath distributed**] i.e. his condition and circumstances of life. **18. Circumcised .. uncircumcised**] Used metaphorically, 'If any Jew has been converted, let him remain a Christian Jew ; if a Gentile is converted, let him not seek to become a Jew, but remain a Christian Gentile.' **19. Circumcision is nothing**] cp. Gal 5 6 6 15 Ro 2 25-29. 'Not nationality but obedience to God determines Christian character' (Stevens). **20. Calling**] not 'occupation in life,' but 'condition in which God's call found him.' St. Paul lays this down, not as a universal, but as a good general rule : cp. vv. 9, 15, 28. **21. But if thou mayest be made free, use it rather**] an ambiguous sentence, like v. 16. 'It' may mean 'slavery' or 'freedom.' Either 'even if you have an opportunity of freedom, remain a slave'—this suits the immediate context—or, 'but if you have an opportunity of freedom, take it.' This would be a parenthetical piece of advice. This is favoured by St. Paul's thought elsewhere. He was proud of his citizenship ; he prefers celibacy because it gives greater freedom to serve God. So does liberty compared with slavery. Slavery was an essential part of the social con-

ditions of the time. The Apostle accepts it as such, but lays down a principle which undermines it, viz. that Christ makes no difference between bond and free. He insists, not on the rights of slaves, but on the duties of masters towards their Christian brethren (Eph 6 5-9 Col 3 22-4 1 1 Tim 6 1, 2, and especially Philemon). The spread of the Christian spirit swept away the worst evils of slavery, before abolishing slavery itself.

22. Freeman] RV 'freedman' ; set free from sin (Jn 8 34-36 Ro 8 2 Gal 5 1), but still owing service to Him who freed him. **Christ's servant**] RV 'bondservant'; bought by Him 'whose service is perfect freedom.' **23. Bought with a price**] cp. 6 20. **Servants**] (RV 'bondservants') **of men**] i.e. slavishly yielding to their desires ; slaves to custom or public opinion : cp. 2 Cor 11 20. **24. With God**] i.e. in His presence, consciously doing His will.

25–38. Marriage of virgins. The Corinthians seem to have asked particularly whether fathers ought to give their daughters in marriage. St. Paul now comes to this point, first, however, going into the question of marriage generally, and giving reasons for preferring celibacy. He says he cannot appeal to any commandment of the Lord, so simply gives his own opinion, assured that he deserves their confidence. He repeats the general rule (cp. v. 17) that it is best for each to remain as he is, considering the early coming of the Lord and the distress preceding it ; so that while there is no sin in marriage, yet celibacy is best, (a) because the married will meet with greater troubles ; (b) because the shortness of the time before the Lord's coming bids all to sit loose to worldly things ; (c) because the unmarried is freer from distraction, and able to serve the Lord more completely. However, he does not want to constrain them, but merely to advise for the best. If a man considers it right to give his daughter in marriage, let him do so ; but he who, feeling no such necessity, resolves to keep her unmarried, does better.

25. Virgins] i.e. unmarried daughters. The Roman law endeavoured to make marriage universal ; and the Jewish view was similar. **No commandment of the Lord**] either laid down by Him while on earth (see on vv. 10–12), or imparted by special revelation. **To be faithful**] i.e. to give a trustworthy opinion, one deserving of confidence, as a steward of the mysteries of God (4 1-2). **26. The present distress**] Perhaps persecution, which, however, is not elsewhere mentioned in this Epistle; more probably the 'distress' Christ had said would precede His return (Lk 21 23), which was thought to be near (v. 29). **So to be**] RV 'to be as he is.' **27. Art thou loosed**] i e. unmarried. **28. Trouble in the flesh**] i.e. in their earthly circumstances. Trouble would fall not only on themselves, but on those dear to them. St. Paul wants to save them such suffering (RV 'and I would spare you').

29. The time is **short: it remaineth, that,** etc.] RV 'the time is shortened that henceforth,' etc. The thought of the nearness of the Lord's coming, when earthly things would pass away, should keep them from being engrossed in present interests. **31. Abusing**] RM 'using it to the full,' as if the sole source of enjoyment : cp. 1 Jn 2 15-17.

32. Without carefulness] RV 'free from cares.' **33, 34.** The exact words and punctuation are doubtful (cp. RM) ; but this does not affect the general sense, viz. that the unmarried are less subject to worldly distractions and anxieties than the married. **35. Cast a snare** (or, 'halter') **upon you**] i.e. not deprive you of liberty ; force you into this course.

Comely] RV 'seemly.' **36. Any man**] i.e. parent or guardian. **Uncomely**] i.e. unfairly, in not seeing her married. **His virgin**] daughter or ward. **Let them**] i.e. the maiden and her suitor. **37. Hath power over** (RV 'as touching') **his own will**] i.e. is able to carry it out. The whole v. shows the need of careful deliberation in the matter ; no hasty resolve. Throughout, according to the social and legal conditions of the time, no account is made of the maiden's own wishes. This is probably due also to the precise question St. Paul had to answer.

In applying this c. to the present day we have to remember, (1) the altered social conditions, (2) that St. Paul's advice is influenced by his regarding the Lord's coming as very near.

39, 40. Remarriage of widows. A widow may remarry after her husband's death, provided it be a Christian marriage ; but St. Paul's opinion is, she will do better to remain a widow.

39. In the Lord] This forbids marriage from unchristian, worldly motives ; and, practically, marriage with a heathen. **40. So abide**] RV 'abide as she is' : cp. 1 Tim 5 3-10, for widows on the Church roll. **Have the Spirit of God**] am guided by Him in what I say, not merely expressing my personal inclinations.

CHAPTERS 8 1–11 1
(b) FOOD OFFERED TO IDOLS

In these chs. St. Paul answers another question of the Corinthians—as to the lawfulness of eating food which had been offered in sacrifice to idols. This was a very urgent question. The whole worship of the heathen was sacrificial, and sacrifices were offered by them whenever a birthday or marriage was celebrated. Only part of the animal was consumed on the altar. Of the remainder, part became the priest's perquisite, and the rest was returned to the sacrificer, and he and

his friends commonly feasted upon it, often in the precincts of the temple. Again, the bond of union between members of a Greek club, or guild, was a feast following a sacrifice. Much, too, of the meat in the market would have been offered in sacrifice, and sold by either priest or offerer. Thus a Corinthian Christian at a feast given by a heathen friend would probably have before him meat which had been offered in sacrifice ; this might be the case even with meat bought in the market ; and continued membership of these guilds meant joining in their sacrificial meals.

The Corinthians found this problem continually confronting them, and had asked St. Paul's advice. Their letter seems to have suggested that as an idol did not represent a real deity, food could not be polluted by being offered to it, and so might lawfully be eaten. St. Paul, however, admitting the truth of their view of idols, tells them that (1) knowledge must be tempered by love, care being taken to avoid injuring another's conscience ; and (2) they must beware of idolatry.

In c. 8 he deals with the general principle, giving caution (1) above. In c. 9 he appeals to his own example, in forbearing, for the sake of others, to exercise rights he actually possessed, and in guarding against self-indulgence in his own life. In c. 10 he warns them against the danger of idolatry, reminding them of the sin and fate of the Israelites, and that the idol feasts mean fellowship with demons (idolatry being a suggestion of the powers of evil), which is inconsistent with the fellowship with and in Christ, bestowed in the Lord's Supper. Finally, he gives the practical advice, not to be needlessly scrupulous oneself, but to respect the scruples of others.

At the Council of Jerusalem, Gentile converts were directed to abstain from things sacrificed to idols (Ac 15 29). St. Paul had himself published these decrees in Syria, etc., but does not mention them here, though he says nothing inconsistent with them. Possibly he saw the Corinthians would be more influenced by argument than by appeal to authority, seeing that they prided themselves on their wisdom (3 18) and their ability to discern spiritual truth (2 13-15 3 1).

CHAPTER 8
(b) FOOD OFFERED TO IDOLS : (i) THE PRINCIPLE OF SELF-DENIAL

Knowledge must be tempered by love. More enlightened Christians must respect the scruples of their weaker brethren in the matter of eating meat which had been offered to idols.

1–13. Paraphrase. 'Your next question relates to meat offered in sacrifice to idols, asking whether it is permissible for a Christian to partake of it. We all know, as you remark, that such food is absolutely harmless to a man's spiritual life ; but we must have regard for the feelings of others, and let love regulate our attitude. (2) Any one who prides himself on his knowledge is but a beginner in learning ; (3) but if a man loves God, He receives His divine approval. (4) We know, of course, that an idol represents no real deity, for there is but one God. (5, 6) The heathen, doubtless, speak of many deities and demigods, but we know that these have no actual existence : we believe in God the Father and the Creator and in Jesus Christ His Son. (7) There are many Christians, however, not so well instructed as we are, who still think, as they have been accustomed, of an idol as representing an existing deity, and are shocked at the idea of eating meat which has been offered to it in sacrifice. (8, 9) Now it is quite true that whether we eat it or not is, in the abstract, a matter of indifference ; it will make us neither better nor worse in the sight of God. But, at the same time, you must take care to do nothing that will shock another's feelings or wound his conscience. (10) If a man who thinks he cannot as a Christian eat in an idol's temple, sees one of you doing so, he may be led to follow your example ; although his conscience, which is not so enlightened as yours, tells him he is doing wrong. (11) He is thus led to act against and stifle his conscience ; and so the man for whom Christ died is brought to moral ruin by your self-confidence and bravado. (12) If you act in this way, offending the consciences of less self-reliant brethren and leading them into temptation, you sin directly against Christ. (13) Rather than thus do the weakest of my brethren spiritual injury, I would eat no flesh as long as I live, if to eat it is to harm another soul.'

1. We all have knowledge] This remark is probably quoted from the letter of the Corinthians. Vv. 2, 3 are St. Paul's comment on it. **Charity**] RV 'love.' **3. Known of him**] 'We can only know God by love... They who love Him are known of Him because they have intercourse with Him, and this mutual intercourse enables them to know him personally' (Sadler): cp. Gal 4⁹. **4. An idol is nothing**] i.e. has no spiritual reality behind it. **6.** 'For us there is but one God the Father, the Source of all things, for whose service we exist, and one Lord Jesus Christ, by whose agency all things were created, and we Christians created anew.' **7. With conscience of the idol unto this hour**] RV 'being used until now to the idol' ; i.e. not having yet been able to shake off the idea that it represents some spiritual power. **Their conscience being weak is defiled**] i.e. they have a sense of moral defilement, because their conscience is not pro-

perly enlightened. **8. But meat,** etc.] It is not such matters that make us well-pleasing to God. **9. This liberty of yours**] i.e. freedom to eat.

10. See thee .. sit at meat in the idol's temple] This was what their boasted liberty had brought them to. Some of the Christians had actually partaken of a feast held in honour of some of the heathen deities. This was a more serious matter than merely eating (at home or at a friend's house) of meat which had been offered to an idol, and more fraught with danger to others. For it involved some sort of recognition of the heathen deity—at least, the weak brethren would naturally think so. **Knowledge**] enlightenment, consciousness that idols do not represent a real deity.

11. Perish] The result of acting against conscience : cp. Ro 14²³. 'Whatsoever is not of faith' (i.e. done without thorough conviction that it is right) 'is sin.' **12. Sin against Christ**] who identifies Himself with His brethren (Ac 9⁴ Mt 25⁴⁰). **13.** Probably this abstaining from flesh would be practised by St. Paul only where circumstances required it, as at Corinth.

CHAPTER 9

(b) FOOD OFFERED TO IDOLS
(ii) ST. PAUL'S OWN EXAMPLE

St. Paul has appealed to the 'enlightened' converts at Corinth to give up for the sake of others a practice which they might otherwise have had no hesitation in indulging. He now strengthens this appeal by pointing to his own example of self-denial. As an Apostle he had the right to maintenance from the Church, but had refrained from exercising it, lest he might be suspected of preaching for gain.

Since his opponents declared that he maintained himself by his own work simply because he knew he was no true Apostle, he begins by proving (vv. 1–3) his claim to the Apostleship, and so (vv. 4–6) to the rights enjoyed by other Apostles. He defends this right (vv. 7–14) by a number of arguments. Then he gives (vv. 15–22) his reasons for not exercising it. His whole conduct has been influenced by the aim of causing no hindrance to the gospel, but of commending it to every man.

1–6. His claim to Apostleship, and consequent right to maintenance.

Paraphrase. '(1) Am not I myself free from outward authority ? For am I not an Apostle, having seen Jesus our Lord ? (2, 3) Why, your very existence as a Christian Church should be to you a sufficient proof of my Apostleship. (4–6) Now other Apostles, the Lord's brethren, and Peter himself, are supported as well as their wives, by the Churches they visit ; have not Barnabas and myself this same right ?'

1. **Am I not free**] (RV puts this question first) i.e. being an Apostle, I am free from man's authority, and could do many things I abstain from doing for your sakes : cp. v. 19.

Have I not seen Jesus] An Apostle's work was to be a witness of the Resurrection (Ac 1 22 2 32) ; therefore he must have seen the risen Lord. This St. Paul had done at his conversion (Ac 22 14 1 Cor 15 8, 9). **2. Unto others**] in their opinion. **The seal**] That which authenticates, or proves true. The existence of the Corinthian Church was a proof of St. Paul's apostolic power. V. 3 probably refers to this, not to what follows, 'If you want a proof of my apostleship, look around you !' **4. Power**] RV 'right.' **To eat and to drink**] as guests of the Church. **5. To lead about a sister, a wife**] RV 'a wife that is a believer'; i.e. to claim support on his journeys for his wife as well as himself. It is implied that the Apostles were mostly married ; Peter's wife's mother is mentioned Mt 8 14. No doubt their wives were of great service in getting access to the women of Eastern cities. **Lead**] as the companion of his travels. He asserts that he could reasonably claim not only support for a wife, but also payment of her travelling expenses as well as his own. **The brethren of the Lord**] cp. Mt 12 46 13 55. They seem here included among the Apostles ; but the title of Apostle was not limited to the Twelve. **6. Barnabas**] was like St. Paul, an Apostle (Ac 14 14), and like him, but unlike the rest, he maintained himself by his own labour. They may have jointly adopted this course on their missionary journeys (Ac 13, 14). We see that Barnabas known to the Corinthians, and still working as a missionary. For St. Paul's self-support see on 4 12.

7-14. Proof of this right. This right is proved (v. 7) from the analogy of soldiers, husbandmen, shepherds ; (vv. 8-10) from the direction in the Law that the ox should not be muzzled (vv. 11, 12) on grounds of common fairness and gratitude ; (vv. 13, 14) from the example of the Jewish priesthood.

7. Who goeth a warfare] The Apostles were spiritual soldiers, husbandmen, shepherds.

8. As a man] RV 'after the manner of men' ; i.e. reasoning only from analogies of common life. **9. For it is written in the law**] RV 'Is it not also written in the law ?' **Thou shalt not muzzle the . . ox**] Dt 25 4. The ox threshed out the corn either by simply walking upon it, or by dragging a heavy sledge over it.

Doth God take care for oxen ?] RV 'Is it for the oxen that God careth ?' i.e. He did not make this law merely for their sake ; He meant the principle to go much further, to be applied to men. This is an instance of St. Paul's use of the allegorical method of interpretation : cp. 2 Cor 3 13 Gal 4 22. **10. Altogether**] or,

'really,' 'certainly.' **He that thresheth in hope, etc.**] RV 'He that thresheth to thresh in hope of partaking.' The same principle which applies to oxen holds good of human labourers, and so of spiritual labourers. **11. Carnal things**] i.e. earthly material support : cp. Ro 15 27. **12. If others be partakers**] This shows that there were some persons receiving support from the Corinthian Church : cp. 2 Cor 11 20.

Power] RV 'right.' **Rather**] RV 'yet more'; i.e. as the instruments of your conversion.

Suffer] RV 'bear.' **Hinder the gospel**] by being suspected of self-interest. **13. Live** (RV 'eat') *of the things* **of the temple**] i.e. its tithes and offerings. **Partakers with the altar**] Part of the offering was burnt on the altar ; part fell to the priest : cp. Nu 18 Dt 18 1-3.

14. Hath the Lord ordained] Mt 10 10 Lk 10 7.

15-23. His own reason for not exercising this right.

Paraphrase. '(15) But I am resolved to maintain my independence. (16-18) It is the one thing I can boast of. I cannot boast of my preaching the gospel, for I am compelled to preach the gospel ; I have no choice in the matter ; but this self-support is of my own free will, and I find its reward in increased opportunities and success. (19-23) To obtain such, I have also been in the habit of adapting myself to the position and circumstances of every class of men in turn.'

15. I have used none of these things] The Apostle was the more free to advocate the principle 'that they who preach the gospel should live of the gospel,' because his own refusal of support kept him free from personal bias. **These things**] i.e. these rights. **Make my glorying void**] deprive me (by supporting me) of my boast of preaching the gospel freely.

17. Willingly . . against my will] RV 'of mine own will . . not of mine own will.' He preached under the constraining influence of the love of Christ. **Reward**] answers to 'glorying': cp. Ro 4 2-5. A voluntary action admits of 'glorying,' and calls for 'reward.' So it was with St. Paul's self-support ; not with his gospel-preaching. **Dispensation**] RV 'stewardship.' **18. That I abuse not my power**] RV 'so as not to use to the full my rights'; viz. of claiming maintenance from his people.

19. Free from all *men*] Under authority or obligation to no man. **Servant unto all**] Accommodating myself to their desires and prejudices as far as possible.

20. I became as a Jew] preaching first in their synagogues ; appealing to their Scriptures, e.g. Ac 13 14, etc. **As under the law**] e.g. circumcising Timothy, who was half a Jew (Ac 16 1-3) ; helping the men who had taken the Nazirite vow (21 23-26) ; keeping the feasts (20 16). RV inserts, 'not being myself under the law': cp. Gal 2 11-19. **21. To them that are**

without law] i.e. Gentiles : cp. Ro 2 12-19. To them he became as **without law** ; e.g. refusing to have Titus, a Gentile, circumcised (Gal 2 3-5) ; mixing freely with Gentiles ; using arguments from natural religion and from Greek literature and philosophy, as at Lystra (Ac 14 15-17) and Athens (17 22-31). **Being not without law to God**] Liberty did not mean licence ; though free from bondage to the Law of Moses, he yielded obedience to the moral law of God as revealed in Christ. **22. The weak**] cp. 8 13 Ro 14, 15. **By all means**] some in one way, some in another. **23. Partaker thereof with you**] RV 'joint partaker thereof,' i.e. share with my converts in its blessings and salvation. This v. forms the transition to the next paragraph. St. Paul practised self-denial for his own sake also.

24–27. The importance of self-discipline. St. Paul illustrates the need of this self-denial which he has been inculcating from the Greek games or athletic sports, some of the most noted of which (the Isthmian) were held near Corinth every two years. The prize was a mere wreath (at Corinth, formed of parsley, afterwards of pine), but the winner was welcomed home to his native city with the honours of a victorious general ; his statue was erected ; his victory was celebrated by a leading poet ; a front seat was assigned him at all festivals and spectacles ; he was frequently relieved from taxation. St. Paul draws lessons for his converts from the earnestness and self-discipline needed in these contests : cp. Phil 3 13,14 2 Tim 2 5 4 7 Heb 12 1. **24. Not** all who start in a race, win ; only the best. In the Christian race there is a crown for all who run their best, but only for such. **25. Striveth for the mastery**] RV 'striveth in the games.' **Temperate in all things**] i.e. under strict 'training' as to food, drink, and exercise. **An incorruptible**] 'a crown of glory that fadeth not away' (1 Pet 5 4). **26. Not as uncertainly**] not hesitating, looking back. **Not as one that beateth the air**] but aiming my blows well. The metaphor changes from running to boxing. **27. Keep under, etc.**] RV 'I buffet my body and bring it into bondage.' The body is the seat of temptation to self-indulgence. One great object of fasting and abstinence is to secure this control over our bodies, so that 'the flesh may be subdued to the spirit.' The illness to which St. Paul was subject, his 'thorn in the flesh' (2 Cor 12 7), must have tempted him often to seek his own ease and comfort and to live a more self-indulgent and less laborious life ; and this temptation he fought against unceasingly. **Preached to others**] like the herald who proclaimed the conditions of the contest and its prizes, and summoned the competitors. **A castaway**] RV 'rejected' ;

disqualified. 'No amount of usefulness to others will save us if we ourselves live not the life of God' (Woodford).

CHAPTER 10

(b) FOOD OFFERED TO IDOLS
(iii) HISTORICAL ILLUSTRATIONS AND PRACTICAL ADVICE

St. Paul has been speaking of the need of earnestness and self-discipline, and the danger of failure ; he now holds out the fate of the Israelites as a warning against self-confidence. The Corinthians were tempted to the very same sins for which Israel suffered.

All of the Israelites received great blessings from God, types of the sacramental privileges Christians enjoy, yet most of them perished in the wilderness because of sin. They accepted the privilege of their high calling, but renounced its responsibility. Their fate should warn his converts against setting their heart on evil things, idolatry, impurity, presuming on God's patience, murmuring.

1. All our fathers] Though most of the Corinthians were Gentiles, yet the Israelites were their spiritual forefathers ; the Christian Church is a continuation of the Jewish. **The cloud . . the sea**] see Ex 13 21, 22 14. The cloud denoting the presence of God was over them, the water of the Red Sea on either side of them. Their passage through the sea was a break with their old life in Egypt ; it definitely committed them to Moses' guidance, was in effect a profession of discipleship to him (Ex 14 31) ; they were thus **baptized unto Moses.** This typified our baptism, which is, (1) deliverance from the bondage of sin and entrance upon a new life ; (2) discipleship to Christ and union with Him. So the **spiritual meat** (the 'manna,' Ex 16) and **spiritual drink** (water from the rock, Ex 17 Nu 20) by which their life was sustained, were types of the Body and Blood of Christ, by which our souls are nourished. Our Lord Himself made the manna a type of Himself, the Living Bread (Jn 6 31-35). Here only in the NT. are the two Sacraments mentioned side by side. This food and drink are called 'spiritual' because, (1) miraculous, (2) typical, (3) assuring the people of God's presence, strengthening their faith. **4. That** (RV 'a') **spiritual Rock that followed them : and that Rock was Christ**] The several visible rocks from which water came were symbols of the one invisible Rock who accompanied them and bestowed these blessings. God is often called a Rock in the OT., e.g. Dt 32 15-18 Ps 18 2, 31. We see St. Paul's recognition of Christ's pre-existence ; the divine power which sustained the Israelites was the power of Christ working on earth before His Incarnation : cp. also Jn 7 37, 38 **5. Many**] RV 'most.' All shared these same blessings, yet most, all, in fact, except Caleb and Joshua, perished in the wilderness. So our sacramental privileges will not save us if we live a careless life. **6. Examples**] to be avoided: cp. Heb 3 7–4 2. **They . . lusted**] after the flesh-pots of Egypt (Nu 11); the Corinthians were inclined to hanker after heathen pleasures.

7. The people sat down, etc.] in honour of the golden calf (Ex 32 6). **Play**] revelling accompanying the idol-worship. **8. Some of them committed**] Nu 25. Fornication was a temptation to the Corinthians (c. 6). It was closely associated with idolatry; at Corinth there were a great number of women attached to the temple of Aphrodite (Venus) and devoted to her shameful service. **9. Tempt Christ**] (RV 'the Lord'; with AV, see on v. 4) i.e. try His patience. **Destroyed of serpents**] Nu 21 5, 6. **10. Murmur**] as some might at losing their old heathen pleasures. **Destroyed of the destroyer**] i.e. the destroying angel inflicting pestilence (Ex 12 23 2 S 24 15, 16 Nu 16 41-49).

11. For ensamples] RV 'by way of example.' **Written for our admonition**] not merely as ancient history : cp. Ro 15 4. **The ends of the world**] RV 'of the ages.' Christians are 'the heirs of all the ages,' living in the final dispensation: cp. Heb 1 2 **13. Such as is common to man**] RV 'such as man can bear.' **God is faithful**] He will not fail you (1 9); so endure, assured that He will support and finally deliver **(make a way to escape)**.

14–22. Partaking of the Holy Communion is morally incompatible with partaking of idolatrous feasts. By partaking of the Eucharist they showed themselves Christians having communion with Christ, and in Him with one another ; by sharing in sacrificial feasts in honour of idols they made themselves pagans, recognising the existence of false gods and forming a brotherhood with idol-worshippers. The two were morally incompatible, an offence against the Lord, who required their whole allegiance.

Paraphrase. '(14) Therefore avoid all connexion with idolatry. (5) Judge for yourselves, ye that are sensible men. (16) The Cup that we bless, the Bread that we break, do they not mean fellowship with Christ through sharing in Christ's Blood and Body ? (17) And we are all made one body in fellowship together by partaking of the one Bread. (18) So among the Jews, eating of the sacrifice means communion with God through (or with) the altar. (19) Now though an idol is a mere nothing, (20) yet we cannot help regarding heathen sacrifices as offered to evil spirits, (21) and it is morally impossible to share both in the Table and Cup of the Lord, and in those of evil spirits ; (22) we cannot afford to provoke the Lord to jealousy.'

14. Flee from idolatry] do not run into temptation by attending these sacrificial feasts. **15. As to wise men**] such as the Corinthians prided themselves on being: cp. 3 18 4 6 8 10. They could judge how incongruous it was, after having by the Eucharist been made partakers of Christ, to share in idol sacrifices, and so enter into fellowship with evil spirits. **16. Cup of blessing**] the cup of wine upon which a blessing was pronounced. **We bless**] i.e. consecrate by thanksgiving and prayer.

Communion of the blood of Christ] In c. 11 St. Paul presents the Eucharist under the aspect of a memorial of Christ's death; here under that of communion with Him ; hence our term 'Holy Communion' for this Sacrament. Partaking of the Cup bestows spiritual communion with Christ, helping those who have faith to receive more and more of His spirit and influence. So partaking of the Bread brings the same spiritual blessings. Both form one act of communion, the only difference being that while partaking of the Cup their thoughts are fixed on Christ's Blood shed for many, and while partaking of the Bread, upon His broken Body. **We break**] following Christ's own institution (Mt 26 26, 27). The Church is spoken of as doing what was actually done by its president (Ac 20 11). **17. For we being many**] better, RM 'Seeing that there is one bread, we who are many are one body.' It is a Sacrament of unity in Christ; partakers of the one Bread, broken and distributed to each, we all partake sacramentally of Christ's Body, and are thus 'members incorporate in His mystical Body, the blessed company of all faithful people.'

18. Israel after the flesh] the natural Israel. We Christians are the true Israel, who do God's will (Gal 6 16). **Partakers of** (RV 'have communion with') **the altar**] i.e. with God, whose share was offered on it: see on 9 13. Or, 'communion (with God) in (by) the altar.' 'The altar on which the victim was given to Jehovah, and from which it was given back to the offerers, was a meeting-place of communion between God and His people' (Evans). **19. That the idol is any thing**] no contradiction of 8 4, 7. **20. They sacrifice to devils** (lit. 'demons'), **and not to God**] an echo of Dt 32 17. St. Paul means that while particular heathen gods have no real existence, yet idolatrous worship is the invention of evil spirits, who instigate the excesses connected with it. To join in idolatrous feasts is to come into contact and fellowship with these spirits. **21. Cannot**] It is morally impossible ; to indulge in the latter makes the former a mere mockery.

22. Provoke the Lord to jealousy] (from Dt 32 16, 21 ; cp. Ex 20 5) by dividing an allegiance. **Are we stronger than he ?**] This was really what the conduct of those who frequented idol-feasts amounted to—a challenge to God. How absurd their conduct when thus analysed !

10 23–11 1. Practical directions. St. Paul has shown the moral danger of joining in what was avowedly a sacrificial, idolatrous feast. He now comes to cases where it was lawful to eat meat that had been offered in sacrifice to idols, provided the feelings of others were considered.

Paraphrase. '(23, 24) In dealing with the limits within which Christian liberty may be exercised, we have to consider not merely whether a thing is permissible, but whether it is helpful to others, as well as to ourselves. (25, 26) You may freely eat, without asking questions, any meat you buy in the market, for all that is in the world is from God, and therefore good. (27) And if you go to a feast at a friend's house, eat, without questioning, whatever is placed before you ; (28, 29) but if told that anything has been offered in sacrifice, abstain from it, so as not to wound the conscience of your informant. (29, 30) Remember it is entirely for his sake that you abstain ; for in the abstract it is not well that another's conscience should be scandalised by the liberty I exercise, or that what I receive as God's good gift should cause me to be maligned. (31) So not only eat and drink, but do everything, to God's glory ; (32) and avoid giving offence to men, whether Jews, or heathen, or fellow-Christians. (33) Remember that I always seek to deny myself for others with a view to their profit and salvation. (11 1) Follow my example in this respect as I follow Christ's.'

23. All things (i.e. things indifferent) **are lawful**] see on 6 12, 13. **Edify**] lit. 'build up' the Christian character. **24. Another's wealth**] RV 'his neighbour's good.' 'Wealth' is old English for 'welfare.' **25. Shambles**] the meat market. **Asking no question for conscience sake**] i.e. so as not to trouble your conscience, or, not stopping to consult conscience. St. Paul does not want to encourage unhealthy scruples. **26. The earth is the Lord's, and the fulness thereof**] i.e. all its contents (Ps 24 1) ; said to have been a Jewish grace before meat. RV omits these words at end of v. 28. **29. Of another**] RV 'by another.' Stevens paraphrases the v., 'Such action would have its entire reason in the weakness of the scrupulous man, for, in itself considered, one's liberty is not determined by some one else's conscience, but by his own.'

30. If I by grace be a partaker] RM, better, 'If I partake with thankfulness' : cp. 1 Tim 4 3-5. **Evil spoken of**] Heathens, or weak Christians, would think it grossly inconsistent to thank God for food offered to idols.

31. Do all to the glory of God] The principle the Apostle has been inculcating in respect of meats has a universal application. **32. None offence**] RV 'no occasion of stumbling.' **33. I please all men**] cp. 9 22, and especially Ro 15 1, 2, 'Let every one of us please his neighbour for his good to edification' : contrast Gal 1 10. **C. 11. 1. Be ye followers of me**] cp. 4 16. For Christ's example cp. Phil 2 4 Ro 15 3, 'even Christ pleased not himself.' This v. is closely joined to the preceding ; 11 2 begins a new section.

CHAPTER 11
DISORDERS IN WORSHIP
2–16. (c) THE VEILING OF WOMEN IN CHURCH

2. Now I praise you] This v. introduces the two following sections. The Apostle begins by praising them, perhaps echoing words from their own letter, for keeping the rules and teaching he had given ; but goes on to rebuke faults that have come to his knowledge. **Keep the ordinances**] RV 'hold fast the traditions' : cp. 2 Th 2 15. **I delivered them to you**] 11 23 15 3. Probably here rules for worship are specially meant.

3–16. Dress of women in public worship. In Greek, as well as in Eastern cities, it was customary for women, except those of bad character, to cover their heads in public. Some of the female Corinthian converts had discontinued this practice in Christian worship, thus practically claiming equality with men. Now St. Paul himself taught that 'there can be no male and female : for ye are all one in Christ Jesus ' (Gal 3 28, written either shortly before or shortly after 1 Cor). By this he meant that salvation is offered to all alike, all are alike in spiritual position ; but these women had taken such teaching to mean that all social subordination to men was also done away. But just as in the case of slavery (see on 7 21), Christianity did not come to abolish existing social conditions. It has done much to improve the condition of women, but has done so gradually. And when all is said, there remains a natural subordination of women to men ; and the conduct of these women in the prevailing circumstances of the age was likely to bring reproach on Christianity.

St. Paul first lays down the principle of subordination. He then speaks of the unseemliness of the practice in question, and of its converse, namely, men covering their heads ; and shows how this matter comes under the above principle, while women are not degraded by this subordination. He next uses corroboratory arguments from nature, and finally appeals to the practice of all other Churches.

Paraphrase. '(3) Every man is subordinate to Christ ; woman, on the other hand, is subordinate to man, just as Christ is subordinate to God. (4) Now, on this principle, if necessary, if any man were to worship with covered head he would disgrace himself, because the covered head is the symbol of inferior position. (5) In the same way every woman who worships without her veil, thus violating the custom among women of good character, acts discreditably and brings shame upon herself. (6) Indeed, she might as well have her hair cut short ; and she knows the shame attaching to that. (7–9) The man, therefore, as receiving his authority directly from God, ought to keep his head uncovered in worship ; whereas the woman should veil her head as the sign that her authority is derived from man. (10) And this is the more necessary when we remember that the angels are witnesses of Christian worship. (11, 12) But, after all, in the Christian life man and woman are dependent upon each other, just as they are in natural life, and in all things they are dependent upon God. (13–15) Now, just say yourselves if it is seemly for a woman to worship unveiled. Why, even nature, by giving her long hair for a natural veil, asserts the contrary. (16) But if any one is still unconvinced, let me say, once for all, that this practice of the unveiling of women is unknown to us and to the Churches of God.'

3. The head of every man is Christ] as the Son of man, the second Adam ; and so the head of all men : cp. Eph 4 15. **The head of the woman**] cp. Eph 5 22, 23. Woman was socially subordinate to man, and this was to be recognised in her behaviour at public worship. **The head of Christ** *is* **God**] He is subordinate to the Father (a) in His humanity, His mediatorial work, (b) as deriving His nature from the Father : see on 3 23. **4. Prophesying**] i.e. uttering a revelation of God's will. **Dishonoureth his head**] because he is wearing the mark of dependence. **5. Dishonoureth her head**] through not wearing the symbol of dependence. **As if she were shaven**] i.e. it is as shameful as if her hair were cut off. **6. Be shorn**] be like men in this also. **A shame**] it was the punishment of an adulteress. **7. Image and glory of God**] displaying most fully the divine perfections (Gn 1 26). **The woman is the glory of the man**] The meaning is that while man's authority is derived directly from God, woman's authority is derived from man. She thus receives not immediate but reflected light, so to speak. **8, 9. Of the man .. for the man**] cp. Gn 2 18-23. **10. Power**] RV 'a sign of authority,' i.e. that she is under authority. **Because of the angels**] The angels were conceived to be present as witnesses of and sharers in Christian worship. The recollection of this

should make the worshippers more reverential : cp. 'With angels and archangels .. we laud and magnify thy glorious name.' **11, 12.** See outline. **14. Nature**] i.e. the natural order of things, and man's sense of its fitness. For such guidance, cp. Ro 2 14.

15. The argument is that God, by providing woman with a natural veil, has taught that she ought to cover her head before Him.

16. Contentious] argumentative ; not open to conviction. **No such custom**] i.e. that women should be unveiled. For similar appeal to the example of other Churches, see on 4 17 7 17 14 33-36 : cp. with the whole passage vv. 3–16, Eph 5 22-24 1 Tim 2 8-15.

17–34. (d) THE PROPER OBSERVANCE OF THE LORD'S SUPPER

Like other societies and guilds in Greek cities, the early Christians used to have a common meal, to which all contributed according to their power, the rich helping their poorer brethren. Being thus a token of brotherly love and Christian fellowship, it was called a 'Love Feast' (Gk. *agapé*, see Jude v. 12 RV). In the earliest times the Eucharist was connected with it, as at the institution of the Lord's Supper, from which perhaps this feast was copied. But later on, perhaps in consequence of such disorders as those here mentioned, the two were separated, the Eucharist being held in the morning, the Love Feast in the evening ; and the latter gradually died out. Here the two are clearly united, and it is not clear whether ' the Lord's Supper' means the whole feast or the memorial service preceding or following the 'Love Feast.'

This feast had been greatly abused by the selfishness and individualism so prevalent at Corinth. Each individual or small clique began at once to consume the food and wine brought by themselves without waiting for the whole community to assemble, and without letting the poorer brethren share with them. What ought to have been an evidence of brotherly love had become an exhibition of selfish greed ; and under these circumstances it was impossible to have an orderly and reverent administration of Holy Communion. See also art. ' The Church in the Apostolic Age.'

St. Paul in this passage denounces this conduct (vv. 17–19). He blames them for the divisions and abuses which desecrated their religious meetings, and shows (vv. 20–22) how this spirit is fatal to the proper observance of the Lord's Supper. He reminds them of the institution and meaning of the Eucharist (vv. 23–26), of the need of partaking in a right spirit, and the sin and penalty of doing otherwise (vv. 27–32). He concludes (vv. 33, 34) with practical recommendations, which he will supplement when he comes.

17–34. Paraphrase. 'I wrote of praising you for keeping my ordinances, but I cannot praise you with regard to your Church meetings, which, as now conducted, do you more harm than good. (18) First I hear of there being factions among you there, and I think there must be some truth in the report. (19) The existence of such parties serves, at all events, to make known true Christians. (20) But the result of this factious spirit is that in your meetings there is no proper observance of the Lord's Supper ; (21) each cares only for himself ; some get too little, some too much. (22) Cannot you satisfy your hunger at home ? Do you dare to treat with contempt the Church of God and your poorer brethren ? (23–25) Call to mind what I taught you, as I myself received it from the Lord, about the most solemn institution of this Sacrament. (26) The observance of it is a constant proclamation of the Lord's death for man till His return ; (27) to partake of it unworthily is to be guilty of insult to the Lord's Body and Blood offered for us. (28) Let every one, then, first examine his motives for coming. (29) Any one not realising the presence of the Lord's Body in this Sacrament brings a judgment on himself, (30) hence the prevalence of sickness and death among you. (31, 32) If we would but judge ourselves, we should not be so judged ; but this judgment is the Lord's chastening, to save us from final condemnation with the world. (33) Therefore avoid this greedy selfishness, (34) and satisfy your appetite at home, that your meetings may not bring down a judgment upon you. Other matters I will settle when I come.'

17. The Apostle had praised them (v. 2) for keeping his instructions ; and had gone on to instruct them further regarding the veiling of women, a subject he had probably not needed to mention before. He now tells them that his praise is qualified. **In this**] RV 'in giving you this charge.' **Ye come together**] for Church meetings. **Not for the better**] which ought to be the result of all religious meetings. **18. In the church**] i.e. as always in the NT., not the building, but the assembly ; RM 'in congregation.' **Divisions**] or, 'schisms,' lit. 'splits.' They split up at their meeting into different sets. **19. There must be also heresies**] cp. Mt 18⁷, 'It must needs be that offences come,' i.e. owing to human weakness and sinfulness. **Heresies**] RM 'factions' : cp. Gal 5²⁰. The word (lit. 'choice,' then 'chosen opinions,' or 'a party holding opinions of their own') is repeatedly used of the sects of the Jews. **That they which are approved, etc.**] i.e. these parties 'are a magnet attracting unsound and unsettled minds, and leaving genuine believers to stand out approved by their constancy' (Findlay). **20.** *This* **is not to eat**] RV 'it is not possible

to eat.' Their selfishness (v. 21) was fatal to the proper spirit of devotion and brotherly love ; it became no more than an ordinary meal. **The Lord's supper**] This name occurs only here in the NT. ; it is uncertain whether it refers here to the Eucharist alone, or to the whole supper, or Love Feast. **21. Every one taketh, etc.**] corrected, v. 33. See introductory remarks on vv. 17–34. **22. Have ye not houses**] cp. v. 34. **Despise ye the church of God**] i.e. by thinking only of yourselves, and not of the welfare of the whole household of God. **Them that have not** (RV 'nothing')] i.e. the poor, who have no food to bring. **I praise** *you* **not**] cp. v. 2. They had not kept *this* 'tradition he had delivered them.'

23. I have received of the Lord] It is doubtful whether this must mean 'by direct revelation,' or whether it may be 'through instruction from others' : cp. 15³. Probably the facts were learnt from older Christians, but their full significance was directly revealed to him by the Lord. St. Paul contrasts here the solemn circumstances of the institution of the Sacrament with the disorderly scenes accompanying its frequent celebration at Corinth. **Which also I delivered unto you**] Instruction about this Sacrament formed part of St. Paul's earliest teaching to his converts. **The** *same* **night in which he was betrayed**] The mention of this calls to mind all the circumstances of the Passion, which we see St. Paul and his readers must have fully known, and so gives force to His last command. The account here of the Institution of the Eucharist agrees closely with that given by St. Luke, who may have been familiar with the words St. Paul used when consecrating ; and differs slightly from the accounts of St. Matthew and St. Mark. The one phrase found only here is, 'This do ye, as oft as ye drink it, in remembrance of me.' **24. Take, eat**] RV omits. In the MSS which have this reading the copyists probably supplied it from St. Matthew's Gospel, for the sake of securing uniformity in the accounts of the institution. **Is broken for you**] RV 'is for you.' St. Luke says, 'which is given for you.' **This do in remembrance of me**] So Lk, not Mt, Mk. **This do**] i.e. all that was done then—'Take, bless, break, distribute,' eat. **In remembrance of me**] or, 'as a memorial of Me' and of My atoning death (v. 26)—one great aspect of the Eucharist. **25. When he had supped**] RV 'after supper.' The bread was taken and distributed by our Lord during the Passover feast : cp. Mt 26²⁶ ; the cup was given at the close of the feast, and may have been the ordinary cup of thanksgiving taken at the conclusion of the Passover feast, set apart by Christ to this special purpose henceforth. **This cup is the new testament** (RV 'covenant') **in**

my blood] So Lk, Mt, Mk, 'this is my blood of the covenant.' Christ's Blood establishes a new covenant between God and man, one of forgiveness and grace : cp. Heb 8 6-13 9 15 f. The cup is a seal or assurance of our being included within this covenant. **26. Ye do show the Lord's death**] The celebration is 'a living sermon.'

27. Eat . . and drink] RV 'eat . . or drink.' This suggests a possible interval between the two : see on v. 25. **Unworthily**] i.e. carelessly, irreverently, as if an ordinary meal, regardless of its sacred meaning. **Guilty of the body and blood**] i.e. he sins against them ; by insulting the Sign, he insults the thing signified. **28. Let a man examine** (RV 'prove') **himself**] i.e. see that he understands the sacrament, and is in a fit moral condition to receive it. **29. Unworthily**] RV omits here, and for **not discerning** reads, 'if he discern not the body,' i.e. if he does not realise that it is not mere bread, but the Lord's Body that is given under the symbol, and if while he partakes of the bread he does not also receive inwardly of Christ's spirit and increase in consciousness of union with Him. **Damnation**] RV 'judgment,' not final condemnation, but God's chastening punishment intended to bring to repentance, and so save from the final condemnation of the ungodly world (v. 32). So vv. 31, 34, where RV reads 'judgment' for 'condemnation.' **30. For this cause**] Their irreverence had led God to punish them by disease and death (**sleep**, i.e. 'in death'). They had been visited with sickness, and St. Paul was enlightened by God to see in this the punishment of this irreverence. It is possible, however, that the words may be used in the spiritual sense, and may refer to the moral condition of the Corinthians. **31. Judge ourselves**] realise our true condition. **33, 34.** These vv. correct abuses described vv. 21, 22.

St. Paul regards the Eucharist as, (1) a means of communion with Christ (10 16, 17) ; (2) a sign of brotherhood by which all Christians are united together (10 17) ; (3) a memorial of Christ and of His death for man (11 24-26) ; and he records Christ's words which describe it as (4) the Seal of the New Covenant. From these chs. we get the phrases 'Holy Communion,' 'Lord's Table,' 'Lord's Supper.'

CHAPTERS 12–14
(e) SPIRITUAL GIFTS

In the early Church various powers, faculties, and graces were bestowed on individual Christians by the Holy Spirit. Some of these were distinctly miraculous, such as prophecy, tongues, power to work miracles ; others were less extraordinary gifts, such as teaching or wisdom : or special graces of Christian character, such as love. The Apostle does not distinguish between these classes all alike come from the same Source, and are to be exercised for the good of all. The Corinthians were inclined to overvalue the more showy gifts, especially that of tongues. Those possessing this gift were tempted to use it for mere display ; those not possessing it envied these others, and undervalued their own gifts.

St. Paul first (c. 12) shows that all these gifts come from the same Spirit, and all alike contribute to the well-being of the Church. But love (c. 13) surpasses them all ; without it they are of no avail. Of these gifts, prophecy (i.e. inspired preaching, revelation of God's will) is better than tongues because it builds up the Church, and produces a better effect upon unbelievers (c. 14). But the exercise of both gifts must be so regulated that all things may be done, (*a*) 'to edifying' ; (*b*) 'decently and in order.'

CHAPTER 12
(e) SPIRITUAL GIFTS
(i) THEIR NATURE AND RELATIONS

1–3. The test of the Spirit's presence is the confession of Jesus as the Lord. It would seem that some members of the Church, carried away by their excitement when speaking in the congregation under the power of the Spirit, as they said, had called Jesus accursed, as if they had been unbelievers. No such utterance, says the Apostle, can proceed from any one who speaks by the Spirit.

2. Gentiles] and so ignorant of all spiritual gifts, and requiring guidance now. **3. Wherefore**] i.e. because these gifts differ from any experience you had when heathens. **Calleth Jesus accursed**] RV 'saith, Jesus is anathema,' as unbelieving Jews would say. **Jesus is the Lord**] cp. Ro 10 9 (RV). This sincere confession is the essence of Christianity, and proves the presence of the Holy Spirit, the possession of a gift from Him. For a similar test cp. 1 Jn 2 1-3. Prof. Stevens paraphrases thus : 'The very first thing to be understood is that the confession of Jesus Christ as Lord is the keynote of all inspired speech. The primary test of the Spirit's inspiration is : Do you acknowledge the Lordship of Christ ?'

4–11. There are many gifts, but all are bestowed by one Spirit.

4, 5, 6. Spirit . . Lord . . God] The doctrine of the Holy Trinity is implied here. **Administrations**] RV 'ministrations' ; ways in which the Lord is served. **Operations**] RV 'workings.' **Which worketh all in all**] i.e. who is the author and instigator of all these activities in all who possess them. **7.** The gift by which the Spirit manifests His presence is given to each for the common good of all. **9. Faith**] i.e. (probably) a great wonder-working faith (13 2 Heb 11 33). **10. Prophecy**] i.e. inspired utterance of God's mind ; not only 'fore-telling,' but 'forth-telling ': see on 14 1. **Discerning of spirits**] power to recognise whether a man were a true or a false prophet. **Tongues .. interpretation**] cp. intro. to c. 14. **11. As he will**] Notice the personality and the freedom of the Spirit.

12–31. The Church is like the human body. It consists of many members, with different functions, but all intended to promote the good of the whole. Thus there is no room for selfish display, envy of others' gifts, contempt of one's own : cp. Ro 12 4, 5 Eph 4 15, 16 ; and the Roman fable of the belly and the members.

12, 13. Stevens paraphrases thus : 'The unity of those who possess the various gifts is analogous to the unity of the body ; they are all one in Christ. Their baptism into Christ signifies their unity in Him, whatever their nationality or social condition.' **12. Are**] i.e. constitute one body. **So also** *is* **Christ**] Christ is regarded here as the personality whose body is the Church. He is so closely connected with the Church that He is almost identified with it. He infuses His Spirit into it, and His Presence interpenetrates it. Every Christian is a member of Christ's body—head, hand, foot, eye, ear, or some other equally essential member. **13. Into one body**] i.e. so as to become one body : cp. Eph 4 4. **Have been all made to drink into** (RV 'of') **one Spirit**] or, perhaps, 'been watered with one Spirit.' He has poured His gifts into us all. **15.** A warning against being envious of others' gifts, negligent of our own. **Is it therefore not of the body ?**] RV 'it is not therefore not of the body'; it does not on this account cease to belong to it.

17 f. If the whole body] Just as the differences of powers and functions are a great advantage to the body, so the existence of different gifts benefits the Church. The position of each individual, his possession of this or that gift, has been ordered by God.

21. I have no need of thee] a rebuke to those who despised those not possessing *their* gifts. **23. Bestow more abundant honour**] i.e. by clothing them. **24. No need**] of clothing. **Tempered .. together**] wrought all into harmony. **Given more abundant honour**] by implanting in men the instinct of v. 23.

25. No schism] contrast 1 10 11 18, where see note. **26. All the members suffer with it**] What is true of the human body, through the nervous connexion of all its parts, should be true of the Church : cp. Ro 12 5.

27–31. Application. The various offices and functions in the Church, Christ's Body. These are by God's assignment ; all do not possess the same gift. **27. Ye are the body of Christ**] true of individual Churches, as here ; and of the Church universal (Eph 1 23).

Members in particular] i.e. each in his place ; RV 'severally members thereof.' **28. First apostles,** etc.] cp. similar list, Eph 4 11. It is a list not so much of distinct offices as of functions and gifts, some of which may be combined in the same man. St. Paul was Apostle, prophet, teacher (Ac 13 1), worked miracles, and spoke with tongues (1 Cor 14 18).

Apostles] commissioned witnesses of Christ's Resurrection, founders or organisers of Churches. **Prophets**] cp. v. 10, inspired revealers of God's mind. **Teachers**] who gave instruction regarding the faith and the bearing of religion upon life and conduct (v. 8).

Helps] including the original work of deacons, ministration to the poor and sick.

Governments] i.e. powers of organisation and administration, including much of the work of presbyters. **Tongues**] are perhaps put last, because overvalued at Corinth.

30. Interpret] i.e. the tongues (v. 10).

31. Covet (RV 'desire') **earnestly the best** (RV 'greater') **gifts**] The lowest have their place, but it is right to aim at possessing the higher. **And yet shew I unto you a more excellent way**] RV 'a still more excellent way show I unto you,' i.e. in which to possess and use them. To have them is good, but it is still more important to use them in a spirit of love.

CHAPTER 13

(e) Spiritual Gifts

(ii) The most excellent Gift of Charity

In this c. we enter into the purest atmosphere and breathe the most fragrant odours. Passing from the previous chs. with their tale of faction and scandal and shame to this passage with its description of Christian love is like passing from the enchanted ground of the 'Pilgrim's Progress' to the land of Beulah within sight of the Celestial Gate.

The Revised Version reads 'love' for **charity** throughout the c. The Gk. word is translated 'love' in most places of the NT., so is the corresponding verb always. The RV change (1) is desirable for consistency ; (2) gives the Apostle's meaning better—love being much more than almsgiving or kindly judgment, which are now the usual meaning of 'charity'; (3) shows St. Paul and St. John are agreed in attaching the highest value to love, thus enforcing the 'great commandment of the Law' as declared by our Lord. The Gk. word translated 'charity' in AV does not exist in classical Greek. It is found first in the Septuagint. The corresponding verb means to desire the good of one whom you esteem ; and the noun is appropriately applied to the spirit which seeks not its own but others' good, and sacrifices itself for others.

1-3. Great gifts (e.g. tongues, prophecy, knowledge, faith) and even good deeds are of no avail without love : cp. Mt 7 22. What a man is, is more important than what he has.

1. Tongues] the gift the Corinthians most valued. **Have not charity**] do not use the gift in a spirit of love. **Sounding brass**] i.e. merely so much noise. **2. All faith**] see on 12 9. **Remove mountains**] Mt 17 20 21 21. St. Paul may have our Lord's words in mind ; but it was a proverbial expression. **3.** These actions would seem works of love, but may spring merely from ostentation or vainglory.

Give my body] A still greater instance of self-devotion. **To be burned**] Some MSS have, 'give my body that I may boast,' in self-approval.

4-7. The character and actions of Love.

4. Vaunteth not itself] does not make a display. **Puffed up**] i.e. conceited. **5. Seeketh not her own**] i.e. her own advantage (10 24, 33).

Thinketh no evil] RV 'taketh not account of evil ' ; does not reckon up her grievances.

6. Rejoiceth not in iniquity] i.e. in hearing or telling of others' faults or follies. **In** (RV ' with ') **the truth**] i.e. in the spread and victory of truth and right. **7. Beareth**] without breaking down. **Believeth all things**] is not suspicious ; puts the best construction on things.

Endureth] without giving up.

8-13. Love is eternal. Other gifts, knowledge, prophecy, tongues serve but a temporary purpose. 'They are only means towards an end. Love remains the completion and perfection of our human being' (F. W. Robertson).

9. In part] partially, imperfectly. **11. When I was a child**] an illustration of v. 10. **Understood**] RV 'felt.' **12. Through a glass**] RV 'in a mirror,' seeing only a reflection, not the actual reality. Ancient mirrors were of metal (cp. Ex 38 8), often reflecting imperfectly.

Darkly] lit. ' in a riddle,' taught by hints and metaphors. Our knowledge of divine things is necessarily imperfect ; much is not revealed, much only partially ; we have to use earthly and human figures and language to express eternal truths. **Know even as also I am known**] ' Then shall I plainly know spiritual things with a knowledge like that of God ' (Stevens) ; or, ' even as God knows me.'

15. Now abideth] Probably meaning not ' these three exist now, but finally love alone will remain '; but, ' the fact is that these three alone are eternal.' **Faith** (confidence in God) will continue in the next life : so will **hope** (expectation of future good) ; for that life will be one of progress not stagnation. **The greatest of these is charity**] RV ' love.' For love is the mainspring of faith and hope ; and ' God is love.'

CHAPTER 14

(e) SPIRITUAL GIFTS

(iii) THE GIFT OF TONGUES SUBORDINATE TO PROPHECY

The Apostle in this c. deals with the abuse of the gift of tongues which characterised the Corinthians, and declares that it is inferior to the gift of prophecy, though valuable enough in itself if kept in proper control. Speaking with tongues is a phenomenon we meet with in the NT. only here and in the Acts of the Apostles. The gift as recorded in Ac 2 seems to have been the power to speak in foreign languages. We are told that Parthians, Medes, and Elamites, as well as dwellers in Asia Minor, Egypt, Rome, Crete, and Arabia heard their own languages spoken by the disciples on the day of Pentecost. In the Corinthian Church the gift of tongues seems to have been manifested in a different way. It took the form of ecstatic utterance. Those who possessed it often burst forth during public worship in a rhapsody of words, unintelligible to others and often to themselves. There were others who had the gift of interpreting these utterances and explaining them to the congregation. But often there was no interpreter present ; and the unedifying spectacle was witnessed of several worshippers speaking at once, and no one understanding a syllable of what was said. This gift, too, as it attracted attention and appealed to the Greek belief in prophetic ecstasy and love of display, was held in high estimation and anxiously sought after : but as the results proved, it was capable of grievous abuse.

The Apostle here points out that the gift of tongues while it is of value to the person who possesses it (v. 4), and of importance as attracting the notice of unbelievers (v. 22), is of no benefit to the Church, because it provides no edification (vv. 2, 5, 11, 12). On the other hand, the gift of prophecy is a benefit to others, for by it the Church receives edifying ; because the speaker declares the secrets of God's dealing with men and reveals to men their need of God's grace, speaking so that all can understand him. Therefore the Apostle, though himself possessed of the gift of tongues in a high degree (v. 18) and desiring that others should have it also (v. 5), declares that prophecy is a far higher gift, because far more useful to the Church (v. 5, 22, 24, 25).

1-19. The gift of prophecy is better than that of tongues, because it edifies believers.

1. Follow after charity] Seek a loving spirit before all things. **And desire**] RV ' yet desire earnestly' (cp. 12 31); do not neglect other gifts. **But rather that**] and more especially that. **Prophesy**] inspired preaching ; declaring God's mind. A prophet in Scripture does not simply foretell the future ; he tells forth the will of God, and speaks for God as His mouthpiece.

Paraphrase. '(2–4) One who has the gift of tongues speaks only to God ; he does not communicate to others the mysterious truths of which he is conscious ; he cultivates only his own spiritual life. But a prophet builds up the spiritual life of the Church by his words of exhortation and encouragement. (5) I do not disparage tongues ; I should like you all to possess that gift ; but it is inferior to prophecy unless the speaker can interpret and so build up the Church. (6) I myself could do you no good by speaking in a tongue, unless I added interpretation and teaching. (7) The melody played upon a musical instrument cannot be recognised unless the notes are distinct ; (8) the bugle-call must be clear if it is to bring men to battle. (9) Similarly, unless it is possible to understand what you say, of what value are your words ? (10, 11) Every language in the world has a meaning ; but the hearer must understand the speaker's language, if they are to communicate with one another. (12) Seek then for the spiritual gifts which are most useful in edifying the Church. (13) Let him who has the gift of tongues seek also the gift of interpretation, (14, 15) so that his understanding may have its part in his prayer and praise, as well as his spirit. (16, 17) How can the ordinary worshipper say "Amen" when you give thanks, if he does not understand what you say ? Your thanksgiving may be earnest and heartfelt, but it is valueless for his comfort and encouragement. (18, 19) I am thankful that I am highly endowed with this gift ; but I would rather in your gatherings for worship say five words that would be helpful to your spiritual life than ten thousand which no one could understand.'

2. An *unknown* **tongue**] RV omits 'unknown' : so throughout the c. In AV it is in italics, merely added as an explanation or interpretation. **4. Edifieth** (RM ' buildeth up ') **himself**] by conscious communion with God. **6. Except I shall speak to you**] i.e. in addition to (or instead of) speaking with tongues. A rhapsody of praise imparts little truth to others. **9. By the tongue**] i.e. with your tongue, the instrument of speech. **10, 11. Kinds of voices**] i.e. languages. **Barbarian**] i.e. foreigner. **12. Excel**] RV 'abound,' i.e. in these gifts. **13. Pray that he may interpret**] i.e. pray for the ability to make known to others the meaning of the impassioned words in which he has poured out his spirit.

14. Is unfruitful] is of no use to myself or to any one else. **16. Bless . . giving of thanks**] Probably no special reference to the Eucharist. It is clear that public worship was largely at least extempore. Every member who was moved to do so, contributed to the edification of the congregation, by psalm, or prayer, or exhortation, or explanation : cp. v. 26.

Occupieth the room (RV ' filleth the place ') **of the unlearned**] RM ' him that is without gifts ' ; probably here, ' any one not understanding your " tongue." ' The (RV) **Amen**] the close of prayers and thanksgivings among both Jews and Christians, expressing the assent of the congregation (Neh 8 6 Ps 106 48.)

19. In the church] i.e. at a Church assembly. St. Paul insists upon Church worship being really ' common prayer,' each worshipper joining intelligently in what is said.

20–25. Prophecy is better than ' tongues ' for convincing unbelievers.

Paraphrase. '(20) Do not reason like children, but like grown men : it is only in regard to knowledge of evil that I wish you to be childlike. So do not overestimate the more pretentious gift. (21) The history of God's dealings with Israel suggests a lesson regarding the use of unintelligible speech. The warning of impending judgment was brought home to the people of Judah when they heard the strange accents of the Assyrians among them. (22) And what is suggested to us is that the utterances of those who have received this gift are a sign to attract the attention of unbelievers and warn them of the presence of the Spirit : whereas, on the other hand, prophecy makes its appeal rather to believers. (23) But if an unbeliever comes into your assembly and hears only words uttered in ecstasy without interpretation, will he not suspect you all of madness ? (24, 25) Whereas if he comes in and finds you prophesying, he is likely to be impressed and converted.'

20. Be not children] who seek the showy rather than the useful : cp. Mt 10 16 Ro 16 19.

21. In the law] i.e. the OT. (Isa 28 11, 12). As God confounded the unbelieving Jews who rejected Isaiah's plain warnings as folly, by bringing upon them invaders (Assyrians) of unintelligible speech, so tongues are meant to impress unbelievers, as a sign of the existence of spiritual influences ; but, as of old, many will be confirmed by them in their unbelief.

22. Tongues] were valuable to unbelievers as a sign of the Spirit's presence, but not for believers, who already were convinced of it, and who could appreciate prophecy. **23. All speak with tongues**] Not necessarily all at once, but one after another, leaving space for nothing else. **Unlearned**] cp. v. 16 ; any one not understanding this gift.

24. He is convinced of all] ' His conscience is aroused and awed by this united testimony to truth' (Massie).

25. In you of a truth] ' among you indeed.'

26–33. Regulations for the exercise of the various gifts.

Paraphrase. '(26) Now, brethren, I hear that there is much disorder in your worship, each of you being eager to utter his psalm, or lesson, or rhapsody, or interpretation, or exhortation, and apt to interrupt the other. Let this disorder cease, and everything be done with a view to strengthening your faith and deepening your spiritual life. (27, 28) Let no more than two or three speak with tongues at any meeting, and let them speak in succession, what they say being interpreted. But if there be no one present to interpret, let them engage in silent prayer and worship. (29–31) So also with the prophets : let two or three speak in succession ; and if some one be moved to speak at any time, let him who is addressing you make way. In this way, you will all get an opportunity of edifying and being edified by one another. (32, 33) The prophet who is truly inspired is to be recognised by his self-restraint ; for God does not inspire men to bring disorder into the Church, but prompts them to do the things that make for peace.'

26. Every one of you] The right of taking the lead in public worship was practically unrestrained at Corinth ; and the need of regulation is here made very manifest. **Hath a psalm]** i.e. to sing (cp. Eph 5¹⁹) ; either from the OT., or else impromptu: cp. the Magnificat, Benedictus, Nunc Dimittis. **Doctrine, revelation]** cp. v. 6, 12²⁸. **27. By two]** i.e. two or, at most, three may speak in succession, if there is an interpreter. **28. Speak to himself, and to God]** i.e. use this gift at home, not in public worship. **29. Let the other** (RV 'others') **judge]** whether the speakers have a message from God : cp. 12¹⁰. **30. Be revealed to another]** The speaker is to conclude if he perceive another has received a sudden revelation. **31. Comforted]** i.e. encouraged, exhorted. **32. The spirits of the prophet,** etc.] So let none maintain he must speak, or cannot stop. 33. *The author*] RV '*a God.*' Not confusion, but peace, is to His mind : cp. Ro 15³³. **As in all churches of the saints]** i.e. all Christian communities. This clause belongs to the whole preceding paragraph, 'Such arrangements are in force elsewhere, and you also ought to adopt them': cp. 11¹⁶ 4¹⁷ note.

34–36. Women are not to speak in Church assemblies : cp. 11³⁻¹⁶ 1 Tim 2¹¹⁻¹⁵. In 11⁵ St. Paul seems to allow, provided the head be covered, what he forbids here. Either (a) on second thoughts he now forbids it altogether ; or, (b) here he is thinking of public services ; there, of more private gatherings : cp. Ac 18²⁶, where Priscilla is associated with Aquila in the teaching of Apollos. See also 16¹⁹.

34. As also saith the law] Gn 3¹⁶ : cp. 1 Tim 2¹³⁻¹⁴. **35. If they will learn any thing]** Perhaps some had expressed their own opinions under cover of seeking information. **Their husbands]** Most would be married ; speaking would be still more unsuitable for the unmarried. **36. Came the word of God out from you?]** RV 'Was it from you that the word of God went forth? or came it unto you alone?'; i.e. you are neither the original nor the only Church ; what are you that you diverge from the general practice and set up a standard of your own? The Apostle here falls back again on the weapon of sarcasm.

37–40. Conclusion of subject.

Paraphrase. '(37) To sum up, then, let those who claim to have these spiritual gifts attend to these regulations, for they express the will of the Lord. (38) But if any one refuse to learn, let him just abide in his ignorance. (39) Do not forbid the exercise of ecstatic utterance ; but encourage prophecy. (40) See that above all you have all orderly and seemly worship.'

37. Spiritual] i.e. possessing spiritual gifts. **Let him acknowledge]** If their claim to have the Spirit is true, they will recognise the authority of these regulations. **The commandments of the Lord]** cp. 7¹⁰ ; contrast 7²⁵, ⁴⁰. **38. Let him be ignorant]** RM 'If any man knoweth not, he is not known,' i.e. God does not recognise him. But perhaps the Apostle means, 'If any man will not learn, then he must just abide in his ignorance, with all its inevitable loss': cp. Rev 22¹¹. **39. Covet to prophesy]** This is to be 'earnestly desired' (RV); tongues are merely allowed. **40. Decently]** i.e. in a becoming and proper way.

The principles St. Paul keeps steadily in view are, (1) Public worship must be edifying to all ; (2) it must be conducted in good order.

CHAPTER 15

(f) The Fact and the Doctrine of the Resurrection of the Dead

Some Corinthians disbelieved in the resurrection of the dead—not, apparently, in Christ's Resurrection, though St. Paul felt this would soon follow, but in their own future resurrection. This occasioned him to write this grand chapter, which has cheered the hearts of so many mourners, read, as the greater part of it is, at the burial of the dead. He first (vv. 1–11) repeats the historical evidence for Christ's Resurrection, a truth taught by all Christian teachers to all their converts ; then shows (vv. 12–19) that the denial of the resurrection of the dead leads logically to the denial of Christ's Resurrection, thus overthrowing the whole Christian faith. He next

(vv. 20–28) speaks of the consequences of Christ's Resurrection ; and (vv. 29–34) the influence of the hope of resurrection upon Christian life and practice.

He then throws light on the nature of the resurrection-body (vv. 35–44), by using the analogy of seed and plant, and reminding his readers of the differences now existing between various bodies. So the resurrection-body will spring from the earthly one, but be far more glorious, a spiritual body, not like Adam's earthly body, but like Christ's glorified one (vv. 45–49). The bodies of the living (vv. 50–52) will experience a similar change. This resurrection change is the final victory over sin and death (vv. 53–58). The Apostle's teaching is to be distinguished from the doctrine of the immortality of the soul taught by the great heathen thinkers like Socrates and Plato. It includes that doctrine, but adds to it the doctrine of the redemption of the body (Ro 8 23) ; and bases the whole doctrine of the resurrection-life upon the fact that Christ is risen from the dead.

The doctrine of resurrection and future life was not clearly revealed in OT. times. Death was commonly regarded not as the end of all things, but as followed by a shadowy existence, not worth calling a life, cut off from all its joys and even from God Himself (Ps 6 5 88 5, 12 Isa 38 18). So the rewards and punishments set before Israel in the Law were temporal ones (Dt 28). But God gradually led His people on to clearer light. (1) Their consciousness of communion with God was so strong that they felt death could not end it (Ps 73 24-26). (2) They felt a future life was required to vindicate God's justice. Isaiah (26 19) speaks of a national resurrection (cp. Ezk 37) ; Daniel (12 2) of an individual one. The hope gradually grew stronger ; in our Lord's day the Pharisees held to it firmly, though the Sadducees denied it (2 Maccabees and the Psalms of Solomon, probably written by Pharisees about 45 B.C., show the prevalence of this hope). But our Lord's Resurrection changed what was previously only partially revealed into a ' sure and certain hope ' : cp. 2 Tim 1 10. Not only did it (1) prove the truth of His claim to be the Son of God (Ro 1 4), and (2) assure men that His sacrifice had been accepted (Ro 4 25) ; it is (3) appealed to by St. Paul as a call to Christians, in virtue of their mystical union with Christ, to live no longer to sin, but to God (Ro 6 4, etc.) ; and (4) it is the pledge that we too shall rise again (here, and 2 Cor 4 14 Ro 8 11, etc.). And what we gather as to the nature of Christ's resurrection-body (Lk 24 Jn 20) throws light upon the change in ours, which will be conformed to the body of His glory (Phil 3 21 RV). It was a real body, bearing the marks of His

former ' natural ' body (Jn 20 27) ; capable of receiving food (Lk 24 43), and of being recognised by those who had formerly known Him, though apparently only when He willed to be recognised : cp. Lk 24 15, 16, 31. Yet it could be transported mysteriously from place to place, passing even through the closed doors. St. Paul uses the analogy of plant and seed to explain the relation of the resurrection-body to the present one. We may infer that the glorified body will have some relation to the natural body, thus preserving personal identity ; but will not be composed of the identical material particles of the body laid to rest ; it will be free from its limitations and imperfections, a fit abode for the perfected spirit.

1–11. The historical evidence for Christ's Resurrection. St. Paul reminds his converts of his original teaching at Corinth—how the Resurrection was one of the essentials of his gospel message. As at Athens (Ac 17 18) he preached ' Jesus and the Resurrection,' and their position as Christians rests upon their adherence to this truth. His great message to them was Christ's atoning death, His burial, and His return from the grave. He mentions five separate appearances of Christ after His Resurrection, and finally mentions the Lord's appearance to himself. He reminds them that, although unworthy to be called an Apostle on account of His former persecution of the Church, God's grace has made him a true Apostle. And he concludes by pointing out that in the matter of proclaiming the Resurrection of Christ he and the other Apostles are at one.

2. Are saved] i.e. are in the way of salvation (see on 1 18), by faith in the crucified and risen Saviour. **Keep in memory**] RV 'hold fast.' **Have believed** (RV 'believed,' i.e. at your conversion and baptism) **in vain**] i.e. without consideration, and so without stability. **3. I delivered . . which I received**] see on 11 2, 23. Probably he ' received ' the accounts of these appearances of the risen Lord on his visit to Jerusalem (Ac 9 27, 28 Gal 1 18, 19), when he saw Peter and James. **First of all**] As most important. **For our sins**] i.e. to atone for them.

According to the scriptures] Not by accident, but in fulfilment of God's plan : cp. Isa 53 Lk 24 44-46. **4. Buried**] This proves the reality of both Death and Resurrection. **5. He was seen**] RV 'appeared to.' Not a complete list. Mary Magdalene, e.g., and the two at Emmaus (Lk 24) are omitted. He mentions those personally known to himself, and whose authority would have weight at Corinth.

Cephas, then of the twelve] Lk 24 33-36.

6. Above five hundred brethren at once] probably on the mountain in Galilee (Mt 28 16, 17). **Some are fallen asleep**] i.e. dead. Twenty-five years at least had elapsed. **Sleep**

is used of death often in OT. (e.g. 1 K 2 10), but Christ, by using it of those He was about to restore to life (Mt 9 24 Jn 11 11-13), and by His own Resurrection, which is the assurance of ours, has given new meaning to it, viz. not merely cessation of the work of life, but a sleep from which we shall awake to new life. **7. James]** The Lord's brother (Gal 1 19 Ac 15 13). This appearance is not mentioned in the Gospels.

All the apostles] probably just before the Ascension, Ac 1 4.

The present passage is the oldest account of the appearances of the risen Lord, written years before any of our Gospels, and only about twenty-five years after the events, while hundreds of witnesses were still living. It is thus a most valuable piece of evidence as to the certainty of our Lord's Resurrection, which would remain firmly attested even if the authenticity of our Gospels were denied.

8. Of me also] on the road to Damascus, at his conversion (Ac 9). **Born out of due time]** Suddenly, without the gradual training of the rest ; as inferior as an immature birth is to a mature one. **9. The least of the apostles]** cp. 1 Tim 1 12-16. **10. I am what I am]** i.e. an Apostle. **Not in vain]** i.e. was justified by its results. His apostolic work, as well as his apostleship itself, was due to **the grace of God. 11. Or they]** i.e. the other Apostles ; Christ's Resurrection was taught by all Christian preachers, accepted by all believers.

12–19. Denial of the resurrection of the dead logically involves the denial of Christ's Resurrection, which would overthrow the whole Christian Faith. The belief in the resurrection of the dead is bound up with the Resurrection of Christ. But His Resurrection shows that resurrection is not an impossibility, and as He is Son of man, 'the spiritual head of humanity,' His Resurrection does not stand by itself ; it is man's resurrection also. The Corinthians accepted the truth of the Resurrection of Christ, and the Apostle asks them how they can logically deny the truth of the resurrection of the dead. He then proceeds to establish the truth of the resurrection of the dead by the method of indirect proof, showing the awful consequences which would result from its denial. The first of these impossible consequences is that Christ is not risen ; another is that they are still unforgiven sinners, their faith being useless ; a third is that the Apostles are proclaiming falsehoods ; and a fourth is that their beloved dead are hopelessly lost to them. He concludes, therefore, that if their hope in Christ has reference only to the present life they are in a pitiable state, for they are cherishing a mere delusion, if there be no truth in the resurrection of the dead.

12. How say some among you, etc.] Their unbelief probably sprang from the philosophical idea that the matter was essentially evil, so that the soul would be better off when set free from the body ; thus the doctrine of the Resurrection was to them a needless difficulty : cp. also 2 Tim 2 17. The Corinthians, however, accepted the Resurrection of Christ as a fact, and the Apostle argues that they cannot logically deny the fact of the resurrection of the dead, as Christ's Resurrection is a particular case of it. **13. Then is Christ not risen]** For if a thing be altogether impossible, there cannot be even one instance of it. In this and the following vv. (see summary) the Apostle shows the logical consequences of disbelief in the resurrection, or, rather, the consequences that would follow were there no resurrection. These consequences, he concludes, are unthinkable or absurd, and, therefore, he argues that the premises which produce them are false.

14. Vain] i.e. there is nothing in it.

15. False witnesses] not merely empty talkers, but positive liars. No thoughtful sceptic now-a-days regards the Apostles as impostors. Their character, as well as their sufferings, forbids this ; but he would say they were victims of a mistake—merely imagined they saw the risen Lord. But the idea of this never enters St. Paul's mind ; it was to him perfectly impossible that they could have been mistaken. **17. Yet in your sins]** not justified from them (Ro 2 25) ; unforgiven, unrenewed. 'Christ's Resurrection is the seal of our justification and the spring of our sanctification' (Findlay). If there be no resurrection, of what avail are forgiveness and salvation ? **18. They also which are fallen asleep]** The Apostle here argues from the natural affections of the human heart. It is impossible to believe that those who died in faith in Christ perished utterly. The inference is : 'But we are sure these things are not so ; therefore Christ has risen ; therefore the resurrection is possible.' He argues from Christian experience. **19. If in this life only we have hope in Christ]** If our hope in Him does not reach beyond this life, we are **most miserable** (RV 'pitiable'), because the hope of future joy and blessing which inspires our toils and sufferings is a mere delusion.

20–28. The fact and the consequences of Christ's Resurrection. Christ is risen as the firstfruits of those who sleep. As death came on all through Adam, so resurrection-life will come to all through Him. But this will only be at His coming, which will be followed by His handing over the Mediatorial Kingdom to the Father, now that all things, even death itself, have been subjected to Him.

20. The firstfruits] The first sheaf accepted by God is a pledge of the coming harvest : cp. Lv 23 10, 11. **21, 22.** The Apostle, as in

Ro 5, contrasts Adam, from whom by natural descent we all derive a corrupt nature, with Christ the second Adam, the Son of man, our spiritual head, by union with whom we receive spiritual life. **All . . all**] The first ' all ' means, of course, all mankind. The second may mean the same, in which case **shall be made alive** simply refers to resurrection, whether to life or to judgment (Jn 5 28, 29 ; cp. Dan 12 2 Ac 24 15). But perhaps more probably it means only, ' all those who are Christ's ' (v. 23), who shall enjoy the ' resurrection of life.' Cp. v. 23, ' Christ the firstfruits : then they that are Christ's.'

23. In his own order] i.e. rank, or place. Christ comes first, the rest long after.

24. Then *cometh* **the end**] Christ's Advent and the Resurrection conclude this dispensation. **When he shall have delivered up the kingdom**] The purpose of the Incarnation will have been accomplished ; Christ will have recovered for His Father the dominion over all things. ' This is no ceasing of Christ's rule, but the inauguration of God's eternal kingdom ' (Findlay). **All rule**] i.e. every opposing power. **25. He must reign**] according to prophecy (Ps 110 1). **26. The last enemy**] ' The first enemy of Christ and of Christians is the devil, who was conquered by Christ on the Cross ; the second is sin, which through the grace of Christ is conquered by Christians in this life ; the third is death, which, as the last of all, will be conquered at the Resurrection ' (quoted by Sadler). **27. For he** (God) **hath put all things under his** (Christ's) **feet**] cp. Ps 8 6 Heb 2 8 Phil 2 9-11. The Father has bestowed upon Him as Son of man dominion over the whole universe. **When he saith, etc.**] RM ' when he shall have said, All things are put in subjection (evidently excepting him that did subject all things unto him), when, *I say*, all things,' etc. ; i.e. when Christ announces His complete victory, which is no infringement of God's sovereignty. **28. Then shall the Son also himself be subject**] see on v. 24. The Son will continue to be subordinate to the Father, as now. This is involved in the very idea of Sonship : cp. 3 23 11 3. **That God may be all in all**] The universe, with all it comprises, will wholly answer to God's will and reflect His mind.

29-34. The practical effects of the doctrine of the Resurrection. The Resurrection alone gives an adequate motive for (*a*) baptism for the dead ; (*b*) running risk of death in Christian work ; or indeed (*c*) abstaining from a life of self-indulgence.

29. Baptized for the dead] a very obscure allusion. There was somewhat later a practice, among certain sects of vicarious baptism ; when a man died unbaptised, a friend would receive baptism in his stead. This may have already existed and be meant here. St. Paul mentions

' baptism for the dead,' without expressing his approval ; but some think the practice sprang up later from a perversion of this passage. Two other views seem possible. (1) That of St. Chrysostom : ' Before baptism we confess our faith in " the resurrection of the dead," and are baptised in hope of this resurrection.' (2) That of Godet, who regards the baptism as the baptism of suffering, the baptism with which those were baptised who have by martyrdom entered the Church invisible. But it can scarcely be denied that, as Dr. Dods says, ' the plain meaning of the words seems to point to a vicarious baptism, in which a living friend received baptism for a person who had died without baptism.'

31. By your rejoicing] RV ' by that glorying in you,' i.e. as surely as I am proud of you : cp. 1 Th 2 19, 20. **I die daily**] am daily in danger of death, and my daily sufferings must end in it : cp. 2 Cor 11 23. **32. After the manner of men**] i.e. from ordinary human motives, for applause or money ; and with no hope of reward in the resurrection life. **I have fought with beasts**] probably a strong metaphor (cp. 4 9) for some plot of the Jews or attack of the mob. His Roman citizenship and influential friends (Ac 19 31) would have saved him from actually having to fight wild beasts in the theatre ; and this, if it had really happened, would probably have been specially mentioned (2 Cor 11 23 f.).

If the dead rise not] RV takes this with the next sentence. **Let us eat and drink**] Isa 22 13. The natural though not the necessary consequence of disbelief in a future life is to care only for self-gratification.

33, 34. Do not associate with those who deny this vital truth. You are in great danger of being corrupted by them. Be aroused to a sense of your condition, and cease from sin. I trust that my words will shame you out of your folly.

33. Evil communications] RV ' evil company,' a quotation from a Greek poet, Menander, warning the Corinthians against the influence of heathen ideas about the future life. The line had probably in St Paul's day become a proverb, as it is still. **34 Some have not the knowledge of God**] hence both unbelief in resurrection, and low moral tone. **To your shame**] i.e. to shame you ; for you ought to surpass the heathen.

35-44. The nature of the Resurrection and the Resurrection body. St. Paul here uses several illustrations of (*a*) the possibility (*b*) the nature of the resurrection change. The seed sown in the ground decays, but gives birth to a new plant. So from the body laid in the grave a nobler one will arise. There are in the world many varieties of animal life, each suited to its surroundings, and, moreover, bodies of heavenly beings as well as earthly far more glorious than they. Moreover, sun, moon, and various stars have different degrees of brightness. So our resurrection body will be far more glorious, adapted to its surroundings. Our body sown in corruption, dishonour, weakness—a mere natural body—will be raised in incorruption, honour, power—a spiritual body : see intro. to this c.

36. *Thou* **fool**] RV 'thou foolish one.' The Apostle is somewhat impatient of objections to his doctrine of the Resurrection, which the analogies of nature readily refute. **That which**] i.e. the seed which. **Is not quickened, except it die**] cp. Jn 12 24. In nature, death leads to higher life. **37. Not that body that shall be, but bare** (RV 'a bare') **grain**] The actual seed sown does not reappear, but something higher, a complete plant, springs from it. **38. His own body**] RV 'a body of its own,' i.e. a plant of the same kind as the seed.

39. There are many different forms of animal life ; so there may be of human life.

40. Celestial bodies] probably this refers to angels, not to sun and moon, etc. But this leads him in the next v. to speak of degrees of glory. **Bodies terrestrial**] i.e. creatures of the earth. **41.** *One* **star differeth**] The primary meaning is the literal one. Some stars are brighter than others. There are great differences between things of the same class ; so also between the natural and the spiritual body.

44. A natural body] (cp. 2 14, 'the natural man') endowed with natural life and fitted for an earthly existence. The **spiritual body** will be filled with spiritual life and adapted for a spiritual existence. The word 'natural' is literally 'soulish,' and suggests the possession of an ordinary human personality ; while the word 'spiritual' suggests a relation to the divine. Man possesses the spiritual life through his union with Christ, and the Apostle asserts that there is a spiritual body fitted for the requirements of this spiritual life, and that he will come into possession of it in the resurrection life

45–49. Our bodies will be like Christ's, no longer like Adam's. Adam, made from the earth, became 'a living soul' ; Christ, who is from heaven, is constituted a life-giving Spirit. We belong to both, and so share the nature of both ; we have borne the image of the earthly man, we shall bear that of the heavenly Man.

45. Was made a living soul] (Gn 2 7). Life was given to him, while Christ is the Giver of life. **The last Adam** *was made*] RV 'became' (i.e. at His Resurrection). **A quickening** (RV 'lifegiving') **spirit**] bestowing resurrection as well as spiritual life : cp. Jn 5 21-29 11 25, 26. **The last Adam**] the new Head of the human race : cp. vv. 21, 22, Ro 5. **47. Of the earth, earthy**] hence subject to decay and death : cp. Gn 3 19, 'out of it' (the ground)

'wast thou taken ; for dust thou art, and unto dust shalt thou return.' **From heaven**] and so, spiritual and eternal. **49. Have borne the image**] i.e. have been made like. Our present body is like Adam's, but it will be conformed to the body of Christ's glory (Phil 3 21).

50–53. The necessity of this change, in which the living will share. Our earthly perishable nature cannot take possession of God's imperishable kingdom. All men will not pass through death, but all alike will be instantaneously transformed. Our mortal nature must clothe itself with immortality.

50. Flesh and blood] i.e. human nature in its present material and perishable condition. **Inherit**] take possession of ; have rightful entrance upon. The argument is, that such a spiritual body as he has been speaking of is absolutely necessary in the kingdom of God. **51. Not all sleep**] for some will be living when Christ comes again. **52. At the last trump**] cp. Mt 24 31 1 Th 4 16—a signal which all will hear : cp. also Ex 19 13. **We**] i.e. those still living ; the quick.

Shall be changed] The Apostle hoped Christ would return in his lifetime. **53. This mortal** (body) *must* **put on immortality**] cp. 2 Cor 5 1-5.

54–58. The Resurrection is the final triumph over sin and death. When this glorious body has been received, then will be the end of death and the grave. Sin, too, shall have disappeared, and the Law will be no longer necessary. Over all God gives us the victory through Christ. Let us therefore praise Him, and seek to abound in His work, which is not in vain if done in Christ.

54, 55. Death is swallowed up, etc.] Isa 25 8. **O death, where** *is* **thy sting,** etc.] from Hos 13 14. **56. The sting of death** *is* **sin**] which brought death into the world (Ro 5 12), and gives it its bitterness : cp. Heb 2 14, 15. **And the strength of sin** *is* **the law**] which reveals sin and, indeed, 'intensifies its power,' without giving power to overcome it (Ro 7 7-13 8 2, 3). But God **giveth us the victory** over sin now (Ro 8 1, 2), and hereafter over death (Ro 8 11).

Through our Lord] because Christ has overcome sin, and through faith in Him we, inspired by His Spirit, overcome it also.

58. Unmoveable] not shaken by false teaching. **Not in vain**] contrast vv. 16–19. **In the Lord**] Christ is regarded as the atmosphere, so to speak, in which their work is done. It is inspired by Him and done for Hi sake : cp. 9 1.

CHAPTER 16

The Collection. Personal Messages and Conclusion

The Apostle in this c. instructs the Corinthians to make a collection for the poor Christians in Judæa, intimates his intention of visiting them at an early date by way of Macedonia, and concludes with kind messages of brotherly love. In v. 8 he mentions his intention to stay in Ephesus till Pentecost. He probably stayed much longer, owing to the troubles that arose in Corinth; for in our Second Epistle (2 Cor 9 2) he speaks of the collection which he here appoints to be made, being ready a year ago. Meanwhile he had probably made the Corinthians a short visit by sea from Ephesus, and returned disappointed. He finally visited them by way of Macedonia, according to his original intention, announced in this c. after their repentance. On the whole circumstances see Intro. to 2 Cor.

(g) 16 1-4. THE COLLECTION

The collection for the Church in Jerusalem was made at St. Paul's request by all the Churches he had founded in the Gentile world, as we learn from his letters and from the list of delegates sent by these Churches to Jerusalem (Ac 20 4). The Church in Jerusalem included many poor (Ac 6 1), and the Gentile Churches were enabled to show alike their gratitude to and their sympathy with the Mother-Church by material aid from their more ample resources.

1. The collection for the saints] cp. 2 Cor 8 and 9, Ro 15 25-28.

To the churches of Galatia] either by messenger, or by a letter not preserved; not in our Epistle to the Galatians. The Churches of Galatia were those he had established in Pisidian Antioch, Iconium, Derbe, and Lystra: see Ac 13 14-14 23. **2. The first** *day* **of the week]** viz. Sunday, already the day for Christian assemblies (Ac 20 7); a fit time for an act of Christian love. This v. is the great scriptural justification of the weekly offertory.

That there be no gatherings (RV 'that no collections be made') **when I come]** i.e. that it may be all your own doing, not mine. **3. By** *your* **letters]** of commendation to the Christians at Jerusalem: cp. 2 Cor 3 1. Delegates would go from Corinth to avoid all suspicion of misappropriation of the money (2 Cor 8 19-21).

(h) 16 5-24. PERSONAL MESSAGES AND CONCLUSION

5. I do pass through Macedonia] i.e. this is my present intention. His original plan had been to go direct to Corinth (2 Cor 1 15, 16), but only for a passing visit. **6. Yea, and winter]** RV 'or even winter.' He stayed three months in Greece (Ac 20 2, 3), when at length he carried out his plan. **Bring me on my journey]** cp. Ro 15 24 Tit 3 13. **8. Pentecost]** one of the three great Jewish feasts, associated under Christianity with the descent of the Holy Spirit. **9. A great door and effectual is opened]**

cp. 2 Cor 2 12 Col 4 3 Rev 3 8. 'I have good openings, and must make full use of them.' **Many adversaries]** Ac 20 19, also 19 23.

10. If Timotheus (RV 'Timothy') come] cp. 4 17. It is not quite certain whether or not he reached Corinth: see Intro. 2 Cor. He was young (cp. 1 Tim 4 12), and seems to have been timid. **11. With the brethren]** the bearers of this letter. **12. Apollos]** Perhaps the Corinthians had asked that he might visit them. His refusal may have arisen from fear of rekindling the party feeling at Corinth. **13, 14.** These vv. sum up the practical teaching of the Epistle. They needed to avoid carelessness, fickleness, and moral feebleness, and to cultivate a spirit of Christian love. **15. The house of Stephanas]** baptised by the Apostle himself (1 16).

The firstfruits of Achaia] There were converts at Athens (Ac 17 34), therefore Achaia must be used in the narrower sense of Southern Greece; or else these were the firstfruits as a household. **Addicted themselves to the ministry]** RV 'have set themselves to minister.' **16. Submit yourselves unto such]** 'esteeming them very highly in love for their work's sake' (1 Th 5 13). **17. Stephanas and Fortunatus and Achaicus]** who had probably brought the letter from the Corinthians (7 1). **That which was lacking on your part they have supplied]** i.e. their visit has made up for your absence. **18. And yours]** for you will be glad to hear of my gladness. **19. Asia]** i.e. the Roman province, of which Ephesus was the capital—the western part of Asia Minor or Turkey in Asia: cp. Ac 19 10, 26 Rev 1 11.

Aquila and Priscilla] cp. Ac 18 2, 3; at Ephesus, Ac 18 18, 19, 26. **The church that is in their house]** Those Christians who assemble there.

20. An holy kiss] a token of Christian brotherhood: cp. Ro 16 16. **21. With mine own hand]** This signature authenticated the letter, which was written by a secretary, perhaps Sosthenes (1 1): cp. Ro 16 22 2 Th 3 17.

22. If any man love not the Lord] Without this love, religion is a delusion or mockery; where this love is the man cannot go far wrong. And love is shown by obedience (Jn 14 15). **Anathema]** a Gk. word, meaning 'accursed,' 'cut off from God.' **Maran-atha]** This expression stands by itself and is not joined to **anathema** as in AV. It is two Aramaic words, meaning either 'the Lord has come' (cp. 1 Jn 5 20), or 'our Lord cometh' (RM), or perhaps 'Lord, come': cp. Phil 4 5 Rev 22 20.

24. My love *be* **with you all]** though I have had to reprove severely, and though some prefer other leaders. **In Christ Jesus]** who inspires all Christian love.

For the subscription see Intro.: v. 8 shows that the Epistle was written from Ephesus.

2 CORINTHIANS

INTRODUCTION

THE problems presented by the Second Epistle to the Corinthians are more numerous and complex than those of the First. In opening this Epistle we find ourselves at once in a different atmosphere from that of the previous one. St. Paul writes in a different tone. He alludes to matters of which there is no mention in the earlier letter. He indicates that a momentous crisis in the relations between himself and the Church has been safely passed. And in reconstructing the situation for ourselves we have nothing but hints and allusions and references to past events in the letter itself to guide us. The difficulties, however, largely disappear if we assume what is regarded by many scholars as proved, viz. that chs. 10–13 were a letter written some time after 1 Cor., and that chs. 1–9 were a third letter written when the Apostle learned the effect produced by chs. 10–13 in the Corinthian Church.

1. Events between the First and Second Epistles.

(*a*) **The reception of the First Epistle at Corinth.** As was mentioned in the Intro. to the First Epistle, when the Apostle heard of the irregularities in doctrine and morals that had arisen in the Church, he announced that Timothy would visit Corinth after he had performed the work entrusted to him in Macedonia, to bring them into remembrance of his ways in Christ (1 Cor 4[17] 16[10]). About the same time he sent the First Epistle by the shorter sea route to Corinth, perhaps by the hands of Titus and another of his companions (12[18]), to whom was also given the duty of organising the collection (1 Cor 16[1, 2]). The mission of Timothy was in the first instance to the Churches of Macedonia, and it is uncertain whether or not he ever reached Corinth. Meanwhile the work of organising the collection, whether by Titus or by others, went on apace, and such favourable reports of the success of the movement reached St. Paul, that he afterwards quoted the Corinthians to the converts of Macedonia as an example of liberality (9[2]). On the completion of these arrangements Titus probably returned to St. Paul at Ephesus and reported the progress made.

(*b*) **The increasing influence of the 'Christ' party.** Very soon after these events there seems to have taken place a considerable increase

in the influence of the party of Christ, which is just mentioned in the First Epistle (1 Cor 1[12]). An attempt, which for a time threatened to prove successful, was made by them to impose upon the Corinthian Church the requirements of the Jewish law, and undermine the influence of St. Paul. We gather the information about this movement, not from any direct statements on the subject, but mainly from the Apostle's defence of his apostleship, and the points on which he dwells in refuting the charges brought against him. The leaders of this party—perhaps recently arrived from Jerusalem—claimed to speak for Christ in a way in which they said that St. Paul could not speak. They were Hebrews (11[22]); they called themselves apostles and ministers of Christ (11[13, 23]); they taught another gospel, inculcated another spirit, preached even another Jesus (11[4]). St. Paul calls them false apostles (11[13]), deceitful workers (ib.), ministers of Satan (11[15]). It would seem that they set up Judaism as the entrance to Christianity. They may not have insisted upon the imposition of the rite of circumcision, but they probably demanded obedience to the ceremonial law, taking their stand upon the teaching and example of Jesus Himself (e.g. Mt 3[15] 5[17]), and insisting upon the maintenance of the legal standard of righteousness. They thus naturally came into conflict with St. Paul, whose doctrine of justification by faith (cp. Ro 4, 5) seemed to them to be destructive of the Law; and perhaps being incensed at the lax morals of some of the Corinthian converts, they traced the irregularities to his teaching, and denounced him as a false apostle. Not content with this, they attributed to him vacillation and cowardice (10[10]), pointed to his refusal of sustenance as a proof of his lack of authority (11[7]), and declared that he was afraid to exercise the power he boasted of in his letters (13[2, 10]). They charged him with cheating his converts (12[14-18]), said that he was puffed up with vanity (10[14]), and even called him a fool (11[16, 21, 23]).

In this way these Judaising teachers sought to discredit the Apostle. They probably attracted those who had been of the party of Peter, and those who had been of the party of Christ at an earlier date, and united them in one strong body which influenced or overawed the whole Church. They called themselves Christ's men, preached Christ as the Messiah according to the flesh, and gloried in their connexion with those who had actually seen the Lord (10^7 11^{23} 12^1).

That they met with great success is evident from the Second Epistle. They turned the Church as a whole against St. Paul. The Corinthians received them without suspicion, listened readily to their charges, and as the result renounced their allegiance to their spiritual father (7^2 $11^{3,4}$ $13^{2,10}$). They submitted even to be victimised by these intruders, and allowed them to do with impunity the very things they counted wrong in St. Paul. The members of the Church were so infatuated with their new teachers that they permitted themselves to be 'brought into bondage, devoured, robbed, struck in the face' (11^{20}). The more the new apostles demanded, the better they were pleased with them. All that St. Paul had done for them was for the time forgotten, and their allegiance transferred to the new-comers, who denounced him as no minister of Christ at all.

(c) **St. Paul's brief (unrecorded) visit to Corinth.**

It was not long before the news of the revolt reached St. Paul. It may be that Timothy coming south to Corinth as the Apostle indicated in the First Epistle (1 Cor 4^{17}) found the Church already in revolt, and that on attempting to deliver a message from his master he was insulted and put to silence (7^{12}. Here 'his cause that suffered wrong' may refer to Timothy). Or it may be that the Apostle heard of the state of matters in some other way, as he had heard of their contentions before writing the First Epistle (1 Cor 1^{11}). In any case, he felt that he must take prompt and resolute action, and accordingly he paid a short visit to Corinth in order to restore his authority and win the Corinthians back to their allegiance.

This visit is not recorded in the book of Acts, nor is its occurrence related in so many words in St. Paul's letters ; but it is frequently referred to in 2 Corinthians and implied in several of the Apostle's statements. In 2^1 he distinctly alludes to a visit which he had paid to the Church 'in sorrow.' In 12^{14} 13^1 he announces that he is coming to them the third time. And as the only visit recorded in the Acts or in 1 Corinthians is the visit made when founding the Church, it is obvious that a second visit must have been paid in the interval before these passages were penned. In 13^2 indeed he distinctly mentions this second visit, and reminds them that he told them on that occasion that if he came again and found them unrepentant he would not spare them. This visit was probably paid as soon as he received the bad news, the journey being made by sea. The Apostle's appearance at Corinth, however, had not the expected effect. The influence of the Judaisers was still supreme : an attack of the illness to which he was subject prostrated him, and it was interpreted by his enemies as a mark of divine disfavour, and used to discredit his apostleship (12^{7-10}). He had to retire to Ephesus baffled and disheartened, having perhaps been insulted and denounced to his face in presence of the Church by some violent member (7^{12}, if the reference is not to Timothy but to himself. But see note).

(d) **The visit of Titus with the 'severe' letter.**

On reaching Ephesus again St. Paul wrote a letter to the recalcitrant Church, in which he sought to bring the members to a sense of their position. This letter is referred to in $2^{3,4}$ 7^8. It was written 'in much affliction with many tears'; it was stern and severe in its tone ; and it was designed to make them sorry and bring them to repentance. So strong were its terms, indeed, that St. Paul for a time regretted having written it. The greater portion of this 'severe' letter, in the view of an increasing number of scholars, is preserved in chs. 10–13. This theory solves many of the problems raised by 2 Corinthians, and best explains the facts as we know them. (For reasons see below, under **2.**)

The 'severe' letter was dispatched from Ephesus by the hands of Titus, who seems to have been regarded by St. Paul as better able to deal with the situation than Timothy. On receiving it the Corinthians were stung by the reproaches of conscience, and repenting of their treatment of St. Paul, cast out of the Church by a majority the man who had given offence by his attack on the Apostle or his messenger (2^6), and acknowledged their founder once more (7^{11}). Titus seems to have aided materially in bringing about the happy change; and, having from the outset realised the responsibility of the charge committed to him, he was overjoyed at the issue of his visit ($7^{6,7}$).

(e) **St. Paul's meeting with Titus.**

Meanwhile St. Paul left Ephesus and crossed the sea to Philippi, sailing along the coast to Troas, and thence taking ship for Europe. Troas offered him a good field for mission work (2^{12}); but, when Titus did not appear as he expected, anxiety about the Corinthians drove him onwards to meet him. At last in Macedonia (perhaps at Philippi) he encountered his messenger (2^{13} $7^{5,6}$), and was relieved and gladdened by the good news he brought. In his delight at the return of the Corinthians to their faithfulness, he proceeded to carry out his purpose of visiting them as announced in the First Epistle (1 Cor 16^5), and first of all sent Titus back to them with a letter expressive of his relief and joy—the Second Epistle, chs. 1–9.

This plan of visiting Corinth after passing through Macedonia was ultimately carried out according to his original intention ; but at one period St. Paul had in mind another plan, which he afterwards disclosed to the Corinthians. This was to cross by the direct route from Ephesus to Corinth, and from thence to visit Macedonia, returning again to Corinth on the way to Jerusalem, thus giving the Corinthians 'a double benefit' ($1^{15, 16}$). Circumstances, however, caused him to revert to his original intention, and pay the visit to Macedonia before going south to Corinth.

(f) **The 'thankful' letter.**

Chs. 1–9 of the Second Epistle seem to constitute the letter written by the Apostle after receiving the good news. This letter was sent by Titus, who is repeatedly referred to in it (2^{13} $7^{6, 13, 14}$ $8^{6, 16, 23}$), and with him were sent other two— the brother whose praise 'is in the gospel throughout all the churches' (8^{18}), and 'our brother whom we have oftentimes proved diligent in many things' (8^{22}). Besides the conveyance of the letter they were entrusted with the reorganisation of the collection for the saints at Jerusalem, which had promised well when it was begun, but had probably fallen into abeyance while the trouble lasted (9^{2-5}). Following in their footsteps, St. Paul soon afterwards himself arrived at Corinth to complete the reconciliation.

2. The Authenticity, Unity, and Date of the Epistle.

(a) That the Second Epistle is a genuine work of St. Paul has seldom been seriously disputed. Allusions to passages in it are found early in the second century in the letters of Polycarp, and it is quoted by the early Christian writers, Irenæus, Athenagoras, and Clement of Alexandria. The evidence from the Epistle itself is stronger. In particular, the personal allusions and references, the details of the Apostle's life and work, the intensely earnest character of its thanksgivings and appeals, confirm its own testimony to the authorship of St. Paul.

(b) The theory that portions of more than one letter of St. Paul to the Corinthians are to be detected in the Second Epistle is supported by the following amongst other arguments :

(1) The thoughtful reader of 2 Corinthians can hardly fail to notice the remarkable change in tone between chs. 1–9 and 10–13. In chs. 1–9 the breach between St. Paul and the Corinthians seems to be completely healed. The section abounds in expressions of love and goodwill, of thanksgiving and confidence : cp. $2^{3, 10}$ 3^2 $7^{4, 7, 9, 11}$ 8^7 $9^{13, 14}$. In chs. 10–13, on the other hand, it is evident that the breach is not yet healed. He

there meets charges brought against him ($10^{2, 10}$ $11^{6, 7}$, etc.), defends his apostleship by an appeal to his work and sufferings (11^{21-33}), declares himself to be in no way 'behind the very chiefest apostles' (12^{11}), and threatens to visit them in severity and not to spare (13^2). The circumstances to which the writer has regard in chs. 1–9 are different from those to which he looks in chs. 10–13. No explanation is so satisfactory as that which dates chs. 10–13 before, and chs. 1–9 after, the causes of strife had been removed.

(2) There are passages in chs. 1–9 which seem to refer to passages in chs. 10–13, and are best explained in the light of them. Cp. 13^2, 'If I come again, I will not spare,' with 1^{23}, 'To spare you I forbore to come to Corinth' ; and 13^{10}, 'I write these things while absent, that I may not when present deal sharply,' with 2^3, 'I wrote this very thing, lest when I came, I should have sorrow': cp. also 10^2 with 8^{22}, 10^6 with 2^9, and $11^{5, 18, 23}$ with 3^1 5^{12}.

(3) In chs. 1–9 there are four references to a former letter apparently severe in tone. (a) It was written 'out of much affliction and anguish of heart with many tears' (2^4) ; (b) after sending it away the Apostle repented of his action (7^8) ; (c) in it he had commended himself 'again' (3^1 5^{12}) ; (d) the Apostle was at the time of writing the former letter meditating a visit to deal sharply with them, which, however, in mercy he did not pay (1^{23} 2^1). These points describe the letter chs. 10–13, and apply to no other letter of the Apostle now extant ; e.g. (a) and (b) cannot refer to the First Epistle, and (c) does not apply either to the First Epistle or to any passage in 2 Cor before 3^1, where he speaks of commending himself 'again.'

(4) Chs. 1–9 were written from Macedonia (2^{13} 7^5 9^2) ; while 10^{16} indicates that the geographical position of the writer of that passage—which speaks of his hope to preach the gospel in the regions beyond them—was on the E. of Corinth rather than on the N., for we know that St. Paul's plan was to visit Rome. This suggests that chs. 10–13 were written from Ephesus, and affords another hint of identification between chs. 10–13 and the 'severe' letter of 2^4 7^8. [A full discussion of the question is given in Dr. J. H. Kennedy's 'The Second and Third Epistles to the Corinthians,' from which the above sections are mainly drawn.]

(c) **The dates** of the two parts of the Second Epistle remains to be fixed. According to the evidence afforded by First and Second Corinthians themselves, the latter was written about eighteen months after the former. In 1 Cor 16 St. Paul gives directions about the collection for the poor in Jerusalem, mentioning such details about the method to be adopted in gathering it as lead us to the conclusion that a beginning was now only being made with it. As the offerings were to be made weekly, and as many of the converts were poor (1 Cor 1 26), it is obvious that some months would have to elapse before the contributions amounted to such a sum as the Church would like to send. In 9 2, however, the Apostle commends them for being ready with their contribution 'a year ago': cp. 8 10. It therefore follows that some months more than a year separate the First Epistle from these passages in the Second. If, therefore, the First Epistle was written in the spring of 55 or 56, it follows that chs. 1–9 of the Second were written in the autumn of 56 or 57. Chs. 10–13 were written in any case only a month or six weeks before chs. 1–9. That about eighteen months thus separated the First and Second Epistles is confirmed by the recollection of the number of events which took place between them. We have to allow time for the transmission of the First Epistle, for the development of the rebellion against St. Paul's authority, for the news to reach the Apostle at Ephesus, for his visit to Corinth and return, for the dispatch of the 'severe' letter by Titus, and for St. Paul's journey to Philippi. Two lines of proof thus converge upon the same conclusion.

It may be briefly mentioned here that some scholars regard the passage 6 14–7 1 as an interpolation, and hold that it is really part of the first (lost) letter of St. Paul to Corinth. The contents of the passage certainly correspond with what the Apostle tells us was contained in that lost letter (1 Cor 5 9); and they break the natural connexion between 6 13 and 7 2. But the case for eliminating the vv. can hardly be said to be proved.

3. Synopsis of Contents.

(A) Chs. 1–9. The thankful letter.

Introduction 1 1–11. Salutation and thanksgiving.

I.   1 12–7 16. Thoughts suggested by the recent crisis.

(a) 1 12–2 2. The sincerity of St. Paul's intention to visit the Church.

(b) 2 3–13. The object and result of the 'severe' letter.

(c) 2 14–5 19. The glory, the comfort, and the inspiration of the ministry.

     (i) 2 14–3 6. The Apostle's true letter of recommendation.

     (ii) 3 7–4 6. The glory of the gospel.

     (iii) 4 7–5 10. The sources of his comfort.

     (iv) 5 11–19. The love of Christ his inspiration.

(d) 5 20–7 1. Appeal for purity of life.

(e) 7 2–16. The Apostle's joy in the Corinthians' repentance.

II.   8 1–9 15. The collection for the poor in Jerusalem.

(a) 8 1–9. The example of the Macedonian Churches.

(b) 8 10–24. The principles of Christian liberality.

(c) 9 1–15. Exhortations to generous giving.

(B) Chs. 10–13. The 'severe' letter. St. Paul's defence of his ministry.

(a) 10 1–18. Answer to the charge of feebleness and cowardice.

(b) 11 1–15. Defence of his gospel and his independence.

(c) 11 16–12 18. The evidences of his apostleship in suffering and service.

(d) 12 19–13 10. Warnings against evil and exhortations to holiness.

(e) 13 11–14. Conclusion and benediction.

4. Outline of the Epistle.

Chs. 1–9. The Apostle sends his salutation to the Corinthian Church, and gives thanks for the comfort which comes through suffering and for the power of sympathy it confers (1 1–11). He then passes to the crisis through which the Church had passed, and gives some thoughts suggested by it. He asserts the sincerity of his intentions to pay the Corinthians another visit, although he has been obliged to change his plans; and he shows that such changes of his plans as he had made, were made with a view to their benefit (1 12–2 2). He had, indeed, written them a severe letter which caused them pain; but he could not regret it because it had brought them to repentance and secured the purity of the Church, and enabled him to forgive the now penitent offender (2 3–13). Next he enlarges upon the joy attending the successful preaching of the gospel (2 14–17). He sees in his converts his true letters of commendation—even, so to speak, letters of Christ Himself, bearing His signature and witnessing to His influence (3 1–4). He remembers, indeed, the great responsibility of his work, but finds comfort in recalling the unfailing supply of strength from God; and he contrasts the old ministry of the law with the new ministry of reconciliation through Christ (3 5–4 6). The glory of the gospel reminds him of the weakness of those to whom its message is entrusted. In themselves they are feeble; but their faith prevails over all difficulties as they look, not on the seen and temporal, but on the unseen and eternal (4 7–18). They know too that death overtakes the mortal body, but they know that God has provided them with an immortal body, and has given them the pledge of eternal life in the gift of His indwelling Spirit (5 1–5).

They are therefore always faithful to the trust committed to them, being constrained by the love of Christ to plead with men to be reconciled to God and to become new creatures in Christ (5 6-21). The Apostle goes on to point to his own conduct as the proof of his claims to be a minister of God, and beseeches the Corinthians to live unspotted from the world (6 1–7 1). He appeals to them by his affection for them to be reconciled to him, and rejoices anew in their repentance (7 2-16).

The Apostle then calls their attention to the collection for the poor in Jerusalem, telling them of the example set by the Churches of Macedonia (8 1-9), enunciating the principles of Christian liberality, and reminding them of the self-sacrifice of Christ (8 10-24), and finally exhorting them to generous and cheerful giving (9 1-15).

Chs. 10–13. St. Paul defends his ministry from the attacks of enemies, and vindicates his apostleship. A charge of vacillation and cowardice had been made against him, and he assures the Corinthians that if strong measures are really necessary to bring them to a right way of thinking, he will not shrink from taking them (10 1-18). He does not wish to boast of his position in reply to his enemies, but he points out that he had maintained his independence among them, and had never been a burden to them (11 1-10). Those who speak against him and boast of their zeal are no true apostles ; in spite of their talk of righteousness they are as false as their master, Satan (11 11-15). But seeing that boasting is the fashion, he also will boast—he will boast of his labours, his sufferings, his anxieties, his visions and revelations, nay, his very thorn in the flesh, in all which he rejoices for Christ's sake (11 16–12 10). He goes on to apologise for this boasting, and for his refusal to receive gifts from them. But he is glad he has maintained his independence, because none can say that he made his converts a source of gain (12 12-21). He finally assures them of his approaching visit, warning them that if need be he will exercise his authority, but pleading rather for their repentance and submission (c. 13).

5. Teaching of the Epistle.

(a) Chs. 1–9. (1) The teaching of this Epistle is based, like the teaching of the First Epistle, on the great thought of the union of Christ and the believer. The sufferings of St. Paul which he endures for the gospel's sake are 'the sufferings of Christ' (1 5), and the consolation he receives 'aboundeth by Christ' (1 5). Those whom he forgives, he forgives 'in Christ' (2 10) ; and the gospel he preaches, he preaches 'in the sight of God in Christ' (2 17). He bears about in his body 'the dying of the Lord Jesus,' and he is 'delivered unto death for Jesus' sake, that the life also of Jesus might

be manifest' in his own life (4 10, 11). This union with Christ, in which he lives himself, is the union he desires for others. 'If any man be in Christ he is a new creature' (5 17), and they themselves are established with him 'in Christ' (1 21).

On the basis of this doctrine he urges them to forgiveness (2 10), encourages them to perseverance (4 15), beseeches them to be reconciled to God (5 20), and exhorts them to a life of purity and holiness (7 1).

(2) A considerable portion of the letter is occupied with the collection. This collection is mentioned first in 1 Cor 16. Its purpose was to provide assistance for the poor Christians in Jerusalem, of whom there had been many from the beginning (Ac 6 1, 3). St. Paul regarded the Church at Jerusalem as the Mother-Church, and sought to interest his converts in the head-quarters of their faith. The collection also enabled the members of the Churches in Galatia (1 Cor 16 1), Macedonia (2 Cor 8 1), and Achaia, to realise their unity as members of one Church, as well as to give evidence of their sympathy with their brethren. The offerings were to be laid aside week by week upon the Lord's Day (1 Cor 16 2), and to be finished before the Apostle arrived. At the end of the time, under his own superintendence, they were to be dispatched to Jerusalem by men chosen by the Church (1 Cor 16 3). In exhorting the Corinthians to liberality he quotes to them the example of the Macedonian Churches, which in this matter (8 2, 3), as well as in others (Phil 4 10-17), were distinguished for generosity : and reminds them of the example of Christ (8 9), who 'though he was rich yet for your sakes became poor.' He urges them to give cheerfully (9 7) and liberally (9 6), according to their means (8 13, 14) ; not holding back through indifference or greed (8 10, 11), nor feeling compelled to give in such a way as to make the offering a burden (8 13), but presenting their gifts out of a willing mind (8 12), and remembering that they may need some help themselves in their day of necessity, which would be gladly given (8 14). And he tells them that this offering has not only a material, but also a religious value ; for it causes the recipients of it to give thanks to God, recognising in it a gift from Him (9 12), and it is a powerful witness to the Christian faith and obedience of those who so freely bestow it (9 13).

(b) Chs. 10–13. These chs. are wholly occupied with St. Paul's reply to his enemies' attack, and are chiefly interesting for the information they give us about the doings of the troublers of the Church, and about the life of the Apostle himself. The former subject has already been touched upon (see I (b)) ; the latter may now be noticed. In 11 22-33 St. Paul mentions several incidents in his career which are not recorded in the sketch of his missionary career given in the Acts of the Apostles. He speaks of five floggings at the hands of the Jews, none of which are mentioned elsewhere. Of the three beatings with rods only one is recorded (Ac 16 23). Of the shipwrecks we know nothing, as the events recorded in Ac 27 did not occur until a later date. It was evidently on the occasion of one of these that he spent a night and a day in the deep, probably on a raft or on wreckage. He tells us also of his escape from Damascus, which is also recorded in Acts (9 25), affording confirmation of the narrative there. These incidental hints suggest the intensely interesting career which full knowledge of the Apostle's travels would have revealed, and show us in some slight degree the privations and dangers and afflictions summed up in that phrase ' the sufferings of Christ ' (1 5).

CHAPTER 1

INTRODUCTORY SECTION

1 1-11. SALUTATION AND THANKSGIVING

After the usual epistolary introduction, St. Paul makes pointed reference to a severe trouble he has lately endured, and gives thanks to God for deliverance from it.

1. By the will of God] He asserts his divine call to office in presence of opposition : cp. 1 Cor 1 1 Gal 1 1, and contrast Phil 1 1 1 Th 1 1, in cases where his relations to the Church were happy. **Saints**] A common designation of the Christian converts. It reminded them of the life to which they were consecrated at baptism. **Achaia**] probably used in a loose popular sense for the country around Corinth : cp. 1 Cor 1 2.

2. Grace . . and peace] i.e. all good wishes for spiritual blessings.

3-7. Paraphrase. ' We give thanks to God, the Father of our Lord Jesus Christ, the Fount of all blessing and comfort, (4) for the comfort and courage He gives us in our trials, whereby we are enabled to comfort and encourage others. (5) For as we are brought into union with Christ by our sufferings for His sake, so are we brought into union with you by the comfort we receive from Christ. (6) And all our experiences both of trial and of comfort are for your spiritual benefit. (7) And we are confident that as ye now suffer as we did, so you will receive the blessing we received.'

5. The sufferings of Christ] Because they are met in Christ's service and borne in Christ's spirit : cp. Phil 3 10. **6. And whether, etc.**] RV ' But whether we be afflicted, it is for your comfort and salvation ; or whether we be comforted, it is for your comfort, which worketh in the patient endurance of the same sufferings which we also suffer.' His sufferings caused

them to repent (cp. 7 7-9), and his joy at their repentance gave them courage to persevere.

8-11. Paraphrase. 'For it is right, my friends, that you should know that I had to undergo very severe suffering in Ephesus, and was even at death's door. (9) This great danger taught me that my life is in the hand of God, (10) for He saved me from the danger, as He saves me continually, (11) even while you prayed for me, that you and many might give thanks for my preservation.'

8. Pressed, etc.] RV ' weighed down exceedingly.' **Our trouble . . life**] The nature of this trouble is not exactly known. A serious illness in Ephesus, aggravated at a critical stage by the startling news of the defection at Corinth, seems best to explain the hints and allusions in this passage. **9. The sentence of death**] RV ' the answer of death.' When he wondered whether the issue would be life or death, his own heart answered, 'Death.' **That we should not trust**] His recovery taught him a stronger faith in God. **10. So great a death**] i.e. death with the consciousness that his work in Corinth had been a failure. **Doth deliver**] RV ' will deliver ' : i.e. in future dangers which he already foresaw.

11. You also helping by prayer. St. Paul asks the prayers of the Corinthians, and tells them that they will thus help in his recovery. The Apostle always attached great importance to the prayers of others on his behalf (Ro 15 30 1 Th 5 25 2 Th 3 1), and made a practice himself of praying for others (1 Cor 1 3 Phil 1 4 1 Th 1 2). He knows, too, that, when praying for him, the Corinthians will be furthering the work he has at heart.

DIVISION I. 1 12-7 16. THOUGHTS SUGGESTED BY THE RECENT CRISIS

(a) **1 12-2 2. THE SINCERITY OF ST. PAUL'S INTENTION TO VISIT THE CHURCH**

12-16. Paraphrase. ' The Apostle bases his expectation of receiving their prayers on the purity and sincerity of his conduct, especially in respect of his treatment of them. (13) He asserts that he writes nothing to them but what is common property, namely, that they mutually understand and glory in one another. (14) Some of them have acknowledged this all along, and he trusts that they will increasingly understand and sympathise with one another until their relations be perfected at the coming of Christ. (15) With this purpose in view he had planned at one time to make two visits to Corinth, (16) one on his way to Macedonia, and the other on his return to Asia by the same route.'

12. Simplicity] RV ' holiness.' **Fleshly wisdom**] mere cunning. **Had our conversation**] RV ' behaved ourselves.' **13. None other things**] St. Paul seems to have been suspected of writing to individual members of the Church that he was not so satisfied with their conduct and attitude as he professed to be in his public letters. **Read or acknowledge**] or, perhaps, 'acknowledge and even maintain,' i.e. that he was now perfectly satisfied with them, and they with him. **14. In part**] Some had been faithful all the time. **The day of the Lord Jesus**] the second coming (cp. 1 Cor 3 13 1 Th 2 19), which the Christians believed to be at hand.

15, 16. The Apostle after his second visit to Corinth (the visit in sorrow, 2 1) had intended to pay another visit to Europe from Ephesus, in the course of which he would come to Corinth twice. His plan had been to sail from Ephesus to Corinth, and from there to go N. to Macedonia, then to turn and retrace his steps back to Corinth, and sail thence to Palestine in charge of the collection in time for the Passover. The Corinthians would thus have received a second benefit, i.e. two visits in the same journey.

17–24. Paraphrase. 'When you find me now writing from Macedonia before you have had a visit at all, you may think me changeable and capricious. (18) But I assure you solemnly I am not easily turned from my purposes. (19) You know that the Christ I preach is true and faithful, (20) for the promises of God which He brought to the world are unchangeable and sure. (21) Well, then, it is God who has appointed us to proclaim these promises (22), and has marked us for his own by the gift of His Spirit. (23) As He is steadfast in purpose, so are we His messengers. (24) For I have no desire to lord it over you, but only to help your Christian life.'

17. Lightness] RV 'fickleness.' **According to the flesh**] deceitfully. Two charges had been brought against the Apostle : (1) that in changing his plans he showed himself fickle, and (2) that he had said one thing while he purposed another. **18, 19.** His word was not deceitful, but was as trustworthy as his gospel. **18. Yea and nay**] i.e. the use of words with a double meaning. **19.** He appeals to his solemn preaching of Christ as the pledge of his sincerity. **Silvanus**] Silas (Ac 18 5). **20. In him** *are* **yea and . . Amen**] Christ is the affirmation (the **yea**) and the fulfilment (the **Amen**) of God's promises. **Amen**] For the general Amen see 1 Cor 14 16. **By us**] as the instruments. **21. Paraphrase.** 'Well, then, it is God who is continually strengthening the spiritual bond which unites both us and you to Christ, and who has set us apart to declare His message.' **21.** The fact that St. Paul (like the Corinthians) was consecrated to God was the guarantee that he would be faithful in all his

dealings with them. **Stablisheth us with you in Christ**] The underlying thought is that of the union of Christ and the Christian : cp. Gal 2 20 Ro 6 3-5, and Intro. **Anointed**] sacramentally set apart to office. **22. Sealed**] **Given the earnest of the Spirit**] bestowed the gift of the Spirit as the pledge and sample of all spiritual blessings to come : cp. Ro 8 23 Eph 1 14.

23. Moreover . . Corinth] Another reason for the Apostle's change of plan was consideration for their feelings. **Record**] RV 'witness.' **To spare you**] i.e. from censure. This refers to 13 2, 'If I come again, I will not spare' ; chs. 10–13 being the earlier severe letter (see Intro.). **Came not as yet**] RV 'forbare to come.' **24. Dominion**] probably refers to an accusation made by the Judaisers that St. Paul was lording it over them. **By faith ye stand**] A difficult phrase ; perhaps it means, ' You need no master over you, for you are grounded in the faith,' or, ' Your faith is a sufficient strength, security, and support.'

C. 2. 1, 2. Continuation of explanation regarding his proposed visit.

1, 2. Paraphrase. ' It was therefore because I desired to spare your feelings that I resolved not to pay you another visit. (2) For such a visit would be painful to us both, because my joy could only be attained through your sorrowful repentance.'

1. Again . . in heaviness] a clear reference to a visit to Corinth, which gave him much pain, subsequent to his writing the First Epistle (see Intro.).

CHAPTER 2

(b) **2** 3-13. The Object and Results of the severe Letter

The Apostle reminds them that to produce this godly sorrow was the object of the letter he wrote before. He then speaks of one man who has caused him pain, asking them to remit the punishment inflicted already and forgive him, and telling them that he had written also to ascertain the extent of their obedience, and that if they were willing to forgive now, so was he. He then relates his anxious desire to hear what had occurred on their receipt of his letter—a desire so great that he had to push southwards to meet Titus and get the news.

3, 4. Paraphrase. ' My reason for writing sternly rather than paying another painful visit was that I wished to have happiness and not sorrow when I came. (4) I wrote the severe rebukes and exhortations with suffering and tears, not that I wished wilfully to grieve you, but that I hoped you would realise the love I bear you.'

3. I wrote] i.e. the painful letter of which chs. 10–13 of the Second Epistle are probably a portion (see Intro.). **In you all**] He speaks thus generously now that he has found his confidence not misplaced.

5–9. Paraphrase. 'Now with regard to the person who has been the occasion of this grief, he has grieved not me only, but to some extent (not to be too harsh) the Church. (6) And the sentence pronounced by the majority is quite sufficient punishment for him. (7) Do not inflict any further punishment, but forgive and encourage him, lest he be driven to despair. (8) Show him that you are actuated by Christian love. (9) For the main purpose of my letter has been accomplished now that you have given proof of your readiness to obey me.'

5. Any] A definite person is meant, but now that punishment has brought him to repentance the Apostle merely hints at him. The same person is indicated in 7¹², where see note. **6. Punishment**] probably excommunication : cp. 1 Cor 5 ⁴,⁵ (a different case). **Of many**] i.e. by the majority. **7. Overmuch sorrow**] The offender had now realised the heinousness of his offence, and the continuance of punishment would serve no good purpose, and might even do harm. **8. Confirm** *your* **love**] by restoring him to the Church.

9. The Apostle valued the act of discipline as much for the proof it afforded of the Corinthians' loyalty as for its effect upon the offender.

10–13. Paraphrase. ' I forgive any one whom you forgive ; for I have no personal feeling in the matter, and it is only for your sakes that I speak of forgiveness at all, and I forgive in the spirit of Christ. (11) I forgive this man lest he be tempted by Satan to deny the faith, for we know that the adversary seeks to prevail against us. (12) I was so anxious to hear what you had done while I was engaged in successful work for Christ in Troas, (13) that I could not remain there when Titus did not come, but pushed on to Macedonia to meet him.'

10. In the person of Christ] either (1) as in His sight, or (2) as in His place, or (3) as having Christ living in me : cp. 1²¹ 2¹⁷. **11. Get an advantage**] by the man being lost to Christ, or by the estrangement of the Apostle and the Corinthians ; perhaps both.

12, 13. St. Paul had gone from Ephesus to Troas on the coast of Asia Minor a short time after dispatching the severe letter to Corinth by Titus. He had expected Titus to meet him there with the news of the condition of the Church and of the way in which his letter had been received ; but not finding him he became anxious and hastened on to Macedonia, where, probably at Philippi, he met Titus bringing good news. **Troas**] for other visits there see Ac 16 ⁸⁻¹⁰ 20 ⁶⁻¹². **A door was opened**]

the preaching of the gospel found ready acceptance.

(c) **2¹⁴–5²¹. The Glory, the Joy, the Comfort, and the Inspiration of his Ministry**

(c) i. **2¹⁴–3⁶. The Apostle's True Letter of Recommendation**

The return of Titus with joyful news suggests thanksgiving to God, who has made the Apostle the means of spreading abroad the gospel message. St. Paul and his fellow-workers proclaim the gospel both to those who accept and to those who reject it. To the former it is a message of life ; to the latter, of death. And no one can bear such a burden of responsibility unless he preaches with a pure purpose, and under a deep sense of accountability to God.

14. Causeth us to triumph] RV ' leadeth us in triumph.' The language is suggested by the triumphal procession of a Roman general. St. Paul thinks of himself as being a willing captive in Christ's train (cp. 10⁵), and as spreading abroad the knowledge of Him like the pervading scent of the incense scattered as the procession moves onward. **16.** The figure of the triumphal procession is continued. 'Some of the conquered enemies were put to death when the procession reached the Capitol ; to them the smell of the incense was " an odour of death unto death " ; to the rest, who were spared. an odour of life unto life " ' (Conybeare and Howson's ' Life of St. Paul '). For the thought suggested in these verses cp. Jn 1¹¹,¹² 9³⁹ 1 Pet 2⁷,⁸ Rev 22¹¹. **Who is sufficient**] the great responsibility of the preacher. The answer to the question is suggested in v. 17.

17. Many] RV ' the many '; i.e. those Judaising preachers of whom they had experience. These men had stirred up strife in the Church at Corinth by denying St. Paul's authority, accusing him of personal interest in the collection, and (what he resented most) impugning his doctrine. They insisted on the observance of the Jewish Law, and as St. Paul preached the gospel to the Gentiles without reference to the Law, they carried on a mission against him in the cities he visited, seeking to gain his converts over to their own narrow views and Jewish prejudices. It was a critical period for the Church both in Corinth and in other places (cp. Gal 1 ⁶⁻⁹ 3¹⁻⁴). 'The true question was no less than this : whether the Catholic Church should be dwarfed into a Jewish sect ; whether the religion of spirit and of truth should be supplanted by the worship of letter and of form ' (Conybeare and Howson). **Corrupt**] Make the gospel a means of personal gain. The opponents of St. Paul seem to have made personal profit out of the

Corinthians (11 20) ; and at the same time to have charged the Apostle with having a personal interest in the money he was raising for the poor at Jerusalem : cp. 8 20 12 17, 18.

As of God] i.e. as God's true servants. **In Christ**] i.e. in union with Christ. St. Paul was so entirely submissive to Christ's influence and inspired by His spirit that he spoke of Christ living in him, and of himself as living in Christ : cp. 1 21 and ref.

CHAPTER 3

This c. is closely connected with what goes before, and carries on the vindication of the Apostle's conduct.

1-6. Paraphrase. 'In speaking thus highly of my motives I am not writing a letter to commend myself, nor do I need (like these opponents of mine) letters of recommendation either to you or from you. (2) You, my converts, are my best recommendation, for I think of you with gratitude as do all who know your faith and works. (3) You are, indeed, a very letter of Christ who has used me as His amanuensis, and bear the writing of the Spirit on your hearts. (4) It is such a result of my work as I see in you that assures me that God is using me as an instrument of Christ, (5) not that I trust in my personal ability, but that I look to God for help ; (6) for it is He who has given me any ability I possess to proclaim the gospel of Christ.'

1. Again] probably refers to the passages in the severe letter (chs. 10-13) in which he defended himself and stated his claims to recognition : see especially 11 22-33 12 1-5 12 16-19.

As some] The Judaising leaders had probably brought letters from Palestine and charged St. Paul with having no such recommendations. **Epistles of commendation**] Such Epistles were commonly used in the early Church to introduce strangers ; for examples see Ro 16 and Philemon, and cp. Ac 15 23-27 18 27.

2. Our epistle] i.e. of commendation. **Known and read**] better, known and acknowledged : the Church was an unmistakable witness to the Apostle's labours. **3.** *Forasmuch as ye are*] omitted in RV. **Ministered by us**] The Apostle regards himself as the scribe of Christ who wrote Christ's words on their hearts. **Not with ink, etc.**] In this v. the figure is slightly changed ; the writing is now that of the Spirit of God on their own hearts. It is no mere matter of paper and ink, but the work of the finger of God ; it is written not like the old Law upon tables of stone, but upon living, human hearts. **4.** Such **trust**] i.e. such confidence in you as our letters of commendation. **Through Christ to God-ward**] my confidence is not in myself, but through Christ in God : i.e. I look to Him for strength and grace through Christ. **5. To**

think any thing as of ourselves] RV 'To account any thing as from ourselves.'

6. Paraphrase. 'All my power in saving men comes from God, who has given me grace to proclaim a new covenant between Himself and His people—a covenant which is not a formal legal system, but an indwelling, spiritual power, for while the old covenant could only condemn the sinner to death owing to his inability to perform its demands, the new covenant inspires to faith and life.'

Sufficiency] i.e. ability. **The new testament**] not the book, but, as RV, 'a new covenant'—a new arrangement made by God for man's welfare to which he must submit himself. **The letter killeth, etc.**] The Law sets up an external standard, which, because we are unable to attain to it, puts us out of heart and makes us despair of success ; the Gospel of Christ proclaiming pardon, and bringing us under Christ's influence, calls forth our faith and love, and inspires us ever upward and onward : cp. Ro 7, 8. **The spirit** is contrasted with the letter. It means the inward inspiring power of the Gospel.

(c) ii. 3 7-4 6. THE GLORY OF THE GOSPEL

The mention of the new covenant suggests a contrast between it and the old. The Gospel is more glorious than the Law, for it is not a lifeless Law but a life-giving Spirit. Therefore its apostles are eager to proclaim it to all. Those who cling to the Law are blind to the truth. But those who receive the Gospel are changed into the likeness of Christ.

7-11. Paraphrase. 'Now if the system which could only declare the sentence of death upon sin was glorious (and glorious it was, for at its giving the very face of Moses was transfigured), (8) the system which brings life and inspiration is more glorious still. (9) I repeat, if the Law was glorious, the Gospel is far more so. (10) For the glory of the Gospel puts the glory of the Law into shadow. (11) For if the transient be glorious, how much more glorious is the permanent !'

7. The ministration of death] i.e. the Law of Moses. **Engraven**] Ex 32 16 34 28. **The face of Moses**] The transfiguration of Moses' face (Ex 34 29) is given as an example of the glory attending the giving of the Law. **To be done away**] The fading of the glory typified the transitoriness of the Law, which was to give place to the Gospel. **8. Rather glorious**] The Gospel was more glorious than the Law because it was a message of forgiveness and not of condemnation, and because it was not a mere legal system, but an inspiring summons.

9. Ministration of righteousness] better, 'of acquittal,' in contrast to 'of condemnation.' The gospel message is one of pardon and reconciliation. **10. That excelleth**] The glory of the Law is completely eclipsed by that of the Gospel, which offers forgiveness instead of condemnation. **11. That which is done away,** etc.] another aspect of the truth stated in v. 10.

12-18. Paraphrase. 'Since our hopes of the future of the gospel are so great, we speak frankly and boldly. (13) We do not seek to conceal anything as Moses concealed his face with a veil lest the people should see the glory fading from it. (14) Those who looked upon the giving of the Law did not understand that it was a temporary measure to convince them of sin; and even now their successors do not realise that it has been superseded by Christ, (15) but think that it still remains in force. (16) When, however, they receive Christ into their hearts, they will know the truth. (17) For Christ is the life-giving Spirit who leads men to the truth and sets them free from bondage. (18) And all we who have received Him, gazing as into a mirror on the glorious Personality of the Lord, are transfigured into His likeness in spirit and character in ever-increasing degrees of perfection, through the influence of the Lord who is the Spirit.'

12 f. The whole of this contrast between the glory of the new and the glory of the old dispensation seems aimed at the retrograde teaching of the Judaisers in Corinth. They sought to retain the rites and restrictions of the Law, and to conceal the full truth of the Gospel which does away with the old legal system.

13. In this and the next two vv. we have a good example of St. Paul's habit of blending the allegorical with the historical interpretation of the OT.: see also Gal 4 22-31. The reference here is to Ex 34 33. **Could not**] RV 'should not.' **The end of that which is abolished**] i.e. the glory fading from his face. **14. Blinded**] RV 'hardened.' **The same vail**] Note the quick transition from history to allegory. The veil with which Moses covered his face to keep the Israelites from seeing the glory fading is typical of the spiritual veil which keeps Jews and Judaising Christians from seeing that the Law is transitory. **Done away in Christ**] i.e. when they will truly come under Christ's influence and power they will see that He has made the Law unnecessary, because they will experience the new spirit He bestows. **15. When Moses is read**] i.e. when the Law is read: cp. Ac 15 21. **16. It**] i.e. their heart. The Law is incomprehensible without Christ.

17. The Lord is that Spirit] RV 'The Lord is the Spirit.' Christ is the life-giving Spirit. There is perhaps a reference to 'the ministration of the Spirit' in v. 8. The Spirit is Christ's Spirit: cp. Ac 16 7 (RV) Ro 8 9 1 Pet 1 11. What is meant is that he who turns to Christ shall receive the illuminating and quickening

Spirit. **Liberty**] freedom from the bondage of the Law is the primary meaning; but perhaps freedom from sin is included: cp. Jn 8 31, 32

18. He who keeps the memory and the example of Christ ever before his mind's eye, and tries to follow Him in his life, will gradually come to show in his own character and life an increasing likeness to his Lord.

CHAPTER 4

1-6. The messengers of this gospel are not afraid to proclaim it, for they preach Christ, who has revealed the glory of God.

1, 2. Paraphrase. 'Having this glorious gospel to preach, we proclaim it boldly. (2) We have nothing to do with methods and practices which cannot bear the light (like those of your false teachers), for we neither seek to undo another's work by unscrupulous hints and disgraceful insinuations, nor try to gain the favour of the Jewish Christians by false teaching about the relation of Christ and the Gospel to the Law of Moses. On the contrary, we proclaim the simple truth, and make our appeal to the conscience as in the sight of God.'

1. As we have received mercy] in his conversion from the blindness of Judaism. **2. The hidden things of dishonesty**] i.e. the disgraceful methods of gaining adherents used by the false teachers: see on 2 17.

3-6. Paraphrase. 'If our gospel is not understood by any, it is only by those (4) whose minds are dulled by sin. (5) For the subject of our preaching is not ourselves, but Christ. (6) As God at first created light, so has He created spiritual light in our hearts, that we might reflect His light, even the knowledge of His love revealed in Christ.'

3. Are lost] RV 'are perishing.' If some will not let the light of the gospel shine into their hearts, it is their own fault. **4. The God of this world**] cp. Jn 12 31 14 30. Worldly men make the devil their god by serving him, and thus serving him become even more worldly. **Lest the light,** etc.] For the thought, cp. Mt 13 13-15. **Image of God**] Christ is the expression of God's character of love and holiness. **5. Not ourselves**] as do the false teachers. **For Jesus' sake**] Love to Jesus is his motive in seeking to serve the Corinthians.

6. For God .. hath shined] RV 'Seeing it is God that said, Light shall shine out of darkness, who shined in our hearts.' The reference is to Gn 1 3. He who gave natural light gave also spiritual light.

(iii) 4 7-5 10. THE SOURCES OF THE APOSTLE'S COMFORT IN THE MINISTRY, AND THE HOPES THAT GIVE HIM COURAGE

7-18. This glorious gospel is entrusted indeed to frail and suffering messengers, but that is in order that the glory may be given not to man but to God. Life is a continual affliction and danger, but it enables the Apostle to learn how to comfort and edify the Corinthian converts, and he gladly suffers that many may learn the salvation of God and glorify His holy name, while he is upheld by the hope of the resurrection life.

7. This treasure] i.e. the work of the ministry. **In earthen vessels**] i.e. in a weakly body. Herodotus tells us that Darius Hystaspis melted his gold into earthen pots, which could be broken when it was wanted. **8.** *We are* **troubled, etc.**] Images are heaped one upon another in picturesque accumulation to express the fact that, in spite of many great trials (cp. 11 26 12 10), the Apostle has grace given him to persevere.

10-12. Paraphrase. 'In suffering for Christ's sake we are drawn into close communion with Him who suffered and died on our behalf ; and thus sharing His experience and " having this mind in us which was also in Him," we are enabled to show forth in our life the power of Christ, whose indwelling influence gives us the victory over the temptations which these trials bring. (11) Indeed, it is for this very purpose that we are constantly brought into peril and affliction ; (12) and the result is that, while we suffer and draw near even to death itself, your spiritual life is strengthened by the spectacle of our spiritual victory.'

10. Bearing about, etc.] He 'dies daily,' he 'stands in jeopardy every hour' (1 Cor 15 30, 31) for Christ's cause, and thus he has learnt 'the fellowship of his sufferings' (Phil 3 10 Col 1 24). **In the body**] cp. 1 5 Gal 6 17.

11. Explaining and emphasising v. 10.

13-15. Paraphrase. '(13) Our faith is like that of the Psalmist, who spoke out of the depths of his inward conviction, and we speak what we verily believe. (14) For we are confident that God who raised Jesus our Lord from the dead will raise us also and unite us with you in the blessings of the resurrection life. (15) And all my experiences are a source of blessing to you, because as the grace of God enables me to overcome my difficulties, many of you are inspired by my testimony to rise to higher levels of Christian life, and to give thanks to God for so many mercies.'

13. The reference is to Ps 116 10. **14. By Jesus**] RV 'with Jesus.' **15.** The AV is here inaccurate. RV 'For all things are for your sakes, that the grace being multiplied through the many, may cause the thanksgiving to abound unto the glory of God.'

16-18. St. Paul goes on to speak of the things that comfort him in the presence of his trials. These are the strengthening of his spirit, the thought that the temporal is transient, and the assurance of a future life.

16 Though our outward man perish, etc.]

These afflictions may weaken the body, but through them the spirit is strengthened. Experience shows us the truth of this in many cases ; e.g. bodily weakness often produces beauty of character, and grey hairs bring wisdom : cp. for the thought, Jn 15 2 Heb 12 11.

17. Our light affliction, etc.] The affliction is light, and vastly outweighed by the glory which it helps to secure ; seen in its true perspective, too, it is but momentary, while the glory is eternal. **18. We look not**] If we look at these afflictions they will loom so large in our view as to shut out the prospect beyond ; therefore we look past them. **The things which are seen**] the material, including these afflictions. **The things . . not seen**] the spiritual, including the results of these afflictions in character and spiritual life.

CHAPTER 5

The subject of c. 4 is continued. St. Paul has been pointing out that amid bodily weakness and decay he is encouraged by the thought that the temporal is transient, while the spiritual is eternal. He now goes on to speak more particularly of the great prospect that sustains him—the replacement of the earthly material body by an eternal heavenly one. He hopes to survive till Christ's coming, and receive the heavenly body without passing through the experience of death : but, if it should be ordered otherwise, he has no fear of being left by death in the disembodied condition so repugnant to the Hebrew mind, for the eternal, spiritual body will still be given him, in which he will be presented to the Lord.

1-5. Paraphrase. 'A further reason for my courage in presence of difficulty and affliction consists in my knowledge that if my body undergo the dissolution of death, I shall be endowed by God with an imperishable heavenly body. (2) My hope, however, and desire is that while still alive and in possession of this earthly body I may simply be transformed at the coming of the Lord, (3) since, if I receive it thus, I shall not be left a disembodied spirit in the state of death. (4) Our material body is a burden under which betimes we groan ; but, however we may be called to part with it, we may confidently cherish the expectation of being endued with something better in its place, i.e. we may hope to be clothed with the heavenly, resurrection body, and not left naked spirits. (5) It is for this very purpose God has wrought in us : besides, He has given us His Spirit as the pledge and instalment of the resurrection life.'

1. For] introduces an additional reason for courage. Even if his earthly tent be taken down, if his body be broken up by death, God has prepared a heavenly mansion for him, a resurrection body which is eternal. **Taber**

nacle] rather, 'tent.' **Building**] contrasted with the temporary tent to which the earthly body is compared. **Of God**] RV 'from God.'

2. In this] i.e. in this present body. **Clothed upon**] St. Paul's idea was that the heavenly body would be superimposed upon the earthly one, at the same time transforming it. Conybeare and Howson render thus : 'Desiring to cover my earthly raiment with the robes of my heavenly mansion': cp. 1 Cor 15 51-54.

3. If so be, etc.] This is a parenthesis explaining **clothed upon** in the previous verse. AV and RV are both rather obscure: better, 'Since, once this heavenly body is assumed, we shall be in no danger of being found disembodied by death.' **Naked**] i.e. disembodied spirits. The shrinking of the ancients, both Jews and Greeks, from the disembodied state as they conceived it, is well known from its expressions in their literature. See, for example, the dreariness of the spirit-world portrayed in the eleventh book of the 'Odyssey.' **4. Burdened**] by the anxiety of uncertainty. **Not . . unclothed**] The Apostle's desire was to gain the resurrection life without dying. He looked on Christ's coming as comparatively near at hand: cp. 1 Cor 4 5 1 Th 4 15. **5. He that hath wrought us**] St. Paul here argues for immortality and the resurrection life from the instinctive longings of the human heart. God has planted these longings there; He has confirmed them by the pledge of His Spirit in conscience, aspiration, and all spiritual blessings; and He will not in the end disappoint us: cp. 'Thou wilt not suffer thine Holy One to see corruption' (Ps 16 10)—

'Thou wilt not leave us in the dust :
   Thou madest man, he knows not why:
   He thinks he was not made to die ;
And Thou hast made him : Thou art just.'
               (Tennyson.)

6–8. Paraphrase. 'With this hope in our hearts we are always courageous. We know that while we live in this mortal body we are away from the Lord, and that when we put off this body we shall be in His presence; (7) (for we live in anticipation, not yet having realised the vision of Christ.) (8) We are courageous, I repeat ; and are even ready to put off this mortal body and to be at home in the presence of the Lord.'

8. Absent from the body] St. Paul here grapples with the possibility of death before the second coming of Christ. To die was 'to be with Christ which is far better' (Phil 1 23). Even death could not separate him from the love of Christ. If he did not then gain the full resurrection life, he would still be in Christ's presence. Perhaps his idea is that suggested in Rev 6 9-11.

9. Present or absent] i.e. living or dead. **Accepted**] RV 'well-pleasing.' **10. Appear**] RV 'be made manifest'; our conduct and character being disclosed. **Receive the things**] i.e. the recompense of them: cp. Mt 16 27 Rev 22 12.

(iv) 5 11-19. THE LOVE OF CHRIST THE APOSTLE'S INSPIRATION

In the recollection of this judgment the Apostle preaches. His motive is wholly unselfish. It is the love of Christ which constrains him. For the love of Christ was shown in His dying for all men in order to transform them into a new life. If any man, therefore, be in Christ, he lives a new life through the mercy of God, who has reconciled us to Himself by sending His Son to be our Saviour, and has given to His Apostles the message of reconciliation.

11–15. Paraphrase. 'Seeing, then, that we realise the awe inspired by Christ our judge, we try to convince men of our faithfulness and unselfishness: to God, indeed, our sincerity is already manifest, and also, I trust, to you in your secret thoughts. (12) Do not think that this is mere self-commendation. Look upon it rather as suggesting the answer you may make to our enemies when they try to belittle our work and boast of their external advantages. (13) For if in our enthusiasm we are mad (as they say), it is for God's glory ; or, if we are sensible, it is for your benefit. (14) For the love of Christ to men is our incentive ; because we are convinced that in Christ's death for the sin of all we all received power to die to sin, (15) so that we should live a new and transformed life, thinking not of our own desires, but of His will who died for us and rose again.'

11. Terror] the reverence or fear inspired by the thought that Christ is judge (v. 10). **We persuade men**] i.e. of our sincerity, with a view to winning them. **In your consciences**] The Corinthians as a Church believed in the Apostle. **12. Glory in appearance**] The false teachers boasted of external advantages (perhaps of having seen the Lord), which were no evidence of character and spiritual life.

13. Beside ourselves] His enemies declared that he was mad ; probably owing to his enthusiasm and vehemence in preaching: cp. Ac 26 24.

14. The love of Christ] i.e. the love Christ has shown towards us. **Judge**] i.e. have come to this conclusion. **One died for all**] i.e. as the head and representative of the race. 'In Christ's saving death the moral transformation of all, which I may call death to sin, was included, and his saving death had this meaning and purpose ; namely, that they who are quickened into a holy life in Him should not live selfishly, but should give themselves up to His service who died and rose to save them' (Stevens).

16-19. Paraphrase. 'Since, therefore, it is holiness alone that is of importance, we, unlike our opponents, pay no attention to men's outward appearance and circumstances ; even in the case of Christ, though I once regarded Him as merely a man and a Jew, yet I look at Him in this way no longer, but rather as my Saviour and Risen Lord. (17) Whoever then knows Christ in this higher way is indeed a new man. He looks on life from a higher point of view. His ideals and aspirations have been transformed : all things are new to him. (18) And this change is due to God, who removed the barrier sin had made between Himself and us, and gave to us his Apostles the message of His saving grace. (19) And that message is this, that in Christ's life and work we see God casting down the barrier that divided us from Him, and proclaiming forgiveness and love to all mankind : and this is the message of reconciliation which He committed to us.'

16. After the flesh] i.e. have regard to what is outward rather than to what is inward, to circumstances and position rather than to character and personality. **Known Christ after the flesh**] St. Paul once looked for a Messiah as a Jewish conqueror, and in the light of this expectation regarded Jesus as (at best) a prophet who had made claims which he was unable to substantiate, and whose career had terminated (perhaps deservedly) at Calvary ; but now he looks on Jesus in the light of His atoning death and glorious resurrection, and sees in Him the Christ of God.

17. A new creature] or, as we would say, a new man. He looks on things from a different standpoint, tries them by a different standard, because he is united to Christ in such a way that he lives always under Christ's indwelling, purifying, and transforming influence. **Are become new**] A new world opens to the new man. **18. All things**] i.e. all these changes. **The ministry of reconciliation**] the whole message of the gospel conveyed by preaching, teaching, the sacraments, and the example of Christians, assuring men of God's love and leading them to accept the will of God as revealed in Christ as their own. **19. God was in Christ, etc.**] When we see Christ teaching, healing, forgiving, comforting, and dying for men, we are to see there the expression of God's love and deep desire. In this atoning work Christ was 'the express image of His Person.' **Reconciling the world unto himself**] The desire for reconciliation came from God.

(d) 5 ²⁰-7 ¹. APPEAL FOR PURITY OF LIFE

As an ambassador of Christ St. Paul entreats them to be reconciled to God. And not only does he make this entreaty in words ; he appeals to them by his life and conduct in all the varied experiences through which he has to pass. He asks them for greater affection towards himself, and reminding them of God's promises to the pure, bids them keep themselves 'unspotted from the world.'

20, 21. Paraphrase. 'We, then, are ambassadors in Christ's place, conveying to you God's message and desire ; we ask you, speaking in Christ's name, to accept this great salvation. (21) It was to secure our salvation that God gave up His sinless Son to death, making Him bear the penalty of our guilt, that we might be made partakers of His divine nature by submitting ourselves wholly to Christ's transforming influence.

20. Be ye reconciled to God] It is not God who needs to be reconciled to man, but man who needs to be reconciled to God. **21. Made him *to be* sin for us**] Christ had to bear not the guilt, but the burden of sin. He bore its penalty not as a punishment, but as the innocent suffers for the guilty ; feeling all its shame and horror, but free from the sense of guilt and degradation. Hence St. Paul says not, 'He hath made Him to be a sinner,' but 'He hath made Him to be sin.' The spectacle of Christ thus bearing our penalty touches the heart and conscience, and makes us respond to the love wherewith He hath loved us : cp. Ro 8 ³, ⁴.

CHAPTER 6

1, 2. Paraphrase. 'Now it is as coöperators with God in this work that we exhort you not to make the grace of God fruitless in your life by continuing in sin. (2) For God has told us in Scripture of a time of grace and of a day of salvation ; and this is that blessed time of grace and that day of salvation.'

1. Workers together *with him*] For the idea cp. 1 Cor 3 ⁹. **In vain**] i.e. by an unholy life.

2. He (i.e. God) **saith**] The v. is a parenthesis. The reference is to Isa 49 ⁸, God's words of comfort to His Suffering Servant. **Behold, now,** etc.] This is St. Paul's comment on the quotation. **Accepted time**] RV 'acceptable time.'

3-10. Paraphrase. 'We avoid all conduct which might bring reproach upon our ministry ; (4) and try, on the contrary, to commend ourselves by acting as true ministers of God. (5) This is our aim in all the trials and persecutions we endure, (6, 7) for we seek to exhibit all the Christian graces both in our life and in our teaching. (8) Whether we are held in honour or defamed our object is the same : (9) we are looked upon as deceivers, but we remain true ; we are obscure, but known by our work ; we are often at death's door, but through God's grace we live ; (10) we are cast down, but are enabled to rejoice through Christ ; in our poverty we enrich many with spiritual blessings ; though having nothing of ourselves we have all through Christ.'

3. Giving no offence] The main sentence beginning in v. 1 is here resumed, these words being in apposition with ' we as workers together with him.' **4. Approving ourselves**] RV ' commending ourselves,' i.e. by our conduct in the various circumstances detailed.

In much patience, etc.] The Apostle's desire to commend himself is shown (*a*) in endurance of hardship and trouble (v. 4) ; (*b*) in the persecutions and dangers incidental to a missionary life (v. 5) ; (*c*) in the purity and sincerity of his Christian life (vv. 6, 7) ; (*d*) by his conduct in presence of friends and enemies (v. 8) ; (*e*) by the manner in which he met the ordinary experiences of his life (vv. 9, 10). **5. Stripes**] cp. Ac 16 ^{23} 2 Cor 11 $^{23-35}$.

Imprisonments] Ac 16 ^{23} 2 Cor 11 ^{23}. **Tumults**] Ac 13 ^{50} 14 ^{5,19} 18 ^{12} 19 ^{23}.

6. By] RV 'in.' The preposition ' in ' is unchanged until the last clause of v. 7, 'by the armour,' etc.

The Holy Ghost] the translation, ' in a holy spirit,' is tempting, as it brings the clause into parallelism with the others. **7. By the word of truth**] i.e. in the preaching of the gospel.

By the power of God] i.e. in his exercise of all the powers entrusted to him by God. **The armour of righteousness, etc.**] The right-hand weapon was the sword for attack, the left the shield for defence. The Apostle's methods were fair and open, whether in attacking idolatry and vice or in defending himself against traducers. **8. As deceivers**] probably refers to the charges of his opponents.

10. Making many rich] i.e. with spiritual gifts. **Possessing all things**] i.e. all things of value for life and character in this world and a rich inheritance in the world to come : cp. 1 Cor 3 $^{22, 23}$ 2 Cor 4 ^{18} 5 ^{1}.

11–13. The Apostle assures them of his deep affection for them before he lays upon them the strict injunctions which might prove unwelcome. **12. Ye are not straitened, etc.**] i.e. there is abundant room in my heart for you, but too little hitherto in yours for me.

Bowels] RV ' affections ' ; as frequently in Scripture. **13. A recompence in the same**] A return for his affection.

14–16. Paraphrase. ' Do not become entangled in alliances of any kind with unbelievers to your spiritual hurt. There is no relation possible between holiness and sin, between light and darkness, (15) between Christ and Satan, between the true and the untrue, (16) between the worship of God and the worship of idols : for we are indeed the very temple of the living God ; and it is of us that He speaks in His Word, promising to dwell in us and to commune with us, making us His peculiar people, and calling us to purify ourselves and

become worthy children of our heavenly Father.'

14. Unequally yoked together with unbelievers] The ever-present and ever-pressing temptation and danger was that they might be led into immorality through the abominable rites of idol-worship : cp. 1 Cor 5 ^{9,11} 6 ^{15} 8 ^{10,11} 10 ^{14}. **Unequally**] better, ' incongruously.'

15. Christ with Belial] For the idea cp. Mt 6 ^{24}.

Belial] Here used as a synonym for the devil. The meaning of this name is doubtful. There is no trace of the worship of any god under this name. It is used in the OT. in such expressions as ' sons of Belial,' 'men of Belial,' meaning ' wicked men' : 1 S 2 ^{12} 25 $^{17, 25}$ 2 S 20 ^{1} 1 K 21 ^{10}. **16. The temple of the living God**] cp. 1 Cor 3 $^{16, 17}$. **Ye**] RV ' we,' according to the best Gk. MSS. **God hath said**] i.e. in the Scriptures : see on Lv 26 ^{12}. **17. Saith the Lord**] The words quoted are from Isa 52 ^{11}, freely rendered (v. 17), with echoes of other OT. passages (v. 18) like 2 S 7 ^{8} Isa 43 ^{6} Hos 1 ^{10}.

C. 7. 1. These promises] given in 6 $^{16-18}$. **Filthiness**] RV ' defilement.' **Of the flesh and spirit**] cp. Ps 24 ^{4}. **Perfecting holiness**] For the thought cp. 3 ^{18} Heb 6 ^{1} 12 ^{14}.

CHAPTER 7

(*e*) **7** $^{2-16}$. **THE APOSTLE'S JOY IN THE CORINTHIANS' REPENTANCE**

St. Paul goes on to ask them to give him their affection, and renews his assurance of purity of deed and motive. He tells them of the suspense in which he had awaited their response to his 'severe' letter, and his joy at the return of Titus with good news. He is now glad that he vexed them by that letter—though he was inclined to regret his action for a time—because of its happy results in their attitude and conduct ; and he concludes by expressing anew his affection for them, and his joy that mutual confidence has been restored.

2–4. Paraphrase. ' Give us your affection ; we have done no man any injury either in influence or in character or in pocket. (3) I am not returning to this subject to blame you again, for whether I live or die I have the deepest affection for you. (4) I speak freely to you as I boast of you freely to others ; I am greatly comforted, and rejoice exceedingly amid all my sufferings.'

2. Receive us] RV ' Open your hearts to us.' **We have wronged .. corrupted .. defrauded no man**] St. Paul is referring to charges that had been brought against him. For hints as to these, cp. 11 $^{4, 7, 8, 9}$ 12 $^{14, 16, 17}$.

4. Glorying of you] i.e. boasting about you : cp. 9 $^{2, 3}$.

Paraphrase. '(5) For when I came to Macedonia looking for your answer to my letter, I was troubled both by conflicts with enemies and by forebodings about you. (6) But God, who comforts those who are in trouble, comforted me by the arrival of my friend Titus. (7) Not only was I cheered by his presence, but by the comfort he communicated to me, which he had derived from your sorrow for your faults and your affection for me ; so that my anxiety was transformed into joy.'

5. 'When I came to Macedonia': see Intro.

6. God, that comforteth] cp. 1 3,4. **Titus**] was the bearer of the letter to the Corinthians mentioned in v. 8 : see Intro. **7. The consolation wherewith,** etc.] Titus was comforted by their repentance, and this comfort he passed on to St. Paul when he gave him the good news.

8. Though I did repent] The Apostle for a time feared his previous letter had been too severe. The letter was probably that of which chs. 10–13 of the Second Epistle form the chief part : see Intro. **10. Godly sorrow,** etc.] The contrast is between repentance and remorse, between sorrow for sin and sorrow for its consequences : cp. St. Peter and Judas.

Repentance to salvation] cp. ' Heart-sorrow and a clear life ensuing ' (Shakespeare). **The sorrow of the world**] i.e. grief that regrets not the sin, but the fact of being found out.

Death] Moral and spiritual ruin.

11, 12. Paraphrase. ' Your own repentance is a case in point. Yours was a godly sorrow, as the results proclaim ; for it made you earnest to amend your ways, anxious to clear yourselves, indignant that you had been misled, afraid of the results of your conduct, anxious to see me, zealous for truth and justice, resolute in purifying the Church. In every respect you showed that you had no share in the offender's guilt, and no desire to shield him. (12) And this was the very purpose of that severe letter, not to secure the punishment of the offender, or to satisfy the resentment of the injured, but to cause you to recognise before God the feelings of affection and devotion with which you really regarded me.'

12. For his cause that had done the wrong .. for his cause that suffered wrong] The reference, of course, was obvious to the readers without particulars ; but we are ignorant of some of the facts. It would seem that on the occasion of his brief visit St. Paul had been attacked and denounced by some leader of the disaffection in the Church, or else that Timothy on the occasion of his visit had been the object of vituperation ; and that in either case St. Paul had insisted upon the punishment of the offender. This had now been done. The doer of the wrong here is this leader of rebellion, and the sufferer either St. Paul or Timothy. This seems the most probable solution of the problem from the knowledge we possess. **Our care for you**] RV ' your earnest

care for us.' The reading of RV is best attested by the MSS, and is more in harmony with the train of thought in v. 11. His letter was written to let them see the real feelings they had towards him, which were concealed for the moment by their irritation.

13–16. Paraphrase. ' Now that all has ended well, I am thankful ; and my joy is increased because Titus also rejoices at your attitude. (14) For all that I said to him in your praise has been justified, and I am not ashamed of my boasting ; (15) and the affection of Titus for you has increased since he visited you and saw your anxiety to do well. (16) I rejoice, therefore, that I have every confidence in you.'

14. Our boasting, etc.] Titus had evidently been rather despondent about the result of his mission with the letter when he started ; but St. Paul had encouraged him by confident forecasts of the Corinthians' repentance.

15. With fear and trembling] not dread of punishment, but anxiety to fulfil their obedience : cp. Phil 2 12.

DIVISION II. 8 1–9 15. THE COLLECTION
FOR THE POOR IN JERUSALEM
CHAPTER 8

(a) 8 1-9. THE EXAMPLE OF MACEDONIA

1–5. Paraphrase. ' I wish you to know how liberally and spontaneously the Churches of Macedonia have contributed to the relief of their fellow-disciples in Jerusalem, having first of all presented themselves to God's service.'

1. Do you to wit] RV ' make known to you.' **The grace of God**] the inspiration to give liberally. **The churches of Macedonia**] i.e. Philippi, Berœa, and Thessalonica, with, perhaps, others unknown to us : cp. Ac 16 12–17 14 20 4. **2. Their deep poverty**] The Christians of Macedonia were very poor, and so their liberality was all the more marked.

3. Beyond *their* **power .. of themselves**] Their giving was bountiful and spontaneous.

4. The RV gives a better meaning : ' Beseeching us with much intreaty in regard of this grace and the fellowship in the ministering to the saints.' They desired the privileges (1) of being allowed to give, and (2) of making common cause in this ministry of kindness. **4. The ministering**] On the collection see Intro. **5. First gave,** etc.] the best of all giving. They surrendered themselves (not their money only) to God's will first, and then to the Apostle's guidance.

6–9. Paraphrase. ' The collection prospered so well here that we asked Titus to complete this work of charity which he organised on his former visit. (7) See, therefore, that you manifest this gift in the same degree as the others in which you abound. (8) I am not laying commands upon you ; I am only telling you what has been suggested by the liberality of others in order to give you the chance of proving your sincerity. (9) But let me remind you of the great love of Christ, who divested Himself of the riches of His glory and became poor for your sakes, that by His self-denial and humility you might inherit eternal salvation.'

6. Titus] He organised the collection after the arrival of our First Epistle, which contained instructions about it : cp. 1 Cor 16 1 2 Cor 2 18. **7. This grace also**] Liberality is a Christian grace as much as these others.

9. The grace of our Lord] the crowning example of liberality : cp. Phil 2 5-8.

(b) **8** 10-24. The Principles of Christian Liberality

The Apostle counsels them to complete their good work, tells them that the purpose of the collection is mutual sympathy and aid, and commends to their care Titus and two brethren who go with him.

10-15. Paraphrase. ' In saying this I am not laying a command upon you, for you have already manifested the spirit and practised the duty of giving this twelvemonth past. (11) Complete the offering according to your means, (12) for the willing mind is shown by gifts in accordance with your ability, and not by foolish prodigality beyond it. (13) My purpose is not to make others a burden upon you, (14) but to get you to supply what they lack, and them to supply what you lack ; (15) thus acting on the principle of equality illustrated in the bestowal of the manna in bygone days, that none should have too much, and none too little.'

10. Advice] or, ' opinion,' i.e. as opposed to ' command.' A command was not needed in their case : cp. 1 Cor 7 6, 25. **A year ago**] A year had elapsed since they had first responded to the Apostle's suggestion of the collection.

11. Perform] better, ' make perfect.'

12. According to that a man hath] the true principle of Christian giving. The best commentary on it is Lk 21 1-4. **14. Their abundance,** etc.] A time might come when the relative positions of the Christians in the two cities would be reversed. **15.** The reference is to Ex 16 18, but the meaning is somewhat different in the two cases. There the equality is the result of a miracle ; here it is the result of mutual love and generosity.

16-24. Paraphrase. ' The zeal of Titus on your account causes us great thankfulness to God, (17) for he did not need my suggestion, but was eager to return to you. (18) With him we send our fellow-labourer, whose work in spreading the gospel is spoken of in all the Churches, (19) and who was chosen by those of Macedonia to accompany us in charge of

this gift, to promote Christ's glory and to satisfy our own desire. (20) And his presence wards off all suspicion of our motives, and silences all criticism of the manner in which we distribute the funds collected ; (21) for we desire to do what is honourable both in the sight of God and in the sight of men. (22) We also send with Titus and his fellow-disciple another brother whom we have learned to trust from much experience, and who is more zealous than ever since he has heard of your enthusiasm. (23) If any one asks about Titus, speak of him as my fellow-labourer among you ; or if any one asks of the other brethren, they are sent by the Churches, and show forth in their lives the love of Christ. (24) Show, therefore, to them and through them to the Churches the proof of your love and the justification of my boast of you.'

18. The brother] His identity is uncertain, but we may look for him in the list given in Ac 20 4 of those who accompanied St. Paul to Jerusalem, excluding the delegates from Asia and including St. Luke, who joined them at Troas (Ac 20 5, 6). Sopater has been suggested, as he is mentioned first in that list, though the representative of the smallest Church.

19. This grace] the collection. **To the glory,** etc.] The Apostle keeps in view that in aiding the poor he is furthering Christ's glory. *Declaration of* **your ready mind**] RV ' to shew our readiness.' The meaning is, ' in accordance with our strongly expressed desire.' The reason of the desire is indicated in v. 20.

20. That no man, etc.] Charges of this kind had already been made against St. Paul. He replied to them in 12 17, 18, which was written previous to this : see Intro. **This abundance**] RV ' *the matter of* this bounty.'

21. Providing for honest things] RV ' For we take thought for things honourable.'

22. Our brother] perhaps St. Luke, if he is not ' the brother ' of v. 18. *I have*] RV ' he hath.'

CHAPTER 9

(c) **9** 1-15. Exhortations to Generous Giving

There is no need to write to you about the purpose and necessity of the collection, for your zeal in the matter is well known, and has been used by me as a stimulus to the Macedonians. I send our friends to you only to make sure that our boast of you has not been vain. Remember that the blessing you receive will be in proportion to your giving, and that much spiritual benefit will come both to you and to them by this interchange of sympathy.

1. The ministering] St. Paul had already written on the collection in general (1 Cor 16 1-4), and had sent instructions by Titus on his first visit (12 18). **The saints**] the Christians in

Jerusalem. **2. The forwardness of your mind**] RV 'your readiness.' **A year ago**] see on 8¹⁰. **Provoked**] RV 'stirred up.'

4. We (that we say not, ye)] He bids them realise how much he would be ashamed before the Macedonian delegates if they were unprepared : at the same time he suggests in passing that he is sure their own shame would not be less than his.

5. Your bounty, whereof ye had notice before] RV 'your aforepromised bounty.'

Bounty, and not . . covetousness] He desired their gift to be ready before he came, that it might be evident to the delegates that they had given it of their own free-will, and did not need to have it dragged out of them through shame in his presence. **7. As he purposeth in his heart,** *so let him give,* etc.] i.e. do not let a man give what he grudges or because he feels that he must do as the others ; let the open hand correspond to the willing spirit.

8–11. Paraphrase. 'And God has power to enrich you with all earthly blessings, that ye may have sufficient for yourselves and the means of helping those who need, (9) and so experience the fulfilment of the promise of God's Word. (10) Now God, who supplies seed to the sower and bread for food, will both provide for your wants and abundantly bless your charity and make it fruitful for good ; (11) for your willingness to give freely of what you have freely received will cause those to whom we bear your bounty to give thanks to God for your thoughtful love.'

8. All grace] every earthly blessing that will give them opportunity of blessing others. **That ye . . may abound**] The purpose of God's gifts to them is that they may share them with others : cp. for the thought 1⁴.

9. As it is written] Ps 112⁹. **His righteousness remaineth**] In return for his generosity, God will give him continually the disposition to be generous ; the charitable man has his reward in becoming more charitable—a true spiritual blessing.

12–15. Paraphrase. 'For this charity has a twofold benefit : it supplies the needs of the brethren in Jerusalem, and it makes them give thanks and praise to God. (13) They give glory to God because they see in this bounty the proof of your obedience to Christ, and they praise Him for your generous gift to them and to others, (14) while they express in prayer their fervent longing that all blessings may be yours. (15) God be praised for this great boon, whose blessedness no tongue can tell.'

12. The exercise of the gift of charity had both a material and a religious value.

13. Whiles by the experiment of this ministration] RV 'Seeing that through the proving

of you by this ministration.' The reception of the collection would be proof to the Church in Jerusalem of the true Christianity of those who called themselves Christians in Corinth : cp. 1 Jn 4²⁰. **15. His unspeakable gift**] The establishment of these happy relations between the Churches, each giving thanks for the others and praying for their growth in all goodness, was a blessing from God beyond the power of words to express.

(B) CHAPTERS 10–13
ST. PAUL'S DEFENCE OF HIS MINISTRY

As explained in the Introduction, this section is regarded as part of the intermediate letter, referred to in 2³,⁴ and 7⁸, in which the Apostle rebuked his converts, and sought to bring them to repentance. It is, therefore, to be taken as earlier in time than chs. 1–9, which were written as the result of the Corinthians' reception of the intermediate or 'severe' letter.

Here the Apostle answers the charges of weakness and cowardice that have been brought against him, defends his preaching and his independence, points to the proofs of his apostleship in suffering and service, and finally warns them against evil and exhorts them to live a pure and holy life.

CHAPTER 10
(a) **10¹⁻¹⁸. ANSWER TO THE CHARGE OF FEEBLENESS AND COWARDICE**

The Apostle beseeches the Corinthians to act in such a way that he will not need to resort to extreme measures on the occasion of his forthcoming visit. He points out that his purpose is to make every man's thoughts subject to the power of Christ, and that he will punish any who are rebellious when the Church as a whole shall have returned to its obedience. He goes on to say that those who have been accusing him of cowardice will soon find themselves mistaken. He will make no boast that his record cannot justify, and he will boast chiefly of his success in converting the Corinthians themselves. This was a field of labour the Apostle had made peculiarly his own ; and he hoped for the assistance of the Church in carrying the gospel further west. But let them not forget that the only glorying that was safe was that which came through seeking the approval of the Lord.

1. Now I Paul] If this is not the beginning of the 'severe' letter, it is evidently the beginning of a new subject. Possibly one leaf of the MS containing this letter was lost at an early date ; and this loss led to the remaining portion being attached in course of time to the longer Epistle consisting of chs. 1–9. **By the meekness and gentleness of Christ**] cp. Phil 2¹. He invokes

Christ's meekness to indicate the spirit in which he wishes to deal with his opponents.

In presence *am* **base, etc.**] This was their story, by which they sought to prejudice him in the eyes of the Church.

2. According to the flesh] i.e. in a worldly spirit. His enemies declared that he was one who sought his own advantage and tried to gain popularity by whatever methods seemed best at the moment. When he was at a distance, he issued commands and declared his authority over the Church; but when he came they found him a poor creature who was overawed by the firmness of the Church against him.

3–6. Paraphrase. 'We live in the flesh, and are subject to its weaknesses and temptations, like others; but we are not prompted by fleshly motives, such as dread of giving offence, or desire of popularity. (4) For we fight not in our own strength, but in the strength of God, and this reliance upon Him enables us to prevail against all opposition and prejudice, however strong or deep-rooted. (5) In this strength we shatter the false reasonings and assertions of our opponents, and bring back your rebellious thoughts into obedience to Christ, (6) while after we secure your submission, we shall certainly punish any who may still resist His will.'

4. Carnal] RV 'of the flesh.' **Through God**] RV 'before God.' **5. Imaginations**] the false reasonings of his enemies. **Every high thing**] All the pride and self-satisfaction and self-delusion which made the Corinthians rebel against him. **Bringing into captivity**] The Apostle describes the Corinthians in a metaphor as rebels in possession of a castle (v. 4) with battlements and high towers, (v. 5) which he must attack in order to capture the defenders. **6. Disobedience**] There may be some contumacious to the bitter end.

7–10. Paraphrase. 'You are too much influenced by appearances. My opponents say that I do not act as an Apostle of Christ, do they? Be sure that I am just as devoted a servant of Christ as any who assert their superiority. (8) Even if I boasted of my authority which Christ has given me, I should still be justified. (9) I write this to show that I am not seeking to terrify you by empty threats, (10) for, according to my opponents, my presence among you and my appeals were alike ineffective.'

7. Do ye look, etc.] RV 'Ye look at the things that are before your face.' **As he** *is* **Christ's, even so** *are* **we**] St. Paul claims that his relation to Christ is as close as that of any of his opponents: cp. 13 3,4. For the Christ party see Intro. 1 (*b*). Some think that the leaders of this party claimed to have known Christ during His earthly life. **10.** *His* **letters**]

They had at this date received at least two from St. Paul, (1) that mentioned in 1 Cor 5 9, and (2) our First Epistle. *His* **bodily presence** *is* **weak**] i.e. his action is feeble when he is present. *His* **speech contemptible**] RV 'of no account'; i.e. produced no effect. Possibly the Apostle pleaded with them rather than asserted his authority. He was an eloquent speaker (Ac 14 12). **11.** *Will we be*] RV 'are we.' **12. We dare not**] RV 'we are not bold': cp. v. 2. His confidence was not based on comparison with his opponents. **Not wise**] RV 'without understanding.' Such a method of self-commendation is useless and foolish.

13–18. Paraphrase. 'Others may boast without reason, but we will make no boast which cannot be justified by our work—a work which includes your conversion. (14) For in claiming you as our converts we are not making too great a boast. (15) And we are not taking credit for other men's labours as our opponents are for ours, but are rather hoping that as your faith increases so also will our influence, (16) that we may be aided to preach the gospel in districts beyond your city, and not seek, as some are doing, to claim credit for success where others have laboured before us. (17) The only safe rule about boasting of success is this: He that glorieth, let him glory in the Lord. (18) For self-praise is no attestation of the work that is done; that attestation is only shown when God's blessing attends and prospers it.'

13. Without *our* **measure**] outside our province. He will only boast of work done by himself, and that included preaching the gospel in Corinth. **The measure of the rule, etc.**] RV 'The measure of the province which God apportioned to us as a measure, to reach even unto you.' St. Paul's province was heathendom, and that included Corinth.

14. We are come] He was the first to preach Christ in Corinth. **15. Not boasting, etc.**] RV 'not glorying beyond *our* measure, *that is*, in other men's labours; but having hope that as your faith groweth, we shall be magnified in you according to our province unto *further* abundance.' **Of other men's labours**] The suggestion is that his opponents do so. **We shall be enlarged**] As their faith increased and their Christian life became more manifest, his name would become better known, his influence would increase, and his sphere of service would be much extended, according to his rule of making a Church the starting-point for further efforts.

16. The *regions* **beyond you**] These chs. were written in Ephesus; hence this would refer to Rome, and perhaps Spain. Rome was already in his mind (Ac 19 21), and soon after this date he wrote of going to Spain

(Ro 15 24, 28). **Not to boast in another man's line of things made ready**] RV 'not to glory in another's province in regard of things ready.' **17**. Cp. Jer 9 23 1 Cor 1 31. **In the Lord**] The only boasting is to be of Him who gives the blessing. **18. Not he that commendeth himself**] Contrast between himself and his accusers is implied. The true test is the success of the work, not the self-advertisement of the workers.

CHAPTER 11

(*b*) **11** 1-15. DEFENCE OF HIS GOSPEL AND OF HIS INDEPENDENCE

St. Paul says that he also will now boast a little, for he is as much an Apostle as those whom they prefer. If he refuses monetary support from them, it is in order to prevent these false teachers charging him with making gain of the ministry.

Paraphrase. '(1) Bear with me a little if I begin to boast foolishly? Yes; do bear with me. (2) My affection for you makes me apprehensive, even as I may say that God also is apprehensive regarding you; for I have as it were betrothed you to Christ, and cannot endure that you should be unfaithful to your troth. (3) I fear lest these false teachers corrupt your minds, even as Satan with his smooth tongue corrupted Eve.'

1. In *my* **folly**] Spoken in irony. They bear with others; why not with him? Possibly they had spoken of his words when with them as folly. **2. Godly jealousy**] lit. 'the jealousy of God.' **I have espoused you**] cp. Eph 5 25-27 2 Jn 1, 13 Rev 19 7 21 2 22 17. **3. The simplicity that is in Christ**] i.e. the pure gospel that salvation is by faith in Christ alone.

4-6. Paraphrase. 'And my fear is not without reason, for you are certainly very favourably inclined towards those who bring quite a different gospel from that which I preached. (5) But if you tolerate them, you can surely tolerate me, for I venture to think that I am quite as good in every way as these very eminent apostles of yours. (6) I may know little of the art of speaking (as they say), but at least I know something of divine truth, as is abundantly clear from my work among you.'

4. He that cometh] i.e. any new arrival claiming to be an Apostle. **Preacheth another Jesus**] These preachers, who were hostile to St. Paul, proclaimed Jesus as a Jewish teacher who demanded strict adherence to the Law, and declared that those who became His followers must observe the rites of Judaism. This was their other gospel, which showed another spirit than that of St. Paul—the spirit of prejudice and exclusiveness. **Ye might well bear**] rather, 'ye bear with him nobly.' The Apostle writes ironically. **5. The very chiefest apostles**] RM 'those preëminent apostles ; i.e. of course not the members of the apostolic band like St. Peter and St. John, but the false teachers to whom he is constantly referring. **6. Rude in speech**] Evidently a stock charge of his enemies : cp. 10 10.

7-9. Paraphrase. 'Is it a fault in your eyes that I took nothing from you while labouring for your spiritual benefit, but gave you the gospel gratuitously ? (8) I took more than their due from others to promote my mission to you, (9) and anything I wanted when among you I received not from any of you, but from the brethren who came from Macedonia. Hitherto I have been independent of your gifts, and so I intend to remain.'

7. An offence] His very independence had been used against him. For his practice cp. 1 Th 2 9 2 Th 3 8. **8. Other churches**] especially the Philippian Church (Phil 4 15, 16).

9. Wanted] RV 'was in want.' His supplies gave out. **The brethren**] perhaps Silas and Timothy (Ac 18 1, 5).

10-15. Paraphrase. 'I assure you, by the truth of Christ within me, that I shall permit no one to interfere with the grounds of this boast in the district of Achaia. (11) And that, too, not because I despise you and contemn your gifts, (12) but because I am determined that my opponents shall have no occasion to charge me with selfishness, but that they may show themselves as disinterested as I am. (13) For they are really hypocrites and deceivers, pretending to be apostles of Christ. (14) Their master, Satan, is accustomed to masquerade as an angel to further his base designs. (15) We cannot wonder, therefore, if his servants pretend to be servants of God ; but their punishment shall be suited to their actions.'

10. As the truth of Christ is in me] an adjuration calculated to impress them : cp. Ro 9 1.

This boasting] of preaching the gospel without cost to them. **11. Because I love you not?**] This was the reason his enemies gave for his independence of the Corinthians. **God knoweth**] that I love you. **12. That wherein they glory, they may be found even as we**] The 'false apostles,' or Judaisers, received support (v. 20) as due to their apostleship. Had St. Paul done so they would have charged him with greed ; but he is determined not to give them the opportunity. And by refusing support he hopes to force them to refuse it also, and thus to cause their other charge—that he feared to take it because he doubted his apostleship—to recoil upon themselves.

13. False apostles] He now exposes them in plain terms. **Transforming themselves**] RV 'fashioning themselves,' and so in next v.

14. Satan himself . . into an angel of light] tempting men by making evil seem good, 'making the worse appear the better reason.'

(c) **11 16–12 18. THE EVIDENCES OF HIS APO-STLESHIP IN SUFFERING AND SERVICE**

The Apostle goes on to show that if he begins to boast, he has far more to boast of than the Judaising teachers. In nationality he is their equal, in labours carried on and sufferings endured for the gospel he is far their superior ; he has had visions and revelations of the Lord which they cannot claim. The only thing in which they might find fault with him was his refusal of support from them. But in that lay his safety in dealing with his enemies : no one could say that either he, or any one sent by him, had made any profit out of the Church.

Paraphrase. '(16) Again I say, Do not think me a fool ; or, if you do think me a fool, let me indulge, like your other apostles, in a fool's boasting. (17) I am not speaking now under the inspiration of Christ ; I am only answering fools according to their folly. (18) Since many other teachers are boasting of their qualifications, I shall boast of mine. (19) For you who are so wise yourselves, have a great appreciation for fools. (20) You are very patient with people who delude and cheat you, and who insult and injure you.'

16. A fool] The repetition of this word so frequently suggests that he had been jeered at as a fool among the members of the Church. This whole passage (vv. 16–20) is full of irony. **17. Not after the Lord**] entirely on his own responsibility. He is very jealous of Christ's honour. **18. After the flesh**] i.e. of their worldly advantages : cp. vv. 22, 23. **19. Suffer**] RV 'bear with.' **20. If a man**] i.e. any of his Jewish opponents. **Bring you into bondage**] to the Ceremonial Law : cp. Gal 2⁴. **Devour**] make money out of you : cp. Mk 12⁴⁰ Lk 22⁴⁷. **Take** *of you*] RV 'taketh you captive.' **Smite you**] may be literal, but is more probably figurative, denoting the extreme of insult and impudence.

21–29. Paraphrase. ' I confess to my shame I was far too weak, as they call it, to act in that way. But if there is to be boasting, I am a fool and can boast too. (22) Are they of the chosen race claiming Abraham as their ancestor ? I am on an equal footing with them. (23) Do they boast of their missionary service ? I am ready to compare my service with theirs, and the comparison will not be in their favour (though, of course, all such boasting is madness). I have been in far more trials and punishments and dangers than they. (24) How cften have I been beaten, (25) scourged, stoned, in danger of my life by shipwreck ! (26) How many risks have I run in the course of my wanderings ! (27) How much suffering and privation have I endured ! (28) And do not forget my daily burden of anxiety in the over-

sight of all the Churches ; (29) for I enter into the feelings of my tempted and sinning brethren.'

21. As concerning reproach] RV 'by way of disparagement.' 'I admit to my own shame that I was incapable of acting as such an one.' The words are, of course, ironical. **22. Hebrews**] by descent. **Israelites**] in privilege. **The seed of Abraham**] in respect of promised blessings. There is probably a climax in the order. **23. I** *am* **more**] i.e. in a higher degree, as I can easily prove. **In deaths**] in danger of death : cp. Ac 14¹⁹. **24. Forty** *stripes* **save one**] A Jewish punishment : cp. Dt 25³. Only thirty-nine were given lest by a miscount the number were exceeded. None of the five cases is mentioned in Acts. **25. With rods**] A Roman scourging, as at Philippi (Ac 16²²). **Stoned**] at Lystra (Ac 14¹⁹). **Shipwreck**] The only instance recorded in Acts was later than this. **In the deep**] floating on wreckage or on a raft. **28. Beside those things that are without**] i.e. besides these exceptional troubles, there is the daily anxiety for the Churches. Or, as others suggest, 'besides all the rest which I do not mention.' **29. And I am not weak**] The Apostle shares the sufferings of others by sympathy. **Offended**] RV 'made to stumble,' i.e. led into sin. **Burn**] i.e. with anger.

30–33. Paraphrase. 'If, however, I must boast in self-defence, I shall boast about my weakness and helplessness ; for I shall thus make it plain what Christ has done by means of such a feeble servant. (31) And God is my witness that I speak the truth. (32) From the very outset I have endured ignominy ; for in Damascus the governor sought my life, (33) and I had to make my escape through the window of a house built on the city wall, being lowered in a basket by night.'

32. Damascus] This event in his career happened either immediately after his conversion, or after his return from his subsequent sojourn in Arabia: cp. Ac 19⁹ and Gal 1¹⁷. **Aretas**] This king (Aretas IV) ruled Arabia Petræa from 9 B.C. to 40 A.D. Damascus was taken by the Romans in 65 B.C., and was retained by them until about the time here mentioned, when it seems to have been restored to Aretas from motives of policy.

CHAPTER 12

HIS PRIVILEGES AND TRIALS

The Apostle unwillingly resumes his boasting and tells of a revelation he received from God ; but returns again to dwell on his weaknesses, and especially on his bodily infirmity, through which Christ's grace was manifested.

Paraphrase. '(1) It is not expedient for me to boast again : I have really been compelled to do it. I will now mention my experiences

of divine visions ana ievelations. (2) Fourteen years ago I experienced such a divine
ecstasy that I knew not whether I was still in
the flesh or whether I had been translated
to another sphere. (3) I repeat, I did not
know in what state of being I was ; (4) but I
had a divine revelation which caused me unspeakable joy and taught me truths too deep
for words to express.'

1. It is not expedient, etc.] RV 'I must
needs glory though it is not expedient'; i.e.
in self-defence. **2. I knew** (RV 'know') **a
man**] St. Paul is speaking of himself, of course,
as v 7 shows. **In Christ**] so much devoted to
Christ and under His influence, that Christ
completely dominated him and, as it were,
lived in him. **Whether in the body .. out of
the body**] The Apostle was in a trance or
ecstatic state in which consciousness of the
outer world was for the time suspended : sight,
hearing, feeling were gone, and he was lost in
contemplation of the divine. His reference to
the experience is too vague for us to draw any
conclusions from it : it must be remembered
that he was not giving information about his
revelations, but only mentioning the facts to
prove that he was 'not a whit behind the very
chiefest Apostles.' **The third heaven**] the
highest state of bliss. **3. And I knew**] repetition of v. 2 for emphasis. **4. Into paradise**] Paradise is used as a synonym for the
third heaven of v. 2. The word is used in the
NT. for the abode of the blessed after death :
cp. Lk 23 43 Rev 2 7. **Lawful**] better, 'possible.'

5, 6. Paraphrase. ' I can boast of these experiences, for they were due to no labours or
merits of my own ; but I will not boast of anything I have done myself, though I may speak
of my weaknesses through which God's grace
toward me has been manifested. (6) For even
if I wanted to boast of all the privileges I
have received, I should be justified, for my
words would be true ; but I am unwilling that
any one should be led to think of me more
highly than my services warrant.'

5. Of such an one] He can boast of these
experiences because they do not glorify him as
an individual. **Of myself**] He will not boast,
as he might, of what he has done.

7-10. Paraphrase. 'And lest I should be
uplifted by spiritual pride as the result of these
revelations, a painful bodily weakness—the
very work of Satan—was inflicted upon me.
(8) I prayed earnestly for the removal of this
affliction ; (9) but the Lord answered me saying, "My grace is sufficient for thee, for my
strength is made perfect in weakness." And
therefore I rejoice in my sufferings, because it
is in enduring them that I realise most clearly
that Christ is helping me. (10) I am glad
when trials and persecutions for Christ's sake
are my lot, for in my moments of greatest

weakness I am strengthened with power from
on high.'

7. A thorn in the flesh] some extremely
painful bodily disease whose symptoms recurred at intervals. Some, like Lightfoot, suggest epilepsy ; others, like Farrar, ophthalmia ;
and Ramsay holds that it was malarial fever :
cp. Gal 4 13-15. **The messenger of Satan**] RV
'a messenger of Satan.' For the idea, cp. Job
2 5-7 Lk 13 16 Ac 10 38. **8. The Lord**] Christ, as v. 9 shows. **Thrice**]
He probably made this ' thorn' the subject of
earnest prayer on three special occasions : cp.
Mt 26 44.

9. My grace, etc.] ' It is enough for thee
that thou hast my grace ; my power makes itself felt when there is no other support'
(Stevens). For the thought, cp. Lk 22 43 Pss
20 6 138 3. The best answer to prayer is the
consciousness of the support of the unseen
Hand. **Rest upon**] RV ' cover.'

11, 12. Paraphrase. 'Well now, you have
compelled me to boast like a fool. I should
not have needed to do so, for you ought to have
spoken in my defence ; but I think I have
shown that insignificant though I be, I am at
least on an equality with these preëminent
apostles of yours. (12) You certainly had all
the proofs of my true apostleship in the work
I did and the conduct I exhibited among you.
(13) For wherein did I treat you differently
from other Churches except in my refusal of
support from you ? Pray forgive me this great
injury.'

11. I ought to have been commended] Instead of listening to his detractors they should
have vigorously defended him. **Though I be
nothing**] i.e. as my enemies say. **12. Signs,
and wonders, and mighty deeds**] miracles in
various aspects. That St. Paul claimed to
have wrought miracles is evident also from
Ro 15 18, 19 : cp. Gal 3 5. **13. Forgive me**] The
verse is ironical.

14-18. Paraphrase. ' I am now about to pay
you a third visit, and, as on former occasions,
I shall accept nothing for my support. It is
not your possessions but your very selves
that I want ; for you are my spiritual children,
and it is not customary for children to lay by
wealth for their parents, but rather for parents
to lay by for their children. (15) And I am
ready to give all I possess to win your souls.
Are you going to continue indifferent to my
love for you ? (16) But some have been saying
that while I took nothing from you directly, I
was cunning enough to rob you indirectly.
(17) Well, I appeal to yourselves. Did any
of the brethren I sent take anything from you ?
(18) When Titus and his companion visited
you, did they not live and act exactly as I had
done ?'

14. The third time] His former visits were,

(1) the visit recorded in Ac 18, when he founded the Church, and (2) the short visit 'in sorrow,' not mentioned in Acts, but referred to in 2¹: see Intro. 1 (c). **I will not be burdensome**] see on 11 7-12. **Not yours, but you**] cp. 8⁵. **The parents for the children**] He wished to act towards them as a self-denying parent: cp. 1 Cor 4 14,15. **15. Though the more abundantly I love you, the less I be loved**] RV 'If I love you more abundantly, am I loved the less?'

16. But be it so] He now meets another insinuation: this one is disposed of.

18. I desired (RV 'exhorted') **Titus**] This visit of Titus must have been made at an earlier period than that referred to in 2¹³ and 7⁶ and that intimated in 8 6,17 as about to be made. There were evidently three visits of Titus to Corinth: (1) that here mentioned and referred to in 8⁶ ('as he had begun'), during which he seems to have organised the collection; (2) that referred to in 2¹³ 7⁶, when he went to quell the rebellion, bearing this very letter (chs. 10–13); (3) that referred to in 8 6,17, when he conveyed chs. 1–9. See Intro.

(d) **12**¹⁹–**13**¹⁰. WARNINGS AGAINST EVIL AND EXHORTATIONS TO HOLINESS

The Apostle reminds them that he is not pleading his cause before them, but writing for their edification.

Paraphrase. '(19) Do you think that all I have been writing is a defence of my conduct to satisfy you? It is not you, but God, who will judge me. What I have written is for the purpose of helping you to strengthen character and raise the standard of Christian life. (20) I am afraid lest when I visit you I find you unrepentant and obstinate, and I have to use severity. I am afraid lest the dark passions and vices I reproved still disfigure the Church, (21) and lest I be distressed and humiliated by the impenitence and shamelessness of those who were given to sensual sins and still continue their evil habits.'

19. Again, think ye] RV 'Ye think all this time that we are excusing ourselves,' i.e. pleading our cause. **In Christ**] as inspired by Christ's Spirit through living in union with him. **For your edifying**] He seeks not their favourable verdict, but their growth in goodness. **21. When I come again**] The 'again' should be joined with the next clause, 'God will again humble me.' He had been humbled at his last visit—the visit 'in heaviness' referred to in 2¹.

CHAPTER 13

The Apostle announces a third visit, and exhorts them to repentance. He expresses his desire for their growth in grace.

Paraphrase. '(1) This is the third visit I am about to pay you. On this occasion I shall proceed to punish these gross sinners after hearing all the evidence. (2) I repeat now what I said on my second visit, that those who persist in sin will find me stern in punishment. (3) And why am I thus severe? Because you demand proof that I possess Christ's authority, though that proof should be found in your own experience. (4) Christ indeed as a helpless man submitted to the death of the Cross, but in the power of God He still lives; and in the same way, in the Spirit of Christ, we have shown a forbearance which you mistook for weakness; but in the power of God we shall exhibit our strength when we come.'

1. The third *time*] see on 12¹⁴. **Two or three witnesses**] Quoted from Dt 19⁵. It seems to mean 'in accordance with the principles of justice I will act.' But some think the three witnesses mean the Apostle's three visits, and that he is interpreting the quotation allegorically, in accordance with his custom elsewhere: cp. 3 12-18 Gal 4 22-31. Thus Prof. Stevens paraphrases: 'I shall visit you a third time, and thus I shall have concerning you a threefold testimony, such as the Law requires to establish a cause.'

2. Which heretofore have sinned] i.e. old offenders still impenitent. **All other**] RV 'all the rest.' **3. Which to you-ward is not weak**] Christ's power had already been made manifest among them: cp. 1 Cor 1 5-8.

4. Through weakness] i.e. in the human weakness he assumed of his own accord: cp. Phil 2 6-8.

5. Paraphrase. 'Do not be so anxious to test me. Test yourselves. Do you not know that Christ's Spirit is in you, guiding your life, unless you are false disciples? I hope, at any rate, that you will learn that I am no false Apostle.'

5. Examine yourselves] i.e. not me. **Reprobates**] counterfeits.

7–10. Paraphrase. 'We pray to God that you may lead a pure and holy life, not to do us credit, but because it is right, even though we be like false apostles. (8) For our authority is given us to advance what is right, and not to hinder it. (9) We rejoice when we have no need to reprove you, for then your Christian life is healthy; and this is what we most earnestly wish, that you become more and more perfect in all Christian graces. (10) It is, believe me, for this reason that I have written to you these earnest remonstrances, because I do not wish to visit you in anger and severity. I have no desire to use the authority that Christ has given me in degrading and punishing you; for its true purpose is to strengthen my hands in helping you to become increasingly pure and holy in spirit and character.'

7. As reprobates] i.e. as if we had no

authority, because we shall not need to show it. **8. Against the truth**] He has no pleasure in their evil-doing, although it gives him opportunity to exercise his authority.

9. When we are weak] i.e. when our authority is in abeyance : cp. v. 4. **10. To edification, and not to destruction**] RV 'for building up, and not for casting down.'

(e) **13**¹¹⁻¹⁴. CONCLUSION AND BENEDICTION

The Apostle gives them his parting greeting, and bids them try to live a pure and holy life. He sends greetings from their Christian brethren, and invokes the blessing of God upon them.

11. Farewell] RM 'rejoice.' A cheerful parting message. **12. An holy kiss**] the token of brotherhood in the early Church : cp. Ro 16¹⁶ 1 Cor 16²⁰ 1 Th 5²⁶ 1 Pet 5¹⁴.

14. The grace, etc.] the fullest of St. Paul's benedictions. **The grace of the Lord Jesus Christ**] see 8⁹. **The love of God**] Perhaps including both the sense of His love for us and the love which He inspires in us. **The communion of the Holy Ghost**] the sense of His presence and guidance. *Be* with you all] The prayer is for all, those who rebelled as well as those who continued faithful.

The subscription in AV, 'The second *Epistle* .. was written from Philippi,' etc., is of no authority whatever. For the places where the two parts were written see Intro.

GALATIANS

INTRODUCTION

1. Authenticity. The Epistle to the Galatians is almost universally recognised as a genuine letter of St. Paul. The few recent attempts to discredit it have met with little favour, and still leave it practically unchallenged. It belongs in spirit, and probably in time, to the great doctrinal or argumentative group of Pauline letters, which includes 1 and 2 Corinthians and Romans. Internally it bears the stamp of the Apostle's personality, and fits in with the course of his life and thought. External evidence of its authenticity is to be found in Polycarp, Irenæus, Clemens Alexandrinus, and Justin Martyr. The first-named quotes 4²⁶ and 6⁷, though without mentioning the source ; the others definitely cite the Epistle as the work of St. Paul.

2. The persons addressed. This question has given rise to considerable controversy, and is even yet being discussed to some extent. (1) Some scholars, taking Galatia to be the pre-Roman kingdom of that name, in the NE. of Asia Minor, maintain that the Epistle was written to Churches founded by St. Paul during his Second Missionary Journey (Ac 16⁶) in its chief cities, Ancyra, Tavium, and Pessinus. Something may be said for this theory, but it is open to many objections : for instance, there is no mention of any of these places in the account of St. Paul's travels in the Acts of the Apostles, and no record of the existence of Churches there until about a century and a half later. (2) It may be safer, therefore, to take the view of others, that Galatia is the Roman province of that name. In St. Paul's time it included, besides the former kingdom properly so called, Paphlagonia, Phrygia, Isauria, and parts of Lycaonia and Pontus. In the southern portion of that large province lay the cities of Pisidian Antioch, Iconium, Derbe, and Lystra. These cities had been visited by St. Paul, and Christian communities founded in them, during his First Missionary Journey (Ac 13¹³⁻14²⁵) ; at the beginning of his Second Journey he had revisited them, and confirmed his converts in their faith. It is assumed, therefore, that the Epistle to the Galatians was addressed to them. Confirmation of this view is given in 2⁵, where the Apostle says that he had contended against the false brethren 'that the truth of the gospel might continue with you.' The only part of Galatia in which we know him to have been before this time is that which contained the cities mentioned in Ac 13, 14 ; consequently the reference is believed to be to them.

The population of these cities was almost entirely heathen (4⁸), and consisted partly of natives of the country, and partly of Greek and Roman colonists. The proportion of Jews was small (Ac 13⁴⁴⁻⁴⁸ 14¹). At Lystra, on the Apostle's first visit, Barnabas was taken for Jupiter, and Paul for Mercury (Ac 14¹¹,¹²). The heathen priests dominated the people, and bound them to the practices of a ceremonial law, as hard as that of the Jews. St. Paul refers to this in his Epistle (4 8), and bids them take care not to be entangled *again* with the yoke of bondage (5 1).

The history of the Galatian Churches is as follows. On his First Missionary Journey St. Paul, accompanied by Barnabas and John Mark (Ac 13 2, 5), after visiting Cyprus, sailed to Perga in Pamphylia. At this point John left them, and during the rest of the tour they were alone. They did not preach in Pamphylia, as seems to have been their original intention (Ac 13 12), but, owing to an illness which befell St. Paul (4 13), left the coast and went up to the higher ground in the interior, visiting in succession and founding Churches in Pisidian Antioch (Ac 13 14), Iconium (Ac 13 51), Lystra (Ac 14 6), and Derbe (Ac 14 20). On their return journey they visited these cities in the reverse order, giving some organisation to the infant Churches, appointing elders over them to watch over their interests and guide them (Ac 14 23), and exhorting the disciples to faithfulness and constancy, especially in presence of suffering and danger (Ac 14 22). On his Second Journey St. Paul, accompanied this time by Silas, again visited these Churches. He had just come from the apostolic council at Jerusalem (Ac 15 6-29), which declared the Gentiles free from the obligations of the Jewish ceremonial Law. He conveyed the message of the council to the Galatian Churches, and infused new life and strength into their members (Ac 16 1-5). During this visit the Apostle saw reasons for anxiety about the future of these ardent but unstable Christians, and warned them carefully against their besetting dangers and the temptations which he foresaw would assail them (1 9 5 2). A third visit to Galatia is mentioned in a word in Ac 18 23, at the beginning of his third great journey. The First Epistle of St. Peter is addressed to the elect in Galatia, as well as in other parts of Asia Minor.

3. **Occasion of the Letter.** Throughout the Church, the question was being keenly canvassed as to whether or not the observance of the Jewish Law was binding upon the Gentiles who became disciples of Christ. For the most part, of course, discussion was confined to the necessity of circumcision ; for this rite was the outward sign of the adoption of Judaism, and the acceptance of it accordingly imposed the obligation of keeping the whole Law. The Churches of Galatia had early felt the stress of this controversy. There was trouble in them from the very beginning (Ac 13, 14). It became greatly accentuated, however, after either the second or third visit of St. Paul. Certain Jewish Christians, or Judaisers, as they are called, appeared amongst them, insisting upon the keeping of the Law, and especially upon circumcision, as necessary to salvation. These seem to have been men of importance,

at least in the eyes of the Galatians (5 10), over whom they soon acquired considerable influence (3 1 5 7). They disparaged the teaching and work of St. Paul (1 12), and asserted his dependence upon other Apostles for his knowledge and authority (2 6, 8, 9). The Galatians yielded to their representations, and began to think of adopting circumcision (5 2, 3), and observing Jewish fasts and feasts (4 9, 10). To St. Paul this was a practical denial of the efficacy of faith in Christ, and the substitution of a doctrine of justification by the works of the Law for the great truth of justification by faith alone (2 16, 21 3 5 5 4, 6). Immediately upon the receipt of the news of the apostasy of the Galatians, the Apostle wrote his letter to them.

4. **Characteristics.** In the writing of his letters St. Paul usually employed an amanuensis (Ro 16 22), and wrote only the concluding salutation himself (1 Cor 16 21 Col 4 18 2 Th 3 17). The Epistle to the Galatians he penned with his own hand (6 11 RV). It is written with feeling and vehemence. The Apostle's anger at the seducers, and his anxiety for the seduced, stand out in every sentence. It is the most biographical of his letters, for the charges brought against his apostleship lead him to justify his authority by an account of his career as a Christian, and of his relations with the other Apostles (1 15–2 14). Doctrinally, the Epistle is related most closely to Romans. In both, the great ideas of St. Paul's theology are prominent. The doctrine of justification by faith is the common corner-stone of their argument : cp. 2 16, 21 3 2, 5, 11 with Ro 1 17 5 1, 9 8 1, 2 10 11, 12. There is the same doctrine of adoption : cp. 4 6 with Ro 8 15. The strife of the flesh with the Spirit is referred to alike in 5 17 and Ro 7 14-25. The illustration of Abraham's faith is used both in c. 3 and Ro 4.

5. **Time of Writing.** Various dates are given by different scholars. If it was after St. Paul's second visit that the trouble arose in the Galatian Churches, he may have heard of it on his arrival at Antioch at the close of that journey (Ac 18 22), in which case the letter would be written from there, probably in 53 A.D. On the other hand, if it was not until after the third visit (Ac 18 23) that the defection took place, the Apostle probably heard of it during his residence in Ephesus (Ac 19 1, 22), and wrote the letter from there, while Timothy was on the visit to Corinth which ended so disastrously, in 55 or 56. Either of these dates may be accepted. Some, however, place it as early as the close of St. Paul's first journey in 49, 50, and others after 2 Corinthians, or even after Romans, in 57, 58 ; but neither of these dates is so probable.

6. **Teaching.** The great subject of the Epistle is the superiority of the Gospel to the Law. The Jewish teachers, who sought

to pervert the Galatians, had themselves embraced Christianity without slackening their grasp of their old religion. To their mind, Jesus was the Messiah and Saviour of the Jewish race, not of the world in general; hence the Gentiles must become Jewish proselytes before they could receive the blessings of Christ. St. Paul's teaching was developed in opposition to this doctrine. He shows that the Law (i.e. the Old Testament revelation with its rules and sanctions) failed to make men righteous (2^{16} 3^{11}), because it did not supply a principle of life (3^{21}), but rather paralysed men's hearts by its rigorous demands (3^{10}). At the same time it had its uses, and fulfilled a purpose. It educated and disciplined men for a better revelation (3^{24}); it made them realise their sin (3^{19}); it caused them to feel their bondage (4^3); and so prepared them to become sons of God ($4^{5, 6}$). The Gospel of Christ, on the other hand, brought men a new principle of life. That principle is faith. Through it, the righteousness is obtained which the Law could not give (2^{16}). It unites a man to Christ, whose righteousness is thereby imparted to him, for Christ lives in him, and he in Christ (2^{20}). He is justified by faith in Christ, as he could not be by the works of the Law; indeed, the effort to live by the Law only weakens his spiritual life by slackening his hold upon Christ (5^{2-4}). The Gospel supplies the spiritual principle, even the moral motive power, lacking in the Law. The impulse derived from the indwelling Christ leads men to love their fellows (5^6); to renounce the works of the flesh ($5^{16, 20, 24}$); to bring forth the fruits of the Spirit ($4^{22, 25}$).

Besides justification by faith, other great truths of Christianity are mentioned incidentally: the Incarnation in 4^4; the Crucifixion in $6^{12, 14}$; the gift of the Holy Spirit, as the experience of the Galatians, in $3^{2, 3, 5}$ 5^{25}.

7. Summary. The Epistle falls naturally into three divisions. (1) An apologetic section (1^1–2^{21}), in which the Apostle defends the validity of his apostleship, by showing that his call was directly from Christ, and that he was absolutely independent of the other Apostles, both as to his teaching and commission. (2) A polemical section (3^1–5^{12}), in which he contrasts faith and works as means of salvation, and proves even from the Old Testament that faith is all-sufficient. (3) A hortatory section (5^{13}–6^{18}), in which he applies the truth he has been establishing to the different relations and duties of life.

The detailed sequence of thought is as follows:

CHAPTER 1

ST. PAUL MAINTAINS THE VALIDITY OF HIS APOSTLESHIP AND THE TRUTH OF HIS GOSPEL

1-5. The Apostle sends greetings from himself and the brethren with him to the Churches of Galatia, reminding them at the same time that his apostolic authority was not of human but of divine origin.

Paraphrase. '(1) I, Paul,—no self-constituted or humanly appointed missionary, but an Apostle divinely called by Christ and by God, who raised Him from the dead—(2) send greetings to the Churches of Galatia, in which all the brethren who are with me join. (3) May all spiritual blessings be yours from God and from Christ, (4) who offered Himself a living sacrifice for our sins, in order to save us from the spiritual bondage of this world and its lusts. (5) May all praise and glory be ascribed to Him eternally. Amen.'

1. An apostle] The title is used in the technical sense, and is introduced by St. Paul to assert his equality with the Twelve which had been challenged. It is always used by him in letters to Churches where his authority was questioned or to which he was unknown in person (Ro 1^1 1 Cor 1^1 2 Cor 1^1 Eph 1^1 Col 1^1); whereas in the cases where the Churches were thoroughly devoted to him he drops it altogether (Phil 1^1 1 Th 1^1 2 Th 1^1). **Not of men**, as source, **neither by** (RV 'through') **man**, as medium. Sanday suggests the illuminative analogy of the Sovereign as the fount of honour, and the ministry as the channel through which the honour is conferred. **But by** (RV 'through') **Jesus Christ, and God the Father**] Both his conversion (Ac 9 4-6 Gal 1 15) and his call to missionary work (Ac 13 2; cp. Ac 22 21) were directly from God and Jesus Christ.

Who raised him] It is the risen Christ from whom St. Paul derives his authority.

2. All the brethren which are with me] Some think this refers to the Apostle's travelling companions. Others hold that it includes the whole Church. If the letter was written from Antioch, it would thus convey the greeting of the Church which was the Mother-Church of the Galatian communities, as from it St. Paul proceeded to them. If it was written from Ephesus, it would inform them of the interest of that Church in their welfare.

Unto the churches] There is no commendation of them, as is usual in his letters (Ro 1 8 1 Cor 1 4 Phil 1 3).

4. Who gave himself up to death **for our sins**] cp. 1 Cor 15 3; on account of them, to atone for them, and to rescue us from their power. **That he might deliver** (recover) **us from** the evil which characterises **this present evil world** (age), **according**, etc.] connect with 'gave himself.' **5.** (The) **glory** due to Him for His gracious action in salvation. **Amen**] = truly, may it be so.

6-10. A sharp rebuke for their speedy departure from the truth (of salvation by grace) under the influence of false teaching. There is but one true gospel; all rival teachings, whether proclaimed by man or angel, are false. Hence the Apostle's boldness and confidence.

Paraphrase. '(6) I am surprised that you should so soon have deserted the truth which I taught you for a spurious gospel. (7) This perversion is due to false teachers. (8, 9) But if we Apostles even—yes, if an angel from heaven—should proclaim any teaching contrary to the doctrine of salvation by grace and faith, I pronounce a curse upon him. (10) I make this strong assertion—and I repeat it— in the knowledge that in my teaching I am not seeking man's favour, but obeying God's will in the service of Christ.'

6. So soon] after their conversion; or better, after the Apostle's last visit. **Him that called**] that is, God. **Another gospel**] RV 'a different gospel'; a (pretended) gospel of a different kind (from mine), that is, false. **7. Which is not another**] i.e. in addition to the true one, since, in the nature of the case, there can be but one. **But there be**] RV 'Only there are'; these heralds of a different doctrine are Jewish Christians who believe that observance of the Mosaic Law is necessary to salvation, and are misleading you through misconceiving and misrepresenting the gospel. **8. Accursed**] the strongest

possible form of condemnation: cp. Ac 23 14 Ro 9 3 1 Cor 12 3 16 22. **9. We**] the epistolary plural, as also in v. 8; on repetition it becomes the emphatic 'I.' **Said before**] in his personal teaching when with them. **Now again**] emphatic and solemn repetition.

11-17. The gospel which St. Paul preached not of human origin. Twofold proof of the fact: (1) the Apostle's whole course of life until his conversion was intensely Jewish, and only by a divine revelation was he made a messenger of Christ; and (2) after his conversion he remained aloof from the men from whom he might have been supposed to receive his message.

Paraphrase. '(11, 12) I solemnly assure you that the doctrine which I have taught was not a human product or derived from any human source, but that it came to me by revelation from Christ Himself. (13, 14) In proof of this, consider how unlikely it is that I, an intense Jewish zealot and a fierce persecutor of the Church, should have been transformed into a preacher of Christ by any merely human means. (15, 16) But when God, who had chosen me from my birth and graciously called me, disclosed Christ to my heart and designated me as His messenger, I did not resort to human authorities in order to learn what my message was to be; (17) I did not visit the primitive Apostles to learn anything from them, but went away into the seclusion of Arabia, and thence returned, not to Jerusalem, but to Damascus.'

11. Certify] RV 'make known'; urge and impress upon you. **The gospel**] the doctrine of salvation by grace through faith. **Not after man**] not human, but divine, in origin and character. **12. I neither received it of man**, any more than the original Twelve received it from man (but from Christ); but I received it **through** (RV) **the revelation of Jesus Christ**] His conversion was a disclosure to him of the Messiahship and Saviourhood of Christ.

13. Ye have heard] a notorious fact. **Beyond measure**] Saul killed, as well as disturbed (Ac 19 24 22 4). **14. Profited**] RV 'I advanced': cp. Ac 22 3. Saul was more devoted than most of his compeers to the customs and traditions of his people and his sect (the Pharisees).

15. Who separated] God determined upon him as an Apostle from the time of his birth: cp. Isa 49 1 Jer 1 5. **And called**] in his experience on the Damascus road. **16. To reveal,** etc.] to disclose in my consciousness—to my soul—the real meaning and saving power of Christ. **That I might,** etc.] This revelation carried with it this result. St. Paul seems to have been absent from Jerusalem during the ministry of Christ, and to have had no direct knowledge of Him before the vision on the

road to Damascus. **17. Neither went I, etc.**]
I did not visit the seat of apostolic influence,
as might have been expected. **Arabia**] This
is not mentioned in Acts, as St. Luke does not
deal with St. Paul's private life except in so
far as is necessary to explain movements in
prosecution of his work. The Apostle retired
to the wilderness in the neighbourhood of
Damascus (which was at that time subject to
the king of Arabia) for thought and prayer.
Perhaps it was there that he saw some of
those visions and revelations of the Lord to
which he refers in 2 Cor 12. **Damascus**] see
also Ac 9 25 2 Cor 11 22, 23, and notes.

18–24. It was a long time before St. Paul
saw any of the original Apostles. When he
did at length visit Jerusalem he saw only
Peter and James. Then he departed to
regions remote from Jerusalem. The Judæan
Christians did not even know him by sight.
Paraphrase. '(18, 19) After my conversion my course was such as to prove my independence of human teachers. It was three
years before I visited Jerusalem ; then I went
to interview Peter, and my stay was a short
one. Of the other Apostles I saw only James.
(20) I solemnly assert the truth of these statements. (21) I next travelled through Syria
and Cilicia to my native province. (22–24)
Up to this time I was personally quite unknown to the Judæan believers ; they had
merely heard that I, the fierce persecutor, had
now become a preacher of the gospel, and
they gave thanks to God for my conversion.'

18. After three years] a long time (though
it probably does not mean, 'at the end of
three years,' but rather, 'in the third year'),
during which he could not have received instruction from the original Apostles. **To see**]
RV 'to visit Cephas' (Peter)—to make his
acquaintance and hear his story. **Fifteen days**]
So short a sojourn could not have served for a
course of instruction in the gospel. Ac 9 26-30
must be read in the light of the first-hand
information given here by St. Paul.

19. James] here called an Apostle in the
secondary sense : cp. 1 Cor 15 7. Barnabas
(Ac 14 14) and Paul were also Apostles, though
not of the Twelve. **20.** To this solemn iteration he is moved, no doubt, by the thought of
the aspersions of his enemies. **21.** St. Luke
says (Ac 9 30) that he went from Jerusalem to
Cæsarea (Roman capital of Judæa) and Tarsus
—a more specific statement. By **Syria and
Cilicia** is meant the Roman province of that
name in which Tarsus was situated. **22. Unknown**] though he had preached in and about
Jerusalem (Ac 9 28), since his labours there
had been among the Greek-speaking Jews.
The Churches . . which were in Christ] not
merely 'the Christian Churches' as opposed
to the Jewish ; but the Churches whose

members were in a living relation to Christ,
who fulfilled the command, 'Abide in me.'

23. They had heard only] that was all the
knowledge they had of me. **Preacheth the
faith**] proclaims the necessity of trust in
Christ as the sole essential to salvation.

24. They glorified, etc.] They considered
Saul's conversion not as a great gain to the
Church, but as a great victory of grace. **In
me**] in my case.

CHAPTER 2

HIS AUTHORITY RECOGNISED BY THE
APOSTLES AT JERUSALEM AND MAIN-
TAINED IN HIS CONFLICT WITH ST. PETER

1–10. It was not until upon the occasion
of a subsequent visit to Jerusalem fourteen
years later that St. Paul had laid his gospel
before the chief authorities there, and they
had approved of all that he had done and
taught.

Paraphrase. '(1) It was fourteen years
before I again visited Jerusalem, in company
with Barnabas and Titus. (2) It was an
impulse from the Spirit which led me to go
and explain my teaching to the leaders there,
that I might see whether they approved it.
(3) That they did so was shown by the fact
that they did not demand the circumcision
of my companion, Titus, Gentile though
he was. (4) Some, no doubt, desired it, but
on account of the Judaisers, who were trying
to bind the burdens of the Law upon us, (5)
I utterly refused, because by allowing it I
should have compromised the truth of the
gospel. (6) But the most influential leaders
of the Jerusalem Church—let their authority
be what it may, that does not concern the
truth or divine approval of my teaching—had
no desire to correct or supplement my views,
(7) but recognised that I had my sphere of
labour among the Gentiles as truly as Peter
had his among the Jews, (8) and that each
was successful in his own sphere. (9) Not
only so, but these leaders, James, Peter, and
John, gave us the right hand of fellowship in
token of their approval and sympathy, and
bade us God-speed in our foreign mission,
while they themselves sought to evangelise
the Jews, (10) only asking us to send contributions for the poor at Jerusalem, which
indeed we were eager to do.'

1. Fourteen years after] i.e. after his conversion (1 16), from which the various subsequent
events are dated : cp. 1 16, 18, 21. **Again**] There
is much difference of opinion as to which of
St. Paul's visits to Jerusalem, as recorded in
the Acts, he here refers. Many scholars hold
that this visit corresponds to that recorded in Ac
15 at the close of the First Missionary Journey.
Others, especially Ramsay, identify this visit
with that recorded in Ac 11 27-30 and 12 25.

Barnabas was his companion on both occasions. Certainly that mentioned in Ac 11 27-30—his second visit—was caused by a revelation—that to Agabus—but the third visit (Ac 15), the direct occasion of which was about the Mosaic Law, seems, from what follows, the one to which the Apostle alludes. **Barnabas**] cp. Ac 4 36 37 11 22 13 2. **Titus**] was perhaps the most trusted of all St. Paul's companions and emissaries. When any specially delicate work had to be done requiring experience and tact, Titus was chosen for the purpose : cp. 2 Cor 7 6 8 6,17,18, and notes there. It is remarkable that his name is never mentioned in Acts.

2. By revelation] in response to a prophetic inspiration. **Them .. of reputation**] cp. v. 9.

Last, etc.] that it might be evident that even in their view he was not labouring in vain.

3. But neither (RV 'not even') **Titus .. was compelled**] This was a crucial instance of the application of the principle at stake. A demand was made by the rigid Judaists that Titus should be circumcised. The demand raised the whole question of the obligation of the Gentiles to observe the Jewish Law, and St. Paul peremptorily refused it. There is an apparent inconsistency between the Apostle's rejection of the demand in this case and his consent to the circumcision of Timothy at Lystra (Ac 16 3) 'because of the Jews which were in these parts.' The inconsistency, however, is only apparent. In the case of Titus St. Paul was opposing the principle that observance of the Jewish Law (and circumcision as the sign of it) was necessary to salvation. This was the doctrine of the Jewish-Christian party, and St. Paul gave no place to them, 'no, not for an hour.' In the case of Timothy there was no such principle at stake. There were no Jewish Christians in question, only Jews, who evidently thought that Timothy, being of Jewish nationality on his mother's side, should bear the outward sign of his nationality. As the matter had only a racial, not a religious, significance, St. Paul circumcised Timothy on grounds of expediency. We may compare his own personal attitude in similar matters (Ac 18 18 20 16 21 23) as showing that he continued to practise some of the Jewish customs, even in religious observances, though he did not regard them as necessary to salvation, or think of imposing them upon others. It is to be remembered also that while Timothy was half a Jew, Titus was a pure Gentile, and the question at issue involved the Christian liberty of the Gentiles. **4. Liberty**] i.e. from the requirements of the Mosaic Law.

5. We maintained our position firmly in order to preserve for you (and for all like you) the distinctive truth of the gospel, viz. that faith in Christ is the one condition of salvation.

6. But of those, etc.] RV 'But from those who were reputed to be somewhat'; those to whom was accorded the greatest influence.

Maketh no matter] does not affect the merits of my claim. **In conference added** (RV 'imparted') **nothing**] did not propose any correction or addition to my teaching. **7.** The reference is not to two different doctrines, but to two different spheres of the Gospel's operation. **8.** God gave to me success in my work, as He had given to Peter success in his.

10. Only *they would*] they made this one stipulation. **The poor**] cp. Ac 11 29, 30 24 17 1 Cor 16 3. **I also was forward**] RV 'zealous'; I was as eager to do this as they were to have me.

11-16. Not only was St. Paul's independence of the Twelve established by the circumstances already mentioned, but on one memorable occasion he had felt obliged to rebuke Peter for inconsistent action (thereby asserting his own independent authority), and at the same time to remind him that it was by faith they themselves had been saved.

Paraphrase. '(11) On another occasion, at Antioch, I similarly maintained my independence of the Judæan Apostles, for I testified against Peter's unworthy action there to his face. (12) When he came at first among the brethren there he joined freely in the love-feasts with the Gentile converts ; but on the arrival of some Jewish Christians from Jerusalem he dissociated himself from the Gentiles owing to a weak dread of criticism. (13) Other Jews, including even Barnabas, were led away by his example. (14) In view of this inconsistency, I publicly challenged Peter thus : If hitherto you have been content to associate freely with the Gentiles and conform to their way of life, why do you now keep aloof as if these brethren ought to adopt the Mosaic Law before you can admit them to your company ? (15) You and I, Jews as we are, and not Gentile outcasts, (16) know from our own experience that it is by faith in Christ that men are saved, and not by works of Law.'

11. Peter] RV 'Cephas.' **To Antioch**] Those who hold that the previous passage (vv. 1-10) refers to St. Paul's second visit to Jerusalem (Ac 11 29, 30), of course place this visit of Peter to Antioch after St. Paul's return there, i.e. between Ac 12 25 and 13 1. Those who take 1 1-10 as referring to the Apostle's third visit (Ac 15), for the most part date this occurrence after the council of Jerusalem, i.e. during the interval mentioned in Ac 15 35 ; though some hold that St. Paul in this passage is not mentioning a later instance of his independence, but merely another illustration of it which was earlier in time than that mentioned in vv. 1-10.

Because he was to be blamed] RV 'because

he stood condemned,' i.e. by the very inconsistency of his acts. **12. He did not eat with the Gentiles**] He would thus be defiled according to the Jewish Law. **Withdrew**] i.e. refused any longer to sit with the Gentile Christians at the love-feasts, and perhaps also in their houses. Peter had evidently forgotten the lesson of his vision at Joppa (Ac 10 9-16), and if this action of his was done after the decision of the council at Jerusalem (Ac 15 14-21), his conduct is placed in a still more unfavourable light. **13. Barnabas also**] RV 'even Barnabas,' whom the Galatians knew as fellow-missionary with St. Paul.

15. Sinners of the Gentiles] St. Paul is here adopting for argument's sake the rigid Jew's contemptuous description of the Gentiles.

16. Even we] i.e. with all our Jewish privileges we are no better than the Gentiles we despise, but must equally with them seek salvation by faith in Christ.

17-21. St. Paul seems here quite imperceptibly to pass from his rebuke to Peter to the broader question of the obligation of the Law and to the impassioned statement of his own living faith.

Paraphrase. '(17) But some one says that in spite of their trust in Christ some have fallen into sin (and therefore require the guidance of the Law). Is Christ then, or the Gospel, the cause of their sin? Whatever conclusion we may draw, that one is manifestly absurd. (18) But whoever goes back to the Law for guidance, after having left it and put his trust in Christ, is the real transgressor. (19) I was led by the Law to know my sin and put my trust in Christ, that I might live unto God; delivered by Him from sin, I was done with the Law—as much so as if I had been dead. (20) Through the power of Christ's Cross I died to my old life; and yet I live in a truer sense than before: rather I should say that it is no longer I who live, it is Christ who lives in me; and if I can speak of living at all, it is in so far as I live by faith in the Son of God, who is the source and support of my life, the indwelling power of a new righteousness. (21) I do not thus make the grace of God of no effect, as I would if I clung to the Law; for if we could be made righteous by the Law, Christ need not have died for our salvation.'

17. But if, etc.] This is a difficult passage. It seems to state an objection of the Judaising party, that faith in Christ is insufficient to keep men from sin. Or possibly it deals with an argument put forth by the Galatians themselves, that their faith in Christ was insufficient to enable them to withstand their temptations, and that adoption of the Law would be a help. In any case St. Paul pushes the argument to its logical conclusion, and shows its absurdity. **God forbid**] lit. 'be it not so,' 'far be it';

St. Paul's usual formula for rebutting an argument: cp. 3 21 Ro 3 4, 6, 31 6 2, 15, etc.

19. Dead] ethically; broke relations with the Law system as by a death. **That I might live**] I died to the old life and relations in order to live to the new.

20. St. Paul passes from the inability of the Law to the ability of Christ to save him.

Crucified with Christ] He identifies himself with Christ in His death. Christ's death means to him the cessation of the old life of sin as well as of legal justification: cp. 6 14 Ro 6 1-11 2 Cor 5 14 Col 3 3. **Nevertheless I live**] RM 'and it is no longer I that live'; my real life is not this natural life, but the life of faith in union with Christ. **By the faith of**] RV 'in faith, the faith which is in the Son of God.' St. Paul here enunciates his doctrine of mystic union with Christ. He is so entirely under the influence of Christ that he regards his thoughts and words and deeds as prompted by the Saviour. All that he is he owes to Christ who abides in Him. The spiritual relation between Christ and himself is so intimate that he can only describe it as Christ living in him: cp. Ro 6 1-11.

CHAPTER 3

JUSTIFICATION IS BY FAITH, NOT WORKS

1-14. The Apostle upbraids the Galatians with their speedy change from faith to legal observances, reminding them of the fact that their reception of the Spirit had not been through the works of the Law, but through faith, and appealing both to the testimony of their own consciences and to the teaching of sacred history in the parallel case of Abraham.

Paraphrase. '(1) You thoughtless Galatians have surely been bewitched. I told you plainly of Christ dying for your sins, and you accepted this salvation for your own. Why have you turned away from the Saviour? (2) Was it by obeying the Jewish Law, or by trusting in Christ, that you received those gifts of the Spirit which were so manifest among you when you first believed? (3) What folly, then, to desert the life of the Spirit for that of outward observance! (4) Why endure persecutions for the Gospel if you so lightly esteem it? (5) Have not all your spiritual gifts and the miraculous powers which are manifest among you been due entirely to your faith? (6) You read in the Scriptures that Abraham was accounted righteous on account of his faith, and your experience is an illustration of the same principle. (7) You want to be sons of Abraham. I tell you that his true spiritual children are those who have a faith like his. (8) In the promise made to him, because of his faith, you hear the principle of the Gospel announced in advance. (9) It is, therefore, those who base their lives on faith who share the blessing assured to him. (10) The Law, on the other hand, has no power to bless, but only to curse ; for it pronounces a curse upon all who do not obey it in every detail. (11) How impossible salvation is on this principle the Scriptures plainly declare. (12) The Law does not rest on faith. It only justifies those who fulfil its works. (13) But Christ has come to redeem us from the curse which the Law pronounces ; and He has accomplished that by taking the curse upon Himself, as His crucifixion makes evident. (14) And the purpose of His saving death was to secure that the Gentiles might receive through their faith the blessing which Abraham received through his, and gain the gift of the Spirit.'

1. Foolish] thoughtless, undiscerning, inconsistent. **Bewitched**] and so perverted you.

Before whose eyes] Paul had vividly (**evidently**, RV ' openly ') portrayed the crucified Christ as Saviour. **2. This only**] one question will reveal your error and inconsistency. **Received ye,** etc.] Of course the latter was the case. **3. Spirit** and **flesh** denote the characteristics of Gospel and Law respectively—the spheres to which they belong : cp. 6 12. The Galatians had begun by putting their trust in Christ, and living a new life under His abiding influence. To forget this beginning and to aim not at living according to the mind of Christ, but at fulfilling the demands of a law, was to forsake the spiritual for the merely human or carnal. **4. Have ye suffered .. in vain**] It was all for naught, and might better not have been endured, unless the gospel is deserving of their consistent adherence. **If** *it be* **yet in vain**] There was still hope that they might be reached and convinced by the appeal now made to them.

5. He that, etc.] i.e. God. **Miracles**] cp. 1 Cor 12. *Doeth he it,* etc.] Of course, in the latter way, or on the latter condition. **6. As Abraham**] a typical case, which the Judaisers could not gainsay : cp. Gn 15 6. St. Paul declares : Our Jewish sacred Scriptures teach salvation by faith. Abraham was blessed because he trusted in God absolutely, and did His will, before the Law even existed. So men are now to trust in Christ the Son of God, living according to His will and having His life in them, now that He has made the Law unnecessary. **7.** Sonship to Abraham, therefore (in the spiritual sense), is determined by faith. **8. Preached before** (RV ' beforehand')] proclaimed long in advance the central principle of the Christian gospel. **9.** The conclusion which follows from vv. 2, 5. **10.** Why men cannot be saved by legal works of merit ; they must be perfect and complete, or they never can be : cp. Dt 27 26 Ro 2 13 3 20 4 4, 5 8 3 10 5.

11, 12. Further scriptural confirmation : cp. Hab 2 4. Even under the Law a man was counted righteous not because he fulfilled the demands of the Law, but because he trusted in God, of whose will the Law was the imperfect expression.

13. Redeemed] a figure drawn from the analogy of ransoming captives. **Us**] i.e. Jews. **The curse**] the condemnation pronounced by the Law upon sin. **Being made**] by submitting to the shame of being crucified : cp. Dt 21 23. The Law declared that any one who died a criminal's death upon a cross was accursed. Christ died thus, and so was accursed. St. Paul associates this curse arising from ceremonial defilement with the curse which rests upon man for sins, and regards Christ as thus bearing the curse on man's behalf. Christ's death in some way availed to ransom men from the curse of the Law. God for Christ's sake then bestowed the blessing of His Spirit on all who put their trust in His Son, and sought to live in union with Him. The Law was a mere outward command, seeking to gain man's obedience by promises of reward and threats of punishment. Christ substituted loyalty to Himself for obedience to Law ; and by thus introducing the personal element of love brought a powerful influence to bear upon His people, and inspired them with a new power to overcome the sin that beset them.

15–22. The principle of the Gospel—salvation by grace on condition of faith—antedates and underlies the Law.

Paraphrase. ' (15) To take a familiar illustration : even a man's will, when ratified, no third party may annul or supplement. (16) Now God's gracious promise to Abraham and his descendants is realised only in and through Christ, in whom all believers are one. (17) The Law system, which arose long after the promise was made to Abraham, cannot change or nullify that promise ; (18) and as salvation (the promised inheritance) must be either by obedience to the Law or by grace, the case of Abraham proves that it is by grace. (19) If, then, the Law could not save, what purpose did it serve ? It had a temporary and educational purpose. It was designed to excite in men's hearts the consciousness of sin, which shows men their need of salvation, and so to point them to Christ ; it was a system given not directly by God to the people, but indirectly through angels to Moses, who in his turn gave it to the nation. (20) Now when a mediator is employed, it means that there are two parties making a bargain ; but in the case of Abraham there was but one party—God— making a promise out of His own free-will. (21) It is evident, then, that the Law cannot affect God's promise. The Law is subordinate to the Gospel, but it serves the ends of the Gospel—otherwise it would have been sufficient of itself, and the Gospel need never

GALATIANS

have been given. (22) And the way in which it serves the ends of the Gospel is by convicting men of sin, and forcing them to realise that they can only be saved by God's mercy through faith in Christ.'

15. Covenant] better as mg. 'testament,' or will. It is an 'inheritance' that is in question (v. 18). According to Ramsay, this word 'will' as understood in the Galatian cities meant 'a provision to maintain the family with its religious obligations. . . The appointment of an heir was the adoption of a son, and was final and irrevocable in the Galatian territory.' **16. Thy seed, which is Christ**] St. Paul here argues from the fact that the singular number is used—'seed,' not 'seeds'; but the verbal reasoning does not affect the argument. The word is collective. He regards Christ as including all who are united to Him by faith, who are the true seed of Abraham. **17. The law . . cannot disannul**] the will of God is irrevocable (as is seen even in the case of the wills of men); the Law, therefore, cannot be contrary to it, but must be explained in some other way. **Four hundred and thirty years**] The giving of the Law is dated 430 years after Abraham's sojourn in Canaan. According to another passage (Ac 7⁶), the sojourn in Egypt alone was to be 400 years. But the length of the time which had elapsed is immaterial to the argument. **18. The inheritance**] the blessings promised to Abraham, here understood in the sense of the spiritual blessing of salvation through Christ. **Of the law . . of promise**] two contrasted dispensations; salvation cannot be by both. Scripture is explicit in favour of the latter. It is better to depend upon a promise of God made unconditionally, and to read all subsequent happenings in the light of that promise, than to rest everything upon a contract made between God and man.

19. Inferior character of the Law shown (1) by its aim to make transgressions abound, cp. Ro 3²⁰ 4¹⁵ 5²⁰ 7⁷; and (2) by its mediation through the angels and Moses: cp. Dt 33² Ac 7⁵³. **Ordained by angels**] an addition of the rabbis to Scripture. St. Paul is justified in bringing it into his argument, as he is dealing with those who accepted the addition. **20.** There is no place for a mediator where there is but one party to a transaction. Now, in issuing His promise to Abraham, God stands forth independent and alone. The point is the contrast between the conditions of the giving of the Law and of the promise. The former depends upon the fulfilling of a contract—and that man failed to do; the other is no contract, but the free gift of God. **21.** It does not follow because the Law and the promise are of different rank that they are contrary.

22. Concluded all] RV 'shut up all things.' The OT. teaches what the Gospel teaches, that all need a gracious salvation. Both Law and Gospel contemplate the same ultimate end. 'The connexion of the argument is, that if the Law could give men spiritual life, and so enable them to fulfil its precepts, it would give them righteousness; but it does not pretend to do this; on the contrary, it shows the impotence of their nature by the contrast of their requirements with their performance'(Conybeare and Howson): cp. Ro 11³².

23-29. The Law had a preparatory and disciplinary office, but it was now being fulfilled in the Gospel.

Paraphrase. '(23) Before Christ's coming it was the office of the Law to imprison men by its condemnation of sin until they should be set free by believing on Him. (24) Thus the Law was like a stern disciplinarian who made us willing and eager to receive the grace of God in the Gospel. (25) But now, in the freedom of faith and of sonship to God, we are exempt from the Law's bondage and discipline. (26, 27) Through faith we are united to Christ and are become God's children, and this is symbolised by our baptism. (28) In Him distinctions of nationality and social condition disappear; (29) in Him all believers alike become heirs of the gracious promise made to Abraham, the man of faith.'

23. Faith] i.e. the Gospel, whose principle is faith. Both Faith and Law are here personified. **Kept**] RV 'kept in ward,' imprisoned by the Law's verdict upon sin, awaiting the time of our deliverance through Christ. **24. Schoolmaster**] cp. Ro 7⁷ᶠ. Tutor, or trainer, who by his chastisement for our faults made us see our need of grace and pardon. St. Paul may have been thinking of the Jewish custom of fathers daily conducting their sons to school. **25.** The Law is the stern jailer or disciplinarian; Faith the liberator from bondage and chastisement. **We**] i.e. the Jews. **26. Ye . . all**] whether Jews or Gentiles, are no longer bondsmen (cp. Ro 8¹⁴ᶠ.), but sons: see v. 16. Vv. 17–25 are a kind of parenthesis.

27. Baptized into Christ] entered by baptism into the relation of fellowship with Christ. The argument is: Baptism means union with Christ, and union with Christ means the liberty of sonship to God. **28.** Such distinctions do not separate true believers. There is a unity in Christ which is deeper than differences of nationality, condition, or sex. The **Greek** is the Galatian. St. Paul shows his tact in using that name, as the more refined natives would probably like it. **29. Abraham's seed**] his spiritual descendants. Not lineal descent from Abraham, but spiritual kinship to him through a faith like his, determines whether we are heirs of the promise made to him.

CHAPTER 4
THE BONDAGE OF THE LAW. FREEDOM IN CHRIST

1–7. Under the Law we were in bondage ; under the Gospel we have received the freedom of sons.

Paraphrase. '(1) The heir before he comes of age can no more enter upon his inheritance than a servant in the family can possess himself of it, (2) but must continue, until the set time, in a subordinate position, and under the authority and training of others. (3) So, when we were under the elementary Law system, we were in a position like that of the heir in his minority ; (4) but when the appointed time arrived, God sent His Son, subject not only to human conditions, but also to the Jewish Law, (5) in order that He might set free all who were in bondage to the Law and put them in possession of full liberty and all the rights of the sons of God. (6) And God also gave us the Spirit of His Son, and imparted to us the sense of sonship, (7) so that we now know ourselves as no longer bondmen to the Law, but freemen, and heirs of the salvation which is our rightful, destined possession.'

1. The heir] is, of course, a son, as v. 2 shows. **A child]** i.e. under age ; a minor.

Differeth nothing] as respects the control of his destined possessions, though, in prospect, lord of all. **2. Tutors]** RV 'guardians '; the regular term for the guardian of a minor. **Governors]** RV 'stewards,' who have the management of his prospective property. **Time** (RV 'term') **appointed]** the time of reaching his majority. Ramsay points out that under the Syrian law, which prevailed in S. Galatia, a child was subject to a 'tutor' until he was 14, after that he could make a will and dispose of his property ; but the management of his estate was under a 'governor' or curator until he reached the age of 25. **3. Children]** in a state of tutelage under the Law. **Elements]** RV 'rudiments' (cp. 4⁹ Col 2⁸) ; elementary religious observances belonging to the outward, visible **world.**

4. Cp. 3¹⁹,²⁴ Ro5²⁰,²¹. **Made]** RV 'born'; entering fully into our human lot. **5. Redeem]** i.e. save us from our bondage in sin under the Law, and introduce us into full sonship to God. **Under the law]** and therefore bound to obey it, and yet guilty of infringing it. **Adoption]** Redemption is followed by the admission of the sinner among the children of grace.

6. This emancipation being accomplished, a new sense of sonship fills the heart. **Abba]** an Aramaic word commonly used in prayer, meaning 'Father.' Christ's love for us exhibited in His incarnation and all that it in-

cludes wins our love, and for His sake we overcome sin. **7. Thou art]** application of the conclusion to the individual. **An heir of God]** RV 'an heir through' (the adopting act of) 'God.'

8–11. In the past the Galatians had been idolators, in bondage to gods that were 'no gods' at all. Now they are going back again to a similar bondage.

Paraphrase. '(8) Before your conversion you Gentiles were victims of idol-worship ; (9) but now, since the true God has revealed Himself to you in Christ, how can you desire to return again to a lower plane of religious knowledge and practice ? (10) This you are doing in taking up the observance of Jewish feast-days and ceremonies. (11) This action causes me to fear lest my labours on your behalf should prove to have been in vain.'

8. Howbeit then] RV 'At that time,' when they were yet unconverted heathen. **No gods]** cp. 1 Cor 8⁵ 10²⁰ ; the so-called divinities of the heathen. **9.** Their lapse into Judaism is a return, not, indeed, into idolatry, but into an imperfect and rudimentary religion. In this point of view only does the Apostle class heathenism and Judaism together. The Law is **weak,** etc., as being powerless to justify and give the assurance of sonship. **Known God, or rather are known of God]** i.e. now that ye have come to know the nature and love of God, or rather that God has recognised you and bestowed upon you His gifts. **10. Days]** Jewish feast- or fast-days. **Months]** new moons : cp. Col 2¹⁶. **Times]** RV 'seasons,' such as Passover, Pentecost, etc. **Years]** e.g. sabbatic years. These observances are 'weak and beggarly elements' (v. 9), because they are matters of dry routine, customs which the Gentiles would adopt without understanding their meaning or catching anything of the spirit which lay behind them. They were of no avail for salvation. **11. Afraid]** anxiously solicitous lest they should repudiate their Christian profession.

12–20. The Apostle appeals to his readers to return to their former allegiance to the gospel.

Paraphrase. '(12) I plead with you to come to my point of view, even as I in renouncing slavery to the Law, have become as a Gentile to you Gentiles. (13) I hope for this result on the ground of your former kindness to me ; you remember that it was in consequence of an illness that I was led to become your Christian teacher, (14) but you did not consider the care of me at that time burdensome, but received and treated me with the greatest honour and deference. (15) How great is the change in you since that time when you would have made any sacrifice for me ! (16) Do you now regard me as hostile to you because I urge you to loyalty to Christ ? (17) The Judaisers are courting your favour only that they may make you their partisans and supporters. (18) It is well to be the object of others' interest in a good cause—and that at all times and not merely when I am with you. (19, 20) I assure you my desire that you should be moulded after Christ's pattern is intense ; and I would fain visit you and adopt a less censorious tone in the hope of winning you back.'

12. As I *am*] loyal to Christ : cp. 1 Cor 11[1].

I *am* **as ye** *are*] cp. 1 Cor 9[19-23]. RV puts a period after ' ye *are*,' and then reads ' Ye did me no wrong ; but *ye* know that because of an infirmity,' etc. **Ye have not injured me**] i.e. I am not personally offended.

13. The first] lit. as RM ' the former time.' The Gk. word, accurately interpreted, indicates that St. Paul had paid the Galatians two visits before the date of this letter. This ' former ' visit is of course that recorded in Ac 13[14]–14[24]. St. Paul probably intended preaching at Perga when he landed there ; but being seized by illness was compelled to leave the low ground of Pamphylia and seek health and strength on the high plateau further inland. His journey brought him first to Pisidian Antioch, then to Iconium, Lystra, and Derbe. On his return to Perga, on his way back to Antioch in Syria, he preached the gospel there, as he had not been able to do it on his outward way : cp. Ac 13[13,14] with 14[25].

14. My temptation which was in my flesh] RV ' That which was a temptation to you in my flesh.' The bodily infirmity which had attacked him had left such traces that they might have been excused for rejecting one whose ' bodily presence was weak ' : see 2 Cor 12[7] and note there. **As an angel**] with even excessive reverence. This spirit had been exhibited towards him in Lystra, even by the heathen (Ac 14[13]) ; and, indeed, in all the cities of Galatia by those who had received his message and become followers of Christ.

15. Blessedness] RV ' Gratulation,' your felicitation of yourselves in my teaching.

Plucked .. eyes] made any sacrifice for me, so great was your former kindness. **17.** RV ' They zealously seek you in no good way ; nay, they desire to shut you out that ye may seek them.' **They**] the Jewish extremists.

Not well] i.e. in a party spirit. **Exclude you**] from the influence of other teachers, especially from my own. **Affect** (RV ' seek ') **them**] cling zealously to them as partisan adherents. **18.** RV ' But it is good to be zealously sought in a good matter at all times.' I am glad that you are the objects of others' zeal and interest, whether I am present or absent, provided your favour is courted in a good cause. **19. I travail in birth again**] RV

' I am again in travail.' In his anxiety and distress he would reconvert them to Christ.

20. Desire] RV ' could wish,' i.e. if such a thing were possible. **Change my voice**] i.e. change my tone, speak more mildly.

21-31. This passage is an example of the rabbinical method of interpretation, which found a hidden sense, embodied and intended, in many parts of Scripture. Here a historical narrative is taken as revealing the truth that those who adhere to the Law are in bondage, and those living by faith in Christ, free.

Paraphrase. ' (21) You who are so zealous for the Law will surely take a lesson from the Law itself. (22) You know the story of Abraham's two children, Ishmael and Isaac, (23) the former the child of the bondwoman, Hagar, the latter of Sarah, born in accordance with a divine promise. (24) These two women represent, in the allegorical application, two covenants, the old and the new. Hagar represents the Law, whose symbol is Mt. Sinai, since her descendants, like the adherents of this old covenant, are born into a state of bondage. (25) Indeed, Hagar is a name of Mt. Sinai in Arabia, and corresponds to Jerusalem, the sacred seat of the Law system, which, again, is a symbol of bondage. (26) But the spiritual Jerusalem, answering to Sarah, is, like her, the mother of freemen. (27, 28) For our spiritual mother has fulfilled the promise of Scripture to the childless, by making us like Isaac, the heirs of God's gracious promise. (29) But just as then, so now, the unspiritual persecutes the spiritual. (30) And as then the Ishmaelites were rejected from the heirship of the promises, so now God will reject the slaves of the Law. (31) It is the Christian believers who are God's true freemen and heirs of His promises.'

21. The very Law in which the Judaisers trust is shown to be against their contentions. **22.** One son, from the circumstances of his birth, typifies bondage ; the other, freedom : cp. Gn 16, 21. **It is written**] This does not introduce a quotation here, but simply indicates the facts as recorded in the Scripture history. **23.** One was born in a relation merely carnal, the other in fulfilment of a special promise of God : cp. Heb 11[11,12]. **24. Are** (RV ' contain ') **an allegory**] i.e. are spoken allegorically. An allegory is a narrative where the literal sense ' half reveals and half conceals' a spiritual meaning. The best example of allegory in the English language is Bunyan's ' Pilgrim's Progress.' Hagar and Sarah represent, respectively, the Law and the Gospel—bondage and freedom. Of the former, Sinai, as the place where the Law was given, is the symbol.

25. Hagar] Some MSS of the Epistle omit this word here, in which case we should render :

'Sinai is a mountain in Arabia' (so RM)—the land of Hagar's descendants. Sinai and Jerusalem mean the same thing—law and bondage ; Hagar typifies both. On St. Paul's use of allegorical interpretation, cp. 1 Cor 9 9, 10 Gal 3 16 2 Cor 3 13, 14. As Hagar corresponds to (Mount Sinai, which is now represented by) the earthly Jerusalem, so Sarah corresponds to the ideal Jerusalem which is in heaven, of which all true Christians are citizens. With the whole passage cp. Heb 12 18-24.

26. Jerusalem .. above] the spiritual commonwealth or city of God, of which believers are citizens. **The mother of us all**] RV ' our mother,' prefigured by Sarah. **27.** This v. in its original context (Isa 54 1) had no reference to the Jerusalem above, only to the actual Jerusalem. It is quite in the rabbinical style for St. Paul to give it another, more spiritual application. **28.** Conclusion and application. We believers stand in a relation to God's promise and favour analogous to the descendants of Sarah, while the Judaisers take the place of the Ishmaelites.

29. Cp. Gn 21 9. The ' mocking ' there mentioned hardly amounts to persecution. Perhaps the general hostility of Hagar's descendants to Israel is referred to : cp. Ps 83 6 1 Ch 5 10, 19. History was now repeating itself in the persecution of the Christians of Galatia by Jews and Judaisers. **30. Cast out**] cp. Gn 21 10, 12. Hagar's spiritual descendants are the Jews and the Judaisers, who are the natural descendants of Sarah ; while the heathen who have accepted Christ are the spiritual descendants of Sarah, and inherit the blessings promised to her children. For similar ideas in the teaching of Jesus cp. Jn 8 31-43. **31. So then**] RV ' Wherefore ' ; since this rejection does not apply to us ; we belong to a higher lineage and order. And as we are thus spiritually free (5 1), let us take care to maintain our freedom.

CHAPTER 5
THE NATURE OF CHRISTIAN LIBERTY

1-12. The futility of seeking justification by attempting to comply with the demands of the Mosaic Law ; the inconsistency of works and faith as methods of salvation.

Paraphrase. ' (1) Since Christ has freed us from the necessity of obeying these legal demands and customs, let us consistently maintain and use our liberty. (2) To receive circumcision as necessary to salvation is to renounce allegiance to Christ, (3) since submission to this rite commits one to the observance of the whole legal system. (4) In taking such a step you would be repudiating the free grace of God; (5) for it is through the operation of the Holy Spirit, not through symbols in our flesh, and in consequence of

our faith in Christ and not of works we perform, that we hope for justification before God. (6) Circumcision is wholly unimportant ; the only condition of salvation is a faith which evinces its vital power in love. (7) You were making good progress in the Christian life ; who has misled you into disloyalty to the gospel ? (8) This teaching by which you have been led astray is not of God ; (9) and though it has so far done only a little mischief, it will spread like leaven. (10) I have good hope, however, that you will now heed my exhortation ; but the leader of this sedition will receive a heavy punishment. (11) As for the accusation that I myself sometimes commend circumcision, were that the case would the Jews still persecute me ? If that were true I should no longer be giving them offence through my preaching of the crucified Christ as the author of salvation. (12) But enough ! I wish that these men who are perverting your faith by insisting upon circumcision would mutilate themselves completely.'

1. Connected closely with preceding section. **Bondage**] to legal observances. **Christ hath made us free**] by fulfilling the Law, and so teaching us to obey it, not in the letter but in the spirit, which we shall do best by living by faith in Him, and having the same mind in us as was also in Him : cp. Mt 5 17-48. **2. Be circumcised**] RV ' Receive circumcision ' as essential to salvation. **Christ .. profit .. nothing**] because you thereby reject Him as sole and sufficient Saviour. **3.** Circumcision is the sign of the system of which it is a part, and its practice indicates that a complete observance of all the Law's requirements is obligatory. **4. Christ is become, etc.**] RV ' Ye are severed from Christ, ye who would be justified,' etc. By resorting to the Law for salvation, as if Christ were not sufficient, you are no longer Christ's people. **Fallen, etc.**] fallen down from the higher plane of grace upon the lower plane of Law. To us now the bondage of the Law has little meaning; but if we come into bondage to sin, we fall from grace as surely as did the Galatians. Christ has given us power to keep from the love of sin and to resist its power ; He has liberated us from its bondage and given us the liberty of the Spirit ; and it is ours to maintain that liberty, and not to return to the works of the flesh, which bring us to slavery.

5. The true mode of salvation, viz. by the agency of the Spirit, on condition of faith alone. **6. Availeth**] for salvation. **Faith which worketh**] an active, energetic faith ; cp. Jas 2 14-26. **7. Run well**] before the Judaisers misled you. **Who did hinder**] a rhetorical question. **8.** *Cometh*] RV ' came.' This dissuasion from loyalty to Christ to which you have yielded does not emanate from God, but is contrary to His will.

9. A little leaven] It would seem that only a few of the Galatian converts were affected by the false teaching; but their influence would soon prove far-reaching and pernicious: cp. 1 Cor 15 33. Leaven is always used in NT. as a symbol of influence. Our Lord uses it to illustrate the influence of the kingdom of God (Mk 8 15 and parallels). St. Paul uses it to describe the penetrating and poisonous power of evil influence: cp. 1 Cor 5 6, 7, 8.

10. The Apostle now adopts a more hopeful tone, and turns from reproof to encouragement. **None otherwise minded**] than as I have taught you. **11. Then is the offence of the cross ceased**] RV 'then has the stumbling-block of the cross been done away.' The Judaisers who had 'troubled' the Galatians had evidently brought against the Apostle the charge that he still preached circumcision himself, although he had dispensed with it in the case of the Galatians. The accusation may have been based on the fact mentioned in Ac 16 3, that on his second visit to Galatia he had circumcised Timothy at Lystra: see on Gal 2 3. He shows that this accusation is inconsistent with the other charge of abolishing the Law, for which they constantly attacked him. If he preached circumcision, why did they persecute him? **12. Were even cut off**] RV 'would even cut themselves off,' RM 'would even mutilate themselves'; i.e. would even go beyond circumcision, like the priests of Cybele, whom the Galatians had formerly worshipped. A bitterly satirical wish. The Apostle was evidently carried away by his righteous wrath at the bitterness of the Judaisers.

13-15. Freedom from the requirements of the Law does not mean disobedience to its spirit, which is that of love to others.

Paraphrase. '(13) Cling, then, to your freedom from legal rules and customs; but remember that freedom means not licence, but loving service. (14) For love is the essence of God's Law, (15) whereas mutual backbiting and hatred can only end in the destruction of one another's spiritual life.'

13. A caution against an easy and common misunderstanding of Christian freedom: cp. Ro 6 15. **14.** The real moral substance of the Mosaic Law was the gospel principle of love: cp. Mt 22 40 Ro 13 10. **15. Bite and devour**] in party strife. **Consumed**] as respects your personal and collective Christian life.

16-26. The spiritual and the carnal life contrasted.

Paraphrase. '(16) In the life which is fostered by the Spirit you will find your true safety against the evils of which I am warning you. (17) For between the pure aspirations of the Spirit and the sinful impulses of the flesh

there is a sharp, irrepressible conflict. (18) If you live under the influence of the Spirit of God, you have no need to seek the guidance of law. (19-20) Contrast the sins which spring from the carnal impulses (21-24) with the virtues which spring from the Spirit's guidance. The former exclude from God's kingdom; the Christian must abjure them; but the latter are not condemned by any law. (25) If, then, we possess the Spirit in our hearts, let our outward action be under His guidance, and (26) let us avoid factious boasting and all attempts to incite others to rivalry and jealousy.'

16. The Spirit] the sanctifying Spirit of God. **Shall not fulfil**] because the Spirit and the flesh are contrary principles. **The flesh**] a general name for the sinful impulses. **17.** The carnal desires are opposed to the Spirit, and the impulses from the Spirit are contrary to these desires. **18. Not under the law**] Those who live under the guidance of the Spirit of God are in no need of the Law. They do what is right not because the Law commands it, or because the Law penalises wrong-doing, but because they live under the influence of Christ and have His Spirit in them; e.g. they refrain from injuring others not because the Law says 'Thou shalt not kill,' but because they love their neighbours in the Spirit of Christ. And so, for the ideal Christian who is perfectly changed into Christ's likeness, the Law might just as well not exist, for he has no need of it.

19-21. Works of the flesh include not merely carnal sins, such as the first three in the list, but evil passions like strife and jealousy and their social effects, such as factions and divisions. **22, 23. Against such** (virtues) **there is no law**] hence there can be no condemnation for those who possess them. But even the Law condemns the works of the flesh. **24. Have crucified**] in the act of uniting themselves to Christ by faith: cp. Gal 2 20 Ro 6 2. **25.** The inner life should rule the outer life. **26. Vainglory**] indulging in rivalry and jealousy. **Provoking**] to strifes of opinion. **Envying**] cherishing grudges.

CHAPTER 6

PRACTICAL EXHORTATIONS. THE APOSTLE'S
GLORYING

1-5. The nature and requirements of the law of love.

Paraphrase. '(1) If sin overcome one of your number, try to correct the fault in a temper of gentleness, remembering that you yourselves may some time need a similar forgiveness. (2) Share each other's cares and sorrows, and so fulfil Christ's law of love. (3) Shun the self-deception which springs from pride; (4, 5) let each man' test his actions on their own merits and not by comparison with other men, for each must bear his own load of responsibility.'

1. Overtaken] as if pursued and caught.

Fault] RV 'trespass,' or transgression, such as the error into which the readers had been beguiled. **Spiritual**] as opposed to 'natural' or 'carnal' : cp. 1 Cor 2^{14} 3$^{1-4}$.

Spirit] i.e. temper. **Lest thou**, etc.] in similar circumstances need a similar sympathy. **2.** Cp. Ro 15^1. **Bear**] in sympathy. **Law of Christ**] cp. Mt 8^{17}. St. Paul has warned them against law ; but there is a law to which they owe obedience and devotion—the new commandment of Christ—the royal law of love : cp. Jas 2^8. **3.** The real greatness of the Christian is found in service : cp. Mt 20^{26}.

4. Prove] test, to see whether it is morally real and genuine. **Work**] life and conduct.

Rejoicing] a ground of satisfaction.

5. Burden] of accountability. The word is different from that used in v. 2.

6–10. The principle of the spiritual harvest. **Paraphrase.** '(6) Share with your teachers. (7, 8) If you refuse to obey the law of love, the result will be a debased moral life ; its observance conducts to a blessed existence. (9, 10) Our reward is sure if we discharge the obligations of love to all men, especially to our Christian brethren.'

6. Communicate] i.e. share, either in general sympathy and friendship, or, more specifically, in contributions to the support of the teacher. **7.** None can escape the application of God's law of the spiritual harvest.

8. He who tills the field of the carnal life or that of the spiritual life reaps, in each case, his appropriate fruitage. **Corruption**] 'a harvest doomed to perish' (Conybeare and Howson). **Life everlasting**] the harvest of which the Spirit gives us the pledge in this life, and of which we shall receive the fruition in the life to come. **9.** An encouragement to persistent spiritual sowing and cultivation.

10. A conclusion from the certainty of reaping if we faint not. **Of the household of faith**] members of the Christian family whose bond of union is faith.

11–18. The true ground of glorying. **Paraphrase.** '(11) Look at my own bold handwriting in which I have written this letter as the proof of my longing for your salvation. (12) To sum up : Those who are insisting on your circumcision are doing so in order to curry favour with the Jews, for (13) as

Christians they do not themselves consistently observe the Law, but are making a show of zeal for it by inducing you to assume its burdens. (14) But the only true ground of glorying is the cross by which I have been put to death to the sinful world. (15) The question of circumcision is indifferent ; new life in Christ is the one important thing. (16) God's favour be upon all such as test their lives by this principle, thereby proving themselves true Israelites. (17, 18) Let me hear no more accusations ! The proof that I am Christ's Apostle is found in the scars which I have received in His service. May blessings from Him fill your heart !'

11. Ye see how large a letter] RV 'See with how large letters.' **Have written**] probably an allusion to the writing of the foregoing letter. St. Paul usually dictated his letters, adding only the closing salutation in his own hand : cp. Ro 16^{22} 1 Cor 16^{21} 2 Th 3^{17}.

12. In the flesh] the sphere to which circumcision belongs. **Lest they should suffer**, etc.] RV 'that they may not,' etc.—a prudential motive underlies their zeal. It must be borne in mind that St. Paul is writing to a Church composed chiefly of Gentiles. They were Christians, having been converted by the Apostle, but they had been influenced by teachers who had strong Jewish sympathies and maintained that the Law was obligatory on all Christians.

14. St. Paul, on the contrary, will glory only in salvation through sacrifice and self-giving. **By whom**] RV 'through which,' etc.; because he died to sin with Christ on His cross: cp. Ro 6$^{2, 8}$ Col 2^{20}. **15. A new creature**] RM 'a new creation.' Salvation is newness of life in Christ, and is in no way dependent upon the question of circumcision. **16. This rule**] the test of acceptance with God mentioned in the previous v. **Israel**] the true spiritual Israel : cp. 3^9 Ro 4$^{13-16}$. **17. Let no man**, etc.] Let these annoying insinuations concerning my apostleship cease. **I bear in my body**, etc.] RV 'I bear branded on my body the marks of Jesus' : cp. 2 Cor 11$^{23-28}$, evidences of the genuineness of his consecration to Christ.

18. The absence of commendation and the severe tone of the letter are noticeable ; yet, quite exceptionally, he adds to the benediction an appellation of personal affection (**brethren**).

EPHESIANS

INTRODUCTION

FOUR questions have to be considered in an Introduction to this Epistle : Author, Recipients, Circumstances, and Contents. And it will be best to take the questions in that order. The answers respecting the recipients and the circumstances depend to a very great extent upon the answer respecting authorship.

1. **The Author of the Epistle.** If the authorship of this letter had not been disputed by competent scholars, it would not be necessary to spend much time upon this point. And the necessity for discussion depends much more upon the weight of the authority of the critics who question or deny the Pauline authorship than upon the weight of the arguments which they employ. Some consideration of their arguments is required : but the result of such consideration will be to confirm us in what was the unanimous belief of Christians for many centuries, that in this Epistle we have what perhaps may be called the richest and most glorious product of the active mind of St. Paul. The only other Epistle of which that might with reason be said is the Epistle to the Romans ; and the fifteenth chapter of that great letter is left incomplete until the Epistle to the Ephesians is added to it. Here we have a full statement of the unity of mankind in Christ, as sons of Him who is their Father and His Father, and of God's purpose for the world through the Church. This completion is worthy of ' Paul the Master-builder.' And it would seem that the objections to the Pauline authorship are being felt to be less serious than they were supposed to be ten or twenty years ago. The Epistle has fewer opponents and more defenders of the first rank than used to be the case : and it is remarkable that Dr. Armitage Robinson in his admirable commentary does not think it necessary to discuss the question of authorship, because he considers that the Epistle has already, by Dr. Hort and others, been sufficiently shown to be the work of St. Paul. One reason for the decrease in important objectors to the Epistle lies very near the surface. It has been found more and more difficult to accept the other Epistles to which Ephesians is inseparably linked as writings of St. Paul and yet deny the Pauline authorship of Ephesians. Philippians, Colossians, Philemon, and Ephesians form a closely connected group. To doubt that the Apostle wrote the exquisite and purely personal letter to Philemon is generally recognised as irrational scepticism ; and most of the critics who doubt or deny the Apostolic authorship of some of the Pauline Epistles, admit Philippians also to be genuine. If Philippians and Philemon are accepted as St. Paul's, some violent hypotheses are needed in order to make it tenable that Colossians is not by him.* And if Philippians, Philemon, and Colossians are all allowed to be his, then the difficulty of excluding Ephesians becomes very great indeed.

The external evidence in favour of Ephesians is very strong. As Renan says, among the Pauline Epistles it ' is perhaps the one of which there are most early quotations as the composition of the Apostle of the Gentiles.' Not only the witnesses between 170 and 220 (Irenæus, Clement of Alexandria, Tertullian, Muratorian Canon) treat it as unquestionably Pauline, but also those who wrote about a century earlier. Marcion (circ. 130) included it in his collection of St. Paul's writings. It is quoted in the Second Epistle of Clement, which may be later than Marcion, and in the ' Shepherd of Hermas,' which may be earlier. It is quoted by Polycarp (circ. 120) and almost certainly by Ignatius, who is a little earlier. Clement of Rome evidently knew the Epistle, and he takes us into the first century (95), within the lifetime of St. John. Above all, it seems to have been known to St. Peter and to St. John, for there are striking parallels between Ephesians and 1 Peter, and between Ephesians and the Revelation. This constitutes a very strong case.

It is the internal evidence which has been supposed to tell against the Epistle, and that mainly on two grounds: (1) the resemblance to Colossians; one Epistle is suspected of being copied from the other by some unknown writer; (2) the form of doctrine. (1) Not much can be made out of the first point. That two letters carried by the same messenger (Tychicus), to Churches in the same part of the world, should often have the same thoughts, and not seldom

---

* For instance, Holtzmann has suggested that some parts of Colossians are genuine ; and he puts together what he supposes to have been the original letter. Some forger took this little letter and expanded it into our Epistle to the Ephesians. Then he was so pleased with the result, that he worked similar additions here and there into the original letter to the Colossians. This patchwork was thought so very superior that it passed at once as St. Paul's, and the genuine letter was lost.

the same language, is just what we might expect ; the salutations, the structure, and the subjects of the two Epistles are very similar ; and there are nearly 80 coincidences of expression in the 155 vv. Compare Huxley's letters written about the same time to different correspondents. On the other hand, assume that only one of the two Epistles is genuine, and that the other is made up from it, and it is impossible to determine which is the original and which is the copy; for in one place Ephesians, and in another place Colossians appears clearly to be original. If both are original, there is no difficulty. (2) Nor is much serious difficulty to be found in the second point. We are told that the kind of Pauline teaching which we find in Ephesians is of a more developed character than the teaching of St. Paul, and therefore belongs to a later age : it reveals a doctrinal standpoint which a disciple of the Apostle might reach, but not St. Paul himself. The doctrine of all Christians making one Church of which Christ is the Head, and of its being through the Spirit (2 22) that Christ abides and works in the Church, is thought to be beyond the earlier teaching of the Apostle. This attempt to put a limit to the amount of growth that would be possible for such a mind as that of St. Paul is arbitrary and uncritical. The advance, as compared with Romans, is not so extraordinary. The equality of Gentiles with Jews in the Church is maintained in both Epistles (Ro 2 1-29 Eph 1 11-15), and in both the universality of the previous corruption is made an argument for the universality of salvation (Ro 3 9-31 Eph 2 1-22). An advance is made in Ephesians, in that here for the first time all Christians are regarded as forming one Ecclesia, or Assembly of God, or Church, of which Christ is the Head (4 3, 4, 12, 13, 15). This development was very natural in one who was writing from Rome, the centre of the civilised world. It does not imply that there are a number of local Churches which all make up one universal Church: that idea might be evidence of a later age: but that, throughout the world, there are many Christian individuals, who are members of a Body, whose Head is Jesus Christ.

2. The Recipients of the Epistle. There is little doubt that Beza was right in supposing that this letter was addressed, not to the Ephesians alone, but to other Churches of Asia also ; and that Archbishop Ussher got still nearer to the truth in regarding it as an encyclical letter, which Tychicus was to take first to Ephesus and then to other Churches, of which Laodicea was one. Our Epistle to the Ephesians is probably ' the Epistle from Laodicea,' which the Colossians were to read, while their own Epistle was to be read at Laodicea (Col 4 16). Our two best MSS (ℵ, B) and the

well-informed corrector of another (67) omit ' at Ephesus ' in Eph 1 1. Origen shows that his text did not contain ' at Ephesus ' ; and St. Basil states that ' at Ephesus ' was omitted both by predecessors of his and in the older MSS. Marcion cannot have had the words. Evidently, from early in the second century, there were copies of the Epistle in which there was a blank after ' to the saints which are,' and the bearer of the letter would fill in the blank according to the place in which he was at the time. Probably each Church made a copy of the letter for its own use before it was sent on, and so large a Church as that of Ephesus would multiply copies, each of them with the words ' at Ephesus ' filled in. This explanation of the omission of 'at Ephesus' in such very early authorities is strongly confirmed by the character of the Epistle itself. It has no local colour, no allusions to special difficulties or dangers, no mention of individuals other than the bearer of the letter. When we consider that St. Paul had lived for three years at Ephesus (Ac 20 31), that he must have been most intimate with the Christians there and their needs, and that not only in earlier letters (as Thessalonians and Corinthians), but also in letters written at the same time as Ephesians (as Colossians and Philemon), he exhibits the keenest interest in local requirements and persons, then the omission of all such things in this Epistle would be inexplicable, if it were addressed to the Ephesians only. If it is addressed to Ephesus and several other Churches, in some of which there were persons who were unknown to him, then the absence of local features is not only natural but necessary. In 1 15 3 2 4 21 he seems to be thinking of people who have not seen him, and perhaps do not know much about him.

3. The Circumstances of the Epistle. St. Paul wrote it when he was ' the prisoner of Christ Jesus ' (3 1), ' the prisoner in the Lord ' (4 1). Does this refer to the two years' imprisonment at Cæsarea, the civil capital of Palestine, or to the two years' imprisonment (which began soon afterwards) at Rome, the capital of the empire ? Such evidence as we have decides for the latter. (1) At Cæsarea the Apostle was in rather close confinement, and strangers would not be likely to come in contact with him. At Rome he lived ' in a hired lodging of his own and received all that went in unto him, preaching the gospel of God .. with all boldness, none forbidding him ' (Ac 28 30, 31). Here Onesimus could easily hear him and be won over to Christianity. Moreover, a runaway slave would be more likely to take refuge in Rome than at Cæsarea. And the imprisonment in which St. Paul converted Onesimus is the imprisonment in which he wrote our Epistle. (2) The whole tone of the Epistle is imperial.

Christ is the Ruler of a world-wide empire, in which every Christian, Jew or Gentile, has equal rights and duties. Such a conception of the Christian commonwealth would arise much more readily in the metropolis of the world, and close to the palace of the Cæsars, than in a provincial town like Cæsarea. The providential purpose of the Roman empire suggests the providential purpose of the Christian Revelation. And thus he writes, not merely to one Christian, as Philemon, and to one particular Church, as Colossæ, but also *urbi et orbi*, to the whole body of Christians ; and one and the same messenger (probably in 63 A.D.) carries these three proofs of the versatility of the Apostle to the Churches of the East.

4. The Contents of the Epistle. After the usual Salutation ($1^{1,2}$), Thanksgiving (1^{3-14}), we have a corresponding Prayer ($1^{15}-2^{10}$), and a Contrast between the unconverted and the converted Gentiles (2^{11-22}). The Apostle's special interest in the Conversion of the Gentiles (3^{1-13}) leads to a return to Prayer for them and a Doxology (3^{14-21}), and then to Exhortations respecting the Unity of the Catholic Church (4^{1-6}) and the Duties of its Members ($4^{7}-6^{9}$), who must be Spiritual Warriors arrayed in the armour of God (6^{10-20}). The Mission of Tychicus ($6^{21,22}$) and the Benediction ($6^{23,24}$) form the conclusion. Let us look at these subjects more closely.

While Colossians sets forth Christ's glory as Head of the Church and of the Universe, Ephesians sets forth the glory of the Church itself, and draws practical conclusions from it. The main idea is the unity of Christians as forming one body with Christ as its unseen Head. All men, whether Jews or Gentiles, are one in the Church, which is the holy Temple of God (2^{20-22}) and the spotless Bride of Christ (5^{25-28}). The existing Church has many imperfections, but the full measure of perfection will at last be realised (4^{13}). And each Christian must labour for this, especially through purified family life ($5^{1}-6^{9}$) ; for the life of the family is a symbol of the life of the Church. Each individual member must have this ideal before him—the perfecting of the unity of the whole body : unless the unity is realised, perfection is impossible. This is what is meant by saying that in this Epistle 'St. Paul has given to his teaching a new centre,' viz. the existence of the Church. Round this the teaching in the Epistle revolves. This new centre is all the more appropriate, when we remember that the Epistle was not addressed to the Ephesians only, but was an open letter to be sent to several Churches in succession.

The Epistle opens with the grand idea of the unity of Creation, which was in God's mind from the first ($1^{4,9,10}$). And this idea is emphasised by the wonderful fact, that the two divisions of the human race, the Jews and the Gentiles, who had hitherto been so bitterly opposed, are henceforth to be blended into one body, with one Head, and one God and Father of all (2^{11-22}). The gospel is not for any one favoured race, but for all mankind. This mystery of the universality of the gospel and of salvation has been revealed to the Apostle (3^{1-13}), who prays that those who accept it may be able to understand it (3^{14-19}). The very thought of such a consummation causes the Apostle to burst out into fervent praise of God, whose glory in the Church and in Christ will continue to grow in successive generations through countless ages ($3^{20,21}$).

To this magnificent idea of unity the Christian life must correspond, by the rightly proportioned and harmonious development of the members of the Christian community, in the body of which Christ is the Head (4^{3-15}). It was not always thus harmonious : the old heathen life (4^{17-19}) was very different from the new Christian life (4^{20-24}). Just consider these particular marks of change for the better ; they are a revolution. There is truthfulness (4^{25}), control of temper ($4^{26,27}$), honest and generous labour (4^{28}), avoidance of bad language and bitterness (4^{29-32}), lovingkindness ($5^{1,2}$), horror of impurity in act or word (5^{3-6}). In short, Christians must be at home, not in darkness and deeds of shame, but in the light which is shed by the presence of Christ (5^{7-14}). This will produce a wise sobriety, in a spirit of thankfulness to God, and of good feeling towards one another (5^{15-21}).

Let us come down to the details of family life ; for the family is the unit of society. Out of families, rather than out of individuals, the Church is built up. There is the duty of wives to husbands and of husband to wives, symbolising the relation between Christ and the Church, just as the family symbolises the Church (5^{22-33}). There is the duty of children to parents and of parents to children (6^{1-4}). And there is the duty of servants to masters and of masters to servants (6^{5-9}). In all these three elements of family life the idea of unity is found once more. Husband and wife, in a mysterious way, are ' one flesh.' The relationship of parent and child, with affectionate education on the one side and affectionate obedience on the other, is ' in the Lord ' ; each is a member of Christ. Both servants and masters have one and the same Master in heaven. And in all three cases there is ' one God and Father of all, who is over all, and through all, and in all.'

But the peacefulness of the family gives only one side of the Christian life ; on another side it is a perpetual warfare against great and unseen powers. Against these spiritual hosts of wickedness the Christian must always be fully armed with weapons equal to the conflict ; and there is a divine equipment of truth and righteousness, faith and salvation, the gospel and the word of God, always at his disposal (6 10-17). But he must not be absorbed in his own contest ; he must remember to pray for all other Christians. Especially let him remember the prisoner that writes this letter, and pray, not that he may be set free, but that even in chains he may have courage to preach the gospel. Tychicus will tell you all about him ; and may God give all of you His grace and love, together with faith to accept these gifts (6 18-24).

The earliest form of the title is 'To the Ephesians'; but even this is not original. Whoever first placed it at the head of the Epistle either made a good guess as to its destination or had 'at Ephesus' (1 1) in his copy. Marcion called it 'To the Laodicenes.'

CHAPTER 1
THANKSGIVING FOR BLESSINGS AND PRAYER FOR WISDOM

1, 2. The salutation. **1.** In the Salutations to the Colossians and to Philemon, written at the same time, 'Timothy the brother' is coupled with St. Paul. He is omitted here because of the general character of the letter. **At Ephesus** was omitted for the same reason (see Intro.). The Apostle takes the whole responsibility of instructing Christians at large respecting 'the whole counsel of God' (Ac 20 27).

2. This is the usual salutation in the Pauline, as in the Petrine Epistles ; 1 and 2 Timothy are exceptions.

3-14. This doxology or thanksgiving should be compared with that in 2 Cor 1 3-11. That is for a special deliverance ; this is for God's general mercy in revealing His purpose to sum up all things in Christ. 'We Jews have long had this promise ; but ye Gentiles also have been sealed with the Holy Spirit as an earnest of the inheritance.' The long sentence, with its accumulated richness of language, shows how difficult St. Paul finds it to express in words the majestic thoughts of which his mind is so full. 'I bless God, who has blessed us with the best of blessings, in virtue of our union with Christ. For this end He selected us from all eternity to live in His presence in holiness and love. All along He destined us to be His sons through the work of Jesus Christ. He did this simply out of His good-will, and to call forth our adoring gratitude. This was His grace to us in Him who is the Beloved, who redeemed us by His death, and freed us from our sins.

What a wealth of grace is this ! It conveys wisdom and understanding ; for He has let us know His secret purpose, which directs and explains the course of ages, to bring all things, both in heaven and on earth, into harmony in Christ. In Christ, I say, in whom we have been chosen as God's portion ; for all along He destined us, according to His all-wise will, that we Jews, who had fixed our hopes on Christ, should live to His glory. And with us Jews, you Gentiles also are now associated by faith in the gospel, and have received the Spirit as a pledge that you are His portion, and that His work of redemption is complete and redounds to His glory.'

3. With **the God of our Lord Jesus Christ** cp. 1 17 Heb 1 9 Jn 20 17 Rev 1 6 3 2, 12. **With all spiritual blessings**] RV 'with every spiritual blessing.' Something much higher than the material, temporal blessings promised in the OT. **In heavenly** *places*] RV 'in the heavenly *places*.' The phrase is found in four other places in Ephesians (1 20 2 6 3 10 6 12), and nowhere else. There is no substantive in the Gk., and we may render, 'among the heavenly things'; the unseen world, in which lie the spiritual forces which oppose us and which help us. Here are the true realities.

4. In history God selected the Jews first, and then the Gentiles ; but the selection of both was made in eternity, independently of time, and through Christ. **In love**] man's love to God and his fellows, not God's love to man (3 17 4 2, 15, 16 5 2). **5.** All are God's children by creation ; but He adopted first the Jews (Ro 9 4), and then believers (Ro 8 15 Gal 4 5), into a special sonship. St. Paul is the only NT. writer who uses this metaphor of adoption, taken from Roman law. **6. To the praise of the glory**] This phrase comes thrice, as a sort of refrain : cp. vv. 12, 14. God's amazing bounty is a glory to be ceaselessly praised.

7. Israel had been redeemed by Jehovah from bondage ; Israelites and Gentiles are redeemed by Christ from sin. **8. Wisdom and prudence**] These are the fruits of God's grace in us ; insight into His counsels and consequent wise conduct : **in all** = in giving us all, etc. **9. Mystery**] In the NT. this means a secret that has been revealed ; a favourite word with St. Paul (3 3, 4, 9 5 32 6 19, etc.) : cp. 2 Esdr 12 36.

10. 'For carrying out a dispensation which was carried out in the fulness of the seasons, so as to gather up in one all things in Christ.' When all the seasons had run out, the final revelation came : cp. 2 Esdr 4 37. **Dispensation**] = (1) office of steward, (2) household management, (3) any provision or arrangement.

13. Ye also] 'ye Gentiles as well as we Jews.' **Sealed with**] 'received the Holy Spirit as a pledge that your deliverance should be complete.' **14.** An **earnest** = Scotch 'arles,' is more than a 'pledge'; it is an instalment handed over in advance, as a guarantee that the remainder will follow (2 Cor 1 ^{22} 5 ^{5}). It is part of the whole to be delivered. **Redemption of the purchased possession**] 'the emancipation of all that God has made His own.'

15.-C. 2 ^{10}. The doxology shades off into prayer that his readers may have wisdom to understand the glory of their inheritance and the great power of God, a power manifested in raising and exalting Christ (vv. 20–23), and in raising and exalting us (2 $^{1-10}$). How great it must be!

15. Heard] This looks as if there were some whom St. Paul had not seen, i.e. others besides Ephesians. **17.** Cp. 2 Esdr 14 $^{22-25}$.

21. The Apostle partly adopts and partly rejects Jewish phraseology about unseen powers. 'Call them what you please, Christ is above them all.' **22.** An echo of Ps 8 $^{5-8}$. If that could be said of man, how much more of Christ! **23.** Cp. the Vine and the branches (Jn 15 ^{5}); Christ is the source of the life and completeness of the Church. But St. Paul seems to mean that Christ is, in a sense, incomplete without the Church. The very idea of Head implies a body. It is doubtful whether the Gk. can mean 'that filleth all in all.' Rather, 'who all in all is being fulfilled, made complete': cp. Col 1 ^{24}.

CHAPTER 2
GENTILES AND JEWS ARE NOW ONE IN CHRIST

1–10. Further illustration of God's power. He raised both Gentiles and Jews from the death of sin and exalted them to Christ's side. **2. The prince of the power of the air**] Jewish phraseology, as in 1 ^{21}. The air is regarded as full of evil powers, with Satan as their prince (6 ^{12} Lk 22 ^{53} Ac 26 ^{18} Col 1 ^{13}). **3. Also we**] 'we Jews were as dead in sins as you Gentiles, and were thus objects of God's wrath' (5 ^{6}).

Had our conversation] RV 'lived.'

5. Quickened us .. with Christ] 'made us, who were morally dead, to share the life of Christ.' **6, 8, 9.** 'No merit of our own has saved us; it is all God's free gift.' **10. Created in Christ Jesus**] He means the new creation, by which the whole human race, reunited in Christ, makes a fresh start (2 ^{14} 4 ^{24} Gal 6 ^{15}). Mankind began as one race; it was split in two; it is now one again.

11–22. 'Ye Gentiles were formerly cut off from Israel and from God's promises. But now Christ's death has broken down the barrier between Gentile and Jew, and reconciled both as one body to God. There are now no strangers: all are fellow-citizens; all are parts of a spiritual temple, in which God, in His Spirit, dwells.'

11. In the flesh] repeated for emphasis;

it was in the flesh that the difference between Jew and Gentile was marked. **Called**] not contemptuous in either place; not 'so-called.' The distinction was real enough, but it has been done away. **12. Without God**] 'Atheists'; the only place where the word occurs in the Bible: the heathen were 'godless.' **13. But now**] The blessed contrast is enlarged upon at four times the length (vv. 13–22) of the original sad condition (vv. 11, 12).

14. He is our peace] emphatic pronoun; 'it is He who is our peace.' **The middle wall of partition** is perhaps an allusion to the warning barrier which marked off the Court of the Gentiles from the higher level of the Court of the Women in the Temple. It was death for a Gentile to pass the barrier. **15.** The Fall of man introduced discord between God and man, and between man and man. The Law revealed this discord. Christ in His humanity fulfilled the Law for man, and set an example of perfect obedience. His humanity united all mankind; His obedience united mankind to God. **16.** A paradox: the Slain slays, and a bloody death, which commonly provokes enmity, slays it. **17.** Exulting repetition of 'peace,' four times in four vv.: cp. Isa 57 ^{19}.

18. Quite incidentally the recognition of Son, Spirit, and Father, comes to the surface: cp. 4 $^{4-6}$ 1 Cor 12 $^{4-6}$ 2 Cor 13 ^{14}. The Apostle habitually thinks of the Godhead as threefold.

19. From the idea of 'Father' he easily passes to that of 'household,' and thence to that of 'a house.' **20.** They are not merely members of the family; they are stones in the structure of the home, in which God Himself dwells: see on 3 ^{5}. **21. All the building**] This is the right meaning: only one building is in the Apostle's mind, as the preceding vv. show. The RV's accuracy is here misleading: cp. 'all' in 1 ^{8} Col 4 ^{12}. **22. Through the Spirit**] RV 'in the Spirit.' It is in the Spirit's dwelling in us that God dwells in us.

CHAPTER 3
REASONS FOR RENEWING THE PRAYER FOR WISDOM

1–13. A digression, which, however, could not be spared. As in 1 ^{15}, he begins to speak of himself, and this time he explains his unique interest in the conversion of the Gentiles. 'Many of his readers had not seen him, but they must have heard of the special work assigned to him by God, of making known to all the mystery of the ages, so that even angelic powers learn through the Church the manysidedness of the Divine counsels.'

1. 'It was worth while becoming a prisoner in such a cause' (Philemon v. 9, 2 Tim 1 ^{8}). **2.** Again the sentence is broken: cp. 1 ^{13} 4 ^{4,5}. His being a prisoner on their behalf suggests a fresh train of thought. If he had been writing to Ephesians only, he could not have said 'if.' Ephesians had heard himself : cp. Col 1 25. **3. Afore in few words**] in the first two chs. **5.** 'The revelation is quite new ; it has been hidden for many generations.' The Apostles and prophets are **holy**, as the readers are **saints** (1 1), as being set apart for God's service ; they had accepted St. Paul's doctrine of salvation for the Gentiles. The prophets are the NT. prophets, as in 2 20 4 11 1 Cor 12 28-31. **6.** This is the mystery that has been revealed.

7. The Apostle of the Gentiles enlarges on the greatness of his special mission. Thrice here he calls it a grace given to him : cp. Gal 2 7-9 Col 1 24. **8. Unsearchable**] inexplorable ; that cannot be traced out. **Riches**] the comprehensiveness and power of the gospel.

9. 'That which for ages has been kept secret from the wisest and holiest is now brought to light for all to see.' **10.** It is an amazing thought that, by means of the Church, God's varied wisdom in the scheme of redemption is made known to heavenly beings. 'Angels desire to look into' 'the manifold grace of God' (1 Pet 1 12 4 10). **11, 12.** God's eternal purpose accomplished in Christ, through faith in whom we have courage to draw near to God. **12.** A repetition of 2 18 : cp. Ro 8 38, 39.

13. That ye faint not] It might mean 'that *I* may not faint.' But St. Paul is not afraid of losing heart ; he rejoiced in tribulations (Ro 5 3), and took pleasure in weaknesses (2 Cor 12 10). He is afraid that the Gentiles may lose heart, when they see him persecuted for helping them : they ought rather to glory in this.

Now he returns to v. 1 after his magnificent digression, and at last gives in fulness the prayer for their enlightenment which he began 1 17. It is a very bold intercession.

14-21. Prayer and doxology. 'May they have great spiritual power, may Christ dwell in their hearts, may they know His incomprehensible love, and be filled up to the measure of God's fulness. To Him, who can give in abundance blessings which we cannot even imagine, be glory for ever.'

14. For this cause] because of their union with the Jews in Christ (2 13-22). The Jews stood to pray (Mt 6 5 Lk 18 11-13), prostration being exceptional ; but Christians are said to kneel (Ac 7 60 9 40 20 36 21 5), perhaps after Lk 22 41.

15. 'All fatherhood, whether earthly or celestial, derives its name from the Fatherhood of God.' **16. The inner man**] is the immaterial part of man's nature, the soul and spirit ; 'the outward man' (2 Cor 4 16) being the flesh.

18. May be able] 'may have *full strength* to comprehend what is really incomprehensible.' The four dimensions represent the *vastness* of

the love of Christ towards us. **19.** An audacious paradox : 'that ye may be filled up to all the fulness of God,' i.e. to the perfection of the Divine attributes (Mt 5 48).

20. The doxology explains the audacity of the prayer. God can give superabundantly quite inconceivable boons. **21. In the Church by Christ Jesus**] RV 'in the Church and in Christ Jesus,' in the Body and in the Head. The Church in this Epistle is always the Church universal, never a local Church. This Church completes the Christ (1 23), reveals God's wisdom to the angels (3 10), is, with Christ, the sphere in which God is glorified. It is indeed a glorious Church (5 27).

CHAPTER 4
UNITY OF THE NEW LIFE. RULES FOR THE NEW LIFE

The Apostle passes, as usual, from doctrinal statements to practical exhortations ; but doctrine is here and there introduced to support exhortation.

1-6. 'Live in humility, in loving forbearance, and in unity, for we have one Body, one Head, and one Heavenly Father.' **1. Prisoner**] This looks back to 3 1. 'He can no longer superintend them : they must walk alone. He lost his liberty in their service : they will do what he asks.' **2.** To a Greek, meekness was a second-rate virtue, and lowliness no virtue at all. The gospel gives both qualities their true position. The nearer man comes to God, the more he feels his own worthlessness, and the member of a vast Church knows his own insignificance. **4.** 'One Body, animated by one Spirit, and cheered by one Hope.'

5. 'One Head, to which each member is united by one Faith and one Baptism.'

6. 'One God, the supreme Source and Sustainer.' **In you all**] RV 'in all.' Throughout the v. the 'all' is vague and may be neuter : we must leave it vague. Note the Trinitarian background : Spirit, Lord, Father.

7-16. 'But the various members have various gifts and functions.'

8. He saith] There is no pronoun in the Greek, and the nominative may be 'it,' 'the Scripture,' viz. Ps 68 18. The important parts of the quotation are 'He ascended' and 'gave gifts.' **Led captivity captive**] i.e. led many captives in His train. These He used as ministers. **9, 10.** The meaning of this obscure passage seems to be this. 'Christ ascended, not to leave His Church an orphan (Jn 14 18), but in order to return to it with the rich gifts of His spiritual presence. The ascent without this subsequent descent would be incomprehensible.' The descent is placed after the ascent, and can hardly refer to either the burial or the descent into Hades. RV omits first.

11. He gave] 'He' is emphatic ; 'He it is

who gave.' **Some, apostles**] RV ' some *to be* apostles '; ' some as Apostles.' ' Some ' is accusative, not dative. St. Paul is speaking of the Church as a whole, and does not mention bishops, presbyters, or deacons, which were local ministers : cp. 1 Cor 12 28 Ro 12 6-8.

12. For .. for .. for] There is a change of preposition, which should be marked in English —*for .. unto .. unto;* and there should be no comma after ' saints.' The saints are perfected with a view to their ministering, to their building up of the Church. **13. Come in the unity**] RV ' attain unto the unity.' A more mature and perfect unity than the Church had at first (2 15), an ideal to work for, resulting in a mature and perfect humanity, endowed with the fulness which Christ, in union with the Church (1 23), has.

14. ' In order to reach this united manhood, we must cease to be a number of unstable children, at the mercy of every scheming teacher.' **15. Speaking the truth in love**] upholding truth without bitterness.

16. Language cannot express the full truth. Christ is the Head. He is also the whole organism. He is also the source of its unity, growth, and energy. Consistency of thought and language is lost in this divine physiology.

17-24. ' How different are the believing Gentiles from the unbelieving ! Believers must beware of retaining anything of the vanity, ignorance, or impurity of the old heathen life.'

17. Walk] He returns from the lofty panegyric of Christian unity to the lower but necessary topic of the Christian ' walk.' He began with ' do ' (4 1) ; here it is nearly all ' do not.'

18. Pagans, ' being darkened in their understanding,' must be alienated from Him in whom is no darkness (1 Jn 1 5). RV substitutes ' hardening ' for **blindness** ; perhaps wrongly.

19. Being past feeling] they ceased to notice the pricks of conscience, and became reckless. In Ro 1 21-24 we have the same sequence : vanity, darkness, uncleanness.

21. Heard him] He is not thinking of the possibility that some of them had heard Christ teach : they ' heard Him ' in listening to the gospel ; heard what He taught on earth. **In Jesus**] St. Paul rarely uses this name by itself ; when he does, he is thinking of the earthly life, death, and rising again. To him Christ is the glorified Christ, ' Jesus Christ,' ' Christ Jesus,' ' the Lord Jesus,' or ' the Lord Jesus Christ.' **22. Put off**] Like filthy, worn-out clothes, the old self had to be put away. **Conversation** has the old meaning of ' manner of life ' (Shakespeare, ' 2 Hen. IV,' v. 5) : cp. 1 Pet 3 2 2 Pet 2 7. **24. The new man which after God hath been created** is that fresh form of humanity, after the first divine pattern, which redemption has produced. **In**

righteousness and true holiness] RV ' in righteousness and holiness of truth.' ' Of truth ' belongs to both substantives.

25-32. Illustrations of the old man : falsehood, vindictiveness, theft, bad language, bad temper ; and, by contrast, of the new.

25. From Zech 8 16. ' How monstrous that members of the same body should deceive one another ! and members of Christ !' **26.** From Ps 4 4. ' Anger may be righteous, but beware of nursing it.' **27. Give place to** means ' give him an opening.' **28.** ' Instead of robbing others, earn something to share with others.'

29. Corrupt communication] bad language of any kind. **To the use of edifying**] RV ' for edifying as the need may be,' i.e. for building up the social fabric as occasion may require, that it may benefit them that hear. **30.** ' The Spirit, who sealed us as His own, is pained when our tongues rebel.' **32.** ' The mercifulness of God forbids our being unmerciful to our brethren : become kind.'

CHAPTER 5
The old Darkness and new Light. Rules for the Married

1, 2. In close connexion with what precedes. ' It is the mark of beloved children to become imitators of a loving Father ; practise the self-sacrifice of Christ, which shows how He loved us and the Father.'

3-14. Special exhortation against covetousness and impurity.

3. But] The five sins mentioned in 4 25-32 are to be put away ; these two are not even to be mentioned : ' saints ' are set apart from such subjects, being consecrated to God. **4.** ' Do not get near these topics for the sake of being amusing.' ' Thanksgiving ' is not an obvious contrast to ' jesting,' but in Gk. there is an alliteration ; not *t*houghtlessness, but *t*hanksgiving. **Convenient**] RV ' befitting.' **5.** ' Those who do these things can have no inheritance in Christ's kingdom.' **6.** ' Sophists tell you that these things are " natural," " venial," " peccadillos." It is just these sins which incur God's wrath.'

7, 8. ' Do not return to your old darkness (4 18) : ye are now light to illuminate others.'

9. Fruit of the Spirit] This comes from Gal 5 22 : ' fruit of the light ' is right here (RV). **10.** ' Those who walk as children of light find out by experience what God's will is : light is always a test.' **11.** Light has ' fruit ' (v. 9), but darkness has only ' fruitless works ' : cp. Gal 5 19,22. **Rather reprove them**] ' rather even expose them,' as light is sure to do. ' Reprove them ' is hardly consistent with the context. In Jn 3 20 ' reproved ' should be ' exposed ' : cp. 1 Cor 14 24. Things so shameful ought not to be passed over.

13. ' But all things when they are exposed

by the light are made manifest ; for whatsoever is made manifest is light.' Light turns darkness into light : this had happened to his readers (v. 8). **14. He saith**] rather, 'it saith ' ='it is said.' The quotation is probably from a Christian hymn, based on Isa 60 1 : cp. 1 Tim 3 16.

15–21. 'Be most careful then in conduct. Beware of folly ; in particular of drunkenness. Prefer spiritual exaltation and an orderly life, each in his own place.'

15. Then or 'therefore' marks the return to exhortation, and **walk** refers back to vv. 2, 8. RV is everywhere better : ' Look therefore carefully how ye walk, not as unwise, but as wise.' **16. Redeeming**] 'buying up for yourselves the opportunity.' **17.** 'Wherefore do not show yourselves fools, but understand.'

18. Excess] RV ' riot ' (as Tit 1 6 1 Pet 4 4), and ' riotous living ' (Lk 15 13). **With the Spirit**] RM ' in spirit ' ; ' not your bodies, but your souls should be full.' **19.** The primitive Church was emphatically a Church of enthusiasm and spiritual emotion (Ac 2 43-47 8 8 16 25 : cp. Col 3 16). **21.** But everything is to ' be done decently and in order ' : enthusiasm is not to lead to anarchy. St. Paul ceaselessly preaches ' submission ' or ' subjection ' to authority (Ro 13 1-7 1 Cor 14 32, 34 16 16 Tit 3 1).

22–33. First illustration of orderly subordination ; the relation between wives and husbands.

22. As unto the Lord] with ' the fear of Christ ' (v. 21) as their motive. **23.** Once more (3 15) a mystical connexion between heavenly and earthly relationships is traced. The forethought of the head preserves the body : control implies obligation to protect.

24. Accepting protection implies submission.

25–33. The love of husbands to their wives corresponds to Christ's love to His Church, for which He sacrificed Himself, to hallow it, to present it to Himself, and to *keep* it holy. Christ and the Church are one in body ; husband and wife are one in body ; hence Christ's love for His Church is that of husband for bride. Of marriage it is wonderfully said that two become one. This is true of Christ and the Church. And as the Church responds to Christ's love with reverential fear, so let the wife have reverential fear of her husband.

25. Government must be unselfish—for the good of the governed : cp. v. 2. **26. Washing of water**] Christian baptism, with perhaps a reference to the bride's bath before marriage.

By the word] RV 'with the word,' to be taken with ' the washing of water ' and meaning the baptismal formula. **27.** 'That He might Himself to Himself present the Church all-glorious ': cp. 2 Cor 11 2, of St. Paul's presenting the Corinthian Church to Christ.

28. RV 'Even so ought husbands also to love their own wives as [being] their own bodies.' Not 'as much as,' or 'as if they were ': their wives *are* their own bodies.

29. The change from ' body ' to ' flesh ' prepares for what is coming. **30.** ' Christ cherishes the Church, because its members are His.' The words ' of His flesh and of His bones ' are an interpolation from Gn 2 23.

32. This is a great mystery] RV ' This mystery is great.' ' It has a deep, wide-reaching meaning ; but I am employing it of Christ and the Church.' **33. Reverence**] RV ' fear.' He returns to the motive stated at the outset, ' the fear of Christ ' (v. 21). Reverential fear, as that of the Church to her Lord, is meant. Subjection without reverence would be servile.

CHAPTER 6

RULES FOR THE FAMILY. THE CHRISTIAN'S ARMOUR

1–4. Second illustration of orderly subordination : the relation between children and parents.

1. As before, those who have to obey and submit are taken first. Cp. **in the Lord** here with ' unto the Lord ' (5 22) and ' unto Christ ' (v. 5). **Right**] both nature and the express Law of God enjoin it. **2. With promise**] the first which is accompanied with a promise : cp. ' *with* the word ' (5 26). We might punctuate, ' the first commandment, with promise that it may be well,' etc. **3.** On the other hand, disobedience to parents is very heinous (Ro 1 30 2 Tim 3 2). **4. And**] 'Parents also have their obligations : they must (1) not be unreasonable in their demands on their children ; (2) give godly discipline.' He says ' fathers,' because mothers would be less likely to be too severe or to control the education.

Nurture] RV ' chastening ' (Heb 12 5, 7, 8, 11) : in 2 Tim 3 16, ' instruction.' **Of the Lord** means ' such as God would provide ': cp. ' of God,' v. 11.

5–9. Third illustration : the relation between servants and masters.

5. Servants] All servants then were *slaves ;* and St. Paul says ' slaves ': ' be obedient to ' might be ' obey,' as in v. 1 : ' according to the flesh ' = earthly. **With fear and trembling**] ' very anxious to do well ': it does not imply a harsh master (2 Cor 7 15 Phil 2 12). **6.** Christianity gives no sanction to rebellion : it elevates and intensifies the duty of obedience. **From the heart**] These words may be taken with what follows ; ' from the soul with good-will doing service.' **7.** ' Obedience must be not only thorough, but hearty : temper is all-important.' **8.** ' Good conduct, whether of slave or lord, will be fully requited by Him who is Lord of both.' **9.** ' Masters, like husbands and parents, have *their* obligations ; they also must have good-temper and good-will, and be God-fearing.' St. Paul does not

965

tell them to emancipate their slaves ;. but he tells them to love them as brethren (Philemon v. 16). This does not free the slave, but it frees slavery of its evils.

10–20. The final charge is, 'Be strong, and find your strength in the Lord. Be armed with God's armour ; for we have to contend, not with earthly foes, but with spiritual powers of great wickedness. Watch and pray ceaselessly for the whole Church and for me, that I may be a courageous missionary, even in prison.'

10. My brethren] an insertion from Phil 3[1]: cp. 2 Cor 13[11] Phil 3[1] 2 Th 3[1]. **Be strong**] lit. 'be strengthened' (Ro 4[20]). **11. Whole armour**] 'Nothing must be missing of the full provision which God makes for our safety.' St. Paul omits the spear or pike and the greaves of the Roman soldier, yet mentions being girded and shod, which most men are, but soldiers must be. **12.** The malignant powers, by which the wiles or stratagems of the devil are carried out, are specified. The passage is tinged by Jewish ideas about the unseen world. **The rulers of the darkness of this world**] This fairly represents the Gk., which means powers of darkness, that are rulers of this world, but not rulers of the universe : cp. 1[21] 3[10] Col 1[16] 2[15]. **In the heavenly places** (RV)] 'In the spiritual world' : but the Jews contemplated the possibility of evil in some of their seven heavens.

13. 'Against these superhuman powers nothing less than the whole armour of God will suffice ; but with that the Christian warrior is safe.' **14.** The Septuagint of Isa 11[5] and 59[17] is in the Apostle's mind : there it is Jehovah who wears the panoply. **15. The preparation**] 'readiness' to preach the good-tidings of peace : cp. Isa 52[7]. The Christian warrior fights to bring peace. **16.** 'Fire-tipt darts' is a metaphor for fierce temptations coming from the outside. Faith in God is a sure protection against them. **17. Take**] 'Receive from God who supplies the panoply, and whose Spirit furnishes the sword, the helmet that is salvation.' He is thinking of Isa 11[4] : cp. Heb 4[12]. **18.** The thought of the sword furnished by the Spirit, 'who

maketh intercession for us' (Ro 8[26]), naturally leads on to the thought of prayer : 'receive this sword, with all prayer and supplication praying in every season (1 Th 5[17]) in the Spirit.' **Watching**] as a trusty warrior should (Lk 21[36]). **19. For me**] RV 'on my behalf,' there being a change of preposition in the Gk. : cp. Col 4[2,3]. **Boldly**] This probably belongs to what follows, as RV 'that utterance may be given unto me in opening my mouth, to make known with boldness,' etc. 'Pray that all this may be granted to me.' **20. Am an ambassador in bonds**] RV 'in chains' : mg. 'in a chain.' The singular *may* refer to the coupling-chain by which he could be attached to the soldier that guarded him. In any case, that an ambassador, whose person was inviolate, should be chained, was a paradox.

21, 22. The Mission of Tychicus : almost verbatim as Col 4[7,8]. Tychicus is the bearer of both letters, and of that to Philemon : cp. Ac 20[4] 2 Tim 4[12] Tit 3[12]. By long service he well earned the title of 'faithful minister.'

23, 24. Concluding Benediction.

Note the omission of all personal salutations and similar details, of which we have eight vv. in the Epistle to the Colossians. This is a circular letter to several Churches, and hence no individuals are mentioned. Note also the change to the third person, 'to the brethren .. all them that love our Lord.' In Colossians, as elsewhere, he says 'you.' In two other points this benediction differs from that in other letters. It is twofold, not single ; **Peace** *be* **to, Grace** *be* **with** ; and 'Peace' is placed before, not after 'Grace.' Contrast Ro 1[7] 1 Cor 1[3] 2 Cor 1[2] Gal 1[3] Col 1[2], etc. An imitator would have copied other Epistles.

24. Sincerity] It is doubtful whether the Gk. can mean this ; better, 'incorruption' (1 Cor 15[42,50,53,54]) or 'incorruptibility.' It is those who love with an imperishable love that are meant : there must be neither decrease nor decay. 'Those who were "chosen in Him before the foundation of the world" (1[4]) retain their love for Him undiminished after the world itself has passed away.'

A worthy conclusion to this immortal Epistle !

PHILIPPIANS

INTRODUCTION

1. Writer and Readers. The community of 'the saints in Christ Jesus' at Philippi had existed ten years or more when this letter was addressed to them, in 61 or 62 A.D. It was founded by the two 'servants of Christ Jesus' whose names head the letter, along with St. Silas (Silvanus, 1 Th 1[1], etc.), St. Paul's colleague on the second of his great missionary journeys (49–53 A.D. : see Ac 15[36]–18[21]).

The graphic story of the coming of the gospel to Philippi in Ac 16 is from the pen of an eye-witness; from v. 10 to v. 16 the narrative runs in the first person plural, which reappears in 20[5,6] at a point six years later, when St. Luke, presumably, re-joined the Apostle at Philippi.

Philippi (in form a Gk. plural)—earlier Crenides—bore the name of Philip, father of Alexander the Great, who gave the place importance. It guarded the eastern frontier of Macedonia, and commanded the pass leading from the interior plains to the Ægean Sea at Neapolis (Ac 16[11]). This was the first station for a traveller from the E. along the Via Egnatia, the Roman highway across the Balkan peninsula; here St. Paul first halted in his invasion of Europe, and the Philippian Church was the earliest fruit of his labours in our continent. The town had given its name to the famous battle, fought in 42 B.C., in which Antony and Octavian crushed the Republicans of Rome under Brutus and Cassius. In commemoration of that victory Philippi was raised to the rank of a military 'colony,' a body of discharged soldiers being settled there. The colonists were free citizens, enjoying exemption from poll-tax and tribute, and the right of holding the land in full ownership. Such communities were regarded as detached portions of the Roman State, and took no little pride in their connexion with the imperial city. The Philippian officials are designated, in Roman style, 'prætors' and 'lictors' in Ac 16 (AV 'magistrates' and 'serjeants'); they beat the prisoners with the Roman 'rods.' 'Being Romans,' the people of Philippi resent the introduction of 'unlawful' Jewish 'customs' (Ac 16[20,21]). Hence also the emphasis and effect with which the Apostle and his companion assert here their Roman citizenship. Though but a fraction of the Church may have belonged to the privileged class holding the Italian franchise, the civil status of the 'colony' affected all its inhabitants; the meanest Philip-

pian was sensible of the dignity of his city. Twice in this letter St. Paul describes the Christian status as a 'citizenship' (1[27] 3[20] : see RV, and mg.). The 'colonial' sentiment of Philippi doubtless heightened the interest with which the readers watched the course of their Apostle's trial and entered into his experiences at Rome.

Behind the offended civic pride of Philippi there lay the vulgar motive of 'gain' (Ac 16[19]), which in the first instance awakened hostility to the Christian teaching in this place. Wherever the gospel won heathen converts, it injured the vested interests of paganism. In Philippi St. Paul silenced a soothsaying slave-girl, and her masters, seeing their unholy property spoilt, dragged the offenders before the rulers and roused the populace against them. The indignities which SS. Paul and Silas suffered under this attack (cp. 1 Th 2[2] with Ac 16), were the beginning of a persecution that has continued to the time of writing; in such experience the Church is identified with its Apostle ; see Phil 1[5, 29, 30] 2[15], and cp. 2 Cor 8[1,2]. From the first it has had to 'struggle for the faith of the gospel' (1[27]).

Judaism counted for little in Philippi. Instead of a synagogue, there was only a *proseucha* ('praying-place')—probably a retired open-air resort—by the river-banks outside the town, where the missionaries found a company of women assembled on the sabbath (Ac 16[13]). Out of this band the first Christian disciple, Lydia of Thyatira, was gained, and probably the women named in 4[2,3] (see note). The circle, it may be presumed, was Jewish only in part. St. Paul gathered his converts and helpers largely from the constituency of intelligent and pious Gentiles (more often women than men) who frequented Jewish worship as 'proselytes' or 'fearers of God,' and had been grounded in the OT. Women took a leading part in the Philippian Church at the outset; Macedonia was distinguished in Greek society by the greater freedom and influence allowed to their sex.

Since the events of Ac 16 and 17, St. Paul had twice traversed Macedonia, and accordingly visited Philippi: first on his way from Ephesus, through Troas, to Corinth toward the end of the Third Missionary Tour in the spring of the year 56 (1 Cor 16[5]); and again on leaving Corinth in the following spring, when he kept

967

Easter there (Ac 20 [1-6]). From 2 Cor 1 [8-11] 2 [12, 13] 7 [4-12] we gather that the Apostle was at the period of the former of these two visits in great trouble, suffering from prostrating bodily sickness and from anxiety about the Corinthian and (probably) the Galatian Churches, whose loyalty at that juncture hung in doubt: see Gal 1 [6-9] 3 [1, 4, 20] 5 [2]; cp. 2 Cor 11 [28]. Arriving in such a plight in Macedonia, Philippi would be his harbour of refuge; there, we imagine, he passed the crisis of his illness, under St. Luke's skilful care (see par. 2 above). These intervening visits, though not recalled in the Epistle, help to account for the intimacy it reveals between writer and readers; they serve to justify the words of 1 [5] implying a continuous intercourse, and give a fuller meaning to the language of 2 [1], which speaks of mutual 'consolation' and 'compassions.'

Although 'Timothy' figures along with 'Paul' in the Address—for the former is with the Apostle at the time of writing and is well known to the readers (2 [22]), and therefore shares in the Salutation—the letter proceeds from St. Paul alone, running in the first person singular throughout (otherwise than in 1 Th and 2 Cor 1–7); St. Timothy is referred to in the course of the letter (2 [19-23]), just like Epaphroditus, in the third person.

The writer is a prisoner awaiting trial, and at Rome; he is in sight of the end of his captivity there, which extended over two years (62 A.D.: see Ac 28 [30, 31]). His 'appeal to Cæsar' is at last to be decided (1 [20] 2 [23, 24]). The Apostle has been long enough in Rome, and free enough despite his 'bonds' (as Ac 28 [15, 16, 30, 31] intimates), to make his influence widely felt in various directions (1 [12-16] 4 [22]). If 'in the prætorium' (1 [13]; see note) means 'amongst the prætorian troops,' the impression made on the army is accounted for by the succession of guards put in charge of the prisoner at his lodging; if it means, as Sir W. M. Ramsay suggests, 'in the prætorian court,' then the judicial trial is proceeding, and the accused has been removed to prison-quarters.

2. Occasion of the Letter. Beyond others, the Philippians were grateful and devoted to the Apostle Paul (1 [5] 4 [15]). Lydia's insistent hospitality at the beginning (Ac 16 [15]) was typical of this Church's character: cp. 2 Cor 8 [1-4]. Twice it had sent aid to St. Paul in Thessalonica on his first departure, and subsequently when he left Macedonia for Achaia; now their care for him has 'blossomed anew'; Epaphroditus had been dispatched with a sum of money for his necessities, under instructions to stay and assist the Apostle in Rome (2 [25, 30] 4 [10-18]). The good man fell dangerously ill upon his errand, and after his recovery is longing for home; St. Paul sends him back therefore, and this letter with him. Epaphroditus

brought tidings from the Philippians in conveying their gift; and further communications had taken place since his arrival, for the Philippians have heard of the illness of their deputy and he is informed of their grief over this (2 [26]). They seem to have written quite recently to St. Paul, expressing their anxiety about his trial, betraying also—to judge from the tone of his reply—some despondency under the protracted afflictions falling on themselves, and some concern about the manner in which their present had been received: see on 4 [10]. We must bear in mind that the extant Epistles are extracts from a larger correspondence; to read them properly, we need to hear the other side and to reproduce by imagination, between the lines, the messages and requests to which the writer is replying.

There was no error of doctrine, no grave faultiness of life to reprove in this Church—only a certain want of harmony amongst its leading members (4 [2, 3]); the removal of this defect will 'fill up' the Apostle's 'joy' (2 [2-5]). The prayer of 1 [9, 10] and the exhortation of 4 [8] (see notes) hint at a deficiency in moral enlightenment and appreciation, such as not unfrequently accompanies religious zeal and lively affections. The warning against Jewish intriguers in 3 [2-11] was prompted by the writer's present experience and by the general peril from this cause, rather than by any Judaising tendency on the part of the readers: see on 3 [1b].

3. Contents of the Letter. The Epistle to the Philippians was strictly a letter, the unconstrained outflow of St. Paul's heart. Hence its delightful desultoriness. It has no burning controversy, no absorbing doctrinal theme, no difficult moral problems to deal with. The recent communications from Philippi supply the starting-point, and are glanced at as occasion serves; but they scarcely control the composition. The Epistle does not admit therefore of formal analysis; its links of association are those of feeling and of memory, not of logic.

The opening phrase of c. 3 divides the writing into its two parts—principal (chs. 1, 2) and supplementary (chs. 3, 4). The latter section runs, beyond the writer's intention, to a length equalling that of the former: the repetition of the 'Finally' of 3 [1] in 4 [8] indicates that his thought has made an excursion.

The division of the first and main half of the letter falls at v. 26 of c. 1. After the prefatory thanksgiving and prayer (1 [3-11]), the Apostle begins by reassuring the Philippians about his own situation (vv. 12–26); with v. 27 he turns from himself to *them*, exhorting them to the behaviour that will cheer him, and ensure their victory in the common conflict. The above three divisions—1 [3-11] 1 [12-26] 1 [27]– 2 [18]—are linked by the thought of 'the gospel,' which is the ground of union between writer and readers : see $1^{5, 12, 27}$ 2^{16} ('word of life').

Having told the Philippians what they wish to hear about him (1^{12-26}), and what he wishes to see in them ($1^{27}-2^{18}$), the Apostle further states what he intends to do for them, by sending Epaphroditus, and then Timothy, hoping himself to come ere long, so that their hearts and his may be mutually refreshed (2^{19-30}).

At 3^1 the Epistle seems to be concluding. Had the writer proceeded at once from this point to c. 4, 3^{2-21} would never have been missed. This long passage is an unpremeditated outburst—by a few critics mistakenly regarded as an editorial interpolation from another letter, by others attributed to some provocation that interrupted the Apostle in the act of writing. Three distinct classes of errorists appear to be stigmatised in c. 3—the first and last being of a virulent type. Vv. 2, 3 denounce St. Paul's old enemies, the zealots for Jewish Law ; vv. 17–21 combat the Gentile tendency to sensual licence. The common reference to the writer's personal example binds these denunciatory paragraphs together (see also 4^9) : against legalist pretensions he sets forth his experience as a Jewish Christian believer (vv. 4–11) ; the sensualists are shamed by the purity and loftiness of the Christian life exhibited in himself and those like-minded (vv. 17–21). The bearing of the intervening paragraph (vv. 12–16) is more difficult to seize : the Judaists are, seemingly, forgotten, the Antinomians not yet in sight ; the Apostle at this point is contrasting himself with pretenders to perfection, with Christians who deem themselves already at the goal, denying the future resurrection (v. 11), and renouncing the aspirations after the heavenly state that were so strongly cherished by St. Paul : see on vv. 3, 12, 15. Nothing could show more affectingly the Apostle's deep communion with the readers and the ascendency of his character, than this frank unlocking of his heart to them and the use he makes for their benefit of his most sacred experiences. So the after-thought forms the most precious part of this Epistle.

The actual conclusion in c. 4 consists of a brief homily, partly personal, partly general in scope (vv. 4–9) ; followed by an acknowledgment of the Philippian bounty (vv. 10–20) —probably the chief subject in the writer's mind when he intended finishing the letter at 3^1 ; and the final good wishes (vv. 21–23). The scheme of the Epistle on which this exposition is based is as follows :—

§ 1. Address and Salutation ($1^{1, 2}$).

I. ACT OF PRAISE AND PRAYER.

§ 2. Thanksgiving for Fellowship in the Gospel (3–8). § 3. Prayer for the perfecting of Love in Knowledge (9–11).

II. ABOUT PAUL'S AFFAIRS.

§ 4. The Gospel furthered by his Troubles ($12-18^a$). § 5. The Twofold Issue confronting him (18^b-26).

III. HOW PAUL'S COMRADES MAY SUPPORT HIM.

§ 6. By brave Loyalty in face of Persecution (27–30). § 7. By a self-effacing Love to each other, fashioned after that of Christ (2^{1-11}). § 8. By working out in his Absence their Salvation, so that his Ministry may be crowned with Joy (12–18).

IV. THE APPROACHING VISITS.

§ 9. The speedy Coming of Timothy—probably of Paul himself after a while (19–24). § 10. The immediate Return of Epaphroditus (25–30).

V. INTERJECTED WARNINGS.

§ 11. St. Paul and his Jewish Rivals (3^{1-6}). § 12. Losing all, to win Christ (7–11). § 13. The Christian Goal (12–16). § 14. The earthward and the heavenward-bent Mind (17–21).

VI. CLOSING EXHORTATIONS.

§ 15. Personal Differences in the Church (4^{1-3}). § 16. The Christian Temper (4–7). § 17. The Largeness of Christian Ethics (8, 9).

VII. ACKNOWLEDGMENT OF THE CONTRIBUTION FROM PHILIPPI.

§ 18. A Bounty welcome to the Apostle, notwithstanding his Independence (10–16). § 19. St. Paul's Reflexions upon the Gift (17–20). § 20. Salutations from Rome, and Benediction (21–23).

4. Character of the Letter, and its place among St. Paul's Writings. This Epistle is a letter of friendship, full of affection, confidence, good counsel and good cheer. It is the happiest of St. Paul's writings, for the Philippians were the dearest of his children in the faith : 'Summa epistolæ,' writes Bengel, 'Gaudeo, gaudete' (One word sums up the Epistle : I rejoice ; do you rejoice !). 'From the first day until now' the communion between the writer and his 'beloved and longed for' has been unbroken and unclouded.

The letter is, therefore, one of self-revelation ; it is a classic of spiritual autobiography. St. Paul writes here at his ease ; he makes those spontaneous disclosures of the inner self which only the tenderest sympathy can elicit. While 2 Corinthians displays the agitations which rent the Apostle's heart in the crucial conflict of his ministry, Philippians reveals the spring of his inward peace and strength. It admits us to St. Paul's prison meditations and communings with his Master. We watch his spirit ripening through the autumn hours when patience fulfilled in him its perfect work. This Epistle holds a cardinal place in the history of

St. Paul's character, such as Galatians holds in the history of his doctrine. It exhibits an unsurpassed picture of selfless devotion, manly fortitude, and joyous Christian hope; well may the writer say, 'I can do all things in Him that enables me!'

While kindred in language and thought to the other Letters of the First Roman Captivity —Ephesians, Colossians, and Philemon—Philippians stands somewhat apart from these three; the question of priority as between it and them is disputed. From the fact that it was written toward the close of the imprisonment when the Apostle had been for a considerable time in Rome (see last par. of I above), and from other indications, we judge that Philippians was the latest of the group. The opening prayer recalls those of Ephesians and Colossians, which also turn on the connexion of *knowledge and love;* vv. 12–16 of ch. 3 (see notes) are best understood as alluding to notions kindred to the Colossian error. The Christological passage of Phil 2 5-11 comes from a mind full of the grand conception of the glory of Christ that St. Paul has developed in Colossians. This paragraph, and the sentence concerning Justification by Faith in 3 9, go to show that the characteristic doctrines of St. Paul's Epistles were as far as possible from being abstract theorems or passing phases of thought due to controversial exigencies. The ideas they express present themselves in a spontaneous, unstudied fashion; for they belonged to the staple of the writer's thought, and were the outcome of his vital experience of salvation through Christ.

C. 3 reminds us rather of the Letters of the Second Group: vv. 14, 17, 18, 21 of 1 Cor; vv. 4–6 of 2 Cor; vv. 2, 16 of Gal; and, above all, vv. 9–11 of Ro. It is for this reason chiefly that some leading scholars place Philippians first in the Third Group of the Epistles, nearest to those just mentioned. The resemblance is explained by the consideration that when touching upon Judaistic questions St. Paul's mind inevitably fell into the vein of Romans and Galatians.

The expressions of 1 23 and 2 16, 17, anticipating the writer's death, are in the vein of 2 Tim, the Apostle's farewell letter; while the simplicity and cordiality pervading Philippians recall the strain of his earliest, the First to the (Macedonian) Thessalonians. Thus Philippians combines traits of most of the other Epistles; it mirrors *the whole Paul.* At once it touches the summits of his loftiest doctrine, and sounds the depths of his mystic consciousness.

The writing and the man are inseparably one. By a consent in which the severest criticism shares, Philippians is ranged with the great quaternion of the Second Group (Romans, 1 and 2 Corinthians, Galatians) as amongst the things most certainly genuine and Pauline. Erasmus' sentence is a sufficient verdict on opinions to the contrary: 'Nemo potest Paulinum pectus effingere' (One cannot feign a heart like Paul's!).

5. St. Polycarp and St. Paul. Some fifty years later the Philippian Church received a letter, that it has preserved, from Polycarp, the martyr-bishop of Smyrna, in which this remarkable testimony is found (3 2): 'Neither I nor any one like me can follow up the wisdom of the blessed and glorious Paul, who when he was amongst you, confronting the men of that day, taught with exactness and sureness the doctrine concerning truth; who also when absent wrote [a] letter[s] to you, by the close study of which you will be able to build yourselves up in the faith that was given you.' St. Polycarp seems to refer, in speaking of *letters*, to more than one Epistle of St. Paul as then extant and used at Philippi —though it is possible, grammatically, that the Gk. plural bore (like *litteræ* in Latin) a singular sense. It is more than likely that the Apostle wrote repeatedly to the Philippians; and if so, several of his letters may well have survived into the 2nd cent., though but one of these found a place in the canonical collection. More important is it to observe the reverence paid to St. Paul by one whom tradition associates with the school of the Apostle John, and whose cast of mind was far from Pauline, and the sense diffused through the Church in the generation following St. Paul of the unique inspiration and authority that attached to his written word: cp. 2 Pet 3 15, 16; also the Epistle of Clement to the Corinthians, chs. 5 and 47; of Ignatius to the Ephesians, 12. 2, and to the Romans, 4. 3. Polycarp's gracious Epistle to the Philippians reads like an echo of the NT.; Paul's Epistle to the Philippians breathes in every line the freshness and power of the original Christian inspiration.

[Note. The writer comments usually on the revised Text, which is accordingly printed in heavy type.]

CHAPTER 1

The Prisoner Apostle in Rome

§ 1. **Address and Salutation** (1 1, 2).

1 1, 2. The form of greeting in 1 1, 2 is that common to the Epistles of the third group.

1. To all the saints] holy persons—consecrated to God as all Christian believers are. This and similar emphatic expressions (in vv. 3, 4, 7, 8, 25, c. 4 2) show that the entire Church, despite differences between its members (2 2,3 4 2), has the Apostle's confidence. Only in this Epistle are the Church officers singled out in the address; probably because they figured in the letter of the Church, to which St. Paul is replying : see Intro. **Bishops and deacons]** ' overseers' and 'attendants'—associated here for the first time in NT.—are the superior and subordinate officers of the local Church. ' Bishops' appear to be the same as the 'presidents' ('those that are over you') of 1 Th 5 12, the 'pastors' of Eph 4 11 (cp. 1 Pet 2 25), and the more familiar 'elders' of Ac 14 23 1 Tim 5 17-19 Tit 1 5-9, etc. : see Ac 20 17,28 (RV), and 1 Pet 5 1-4, for the identity. The same persons might be called 'elders' in respect of status, and ' overseers' in respect of duty. At this early stage of development, there was no strict uniformity of title or function in the offices held in various Churches. *Episkopos* (bishop) was a name for persons charged with administrative or financial responsibility in Greek communities ; and this title may have been adopted by the Hellenic Churches. ' Deacon' (*diakonos*) represents the every-day word for ' servant,' 'attendant,' as in Mt 20 26 Ro 13 4, etc. For further elucidation, see notes on these words in the Pastoral Epistles. **2. Grace]** is God's forgiving and redeeming love to men : see Ro 4 24–5 2, 17-21 Eph 1 6,7 2 7,8, etc.

I. ACT OF PRAISE AND PRAYER (1 3-11)

§ 2. 1 3-8. The characteristically Pauline Thanksgiving, vv. 3-6, runs into a chain of participial sentences loaded with adverbial clauses, the connexion of which is not always certain. V. 5 accounts for the **joy** attending St. Paul's supplications for his readers as due to their unbroken **fellowship** with him ; and v. 6 declares the assurance of complete success that animates his prayers. The rendering **of this very thing**, in v. 6, is difficult to justify ; say rather, 'being confident on this very account—viz. because of your steadfast fellowship with me—that God will consummate in you what He has so signally begun.'

7. The assurance above expressed is supported by the reflexion that **it is right to cherish these thoughts**—of thankfulness, joy, trust—about you all, **since I hold you in my heart . . as being all of you fellow-partakers with me in grace:** i.e. the Philippians are so entirely bound up with the Apostle in the cause of the gospel, that it would be wrong and an ill-requital of their devotion to entertain any other thoughts of them. He is conscious of their communion **both in his bonds**, which they share by sympathy and by the presence of Epaphroditus (2 25, 30), **and in the defence and confirmation of the gospel**—the negative and positive sides of his ministry in Rome, where he both vindicates the cause of Christ and demonstrates its saving power : cp. Eph 6 19, 20. **8.** A solemn attestation of the heart-union just declared. To **yearn over** one **in the heart of Christ Jesus is** to love him with the depth and tenderness

of His affection : cp. Jn 13 34, and on 4 1. **Bowels]** RV 'tender mercies.'

§ 3. 1 9-11. The Prayer of vv. 9–11 recognises the **love** exhibited in the 'fellowship' of the readers with St. Paul (v. 5), desiring that it may be enriched by intelligence and moral tact. The Gk. term here used for **knowledge,** characteristic of the letters of this group, signifies 'advanced, thorough knowledge' ; the word rendered **discernment** (RV)—here only in NT.—containing the root of 'æsthetics,' belongs to the region of taste, rather than **judgment** (AV). Strong in affection and zeal, the Philippians needed a more enlightened conscience (see on 4 8), in order to **prove the things that differ** (RM : cp. 1 Th 5 21 Heb 5 12).

Sincere] (= clear, translucent) implies purity of disposition ; **void of offence,** faultlessness of conduct : for attaining such perfection, approved at **the day of Christ,** a fine moral intelligence, as well as a right intention, is needful. The emphasis of v. 11 rests on **filled** (made complete) ; and **fruit of righteousness** embraces all the moral issues of the righteousness of faith (see 3 9), abounding to **the glory . . of God** (cp. Jn 15 8).

II. ABOUT PAUL'S AFFAIRS (1 12-26)

§ 4. 1 12-18 a. The supreme interest of writer and readers alike (cp. vv. 5-7) lies in 'the progress of the gospel.' The news from Rome about St. Paul troubled the Philippians on this account, and their alarm had been expressed in their recent letter : see Intro. He hastens to reassure them : **the things that have befallen me have turned out rather to the progress of the gospel. 13. My bonds have become manifest in Christ]** means that the writer, instead of being thrust out of sight, as the Philippians fear, is conspicuous at Rome as Christ's messenger : cp. Eph 6 20. His prison-lodging has become a vantage-ground : see Ac 28 30, 31; his trial is favourably advertising the gospel. **The whole Prætorian guard]** ('all the palace,' wrongly, AV ; RM ' the whole Prætorium') the corps of troops attached to the imperial head-quarters—had heard of it, presumably through the men told off in turn to guard the prisoner, who was chained by the wrist to his keeper **night and day ; all the rest** signifies the Roman public, who freely visited the distinguished prisoner.

Vv. 14–18 describe the effect of this turn of events on the Roman Church. Some of its members may have been discouraged ; but **most of the brethren in the Lord . . are more abundantly bold,** etc. St. Paul's cheerful confidence, at the same time the respect shown to him in his captivity and the likelihood of his acquittal, encouraged the majority; his trial, so far, went to clear Christianity **of** anything criminal in the eyes of the State. Hence the Roman Christians, beyond expectation, have gained confidence by his bonds.

St. Paul's presence stimulates Christian work at Rome in two opposite ways. **15.** Some in their bolder testimony are actuated by **envy and strife ; some by good will**—he rejoices in the activity of both parties! (v. 18ᵃ). Both, it is clear, are proclaiming a true gospel, and the Apostle's ill-wishers cannot have been preaching the 'other (Judaising) gospel' condemned in Gal 1⁶. Personal dislike actuated the latter ; they were jealous of St. Paul's ascendency, and regarded him as an interloper —a disposition only too natural in a Church of which he was not the founder: cp. Ro 15¹⁵⁻¹⁸. These rivals meanly **think to add affliction to his bonds**—supposing that he would be chagrined by their success ! They **proclaim Christ** therefore **not sincerely** (not in a pure spirit), but **in pretence** (vv. 16, 18) ; and St. Paul, though glad that their work is making Christ's name more widely known, censures its motives. The better sort preach **of love and in truth** (with consistent motives), recognising in the prisoner-apostle the champion of the gospel. Observe the reversal in vv. 16, 17, according to RV, of the order of the two parties distinguished in v. 15.

§ 5. ₁¹⁸ᵇ⁻²⁶. With the last clause of v. 18 (before which it is better to place a full stop) St. Paul turns from the present to the future: **Yes, and I will rejoice ; for I know,** etc. **This** (v. 19), like **therein** (v. 18), embraces the whole situation described in vv. 12–18, which while furthering the gospel (v. 12) **will turn to** St. Paul's final **salvation:** cp. 1 Cor 9²³ 2 Tim 4¹⁸. In his humility, the Apostle regards this issue as depending on **your supplication and ministry of the Spirit of Jesus Christ** (cp. Gal 3⁵), of whose influence his friends' prayers bring him richer supplies: cp. 2 Th 3¹¹. **20.** The above result accords with the writer's **eager expectation and hope,** that in any event **Christ will be magnified** in his person as hitherto : he lives, and will die, for this alone. Whatever happens to **my body,** the essential interests are safe.

Vv. 21–26 weigh the alternatives of **life or death** (v. 20) depending on the verdict awaited at Cæsar's bar. **21. To live]** as distinguished from **to live in the flesh** (v. 22), means 'life essential': cp. 1 Tim 6¹⁹. Col 3¹⁻⁴ is the true commentary on v. 21ᵃ : 'Your life is hid with Christ in God'—'Christ, who is our life.'

For to me, to live is Christ] i.e. life consists of and is rooted in Him : see Ro 8³⁵⁻³⁹ Gal 2²⁰. Hence, **to die is gain** ; for dying would bring the Apostle nearer to Christ : see v. 23 and 2 Cor 5⁶⁻⁸. (How the expectation of **being with Christ** immediately after death agrees with the conception of an intermediate state, indicated

in 1 Th 4¹⁴,¹⁶ and 1 Cor 15⁵¹,⁵², is not evident ; our best notions of the other world are dim and confused : see 1 Cor 13¹².)

22. There is gain also on the opposite side **If to live in the flesh be my lot** (RM ; the Gk. is highly elliptical, as Paul's language often becomes under excitement), **this means for me fruit of work,** i.e. continued labour and a richer reward. The writer **knows not which he shall choose** ; advantages are balanced.

23, 24. His heart prompts the wish to go ; his judgment, guided by his friends' need, advises staying ; that he will so **abide in the flesh for** their **progress and joy in the faith,** St. Paul is persuaded (vv. 25, 26). This outcome of the pending trial will bring exceeding joy, as well as spiritual benefit, to the Philippians. The peculiar Gk. word for **depart** (v. 23), also used in 2 Tim 4⁶, means 'loosing the tent-peg': cp. the metaphor of 2 Cor 5¹. The **glorying** (AV 'rejoicing') anticipated in v. 26 is the exultation of the Philippians in the Apostle's escape and the resulting gain to the Christian cause.

III. How Paul's Comrades may support Him (1²⁷–2¹⁸)

§ 6. ₁²⁷⁻³⁰. With v. 27 the Apostle turns upon his readers, as much as to say, 'I have told you how it fares with me ; what about yourselves ? My happiness depends on you.' The transitional **Only** implies a possible qualification—a cloud that might darken the bright prospect of vv. 25, 26 : cp. 1 Th 3⁸.

The manner of life (AV 'conversation') expected is defined by a Gk. term familiar to 'colonials' (see Intro.), which recurs in 3²¹ : **hold your citizenship in a manner worthy of the gospel of Christ:** cp. Eph 2¹⁹. 'The gospel' supplies in itself the motives for a worthy life ; the Apostle's presence or absence should not affect his fellow-believers' loyalty. Steadfastness is the chief quality desired in them, that **ye stand fast**—a characteristic of the citizen-soldier. **In one spirit** signifies unity of religious principles and purpose ; **with one soul** (RV) unity of feeling and effort. **The faith of the gospel** does not mean Christian doctrine, the contents of faith, but faith as a conscious power in the soul, 'striving like one man to maintain and carry into effect your faith in the gospel': cp. Jude v. 3.

28. Steadfastness meant, especially for this Church, **not to be daunted** by persecution. They are Paul's comrades in **the conflict** which he underwent at Philippi formerly, and now endures in Rome (v. 30). Let them understand that their courage is itself **a token** of their adversaries' **perdition** (ruin) and their **salvation**— a sign that God is with them (cp. vv. 19, 20, in this connexion) ; **for indeed** (v. 29) their sufferings are a bounty of divine grace (cp. Mt 5¹² 1 Pet 4¹¹⁻¹³) shared with their Apostle (cp. **v. 7** ;

also Col 1 [24] Eph 3 [1, 13])—a favour directly consequent on their believing in Christ. To suffer in His behalf, as representing Christ amid an evil world (cp. Jn 15 [18-20]), is indeed an honour.

CHAPTER 2

THE MUTUAL SERVICE OF PAUL AND THE PHILIPPIAN CHURCH

§ 7. 2 [1-11]. In view of what has just been said, therefore the Apostle entreats his readers, under all the obligations arising from past fellowship (v. 1), to make his joy complete by a thorough concord (v. 2). This will be attained through self-effacing regard for each other (vv. 3, 4), of which Christ is the ground and example (vv. 5–8).

1. St. Paul invokes four bonds of friendship : exhortation (i.e. encouragement) in Christ, given on his part ; consolation of love, fellowship in the Spirit (cp. 1 [19]), tender mercies and compassions, mutually exhibited ; if there be any such things—or if they count for anything as between us (the sentence is elliptical, and the text a little doubtful)—this entreaty will prevail.

2. That ye be of the same mind (v. 2) imports oneness of sentiment and aim, to be realised in having the same love—i.e. cherishing a uniform reciprocal affection—as men conjoined in soul (' of one accord,' RV ; cp. 1 [27], 'with one soul'), minding the one thing (cp. Col 3 [2] RV). In rendering the last clause of one mind, AV ignores the Gk. definite article : St. Paul's ' one thing needful ' (cp. Lk 10 [42]) is nothing else than ' the gospel ' (see 1 [5, 8, 27]) ; concentration upon this is the guarantee of unity.

3, 4. Such oneness of soul means doing nothing in a factious or vainglorious way, each man in lowliness of mind counting the other better than himself, and keeping an eye not for his own interests but for those of his neighbour. In short, love and humility together overcome all divisive influences, and bring about the perfect socialism of the Spirit.

V. 5 goes on to say that this altruism is the proper Christian way of thinking : Have this mind in you, which is indeed (the mind) in Christ Jesus—i.e. the mind grounded in Him. The Pauline phrase ' in Christ Jesus ' signifies the mystical union : not the Jesus Christ who ' was ' (the verb of AV is wanting in the Gk.), but the Christ Jesus who ' is,' inspires this way of thinking.

Vv. 6–8 lead back from the present to the past, exhibiting the Christian altruistic mind as it wrought first in the Founder ; St. Paul relates the experience of the Head to teach the members a lowly, self-renouncing love. For this purpose he must show how much Christ had to forgo and to what lengths His abnegation went. The difficult expressions of this profound passage are, especially, the synonymous connected phrases form (of God, of a bondman), on an equality (with God), likeness (of men), in fashion (as a man), which denote resemblance in different aspects or degrees. The first signifies essential form, the mode of existence proper to the person in question ; the second, the footing on which he stands, or might stand ; the third, his visible features ; the fourth, the guise, or habit of life, in which he moves. The verbs of vv. 7, 8—emptied (RV), and humbled Himself —affirm respectively a negative self-deprivation or depotentiation, and a positive self-humiliation based upon the former ; the latter act has its antithesis in the exalting of Christ by God spoken of in v. 9, and the former in the granting to Him of the name above every name. The rare verbal noun of v. 6, (counted it not) a prize (RV ; AV ' robbery '), meant first ' the act of grasping ' or ' clutching,' and then ' a thing to be clutched.' We take the sense of the passage to be, that Christ, while divine in His proper nature, did not, when the call came to serve others, hold fast in self-assertion His God-like state, but divested Himself of this by assuming a servant's form (adding to His divine a human being, which eclipsed the Godhead in Him) and leading an earthly life such as our own (vv. 6, 7 [a]). But He went lower still ; having stooped from His Godhead to man's condition, He traversed all the stages of obedience down to the humiliation of death (cp. 3 [21]), and of death in its uttermost shame (vv. 7 [b], 8). Such was the devotion of the Son of God to men ; and every man who is in Christ Jesus shares this mind.

The verb ' emptied ' in v. 7 supplies the theological term *kenosis* for the deprivation of divine attributes or powers involved in the incarnation of our Lord. However far this diminution went—and we cannot pretend to define its limits—since it was a *self*-emptying, an act of our Lord's sovereignty, it involved no forfeiture of intrinsic Deity.

At v. 8 the illustration properly ends ; but St. Paul cannot leave his Master on the cross, nor have it supposed that self-abnegation is real loss : cp. Mt 10 [39] Jn 12 [24]. By a divine recompense, Christ was lifted up from the death of the cross to the Messianic dominion, with glory added to His primal glory (vv. 9–11) : Wherefore indeed God more highly exalted him, and granted to him the name that is above every name : cp. Eph 1 [20-22]. This ' name ' is the completed title, THE LORD JESUS CHRIST, under which our Saviour will be adored throughout the universe. Things under the earth was a Gk. euphemism for the dead : cp. Ro 14 [9] Eph 4 [9].

Vv. 10, 11 appropriate for Jesus the language of Isa 45 [23], which foretold the worship to be paid to Israel's God by all mankind. The **glory of the Father** will be realised in the universal acknowledgment of the Lordship of the Son whom He enthroned : cp. 1 Cor 15 [24-28].

§ 8. **2** [12-18]. The connexion of the third exhortation, to thoroughness in the pursuit of **salvation** (vv. 12–18), with the two foregoing paragraphs may be brought out thus : And so, my beloved—since Christ's triumph, won by self-forgetting love, is sure (§ 7), and since you are my fellow-soldiers in His war (§ 6)—**as you have always answered to my challenge,** I expect that **now in my absence**—when you depend on yourselves—**much more than in my presence, with fear and trembling you will** prosecute **the work of your salvation ; for God is he that worketh in you both the willing and the working** (contrast Ro 7 [18]), **for his good-pleasure's sake** (v. 13). God's working in the Philippians is alleged not to enforce the **fear and trembling** (which St. Paul assumes and approves in them), but as a strong encouragement : ' Whatever human aid is wanting, God is with you—in you !' cp. 1 [6, 28] ; also Eph 3 [20] Col 1 [29] Ac 20 [32]. That God is thus working in the readers in the interests of His good pleasure, implies that their life-work is taken into God's plan for the kingdom of His Son; see vv. 9–11, 1 [29]; also Lk 12 [32] 2 Th 1 [11, 12].

14. The consciousness of God's sovereign grace operating in the Philippian Christians will prevent their work being marred by **murmurings** and **reasonings** against their lot (cp. 1 [29] 4 [6]; also 1 Pet 4 [12-14]); in this confidence they will bear themselves as **God's children** (vv. 15,16[a]) amid an evil world, where they are set to **shine as luminaries, holding forth** in its lustre **the word of life**: cp. 1 Th 1 [8-10]; also Mt 5 [14-16] Jn 1 [6-8] 5 [35]. For salvation-seeking is not egoism ; Christian excellence is that of a lamp, the more radiant as it is better trimmed.

16[b]. The writer, too, will gain much by the advancing salvation and luminous witness of his converts : this will be **for a glorying to myself against the day of Christ**, as showing **that I have not run in vain nor toiled in vain**: cp. 1 Th 3 [5] Gal 2 [2].

17, 18. Supposing the worst fears of the Philippians realised by his condemnation to death, their **faith** will turn this into a glad offering on the Apostle's part to God. Even in this issue, he **joys and rejoices with** them, and calls on them to **joy and rejoice with** him ! While he and they are true to Christ, nothing can take away their common joy : cp. 1 [20] Ro 8 [31-39]. St. Paul represents his death under the figure of a libation, or **drink-offering** (RM) : his blood, shed for the salvation of the Gentiles (Ro 15 [16] Col 1 [24], etc.), would be **poured out over the sacrifice and service** rendered to God by the faith of his Churches—a shower that will feed the sacrificial flame.

iv. The Approaching Visits (2 [19-30])

§ 9. **2** [19-24]. The Apostle **hopes however in the Lord Jesus** (under His sovereign direction) that events will take a different course ; he will **send Timothy forthwith** to Philippi, **so soon as** the outlook is clear, purposing himself to follow when free (vv. 23, 24) : cp. 1 [25, 26]. The motive for sending is, **that I too** (as well as you) **may be of good cheer through learning the news about you** (as you through hearing about me) ; and the reasons for sending *Timothy* are, on the one hand, his **genuine care** for the Philippians and the absence of any one else **like-minded** (lit. 'equal-souled '), and on the other hand the **knowledge** the Philippians have of his character and intimacy with his master (v. 22). In the hard saying, **they all seek their own, not the things of Jesus Christ** (RV), ' all ' is limited by the context, and by the Gk. definite article, to St. Paul's available helpers. Some of his companions were busy elsewhere ; others decline the errand through motives that he regards as selfish (vv. 20, 21).

§ 10. **2** [25-30]. **Epaphroditus** returns forthwith, carrying this letter (v. 25); see Intro. The Apostle heaps commendation upon him, apprehending seemingly that he might have a cool reception (see vv. 29, 30), since he is going home prematurely and without having rendered all the service expected. To St. Paul he has proved **my brother and fellow-worker and fellow-soldier,** having shared the Apostle's toils and labours to the best of his power ; on behalf of the Philippians, **your apostle** (deputy-messenger) and **minister** (minister-insacred-things : this word is repeated in the **service** of v. 30) **to my need.** The Apostle sends him back thus early because of his homesickness, which was aggravated by news of the grief of his friends at his recent illness (v. 26)— an illness threatening **death**, which God had averted in **mercy** both to himself and to Paul ; his immediate return, under these circumstances, is happier for all parties (vv. 27, 28) : Epaphroditus, it seems, had fallen into sickness through some venture, beyond the common risks of travel, in which he had **hazarded** (the rare Gk. verb means ' gambling with') **his life**— ' setting his life upon a cast '—to serve the Apostle on behalf of the Philippians in promoting **the work of Christ** (v. 30). How this came about, it is idle to conjecture.

CHAPTER 3
Dangers and Hopes of the Present Situation

v. Interjected Warnings (3 [1-21])

§ 11. **3** [1-6]. **Finally** (lit. 'For the rest'), **my brethren,** brings the close of the letter in sight (see Intro.) ; the Apostle has only a few supplementary counsels to give—prefaced by the Rejoice in the Lord, which is the prevalent note of the Epistle (1 4, 18, 26 2 2, 17, 18)—and to make acknowledgment of the contribution sent through Epaphroditus. But the admonition of v. 2 strikes a chord of feeling in his breast which vibrates too strongly to be soon arrested. From v. 4 onwards, c. 3 is a diversion in the Epistle, but such as answers his underlying purpose, since it opens St. Paul's heart to his readers and makes them more than ever 'partakers of' his 'grace' (1 7).

The observation of v. 1b relates to vv. 2, 3 ; St. Paul is writing the same things about the seductions of Judaism that he has said or written before : this was a chronic danger to his Churches. Though Philippi contained few Jewish settlers, its situation (see Intro.) exposed this Church to the visits of Jewish emissaries. The dogs, the evil workers, the concision (mutilation) form one class of adversaries, who receive the last epithet by way of scornful play upon the boasted name of 'the circumcision.' The Abrahamic covenant-seal has become null and void for rejecters of Christ, and no better than any other 'cutting' of the body ; so the Apostle transfers its name to the Church, upon which the OT. inheritance devolves : see Ro 2 25-29 4 12 11 17 Gal 3 7 6 16 Eph 2 11-19 3 6 Col 2 11-13 ; also Mt 21 43. These same men are dogs, raging against and ready to devour the Apostle of the Gentiles (cp. Ps 22 16, 20) ; ill-workers, because of their mischievous and unscrupulous activity : cp. 2 Cor 11 13. As in 1 Th 2 14-16, unbelieving Jews are here intended, radically opposed to the gospel ; not, as in Galatians and 2 Corinthians, Christian Jews who pervert it. Jewish hostility was violent beyond measure in Macedonia : see Ac 17.

3. By contrast with anti-Christian Jews, we are the circumcision, who worship by the Spirit of God (whose worship is inspired by the Holy Spirit), and glory in Christ Jesus (not in Moses, the Temple, etc.), and have no confidence in flesh (in any external privilege or performance). Here the Apostle strikes into the current of his own experience, which carries him away for the rest of the c. 4. Though I (one of the emphasised 'we' of v. 3) might have confidence indeed in the flesh—who had a better right to presume upon outward prerogative ? Amongst the seven points of superiority enumerated in vv. 5, 6, four came to Saul by birth, three by acquisition. The eighth day was the proper date for the infant's circumcision (Gn 17 12) ; Israel, the covenant-name of Jehovah's people ; Benjamin, the tribe eminent as supplying the first king of Israel, and subsequently remaining faithful to the throne of David ; a Hebrew sprung from Hebrews, one whose family preserved the home-language : see Ac 21 40. The fact that he had been a persecutor of the Church, combined with his Pharisaic professions and legal blamelessness, raised Saul's reputation to the highest pitch : cp. 2 Cor 11 22 Gal 1 13, 14 Ac 22 3-5.

§ 12. 3 7-11. The treasured gains of Saul of Tarsus, Paul the Apostle has counted loss because of the Christ, content to lose them if he might gain Christ (cp. Gal 6 14) ; there is no treasure that he would not hold cheap in this exchange—I count all things to be loss for the surpassing worth of the knowledge of Christ Jesus my Lord (v. 8). And this is no untried vaunt : For whose sake I have suffered the loss of all things—home, ease, honour, everything that men count dear (cp. Ac 20 24)—and count them refuse ! So contemptible had the world's wealth become to him through knowing Christ ; he wins infinite riches in exchange for dross !

The last clause of v. 8 is completed by v. 9 which unfolds St. Paul's distinctive conception of the believer's relation to his Saviour : that I may gain Christ and be found in him, not having a righteousness of my own, that which comes of law, but that which comes through faith in Christ, the righteousness which is of God, resting upon faith. These words sum up the doctrine of salvation taught in Romans and Galatians : the Apostle has not 'gained Christ' as an outward possession, but so as to be planted in Him and recognised as one with Him ; so that even his 'righteousness'—the moral worth that gives value to his existence—is not claimed for his own, as though it had been won by law-keeping, for it accrues to him through faith in Christ, and thus has its fountain in God ; it is built not, like the Pharisee's righteousness, upon human efforts and strivings, but upon faith in God and Christ.

Vv. 10, 11 are parallel to v. 9, setting forth objectively, as that defined subjectively, the Apostle's 'gain' in Christ. As v. 9 expanded the for whom of v. 8, so vv. 10, 11 take up and enlarge upon the foregoing phrase, the knowledge of Christ Jesus my Lord ; the entire sentence (vv. 8–11) is symmetrical :

I count all things to be loss, for the excellency of the knowledge of Christ Jesus my Lord,
 For whom I suffered the loss of all things, etc.,
 That I may gain Christ, and be found in Him, etc.,
So that I may know Him, and the power of His resurrection, etc.

10, 11. Three points are specified in St. Paul's 'knowledge of Christ': (a) The power of His resurrection, which came on Saul in the Damascus revelation. The resurrection of Jesus Christ which manifested Him as the Son of God, at the same time revealed in Him 'the power of God' working 'unto salvation' : see Ro 1 4, 16 4 24, 25 Eph 1 19, 20. The whole faith of the gospel turned upon Christ's resurrection (see 1 Cor 15[1-4,12-25] Ro 10[9]); the new life of the believer springs from His opened grave (Ro 6[4-11] 1 Cor 15[20, 21, 45-49]). (b) In contrast with the power of the Lord's resurrection-life stands the fellowship of His sufferings (2 Cor 13[4]), to which St. Paul was admitted from the outset: see Ac 9[16]. The present situation sets his ministry in this light: see Col 1[24] Eph 3[13] 2 Cor 4[10] 2 Tim 2[11, 12], and cp. Mt 16[24] 20[22, 23]. This fellowship goes to the length of being conformed to His death (a continued process); for the disciple is following his cross-bearing Master (Mt 10[38], etc.), and his daily course is as a march to Calvary: cp. 1 Cor 15[3] 2 Cor 4[10] Gal 2[19, 20] 6[14]. (c) St. Paul's knowledge of Christ will culminate in his attaining unto (arriving at) the full (or final) resurrection from the dead; hitherto he 'knows in part,' then he will 'know as' he 'is known' (1 Cor 13[9-11]). If by any means bespeaks humility rather than misgiving; St. Paul cannot look with steady eye on the dazzling prospect: cp. 3[20] 1 Jn 3[2]. For 'resurrection' a unique intensive Gk. compound is here used, signifying completeness, finality—a resurrection that leaves mortality for ever behind: cp. 2 Cor 5[4].

§ 13. 3[12-16]. The goal of the Apostle's career lies beyond this world; hence he proceeds: Not that I have already obtained the 'gain' secured to me in Christ (cp. 1[21]), or am already made perfect; but I am pressing on, if so be that I may apprehend (lay fast hold of) that for which I was apprehended (laid fast hold of) by Christ Jesus. In this disclaimer, emphatically resumed in v. 13, St. Paul contrasts himself with Christians holding mistaken notions of perfection similar, probably, to those attributed to 'Hymenæus and Philetus' in 2 Tim 2[16-18], who taught that 'the resurrection is already past' (scil. in the regeneration of the soul) and denied 'the redemption of the body' with all that this implies: see Ro 8[18-23]; cp. 1 Cor 15[12]. Challenging these perfectionists, who imagined that Christ in their present state had reached the goal of His work of redemption, St. Paul protests: Brethren, for my part I do not reckon myself as yet to have apprehended; but one thing—! (v. 13) Here he breaks off; 'one thing I do' (AV) supplies the aposiopesis: forgetting the things behind and straining out unto the things before, I press on towards the mark, to reach the prize of the upward calling of God in Christ Jesus (v. 14): cp. Heb 3[1] 1 Th 2[12]. 'The prize' is the heavenly life of the redeemed (vv. 11, 20, 21),—'our perfect consummation and bliss both in body and soul'; 'God calls' men to this in Christ Jesus, since Christ conveys the call and supplies in His person its mark (v. 21; cp. Ro 8[29]). The Apostle depicts himself as a racer straining every nerve to reach the goal and wasting not an instant in looking backward.

The Gk. adjective perfect (i.e. 'full-grown, 'mature': see 1 Cor 14[20] Eph 4[13]) appearing in vv. 12 and 15, was used of initiates into the religious 'mysteries' of the time, at the final stage of qualification'; the party in view claimed, under this designation, to have acquired an esoteric 'knowledge' of Christianity going deeper than simple 'faith': see Col 2[4, 8] 1 Tim 6[20, 21]. This Gnosticising tendency, so strongly evidenced by the Colossian heresy, was widespread and manifold in form; it greatly exercised the Apostle's mind at this time. 15. Let us, so many as be perfect (the true 'initiates,' in contrast with those alluded to in v. 12), be thus minded—as much as to say, 'Those really deep in Christian knowledge will think in this way' (vv. 10–14). The perfect recognise the distance of the goal; they are the last to count themselves perfect: cp. the treatment of Gk. conceit of wisdom in 1 Cor 2[6-16] 8[1, 2] 14[37, 38].

15[b], 16. Some members of this Church are otherwise minded—unable to follow what St. Paul has just said; knowing their loyalty, he can wait confidently for their enlightenment— God will reveal this also unto you (cp. 1 Cor 2[10-15])—provided that they faithfully practise the truth already grasped: whereunto we have attained, by that same rule let us walk (RV): cp. Gal 6[16] Jn 7[17]. Omit 'let us mind,' etc. (AV).

§ 14. 3[17-21]. Against the third class of opponents (see Intro.)—in some instances identical with the second, for spiritual conceit and moral depravity may be found together (see 1 Tim 6[3-5])—St. Paul adduces his example and that of others of like behaviour, as against the two former he cited his religious experience. 18, 19. Their character is notorious: the Apostle has spoken of them often, and weeps over them as he writes now. These are peculiarly the enemies of the cross of Christ—not Jews who 'stumble at' the cross (Gal 6[12] 1 Cor 1[23]), but professed Christians whose walk tends to its subversion; men whose end is perdition—like that of 'the adversaries' of 1[28] (see 2 Cor 11[15] 2 Pet 2[1-3])—for their god is the belly (they honour sensual appetite like a god: see Ro 13[13, 14] 16[18] 2 Tim 3[4]), and their glory is in their shame (they pride themselves on sensuality: see Eph 4[19] Ro 1[32] 2 Pet 2[13, 14]); who mind earthly things! (cp. Ro 8[5-7])—the delineation ends in amazement. These men are Antinomians, accepting Paul's gospel only to 'continue in sin that grace may abound,' and 'using liberty for an occasion to the flesh' (see Ro 6[1, 12] Gal 5[13] Jude v. 4). They were the reproach and grief of the Apostle's ministry. One hardly supposes that the writer has such enemies amongst the Philippians (see 1[3-8]); but libertine Christians were numerous, and might travel that way.

20, 21. Against the earthly is set the heavenly

mind and walk, described by a word appealing to the Philippian civic consciousness (see Intro., and cp. 1²⁷): our citizenship (AV ' conversation ') is in heaven! (cp. Rev 21²). As the distant Philippian ' colonus ' belonged to Rome, so the Christian sojourning on earth is a citizen of heaven; his home lies 'where Christ is' (Col 3¹⁻³ Eph 2¹⁹ 2 Cor 5¹⁻⁹ Heb 11¹³⁻¹⁶ Mt 6²¹ Jn 14²,³). From this region, ours already by affinity, we await a Saviour (see 1 Th 1¹⁰ 4¹⁶,¹⁷ 1 Cor 1⁷ 15²³) .. who will re-fashion the body of our humiliation ('vile body,' AV, is a mistranslation), that it may be conformable to the body of his glory. The Gk. adjective rendered 'conformable' appeared in Ro 8²⁹ — 'conformed to the image of God's Son': conformity of bodily state completes conformity of character. Upon this metamorphosis, see 1 Cor 15⁵¹⁻⁵⁴ and 1 Th 4¹⁴⁻¹⁷. The Apostle keenly felt the 'humiliation' of man's mortal state: see 2 Cor 4⁷⁻5⁵. The idea of 'the body of glory' was given him by the form of heavenly splendour in which he had seen the Lord Jesus on the Damascus road: cp. 2 Cor 4⁴⁻⁶, also Rev 1¹³⁻¹⁷.

This transformation of the saints will be the supreme act of that mighty working in which Jesus displays His power, as Lord of God's kingdom, to subjugate all things unto Himself: cp. 2¹⁰,¹¹ and Mt 28¹⁸. The human body is, from first to last, the object of His miracles. Read 1 Cor 15²⁴⁻²⁸ in this connexion.

CHAPTER 4
FINAL CHARGE. ACKNOWLEDGMENT OF PHILIPPIAN BOUNTY
VI. CLOSING EXHORTATIONS (4¹⁻⁹)

§ 15. 4¹⁻³. With heightened feeling St. Paul resumes the vein of exhortation commenced in 3¹: Wherefore (in view of the grand hope of our calling) .. so stand fast in the Lord (see 1²⁷)—'so,' i.e. in 'imitating' the Apostle and 'marking those' of like 'walk' (3¹⁷); this appeal sums up the foregoing homily. For the endearing epithets accumulated here, cp. 1³⁻⁸ 2¹⁶,¹⁷, also 1 Th 2¹⁹,²⁰.

2. The entreaty to Euodia and Syntyche to be of one mind in the Lord, is a pointed application of 1²⁷ and 2¹⁻⁵; they have a serious difference of judgment in carrying out the will of Christ. These ladies bear good Greek names; one of them is, possibly, the same as the Lydia of Ac ¹6, the latter name in that case being an ethnic appellation (' the Lydian'). As at Thessalonica (Ac 17⁴), women were conspicuous amongst the earliest converts in Philippi: see Intro.

3. The Gk. 'Synzygos' (yoke-fellow) is better read as a proper name, on which the Apostle plays, as upon 'Onesimus' (serviceable) in Philemon v. 11: Yea, I ask also thee, true Synzygos—worthy of thy name—help them

(Euodia and Syntyche) to come to an understanding. Others suppose Epaphroditus to be addressed as 'yokefellow': cp. 2²⁵. The disagreeing women had shared St. Paul's struggles (this Gk. verb is rendered striving together in 1²⁷) in the gospel,—a fact which makes him specially anxious for their reconciliation. With these former comrades St. Paul associates a certain Clement otherwise unknown (hardly the Clement of Rome, famous a generation later), and the rest of my fellow-workers, whose names are in the book of life (see Rev 3⁵, etc., Lk 10²⁰ Heb 12²³),—and therefore need not be enumerated here.

§ 16. 4⁴⁻⁷. Joy in the Lord, and the peace of God, are the sovereign factors in the Christian temper (vv. 4, 7); these manifest themselves in gentleness (RM; AV 'moderation') toward men, and serenity (In nothing be anxious, RV) in all events, maintained by continual prayer and thanksgiving. V. 4 repeats, with resolute emphasis, the command of 3¹: see note.

5. Gentleness (ascribed, under the same word, to Christ in 2 Cor 10¹) is the opposite of self-assertion and rivalry. Like 'patience' in Jas 5⁸, it is enforced by the nearness of the Lord's advent, the prospect of which quenches worldly passions: cp. 1 Cor 7²⁹⁻³¹ Lk 12²⁹⁻⁴⁰. Though we may not think of the second coming of Christ as at hand in the sense in which the first Christians did, our appearance at His judgment-seat is no less certain, and the thought of it should affect us in the same way.

6. Anxiety is precluded by the direction, let your requests be made known unto God—since 'he careth for you' (1 Pet 5⁷; cp. Mt 6³¹,³²). Prayer is devout address to God in general, supplication the specific appeal for help, and request the particular petition made. In everything includes temporal with spiritual needs, covering all occasions of anxiety.

7. The peace of God is that which ensues on reconciliation through Christ and the bestowment of the Holy Spirit, who breathes the Father's love into the heart: see Ro 5¹,²,⁸⁻¹¹ Eph 2¹³⁻¹⁸. The consciousness of this fortifies the mind against trouble: it shall guard (or garrison) your hearts and your thoughts in Christ Jesus. God's peace surpasses (AV 'passes': the same word was rendered 'better than' in 2³, and 'excellency' in 3⁸) all reason (Gk. nous) in its fortifying power. Greek philosophy sought in Reason the prophylactic against care and fear; the true remedy is found in Christ.

§ 17. 4⁸,⁹. The real Finally is now reached: see on 3¹. The list of virtues here commended is unique in St. Paul's writings, resembling the catalogues of Greek moralists; its items belong to natural ethics. These things, St. Paul says, take account of (RM); i.e. reckon and allow for (the verb of 3¹³ 1 Cor 4¹ 13⁵, etc.): he desiderates in the readers a larger appreciation of goodness, a catholic moral taste—mark the reiterated whatsoever. This Church was intensely devoted, but intellectually narrow (see on 1⁹),—a defect naturally aggravated by persecution. Hence the stress laid on 'gentleness' in v. 5, and on the amenities of life in v. 8. Things true and honourable (to be revered) constitute the integrities of personal character; things pure and just represent the moralities, and things amiable and winning the graces, of social life. The further expressions, if there be any virtue and if there be any praise (aught to be praised), bring in every conceivable form and instance of moral excellence. Virtue—the ruling category of heathen ethics—figures only in this passage of St. Paul; the Apostle is seeking common ethical ground as between the Church and Gentile society. The Christian man must prize every fragment of human worth, claiming it for God.

9. So much for reflexion and appreciation; for practice, the writer points once more, as in c. 3, to himself,—to his personal teaching (what things you both learned and received) and behaviour (and heard of and saw in me). The God of peace shall be with you is a virtual repetition of v. 7: men of large-hearted charity and steadfast loyalty dwell in God's peace amidst all storms.

VII. Acknowledgment of the Contribution from Philippi (4¹⁰⁻²⁰)

§ 18. 4¹⁰⁻¹⁶. With the Benediction of v. 9 (cp. Ro 15³³) the letter might have ended; but St. Paul in sending back Epaphroditus (2²⁵⁻³⁰) desires to make ample recognition of the gift conveyed by him, and has reserved this matter to the last. The remittance had surely been acknowledged earlier; communications had been exchanged since Epaphroditus' arrival in Rome: see Intro. It looks as though the Philippians had been grieved in some way over the reception of their contribution. Perhaps the Apostle's former acknowledgment through its brevity was open to misconstruction. With care and earnestness he now endeavours to set himself right with his friends :—

'Greatly was I gladdened,' he writes, ' that now once again you have blossomed out in your thoughtfulness for me; indeed, you were thinking of me in this way before, but you lacked opportunity to show it.' The recent gift was the revival of the care for the Apostle's wants shown by the Philippians at an earlier time; no other Church had so markedly proved its gratitude in this kind (v. 15). The readers are aware of this fact (Moreover ye yourselves know, ye Philippians); they had probably referred to it, in their Church letter, with pardonable pride. In the beginning of the gospel means at the time of its coming to

these regions (cp. 1⁵); in the matter of giving and receiving (RV) might be rendered 'by way of credit and debit account' (cp. 1 Cor 9¹¹ Gal 6⁶ Philemon vv. 18, 19)—a mercantile idiom When I went out from Macedonia refers to contributions sent to the writer at Athens or Corinth (see 2 Cor 11⁷⁻¹⁰); even before this, during the short time he stayed in Thessalonica, they had helped him once and again (v. 16).

In the intervening passage (vv. 11–14) St. Paul explains his attitude. He does not speak as though in want and dependent on such support; he has learned to be self-sufficient (content) under all conditions. I know, he continues, how to be abased (by poverty: see 1 Cor 4¹¹ 2 Cor 11⁹, ²⁷ Ac 20³⁴), and I know also how to be in affluence; in every variety of state and circumstance, I have become versed (lit. 'initiated') both in feasting and hungering, both in affluence and destitution. Thrice St. Paul speaks of his 'abundance' (vv. 12 and 18); and this bears out the conjecture of Sir W. M. Ramsay, suggested by the heavy cost entailed in the 'appeal to Cæsar' (Ac 25¹¹, ¹²) and the unlikelihood of his taxing the Churches for this purpose, that he had by this time come into the inheritance of property and is no longer a poor man. If this was so, then St. Paul is thinking of the trials of both estates when he says, I am equal to everything, in him that enables me (v. 13): cp. 2 Cor 12⁹, ¹⁰ Eph 3²⁰ Col 1²⁹. He rejoices, therefore, in the gift of the Philippians for their sake rather than his own (v. 14): Howbeit ye did well, that ye had fellowship with my affliction (showed sympathy with my persecuted condition)—not, as 'in Thessalonica,' with 'my need' (v. 16).

§ 19. 4¹⁷⁻²⁰. Hence the Apostle was not eager for the gift (as a boon to himself), but for the evidence it afforded of God's grace in the givers (cp. 1¹¹ 2 Cor 9⁶⁻¹¹ Eph 5⁹)—the fruit that increaseth to your account. But I have enough and to spare; I am filled full—in satisfaction of mind as of bodily wants (cp. 2² 2 Cor 7⁴)—now that I have received from Epaphroditus what you have sent,—a fragrant savour, an acceptable sacrifice, well-pleasing to God (cp. Heb 13¹⁶): the religious, not the material value of the gift weighs with its receiver.

19. Since the offering is a sacrifice to God, He will recompense it (cp. Heb 6¹⁰ Prov 19¹⁷): my God will fill up every need of yours—as you have striven to meet His servant's need—according to his riches. Temporal and spiritual needs are together included in the promise; God's 'wealth' contains all kinds of treasure. In glory points to the heavenly consummation (cp. Ro 2⁴, ⁷ Eph 1⁷, ¹⁸), in Christ Jesus to the ground and channel of divine supplies.

20. The Doxology (cp. 2 Cor 9¹⁵, in relation to its context) magnifies the bountiful Giver as our Father: see Mt 6⁸, ³².

§ 20. **4** [21-23]. In conclusion, the Apostle bids a greeting to **every saint in Christ Jesus**—his good will knows no exception: see 1 [1, 4, 7, 8]. With his own he sends greetings from his companions, from the whole Roman Church, and particularly from **those of Cæsar's household** (to think of Christians in *Nero's* house !) —the latter singled out because their saluta-

tion would peculiarly touch the Philippians: see Intro. The circumstances of his captivity and trial brought the Apostle into contact with the palace and the imperial attendants ; friends in that quarter were specially serviceable to him.

23. The Benediction (RV) is nearly identical with that of Galatians, Philemon, and 2 Timothy.

COLOSSIANS

INTRODUCTION

1. COLOSSÆ was a town of Phrygia in Asia Minor, situated upon the S. bank of the Lycus, a tributary of the Mæander. Laodicea (2 [1] 4 [13, 15, 16] Rev 1 [11] 3 [14]) and Hierapolis (4 [13]) were distant from it eleven and thirteen miles respectively. As these cities grew, Colossæ seems to have declined ; for, though Herodotus speaks of it as 'a city of great size,' and Xenophon as ' a populous city, prosperous and great,' about the beginning of the Christian era it is mentioned by Strabo as 'a small town.' In St. Paul's time, Pliny classes it among the 'most famous towns' of the district ; but he was probably thinking mostly of its past consequence. It is to the Christians in this town that the present Epistle is addressed ; and some discussion has arisen as to St. Paul's previous relations with them. He seems to have written an earlier letter to them (4 [10]) to which Epaphras had brought a reply (1 [7]) ; but whether he had himself actually visited Colossæ at any time is a matter of doubt. He may have done so on his Third Missionary Journey, when ' he went over all the country of Galatia and Phrygia in order ' (Ac 18 [23]), or even during his three years' stay at Ephesus, when ' all they which dwelt in Asia heard the word ' (Ac 19 [10]), but it is tolerably clear that he had never made a prolonged stay in Colossæ, and was not directly the founder of its Church (1 [4] 2 [1]). Christianity was probably introduced into Colossæ by one of his converts, and Epaphras (1 [7] 4 [12, 13]) generally has the honour accorded to him.

2. Occasion of the Epistle. The present letter, which was taken by Tychicus, who was accompanied by Onesimus, Philemon's runaway slave (4 [7, 9]), was called forth by a serious danger that threatened the faith of the Colossian Church. The danger arose from a type of false teaching, essentially Jewish in character. It emphasised the importance of sacred seasons, the sabbath, the new moon, the feast

day ; it laid down certain restrictions as to meats and drinks, made much of circumcision and the Law, and gave an important place to the tradition of men. It insisted on severity to the body, and perhaps claimed to rest upon vision. By its worship of the angels it degraded Christ from His true position as the Head of the body. While the teachers thought too meanly of themselves to seek fellowship with God, and therefore worshipped the angels, they were puffed up with conceit towards men, professing to put a philosophical view of religion in place of the elementary teaching the Colossians had received (2 [16-23]).

The modern reader will find the Epistle easier to understand if he gains some acquaintance with the doctrine of angels current in the Judaism of St. Paul's time. This doctrine had received a great development in the centuries immediately preceding the birth of Christ. The world was imagined to be full of angels and demons, who presided over all the operations of nature and entered into the closest relations with the life of man. Every blade of grass had its angel, much more the mightier forces and elements of nature. Each nation had its angel, who guided its destiny and fought its battles. The common view that the angels are sinless was unknown, and even the best were not regarded as free from moral imperfections. Owing to the distance which later Jewish theology set between God and the world, it was natural that many should turn for help to the angels, who were ever close at hand and were the actual controllers of the ordinary course of nature and human affairs. It is probable that by ' the elements of the world ' (2 [8, 20] RV) St. Paul means the elemental spirits, and he considers the whole race of man, both Jewish and Gentile, to have been in subjection to these 'elements,' 'which by nature were no gods' (Gal 4 [3-10]). This angelic rule found one expression in the life of Israel which is of great importance for our purpose. It was a tenet of Judaism, endorsed also in the New Testament (Ac 7 53 ; cp. Ac 7 38 Gal 3 19 Heb 2 2), that the Law had been given through the angels ; accordingly subjection to it meant subjection to them

A large section of Epaphras' converts at Colossæ had given their adhesion to the false teaching, and no doubt the sounder portion had written for advice to Epaphras or even to St. Paul, and hence the Epistle before us.

St. Paul does not meet the Colossian heresy by an appeal to the Old Testament, which might have been set aside by allegorical interpretation. He meets it by an appeal to their own experience, and by a statement of the Person and work of Christ, the Son of God and all-sufficient Saviour, and he dwells on them as contradictory to and incompatible with the conceptions entertained by the false teachers. In the Son, who had condescended to become man, there resides, he says, the totality of the divine qualities and powers. Of Himself He is sufficient to form the link uniting God and man together. Where, then, is there room for angelic and other mediators intruding between the lowliness of man and the majesty of God ? Christ suffices to bridge the chasm. And how insufficient are angelic beings for such an end ! Christ, acting for His Father, has created the universe and is its Head—not any angel. The angels were indeed His creatures. Christ—not any angel—is also the Head of the Church. The Old Dispensation, indeed, had been 'ordained by angels' (Gal 3 19), and was under their supervision. But their Dispensation, with its ordinances and rules and observances, was done away with (Eph 2 15). Christ had taken the bond of the Old Dispensation (and of every other religion which founds itself on outward observances) and had nailed it to His Cross, superseding by His own operation the inferior work which had been entrusted to the agency of angels. How can it be right to descend to the adoration of angels from the worship of the Lord and Creator of angels, who had shown His superiority to their 'principalities and powers,' and had 'openly triumphed' over the Dispensation which they had been allowed to superintend, by the Dispensation inaugurated by the Cross (2 14, 15). Such an adoration is no sign of humility, but a superstition dishonouring to the gospel and arising from an inability to realise the true relation between God and man, as man is reconciled and adopted in Christ (2 18). As to the rules of outward observances in which Judaism delighted, and the injunctions of asceticism which perhaps followed from the misapprehension of the nature of matter, they are of no use as restraints to the flesh, and only lead to a self-conceit which applauds itself for its humility.

The overmastering idea of the greatness of Christ gives their form to some of the practical exhortations which succeed to the argument— 'Christ sitteth upon the right hand of God' 'your life is hid with Christ in God' : 'Christ our life' : 'Christ is all in all' : as is fit in the Lord' : 'as to the Lord, and not unto men' : the Lord Christ' : 'the mystery of Christ' : 'Epaphras, a servant of Christ' (3 1, 3. 4, 11, 18, 23, 24 4 3, 12).

3. Authorship. There need be no misgiving in accepting the Pauline authorship of the Epistle. The doubts formerly entertained by critics have largely disappeared, and the number continually increases of those who only admit its genuineness. The time is probably not far distant when this will be regarded as settled by common consent. It used to be said that the false teaching alluded to by St. Paul was a form of that large class of beliefs grouped together under the name of Gnosticism, and therefore that it could not be earlier than the second century. The present writer is convinced that there is not a trace of specific Gnosticism in the Epistle, but even if there were we have good reason to believe that the Gnostic systems of the second century struck their roots into a much earlier time. He also believes that the Essene features found by many scholars in the false teaching are quite imaginary. There is absolutely nothing in that teaching which could not have been given in Colossæ by 59 A.D. or even earlier. Nor is there anything in the writer's own exposition that contradicts Pauline authorship. His doctrine of Christ and the angels can be matched in nearly every point from St. Paul's generally accepted Epistles. The style, it is true, differs from that of Galatians, Corinthians, and Romans, but a letter written in the meditative seclusion of a prison is not likely to have the same rapidity of movement or passionate intensity as a letter like Galatians, dashed off at white heat by a missionary immersed in the most distracting activities and fighting with his back to the wall in defence of the gospel. The Epistle was written at the same time as Ephesians and Philemon, possibly during the Apostle's imprisonment at Cæsarea, but much more probably at Rome. It was in the earlier part of his imprisonment, and also, we may say with tolerable confidence, before the composition of Philippians. The precise date is uncertain, probably 59 A.D. is not far from the mark.

CHAPTER 1
THE SUPREMACY AND ALL-SUFFICIENCY OF CHRIST

1–8. Salutation to the Colossian Christians. and thanksgiving for the news of their spiritual state.

Paraphrase. '(1, 2) Paul and Timothy salute the saints and believers in Colossæ. (3–5) We always thank God, when we pray for you, on account of your faith and the love you display in hope of the heavenly reward, of which you heard when the gospel was first proclaimed to you. (6–8) This gospel is the word of truth which approves itself by its universal diffusion and success, and has from the very first achieved a similar success among yourselves, taught you as it has been in its genuine reality by Epaphras, who has ministered to you in my place and has made known your love to me.'

2. Faithful] better, 'believing.' **And the Lord Jesus Christ]** RV rightly omits.

3. Better, 'We always give thanks to God the Father of our Lord Jesus Christ when we pray for you.' **5. For the hope]** i.e. based on the hope. **6, 7.** It is the gospel as Epaphras taught it them, not that urged on them by the false teachers, which is exercising this world-wide influence. The universal corrects the local. **7^{b}.** RV 'who is a faithful minister of Christ on our behalf' is probably right. The Apostle of the Gentiles could not himself visit Colossæ. Epaphras has done this part of his work for him. Epaphras is not to be identified with Epaphroditus (Phil 2 $^{25-30}$ 4 ^{18}).

9–14. St. Paul's prayer that the Colossians may be filled with wisdom, strength, and thanksgiving.

Paraphrase. '(9) Since we heard the glad report, as you pray for us so we pray without ceasing for you, that you may be filled with a knowledge of God's will touching your conduct, a knowledge characterised by wisdom and insight. (10) Such knowledge is not indeed an end in itself. It must lead to a life well pleasing to Christ; you must bear fruit and increase in every good work by means of your knowledge of God. (11) This you can do only as God Himself strengthens you, and this He will do not simply according to your need, but in the measure of His own power. Thus you will be strengthened for the supreme test, the trial of steadfastness and forbearance, which you will meet with joy. (12–14) Give thanks also to the Father, who qualified you to share in the lot of the saints which is situated in the realm of light, by rescuing you from the dominion of darkness and translating you into the kingdom of that Son on whom His love rests, in whom we possess deliverance, the forgiveness of our sins.'

9. In all wisdom, etc.] RV 'in all spiritual wisdom and understanding.' **10.** RM 'by the knowledge.' **12. Made us meet]** better, 'qualified you.' Usually the saints in light is taken as a single phrase meaning 'saints in heaven.' But 'in light' should be connected with 'the lot.' It defines its situation. 'The

lot' (AV **inheritance**) 'of the saints' is the blessedness awaiting them. **13. His dear Son]** RV 'the Son of his love.' **14. Redemption]** The view that the word means ransom is very dubious. 'Deliverance' is the best translation. Omit **through his blood.**

15–23. The supremacy of the Son in the universe and the Church.

Paraphrase. '(15) This Son of God's love, in whom we have our deliverance, the pardon of our sins, is the exact image of God, so that while God is the invisible, He is manifested to us in His Son. (16) The Son also possesses the first-born's dominion over every creature in virtue of the fact that the creation of all things depended on Him, whether in heaven or on earth, whether visible or invisible. Let it be specially observed that in the 'all things' thus created must be included the Angelic powers of the loftiest orders. All things I say have come into existence by His agency, and He is the goal for which they have been created. (17) He is before all things and the principle of their cohesion. (18) And this preëminence in the universe is matched by His preëminence in the Church. He is the Head of the body, inasmuch as He is the ruler who has passed to His dominion from the dead, in order that He who is from the first supreme in the universe may become supreme in the Church, and thus be supreme in every sphere. (19, 20) This position He attained because God was well pleased that all the fulness of His Grace should dwell in His Son, and thus reconcile through Him all things to Himself. It was through the blood shed on His Cross that peace was thus made. And the scope of this reconciliation was universal, it embraced not things in earth alone, but those in the heavens; (21) aye, and you Colossians, too, once estranged from God and hostile to Him though you were. (22, 23) Now you have been reconciled in the Son's fleshly body through His death, to present yourselves blameless before God, if you stand unshaken in the Gospel.'

The aim of this great exposition of the nature and work of the Son is to accord to Him the supreme position alike in the world and the Church, and sweep away the false teaching which assigned to angelic mediators the position and functions of the Son. He and not they created, sustains, and rules the universe; they, even the loftiest, are merely His creatures. He, and not they, is the Redeemer, they are among the redeemed.

15. The **image** perfectly resembles and reveals the original. **First born]** The word expresses priority to and then supremacy over. Probably the latter only is meant here. **Every creature]** better than RV 'all creation.'

16. By him] RV 'in him.' **Thrones, etc.]**

various ranks of higher angels. **17. Consist**] RM 'That is, hold together.' The Son is the centre of unity for the universe. **19.** RV 'For it was the good pleasure of the Father that in him should all the fulness dwell.' A very difficult v., but probably this is more correct than RM, 'For the whole fulness of God was pleased to dwell in him.' The fulness is not as in 2⁹, the fulness of Godhead, but the fulness of grace possessed by the Son in His incarnate state. **20.** The Son's atoning death availed for the whole angelic world, as well as for the world of men, since the Son is Head of both.

20–22. Very difficult, but probably a full stop should be placed at the end of v. 21. We may translate, 'And through him to reconcile all things unto himself, having made peace through the blood cf his Cross, through him, whether the things on earth or the things in the heavens, you also who once were alienated and enemies in mind in evil works. But now ye have been reconciled in the body of his flesh,' etc. **22. Body of his flesh**] as against the false teachers who thought non-incarnate angels could redeem.

24—C. 2³. Paul's sufferings, labours, and anxieties for the Church.

Paraphrase. '(24–26) I rejoice in the sufferings I endure for your sake, and fill up the measure of afflictions Christ has still to endure in my flesh on behalf of His body, the Church, which I serve in my office of stewardship entrusted to me by God, to set forth the gospel in its universal scope, that secret hidden from eternity but now revealed to His saints. (27) To them God has willed to make known how rich is the glory of this mystery among the Gentiles which is none other than the indwelling Christ, the pledge of your participation in the heavenly glory. (28, 29) This Christ we proclaim to all, that we may present each perfect in Him—an end to which I devote all the energy which He has made to work so mightily in me. (C. 2. 1–3) For let me assure you how intense is my inward struggle for you and the Laodiceans, personally unknown to me though you are, that you may be strengthened and knit together in love to attain all rich fulness of insight, a full knowledge of Christ the divine mystery, in whom exist all the treasures of wisdom and knowledge, not on the surface, but concealed where they must be discovered by earnest search.'

24. Christ suffers in His members in virtue of their union with Him, and the afflictions Paul undergoes in prison are filling up the measure of suffering Christ has still to endure in him.

25. Dispensation] RM 'stewardship.'

26. Mystery] truth not to be discovered by man's unaided power, and therefore known only through divine revelation. This mystery was concealed from the ages before the world and the generations of mankind, in other words from angels and from men.

C. 2. 1. Paul was personally unknown both to the Colossians and the Laodiceans.

2. Full assurance] RM 'fulness.' **To the acknowledgement,** etc.] RV, better, 'that they may know the mystery of God, *even* Christ.' The wealth of full understanding consists in knowledge of the mystery of God, and this mystery of God is no other than Christ Himself, since in Him God's eternal purpose is realised and revealed. They need not go to other sources as the false teachers advise, all is contained in Christ.

CHAPTER 2
The False Teaching and its Refutation

4–15. Hold fast to Christ the All-sufficient Saviour.

Paraphrase. '(4) I emphasise these truths about Christ lest you should be beguiled by plausible persuasions. (5) While I am physically absent from you, I am with you in spirit, rejoicing with you and beholding your order and the firm foundation of your faith in Christ. (6, 7) Let your moral life in Christ Jesus be in harmony with the teaching through which you received Him as Lord ; be firmly rooted and built up in Him, established in faith as you were taught, abounding in thankfulness. (8) Let no one lead you away as his prey by any empty sham that he may recommend as 'philosophy' drawn from human tradition, with the elemental spirits of the world and not Christ for its content. (9, 10) For it is in Christ, not in them, that all the fulness of Godhead dwells, and dwells as an organic whole ; and it is in Him that you find every spiritual need completely met, in Him the Head of the angelic powers. (11) You need no physical circumcision, for in your conversion you received a spiritual circumcision, not the mere cutting away of a fragment of the body, but the removal of the whole carnal nature. Really this went back to the death of Christ in which He underwent this spiritual circumcision ; (12) and you have not only shared Christ's burial in baptism, but also His resurrection through faith in the working of God who raised Him from the dead. (13) You too, though spiritually dead by reason of your trespasses with your carnal nature unremoved by spiritual circumcision ; you did God quicken along with Christ, forgiving us all our trespasses (I say 'us,' not 'you,' for I cannot be silent about God's forgiving love to me), because He had cancelled the bond which was against us by its ordinances, the Law which was hostile to us. (14) And He has taken it out of the way, annulling it by nailing it to Christ's Cross that it might be put to death with Him. (15) He despoiled the angelic forces, and showed them frankly in their true position as givers of an abrogated Law, and rulers of elements to which Christians have died, triumphing over them on the Cross.'

8. Paul is not condemning philosophy properly so called, but the empty doctrines which the false teachers dignified by that name. **Spoil**] RV 'maketh spoil of you'; the word means to lead away as prey. **The rudiments of the world**] better, as mg., 'the elements of the world.' This cannot be the first principles of religion, which could not be well called 'weak and beggarly' (Gal 4⁹), were not strictly common to Jews and heathen, nor an apt description of the false teaching which was something very different. Here they are contrasted with Christ; in Gal 4⁸,⁹ they are identified with those who by nature are not gods; and in Gal 4³ compared with 'guardians and stewards.' They must then be personal beings, not however the spirits of the stars, but the elemental spirits that animate the material world. The false 'philosophy' had these angels not Christ for its subject-matter.

9. The reference is to the exalted Christ. **Bodily**] usually explained to mean in bodily fashion. Probably we should render 'in the form of a body,' and explain it to mean as an organic whole. The fulness of the Godhead is not distributed among the angels, but exists in all its completeness in Christ. **11. The body of the sins of the flesh**] RV 'the body of the flesh.' The carnal nature, the old self, is meant. **The circumcision of Christ**] probably an expression for the death of Christ, in which the Christian ideally died to sin.

12. RV 'Through faith in the working of God.' **13. The uncircumcision of your flesh**] not physical, as if he meant, 'because you were uncircumcised Gentiles,' for the circumcised Jews also were, in Paul's judgment, spiritually dead. He means the spiritual uncircumcision, which consisted in the possession of a carnal nature. **Forgiven you**] RV 'forgiven us.' Paul cannot leave himself out. **14. Handwriting of ordinances, that was against us**] RM 'the bond that was against us by its ordinances.'

15. Principalities and power] mean here precisely what they mean elsewhere in this Epistle. They are not evil spirits, but the angels who gave the Law that brought Christ to His death, and that rule over the material elements. God is the subject throughout the passage.

16–23. Hold fast the treasure of which the false teachers would rob you.

Paraphrase. '(16) Since then the Law no longer exists for you, and the angels have been deposed from their rule, let no one pass judgment on you in the matter of food or sacred seasons. (17) These things are a mere shadow; it is Christ who possesses the substance. (18) Let no one give judgment against you in the matter of gratuitous humility and angel worship, vainly speculating and inflated with fleshly pride. (19) Such a man has no firm grasp of Christ the Head, from whom the whole body of the Church draws and maintains its unity by the joints and ligaments and grows with such growth as God requires. (20) If your conversion meant that in union with Christ you died to the elemental spirits that ruled the old order, why do you act as if you still belonged to it and were subject to them, and permit yourselves to be dictated to in such terms as these, (21) 'You must not handle nor taste nor even touch'? (22) What folly, when every one of the things prohibited is so unimportant that we annihilate it in the very act of use! These prohibitions have their source not in divine, but in human precepts and teachings. (23) They confer, it is true, a reputation for wisdom in respect of gratuitous worship of the angels and humility and ascetic severity to the body, but confer no true honour, and tend to the indulgence of the flesh.'

16. The Jewish character of the false teaching comes very plainly into view here.

17. In Christ they have all in reality which they think they have in Judaism. This v. might almost serve as a text for the Epistle to the Hebrews, which sees in Christianity the religion of eternity realised in time in the person and work of Jesus, but casting its shadow before it into the world in the form of Judaism.

18. Text and translation are alike very uncertain. We should probably correct the text and render : 'Let no one give judgment against you in voluntary humility and worship of the angels, treading the void of air, groundlessly puffed up by the mind of his flesh.' **Intruding into**] If the text is right, 'investigating' would be a better rendering. **Which he hath not seen**] The negative should certainly be omitted with the best MSS. If the text is right, the meaning of the clause seems to be, 'investigating his visions,' but the text is probably incorrect, and we should read with a very slight alteration of the Gk., 'treading the void of air.' They leave the solid ground of fact and experience for the insubstantial bubbles of speculation. **Fleshly mind**] a sharp warning to men who fancied they were achieving the destruction of the flesh by worshipping angels and severity to the body; these practices had their origin in the flesh, which dominated their whole nature, mind and all.

19. Severance from the Head cuts off the supply of spiritual life. **20.** Death with Christ is death to the old order of things, to the world and the Law and the angels who ruled them both. The false teachers would have them revert to a stage they have left below them. **21.** Precepts of the false teachers. **23. Shew of wisdom**] better, 'reputation for wisdom.' **Will worship**] a worship not required of them, the worship of angels. **Neglecting of**] RV 'severity to.' **Not in any honour, etc.**] This clause is extremely difficult, and no satisfactory explanation has been given. The RV rendering, 'but are not of any value against the indulgence of the flesh,' is highly questionable. Hort, our chief textual critic, and Haupt, the best commentator on the Epistle, are agreed that the text is corrupt. Perhaps some words have been accidentally omitted.

CHAPTER 3

THE CHRISTIAN'S RISEN LIFE AND THE DUTIES IT ENTAILS

1-4. Resurrection with Christ and the heavenly life.

Paraphrase] '(1) Seeing then that at your conversion you shared not Christ's death only, but His resurrection, go on to participate in His heavenly life, in that heaven where He is, and where He sits at God's right hand. (2) Let your whole thought be set on heavenly, not on earthly things. (3) For you died with Christ, and your life in union with Him is a hidden life in God. (4) It is not always to remain hidden, for at Christ's second coming it will be revealed; for Christ is our very life, so that His manifestation involves ours.'

2. Affection] RV 'mind.' **3. For ye are dead**] RV 'Ye died,' i.e. at conversion.

5-16. The moral life of the Christian.

Paraphrase. '(5, 6) Since you died and rose with Christ and your life is hidden with Him in God, realise these experiences already ideally yours in putting your sins to death, impurity and covetousness, (7) those heathen vices which draw down God's wrath, which you also once practised. (8) Put away anger, malice, abusive speech, (9) lying, for the old self has been discarded, (10) and the new self has been put on, which is being renewed with a view to deeper knowledge in conformity to the Creator's image. (11) Where there is such a new nature, all distinctions of race, social position, and religion are annulled, and Christ is all and in all the relations of life. (12-14) Be kind, forbearing, and forgiving as Christ forgave you, and let love, which binds all Christians in one, do its perfect work. (15) Let the peace of Christ control your life, do nothing to ruffle it, and be thankful. (16) Let the gospel dwell within you, wisely teach and warn each other in songs of praise, let all your life be lived in Christ's name, and express through Him your thankfulness to God.'

8. Blasphemy] RV 'railing.' **Filthy communication**] rather, 'abusive speech.' **10. In knowledge**] RV 'unto knowledge.' **11. Is**] RV 'cannot be.' **Scythian**] the extreme barbarian. **14. Charity**] RV 'love.' **Bond of perfectness**] the bond in which perfection consists. Love is the bond, in the sense that it binds Christians together (not the virtues).

18-C. 4¹. Reciprocal duties of wives and husbands, children and fathers, slaves and masters.

22. The case of slaves is treated more fully, since the case of Onesimus was engaging Paul's attention. But he wished to keep the gospel clear of any attempt to revolutionise society. It was to be leaven, not dynamite. **Eye-service**] i.e. service most zealously performed when the slave is under observation. **25.** The meaning is probably that the Christian slave must not suppose, because he is a Christian, that God will deal leniently with his misconduct.

CHAPTER 4

EXHORTATION AND GREETING

2-6. Exhortation to prayer and wisdom in dealing with heathen.

6. Grace, not divine grace, but graciousness. Their speech must be winning and wise, **seasoned with salt.**

7-18. Commendation of bearers of the letter, and salutations.

8. I have sent] i.e. I am (now) sending.

He might know your estate] RV 'that ye may know our estate.' **10. Sister's son**] RV 'cousin.' They must have received these commands at an earlier time. **14.** From this v., compared with v. 11, it is clear that Luke was a Gentile. **15.** Probably we should substitute 'Nymphas' and 'her house.' **16. The** *epistle* **from Laodicea**] perhaps our Epistle to the Ephesians.

18. Paul dictated the letter, as was his custom, and signed it with his chained hand. **Remember**] in your prayers.

1 AND 2 THESSALONIANS

INTRODUCTION

THE Epistles of St. Paul fall naturally into four groups, each divided from the others by a considerable interval of time. In the earliest of these groups, written during the Second Missionary Journey, the great central thought is the coming of Christ to judge the world. The second group (1 and 2 Corinthians, Galatians, Romans), written during the Third Missionary Journey, has for its leading theme the reconciliation of man with God and with his fellow-man by means of the Cross of Christ. The third group (Philippians, Colossians, Ephesians, Philemon), written during the first Roman captivity, dwells on the thought of Christ as the great King and Head of the Church. The fourth group (1 and 2 Timothy, Titus), written at the close of the Apostle's life, deals with practical questions of Church organisation. The two Epistles to the Thessalonians together form the first group. In them we have the earliest of St. Paul's writings, and, with the probable exception of the Epistle of St. James, the earliest books of the New Testament.

1. The Persons Addressed. The Thessalonians inhabited the chief city of Macedonia. Macedonia was the first European country in which St. Paul preached, and he always regarded it with peculiar affection. In Ac 16, 17 we have St. Luke's wonderfully vivid narrative of the bringing of the Gospel to Macedonia. After some stay at Philippi the Apostle went through Amphipolis and Apollonia to Thessalonica, where he stayed for some six months (Ac 17 1-9), preaching first to the Jews as usual, and afterwards winning many converts among Gentile proselytes and women as well as among the heathen. Jewish intrigue at length drove him away. This famous city of Thessalonica, originally called Therma, had been re-founded by Cassander about 315 B.C., and, owing to its natural advantages, had grown and flourished. After the Roman conquest the great military road, the Via Egnatia, connected it with Italy and the East, while its fine harbour made it a great commercial centre. It was made a Free City by Augustus, with the privilege of self-government (Ac 17 6). At the present time, under the slightly altered name of Saloniki, it is the second city of the Turkish empire, with a population of 70,000. It contained (and still contains) a considerable number of Jews, and had a large native

population. It was from this latter class that St. Paul's converts were chiefly drawn (cp. 1 Th 1 9 2 14, and observe the absence of OT. quotations), and it is plain that they had the characteristic virtues, as well as some of the characteristic defects, of their race, which was brave, independent, persevering, and liberty-loving. But the Thessalonian converts sometimes allowed their independence to degenerate into undue self-assertion and disregard of authority (1 Th 5 14 2 Th 3 6, 7). Yet, on the whole, St. Paul was proud and fond of them. Notwithstanding terrible persecution, they had remained firm (1 Th 1 6 2 8, 14 2 Th 1 4-7). Though poor they were generous (2 Cor 8 1-5). Their influence was felt throughout Macedonia and Greece (1 Th 1 8). Their faith, hope, and love filled the Apostle's heart with joy (1 Th 1 2, 3).

2. Time and Place of Writing. The First Epistle was written towards the close of the Second Missionary Journey (? 51 A.D.), some time about the middle of the eighteen months' stay at Corinth (Ac 18). St. Paul had not long left Thessalonica (1 Th 2 17), but had had time to visit Athens (1 Th 3 1). Timothy had been to Macedonia and back (1 Th 3 6), and Silas (Silvanus) who is never mentioned after the Second Missionary Journey, is now the Apostle's companion (1 Th 1 1). There had been time for the influence of the Thessalonian Church to make itself felt (1 Th 1 7, 8). Some members of the Christian community had died (1 Th 4 13). The Second Epistle must have been written towards the close of the same Corinthian stay, when St. Paul had received news that the teaching of his first letter had been misrepresented and misunderstood (2 Th 2 2). Silvanus and Timothy were still with him (2 Th 1 1). Persecution was still raging (2 Th 1 4), and there was much excitement and increasing disorder on account of expectation of an immediate coming of Christ (2 Th 2 2, 3).

3. Reception in the Church. These Epistles are quoted or alluded to from very early times. Ignatius, Polycarp, Irenæus, Justin Martyr, and Tertullian refer to them. They are included in Marcion's Canon (circ. 140 A.D.), and are found in the early list of the books of the NT. known as the Muratorian Canon (circ. 190 A.D.). The internal evidence is also strong. Passages like 1 Th 1 5-9 2 1-12 4 15 5 27 2 Th 3 8, 9, and the style and language, the personal touches, the intercessions and requests for the prayers of the Thessalonians, are characteristically Pauline. The only serious objections to the genuineness of the Epistles are connected with the section about the Man of Sin (2 Th 2 1-12), which is said by some to be un-Pauline and founded on the Revelation of St. John. But when we remember the large place occupied by Apocalyptic questions in Jewish and early Christian thought, the evident interest which they had for the Thessalonians, and the great prophecy of His coming uttered by our Lord Himself, we shall have no difficulty in coming to the conclusion that St. Paul would naturally deal with the subject quite independently of St. John or any other NT. writer.

4. Value and Importance. These earliest of St. Paul's Epistles, short as they are, contain much of extreme interest to Bible students. They show us how St. Paul presented the gospel to heathen converts. They give us a vivid picture of Christian life in the first days before dissensions and false beliefs had vexed the peace of the Church, when teachers and taught loved each other, and faith and zeal were yet glowing. Incidentally they reveal to us much of the writer's mind and character (1 Th 3 5-10, 11-13 2 Th 3 7-12). But, most important of all, they tell us what were the doctrines held and taught some twenty years after the Ascension. (a) Christ is frequently called 'the Lord,' 'our Lord.' He is addressed in prayer (1 Th 3 11 2 Th 2 16, 17). He died (1 Th 2 15), rose again (1 Th 1 10), is in Heaven (1 Th 4 16), and shall come to judge the world (1 Th 4 14-18). He is the Redeemer and Deliverer (1 Th 5 9, 10). (b) The Holy Spirit is given to Christians (1 Th 1 5, 6 4 8 5 19). (c) The Church is already organised. The Apostles have authority (1 Th 5 27 2 Th 3 14). There is a regular ministry (1 Th 5 12, 13). Baptism may be alluded to in 1 Th 4 8. There were already meetings, probably for communion, where the 'holy kiss' was used (1 Th 5 26, 27, Justin's 'Apology,' I. 65). The local Church was united in bonds of brotherhood with other Churches (1 Th 1 8 2 14 4 10), and with the faithful departed (1 Th 4 13, 17). Thus, these Epistles, besides giving a picture of Church life in early days, testify to the main articles of the Creed.

5. Analysis. First Epistle. Two main divisions : (a) Personal, 1 1-3 13; (b) Hortatory, 4 1-5 28. 1 1-10, Salutation and thanksgiving for their conversion and progress. 2 1-12, Sketch of the Apostle's own work at Thessalonica : cp. Ac 17 1-10. 2 13-16, A second thanksgiving, with special reference to their persecutions. 2 17-3 10, His anxiety about the Thessalonians, and the joy with which he had received the good news about them brought by Timothy. 3 11-13, A solemn prayer for them to Christ as God.

4 1-12, Exhortations to purity of life, brotherly love, quietness and industry. 4 13-5 11, The chief subject of the Epistle (alluded to in 1 10 and 3 13), the Second Advent. The faithful departed, about whom the Thessalonians were anxious, shall rise by virtue of their union with Christ, and shall rise before those who are now alive. But the time is uncertain ('Watch, therefore, and be sober'). 5 12-22, Practical exhortation : (a) vv. 12-15, Social duties ; (b) vv. 16-22, Spiritual duties (joy, prayer, thanksgiving, etc.). 5 23-28, Concluding prayer, injunctions, and benediction.

Second Epistle. 1 1-4, Salutation and thanksgiving. 1 5-2 14, The Second Advent. 'You have suffered persecution, but God is just, and will requite both you and your enemies at the coming of Christ. I pray you may be found ready for it. But this coming will not be till after the great Apostasy and the revelation and destruction of the Man of Sin and all those whom he has deceived. I thank God you have been saved from this fate.' 2 15-17, 'Hold fast the Faith. I pray Christ and God the Father to comfort and strengthen you.' 3 1-15, Exhortation to intercessory prayer (cp. 1 Th 5 25), hopes for their progress, rebukes to the idle and disorderly. 3 16-18, Concluding prayer and benediction.

The Second Epistle presupposes the First : cp. 2 Th 2 15 3 6 with 1 Th 4 1-8, 11 ; and there is a great similarity in structure between the two (1 Th 1 1, 2 3 11 5 23 2 Th 1 1-3 2 16 3 16).

6. The **chief subject of the Epistle** is, as has been said, **the Coming** (or, as St. Paul calls it, the Presence) **of Christ—the Second Advent.** And although he nowhere speaks definitely as to the time of this Coming (which no man knows, Mt 24 36), he certainly uses language which suggests that 'there was a reasonable expectation of the Lord's appearing soon.' The expectation is doubtless based on our Lord's great prophecy of the destruction of Jerusalem and of Judaism found in Mt 24 and elsewhere. In the Second Epistle especially the language used often recalls that of our Lord (2 Th 2 1-4, 7, 9 Mt 24 6, 10-13, 15, 24), and the final Coming seems to be closely connected in St. Paul's mind with the overthrow of Judaism. In so far as he expected that these two events would happen together, or that the Final Coming would be soon after the overthrow of Judaism, he was doubtless mistaken. But it is to be observed that (a) the overthrow of Judaism by the destruction of Jerusalem and the Temple was in very truth a Coming of Christ to Judgment. 'The destruction of Jerusalem was an event which has no parallel in history. It was the outward and visible sign of a great epoch in the divine government of the world. It marked the inauguration of a new order of things. The Messianic kingdom was now fully come. The final act of the King was to sit upon the throne of His glory and judge His people.' (b) St. Paul's mistake, if mistake it be, does not in the least affect the value of his ethical teaching on the subject. For he points out to the Thessalonians the true way of preparing for the Final Advent which Christ meant His Church to expect. They were to make ready for it, not by feverish excitement and restlessness, but by the quiet, steady performance of everyday duty as in His sight, with the assurance that His followers, whether living or asleep in Him, were in His safe keeping.

1 THESSALONIANS

CHAPTER 1

SALUTATION AND THANKSGIVING

1. Salutation. For **Silvanus** (Silas) see Ac 15 22 16 20,37,38. Timothy was one of St. Paul's most constant companions (Ac 16 1 Ro 16 21 1 Cor 4 14-17 2 Cor 1 19 Phil 1 1 2 19-24 2 Tim 1 5 3 14). **The church .. which is in God,** etc.] a phrase peculiar to this Epistle. The Church is in living union with God and Christ (Col 2 19).

2–10. Fervent thanksgiving for their conversion and growth in grace.

4. Better, 'Knowing, brethren beloved of God, your election, how that,' etc. 'Election,' i.e. to Christian and Church privileges (2 Tim 2 10). **5. Assurance**] RVmg. 'fulness.' They preached with deep conviction of the truth and power of the message entrusted to them. **6. Affliction**] referring to the persecution and suffering recorded in Ac 17 10-13. **Joy of**] i.e. joy inspired by the Holy Ghost. **7. In Macedonia**] of which Thessalonica was the capital. **And Achaia**] of which Corinth, where the Apostle was, was capital. **Achaia**, the Roman province (= Greece). **8. To speak anything**] i.e. to recount their faith. **9. They themselves**] i.e. the dwellers in all the places the Apostle and his companions had visited or heard from. **The living and true God**] better, 'a living and true God.' The Thessalonian converts had, as a rule, been heathens, though some were proselytes (i.e. Jews by religion), Ac 17 4. **10. To wait**] to look for the Second Coming. **Jesus, which delivered us from the wrath to come**] better, 'delivereth us from the wrath which is approaching.'

CHAPTER 2

THE NATURE OF ST. PAUL'S LIFE AND WORK AT THESSALONICA

2. The persecution at the Roman garrison-town of Philippi made a deep impression on St. Paul the Roman citizen (Ac 16 19-40 Phil 1 30). It was the indignity that hurt him. **Contention**] better, 'conflict.' **3.** It would ▸ em that St. Paul was at first looked upon by some as an impostor, seeking his own ends. He declares that he came with a sincere desire for their salvation only. **Deceit**] better, 'error.' **Uncleanness**] Impurity was often associated with heathen worship, and this was especially the case at Thessalonica and Corinth.

4. Allowed] better, 'approved.' **5. Cloke of covetousness**] i.e. covering to conceal avarice. **6-11.** St. Paul says that he might have made a display of apostolic authority and have demanded pecuniary support : see 1 Cor 9. But he was like a babe (better than 'gentle'), or like a mother who nurses her own children, or a father who guides and directs his son. At the same time he supported himself by tentmaking (Ac 18 3 20 34).

13-16. A second thanksgiving for their faith and patience under persecution.

14. The (Gentile) Thessalonian Church had suffered much at the hands of their fellow-countrymen, just as the Jewish Church had suffered from the unbelieving Jews. Here was a bond of union and sympathy between the two. **15, 16.** A characteristic outburst. The Jews had followed St. Paul with unceasing hostility in Europe as well as in Asia. They have driven him from Thessalonica and Beroea, and were doing their utmost against him at Corinth. Their narrow exclusiveness (**forbidding us to speak to the Gentiles**) and hatred of other nations (**contrary to all men**) were a bitter trial to a patriot like St. Paul. **To the uttermost**] i.e. there was no longer any hope of their repentance or escape from their doom (Mt 23 32). The end was close at hand.

17–C. 3 16. 'Till Timothy's good report of you reached us, we were anxious about you, but now we rejoice and bless God for the news he brings, that you have stood firm under persecution.' **18.** St. Paul generally uses the 1st person plural in these Epistles, including Silvanus and Timothy with himself. Here, however, he speaks for himself. The hindrance may have been an illness—probably malarial fever (2 Cor 12 7), or Jewish hostility. To St. Paul **Satan** is a real person (Ro 16 20 2 Cor 11 14 1 Tim 1 20). **19.** The prospect of presenting his converts to Christ fills the Apostle with joy.

CHAPTER 3

THE APOSTLE'S ANXIETY ABOUT HIS CONVERTS

1. Forbear] better, 'endure the suspense.' **2. Our fellow-labourer**] better, 'God's fellow-worker' or 'minister,' RV. **3. Should be moved**] better, 'led astray.' **Afflictions**] at the hands of Jews and Gentiles : see Ac 17 5 f.

6. Now when] better, 'as soon as.' **Charity**] RV 'love.' **8. We live**] it puts new life in us. **If ye stand fast**] better, 'if only ye stand fast.' The Gk. expresses some doubt and anxiety. **10.** 'I pray unceasingly and urgently to the end that I may see you again and correct your shortcomings.' The prayer was answered after some years (Ac 20 1, 2).

11–13. A prayer to Christ as co-equal with the Father, with which the first section of the Epistle ends : cp. 2 Th 2 16.

11. The verb is in the singular, emphasising the reference to Christ, who is also called 'the Lord' in v. 12. The key-note of these Epistles is again struck at the concluding words of the prayer, 'at the coming' (lit. 'presence') 'of our Lord Jesus Christ with all His saints' (cp. 2 19).

CHAPTER 4

EXHORTATION TO PURITY AND BROTHERLY LOVE. THE SECOND ADVENT

1. 'You are already walking in the right path. I want you to advance in it more and more.'

3, 4. Translate, 'For this is a thing willed by God, even your sanctification, that ye shall abstain from fornication (cp. Ac 15 20), that each one of you should learn to win his body to a state of purity and honour.' **Vessel**] i.e. body. Some think the word means 'wife,' but this is not so likely. **5. Lust of concupiscence**] RV 'passion of lust.' **6. Go beyond and defraud**] RV 'overreach (mg.), and wrong' (i.e. by his sin). *Any*] should certainly be 'this.' **7.** Better, 'For God called us not for uncleanness, but to be in a state of purity.' **Who hath also given**] better, 'who is ever giving' (present tense).

This passage (vv. 3–8) contains in brief a statement of the Christian doctrine of purity. Impurity is, (1) (from the point of view of the man himself) a dishonouring of the temple of the Holy Ghost (1 Cor 3 16) : since He takes up His abode in it, and since Christ has become incarnate, and the body is to rise again, we must honour the body, not defile it; (2) (from the point of view of our brothers and sisters) a violation of the law of love—a fraud and a cheat. Sins of the flesh were very lightly regarded by the heathen world.

9. Brotherly love] better, 'love of the brethren' ; i.e. the special love to be shown towards all the members of the Church.

10. In all Macedonia] These words imply that there were other Churches there besides those of which we read in the Acts. They also show that these Churches were not isolated. The idea of a Catholic Church is growing. **11. Study**] better, 'strive earnestly.' Religious excitement, especially in view of the expected coming of Christ, was a danger to the Thessalonian Church (2 Th 3 12). It caused neglect of 'the duty of every day.' **12. Work** would give them, (1) respect in the eyes of their heathen neighbours (**them that are without**) ; (2) independence (Eph 4 28). **Honestly**] or, as we should now say, 'honourably.'

4 13–5 11. The Second Advent. The dead in Christ will rise before the living, and both alike will share in the life everlasting. But the time of the Advent is uncertain. Let us therefore watch and be sober.

13. Are asleep] better, 'are lying asleep.' The Thessalonians were anxious as to the part which those who had died in the Faith would take in the Second Advent, which was believed to be near at hand. **Others**] better, 'all the rest,' i.e. the heathen who, even if they believed in some sort of an existence after death, had no hope of immortality. **14. Which sleep in Jesus**] better, 'that are fallen asleep through Jesus,' i.e. in communion with Him. **15. Prevent**] better, 'be before,' i.e. the dead, about whom you are anxious, will be at no disadvantage at the Advent, so far as its blessedness is concerned.

16. Cp. Mt 24 30, 31. At the Resurrection of the Just the dead will rise before the living : see 1 Cor 15 51, 52 regarding the spiritual body.

CHAPTER 5

THE NEED OF WATCHFULNESS. FINAL INJUNCTIONS

1. Times and seasons] St. Paul always lays stress on the uncertainty as to the time of the Advent (2 Th 2 2 ; cp. 2 Pet 3 3, 4). **3. When they shall say**] i.e. when people are saying. **4, 5. Thief**] better, 'as thieves.' Thieves work in darkness. You are all children of light. Live up to your birthright. **6. Let us not sleep**] i.e. in carelessness and sin. **Others**] better, 'the others.'

8–10. Mason paraphrases, 'Let us arm ourselves with a brave hope of our salvation, for it will be against God's will if we perish. He means us to save ourselves by union with Him who put an end to death for us by dying, and made all who wait for His coming to live, whether they be in the world's sense dead or alive.'

8. A new metaphor (cp. Eph 6 13-17 Isa 59 17), but suggested by the idea of watchfulness.

9. To obtain salvation] (Phil 2 12, 13) or, perhaps, 'for the adoption which consists in salvation' : cp. 2 Th 2 14. **10. Whether we wake or sleep**] i.e. whether we are alive or dead at the Advent.

11. Edify] better, 'build up.' **As also ye do**] St. Paul always praises and encourages where he can.

12–28. Exhortations to respect for their clergy, orderly living, prayer and other spiritual duties, and conclusion. **12. Know**] better, ' value.' The probable reference is to the presbyters sometimes called (in allusion to their duties) ' overseers ' (1 Tim 5 17). **14. Feebleminded**] better, 'fainthearted.' **The weak**] i.e. in faith, Ro 15 1. **15.** Cp. Mt 5 39 1 Pet 3 8, 9. **16. Evermore**] better, 'always.' Joy is a necessary part of the Christian character (Ro 14 17 Phil 2 18 3 1 4 4), and a Christian duty. **18.** Cp. Eph 5 20. Prayer is put between joy and thanksgiving, because it is only by constant prayer that we are enabled to feel true joy or gratitude. God's will towards us is that we should be always joyful, prayerful, grateful, and (3 3) pure in life.

20. The Christian prophets were an order of men specially inspired to reveal the will of God to others ('mission-preachers '), who might sometimes (Ac 11 27, 28 21 10, 11) be charged to foretell the future : see 1 Cor 11 4, 5 14 5 Eph 4 11 3 5 1 Tim 1 18 4 14. 'Prophets' are also mentioned in the early Christian tract known as the ' Didache,' or ' Teaching of the Twelve Apostles.' The Thessalonians seem to have been disposed to check enthusiasm. **21. Prove**] better, 'test.' You must test all these thoughts by spiritual standards, since there is an inspiration which is false (1 Jn 4 1). **22. All appearance**] better, ' every form.' Good is one ; evil is manifold.

23. May your spirit (by which man maintains communion with God) **and soul** (the feelings and emotions) **and body** (which is to rise again) be preserved entire and without blame, and be so found at the Advent. **24. Will do it**] i.e. will preserve your spirit, soul, and body.

25, 26. The duty of intercessory prayer (? especially at the Eucharist, where the **holy kiss** was a part of the rites from very early times). **27. I charge**] better, 'I adjure.' The reading was probably to be at the Eucharist (Justin Martyr, 'Apol.' 1. 65–67). St. Paul wishes his earliest letter to be read to **all** without any suppression or omissions, otherwise a wrong use might be made of his authority.

---

2 THESSALONIANS

CHAPTER 1

SALUTATIONS. THE SECOND ADVENT

1–4. Greeting and thanksgiving for their constant faith and love and patience under persecution : cp. 1 Th 1 3.

5–C. 2 17. The Coming of Christ to judgment. Much is to happen before Christ comes.

5. A manifest token] The words refer to their sufferings and their patience. If God is righteous there must come a time when wrongs such as theirs shall be righted, and patience like theirs be rewarded. Thus the sufferings and patience of the Thessalonians become a proof that there is a judgment to come (Phil 1 8). **7. Rest**] better, 'relief.' The true rest and relief comes to the faithful when Christ comes.

8. Taking vengeance] better, ' awarding retribution.' **Them that know not God, and that obey not**] better, (1) 'them that know not, and (2) them that obey not.' Possibly (1) Gentiles and (2) Jews.

9. The **everlasting destruction** (only here) consists in exclusion from God's presence.

11. Calling] cp. Phil 3 14, Heb 3 1. **All the good pleasure of** *his* **goodness**] better, ' all delight in well-doing.'

CHAPTER 2

THE GREAT APOSTASY

2. Spirit] i.e. a pretended revelation uttered by a false prophet. **Letter as from us**] perhaps a forged letter (the probable meaning), cp. 3 17, or a misunderstanding of the First Epistle.

3–10. It will be convenient to treat this difficult passage as a whole. Literally translated, it runs thus : ' Let no man deceive you in any wise : for [the Final Presence of our Lord shall not be] except (or till) the falling away come first and the Man of Lawlessness be revealed, the son of perdition, he that opposeth and exalted himself against all that is called God or an object of worship, so that he sitteth in the Sanctuary of God, setting himself forth as God (Do ye not remember that, when I was yet with you, I told you these things?) And now ye know about that (power) which restraineth, to the end that he may be revealed to his own season. For the mystery of lawlessness is already working, only there is one that restraineth now till he be taken out of the way. And then shall the Lawless one be revealed, whom the Lord Jesus shall slay with the breath of His mouth, and bring to naught by the Epiphany of His Presence—

even him whose presence is according to the working of Satan, in all power and signs and wonders of falsehood, and in every deceit of unrighteousness for the ruin of those who are perishing because they received not the love of the truth, that they might be saved.'

In the first place, we must remember that St. Paul is here speaking of something which is already at work, and the overthrow of which is to precede that Final Presence of the Lord which the Thessalonians thought to be immediately impending. Realising this, we shall at once reject all those interpretations which see in the Man of Sin (Lawlessness) some historical character (e.g. one of the Popes, or of Napoleon I) who lived after St. Paul's time. We must also remember that the Thessalonians had the key to the interpretation of the passage which we do not possess, since they had been orally instructed by St. Paul on the subject. But, though certainty is now impossible, we may be guided to a probable solution by studying the passage in connexion with the Revelation of St. John, and (especially) our Lord's great prophecy recorded in Mt 24 Mk 13 and Lk 21. When, further, we remember how bitterly St. Paul felt the opposition of his fellow-countrymen to Christ (1 Th 2 15, 16), and how full the Gospels are of denunciation of Jewish sins, we shall be led to the conclusion that 'the Apostasy' is the Jewish apostasy, and that the 'Man of Sin (Lawlessness)' is either some false Christ (Mt 24 24), many of whom appeared among the Jews about this time, or (more probably) the spirit of Judaism personified. (A somewhat similar personification may be found in Rev 2, 3, where 'the angel' of each of the seven churches seems to denote, not any official, but the Church itself.) The Jews had been chosen of God to bear witness to Him, and they had betrayed their trust. Their worship was a lie (Mt 23 16-22). They were 'a synagogue of Satan' (Rev 2 9 3 9). They had made the Temple a den of robbers (Mt 21 13). Some of them could perform lying wonders (Mt 12 27 Mk 13 22 Ac 19 13). They were persecuting the Church of Christ and opposing the truth (Ac 13 6, 45 14 19 17 5-13 18 12 22 22 23 12). And so their apostasy was to be revealed and punished by the utter (but not final, Ro 11 25-27) overthrow of Judaism, and the destruction of the Holy City and the Temple in 70 A.D. by the Romans. This great event would come before the final advent, which the Thessalonians were expecting immediately. The further question who, or what, is the Person or Power that restrains the Man of Lawlessness, is one of considerable difficulty. The usual answer is 'the authority of the Roman empire, or perhaps the reigning Roman Emperor Claudius' (41-54 A.D.). In the very earliest days of Christianity the Romans did protect the Chris-

tians from Jewish violence (Ac 18 14, 15 23 23, 24 25 14-21). But soon, under the Emperor Nero, this attitude was exchanged for one of hostility, after the fire at Rome in 64 A.D. And it is hard to see how the words 'until he be taken out of the way' can apply to a Roman emperor or to the Roman empire in its dealings with Judaism. It is possible that by the Restrainer St. Paul means the Christian Church in Jerusalem—the Mother-Church of which the Thessalonians 'became imitators' (1 Th 2 14). We know that St. James, the head of that Church, had great influence over his unbelieving fellow-countrymen, and may well have exercised a restraining power over them. Some Jews even appear to have seen in the siege of Jerusalem the punishment for his murder by the high priest Ananus. It is to be noted that the Jerusalem Church, obeying the Lord's command (Mt 24 15, 16), left the doomed city on the approach of the Roman army and fled to Pella. Thus she might be said to be 'taken out of the way' of the evil to come.

3. Falling away] Gk. 'apostasy.' **4.** The reference is to the pretensions of a false Messiah.

7. Mystery] This word in NT. always denotes something once hidden, but now revealed, or soon to be revealed (1 Cor 4 1 Col 2 2 4 3 Eph 6 19). **8. Brightness,** etc.] rather, 'manifestation of His presence.' **11. Strong delusion**] better, 'inner working of error.' Those who obstinately refuse the truth at last become incapable of receiving it. **12. Damned**] RV 'judged.' **13. From the beginning**] perhaps (with the oldest MS), 'as firstfruits.' **15. The traditions**] i.e. the truths taught, whether orally or by writing.

CHAPTER 3
EXHORTATIONS, REBUKES, AND BENEDICTION

2. Unreasonable] almost 'outrageous.' **Faith**] better, 'the Faith.' **3. Evil**] RV 'the evil one.' **5. Patient waiting for**] better, 'the patience of.' **6.** Evidently disorder in the Church had increased since the First Epistle was written. **Withdraw yourselves**] or, 'shun.'

8. Cp. 1 Th 2 9. **9. Power**] better, 'the right.' We have the right to be supported, but for the sake of example we waived it in your case (1 Cor 9 3-18). **11. Working not at all .. busybodies**] i.e. neglecting their own work (in view of a supposed immediate Advent), but interfering with that of others. **16. By all means**] better, 'in all places,' or, 'in all ways.' **17.** St. Paul wrote the body of his letters through a secretary, but he added a few words in his own large handwriting, in order that his correspondents might know them to be genuine (1 Cor 16 21 2 Th 2 2 Col 4 18). **So I write**] better, 'this is my handwriting.'

THE PASTORAL EPISTLES

GENERAL INTRODUCTION

THE two Epistles to Timothy and the Epistle to Titus constitute a group by themselves, and are usually called 'The Pastoral Epistles,' because they deal to a large extent with matters of Church organisation and government. That they were all written by one author is generally agreed, not only by those who accept the tradition that St. Paul was the writer, but also by those who reject it. It will be convenient, therefore, to discuss the points common to all three, before dealing with each in detail.

1. Authorship. The authorship of these Epistles is one of the questions of NT. criticism upon which scholars are sharply divided. The objections urged against the Pauline authorship are of different kinds and varying degrees of weight, and may be briefly enumerated as follows : (a) Historical difficulties ; (b) References to heresies ; (c) Church organisation ; (d) The description of St. Paul in the salutations ; (e) Language and style.

(a) **Historical Difficulties.** It is impossible to find a place for these Epistles in the scheme of St. Paul's life, which is derived from the narrative in Acts and the references in the acknowledged Epistles. The journeys to which the Apostle makes reference are inconsistent with his movements as recorded in Acts. According to 1 Tim 1 3, Timothy had been left at Ephesus while Paul proceeded to Macedonia ; but in Ac 19 22 20 1 Timothy was sent from Ephesus to Macedonia in advance of St. Paul. In 1 Tim 3 14 the Apostle intended to return to Timothy at Ephesus ; but in Ac 20 4 Timothy was with him in Greece, and in 20 14,17 St. Paul did not go to Ephesus, but sent for the Ephesian elders to meet him at Miletus. So in 2 Tim 4 20 the reference to Trophimus cannot relate to the journey recorded in Ac 20 17-21 8, for Trophimus accompanied the Apostle to Jerusalem (Ac 21 29). Again, the references in Tit 1 5 3 12, where St. Paul speaks of leaving Titus in Crete and asks him to meet him at Nicopolis, cannot be connected with the only occasion on which the Apostle visited Crete according to Acts (27 8), viz. when he was a prisoner en route for Rome, where Acts leaves him still under arrest.

These difficulties, however, are obviated when the tradition is accepted that St. Paul after his first imprisonment (Ac 28 30 Phil 1 13)

was set free in 62 or 63 A.D., and arrested again in 66 or 67. In the First Epistle of Clement of Rome to the Corinthians (about 97 A.D.) the writer speaks of St. Paul having 'gone to the extreme limit of the west.' This expression in a letter written at Rome seems to point to Spain. St. Paul had once hoped to visit that country (Ro 15 24) ; and in the 'Muratorian Fragment,' a document of date about 200 A.D., it is indicated that he had done so : a tradition which is mentioned later by Eusebius in the 4th cent., and Chrysostom in the 5th cent. If the genuineness of the Pastoral Epistles is established on other grounds, they give powerful testimony to St. Paul's activity during the period after Acts.

(b) **References to Heresies.** Many critics see in these Epistles, and especially in 1 Tim (1 4 4 1-3 6 20), references to heresies which prevailed widely in the Church during the 2nd cent., and are classed under the name of Gnosticism. These heresies dealt with solutions of the problem of evil ; they combined ideas from Jewish and heathen sources with Christian truth ; they tended to represent Christ's earthly career and sufferings as only seeming, not real (Docetism) ; and they exalted knowledge (gnosis, whence the name) as a special privilege of the few, and superior to faith, the possession of the many.

The references to heresies in the Pastoral Epistles, however, are extremely vague and indefinite. There is no reference to Docetism, such as we find in 1 John (4 1-3), supposed to have been written at Ephesus before 100 A.D. ; and the references to false doctrines in 1 Tim 4 1-4 6 20 do not seem to require a 2nd-cent. date, or to conflict with the Pauline authorship any more than the references to heresies in Col 2 8,18,23 require that Epistle to be denied to St. Paul, and assigned to the 2nd cent. In the early Church, composed, as almost every congregation was, of elements diverse in race, education, and religion, it is not surprising to find the germs of false doctrine from the beginning, showing themselves sometimes in tendencies towards Jewish legalism (1 Tim 1 7 Tit 1 14 3 9), as was the case among the Galatians at an earlier date ; sometimes in philosophical speculations drawn from heathen sources (1 Tim 4 7 6 20), as was previously the case among the Colossians. The heresies indicated in the Pastoral Epistles seem largely Jewish in origin. They are speculations about the Law (1 Tim 1 7-10; cp. 2 Tim 3 14-17), about genealogies (1 Tim 1 4 Tit 3 9), about Jewish fables (Tit 1 14, and probably also 1 Tim 1 4 4 7); and while the ascetic practices (1 Tim 4 1-4) which some taught may have had some heathen elements, they are quite as likely to have been suggested by exaggerations of Jewish ceremonialism: see Ro 14 3 1 Cor 8 Col 2 16, and cp. 1 Tim 4 4 with Ac 10 11-15.

(c) **Church Organisation.** It has been objected to St. Paul's authorship of these letters that the indications of Church organisation are such as point to a time later than that of St. Paul. Titus was appointed to 'ordain elders in every city' (1 5) in Crete; and both he and Timothy were instructed as to the qualifications of 'the bishop' (Tit 1 7-9 1 Tim 3 1-7). Timothy was also given instructions regarding the deacons (1 Tim 3 8-10). The organisation, however, does not seem when examined to be more developed than was necessary in the Churches almost from the beginning. Deacons had to be appointed at a very early date in the Church at Jerusalem— although the name was not then given them, the corresponding verb is used of their work —(Ac 6 4); and elders were appointed by St. Paul in every Church in Galatia on his first missionary journey (Ac 14 23); while at Ephesus, at the end of his third journey, they were evidently a recognised body (Ac 20 17) entrusted with the duties of overseeing and teaching the flock (20 28). Nor is the term 'the bishop' (1 Tim 3 2 Tit 1 7) necessarily an indication of a post-apostolic date. For (1) it is largely held that the terms 'bishop' (*episcopos*) and 'elder' (*presbuteros*) are used synonymously in these Epistles, as they undoubtedly were at an earlier period (Ac 20 28; cp. Phil 1 1); and (2) even if, as is also influentially maintained, 'the bishop' here means the principal minister of the Church, it would still be hazardous to pronounce the Epistles non-Pauline. Many good authorities trace back the beginnings of episcopacy to the apostolic age, and so it is by no means impossible that in an apostolic Epistle, written as late as 65–67 A.D., the term 'bishop' might occur in its later sense.

(d) **Paul an Apostle.** Another objection has been found in the fact that, in letters written to intimate friends and disciples, the writer should emphatically assert his apostleship. This trait, it is said, indicates that they were written by some one who was using the Apostle's name at a later time, as the Apostle himself did not mention his apostleship in letters written to those with whom he was on friendly terms, whether churches or individuals (Phil 1 1 Philemon v. 1). But these Pastoral Epistles are not, properly speaking, private letters. They were probably intended to be

read to the Churches: 'the author is writing with his eye on the community'; and the fact that heresy and incipient faction were to be guarded against, sufficiently explains the assertion of apostolic dignity.

(e) **Language and Style.** The difference in language and style which exists between these Epistles and the undoubted letters of the Apostle is felt by many to be a serious objection to their genuineness. It is impossible here to enter into details; but there are a great many words and phrases found in these books, which are absent from the other writings of St. Paul, and there are over a hundred and seventy words used which are not elsewhere present in NT. A number of these words are, of course, necessitated by the fact that new subjects are here discussed; but there are many which cannot be thus explained. And on this ground alone many refer the Epistles to a later writer, who, according to some, has incorporated in them (especially in 2 Tim) fragments of genuine lost letters of St. Paul.

The argument from language, however, is by no means conclusive. The differences from the other Pauline Epistles in language and style may be the consequence of lapse of time. As the Apostle became older and travelled over new ground, meeting with new experiences, and making new converts, it would not be wonderful if he gained a wider command of language, and adopted a different mode of expression, according to the necessities of the case. As Farrar points out ('St. Paul': Excursus 27), 'St. Paul was the main creator of theological language.' He 'had to find the correct and adequate expression for conceptions which as yet were extremely unfamiliar. Every year would add to the vocabulary, and the harvest of new expressions would always be most rich where truths already familiar were brought into collision with heresies altogether new.'

It has recently been ascertained by an examination in detail of about two hundred words which are not elsewhere found in the NT. that none of them had its origin later than St. Paul, that nearly half of them are found in the Septuagint, that over fifty are found in classical writers and writers who flourished not later than St. Paul, and that almost all the rest can be explained as necessitated by new subjects, or formed from Pauline or biblical words, or as otherwise consistent with the apostolic authorship. The argument from language would be valid and conclusive had it been shown that a number of words used in these Epistles did not come into use until after St. Paul's day. The fact that none can be shown to be of later date, but that almost all can be proved to be contemporaneous with the Apostle, indicates that there is nothing in the language of the Pastorals to conflict with their claims to be St. Paul's. It may be added that even critics adverse to the Pauline authorship recognise in these letters the reflexions of thoughts and ideas characteristic of the Apostle. Many think they see incorporated in them reminiscences of the Apostle and private notes he had written to companions and friends (e.g. 2 Tim 1 15-18 4 6-22 Tit 3 12, 13), and describe them as Pauline, though not by the Apostle himself. Advocates of a 2nd-cent. date admit that a detailed comparison of the Pastorals with the letters of Clement of Rome, Ignatius, and Polycarp, exhibits the former as 'astonishingly superior': and acknowledge that the writer was saturated with the contents of the genuine Epistles of St. Paul. Apart, therefore, from the historical and internal difficulties which have been dealt with, the Epistles suggest the apostolic authorship, and bear the marks of St. Paul's personality; and as these difficulties seem all to be capable of explanation, we need have little hesitation in receiving them for what they profess to be.

2. The External Evidence for the Pastorals is both early and good. They were probably made use of in the Epistles of Ignatius and Polycarp in the first quarter of the 2nd cent.; Irenæus (circ. 180) quotes from 1 Tim as a genuine letter of St. Paul; and they seemed to have been known to the writer of the letter from Vienne and Lyons about the same date. Tertullian and Clement of Alexandria, the African contemporaries of Irenæus, also speak of them as St. Paul's. Clement of Rome, who flourished in the end of the 1st and beginning of the 2nd cent., has many parallels to passages in the Pastorals; and, though some scholars think that this arises from their origin in a similar atmosphere, and amid a common phraseology, it is quite as likely that the similarities are due to Clement's acquaintance with the contents of these letters. Marcion, the Gnostic of the 2nd cent., omits these Epistles from his collection of authoritative Christian writings, and that, too, although he was 'a Pauline enthusiast,' accepting only St. Luke's Gospel and the other ten Epistles of St. Paul. But Marcion was bound to reject these letters, if he was to save his doctrine, which they condemned by implication, root and branch; and no argument against their genuineness can be based upon the evidence of so interested and so prejudiced a witness. The external evidence therefore goes to support the view that St. Paul was the author.

3. Date. Accepting the Pauline authorship, we may conclude that these Epistles were written during the interval between the first and the second imprisonment of St. Paul at

Rome. The Apostle arrived in Rome (Ac 28 16) probably early in the year 59. He was a prisoner there, dwelling in his own hired house (Ac 28 16, 30) for two years. There the Acts of the Apostles leaves him. His appeal, however, seems to have been sustained and himself afterwards set at liberty. If he visited Spain, it must have been immediately after his release. Subsequently he revisited the scene of his earlier labours in Macedonia, and possibly in Ephesus (1 Tim 1 3). Timothy had been in Ephesus for some time, and the Apostle asked him to remain there for a longer period. To instruct him further regarding his action in the difficult situation he had to face, St. Paul wrote the First Epistle to him from Macedonia, perhaps in 65 or 66. About the same time, or very soon after, he wrote the Epistle to Titus. From it we learn that Titus was in Crete, where he had been left by the Apostle (1 5), who had visited the island probably on his way to Macedonia. St. Paul asked him to join him in the winter of the same year at Nicopolis. From Nicopolis St. Paul returned to Rome, whether under arrest or of his own will we cannot tell; but if he arrived a free man he was very soon a prisoner. From prison he wrote the Second Epistle to Timothy asking him to come to him (4 9). Where Timothy was at that time does not appear. He seems to have left Ephesus, otherwise he would have known of Trophimus having been invalided at Miletus, which was close by, and also of the visit of Tychicus (2 Tim 4 12, 20). The Apostle felt that he was nearing his end (4 6, 7); he had already appeared before his judges (4 16), but he evidently expected to be condemned. The Second Epistle to Timothy was thus written shortly before the Apostle's martyrdom in 67 or 68.

4. Church Organisation. The state of Church organisation exhibited in these Epistles is exactly what might be expected to have existed in the later years of St. Paul's life. When the Apostle in his first missionary operations had made a number of converts in any town or district sufficient to constitute a congregation, he appointed presbyters to minister and rule in it (Ac 14 23), perhaps also, as many maintain, a leading or presiding presbyter (*episcopos*) with special authority—all of them looking to the Apostle as their superior. When he, however, was no longer able himself to visit and control the various presbyters, and set in order the things that might be amiss, he selected one of his companions and assistants to act in his stead. This was the state of things in Ephesus (1 Tim 1 3) and Crete (Tit 1 5). St. Paul had appointed Timothy and Titus to be his delegates in these places, though their duty in that capacity may only have been temporary (2 Tim 4 9, 21 Tit 3 12).

One of their duties was to appoint presbyters (elders) and (if presiding presbyters had been already introduced) bishops in these Churches (1 Tim 3 1-7 Tit 1 3-9), who were to bear rule over the brethren (1 Tim 5 17), and to teach and preach (1 Tim 5 17 Tit 1 9). The functions of these officers, however, are not minutely detailed : it is their character upon which the Apostle dwells. The qualities in which they are to be preëminent are moral qualities, and they are to be held in honour in proportion to their diligence in duty and faithfulness in teaching (1 Tim 5 17).

Besides them, there were to be deacons appointed, whose duties would be much the same as those of the deacons appointed in Jerusalem in the earliest days of the Church (Ac 6 1-6). They would have charge of the temporal affairs of the Church, but might, like Stephen, also have part in purely spiritual work. The Apostle in their case also dwells not upon their functions, but upon their character (1 Tim 3 8). Perhaps also deaconesses were appointed, charged with the care of the women in the Church and with the duty of commending the gospel to women outside its pale (1 Tim 3 11, where many translate 'their wives,' RV 'women,' as 'deaconesses' : see note there).

5. Christian Doctrine. Much stress is laid by the Apostle upon the proclamation of the true faith. Exception has been taken to the genuineness of the Epistle on the ground of the Apostle's insistence upon sound doctrine.

But nothing could be more natural, as nothing was more necessary, than that emphasis should be laid upon doctrine, when heresy was rampant, and that the importance of the truth should be asserted in presence of false teaching. In any case, the doctrines taught are doctrines which St. Paul was continually insisting upon : God's desire that all men should be saved (cp 1 Tim 2 4 with Ro 3 29 10 12); Christ's manifestation as our Saviour, and His giving Himself as a ransom (1 Tim 2 6); His death and resurrection (2 Tim 2 8, 11 4 8); our spiritual union with Him (2 Tim 2 11, 12 3 11); salvation not of works, but of free grace (Tit 3 5), etc. So in characteristically Pauline fashion practical teaching is closely connected with doctrinal, and the moral aspect of faith in Christ is impressed upon the recipients of the letters. It is doubtless important to 'hold fast the form of sound words,' but it is because the results of 'sound doctrine' are manifest in life and conduct (1 Tim 1 9, 10 2 Tim 4 3 Tit 2 1, 2). A feature of the Epistles is the recurrence of the phrase 'Faithful is the saying,' used to introduce maxims of truth or duty. This expression occurs five times, viz. 1 Tim 1 15 3 1 4 9 2 Tim 2 11 Tit 3 8. It would seem to point to the fact that favourite sayings or watchwords were current among the Christians by this time—perhaps extracts from manuals of instruction, which had already begun to be prepared for the use of the presbyters in preparing converts for baptism—which were quoted by the Apostle.

1 TIMOTHY

INTRODUCTION

1. Authenticity. The First Epistle to Timothy is the first letter of the group called the Pastoral Epistles. Until the beginning of the 19th cent. no doubt was ever expressed as to the Epistle being written by St. Paul, except by the Gnostics ; who, as is stated by Tertullian ('Adv. Marc,' v. 21), Clement of Alexandria ('Strom.' ii, 11), and Jerome ('Prol. ad Titum '), rejected all the Pastoral Epistles simply because the teaching contained in them was opposed to their peculiar doctrines. The external evidence, therefore, may be regarded as perfectly satisfactory, passages being quoted from it or alluded to by Clement of Rome, Hegesippus, Athenagoras, Theophilus, and the Pauline authorship directly declared by Irenæus, Clement of Alexandria, and Tertullian,

and accepted without demur till a hundred years ago, when T. E. C. Schmid for the first time (1804), followed by Schleiermacher (1807), Eichhorn (1812), De Witte (1826), Baur (1835), denied its genuineness, arguing entirely from internal evidence.

The internal evidence to which the opponents of the authenticity of the Epistles have appealed is the character of the heresies controverted in them, which, they say, were of a later date than St. Paul, and the use of a number of words and phrases not employed by St. Paul in his other Epistles. The answer to these objections is that the writers in question are mistaken in identifying the heresies denounced by St. Paul with the full-grown Gnostic system of the 2nd cent. ; and that it is natural that a man writing a letter or letters many years after his earlier letters, and on a different subject, should use words which do not occur in those earlier letters.

2. Reader. Timothy, or Timotheus. Timothy was possibly converted to Christianity by St. Paul in his First Missionary Journey, when he visited Lystra, 47 A.D. He was the son of a Jewess named Eunice (Ac 16 [1] 2 Tim 1 [5]), who was married to a Greek husband, and was herself also a convert to Christianity together with her mother Lois. We first hear of him at Lystra on St. Paul's Second Missionary Journey, when he is described as already a disciple (Ac 16 [1]). St. Paul took him as his companion from Lystra as far as Berœa, where he remained with Silas for a short time after St. Paul's departure (Ac 17 [14]), and later on rejoined the Apostle at Corinth (Ac 18 [5]). It is probable that he accompanied St. Paul on his return journey as far as Ephesus, where we find him 'ministering' to St. Paul in his Third Missionary Journey, 55 A.D. From thence he was sent forward by St. Paul to Macedonia (Ac 19 [22]), where the Apostle joined him shortly afterwards; and he was one of those who accompanied his master on his last visit to Jerusalem (Ac 20 [4]). Later he was with St. Paul in Rome during his imprisonment, and is associated with him in the Epistles to the Colossians and Philippians. According to this Epistle, St. Paul seems to have paid another visit to Ephesus, 65 A.D., and on his departure left Timothy in charge of the Church of Ephesus as his deputy (1 Tim 1 [3]), and soon afterwards wrote to him the First Epistle to instruct him fully in his duties. In the following year he addressed to him the pathetic letter known as the Second Epistle, begging him to come and be with him in his last imprisonment. Whether he was able to fulfil this longing of his master we do not know. Tradition says that the rest of his life was spent at Ephesus as its bishop, subject to the apostolic authority of St. John exercised throughout proconsular Asia. We find from the book of the Revelation that the Church of Ephesus had striven manfully against those 'which say that they are apostles and are not' in fulfilment of St. Paul's last injunctions, but had now 'left its first love' (Rev 2 [4]). We may well suppose that Timothy's ministry was marked by the first characteristic, and that it was on his death that the Ephesian Christians fell from their first love. We learn from the two Epistles that Timothy was ordained by the laying on of hands of St. Paul and some presbyters, but when this occurred we do not know.

3. Date and Place of Composition. It was either written from Macedonia or some other point in the Apostle's last journey, 65 or 66 A.D. (1 Tim 1 [3]).

4. Contents and Purpose. The Epistle may be regarded as an Apostolic Charge. Its chief purpose is to instruct Timothy as to his attitude to the forms of heresy which were prevalent, and to direct him in his choice of presbyters. The immediate assailants of the faith were a sect, the growth of which we can trace through St. Paul's Epistles. When he wrote the Epistle to the Galatians, 55 A.D., his adversaries were Jews proper, who had embraced Christianity but desired to combine with the gospel the practices and tenets of Judaism. When he wrote to the Colossians, 60 A.D., the sect had imbibed a number of speculative opinions, known later as Gnostic, which were derogatory to Christ, and added them to their previous tenets. When we reach the date of the Pastoral Epistles, 67 A.D., the Jewish basis still remained, but the most prominent feature of the belief was a more developed form of the Colossian heresy, which departed from faith in Christ and attached importance to 'knowledge falsely so called.' After the fall of Jerusalem, 70 A.D., the Jewish element grew weaker and weaker till it was either eliminated or merged in pure Gnosticism (from Gk. *gnosis*, 'knowledge'), which was a philosophy which attempted to explain the existence of evil by declaring evil to be a necessary quality of matter, denied the reality of Christ's sufferings, and too often found excuses for and was associated with a low state of morality. St. Paul here instructs Timothy to be bold in his opposition to the false teachers, whose doctrine at this time was evidently destructive of both faith and morals.

A secondary object of the Epistle is to give Timothy instructions as to the organisation of the Church, and as to the kind of men whom he should ordain as presbyters and deacons. Its contents are nine charges to Timothy, interspersed with exhortations to him.

CHAPTER 1

TIMOTHY REMINDED OF HIS COMMISSION, AND EXHORTED TO EARNESTNESS

1, 2. Salutation. An apostle] St. Peter and St. John, with regard to whose position no question was raised, are content to call themselves presbyters (2 and 3 John, 1 Pet 5 [1]), but St. Paul usually designates himself as an Apostle owing to the peculiarity of his call to the apostleship which led his adversaries to deny him the title; and for the same reason he claims that he holds his apostleship by the commandment of God the Father and the Lord Jesus Christ. **God our Saviour]** The full force that the Apostle assigned to the expression is shown in 2 [3]: 'God our Saviour, who willeth that all men should be saved and come to the knowledge of the truth.' **Christ, which is our hope]** so designated because it is through Christ that we have the hope of future salvation. **2.** *My* **own son in the faith**] see 3¹³ and Tit 1⁴. St. Paul speaks of Onesimus in like terms as 'my son whom I have begotten in my bonds' (Philemon v. 10).

3–20. The first charge to Timothy. To remember and act upon the instructions already given him by St. Paul, which were to be firm in resisting the heterodox teachers in Ephesus, as the Apostle had been himself, and to promote love, purity, uprightness, and faith.

3. As I besought thee] The words 'so do' (i.e. remember and act upon my instructions), or 'so I do now,' RV, i.e. 'I repeat my charge to you,' must be supplied. **When I went**] RV 'when I was going.' It is probable that the charge was given to Timothy by St. Paul in Ephesus when he left that city himself. This journey he took in the interval between his first and second imprisonment. **That they teach no other doctrine**] RV 'not to teach a different doctrine'; better, 'not to teach heterodox doctrine.' **4. Fables and endless genealogies**] not the Gnostic stories of emanations and æons, but idle Jewish legends and genealogical claims, as is shown by Tit 1¹⁴ 3⁹.

Minister questions, rather than godly edification] RV 'minister questions rather than a dispensation of God.' This would mean one of two things, either that the heterodox teaching led to futile speculation and not to the spread of the knowledge of the dispensation of the gospel, or that it made men idle disputants instead of faithful dispensers of God's truth.

5–7. The end of the commandment] RV 'the end of the charge,' i.e. the aim of all true teaching as contrasted with 'fables and endless genealogies.' The gospel which Timothy had to preach consists of **charity** or 'love,' RV, springing from purity of heart, an enlightened conscience, and a sure faith. This was not the gospel preached by the heterodox teachers, whose doctrine consisted in quibbling subtleties, like those of the rabbis, and misrepresentations of the Law, the meaning of which they did not understand.

8–11. St. Paul guards himself against seeming to minimise the value of the Law. Properly understood, it was of the utmost use as a restraint of evil-doers. This he preached 'according to the gospel committed to his trust,' i.e. as a part of Christian teaching.

12–17. That the preaching of the gospel had been committed to him, leads him to offer a fervent thanksgiving for the grace so bestowed upon him, unworthy as he was.

12. Putting me into the ministry] RV 'appointing me to his service.' **13. I did** *it* **ignorantly**] St. Paul's is an instance of that form of ignorance which excuses acts done through it, i.e. ignorance of fact, not of a

moral principle. **14. Grace .. was .. abundant with faith and love**] The act of God (grace) is accompanied and supplemented by man's loving acceptance of it in faith.

15. This *is* **a faithful saying**] For this formula, peculiar to the Pastoral Epistles (cp. 1 Tim 4⁹ 3¹ 2 Tim 2¹¹ Tit 3⁸), see General Intro. St. Paul's case is covered by the general principle that **Christ came to save sinners.**

16. First] St. Paul was in his own estimation first in sinfulness (v. 15), and first forgiven, as an example to other sinners to hope for pardon. **17.** A doxology of thanks to God for what He had done for him : cp. Ro 16²⁵. **King**] This title is applied to God only here and in 1 Tim 6¹⁵ and Mt 5³⁵. **Eternal**] lit. 'of the ages,' but meaning 'eternal.' The original has 'king of the æons.' Had the doctrine of the Gnostic æons been in existence when the Epistle was written, this expression would not have been used without some contradiction of that theory or explanation of the words. This is an incidental proof of the early date of the Epistle.

18–20. He returns from the digression respecting himself to the subject of the charge previously given to Timothy, to resist heresy (v. 3), and to promote charity, purity, uprightness, and faith (v. 5).

18. I commit unto thee] The duty of maintaining the truth whereby to resist heresy is a trust committed to Timothy : see 1 Tim 6²⁰ 2 Tim 1¹⁴. **According to the prophecies**] This trust he would fulfil in pursuance of declarations made respecting him by the 'prophets' of the Church at the time of his ordination. The 'prophets' are very prominent in the Apostolic Age : see Ac 13¹ 1 Cor 12. **By them**] in accordance with the anticipation of the 'prophets.' **19. Which**] the guidance of their conscience. **Concerning faith,** etc.] RV 'made shipwreck concerning the faith'; not their own belief, but the substance of the revealed truth.

20. There are two instances of excommunication in Scripture, (1) that of the Corinthian for immorality (1 Cor 5), (2) of Hymenæus and Alexander for heresy. We learn from 2 Tim 2¹⁹ that Philetus was one of Hymenæus' associates, but whether Timothy followed St. Paul's example and excommunicated him, we do not know. It is probable that the Alexander here mentioned is the same as 'Alexander the coppersmith' of 2 Tim 4¹⁴, who may have 'done' St. Paul 'much evil' at Rome during his trial, in consequence of the excommunication pronounced upon him by the Apostle at Ephesus. He may also have been the Alexander of Ac 19³³. **Delivered unto Satan**] because relegated from the Church to the world, from the kingdom of God on earth to the empire of Satan (Ac 26¹⁸).

CHAPTER 2

CONCERNING PRAYER, THANKSGIVING, AND THE PLACE OF WOMEN

1-8. The second charge to Timothy—to teach those over whom he was set to use public prayer and intercession.

1. Therefore] in the sense of ' well then.'

First of all] His first exhortation as to Christian men is that they should pray. **Supplications, prayers, intercessions, thanksgivings]** The duty of the Christian Church in the matter of intercession is to offer prayers for others, and to give thanks for good things happening to others, and for events relating to others which may be a blessing to herself. **For all men]** Christian charity and good-will excludes none. **2. For kings]** Nero was at this time emperor. The Apostle's instruction, therefore, shows that the prayers of the Church are to be offered for bad rulers as well as good. *For* **all that are in authority]** that they may be so directed as to further the peace and prosperity of Christ's Church.

That we may lead a quiet and peaceable life in all godliness] cp. the Prayer for the Church Militant, 'that under him we may be godly and quietly governed.' **3. This** *is* **good]** that is, the public offering of intercessory prayers. **God our Saviour]** see 1¹. **4. Will have, etc.]** RV 'willeth that all men should.'

5-7. A summary statement of the gospel which St. Paul preached. It is introduced in connexion with the doctrine of God's will that all men should be saved. Surely that is His will, is the Apostle's argument, for He is the God of all (there is no other), and Christ, Himself Man, is the Mediator of all (there is no other), and He is the Redeemer of all, as was shown to be the case, when the due time came, by the means appointed by God, one of which means was St. Paul's own preaching and his apostleship of the Gentiles. **7. I speak the truth]** St. Paul does not forget that his apostleship had been denied, and takes occasion to reaffirm it : see 1 Cor 9¹ 2 Cor 12¹². **Teacher of the Gentiles]** Gal 2⁹. **In faith and verity]** The faith, which was also the truth, was the subject of his teaching to the Gentiles.

8. As to men (contrasted with women, about whom he is about to give a different charge), they are not to quarrel and dispute, but, wherever they are, they are to pray. **Men]** RV ' the men,' that is, the male members of the Church. **Doubting]** RV 'disputing.' **Lifting up holy hands]** the gesture of the early Christians, and perhaps the most natural gesture in very earnest prayer.

9-15. The third charge to Timothy, as to the comely behaviour of women, and their place in the Church.

9, 10. In like manner] rather, 'so also'; there is no likeness in the conduct enjoined on women to what has gone before. The first rule is, that their ornament is not to be braiding of hair or wearing of jewels or fine dresses, but good works and modesty and serenity of life. There is no prohibition of women wearing jewels and head-dresses and handsome gowns here, but they are not to regard them as their real ornaments in comparison with good life. **11, 12.** The second rule is, that they are not to teach in the congregation, and are to be submissive. **13, 14.** Two reasons which show, not cause, inferiority on the part of the woman. Man was created before woman, who was formed to be a helpmeet for him ; and woman was the first transgressor, showing that her weakness more readily yielded to temptation. **15. In childbearing]** i.e. by keeping faithfully and simply to her allotted sphere as wife and mother.

CHAPTER 3

CONCERNING THE OFFICERS OF THE CHURCH

1-7. The fourth charge to Timothy, in respect to presbyters.

1. Desireth a good work] i.e. a noble occupation.

2. A bishop] RV 'the bishop,' RM 'overseer.' Some think (see General Intro.) that the terms 'bishop' and 'elder' are used interchangeably in these Epistles, as they seem to have been at an earlier date (Ac 20²⁸ Phil 1¹). Others, however, think that, at the close of the apostolic age, to which these Epistles belong, the term 'bishop' was coming into use in the sense of a chief ruler of the Church, or presiding elder, and that that is the meaning here. In favour of the latter view it is urged that 'bishop' in these Epistles occurs only in the singular, and always with the definite article (' the bishop' : see RV Tit 1⁷), whereas 'elder' is found in the plural, and where it occurs in the singular has no article (1 Tim 5¹,¹⁷,¹⁹ Tit 1⁵). The question, however, requires to be handled with caution, owing to the limited and imperfect knowledge we have of the development of Church organisation in the first century.

The husband of one wife] lit. 'a man of one woman.' Four meanings have been attached to the words : (*a*) The presbyter is not to be a Christianised Jew, who, in accordance with the Law of Moses, had previously taken two wives. (*b*) He is not to take a second wife after the death of the first. (*c*) He is not to marry again while his divorced wife lives. (*d*) He is to be faithful to his wife, 'a man of one woman,' and 'keep himself only unto her so long as they both should live,' whether it were a first wife or a second wife. The last is probably the right exposition, as set forth by

Theodore of Mopsuestia and Theodoret. In any case the presbyter or bishop is contemplated as a married man. **Given to hospitality]** This injunction was most necessary for the sake of travellers when inns in the modern sense did not exist : see 3 Jn v. 5.

4. Having his children in subjection] more exactly, 'having children (who are) in subjection.' **6. Novice]** i.e. a recent convert. A 'bishop' or 'presbyter' must have Christian experience. **Lifted up]** The young presbyter's danger is the pride which led to the condemnation of the devil, and is the snare laid for him by the devil.

8–13. Fifth charge to Timothy—as to deacons and deaconesses.

8. Greedy of filthy lucre] Part of the office of the deacon was to 'serve tables' and administer relief to the poor, so that he had opportunity for peculation and base gains.

9. The mystery of the faith] the Christian faith, which, having once been hidden, is now revealed : cp. v. 16.

11. *Their* **wives]** RV 'women': but instructions about women in general would not be thus parenthetically inserted. Both Lightfoot and Ellicott translate 'deaconesses.' Such an order, which, it is certain, came into existence at a very early date, was especially necessary in the East owing to the strict seclusion of the female sex, who were thus debarred from the ministrations of men. Deaconesses were admitted to their order by the laying on of the bishop's hands ('Apost. Const.' iii. 15, viii. 19). They were not allowed to marry (Can. 15 of Chalcedon). Their duties were to minister generally to women, to assist at the baptism of women, to stand at the women's door of the church, to act as go-between between the clergy and women ('Apost. Const.' iii. 15, ii. 26, ii. 57, ii. 26). There were 40 deaconesses attached to the great Church of Constantinople in the time of St. Chrysostom. The order practically became extinct in the West, perhaps very gradually, after the tenth century, and lingered on rather longer in the East. But in the West it never completely died out in the Church of France, where to this day Benedictine abbesses receive the ordination of a deaconess. Both in England and Scotland it is now revived, and forms a most wholesome and scriptural channel through which organised women's work can be carried on.

12. Husbands of one wife] see on v. 2.

13. Purchase] RV 'gain.' **A good degree]** RV 'standing,' a high position in estimation and influence.

14–16. Importance of the above charges, for the purpose of instructing Timothy how to act as a minister of God's Church—an institution which God has established to hold up the truth as a pillar supports a roof, and to keep it unshaken as a firm foundation gives security to a building. Were it not for the support and steadiness given to truth by the society of faithful men which maintains it, it would ere now have vanished from the earth.

16. Without controversy] rather, 'as we confess'; and then the Apostle quotes some words of an early confession of the Christian faith : 'He who was incarnate ; whose righteousness was made manifest ; who was an object of open vision to angels ; whom the Apostles preached to the world ; whom the faithful believed in ; who at the end of His ministry was taken up into heaven.' The reading is apparently not **God was manifest** (AV), but 'He who was manifest' (RV). **Mystery]** The hidden secret now revealed in Christ, which is the basis of holiness : cp. v. 9.

CHAPTER 4
VARIOUS DIRECTIONS AND EXHORTATIONS

1–10. A return to, and emphatic reiteration of, the first charge to Timothy (1 3-20) against heterodoxy and in favour of true godliness. This form of heterodoxy which he would have to oppose was an asceticism which taught that there was merit in abstaining from meats, and forbade conjugal intercourse as on a lower moral level than celibacy.

1. The Spirit speaketh (RV 'saith')] possibly in some definite prophecy of OT., or of our Lord, or of the Apostles, but more probably in the general prophetic testimony of the Church, and particularly in the present and former words of St. Paul himself (cp. Ac 20 29). **In the latter times]** RV 'in later times.' **2. Seared]** RV 'branded.' Their consciences were not made incapable of feeling, but false principles were burnt into them. **3. From meats]** cp. Col 2 16. **4.** If we partake of food and accept other such blessings with gratitude to the Giver, which naturally shows itself in words of thanksgiving, that food and those blessings are thereby hallowed to us ; so that it is not only a mistake, but a sin, to refuse them.

6. Minister] The word *diaconus* is still used in its general sense (cp. Eph 3 7) as well as specifically (3 8). **7. Old wives' fables]** such as those which are recorded in the apocryphal books of the 2nd cent., and became the mythology of the Middle Ages.

8. We are to train the body and exercise self-denial, which will help us to control our lower nature, and is often necessary to be practised that we may help others. It is 'profitable for a little' (RV)—that is, up to a certain point—as it is a help towards, and a part of, piety ; but it does not lay up merit for us, and it does not procure for us the blessedness which is the promised result of piety in this and in the future life. **9.** This v. is parenthetical

There was a Christian 'saying, the Apostle reminds Timothy, to the same effect as what he had written in the last verse. **10. For**] This word refers us back to the promise of the future life in v. 8 : 'For,' says the Apostle, 'it is in hope of the future salvation, offered by God to all and attained by believers, that we bear toil and suffering.'

11-16. Sixth charge to Timothy—personal to himself.

12. Thy youth] Timothy was probably at this time between 35 and 40—an early age to be placed over other presbyters, all of whom were comparatively elderly men, as St. Paul's deputy. St. Paul was called a young man when his age was about the same (Ac 7 58).

13. Reading . . exhortation . . doctrine] i.e. the public reading of Scripture in church and sermons hortative and doctrinal. **14. By prophecy**] through the medium of prophecy : cp. Ac 13 1,2 for a parallel. This is a second reference to Timothy's ordination, and we see that in it the 'prophets' (preachers), presbyters, and St. Paul took part (1 18 2 Tim 1 6). It is probably owing to this precedent that the presbytery alone, or in association with the bishop, according to the form of Church polity in use, has to do with laying hands on a presbyter at his ordination. **16. Thou shalt . . save**] i.e. be the salvation of, or the means of, saving.

CHAPTER 5
REGARDING WIDOWS AND ACCUSATIONS AGAINST ELDERS

1. Rebuke] This shows the authority which Timothy exercised. **An elder**] i.e. an elderly man, not one officially so named.

3-16. The seventh charge to Timothy—as to widows.

3. Widows indeed] Each local Church kept a list of the widows belonging to the congregation, who were supported by the alms of the faithful if they were widows indeed, that is, if they had none to help them (vv. 4, 5). In return, they did what services they could to the brethren. **4. Nephews**] RV 'grandchildren,' whose duty it was to take charge of their relations. **Them**] i.e. the children or nephews. **7. Blameless**] RV 'without reproach,' that the Church widows may not be spoken ill of as women whom their relatives ought to support. **9, 10.** The qualifications for being put on the widows' list, besides being destitute, are, (1) to be 60 years of age ; (2) to have been faithful to her husband or husbands (a 'woman of one man ') ; (3) to be of good reputation ; (4) to have brought up her children well ; (5) to have shown hospitality to strangers (cp. 3 Jn v. 5) ; (6) to have washed the saints' feet (i.e. humbly ministered to her fellow-Christians ; (7) helped any in distress ; (8) to be fruitful of good works.

11-15. Reasons against admitting younger widows. After devoting themselves to the service of Christ in their first grief, they may afterwards marry and give up their work, in spite of the promise they made at the beginning, and if not that, they may become gossips and scandal-mongers. It is better that they should marry again, and occupy themselves with the cares of a household. From this we see that St. Paul was no enemy to second marriages, and he would not, therefore, have excluded elderly women from the widows' company because they had been twice married. This view confirms the meaning already given to 'wife of one man ' (v. 9). **12. Having damnation**] or, 'condemnation '; rather, 'incurring severe judgment.' **15. Some**] i.e. some widows. The enthusiasm with which they had embraced Christianity and received St. Paul's gospel had already worn off. With some temperaments it takes but a short time for this to occur—a shorter time generally in women than in men. They had turned aside out of the right path, and were, therefore, going after Satan. **16. Any man or woman that believeth**] RV 'any woman that believeth.' Not only children and grandchildren, but other relatives likewise, are to support aged widows, and so spare the Church's fund. The injunction must apply to men as well as women, though the RV reading stands on the better authority of MSS.

17-25. Resumption of charge to Timothy as to presbyters. (1) Presbyters distinguished by their zeal, specially those distinguished in preaching and catechising, are to have higher honour and a larger stipend than the rest. (2) An accusation against presbyters is not to be entertained by their superior officer (apostolic deputy, possibly bishop) sitting by himself and listening to reports, but only before (AV), 'at the mouth of ' (RV), two or three witnesses, who would confirm each other's statements (Dt 19 15), and also make the case to be publicly known to the Church. (3) Presbyters must not be appointed hastily, or those who admit them into the ministry will be answerable for their ill-doing.

17. Elders] In v. 1 this word had meant elderly men ; here it means presbyters. This order of the ministry consisted at the time of elderly men, whence they had the name of elders or presbyters. **18. Thou shalt not muzzle the ox**] Dt 25 4 1 Cor 9 9 **And, The labourer** is **worthy of his hire**] read, ' And the,' etc. The words seem St. Paul's, not a quotation. **20. Them that sin**] Their punishment is to be public, not kept secret for fear of scandal.

21. The solemnity of St. Paul's words emphasises the responsibility of imposing penalties on a presbyter. **The elect angels**] not a particular class of angels, but the angels who are chosen by God as His ministers. **22. Lay hands**] It was Timothy's office now, as it had been St. Paul's previously (2 Tim 1 6), and that of the presbytery or bishops (at least afterwards), to appoint presbyters by the laying on of hands. Some find here a reference to the absolution of offenders or heretics.

23. A continuation of the personal charge to Timothy. St. Paul seems to have been reminded to give the present injunction by the evident necessity of Timothy's taking care of his bodily health, if he is to carry out the work of his office satisfactorily. He, therefore, inserts it parenthetically. It teaches us that if the body needs the stimulant of wine, it is right to take it in moderation.

24, 25. Some men's sins] Return to the subject of laying on of hands. Some candidates for ordination have characters so evidently bad that their unfitness is plain before probation ; in others it comes out later. And the same may be said of worthy candidates ; some are plainly fit at first sight, others will be found fit on looking below the surface. So that Timothy must exercise his judicial functions on presbyters and candidates for orders very cautiously. **25. They that are otherwise**] The character of those who differ from the class just mentioned by their goodness not being self-evident, will yet certainly come out in a short time.

CHAPTER 6
Concerning Servants, the Rich, and corrupt Teachers

1, 2. The eighth charge to Timothy, as to bondservants or slaves. We have here an indication of the way in which Christianity abolished slavery—not by denouncing it, but by implanting the idea of Christian brotherhood, which was incompatible with it : see Intro. to Philemon. If a Christian were the slave of an unbeliever, his submissiveness was to be such as to earn credit for his profession. If he had a Christian master, he was to be the more zealous in his service, inasmuch as his master, who derived benefit from it, was a believer like himself, and therefore an object of love.

2. Because they are faithful and beloved, partakers of the benefit] RV 'because they that partake of the benefit of their service are believing and beloved.'

3–10. Resumption of the charge against heterodox teachers. They had all the faults already mentioned, and in addition they made use of religion as a means of getting money, or, as they expressed it, of 'gain.' Reproving them, St. Paul points out in what sense religion is a 'gain,' namely, that it produces resignation and contentment of mind, which

prevent the disquieting effects of covetousness, whereas the desire of 'gain,' in the sense of money-getting, leads to every kind of evil-doing.

3. Wholesome words] RV 'sound words.' *Even* **the words of our Lord Jesus Christ**] His teaching in the Gospels. **5. Supposing that gain is godliness**] RV 'supposing that godliness is a way of gain.' **8. Raiment**] RV 'covering.' Houses may be included as well as clothes. **9, 10.** Similarly Seneca, 'Ep.' 87, 'While we wish to gain riches we fall into many evils.'

11–16. Resumption of personal charge to Timothy. Timothy's conduct was to be in absolute contrast with that of the heterodox teachers, who valued religion as a source of gain. He must be faithful, as he had promised when he made his confession of faith, and as Christ faithfully made His confession before Pontius Pilate. This faithfulness Timothy was especially to show in keeping safe the truth committed to him by St. Paul, which he was to do his part in maintaining uncorrupted till the Second Coming of Christ, which God would manifest at His own time.

11. O man of God] cp. 1 S 2 27 1 K 12 22.

12. Art .. called] RV 'wast called.' **A good confession**] RV 'the good confession,' made when he was admitted into the Church, or possibly when he was brought before a Roman magistrate to answer for his faith (Heb 13 23).

14. *This* **commandment**] i.e. the sum of the charges contained in the Epistle. **Without spot, unrebukeable**] Timothy's faith is to be without spot, so that he should be without reproach. **Until the appearing**] These words do not necessarily indicate a belief on St. Paul's part th t the Coming of the Lord would be in Timothy's lifetime. It might be, and then Timothy would have kept his deposit to the end if he were faithful; it might be later, and then he would have done his part in keeping it in his generation. The Return of the Lord is to take place in God's time, which 'He hath placed in His own power' (Ac 1 7).

15, 16. Probably an ascription of praise in use in the Apostolic Church.

17–19. The ninth charge to Timothy, arising out of vv. 6–10, respecting the rich. He is to instruct them not to trust in their riches and grow conceited, but to be ready to give to others, so laying up for themselves a treasure in heaven. The right use of wealth, as of all other of God's gifts, while it will not earn eternal life, will yet conduce to our attainment of it, good works not being the cause, but being nevertheless, in adults, a condition of salvation.

18. Ready .. to communicate] i.e. to contribute generously of their substance.

19. Laying up in store] see Mt 6 19 Lk 16 9. **Eternal life**] RV 'life u deed,' following a reading which has slightly the better authority of the two.

20–22. Final and impassioned appeal to Timothy. The faith is a 'deposit' (RV) which St. Paul has **committed** to Timothy (2 Tim 1 13, 14), and which it is his office, as it is now the office of the Church, to keep safe and uncorrupted for the salvation of the world in spite of gnostic or agnostic speculations and theories. ' Who at this day,' says Vincentius Lerinensis, ' is Timothy but either generally the whole Church, or especially the whole body of prelates, who ought either themselves to have a sound knowledge of divine religion, or to infuse it into others ? What is meant by keeping the *depositum*? Keep it, quoth he, for fear of thieves, for danger of enemies, lest when men be asleep they oversow cockle among that good seed of wheat which the Son of man hath sowed in His field. Keep, quoth he, the *depositum*. What is meant by this *depositum*? It is that which is committed to them, not that which is invented by thee ; that which thou hast received, not that which thou hast devised ; a thing not of wit, but of learning ; not of private assumption, but of public tradition ; a thing brought to thee, not brought forth of thee ; wherein thou must not be an author, but a keeper ; not a founder, but an observer ; not a leader, but a follower. Keep the *depositum*, quoth he ; preserve the talent of the Catholic Faith safe and undiminished ; that which is committed to thee, let that remain with thee, and that deliver. Thou hast received gold, render thou gold ; I will not have one thing for another. O Timothy, O Priest, O Teacher, O Doctor, if God's gift hath made thee meet and sufficient, for thy wit, exercise, and learning .. let them that come after you rejoice at arriving at the understanding of that, by thy means, which antiquity, without that understanding, had in veneration. Yet for all this, in such sort deliver the same things which thou hast learnt, that albeit thou teachest after a new manner, yet thou never teach new things' (c. 22). No one has better grasped and expressed the underlying thought and purpose of St. Paul's appeal to Timothy than Vincentius.

---

2 TIMOTHY

INTRODUCTION

1. Authorship. There can be no doubt that the author of 1 Timothy is the author of 2 Timothy. The evidence, external and internal, is almost the same for each, and the similarity of style and subject is unmistakable. If, therefore, St. Paul is the author of 1 Timothy, he is the author of 2 Timothy.

2. Reader. Undoubtedly the same as in the case of 1 Timothy.

3. Date and place of composition. It was written shortly before the Apostle's martyrdom from his prison in Rome, probably in the early part of 67 or 68 A.D.

4. Contents and purpose. The Apostle's primary object in the Epistle is to beg Timothy to come to him, as he was in prison and forlorn, most of his ordinary companions being gone elsewhere, and he needed the human comfort of a friend. The secondary purpose of the Epistle is to urge Timothy, once again, to maintain the faith entrusted to him for safe custody. It may be argued that the teaching of the two Epistles is compatible with a theory of legitimate development, but it certainly is not with any theory which would justify external additions to the once for all delivered

faith, or subtractions from it, or any rearrangement of it which should throw the truths insisted upon by the Apostles into the background, and open the way for new dogmas.

A third object of the Epistle is to give further instructions as to Church organisation, similar in kind to those already given in the earlier letter. The position of Timothy and Titus was such as peculiarly to demand these apostolic instructions. They are the link between the Apostles and the local Church officers, and their appointment may be regarded as indicating a transition stage between government by Apostles and government by diocesan bishops. Episcopacy seems to have arisen in two ways : (1) From within the body of presbyters, by the appointment of ? permanent president, to whom the title of ' bishop ' or ' overseer,' originally shared by all the presbyters (Ac 20 28 Phil 1 1), was gradually restricted. Whether this development took place within the apostolic age, or a little later, is a disputed question. It was, at any rate, well advanced by the beginning of the second century. (2) By the gradual settlement in local Churches of apostles, prophets, evangelists, and other apostolic men, naturally more highly regarded than presbyters. Thus St. John is said to have settled in Asia, St. Mark at Alexandria, Titus in Crete. The 'Didache,' which belongs to the first, or early part of the second, century, contemplates the possibility of the settlement of a 'prophet' in a local Church, where he was honoured as a 'chief priest,' and received the first-fruits of all produce (ch. xiii). If this dual origin of the episcopate be admitted, it furnishes an explanation of the fact that there was some hesitation in the early Church as to whether bishops were an order completely distinct from presbyters. In those Churches in which the episcopate had its origin within the presbyterate, there would be a tendency to regard the bishop as of one order with the presbyters, and of comparatively limited authority ; but in those Churches in which the episcopate had originated in the settlement of an apostle or apostolic man such as Timothy or Titus, there would be a tendency to regard the bishop as of a higher order than the presbyters, and to assign to him a distinctive position and authority.

CHAPTER 1
EXPRESSIONS OF AFFECTION AND EXHORTATIONS TO FAITHFULNESS

1, 2. Salutation. According to the promise of life] St. Paul declares himself appointed an Apostle with the view of his spreading the knowledge of the life which had been pro mised and was now being enjoyed by Christians adopted in Christ.

3-5. The happy assurance of Timothy's faithfulness which St. Paul's recollections of past years supply him with. **3. I thank God]** The construction is involved. What St. Paul thanks God for is Timothy's **unfeigned faith** which he remembers night and day, thinking of their last sad parting and hoping to see him again. **5. Eunice]** is simply described in Ac 16¹ as 'a woman that was a Jewess.' She was Lois' daughter. Timothy's father was a Greek.

6-14. Exhortation to firmness in his glorious calling.

6. Stir up] as a fire that is beginning to die down. **The gift of God]** which he received at his ordination by the laying on of the hands of St. Paul and the presbyters of Ephesus (1 Tim 4¹⁴). **7. Fear]** indicating a certain timidity in Timothy, like the 'Be not ashamed' of v. 8. **A sound mind]** RV 'discipline.' It means self-discipline, self-control. **8. His prisoner]** St. Paul was now undergoing his last imprisonment in Rome. He refers in like manner to his first imprisonment in Eph 3¹ 4¹ Philemon v. 9. **Partaker of the afflictions of the gospel]** RV 'suffer hardship with the gospel'; better, 'suffer hardship with me for the gospel.'

9. Hath saved] RV more exactly, 'saved.' God by His free grace and mercy called, and still calls us into a state of salvation, not for our work's sake (which is a false view of justification), but according to His own purpose and by the grace of adoption given us in Christ in eternity. How can the grace of our adoption be said to have been given us in eternity ? Because what God determines is regarded as done. That grace and purpose, resolved on in eternity, was first exhibited to the world at the manifestation of Christ in the flesh, who by His death and resurrection made death as a power of no effect, and threw new light upon life and immortality by His gospel. **10. Abolished death]** The resurrection of Christ showed that death was under control, and delivered believers from its fear. **12. I .. suffer these things]** this imprisonment, etc. **Whom I have believed]** i.e. trusted. **That which I have committed unto him]** himself and all his hopes.

13, 14. As God will keep safe that which is committed to Him, so Timothy is by the help of the Holy Ghost to **keep the good thing committed unto thee,** and that good thing is **the form of sound words, which thou hast heard of** (from) **me.** There is nothing so near the heart of the aged Apostle, who knew that he was himself about to depart from the world, as that the faith which he had himself received and preached should be regarded and treasured as a sacred deposit, left in charge of the Church for the salvation of mankind. The First Epistle ends with an earnest appeal to keep the deposit, and the Second Epistle begins with the same charge. For it is one of the chief duties of bishops and rulers of the Church to recall their clergy, straying into error, to the primitive 'pattern' (RV) of doctrine which is set before us in the sound words of the gospel.

15-18. Urging Timothy to be faithful to what he had taught him, St. Paul points to two cases, in the first of which his converts had shown unfaithfulness, and in the second courage. The Asiatic Christians, that is, some —in his bitter disappointment St. Paul says **all**—of those who lived in proconsular Asia, represented by **Phygelus** (this seems to have been the spelling of the name) and **Hermogenes,** of whom we know nothing more, had repudiated St. Paul's authority. On the other hand, **Onesiphorus** had bravely ministered to him in his imprisonment in Rome, and before that at Ephesus. In memory of his kindness St. Paul prays that God may bless his family and utters an aspiration that mercy may be shown to him at the last day. From the form of the expression, and the fact that both here and in 4¹⁹ only the household of Onesiphorus is mentioned, it has been inferred with considerable probability that Onesiphorus was dead. On this supposition many Protestant scholars find in the utterance of St. Paul an instance of prayer for a deceased person, but others regard it only as a pious hope or wish.

CHAPTER 2
Exhortations to Firmness, Uncontentiousness, and Perseverance

1–26. The duties of God's ministers are, (1) to maintain the faith against assailants and seducers (vv. 1, 2, 14–21, 26), and, (2) to be brave and patient (vv. 3–13, 22–25).

1. Therefore] will then. **Be strong**] show the strength which is yours as a Christian and as a minister of Christ. **2.** The Apostle refers especially to the charge that he had given to Timothy at his ordination in the presence of the presbyters and others who assisted at it. This charge contained a summary of the faith, which in turn Timothy was to hand on to others. **Teach others**] probably, ' teach them to others.' They have now been stereotyped in the Scriptures of the NT. and in the Creeds.

3–6. Endure hardness] RV ' suffer hardship with me.' **A good soldier**] The soldier's virtue is to be shown in resisting, (1) the enemies of the faith, (2) all evil ; and with this end in view he will not devote himself to other occupations, but observes the rules of his service. God's minister must be like him, and like the labourer who works hard in the field. In which case, St. Paul adds, he has, like the husbandman, a right to a living wage.

7. If Timothy thinks it over, he will see that it is only reasonable that the presbyter should be supported by a stipend, answering to the labourer's wages. **8.** Timothy is to be firm and unflinching in maintaining the doctrines of the Incarnation and Resurrection of Christ, which his adversaries denied.

9, 10. As an evil doer] St. Paul was now probably imprisoned on the charge of setting fire to Rome with the other Christians. He was willing to endure that or anything else provided that so he might make known the salvation in Christ to those whom God had chosen to know it ; if the preacher was in chains, the word he preached was unfettered and had free course. St. Paul says this in part as an encouragement to Timothy to suffer with him (v. 3).

11–13. The Apostle quotes a saying or hymn in use among Christians, which is applicable from its reference to endurance. **11. A faithful saying**] 1 Tim 1 [5] 4 [9]. **13. He abideth faithful**] We have been admitted into covenant with Him, and whatever we may do, He will observe the terms of the agreement, whether they bring us good or evil.

14–21. Urgent charge to Timothy to resist the heterodox teaching.

15. Rightly dividing the word of truth] The original word means either cutting a straight path for it, or dealing in a straightforward way with it. **16. They**] the heterodox teachers.

17, 18. Hymenæus] 1 Tim 1 [20]. Of **Philetus** nothing more is known. Their heresy may have been an allegorical explanation of the Resurrection as the new life of the soul which had been imparted to it by faith in Christ. The belief that ' the resurrection is past already' may have been that Christ's Resurrection was the only one that was to be. A belief like this seems to have prevailed at Corinth : cp. 1 Cor 15 [12, 16, 20]. **19.** The doctrine of the Resurrection is **the sure foundation of God,** which stands as a fundamental article of the Christian faith. When the time comes, the Lord will show that He **knoweth them that are his,** who will be those that during their life on earth have, as Christians, departed from iniquity. **This seal**] the inscription stamped upon the foundation stone of the faith.

20, 21. In the visible Church there would be some hearts of gold incapable of being seduced, but there would also be some of less precious material liable to be led away by the heterodox teachers ; if the latter **purged themselves from their** false teachers by rejecting their doctrine and ministry, they too would become **vessels unto honour.**

22–25. Personal to Timothy.

22. Flee . . youthful lusts] avoid a young man's desires after novelty in teaching. (There is apparently no reference to the desires of the flesh.) Avoid **foolish questions** or speculations **which gender strife,** and pursue a steadfast course of piety with sincere believers, not entering into controversial disputations, but correcting opponents with gentleness and meekness, not for the sake of victory, but for their good. **Also**] RV ' but.' **26.** St. Paul's thought passes from Timothy's behaviour towards the heterodox to what may be the results of it to themselves namely, their recovery.

CHAPTER 3
Warnings and Exhortations regarding the Last Days

1–9. In the days immediately preceding the Second Coming, the Lord had taught that iniquity would abound. St. Paul reminds Timothy of this truth as a warning to him, for when those days would come neither he nor any one on earth knew ; they might be close at hand, and the existing wickedness might be the commencement of the final iniquity. The depravity then would be terrible, and already in its degree it existed, and must be resisted.

1. In the last days] ' But of that day and

that hour knoweth no man' (Mk 13 32), not a St. Paul, not a St. John (1 Jn 2 18). **5. A form of godliness**] an outside appearance of it. **Denying the power thereof**] the outward form of piety not having power to influence their lives for good. **6. Creep into houses**] the constant habit of proselytisers to evil, who do not shrink from crooked and base means of accomplishing their purpose. **Lead captive**] having lost all freedom of will, like prisoners taken in war. **7. Ever learning, and never able to come to the knowledge of the truth**] an exquisite description of that restlessness of mind, which leads to excessive curiosity upon religious subjects, but does not minister to genuine knowledge or faith.

8. These] the teachers who are leading men and women on to this depravity and weakness. **Jannes and Jambres**] the names of the Egyptian magicians in Ex 7 11-22, according to Jewish tradition. **9. They shall proceed no further**] they shall not be able to continue to resist Timothy with success, any more than the magicians were capable of finally resisting Moses (Ex 8 18 9 11).

10-17. Exhortation. Timothy was well instructed in the OT. and in the gospel preached by St. Paul, and he must 'abide in the things that he had learnt and been assured of.'

10. Hast fully known] RV 'didst follow.' **11.** Timothy was well acquainted with all that happened to St. Paul at Antioch of Pisidia, Iconium, and Lystra in his First Missionary Journey, when he was himself converted to Christianity (Ac 13 50 16 1). **14. Of whom thou hast learned them**] From Eunice and Lois. **15. The holy scriptures**] RV 'the sacred writings,' i.e. the OT., which, when read in the light of the faith of Christ Jesus and with trust in Him, gave sufficient instruction for his salvation.

16. All scripture] RV 'every scripture.' The AV is right, because St. Paul is here contemplating the OT. not as a work made up of many writings, but as one book. So in Eph 3 15, 'the whole family in heaven' (AV) is right, not 'every family' (RV); Eph 2 21, 'all the building groweth' (AV), not 'each several building' (RV); Ac 2 36, 'Let all the house of Israel know' (AV and RV); Ac 7 22, 'all the wisdom of the Egyptians' (AV and RV), because contemplated as one subject; Mt 2 3, 'all Jerusalem' (AV and RV). **All scripture**] In this passage the 'scripture' denoted is the OT. only, but when the expression is afterwards applied to the NT. (2 Pet 3 16), it implies that the same characteristics will be found in the NT. as are here enumerated in reference to the OT. **Scripture** *is* **given by inspiration of God, and** *is* **profitable**] RV 'scripture inspired of God *is* also profitable.' There is nothing whatever to show which of these renderings is

the better. The profitableness of Scripture consists in its teaching, convicting, correcting, training. It is profitable both for faith and piety.

The assurance which St. Paul has of Timothy's piety leads up to his final appeal in the next chapter.

CHAPTER 4

St. Paul's last Messages and Counsels

1-8. The Apostle, knowing that his days are fast drawing to a close, exhorts Timothy to increased diligence and earnestness in his teaching, in view of the imminence of a time of error and excitement. He refers to his approaching martyrdom, expressing his readiness for whatever may await him, and his confidence in the reward of his faithfulness.

1. I charge *thee*] cp. 1 Tim 5 21. **And the Lord Jesus Christ**] RV 'and of Christ Jesus.' **At his appearing, etc.**] RV 'and by his appearing and his kingdom.' The Second Coming and the glorious kingdom of Christ are invoked to remind Timothy of the greatness of his responsibility. **2. In season, out of season**] This has been well rendered, 'Take opportunity, or make it.' **With all longsuffering and doctrine**] i.e. ever patient and ready to teach.

3. False views of Christian truth would gain credence in the future as they had done in the past (cp. 2 Cor 11 4, 12-15 Col 2 8, 18); and it would be well that the converts should be prepared against the day of trial. **After their own lusts**] They would prefer teaching which agreed with their selfish desires to the pure truth of the gospel condemning their evil habits and awakening their consciences: cp. Jer 5 31.

5. The work of an evangelist] i.e. of preaching the gospel. **Make full proof of thy ministry**] i.e. neglect no aspect of the work.

6. For I, etc.] The 'I' is emphatic, in contrast to the 'Thou' of v. 5. St. Paul's day is almost over, Timothy must wage his warfare alone. **Ready to be offered**] lit. 'being poured out as a drink offering': a reference to the shedding of his own blood in his approaching martyr's death: cp. Phil 2 17, where the same word is used. **7. A good fight**] rather, 'I have contested the good contest.' The reference is not to a battle, but to a contest in the games: cp. 1 Cor 9 25. **Kept the faith**] 'The faith' is here regarded as a precious treasure entrusted to him: cp. 1 Tim 1 11 6 20 2 Tim 1 13, 14. **8. A crown**] RV 'the crown,' the reward for righteousness. St. Paul here carries on the metaphor of the contest in the games, which he had dropped for the moment in the last clause of v. 7. **At that day**] i.e. the day of judgment.

9-15. St. Paul bids Timothy endeavour to come to him quickly, for some of his com panions have left him and others have been sent on missions to the Churches. He asks him to bring some things of which he is in want, and warns him against an enemy who has done the Apostle much harm.

10. Demas] mentioned as a companion of St. Paul in Col 4 14 Philemon v. 24. **Crescens]** nowhere else mentioned in NT. **Titus]** frequently mentioned in 2 Cor and elsewhere as one of the Apostle's most trusted lieutenants. He had evidently gone to Dalmatia on the E. coast of the Adriatic on a mission from St. Paul.

11. Luke] 'the beloved physician,' Col 4 14. **Mark]** was with the Apostle on his First Missionary Journey (Ac 12 25), but St. Paul lost confidence in him and refused to take him on the Second Journey (Ac 15 37-40). Mark, however, afterwards redeemed his reputation, and we find him with the Apostle in Rome when the Epistle to the Colossians was written (Col 4 10).

12. Tychicus] see Ac 22 5 Eph 6 21 Col 4 7.

13. The cloke] Probably a long thick mantle which the approach of winter (v. 21) would render necessary to the Apostle in prison.

The books] It is impossible to conjecture what these were. **The parchments]** may have been some of the books of Scripture.

14. Alexander] may be the same as the Alexander mentioned (1 Tim 1 20) in conjunction with Hymenæus. He had evidently been an opponent of St. Paul's teaching.

16–22. The Apostle mentions the circumstances of his first appearance before his judges, declares his abiding trust in the Lord, sends salutations to friends, and prays for a blessing on Timothy.

16. My first answer] It would seem that St. Paul's case had been partly heard, but the evidence had been insufficient for condemnation, and the hearing had been adjourned.

19. Prisca and Aquila] see Ac 18 2. **Onesiphorus]** cp. 2 Tim 1 16.

20. Erastus] perhaps 'the chamberlain of the city' of Corinth mentioned in Ro 16 23 : see also Ac 19 22. **Trophimus]** see Ac 20 4 21 29.

21. The names in this v. are those of members of the Church in Rome. **Linus]** There was a Linus bishop of the Church of Rome a little later, and this is probably the same person.

22. The first blessing is for Timothy : the second for him and all who are with him (**you** being plural).

The subscription has no authority, though possibly quite correct.

TITUS

INTRODUCTION

1. Contents. The writer, professing to be Paul the Apostle and maintaining his right to be an Apostle, sends an affectionate greeting to his son in the faith, Titus (1 1-5). He reminds Titus that he left him in Crete to perfect the organisation of the Church in the island, by ordaining presbyters ; and he now dwells on the moral qualifications and loyalty to the faith which these Church officers must have (1 6-9). He points out that the Cretans, a volatile folk, need sharp teaching to keep them accurate in speech and pure in life (1 10-16). The old should preserve a Christian dignity, not only for their own sake, but also as a sound example for the young, that they too may be good and true (2 1-6). Nor should Titus forget that his own example is paramount (2 7,8). Servants must find in obedience to their earthly masters a way to obey God (2 9,10). All need to be on their guard, for all alike are waiting for the quick return of Christ, the Redeemer (2 11-15). Titus must further remind the Cretan Christians that they have a

duty also to the un-Christian world about them ; they must be good citizens and good neighbours (3 1,2) ; for as, by no merit of ours, God raised us from a heathen to a Christian life, so we should try by an attractive goodness to win others (3 3-8). He urges Titus not to argue, but if a man is a 'heretic,' to give him two warnings, and then shun him (3 9-11). With a few personal words about his own plans, a final word of advice, and a reverent farewell, the letter closes.

2. Value of the Epistle. It will be seen that the chief value of the Epistle lies in its common-sense and spirituality, and is not dependent upon date or authorship. Even those critics who believe it pseudonymous explain that, in an age of different literary ethics from ours, a pupil honoured his master by writing in his name what he believed his master would write were he still alive. As the Epistle has, all through Christian history, been a store-house of good advice for Church officers, so it must continue to be, whatever the outcome of modern scholarship about it. We catch a glimpse of the development of the ministry, and of a growing insistence on orthodoxy, which seem to some recent scholars beyond what we see in former writings of St. Paul. This contention cannot be granted without serious qualification ; for even those most willing to question the early crystallisation of Christian tradition are now more and more tending to admit that, before the last decades of the 1st cent., Christianity was definitely organised ; and the movement towards an intellectual basis for faith was certainly well within St. Paul's active career—even if ' faith ' to him was ordinarily ' a firm hold upon spiritual realities,' it often stood squarely for ' the Christian system,' whether doctrinal or institutional (e.g. Ro 1 ^{5} Gal 1 ^{23} Phil 1 ^{27} ; cp. also Ac 6 ^{7} 13 ^{8} 14 ^{22} 16 ^{5} 24 ^{24}). Moreover, even in this Epistle, soundness in doctrine means soundness in morality rather than soundness in creed (see on 2 ^{1}). However, though we grant the most radical view of this advance of organisation and doctrine, the questions arising from it are no longer of first importance ; because those who look to primitive authority for ministry and creed are increasingly assured that the development as well as the inception of Christianity is a divine act, so that for them the divine authority of ministry and creed is not weakened if a document be proved of somewhat later date than it was formerly thought to be. For all readers, therefore, the interest of the Epistle is not so much historical or controversial, as practical and spiritual. Once admitted to canonical Scripture, it holds its place on its own merits.

3. Authorship and Date. Till recent times, with essential unanimity, this Epistle was ascribed to St. Paul. It is true that the heretic Marcion omitted it from his list of St. Paul's Epistles, but his doctrinal reasons for this are so evident as to rob his omission of significance. In the last cent., when biblical criticism began, Titus was set down as a forgery of the 2nd cent. To-day critics are finding in it what they believe undoubted fragments of St. Paul, and are calling it ' sub-Pauline,' with a date between 90 and 120 A.D. The trend even among radical scholars is, therefore, *toward* the traditional view of authorship.

The authorship is wisely left more or less open. The discovery of a few pages of early Christian MS might turn the question one way or the other. A few points are becoming clear ; the first of which is that if St. Paul is the author, he was released from his first Roman imprisonment, and, in the interval before his final imprisonment, visited some of his Churches. We may safely say that if the Epistle is his, he wrote it about 64 A.D. If authentic, this Epistle (with 1 and 2 Tim) practically proves that St. Paul was released after the imprisonment recorded in the Acts. There is much in known Roman procedure to commend such a theory ; the argument from silence is the most formidable obstacle.

The difficulties attending the ascription of the Epistle to St. Paul are important in the aggregate rather than separately. A fairly good answer can be made to each objection. (1) Writing personally to an intimate friend, the author asserts his apostleship too strenuously ; but St. Paul was old and worn, and one who, younger, wrote Galatians, would, even to an intimate, be apt to say what we find in the opening words of Titus : old men much in the public eye are always quite aware that private correspondence, not strictly confidential, is wont to reach many persons. (2) If the author was St. Paul, he put an emphasis upon organisation and orthodoxy quite unlike himself in his other Epistles. But St. Paul was older, new experiences drive to new moods, the exigencies of the Church created new needs, therefore there would be reason for conservatism. Men now, with sense of responsibility, tend to become conservative in age, however radical in youth. Besides, organisation and orthodoxy in this Epistle are stressed only for moral and spiritual ends : they seem to have little value in themselves. There is only slight advance upon St. Paul's other Epistles here. (3) The facts of Church organisation implied in both Titus and 1 and 2 Timothy seem too far beyond the facts revealed in St. Paul's earlier Epistles ; but the most ardent believer in organisation can find in these Epistles only a still indefinite organisation, the functions of the officers are not clear, and the bishop seems at most only emerging from among the presbyters ; certainly he is very far from the official described by Ignatius. Knowing the development that came later, we should expect the ministry in the year 64 to be much like this fluid picture in the Pastoral Epistles. (4) The most serious difficulty is the change in language and style from St. Paul's former modes of expression. In 46 verses are 26 words not used in any other known Epistles of St. Paul. Favourite words and particles are quite absent, and other expressions and turns (common to Titus and 1 and 2 Timothy) take their place. Even the lapse of several years seems inadequate to explain the change of style ; but the spirit of St. Paul, more subtle than language, is evident ; so that the best explanation if we ascribe the Epistle to St. Paul, is to say that he left unusual liberty to his amanuensis. For a fuller discussion see ' General Intro. to the Pastoral Epistles.'

CHAPTER 1

Greeting. Directions for Organising the Cretan Church

1-16. 'Paul an Apostle, to Titus his own son in the faith. In appointing elders in the towns of Crete, see to their character, and be sure that they keep the faith. There are Judaisers in the island, and the Cretans are liars ; so Church officers must be especially careful that their discourse may be sound.' **1. Paul, a servant of God**] St. Paul does not elsewhere use this designation in his superscriptions ; so an imitator would be unlikely to use it. **According to the faith, etc.**] i.e. to promote the true faith. **Which is after godliness**] i.e. which leads to godliness.

2. That cannot lie] A bad translation. The single Gk. word means 'absolutely truthful.' It is irreverent to say of the One Self-determined Being, 'cannot' ; 'will not' is sufficient and final. Here AV and RV both add an idea not in the original, borrowing, doubtless, from Heb 6 18 : cp. Ro 3 4 and 1 Cor 1 9. **Before the world began**] lit. (as RV) 'Before times eternal.' **3.** RV 'But in his own seasons manifested his word in the message' (proclamation) 'wherewith I was entrusted,' etc. **His word**] To the Hebrew, 'word' or 'name' stood for the being whose it was ; so we might safely translate, 'himself.' St. Augustine interpreted it definitely 'Christ.'

4. Son after the common faith] i.e. his pupil in the faith which they shared together. Titus is not mentioned in Acts, but from St. Paul's Epistles we gather the following details : he was a Greek (Gal 2 3) ; neither at his conversion nor (probably) later was he circumcised (ib.) ; he went on missionary journeys with and for St. Paul (Gal 2 1 2 Cor 7 6 f., 13-15 8 6, 16-18). We know nothing more till we find him here. **5.** Though in a personal letter, these words are so explicit that, should the Cretans resist Titus' authority, he might read to them what the great master himself had said. We are wont to say, 'If you have trouble, show this letter.' St. Paul, perhaps, implied this here.

Left I thee in Crete] This cannot be identified with the only visit of St. Paul to Crete elsewhere recorded (Ac 27 7 f.). The visit when he left Titus there was after the Roman imprisonment : see Intro. There were many Jews in Crete, and there were Cretans in Jerusalem at Pentecost (Ac 2 11), but we do not know how Christianity was planted in the island. **Elders**] Gk. 'presbyters.' Rectors, or pastors, we should say to-day. **6. The husband of one wife**] not necessarily of any wife, but of not more than one. Probably not an objection to polygamy, which was rare, but to divorce and remarriage, which was common. It is hardly likely that

remarriage, after the death of a first wife, was to be a disqualification for office : cp. 1 Tim 3 2. **Faithful children**] i.e. brought up as Christians. **7. A bishop**] This officer seems simply to be one of the 'elders' in v. 5 : though the difference in name and number may suggest the beginning of a distinction between them. At any rate, the Church is here more highly organised than when St. Paul wrote, e.g. 1 Cor, but not nearly so much so as when Ignatius wrote, e.g. to the Ephesians, circ. 115 A.D. : cp. 1 Tim 3 1. **8. Lover of good men**] better (as RV), 'lover of good,' including both men and things. **9. As he hath been taught**] RV (which is lit.) 'according to the teaching' ; i.e. the teaching which he has received, perhaps referring to a gradually forming statement of the essentials of the faith, such as culminated, in the 2nd cent., in the 'Roman symbol,' or early form of the Apostles' Creed.

10. Here begins the arraignment of the false teachings which the elders will have to meet (vv. 10-16). **They of the circumcision**] i.e Jewish converts who insisted that to be a Christian one must also submit to Jewish ordinances.

12. One of themselves] i.e. one of the Cretans. The reference is to Epimenides, a poet, circ. 600 B.C. St. Paul calls him a prophet because, (1) poets and prophets were apt to be classed together, and (2) his 'witness' was still true in St. Paul's day. One reason why the Cretans were called liars was because they said that Zeus was buried in Crete. **Slow bellies**] i.e. gross and corpulent through self-indulgence. **14. Jewish fables**] e.g. the sort of rules, for maintaining which our Lord condemned the Pharisees (Mt 15, 23, etc.).

15. Unto the pure all things are pure] St. Chrysostom said, 'God made nothing impure.' Used, not abused, all things are right ; abused, the seemingly innocent thing is sin. St. Paul does not mean to limit this principle to ceremonial distinctions (about meats, etc.), with which the Judaisers would be apt to vex the Cretans. **Their mind and conscience is defiled**] cp. Mt 15 4-8. **16. They profess**] Not mere pretence, but blatant self-confidence.

CHAPTER 2

Various Instructions for Christian Life and Doctrine

1-15. 'In giving sound doctrine, to offset false teaching, put the first emphasis on the need of character, because Christ is our reward, and very soon. And do thou, Titus, set a good example, and maintain thine own authority.'

1. Sound doctrine] cp. 2 2, 'sound in faith.' The context shows that this is soundness not in intellectual opinions, but in the inculcation of uprightness of life. In Christ's day 'faith' was always regarded as spiritual ; in the apostolic age, nearly always so ; but in the apostolic age the tendency unquestionably began to identify 'faith' with a system. It is important to mark that faith and doctrine as used in this Epistle are not far from the earlier use : cp. Intro. § 2.

2. The aged men] Not the elders in an official sense, but simply the old men. **3. Behaviour**] All outward deportment ; not simply dress on the one hand ; not inner thoughts on the other. **Not given to much wine**] RV ' enslaved to much wine.' Cretans, both men and women, were notorious drinkers : cp. 1 ¹².

4. Teach] RV ' train,' a much better word.

5. Keepers at home] Another Gk. text (adopted in RV) gives ' workers at home.'

Blasphemed] The Cretans would say, ' See how they treat their husbands, *that* is Christianity !'

7. St. Paul now turns to Titus personally. Even if he had recently seen him, it was not unnatural to press a warning upon ' his child in the faith.' **Sincerity**] Rightly omitted in RV, since it is lacking in the best MSS.

9. Servants] i.e. ' slaves.' Slaves made up a considerable proportion of early Christian congregations ; and, often being more intelligent than their masters, could influence them in spiritual things. **11.** The RV is again more accurate than AV : ' For the grace of God hath appeared, bringing salvation to all men.'

12. Teaching] better, ' disciplining,' or even (as Luther), ' chastising.' **That**] purpose, ' in order that.' **This present world**] lit. ' this present age '; i.e. before Christ's reappearing.

13. The **blessed hope** is ' the appearing.' The apostolic age cannot be understood without constantly keeping in mind that the Christians expected Christ's return in glory within their generation. **Glorious appearing**] This should be (as in RV), ' appearing of the glory.' The ' glory ' is the visible majesty of the divine. The Jews called it the ' shekinah.' **The great God and our Saviour Jesus Christ**] RV ' our great God and Saviour Jesus Christ.' Scholars have always been divided whether the Father and Christ both are meant, or only Christ. The most skilful escape from the difficulty is to say that Christ will appear in both His own glory and His Father's. If it is to be interpreted ' our God .. Christ,' the expression is unique in the NT., unless we take RM for Jn 1¹⁸, ' God only begotten.' **14. For us**] Not ' in our stead,' but ' for our sake.' However, the next words suggest both meanings. **Redeem**] lit. ' set free by means of a ransom.' **A peculiar people**] An OT. expression : ' a chosen, favoured, superior people.' ' *His own* people ' is perhaps the best rendering. **15. Let no man despise thee**] i.e. push these counsels home so gravely and thoroughly that men will heed thee : cp. 1 Tim 4¹².

CHAPTER 3

THE SUBSTANCE AND MANNER OF THE TEACHING TO BE GIVEN. FAREWELL

1–15. ' Remind the Cretans to be loyal citizens, good neighbours. As, through no merit of ours, God won us to Himself, so we must live good lives. Never argue with stubborn-hearted people. Warn a heretic twice ; then drop him. Come to me at Nicopolis, when Artemas or Tychicus leaves me, and see that Zenas and Apollos get well started on their missionary journey. We all greet you all.'

1. To principalities and powers] better (as RV), ' to rulers, to authorities.' We should be apt to say, ' to the government.' **To obey magistrates**] The original meaning of the Gk. word is ' to obey one's superiors ' : ' to obey ' or ' to be obedient ' (RV) is, therefore, a better translation. **3. We ourselves**] i.e. we Christians. **Were sometimes**] ' Were ' (standing first in the Gk. sentence is emphatic) ' at one time ' (RV ' aforetime ').

4. Alford translates this v., ' But when the goodness and love-toward-men ' (one Gk. word) ' of our Saviour, God, was manifested.' **God our Saviour**] the Father. **Appeared**] ' was manifested ' ; i.e. in the coming, life, and death of Christ. **5. By the washing of regeneration**] For ' washing,' ' laver ' (i.e. place where the washing took place) is better. Baptism is referred to here. **Renewing of the Holy Ghost**] The baptism to be efficient must be both by water and by the Spirit. It is not a mere outward act. **6. Which he shed on us**] When ? At Pentecost, or, generally, to each individual ? Probably both meanings should be included. **7. Heirs according to the hope of eternal life**] better (as RM), ' heirs, according to hope, of eternal life.'

8. Faithful saying] i.e. a condensed reflection, an axiom in rhythmical form, a Christian proverb. Scholars disagree whether the ' faithful saying ' here includes vv. 4–7 or only v. 7. The presence of ' faithful sayings ' shows that a religious movement is no longer in its infancy : men have reflected about it for some time : cp. 1 Tim 1¹⁵ 3¹ 4⁸ 2 Tim 2¹¹. **Believed in God**] better (as RV), ' believed God ' ; i.e. trusted His word.

9. Every Christian minister learns the futility of arguments to persuade the prejudiced. Living reasonable lives, teaching positively and reasonably, we convince men ; not otherwise.

10. Heretick] A heretic, to St. Paul, was never one who held erroneous opinions only, but one whose error sprang from moral crookedness, issuing at last in evil life. There seems always a sensual element in what St. Paul calls heresy ; for he classes it with the sins of the flesh (Gal 5²⁰). The heresies of the Corinthian Church were moral rather than intellectual (1 Cor 11 19). Eph 4 18 f. exactly describes heresy, though the word itself is not mentioned. It is not important, but interesting to note that the word 'heretic' occurs only here in the NT. 'Heresy' is common. **Reject**] This is not excommunication. 'Refuse,' 'avoid,' 'shun,' 'decline to have intercourse with,' have been suggested as better translations.

12. Artemas] Nothing is known of him beyond this mention. Tradition says that he was later bishop of Lystra. **Tychicus**] cp. Ac 20 4 Eph 6 21 Col 4 7 2 Tim 4 12. **Nicopolis**] Several towns had this name. This may be the one in Epirus. **13. Zenas .. and Apollos**] Perhaps the bearers of the Epistle. Zenas was probably a Jewish scribe. For Apollos see Ac 18 24 1 Cor 1 12 16 12. The mingling of old names with new is a strong critical argument for the Pauline authorship; a pupil wishing to imitate would hardly be apt to mention any but well-known names. **14. Our's**] 'our people' (RV); i.e. the Christian community in Crete. **For necessary uses**] i.e. for helping such persons as Zenas and Apollos to give their time to Church extension. We should say, 'See that the people of the different congregations give good missionary offerings.'

15. In the faith] lit. 'in faith.'

The subscription appended to the Epistle in the AV is certainly spurious.

PHILEMON

INTRODUCTION

The Epistle of Paul to Philemon is a personal letter to a friend, called out by a situation probably not infrequent in antiquity. A letter of Pliny on a similar occasion ('Ep.' ix. 21, see translation in Lightfoot, ' Comm. on Philemon,' pp. 316 f.) has been preserved.

1. Recipients and Occasion. Philemon was a resident of Colossæ in Phrygia (cp. Col 4 9 with Philemon v. 11). He owed his conversion to Paul (v. 19), having perhaps heard the gospel on some visit to Ephesus during the three years of Paul's stay there (Ac 19). A man of wealth, he had distinguished himself by deeds of charity (vv. 5–7), as well as by zeal in spreading the gospel (v. 1), and his house was the habitual meeting-place of a group of Colossian Christians (v. 2). He may be compared with Stephanas of Corinth (1 Cor 16 15-18). **Apphia** (v. 2), also a Christian, bearing a characteristic native Phrygian name, was doubtless Philemon's wife, and the subject of the letter concerned her too. **Archippus** may have been their son. He had a 'ministry' (perhaps as presbyter or evangelist) at Laodicea (Col 4 15-17). **Onesimus** (a name often borne by Greek slaves at this period) was a slave (doubtless a house-slave) of Philemon, who had run away, probably robbing his master at the same time. Reaching Rome (or, according to some, Cæsarea), he had somehow found his master's friend Paul. Such a chance would not be surprising in a great and compactly populated city. In his desperate case, liable to arrest and the severest punishment, he may have voluntarily sought the Apostle's aid. At any rate he met with kindness, was brought to faith in Christ, and served Paul with grateful devotion. When Tychicus went to Asia Minor (Col 4 7-9), Paul took the occasion to send back Onesimus, now ' the faithful and beloved brother,' with general commendation to the Colossian Christians, and with this special letter of intercession to Philemon.

The letter was thus written in the same circumstances, and sent at the same time, as Colossians (cp. Col 4 9 with vv. 12, 17) : see, however, Col 4 10, and on v. 23. The place of writing was probably Rome, where Paul was imprisoned. The escaped slave may well have tried to lose himself in the throngs of the capital, and would have been at least as well able to secure transportation thither as to Cæsarea.

2. Attitude to Slavery. Paul in this letter is in accord with early Christianity generally in accepting slavery without criticism, and he assumes the property right of the slave-owner ; but he recognises the slave as a brother in Christ, to whom is due not merely forgiveness but Christian friendship. Compare what he says of a sphere of life in which neither bondage nor freedom has any place (1 Cor 7 20-24 12 13 Gal 3 28 Col 3 11), and his directions to masters and slaves in Eph 6 5-9 and Col 3 22–4 1. Whether or not in 1 Cor 7 21 he meant to advise a slave to use lawful opportunities of securing his freedom, is a disputed question. The effect of Jesus Christ's principle of the essential worth of the human soul (Mt 6 26 f. 10 30 f. 12 12 Lk 15) a principle which Paul recognised, is to be seen in the attitude of the modern Christian world toward slavery itself. On ancient slavery, which, especially under Roman law, gave the owner absolute authority over the person and life of the slave, and was full of cruelty, vice, and every horror, see Becker, 'Gallus'; Lecky, 'History of European Morals,' chs. ii. and iv. ; Vincent, 'Commentary on Philemon,' pp. 162–168.

3. Genuineness. Philemon was included in Marcion's collection of Pauline Epistles, circ. 150 A.D. Its perfect adaptation to the concrete situation everywhere consistently presupposed, its freshness and charm, and the rare delicacy and tact which it reveals are good grounds for holding it genuine ; and when to these considerations is added its close resemblance in style and expression to the other Epistles of Paul, the evidence supporting its own claim (v. 1) to Pauline authorship is conclusive. On this view, the interest of this beautiful little Epistle is immensely increased, as affording a glimpse into the Apostle's private life, and exhibiting his great tenderness and delicacy of feeling.

The intimate connexion of Philemon with Colossians has led some scholars to deny its genuineness, but neither by the frigid allegories suggested (e.g. 'What man loses in this world he regains for ever in Christianity'), nor by the theory that it is an ethical tract on slavery, has it been possible satisfactorily to explain the origin of the Epistle. For an account of such views see art. 'Philemon, Epistle to,' in 'Encyclopædia Biblica.'

4. Contents.

I. Vv. 1–3. Greeting.

II. Vv. 4–7. Epistolary thanksgiving (for Philemon's faith and love) and prayer (that these may be crowned with understanding of the significance of God's gift to men).

III. Vv. 8–21. Request for kind treatment to Onesimus.

IV. V. 22. Paul hopes to be set free and to visit Colossæ.

V. Vv. 23, 24. Salutations from friends.

VI. V. 25. Farewell benediction.

1. A prisoner of Christ Jesus] Paul thus describes himself because his bonds (which are to be here understood literally) have been incurred in the service of Christ : cp. v. 9 (and v. 23) and Eph 3[1] 4[1]. The usual claim to be an Apostle is here unnecessary ; so Phil 1[1], in that Epistle of Paul which stands next to Philemon in its tender intimacy.

Timothy] with Paul in Ephesus (Ac 19[22]), and doubtless known to Philemon : cp. Phil 1[1] 2[19] Col 1[1]. **Our brother**] 'my fellow-Christian': cp. 1 Cor 5[11], also 2 Cor 1[1] Col 1[1] 1 Th 3[2]. So v. 2, 'sister': cp. Ro 16[1]. **Beloved**] as in

the English epistolary 'My dear.' Here probably with a certain emphasis: cp. 3 Jn v. 1.

Fellowlabourer] RV 'fellow-worker': i.e. in the gospel : cp. vv. 2, 24, Ro 16[3] 2 Cor 8[23] Phil 2[25], etc. **2. Fellowsoldier**] i.e. of Christ: cp. Phil 2[25] and 2 Tim 2[3]. **The church in thy house**] see on Ro 16[5] 1 Cor 16[19] Col 4[15] (Laodicea), Ac 12[12]. A constituent part of the body mentioned in Col 1[2]. **3.** Paul's usual greeting : see on Ro 1[7]. **You**] the whole group of vv. 1, 2 : cp. vv. 22, 25. Note vv. 4–23, 'thee,' 'thy,' 'thou,' referring to Philemon only.

4. I thank my God .. always, etc.] the usual thanksgiving, congratulation, and prayer: cp. Ro 1[8 f.] Eph 1[3, 15-17] Phil 1[3-5, 9] Col 1[3 f., 9 f.], etc.; and see on v. 20. For illustrations of this conventional element of a Greek letter, see J R. Harris, 'A Study in Letter-writing,' 'Expositor,' 5th series, vol. viii. 1898, pp. 161–167.

5. Hearing] introduces the special reasons for thanksgiving, viz. Philemon's love and faith. **Of thy love and faith**] RM 'of thy love, and of the faith' is a better rendering. The faith is toward the Lord Jesus, the love toward all the saints. The order of clauses is inverted (as in Gal 4[4 f.]): cp. Gal 5[6] Eph 1[15] Col 1[4] 1 Th 1[3] 3[6]. **Faith .. toward**] the same as 'faith in.'

6. That] introduces mention of that for which Paul prays (v. 4), viz. recognition by Philemon of the greatness of God's gift to men. **The communication** (RV 'fellowship') **of thy faith** is perhaps best taken in the sense, 'the generous charity which has proceeded from thy faith.' So in Phil 1[9] love is to culminate in knowledge; and in the parallel to our v. in Col 1[9-11], references to conduct and to knowledge are interwoven: cp. Col 3[10]. The word for fellowship (*koinōnia*) is used of a charitable contribution : cp. Ro 15[26] 2 Cor 8[4] 9[13] Heb 13[16]. In 'the fellowship of thy faith' both the love and the faith of v. 5 are included. The love is emphasised again in v. 7. Another possible rendering is, 'thy participation (i.e. with us and all Christians) in our (Gk. 'the') faith': cp. v. 17. **Effectual by the acknowledging** (RV 'in the knowledge'), etc.] means, 'effectual in leading to the recognition on Philemon's part of all the blessings which Christians have.' 'In you' (or, better, RM 'in us') includes both 'already in your possession' and 'within your reach.' What Paul has in mind is made clear by the parallel, Eph 1[18 f.]: cp. Eph 3[18 f.], also Phil 1[9 f.] Col 1[9]. An understanding of how exalted is the privilege of salvation through Christ is the crown and culmination of faith, and involves a knowledge of the deeper mysteries of God. It is, moreover, essential to soundness of Christian life and to the Christian enthusiasm on which security against temptation depends. **In** (RV unto ') **Christ**] loosely added, without exact indication of relation to the preceding, in order to point out that as the object of faith is Christ, so only through a relation to Christ is love active or knowledge possible, or ' every good thing,' which is the object of knowledge, to be valued. **7. For**] introduces another statement of Paul's reason for thanking God (v. 4).

Bowels .. are refreshed] RV ' Hearts.. have been refreshed '; i.e. through the charitable acts prompted by Philemon's ' love.' The ' heart ' (Gk. ' bowels ') is the seat of grief and despondency and of joy and courage : cp. v. 20.

The Saints] means merely ' the Christians,' without regard to eminent attainments in character.

8. Wherefore] In view of this evidence of faith and love Paul adopts a tone of request, not of command. **All** (Gk. ' much ') **boldness in Christ**] means, ' abundant readiness to adopt freedom of speech, by reason of my own and of thy relation to Christ and so of our relation to each other.' ç. **For love's sake**] or, ' in the name of love.' Philemon's response is to be a matter of love, not of mere obedience. Paul chooses to put the matter on the highest possible plane. **Paul the aged**] Paul may have been over sixty years old at this time. At the time of his conversion, about thirty years earlier, he is called a ' young man ' (Ac 7[58]), a term applied to persons between the ages of twenty-four and forty. With this rendering these and the following words have a touch of pathos befitting the whole tone of the passage. If the rendering of RM ' an ambassador ' is preferred (cp. Eph 6[20]), the words would seem to imply an attitude of command. **Also a prisoner of Christ Jesus**] cp. v. 1. **10. My son**] RV ' my child '; cp. 1 Cor 4[14, 15, 17] Gal 4[19]. Cp. Mishna, ' Sanhedrin,' fol. 19, 2, ' If one teaches the son of his neighbour the law, the Scripture reckons this the same as though he had begotten him.'

11. Unprofitable .. profitable] A play on the name Onesimus, which means ' helpful,' ' profitable.' **To me**] valuable to Paul, as to Philemon, because of both his personal service (v. 13) and his Christian friendship. **12. I have sent**] better, ' I send,' as the same tense is translated in vv. 19, 21, ' I write.' **13. In thy stead** (RV ' behalf ')] Since Onesimus was Philemon's slave, his service to Paul was a gift from Philemon. ' In thy behalf ' does not mean ' in thy place.' **In the bonds of the gospel**] ' in this imprisonment incurred through preaching the gospel ': cp. vv. 1, 9, 23.

14. Without thy mind] a common Greek expression for ' without thy consent.' **As .. of necessity**] Paul shrinks from saying outright that if he had kept Onesimus that

would have been extracting from Philemon an obligation which he would have resented or grudged.

15. For] introduces a further consideration in favour of sending the slave back. **He therefore departed**] RV ' was therefore parted from thee ' ; in the providence of God : cp. (so Chrysostom) Gn 45[5, 8]. ' Therefore ' refers to the divine purpose, ' that thou shouldest have him for ever.' **For ever**] an eternal possession, not by legal bond, but by Christian friendship.

16. Servant] ' slave.' **In the flesh**] ' in human relations ' : cp. Ro 1[3] Eph 6[5] Col 3[22]. This seems to imply that in the past Onesimus had had kindly treatment and friendship. These old associations should now, in his repentance, make him even more dear to Philemon than he can be to Paul. This is said in order to make bitterness toward the former ungrateful runaway an impossibility. **In the Lord**] ' through your common relation to Christ.'

17. A partner] one who shares : cp. 2 Cor 8[23]. This partnership is further described in 1 Cor 1[9], ' partnership in common relation to His Son Jesus Christ ' ; 2 Cor 13[14], ' participation in the Holy Spirit ' ; Phil 2[1] 1 Jn 1[3, 7].

19. I Paul have written *it* **with mine own hand**] This formal language is meant to suggest the phraseology of a legally binding note. ' I Paul ' corresponds to the usual method of an ancient signature : cp. 1 Cor 16[21] Col 4[18] 2 Th 3[17]. The whole letter was probably an autograph : see on Gal 6[11]. **20. Let me have joy of thee**] a somewhat common Greek expression, especially with reference to children and friends. Here **in the Lord** marks the relation as a Christian one. So **in Christ**, v. 23. **Refresh my bowels** (RV ' heart ')] see on verse 7.

21. Do more than I say] RV ' even beyond what I say.' This need not imply the actual releasing of Onesimus from slavery.

22. A lodging] cp. Phil 1[25] 2[24] for Paul's plan for a journey to the East. The ' lodging ' might be at Philemon's house or at an inn.

Through your prayers] cp 2 Cor 1[11].

23. Epaphras, my fellow-prisoner] in Col 4[10] Aristarchus was Paul's fellow-prisoner. Apparently his friends took turns in sharing his imprisonment and ministering to his needs. Epaphras (Col 4[12]) was of Colossæ, and had brought the gospel to that city (Col 1[7]). **24. Mark, Aristarchus, Demas, Luke**] cp. Col 4[10, 14], Jesus Justus, perhaps as not personally known to Philemon and his circle, is here passed over. For Mark, cp. also Ac 12[12, 25] 13[5, 13] 15[37-39] 2 Tim 4[11] 1 Pet 5[13] ; Aristarchus (of Thessalonica), Ac 19[29] 20[4] 27[2] ; Demas, Luke, 2 Tim 4[10, 11]. **My fellowlabourers**] see on v. 1.

25. Farewell benediction. Cp. Gal 6[18] Phil 4[23] ; also 2 Tim 4[22].

HEBREWS

INTRODUCTION

1. Authorship. The Epistle to the Hebrews is an anonymous work. It is ascribed to St. Paul in our English Bibles—even in the Revised Version unfortunately; but this is only in the title, which was not a part of the original autograph. All St. Paul's acknowledged Epistles have his name as part of the opening salutation according to the usual custom with ancient letters; but that is not the case with this Epistle, which begins without any salutation. Therefore, if we do not ascribe it to the Apostle that is not to charge the author with 'forgery,' nor in the milder modern phrase with 'pseudepigraphy.' There is no evidence that he ever intended to have St. Paul's name associated with it. The title in the oldest MSS is simply 'To the Hebrews.'

How, then, does the Epistle come to bear St. Paul's name in our English Bibles? The reason is that the fuller title is found in the later Gk. MSS, from some of which it passed into the Latin Bible, the Vulgate. We can easily understand how this came about. There was a tendency in the early Church to inscribe great names on anonymous works in order to further their currency. No greater name than that of the Apostle to the Gentiles could be found for this letter to the Hebrews, which might well be accounted worthy of no less a personage. And if it was to be brought within the circle of the chief inspired teachings of the apostolic age, this narrowed the possibilities of authorship to a comparatively small group. Then, like St. Paul, the writer is emancipated from the Jewish Law; he exalts Christ specifically as the 'Son of God,' St. Paul's most significant name for our Lord; he elaborates the thought of the Atonement by the death of Christ; he glorifies faith. On the other hand, his style and diction are quite unlike St. Paul's; instead of the Apostle's simple, direct, rugged speech, we have here rhetorical phraseology in rounded periods. Of more importance is the theological attitude of the writer, which is very different from that of St. Paul. The Apostle combats legalism, but in the interest of justification—a legal condition; our author is concerned with the Tabernacle ritual of the Old Testament, and his aim is to show the way of approach to God through purification, so that while St. Paul treats of the gospel in opposition to the Pharisees and their casuistry, the unknown author of Hebrews is interested in its relation to the priests and their sacrifices.

The authorship of this Epistle was much discussed in early ages; but Origen, the most learned of the early teachers, concluded his examination of the question with the words, 'Who wrote the Epistle God only knows.' About the same time another Church father, Tertullian, referred to it as 'the Epistle of Barnabas,' taking for granted that Barnabas was its author. It is a significant fact that this is the oldest positive and definite ascription of any name to it that has reached us; and there is much in the character and position of Barnabas to agree with it. Others have suggested Apollos, Clement of Rome, St. Luke. The latest proposal is the brilliant suggestion of Harnack that the author was Priscilla. If it were written by a woman it might have been thought in that unenlightened age not wise to give her name. Priscilla was the chief teacher of Apollos, an Alexandrian, and there is evidence of Alexandrian influences in the contents of the Epistle. But the question cannot be definitely determined.

2. Alexandrian Influences. This point is of great interest for our right understanding of the Epistle, as well as with regard to the problem of its authorship. There can be no question that the author was more or less imbued with the literary and theological methods pursued by Jewish scholars at Alexandria. Those methods included a highly allegorical treatment of the Old Testament, and it is quite Alexandrian for our author to regard the Levitical dispensation as a shadow of the spiritual realities that are to be found in the heavenly tabernacle and its ordinances. The very forms of introduction in which passages from the Old Testament are quoted are precisely those used by Philo, the famous Alexandrian Jewish philosopher, but quite unlike the forms employed by St. Paul or any other New Testament writer. Elsewhere we meet with such expressions as, 'it is written,' 'the Scripture says,' 'David says,' 'Moses says,' 'Isaiah says.' These expressions are never met with in Hebrews, where, as in Philo, no human authors are named—although in a single instance we have the periphrasis 'one hath somewhere testified' (2^6); but the utterances cited are attributed immediately to God or the Holy Spirit, in such terms as, ' He saith'

(1^7), 'the Holy Ghost saith' (3^7). Further, there are certain phrases and images found nowhere else in the Bible which Hebrews shares with Alexandrian writers. Thus the rare form rendered 'at sundry times' (1^1), or, better, as in the Revised Version, 'in divers portions,' is also in the book of Wisdom (7^{22}) —an Alexandrian work. Then the peculiar expression 'effulgence,' applied to God's glory in Hebrews (1^3), is referred to Wisdom in the book of that name (Wisd 7^{26}), and it is quite a favourite word with Philo. Again, the word rendered 'substance' in the same v. of Hebrews is also found in Wisd 16^{21}, probably in the same sense, though here the reading, and therefore the rendering, is doubtful. Lastly, the rare expression for death rendered 'the issue of their life' in Hebrews (13^7) can be traced to Wisd 2^{17}. But we are not left to depend on such comparisons of words and phrases. The whole spirit and atmosphere of Hebrews is Alexandrian rather than Palestinian.

3. Recipients and probable Date. Brushing aside less probable conjectures—as that the Alexandrianism of the Epistle implies that it was destined for Alexandria, a curious inversion of ideas—we have two contending theories of its destination—one pointing to a Palestinian Church, the other claiming Rome as the residence of the recipients. We should expect an Epistle to Hebrews to go to the district where Hebrew (or, rather, Aramaic) speaking Jews lived, and the whole argument on the Levitical system would seem to indicate this region. Jerusalem could not be the place, because the readers were not the first gospel converts (2^3), and perhaps, too, because Jerusalem was a poor Church needing help from the more prosperous Churches, whereas the Church here addressed is praised for its bountifulness (10^{34}). Cæsarea and Antioch have been suggested as possible places for the Epistle to have been directed to. But there is a strong inclination to locate the Church addressed at Rome, where there was a large Jewish community, and where Clement (95 A.D.) was familiar with it. Some think the sufferings referred to in $10^{32\text{-}35}$ were those of Nero's persecution. Rome would be interested in a salutation from Italians (13^{24}). A more serious question is as to the nationality of the recipients. It has been denied that they were Jews, chiefly because their apostasy is described as departure from 'the living God'—not merely from Christ. But the author might well think that to abandon the faith of Christ was for Christians to give up everything— God and all. On the other hand, the minute discussion of the tabernacle ritual points most probably to Jews. The **date** cannot be fixed with certainty. But since the writer, while arguing for the temporary character of the Levitical system, makes no reference to the destruction of Jerusalem—the vast cataclysm in which that system was swept away—it is to be inferred that an event which would so immensely have strengthened his position if he had appealed to it could not have happened before he was writing. Perhaps we may assign the Epistle to about 68 A.D., when Jewish zealots would be urging all men of Hebrew blood to make common cause with the defenders of the ancient faith against the Roman enemy.

4. Aim and Object. It must be clear to every careful reader that this Epistle was written with one definite end in view. There is a unity in its composition that we do not recognise in any other NT. book. The author makes straight for his goal from start to finish. Even the exhortations that are so characteristic of the work, while they break the thread of the argument, are not digressions from the main object, but rather direct means for attaining it. They are applications of each stage of the discussion to the one great aim that is kept steadily in view throughout. It is in these exhortations that we see most clearly what that aim is. The Christians addressed are evidently in danger of falling away from their faith and apostatising altogether. So desperate does their condition appear to the author, that he feels it necessary to expostulate in the gravest terms. It is no fascination of the world luring them away from their original consecration that occasions this danger. The Hebrews are discouraged to almost the extent of despair, because they do not see how the gospel can offer them anything like compensation for what they have lost in being cast out of the synagogue on account of their confession of the Nazarene. This is the condition that the Epistle has to face. The method of meeting it is to boldly challenge the vaunted, venerable Judaism in its very citadel, the Levitical Law. The author institutes a comparison between Christianity and Judaism, or rather between Christ and the chief personages of Judaism—for with him 'Christianity is Christ'—in order to show that Christ is their superior in their very points of excellency, and that the gospel gives us the very things that the Law professed to give, but much more effectually. It has all that Judaism had ; and it has this in a higher form, in a larger measure ; nay, it alone really has this, for Judaism failed—Judaism could not do what it was relied upon to accomplish. The reason for this failure was that it had no substance. It was only the earthly shadow of those heavenly realities that Jesus Christ came to establish and bring within our reach. This position being proved all along the line, point by point, the conclusion is that it would be fatal folly to return from Christ to Judaism, and thus the readers are urged to be loyal to the New Covenant with its paramount privileges.

5. Theology. The author assumes the Jewish faith in God, but advances to the richer Christian ideas of the divine nature. The holiness of God is profoundly felt as the reason for a more effective cleansing before approaching Him than Judaism provided, and the gravity of apostasy is emphasised by the thought that we dare not trifle with God's demands, since He is a ' consuming fire' (12^{29}). On the other hand, it is also taken for granted that to come near to God is the one thing to be supremely sought after in religion (4^{16}). The Epistle reaches a climax in showing how this may be done through Christ as it could not be done by means of the Levitical system (10^{19-22}). Then the Fatherhood of God is expounded with a fulness and emphasis that we meet with nowhere else except in the teachings of Jesus Christ (12^{5-10}). There is a very lofty conception of our Lord as specifically ' the Son' who as such is higher than all other beings, angels as well as men, and also expresses to us the character and the very being of God ($1^{2,3}$). Nevertheless the Incarnation was a reality, and our Epistle uses language of remarkable strength and clearness concerning the human experience of Christ ($5^{7,8}$). In His work He is chiefly regarded as the High Priest of the Heavenly Tabernacle (3^1). Hebrews is the only New Testament book that gives us a distinct conception of the priesthood of Christ. This is exercised after His Resurrection and Ascension. His sacrifice on the Cross is actually presented to God in heaven. To our author the whole present interest in Christ is in that later sphere of His heavenly life—in what He is now as our priest and intercessor, though that rests on what He was on earth in His obedience and sacrifice. The death of Christ is the one sacrifice for sin (9^{12}). This is not discussed under the figure of acquittal in a court of law, after the manner of St. Paul; it is treated with reference to the tabernacle worshipper who knows himself to be unfit to enter the presence of God owing to defilement (9^{19}). Christ's sacrifice removes this defilement (10^{22}). The sacrifice consists in His offering Himself to God in death by ' the Eternal Spirit' (9^{14}), i.e. apparently, in virtue of His divine spiritual nature, which being eternal confers eternal efficacy. The essence of the sacrifice consists in the attitude of Christ's will, namely in His delighting to obey God's will, even to the extent of dying when the course of obedience involves that extremity. It is not too much to say that we have the clearest New Testament exposition of the very heart and essence of the Atonement in the statement

of this truth (10^{8-10}). Lastly, His great act of obedience in death was offered as the deed, not of *a* man, but of the leader and high priest of men, whereby He enables us to participate with Himself in doing the will of God, in which will our sanctification stands. Still, this is only to be enjoyed on condition of trust and fidelity; and the counterpart to Christ's sacrifice is His people's faith, the triumphs of which are celebrated as a conclusion of the whole argument (c. 11). Thus the New Covenant predicted by Jeremiah is established by Christ.

6. Analysis of the Epistle.

1^{1-3}. THE TWO METHODS OF REVELATION CONTRASTED

Judaism rested on the OT. as its authority; Christianity rests on the revelation in Christ. The earlier revelation was fragmentary, and limited by the limited human nature of the prophets through whom it came; the later revelation is a unity coming through that one Person in whom Sonship to God has been perfected, and who therefore most adequately represents the divine nature.

1^4-4^{13}. THE SUPREMACY OF CHRIST

The OT. itself testifies to His supremacy as God's Son over its chief personages—first, the angels, through whom the Jews believed that creation had been effected and the law given (1^4-2^4); nevertheless Jesus, though thus really superior to the angels by nature, is temporarily in a lower state that He may learn sympathy with us, taking our nature upon Him in order to become our adequate High Priest (2^{5-18}). Jesus is also superior to Moses, the founder of the national religion, yet only a servant, while He is the Son (3^{1-6}); Christ has a rest to give which we are warned not to miss by unfaithfulness as Israel missed its rest by provoking God in the wilderness (3^7-4^7). This promised rest which Joshua, the Jesus of the OT., could not give remains for another to confer. We therefore must labour to enter into it, considering how penetrating is God's word which promises the rest but also threatens punishment for unfaithfulness (4^{8-13}). Again turning to the high-priesthood of Christ, who is Jesus the Saviour indeed, the author prepares for his full discussion of it by a reference to the privilege it confers on us (4^{14-16}).

$5-7^{4-10}$. THE HIGH PRIESTHOOD OF CHRIST

The introduction of the High Priest ends the historical survey which had been brought down from the creation, through Moses and then Joshua. At this point the argument resolves itself into a discussion of Christ's priesthood in comparison with the Levitical priesthood, which is developed as the dominant theme of the Epistle. First we have Christ's resemblance to Aaron briefly stated, so as to show that He is at least as true a priest. Christ fulfilled the two requisite conditions that were seen in the case of Aaron—human brotherhood, essential to the representative character of priesthood (5$^{1-3}$), and divine appointment, essential to its authority (5^{4,5}). A quotation from Ps 110 referred to as proof of God's appointment of Christ to the priesthood introduces the name of Melchizedek (5^6). This starts a fruitful line of suggestions. In His humanity Jesus suffered grievously, but, by teaching Him obedience, that awful suffering perfected Him as a priest 'after the order of Melchizedek,' so that He became the author of eternal salvation to those who obey Him (5$^{7-10}$). Realising that his discussion is becoming difficult, the author breaks off to deplore the dulness of his readers and their infantile backwardness. They can only take milk ; they are not yet fit for strong men's meat (5$^{11-14}$). But he feels that not to advance is to be in danger of going back, and therefore while encouraging diligent progress he points out the dreadful condition to which apostasy reduces men (6$^{1-12}$), over against which he sets the encouragement of God's promise to Abraham, confirmed by oath (6$^{13-20}$). This brings us back to Melchizedek, who is now more minutely studied as he appears in the Genesis narrative. In his high titles and his uniqueness of kingly priesthood, independent of priestly descent as in the case of the Levitical priesthood, he is like Christ (7$^{1-3}$). He must be reckoned greater than the Levitical priests because he took tithes—the priests' privilege under the Law—from no less a personage than their ancestor Abraham. The conclusion to which all this points is that since Melchizedek is so superior to the Levitical priests, Christ, who is of the order of Melchizedek, must also be superior in His high-priesthood (7$^{4-10}$).

7^{11}–8^{13}. THE NEW COVENANT

The argument now takes a further step forward. Since God promised a new priesthood (in Ps 100), this must supersede and abolish the old priesthood, which had failed through not effecting its purpose, which was to secure perfection ; but that implies that the conditions of the old covenant, from which the Levitical priesthood derived its authority, are also annulled, and that conditions of a new covenant are introduced to take its place, with Jesus as its surety. This covenant and its priesthood will never in its turn be superseded by yet another ; because the eternity of the priest, indicated by Ps 110^4, secured the eternity of the covenant, rich privileges on which the author enthusiastically enlarges (7$^{11-28}$).

It is under the new covenant that Jesus appears as a priest, for He could claim no priesthood under the old law. This covenant is superior to and supersedes that of the Levitical system, because it concerns priesthood in the heavenly tabernacle, which was the pattern for the merely earthly tabernacle that Moses saw on the Mount (8$^{1-7}$). It is confirmed by Jeremiah's great prophecy (8$^{8-13}$).

9^1–10^{39}. THE SACRIFICE OF CHRIST

We now approach the very heart of the Epistle and its most profound teachings. Under the first covenant there was a variety of Temple furniture and an elaborate ceremonial, with a continual series of sacrifices. This reached a climax in the annual visit of the high priest to the inner chamber of the tabernacle with sacrificial blood. The very ceremony of reconciliation signified God's separation from the people. All these ceremonies were unable to make the worshipper 'perfect,' i.e. like a fully initiated person fit to participate in the mysteries (9$^{1-10}$). But now, what those mere animal sacrifices, so often repeated, could never effect, Jesus accomplished when He entered the heavenly tabernacle with His own blood, i.e. when He presented Himself in the presence of God after His crucifixion. A covenant is designated in the Bible by a Gk. word (*diathekē*) which in the classics means a 'will.' Now, a will only comes into effect through the death of the testator. Similarly, the new covenant is like Christ's will; its validity is due to His death. This death being by voluntary surrender of His life, as a free act of His spirit, is of real value in the sight of God (9$^{11-22}$). It is enough for such a sacrifice to be offered once for all (9$^{23-28}$). Thus over against the failure of the old, proved by the necessity of repetition, is the success of the new. This is illustrated by a passage from Ps 40, which shows us that the essence of sacrifice is obedience to the will of God (10$^{1-18}$). On the ground of the cleansing thus accomplished by Christ follow exhortations (10$^{19-25}$), admonitions (10$^{26-31}$), and encouragements (10$^{32-39}$).

C. 11. THE ACHIEVEMENTS OF FAITH

These are illustrated from the annals of Israel, beginning with the patriarchs and coming down to the martyrs.

The recital is introduced by a description of faith as giving assurance for hope and proving the reality of the unseen, and so accounting for the success of the ancients of Israel (vv. 1, 2). It enables us to see the divine source of creation (v. 3). Abel, Enoch, Noah, Abraham, Sara, all succeeded through faith (vv. 4–12). The reason was their pilgrim attitude in seeking for a better country (vv. 13–16). Resuming the survey we see faith in Abraham offering Isaac, in Isaac, Jacob, Moses, and the conduct of the exodus ; in the fall of Jericho, and the conduct of Rahab ; in the heroism of the judges, and the endurance of the martyrs (vv. 17–40).

12¹–end. FURTHER ENCOURAGEMENT
AND WARNINGS

The heroes of faith are witnesses of our race, the thought of whom should stimulate us, while we look to our leader, Jesus, for the beginning and ending of our faith (12¹⁻³).

Suffering should be borne patiently, since

CHAPTERS 1–4¹³

The Supremacy of Christ. The OT. itself testifies to His supremacy as God's Son over its own chief personages : (*a*) first the angels, through whom the Jews believed that creation had been effected and the Law given (1⁴–2¹⁸).

He is also superior (*b*) to Moses, the founder of the national religion, yet only a servant, whereas He is a Son (3¹⁻⁶). He is superior (*c*) to Joshua. He has rest to give, which Christians are warned not to miss by unfaithfulness, as Israel missed the rest of Canaan, which was a type of the true rest of Christ's kingdom, and which they lost by provoking God in the wilderness. For there is no escape from God's judgments (3⁷–4¹³).

CHAPTER 1

THE FINAL REVELATION IN THE SON

1-4. Introduction. God of old revealed Himself to the fathers of the race, but the revelation was not complete or final. In our own day He has given a direct revelation in the person of His own Son, the Lord and Creator of the universe, the perfect expression of the divine nature, who after His temporary humiliation upon earth, now occupies the highest place in the heavenly courts. **1. At sundry times and in divers manners]** RV ' by divers portions and in divers manners.' The first clause refers to the fragmentariness of the previous revelation at any one time ; it was given bit by bit ; the second to the various forms in which it was conveyed, such as commandment, prophecy, ceremonial, etc. **By the prophets]** RV ' in the prophets,' a general term including the whole of the OT. **2. In these last days]** RV ' At the end of these days.' The phrase that in OT. commonly indicates the Messianic age, is here varied so as to imply that the gospel times were the transition to that age. **By** *his* **son]** lit. ' in a Son ' ; i.e. in One who is by nature a Son : cp. 3⁶ 5⁸ 7²⁸. **Heir of all things]** cp. 2⁸. The lordship of Christ over the universe was determined

it is God's fatherly discipline. If we did not have it this would be a sign that we were not true sons (12⁴⁻¹³) ; care must be taken not to fall like Esau (12¹⁴⁻¹⁷) ; our greater privileges entail greater responsibilities than those of the Israelites at Sinai (12¹⁸⁻²⁸). Therefore, brotherly love and pure living should be cultivated (13¹⁻⁶) ; respect for the rulers of the Church is enjoined, and courage to break away from even the dearest ties for Christ's sake and in union with Him (13⁷⁻¹⁷). Final exhortations, benedictions, and salutations bring the Epistle—which did not open as such—to the usual conclusion of a letter.

'before all worlds,' and though it is not yet fully realised (2⁸ᶠ·), His session now at the right hand of God is the pledge of its ultimate realisation. **Made the worlds]** lit. ' the ages,' but not to be distinguished from ' all things ' : cp. Col 1¹⁶. The expression, however, implies the idea of an historical manifestation of the creative energy.

3. Brightness] RV ' effulgence.' A favourite word in the language of philosophical schools of Alexandria : cp. Wisd 7²⁵ᶠ. It contains the double notion of derivation and manifestation.

Express image of his person] RV ' very image of His substance.' The word rendered ' image ' is the Gk. word ' character,' meaning an impression such as a seal leaves on wax, an exact reproduction of the original. The word ' substance ' implies nothing material, but is nearly equivalent to ' nature ' or ' essence.' Christ is the exact reproduction of the Divine Essence. He is the counterpart or facsimile of the Father. **Being . . upholding]** Both participles seem most properly to refer to the pre-incarnate life of the Son. **On the right hand]** the place of dignity and authority : cp. 8¹ Mt 28¹⁸. The ' sitting ' indicates the completion of the earthly course of the redemptive work. The solemnity of the introductory paragraph is heightened by the use of the phrase ' the Majesty on high.' **4. Being made]** RV ' having become,' i.e. by His exaltation.

Better] a characteristic word of the whole Epistle, which is designed to show the superiority in all points of the new dispensation to the old. Cp. a ' better hope,' 7¹⁹ ; ' better covenant,' ' better ministry,' ' better promises,' 8⁶ ; ' better tabernacle,' 9¹¹ ; ' better sacrifices,' 9²³ ; ' better possession,' 10³⁴ ; ' better country,' 11¹⁶ ; ' better resurrection,' 11³⁵ ; ' better thing,' 11⁴⁰ ; ' better things,' 12²⁴.

5-14. Christ is superior to the angels. They are not addressed by God as ' sons,' but are expressly commanded to worship the Son. The angels are servants doing the will of God in the lower sphere of the material world, and ministering to those who shall inherit salvation. And their power and dignity are not, as His, changeless and eternal.

5. Unto which of the angels] Angels are sometimes in the OT. called 'sons of Elohim,' e.g. in Job 1⁶, i.e. belonging to the class 'Elohim': cp. 'sons of the prophets,' i.e. members of the prophetical class. 'Elohim,' at first a plural, meaning spiritual beings, was used as a singular to signify the one God. As used of the angels, the term does not imply sonship in the unique sense in which it is used of Christ. The first citation is from Ps 2⁷, commonly interpreted as Messianic, and accepted as such by the writer and his readers. The second is from 2 S 7¹⁴ and Ps 89²⁶. God's promise to the line of Davidic kings is here applied to Messiah, as Son of David.

6. RV 'When he again bringeth in'; or, rather, 'shall have brought in.' The position of the adverb **again** indicates that it is to be connected with the verb, and is not a rhetorical particle introducing a new quotation. The reference is to a future event, evidently the Second Advent **7.** From Ps 104⁴, according to LXX. The angels are not sons but servants, 'doing His pleasure' in the material world.

8. From Ps 45⁶, ⁷, here interpreted Messianically. The dominion of Christ, unlike that of the angels, is eternal. The Son is addressed as 'God,' but there is some difficulty in regard to the exact reading of the first clause in the original. Some propose to read, 'Thy throne is God for ever and ever.' But this is harsh, and in any case the writer means to assert the unity of the Son with God.

9. Anointed] i.e. set in royal dignity. **Thy fellows**] The angels are meant here. As 'sons of Elohim' (see on v. 5), they consort with the Son, though immeasurably inferior to Him.

10-12. From Ps 102²⁵ᶠ. The Son is the Creator of the world (cp. v. 2), and is above all change and decay. The reference to the material world here is perhaps facilitated by the close connexion of the angels with material phenomena (see v. 7), and by the statement in v. 2 that the worlds were created by the Son.

13, 14. The climax of the argument in vv. 4-12, and the scriptural corroboration of the statement in v. 3 f. that Christ is Lord of all, and shares the dignity of the throne of God.

Ministering spirits] The angels do not rule ; they only 'stand and wait.' They are the servants of God and of Christ, and that for the sake of all in OT. or NT. times who were to be heirs of salvation. The Son is the Author of the salvation to which Christians are destined ; the angels are His agents and ministers.

CHAPTER 2
JESUS EXALTED IN HUMILIATION

1-4. The former dispensation, even though mediated by comparatively inferior beings such as the angels, was yet so sacred that all neglect of it was severely punished. This being so, a far more terrible fate must now be theirs who neglect the revelation brought by the Son of God Himself, delivered to us by eye-witnesses, and authenticated by miracles and gifts of the Holy Ghost.

1. Let *them* **slip**] RV 'drift away from them,' as a ship from its moorings. This was what the readers were in danger of doing : see Intro. 'Aim and Object.' **2. Spoken by angels**] RV 'through angels.' Angels were the mediators of the Law : see Dt 33² Ac 7⁵³ Gal 3¹⁹.

Was stedfast] RV 'proved stedfast,' i.e. was authoritative while it lasted. **4. Gifts**] RM 'distributions.' The word implies variety of spiritual endowments : cp. 1 Cor 12⁴⁻¹¹ Ro 12⁶ Eph 4⁷.

5-18. It is no objection to the supremacy of Christ to say that by assuming human nature He became therefore lower than the angels. His humiliation was temporary, and undergone for purposes of redemption, His sufferings and death constituting Him an adequate High Priest through His oneness with humanity. And it is man (not angels) who is lord of the world to come. The lordship of humanity is not yet indeed realised, but the exaltation of Christ is the pledge of it.

5. RV 'not unto angels did he subject.' The position of the negative is emphatic.

The world to come, whereof we speak] i.e. the new dispensation, which is the theme of our Epistle. In the world to come the rule of the angels is ended. **6.** The quotation is from Ps 8⁴⁻⁶. **7. A little lower**] This is the meaning of the Heb., but the rendering 'for a little lower' (RM) seems to be required for the argument. Man's inferiority to the angels is only temporary. **8. He left nothing**] nothing will be left for angels to rule over.

9. Jesus .. made a little lower than the angels] The words imply the doctrine of the Incarnation of One who was essentially and previously higher than the angels. **For the suffering of death**] RV 'because of.' The clause is to be connected with what follows. The exaltation seems to be regarded here as the consequence or reward of the humiliation. Cp. Phil 2⁶⁻¹¹, and especially v. 9, 'wherefore God highly exalted him': see on 12². **Taste death**] i.e. experience its full bitterness : see on 6⁴.

10. It became him (sc. God)] i.e. it was in accordance with His gracious nature : cp. v. 9, 'by the grace of God.' **Captain of their salvation**] lit. 'leader,' i.e. not only originator, but the sharer of their lot, leading the way to glory. **Make .. perfect**] a characteristic word of the Epistle. In the new dispensation everything is perfect. The word means, to bring to its destined or appropriate consummation. Here the thought is, that by sharing the sufferings of humanity Christ was enabled to effect a perfect salvation for the sons of God, and attain that supremacy which is rightfully His: cp. 1³ 2⁹. **11. Of one**] i.e. God. Christ and Christians, the Captain and the host whom He leads to glory, are all sons of the one Father—He by nature, they by grace. Hence he calls them brethren.

14. Destroy] RV 'bring to nought,' i.e. render powerless. Death and the devil still exist, but their power is broken. **The power of death**] Death being the direct consequence of sin (Ro 5¹² 6²³), the devil may be said to have the power of death in so far as he tempts men to sin, and so keeps sharp the sting of death (1 Cor 15⁵⁶). **16.** RV 'not of angels doth he take hold.' The word does not mean (as in AV) to assume the nature of, but to put out a hand in order to support or help. 'Christ took in hand to save not angels but you, my Hebrew brethren' (Bruce). The **seed of Abraham** are the Hebrew race, the representative or priestly race, through which Jesus came to redeem mankind : cp. Ro 9⁵. The writer believes, at the same time, that Christ tasted death 'for every man' (v. 5).

17. In all things] i.e. in participation of flesh and blood and experience of death. **That he might be**] Gk. 'might become.' Christ became High Priest when He offered His sacrifice, which He did by His death on the Cross: cp. 9²⁴, ²⁵. **Merciful**] cp. 5². **Reconciliation**] RV 'propitiation': cp. 5³. To 'purge sins' and to 'make propitiation for sins' describe the same act from different points of view. In the former case what is in view is the removal of uncleanness ; in the latter, of the alienation from God caused by sin.

18. RM 'having been himself tempted in that wherein he hath suffered.' This is the simplest rendering of a difficult passage. Christ's temptations arose out of His sufferings (not conversely, as AV seems to suggest) ; hence He is able to succour the Hebrews who are tempted by their hardships : see 12³ᶠ. As High Priest Christ, therefore, not only effects reconciliation between God and man, but brings men safe through all hardships to the inheritance appointed for them. Cp. for the same combination of propitiation and succour, Ps 79⁹.

CHAPTER 3
JESUS CHRIST, LORD OF THE HOUSEHOLD OF GOD

(*b*) **Christ is superior also to Moses**; for He is Son over the house of God, whereas Moses was only a servant in it.

1. Wherefore] A new section begins here,

in which argument and exhortation are blended. The connexion with the preceding is not quite plain. It may lie in the fact that Christ has been described (2¹⁰) as a Leader of salvation, conducting God's children to glory, suggesting a similar function performed by Moses, the Leader of God's people to the rest of Canaan. Christ is the Apostle and High Priest of the new profession, as Moses was of the old. But all those who set out under the leadership of Moses did not enter into the promised rest. Hence the warning against unbelief and falling away from the living God (v. 12: cp. 2¹⁻³). **Holy brethren**] They are consecrated to God, as Israel was : cp. Ex 19⁶ ; and see on 2¹¹. **The heavenly calling**] RV 'a heavenly calling,' as distinguished from the calling of Israel to an earthly Canaan. **Apostle and High Priest**] Christ is both the messenger (cp. 1²) or representative of God to man, and the representative of man before God.

2. In all his house] i.e. God's house : see Nu 12⁷. Christ and Moses both set an example of faithfulness, which the Hebrews will do well to copy ; but Christ's sphere is higher than that of Moses, for while Moses was a servant in the house, Christ, as Son of God, made the house : cp. 1². **5. For a testimony**] i.e. to bear testimony to the revelation afterwards made in the Law : cp. 1¹. **6. If we hold fast**] Transition to the warning in v. 7–4¹³. The condition of remaining in the house of God is steadfast faith. **7. Wherefore**] In AV the long quotation from Ps 95 is treated as a parenthesis, and 'Wherefore' is connected with 'Take heed' in v. 12. This is probably correct, but owing to the length of the parenthesis, the connexion becomes broken and a new sentence begins at v. 12. **The Holy Ghost saith**] cp. 10¹⁵ Ac 1¹⁶ 2 Pet 1²¹. **8. Provocation** and **temptation** are translations of the Heb. proper names, Massah and Meribah. For the instances of unbelief and apostasy connected with these places see Ex 17¹⁻⁷ Nu 20¹¹⁻¹³ Dt 33⁸. **9. Proved me**] RV 'by proving me,' i.e. by presumptuously putting to the proof. **Saw my works**] 'my works of judgment following on their unbelief,' or, more probably, 'in spite of their experience of my works of deliverance and mercy.'

13. Deceitfulness of sin] The sin in view is unbelief culminating in apostasy, for which no doubt many specious reasons were forthcoming. **15. While it is said**] This is best taken in connexion with the preceding v. to mean 'in view of the saying,' 'seeing we have received this warning.'

16. RV rightly takes this v., like the two following, interrogatively. 'For who, when they heard, did provoke ? Nay, did not all they that came out of Egypt by Moses ? And with whom was he displeased forty years ?

Was it not with them that sinned..? And to whom sware he.. but to them that were disobedient?' Israel's apostasy was universal in spite of the fact that they had heard the words and seen the works of the Lord, and had such a leader as Moses. The inference is the same as in 2 1-3.

CHAPTER 4

JESUS CHRIST, GIVER OF THE PROMISED REST, AND HIGH PRIEST TO BRING MEN TO GOD

1-13. Israel through unbelief failed to enter into the promised rest. The rest, therefore, remains open and a promise of entrance is made to us. Let us not make the same mistake and fail to enter in because of unbelief. For by no possibility can the most secret unbelief escape the searching eye of the living God.

1. Being left] God's promise of rest cannot fail. Israel having failed to enter into it, the promise remains unfulfilled, and therefore it is open for us to enter in, if we keep the faith. **Should seem**] either a milder form of expression, or, as the words may be rendered, 'should be found to have come short,' when the time comes. The latter is the more forcible interpretation.

2. The gospel] RV 'Good tidings,' i.e. a promise of the rest of God. **Not being mixed with faith**] RV adopts AVmg. 'because they were not united by faith with them that heard.' which is the rendering of a well-attested various reading. This makes a distinction between 'those who heard' (i.e. believed and obeyed), who must be Joshua and Caleb, and those who believed not. But in 3 16 it is assumed that all believed not. The rendering of AV gives good sense. Faith is the means whereby the word that is heard is vitally appropriated and realised in action. **3.** The promise of rest applies to us who are Christians, seeing that those to whom the promise was made failed to attain to it. And their failure was not due to the fact that the rest was not prepared, because it existed since the day that God finished His work of creation. This is proved by the words 'and God rested' in one place, and the words 'my rest' in another. God's rest is therefore a fact, and it is clearly His purpose that some shall enter into it.

7. After so long a time] i.e. the time between Moses and David. In David's time the rest continued open, and therefore it is concluded that it is open still. **8. Jesus**] RV, rightly, 'Joshua.' The Gk. for both names is the same. If the entry into Canaan under Joshua had been the fulfilment of the divine promise of rest, there would have been no mention centuries later in the Psalm of a rest still

remaining ; hence, 'there remaineth a rest for the people of God.' **9. A rest**] RV 'a sabbath rest.' The rest that remaineth is also of a different character from the rest of Canaan. It is God's rest, a holy and eternal satisfaction. **10. His rest**] i.e. God's rest. **12. Quick, and powerful**] RV 'living, and active.' It does not die when uttered, but continues vital and operative, and, like a sharp sword, penetrates to the inmost recesses of the heart and life. **A discerner**] RV 'quick to discern,' lit 'critical,' i.e. able to judge.

14-16. A summary of what has been said, forming a transition to the treatment of Christ's supremacy as High Priest, which takes up the main body of the Epistle.

14. Seeing then] The connexion is with 2 17 3 1. **Into the heavens**] RV 'through the heavens.' In Jewish theology there were several heavens: cp. 2 Cor 12 2. Jesus has passed through all the outer courts into the Holy of Holies : cp. 9 24. He occupies the highest place in heaven (1 3). **15.** However highly Christ is exalted He sympathises with us, having experienced the trials and temptations of humanity. This combination in Him of suffering and sinlessness is the ground of our confidence in Him : cp. 7 26. *Yet* **without sin**] i.e. His trials and temptations never resulted in sin. **16. Come boldly**] RV 'draw near.' This privilege of access is one of many points of superiority in the new dispensation as compared with the old : cp. 10 19-22 12 18-24 Eph 2 13, 18.

CHAPTER 5

HUMAN BROTHERHOOD AND DIVINE APPOINTMENT

The High Priesthood of Christ. The argument now resolves itself into a discussion of Christ's priesthood in comparison with the Levitical priesthood, which is developed as the dominant theme of the Epistle. Christ's qualifications as our High Priest are noted. First, we have His resemblance to Aaron briefly stated so as to show that He was at least as true a priest. Christ fulfilled the two requisite conditions that were seen in the case of Aaron, viz. human brotherhood, essential to the representative character of priesthood (vv. 1-3), and divine appointment, essential to its authority, as evidenced by Ps 110 (vv. 4-6). In His humanity, too, Jesus suffered grievously, but by teaching Him obedience that awful suffering perfected Him as a priest, so that He became the author of eternal salvation to those who obey Him (vv. 7-10).

1-3. First qualification—human brotherhood. **1. Gifts and sacrifices**] The former are the vegetable, the latter the animal, sacrifices. Together they describe all kinds of offerings. **2. Have compassion**] RV 'bear gently.' The word means to be moderate in the passions, to have well-balanced emotions. **Ignorant . . out of the way**] RV 'ignorant and erring.' For high-handed sins against the covenant no atonement was provided in the Law : see Lv 5¹⁴ᶠ. Nu 15³⁰, and see on 10²⁶. **3.** See Lv 16⁶,¹¹. In this respect Christ might not seem to resemble the Levitical priest. Yet as He took our sin upon Him, there is a sense in which He offered sacrifice for Himself with us.

4–6. The second qualification—divine appointment. **6.** This is developed in c. 7 : see notes there.

7–10. The way in which Christ was perfected as a priest, the way of suffering and obedience.

7. Days of his flesh] The expression denotes, of course, His earthly life, but with the implied suggestion of humiliation and weakness.

Prayers and supplications] The reference is clearly to the Agony in Gethsemane. **To save him from death**] lit. 'out of death.' If Jesus prayed to be saved from death, it could not be said that His petition was granted. He prayed to be saved ' out of death,' and the answer to His prayer consisted in His victory over death— His resurrection. **In that he feared**] RV 'for his godly fear,' lit. 'from His fear.' The statement that Christ ' was heard from His fear ' is taken by some as a pregnant construction equivalent to 'was heard and delivered from His fear (of death).' But this sense of the word rendered 'fear' is unusual ; it means reverence or piety ; and if the interpretation of the prayer given above is accepted, Christ showed His godly fear in His submission, expressed in the words, ' Not My will, but Thine be done.' **8. Learned he obedience**] The phrase does not imply any previous unwillingness to obey ; but His obedience grew deeper and deeper, till it reached perfection on the Cross : cp. Lk 2⁴⁰ Phil 2⁸. **9. Being made perfect**] see on 2¹⁰. **Eternal salvation**] as distinguished from the temporary deliverance from the results of sin effected by the Levitical Law : cp. 9¹².

11–14. The author recognises the difficulty of his subject, and breaks off to deplore the inattention and childish ignorance of his readers. But he feels that not to advance is to be in danger of going back, and therefore, while encouraging diligent progress, he points out the dreadful condition to which apostasy reduces men (6¹⁻¹²), and sets before them God's promise to Abraham, confirmed by oath, to persuade them to constancy (6¹³⁻²⁰).

12. For the time] i.e. considering the length of time they had been Christians : cp. 10³².

Oracles of God] not, as commonly, the revelation contained in the OT., but the doctrines of the Christian faith. The ' first principles ' are probably those enumerated in 6¹,².

Strong meat] RV 'solid food': cp. 1 Cor

3¹,². **13. Unskilful in**] RV 'without experience of.' It is uncertain what precisely is meant by the **word of righteousness.** It may mean correct or rational discourse in general, or Christian truth in particular, or, since the same Gk. word means 'word' and ' reason,' something like ' the reason of the hope that is in' Christians may be implied.

CHAPTER 6
WARNING AND ENCOURAGEMENT

1. Leaving . . let us go on] RV 'let us cease to speak of . . and press on.' The words are either an exhortation to the readers to advance beyond the elementary stage of Christian doctrine, or a resolution on the part of the writer to omit the discussion of rudimentary truths and to proceed to more advanced subjects. The latter is probably correct, in which case the ' us ' is that of authorship. But though he determines to omit the treatment of elementary doctrines, he mentions what they are under six headings arranged in three pairs. The first are ' repentance from dead works and faith toward God,' the first steps to be taken in the Christian life : cp. Mk 1¹⁵ Ac 20²¹ 17³⁰ ; see on 9¹⁴. **Dead works**] i.e. sinful works, the wages of which is death (Ro 6²³). **2.** The second pair comprises the ' teaching of baptisms and of laying on of hands,' which constitute the next step in the Christian life. Baptism is for the remission of sins, and laying on of hands for the reception of the Holy Ghost : see Ac 2³⁸ 8¹⁶,¹⁷. The plural ('baptisms') is employed probably because instruction with regard to Christian baptism would necessitate a comparison with Jewish baptism and other ceremonial washings. The third pair is 'resurrection and eternal judgment,' also fundamental doctrines of the Christian faith, and dealt with in apostolic preaching : see Ac 4²,³³ 10⁴² 17³¹ 24²⁵.

4–8. Any attempt to lay the foundations of Christian doctrine afresh for those who, after accepting them, have rejected them and are in a hopeless condition, is (to the author and his readers at any rate) in vain : see on 12¹⁷.

4. Tasted] i.e. had full experience of : cp. 2⁹. The **heavenly gift,** if it is not a general expression denoting the whole contents of the grace of God, will mean either the forgiveness of sin or the gift of the Holy Ghost. Of these two the former is the most probable, seeing the latter is expressly mentioned in the next clause. **5. Powers of the age to come**] so RV. Either the miraculous gifts referred to in 2⁴, or more probably the fortifying influences of God's sure promises concerning the future.

6. Crucify . . afresh] They take the part of those unbelieving Jews who rejected Christ and openly reviled Him : cp. 10 29. **7. The earth**] rather, 'the land' or 'the field' that makes a good use of God's gift of rain is blessed by Him ; but 'the field' that responds to His goodness with a crop of thorns and thistles is destroyed. The parable is a warning against the wilful misuse of those gifts of God referred to in vv. 4, 5 : cp. Ro 2 4-9.

9. Beloved] only used here in this Epistle. The word expresses the writer's solicitude for his readers in view of even the remote possibility in their case of such an awful fate as has been described. **Accompany salvation**] are intimately connected with it, leading to it.

11. The same diligence] i.e. be as zealous in maintaining the fulness of their own hope as they have been in ministering to their brethren. **12. Inherit**] i.e. enter into possession of what is promised. The verb is in the participial mood, and refers equally to the past and present. The writer is thinking of the class of persons who may be described as 'inheritors of the promises.' **Patience**] means patient waiting.

13–20. The example of Abraham is an encouragement in this respect. God's promise to him was confirmed by an oath, and the Christian hope is no less sure, because not only has God given promise of the heavenly inheritance, but Christ has entered within the veil as High Priest and Forerunner.

13. See Gn 22 16, 17. **15. He obtained the promise**] i.e had the promise made to him : cp. Gn 22 16 f. What Abraham actually saw in his lifetime was only the beginning of the fulfilment : cp. 11 39, 40. **16.** RV 'and in every dispute of theirs the oath is final for confirmation.' **17. Wherein**] i.e. this being the case among men. **Confirmed** *it* **by an oath**] RV 'interposed' (RM 'mediated') 'with an oath.' The idea is that as there was no greater who could be called in as a third party or surety for the fulfilment of the promise, God made Himself the surety by means of the oath by Himself. **18. Two immutable things**] viz. the promise. which, because it was God's promise, was immutable, and the oath, which, though not necessary in this case, was added for confirmation of men's faith. **Consolation**] RV 'encouragement.'

19. Sure and stedfast, and which entereth] RV inserts 'a hope' before these adjectival terms, thus confining the metaphor of the **anchor** to the one clause, 'as an anchor of the soul,' and taking the three expressions as descriptive not of the anchor, but of the hope. This simplifies matters in so far as it gets rid of the somewhat incongruous idea of an anchor entering within the veil. There may be, however, a mingling of fact and figure. The first two epithets are certainly suggested by the anchor, if they do not directly apply to it. The general

idea is sufficiently clear. The Christian hope is infallible, because it is fixed on Christ, who, as High Priest and Forerunner, is now within the veil. **The veil**] The entry of the High Priest through the veil into the Holy of Holies was the climax of his ministry on the Day of Atonement : see Lv 16 2, 12 f.

20. The discussion is brought round to the point where it was interrupted (5 10) by the warning against the danger of spiritual dulness and apostasy.

CHAPTER 7
PRIESTHOOD AFTER THE ORDER OF AARON AND OF MELCHIZEDEK

The theme of Christ's superiority to the Levitical priesthood is here resumed. In 5 1-10 it has been shown that Christ possesses all the characteristics of a true High Priest, and moreover that He is called of God 'an High Priest for ever after the order of Melchisedec.' Now the priesthood of Melchizedek was perpetual, and in this respect he is a type of Christ. His greatness is shown by the fact that he received tithes from Abraham, and as Levi was descended from Abraham, it follows by implication that the Melchizedek priesthood is superior to the Levitical (7 1-10).

1–3. Melchisedec] a type of Christ in his high titles, independence of priestly descent, and especially in respect that his priesthood is eternal.

1. The main statement is, 'This Melchisedec .. abideth a priest continually.' Every feature in his history as recorded in Gn 14 is turned to account in the comparison instituted here between him and Christ. He is King of Salem, i.e. Jerusalem. But Salem means 'peace,' and Christ is Prince of Peace (Isa 9 6). His name Melchizedek means 'King of Righteousness,' and righteousness is a characteristic of Christ's kingdom (Ps 62 12 Isa 9 7 32 1 : see on 1 8, 9). Unlike the Levitical priest who must be able to trace his descent from Levi, Melchizedek is without genealogy, connected with no priestly family, and he has no successor. He is 'a priest for ever.'

3. Without father, without mother, without descent (RV 'genealogy')] The writer bases his argument on the silence of Scripture with regard to Melchizedek's origin. He appears suddenly in the narrative of Gn 14, and disappears in a similarly mysterious way. In respect that his priesthood does not rest on his pedigree, he stands in emphatic contrast with the Levitical priests. He is 'made like unto the Son of God,' i.e. is described in the narrative in such terms that they suggest the eternal Son who exists from eternity and lives for ever (1 2, 10-12).

4. Melchizedek was superior to Abraham, because he took tithes from Abraham (Gn 14 20), and he also gave him his priestly benediction (Gn 14 19, 20).

5–7. He is much more superior to the Levitical priests who take tithes from their Israelite brethren, but who, in Abraham their progenitor, paid tithes to Melchizedek (vv. 9,10).

8. He is superior to them, further, in respect that the Levitical priests are men who die. What Scripture witnesses to concerning Melchizedek is just his life. Its silence as to his family and death points to the endless life of the divine inheritor of his priesthood.

11–28. The argument now takes a further step forward. Since God promised a new priesthood (in Ps 110), this must supersede and abolish the old. But this substitution would not have been made were it not that the old priesthood had failed to accomplish its purpose, viz. to reconcile man to God. A new covenant is therefore introduced, with Jesus as the surety for its fulfilment. It is eternal because He is eternal ; and it secures salvation to the uttermost, because the Priest is One who ever liveth to intercede for those who draw near to God through Him.

11–19. The introduction of a new priesthood, and consequently of a new law, implies the imperfection of the old. **11. If therefore]** RV 'Now if': the beginning of a new argument. The priesthood is designed to reconcile men to God by removing the barrier between them, viz. sin. **Not . . after the order of Aaron]** but after the order of Melchizedek, who was independent of Levitical descent, being anterior to it. **13.** He of whom these things (i.e. Ps 110⁴) are spoken is Jesus, who belonged to the tribe of Judah, in which the old Law recognises no priests. **15.** RV 'And what we say is yet more abundantly evident,' viz. the statement that a change of law is involved in a change of priesthood. **16.** Under the old Law priesthood was a matter of physical descent—it was **the law of a carnal commandment ;** but the priesthood of Jesus rests on the **power of an indissoluble life** (so RV). What constitutes Him priest is not an external commandment, but a power inherent in Him as the eternal Son, who, though as incarnate He died, nevertheless rose from the dead and liveth for ever (vv. 24, 25). His qualifications were personal, not official.

18, 19. Read, 'For there is a disannulling of a preliminary [or, provisional] commandment [viz. that constituting the Levitical priesthood] on account of its weakness and unprofitableness [i.e. its inability to effect atonement for men's sins] (for the law made nothing perfect), and there is the subsequent introduction of a better hope through which we draw near to God.' The words 'for the law made nothing perfect' are a parenthesis. The particular commandment in question was of a piece with the whole Law, which made nothing perfect, i.e. failed in every respect to attain its object, viz. to bring men near to God in reconciliation.

20. The fact that Jesus was made priest with an oath guarantees that the covenant He mediates is better than the former (in which there was no such oath) and also that it is eternal : cp. 6¹⁶⁻¹⁸. **22. Surety]** The word is not found elsewhere in the Greek canonical Scriptures. It means one who gives security for the fulfilment of an agreement between two other parties, a guarantor or sponsor. The word usually employed is that rendered 'mediator' in 8⁶.

23. The Levitical priesthood was a succession of different priests, because those filling the office were mortal men. Christ's priesthood does not pass to any other ; it is continuous and unchangeable ; hence 'He is able to save to the uttermost.' **Were not suffered]** RV 'are hindered.' **24. Unchangeable]** lit. 'that does not pass by succession from one to another.'

25. To the uttermost] Either of time, 'from one generation to another' ; or, more probably, of extent, 'perfectly.' **Come unto God]** RV 'draw near unto God through Him,' i.e. avail themselves of His mediating agency as High Priest. The object of all priesthood is to bring men to God in spiritual communion. What the Levitical priesthood was unable to effect (v. 18), Christ, the Melchizedek-High-Priest, has completely secured. **Make intercession]** not offering, which has been made once for all, but a continual representation on the ground of the completed offering.

26–28. A summary of the characteristics of Christ as High Priest, which make Him such an adequate High Priest as we need.

26. Became us] i.e. suited our condition.

Holy] denotes His relation to God, consecrated. **Harmless]** denotes His personal character ; the word usually means 'without guile.' **Undefiled]** denotes His official qualification, having no ceremonial flaw or impediment : cp. Lv 21²¹. **Separate]** RV 'separated,' not by sinlessness (as AV seems to suggest), but by being withdrawn from men and exalted to the right hand of the Majesty on high. The clause is to be taken along with the following : cp. 4¹⁴. **27. First for his own sins]** see Lv 16 5, 6, 11, 15, and see on 5³. **Once]** i.e. once for all. **He offered up himself]** see on 9¹¹⁻¹⁴, 25-28 10¹¹⁻¹⁴. **28. Since the law]** RV 'after the law,' and disannulling it : cp. vv. 18, 19. **The Son]** rather, 'a Son,' i.e. one who is a Son, perfected for evermore : see 2¹⁰ 5⁸, ⁹.

CHAPTER 8

THE HIGH PRIEST OF THE HEAVENLY SANCTUARY AND THE FULFILMENT OF JEREMIAH'S PROPHECY

Christ, as Melchizedek-High-Priest, has a

higher ministry than the Levitical priesthood, because He ministers in the true Tabernacle in heaven which indeed was the pattern for the earthly tabernacle (vv. 1–5). Besides He is superior in proportion as the new covenant is better than the first (vv. 6–13).

1. The sum] RV 'the chief point.'

2. A minister] i.e. an officiating high priest. **The sanctuary**] corresponds to the innermost chamber of the tabernacle, which is a general name for the whole place of ministry. It is called the 'true' tabernacle, i.e. authentic or primary, that on earth being secondary, a copy of the heavenly (v. 5). **3. Gifts and sacrifices**] see on 5 1. A high priest implies an offering, and this Christ has : see on 7 27 and references there.

4. The connexion is with v. 2. Christ's ministry must be in the heavenly tabernacle, for there is already a priesthood on earth ; the office on earth is preoccupied. 'He would not be a priest at all' (so RV), much less a high priest. It has been inferred from this v. that the Epistle was written while the Levitical priesthood was still in existence, i.e. before the destruction of Jerusalem : see Intro. § 3, 'Recipients and Probable Date.' Otherwise it must be supposed that the writer is speaking generally from the view-point of the OT.

5. Example] RV 'copy,' implying that there is an original in heaven. Observe that the heavenly is the real ; the earthly is the copy and shadow. The reference is to Ex 25 40 : cp. Ac 7 44. **6. Now**] is logical, not temporal, and means, 'this being so.' **Better promises**] see vv. 10–12.

8–12. The promise is taken from Jer 31 31-34.

9. Regarded them not] i.e. rejected them after they had broken the covenant ; or, let them alone : cp. Mt 23 38 RM.

10–12. The second covenant is better than the first, because, (1) it is an internal principle instead of an external code ; (2) it is universally realised; every member of the covenant is in direct and personal communion with God ; (3) it secures real righteousness. This is the ground of the two preceding promises.

13. Even in the time of Jeremiah mention was made of a new covenant, showing that the first was destined to be superseded. Since then it has actually vanished away.

CHAPTER 9
THE NEW COVENANT AND THE SACRIFICE OF CHRIST

9 1–10 39. The writer now proceeds to elaborate in greater detail the contrast between the old covenant and the new. The old covenant had its tabernacle with furniture and elaborate ceremonial and continual series of sacrifices, culminating in the annual visit of the high priest to the inner chamber of the tabernacle with sacrificial blood. But these very ceremonies implied the impossibility of communion with God, and were unable to make the worshipper 'perfect,' i.e. fit to participate in the mysteries (9 1-10). But now, what these mere animal sacrifices, the ineffectiveness of which was signified by the necessity of their repetition, failed to do, Jesus accomplished when He entered the heavenly tabernacle with His own blood, i.e. when He presented Himself in the presence of God after His crucifixion, having obtained eternal redemption. As Mediator of a new covenant He does this by His death. For a covenant, or will, only comes into effect through the death of the testator. Similarly, the new covenant becomes valid through the death of Christ, which, being a voluntary surrender of His life, as a free act of His Spirit, is of real value in the sight of God (9 11-22). It is enough for such a sacrifice to be offered once for all (9 23-28). Thus over against the failure of the old, proved by the necessity of repetition, is the success of the new. This is illustrated by a passage from Ps 40, which shows that the essence of sacrifice is obedience to the will of God (10 1-18). On the ground of the cleansing thus accomplished by Christ follow exhortations (10 19-25), admonitions (10 26-31), and encouragements (10 32-39).

1–10. The Tabernacle Ministry.

1. A worldly sanctuary] RV 'its sanctuary, a sanctuary of this world,' and therefore inferior to the 'true' tabernacle in the heavens (8 2), of which it was but a copy. **2. A tabernacle**] This term is applied to each of the two chambers into which the whole tent was divided ; the outer chamber being the Holy Place, the inner being the Holy of Holies : see Ex 26. **Candlestick**] or lampstand : see Ex 25 31-40. **The table**] see Ex 25 23-30. **The shewbread**] see Ex 25 30 Lv 24 5-9. **3. The second veil**] so called because a veil hung also before the Holy Place. Elsewhere the second veil is called simply 'the veil' : see 10 20, and cp. Ex 26 31-33. **Holiest of all**] i.e. according to a Hebrew idiom, the Most Holy Place.

4. Censer] The word may mean 'altar of incense' (Ex 30 1-10). This, however, stood in the Holy Place, though the writer did not mention it among the furniture in v. 2. But as the Most Holy Place was never entered without incense (Lv 16 12) it might be described as 'having the altar of incense.' **Ark of the covenant**] the chest containing the tables of the Law : Ex 25 10-22. **Pot..manna**] see Ex 16 32-34. On **Aaron's rod**, see Nu 17 1-10.

5. Cherubims] RV 'cherubim,' the Heb. plural of 'cherub' : see Ex 25 17-22 37 6-9. The **mercy-seat**, or propitiatory, was the golden lid of the ark (Ex 25 17, 21) on which the blood

was sprinkled on the Day of Atonement :
Lv 16 14, 15. **Particularly**] RV ' severally.'

7, 8. The point is, that entrance into the
presence of God was restricted to the high
priest alone, and that only once a year, and
that it was altogether denied to the people
and even to the ordinary priests. The argument of this whole section is that the Levitical
system did not and could not provide real
access to God. **Holiest of all**] RV ' the holy
place,' meaning here, probably, the real presence of God, the heavenly sanctuary, as in
v. 12. **9. Which** (i.e. the Holy Place) *was* **a
figure for the time then present**] meaning that
it pointed the worshippers of that time forward
to the dawning of a better time to come.

Figure] RV ' parable.' **In which**] RV ' According to which,' sc. parable. **Him that did
the service**] RV ' the worshipper.'

11–14. The superiority of Christ's Ministry,
which does cleanse the conscience, being discharged in a heavenly tabernacle (v. 11) and
mediated through the sacrifice of Himself
(vv. 12–14).

11. Not of this building] RV ' not of this
creation,' i.e. of this material creation, but a
heavenly sanctuary. **12. Once**] i.e. once for
all, unlike the high priest in the earthly tabernacle who entered once a year (v. 7). Repetition is unnecessary, seeing the redemption he
obtained is an ' eternal redemption,' being
effectual for ever. The word **obtained** implies
the expenditure of effort.

13. Bulls and goats] refer to the sacrifices
offered on the Day of Atonement (Lv 16),
heifer to the ceremonial described in Nu 19

Purifying of the flesh] i.e. the removal of
ceremonial defilement, so as to permit the
worshipper to take part again in the services of
the tabernacle. It is admitted that a limited
efficacy is possessed by the Levitical sacrifices,
and therefore Christ's offering, being immeasurably nobler and being voluntary, has
immeasurably greater efficacy.

14. Through the eternal Spirit] So AV and
RV, suggesting that the Third Person of the
Trinity is referred to. In the original the
article is wanting, which emphasises the operation rather than the personal being of the
Spirit. The **spirit** is Christ's own spirit, or
the Holy Spirit in Christ, and the closest
parallels to the expression used here are in
7 16 and 1 Pet 4 6 (see note there). The word
' spirit ' is employed to contrast the nature and
sphere of the operation of Christ's offering
with those of the Levitical sacrifices. The
latter operate in the region of the flesh (cp.
v. 13), and are temporary in their effect (see
on v. 12) ; the former belongs to the sphere
of the spirit and will, effects an inner cleansing of th conscience, and is eternal. **Offered
himself**] 'Himself ' is emphatic, being one of

the points of contrast. What He offered was
His own body on the Cross: see on 10 10. **Dead
works**] see on 6 1. To cleanse from dead
works is to cleanse from the defilement (and
the consequences of it) caused by such works,
and so to enable the sinner to engage in the
service of God.

15. ' By offering Himself Christ has become
the Mediator of a new covenant, in order that
those who have been called may receive the
eternal inheritance that is promised, and the
necessary condition of this was the redemption
of the transgressions that were under the first
covenant by means of a death.' Christ's sacrifice is here represented as having a retrospec-
tive efficacy, operating not merely on the past
sins of the Hebrew Christians, but on the sins
of the OT. saints who lived under the first
covenant, and who could not inherit the
promises because the first covenant could not
remove their transgressions.

16. Testament] The Gk. word (*diathekē*)
means either covenant or testament (i.e. will),
and in this v. the writer passes from the former
to the latter sense. For the operation of the
terms of a testament the death of the testator
is undoubtedly necessary. Is it also necessary
in the case of a covenant ? So the writer
asserts in vv. 18–20, where he reverts to the
former sense of *diathekē* as covenant. He says
that any *diathekē* involves death, and cites the
Mosaic covenant as an instance. This must be
on the supposition that the covenanter is represented by the victim which died in the sacrifice which usually accompanied any serious
covenant. The death of the victim represented
the inability of the covenanter to retract. It
was the solemn ratification of the terms of the
covenant.

17. After men are dead] RV ' where there
hath been a death.' The Gk. is lit. ' over dead.'
18. Whereupon] RV ' wherefore.' **Neither
the first**] RV ' even the first . . not,' imperfect
and temporary though it was. **19, 20.** See Ex
24 3-8. **20. Testament**] RV ' covenant ': see
on v. 16. **21.** This is not recorded in Exodus,
but is mentioned by Josephus. It rested probably on some Jewish tradition.

23. Patterns] RV ' copies,' i.e. the earthly
things which were made according to the pattern of the heavenly : see 8 5. In the view of
the writer, the heavenly original needed purifying just as the earthly copies, only with better
sacrifices. It is not necessary to supply a different predicate in the second clause, such as
' should be dedicated.' To enable men to draw
near to God, however imperfectly, on earth, it
was necessary that both they and the tabernacle
be sprinkled with the blood of sacrifice ; and
the inference is that in order to enable men
perfectly to hold communion with God above,
both they and the heavenly places must in like

manner be sprinkled with the blood of a better sacrifice, viz. that of Christ.

24. To appear] lit. ' to be manifested before the face of God,' i.e. to show Himself to God : cp. 7 25. The earthly ' copy ' of this act is that of the high priest who once a year presented himself before God in the Holy of Holies on behalf of the people. In the OT. to ' appear before God ' means to go into the Temple to worship Him : cp. Ex 23 17 Pss 42 2 84 7.

26. End of the world] The Second Coming is regarded as imminent : cp. 10 37. **Appeared**] lit. ' been manifested,' i.e. in the flesh to men : cp. v. 24, where the verb, though different, is from the same root.

27. In the case of men, death is a single event, the definite close of a stage in their career. So Christ's death is one final achievement. And as in the former case death is followed by **judgment**, so Christ's death is followed by His reappearing for the **salvation** of His people. Moreover, as death and judgment are connected as cause and effect, so Christ's death and His people's salvation are similarly connected : cp. Ro 5 18. **28. Apart from sin**] So RV. His First Coming was in connexion with sin ; He came because of sin, and bearing sin to put it away (v. 26) ; but His Second Coming will be ' apart from sin,' since in dying He did put away sin, actually for Himself, for men by anticipation in faith.

Them that look for him] RV ' that wait for him.' The reappearing of the high priest from out the Holy of Holies on the Day of Atonement would be waited for with anxious expectancy by the people as the sign that all that was needful for their reconciliation with God had been done, and that the offering had been accepted by Him : cp. Lk 1 21, and see Ro 8 19, 23 1 Cor 1 7 1 Th 1 10 2 Tim 4 8.

CHAPTER 10
SACRIFICE COMPLETE IN THE FULFILMENT OF GOD'S WILL. THE OPEN WAY TO GOD

Recapitulation and close of the argument. The sacrifices of the Law were ineffective to cleanse the conscience, as shown by their continual repetition (vv. 1–4). In the mind of God they were temporary. But the offering of Christ is a sacrifice that accomplishes the will of God and consecrates us as the people of a new covenant (vv. 5–10). That it is efficacious and final is also proved by the session of Christ at God's right hand. Unlike the Levitical priests, who continually stand to offer sacrifices, Christ having made one perfect sacrifice is now set down, waiting the final triumph over all His foes (vv. 11–14). The finality of His sacrifice is also confirmed by the prophecy which foretells that under the new covenant God will remember the people's

sins no more, implying that sin has been dealt with finally and for ever (vv. 15–18).

1. The shadow is unsubstantial, lacking all the qualities of the original except perhaps outlined form ; the **very image** is an exact reproduction of the original. **Continually**] is perhaps best taken with the preceding verb, ' offered.' **Comers thereunto**] see on 7 25.

2. Conscience of sin] i.e. consciousness of sin, sense of guilt : cp. 9 9. **3.** The continual repetition of the sacrifices served only to remind the worshippers of the continuity of the need of cleansing.

5. The quotation is from Ps 40 6-8, according to the LXX, which reads, ' a body thou hast prepared for me,' where the Hebrew has, ' mine ears thou hast opened,' meaning that God has opened the ears of His servant to hear and obey His will. The LXX may be due to an early corruption of the text, or it may be a free reproduction of the sense. As used here the words refer to the Incarnation, and are taken to indicate the superiority of Christ's sacrifice over the animal sacrifices of the Law in respect that His offering was voluntary and moral. It was a sacrifice of obedience (v. 7), the voluntary and glad (cp. 12 2) surrender of His own life to God. **9. He taketh away**] i.e. Christ supersedes the legal and ineffectual mode of reconciliation by His own sacrifice, in accordance with God's will. **10. Sanctified**] i.e. cleansed from the defilement of sin and enabled to draw near to God.

11–14. Further proof of the finality of Christ's sacrifice : see analysis at the beginning of this chapter. The ineffectiveness of the legal ordinances is brought out forcibly by the accumulation of the words, **standeth daily . . oftentimes . . the same sacrifices.** There is no cessation, no ' sitting down,' as in the case of Christ. **13, 14.** His people are finally sanctified ; His enemies are the only class remaining to be dealt with.

15–18. See analysis above.

19–25. Practical exhortation to hold fast the superior benefits and privileges of the new covenant.

19. Boldness to enter into the holiest] a privilege denied to the worshipper under the old covenant. **20.** The way is **new,** i.e. lately opened up, and it is **living,** either because it is effective (cp. 4 12), or because Christ is living : cp. Jn 14 6, where Christ says that He is the Way, and the Truth, and the Life. **Through the veil**] During His earthly life His flesh stood between Him and the entrance into the heavenly sanctuary. By the rending of that veil, i.e. His death, He has entered in, opening the way for His people.

22. The First Exhortation. Draw near] i.e. in worship and service : see on 7 25.

Bodies washed] There may be here **a re**

ference to baptism, but the two clauses together denote the purification of the whole man, within and without : see Ex 19 10 29 4, and cp. Eph 6 5, 6. **23.** The Second Exhortation, to 'hold fast the confession of our hope ' (so RV): cp. 3 6, 14. **24.** The Third Exhortation, to ' encourage each other to love and good works.'

Provoke] The word is used in the good sense equivalent to stimulate.

25. Assembling of ourselves] i.e. the meeting of Christians which gives the opportunity to exercise the love and good works already recommended, and also to make the confession of the Christian faith and hope which is to be held fast. **The day**] is the Day of the Lord, the Day of His Second Coming : cp. on 9 26.

26-31. A warning against unbelief and apostasy, suggested by the thought that the Day of the Lord which is approaching will be a day of judgment to some, especially to those who, after having been enlightened, have **fallen away**: cp. the warning in 6 1-8. **26. Sin wilfully**] The participial form of this condition expresses not a single act, but a deliberate and persistent state. The Levitical Law made no provision for the atonement of sins done with a high hand : see on 5 2. **No more sacrifice**] Christ's sacrifice is final : see on vv. 13, 14.

28-30. For the form of the argument cp. 2 1-4. **28. Under**] RV ' at the word of ' : see Dt 17 2-7.

32-39. An exhortation to exhibit the same steadfastness under the present trials as they had shown in a previous time of affliction : cp. the similar change from a tone of warning to one of hope of better things in 6 9f.

32. Were illuminated] RV ' enlightened,' i.e. became Christians : cp. 6 4. **Fight of afflictions**] see Intro. § 3, ' Recipients and Probable Date.' **33. Companions**] i.e. voluntary partners and sympathisers with those who suffered : cp. 6 10. **34.** RV ' had compassion on them that were in bonds.' This is the better attested reading, though the other has good support. **In yourselves**] It is possible to render, ' Knowing that ye have your own selves for a better possession,' a similar thought to that in Lk 9 25 21 19 RV, and in v. 39.

35. Recompence of reward] cp. the other aspect of ' just recompence ' in 2 2.

37. A quotation from Hab 2 3, 4, with the addition of the introductory clause ' yet a little while,' reminiscent of Isa 26 20. In Habakkuk the idea is that steadfast adherence to God is needed by the righteous man in view of the perplexing anomalies visible at present in God's method of providence. Here the idea is much the same ; the Coming of the Lord being regarded as the chief ground why Christians should not draw back, and so fail to enter upon the promised inheritance. **38. The just**] RV ' my righteous one.' The Speaker

is God. **39. But we**] The writer is unwilling to believe that his readers will abandon their faith : cp. 6 9. **The saving**] lit. ' gaining,' or ' winning ': see on v. 34.

CHAPTER 11
HEROES OF FAITH

The Achievements of Faith, illustrated from the annals of Israel, beginning with the patriarchs and coming down to the martyrs. The writer has already mentioned faith as a necessary condition of a righteous life, and he now proceeds to illustrate the fact that it was by faith that the fathers of the race were able to work righteousness and to endure their trials. Their heroic example ought to encourage the Hebrews to stand fast. The primary purpose, therefore, of this long passage is a practical one. But it has also a place in the main argument of the Epistle. It has been shown that the earthly and visible things are but the types, copies, or shadows of heavenly realities : see 8 5 9 22, 23 10 1. The underlying thought of the preceding chapters is that, contrary to the ordinary way of thinking, it is the heavenly that is the real. But how are heavenly and invisible things to be realised with any assurance ? It is by the operation of faith. Faith is that by which the invisible becomes real and the future becomes present. ' Faith gives a reality to things hoped for, and puts to the test things for the present unseen.' It is no new principle in the world, because it was faith that inspired the heroism and self-sacrifice of the saints who lived under the old dispensation. We, having better promises and a better covenant than they, ought not to fall behind in the exercise of the same faith by which they lived.

1. RV renders, ' Now faith is the assurance of things hoped for, the proving of things not seen.' The word represented here by ' assurance ' is rendered 'substance ' in 1 3 RV and ' confidence ' in 3 14. What is meant is that faith is that which gives assurance or certainty of things still in the future. They exist apart from faith, but it is by faith that they are realised. ' Proving ' means testing resulting in conviction.

2. The elders] i.e. the faithful men under the old dispensation. **Obtained a good report**] RV ' had witness borne to them,' sc. by God in the Scriptures. **3.** Faith enables us to perceive the invisible cause of the phenomenal world : cp. Ro 1 20. The writer begins with Gn 1 before proceeding to give examples of the realising faith of the fathers. **4. Abel**] The writer says that the greater excellence of Abel's sacrifice was due to his faith, but in what particular the faith was manifested he does not say. It may have been a ' fuller consciousness of the claim of God to the best.'

Yet speaketh] 'Yet,' i.e. still to us. The reference is to Gn 4¹⁰, where Abel's blood is represented as crying from the ground after his death. By faith he overcame death.

5, 6. Enoch] The writer here follows the Greek Version of the OT. Enoch's faith is an inference from the statement in Genesis that he 'walked with God' (Gk. 'pleased God'), and his 'translation' was the reward of his faith. **7. Noah**] His faith rested on a direct revelation of 'things not seen as yet,' viz. the destruction of the world and the means of salvation. **Fear**] is 'godly fear,' as in 5⁷. **He condemned the world**] i.e. either because he warned the world of the impending doom (see 1 Pet 3²⁰ 2 Pet 2⁵); or because his example took away from them any ground of excuse : cp. Mt 12⁴¹. **8. Abraham**] By faith he realised the promises, and made a great surrender in obedience to God's call. He was preeminently a man of faith, the first whose faith is definitely mentioned in the OT. (Gn 15⁶) ; he is the 'father of the faithful.' All his life he 'sojourned, dwelling in tents,' i.e. not actually receiving the promises, but waiting patiently for their fulfilment, and making therefore no attempt to settle permanently in Canaan. He looked for the invisible and heavenly 'city of God,' as the fulfilment of the ideal which was to him the real. **11. Sara**] RV 'Even Sarah herself,' i.e. in spite of her earlier and natural incredulity : see Gn 18¹⁰⁻¹⁵. **12. Of one**] i.e. Abraham.

13. The promises] i.e. the fulfilment of them. **Persuaded of** *them*, **and embraced** *them*] RV 'greeted them from afar.' They looked forward by faith and saw the promises and 'saluted them,' or hailed them, from afar, and lived here as in a foreign land, conscious that their true fatherland was not here, but in heaven. And God rewarded their faith by acknowledging them as His people, and providing a 'city' for them above.

17. Abraham's faith in offering Isaac : see Gn 22. This was the supreme trial of Abraham's faith. He was not allowed to slay Isaac, but he did actually offer him, i.e. surrender him to God, although he was the 'only-begotten,' the child of promise and the only link in the chain of the promise. But faith in God's promise made him superior to all seeming impossibilities in the way of realising the promises.

20-22. Isaac, Jacob, and Joseph were all alike in the fact that on their death-beds they looked by faith beyond death, and were confident of the future. **21. Top of his staff**] The Heb. in Gn 47³¹ reads, 'the head of his bed.' The difference is due to the same consonants being read with different vowels, *mittah* being 'bed,' and *matteh* being 'staff.'

23-28. The faith of Moses and his parents. **23. Proper**] i.e. goodly or beautiful. The appearance of the child is said here to have quickened their faith in God that He had destined the child for some great purpose, and their faith was shown in their daring disregard of the king's commandment : see Ex 1¹⁶⁻²².

24. Moses' faith was shown in his renunciation of all preferments at the court of Pharaoh, and in his espousing the cause of his afflicted brethren. The **pleasures of sin** were not vicious courses in themselves, but a life of worldly success, which would have been sin for him, conscious as he was of a call to a higher and harder life of duty.

26. The reproach of Christ] cp. 13¹³ Ro 15³. The same reproach as Christ suffered in delivering His people : cp. 2¹⁰. There may, however, here be the deeper thought not merely of similarity, but of identity of suffering. Christ, who was from all eternity, may be conceived as actually the deliverer of Israel by the agency of Moses, and so as suffering Himself what Moses had to endure. **The recompence of the reward**] see on v. 1, and cp. the next v. **28.** The keeping of the Passover was an act of faith, because it was the appointed means of deliverance from death, and the performance of it implied faith in God's promise of safety.

31. Them that believed not] i.e. the people of Jericho who knew what Jehovah had done for Israel : see Josh 2⁹, ¹⁰. **33. Obtained promises**] cp. 6¹⁵. **35. Raised to life again**] RV 'by a resurrection.' This literal rendering of the original is necessary to bring out the contrast expressed in the words at the end of the v., 'a better resurrection,' i.e. one to a life which would not, as in the former case, be again interrupted by death. **39. A good report**] see on v. 2.

40. There is here the answer to an implied objection, that the faith of these suffering heroes was all in vain, seeing they did not receive the fulfilment of the promises. But, the writer says, this is a wrong inference, the truth being that God has merely deferred their reward in order that they may enter along with us of a later age upon the realisation of the promised inheritance. They are waiting for us so that the whole number of the faithful may be perfected together. Cp. the petition in the Burial Service, 'beseeching Thee . . shortly to accomplish the number of Thine elect, and to hasten Thy kingdom ; that we, with all those that are departed in the true faith of Thy holy Name, may have our perfect consummation and bliss. . .'

CHAPTER 12

The Contest. Endurance, Holiness, and Divine Communion proposed to the Sons of God

Inspired by the example of those victorious

heroes of faith who now encompass us, we ought to run our race patiently, looking to Jesus the supreme example of patient endurance (vv. 1, 2). The present sufferings are the discipline of a loving Father, and are actually evidence of our being His children. Be brave, therefore, and help others to be the same (vv. 3–13). Beware of strife and impurity, taking warning from the case of Esau, who irretrievably forfeited his blessing (vv. 14–17). Our greater privileges entail greater responsibilities and call for greater watchfulness (vv. 18–29).

1. Witnesses] The Gk. word is *martyres*. The word means primarily 'one who bears witness' to something he has seen or experienced. Here the witnesses are those who have borne testimony to the victorious power of faith. But the word passes easily over to the further sense of 'spectators,' which is also implied in this whole passage. The writer conceives these heroes as surrounding in a **cloud,** or dense mass, the arena in which the present generation of God's people are running their race. Once they were themselves runners; now they are promoted to the rank of spectators. Their presence and example ought to be a stimulus to those running now.

Every weight] mg. 'all cumbrance.' The word may refer to anything that impedes free running, such as loose garments. But it is used in a special sense to denote the superfluous flesh which an athlete seeks to get rid of by strict training : cp. 1 Cor 9 24-27.

Which doth so easily beset *us*] The meaning of this phrase, represented in the original by a single adjective, is doubtful, and the Revisers have not seen fit to change the translation in the text. But they give in the margin the two other possible renderings : (1) 'that doth closely cling to us,' i.e. like a clinging garment (cp. the common Oriental phrase, 'to gird up the loins,' i.e. to tuck the loose ends of the outer flowing robe under the girdle as a preparation for any exertion); or (2) 'that is admired of many,' lit. 'well-surrounded' by an admiring throng. The former, which is virtually identical with the accepted rendering of AV, is the easier, and is appropriate to the idea of a runner divesting himself of all *impedimenta*. It is to be observed that 'the sin' spoken of is not a particular sin (as the common use of the phrase 'besetting sin' suggests), but sin in general, all sin, the definite article being the 'generic' article.

2. Looking unto] The Gk. word is used of an artist who looks at his model. Jesus is the Great Exemplar, on whom, rather than on the cloud of witnesses, the runners are to fix their eyes. **Author and perfecter**] so RV : cp. 2 10, where the word 'author' is rendered 'captain' in AV. *Our* **faith** suggests a system of Christian

doctrine. But there is no word representing 'our' in the original. Jesus is leader in the way of faith, and He leads to the very end, exhibiting the perfection and triumph of faith.

For the joy] may mean 'instead of the joy,' i.e. renouncing it; but more likely 'in view of the joy,' i.e. the recompence of reward, as in 11 26 : cp. 11 1.

3. Against himself] RV 'against themselves.' A more difficult, but well-attested reading. If correct, it will mean that sinners sin against themselves, either by wronging their own souls (see Prov 8 36) or by contradicting their better selves. **4. The struggle** has not yet been severe. A mild reproach of faint-heartedness is implied : cp. Prov 24 10 Jer 12 5. **5.** The quotation is from Prov 3 11, 12. **7.** RV 'It is for chastening ye endure,' i.e. your sufferings are designed as a discipline or means of education. God dealeth with you as with sons. **8. All are partakers**] The clause refers to v. 6.

11. Peaceable fruit of righteousness] i.e. the fruit which is righteousness. The result of discipline is called 'peaceable,' or 'peaceful,' in contrast to the 'painfulness' of the process spoken of in the previous part of the v.

13. Straight paths] better, 'even' or 'smooth paths,' containing no stumbling-blocks that may injure the lame. The strong are to encourage the weak. **Turned out of the way**] RM 'put out of joint.' The reference to lameness and healing suggests that this is the right rendering. If they do not remove the stumbling-blocks from the paths, lameness may become dislocation. But by making the paths 'even,' the lameness may be healed.

15. Fail of] RV 'fall short of.' **Root of bitterness**] cp. Dt 29 18. **16. Any fornicator**] In the OT. apostasy from Jehovah is frequently described as adultery or fornication, being a breach of covenant ; but here the word should perhaps be understood in the literal sense : cp. 13 4. **Profane**] The word is the antithesis of 'hallowed' or 'consecrated,' and means 'common,' 'unspiritual,' 'secular.' Esau's defect was a want of appreciation of spiritual blessings. He 'despised his birthright' (see Gn 25 34), which implied not merely material advantage, but the spiritual heritage of the covenant promises. **17. Would have inherited**] The RV removes the ambiguity of these words by rendering 'when he afterward desired to inherit.' **He sought it**] i.e. the blessing, not the repentance. When Esau is said to have 'found no place of repentance,' this does not mean that he found it impossible to repent—a thing contrary to all the doctrine of Scripture. In 6 4-6 the author does not say 'they cannot repent,' but 'we cannot make them repent.' What is meant is that when he afterward wished to inherit the blessing he found it irretrievably beyond his reach. He found no way of undoing the consequence of his own act : see Gn 27 34-36.

18-24. Appeal for greater watchfulness based on a contrast between the new covenant and the old : cp. 2 1-4 10 28-31.

18. Unto the mount] This balances the words 'unto mount Zion' in v. 22. But the best MSS omit the word 'mount' here, and read 'unto a palpable (i.e. material) and kindled fire.' For the whole description of the former manifestation see Ex 19 12,13,18,19 20 18 Dt 4 11. The old revelation was given with material and terrifying accompaniments ; the new is a revelation of grace and peace, introducing its recipients to a spiritual society with spiritual privileges. But so much the more does it call for obedience (v. 25) and consecration (v. 28). **Ye are not come**] Even here and now they are members of this heavenly community and enjoy these spiritual privileges, although the fulness of the inheritance is reserved for the future.

22. Mount Sion] the heavenly city, the New Jerusalem, the eternal and ideal sphere, the abode of God and the angels and the spirits of the OT. saints. **23. General assembly**] a word commonly applied to the Greek festal assemblies, such as at the Olympian Games. **Church of the firstborn, who are enrolled in heaven**] so RV. Seeing that human beings are mentioned at the close of the v., these words are best taken as referring to the angels, who were created before man and may be appropriately described as 'first-born': cp. Job 38 7. In this case the word 'church' is used in its original sense of 'convocation,' or 'congregation.'

And to God] whose manifestation is direct and immediate. There is a suggestion of warning in the epithet **Judge of all. Just men**] i.e. the saints of the OT. dispensation, who are in one sense 'perfected,' though in another they still wait their final consummation of bliss: see 11 40. **24. To Jesus**] whose mediating has assured all these privileges. **Speaketh better things**] Abel's blood cried for vengeance (see on 11 4); that of Jesus appeals to God for pardon and reconciliation. **25. Him that speaketh**] i.e. God, who spoke both at Sinai and now from heaven in the new manifestation. **26. Then**] i.e. at the giving of the Law: see Ex 19 18. The quotation is from Hag 2 6,21, which is here applied as a prediction of the Second Coming, regarded as imminent. **27. Yet once more**] i.e. once for all, finally. What follows the shaking and removal of the created and sensible world will be stable and imperishable. **28. Let us have grace**] RM 'thankfulness'; but cp. v. 15. **29. A consuming fire**] cp. Dt 4 24. A solemn warning against presumption.

CHAPTER 13

ADVICE, MEMORIES, PRAYERS, GREETINGS

The Epistle concludes with various exhortations in regard to the social life (vv. 1-3), private life (vv. 4-6), the religious life (vv. 7-17), in which connexion the readers are exhorted to follow steadfastly the example and doctrine of their former teachers (vv. 7-16), and to respect the authority of their present rulers (v. 17). The writer requests their prayers (vv. 18, 19); he prays himself on their behalf (vv. 20, 21); he sends greetings, and utters his benediction (vv. 22-25).

1-3. Duties of social life, viz. brotherly love, hospitality, and sympathy with those who suffer for Christ's sake.

2. Strangers] Christian brethren from other places are meant: cp. 6 10. **Angels unawares**] cp. Gn 18, 19 Jg 6 11-24 13 2-23.

3. Yourselves also in the body] and liable therefore to the same sufferings : cp. 10 32-34.

4-6. Duties of the private life, viz. chastity and contentment.

4. Marriage is] RV 'Let marriage,' etc.: the words are an exhortation. **5. Conversation**] i.e. manner of life. RV simply, 'be ye free from the love of money.'

7-16. Duty of steadfastly adhering to the doctrine of their departed teachers.

7. Which have the rule] RV 'that had the rule .. which spake.' The words **end of their conversation** (see v. 8) indicate that they were no longer living. RV renders, 'issue of their life.' **8.** AV suggests that the 'end of their conversation' was Jesus Christ, but He can hardly be called the 'issue of their life.' This v. is a distinct sentence, and is introduced as an argument for steadfast adherence to the faith of the former teachers. Christ is the same now as when their teachers first taught them, so that they have no reason to go after divers and strange teachings (v. 9).

9. Carried about] RV 'carried away.' The **strange doctrines** seem to have been connected with the ritual of 'meats,' or sacrificial meals (v. 10).

10-14. We Christians **have** certainly **an altar**, the Cross of Christ, but as on the Day of Atonement the blood of the sacrifice was carried into the Most Holy Place, while the flesh of the victim was not eaten but burned outside the camp, so those who wish to participate in the benefits of the Christian sacrifice must not remain within the camp of Judaism, but utterly renounce all its 'carnal ordinances,' even though that entail bearing reproach for Christ's sake. We may be rendered homeless here below, but we have an abiding city above (11 10 12 22).

15, 16. Christ having offered Himself once for all as the great sacrifice of atonement, the only sacrifice Christians can now offer is that of thanksgiving (cp. Ps 116[17] 1 Pet 2[5, 11]), **the fruit of lips** (cp. Hos 14[2]) **which make confession of his name,** and also that of **mercy** with which God is well pleased (Hos 6[6]).

The sacrifice of praise or thanksgiving had been the highest form of peace-offering under the Levitical Law (Lv 7[12] 22[29]; the words in the LXX which our author used are exactly quoted by him here), and the Psalmists had adopted the term to describe that truly spiritual worship which the atoning sacrifice of Christ does not supersede, but deepens and assures (Pss 107[22] 116[17]). His sacrifice of atonement shall never be repeated; but an offering to God is, in its highest form, sacrifice or sacred service, whether it be of words or charity (cp. Hos 14[2] 6[6]), or of the duties of ordinary life (Ro 12[1]: cp. 1 Pet 2[5, 11]). Such sacrifice of thanksgiving is now to be offered continually, not as of old at merely ceremonial times or after separate acts of imperfect atonement; and through the one true High Priest, who has really opened the way for such worship to be brought to God, by the one real sacrifice of atonement which is effectual for ever.

17. Duty of obedience to present rulers.

Watch for (i.e. in behalf of) **your souls**] like sleepless shepherds who feel their responsibility to God for the flock. **Do it with joy**] i.e. watch with joy, feeling their duty to be a delight not a burden, for in the latter case the flock would suffer. **18. Pray for us**] The plural denotes that the writer identifies himself with the rulers of the Church, on whom some suspicion has fallen, and he therefore in their name protests their integrity. **19.** The singular number indicates that the writer stood in some special relationship to his readers from whom he is for the present separated for some reason not given. It seems not to have been imprisonment (see v. 23), and the separation is regarded as only temporary.

20, 21. Prayer for the readers.

20. God of peace] i.e. the God who makes peace: cp. Ro 15[33] 16[20] 2 Cor 13[11] Phil 4[9], and see on v. 14. **Brought . . from the dead**] The words refer not so much to the Resurrection of Christ as to His entrance into the heavenly sanctuary 'with the blood of the everlasting covenant,' and His exaltation as Head over the household of God (3[1-6]): cp. Isa 63[11]. **21.** Cp. Phil 2[12, 13].

22. Word of exhortation] the whole Epistle. The apologetic tone indicates some doubt as to the manner of its reception (cp. v. 18), and also a consciousness that the subject has been treated more briefly than it deserves ('in few words').

23. *Our* **brother Timothy**] The reference does not point conclusively to St. Paul as the writer, but indicates that he was intimately connected with the Pauline circle. We have no other knowledge of Timothy's imprisonment. **If he come**] Timothy is elsewhere at present.

24. The salutation shows that the Epistle was not addressed to the rulers, but primarily to the whole community. **They of Italy**] i.e. those from Italy, those belonging to Italy. The phrase is most naturally taken to indicate that the Epistle was written outside Italy at some place where Italian Christians had settled. If the Epistle was sent to Rome, these Italian Christians would naturally wish to join in the salutation. See Intro. § 3, 'Recipients and Probable Date.'

25. Cp. Col 4[18] 1 Tim 6[21] 2 Tim 4[22] Tit 3[15].

JAMES

INTRODUCTION

1. The Author. In the New Testament we meet with four persons named James (Jacob): (1) the father, or, possibly, brother of Jude; (2) the son of Alphæus; (3) the brother of John; (4) the brother of the Lord and head of the Church at Jerusalem (Ac 1 14 12 2-17 15 13-21 21 18-25 Gal 1 19 2 12). Of these four, we know nothing but the names about (1) and (2); (3) was put to death by Herod Agrippa I in 44 A.D., some time before the earliest date usually assigned to our Epistle. We are, therefore, almost driven to the conclusion that the author is (4), James the Lord's brother, whom we meet in the Acts as head of the Church at Jerusalem. And this conclusion, reasonable in itself, is confirmed by all the evidence at our disposal. Besides the positive statement of St. Jerome ('Vir. Ill.' 2) that 'James called the brother of the Lord' wrote it, we have the striking correspondence in the thoughts and language of the Epistle to what we know of the character of the head of the Jerusalem Church. In the first place, there is the tone of authority which we find in the Epistle, natural to one in the position of St. James. Then there are the frequent references to the Old Testament, and to books like the Wisdom of Solomon and the Wisdom of Jesus son of Sirach (called in our version 'Ecclesiasticus'), which to a devout Jew like St. James would be very familiar. [Observe the allusions to Genesis 1 (1 18), Abraham (2 21), Rahab (2 25), Deuteronomy 6 4 (cp. Jas 2 19), Job (5 11), Elijah (5 17), and compare Jas 1 2-4, 5-8, 12-17, 23-25 with Ecclus 1 26 2 1-15 7 10 12 11 14 23 15 11 Wisd 7 18, etc. See also Job 28 12 (Jas 3 13), Prov 3 34 (Jas 4 7-11), Prov 10 12 (Jas 5 20), Isa 40 7 (Jas 1 11).] Then, again, the language of the Epistle is similar to that found in the speech of St. James, and in his circular letter (Ac 15). We conclude, therefore, that the well-nigh unanimous opinion, which assigns the Epistle to the brother of the Lord, is the only reasonable one. For the relationship implied by 'brother' see on Mt 12 46.

Of the personality of this great man we can form a tolerably clear idea from the New Testament and early Church tradition. Refusing to accept Christ as Messiah during His earthly life, he was converted by a special appearance to him of the Risen Lord (1 Cor 15 7). We can well believe that in the Nazareth home he was carefully trained in all the precepts and practices of the Jewish faith, and to that faith he clung with deep devotion all through his life. We must picture him to ourselves, not as one of those false Jews whose observances were merely formal and external, but as one of those true and earnest Jews whose obedience to the Law was a joy and an inspiration—whose life was lived in the spirit of Ps 119. His sincere and spiritual Judaism would be a guide to lead him to Christ, the 'fulfiller' of the Law (Mt 5 17). The good Jew would make a good Christian. And in those early days it was possible to combine observance of the Law with obedience to the 'Royal Law' of Christ. To St. James Christianity presents itself primarily as a Law (1 25 2 12 4 11, 12). This idea is found elsewhere in the New Testament (Ro 8 2 Heb 8 7-13). The time had not yet come when (as in the crisis which called forth the Epistle to the Hebrews) it was necessary to choose between Judaism and Christianity. And so, even as 'bishop' of Jerusalem, St. James went on keeping the whole Law, although he was ready to grant the fullest liberty to those Gentile converts who had never been Jews by religion (Ac 15). He combined strong personal convictions with the widest sympathy with the views of others. Hence, although himself a strict Jew, he could act cordially with St. Paul, the champion of Gentile liberty. At the end of each of his three missionary journeys the Apostle of the Gentiles went up to Jerusalem to report progress to St. James (Ac 15, 18 22 21 18), and it was at his suggestion that St. Paul undertook the Nazirite vow in the Temple which led to the attack on him of the unbelieving Jews. At this point the narrative of the Acts leaves St. James; but from the Jewish historian Josephus, and the converted Jew Hegesippus, we get accounts of his death which, though they differ in details, agree in their main facts. From these we learn that he was held in great esteem by his fellow-countrymen, and even permitted to enter the Temple. A Sadducean high priest, Ananus, brought him before the Sanhedrin, and caused him to be put to death by stoning, spite of the remonstrances of all the better sort of Jews. James 'the Just' (as he was called by his fellow-countrymen) died praying, like St. Stephen, for his murderers, a few years before the final overthrow of Judaism by the Romans. In very truth he was taken away from the evil to come. Some have seen in St. James the Restrainer of 2 Th 2 7, after whose removal the Jewish apostasy would stand revealed, and receive its due reward in the overthrow of the nation and the religion of the Jews.

2. The Readers. The Epistle is addressed

'to the twelve tribes which are scattered abroad,' not exclusively to Christian Jews, nor even to the Jews of Jerusalem or Palestine only, but to all Jews scattered throughout the world. It is important to realise this at the outset, since it will help to explain what might otherwise be a difficulty—the absence from the Epistle of any distinctively Christian doctrine. Christianity is there indeed. St. James is 'the servant of the Lord Jesus Christ.' His faith is 'the faith of our Lord Jesus Christ.' But all through the Epistle his appeal is chiefly to that which was common to unconverted Jews and Christian Jews alike —the belief in one God, and reverence for the Old Testament Scriptures. No doubt there are special messages of consolation and encouragement to the devout remnant who had accepted Christ as their Saviour and Messiah; but he evidently hoped that his letter would be read by a wider circle, and that it would appeal to all earnest souls among his fellow-countrymen. The sins he denounces are those to which Jews were specially tempted—love of money, oppression of the poor, profession without practice, and the like. The tone and atmosphere of the Epistle are Jewish. Even the allusions to natural phenomena are drawn from those of Palestine.

3. Date. This Jewish tone, and the absence of any allusion to the controversies which afterwards distracted the Church, combined with the simplicity of thought and the absence of any discussion of exclusively Christian topics, points to an early date, somewhere between 45 A.D. and 49 A.D. If that conclusion be correct we shall see in the Epistle a 'golden bridge connecting the Old and New Testaments.' Some scholars, however, have assigned it to a later date in the life of St. James, i.e. about 60 A.D. or a little later, chiefly on the ground that in certain passages he appears to be correcting an exaggerated view of the teaching of St. Paul contained in Ro 4 and Gal 3. Certainly there does appear to be a resemblance between these chs. and Jas 2, but it must be remembered, (1) that the questions discussed were common subjects of debate among the Jews, and might therefore be dealt with by the two writers quite independently of one another; and (2) that the resemblance may be explained on the theory that St. Paul was acquainted with our Epistle. Professor J. B. Mayer, indeed, considers that in passages like Ro 5 3-5 7 23 St. Paul has borrowed from St. James. On the whole, therefore, the earlier date seems the more probable.

4. Reception in the Church. In the first ages of the Church our Epistle does not seem to have been widely known. St. Clement of Rome (about 95 A.D.) appears to have been acquainted with it, and Hermas (130–160 A.D.) has various allusions to it. The ancient Jew-Christian tract known as the 'Didache' (? 100 A.D.) has two or three passages which may refer to it. But it was not included in the list of books of the New Testament known as the Muratorian Canon (? 180 A.D.), and Eusebius of Cæsarea (4th cent.) says that, although it was generally received, there were doubts about its genuineness. In the East it was (as we should expect) well known. It is found in the ancient Peshitta Syriac version as well as in the oldest Egyptian versions. St. Jerome had no doubts about it, and eventually it was universally accepted. Any hesitation there may have been about admitting it into the Canon of the New Testament is easily understood when we remember that it was a short letter addressed to Jews, and that there was in some quarters an idea, plausible but false, that there was antagonism between St. Paul and St. James. There is, therefore, no valid reason, either in the character of the Epistle or in its reception by the Church, for doubting the opinion of the vast majority of Christians that it is the genuine work of the brother of the Lord, and, probably, the earliest of the writings of the New Testament. Even those who assign to it a somewhat later date would agree with Dean Stanley in his remark that it is 'the earliest in spirit' if not in time.

5. Character and Contents. Allusion has already been made to the Jewish tone and undeveloped theology of the Epistle, as well as to the numerous references to the Old Testament and the Apocrypha which meet us at every turn. The question may therefore be asked, What is the special value to us Christians of to-day of this brief Judaic Epistle with its somewhat narrow range and limited outlook? If we approach the study of it from the right point of view, not regarding it as a treatise on Christian theology, but rather as a practical letter on Christian ethics treated from the standpoint of a devout Jew, we shall find it both interesting and deeply instructive. It occupies somewhat the same position in regard to the other Epistles as the teaching of St. John Baptist does in the gospel narrative: cp. Jas 1 22-27 2 15,16 5 1-6 with Mt 3 8-12 Lk 3 11. It is a call to repentance, and wholeheartedness and reality in religion. But it goes further than this. Everywhere we find the teaching of Christ reproduced, often in almost the very words of the Master: cp., for instance, Mt 5 34-37 6 19 7 2,16 10 22 12 36 18 4 with Jas 5 12 5 2,3 2 13 3 12 1 12 3 1,2 1 9-10. Notice also the resemblance between the Magnificat (Lk 1 50-53) and Jas 4 6. No doubt the sins rebuked are those to which outwardly respectable Jews were very prone, but they are sins which in this age of the Church's history also seem specially prevalent. The dangers of the possession of wealth, and the temptations which easily beset the rich man, the perils of half-heartedness and of the attempt to combine the service of God with the service of the world, the undue respect for mere rank and wealth, the anxiety to teach instead of to learn, sins of speech, and harsh and hasty judgments of others—all these things confront us to-day in other, but not less dangerous, forms than those which St. James attacked. So that we shall find that the Epistle is in many respects singularly modern in tone, and specially helpful to us in dealing with modern problems, which after all are only the old problems in a new guise.

6. Analysis. It is not easy to give an analysis of an Epistle which, at first sight, seems to be rather a collection of ethical precepts than a connected whole. But, if we look closer, we shall find one great leading thought underlying the whole and binding together its various sections. And that thought is the central doctrine of the Old Testament, 'Hear, O Israel, the Lord our God is one Lord' (Dt 6⁴). That was the creed of every devout Jew, and that is the text of St. James's homily. If God is one—one in Himself as well as the one true God—then His children, made in His image (Gn 1²⁶), must strive to be like Him. In God there is no change (1¹⁷). He is 'the same yesterday and to-day and for ever' (Heb 13⁸). He is wholly good. He demands from His children complete sincerity and whole-hearted love and obedience ; hence the heinousness of sins like want of faith (1⁶), hearing without doing (1²²), inconsistency in religious observances (1²⁶ 2¹), partial obedience (2¹⁰), using the tongue for cursing as well as blessing (3⁹), the attempt to combine the service of God with the service of the world (4²). With this clue in our hands we can proceed to an analysis of the Epistle.

(Probably the author of the Epistle to the Hebrews alludes here and elsewhere to St. James : cp. Heb 11³¹ 12¹¹ with Jas 3¹⁸ 2²⁵. Possibly Heb 11 starts with a definition of faith because of the difficulties raised by Jas 2¹⁴⁻²⁶. Heb 13⁷ is supposed by many to contain an allusion to the death of St. James.)

C. 1. 1. Salutation. 2–8. Trial from without, a source of joy to the man of prayer and faith. 9–12. Poverty is an example of those trials which may become joys. The reward of patient endurance. 13–18. Trial from within (= temptation) ; not from God, but from a man's own sinful inclinations. God, our Maker, the author of good and never of evil. 19–25. We must be ready to listen and to receive the Word. But we must not be mere listeners ; we must be doers. 26, 27. Our religious service must be real and practical. We must carry our worship into life by showing love and sympathy to others.

C. 2. 1–7. An instance of that inconsistency of life which is unworthy of a child of God— undue respect for wealth and position. 8–13. As God is one, so is His Law one. You cannot break a part without violating the whole Law. 14–26. Another instance of inconsistency—'faith' without practice, which is really no faith at all.

C. 3. 1, 2. Warning against the excessive desire to become teachers of others. The teacher's work is one of great responsibility. 3–12. All are liable to err, especially in speech. The tongue is a terrible power for mischief, and often leads to inconsistency. With the same tongue we bless God and curse men. 13–18. The true wisdom contrasted with the false.

C. 4. 1–4. Stern denunciation of those who pursue worldly pleasure. Such pursuit leads to crime and marks a man as the enemy of God. He is a jealous God. 5–10. God resists the proud and gives grace to the humble. Therefore surrender your wills to Him, and in His strength fight the devil. Repent of your sins and inconsistency of life, and then God will exalt you. 11, 12. Show humility by refraining from speaking evil of your brethren. By so speaking you sit in judgment upon and condemn the Law of God, and even the Lawgiver Himself. 13–17. Stern prophetic denunciation of those who form schemes of money-getting without any thought of God.

C. 5. 1–6. Denunciation of the tyranny and injustice of the rich. 7–11. Exhortation to the Christian Jews to be patient and uncomplaining. The Judge who will right all wrong is at hand. 12–20. Postscript. Warning against swearing. The right use of sorrow and joy. The sick man is to confess to the 'elders of the Church,' who will intercede for him with God. The value of intercessory prayer, especially for the diseases of the soul. The man who saves a soul from death brings a blessing to himself as well as to others.

[The changes of tone from stern denunciation to tenderness in the last chs. are most likely due to the fact that St. James is sometimes addressing non-Christian Jews and sometimes his 'beloved brethren' in Christ. It is to be observed that the sections of greatest severity (4¹⁻⁴, ¹³⁻¹⁷ 5¹⁻⁶) never employ the words 'brethren,' 'my brethren,' which are characteristic of the rest of the Epistle. In the little Christian communities of the East there would not be many rich men. Indeed, the Church of Jerusalem was notoriously poor (Ac 11²⁹ Ro 15²⁶ 1 Cor 16¹⁻³). Probably many of the Jew-Christians were in the employment of their rich fellow-countrymen, who would cheat them of their wages and oppress them (2⁶ 5⁴.)]

CHAPTER 1

THE POWER OF FAITH UNDER TEMPTATION

1. Servant] better, ' slave.' The word does not suggest any degradation, but only absolute surrender to the Master. St. James's humility prevents the mention of the earthly relationship. **Scattered abroad**] RV ' of the Dispersion.' Jews were found (sometimes in great numbers) in all the cities of the Roman empire. They kept up their connexion with the mother-country by going up to the great Jewish feasts. **Greeting**] better, ' joy be with you.' This form of salutation is found elsewhere only in Ac 15²³.

2. Temptations] better, ' trials ' (from without). Trials, rightly borne, bring joy. The Christian is bidden to pray ' lead us not into temptation ' (= trial); but for him, trial, when it comes, may be made to yield ' peaceable fruit ' (Heb 12¹¹). Out of bitter may come sweet. **3. Trying**] RV ' proof,' or ' process of testing.' **4. Perfect and entire**] better, ' full grown ' (Eph 4¹³), and ' complete ' (1 Th 5²³). **6. Wavereth**] RV ' doubteth.' **Wave**] RV ' surge.' St. James is thinking of the sudden storms on the lake of Galilee. This is the first of the eleven metaphors drawn from the natural phenomena of Palestine which recall our Lord's earlier parables, and show St. James as a keen observer of nature. **8. A double-minded man** *is* **unstable**] better, ' he is a double-minded man, unstable,' etc. ' Double-minded ' is one of the key-words of the Epistle. It implies half-hearted allegiance—an attempt to combine the service of God with the service of self and the world (Mt 6²⁴).

9. Rejoice] better, ' exult.' Poverty is an instance of those trials which may become joys. The poor man is to exult in his high estate as a Christian : the rich man is to glory in the loss of those riches which are so dangerous and so fleeting. **11. Burning heat**] better, ' sirocco,' the hot wind of Palestine which parches vegetation. **Ways**] better, ' goings '; perhaps used of the journeyings of rich merchants (4¹³). **12. When he is tried**] RV ' when he hath been approved.' **Crown**] the wreath that crowns the victor (2 Tim 4⁸ Rev 2¹⁰).

13–15. Trials from within (= temptations). The Jews seem to have sometimes believed (from a mistaken interpretation of passages like 2 S 24¹) that God sent temptations, and that it was therefore impossible to resist them (Ro 9¹⁹). This error was fatal, alike to any true conception of God and to any realisation of human responsibility. It made the one God inconsistent with Himself. God is insusceptible to evil, and never tempts to sin, though He may permit temptation, in order

that we may be made stronger by resisting it. Temptation comes from a man's own heart, with its evil desire, that draws him from the right path. Desire becomes the mother of sin. Sin grows up and has a child—death.

17. God is the source of good, and of good only. Every good gift and every perfect boon (not ' gift,' as AV) comes from Him, who is the creator of the sun, moon, and stars. But, while they change and vary, and, as they revolve, are sometimes in shadow, He is always the same. **Shadow of turning**] RV ' shadow that is cast by turning.' **18. Begat**] RV ' brought forth.' It seems at first sight natural to see in this v. a reference to the new birth of baptism, or to the regenerating power of the gospel (1 Pet 1²³). But such ideas are foreign to the simplicity of St. James's theological thought. The **word of truth** is the divine word which brought about the creation of man in God's image (Gn 1²⁶). **Firstfruits**] see Nu 15²¹ Dt 18³,⁴ Ro 11¹⁶.

19. Wherefore] RV ' ye know this.' **20.** The bitter words and angry passions of men will never bring about that righteousness—that entire and loving obedience to His divine will—which God requires from His children.

21. Superfluity of naughtiness] better, ' overflowing of malice.' The much-speaking of the Jews often ended in evil-speaking. **Engrafted**] RV ' implanted.' The Word is like a seed lying in the heart, which, under favourable conditions, would grow and bear fruit in life. **22–25.** Hearing without doing is useless. A mere hearer is like a man who glances at his natural face in a mirror (1 Cor 13¹²), and then goes away and at once forgets what he looks like. But the man who practises as well as hears stoops down and gazes into the perfect Law of Christ, obedience to which is perfect freedom. He remembers the ideal of Christian manhood he sees there, and strives to realise it in life. Thus he wins blessing. See on 2¹². **26. Religion**] better, ' religious observance, the outward service of God.' In order that the service and worship of God may be acceptable, the man who offers it must (1) show practical love and sympathy, and (2) strive after personal holiness (Pss 40⁶⁻⁸ 51¹⁶,¹⁷ Isa 1¹⁰⁻²⁰); otherwise he is inconsistent.

CHAPTER 2

WARNINGS AGAINST RESPECT OF PERSONS. BELIEF AND PRACTICE

1. Another instance of inconsistency. **Jesus Christ** *the Lord* **of glory**] better, ' Jesus Christ the glory,' or ' the glorious one.' One of the rare passages in which St. James breaks through his habitual reserve in speaking of the Master, and shows us something of his devotion to Christ. Such reserve was natural to a Jew. **2.** In the Jewish-Christian Church the place for worship is still the synagogue (Heb 10 25). At first strangers would be admitted (1 Cor 14 16). **4. Partial**] better, 'divided' between Christian duty and worldly interests.

Judges of evil thoughts] better, 'evil-thinking judges.' By showing undue preference to the rich man you judge, and judge wrongly, as to the relative merits of the rich and the poor man (see 4 11). God, the Just Judge, gives greater honour to the pious poor man. He is an heir of the kingdom (1 9).

6. Josephus ('Ant.' 28.8) speaks of the cruelty of the rich Sadducees to the poor in Jerusalem : cp. also Isa 3 15 Am 4 1, and many other passages from the prophets of the OT. denouncing the cruelty and oppression of the rich. **7. Worthy name**] RV 'honourable name.' For baptism into the name of Christ see Ac 2 38. For the expression cp. Ac 5 41 (RV) Phil 2 9. **By the which ye are called**] better, 'which was called over you,' i.e. probably at baptism.

8. Royal law] see Lv 19 18 and Mt 5 43-47.

10. It might be said that, even if a man transgressed the Law of Christ in the matter of respect of persons, he was only breaking a small part of that Law. Not so. The Law, like the Lawgiver, is one. To break any commandment is to violate the whole Law of love, the unity of which is marred by any disobedience.

12. The law of liberty] better, 'a law of liberty.' There can be no true liberty without obedience. A Law of liberty is one which a man obeys freely, not because he must, but because it is a Law of love, which is gladly obeyed. To serve the Master, Christ, is 'perfect freedom.' To St. James even the OT. Law —though imperfect—was something higher than a mere code. He saw in it the underlying principle of love. Thus he was led on to find in the Law of Christ the fulfilment of the old Law. **13.** The meaning of the last phrase probably is, The unmerciful and unloving man is condemned without pity (Mt 18 21-35), but the merciful man is triumphantly acquitted. The man who loves is 'justified' by God.

14. A third instance of inconsistency—great profession of belief without practice. In order to understand this passage we must bear in mind that St. James is here using the word 'faith' in a sense opposite to that of 1 3, 6, and different also from that in which St. Paul uses it. To St. Paul faith is always living and loving belief in Christ. To St. James (in this passage) faith is a kind of 'otiose assent,' or at any rate a 'barren orthodoxy, untouched by love.' Similarly, to St. Paul 'works' are the works of the Law—the fulfilment of certain obligations quite apart from faith. To St. James 'works' are the necessary fruits of Faith, without which Faith in any true sense cannot exist. That the two writers are in substantial agreement is shown by passages like 2 Cor 9 8 Eph 2 10 2 Th 2 17 1 Tim 2 10 5 10 6 18 2 Tim 3 17 Tit 2 7, 14 3 8. (St. James's 'faith' would be represented in St. Paul's language by 'knowledge,' and his 'works' by 'the fruits of the Spirit.') The difference is 'merely a difference in method of stating the truth.' The two writers, 'like trains on different pairs of rails, cannot collide, though they may seem to be in danger of doing so.' The further question whether, if either was acquainted with the writings of the other, he would have used phrases liable to be misunderstood, is one not easy to answer with certainty ; but at least we may say that it cannot be regarded as proved that either of the two had read the work of the other. It is, at any rate, unlikely that St. James had read St. Paul.

15-17. Faith without practical love of the brethren is dead. The reference may be to the famine of Ac 11 28-30. **Being alone**] RV 'in itself.' **18.** If you have 'faith' without active piety to be its evidence, it is impossible for any one to be sure that you have faith at all. **19. Tremble**] better, 'shudder.' Even the evil spirits have a kind of 'faith'; and their faith bears fruit of a sort. It causes them profound fear : Mk 1 24 Lk 8 28. No doubt St. James has in his mind these incidents recorded in the Gospels.

20-25. The appeal to Scripture. Abraham's readiness to sacrifice his only son was the crowning act of a life of faith which began when he left home and country. By that faith he was 'justified' (i.e. acquitted at the bar of God's judgment), and called God's friend (Isa 41 8). So also, when Rahab received Joshua's spies and saved their lives, her faith was practical (Josh 2 7 Heb 11 31 1 Clem 12). Rahab, though a Gentile and an outsider, was sure that the God of Israel was the one true God, and that His people would be victorious. And she had the courage of her convictions. She showed in a practical way that she was on the Lord's side, and so was rewarded by becoming an ancestress of Christ Himself after the flesh (Mt 1 5).

26. Without] better, 'apart from'

CHAPTER 3
THE CONTROL OF THE TONGUE

1, 2. Warning against undue eagerness to teach : cp. Mt 12 37 23 7 Ro 2 19, 20 1 Cor 12 28 14 26-40 Eph 4 11. **Masters**] better, 'teachers.' The position of a teacher is one of great responsibility. **Greater condemnation**] RV 'heavier judgement' (Lk 12 48). We all frequently err (RV 'stumble,' better than AV offend). There is no such thing as human infallibility. That which is most likely to cause us to err is the tongue (vv. 3–12). **4. Governor]** RV 'steersman.'

5. Great power is exercised by small things like a horse's bridle and a rudder. So also the tongue, although small, is very powerful, and generally for evil rather than for good. **How great a matter]** better, 'how great a wood.' A tiny spark can set on fire a great forest.

6. The tongue is .. **a world of iniquity]** better, 'the tongue maketh itself (or, becometh) like the wicked world.' The idea conveyed in this difficult passage seems to be that, while other members can sin only to a limited extent, the tongue can inspire and cause a whole cycle of wickedness—a whole world of evil. 'There is no divine law which the tongue cannot break' (R. W. Dale, 'Epistle of James,' 94). **Course of nature]** perhaps, 'the wheel of nature '— the whole circle or sphere of life.

Set on fire of hell (RV ' by hell ')] i.e. the source from which this evil activity of the tongue springs is hell, the Gehenna of Fire.

8. Unruly] better, 'restless,' 'unstable,' 'never still.'

9–12. 'The tongue is not only mischievous, but also gives rise to inconsistency. With it we bless the God of love (and thereby profess that we are striving to be like Him), and in the same breath curse our fellow-men, made in His image. Nature should teach us to avoid such inconsistency. The purposes of nature are clear and single. Fig trees bear figs, and vines grapes. Salt water does not yield fresh.' The last clause means that, just as a fountain of bitter water cannot yield any that is sweet, so the man who speaks bitter words against his fellow-men cannot truly praise or love God (1 Jn 4 20).

13. Here St. James returns from the digression of vv. 3–12 to the subject of vv. 1, 2. His readers desired to become teachers. But the first qualification for a teacher is wisdom. True wisdom defined, and contrasted with its counterfeit. **Out of a good conversation]** RV 'by his good life.' True wisdom is practical and gentle ; false wisdom shows itself in strife and party spirit. If a contentious man boasts of his wisdom he is a liar. **15. Sensual]** better, 'carnal,' 'belonging to the natural man' (1 Cor 2 14 15 44). **17. Easy to be intreated]** better, 'teachable,' ready to welcome truth from whatever quarter it may come, not refusing the guidance of others. **Without partiality]** better, 'free from double-mindedness.'

18. Of them that make peace] better, 'by peacemakers.' The wise man is a peacemaker who sows good seed that in God's time will bear precious fruit.

To sum up. The heavenly wisdom is, (1) chaste, pure (in relation to its possessor) ; (2)

peaceable (in its relation to others), (a) actively, 'reasonable,' (b) passively, 'easy to be persuaded ' ; (3) practical, 'full of pity and good works ' ; (4) certain of itself, 'without doubtfulness,' and therefore 'without hypocrisy.' Wisdom, in St. James's view, is moral rather than an intellectual quality.

CHAPTER 4
DENUNCIATION OF GREED AND LOVE OF PLEASURE

1. Lusts] better, 'pleasures.' **2.** 'You eagerly desire something which another has and you have not. This unregulated desire may lead to hate and even murder (cp. Ahab, 1 K 21), but even so your covetous desires go on ; they grow by what they feed on. Still you have not got your desire. Then comes the wholesale murder of unjust war ; and yet you are unsatisfied, because you try to get things for yourselves, instead of asking God for them.' The chief difficulty of this passage lies in the words ' ye kill.' It has been argued that the words as they stand are out of place, and that the early Christians of St. James's time could not have been guilty of murder. It has been suggested that the true reading is a word translated ' ye are envious.' But, (1) while a Christian in these first days might not have been guilty of actual murder, he might well have given way to those feelings of hate which lead to murder ('Whosoever hateth his brother is a murderer,' 1 Jn 3 15) ; and, (2) the Epistle was not meant exclusively for Christian Jews. In the Jewish society of St. James's day murder was frequently the first means by which a man sought to gratify his desires (Mk 15 7 Ac 21 38 23 14). With a passionate people like the Jews there was always a danger of a sudden attack and murder.

4. Adulterers and adulteresses] RV 'adulteresses ' (without ' adulterers and '), meaning, of course, those who have forsaken God. The thought is very common in the OT. (Isa 57 3-9 Jer 3 20 Ezk 16 Hos 2). It is also found in Mt 12 39. The metaphor of the Church as the bride of Christ occurs in Eph 5 22 and other passages of the NT.

5. The spirit that dwelleth in us lusteth to envy] better, 'God longeth eagerly for the spirit that He planted in us.' St. James is here alluding to several passages in the OT. rather than quoting accurately. The thought is found in Ex 20 5 34 14 Dt 4 24. 'God is a jealous God, but His jealous love is very different from that of man. It shows itself in the good gift of more grace. He longs that the spirit of man should be drawn more closely to Him, and become like Him.' The above is the best rendering of a disputed passage. Others translate, 'The (Holy) Spirit which He made to dwell in us yearns for us.' But there does not seem to be any specific reference to the work of the Holy Spirit in this passage.

7-12. Duty to God—humility, sincerity, repentance. Duty to man—to live in love, and refrain from slander and fault-finding.

8. Double minded] Notice the recurrence of the key-note struck in 1^8. **9. Heaviness**] better, 'dejection.' **11.** When a man speaks against his brother he is practically condemning the Law of Love, and thus arrogating to himself the office of a judge. In criticising that Law he is virtually criticising the divine Lawgiver.

13-C. 5^6. Stern denunciation of the presumption and tyranny of the rich. From the Old and NT. it may be gathered that, on the whole, wealth was misused by the Jews, and that therefore the 'mammon of unrighteousness' was an occasion of sin and a terrible temptation. St. James's teaching about wealth is put in a brief, uncompromising form, without limitations or exceptions. The possession of riches is regarded as a danger. But that a Christian might possess wealth, if only he recognised that he was a steward of it (Lk 16^{1-12}), is clear from passages like 1 Tim 6^{17-19}. Zacchæus (Lk 19^{1-9}) and Joseph of Arimathæa (Mt 27^{57}) were both rich, and both disciples.

13. Such a city] RV 'this city.' The presumption rebuked is that of the rich (? non-Christian) Jewish merchant who travelled for purposes of gain. **14. What** *is* **your life? It is even a vapour**] RV 'Ye are a vapour.'

CHAPTER 5

REBUKE AND ENCOURAGEMENT

2. Are corrupted, etc.] prophetic tense, in which the future is spoken of as though it were already come to pass. **3. For the last days**] RV '*in* the last days.' The warning was fulfilled during the siege of Jerusalem, when many rich Jews were slain by Zealots (Jos. 'Wars,' 5. 10). **4. Lord of Sabaoth**] an OT. phrase = 'Lord of Hosts.' It is not found elsewhere in the NT., except once in a quotation (Ro 9^{29}). **5. As in a day of slaughter**] omit 'as,' and cp. Jer 12^3 25^{34}. **6. The just**] RV 'righteous one,' may refer (as Ac 3^{14} 7^{52}) to our Lord, but is perhaps a general statement, although in that case the plural rather than the singular would naturally be used.

7-11. A message of patience and hope to the persecuted Christians.

7. There will be a final Judgment, when justice will be done. Therefore **be patient** (better, 'longsuffering,' Ro 2^4). **8. The coming of the Lord**] here clearly the reference is to the Lord Christ, to whom St. James applies the sacred Name given by the Jews to God the Father. To a Christian Jew the promise was fulfilled in the siege and destruction of Jerusalem. **Early and latter rain**] Another illustration from Palestine (Dt 11^{14} Jer 5^{24} Joel 2^{23} Zech 10^1). **9.** Do not let your irritation and soreness at outside oppression vent itself in impatience and grumbling towards one another.

11. Patience] better, 'endurance.' This is the only NT. reference to Job, though the book is quoted 1 Cor 3^{19}. **End of the Lord**] In the end God turned Job's sorrow into joy, and showed that He is full of compassion and mercy.

12. See Mt 5^{33-37}. It was a common Jewish sin to confirm statements by an oath or curse (Mt 23^{16} Mk 14^{71}). The question of judicial oaths is not touched either here or in the Gospels. **Above all things**] i.e. in your controversies and quarrels (referring back to v. 9) 'avoid especially the use of an oath to strengthen your assertions in ordinary conversation.' The use of oaths when seriously taken as in the presence of God was allowed both by the Old and the NT. (Dt 6^{13} Ps 63^{11} Isa 65^{16} Jer 4^2 Ro 1^9 9^1 2 Cor 1^{23} 11^{31}, etc). **13.** The true means of sanctifying times of excitement, whether joyful or sorrowful. We must make the worship of God the outlet for our emotion.

14-16. In order to understand this passage, round which much controversy has raged, we must remember that it was, and is, a Jewish custom for a sick man to make his confession to some rabbi or rabbis. Elaborate rules to guide those who receive such clinical confessions are found in the Talmud. St. James is telling his readers that this custom was to be continued by Christian Jews, and that the confession of the sick man was to be made to the clergy ('presbyters') of the Church. They would then (1) pray over him for the pardon of his sins, and (2) anoint him with oil (the recognised remedy, Isa 1^6 Mk 6^{13} Lk 10^{34}). By these means he would obtain forgiveness of his sins, and (if it were God's will) recover from his sickness. It is scarcely necessary to point out that the Roman Catholic doctrine of Extreme Unction receives no justification from this passage. In the Prayer-Book ('Office for the Visitation of the Sick') the lines laid down by St. James are closely followed. To a Jew sickness and sin were associated (Jn 9^2).

16. Confess *your* **faults**] RV 'Confess *therefore* your sins,' referring back to the previous vv. St. James is throughout talking about the confession of a sick man to the elders. He does not touch upon the wider question of the lawfulness of confession generally.

The effectual fervent prayer of a righteous man] better, 'the supplication of a just man availeth much in its working.' Once more St James draws his illustration from the OT. Elijah, though a great and holy man, was yet a man of like nature with any other man. But, being holy, he was mighty in intercession. His intercessions not only removed the national trouble, sent as a punishment for national sins, but also (for the time, at least), brought about a national repentance and therefore the divine pardon. The supplication of Elijah for the sick nation is analogous to the supplication of the presbyter for the sick man.

19. The glorious privilege of the man who brings a human soul to repent and believe.

He saves a soul from spiritual death, and is himself blessed.

20. The concluding words (quoted from Prov 10 ^{12} and found also in 1 Pet 4 ^{8}) are usually referred to the sinner. But passages like Ecclus 3 ^{30} Dan 4 ^{27} Tob 4 ^{10} 12 ^{9} show that the later Jews held that good deeds blot out the sins of those who do them. Probably St. James has these passages in his mind, and teaches that he who waters others shall be watered also himself—that, in covering the sins of another a man may be covering his own.

1 PETER

INTRODUCTION

1. Author. The author describes himself as ' Peter an apostle of Jesus Christ ' throughout, and there is no reason to doubt the truth of his claim. The Christian writers who lived nearest to apostolic times knew the Epistle, and did not question its authorship, and, as soon as collections of apostolic books were formed, we find it included in them. Only in modern times have objections been raised, on the ground that such widespread and severe persecution as the letter implies was unknown during St. Peter's lifetime, and that the author is more indebted to St. Paul's Epistles than St. Peter was likely to be. These objections disappear when the Epistle itself and the relations of St. Peter to St. Paul are carefully studied.

2. Occasion and Contents. That both writer and readers were expecting a severe persecution is the first and strongest impression which the letter leaves on us. But this ' fiery trial ' is only expected ; it is not even certain that it will come at all (3 $^{14-17}$). As yet there has been suffering from slander and isolation, but now something worse is certainly looked for. What had caused this expectation? In 64 A.D. there had been a great fire at Rome, which the Emperor Nero was suspected of having caused. He directly afterwards put to death a large number of Christians in order to quiet the people. Trustworthy tradition says that both St. Paul and St. Peter were slain in the persecution that thus began ; it is, however, not improbable that St. Paul suffered some years before St Peter. This news would soon spread to the Christians in all parts of the empire, who would naturally begin to fear for themselves. The Christians to whom this Epistle was written dwelt in districts of Asia

Minor, all of which probably, and two of which certainly, were connected with St. Paul. It was carried by Silvanus, the friend of St Paul. It is then reasonable to suppose that St. Peter wrote to these people soon after St. Paul's martyrdom, being himself at the time in Rome, surrounded by the sorrows and dangers of a terrible persecution, to encourage them to meet the trial steadfastly, if, as they feared, it should reach them. Silvanus would tell them all there was to tell about their master Paul. The letter from St. Peter would show that they were still cared for by an Apostle, to whom some of them probably owed their conversion on the first Whit Sunday : cp. Ac 2 $^{9f.}$ and 1 Pet 1 ^{1}. It contained too encouragement of a deeper kind. St. Peter begins by greeting them in the name of the Holy Trinity ; reminds them that all events have their source in God's foreknowledge ; that this trial is part of His eternal purpose, and that they are therefore sure of His protection ; that, if the veil were lifted, as one day it will be, they would see the divine power and glory surrounding them ; that Christ's work was done through suffering, and that suffering is the proper state of Christians, and the condition of their happiness and hope, for safety from the perils of this life is a little matter to those who are heirs of eternal safety ; that the Holy Spirit, who in times past gave ancient Israel its Messianic hope, is with them still, making them the people of Christ, the manifested Messiah, binding together the whole brotherhood throughout the world for the fulfilment of God's single purpose, and enabling them to live as a consecrated people should. ' In quietness and confidence shall be your strength ' is the sum of his encouragement. Those whom the heathen scorn as ' Christians ' must live, and, if need be, suffer, as men would who are like Christ, being holy, gentle, courteous, loyal, giving no occasion for real offence. Even the imperial authority is to be respected ; whatever Nero's conduct may be, his office is of divine appointment. But more than that : Christ's sufferings were sacrificial ; through them He saved sinners, and through death the scope of His redeeming work was enlarged. So through their sufferings—to which they have been consecrated by the sprinkling of Christ's Blood—these Christians may be the means of bringing even their persecutors to salvation.

3. General Remarks on the Epistle. No one was better fitted than St. Peter to write such an Epistle. The Lord had named him Peter the Rock ; and though his conduct in gospel days may sometimes have seemed to belie the name, yet his later life showed that Christ had judged his character aright, and had by His discipline 'stablished and strengthened' his steadfastness. He stood firm in Jerusalem before persecuting rulers, and knew how persecution should be met.

His speeches, as recorded in Acts, show that he was sustained in those days by the same kind of thoughts as he expresses in this Epistle —obedience is the great duty ; the sufferings of Christ were appointed by God, and were not the chance triumph of His enemies ; they involved humiliation, rejection, and the curse of the Tree ; they led to the Resurrection which was due to the act of the Father, and is the source of Christian hope ; now He sits supreme at the right hand of God, and has poured forth upon His people the Holy Spirit of whom He had received the promise from the Father : from thence He shall come at the time of the restoration of all things to judge the quick and dead. Jesus of Nazareth is the Messiah, of whom prophets spoke, and for whom Israel hoped. Forgiveness and repentance come from Him, and through faith in His name is safety and salvation. The Apostles are His witnesses, and so is the Holy Spirit in His people. All that has happened since He came is the outcome of past history, and there has been no break in the life of the people who are God's peculiar care ; among them the believing Gentiles are also reckoned.

There has however been some progress in the Apostle's mind between the speeches and the Epistle. Christ's sufferings, once his stumbling-block, had become reasonable to him after the Resurrection ; now he sees that they are the beginning of His glory and the great means of His salvation. Now he understands, as he scarcely did then, their sacrificial character, and therefore lays more stress than he

did on the Christian privilege of suffering for others, and aiding to advance the salvation of the world. It is remarkable that Ac 2 31 is the closest parallel that can be found in NT. to 1 Pet 3 18 f., but that, whereas in the speech Christ's continued life in the spirit is alone mentioned, in the Epistle the subject is the extension of His redeeming work to those who seemed to have perished beyond hope.

This development is natural in an Apostle who had for years been testing by experience the power of the gospel, but it is likely that St. Paul had been a special aid to him. From Gal 2 11-14 some have imagined that there was the same continued opposition between them as there was between St. Paul and the narrow Judaising conservatives who ' came from James.' But the broad lesson of NT. is that the Apostles, in spite of differences of training and temperament, were agreed on all important points, and were strong enough to overcome the scruples and opposition of these Judaisers.

This Epistle seems to have been written to Churches which were mainly composed of Gentile Christians ; but the old disputes about the Law have long ago been settled ; there is no trace of them here ; the Church is no longer divided ; all Christians alike are simply the inheritors of ancient Israel. There is then nothing strange in finding, as we certainly do, that St. Peter has studied Epistles of St. Paul with care. With Romans and Ephesians in particular, it is plain that he is thoroughly familiar. To quote detached verses would hardly be convincing. Most of the parallels are pointed out in the notes, and it will be seen that the thoughts of whole passages are reproduced with just that kind of difference which would be expected if the resemblance were due to memory, not copying. St. Peter has borrowed nothing which he has not made his own. He does not follow St. Paul in his use of ' flesh ' for man's lower, corrupt nature, or of ' soul ' for that part of man's compound being which he shares with all that lives, but gives to these words the simple meaning which they bear in the Gospels. Nor does he speak of faith quite as St. Paul does ; *faith* in this Epistle, as in Hebrews, is akin to *hope ;* it is belief in that which shall at last be revealed. He twice uses the phrase ' in Christ,' but does not, like St. Paul, make it the very centre of his theology. The doctrine which it implies, and which was derived from our Lord Himself, is found indeed in St. Peter, but he lays on the whole more stress on following Christ as a leader than on the mystical union with Christ, which St. Paul realised vividly. In Ephesians the immediate coming of Christ seems to be no longer expected ; a long course of development in the Church is looked for. But St. Peter, with the fearful signs of the changed time before him, writes, 'The end of all things is at hand.' He never applies the title of Church, so frequent in that Epistle, to the Christian community.

That the Epistle of St. James had been studied also by St. Peter seems certain, and if this was written at an early date in Palestine, he may have done so in his Palestinian days. Cp. 1 Pet 1 7, 12, 24 4 8 5 5 with Jas 1 3, 11, 25 4 6 5 20.

He presents us indeed in this Epistle with

'Thoughts, sometimes new and rare, but chiefly drawn

Out of the treasure-house of memories dear,'

and the dearest of those memories are of his Lord. Christ's sufferings; the new life of hope which began with the Resurrection; the restoration of the fallen Apostle when Christ bade him 'Feed, tend, My sheep, My lambs'; the Saviour washing the disciples' feet with the towel knotted round Him; the Apostle's own confession that Jesus was the Christ, and the Lord's answer, 'Happy art thou, Simon' —these are some of the gospel memories which he unobtrusively introduces into his letter, and all through it we perceive his longing to see his beloved Lord again.

4. Two points remain for special notice. (1) If St. Peter wrote from Rome why does he say 'She that is in Babylon saluteth you' (5 13 RV)? In Revelation Babylon means Rome. It is not unlikely that St. Peter should have applied the name, even at an earlier time, to the city which was already being stained with the blood of the saints. That title for Rome would correspond with the Jewish titles which he gives to the Gentile Christians. There is no trustworthy evidence that he ever went to the real Babylon. St. Mark, from whom greeting is sent, was summoned to Rome by St. Paul just before his martyrdom (2 Tim 4 11). The order in which the districts are named can only be explained if the letter was sent by sea. The two Epistles of St. Paul which have particularly influenced its thought and language were connected with Rome; so was, probably, the Epistle to the Hebrews, which has much in common with 1 Pet. Everything points in the same direction—that by Babylon St. Peter means Rome, and probably Rome become fearful by Nero's persecution. See also on 5 12, 13.

(2) The Epistle is written in remarkably good Greek, and is more like the work of a careful student than of a Galilean fisherman. We feel, as we read it, the same surprise as the rulers did when they found that St. Peter and St. John were 'unlearned and ignorant men' (Ac 4 13). But Greek was much used in Palestine, and even a fisherman of Galilee would know how to speak it tolerably. The rulers in their amazement 'took knowledge of them that they had been with Jesus,' and the

companionship of a great character does raise a man's style. So does familiarity with such books as the OT. Scriptures and the Epistles of St. Paul; nor does the greatness of his theme itself fail to affect the writer. If further explanation is needed, it may perhaps be found in 1 Pet 5 12, where the meaning may quite well be, 'I have used Silvanus as my secretary; he has, I am sure, given my thoughts faithfully, though he has written them out in his own language.'

CHAPTER 1

GREETING IN THE NAME OF THE HOLY TRINITY. ENCOURAGEMENT TO HOPE IN FAITH AND OBEDIENCE

1, 2. To the strangers scattered throughout .. elect] RV 'to the elect who are sojourners of the Dispersion in,' etc. The RV order shows that the present circumstances of his readers, as well as their election and his own apostleship, are all according to the foreknowledge of God. **Elect**] i.e. chosen. Christians, like Israel of old, are God's chosen people. The 'Dispersion' was a term used to describe the Jews who had been scattered among the nations since the time of the captivity: cp. Isa 11 12 Zeph 3 10 Jn 7 35 Jas 1 1. **Pontus, Galatia, etc.**] These names include the whole of what we call Asia Minor, N. and W. of the Taurus range. The order is natural if we suppose St. Peter's messenger carried the letter from Rome to a port of Pontus, then made a circuit with it, and returned to the same port. St. Paul had preached in part of this country: cp. Ac 16 6. There were men from Cappadocia, Pontus, and Asia at Jerusalem on the day of Pentecost (Ac 2 9). **2. The foreknowledge of God**] cp. 1 20 RV. The whole course of events which are gradually revealed to man is known to God from everlasting: cp. Ro 4 17 and 8 29 Heb 11 40 (RM) Rev 4 11 (RV). **Through sanctification**] RV 'in sanctification.' God's chosen people are surrounded by the influences of the Holy Spirit. By these they are brought to consecration and guided afterwards to more and more perfect obedience.

Sprinkling of the blood] Sacrificial sprinkling is meant: cp. Heb 9 13, 19, 21 10 22 12 24. The expression is peculiar to these two Epistles, and the reference in both is to the sacrifices at the giving of the Law at Sinai (Ex 24 3-8), where sprinkling with the blood of slain victims was the means of purifying and consecrating the people for entering on the divine covenant, in which they were, on the one hand, accepted as Jehovah's people, on the other, obliged to obedience. So God's foreknowledge, working in the Spirit's sanctification, has chosen a people to be consecrated to fellowship and obedience in the new covenant. But the sprinkling with *this* Blood is no mere symbol:

the blood is the life which has been perfect by death (cp. Lv 17 11), and when the Christian is sprinkled with Christ's Blood, he is made to share His life, and, at the same time, consecrated to an obedience which may have to be unto death. **Grace .. and peace**] An apostolic salutation, perhaps suggested by the priestly blessing in Nu 6 22-27. In the word 'grace' is gathered up 'all that may be supposed to be expressed in the smile of a heavenly King looking down upon His people' (Hort).

In this greeting we have, as it were, the ends of the threads which are presently interwoven to make the texture of the Epistle. 'Elect who are sojourners' sums up in an epigram the contrast between the outward uncertainty which was the occasion, and the inward assurance of peace and duty which is the teaching of the whole Epistle. Thus the doctrine of the Holy Trinity on which the greeting is based, becomes the text of the Apostle's exhortations. From 1 3–2 10 the sanctification of the Spirit issuing in the Christian life of faith and obedience is the main theme. From 2 11–4 11 the sufferings of Christ are presented as the example and purification of those whose ordinary lot is to suffer. From 4 12–5 11 the special and fiercer trial which is about to begin is shown to be part of the foreknowledge and counsel of God.

1 3–2 10. The first division of the letter : *A* (i), 1 3-9, the faith of Christians, (ii), 1 10-12, its connexion with the faith of ancient Israel ; *B* (i), 1 13-21, the life of obedience to which their faith devotes them is (ii), 1 22-25, a new life, (iii), 2 1-10, which is nevertheless the fulfilment of the ideal of the Jewish Church.

A (i). **1 3-9.** 'Blessed be God who has begotten us to a living hope through the Resurrection. Laying hold of this hope by faith, you know that you are being kept safe, though trials beset you. These trials but purify your faith, enriching it with joyful love for Jesus Christ, the earnest of the perfect salvation, which shall be revealed when He is revealed.'

3. Hath begotten] RV 'begat': the RV rendering brings the moment of begetting before us. The Resurrection must have been to all the Eleven, and to St. Peter especially, such a change from despair to hope as could only be expressed as a beginning of new life : cp. Ro 6 4 Eph 2 5 Phil 3 10. **4. Inheritance**] The land of promise (Heb 11 9) was the inheritance of Israel. During all their wanderings this was **reserved** for them, but they were taught in many ways that it was a type of a better inheritance. This inheritance is reserved for the true Israel in heaven. It cannot be corrupted, as the earth was in the days of Noah (Gn 6 11), or defiled as Canaan was by abomina-

tions (Lv 18 27 Dt 21 23 Jer 2 7), and the Temple by the heathen (Ps 79 1), nor do its flowers or fruits fade away (Isa 32 15 60 13, 61 11): cp. 2 Pet 3 13. **5. Kept**] RV 'guarded': cp. Gal 3 23 Phil 4 7. **Salvation**] RV 'a salvation.' The Gk means 'safety,' 'health,' and is so used in Ac 27 34 Heb 11 7. It must have had to all early Christians some of the freshness of a metaphor (cp. The Order of the Visitation of the Sick : 'in whom, and through whom, thou mayest receive health and salvation'), and here, as in Ac 4 12, St. Peter seems to pass from the simple to the deeper significance. **In the last time**] The Gk. might be rendered, 'in a time of extremity,' i.e. when things are at the worst : cp. Dan 12 1.

6. Ye greatly rejoice] as the Lord bade His disciples to do in tribulation (Jn 16 33; cp. 15 11 16 24). Joyfulness characterised the earliest disciples. **Temptations**] RM 'trials.'

7. The trial of your faith] RV 'The proof of your faith.' St. Peter means it is worth while to purify even perishable gold, much more your faith (cp. Job 23 10 Ps 66 10 Prov 17 3 Zech 13 9, and especially Isa 48 10 Ecclus 2 5); but he expresses it a little inaccurately, as though the proof, not the thing proved, were precious : cp. Jas 1 2. It is St. Peter's habit to speak somewhat scornfully of gold : cp. 1 18 3 3 5 2 Ac 3 6. **8. A generous touch.** The Apostle who has seen admires the love and joy of believers who have not seen the Lord ; cp. Jn 20 29. **Full of glory**] in which God dwells : cp. Ex 34 29 f. 1 Tim 6 16. Faith leads into the presence of God, and adds to joy something which is unspeakable and divine : cp. Phil 4 7. **9. The end of your faith**] i.e. the final result of it, which they are already in process of receiving, though it is not yet fully theirs. **The salvation of** *your* **souls**] There is no word for 'your' in the Gk. St. Peter directs the thoughts of his readers beyond their own small circle : cp. 5 9 2 Pet 1 7 (RV). Throughout this Epistle, except perhaps in the quotation 3 20, 'soul' means the true life, the very self : cp. 1 22 2 11,25 4 19 2 Pet 2 8, 14.

A (ii). **1 10-12.** This salvation is no new thing. The prophets knew something of it, and sought to learn more. In them, as in kings and priests, and to some extent in the whole nation, there was the Messianic Spirit, and they understood that sufferings and glories were destined for the Messiah. The exact time when these should be fulfilled they could not tell, but so much at least was revealed to them—that they were serving God for generations yet to come. What the Spirit in them dimly showed, those who have preached to you by the same Spirit have plainly announced ; what is still to follow, angels are looking forth from heaven to see.

10. Searched diligently] studying the sacred writings that already existed, observing the signs of the times, meditating on the spiritual significance of worship, and trying to discern God's true will in the inward impulses by which they were themselves moved : cp. Jer 15 19. Thus they 'tested things not seen' (Heb 11 1 RM). **11. What, or what manner of time**] the second expression corrects the first. The prophets learnt not to expect too definite a message. **The sufferings of Christ**] RM 'unto Christ,' i.e. that should come unto Christ. **12. From heaven**] as in v. 4, represented as a place. The visible heavens are a symbol of the spiritual heaven, which, without such a symbol, we can hardly think of at all ; but our Lord's words in Lk 17 21 warn us not to press human language too far : cp. 3 19, 22. **To look into**] The Gk. word means 'to look as out of a window.' The angels from the heights of heaven, if we may thus carry on the symbolic language, have a wider view than ours, and watch the results of Christ's redeeming work coming one after another into view.

B (i). 1 13-22. 'Such faith and hope belong to your life of sanctification ; but so does obedience. Sanctification indeed means a holy life. Christ's redemption has allowed you to call the Judge of all men Father ; but you may not therefore fear Him less ; indeed, life becomes more awful when you think of the price and mystery of that redemption, which has been designed from eternity to direct your faith and hope to God Himself.'

13. Gird up the loins of your mind] in preparation for the strenuous life of obedience : cp. Dt 10 16 1 K 18 46. **Be sober**] cp. 4 7 5 8 1 Th 5 6, 8. Christians among heathen must be self-restrained, like sober men among drunkards. **To the end**] or, as AV mg. and RV, 'perfectly.' **14. Obedient children**] RV 'children of obedience,' a Hebrew mode of expression (cp. Eph 2 2 5 6), which implies that obedience was the ruling passion of their lives. **15. Conversation**] RV 'manner of life': cp. v. 18 2 12 3 1 f. 3 16. **16. Because it is written**] It was a habit of St. Peter to clench his words in this way. From the sacred writings he recognised no appeal : cp. 1 24 2 6 3 5, 10 4 8, 17 5 5 Ac 1 20 2 17, 25 3 22-24 10 43; cp. 2 Pet 3 2. The words quoted occur several times in Leviticus (11 44 19 2 20 26). The latter half of the quotation shows that the Law was intended to produce something much deeper than mere ceremonial holiness. The Christian must live as the Jew was meant to live, a consecrated life. **17. Call on the Father**] RV 'call on him as Father' : cp. Jer 3 19 and Mt 6 9, which is the fulfilment of the prophetic promise.

Without respect of persons] cp. Ro 2 10 f. and St. Peter's speech at Cæsarea, Ac 10 34 ; also Jas 2 1. But the expression comes from the OT., Dt 10 17. **Judgeth**] a real present. God is judging men according to their works every day : cp. Ps 7 11 Jn 12 31. There is a sense in which men shall be judged according to their works at the last day : see Mt 16 27 Ro 2 6 14 12 2 Cor 5 10 Rev 2 23 20 12 22 12. Of this continuous judgment we have present experience, of the last judgment Holy Scripture gives us a dim outline. Sometimes God is spoken of as the judge, sometimes Christ ; e.g. Mt 16 27 Ac 10 42 17 31 2 Cor 5 10 : cp. Jn 5 22-27. The phrase 'according to their works' is probably derived from OT. (cp. Ps 62 12), but that very passage shows that it does not exclude God's mercy through Christ : cp. Ac 10 43. What is meant is what St. Peter says here, and St. James insists on in his Epistle—God is no respecter of persons ; a mere profession of faith will assure no man of salvation. The very idea that it would, becomes impossible, as soon as we combine what is said in Holy Scripture about the continuous present judgment with the other passages in which a future judgment is spoken of. A man who has been untrue to his Christian profession knows that he is being judged ; he knows also, however, that he may again pass 'out of death into life,' and so not 'come into judgment,' Jn 5 24. God's judgment is not a legal process. Whenever the heart is wrong judgment must ensue. It is to be noticed that, except in Mk 16 16, it is never written in NT. that man shall be condemned by God, though it appears otherwise in AV.

18. Cp. v. 15. Vain] i.e. empty, purposeless : cp. 4 2 f. Eph 4 17. *Received* **by tradition**] Heathen as well as Jews would have many traditions to break with when they became 'obedient': cp. 4 4. **19. The . . blood of Christ**] is here regarded as a precious price paid for His redeemed. **20. In these last times**] RV 'at the end of the times.' Christ came at the end of the old, His death and Resurrection began the new, era : cp. Heb 1 2 2 5.

B (ii). 1 22-25. 'Having entered on the sanctified life of obedience, you have entered a brotherhood which is bound together by a more mysterious and eternal relationship than can come through natural generation. Such brothers must indeed love one another sincerely. Their life is the lovely and eternal life which God promises through the prophet to the restored Israel.'

22. Truth is the substance of the gospel (Gal 2 5, 14 Col 1 5 ; cp. 2 Pet 1 12), for Christ is the Truth (Jn 14 6), and sanctified Himself that His people might be 'sanctified in truth' (Jn 17 19). **23. Being born again**] RV 'having been begotten again ' : cp. 7. 3. **Not of corruptible seed, but of incorruptible**] cp. Jn 1 12 f. 1 Jn 3 9. **By the word**] We need not discuss whether ' the word ' means Christ, or the word of the gospel preached or written ; or, again, the word that is heard in each man's conscience. All forms of God's speech are summed up in Christ, who is the Truth : cp. Heb 1 2. **The word of God, which liveth**] RM ' or, God who liveth ' : cp. Dan 6 26. **24. For**] Once more St. Peter clenches his argument by the authority of Scripture. The quotation is taken from Isa 40 6, where the section of the book of Isaiah begins, in which the new life of the forgiven and restored nation is proclaimed.

CHAPTER 2

NEW LIFE ACCORDING TO THE ANCIENT PROMISE, AND AFTER THE EXAMPLE OF CHRIST

B (iii). **2 1-10**. St. Peter considers that the Christian is the continuation of the Jewish Church. Christ's coming has been a time of reformation (Heb 9 10), but there has been no break with the past. After setting forth the doctrine of salvation (1 3-9), he went on to show that it was the fulfilment of the doctrine of the prophets (1 10-12). Now, after writing about the new life of Christians (1 13-22), and showing that it also had been promised in prophecy (1 24), he bids his readers in the half-playful language of metaphor (cp. Heb 5 12-14) to live simply, like new-born babes, nourished on simple, spiritual food, which the Lord Himself gives them, as has been signified in OT. (2 1-3). He then shows that the Lord named in his quotation has been manifested in Jesus Christ, who is the corner-stone, spoken of in the Psalm, of the spiritual Temple which is being built up of His people to take the place of the old Jewish Temple with its imperfect sacrifices (2 4-6). Obedience to the faith, not privilege of race, is the means by which this union with Christ in the new Temple is effected (2 7 f.). Finally, he brings title after title of the chosen people from OT., and applies them to his readers, teaching them how their new position makes them God's royal priests and prophets to the world, and closes with a quotation from Hosea, the prophet of God's lovingkindness, which must touch their hearts, and commend all that he has said (2 9 f.).

1. Malice] RV ' wickedness.' A general word, as, beginning a new life, they must turn from worldly vices and become as little children (Mt 18 3). With this and the following v. cp. Jas 1 21. **2. The sincere milk of the word**] RV ' The spiritual milk which is without guile.' **Grow thereby**] RV adds ' unto salvation,' which was omitted in the MSS which the AV translators followed. **3. If . . ye have tasted**, etc.] from Ps 34 8 : cp. Heb 6 5.

The Lord in the Psalm is Jehovah. As in other places in NT., words spoken of Him are applied to Christ, through whom God is manifested to man (Heb 1 10). **4.** The references in this v., as in v. 7, are to Ps 118 22 : cp. St Peter's speech, Ac 4 11. In v. 6 a passage from Isa 28 16, on the same subject, is quoted from the Septuagint. **Precious**] RM ' honourable,' in contrast to ' disallowed.' **5. Lively stones**] RV ' living stones,' as in v. 4. The whole process of salvation is a process of life : cp. Jn 1 4 4 10 6 35 11 25 14 6 Ro 12 1 Heb 10 20 and 1 Pet 1 23 (RM). **Are built up**] i.e. are being built up. **6. Wherefore**] RV ' because.' **7. Which be disobedient**] RV ' disbelieve.' **8.** The reference is to Isa 8 14 f. **Whereunto also they were appointed**] as the words of Isaiah show. God has indeed appointed the disobedient unto stumbling, but also His royal priesthood for their recovery. **9. A chosen generation**] RV ' an elect race ' : cp. Isa 43 20. **A peculiar people**] RV ' a people for God's own possession ' : cp. Ex 19 5 f. **Praises**] RV ' excellencies ' ; AVmg. ' virtues ' : cp. Phil 4 8 2 Pet 1 3, 5. St. Peter repeats the teaching of the prophet (cp. Isa 43 21) that men are elect, not for their own sakes only, but to be God's priests and prophets to the world, so as to tell of Him to others, and to present, as spiritual sacrifices, in union with the sacrifice of Christ, not only themselves (Ro 12 1), their praise and alms (Heb 13 15 f.), but also the heathen (Ro 15 16 ; cp. Phil 2 17), whom they win for God. **Into his marvellous light**] in which God dwells. It is unapproachable (1 Tim 6 16), yet He, with whom all things are possible, has called us into it : cp. Isa 57 15, and see on 5 10. **10.** From Hos 1 6-9 2 1, 23 : cp. Ro 9 25 f.

2 11-4 11. With the word ' beloved,' St. Peter begins each of the two following divisions of his letter. The keynote to this division is given in the references to Christ as suffering patiently, for the sake of others, to take away sin, and as having triumphed through suffering. He is the example and protector of these sojourners, whose life among an estranged population is one of constant suffering, under which they ought to be patient, gentle, and good, holding faster to one another in love, not, however, forgetting that they live and suffer on behalf of the heathen among whom they dwell.

The whole may be subdivided into four parts : *A*, 2 11 f., introductory ; *B*, 2 13-3 12, their duty as subjects—as, in particular, servants, wives, husbands ; and again, in general, as members of a Christian community ; *C*, 3 13-4 6, encouragement for their dangers and sufferings, the purpose of which is explained ; *D*, 4 7-11, exhortation to a sober, spiritual, and loving Christian life, to the glory of God.

A. 2¹¹ᶠ. Introduction, which sketches the thought of the whole section.

11. **Strangers** (RV 'sojourners') **and pilgrims**] from Gn23³ and Ps39¹²; cp. Heb 11¹³. **Fleshly lusts**] the desires of the body, which, though innocent when under restraint, were always a source of temptation among the heathen. 12. **Conversation honest**] RV 'behaviour seemly': cp. 1¹⁵. **In the day of visitation**] (from Isa10³) when God shall no longer overlook the heathen ignorance: cp. Ac17³⁰. Then the good lives of the Christians, even though seen in memory only, may help them at last to glorify God.

B. 2¹³–3¹². The duties of the Christians, as a body and in particular classes.

B (i). 2¹³⁻¹⁷. 'You are all subjects of the government, and must live as such. The government, though it might seem to be a mere human institution, is really created by God, and you see God's will working through it, as through the rest of the creation. God's will is that you should do well, and be at last delivered from the misconstructions of your ignorant neighbours. The government, by its repression of evil and encouragement of well-doing, is acting towards both these ends. When you recognise that such submission is submission to God's will, then submission becomes part of that freedom to which you have been brought by redemption—a freedom which those only know who have become slaves of God. This freedom obliges you to have a wide and noble rule of courtesy. Honour all men: only so can you keep the private rule of your community to love the brotherhood. In the same way honour to the king must follow fear towards God, by whom kings rule: as indeed Holy Scripture teaches you.'

With this paragraph cp. Ro13¹⁻⁷ Tit3¹ᶠ.

13. **Ordinance**] RM 'Gr. creation': cp. 4¹⁹. **The king**] i.e. the Roman emperor. 14. **Governors**] i.e. of provinces. 16. The licence of the heathen, unlike the freedom of the Christian, could be used as a **cloke,** or pretext, for wickedness (see RV); they would do what they chose, considering it no one's business but their own. 17. **Fear God. Honour the king**] cp. Prov24²¹.

B (ii). 2¹⁸⁻²⁵. Another ordinance of man, yet also of God's creation, is the family, which includes servants, wives, and husbands. Hitherto in this section St. Peter has rather hinted at than spoken plainly of suffering. Now he comes to a class who are sufferers indeed—the slaves of the household. He makes no more complaint against slavery than against the emperor, but his tender heart goes out to these ill-treated slaves, and he honours them above all their fellow-Christians by presenting to them, as their example in a special manner, Christ suffering innocently, patiently, trustfully, offering Himself in His sufferings as a sacrifice for the sins of us all. Thus these slaves, who are, like Christ, 'despised and rejected,' have a glory and grace which is specially their own, and are a special care of Christ.

19. **Thankworthy**] RV 'acceptable'; RM 'Gr. grace.' The Gk. for 'grace' and 'thankfulness' is the same. As joy in suffering partakes of the divine glory (cp. 1⁸), so thankfulness and cheerfulness reflect the gracious light of God's countenance: see on 1².

22–25. This picture of Christ is taken from the description of the suffering servant of Jehovah in Isa53. 24. **Bare our sins.. on**] RM 'carried up.. to.' A sacrificial term is here used: cp. Heb7²⁷ 9²⁸ 13¹⁵. **The tree**] i.e. the Cross: cp. Dt21²²ᶠ. Ac5³⁰ 10³⁹ 13²⁹ Gal3¹³. 25. **Shepherd**] suggested by Isa53⁶: cp. Isa40¹¹ and 1Pet5⁴. **Bishop**] RM 'overseer': cp. Ac1²⁰ (AV and RM). The overseer or bishop is an officer of the Church in the Pastoral Epistles: cp. Ac20²⁸ Phil1¹. Here the reference may be to the officer of the household who is set over the servants (cp. Lk12⁴²⁻⁴⁶); he may have no interest in them except as chattels, but they have an unseen overseer who cares for their very selves.

CHAPTER 3

The Blessedness of Christ's People, though they should suffer like Christ

B (iii). 3¹⁻⁶. Another divinely created ordinance of man is marriage. One of the purposes of Christianity was to teach chivalry towards women: this is part of the 'grace' which men can exercise. But to this must correspond the modesty and graciousness of women. The Israelites had already been taught that; and women, when they enter the Christian society, become daughters of Abraham, heirs both of the honour and of the womanliness of the women of the Jewish Church. A quiet and holy married life tends, like all other parts of Christian life, to the salvation of the heathen.

With this and the next paragraph cp. Eph 5²²⁻³³ Col3¹⁸ᶠ.

1. **Likewise**] cp. v. 7, the whole household is to be one family; the subjection of servants to masters has a like excellence with the subjection of wives to husbands. **Without the word**] 'Perhaps the Spirit of Christ pours itself abroad more widely than our interpretations allow.' (Erasmus). 4. **The hidden man of the heart**] cp. Ro7²² 2Cor4¹⁶ Eph3¹⁶.

In that which is not corruptible, *even the ornament* **of a meek and quiet spirit**] RV 'in the incorruptible *apparel* of a meek and quiet spirit.' **5. Trusted**] RV 'hoped.' Hope, the Messianic spirit, was characteristic of the OT. saints. **6. Lord**] RV 'lord' : cp. Gn 18 12.

Ye are] RV 'ye now are'; RM 'ye are become.' They became Abraham's daughters when they became Christians, but, if they are to continue such, perseverance is required, which the coming persecution will make difficult : cp. 2 Pet 1 5f. **Afraid with any amazement**] RV 'put in fear by any terror': cp. Prov 3 25.

B (iv). 3 7. Husbands, in like manner, must be chivalrous and chaste. Nature itself teaches all men that, but Christians have a deeper insight into the grace and dignity of life, and an eternal hope in their marriage.

7. The weaker vessel] cp. 2 Cor 4 7 1 Th 4 4. It would appear from 2 Esdr 4 11 and 7 [88] RV, that the human body is meant by 'the vessel.' **The grace of life**] is the loveliness, partaking of the divine, which God adds to His servants' life. **That your prayers be not hindered**] RV 'to the end that,' etc. Prayer is access to God, which is the aim of all Christian life. All faults in married life hinder it : cp. 1 Cor 7 5 Col 3 19.

B (v). 3 8-12. The general behaviour of the whole body of Christians is summed up in the love which makes them consider others more than themselves, hold fast together in their brotherhood, and be patient towards those without. By peace-making they inherit the blessing which was promised to them in the Psalm.

With this paragraph cp. Ro 12 14-21 and Jas 3.

8. Having compassion one of another] RV 'compassionate' ; RM 'Gr. sympathetic' : cp. Heb 4 15 10 34. Tenderness towards even the feelings of others is implied.

10-12. Quoted from Ps 34, in v. 8 of which blessing is promised to the man that trusts in God. The whole Psalm promises salvation in persecution, and describes just the situation in which St. Peter's faith sees his readers placed—in danger, but with the angel of the Lord encamping round about them, and all things working out a blessing for them if they trust in Him.

11. Eschew] RV 'turn away from.' **Ensue**] RV 'pursue.' **12. Over .. against**] RV 'upon .. upon.' God's aspect is the same to each, it is man who turns 'grace' into 'wrath': cp. Ex 14 24.

C (i) 3 13-22, deals chiefly with faith, (ii) 4 1-6 with conduct. It brings out deeper and deeper doctrine as it proceeds about the purpose and meaning of suffering. 'Who will harm you if you are zealous for the good ? Even if you should suffer for the righteous cause you would be blessed. Take the ancient

encouragement of Israel to yourselves. Enter into its fullest meaning by using the interpretation of the old words which Christ's life has given, and sanctify Him in your hearts, though in visible form you cannot see Him, as the Lord of whom the Psalmist spoke. Be ready to give answer to any one that asks you about this hope which is in you, and which seems so strange to him ; but answer meekly, and remember that though you need not fear him, you do fear God. Have therefore a good conscience. Your own hope will die away if you have not that, but with it you will find that the very slanders you suffer from will turn out to be the means of doing good to your enemies. Even as Christ did, for He suffered, the just for the unjust, that He might thus bring us who were among the unjust to God. His sufferings were the means of His doing so. Through suffering death in His flesh He entered into a wider life in His spirit, and went a journey that none could go in the flesh, and as a spirit preached to spirits. For us another way of salvation is appointed. The time when those spirits lived on earth prefigured the times of Christ. As then God prepared a place of safety from destruction, by directing Noah to build an ark into which eight persons were brought into safety through the dangerous waters of the flood, so now we have the fellowship of Christ into which we are brought by baptism, that is, through the resurrection of Christ which was the outcome of His painful death. Baptism, itself a painful step for the convert in a heathen land to take, is indeed our sharing in Christ's death and resurrection ; not so, however, if we look upon it as a mere form, but truly so, if we receive it with a good conscience, which, as we submit to the symbolic washing, appeals to God to accept it through the resurrection of Jesus Christ, who has completed His redeeming work by ascending into heaven in the perfection of His human and divine nature, and sits supreme, as the Psalmist prophesied, at the right hand of God.'

14. If ye suffer] RV 'if ye should suffer.' The persecution has not yet begun : cp. v. 17.

15. Sanctify the Lord God in your hearts] RV 'sanctify in your hearts Christ as Lord' : cp. Isa 8 12f. **17. If the will of God be so**] RV 'if the will of God should so will'—a rugged but emphatic expression. **18. Once**] i.e. once for all : cp. Heb 9 26, 28. **That he might bring us to God**] cp. Ro 5 2. Access to God was the end to which all the Levitical sacrifices were directed, but till Christ offered Himself this end was never attained ; as the Epistle to the Hebrews teaches. **Quickened**] i.e. made to live. **By the Spirit**] RV 'in the spirit.' This fuller life came to Christ through, or in the sphere of, His human spirit : cp. 4 6 Lk 23 46.

19. By whicn] RV 'in which.'   **In prison]** cp. Rev 20[7], i.e. the place where such disembodied spirits were kept waiting for the end of the present order of things : see on 'heaven,' 1[4]. This is the hell, or Sheol, of OT. : cp Ps 16[10] 49[14] (RV) Isa 14[9]. Our Lord refers to it, Lk 23[43], and in Lk 16[22f], where the blessed dead are described as separated from the 'disobedient.'   **20. Sometime]** RV 'aforetime.'

The whole passage clearly means that Christ, as a spirit, preached to certain spirits, who had been disobedient to the end of their earthly life. This preaching took place between His death and resurrection, and its purpose was that, by hearing the gospel, these men might have an opportunity of repentance. St. Peter does not say that a place of repentance is still left for men after death. That is neither affirmed nor denied in NT. ; but this passage makes rather against than for such a hope ; for the point is that these men did receive such an opportunity, because they had not heard the gospel in their earthly life. St. Peter considered that the Jews, unlike the men of Noah's time, had known something of Christ : cp. 1[10f]. It should, however, be noticed that 'once,' which in AV seems to limit the reference very strictly, is omitted in RV, and perhaps that time is specially mentioned because it affords a type of baptism.

Wherein few .. were saved by water] RM 'into which few .. were brought safely through water.'

21. The like figure, etc.] RV 'which also after a true likeness' (RM 'in the antitype') 'doth now save you, even baptism, not the putting away of the filth of the flesh, but the interrogation' (RM 'inquiry *or* appeal') 'of a good conscience toward God, through the resurrection.' 'The like figure' = Gk. 'antitype.' The type is the seal, the antitype the impression. Here we think most of the impression as the purpose or reality of the seal, in Heb 9[24] of the seal as the origin of the impression. **The interrogation** (RV) **of a good conscience** may refer to the question asked of the convert before baptism : cp. Ac 8[37] (AV and RM), Hooker, V. lxiii. 3 ; but RM makes better sense—the appeal of the convert to God might be expressed in the gospel words, 'I believe, help thou mine unbelief' : cp. 1 Jn 3[20]. **By** (RV 'through') **the resurrection** should be taken with the whole v., not with 'the appeal' nor with 'doth save' alone : cp. Ro 6[4f], Col 2[12]. It corresponds to 'through water,' v. 20 ; in each case that which seemed to be destruction proved the means of safety.

22. On the right hand of God] from Ps 110[1]. The words that follow show that St. Peter has Eph 1[20f]. in his mind. Like St. Paul, he speaks in general terms of the heavenly powers, which the Jews of those days described with unwarrantable detail : cp. Eph 1[21] Col 2[18].

CHAPTER 4

The security of the Faithful in the approaching Judgment

C (ii). 4[1-6]. 'This is your faith : live then in accordance with it. Arm yourselves against your troubles by resolving to be like Christ in suffering. Suffering gives rest from sin, and the results of what you have already endured should be a life henceforth in accordance with God's will. You have lived the heathen life long enough in the past to have learnt its wretchedness. The heathen are surprised now at your estrangement from them, and speak evil of you and of God. But think not that it is as they say, and that no one cares how a man lives. They shall give account to Him who is judging promptly and certainly as each man makes his choice, whether he be living or dead. For even the dead have had their chance. That was why the gospel was preached even to the dead, that they might be able through judgment to enjoy life.'

1. Hath ceased from sin] cp. Ro 6[2,11]. Suffering braces a man's mind, so that temptation loses its power over him, and the opposition of the heathen compelled Christians to be strangers to their mode of life : cp. Eccl 7[3f].

3. Will] RV 'desire,' contrasted with the will of God. **4. Speaking evil of** *you*] 'Of you,' as RV shows, is not in the Gk. These men spoke the same kind of blasphemy as the mockers in 2 Pet 3[3f].

6. This v. refers back to 3[19f]. The dead are the same persons in each place. Judgment does not mean punishment, but separation, and man, by choosing His side, coöperates with God's judgment. This choice and separation could not, St. Peter considers, be made until the gospel had been heard. Thus the judgment of these dead men did not take place till Christ preached in the spirit to them. Then they could choose their side, for or against Him. St. Peter, however, does not claim to penetrate the depths of the mystery of judgment, and leaves the subject with a statement containing, like that of St. Paul in Phil 2[12f], two parts which we cannot reconcile, but which he assures us will be reconciled— they must be judged as all men must, in the flesh, i.e. by what they did in their earthly life, and yet they may live, as God lives, in the spirit, i.e. by the choice they make in their disembodied state.

D. 4[7-11]. 'But all these present judgments are about to be completed by that great judgment which is the end of the whole present order of things. Be then sober, diligent, devout, aiming in all things at God's glory through Jesus Christ.'

With this paragraph cp. Ro 12 3-21.

7. Prayer] RM 'Gr. prayers.' Neither the sensible conduct of affairs nor the regular course of the Church's devotions is to be changed. **8. Have fervent charity**] RV 'being fervent in your love,' lit. 'intense'; perseverance and vigour, not excitement, is implied.

Shall cover the multitude of sins] 'covereth a multitude of sins,' from Prov 10 12, which is also quoted Jas 5 20. St. Peter gives, following our Lord's teaching (cp. Lk 7 47), a deeper meaning to the OT. words. If the Christians have love, they are not likely to have much sin among them : cp. Heb 6 9 f. **11.** *Let him speak* **as the oracles of God**] RV '*speaking* as it were oracles of God,' i.e. God's solemn utterances, such as the prophets used to introduce by 'thus saith the Lord.' God's oracles had always been entrusted to His people to minister to others : cp. Ac 7 38 Ro 3 2 Heb 5 12.

Amen] a Heb. word used by our Lord (and translated 'verily') when He wished to assert anything with special emphasis : cp. Mt 26 34 Lk 23 43. Such sayings might be called His 'oracles.'

4 12-5 14. With this second 'Beloved' the last section of the Epistle begins. In it the Apostle encourages the readers to meet with courage and trust the severer persecution which is threatening them. As good discipline in their community will help them to do this, he gives precepts for rulers and ruled, and then brings their thoughts back to God the Father, in whose keeping their lives and the course of the whole world are secure. He adds a prayer to God for His support, and ends with greetings and a blessing.

The section falls into five parts : *A*, 4 12-19, the fiery trial ; *B*, 5 1-5, discipline ; *C*, 5 6-11, trust and hope in God ; *D*, 5 12-14a, greetings ; *E*, 5 14 b, blessing.

A. 4 12-19. 'Beloved, the trial that is coming is not a strange one for Christians to endure, for it will prove you as God's gold must be proved, and will enable you to share Christ's sufferings and glory—that glory which is surrounding you even now, though you cannot see it yet. Suffering and reproach for the name of Christ are blessings : like Israel of old you thus partake in the lot and in the spirit of God's Anointed One. If they call you Christians in mockery, be worthy of that holy name, and give them no more real cause of offence. Judgment is about to begin, as it did at the fall of Jerusalem, from the house of God. You are that house, do not risk by disobedience the more fearful fate of those outside it. Those who suffer according to

the will of God may do what their Lord did when He suffered, and commit their souls unto God, confident that He who created will also support : but, I insist, let it be in well-doing.'

14. If ye be reproached] RV 'are reproached.' This part of their trial had already come. Cp. Ps 89 51. **The spirit of glory and of God**] RV 'the *Spirit* of glory and the Spirit of God,' double title of the one Spirit. **16. Christian**] a name which the heathen first gave the disciples : see Ac 11 26 26 28. **On this behalf**] RV 'in this name.' **17.** Cp. Ezk 9 6. **18.** Cp. Prov 11 31.

CHAPTER 5

ENCOURAGEMENTS TO SHEPHERDS AND TO FLOCK. PROMISE OF GOD'S PROTECTION. FAREWELLS

B. 5 1-5. 'To behave well in this trial you must preserve discipline. Let old and young, rulers and ruled, do their duty in love and humility, as men who have an eternal hope and a supreme invisible Lord.'

1. Elders] An official title among the Jews and in the early Church. From the Gk. for 'elder' 'priest' is derived, and from the Gk. for 'overseer' 'bishop.' In NT. however elders are not distinguished from bishops, as they soon afterwards were : cp. Ac 20 17, 28 Tit 1 5, 7. **A witness**] Gk. 'martyr,' not merely one who has seen, but one who bears witness to what he has seen : cp. Heb 12 1. The Apostles were to be witnesses : see Ac 1 8, 22 Jn 15 27 ; cp. Ac 22 20 26 16 Rev 2 13 11 3 17 6 and Rev 1 5 3 14, where Jesus Christ Himself is called 'the faithful witness.' **2. Feed**] RV 'tend' : cp. Jn 21 16 (RV). **3. Being lords over**] RV 'lording it over' : cp. Lk 22 25. *God's* **heritage**] RV 'the charge allotted to you.' From the Gk. word 'clergy' is derived. **Being ensamples**] RV 'making yourselves,' etc.

4. The chief Shepherd] cp. 2 25 Jn 10 11.

A crown] RV 'the crown,' i.e. the wreath with which victors in such a contest as these elders expect to endure, may hope to be crowned : cp. 1 Cor 9 25 2 Tim 2 5 4 8 Rev 2 10.

5. Ye younger . . the elder] in the early Christian communities their actual age was a reason for the respect which the clergy received (1 Tim 4 12 5 1 Philemon v. 9). **Be subject one to another, and be clothed with humility**] RV 'gird yourselves with humility, to serve one another.' An unusual word is used here, which might be translated 'knot round you.' Does St. Peter remember the Lord washing His disciples' feet with the towel knotted round Him (Jn 13 4 f.) ? **God resisteth, etc.**] from Prov 3 34, quoted also in Jas 4 6.

C. 5 6-11. 'Humble yourselves, therefore, under the hand of God, whose might will be proved in the coming trial. Trust is part of humility. You have been taught to cast your burden of anxiety upon God (cp. Ps 55 22) : cast it all. Watch well. The real adversary you have to guard against is the great accuser, who with restless activity (cp. Job 1 7 2 2) seeks to terrify you into your ruin. Resist him bravely in the trustful faith that your brothers throughout this world are joined with you in accomplishing the one divine purpose of all these sufferings. The trial, though sharp, is short, and through it God, whose gracious face is ever turned to you, and whose supremacy is eternal, shall bring you to perfection and security.'

D. 5 12, 13. 'By Silvanus I have written this letter to you. I recommend him to you as one whom I account worthy to be called the faithful brother. The letter is a short one ; for, indeed, my affectionate exhortation, and my testimony as an Elder and Apostle can all be put thus briefly. The true grace of God is manifested in the faithful conduct I have prescribed for you : stand fast therein. The people of God who are in this city like the captives in Babylon, yet in the purpose of God are one with you, send greeting, so does Mark, my spiritual son. Salute one another

with the kiss which is the symbol of our Christian love.'

12. Silvanus] called Silas in Acts ; the friend of St. Paul : see Ac 15, 16, 17 and 18, 2 Cor 1 19 1 Th 1 1 2 Th 1 1. Wherein ye stand] RV 'stand ye fast therein' : cp. Gal 5 1. 13. The church that is at Babylon] RV 'She that is in Babylon' ; RM 'That is, The church, or, The sister.' The community, not a person, is probably meant : cp. 2 Jn 1. The Gk. has simply 'the.' Marcus] RV 'Mark.' John Mark the evangelist is no doubt meant, who became, according to tradition, St. Peter's companion and interpreter. My son] cp. 1 Tim 1 2, 18 2 Tim 1 2 Gal 4 19.

14. A kiss of charity] RV 'a kiss of love' ; cp. Ro 16 16 1 Cor 16 20 2 Cor 13 12 1 Th 5 26.

E. 5 14. Final blessing in which St. Peter uses the old Hebrew prayer for peace. This was the blessing he had heard his Lord use : cp. Mt 10 12 f. Mk 5 34 Lk 2 14, 29 Jn 20 19, 21, 26.

In Christ Jesus] RV 'Christ.' 'Christ Jesus,' so frequent in St. Paul's Epistles, is not used by St. Peter. For 'in Christ' see Intro. Amen] RV omits.

2 PETER AND JUDE

INTRODUCTION

1. Connexion of 2 Peter and Jude, and difference between them. These Epistles are closely connected. Both were written to meet a sudden danger to the faith which had arisen in some unnamed Churches. Both authors seem to have intended to write an ordinary pastoral letter. St. Jude says so (v. 3 RV), and in 2 Pet part of the intended letter is given (c. 3). Both, however, have been compelled by the sudden peril to send a special warning. It seems plain that one had read the letter of the other, or even that the first letter had opened the eyes of the second writer to the danger.

Yet the one Epistle is by no means a mere repetition of the other. St. Jude writes with a stern sense of honour, and the joy of a theologian in the deep mysteries of the creed. 'Contend for the faith once for all (RV) delivered' is his command, which, however, he softens with a touch of pity here and there for those who are falling. The enemies of the faith he scorns too much to allow them the name of teachers. The author of 2 Pet

has a simpler mind, though by no means a less thorough faith in Christ as God. 'Hope on and do your duty more and more' is his message. The tone of almost diffident love and admiration with which he speaks of St. Paul (3 15, 16) gives us a glimpse into a very gentle heart.

2. Connexion between 2 Peter and 1 Peter. Which letter was written first ? Most say St. Jude's. This is partly because there would otherwise be little original matter in his Epistle ; but if the need were urgent he would not have delayed in order to be original. There are, however, some things in 2 Pet which tend to raise suspicion that it is not only founded upon Jude, but is a much later piece, written not by, but only in the name of, St. Peter. Thus the prophecy about the mockers in 2 Pet 3 2 f. looks as if it were designed as an imaginary explanation of the reference to such a prophecy in Jude vv. 17 f. But the passage takes another colour in RV : it is itself a reference to a prophecy. Again, the references to events in the life of St. Peter in 2 Pet 1 (vv. 14, 16–18)

are perhaps more obvious than natural : yet St. Peter might have written in this way. The style of 2 Pet differs from that of 1 Pet : but again, this may be accounted for by the difference in subject, or perhaps by a change of secretary. Resemblances in language between 2 Pet and 1 Pet must not be pressed too much in either direction, since an imitator might have designed them ; or, if St. Peter did employ secretaries to shape his letters for him, mere resemblance in language would not be important. Resemblances of thought, which betray the mind of the author, would mean more, and there are such. No one can fail to notice that, while in Jude there are several thoughts and expressions which remind us of the deep and mysterious mind of St. Paul ; in 2 Pet, as in 1 Pet, spite of many resemblances to St. Paul in words, there is a marked difference in the habit of thought. The reference to St. Paul at the end of 2 Pet is just what the author of 1 Pet would agree with.

3. Ancient Opinion about Authorship of 2 Peter and Jude. Objections to Apostolic Authorship, especially of 2 Peter. The genuineness of both Epistles has been questioned even in early times. But the wide acceptance of Jude at the beginning of the third century, justifies us in accepting with little hesitation the final verdict of the Church in its favour, especially as there is really nothing in it which might not have been written in the apostolic age. It is not quite the same with 2 Pet. Not only were doubts expressed in various places for a long time about it, but no certain traces of its existence can be found in Christian literature before the end of the second century. Yet this could be explained if the Epistle had but a small circulation in the earliest years, and in any case its peculiar subject and its shortness would prevent its being often quoted. If it could be proved that 2 Pet is copied in Jude, the whole aspect of the case would be changed, and the apostolic authorship would be supported by practically contemporary evidence. This cannot be proved, and a comparison of the two Epistles leaves a different impression on different minds. This, however, may be said. When one document is founded on another, the later one has generally been made smoother and clearer, and some rugged but forcible phrases have been lost in the process. It looks as if this might have happened in the composition of Jude : cp., for instance, 2 Pet 2¹⁷ with Jude vv. 12 f. Here Jude is certainly smoother and clearer, but the fine expression 'mists driven by a storm' (RV) is wanting. In 2 Pet the sentence ends awkwardly but

forcibly with 'for whom the blackness of darkness hath been reserved,' where the antecedent to 'whom' is not 'springs' or 'mists,' but 'these men.' In Jude this fits easily and obviously into the sentence through the addition of 'wandering stars.'

Even granting this, however, we should still have a difficulty about the date. The Jude who wrote the Epistle does not call himself an Apostle, but 'brother of James.' He was, therefore, the Jude who was one of the brothers of the Lord (Mt 13⁵⁵ Mk 6³). He may have lived till about 80 A.D. But tradition says that St. Peter was put to death by Nero about the same time as St. Paul. Now if 2 Pet 3¹— 'this is the second epistle that I write unto you '—is really a reference to our First Epistle, and if 1 Pet was written during the Neronian persecution, it is strange, but not impossible, that a letter so different, and dealing with a danger almost incompatible with the danger of persecution which the First Epistle foretells, should have been written almost directly afterwards to the same readers. We do not know for certain that St. Peter did not live longer — even much longer, and we cannot be sure that the reference is not to quite another Epistle, written to different people, earlier in St. Peter's life. Then 2 Pet would be earlier than 1 Pet, which, however, is not an easy supposition to those who notice affinities between 2 Pet and the Pastoral Epistles.

4. If copied from Jude, 2 Peter was probably written in the second century, yet in good faith. If it could be proved that 2 Pet was copied from Jude, it would be almost necessary to think that it is a work of the second century, written in the Apostle's name. No fraud need have been designed. The book would be a kind of religious fiction, intended for the instruction of readers who would be interested, but not deceived, by the imaginary setting. It must be remembered that this was what many in the early Church did believe it to be. There are, however, many such works, not a few being in St. Peter's name, and the difference in earnestness and spiritual power between the best of them and 2 Pet is remarkable. If 2 Pet is a fiction, it alone among such works carries with it the distinction of the apostolic age. The question cannot be decided on the limited evidence we have. The doubts of the early Church, and the probable silence of the first and second centuries, are not to be disregarded ; on the other hand, the critical suspicions of our own age ought not by themselves to be allowed an exaggerated importance.

2 PETER

The Epistle falls into three divisions: c. 1, Introduction; c. 2, warning against the false teachers; c. 3, answer to the mockery of those who denied the Second Coming of Christ.

CHAPTER 1

GREETING. THANKSGIVING. EXHORTATION TO PROGRESS IN RIGHTEOUSNESS FROM ONE WHO REMEMBERS JESUS CHRIST

C. 1 may be subdivided into two parts: (a) vv. 1–11, greeting followed by a declaration of the glory and virtue of the Christian life, which is a life of continual growth and progress, and requires diligent effort in those who would lead it; (b) vv. 12–21, declaration of the Apostle's care and authority to provide for his readers' remembrance of these truths—he, who saw the glory of the Transfiguration, is certain of the present power and future return of Jesus Christ, and his testimony completes the testimony of prophecy.

1. Simon] RM 'Symeon,' the more distinctly Jewish form of the name: cp. Ac 15 14. **God and our Saviour Jesus Christ**] RV 'our God and Saviour Jesus Christ.' Both titles are given to Christ: cp. Ro 9 5 Heb 1 8, and Tit 2 13 (RV). **3. His divine power**] i.e. Christ's: cp. 1 16. **Him that hath called us**] i.e. the Father, as in 1 Pet 5 10. **To glory and virtue**] RM 'through glory and virtue.' The Christian advances towards the eternal kingdom through an earthly life which is touched with the divine glory and virtue. **4. Whereby**] i.e. by glory and virtue. **Might be**] RV 'may become'; such partaking is not yet completed.

5. And beside this, giving all diligence] RV 'Yea, and for this very cause adding on your part all diligence.' God has granted all things, and for that very reason we must be diligent: cp. v. 10 and Phil 2 12 f. Virtue must answer to glory, duty to grace. All this is just in the spirit of 1 Pet 1. **Add to your faith virtue**] RV 'in your faith supply virtue': cp. v. 11 (RV). The Christian life is not a mere adding of qualities together, but a growth. Virtue is *in* faith, as the flower is in the seed; the complete fruit is love: cp. 1 Tim 1 5. **6. Temperance**] RM 'self-control.' **7. Brotherly kindness**] RV 'love of the brethren,' i.e. the Christians: cp. 1 Pet 3 8. **Charity**] RV 'love,' which goes beyond the Christian circle to God and all that He has made.

9. Blind, and cannot see far off] As in 1 Pet 1 11, the first statement is less exact than the second. He who cares not to progress loses his spiritual vision; the cleansing he received

in baptism, and the eternal kingdom into which he is entering, are out of his sight.

11. An entrance .. ministered .. abundantly] RV 'the entrance .. richly supplied': cp. Col 1 13. Life is a progress into that eternal kingdom to which we already belong.

12. The present truth] RV 'the truth which is with *you*.' **13. Tabernacle**] or 'tent,' i.e. the body (cp. 2 Cor 5 1)—a fit thought for those who are sojourners and pilgrims on earth: cp. 1 Pet 1 1 2 11. **14. Shortly must put off *this* my tabernacle**] RV 'the putting off of my tabernacle cometh swiftly.' His death was to be violent, and therefore sudden: cp. Jn 21 18. There will be no time then for admonitions, therefore he will be diligent now, and will leave his words in writing, that they may help the readers after his **decease.** This word, like 'tabernacle,' reminds us of the Transfiguration (cp. Lk 9 31), of which the Apostle goes on to speak. The reference in v. 15 seems to be to more than this one letter. Tradition says that St. Mark gave St. Peter's teaching in his Gospel, and this Gospel may be the promised means of remembrance.

16. Coming] i.e. Second Coming, in that glory of which a glimpse was given at the Transfiguration.

19. We have also a more sure word of prophecy] RV 'And we have the word of prophecy made more sure,' i.e. OT. prophecy, which is confirmed by this sight and sound: cp. 3 2.

A light that shineth in a dark place] RM 'a lamp shining in a squalid place.' The word 'squalid' prepares the reader for the bad state of things described in the next c. **Until the day dawn, etc.**] cp. Song 2 17 4 6. The Second Coming of Christ is meant.

20 f. God gave prophecy of old, not to this or that man, but to the whole Jewish Church; so now it belongs to, and must be interpreted by, the whole Church, under the direction of the Holy Spirit, not by the private, contested opinions of individuals.

CHAPTER 2

WARNING AGAINST A THREATENED PLAGUE OF BRUTAL FALSE TEACHERS

As of old there were false as well as true prophets, so it will be now. This leads the Apostle to speak about the false teachers, who —if they have not already begun—he expects will trouble his readers. Prophets were important persons in the early Church: cp. Ac 11 27 1 Cor 12 28 f. 14 29 f. Eph 2 20 3 5 4 11. These teachers, who had doubtless been baptised, claimed, it would seem, to be prophets, and therefore to be outside ordinary rules and discipline: they put a 'private interpretation' on such matters. Hence they fell into the sin of pride, and rebelled against official authority; and of lust and covetousness, despising the laws of morality. The Apostle shows, by the example of the angels that sinned, and of the cities of Sodom and Gomorrah, that sure punishment is ready for them, but that God will preserve the faithful from their seductions. He writes in strong but very spiritual language, and is in accord with the rest of the NT. in teaching that the destruction of the unrepentant sinner is continuance in sin: see vv. 12 f. (RV), 19 f.; and cp. Mk 3 29 (RV) Ro 1 28 2 Th 2 11 f. (RV) Heb 6 6.

This c. should be carefully compared with St. Jude's Epistle.

1. Damnable heresies] RV 'destructive heresies.' The word 'heresy' is passing here from its older meaning of a 'school' or 'sect' (RM) to the modern meaning of 'false doctrine': cp. Ac 24 14 1 Cor 11 19 Gal 5 20. **Even denying the Lord**] RV 'denying even the Master'; their evil lives were a denial of Christ's authority. **2. Pernicious ways**] RV 'lascivious doings.' **3. Damnation**] RV 'destruction': cp. v. 12, 3 7. With the rude but vigorous style of this and other vv. in the c. cp. 1 Pet 3 17. St. Jude is more polished, but less strong.

4. The Apostle here follows Jewish tradition (cp. Rev 20 1-3), as it is given in the book of Enoch, from which St. Jude expressly quotes. **5. Noah the eighth** *person*] RV 'Noah with seven others': cp. 1 Pet 3 20. **6.** Neither here nor elsewhere in Holy Scripture is it said that these cities were submerged. Zeph 2 9 is against such a belief. **7. Vexed with the filthy conversation**] RV 'sore distressed by the lascivious life.' **9. Unto the day of judgment to be punished**] RV 'under punishment unto the day of judgement.' God's punishment is remedial, and this v. gives just a gleam of hope for the false teachers.

11. Comparison with Jude v. 9 would suggest that the Apostle is here too referring to an apocryphal book, but if we did not know that Epistle we should more naturally think of Job 1 or Zech 3. **12. Natural brute beasts, made to be taken**] RV 'creatures without reason, born mere animals to be taken.' **Shall utterly perish in their own corruption, and shall receive the reward of unrighteousness**] RV 'shall in their destroying surely be destroyed, suffering wrong as the hire of wrongdoing.' **13. Sporting themselves with their own deceivings**] RV 'revelling in their love-feasts.' Such a love-feast or common meal of the Christians is described in 1 Cor 11 20 f. The

abuses for which the Corinthians were rebuked led to the separation of the Holy Communion from such feasts. But though St. Jude has 'love-feasts' in the parallel passage, it is more than possible that 'deceivings' of AV and RM is right here. The Gk. words only differ by two letters, and if St. Jude used this Epistle he might well correct a difficult to a seemingly easy expression.

14. Cursed children] RV 'children of cursing,' a Hebrew mode of expression: cp. 1 Pet 1 14; it means that their whole character is worthy of execration. **15. Bosor**] RV 'Beor,' as in Nu 22 5. Balaam, as we learn from Rev 2 14, taught Balak to try and ruin the Israelites by tempting them to uncleanness, and Balak had already offered him rewards (Nu 22 7,17). Thus he was like the false teachers in two respects **16. Forbad**] RV 'stayed.'

17. Wells without water, etc.] RV 'springs without water, and mists driven by a storm; for whom the blackness of darkness hath been reserved.' The false teachers are as disappointing as springs without water, or as mists which promise moisture but are scattered by the wind: cp. Wisd 2 4 and Eph 4 14. The Day of the Lord will come to them, as Joel saw it (Joel 2 1 f.), 'with clouds and thick darkness'—a storm which will truly satisfy the thirsty land: see Intro.

18. *Through much* **wantonness**] RV 'by lasciviousness.' The repetition of this word points to the character of the false teachers. Repetition of this kind is frequent in 1 Pet.

Those that were clean escaped] RV 'those who are just escaping'; i.e. those who have become Christians, but are not far advanced in the Christian life; 'new-born babes,' as they are called in 1 Pet, who have still to 'grow unto salvation.' **19.** Cp. Jn 8 34 Ro 6 16. **20.** Knowledge of Christ is both the beginning and the end of Christian life: cp. 1 8 (RV). **Latter end**] RV 'last state': cp. Mt 12 45 and Heb 6 4-6 10 26 f. **21. Turn**] RV 'turn back.' **22.** The second proverb is not in Holy Scripture; the first comes from Prov 26 11.

CHAPTER 3

ANTIDOTE AGAINST DESPISING THE DAY OF THE LORD. EXHORTATION. DOXOLOGY

C. 3 may be subdivided into three parts: (*a*) vv. 1–7. 'This Second Epistle is a reminder of what prophets and apostles said. Those who would understand it must first know that, though mockers will deny this, there will be an end of the present world by fire, as once it was overwhelmed by water. This will be a day of judgment and destruction for the ungodly. (*b*) vv. 8–13. As for the delay, which induces some to doubt this, time to God is not what it is to us, and His delay is due to His longsuffering will that men should be saved. When the day does come, it will be sudden, and since it is surely approaching, we ought to be preparing the way for it by holy living. (c) vv. 14–18. Be holy then, and consider that God's longsuffering is a means of attaining spiritual health. This is the teaching of St. Paul's letters, though some mischievously pervert their meaning. Do you keep free from error and grow in grace and knowledge of Jesus Christ, to whom be glory now and when that day of eternity shall come.' The mockers may be different persons, but are probably the same as the false teachers. Here, as in c. 2, the Apostle speaks of an evil which is expected in the future, but of which he already sees the signs: cp. Ac 20 30 1 Tim 4 1-5 2 Tim 3 1-9.

1. This second epistle .. I now write] RV 'This is now .. the second epistle that I write': see Intro. **Your pure minds by way of remembrance]** RV 'your sincere mind by putting you in remembrance.' **2. Us the apostles of the Lord and Saviour]** RV ' of the Lord and Saviour through your apostles.' Prophets of old and Apostles now have alike uttered the commandment of Christ: cp. 1 Pet 1 11 f.

3. Shall come .. scoffers] RV 'mockers shall come with mockery,' a repetition in the style of 1 Pet. **4. The fathers]** i.e. the men of Old Testament times: cp. Ro 9 5 Heb 1 1. **5. Willingly are ignorant of]** RV 'wilfully forget.' **That by the word of God, etc.]** RM 'that there were heavens from of old, and an earth compacted out of water and through water, by the word of God' (cp. Gn 1 2); a thing is made both out of and through its material. What the mockers forgot was that God who made can also break up what He has made by His word. Note the emphatic position: cp. Heb 11 3. **6. Whereby]** i.e. by means of the water and of the word: cp. v. 7, 'word' and 'fire.'

8. Be not ignorant] RV 'forget not': cp. v. 5. Another characteristic repetition. **That one day, etc.]** from Ps 90 4. **9. Not willing]** RV 'not wishing'; in spite of this different word we are reminded of 1 Tim 2 4.

10. As a thief in the night] cp. 1 Th 5 2. RV 'as a thief': cp. Mt 24 43. All through this passage the Apostle has in mind the prophecy of our Lord which is recorded in that c. **The**

elements] the parts into which we might, roughly speaking, divide the world, e.g. earth, sea, sky. But the heavenly bodies (RM) may be meant. **The works that are therein]** i.e. the processes of nature. Hence the expression, 'shall be discovered' (RM), is quite appropriate: cp. 1 Pet 1 7.

11. Conversation] RV 'living.' **12. Hasting unto]** RV 'earnestly desiring,' RM 'hastening.' It is written in the Talmud, 'If Jews exercised penitence for one day, Messiah would straightway come.' **Wherein]** RV ' by reason of which.' The Day of God is the cause. 'There will be a judgment,' not, 'the world will come to an end,' is the point of this c.

13. According to his promise] given in Isa 65 17. After all, the world will be renewed rather than destroyed: cp. Rev 21 5. **Wherein dwelleth righteousness]** cp. Rev 22 3. **14. Such things]** RV 'these things,' i.e. new heavens, new earth, righteousness.

That ye may be found] the same word as that which is translated 'discovered' in v. 10 (RM). There may be a reference back to it: whatever the earth and the works therein may be found to be, take care that you are found in peace.

15. Hath written] RV 'wrote.' Such teaching is found in Romans and in the Pastoral Epistles (Ro 2 4; cp. Ac 17 30 1 Tim 2 4), but the letters referred to in this v. may not be preserved in our collection of St. Paul's Epistles. As the author of this Epistle has noticed, patience and confidence in God's patient working out of His purpose is everywhere characteristic of St. Paul.

16. The other Scriptures] RV '.. scriptures.' The Scriptures proper of the Apostolic Church were the books of the OT. But the letters of the Apostles were read publicly in the churches to whom they were addressed, and in others: see Col 4 16. Hence they would gradually come to be called 'scriptures' also. Here, as perhaps in 2 Tim 3 16, we discern the beginning of this habit.

18. Grow in grace, and *in* **the knowledge of]** RV 'grow in the grace and knowledge of.' Grace is the gift of, as knowledge is directed towards, Christ. 'Grow' sums up in one word the admonitions of 1 and 2 Pet. **For ever]** RM 'unto the day of eternity.' This is the goal of hope in both Epistles.

1 JOHN

INTRODUCTION

1. Authorship. The question is bound up with that of the authorship of the other Johannine books, both as regards internal and external evidence: see especially Introductions to the Gospel and to the Second and Third Epistles.

(*a*) **Internal Evidence.** The witness of the book itself to its authorship is sufficiently strong. The writer speaks with authority, as an Apostle would. He claims to have first-hand knowledge of the facts which underlie the gospel message (1 1-3). The tone and teaching of the letter suit the circumstances to which Christian tradition assigns it; they are such as we should expect from the aged St. John, writing to his disciples a last message regarding the truths enshrined in his Gospel.

When the Epistle is compared with the Gospel of St. John, the conclusion that the two books are the work of one hand is well-nigh irresistible. The style, the language, the thought of the Epistle reflect the features of the corresponding elements of the Gospel. The resemblance and agreement between the two are so great and so consistent as to establish, to the satisfaction of most minds, an identity of authorship.

Of these resemblances, the most obvious are certain verbal correspondences of language, of which the following examples will repay comparison. (1) Characteristic words used in a peculiar sense: 'life' (1 1,2 3 14; cp. Jn 1 4 6 33,51); 'light' (1 5 7 2 8; cp. Jn 1 4, 5, 7-9); 'darkness' (1 6 2 11; cp. Jn 8 12 12 35); 'world' (2 15-17 4 4,5; cp. Jn 1 10 12 31 14 17). (2) Characteristic expressions: 'eternal life' (1 2 3 15; cp. Jn 3 15,16 6 40 17 3); 'a new commandment' (2 8; cp. Jn 13 34); 'only begotten Son' (4 9; cp. Jn 1 18 3 16); 'know God' (2 3,4 4 6; cp. Jn 17 3,25); 'abide in Christ' (2 6 3 24; cp. Jn 6 56 15 4,5.) (3) Identical phrases: 'that your joy may be full' (1 4; cp. Jn 16 24); 'walketh in darkness, and knoweth not whither he goeth' (2 11; cp. Jn 12 35); (*are*) 'passed from death unto life' (3 14; cp. Jn 5 24); 'know him that is true' (5 20 (RV); cp. Jn 17 3). Besides these and other like examples, a general similarity of style and thought gives evidence almost the strongest of its kind to show that if St. John wrote the Gospel which bears his name, he wrote the Epistle also.

(*b*) **External Evidence.** The witness afforded by the book itself to its authorship is amply supported by the testimony of ancient writers. The Epistle is evidently quoted (though without mention of the fact) by Polycarp (116 A.D.), who was, according to Irenæus, a disciple of St. John. It was used, Eusebius tells us, by Papias (120 A.D.), an associate of Polycarp, also said to have been a hearer of St. John. It is quoted and referred to as St. John's Epistle by Irenæus (180 A.D.), Polycarp's disciple, by Clement of Alexandria (190 A.D.), Tertullian (200 A.D.), Origen (230 A.D.), and others.

2. Date and Destination. These questions are involved in more uncertainty, though fairly satisfactory inferences regarding them may be drawn both from tradition and from the book itself.

(*a*) **When was it written?** St. John is said to have written his Gospel at Ephesus (Iren. 'Adv. Hær.' iii. 1, 1), probably between 80 and 90 A.D. As to the date of the Epistle we have no direct evidence. It is commonly believed, however, that the two writings are closely connected in time, the prevailing opinion perhaps being that the Epistle was written subsequently to the Gospel, whether as a supplement or as an independent composition.

The idea of an original connection with the Gospel has been supposed to find support from the place which the Epistle occupies in the Muratorian Fragment on the Canon (circ. 170), a witness for the authenticity of the Epistle not included in the authorities mentioned above. In this document, which contains (incomplete in its extant form, as the name implies) an annotated list of the books of the New Testament, the First Epistle of St. John is placed directly after the Gospel, and not with the two minor Epistles. This, it has been conjectured, was the position which it originally occupied as a supplement or post-script to the Gospel, and from which it was subsequently removed when the books of the New Testament were grouped in their present order. However this may be, as the Epistle contains no reference to persecutions, such as took place during the reigns of Domitian and Trajan, it can hardly have been issued much later than 90 A.D.

(*b*) **For what Readers was it intended?** In this there is involved a prior question as to the character of the composition itself. Is it

1053

an Epistle at all ? Of all the New Testament Epistles, this and the Epistle to the Hebrews alone begin without any epistolary form of address. Moreover, this contains no salutations or messages to individuals, such as are found in Hebrews and in nearly all the other Epistles. Some, therefore, have regarded it as a treatise rather than a letter.

While, however, this book is not written in epistolary form, it contains the substance of an Epistle. Its epistolary character is also seen in the constant use of the second person (1^3 and onwards), the terms 'little children,' 'fathers,' 'young men,' 'beloved,' by which the readers are addressed, and the frequent use of the expression, 'I write unto you' (2^{12-14} 3^2, etc.). The opinion, therefore, is probably not far wrong which regards the work as a pastoral or circular letter, addressed to the Churches in the province of Asia with which St. John is definitely connected in c. 1 of the Apocalypse, and having reference primarily to the peculiar circumstances of those Churches and the particular spiritual dangers to which they were exposed.

At the same time, the absence of local colour makes it possible that a wider circle is addressed. It is most natural, however, to infer a distinctly Gentile community, as well from the warning against idolatry with which the book concludes as from the absence of the Hebrew element so manifest throughout the Gospel, and of any quotations from or allusions to the Old Testament.

3. **Contents.** The theme of the Epistle is fellowship with God ; its object, to bring its readers into that fellowship and to secure them against losing it.

This purpose finds expression at the opening of the Epistle, and again near its close. 'That which we have seen and heard declare we unto you, that ye also may have fellowship with us : and truly our fellowship is with the Father, and with His Son Jesus Christ. And these things write we unto you, that your joy may be full' ($1^{3,4}$). 'These things have I written unto you that believe on the name of the Son of God ; that ye may know that ye have eternal life, and that ye may believe on the name of the Son of God' (5^{13}). There is thus a distinct difference between the object of the Epistle and that of the Gospel (see Jn 20^{31}), the object of the one being to promote faith in Christ, that of the other to confirm the faith and develop the religious life of those who already believe.

The writer's thought revolves about certain fundamental watchwords regarding the nature of God. The three great watchwords which occupy the pivotal places in the plan of the Epistle (see analysis below) are, 'God is light,' 'God is righteous,' 'God is love.' Corre

sponding to these are the Christian graces of faith, obedience, love, and the Christian duties of confessing Christ, keeping the commandments, and loving the brethren. Together with the positive inculcation of these truths and duties is combined a recognition of their opposites. Underlying all the thought of the Epistle is the conception of the irreconcilable antagonism which exists between Christ and the world ; hence the statement of truth or duty is strengthened or expanded by a denial of or warning against its opposite. The active presence of error and evil among those addressed accounts for the polemical element in the Epistle, and the warnings against evil influences and wrong ways of thinking and living with which it abounds.

The particular heresy which the writer combats appears to have been an incipient form of one of the various systems which, as developed in the 2nd cent., are included under the general name of Gnosticism, in all of which there was involved a denial of the reality of the Incarnation : cp. 4^2 2 Jn v. 7. This subject is more fully treated in Intro. to Second and Third Epistles. The polemical element is, however, subordinate to the main object of the Epistle, which is to promote the spiritual life of believers by bringing them into a living union with Christ and confirming them therein.

The plan of the Epistle is difficult to follow, and has been differently understood, some failing to recognise any regular plan at all. In the following **Synopsis,** the minor sections are grouped about the three fundamental statements mentioned above.

1^{1-4}. **Introduction.** The fundamental scheme of the Epistle : God manifested in Jesus Christ, that man may have fellowship with the Father through the Son.

1^5-2^{28}. **I. God is Light,** hence fellowship with Him means walking in the light and realising a sense of brotherhood and the forgiveness of sins (v. 7).

  (i) This involves, (a) confession of sin (vv. 8-10), (b) keeping His commandments (2^{3-6}), (c) in particular, loving the brethren (vv. 7-11).

  (ii) (a) Reasons for writing, as regards the spiritual condition of the readers (vv. 12-16).

    (b) Things and persons to avoid. (1) The love of the world (vv. 15-17). (2) Fellowship with false teachers (vv. 18-26).

    (c) The believer's security and hope (vv. 27, 28).

2 ²⁹–4 ⁶.   II. **God is Righteous,** hence fellowship with Him involves doing righteousness, and this is an evidence of divine sonship (v. 29).

    (i) Sonship a motive to righteousness (3 ¹⁻⁹).

    (ii) Sonship the root of brotherly love (vv. 10–18).

    (iii) Sonship resulting in glorious privileges :

        (*a*) assurance (vv. 19–21), (*b*) answer to prayer (v. 22), (*c*) fellowship, realised through the gift of the Spirit (v. 24), (*d*) discernment of truth and error (4 ¹⁻⁶).

4 ⁷–5 ¹².   III. **God is Love,** hence fellowship with Him involves walking in love (vv. 7, 8).

    (i) How God's love to us was manifested (vv. 9, 10).

    (ii) Our rightful response to it, brotherly love (vv. 11, 12).

    (iii) The proofs of fellowship, (*a*) the indwelling Spirit (v. 13), (*b*) confessing Jesus (vv. 14, 15), (*c*) abiding in love (v. 16).

    (iv) Perfect love casts out fear (vv. 17, 18).

    (v) Brotherly love the test of love to God (vv. 19–21).

    (vi) Love finds expression in obedience (5 ¹⁻⁴).

    (vii) Obedience rests on faith in and fellowship with Christ (vv. 5–12).

5 ¹³⁻²¹.   **Conclusion.**

    (i) Reason for writing restated in different form (v. 13).

    (ii) The assurance which believers may have : (*a*) of the efficacy of prayer (vv. 14–17), (*b*) of the guardianship of God (v. 18), (*c*) of divine sonship (v. 19), (*d*) of the reality of the divine manifestation and the fellowship resulting from it (v. 20).

    (iii) Final warning (v. 21).

CHAPTER 1
FELLOWSHIP WITH GOD IN LIGHT

1. Observe the grammatical form of vv. 1–3. In v. 1 a sentence is begun which, interrupted by the parenthesis in v. 2, is continued in v. 3. The sense is, 'We declare unto you that which was from the beginning, that which we have heard, etc., concerning the Word of Life.' **From the beginning**] cp. Jn 1 ¹. **Heard . . handled**] the evidence of eyewitness. The Docetists taught that Christ was

a mere phantom : cp. Lk 24 ³⁹. **Of the Word of life**] RV 'concerning the Word of life': cp. 'bread of life,' Jn 6 ³⁵. For 'the Word' (*Logos*) see on Jn 1 ¹.

2. This v. is parenthetical, reiterating the fact that the preëxistent Eternal Word was manifested to men. In v. 3 this manifestation is said to determine man's relation to God.

3. Declare we unto you] RV adds 'also.' **Fellowship with us**] i.e. union with us in Christian fellowship. **And truly**] RV 'yea, and.' Fellowship with Christian teachers involves fellowship with God in Christ.

4. That your joy may be full] RV 'that our joy may be fulfilled.' 'Fellowship with Christ and with the brethren is the measure of the fulness of joy' (Westcott).

5. Light . . darkness] The one suggests truth and goodness, the other falsehood and evil. All truth and goodness emanate from God. To walk in the light, therefore, i.e. to possess and practise these, is to have fellowship with Him. On the other hand, to be without these is to be without God (v. 6). **7. One with another**] i.e. with other Christians, the result of fellowship with God. **The blood of Jesus Christ**] RV omits 'Christ.' Only those who 'walk in the light' can appropriate the cleansing efficacy of the life laid down upon the Cross. **Cleanseth**] The present tense denotes a continuous process—the progressive sanctification of the believer's soul : cp. Jn 13 ¹⁰.

8. Deceive ourselves] lit. 'lead ourselves astray.' **9. Just**] RV 'righteous.'

Forgive . . cleanse] 'Forgive' refers to the remission of punishment, 'cleanse' to the removal of pollution.

CHAPTER 2
THE ADVOCACY OF CHRIST AND THE OBLIGATIONS OF BELIEVERS

1. My little children] The diminutive implies the fatherly care which the aged Apostle felt for his disciples. **Advocate**] The word thus translated is used by St. John alone of the NT. writers. Elsewhere (Jn 14 ^{16, 25} 15 ²⁶ 16 ⁷) it is rendered 'Comforter.' Literally it means one who is called to the side of another for counsel and help. The rendering 'Advocate' suits the passages in the Gospel (see RM *in loco*). The Son and the Holy Spirit both act as Advocate with the Father : cp. Ro 8 ^{26, 27, 34}. The Redeemer's work calls for the mercy which 'rejoiceth against judgment.'

2. Propitiation] the act or offering which makes an injured person favourable to the offender. Christ is the propitiation as well as the propitiator : the offering itself as well as the sacrificing priest who makes it. **The whole world**] cp. Jn 1 ²⁹ 4 ²⁴ 17 ²⁰⁻²³. The work of Christ was wrought for all, not for a chosen few. There are none who **may**

not share its benefits if they will. **5. The love of God**] i.e. man's love to God : cp. 4 12. An ideal condition is here presented. Perfect obedience is evidence of perfect love.

7. An old commandment] cp. 2 Jn v. 5. Old, because they have known it from the beginning of their Christian life. **Which ye had from the beginning**] RV 'which ye heard.'

8. A new commandment] The commandment of love, old as it now is in one sense, is in another new, as it ever gains fresh light and meaning. **The darkness, etc.**] RV 'the darkness is passing away, and the true light already shineth.' **10. Occasion of stumbling**] lit. 'stumbling-block,' that which may cause himself or others to fall, in this case probably (see next v.) himself. Without love no one can walk in the light of God's truth.

12–14. In these vv. the readers are addressed, twice over, as (1) 'little children,' (2) 'fathers,' (3) 'young men.' Probably the first of these is the term of endearment already used (v. 1), including the whole community. Next, the old and the young are respectively addressed as 'fathers,' 'young men.' Corresponding to the two series of personal addresses is a change in the tense of the verb from 'I write' to 'I wrote,' or 'I have written': see RV, noting change in v. 13. Perhaps 'I write' refers to the Epistle, 'I wrote' to the Gospel ; or else the change is made for variety, the present being used from the writer's standpoint, the past from that of the readers, when the message would reach them.

15. Love not the world] The 'world' here is not the world of nature, nor the world of humanity which 'God so loved' (Jn 3 16). It means all in the present order of things which appeals to the soul as an object of desire apart from and in rivalry to God. **16.** All that is thus antagonistic to God is summed up under three heads, the separate avenues through which the world-spirit reaches the soul. While the classification is hardly exhaustive, as a category covering all kinds of evil it is very comprehensive, and corresponds to the three elements which appear in the temptation of Eve (Gn 3 6) and in the temptation of our Lord (Lk 4 3-12).

18. The last time] RV 'the last hour.' The Apostles undoubtedly anticipated a coming of Christ in the near future as a vital possibility, and all generations are enjoined by our Lord's teaching to do the same. The dispensation which immediately precedes that great event, the time of which is known only to the Father (Mk 13 32), is rightly called, whatever its length may prove to be, the 'last hour.' **Antichrist shall come**] RV 'Antichrist cometh.' The hostile influence described as Antichrist is further defined in v. 22, 4 3 2 Jn v. 7, as the Spirit which denies the Incarnation, and is regarded

as a sign of the last days : cp. 2 Th 2 3-10. The term 'Antichrist' suggests the ideas of opposition and rivalry to Christ. St. John regards as embodiments of this spirit all the false teachers who had already (v. 19) gone out from the Church because they did not really possess the Spirit of Christ.

20. An unction] RV 'an anointing' : cp. 2 Cor 1 21. Oil is the sacred symbol of the Spirit's operations. The anointing here represents the gift of the Spirit, whereby believers are endowed with spiritual discernment (Jn 14 26 16 13). **The Holy one**] probably Christ.

23. 'The denial of the Son involves the loss of the Father, not only because the ideas of sonship and fatherhood are correlative, but because the Son alone can reveal the Father.'

28. When he shall appear] RV 'if he shall be manifested.' The 'if' implies no doubt as to the fact, but only uncertainty as to the time. **Confidence**] RV 'boldness,' lit. 'freedom or readiness of speech.' **29. Is born of him**] lit. 'hath been begotten from him.' 'The presence of righteous action is the sure sign of the reality of the divine birth' (Westcott).

CHAPTER 3

The Righteousness of God and the Duties and Privileges of Sonship

1. The sons of God] RV 'children of God,' adding the words, 'and *such* we are.' The word translated 'children' here is characteristic of St. John, and implies community of nature, whereas the term 'sons' as used by St. Paul suggests the privileged condition of heirship. **2.** Note changes in RV. **3. This hope**] of being hereafter like God in Christ.

In him] RV 'set on him.' **Purifieth himself**] 'He who looks forward to becoming like God hereafter must strive after His likeness now' (Westcott).

6. Sinneth not] That the possibility of sinlessness in present experience is not taught here is clear from 1 8, 9. St. John's thought moves in the region of the ideal. The divine life and the life of sin are in idea mutually exclusive. Sin in the Christian is either involuntary or in acknowledged contradiction to the ruling principle of his life. The commission of it is to that extent a failure perfectly to abide in Christ. **8. He that committeth sin**] RV 'he that doeth sin.' The present tense implies that which is habitual, which results from a ruling principle. **9.** RV 'Whosoever is begotten of God doeth no sin, because his seed abideth in him.' The same principles of interpretation apply here as in the foregoing vv. A perfect realisation of the filial relationship to God excludes sin. **His seed remaineth in him**] The germinal principle from which his new life has sprung.

12. Cain] The typical example of hatred, inspired by the Evil One, and resulting in murder, the germ of which is hatred (v. 15).

16. Hereby perceive we the love *of God*] RV 'hereby know we love,' i.e. wnat love is.

He . . we] The pronouns are emphatic.

17. This world's good] RV 'the world's goods,' lit. 'the world's life,' i.e. that which supports life.

19. Hereby] i.e. by loving in deed and truth. **20.** In RV v. 19 ends with a comma, then follows, 'whereinsoever our heart condemn us ; because God,' etc. **God is greater**] He is a more perfect judge. Are these words meant to inspire awe or to afford consolation ? Is God regarded as more exacting or more merciful than conscience ? Opinion is much divided. The contrast in v. 21 suggests the former alternative, but the whole context rather favours the latter. 'We shall then still our heart in whatsoever it may condemn us, because we are in fellowship with God, and that fact assures us of His sovereign mercy' (Westcott). **22.** See 5 15.

24. The spirit which he hath given us] RV 'the Spirit which he gave us,' i.e. when we became Christians. The indwelling Spirit, from whom springs the Christian's love to God and man, is his assurance of fellowship with God. The test of having the Spirit of God, and not the spirit of Antichrist, is treated in the six following verses.

CHAPTER 4
FELLOWSHIP WITH GOD IN LOVE

1. Try the spirits] RV 'Prove the spirits.' The verb is used of testing metals. **2, 3.** See on 2 Jn v. 7. **3. Confesseth not that Jesus Christ is come in the flesh**] RV 'confesseth not Jesus.' **4. He that is in the world**] the Devil : cp. 3 10 Jn 8 44 12 31. **5. They**] the false prophets. **6. We**] the Christian teachers.

8. God is love] the third fundamental maxim (see Intro.). Love is not merely an attribute of God, it is His very Being. Hence to be without love is to be without God : cp. v. 16. **9.** See Jn 3 16. **11. We ought also**] RV 'we also ought.' **12. Hath seen God**] RV 'hath beheld God.' **His love**] i.e. our love to Him. If we love one another we have proof both of His presence with us and of our love to Him.

17. Herein is our love made perfect] RV 'herein is love made perfect with us,' i.e. in the double communion spoken of in the preceding v. **As he is, so are we**] We, as we are in this world, are like Christ, who shares our human nature. The sense of likeness to Him gives us confidence. **18. No fear in love**] not the rightful awe which pertains to reverence, but servile or guilty fear. **19. We love**

him] RV 'we love.' Possibly the verb should be rendered 'let us love.'

CHAPTER 5
THE LOVE, OBEDIENCE, AND ASSURANCE OF BELIEVERS

1. The reason for brotherly love. **2.** This is the converse of 4 19-21. Love to God and love to the brethren being inseparable, each is the test of the other. **4. Whatsoever**] not 'whosoever.' 'It is not the man, but his birth from God, which conquers' (Plummer).

6. This is he that came by water and blood] According to the most generally accepted interpretation of this difficult passage, the reference is primarily to our Lord's baptism in Jordan and His death upon the Cross —the baptism of water and the baptism of blood, which together sum up His redemptive work and represent its cleansing and atoning power. There is, perhaps, some allusion also to the 'blood and water' to which St. John bore witness at the Cross (Jn 19 34). besides a symbolical reference to the two sacraments.

7, 8. All the words between **that bear record** in v. 7 and **the spirit** in v. 8 are omitted in RV. It is quite certain that these words did not belong to the original text. They are found in no Gk. MS earlier than the 14th cent., and are quoted by none of the Fathers before the middle of the 5th cent. The Fathers understood the passage in its original form to symbolise the Trinity, an interpretation which may have been inserted at first as a marginal note and afterwards found its way into the text.

14, 15. The prayer of faith prevails when it is in accordance with God's will. Thus offered it is surely heard, and, though it may not have any visible effect, receives its answer. He who trusts God's love knows that the answer he receives is the best.

16, 17. There is a sin unto death] RM 'There is sin unto death,' not any special sin which can be recognised as 'unto death.' Sin cannot be divided into 'mortal' and 'venial' on the authority of this passage. Sin may be of such a character as to lead to total separation from Christ, which is spiritual death. '"Sin unto death" is not any *act* of sin, however heinous, but a *state* or *habit* of sin wilfully chosen and persisted in : it is constant and consummate opposition to God' (Plummer).

18. He that is begotten of God keepeth himself] RV 'he that was begotten of God (i.e. Christ) keepeth him.' **21.** Taken comprehensively, this warning is directed against all that takes the place of God in man's affections.

If, as seems likely, the Epistle is St. John's latest work, these are, in point of time, the last words of Holy Scripture.

2 AND 3 JOHN

INTRODUCTION

1. Authorship. The majority of the Epistles of the New Testament are catholic, that is, they are addressed not to individuals but to Churches of this and that locality. There are references to letters of this kind which are now lost. Thus St. Paul says, 'I wrote unto you in an epistle not to keep company with fornicators' (1 Cor 5⁹). And he directs the Colossian Church to exchange Epistles with the Church at Laodicea (Col 4¹⁶); this being the only mention we have of a Laodicean Epistle. But there are several private letters in the New Testament, each bearing the vivid stamp of an occasion. And these must have constituted but a small part of the correspondence of the early Christian writers. St. Paul speaks of 'epistles of commendation' (2 Cor 3¹), personal letters of introduction, as passing frequently among the Churches. Undoubtedly, then, many private letters by the authors of the New Testament have been lost.

This adds special interest to the Second and Third Epistles of St. John ; for here we have two letters of unquestionably early date, revealing each a section of the Christian community in the colours of life. They are almost universally allowed to be by the same hand ; by the hand, most commentators add, of John the Apostle. The direct external evidence for their authenticity is not extensive. This may be perhaps on account of their brevity and their private character, which would render them not likely to be mentioned frequently by the Fathers. Yet there are several references to them in the first four centuries. It is said in the Muratorian Canon (170 A.D.) that John wrote at least two Epistles. Irenæus (180 A.D.) twice ascribes the Second Epistle to St. John. The Old Italic Version (180 A.D.) has both Epistles. Clement of Alexandria (190 A.D.) refers to the First Epistle as 'the larger Epistle,' implying that he knows another which is shorter ; and again he speaks of a Second Epistle of John, addressed 'to a Babylonian lady by name Electa.' Both Epistles, the Second and Third, are mentioned by Origen (230 A.D.), and by Dionysius of Alexandria (245 A.D.). Eusebius (325 A.D.) in speaking of them places them among the books whose right to a position in the Canon is disputed. The Second

Epistle is referred to by Cyprian (248 A.D.) ; and both are acknowledged by the Councils of Laodicea (363 A.D.), of Hippo (393 A.D.), and the Third Council of Carthage (397 A.D.).

The internal evidence is stronger. According to the contents, the author is a person of apostolic, or at least authoritative, position. There is no ground for doubting that such was the case, for there is no motive conceivable for forgery. Moreover, if the attempt had been made to pass off the work of an obscure author for that of a prominent one, a more definite and authority-giving title than that which heads both Epistles—'the Presbyter'—would have been assigned the writer. Their style, form, and contents are so alike that their unity of authorship can hardly be questioned. In each case the opening address (cp. 2 Jn v. 1, 3 Jn v. 1), the writer's joy in the conduct of his friends (cp. 2 Jn v. 4, 3 Jn v. 4), and the conclusion (cp. 2 Jn v. 12, 3 Jn vv. 13, 14), is the same. Similarity in the words, ideas, style, character, binds them also to the First Epistle. 'Love' and 'truth' glow as fundamental conceptions in all three. (Among instances of similar treatment of the same themes, are the following : cp. 2 Jn vv. 4, 6, 1 Jn 6⁷, 2 Jn vv. 6, 11 ; cp. 2 Jn v. 5, 1 Jn 2⁷ ; cp. 2 Jn v. 6, 1 Jn 5³ ; cp. 2 Jn v. 7, 1 Jn 2²² ; cp. 2 Jn v. 7, 1 Jn 4¹⁻³ ; cp. 2 Jn v. 9, 1 Jn 2²³ ; cp. 2 Jn v. 12, 1 Jn 1⁴ ; cp. 3 Jn v. 11, 1 Jn 3¹⁰. Of the thirteen vv. of the Second Epistle eight are thus found in essentially the same form in the First.) In all of them the centre of Christianity is the recognition of Jesus as the Christ and the authoritative revealer of God, and walking in love and truth as the soul's mode of union with Him. The prominence given to Christ leads to warnings against 'antichrist,' an expression found in the New Testament in the First and Second Epistles of John only (1 Jn 2¹⁸,²² 4³ 2 Jn v. 7). The First Epistle utters three clear and weighty warnings against the dangers of the time—the danger of denying the true Christ, of failing in love to the brethren, and of not observing Christ's commandments. These same three warnings constitute the body of thought of the Second Epistle (2 Jn vv. 7, 9, 5, 6). The connexion between the First Epistle and the Second and Third is so close that the arguments for the Johannine authorship of the last two are in the main the same as for the First, and may be found at length in commentaries on that Epistle. Whether this connexion involves unity of authorship with the Fourth Gospel and the Revelation, is a question too large to be entered upon here.

It has been held that the title which the author of the Second and Third Epistles gives himself—'the Presbyter' or 'Elder'—excludes Johannine authorship. For this, it is maintained, is the official designation of the minister of a particular Church, and therefore cannot have been assumed by one having the apostolic position of St. John. This opinion is supported by a passage in Eusebius, in which Papias is quoted as mentioning a John the Presbyter. 'If I met with any one who had been a follower of the Presbyters, I made it a point to enquire what were the declarations of the Presbyters; what was said by Andrew or by Peter or by Philip or by Thomas or by James or by John or by Matthew or any of the Lord's disciples; and what Aristion and the Presbyter John, the disciples of the Lord, say.' Of this statement of Papias, Eusebius says: 'It is proper to observe that the name of John occurs twice. The one John he mentions with Peter and James and Matthew and the other Apostles. But in a separate part of his discourse he ranks the other John with the rest not included in the number of the Apostles, placing Aristion before him. · He distinguishes him plainly by the name of Presbyter.' Eusebius therefore infers that there were two Johns—John the Apostle and John the Presbyter. Cp. Euseb. 'Hist. Eccles.,' VII, 25. But apart from the fact that it is somewhat uncertain whether Papias in this passage refers to a different person from John the Apostle, this is the only place in Christian history down to the time of Eusebius in which such a person as John the Presbyter is mentioned. Moreover, it is an assumption that 'the Presbyter' must necessarily be the technical and official title of the minister of a special Church; for in the very passage quoted, Papias calls seven of the Apostles Presbyters. It is more probable, therefore, that 'Presbyter,' at the beginning of the Second and Third Epistles of John, is not an official title, but a descriptive appellation, as it is translated in both AV and RV—'the Elder.' The term therefore claims for the author a position of dignity and authority in the Christian community; not necessarily implying apostleship, but not excluding it.

2. Occasion. We have said that the background of thought of the Second and Third Epistles is the same as that of the First, and that this contained three warnings against dangers of the time. These dangers resulted from the great main problem which lay at the

foundation of all Oriental religions—the relation of finite man to the infinite God. How could that chasm be crossed? how had it been crossed in the work of creation? how were spirit and matter related? how did evil enter the world, and what was evil? Almost all early thinkers were driven by these questions into some form of Dualism. There were, they must believe, two Powers in conflict. Since spirit was the higher, matter was evil; it was the work of the inferior god. The material, the natural, was therefore to be fought against; the spiritual man could have nothing to do with it. Indeed, so far as he was truly spiritual, he was already freed from and above it. Hebrew religion, in its moments of clearest insight, set itself against this Dualism. The creation, it declared, was not the work of an inferior deity or deities, but both worlds, those of spirit and matter, were called into being by one and the same infinite God. 'In the beginning God created the heaven and the earth.' The Prophet of the Exile was so daring indeed in his proclamation of Monism, that he did not hesitate to declare Jehovah to be the author of evil itself. 'I form the light and create darkness; I make peace and create evil. I, the Lord, do all these things' (Isa 45⁷).

Of course this problem laid its heaviest grasp upon the early Christians in relation to the person and work of Jesus Christ. Starting from the same ground—the essentially evil nature of matter—two opposite schools of thought arose. The one—that of Cerinthus—held that Jesus, as the true son of Joseph and Mary, was, like His fellow-men, tainted with sin, though more righteous than others. The divine Logos, however, was at His baptism joined with Him; and these two continued together in the human body of Jesus, until at His death He cast off His flesh and became pure spirit. Dualism was thus seated in the very person of Christ. The other school, that of the Docetists, denied altogether the fleshly, i.e. evil, nature of Jesus, and maintained that He was human in appearance only, having no real human nature, but a wholly spiritual one. This too established a dualism in Christ, through the failure of the different elements in Him to constitute a unity. Round this problem, thus insoluble—to keep Jesus in touch with humanity, to assert His freedom from the taint of sin, and to proclaim at the same time the essential distinction between human and divine, and the inherent evil of the human—over and about this the currents of thought flowed for centuries hopelessly. Ideas, speculations, fancies, from sources Christian, Jewish, Oriental, classical, magical, all combined in the many and strange systems which came to be known as Gnosticism. Dualism stamped itself deep even upon Christianity, and it came to be taken for granted that there was a necessary opposition between faith and reason, grace and nature, supernatural and natural, the priest and the man, the Church and the world.

Such opinions could not remain speculative only. They involved a denial of that which to St. John was life's most precious possession— the conviction that Jesus was the authentic revelation of the infinite God; and this denial again gave birth to a disbelief in any ultimate standard, which resulted in antinomianism and immorality, and to a disregard of the corporate nature of religion, which then became gross selfishness. One who can see Jesus Christ, and yet not welcome in Him the ideal of God and man, can do so, in St. John's view, only by denying his own moral perceptions. And so the Apostle bursts out into the exclamation which is the central thought of all his Epistles, ' Who is a liar but he that denieth that Jesus is the Christ !' (1 Jn 2 22).

3. Date. If we are correct in assigning these Epistles to St. John, they belong to the last quarter of the 1st cent. The Christian Church had not yet attained that definiteness of organisation which was the work of the 2nd cent. The Churches of different localities were connected by ties of friendship and spiritual communion rather than by the authoritative bonds of organised ecclesiasticism. Yet the tendency to centralisation had begun. A unified system not only of belief, but of conduct, organisation, and discipline was growing up. Importance began to be laid on doctrinal unity. The authority of some prominent man, one of the Twelve (1 Cor 1 12 3 Jn v. 9), or of the other Apostles (1 Cor 7 17 Ro 16 7), would be recognised by a Church or group of Churches. He would often give letters of recommendation to the evangelists or messengers, or to the brethren travelling on private business from one community to another. To receive and entertain these was a duty for every Church. An interesting document of the next century, ' The Teaching of the Twelve Apostles ' (circ. 120 A.D.), lays down rules for the prevention of the abuse of this hospitality. ' With regard to Apostles and prophets, do with them according to the ordinance of the gospel. Let every Apostle who cometh to you be received as the Lord. He shall not overstay one day, though, if need be, the next ; but if he remain three days, he is a false prophet. And let not the Apostle, on departing, take aught save bread till he come to a stopping-place ; and if he ask money, he is a false prophet. And the prophet that speaketh in the spirit you shall not question nor judge, for every offence shall be forgiven, but this offence shall not be forgiven. Not every one that speaketh in the spirit is a prophet, unless he have the ways of the Lord. By their ways, then, shall the false prophet

and the prophet be known. And no prophet who in the spirit appointeth a feast eateth thereof, unless he be a false prophet ; and any prophet who teacheth the truth, if what he teacheth he do not, is a false prophet. . . And whoso saith in the spirit, Give me moneys or other things, you shall not hearken to him ; but if for others in straits he say, Give, let no one judge him.' In the Second and Third Epistles we see these itinerant teachers and brethren on their way from Church to Church (2 Jn vv. 7, 9–12, 3 Jn vv. 5, 6, 8–13). We find there are many ' deceivers ' among them ; while there are in the Churches lordly officials inflated with power, refusing recognition to the Apostle's messengers, and, on the other hand, warm-hearted and influential laymen, who delight to serve the Christian community by entertaining its representatives. We see the little congregation in this place and a congregation of strangers distant in that place finding themselves at one through loyalty to a common Master. We see the knitting of those ties which are soon to become the great fellowship of the Christian Church. Short as these two Epistles are, they furnish a glimpse, clear and vivid, of the life of the Christian community near the close of the 1st cent., and of the means for securing that unity of belief and organisation which in the course of the next century was to develop the great Catholic Church.

4. Contents of the Epistles. In the Second Epistle the author sends his greeting to ' the elect lady ' and her children, dwelling upon the ground of their mutual friendship—their fellowship in ' the truth.' He has met with some of her children (or some members of the Church addressed), and has been glad to find them living as they ought, in the way of God's commandment. This commandment is nothing new, but is as old as religion itself. It is simply love as the law of life. The writer gives some of his characteristic definitions. The commandment is to love, and love means to keep the commandments. Then comes a warning against false teachers. The test by which the true teacher may be known is his recognition of Jesus Christ as historic and authoritative, and his following of the teaching of Christ. ' Erroneous ideas ' on this subject are not to be tolerated, and kindness shown to any one who does not meet this test is mistaken charity and participation in evil. There is much more which the author has in mind to say ; but he will write no more at present, for he hopes to visit his readers soon, to the fulfilment of their mutual satisfaction. A closing salutation is sent to the recipient of the letter by the children of her elect sister.

The **Third Epistle** opens with the same form of greeting as the Second. In this case it is to a certain Gaius ; who is dear to the writer as a member of the Christian community—he is ' in the truth '—and for his own large, generous character. If his body is as vigorous as his soul, the writer will rejoice. For messengers have recently come from the Church to which Gaius belongs, and reported that he is conducting himself as a worthy member of the fellowship of Christ—' walking in the truth '—and especially that he is most hospitable to all, both friends and strangers, who are serving the Cause. Such praiseworthy conduct is in marked contrast with that of an official of the same Church, Diotrephes, who had recently refused to receive messengers with a letter from ' the Elder,' and had threatened excommunication to those who wished to welcome them. The members of the Church are warned not to imitate such evil conduct ; which suggests, by contrast, that of a certain Demetrius, whom the writer warmly commends to them. This man has the threefold witness —of general approval, of membership in ' the truth,' and that of the Apostle himself. As in the preceding letter, further discourse is postponed to the personal meeting which he hopes will shortly take place. The Epistle closes with salutations from the Apostle and his friends to Gaius and his friends.

---

2 JOHN

1. The elder] cp. Intro.

The elect lady] Gk. *eklektē kuriā.* The question who is meant by this designation has given rise to much discussion. The various opinions are as follows : (1) Some regard the second word of the phrase as a proper name, and translate, ' To the lady Electa.' This is not likely ; because if it had been intended, the Greek would probably have been different ; because we should then be obliged to translate Electa as a proper name in v. 13 also, in spite of the unlikelihood that two sisters would have the same name ; and because St. Paul uses the word (Ro 16 13) plainly not as a name, but as a descriptive adjective. (2) The third word is a proper name—' the elect Kyria.' This opinion has in its favour the fact that Kyria was a common name among the Greeks, being the feminine of ' Cyrus.' The analogy of 3 Jn v. 1 is also in favour of an address by name. But this same analogy would lead us to expect a different order of words. Again, if Kyria were the lady addressed, and if she was known and loved by ' all that have known the truth ' (v. 1), it would perhaps be strange that we have no other mention of so prominent a person. This, with other considerations, has led to the opinion (3) that not a person but the Church in general is meant. This seems inconsistent with the Apostle's expectation (v. 12) of visiting her and seeing her face to face. Others hold (4) that it is not the Church universal, but some particular Church, to which the Apostle writes of his approaching visit. Others still find here no proper name and no metaphor, but translate (5), ' To the elect lady ' ; while some who agree in the main with this position point out (6) that there is in the Greek no definite article, and therefore translate, ' To an elect lady.' The weight of evidence seems in favour of the last opinion in one of its forms, (5) or (6) ; though the case is best summed up in the words of

Bp. Westcott : ' No solution of the problem offered by *eklektē kuriā* is satisfactory.'

The truth in this and the following Epistle has come to have almost a technical meaning, implying not only the eternal principle, but also the organisation which embodies it—the Church. Cp. in Acts the use of ' the Way ' : Ac 9 2 19 9, 23 22 4 24 22. **3. With you**] The better text reads ' with us.' Cp. Westcott and Hort. **4. I found of thy children**] This shows that the lady must have had at least three children. Some have seen in it a sad, gentle hint that there were others of her children who did not walk in the truth.

5–8. Note the distinctively Johannine characteristics here: (1) He is giving his hearers a new commandment: cp. Jn 13 34 15 12. (2) The commandment is to love one another: cp. Jn 13 35 1 Jn 3 23. (3) Love means walking according to the commandments of God: cp. Jn 14 15, 21 1 Jn 2 5 5 3. (4) The central fact of Christianity is the recognition of Jesus as the Christ: cp. 1 Jn 2 22 4 2, 3. Note also a peculiarity of the Johannine (a) thought and (b) style: (a) the habit—logical, un-Hebraic —of giving definitions, e.g. ' love,' ' the commandment,' ' antichrist '; (b) the use of a demonstrative pronoun or adverb pointing forward to the definition coming in the next clause; e.g. **This is love, that we walk after His commandments. This is the commandment, That, as ye have heard from the beginning, ye should walk in love.** Cp. Jn 15 8 17 3 1 Jn 2 3 3 16.

6. In it] better to make ' it ' refer not to the nearest noun, ' commandment,' but to ' love.' **7. Are entered into the world**] rather, ' are gone out into the world ': cp. RV; i.e. they were formerly members of the Church, but have apostatised: cp. 1 Jn 2 19. To confess that Jesus Christ is come in the flesh is with St. John the central fact of Christian belief. Not to recognise in Jesus the authentic revelation of the infinite God and the highest ideal of humanity, can, in his opinion, imply only moral depravity.

9. Whosoever, not transgresseth, but 'has erroneous ideas.' No claim of superior knowledge can be allowed which sets aside what Christ taught. **Doctrine in the NT.** is never synonymous with 'dogma,' but means 'teaching.'

10. 'This verse reminds us that the Gospel has its intolerance as well as tolerance' (Bp. Alexander). Ordinary courtesy is not forbidden, but to extend the right hand of fellowship would be to condone and further false doctrine and to share the guilt of disloyalty.

11. Biddeth him God speed] 'The three salutations are eminently characteristic of the general view of life and its aim entertained

by the three races. The Roman, to whom health and strength seemed all in all, said *Salve*, "health." The Greek, whose existence aimed supremely at sweetness and light, said *Chairē*, looking upon "joy" as the highest aim. The Hebrew, who had a revelation, and knew the blessedness of reconciliation with God and conscience, said *Shalon*, "peace"' (Bp. Alexander).

13. The writer may have been staying at this second matron's house. If the Epistle was written to an individual, the transmission of this trivial message from children to an aunt is an interesting note of the simplicity and courtesy of the writer of high station—Elder, Apostle, personal friend of Jesus, whoever he may have been.

---

3 JOHN

1. Gaius] A Gaius or Caius—the common Latin form of the name—is mentioned in four other places in the NT. (Ac 19 29 20 4 Ro 16 23 1 Cor 1 14). The trait of character indicated here is in line with the generous hospitality referred to in the third of these passages. It is hardly likely, however, that one who was sufficiently prominent in the Church of Corinth to be a general host about the year 50, would be still exercising the same function some thirty years later. The identification therefore of the Gaius to whom the Third Epistle is addressed, with St. Paul's host, or with any of the others mentioned, is more than doubtful. **In the truth**] see on 2 Jn v. 1.

2. I wish] better, 'I pray.' This may imply that Gaius had been ill. **3. Thou**] In the Gk., emphatic; in contrast with others, like Diotrephes, of whom this could not be said. **4. Greater**] In the Gk., a double comparative, as in English 'betterer' would be. This may indicate that the author was not a classical Greek scholar, or the usage may be intentional, for emphasis, like the comparative formed on a superlative in Eph 3 8. Cp. also, 'How much more elder art thou than thy looks!' ('Merchant of Venice,' IV, i).

5. Doest .. doest] The second verb is different in the Gk. from the first, and implies more of toilful labour. **And to strangers**] Much stronger in the best text—'and that too to strangers.' 'The duty of entertaining Christians on their travels was of peculiar importance in early times, (1) from the length of time which travelling required, (2) from the poverty of the Christians, (3) from the kind of society they would meet at public inns' (Sinclair). **6. Bring forward**] i.e. with practical assistance—money, provisions, escort, etc.

7. Taking nothing of the Gentiles] The

missionaries whom Gaius had entertained had not been willing to receive assistance from the non-Christians among whom they had been labouring. While they might properly receive from those who had long been Christians, it would be of great importance that there should be not the least suggestion of selling the truth.

9. I wrote, etc.] The Gk. makes the statement more exact by inserting an object of the verb—'I wrote somewhat to the Church.' Of this letter we have no further knowledge. Possibly a part of the offence of Diotrephes had been its suppression; so that this may be a hint to Gaius that the contents of this letter at least should be made known to the Church.

We know no more of Diotrephes. V. 10 may imply that he had the power of excommunication, and therefore was the official head of the Church to which Gaius belonged. It may, however, only imply that he had sufficient social influence to exclude the brethren from the Christian society of the place. His fondness for being preëminent had, at all events, brought him a certain local power.

11. Hath not seen God] a truly Johannine thought: cp. 1 Jn 3 6.

12. Nothing further is known certainly of Demetrius. But as both he and the mobleader of the same name (Ac 19 24) lived apparently in or near Ephesus, there is nothing impossible in the suggestion that the agitator had become a disciple, and that both references, therefore, are to the same person. He may have been the bearer of this Epistle. The thought of a threefold witness—in this case, general report, the truth, and the Apostle himself—is characteristic of St. John: cp. 1 Jn 5 6-10.

13, 14. The conclusion is the same as that of the Second Epistle. Possibly the journey contemplated in both is the same.

JUDE

See General Introduction to 2 Peter and Jude.

Contents.

ı. Vv. 1, 2. Greeting.

ıı. Vv. 3–16. The ungodly men.

(a) 3, 4. 'I was writing a pastoral letter to you when the news that certain ungodly men have crept in obliged me to address you with a special admonition.'

(b) 5–7. 'I would remind you—though as Christians you already know all I can tell you—that the examples of Israel and of the angels prove that it is possible to fall away from grace, and that a punishment—of which the destruction of the cities of the plain is a visible demonstration—assuredly follows.'

(c) 8–13. 'So it is with these men, who now show themselves so insolent, ignorant, and bestial. That which is most dreary, desolate, and disappointing in nature is a type of their hypocrisy, and, like wandering comets, they are destined for darkness at last, from which they shall never again come forth.'

(d) 14–16. 'It is to them that Enoch's prophecy of judgment applies—to these selfish schemers who abuse the gift of speech.'

ııı. Vv. 17–23. 'Remember the mockers of whom the Apostle forewarned you. Here they are—these unspiritual men who make separations among the believers. Do you abide in the one faith, with prayer in the Holy Spirit, trust in the love of God, and hope of Christ's mercy. And in that hope have mercy yourselves as far as may be on those who are falling victims to this plague which is among you.'

ıv. Vv. 24, 25. 'May the only God our Saviour keep you firm, to whom be glory through Christ.'

GREETING WHICH INTRODUCES A PASTORAL LETTER WRITTEN TO MEET AN INROAD OF BLASPHEMOUS FALSE TEACHING. EXHORTATION. DOXOLOGY

1. To them that are sanctified by God the Father, and preserved in Jesus Christ, and called] RV 'to them that are called, beloved in God the Father, and kept for Jesus Christ.'

To them that are sanctified (RV 'called')] One word in the Gk., which, like 'saints' in v. 3, is used as a name for Christians. This greeting, taken together with vv. 20 f., shows that our most holy faith, which was once for all delivered unto the saints, is based upon the doctrine of the Holy Trinity. The Holy Spirit is not expressly named in the greeting, but His

agency is implied. It is He who has kept and will keep the readers for Christ; He makes them live in the Father, who is the source of love, as Christ is of mercy, and as the Holy Spirit Himself is of peace. **In (RV) God]** In Him all men live and move and have their being (Ac 17 28), and in Him the life of Christians is hid with Christ (Col 3 3). God's love embraces in Himself those whom He loves. The expression is difficult, but the thought is deep. Here, as in much else that he says, St. Jude shows a mind near akin to St. Paul's. **2.** As St. Paul in his two Epistles to Timothy, so St. Jude adds **mercy** to the 'grace and peace' of the ordinary apostolic salutation.

3. When I gave .. it was needful] RV 'while I was giving .. I was constrained': see Intro. **Our (RV) common salvation** is the result of Christ's work, which is a fact that nothing can alter, on which all alike, Apostle and disciple, strong and weak, may base their life: **the faith which was once for all (RV) delivered to the saints** is the declaration of this fact, and must be defended, or it may be forgotten or denied. **4.** From this v. to v. 19 this Epistle must be compared with 2 Pet. **The only Lord God, and our Lord Jesus Christ]** RV 'our only Master and Lord, Jesus Christ.' These men did not refuse to believe in God, though they rebelled against Him, and by their lasciviousness abused His grace. In Christ, as Master and Lord, they would not believe. Their unbelief, rebellion, and lasciviousness correspond to the unbelief of Israel, the rebellion of the angels, and the lasciviousness of the cities of the plain (vv. 5–7).

5. Though ye once knew this] RV 'though ye know all things once for all,' i.e. because they are Christians, and have learnt the whole Christian creed (cp. Heb 6 2); or perhaps (a deeper thought) because they have as Christians 'the Spirit in their mind' (cp. Eph 4 17, 23), and 'need not that any man teach them' (1 Jn 2 27).

A curious reading of some MSS is noticed in RM—'Jesus' for the Lord. It recalls Heb 4 8, as the rest of the v. does Heb 3 17-19.

6. First estate] RV 'principality.' **7. Vengeance]** RV 'punishment.' The fire may be called eternal, because the destruction wrought by it remains. The Gk., however, would allow us to take **example** with **of eternal fire**—'as an example of eternal fire, suffering punishment' (RM).

8. Likewise] RV 'Yet,' i.e. in spite of such a warning. **Also these _filthy_ dreamers]** RV 'these also in their dreamings,' i.e. their perverted faith and life is like a dream, sentimental and unpractical. **9.** With this v. cp. 2 Pet 2 11. St. Jude, however, does not say at all the same thing, and refers to a certain apocryphal Jewish book called 'The Assumption of Moses'; cp. vv. 11, 14, and 2 Tim 3 8. Though he refers to such books, he does not necessarily imply that the stories he read in them are true. Even in sermons we sometimes hear references to stories or speeches in Shakespeare or Milton, which we listen to as illustrations, not as being true to fact.

10. As brute beasts] RV 'like the creatures without reason.' **11. Cain**] The Jews spoke of Cain as the first 'freethinker,' and these unbelievers would be his followers in that respect. Holy Scripture, however, tells us that Cain destroyed his brother, and these men were doing the same. The mention of Balaam brings in a new fault—their treacherous, hypocritical greed. **Core**] RV 'Korah': cp. Nu 16. **12. Feasts of charity**] RV 'love feasts': cp. 2 Pet 2 13. **Feeding themselves**] RV 'shepherds that feed themselves': cp. Ezk 34 8. **Trees whose fruit withereth**] RV 'autumn trees'; they are **twice dead,** for the dying year is a symbol of death, and being plucked up by the roots is a symbol of the second death, from which there is no return to life: cp. Rev 21 8. **13. Raging waves**] RV 'wild waves.' **Wandering stars**] i.e. comets, whose return no man sees.

14. Enoch also .. prophesied of these] RV 'To these also Enoch .. prophesied,' i.e. to these as well as to the men to whom the prophecy is addressed in the apocryphal book of Enoch. **Cometh**] RV 'came.'
Ten thousands of his saints] RM 'his holy

myriads': cp. Dt 33 2 Zech 14 5. **15. Convince**] RV 'convict.' **16. Having men's persons in admiration because of advantage**] RV 'shewing respect of persons for the sake of advantage.'

17. Of the apostles] RV 'by the apostles': cp. 2 Pet 3 2 f. **19. Separate themselves**] RV 'make separations,' i.e. they break up the Church into parties and sects : cp. 1 Cor 1 12 f.
Sensual] RM 'natural or animal': cp. v. 10. **Spirit**] RV 'Spirit,' i.e. the Holy Spirit. **22, 23. And of some,** etc.] RV 'and on some have mercy, who are in doubt ; and some save, snatching them out of the fire ; and on some have mercy with fear'; but RM, 'the Greek text in this passage ("and .. fire") is somewhat uncertain.' **The garment spotted by the flesh**] cp. Zech 3 2 f. and Lv 13 47-59. There is contagion in their error like that of a plague. In their efforts to save others they must beware of this.

24. Falling] RV 'stumbling': cp. Ro 11 11 1 Pet 2 8. **Faultless**] RV 'without blemish': cp. Eph 1 4 (RV) Col 1 22 (RV) Heb 9 14 (RV) 1 Pet 1 19. **25. The only wise God our Saviour**] (cp. Ro 16 27 RV). RV 'the only God our Saviour.' God is called Saviour elsewhere in NT. only in 1 Tim 1 1 2 3 4 10 Tit 1 3 2 10 3 4, and Lk 1 47 (from OT.). **Now and ever**] RV 'before all time, and now, and for evermore.'

The word for 'be' is not expressed in the Gk., but may rightly be supplied, though at first sight it does not seem to go well with 'before all time' (RV). 'Is,' however, would be less forcible, for in this blessing St. Jude 'contends for the faith which was once for all delivered to the saints.' Whatever ungodly men may think, he says, 'Let God's proper glory be rendered to Him.'

REVELATION

INTRODUCTION

1. The Title. The title of the book varies in the later MSS, though all ascribe it to John. One MS of the 11th cent. has ' the Revelation of Jesus Christ given to the theologian John.' The word ' divine ' in AV and RV is used in the sense of ' theologian,' ' one who writes on God and the divine nature.' The title in the oldest MSS is ' the Revelation (Gk. *Apocalypsis*) of John.' The writer calls the book ' Apocalypse,' or ' Revelation,' only in 1¹. Elsewhere he speaks of it as ' prophecy ' (cp. 1³ 22⁷, ¹⁰, ¹⁸ᶠ·), and of himself as a ' prophet ' (cp. 10¹¹ 22³,⁹). Yet the form which the prophecy has taken is rightly described by the title ' Apocalypse.'

' Apocalypse ' (i.e. ' uncovering,' ' unveiling ') is a technical term used to denote a particular kind of writing which sprang up among the Jews mainly during the two centuries before Christ. It had its antecedents in such eschatological passages (i.e. passages foretelling the end of the present order of things) as Isa 24–27, Joel, and Zech 12–14. The thoughts and images of such passages as these were dwelt upon and developed in later times into apocalypses. The book of Daniel is an apocalypse. Other writings of an apocalyptic kind are, the ' Apocalypse of Baruch,' the Ethiopic ' Book of Enoch,' the Slavonic ' Book of Enoch,' the ' Ascension of Isaiah,' the ' Book of Jubilees,' the ' Assumption of Moses,' the ' Testaments of the Twelve Patriarchs,' the ' Psalms of Solomon,' the ' Sibylline Oracles.'

Apocalypses were written at times when the righteous suffered oppression by a foreign power. The message of the apocalypse was that deliverance was coming, and that the righteous were to wait for it in patience. In this sense an apocalypse differed from prophecy, which, for the most part, warned unfaithful and wicked Israel of the coming of a ' Day of the Lord,' and called for repentance. Moreover, the apocalypse saw in the evil plight of the righteous a sign of the power of Satan in the world, which made it certain that God would soon intervene to overthrow the evil. Apocalypses were written when men were troubled because the promises of good made by the prophets seemed to be unfulfilled. Accordingly, the apocalyptic writer set out to justify the dealings of God. He ' sketched in outline the history of the world and of mankind, the origin of evil and its course, and the consummation of all things... The righteous

as a nation should yet possess the earth, either in an eternal or in a temporary Messianic kingdom, and the destiny of the righteous individual should be finally determined according to his works. For though amid the world's disorders he might perish untimely, he would not fail to attain through the resurrection the recompense that was his due, in the Messianic kingdom, or in heaven itself ' (R. H. Charles, HDB.).

Apocalypses were characterised by strange and mysterious figures, seen in visions and explained by angels. Sometimes these figures were new, and shaped to represent persons or events of the time. Sometimes they were borrowed or adapted from older apocalypses, or from the OT., or even from remote tradition. It is thought that some of these last traditionary figures may have gradually developed out of creation myths.

Apocalypses were pseudonymous, i.e. they were given forth under the name of some great person of the past, such as Enoch or Moses. It has been suggested that this was caused by the general feeling of despair with which the times were viewed. Prophecy had ceased, and perhaps no living person could hope for a hearing. But the pseudonym may have had a better justification. The figures and traditions which were used may have been so connected with those old great names, that the apocalyptic writer looked upon his writings as proceeding rather from the heroic saint he reverenced than from himself (see HDB. arts. ' Apocalyptic Literature ' and ' Revelation, Book of ').

But although the book we call ' the Revelation of St. John ' is one of a class, it does not follow that it has no deeper value for us than the others of its class. The fact that it has been taken into the Canon of Scripture, while they have been rejected, shows that it outshines them all. In this ' the Revelation ' is like other books of the Bible. The histories, the Psalms, the Wisdom books of the OT., have been distinguished from others which are left outside the Canon. And Lk 1¹ shows that our Gospels were not the only memoirs of the life of Christ which existed in the earliest Christian age. Again, the title of the book is evidence that, as regards other apocalypses, it claims to stand above them all. Other apocalypses, as has been said above, professed to come from some great man of the

past, as Enoch, and we know that only in a
very loose sense could such a profession be
justified. Our Apocalypse does not go back
to some far distant and hardly more than
nominal author. It is not even, as in the
title, the Apocalypse of John, for that title
is of uncertain date. The true title is given
in 1[1]. The book is 'The Revelation of Jesus
Christ.' The book claims to have Jesus
Christ as the author of the revelation it
contains. The place St. John assigns to
himself is that of a prophet who is able to
receive from Christ a revelation and to communicate it to others. Christian believers
may be unable to see how there can be any
true connexion between Enoch and the book
which bears his name. But they do not doubt
the reality of the gift of prophecy, or the fact
that Christ could and did reveal Himself to
His Apostles.

2. Purpose. The Christians in the western
part of Asia Minor, for whom, during the
latter part of the 1st cent., the book was
specially written, had evidently been undergoing great trials. The purity of their
Churches was sullied by teaching which con-
doned immoral and heathen practices, and by
growing worldliness: cp. 3[2, 17 f.] They had
experienced persecution, both from the religious hatred of the Jews (cp. 2[9] 3[9]) and from
the Roman government. Under the Roman
government, religion had become largely identified with Imperialism. Temples had been
dedicated, in various places, to Rome and the
emperor, and the emperor had been called
'Lord and God.' To a Christian, worship
such as this was blasphemy (cp. 13[1, 12, 14 f.]), and,
rather than join in it, many had died: cp.
2[13] 6[9] 13[15] 17[6] 18[20]. The book was written
during a lull in the persecution, which would,
however, be temporary: cp. 2[10] 6[11] 11[7 f.]
Thus the times were dark and threatening for
the Christian Church. Christians were not
only shut out from all the splendour and glory
of life, from the honours and ambitions, from
the riches and festivities which they saw daily
in surrounding heathen society, but which they
must not taste. They were not even allowed
to live their simple lives in their own way.
All the power of the empire was being directed
upon them in inflexible hostility, and if they
would not yield it seemed as if they must be
crushed. Christ had promised His perpetual
Presence, but they felt no lifting of the weight
of the Roman hand. Christ had promised to
come again, and they yearned for His coming
that He might deliver them, but it seemed as
if they yearned in vain. And in this strain
and stress came the seducing advice of 'Jeze-
bels' (cp. 2[20]), who bade them save their lives
and win security by outward conformity to
heathen requirements and heathen ways.

So, to brace them to endurance, came the
message of the Revelation. The things which
were seen, rich and mighty though they
appeared, were temporal, about to pass away;
but the things which were not seen were
eternal and to abide for ever. God was on
His throne, and the future of the world was in
the hand of Christ. The persecuting empire
was inspired and supported by Satan, but God
was stronger than Satan. Satan had already
been conquered, essentially, by the work of
Christ, and his overthrow, and the overthrow
of his instruments, would soon be seen openly
on earth. Rome, the persecuting empire, the
heathen worship and priesthood, and the
wicked of the earth, were all to fall before the
conquering Christ. Last of all would be the
general judgment, and then the incomparable
and eternal bliss of the New Jerusalem. In
these ways Christ would come, and come
quickly.

Therefore let Christians bear manfully their
perils and pains. There was nothing strange
in the demand that was made upon them.
Christ Himself had endured before them. It
was by death that He had won His victory,
and their victory was to be won in the same
manner. Therefore death for Christ was not
defeat but overcoming, and great glory with
Christ would be the reward of those who so
overcame.

3. Interpretation. Our interpretation of
Revelation depends upon what view we take as
to the period of the Church's history to which
the figures and scenes preparatory to the
climax of the book refer. There have been
three chief schools of interpretation. One
school (called the 'Futurist') regards the book
as dealing with the end of the world, and with
events and persons which will immediately
precede that end. The 'Historical' school
sees in the book a summary of the Church's
history from early days until the end. The
'Preterists' look back to the past, and interpret
the book as having to do with the times in
which it originated. A fourth method sees in
the book symbolical representations of good
and evil principles, common to every age, and
to be understood spiritually. According to
this last method, the New Jerusalem, e.g.,
would be explained as representing the blessedness, even in this earthly state, of true believers
whose lives are hid with Christ in God.

The sketch of the purpose of the book will
have shown that the 'Preterist' view is at the
basis of the present Commentary. The probability of this view is supported by the analogy of other apocalypses. And it seems
natural to suppose that the book would be
meant to be intelligible by those to whom it
was addressed, and would have arisen out of
the circumstances of their state. Moreover,

the language and the figures of the book are found to fit the condition of the early days of Christianity, and to yield, on this system, a consistent and unforced interpretation. The advocates of the other systems have differed widely among themselves, e.g. explaining the woman (c. 17) and the beasts, now to mean the Roman Church and the Pope, now the Turks and Mohammed, now the French Revolution and Napoleon. But while this Commentary adapts the Preterist view, it is not denied that, the principles of God's government of the world being always the same, practical use may be made of visions and figures which refer to past circumstances by applying the principles which they reveal to the events with which we ourselves have to do.

The question remains whether those predictions which have to do with the millennium, i.e. the thousand years during which Christ would reign on earth (cp. $20^{4f.}$), were meant to be understood literally or spiritually. The earliest interpretation was literal. Those who accepted the book expected a literal reign of Christ on earth. It was for this reason that many, not believing in a literal millennium, would not accept the book as canonical. It was only the spread of spiritual interpretation, by which the 'thousand years' denoted the present period of the Church, the view advocated by Jerome and Augustine, that enabled the Church as a whole to receive the book.

4. Unity. The structure of Revelation is not what might have been expected. We might have expected a prophecy which passed on in regular course, developing evenly from stage to stage until the end was reached. Instead of this we find progression indeed, but of a rough and uneven nature, and a number of dissimilar and abrupt visions and figures, often not so much flowing one out of another as piled one upon another. During the last twenty years some critics have attempted to account for these features by supposing, either that the book is composed of two or three earlier apocalypses, worked over and fitted together by a Christian editor, or else that the author drew upon various older materials, fragmentary in character, which he has used and incorporated.

The former of these theories seems to be improbable. The book certainly follows out a plan, even though it be roughly. And critics have not agreed in the results of their attempts to dissect the book and to display the joints and lines of union. But it seems more likely that the writer made some use of older materials. It is certain that he made large use of the OT., especially of Ezekiel and Daniel, e.g. cp. 1^{13} $4^{6f.}$ $13^{1f.}$ $18^{9f.}$ It is not, on the face of it, unlikely that some of the figures which cannot be traced to OT. sources may have been derived from lost or traditional materials, eg. chs. 11 f. We can see, indeed, that Jewish, and even heathen, ideas and beliefs were so used by the writer, and were given a Christian meaning : cp. 2^{17} $9^{1f., 14}$ $13^{3, 18}$ $16^{5, 7}$ 17^{16} 20^{2-4}. However, if this theory be true, we should suppose that the writer's use of such materials would be parallel to his use of the OT. He never slavishly copied from the OT., but employed and adapted OT. language and figures as if they were so familiar to him that he naturally expressed himself by their means. Similarly he may have pondered upon existing apocalyptic materials until they had become part of the furniture of his mind. The striking parallels of Rev. with Mt 24 = Mk 13 = Lk 21, 17^{20-37} 12^{35-48}, seem to show the dependence of the author of Rev. upon the discourse of Christ on the Mount of Olives. E.g. cp 1^1, 'which God gave unto Him,' with $Mt 24^{36}$; 'shortly come to pass,' with $Mt 24^{34}$; while chs. 2 f. show that the situation foretold in $Mt 24^{9-14}$ is present. Cp. also 6^{1-8} with $Mt 24^{3-14}$; 6^{12-17} with $Mt 24^{29-31}$; 8^1 with $Mt 24^{31}$; 8^{7-12} with $Mt 24^{29}$ $Lk 21^{25}$.

5. The Visions. Supposing that some part of the theories mentioned in the last section be true, how can it be said that St. John received the contents of the book in a vision ? The answer is threefold. (1) It is not necessary to understand the book as claiming to have been wholly received, as it stands, in one vision at one time. The first vision was received in Patmos. Others may have followed at subsequent times. (2) It is not necessary to suppose that the very words of the book were taken down, as if from dictation, by the writer. The writer claims to be a prophet (cp. 10^{11} $22^{6,9}$), and in the exercise of his gift he may have developed afterwards the facts which were revealed to him by vision. (3) The memory of previously acquired knowledge cannot but have a large share in the apprehension of truths divinely received. Such truths must be rendered into a language previously learned ; and if they are rendered into figures previously assimilated, that is only another form of the same process. And the vision itself may, perhaps, be divinely adapted to the language and figures which are already contained in the mind of the recipient of the vision.

6. Authorship. The writer of the book calls himself 'John': cp. $1^{1,4,9}$ 22^8. No other description or definition is given. To the early Christian Church, 'John' would signify John the Apostle. Besides this, the writer was of account among the Churches of the Roman province of Asia, and was in exile in Patmos. Early Christian tradition asserts both these things of St. John. It would seem, therefore, that the book was written either by the Apostle, or by some one who wished it to be thought the work of the Apostle.

The external evidence for the apostolic authorship is very strong, coming from Fathers in all parts of the Church. The earliest witnesses are Justin Martyr (circ. 140 A.D.), and probably Melito, bishop of Sardis (circ. 170), and Theophilus, bishop of Antioch (circ. 180). Irenæus, bishop of Lyons (circ. 180), who had known Polycarp the disciple of St. John, distinctly says that it was written by the Apostle. The apostolic authorship is also witnessed to by the Muratorian Fragment (circ. 200), Tertullian (circ. 220), Hippolytus, bishop of Ostia (circ. 240), Clement of Alexandria (circ. 200), Origen (circ. 233), and Victorinus, who wrote the earliest extant commentary on Rev., and who was martyred under Diocletian (303).

On the other hand, an Asiatic sect of the end of the 2nd cent., known as the 'Alogi,' rejected all the writings of St. John, and among them Rev. They did not appeal to any knowledge or tradition as to the authorship, but said that they found the book unprofitable, and that there was no Church at Thyatira. Their rejection of St. John's writings was probably caused by their doctrinal views. Caius, a presbyter of Rome (circ. 200), ascribed the book to Cerinthus, a heretical teacher, who lived at Ephesus in the reign of Domitian, in whose system were combined elements derived from Judaism, Christianity, and Oriental speculation, and whose tenets seem to be opposed in the Gospel and Epistles of St. John. Both the Alogi and Caius opposed the Montanists, who appealed to Rev. in support of their views.

Dionysius of Alexandria (circ. 250) denied the apostolic authorship, but wholly on critical grounds, arguing from the language of the book, and from its unlikeness to the Gospel and to the First Epistle. He thought it must have been written by another John, perhaps John Mark, and said that he had heard that there were two tombs at Ephesus, each called that of John. Eusebius of Cæsarea tells us that Papias spoke of a 'John the Presbyter,' distinguishing him from the Apostle, and he hazards a guess that possibly this Presbyter was the John of Revelation.

It will be seen that the evidence of tradition is altogether in favour of the apostolic authorship of the book. Those who rejected it did so on grounds of internal evidence, which we are as competent to judge as they were. The internal evidence, i.e. the matter and style of the book, does at first sight make it difficult to accept the apostolic authorship. The Greek of the other writings of St. John in the NT.

is smooth and free from barbarism, while that of Rev. is the reverse. But this may be accounted for by the character of the books. The Gospel and Epistles were probably written calmly and meditatively, repeating much that the Apostle had been in the habit, for years, of saying to his flock in Greek-speaking Ephesus. But St. John was a Jew, although a Greek dress had come to surround his thought. In Rev. he is borne along by the rapture of his visions, and the Jew that he was by nature and by upbringing might, not unnaturally, have burst through the Greek veneer. Besides this, it is plain that the writer's mind, at the time of writing, was filled with the Jewish Scriptures, and with Jewish apocalypses, and it may have seemed to him fitting that the style of the new Apocalypse he was producing should be in harmony with other apocalypses which both he and his first readers knew. The Hebraic style may have seemed to him to be almost as much a necessity for an apocalypse as the symbolic and figurative material. There would be nothing forced or unreal about this, for Hebrew was native to St. John, while Greek must have been to him always more or less artificial. This consideration will increase in force if, as is quite likely, eighteen or twenty years were spent by St. John in Greek-speaking Ephesus between the writing of Revelation and the writing of the Gospel and Epistles.

As to the language. It is true that characteristic words and thoughts of the Gospel do not appear in Rev. On the other hand, it is only in the Gospel and First Epistle of St. John and in Rev. that Christ is called 'the Word' (cp. Jn 1 1 Rev 19 13). The title 'Lamb,' so frequently applied to Christ in Rev., reminds us of Jn 1 29, 36, though the form of the word is slightly different; the symbol of the Shepherd applied to Christ (cp. Rev 7 17 Jn 10 1, 27 f. 21 16), and the figure of living water, or water of life, are common to Gospel and Rev.; and there are other striking likenesses, such as the words translated 'true' (Rev 3 7, etc.), 'overcome,' 'keep,' 'witness,' 'testimony.'

On the whole, the difference between the style of the Gospel and Rev., though great, can be accounted for, and does not seem to outweigh the very strong and early testimony to the apostolic authorship of Revelation.

The doctrinal teaching of Rev. may be regarded as that of the Fourth Gospel at an earlier stage. Westcott pointed out that 'the main idea of both is the same. Both present a view of a supreme conflict between the powers of good and evil. . . In the Gospel the opposing forces are regarded under abstract forms, as light and darkness, love and hatred: in the Apocalypse under concrete and de finite forms; God, Christ, and the Church warring with the devil, the false prophet, and the beast.' In both books history and vision lead to the victory of Christ, and His Person and work are the ground of triumph. Both books lay stress on personal 'witness.' Both present the abiding of God with man as the issue of Christ's work (Jn 14 23 Rev 3 20 21 3).

But there are important contrasts. In Rev. Christ's coming is outward ; while in the Gospel it is spiritual, and judgment is self-executing. In Rev. the 'future' is historical ; in the Gospel it is present and eternal. In Rev. the conception of God follows the lines of the OT. ; in the Gospel God is revealed as the Father, and specially in connexion with the work of redemption.

The portrayal of Christ in Rev. is in harmony with that in the Gospel. His humanity and His redemptive work are recognised (1 5, 7 5 5, 9 7 14 11 8 12 11 14 3 f. 22 16), followed by His exaltation. Christ is wholly separated from creatures. He possesses divine knowledge (2 2, 9, 13, 19, 23), and divine power (11 15 12 10 17 14 19 16). 'He receives divine honour (5 8 f. 20 6), and is joined with God (3 2 5 13 6 16 f. 7 10 14 4 21 22 22 1, 3), so that with God He is spoken of as one (11 15 20 6 22 3) ; He shares also in part the divine titles (1 7 3 7 19 11).' His pre-existence is recognised in passages (1 17 2 8 3 14 19 13) in which we have an earlier form of the truth unfolded in Jn 1 14 : see Westcott, 'Intro. St. John,' pp. lxxxiv f.

7. Date. The state of the Churches at the time of writing (chs. 2 f.) was such that we should suppose that some considerable time had elapsed since their foundation. They were infected by heresy and by worldliness. The connexion of St. Paul with Ephesus seems to have been a thing of the past, and his martyrdom is, perhaps, referred to in 18 20. Persecution had been violent, Rome was 'drunk with the blood of the saints' (17 6) ; and fiercer persecution was expected (3 10 13 7, 15 f.). All this seems to point to a date after the persecution of Nero, 68 A.D., and before that of Domitian, 95 A.D. Professor Ramsay argues that the character of the persecution referred to in Rev., in which the Christians seem to have suffered, not under accusation of specific crimes, but 'for the Name' (cp. 2 13 6 9 12 11 17 6), demands that Rev. should be dated, not under Nero, but under Domitian. However, 'the testimony of Jesus' does not mean 'witness borne to Him,' but 'the revelation made by Him.' The use probably made of the popular expectation of the return of Nero from hell (13 3 17 8, 11) would imply that some years had elapsed since Nero's death.

If 11 1 f. is to be literally understood, the book would have to be dated before the destruction of Jerusalem, 70 A.D. But the passage, probably, should have, in its present context, another interpretation : see notes.

C. 17 7-12 (see notes) seems clearly to indicate that the book was written in the reign of Vespasian (69–79). With this most of the considerations referred to above agree. We suppose, therefore, that the book was written about 77 A.D.

On the other hand, primitive tradition asserts that the book was written towards the end of the reign of Domitian, circ. 95 A.D. This tradition probably rests on the statement of Irenæus, circ. 180. Either Irenæus was mistaken, or else in c. 17 St. John was making use of an earlier apocalypse, perhaps that which was the original of part of c. 11.

8. Canonicity. More evidence exists for the early use of Rev. than for any other book of the NT. In the section on 'authorship' early authorities have been quoted. Besides these, Papias, a friend of Polycarp the disciple of St. John, bishop of Hierapolis in Phrygia in the early part of the 2nd cent., probably used the book. Andreas, a bishop of the 9th cent., who wrote a commentary on Rev., states that Papias maintained 'the divine inspiration' of Rev., and Eusebius says that Papias expected an earthly reign of Christ for 1,000 years, 'not understanding correctly those matters which (the apostolic narrations) propounded mystically in their representations' (Euseb. III. 39).

The Churches in Lyons and Vienne (177) regarded Rev. as Scripture. Apollonius (circ. 210), who was perhaps a bishop of Ephesus, is said by Eusebius to have made use of testimonies from Revelation.

But while the Western Church always accepted Rev., doubts about it sprung up in the Eastern Church. This attitude was probably influenced by opposition to the advocates of a literal millennium (or reign of Christ on earth for 1,000 years), and to the Montanists, all of whom were warm upholders of the book. Dionysius of Alexandria, who concluded on critical grounds that St. John was not the author of the book, has been referred to above ; Eusebius was inclined to agree with Dionysius. 'The first Eastern commentary belongs to the 5th cent., the next to the 9th. Each begins with a defence against doubts as to the canonicity of the book.'

It was only gradually that it came to be received generally, and, owing to the difficulty of its interpretation, its reception in modern times has not been so unqualified as that of the rest of the NT. Luther was at first strongly averse from the book, though, later, he printed it with Hebrews, James, and Jude in an appendix to his NT. Zwingli regarded it as non-biblical, and Calvin did not comment upon it.

9. Contents.

1 1-3. **Introduction,** describing the contents of the book as an apocalypse, given by God to Jesus Christ, and signified by Him to John through an angel.

1 4-8. **Salutation,** in which the distressed Church is pointed to God.

1 9-20. Account of the vision of the glorified Christ, who bade St. John write to the Seven Churches the things which he saw.

Chs. 2, 3. Letters to the Seven Churches.

2 1-7. The Church in Ephesus is praised for her steadfastness against false teachers and heathen persecutors, but called upon to repent of the coldness of her love. 2 8-11. The Church in Smyrna is about to suffer persecution. Let her endure it boldly, for it cannot hurt her true life. 2 12-17. The Church in Pergamum has been faithful in persecution. But she has been tolerant of immoral teachers, and of this she must repent. 2 18-29. The Church in Thyatira is increasing in faith and endurance, and in love to God and man. But a party in the Church have led unfaithful lives, and they will be punished unless they repent. Let the rest of the Church continue faithful.

3 1-6. The Church in Sardis is sternly rebuked for her lack of earnestness. Unless she repents she must endure Christ's judgment. The few in Sardis who have kept themselves unspotted from the world shall enjoy the companionship of Christ in glory. 3 7-13. The Church in Philadelphia is small and weak. But she has been faithful in persecution, and she is promised many converts, especially from among the Jews. Christ will guard this Church from the time of trial that is coming. 3 14-22. The Church in Laodicea is lukewarm and self-satisfied. Let her see herself as she is, and humbly seek from Christ the supply of her needs. If she does so, He will richly bless her.

Chs. 4, 5. The Lord and Ruler of all.

4 1f. Vision of the Almighty, enthroned in glory and mercy, receiving the worship of heaven.

5 1f. The course of the future, predetermined by God in His secret counsel, is represented by a book, covered with writing and close-sealed, resting on the outstretched hand of the Almighty. It has been committed to Christ to make known and to carry out God's will for the future, and this because of His death.

C. 6. The Seals—Judgment pictured.

6 1-8. The first four seals are opened. The victorious spread of the gospel is shown, and then the coming of war, famine, and pestilence. 6 9-11. The fifth seal. Judgment delayed, and the reason. The martyrs are not forgotten by God. He gives them gladness and rest. But His judgment will fall upon the wicked world that slew them, when it has fulfilled its wickedness by slaying those who are yet to die for Christ. 6 12-17. The sixth seal. Judgment at last on the point of falling, at the day of the wrath of God and of the Lamb.

C. 7. Parenthesis—the Church's safety.

7 1-8. The judgments of 6 3-8, spoken of here as 'the four winds,' will not hurt God's elect, every one of whom is marked out by Him, and their full number known. 7 9-17. Neither does the great persecution hurt God's people, for death brings them to glory.

Chs. 8, 9. The Trumpets—Judgment proclaimed.

8 1,2. The seventh seal shows the trumpets which herald Judgment, given to seven angels.

8 3-5. The prayers of the saints do reach God, and the Judgment about to fall on the earth is His answer.

8 6-13. The first four trumpets announce convulsions of nature, which portend the approach of the Day of Christ.

9 1-12. The fifth trumpet, and the first woe, by the figure of stinging locusts from the abyss, proclaims that the wicked world shall suffer the spiritual torment which follows sin.

9 13-21. The sixth trumpet, and second woe, proclaims ravages upon the idolatrous world by devastating armies.

10 1-11 14. Parenthesis—the Church's safety.

10 1f. After 'seven thunders,' which St. John is bidden to keep secret, he receives a fresh revelation, signified by a little book, which probably consists of c. 12 f.

11 1,2. The Christian Church, represented by the Temple, is to be preserved, although Judaism, represented by the outer part of the Temple buildings, is overthrown. 11 3-14. Yet it will be by death that the people of Christ, now represented by two witnesses, will be preserved. The Roman power will persecute and dishonour them. Yet in this they will be like Christ, and will share His glorified life.

11 15-19. The seventh trumpet, proclaiming the consummation of mercy and judgment.

Chs. 12–14. Parenthesis—the Church's enemies.

12 1-6. Under the figure of a woman opposed by a dragon, it is shown that the great enemy of the Church is Satan, and that it is his power which impels the Roman empire to persecute. He persecuted the Church of God before the birth of Christ, he persecuted Christ, and he persecuted the young Christian Church of Palestine. But Christ and His Church were preserved by God. 12 7-12. By the figure of a war in heaven, the Church is assured that she need not fear Satan, for by the work of Christ

he has been conquered. 12 13-17. The persecution of the Gentile Church is the natural sequence of Satan's failure against the Church in Palestine.

13 1-10. The second great enemy of the Church is the Roman power, signified by a beast. The power and dominion of the beast come from Satan, yet men worship both. For a limited time the beast is allowed by God to triumph over the Church. 13 11-18. The third enemy of the Church, the government of the Province of Asia, both civil and religious, is figured by a second beast, who causes all who will not join in idolatrous worship to be put to death.

C. 14. The enemies of the Church have been shown in the true evil character which underlay the glory and power of the empire. Now the Church is bid to contrast with the false glory of the empire the true glory of Christ and His people in heaven (vv. 1-5), to hearken to the good news of the approaching manifestation of God, and of the fall of wicked Rome (vv. 6-8), and to beware lest any fail of steadfastness, and fall away to the beast, for great will be the misery of such, while those who die in Christ are blessed (vv. 9-13). Christ will gather in His own (vv. 14-16), but the wicked will perish under the wrath of God (vv. 17-20).

Chs. 15, 16. **The Bowls—Judgment poured out.**

15 1-5. The wrath of God is about to be manifested. During a pause before it is launched, is heard the triumphant praise of those who have come victorious from the beast.

15 6-8. Then the seven angels file forth from the heavenly Temple and receive seven bowls, full of the wrath of God, which they are to pour out on the earth.

16 1-9. The first four bowls. Convulsions of nature afflict the ungodly, preliminary to the overthrow of the enemies of Christ.

16 10,11. The fifth bowl. The idolatrous people, instead of repenting at God's judgments, become full of blasphemous rebellion.

16 12-16. The sixth bowl. The evil influence of the dragon and of the two beasts stirs up the rulers of the world to gather to battle against Christ.

16 17-21. The seventh bowl. The end of the preparatory judgments is reached. All earthly powers are shaken, as the wrath of God is manifested to overwhelm the enemies of Christ, and, first among them, the city of Rome (Babylon).

Chs. 17, 18. **The Overthrow of Rome.**

17 1f. The city of Rome, pictured as a harlot, magnificently attired, enthroned upon the beast, and drunken with the blood of the martyrs, will be destroyed and burnt by the kings of the earth and by the beast.

18 1-3. The Fall of Rome is announced.

18 4-8. God's people are warned to quit her.

18 9-19. The dirge over Babylon of those who loved her. 18 20. The exultation of those she has persecuted. 18 21-24. Renewed prediction of her Fall.

Chs. 19, 20. **The overthrow of the Empire and its Asian idolatry, and of Satan, and the last Judgment of the wicked.**

19 1-10. Heaven glorifies God because of the overthrow of wicked Rome (vv. 1-4), and because the marriage of the Lamb is come (vv. 5-10). 19 11-16. But before the marriage Christ comes forth to triumph over His remaining enemies. 19 17,18. The completeness of Christ's coming victory signified by a cry to the vultures to gather to the prey.

19 19-21. All the power of the Roman empire is concentrated against Christ, and the Pagan empire and its religion are overthrown.

20 1-3. The devil remains, but for a period of rest and happiness he will be prevented from inspiring a general attack upon Christianity. 20 4-6. This time of earthly rest was not for the Christians of St. John's day. Yet for them would be triumph and happiness with Christ after death, while the wicked were kept for the Last Judgment. 20 7-10. Once more, in the future, Satan's power will break forth in a final attack upon the Church. For the last time God will overthrow these enemies, and then the power of Satan will perish for ever. 20 11-15. Then will come the last Judgment of the wicked, after which there will be no more death.

21 1-22 5. **The Eternal Bliss of Heaven.**

21 1-8. St. John sees, as if from a distance, the heavenly home of the Redeemed coming down upon the new earth, and hears a description of its blessedness. 21 9-27. He is brought near, by one of the seven angels, to the 'New Jerusalem,' the Bride, so that he can view her in her security and beauty and holiness as the resting-place of God's glory and the home of the Church.

22 1-5. Finally he is shown the inner life of the heavenly Jerusalem.

22 6-21. **Closing Section.**

22 6-9. The angel affirms the truth of the visions. 22 10-15. The prophecy now completed is to be used. The time is short. Blessed are they who shall share in the glories revealed.

22 16,17. Christ declares that the Revelation has been sent by Him for the use of the Church. The Spirit in the Church, hearing Christ's voice, calls for His Advent.

22 18,19. St. John warns those who hear the book read in the services of the Church that it is not to be falsified. 22 20. Christ repeats the promise of His coming, and St. John prays for it.

22 21. Benedictory prayer

CHAPTER 1

THE VISION OF THE SON OF MAN

St. John addresses ' the seven churches which are in Asia,' telling them of a vision of Christ, who bade him write in a book what he saw and send it to them.

1–3. Introduction, describing the book as an 'apocalypse,' the Gk. word which signifies ' unveiling' or ' revelation.' This does not mean here the unveiling of Christ at His Coming, as in 1 Cor 1⁷ 2 Th 1⁷ 1 Pet 1⁷,¹³ 4¹³, but the Revelation given by Christ. The book is, at the same time, a prophecy (cp. v. 3), because divinely communicated, and because of its exhortations which must be kept. It is, also, in the form of a letter : cp. 1⁴ 22²¹. Notice in this section the threefold arrangement of ideas, so common in the book.

1. Of] i.e. Christ is the real author.

Shortly] the events were in the near future.

2. Record] RV ' witness.' **Word of God**] i.e. the revelation which God gave to Jesus Christ (v. 1). **Testimony of Jesus**] i.e. the witness which Jesus bore, the word of God which Jesus communicated : cp. 6⁹ 12¹⁷ 19¹⁰.

And of all] RV ' even of all.' **3. Readeth**] i.e. aloud, before the congregation. **Prophecy**] The writer is a prophet, i.e. his utterances proceed from the illumination of the Holy Spirit : cp. 22⁷,¹⁰ Ac 13¹ 1 Cor 12²⁸ 13² 14³ Eph 4¹¹. An Apostle could be a prophet : cp. Eph 3³ᶠ.

4–8. Salutation, which sounds the keynote of the book, by proclaiming to the distressed Church the eternal power of God, the omnipresent and penetrating energy of the Spirit, and the redeeming Lordship of Christ, who will return to overcome His enemies.

4. John] We know of no John, except the Apostle, who had authority to address seven Churches. **Seven**] the number which signifies completeness. These seven Churches stand also for the whole Church of Christ. **Asia**] i.e. the Roman province of that name, which was the western part of what is now called Asia Minor. It included Mysia, Lydia, Caria, part of Phrygia, and islands off the coast.

Which is, etc.] i.e. the Eternal : cp. Ex 3¹⁴.

Seven Spirits] i.e. the Holy Spirit in His complete working : cp. 4⁵ 5⁶. **5. Witness**] cp. v. 2, 3¹⁴ Ps 89³⁷ Jn 18³⁷. **First begotten**] RV ' firstborn,' i.e. the first of the dead to enter life : cp. Col 1¹⁸ Ps 89²⁷. **Washed**] RV ' loosed,' i.e. as the Redeemer of slaves. **In his own**] RV ' by his.' **6. Kings**] RV ' to be a kingdom,' i.e. a society under His kingship : cp. Ex 19⁶ 1 Pet 2⁹. **Priests**] to offer spiritual sacrifices : cp. Heb 13¹⁵ᶠ· 1 Pet 2⁵. **Unto God,** etc.] i.e. belonging to God and engaged in His service. RV ' unto his God and Father'; spoken of Christ in His humanity : cp. 3² (RV) ¹²

Mt 27⁴⁶ Jn 20¹⁷. For doxologies addressed to Christ, cp. Ro 16²⁷ 2 Tim 4¹⁸ Heb 13²¹ 1 Pet 4¹¹.

7. Behold, etc.] from Dan 7¹³. **Cometh**] i.e. at the Judgment : cp. Mt 24³⁰ 26⁶⁴. **Every eye,** etc.] from Zech 12¹⁰ : cp. Jn 19³⁷. **Kindreds,** etc.] RV ' the tribes of the earth': contrasted with the ' saints,' the people of Christ.

Wail because of] RV ' mourn over.'

8. Alpha and Omega] RV ' the Alpha and the Omega'; i.e. the Eternal One: cp. 21⁶ Isa 44⁶. In 22¹³ the title is applied to Christ. Alpha and Omega are the first and last letters of the Gk. alphabet. **Lord**] RV ' Lord God.' **The Almighty**] i.e. He who rules over all. The Gk. word is the LXX rendering of ' God of hosts,' i.e. God of the universe : cp. Am 4¹³.

9–20. The vision John received of Christ in glory. Christ is described in language which is drawn from the OT., especially from Daniel, and which is to be understood figuratively of the majesty and power of Christ. He is revealed as present, though unseen by men, in the midst of the Churches. His triumph after suffering and His present care are to nerve them to endure their tribulation victoriously.

9. Companion] RV ' partaker with you.'

Tribulation, etc.] RV ' the tribulation and kingdom and patience.' **Patience**] i.e. brave endurance. **Of Jesus Christ**] RV ' which are in Jesus.' Tribulation, kingdom, and patience are all found in union with Christ, and as such are to St. John the characteristic elements of the life of the Church. **Patmos**] a small, bare volcanic island in the Ægean Sea, about 15 m. from Ephesus. **For the word of God,** etc.] i.e. probably he had been banished in punishment for his Christian preaching. ' It was the common practice to send exiles to the most rocky and desolate islands.' **10. Spirit**] RV ' Spirit.' John was in a prophetic trance : cp. Ac 10¹⁰ᶠ· 2 Cor 12². **Lord's day**] the earliest known use of the term for ' Sunday ' : cp. Ac 20⁷ 1 Cor 16².

As of a trumpet] Archbp. Benson pointed out (' The Apocalypse ') that this voice is that of the herald angel who called St. John to his work. This has been obscured by the false reading in v. 11. The angel's trumpet-voice is recorded again in 4¹. The angel directs St. John by his voice from afar in the first part of Rev. (cp. 10⁴,⁸ 11¹ 14¹³), but after 17¹ accompanies him. ' As an angel of the Presence (cp. 8² 15¹,⁵ᶠ·), he is called Christ's angel and God's angel (cp. 1¹ 22⁶), and his voice has been " out of heaven." ' This angel speaks in 19⁹ 21⁵ᵇ,⁹, is referred to in 21¹⁵ 22¹, and speaks again in 22⁶,¹⁰.

Other voices to be noted are, the ' great voice ' of the Almighty (11¹² 16¹⁷ 21³,⁵ᶠ·); the voice of Christ, ' as the voice of many waters ' (vv. 15, 17 f., 14² 16¹⁵ 19⁶ 22⁷,¹²⁻¹⁵,¹⁶,²⁰);

the voice of the living creatures, 'as a voice of thunder' (6^1 19^6); the voice of the elders, 'as the voice of harpers harping with their harps' (5^8 14^2); and the voice of the saints before God's throne, 'as it were the voice of a great multitude' ($7^{9f.}$ $19^{1,6}$).

11. I . . last: and] RV omits. **12. Candlesticks**] see on v. 20. **13. The Son**] RV 'a son': see on 14^{14}, Dan 7^{13}. **To the foot**] i.e. of kingly or priestly dignity. **Girdle**] cp. Dan 10^5. **14. White**] denoting the purity and majesty of God: cp. Dan 7^9. **15. Fine**] RV 'burnished': cp. Ezk 1^7 Dan 10^6. **Waters**] cp. Ezk 1^{24}. **16. Stars**] see on v. 20. **Sword**] A comparison with Isa 11^4 2Th 2^8 shows that this probably signifies that Christ has but to 'speak the word' and His enemies will be destroyed. He has absolute authority.

18. I am he that, etc.] RV 'and the Living one; and I was dead'; 'Living,' i.e. eternally, both before and after the Incarnation: cp. Jn $1^{1,4}$, and OT. phrase 'living God.' The persecuted need not fear death, for Christ had died. **Hell and of death**] RV 'death and of Hades.' 'Hades' = OT. 'Sheol,' the world of the dead, not the place of punishment: cp. Isa 14^9 (RM) 38^{10} (RM) Mt 16^{18}. He has the 'keys' because the time and manner of the death of each person are under His control. To think of this would give heart to the persecuted.

19. Hast seen] RV 'sawest,' i.e. this vision. **Which are**] i.e. the state of the Churches. **Be**] RV 'come to pass.' **20. The mystery**] i.e. concerning the mystery; 'mystery' = a hidden thing now revealed. **Stars**] i.e. lights in heaven.

Candlesticks] lights on earth. The Churches are represented by candlesticks (or 'lampstands'), because they are made to shed the light of truth and goodness derived from Christ, the light of the world, upon the world around them. The flame is supported by the oil of the Holy Spirit: cp. Ex 25^{31} Zech 4^2 Mt $5^{14f.}$

Angels] Each letter is addressed to the 'angel,' and the 'angel' is praised or blamed for the state of the Church. Many have thought 'angel' here = 'bishop,' but such a meaning is unknown elsewhere. Its 'angel' is to each 'church' as the 'star' is to the 'lamp,' i.e. its heavenly counterpart. The angel, therefore, is a heavenly existence, corresponding to the Church on earth, but nearer to God. We need not suppose that each Church literally has such a being in connexion with it. St. John was writing in symbols, and using symbols which he found ready made. Translated from symbolic language into prose, 'angel' here probably means 'that perfect ideal which the Church imperfectly fulfils.'

CHAPTER 2

THE EPISTLES TO THE SEVEN CHURCHES (2^1–3^{22})

Since 'seven' is the perfect number, the 'seven churches' represent all the Churches of the province of Asia. At the same time, the special circumstances of each Church are faithfully pictured in each epistle. Ramsay points out that St. John alludes, as well, to the special circumstances of each city. He suggests that the Churches are mentioned in the order in which a messenger carrying letters would travel. The letters, however, were not to be sent separately to the Churches. The book was to be taken as a whole. St. John adopted the familiar form of an 'apocalypse' through which to deliver his message, and added to that the equally familiar form of 'letters.'

In every epistle Christ is described under an aspect, mostly drawn from $1^{12f.}$, suited to the special needs of the Church addressed. Each Church is then assured that Christ knows it, whether for praise or blame, but always with love, and receives the exhortation suited to it, followed by a special promise with a special token.

The main purpose of the epistles is to give courage to the Church to pass victoriously through its trials. For this reason it is told of Christ's presence and help, and bid to look forward to the glory that Christ will soon give to those who overcome. The chief trials of the Church consist in persecution from heathen and Jews, and in corrupt teaching within. The false teaching is of the character denounced in 2 Pet. and Jude. It seems to have desired that Christians should be permitted to take part in the clubs and organisations of the heathen society around them, and in their festivals, permeated though they were with idolatrous observances.

1–7. To the Church in Ephesus Christ speaks as He who is present with the Churches (v. 1). The Church is praised for its work for Christ, its endurance of suffering, and its faithfulness to the truth (vv. 2, 3), yet it is blamed, not because of its deeds, but because the love which used to animate them has cooled (v. 4). Even for this fault repentance is necessary; a Church without love must perish (v. 5). To those members of the Church who pass victoriously through their trials, eternal life with God is promised (v. 7).

1. Ephesus] the metropolis and great commercial centre of the province of Asia, famous for a temple to Diana. After St. Paul's work in Asia was ended, Timothy was stationed there for a time (cp. 1 Tim 1^3), with general authority, till 2 Tim 4^9. Soon afterwards became the home of St. John. **After Rom**

times, the harbour of Ephesus, 3 m. from the sea, silted up, and the place decayed. Except for a small Turkish village, only ruins remain.

2. Apostles] i.e. travelling envoys representative of Christ, in a sense not limited to the twelve : see on Ro 16⁷. The title was claimed by some to whom it was not due. **Hast . . liars**] RV 'didst find them false' : cp. 2 Cor 11³,¹³ᶠ.

4. First] i.e. at the beginning of their Christian course. **5. First works**] i.e. such as those inspired by their early love. **I will come . . quickly**] RV 'I come to thee.' **Remove thy candlestick**] If the flame of Christian love dies down, the candlestick will be put away as useless, i.e. the organised Church will come to an end : cp. Jn 15⁶. The Church in Ephesus flourished for centuries, so we may presume that it did repent.

6. Nicolaitanes] Mentioned again in the letter to Pergamum, in connexion with Balaam (vv. 14ᶠ.), and probably referred to in the letter to Thyatira (vv. 20ᶠ.). It has been supposed, from the mention of Balaam, that they were Antinomians, i.e. men who held that Christians were not bound by the moral law, and that sin was no sin for those who had faith : cp. 1 Cor 6¹³ᶠ. 8⁹ᶠ. 10²⁸ Gal 5¹³ 2 Pet 2¹ᶠ·¹⁴ᶠ. Jude vv. 4, 11 f. It has also been suggested that they may have claimed the authority of the deacon Nicolas (cp. Ac 6⁵) ; but perhaps St. John used the term 'Nicolaitan' as a Greek word representing the Hebrew 'Balaam.' Ramsay thinks that the 'Nicolaitans' were some who attempted to effect a compromise with the established usages of Græco-Roman society, permeated with luxury and tainted with idolatry though these were, and that they also wished to comply with the State's demand, and show their loyalty by burning incense before the emperor's statue. St. John saw, as St. Paul did in 1 Cor., that the Church must conquer the imperial idolatry, or be itself destroyed (Ramsay, 'Letters to the Seven Churches,' pp. 299 f.). By 115 A.D. Ignatius wrote to the Ephesians, 'in your midst no heresy has its dwelling.'

7. He that hath, etc.] cp. Christ's words, Mt 11¹⁵, etc. **The Spirit**] John was under the influence of the Spirit : cp. 1¹⁰. **Overcometh**] i.e. continuously. The Christian life is a continual fight against sin and tribulation, and this book's purpose is to give heart to overcome.

To eat of, etc.] i.e. he shall have eternal life : cp. 22² Gn 2⁹. **Paradise**] a Persian word for 'garden,' used in LXX for the garden of Eden. The later Jews employed the word to denote various ideas of heavenly blessedness : cp. Lk 23⁴³ 2 Cor 12⁴. Here it is equivalent to the New Jerusalem of chs. 21 f.

8–11. To the Church in Smyrna Christ speaks as the Eternal, who tasted death, and whose death ended in life (v. 8). There is no blame for this Church. It is praised for its endurance of tribulation and poverty, and for its spiritual condition (v. 9). More persecution is to be expected, which may be borne without fear. After death for Christ, nothing but life will follow (vv. 10 f.).

8. Smyrna] about 50 m. N. of Ephesus, was a wealthy port and the most splendid city in the province of Asia. In 26 A.D. a temple was founded there in honour of Tiberius. Polycarp, its bishop, was martyred 155 A.D., when he had served Christ 86 years. Smyrna was the last stronghold of Christianity in Asia Minor, and even now is called by the Turks 'Infidel Smyrna' (HDB.). **Is alive**] RV 'lived again.' **9. Works, and**] RV omits. **Rich**] i.e. spiritually : cp. Mt 6¹⁹ Jas 2⁵. **Blasphemy**] RM 'calumny,' i.e. which thou sufferest.

Say they are Jews] i.e. they are Jews in name only : cp. 3⁹ Ro 2²⁹. The Apostle uses the name as an honourable one, equivalent to 'those who are not Gentiles, but are the people of God.' By their enmity to God's will and word, these men, Jews by race, had forfeited their position of privilege, and had become as bad as Gentiles. It is implied that it is the Christian Church in Smyrna which has succeeded to the privilege : cp. Ro 2²⁸ᶠ. Jews joined in the martyrdom of Polycarp. **Synagogue**] i.e. congregation : cp. Nu 20⁴ 31¹⁶. **Of Satan**] i.e. they called themselves God's, but were serving Satan.

10. Devil] Persecution is prompted by the devil : cp. 12¹⁷ 13⁴ 1 Pet 5⁸ᶠ. **Prison**] i.e. as a prelude to execution. **Tried**] cp. Jas 1³,¹² 1 Pet 1⁷ 4¹². **Ten days**] not lit.; the persecution would be short and sharp. **Faithful**] Ramsay suggests that here, as in each letter, St. John refers to the local history of the city. Smyrna was honoured for its faithfulness to Rome, Cicero calling it 'the most faithful of our allies.' It was also proud of its 'Crown,' which was 'the garland of splendid buildings encircling the rounded hill Pagos.' **A crown**] RV 'the crown,' i.e. eternal life will crown your victorious death. **11. Second death**] a Jewish phrase for the final condemnation of sinners : cp. 20⁶,¹⁴ 21⁸ Mt 10²⁸.

12–17. To the Church in Pergamum Christ speaks as He who destroys the wicked (v. 12). The Church is praised for faithfulness during a time when Christians might be called upon to deny Christ and worship the emperor. One of the Church, at least, had confessed Christ at the cost of his life (v. 13). Yet even this Church was corrupted by immoral teaching (vv. 14 f.), and must repent, for a corrupt Church will suffer Christ's judgment (v. 16). Those who live victoriouly are promised heavenly food, and knowledge of Christ in their secret souls (v. 17).

12. Pergamos] RV 'Pergamum,' about 50

m. N. of Smyrna. Under the Roman empire it was resorted to by invalids, who attended for healing at the temple of Æsculapius. Until the 2nd cent. A.D. it was regarded as the capital of the province of Asia. Under Augustus a temple was built at Pergamum, probably 29 B.C., and dedicated to Rome and Augustus, and Pergamum became the centre of the imperial worship and 'Satan's throne.' ' It has continued to be a place of some consequence, preserving the ancient name Bergama, down to the present day' (HDB.).

Sword] As the centre of the worship of the emperor, Pergamum must have been the seat of authority, and the sword was the symbol of the highest order of authority. The message is that in the city in which the Roman proconsul has the power of life and death, Christ has power and authority greater than his (Ramsay).

13. Satan] i.e. the official authority opposing the Church. **Seat**] RV 'throne,' in the temple at Pergamum. **Name**] Christians had to conform to the State religion or suffer death. **Even in those**, etc.] RV 'even in the days of Antipas my witness, my faithful one.' **14.** Cp. Nu 25$^{1f.}$ 31^{16} Ac 15^{28} 1 Cor 8$^{9f.}$ 10 Jude v. 11. **14, 15. Them**] RV 'some.' **Doctrine**] RV 'teaching.' **15. Nicolaitanes**] RV 'Nicolaitans in like manner,' i.e. the Nicolaitans held the teaching of Balaam : see on 2^6. **Which thing I hate**] RV omits. **16. Repent**] RV 'Repent therefore,' i.e. by casting out the Nicolaitans.

17. To eat] RV omits. **Hidden manna**] cp. Ex 16^{33} Heb 9^4. Jewish tradition held that the ark and its contents, including the pot of manna, were hidden by Jeremiah, and that they would be restored when the Messiah came. This tradition is used here to symbolise the bread of life: cp. Jn 6$^{31f.}$

White stone] Ramsay explains this as a 'tessera,' i.e. a little cube of stone, ivory, or other substance, with words or symbols engraved on one or more faces. Here the ' stone' is simply to bear the name, and the stress of the passage is on the name. It is a stone, imperishable, because that which is to last is put on imperishable material ; and it is white, as the fortunate colour.

New name] A new name implied entrance on a new life: cp. the new name given in baptism. So by this ' new name ' is meant that the victorious Christian will enter upon a new and higher stage of existence. But the name is also the secret name of God (cp. 3^{12}), and it was anciently supposed that the knowledge of the name of God gave power over spirits. So the Christian, triumphant over persecution, will enter into life, and have new knowledge of God and new power.

18–29. To the Church in Thyatira Christ

speaks in His majesty as Son of God (v. 18). The Church is praised for its increase in love and faith and the service of others, and its patience under trials (v. 19). Yet it harbours corrupt teaching (v. 20), and those who follow such teaching without repentance must suffer under Christ's chastening hand. Every member of the Church must be judged by what he himself does (vv. 21f.). But he who wins the victory over the temptations of Christ, will share in Christ's glorious reign in light (vv. 24f.).

18. Thyatira] a busy commercial city in the northern part of Lydia, between Pergamum and Sardis. **Fine**] RV ' burnished.'

19. Charity] RV 'love.' **Service**] RV 'ministry,' i.e. towards men : cp. Mk 10$^{43f.}$ **And thy works; and,** etc.] RV ' and that thy last works are more than the first,' i.e. the Church was even more faithful and earnest than at the time when it was founded : see on v. 4f. **20. Notwithstanding**, etc.] RV 'But I have this against thee, that.'

Jezebel] probably so called because she led astray Christians, as the wife of Ahab had led astray Israel. She seems to have been a prophetess, who taught that it was possible to be a Christian while remaining in ordinary pagan society and belonging to the social clubs which were characteristic of pagan life. These were idolatrous and luxurious, celebrating in a corporate manner the pagan religion and joining in common banquets carried out with revelry. This 'Jezebel' sanctioned. The minority of the Church who were against this teaching, yet tolerated ' Jezebel ' (' sufferest '): see on 2^6. (See HDB.) **To teach,** etc.] RV ' and she teacheth and seduceth.'

22. Bed] i.e. the couch of the feasts, now changed into a couch of tribulation. **Adultery**] i.e. unfaithfulness to God. **23. Death**] RM ' pestilence.' **Reins**, etc.] i.e. the inner thoughts and desires : cp. Ps 7^9 Jer 17^{10}.

24. And unto the rest] RV ' to the rest.' **Doctrine**] RV ' teaching.' **Depths**] RV ' deep things.' **Speak**] RV ' say'; i.e. these misguided Christians called their philosophical arguments ' deep things of God ' (cp. 1 Cor 2^{10}), but they were really ' deep things of Satan ' : cp. 2^9. **None other burden**] probably a reference to the letter from Jerusalem : cp. Ac 15^{28}. The directions of that letter would guide them in the difficulties as to their relations with pagan society.

25. That which ye have] i.e. the faithfulness, etc.: cp. v. 19. **Hold fast**] because the Deliverer is near.

26. Power] RV ' authority': cp. Ps 2$^{8f.}$ Christ's disciples will share in His kingdom: cp. 20$^{4, 6}$ 22^5. **27. Rule**, etc.] quotation from Ps 2^9. A figurative description of the victory of the Messiah in which His people would share. At this time 'Rome was the only Power on earth that exercised authority over the nations, and ruled them with a rod of iron, and smashed them like potsherds' (Ramsay). But the Christian, victorious through death, will be stronger than Rome and conquer Rome. **Received**] cp. Jn 10 18. **28. Morning star**] i.e. the glory of Christ, who brings in the perfect day: cp. 1 16,20 22 16 Nu 24 17 2 Pet 1 19.

CHAPTER 3

THE EPISTLES TO THE SEVEN CHURCHES
(concluded)

1–6. To the Church in Sardis Christ speaks as He who gives the spirit and looks for spiritual life. There is no praise for this Church. Its life is without spiritual reality (v. 1). Yet, even now, awakening is within its power. But if it continue to sleep, Christ will come in sudden judgment (vv. 2 f.). A few individuals have remained faithful. To them, and to all such, Christ promises gladness and life, and that He will acknowledge them as His (vv. 3 f.).

1. Sardis] about 35 m. S. of Thyatira. When there was a kingdom of Lydia, before 549 B.C., Sardis was its capital. It was still an important city at the time of the Apocalypse, but is now only a ruin. **Spirits**] cp. 1 4 Ro 8 9. **Name**] i.e. its Christianity was nominal. **2. Not found thy works perfect**] RV 'found no works of thine fulfilled,' i.e. up to the proper standard. **3. Received**] i.e. the gospel: cp. 1 Th 2 13. **Heard**] RV 'didst hear'; Christ appeals to the memory of their conversion: cp. Gal 3 1 f. **As a thief**] cp. 16 15 Mt 24 43 f. **4. Names**] i.e. persons: cp. Ac 1 15. **Have not defiled**] RV 'did not defile,' i.e. at some crisis of persecution, when most yielded: cp. 7 14. **Walk**] i.e. spend their life. **White**] the colour of victory: cp. vv. 5, 18, 6 11 7 9. **5. The same shall be clothed**] RV 'shall thus be arrayed'; 'thus' = 'as I am': cp. 1 13 f. **Book of life**] i.e. the number of Christ's people: cp. 13 8 17 8 20 12,15 Ex 32 32 Lk 10 20 Phil 4 3.

7–13. To the Church in Philadelphia Christ speaks as He by whom alone comes entrance into the Church, the spiritual house of God (v. 7). The Church is praised for its faithfulness in persecution. Its own power is small, but Christ is with it, and He is giving it an opportunity for the conversion of some of those Jews who have aided the persecutors (vv. 8 f.). The Church shall be brought safely out of the coming trial (v. 10). Christ will quickly come, therefore let the Church endure a little longer (v. 11). Those who 'overcome' shall have an honourable place in the heavenly sanctuary and a joyful knowledge of Christ (v. 12).

7. Philadelphia] 28 m. SE. from Sardis, a rather rich and powerful city. 'It had the most glorious history of all the cities of Asia Minor in the long struggles against the Turks' (Ramsay). It is still to a large extent Christian. **Key of David**] a reference to Isa 22 22. As authority over the royal house was conferred upon Eliakim, so Christ has authority in the Church, above all earthly ministers, and it is really He who admits or excludes, who gives the 'open door' of vv. 8 f.: cp. Jn 10 9 14 6. **8. An open door**] i.e. the Church shall win converts: cp. 1 Cor 16 9 2 Cor 2 12 Col 4 3, perhaps from the persecuting Jews (cp. v. 9), and perhaps also from the Phrygian land on the road to which Philadelphia lay. **Hast not denied**] RV 'didst not deny,' i.e. in a time of persecution. **9. I will make**] RV 'I give.' **Synagogue**] see on 2 9. Evidently, here, Jews proud of their national privileges, and powerful in numbers and in wealth. No doubt they despised the Jewish Christians as traitors. **Loved thee**] cp. Isa 43 4. **10. The word,** etc.] i.e. the message which sets forth 'patience,' i.e. steadfast endurance, as part of Christ's life and of the life of His people. **Temptation**] RV 'trial': a general persecution is foretold, but the Philadelphian Church will be so kept that, though they may suffer in outward matters, their life in Christ will be unharmed: cp. Lk 21 18 f. (RV). **12. A pillar**] i.e. he shall have a permanent place in the 'temple,' i.e. the Church, here the glorified Church: cp. 1 K 7 21 Gal 2 9 Eph 2 20 f. 1 Pet 2 5. **Temple**] cp. 1 Cor 3 16 f. **Named,** etc.] i.e. he shall receive the full knowledge and blessing of belonging to God, to the kingdom of Glory and to Christ: cp. 2 17 19 12-16.

New name] Ramsay points out that about 17 A.D. Philadelphia had taken the name 'Neokaisareia,' that is, city of young Cæsar, and disused its own. No doubt at the same time a shrine of the young Cæsar, with priest and ritual, was established. Thus it wrote on itself the name of this imperial god, and called itself the city of the imperial god. With this St. John contrasts what Christ will do for His own. There will be a name written on the victorious Christian, which will be the name of God and the name of the 'Church,' and the new name of Christ: see on 2 17.

14–22. To the Church in Laodicea Christ speaks as He through whom alone comes true life with its riches and blessings (v. 14). The Church is blamed for lukewarmness, self-satisfaction and worldliness (vv. 15 f.). Instead of trusting in itself let it turn to Christ for the true riches (v. 18). He chastens the Church because He loves it. What it needs is zeal (v. 19). Even in this proud Church Christ humbly knocks at the door of each heart, and is ready to enter with blessing (v. 20). Those who share Christ's victory over the world shall share Christ's honour (v. 21).

14. Laodicea] SE. of Philadelphia and E. of Ephesus. Its site is now utterly deserted. In 60 A.D. Laodicea was destroyed by an earthquake, but did not accept help from the emperor for the rebuilding, as many cities did. It was a great banking centre. It was also famous for the glossy black wool of its sheep, and did a large trade in the garments made from the wool: cp. vv. 17f. An article called ' Phrygian powder,' used to cure weakness of the eyes, may be alluded to in v. 18. A bishop of Laodicea was martyred 166 A.D.

14. Amen] i.e. Truth (cp. Isa 65^{16} RM); He is the Reality behind all passing things; His life is the life which is life indeed; His promises are sure; He can be trusted utterly. **Witness**] see on 1^5. **The beginning, etc.**] i.e. He who is the source of all life: cp. Col 1^{18}. **15.** Cp. Mt 21^{31}. **16.** An allusion to the nauseating effect of lukewarm water. **17.** Cp. Hos 12^8 Mt 23^{12} Lk 1^{52} Jas 2^{1f}. **18. Buy**] cp. Isa 55^1. **Raiment**] RV 'garments': cp. vv. 4f. Mt 22^{11f}. **Anoint .. eyesalve**] RV 'eyesalve to anoint thine eyes.' **See**] cp. Jn 9^{40f}. **19.** Cp. Prov 3^{12} Heb 12^6. **20. Knock**] cp. Song 5^2 Lk 12^{36}. **Hear**] cp. Jn 10^{4,28}. **Come in**] cp. Jn 14^{23}. **Sup**] The blessings which Christ gives, both here and hereafter, are often spoken of under the figure of a feast: cp. 19^9 Mt 25^1 Lk 22^{29f}. **With him .. me**] cp. Jn 15^4 17^{21f}.

21. Cp. Jn 16^{33} 17^{24}.

CHAPTER 4
THE GLORY OF GOD

The Church has been encouraged in the midst of her tribulation and temptation by the vision of the presence and support of Christ. Now (chs. 4, 5) a further series of visions begins, in which are shown, under figures, the forces by which the life of the Church is affected, or, in other words, those who are for her and those who are against her. She is shown God and the Lamb, and she is shown the devil, the beast, the false prophet, and the apostate city. Then she is shown the victory of Christ, and the eternal defeat of the powers of evil.

In c. 4, for the comfort of the Church, the greatness and majesty of God the Father is shown in language adapted from Isa 6 and Ezk 1, 10. He is portrayed, on His heavenly throne, sitting ' above the water floods,' surrounded by beings representative of the angelic creation and of the Church. These beings ceaselessly watch Him to do His will, and worship Him as Creator.

We are not to understand the imagery as literally descriptive of heaven, but as pictorial symbols of spiritual things: see on 5$^{5-7}$.

1. First voice] i.e. the voice of 1^{16}.

3. Jasper] i.e. according to some, the diamond; but according to Flinders Petrie (HDB. ' Stones, Precious '), the green jasper: cp. 21^{11}. The diamond would be emblematic of God's purity, the green jasper of His mercy. **Sardine stone**] RV 'sardius,' i.e. according to F. P., red jasper; emblematic of God's judgments. **Rainbow**] the sign of mercy: cp. Ezk 1^{27}.

Emerald] F. P. thinks the word translated ' emerald ' means rock crystal, which could show a rainbow of prismatic colours. **4. Seats**] RV 'thrones.' **Elders**] either representative of the Church of both dispensations (OT. and NT.); or, as some think, angelic beings: cp. Isa 24^{23} Col 1^{16}. **5. Lightnings, etc.**] signifying awe-inspiring majesty and power: cp. Ex 19^{16}. **Seven Spirits**] see on 1^4.

6. *There was* a sea of glass] RV 'as it were a glassy sea,' perhaps representing the waters that were above the firmament, Gn 1^7. Over this the throne of God is looked upon as set: cp. Ezk 1^{22}. **In the midst of, etc.**] i.e. probably, supporting the throne. **Beasts**] RV ' living creatures ': cp. Ezk 1^{5f}. ; in Ezk 10$^{1-20}$ identified with the ' cherubim.' The ' cherubim ' seem to have been emblematic of the forces of nature, especially of the storm-cloud: cp. Gn 3^{24} (' sword ' perhaps = ' lightning '), Ps 18^{10}. ' To the Heb. poet the cherubim are not only the attendants of Jehovah, but the bearers and upholders of His throne. The thunderclouds are the dark wings of these ministers of God: cp. 2 K 19^{15} Pss 80^1 99^1 Isa 37^{16}. . . In later Jewish theology the cherubim take their place among the highest angels of heaven ' (HDB.). **Full of eyes**] symbolising their unceasing watchfulness: cp. Ezk 10^{12}.

7. Beast] RV ' creature.' The four creatures were anciently taken as emblems of the four evangelists. **8. Beasts**] RV ' living creatures.' **Rest not**] RV ' have no rest '; cp. ' watchers ' as title of angels, Dan 4^{13}. **Holy, etc.**] see on 1^4 and 1^8 Isa 6^3. **9. Those beasts**] RV ' the living creatures.' **Give**] RV ' shall give,' i.e. whenever they give. **11. Hast created**] RV ' didst create.' **For thy pleasure**] RV ' because of thy will.' **Are**] RV ' were,' i.e. existed ' in His idea from all eternity; and when the appointed moment came, they ere created ' (Milligan).

CHAPTER 5
THE GLORY OF THE LAMB

The Church is shown that Christ is on her side. He has overcome by suffering. Now the future is for Him and His people, and He is worshipped with the Father.

1-4. A roll of a book, covered with writing on both sides, signifying the full contents of God's purposes for the future (cp. Ezk 2^{9f}.)

'close sealed' (RV) with seven seals, i.e. completely hidden from the knowledge of angels and men, rests on the outstretched right hand of 'Him that sitteth on the throne,' signifying that God offers His will to be made known and His purposes to be worked out (v. 1). But no created being (RV 'no one') is fit to receive so high a mission (vv. 2 f.), and St. John weeps, fearing lest the promise of 4¹ should fail (v. 4).

5–7. St. John is told that the victory which Christ has won has fitted Him to take and open the book. Christ in His royal power and strength is spoken of as 'the Lion that is of the tribe of Judah' (RV), a reference to Gn 49⁹, which was interpreted by the Jews of the Messiah (cp. Heb 7¹⁴), and as the 'Root of David,' i.e. the stem or 'Branch' coming from the root (cp. 22¹⁶ Isa 11¹, ¹⁰ Jer 23⁵ Zech 3⁸), another accepted designation of the Messianic King (v. 5). St. John looks for the Lion and sees a Lamb (cp. Jn 1²⁹, ³⁶), 'standing, as though it had been slain' (RV), i.e. recently slaughtered or sacrificed. The reference is to Isa 53, and the meaning is that it was by His sacrifice that Christ had won His victory. By the Cross, the devil and the world were already essentially overcome (cp. Jn 12³¹ᶠ. 16¹¹, ³³ Col 2¹⁵); and God's purposes for man, which depended on the Atonement of Christ, could now be carried out. It is implied that the persecuted saints, for whom this was written, were not to fear tribulation, because it was for them also the appointed means by which they should 'overcome.' The Lamb has seven horns and seven eyes, signifying the complete power and searching insight of the Spirit by which He rules His people and overthrows His enemies and carries out the divine purpose (v. 6): see on 1⁴; cp. 4⁶, ⁸ 1S 2¹⁰ Dan 7⁷, ²⁰ Zech 3⁹. Then the Lamb takes the book (v. 7).

We are not to understand that Christ literally has the form of a Lamb. The figures of a Lamb, and of horns and eyes, were familiar to all students of the OT., and the truth about Christ was expressed to St. John's mind in vision under this familiar imagery, just as it might have been expressed solely by words. If figures and words were equally expressive of spiritual realities, either might be employed.

5. Prevailed] RV 'overcome.' **6. In the midst]** i.e. in front of the throne. **Beasts]** RV 'living creatures.'

8–14. The Church, in her praise and prayer, sings the glory of the conquering Lamb. All angels and all creation join their chorus.

8. Vials] RV 'bowls'; as used in the Temple for incense. **Odours]** RV 'incense': cp. 8³ Ps 141². **Saints]** RV 'the saints,' i.e. the true people of God. **9. Sung]** RV 'sing.'

New] because belonging to the 'new' state of Redemption: see on 2¹⁷; cp. 14³. **Hast redeemed,** etc.] RV 'didst purchase unto God with thy blood men of every tribe, and tongue,' etc.: cp. Ac 20²⁸. **10. Kings]** RV 'a kingdom': see on 1⁶. **Reign]** i.e. have power over tribulation and sin: cp. Eph 2⁶ 1 Pet 2⁹. **12.** Sevenfold praise is rendered. **13.** The chorus of praise becomes universal. **Creature]** RV 'created thing.'

CHAPTER 6
THE SIX SEALS

The afflicted Church has been reminded in chs. 4 f. that God is over all, and that the future is committed to the Lamb. Now (chs. 6–8¹) she is shown that future, unrolling to its appointed end, i.e. the judgment of the enemies of God and the triumph of those who 'overcome.' The Lamb opens the seven seals. Apparently we are to understand that, as each seal is opened, a portion of that which is written in the book is revealed pictorially. C. 7 contains an episode between seals six and seven.

The first six seals. The key to this vision is the prophecy of Christ in Mt 24³⁻³¹. In that prophecy, vv. 4–14 foretell the signs preceding the destruction of Jerusalem, vv. 15–28 the destruction of Jerusalem, and vv. 29–31 the signs which will precede the coming of Christ. There is the same threefold division in this c., but in place of the destruction of Jerusalem is the appeal of the martyrs to God, while the whole looks forward to the coming of Christ.

St. John had, doubtless, thought long on the prophecy recorded for us in Mt 24. It was a natural effect of his memory that that vision should follow the lines of that prophecy; and, at the same time, our Lord saw fit to make further use of the thoughts already implanted in the Apostle's mind. The working of the same prophecy appears in the visions of the trumpets and the bowls.

1–8. Four riders are summoned, each by the word 'come' (RV omits 'and see'); cp. Zech 6¹ᶠ., where the horses stand for the four winds, symbolising the divine judgments (v. 1).

The white horse and the crown of the first rider are symbols of victory, and for the bow cp. Ps 45⁴ᶠ. The victorious progress of the gospel is perhaps represented (cp. Mt 24¹⁴), or, as many think, Christ: cp. 19¹¹ (v. 2).

The second and third riders represent war and famine respectively (vv. 3–5). A 'penny' (cp. Mt 18²⁸ RM) was the wages of a labourer for a day's work (cp. Mt 20²ᶠ.); the 'measure' contained two pints. Judgment is tempered with mercy, for the wheat and the barley are not to be wholly destroyed, and the oil and the wine are to be uninjured (v. 6).

Then Death and Hell (RV 'Hades,' i.e. the 'underworld' of the dead) come to claim a fourth part, i.e. not the whole, of the ungodly, by God's four judgments of sword, famine, death (i.e. pestilence), and wild beasts: cp. Ezk 14 21 (v. 8).

9-11. The opening of the fifth seal reveals that the death of the martyrs is not unregarded by God. As they sacrificed their lives, they are represented as having been offered on a heavenly altar, at the foot of which their blood (or 'souls,' or 'lives': cp. Lv 17 11) has been poured out: cp. Ex 29 12 (v. 9). Their blood is said to call out upon God, as Abel's did (cp. Gn 4 10), and as every crime does, for punishment (v. 10). God is not unheeding, but the final judgment must wait till the number of the martyrs is fulfilled. Meanwhile these, having overcome (cp. 3 4 f.), are given robes of victory (v. 11).

10. Lord] RV 'Master.'

12-17. At the opening of the sixth seal the day of the wrath of God and of the Lamb is impending. The description is founded on the words of Christ: cp. Mt 24 29 f. The prophets had expressed the awfulness of the 'day of the Lord,' by associating it with terrible catastrophes, and these are heaped together in this passage to create a picture of fear and ruin. The details are not to be literally understood: cp. Isa 2 10 f. 34 4 50 3 Jer 4 24 Am 8 9 Nah 1 5 f. Hag 2 6 f. Lk 23 30 Heb 12 26.

The picture seems to be, as it were, foreshortened to the Apostle, so that he is not able to see the length of the interval which separates the Fall of Jerusalem from the conquest of the empire by Christianity, nor of the interval which separates that conquest from the Day of Judgment. So throughout the book, yet see the 'thousand years' of c. 20.

17. His] RV 'their.'

CHAPTER 7
THE REDEEMED

Two visions interposed between the sixth and seventh seals. There are similar episodes between the sixth and seventh trumpets and bowls.

1-3. Four angels are holding in check the four winds of God's judgments (v. 1), and are ordered not to release them until God's servants are sealed, i.e. marked as His: cp. Ezk 9 4 Eph 1 13 4 30 2 Tim 2 19 (vv. 2 f.). These four winds may be the horsemen of 6 1 f. The meaning is, that Christians need not fear the judgments of c. 6. Not a hair of their head shall perish (Lk 21 18).

4-8. The complete number of God's people (see on 21 15 f.), and that a large one (144,000 is the square of 12 a thousandfold), is being gathered together for everlasting safety. The Church of Christ is spoken of in OT. language:

cp. Ro 2 28 f. The tribe of Dan is not mentioned, perhaps because of a Jewish tradition that Antichrist was to come from that tribe.

9-17. St. John sees, in another vision, how the saints, the '144,000,' are preserved. They may not be delivered *from* death, but they will be delivered *by* death: cp. Lk 21 16 f. Robes and palms of victory (vv. 9 f.) are for those who 'overcome,' and they are enabled to overcome by the 'blood,' i.e. by the communicated power of the sacrificed life of the Lamb: cp. 12 11 (v. 14). Their blessed state is pictured in sweet imagery drawn from the OT. (vv. 15-17).

10. Salvation] i.e. victory : cp. Ps 3 8 RM.

11. Beasts] RV 'living creatures.'

12. Sevenfold praise. **14.** Sir] RV 'My lord.' **Great**] RV 'the great.' **Washed**] cp. 22 14 RV. **15.** Dwell among] RV 'spread his tabernacle over': cp. Lv 16 2 26 11 Ezk 10 3 f. 37 27. **16.** Cp. Isa 49 10. **17.** Feed] RV 'be their shepherd': cp. Ps 23 1 f. Ezk 34 23. **Living fountains of waters**] RV 'fountains of waters of life': cp. 21 6 22 1, 17 Jer 2 13 Jn 4 10 7 37.

Wipe away] cp. Isa 25 8.

CHAPTER 8
THE SEVENTH SEAL. THE FOUR TRUMPETS

1. The seventh seal is opened. Heaven waits in hushed awe for a brief period.

8 2**-11** 19**.** The Seven Trumpets.

2. The seven angels, regarded in later Jewish belief as having a special position in God's presence (cp. Tob 12 15 Lk 1 19), are given **seven trumpets**, symbols of judgment: cp. Mt 24 31 1 Cor 15 52 1 Th 4 16. It is best to understand the vision of the trumpets as being the contents of the seventh seal. This appears from the character of the events belonging to the first four trumpets, which spring from the third division of Christ's prophecy (Mt 24 29 f. Lk 21 25 f.), and are parallel with the sixth seal: see on c. 6. Therefore the trumpets represent the judgments on the heathen world, especially on the Roman empire, to come after the Fall of Jerusalem. It will be noticed that the arrangement of the trumpets is parallel to that of the seals, and that there is an episode of two visions between the sixth and seventh trumpets as there was between the sixth and seventh seals

3-5. The incense of the prayer of heaven is joined to the Church's prayer that Christ will not tarry, cp. 6 10 Ro 8 26 (vv. 3 f.), and, in answer, the fire of God's judgment is cast on the earth, cp. Ezk 10 2 (v. 5), after which the sounding of the trumpets begins.

3. Offer *it* with] RV 'add it unto.'

4. *Which came*] RV omits. **5.** Were] RV 'followed.'

6-13. The first four trumpets announce convulsions of nature, affecting earth, sea, rivers and the heavenly bodies. The language is in part borrowed from the narrative of the plagues of Egypt, but the whole fourfold vision looks like the picture of a volcanic eruption. Destruction comes upon one-third only, i.e. the mercy is greater than the judgment. The details are not to be pressed. The general idea is that the convulsions of nature are the shadow cast before by the approach of the terrible day of Christ (vv. 6–12).

After the fourth trumpet, an eagle (not 'angel,' as AV), whose swoop upon the prey is another symbol of judgment (cp. Hos 8 1 Mt 24 28), announces three woes upon the ungodly (v. 13). Each of the last three trumpets heralds one of these woes.

7. Hail and fire mingled, etc.] RV ' hail and fire, mingled,' etc. **Upon the earth**] RV adds, ' and the third part of the earth was burnt up.'

10. As it were a lamp] RV 'as a torch.' **13. Angel**] RV ' eagle.'

CHAPTER 9
The Fifth and Sixth Trumpets

These herald woes upon the ungodly and idolatrous, inflicted both by demonic and by human agency.

1–12. The fifth trumpet initiates the first of the three woes. A star fallen to the earth, i.e. an angel who has descended from heaven (cp. 1 20), not necessarily an evil angel (v. 1), opens the pit of the abyss. The ' abyss ' is the abode of evil spirits or demons, and the ' pit ' is the shaft which was supposed to lead to it. St. John uses this Jewish idea, which may have been derived from volcanoes, as a figure of spiritual things. At the opening of the pit smoke pours forth (v. 2), and from the smoke issue evil spirits with the appearance of locusts (v. 3). They are not to hurt green things, for they are not really locusts ; but, besides being like locusts in their numbers and their devastating power, they are to be like scorpions in that they give pain to men, but only for a limited period—a visitation of locusts was usually limited to five months, from May to September. They are to afflict those who are not sealed : see on 7 1f. (v. 4 f.). The description of the locusts is partly taken from Joel 1 6 2 1f. No special significance need be sought in the details, which probably are only meant to increase the vivid terror of the picture (vv. 7 f.). Unlike the locusts of Prov 30 27 they have a king, Abaddon or Apollyon, i.e. 'Destroyer' (cp. Job 26 6 RV Prov 15 11 RV) : names which at first signified the place of the lost, and afterwards, as here, the ruler of the hosts of evil (v. 11). This vision may be regarded as a picture of the mental and spiritual misery which follows sin. It is a contrast to the fifth seal ; cp. v. 6, ' seek death and in no wise find it,' with 6 11, ' rest ': cp. Isa 48 22.

1. Fall from heaven] RV ' from heaven fallen.' **1, 2. Bottomless pit**] RV ' pit of the abyss.' **9.** RV inserts a comma after **chariots.**

10. And there were stings, etc.] RV ' and stings ; and in their tails is their power to hurt men five months.' **11.** RV ' They have over them as king the angel of the abyss,' etc.

13–21. The sixth trumpet sounds, and a voice from the altar answers the prayers of the martyrs crying for vengeance, cp. 6 9f. 8 3 (v. 13), by commanding the four angels, bound at the Euphrates, to be loosed (v. 14). Immense armies of horsemen issue forth, and kill the third part, i.e. a large number, but not the whole, of the ungodly : cp. vv. 20 f. The Euphrates is the river of Babylon, and Babylon in this book represents Rome. Perhaps, therefore, this vision speaks of devastation caused by Roman armies, possibly in the civil wars that followed the death of Nero.

In the ' four angels bound,' St. John uses a familiar Jewish apocalyptic idea. Each country was supposed to have its angel or angels (cp. Dan 10 13, 20), ' Prince of Persia,' ' Prince of Greece,' and see on 1 20. The four angels would be the invisible representatives of the hosts of ' Babylon,' i.e. Rome, and their ' binding ' or ' loosing ' would represent the spiritual cause of the restraint or letting loose of the armies. The angels were held in leash until the exact moment foreordained by God (v. 15). As with the locusts, the details of the description probably have no special meaning.

14. In] RV 'at.' **15. Were prepared**] RV ' had been prepared.' **An hour, etc.**] RV ' the hour and day and month and year.'

17. Jacinth] RV ' hyacinth,' i.e. smoky blue. **20. Works of their hands**] i.e. idols : cp. Ps 115 4 Isa 17 8 Dan 5 3 f.

CHAPTER 10
The Little Book

Between the sixth and seventh trumpets, as between the sixth and seventh seals, is an episode consisting of two visions. The first vision is related in this c.

Another mighty angel (cp. 5 2), depicted as clothed with God's power and mercy, which he is commissioned to minister, comes from heaven (v. 1), holding a little book open in his hand. The book is different from that of c. 5, and contains a special revelation for St. John to make : cp. v. 11 (v. 2). Seven thunders utter their voices, apparently signifying that there will be a cycle of judgments not included in the seals, trumpets, and bowls (v. 3), but these St. John is forbidden by the herald angel (cp. 1 10) to record : cp. Dan 12 4 (v. 4). The angel of v. 1 (v. 5) now declares (cp. Dan 12 7) that the ' little time ' of 6 11 shall be brought to an end (v. 6) in the days of the seventh trumpet, when God's eternal purpose of salvation, the revelation of which had gladdened the prophets of both dispensations (cp. Dan 9 6, 10 Zech 1 6 Ro 1 1), shall be fulfilled (v. 7). At the command of the herald-angel, St. John takes the book (v. 8), and eats it. It is sweet in his mouth, but bitter in his belly (cp. Ps 119 103 Ezk 2 8 f. 3 1 f.), signifying that it is sweet to him to receive God's revelation, but that its wrath and judgment fill him with sorrow (vv. 9 f.). The two angels bid him announce the contents of this new revelation, which are, probably, to be found in chs. 12 f. (v. 11).

3. Seven] RV 'the seven.' **7. Shall begin**] RV 'is about.' **Mystery**] cp. Ro 16 25 f. **As he hath declared**] RV 'according to the good tidings which he declared.'

CHAPTER 11
The Two Witnesses. The Seventh Trumpet

1-14. Second episode. There is much difference of opinion as to the meaning of this vision. Perhaps the key may be found in the parallelism of the book. There were two episodical visions after the sixth seal (see on c. 7), the first signifying that Christ's people were separated and preserved from God's judgments, the second that they were preserved not *from* but *through* death. The same meaning may be found here.

1, 2. The sanctuary and altar of Jerusalem, with the worshippers, are to be measured, i.e. with a view to preservation : cp. 2 S 8 2 Ezk 40 3 f. (v. 1). But the court of the Gentiles has been given over, with the rest of the city, to the nations (v. 2). This is plainly a reference to, or prophecy of, the siege and capture of Jerusalem, 70 A.D., as foretold by Christ : cp. Lk 21 24. But it is to be interpreted symbolically. The temple, altar, and worshippers signify the Christian Church and its worship (cp. 1 Cor 3 16), which have arisen in the midst of Judaism, and which are to be preserved, although Judaism is doomed. The time named, 42 months, i.e. 3½ years (v. 2), the half of seven the holy number, is not to be understood literally. It was the duration of the persecution of Antiochus Epiphanes, and signifies a period, of whatever extent, in which evil had power : cp. v. 3, 12 6 13 5 Dan 7 25 12 7.

3-14. But the people of Christ, although to be preserved, will be preserved through death. They are represented now under the figure of two 'witnesses' (cp. Ac 1 8), prophesying during the period of evil (v. 3). They are compared to the olive trees and candlesticks (Zerubbabel and Joshua) of Zech 4, because they give forth the light of the truth of Christ and are fed with the oil of divine grace (v. 4). They are also compared, in language which is meant to assure them of God's special favour and protection, to Elijah and Moses (vv. 5 f.). Yet God's favour will be shown in preserving them not *from* but *through* death. The 'beast,' i.e. the Roman power (cp. 13 1 note, 17 8) will persecute them to the death (v. 7). There is, perhaps, an allusion to the death of two godly men in Jerusalem, of whom James, the Lord's brother, may have been one. As their dead bodies were treated with dishonour by the Jews, so, too, will the heathen dishonour the martyred Christians. But in all this they are identified with Christ (vv. 8 f.), and will share His life with God (vv. 11 f.). In the judgment which falls upon the wicked world, of which Jerusalem, now that the Christian Church has been separated from her (vv. 1 f.), has become a figure ('Sodom,' 'Egypt,' 'great city,' v. 8 ; see on 14 8), many are converted : cp. Ac 2 23 37 f. (vv 13 f.).

1. The angel stood, saying] RV 'one said.' **2. Out**] RV 'without.' **3.** RV 'And I will give unto my two witnesses, and they shall prophesy '—a Hebraism for ' cause them to prophesy.' **5 f.** Cp. Ex 7 19 1 K 17 1 f. 2 K 1 10 Lk 4 25. **5. Will .. will**] RV 'desireth to .. shall desire to.' **7. Bottomless pit**] RV 'abyss': see on 9 2. Cp. Dan 7 3, 7 f. 21. **8. Our**] RV 'their.' **9.** RV 'And from among the peoples and tribes and tongues and nations do men look upon their dead bodies .. and suffer not,' etc. **10. They .. earth**] i.e. the ungodly. **11. The Spirit**] RV 'the breath': cp. Ezk 37 5, 10. **12. A great voice**] i.e. God's: cp. 2 K 2 11. **13. Earthquake**] see on 6 12.

15-19. The seventh trumpet sounds. This will bring about the consummation (cp. 10 7), and therefore the rest of the book is developed out of it. Instead of a silence in heaven, such as that which followed the opening of the seventh seal, St. John hears a heavenly chorus anticipating and celebrating the victory of the Kingdom which the seventh trumpet is to bring, and which is related in chs. 12-20 (vv. 15-18). Now is opened the temple of God in heaven, and in it is seen the ark of the covenant of mercy, and from it proceed lightnings and thunderings of judgment (cp. 8 5 16 18, 'seals' and 'bowls') (v. 15). Of this mercy and judgment the following chs. narrate the exercise.

15. Kingdoms of this world] RV 'kingdom of the world': cp. Ps 2 2. **16. Seats**] RV 'thrones.' **17. And wast, and art to come**] RV ' and which wast.' **To thee**] RV omits. **Hast reigned**] RV ' didst reign.' **18. Angry**] RV 'wroth.' **Is come**] RV 'came.' **19. Testament**] RV 'covenant.'

CHAPTER 12
The Woman and the Man-Child. The Dragon

The persecution which the Church had

already suffered, and which was about to burst forth again, is the great fact which underlies the whole ' Revelation.' The sufferings of the Church and its members have been referred to again and again, particularly in 11 1-13. In the ' seals' and the ' trumpets' the Church has been assured, in a broad and general manner, that God's judgments will fall upon the world of wickedness, and that the ungodly will bow before the power of the Lamb. In the remainder of the book (chs. 12–22), the victory of Christ and His Church is foretold in more definite detail. The great enemies of Christ are brought forward, under the personifications of the Dragon (c. 12), the two Beasts (chs. 13 f.), and the harlot City (c. 17). Then we are shown Christ's battle against them, and the complete overthrow both of them and of all evil (chs. 18–20), after which the book ends with the glorious and everlasting blessedness of the New Jerusalem (chs. 21 f.).

The first great enemy of Christ's Church, the cause of all the hostility against her, is Satan. Christ suffered his enmity, but passed through it triumphantly (vv. 1–6). Satan is already conquered in principle (vv. 7–9), though for a short time the Christian Church experiences his malignity (vv. 10–17).

1-6. The Church, of both the OT. and NT. covenants, is shown under the figure of a woman, clothed with heavenly glory (v. 1) from whom the Messiah is about to come : cp. Isa 66 19 Mic 4 10. She is opposed by the devil (v. 9), pictured as a dragon, red with the blood of the saints : cp. 17 3 f. (v. 3). His seven heads and ten horns (cp. Dan 7 7) represent the Roman emperors through whom he exercised his power. The seven crowned heads perhaps signify the seven emperors, from Augustus to Titus, who had really reigned. The ten horns may stand for the same emperors with the addition of Galba, Otho, and Vitellius : cp. 13 1 17 10 f. (see C. A. Scott, ' Century Bible : Revelation,' p. 53). The dragon waits to attack the Messiah (v. 4), but when He is born (cp. Ps 2 8 f.), the dragon has no power over Him, and He is exalted to God's throne : cp. Phil 2 9 (v. 5). The Church escapes from the dragon, as the Church of Israel escaped from Pharaoh into the wilderness, to be kept during a time of trouble : see on 11 2 (v. 6). The reference here may be to seasons of rest which the Palestinian Church experienced during the troubles which ended in the destruction of Jerusalem (cp. Ac 9 31), and to the escape of the Christians of Jerusalem to Pella before the siege : cp. Mt 24 16.

1, 3. Wonder] RV 'sign.' 3. Crowns] RV ' diadems,' i.e. kingly crowns. 4. Tail, etc.] i.e. he was huge and mighty : cp. Dan 8 10.

6. Feed] RV ' nourish.'

7-9. The Christians for whom St. John wrote were beginning to experience persecution : cp. 2 3, 10 f. 13 3 4 note, 10. Yet their victory is assured. This is symbolically expressed under the figure of a war in heaven between good and evil angels (v. 7) in which Satan and his host are conquered and cast down from heaven (vv. 8 f.). The figure is derived from Jewish apocalyptic ideas, but the meaning for Christians is that in the Death and Resurrection and Ascension of Christ, Satan was already essentially conquered : cp. Jn 12 31 f. 16 33.

7. Michael] one of the four archangels : cp. Dan 10 13 12 1 Jude v. 9. 9. Out] RV ' down.' Serpent] cp. Gn 3 1. Satan] i.e. 'adversary' (Heb.), or ' devil' (diabolos, Gk.) : cp. Job 1 6 Ps 109 6 Zech 3 1 f. Deceiveth] cp. Jn 8 44.

10-12. Satan being already potentially conquered, heaven celebrates in anticipation the victory which the persecuted saints will win because Christ died for them and gives them strength to die.

10. Accused] cp. 1 Tim 3 6 f. 11. By] RV ' because of ' (twice). Word of, etc.] i.e. the word of Christ to which they testify.

13-17. The devil is not able to hurt a section of the Church, perhaps the Palestinian Church at Pella is meant, for God protects her. God's protection is described in terms of the deliverance of the exodus, when Israel was borne by God on eagles' wings, cp. Ex 19 4 (v. 14), and escaped from Pharaoh into the wilderness, passing safely through the Red Sea (' water as a river,' vv. 15 f.). This being so, Satan turns against the Church in Gentile lands (v. 17).

In this c. St. John used figures which were frequently employed in Jewish apocalypses. These may have been derived originally from the ancient myth of the fight between the sun and darkness. Whatever was their original meaning, here they are symbolical of Christian truth : cp. note, c. 6, on St. John's use of the prophecy in Mt 24.

15. Flood . . flood] RV ' river . . stream.' 16. Flood] RV ' river.' 17. Was] RV ' waxed.' Seed] cp. Gal 4 26. Have] RV ' hold.'

CHAPTER 13
THE TWO BEASTS

Personification of the two powers inspired by the devil to persecute the Church.

1-10. The dragon stands by the sea (i.e. the Ægean Sea), from which there rises to meet him a ' beast,' i.e. something inhuman : signifying the Roman empire, which came to the Province of Asia, in which were the Churches addressed in Rev., from the sea. The beast has ten horns and seven heads : cp. Dan 7. On the horns are diadems and on the heads ' names of blasphemy,' i.e. blasphemous titles : cp. 17 3. The ten horns (see on 12 3) are the ten emperors from Augustus to Titus. The seven horns are those of the ten who had reigned long enough for worship to be paid to them, i.e. omitting Galba, Otho, and Vitellius. The 'names' were, probably, 'Augustus' or 'Sebastos,' i.e. 'reverenced,' under which the emperors were worshipped : cp. vv. 12 f., 2 13 note (v. 1).

'The emperor represented the majesty, the wisdom, and the beneficent power of Rome : he was in many cases actually represented in different parts of the empire as an incarnation of the god worshipped in that district... Domitian .. delighted .. to be idolised as the Divine Providence in human form ; and it is recorded that Caligula, Domitian, and Diocletian were the three emperors who delighted to be styled *dominus et deus*' (Ramsay, 'Church in Rom. Empire,' pp. 191, 275).

The monster combines the powers of the four beasts in Dan 7 (v. 2). One head is smitten unto death, but the death stroke is healed. This head probably represents Nero (54–68 A.D.), of whom popular report said that he was not dead, or that if dead he would return to life (Tacitus, 'Hist.' ii. 8, Suetonius, 'Nero,' 57): cp. 17 8 f. The word translated **wounded**, RV 'smitten,' is that translated 'slain,' of the Lamb, 5 6. It is implied that Nero, both as the head of the world kingdom, and in his death and return to life, was the counterpart of Christ in God's kingdom. St. John took this Nero superstition, and used it to symbolise the breaking out again of Nero's persecuting spirit in Domitian, 81–96 A.D. (v. 3). As Nero is represented as the counterpart of Christ, so the worship of the dragon and the beast is the evil counterpart of the worship of God : cp. 'who is like,' etc., with Ex 15 11 (v. 4). The beast blasphemes God and His tabernacle (i.e. the Church, the dwelling-place of God) by the assumption of divine honour and by imputing evil practices to Christianity : cp. 1 Pet 2 12 (vv. 5 f.). He is appointed (i.e. by God, who overrules the work of evil men to His glory) to war against the 'saints' in world-wide power (v. 7), and worship is offered to him by the ungodly (vv. 8 f.). The description of the beast ends with an injunction to the saints to submit to God's will in unresisting patience (v. 10).

1. I stood] RV 'he stood.' **Saw**] RV 'I saw.' **Crowns**] RV 'diadems,' i.e. kingly crowns. **The name**] RV 'names.' **4. Which gave power**] RV 'because he gave his authority.' **5. Forty** *and* **two months**] see on 11 2.

6. And them, etc.] RV 'even them.' Christians are themselves God's 'tabernacle,' because He is 'in the midst of' them : cp. 21 3.

Dwell] Gk. 'tabernacle.' **In heaven**] Christians are here said to dwell in heaven, because they belong to the kingdom of heaven on earth and because in Christ they have begun to live the heavenly life : cp. Eph 2 6.

7. All kindreds, etc.] The Roman empire was world-wide. **8. Book of Life**] see on 3 5.

From the foundation, etc.] i.e. in God's eternal counsel : cp. 1 Pet 1 19 f. **10.** RV 'If any man is for captivity, into captivity he goeth' (i.e. his captivity is by God's will) : 'if any man shall kill with the sword, with the sword must he be killed,' i.e. Christians are not to fight against the persecutors, but are to submit to God's will : cp. Mt 26 52.

A second beast is seen. It comes out of the earth (contrast v. 1), because it belongs to the Province of Asia, the land of the writer and first readers of this book. This beast represented 'the Province of Asia, in its double aspect of civil and religious administration, the Proconsul and the Commune. It had two horns, corresponding to this double aspect, and was like a lamb, for Asia was a peaceful country where no army was needed' (Ramsay). Yet it spake as a dragon, i.e. it made the same blasphemous assertions and demands as those which the first beast had learnt from the dragon : cp. v. 5 f. (v. 11). The authority of the Imperial Government had been delegated to the Provincial Government, which used its authority in enforcing the worship of the emperor. As the persecuting spirit of the empire was incarnate in Nero, the Imperial Government is identified with Nero himself, restored to life ; i.e. the succeeding emperors will act in the spirit of Nero (v. 12). The worship of the emperor's image is recommended to the credulous populace by the aid of trickery and conjuring (v. 13 f.), and by ventriloquism. (Hence the beast is also called the 'false prophet,' cp. 16 13 19 20 20 10.) The punishment for refusing to worship the image is death (v. 15). No one in the Province is allowed to buy or sell, who cannot produce a certificate, under Imperial seal ('the mark, *even* the name of the beast,' RV), showing that he has joined in the worship of the emperor. Or the meaning may be that all must offer incense with the hand, or bow the head, to the image, before they are allowed to trade (v. 16 f.). The name of the beast, i.e. of the smitten head, is given as 666 (v. 18). The reference is to the numerical value of letters. In both Greek and Hebrew, letters of the alphabet were used as numbers. It has been found that if 'Neron Cæsar' be written in Hebrew letters, the sum of the letters is 666. This is generally accepted at present, although, to get 666, 'Cæsar' has to be written defectively. If spelt 'Nero Cæsar,' the sum of the letters is 616, which is the reading of some MSS. Some hold that 616 is the original reading, and that it represents 'Gaios Cæsar,' i.e. Caligula. Irenæus took the number as standing for 'Lateinos,' i.e. 'the Latin.' Another interpretation sees in the number simply a continuation of the contrast with Christ of v. 11. The number of the name 'Jesus' in Gk. is 888 ; and, according to this interpretation, the meaning is that the beast falls as far short of 'seven' (i.e. perfection and holiness) as Jesus goes beyond it.

13. Wonders] RV 'signs': cp. 12 [1]. **Fire]** The false prophet is a travesty of Elijah: cp. 1 K 18 [38] 2 K 1 [10 f.] **14. Miracles]** RV 'signs.' **15. Life]** RV 'breath,' i.e. apparently ; perhaps by ventriloquism. **18. Here is wisdom]** i.e. wisdom is needed to interpret that which follows: cp. 17 [9].

CHAPTER 14
The Lamb and His Followers. Judgment on His Enemies

In the last two chs. were seen the enemies of the Church, and their fierce power. Now, by way of contrast, and to encourage the Church to resist her enemies with complete certainty of victory, pictures are shown of the blessedness of those who witness a true confession for Christ, and of God's judgment on the ungodly.

1-5. The Lamb (cp. 5 [6], etc.) is seen on Mount Zion, i.e. the true and heavenly home of the Church: cp. Heb 12 [22]. With Him are the perfect number (cp. 7 [4]) of those who had been marked with His name and the name of His Father, instead of with the mark of the beast: see on 3 [12], and cp. 7 [3] 13 [16 f.] Both here, and in 7 [4], '144,000' is a figurative expression for the whole number of the Redeemed (v. 1). A heavenly chorus is heard, in which the voice of Christ is followed by the voices of the living creatures and of the elders (v. 2). The Redeemed join in the strain (v. 3). They are described as undefiled by idolatry, which is often described in Scripture as adultery against God, and which was itself commonly allied with impurity ; as following the Lamb through suffering to glory ; as a choice offering to God (v. 4) ; as having confessed the true God and not the lying idol (**guile,** RV 'lie') ; and as an undefiled (**fault,** RV 'blemish') sacrifice, perhaps with an allusion to the death of the martyrs : cp. Heb 9 [14] 1 Pet 1 [19] (v. 5).

1. Looked] RV 'saw.' **A Lamb]** RV 'the Lamb.' **His Father's name]** RV 'his name, and the name of his Father.' **2. A voice]** see on 1 [10]. **I heard the voice of]** RV 'the voice which I heard was as the voice of.' **3. They]** i.e. the 144,000. **Beasts]** RV 'living creatures.' **4. Being]** RV 'to be.'

6 f. An angel announces the glad tidings for those who fear God, that He is about to be manifested for the salvation of His oppressed people.

6. Heaven] i.e. the sky. **8. The Fall of**

Babylon, i.e. Rome (see on 17 [5] 18), is spoken of as if it had already taken place. RV 'Fallen, fallen is Babylon the great, which hath made,' etc. : cp. Isa 21 [9] Dan 4 [30]. **The wrath of her fornication]** i.e. the wrath of God incurred by her unfaithfulness to God in which they had shared : cp. 17 [2] Jer 51 [7].

9-13. God's wrath is denounced on any who fall away from the Lamb to the beast (v. 9). Their woe is described in language drawn from Isa 34 [8 f.], and from the account of the destruction of Sodom and Gomorrah (vv 10 f.). The wrath of God is more terrible than that of the beast, hence the endurance of the 'saints' is justified (v. 12). Therefore, also, it is well with those who have died in persecution in the faith of Christ ; for while death brings no rest to those who worship the beast (cp. v. 11), the death of the saints brings rest from their labours and sorrows (v. 13).

9. See on 13 [16 f.] **10. Poured out without mixture into]** RV 'prepared unmixed in,' i.e. it is of full strength : cp. Ps 75 [8] Isa 51 [17]. **13. A voice]** see on 1 [10].

14-20. St. John sees one 'like unto a son of man' (RV). The expression is derived from Dan 7 [13], where it meant one in human form, as contrasted with the beasts. The title was interpreted of the Messiah, and the Jewish 'Book of Enoch' shows that under it the Messiah was regarded as a supernatural person. This was the significance of the term when our Lord applied it to Himself, and He joined to it the conception of the 'man of sorrows' of Isa 53. Now, after His sorrows, He is throned on a 'white cloud' (representing the glory of God, cp. Ex 40 [34] 1 K 8 [10] Mt 17 [5] Mk 14 [62]), and crowned as king : cp. 19 [12] (v. 14). He casts His sickle down to the earth, and the harvest of the saints is gathered (vv. 15 f.).

Then the angel of the fire on God's altar (cp. 9 [14] 16 [5]), the fire of God's judgments (cp. 8 [5]), calls for the gathering of the wicked for the winepress of God's wrath : cp. 19 [15] Isa 63 [1 f.] Joel 3 [13 f.] (vv. 17 f.). Those who are judged (v. 19) are separated from the heavenly state of the redeemed ('without the city,' cp. Zech 14 [4, 10] Heb 13 [11 f.]). The awfulness of the judgment is described in language similar to that of a description of judgment in the 'Book of Enoch' ; and its universality, by the extent of land covered by blood. 'Four' is the number symbolical of the earth, and 1600 is a thousand times the square of 4 : cp. '144,000,' the number expressing the people of God (v. 20).

15. Temple] cp. 11 [19]. **Crying .. to him]** i.e. the will of the Father is communicated to Christ. **Thrust in]** RV 'send forth' (and v. 18). **For thee]** RV omits. **Ripe]** RV 'overripe.' **16, 19. Thrust in]** RV 'cast.' **18. Vine]** RV 'vintage.' **20. By the space of]** RV 'as far as.'

CHAPTER 15

THE SEVEN ANGELS OF THE BOWLS

The crisis of the book is drawing near. The enemies of Christ and His Church—Satan, the empire, and the Provincial Government— have been shown in their power and cruelty. In c. 14 these were left standing in their might, while the blessed safety of the people of God was pictured. In this c. is described the approach of the judgments which are about to fall on the empire and on the heathen world.

1-4. Seven angels appear, they to whom are committed the 'plagues,' i.e. scourging punishments, 'which are the last' (RV), because in them the temporal judgments of God are fully carried out (RV 'finished'). But yet once more there is a pause, as if the safety of God's people in the midst of all this sin and judgment could not be insisted on sufficiently, and a vision is granted of the blessedness of those who by faithfulness even unto death have conquered the beast. They stand by the 'glassy sea' (RV), i.e. the firmament (see on 4⁶), having harps of God, i.e. harps such as are suited to the heavenly worship of God (v. 2). They sing 'the song of Moses and the song of the Lamb,' i.e. a song called out by the deliverance wrought by Christ, as the song of Ex 15 was called out by the deliverance from Egypt—a song in praise of God who from the time of Moses to the time of Christ has never forgotten His oppressed people (vv. 3 f.).

3. Cp. Pss 98¹ 111² 139¹⁴ 145¹⁷ Jer 10⁷. **Saints**] RV 'the ages': cp. 1 Tim 1¹⁷ (RM). **4.** Cp. Ps 86⁹ Isa 66²³. **Judgments**] RV 'righteous acts': cp. Ps 51⁴ Ro 5¹⁸.

5-8. Again, as in 11¹⁹, is opened the sanctuary of the heavenly tabernacle, by which is symbolised that presence of God to which the worship of heaven is directed, and from which the actions of heaven proceed, and which was typified on earth by the earthly tabernacle. In 11¹⁹ it was God's mercy, represented by the ark of the covenant, which was manifested; now it is the declaration of His holy will, represented by the 'testimony,' i.e. the ten commandments, which is to be enforced (v. 5). From the Divine Presence come forth the angels of the plagues, as priests, but arrayed with flashing gems (v. 6). To them are given golden 'bowls' (RV), corresponding to the basons used by the priests for the blood in the sacrificial ritual (cp. Ex 27³) full of God's wrath (v. 7). The Presence of God, sanctioning the service, is manifested by the smoke of His glory: cp. Ex 40³⁵ 1 K 8¹⁰f. Isa 6⁴ (v. 8).

6. Clothed .. linen] RV 'arrayed with precious stone, pure and bright.' **7. Beasts**] RV 'living creatures.'

CHAPTER 16

THE SEVEN BOWLS

In the last c. there was a pause of suspense, during which the angels of the 'plagues' were seen coming forth from the Presence of God to pour out His wrath. In this c. the suspense is ended, and the angels pour out God's wrath into the earth.

1-9. The vision of the 'bowls' (RV) is parallel with that of the 'trumpets' (chs. 8 f.). In each vision there are four preparatory judgments, falling upon the earth, the sea, the rivers and fountains, and the sun. But, in the 'trumpets,' it is the 'third part' that is affected; while in the 'bowls' it is the whole. At the fourth trumpet, the third part of the heavenly bodies are darkened; while at the fourth bowl, the sun blazes out with scorching heat. These differences are in harmony with the figure employed. The 'trumpets' herald the judgments, and give anticipations and warnings of them by calamities which foreshadow others. The first four trumpets and the first four bowls are parallel with the sixth seal (6¹²f.) and with Mt 24²⁹f. They foretell judgments to fall upon the heathen world of the Roman empire (cp. v. 2) before, and leading up to, the destruction of Rome. As in the 'trumpets,' the description is partly derived from the plagues of Egypt. It is to be understood, not literally, but as figuring a time of intense calamity and terror.

1. A great voice] i.e. God's: see on 1¹⁰. **5. Angel of the waters**] As Churches (cp. 1²⁰), and nations and armies (cp. 9¹⁴f.), so also the elements of nature (cp. 7¹ 14¹⁸) are in Rev. represented as having a spiritual counterpart. The exact idea occurs nowhere else in the Bible, though for what, possibly, may be approaches to it, cp. Job 4¹⁸ 25³,⁵ Ps 104⁴ Isa 24²¹f. Dan 10¹³,²⁰f. Mt 18¹⁰ Ac 12¹⁵ Heb 1⁷ (RV). In so poetical a book as Rev., it is difficult to decide whether these angels of water, fire, etc., are meant to be understood as real beings or merely as poetical personifications. **7. Another out of the altar**] RV 'the altar': cp. 6⁹ 8³. The altar is personified: see previous note. **9. God, which**] RV 'the God which.'

10 f. The fifth bowl is poured in judgment upon the city of Rome, the seat of empire. The heathen world governed by Rome becomes full of the darkness of terror and rebellion at God's judgments. This is parallel to the spiritual torments threatened at the fifth trumpet: cp. 9¹f. It is in contrast to the fifth seal (cp. 6⁹f.), where the martyrs, who have suffered, call on God, while here the subjects of the beast blaspheme God because of their pains. **10. Seat**] RV 'throne.'

12-16. The sixth bowl is poured out upon

the Euphrates, the river of Babylon, i.e. Rome: see on 17⁵. At the sixth trumpet (9¹³ᶠ·) armies were to come from the 'Euphrates.' Here the 'Euphrates' is to be dried up, to make a way for the kings from the sunrising, i.e. that they may be able to capture Rome; see on 17¹⁶ (v. 12). The drying up of the Euphrates refers to the manner in which Cyrus took the literal Babylon by diverting the course of the river. The capture of Rome is preparatory to the final battle of the 'kings of the world,' i.e. ungodly nations, against the Lamb at Har-Magedon (RV): cp. 17¹²ᶠ· (vv. 14–16). Har-Magedon probably means 'the Mount of Megiddo,' and signifies that the future battle is typified by the defeat of the kings of Canaan (Jg 5¹⁹; cp. Zech 12¹¹). The kings of the earth are stirred up to fight against the Lamb by the influence of the Lamb's three great enemies: cp. 1 K 22²⁰. Their evil influence is shown under the figure of frogs (cp. Ex 8⁷), because it was by producing frogs that the magicians deceived Pharaoh (vv. 13 f.).

13. False prophet, i.e. the second beast: see on 13¹¹. **15.** The voice of Christ breaks in: cp. 22⁷,¹²⁻¹⁵. **Keepeth his garments**] i.e. let not the power and attractiveness of the coming evil rob any Christian of the strict purity of his Christian life: cp. 3¹⁸ 7¹⁴. **16. He**] RV 'they,' i.e. the frog-like spirits.

17–21. The seventh bowl is poured out, and the voice of God announces that the end of the preparatory judgments is reached (v. 17). With the lightnings and thunderings and voices which close each vision (cp. 8⁵ 11¹⁹), comes now a great earthquake (v. 18), which splits Babylon (Rome) into three, and overthrows other worldly powers (v. 19). Some have understood this as a literal prediction that Rome was to be destroyed by an earthquake. More probably the earthquake represents the shaking of all earthly institutions when God comes to judgment: cp. 6¹² 8⁵ 11¹⁹. The judgments of the bowls end with a picture, expressed in physical figures, of the upheaval and destruction which accompany the manifestation of the wrath of God: cp. 6¹⁴ 11¹⁹ 20¹¹ (vv. 20 f.). **The cup**] see on 14⁸.

CHAPTER 17
BABYLON THE GREAT HARLOT

The judgment on Rome, which had been announced before, is now shown in detail. The identification of 'Babylon' with Rome, here and elsewhere in Rev., is supported (HDB.) by the following considerations :— The name Babylon in 17⁵ 'is described as *mystery*, i.e. a name to be allegorically interpreted... B. is described (1) as "the harlot"; the supreme antithesis of "the bride," "the holy city," "the new Jerus."; (2) as the centre and ruler of the nations, 14⁸ 17¹ᶠ·,¹⁵,¹⁸; (3)

as seated on "seven mountains," 17⁹; (4) as the source of idolatry and impurity, 17²ᶠ· 18² 19²... (5) as a great trading centre, 18³,¹¹⁻¹⁹; (6) as enervated by luxury, 18⁷,¹²ᶠ·²²; (7) as the arch-persecutor of the saints and of "the witnesses of Jesus," 17⁶ 19².' Babylon, as the seat of world-empire, and the ancient and persistent enemy of the people of God, was a striking type of Rome. Many think Rome is meant in 1 Pet 5¹³.

1 f. Rome is spoken of by the herald angel of the bowls as a harlot, cp. Isa 23¹⁵ᶠ· (Tyre), Nah 3⁴ (Nineveh), sitting on many waters, cp. Jer 51¹³ (Babylon), which signify the peoples over whom Rome ruled, cp. v. 15. **1. Vials**] RV 'bowls.'

3–6. St. John is taken to a wilderness to see the harlot city, as in Isa 21¹ the vision of Babylon's fall was declared from a wilderness. She is sitting on a beast, i.e. the Roman empire: cp. 13¹ᶠ·. The beast is scarlet, because of the blood shed by Rome. It is full of names of blasphemy (e.g. Sebastos; see on 13¹), for in coins and seals and statues and temples the empire was full of such names. It has seven heads and ten horns, explained in vv. 9, 12 (v. 3). The woman, i.e. the city, is clothed with luxury, and she has in her hand a golden cup, signifying debauchery: cp. 14⁸ Jer 51⁷ (v. 4). On her forehead, after the custom of Roman harlots, is a label with her name (v. 5). She is drunken with the blood shed in the persecution of Nero. St. John wonders at her iniquity (v. 6). **6. Admiration**] RV 'wonder.'

For some description of the condition of Rome, see Intro. Romans. The state of society at Rome, at the time of the Rev., was probably the worst the world had ever seen. The aristocracy, which alone had any voice in public affairs, was, with few exceptions, utterly given over to the most shameless wickedness. Vast wealth was in their hands, which was spent in unbridled luxury and debauchery. Their continual craving for new sensations was ministered to by foreign parasites, who introduced new vices and flagrant superstitions. With no feeling for others, their cruelty was appalling. With their appetite for life jaded by the pursuit of pleasure, suicide became common. The herded masses of the people were sunk in ignorance and pauperism. The public distribution of corn confirmed them in idleness, and the public shows helped to harden their hearts and to corrupt their feelings. The State religion was not believed in by the educated, while it had no moral teaching to provide for those who did believe in it, and there was no system of public education.

The Christians were accused of having caused the great fire which raged in Rome for nine days (64 A.D.) According to Tacitus, a great multitude were convicted, not only of incendiarism, but of hatred of mankind. Some were covered with the hides of wild beasts and worried to death by dogs ; others were covered with pitch and set on fire at nightfall to illuminate the imperial gardens. For some years Christians were punished on the accusation of horrible crimes. Afterwards, certainly by the time of Domitian, the mere profession of Christianity became punishable.

7-18. The angel interprets the mystery (v. 7). The beast, which has previously represented the empire, now stands for Nero, in whom the cruelty of the empire had been personified : see on 13³. He shall come up out of the 'abyss' (RV), cp. 9¹ note, 11⁷, i.e. return to life, and then go to perdition : cp. 19²⁰ Mt7¹³ (v. 8). The seven heads have two significations. They represent the seven hills of Rome on which the city sits (v. 9). They also represent seven kings, i.e. probably Augustus (27 B.C.–14 A.D.), Tiberius (14–37), Caligula (37–41), Claudius (41–54), Nero (54–68), Vespasian (69–79), Titus (79–81). Five are dead ; therefore, apparently, the prophecy was written in the reign of Vespasian. Titus is about to come (v. 10). Then Domitian (81–96) will reign. Besides being the eighth king, he will be 'Nero,' because in him the persecuting spirit of Nero will have returned (v. 11). The ten horns are given an interpretation different from that in c. 13. Now they signify 'the kings from the sun-rising' of 16¹² (v. 12). These are to join with the beast in war against the Lamb, and the Lamb will overcome them : cp. 16¹⁶ 19¹⁹ᶠ. (vv. 13f.). In one sense, the Lamb overcame them when not even death could make Christ's people unfaithful to Him ; in another sense, when the empire became converted to Christ. The kings of the earth, joined to the beast, will turn against the city, and destroy and burn her. In v. 16 use is made of the common expectations that Nero, returned to life, and in alliance with the Parthians, would take signal vengeance on Rome for her rebellion against him (vv. 16f.). In v. 18 the city is identified with Rome. It is clear that the prophecy of the destruction of Rome, of which this c. forms part, has not been fulfilled. It has been suggested that the rapid spread of Christianity in Rome altered the character of the city, and that, for this reason, God withheld the threatened judgment : cp. Gn18²⁶ᶠ. (Sodom), Jon3¹⁰ (Nineveh).

8. That was] RV 'how that he was.' **Yet is**] RV 'shall come.' **9. Here** *is* **the mind,** etc.] i.e. a wise man will be able to understand that which follows. The expression challenges the reader's attention : cp. 13⁸.

10. There] RV 'they.' **10f. He must continue,** etc.] With a different punctuation of the Greek this might be rendered, 'he must continue a little while, and (so must) the beast which was and is not. And he himself is also an eighth,' etc. With this rendering, the beast is not identified with one of his horns. **11. Even he is the eighth**] RV 'is himself also an eighth.' **12. One hour**] i.e. a very short time. **14. And they . . called**] RV 'and they also shall overcome that are with him, called.' **16. Upon**] RV 'and.'

CHAPTER 18
The Fall of Babylon

In the last c., the fall of Rome, and the manner of its fall, were prophetically announced. In this c., the greatness of the tragedy is shown by songs of thanksgiving and of lamentation which it calls forth.

As was suggested on c. 17, we may believe that the songs of the joy of angels over sinners that repent have taken the place of these songs. Yet they serve their purpose in encouraging God's people to faith and endurance when at any time wickedness and worldliness seem to be triumphant.

The language of the prophets of the OT. is freely used. From the human side, we may say that the mind of the writer was so saturated with the old Scriptures that he naturally employed their language. From the divine side, we are to learn that 'no prophecy . . is of any private interpretation,' 2 Pet1²⁰, and that God looks on worldly wickedness at any time according to the same principles with which he regarded Babylon and Tyre of old.

1-3. Proclamation of the Fall of Rome.

2. Fallen] cp. 14⁸ Isa21⁹. **Habitation**] cp. Isa13²¹ 34¹³ᶠ. **Cage**] RV 'hold,' i.e. prison. **3.** RV 'For by the wine of . . all the nations are fallen' : cp. 14⁸ 17². **Abundance of her delicacies**] RV 'power of her wantonness.'

4-8. God's people are commanded to come out of Babylon as, before, they were warned to quit Jerusalem : cp. Jer51⁴⁵ Mt24¹⁶. So, spiritually, God's people are to take care that the pleasures of wickedness do not entice them to have fellowship with it.

5. Remembered] cp. 16¹⁹. **6. Reward her**] RV 'Render unto her' : a command to the ministers of God's wrath. **Rewarded you**] RV 'rendered' : cp. Ps137⁸. **Double**] i.e. very great sin calls forth very great punishment : cp. Jer16¹⁸. **7. Lived deliciously**] RV 'waxed wanton.' **Saith**] cp. Isa47⁵ᶠ.

9-20. Dirge of those who loved the wicked city. The writer evidently had in his mind Ezek26ᶠ. (of Tyre). The dirge is suddenly overmastered (v. 20) by the exultation of those she has oppressed.

9. Deliciously] RV 'wantonly.' **11.** Rome was not a trading city, but must have been a great buyer of luxuries. **12. Thyine wood**] a very hard, fragrant wood, specially valued by the Greeks and Romans as a material for tables (HDB.).

13. Cinnamon] RV 'cinnamon, and spice.' **Odours**] RV 'incense.' **Beasts**] RV 'cattle.'
14. Goodly] RV 'sumptuous.' **20.** *Ye holy apostles*] RV 'ye saints, and ye apostles,'—SS. Peter and Paul were put to death at Rome. **Avenged you**] RV 'judged your judgment.'
21–24. An angel compares the casting down of Babylon to the casting down of a millstone into the sea, i.e. it shall be sudden, and 'with no restoration in the future' (Benson).

CHAPTER 19
CHRIST AND HIS ARMIES CONQUER THE BEAST AND HIS PROPHET

The harlot city having been destroyed, the marriage of the Lamb with the glorified Church is announced. But before this can take place, the other enemies of the Lamb must be overcome, and St. John sees in a vision the overthrow of the beast and of the false prophet.

1–4. The great multitude of the saints in heaven (see on 1 10) praises God (v. 1) because the wicked city, which corrupted the earth, and shed the blood of God's servants, is judged (vv. 2 f.). The living creatures and the elders join in the worship and praise (v. 4).

1. Alleluia] RV 'Hallelujah,' lit. 'praise ye the Lord.' The word, which occurs only here in the NT., is common in the Psalms.

5–10. A voice calls on all God's servants to praise Him (v. 5). In response, a vast hymn of praise from Christ, the living creatures, and the saints (see on 1 10) is heard, announcing the marriage of the Lamb (vv. 6 f.). In this way, as so often, the writer brings forward a new thought, which is to be developed later (see on 21 1 f.). The bride, the New Jerusalem, is to be arrayed in the pure linen of righteous acts, in contrast to the harlot's red garment of sin : cp. 18 5 (v. 8). The herald angel declares the blessedness of those who are called (RV 'bidden') to the marriage supper : cp. 3 20 17 14 Mt 22 3 f. Lk 14 15 (v. 9). Of course, except in idea, 'the bride' and those 'called,' i.e. the Church and its members, are identical. Filled with wonder and joy, St. John falls down to worship the angel : cp. 22 8 f. But the angel checks him, saying that worship is for God alone (cp. Col 2 18), and that the fact that the testimony of Jesus, i.e. probably the Revelation made by Jesus, is ministered both by the angel and by Christian prophets and saints, is a sign that they are fellow-servants (v. 10).

5. Out of] RV 'forth from.' The voice does not seem to be God's. Perhaps it is the throne which speaks : see on 16 7. **Servants, and ye**] RV 'servants, ye.' **8. Be arrayed**] RV 'array herself.' **Clean and white**] RV 'bright and pure.' **Righteousness**] RV 'right-

eous acts.' These 'righteous acts' are not the cause of salvation, but its consequence.

10. For the testimony, etc.] probably a comment made by St. John. **Spirit of prophecy**] i.e. the inspiring force of all prophecy.

11–16. Before the fulfilment of the marriage, the Lamb's enemies must be overcome. Christ comes forth as a warrior (cp. Ps 45 3 f.), riding the white horse of victory. His crowns show Him to be King of kings : cp. v. 16. He alone knows His name, i.e. He is greater than any one can say or understand : cp. 2 17 3 12 Mt 11 27. Yet, as coming forth from the Father, He is called the Word of God (cp. Jn 1, 1 Jn 1) ; and when He conquers and rules the nations He is called King of kings and Lord of lords : cp. 17 14. His garments are sprinkled with blood, i.e. His enemies perish before Him : cp. Isa 63 1 f. (vv. 11–13). The heavenly hosts of angels (cp. 1 K 22 19) follow Him, but no blood is on their garments, for He alone overcomes the enemies, cp. v. 21 (v. 14), which He does by the word of His mouth : cp. 1 16 2 12 Isa 11 4 Jn 12 48 Heb 4 12. He treads God's enemies in the winepress of God's anger (a change of figure) : cp. 14 19 f. Isa 63 3 (v. 15).

11. Heaven] RV 'the heaven,' i.e. the sky. **White horse**] cp. 6 2. **12. Crowns**] RV 'diadems.' **13. Dipped in**] RV 'sprinkled with.' **14. Clean**] RV 'pure.' **15. Rule**] cp. 2 27 12 5 Ps 2 9. **Fierceness and wrath**] RV 'fierceness of the wrath.'

17 f. The greatness of the coming victory is foretold by a cry to birds of prey to eat the flesh of the slain : cp. Ezk 39 17 f.

17. In the sun] i.e. in mid heaven ; a central station to call to the vultures. **Fowls**] RV 'birds.' **The supper,** etc.] RV 'the great supper of God,' i.e. the supper which God has prepared.

19–21. The persecuting empire gathers all its forces to overcome Christ, cp.16 14, 16 note, 17 12 f. (v. 19), but is itself overcome, together with the Asian Emperor-worship, figured by the beast and the false prophet or second beast : cp. 13 11 f. note, 16 13. Both empire and Emperor-worship are cast into the lake of fire (v. 20) The 'lake of fire' (cp. 20 10, 14, 15 21 8) is Gehenna, cp. Mt 18 9 (RM) Mk 9 43 (RM), etc., i.e. 'the valley of Hinnom.' This is a valley outside Jerusalem, and was the place of idolatrous sacrifices to Molech : cp. 2 K 16 3 21 6 Jer 7 31 f. 19 11. It came to be regarded as a figure of the place of punishment of the wicked : cp. Isa 66 24 2 Esdr 7 36 f. Mt 5 29 (RM) 10 28 (RM) : see HDB. Evidently the casting of empire and idolatry into such a place can only be a figure for the complete destruction of the persecuting and wicked systems. The 'rest' (RV), i.e. the kings of the earth and their armies, were killed with the sword of Christ's mouth (v. 21). The distinction between their fate and that of the two beasts appears to have been made, partly because destruction by the lake of fire could not be the end of any human being before the Judgment, partly because the slaughter is symbolical. Christ overcomes men who are His enemies, in one way by strengthening His people to endure their assaults, in another way by converting them. But it is not so much individuals who are spoken of here, as the systems and principles of evil which succeeding generations of individuals nourish and carry out. It is those systems and principles which are conquered by Christ. The weapons which they turn against Him and His people are persecution, 'the lust of the flesh, the lust of the eye, and the pride of life,' the spirit of materialism, etc. This spirit of the world is conquered by the preaching of the gospel of Christ, and by the Spirit of Christ in the hearts of men. This is the battle of Har-Magedon.

20. Miracles] RV 'the signs,' i.e. those spoken of in 13$^{14f.}$, where see notes.

CHAPTER 20

SATAN CONQUERED. THE LAST JUDGMENT

In this c. the visions of the overthrow of Christ's enemies are continued. The devil is bound for 1,000 years (vv. 1–3); the martyrs reign with Christ for 1,000 years (vv. 4–6). It is foretold that, at the end of the 1,000 years, Satan will be loosed, and will make a last assault against the saints, after which he is cast into the lake of fire (vv. 7–10). A vision of the Last Judgment follows (vv. 11–15).

The binding of Satan and the reign of the saints with Christ, both for 1,000 years, is known as 'the Millennium.' Many of the later Jews expected that the Messianic kingdom, of which the prophets spoke, would come in the present age, and they distinguished it from the Final Judgment and new heaven of righteousness which would follow. By some it was said that the Messianic kingdom would last 1,000 years, though other periods were also named.

It is plain that St. John made use of this Jewish expectation in his prophecy. But it does not follow that he meant it to be understood literally. It is more in harmony with the character of the book to suppose that he meant this Jewish apocalyptic expectation to be understood spiritually. The same conclusion seems probable from the general circumstances. The Christians had just been told that the persecuting city and empire would be overcome. They might ask whether the devil, the author of all evil,

would not raise up fresh enemies against them.

1–3. For a thousand years the devil will be bound and shut up in the abode of spiritual evil (the 'abyss,' see on 9^1, not 'the lake of fire,' which is the place of final punishment, see on 19^{20}). The meaning is, that for '1,000 years' the power of evil would not be able to gather itself into an organised attack upon Christianity. The '1,000 years' are not to be understood numerically, but as a period of rest and happiness. For 1,000 is a multiple of 10, which was regarded as a sacred number because the commandments are 10; and it is the number which was considered to stand for the sabbath in the history of the world, 1,000 years' rest coming after 6,000 years' toil: cp. Ps 90^4.

4–6. The Christians for whom St. John wrote would ask what share they had in these joyful tidings. Although generations to come would enjoy rest and peace, it was not to be in their day, and many of them must suffer death. So they are told that good things are in store for them. Although they die, yet their souls will live and reign with Christ (v. 4). 'The rest of the dead,' i.e. the ungodly dead, the men of the earth, 'lived not,' i.e. did not share in the presence of Christ, but remained for the Judgment: cp. v. 11. The life of the saints with Christ is called 'the first resurrection' (cp. Jn 5^{25}), because it depends upon the resurrection from the death of sin to the life of righteousness. As such, it belongs to all who are Christ's, whether on earth or in paradise (v. 5). Over them 'the second death' (cp. v. 14, 21^8) has no power, because they 'have passed from death unto life,' 1 Jn 3^{14} (v. 6).

7–10. After the time of rest, and when the Final Judgment is near, the power of evil will gather force again (v. 7). Gog and Magog, i.e. the world hostile to God's people, cp. Ezk 38 f. (v. 8), will assail the Church (the 'camp of the saints and the beloved city,' i.e. the spiritual Jerusalem). But God will overthrow these last enemies (v. 9), and the devil will be cast into the lake of fire, i.e. the power of evil will be destroyed for ever (v. 10).

11–15. God sits on a 'great white throne,' i.e. in glory and purity (v. 11), to judge the wicked dead. They are not written 'in the book of life' (cp. 3^5 13^8 17^8 21^{27}), and they are judged according to their works (vv. 12 f.), and 'cast into the lake of fire.' Into the lake of fire, Death and Hades (i.e. the abode of the dead) are also cast, for 'the last enemy that shall be destroyed is death' (1 Cor 5^{26}; cp. 21^4). This is the 'second death,' for it is the final separation from eternal life (vv. 14 f.). This judgment does not apply to Christ's people : cp. Jn 5 24. They are in the book of life. They already 'live' (cp. v. 4), and, therefore, are not reckoned among the 'dead' of v. 11.

It is plain that St. John's view is, as it were, foreshortened. He sees the overthrow of the anti-Christian persecution. He sees, farther on, the Last Judgment. But he does not specify the length of the time of rest and then of conflict for the Church which lies between.

1, 3. Bottomless pit] RV 'abyss.' **3. Him up**] RV 'it.' **Set a seal upon him**] RV 'sealed it over him.' **Deceive**] i.e. into attacking the Church: cp. vv. 8, 10, 19 20 Gn 2 Jn 8 12, 44.

Fulfilled] RV 'finished.'

4. Thrones] cp. Dan 7 9, 22 Mt 19 28. **They**] i.e. the martyrs.

Witness] RV 'testimony,' i.e. the revelation made by Christ, 'the faithful witness': cp. 1 5, 9 12 17 19 10. **Mark**] cp. 13 14 f. **Reigned**] The saints share Christ's triumph over sin and death, and also, in ways which we know not, share the glories of His kingdom: cp. 5 10 Ro 8 17.

6. Priests] cp. 1 6 note, 5 10. **8. Deceive**] see on v. 3. **10. Shall be**] RV 'they shall be.' **11. Throne**] cp. Isa 6 1 Dan 7 9.

12. The books] RV 'books ': cp. Dan 7 10. **Works**] cp. Mt 16 27 Ro 2 6.

13, 14. Hell] RV 'Hades.'

14. The second death] RV 'the second death, even the lake of fire ': cp. 2 11 Mt 25 41.

CHAPTER 21
THE HOLY CITY

The enemies of the Lamb have been conquered. The Judgment is over. The old condition of things has passed away : cp. 20 11. Now St. John sees in a vision the blissful glory of heaven, in which the Lamb's redeemed people will dwell for ever.

1-8. The eternal dwelling-place prepared for the redeemed is seen from a distance (vv. 1 f.), and the voice of God declares what it means (vv. 3-6), and for whom its glories are (vv. 7 f.).

Three points come out in the description. (1) The Presence of God with the Jew, symbolised by the tabernacle in the wilderness, will now be perfected by His dwelling ('dwell,' lit. 'tabernacle,' v. 3 ; cp. Jn 1 14 RM) with the redeemed of all races ('men,' v. 3). The 'peoples,' i.e. Gentiles, have become 'His peoples' (v. 3 RV), and He their Emmanuel ('God .. with them,' v. 3): cp. Isa 7 14 Mt 1 23. He will take from them, and keep from them, all sorrow, pain, and death (cp. 7 17 Isa 25 8 35 10 65 16 f.), because these belonged to the first dispensation, while now, (2) all things are new. There is a new heaven, i.e. sky, and a new earth (cp. Isa 65 17 66 22), from which the sea, emblem of unrest and of separation, has de-

parted (v. 1) ; there is a new society, 'new Jerusalem' (v. 2) ; and 'all things,' i.e. all ways and thoughts and circumstances of existence, are new : cp. 2 Cor 5 17 (v. 5). The word translated 'new' does not signify 'that which has never existed before,' but 'fresh,' 'that which has not been used or worn '; so it may be taken as meaning 'undimmed,' 'unspoilt.' The term 'new Jerusalem' is used figuratively for the divine society of the redeemed in glory, as 'Jerusalem' represents the society of the redeemed on earth : cp. 20 9 Gal 4 26. It is a 'city' in the sense of being an organised community : cp. Eph 2 19 Heb 11 16. The New Jerusalem is compared to a bride (vv. 2-9 ; contrast 17 1-5), to denote that the happiness of the redeemed springs from their union with Christ : cp. Isa 61 10 f. 62 1 f. Mt 22 3 25 10 Lk 12 36 Eph 5 25 f. (3) Those for whom these blessed things are in store : those who thirst for, i.e. intensely desire, God, righteousness, and eternal life, cp. Isa 55 1 Mt 5 6 Jn 7 37 Ro 2 7 (v. 6), and who 'overcome' (v. 7). Thus the chief purpose of the book, in encouraging the tempted and persecuted to overcome by resistance unto death, is maintained to the end. The 'city' is not for those who are too cowardly to endure, who fall from faith and join in heathen abominations (v. 8).

3. A great voice] i.e. God's. **Heaven**] RV 'the throne': cp. 19 5.

4. Former] RV 'first.'

5. He said] i.e. the herald angel. **6. He said**] i.e. God. **It is done**] RV 'They are come to pass '; 'they '= 'these words' (v. 5).

7. All] RV 'these.'

8. Abominable] i.e. those who join in heathen debaucheries : cp. 17 4.

Sorcerers] lit. 'poisoners': cp. 18 23 22 15 Gal 5 20 RV. There was much magic in heathenism, and it dealt in philtres and poisons. **The lake**] see on 19 20. **Second death**] see on 20 6.

9-27. Further description of the city. St. John has seen the city descending in the distance. Now it is shown him in full view by one of the angels of the bowls (vv. 9 f.), probably the herald angel: cp. 17 1, see on 1 10. The visible cloud of God's glory is in the city (cp. vv. 3, 23 Ezk 43 2 f. Heb 9 5), and causes her to shine with glory as she descends (v. 11). Her walls represent her beauty and security, and, with the gates and foundations (cp. Nu 2 Ezk 48 Eph 2 20), signify also that she is the home of the Church of both OT. and NT. The twelve Apostles are mentioned as a body, so that we need not ask whether the twelfth was Matthias or Paul (vv. 12-14). The city is measured, but as the city is figurative, so are the measurements. All the dimensions are compounded of 12, the number of the OT. and the NT. (cp. 7 4 f.), the number which signifies that God is in the midst of His people : see on v 12. The city is a cube, which, taken literally, would be monstrous, but in its symbolical meaning says that the whole city is a sanctuary like the Holy of Holies in the Tabernacle (vv. 15–17). The magnificence of the city is figured by the most beautiful and precious things (vv. 18–21). Her spiritual perfection is such that no special sanctuary is needed: cp. Jn 4 21. There is no one in the city who is not at one with God. All her people are united in His service. Thus 'there is no temple, because the city is all temple' (C. A. Scott) (v. 22). Earthly light and knowledge, which are imperfect and partial, have vanished in the full light and knowledge of God: cp. Isa 60 19 Jn 8 12 1 Cor 13 9 f. (v. 23). The prophecies of the gathering in of the Gentiles (cp. Isa 60.3) are fulfilled (v. 24), and redeemed humanity worships God within the open gates of the city (cp. Isa 60 11) in perpetual light and security (vv. 25 f.); those only being shut out who are unclean through their separation from God to the service of the devil's agents (v. 27).

9. Vials] RV 'bowls.' Full of] RV 'Who were laden with.' 10. Spirit] RV 'Spirit': cp. 17 3. Mountain] cp. Ezk 40 2 f. Mt 4 8.

11. Jasper] see on 4 3.

12. Twelve gates] 'Four is the number which is the symbol of the world, three that of God. Twelve, therefore, is the signature of the covenant people among whom God dwells. The enclosure of the Tabernacle was a square space, three tribes being over against each of the four sides. Thus we have a square with the Tabernacle in the midst, expressive of God in the midst of His people' (Currey).

15. Cp. Ezk 40 3 f. 17. The wall] i.e. the thickness of the wall: cp. Jer 51 58. The angel] RV 'an angel,' i.e. the angelic cubit was of the same length as a human cubit.

19 f. The stones are, with exceptions, the same as those in the high priest's breastplate (cp. Ex 28 17 f. 39 10 f.), and those ascribed to the king of Tyre (Ezk 28 13). Flinders Petrie (HDB.) says that precious stones were not so exactly distinguished from one another in ancient days as they are now. 'Jasper' was, according to him, green jasper; the 'sapphire' was our lapis-lazuli; the 'chalcedony' was dioptase (silicate of copper); the 'emerald' should be rock-crystal, cp. 4 3 note; 'sardonyx' was the red and white onyx; the 'sardius' was red jasper; the 'chrysolite' in St. John's time was the present topaz; the 'beryl' was either beryl, i.e. an opaque emerald, or green felspar; the 'topaz' was peridot; the 'chrysoprasus' was, probably, the green chalcedony; the 'jacinth' was the sapphire; the 'amethyst' was the modern amethyst.

24. Of them which are saved] RV omits.

27. That defileth] RV 'unclean,' lit. 'com-

mon': cp v. 8 Isa 52 1 Ezk 44 9. Worketh, etc.] RV 'maketh an abomination and a lie.' Book of life] cp. 3 5 13 8 20 12.

CHAPTER 22

THE VISION ENDED. THE LORD IS AT HAND

The inner life of the heavenly Jerusalem is described. Then the 'Revelation' closes with the repeated assurance that Christ is at hand, and with the yearnings of the Church and of St. John for the joy of His advent.

1–5. In the New Jerusalem, the blessed life of Eden is more than restored. There is a river of life (cp. Gn 2 10), i.e. the Holy Spirit: cp. Jn 4 14 7 37. Cp. also Ezk 47 1 Joel 3 18 Zech 14 8, in which prophecies the waters come from the Temple: here there is no Temple, and the waters flow from the throne of God, i.e. they are the result of God's immediate presence, and of His fully accepted government (v. 1). On either side of the river as it flows in the midst of the street is a grove of trees, the tree of life: cp. Gn 2 9 Ezk 47 12. The fruit is always available, for there is a fresh crop every month: cp. the manna, Jn 6 31 f. The leaves healed the sin of the 'nations' within the city, and the fruit nourishes their life. In the tree we see the cross on which Christ hung as precious fruit (v. 2). Now, too, as He became 'a curse for us' (Gal 3 13), the curse of Eden (cp. Gn 3 17, 22 f.) is taken away: cp. Zech 14 11. Over the 'sweet societies' of the Redeemed, God and the Lamb reign for ever. The Redeemed offer up worship face to face with God (the 'beatific vision') (cp. Ps 17 15 Mt 5 8, 1 Cor 13 12 1 Jn 3 2) and receive His Name, i.e. are marked as His (see on 7 3 and 14 1), and transformed into His likeness (vv. 3 f.). And as His glory thus shines upon and enters into them, they 'reign,' i.e. their life can develop and expand to its fullest powers, there being no evil ('curse,' v. 3) in them to be restrained, nor hindering circumstances without to restrain them (v. 5).

1. Clear] RV 'bright.' 1 f. And of the Lamb. In the midst of the street .. river] RV 'and of the Lamb, in the midst of the street thereof. And on this side of the river and on that.' 2. Manner] RM 'crops.'

5. Candle] RV 'light of lamp.'

6–9. Affirmation of the truth of the vision which is now concluded, and of the near approach of that of which it tells (vv. 6, 7). St. John, knowing the angel has finished his task and is about to leave him, falls before him in worship, as in 19 10, but is again charged to worship God alone (vv. 8 f.).

6. The Lord God of the holy prophets] RV 'the Lord, the God of the spirits of the

prophets': cp. 1 Cor 14 32. The meaning is that the words of the Christian prophets do not speak their own mind, but God's. **7.** Christ's voice breaks in : cp. 16 15.

8. RV 'And I John am he that heard and saw these things.'

10–15. The vision is not to be sealed, as was Daniel's (cp. Dan 12 4), because it is for immediate use (v. 10). Those who 'will not turn and repent because of the Revelation which Christ has now completed, will not, cannot have any greater power brought to bear on them before He comes again : cp. Lk 16 31' (Benson) (vv. 11–13). Happy are they who are purified, through faith, by His blood (cp. 7 14), for the life and joy of the city are for them (vv. 14 f.).

10. Seal not] RV 'seal not up' : cp. 10 4.

11. Cp. Ezk 3 27 20 39 Dan 12 10. **Unjust**] RV 'unrighteous.' **Be unjust**] RV 'do unrighteousness.' **Be filthy**] RV 'be made filthy.' **Be righteous**] RV 'do righteousness.' **Be holy**] RV 'be made holy.'

12–15. Spoken by Christ : cp. v. 7, 16 15.

14. Do his commandments] RV 'wash their robes.' **Right**] RV 'the right to come.'

16 f. The Messiah attests the Revelation (v. 16). The Holy Spirit in the Church (cp. Ro 8 16), and the Church herself, hearing His voice, call for His advent, and, at the same time, invite all who will to take part with the Church in this joyful expectation (v. 17).

16. The root, etc.] The reference is to the Messiahship of our Lord, as son of David, and as the 'star' of Balaam's prophecy : cp. 2 28 5 5 Nu 24 17 Isa 11 1, 10 Mt 11 22 42. **17. Bride**] see on 21 2. **Heareth**] see on 1 3. **Athirst**] cp. 21 6. **Freely**] cp. Isa 55 1.

18 f. A warning that the book is not to be falsified by addition or excision : cp. Dt 4 2 12 32. **19. Book of life**] RV 'tree of life.'

And *from* **the things**] RV omits.

20 f. Christ sums up the book by announcing His speedy advent, and St. John prays for it (v. 20). The book, and with it the Bible, closes in prayer for that in which all its blessings are contained, 'the grace,' i.e. the manifested love, 'of the Lord Jesus' (v. 21).

THE END

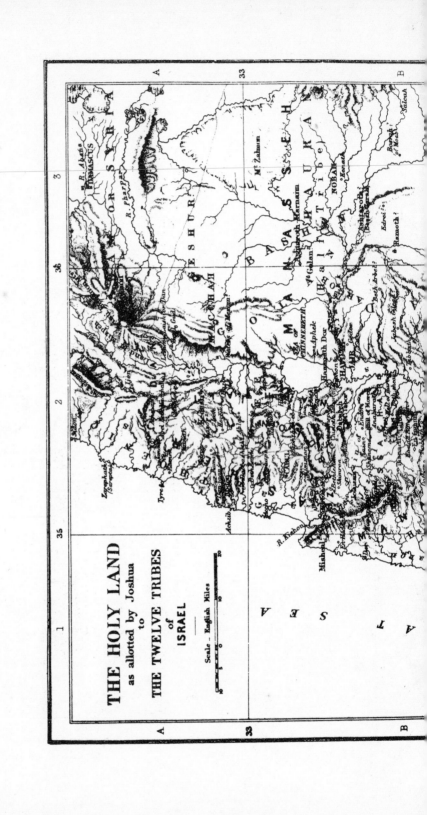

THE HOLY LAND
as allotted by Joshua
to
THE TWELVE TRIBES
of
ISRAEL

Scale - English Miles

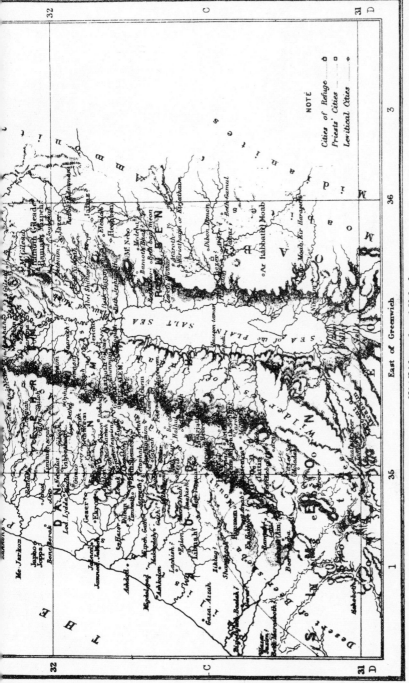

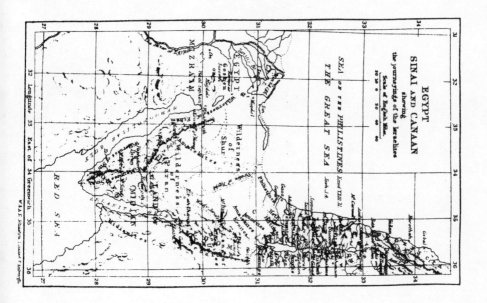

EGYPT
SINAI AND CANAAN
shewing
the journeyings of the Israelites
Scale of English Miles

SEA OF THE PHILISTINES Exod. XIII.21

THE GREAT SEA Josh. I.4

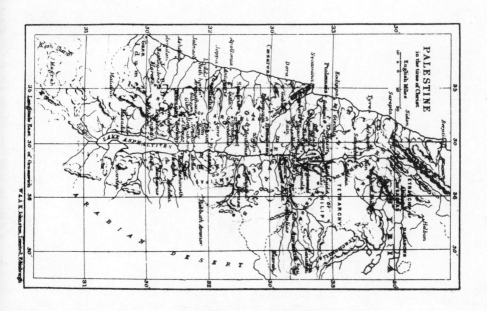

PALESTINE
in the time of Christ

English Miles

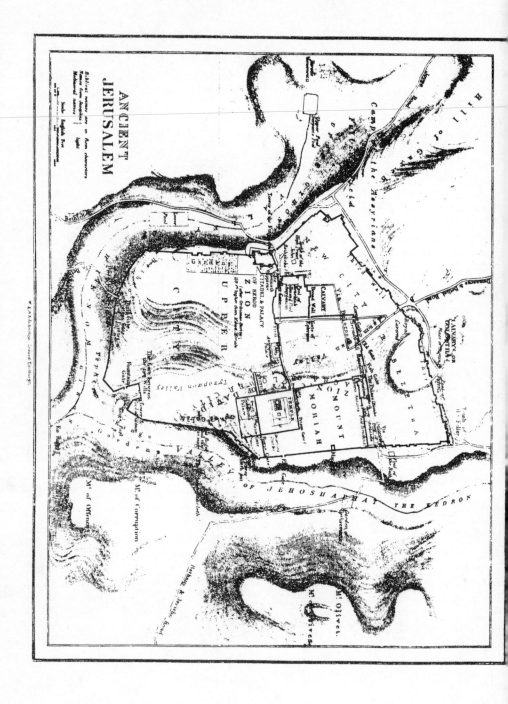

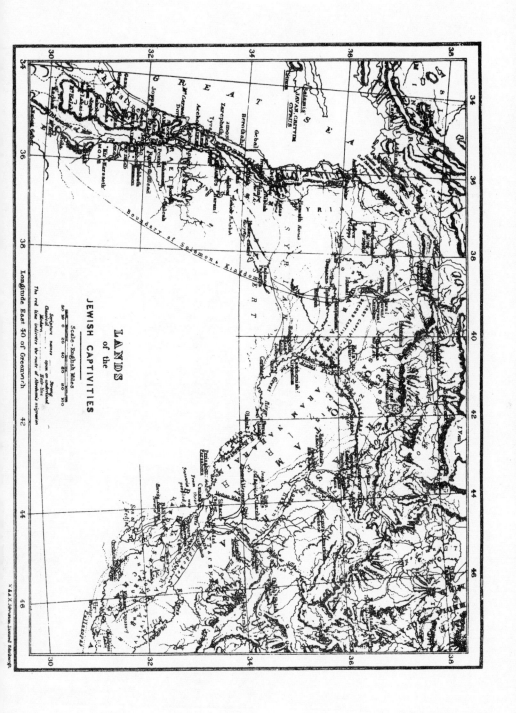

LANDS
of the
JEWISH CAPTIVITIES

Scale - English Miles

Scripture names
Classical _____ open
Modern _____

The red line indicates the route of Abraham's migration

Longitude East 40 of Greenwich

W. & A. K. Johnston, Limited, Edinburgh.

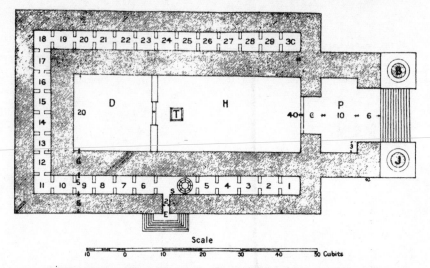

GROUND PLAN OF SOLOMON'S TEMPLE.

B and J = Boaz and Jachin—the pillars.   P = the porch.   H = the *hēkāl* or Holy Place.   D = the *debīr* or Most Holy Place.   T = the table of shewbread.   S = the stairway to the upper chambers.   E = the entrance to the chambers.   1-30 = the chambers after Ezekiel's temple.

Reproduced by permission of Messrs T. & T. Clark from Dr. Hastings' "Dictionary of the Bible."

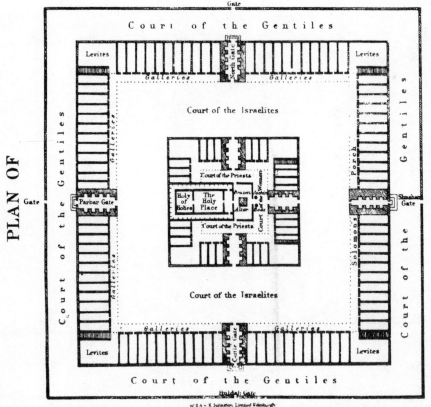

PLAN OF   HEROD'S TEMPLE

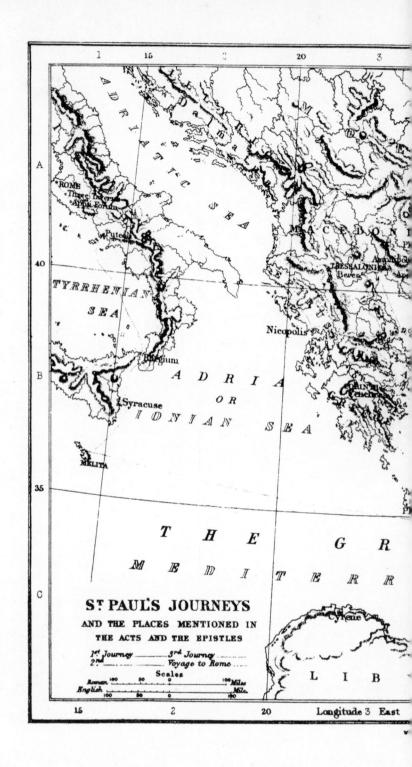

ST PAUL'S JOURNEYS

AND THE PLACES MENTIONED IN
THE ACTS AND THE EPISTLES

1st Journey .... 3rd Journey ....
2nd ——————— Voyage to Rome ....

Scales